Sunday EXPRESS
WORDMASTER

J A Coleman

ERIC DOBBY REFERENCE BOOKS

First published in Great Britain 1994
by Eric Dobby Publishing Limited
12 Warnford Road
Orpington, Kent, BR6 6LW

ISBN 1-85882-025-1

Text typeset in Times New Roman by Kevin O'Connor, Poole
Printed and bound in Great Britain by
BPC Hazell Books Ltd
A member of
The British Printing Company Ltd

INTRODUCTION

To say that we use a dictionary to look up a word is only an approximation of the truth. Almost invariably we know the word exists and we turn to that word in the dictionary to find some information about it such as its correct pronunciation, meaning, derivation and so on. But what if we do not already know the word or - a familiar enough experience to most of us - know that we know it but cannot call it to mind? 'My brother is a ... what d'ya call it? He collects coins'. You knew it was 'numismatist' all along but you could not look up 'coin collector' or 'collector of coins' because standard dictionaries don't work that way. You need a dictionary that does work that way - from the definition to the word. You need a reverse dictionary.

Crossword enthusiasts need such a dictionary more than other people. The compiler has a marked advantage; he enters words in his grid asking only that they fit. Then he uses a standard dictionary to find meanings around which he can concoct his devious clues. The solver must work the other way round - from the definition in the clue to the word itself. For this he needs a reverse dictionary.

The standard type of dictionary has been with us for over 200 years. It was not until 1989 that the first reverse dictionary (published by Readers Digest) appeared. *Wordmaster* has its origins a little earlier. I had always felt the need for a dictionary of this sort when struggling with a crossword, such as *The Sunday Times* Mephisto, which regularly uses many words not found in the average solver's vocabulary and the lists appearing in the *Crossword Dictionary* published by Collins over my name constitute a form of reverse dictionary. Since that book contains, in addition to the lists, much material specifically related to crosswords, it was referred to as a Crossword Dictionary rather than a Reverse Dictionary. *Wordmaster* reproduces many of the lists from the Collins book but it has a far wider coverage in both the original subjects and in the range of subjects dealt with. The crossword-specific material has been omitted, leaving only the definition-leading-to-the-word format. Now, if you are stuck for the word for 'Sikh temple', you can turn to the headword Sikh, run down the list to find 'temple' and then across to GURDWARA. It's as simple as that. And if you choose to approach it from the 'temple' end rather than the 'Sikh' end, you will be referred to church buildings where there is a sub-section listing various types of 'temple', including the one you want.

So, if you want to know what Shakespeare called a footpad or which word Spenser might have used for a bull's-eye, you will find the answer here together with many, many more - about 80,000 more.

Many of the definitions are based on those used in the 1977 edition of the *Chambers 20th Century Dictionary* and I am grateful to the publishers for permission to use this material. Thanks are also due to Collins for their generosity in allowing the reproduction of some lists from the *Crossword Dictionary*.

James Coleman
Penkridge

James Coleman was born in 1920 in the Cotswolds. He entered local government after leaving school but found his professional studies interrupted by World War II. After 6 years with the Grenadier Guards (serving in North Africa and Italian campaigns) he took up his career again, qualifying as a chartered surveyor and becoming Engineer and Surveyor to the former Cannock RDC, a post from which he retired in 1974 to set up his own architectural and town-planning practice. He finally gave up work in 1986 to 'play about with words'; the results of this playing appear in *Wordmaster* and his earlier books, *The Complete Guide to Cryptic Crosswords* (soon to be republished by Eric Dobby Publications) and the large *Crossword Dictionary*, both originally published by Collins.

Index of headwords

Entries in the book are under main headwords and many are also cross-referenced. This Index provides a listing of those main headwords and their cross-references with some additional cross-referencing under general categories such as 'sport' or 'food'.

aborigine words   (*see* Australia)
absence of   (*see* without)
Abyssinian
acids
Adam
addiction to   (*see* love)
address
Afghan(istan)
African
Afrikaans   (*see* African)
agent
aircraft
airlines
airports
Albania
alchemy
Alderney
Algeria
alloys
alphabet
American
American football
amino-acid   (*see* acids)
anatomist   (*see* physician)
ancient words   (*see* old[1])
Andorra
Angola
animals   (*see* antelopes, bats, birds, butterfly, cats, cattle, deer, dogs, duck, fish, goats, goose, greyhound, hens, horse, insects, lizards, monkeys, ox, pigs, pigeon, rabbit, sheep, shellfish, snakes, whale)
anniversaries
antelopes
anthropology
Apostles
apparition   (*see* spirit)
apples
Arabia
archaeology
archaeologists   (*see* archaeology)
archaic words   (*see* old[1])

architects
architectural features
     (*see also* building construction)
architectural styles
Argentina
Armenia
armour
army
     (*see also* military, soldiers, weapon)
art
Asian
asteroids   (*see* astronomy)
astrology
astronomy
athletes
     (*see also* games)
atmosphere   (*see* meteorology)
Australia
Austria
authority of   (*see* power)
aversion to   (*see* fear)
bachelor
bacteriology   (*see* biology)
Bahamas
Bahrain
Balearic Islands
ballet
balsam   (*see* gum)
Bangladesh
Barbados
Barbary
baseball
Basque
bats
battles
bearing
     (*see also* having)
Bechuanaland
     (*see also* Botswana)
becoming
beginning
Belgium

Index of headwords

beliefs
    (*see also* worship)
Belize
Bengal
Benin
Biblical language   (*see* old[1])
biology
birds
    (*see also* duck, goose, hen, pigeon)
biscuits
blood   (*see* circulation)
boats
Bolivia
bone
books
botany   (*see* biology)
Botswana
bottle
bowls
boxing
brain
Brazil
bread
breeding   (*see* bearing)
bridge
British
Browning, Robert
Brunei
Buddhist
building construction
    (*see also* architectural features)
buildings   (*see* architects)
Bulgaria
bullfighting
Burkina Faso
Burma
Burns, Robert
    (*see also* Scottish)
Burundi
butterfly
Byzantine
cacti
cakes
Cambodia
camera   (*see* photography)
Cameroon
Canada
Canary Islands
Cape Verde Islands
capes
card games
carriages
carrying   (*see* bearing)
cart   (*see* carriages)
coach   (*see* carriages)
cats

cattle
    (*see also* ox)
cattle diseases
Celebes   (Sulawesi)
    (*see also* Indonesia, East Indies)
Celtic
    (*see also* Ireland, Scottish)
Central African Republic
Central America
    (*see also* South America)
cereal
    (*see also* grasses)
Ceylon
Chad
Chaldean
Channel Islands
cheese
cheese dishes
chemistry
chess
chief magistrate   (*see* magistrate)
Chile
china
China
church — building
church — personnel
church — terms
church — vestments
    (*see also* belief, garments, prayer, worship)
cinema
circulation
city
    (*see also* street, square)
classical Greek   (*see* Greece)
clergy   (*see* church—personnel)
climate   (*see* meteorology)
clothes
    (*see also* footwear, garments, headgear)
clouds   (*see* meteorology)
club
Cockney rhyming slang
cocktails
    (*see also* drinks, wine)
coffee
coins
collecting
collection of   (*see* group)
Colombia
colour
commander   (*see* leader)
complaint   (*see* diseases)
composers   (*see* musicians)
computing
concerning   (*see* pertaining)
condition   (*see* diseases)
Congo

constellations
  (*see also* astronomy)
cookery
Coptic
Costa Rica
counties
cricket
cross
  (*see also* decorations)
Cuba
cultivation   (*see* bearing)
cycling
Cyprus
Czechoslovakia
dance
decorations
deer
  (*see also* antelopes)
deficiency of   (*see* without)
demon   (*see* spirit)
Denmark
department
description of   (*see* write)
desert
dessert
detectives, fictional
dialects (English dialect words)
digestive system
dinosaur   (*see* lizards)
discoveries
  (*see also* first, inventor)
diseases
  (*see also* cattle diseases, horse diseases, plant
  diseases)
disorder   (*see* diseases)
divers   (*see* swimming)
divination
diving   (*see* swimming)
Doctors of
dogs
Dominica
Dominican Republic
dove   (*see* pigeon)
dramatists
  (*see also* Shakespeare)
drawing (of)   (*see* write)
drinks
drugs
duck
Dutch
dyes
ear
earth   (*see* geography)
earthquake
East Indian

eastern
  (*see also* Oriental)
eat
economics
Ecuador
egg
Egypt
eight
eighteen
eighth
eighty
El Salvador
electric
  (*see also* physics)
elements
  (*see also* physics)
eleven
embroidery   (*see* sewing)
engineers   (*see* architects)
English
engraving   (*see* write)
enzymes
equal
Eskimo
Ethiopia   (*see* Abyssinian)
Europe
excessive love for   (*see* love)
explorer
explosives
eyes
fabric
fabulous
  (*see also* monsters)
Faeroe Islands
failure of   (*see* without)
farewell
fastdays   (*see* holidays)
fastest
Fates
fear
feastdays   (*see* holidays)
feathers
feet
fences
fencing
ferns
festivals   (*see* holidays)
feudal   (*see* mediaeval)
fifty
figures of speech   (*see* rhetoric)
Fiji
films   (*see* cinema)
Finland
first
fish
fish dishes

Index of headwords

fishing
five
flags
flower
    (*see also* plants)
food   (*see* apples, biscuits, bread, cakes, cereal,
    cheese, cheese dishes, cookery, dessert, egg, fish
    dishes, fruit, fungi, grape, herb, meat, meat
    dishes, menu, pasta, pasta dishes, pastry, poultry
    dishes, pulses, rice, sauce, sausage, shellfish,
    soup, spice, stew, sugar, tea, vegetable, vegetable
    dishes, vitamin)
football
footwear
fortifications
forty
four
fourteen
fourth
France
French
fruit
fungi
    (*see also* biology)
fur
Furies
furniture
Gabon
Gaelic
    (*see also* Ireland)
Gambia
games[1]
games[2] (terms)
game (birds)   (*see* poultry dishes)
garments
gases
gazelles   (*see* antelopes)
gems
genetics   (*see* biology)
geography
    (*see also* capes, counties, desert, earthquake,
    explorer, lakes, mountain, oceanography, rock,
    rivers, stone, swamp, volcano, waterfall, wind,
    zoological regions)
geology   (*see* geography)
German
Ghana
ghost   (*see* spirit)
Gibraltar
girls
    (*see also* woman)
gland
glass
goats
gods
goddesses

golf
goose
government by   (*see* power)
governor
    (*see also* leader, power)
Graces
grammar   (*see* rhetoric)
grape
    (*see also* wine)
graph   (*see* write)
grass
    (*see also* cereal)
Greece
    (*see also* mythology)
Grenada
Grenadines
greyhound
group
Guatemala
Guernsey
gum
gun
Guyana
gymnastics
gypsy
hair
Haiti
harness   (*see* horse)
Harpies
hat   (*see* headgear)
hatred of   (*see* fear)
having
Hawaii
head
headgear
heart   (*see* circulation)
Hebrew
Hell
hens
Her
heraldic beasts   (*see* monsters)
heraldry
herb
heresies   (*see* beliefs)
hills   (*see* mountain)
Hindu
    (*see also* Indian)
His
historians
historical words   (*see* old[1])
holidays
Holland   (*see* Dutch)
holy
hominids   (*see* anthropology)
Honduras
Hong Kong

hormone
horse[1] (breeds)
horse[2] (terms and tackle)
horse diseases
horse racing
house
hundred
Hungary
hybrid
Iceland
illness   (*see* diseases)
India
   (*see also* Hindu, Sikh)
Indonesia
indoor sports   (*see* games[1])
insects[1]
insects[2] (terms)
institute/institution
instrument   (*see* instrument of torture,
   measuring instrument, musical instrument)
instrument of torture
international
inventors
   (*see also* discoveries, first)
Iran
   (*see also* Persia)
Iraq
Ireland
Islam   (*see* Moslem)
Isle of Man
Isle of Wight
Israel
   (*see also* Hebrew)
Italy
Ivory Coast
Jamaica
Japan
Javanese
Jersey
Jesus
jewellery
   (*see also* gems)
Jewish   (*see* Hebrew)
Jordan
judge   (*see* magistrate)
June
Kampuchea   (*see* Cambodia)
Kenya
kill
kings[1] (general)
kings[2] (British)
knife
knight
knot
knowledge of   (*see* study)
Korea

Kuala Lumpur
Kuwait
lack of   (*see* without)
lacking   (*see* without)
lake
Lamb (Charles)
language
   (*see also* rhetoric)
Laos
Latin
   (*see also* Roman)
law[1] (terms)
law[2] (describing, governing, stating that)
   (*see also* electric, physics)
leader
   (*see also* nobles, power)
leaf
leather
Lebanon
Lesotho
Liberia
library
Libya
   (*see also* Arab)
Licentiate
lichen   (*see* fungi)
Liechtenstein
life symbol
lifestyle
like   (*see* pertaining)
literature
lizards
logic
London
lord
   (*see also* leaders, nobles)
loss of   (*see* without)
Louis XIV
love
lover of   (*see* love)
low
Luxembourg
lymph   (*see* circulation)
Madagascar
magistrate
Malagasy   (*see* Madagascar)
Malawi
Malaya
Malaysia
Mali
Malta
mania for   (*see* love)
Manx
many
Maori   (*see* New Zealand)
martial arts   (*see* games)

Index of headwords

masonry   (*see* architectural features)
mass of   (*see* group)
master
material   (*see* fabrics)
mathematics
Mauritania
Mauritius
May
measures
measuring instrument
     (*see also* scientific instruments)
meat
 meat dishes
     (*see also* cookery, menu)
medal   (*see* decorations)
medi(a)eval
medical
     (*see also* diseases, physicians, surgery)
medical instruments   (*see* surgery)
medicines   (*see* drugs)
Mediterranean
member
menu
merchant
meteor   (*see* astronomy)
meteorology
metric weights   (*see* French)
Mexico
military
     (*see also* fortifications, soldier)
million
Milton, John
mineral
mineralogy   (*see* geography)
minus   (*see* without)
Miss
     (*see also* girl)
missile
     (*see also* space)
mites   (*see* insects[1])
Mongolia
monkeys
monsters
moons   (*see* astronomy)
Moor
     (*see also* Morocco)
Morocco
Moslem
moths
motor car
motorcycle
motor racing
motor rallying
mountain
mountaineers   (*see* mountain)
Mozambique

Mrs
muscle
Muses
mushroom   (*see* fungi)
music
musical instruments
musicals
musicians
Muslim   (*see* Moslem)
Myanmar   (*see* Burma)
mythical beasts   (*see* monsters)
mythology
     (*see also* gods, goddesses)
names
Namibia
national
naturalists   (*see* biology)
Navy
     (*see also* sailor)
needlepoint   (*see* sewing)
Nepal
nerve
Netherlands
     (*see also* Dutch)
New
New Zealand
newspaper
Nicaragua
nicknames
     (*see also* boxing, football)
Niger
Nigeria
nine
nineteenth
ninety
nobles
     (*see also* leader)
Norse
     (*see also* mythology, Scandinavia)
north
Norway
     (*see also* Norse, Scandinavia)
nose
Nova Scotia
nuclear reactors
numbers   (*see* mathematics)
nut
nymph(s)
observatory
obsession with   (*see* love)
obsolete words   (*see* old[1])
oceanography
of   (*see* pertaining)
of the nature of   (*see* pertaining)
old[1]
old[2] (former)

Olympians   (*see* gods, goddesses)
Oman
one
opera
operetta   (*see* musicals)
Order
   (*see also* decorations)
orders, religious   (*see* beliefs)
Ordinary
Ordnance
organ stops
Organisation
oriental
   (*see also* Eastern)
origins (of)   (*see* beginning)
ox
   (*see also* cattle)
pain   (*see* diseases)
painting
   (*see also* art)
Pakistan
palaeontology   (*see* archaeology)
Palestine
palm
Panama
Papal
Papua New Guinea
Paraguay
parliament
Parliamentary
particle
   (*see also* physics)
parts of the body   (*see* bone, brain, circulation,
   digestive system, ear, enzymes, eyes, feet, gland,
   hair, head, hormone, muscle, nerve, nose,
   respiratory system, teeth, toes)
pasta
pasta dishes
pastimes   (*see* games[1])
pastry
perfume
Persian
pertaining
Peru
Pharmaceutical Society
Pharmacopoeia Britannica
Philippines
Philological Society
philosophy
   (*see also* belief)
Philosophy, Politics and Economics
phobias   (*see* fear)
photograph (of)   (*see* write)
photography
physician
   (*see also* diseases, surgery)

physiologist   (*see* physician)
physics
pigs
pigeon
pigments   (*see* dyes)
pilot
pirate
Planck's constant
planets   (*see* astronomy)
plants
   (*see also* cacti, cereal, ferns, flower, fungi,
   grasses, palm, pulses, seaweed, shrubs, timber,
   trees)
plant diseases
plant pests   (*see* plant diseases)
playwrights   (*see* dramatists)
poetic
   (*see also* Burns, Milton, old, Scott, Shakespeare,
   Spenser)
poets
poison
Poland
police
Polynesian
porcelain   (*see* china)
Portugal
potato   (*see* vegetables)
potentate   (*see* leader)
poultry dishes
power
prayer
   (*see also* beliefs)
precious stones   (*see* gems, minerals)
presidents (US)
prime ministers (UK)
prince   (*see* leader)
printing
   (*see also* write)
producing   (*see* bearing)
proposer of   (*see* discoveries)
proteins
psychiatry   (*see* psychology)
psychology
public
Puerto Rico
pulses
Qatar
quarter
quasi-stellar object
Quebec
queen
rabbit
radio
railway
rearing
record (of)   (*see* write)

Index of headwords

Red Indian
relating to   (*see* pertaining)
religions   (*see* beliefs)
religious leader   (*see* church — personnel, leader)
reproduction (of)   (*see* beginning)
resident
resin   (*see* gum)
respiratory system
reverence for   (*see* worship)
rhetoric
(*see also* language)
Rhodesia
(*see also* Zimbabwe)
rice
rivers
rock
(*see also* geography, mineral, stone)
rockets   (*see* missiles, space)
Roman
(*see also* Latin)
Romania
room
rope
Royal
Royal Air Force
royal family   (*see* house)
Royal Marines
Royal Navy
rubber
rug
Rugby football
rule (by)   (*see* power)
ruler   (*see* leader)
Russia
Rwanda
sacred
sailor
(*see also* Royal Navy)
St Lucia
St Vincent
saint's day   (*see* holidays)
salad   (*see* vegetables)
Sanskrit
(*see also* Hindu, Indian)
Sao Tome
satellites, artificial   (*see* space)
satellites, natural   (*see* astronomy)
sauce
Saudi Arabia   (*see* Arabia)
sausage
Scandinavian
(*see also* Norse)
science   (*see* acids, anthropology, archaeology, astronomy, biology, chemistry, computing, discoveries, economics, electric, elements,

enzymes, gases, geography, inventors, law[2], mathematics, measuring instrument, meteorology, nuclear reactors, observatory, oceanography, physics, psychology, radio, scientific instrument, space, surgery)
science of   (*see* study)
scientific instrument
(*see also* measuring instruments)
Scotland
(*see also* Scottish)
Scott, Sir Walter
Scottish
script   (*see* alphabet)
sculpture
seaweed
secret
semi-precious stones   (*see* gems)
Senegal
senior
sergeant
servant
seven
seventy
sewing
Seychelles
Shakespeare
Shakespeare's people
Shakespeare's plays (titles and characters)
shapes
sheep
shellfish
Shinto
(*see also* Japanese)
ship[1] (types)
ship[2] (terms)
(*see also* rope, boats, sailor)
shoes   (*see* footwear)
showjumping
shrubs
Siamese
Sierra Leone
Sikh
(*see also* belief, Indian)
Singapore
six
sixteen
sixth
sixty
skating
skiing
snakes
snooker
soccer   (*see* football)
Society
soldier
solicitor

Somalia
son of
soup
South Africa
    (*see also* African)
South America
South Australia
South Island
South Pole
Soviet Union
    (*see also* Russia)
space
Spain
Spanish
special
speech   (*see* language, rhetoric)
Spenser, Edmund
spice
spiders   (*see* insects[1])
spirit
spectre   (*see* spirit)
sport   (*see* American football, athletes, baseball,
    boxing, bullfighting, chess, cricket, cycling,
    fencing, fishing, games, golf, gymnastics, motor
    racing, motor rallying, mountain, showjumping,
    skating, skiing, snooker, surfing, swimming,
    tennis, yachting)
square
Sri Lanka   (*see* Ceylon)
standard
stars
state[1]
state[2] (USA)
stew
stone
    (*see also* building construction, minerals, rocks)
street
student
study
    (*see also* pertaining, write)
Sudan
sugar
Sun   (*see* astronomy)
surfing
surgeon   (*see* physician)
surgery
surgical instruments   (*see* surgery)
Surinam(e)
swamp
Swaziland
Sweden
sweets
swimming
Swiss
Switzerland
sword

Syriac
Syrian
Taiwan
Tanganyika
tanks
Tanzania
tea
teeth
telescope   (*see* observatory)
temple   (*see* church—buildings)
ten
tennis
tenth
Thailand
    (*see also* Siamese)
theatre
theologian
    (*see also* church—personnel)
thirteen
thirty
thousand
three
Tibetan
timber
Titans   (*see* gods)
toasts
toes
Togo
Tonga
tools
Uganda
Ulster
united
universal
university
Uruguay
US(A)   (*see* America, states)
USSR
    (*see also* Russia)
Vanuatu
vegetable
vegetable dishes
vehicle
    (*see also* motor car)
veins   (*see* circulation)
Venetian
Venezuela
verse
vestments   (*see* church — garments)
Victoria
video
Vietnam
virtues
violin
vitamin
volcano

Index of headwords

volunteer
Wales
want of, etc   (*see* without)
water sports   (*see* games[1])
waterfall
weapon
weather   (*see* meteorology)
weight
Welsh
West Indian
Western Samoa
whale
which
wind
wine
winter sports   (*see* games[1]))
Wise Men
without
woman
   (*see also* girls)
words   (*see* rhetoric)
   (*see also* language)
world
worship
   (*see also* belief)
write
writers

A

Abyssinian

baboon	GELADA
capital	ADDIS ABABA
cereal	TOCUSSO
coin	BIRR, CENT, TALARI
grass	TEF(F)
insect	ZEBIB, ZIMB
king	NEGUS
language	AMHARIC, GEEZ, GIZ
measures	
—1 oz	OKET
—2 lb	NATR
—100 lb	KANTAR
parliament	SHENGO
patriarch	ABUNA
prince	RAS
self-governing towns	KABELE, KEBELE

acids

abscisic acid	ABSCISIN, DORMIN
acetic acid	ETHANOIC ACID
acetylsalicylic acid	ASPIRIN
acid linking chains	
in proteins	AMINO-ACID
amino-acetic acid	GLYCIN(E), GLYCOCOLL
amino-acid	ALANINE, ARGININE
	ASPARAGINE, ASPARTIC, CYSTEINE
	CYSTINE, GLUTAMIC, GLUTAMINE
	GLYCINE, HISTIDINE, ISO-LEUCINE
	LEUCINE, LYSINE, METHIONINE
	PHENYLALANINE, PROLINE, SERINE
	THREONINE, TYROSINE
	TRYPTOPHAN, VALINE
—in	
casein	METHIONINE
eggs	PHENYLALANINE
fish	HISTIDINE
milk	PHENYLALANINE
proteins	PROLINE
thyroid	THYROXIN(E)
wool	METHIONINE
amino-succinic acid	ASPARAGINIC ACID
	ASPARTIC ACID
aqua fortis	NITRIC ACID
aqueous sulphuric acid	AQ
ascorbic acid	CEVITAMIC ACID
	VITAMIN C
asparaginic acid	AMINOSUCCINIC ACID
	ASPARTIC ACID

aspartic acid	AMINOSUCCINIC ACID
	ASPARAGINIC ACID
aspirin	(ACETYL)SALICYLIC ACID
azoimide	HYDRAZOIC ACID
baking powder	TARTARIC
barbital	DIETHYLBARBITURIC ACID
	VERONAL
based on sulphur	THIO-ACID
	THIOCYANIC ACID
	THIOSULPHURIC ACID
bases forming amino-acid	TRIPLET
behenic acid	DOCOSANOIC ACID
benzoic acid	BENZENECARBOXYLIC ACID
boracic acid	(ORTHO)BORIC ACID
boric acid	BORACIC ACID
both acid and base	AMPHOTERIC
breaks down glucose	PYRUVIC ACID
butanedioic acid	SUCCINIC ACID
butanoic acid	BUTYRIC ACID
butenoic acid	CROTONIC ACID
cacodylic acid	DIMETHYL ARSINIC ACID
caproic acid	HEXANOIC ACID
carbolic acid	PHENOL
carbon dioxide and	
water	CARBONIC ACID
Caro's acid	PER(MONO)SULPHURIC ACID
cevitamic acid	ASCORBIC ACID, VITAMIN C
chain of	
—amino-acids	POLYPEPTIDE
—nucleotides	NUCLEIC ACID
chrysophanic acid	RHEIN
citric acid cycle	KREBS CYCLE
colourless solid	LACTIC ACID
	METAPHOSPHORIC ACID
compound of	
—tin	STANNIC ACID
—two amino-acids	PEPTIDE
—several amino-acids	POLYPEPTIDE
container for	CARBOY
containing carboxyl	
group(s)	(DI)CARBOXYLIC ACID
copper sulphate	BLUE VITRIOL
corrosive	AQUA FORTIS, AQUA REGIA
	HYDROCHLORIC, METHACRYLIC
	NITRIC, SELENIC, SULPHURIC
crotonic acid	BUTENOIC ACID
cyanuric acid	TRICYANIC ACID
description of acids	
based on valency	LEWIS ACID
diethylbarbituric acid	BARBITOL, VERONAL
dimethyl arsenic acid	CACODYLIC ACID
disinfectant	CARBOLIC ACID, PHENOL
docosanoic acid	BEHENIC ACID
dodecanoic acid	LAURIC ACID
dormin	ABSCISIC ACID, ABSCISIN
ethanedioic acid	OXALIC ACID

ethanoic acid	ACETIC ACID
excreted by primates, birds and reptiles	URIC ACID
fatty acid	ERUCIC ACID, PROPANOIC ACID PROPIONIC ACID, PROSTAGLANDIN STEARIC ACID, TRIGLYCERIDE
ferrous sulphate	GREEN VITRIOL
folic acid	PTEROYLGLUTAMIC ACID
formic acid	METHANOIC ACID
from/in	
—animal tissues	PANTOTHENIC ACID
—ants	FORMIC ACID
—apples	MALIC ACID
—argol	TARTARIC ACID
—bacterial metabolism	LACTIC ACID
—bile	GLYCOCHOLIC ACID TAUROCHOLIC ACID
—bran	PANTOTHENIC ACID
—breakdown of glucose	LACTIC ACID
—carbohydrates	LAEVULI(NI)C ACID
—castor oil	RICINOLEIC ACID SUBERIC ACID
—cells	DEOXYRIBONUCLEIC ACID, DNA RIBONUCLEIC ACID, RNA
—in DNA	NUCLEIC ACID
—electrolysis of brine	HYDROCHLORIC ACID MURIATIC ACID SPIRITS OF SALT
—ergot	LYSERGIC ACID
—fruit	CITRIC ACID
—fumitory	FUMARIC ACID HYDROXYSUCCINIC ACID MALIC ACID
—fungi	GIBBERELLIC ACID
—galactose	MUCIC ACID
—gallnuts	TANNIC ACID, TANNIN
—genes	DEOXYRIBONUCLEIC ACID DNA
—glucose	GLUCONIC ACID
—glycerides	OELIC ACID
—glycerol	GLYCERIC ACID
—gouty joints	URIC ACID
—grapes	TARTARIC ACID
—gum	MUCIC ACID
—hydrogen chloride	HYDROCHLORIC ACID
—malic acid	MALEIC ACID
—milk	LACTIC ACID
—mustard seed	ERUCIC ACID
—naphthalene	PHTHALIC ACID
—palm-oil	PALMITIC ACID
—peanut oil	ARACH(ID)IC ACID
—phosphorus pentoxide	PYROPHOSPHORIC ACID
—plants	FORMIC ACID PANTOTHENIC ACID
—rancid butter	BUTANOIC ACID BUTYRIC ACID
—rape seed	ERUCIC ACID
—rice	PANTOTHENIC ACID
—seaweed	ALGINIC ACID
—sugar beet	AMINOSUCCINIC ACID ASPARAGINIC ACID ASPARTIC ACID
—sumach	TANNIC ACID, TANNIN
—tea	TANNIC ACID
—thymus	THYMONUCLEIC ACID
—urine	URIC ACID
—vegetable oils	LINOLE(N)IC ACID
—vinegar	ACETIC
—wallflowers	ERUCIC ACID
—wood	PYROLIGNEOUS ACID
—wood sorrel	OXALIC ACID
fuming sulphuric acid	OLEUM
gallic acid	TRIHYDROXYBENZOIC ACID
gelatinous mixture from silicate	SILICIC ACID
glycin(e)	AMINOACETIC ACID AMINOETHANOIC ACID GLYCOCOLL
glycocoll	AMINOACETIC ACID AMINOETHANOIC ACID, GLYCIN(E)
growth	
—acid	OROTIC ACID, VITAMIN B
—regulator	GIBBERELLIC ACID
growth-inhibiting hormone in plants	ABSCISIC ACID ABSCISIN, DORMIN
having	
—one hydrogen atom	MONOBASIC ACID
—two hydrogen atoms	DIBASIC ACID
—three hydrogen atoms	TRIBASIC ACID
hexadecanoic acid	PALMITIC ACID
hexanoic acid	CAPROIC ACID
hydrated tungsten trioxide	TUNGSTIC ACID
hydrazoic acid	AZOIMIDE
hydrochloric acid	MURIATIC ACID SPIRITS OF SALT
—with nitric acid	AQUA REGIA
hydrocyanic acid	HYDROGEN CYANIDE PRUSSIC ACID
hydrogen	
—bromide dissolved in water	HYDROBROMIC ACID
—cyanide	HYDROCYANIC ACID PRUSSIC ACID
—fluoride dissolved in water	HYDROFLUORIC ACID
—iodide dissolved in water	HYDRIODIC ACID
hydroxypropanoic acid	LACTIC ACID
hydroxysuccinic acid	MALIC ACID

hygroscopic liquid	PERCHLORIC ACID
hypothetical	CHLORIC ACID
	CHLOROUS ACID, CHROMIC ACID
	ISOCYANIC ACID, MANGANIC ACID
	PERBORIC ACID, PERMANGANIC ACID
indicator of	LITMUS PAPER
iodine and nitric acid	IODIC ACID
isomer of maleic acid	FUMARIC ACID
lactic acid	HYDROXYPROPANOIC ACIC
lauric acid	DODECANOIC ACID
linole(n)ic acid	VITAMIN F
malic acid	HYDROXYSUCCINIC ACID
malonyl urea	BARBITURIC ACID
methanoic acid	FORMIC ACID
molecule containing	
genetic code	NUCLEIC ACID
muriatic acid	HYDROCHLORIC ACID
	SPIRITS OF SALT
neutraliser	ALKALI
niacin	NICOTINIC ACID, P-P FACTOR
nicotinic acid	NIACIN, P-P FACTOR
nitric acid	AQUA FORTIS
nonanoic acid	PELARGONIC ACID
nucleic acid with	
—protein	NUCLEO-PROTEIN
—ribose	RIBONUCLEIC ACID, RNA
octadecanoic acid	STEARIC ACID
oil of vitriol	SULPHURIC ACID
	VITRIOL
organic acids	FATTY ACIDS
orotic acid	VITAMIN B
orthoboric acid	BORACIC ACID
oxalic acid	ETHANEDIOIC ACID
palmitic acid	HEXADECANOIC ACID
pantothenic acid	VITAMIN B
pelargonic acid	NONANOIC ACID
pentanoic acid	VALERIC ACID
permonosulphic acid	CARO'S ACID
phenol	CARBOLIC ACID
picric acid	TRINITROPHENOL
poison	HYDROCYANIC, PRUSSIC
—gas	CYANIC ACID, CYANOGEN
P-P factor	NIACIN, NICOTINIC ACID
propanoic acid	PROPIONIC ACID
prussic acid	HYDROCYANIC ACID
	HYDROGEN CYANIDE
pteroylglutamic acid	FOLIC ACID
rhein	CHRYSOPHANIC ACID
smelling like	
—bitter almonds	HYDROCYANIC ACID
	HYDROGEN CYANIDE
	PRUSSIC ACID
—cheese	CAPROIC ACID
	HEXANOIC ACID
spirits of salt	HYDROCHLORIC ACID
	MURIATIC ACID

stearic acid	OCTADECANOIC ACID
	TRISTEARIN
succinic acid	BUTANEDIOIC ACID
sugar of lead	LEAD ACETATE
sulphur dioxide in water	SULPHUROUS ACID
sulphuric acid	(OIL OF) VITRIOL
tautomer of cyanic acid	ISOCYANIC ACID
tricyanic acid	CYANURIC CID
trihydroxybenzoic acid	GALLIC ACID
trinitrophenol	PICRIC ACID
tristearin	STEARIC ACID
universal solvent	ALCAHEST, ALKAHEST
unstable acids	PERIODIC ACIDS
used	
—as	
antiseptic	BORACIC ACID
	MANDELIC ACID
	(ORTHO)BORIC ACID
	SALICYLIC ACID
aspirin	SALICYLIC ACID
disinfectant	CARBOLIC ACID
	FLUOROSILICIC ACID
	HYDROFLUOROSILICIC ACID
	PHENOL
flavouring	BUTANOIC ACID
	BUTYRIC ACID, CAPROIC ACID
	GLUTAMIC ACID
	HEXANOIC ACID
food-preservative	BENZOIC ACID
oxidising agent	BROMIC ACID
	CARO'S ACID
	PER(MONO)SULPHURIC ACID
preservative	MALEIC ACID
reducing	
agent	HYPOPHOSPHOROUS ACID
rocket	
propellant	FUMING NITRIC ACID
solvent	PHENYL(ACETIC) ACID
stain in microscopy	OSMIC ACID
wart-remover	CHLOR(O)ACETIC ACID
weedkiller	CACODYLIC ACID
	DIMETHYL ARSINIC ACID
wood preservative	FLUOROSILICIC ACID
	HYDROFLUOROSILICIC ACID
—for	
cleaning metals	GLUCONIC ACID
flavouring	
drinks	ORTHOPHOSPHORIC ACID
glass-etching	HYDROFLUORIC ACID
	MORDANT
stimulating growth	
of plants	GIBBERELLIC ACID
treating	
—anaemia	FOLIC ACID
	PTEROYLGLUTAMIC ACID
	MORDANT

—burns	PICRIC ACID
—in	
acrylic resins	ACRYLIC ACID
baking powder	FUMARIC ACID
	TARTARIC ACID
barbiturates	MALONIC ACID
bleaching	HYPOCHLOROUS ACID
	OXALIC ACID
calico-printing	TARTARIC ACID
candles	STEARIC ACID
cosmetics	BEHENIC ACID
	DOCOSANOIC ACID
	DODECANOIC ACID
	LAURIC ACID, STEARIC ACID
detergents	DODECANOIC ACID
	LAURIC ACID
dyes	CACODYLIC ACID
	CARBOLIC ACID
	CHLOR(O)ACTIC ACID
	DIMETHYL ARSENIC ACID
	FORMIC ACID, LACTIC ACID
	MALEIC ACID, OXALIC ACID
	PHENOL, PICRIC ACID
	PHTHALIC ACID, SUCCINIC ACID
	SULPHANILIC ACID
	TARTARIC ACID
effervescent	
—drinks	TARTARIC ACID
—salts	CITRIC ACID
electroplating	FORMIC ACID
explosives	FUMING SULPHURIC ACID
	OLEUM, PICRIC ACID
fertilisers	ORTHOPHOSPHORIC ACID
histamines	HISTIDINE
hydrogen	
peroxide	PERDISULPHURIC ACID
ink	GALLIC ACID
	TRIHYDROXYBENZOIC ACID
	OXALIC ACID, TANNIC ACID
	TANNIN
lacquers	SUCCINIC ACID
lamp filaments	TUNGSTIC ACID
lead accumulators	SULPHURIC ACID
LSD	LYSERGIC ACID
lubricants	ARACH(ID)IC ACID
medicine	PHTHALIC ACID
metal polish	OXALIC ACID
nylon	ADIPIC ACID
organic synthesis	FUMING NITRIC ACID
perfume	CINNAMIC ACID
	PENTANOIC ACID
	VALERIC ACID
	PHTHALIC ACID
phosphites	PHOSPHOROUS ACID
plasticisers	ISOPHTHALIC ACID
	SEBACIC ACID

plastics	CARBOLIC ACID
	LAEVULI(NI)C ACID, PHENOL
	SUBERIC ACID
resins	FUMARIC ACID, MALEIC ACID
	SEBACIC ACID
	TEREPHTHALIC ACID
soap	DODECANOIC ACID, LAURIC ACID
	PALMITIC ACID, RICINOLEIC ACID
	STEARIC ACID
synthetic resins	ISOPHTHALIC ACID
synthesis	MUCIC ACID, TOLUIC ACID
—of	
barbiturates	BARBITURIC ACID
organic	
substances	BUTENOIC ACID
	CROTONIC ACID
	CYANURIC ACID
	TRICYANIC ACID
synthetic fibres	TEREPHTHALIC ACID
tanning	FORMIC ACID
	GALLIC ACID, LACTIC ACID
	TANNIC ACID, TANNIN
	TRIHYDROXYBENZOIC ACID
waxes	BEHENIC ACID
	DOCOSANOIC ACID
—to	
flavour drinks	ORTHOPHOSPHORIC ACID
stimulate plant	
growth	GIBBERELLIC ACID
treat anaemia	FOLIC ACID
	PTEROYLGLUTAMIC ACID
valeric acid	PENTANOIC ACID
veronal	BARBITAL
	DIETHYLBARBITURIC ACID
vinegar	ACETIC ACID, ETHANOIC ACID
vitamin A	RETINOIC ACID
B	FOLIC ACID
	OROTOIC ACID
	PANTOTHENIC ACID
	PTEROYLGLUTAMIC ACID
C	ASCORBIC ACID
F	LINOLE(N)IC ACID
M	FOLIC ACID
	PTEROYLGLUTAMIC ACID
vitriol	OIL OF VITRIOL
	SULPHURIC ACID
—blue	COPPER SULPHATE
—green	FERROUS SULPHATE
—white	ZINC SULPHATE
white	
—crystalline	MARONIC ACID
—vitriol	ZINC SULPHATE
yellow	
—crystal	PICRIC ACID, VANADIC ACID
—crystalline substance	MOLYBDIC ACID
—powder	IODIC ACID

zinc sulphate	WHITE VITRIOL
	(*see also* **chemistry** — salt of)

Adam

Adam (and Eve)	BELIEVE
Adam's ale/wine	WATER
Adam's first wife	LILITH
Adam's apple	LARYNX

address

mode of address for notables:

ambassador	EXCELLENCY, HE
archbishop	GRACE
archdeacon	VEN(ERABLE)
baron	LORD
bishop	LORD
cardinal	EMINENCE
—old	MOST ILLUSTRIOUS
dean	VERY REV(EREND)
duke	GRACE
earl	LORD
judge	LORD
king	MAJESTY
knight	SIR
magistrate	HONOUR
marquess	LORD MARQUESS
mayor	WORSHIP
Member of Parliament	HON(OURABLE)
pope	HOLINESS
prince	HIGHNESS
Privy Councillor	RIGHT HON(OURABLE)
queen	MAJESTY
vicar	REV(EREND)

Afghan(istan) AFG, PATHAN

capital	KABUL
clan	KHEL
coins	AFGHANI, AMANIA, PULS
greatcoat	POS(H)TEEN
language	PASHTO, PASHTU
	PAKHTO, PAKHTU
	PUSHTO(O), PUSHTU
native tribe	AFRIDI, KAFIR, PATHAN
sport	BUZ KASHI

African

including: Afrikaans

aardvark	ANT-BEAR, EARTH-HOG
	GROUND-HOG
aardwolf	EARTHWOLF
acacia	DOORN-BOOM
Afrikaans	TAAL
Afrikaner	BOER, BOOR, DUTCHMAN
airline	AIR AFRIQUE, SAA, ZAS
amaryllis	BELLADONNA
amulet	GREEGREE, GRI(S)GRI(S)
ant	
—bear	AARDVARK, EARTH-HOG
	GROUND-HOG
—eater	PANGOLIN

ape	CHIMPANZEE, GORILLA
aromatic seeds	GRAINS OF PARADISE
ass (extinct)	QUAGGA
assembly	RAAD
—of elders	KGLOTA
back of beyond	BUNDU
badger	RATEL
barbecue	BRAAIVLEIS
baobab	CREAM-OF-TARTAR TREE
	MONKEY-BREAD
bay	BAAI
beer	POMBE
begone!	VOETSAK
beryl	HELIODOR
bird	AASVOGEL, ADJUTANT-BIRD
	BALAENICEPS, BEEFEATER, BUPHAGA
	CAPE PIGEON, COUNCAL
	GUINEA-FOWL, HAMMERHEAD
	HAMMERKOP, HONEY-BIRD
	HONEY-GUIDE, LARK-HEELED CUCKOO
	MARABOU(T), MESSENGER, OSTRICH
	OX-PECKER, PRINIA, PLANTAIN-EATER
	SECRETARY-BIRD, SENEGAL, SHOE-BILL
	T(O)URACO, UMBER(-BIRD), UMBRETTE
	WHALE-HEAD, WHIDAH-BIRD
	WHYDAH-BIRD, WIDOW-BIRD
biscuit	SOETKOEKIE
biting spider	TARANTULA
blood-flower	HAEMANTHUS
body of warriors	IMPI
bracelet (money)	MANILLA
brandy	CAPE SMOKE, DOP
bread	KISRA
Briton	UITLANDER
bucket	EMMER
bugbear	MUMBO-JUMBO
bustard	DIKKOP, PAAUW, PAU
butter-tree	KANYA, KARITE, SHEA
camp	BOMA, LAAGER, LAER
cape	KAAP
Cape	
—Dutch	TAAL
—gooseberry	GOLDENBERRY, PHYSALIS
—hyrax	KLIPDAS, ROCK-BADGER
—Province	CP
carrier by wagon	TRANSPORT-RIDER
castle	CASBAH, KASBA(H)
cattle	ANKOLE
—disease	NAGANA
—pound	SCHUT
channel	SLOOT, SLUIT
charm	GREEGREE
	GRI(S)GRI(S), JU-JU
chief	CAID, KAID
civet	LINSANG, MEERCAT
	MEERKAT, NANDINE, SURICATE

cloak	JELLABA
	(*see also* **Arabia**)
clout	LAP(PIE), LAPJE
club	KERRIE, KIERIE, KIRI
	KNOBKERRIE
coin	(KRUGER)RAND, RD
—threepenny bit	TICK(E)Y
col	NEK
coney	DASSIE
coral	ZEETAK
—tree	KAFFIR-BOOM
cormorant	DUIKER, DUYKER
corral	KRAAL
cotton dress	KANGA
coucal	SWAMP PHEASANT
crown of rock on	
mountain top	KRANS, KRAN(T)Z
cup	BEKER
dead person still drawing	
wages as if alive	DIEMAN
deity of the python	ZOMBI(E)
delicious	LEKKER
deposit	LAY-BY(E)
desert plant	CAMEL'S THORN
detect by witchcraft	SMELL OUT
diseases	(*see* **disease**)
dish	COUSCOUS(OU), CUSCUS
	KHUSKHUS
ditch	SLOOT
dog	BASENJI
	RHODESIAN RIDGEBACK
domesticated animal	CAMEL
dove	NAMAQUA
dried	
—apricots	MEBOS
—meat	BILTONG
drink	POMBE, SKOKIAAN
	TOMBO
—after sunset	SUNDOWNER
drug	CAPE DAGGA
	RED DAGGA
durra	GUINEA-CORN
Dutch/English	KITCHEN DUTCH
eagle	BATELEUR, BERGHAAN
ear of maize	MEALIE
earth-wolf	AARDWOLF
edible	
—pods	OKRA
—tuber	ELEPHANT'S-FOOT
	HOTTENTOT BREAD
Englishman (soldier)	ROOINEK
esparto-grass	(H)ALFA
expedition	SAFARI, TREK
extinct wild ass	QUAGGA
farm cart	SCOTCH CART
fenced enclosure	BOMA

fetish	GREE-GREE
	GRI(S)GRI(S), JU-JU
fine	MOOI
fish	BARRACOUTA, DORAS
	KABELJOU(W), PANCHAX
	POLYPTERUS, SNOEK, SNOOK
	TILAPIA
florin	SCOTCHMAN
flowers	CHINCHERINCHEE
	CHINKERINCHEE
	CINERARIA, NEMESIA
	NERINE, STRELITZIA
fly	BROMMER, BRUMMER
	KIVU, TSETSE
folk-music	KWELA
ford	DRIFT
foreigner	UITLANDER
fort	CASBAH, KASBA(H), SCHANS
fox	FENNEC, ZERDA
freedom	UHURU
French soldier's hat	CHECHIA
frog	CAPE NIGHTINGALE
	PLATANNA
fruit	A(C)KEE, BITO, DIKA
	HOTTENTOT FIG, NAARTIE
	NAR(R)AS, NARTJIE
	SHEA-NUT, WILD MANGO
garden plot	ERF
garment	KANZU
gin	SQUARE-FACE
glass beads	AGGRI, AGGRY
go away!	VOETSEK
gorge	KLOOF
god	MUMBO-JUMBO
gold ore	BANKET
good	MOOI
goosefoot	AIZOON
government	SERKALI
grain	C(O)USC(O)S, FUNDI
grape	H(A)ANEPOOT, HONEYPOT
grass	FUNDI, GUINEA-GRASS
	MILLET PENNISETUM
—country	VELD(T)
green rock	VERDITE
greet	WISH
greeting	JAMBO
ground	FLOOR
guitar	SANCHO, SANKO
gully	DONGA
gum-resin	OLIBANUM
gun	ROER
hair ornament	HEAD-RING
headman	CABOCEER
hemp	IFE, SISAL
heron/stork	HAMMERKOP, UMBRETTE
high grassland	KAR(R)OO

hill	BERG, KOP(PIE), KOPJE
hippopotamus	RIVER-HORSE, ZEEKOE
honey-badger	RATEL
hooligan	TSOTSI
horse disease	NAGANA
horse's canter	TRIPPLE
Hottentot	
—fig	MESEMBRIANTHEMUM
	MESEMBRYANTHEMUM
—god	PRAYING MANTIS
hut	KRAAL, KYA, RONDAVEL
hyena	TIGER-WOLF
hyrax	DASSIE
immature locust	VOETGANGER
Indian	GOAN
infantryman	VOETGANGER
insect	GOGGA
insectivore	ELEPHANT SHREW
	GOLDEN MOLE, OTTER-SHREW
iris	FREESIA
island(s)	EILAND(EN)
it is not	AIKONA
ivory	PANGANI
jackal	DIEB
jam	KONFYT
javelin	ASSAGAI, ASSEGAI, ASSEGAY
kaffir	
—boom	ERYTHRINA
—bread	PALM-PITH
—English	KITCHEN KAFFIR
knife	PANGA
lake	MEER, NYANZA
language	AFRIKAANS, BANTU, BASUTO
	BASUTU, CAFFRE, CAPE DUTCH
	HERERO, HOTTENTOT, IBO, KABYLE
	KAFFER, KAF(F)IR, MANDINGO
	SWAHILI, TAAL, TSWANA, TUAREG
	TWI, (UNION)SHONA, X(H)OSA
	YORUBA, ZULU
	(*see also* races *below*)
	(*see also separate entry*)
legislative assembly	VOLKSRAAD
lemur	AGWANTIBO, POTTO
leopard	TIGER
liberal	VERLIGTE
lieutenant	FIELD-CORNET
lily of the Nile	PIG-LILY
lizard	GECKO, (I)GUANA
	MONITOR, SKINK
locust before wings grow	VOETGANGER
look out	PAS OP
loose tunic	DASHIKI, KANZU
Lord's supper	NACHTMAAL, NAGMAAL
low-lying ground	VLEI, VLY
lynx	CARACAL
mackerel	ALBACORE, ALBICORE

magistrate	FIELD-CORNET, LANDDROS(T)
maize	MEALIES
mango	DIKA
mantis	HOTTENTOT'S GOD
master	BAAS, BWANA
—race theory	APARTHEID, BAASKAP
measures	
—2 acres	MORGEN
—7½ gallons	ANKER
—31 gallons	AUM
—3 bushels	MUID
—cloth	JACKTAN
medicinal plant	BUCHU, BUCKU, CALUMBA
millet	DARI, D(O)URA, D(H)URRA
mixed race	BASTARD, BASTER
	(CAPE) COLOURED, GRIQUA
mongoose	MEERCAT, MEERKAT
Moslem	SENUSSI
mountain	BERG
—pass	NEK, POORT
—range	GEBERGTE
mud hut	TEMBE
multi-coloured	BONT
musical instrument	BALAFON, GORA(H)
	GOURA, KONA
	KORA, HARP-LUTE, ZANZE
narrow water-channel	SLUIT
national independence	UHURU
native	
—hut	RONDAVEL
—soldiers	ASKARI, IMPI
Negrito	NEGRILLO
no	AIKONA
nomadic race	TUAREG
nothing at all	NIKS-NIE, NIX-NIE
nut-tree	COLA, KOLA
object of superstition	JU-JU
open country	VELD(T)
open-sided bus	MAMMY-WAGON
one of	
—conservative views	VERKRAMPTE
—liberal views	VERLIGTE
orange	NAARTJE, NARTJIE
orchid	DISA
ostrich	STRUTHIO
ox-pecker	BEEF-EATER, BUPHAGA
palm	DOOM-PALM, D(O)UM-PALM
	PALMYRA
	(*see also separate entry*)
—civet	NANDINE
—wine	TOMBO
pangolin	MANIS
parliament	RAAD
pass	NEK, POORT
—book	REFERENCE BOOK
peasant	KOPI

pedestrian	VOETGANGER	—horse	HIPPOPOTAMUS
pedlar	SMOUCH, SMOUS(E)	riverside plant	PALMIET
	SMOUSER	robe	KANZU
perennial herb	LASERPICIUM	rock-badger	CAPE HYRAX, KLIPDAS
periwinkle	STROPHANTHUS	rue	HARMALA, HARMEL
petrel	CAPE PIGEON	rug	CAROSSE, KAROSS
pheasant	FRANCOLIN	Rugby player	SPRINGBOK
pioneer	VOORTREKKER	runner	CHEETAH, OSTRICH
plain	VELD(T)	sacrament	NACHTMAAL, NAGMAAL
plant	GOA BEAN, GRAPPLE-PLANT	sausage	BOEREWORS
	ROSE OF JERICHO	scaly ant-eater	MANIS, PANGOLIN
	WELWITSCHIA	scram!	VOETSEK
—extract	NIGER-OIL	sea	MEER
plateau	PLATO	secretary-bird	MESSENGER
platform	STOEP	segregation of races	APARTHEID
pole for crossing river	RIVER-HORSE	separate development	APARTHEID
policeman	ASKARI	series of strata	KAR(R)OO
pool	VLEI, VLY	sesame	BENNE
porch	STOEP	shea-tree	KARITE
pounded maize	STAMP	sheriff	LANDDROS(T)
preacher	PREDIKANT	shrub	BUAZE, BUCHU, BUCKU, BWAZI
precipice	KRANS, KRAN(T)Z		PENTZIA, PROTEA
preserved fruit	KONFYT		SPEKBOOM, TEA-TREE
prickly pear	JOINTED CACTUS	sir	BWANA
public house	CANTEEN	sitting up (courtship)	UPSITTING
purslane tree	SPEKBOOM	skin blanket	CAROSSE, KAROSS
pygmy	NEGRITO	skunk	ZORILLA, ZORIL(LE)
pyrethrum	PELLITORY	small	
race	BANTU, BASUTO, BASUTU, BEJA	—garden	ERF
	BERBER, BUSHMEN, CAFFRE	—gift	BONSELLA
	GALLA, GRIQUA, HADENDOA	—orange	NA(A)RTJE
	HAMITE, HAUS(S)A, HERERO	—parrot	LOVE-BIRD
	HOTTENTOT, IBO, KABYLE	—piece of ground	ERF
	KAFFER, KAF(FIR), KIKUYU	snake	(see snakes)
	KROO, KRU, MASAI, MATABELE	snake-eating bird	SECRETARY-BIRD
	MANDINGO, SWANA	soldier	ASKARI, SPAHI
—theory	APARTHEID, BAASKAP	soldiers	IMPI
rag	LAP(PIE), LAPJE	sorghum	KAFFIR-CORN
rascal	SCHELM, SKELM	spear	ASSAGAI, ASSEGAI, ASSEGAY
ratel	HONEY-BADGER	spell	GREEGREE, GRI(S)GRI(S), JU-JU
ravine	DONGA, KLOOF	spider	BUTTON SPIDER
rawhide		spotted hyena	NANDI BEAR
—shoe	VELDSCHOEN, VEL(D)SKOEN	spring	BRON, FONTEIN
—string	RIEMPIE	squatter	BIWONER, BYWONER
—thong	REIM	squirrel	XERUS
remote country	BACK VELD(T), BUNDU	stinking flower	CARRION-FLOWER
resin	SANDARIC	stockade	BOMA
reward	BONSELLA	stork	MARABOU(T), SIMBIL
rhinoceros	KEITLOA	strawberry-tomato	CAPE GOOSEBERRY
ridge overlooking valley	RAND	tableland	KAR(R)OO
rifle-shooting competition	WAPINS(C)HAW	taffeta	ARIDAS
	WEAPON-S(C)HAW	tallow	ROKA
	WA(P)PENS(C)HAW	Teddy boy	DUCKTAIL
river	RIVIER	thorn	DOORN
	(see also rivers)	thorny plant	WAIT-A-BIT, WAIT-A-WHILE
—fish	POLYPTERUS		WAG-'N-BIETJIE

thug	TSOTSI	—dog	HYENA-DOG
tick	TAMPAN	—hog	WART-HOG
tiger-cat	BUSH-CAT, SERVAL	—pig	RIVER-HOG
timber	(*see separate entry*)	wine	CONSTANTIA
tip	BONSELLA	witch doctor	INYANGA, SANGOMA
toad	XENOPUS	woman's dress	KANGA
trade as pedlar	SMOUCH, SMOUS(E)	wooded veld	BUSHVELD(T), BOSCHVELD(T)
transport	KURVEY	Zulu king	CETEWAYO, CHAL(K)A, CHAKA
—rider	KURVEYOR		TCHAKA, INKOS, (I)NKOSI

tree ALOE, A(C)KEE, AMBATCH
BAOBAB, BERG-CEDAR, BITO
BOOM, BUBINGA, CAMWOOD, COLA
DATE PALM, FUNTUMIA, GUMBO
KOLA, LOTE, LOTOS, LOTUS
MOLI, MONKEY-BREAD TREE
MVULE, OBECHE, OKRA
PITH-TREE, PROTEA, SHEA
SILVER-TREE, SNEEZEWOOD
SOUR-GOURD, TARFA, TEAK
WA(GEN)BOOM, WILD MANGO
(*see also* **timber**)

trek-wagon	BUCK-WAGON	**agent**	AGT, SPY
tribal		administering estate	TRUSTEE
—conference	INDABA	acting in	
—councillor	INDUNA	—court	ADVOCATE, ATTORNEY
tribe	(*see* race *above*)		BARRISTER, PROCURATOR
tuber	ELEPHANT'S FOOT		SOLICITOR
	HOTTENTOT BREAD, TANIA	—spiritual court	PROCTOR
tulip-tree	SPATHODEA	agent Orange	DEFOLIATOR
turaco	LORY	agent's fee	COMMISSION
ultra-conservative	VERKRAMPTE	American	G-MAN
uncle	OOM	dealing in property	ESTATE AGENT, REALTOR
unknown animal	CATOBLEPAS	document authorising	
valley	DAL	agent	POWER OF ATTORNEY
vegetable	DOODY	deputy ruler	VICEGERENT, VICEREGENT
vehicle	CAPE CART		VICEREINE, VICEROY
verandah	STOEP	FBI	G-MAN
village	DORP, KRAAL	financial agent (Roman)	PROCURATOR
violet	SAINTPAULIA		QUAESTOR
viper	RIVER-JACK	go-between	INTERMEDIARY, PANDER(ER)
vulture	AASVOGEL		PIMP, PROCURER
wagon-trip	TREK	government agent	AMBASSADOR, EMISSARY
watercourse	SLOOT, SLUIT, SPRUIT	legal representative	
weaver-bird	GRENADIER, OX-BIRD	of company etc	SYNDIC
	QUELEA, TAHA, WHIDAH-BIRD	—at meetings	DELEGATE, PROXY
	WHYDAH-BIRD, WIDOW-BIRD	manager	
weight	OKA, ROTL	—for another	PROC(URA)TOR
well of water	BRON	—of estate	BAILIFF, REEVE, STEWARD
what's his name	DINGES, DINGUS	middleman	BROKER, FACTOR
whip	(S)JAMBOK	representative of	
white		—Australian state or	
—rulers	SERKALI	Canadian province	AGENT-GENERAL
—Teddy girl	SHEILA	—clergy	PROCTOR
wife purchase	LOBOLA	—principal	ASSIGNEE, COMMISSARY
wild			DEPUTY, PROXY, VICAR
—cat	CHAUS, CIVET	secret agent	DOUBLE AGENT, SPY
		secretly representing another	DUMMY, FRONT

aircraft
bombers/strike aircraft
—American BOSTON, BRONCO
DAUNTLESS, FLYING FORTRESS
HAVOC, HUDSON, HUSTLER, INTRUDER
KEYSTONE, LIBERATOR, MITCHELL
MUSTANG, PACKARD, SKYHAWK
STANDARD, STEALTH
STRATOFORTRESS, SUPERFORTRESS
THOMAS MORSE, THUNDERBOLT
THUNDERCHIEF, VIGILANTE

—British   AIRCO, AVRO, BATTLE
BLENHEIM, BUCCANEER, CANBERRA
CUCKOO, FOX, GUNBUS, HALIFAX
HANDLEY-PAGE, HARRIER, HAWK
LANCASTER, LINCOLN, MOSQUITO
STIRLING, SWORDFISH, VALIANT
VICTOR, VIMY, VULCAN
WELLESLEY, WELLINGTON
WIGHT
—European   EFA, TORNADO
—French   ALPHA JET, AMIOT, BLERIOT
BREGUET, CAUDRON, ETENDARD
FARMAN, MIRAGE, POTEZ
—German   AEG, DORNIER
FRIEDRICHSHAFEN, GOTHA
HEINKEL, JUNKERS, LVG, STUKA
STORMBIRD, STURMVOGEL, VAK
—Italian   ANSALDO, CAPRONI, POMILIO
SAVOIA, SIA
—Japanese   NAKAJIMA, VAL
—Russian   BACKFIRE, BADGER
BLACKJACK, BLINDER
BREWER, FIDDLER, FITTER
ILYA MOUROMETZ, ILYUSHIN
SUKHOI, TUPOLEV
—Spanish   HISPANO
—Yugoslav   GALEB, GULL
civil
—American   ARAVA, ATB
BEECH, BOEING, COMMUTER
CONVAIR, DAKOTA, DOUGLAS
ELECTRA, GULFSTREAM, JUMBO
LEARJET, MALLARD
MCDONNELL, MERLIN
METRO, STRATOLINER
(SUPER-)CONSTELLATION
TRISTAR, VEGA
—Australian   NOMAD
—Brazilian   BANDEIRANTE, BRASILIA
VECTOR
—British   AEROVAN, ALBATROSS
BRABAZON, BRITANNIA, CHALLENGER
(CANADA)DASH, CITATION, COMET
CONCORD, DOVE, ENSIGN
GEMINI, GULFSTREAM, HASTINGS
HERALD, HERMES, ISLANDER
JETSTREAM, ONE-ELEVEN, PHOENIX
RAPIDE, STATESMAN, TRIDENT
TRILANDER, TUDOR
VIKING, VISCOUNT
—Canadian   TWIN OTTER
—Czech   TURBOLET
—Dutch   FELLOWSHIP, FRIENDSHIP
—French   CARAVELLE, CONCORDE
CORVETTE, FALCON
FREGATE, MERCURE

—German   DORNIER, FOKKER
HANSA FAN JET, SKYSERVANT
—international   AIRBUS, AIRTECH
SAAB-FAIRCHILD
—Israeli   COMMODORE
—Russian   ANTONOV, BERIEV, CARELESS
CHARGER, CODLING, CONCORDSKI
FOXHOUND, ILYUSHIN
TUPOLEV, YAKOVLEV
—Spanish   AVIOCAR
early planes   ANTOINETTE, BLERIOT
DEMOISELLE, (GOLDEN) FLYER
JUNE BUG, PTERODACTYL, VOISIN
engine manufacturers
—American   GENERAL ELECTRIC
PRATT AND WHITNEY
—British   ROLLS-ROYCE
—French   SNECMA
—German   DAIMLER-BENZ
—Russian   SOLOVIEV
famous planes
—American president   AIR FORCE ONE
—dropped atom bomb   ENOLA GAY
—first
    commercial jetliner   COMET
    supersonic jetliner   CONCORD(E)
—Howard Hughes   SPRUCE GOOSE
—Jim Mollison   THE HEART'S CONTENT
—Kingsford Smith   SOUTHERN CROSS
—Lindbergh   SPIRIT OF ST LOUIS
—Lord Rothermere   BRITAIN FIRST
—solar-powered   SOLAR CHALLENGER
—Wiley Post   WINNIE MAY
—Wright brothers   FLYER
fighters/interceptors
—American   AIRABONITA, AIRACOBRA
AIRACOMET, AIRACUDA
BLACK WIDOW, BUFFALO
CORSAIR, CRUSADER
DELTA DART, EAGLE, FALCON
FREEDOM FIGHTER, HELLCAT
HORNET, KINGCOBRA, KITTYHAWK
LANCER, LUSAC, MOHAWK, MORSE
MUSTANG, PEASHOOTER, PHANTOM
SABRE, SHRIKE, STARFIGHTER
THUNDERBOLT, THUNDERCHIEF
TIGERCAT, TIGERSHARK, TOMCAT
WARHAWK, WILD WEASEL
—Argentinian   PUCARA
—Australian   BOOMERANG
—British   AIRCO, AVOCET, BAGSHOT
BEARDMORE, BEAUFIGHTER
BRISTOL BULLDOG, CAMEL
DEFIANT, DEMON, DESTROYER
DOLPHIN, FIREFLY, FURY, GAMECOCK
GAUNTLET, GLADIATOR, GREBE

HARRIER, HIPPO, HORNET, HOTSPUR
HUNTER, HURRICANE, KANGAROO
LIGHTNING, LINCOCK, MARTINSYDE
METEOR, NIGHTHAWK, PTERODACTYL
PUP, SALAMANDER, SCOUT, SE
SEA HAWK, SEA VIXEN, SEAFIRE
SISKIN, SNARK, SOPWITH, SNIPE
SPITFIRE, TEMPEST, TORNADO
TYPHOON, VAMPIRE, VENOM, WELKIN
WESTBURY, WHIRLWIND, WOODCOCK
—Czech   AVIA
—Dutch   KOOLHAVEN
—European   JAGUAR
—French   BEBE, BLOCH, CORSAIRE
DELANNE, HANRIOT, MILAN, MIRAGE
MORANE(-SAULNIER), NIEUPORT
PARASOL, RAFALE, SALMSON
(SUPER) ETENDARD
(SUPER) MIRAGE, SPAD SCOUT
VOISIN, WIBAULT
—German   ALBATROS(S), ARADO
ARROW, AVIATIK, BRANDENBERG
DFW, EINDEKKER, FALCON
FOCKE-WULF, FOKKER, HALBERSTADT
HANNOVER, KOMET, MESSERSCHMITT
MOSKITO, NATTER, OWL, PFALZ
PFIEL, PHONIX, ROLAND
RUMPLER, SALAMANDER
SCHWALBE, SIEMENS-(SCHUCKERT)
STARSTRUTTER, SWALLOW, TAUBE
UFAG, UHU, VIPER, VOLKSJAGER
—Italian   AMBROSINI, ANSALDO, CAPRONI
DARDO, FIAT, FALCO, FOLGORE
MERIDIONALI, PIAGGIO
REGGIANE, VIZZOLA
—Japanese   AURORA, BOLT OF LIGHT
DENKO, DRAGON KILLER, GALE
GEKKO, HAYABUSA, HAYATE, HIEN
HURRICANE, KIKKA, KYOKKO
MOONLIGHT, ORANGE BLOSSOM
PEREGRINE FALCON, RAIDEN
REPPU, SHIDEN(-KAI), SHUSUI
SWALLOW, SWINGING SWORD
THUNDERBOLT, TORYU
VIOLET LIGHTNING, ZERO(-SEN)
—South African   CHEETAH
—Swedish   DRAKEN, GRIPEN, VIGGEN
—Russian   ANADE, ANATRA, BEREZNIAK
FIDDLER, FIREBAR, FISHBED
FITTER, FLAGON, FLOGGER
FOXBAT, LAVOCHKIN
MIG, MIKOYAN
POLIKARPOV, SUKHOI
SHTURMOULK, YAK
—Yugoslav   IKARUS-ROGOZARSKI
HAWK, JASTREB

flying-boats
—American   BOEING, CATALINA
CURTISS, LARGE AMERICA
MALLARD, MARTIN
—British   EMPIRE, FELIXSTOWE
NORMAN THOMPSON
SUNDERLAND, WALRUS
—Canadian   CANADAIR
—German   DORNIER
—Japanese   SHIN MEIWA
—Russian   BERIEV, TCHAIKA
helicopters
—American   APACHE, BELL, BLACKHAWK
CHINOOK, COBRA
FAIRCHILD HILLER
HUGHES, HUEYCOBRA, IROQUOIS
JETRANGER, KAMAN SEASPRITE
MOJAVE, RANGER, SEABAT
SHAWNEE, SIKORSKY
SKYCRANE, TWIN TWO-TWELVE
VERTOL, WHIRLAWAY, WORK-HORSE
—Austrian   LOHNER
—British   AIRMARK WALLIS, AVRO
BELVEDERE, BRISTOL
CAMPBELL CRICKET
CIERVA ROTORCRAFT
DRAGONFLY, GYRODYNE
HELIPLANE, HOVERFLY, LYNX
ROTODYNE, SEAKING, SQUIRREL
SYCAMORE, WESTLAND
WHIRLWIND
—French   ALOUETTE, ARIEL
ASTAZOU, CHEETAH, DE MICHEN
DJINN, FRELON, GAZELLE
GYROPLANE, LAMA, PUMA, SPRITE
—German   BACHSTEIZE, DOBLHOFF
DRACHE, FLEITNER
FOCKE(-WULF)
—Russian   HIP, HIND, HOMER
HOODLUM, HOOK, HOPLITE
HORMONE, KAMOV
MIL, SWIDNIK, YAKOVLEV
—Spanish   AIR HORSE, CIERVA
PESCARA
light aircraft
—American   AEROSTAR, BEECHCRAFT
CESSNA, CITATION
GOLDEN EAGLE
LEARJET, MUSKETEER
PIPER NAVAJO, MERLIN
—Brazilian   IPANEMA
—British   FLYING FLEA, GIANT MOTH
GYPSY MOTH, ISLANDER
MEW GULL, NYMPH, PUSS MOTH
SILVER STREAK, TIGER MOTH
—Czech   TURBOLET, ZLIN

—French	DIPLOMATE, FALCON
	RALLYE
—German	HANSA FAN JET
—Italian	BRAVO, MARCHETTI
	OSCAR, PARTENAVIA
—New Zealand	AIRTOURER
—Romanian	IRMA
—Russian	SUKHOI
—Swedish	MFI
—Swiss	BRAVO
—very light and small	(HANG) GLIDER
	MICROLIGHT

manufacturers

—American	BELL, BOEING, BREWSTER
	CONSOLIDATED, CONVAIR, CURTISS
	DOUGLAS, FAIRCHILD, FARMAN
	GATES, GENERAL DYNAMICS
	GOODYEAR, GRUMMAN, LOCKHEED
	MCDONNELL, MORSE
	NORTH AMERICAN, NORTHROP
	PACKARD, PIPER, REPUBLIC
	ROCKWELL, SEVERSKY, SIKORSKY
	SWEARINGEN, VOUGHT, WRIGHT
—Australian	GAF
—Brazilian	EMBRAER
—British	AIRMARK
	ARMSTRONG WHITWORTH
	AVRO, BEARDMORE, BLACKBURN
	BRISTOL, BRITTEN-NORMAN
	CAMPBELL, CIERVA, DE HAVILLAND
	FAIREY, FARNELL, GLOSTER
	HANDLEY-PAGE, HAWKER SIDDELEY
	PERCIVAL, SAGE, SAUNDERS-ROE
	SHORT, SOPWITH, SUPERMARINE
	VICKERS, WESTLAND
—Canadian	BOMBARDIER, CANADAIR
—Czech	LET
—French	AEROSPATIALE, BLERIOT
	BREGUET, BLOCH, DASSAULT
	DEWOITINE, NIEUPORT
	NORD, SALMSON
	SOCATA, SPAD
	SUD-AVIATION, SUD-EST
—German	BLOHM UND VOSS, DORNIER
	FOCKE-WULF, FOKKER, GOTHA
	HEINKEL, JUNKERS, MBB
	MESSERSCHMITT, PFALZ
—Indian	HAL
—Italian	AERMACCHI, FIAT
	REGGIANE, PARTENAVIA
	SAVOIA-MARCHETTI
—Japanese	AICHI, KAWANISHI
	KAWASAKI, KYUSHU
	MITSUBISHI, NAKAJIMA, NAMC
	SHIN MEIWA, TACHIKAW
	YOKOSUKA

—Russian	ANTONOV, ILYUSHIN
	MIKOYAN, SIKORSKY
	YAKOVLEV
—Spanish	HISPANO
—Swedish	SAAB, SVENSKA
—Yugoslav	SOKO
pilotless	DRONE

pilots

—American	BONG, BOYINGTON, BYRD
	CASTLE, CUNNINGHAM, EARHART
	GABRESKI, GENTILE, IACCACI
	JOHNSON, LAMBERT
	LEMAY, LEPPLA
	LINDBERGH, LUFBERY, LUKE
	MITCHELL, O'HARE, POST
	RICKENBACKER
	WRIGHT, YEAGER
commanders	CHENNAULT, MITCHELL
	SPAATZ
—Australian	HINKLER
—Austro-Hungarian	ARIGI, BRUMOWSKI
	FIALA, LINKE-CRAWFORD
—Belgian	COPPENS, JACQUES
	MEULEMEESTER, THIEFFRY
—British	AARON, ALCOCK, BADER
	BALL, BEACHAMP-PROCTOR
	BEAMONT, BOOTHMAN, BROWN
	BULMAN, CARMICHAEL, CHESHIRE
	COBHAM, COLLISHAW, CUNNINGHAM
	DUKE, GIBSON, GREENWOOD
	HAWKER, JOHNSON
	KINGSFORD-SMITH
	MACLAREN, MANNOCK
	MCCUDDEN, MOLLISON, SAMSON
	SHORT, STAINFORTH, TRUBSHAW
	TUCK, WAGHORN
commanders	BARRATT
	BROOKE-POPHAM, DOWDING
	HARRIS, PARK, PORTAL
	SLESSOR, TEDDER, TRENCHARD
display team	RED ARROWS
—Canadian	BARKER, BISHOP, KENT
display team	SNOWBIRDS
—Finnish	LUUKKANEN
—French	BOYAU, CLOSTERMANN
	FARMAN, GARROS
	LE GLOAN, GUYNEMER
	MADON, NUNGESSER, PONCK
display team	PATROUILLE DE FRANCE
—German	BAR, BECKER, BERTHOLD
	BOELCKE, GALLAND, GOERING
	HARTMANN, HEINRICH, IMMELMANN
	LENT, LOERZER, LOWENHARDT
	MARSEILLE, MEYER, OSTERKAMP
	RICHTHOFEN, RUDEL, RUMEY
	SCHAUFER, TRATT, UDET, VOSS

commanders	GALLAND, GOERING
	LOHR, RICHTHOFEN
—Italian	BARACCA, BARRACHINI
	PICCIO, SCARONI
display team	TRICOLORI
—Japanese	FUCHIDA, IWAMOTO
	NISHIZAWA, SAKAI, SUGITA
—New Zealand	DEERE
—Polish	BRUMOWSKI
	LINK-CRAWFORD
—Portuguese display team	ASAS
—Russian	AVDYEYEV, D'ARGUEEFF
	KAZAKOV, SEVERSKY
	SMIRNOFF
—South African	MALAN, PATTLE
—Spanish display team	PATRULLA AGUILA
—Swiss	RUBENSDORFFER
display team	PATROUILLE SUISSE
pioneers	BLERIOT, BRABAZON
	CODY, FAIRCHILD, FARMAN
	GARROS, LILIENTHAL, NORTHROP
	SOPWITH, WRIGHT
reconnaissance planes	
—American	BLACKBIRD, HAWKEYE
	ORION, PROWLER, RAVEN
	SENTRY, VIGILANTE, VIKING
—British	BUCCANEER, HARRIER
	LYSANDER, NIMROD
	SHACKLETON
—French	ATLANTIC, BLERIOT
	CAUDRON, FARMAN
	LONGHORN, SHORTHORN
—German	AGO, BRANDENBERG, DFW
	HALBERSTADT, LOHNER, LVG
	RUMPLER, STEISLER
	STORCH, VAK
—Italian	SAML, SIA
—Russian	BLINDER, BREWER
	FIDDLER, TUPOLEV
seaplanes	
—American	BOEING
—British	CAMPANIA, SHORT
	SUPERMARINE, SWORDFISH
	WIGHT
—German	SABLATNIG
spy plane	BLACKBIRD, U2
terms	
—accident	PRANG
—advanced technology	
bomber	ATB, STEALTH
—air deflector	AIR-BRAKE, SPOILER
	WIND-BRAKE
—angle of wing	ANHEDRAL, DIHEDRAL
—baggage conveyor	CAROUSEL
—body	FUSELAGE
—bombing raid	MISSION

—cargo	PAYLOAD
—circular course	
over airfield	HOLDING PATTERN
—cockpit cover	CANOPY
—control	
stick	COLUMN, JOYSTICK
surface	AEROFOIL, ELEVATOR
	FLAP, RUDDER
—course	VECTOR
—curve of wing	CAMBER
—decrepit plane	CRATE
—ejecting cockpit	CAPSULE
—enemy aircraft	BANDITS
—engine housing	NACELLE
—experimental stealth	
technology	XST
—faster than sound	SST, SUPERSONIC
—fault (often inexplicable)	GREMLIN
—flight recorder	BLACK BOX
—fly across the wind	CRAB
in vertical circle	LOOP(-THE-LOOP)
low	HEDGE HOP
without power	GLIDE, VOLPLANE
—forecourt	APRON
—height recorder	ALTIMETER
—jet-assisted take-off	JATO
—land	TOUCH DOWN
beyond runway	OVERSHOOT
in the sea	DITCH
short of runway	UNDERSHOOT
—landing surface	RUNWAY, TARMAC
—lifting surface	AEROFOIL
—lose speed and fall	STALL
—mission	SORTIE
—move aircraft on land	TAXI
—navigation system	DECCA, TACAN
—operations centre	CONTROL TOWER
—passenger-carrying	
jet plane	JETLINER
—raid	SORTIE
—route	FLIGHT PATH
	FLIGHT PLAN
—shock wave	SONIC BOOM
—short take-off and landing	STOL
—speed recorder	MACHMETER
—start flight	TAKE OFF
—tail sections	EMPENNAGE
—take off quickly	SCRAMBLE
—testing chamber	WIND TUNNEL
—tilt sideways	BANK
—towed target	DROGUE
—training machine	SIMULATOR
—triangle-shaped	DELTA-WING
—vertical take-off and landing	VTOL
—visible trail in sky	CONTRAIL
	VAPOUR TRAIL

—waiting	
area	CONCOURSE
room	TRANSIT LOUNGE
—wheel cover	SPAT
—wind indicator	WIND CORE, WIND SLEEVE
	WINDSOCK
—wing	
or tailplane	AEROFOIL
storage attachment	POD
—with	
moveable wings	SWING-WING
	SWIVEL-WING
rotors on wings	TILT-ROTOR
training planes	
—British	AUSTER, AVRO, BULLDOG
	GNAT, HAWK, PROVOST
	STRIKEMASTER
—Canadian	TUTOR
—Czech	AERO, SKYDEVIL, ZLIN
—French	ALPHAJET, STAMPE
—Indian	MARUT
—Italian	AEROMACCHI, MARCHETTI
—Swedish	SAAB
—Swiss	BRAVO
—Yugoslav	GALEB
transport planes	
—American	CONSTELLATION, DAKOTA
	EXTENDER, GALAXY, HERCULES
	LOCKHEED, STARLIFTER
	STRATOCRUISER
—British	SKYVAN
—Canadian	BUFFALO, TWIN OTTER
—European	TRANSALL
—French	CARAVELLE
—Israeli	ARAVA
—Italian	FIAT
—Russian	ANTEI, ANTONOV
	ILYUSHIN, TUPOLEV
—Spanish	AVIOCAR
—Swiss	PILATUS PORTER
airlines	
Africa	AIR AFRIQUE, SAA
Alaska	WIEN AIR
America	AIR CAL, AMERICAN, APOLLO
	ARIZONA AIR, ARROW, BRANIFF
	CONTINENTAL, DELTA
	EAGLE, EASTERN
	FRONTIER, IMPERIAL, NORTHWEST
	OZARK, PANAM(ERICAN), PIEDMONT
	REPUBLIC, TRANSAIR, TRANSWORLD
	(TWA), UNITED, US AIRLINES
	WESTERN, WORLD AIRWAYS
Arabia	SAUDIA
Australia	QANTAS
Belgium	SABENA
Brazil	VARIG INTERNATIONAL

Britain	AIR EUROPE
	AIR UK, BA, BAC, BCAL, BEA
	BIRMINGHAM EUROPEAN
	BOAC, BRITISH CALEDONIAN
	BRITISH MIDLANDS, BRITANNIA
	BRYMON, DANAIR, FLEXAIR
	IMPERIAL AIRWAYS
	JERSEY EUROPEAN, LOGANAIR
	LONDON CITY AIRWAYS
	MANX AIRLINES, ORION
	PARAMOUNT, VIRGIN
Canada	AIR CANADA, AIR ONTARIO
	CP AIR, WARDAIR
Chile	LAN(CHILE)
China	CACC
Cuba	CUBANA DE AVIACION
Dominica	AEROMAR
Ecuador	ECUATORIANA
Egypt	ZAS
El Salvador	TACA
Finland	FINNAIR
France	AIR FRANCE, UTA
Germany	INTERFLUG, LUFTHANSA
Greece	OLYMPIC
Guatemala	AVIETECA
Gulf States	EMIRATES, GULF AIR
Hawaii	ALOHA, HAWAIIAN AIR
Honduras	AEREO (DE HONDURAS)
	SERVICEO
Hong Kong	CATHAY PACIFIC
India	AIR INDIA
Indonesia	GARUDA INDONESIA
Ireland	AER LINGUS, RYAN AIR
Israel	EL AL
Italy	ALITALIA
Japan	ALL NIPPON, ANA
	JAL, NAGASAKI
	NIHON KINKYOR, TOA
Jordan	ALIA, ARAB WING
	ROYAL JORDANIAN AIRLINES
Korea	KOREAN AIRLINES
Luxemburg	LUXAIR
Malaysia	MALAYSIAN AIR SERVICES
Mexico	AEROMEXICO
Netherlands	KLM, ROYAL DUTCH
New Zealand	AIR NEW ZEALAND
Pakistan	PAKISTAN INTERNATIONAL
Poland	LOT
Portugal	TAP
Romania	TAROM
Russia	AEROFLOT
Scandinavia	CONAIR
Singapore	SINGAPORE INTERNATIONAL
South Africa	SAA
Spain	IBERIA, SPANTAX
Sweden	LINJEFLYG

Switzerland	SWISSAIR
Thailand	THAI INTERNATIONAL
Venezuela	VIASA
Yugoslavia	JAT

airports

America	
—Alaska	HARTFIELD INTERNATIONAL
—Boston	LOGAN INTERNATIONAL
—California	LOS ANGELES INTERNATIONAL
	SAN FRANCISCO INTERNATIONAL
—Chicago	O'HARE
—Dallas	DALLAS-FORT WORTH
	LOVE FIELD, REDBIRD
—Denver	STAPLETON INTERNATIONAL
—Florida	MIAMI INTERNATIONAL
—Hawaii	HONOLULU INTERNATIONAL
—New York	JOHN F KENNEDY
	LA GUARDIA, NEWARK
—St Louis	LAMBERT
—Texas	DALLAS/FORT WORTH REGIONAL
—Washington	WASHINGTON
	INTERNATIONAL
England	BIGGIN HILL, BIRMINGHAM
	EAST MIDLANDS, EXETER, GATWICK
	HEATHROW, HUMBERSIDE
	LEEDS/BRADFORD, LIVERPOOL
	LUTON, MANCHESTER, NEWCASTLE
	NORWICH, SOUTHAMPTON, SOUTHEND
	SPEKE, STANSTED
France	AEROPORT DE PARIS
	CHARLES DE GAULLE
	LE TOUQUET, ORLY
Canada	
—Toronto	PEARSON
Germany	
—Berlin	TEGEL, TEMPELHOF
—Frankfurt	FLUGHAFEN FRANKFURT MAIN
Holland	SCHIPHOL
Hong Kong	KAI TAK
Ireland	DUBLIN, COLLINS, SHANNON
Israel	BEN GURION
Italy	ROMA
Japan	
—Osaka	OSAKA INTERNATIONAL
—Tokyo	HAMEDA
	TOKYO INTERNATIONAL
Russia	SHEREMETEVA
Scotland	ABERDEEN, EDINBURGH
	GLASGOW, PRESTWICK
Singapore	AIRTROPOLIS, CHANGI

Albania   AL

brigand	KLEPHT
capital	TIRANA, TIRANE
cavalryman	SPAHI
coin	GROSH, LEK, QINDARKA
	QUINT(AR)
dialect	CHAM, TOSK
kilt	FUSTANELLA
mountaineer	ARNA(O)UT
ruler	MPRET
secret police	SIGURIMI
soldier	ARNA(O)UT, PALIKAR

alchemy

alchemist	STAGYRIST
—Arabic	ALHAZEN, GEBER
	JABIR IBN-HAYYAN
—Dutch	VAN HELMONT
—Italian	DELLA PORTA
—Swiss	PARACELSUS
	VON HOHENHEIM
—Syrian	CALLINICUS
black(ish) compound	ETHIOPS
distilling flask	ALEMBIC
element involved in combustion	PHLOGISTON
furnace	ATHANOR
gold	SOL
mercury	AZOTH
—ammonal chloride	SAL ALEMBROTH
process in search of	
philosopher's stone	OLBATION, CIBAT
red	
—or black tincture	SERICON
—powder	COLCOTHAR
	CROCUS OF MARS
salt of wisdom	SAL ALEMBROTH
secret remedy	ARCANUM
silver	LUNA
solvent	MENSTRUUM
substance giving eternal life	ELIXIR
textbook	ALMAGEST
transmuting agent	ELIXIR, MAGISTERY
	PHILOSOPHER'S STONE
	SERICON
universal	
—remedy	ELIXIR, PANACEA
—solvent	ALCAHEST, ALKAHEST
vital principle	ARCH(A)EUS

Alderney   GBA

Algeria   ALG, DZ

capital	ALG(I)ERS, EL DJAZAIR
castle	CASBAH, KASBA(H)
cavalryman	SPAHEE, SPAHI
cheese	CAPRINO
coin	CENTIME, DINAR
dish	COUSCOUS(OU), CUSCUS
	KHUSKHUS
drink	AGRAS
fort	CASBAH, KASBA(H)
governor	DEY
infantryman	TURCO, ZOUAVE
measure	PIK
raid	ROZZIA

reedy grass	DISS		etc	OREIDE, OROIDE
ship	XEBEC(K), ZEBEC(K)			ORMOLU, PLATINOID, POTIN
shrub	BRIAR, BRIER			TOMBAC, TOMBAK
soldier	SOUAVE, TURCO, ZOUAVE			YELLOW-METAL
weight	ROTL		iron	DELTA METAL
wine	PINARD		nickel	GERMAN SILVER
alloys			tin	ORMULU
aluminium			Egyptian	ASEM
—and			emitting sparks	
brass	ALUMINIUM BRASS		when struck	PYROPHORIC ALLOY
copper	ALUMINIUM BRONZE		for joining metals	SOLDER
—zinc	AERO METAL		gold and	
magnesium	MAGNALIUM		—brass	TALMI GOLD
—hard	DURALUMIN(IUM)		—nickel	WHITE GOLD
anti-friction alloy	BABBIT(T'S) METAL		—palladium	WHITE GOLD
bismuth and			—silver	ASEM, CARACOLY, EGYP
—cadmium, lead, tin	WOOD'S METAL			ELECTRUM
	LIPOWITZ'S ALLOY		gold-coloured	ORICHALC
—lead, tin	FUSIBLE METAL		imitating gold and silver	LEAF-METAL
	ROSE'S METAL		imitation gold	PINCHBECK
brass	LATTEN, ORICHALC		iridium and osmium	IRIDOSMINE
—and manganese	MANGANESE BRONZE			IRIDOSMIUM, OSMIRIDIUM
Britannia metal	TUTANIA		iron and	
bronze and tin	WHITE BRONZE		—carbon	STEEL
cast iron with nickel etc	NICROSILAL		—chromium, carbon	STAINLESS STEEL
ceramic and metal	CER(A)MET		—manganese and carbon	SPIEGEL(EISEN)
cerium with iron			—nickel	PERMALLOY
and rare earths	MISCHMETAL		carbon	INVAR
cobalt and			—other metal	FERRO-ALLOY
—chromium, tungsten etc	STELLITE		—with another metal	FERRO-ALLOY
—iron, nickel	KOVAR		kind of Britannia metal	TUTANIA
commercial zinc	SPELTER		lead and	
copper and			—antimony, tin	TYPE METAL
—aluminium, zinc	DEVARDA'S ALLOY		—tin	CALIN, TERNE(-METAL)
—arsenic	TOMBAC, TOMBAK		copper, etc	PEWTER
—manganese, nickel	MANGANIN		light-coloured copper	WHITE COPPER
—nickel	CONSTANTAN		magnesium	
	CUPRO-NICKEL		—alloy used as sheath	
iron, etc	MONEL METAL		for uranium rods	MAGNOX
tungsten, zinc	PLATINOID		—and aluminium	MAGNALIUM
zinc	GERMAN SILVER		magnetic alloys of	
	NICKEL SILVER		copper, manganese,	
—tin	BRONZE, GUN METAL		aluminium	HEUSLER'S ALLOYS
	SPECULUM METAL		manganese and nitrogen	MEAN STEEL
phosphorus	PHOSPHOR BRONZE		mercury alloy	AMALGAM
zinc	GUN-METAL		misch metal and iron	AUER METAL
	MOSAIC GOLD, MUNTZ METAL		nickel	
	PINCHBECK, PRINCE'S METAL		—and	
	WHITE BRASS		chrome	NICHROME
—zinc	BRASS, DUTCH METAL		copper	CONSTANTIN
	MANGANESE BRASS		iron, copper, manganese	MUMETAL
	MANGANESE BRONZE		steel	INVAR
	MOSAIC GOLD		—based	MONEL METAL
	MUNTZ METAL, PINCHBECK		non-ferrous	TULA
	PRINCE'S METAL, SIMILOR		osmium and iridium etc	OSMIRIDIUM
	WHITE BRASS		pewter	BIDRI, TRIFLE

silver and
—copper   SHIBIUCHI
etc   BILLON, VELLON
—nickel   ALFENIDE
silvery   OCCAMY
steel and
—chromium   STAINLESS STEEL
—manganese   MANGANESE STEEL
—nickel   NICKEL STEEL
and chromium   ELINVAR
—silicon   STALLOY
tin
—and
copper, etc   BRITANNIA METAL
   BABBIT(T'S) METAL
   TUTANIA
lead, antimony   PEWTER
—based   WHITE METAL
tutania   BRITANNIA METAL
used in dentistry   AMALGAM
yellow   SIMILOR
zinc and
—copper etc   TUTENAG
—lead etc   COMMERCIAL ZINC, SPELTER

alphabet
any based on syllables   SYLLABARY
Arabic   CUFIC, KUFIC
—script   NASK(H)I, NESK(H)I
Assyrian and Babylonian   CUNEIFORM
Bulgarian   CYRILLIC
Celtic   OG(H)AM
Chinese   HAN CHARACTERS
   IDEOGRAMS
   IDEOGRAPHY, PINYIN(ZIMU)
code words for letters   PHONETIC ALPHABET
Cretan   LINEAR A, LINEAR B
Egyptian
—pictorial   HIEROGLYPHICS
—religious   HIERATIC
—secular   DEMOTIC
for the blind   BRAILLE, MOONTYPE
games   LEXICON, SCRABBLE
Greek   LINEAR B
   (*see also* **Greek**)
Hebrew   (*see* **Hebrew**)
Hindu   DEVANAGARI
Indian   DEVANAGARI
—group   NAGARI
international   IPA
Iranian   PAHLAVI, PEHLAVI
Irish   OG(H)AM
Italian (old)   CHALCIDIAN
Japanese   HIRAGANA, KANJI, KATAKANA
joined letters   CURSIVE
medieval   CAROLINGIAN, RUSTIC
   UNCIAL

old characters   EDH, ETH
   SCHARFES S, THORN, YOGH
Persian script   NASTALIK, NASTALIQ
   NASTAUK, NASTAUQ
phonetic   GLOSSIC, IPA, ROMIC
—signalling   ALPHA, BRAVO, CHARLIE
   DELTA, ECHO, FOXTROT, GOLF
   HOTEL, INDIA, JULIET, KILO
   LIMA, MIKE, NOVEMBER, OSCAR
   PAPA, QUEBEC, ROMEO, SIERRA
   TANGO, UNIFORM, VICTOR, WHISKY
   X-RAY, YANKEE, ZULU
pictorial   HIEROGLYPHICS, IDEOGRAMS
   PICTOGRAMS
Romany   ROMAJI
rounded script   UNCIAL
runic   FUTHARK, FUTHORC, FUTHORK
Russian   CYRILLIC
   (*see also* **Russian** — letters)
Sanskrit   (DEVA)NAGARI
Sicilian (old)   CHALCIDIAN
signaller's   MORSE CODE, SEMAPHORE
Sikh   GURMUKHI
Slavonic   GLAGOL(ITIC)
sloping script   ITALIC
standard   ROMAN
Sumerian   CUNEIFORM
Syriac   ESTRANG(H)ELO
teaching   ITA
upright script   ROMAN
wedge-shaped   CUNEIFORM

American
aboriginal   AMERIND, ESKIMO
   (RED) INDIAN, INUIT
accessories   FINDING
accustomed   WONTED
act as paid dance partner   HOSTESS
address of welcome   SALUTATORY
adherent of British
government   ROYALIST
administrative district   TOWNSHIP
administrator of local
school system   SUPERINTENDENT
admiring looks   EYE SERVICE
advertising leaflet   DODGER
advocate, council   MOUTHPIECE
affair   SHEBANG
agency
—intelligence   CIA
—security   FBI
agitated   HET UP
agrimony   BONE-SET
air control   CAB
aircraft navigation system   VOR
airline   PAN AM, TWA
alert   HEADS-UP

all	
—clear	COPACETIC, COPESETTIC
—right	HUNKY(-DORY)
allowable	RULABLE
alluvial deposits	BOTTOM-LAND
almost	MOST
aloe	AGAVE, MAGUEY
alter	BUSHEL
ambassador	EMBASSADOR
Amelanchier	JUNEBERRY, SHADBUSH
anxious	ANTSY
American people	UNCLE SAM
animal	CRITTER, CRITTUR
anti	
—British Association	FENIAN
—cartel worker	TRUST-BUSTER
—fraud laws	BLUE SKY LAWS
antiquated	FOGRAM
anxious	ANTSY
any labiate plant	MINT
anything, something	
—dishonestly obtained	MAVERICK
—done for applause	HOKUM
—large	SCROUGER
—of little value	SMALL POTATOES
—rented or hired	RENTAL
—superfluous	BLITVIT
—very big	SLOCKDOLAGER
	SOC(K)DOLAGER, SOCDOLIGER
	SOCDOLOGER, SOGDOLAGER
	SOGDOLIGER, SOGDOLOGER
Apocynum	INDIAN HEMP
applaud	ROOT
apple	BALDWIN, JONATHAN
—brandy	APPLE-JACK
—pie or pudding	PANDOWDY
aquatic rodent	MUSK-RAT, MUSQUASH
area of	
—dark soil	BLACK-BELT
—negro population	BLACK BELT
armed right wing	
organisation	MINUTEMEN
army quartermaster	PAYMASTER GENERAL
arrest	BUST
arrogant	TOPPING
art gallery	MUSEUM
Artemisia	SAGEBRUSH
assistant purser	MUD-CLERK
astonished	BUG-EYED
Astragalus	LOCO(-PLANT)
	LOCO-WEED
asylum	BUG-HOUSE
at	
—any rate	LEASTWAYS, LEASTWISE
—odds	AT OUTS
—present	PRESENTLY

attend	
—class	AUDIT
—to	TEND OUT ON
audition	CATTLE CALL
autumn	FALL
aware of	KNOWING TO
awkward fellow	JAY
axolotl	MUD-PUPPY
baby's	
—dummy	PACIFIER
—nappy	DIAPER
backwoodsman	BUCKSKIN
back yard	DOOR-YARD
bad whiskey	TARANTULA JUICE
badge of naval rank	SHOULDER-MARK
badger	TAXEL
bag	
—from which gifts	
are drawn	GRAB-BAG
—net	FYKE
baggage to be laid down	
at a railway station	WAY-BAGGAGE
bait	HELLGRAM(M)ITE
baited line	TRAWL
bald eagle	WHITE-HEADED EAGLE
ball	FANDANGO
Baltimore oriole	FIRE-BIRD, HANGBIRD
	ICTERUS
bank	
—governor	PRESIDENT
—note	BILL
—rate	DISCOUNT RATE
Baptist sect	DUNKERS
barbecue	COOK-OUT
bar-room	EXCHANGE
bargaining	DICKER
baseball	(see separate entry)
bass	GROWLER
bat	MORMOPS
batter pudding	POPOVER
be	
—a school-teacher	TEACH SCHOOL
—furiously angry	STAMP
—in domestic service	LIVE OUT
—the guest of	VISIT WITH
bean	TEPARY
bear	CINNAMON-BEAR, GRIZZLY
	KODIAK, MUSQUAW
—berry	MANZANITA
beat	SHELL
beaten path	TRACE
beating the bounds	PROCESSIONING
bed	
—bug	CHINCH
—quilt	COMFORTABLE
	COMFORTER

—room over hall	HALL-BEDROOM
bedded oyster	PLANT
bee	
—hive	GUM
—line	AIRLINE
beer jug	GROWLER
beg	PANHANDLE
beggar	PANHANDLER, SCHNORRER
believe	GUESS
bird	APHRIZA, BALTIMORE (ORIOLE)
	BLACK-THROATED BUNTING
	BLUE-BIRD, BOBOLINK, BOBWHITE
	BUFFLEHEAD, BUSH-TIT
	CHAPARRAL COCK
	COW (BLACK-)BIRD
	DICKCISSEL, FIELD-LARK
	FIREBIRD, GOATSUCKER, GRA(CK)LE
	GREENLET, GROUND-ROBIN, HANGBIRD
	HANGNEST, MARSH-ROBIN
	MEADOW-LARK, MELOPSIZA
	MOCKING-THRUSH, PURPLE FINCH
	RAIL, REED-BIRD, RICE-BIRD
	ROAD-RUNNER, SCISSOR-TAIL
	SHARP-TAILED GROUSE, SKUNK-BIRD
	SNOW-GOOSE, SONG-SPARROW, SORA
	SPIRIT-DUCK, STONE-CURLEW, SURF-BIRD
	TATTLER, THRASHER, THRESHER
	TOWHEE, TURKEY-VULTURE
	TYRANT-BIRD, TYRANT-FLYCATCHER
	VEERY, VELVET SCOTER, VIREO
	WAV(E)Y, WHIP-POOR-WILL
	WHITEWING, WILLET, WOOD-THRUSH
	WOOD-WARBLER, WREN-TIT, ZOPILOTE
bird-catching spider	MYGALE
bison	BUFFALO
black	
—bass	GROWLER
—bird	GRA(C)KLE
—tailed deer	JUMPING DEER
—vulture	CARRION CROW
blackmail	STRIKE
bladder-campion	CAROLINA PINK, PINKROOT
bland	MICKEY
blarney	TAFFY
blind fish	AMBLYOPSIS
block of	
—buildings	SQUARE
—public land	TOWNSHIP
blockhead	MUTT
bloodroot	PUCCOON
blue-winged snow-goose	WHITEHEAD
board on which fish is cooked	PLANK
boat	DORY
bobolink	REED-BIRD, RICE-BIRD
	SKUNK-BIRD
bobwhite	QUAIL

boiled	
—flour dumpling	DOUGH-BOY
—maize	HOMINY
boiler-suit	COVERALL
bony pike	GARFISH
boo	BRONX CHEER
bookmaker's book of bets	HANDBOOK
boot of car	TRUNK
boring	
—old fool	FOGRAM
—person	SCHMO
boss	HONCHO
botch	FLUB, MUX
bottle of dark glass	JUNK-BOTTLE
bottom-drawer	HOPE-CHEST
bowfin	LAKE-LAWYER
Bowie knife	TOOTH-PICK
bowler hat	DERBY
bowls	TEN-PINS
box-wagon	BOX-CAR
Boxing Association	WBA
boy	BUB(BY)
braces	SUSPENDERS
branch post-office	STATION
brawl	ROUGH-HOUSE
brawn	HEADCHEESE
breach of river bank	CREVASSE
bread (maize)	CORN-BREAD
—root	PRAIRIE-TURNIP
breakdown truck	WRECKER
bribe	KICKBACK
bridesmaid	MAID OF HONOUR
bring up	FETCH UP
brisk run	BRUSH
brittle	BRASH
broad-brimmed hat	SUNDOWN
broadcasters	CBS, CNN, RCA
broken tree	RAMPICK, RAMPIKE
brook	CREEK, RILL
brother	BUD(DY)
brownish-yellow	CLAY-BANK
brown-paper patch	SHIN-PLASTER
brushwood thicket	CHAPARRAL
buckthorn	CEANOTHUS, WAHOO
buffalo-nut	OILNUT
buffalo/cow hybrid	BEEFALO
building	
—earning money to pay taxes	TAX-PAYER
—stone	BROWNSTONE, FIELDSTONE
bulge	BUG
bulrush	SCIRPUS, TULE
bumpkin	YAP
bunk	HOKUM
buoyed line with hooks	TRAWL
burbot	LAKE-LAWYER

burglar	YEGG(MAN)	cart	DEMOCRAT(-WAGON)
burning bush	WAHOO	cast	MOLT
burrowing		catapult	SLING-SHOT
—animal	(POCKET-)GOPHER	catch	
—snake	GOPHER	—fish with seine-net	TRAWL
bus with low fares	JITNEY	—of fish	MESS
bush	CHAPARRAL	caterpillar	WEBWORM
	CREOSOTE-PLANT	catfish	HORN(ED)-POUT
business	INC		MUD-CAT, SILURE
bustle	RUSTLE	cattle-drover	PUNCHER
butter-nut	OILNUT	cause to fall	FALL
buzzard	RED-TAIL	censorious	NEGATIVE
by short cuts	ACROSS LOTS	central reservation	PARKING
bye-law	ORDINANCE	cereal	INDIAN CORN, MAIZE
cabinet	OFFICIAL FAMILY		MEALIES
cake	CORN-CAKE, CORN-DODGER	ceremony	EXERCISE
	FRIEDCAKE, HOE-CAKE	certainly	SURE
	LOAF-CAKE, SHORTCAKE	chairman of company	PRESIDENT
Californian		challenge to perform a feat	STUMP
—buckthorn bark	CASCARA	change	
—plant	FOUR-O'CLOCK	--over	TRANSFER
—shrub	CHAMISE, CHAMISO	—in nature or politics	FLOP
—white oak	ROBLE	changing hut	CABANA
call on	GAM	chaos	SNAFU
camp		chaotic	SNAFU
--follower	BUMMER	charivari	SHIVAREE
—kettle	DIXIE	chat	VISIT
camping kit	DUFFEL, DUFFLE	chat with	VISIT WITH
Canadian	CANUCK, KANUCK	cheap	JITNEY
candlefish	EULACHON, OOLAKAN	—cigar	LONG NINE
	OULACHON, OULAKAN	—hotel	FLOPHOUSE
candy floss	CANDY-COTTON	checker-berry	PARTRIDGE-BERRY
	COTTON CANDY	cheeky	SASSY
	FLUKUM, SPUN SUGAR	cheer	ROOT
canvasser	SALESMAN, SOLICITOR	chemist	DRUGGIST
capital	WASHINGTON (DC)	chemist's shop	DRUG-STORE
car	AUTO(MOBILE)	cheque	CHECK
—body (rear)	TONNEAU	cherry-laurel	MOCK-ORANGE
—bonnet	HOOD	chest of drawers	DRESSER
—boot	TRUNK	chest-strap for carrying	TUMP-LINE
—park	PARKING LOT	chevrotain	MOUSE-DEER
—silencer	MUFFLER	chewink	GROUND-ROBIN
—wing	FENDER	child's	
carbine	ESCOPETTE	—apron	TIER
card-game	EUCHRE	—garment	PANTY-WAIST
cardigan	WAM(M)US, WAMPUS	chipmunk	GROUND-SQUIRREL
cargo ship	LIBERTY SHIP	chiropodist	PODIATRIST
caribou	REINDEER	choice specimen	PEACHERINO
Carolina		chopped bait	TOLL-BAIT
--allspice	CALYCANTHUS	cicada	HARVEST-FLY
—jasmine	GELSEMIUM	cigar(ette) end	SNIPE
carriage	BUCKBOARD, BUCKCART, BUGGY	circular saw	BUZZ-SAW
	HERDIC, ROCKAWAY, SURREY	civil	
carry	TOTE	—law officer	MARSHAL
—on the hip	HIP	—War	WAR OF SECESSION
—out	FILL	civilian	CITIZEN

clam	COHOG, QUAHOG, QUAHAUG
claptrap	HOKUM
class-room	RECITATION-ROOM
clear by felling trees	SLASH
clergyman	DOMINIE
clever	HEADS-UP
cliff-sided hill	BUTTE
climbing plant	GELSEMIUM
	CLUSIA, STAR-OF-THE-NIGHT
cloak-room	CHECK(ING)-ROOM
clot of dirt or colour	SPLATCH
clump of trees	MOT, MOTT(E)
clumsy person	SCHLEMIEL, SCHEMIHL
coalition	FUSION
cock's-foot grass	ORCHARD-GRASS
coffin	CASKET
coin	ROCK
—old (Spanish)	PISTAREEN, REAL
—cent	PENNY
—5 cents	JITNEY, NICKEL
—6½ cents (old)	PICAYUNE
—10 cents	DIME
—12 cents	BIT
—17 cents (silver)	PINE-TREE MONEY
—25 cents	QUARTER, TWO BITS
—50 cents	HALF-DOLLAR
—100 cents	DOLLAR
—dollar	BUCK, GREENBACK, WHEEL
—5 dollars	ABE'S CABE, FIN
—10-dollar bill	SAWBUCK, TENSPOT
—10 dollars	EAGLE
—20 dollars (gold)	DOUBLE EAGLE
—500 dollars	MONKEY
—proposed	MILL
—small	PICAYUNE
—unit	CENT
college	
—dance	PROMENADE
—lecturer	INSTRUCTOR
coloured nurse	MAMMY
comedy drama	DRAMEDY
comics in newspaper	FUNNIES
commercial traveller	DRUMMER
	SALESMAN
commotion	RUCKUS
company	CAHOOT, CORPORATION
—working together	OUTFIT
compass-plant	SILPHIUM
computer	ENIAC
concede	ALLOW
concerned with administration	PRUDENTIAL
conclusive argument	SLOCKDOLAGER
	SOCDOLIGER, SOCDOLOGER
	SOC(K)DOLAGER, SOGDOLAGER
	SOGDOLIGER, SOGDOLOGER
conduct in court, as a lawyer	TRY

conductor	LEADER
confectionery	CANDY
confederacy of Indian tribes	FIVE NATIONS
Confederated States	CFA
confer degree on	GRADUATE
confidence trick	BUNCO, BUNKO
confounded	BLAME(D)
confused	STREAKED
confused conflict	MUSS(LE)
congregation	PARISH
Congressman	SOLON
connecting-rod	PITMAN
conscription	DRAFT
conservative person	HUNKER
considerable	SMART
constituency	DISTRICT
constrain	OBLIGATE
con-trick	BUNCO, BUNKO
controller	HONCHO
convey rapidly	GIGGIT
conveyance	PROTOCOL
cook on a board	PLANK
coral-snake	ELAPS
corn	MAIZE
cornflour	CORNSTARCH
corny	MICKEY
cotton	
—cloth for shorts	MUSLIN
—stripping machine	LINTER
cougar	CATAMOUNT, PANTHER
	PUMA, PAINTER
courgette	ZUCCHINI
councillor	COUNCILMAN
country	
—dance	HOEDOWN, VIRGINIA REEL
—lout	JAKE
—music	STAR-SPANGLED BANNER
covered wagon	PRAIRIE-SCHOONER
cowardly man	PANTY-WAIST
cowboy	BUCKAROO, COWPOKE
	COWPUNCHER
—hat	STETSON, TEN-GALLON HAT
—leggings	CHAPS, SHAPS
cowcatcher	PILOT
coyote	PRAIRIE-WOLF
crack-shot	DEAD-EYE
crazy person	SCREWBALL
crib	HORSE, PONY, TROT
crime	HEIST
cripple confined to house	SHUT-IN
critical onlooker	KIBITZER
croquet	ROQUE
cross of twigs	GOD'S EYE
crossing with underpass	GRADE SEPARATION
crowd	RAFT

crushed	CHAWED UP	disconcert	DISCOMBOBERATE
cuckoo	COW-BIRD		DISCOMBOBULATE
cure and brown	DUN	discontented person	SOREHEAD
curtain	DRAPE	discounter	NOTE-SHAVER
customs-officer	'NAVAL OFFICER	disgusting	SCUZZY
cycad	COONTIE, COONTY	—person	SCUZZBALL
cyclist	CYCLER	dismissal	BOUNCE
dabchick	DIPPER	dissolute	BUM
dagga	MARIJUANA	distillery	STILL-HOUSE
dainty	CUNNING	district	SECTION
dairy over stream	SPRING-HOUSE	—juicy with bribes	TENDER-LOIN
damnation	(TAR)NATION	disturbance	ROUGH-HOUSE, RUCKUS
damned	BLAME(D)	diving duck	BUFFLEHEAD
dance	(see dance)	do menial work	STRIKE
dandy	DUDE	dock (plant)	CANAIGRE
dare	STUMP	docker	LONGSHOREMAN
dark sandstone	BROWNSTONE	doctor's consulting-room	OFFICE
dead		dogbane	FLY-TRAP
—person	DECEDENT		INDIAN HEMP
—tree	RAMPICK, RAMPIKE	dollar	BUCK, WHEEL
debris of trees	SLASH	—bill	SCRIP
debutante	BUD	dolt	CLUNK
decamp	ABSQUATULATE, DIG OUT	domestication of animals	ZOOCULTURE
decayed tree	RAMPICK, RAMPIKE	doss-house	FLOPHOUSE
decision of council	REBOUND	double plough	LISTER
decisive blow	SLOCKDOLAGER	doughnut	CRULLER, OLYCOOK
	SOCDOLIGER, SOCDOLOGER		OLYKOEK, SINKER
	SOC(K)DOLAGER, SOGDOLAGER	downright	UP-AND-DOWN
	SOGDOLIGER, SOGDOLOGER	drag	SCHLEP, TUMP
decoration for wounds	PURPLE HEART	drawback	OUT
decoy	TOLE, TOLL	drawer (of chest)	DRAW
deer	(see antelope)	drawing-pin	THUMB-TACK
deer-mouse	WHITE-FOOTED MOUSE	dress up	GUSSY UP, RAG
defeat		dressing	
—by small margin	EDGE	—gown	BATH-ROBE
—totally	CHAW-UP, SKUNK	—table	DRESSER, LOW-BOY
defeatist	NEGATIVE	drink	MINT-JULEP
deficiency	WANTAGE	drinking	
denim trousers	CHINOS	—bar	SALOON
denomination	PARISH	—fountain on	
denominational	PAROCHIAL	ship	SCUTTLEBUTT
dentist	DOCTOR	—resort	DOGGERY
dentures	STORE TEETH	drive	
derail	DITCH	—cattle	PUNCH
desert	BUG-OUT	—fast	BARREL
destroy political influence of	SCALP	driving turnout	RIG
detective	FED, G-MAN	drought area	DUST-BOWL
	JACK, SHAMUS	druggist	DOCTOR
detectives	FBI	drunk	JAGGED
diagram	PLAT	drunkard	SOUSE
difficulty	NINE HOLES	duck	CANVAS-BACK
dinner-jacket	TUXEDO	dull	
disadvantage	OUT	—person	FLAT TYRE
disaster	PROVIDENCE	—town	BOHUNK, HICKSVILLE
discharge from armed forces	MUSTER OUT	dummy	PACIFIER
discompose	FAZE, PHASE	dumpling	CORN DODGER

dung-beetle	TUMBLE-BUG
	TUMBLE-DUNG
dust	
—bin	GARBAGE CAN, (TR)ASH-CAN
—coat	DUSTER
—man	GARBAGEMAN
Dutch rush	SCOURING-RUSH
dwarf	
—cherry	SAND-CHERRY
—chestnut	CHINCAPIN, CHINKAPIN
	CHINQUAPIN
early civilisation	ADENA, HOPEWELL
	MISSISSIPPIAN
eastern	
—Indian	MOUND-BUILDER
—New York	EAST SIDE
easy educational course	CAKE COURSE
eccentric	DIFFERENT DRUMMER
	SCREWBALL
eczema	SALT-RHEUM
edible berry	SAL(L)AL-BERRY
—bulb	CAMAS(S), CAMASH
	QUAMASH
—caterpillar	PUXI
—fungus	TUCKAHOE
—part of anything	MEAT
educational meeting	CHAUTAUQUA
effeminate man	PANTY-WAIST
elderly man	UNCLE
election	
—scrutiny	CANVASS
—with disputed	
result	CONTESTED ELECTION
elementary school	COMMON SCHOOL, GRADE
elk	MOOSE
elm	WAHOO
embezzle	KNOCK DOWN
encourage	ROOT
end of whiplash	SNAPPER
engine	
—driver	ENGINEER
—house with turntable	ROUND-HOUSE
enlist	MUSTER IN
—into military	INDUCT
enroll	MUSTER IN
entertain as guest	HOST
entrance	
—fee	INITIATION FEE
—hall	HALLWAY
enunciation	DICTION
equinoctial storm	LINE-STORM
estate agent	REALTOR
eternal	TARNAL
evangelist	RELIGIONIST
evening just past	OVERNIGHT
evening primrose	SUN-DROPS

evergreen	LIVE-OAK, MADRONA
	MADRONO, MOUNTAIN-TEA
ewer	PITCHER
ex-directory	UNLISTED
ex-serviceman	VET(ERAN)
excellent	COPACETIC, COPESETTIC
excessively enthusiastic	GUNG-HO
exchange courtesies with	GAM
exclusive social set	THE FOUR HUNDRED
exclusively fashionable	PINK
expert shot	DEAD-EYE
exploratory well	WILD-CAT
expression of	
—admiration	SOME POTATOES
—disgust	BLECH, BLEGH
—vexation	DOG ON IT, DOGGONE IT
expressway	THROUGHWAY, THRUWAY
exquisite	PINK
extinct bird	HEATH-HEN
	PASSENGER-PIGEON
exuberant	FEISTY
fail at	FLUB
false teeth	STORE TEETH
familiar	GAY
fancy dishes or adjuncts	DOINGS
fanlight	TRANSOM
farewell oration	VALEDICTORY
farm	BOWERY
—boundary fence	LINE-FENCE
fast car	HOT ROD
feign death	PLAY POSSUM
fellow	GUY, JACK
—lodger	ROOM-MATE
female night-club singer	CHANTEUSE
fence of pales	PICKET-FENCE
fight	MIX-IN
figure with	
—no sides parallel	TRAPEZIUM
—two sides parallel	TRAPEZOID
finch	CARDINAL-BIRD, CHEWINK
	GROUND-ROBIN, INDIGO BIRD
	PINE-FINCH, SNOW-BIRD
	TOWHEE
fine	SWELL
fireman's ladder	BIG STICK
firmness of character	SAND
first	
—Monday in September	LABOR DAY
—display of new	
season's goods	OPENING
fish	ALE-WIFE, BLACK BASS
	BLUE-FISH, BOWFIN, CAP(E)LIN
	CAVALLA, CAVALLY, CISCO, CONNER
	CUNNER, DARTER, DOLLY VARDEN
	GROUPER, HORNYHEAD, JEW-FISH
	LAKE-HERRING, MASKALONG

MASKEL(L)ONGE, MASKINONGE
MENHADEN, MISSISSIPPI STURGEON
MUSKELLUNGE, PIG-FISH
POMPANO, ROBALO, RONCADOR
SCUP(PAUG), SEA-ROBIN
SHEEP'S-HEAD, SHOVEL-HEAD
SPECK, SQUETEAGUE, SUCKER
SURF-FISH, TAUTOG, TILEFISH
TOGUE, TORSK, TUNA, TUNNY
WALL-EYE, WHITEBASS
YELLOW-CAT

—bait	TOLL-BAIT
—split for cooking	SCROD
fit out	STAKE
fix	NINE HOLES
flag	OLD GLORY
	STARS AND STRIPES
—awarded for victory in games	PENNANT
—day	TAG-DAY
flapjack	SLAPJACK
flat	APARTMENT
—railway wagon	GONDOLA
—region	PLAT
flat-bottomed boat	MACKINAW
flat-sided	SLAB-SIDED
flattery	SOFT SAWDER, TAFFY
fliers	USAAF
flirt	CHIPPY
floating tree	SAWYER
floor behind theatre stalls	PARQUET CIRCLE
flounder	LIMANDA
flow	PUT
flower	COSMOS, INDIAN PIPE
	PENSTEMON, RUDBECKIA
	TARWEED, TRILLIUM, WAKE-ROBIN
fly	
—larvae used as bait	HELLGRAM(M)ITE
—catcher	KING-BIRD, SCISSOR-TAIL
—catching thrush	SOLITAIRE
folk concert	HOOTANANNY, HOOT(E)NANNY
	HOOTANANNIE, HOOT(E)NANNIE
fool	YAP
foolish	FOOL
football	(see separate entry)
fop	DUDE
forage grass	GAMA-GRASS
forbid	ENJOIN
forehead strap for carrying loads	TUMP-LINE
forest	
—clearing	SLASH
—land	TIMBER
formal proceeding	EXERCISE
forward	FORTH-PUTTING

fourth-year student	SENIOR
fowl	RHODE ISLAND RED
fox	VORCYRON
free admission	CUFFO
freeze	TAKE
French bean	STRING BEAN
fresh vegetables	TRUCK
freshwater	
—fish	ETHEOSTOMA, GOLDEYE
	LAKE-LAWYER, MOON-EYE
—mussel	DEER HORN
friction match	LOCOFOCO
fried	
—ball of dough	HUSH PUPPY
—cake	CRULLER
—chicken	BARNYARD PIMP
friend	BUD(DY), PAISANO, SIDEKICK
fringe	BANG
fruit	BLUEBERRY, CHOKEBERRY
	CRANBERRY, DEERBERRY
	HUCKLEBERRY, JUNEBERRY
	MARIONBERRY, MAY APPLE
	MIN(N)EOLA, SAL(L)AL-BERRY
	SASKATOON, SHADBERRY
—juice and vinegar	SHRUB
frying-pan	SKILLET
fudge	PENUCHE
full of	
—speed	NIP AND TUCK
—stumps	STUMPY
fun	MUSIC
funeral director	MORTICIAN
furnish	STAKE
furrow made with lister	LIST
galoshes	GUMSHOES
game	ROQUE
garden	
—party	LAWN-PARTY
—produce	TRUCK
gathering	
—for husking corn	HUSKING(-BEE)
—to help raise house-frame	RAISING-BEE
genuine	SURE-ENOUGH
German	DUTCH
get up (to horse)	HUDDUP
ghost	HAUNT
giant cactus	SAGUARO
girl	BABE, BROAD, DAME, QUAIL
give notice of mining claim	DENOUNCE
glance	SLANT
glassy (surface)	GLARE
goal or base in game	HUNK
goat/antelope	ROCKY MOUNTAIN GOAT
goatsucker	BULLBAT
gobstopper	JAWBREAKER

gold-seeker	FORTY-NINER
good	
—condition	KELTER, KILTER
—deal more	SOME
—hand at cards	PAT
—natured	CLEVER
goods	
—van or wagon	FREIGHT-CAR
—wagon	FREIGHTER
gooseberry	WORCESTER-BERRY
gopher	CAMASS-RAT
gorge	BARRANCA, BARRANCO
gossip	SCHMOOSE, SCHMOOZE
	SCUTTLEBUTT
got	GOTTEN
government	
—certificate for acquisition of	
public land	LAND-SCRIP
—dockyard	NAVY YARD
—exhortation to restrain wages	JAWBONE
—money for improvements	PORK
—office as reward	PLUM
—official who practises	
outside office	SUNDOWNER
grackle	BLACKBIRD
graduand giving address	SALUTATORIAN
grain pest	JOINT-WORM
gramophone	PHONOGRAPH
grape	CATAWBA, FOX-GRAPE
	SCUPPERNONG
grass	GRAMA, PASPALUM
	SPIKE-GRASS, UNIOLA, XYRIS
	YELLOW-EYED GRASS
grasshopper	KATYDID
gratuity	LAGNIAPPE
great	
—Bear	BIG DIPPER
—deal	SOME
grey wolf	TIMBER-WOLF
griddle-cake	SLAPJACK
groin	GROYNE
gromwell	PUCCOON
ground	
—cuckoo	CHAPARRAL-COCK
—floor	FIRST FLOOR
—hog	MARMOT, WOODCHUCK
—squirrel	FLICKERTAIL, GOPHER
grouse	PRAIRIE-CHICKEN
	SAGE-COCK, SAGE-GROUSE
guard (railway)	CONDUCTOR
guard's van	CABOOSE
guelder-bark	CRAMP-BARK
guelder-rose	CRANBERRY-TREE
gully	GULCH
gum tree	TUPELO
gunman	GUNSEL

habituated	WONTED
hackberry	HAGBERRY
hackee	GROUND-SQUIRREL
hagberry	HACKBERRY
haggling	DICKER
hair grip	BOBBY PIN
hairy creature (supposed)	BIGFOOT
	SUSQUATCH
hamlet	CROSSROAD
hand of welcome	GLAD HAND
handbag	CABA, POCKET-BOOK
	PURSE
handbill freely distributed	THROW-AWAY
handicraft article	BOONDOGGLE
hard blow	SLOCKDOLAGER
	SOC(K)DOLAGER, SOCDOLIGER
	SOCDOLOGER, SOGDOLGER
	SOGDOLIGER, SOGDOLOGER
hare	JACK-RABBIT
	SNOW-SHOE RABBIT
herald	OLD SQUAW
harmless snake	RING-SNAKE
harness horse	HITCH
harvest-mite larva	CHIGGER, CHIGOE
	CHIGRE, JIGGER
hat	STETSON
haul of fish	MESS
have done	BE THROUGH
headmaster	PRINCIPAL
head of	
—fire brigade	FIRE-MARSHAL
—organisation	PRESIDENT
—police or fire brigade	MARSHAL
hearing of prepared lesson	RECITATION
heat anew	WARMED-OVER
heated	HET
hedge-tree	OSAGE ORANGE
height of room	STUD
helicopter	CHOPPER, HOVER
hellbender	MUD-PUPPY
helping	ORDER
hemp-agrimony	MIST-FLOWER
hen	PLYMOUTH ROCK
	RHODE ISLAND RED
herd of saddle horses	REMUDA
herdsman	WRANGLER
herdsmen's hut or village	RANCHERIA
herring	MENHADEN
hickory	PECAN(-TREE)
hiding-place	HIDY-HOLE
highwayman	ROAD-AGENT
hill-country rustic	HILL-BILLY
hillside terrace	OFF-SET
hilly upland region	COTEAU
hire purchase	INSTALLMENT PLAN
hired thug	GOON

hold	HOLT
holiday	LABOR DAY
hollo	HOLLER
home run	HOMER, TATER
homely philosophy	CRACKER-BARREL
hooligan	ROUGH-NECK
horse	
—breaker	WRANGLER
—chestnut	BUCKEYE
—Indian	CAYUSE
—piebald	PINTO
—poor	TACKY
—race	KENTUCKY DERBY
—riding	SADDLER
—sprinter	QUARTER-HORSE
—thin	RACKABONES
—wild	BRONC(H)O, MUSTANG
horsetail	SCOURING-RUSH
house	SHEBANG
—man	INTERN(E)
—of Congress	CAPITOL
—warming	INFARE
—with rooms to let	ROOMING-HOUSE
household goods	PLUNDER
however	LEASTWAYS, LEASTWISE
huckster	PITCHPERSON
humbug	GUM
Hungarian	BOHUNK, HUN(KY)
husband during wife's lying-in	GANDER-MOONER
husk	SHUCK
hut	SHEBANG
ice-cream counter	SODA-FOUNTAIN
icy surface	GLARE
idiot	AIRHEAD, APPLEHEAD
ill-conditioned person	TACKY
illegal Mexican immigrant	WETBACK
illicit liquor shop	SPEAK-EASY
immediately	LICKETY-SPLIT
impetuous	BRASH
impose on by talking	GAS
in	
—advantageous position	IN THE CATBIRD SEAT
—America	STATESIDE
—collusion	IN CAHOOTS
—good condition	THRIFTY
—good position	HUNKY(-DORY)
—less than	INSIDE OF
—partnership	IN CAHOOTS
—proper manner	ABOUT EAST
—the evening	EVENINGS
inclined or level stretch of road or railway	GRADE
inconclusive trial	MISTRIAL
increase	LIFT

Indian	AMERINO, RED INDIAN, REDSKIN
—corn meal	NOCAKE
—meal cake	HOE-CAKE
—Negro	GRIFF(E)
—poke	ITCHWEED
	(*see also* **Red Indian**)
indoor fair	KERMESS, KERMIS(S)
ineffectual person	LUNCH GUY
inefficient person	SLOUCH
inexperienced youth	GUNSEL
infant	CARPET-APE, RUG-APE
	RUG-RAT
infantryman	DOUGH-BOY
inferior	JAY, SCHLOCK
influence	DRAG
inform	CUE IN
informed of	KNOWING TO
informer	FINK
innkeeper	INNHOLDER
insect	GOLD-BEETLE, GOLD-BUG
	KATYDID
insectivorous plant	DIONAEA
	SARRACENIA
	SIDE-SADDLE FLOWER
	VENUS'S FLY-TRAP
insincere work	EYE SERVICE
inspecting policeman	ROUNDSMAN
intelligence	CIA
interjection	GEE, SON OF A GUN, ZOWIE
intermediate station	WAY-STATION
interpreter	LING(UI)STER, LINKSTER
into	
—confusion	GALLEY-WEST
—New England	DOWN EAST
—unconsciousness	GALLEY-WEST
intoxicating liquor	RUM, TANGLEFOOT
invalid confined to house	SHUT-IN
investigators	CIA, FBI
ivy	ANGELICA-TREE
jaguar	(AMERICAN) TIGER
jail	HOOS(E)GOW
jam tart	CUPID
Japanese immigrant	ISSEI, NISEI
jargon	BAFFLEGAB
jay	XANTH(O)URA
jubilee	SEMI-CENTENNIAL
jug	PITCHER
July 4th	INDEPENDENCE DAY
jumble	WUZZLE
June 14th	FLAG-DAY
Juneberry	AMELANCHIER, SHADBUSH
jury	
—man	VENIREMAN
—writ	VENIRE (FACIAS)
kaput	KABLOOEY, (KER)FLOOEY
Kentuckian	CORNCRACKER

key	HORSE, PONY, TROT	—or register of business	
keyless watch	STEMWINDER	to be transacted	DOCKET
kind	STRIPE	literal translation	TROT
king-bird	PETCHARY	litter-bin	TRASH-CAN
knitted jacket	WAM(M)US	little finger	PINKIE, PINKY
lake fish	MENOMINEE	lizard	UTA
land allotted to settler	HOMESTEAD	loaf	BUM
landsman	SHORESMAN	—around	SLOSH
larch	HACKMATACK	lobelia	INDIAN TOBACCO
	TAMARACK	—red	CARDINAL-FLOWER
larder over stream	SPRING-HOUSE	lobster fat	TOMALLEY
large		local councillor	SELECT-MAN
—estate	PLANTATION	lodge of Order of Patrons	
—fish	TARPON	of Husbandry	GRANGE
—quantity	SLATHER	lodge(r)	ROOM(ER)
—sandwich	HERO, SUBMARINE	lodging-house	ROOMING-HOUSE
larva of ant-lion	DOODLEBUG	long	
laurel	KALMIA	—jump	BROAD JUMP
lawless backwoodsman	ROWDY	—television programme	TELETHON
lawyer	COUNSELLOR	look	GANDER
	DA, JURIST	—out!	HEADS-UP
lax in law-enforcement	WIDE-OPEN	loose jacket	VAREUSE
leaf-nosed bat	MORMOPS	lorry	TRUCK
lean hog	LAND SHARK	Louisiana French or Spanish	CREOLE
leather support-strap		Louisianan of French descent	HABITANT
of carriage	THOROUGHBRACE	low	
leave		—public-house	GROGGERY
—hastily	BUG OUT	—sled	STONE-BOAT
—military	FURLOUGH	lower very slightly	SHADE
leaves round maize ear	CORN-HUSK	lucerne	ALFALFA
	CORN-SHUCK	luggage	
legislature	CONGRESS	—compartment of car	TRUNK
lending library	RENTAL LIBRARY	—room	CHECK(ING)-ROOM
leopard	OCELOT	—van	FREIGHT-CAR
lesson	RECITATION	lumberman	RAIL-SPLITTER
letter		lumberman's hook	PEAV(E)Y
—box	MAILBOX	lure	TOLE, TOLL
—for local delivery	DROP LETTER	lynx	BOBCAT, CATAMOUNT
level		mad	LOCO(ED)
—crossing	GRADE CROSSING	made to order	CUSTOM
—tract	BENCH	mafia	COSA NOSTRA
by river	INTERVALE	magnolia	CUCUMBER(-TREE)
licensing law	EXCISE LAW		SWEET-BAY
lift	ELEVATOR	main road	PIKE
light cart	BUCKBOARD	maize	CORN
lighter	GONDOLA	—bread	INDIAN BREAD
lights out	TAPS	—drink	CORN WHISKEY
lily	CAMAS(S), CAMASH	—dumpling	CORN-DODGER
	MEDEOLA, QUAMASH	—exchange mart	CORN-PIT
limitation of debate	CLOTURE	—loaf	CONE-PONE
linden tree	BEE-TREE	—plantation	CORN-BRAKE
liquor	RUM	majority over any other	PLURALITY
—law	EXCISE LAW	make	
—shop	GROCERY	—a plan of	PLAT
list		—up (prescription)	FILL
—of candidates	TICKET	—use of	IMPROVE

male	
—homosexual	FRUIT
—Indian	BUCK
—negro	BUCK
malicious damage	MAYHEM
man	BO, GUY, JACK
—living apart from his wife	GANDER
marine	LEATHERNECK
market	
—garden produce	TRUCK
—gardener	TRUCK-FARMER
marmot	GROUND-HOG, WOODCHUCK
	PRAIRIE-DOG
marsh-marigold	COWSLIP
marshland creek	SLOUGH
marshy river or lake	BAYOU
marsupial	(O)POSSUM
marten	BLACKCAT, BLACKFOX
	FISHER, PEKAN
	WOODSHOCK
mass of floating waterfowl	RAFT
matter	SHEBANG
mean customer	DRAGGER
measures	
—1¼ acres	ARPENT
—¹⁄₁₆ pint	FLUID OUNCE
—6 fl. oz.	PINT
—473-551cc	PINT
meat closest to the bone	TENDER-LOIN
mechanic	GREASE-MONKEY
medicinal root	DRAGON-ROOT
meeting of	
—delegates	CAUCUS
—voters	TOWN-MEETING
melon	CANTALOUP
member of	
—Chinese secret society	HIGHBINDER
—gymnastic club	TURNER
—incorporated company	INCORPORATOR
—Ku-Klux-Klan	NIGHT-RIDERS
—lynch party	NIGHT-RIDERS
—People's Party	POPULIST
—secret	
fraternity	MOOSE
party	KNOW-NOTHING
memorial tablet	MARKER
men's outfitter	HABERDASHER
mercenary soldier	HESSIAN
merge	MELD
merry-go-round	CAR(R)OUSEL
mess	JACKPOT, MUX
messenger in Congress	PAGE
Mexican	GREASER
middle	CENTER
military	
—decoration	PURPLE HEART
—HQ	PENTAGON
—policeman	SNOWDROP
militiaman	MINUTEMAN
milkweed	PLEURISY-ROOT
milkwort	SENEGA
mink	VISON
miscellaneous lot	RAFT
Mississippi sturgeon	SHOVEL-HEAD
mock serenade	HORNING, SHIVAREE
mocking-bird	MIMUS
mole	STAR-NOSE
money	JACK, SCRIP, SPONDULICKS
mongrel	MUTT
monkey	MARMOSET
month of lying-in	GANDER-MOON
more than	THE RISE OF
mosquito	GALLINIPPER, SKEETER
mother-in-law	MADAM
motherless calf	DOGIE, DOGY
motor junk yard	POT LOT, IRON LOT
mottled	PINTO
mountain	
—bear	GRIZZLY
—foothill region	PIEDMONT
—mocking-bird	SAGE-THRASHER
—valley	PARK
mountains	ROCKIES
mounted policeman	TROOPER
mouse	DEER-MOUSE
—deer	CHEVROTAIN
move rapidly	GIGGIT
mugger of women	MOLL BUZZER
municipal	
—division of county	TOWN
—police	MP
mush	SCHMALTZ
musk-rat	WATER-RAT
musquash	ONDATRA
name-plate	SHINGLE
nappy	DIAPER
narrow, rocky valley	GULCH
National	
—Broadcasting Company	NBC
—Bureau of Standards	NBS
—emblem	BALD EAGLE
	WHITE-HEADED EAGLE
—flag	OLD GLORY
	STARS AND STRIPES
—Guard	MILITIA
—holiday	FOURTH OF JULY
	INDEPENDENCE DAY
	THANKSGIVING
native of	
—Illinois	SUCKER
—Nova Scotia	BLUENOSE
—Virginia	TUCKAHOE

naval	
—engineer	SEABEE
—petty-officer	QUARTER-GUNNER
—quartermaster	PAYMASTER GENERAL
—warrant officer	SAILING-MASTER
neck and neck	NIP AND TUCK
negative	NOPE
negro	MOKE
—in south-east	GULLAH
—patois in Louisiana	GUMBO
—song	SECULAR, SPIRITUAL
neighbouring	NEIGHBO(U)R
New York	BIG APPLE, GOTHAM
New Yorker	GOTHAMITE
	KNICKERBOCKER
news	
—agent	NEWS-DEALER
—boy	NEWSHAWK, NEWSY
night	
—hawk	BULLBAT
—jar	POORWILL
—train	OWL-TRAIN
—tram-car	OWL-CAR
—watchman of remuda	NIGHTHAWK
nincompoop	APPLEHEAD
Nissen hut	QUONSET HUT
non-venomous snake	GARTER-SNAKE
North Carolinian	TAR-HEEL
north-south strip	RANGE
northern sea-duck	OLD SQUAW
nose-bleed	YARROW
not	
—Mormon	GENTILE
—one	NARY
—surveyed or marked off	UNLOCATED
—trade union member	YELLOW DOG
note down for nomination	SLATE
notecase	BILLFOLD
noughts and crosses	TICK-TACK-TOE
now	PRESENTLY
numbers in lottery	POLICY
nut	HICKORY, PECAN
	PICHURIM BEAN, SASSAFRAS NUT
—tree	HICKORY, PECAN
oak	QUERCITRON
obtain	
—on credit	RUN ONE'S FACE
—right of pre-emption	ENTER
occupy	IMPROVE
occurring now and then	SEMI-OCCASIONAL
odd-job man	ROUSTABOUT
officer	
—who determines	
boundaries	PROCESSIONER
—of lowest rank	ENSIGN
oilskin	SLICKER

old	
—Democrat	LOCOFOCO
—fashioned	FOGRAM, SCHMALTZY
—man on a station	ROUSTABOUT
—negro	UNCLE TOM
—New York democrat	HUNKER
—political party	WHIG
olive tree	FRINGE TREE
on the same level	AT GRADE
one	
—from same area	PAISANO
—of Mexican descent	CHICANO
—out to make up to	
all and sundry	GLAD-HANDER
—prevented from winning	SHUTOUT
—who	
carries by pack	PACKER
conducts log rafts	RIVER-DRIVER
does	
—not conform	MAVERICK
—public work	ENGINEER
has been a JP	SQUIRE
plays hand as dealt	STAND-PATTER
serves ice-cream etc	SODA-JERKER
splits logs for fencing	RAIL-SPLITTER
open-air seating	BLEACHERS
opening with grille	WICKET
opossum	DIDELPHYS
optional	ELECTIVE
—subject of study	ELECTIVE
oral examination	QUIZ
ordinary	ORNERY
out	
—and-out	REGULAR, STRAIGHT-OUT
—of	
date	FOGRAM, LUNCHY
sorts	MEAN
outlying trading-station	FORT
outmoded	SCHMALTZY
outwit	EUCHRE
overhead railway	EL
overshoe	ARCTIC, RUBBER
owl	SAW-WHET, WAPACUT
pack saddle	KYACK
packed in jars	CANNED
paddle-steamer	STERN-WHEELER
page torn out for reference	TEAR-SHEET
pair of valves or transistors	FLIP-FLOP
pal	BUD(DY), SIDEKICK
paling	PICKET-FENCE
paltry	JITNEY
papa	POPPA, POPPER
paper money	SCRIP, SHIN-PLASTER
paraffin	KEROSENE
parched Indian corn	NOCAKE, PINOLE
parlour	SPARE ROOM

part of Corn Exchange floor	PIT
particular sort	STRIPE
partly burned tree	RAMPICK, RAMPIKE
partner	PARD(NER)
partnership	CAHOOT(S)
party	HOEDOWN
—at which gifts are given	SHOWER
pass over in favour of another	OVERSLAUGH
passé	FOGRAM, LUNCHY
passenger	PAX
path	TRACE
patriot	HUNDRED-PERCENTER
paved road	PAVEMENT
pavement	FOOTWAY, PAVE, SIDEWALK
payment	COMPENSATION
penitent at revival meeting	MOURNER
perch-pike	SAUGER
peregrine falcon	DUCK-HAWK
period of slackening business	ROLLING ADJUSTMENT
permission to go out	OUT
personal	
—announcement in newspaper	CARD
—goods	PLUNDER
pertaining to woods	WOODSY
perturb	FAZE, PHASE
petrol	COAL-OIL, GAS(OLENE) GASOLINE
pharmacist	DRUGGIST
philop(o)ena (game)	FILLIPEEN
Phytolacca	POKEBERRY, POKEWEED
pickerel-weed	PONTEDERIA
picket fence	RAIL-FENCE
picnic	CLAMBAKE
piebald horse	PINTO
pie-plant	RHUBARB
pig-sty	HOG-PEN
pigeon	GROUND-PIGEON GROUND-DOVE MOURNING-DOVE
—berry	GARGET, POKEWEED
piggin	PIPKIN
pike	PICKEREL, SAUGER
pinafore	TIRE
—dress	JUMPER
pine	LOBLOLLY(PINE)
pistol	DERRINGER, GAT, IRON, ROD
pitcher-plant	DARLINGTONIA
plain	HOMELY, ORNERY
plan	PLAT
plane-tree	BUTTON-WOOD, SYCAMORE
plant	CHECKERBERRY EVENING-PRIMROSE GODETIA, GOLDEN-SEAL JACK-IN-THE-PULPIT PARTRIDGE-BERRY

	PHLOX, RAGWEED SEGO, SNEEZEWEED SNOW-PLANT, WINTER-CLOVER WINTERGREEN
—fraudulent voters	COLONISE, COLONIZE
plateau	BARREN
play	
—hand as dealt	STAND PAT
—pizzicato	PINCH
pleaded	PLED
pliable	DOUGH-FACED
plot out	PLAT
plover	KILLDEE(R), STONE-SNIPE
pluck	PINCH
plum suitable for drying	PRUNE
pocket-gopher	POUCHED-RAT
pod	SHUCK
poison-oak	SUMAC(H)
poisoned by locoweed	LOCOED
pokeweed	GARGET, PIGEON-BERRY
police	
—patrol car	PROWL CAR
—station	STATION-HOUSE
policeman	BULL
—on the beat	PATROLMAN
—without rank	PATROLMAN
policeman's	
—badge	SHIELD
—stick	NIGHT-STICK
policy involving spending on improvements	PORK-BARREL
political	
—conference	CONVENTION
—division of county	TOWN
—funds	BARREL
—party machine	ORGANISATION
—party organisation	MACHINE
—speaker	STUMP-ORATOR
—wire-puller	PIPE-LAYER
pond	TANK
Pontederia	PICKEREL-WEED
poor	
—horse	CAYUSE, TACKY
—whisky	REDEYE
—white	CONCH, CORN-CRACKER LOW-DOWNER
—whites	TRASH
porch	STOOP
porter	RED-CAP
portion	GRIST, ORDER
postal code	ZIP CODE
postcard	MAILING-CARD, POSTAL(-CARD)
potassium bicarbonate	SALERATUS
potato pest	COLORADO BEETLE
pot-hole	THANK-YOU-MA'AM
pouched-rat	(POCKET-)GOPHER

poultry	PLYMOUTH ROCK	quaintly pleasing	CLEVER
	RHODE ISLAND RED	Quaker City	PHILADELPHIA
prairie		quantity	GRIST, MESS
—chicken	GROUSE	quickly	LICKETY-SPLIT
—dog	MARMOT, WISHTONWISH	quite	REAL
—grass	BUFFALO GRASS	—as much as	RISING
—oyster	RAW EGG	rabbit	COTTONTAIL
—schooner	COVERED WAGON	rac(c)oon	COON, PROCYON
—turnip	BREADROOT	radio broadcast	DOPE
—wolf	COYOTE	Radio Corporation	RCA
president	PREXY	railway	AMTRAK, EL
—of college	PREX		RAILROAD, ROAD
press-stud	SNAP FASTENER	—buffer	BUMPER
pretty girl	DOLL, PEACHERINO, QUAIL	—carriage	RAIL(ROAD)-CAR
primrose	SUN-DROP	—coach connection	VESTIBULE
prison	BRIG, CALABOOSE, CAN	—porter	RED-CAP
	HOOS(E)GOW, LOG-HOUSE	—saloon	PARLOUR-CAR
	PENITENTIARY	—signal	TARGET
—cell	TANK	—sleeper	TIE
—enclosure	BULL-PEN	—station	DEPOT
—van	PATROL-WAGON	—van or truck	RAILROAD CAR
private		—worker	RAILROADER
—compartment on train	DRAWING-ROOM	ramify	SPRANGLE
—detective	PINKERTON	rapid	SA(U)LT
probable customer	PROSPECT	rapids in a gorge	DALLE
professional killer	GUN(SEL)	rascal	SKEESICKS
Progne	SWALLOW	raspberry	SALMON-BERRY
prohibit by injunction	ENJOIN	ravine	COULEE, FLUME, GULCH
promiscuous woman	CHIPPY, HOOKER		PURGATORY
promise to accept		raw egg	PRAIRIE-OYSTER
later invitation	RAIN-CHECK	ray	STINGAREE
promoter	PITCHPERSON	re-enlisted soldier	VETERAN
promptly	IN SHORT ORDER	reactionary	BOURBON
prosecutor	DA	real	SURE-ENOUGH
prosperous	THRIFTY	really	REAL
protection money	KICKBACK	rear	FETCH UP
provisions given for share in finds	GRUB-STAKE	rebuke	SCORE
public		reckless	BRASH
—auction sale	VENDUE	—youth	HOT-RODDER
—lavatory	COMFORT STATION	record of land transfer	PROTOCOL
—service	UTILITY	recovery-vehicle	WRECKER
pucker	POCKET	recurring spree	PERIODICAL
puddle	LOBLOLLY	red squirrel	BOOMER, CHICKAREE
Pueblo Indian	ZUNI		S(E)WELLEL
pull	SCHLEP	red-breasted thrush	AMERICAN ROBIN
puma	CATAMOUNT, COUGAR	redtop (grass)	HERD('S) GRASS
	PAINTER, PANTHER, (RED)TIGER	reed-bird	BOBOLINK
pumpkin	CASHAW	refrigerator	COOLER
pupil at kindergarten	KINDERGARTENER	refuge	HOLT
pupil's mark	GRADE	refuse container	(TR)ASH-CAN
puritanical person	BLUENOSE	region	SECTION
purple medick	ALFALFA	register	LEDGER
purpose	CALCULATE	registrar	REGISTER
put in danger	JEOPARD	reheated	WARMED-OVER
quail	BOB-WHITE, COLIN	reindeer	CARIBOU
	ODONTOPHORUS, ORTYX	religious excitement	ROUSEMENT

Remembrance Day	DECORATION DAY	rustic	HICK, RUBE
	MEMORIAL DAY	saddle	
remove shell or husk	SHUCK	—girth	CINCH
remuneration	COMPENSATION	—horse	SADDLER
rented farm-land	MANOR	safe-breaker	YEGG(MAN)
repertory company	STOCK COMPANY	sailor in Navy	GOB
representing whole area	AT LARGE	salal	GAULTHERIA
reprimanded	CHAWED UP	salamander	HELL-BENDER, MENOPOME
request to accept			MUD-PUPPY
later invitation	RAIN-CHECK	saloon car	SEDAN
reservation	HOLD	sand	
residential part of town	UP TOWN	—bar	OVERSLAUGH
residing in college	PARIETAL	—piper/stint	SAND-PEEP
resolute	FLAT-FOOTED	sans-serif type	GOTHIC
return	ROUND-TRIP	saucy	SASSY
reverse charges call	COLLECT CALL	saunter	MOSEY
revolver	COLT, GAT, IRON, ROD	school	
rhododendron	RHODORA	—dance	PROMENADE
rhubarb	PIE-PLANT	—imposition	PENSUM
rice-bird	BOBOLINK	—mistress	SCHOOL-MA'AM
ridge or hollow in road	THANK-YOU-MA'AM	scion	CION
riding-horse	SADDLER	Scout's leather cord	BOONDOGGLE
rifle	WINCHESTER	scrutinise	CANVASS
right of state to oppose		sea	
federal government	INTERPOSITION	—board	TIDE-WATER
ringplover	KILLDEE(R)	—bream	PORGIE, PORGY
ringtail(-cat)	CACOMISTLE, CACOMIXL	—lavender	SEA-ROSEMARY
risen	RIZ	season ticket	COMMUTATION TICKET
river		seclusion	RETIRACY
—fish	GROWLER	second-year student	SOPHOMORE
—mussel	NIGGER-HEAD	secret organisation	KU-KLUX(KLAN)
—sides	UPLAND	Secretary of State	PREMIER
—water affected by tides	TIDE-WATER	sedge	CHUFA, NUT-GRASS
rivers	(see separate entry)		TIGER-NUT
riverside embankment	LEVEE	see-saw	TEETER(-BOARD)
robbery	HEIST	seize without right	MAVERICK
rocket fuel	HYDYNE	self	
Rocky Mountain sheep	BIGHORN	—appointed	
rodent	JUMPING-MOUSE	peace-keepers	LYNCH MOB
	KANGAROO-RAT, MARMOT		VIGILANCE COMMITTEE
MOUNTAIN-BEAVER, POUCHED-MOUSE			VIGILANTES
	S(E)WELLEL, WOODCHUCK	—possession	COOL
rodeo performer	COWBOY	sell tickets at inflated prices	SCALP
roll	BAGEL	semibreve	WHOLE NOTE
room	SHEBANG	send (on passenger ticket)	CHECK
—attached to shop	PARLOUR	sentimentality	SCHMALTZ
rose	RIZ	sergeant-fish	COBIA, CRAB-EATER
—pest	ROSE-BUG	settle	LOCATE
rough country	BOONDOCKS	shadbush	AMELANCHIER, JUNEBERRY
roundabout	CAR(R)OUSEL		SASKATOON, SERVICE-BERRY
routine flight	MILK-RUN	shallow section of river	RIFFLE
rubber overshoe	GUM(SHOE)	sharp-tailed grouse	PRAIRIE-CHICKEN
ruffed grouse	PARTRIDGE	shebeen	SPEAK-EASY
rumour	SCUTTLEBUTT	shell	SHUCK
running on thin ice	KITTLY-BENDERS	shoe	TIE
rural area	STICKS	—lace	(SHOE-)STRING

shop	SHEBANG	—gathering	HOEDOWN
—assistant	(SALES-)CLERK	—intercourse	GAM
—keeper	STOREKEEPER	soda-fountain worker	SODA-JERK(ER)
short jacket	ROUNDABOUT	sodium bicarbonate	SALERATUS
shortage	WANTAGE	soft drink	SARSAPARILLA
shout	ROOT	soil, sticky when wet	GUMBO
show spirit	SPUNK	soldier	DOUGH-BOY, GI, SAMMY
showy production	SCHMALTZ	—of both world wars	RETREAD
shrewd	HEADS-UP	solicit orders	DRUM
shrub	BUTTON-BUSH, BUFFALO-BERRY	sound	COPACETIC
	BUFFALO-NUT, CALICO-BUSH		COPESETTIC
	CANDLEBERRY-TREE, CORAL-BERRY	source of patronage, etc	PIE-COUNTER
	FRANGIPANI, GREASEWOOD	Southerner who co-operated	
	HAMAMELIS, HOP-TREE	with Republicans	SCAL(L)AWAG
	HUCKLEBERRY, KALMIA		SCALLYWAG
	MOUNTAIN-LAUREL	Spanish-American	GREASER
	RED-JASMINE, SAL(L)AL	—half-caste	MESTIZO
	SNOWBERRY, SPICE-BUSH	—speaking district	BARRIO
	STAFF-TREE, STRAWBERRY-TREE	sparrow	SAVANNA-SPARROW
	SYMPHORICARPUS, WAX-MYRTLE	speaker of farewell	VALEDICTORIAN
	WINTER-BERRY, WITCH-ALDER	special subject	MAJOR
	WITCH-HAZEL, WITHE-ROD	specialise at college	MAJOR
	YA(U)PON, YUPON	spectacles	CHEATERS
side		speculative scheme	WILD-CAT
—in billiards	ENGLISH	speculator	WILD-CAT
—of valley	COTEAU	speedwell	NECK-WEED
sightsee(r)	RUBBER-NECK(ER)	spelling competition	SPELL-DOWN
sign-board	SHINGLE	spice-bush	BENJAMIN-TREE
sign language	AMESIAN	spider	BLACK WIDOW
simpleton	FLATHEAD	spies	CIA
sir(rah)	SIRREE	spill	LAMP-LIGHTER
six-mile width of town	RANGE	spindle-tree	BURNING BUSH
skipping	JUMP-ROPE	spiny	
skittles	TEN-PINS	—fish	SCULPIN
skunk	SEE-CAWK	—lizard	HORNED TOAD
—bird	BOBOLINK	Spiraea	HARD-HACK
Slav	BOHUNK	spiritless person	FLAT TYRE
sloppy	SOZZLY	spittoon	CUSPIDOR(E)
slops	SOZZLE	splash	SOZZLE
slush	SPOSH	—of dirt or colour	SPLATCH
small		splotch	SPLATCH
—college	FRESHWATER COLLEGE	spoil	MUX
—lizard	FENCE-LIZARD	sponge	BUM
—loaf (maize)	CORN-DODGER	sporting kit	DUFFEL, DUFFLE
—river	CREEK	spotted sandpiper	PEETWEET
—township	VILLAGE	sprawl	SPRANGLE
smoker's haze	SMAZE	spree	BUM
snack	LUNCH	sprinter (horse)	QUARTER-HORSE
snake	HOG-NOSE, PIT-VIPER	spruce	HEMLOCK
snipe	SHAD-BIRD, WILLET	spy	FINK
snow		squalid	SCUZZY
—bird	JUNCO	squat	ABSQUATULATE
—goose	WAV(E)Y	squirrel	CHIPMUCK, CHIPMUNK
—up	STALL		GROUND-SQUIRREL, HACKEE
social	SOCIABLE		S(E)WELLEL
—blunder	BREAK	St John's-wort	ORANGE-GRASS

stag		suppose	CALCULATE, GUESS
—beetle	HORNBUG	surmount	RISE
—party	STAG	suspect	SUSPICION
stage-coach	THOROUGHBRACE	swallow	PROGNE
stalk	STILL-HUNT	—hole	SINK-HOLE
starchy tuber	INDIAN TURNIP	swamp	DISMAL, PURGATORY, VLEI, VLY
start	JUMP-OFF	swan	TRUMPETER
state		swede	RUTABAGA
—governor's deputy	LIEUTENANT-GENERAL	sweet	
—militia	NATIONAL GUARD	—friedcake	CRULLER, WONDER
states	(see separate entry)	—popcorn	CORNBALL
—without slavery	FREE STATES	—potato	YAM
steal cattle	RUSTLE	—seller on train	BUTCHER
stevedore	LONGSHOREMAN	sweets	CANDIES
stew	BURGOO	swerving throw at baseball	SCREWBALL
—of corn and beans	SUCCOTASH	swift	CHIMNEY SWALLOW
stewed fruit	SAUCE	swimming-pool	NATATORIUM
stock		swindler's helper	BUNCO-STEERER
—of a commodity	INVENTORY	Swiss roll	JELLY ROLL
—farm	RANCH	swot	POLER
stopping train	WAY-TRAIN	symbol of luck	GOD'S EYE
straggle	SPRANGLE	take	
straight dress	SHIRTWAISTER	—a holiday	VACATION
strawberry shrub	CALYCANTHUS	—up residence	LOCATE
stray animal	MAVERICK	talk	
stream	CREEK, KILL	—bluntly	TALK TURKEY
street		—business	TALK TURKEY
—boy	TAD	—nonsense	BLATHER
—car	HORSECAR	talker of nonsense	BLATHERSKITE
—charges	STREETAGE	tall hat	STOVEPIPE
—ruffian	PLUG-UGLY	tallboy	HIGHBOY
—vendor's barrow	PUSH-CART	tap	FAUCET
strip		teacher	SCHOOLMAN
—occupied by railway		teal	BLUE-WING
track or road	RIGHT-OF-WAY	team gathering	HUDDLE
—off	SHUCK	telephone	
strong jacket	WAM(M)US, WAMPUS	—call-box	PAY-STATION
struggle	SPRANGLE	—circuit	TRUNK
student	SOPHOMORE	television	VIDEO
stunning girl	PEACHERINO	—award	EMMY
stupid	DUMB, JAY	temporary school	INSTITUTE
—fellow, person	APPLEHEAD, BOB	tender	PROPOSAL
	BUFFLEHEAD, DUMB-BELL, JAY	tenderfoot	GREENHORN
	KNUCKLE-DRUGGER, LUNKHEAD	—in Alaska	CHE(E)CHAKO
	LUNCH GUY, SCHMO(CK)		CHEECHALKO, CHECHAQUO
	SCHMUCK, SCHNOOK	term	SEMESTER
—youth	GUNSEL	—of endearment	HONEY-CHILE
sturdy fellow	HUSKY	termite	WOOD-LOUSE
sub-division of county	TOWNSHIP	theatre stalls	PARQUET
submarine	PIG-BOAT	theatrical award	TONY
suburbs	BOONDOCKS	theological student	THEOLOGUE
sulky	STUFFY	thick soup	BURGOO
sumac	POISON-OAK	thicket of canes	CANE-BRAKE
summer residence	COTTAGE	thin person or horse	RACKABONES
sunfish	CRAPPIE	thingummy	HOOT(E)NANNY
supply	GRIST, STAKE		IIOOTANANNY

think	CALCULATE, GUESS
third-year student	JUNIOR
thorn	
—apple	JIM(P)SON WEED
	JAMESTOWN WEED
—bush	MESQUITE
thorough	REGULAR
thoroughly	ALL TO PIECES
—acquainted with	NEXT TO
thousand	
—dollars	GRAND
—million	BILLION
—to	
fourth power	TRILLION
fifth power	QUADRILLION
sixth power	QUINTILLION
through and through	ALL TO PIECES
thrush	CAT-BIRD, VEERY
ticket given for future use	RAIN-CHECK
tidy up	PICK
tiger-nut	CHUFA
timber	LUMBER
	(*see also separate entry*)
—wolf	GREY WOLF
timothy (grass)	HERD('S) GRASS
tiny	TEENTY
titmouse	CHICKADEE
toady	BOOTLICK
tobacco	PERIQUE
toffee	TAFFY
toll for street facilities	STREETAGE
toll-free road	FREEWAY
top-hat	PLUG-HAT
tortoise	GOPHER, TERRAPIN
totalisator/tote	PARIMUTUEL
tough	ROUGH-NECK
towhee	GROUND-ROBIN
town	BURG
townsman	COCKNEY, DUDE
track	SIGN
trade union branch	LOCAL
trader with Indians	COMANCHERO
trader's jargon	CHINOOK
trail	SIGN
trailing plant	PARTRIDGE-BERRY
train with limited	
number of passengers	LIMITED EXPRESS
tram	STREET-CAR
—car	TROLLEY(-CAR)
—ticket	TRIP SLIP
tramp	HOBO
—light	SLUT LAMP
translation	HORSE, PONY, TROT
transport	HAUL
transportation of freight	
containers by ship or barge	FISHYBACK

transporting agent	FREIGHTER
travel bag	GRIP(SACK)
travelling trunk	SARATOGA(TRUNK)
tread softly	CATFOOT
tree	BLACK WALNUT, CATALPA
	DOUGLAS FIR, DYER'S OAK
	FRINGE-TREE, HALESIA
	HEADACHE TREE, HONEY-LOCUST
	JACK-PINE, JOJOBA, LIQUIDAMBAR
	LOBLOLLY(-PINE), OSAGE ORANGE
	PITCHPINE, QUERCITRON, SASSAFRAS
	SEQUOIA, SHAWNEE-WOOD, SILVER-BELL
	SLIPPERY ELM, SNOWDROP-TREE
	SUGAR-MAPLE, SUGAR-PINE
	SWAMP CYPRESS, TAXODIUM
	TULIP-TREE, WASHINGTONIA
	YELLOW-BARKED OAK
	YELLOW-WOOD
—allied to elm	HACKBERRY
—Gordonia	LOBLOLLY-BAY
—leathery-leaved	LOBLOLLY-TREE
—Tsuga	HEMLOCK
tree-frog	PEEPER
trilby	FEDORA
trite	MICKEY
trounce	SHELL
trouser turn-up	CUFF
trousers	HIP-HUGGERS, PANTS
trout	LAKER, TOGUE
truant	HOOKEY
truck-driver	TEAMSTER
truckling	DOUGH-FACED
truncheon	NIGHT-STICK
trunk	SARATOGA
—call	TOLL-CALL
tufted grouse	PHEASANT
tulip-tree	CUCUMBER-TREE, POPLAR
tumbleweed	WILD-INDIGO
turn-out	TEAM
turtle-dove	MOURNING-DOVE
tussock in swamp	NIGGER-HEAD
twilled cotton	CHINO
tyrant flycatcher	KING-BIRD, PETCHARY
ugly	HOMELY
unbranded animal	MAVERICK
uncomfortable	MEAN
underground railway	SUBWAY
undertaker	MORTICIAN
undue forwardness	FORTH-PUTTING
unduly familiar	GAY
unfounded story	MALARK(E)Y
uniform colour	OLIVE-DRAB
unit trusts	MUTUAL FUNDS
United States	UNCLE SAM
university calendar	CATALOG
unlucky person	S(C)HLIMAZEL

unmade road	DIRT-ROAD	—weed	ANACHARIS, ELODEA
unmanageable animal	OUTLAW	waxwing	CEDAR-BIRD
unmannerly lout	ROUGH-NECK	wayfaring-tree	HOBBLE-BUSH
unruly	TORN-DOWN	weasel	CARCAJOU, GLUTTON
unsaleable article	STOREKEEPER		WOLVERENE, WOLVERINE
unsound financial scheme	WILD-CAT	wedding gifts	SHOWER
until the end of	THROUGH	weed	SPANISH NEEDLES
unyielding	ROCK-RIBBED	weight	HEFT
up to and including	THROUGH	—25lb	QUARTER
upper		—100lb	CENTAL
—floor	LOFT		HUNDREDWEIGHT
—part of river-steamer	TEXAS	—750-1200lb (tobacco)	HOGSHEAD
unskilled worker	HUNKY	—2000lb	SHORT TON
usurer	NOTE-SHAVER	—2240lb	LONG TON
utterly	PLUMB	well off	FOREHANDED
valley side	COTEAU	wharf labourer	ROUSTABOUT
vegetable		wheat pest	HESSIAN FLY
—marrow	MARROW-SQUASH	whippoorwill	WISHTONWISH
—seller	SAUCEMAN	whisky	BOURBON, TANGLEFOOT
vegetables eaten with meat	SAUCE	—and soda	HIGHBALL
vehicle	SHEBANG, SURREY	white	
—for hire	HACK	—fish	ROUND-FISH
verandah	PIAZZA, PORCH, STOOP	—headed eagle	BALD EAGLE
veritably	REAL	—hellebore	INDIAN POKE
very much	SOME	—wash	SKUNK
—indeed	AND HOW	Whitsuntide	PINKSTER, PINXSTER
vice	VISE	whopper	SCROUGER, SLOCKDOLAGER
Virginian	TUCKAHOE		SOCDOLIGER, SOCDOLOGER
—fungus	INDIAN BREAD		SOC(K)DOLAGER, SOGDOLOGER
—quail	PARTRIDGE		SOGDOLAGER, SOGDOLIGER
visit at sea	GAM	wild	
vote illegally more		—cat	CATAMOUNT
than once	REPEAT	—horse	BRONC(H)O, MUSTANG
voters' meeting to		window	
nominate candidate	PRIMARY	—blind	SHADE
vow	VUM	—dressing	TRIM
vulture	TURKEY-BUZZARD	windscreen	WINDSHIELD
waistcoat	VEST	wine	CATAWBA, SCUPPERNONG
waiter	BUS-BOY, GOSSOON	wing	
waitress	BUS-GIRL	—making ell-shape	EL
walk	PASEAR	—or annex of house	EXTENSION
walking boundaries	PROCESSIONING	wintergreen	CHECKER-BERRY
wallet	BILLFOLD		GAULTHERIA
walnut	BUTTERNUT, CARYOCAR	wireless news bulletin	DOPE
warbler	REDSTART	witch	
warn not to pay or		—alder	FOTHERGILLA
give up goods	FACTORISE	—hazel	FOTHERGILLA, HAMAMELIS
warship	USS	with ice cream	A LA MODE
water		withhold support	BOLT
—cask	SCUTTLEBUTT	witness-box	CHAIR, STAND
—fall	SA(U)LT	witty thought after	
—lily	SPATTER-DOCK	the occasion	LATTER-WIT
leaf	PAD	woman	BROAD, DAME, DOLL(Y)
—proof	SLICKER		FRAIL, SKIRT
—shed	DIVIDE	women's	
—thrush	WAGTAIL	—academic society	SORORITY

—blouse	SHIRTWAIST
or bodice	WAIST
—club	SOROSIS
—widebrimmed hat	SUNDOWN
wonderful	BOFFO
wood	
—land	TIMBER
—louse	TERMITE
—shavings	EXCELSIOR
wooden bowl or pail	PIPKIN
woodpecker	FLICKER, YUCKER
work	LABOR
—basket	CABA
—of little value	BOONDOGGLE
worker in compressed air	SAND-HOG
workman's railcar	HANDCAR
workshop worker	SHOPMAN
worm-fence	SNAKE-FENCE
worry	FAZE, PHASE
worthless (fellow)	BUM
wrecking clause in document	JOKER
wrestle and throw	BULLDOG
wring evidence or	
confession from	SWEAT
writ issued by sheriff	VENIRE(FACIAS)
yard outside entrance	DOORYARD
yarrow	NOSE-BLEED
yearly stage in education	GRADE
yell to supplement a cheer	TIGER
yellow-wood	GOPHER
yes	YEP
—certainly	AND HOW
yodel	WARBLE
yokel	CORNBALL, HICK, JAKE, RUBE
young	
—man	GOSSOON
—townsman	MUCKER
zero score	GOOSE-EGG

American football

act of violence	PERSONAL FOUL
area behind goal-line	END ZONE
attempt to	
—progress	DOWN, PLAY
—sack quarterback	BLITZ, DOGGING
	PASS RUSH
catching quarterback in	
possession of ball	SACKING
distance a punted ball is	
carried after catching	PUNT RETURN
downfield kick	PUNT
dropping ball	FUMBLING
extra time	OVERTIME
famous players	ANDERSEN, BLANDA
	BROWN, CRAIG, DAVIS
	DEMPSEY, ELWAY, HALAS, HIRSCH
	JAWORSKI, JOHNSON, JONES
	LARGENT, LOMBARDI, MARTIN
	MONTANA, NAMATH, NEALE
	PAYTON, PERRY, SIMPSON
	SINGH, SMITH, TAYLOR
final match	SUPERBOWL
formations	
—attacking	I-FORMATION, MAN IN MOTION
	SHORT YARDAGE, SHOTGUN, SPLIT
	STANDARD PRO SET
	T-FORMATION, TWIN SET
—defending	BLITZ, DOG, FOUR-THREE
	SHORT YARDAGE
	THREE-FOUR
grouping to discuss tactics	HUDDLE
illegal	
—blocking	CLIPPING
—move in scrimmage	ENCROACHING
—throw to	
ground	INTENTIONAL GROUNDING
lateral running at	
scrimmage	IN MOTION
leagues	AMERICAN FOOTBALL
	CONFERENCE
	NATIONAL FOOTBALL CONFERENCE
line	ENDLINE, GOAL-LINE
	SIDELINE
—halfway mark	MIDFIELD STRIPE
—outside playing area	RESTRAINT LINE
—where ball is	
spotted	LINE OF SCRIMMAGE
—yard marker	HASH MARK
loss of (control of) ball	FUMBLING
movement to gain ground	PASSING
	RUSHING
obstruction	BLOCKING
officials	BACK JUDGE, FIELD JUDGE
	HEAD LINESMAN, LINE JUDGE
	REFEREE, SIDE JUDGE, UMPIRE
pass that is caught	COMPLETION
pitch	GRIDIRON
positions	CENTER, CORNER BACK
	END, GUARD, LINEBACKER
	QUARTERBACK, RUNNING BACK
	SAFETY, WIDE RECEIVER
progress towards goal	DRIVE
restart	
—after dropped ball	SCRIMMAGE
—between plays	SNAP
—out of bounds	SCRIMMAGE
scoring	
—1 point	CONVERSION, POINT AFTER
—2 points	SAFETY
—3 points	FIELD GOAL
—6 points	TOUCHDOWN
sign of foul	YELLOW FLAG
	YELLOW HANDKERCHIEF

space between teams	
at scrimmage	NEUTRAL ZONE
start	KICK-OFF
stoppage	TIME-OUT
—by referee	TWO-MINUTE WARNING
supervisory	
body	NATIONAL FOOTBALL LEAGUE, NFL
team	
—on field	ELEVEN
—total	FORTY-FIVE
teams	
—Atlanta	FALCONS
—Buffalo	BILLS
—Chicago	BEARS
—Cincinnati	BENGALS
—Cleveland	BROWNS
—Dallas	COWBOYS
—Denver	BRONCOS
—Detroit	LIONS
—Houston	OILERS
—Indianapolis	COLTS
—Kansas City	CHIEFS
—Los Angeles	RAIDERS, RAMS
—Miami	DOLPHINS
—Minnesota	VIKINGS
—New England	PATRIOTS
—New York	GIANTS, JETS
—Philadelphia	EAGLES
—Phoenix	CARDINALS
—Pittsburgh	STEELERS
—San Diego	CHARGERS
—San Francisco	FORTY-NINERS
—Seattle	SEAHAWKS
—Tampa Bay	BUCCANEERS
—Washington	REDSKINS
through-the-legs pass	
at start of play	SNAP
time ball is in air after a punt	HANG TIME
transfer of possession of	
ball to opponents	TURNOVER
trophy	AMERICAN BOWL
	LOMBARD TROPHY
	PRO-BOWL, SUPERBOWL TROPHY
unit of game	DOWN, PLAY
amino-acid	(*see* **acids**)
anatomist	(*see* **physician**)
Andorra	AND
capital	ANDORRA LA VELLA
Angola	
capital	LUANDA
coin	ANGOLAR, KWANZA, LWEI
sheep	ZUNA
anniversaries	
2 years	BIENNIAL
3 years	TRIENNIAL
4 years	QUADR(I)ENNIAL

5 years	QUINQUENNIAL
6 years	SEXENNIAL
7 years	SEPTENNIAL
8 years	OCTENNIAL
9 years	NOVENNIAL
10 years	DECENNIAL
100 years	CENTENNIAL
200 years	BICENTENNIAL
300 years	TERCENTENNIAL
	TRICENTENNIAL
400 years	QUADRICENTENNIAL
	QUATERCENTENNIAL
500 years	QUINCENTENNIAL
1000 years	MILLENNIUM
—wedding anniversary	
1 year	COTTON
2 years	PAPER
3 years	LEATHER
4 years	FLOWER, FRUIT
5 years	WOOD
6 years	IRON, SUGAR CANDY
7 years	WOOL
8 years	BRONZE
9 years	COPPER, POTTERY
10 years	TIN
11 years	STEEL
12 years	LINEN, SILK
13 years	LACE
14 years	IVORY
15 years	CRYSTAL
20 years	CHINA
25 years	SILVER
30 years	PEARL
35 years	CORAL
40 years	RUBY
45 years	SAPPHIRE
50 years	GOLD(EN)
55 years	EMERALD
60 years	DIAMOND
65 years	DIAMOND
antelopes	
including: deer	
gazelles	
Abyssinia	MADOQUA
Alpine ibex	STEINBOCK
Africa	ADDAX, ADMI, ARIEL, BISA
	BLAUWBOK, BLESBOK, BLOUBOK
	BLUE-BUCK, BONGO, BONTEBOK,
	BOS(SH)BO, BOTIGO, BUBALIS
	BUSHBOK, BUSHBUCK, CAMA
	CHEVROTAIN, COBA, DAMA, DIBITAG
	DIK-DIK, DUIKER, DUYKER, ELAND
	GEMSBOK, GNU, GRYSBOK, GUIB
	HARNESSED ANTELOPE, HARTEBEEST
	IMPALA, IMPOPO, (I)NYALA, KAAMA
	KLIPSPRINGER, KOB(O), KOODOO

	KORIN, KUDO, LECHWE, MHORR, MOHR
	NAGOR, NAKONG, ORIBI, ORYX, OUREBI
	OX-ANTELOPE, PALA, PALEBUCK
	PALLAH, POKU, POOKOO, PUKU
	PYGARG, REEBOK
	REITBOK, RHEBOK, RIETBOK, SABLE
	SASSABY, SPRINGBOK, SPRINGBUCK
	STEENBOK, STEINBOCK, STEMBOK
	STEMBUCK, SUNI, TOPI, TORA
	TSESSEBE, WATER-BUCK
	WATER-DEER, WILDEBEEST
America	CABRIE, CABRIT, CARIACOU
	CARIBOU, CARCAJOU, ELK, MOOSE
	MULE-DEER, PRONGBUCK
	PRONGHORN
	ROCKY-MOUNTAIN GOAT
	VIRGINIAN DEER, WAPITI
Asia	AHU, ARIEL, AXIS, BARKING-DEER
	CHITAL, DZEREN, ELK, GAZEL(LE)
	HANGUL, KAKAR, MAHA, MUNTJAC
	MUNTJAK, MUSK-DEER, NAPU
	RATWA, RUSA, SAIGA, SAMBOO
	SAMBHUR, SAMB(O)UR
	SAMB(W)AR
Burma	THAMENG, THAMIN
China	MUSK-DEER, WATER-DEER
chamois	RUBICAPRA
East Indies	RUCERVUS
Europe	CHAMOIS, ELK, IBEX, IZZARD
female	DOE, ROE
Himalayas	GORAL, SEROW
India	AXIS, BLACKBUCK, CHI(N)KARA
	CHIRU, CHITAL, NILGAI, NYLG(H)AU
	RUSA, SAMBOO
	SAMBHUR, SAMB(O)UR
	SAMB(W)AR, SASIN, SEROW
Japan	SIKA
male	BUCK, STAG
Mongolia	DZEREN, DZERON
mouse-deer	CHEVROTAIN
puff-nosed	SAIGA
Pyrenees	IBEX, IZZARD
Russia	SAIGA
sable antelope	POTOQUANE
Senegal	NAGOR
South America	ALPACA, GUANACO
	HUANACO, LLAMA, PACO, PUDU
striped	HARNESSED-ANTELOPE
Tibet	GOA
white-bellied	LECHWE
young	FAWN

(see also **deer***)*

anthropology

ages of human culture
—earliest	EOLITHIC
—Old Stone Age	PALAEOLITHIC
Early Palaeolithic	CHELLEAN
	OLDOWAN, ACHEULEAN
	ACHEULIAN, MOUSTERIAN
Upper Palaeolithic	AURIGNACIAN
	CHATEL PERONIAN
	PE RIGORDIAN, GRAVETTIAN
	SOLUTREAN, SOLUTRIAN
	MAGDALENIAN
—Middle Stone Age	AZILIAN, MESOLITHIC
	EPIPALAEOLITHIC
—New Stone Age	NEOLITHIC
	ACERAMIC, CERAMIC
—transitional	AENOLITHIC
—Copper Age	CHALCOLITHIC
—later	BRONZE AGE
	HALLSTATT
	IRON AGE

anthropologists
—American	BENEDICT, GEERTZ
	HERSKOVITS, KROEBER
	LINTON, MALINOWSKI
	REDFIELD, VANTINA
	WARNER
—Belgian	VANTINA
—British	BATES, DALTON, GALTON
	LEAKEY, PERRY
	RADCLIFFE-BROWN, TYLOR
—French	LEVI-STRAUSS
	TEILHARD DE CHARDIN
—Polish	MALINOWSKI
—Spanish	BAROJA
biology of humans	ANTHROPOBIOLOGY

body types
—long, lean	ECTOMORPH
—muscular	MESOMORPH
—short	
rounded	ENDOMORPH
stocky	AMPLOSOME

civilisations
(earliest first)	EGYPTIAN
	SUMERIAN
	INDIC
	MAYAN
	MINOAN
	HITTITE
	CHINESE, SINIC
	BABYLONIAN
	GREEK, HELLENIC
	SYRIAC
	ESKIMO
	GREEK, SPARTAN
	POLYNESIAN
	ANDEAN
	KHMER
	JAPANESE, KOREAN
	WESTERN

	ORTHODOX CHRISTIAN
	HINDU
	RUSSIAN CHRISTIAN
	ARABIC
	MEXICAN
	OTTOMAN
	ISLAMIC
dawn man (hoax)	EOANTHROPUS
	PILTDOWN MAN
human ancestors	
(earliest first)	PRE-ADAMITE
—Oligocene	
Egypt	PROLIOPITHECUS
—Miocene	
East Africa	SIVAPITHECUS
	LIMNOPITHECUS
	PROCONSUL
India	PALAEOSIMIA
	SIVAPITHECUS
Europe	PLIOPITHECUS
India	DRYOPITHECUS
Africa	KENYAPITHECUS
India	RAMAPITHECUS
—Pliocene	
Europe	OREOPITHECUS
	DRYOPITHECUS
Asia	PLIOPITHECUS
Ethiopia	AUSTRALOPITHECUS
—Pleistocene	
Lower	
—Africa	HOMO HABILIS
	OLDUVAI MAN
	NUTCRACKER MAN
	ZINJANTHROPUS
	PLEISANTHROPUS
—Java	JAVA MAN, HOMO ERECTUS
	PITHECANTHROPUS
Middle	
—Africa	PARANTHROPUS
	ATLANTHROPUS
—China	PEKING(G) MAN
	HOMO ERECTUS
	PITHECANTHROPUS
	SINANTHROPUS
—Europe	SWANSCOMBE MAN
	STEINHEIM MAN
Upper	
—Europe	FONTECHEVADE
—Africa	SALDANHA
—Israel	MOUNT CARMEL MAN
—Europe	NEANDERTHAL MAN
—Java	SOLO MAN, HOMO SOLENSIS
—Africa	BROKEN HILL MAN
	RHODESIAN MAN
—Europe	CRO-MAGNON MAN
—Holocene (Recent)	HOMO SAPIENS

manlike	ANTHROPOID
measurement of	
—body	ANTHROPOMETRY
—head shape	CRANIOMETRY
primitive primate	ADAPID, OMOMYID
races	AFRICAN, ASIATIC
	AMERINDIAN, AUSTRALOID
	CAUCASOID, INDIC
	MELANESIAN, MELANOCHROI
	MICRONESIAN, MONGOLOID
	NEGROID, POLYNESIAN
study of	
—ancient blood groups	PALAEOSEROLOGY
—distribution of	
mankind	ANTHROPO(GEO)GRAPHY
—man	ANTHROPOLOGY
—origins of man	ANTHROPOGENESIS
	ANTHROPOGENY
	ANTHROPOGONY
—remains of ancient	
man	PALAEOPATHOLOGY
transformation to shape	
of human	ANTHROPOMORPHOSIS
worship of man	ANTHROPOLATRY
Apostles	
Apostle of Northumbria	CUTHBERT
Apostles of Christ	(*see* **twelve**)
apples	ARTHUR TURNER
	ASHMEAD'S KERNEL
	BAKER'S DELICIOUS, BEAUTY OF BATH
	BESS POOL, BIFFIN, BLENHEIM (ORANGE)
	BRAEBURN, BRAMLEY SEEDLING
	BRAEBURN, CHARLES ROSS
	CHIVER'S DELIGHT
	CLAYGATE PEARMAIN, CODLIN(G),
	COSTARD, COX'S ORANGE (PIPPIN)
	CRIMSON COSTARD, D'ARCY SPICE,
	DEVONSHIRE QUARRENDON
	DISCOVERY, DUMELOW SEEDLING
	EARLY VICTORIA, EGREMONT RUSSET
	ELLISON ORANGE, EMNETH EARLY
	ENSTAR, FIESTA, FORGE, FORTUNE
	GEORGE CAVE, GOLDEN DELICIOUS
	GRANNY SMITH, GREENSLEEVES
	GRENADIER, IDARED, INGRID
	JAMES GRIEVE, JONATHAN
	KATY, KING OF THE PIPPINS
	LADY SUDELEY, (LANE'S) PRINCE ALBERT
	LAXTON'S FORTUNE, LAXTON'S SUPERB
	LITTLE HOG SNOUT, LORD BURGHLEY
	LORD DERBY, LORD HINDLIP
	LORD LAMBOURNE, MARIE
	MICHAELMAS STUBBARD
	NEWTON WONDER, NORFOLK ROYAL
	OLD FRED, PEASGOOD NONSUCH
	PIG'S NOSE PIPPIN

PITMASTON PINEAPPLE, QUEEN COX
RED ELLISON, RIBSTON PIPPIN
ROYAL GALA, RUSSET
ST EDMUND'S PIPPIN, SPARTAN
STAR OF DEVON, STAR KING
STURMER PIPPIN, SUNSET
SUNTAN, TIDEMAN'S LATE ORANGE
TOM PUTT, WARNER'S KING
WHITE MELROSE
(WORCESTER) PEARMAIN

America	BALDWIN, JONAGOLD, JONATHAN
	WASHINGTON RED
Australia	COLANE
Canada	MACINTOSH RED, SPARTAN
France	GOLDEN DELICIOUS
	ORLEANS REINETTE, RED DESSERT
Germany	HOLSTEIN
green-skinned	GREENLING
Holland	BELLE DE BOSKOOP
Japan	CRISPIN
New Zealand	GALA, KIDD'S ORANGE RED
old	JENNETING, LEATHER-COATS
	POM(E)ROY, POMEWATER
	RENNET, SWEETING
Sweden	KATY
Arabia	UAR
anchorage	BANDAR, MARSA, MERSA
ancient people	HIMYARITE, SABA, SHEBA
ascetic	DERVISH
banker	SCHROFF
bay	BAHR, GHUBBAT
	KHALIG, KHALIJ
camel	DROMEDARY
—train	CAF(F)ILA, KAFILA
camp	D(O)UAR, DOWAR
canal	BAHR
cape	RAS
capital (Saudi)	AR RIYAD, RIYADH
chapter of Koran	SURA(H)
cherry	MAHALEB
chief	AMEER, AMIR, CAID, EMEER
	EMIR, KAID, RAIS, SA(Y)ID
	SAYYID, SCHIEK, SHEIK(H)
Christ's thorn	NABK, NEBBUK, NEBE(C)K
Christian	COPT
cistern	THAMAD
city	MADINAT
cloak	ABA, BERNOUS(E), BURNOUS(E)
	BURNOOSE, BOURK(H)A
	BURK(H)A, CAFTAN, (D)JIBBAH
	DJELLABA, GAL(L)ABEA(H), GALABIA
	GAL(L)ABI(Y)AH, GAL(L)ABI(Y)EH
	JUBBAH, KAFTAN, HAI(C)K
	HAIQUE, HYKE
coffee-cup without a handle	FINGAN, FINJAN

coins	BUCKSHA, DINAR, HALALAH
	QURSH, RIYAL, SAUDI
commando(s)	FEDAYEE(N)
courtyard	HOSH
cove	SHARM
cup-holder	ZARF, ZURF
dam	SADD
dancing-girl	ALMA(H), ALME(H)
demon	AFREET, AFRIT, MAHOUN(D)
depression	BAT(I)N, QA(RARAT)
dervish	SANTON
desert	BADIYAH, ERG
	NAFAD, SAHRA
—plant	CAMEL'S THORN
—rat	JERBOA
devil	SHAITAN
dish	COUSCOUS(OU), CUSCUS
	KHUSKHUS
dog	SALUKI
domed tomb	QUBBAH
domesticated animal	CAMEL
drink	BOSA, BOZA(H), LEBAN
	SHRAB
drug	BHANG, BENJ, HASHEESH
	HASHISH
dry river-bed	OUED, WADI, WADY
dune	NAFAD
dust-storm	SHAITAN
dynasty	ABBASSID, ALMORAVIDES
	AMMIAD, FATIMIDS, UMAYYAD
encampment	D(O)UAR, DOWAR
enclosed balcony	MOUCHARABY
estuary	MASABB
eye shadow	KOHL
fate	KISMET
father	ABU
fort	CASBAH, HISN, KASBAH
fortified camp	ZAREBA
girl	BINT
go away!	IMSHI, IMSHY
grain	TOMAND
gravel plain	JIDDAT, SAYH
gulf	KHALIG, KHALIJ
gum-resin	FRANKINCENSE, OLIBANUM
habit	(*see* cloak *below*)
harbour	BANDAR, MINA
head-dress	CHECHIA, FEZ, KAFFIYEH
	KEFFIYEH, TARBOOSH
	TARB(O)USH
—cord	AGAL
headman	MOCUDDUM, MOKADDAM
	MUQADDAM
hill	BARQA, CHEBKA, GARET, ILW, KEREB
	KULET, MINQAR, NASB, QARET, QOZ
	RIJM, RUJM, TEL(L), TILAT
	TALL(AT), TARAQ

hills	MANAQIR, QUR(AYYAT), QURUN		—lake	CHOTT
	TALL(AT), TARAQ, TULUL		sand	
holy			—dunes	IDHAN, GHARD, HADH(AT)
—building (Mecca)	KAABA			IRQ, KATHI
—litter sent to Mecca	MAHMAL		—storm	HABOOB
in the name of Allah	BISMILLAH		sands	RAMLAT
jinni	MARID		script	CUFIC, KUFIC
language	ARABIC			NASK(H)I, NESK(H)I
look	SHUFTI		sea-captain	NOCADAH
magistrate	CADI, CAID, KADI, KAID		shawl	KAFFIYEH, KEFFIYEH
	SHEREEF, SHERIF		ship	BAGGALA, D(H)OW
market	SUQ, SOUK			FELUCCA, SAIC
marsh	CHOTT		shirt	CAMESE, CAMIS(E)
measure	ARDEB, COVID(O), DEN			CAMISO, KAMIS
merchant	HOWADJI		shrine	CAABA, KAABA
millet grain	COUSCOUS(OU), CUSCUS		shrub	K(H)AT, NABK
	KHUSKHUS			NEBBUK, NEBE(C)K
mosque	MASJED, MASJID, MESJID		sign of glottal stop	HAMZA(H)
mound	TEL(L)		skull-cap	CHECHIA
mountain	(D)JEBEL, GEBEL, IDWET		slave	MAMELUKE
	JABAL, J(E)BEL, HASHM, NASB		smoking(hookah)	CHILLUM
musical form	MAQAM		Socialist party	BA'ATH
native quarter	MEDINA		spirit	DJINNI, GENIE, GH(O)UL
nomad	BEDAWIN, BEDOUIN			GINNI, JANN, JINNEE
	SARACEN, TUAREG			JINNI, MARID
oasis	WAHAT		spring	AIN, AYN
ornamental holder	ZARF, ZURF		spur	RIJM, RUJM
pass	AQABAT, MAMARR, NAQB		state of bliss	KEF
	TENIET, TIZI		stockade	ZARE(E)BA, ZEREBA
physician	HAKEEM, HAKIM			ZERIBA
pilgrim	HADJI, HAJJI		strait	BAB
pilgrimage	HADJ, HAJJ		stream	BAHR
plain	HADABAT, HAMMADAH		street	SHARI
	HAMMADAT, SAHL, SUHUL		surrender	ISLAM
plateau	HAMADA, HAMEDET		tariff	ZABETA
	HAZM, TASSILI		tea	K(H)AT, QAT
poem	GAZEL, GHAZAL, GHAZEL		tent village	D(O)UAR, DOWAR
pool	BIRK-AT, BIRK-ET		thorn hedge	ZARE(E)BA, ZEREBA
race	BERBER			ZERIBA
racing camel	DELOUL, MEHARI		title	SIDI
raider	FEDAYEEN		tomb	MASTABET, QABR
rainpools	KHABARI		town	MADINAT, MEDINA
ravine	KHOR, WADI, WADY		tree	ALHAGI
reed pipe	ARGHOOL		trough in sands	KHABB, SHAQQAT
religion	ISLAM, MOHAMMEDANISM			SHIQAQ, SHUQQAT
	MOSLEM, MUSLIM		unbeliever	CAFFRE, KAFIR
religious			underground water	
—ceremony	DOSEH		channel	QANAT
—philosophy	AVERR(H)OISM		uprising	INTIFADA
resurgence	BA'ATH		verse form	G(H)AZAL, GHAZEL
ridge	JAL, KEREB		water	
river	NAHR, SHATT		—course	CHALB, FAJJ, FULAYJ
—mouth	SHATT			GHADFAT, IRHZER
rocky plateau	HAMMADAH, HAMMADAT			SHAIB(AN), WADI
salt			—hole	BID, KHABRAH, KHABRAT
—flat	SABKHAT, SEBKRA		—pipe	CHILLUM, HOOKA(H)

—skin   KIRBEH
—wheel   SAKIA, SAKI(Y)EH
weak jinni   JANN
weight   KELA, ROTL, ROT(T)OLO
well   AGUELT, AIN, ANOU, AYN
     BIR, BIRK-AT, BIRK-ET
     GHADIR, GUELTA, HASSI, HASY
     IDD, KARIF, MASHASH, MATAN
     MISHASH, MUSHASH, OGLA, OGLET
     QALAMAT, QALIB, SANIYAT
     THAMAD, UQLAT
whip   K(O)URBASH

archaeology
   including: archaeologists
     palaeontology
ages of earth   (*see* **geography**)
archaeologists/palaeontologists
—American   GOULD, SEPKOSKI
—British   BROOM, BURTON, CRAWFORD
     EVANS, KEITH, LAWRENCE
     LAYARD, LEAKEY, MARSHALL
     PETRIE, RAWLINSON, SMITH
     WHEELER, WOODWARD, WOOLLEY
—Danish   STENNO, THOMSEN, WORSAAE
—Dutch   DUBOIS, KOENIGSWALD
—French   BOULE, BREUIL, CUVIER
     LARTET, NOUVEL, PERTHES
     POIDEBARD
—German   SCHLIEMANN
Bronze Age
—axe   PALSTAFF, PALSTAVE
—building (Greek)   MEGARON
—cemetery   URNFIELD
—ornament   LUNULA
burial
—mound   BARROW, TUMULUS
—place   BEEHIVE TOMB
Celtic necklace   TORC, TORQUE
civilisations   (*see* **anthropology**)
classification of artefacts   TYPOLOGY
coffin (stone, lead, etc)   SARCOPHAGUS
dating by
—artefacts   TYPOLOGY
—astronomy   ORBITAL DATING
—depth of strata   SEQUENCE DATING
     STRATIGRAPHY
—electrons   ELECTRON SPIN RESONANCE
     ESR
—heating   THERMOLUMINESCENCE, TL
—magnetism   ARCHAEOMAGNETISM
     MAGNETIC STRATIGRAPHY
—radioactivity   ARGON-ARGON DATING
     CARBON(-14) DATING
     POTASSIUM-ARGON DATING
     RADIOCARBON DATING
     RADIOMETRIC DATING

—sediment layers   VARVE DATING
—tree rings   DENDROCHRONOLOGY
deposit under pile-
   dwelling (Italy)   TERRA MARA
chamber in chalk   DENE-HOLE
cold period of
   Pleistocene   GLACIAL PERIOD, ICE AGE
double axe   LABRYS
embalmed body   MUMMY
exploration by measuring
   sub-soil resistance   RESISTIVITY SURVEYING
flint tool   BURIN
fortified island   CRANNOG
fossil
—animal   PALAEOTHERIUM
     SIVATHERIUM
—amphibians   LABYRINTHODONTIA
     STEGOCEPHALIA
—arachnid   EURYPTERIDA
—arthropod   TRILOBITE
—bird   (A)EPYORNIS, ARCHAEOPTERYX
     ARCHAEORNIS, ICTHYORNIS
     ODONTORNITHES, SAURURAE
—bone   ODONTOLITE
—cephalopod   AMMONITE, BACULITE
—dung   COPROLITE
—fish   ACANTHODII, OSTEOLEPSIS
     PLACODERMI
—fish-spine   ICTHYODORULITE
     ICTHYODORYLITE
—fruit   LEPIDOSTROBUS
—horse   HIPPARION
—Hydrozoa   GRAPTOLITES
—plant(s)   CALAMITE, PSILOPHYTALES
     SPHENOPHYTALES
     PTERIDOSPERM(AE)
—reptiles   DINOSAURS
     ICTHYOSAURIA, ORNITHISCHIA
     SAURISCHIA, SAUROPTERYGIA
     THERAPSIDA, THERIODONTIA
     THERIOMORPHA
     (*see also* **lizards**)
—resin   IXOLITE
—tooth   ODONTOLITE
—trees   GINKGOALES, LEPIDENDRON
—ungulate   UINTATHERIUM
—whale   ZEUGODON(T)
fragment of pottery   (POT)SHERD, SHARD
hill-fort (Irish)   RATH
Iron Age tower (Scot.)   BROCH, BRO(U)GH
lake-dwelling   CRANNOG, PALAFITTE
mound   TEL(L)
rubbish-heap   KITCHEN-MIDDEN
seasonal deposit in still water   VARVE
shelter on piles   LAKE DWELLING
spread of cultures   DIFFUSION

stone	
—circle	CROMLECH, HENGE
	PERISTALITH
—column	OBELISK
—implement (small)	MICROLITH
—large	MEGALITH
—monument	CROMLECH, DOLMEN
	MENHIR, NAVETA
Balearic Islands	TALAYOT, TAULA
—standing	MEGALITH,MENHIR
	MONOLITH
—table	DOLMEN
—tower (Scot.)	BROCH
—upright	
slab	STELA, STELE
stones with slab on top	DOLMEN
	TRILITH(ON)
Stone Age	
—axe	COUP DE POING
—tool (small)	MICROLITH
straight line between	
features of landscape etc	LEY (LINE)
study of	
—ancient inscriptions	EPIGRAPHY
—fossil animals	PALAEOZOOLOGY
—fossils	PALAEONTOLOGY
—human	
antiquities	ARCHAEOLOGY
blood groups	PALAEOSEROLOGY
remains	PALAEOPATHOLOGY
terrace in hillside	LINCH(ET), LYNCHET
tomb	
—earth-covered	BARROW, TUMULUS
—Egyptian	MASTABA, PYRAMID
—stone slabs	DOLMEN
vertical shaft	DENE-HOLE

architects

including: buildings	
engineers	
American	FULLER, JENNEY, JOHNSON
	KIESLER, MEIER, PEI, RICHARDSON
	STEIN, SULLIVAN, WRIGHT
Austrian	ACHLEITNER, HOFFMANN
	KIESLER
Belgian	HORTA, VAN DE VELDE
Brazilian	NEIMEYER
British	BARRY, BRUNEL, BURLINGTON
	BURTON, CHAMBERS, CULLEN
	DANCE, DARBY, FARRELL
	FOSTER, GIBBERD
	GIBBS, HAWKSMOOR, INIGO JONES
	KENT, LASDUN, LUBETKIN
	LUTYENS, NASH, PETO
	PARRY, PAXTON, PENTY, PUGIN
	ROGERS, RUSKIN, SCOTT, SEIFERT
	SHAW, SMITHSON, SOANE, SPENCE

	STIRLING, STREET, TELFORD
	VANBRUGH, VENTRIS, VOYSEY
	WEBB, WILSON, WREN, WYATT
Chinese	PEI
Danish	SPRECKELSEN
designer of	
—Albert Dock, Liverpool	HARTLEY
—Albert Memorial, London	SCOTT
—Alton Towers, Staffs	PUGIN
—Arche de la Défense, Paris	SPRECKELSEN
—Ashmolean Museum, Oxford	COCKERELL
—Athenaeum, London	BURTON
—Balmoral	SMITH
—Bank of England	SOANE
—Banqueting Hall, Whitehall	JONES
—Bastille opera, Paris	OTT
—Battersea Power Station	SCOTT
—Blenheim Palace	VANBRUGH
—Brandenburg Gate, Berlin	LANGHANS
—Brighton Pavilion	NASH
—British Library	WILSON
—Castle Howard	VANBRUGH
—Centre Point, London	SEIFERT
—Charles de Gaulle airport	ANDREV
—Chatsworth, Derbyshire	PAXTON
—Clore Gallery, London	STIRLING
—Coventry Cathedral	SPENCE
—Crystal Palace, London	PAXTON
—Edinburgh University	ADAM
—Euston Arch, London	HARDWICK
—Foreign Office, London	SCOTT
—Free Trade Hall, Manchester	WALTER
—glass pyramids, Louvre	PEI
—Grand Hotel, Scarborough	BRODRICK
—Greenwich Hospital	WREN
—Guggenheim Museum, New York	WRIGHT
—Harrods, London	HUNT/STEVENS
—Holloway Prison	BUNNING
—Hong Kong and	
Shanghai Bank	FOSTER
—Houses of Parliament	BARRY, PETO
	PUGIN
—Irish National Gallery, Dublin	FOWKES
—iron bridge, Telford	DARBY
—Keddlestone Hall	ADAM
—King's Cross Station, London	CUBITT
—Law Courts, London	STREET
—Les Invalides	MANSART
—Liverpool Cathedral	
Anglican	SCOTT
Roman Catholic	GIBBERD
—Mansion House	DANCE
—Menai Bridge	STEPHENSON
—Mentmore Towers	PAXTON
—Midland Hotel, Manchester	TRUBSHAW
—Natural History Museum	WATERHOUSE

architects

—Nelson's column, London	PETO
—Newgate gaol	DANCE
—New Scotland Yard	SHAW
—Osborne House, IoW	CUBITT
—Paddington Station	BRUNEL/WYATT
—Palm House, Kew	BURTON/TURNER
—Pompidou Centre, Paris	FOSTER
—Port Sunlight	OWEN
—Queen's House, Greenwich	JONES
—Radcliffe library	GIBBS
—Reform Club, London	BARRY
—Royal Crescent, Bath	WOOD
—Royal Infirmary, Edinburgh	BRYCE
—Royal Opera House, London	BARRY
—Royal Pavilion, Brighton	NASH
—St Martin-in-the-Fields	GIBBS
—St Pancras Station, London	BARLOW/ORDISH/SCOTT
—St Paul's Cathedral	WREN
—St Peter's, Rome	BRAMANTE BRUNELLESCHI, MICHELANGELO
—Savoy Hotel, London	COLLCUTT/MACKMURDO
—Scotland Yard	SHAW
—Scott Memorial, Edinburgh	KEMP
—Scottish National Gallery	PLAYFAIR
—Seagram Building, New York	MIES
—Somerset House	JONES, CHAMBERS
—Stuttgart Museum	STIRLING
—Suspension Bridge, Clifton	BRUNEL
—Sydney Opera House	UTZON
—Tower, Blackpool	MAXWELL/TUKE
—Tower Bridge, London	JONES/PARRY
—Town Hall	
Leeds	BRODRIC
Manchester	WATERHOUSE
Sheffield	MOUNTFIELD
—University of Glasgow	SCOTT
—Versailles	LE VAN, MANSART
—Viceroy's House, Delhi	LUTYENS
—Villa Savoie	CORBUSIER
—Westminster Abbey towers	HAWKSMOOR
—Westminster Cathedral	BENTLEY
—West Pier, Brighton	BIRCH
—Whitehall Court, London	ARCHER, GREEN
Dutch	DE VRIENDT, RIETVELD VAN EYCK, VAN NOORT VAN ZOYE
Finnish	AALTO, ENGEL, SAARINEN SONCK
French	BULLANT, DE L'ORME EIFFEL, FRIEDMAN, GUINARD LE CORBUSIER, LE VAU, LESCET MALLET-STEVENS, MANSART PERRET, ROUX-SPITZ, SEGUIN VIOLLET

architectural features

German	BEHRENS, GROPIUS MEYER, MENDELSOHN MIES (VAN DER ROHE) MUTHESIUS, SCHINKEL SCHULTZE-NAUBURG, TAUT
—school	BAUHAUS
Greek	DOXIDIAS
Italian	ALBERTI, BERNINI BORROMINI, BRAMANTE BRUNELLESCHI, MADERNA MICHELANGELO, NERVI PALLADIO, SANSOVINO SANTELIA
Mexican	CANDELA
Russian	LUBETKIN
Scottish	ADAM, CAMPBELL GIBBS, MACKINTOSH
Spanish	BERRUGUETE, CANDELA DE HERRARA, GAUDI SORIA Y MATA
Swedish	MAILLART
Swiss	BILL, LE CORBUSIER, MEYER
Venetian	PALLADIO

architectural features

apex of building	FASTIGIUM
apse	CONCHA
arc of arch	HANCE, HAUNCH
arcade over aisle	TRIFORIUM
arch	
—across interior angle	SQUINCH
—linked to buttress	ARC BOUTANT FLYING BUTTRESS
—over gate	PORTAL
—springing from above capital	STILTED ARCH
—stone	VOUSSOIR
arched	
—roof	VAULT
—walkway	ARCADE
architrave	EPISTYLE
arm	BRACE
arrangement of small arcs and cusps	FEATHERING
astragal moulding	FUSAROL(E)
ball	
—on pillar	BALLOON
—shaped finial	POMMEL
band used with moulding	FILLET
base of pillar	DADO, PATTEN
bay	
—resting on brackets	ORIEL
—window	JUT-WINDOW
beam	
—at foot of	
—opening	SILL

—rafters	JOIST, WALL-PLATE
mid-point of rafters	COLLAR
or near foot of rafters	HAMMERBEAM
—forming ridge	RIDGE POLE
—over	
columns	ARCHITRAVE
door or window	LINTEL
—supporting	
joists, etc	BREASTSUMMER
	BRESSUMMER, SUMMERBEAM
rafters	PURLIN
belltower	CAMPANILE
board	
—at eaves	FA(S)CIA
—covering verge	BARGEBOARD
—under eaves	SOFFIT(E)
body of Corinthian capital	VASE
bottom stone of arch	SPRINGER
bracket under cornice	MODILLION
broad flat band	FASCIA
burial chamber	TOMB, VAULT
buttress supported	
by a corbel	HANGING BUTTRESS
cap of pier	CUSHION
capitals (Egypt)	(CLUSTERED) LOTUS BUDS
	HATHOR-HEADED
	INVERTED BELL, PALM
carved basket	CORBEIL
central stone of arch	KEYSTONE
chancel	ADYTUM
chapel	
—at west end of church	GALILEE
—of prothesis	PARABEMA
—within church	SACELLUM
chevron moulding	DANCETTE
choir-screen	REREDOS(SE)
	REREDORSE
church	(see separate entry)
clawlike ornament	GRIFF(E)
close-set columns	PYCNOSTYLE
colonnade	PORCH, PORTICO, STOA
column	
—base	PEDIMENT, PLINTH
—female figure	CARYATID
—fillet round column	ANNULET
—flat tablet on capital	ABACUS
—groove in shaft	FLUTE, FLUTING
—lower part of capital	NECK
—male figure(s)	ATLAS (ATLANTES)
	TELAMON(ES)
—moulding	
at base	TORUS
below abacus	ECHINUS
—section of shaft	DRUM, FRUSTRUM
—shaft	FUST, SCAPE, SCAPUS
	TIGE, TRUNK, VERGE

—spiral decoration	
on capital	HELIX, SCROLL, VOLUTE
—styles	COMPOSITE, CORINTHIAN
	DORIC, IONIC, TUSCAN
—top	CAPITAL
combination of	
—beams	TRABEATION
—truncated gable	
and lipped roof	JERKINHEAD
concave ceiling	CUPOLA
concave moulding	TROCHILUS
continuous	
—arch	BARREL VAULT
—pedestal	PODIUM
convex	
—projecting moulding	ECHINUS
—surface of arch	EXTRADOS
corner	
—of coping	SKEW-CORBEL
	SKEW-PUT, SKEW-TABLE
—stone	QUOIN
cornice above base of	
pedestal	SURBASE
covered	
—arcade	CLOISTER, LOGGIA
—colonnade	STOA
—entrance	PORTE COCHERE
—portico	XYST(OS), XYSTUS
—walkway	AMBULATORY, ARCADE
	PAWN
crescent-shaped space	LUNETTE
cresting	BRATTICING
	BRATTISHING
cross	
—beam	TRANSOM
—rib in vaulting	LIERNE
crossed fillets	STRAP-WORK
cupola	THOLOS, THOLUS
curve where	
—column merges	APOPHYGE
—vaults merge	GROIN
curved	
—timber roof support	CRUCK
—wall/ceiling junction	COVE
cylindrical part of dome	DRUM
cyma recta moulding	DOUCINE
decorated	
—band at top of wall	FRIEZE
—with leaves	FOLIATED
decoration in	
—moulding	LINEN-SCROLL
—panels	LINENFOLD
decorative scroll	CARTOUCHE
detached support	PILLAR
diagonal rib of vault	OGIVE
die of a pedestal	SOLIUM

disguised door	JIB-DOOR
dome	CUPOLA, THOLOS, THOLUS
doorway	PORTAL
—enclosure	PORCH
—surround	ARCHITRAVE
Doric order	MALE ORDER
dormer-window	LUCARNE
double-grooved ornament	DIGLYPH
dripstone	LABEL, LARMIER
droplike feature	GUTTA
dual-pitched roof	MANSARD(-ROOF)
east end of church	CHEVET
elliptical auditorium	SPHENDONE
enclosed space	CLOISTER
—of church	PARVIS(E)
enclosing wall of precinct	PERIBOLOS
	PERIBOLUS
entablature	TRABEATION
—highest part	CORNICE
—lowest part	ARCHITRAVE
—middle part	FRIEZE
—projecting part of cornice	CORONA
—underside	SOFFIT
entrance	PORTAL
—admitting carriage	PORTE-COCHERE
entresol	MEZZANINE
extension of church	
behind the altar	RETROCHOIR
external	
—curve of voussoir	EXTRADOS
—steps	PERRON
fascia	PLATBAND
female figure	
—used as column	CARYATID
—with basket	
on the head	CANEPHOR(A)
	CANEPHORE, CANEPHORUS
fillet	LIST
—above architrave	TAENIA
—below triglyph	REGULA
—between flutes	STRIA
finial	CROP
five-petalled feature	CINQUE-FOIL
flat	
—arch	PLATBAND
—fillet	BANDELET
—moulding	PLATBAND
—narrow moulding	REGLET
—on top floor	PENTHOUSE
—ornament	PATERA
floor	PLANCH
flower bud as ornament	KNOSP
flower-like ornament	FLEURON
four-lobed ornament	QUATREFOIL
	QUATREFEUILLE
French window fastener	ESPAGNOLETTE

front of building	FACADE
gable	FASTIGIUM
—coping stone	SKEW
gallery	PAWN
—over aisle	TRIFORIUM
garret	SOL(L)AR, SOL(L)ER
gate	PORTAL
—pillar	PIER
gateway	
—of Egyptian temple	PYLON
—to temple	PROPYLAEUM
	PROPYLON
glazed structure on roof	LANTERN
	ROOFLIGHT, SKYLIGHT
groove between neck of	
capital and shaft	HYPOTRACHELION
grooved border	SWAGE
grotesque ornamentation	BABERY
half-round moulding	ASTRAGAL
having	
—1 column	MONOSTYLE
—1 row of columns	PERIPTERAL
—2 columns	DISTYLE
—4 columns	TETRASTYLE
—5 columns	PENTASTYLE
—6 columns	HEXASTYLE
—8 columns	OCTASTYLE, OCTOSTYLE
—9 columns	ENNEASTYLE
—10 columns	DECASTYLE
—12 columns	DODECASTYLE
—many columns	POLYSTYLAR
—not more than four columns	PROSTYLE
head of column	
supporting arch	CHAPITER, CHAPTREL
hemispherical roof	CUPOLA, DOME
high narrow arch	LANCET ARCH
hollow moulding	CASEMENT, CAVETTO
	SCOTIA
horizontal	
—block	IMPOST
—division of window	TRANSOM
—member on wall	WALL-PLATE
inclined surface	SKEW-BACK
inner	
—chamber of temple	CELLA, NAOS
—fortified retreat	REDUIT
intercolumniation of	
—1½ diameters	PYCNOSTYLE
—2 diameters	SYSTYLE
—2¼ diameters	EUSTYLE
—3 diameters	DIASTYLE
—2-4 diameters	AR(A)EOSYSTYLE
—4 diameters	AR(A)EOSTYLE
internal part of dome	CUPOLA
internally splayed opening	EMBRASURE
	EMBRAZURE

intersection of vaults	GROIN
key	
—pattern	FRET
—stone	QUOIN, SAGITTA
lantern on dome	CUPOLA
level tablet	ABACUS
like silversmith's work	PLATERESQUE
lintel	PLATBAND, TRANSOM
—on corbels	SHOULDERED ARCH
little	
—chapel	SACELLUM
—round window	OEIL-DE-BOEUF
long lintel	BRESSUMMER
	(BREAST)SUMMER
longitudinal groove	FLUTE
low	
—side window	LYCHNOSCOPE
—spherical vault	CUL-DE-FOUR, CUPOLA
—storey between	
main storeys	ENTRESOL, MEZZANINE
—wall	STYLOBATE
lower part of	
—cupola or dome	DRUM
—internal wall surface	DADO, WAINSCOT
main body of church	NAVE
male figure(s) used	
as column(s)	ATLAS(ATLANTES)
	PERSIAN, TELAMON
mansard roof	GAMBREL ROOF
masonry	
—filled with rubble	EMPLECTON
	EMPLECTUM
—rough-faced	RUSTICATED
—smooth	ASHLAR
—uncoursed	(RANDOM) RUBBLE
—uniformly coursed	ISODOMON
	ISODOMUM
—with sunken joints	RUSTICATED
measure of proportion	MODULE
moulded border	SWAGE
moulding	
—above base of pedestal	SURBASE
—at	
base of column	TORUS
junction of	
shaft and capital	NECK-MOULDING
—hollow	CAVETTO
—ogee	CYMA, TALON
concave	CYMA RECTA
convex	CYMA REVERSA
—round door or wondow	ARCHITRAVE
—S-shaped	OGEE
narrow band	FILLET
neck of capital	HYPOTRACHELION
Norman moulding	DOG-TOOTH
notch in parapet	CRENEL

oblique opening	SQUINT
open	
—colonnade	XYST(OS), XYSTUS
—sided pavilion	BELVEDERE
opening for cannon	EMBRASURE
	EMBRAZURE
orders	CORINTHIAN, DORIC
	IONIC
ornament	
—in the form of	
basket	MODILLION
beads	PATERNOSTER
conventionalised leaf	ACANTHUS
curled leaf	CROCKET
festoon of flowers	SWAG
flower	CROCKET, FLEURON
—bud	KNOSP
—with	
3 petals	TREFOIL
4 petals	QUATREFEUILLE
	QUATREFOIL
5 petals	CINQUEFOIL
6 petals	SEXFOIL
garland	FESTOON
palm-leaf	PALMETTE
scroll	CARTOUCHE
waterlily	LOTE, LOTOS, LOTUS
—on	
capital	WATER-LEAF
gable	FINIAL
mouldings	EGG-AND-ANCHOR
	EGG-AND DART
pediment	ACROTER(ION)
	ACROTERIUM
pinnacle	CROCKET
—rose-shaped	ROSETTE
ornamental	
—bracket	MODILLION
—channel or fluting	GLYPH
—openwork	TRACERY
panelling	
—behind altar or seat	REREDORSE
	REREDOS(SE)
—on internal wall	DADO, WAINSCOT
part of jamb	SCONCHEON, SCUNCHEON
	SCONTION
partitioning	QUARTERING
pedestal	ACROTERION, ACROTERIUM
—base	DADO
pediment	ACROTER(ION)
	ACROTERIUM
pillar	
—between two	
openings	PIER, TRUMEAU
—supporting arch	PIER
—upper part	IMPOST

plain	
—face	
at base of wall	SOCLE
of plinth	SOCLE, ZOCCO(LO)
—plinth	SOCLE
plaster	
—cast in low relief	PRINT
—moulding	CORNICE, COVE
—wall coating	STUCCO
plate supporting end of beam	TASSEL, TORSEL
plinth at base of wall	SOCLE, ZOCCO(LO)
pointed dome	IMPERIAL
porch	STOA
—at west end of church	GALILEE
portico	PORCH
post placed against wall	PENDANT-POST
precinct	PERIBOLOS
	PERIBOLUS
privy behind monastic	
dormitory	REREDORTER
projecting	
—arch stone	CROSSETTE
—band at bottom of wall	PLINTH
—carved spout	GARGOYLE
—course	STRING (COURSE)
—gallery	MACHICOLATION
—mould	HOOD-MOULD(ING)
—moulding	CORNICE
—part	JUTTY
—support pillar	BUTTRESS
—window	BAY, BOW, ORIEL
	SHOT-WINDOW
projection	CORBEL
—in carving	BOSS
—of cornice	CORONA
—on impost	CROSSETTE
raised area at entrance	PERRON
range of columns	COLONNADE
	PORTICO
—round building or	
square	PERISTYLE
recess	APSE, APSIS
recessed face of pediment	TYMPANUM
reinforcing pier	BUTTRESS
relief	RILIEVO
rib at intersection	GROIN
roof	
—arched	VAULT
—gutter	CULLIS
—supported by pillars	HYPOSTYLE
—tile	TEGULA
—with	
equal slopes	SPAN-ROOF
insulation above	
structure	INVERTED ROOF
one slope	MONOPITCH
steeply pitched glazing	NORTH-LIGHT
two slopes each side	MANSARD
roofed over	CL(E)ITHRAL
rose-window	CATHERINE-WHEEL, ROSACE
rosette	PATERA, ROSACE
round building	THOLOS, THOLUS
row of	
—arches	ARCADE
—corbels	CORBEL-TABLE
S-shaped moulding	OGEE
sacristy	DIACONICON, PARABEMA
screen behind altar	
or seat	REREDORSE, REREDOS(SE)
scroll ornament	CARTOUCHE
sculptured basket	PANNIER
secondary beam or joist	SOLIVE
semi-	
—circular recess	APSE, APSIS
—dome	CONCHA
—elliptical auditorium	SPHENDONE
sepulchral monument	CENOTAPH
shaft of column	FUST, SCAPE, SCAPUS
	TIGE, TRUNK, VERGE
shallow dome	SAUCER DOME
sharp-edged groove	QUIRK
shoulder in arch-stone	CROSSETTE
shrine for standards	SACELLUM
side of dormer	CHEEK
—surface of recess	REVEAL
six-lobed design	SEXFOIL
skirting	DADO
slab in frieze	METOPE
slope on top of moulding	WEATHERING
small column	COLUMEL
—fillet	ANNULET, LISTEL
—gable	GABLET
—low window	MEZZANINE
—moulding	BAGUETTE, REED
soffit	INTRADOS
space	
—between	
arch and moulding	SPANDREL, SPANDRIL
bed and wall	ROUELLE
columns	INTERCOLUMNIATION
corbels	MACHICOLATION
lintel and arch	TYMPANUM
pilasters	INTERPILASTER
pillars or windows	BAY
temple cell and pillars	PERIDROME
—for two triglyphs	DITRIGLYPH
—in Doric frieze	METOPE
spherical triangle formed	
by dome on square base	PENDENTIVE
spire	FLECHE
—or lantern formed by	
flying buttresses	CROWN

square	
—block	
at base of column	PLINTH
in moulding	DENTEL, DENTIL
—column against wall	PILASTER
—flat bracket	MUTULE
—pilaster	ANTA
—pilasters	ATTIC ORDER
stone	
—forming part of arch	HEADSTONE
	KEYSTONE, QUOIN
	VOUSSOIR
—pillar	OBELISK
storey over aisle	TRIFORIUM
sunken panel	COFFER, LACUNAR
stylobate	PODIUM
subordinate rib	TIERCERON
substructure of	
—dome	THOLOBATE
—row of columns	STYLOBATE
sunken panel	LACUNAR
support for	
—column	PEDESTAL
—inner part	
of wall	REAR-ARCH, RERE-ARCH
—roof	HAMMER BEAM, KING-POST
	PURLIN, QUEEN-POST
	RAFTER, SUMMER-BEAM, TRUSS
—wall	(FLYING)BUTTRESS
supporting	
—bracket	CORBEL
—pillar	BUTTRESS
swelling outline of column	ENTASIS
tall	
—building	POINT BLOCK, SKYSCRAPER
	TOWER BLOCK
—narrow	
pillar	OBELISK
window	LANCET WINDOW
temple gateway	PROPYLAEUM, PROPYLON
ten-column portico	DECASTYLE
three	
—grooved tablet	TRIGLYPH
—lobed tracery	TREFOIL
timber cladding	CLAPBOARD
	WEATHERBOARD
tomb	THOLOS, THOLUS
—as chapel	SACELLUM
toothlike ornament	CUSP
top of	
—column	CAPITAL
—entablature	CORNICE
tower	MINAR
—bell	CAMPANILE
—fort	MARTELLO
—mosque	MINARET

tracery on vault	FAN TRACERY
	FAN VAULTING
triangular	
—part of external wall	GABLE
—roof support	TRUSS
—structure over porch	PEDIMENT
twist in capital	HELIX
type of classical architecture	ORDER
under-curve of arch	ARCHIVOLT
underside of	
—arch	INTRADOS, SOFFIT
—eaves, stairs, etc	SOFFIT
uniformly coursed blocks	ISODOMON
	ISODOMUM
upper	
—lighted storey	CLEARSTORY
	CLERESTORY
—part of pillar	IMPOST
—room	SOL(L)AR, SOL(L)ER
upright	
—in roof truss	KING-POST, QUEEN-POST
—part of cupola	DRUM
ventilator	FEMERALL, FEMERELL
vertical member	MONTANT, MUNTIN
	STILE
voussoir	QUOIN
wall	
—between two openings	TRUMEAU
—panelling	DADO, WAINSCOT
weatherproof joint covering	FLASHING, SOAKER
wedge-shaped arch stone	VOUSSOIR
windows	
—bottom-hung	HOPPER
—centre-hung	PIVOT WINDOW
—circular	BULL'S-EYE
	CATHERINE WHEEL
	OEIL DE BOEUF
	PORTHOLE, ROSE
—curved head	EYEBROW WINDOW
—dormer	LUCARNE
—French	FENETRE
—full-length	
opening out	FRENCH WINDOW
sliding	PATIO DOOR
—high and shallow	CLERESTORY
—in	
roof	DORMER, LUCARNE
	ROOFLIGHT, SKYLIGHT
spire	LUCARNE
—opening at high level	FANLIGHT
—over door	FANLIGHT
—projecting	BAY, BOW, COMPASS
	JUT, ORIEL, SHOT
—side-hung	CASEMENT
—sliding	SASH
—small and low	MEZZANINE

—Spanish	VENTANA
—tall and pointed	LANCET
—wide	LANDSCAPE WINDOW
	PICTURE WINDOW
—with	
diamond-shaped panes	LATTICE
hinged shutter	SHOT-WINDOW
with flame-like tracery	FLAMBOYANT
wooden beam with steel tie	TRUSS-BEAM
zigzag moulding	DANCETTE

architectural styles (*see also* **building construction**)

5th c	BYZANTINE
pre 1066	PRE-CONQUEST, SAXON
11th c	NORMAN, ROMANESQUE
12th c	EARLY ENGLISH
12th-13th c	TRANSITIONAL
12th-16th c	GOTHIC
13th c	DECORATED
14th c	PERPENDICULAR
15th-16th c	RENAISSANCE, TUDOR
16th c	ELIZABETHAN, PALLADIAN
early 17th c	JACOBEAN
17th c	BAROQUE, CLASSICAL
early 18th c	QUEEN ANNE
18th c	GEORGIAN, NEO-CLASSIC(AL)
	PALLADIAN, ROCOCO
early 19th c	REGENCY
19th c	VICTORIAN
20th c	BRUTALIST, FUNCTIONALIST
	INTERNATIONAL, MODERNIST
	POSTMODERNIST
American	COLONIAL
—19th c	CHICAGO SCHOOL
classical architecture	
—Greek	CORINTHIAN, DORIC, IONIC
and Roman	CLASSICAL
—Roman	TUSCAN
formal based on classical styles	BEAUX ARTS
half-timbered	ELIZABETHAN, TUDOR
highly decorative style	BAROQUE, ROCOCO
of a particular place or time	VERNACULAR
with	
—pointed arches	GOTHIC
—semi-circular arches	ROMAN, NORMAN

Argentina	RA
barbecue	ASADO
capital	BUENOS AIRES
coin	AUSTRAL, CENTAVO, PESO
cowboy	GAUCHO
dance	TANGO
flower	PLATE
plain	CHACO, LLANO, PAMPA
tree	TALA
weight	GRANO, QUINTAL
Armenia	ARM, HAIKH
capital	(Y)EREVAN

armour	MAIL
air-hole	AVENTAIL(E)
breastplate	BYRNIE, CORS(E)LET
	CUIRASS, FELTRE
	PLACKET
—under hauberk	PLASTRON
buckler	PELTA, SHIELD
coat-of-mail	BRIGANDINE, BRIGANTINE
	HABERGEON, HAUBERK
contrivance on breastplate	REST
covering	
—arm	BRASSARD, BRASSART
	BRASSET, CORIUM
—body	BRIGANDINE, BRIGANTINE
	HAUBERK
—breast	BYRNIE, CORSELET
	CUIRASS, PECTORAL
	PLACKART, PLACKET
—chin and throat	MENTONNIERE
—crotch	FA(U)LD
—elbow	COP, COUDIERE
	COUTE(R), UBITIERE
—face	BEAVER, MESAIL, MEZAIL
	UMBREL, UMBR(I)ERE
	UMBRIL, VISOR, VIZOR
—foot	SABATON, SOLARET, SOLLERET
—forearm	LOWER CANNON
	VAMBRACE, VANTBRACE
—hand	GAUNTLET
—head	HELM(ET)
—hips	CULET(TE), FAULD
—horse's	
breast	PECTORAL, POITREL
head	CHAFFRON, CHAMFROM
	CHAMFRAIN
—joint	GUSSET
—knee	GENOUILLERE, POLEYN
—leg	CHAUSSES, GREAVE
	JAMB(E), JAMBEAU
—neck	BEVOR, HAUBERK
and shoulder	GORGET
—shoulder	AILETTE, BESADEUR
	GARDBRACE, PALLETTE
	PAULDRON, POULDRON, SPAUDIER
—stomach	PANSER
—thigh	CULET, TASSET
—throat	GORGET
—upper	
arm	MONION, REREBRACE
body	(PEASCOD-)CUIRASS
leg	CUISSE
crest of helmet	COMB
face-cover	VISOR, VIZOR
for	
—horse	BARBE, BARDCHANFRAN
	CRUPPER, HARNESS, SHANFRON

—man	BARD, HARNESS, MAIL
full suit of armour	PANOPLY
hand-shield on lance	VAMPLATE, VAMPLET
helmet	ARMET, BASINET, BURGANET
	BURGONET, CASK, CASQUE
	MORIAN, MOR(R)ION
	SALADE, SAL(L)ET
knee-piece	GENOUILLERE
leather	
—arm-piece	CORIUM
—coat	GAMBESON, JACK
—corselet	LORICA
—doublet with	
steel strips	PLACCATE, PLACKET
—Roman	LORICA
light headpiece	BASINET
long coat of chain-mail	HAUBERK
lozenge-shaped plate	MASCLE
mail-coat	BYRNIE
massive helmet	HEAUME
movable front	
of helmet	VENTAIL, VENTAYLE
open helmet	MOR(R)ION
overlapping piece	TACE, TASLET, TASSE(T)
padded	
—breast-shield	PLASTRON
—jacket	ACTON, GAMBESON
	HA(C)QUETON, (H)AKETON
part of skirt	TACE, TASLET, TASSE(T)
plate below tasses	TUILLE(TTE)
quilted coat	GAMBESON
set of armour	GARNITURE
shield	
—large	PAVIS(E)
—small	BUCKLER, PELTA
—worn on left gauntlet	GLOVE-SHIELD
shoulder-plate	AILETTE, PAULDRON
	POULDRON
skull-cap	CAPELINE
sleeveless mail-coat	HABERGEON
spear rest	FEWTER
splint armour	JAZERANT, JESSERANT
steel plates worn skirt-like	LAMBOYS
suit of mail	CATAPHRACT
thin metal plate	LAME
veil over helmet	LAMBREQUIN
visor/vizor	MESAIL, MEZAIL
	UMBREL, UMBRIL, VOLBR(I)ERE

army

chaplains	HCF, OCF
dentists	RADC
doctors	RAMC
paymasters	RAPC
ranks (lowest first)	
—other ranks	OR
	RECRUIT, ROOKIE

	(BANDSMAN, GUARDSMAN, GNR
	(GUNNER, PRIVATE, PTE
	(SAPPER, SIGNALMAN, TROOPER
—non-commissioned	
	LANCE-BOMBARDIER
	LANCE-CORPORAL
	BOMBARDIER, CORPORAL, CPL
	LANCE-SERGEANT, SERGEANT, SGT
—warrant officer I	STAFF SERGEANT
COMPANY QUARTERMASTER-SERGEANT	
	CQMS
	COMPANY SERGEANT-MAJOR, CSM
—warrant officer II	DRILL SERGEANT
	REGIMENTAL
QUARTERMASTER-SERGEANT	
	RQMS
	REGIMENTAL SERGEANT MAJOR, RSM
—commissioned rank	SECOND LIEUTENANT
	LT, LIEUTENANT
	CAPT, CAPTAIN
	MAJ, MAJOR
	LIEUTENANT-COLONEL, LT-COL
	COL, COLONEL
	BRIG, BRIGADIER
	MAJ-GEN, MAJOR-GENERAL
	LIEUTENANT-GENERAL, LT-GEN
	GEN, GENERAL
	FIELD MARSHAL, FM
teachers	RAEC
technicians	REME
vets	RAVC
	(*see also* **military, soldiers**)

art

amateur	DABBLER, DILETTANTE
art lover	AESTHETE
art movements	
—15th c Italian	QUATTROCENTO
—16th c Italian	MANNERISM
—17th/18th c	BAROQUE
—18th/19th c	NEO-CLASSICISM
	ROMANTICISM
—1848	PRE-RAPHAELITISM
—1890s	ART NOUVEAU
—19th c	REALISM
—19th c French	BARBIZON SCHOOL
	IMPRESSIONISM
—1920s and 1930s	ART DECO
—20th c	ABSTRACT EXPRESSIONISM
	CUBISM, DADAISM
	EXPRESSIONISM, FAUVISM
	OP ART, SURREALISM
British	VORTICISM
Dutch	DE STIJL, THE STYLE
German	BAUHAUS
Italian	FUTURISM
Russian	CONSTRUCTIVISM

—based on classical design	BEAUX ARTS
—characterised by	
depiction of life objectively	REALISM
depiction of machine	
age	FUTURISM
	VORTICISM
distortion of human figure	MANNERISM
dots of colour	POINTILLISM(E)
exploration of dreams and	
the unconscious	SURREALISM
expression of spiritual	
significance	NABIS, SYMBOLISM
extreme abstraction	DE STIJL
	THE STYLE
function dictating shape	BAUHAUS
geometric shapes	ART DECO
	CONSTRUCTIVISM
	CUBISM
	OP ART
immediate visual impact	
of the subject	IMPRESSIONISM
landscape	
for its own sake	BARBIZON SCHOOL
ornate shapes	BAROQUE
rejection of	
—classicism	ROMANTICISM
—impressionism	EXPRESSIONISM
—rationality	DADAISM
representation as two-	
dimensional decoration	FAUVISM
revival of classical	
proportions	NEO-CLASSICISM
style ahead of the times	AVANT GARDE
swirling shapes	ART NOUVEAU
use (in 19th c) of style	
of 15th c artists	PRE-RAPHAELITISM
visual illusion	OP ART
artists	(see **painting**)
artist's complete works	CORPUS, OEUVRE
—workroom	ATELIER, STUDIO
artistic circle	CLIQUE, COTERIE
—rebirth	RENAISSANCE
	RENASCENCE
artistically impressive object	OBJET 'DART
drawing showing exposed	
muscles	ECORCHE
exhibition covering many	
years of artist's work	RETROSPECTIVE
natural object displayed	
as a work of art	OBJET TROUVE
official exhibition	SALON
optical	
—aid	CAMERA LUCIDA
—illusion	TROMPE L'OEIL
ornamentation of metal by	
engraving etc	NIELLO

representation of human	
form	ANTHROPOMORPH
unconventional artist	BOHEMIAN
Asian	
anteater	PANGOLIN
bean(-plant)	SOJA, SOY(A)
bird	FROGMOUTH, MANDARIN DUCK
	MYNA(H), PEACOCK-PHEASANT
	PITTA, SIRGANG, TAILOR-BIRD
	TRAGOPAN
cattle	YAK, ZEBU, Z(H)O
	(see also **ox**)
cereal	JAPANESE MILLET
chief	CHAGAN, CHAM, KHAN
civet	PARADOXURE, ZIBET
climbing pepper	BETEL
day-lilies	FUNKIA
doctor/priest	SHAMAN
domesticated animal	CAMEL
desert plant	CAMEL'S THORN
durra	GUINEA-CORN
dziggetai	HEMIONE
evergreen shrub	CAMELLIA
falcon	LUGGER, SHAHIN
felt tent	KIBITKA
fibre	RAMIE
fish	PANCHAX
—hook money	LARI(N), LARREE
fowl	LANGSHAN
fox	ADIVE, CORSAC, CORSAK
fruit	BITO, WAMPEE
goat	JAGLA
hawk	SHIKRA
hemp	PUA
hornless deer	MUSK-DEER
horse	PRZEWALSKI'S HORSE
—disease	SURRA
kebabs	SATAY, SATE
kiang	HEMIONE
legume	COW-PEA
lizard	MONITOR
magician	SHAMAN
nut	PISTACHIO
orchestra	GAMELAN
orchid	DENDROBIUM
pangolin	MANIS
paradoxure	MUSANG
partridge	SEESEE
perennial herb	LASERPICIUM
periwinkle	STRIPHANTHUS
pheasant	TRAGOPAN
piping hare	PICA
plant	ABELMOSK, GOA BEAN
	HOSTA, LICORICE
	LIQUORICE
primitive heartland	ANGARALAND

Asian

prince	CHAGAN, CHAM, KHAN
pygmy negroid	NEGRITO
religion	SHAMANISM
rodent	GERBIL
scaly ant-eater	MANIS
sheep	*(see separate entry)*
shrub	PATCHOULI, PATCHOULY
	SKIMMIA, TCHE, TEA
snake	KING-COBRA
snow-leopard	OUNCE
tailless hare	OCHOTONA, PICA
tree	ACLE, AILANTO, ASAK, ASOK(A)
	BITO, CAL(L)IATOUR
	CAL(L)IATURE, DATE PALM
	DIYA, LIQUIDAMBAR
	PAPER-MULBERRY, RED SANDERS
	(RED) SANDAL(-WOOD)
	SAKSAUL, SAXAUL, SIRIS
	TREE-OF-HEAVEN
tribes	KALMUK, KIPCHAK, TA(R)TAR
trousers	SHERWAL, SHERRYVALLIES
wild	
—ass	DZIGGETAI, HEMIONE
	KIANG, KYANG, ONAGER
—dog	RAC(C)OON-DOG
—goat	MARKHOR, SERPENT-EATER
—horse	PRZEWALSKI'S HORSE
asteroids	*(see astronomy)*
astrology	
apparent meeting of stars or planets	CONJUNCTION
astrologers	
—Austrian	MESMER
—French	NOSTRODAMUS
benign	TRINE
diagram of heavens at moment of one's birth	HOROSCOPE
coincident influences	SYNASTRY
comparison of horoscopes	SYNASTRY
division	
--between signs of the zodiac	CUSP
—of the zodiac	HOUSE, MANSION, SIGN
force from stars etc alleged to affect actions	INFLUENCE
forecast based on diagram of heavens	HOROSCOPE, NATIVITY
horoscope	NATIVITY
imaginary belt of the heavens	ZODIAC
overlapping of stars or planets	CONJUNCTION
part of the ecliptic just risen above horizon	ASCENDANT
planet	
—in conjunction with or near the sun	COMBUST

—ruling at birth	HYLEG
	(see also astronomy)
point on the ecliptic opposite to the ascendant	DESCENDANT
relative positioning of stars or planets	CONSTELLATION
—at	
72° apart	QUINTILE
120° apart	TRINE
moment of birth	HOROSCOPE
set of three signs 120° apart	TRIGON, TRIPLICITY
signs of zodiac	*(see zodiac)*
situation of one planet with respect to another	ASPECT
trigon	
—1st: Cancer, Scorpio, Pisces	WATERY TRIGON
—2nd: Taurus, Virgo, Capricorn	EARTHLY TRIGON
—3rd: Gemini, Libra, Aquarius	AIRY TRIGON
—4th: Aries, Leo, Sagittarius	FIERY TRIGON
astronomy	URANOLOGY
age of Moon at start of calendar year	EPACT
alignment of heavenly body with Sun and Earth	CONJUNCTION
angle between	
—Earth and Sun as seen from space	PHASE ANGLE
—planet and its last perihelion	ANOMALY
angular distance from celestial equator	DECLINATION
pole	AZIMUTH
apparent	
—displacement of star	ABERRATION
—movement of body resulting from movement of observer	PARALLAX
—path of Sun	ECLIPTIC
asteroids	ACHILLES, ABANDERADA
	ADONIS, AMOR, APOLLO, ASTRAEA,
	BAMBERGA, BETTINA, CAMILLA
	CERES, CHIRON, CYBELE
	DAVIDA, EGERIA, EKARD, EROS
	EUGENIA, EUNOMIA, EUPHROSYNE
	EUROPA, HALAWE, HAPAG, HERMES
	HIDALGO, HYGEIA, ICARUS
	INTEROMNIA, JUNO, LORELEI
	MELPOMENE, NORC, PALLAS
	PATENTIA, PSYCHE, SYLVIA
	THEMIS, TORO, VESTA
astronomers	
—Alexandrian	PTOLEMY

—American   ADAMS, BAADE, BARNARD
BOLTON, BOND, BOWEN, CHANDLER
DOUGLAS, DUNHAM, DYCE, EDDY
EWEN, GOLDSTEIN, GREENSTEIN, HALE
HERBIG, HEWITT, HUBBLE, HUMASON
JANSKY, KEELER, KOWAL, LANGLEY
LEAVITT, LOWELL, MENZEL
MINKOWSKI, MORGAN, MOULTON
NINNINGER, PARKER
PENZIAS, PICKERING, PURCELL, REBER
RUSSEL, SAGAN, SANDAGE, SCHABERLE
SCHMIDT, SEYFERT, SHAPLEY
SHOEMAKER, SLIPHER
TERRILE, TERRY, TOMBAUGH
TRUMPLER, TUCKER, VAN DE KAMP
WHIPPLE, WILDT, WILSON, ZWICKY
—Arabian   AL BATTANI, ARZACHEL
—Australian   CRAFORD, HAZARD
—Austrian   LITTROW
—Belgian LEMAITRE, SWINGS, WENDELIN
—British   ABNEY, ADAMS, AIRY, BOND
BONNOR, BRADLEY, DARWEN
EDDINGTON, FLAMSTEED, GILL
GOLD, GOODRICKE, HALLEY
HENDERSON, HERSCHEL, HOOKE
HOYLE, HUGGINS, HUSSEY, JEANS
JEFFREYS, LOCKYER, LOVELL, MOORE
NAPIER, NEWTON, PARSONS, POGSON
RYLE, WREN, WOOLFSON
—Chinese   HONG-YEE CHIU
—Danish   BOK, BRAHE, HERTZSPRUNG
KUIPER, ROEMER
—Dutch   DE SITTER, FABRICIUS
HUYGENS, KAPTEYN, OORT
SNEL VAN ROYEN, SNELLIUS
VAN DE CAMP, VAN DE HULST
—Egyptian   SOSIGENES
—Estonian   OPIK
—French   CASSINI, FLAMMARION
JANSSEN, LAPLACE, LE VERRIER
LYOT, MESSIER, RICHER
—German   BAADE, BESSEL, BODE
CLAVIUS, ENCKE, GALLE
HARTMANN, HERSCHEL, KEPLER
MARIUS, SCHWABE, SCHWARZCHILD
VOGEL, VON STRUVE, WEIZSACKER
WILDT, WITT, WURM
—Greek   ARISTARCHUS, ERATOSTHENES
HIPPARCHUS, KAL(L)IPPOS
METON, POSIDONIUS
—Indian   CHANDRASEKHAR
—Irish   OPIK
—Italian   BIANCHINI, GALILEO
GRIMALDI, MAFFEI
RICCIOLI, SCHIAPARELLI
SECCHI

—Polish   COPERNICUS, HELVETIUS
—Russian   KARDASHEV, KOSYREV
SAFFRONOV, SHKLOVSHY
VON STRUVE
—Spanish   DE FERRER
—Sri Lankan   WICKRAMASINGHE
—Swedish ALFVEN, ANGSTROM, CELSIUS
LUNDMARK, SWEDENBORG
—Swiss   TRUMPLER, ZWICKY
—Uruguayan   FERNANDEZ
bands of darkness before
  and after solar eclipse   SHADOW BANDS
Big Bang theory   SUPERDENSE THEORY
blocking of light from
  one body by another   OCCULTATION
blue star with large
  red shift   BLUE STELLAR OBJECT, BSO
bright spots seen
  at total eclipse   BAILY'S BEADS
brightest star   SIRIUS
cascade shower   COSMIC RAY SHOWER
circle
  —of altitude   ALMACANTAR
  —through poles   MERIDIAN
classification of stars
  by spectra   HARVARD CLASSIFICATION
SPECTRAL CLASS, SPECTRAL TYPE
clockwork model of Solar System   ORRERY
cloud of gaseous matter   NEBULA
collapse of universe   BIG CRUNCH
coloured lights in
  sky over Poles   AURORA AUSTRALIS
AURORA BOREALIS
comets   BENNETT, BIELA, BROOKS
CHIRON, CHURIUMOV-GERASIMENKE
CROMMELIN, D'ARREST
DONATI, DUTOIT-HARTLEY
ENCKE, FINLAY, GIACOBINNI-SINNER
GREAT, HALLEY, HARTLEY
HUMASON, LEVY, LEXELL'S, KOHOUTEK
MRKOS, TEMPEL, TUTTLE
WHIPPLE, WIRTANEN
conjunction (old)   SYNOD
constellations   (*see separate entry*)
cosmic ray shower   AUGER SHOWER
CASCADE SHOWER
PENETRATING SHOWER
SOFT SHOWER
critical mass of star that
  can become a white
  dwarf   CHANDRASEKHAR'S LIMIT
cycle of moon phases   CAL(L)IPPIC CYCLE
METONIC CYCLE
distance
  —Earth to Sun   ASTRONOMICAL UNIT
  —parallax of 1 sec of arc   PARSEC

distant group of stars	NEBULA	—gas clouds	COALSACK
extremity of major axis of orbit	APSIS	—nebula	CRAB, HORSEHEAD NEBULA
final stage of star	NEUTRON STAR	large meteor	BOLIDE
fluctuation of		laws governing movements	
—Earth's movement		of planets	KEPLER'S LAWS
round celestial pole	NUTATION	light emitted by star	LUMINOSITY
—equinoctial points along		line between	
the ecliptic	PRECESSION(AL) MOTION	—focus and	
galaxy		point on orbit	RADIUS VECTOR
—extremely bright	SEYFERT GALAXY	—light and dark	
—including Earth	MILKY WAY	areas of planet or moon	TERMINATOR
—nearest	MAGELLANIC CLOUDS	lining up of	
—with arms in spiral form	SPIRAL GALAXY	celestial bodies	CONJUNCTION
	SPIRAL NEBULA	Earth between planet	
gas cloud	NEBULA	and Sun	OPPOSITION
glare in sky	GEGENSCHEIN	luminous	
	ZODIACAL LIGHT	—patch	NEBULA
graph of main sequence		in	
of stars	HERTZSPRUNG DIAGRAM	—east at sunrise	ZODIACAL LIGHT
great circle		—west at sunset	ZODIACAL LIGHT
—in the heavens	ECLIPTIC	—ring round the Moon	BROCH, MACULA
—through poles	CELESTIAL MERIDIAN	magnitude of star	LUMINOSITY
group of stars		measure of	
—in recognised pattern	CONSTELLATION	—elongation of	
—with common motion	OPEN CLUSTER	ellipse	ECCENTRICITY
halo round		—star's brightness	MAGNITUDE
—head of comet	COMA	meteors	ANDROMEDID, AQUARID
—Sun or moon	CORONA		BIELID, GEMINID, LEONID
happening at sunrise	COSMIC(AL)		LYRID, ORIONID, PERSEID
hazy patch in sky	NEBULA		QUADRANTID, TAURID, URSID
highest point in heavens	VERTEX, ZENITH	—large, bright	BOLIDE
horizontal bearing of		—nickel-iron	SIDERITE
celestial body	AZIMUTH	—stone	AEROLITE, AEROLITH
hypothetical one-		meteor craters	
dimensional warp	COSMIC STRING	—Africa	ASHANTI CRATER
imaginary sphere containing			BOSUMTIBI, VREDEFORT RING
heavenly bodies	CELESTIAL SPHERE	—America	BARRINGER CRATER
instrument for			COON BUTTE
—detecting radio frequencies			MANSON, SERPENT MOUND
of stars etc	RADIO TELESCOPE		WELLS CREEK, WINSLOW
—determining star's		—Australia	GOSSES BLUFF
passage	ALMACANTAR		WOLF'S CREEK
	ALMACANTUR	—Brazil	ARAGUAINHA DOME
—following movement		—Canada	BRENT CRATER, CARSWELL
of stars etc	COELOSTAT		CHARLEVOIX, CHUBB CRATER
—measuring altitudes	ASTROLABE		CLEARWATER LAKES
—observing meridian			DEEP BAY, HAUGHTON DOME
passage	DIPLEIDOSCOPE		HOLLEFORD, MANICOUAGAN
intense gravitational field			MISTATIN, NEW QUEBEC
preventing escape even			STEEN RIVER, SUDBURY
of light	BLACK HOLE	—France	ROCHECHOUART
intersection of plane of		—Germany	(NORDLINGER) RIES
Equator with		—Iraq	AL UMCHAIMIN
celestial sphere	CELESTIAL EQUATOR	—Russia	KAMENSK, VLADIVOSTOK
interstellar		—Siberia	TUNGUSKA
—dust	COSMIC DUST	—Sweden	SILJAN

meteoric scar	ASTROBLEME
meteorite	AEROLITE, SIDER(OL)ITE
	THUNDERSTONE
—iron	AEROSIDERITE
—probable	AUSTRALITE, TEKTITE
—stony	CHONDRITE
Milky Way	WATLING STREET
minor planet	ASTEROID
moment when the Sun is	
—farthest	
north from the	
Equator	SUMMER SOLSTICE
south from the	
Equator	WINTER SOLSTICE
—overhead at the Equator	EQUINOX
Moon	LUNA, OLIVER
—area of high gravity	MASCON
—bays	ASTRONAUTS BAY
Bay of	
—Billows	SINUS AESTUUM
—Dew	SINUS RORIS
—Rainbows	SINUS IRIDUM
Central Bay	SINUS MEDII
—craters	ALPHONSUS, ARCHIMEDES
	ARISTARCHUS, ARISTOTELES
	ATLAS, BIANCHINI, COPERNICUS
	FLAMSTEED, GRIMALDI, HERCULES
	HIPPARCHUS, JOLIOT-CURIE
	LOMONOSOV, PLATO
	PTOLEMAEUS
—full moon	PLENILUNE
—inhabitant	LUNARIAN, SELENITE
—mock moon	PARASELENE
—mountains	ALTAI, CAUCASUS
	JURA, LEIBNITZ
—oscillation	LIBRATION
—period between	
new moons	LUNATION
	SYNODIC MONTH
—phases	NEW MOON
	FIRST QUARTER
	FULL MOON
	THIRD QUARTER
—seas	MOSCOW SEA
Ocean of Storms	OCEANUS
	PROCELLARUM
Sea of	
—Clouds	MARE NUBIUM
—Cold	MARE FRIGORIS
—Crises	MARE CRISIUM
—Fecundity	MARE FECUNDITATIS
—Humboldt	MARE HUMBOLDTIANUM
—Moisture	MARE HUMORUM
—Nectar	MARE NECTARIS
—Rains	MARE IMBRIUM
—Serenity	MARE SERENITATIS

—Tranquillity	MARE TRANQUILLITATIS
—Vapours	MARE VAPORUM
—sunlight reflected	
from Earth	EARTHSHINE
moons	
—Earth	LUNA, MOON
—Jupiter	ADASTREA, AMALTHEA
	ANANKE, CALLISTO, CARME
	ELARA, EUROPA
	GANYMEDE, HIMALIA, IO
	LEDA, LYSITHEA, METIS
	PASIPHAE, THEBE, SINOPE
—Mars	DEIMOS, PHOBOS
—Neptune	NEREID, TRITON
—Pluto	CHARON
—Saturn	ATLAS, CALYPSO, DIONE
	ENCELADUS, EPIMETHEUS
	HYPERION, IAPETUS, JANUS
	MIMAS, PHOEBE, RHEA, SPAHN
	SPONHOLZ, TELESTO, TETHYS
	TITAN
—Uranus	ARIEL, CORDELIA
	MIRANDA, OBERON, OPHELIA
	TITANIA, UMBRIEL
movement	
—across meridian	MERIDIAN PASSAGE
—from east to west	REGRESSION
—of	
equinoctial points	PRECESSION
lines on spectrum due to	
—approach of star	BLUE SHIFT
—recession of source	RED SHIFT
star across line	
of sight	PROPER MOTION
nearest star	PROXIMA CENTAURI
nebulous head of comet	CHEVELURE, COMA
non-distorting telescope	SCHMIDT CAMERA
Northern Lights	AURORA BOREALIS
	AURORA SEPTENTRIONALIS
observatory	(see separate entry)
occlusion of one body	
by another	ECLIPSE
optical representation of	
celestial bodies in dome	PLANETARIUM
orbit of planet round circle	EPICYCLE
oscillation of	
—axis of Earth	CHANDLER'S WOBBLE
—pole of Earth	NUTATION
—surface of Moon	LIBRATION
pair of stars	BINARY STAR
	DOUBLE STAR
path of one body round another	ORBIT
period	
—between successive	
conjunctions of a	
planet with sun	SYNODIC PERIOD

new moons	LUNATION	quasar which is not a	
	SYNODIC MONTH	radio source	QUASI-STELLAR GALAXY
—of complete obliteration			QSG
during an eclipse	ROTALITY	quasi-stellar radio source	QUASAR
—of Earth's rotation	SIDEREAL DAY	radiation from space	COSMIC RAYS
planets	EARTH, JUPITER, MARS	radio source	LACERTAE OBJECT
	MERCURY, NEPTUNE, PLUTO		QUASAR
	SATURN, URANUS, VENUS	rising with the Sun	COSMIC(AL)
—blue planet	EARTH	rounded granule in meteorite, etc	CHONDRULE
—brightest	VENUS	search for other life in	
—closer to Sun than Earth is	INFERIOR	the universe	BIOASTRONOMY
—farther from Sun than		shadow cast in eclipse	
Earth is	SUPERIOR	—darker part	UMBRA
—largest	JUPITER	—lighter part	PENUMBRA
—minor	ASTEROID	shape of	
	CERES, PALLAS, VESTA	—body between half and	
—mythical (Hindu)	RAHU	full phase	GIBBOUS
—nearest	VENUS	—Moon seen from Earth	PHASE
—orbital point		shower	
farthest from sun	PERIHELION	—extending over wide	
nearest to sun	APHELION	area	AUGER SHOWER
—red planet	MARS	—of	
—smallest	PLUTO	electrons etc	CASCADE SHOWER
—Venus	(see below)		SOFT SHOWER
—watery planet	EARTH	nucleons etc	PENETRATING SHOWER
point		situation of heavenly body	
—directly above observer	VERTEX, ZENITH	—lined up with another	CONJUNCTION
—directly below observer	NADIR	—opposite another	OPPOSITION
—of		skeleton sphere showing	
conjunction or opposition	SYZYGY	motions of stars etc	ARMILLARY SPHERE
infinite gravity	SINGULARITY	small body	
orbit		—reaching Earth's surface	AEROLITE
—farthest from			AEROLITH
Earth	APOGEE		METEORITE
Moon	APOCYNTHION	—travelling through space	ASTEROID
Sun	APHELION		COMET, METEOR
—nearest			SHOOTING-STAR
Earth	PERIGEE	source of high radiation	QUASAR
Moon	PERICYNTHION	Southern Lights	AURORA AUSTRALIS
	PERILUNE	space	(see separate entry)
Sun	PERIHELION	space dust	COSMIC DUST
—of very strong gravity	BLACK HOLE	speed of	
—in heavens opposite		—approach or recession	
nadir	VERTEX, ZENITH	of heavenly body	RADIAL VELOCITY
zenith	NADIR	—light	C
—where		—recession proportional	
orbit intersects ecliptic	NODE	to distance	HUBBLE'S LAW
Sun crosses celestial		star	(see separate entry)
equator	EQUINOX	study of	
position		—orbits and	
—at 90°	QUADRATURE	trajectories	CELESTIAL MECHANICS
—of planet in orbit	ANOMALY	—origins of universe	COSMOLOGY
presumed site of collapsed		Sun	
star	BLACK HOLE	—absorption lines in	
pulsating star	PULSAR	spectrum	FRAUNHOFER LINES
quartile aspect	SQUARE	—apparent path	ECLIPTIC

—appearance above horizon	DAWN
	SUNRISE
—bright area in	
chromosphere	SOLAR FLARE
photosphere	FACULA
—dark area on surface	MACULA
	SUNSPOT
—disappearance	
below horizon	SUNSET
during eclipse	TOTALITY
—fictitious, used in timekeeping	MEAN SUN
—halo	CORONA
—having Sun as centre	HELIOCENTRIC
—incandescent gas	
layer	CHROM(AT)OSPHERE
—intensity of radiation	SOLAR CONSTANT
—large flare of	
solar gas	(SOLAR) PROMINENCE
—light reflected by Earth	
to dark side of Moon	EARTHSHINE
—luminous envelope	PHOTOSPHERE
—mid-point on ecliptic	
between equinoxes	SOLSTICE
—mock sun	PARAHELION
—outbursts of high	
temperature	SOLAR FLARE
—stream of particles	
emitted by solar flares	SOLAR WIND
—study	HELIOLOGY
—time	
between successive	
returns of Sun to meridian	SOLAR DAY
of greatest declination	SOLSTICE
—ultra-violet rays	ACTINIC RAYS
—visible at night in	
polar regions	MIDNIGHT SUN
—worship	HELIOLATRY
superdense theory	BIG BANG THEORY
system of galaxies	METAGALAXY
table of astronomical data	EPHEMERIS
telescopes	(*see* **observatory**)
theory of	
—Earth as centre of	
Solar System	COPERNICAN THEORY
	GEOCENTRIC THEORY
—origin of universe	BIG BANG THEORY
	PULSATING UNIVERSE
	STEADY STATE THEORY
	SUPERDENSE THEORY
—planet formation	PLANETESIMAL
	HYPOTHESIS
	TIDAL HYPOTHESIS
—star formation	NEBULAR HYPOTHESIS
—Sun as centre of	
solar system	HELIOCENTRIC THEORY
	PTOLEMAIC THEORY

time	
—difference between lunar	
and solar year	EPACT
—measured from movements	
of planets	EPHEMERIS TIME
twelfth of diameter of Moon	
or Sun	DIGIT
two stars with common	
centre of gravity	BINARY STARS
two-star system that can be	
resolved with optical	
telescope	VISUAL BINARY
universe as system of galaxies	METAGALAXY
value which determines	
elliptic orbit	ELEMENT
variation in	
—apparent motion	
of heavenly body	ABERRATION
—orbit caused by mutual	
gravitational attraction	PERTURBATION
Venus	
—as	
evening star	HESPERUS, VESPER
morning star	LUCIFER
—mountainous region	BETA REGIO
—plain	GUINEVERE PLANITO
	ISHTAR TERRA
—volcano	THEIA MONTES
vertical angle of celestial body	ALTITUDE
Watling Street	MILKY WAY
zone containing orbits of Sun,	
Moon and planets	ZODIAC
athletes	(*see also* **games**)
(f) indicates women athletes	
decathletes	
—American	JENNER, JOHNSON
	MATHIAS, TOOMEY
—British	KRUGER, THOMPSON
	THORPE
—Canadian	SMITH
—Finnish	JARVINEN, YRJOLA
—German	EBERLE, HINGSEN
—Russian	AVILOV, KUTSENKO
	KUZNETSOV
—Swedish	LOMBERG, OHLSON
discus throwers	
—American (m)	HOUSER, OERTER
	ROSE, WILKINS
(f)	COPELAND
—British (f)	PICTON
—Bulgarian (f)	PETKOVA, VERGOVA
—Canadian	LAZDINS
—Czech (m)	BUGAR, DANEK
(f)	FIKATOVA
—Dutch (f)	STALMAN
—French (f)	MAZEAS, OSTERMEYER

—German (m)	DANNENBERG, SCHMIDT	—German (m)	SCHMIDT
(f)	JAHL, SCHLAAK	(f)	BALZER, ERHART
—Polish (f)	WAJSOWNA		OSCHKENAT, SCHALLER
—Romanian (f)	MANOLIU, MENIS	—Irish	BEATTIE
—Russian (m)	BARTES, RASSOHUPKIN	—Italian (f)	VALLA
(f)	MELNIK, PRESS	—Monégasque (f)	MOUTAWAKEO
	ROMASHKOVA	—Russian (f)	KOMISOVA, PRESS
hammer-throwers			STEPANOVA
—American	FLANAGAN, ROSE	javelin-throwers	
—British	SMITH	—American (m)	MILLER, OBERST, YOUNG
—Finnish	TAIANEN	(f)	DIDRIKSON
—Irish	O'CALLAGHAN	—Austrian (f)	BAUMA
—Russian	BONDARCHUK, SEDYCH	—British (m)	BACKLEY, BEVAN, OTLEY
heptathletes (f)		(f)	SANDERSON, WHITBREAD
—American	JOYNER-KERSEE	—Czech (m)	ZELEZNY
—Australian	FLEMMING, NUNN	(f)	ZATOPKOVA
—British	HAGGER, SIMPSON	—Finnish	HAERFOENEN, JARVINEN
—German	BEHMER		MYRRA, RATY
—Russian	NIKITINA	—German (m)	TAFELMEIER
high-jumpers		(f)	FELKE
—American (m)	EWRY, FOSBURY, OSBORN	—Hungarian (m)	NEMETH
(f)	COACHMAN, DIDRIKSON	(f)	NEMETH
	MCDANIEL	—Japanese	MIZOGUCHI
—Australian (f)	STANTON	—Romanian (f)	PENES
—British (m)	GRANT	—Russian (m)	KULA, MAKAROV
(f)	LERWILL, TYLER	(f)	OZOLINA, YAUNZEME
—Bulgarian (f)	KOSTADINOVA	—Swedish	BODEN, LEMMING
—Canadian (m)	MCNAUGHTON, OTTEY	long-jumpers	
(f)	CATHERWOOD	—American (m)	BEAMON, EWRY
—Cuban	SOTOMAYOR		LEWIS, PRINSTEIN
—Czech (f)	REZKOVA	(f)	WHITE
—German (m)	MOERGENBERG, WESSIG	—Australian	HONEY
(f)	ACKERMAN, MEYFARTH	—British (m)	DAVIES
—Hungarian (f)	CZAK	(f)	CAWLEY, MAY, RAND
—Italian (f)	SIMEONI	—German (f)	DRESCHLER, ROSENDAHL
—Romanian (f)	BALAS		VOIGT
—Russian	PAKLIN	—Hungarian (f)	GYARMATI
hurdlers		—New Zealand (f)	MOFFITT, WILLIAMS
—American (m)	CALHOUN, DAVIS	—Polish (f)	KRZESINSKA, SZEWINSKA
	DILLARD, KINGDOM	—Romanian (f)	STANCUI
	KRAENZLEIN, MOSES	—Russian (m)	EMMIYAN
	NEHEMIAH, TEWKSBURY	(f)	KOLPAKOVA, KREPKINA
(f)	DIDRIKSON	marathon runners	
	FARMER-PATRICK	—American (m)	COREY, HAYES, HICKS
	FITZGERALD-BROWN	(f)	BENOIT, LARRIEN-SMITH
—Australian (f)	CAIRD		WIEDENBACH
	FLINTHOFF-KING	—Australian (m)	DE CASTELLA, MARTIN
	STRICKLAND		MONEGHETTI
—British (m)	AKABUSI, BURGHLEY	(f)	MARTIN
	HEMERY, JACKSON	—British	DAVIES-HALE, FERRIS
(f)	GUNNELL, MORLEY		HARPER, HEATLEY, HUTTON
—Bulgarian (f)	DONKOVA		JONES, MILOVSOROV, PETERS
—Canadian (m)	MCKOY		SPEDDING, THACKERY
(f)	ROCHELEAU	—Chilean	PLAZA
—Dutch (f)	BLANKERS-KOEN	—Chinese (f)	YOUFENG
—French	CARISTON	—Czech	ZATOPEK

—Estonian	LOSSMAN
—Ethiopian	BIKILA, DENSIMO, WOLDE
—Finnish	KOLEHMAINEN, STENROOS
—French	EL OUAFI, MIMOUN, TEATRO
—Italian	BERTINI, BETTIOL
	BORDIN, PETRI
—Japanese	SON, TANIGUCHI
—Kenyan	WAKIIHURI
—New Zealand	RYAN
—Norwegian (f)	KRISTIANSEN, WAITZ
—Polish (f)	PANFIL
—Portuguese (m)	LOPES
(f)	MOTA
—Russian (m)	KOTOV, TOLSTIKOV
(f)	KLOCHKO
—Tanzanian	INKANGAA

middle-distance runners

—American (m)	CUNNINGHAM, EVANS
	LIGHTBODY, PETTIGREW
	REYNOLDS, SHEPPARD
	WHITFIELD, WHOTTLE
(f)	BABER, BRISCO-HOOKS
	MANNING
—Australian (m)	ELLIOTT, FLACK
	LANDY, CLARKE
(f)	FLINTHOFF-KING
—Belgian	MOENS, PUTTEMANS, RIEFF
—Brazilian	CRUZ, JUANTORENA
—British (m)	BANNISTER, BLACK, BILLY
	BUCKNER, CHATAWAY, COE, CRAM
	ELLIOT, FOSTER, HILL
	IBBOTSON, LOWE, MCKEAN
	MOORCROFT, OVETT, PIRIE
	REDMOND, SOLLY, WOODERSON
(f)	COOK, EDWARDS, HUNTER
	LYNCH, MCCOLGAN, MURRAY
	PACKER, WADE
—Canadian (m)	CUNNINGHAM
(f)	WILLIAMS
—Cuban (f)	QUIROT
—Czech (m)	ZATOPEK
(f)	KRATOCHVILOVA
—Dutch (f)	BLANKERS-KOEN
—Ethiopian	WOLDE, YIFTER
—Finnish	LARVA, NURMI, RITOLA
	VIREN, VIRTANEN
—French	MIMOUN
—German (m)	HOFFMEISTER
(f)	KOCH, ZINN
—Irish	DELANEY
—Italian (m)	MEI
(f)	CACCHI, DORIO
—Kenyan	BIWOTT, BOIT, ERENG, KEINO
	KIBET, KIBOR, KIROCHI
	KIPRIGUT, KONCHELLAH
	NGUGU, ONDIEKI, RONO, SIGEI

—Luxemburg	BARTHEL
—Moroccan	AOUITA
—New Zealand (m)	HALBERG, LOVELOCK
	QUAY, SNELL, WALKER
(f)	AUDAIN
—Nigerian	EGBUNIKE
—Norwegian (f)	KRISTIANSEN
—Romanian (f)	IVAN, MELINTE, PUICA
—Russian (m)	BOLOTNIKOV, KIROV, KUTS
(f)	AGLETDINOVA, BARGINA
	BOUDARENKO, KAZANKINA
	OLIZARENKO
—Somali	BILE
—South African (f)	BUDD
—Swedish	BACKMAN, WIDE
—Tunisian	GAMMOUDI

pentathletes

—American (m)	LEONARD, MAYO, THORPE
—British (f)	PETERS, RAND
—German (m)	HANDRICK, KAHL
(f)	BECKER, LASER
	ROSENTHAL, SIEGL
—Hungarian (m)	BALCZO, NAGY, NEMETH
(f)	KOVACS
—Russian (m)	LEDNEV, ONISHENKO
	STAROSTIN
(f)	PRESS, TKACHENKO
—Swedish (m)	DYRSSEN, HALL, LINDMAN

pole-vaulters

—American	HANSON, HOYT, RICHARDS
—Australian	ARKELL
—British	ASHURST
—French	QUINON
—German	NORDWIG
—Polish	KOSAKIEWICZ, SLUSARSKI
—Russian	BUBKA, GATAULLIN
	VOLKOV

shot-putters

—American	MATSON, O'BRIEN
	ROSE, WOODS
—Australian	MARTIN
—British	CAPES, COLE
—Bulgarian	CHRISTOVA
—French (f)	OSTERMEYER
—German (f)	BEYER, GUMMEL, KRIEGER
	LOSCH, SLUPIANEK, WERNER
—Italian	ANDRES
—Russian (m)	KISELYOV
(f)	PRESS, ZYBINA

sprinters

—American (m)	DILLARD, EVANS, HAHN
	HAYES, HINES, LEWIS
	MORROW, OWENS, SMITH
	TEWKSBURY, TOLAN
(f)	ASHFORD, CUTHBERT
	GRIFFITHS-JOYNER

	RUDOLF, SOWELL, TYUS
	WALSH
—Australian (m)	FLINTHOFF
(f)	BOYLE, CUTHBERT
	JACKSON, STRICKLAND
—Brazilian	DA SILVA
—British (m)	ABRAHAMS, BLACK
	CHRISTIE, LIDDELL, MAFE
	RADFORD, REGIS, WELLS
(f)	COOK, DOUGLAS
	OAKES, PACKER, SIMPSON
—Bulgarian	PETROV
—Canadian (m)	ANDERSON, DWYER
	JOHNSON, MAHORN, WILLIAMS
(f)	ISSAJENKO
—Dutch (f)	BLANKERS-KOEN
—French (f)	BRESSON
—German (m)	SCHMIDT
(f)	DRESCHLER, ECKERT
	GOEHR, KOCH, RICHTER
	STECHER, WOCKEL, ZEHRT
—Italian	BERUTTI, ENNEA
—Jamaican (m)	MCKENLEY, MILLER
	QUARRIE, STEWART, WINT
(f)	JACKSON, OTTEY
—Russian (m)	BORZOV, KRYLOV, MARKIN
(f)	KONDRATYEVA
steeplechasers	
—American	ASHENFELTER, LIGHTBODY
	MARSH
—British	BRASHER, DALY, DISLEY
	HODGE
—Canadian	FELL, ORTON
—Finnish	NURMI
—German	METZER
—Kenyan	BIWOTT, JIPCHO
	KEINO, KORIR
—Polish	MALINOWSKI
—Russian	MALINOWSKI, SOKOLOV
—Swedish	GARDERUD, SJOSTRAND
—Tanzanian	BAYI
triple jumpers	
—American	EWRY, JOYNER, PRINSTEIN
—Brazilian	DA SILVA
—British	HERBERT
—Bulgarian	MARKOV
—Japanese	ODA
—Polish	SZMIDT
—Russian	SANEEV, UNDMAE
atmosphere	(*see* **meteorology**)
Australia	AUS, DOWN UNDER, OZ
including aborigine words:	
aborigine	ABO, BINGHI
	BLACKFELLOW, MYALL
—dance	CORROBOREE
—drum	UBAR

—hut	GOONDIE, GUNYA(H), HUMPY
	MIAM(IA), MIMI, WURL(E)Y
—woman	GIN, LUBRA
absurd story	FURPHY
acacia	GIDGEE, GIDJEE
	MULGA, MYALL
	RASPBERRY-JAM TREE
	SALLEE, SALLY, WATTLE
afternoon	ARVO
agricultural worker	STATION-HAND
air force	RAAF
airline	QUANTAS
alcoholic drink	GROG
amulet	CHURINGA
angry	CROOK
animal	KANGAROO, KOALA
	(O)POSSUM, PLATYPUS
	WALLABY, WOMBAT
—that has run wild	SCRUBBER
ant-eater	ECHIDNA, NUMBAT
apple	COLANE
aquatic rodents	HYDROMYS
arboreal marsupial	KOALA, PHALANGER
area outside towns	OUTSIDE COUNTRY
arm	WARDEN'S FARM
assembly	ROLL-UP
Australian	AUSSIE, DIGGER, OZZIE
—soldier	ANZAC, DIGGER
back-country	OUTBACK
bad	ONCUS, ONKUS
bag	DILLY
bandit	BUSHRANGER
barbecue	BARBIE
be itinerant	HUMP THE BLUEY
bear	KOALA
become involved in	BUY INTO
beefwood	FOREST-OAK
beer	AMBER, FROSTY, GROG
—can	TUBE
—glass	MIDDY
best thing or person	RINGER
bird	ANT-THRUSH, BELL-BIRD
	BITTERN, BLACK SWAN
	BLOOD-BIRD, BOWER-BIRD
	BROLGA, BUDGERIGAR
	CASSOWARY, CAT-BIRD
	COACHWHIP-BIRD, COOEE
	COOEY, COUCAL, CURRAWONG
	DRONGO, EM(E)U, EMU-WREN
	FANTAIL, FROGMOUTH
	GALAH, HONEY-EATER
	KOEL, KOOKABURRA
	LARK-HEELED CUCKOO
	LEIPOA, LORIKEET, LORY
	LYRE-BIRD, MOPEHAWK
	MOPOKE, MOREPORK

	MOUND-BIRD, QUARRIAN
	REGENT-BIRD, RHIPIDURA
	RIFLE(MAN)-BIRD
	SATIN-BIRD, SCRUB-BIRD
	SWALLOW-SHRIKE, THICKHEAD
	WATTLE-BIRD, WOOD-SWALLOW
	ZEBRA-PAR(R)AKEET
blanket bundle	BLUEY
blind mole	NOTOCYTES
boast	SKITE
boaster	GALAH
boiling-pan	BILLY(-CAN), BILLIE
boomerang	KARLI, KILIE, KYLEY
	KYLIE, TURRAMA
bottom drawer	GLORY BOX
boulder	GIBBER
bower-bird	REGENT-BIRD, SATIN-BIRD
bread	DAMPER
break for a smoke	SMOKE-HO, SMOKO
breakdown-lorry driver	TOWIE
brook	CREEK
buddy	COBBER
bullroarer	CHURINGA
	THUNDERSTICK
	TU(R)NDUN
bundle	BLUEY, DRUM, SWAG
burrowing marsupial	NOTOCYTES, WOMBAT
bush	
—country	MALLEE
—tramp	DRUMMER
—turkey	VULTURN
bushman's swag	MATILDA
cadge	HUM
can of beer	TUBE
capital	CANBERRA
—Territory	ACT
carpet shark	WOBBEGONG
carry on back	HUMP
cattleman	STOCKMAN
cheap covered seats	BLEACHERS
chestnut tree	CASTANOSPERMUM
chicken	CHOOK
child	ANKLE-BITER
children's cricket	KANGA CRICKET
chocolate-covered cake	LAMINGTON
clergyman	JOSSER
club	DOWAK, NULLA(-NULLA)
	WADDIE, WADDY
cockatoo	CORELLA, GALAH
coin	DOLLAR
—5cents	ZACK
—sixpence	ZACK
coin-tossing game	TWO-UP
cold beer	FROSTY
collie	KELPIE, KELPY
conversation	YABBER

cool-box for food, etc	COOLGARDIE SAFE
	ESKY
coucal	SWAMP PHEASANT
countryside	BACK BLOCKS, OUTBACK
courgette	ZUCCHINI
cowboy	WADDIE, WADDY
crane (bird)	BROLGA
crayfish	YABBY
creditor	ORNITHORHYNCUS
crowd	MOB
currant bread	BROWNIE
cut-off river loop	BILLABONG
cyclone	WILLY-WILLY
dairy farmer	COW-COCKY
dance festival	CORROBOREE
decrepit	WARBY
defeat	TOSS
delinquent youth	BODGIE
desert-pea	GLORY-PEA
detective	DEMON
dewpond	GHILGAI
diarrhoea	WOG GUT
difficult situation	(FAIR) COW
dingo	WARRAGAL, WARRIGAL
dip sheep's	
hindquarters	CRUTCH
dislike	DERRY
disordered	ONCUS, ONKUS
disreputable person	QUANDONG
dog	KELPIE, KELPY
dream time	ALCHERINGA
drive herds across country	OVERLAND
driver of team	PUNCHER
drunk	ON THE SHICKER
dwarf eucalyptus	MALLEE
ear	SHELL-LIKE
edible	
—drupe	NATIVE PEACH
—fern	NARDOO
—grubs	WITCHETTY
effeminate man	PUNCE
egg-laying	
mammal	DUCKBILL(ED PLATYPUS)
	DUCK-MOLE, ECHIDNA
enclosed field	PADDOCK
Englishman	POM
eucalyptus	COOLABAH, GUM, IRON-BARK
	MALLEE, SALLEE, SALLY
	TEWART, TOOART, TUART
excel	RING
expert (shearer)	RINGER
false report	FURPHY
fern	NARDOO
festive gathering	CORROBOREE
fibre	
—bag	DILLY BAG

—plant	HEMP-BUSH
fish	BARRAMUNDA, BARRAMUNDI
	CARANX, GROPER, JEW-FISH
	MORWONG, PAGROSOMUS, PEGASUS
	PIG-FISH, ROCK-COD, S(CH)NAPPER
	TREVALLY
—like sea-horse	PEGASUS
flashily dressed	LAIRED UP
—man	LAIR
fliers	RAAF
flock	MOB
fly-catcher	WAGTAIL
fodder grass	KANGAROO-GRASS
food	TUCKER
fool(ish)	DILL, DRONGO, GALAH, NONG
football	RULES
forest	BRUSH
forlorn hope	BUCKLEYS
free immigrant	SQUARE-HEAD
friar-bird	LEATHER-HEAD
friend	COBBER
frogmouth	MOPEHAWK, MOPOKE
	MOREPORK
fruit	NONDA, QUANDONG
gang of convicts	PUSH
genuine	DINKUM, DINKY-DI
germ	WOG
ginger-haired (person)	BLUEY
girl	SHELAH, SHEILA
glass of beer	MIDDY
glory-pea	(STURT'S) DESERT PEA
golden age	ALCHERINGA, DREAMTIME
good	BONZER, BUDGEREE
grass	BARCOO, SPINIFEX
—bag	DILLY BAG
—tree	BLACKBOY
Great Britain	OLD DART
gum tree	EUCALYPTUS, KARRI
	STRINGY-BARK, WANDOO
	YARRAH
half-beak	GARFISH
hard work	YACKER, YAKKA, YAKKER
head-frame for cows	BAIL, BAYLE
heath-like plant	EPACRIS
hen	AUSTRALORP
herd	MOB
herdsman	STOCKMAN
hibiscus	COTTON-TREE
hold-up	BAIL UP
honest	DINKUM, DINKY-DI
honey	
—eater	BLUE-EYE, FRIAR-BIRD
	WATTLE-BIRD
—mouse	TARSIPES
—possum	TAIT
hooligan	LAR(R)IKIN

hornless	POLEY
horse	WALER
—jump from all four legs	PIG-JUMP
hot places	BOOLIGAL, HAY-HELL
house on farm	HEAD-STATION
hut	(*see* aborigine *above*)
ice-lolly	ICEBLOCK
ill	CRONK, CROOK
illicit	SLY
immigrant from Britain	POM(MY)
impostor	BUNYIP
in funds	RIBBED UP
influenza	DOG'S DISEASE
informer	FIZ(Z)GIG
initiation rite	BORA
insect	LAAP, PERP, WITCHETTY
insignificant twerp	DRONGO
instrument	DIDGERIDOO
	WOBBLE BOARD
insulated box	COOLGARDIE SAFE, ESKY
interfering person	BOT
interior of station	BACK-BLOCKS
itinerant worker	SWAGMAN
jabber	YABBER
jackpot win	MOTSER, MOTZA
journey	WALKABOUT
jumping chicken	AUSTRALORP
kangaroo	BOOMER, ROO
—big	FORESTER
killjoy	WOWSER
kingfisher	KOOKABURRA
kitchen-midden	MIRRYONG
ladybird	VEDALIA
lager	AMBER, FROSTY
landowners	SQUATTOCRACY
language	STRINE
large	
—amount of money	MOTSER, MOTZA
—kangaroo	EURO, WALLAROO
—landowner	PASTORALIST, SQUATTER
laughing jackass	GOBURRA, KOOKABURRA
lavatory	DUNNY
learner	COLONIAL EXPERIENCE MAN
	JACKAROO, JACKEROO
leaves used for tea	MANUKA
liquor	NECK OIL
live monotonous life	VEG OUT
lizard	BLUE TONGUE, GO(H)ANNA
	MOLOCH, MONITOR
	PERENTIE, THORN-DEVIL
loafer	SUNDOWNER
look	CAPTAIN COOK
loop in river	ANABRANCH
lose one's temper	PERFORM
lottery agency	TATTERSALLS
lout	LAIR

lung-fish	BARRAMUNDA, BURNET SALMON, CERATODUS
lyre-bird	PHEASANT
mad	DILL, DRONGO, GALAH, NONG
magpie	PIPING CROW
marine animal	CUNJEVOI
marsupial	BANDICOOT, CUSCUS, DASYURE DENDROGALUS, EURO, KANGAROO KOALA, NUMBAT, PHALANGER QUOKKA, TAIT, TASMANIAN DEVIL TREE-KANGAROO, WALLABY WALLAROO, WOMBAT
marvellous	BEAUT
mate	COBBER
mean	HUNGRY
meeting	ROLL UP
midget kangaroo	QUOKKA
miner	HATTER
mining gleaner	FOSSICKER
mix	BOX
mixed collection	MOB
monkey-puzzle tree	BUNYA(-BUNYA)
monotreme	(DUCKBILLED-)PLATYPUS
monster	BUNYIP
most excellent thing or person	RINGER
moth	BOGONG, BUGONG
mound-bird	BRUSH TURKEY, LEIPOA MALLEE-BIRD, MALLEE-FOWL MALLEE-HEN, SCRUB-TURKEY
mountain	RANGE
mountainous	RANGY
mounted	
—herdsman	STOCK-RIDER
—policeman	TROOPER
native	
—dance/song	CORROBOREE
—dog	DINGO
—hut	GOONDIE, GUNYAH, HUMPY
Navy	RAN
nest	WURLEY
newcomer on sheep station	JACKAROO JACKEROO, JILLAROO
newly-arrived	YOUNG
New South Wales person	CORNSTALK
New Zealand(er)	ENZED(DER)
nitwit	DRONGO
no	
—chance at all	BUCKLEY'S (CHANCE)
—good	CROOK
north Queensland	NEVER-NEVER-LAND
nut	QUANDONG-NUT QUEENSLAND-NUT
objectionable person or thing	COW
odd-job man	KNOCKABOUT

old man on a station	ROUSEABOUT ROUSTABOUT
on the move	WALKABOUT
out of season	MURKEN
owl	BOOBOOK
owner of livestock	STOCKHOLDER
pack-animal	PACKER
parakeet	ROSELLA
parliamentary obstruction	STONEWALL
parrot	COCKATOO, COCKATEEL COCKATIEL, CORELLA LORIKEET, LORY
pest	BOT
petrel	TITI
phalanger	OPOSSUM, TAGUAN, TAIT TARSIPES, VULPINE OPOSSUM
pick-up truck	UTE
pigeon	BRONZE-WING WONGA(-WONGA)
pioneer	SAND-GROPER
plan	DART
plant	BANKSIA, BINDI-EYE BOTTLEBRUSH, CONJUVOI GRASS-TREE, HOYA, KANGAROO PAW LAPORTEA, LOGANIA, NETTLE-TREE PINK HEATH, SPIDER FLOWER SPIGELIA, STURT DESERT PEA WARATAN, WATTLE WAX-FLOWER
political union	ANZUS
pond	BILLABONG
poor quality	CRONK
porcupine-grass	SPINIFEX
posse	MUSTER-PARTY
potoroo	RAT-KANGAROO
prejudice	DERRY
prospect	FOSSICK
prude	WOWSER
Queensland hemp	SIDA
quickest sheep-shearer	RINGER
racket	RORT
rail serving as gate	SLIP-RAIL
rat-kangaroo	POTOROO
ray	STINGAREE
real	DINKUM, DINKY-DI
recent immigrant	NEW CHUM
regent-bird	BOWER-BIRD
relative	DISTANT COUSIN
reprove	ROUSE ON
right	APPLES
river	
—effluent	BILLABONG
—flowing full	BANKER
robber of diggings by night	NIGHT-FOSSICKER
rock hole in desert	GNAMMA HOLE

rodent	WATER-MOUSE
rough	LARRIKIN
round-up	MUSTER
Rugby player	WALLABY
rules	FOOTBALL
running bird	EM(E)U
rural area	OUTBACK
rush bag	DILLI, DILLY(-BAG)
savage	WARRAGAL, WARRIGAL
scheme	DART
scrounge	HUM
sea-berry	HALORAGIS
—bream	TARWHINE
—horse	SEA-DRAGON
search for profit	FOSSICK
shark	MAKO
shearwater	MUTTON-BIRD
shed	HUMPY
sheep	JUMBU(C)K, MONKEY
—dog	KELPIE
--shearer (quickest)	RINGER
shelter in the bush	GUNYAH
shield	HIELAMAN
shoulder	HUMP
shrub	BANKSIA, CLIANTUS
	LIGNUM(-SCRUB), PITURI
	PROTEA, SALT-BUSH
	TEA-TREE, TELOPEA, WARATAH
sick	CROOK
single-storey house	COTTAGE
site for town	TOWNSHIP
slice of chocolate cake	LAMINGTON
small	
—bottle	STUBBY
—farmer	COCKY
—kangaroo	WALLABY
—marsupial	HONEY-MOUSE
	POUCHED-MOUSE
—parrot	LORIKEET
—river	CREEK
—settlement	TOWNSHIP
soldier	ANZAC, DIGGER
—of both World Wars	RETREAD
something extremely good	PURLER
spear-thrower	WOOMERA
speech	STRINE, YABBER
spider	KATIPO, NIGHT STINGER
	TARANTULA
spinifex	PORCUPINE-GRASS
spit	WOG
spiv	RORTER
spoilsport	WOWSER
spore-case used as food	NARDOO
square	DINKUM, DINKY-DI
squatter	JACKEROO
stampede	BREAKAWAY

stampeding animal	BREAKAWAY
state/territory	AUSTRALIAN CAPITAL
	TERRITORY
	NEW SOUTH WALES
	NORTHERN TERRITORY
	QUEENSLAND
	SOUTH AUSTRALIA
	TASMANIA, VICTORIA
	WESTERN AUSTRALIA
—governor's deputy	LIEUTENANT-GENERAL
stick used in two-up	KIP
stingy	HUNGRY
stock	
—farm	STATION
—man	RINGER, STATION-HAND
stone polished by wind	GIBBER
stop suddenly (horse)	PROP
straight-haired	CURLY
strike with club or stick	WADDIE, WADDY
strong	
—drink	SHICKER
—tobacco	NAIL-ROD
stupid	DILL, DRONGO
	GALAH, NONG
submerged reef	BOMBORA
supplementary spouse	PIRRAURU
surfer	LEMONHEAD
surrender	BAIL UP
swag	MATILDA
sweepstake agency	TATTERSALLS
swimming costume	COSSIE
take up Crown land	FREE-SELECT
talk	YABBER
tall thin person	CORNSTALK
Tasmanian devil/wolf	DASYURE
tea	
—break	TEA-HO
—pot	BILLY(-CAN), BILLIE
—tree	TI
tease	CHYAK
tektite	AUSTRALITE
tend	TAIL
termite-eater	NUMBAT
thicket	DEAD-FINISH
	MALLEE-SCRUB
throwing-stick	BOOMERANG
	WO(O)MERA, WOOMERANG
thunderstick	(see bullroarer above)
till	PETER
timber-cart	JINKER
time of creation	ALCHERINGA, DREAMTIME
tramp	SWAGGER, SWAGMAN
tramp's bundle	BLUEY, SHIRALEE
	SWAG, SWAGGIE
travelling through	
the bush	ON THE WALLABY (TRACK)

Australia   Austria

tree	BEEF-WOOD, BELAH, BELAR, BILLA
	BOTTLE-TREE, CASUARINA
	CREAM-OF-TARTAR TREE, EUCALYPTUS
	FLINDERSIA, GEEBUNG, GIDYA
	HORSE-RADISH TREE, JARRAH
	KARRI, KURRAJONG, MANUKA
	MORETON BAY CHESTNUT, MULGA
	PENDA, PROTEA, QUANDONG
	QUEENSLAND-NUT, SHE-OAK
	SOUR-GOURD, SPEAR-WOOD
	SWAMP-OAK, TEWART
	TUART, TOOART, WADDYWOOD
	WHITE TEAK, WOODEN PEAR
—snake	DENDROPHIS
true	DINKUM, DINKY-DI
trunk for trousseau	GLORY BOX
try to deceive	COME THE RAW PRAWN
tulip	WARATAH
turkey	VULTURN
U-turn	UEY
unbranded animal	CLEAR-SKIN
uncultured man	OCKER
undermine another's claim	FOSSICK
unmanageable	ROP(E)ABLE
useless person	GALAH
vagrant	SWAGGER, SWAGMAN
very	
—angry	ROP(E)ABLE
—good	APPLES, BEAUT, BONZER
	BOSHTA, BOSHTER
	BOSKER, BUDGEREE
virus	WOG
vomit	CHUNDER, HURL
	LIQUID, LAUGH,
	TECHNICOLOUR YAWN
walk with swag on back	HUMP
	WALK MATILDA
	WALTZ MATILDA
walking-stick	WADDIE, WADDY
wallaby	BRUSH-KANGAROO
	PAD(D)YMELON, PADEMELON
wandering	WALKABOUT
war-club	WADDIE, WADDY
water-cart	FURPHY
waterproof coat	DRIZA BONE
wattle tree	BOREE, WAIT-A-WHILE

weapon	LILLIL, NULLANULLA
welsher	SHICER
West Australian	SAND-GROPER
white man	GUB(B)AH
—with aboriginal wife	COMBO
wild	ROP(E)ABLE
	WARRAGAL, WARRIGAL
—aboriginal	MYALL
—cat	DASYURE
—dog	DINGO, WARRAGAL
	WARRIGAL
—horse	BRUMBY, WARRAGAL
	WARRIGAL
—young bull	MICK(E)(Y)
win shearing competition	RING THE SHED
witch doctor	BOYLA
wool	BOTANY
work	
—alone	HAT
—over waste ore	FOSSICK
worn out	WARBY
wrasse	PIG-FISH
young	
—animal	JOEY
—kangaroo	JOEY
—pig	SLIP
zoological region	NOTOGAEA
Austria	A
capital	VIENNA, WIEN
coin	
—100 groschen	SCH, SCHILLING
—20 kreutzers	ZWANZIGER
—100 kreutzers	FLORIN
—100 heller	KRONE
—money of account	GULDEN
dance	WALTZ
dynasty	HABSBURG, HAPSBURG
flower	EDELWEISS
measure	FASS, MUTH
noble	HERTZOG
provinces	BURGENLAND,
	NIEDER OSTERREICH, KARNTEN
	OBER OSTERREICH, OST TIROL
	SALZBURG, STEIERMARK
	TIROL(TYROL), VORARLBERG
soldier	PANDOOR, PAND(O)UR
weight	UNZE

B

bachelor	B, BA, BACH
of	
—Arts	AB, BA
—Civil Law	BCL
—Commerce	BCOM(M)
—Dental Surgery	BDS
—Divinity	BD
—Education	BED, EDB
—Engineering	BAI, BE, BENG
—Law	BL, LLB
—Letters	BL
—Literature	BLITT
—Medicine	BM, MB
—Music	BMUSc
—Philosophy	PHB
—Science	BS, BSC, SCB
—Surgery	BCH, BS, CHB
bacteriology	(*see* **biology**)
Bahamas	
capital	NASSAU
coin	DOLLAR
Bahrain	BRN
capital	MANANA
coin	DOLLAR, FILS
Balearic Islands	E
ballet	
ballets	COPPELIA, DAPHNIS AND CHLOE
	FIREBIRD, GISELLE, LA BAYADERE
	LA FILLE MAL GARDEE, LA SYLPHIDE
	NUTCRACKER, ONDINE, PETRUSHKA
	ROMEO AND JULIET, LES SYLPHIDES
	SLEEPING BEAUTY, SWAN LAKE
characters	
—Coppelia	COPPELIUS, FRANZ
	SWANHILDA
—Giselle	ALBRECHT, BATHILDE
	GISELLE, HILARION
	LOYS, MYRTHA
—La Bayadère	GAMZATTI
	HIGH BRAHMIN
	NIKIYA, RAJAH, SOLOR
—La Fille mal Gardée	ALAIN, COLAS
	LISE, SIMONE, TOMAS
—La Sylphide	EFFIE, GURN, JAMES
	MADGE
—Nutcracker	CLARA
—Ondine	BERTA, ONDINE
	PALEMON, TIRRENIO

—Romeo and Juliet	FRAY LAWRENCE
	JULIET, ROMEO
—Sleeping Beauty	AURORA, CARABOSSE
	LILAC
—Swan Lake	ODETTE, ODILE
	SIEGFRIED
	VON ROTHBART
choreographers	ASHTON, BALANCHINE
	BEJART, CUNNINGHAM
	DE VALOIS, DIAGHILEV
	DOLIN, HELPMANN
	MACMILLAN
company	AMERICAN BALLET THEATRE
	BALLET JOOSS, BALLETS RUSSES
	BOLSHOI, BOROVANKSY, KIROV
	PARIS OPERA BALLET, RAMBERT
	ROYAL BALLET, SADLER'S WELLS
dancers	
—background dancer	FIGURANT(E)
—female	BARBIERI, BERIOSOVA
	DANILOVA, FONTEYN
	GUILLEM, JONES, KATRAK
	MAKAROVA, MARKOVA
	PAVLOVA, PENNEY
	SEYMOUR, SPIRA-CAPAB
	TUCKER, ULANOVA
	VAN PRAAGH
—in group	CORYPHEE
—male	ASHTON, BEJART, BLAIR
	DOLIN, DOWELL, HELPMANN
	LIEPA, MUKHAMEDOV
	NIJINKSY, NUREYEV, PRICE
	SCHAUFFUSS, RUZIMATOV
	WELCH
—supporting group	CORPS DE BALLET
direction of body	
—away from audience	(EN) ECARTE
	EN EFFACE
—bent	EN FONDU
—facing front	EN FACE
—leaning	PENCHEE
—legs crossed	EN CROISE
—turning	
inwards	EN DEDANS
outwards	EN DEHORS
movements	
—at slower tempo	SOUTENU
—basic	
jump	JETE, SAUT
step	PAS
—close to floor	A TERRE
—exercises	BATTEMENT, CAMBRE
	COUP DE PIED, DEMI PLIE
	DEVELOPPE, GRAND BATTEMENT
	GRAND PLIE, PENCHE, RELEVE
	RETIRE, ROND DE JAMBE

—leaps	ASSEMBLE, BALLON, BATTERIE
	BATTU, CABRIOLE, CAPRIOLE
	CHANGEMENT, ECHAPPE
	ENTRECHAT, GRAND JETE (EN AVANT)
	JETE (FOUTTE), (PAS) CISEAUX
	(PAS DE)BRAISE, REVOLTADE
	RIVOLTADE, SAUT, SOUBRESANT,
	TEMPS DE POISSON, TEMPS LEVE
	TOURS EN L'AIR
—move	
holding partner above	
head on one straight arm	STULCHAK
on floor	SPLITS
—positions	ARABESQUE, ATTITUDE
	BRAS BAS, CROISE, DEMI-BRAS
	DEMI-SECONDE, ECARTE
	EPAULEMENT, EFFACE, EN FACE
	PORT DE BRAS
—quickstep	PAS DE DOUBLE
—steps	ASSEMBLEE, GALOP, GLISSADE
	JETE, PAS BALIONE, PAS BRISE
	(PAS) CHASSE, PAS DE BOURREE
	PAS DE CHAT, PAS DE CHEVAL
	PAS DE CISEAUX, SISSONNES
—swaying	BALANCE DE COTE
—turns	FOUETTE, PIROUETTE
terms	
—ability to leap high	ELEVATION
—ankle	COU-DE-PIED
—bar	BARRE
—beaten	FRAPPE
—bow	REVERENCE
—classic costume	TUTU
—coach	REPETITEUR
—curtsey	REVERENCE
—dance for two	PAS DE DEUX
—director	REGISSEUR
—exercise rail	BARRE
—gliding	GLISSE
—interlude	DIVERTIMENTO
	DIVERTISSEMENT
—on toe	(SUR LES) POINTES
—practice dress	LEOTARD
—producer	REGISSEUR
—running steps together	ASSEMBLE
	ENCHAINEMENT
—scissors	CISEAUX
—senior dancer	CORYPHEE
—sliding	GLISSE
—solo dance	PAS DE SEUL
for male	VARIATION
—staccato	PIQUE
—stand on	
ball of foot	DEMI-POINTE
toe	POINTE
—step	PAS, POSE

—teaching of slow movements	ADAGE
Bangladesh	BD
capital	DACCA, DHAKA
coin	PAISA, TAKA
Barbados	BDS
Barbados pride	(RED)SANDALWOOD
capital	BRIDGETOWN
coin	CENT, DOLLAR
Barbary	MAGHREB
ape	MAGOT
privateer	CORSAIR
ship	SANDAL, SETTEE, XEBEC(K)
baseball	
abandoned game	CALLED GAME
aiming mark	PLATE
all bases full	BASES LOADED
ambidextrous batter	SWITCH-HITTER
area	
—between foul lines	FAIR TERRITORY
—inside four bases	INFIELD
—outside	
foul lines	FOUL TERRITORY
four bases	OUTFIELD
—over plate between knee	
and armpit	STRIKE ZONE
attempt to hit the ball	STRIKE
ball	
—hit into	
fair territory	FAIR BALL
foul territory	FOUL BALL
—skied from bat	FLY BALL
—thrower	PITCHER
bat	CLUB
batting	
—area	BATTER'S BOX
—position	PLATE
conceded out	SACRIFICE
corner of diamond	BASE
credit to fielder	ASSIST
deliberate pitching of	
four balls	INTENTIONAL WALK
dismiss	
—three men at once	TRIPLE PLAY
—two men at once	DOUBLE PLAY
dismissal	
—after three strikes	STRIKE OUT
—when two men occupy	
one base	FORCE PLAY
extra batter	DESIGNATED HITTER, DH
glove	MITT
hit	
—bringing four runs	GRAND SLAM
—over boundary fence	HOME RUN, HOMER
—resulting in run	BASE HIT, DOUBLE
	SINGLE, TATER, TRIPLE
leagues	AMERICAN, NATIONAL

number of balls or strikes	COUNT
old name	CHERMANY
pitch (ball)	CURVEBALL, FASTBALL
	FORKBALL, KNUCKLEBALL
	SCREWBALL, SCUFFBALL
	SLIDER, SPITBALL
—illegal	BALK
—in strike zone, not hit	STRIKE
—not stopped by catcher	PASSED BALL
—outside strike zone	BALL
—wide	WILD PITCH
players	
—batters	AARON, BANKS, BOONE
	CANESCO, COBB, DI MAGGIO
	DYKSTRA, GEHRIG, HORNSBY
	JACKSON, MANTLE, MATTHEWSON
	MAYS, PAIGE, REECE, ROBINSON
	ROSE, RUTH, RYAN, VALENZUELA
	WAGNER, YOUNT
—catchers	CARTER, FISK
—pitchers	BOUGH, CARLTON, CLEMENS
	FIDRYCH, GEDMAN, GOODEN
	MORRIS, NIERRO
	RYAN, SCOTT, YOUNG
playing	
—area	DIAMOND
—positions	CATCHER, CENTRE FIELD
	FIRST BASE, LEFT FIELD
	PITCHER, RIGHT FIELD
	SECOND BASE, SHORT STOP
	THIRD BASE
public seating	BLEACHERS
push ball with bat	BUNT
substitute batter	PINCH HITTER
team	NINE
teams	
—Atlanta	BRAVES
—Baltimore	ORIOLES
—Boston	RED SOX
—California	ANGELS
—Chicago	CUBS, WHITE SOX
—Cincinnati	REDS
—Cleveland	INDIANS
—Detroit	TIGERS
—Houston	ASTROS
—Kansas City	ROYALS
—Los Angeles	DODGERS
—Milwaukie	BREWERS
—Minnesota	TWINS
—Montreal	EXPOS
—New York	METS, YANKEES
—Oakland	ATHLETES
—Philadelphia	PHILLIES
—Pittsburgh	PIRATES
—St Louis	CARDINALS
—San Diego	PADRES

—San Francisco	GIANTS
—Seattle	MARINERS
—Texas	RANGERS
—Toronto	BLUE JAYS
touch player with ball	TAG
two games at one session	DOUBLE HEADER
umpire	HONCHO
—for	
major games	SIX
other games	FOUR
warm-up area	BULLPEN
Basque	
dish	PIPERADE
game	PELOTA
language	EUSKARA
region	PYRENEES
bats	HORSESHOE, NOCTULE
	PIPISTRELLE, SEROTINE, VAMPIRE
battles	
Abyssinia/Italy	ADOWA
Afghanistan/Britain	MAIWAND
America/Germany - WW1	BELLEAU WOOD
	CANTIGNY
/Japan	GUADALCANAL, IWO JIMA
	LEYTE, LUZON
	OKINAWA, TARAWA
—naval	BISMARCK SEA
	CAPE ESPERANCE, CORAL SEA
	JAVA SEA, LEYTE GULF
	MIDWAY, PEARL HARBOUR
	PHILIPPINE SEA
	SAN BERNARDINO STRAIT
	SANTA CRUZ, SURIGAO STRAIT
	TASSAFARONGA
American	
—civil war	BALL'S BLUFF
	BELMONT, BULL RUN, CARRICK'S FORD
	CEDAR MOUNTAIN, CHAMPION HILL
	CHANCELLORSVILLE
	CHICKAMAUGA VALLEY
	CHICKASAW BLUFFS, CORINTH
	CRAMPTON GAP, ELKHORN TAVERN
	FAIROAKS, FOUR OAKS
	FREDERICKSBURG, GETTYSBURG
	IUKA, MANASSAS (JUNCTION)
	MALVERN HILL, MARYE'S HEIGHTS
	MILL SPRINGS, MISSIONARY RIDGE
	MURPHREESBORO, PEA RIDGE
	PETERSBURG, PRAIRIE GROVE
	RICH MOUNTAIN, RICHMOND
	SEVEN PINES, SHARPSBURG, SHILOH
	SOUTH MOUNTAIN, STONE RIVER
	THE ANTIETAM, TURNER'S GAP
	VICKSBURG, WILLIAMSBURG
	WILSON'S CREEK
	WOGAN'S CROSS ROADS

—Indian war	LITTLE BIGHORN
	WOUNDED KNEE
—Revolution	BEMIS'S HEIGHT
	BRANDYWINE, BUNKERS HILL
	CHARLESTON, CHATTERTON HILL
	CONCORD, EUTAW SPRINGS
	FREEMAN'S FARM, GERMANTOWN
	GREEN SPRING, GREENSBORO
	HANGING ROCK, HARLEM HEIGHTS
	KING'S MOUNTAIN, LEXINGTON
	LONG ISLAND, MONMOUTH, NEWTOWN
	NINETY-SIX, ROCKY MOUNT
	SARATOGA, STILLWATER,
	TICONDEROGA, TRENTON, VINCENNES
	WHITE PLAINS, YORKTOWN
—naval	CHESAPEAKE BAY
Arabs/Byzantium	YARMUK
/French	POITIERS
/Persians	KADESSIA, NEHAVEND
	QADISIYA
/Spanish	NAVAS DA TOLOSA
Athens/Sparta	ARGINUSAE, AEGOSPOTAMI
Austria/Britain	ALMANZA
/Italy	ASIAGO, CAPORETTO, ISONZO
	PIAVE RIVER, VITTORIO VENETO
/France	AUSTERLITZ
	HOHENLINDEN, MARENGO
	PAVIA, ULM, VALMY, WAGRAM
/Prussia	KOLIN, SADOWA
/Serbia	JADAR RIVER
	KOLUBRA RIVER
/Swiss	MORGATEN
/Turks	ZENTA
Bavarians/Magyars	PRESSBURG
Belgium/Germany	LIEGE
Britain/Denmark — naval	COPENHAGEN
/France	ALBUERA, BADAJOZ
	BAROSSA, BAYLEN, CORUNNA
	FONTENOY, HASTENBECK
	LAUFFELDT, MAIDA, MINDEN
	SALAMANCA, TALAVERA
	VIMIERA, VITTORIA
	WANDEWASH, WATERLOO
—naval	ABOUKIR, LAGOS
	LES SAINTES, QUIBERON BAY
	THE NILE, TRAFALGAR, USHANT
/Germany - WW1	AISNE, ARDENNES
	ARRAS, ARTOIS(-LOOS), CAMBRAI
	FESTUBERT, FRONTIERS, LE CATEAU
	LORRAINE, LOOS, MARNE, MESSINES
	MONS, NEUVE CHAPELLE
	PASSCHENDAELE, SAMBRE, SOMME
	VERDUN, VIMY RIDGE, YPRES
—naval	CORONEL
	DOGGER BANK
	FALKLAND ISLANDS
	HELIGOLAND BIGHT
	JUTLAND
/Germany - WW2	ANZIO, ARDENNES
	ARNHEM, CASSINO, EL ALAMEIN
	FALAISE GAP, GAZALA, KASSERINE
	MEDENINE, MORTAIN, ST LO
	SANGRO, SIDI REZEGH
	THE BULGE, TOBRUK
—air	BRITAIN
—naval	ATLANTIC
	RIVER PLATE
/Holland —naval	CAMPERDOWN
/India	ASSAYE, BUXAR
	CHILIANWALA, LASWARI
	MIANI, PANIPAT, PLASSEY
	SOBRAON
/Italy - WW2	GAZALA, SIDI REZEGH
—naval	CAPE MATAPAN
/Japan - WW2	IMPHAL, KOHIMA
/Russia	ALMA, BALACLAVA
	INKERMAN
/South Africa	MAGERSFONTEIN
	MAJUBA HILL, SPION KOP
	STORMBERG
/Spain - naval	CAPE PASSARO
	CAPE ST VINCENT
	ST JUAN DE ULLUA
/Sudan	ABU KLEA, OMDURMAN
/Turks	CTESIPHON, GALLIPOLI
	GAZA, MEGIDDO, RAFA
	RAMADI, ROMANI, SHARQAT
—naval	NAVARINO
	(*see also* England *below*)
/Zulus	ISANDHLWANA
	RORKE'S DRIFT, ULUNDI
Britons/Saxons	DYRHAM, MOUNT BADON
Byzantium/Arabs	YARMUK
/Persia	NINEVEH
/Turks	MANZIKERT, MELASGRID
Carthage/Rome	CANNAE, ZAMA
Christians/Moors	LAS NAVAS DE TOLOSA
Denmark/Spain	LUTTER
/Sweden	LUND
Egypt/Hittites	QADESH
/Romans - naval	ACTIUM
/Syria	MEGIDDO
England/Arabs	ACRE
/France	AGINCOURT, BAUGE
	BEACHY HEAD, BRIHUEGA
	CASTILLON, COURTRAI, CRECY
	DENAIN, LANDEN, LEIPZIG
	MALPLAQUET, NAJERA, NAMUR
	OUDENARDE, POITIERS
	RAMILLIES, SPURS, STEENKIRK
-naval	LA HOGUE, MALAGA
	SLUYS

/Ireland	AUGHRIM, BOYNE
	RATHMINES, YELLOW FORD
/Scotland	BANNOCKBURN
	BRANHAM MOOR, CHEVY CHASE
	CULLODEN, FLODDEN, GLENCOE
	HALIDON HILL, HARLAW
	HOMILDON HILL, KILLIECRANKIE
	NECTANSMERE, NEVILLE'S CROSS
	NORTHALLERTON, PINKIE
	PRESTON PANS, SOLWAY MOSS
/Spain - naval	AZORES
English civil war	ADWALTON MOOR
	BARNET, BENBERB, BOTHWELL BRIG
	BRADDOCK DOWN, CROPEDY
	DUNBAR, EDGEHILL, LANGPORT
	LOSECOAT, LOSTWITHIEL
	MARSTON MOOR, NASEBY
	NEWBURY, PRESTON
	SEDGEMOOOR, STRATTON
	WINCEBY, WORCESTER
English/Danes	ASHDOWN, ASHINGDON
	EDINGTON, MALDON
/Normans	HASTINGS
	TENCHEBRAI
/Norse	BRUNANBURH, FULFORD
	STAINMORE, STAMFORD BRIDGE
final battle, good/evil	ARMAGEDDON
	RAGNAROK
France/Austria	MAGENTA, SOLFERINO
/Germany	CHAMPAGNE, MULHOUSE
	SEDAN, VERDUN
/Italy	FORNOVO, RAVENNA
/Netherlands	BOUVINES
/Russia	EYLAU, FRIEDLAND
/Prussia	JENA, METZ, ROSSBACH
	SEDAN
/Spain	ST QUENTIN
/Switzerland	MARIGNANO
Franks/Huns	TROYES
/Visigoths	VOVILLE
Germans, Poles/Mongols	LEIGNITZ
Germans/Magyars	RIVER LECH
Germany/Italy	CAPORETTO
/Russia - WW1	GUMBINNEN, LODZ
	MASURIAN LAKES
	NAROCH LAKE
	STALLPONEN
	TANNENBERG
—WW2	BERLIN, KURSK
	STALINGRAD
/Sweden	LUTZEN
Greeks/Macedonia	CHAERONEA
/Persians	ISSUS, MARATHON
	PLATAEA
—naval	SALAMIS
/Romans	CYNOSCEPHALAE, PYDNA

Hungary/Russia	SEGESVAR
/Turks	NICOPOLIS
Irish/Norse	CLONTARF
Japan/Russia - naval	TSUSHIMA
Macedonia/Persians	ARBELA, GRANICUS
Mexico/Texas	ALAMO
Mongols/Turks	ANKARA
Poles/Teutonic Knights	TANNENBERG
Portugal/Spain	ALJUBAROTTA
Prussia/Sweden	FEHRBELLIN
Rome/Carthage	CANNAE, ZAMA
/Egypt - naval	ACTIUM
/Epirus	HERACLES
/Goths	ADRIANOPLE
/Huns	CATALAUNIAN FIELDS
/Persia	MAGNESIA
/Syria	MAGNESIA
Russia/Sweden	NARVA
/Turkey	ERZINCIAN, SARIKAMISH
	SINOPE
Serbia/Turks	KOSSOVO
Spain/Turks	LEPANTO
Sparta/Thebes	LEUCTRA
Wars of the Roses	BARNET, BLORE HEATH
	BOSWORTH, EDGECOTE
	HEDGELEY MOOR, HEXHAM
	LUDLOW, MORTIMER'S CROSS
	ST ALBANS, TEWKESBURY
	WAKEFIELD
with the gods	THEOMACHY

bearing
meaning: carrying
    producing

acorns	GLANDIFEROUS
all kinds	OMNIFEROUS
aluminium	ALUMINIFEROUS
apples	POMIFEROUS
arms	ARMIGEROUS
balsam	BALSAMIFEROUS
beans	LEGUMINOUS
berries	BACCIFEROUS
blood	SANGUIFEROUS
bones	OSSIFEROUS
bracts	GLUMIFEROUS
breasts	MAMMIFEROUS
bristles	CHAETIFEROUS
	CHAETOPHOROUS, STYLIFEROUS
catkins	AMENTIFEROUS
cells	CELLIFEROUS
claws	CHELIFEROUS
cloud	NUBIFEROUS, NUBIGINOUS
clubs	CLAVIGEROUS
coal	CARBONIFEROUS
copper	CUPRIFEROUS
coral	CORALLIFEROUS, CORALLIGENOUS
cross	CRUCIFEROUS

culm (coal)	CULMIFEROUS
cupules	CUPULIFEROUS
death	LETHIFEROUS
diamonds	DIAMONDIFEROUS
	DIAMANTIFEROUS
disease	MORBIFEROUS
drops	GUTTIFEROUS
eggs	OVIFEROUS, OVIGEROUS
excess hair	CHAETIFEROUS
	CHAETOPHOROUS
fatty matter	SEBIFEROUS
feathers	PLUMIGEROUS
flame	FLAMMIFEROUS
flowers	FLORIFEROUS
forked appendage	FURCIFEROUS
fossils	FOSSILIFEROUS
fossil reptiles	REPTILIFEROUS
fruit	FERACIOUS, FRUCTIFEROUS
	FRUGIFEROUS, POMIFEROUS
garnet	GARNETIFEROUS
glands	GLANDIFEROUS
glumes	GLUMIFEROUS
god	DEIPAROUS
gold	AURIFEROUS
good health	SALUTIFEROUS
granules	GRANULIFEROUS
grass stems	CULMIFEROUS
guano	GUANIFEROUS
gum	GUMMIFEROUS
hair	CRINIGEROUS, PILIFEROUS
honey	MELLIFEROUS
horn	KERATOGENOUS
horns	CORNIGEROUS
hornstone	CORNIFEROUS
incense	THURIFEROUS
iron	FERRIFEROUS
keratin	KERATOGENOUS
keys	CLAVIGEROUS
lead	PLUMBIFEROUS
leaves	FRONDIFEROUS
lime	CALCIFEROUS, CALCIGEROUS
light	LUCIFEROUS, LUMINIFEROUS
manganese	MANGANIFEROUS
manna	MANNIFEROUS
metal	METALLIFEROUS
milk	GALACTOPHOROUS
	LACTIFIC, LACTIFEROUS
monsters	TERATOGENIC
mucus	MUCIFEROUS
musk	MOSCHIFEROUS
nectar	NECTARIFEROUS
nipple-like projections	PAPILLIFEROUS
nuts	GLANDIFEROUS, NUCIFEROUS
oil (as seeds)	OLEIFEROUS
ovules	OVULIFEROUS
oxide of yttrium	YTTRIFEROUS

partitions	SEPTIFEROUS
pearl	MARGARITIFEROUS
pears	POMIFEROUS
peas	LEGUMINOUS
pests	PESTIFEROUS
petrol	PETROLIFEROUS
platinum	PLATINIFEROUS
pods	LEGUMINOUS
pulses	LEGUMINOUS
pupa case	PUPIGEROUS
pyrites	PYRITIFEROUS
quartz	QUARTZIFEROUS
salt	SALIFEROUS
seed	SEMINIFEROUS
shade	UMBRIFEROUS
shaft of column	SCAPIGEROUS
shells	CONCHIFEROUS
silica	SILICIFEROUS
silver	ARGENTIFEROUS
sleep	SOMNIFIC, SOMNIFEROUS
	SOPORIFEROUS, SOPORIFIC
small	
—cells	CELLULIFEROUS
—glands	GLANDULIFEROUS
—globes	GLOBULIFEROUS
—holes	FORAMINIFEROUS
—nipples	PAPILLIFEROUS
—round particles	GLOBULIFEROUS
—spines	SPINULIFEROUS
spines	SPINIFEROUS
	SPINIGEROUS
spirally shaped parts	STROMBULIFEROUS
spots	GUTTIFEROUS
stars	STELLIFEROUS
stigmas	STIGMATIFEROUS
style	STYLIFEROUS
suckers	STOLONIFEROUS
sweat	SUDORIFEROUS
teeth	DENTIGEROUS
thorns	SPINIFEROUS, SPINIGEROUS
tin	STANNIFEROUS
titanium	TITANIFEROUS
tubers	TUBERIFEROUS
urine	URINIFEROUS
vines	VITIFEROUS
well-being	SALUTIFEROUS
whip	FLAGELLIFEROUS
	MASTIGOPHOROUS
wool	LANIFEROUS
yolk	VITELLIGENOUS
young	
—from eggs	OVIPAROUS
inside body	OVOVIVIPAROUS
—live	VIVIPAROUS
zinc	ZINKIFEROUS
	(see also **having**)

Bechuanaland	(*see* **Botswana**)
becoming	
adult	ADOLESCENT
apparently cooler	DECALESCENT
atrophied	CONTABESCENT
better frame of mind	RESIPISCENT
big	TURGESCENT
bigger	ACCRESCENT
black	NIGRESCENT
born anew	RENASCENT
branched	DELIQUESCENT
bubbly	EFFERVESCENT
cooler	DEFERVESCENT
dark	NIGRESCENT
dry	ARESCENT
faded	EVANESCENT
flowers	FLORESCENT
glass	VITRESCENT
green	VIRIDESCENT, VIRESCENT
healthy	CONVALESCENT
hidden	DELITESCENT
hot	FERVESCENT
into being	NASCENT
latent	LATESCENT
leafy	FRONDESCENT
less	DECRESCENT
light	LUMINESCENT
liquid	(COL)LIQUESCENT
	DELIQUESCENT
luminous with heat	INCANDESCENT
male	VIRILESCENT
milk	LACTESCENT
milky	OPALESCENT
obsolete	OBSOLESCENT
old	SENESCENT
pale	PALLESCENT
quiet	QUIESCENT
rainbow-coloured	IRIDESCENT
red	ERUBESCENT, RUFESCENT
revived	REVIVESCENT, REVIVISCENT
rotten	PUTRESCENT
sexually mature	PUBESCENT
shrivelled	TABESCENT
sleepy	SOMNOLESCENT
stem-like	CAULESCENT
stone	LAPIDESCENT
swollen	(IN)TUMESCENT, TURGESCENT
together	COALESCENT, CONCRESCENT
tree-like	ARBORESCENT
warm	INCALESCENT
wasted	TABESCENT
white	ALBESCENT, CANESCENT
white-hot	(IN)CANDESCENT
withered	MARCESCENT
yellow	FLAVESCENT, LUTESCENT
youthful	JUVENESCENT

beginning	
meaning: origins (of)	
reproduction (of)	
according to laws of nature	NOMOGENY
all cells contributing to heredity	PANGENESIS
alternation	METAGENESIS
alternative	HETEROGENESIS
asexual	MONOGENESIS, MONOGONY
blood formation	HAEMATOGENESIS
bones	OSTEOGENESIS, OSTEOGENY
by	
—budding	BLASTOGENESIS
—fission	SCHIZOGENESIS
—radioactive disintegration	RADIOGENIC
cancer	CARCINOGENESIS
cartilage	CHONDROGENESIS
cells	CYTOGENESIS
continent-building	EPEIROGENESIS
cross-fertilisation	ALLOGAMY
crystals	CRYSTALLOGENESIS
cyclones	CYCLOGENESIS
determinate variation	ORTHOGENESIS
development of form	MORPHOGENESIS
different genes	ALLOGENESIS
differentiation	HISTOGENESIS
	HISTOGENY
disease	PATHOGENESIS, PATHOGENY
distinctive form	MORPHOGENESIS
doubling of parts	DIPLOGENESIS
eggs	OOGENESIS
evolutionary pedigree	PHYLOGENESIS
	PHYLOGENY
fission	SCHIZOGONY
from	
—like parents	HOMOGENESIS
—living things	BIOGENESIS
—male and female	SYNGENESIS
—non-living matter	ABIOGENESIS
	BIOPOIESIS
—nothing	ABIOGENESIS
	SPONTANEOUS GENERATION
—unfertilised ovum	PARTHENOGENESIS
gametes	GAMETOGENESIS
gods	THEOGONY
gradual production	EPIGENESIS
heat	THERMOGENESIS
human beings	ANTHROPOGENESIS
	ANTHROPOGENY
	ANTHROPOGONY
hypnotic state	HYPNOGENESIS
	HYPNOGENY
imperfect development	AGENESIS
in larval state	PAEDOGENESIS
individual development	ONTOGENESIS
involving all cells	PANGENESIS
like origins	ISOGENY

living	
—beings	ZOOGENY, ZOOGONY
—organisms	ORGANOGENESIS
many origins	POLYGENESIS, POLYGENY
mind	NOOGENESIS
	PSYCHOGENESIS
	PSYCHOGONY
minerals	PARAGENESIS
miraculous origin	THAUMATOGENY
mixed origins	MISCEGENATION
monsters	TERATOGENY
mountains	OROGENESIS
multiple origins	POLYGENESIS, POLYGENY
myths	MYTHOGENESIS
naturally	NOMOGENY
nervous activity	DYNAMOGENESIS
new birth	PALINGENESIS
	PALINGENESIA
	PALINGENESY
of parts	MEROGENESIS
organic evolution	BIOGENESIS
outside the body	ECTOGENESIS
ovum development	OOGENESIS, OOGENY
phantasms	PHANTASMOGENESIS
plants	PHYTOGENESIS, PHYTOGENY
rock from sediments	DIAGENESIS
segmentation	MEROGENESIS
self-fertilisation	AUTOGAMY
sexual reproduction	AMPHIMYXIS
	GAMOGENESIS
similar genes	ISOGENESIS, ISOGENY
	SYNGENESIS
soil	PEDOGENESIS
soul	PSYCHOGONY
species	SPECIATION
sperm	SPERMATOGENESIS
	SPERMATOGENY
spontaneous	ABIOGENESIS
	HETEROGENESIS
spores	SPOROGENESIS, SPOROGENY
systematic evolution	ORTHOGENESIS
teeth	ODONTOGENY
tissues	HISTOGENESIS, HISTOGENY
transmission of vibrations	PERIGENESIS
unlike parents	XENOGENESIS
virgin birth	PARTHENOGENESIS
weather front	FRONTOGENESIS
without fertilisation	APOMYXIS
Belgium	B, BELG
airline	SABENA
capital	BRUSSELS, BRUXELLES
coin	BELGA, CENTIME
	FRANC, MITE
language	FLEMISH, FRENCH
	WALLOON
races	FLEMISH, WALLOON

beliefs	
including: founders	
followers	
heresies	
orders	
religions	
1000 years of Christ's	
rule	CHILIASM, MILLENARIANISM
	MILLENIALISM
acceptance of complete	
divinity of Christ	APOLLINARIANISM
adult baptism	ANABAPTISTS
African Christian	DONATISM
—heretics	ABELITES, ABEL(OR)IANS
all gods	PANTHEISM
allegorical interpretation	ORIGENISM
Alpine Christian	VALDENSIAN, WALDENSIAN
American	AMISH, MORMONISM
—Assemblies of God	HOLY ROLLERS
	PENTECOSTAL CHURCH
—Quakers	SHAKERS
	UNITED SOCIETY OF BELIEVERS
Anabaptists	AMISH, HUTTERITES
	MENNONITES
Anglo-Catholics with leaning	
towards Rome	NEO-CATHOLICS
Arab	
—philosophy	AVERR(H)OISM
—religion	ISLAM, SHI'ISM
	SUFISM, SUNNISM, WAHABISM
Armenian sect	YEZIDEE, YEZ(I)DI
	ZEZIDEE
Arminian Methodism	WESLEYISM
ascribing	
—to God human	
feelings	ANTHROPOPATHISM
mind or	
soul	ANTHROPOPSYCHISM
nature	ANTHROPOPHUISM
—human characteristics	
to non-human	ANTHROPOMORPHISM
Asian	BUDDHISM, HINDUISM
	SHAMANISM
assertion of God's justice	THEODICY
attribution of soul	
to material objects	ANIMISM
Babylonia	MANDAEAN, MENDAITES
	NASOREAN, SABIANISM
	ZABIANIAM
baptism by immersion	BAPTISTS
baptist heretic	CATABAPTIST
	PEDOPABTIST, SE-BAPTIST
based on	
—Bible	BARTHIANISM
—Gospels	EVANGELICALISM
—spiritual healing	CHRISTIAN SCIENCE

bearing name of god	THEOPHORIC
beasts as gods	THERIOMORPHISM
belief in	
—Allah	ISLAM, MOHAMMEDANISM
	MOSLEM, MUSLIM
—Brahma	BRAHMANISM, BRAHMINISM
—Buddha	BUDDHISM
—god	DEISM, THEISM
—Jehovah	JUDAISM
—many gods	POLYTHEISM
—Mazda	ZOROASTRIANISM
—one god	MONOTHEISM
—two gods	DITHEISM
Benedictine	OLIVETAN, TIRONENSIAN
	TYRONENSIAN
birth and descent of gods	THEOGONY
Blackfriar	DOMINICAN
blending of religions	SYNCRETISM
Buddhism	
—Burma	MON
—China	CHAN, FOISM
—forms	HINAYANA, MAHAYANA
	THERAVADA, VAJRAYANA
—Japan	ZEN
—Tibet	GELUK PA, SAKYA PA, LAMAISM
	(see also **Buddhist**)
Bulgarian Moslem	POMAK
Burmese Buddhist	MON
Calixtin(e)	HUSSITE, UTRAQUIST
Calvinism	GENEVANISM
Canadian sect	D(O)UKHOBOR
Carmelite	WHITE FRIAR
Cathar(ist)	ALBIGENSIAN, MANICHAEAN
Catholic	
—Apostolic Church	IRVINGISM, IRVINGITES
—revival	OXFORDISM
	OXFORD MOVEMENT
	TRACTARIANISM
Children of God	SHAKERS
Chinese	CONFUCIANISM, FOISM, TAOISM
Christ	
—was a mere man	ARIANISM
	PSILANTHROPISM
—with one nature	COPTS
	MONOPHYSITES
	THEOPASCHITES
Christ's	
—body merged into Deity	
at Ascension	METAMORPHISTS
—divinity and humanity	
separate	NESTORIANISM
—second	
coming	(SEVENTH DAY) ADVENTISTS
Christianity as affected	
by war, etc	CRISIS THEOLOGY
	DIALECTICAL THEOLOGY

Church of	
—Christ	CHRISTIAN SCIENTISTS
—England	ANGLICANISM
Close Brethren	EXCLUSIVE BRETHREN
	PLYMOUTH BRETHREN
common ownership of	
property	SHAKERS
complete scepticism	PYRRHONISM
conditional mortality	CHRISTADELPHIANS
	THOMASITES
Darbyites	PLYMOUTH BRETHREN
denial of	
—Christ's divinity	ARIANISM
	PSILANTHROPISM
—existence of God	ANTITHEISM, ATHEISM
—marriage and priests	LIPOVANIANS
—original sin	PELAGIANISM
—predestination	ARMINIANISM
Devil worship	DEMONISM, SATANISM
devotion to	
—bishops	EPISCOPALIANISM
—Haile Selassie	RASTA(MAN)
	RASTAFARIAN
—priests	SACERDOTALISM
direct experience of the divine	MYSTICISM
discussion of	
Eucharist	EUCHARISTIC THEOLOGY
dissenter	RECUSANT
divine	
—abnegation	KENOSIS
—inspiration	THEOSOPHY
divinity made manifest	PANTHOS
doctrine	
—of	
last things	ESCHATOLOGY
life and work of Christ	CHRISTOLOGY
—that knowledge is from faith	FIDEISM
Dominican	BLACKFRIAR
Dutch Arminian	REMONSTRANT
early	
—Christian esoteric religion	GNOSTICISM
—heretic	CERINTHIAN
East European Catholic	UNIATE
Eastern	
—Orthodox sect	UNIATS
—sorcery	MAG(IAN)ISM
Egyptian Christian	COPT
English monks (13th c)	BETHLEHEMITES
ethico-dualistic philosophy	MARCIONITE
Evangelical Union	MORISONIANS
Exclusive Brethren	CLOSE BRETHREN
	PLYMOUTH BRETHREN
Father and Son of	
—of	
similar essence	HOMOIOUSIAN
the same essence	HOMOOUSIAN

—and Holy Ghost
  are one   SABELLIANISM
faith alone necessary   SOLIFIDIANISM
founded by
  —Annie Besant   THEOSOPHICAL SOCIETY
                    THEOSOPHY
  —anti-pope   NOVATIONISM
  —Apollinaris   APOLLINARIANISM
  —Aquinas   THOMISM
  —Arius   ARIANISM
  —Arminius   ARMIN(IAN)ISM
  —Bab-ed-Sin   BABEEISM, BAHAI(I)SM
  —Baha-Ullah   BAHAISM
  —Bishop of Laodicea   APOLLINARIANISM
  —Buddha   BUDDHISM
  —Charles Russell   JEHOVAH'S WITNESSES
                  RUSSELLITES
  —Christ   CHRISTIANITY
  —Cornelius Jansen   JANSENISM
  —Emmanuel Swedenborg NEW JERUSALEM
                  CHURCH
           SWEDENBORGIANISM
  —Erastus   ERASTIANISM
  —Francis Barham   ALISM
  —Gautama   BUDDHISM
  —Georg Calixtus CALIXTIN(E), SYNCRETISM
  —George Fox   QUAKERISM
         SOCIETY OF FRIENDS
  —George Rapp   RAPPISTS, RAPPITES
  —Ghulam Ahmad   AHMADIYYA
  —Ignatius Loyola   JESUITISM
         JESUITRY, JESUITS
        SOCIETY OF JESUS
  —James Morison   MORISONIANISM
  —J H Newman   OXFORDISM
        OXFORD MOVEMENT
          TRACTARIANISM
  —J N Darby   DARBYITES
  —John Calvin CALVINISM, GENEVANISM
          PRESBYTERIANISM
             PURITANISM
  —John Glas   GLASSITES
  —John Hus HUSSITES, MORAVIANS
  —John Maron   MARONITE
  —John Thomas   CHRISTADELPHIANS
            THOMASITES
  —John Wesley   METHODISM
  —John Wycliffe   LOLLARDISM
           LOLLARD(R)Y
  —Joseph Smith   MORMONISM
  —Kaspar v. Schwenkfeld SCHWENKFELDERS
  —Kong Qiu (Confucius) CONFUCIANISM
  —Lao-tzu   TAOISM
  —Madame
    Blavatsky THEOSOPHICAL SOCIETY
                  THEOSOPHY

  —Mahavira   JAINISM
  —Mohammed (Mahomet)   ISLAM
        MOHAMMED(AN)ISM
        MOSLEM, MUSLIM
  —Mani(chaeus)   MANICHAEANISM
  —Marcion of Sinope   MARCIONITES
  —Martin Luther   LUTHER(AN)ISM
          PROTESTANTISM
  —Mary Baker Eddy CHRISTIAN SCIENCE
  —Melanchthon   SYNERGISM
  —Menno Simons   MENNONITES
  —Mo-zi   MOHISTS
  —Nanak   SIKHISM
  —Nestorius   NESTORIANISM
  —Novaticinus   NOVATIONISM
  —Peter Waldo VALDENSES, WALDENSES
             WALDENSIANS
  —Pyrrho of Elis   PYRRHONISM
  —Richard Cameron   CAMERONIAN
  —Robert Sandeman   SANDEMANIANS
  —Ron Hubbard   SCIENTOLOGY
  —Rudolf Steiner   ANTHROPOSOPHY
  —Sabellius   MODALISM
  —St Columba COLUMBAN (CELTIC) CHURCH
  —St Maron   MARONITE
  —St Vincent de Paul   LAZARISM
  —Sakyamuni   BUDDHISM
  —Saraswati   ARYA SAMAJ
  —Shirazi   BABISM, BAHAISM
  —Søren Kierkegaard   CHRISTIAN
         EXISTENTIALISM
     EXISTENTIAL THEOLOGY
  —Sun Myung Moon   MOONIES
     UNIFICATION CHURCH
  —Thomas Erastus   ERASTIANISM
  —Ulrich Zwingli   ZWINGLIANISM
  —William Booth   SALVATION ARMY
  —William J Seymour PENTECOSTAL CHURCH
  —Zarathustra   ZOROASTRIANISM
founded in
  —America   (SEVENTH DAY) ADVENTISTS
             MORMONISM
      RAPPISTS, RAPPITES
  —Dublin   PLYMOUTH BRETHREN
            PLYMOUTHISM
  —Geneva   CALVINISM
  —India   THEOSOPHY
  —Korea   MOONIES
     UNIFICATION CHURCH
  —Pennsylvania JEHOVAH'S WITNESSES
Franciscan   CAPUCHIN, CORDELIER
      GREYFRIAR, MINORITE
Free Presbyterian Church   WEE FREES
French
  —Gnosticism (13th c)   ALBIGENSIAN
            CATHARIST

—Protestant	CAMISARD, HUGUENOT
—Revolutionary	
creed	THEOPHILANTHROPY
fundamentalist	
Christians	JEHOVAH'S WITNESSES
	PENTECOSTALISTS, RUSSELLITES
fusion of religions	SYNCRETISM
Genevanism	CALVINISM
German	
—American Baptists	DUNKERS
—Jews	ASHKENAZIM
—Protestant	ANABAPTIST
	LUTHER(AN)ISM
gift of the Holy	
Spirit	CHARISMATIC MOVEMENT
	PENTECOSTAL CHURCH
Glassite	SANDEMANIAN
Gnostic creator	DEMIURGE
god	THEISM
—and devil	YEZIDEE, YEZ(I)DI
	ZEZIDEE
—as	
sole sovereign	THEOCRACY, THEISM
trinity	TRINITARIAN
unity	UNITARIAN
universe	PANTHEISM
—identified with cosmos	COSMOTHEISM
	PANTHEISM
—with	
one will	MONOTHELETISM
two wills	DITHELETISM
	(see also **gods***)*
gospel-preaching	EVANGELICALISM
government by bishops	EPISCOPACY
	EPISCOPAL(IAN)ISM
Greek	
—Catholics in the Middle East	MELCHITES
—Christian Church	GREEK ORTHODOX
Greyfriar	FRANCISCAN
Harmonists	SECOND ADVENTISTS
Hebrew	JUDAISM
—asceticism	ESSENISM
	(see also **Hebrew***)*
Hemerobaptist	MANDAEAN
High Church principles	PUSEYISM
Hindu	BRAHMANISM, S(H)IVAISM
	(see also **Hindu***)*
host of heaven	SABAISM
Hussite	CALIXTIN(E), TABORITE
	UTRAQUIST
identifying one god	
as another	THEOCRASIA, THEOCRASY
idols	IDOLATRY
image	
—breaker	ICONOCLAST
—worshipper	ICONODULE
imminent end	
of the world	JEHOVAH'S WITNESSES
	RUSSELLITES
	(SEVENTH DAY) ADVENTISTS
in the likeness of a	
god	THEOMORPHIC
Indian	
—Moslems	COSSAS
—Parsees	ZOROASTRIANISM
—religions	BUDDHISM, HINDUISM
	ISLAM, JAINISM, SIKHISM
infallibility of Bible	FUNDAMENTALISM
inspired by god	THEOPNEUST(IC)
Iranian Guebres	ZOROASTRIANISM
Irvingism	CATHOLIC APOSTOLIC CHURCH
Islam	MOHAMMED(AN)ISM
	MOSLEM, MUSLIM
	(see also **Moslem***)*
Italian	
—Gnosticism (13th c)	ALBIGENSIAN
	CATHARIST
—Unitarians	SOCINIANISM
Jamaican	RASTAFARIANISM
Japan	BUDDHISM, SHINTOISM
Japanese Buddhists	AMIDA, AMITA
	SOKA GAKKAI, ZEN
Jehovah	HEBREW, JEWISH, JUDAISM
Jesuits	SOCIETY OF JESUS
Jewish	
—Christian	NAZARENE
—formalist	PHARISEE
—sceptic	SADDUCEE
—sect	(C)HAS(S)ID(IC), ESSENE
performing daily	
ablutions	HEMEROBAPTISTS
last or final things	ESCHATOLOGY
Latter Day Saints	MORMONS
Lebanese	DRUSE, DRUZ(E)
	MARONITE
liberal	
—belief	LATITUDINARIANISM
—Catholic	NEO-CATHOLIC
literal truth of Bible	FUNDAMENTALISM
Logos in lieu of soul	APOLLINARIANISM
loss of belief	ANOMIE
Manichaean	CATHAR(IST), PATARIN(E)
manifestation of god	THEOPHANY
many gods	POLYTHEISM
—each supreme	KATHENOTHEISM
Maronite	UNIAT(E)
material good arriving with	
spirits of the dead	CARGO CULT
meditation	MYSTICISM
Middle Eastern Christian	
Church	EASTERN ORTHODOX
Milanese heretic	PATARIN(E)

missionary Protestants	MORAVIANS
	UNITED BRETHREN
mixture of religions	THEOCRASIA
	THEOCRASY
moderate Hussite	CALIXTIN(E), UTRAQUIST
Moonies	UNIFICATION CHURCH
Moravians	UNITED BRETHREN
Morisonians	EVANGELICAL UNION
Mormons	LATTER-DAY SAINTS
Moslem	
—mysticism	SOF(I)ISM, SUF(I)ISM
—sect	AHMADIYYA, IMAMITES
	ISMAILITES, KHARIJITES
	SHIA(H), SUNNI, WAHABEE
	WAHABI
—traditional teaching	SUNNA
mother of God	THEOTOKOS
	VIRGIN MARY
mystic religion	ALISM, SANTERIA
nature-worship	PAN(EN)THEISM
New Jerusalem Church	SWEDENBORGIANISM
non-belief	AGNOSTICISM, ATHEISM
	HEATHENISM, HUMANISM
	PAGANISM
non-believer	INFIDEL
non-Christian	PA(I)NIM, PAYNIM
one god	HENOTHEISM, MONOTHEISM
opposed to	
—marriage of priests	PATARIN(E)
—military service	DUNKERS
	D(O)UKHOBOR
order	
—founded at	
Camaldoli	CAMALDOLITES
Cassino	BENEDICTINE
Chartreuse	CARTHUSIAN
Citeaux	BENEDICTINE
	BERNARDINE
	CISTERCIAN
Cluny	BENEDICTINE, CLUNIAC
Monte Oliveto	OLIVETANS
Mount Carmel	CARMELITES
	WHITE FRIARS
Palestine	CARMELITE, WHITE FRIARS
Premontre	NORBERTINE
	PREMONSTRATENSIANS
	WHITE CANONS
T(h)iron	TIRONENSIANS
	TYRONENSIANS
—founded by	
Bernard of Clairvaux	BERNADINE
	CISTERCIAN
John Peter Caraffa	THEATINE
Pietro da Morrone	CELESTINE
St Augustine	AUGUSTINIAN
	AUSTIN FRIARS

St Bruno	CARTHUSIAN
St Dominic	BLACK FRIARS
	DOMINICAN
St Francis of Assisi	FRANCISCAN
	GREY FRIARS
St Francis of Paola	MINIMS
St Francis of Sales	SALESIANS, VISITANTS
St Ignatius of Loyola	JESUITS
St Norbert	NORBERTINE
	PREMONSTRATENSIANS
	WHITE CANONS
St Romuald	CAMALDOLITES
—wearing the sign	
of the Cross	CROSSED FRIARS
	CROUCHED FRIARS
	CRUTCHED FRIARS
orthodox	
—Jews	(C)HAS(S)ID(IC)
—Roman Catholic	TRIDENTINE
Oxford Movement	TRACTARIANISM
Papism	ROMAN CATHOLICISM
Parsee	ZOROASTRIAN
passionate belief	FUNDAMENTALISM
Pentecostalists	ASSEMBLIES OF GOD
	HOLY ROLLERS
Persian	BABEEISM, BAB(I)ISM
	BAHAISM, IMAMISM, MAGISM
	MANICH(A)EANISM, MAZDEISM
	MAZDAISM, MITHRAISM
	PARSEEISM, PARSIISM
	ZOROASTRIANISM
philosophical Taoism	TAO-CHIA
philosophy of God's justice	THEODICY
Plymouth Brethren	CLOSE BRETHREN
	DARBYITES
	EXCLUSIVE BRETHREN
Polish Jews	ASHKENAZIM
polytheism with each	
god supreme	KATHENOTHEISM
Portuguese Jews	SEPHARDIM
—converted to Christianity	MARRANOS
Protestant sect	MENNONITES
Protestantism	METHODISM
Quakers	SOCIETY OF FRIENDS
—sect	SHAKERS
reason, not authority	RATIONALISM
reasserting the influence	
of the Holy Ghost	CHARISMATICS
reconciling religion	
with science	PROCESS THEOLOGY
	SECULAR CHRISTIANITY
Reformed	
—Church	PROTESTANTISM
—Presbyterian Church	CAMERONIAN
regeneration is the work of	
the Holy Ghost	MONERGISM

reincarnation	THEOSOPHICAL SOCIETY
rejection of	
—Holy Trinity	CHRISTADELPHIANS
	D(O)UKHOBOR
—jurisdiction of bishops	ACEPHALITES
—religion	ATHEISM, HUMANISM
	SECULARISM
religion	
—in relation to	
ethics	MORAL THEOLOGY
science	PROCESS THEOLOGY
	SECULAR CHRISTIANITY
wars, etc	CRISIS THEOLOGY
—without a god	NON-THEISM
religious	
—emotion	THEOPATHY
—legalism	NOMISM
representation of God in	
human form	ANTHROPOMORPHISM
reverence for witch-doctors	SHAMANISM
Roman Catholic	JEBUSITE
	PAPISM, ROMANISM
rule of God	THEONOMY
Russian	
—Christian	UNIAT(E)
—Christian Church	EASTERN ORTHODOX
—sect	D(O)UKHOBOR, LIPOVANIANS
Salesian	VISITANT
salvation	
—by individual redeemer	MESSIANISM
—depends on faith alone	ANTINOMIAN
—doctrine	SOTEROLOGY
—through	
God's grace	CALVINIS
special knowledge of God	GNOSTICISM
Sandemanian	GLASSITE
Saudi Arabia	WAHABISM, ISLAM
scepticism	SADDUC(EE)ISM
Scottish	COLUMBAN CHURCH
—Free Church	WEE FREES
—monk (8th c)	CULDEE
—Presbyterian	CAMERONIAN
	WHIGGAMORE
Second Adventist	HARMONIST, HARMONITE
self	
—baptizing	SE-BAPTISTS
—subsistence of God	AUTOTHEISM
Siberian	SHAMANISM
sleep of soul after death	PYSCHEPANNYCHISM
snake-worship	OPHITISM
Society of	
—Friends	QUAKERS, SHAKERS
—Jesus	JESUITS
sole truth of the Bible	PLYMOUTH BRETHREN
Spanish	
—Jews	SEPHARDIM

converted to Christianity	MARRANOS
—sect	ILLUMINATI
	MOZARABS
speaking in	
tongues	CHARISMATIC MOVEMENT
spirit worship	SHAMANISM, VOODOOISM
spiritual marriage	AGAPEMONE
spiritualism	ANTHROPOSOPHY
State control of Church	ERASTIANISM
strange	
—beliefs	ESOTERISM
—gods	ALLOTHEISM
strict Catharists	PERFECTI
study of religion	THEOLOGY
Sunday as day of	
rest	LORD'S DAY OBSERVANCE SOCIETY
	SABBATARIANS
Supreme God and devil	YEZIDEE, YEZ(I)DI
	ZEZIDEE
Sweden(borgian)	NEW JERUSALEM CHURCH
Swedish	SWEDENBORGIANISM
Swiss Protestant sect	ZWINGLIANS
Syrian	DRUSE, DRUZ(E)
Taborite	HUSSITE
teetotallers	RECHABITES
that one is God	THEOMANIA
three gods	TRITHEISM
Tibetan	BUDDHISM, LAMAISM
Tractarianism	OXFORD MOVEMENT
transubstantiation	CAPERNAITE
tribal religions	PRIMITIVISM
Trinity as manifestations	
of one God	MODALISM
Turkish Muslim	KARMATHIAN, SALAR
two gods	DITHEISM
unbeliever	AGNOSTIC, ATHEIST
	HEATHEN
—Eastern	ZENDIK
Uniat(e)	MARONITE
Unification Church	MOONIES
United Brethren	MORAVIANS
unity of	
—churches	ECUMEN(ICAL)ISM
—God	ARIANISM
	UNITARIANISM
universal salvation	UNIVERSALISM
universe is the Logos	PANLOGISM
unorthodoxy	HERESY, HETERODOXY
Utraquist	CALIXTIN(E), HUSSITE
vision of God	THEOPHANY
Visitant	SALESIAN
war of the gods	THEOMACHY
West Indies	OBEAHISM, OBEISM
	OBIISM, VOODOOISM
	VOUDOUISM
White Friar	CARMELITE

will not free	DETERMINISM, FATALISM
	NECESSARIANISM
	PREDESTINATION
wisdom of	
—God	THEOSOPHY
—man	ANTHROPOSOPHY
	(*see also* **worship**)
Belize	BH
capital	BELMOPAN
coin	CENT, DOLLAR
former name	BRITISH HONDURAS
Bengal	
beggar	BAUL
bison	GAUR
boat	BATEL, BAULEA(H)
cotton cloth	BEZAN
measure	BEGA, CHATTACK, COTTA(H)
tree	BOLA
Benin	DY
capital	PORTO NOVO
coin	FRANC
biology	
including: bacteriology	
botany	
genetics	
abdominal	
—appendage	UROPOD
—cavity	PERITONEAL CAVITY
—segment	UROMERE
ability to	
—change colour	METACHROSIS
—resemble another animal	
or plant	MIMICRY
abnormal	
—elongation of axis	DIAPHYSIS
—growth	HYPERTROPHY
abrupt change	SALTATION
—in DNA of chromosomes	MUTATION
absence of pigments in skin,	
etc	ALBINISM
absorbing part of	
root	PILIFEROUS LAYER
acid linking chains	
in proteins	AMINO-ACID
actively dividing part of plant	MERISTEM
Adam's apple	LARYNX
adapted for walking	GRESSORIAL
additional calyx	EPICALYX
adjustments to focus	
of eye	ACCOMMODATION
aerophyte	EPIPHYTE
affecting more than one	
characteristic	PLE(I)OTROPIC
affinity of organism and	
its parts	HOMOLOGY
Agnatha	CYCLOSTOMATA

air	
—plant	EPIPHYTE
—sac in lung	ALVEOLUS
—tube	
large	BRONCHUS
small	BRONCHIOLE
alcohol compound in animals	
and plants	STEROL
algae	ANTHOPHYTA
BACILLARIOPHYTA, CHAROPHYTA	
CHLORELLA, CHLOROPHYTA	
CHRYPTOPHYTA, CRYSOPHYTA,	
EUGLENOPHYTA, PHAEOPHYTA	
PYRROPHYTA, RHODOPHYTA	
—and fungus in symbiosis	LICHEN
—bacteria and fungi	THALLOPHYTES
—blue-green CYANOPHYTA, MYXOPHYTA	
	SCHIZOPHYCEAE
—filamentous	CONFERVA
	HETEROCONTAE
—forming chain	DESMID
—living in sea	SEAWEED
	(*see also* **seaweed**)
—unicellular	DESMID
algal	
—cell in lichen	CHROMIDIUM
—part of lichen	PHYCOBIONT
alimentary canal	ENTERIC CANAL, GUT
alligators and crocodiles	CROCODILIA
alternation of	
—day and night	PHOTOPERIODISM
—methods of	
reproduction	HETEROGAMY
alternative forms of	
a gene	ALLEL(E), ALLELOMORPH
amino-acid	(*see* **acids**)
Amphibia	ANURA, APODA
GYMNOPHIONA, SALIENTIA	
	URODELA
anaerobic respiration	FERMENTATION
Angiospermae	DICOTYL(EDONE)AE
	MONOCOTYL(EDONE)AE
Angiosperms and	
Gymnosperms	PHANEROGAMIA
angle between leaf and stem	AXIL
animal(s)	
—attached to a surface	SESSILE
—cell undergoing meiosis	SPERMATOCYTE
—developing young	
in the uterus	DIDELPHIA
	MARSUPIALIA
	METATHERIA
—eating	
all foods	OMNIVORE
flesh	CARNIVORE
grass	HERBIVORE

—egg in shell   CLEIDOIC EGG
—feeding on others   CARNIVORE, PREDATOR
—forming part of colony   ZOOID
—kept by ants as guest   SYMPHILE
   SYNOECETE
—living
   on land or in water   AMPHIBIAN
   under stones, etc   CRYPTOZOIC
—many-celled   METAZOA
—single-celled   AMOEBA(AMOEBAE)
   PROTOZOON(PROTOZOA)
—starch   GLYCOGEN
—suckling
   partly-developed young   MARSUPIAL
   well-developed young   MAMMAL
—swallowing food for later
   digestion   RUMINANT
—with
   backbones   CHORDATA, VERTEBRATA
   VERTEBRATES
   combined digestive and
     genital opening   MONOTREMATA
   MONOTREMES
   PROTOTHERIA
   diploid nuclei   DIPLONT
   four limbs   TETRAPODA, TETRAPODS
   hoofs   UNGULATA, UNGULATES
   many arms   HYDRANTH, POLYP(E)
   padded feet   TYLOPODA
   segmented bodies   ARTHROPODA
   slender toes   LEPTODACTYL
   solid hoofs   SOLIPED
   two-part shell   BIVALVE
   webbed feet   PALMIPED(E)
   winged feet   ALIPED
—without
   backbones   INVERTEBRATA
   INVERTEBRATES
   teeth   EDENTATA
   —aardvarks   TUBULIDENTATA
   —scaly anteaters   PHOLIDOTA
   —sloths, etc   XENARTHRA
animalcules in moss etc   TARDIGRADA
animals and plants
   of sea-bottom   BENTHOS
Annelida   CHAETOPODA, GEPHYREA
   HIRUDINEA, LEECHES
   OLIGOCHAETA
Anthropoidea   PITHECOIDEA
antibody which catalyses
   target   ABZYME
apes, monkeys and man   ANTHROPOIDEA
   PITHECOIDEA
   PRIMATES
apoda   GYMNOPHIONA
appendage for cleaning antennae   STRIGIL

area
—in which trees are grown   ARBORETUM
—of vegetation for study   QUADRAT
—retaining character in period
   of general change   REFUGIUM
arrangement of
—folding in flower-bud   AESTIVATION
—organs to prevent self-
   fertilisation   HERCOGAMY
   HERKOGAMY
arrow-worms   CHAETOGNATHA
artery   (*see* **circulation**)
Arthropoda   ARACHNIDA, CHILOPODA
   CRUSTACEA, DIPLOPODA
   INSECTA, MYRIAPODA
   ONYCHOPHORA, SYMPHILA
   TRILOBITA
artificial insemination   AI
—gamete intra-fallopian
   transfer   GIFT
—zygote intra-fallopian
   transfer   ZIFT
artificially produced
   variety of plant   CULTIVAR
asexual
—fungal spore   CONIDIUM
—reproduction   APOGAMY, APOMIXIS
   APOSPORY, BUDDING, FISSION
   GEMMATION, PARTHENOGENESIS
   VEGETATIVE REPRODUCTION
—reproductive unit   SPORE
—spore of algae etc   APLANOSPORE
asexually reproduced descendant
   of sexually produced individual   CLONE
association of
—interdependent organisms   BIOCOENOSIS
—organisms for mutual
   benefit   SYMBIOSIS
atrophy   INVOLUTION
attachment of ovum to
   wall of womb   IMPLANTATION
axis
—of
   compound leaf   R(H)ACIS
   grass spike   RACHILLA
   inflorescence   R(H)ACIS
—producing buds and leaves   STEM
back-plate of arthropod   TERGUM
bacteria   (*see* micro-organisms *below*)
bacterial disease of plants   BACTERIOSIS
bacterium   SCHIZOMYCOPHYTE
baleen   WHALEBONE
barnacles   CIRRIPEDIA
Barr body   SEX CHROMATIN
base(s)
—forming amino-acid   TRIPLET

—of	
DNA	ADENINE, CYTOSINE
	GUANINE, THYMINE
ovule	CHALAZA
RNA	ADENINE, CYTOSINE
	GUANINE, URACIL
based on similarity of	
—evolution	PHYL(OGEN)ETIC
—individuals	PHENETIC
basic	
—entity	PRION
—living matter	PROTOPLASM
batrachia	AMPHIBIA
bats	CHIROPTERA
bear-animalcules	TARDIGRADA
bee	
—fertile female	QUEEN
—glue	PROPOLIS
—male	DRONE
—sterile female	WORKER
beginning of growth	GERMINATION
belly	ABDOMEN
belonging to the stem	CAULINARY, CAULINE
belt or saddle on worm	CLITELLUM
big toe	HALLUX
bile sac	GALL BLADDER
binomial nomenclature	LINNAEAN SYSTEM
biochemical reaction in	
cells	CITRIC ACID CYCLE
	KREBS CYCLE
biogenous	PARASITIC
biological cycle	CIRCADIAN RHYTHM
	DIURNAL RHYTHM
biologists etc	
—American	AVERY, BEADLE, BECKWITH
	BITTNER, BORLANG, BURBANK
	COHEN, COHN, CORBETT
	CRAIG, DAVIS, DOBZHANSKY
	DOISY, DUBOS, ELVEHJEM, ENDERS
	EVANS, GRAFF, GREEN, HALBERG
	HARARY, HARRISON, HERSHEY
	HOLMES, HUBEL, KING, LEDERBERG
	LETTVIN, LILLY, MAYER, MAYR
	MCCOLLUM, MENDEL, MORGAN
	MULLER, NATHAN, OCHOA,
	RASMUSSEN, REED
	RICKETTS, ROSE, SABIN, SALK
	SCHOENHEIMER, SCOTT
	SINSHEIMER, SMITH, SPALDING
	STANLEY, STURTEVANT
	SUTTON, TATUM, WALD, WATSON
	WIESEL, WILLIAMS
—Argentinian	HOUSSAC
—Australian	BURNET, MILLER
—Austrian	BERTALANFFY, LORENZ
	MENDEL, PERUTZ, VON TSCHERMAK

—Belgian	BORDET, CLAUDE
	VAN BEDENEN
—Brazilian	MEDAWAR
—British	BALFOUR, BATESON, BAWDEN
	BROWN, CHAIN, CRICK, DARWIN
	DRUMMOND, ELFORD, FISHER
	FLEMING, FLOREY, FORBES, GEDDES
	GOSSE, GRIFFITH, HALDANE, HARDY
	HODGKIN, HOPKINS, HUTTON
	HUXLEY, ISAACS, LUBBOCK
	MEDAWAR, MOORE, MORRIS
	NEEDHAM, OWEN, PERUTZ, PETERS
	PIRIE, ROSENHEIM, THOMPSON
	THOMSON, TWORT, WADDINGTON,
	WALLACE, WEBSTER, WELDON
	WILLCOCK, WOODGER
—Canadian	AVERY, BERTALANFFY
	D'HERELLE
—Chilean	MATURANA
—Danish	DAM, GRAM, JOHANNSEN
	MULLER
—Dutch	BEIJERINCK, DE VRIES
	DONATH, JANSEN, KYLSTRA
	STAPEL, SWAMMERDAM
—Finnish	WILSKA
—French	CAREL, CUVIER, DE BUFFON
	DUBOS, DU POUY
	JACOB, LAMARCK, LAVERAN
	MILLER, MONOD, NICOLLE
	PASTEUR, RAMON, RUEL
—German	ASCHHEIM, BAER, BAUMANN
	BENDA, BUETENANDT, CHAIN, COHN
	CORRENS, DREISCH, FLEMMING
	EHRLICH, HAECKEL, KOCH, LOFFLER
	LOHMANN, KRUSE, MAYR
	PFEFFER, SCHLEIDEN, SCHOENHEIMER
	SCHWANN, SIEBOLD, SPEMANN
	STENT, VIRCHOW, VON MAYER
	VON MOHL, VON SACHS, WASSERMANN
	WEISMANN, WILSTATTER, ZONDEK
—Greek	THEOPHRASTUS
—Hungarian	SZENT-GYORGI
—Italian	FRASCATORI, MARSIGLI
	SPALLANZANI, STELLUTI
—Japanese	OHDAKE, SHIMAMURA, SUZUKI
—New Zealand	WILKINS
—Norwegian	GUNNERA
—Polish	FUNK, REICHSTEIN, SABIN
—Russian	DOBZHANSKY, IVANOVSKI
	LYSENKO, METCHNIKOFF, OPARIN
	PALADE, PAVLOV, TSVETT, VAVILOV
—South African	THEILE
—Spanish	OCHOA
—Swedish	LINNAEUS, RUDBECK
—Swiss	AGASSIZ, BONNET, CANDOLLE
	MEISCHER, REICHSTEIN, VON NAGELI

birds	AVES	—spike	(STERILE) GLUME
	(*see separate entry*)	spadix	SPATHE
—and reptiles	SAUROPSIDA	—growing round inflorescence	PHYLLARY
—mammals, reptiles	AMNIOTA	brain	(*see separate entry*)
bisexual	HERMAPHRODITE	branch acting as leaf	CLADODE
biting			PHYLLOCLADE
—pincers	CHELICERA(E)	branching part of neurone	DENDRITE
—animal	GYNANDROMORPH	breaking into spores	SPORULATION
bivalves	LAMELLIBRANCHI(AT)A	breaking down	
	PELECYPODA	—and synthesis of organic	
bladder near liver	GALL-BLADDER	compounds internally	METABOLISM
blood	(*see* **circulation**)	—by bacteria	BIODEGRADATION
blotched	CENTONATE		BIODESTRUCTION
body and temperament type	SOMA(TO)TYPE		BIODETERIORATION
—muscular and aggressive	SOMATONIA	—in metabolism	CATABOLISM
body	SOMA		KATABOLISM
—division(s)	TAGMA(TA)	—of food by oxygen	RESPIRATION
—in cell			(*see also* decomposition *below*)
carrying		breathing	RESPIRATION
—chlorophyll	CHLOROPLAST	—organ of aquatic animal	GILL
—food reserve	PLASTID	—pore in	
—genes	CHROMOSOME	animal	SPIRACLE
—pigment	PLASTID	bark	LENTICEL
formed at mitosis	SPINDLE	bringing forth of young	PARTURITION
forming starch	LEUCOPLAST(ID)	bristle	
involved in secretion	GOLGI APPARATUS	—of	
	GOLGI BODY	insect	SCOP(UL)A
	GOLGI MATERIAL	invertebrate	SETA
protoplasm	CENTROSOME	—on	
—in		grass, corn, etc	ARISTA, AWN
cytoplasm	CHONDRIOSOME	some worms	CHAETA
	MITOCHONDRIA	brittle-stars	OPHIUROIDEA
nucleus		brood-pouch	OVISAC
—containing RNA	NUCLEOLUS	Bryophyta ANTHERCEROTAE, HEPATICAE	
—layers	ECTODERM, ENDODERM		LIVERWORTS, MUSCI
	MESODERM	Bryozoa	POLYZOA
—of tapeworm	STROBILA	building up in metabolism	ANABOLISM
—segment	ARTHROMERE, MERO(SO)ME	buoyancy organ in fish	SWIM-BLADDER
	METAMERE, SOMITE	burning of leaves by sun	HELIOSIS
of insect		bursting open of pods	DEHISCENCE
—fore	PROTHORAX	cactus, house-leek, etc	SUCCULENT
—middle	THORAX	calcium carbonate from	
—rear	ABDOMEN	marine skeletons	CORAL
—substance to fight antigen	ANTIBODY	calyx and corolla of flower	PERIANTH
—which can separate and become		camouflage in	
new individual in		animals	CRYPTIC COLO(U)RATION
plants	GEMMA	cancer-producing	CARCINOGENIC
sponges	GEMMULE		ONCOGENIC
bonding to parent	ATTACHMENT	capsule opening with circular	
bone	(*see separate entry*)	detachable lid	PYXIDIUM
—marrow	MEDULLA	carbohydrate	
bottom(s) of hollow organ(s)	FUNDUS(FUNDI)	—in	
bract		plant cell-walls	(HEMI)CELLULOSE
—enclosing		wood cells	LIGNIN
grass		—sticky	MUCILAGE
—flower	LEMMA, PALEA	—stored as food	STARCH

carbon-based ORGANIC
carpels collectively GYNAECEUM
GYN(O)ECIUM
case
  —holding
    few spores SPORANGIOLE
SPORANGIOLUM
    spermatia SPERMAGONE
SPERMAGONIUM, SPERMOGENE
SPERMOGENIUM
    spermatozoa SPERMATOPHORE
    spores SPORANGIUM
  —of protozoa, etc LORICA
category within species FORM
cats, dogs, lions, etc CARNIVORES
causing abnormalities in embryo TERATOGENIC
cavity
  —between intestines and
    wall of body CELOM, COELOM(E)
  —containing
    blood HAEMOCOEL
    digestive organs ABDOMEN, BELLY
    heart and lungs CHEST, THORAX
  —in protoplasm VACUOLE
  —of mouth BUCCAL CAVITY
  —serving as gut COELENTERON
  —where intestinal and urinary
    tracts discharge CLOACA
cell(s) CYTE(S), ENERGID
  —body PERICARYON, PERIKARYON
  —containing pigment CHROMATOPHORE
  —cycle G PHASE, M PHASE
MITOSIS, MITOTIC PHASE, S PHASE
  —division MEIOSIS, MITOSIS
    of diploid cells MITOSIS
    producing haploid cells MEIOSIS
    without mitosis AMITOSIS
  —formation CYTOGENESIS
  —forming
    fibrous tissue FIBROBLAST, FIBROCYTE
    stoma GUARD-CELLS
    structure of organism SOMATIC CELL
    tissues HISTOBLAST
  —found in connective
    tissue FIBROBLAST, FIBROCYTE
  —from
    fertilised egg BLASTOMERE
    which gamete is formed GAMETOCYTE
  —in
    fungus in which spores
     are produced ASCUS
    insect with symbiotic
     micro-organisms MYCETOCYTE
    pancreas secreting insulin
     and glucagon ISLETS OF LANGERHANS
    resting state ARTHROSPORE

  —layer responsible for
    leaf-fall ABSCISS(ION) LAYER
  —layers in body ECTODERM, ENDODERM
MESODERM
  —movement in embryo GASTRULATION
  —multinucleate SYNCYTIUM
  —nucleus
    with membrane EUCARYON
EUKARYON
    without membrane PROCARYON
PROKARYON
  —particle
    reproducing like a gene PLASMAGENE
    which assembles protein RIBOSOME
  —prepared for examination TISSUE CULTURE
  —produced by division
    of single cell DAUGHTER CELLS
D NUCLEI
  —producing
    spermatocytes SPERMATOGONIUM
    spermatozoa SPERMATID
SPERMATOCYTE
    spores ARCHESPORIUM
  —wall envelope in bacteria CAPSULE
  —which
    can store foreign matter ATHROCYTE
    destroys bone OSTEOCLAST
    develops into an organ BLASTEMA
    forms
     —bone OSTEOBLAST
     —gametes GAMETOCYTE
     —ovum OOCYTE
  —with
    distinct form IDIOBLAST
    several nuclei SYNCYTIUM
    —of different
     genetic makeup HETEROCARYON
HETEROKARYON
    —of same genetic
     makeup HOMOCARYON
HOMOKARYON
    thick walls SCLEREID(E)
centipedes CHILOPODA
central
  —column of root or branch STELE
VASCULAR CYLINDER
  —part of
    organ MEDULLA
    ovule NUCELLUS
    tree HEARTWOOD
Cephalopoda SIPHONOPODA
chaffy scale RAMENTUM
chain of
  —amino-acids POLYPEPTIDE
  —nucleotides NUCLEIC ACID
POLYNUCLEOTIDE

—segments STROBILA
change from larva to adult METAMORPHOSIS
changes in life-span of cell CELL CYCLE
character due to mutated gene MUTANT
characteristics of organism PHENOTYPE
chemical
—basis of
genes (DEOXY)RIBONUCLEIC ACID
DNA, RNA
—change in
living organisms METABOLISM
make-up of genes MUTATION
—inhibiting action of auxin ANTIAUXIN
—involved in storage
of light-energy ADP
ADENINE DIPHOSPHATE
ATP, ADENINE TRIPHOSPHATE
—produced to evoke response
from other animals PHEROMONE
—required by plants in
large quantities MACRONUTRIENT
small quantities MICRONUTRIENT
—which kills
algae ALGICIDE
fungi FUNGICIDE
insects INSECTICIDE
plants HERBICIDE
rodents RODENTICIDE
worms ANTHELMINTHIC, VERMIFUGE
VERMICIDE
chemistry of tissues HISTOCHEMISTRY
chemotaxis CHEMOTROPISM
chest PLEURAL CAVITY, THORAX
chin MENTAL PROMINENCE
Choanata AMPHIBIA, AVES
CHOANICHTHYES, MAMMALIA
REPTILIA
chondriosomes MITOCHONDRIA
chromosome
—carrying genetic
instructions SEX CHROMOSOME
—of a species GENOM(E)
—other than sex chromosome AUTOSOME
chrysalis PUPA
Ciliophora INFUSORIA, PROTOZOA
circle of nitrogen use
in nature NITROGEN CYCLE
circular laboratory dish PETRI DISH
circulation of
—blood (*see* **circulation**)
—carbon by living things CARBON CYCLE
—protoplasm CYCLOSIS
citric acid cycle KREBS CYCLE
classification TAXONOMY
—based on chromosome
characteristics CYTOTAXONOMY

—group(s) TAXON(TAXA)
—order of groups (smallest first) SUB-SPECIES
SPECIES
GENUS
TRIBE
SUB-FAMILY
FAMILY
SUPER-FAMILY
SUB-ORDER
ORDER
SUPER-ORDER
COHORT
INFRA-CLASS
SUB-CLASS
CLASS
SUPER-CLASS
SUB-PHYLUM
DIVISION, PHYLUM
SUB-KINGDOM
KINGDOM
—system LINNAEAN SYSTEM
RAUNKIAER'S LIFE FORMS
claw(s) of arthropod CHELA(E)
clear area in bacterial culture PLAQUE
climbing organ of plant TENDRIL
climbing plant of the tropics LIANA, LIANE
cloning from minute
particles of bud MICROCLONING
club mosses LYCOPODIALES
cnidoblast THREAD CELL
coat of seed INTEGUMENT
code of inherited characteristics GENETIC CODE
Coelenterata HYDROZOA
cold-bloodedness POIKILOTHERMY
collagen band connecting
bones at joint LIGAMENT
collection of dried plants HERBARIUM
colony of algae etc COENOBIUM
coloured
—covering of some seeds ARIL
—part of eye IRIS
colourless
—algae LEUCOPHYTE
—plastid LEUCOPLAST
community of organisms and
its environment ECOSYSTEM
component part of
nucleic acid NUCLEOTIDE
compound
—making wood fibres rigid LIGNIN
—of
similar molecules
but different atoms ISOLOGUE
sugar etc in cells NUCLEOTIDE
—with amino and acidic
carboxyl groups AMINO-ACID

concept of living things only
  from germ-cells — GERM THEORY
condition
  —in which
    different gametes are
     present — ANISOGAMY
    similar gametes are present — ISOGAMY
    unlike gametes reproduce — ANISOGAMY
     HETEROGAMY
  —where male and female parts
    mature at the same time — HOMOGAMY
conditions determined by
  characteristics
  of the soil — EDAPHIC FACTORS
conduction of food etc
  in plant — TRANSLOCATION
conidium — ARTHROSPORE
conjugation — ZYGOSIS
  —of similar gametes — ISOGAMY
connective tissue — ADIPOSE TISSUE
  —attaching
    embryo to placenta — UMBILICAL CORD
    UMBILICUS
    muscle to bone, etc — TENDON
  —supporting an organ — CAPSULE
constituent of cell walls — CELLULOSE
container for
  —nectar — NECTARY
  —pollen — POLLEN SAC
  —seeds — OVARY
containing several
  antibodies — POLYVALENT
contraction
  —in tubular organs — PERISTALSIS
  —of nucleus — PYCNOSIS, PYKNOSIS
control of functions by
  electronic monitoring — BIOFEEDBACK
conversion of
  —atmospheric
    nitrogen — NITROGEN-FIXATION
  —glucose to lactic acid — GLYCOLYSIS
  —plant food by light — PHOTOSYNTHESIS
  —soil compounds to
    nitrates — NITRIFICATION
    keratin — CORNIFICATION
coral with many pores — MILLEPORE
corals etc — ACTINOZOA
corium — DERMIS
cork — PHELLEM
  —cambium — PERIDERM, PHELLEGEN
cotyledon of embryo
  of grass — SCUTELLUM
cover of gill-slits — OPERCULUM
covering
  —layer — INTEGUMENT
  —of seed coat — TEGMEN

cows, goats, sheep, etc — ARTIODACTYLA
crabs, lobsters, etc — DECAPODA
creation (alleged) from non-living
  matter — BIOPOIESIS
creeping stem
  —that roots — FLAGELLUM, RUNNER
    STOLON
  —underground — SOBOLE
criteria connecting
  illness to cause — KOCH'S POSTULATES
crop ploughed into soil — GREEN MANURE
cross
  —1st filial generation — F1 GENERATION
    F1 HYBRID
  —2nd filial generation — F2 GENERATION
    F2 HYBRID
  —between unlike parents — HYBRID
  —fertilisation — ALLOGAMY
  —of hybrid offspring
    with parent — BACKCROSS
crossing of
  —related individuals — INBREEDING
  —unrelated individuals — OUTBREEDING
Crustacea — AMPHIPODA, CLADOCERA
  COPEPODA, DECAPODA
  ISOPODA, PHYLLOPODA
crustacean's organ of
  propulsion — SWIMMERET
Cryptogamia — BRYOPHYTA
  PTERIDOPHYTA, THALLOPHYTA
cultivation in water — HYDROPONICS
curving
  —at touch — HAPTOTROPIC
    THIGMOTROPIC
  —of organ
    downward — EPINASTY
    upward — HYPONASTY
cutting
  —back to trunk — POLLARDING
  —grafted on to another plant — SCION
  —trees to ground level — COPPICING
cycle of biological changes — BIORHYTHM
  CIRCADIAN RHYTHM
cyesis — PREGNANCY
cyst
  —of tapeworm larva — HYDATID (CYST)
  —produced by sporulation — SPOROCYST
cytoplasm
  —containing centriole — CENTROSOME
  —forming nerve-cell — CELL-BODY
    PERICARYON
    PERIKARYON
danger from living things — BIOHAZARD
dark phase of daily rhythm — SKOTOPHILE
dead tree cells — CORK, PHELLEM
death of part of plant or animal — NECROSIS

decomposition/destruction/ dissolution	
—by	
acid	ACIDOLYSIS
electricity	ELECTROLYSIS
enzymes	FERMENTATION
	ZYMOLYSIS
heat	PYROLYSIS
water	HYDROLYSIS
—of	
bacteria	BACTERIOLYSIS
cells	CYTOLYSIS, LYSIS
proteins	PROTEOLYSIS
substance catalysed by enzymes	ENZYMOLYSIS
tissues	HISTOLYSIS
—after death	AUTOLYSIS
decrease in size	
of organ	ATROPHY, INVOLUTION
defensive protein produced in response to an antigen	ANTIBODY
deglutition	SWALLOWING
dependence on organic foodstuffs	HETEROTROPHISM
destruction	(see decomposition above)
dermis	CORIUM
detachable joint in tapeworm	PROGLOTTIS
detached bud of water plant	TURION
depression where ducts etc enter organ	HILUM
deutoplasm	YOLK
development	
—from different kinds of cells	HETEROBLASTY
—of	
different characteristics from one gene	PLEIOTROPY
	PLEIOTROPISM
group of organisms	PHYLOGENESIS
	PHILOGENY
individual organism	ONTOGENESIS
	ONTOGENY
ovum without fertilisation	PARTHENOGENESIS
—towards specialised functions	DIFFERENTIATION
device for cutting very thin slices	MICROTOME
diagram of	
—parts of flower	FLORAL DIAGRAM
—resemblances of individuals in group	DENDOGRAM
diatom cell	FRUSTULE
diatoms	BACILLARIOPHYTA
dicotyledon (old)	EXOGEN

Didelphia	MARSUPIALIA
	METATHERIA
difference in	
—arrangement of mutations in chromosomes	CIS-TRANS EFFECT
—colour, etc	VARIEGATION
differentiation	VARIATION
diffusion of particles through membrane	OSMOSIS
digestive	
—fluid	BILE
—juice	SUCCUS ENTERICUS
—system	(see separate entry)
dilated part of oesophagus or gut used as food store	CROP
dioecious	UNISEXUAL
diploid number of chromosomes	ZYGOTIC NUMBER
directional growth in plant	TROPISM
disc producing styles	STYLOPODIUM
diseases of plants	(see **plant diseases**)
displacement of island species by mainland species	SETON'S LAW
dissolution	(see decomposition above)
distributed throughout	SYSTEMIC
division of	
—algae	BACILLARIOPHYTA
	CHAROPHYTA, CHLOROPHYTA
	CHRYSOPHYTA, CRYPTOPHYTA
	EUGLENOPHYTA, PYRROPHYTA
—birds and reptiles	SAUROPSIDA
—body	(METAMERIC) SEGMENTATION
—cell producing	
diploid daughter-cells	KARYOKINESIS
	MITOSIS
haploid daughter-cells	MEIOSIS
	REDUCTION DIVISION
—extinct reptiles	THERAPSIDA
—mammals	THEROPSIDA
—plant kingdom	BRYOPHYTA
—primitive plants	THALLOPHYTA
dizygotic twins	FRATERNAL TWINS
DNA	
—bases	ADENINE, CYTOSINE
	GUANINE, THYMINE
—purines	ADENINE, GUANINE
—pyrimidines	CYTOSINE, THYMINE
dormancy during	
—summer	AESTIVATION
—winter	HIBERNATION
doubling of chromosomes with cell-division	ENDOMITOSIS
drifting animals and plants	PLANKTON
dry	
—fruit with hard shell	NUT
—one-seeded fruit	ACH(A)ENIUM, ACHENE

duct
—carrying ovum from
  ovary to uterus   FALLOPIAN TUBE
                            UTERINE TUBE

—from
  coelom to exterior   COELOMODUCT
  liver to intestine   BILE DUCT
ductless gland   ENDOCRINE GLAND
due to common ancestry   PATRISTIC
duplicate of specimen   ISOTYPE
earliest stage of plant or animal   EMBRYO
early stage of embryo   BLASTULA
                           GASTRULA
ecdysis   MOULTING
Echinodermata   ASTEROIDEA
     CRINOIDEA, ECHINOIDEA
     HOLOTHUROIDEA, OPHIUROIDEA
ecology of
—community   SYNECOLOGY
—species   AUTECOLOGY
ecosystem
—in terms of crops per
  unit area   TROPHIC STRUCTURE
—of animals with same food
  chain   TROPHIC LEVEL
effect of osmosis on cell   PLASMOLYSIS
egg
—capsule   NIDAMENTUM, OVISAC
—of louse   NIT
—producing organ   OVARY
—production   OVULATION
—requiring dormant period   RESTING EGG
                           WINTER EGG
—shell   AMPHIONT
—tube in insect   OVIAROLE
—white   ALBUMEN
eight-armed creatures   OCTOPODA
electricity in living things   BIOELECTRICITY
elephants   PROBOSCIDEA
embryo
—during cleavage stage   MORULA
—in mammal   FOETUS
—tapeworm   HEXACANTH
                           ONCHOSPHERE
embryonic reproductive tract
—female   MULLERIAN DUCT
—male   WOLFFIAN DUCT
Embryophyta   METAPHYTA
end of
—axis carrying flower   RECEPTACLE
—stamen   ANTHER
endocrine gland   DUCTLESS GLAND
endogamy   INBREEDING
enteric canal   ALIMENTARY CANAL, GUT
enzyme   (*see separate entry*)
epiphytes   AEROPHYTES, PSILOTALES

essential organic
  substance in food   VITAMIN
evolution
—by
  natural selection   DARWINISM
  inherited characteristics   LAMARCKISM
                           LYSENKOISM
  several forms   ADAPTIVE RADIATION
—of
  group   PHYLOGENY
  individual   ONTOGENY
—producing greater differences   DIVERGENCE
—producing greater
  similarity   CONVERGENCE
evolutionary pedigree   PHYLOGENY
excessive cell-growth   HYPERPLASIA
exchange of food in
  symbiosis   TROPHOBIOSIS
                           TROPHOLLAXIS
excreting
—urea   UREOTELIC
—uric acid   URICOTELIC
excretory organ   KIDNEY
existence in two forms   DIMORPHISM
exogamy   OUTBREEDING
explanation of biological
phenomena in
—physical terms   MECHANISTIC THEORY
—terms of vital
  force   VITALISTIC THEORY
explantation   TISSUE CULTURE
expression describing
  construction of a flower   FLORAL FORMULA
extension of
—axis of flower
  between carpels   CARPOPHORE
—receptacle bearing
  carpels   GYNOPHORE
—stamen receptacle   ANDROPHORE
exudation of water drops by plant   GUTTATION
eye   (*see separate entry*)
factor controlling
acceptance of
  foreign cells   HISTOCOMPATIBILITY
falling off early   CADUCOUS
Fallopian tube   UTERINE TUBE
false aril   CARUNCLE
fatty tissue   ADIPOSE TISSUE
—in whales, etc   BLUBBER
—secretion   SEBUM
—substance from animal
  decomposition   ADIPOCERE
feather   (*see separate entry*)
feeding
—by filtering with
  thread-like lashes   CILIARY FEEDING

—like	
an animal	HOLOZOIC
a plant	HOLOPHYTIC
—on	
dead matter	SAPROBIOTIC
	SAPROPHAGOUS, SAPROZOIC
other animals	CARNIVOROUS
plants	HERBIVOROUS
various foods	OMNIVOROUS
feeler(s)	PALP, PALPUS(PALPI)
female	PISTILLATE
—gamete	MACROGAMETE
	MEGAGAMETE, OOCYTE
produced from oocyte	OVUM
—organs of flower	CARPEL, GYNAECEUM
	GYN(O)ECIUM, PISTIL
—sex organ	
algae and fungi	OOGONIUM
animals	OVARY, UTERUS
moss, etc	ARCHEGONIUM
seaweed	CARPOGONIUM, OOGONIUM
ferment	ZYME
fermentation	ZYMOSIS
fermentor	ZYMOGEN
ferns	FILICALES
—horsetails, clubmosses	PTERIDOPHYTA
fertilisation	
—by	
pollen	POLLINATION
two male	
gametes	DOUBLE FERTILISATION
—of large egg by	
small gamete	OOGENY
fertilised egg	AMPHIONT, SEED, ZYGOTE
fertilising microspores	POLLEN
fibres in larynx	
producing sound	VOCAL C(H)ORDS
filament in	
—algae	TRICHOME
—fungi	HYPHA
filtering through serous membrane	DIALYSIS
finger	DIGIT
fire algae	PYRROPHYTA
first	
—abdominal section	PROPODEON
—segment of insect	PROTHORAX
—stage of cell-division	PROPHASE
fishes	(see separate entry)
five-fingered limb	PENTADACTYL LIMB
fixed in position (animals)	SESSILE
flap of	
—cartilage at base of tongue	EPIGLOTTIS
—membranous tissue	LOMA
flask-shaped fungal	
fruit-body	PERITHECIUM
flesh-eating animals	CARNIVORES

flora and fauna	BIOTA
flower	
—receptacle	TORUS
—stalk	PEDICEL
—whorl	COROLLA
flowering	
—only once	MONOCARPIC
—plants	ANGIOSPERMS
	DICOTYL(EDON)AE
GYMNOSPERMS, MONOCOTYL(EDON)AE
PHANEROGAMAE, PHANEROGAMIA
SPERMA(TO)PHYTA, SPERMOPHYTA
—shoot	INFLORESCENCE
flowerless plants	CRYPTOGAMIA
fluid	
—filled spaces	VASCULAR SYSTEM
—from	
animal tissues	LYMPH
gland	SUCCUS
—in	
brain and spine	
cavities	CEREBROSPINAL FLUID
joints	SYNOVA, SYNOVIAL FLUID
—secreted from	
endocrine glands	HORMONE
glands in mouth	SALIVA
skin glands	PERSPIRATION
	SEBUM, SWEAT
flukes (trematodes), cestodes	
and turbellarians	PLATYHELMINTHES
foetal envelope	CHORION
fold	
—in peritoneum	EPIPLOON, OMENTUM
—of skin producing shell	
in molluscs	MANTLE
food material	
—of plants	STARCH
—stored in seeds	ENDOSPERM
foot of hind leg	PES
forcing of liquid through tissues	PERFUSION
foreign substance in body	ANTIGEN
forewing	TEGMEN
form derived from	
—adaptation	ECAD
—mutation	MUTANT
—variation	SPORT, VARIANT
formation of	
—egg	OOGENESIS
—fruit without fertilisation	PARTHENOCARPY
—more than one embryo	
from one ovum	POLYEMBRYONY
—polymorphs	GRANULOPOIESIS
—species	SPECIATION
formative plant tissue	MERISTEM
four-footed animals	TETRAPODA
fraternal twins	DIZYGOTIC TWINS

free from micro-organisms	ASEPTIC
frequency of manifestation of dominant gene	PENETRANCE
fresh-water algae	CHLAMYDOMONAS
fringe round mouth of moss capsule	PERISTOME
frogs and toads	ANURA, SALIENTIA
front of tapeworm's head	ROSTELLUM
fruit	(see separate entry)
—body of fungus	APOTHECIUM ASCOCARP, CLEISTOCARP PERITHECIUM
—flies	DROSOPHILA
—of	
Compositae	CYPSELA
grasses	CARYOPSIS
fruiting	
—after cross-fertilisation	ALLOCARPY
—only once	MONOCARPIC
functional unit of animal or plant	ORGAN
fungi	(see separate entry)
fungus in symbiotic relationship with	
—alga	LICHEN
—roots of higher plant	MYCOR(R)HIZA
fused head and thorax	CEPHALOTHORAX
fusion of	
—cytoplasm	PLASMOGAMY
—flowers	SYNANTHY
—gametes	AMPHIMIXIS
—parts	SYMPHYSIS
—petals	COROLLA TUBE
gamete	GERM-CELL
—capable of movement	PLANOGAMETE
—non-motile	APLANOGAMETE
gametophyte in ferns, mosses, etc	OOPHYTE
gap in skull	FONTANELLE
gene	
—combination not present in parents	RECOMBINATION
—controlling	
actions of operon	REGULATOR GENE
biological rhythms	CLOCK GENE
single action at many points	POLYGENE
—not included in chromosome	PLASMAGENE
—over-ridden by dominant gene	RECESSIVE
—producing particular characteristic to the exclusion of others	DOMINANT
—suppression	EPISTASIS
—terminating life of bacteria	SUICIDE GENE

—which	
can reproduce without chromosome reproduction	EPISOME
has undergone change	MUTANT
genealogical history of	
—group	PHYLOGENESIS PHYLOGENY
—individual	ONTOGENESIS ONTOGENY
generation of living from non-living	BIOPOIESIS
genetic	
—element	EPISOME
in bacterial cell	
—autonomous	PLASMID
or integrated	EPISOME
—make-up of individual or group	GENOTYPE
genital passage in females	VAGINA
genus	
—of	
arthropods	PERIPATUS
diatoms	NAVICULA
Diptera	DROSOPHILA
Foraminifera	GLOBIGERINA
Protozoa	TRYPANOSOMA
—which includes man	HOMO
germ	
—cell	GAMETE, OVUM, SPERM(ATOZOON)
—layer	ECTODERM, ENDODERM MESODERM
—tube of fungus spore	PROMYCELIUM
germination	ECESIS
gizzard in insect	PROVENTRICULUS
gland	(see separate entry)
—in head of insect	CORPORATA ALLATA
—on leaf excreting water	HYDATHODE
—secreting nectar	NECTARY
globular bacterium	COCCUS
glycoprotein	MUCROPROTEIN
gnawing animal	RODENT
—hare, rabbit	LAGOMORPHA
—rat, squirrel	RODENTIA
golden-brown algae	CHRYSOPHYTA
gradation of form, etc	CLINE
graft	
—from	
another individual	ISOGRAFT
same individual	AUTOGRAFT HOMOGRAFT
same species	HOMOGRAFT
—with different genetic makeup	ALLOGRAFT
grafting of bud to stock	BUDDING
granule moving freely in statocyst	OTOLITH, STATOLITH
grazing animal	ARTIODACTYLA RUMINANT

green	
—algae	CHLOROPHYTA
—pigment converting light	CHLOROPHYLL
gristle	CARTILAGE
group	
—adapted to particular	
environment	ECODEME, ECOTYPE
—of	
animal kingdom	METAZOA, PARAZOA
	PROTOZOA
Anthropoidea	CATARRHINI
	PLATYRRHINI
antigens in blood-cells	
of some monkeys	RH(ESUS) FACTOR
cells	
—controlling rhythm of	
heart, etc	PACEMAKER
—from division of	
ovum	BLASTOSPHERE
	BLASTULA
closely related organisms	DEME
ecotypes	ECOSPECIES
fish	TELEOSTOMI
flowers on one stalk	INFLORESCENCE
fungi	ASCOMYCETES
	BASIDIOMYCETES
genes controlling	
synthesis of enzymes	OPERON
joined stamens	SYNANDRIUM
organisms with same	
characteristics	PHENOTYPE
Protozoa	FORAMINIFERA
sporangia	SORUS, SYNANGIUM
spores formed by meiosis	TETRAD
vertebrate classes	CHOANATA
—sharing same habitat	COMMUNITY
	TOPODEME
—which can interbreed	GAMODEME
	SPECIES
—with same genetic make-up	GENOTYPE
growing	
—by external additions	EXOGENOUS
—close to the ground	EPIG(A)EAL
—from root	RADICAL
—in sunlight	HELIOPHYTE
or shade	HELIOSCIOPHYTE
—just below the soil	HEMICRYPTOPHYTE
—on	
acid soil	CALCIFUGE
another plant	EPIPHYTE
chalky soil	CALCICOLE
dead matter	SAPROGENIC
	SAPROGENOUS, SAPROPHYTE
dry ground	GLARIAL
gravel	GLAREOUS
ice	CRYOPHYTE

rocks	LITHOPHYTE
	RUPICOLINE, RUPICOLOUS
salty soil	SALSIGINOUS
silica	SILICICOLOUS
snow	CRYOPHYTE
stem	CAULICOLOUS
top of	
—ovary	EPIGYNOUS
—petal	EPIPETALOUS
—sepal	EPISEPALOUS
—pale for lack of light	ETIOLATION
—point or root	
or stem	APICAL MERISTEM
—together of stems	FASCIATION
—towards the	
apex	ACROPETAL
base	BASIPETAL
—underground	HYPOG(A)EAL
gut	ALIMENTARY CANAL
	ENTERIC CANAL
—between	
mouth and oesophagus	PHARYNX
pharynx and stomach	(O)ESOPHAGUS
—breathing animal	ENTEROPNEUST
Gymnophiona	APODA
Gymnospermae	CONIFERALES, CYCADALES
	GINKGOALES, GNETALES
—extinct	CORDIATALES
	CYCADOFILICALES
gynaecium and androecium	
united	GYNOSTEMIUM
hair(s)	
—like appendages on	
bacteria cells	PILI
—used for propulsion	CILIUM(CILIA)
	FLAGELLUM(FLAGELLA)
hallux	BIG TOE
halves of frustule	EPITHECA, HYPOTHECA
hand	MANUS
hanging inflorescence	CATKIN
hard	
—layer of skin	SCLERODERM
—tissue resulting from wound	CALLUS
having	
—ability to form antibodies	IMMUNOGENIC
—anthers	
in form of tube	SYNANTHEROUS
	SYNGENESIOUS
maturing	
—after carpels	PROTOGYNOUS
—at different time	
from stigma	DICHOGAMOUS
—at same time as carpel	HOMOGAMOUS
—before carpels	PROTANDROUS
—all teeth the same	HOMODONT
—backbone	VERTEBRATE

—body with
   three layers of cells   TRIPLOBLASTIC
   two layers of cells   DIPLOBLASTIC
—bushy habit of growth   DUMOSE, DUMOUS
—claws   UNGUAL
    UNGUICULATE(D)
—cloven hoofs   BISULCATE
—cotyledons above ground   EPIG(A)EAL
—different
   areas of distribution   ALLOPATRIC
   forms   PLE(I)OMORPHIC
    POLYMORPHIC
   genes   HETEROZYGOUS
   kinds of teeth   HETERODONT
   set of genes   ALLOGEN(E)IC
—diploid number   ZYGOTIC
—downy covering   PUBESCENT
    TOMENTOSE
—eight times the normal
   number of chromosomes   OCTAPLOID
—embryos which develop
   in eggs   OVIPAROUS
   internally   VIVIPAROUS
   —in eggs   OVOVIPAROUS
—equal numbers of petals
   and sepals   ISOSTEMONOUS
—even number of toes   ARTIODACTYL(IC)
    ARTIODACTYLATE
    ARTIODACTYLOUS
—exact multiple of haploid
   number   EUPLOID
—eyes on stalks   PODOPHTHALMOUS
—female and hermaphrodite
   flowers on
    same plant   GYNODIOECIOUS
    separate plants   GYNOMONDECIOUS
—flower(s)
   parts
    —below gynaeceum   HYPOGYNOUS
    —enclosing gynaeceum   EPIGYNOUS
    —round gynaeceum   PERIGYNOUS
   which
    —do not open   CLEISTOGAMIC
    CLEISTOGAMOUS
    —open   CHASMOGAMIC
    CHASMOGAMOUS
—four
   long, two short stamens TETRADYNAMOUS
   times haploid number of
    chromosomes   TETRAPLOID
—fringe of hairs   CILIATE
—full quota of chromosomes   DIPLOID
—fused
   anthers   SYNANTHEROUS
    SYNGENESIOUS
   carpels   SYNCARPOUS

   digits   SYNDACTYL(OUS)
   petals   GAMOPETALOUS
   sepals   GAMOSEPALOUS
   stamens   SYNANDROUS
—hard
   dry stem   SCLEROCAULY
   skin   SCLERODERMIC
    SCLERODERMOUS
   stiff leaves   SCLEROPHYLLOUS
    SCLEROPHYLLY
—hoofs   UNGULATE
—identical genes   HOMOZYGOUS
—lobes pointing backward   RUNCINATE
—male and female organs on
   different flowers   DECLINY
    DIOECIOUS
   same plant   HERMAPHRODITE
    MONOECIOUS
—male and hermaphrodite
   flowers on
    same plant   ANDROMONOECIOUS
    separate plants   ANDRODIOECIOUS
—many
   cells   MULTICELLULAR
   nuclei   MULTINUCLEATE
—more than
   normal number of digits POLYDACTYLOUS
   twice haploid number
    of chromosomes   POLYPLOID
—no
   coelom   ACOELOMATE
   flowers or sepals   ACHLAMYDEOUS
   skull, brain etc   ACRANIAL
   stalk   SESSILE
   stamens   ANANDROUS
—odd number of toes   PERISSODACTYL(IC)
    PERISSODACTYLATE
    PERISSODACTYLOUS
—one
   bundle of stamens   MONADELPHOUS
   cell   UNICELLULAR
   chromosome
   instead of two   MONOSOME
   cotyledon MONOCOTYLEDENOUS
   kind of spore   ISOSPOROUS
   perianth whorl   HAPLOCHLAMYDEOUS
    HOMOCHLAMYDEOUS
    MONOCHLAMYDEOUS
—open flowers   CHASMOGAMIC
—paired chromosomes
   in nucleus   DIPLOID
—parts in threes   TRIMEROUS
—perianth with
   one whorl   HAPLOCHLAMYDEOUS
    HOMOCHLAMYDEOUS
    MONOCHLAMYDEOUS

two whorls	DI(PLO)CHLAMYDEOUS
—pistils but no stamens	PISTILLATE
—same	
areas of distribution	SYMPATRIC
genes	ISOGEN(E)IC
	SYNGEN(E)IC
—separate	
carpels	APOCARPOUS
male and female	
individuals	DIOECIOUS, UNISEXUAL
petals	POLYPETALOUS
sepals	POLYSEPALOUS
—several stamen groups	POLYADELPHOUS
—sharp points	APICULATE
—single	
eye in centre	CYCLOPIA
set of chromosomes	HAPLOID
—stalk attached near	
centre of leaf	PELTATE
—stigma	STIGMAFEROUS
—spores of different kinds	HETEROSPOROUS
—stamens and carpels	BI-SEXUAL
	HERMAPHRODITE
in separate flowers	UNISEXUAL
—stamens in	
two groups	DIDELPHOUS
two alternating	
whorls	OBDIPLOSTEMONOUS
—sucker both ends	AMPHISTOMOUS
—sucking proboscis	HAUSTELLATE
	SUCTORIAL
—three	
chromosomes instead of two	TRISOME
or more times haploid	
number	POLYPLOID
parts	TRIMEROUS
times haploid number	TRIPLOID
—tubular flowers	TUBERLIFLOROUS
—two	
carpels	DICARPELLARY
cotyledons	DICOTYLEDENOUS
equal flagella	ISOKONT
or more	
—arrangements of	
reproductive parts	HETEROSTYLOUS
—leaf types	HETEROPHYLLOUS
pairs of stamens	DIDYNAMOUS
perianth whorls	HETEROCHLAMYDEOUS
—unbalanced number of	
chromosomes	ANEUPLOID
—uncloven hoofs	SOLIDUNGULATE
—unlike gametes	ANISOGAMY
—unpaired chromosomes	HAPLOID
head of tapeworm	SCOLEX
heart	(see circulation)
heart-urchins	SPANTANGUS

hedgehogs, moles, shrews, etc	INSECTIVORA
helmet-shaped part	GALEA
helminth	WORM
Hepaticae	LIVERWORTS
heredity factor	GENE
hermaphrodite	BISEXUAL
hermaphroditism	GYNANDRYISM
	GYNANDRY
heterosis	HYBRID VIGOUR
hind toe	HALLUX
Hirudinea	LEECHES
histiocyte	MACROPHAGE
holding palm	
—downward and	
backward	PRONATION
—forward and upward	SUPINATION
hollow	
—appendages in starfish etc	PODIA
	TUBE-FEET
—ball of cells	BLASTULA
holotype	TYPE SPECIMEN
hominid	(see separate entry)
homoiothermic	WARM-BLOODED
hoofed animals	UNGULATA, UNGULATES
hormone	(see separate entry)
hornworts	ANTHEROCEROTAE
horse	(see separate entry)
horses, etc	EQUIDAE, EQUUS
	PERISSODACTYLA
horsetails	EQUISETALES
human biology	ANTHROPOBIOLOGY
hybrid	
—from offspring of first	
filial generation	F2
	SECOND FILIAL GENERATION
starting generation	F1
	FIRST FILIAL GENERATION
—vigour	HETEROSIS
hypha-bearing	
sporangia	SPORANGIOPHORE
hypothetical	
—hereditary particle	GEMMULE
—unit of living matter	BIOGEN
	BIOPHORE, MICELLA
	MICELLE, MONAD
identical twins	MONOZYGOTIC TWINS
	UNIOVULAR TWINS
immature	
—flower	BUD
—form of animal	LARVA
—ovum	OOCYTE
impermeable area in	
some cells	CASPARIAN STRIP
inability	
—of hybrids to inter-	
breed	HYBRID STERILITY

—to
   regulate body
     temperature   POIKILOTHERMY
   self-fertilise   SELF-INCOMPATIBILITY
inbreeding   ENDOGAMY, HOMOGAMY
incomplete zygote   MEROZYGOTE
incorporation by digestion   ASSIMILATION
increased
   —diameter due to cell
     division   SECONDARY GROWTH
   —number of parts by
     branching   CHORISIS
   —numbers of plankton   BLOOM
   —size
     due to cell division   PRIMARY GROWTH
     of organ etc to
       compensate for other
       loss   COMPENSATORY HYPERTROPHY
   —vigour as result of
     crossing   HETEROSIS
       HYBRID VIGOUR
increasing thickness of cell walls   APPOSITION
individual
   —clone   RAMET
   —giving tissue for transfer   DONOR
   —intermediate between male
     and female   INTERSEX
inflorescence
   —types   BOSTRYX, CAPITULUM, CATKIN
     CINCINNUS, CORYMB, CYME
     DICHASIUM, HELICOID CYME
     MONOCHASIUM, PANICLE, RACEME
     RHIPIDIUM, SPADIX, SPIKE, STROBILUS
     UMBEL
   —definite   CYMOSE
   —highly condensed   VERTICILLASTER
   —indefinite   RACEMOSE
inflow of water by osmosis   ENDOSMOSIS
Infusoria   CILIOPHORA
ingrowth from another cell   T(H)YLOSIS
inhabited part of Earth
 and atmosphere   BIOSPHERE
inhabiting deep water   ABYSSAL
inhibition of bacterial growth   BACTERIOSTASIS
inimical relationship
 between organisms   ANTIBIOSIS
inner
   —digit   POLLEX
   —layer of
     bark   BAST, PHLOEM
     fruit wall   ENDOCARP
   —part of cytoplasm   ENDOPLASM
insects   (*see separate entry*)
insect-eaters   INSECTIVORES
integument   TUNIC
interbreeding   SYNGAMY

internal
   —opening of nasal cavity   CHOANA
     INTERNAL NARE
   —secretion having specific effect   HORMONE
intestine   (*see* **digestion**)
intolerant of
   —high temperature   STENOTHERMOUS
   —variable osmotic
     pressure   STENOHALINE
involution   ATROPHY
jaws and nose of animal   MUZZLE
jellyfish
   —corals etc   CNIDARIA, COELENTERATA
   —in polyp stage   SCYPHISTOMA
   —stinging organ   CNIDA, NEMATOCYST
junction between plates
 in insect   SUTURE
karyokinesis   MITOSIS
kidney filtering unit   MALPIGHIAN BODY
     MALPIGHIAN CORPUSCLE
kingdoms
   —many-celled animals   METAZOA
   —micro-organisms without
     nucleus   PROCARYOTA
   —microscopic protozoa   PROTISTA
   —single-celled animals   PROTOZOA
Krebs cycle   CITRIC ACID CYCLE
lachrymal gland   TEAR GLAND
lacking
   —coelom   ACOELOMATE
   —reproductive organs   NEUTER
lamp shells   BRACHIOPODA
lampreys, hagfish, etc   CYCLOSTOMATA
lancelet   AMPHIOXUS
large
   —ecological community   BIOME
   —molecule   MACROMOLECULE
     containing ribose   RIBONUCLEIC ACID
     RNA
larva of
   —butterfly, moth   CATERPILLAR
   —coelenterates, etc   PLANULA
   —crustacean   NAUPLIUS, ZOAEA
   —fluke   CERCARIA, REDIA
   —fly   MAGGOT
   —lamprey   AMMOCOETE
   —sea-urchin etc   PLUTEUS
   —tapeworm   BLADDER WORM
     CYSTICERCUS
last
   —segment of insect's body   METATHORAX
   —stage of cell-division   TELOPHASE
layer
   —of
     cells
       —below epidermis   HYPODERMIS

—in embryo	GERM-LAYER
—lining cavities and covering surfaces of body	EPITHELIUM
cortex formed by phellogen	PHELLODERM
epidermis	MALPIGHIAN LAYER
food cells round spore-cells	TAPETUM
wood in tree laid down in one year	ANNUAL RING GROWTH RING
—on epidermis of plant	CUTICLE
—which forms cork	PHELLOGEN
produces skin	DERMATOGEN
leaf	(*see separate entry*)
—like structure	BRACT
—of corolla	PETAL
—stalk	PETIOLE
leafless flower stem	SCAPE
leeches	HIRUDINEA
lid of capsule or egg	OPERCULUM
life	
—begets life	BIOGENESIS
—cycle of flower	ANTHESIS
light-production by living organisms	BIOLUMINESCENCE
line	
—of fusion of carpels	SUTURE
—separating areas of Australian and Oriental animals	WALLACE'S LINE
lining of	
—abdominal cavity	PERITONEUM
—blood-vessel	INTIMA
—chest cavity	PLEURA
—uterus	ENDOMETRIUM
linking of nucleic acid strands	BASE PAIRING
Linnaean system	BINOMIAL NOMENCLATURE
lip of plant or insect	LABIUM
liquid carrying plant nutrients	SAP
little beak	ROSTELLUM
liver secretion	BILE
liverworts	HEPATICAE
living	
—above ground	EPIG(A)EAL
—in mountains	MONTICOLOUS
mud	LIMICOLOUS
rocks	RUPICOLINE, RUPICOLOUS
soil	TERRICOLOUS
tubes	TUBICOLOUS
—on land and in water	AMPHIBIOUS
sea floor	DEMERSAL
—under stones	LAPIDICOLOUS

—without free oxygen	ANAEROBIC
lizards	LACERTILIA
—and snakes	SQUAMATA
	(*see also separate entry*)
local remains of wider distribution	RELIC(T) DISTRIBUTION RELIC(T) FAUNA, RELIC(T) FLORA
long	
—cells with thickened walls	COLLENCHYMA
—pod	SILIQUA
loss of	
—nitrogen from soil	DENITRIFICATION
—water through leaves, etc	TRANSPIRATION
lower	
—jaw of animal	MANDIBLE
—part of body	PERIN(A)EUM
—petals in orchid	LABELLUM
pea-flower	KEEL
lymph	(*see* **circulation**)
lymphoid tissue in pharynx	ADENOIDS, TONSILS
macrophage	HISTIOCYTE
main	
—habitat	METROPOLIS
—lymph vessel	THORACIC DUCT
—vertical root	TAP ROOT
maintenance of constant internal enviroment	HOMEOSTASIS
male	
—cell producing spermatozoa	SPERMATOCYTE
—component of flower	ANDROECIUM
—gamete	MICROGAMETE SPERM(ATOZOID) SPERMATOZOON
—reproductive organ	PENIS, TESTIS
—sex organ of algae etc	ANTHERIDIUM
flower	ANTHER, STAMEN
seaweed	SPERMATIUM
Mammalia	ARTIODACTYLA, CARNIVORA CETACEA, CH(E)IROPTERA EUTHERIA, MARSUPIALIA MONOTREMATA, PLACENTALIA THEROPSIDA
mammal-like reptiles	THEROPSIDA
mammary gland in animals	UDDER
manatees, sea-cows, etc	SIRENIA
mantis-shrimps	STOMATOPODA
manufacture of food from carbon dioxide and sunlight	PHOTOSYNTHESIS
marine	
—animals	ENTEROPNEUSTA HEMICHORDATA
with shells of lime	FORAMINIFERA

—burrowing worms GEPHYREA
—Protozoa with shells of silica RADIOLARIA
mark on
—petal guiding insects to
  nectaries HONEY GUIDE
—seed coat showing former
  attachment HILUM
marsupials DIDELPHIA
METATHERIA
mass of
—amoeboid protoplasm PLASMODIUM
—hyphae in fungus MYCELIUM
—pollen POLLINIUM
—tissue in
  one membrane SYNCYTIUM
  ovule NUCELLUS
—twigs produced in
  response to
  fungal attack WITCHES' BROOM
maternal milk produced
  after childbirth COLOSTRUM
mature insect IMAGO
maximum height of plant DEFINITE GROWTH
meat-eating animal CARNIVORE
meatus PASSAGE
mechanism of
  evolution NATURAL SELECTION
meiosis REDUCTION DIVISION
membrane(s) TUNIC
—between chest and abdomen DIAPHRAGM
—covering plant
  cells PLASMA MEMBRANE
PLASMALEMMA
—enclosing embryo AMNION
—in egg PUTAMEN
—lining
  abdominal cavity PERITONEUM
  chest cavity PLEURA
  inside of body-wall PARIETAL
  tendons SYNOVIAL MEMBRANE
  tubular cavity MUCOUS MEMBRANE
—mucous MUCOSA(E)
—nourishing foetus PLACENTA
—round ovum CHORION
VITELLINE MEMBRANE
ZONA PELLUCIDA
metabolic regulator
  produced by
  endocrine gland HORMONE
metabolism METASTASIS
—of
  complex substances
    from simpler ones ANABOLISM
  decomposition CATABOLISM
KATABOLISM
Metaphyta EMBRYOPHYTA

Metatheria DIDELPHIA, MARSUPIALIA
micro-organism GERM, MICROBE
—bacteria SCHIZOMYCETES
  diverse group EUBACTERIA
  globular COCCUS
  gram-positive ACTINOMYCETE
  in soil DENITRIFYING BACTERIA
  ovoid CLOSTRIDIUM
  rod-shaped BACILLUS
MYXOBACTERIUM
RICKETTSIA, SHIGELLA
  spindle-shaped CLOSTRIDIUM
  spiral SPIRILLUM, SPIROCHAETE
VIBRIO
  twisted chains STREPTOCOCCI
—causing
  disease PATHOGEN
  respiratory and
  intestinal disease ECHO VIRUS
—chemical pathogen which
  multiplies in cells VIRUS
—converting
  ammonium to nitrites NITROBACTERIA
  carbohydrates to
  lactic acid LACTOBACILLUS
  copper sulphide to
  sulphate
THIOBACILLUS CUPRO-OXIDANS
—floating in air AEROPLANKTON
—like yeast TORULA
—mature virus VIRION
—not requiring oxygen ANAEROBE
—requiring oxygen AEROBE
—unclassified MYCOPLASMAS
—virus
  cancer-forming PAPOVAVIRUS
  causing disease PARVOVIRUS
  outer shell CAPSID
  parasitic on bacteria PHAGE
—viruses and
  rickettsias MICROTATOBISTES
microscopic organism GERM, MICROBE
MICRO-ORGANISM
middle
—layer of fruit wall MESOCARP
—segment of thorax of insect MESOTHORAX
mildew MOULD
milk
—production LACTATION
—secreting
  animal MAMMAL
  gland MAMMARY GLAND
milky fluid exuded by
  cut surface of some plants LATEX
millipedes, etc DIPLOPODA
mitochondria CHONDRIOSOMES

97

mitosis	KARYOKINESIS
mode of evolution	NATURAL SELECTION
	SEXUAL SELECTION
modified	
—hind-wing of fly	HALTERE
—inflorescence	TENDRIL
—leaf	BRACT
—wing(s) of beetle	ELYTRUM(ELYTRA)
moist lining membrane	MUCOUS MEMBRANE
molecule containing genetic	
code	NUCLEIC ACID
Mollusca	AMPHINEURA, CEPHALOPODA
	GASTROPODA
	LAMELLIBRANCHI(AT)A
	SCAPHOPODA, SIPHONOPODA
—with lungs	PULMONATA
monochlamydeous	HAPLOCHLAMYDEOUS
monozygotic twins	IDENTICAL TWINS
	UNIOVULAR TWINS
monthly cycle of ovum	
reproduction	MENSTRUAL CYCLE
mosses	MUSCI
mould	MILDEW
moulting	ECDYSIS
mouth-part	LABRUM, LABIUM
—of insect	MANDIBLE, MAXILLA
movement	
—curving	
downward	EPINASTY
upward	HYPONASTY
—in response to stimuli	(see response below)
—of population	MIGRATION
moving cell in blood of	
invertebrates	AMOEBOCYTE
mucroprotein	GLYCOPROTEIN
multicelled animals	METAZOA
multinucleate cell	SYNCYTIUM
Musci	MOSSES
muscle	(see separate entry)
mushroom	(see fungus)
mussels etc	MOLLUSCA
mutated gene	MUTANT
mutation	SPORT
Mycophyta	FUNGI
Myriapoda	CHILOPODA, DIPLOPODA
naked cell	MYXAMOEBA
name	
—which is the same	
in generic and	
specific forms	TAUTONYM
—without description	NOMEN NUDUM
naming system	BINOMIAL NOMENCLATURE
	LINNAEAN SYSTEM
narrow-mouthed	ANGIOSTOM(AT)OUS
navel	UMBILICUS
—string	UMBILICAL CORD

nematode	EELWORM, HOOKWORM
nerve	(see separate entry)
nest-building	NIDULATION
newts, salamanders	URODELA
non-cellular covering of	
animal or plant	CUTICLE
non-motile	
—gamete	APLANOGAMETE
—spore	APLANOSPORE
non-parasitic	
—animal living on another	EPIZOITE
—plant living on another	EPIPHYTE
nostrils	NARES
not	
—affected by environment	BIOSTABLE
—caused by genes	EXOGENETIC
—divided into cells	ACELLULAR
—splitting spontaneously	INDEHISCENT
nucleic acid	
—and protein compound	
in cell	NUCLEOPROTEIN
—containing ribose	RIBONUCLEIC ACID
	RNA
—deoxyribose	DEOXYRIBONUCLEIC ACID
	DNA
nucleolus	PLASMOSOME
nutritive tissue round	
embryo in plants	ENDOSPERM
obtaining energy	
—by	
chemical reactions	CHEMOTROPHIC
photosynthesis	PHOTOTROPHIC
—from	
external sources	HETEROTROPHIC
internal sources	AUTOTROPHIC
light	PHOTOTROPHIC
octopuses, squids, etc	CEPHALOPODA
	SIPHONOPODA
offspring of same parents	SIBLINGS, SIBS
one of two strands into	
which chromosome splits	CHROMATID
opening	
—in skull for spinal column	FORAMEN
—into pharynx	GLOTTIS
—to discharge seeds	DEHISCENT
organ	
—acting as kidney in	
invertebrates, etc	NEPHRIDIUM
—adapted for stimuli	RECEPTOR
—containing spores	
in mosses, etc	CAPSULE
—linking embryo to uterus	PLACENTA
—of	
balance in Crustacea etc	OTOCYST
hearing	EAR
sight	EYE, STATOCYST

smell	NOSE
	OLFACTORY ORGAN
—producing	
lymphocytes	SPLEEN
secretions	GLAND
sex-cells	GONAD
silk	SPINNERET
organ(s) of abdomen	VISCUS(VISCERA)
organic	
—compound	
from distillation of alcohol and acid	ESTER
which hydrolyses into	
amino acids	PROTEIN
—material spread over soil	MULCH
—secretion of plant or insect	RESIN
organism	
—airborne	AEROPLANKTON
—bearing altered gene(s)	MUTANT
—in diploid stage	DIPLONT
—living	
in	
—dirty water	SAPROBE
—sea	
floating	PLANKTON, SESTON
swimming	NEKTON
on	
—sea-bottom	BENTHOS
—the	
inside of	
another	ENDOPARASITE
outside of another	ECTOPARASITE
—made of cells which can	
germinate	SPORIDESM
—which	
lives in symbiosis	SYMBIONT
occurs in different	
forms	POLYMORPH
seeks	
—light	PHOTOPHIL(E)
—shade	SKOTOPHIL(E)
tolerates heat and cold	EURYTHERM
—with	
chromosomes from two	
different species	ALLOPOLYPLOID
eight tentacles	ALCYONARIA
two or more genetically	
different tissues	CHIM(A)ERA
orientation in response	
to gravity	GEOTROPISM
origin of parts of organisms	MORPHOGENESIS
	MORPHOGENY
outbreeding	EXOGAMY
outer	
—coat of	
fruit body in fungi	PERIDIUM
seed	EPISPERM

virus	CAPSID
—covering of seed	TESTA
—envelope round embryo	CHORION
—layer of	CORTEX
cells	EPIDERMIS
cytoplasm	ECTOPLASM
flower	PERIANTH
fruit wall	EPICARP, EXOCARP
meristem	CAMBIUM
ovule	PRIMINE
plant	PERIDERM
root	EXODERM(IS)
tree	BARK
wall of spore	EXOSPORE
xylem	SAPWOOD
—part of	
flower	CALYX
fruit	PERICARP
limb of crustacean	EXOPOD(ITE)
—wall of body	SOMATOPLEURE
outgrowth on	
—fruit	ALA
—seeds	CARUNCLE, STROPHIOLE
ovary	
—and stigma	CARPEL
—of plant (old)	GERM(EN), GERMIN
—stigma and style	GYNAECEUM
	GYNOECIUM, PISTIL
ovum	GERM-CELL
paired chromosomes in meiosis	TETRAD
pairing of parental	
chromosomes	SYNAPSIS, SYNDESIS
pancreas	SWEETBREAD
parachute of wind-borne seed	PAPPUS
parasite on	
—living organism	OBLIGATE PARASITE
—living or dead	
host	FACULTATIVE PARASITE
parasitic	BIOGENOUS
—on insects	ENTOMOGENOUS
—plant genus	VISCUM
—Protozoa	SPOROZOA
part of	
—animal nearest to head	ANTERIOR
—animal's alimentary canal	GIZZARD
—bird's stomach	PROVENTRICULUS
—body between chest	
and pelvis	ABDOMEN
—calyx	SEPAL
—capsule after dehiscence	VALVE
—cell nucleus easily	
stained	CHROMATIN
	GOLGI BODY
—embryonic digestive	
system	STOMATADAEUM
	STOMATOD(A)EUM

—egg undergoing division	BLASTODERM
—flower	BRACT, CARPEL, OVULE
	PETAL, RECEPTACLE, SEPAL
	STAMEN, STIGMA, STYLE
farthest from axis	ANTERIOR
—kidney	BOWMAN'S CAPSULE
—ovary bearing ovules	PLACENTA
—parasite attached to host	HAUSTORIUM
—perianth	TEPAL
—plant	
carrying	
—leaves, etc	STEM
—reproductive organs	RECEPTACLE
capable of growing into	
new individual	PROPAGULE
harbouring mites, etc	DOMATIUM
where differentiation occurs	HISTOGEN
—respiratory system	
in birds	AIR SAC
—seed which turns	
into root	RADICLE
—sperm head	ACROSOME
—style receiving pollen	STIGMA
partial sterilisation	PASTEURISATION
particle in cell	RIBOSOME
partition(s)	REPLUM(REPLA)
	SEPTUM(SEPTA)
passive stage between	
larva and adult	CHRYSALIS, PUPA
pathogenic agent requiring	
host cell for multiplication	VIRUS
pattern of	
—leaves in bud	VERNATION
—veins	VENATION
pertaining to the	
—body	SOMATIC
—effect of	
psychological factors	
on physiology	PSYCHOSOMATIC
period of pregnancy	GESTATION PERIOD
petals of flower	COROLLA
phellegen	CORK CAMBIUM
phellem	CORK
phosphorescent tunicates	PYROSOMA
photosynthetic pigment	CHLOROPHYLL
phylum	
—of	
animals	ANNELIDA, ARTHROPODA
	MOLLUSCA, VERTEBRATA
—with primitive spinal	
—column	CRANIATA
	(PROTO)CHORDATA
	VERTEBRATA
aquatic animals	CNIDARIA
	COELENTERATA
	ECHINODERMATA

physiological race	BIOTYPE
pincer(s)	CHELA(E)
pit of stomach	EPIGASTRIUM
pith	MEDULLA
placental mammals	EUTHERIA
plankton	
—animals	ZOOPLANKTON
—plants	PHYTOPLANKTON
plant	
—adapted to its environment	ECAD
—bud	GEMMA
—community over	
large area	FORMATION
—disease	(see separate entry)
—growing where not wanted	WEED
—hormone	AUXIN, PHYTAMIN
—living on dead matter	SAPROPHYTE
—of	
pea family	LEGUME
Gramineae family	CEREAL
—producing	
gametes	GAMETOPHYTE
zygospores	ZYGOPHYTE
—receiving graft	STOCK
—tissue giving	
mechanical support	SCLERENCHYMA
—which	
has adapted to its environment	ECAD
is tolerant of dry conditions	CACTUS
	SUCCULENT
reproduces by fission	SCHIZOPHYTE
stores water in	
its tissues	SUCCULENT
trails along the ground	PROCUMBENT
—with	
buds	
—above ground	PHANEROPHYTE
—below ground	CRYPTOPHYTE
diploid nucleus	DIPLONT
long life	PERENNIAL
net-veined leaves (old)	DICTYOGEN
one-year life-cycle	ANNUAL
radiating leaves	ROSETTE PLANT
recurring life-cycle	PERENNIAL
seeds not in ovary	GYMNOSPERM
stem, leaf and root	CORMOPHYTE
two-year life-cycle	BIENNIAL
—without chlorophyll	FUNGUS
plants	(see separate entry)
plastid storing oil	ELAIOPLAST
plate on insect	SCUTE, SCUT(ELL)UM
Platyhelminthes	CESTODA, FLUKES
	(TREMATODA) TURBELLARIA
podia	TUBE FEET
poikilothermic	COLD-BLOODED
point from which leaves develop	NODE

pointed outgrowth from epidermis	PRICKLE, THORN
poisonous to cells	CYTOTOXIC
pollen	
—brush in bees	SCOPA
—producing organ	STAMEN
pollex	THUMB
pollination by	
—birds	ORNITHOPHILY
—insects	ENTOMOPHILY
—pollen from same plant	SELF-POLLINATION
—snails	MALACOPHILY
—water	HYDROPHILY
—wind action	ANEMOPHILY
polyploid with all chromosomes from same species	AUTOPOLYPLOID
polysaccharide in food reserve in algae	CHRYSOLAMINARIN LEUCOSIN
Polyzoa	ECTOPROCTA
population of	
—animals	FAUNA
—plants	FLORA
pore(s)	SPIRACLE, STIGMA
—in plants	STOM(AT)A
—large	OSCULUM
—small	OSTIUM
pouch	
—containing testes	SCROTUM
—of marsupial	MARSUPIUM
pregnancy	CYESIS
prehensile claw(s)	CHELA(E)
premature flowering and seeding	BOLTING
preparation of micro-organisms used to stimulate immunity	VACCINE
pressure of sap, etc on cell walls	TURGOR
primitive	
—seed plants	CYCADALES
—spinal column	NOTOCHORD
—stele	PROTOSTELE
produced by	
—external stimuli	PARATONIC
—insertion of genes from one species to another	TRANSGENIC
producing	
—cells which form yolk	MEROISIC
—either male or female gametes	UNISEXUAL
—leaves	
after flowers	HISTERANTHOUS
and flowers together	SYNANTHOUS
—ova	OVULATION
—two offspring at a time	DITOKOUS

—young	
born alive	VIVIPAROUS
in eggs	OVIPAROUS
—hatched internally	OVOVIVIPAROUS
product of fusion of gametes	ZYGOTE
production of	
—chemicals by organisms	BIOSYNTHESIS
—enzymes by chemicals added to cell	INDUCTION
—fruit without fertilisation	PARTHENOCARPY
—milk	LACTATION
—new tissues by stimulus	INDUCTION
—small flowers that fail to open	CL(E)ISTOGAMY
—sound by insects	STRIDULATION
—spores by constricting stalk	ABSTRICTION
programmed cell death	APOPTOSIS
projection(s)	
—from root	ROOT-HAIR, ROOT-NODULE
—in intestine	VILLUS, (VILLI)
—of dermis	DERMAL PAPILLA(E)
—on	
body of fish	FIN
leaf	AURICLE
tongue containing taste-buds	TONGUE PAPILLA(E)
propagule	CUTTING, GEMMA SEED, SPORE
protective covering	
—of	
larvae etc	COCOON
plant embryo	SEED COAT, TESTA
—on growing point of root	ROOT-CAP
protein	(see separate entry)
—acting as catalyst	ENZYME
—and lipid in plant cell membrane	LIPOPROTEIN
—produced in the body to counter antigen	ANTIBODY
protoplasm	BIOPLASM
—from cell-division in fungi, etc	COENOCYTE
—in cell nucleus	CARYOPLASM KARYOPLASM
—of body cells	SOMATOPLASM
—outside nucleus of cell	CYTODE CYTOPLASM
—suggested as responsible for heredity	GERM-PLASM
—unit	ENERGID
Protozoa	FLAGELLATA MASTIGOPHORA RHIZOPODA, SARCODINA

Pteridophyta
—clubmosses   LYCOPODIALES
—epiphytes   PSILOTALES
—ferns   FILICALES
—horsetails   EQUISITALES
pupa   CHRYSALIS
pure culture   AXENIC
quantity of living material   BIOMASS
                                     STANDING CROP
rabbits and hares   LAGOMORPHA
rasping organ in
  molluscs   ODONTOPHORE, RADULA
ratio of
  carbon dioxide
    expired to oxygen
    inspired   RESPIRATORY QUOTIENT
  male to female   SEX RATIO
rats, mice, squirrels, etc   RODENTIA
Raunkiaer's Life Forms
—woody plant with
  high buds   PHANEROPHYTE
  medium tree   MESOPHANEROPHYTE
  shrub   NANOPHANEROPHYTE
  small tree   MICROPHANEROPHYTE
  tall tree   MEGAPHANEROPHYTE
—woody plant with
  low buds   CHAMAEOPHYTE
—herb
  surviving winter as seed   THEROPHYTE
  with buds
    —at soil level   HEMICRYPTOPHYTE
    —below soil   GEOPHYTE
    —in
      mud   HELOPHYTE
      water   HYDROPHYTE
rear
—section of thorax of insect   METATHORAX
—segment of
  abdomen   TELSON
  arthropod   ABDOMEN
receptacle
—of flower   THALAMUS
—in fungus   PYCNIDIUM
receptor for taste   TASTE-BUD
recess   SINUS
recombination of genes
  on same chromosome   CROSSING OVER
region of active cells
  forming new tissue   CAMBIUM, MERISTEM
regrowth of missing part   REGENERATION
—from remaining tissue   MORPHALLAXIS
relationship
—between sex and inherited
  characteristics   SEX LINKAGE
—of mutual benefit to
  organisms living together   SYMBIOSIS

—where one organism is
  dependent upon another   PARASITISM
remains of organism
  found in rocks   FOSSIL
                                     (see **archaeology**)
repeated splitting
  after fertilisation   CLEAVAGE
                                     SEGMENTATION
reproduction
—by
  budding   BLASTOGENESIS
  fission   SCHIZOGENESIS
  grafting bud   BUDDING
  inserting part cut from
    one plant into
    —another   GRAFTING
    —soil   CUTTING
  part taken from parent
    plant   VEGETATIVE REPRODUCTION
  pegging down
    —growing stem   LAYERING
    —leaf   LEAF CUTTING
  splitting large plant   FRAGMENTATION
  transfer of pollen   CROSS-POLLINATION
  transmission of
    vibrations   PERIGENESIS
—from small part of ovum   MEROGONY
—in pre-adult form   PAEDOGENESIS
—of
  exact copies   CLONING, REPLICATION
  living young   VIVIPARITY
  —in plants   VIVIPARY
—without fertilisation   AGAMOSPERMY
                                     APOMIXIS
                          ASEXUAL REPRODUCTION
                          PARTHENOGENESIS
reproductive
—asexual body   SPORE
—cell   GAMETE, GERM CELL
—cycle   OESTROUS CYCLE
—organ
  animal
    —female   OVARY, UTERUS, WOMB
    —male   PENIS, TESTES
  flowering plant
    —female   CARPEL, OVARY, STIGMA
    —male   ANTHER, STAMEN
  red algae
    —female   CARPOGONIUM
—sexual body   OVULE, OVUM
                          POLLEN, SPERM
—unit of Angiosperm   FLOWER
reptiles   REPTILIA
—crocodiles   CROCODILIA
—lizards   LACERTILIA
  and snakes   SQUAMATA

—snakes ANGUIFAUNA, OPHIDIA
—tortoises and turtles CHELONIA
—tuatara RHYNCOCEPHALIA
respiration of
—free oxygen AEROBIC RESPIRATION
—plants in light PHOTORESPIRATION
respiratory
—organ in
fish etc GILL
mammals LUNG
—root of plants growing
in swamps PNEUMATOPHORE
—tissue ARENCHYMA
response to
—alternation of day
and night NYCTINASTY
—chemical stimulus CHEMOTAXIS
TROPHOTROPISM
—directional stimulus TAXIS
—food stimulus TROPHOTAXIS
—general temperature
change THERMONASTY
—gravity GEOTAXIS
PLAGIOGEOTROPISM
at right angles IAGEOTROPISM
—heat THERMONASTY
—light PHOTONASTY
PHOTOTAXIS
—local contact HAPTOTROPISM
—mechanical
stimulus THIGMORPHOGENESIS
—night NYCTINASTY
NYCTITROPISM
—non-directional light PHOTONASTY
—shock SEISMONASTY
—stimulus AROUSAL, KINESIS
TAXIS, (THIGMO)TROPISM
independent of
direction NASTIC MOVEMENT
NASTY
—sunlight HELIOTAXIS, HELIOTROPISM
resting stage of cell INTERPHASE
retaining
—larval features
into adult stage NEOTEINIA, NEOTENY
—leaves all year round EVERGREEN
reversion to characteristics
of ancestral type ATAVISM
ridge on ovule RAPHE
ring of
—petals PERIANTH
—similar parts of plant WHORL
ripened ovary with seeds FRUIT
ripening of male and
female flowers at
different times DICHOGAMY

rise in respiration rate CLIMACTERIC
RNA bases ADENINE, CYTOSINE
GUANINE, URACIL
rod-shaped
—bacterium BACILLUS
—body in cell producing
spindle CENTRIOLE
roof of mouth PALATE, URANISCUS
root RADICAL
—above ground AERIAL ROOT
—as food store TAP-ROOT
—from base of stem SEMINAL ROOT
—like bulb CORM
—of
embryo RADICLE
fungus RHIZOMORPH
moss etc, RHIZOID
—penetrating deep TAP-ROOT
—small RADICLE
—underground
bud BULB
stem RHIZOME
—rooting at nodes STOLON
—swollen TUBER
—which pulls bulb into
ground CONTRACTILE ROOT
rudimentary
—legs of caterpillar PROLEGS
—organism GERM
rule governing origin of
living things from
similar parents PRINCIPLE OF BIOGENESIS
runner SARMENTUM
rust fungi URIDINALES
sac
—for
bile GALL BLADDER
urine BLADDER
—of secreting cells
in gland duct ALVEOLUS
saline solution used to sustain
biological specimens RINGER'S FLUID
scale(s) SQUAMA(E), SQUAME
—chaffy RAMENTUM
—on bird's foot SCUTELLUM
scent organ on butterfly wing PLUMULE
scientific naming
of species BINOMIAL NOMENCLATURE
LINNAEAN SYSTEM
TRINOMIAL SYSTEM
sea
—anemones etc ANTHOZOA (ACTINOZOA)
—butterflies PTEROPODA
—gooseberries, etc CTENOPHORA
—mats BRYOZOA, ECTOPROCTA
POLYZOA

—spiders   PYCNOGONIDA, PYKNOGONIDA
—squirts   TUNICATA, UROCHORDATA
—urchins, starfish, etc   ECHINODERMATA
—weed   (*see separate entry*)
seals, walruses, etc   PINNIPEDIA
seasonal variant   FORM
second stomach in bird   GIZZARD
secondary layer formed
  by phellogen   PHELLODERM
secreted fluid fed by
  pigeons to young   CROPMILK
                     PIGEON'S MILK
secretion of
—endocrine gland   HORMONE
—gland   SUCCUS
—liver   BILE
—pancreas   PANCREATIC JUICE
                     PANCREATIN
—sebaceous gland   SEBUM
secretory organ   GLAND
section of DNA
—between exons   INTRON
—controlling
    protein synthesis   EXON
    structures in embryo   HOMEOBOX
sedentary (animals)   SESSILE
seed   SPERM
—coat   TESTA
—covering in sedge   PERIGONE
—leaf   COTYLEDON
—plant
    with ovary   ANGIOSPERM
    without ovary   GYMNOSPERM
segmentation   MEROGENESIS
self
—amputation   AUTOTOMY
—fertilisation in plants   AUTOGAMY
—pollination within
    unopened flower   CL(E)ISTOGAMY
sense organ   RECEPTOR
sensory
—appendage
    at rear end of insect   CERCUS
    of insects etc   ANTENNA, ANTENNULE
—hair of thread cell   CNIDOCIL
—system   SENSORIUM
sepals collectively   CALYX
sequence of
—amino-acids and nucleotides   GENETIC CODE
—nucleotides determining
    amino-acid   CODON
sex
—chromatin   BARR BODY
—chromosome   X, Y
sexual
—impulse   OESTRUM, OESTRUS

—reproduction   AMPHIMIXIS
sharing of chromosomes   SEGREGATION
sharp-pointed   ACEROSE
sheath round
—central cylinder of plant   ENDODERMIS
—grass
    plumule   COLEOPTILE
    radicle   COLEORHIZA
shedding
—leaves   ABSCISSION, DECIDUOUS
—outer skin   ECDYSIS
shell of
—crabs, etc   CARAPACE
—insect's egg   CHORION
—slug   LIMACEL
ship-worm (a mollusc)   TEREDO
shoot   TENDRON
—from
    base of cut-back stem   TILLER
    below ground   OFFSET, STOLON
                     SUCKER
—grafted on to another plant   SCION
—in embryo   PLUMULE
—pegged down to propagate   LAYER
showing recent origin
  from common stock   CLADISTIC
shrimps, etc   BRANCHIOPODA
                     CRUSTACEA
shrinkage of cell from
  osmosis   PLASMOLYSIS
Siamese twins   PARABIOTIC TWINS
side
—petal (pea)   ALA
—sepal (milkwort)   ALA
—shoot of grasses   TILLER
—wall of thorax   PLEURON
single
—breeding group   SPECIES
—celled
    animals   AMOEBA, PROTOZOA
    fungi   YEASTS
    micro-organism   BACTERIUM
    organisms   CILIATA, CILIOPHORA
                   PROTISTA, SUCTORIA
    plants   ALGAE, BACILLARIOPHYTA
skeleton
—inside body   ENDOSKELETON
—outside body   EXOSKELETON
—small marine animals   CORAL
skin   CUTIS
—cell producing melanin   MELANOCYTE
—dead skin round nail   CUTICLE
—outer skin   CUTICLE
—pattern   DERMATOGLYPHIC
—true skin   DERM(A), DERMIS
slime moulds   ACRASIALES

slipper-animalcule	PARAMECIUM
slow-moving animals	TARDIGRADA
small	
—bract	BRACTEOLE
—bulb	BULBIL
—energy-producing body	
(bodies) in cytoplasm	MITOCHONDRION
	(MITOCHONDRIA)
—flower	FLORET
—fungus	MOULD
—gill-slit in fish	SPIRACLE
—particle in cytoplasm	MICROSOME
—portion of protoplasm	BIOPLAST
—sac	FOLLICLE
—scale(s)	SQUAMELLA(E)
—spore	SPORULE
smallest group in	
classification of plants	FORM
snakes	(see separate entry)
social hierarchy	PECKING ORDER
soft	
—corals, etc	ALCYONARIA
—plant tissue	PARENCHYMA
at centre	PITH
soil surrounding roots	RHIZOSPHERE
sound	
—producing organ in birds	SYRINX
—production in	
grasshoppers, etc	STRIDULATION
space between	
—lobes	SINUS
—viscera and	
body-wall	COELOM(E)
	PERIVISCERAL CAVITY
species that	
—can form fertile hybrids	COENSPECIES
—developed in isolation	VICAR
specimen used to	
describe new species	HOLOTYPE
	TYPE SPECIMEN
sperm	GERM-CELL
—duct	VAS DEFERENS
	VAS EFFERENS
—storing organ in	
insect	SPERMA(TO)THECA
spermatid	SPERMATOBLAST
spherical bacterium	COCCUS
spiders, etc	ARACHNIDAE
spindle-attachment	CENTROMERE
spinning organ	SPINNERET
sponges	PARAZOA, PORIFERA
spongy	
—animal tissue	PARENCHYMA
—tissue in skull	DIPLOE
spontaneous generation	ABIOGENESIS
	PARTHENOGENESIS

spore	
—bearing structure	SPOROPHORE
—case	SPORANGIUM
—formation	SPORULATION
—forming organ	SPOROCARP
—in red algae produced	
sexually	CARPOSPORE
—non-motile	APLANOSPORE
—not produced in a sporangium	CONIDIUM
—of rust-fungi	TELEUTOSPORE
—on promycelium	SPORIDIUM
—produced by abstriction	EXOSPORE
—produced by rust fungus	URED(INI)OSPORE
—produced in an ascus	ASCOSPORE
—producing bacterium	BACILLUS
—with thick wall	CHLAMYDOSPORE
sprout	TENDRON
squids, cuttlefish, etc	DECAPODA
stage of	
—cell-division	ANAPHASE
	DIPLOTENE, LEPTOTENE
	METAPHASE, ZYGOTENE
—development	
of embryo	BLASTULA, GASTRULA
stain for bacterial cultures	GRAM'S STAIN
staining	
—method of classifying	
bacteria	GRAM'S METHOD
—of tissue sections	FEULGEN METHOD
stalk(s)	SPIRE, STIPE(STIPITES)
—attaching ovule to placenta	FUNICLE
—carrying stigma	STYLE
—in mosses, etc	SETA
—looking and acting like a leaf	PHYLLODE
—of	
inflorescence	PEDUNCLE
leaf	PETIOLE
sedentary animal	PEDUNCLE
single flower	PEDUNCLE
—in inflorescence	PEDICEL
spore	STERIGMA
stalkless	SESSILE
stamens collectively	ANDROECIUM
start of growth	GERMINATION
state of paleness from	
lack of chlorophyll	ETIOLATION
stem	
—growing without being	
supplanted	MONOPODIUM
—leafless	SCAPE
—looking like and acting as leaf	CLADODE
	PHYLLOCLADE
—of	
plant	CAULIS
seedling between	
—cotyledon and leaf	EPICOTYL

—cotyledon and root	HYPOCOTYL
tree	CAUDEX
—rudimentary	CAULICLE
—secondary	CAULICULUS
—structures collectively	CAULOME
—with successive branches	
supporting main stem	SYMPODIUM
sterile stamen	STAMINODE
steroid promoting maleness	ANDROGEN
sterol in bloodstream	CHOLESTERIN
	CHOLESTEROL
stimulus-provoking	
instinctive reaction	RELEASER
stolon which forms	
new plant at	
growing tip	RUNNER, SARMENTUM
stomach in ruminants	
—first	PAUNCH, RUMEN
—second	BONNET, RETICULUM
—third	BIBLE, OMASUM
—fourth	ABOMASUM, ABOMASUS
	MAW
in calf	VELL
store of food in egg	YOLK
strand	
—from duplication	
of chromosome	CHROMATID
—of vascular tissue	VASCULAR BUNDLE
strap-shaped corolla	LIGULE
strengthening tissue in	
cells	COLLENCHYMA
string of albumen in egg	CHALAZA
structure	
—developed from	
fertilised ovule	SEED
ovum	EGG
zygote	EMBRYO
—of DNA	DOUBLE HELIX
—on cell surface to	
which chemicals attach	RECEPTOR
study of	
—cells	CYTOLOGY
—diseases of plants	PHYTOPATHOLOGY
—distribution of	
plants	PHYTOGEOGRAPHY
—form of organisms	MORPHOLOGY
—heredity	(CYTO)GENETICS
—light as affecting	
organisms	PHOTOBIOLOGY
—living things	BIOLOGY
—metabolism	BIOCHEMISTRY
—micro-organisms	BACTERIOLOGY
—organisms as affected	
by weather	PHENOLOGY
—plants	BOTANY
—viruses	VIROLOGY

sub-class of	
—Crustacea	BRANCHIOPODA
	CIRRIPEDIA, COPEPODA
—fish	TELEOSTEI
—Gasterododa	EUTHYNEURA
—Infusoria	CILIATA
—Mammalia	EUTHERIA
	PLACENTAL MAMMALS
	PLACENTALIA
sub-order of Polyzoa	CYCLOSTOMATA
sub-phylum of	
—Chordata	ACRANIA
	CEPHALOCHORDATA
	CRANIATA, VERTEBRATA
—Coelenterata	CNIDARIA, CTENOPHORA
substance	
—acting	
in conjunction with	
enzyme in catalysis	COENZYME
on embryonic cells to	
determine structure	MORPHOGEN
—causing	
cancer	CARCINOGEN
mutation	MUTAGEN
—controlling	
mitosis	CHALONE
plant growth	CYTOKININ
—forming	
cartilage	CHONDRIN
cuticle in plants	CUTIN
hard outer parts of insects etc	CHITIN
horn, etc	KERATIN
—found in cell-sap	TANNIN
—in cell aiding oxidation	CYTOCHROME
—inimical to body,	
stimulating formation	
of antibodies	ANTIGEN
—involved in metabolic	
process	METABOLITE
—of which living things	
are made	TISSUE
—on which enzymes act	SUBSTRATE
—produced by organisms	
which is inimical to	
other species	ANTIBIOTIC
—promoting plant growth	AUXIN
	PHYTAMIN
—released by animal affecting	
behaviour of others	PHEROMONE
—secreted by mucous	
membrane	MUCIGEN, MUCIN
	MUCUS
—which is foreign	
to the body	ANTIGEN
succession of communities	
of plants	SERE

—in	
dry spots	XEROSERE
water	HYDROSERE
—on rocks	LITHOSERE
sucking proboscis	HAUSTELLUM
sugary solution from plant	NECTAR
sun-animalcules	HELIOZOA
supposed force directing evolution	BATHISM
surface	
—farthest from spine	VENTRAL
—nearest to spine	DORSAL
—secreting mucus	MUCOUS MEMBRANE
survival from year	
to year	PERENNATION
suspended development	
in insects	DIAPAUSE
swallowing	DEGLUTITION
sweetbread	PANCREAS
swelling caused by	
—nitrogen-fixing	
bacteria	ROOT NODULE
—parasites	GALL
symmetrical about one	
plane (flowers)	ZYGOMORPHIC
	ZYGOMORPHOUS
synthesis	
—by chlorophyll using	
energy of light	PHOTOSYNTHESIS
—in metabolism	ANABOLISM
tactile organ on	
—head of worm	PALP
—mouth of mollusc	PALP
tail part of crustacean	TELSON
taking in of oxygen and	
expiration of CO_2	RESPIRATION
tapeworms	CESTODA
	(see also worms below)
tear-pit	LARMIER
technique of growing	
cells etc	EXPLANTATION
	TISSUE CULTURE
terminal bud	PLUMULE
termination of trachea	
in insect	TRACHEOLE
tetrapods	AMPHIBIA, ANIMALS
	BIRDS, MAMMALS
theory	
—of	
directed evolution	BATHISM
evolution by	
—natural selection	DARWINISM
—acquired	
characteristics	LAMARCKIS
in USSR	LYSENKOISM
gradual development of	
the embryo	EPIGENESIS

heredity	MENDELISM
reappearance of	
throwbacks	ATAVISM
—that life is due to some	
vital force	VITALISTIC THEORY
thorax of crustacean	PEREION
thread	
—cell	CNIDOBLAST
—like lash(es) on cell	CILIUM(CILIA)
—of protoplasm	PLASMODESM
—shaped body in cell	
nucleus carrying genetic	
instructions	CHROMOSOME
thumb	POLLEX
time between conception	
and birth	GESTATION (PERIOD)
tissue	
—between gill-slits	GILL-BAR
—cells	SOMA, SOMATIC CELLS
—culture	EXPLANTATION
—forming over wound	CALLUS
—of	
cells of aquatic plant roots	AERENCHYMA
plants	PARENCHYMA
thick-walled cells	SCLERENCHYMA
toad used in pregnancy	
testing	AFRICAN CLAWED TOAD
	XENOPUS
toe	DIGIT
tolerating variation of	
—osmotic pressure	EURYHALINE
—temperature	EURYTHERMOUS
tongue of gastropod mollusc	RADULA
tortoises and turtles	CHELONIA
touch receptors of bristle	VIBRISSAE
trace element	MICRONUTRIENT
transformation of	
—flower part to leaf-like structure	PHYLLODY
—tissue	METAPLASIA
translucent marine vertebrate	LANCELET
transmission of parental	
characteristics together	LINKAGE
treatment of plants to	
induce flowering	VERNALISATION
tree	
—retaining leaves	CONIFER, EVERGREEN
—shedding leaves	DECIDUOUS
	(see also separate entry)
tropical climber	LIANA, LIANE
true skin	CORIUM, DERMIS
trumpet-like part of flower	CORONA
tuatara	RHYNCOCEPHALIA
tube	
—connecting embryo	
and placenta	NAVEL-STRING
	UMBILICAL CORD

—feet	PODIA
—from throat to lungs	TRACHEA, WIND-PIPE
tunic	INTEGUMENT
	MEMBRANE
turning towards stimulus	TROPISM
twig	SARMENTUM
twin	
—from	
same ovum	MONOZYGOTIC TWIN
two ova	DIZYGOTIC TWIN
	FRATERNAL TWIN
—sterile female in cattle	FREE-MARTIN
type specimen	HOLOTYPE
typical species	GENOTYPE
underground	
—bud	BULB, TURION
—section of plant	ROOT
—stem	CORM, RHIZOME, SOBOLE
undifferentiated	
—perianth	PERIGONE
—plant-body	THALLUS
ungulates with	
—even number of toes	ARTIODACTYLA
—odd number of toes	PERISSODACTYLA
union of gametes	CONJUGATION
	FERTILISATION
	OOGAMY, SYNGAMY
unisexual	DIOECIOUS
unit	
—of	
corolla	PETAL
DNA in chromosome	GENE
	HEREDITY FACTOR
flower calyx	SEPAL
genetic information	CISTRON
living animal matter	CELL
—protoplasm	ENERAID, ENERGID
—in taxonomy	DEME
unopened flower-bud	KNOSP
urine	
—duct	
bladder to exterior	URETHRA
kidney to bladder	URETER
—sac	BLADDER
variant from normal	PARAMORPH, ROGUE
	SPORT
variation	DIFFERENTIATION
vascular	
—bundle in leaf	VEIN
—cylinder	STELE
—tissue in plant	WOOD, XYLEM
transporting nutrients	BAST, PHLOEM
veins	(*see* **circulation**)
vertebrate	
—adapted to land or water	AMPHIBIA
—birds	AVES
—groups	AMNIOTA, ANAMNIOTA
—with	
jaws	GNATHOSTOMATA
skull	CRANIATA
—without jaws	AGNATHA
verticil	WHORL
vesicle containing	
ovum	GRAAFIAN FOLLICLE
vessel conducting food	
etc in trees	TRACHEA
vibrating element in larynx	VOCAL C(H)ORD
virus	
—parasitic on	
bacteria	BACTERIOPHAGE
—used in studies	TOBACCO MOSAIC VIRUS
visceral arch	
in fish	BRANCHEAL ARCH
visual purple	RHODOPSIN
walking on	
—back of toes	DORSIGRADE
—soles of feet	PLANTIGRADE
—tips of hooves	UNGULIGRADE
—toes	DIGITIGRADE
wall of fruit	PERICARP
warm-blooded	IDIOTHERMIC
warning coloration	SYNAPOSEMATISM
waste product	DUNG, EXCREMENT, FAECES
	UREA, URIC ACID, URINE
wasting of	
—an organ	ATROPHY
—minerals from soil	LEACHING
water	
—absorbing layer	
on aerial root	VELAMEN
—conducting system	
in plants	VASCULAR SYSTEM
—fleas	CLADOCERA
—pressure in plants	ROOT PRESSURE
waxy sterol present in body	CHOLESTEROL
weak twig	SARMENTUM
web-forming organ in spider	SPINNERET
weight of all organisms	
in a system	BIOMASS
well supplied with	
nutrients	EUTROPHIC
whalebone	BALEEN
whales, porpoises, etc	CETACEA
wheel-animalcules	ROTIFERA
whip-like thread used	
for propulsion	FLAGELLUM
whorl round sex organs	
of mosses	PERICHAETIUM
wind-pipe	TRACHEA
winged	
—fruit	SAMARA
—growth on fruit	ALA

without	
—backbone	INVERTEBRATE
—leaves	APHYLLOUS
—petals	APETALOUS
—stalk	SESSILE
womb	UTERUS
wood	XYLEM
worm(s)	(see separate entry)
xylem	WOOD
yellow-green algae	XANTHOPHYTA
yolk	DEUTOPLASM
young	
—animal when parts are distinct	F(O)ETUS
—plant	SEEDLING
or animal after fertilisation	EMBRYO
—tree	SAPLING
youngest at	
—base, oldest at top	BASIPETAL
—top, oldest at base	ACROPETAL
zygote	AMPHIONT, SEED
birds	AVES, AVIFAUNA, ORNIS
including: alternative names	
classification	
group names	
able to leave nest at once	PRAECOCES
accentor	DUNNOCK
	HEDGE-SPARROW
—accentors	PRUNELLIDAE
Accipiter	SPARROW-HAWK
Alauda	(SKY)LARK
albatross	ALCATRAS, GOONEY(-BIRD)
—albatrosses	PROCELLARIIFORMES
Alca	SEA-AUKS
Alcatras	ALBATROSS, FRIGATE-BIRD
	GANNET, PELICAN
Alpine	SNOW-FINCH
Anas	GADWALL, TEAL, WI(D)GEON
annet	KITTIWAKE
Anous	NODDY
ant-thrush	PITTA
Antarctic	PENGUIN
Anthus	PIPIT
Arctic	SNOW-BUNTING, SNOW-GOOSE
Arenaria	STREPSILAS, TURNSTONE
ariel	PETREL, SWALLOW, TOUCAN
Astur	GOSHAWK
auk	DIVER, RAZOR-BILL
—auks	CHARADRIIFORMES
avocet	AVOSET
—avocets	CHARADRIIFORMES
	RECURVIROSTRIDAE
babbler	THRUSH
bald eagle	OSSIFRAGE
Baltimore oriole	HANGBIRD
bantam	DANDY-COCK, DANDY-HEN
bargoose	SHELDUCK
bar-tailed godwit	SCAMEL
barn owl	MADGE, SCREECH-OWL
barnacle goose	BARNACLE
	BERNICE-GOOSE, CLAIK
bats	(see separate entry)
bearded	
—tit(mouse)	REEDLING, REED-PHEASANT
—vulture	LAMMERGEIER
	LAMMERGEYER
bee-eater	MEROPIDIAN
bird of	
—paradise	STANDARD-WING
—prey	RAPTOR
bittern	ARDEA, BUTTER-BUMP
	MIRE-DRUM
—bitterns	ARDEIDAE
—group	SEDGE
black	
—backed gull	SWART-BACK
—bird	AMSEL, AMZEL, MERLE
	OUSEL(COCK), OUZEL
blackbirds	TURDIDAE
—cap	WARBLER
blackcaps	SYLVIIDAE
—cock	BLACK GROUSE
—grouse	BLACKCOCK, MOORCOCK
	MOORFOWL, HEATH BIRD
	HEATH FOWL
—guillemot	DOVEKIE, SEA-TURTLE
—headed gull (Scot.)	PICKMAW
blue penguin	KORORA
blue tit	BLUECAP, NUN, PINCHEM
	PINNOCK, TOMTIT, YAUP
Bombycilla	WAX-WING
bramblings	FRINGILLIDAE
brantail	REDSTART, RUTICULA
brent goose	BRANT-GOOSE
	BRENT-BARNACLE, QUINT GOOSE
brown owl	WOOD-OWL
Bucephala	GOLDENEYE
budgerigar	SHELL-PARAKEET
	SHELL-PARROT
	ZEBRA-PAR(R)AKEET
bullfinch	MONK, SHIRLEY
bunting	CIRL, ORTOLAN
—buntings	FRINGILLIDAE
bustard	OTIS
—bustards	GRUIFORMES
butcher-bird	SHRIKE
buzzard	PUTTOCK
—buzzards	FALCONIDAE
Calidris	KNOT
Cape pigeon	PINTADO
Capella	GALINAGO, SNIPE

capercaillie	CAPERCAILZIE, WOOD-GROUSE
—capercaillies	TETRAONIDAE
carrion	
—crow	GORCROW
—eater	VULTURE
cassowaries	CASUARIFORMES
Certhia	TREE-CREEPER
chaffinch	NAPPY, PINK, ROBINET
	SCOBBY, SPINK, WHEAT-BIRD
Charadrius	DOTTEREL, PLOVER
chats	SAXICOLA
chiff-chaff	WARBLER
Chinese	GOLDEN PHEASANT
	SILVER PHEASANT, SWAN-GOOSE
chough	CHEWET, SEA-CROW
—choughs	CORVIDAE
—group	CHATTERING
Ciconia	STORK
Circus	HARRIER
climbing	SCANSORES
coal-tit	COAL-MOUSE, COLE-MOUSE
	COLE-TIT
coastal bird	ROCK-PIPIT
Collocalia	SWIFTLET
common	
—eagle	GOLDEN EAGLE
—harrier	HEN-HARRIER
—kite (obs)	GLED(E)
—lark	SKYLARK
—swan	MUTE SWAN
—wild goose	GREY GOOSE, GREYLAG
coots	GRUIFORMES, RALLIDAE
—group	COVERT, RAFT
Coracias	ROLLER
cormorant	SEA-CROW, SEA-RAVEN, URILE
—cormorants	PHALACROCORACIDAE
	PELECANIFORMES
—Scottish	SCART(H), SKART(H)
corncrake	CRECK, CREX, LANDRAIL
	RAIL, RALLUS
—corncrakes	RALLIDAE
Corvus	CROW, JACKDAW, RAVEN, ROOK
covered with down	
at birth	PRAECOCES
crake	PORZANA
crane	DEMOISELLE
—cranes	GRUIDAE
—genus	GRUS
—group	HERD, SIEGE
creeper	CERTHIA
crest on head	COPPLE
crested	
—European bird	HOOPOE
—grebe	CARGOOSE
—heron	SQUACCO
—penguin	ROCK-HOPPER

—screamer	SERIEMA
Crex	CORNCRAKE, LANDRAIL
crocodile-bird	PLOVER, TROCHILUS
crossbill	LOXIA
—crossbills	FRINGILLIDAE
crow	CORVUS
—crows	CORVIDAE
—group	HOVER, MURDER
cuckoo	COUCAL
—cuckoos	CUCULIDAE, CUCULIFORMES
curlew	TITTEREL, (GREAT) WHAUP
—curlews	CHARADRIIFORMES
	SCOLOPACIDAE
Cuthbert's duck	EIDER DUCK
Cygnus	SWAN
Cypselus	APUS, SWIFT
dabchick	DIDAPPER, DIPCHICK
	DIPPER, DOBCHICK
	LITTLE GREBE
—dabchicks	PODICIPITIDAE
Dafila	PINTAIL
darcock	RALLUS, WATER-RAIL
darter	PLOTUS, SNAKE-BIRD
	WRYNECK
didapper	DOPPER
dipper	WATER-OUZEL
—dippers	CINCLIDAE
diseases	AVIAN TUBERCULOSIS
	COCCIDIOSIS, PARROT DISEASE
	PARROT FEVER, PSITTACOSIS
diver	GAVIA
—divers	GAVIIDAE, GAVIFORMES
diving bird	LOON
domestic duck	INDIAN RUNNER
dorbie	DUNLIN
dotterels	CHARADRIIDAE
dove	CULVER, PIGEON
—doves	COLUMBIDAE
—group	DOLE, DULE, FLIGHT
	PITYING, PRETTYING
duck	GARROT
—ducks	ANATIDAE, ANSERIFORMES
	TADORNA
—group	BADELYNGE, BAD(D)LING
	DOPPING, FLUSH, PLUMP, TEAM
	SMEATH, SMEE(TH)
dun-diver	MERGANSER
dunbird	POCHARD
dunlin	DORBIE, OX-BIRD, OX-PECKER
	PURRE, SEA-MOUSE
	SEA-PECK, STINT
—dunlins	SCOLOPACIDAE
dunnock	(HEDGE-)ACCENTOR
	HEDGE-SPARROW
eagle	ERNE
—eagles	FALCONIDAE

—group	CONVOCATION
—owl	BUBO
Eastern dwarf goose	GOSLET
edible-nest builder	COLLOCALIA
	SALANGANE, SWIFTLET
eider duck	(ST)CUTHBERT'S DUCK
	SOMATERIA
emus	CASUARIFORMES
erne	SEA-EAGLE
European vulture	GRIFFON VULTURE
eve-chur	NIGHTJAR
eve-jar	NIGHTJAR
excrement of sea-birds	GUANO
extinct	DODO, MOA
	PASSENGER PIGEON
fabulous	HARPY, HUMA, PHOENIX
	ROC, ROK, RUC, RUKH
	SIMORG, SIMURG(H), WHISTLER
	(see also **monsters**)
falcon	GERFALCON, HAWK, PEREGRINE
	SACRE, SAKER(ET), STONE-HAWK
	TASSEL-GENT(LE), TERCEL-GENTLE
	TERCEL-JERKIN
—falcons	FALCONIDAE
—group	CAST
Falkland Islands penguin	GENTOO
female	
—black grouse	HEATH-HEN
—blackcock	GREYHEN
—falcon	LANNER
—grouse	GORHEN, GREY-HEN
—moorfowl	MOORHEN
—peregrine	FALCON-GENTIL
	FALCON-GENTLE
—pochard	DUNBIRD
—ruff	REE(VE)
—sandpiper	REEVE
—swan	PEN
fen-owl	NIGHTJAR
fern-owl	NIGHTJAR
fieldfares	TURDIDAE
fig-pecker	BECCAFICO
finch	BRAMBLING, BUNTING, CIRL
	CITRIL, LINNET, SPINK
—finches	FRINGILLIDAE
—group	TREMBLING, TRIMMING
firecrest	REGULUS
flamingoes	CICONIIFORMES
fledgling	QUILLER
flightless	
—bird	CASSOWARY, EM(E)U, KIWI
	OSTRICH, PENGUIN, PINGUIN
	RATITAE, RATITES, RHEA
	STRUTHIONES
—pigeon (old)	SOLITAIRE
flycatcher	MUSCICAPA

—flycatchers	MUSCICAPIDAE
flying reptiles	(see **lizards**)
fork-tailed gulls	XEMA
fossil	(see **archaeology**)
Fratercula	PUFFIN
Fregata	FRIGATE-BIRD
freshwater diver	GREBE
friar-bird	FOUR O'CLOCK
frigate-bird	ALCATRAS
	MAN-OF-WAR(BIRD)
—frigate birds	FREGATIDAE
	PELECANIFORMES
frogmouth	PODARGUS
—frogmouths	CAPRIMULGIFORMES
fully-webbed	STEGANOPOD(ES)
fulmar	MALLEMUCK, MOLLYMAWK
—fulmars	PROCELLARIIDAE
gadwall	RADGE, RODGE
Gallicrex	KORA, WATER-COCK
Gallinago	CAPELLA, SNIPE
game bird	GROUSE, PARTRIDGE
	PHEASANT, QUAIL
	WOODCOCK
—game birds	GALLIFORMES
gannet	ALCANTRAS, BOOBY
	SOLAN(D)
—gannets	SULIDAE, PELECANIFORMES
garden warbler	REELER
garganey	ANAS
—garganeys	ANATIDAE
Gavia	DIVER
Garrulus	JAY
geese	
—flying group	SKEIN
—geese	ANATIDAE, ANSERIFORMES
—group	FLOCK, GAGGLE, NIDE
giant fulmar	OSSIFRAGA
goat-owl	NIGHTJAR
goatsucker	FROGMOUTH, MOTH-HUNTER
	NIGHT-HAWK
—goatsuckers	CAPRIMULGIDAE
	CAPRIMULGIFORMES
godwit	SCAMEL
—godwits	SCOLOPACIDAE
goldcrest	GOLDEN-CRESTED WREN
	KINGLET, REGULUS, ROITELET
—goldcrests	REGULIDAE
golden	
—crested wren	GOLDCREST, KINGLET
	REGULUS, ROITELET
—eagle	AQUILA
—eye	BUCEPHALA
goldeneyes	ANATIDAE
—oriole	LORIOT, WITWALL
	WOODWALE, YELLOW-BIRD
	WOODWALL

goldfinch	GOLDSPINK, GOUDIE
	GOWDSPINK, RED-CAP
—group	CHARM, CHATTERING
	CHIRM, DRUM, TROUBLING
goosander	MERGANSER
—goosanders	ANATIDAE
goose	SADDLEBACK
gorcock	RED GROUSE
gorcrow	CARRION CROW
gorse-frequenting	WHINCHAT
grasshopper-warbler	REELER
great	
—auk	GAREFOWL, GAIRFOWL
—black-backed gull	SADDLEBACK
—northern diver	EMBER-GOOSE
—tit	OX-EYE
greater	
—shearwater	HACKBOLT, HAGBOLT
	HAGDEN, HAGDO(W)N
—spotted woodpecker	WITWALL
	WOODWALE, WOODWALL
grebe	DIVER
—grebes	PODICIPITIDAE
	PODICIPEDIFORMES
green	
—cormorant	SHAG
—finch	GREEN LINNET
—linnet	GREENFINCH
—shanks	SCOLOPACIDAE
—woodpecker	HICKWALL, WITWALL
	WOOD-SPITE, WOODWALE
	WOODWALL, YAFFLE
grey	
—duck	GADWALL, RADGE, RODGE
—lag	GOOSE
—parrot	PSITTACUS
grosbeak	HAWFINCH, PINE-FINCH
group of waterfowl	PLUMP
grouse	BLACKCOCK, BLACK GAME
	CAPERCAILLIE, CAPERCAILZIE
—female	GORHEN, GREY-HEN
—group	COVEY
—grouse	TETRAONIDAE
—male	GORCOCK
guillemot	MARROT, MURRE
	SEA-HEN, WILLOCK
—guillemots	ALCIDAE
guinea-fowl	GUINEA-HEN, PINTADO
gull	SCAURY, SEA-COB, (SEA-)MAW
	(SEA-)MEW, WAGGEL
—gulls	CHARADRIIFORMES, LARIDAE
—group	COLONY
haggard	HAWK
hareld	OLD WIFE
hatching	
—partly developed	NIDICOLOUS

—well developed	NIDIFUGOUS
having crossed	
mandibles	METAGNATHOUS
hawfinch	GROSBEAK
Hawaiian goose	NENE
hawk	BOWESS, GAVILAN
	HAGGARD, LANNER
	TARSEL, TASSEL(L)
	T(I)ERCEL(ET)
—group	CAST, LEASH
—hawks	FALCONIDAE
	FALCONIFORMES
—short-winged	GOSHAWK
heathcock	GROUSE
hedge-sparrow	DUNNOCK
	(HEDGE-)ACCENTOR
	PINNOCK, TITLING
—hedge sparrows	PRUNELLIDAE
hen	
—harrier	HEN-DRIVER
—like	GALLINACEOUS
heron	ARDEA, HERN
—group	SEDGE, SIEGE
—herons	ARDEIDAE, CICONIFORMES
—type	BOATBILL
hickwall	WOODPECKER
Himalayan pheasant	MONA(U)L
Himantopus	STILT(-PLOVER)
Hirundo	SWALLOW
hobbies	FALCONIDAE
honey	
—buzzard	PERN(IS)
—guide	INDICATOR
hooded	
—crow	HOODIE-CROW
	ROYSTON CROW
—pigeon	CAPUCHIN, JACOBIN
hoopoe	UPUPA
—hoopoes	CORACIIFORMES, UPUPIDAE
hornbills	CORACIIFORMES
humming-bird	RACKET-TAIL, COLIBRI
—group	CHARM, CHATTERING
	DRUM, TROUBLING
—humming birds	APODIFORMES
ibises	CICONIIFORMES
`	PLATALEIDAE
Iceland falcon	ICELANDER
Icterus	TROOPIAL, TROUPIAL
imaginary (Liverpool)	LIVER(BIRD)
	(*see also* fabulous)
jacinth	PIGEON
jackdaw	JACK, KAE
—jackdaws	CORVIDAE
ja(e)ger	SKUA
jar-owl	NIGHTJAR
jay	GARRULUS

—group	BAND, PARTY
—jays	CORVIDAE
Jynx	WRYNECK
kestrel	STALLION, STANN(I)EL
	STAN(N)YEL
—kestrels	FALCONIDAE
kingfisher	ALCEDO, (H)ALCYON
—kingfishers	ALCEDINIDAE
	CORACIIFORMES
kinglet	FIRE-CREST(ED WREN)
—kinglets	REGULIDAE
kite	ELANET, FORK-TAIL
	MILVUS, PUTTOCK
—kites	FALCONIDAE
kittiwake	ANNET, HACKLET, HAGLET
—kittiwakes	LARIDAE
kiwis	APTERYGIFORMES
knot	CALIDRIS
—knots	SCOLOPACIDAE
kora	GALLICREX, WATER-COCK
Lagopus	PTARMIGAN
lammergeier	OSSIFRAGE
land-rail	CORNCRAKE, RALLUS
lapwing	PE(E)WIT, PIE-WIFE, PLOVER
	TIRWIT, TEW(H)IT
—group	DECEIT, DESERT
—lapwings	CHARADRIIDAE
—Scottish	PEASEWEEP, PEESWEEP
	PEEWEE, TEUCHAT
large	
—billed bird	PELICAN
—crow	RAVEN
—duck	GOOSANDER
—gull	BLACK-BACKED GULL
	HERRING-GULL
—running birds	STRUTHIONIDAE
	STRUTHIONIFORMES
—sea-bird	NELLY
—thrush	MISSEL
largest bird	OSTRICH
Laridae	GULLS
lark	GAVILAN, LAVEROCK
—group	BEVY, EXALTATION
—larks	ALAUDIDAE
leaving nest	
—immediately	NIDIFUGOUS
—later	NIDICOLOUS
Limosa	GODWIT
linnet	
—linnets	FRINGILLIDAE
—type	REDPOLL
litch-fowl	NIGHTJAR
little	
—auk	DOVEKIE, ICE-BIRD, ROCH
	ROTCH(E), SEA-DOVE
Scottish	DOVEKIE

—auks	ALCIDAE
—grebe	DABCHICK
living birds (except the	
flightless)	CARINATES
long	
—tailed duck	HARELD, OLD WIFE
—tailed tit	MAG
—winged seabird	TERN
loon	DIVER
loriot	(GOLDEN) ORIOLE
magpie	MADGE, MAG, PIE
—group	TIDING, TITTERING
male	
—black grouse	HEATHCOCK
—duck	DRAKE
—lanner	LANNERET
—peregrine	TERCEL-GENTLE
—red grouse	GORCOCK
—redstart	WHITECAP
—sandpiper	RUFF
—sparrow-hawk	MUSKET
—swan	COB
—thrush	THROSTLE-COCK
—turkey	STAG
mallard	
—group	FLUSH, PUDDLING, SORD, SUTE
—mallards	ANATIDAE
mallemuck	FULMAR, MOLLYMAWK
Mareca	WI(D)GEON
marsh	
—bird	BITTERN
—harrier	DUCK-HAWK, MOOR-BUZZARD
martin	MARTLET
—martins	HIRUNDINIDAE
mavis	(SONG-)THRUSH, THROSTLE
meadow-pipit	ANTHUS, TIT-LARK, TITLING
Meleagris	TURKEY
merganser	DUN-DIVER, SERULA
	SAW-BILL, SMEW
—mergansers	ANATIDAE
merlin	ROCK-HAWK
—merlins	FALCONIDAE
Milvus	KITE
missel-thrush	MISTLE-THRUSH
	SCREECH-THRUSH
	STORM-COCK, WOOD-THRUSH
moa	DIORNIS
mocking birds	MIMUS
mollymawk	FULMAR, MALLEMUCK
moor	
—buzzard	DUCK-HAWK
—fowl	GROUSE
—hen	WATER-HEN
moorhens	RALLIDAE
Motacillidae	WAGTAILS
mothhawk	NIGHTJAR

moth-hunter	GOATSUCKER
Mother Carey's chicken	STORM(Y) PETREL
mountain	
—dwelling grouse	PTARMIGAN
—linnet	TWITE
mousebirds	COLIIFORMES
Muscicapa	FLYCATCHER
myna	BOAT-TAIL, GRA(C)KLE
Nettapus	GOSLET
night-hawk	GOATSUCKER, NIGHTJAR
nightingale	PHILOMEL(A), PHILOMENE
	PROGNE
—group	WATCH
—nightingales	TURDIDAE
—type	BLUEBREAST, BLUETHROAT
nightjar	CHURN-OWL, DORHAWK
	EVE-CHUR, EVEJAR, FEN-OWL
	FERN-OWL, GOAT-OWL
	GOATSUCKER, JAR-OWL
	LITCH-FOWL, MOTHHAWK
	NIGHTHAWK, PICK(ERIDGE) BIRD
	SCREECH-HAWK, WHEELBIRD
—nightjars	CAPRIMULGIDAE
	CAPRIMULGIFORMES
northern	
—falcon	GERFALCON
	GYRFALCON, JERFALCON
—freshwater duck	GADWALL
—grouse	WILLOW-GROUSE
—sea-duck	EIDER(-DUCK), GOLDEN-EYE
	HARELD, OLD WIFE
	OEDEMIA, SCOTER
Nucifraga	NUTCRACKER
Numida	GUINEA-FOWL
nut	
—cracker	NUCIFRAGA
—hatch	SITTA
nuthatches	SITTIDAE
—jobber	SITTA
—pecker	SITTA
Oedemia	NORTHERN SEA-DUCK
	SCOTER
Oenanthe	WHEATEAR
oriole	LORIOT
—orioles	ORIOLIDAE
osprey	OSSIFRAGE, PANDION
	SEA-EAGLE, SEA-HAWK
—ospreys	FALCONIDAE
ossifrage	GIANT FULMAR, LAMMERGEIER
	OSPREY, BALD EAGLE
ostriches	STRUTHIONIFORMES
oven-tit	WILLOW-WARBLER
owl	JENNY, SCOPS, STRICK
—group	PARLIAMENT, STARE
—owls	STRIGES, STRIGIDAE
	STRIGIFORMES

ox	
—bird	DUNLIN, BEEFEATER
—pecker	DUNLIN, BUFFALO-BIRD
oyster-catcher	SEA-PIE
—oyster-catchers	CHARADRIIFORMES
	HAEMATOPODIDAE
Pandion	OSPREY
parakeet	BUDGERIGAR
parrots	PSITTACIFORMES
partridge	FRANCOLIN
—group	COVEY
—partridges	PHASIANIDAE
—quail cross	PERCOLIN
Parus	TITMOUSE
Passer	SPARROW
Pavo	PEACOCK
peacock	PAVO
—group	MUSTER, OSTENTATION
pecking birds	PICARIAE
—old	RASORES
peewit	LAPWING, PLOVER
pelican	ALCATRAS
—pelicans	PELECANIFORMES
	STEGANOPODES
penguin	
—group	COLONY, ROOKERY
—penguins	SPHENISCIFORMES
perching birds	PASSERIFORMES
—old	INSESSORES, PASSERES
	PASSERINES
Perdix	PARTRIDGE
peregrine	FALCON, GENTLE
pern	HONEY-BUZZARD
petrel	ARIEL, FULMAR, NELLY
	PINTADO, PROCELLARIA
	STORM-BIRD
—petrels	PROCELLARIIDAE
	PROCELLARIIFORMES
Petronia	ROCK-SPARROW
phalaropes	PHALAROPODIDAE
pheasants	
—group	BOUQUET, NYE
—pheasants	PHASIANIDAE
philip	SPARROW
Philomachus	RUFF, REE(VE)
Pica	MAGPIE
Picidae	WOODPECKERS
pick(eridge) bird	NIGHTJAR
pie	MAGPIE
pied wagtail	WATER-WAGTAIL
pigeon	*(see separate entry)*
pink	CHAFFINCH
—footed bird	GOOSE
pinnock	BLUE TIT, HEDGE-SPARROW
pintado	CAPE PIGEON, GUINEA-FOWL
	PETREL

pintail	DAFILA, SAND-GROUSE
	SMEATH, SMEE(TH)
—pintails	ANATIDAE
piping crow	FLUTE-BIRD
pipit	ANTHUS, TITLARK
—pipits	MOTACILLIDAE
Pitta	ANT-THRUSH
Plataleidae	SPOONBILL
plover	CHARADRIUS, DOTT(E)REL
	LAPWING, PEEWIT, SURF-BIRD
—group	CONGREGATION, LEASH, WING
—like	PRATINCOLE
—plovers	CHARADRIIDAE
	CHARADRIIFORMES
pochard	SCAUP-DUCK, SEA-DUCK
	SMEATH, SMEE(TH)
—pochards	ANATIDAE
Podargus	FROGMOUTH
Podiceps	GREBE
Porphyrio	PURPLE COOT
porzana	CRAKE, WATER-RAIL
prehistoric	(see **archaeology**)
Procellaria	PETREL
Progne	NIGHTINGALE, SWALLOW
Psittacus	(GREY) PARROT
ptarmigan	LAGOPUS, RYPE
	WILLOW-GROUSE
—ptarmigans	TETRAONIDAE
Pterocles	SAND-GROUSE
puffin	FRATERCULA, SEA-PARROT
	TOM NODDY
—puffins	ALCIDAE
—Scottish	TAMMIE NORIE
Puffinus	SHEARWATER
purple coot	PORPHYRIO, SULTAN
quail	
—group	BEVY, COVEY
—quails	PHASIANIDAE
Quaker-bird	SOOTY ALBATROSS
quint-goose	BRENT-GOOSE
racket-tail	HUMMING-BIRD
rafter-bird	SPOTTED FLYCATCHER
rails	GRUIFORMES, RALLIDAE
Rallus	CORNCRAKE
	(WATER-)RAIL
rapacious bird	KITE
rare bird	RARA AVIS
raven	
—group	UNKINDNESS
—ravens	CORVIDAE
razorbill	AUK, MURRE
—razorbills	ALCIDAE
red	
—backed sandpiper	DUNLIN
—breast	RADDOCK, ROBIN
	RUDDOCK, RUBECULA
—breasted merganser	HERALD(-DUCK)
—cap	GOLDFINCH
—grouse	MOORCOCK, MOORFOWL
male	GORCOCK
—headed duck	POCHARD, POCKARD
	POKER
—legged crow	CHOUGH
—polls	FRINGILLIDAE
—shank	GAMBET, SANDPIPER
	TAT(T)LER, TOTANUS
redshanks	SCOLOPACIDAE
—start	BRANTAIL, RUTICILLA
male	WHITECAP
redstarts	TURDIDAE
—wings	TURDIDAE
reed	
—bunting	JUNCO, REED-SPARROW
—pheasant	BEARDED TITMOUSE
—sparrow	REED-BUNTING
—thrush	REED-WARBLER
—warbler	REED-THRUSH, REED-WREN
—wren	REED-WARBLER
reedling	BEARDED-TIT
reeler	GRASSHOPPER-WARBLER
Regulus	FIRECREST, GOLDCREST
rheas	RHEIFORMES
Rhyncops	SKIMMER
ring	
—dove	CUSHAT
—ousels	TURDIDAE
robin	RADDOCK, REDBREAST
	RUBECULA, RUDDOCK
—robins	TURDIDAE
rock	
—bird	PUFFIN
—hopper	CRESTED PENGUIN
—lark	ROCK-PIPIT
—pipit	ROCK-LARK, SEA-LARK
—sparrow	PETRONIA
roller	CANARY, CORACIAS, PIGEON
rooks	
—group	BUILDING, PARLIAMENT
—rooks	CORVIDAE
rose-coloured starling	PASTOR
rotche	DOVEKIE
ruddock	REDBREAST, ROBIN
ruffed grouse	HAZEL GROUSE
—female	HAZEL HEN
ruffs	SCOLOPACIDAE
running	
—bird	EM(E)U, OSTRICH
	ROAD-RUNNER
—birds	CURSORES
rype	PTARMIGAN
St Cuthbert's duck	EIDER DUCK
saddleback	GOOSE, GULL

sand	
—grouse	PINTAIL
	PTEROCLES, SYRRHAPTES
—lark	SANDPIPER
—piper	DUNLIN, GREENSHANK, KNOT
	SAND-LARK, SANDERLING
	SEA-LARK, SEA-SNIPE
	SUMMER SNIPE, SURF-BIRD
	TAT(T)LER
female	REE(VE)
male	RUFF
sanderling	SANDPIPER
—sanderlings	CHARADRIIFORMES
	SCOLOPACIDAE
Saxicola	STONECHAT, WHEATEAR
	WHINCHAT
scaup(-duck)	POCHARD
scissor-bill	SKIMMER
Scolopax	WOODCOCK
Scops	OWL
scoter	NORTHERN SEA-DUCK
	OEDEMIA, SURF-DUCK, WHILK
—scoters	ANATIDAE
scraping birds	RASORES
scray(e)	TERN
screamers	ANSERIFORMES
screech	
—hawk	NIGHTJAR
—martin	SWIFT
—owl	BARN-OWL, LICH-OWL
	SHRIEK-OWL
—thrush	MISSEL-THRUSH
	MISTLE THRUSH
screecher	SWIFT
sea	
—auks	ALCA
—bar	TERN
—bird	TARROCK
—cob	SEAGULL
—crow	SKUA
—dotterel	TURNSTONE
—dove	ICE-BIRD, LITTLE AUK
—duck	POCHARD
—eagle	ERNE, OSPREY
—gull	SEA-COB, (SEA-)MAW
	(SEA-)MEW
—hawk	OSPREY, SKUA
—hen	GUILLEMOT
—lark	ROCK-PIPIT, SANDPIPER
—maw	GULL, SEA-MEW
—mew	GULL, SEA-MAW
—parrot	PUFFIN
—pie	OYSTER-CATCHER
—quail	TURNSTONE
—snipe	SANDPIPER
—swallow	STORM PETREL, TERN

—turtle	BLACK GUILLEMOT
secretary-bird	SERPENT-EATER
—secretary birds	FALCONIFORMES
sedge	
—bird	SEDGE-WARBLER, SEDGE-WREN
—warbler	REED-SPARROW
serin	CANARY
serpent-eater	SECRETARY-BIRD
shag	GREEN CORMORANT
—shags	PHALACROCORACIDAE
shearwater	HACKLET, HAGLET
	PUFFINUS
—shearwaters	PROCELLARIIDAE
	PROCELLARIIFORMES
shel(l)duck	BARGOOSE, TADORNA
sheldrake	BERGANDER, BURROW-DUCK
—group	DOPPING
shell-parrot	BUDGERIGAR
shoebills	CICONIIFORMES
shore bird	SAND-LARK
short-winged hawk	GOSHAWK
shovel(l)er	SPATULA
—shovelers	ANATIDAE
shrike	BUTCHER-BIRD, WOOD-CHAT
—shrikes	LANIIDAE
siskin	ABERDEVINE, TARIN
—siskins	FRINGILLIDAE
Sitta	NUTHATCH, NUTJOBBER
	NUTPECKER
skimmer	RHYNCOPS, SCAUP(-DUCK)
	SCISSOR-BILL
—skimmers	CHARADRIIFORMES
skua	BOATSWAIN, BONXIE, BOS(U)N
	JA(E)GER, SEA-CROW, SEA-HAWK
	STERCORARIUS
—skuas	CHARADRIIFORMES
	STERCORARIIDAE
skylark	ALAUDA
small	
—canary	SERIN
—crested heron	SQUACCO
—curlew	W(H)IMBREL
—falcon	HOBBY, KESTREL, MERLIN
—parrot	LOVE-BIRD, PAR(R)AKEET
—partridge	QUAIL
—sandpiper	DUNLIN, STINT
—sea-bird	MURRELET
—snipe	JACK SNIPE
smallest	FIRECREST, GOLDCREST
—web-footed	STORM(Y) PETREL
smew	MERGANSER, SMEATH
	SMEE(TH)
snake-bird	DARTER, WRYNECK
snipe	CAPELLA, GALINAGO
	JEDCOCK, MIRE-SNIPE
—group	WALK, WHISPER, WISP

—snipe	CHARADRIIFORMES
	SCOLOPACIDAE
—type	PAINTED SNIPE
snow	
—bunting	SNOWFLAKE, SNOWFLECK
	SNOWFLICK
	WAV(E)Y
—goose	GANNET
solan(d)	EIDER DUCK
Somateria	
song	
—birds	OSCINES
—thrush	MAVIS, THROSTLE
sooty	
—albatross	QUAKER-BIRD
—tern	EGG-BIRD
sparrow	PASSER, PHILIP, SP(R)UG
—group	HOST, QUARREL, TRIBE
—sparrows	PLOCEIDAE
sparrow-hawk	ACCIPITER
sparrow-like	HEDGE-WARBLER
Spatula	SHOVEL(L)ER
spoonbill	PLATALEIDAE
—spoonbills	CICONIIFORMES
	PLATALEIDAE
spotted flycatcher	RAFTER-BIRD
sprug	SPARROW
spug	SPARROW
squacco	CRESTED HERON
starling	STURNUS
—group	MURMURATION
—starlings	STURNIDAE
Stercorarius	SKUA
stilt(-plover)	HIMANTOPUS
—stilts	RECURVIROSTRIDAE
stint	DUNLIN
stone	
—chat	STONE-CHATTER
stonechats	TURDIDAE
—curlew	STONE-PLOVER
	THICK-KNEE
stone curlews	BURHINIDAE
—hawk	FALSON
stork	CICONIA
—storks	CICONIIFORMES
storm	
—bird	PETREL
—cock	MISSEL-THRUSH
—petrel	MOTHER CAREY'S CHICKEN
	MOTHER CAREY'S GOOSE
	SEA-SWALLOW
Strepsilas	ARENARIA, TURNSTONE
Streptopelia	TURTLE-DOVE, TURTUR
stupid	NODDY
Sturnus	STARLING
Sulidae	GANNETS
sultan	PURPLE COOT

summer	
—snipe	SANDPIPER
—teal	GARGANEY
—visitor	WHEATEAR
—warbler	YELLOW-BIRD
swallow	ARIEL, HIRUNDO, PROCNE
—swallows	HIRUNDINIDAE
swallow-like	MARTIN(ET)
swallow-tailed	KITE
swan	CYGNUS, MUTE, WHOOPER
	WHOOPING-SWAN
—female	PEN
—goose	CHINA GOOSE
—group	BANK, BEVY, GAME, HEAD
	SQUADRON, WEDGE, WHITENESS
—male	COB
—swans	ANATIDAE, ANSERIFORMES
—young	CYGNET
swart-back	BLACK-BACKED GULL
swift	APUS, CYPSELUS
	SCREECHER
	SCREECH-MARTIN, SENEX
—swifts	APODIDAE, APODIFORMES
swiftlet	COLLOCALIA
Sylvia	WARBLER
Syrrhaptes	SAND-GROUSE
Tadorna	SHEL(L)DUCK, SHIELDUCK
Tantalus	WOOD-IBIS
tat(t)ler	REDSHANK, SANDPIPER
	WOOD-SANDPIPER, TOTANUS
tawny owl	BROWN OWL, GREY OWL
teal	ANAS
—group	COIL, KNOB, RAFT, SPRING
—teal	ANATIDAE
tern	KIP(P), SCRAY(E), EGG-BIRD
	SEA-BAR, SEA-SWALLOW
—terns	CHARADRIIFORMES, LARIDAE
thick-knee	STONE-CURLEW
	STONE-PLOVER
throstle	MAVIS, (SONG-)THRUSH
thrush	BABBLER, MAVIS
	THROSTLE, TURDUS
—group	MUTATION
—thrushes	TURDIDAE
—type	FIELDFARE, REDWING
	RING OUSEL
tinamous	TINAMIFORMES
titlark	PIPIT
titling	HEDGE-SPARROW
	MEADOW-PIPIT
titmouse	PARUS
—titmice/tits	PARIDAE
Tom Noddy	PUFFIN
tomtit	BLUE-TIT, PINNOCK
Totanus	REDSHANK, SANDPIPER
	TAT(T)LER

toucan	ARIEL	—ousel	DIPPER
—toucans	PICIFORMES	water ousels	CINCLIDAE
trained falcon	GENTLE	—rail	DARCOCK, PORZANA, RALLUS
tree-creeper	CERTHIA	—wagtail	PIED WAGTAIL
—tree-creepers	CERTHIDAE	wax	
Trochilus	CROCODILE-BIRD	—bill	WEAVER-BIRD
Troglodytes	WREN	—wing	BOMBYCILLA, CHATTERER
trogons	TROGONIFORMES	waxwings	BOMBYCILLIDAE
troopial	ICTERUS	weaver-bird	BISHOP-BIRD, WAX-BILL
tropic-bird	BOATSWAIN-BIRD	web-footed	PALMIPED(E)
trumpeters	GRUIFORMES	whaup (Scot.)	CURLEW
tumbler pigeon	ROLLER	wheat	
Turdus	BLACKBIRD, FIELDFARE	—bird	CHAFFINCH
	RING OUSEL, THRUSH	—ear	OENANTHE
turkey-buzzard	GALLINAZO	wheatears	TURDIDAE
turkeys - group	DOLE, DULE, FLOCK	wheelbird	NIGHTJAR
	RAFTER, RUFFLE	whimbrel	
turnstone	ARENARIA, STREPSILAS	—Scottish	LITTLE WHAUP
	SEA-DOTTEREL	—whimbrels	SCOLOPACIDAE
—turnstones	CHARADRIIDAE	whinchats	TURDIDAE
turtle-dove	STREPTOPELIA, TURTUR	white	
Turtur	STREPTOPELIA, TURTLE-DOVE	—gerfalcon	ICELAND FALCON
twite	MOUNTAIN LINNET	—heron	EGRET
—twites	FRINGILLIDAE	—owl	SNOWY OWL
umbrella	DRAGOON-BIRD	—throat	BEARDIE, PEGGY
unfledged		whitethroats	SYLVIIDAE
—hawk	EYAS	—throated thrush	RING-OUZEL
—male hawk	EYAS-MUSKET	whooper	SWAN
untamed hawk	HAGGARD	wi(d)geon	ANAS, MARECA, SMEATH
Upupa	HOOPOE		SMEE(TH), WHEWER
Uria	GUILLEMOT	—group	BUNCH, COIL, COMPANY, KNOB
variegated duck	HARLEQUIN DUCK	—wi(d)geons	ANATIDAE
velvet-duck	VELVET-SCOTER	wild	
vulture	GRIPE	—duck	BALDPATE, MALLARD
—bearded	LAMMERGEIER	group	PLUMP
	LAMMERGEYER	—pigeon	ROCK-DOVE, ROCK-PIGEON
—European	GRIFFON VULTURE	willow	
—French	BOULDRAS	—grouse	PTARMIGAN
—North American	TURKEY-BUZZARD	—warbler	OVEN-TIT, WILLOW-WREN
—South American	CONDOR		WOOD-WREN
—vultures	FALCONIFORMES	—wren	WILLOW-WARBLER
wading		wisp	SNIPE
—bird	IBIS, KNOT, PHALAROPE	witwall	WOODPECKER
—birds	GRALLAE, GRALLATORES	wood	
	SCORPUS	—chat	SHRIKE, WOODPECKER
wagtail	MOLLY, SEED-BIRD, TROTTY	—cock	SCOLOPAX
—group	WALK	group	CALL, FALL, PLUMP
—wagtails	MOTACILLIDAE	woodcocks	SCOLOPACIDAE
warbler	FAUVETTE, PEGGY	—grouse	CAPERCAILLIE, CAPERCAILZIE
	PETTICHAPS, PETTY-CHAPS	—ibis	TANTALUS
	SYLVIA	—owl	BROWN OWL
—warblers	SYLVIIDAE	—pecker	AWL-BIRD, HICKWALL
water			WHETTLE, WITWALL, WOODCHAT
—bird	COOT, MOORHEN		WOODWALE, WOODWALL, YAFFLE
—cock	GALLICREX, KORA	woodpeckers	PICARIAE, PICIDAE
—hen	MOORHEN		PICIFORMES

—pigeon	CULVER, CUSHAT
	QUINCE(TY-COCK)
—sandpiper	TAT(T)LER
—spite	GREEN WOODPECKER
—thrush	MISSEL-THRUSH
—wale	(GREEN) WOODPECKER
—wren	WILLOW-WARBLER
	WOOD-WARBLER
wren	BUMBARREL, TROGLODYTES
—wrens	TROGLODYTIDAE
wryneck	DARTER, JYNX, SNAKE-BIRD
yaffle	GREEN WOODPECKER
yaup	BLUE TIT
yellow	
—bunting	YELLOW-HAMMER, YITE
—hammer	SCRIBBLING-SCHOOLMASTER
	YELDRIN, YELDROCK
	YELLOW-BUNTING, YELLOW-YITE
	YOLDRING, YORLING, YOWLEY
	ZIVOLA
—willow-warbler	WOOD-WARBLER
yellowish-green finch	SISKIN
yite	YELLOW BUNTING
young	BRANCHER, NESTLING, PEEPER
—black grouse	HEATH-POULT
—goose	GOSLING, GREEN GOOSE
—gull	SCAURY
—hawk	EYAS(-MUSKET)
—hen	PULLET
—heron	HERONSEW, HER(O)NSHAW
—owl	(H)OWLET
—partridge	FLAPPER
—wild duck	FLAPPER
zebra-par(r)akeet	BUDGERIGAR
zivola	YELLOW-HAMMER

biscuits

almond-flavoured	MACAROON, RATAFIA
American	(BOSTON)BROWNIE
	COOKIE, COOKY
	CRACKER
bread baked crisp	RUSK
brittle	SHORTBREAD, SNAP
caraway	ABERNETHY
chocolate	
—flavoured	BOURBON
—nuts and fruit	FLORENTINE
circular semi-sweet	DIGESTIVE
coconut	MACAROON
coffee-flavoured	COFFEE KISSES
Cornish	CORNISH FAIRINGS
cracker	COSAQUE
—salted	SALTINE
—unsweetened	WATER BISCUIT
crisp	
—cheese biscuit	(CREAM) CRACKER
—salted	PRETZEL
—sweet	SHORTBREAD, SHORTCAKE
currant	GARIBALDI
dry, unsweetened	CRACKER, CRACKNEL
	CRISPBREAD
finger-shaped	LANGUE-DE-CHAT
ginger	
—cylindrical	BRANDY SNAP
—flat	(GRANTHAM)GINGERBREAD
	GINGERNUT, GINGERSNAP
hard	BROWN GEORGE
—unflavoured	HARDTACK
	SHIP('S) BISCUIT
Italian	AMARETTI
knot-shaped	PRETZEL
made with sour milk	SODA BISCUIT
marzipan	PETIT FOURS
nuts	FLORENTINES, NUT ROCK
oatmeal	
—Scottish	FARL(E), OATCAKE
—and syrup	FLAPJACK
plain	OSBORNE
ship's biscuit	HARDTACK, SEA BISCUIT
small, fancy	PETIT FOUR
South African	SOETKOEKIE
spiced (US)	HERMIT
sweet	NICE, SHORTBREAD
	SHORTCAKE
—US	GRAHAM CRACKER
thin crisp ring	JUMBLE, JUMBAL
unsweetened	BATH OLIVER
with printed motto	FORTUNE COOKIE
blood	(*see* **circulation**)

boats

admiral's boat	BARGE
Annamese	GAY-YOU
barge	GABBARD, GABBART
bark-covered	CANOE
canal boat	BARGE, FLY(-BOAT)
	LONGBOAT, NARROWBOAT
Chinese	JUNK, SAMPAN, SANPAN
collapsible	BERTHON-BOAT
—rubber boat	DINGEY, DING(H)Y
coracle	GOPHER
Eskimo	KAYAK, UMIAK
Eton oarsman	WET BOB
fisherman's	COB(B)LE, CORACLE
flat-bottomed	MACKINAW, PUNT
fulcrum for oar	ROLLOCK, ROWLOCK
	RULLOCK
gopher	CORACLE
having	
—1 hull	MONOHULL
—2 banks of oars	BIREME
—2 hulls	CATAMARAN
—3 banks of oars	TRIREME
—3 hulls	TRIMARAN

—3 oars	RANDAN	—tender	PINNACE
—4 banks of oars	QUADRIREME	Welsh	CORACLE
—5 banks of oars	QUINQUEREME	with strakes	
—5 oars	WHALER	—abutting	CARVEL-BUILT
—8 oars	PINNACE	—overlapping	CLINKER-BUILT
—30 oars	TRIACONTER	**Bolivia**	BOL
—50 oars	PENTACONTER	capital	LA PAZ
hollowed tree-trunk	DUGOUT (CANOE)	coins	
	MONOXYLON	—unit	CENTAVO
Indian		—100 centavos	DOLLAR
—Ganges	PULWAR	measure	CELEMIN, LEAGUE
—surf-boat	MASOOLAH, MASSOOLA	musical instrument	CHARANGA
	MASULA	ruminant	LLAMA, VICUNA
Irish	CURRACH, CURRAGH	weight	LIBRA
Italian	BARCA, GONDOLA	**bone**	OS
light rowing-boat	GIG, SHELL, WHERRY	abnormal outgrowth	OUTGROWTH
Malayan	COROCORE, COROCORO	ankle	ASTRAGALUS, TALUS
	PRA(H)U, PROA	back	
Maldives	DHONI	—bone	SPINAL COLUMN
Maltese	DGHAJSA		VERTEBRAL COLUMN
motor-powered	POWERBOAT, SPEEDBOAT	—of skull	OCCIPUT
motors	INBOARD, OUTBOARD	basis of bone	OSSEIN
open rowing-boat	GALLEY	become bone	OSSIFY
pin retaining oar	THOLE(-PIN), THOW(E)L	beneath the tail (fish)	HYPURAL BONE
pointed at both ends	WHALER	bone-destroying cell	OSTEOBLAST
propelled by		bone-formation	OSTEOGENESIS
—pedals	PEDALO		OSTEOGENY
—pole	PUNT	bone-forming	
punt pole	QUANT	—cell	OSTEOBLAST
race meeting	REGATTA	—material	CARTILAGE
racing boat	OUTRIGGER, SHELL	bone-marrow	MEDULLA
Red Indian	(BIRCH-BARK) CANOE	—cell	ERYTHROBLAST
rowing with odd		bone(s) in	
number of oars	CUT-THROAT ROWING	—ankle	ASTRALAGUS, MALLEOLUS
Scottish	COB(B)LE		TALUS
ship's boat	BARGE, CUTTER, JOLLYBOAT	—back	LUMBAR VERTEBRA(E)
	LAUNCH, WHALER	—bottom of spine	COCCYX
side plank	STRAKE, STRAIK	—chest	(EPI)STERNUM
skiff of galley	CAIQUE		(INTER)CLAVICLE
skin-covered	CANOE, CORACLE, CURRACH		MANUBRIUM, PECTORAL GIRDLE
	CURRAGH, KAYAK, UMIAK		PRESTERNUM, RIBS, STERNUM
small rowing-boat	DINGEY, DING(H)Y		THORACIC VERTEBRA(E)
	GIG, PINNACE, SCULL(ER)		XIPHISTERNUM
	SHALLOP, SKIFF	—chin	MENTAL PROMINENCE
South American		—ear	AUDITORY OSSICLE, INCUS
dugout canoe	PERIAGUA, PIRAGUA		MALLEUS, PERIOTIC, STAPES
	PIROGUE	birds, reptiles	COLUMELLA AURIS
state barge	GALLEY-FOIST	—elbow	FUNNY BONE, OLECRANON
Turkish skiff	CAIQUE	—embryo	DERMAL BONE
used			MEMBRANE BONE
—in loading etc	LIGHTER	—foot	CALCANEUM, CUBOID
—on the Bosporus	CAIQUE		CUNEIFORM, (META)TARSALS
—to bring fruit etc to ship	BUM-BOAT		NAVICULAR, PHALANGES
Venetian	GONDOLA		TALUS, TARSUS
warship's		—forearm	RADIUS, ULNA
—second boat	BARGE	—foreleg of horse	METACARPUS

—hand and wrist	CAPITATE, CARPUS
	HAMATE, LUNAE, (META)CARPALS
	NAVICULAR, PHALANGES
	PISIFORM, RADIALE
	SCAPHOID, TRAPEZIUM
	TRIQUETAL, ULNARE
—head	BREGMA(TA), CHEEKBONE
	CRANIUM, ETHMOID, FRONTAL
	JUGAL, LACRIMAL, MALAR
	MANDIBLE, MASTOID PROCESS
	MAXILLA, OCCIPITAL
	PALATINE, PARAQUADRATE
	(PARA)SPHENOID, PARIETAL
	SKULL, SQUAMOSAL, TEMPORAL
	TRIQUETRUM, VOMER
	WORMIAN, ZYGOMA(TIC)
	(*see also* skull *below*)
—hip	HIP GIRDLE, ILIUM
	INOMINATE, ISCHIUM
	PELVIC GIRDLE, PELVIS, PUBIS
—hoof of horse	COFFIN BONE, PEDAL BONE
—hyoid arch (fish)	HYOMANDIBULA
—jaw	ARTICULAR, DENTARY
	MANDIBLE, (PRE)MAXILLA
	PTERYGOID, QUADRATE
—knee	KNEE-CAP, KNEE-PAN
	PATELLA, ROTULA
—lower leg	FIBULA, PERONE, TIBIA
—neck	CERVICAL VERTEBRA(E)
—nose	ETHMOID, NASAL(CONCHAE)
	PINNA
—pelvis	ILIUM, INNOMINATE BONE
	ISCHIUM, PUBIS, SACRUM
—shoulder	CORACOID, SCAPULA
—spine	VERTEBRA(E)
—tail of bird	PYGOSTYLE
—tendon	SESAMOID BONE
—thigh	FEMUR
—tongue (base)	HYOID
—upper arm	HUMERUS
—wing of bird	CARPOMETACARPUS
bone-store	OSSARIUM, OSSUARY
bony	
—fishes	OSTEICHTHYES
	OSTEOGLOSSIDAE
—outgrowth	OSTEOPHYTE
—plate	OSTEODERM, PLACOID
bottom of spine	COCCYX
breaking bone in surgery	OSTEOCLASIS
breastbone	STERNUM
—of bird	WISHBONE
brittleness of bones	OSTEOPOROSIS
cartilage of ribs	TENDRON
cartilaginous skull	CHONDROCRANIUM
cavity in	
—jawbone	ALVEOLUS

—skull bones	SINUS
for eye	ORBIT
cell	
—destroying bone	OSTEOCLAST
—producing bone	OSTEOBLAST
changing to bone	OSSIFICATION
channel in bone	HAVERSIAN CANAL
collarbone	CLAVICLE
connection of bones by	
—cartilage	SYNCHONDROSIS
—ligaments	SYNDESMOSIS
—muscle	SYSSARCOSIS
—tendons	SYNTENOSIS
container for bones	OSSUARY
cutting of bone	OSTEOTOMY
cuttle bone	SEPIOST(AIRE), SEPIUM
decay of bone	CARIES
dermal plate	OSTEODERM
description of bones	OSTEOGRAPHY
diseases of bones	(*see* **disease**)
dorsal process of vertebra	DIAPOPHYSIS
eating bones	OSSIVOROUS
fibula	PERONE
flat and winglike	ALA
fluid in joints	SINOVIA
forepart of skull	SINCIPUT
formation of bone	OSSIFICATION
	OSTEOGENESIS, OSTEOGENY
fracture	OSTEOCLASIS
—clean break	SIMPLE
—with bone(s)	
crushed	COMMINUTED
exposed	COMPOUND
forced together	IMPACTED
split	GREENSTICK
funny bone	OLECRANON
fusion of bones	SYMPHYSIS
	SYNOSTOSIS
gap between bones	FONTANEL(LE)
gill-cover bone (fish)	SUBOPERCULUM
head of bone turning in socket	WHIRL-BONE
heel	CALCANEUS
hip	
—girdle	PELVIC GIRDLE
—joint	COXA
—socket	ACETABULUM
holding teeth	ALVEOLAR ARCH
	DENTARY, (PRE)MAXILLA
hole in bone	FORAMEN
hollow in bone	ANTRUM, FOSSA
	FOVEA
jawbone	
—lower	MAXILLA
—upper	MANDIBLE
joint	
—moving in one plane	GINGLYMUS

—with one bone in
   groove of another   SCHINDYLESIS
junction of bone   SUTURE
kneecap   PATELLA, WHIRL-BONE
knob on end of bone   CONDYLE
  —in socket   WHIRL-BONE
little bone   OSSICLE
loss of calcium   OSTEOPOROSIS
lowest part of spine   COCCYX
manipulation of bones   CHIROPRACTIC
                    OSTEOPATHY
membrane covering bone   PERIOSTEUM
movement of joint   ARTICULATION
neural arch (snakes)   ZYGANTRUM
                 ZYGOSPHENE
part of
  —bone having its own
     ossification centre   EPIPHYSIS
  —sternum   MANUBRIUM
  —temporal bone   SQUAMOSAL
  —vertebra   CENTRUM, DIAPHYSIS
                NEURAL ARCH
              NEURAL SPINE
plate for closing skull   OPERCULUM
projecting part   PROCESS
projection on
  —axis   ODONTOID PROCESS
  —breastbone (birds)   CARINA, KEEL
  —end of bone   CONDYLE
  —hip girdle   PUBIS
  —scapula ACROMION, ACROMIUM
  —skull   BULLA, OCCIPITAL CONDYLE
  —thigh   TROCHANTER
  —ulna   OLECRANON
  —vertebra   PLEUROPOPHYSIS
rib   COSTA, PLEUROPOPHYSIS
segment(s) of
  —breastbone   STERNEBRA(E)
  —spine   VERTEBRA(E)
shaft of long bone   DIAPHYSIS
shin   TIBIA
shoulder
  —blade   SCAPULA
  —girdle   PECTORAL GIRDLE
  —point   ACROMION
skeletal
  —bars (fish)   BRANCHIAL ARCH
          HYOID ARCH
    MANDIBULAR ARCH
      VISCERAL ARCH
  —element   SCLERE
  —plate   SCLERITE
  —rod   NOTOCHORD
  —tissue CARTILAGE, SCLERENCHYMA
skeleton
  —external   EXOSKELETON

—internal   ENDOSKELETON
skull
  —brain and ear   NEUROCRANIUM
  —cavity for eyeball   ORBIT
  —enclosing ear AUDITORY CAPSULE
  —forepart   SINCIPUT
  —in embryo CHONDROCRANIUM
  —jaws SPLANCHNOCRANIUM
  —knob at back OCCIPITAL CONDYLE
  —membrane bone   SQUAMOSAL
  —plate for closing OPERCULUM
  —projecting part round ear BULLA
  —rear part   OCCIPUT
small bone   OSSICLE
  —in sea-urchin   EPIPHYSIS
socket receiving head of
  —femur   GLENOID CAVITY
  —humerus   ACETABULUM
soft tissue in bone cavity   MARROW
softening of bones OSTEOMALACIA
spine   SPINAL COLUMN
   VERTEBRAL COLUMN
  —bottom section   COCCYX
  —section(s)   VERTEBRA(E)
spiny process of temporal bone STYLOID
study of bones   OSTEOLOGY
surgery on bones OSTEOPLASTY
   OSTEOTOMY
thin layer of bone   LAMELLA
tumour of bone   OSTEOMA
union of bones   SYNOSTOSIS
vertebra   SPONDYL
vertebrae
  —first   ATLAS
  —second   AXIS
  —situated in
    chest THORACIC VERTEBRAE
    hip region SACRAL VERTEBRAE
    neck CERVICAL VERTEBRAE
    waist region LUMBAR VERTEBRAE
  —supporting skull ATLAS, AXIS
whalebone   BALEEN
wishbone FOURCHETTE, FURCULA
with cartilage precursor CARTILAGE BONE
   REPLACING BONE
without cartilage
  precursor   DERMAL BONE
wrist   CARPUS
yoke-piece of vertebra ZYGAPOPHYSIS

books
additional material   ADDENDUM
   APPENDIX
annual   ALMANAC(K)
author's early   JUVENILIA
bible
  —Chaldean   TARGUM

—Christian	
earliest gospel	
translation	LINDISFARNE GOSPELS
first five books	PENTATEUCH
first seven books	HEPTATEUCH
in four versions	TETRAPLA
versions	AMERICAN STANDARD
	AUTHORISED, BISHOP'S
	BREECHES, COVERDALE'S
	GENEVA, GOOD NEWS
	GREAT, JERUSALEM
	KING JAMES'S, MASSACHUSETTS
	MATTHEW'S, NEW ENGLAND
	REVISED, RHEIMS AND DOUAI
	TAVERNER'S, TYNDALE'S
—Hebrew	T(H)ORAH
—Latin translation	VULGATE
—Moslem	ALCORAN, (AL)KORAN
	QORAN, QURAN
—Syrian	PESHIT(T)A, PESHIT(T)O
blank leaf in book	FLYLEAF
book	
—binder	BIBLIOPEGIST
—hater	BIBLIOPHOBE
—lover	BIBLIOMANIAC, BIBLIOPHILE
—seller	BIBLIOPOLE
bookmaker's book of bets	HANDBOOK
brief description	BLURB
cased book	HARDBACK
catalogue of books	BIBLIOTHECA
censor's permission to publish	NIHIL OBSTAT
cheap novel	PAPERBACK, PULP
church rules	PIE, PYE
collection of	
— bible readings	LEGEND
—church lessons	LECTIONARY
—cuttings	SCRAPBOOK
—formulae	FORMULARY
—homilies	POSTIL
—hymns	HYMNAL
—learned papers	FESTSCHRIFT
—lessons	LECTIONARY
—maps	ATLAS
—plants	HERBAL
—prayers	MASS BOOK
—precedents	FORMULARY
—psalms	PSALTER
—related subjects	OMNIBUS
—rituals	FORMULARY
—words	DICTIONARY, GLOSSARY
	LEXICON, THESAURUS
—writings	ANTHOLOGY, OMNIBUS
complete condensed treatise	COMPENDIUM
comprehensive book of	
reference	(EN)CYCLOPAEDIA
	PANDECT

condensed treatise	COMPENDIUM
correct use of language	GRAMMAR
corrections	CORRIGENDA, ERRATA
dates	ALMANAC, CALENDAR
day-book	DIARY, JOURNAL
dealing with	
—earlier events	PREQUEL
—later events	SEQUEL
detective story	ROMAN POLICIER
	WHODUNNIT
diary	JOURNAL INTIME
dictionary of	
—derivations	ETYMOLOGICON
—names	ONOMASTICON
displaying photographs, etc	ALBUM
drugs	DISPENSATORY
	FORMULARY, HERBAL
	MIMS, PHARMACOPOEIA
early illustrated book	BLOCK-BOOK
early printed book	INCUNABULA
exercise book	CAHIER
fiction	NOVEL
financial	JOURNAL, LEDGER
first textbook	HORNBOOK, PRIMER
flowers	CYBELE, FLORA
form of publication	EDITION
formal study	TREATISE
geographical index	GAZETTEER
grammar	DONAT, DONET
guide book	BAEDEKER
handbook	VADE MECUM
handwritten	MANUSCRIPT
having sheets folded into	
—8 leaves	OCTAVO
—12 leaves	DUODECIMO
—16 leaves	SEXTODECIMO, SIXTEENMO
—18 leaves	OCTODECIMO, EIGHTEENMO
heraldry	ARMORIAL
illustration at front of	
book	FRONTISPIECE
Indian book of sayings	SUTRA
introductory piece	FOREWORD, PREFACE
large book	TOME
left-hand page	VERSO
licence to print or publish	IMPRIMATUR
librarian	BIBLIOTHECARY
library	BIBLIOTHECA
list of	
—baronets	BARONETAGE
—books	BIBLIOGRAPHY
	BIBLIOTHECA
—clergy	CROCKFORD'S
—goods	CATALOGUE
—important people	WHO'S WHO
—peers	BURKE'S PEERAGE
—train times	BRADSHAW

—words and meanings	DICTIONARY	reference book	(EN)CYCLOPEDIA
	GLOSSARY, LEXICON		TEXTBOOK, TOME
	THESAURUS		TREATISE, VADE MECUM
magazine	JOURNAL	, —on heraldry	ORDINARY
manual	ENCH(E)IRIDION	register	CARTULARY
	HANDBOOK, TEXTBOOK	religious instruction	CATECHISM
manuscript volume	CODEX	repository for books	BIBLIOTHECA
medieval			LIBRARY
—before 1501	INCUNABLE, INCUNABULUM	right-hand page of book	RECTO
—on		Roman law digest	PANDECT
alchemy	ALMAGEST	rule book	ORDINAND
animals	BESTIARY	scriptures	(*see* bible *above*)
mixed fact and fiction	FACTION	section of book	
navigator's manual	PORTOLANO	published separately	FASCIC(U)LE
New Testament books			FASCICULUS
—originally not accepted	ANTILOGOMENA	selections for beginners	CHRESTOMATHY
—taken as authentic	HOMOLOG(O)UMENA	sequence of events	CHRONICLE
notebook	COMMONPLACE BOOK	service-book	TE IGITUR
novel		small book	BOOKLET, DUODECIMO
—about successive			MONOGRAPH, PAMPHLET
generations	ROMAN FLEUVE		SEXTODECIMO, SIXTEENMO
—short	NOVELLA	stamp book	ALBUM
—with		study of books	BIBLIOGRAPHY
a theme	ROMAN A THESE		BIBLIOLOGY
disguised names	ROMAN A CLEF	summary of contents	PRECIS, SYNOPSIS
number of copies at one printing	EDITION	surplus book	REMAINDER
Old Testament	HAGIOGRAPHA	text	
—Greek	SEPTUAGINT	—of oper(ett)a	LIBRETTO
one of a series	VOLUME	—with notes of editors	VARIORUM
page pasted to cover	END-PAPER	travel guide	BAEDEKER
parliamentary		treatise	
—proceedings	HANSARD	—on ecclesiastical	
—report	BLUE BOOK	festivals	FESTILOGY, FESTOLOGY
part of book published in		—political or religious	TRACT
—instalments	HEFT	two pages of open book	SPREAD
—volumes	LIVRAISON	typed	TYPESCRIPT
periodical	JOURNAL, MAGAZINE	with	
personal book	COMMONPLACE BOOK	—editorial annotations	VARIORUM
	DIARY, JOURNAL, SCRAPBOOK	—soft covers	PAPERBACK
pocket companion	VADE MECUM	—stiff covers	HARDBACK
popular book or		written in author's own hand	HOLOGRAPH
pamphlet	CHAPBOOK		(*see also* **literature**)
prayer book	BREVIARY, EUCHOLOGION	**botany**	(*see* **biology**)
	EUCHOLOGY, FORMULARY	**Botswana**	RB
	MISSAL, ORARIUM	capital	GABARONE
—Hebrew	MA(C)HZOR, SIDDUR	coin	
primer	DONAT, DONE	—unit	PULA
printed by Caxton	CAXTON	—100 pula	THEBE
promotional material	BLURB, FLYER	former name	BECHUANALAND
prophetic	SIBYLLINE	**bottle**	
Psalms	PSALTER	American - dark glass	JUNK-BOTTLE
quickly written book	POTBOILER	Australian - small	STUBBY
record of proceedings of		eared bottle	COSTREL
—meetings	MINUTE(BOOK)	empty	DEAD MAN
—parliament	HANSARD	Franconian	BOCKSBEUTEL
records	ANNALS, JOURNAL	Greek	AMPHORA, LEKYTHOS

Italian	FIASCO
large bottle	FLAGON, DEMIJOHN
	(*see also* **measures**-capacity)
leather	JACK
narrow-necked	LAGEN(A), LEKYTHOS
pilgrim's bottle	AMPULLA, COSTREL
quarter-bottle	SPLIT
Roman	AMPHORA, AMPULLA
small bottle	CRUSE, FLACON, PHIAL
	SPLIT, STUBBY, VIAL
	VINAIGRETTE
tear-bottle	LACRIMAL URN
	LACR(H)YMAL URN
used for growing plants	TERRARIUM
water bottle	CARAFE
whisky bottle	AULD KIRK
wine bottle	CARAFE
—with descending spout	PORRON

bowls

area of green	RINK
captain	SKIP
part of team	RINK
players	
—Australian	PARELLA, SCHUBACK
—English (m)	ALLCOCK, BRYANT
	HEPPELL, SEKJER, SMITH
(f)	LINE
—Northern Irish	BAKER, CORKILL
(f)	JOHNSTON
—Scottish (m)	CORSIE, DICKINSON
	THOMSON, WOOD
(f)	MCCRONE
—Welsh (m)	PRICE, THOMAS, WEALE
(f)	ACKLAND
session of play	END
target	JACK

boxing

arena	RING
attendant	SECOND
boundaries of ring	ROPES
boxers	
—American	ALI, ARMSTRONG, BAER
	BAKSI, BERBICK, BRADDOCK
	CHARLES, CLAY, CONN, CORBETT
	CURRY, DEMPSEY, DOKES, FOREMAN
	FOSTER, FRAZIER, FULLMER
	GRAZIANO, GREB, HAGLER
	HEARNS, HOLMES, JOHNSON, KETCHEL
	LA MOTTA, LEONARD, LESNEVICH
	LEVINSY, LEWIS, LISTON, LOUGHRAN
	LOUIS, MARCIANO, MAXIM, MOORE
	NORTON, NOVA, OLIN, PAGE
	PASTRANO, PATTERSON, PENDER
	PEP, QUARRY, ROBINSON, ROSENBLOOM
	SADLER, SAVOLD, SHARKEY, SMITH
	SPINKS, STRIBLING, SULLIVAN

	THOMAS, TUNNEY, TYSON, WALCOTT
	WEAVER, WILLARD, ZALE
—British	BECKETT, BERG, BODELL, BOON
	BRUNO, BUGNER, BYGRAVES
	COCKELL, CONTEH, COOPER
	CRAWLEY, DOWNES, DUNN, ERSKINE
	FITZSIMMONS, GAINS, GARDNER
	GREEN, HARVEY, HOOD
	JOHNSON, KANE, KAYLOR, LEWIS
	LONDON, MACAVOY, MILLS, MINTER
	NOTICE, PETERSEN, PHILLIPS
	PRESCOTT, SCOTT, SIBSON, STACEY
	TARLETON, TURPIN, WALKER
	WALSH, WOODCOCK
—Cuban	GAVILAN, LEGRA, PARET
—French	CARPENTIER, CERDAN, THIL
—German	NEUSEL, SCHMELLING
—Ghanaian	NELSON
—Irish	FINNEGAN, GILROY, KELLY
	MCGUIGAN, MONAGHAN
—Italian	CARNERA, MITRI
—Mexican	SALDIVAR
—Nicaraguan	ARGUELLO
—Panamanian	DURAN
—Scottish	BUCHANAN, LYNCH
	MCGOWAN, PATERSON
	WATT
—South African	COETZEE, FOORD
	MCCORKINGDALE
—Swedish	JOHANNSON
—Welsh	DOWER, DRISCOLL, FARR
	WELSH, WILDE, WINSTONE
floor of ring	CANVAS
governing body	WORLD BOXING ASSOCIATION
	WORLD BOXING COUNCIL
	WORLD BOXING FEDERATION
illegal blow	BELOW THE BELT
	KIDNEY PUNCH
	RABBIT PUNCH
knock down	PUT ON THE CANVAS
methods of winning	KNOCK-OUT, KO
	(ON) POINTS
	TECHNICAL KNOCK-OUT
mouth protector	GUM SHIELD
nicknames	
—Ali, Cassius Clay	LOUISVILLE LIP
—Baer	CLOWN PRINCE
—Corbett	GENTLEMAN JIM
—Dempsey	MANASSA MAULER
—Duran	MAN OF STONE, EL ANIMAL
—Hearns	HIT MAN
—Jake La Motta	RAGING BULL
—Louis	BROWN BOMBER
—Sullivan	STRONG BOY
—Tyson	IRON MIKE
—Wilde	MIGHTY ATOM

officials	JUDGE, REFEREE, TIME-KEEPER
punches	BOLO, CROSS, HOOK, LEFT
	RIGHT, STRAIGHT, SWING
	UPPERCUT
session of boxing	ROUND
venues	
—America	
Atlantic City	CONVENTION CENTRE
New York	MADISON SQUARE GARDENS
	POLO GROUNDS
	YANKEE STADIUM
—Britain	ALBERT HALL, WHITE CITY
weights	
< 108 lb	STRAW-WEIGHT
108	LIGHT-FLYWEIGHT
112	FLYWEIGHT
115	SUPER FLYWEIGHT
118	BANTAMWEIGHT
122	LIGHT-FEATHERWEIGHT
126	FEATHERWEIGHT
130	JUNIOR LIGHTWEIGHT
135	LIGHTWEIGHT
140	LIGHT-WELTERWEIGHT
147	WELTERWIGHT
153½	LIGHT-MIDDLEWEIGHT
160	MIDDLEWEIGHT
175	LIGHT-HEAVYWEIGHT
190	CRUISERWEIGHT
> 190	HEAVYWEIGHT

brain

	ENCEPHALON
action of	CEREBRATION
active part	GREY MATTER
brain-shaped	CEREBRIFORM
brain-waves	ALPHA RHYTHM
	BETA WAVES
cavity	AQUEDUCT OF SILVIUS
	FORAMEN OF MONRO
	VENTRICLE
central lobe of cerebellum	VERMIS
connecting cortex and	
hypothalamus	LIMBIC SYSTEM
connective tissue	DURA MATER
disorders of brain	(see **disease**)
fibres joining hemispheres	PONS VAROLII
ganglion of forebrain	STRIATUM
grey matter	BASAL GANGLIA
	BASAL NUCLEI
H-shaped fissure	ZYGON
half of brain	HEMISPHERE
lobes of brain	AMYGDALA, INSULA
	OCCIPITAL, OLFACTORY
	OPTIC, PARIETAL
	(PRE-)FRONTAL, REIL'S ISLAND
	TEMPORAL, VERMIS
mass of cells related	
to a function	NUCLEUS

membrane(s)	ARACHNOID, DURA MATER
	MENINX(MENINGES)
	PIA MATER
—sheet of dura mater	TENTORIUM
nerve cell fibres	WHITE MATTER
old	HARN(ES)
olfactory lobe	RHINENCEPHALON
operations on brain	LEUCOTOMY
	LOBOTOMY
part controlling	
—appetite	HYPOTHALAMUS
—autonomic nervous	
system	HYPOTHALAMUS
—basic	
activities	VITAL CENTRE
emotions	LIMBIC SYSTEM
—blood flow	HYPOTHALAMUS
—co-ordination	NEOPALLIUM
	THALAMUS
—crude sensations	THALAMUS
—emotions	HYPOTHALAMUS
—endocrine glands	PITUITARY
—muscle action	BASAL GANGLIA
—reflex actions	CEREBELLUM
—response to	
stimuli	RETICULAR FORMATION
—sensation	CEREBRAL CORTEX
	SENSORIUM
—sight and hearing	MESENCEPHALON
—striped muscles	MOTOR CORTEX
—temperature	HYPOTHALAMUS
—thirst	HYPOTHALAMUS
—voluntary movement	CEREBRAL CORTEX
parts of	
—brain	
forebrain	CEREBRUM
	PROSENCEPHALON
glands	PINEAL, PITUITARY
hind-brain	CEREBELLUM
	EPENCEPHALON
	RHOMBENCEPHALON
joining hemispheres	CORPUS CALLOSUM
midbrain	MESENCEPHALON
where optic nerve	
emerges	OPTIC THALAMUS
—brainstem	PONS (VAROLII)
—cerebellum	VERMIS
—cerebrum	CAUDATE
	CEREBRAL CORTEX
	NEOCORTEX, (NEO-)PALLIUM
	PUTAMEN
half of	HEMISPHERE
—corpus callosum	SPLENIUM
—forebrain	DIENCEPHALON
—optic thalami	PINEAL BODY
—spinal cord	MEDULLA OBLONGATA

pituitary gland	HYPOPHYSIS
projection	
—into ventricle	CHOR(I)OID PLEXUS
—on optic thalamus	PULVINAR
raised curved trace in	
lateral ventricle	BIRD'S SPUR
	CALCAR AVIS
	HIPPOCAMPUS
ridge in surface	CONVOLUTION, GYRUS
supporting tissue	NEUROGLIA
ventricles	FOURTH, LATERAL, THIRD

Brazil

ant	TUCANDERA
armadillo	TATOU, TATU
bird	CARACARA, GUAN, KAMICHI
biting-fly	MOTUCA, MUTUCA, PIUM
canoe-waterway	IGARAPE
capital	BRASILIA
club-moss	PILLIGAN
cocoa	GUARANA
coffee	BAHIA
coins	
—old coins	LEMPIRA, REIS
—1000 reis	MILREIS
—unit	CENTAVO
—100 centavos	CRUIZERO, CRUSADO
—1000 cruizeros	CONTO
dance	BATUQUE, BOSSA NOVA
	CARIOCA, MAXIXE, SAMBA
drink	ASSAI
drug	JABORANDI, PAREIRA
fish	PERAI, PIABA, PIRAL
	PIRAN(H)A, PIRAYA
flower	GLOXINIA, TREE-LILY
	VELLOZIA
flycatcher	YETAPA
grass	PARA-GRASS
—land	CAMPO
half-caste	MAMELUCO
hare	TAPETI
heron	SOCO
log canoe	MONTARIA
macaw	ARARA, MARACAN
monkey	SAI
negro	MINA
nut	COQUILLA, PARA-NUT
	SAPUCAIA
offspring of European	
and Indian	MAMELUCO
open forest	CAATINGA
opossum	SARIGUE
palm	(see separate entry)
parrot	ARA
piassava	PARA GRASS
plain	CAMPO, SAVANNAH
plant	IPECAC(UANHA), PIPI

pods used in tanning	PIPI
provinces	ACRE, AMAPA, AMAZONAS
	BAHIA, CEARA, GOIAS, MARANHAO
	MATO GROSSO, MATO GROSSO DO SUL
	MINAS GERAIS, PARA, PARAIBA
	PARANA, PERNAMBUCO, PIAVI
	RIO GRANDE DO SUL
	RIO GRANDE DO NORTE, RONDONIA
	RORAIMA, SANTA CATARINA
	SAO PAULO
rabbit	TAPETI
river	AMAZON
rodent	CAPIBARA, CAPYBARA
rosewood	PALISANDER
rubber	CAUCHO, (H)ULE, PARA
—tree	MANGABEIRA, SERINGA
sirenian	MANATEE, MANATI
snakes	(see separate entry)
soap-tree	TINGI, TINGUY
stork	JABIRU
timber	(see separate entry)
trade jargon	ERAL, LINGOA
tree	ANDA, APA, ARAROB, BARBATIMEO
	BRAUNA, DALI, GOMAEL, GUARABUA
	HERCULES CUB, LECYTHIS
	MACERANDUBA, MANGABEIRA
	MASSARANDUBA, MASSERANDUBA
	MUSTAIBA, PARANA PINE
	PRICKLY-ASH, SAPUCAIA, TINGUY
	TOOTHACHE-TREE, WALLABA
	XANTHOXYLUM
water-lily	VICTORIA
weight	
—1 lb	LIBRA
—32 lb	ARROBA

bread

American	CORN PONE, JOHNNYCAKE
	QUICK BREAD
Australian	DAMPER
—currant bread	BROWNIE
browned by grilling	TOAST
casing with fruit	
filling	SUMMER PUDDING
coarse dark bread	BLACK BREAD
coated with egg and fried	FRENCH TOAST
containing baking powder	SODA BREAD
crescent-shaped	CROISSANT
crumbs from stale bread	RASPINGS
crumpet	PIKELET
date and sultana	TURKESTAN
desserts	BREAD (AND BUTTER) PUDDING
	SUMMER PUDDING
dough reserved as leaven	
for next batch	SOURDOUGH
dry, unsweetened biscuit	CRISPBREAD
finest bread	MANCHET

finger of hard dry toast	RUSK
flat	
—cake, unleavened	ROTI
—loaf	STOTY CAKE
for fillings	
—French	PISSALADIERE
—Italian	PIZZA
French	
—bread	PAIN
—long loaf	BAGUETTE, FICELLE
—roll	BRIOCHE, CROISSANT
German	
—bread	BROT
—crusty roll	BREZEL, PRE(T)ZEL
—rye bread	PUMPERNICKEL
—sweet bread	
toasted	ZWIEBACK
with fruit	STOLLEN
Greek	PIT(T)A
hard exterior of loaf	CRUST
Hebrew	
—rich	CHOLLA PLAIT
—ring	BAGEL
—unleavened	MATZA(H), MATZO(H)
	PASSOVER BREAD
—with poppy seeds	CHALLA(H)
Indian	CHAPAT(T)I, CHUPAT(T)I
	NA(A)N, PARAT(H)A
	PURI, ROTI
Irish	BARMBRACK, POTATO BREAD
	SCOFA, SODA BREAD
Italian	
—bread	PANE
sticks	GRISSINI
—flat loaf	FOCACCIA
—made with olive oil	CIABATTA
large	
—flat roll	BAP
—piece with savoury topping	CROUTE
—roll with filling	SUBMARINE
light soft loaf or roll	BRIOCHE
Lincolnshire	PLUM BREAD
loaf	
—offered in honour of	
the Virgin	PAN(H)AGIA
—shapes	BLOOMER, COTTAGE, ROLL
	SPLIT TIN, STICK, TIN
long	
—roll	HUFFER
—white loaf	FRENCH LOAF, FRENCH STICK
	OATIE BATON, VIENNA LOAF
with filling	HUFFER
made from	
—cornmeal	CORNBREAD
—finest flour	MANCHET
	WASTEL(-BREAD)
—maize	CORN PONE, JOHNNYCAKE
	SPOON BREAD, TORTILLA
—rye	RYEBREAD
—seaweed	LAVER BREAD
—unbleached flour	BROWN BREAD
—unsweetened rye	
or wheat	CRISPBREAD
—wholemeal flour	RAVEL(LED) BREAD
—whole wheat	GRANARY BREAD
	WHEATMEAL, WHOLEMEAL
Middle Eastern	PIT(T)A
New Zealand currant bread	BROWNIE
oat-bread	JANNOCK
open sandwich	SMORREBROD
outer part of loaf	CRUST
penny roll	TOMMY
poorest flour	RED-DOG
porous cake	CRUMPET
raised with sodium	
bicarbonate	SODA BREAD
round case for filling	PIZZA
sandwich with three	
slices	THREE-DECKER
Scottish flat bread	BANNOCK
ship's bread	HARD TACK
singed	TOAST
slice	ROUND
—baked crisp	RUSK
—browned by heat	TOAST
—on which food was placed	TRENCHER
slightly leavened	PITTA
small	
—cube crisply fried	CROUTON
—fragment	CRUMB
—piece	
as garnish	SIPPET
served with soup etc	CROUTON
with savoury topping	CANAPE
—portions in various	
shapes	ROLLS
-roll	FINGER ROLL, BRIDGE ROLL
soft	
—maize bread	SPOON BREAD
—roll	BARM CAKE
	DEVONSHIRE SPLIT
	OVEN BOTTOM
Spanish bread	PAN
stick(s)	GRISSINO (GRISSINI)
sweet	
—bread	SALLY LUNN, TEA BREAD
with currants	TEA CAKE
—roll	BRIOCHE
—sliced and toasted crisp	ZWIEBACK
thin loaf	FRENCH STICK
toasted	
—one side	FRENCH TOAST

—slice for savouries	CROUTE
—very thin	MELBA TOAST
two slices with filling	SANDWICH
unleavened bread	MATZA(H), MATZO(H)
	PASSOVER BREAD
used in Eucharist	HOST
Welsh	BARA BRITH
West Indian	COO-COO
wholemeal	PUMPERNICKEL
	RAVEL(LED) BREAD

bridge

built	
—from stone slabs	CLAPPER BRIDGE
—with open girders	LATTICE BRIDGE
curved	ARCH BRIDGE
end support of bridge	ABUTMENT, PIER
famous bridges	
—Anglesey/	
Wales	MENAI SUSPENSION BRIDGE
—Avon	CLIFTON SUSPENSION BRIDGE
	SEVERN ESTUARY BRIDGE
—Australia	SYDNEY HARBOUR BRIDGE
—Bayonne, USA	KILL VAN KULL BRIDGE
—Berlin	GLIENICKER BRIDGE
—Budapest	ARPAD BRIDGE, CHAIN BRIDGE
—Cairo	AL GALA BRIDGE
	AL GAMMA BRIDGE
	SAYALA BRIDGE
	SIXTH OF JULY BRIDGE
	SIXTH OF OCTOBER BRIDGE
	TAHRIR BRIDGE
—Calcutta	HOWRAH BRIDGE
—Chester, USA	COMMODORE BARRY
	BRIDGE
—Czechoslovakia	ZDAKOV BRIDGE
—Denmark	LILLEBAELT BRIDGE
—Devon	TAMAR BRIDGE
—Dublin	O'CONNELL BRIDGE
—Fayetteville	NEW RIVER GORGE BRIDGE
—Florence	PONTE VECCHIO
—Humberside	HUMBER ESTUARY BRIDGE
—Ipswich	ORWELL BRIDGE
—Istanbul	ATATURK BRIDGE
	BOSPHORUS BRIDGE
	GALATA BRIDGE
—Japan	AKASHI-KAIKYO BRIDGE
	INNOSHIMA BRIDGE
	KAMMON STRAITS BRIDGE
	OHNARUTO BRIDGE
—Key West	SEVEN-MILE BRIDGE
—Lancashire	RUNCORN-WIDNES BRIDGE
—Le Havre	TANKARVILLE BRIDGE
—Lisbon	PONTE 25 ABRIL
—London	BATTERSEA BRIDGE
	BLACKFRIARS BRIDGE
	LONDON BRIDGE

	PUTNEY BRIDGE
	TOWER BRIDGE
	VAUXHALL BRIDGE
	WATERLOO BRIDGE
	WESTMINSTER BRIDGE
—Louisiana	BATON ROUGE BRIDGE
	GREATER NEW ORLEANS BRIDGE
—Madrid	PUENTE DE TOLEDO
—Maryland	BALTIMORE BRIDGE
—Michigan	MACKINAS STRAITS BRIDGE
—Moscow	MOSKVORETSKIY BRIDGE
—Nagasaki	SPECTACLES BRIDGE
—New Orleans	HUEY LONG BRIDGE
—New York	BRONX-WHITESTONE
	BRIDGE
	BROOKLYN BRIDGE
	GEORGE WASHINGTON BRIDGE
	MANHATTAN BRIDGE
	MARINE PARKWAY BRIDGE
	NYACK-TARRYTOWN BRIDGE
	QUEENSBORO BRIDGE
	TAPPAN-ZEE BRIDGE
	VERRAZANO NARROWS BRIDGE
	WILLIAMSBURG BRIDGE
—Newcastle	CLEVELAND BRIDGE
—Oregon	ASTORIA BRIDGE
	FREMONT BRIDGE
—Osaka	MINATO BRIDGE
—Panama	THATCHER FERRY BRIDGE
—Paris	PETIT PONT, PONT AU CHANGE
	PONT AU DOUBLE
	PONT D'ARCOLE
	PONT DE L'ARCHEVECHE
	PONT DE LA TOURNELLE
	PONT DE SULLY
	PONT LOUIS PHILIPPE
	PONT MARIE
	PONT NEUF, PONT NOTRE DAME
	PONT ST MICHEL
—Philadelphia	WALT WHITMAN BRIDGE
—Prague	CHARLES'S BRIDGE
	FIRST OF MAY BRIDGE
—Quebec	LA VIOLETTE BRIDGE
	PIERRE LAPORTE BRIDGE
	QUEBEC BRIDGE
—Rhodesia	BIRCHENOUGH BRIDGE
—Rio de Janeiro	PONTE RIO NITEROI
—Rome	PONTE CAVOUR
	PONTE GARIBALDI
	PONTE MARGHERITA
	PONTE MAZZINI
	PONTE PALATINO
	PONTE SISTO
	PONTE SUBLICIO
	PONTE VITTORIO EMMANUELE
—St Petersburg	KIROV BRIDGE

—San Francisco	CARQUINES STRAIT BRIDGE	
	GOLDEN GATE BRIDGE	
	OAKLAND BRIDGE	
	SAN MATEO BRIDGE	
	(TRANS)BAY BRIDGE	
—Scotland	FORTH BRIDGE, TAY BRIDGE	
—Shropshire	FREE BRIDGE	
	IRON BRIDGE	
—Vancouver	LIONS GATE BRIDGE	
	PORT MANN BRIDGE	
	SECOND NARROWS BRIDGE	
—Venezuela	ANGOSTURA BRIDGE	
—Venice	RIALTO	
—Vienna	ASPERN BRIDGE	
	AUGARTEN BRIDGE	
	FRANZENS BRIDGE	
	MARIEN BRIDGE	
	ROTUNDEN BRIDGE	
	SCHWEDEN BRIDGE	
—Washington	LONGVIEW BRIDGE	
	TACOMA NARROWS BRIDGE	
—Wilmington	DELAWARE MEMORIAL BRIDGE	
floating bridge	PONTOON	
French	PONT	
German	BRUCKE	
hinged bridge	BASCULE, DRAWBRIDGE	
Italian	PONTE	
narrow with recesses	PACK BRIDGE	
pivoting	SWING BRIDGE	
rail bridge	VIADUCT	
rising	BASCULE BRIDGE	
road bridge	FLYOVER, OVERPASS, VIADUCT	
Spanish	PUENTE	
steeply curved	HUMPBACKED BRIDGE	
suspended from		
—cables	SUSPENSION BRIDGE	
—chains	CHAIN BRIDGE	
temporary bridge	BAILEY BRIDGE	
types	ARCH, BAILEY, BASCULE	
	CABLE STAY, CANTILEVER	
	PIVOT, PONTOON, SUSPENSION	
	SWING, TRANSPORTER, TRESTLE	
	TRUSSED	
water bridge	AQUEDUCT	
with		
—arms built out from piers	CANTILEVER	
—lifting arms	BASCULE	
—travelling carriage	TRANSPORTER	

British

Academy	BA
Airways	BA
Association	BA
Broadcasting Corporation	BBC
capital	LONDON
Columbia	BC
company	BL
Empire Medal	BEM
Home Stores	BHS
Honduras	BH
Institute of	
—Management	BIM
—Radiology	BIR
Legion	BL
Library	BL
Medical Journal	BMJ
Museum	BM
—Library	BML
Optical Association	BOA
Oxygen Company	BOC
Pharmacopoeia	BP
Pharmaceutical Codex	BPC
Petroleum	BP
Printing Corporation	BPC
Rail	BR
Red Cross Society	BRCS
Road Services	BRS
Shipbuilders	BS
Standards (Institution)	BS(I)
Steel (Corporation)	BS(C)
Sugar Corporation	BSC
Summer Time	BST
Thermal Unit	BT(H)U

Browning

words used by:	
bombast	AMPOLLOSITY
dandruff	FURFAIR
debate	DISCEPT
dispute	DISCEPT
drive away	AROINT, AROYNT
frighten away	AROINT, AROYNT
greatest astrologer	ARCH-GENETHLIAC
horse's mane	ENCOLURE
instrument of torture	GADGE
lucerne	LUZERN
needed amount	EXIGENT
play antics	ANTICISE
spat upon	BESPATE
turgidity	AMPOLLOSITY

Brunei   BRU

capital	BANDAR SERI BEGAWAN
coin	CENT, DOLLAR

Buddhist

blissful state	NIBBANA, NIRVANA
branches	(see belief)
Book of the Dead	BARDO THODOL
canonical writings	TRIPITAKA
Chinese sect	CHAN
circle	MANDALA
column	LAT
compassion	KARUNA
concentration	SAMADHI

cross	SWASTIKA
demon	MARA
device	UPAYA
disciple	CHELA
discipline	VINAYA
discourse for laity	SUTRA
enlightenment	BODHI, NIBBANA, NIRVANA
ethical conduct	SHILA
evil spirit	MARA
faith	SHRADDHA
fate	KARMA
fertility spirit	YAKSHA, YAKSHI
finial of dagoba	TEE
form	RUPA
function	YUNG
future Buddha	BODHISATTVA
gateway	TORAN(A)
giving	DANA
highest	
—priest	DALAI LAMA
—state	NIRVANA
holy day	UPOSATHA
impermanence	ANICCA
inevitable consequence	KARMA
Japanese sect	AMIDA, AMITA
	SOKA GAKKAI, ZEN
law	DHARMA
—of effect	KARMA
liberation	NIBBANA, NIRVANA
means	UPAYA
meditation	BHAVANA
memorial shrine	STUPA, TOPE
—Sri Lanka	D(H)AGOBA
metaphysics	ABHIDHARMA
method	UPAYA
mind	CHITTA
monastery	LAMASERY, VIHARA
monk	AR(A)HAT, BO, BONZE
	LAMA, TALAPOIN
mound	STUPA, TOPE
—Sri Lanka	D(H)AGOBA
nativity	JATAKA
'no-self' doctrine	ANATTA
novice	CHELA
perfection	SIDDHA, SIDDHI
pillar	LAT
plane between life and death	BARDO
precinct	VIHARA
priest	BONZE, LAMA, PONGYI
reality	TATHATA
reincarnated person	TULKU
relic	STUPA
religious	
—book	PITAKA
—leader	DALAI LAMA, PANCHEN LAMA
—painting	TANKA

sacred	
—language	PALI
—lotus	PADMA
—mountain	OMEI
—text	SUTRA
—tree	BO, BODHI, PEEPUL
—verse	MANTRA
scripture	SUTRA, SUTTA, (TI)PITAKA
seed	BIJA
sermons of Buddha	SUTRA
shrine	DAGABA, DAGO(U)BA
	D(H)AGOBA, STUPA, TOPE
spiritual leader	DALAI LAMA
	PANCHEN LAMA
sudden enlightenment	SATORI
symbol	TRISUL(A)
—of the universe	MANDALA
teaching	SHASTRAS
temple	SANGHA, TERA, VIHARA
—hall	CHAITYA
three bodies of Buddha	TRIKAYA
throne	ASANA
Tibetan sect	GELUK PA, SAKYA PA
title	MAHATMA
tree nymph	YAKSHI
umbrella-shaped finial	TEE
unsatisfactoriness	DUKKHA
wheel of becoming	SAMSARA
wisdom	PRAJNA
world	LOKA
building construction	
arch	FLAT, SEGMENTAL
	SEMI-CIRCULAR
arrangement of bricks in wall	BOND
beam over opening	LINTEL
block materials	AERATED CONCRETE
	CLAY, CLINKER
	FOAMED CONCRETE
brick	
—cut to form arch	GAUGED BRICK
—laid	
flat	
—end showing	HEADER
—side showing	STRETCHER
on end, side showing	BRICK-ON-END
	SOLDIER COURSE
on side, end showing	BRICK-ON-EDGE
—part	BAT
cut diagonally	BEVELLED CLOSER
half, lengthwise	QUEEN CLOSER
with corner cut off	KING CLOSER
—shape having	
bevelled long edge	PLINTH BRICK
cavities	AIRBRICK
	CELLULAR BRICK
double rounded end	COWNOSE

grooved sides	KEYED
rounded end	BULLNOSE
various angles	SQUINT QUOIN
brick materials	CLAY, CONCRETE
	SAND-LIME
brickwork	
—bedding material	CEMENT(-LIME)MORTAR
	COMPO, MORTAR
—bonds	
all	
—headers	HEADER BOND
	HEADING BOND
—stretchers	STRETCHER BOND
	STRETCHING
alternate	
—courses of headers	
and stretchers	ENGLISH
—headers and	
stretchers in course	FLEMISH
one	
—stretcher course to	
several header	
courses	ENGLISH GARDEN WALL
—stretcher, several	
headers per	
course	FLEMISH GARDEN WALL
—joints	FLAT, FLUSH, KEYED
	RAKED, RECESSED
	TUCK(BASTARD), WEATHERED
horizontal	BED JOINTS
vertical	PERPENDS
cladding materials	ASBESTOS-CEMENT
	CONCRETE, FIBREGLASS
	GALVANISED IRON, PLASTIC
	SHEET STEEL, TIMBER
—fixed to frame	CURTAIN WALLING
concrete	PLAIN, REINFORCED
	PRESTRESSED
copper pipe joints	CAPILLARY, COMPRESSION
course of brick, stone,	
etc on top of wall	COPING
damp-proof	
—course	DPC
materials	BITUMEN FELT, COPPER
	LEAD, POLYTHENE, SLATE
—membrane	DPM
door types	FLUSH
	FRAMED, LEDGED AND BRACED
	LEDGED, LEDGED AND BRACED
	PANELLED, SLIDING
drainage	
—access points	INSPECTION CHAMBER
	MANHOLE, RODDING-EYE
—materials	ASBESTOS-CEMENT
	CAST-IRON, PITCH-FIBRE
	PLASTIC, SALT-GLAZED CLAY

—pipe	
horizontal	DRAIN, SEWER
preventing siphonage	ANTI-SIPHON PIPE
providing ventilation	VENT PIPE
taking	
—flow from sanitary	
fittings	FOUL DRAIN
—rain water	STORM(WATER) DRAIN
—waste water	
only	WASTE-PIPE
vertical	SOIL-PIPE
—tank	CESSPOOL, SEPTIC TANK
film on surface of concrete	LAITANCE
flue lining	PARGING
foundations	PILES, RAFT, STRIP
	TRENCHFILL
glass	
—fixing material	GLAZING BEAD
	PUTT, SPRIG
—type	ARMOURED, CAST, DIFFUSING
	FLOAT, GEORGIAN, LAMINATED
	OBSCURE, OPAQUE, PLAIN
	REEDED, ROLLED, SHEET
	TOUGHENED, WIRED
hot-water storage	CYLINDER
insulating materials	FIBREGLASS
	PERLITE, POLYSTYRENE
	VERMICULITE
lead joints	LEAD-BURNED, SPIGOT
	TAFT, WIPED
mortar	COMPO
—behind kerbs	HAUNCHING
—in	
angle	FILLET
manholes	HAUNCHING
—lining flue	PARGING
—round chimney pot	FLAUNCHING
—sealing tiles	PARGING
painting	
—coats	
first	PRIMER
intermediate	UNDERCOAT
final	FINISHING COAT
	GLOSS COAT, TOP COAT
—materials	BITUMEN PAINT
	CEMENT PAINT, DISTEMPER
	EGGSHELL, EMULSION
	EPOXIDE RESIN PAIN, FLAT PAINT
	GLOSS PAINT, MATT PAINT
	PLASTIC PAINT, PRIMER
	SILICATE PAINT, STONE PAINT
	THIXOTROPIC PAINT
	UNDERCOAT, VARNISH
—technique	BRUSH, ROLLER, SPRAY
piles	BEARING, BORED, DRIVEN
	FRICTION

plastering
—external   PEBBLE-DASH, RENDERING
  ROUGHCAST
machine-applied   TYROLEAN
—layers
  first   RENDER(ING) COAT
  second   FLOATING COAT
  top   SETTING COAT
—materials   CEMENT, GYPSUM, LIME
  SAND
—types   ANHYDRITE, ANHYDROUS
  KEENE'S, PARIAN, PLASTER OF PARIS
  RETARDED HEMIHYDRATE
rainwater fittings   GUTTER, DOWNPIPE
  DROP OUTLET, STOPEND
reinforced concrete   FERROCONCRETE
roof
—covering materials   ASBESTOS-CEMENT
  ASPHALT, BITUMINOUS FELT
  BUTYL RUBBER, COPPER
  GALVANISED IRON, LEAD
  NURALITE, SLATE, TILES, ZINC
—edge
  bottom   EAVES
  side   VERGE
  top   RIDGE
—frame   TRUSS, TRUSSED RAFTER
—slate
  sizes: 12"x6"   SMALL
    13"x7"   DOUBLE
    16"x8"   LADY
    20"x10"   COUNTESS
    24"x12"   DUCHESS
    24"x14"   PRINCESS
    26"x16"   EMPRESS
  spacing   GAUGE, LAP
  types   COTSWOLD, CUMBERLAND
  WELSH
—tiles
  materials   ASBESTOS-CEMENT
  CLAY, CONCRETE, STONE
  spacing   GAUGE, LAP
  specials   ARRIS HIP TILES
  BONNET HIP TILES, EAVES TILES
  RIDGE TILES, VALLEY TILES
  types   INTERLOCKING, PLAIN
  ROMAN, SPANISH
—types   COLLAR, COUPLE
  COUPLE CLOSE, KING-POST
  LEAN-TO, MANSARD
  MONOPITCH, NORTH-LIGHT
  PURLIN, QUEEN-POST
sanitary fittings   BATH
  BIDET, LAVATORY BASIN
  (SLOP-)SINK, SHOWER
  URINAL, WATER-CLOSET

scaffolding parts   BRIDLE, CLIP, COUPLING
  CROSS-BRACE, DIAGONAL BRACE
  GUARD RAIL, LEDGER, STANDARD
  TOE-BOARD, TRANSOM
sheet materials   ASBESTOS-CEMENT
  BLOCKBOARD, CHIPBOARD
  FIBREBOARD, HARDBOARD
  LAMINBOARD, PEGBOARD
  PLASTERBOARD
  PLASTIC LAMINATE
  PLYWOOD, SOFTBOARD
stairs
—diagonal step   WINDER
—parts   BALUSTER, BA(N)NISTER
  CARRIAGE, HANDRAIL, NEWEL
  NOSING, RISER, STRING, TREAD
—types   CIRCULAR, DOGLEG
  GEOMETRICAL, HELICAL
  OPEN WELL, SPIRAL, STRAIGHT
stone
—Cornwall   DE LANK, LAMORNA
—Derbyshire   BOLSOVER MOOR
  DARLEYDALE, HOPTON WOOD
—Dorset   PORTLAND
  PURBECK MARBLE
—Gloucestershire   PENNANT
—Kent   RAG
—Leicestershire   MOUNTSORREL
—Lincolnshire   ANCASTER, CLIPSHAM
—Nottinghamshire   MANSFIELD
—Scotland   CORRENNIE, CRETOWN
—Somerset   BATH
—Warwickshire   HORNTON
—Westmorland   SHAP
—Wiltshire   CHILLMARK
—without planes   FREESTONE
stone
—finishes   BOASTED, COMBED
  DRAGGED, DROVED, FURROWED
  HAMMER-DRESSED, MOULDED
  PLAIN WORK, RETICULATED
  RUBBED WORK, SCABBLED
  SCAPPLED, SUNK WORK
  TOOLED, VERMICULATED
—rubble   MOELLON
—walling
  rubble   COURSED RUBBLE, FLINT
  KENTISH RAG
  RANDOM RUBBLE (BUILT TO COURSES)
  SNECKED RUBBLE, SQUARED RUBBLE
  UNCOURSED RUBBLE
  dressed   ASHLAR, BLOCK IN COURSE
tie for
—brickwork   BUTTERFLY TIE, WALL-TIE
—stonework   ANCHOR BOLT, CRAMP
  JOGGLE, TAILING IRON

timber	
curved roof support	CRUCK
—for	
concrete	FORMWORK
trenches	POLING, PROP
	PUNCHEON, RUNNER, SOLDIER
	STRETCHER, STRINGER
	STRUT, WALING
—in	
floor	JOIST, NOGGIN(G)
panelling	
—horizontal	STRETCHER
—vertical	MUNTIN
partitions	STUDDING
roof	
—at	
eaves	FA(S)CIA, SOFFIT
verge	BARGE-BOARD
—structural	BINDER, COLLAR
	DRAGON-TIE, HANGER, JOIST
	KING-POST, PURLIN, QUEEN-POST
	RAFTER, TIE, WALLPLATE
—supporting tiles	BATTENS
—joints	BARE-FACED MORTICE
	CHASE MORTICE, COGGED, COMBED
	CORNER LOCKING, CROSS-TONGUE
	DOVETAIL, DOWELLED
	HALVED, HOUSED, MITRE
	MORTICE AND TENON
	SCARF, STUB TENON, TUSK TENON
—round	
door frames, etc	ARCHITRAVE
openings	LINING
walls	
—door-head level	PICTURE RAIL
—floor level	SKIRTING
—lower half	DADO
—waist level	CHAIR RAIL
—temporary support	
opening	NEEDLE
overstressed walls	SHORE
—types	(*see separate entry*)
walling materials	BRICK, CONCRETE
	FAIENCE, STONE
	TERRA-COTTA, TIMBER
weatherproofing round	
stack, etc	FLASHING, SOAKER
window	
—materials	ALUMINIUM, IRON
	PLASTIC, (STAINLESS)STEEL
	TIMBER
—parts	
bottom	SILL
horizontal member	TRANSOME
small dividing bar	GLAZING BAR
vertical member	MULLION

top	HEAD
—types	CASEMENT, DORMER
	FRENCH, HOPPER, ORIEL
	PATIO, PIVOT, SASH, SLIDING
	SPRING BALANCE
	(*see also* **architectural features**)
Bulgaria	BG, BULG
capital	SOFI(Y)A
coins	LEV, LEY, STOTINKA
head of church	EXARCH
king	CZAR, TSAR, TZAR
measure	KRINE, LEKHA
	OKA, OKE
Moslem	POMAK
national assembly	SOBRANJE, SOBRANYE
revolutionary	COMITAJI, KOMITAJI
weight	OKA, OKE, TOVAR
bullfighting	TAUROMACHY
arena	PLAZA DE TOROS
assistant bullfighter	
—Portugal	FORCADO
—Spain	BANDERILLERO
bullfight	CORRIDA
—France	COMBATS DE TAUREAUX
—Portugal	CORRIDA DE TOUROS
—Spain	CORRIDA DE TOROS
bullfighter	ESPADA, MATADOR
	TOREADOR, TORERO
bullfighters	BAES, BIENVENIDA
	DOMINGUIN, EL CORDOBES
	EL LITRI, HIGGINS
	LAGARTIJO, MANOLETE
	MOLINA, PEREZ, ROMERO
bullpen	TORIL
cape	MULETA
dart	BANDERILLA
devotee	AFICIONADO
fence round bullring	BURLADERO
flourish of cape	PASE, PASS, VERONICA
hat	MONTERA
kill	
—final thrust	MOMENT OF TRUTH
—man and bull moving	ZAL VOLAPIE
—torero standing still	RECIBIENDO
mounted	
—bailiff	ALGUACILE
—fighters	
Portugal	CAVALEIRO
Spain	PICADOR, TOREADOR
part of session	TERCIO
session	CORRIDA
troupe	CAUDRILLA
Burkina Faso	
capital	OUAGADOUGOU
coin	FRANC
previous name	UPPER VOLTA

Burma   BUR

  borderer   SHAN

  Buddhist priest   PONGYI

  capital   RANGOON, YANGON

  civet   LINSANG

  coin   KYAT, PYA

  devil   NAT

  garment   TAMEIN

  girl   MINA

  governor   WOON, WUN

  guerrilla   CHINDIT

  hill-dweller   LAI

  knife   DA(H), DHAR, DOUT, DOW

  language   KAREN, SHAN

  measure   BYEE, DAIN, DHA

          LAN, PALGAT, TENG

  modern name   MYANMAR

  prostrate veneration   SHIKO

  river   IRRAWADDY

  robber   DACOIT, DAKOIT

  robbery   DACOITAGE

        DACOITI, DACOITY

  shrimp   NAPEE

  state carriage   RATH

  timber   (*see* **timber**)

  tree   IRONWOOD, PADAUK

       PADOUK, PYENGADU

  tribe   CHIN, KACHIN, KAREN(NI)

       LAI, MON, SHAN

  violin   TURR

  weight   KAIT, KYAT, MAT, TICUL, VIS(S)

Burns

  words used by:

  angle of wooden dish   LAGGEN, LAGGIN

  beast not housed   OUTLER

  bonny   BONIE

  determine   LAW

  dwarfish person   (K)NURL

  fine linen   SEVENTEEN-HUNDER

  get   FALL

  highest character   ACE

  hoop at bottom of wooden

    vessel   LAGGEN-GIRD

  hot ashes   AIZLE, EASLE

  one out of office   OUTLER

       (*see also* **Scots**)

            RU

Burundi

  capital   BUJUMBURA

  coin   CENTIME, FRANC

  language   KIRUNDI

butterfly   PSYCHE

  black and scarlet   RED ADMIRAL

black-spotted   FRITILLARY

black with white spots   DINGY SKIPPER

       GRIZZLED SKIPPER

       WHITE ADMIRAL

blue   ADONIS, CHALKHILL BLUE

     COMMON BLUE, HOLLY BLUE

     LARGE BLUE, LONG-TAILED BLUE

     SHORT-TAILED BLUE, SMALL BLUE

brown   ARGUS, GATEKEEPER, GRAYLING

     HEATH, LULWORTH SKIPPER

       MEADOW BROWN

chocolate-brown with

  yellow edges   CAMBERWELL BEAUTY

copper   LARGE COPPER, SMALL COPPER

dark brown   ARGUS, RINGLET

  groupings   LYCAENIDAE, NYMPHALIDAE

       PAPILIO, PIERIDAE

     RHOPALOCERA, SATYRIDAE

       THECLA, VANESSA

marbled   MARBLED WHITE

multi-coloured   SWALLOWTAIL

       TORTOISESHELL

purple   PURPLE EMPEROR

purplish-blue   MAZARINE BLUE

reddish-brown with

  'eyes'   PEACOCK

tawny-orange   CHEQUERED SKIPPER

       ESSEX SKIPPER

   LARGE SKIPPER, PAINTED LADY

     SILVER-SPOTTED SKIPPER

       SMALL SKIPPER

various colours   HAIRSTREAK

white   BATH WHITE

     BLACK-VEINED WHITE

     CABBAGE(-WHITE)

     GREEN-VEINED WHITE

   LARGE WHITE, SMALL WHITE

       WOOD WHITE

white-marked   COMMA, POLYGONIA

white with tipped wings   ORANGE-TIP

yellow   BRIMSTONE

       CLOUDED YELLOW

Byzantine

  capital   BYZANTIUM

       CONSTANTINOPLE

  chancellor   LOGOTHETE

  gold coin   BEZANT, BYZANT

       SOLIDUS

  governor   CATAPAN, EXARCH

  guard   PROTOSPATHARIUS

  head of guard   ACOLOUTHOS

       AKOL(O)UTHOS

C

cacti

including: succulents	
bishop's cap	ASTROPHYTUM
brain cactus	ECHINOFOSSULOCACTUS
bunny ears	OPUNTIA
burro's tail	SEDUM
candle plant	KLEINIA
Cape hart's tongue	GASTERIA
chain cactus	RHIPSALIS
Christmas cactus	SCHLUMBERGERA
	ZYGOCACTUS
cinnamon cactus	OPUNTIA
column cactus	CEREUS
Easter cactus	RHIPSALIDOPSIS
	SCHLUMBERGERA
fish hook cactus	FEROCACTUS
ghost plant	GRAPTOPETALUM
giant	SAGUARO
goat's horn	ASTROPHYTUM
golden barrel	ECHINOCACTUS
—lily	LOBIVIA
hen and chickens	SEMPERVIVUM
houseleek	SEMPERVIVUM
jelly bean plant	SEDUM
leaf cactus	PERESKIA
living stones	LITHOPS
Mexican sunball	REBUTIA
milk bush	EUPHORBIA
mistletoe cactus	RHIPSALIS
old man cactus	CEPHALOCEREUS
—of the Andes	OREOCEREUS
orchid cactus	EPIPHYLLUM
panda plant	KALANCHOE
peanut cactus	CHAMAECEREUS
pearl plant	HAWORTHIA
Peruvian old man	ESPOSTOA
pincushion cactus	MAMMILLARIA
rat's tail cactus	APOROCACTUS
silver torch cactus	CLEISTOCACTUS
South American	EASTER CACTUS
star window plant	HAWORTHIA
string of beads	SENECIO
sugar almond plant	PACHYPHYTUM
sunset cactus	LOBIVIA
tiger's jaws	FORCARIA
Tom Thumb cactus	PARODIA
Turkish temple	EUPHORBIA
velvet leaf	KALANCHOE

wart plant	HAWORTHIA

cakes

almond	ANGEL CAKE, FRANGIPANE
	FRANGIPANI, MACAROON
	MAID OF HONOUR, MANDELBROT
	RATAFIA, TRUFFLE CAKE
American	BROWNIE, CORN-CAKE
	CORN-DODGER, CRULLER, FRIEDCAKE
	GINGER MUFFIN, HOE-CAKE
	JELLY ROLL, JOHNNYCAKE
	LOAF-CAKE, MISSISSIPPI MUDCAKE
	OLYCOOK, OLYKOEK, SHORTCAKE
	SINKER
Austrian	(SACHER)TORTE
batter cake	GAUFFRE, WAFFLE
bread-like with currants	LARD(Y) CAKE
brittle, made of	
flour and butter	SHORTBREAD
	SHORTCAKE
cherries	GENOA CAKE
chocolate	DOBOZ TORTE, SACHERTORTE
—and	
cream	DEVIL'S FOOD CAKE
fruit	TORTE
nuts	BROWNIE, FLORENTINE
—Christmas roll	YULE LOG
—coated	LAMINGTON
coconut	COCONUT PYRAMID, MACAROON
—coated	MADELEINE
cream	(BLACK FOREST) GATEAU
	BRANDY SNAP, CHERUB CAKE
	CREAM HORN, CREAM PUFF
	ECLAIR, MERINGUE, PALMIER
—bun	CHOU
crumpet	PIKELET
currant	
—bun	BARMBRACK, CHELSEA BUN
	ROCK BUN, SINGIN(G) HINNY
cake	BANBURY CAKE, ECCLES CAKE
	QUEEN CAKE
doughnut (US)	CRULLER, OLYCOOK
	OLYKOEK, SINKER
Easter	
—bun	HOT-CROSS BUN
—cake	SIMNEL CAKE
—Russian	PASHKA
egg-white and sugar	MERINGUE
fancy cake	GATEAU, TORTE
fatty	LARD(Y) CAKE
finger-shaped	LANGUE DE CHAT
flaky pastry	DANISH PASTRY
	MILLEFEUILLE(S)
	PALMIER, VANILLA SLICE
flat	DROP(PED) SCONE, FARL(E)
	GRIDDLE CAKE, PATTIE, PATTY
	SCOTCH PANCAKE, STOTTY CAKE

French	SAVARIN
fried in fat	DOUGHNUT
fruit baked with shell on top and served fruit side up	UPSIDE-DOWN CAKE
fruit cake	BANANA, CHERRY
	DUNDEE, FARMHOUSE
	GENOA, PARADISE, POUND CAKE
	TYROL, VINEGAR CAKE
gateau	TORTE
German	BLACK FOREST GATEAU
	KUCHEN, MOHNKUCHEN
	POPPYSEED CAKE
	SCHWARZWALDER KIRSCHTORTE
	STOLLEN
ginger	GINGERBREAD, PARKIN, PERKIN
Greek	FINIKIA
Hebrew	
—almond	MANDELBROT
—sponge	PLAVA
iced	FANCY CAKE
—bun	BELGIAN BUN
	JEFFERSON (BUN)
—cake	BIRTHDAY CAKE
	CHRISTMAS CAKE, NAPOLEON
	RUSSIAN, WEDDING CAKE
—pastry	VANILLA SLICE
—small	PETIT FOURS
Italian	PANETTONE
Japanese	MANJU
layers	
—cream and pastry	MILLE FEUILLE(S)
—meringue, cream, fruit	VACHERIN
—various mixes	LAYER CAKE
light sweet cake	ANGEL CAKE
	SPONGE (CAKE)
maize meal (US)	JOHNNY CAKE
marzipan	BATTENBERG CAKE
	PETIT FOURS
mottled	MARBLE CAKE
muffin	PIKELET, POPOVER
pancake	CARCAKE
—with wheat flour	WHEAT CAKE
pastry with	
—sweet filling	DANISH PASTRY
—spices	VIENNA PASTRY
plain	
—bun	ROCK BUN, SCONE
—cake	BATCH CAKE, SAND CAKE
—with raising agent	TEA BREAD
and currants	TEA CAKE
porous	MUFFIN
potato cake	GALETTE
rich cake	BROWNIE, CHRISTMAS CAKE
	DARIOLE, FUDGE, POUND CAKE
	SPICE CAKE
ring-shaped	DOUGHNUT, JUMBAL
	JUMBLE, SAVARIN
rum-flavoured	BABA AU RHUM
	(RUM) BABA
Russian	PASAHKA
sandwich with jam and jelly filling	WASHINGTON PIE
Scottish	BANNOCK, BLACK BUN
	BUTTER-BAKE, CARCAKE
	COOKIE, COOKY, FARL(E)
	FARTHEL, SCOTCH BUN
—Shrove Tuesday cake	CARCAKE
shell-shaped	MADELEINE
shortbread with cream, etc	SHORTCAKE
small	
—currant bun	ROCK BUN, ROCK CAKE
—plain cake with raising agent	SCONE
—sponge cake	MADELEINE
—sweet cake	MADELEINE, PETIT FOUR
	QUEEN CAKE, VIENNESE TART
Spanish	BRAZO DE GITANO
spicy	COBURG
sponge	CARIBBEAN, GENOESE
—cylindrical	SWISS ROLL
—lemon flavour	MADEIRA
—light	ANGEL-CAKE, ANGEL-FOOD
—roll with chocolate coating	YULE LOG
—with fat	VICTORIA SPONGE
sweet bun	BATH BUN, CHELSEA BUN
	SALLY LUNN
Swiss roll with jelly (jam)	JELLY ROLL
tea-cake	CRUMPET, MUFFIN
	PIKELET, SALLY LUNN
—Kent	HUFFKIN
thin	
—crisp sponge	SPONGE FINGER
—sweet cake	JUMBAL, JUMBLE
Twelfth Night cake	GALETTE
unsweetened griddlecake	CRUMPET
vegetable	CARROT CAKE
	GALETTE
wheat cake (Ind.)	PURI
Cambodia	K
capital	PHNOM-PENH
coin	RIEL
language	KHMER
modern name	KAMPUCHEA
	KHMER REPUBLIC
people	KHMER
camera	(*see* **photography**)
Cameroon	
capital	YAOUNDE
coin	FRANC
Canada	CDN
Air Force	RCAF
alewife (fish)	GASPEREAU

birds	HAIRY WOODPECKER	—Yukon Territory	YT
	SAW-WHET OWL	ravine	COULEE
	SHARP-TAILED GROUSE	rice	INDIAN RICE
	STELLER'S JAY	river	FRASER, NELSON
bog	MUSKEG		ST LAWRENCE
Canadian	CANUCK, KANUCK	Royal Academy	CRA
—of French descent	HABITANT	ruminant	MUSK-OX, MUSK-STEER
capital	OTTAWA	sailors	RCN
coin	CENT, DOLLAR	sea-bird	MURRELET
cut grain	SWATHE	sledge	TRAIN
dog	NEWFOUNDLAND	sluice-gate	ALBOLDEAU
dried skin	PARFLECHE	soldiers	CEF
fingers	BREAD HOOKS	swamp	MUSKEG
fliers	RCAF	tenderfoot	CHE(E)CHAKO
freeze	TAKE		CHEECHALKO, CHECHAQUO
half-caste	METIF	timber	LUMBER
hare	SNOW-SHOE RABBIT		(see also **timber**)
houseboat for loggers	WAN(I)GAN, WANGUN	travel with dogs over snow	MUSH
Indian		waterweed	ELODEA
—language	ALGONKIN, ALGONQUIN	windproof garment	PARKA, PARKEE
	MICMAC	**Canary Islands**	E
—tribes	ALGONKIN, ALGONQUIN	**Cape Verde Islands**	P
	BEAVER, BEDTHUK, BLACKFOOT	**capes**	
	CARRIER, CREE, DOGRIB, ESKIMO	including: cape	
	HAIDA, HAN, HARE, INGALIK	head	
	INNU, KASKA, KOYUKON	point	
	KUTCHIN, KWAKIUTL, MANDAN	promontory	
	MICMAC, MONTAGNAIS-NASKAPI	etc	
	SARCEE, SHUSWAP, TANANA	Alaska	HALKETT, LISBURNE
	TLINGIT, TSIMSHIAN, TUTCHONE		PRINCE OF WALES, ROMANZOF
jay	WHISKY-JACK, WHISKY-JOHN	Albania	GJUHEZES
lumber-camp supply chest	WAN(I)GAN	Algeria	CARBON, DE FER, FIGALO
	WANGUN		MATIFOU, ROSA
marsh	MUSKEG	Angola	DAS PALMAS, DAS SALINAS
mounted police	MOUNTIES, RCMP		DE S BRAZ, DE STA MARTA
national emblem	MAPLE LEAF		DO DANDE
—Railway	CNR	Arabia	AL HADD, AL QAIB, ASWAD
navy	RCN		FARTAK, HATIBA, JIBSH, KURKUMA
old-timer	SOURDOUGH		MADRAKAH, SAJAR, SAWQIRAH
Pacific Railway	CPR	Argentina	BERMEJO, BLANCO
pay office	WAN(I)GAN, WANGUN		BUEN TEMPO, CORRIENTES
police force	MOUNTIES, RCMP		DE MOSTARDAS, DEL ESTE
pondweed	WATER-THYME		DELGADA, DOS BAHIAS, GUARDIAN
porcupine	URSON		LA PALOMA, LOBOS, MEDANOSA
provinces/territories			PASO, POLONZO, RASA
—Alberta	ALBA, ALTA		SAN ANTONIO
—British Columbia	BC		SAN FRANCISCO, STA MARIA
—Manitoba	MAN	Australia	ARNHEM, BYRON
—New Brunswick	NB		CATASTROPHE
—Newfoundland	NF(D)		D'ENTRECASTEAUX, DIRECTION
—Nova Scotia	NS		DUIFREN, FLATTERY, GRENVILLE
—Ontario	ONT		HAWKE, HOWE, KNOB, LEEUWIN
—Northwest Territories	NWT		LEVEQUE, LONDONDERRY
—Prince Edward Island	PEI		MELVILLE, NATURALISTE
—Quebec	PQ, Q, QUE		NORTH-WEST, OTWAY, PAISLEY
—Saskatchewan	SASK		WILSON'S, YORK

Brazil	CACIPORE, CORUMBA	Honduras	CAMERON, GRACIAS A DIOS
	DE ATALAIA, DE SAO ROQUE		HONDURAS
	DO BALEIA, DO TOPAGE	India	CALIMERE, CORMORIN
	DOS PASTOS, MACEIO		MALAN, MONZE, NUH, PISHKAN
	MAGUARINHO, MANGUES VERDES	Iran	MAIDUNI
	ORANGE, RASO, REDONDA	Ireland	BLOOD, CARNSORE, ERRIS
Burma	NEGRAIS		FORELAND, MALIN
Canada	BATHURST, BRETON, CANSO		OLD HEAD OF KINSALE
	CHARLES, CHIDLEY, ESKIMO		ROSSAN, SLYNEHD, WICKLOW
	GASPE, HATTON, HENRIETTA MARIA	Isle of Man	POINT OF AYRE
	KELLET, M'CLURE, NORTH	Isle of Wight	ST CATHERINE'S
	PRINCE ALBERT, RAGE, RAY	Italy	CIRCEO, COLONNE, LICOSA
	ST LEWIS, SABLE, SCOTT		RIZZUTO, S MARIA DI LEUCA
	WALSINGHAM, , WOLSTENHOLME		S VITO, SPARTIVENTO, VATICANO
Chile	ALLENA, ANGAMOS, CARRANZA	Liberia	PALMAS
	CARRIZAL, DE LOS LOBOS	Libya	MISURATA
	GORDA, GRUESTIA, LENGUA DE VACA	Mauretania	BLANC
	MORRO, PILAR, PLATA, QUILAN	Mexico	ANGEL, CATOCHE, CORRIENTES
	SAN PEDRO, SAN VEDRA, TAITAO		DE HUATULCO, HERRERO
	TETAS, TOPOCAIMA		S TELMO
Colombia	CHIRAMBIRA, CORRIENTES	Morocco	ALMINA, TRES FORCAS, YUBI
	CRUCES, ESTRELLA, GALLINAS	Mozambique	DA BURRA FALSA
	GUASCAMA, MANGLARES, MARZO	Namibia	CROSS, DOLPHIN, ELIZABETH
Crete	KRIOS, LITHINON, SIDHEROS		FRIO, PALGRAVE
	SPATHA, STAVROS, TRIPTII	New Guinea	D'URVILLE, DE JONG'S
Cyprus	ARNAUTI, ASPRO, GATA		VALSCH
	GRECO, KORMAKITI, PLAKOTI	New Zealand	ABUT, BRETT, CAMPBELL
	POMOS, ST ANDREAS, , ZEVGHARI		CASCADE, COLVILLE, EGMONT
Denmark	SKAGENS, THE SKAW		FAREWELL, FOUL WIND, JACKSON
Ecuador	GALERA, LORENZO, PASADA		KAHUTARA, KIDNAPPER'S, NORTH
Egypt	ABU DARA, BENAS, EL KENAYIS		PALLISER, PROVIDENCE, PUYSEGUR
	KASAR, OLBA, RAWAI		ROCK, RUNAWAY, SOUTH-WEST
England	BEACHY, DODMAN		TAUROA, TURNAGAIN
	FLAMBOROUGH, FORMBY	Nicaragua	GORDA
	HARTLAND, LAND'S END	Norway	LINDESNES, NORDKAPP
	LIZARD, NORTH FORELAND		NORTH, THE NALE
	PORTLAND BILL, ST ALBAN'S	Panama	MALA, MANZANILLO
	ST BEES, SPURN, START, TINTAGEL		ARIATO, S BLAS
France	COURONNE, DE GRAVE	Peru	AGUJA, BLANCO, CHALA
	DE LA COUBRE, DE LA HAGUE		CHICHAMA, DE CHILCA, DE COLES
	DE LA HEVE, DE L'AIGUILLE		PARINAS, PESCADORES, STA MARIA
	DE PENMARCH, GRIS NEZ		SALINAS
	ST GILDA'S	Philippines	BOJEADOR, ENGANO
Gabon	LOPEZ, MATOUTT		MAIRARIRA, NEGRA, TINACA
	STE CATHERINE, TSHIBOBO	Russia	SARYCH
Ghana	THREE POINTS	Scotland	BUCHAN, DUNCANSBY
Greece	AKRITAS, DORO, KAFIREUS		KINNAIRD, MULL OF GALLOWAY
	KANASTRAION, KIMI, MALEA		MULL OF KINTYRE, ST ABB'S
	MASTIKHO, MATAPAN, MESTA		WRATH
	PAPAC, SKILLAION, TAINARON	Senegal	VERDE, VERT
Guinea	VERGA	Sicily	CALAVA, S VITO
Hawaii	APUA, BARBER'S, KA LAE	Sierra Leone	ST ANN, SIERRA LEONE
	KAENA, KAUNA, KEEHOLE, KOKO	Somalia	GARDAFUI
	KUHUKU, KUMUKAHI, LELEIWI	South Africa	AGULHAS, CAPE POINT
	MAKAPUU, PEPEEKEO, UPOLU		DANGER, GOOD HOPE, HANGKLIP
Hebrides	BARRA		ST FRANCIS, ST LUCIA, STONY

Spain	CALA BURRAS, CARVUEIRO
	DE CREUS, DE GATA, DE LA NAO
	DE LAS ENTINAS, DE PALOS
	DE SALOU, DE TORTOSA, ESPICHEL
	FINISTERRE, MACHICHACO
	MARROQUI, ORTEGAL, ROSA
	ST MARIA, ST VINCENT, SINES
	TINOSO, TORINANA, TRAFALGAR
Spanish Sahara	BARBAS, BOJADOR
Sri Lanka	DEVIL'S, DONDRA
	PAUL, PEDRO
Tanzania	DELGADO
Tasmania	GRIM, SOUTH-EAST
	SOUTH-WEST
Thailand	LIANT
Tierra del Fuego	SAN DIEGO, SAN JUAN
	SAN PABLO
Tunis	CAP BON
Turkey	BABA, KORAKA
USA	BANDA, BLANCO, CANAVERAL
	CHARLES, COD, COLNETT
	CONCEPTION, DISAPPOINTMENT
	EUGENIA, FALSO, FEAR, FLORIDA
	HATTERAS, LOOKOUT, MAY
	MENDOCINO, MONTAUK, S LAZARO
	S LUCAS, SABLE, SAN BLAS
Venezuela	BARIMA
Wales	BRAICH Y PWLL, GREAT ORME
	LITTLE ORME, NASH, ORMES
	ST BRIDE'S, ST DAVID'S
	ST GOWAN'S, STUMBLE, WORMS
Zaire	NOIRE, PADRAO
card games	ALL FOURS, BANK CRAPS
	BANKER, BEZIQUE, BLIND HOOKEY
	BRAG, CAS(S)INO, CATCH-THE-TEN
	CRIB(BAGE), GRAB, HEARTS
	KALABRIAS, KLABBERJASS
	KLOB(IOSH), LANTERLOO
	LONG WHIST, LOO, MATRIMONY
	NAP(OLEON), NEWMARKET
	NODDY, OLD FOURS
	ONE-AND-THIRTY, PAM
	PITCH, (PROGRESSIVE) WHIST
	RUFF (AND HONOURS)
	SANCHO-PEDRO, SETBACK
	SHORT WHIST, SLAM, SOLO WHIST
	SPECULATION, SPOIL-FIVE, TRUMP
32 cards	PICQUET
40 cards	COON CAN, MONTE, OMBRE
	QUADRILLE, SEVEN AND A HALF
	ZIGINETTE
45 cards	FARMER
48 cards	CRAP CARDS
ace of	
—clubs (quadrille)	BASTO
—trumps (gleek)	TIB

American game	EUCHRE, FARO
	PINOCHLE, POKER
bluff with four of same suit	FOUR FLUSH
bridge	AUCTION, CHICAGO
	CLUB, CONTRACT, FOUR-DEAL
card winning part of stakes	
for holder (old whist)	SWAB
children's game	BEGGAR-MY-NEIGHBOUR
	HAPPY FAMILIES
	MUGGINS, OLD MAID, SNAP
	SNIP-SNAP-SNORUM
declaration in bezique	MARRIAGE
European	KABARIATZ, KALIBRIZ
	(KLABER) JASS, SMOOSJASS
faro variants	BUCKING THE TIGER
	(CHINESE) FAN-TAN, FAROBANK
	JEWISH FARO, MONTE (BANK)
	PUT AND TAKE, RED DOG, SKIN
	STUSS, ZIGINETTE
fortune-telling	TAROK, TAROT
four aces etc in a hand	MOURNIVAL
French game	BACCARAT, BOUILLOTTE
	CHEMIN DE FER, ECARTE
	QUINZE, ROUGE-ET-NOIR
	TRENTE-ET-QUARANTE
	VINGT-ET-UN
hand	
—played with cards laid out	DUMMY
euchre	JAMBONE
solo whist	MISERE OUVERT
	OPEN MISERE
	ABONDANCE DECLAREE
	ABUNDANCE DECLARED
—with five highest	
cards (euchre)	JAMBOREE
—without trumps	CHICANE
highest card in loo	PAM
knave	JACK
—of clubs	KLABER JASS, PAM
like	
—bezique	PINOC(H)LE
—nap	PAM, PUT(T)
Mexican	THREE-CARD MONTE
old	BASSET, BINOCHLE, BRISCAN
	BRUSQUEMBILLE, CINQ CENTS
	FIVE HUNDRED, FLAKERNOBLE
	LANSQUENET, MARRIAGE, NODDY
	PRIMERO, REVERSIS
—Scottish	PENNEECH, PENNEECK
patience	KLONDIKE, KLONDYKE
	SOLITAIRE
pinochle variants	AEROPLANE, AUCTION
	CUTTHROAT, CHECK, CONTRACT
	FIREHOUSE, HARTFORD
	NEW ENGLAND
	(RADIO) PARTNERSHIP, TURN-UP

poker | DRAW, STUD
—variants | ACEY-DEUCY, ALBEMARLE
ANACONDA, BASEBALL
BASKETBALL, BEAT IT
BEAT YOUR NEIGHBOUR
BLAZER, BLIND ANTE
BLIND OPENERS, BLUFF, BULL
CANADIAN, CINCINNATI
CONFUSION, CRAZY, CRISS CROSS
DOUBLE BARTER, DOUBLE UP
DR PEPPER, ENGLISH, FAIRVIEW
FIVE BETS, FIVE-CARD
FIVES AND TENS, FLIP
FOLLOW MARY, FOLLOW THE KING
FOLLOW THE QUEEN, FOOTBALL
FOUR FORTY-FOUR, FREEZE-OUT
HEINZ, HIGH-LOW, HOLD 'EM
JACKPOT, KANAKEE, KLONDIKE (BOB)
LAINO, LAME BRAIN (PETE)
LEG, LOWBALL, MISTIGRIS
MONTEREY, NEW YORK
NIGHT BASEBALL, NO LOOKIE
NO PEEKIE, OMAHA
PASS THE GARBAGE
PIG (IN A POKE), PROGRESSIVE
PUT AND TAKE, ROCKLEIGH
ROLL 'EM, ROLL OVER
ROUND THE WORLD, RUM
SCREW YOUR NEIGHBOUR
SCREWY LOUIE, SHIFTING SANDS
SHOWDOWN, SKARNEY, SKEETS
SPANISH, SPIT IN THE OCEAN
ST LOUIS, STORMY WEATHER
THREE FORTY-FIVE, TIGER
TURN-UP, TWIN BEDS, TWO-LEG
WHISKY, WILD WIDOW, WOOLWORTH

pontoon | VINGT-ET-UN
—variants | ACE-DEUCE-JACK
ACE LOW, BACCARAT (BANQUE)
BANGO, BANKER AND BROKER
BLACKJACK, CHEMIN-DE-FER
CHEMMY, FARMER, FIFTEEN
HORSE RACE, PONTOON
QUINCE, SEVEN-AND-A-HALF
SHIMMY, SLOGGER, THIRTY-FIVE
TWENTY-ONE, VANJOHN
VINGT-ET-UN, YOU CALL 'EM

rummy | GIN
—variants | BANKERS, BLOCK, BOAT HOUSE
CALOOCHI, CANASTA, CAPTAINS
CAROUSEL, CINCINNATI, COMBINATION
CONTINENTAL, COON CAN, DIZZY
ELIMINATION, FORTUNE, FREEZE OUT
GIN, JAVA, JERSEY GIN
INDIAN CRAPS, KALOOKI, KNOCK
LIVERPOOL, MICHIGAN, MISSISSIPPI

OKLAHOMA, OLD-FASHIONED, PAN
PARTNERSHIP, PERSIAN, PIF-PAF
PROGRESSIVE, QUEEN CITY, RAMINO
ROUND ROBIN, ROUND-THE-CORNER
SKARNEY, SKIP, STANDARD HOLLYWOOD
SUPER GIN, TONK, TURN-UP

Russian game | VINT
second highest card | MANILLE
sequence of three cards
of same suit | TIERCE
series of games (bridge) | RUBBER
sevenfold increase in
stake at basset | SEPTLEVA
signal for trumps | PETER
silent game | MUMCHANCE
single-handed game | PATIENCE, SOLITAIRE
Spanish game | COON-CAN
stake at poker | ANTE
three-handed game | CUT-THROAT (BRIDGE)
GLEEK, OMBRE
SKAT, TRED(D)ILLE

tricks
—no tricks (solo whist) | MISERE
with exposed hand | MISERE OUVERT
OPEN MISERE
—5 tricks (solo whist) | SOLO
—12 tricks
bridge | LITTLE SLAM
whist | SWAB
—13 tricks
bridge | GRAND SLAM
solo whist | ABONDANCE
ABUNDONCE
BUNDLE
—with exposed
hand | ABONDANCE DECLAREE
ABUNDANCE DECLARED
unscientific whist | BUMBLE-PUPPY
Venetian game | BASSET

carriages
including: cart
coach
2-wheeled | BANDY, BUGGY, CABRIOLET
CHARIOT, CURRICLE, DENNET
DOG-CART, DESOBLIGEANTE
GIG, GOVERNESS CART
GUINGUETTE, HANSOM CAB
JAUNTING-CAR, JAUNTY
(JIN)RICKSHAW, QUADRIGA
SCOTCH CART, SCURRY
STANHOPE, SULKY, TILBURY
TONGA, TRAP
TUMBREL, TUMBRIL
3-wheeled
—pedal-car | TRISHAW
—for hire | PEDICAB

4-wheeled	BAROUCHE, BERLIN, BRAKE
	BREAK, BROUGHAM,
	BUCKBOARD, BUGGY
	CART, CHUCK-WAGON
	CLARENCE, COACH
	CONESTOGA WAGON
	COUPE, DILIGENCE
	DOS-A-DOS, DRAY, DROS(H)KY
	FIACRE, FLY, GROWLER
	HACKNEY CARRIAGE
	HACKNEY COACH, HERDIC
	PHAETON, PRAIRIE SCHOONER
	ROCKAWAY, SURREY
	VIS-A-VIS, WAG(G)ON, WAIN
—coach	FOUR-IN-HAND
—folding hood	CALASH, LANDAU
	VICTORIA
—(US)	BUGGY
	CHUCK-WAGON, HERDIC
	PRAIRIE SCHOONER
African	SCOTCH CART
agricultural	WAG(G)ON
baggage-wagon	FOURGON
bullock-cart (Indian)	BANDY
Burmese state carriage	RATH
cart	DRAY, WAG(G)ON, WAIN
Chinese	(JIN)RICKSHAW
coach	FOUR-IN-HAND
Continental stage-coach	DILIGENCE
closed	BROUGHAM
—covered	JINGLE, (HANSOM-)CAB
—military	TUMBREL, TUMBRIL
—US	HERDIC
dung-cart	TUMBREL, TUMBRIL
fast stagecoach	FLY
four-horse	FOUR-IN-HAND
French	DILIGENCE, FIACRE
	TUMBREL, TUMBRIL
gig	DENNET, GUINGETTE
	TILBURY, SPIDER
high-wheeled	
hired coach	HACKNEY-CARRIAGE
Indian	BANDY, BUGGY, EKKA
	GHARRI, GHARRY, TONGA
Irish	BIANCONI, GINGLE
	JAUNTING-CAR, JAUNTY
Italian	VETTURA
light	
—carriage	CHAISE(-CART), TRAP
—cart	SHANDRY(DAN)
—gig	(TIM-)WHISK(E)Y
long and open	DRAG
mail-coach	POST
old-fashioned chaise	SHANDRYDAN
one	
—horse	EKKA, FLY

—person	DESOBLIGEANTE, SULKY
—seater	STANHOPE
open carriage	WAGONETTE
passenger coach	STAGE-COACH
rickety vehicle	SHANDRYDAN
Roman	BIGA, CHARIOT, QUADRIGA
Russian	DROS(H)KY, TROIKA
—wagon	AR(A)BA, KIBITKA, TELEGA
small landau	LANDAULET(TE)
Spanish, covered	TARTANA
tip-cart	TUMBREL, TUMBRIL
wagonette	BRAKE, BREAK
with facing seats	VIS-A-VIS

cats

American	MAINE COON
curly-coated	REX
disappearing cat	CHESHIRE
Eliot's book of	OLD POSSUM'S
fighting cat	KILKENNY
French cat	CHAT
German cat	KATZE
grinning cat	CHESHIRE
in Reynard the Fox	TIBERT
Italian	VETTURA
large	MAINE COON
long hair	ANGORA, BALINESE, BIRMAN
	MAINE COON, PERSIAN
	RAGDOLL, TURKISH
mythical	KELLAS CATS
Norwegian	SKOGCATT
old	GIB, GRIMALKIN
proverbial cat	KILKENNY
Samuel Johnson's cat	HODGE
Sancho Panza's cat	BAVIECA
Scottish cat	BAUDRONS
she-cat	TIB(CAT)
short hair	ABYSSINIAN, BOMBAY
	BURMESE, DEVON REX, EGYPTIAN
	EXOTIC, HAVANA, JAPANESE BOBTAIL
	KORAT, MANX, RUSSIAN BLUE
	SIAMESE, SINGAPURA, SNOWSHOE
	SOMALI, SPHYNX, TONKINESE
	WIREHAIR
slang	MOG(GIE), MOGGY
smiling cat	CHESHIRE
Spanish cat	GATA, GATO
swimming cat	TURKISH VAN
tailless	MANX
theatre cat	GUS, PUSS-IN-BOOTS
yellow and black	TORTOISE-SHELL

cattle

African	AFRICANDER, ANKOLE, BAHEMI
	BAPEDI, BASHI, BORAN
	DRAKENSBERGER, KIGEZI, KURI
	LANDIM, N'DAMA
	NGUNI, WATUSI, WHITE FULANI

American	BEEFALO, BRAHMAN	
	BRANGUS, HOLSTEIN-FRIESIAN	
	SANTA GERTRUDIS	
	TEXAS LONGHORN	
Australian	DROUGHTMASTER	
	MURRAY GREY	
	TASMANIAN GREY	
Austrian	PINZGAU(E)R	
Belgian	BELGIAN BLUE	
Canadian	HOLSTEIN-FRIESIAN	
	RED AND WHITE FRIESIAN	
castrated male	BULLOCK, OX, STEER	
Channel Islands	ALDERNEY, GUERNSEY	
	JERSEY	
Danish	DANISH RED	
dehorned	MUL(L)EY	
English	BRITISH WHITE, DEVON	
	GLOUCESTER, HEREFORD	
	LINCOLN RED, LONGHORN	
	RED AND WHITE FRIESIAN	
	SHORTHORN, SOUTH DEVON	
	SUSSEX, TEESWATER	
	(WILD) WHITE PARK	
Egyptian	BALADI, DAMIETTA	
	MARYUTI, SAIDI	
female	COW, HEIFER, OX	
—sterile	FREE-MARTIN	
Finnish	FINNCATTLE	
	FINNISH AYRSHIRE	
French	AUBRAC, BLONDE D'AQUITAINE	
	CHAROL(L)AIS, GASCONNE	
	LIMOUSIN, MAINE-ANJOU	
	NORMANDY, PIE ROUGE DE L'EST	
	SALERS, SIMMENTAL, TARENTAISE	
German	ANGELN, FLECKVIEH	
	GERMAN RED PIED	
	GERMAN YELLOW, HOLSTEIN	
heavy breed	FRI(E)SIAN	
Hebrides	KYLOE	
heifer (Scottish)	QUEY	
hornless	REDPOLL	
Indian	GIR KANKREJ KHILLARI	
	RED SINDHI THARPARKAR	
Irish	DEXTER, IRISH MOILED, KERRY	
Italian	CHIANINA MARCHIGIANA	
	PIE(D)MONTESE, ROMAGNOLA	
male	BULL, BULLOCK, OX, STEER	
Netherlandish	DUTCH FRIESIAN	
	GRONINGEN	
	MEUSE-RHINE-IJSSEL	
Norwegian	BLACKSIDED TRONDHEIM	
	TELEMARK	
old		
—breed	BLUE ALBION	
—terms	AVER, FEE, NEAT	
Portuguese	BARROSA, GALEGA, MIRANDA	

Russian	ALA TAU, KHOL MOGOR	
	KOSTROMA, RED STEPPE	
Scottish	ABERDEEN ANGUS, AYRSHIRE	
	BELTED GALLOWAY, GALLOWAY	
	HIGHLAND CATTLE, LUING	
	SHETLAND, WEST HIGHLAND	
	(see also **Scottish**)	
short-horned	DURHAM	
Spanish	ANDALUSIAN, FIGHTING BULL	
	GALICIAN BLOND	
Swiss	BROWN SWISS, SIMMENTAL	
Texan	LONGHORN	
Welsh	WELSH BLACK	
West Country	DEVON	
West Indian	JAMAICA HOPE	
white-faced	HAWKEY, HAWKIE, HEREFORD	
young	CALF, HEIFER, STEERLING	
	STIRK	
	(see also **ox**)	
cattle diseases	ANTHRAX, BLACK QUARTER	
	BLACKWATER, BLUE TONGUE	
	BRUCELLOSIS, REDWATER	
actinobacillosis	WOODY-TONGUE	
actinomycosis	LUMPY JAW	
bacterial	ANTHRAX, JOINT-ILL	
	LEPTOSPIROSIS, NAVEL-ILL	
	PLEURO-PNEUMONIA	
	SALMONELLOSIS	
	TUBERCULOSIS	
bovine spongiform		
encephalitis	BST	
cattle plague	RINDERPEST	
	STEPPE MURRAIN	
contagious abortion	BRUCELLOSIS	
deficiency disease	ACETONAEMIA	
	HYPOMAGNESAEMIA	
	KETOSIS	
eye disease	KERATOCONJUNCTIVITIS	
	NEW FOREST EYE	
foot		
—disease	FOOT AND MOUTH	
	FOUL IN THE FOOT	
	LAMINITIS	
—and mouth disease	APHTHOUS FEVER	
fungal	ACTINOMYCOSIS	
	RINGWORM	
gas in the stomach	BLOAT	
grass staggers	HYPOMAGNESAEMIA	
	TETANY	
husk	LUNGWORM	
hypocalcaemia	MILK FEVER	
hypomagnesaemia	GRASS STAGGERS, TETANY	
inflammation of		
—foot	LAMITIS	
—throat	GARGET	
—udder	GARGET, MAMMITIS	

intestinal	JOHNES DISEASE
lumpy jaw	ACTINOMYCOSIS
mad cow disease	BSE
	BOVINE SPONGIFORM ENCEPHALITIS
milk fever	HYPOCALCAEMIA
parasitic	HUSK, LIVER FLUKE
	LUNGWORM, ROUNDWORM
	TAPEWORM, WARBLE-FLY
rinderpest	CATTLE PLAGUE
	STEPPE MURRAIN
steppe murrain	CATTLE PLAGUE
	RINDERPEST
tetany	GRASS STAGGERS
	HYPOMAGNESAEMIA
tuberculosis	PEARL DISEASE
udder disease	MASTITIS
viral	EBL, ENZOOTIC BOVINE LEUCOSIS
	IBR
	INFECTIOUS BOVINE RHINOTRACHETIS
woody tongue	ACTINOBACILLOSIS

Celebes (Sulawesi)

wild hog	BABIR(O)USA
	DEER HOG, HORNED HOG

Celtic

alphabet	OG(H)AM
festival	BELTANE
harp	CLAIRSCHACH, CLARSACH
high steward	MORMAOR
noble	TAOISEACH
sword	CLAYMORE, CLEDDYO

Central African Republic — CAR, RCA

capital	BANGUI
coin	FRANC

Central America

agave	SISAL
ant	KELEP
bird	MOTMOT, SAWBILL
coin	COLON
early civilisation	AZTEC, MAYA
	TOLTEC, ZAPOTEC
lapwing	TERU-TERO
Maya calendar cycle	
—1 day	KIN
—20 days	UINAL
—360 days	TUN
—7200 days	KATUN
—144,000 days	BAKTUN
measure	VARA
races	CORA, CUNA, GUAYMI, HUASTEC
	HUICHOL, LENCA, MISKITO, MIXTEC
	NAHUATL, NICARAO, PAYA, ZAPOTEC
rubber (tree)	(H)ULE
tree	AMATE, EBO(E), S(A)OUARI
	(see also **South America***)*

cereal

African	MEALIE, TEFF(GRASS)

barley	
—shaped by grinding	PEARL BARLEY
—with husks removed	POT BARLEY
	SCOTCH BARLEY
boiled oatmeal	PORRIDGE
coarsely ground	GROATS, GROUT, MEAL
—maize	HOMINY(GRITS), SAMP
—oats	GRITS
ear of maize	CORNCOB
Eastern	JAPANESE MILLET
farina porridge	POLENTA
finely ground	FARINA, FLOUR
Indian	
—corn	MAIZE
—millet	RAGGEE, RAGGY, RAGI
inner husks	BRAN
Irish porridge	STIRABOUT
Italian porridge	POLENTA
lentil flour	ERVALENTA, REVALENTA
maize	INDIAN CORN, SWEETCORN
—Mexican dish	TAMAL(E), TOMALLEY
—porridge	MUSH
American	SAMP
mixed cereals	MASHLAM, MASHLIM
	MASHLIN, MASHLUM
	MASHLOCH, MASLIN
oatmeal and water	DRAMMACH, DRAMMOCH
oats, fruit, etc	MUESLI
other cereal dishes	BURGOO, CORNFLAKES
	CORN ON THE COB
	COUSCOUS, ENCHILADA
	KUSKUS, OATMEAL
	PEARL BARLEY, POT BARLEY
	SEMOLINA, SOWANS, SUCCOTASH
	TABBOULEH, TABBOULI, TAHINA
	TAHINI, TORTILLA
	(see also **rice***)*
parched maize	NO-CAKE, PINOLE, POPCORN
products	CORNFLAKES, CORNFLOUR
	CORNMEAL, RICE CRISPIES
	SHREDDED WHEAT
Red Indian maize dish	SAMP, SUCCOTASH
	SUP(P)AWN
semolina porridge	POLENTA
South African maize	MEALIES
thin porridge	GRUEL
types	BARLEY, BUCKWHEAT, MAIZE
	MILLET, OATS, RICE, RYE
	SWEETCORN, TRITICALE, WHEAT
—buckwheat	SARRASIN, SARRAZIN
	TURKEY WHEAT
wheat	AMELCORN, EMMER
	TRITICOM
—boiled in milk, etc	FRUMENTY, FURMETY
—inferior	SPELT(Z)
—primitive	EINKORN

—rye hybrid	TRITICALE
—spring	DURUM
—wild	EMMER
young corn ears	GREEN CORN
Ceylon	SRI LANKA
aboriginal race	VEDDA(H)
bandicoot	PIG-RAT
Buddhist shrine	DAGOBA
capital	COLOMBO
coin	CENT
finial of dagoba	TEE
form of marriage	BEENAH
grass	CITRONELLA
language	PALI, SIN(G)HALESE, TAMIL
lemur	LORIS
milkweed	COW-PLANT
modern name	SRI LANKA
palm	CORYPHA, TALIPAT, TALIPOT
—leaf book	OCA
people	CINGALESE, SINHALA
	SIN(G)HALESE, TAMIL
pig-rat	BANDICOOT
spice	CINNAMON
timber	CALAMANDER, COROMANDEL
	(*see also* **timber**)
umbrella-shaped finial	TEE
Chad	
capital	NDJAMENA
coin	FRANC
people	TUAREG
Chaldean	
bible	TARGUM
city	UR OF THE CHALDEES
Channel Islands	CI
islands	ALDERNEY, GUERNSEY
	HERM, JERSEY, SARK
coin	DOUBLE
cheese	
American	
—cottage	POT CHEESE
—processed	CLUB CHEESE
—soft	PHILADELPHIA
Ayrshire	DUNLOP
Belgian	LIMBURGER
Cornish	YARG
covered with grape	
seeds	TOME AU RAISIN
Cypriot	HALLOUMIS
Danish	BLUE CASTELLO, BOUCLET
	DANABLU, DANBO
	DANISH BLUE, ESROM, HARVARTI
	JUTLAND BLUE, LE MIDI
	ORANGE ROLL, SAMSOE, SATIA
	SVENBO, TOLKO, TYBO
Dorset	BLUE VINNEY
Dutch	EDAM, GOUDA

English	ADMIRAL'S, APPLEWOOD
	BEAMERDALE, BEL(L)SHIRE
	BLUE VINNEY, BOTTON, CHARNWOOD
	CHEDDAR, CHESHIRE, COTSWOLD
	COUNTY, CURD, DERBY
	DOUBLE GLOUCESTER, HUNTSMAN
	LANCASHIRE, LEICESTER
	LYMESWOLD, MORVEN, NUTWOOD
	PEPPERVALE, RUTLAND
	SAGE DERBY, SHERWOOD, SOMERTON
	SHROPSHIRE BLUE, STILTON
	WALGROVE, WALTON, WENSLEYDALE
	WHIRL, WINDSOR (RED)
French	BABYBEL, BANON, BEAUFORT
	BLANC DES CHAMPS, BLEU D'AUVERGNE
	BLEU DE BRESSE, BOMBEL
	BOULETTE, BOURSAULT
	BOURSIN, BREBIS DES PYRENEES
	BRIE(DE MEAUX), CABECOU
	CAMEMBERT, CANTAL, COULOMMIERS
	D'ANVESNES, DOUX DE MONTAGNE
	ETORKI, FOURME D'AMBERT
	FROMAGE (BLANC), FROMAGE FRAIS
	GERVAIS, GORMANDISE, IRATY
	LARUNS, LE ROULE, LIVAROT
	MEULE D'OR, MUNSTER, NEUCHATEL
	OSSAU, PETIT SUISSE, PIP CREM(E)
	PONT L'EVEQUE, PORT SALUT
	RAMBOL PEPPER, REBLOCHON
	RIGOTTE, RONDELLE, ROQUEFORT
	ST AGUR, ST CHEVRIER
	ST HECLAIRE, ST JULIEN
	ST MAURE, ST NECTAIRE
	ST PAULIN, TARTARE
	TERRES D'OR, TOMME DE CHANTAL
	VALBRESO, VALENCAY, VIEUX PANE
from	
—ewe's milk	BREBIS DES PYRENEES
	ETORKI, EWE-CHEESE, FETA
	HAL(O)UMI, IDIAZIBAL, IRATY
	LARUNS, MANCHEGO, OSSAU
	PARAMO DE GUSMAN, PECORINI
	ROQUEFORT, SERPA, SERRA
	VALBRESO
—goat's milk	CABECOU, CAW'S CARON
	CHEVRE, CHEVROTIN, FETA
	LOS BALACHARES, PANT-YS-GAWN
	PEN-Y-BONT, ST MAURE, VALENCAY
—soya bean milk	TOFU
garlic-flavoured	HRAMSA
German	ALLGAU, BLOU BAY
	BRUDER BASIL, CAMBOZOLA
	EMMENT(H)AL(ER)
	FRUHSTUCKSKASE, GRUNLAND
	HANDKASE, HARZ, LIMBURGER
	MAINZ, MIREE, MUNSTER, PIKADOR

	PILZKASE, QUARK, ROMADUR, RUPP
	SBRINZ, TILSIT(ER)
Greek	AGRAFA, FETA, KEFALOTYRI
high-fat	CREAM CHEESE
Indian	PANEER
indifferent	MOUSETRAP
Irish	CASHEL BLUE, GUBBEEN
	MILLEENS
Italian	BEL PAESE, CACIOCAVALLA
	DOLCELATTE, FONTINA
	GORGONZOLA, GRANO PADANO
	MASCARPONE, MASCHERPONE
	MOZZARELLA, PARMESAN
	PECORINO, PROVOLONE
	RICOTTO, ROBIOLA, ROMANO
	STRACCHINO, TALEGGIO
	TARTUFELLE
	TORTA SAN GAUDENZIO
	VENETO
lightly-salted	DEMI-SEL
low-fat	COTTAGE CHEESE
moulded by hand	HAND-CHEESE
Norwegian	JARL(E)SBERG, MYSOST
Portuguese	SERPA, SERRA
Scottish	CABOC, CROWDIE, DUNLOP
	KEBBOCK, KEBBUCK, ORKNEY
Somerset	CHEDDAR
Spanish	CABREALES, IDIAZABAL
	LOS BALACHARES, MAHON
	MANCHEGO, PARAMO DE GUSMAN
	TETILLA
Swiss	APPENZELL, EMMENT(H)AL(ER)
	GRUYERE, SAPSAGO, TILSIT
	TOGGENBURGER KASE
	VACHERIN
unripe soft cheese	COOK CHEESE
Welsh	ACORN, CAERPHILLY
	CARDIGAN, CAW'S CARON
	CAW'S CENARTH
	LLANBOIDY, MERLIN
	PANT-YS-GAWN, PENCAR(R)EG
	PEN-Y-BONT, SKIRRID, TEIFI

cheese dishes

—cheese and ham	
sandwich	CROQUE-MONSIEUR
—cooked	FONDUE
on toast	BUCK RABBIT
	WELSH RAREBIT, WELSH RABBIT
—individual	RAMAKIN, RAMEKIN
	RAMEQUIN
—melted (Swiss)	RACLETTE
—other	ALPINE EGG, CHEESE SOUFFLE
	CHEESECAKE, DUTCH OMELETTE
	FONDUE, PIZZA, ROMAN GNOCCHI
	ROQUEFORT QUICHE
	QUICHE LORRAINE

chemistry

absorption of	
—gas by solid	OCCLUSION
—water by solid	DELIQUESCENCE
acetylene	ETHYNE
acid	(*see separate entry*)
acting as acid to bases	
and vice versa	AMPHOTERIC
addition of	
—acetyl group	ACETYLATION
—halogen atoms	HALOGENTAION
—hydrogen	HYDROGENATION
	REDUCTION
—hydroxyls	HYDROXYLATION
—impurities to crystal	DOPING
—methyl	METHYLATION
—negative catalyst to	
prevent decomposition	STABILISATION
—nitro group	NITRATION
—oxygen	OXIDATION
—water	HYDRATION
alcohol	ETHANOL
	ETHYL ALCOHOL
alcoholic extract	TINCTURE
alkene	OLEFIN(E)
allotrope of oxygen	OZONE
alternative form	ALLOTOPE
aluminium oxide	CORUNDUM
ammonia and cupric	
hydroxide solution	SCHWEITZER'S REAGENT
amyl acetate	BANANA OIL
	PENTYL ACETATE
amylum	STARCH
analysis by	
—adsorption	CHROMATOGRAPHY
—use of reagents	TITRATION
anomalous water	POLYWATER
aromatic	
—hydrocarbon	TERPENE
—used as indicator	PHENOLPHTHALEIN
—with one or more	
hydroxyl groups	PHENOL
arrangement of elements	
by atomic weight	PERIODIC TABLE
arsenic	
—disulphide	REALGAR
—trioxide	WHITE ARSENIC
artificial water softener	ZEOLITE
atom with	
—free valency	RADICAL
—same	
atomic	
—mass as atom of	
another element	ISOBARE
—number and mass	
but different energy state	ISOMER

proton but different neutron number	ISOTOPE
—unpaired electrons	FREE RADICAL
—with added or missing electrons	ION
atomic weight of isotope	MASS NUMBER
average mass of atoms	ATOMIC WEIGHT
banana oil	AMYL ACETATE
	PENTYL ACETATE
base able to neutralise acid	ALKALI
benzene	PHENE
binary compound of	
—iodine	IODIDE
—oxygen	OXIDE
—sulphur	SULPHIDE
bond where	
—hydrogen atom is bonded to two electronegative atoms	HYDROGEN BOND
—two electrons are donated	SEMIPOLAR BOND
Brunswick green	COPPER OXIDE CHLORIDE
calamine	ZINC CARBONATE
calcium	
—carbonate	CHALK, LIMESTONE
—hydride	HYDROLITH
—hydroxide	LIME WATER, SLAKED LIME
—sulphate	GYPSUM
calomel	MERCUROUS CHLORIDE
carbamide	UREA
carbohydrate	
—in cell walls	CELLULOSE
—with	
5 carbon atoms	PENTOSE
6 carbon atoms	HEXOSE
carbon	
—based	ORGANIC
—dioxide	FIXED AIR
carbylamide	ISOCYANIDE, ISONITRILE
catalyst in polymerisation of ethylene and propylene	ZIEGLER CATALYST
caustic soda	SODIUM HYDROXIDE
chain of two or more amino-acids	PEPTIDE
change	
—caused by enzyme	FERMENTATION
—direct from solid to gas	SUBLIMATION
—in atomic nucleus	NUCLEAR TRANSITION
—of colour induced by light	PHOTOCHROMISM
	PHOTOTROPISM
—to stony structure	PETRIFACTION
chemical	
—analysis by current-voltage curves	POLAROGRAPHY

—attraction	AFFINITY
—bond	VALANCE, VALENCY
—formula showing arrangement of atoms	STRUCTURAL FORMULA
—influence	CATALYSIS
—reaction building compounds from simpler units	SYNTHESIS
chemically inactive	INERT
chemist	DRUGGIST, PHARMACIST
—American	ADAMS, ANFINSEN, ARNON
	AVERY, BAEKELAND, BENEDICT
	BERG, BIGELEISEN, BLOCH
	BRAND, BROWN, CALVIN
	CAROTHERS, CECH, CHARGAFF
	CHASE, CLEMENTI, COLLINS
	CORI, COREY
	CRAFTS, CRAM, DEBYE
	DOERING, FLORY, FOX, FRUTON
	GAIUQUE, GILBERT, HARKINS
	HAUPTMAN, HOAGLAND, HOFFMANN
	INGRAM, KAMEN, KARLE, KHORANA
	KOHMAN, LANGMUIR, LEVENE, LEWIS
	LIBBY, LIPMANN, LIPSCOMB
	MACLEOD, MATTHAE, MERRIFIELD
	MILLER, MIRSKY, MOORE, MCCARTHY
	MCCOY, MIDGLEY, MILLER
	MORLEY, MULLIKEN, NIRENBERG
	NORTHROP,, ONSAGER, ORO
	PALADE, PAULING, PEDERSEN
	RABINOWITCH, RICHARDS
	ROSE, ROSS, RUBEN, SAGER
	SCHAEFER, SEABORG, SHEMIN
	SILLIMAN, SPEDDING, STEIN
	SUMNER, TAUBE, UREY, VIGNEAUD
	WATSON, WHARTON, WILLIAMS
	WOLFGANG, WOODWARD
—Argentinian	LELOIR
—Australian	CORNFORTH, EDMAN
—Austrian	HARTECK, KUHN, PERUTZ
	PREGL, ZSIGMONDY
—Belgian	BAEKELAND, PRIGOGINE, STAS
—British	ABEL, ANDREWS, ASTBURY
	BARTLETT, BARTON, BLACK, BOYLE
	CORNFORTH, COUPER, CRICK, CROSS
	CULLEN, DALTON, DAVY, DEWAR
	GRAHAM, HODGKIN, HOWARTH, JOULE
	KEILIN, KENDREW, KIPPING, LOWRY
	MANN, MARTIN, MINSHELWOOD
	MITCHELL, NEWLANDS, NORRISH
	ORGELL, PARKES, PERKIN
	PERUTZ, PETERS, POLANYI
	POPE, PORTER, RAMSAY
	ROBINSON, RUTHERFORD, SANGER
	SODDY, SYNGE, TENNANT, TODD
	WESTALL, WILKINS, WILKINSON
	WOLLASTON

—Canadian   BAKER, BARTLETT
                       HERTZBERG, HODSON
—Ceylonese   PONNAMPERUMA
—Croatian   RUZICKA
—Czech   HEYROVSKY
—Danish   BRONSTED
—Dutch   DEBYE, DE LA BOE, MULDER
           VAN HELMONT, VAN 'T HOFF
—Finnish   GADOLIN
—French   BERTHELOT, BOUCHARDAT
       BRACCONOT, BRANDENBERGER
          CAVENTON, CHARDONNET
       CHEVREUL, CLAUDE, CURIE
   DE BOISBAUDRAN, DUFAY, DUMAS
     FRIEDEL, GRIGNARD, HERAULT
   LAVOISIER, LE BEL, LEHN, MACQUER
        MOISSON, MORVEAU, PASTEUR
         PAYEN, PELLETIER, PEREY
   PERSOZ, PROUST, REGNAULT, SABATIER
        STAUDINGER, URBAIN, VILLARD
—German   ALDER, BAEYER, BERGMAN
           BLOCH, BOSCH, BRAND
         BUCHNER, BUNSEN, DIELS
         DOBEREINER, DOGMAGK
     EIGEN, EULER-HELPIN, FISCHER
       FRAENKEL-CONRAT, FUELGEN
         GRAEBE, HABER, HOFMANN
     HOPPE-SEYLER, INGRAM, KEKULE
              KILIANI, KIRCHHOFF
     KLAPROTH, KNOOP, KOLBE, KOSSEL
       KREBS, LIEBIG, LIPMANN, LUNGE
      LYNEN, MAYER, MEYER, MEYERHOF
     MORNER, NERNST, OSTWALD, PANETH
         STAHL, STAUDINGER, THIELE
        VON STRADONITZ, WALLACH
              WARBURG, WERNER
       WIELAND, WILLSTATER, WINDAUS
      WINKLER, WISLICENUS, WITTIG
     WOHLER, WOLFGANG, ZIEGLER
—Hungarian   HEVESY
—Indian   KHORANI
—Irish   ANDREWS, BOYLE
—Israeli   KATCHALSKI, WEIZMAN
—Italian   AVOGADRO, CANNIZZARO
         CLEMENTI, MENGHINI, NATTA
             SEGRE, SOBRERO
—Japanese   FUKUI, TAKAMINE, YAGI
—Norwegian   HASSEL
—Polish   ARNON, FRUTON
                       SKLODOWSKA
—Russian   KIRCHHOFF, LEVENE
       LOMONOSOV, MENDELEEV
     OSTWALD, POPOV, RABINOWITCH
                       SEMENOV
—South African   KLUG
—Spanish   OCHOA, ORO

—Swedish   ARRHENIUS, BERZELIUS
        CASPERSSON, EDMAN, GAHN
       MOSANDER, NILSON, SCHEELE
             SVEDBERG, TISELIUS
—Swiss   ABDERHALDEN, BOVET
        DE SAUSSURE, EULER-CHELPIN
         KARRER, MIESCHER, MULLER
             PRELOG, SCHONBEIN
—Yugoslav   PRELOG
chemistry of carbon
  compounds   ORGANIC CHEMISTRY
circulation of carbon
  by living things   CARBON CYCLE
citric acid cycle   KREBS CYCLE
coagulation of fine
  particles into larger   FLOCCULATION
colloid
  —in form of jelly   GEL
  —of
    gel in water   HYDROGEL
    one liquid in another   EMULSION
  —particle   MICELLA, MICELLE
colloidal suspension   SOL
combination of
  —metals   ALLOY
  —molecules of solvent and solute   SOLVATION
  —oxygen   OXIDATION
  —two or more polymers   COPOLYMER
                              DIMER
combining
  —power of atom   VALENCY
  —with
    hydrogen   HYDROGENATION
                         REDUCTION
    oxygen   OXIDATION
common salt   SODIUM CHLORIDE
compound
  —between alcohol and
    glycerine   GLYCOL
  —containing
    carbon   ORGANIC COMPOUND
    iron   FERRIC COMPOUND
                   FERROUS COMPOUND
    oxygen bound to two
      other atoms   EPOXY
    water   HYDRATE
  —formed from
    condensation
      of alcohol and an acid   ESTER
    molecules of solvent and solute   SOLVATE
    replacement of hydrogen
      in acid by a metal   SALT
    union of molecules into
      larger molecules   POLYMER
  —like alcohol but with two
    fewer hydrogen atoms   ALDEHYDE

—of
amino-acids   PEPTIDE
carbon
  —and hydrogen   HYDROCARBON
     ORGANIC COMPOUND
  —hydrogen and
    oxygen   CARBOHYDRATE
cellulose, starch, sugar   CARBOHYDRATE
mercury   AMALGAM
metal with
  —halogen   HALIDE
  —nitrogen   NITRIDE
nitrogen with
  —another element   NITRIDE
  —sugar   NUCLEOSIDE
oxygen with
  —another element   OXIDE
  —two alkyl groups   ETHER
sulphur with another
   element   SULPHIDE
three elements   TERNARY COMPOUND
two elements   BINARY COMPOUND
—which
can form further
   compounds   UNSATURATED COMPOUND
can give up proton
   to a base   ORGANIC ACID
will not undergo further
   reaction   SATURATED COMPOUND
—with
atoms linked with
  —one bond   SATURATED BOND
  —two or more
    bonds   UNSATURATED COMPOUND
chains of molecules   POLYMER
metallic ion bonded to
   two or more atoms   CHELATE
molecules comprising three
   monomer molecules   TRIMER
one component enclosed
   in cavities of another   CLATHRATE
single molecules   MONOMER
concentration in solution   TITRE
constituents of air   CARBON DIOXIDE
    NITROGEN, OXYGEN
containing
  —bivalent tin   STANNOUS
  —hexavalent tellurium   TELLURIC
  —tetravalent
    tellurium   TELLUROUS
    tin   STANNIC
    titanium   TITANIC
    uranium   URANIC
  —trivalent
    thallium   THALLIC
    titanium   TITANOUS

   uranium   URANOUS
—univalent thallium   THALLOUS
conversion of
—atmospheric nitrogen   NITROGEN FIXATION
—liquid to vapour below
   boiling point   EVAPORATION
—nitrogen by soil bacteria   NITRIFICATION
—soil compounds to
   nitrates   NITRIFICATION
—solid
   directly to vapour   SUBLIMATION
   or liquid to gas   GASIFICATION
—vapour to liquid   CONDENSATION
convertible isomer   TAUTOMER
copper
—carbonate   AZURITE, VERDIGRIS
—oxide chloride   BRUNSWICK GREEN
—sulphate   BORDEAUX MIXTURE
copperas   FERROUS SULPHATE
    GREEN VITRIOL
corundum   ALUMINIUM OXIDE
covalent bond   HOME-POLAR BOND
cracking   PYOLYSIS
crystal with
—many branches   DENDRITE
—regular lattice
   and no defects   IDEAL CRYSTAL
crystallisation by loss of
   water   EFFLORESENCE
dative bond   COORDINATE BOND
decomposition/dissolution
—by
   acid   ACIDOLYSIS
   electricity   ELECTROLYSIS
   enzyme   FERMENTATION
    ZYMOLYSIS
   heat   ABLATION, CRACKING
    PYROLYSIS, THERMOLYSIS
   irradiation   RADIOLYSIS
   light   PHOTOLYSIS
   micro-organisms   FERMENTATION
   radiant energy   PHOTODISSOCIATION
   water   HYDROLYSIS
—of
substance catalysed
   by enzymes   ENZYMOLYSIS
two compounds   DOUBLE DECOMPOSITION
    METATHESIS
    STEROID, STEROL
derived lipid
description of process
   of electrolysis   IONIC HYPOTHESIS
deuterium   DIPLOGEN
    HEAVY HYDROGEN
—oxide   HEAVY WATER
device for separating
   solid from liquid   FILTER

diagram of benzene ring	KEKULE FORMULA
diatomaceous earth	KIESELGUHR
dichlordiethyl sulphide	MUSTARD GAS
different form of element	ALLOTROPE
diffusion through porous membrane	OSMOSIS
dimethylbenzene	XYLENE, XYLOL
diplogen	DEUTERIUM
	HEAVY HYDROGEN
disorder of a system	ENTROPY
double	
—benzene ring	NAPHTHALENE
—decomposition	METATHESIS
easily melted	EUTECTIC
eau de Javelle	JAVELLE WATER
effect of catalyst on chemical reaction	CATALYSIS
electrically	
—charged particle	ELECTRON, ION, PROTON
—neutral particle	NEUTRON
electrode	
—negative	CATHODE
—positive	ANODE
electrons in outer shell	VALENCY ELECTRONS
electrovalent bond	(HETERO-)POLAR BOND
	IONIC BOND
element	
—of seventh group of periodic table	HALOGEN
—with atomic number above 92	TRANSURANIC ELEMENT
incomplete electron shell	TRANSITION ELEMENT
valency of	
—one	MONAD
—two	DYAD
—three	TRIAD
—four	TETRAD
ester of	
—fatty acids	LIPID
—gycerol	GLYCERIDE
ethanol	(ETHYL) ALCHOHOL
	SPIRITS OF WINE
	WOOD NAPHTHA
ethene	ETHYLENE
ethenyl	VYNIL
ether	DIETHYL ETHER
	DIETHYL OXIDE
ethyne	ACETYLENE
existence in	
—several forms	POLYMORPHISM
—two or more forms	ALLOTROPY
fats and oils	SIMPLE LIPIDS
ferrous sulphate	COPPERAS
	GREEN VITRIOL
fine particles suspended in air	AEROSOL
fixed air	CARBON DIOXIDE
fluid used in cooling systems	REFRIGERANT
force	
—acting between	
masses	GRAVITY
molecules	VAN DER WAAL'S BOND
nucleons	STRONG NUCLEAR FORCE
particles in atoms	ELECTRIC FORCE
	WEAK FORCE
—which binds atoms	AFFINITY
	CHEMICAL BOND
formation of	
—compounds	SYNTHESIS
—crystals by evaporation	EFFLORESCENCE
—ions	IONISATION
—soap	SAPONIFICATION
formula indicating structure of	
—composition of a molecule in a compound	MOLECULAR FORMULA
—molecule	STRUCTURAL FORMULA
—simple test of ratio between molecule's atoms	EMPIRICAL FORMULA
fractional distillation	RESTIFICATION
fusion by heat	SINTERING
gain of electrons by an atom	REDUCTION
gas	(*see separate entry*)
giving different colours when reacting with acid or base	AMPHICHRO(MAT)IC
Glauber's salts	SALTCAKE
	SODIUM SULPHATE
glycol	DIOL
grease remover	DETERGENT
green vitriol	COPPERAS
	FERROUS SULPHATE
group of atoms	
—forming molecular chain	MICELLA, MICELLE
stable entity	MOLECULE
—unchanged in various compounds	RADICAL, RADICLE
—VII elements	HALOGENS
halogen group	ASTATINE, BROMINE
	CHLORINE
	FLUORINE, IODINE
having	
—affinity for water	HYDROPHILIC
—different properties in different directions	AEOLOTROPIC
	ANISOTROPIC

structure but same composition	ALLOMORPHOUS
—isomerism resulting from different arrangement of atoms	STEREOISOMERISM
mirror-imaging	ENANTIOMERISM
—no affinity for water	HYDROPHOBIC
—same crystal structure	ISOMORPHOUS
form	ISOMER
—but different composition	HOMEOMORPHOUS
number of atoms	ISOTERIC
osmotic pressure	ISOTONIC
—similar structure but different composition	ALLOMERISM
—three atoms per molecule	TRIATOMIC
—two atoms per molecule	DIATOMIC
—valency of more than one	POLYVALENT
one	MONOVALENT
	UNIVALENT
two	BIVALENT, DIVALENT
three	TRIVALENT
four	TETRAVALENT
	QUADRIVALENT
five	PENTAVALENT
	QUINQUEVALENT
six	HEXAVALENT
	SEXIVALENT
seven	HEPTAVALENT
	SEPTIVALENT
heat —absorbed or released during change of state	LATENT HEAT
—content per unit mass	ENTHALPY
—required to raise unit mass through one degree	SPECIFIC HEAT
heavy —hydrogen	DEUTERIUM, DIPLOGEN
—water	DEUTERIUM OXIDE
hetero-polar bond	ELECTRO-VALENT BOND
homovalent bond	COVALENT BOND
horizontal series in periodic table	PERIOD
hydrated —ferric oxide	OCHRE
—silicate of calcium and aluminium	ZEOLITE
hydrocarbon —in essential oils	TERPENE
—series	PARAFFIN SERIES
—with closed carbon chain	AROMATIC
fluorine replacing hydrogen	FLUOROCARBON

one —double bond	ALKENE
—triple bond	ALKYNE
open carbon chain	ALIPHATIC
rings	NAPHTHENE
straight chains	ALKANE
	(see also organic below)
hydrogen —combined with another element	HYDRIDE
—isotopes	PROTIUM, DEUTERIUM
	TRITIUM
hydrolith	CALCIUM HYDRIDE
hydrolysis of an ester	SAPONIFICATION
indicator of pH value	LITMUS (PAPER)
inert gas	NOBLE GAS
insoluble substance deposited from solution	PRECIPITATE
introduction of —halogen atoms	HALOGENATION
—nitro group	NITRATION
ionic bond	ELECTROVALENT BOND
isomer —differing in position of attached atoms	EPIMER
—readily interchangeable	TAUTOMER
isonitrile	CARBYLAMIDE
	ISOCYANIDE
isotopes of radioactive substances containing thorium	THORIDES
Javelle water	EAU DE JAVELLE
jelly-like colloid	GEL
law governing —atomic weights	PERIODIC LAW
—dissociation	OSTWALD'S DILUTION LAW
—heat produced in chemical reactions	HESS'S LAW
lead —antimoniate	NAPLES-YELLOW
—carbonate	WHITE LEAD
—monoxide	LITHARGE
letter(s) representing an atom of element	SYMBOL
lime water	CALCIUM HYDROXIDE
linkage by —one covalent and one electrovalent bond	SEMIPOLAR BOND
—shared electrons	COVALENT BOND
	HOMO-POLAR BOND
—transfer of electrons	ELECTRO-VALENT BOND
	HETERO-POLAR BOND
—two pairs of electrons	DOUBLE BOND
liquid —after elution	ELUATE

filtration   FILTRATE
—remaining after crystallisation
  of salt from brine   BITTERN
—used for elution   ELUANT
litharge   LEAD MONOXIDE
loss of electron(s)   OXIDATION
lowering of positive valency   REDUCTION
lunar caustic   SILVER NITRATE
material capable of resisting
 high temperature   REFRACTORY
measure of unsaturated fatty
 acid   IODINE VALUE
measurement of strength
 of a solution   TITRATION
mercaptan   THIOL
mercuric sulphide   VERMILION
mercurous chloride   CALOMEL
metathesis   DOUBLE DECOMPOSITION
methanol   METHYL ALCOHOL
     WOOD SPIRIT, WOOD NAPHTHA
methyl
—alcohol   METHANOL
     WOOD SPIRIT
—benzene   TOLUENE, TOLUOL
minium   RED LEAD
mixture of
—acid or alkali with salt   BUFFER
—calcium phosphate and
  sulphate   SUPERPHOSPHATE
—liquids or liquids
  and solids   SOLUTION
  by random motion of particles   DIFFUSION
  that
   —cannot be separated
    by distillation   AZEOTROPE
   —freeze simultaneously   EUTECTIC
  with
   —dense particles   SUSPENSION
   —fine particles   COLLOID
molecular mixture of substances   SOLUTION
molecule
—consisting of
  one atom   MONATOMIC MOLECULE
—large   MACROMOLECULE
—with
  free valency   RADICAL
  lone electrons that can
    combine with proton   BASE
movement
—caused by random motion
  of particles   DIFFUSION
—of
  amino group between
    compounds   TRANSAMINATION
  liquid through
    semipermeable membrane   OSMOSIS

name that
—conveys details
  of atomic structure   SYSTEMATIC NAME
—gives no details
  of atomic structure   TRIVIAL NAME
Naples-yellow   LEAD ANTIMONIATE
natural or synthetic polymer   RESIN
naturally occurring
—hydrocarbons   CRUDE OIL
—polymer of glucose   STARCH
negatively charged
—ion   ANION
—particle   ELECTRON
neither acid nor alkaline   NEUTRAL
nitre   POTASSIUM NITRATE
     SALTPETRE
nitrogen   AZOTE
—trichloride   AGENE
nitrogenous substance   PROTEIN
noble gas   ARGON, HELIUM, KRYPTON
     NEON, RADON, XENON
non-carbon compounds   INORGANIC
number of
—hydrogen atoms with
  which an atom will combine   VALENCY
—particles in one
  mole   AVOGADRO'S NUMBER
—protons in nucleus   ATOMIC NUMBER
olefin(e)   ALKENE
organic compound
—aliphatic hydrocarbon   ALKENE
—aromatic hydrocarbon   ARYL
—based on
  ammonia   AMIDE, AMINE
     AMINO-ACID
  benzene ring   AROMATIC
  sterol   CHOLESTEROL
—containing
  alkyd group attached to
    carboxyl group   FATTY ACID
  carbon atoms in chains   ALIPHATIC
  carboxyl group   CARBOXYLIC ACID
   —and alkyd radicals   KETONE
  chains of amino-acids   PROTEIN
  oxygen, hydrogen, carbon   OXIME
  sulphur and oxygen   MERCAPTAN
     THIOL
  two
   —double bonds   DIENE
   —ketone groups   DIKETONE
—derived from silicon   SILICONE
—hydroxyl groups and carbon   ALCOHOL
—in
  petroleum   ALKYL, ALKANE
  plants   CHLOROPHYLL
—related to indigo   INDOL(E)

—which reduces surface
 tension SURFACE ACTIVE AGENT
         SURFACTANT
    (*see also* hydrocarbon *above*)
organic cyanide   NITRILE
oscillation of electrons
 between atoms   RESONANCE
oxidation state   VALENCY
oxide of iron   RUST
oxygen with three atoms per molecule OZONE
paraffin series   ALKANES
 —gases   BUTANE, ETHANE
     METHANE, PROPANE
 —liquids DECANE, HEPTANE, HEXANE
    NONANE, OCTANE, PENTANE
partial sterilisation PASTEURISATION
particles   (*see separate entry*)
passage of gas through
 small apertures   EFFUSION
pentyl acetate   AMYL ACETATE
       BANANA OIL
percentage of iso-octane OCTANE NUMBER
phenylethylene   STYRENE
phospholipids etc COMPOUND LIPIDS
plastic
 —hardening with heat THERMOSETTING
 —softening with heat THERMOPLASTIC
poison   (*see separate entry*)
polar bond ELECTROVALENT BOND
polymeric siloxane   SILICONE
polymerised glucose   CELLULOSE
porcelain filter CHAMBERLAND CANDLE
positively charged
 —ion   CATION
 —particle   PROTON
potassium
 —bicarbonate   POTASH
 —ferric ferrocyanide PRUSSIAN BLUE
 —nitrate NITRE, SALTPETRE
 —sodium tartrate ROCHELLE SALT
power of atom to
 attract electron ELECTRONEGATIVITY
preparation of nitrogenous
 fertiliser   HABER PROCESS
pressure needed to prevent
 osmotic flow OSMOTIC PRESSURE
process
 —by which atoms become
  attached to surface ADSORPTION
 —for making
  salt LEBLANC PROCESS
  washing soda SOLVAY PROCESS
 —in which
  crystals are produced from
  solution
  (FRACTIONAL) CRYSTALLISATION

product of one reaction
 takes part in another CHAIN REACTION
 two molecules react to
 form one plus
 water CONDENSATION REACTION
—not involving heat
 transfer   ADIABATIC
product of combustion
 —complete CARBON DIOXIDE
 —incomplete CARBON MONOXIDE
 —of wood   CHARCOAL
production of chemicals
 by organisms BIOSYNTHESIS
Prussian
 blue
  POTASSIUM FERRIC FERROCYANIDE
purification by
 distillation   RECTIFICATION
pyrimidines CYTOSINE, THYMINE
        URACIL
pyrolysis   CRACKING
racemic acid TARTARIC ACID
radioactive chemicals ACTINIDES
rare-earth elements LANTHANIDES
ratio of mass to mass
 of carbon MOLECULAR WEIGHT
re-freezing of ice after
 melting under pressure REGELATION
reaction
 —in which
  carbon bonds are
  saturated ADDITION REACTION
  heat is
  —absorbed ENDOTHERMIC
  —produced EXOTHERMIC
 —influenced by
  light PHOTOCHEMICAL REACTION
 —requiring energy ENDERGONIC
 —where one reagent
  is reduced and
  another oxidised REDOX (REACTION)
 —yielding energy EXERGONIC
realgar ARSENIC DISULPHIDE
red lead   MINIUM
reduction of viscosity by
 physical disturbance THIXOTROPY
regular structure of crystal LATTICE
relating to crystallisation
 with axes at right angles ISOMETRIC
removal of
 —amino group DEAMINATION
 —oxygen   REDUCTION
 —water   DEHYDRATION
rock salt SODIUM CHLORIDE
rotating polarised
 light to the left LAEVOROTATORY

rules describing formation of valency bonds	RULES OF FAJANS
rust	OXIDE OF IRON
salt of	
—alginic acid	ALGINATE
—aluminium hydroxide	ALUMINATE
—boric acid	BORATE
—bromic acid	BROMATE
—carbonic acid	CARBONATE
—chloric acid	CHLORATE
—chromic acid	CHROMATE
—cyanic acid	CYANATE
—fatty acid	SOAP
—ferric acid	FERRATE
—isocyanic acid	ISOCYANATE
—manganic acid	MANGANATE
—mucic acid	MUCATE
—nitric acid	NITRATE
—nitrous acid	NITRITE
—oxalic acid	OXALATE
—palmitic acid	PALMITATE
—permanganic acid	PERMANGANATE
—phenol	PHENOLATE
—phosphoric acid	PHOSPHATE
—phthalic acid	PHTHALATE
—propionic acid	PROPIONATE
—silicic acid	SILICATE
—stearic acid	STEARATE
—sulphuric acid	SULPHATE
—sulphurous acid	SULPHITE
—telluric acid	TELLURATE
saltcake	GLAUBER'S SALTS
	SODIUM SULPHATE
saltpetre	NITRE
	POTASSIUM NITRATE
seeding with small crystal	IMPING
separate part	PHASE
separation	
—by	
evaporation and recondensation	DISTILLATION
	FRACTIONATION
fractional distillation	RECTIFICATION
melting	LIQUATION
washing	ELUTION
—into constituent elements	ANALYSIS
—of	
colloids	DIALYSIS
liquid from a gel	SYN(A)ERESIS
series of elements in order of potential for oxidation	ELECTROCHEMICAL SERIES
shape of molecule resulting from position	CONFORMATION
silver nitrate	LUNAR CAUSTIC
similar compound	METAMER

simultaneous oxidation and reduction	REDOX
small particles in solution which cannot pass through a membrane	COLLOID
smallest particle showing characteristics of a substance	MOLECULE
sodium	
—carbonate	WASHING SODA
—chloride	(COMMON) SALT, ROCK SALT
—hydroxide	CAUSTIC SODA
—silicate	WATER GLASS
—sulphate	GLAUBER'S SALT
	SALTCAKE
solid	
—carbon dioxide	DRY ICE
—condensed from vapour of solid without liquid phase	SUBLIMATE
—mixture of several substances	SOLID SOLUTION
—particles in liquid medium	SUSPENSION
—with regular structural shape	CRYSTAL
solution	
—acting as electrical conductor	ELECTROLYTE
—holding maximum amount of solute	SATURATED SOLUTION
—in alcohol	TINCTURE
—maintaining pH level	BUFFER
—of	
hydrochloric acid	SPIRITS OF SALT
salt	BRINE
—used to test for	
ammonia	NESSLER'S SOLUTION
sugars	FEHLING'S SOLUTION
—with potassium hypochlorite	EAU DE JAVELLE
	JAVELLE WATER
space of missing electron	HOLE
spirits of wine	ETHANOL
	ETHYL ALCOHOL
spontaneous breaking up of compound	DISSOLUTION
starch	AMYLUM
—component with glucose chains	AMYLOPECTIN
	AMYLOSE
steroids	DERIVED LIPIDS
styrene	PHENYLETHYLENE
substance	
—acting in conjunction with enzyme in catalysis	COENZYME
opposite ways (acid/base, positive/negative)	AMPHIPROTIC
	AMPHOTERIC

—adding hydrogen to
　another　　　　　　　　REDUCING AGENT
—affecting rate of chemical
　reaction　　　　　　　　CATALYST
—assisting fusion of others　　　FLUX
—causing oxidation　　OXIDIZING AGENT
—combining with base to
　form a salt　　　　　　　ACID
—composed entirely of
　similar atoms　　　　　　ELEMENT
—deposited from solution
　or suspension　　　　　PRECIPITATE
—dissolved in a solvent　　　SOLUTE
—dissolving another　　　　SOLVENT
—donating electrons
　to another　　　　　REDUCING AGENT
—existing in
　　only one form　　　MONOTROPISM
　　several forms　　POLYMORPHISM
—fluorescing green　　FLUORESCEIN
—forming lather with water　SAPONIN
—interfering with
　chemical reactions　　　INHIBITOR
—liberating hydrogen ions　　ACID
—marking end of reaction
　by colour change　　　INDICATOR
—more active in
　reactions than in
　normal state　　NASCENT ELEMENT
—produced by the action
　of pepsin on proteins　　PEPTONE
—producing chemical reaction　REAGENT
—reacting with acid
　to form salt　　　　　　BASE
—reducing surface tension　WETTING AGENT
—removing oxygen from
　another　　　　　REDUCING AGENT
—speeding chemical
　reaction　　　　　　CATALYST
—supplying oxygen
　to a reaction　　OXIDANT, OXYDANT
—taking part in
　chemical reaction　　　REACTANT
—transferring a proton to another　ACID
—turning vegetable blues red　ACID
—used
　in
　　—chemical tests　　　REAGENT
　　—dying　　ALUM, ANILINE
　　—paints, etc　　　　ALKYD
　　—papermaking　　　ALUM
　to
　　—adulterate another to
　　　change its properties　DOPANT
　　—seed clouds to
　　　produce rain　SILVER IODIDE

—show condition by
　colour change　　　INDICATOR
—signal end of titration　INDICATOR
—with
　atoms all of the
　　same atomic number　ELEMENT
　elastic properties　ELASTOMER
　pH value
　　—greater than 7　　ALKALI
　　—less than 7　　　ACID
　same
　　—arrangement of atoms but
　　　different molecular
　　　weight　　POLYMER(IDE)
　　—atomic number but
　　　different mass number　ISOTOPE
　　—molecular weight but
　　　different arrangement of atoms　ISOMER
sulphides of metals　　　PYRITES
surface-active agent for cleaning　DETERGENT
synthetic resin　　　　ALKYD
table of elements　PERIODIC TABLE
tartaric acid　　　RACEMIC ACID
temperature
—at which
　element changes
　　state　　TRANSITION POINT
　　　TRANSITION TEMPERATURE
　ignition occurs　FLASH POINT
　substance can exist in all
　　three states　TRIPLE POINT
—on Kelvin
　scale　ABSOLUTE TEMPERATURE
temporary, reversible
　decomposition　　DISSOCIATION
test for
　—acidity　　LITMUS (PAPER)
　—arsenic　　MARSH'S TEST
　—phenols　　MILLON'S TEST
　—proteins in solution　BIURET REACTION
thiol　　　　　MERCAPTAN
three covalent bonds　TRIPLE BOND
titanic oxide　　　　TITANIA
　　　　TITANIUM OXIDE
titanium oxide　　　ANATASE
toluene　　METHYL BENZENE
　　　　　　TOLUOL
treatment
—of illness with
　chemicals　CHEMOTHERAPEUTICS
　　　　CHEMOTHERAPY
—with nitric acid　NITRIFICATION
trihydric alcohol　　GLYCERIN(E)
　　　　　　GLYCEROL
two or more elements
　combined　　　COMPOUND

unavailable energy in system	ENTROPY
urea	CARBAMIDE
use of micro-organisms to break down substance	FERMENTATION
valency of one covalent and one electrovalent bond	SEMIPOLAR BOND
vapour existing in equilibrium with the liquid form	SATURATED VAPOUR
verdigris	COPPER CARBONATE
vermilion	MERCURIC SULPHIDE
vertical column in periodic table	GROUP
vessel used for	
—cultures	PETRI DISH
—incineration	CRUCIBLE
washing	
—soda	SODIUM CARBONATE
—to effect separation	ELUTION
	LIXIVIATION
water	AQ, OXYGEN HYDRIDE
—glass	SODIUM SILICATE
weight of unit mass compared with water	SPECIFIC GRAVITY
white	
—arsenic	ARSENIC TRIOXIDE
—lead	LEAD CARBONATE
wood naphtha	ETHANOL, METHANOL
wood spirit	METHANOL
	METHYL ALCOHOL
xylene	DIMETHYLBENZENE
	XYLOL
zinc	
—carbonate	CALAMINE
—zinc oxide	ZINCITE
zincite	ZINC OXIDE
zirconia	ZIRCONIUM DIOXIDE

chess

alternating checks	SEE-SAW
attack	GREB'S
	NIMZOWITSCH-LARSEN
	RICHTER, TORRE
	TROMPOWSKY
—on two pieces	FORK, SKEWER
bishop hemmed in	BAD BISHOP
bishops on adjoining diagonals	HARROWITZ BISHOPS
blockaded position	TREBUCHET
	ZUGZWANG
check	
—by two pieces	DOUBLE CHECK
—from stationary piece	DISCOVERED CHECK
—in reply to check	CROSS-CHECK
controlling body	FIDE

defence	ALAPIN'S, ALEKHINE'S
	AMBUSH, BENONI, BERLIN
	BIRD'S, BOGOLJUBOW, CARO-KAUN
	CENTRE, CHIGORIN'S, CLASSICAL
	COONTER, COZIO'S, DAMIANO'S
	DORY'S, DUTCH, FIANCHETTO
	FRANCO-INDIAN, FRENCH, GRUNFELD
	HUNGARIAN, KERES, KING'S INDIAN
	MARSHALL'S, NIMIZOWITSCH
	NIMZO-INDIAN, OLD INDIAN
	ORTHODOX, PETROFF'S, PHILIDOR'S
	PIRC, POLISH, QUEEN'S INDIAN
	ROBATSCH, RUSSIAN, (SEMI-)SLAV
	SCHLIEMAN, SICILIAN, SMYSLOV'S
	STEINITZ, SYMMETRICAL, TARRASCH
	TWO KNIGHTS GAME, WESTPHALIA
ending with king not in check	STALEMATE
famous games	EVERGREEN, IMMORTAL
	POLISH IMMORTAL
file with no pawn	OPEN FILE
gambit/opening	ANDERSSEN'S, BENKO
	BIRD'S, BISHOP'S, BLACKMAR
	CATALAN, COLLE SYSTEM, DANISH
	ENGLISH, EVANS, FOUR KNIGHTS GAME
	GIUCO PIANO, GREB'S, KING'S
	KING'S FIANCHETTO, LATVIAN
	PONZIANI'S, QUEEN'S, RETI
	RUY LOPEZ, SARAGOSSA
	SCOTCH GAME, STAUNTON
	STONEWALL SYSTEM
	VAN'T KRUYS, VIENNA GAME
	VOLGA
games	CIRCE, COURIER, DOUBLE-MOVE
	FOUR-HANDED, KAMIKAZE
	KRIEGSPIEL, LOSING GAME
	MARSEILLES, MUST-CAPTURE
	NO-CAPTURE, PROGRESSIVE
	RANDOMISED, REFUSAL, RIFLE
	SCOTCH, THREE-DIMENSIONAL
—high speed	LIGHTNING CHESS
—using people as pieces	LIVING CHESS
immobilisation of piece	PIN
in danger of capture	EN PRISE
intermediate move	ZWISCHENZUG
knight's pawn early move	FIANCHETTO
machines	
—electronic	CHAOS-MASTER
	DEEP THOUGHT, FREEDOM
	HITECH, KAISSA
	MEPHISTO(-PORTOROSE)
	OSTRICH, PAPA, RABBIT, TELL
—mechanical	AJEEB, KEMPELEN'S TURK
	WIENER-SCHACHZEITUNG
mate of king surrounded by his own pieces	SMOTHERED MATE

move taking pawn which has moved two squares	EN PASSANT
moves taking in every square of board	KNIGHT'S TOUR
muse of chess	CAISSA
notation	ALGEBRAIC, DESCRIPTIVE FORSYTH
offered sacrifice in opening	GAMBIT
old names	
—Arabian	SHATRANJ
—Greek	ZATRIKION
—Indian	CHATRANGA
—Persian	CHATANG
pawn	
—not opposed	PASSED PAWN
—placed diagonally	PAWN CHAIN
piece	MAN
—in opponent's half supported by pawn	OUTPOST
pieces	BISHOP, CASTLE, KING KNIGHT, PAWN, QUEEN, ROOK
players	
—American	BROWNE, BENJAMIN CHRISTIANSEN, DE FIRMIAN DENHER, FINE, FISCHER, GULKO IVANOV, MARSHALL, MORPHY PILLSBURY, PINHUS, RESHEVSKY SEIRAWAN
—ancients	ALADDIN, AL-ADLI, ALFONSO AS-SULI, DAMIANO, LEONARDO
—Argentinian	NAJDORF, PANNO SANGUINETI
—Australian	KOSHNITSKY, PURDY
—Austrian	ALIGAIER, GRUNFELD ROBATSCH, SCHLECHER SPIELMAN, STEINITZ
—Belgian	COLLE, KOLTANOWSKI
—Brazilian	GERMAN, MECKING
—British	ABRAHAMS, ADAMS ALEXANDER, ATKINS, CHANDLER GOLOMBEK, GUNSBERG, HODGSON KEENE, KING, KOSTEL, MESTEL NORWOOD, NUNN, PENROSE, SHORT SPEELMAN, STAUNTON, SUBA WINTER, ZUKERTORT
—Bulgarian	BOBOTSOV, PADEVSKY RADULOV, TRINGOV
—Canadian	MORRISON, SPRAGGETT SUTTLES, YANOFSKY
—Colombian	CASTRO, ROJAS
—Cuban	CAPABLANCA, GARCIA
—Czech	DURAS, FLOHR, JANSA PACHMAN, RETI, RICHTER SMEJKAL
—Danish	ANDERSEN, LARSEN MORTENSEN
—Dutch	DONNER, EUWE, TIMMAN
—Estonian	KERES, MIKENAS
—Finnish	BOOK, YRIOLA
—French	DESCHAPELLES, JANOWSKI LA BOURDONNAIS, LAUTIER PHILIDOR, SAIT-AMANT TARTAKOWER
—German	AHUES, ANDERSSEN BOGOLJUBOW, HUBNER LASKER, UHLMANN, UNZICKER
—Hungarian	ADORJAN, BARCZA(Y) BREYER, GUNSBERG, POLGAR PORTISCH, RETI, SAX SZABO, TARRASCH
—Icelandic	HJARTARSON, OLAFSSON PETRURSSON, THORSTEINS
—Indian	AARON, SULTAN KHAN
—Iranian	HRANDI, SHARIF
—Irish	MCDONNELL, O'HANLON REILLY
—Israeli	OZERNIAK, PORATH
—Italian	MARIOTTI
—Latvian	BEHTING, MATTISON NI(E)MZOWITSCH PETROV, TAL
—Mexican	ARAIZA, TORRES
—New Zealand	SRAPU, SUTTON
—Norwegian	ADGESTEIN, BARDA DE LANGE, HOEN JOHANNESSEN, WIBE
—Peruvian	CANAL, QUINONES RODRIGUEZ
—Philippine	BALINAS, TORRE
—Polish	JANOWSKI, PERLIS RUBINSTEIN, SLIWA TARTAKOWER, WINAWER
—Portuguese	DA SILVA, DURAO
—Puerto Rican	KAPLAN
—Romanian	ALBIN, CIOCALTEA GEORGHIU, MARCO TROIANESCU
—Russian	ALBURT, ALEKHINE BOGOLJUBOW, BOTVINNIK CHIGORIN, DOLMATOV, DREEV EINGORN, GUREVICH, HALPRIN IVANCHUK, KARPOV, KASPAROV KORCHNOI, PETROSIAN, SMYSLOV SOKOLOV, SPASSKY, YUSUPOV
(f)	ALEXANDRIA GAPRINDASHVILI, MENCHIK
—Singaporean	TAN
—South African	FRIEDGOOD, HEIDENFELD KIRBY
—Spanish	ILLESCAS, LOPEZ
—Swedish	ANDERSSEN, HELLERS LUNDIN, STAHLBERG, STOLZ

—Syrian	STAMMA	vessel	BLUNGER
—Tunisian	BELKADI, BOUAZIZ	coarse ware	SAXON STONE
—Turkish	ONAT, SUER		SEMI-PORCELAIN
—Welsh	EVANS, HUTCHINGS		STONE CHINA
	WILLIAMS	coloured pottery	SGRAFFITO
—Yugoslav	NIKOLIC, PIRC	colourful glazed pottery	FAIENCE
	UDOVCIC, VIDMAR	crazed glaze	CRACKLE (WARE)
playing-strength rating	BCF SYSTEM	cream Wedgwood	QUEEN'S WARE
	ELO SCALE	Danish	COPENHAGEN
	INGO(-HARNESS) SYSTEM	decoration applied	
row of squares		before firing	UNDERGLAZE
—across board	RANK	Dutch	DELF(T)
—up and down board	FILE	earthenware	CHOAM, FIGULINE
sacrifice of bishop	GREEK GIFT	English	AYNSLEY, BOW, BRISTOL
threat to king	CHECK		CHELSEA, COALPORT, COPELAND
three pawns in one file	TRIPLED PAWNS		CROUCHWARE, (CROWN) DERBY
tie-break system	BUCHHOLTZ SYSTEM		DAVENTRY, DOULTON, LIVERPOOL
	SONNEBORN-BERGER'S SYSTEM		LOWESTOFT, MOORCROFT, MINTON
	SWISS SYSTEM		ROCKINGHAM, SPODE
titles	GRAND MASTER		STAFFORDSHIRE, SUNDERLAND
	INTERNATIONAL MASTER		SWANSEA, WEDGWOOD
	MASTER		WORCESTER
trophy	BRILLIANCY TROPHY	enamelled earthenware	MAJOLICA
	PIATIGORSKY CUP	—terra-cotta	DELLA-ROBBIA
two pawns in one file	DOUBLED PAWNS	felspar porcelain	PARIAN
unsupported pawn	HANGING PAWN	fine	
voluntary surrender		—glaze	SMEAR
of piece	SACRIFICE	—pottery	PEBBLEWARE
winning move	(CHECK)MATE	fireclay case for firing	SAGGAR
Chile	RCH	French	CHANTILLY, LIMOGES
capital	SANTIAGO		MARSEILLES, PARIS, SEVRES
coin	CENTAVO, CONDOR	German	ANSBACH, DRESDEN
	DOBLON, PESO		FRANKFURT, MEISSEN
flower	SCHIZANTHUS	green pattern	FAMILLE VERTE
fruit	LUCAMA	grey	
palm	COQUITO	—blue glazed pottery	CLAIR DE LUNE
saltpetre	CALICHE	—green glazed pottery	CELADON WARE
shrub	MAQUI	hard	
tree	ALERCE	—porcelain	JASPERWARE
china	CERAMIC, PORCELAIN	—white pottery	IRONSTONE
	POTTERY	heavy pottery	STONEWARE
American	REDWARE	Italian	CAPODIMONTE, FAENZA
Austrian	VIENNA		FAIENCE, MAIOLICA
Belgian	TOURNAI		NAPLES, PESARO
black		Japanese	ARITA, HAMADA, IMARI
—background	FAMILLE NOIR		KAKIEMON, SATSUMA, SHOJI
—unglazed pottery	BASALT WARE	lead glaze	GLOST
brown terra-cotta	RUSTIC-WARE	liquid clay	SLIP
Chinese	BLANC-DE-CHINE, CANTON	made of	
	CELADON, CHUN, HAN, JU(AN)	—clay or earthenware	CLOAM
	KO, MING, NANKEEN, QING	—different coloured clays	PEBBLEWARE
	SUNG, TING, YUAN		SCRODDLED
clay	ARGIL, CHOAM, KAOLIN(E)	matt-surfaced stoneware	JASPERWARE
—mixing		pebbleware on gold or	
machine	BLUNGER	blue	LAPIS LAZULI WARE
tool	BALLET	pink pattern	FAMILLE ROSE

Polynesian pottery	LAPITA WARE
refined earthenware	CREAMWARE
salt-glazed stoneware	CROUCH-WARE
scalloped edging	LAMBREQUIN
semi-translucent	BONE CHINA
sold at fairs	FAIRINGS
Switzerland	ZURICH
translucent	EGGSHELL
transparent with pictures	
showing through	LITHOPHANE
unglazed pottery	BISCUIT, BISQUE
	TERRACOTTA
very thin	EGGSHELL
white	
—china trinkets	
sold as mementos	GOSS
sold or given as prizes	
at fairs etc	FAIRINGS
—earthenware	IRONSTONE CHINA
—porcelain	PARIAN (WARE)
raised pattern	CAMEO WARE
	JASPER WARE
	PORCELAIN
with calcium phosphate	BONE-CHINA
yellow background	FAMILLE JAUNE
China	CATHAY, CH, CHIN
	MIDDLE KINGDOM
abacus	S(H)WANPAN
aborigines	LOLOS, MAIOTSE, MANS
	MANZU, YAO(-MIN)
agricultural worker	
with medical training	BAREFOOT DOCTOR
alphabetical system for	
translation	PINYIN, ZIMU
arch	PAILOU
archipelago	QUNDAO
assembly	HUI
association	TONG
bamboo stick	WHANGEE
barge carrying sewage	FOO-FOO BARGE
basin	PENDI
bay	AO, WAN
bean	ADZUKI, MUNG
best quality	FIRST CHOP
bird	SILVER-PHEASANT
	SWAN-GOOSE
boat	JUNK, SAMPAN
	SANPAN, TONGKANG
boat population	TANK(I)A
brand	CHOP
bridge	QIAO
bronze bowl	GUI
Buddha	FO(H)
Buddhist	
—paradise	CHINGTU
—priest	BONZE

—sect	CHAN
business	PIDGIN
cabbage	BOKCHOY, PAKCHOI
canal	YUNHE
cane	WHANGEE
cape (headland)	JIAO, ZUI
capital	BEIJING, PEKING
carriage	(JIN)RICKSHA(W)
chestnut	LING
Chinaman	CATAIAN, CAT(H)AYAN
	CHINK, CHOW
Chinese	CHIN, SERIC, SINAEAN
	SINIC, SINO
club (group)	TONG
coat	MANDARIN
coins	
—small coin	CASH, CHIAO, FEN
—unit	CHIAO
—10 chiao	YUAN
—silver bar	LIANG, SYCEE, TAEL
condiment	NAPEE
cooking pan	WOK
commune	GONGSHE
county	XIAN
crab	HA, MITTEN-CRAB
criminal society	TRIAD
cyclone	TYPHOON
dark principle	YIN
date-plum	KAKI
deities	(see **gods, goddesses**)
department	FOO
desert	SHAMO
dialect	CANTONESE, HAKKA
	MANDARIN
	PEKIN(G)ESE, WU
dish	CHOP-SUEY, CHOW-MEIN
	DIM SUM, WO MEIN, WONTON
divination system	I CHING
dress	CHEONG-SAM, SAMFOO
	SAMFU
drink	KAOLIANG, MAO-TAI
drug	GINSENG
duck	AP, MANDARIN
—eggs in brine	PIDAN
dynasty	CH'IN(G), CHOU
	HAN, MING, QIN(G), SHANG
	SUI, SUNG, TANG, XIA
	YIN, YUA, ZHOU
eating utensils	CHOP-STICKS
egg noodles	WO MEIN
exercise and mental	
training	QIGONG, TAI CHI(CHUAN)
fabulous	
—animal	KYLIN
—bird	FUM, FUNG
factory	HONG

feminine principle	YIN
fibre	CHINA-JUTE
fish	CARP, GOLDFISH
	PARADISE-FISH, TREPANG
foreign mercantile house	HONG
fried	
—noodles	CHOW MEIN
—rice	CHOW FAAHN
frying pan	WO(C)K
fruit	CUMQUAT, KUMQUAT
	LEECHEE, LITCHI, LYCHEE
	LONGAN, LOQUAT, WAMPEE
game	FAN-TAN, MAH-JONG(G), PUTZI
ginger	CURCCUMA, ZEDOARY
gorge	XIA
grass	RAMEE, RAMI(E), WHANGEE
grotesque figure	MAGOT
guild	HUI, TONG
harbour	GANG
hen	BRAHMA, LANGSHAN
herb	GINSENG
house-boat	TANKA-BOAT
idol	JOSS
incense	JOSS-STICK
instrument	KIN
island	DAO, HSU, TAO
jacket	MAKWA
jade	YU(-STONE)
jargon	PIDGIN ENGLISH
jigsaw	TANGRAM
jute	ABUTILON
labourer	COOLIE, COOLY
lacquered screen	COROMANDEL SCREEN
lake	HU
language	CANTONESE, KUO-YO
	MANCHOO, MANCHU
	MANDARIN
life-energy	QI
light principle	YANG
liquor	KAOLIANG
lobster	LUNG HA
magnolia	YULAN
mandarin's house	YAMEN, YAMUN
martial art	KUNG-FU
masculine principle	YANG
measures	
—1 inch	TSUN
—1 foot	CHIH
—12 feet	CHANG
—1/3 mile	LI
—15 galls	PARAH
military	
—district	COMMANDERY
—governor	TUCHUN
minister	AMBAN

mixed condiment	CHOW-CHOW
mountain	SHAN
—range	LING, SHANMAI
mouth organ	SANG
mustard relish	CHOW-CHOW
National People's Party	KUOMINTANG
negative principle	YIN
news agency	XINHUA
no good	NO CHOP
obeisance	COTTOW, KOWTOW
office	YAMEN, YAMUN
official	MANDARIN, TAO-TAI
	TAOYAN
oil	TUNG
old military race	MANCHOO, MANCHU
orange	TAEL
overseer	HOPPO
pagoda	TAA
pass	GUAN, SHANKOU
peak	FENG
Peking duck	KAO YA
peninsula	BANDAO
pheasant	TRAGOPAN
philosophy	CONFUCIANISM
pickled eggs	PIDAN
pillory	CANG(UE)
plain	PINGYUAN
poor quality	NO CHOP
porcelain	MING
pork	JU
positive principle	YANG
prefecture	FU
preserved fruits	CHOW-CHOW
promptly	CHOP-CHOP
prostration	KO(W)TOW
province	SHENG
provinces	ANHUI, FUJIAN, GANSU
	GUANGDON, GUANGXI, GUIZHOU
	HEBEI, HEILONGJIANG, HENAN
	HUNAN, JIANGSU, JIANGXI
	JILIN, LIAONING, NINGXIA
	QINGHAI, SHANDONG, SHA(A)NXI
	SICHUAN, XINJIAN
	YUNNAN, ZHEJIANG
puzzle	TANGRAM
quickly	CHOP-CHOP
raspberry	WINE-BERRY
rebel	TAIPING
reed instrument	CHENG
region	DIQU
religion	BUDDHISM, CONFUCIANISM
	TAOISM
resident official	AMBAN
rice spirit	SAMSHOO, SAMSHU
river	HE, JIANG
rodent	JUMPING-MOUSE

ruler	MANCHOO, MANCHU
	YAO(U), YAU
sauce	SOY
sea	HAI
seal (impression)	CHOP
secret society	BOXER, HOEY
	TONG, TRIAD
self-defence system	KUNG-FU
shark's fin soup	YU TSI TANG
ship	JUNK, SAMPAN, SANPAN
shop	TOKO
silkworm	AILANTHUS, SINA
	TASAR, TUSSAH
silver	PAKFONG, PAKTONG
sleeping platform	KANG
snack	DIM SUM
sorghum	KAOLIANG
spring	QUAN, YUAN
squid	YO YI
statuette of seated figure	MANDARIN
steamed dumplings	DIM SUM
stir-fried vegetables	CHOW CHOI
sugar cane	SWEET SORGHUM
swivel-musket	GINGAL(L), JINGAL
tax	LIKIN
temple	PAGOD(A), TAA
tip	CUMSHAW
toy	TANGRAM
trade intermediary	COMPRADOR(E)
transit duty	LIKIN
tree	GINGKO, GINKGO, LITCHEE
	LITCHI, LONGAN, LOQUAT
	MAIDENHAIR-TREE, PAULOWNIA
	TUNG-TREE, VARNISH-TREE
tuber	KUDZOO, KUDZU
umbrella	TEE
unarmed combat system	KUNG-FU
vegetable dishes	BAMBOO SHOOTS
	BEAN SPROUTS
vehicle	JINRICKISHA
	(JIN)RICKSHA(W)
	TRISHAW
village	CUN
warehouse	HONG
warlord	TUCHUN
water	
—chestnut	MAH TAI
—jar	KANG
wax insect	TELA
weights	
—1oz	LIANG, TAEL
—1lb	CATTY, CHIEN, KIN
—133lb	PECUL, PICUL, PIKUL, TAN
well	JING
wormwood	MOXA
yellow dye	WONGSHY

years (12-year cycle)	BAT, OX, TIGER
	HARE or RABBIT, DRAGON
	SNAKE, HORSE, SHEEP or GOAT
	MONKEY, ROOSTER, DOG, PIG
yoke	CANG(UE)

church — building

abbey church	MINSTER
aisle at east end	AMBULATORY
apse in basilica	BEMA
arcade in monastery	CLOISTER
beam supporting cross	ROOD BEAM
bell	
—screen	LOUVRE
—tower	BELFRY, CAMPANILE
bishop's seat	FALDISTORY, FALDSTOOL
—behind altar	SYNTHRONUS
body of church	NAVE
burial chamber	TOMB, VAULT
canopy over throne, etc	BALDACHIN
	BALDACCHINO
	BALDAQUIN
cathedral	MINSTER
cells in hermitage	LAURA
central part	NAVE
chancel	
—of church	ADYTUM
—in basilica	BEMA
chapel	BETHEL, BETHESDA
	EBENEZER
—at west end of church	GALILEE
—Byzantine	PARABEMA
—dedicated to Virgin	LADY CHAPEL
—for eucharist table	PROTHESIS
—in church	LADY CHAPEL, SACELLUM
—of prothesis	PARABEMA
choir	SCHOLA CANTORUM
—screen	REREDOS(E), REREDORSE
church	
—attached to house	CHAPEL
—with font	DELUBRUM
clergyman's house	MANSE, PARSONAGE
	RECTORY, VICARAGE
colonnade	ATRIUM
courtyard	ATRIUM, PARVIS(E)
cross	ROOD
	(see also separate entry)
desk	FALDSTOOL
detached from main church	CHAPEL OF EASE
dissenters' church	CHAPEL
division of nave	AISLE
east end	CHANCEL, CHEVET
	CHOIR, PRESBYTERY
	SACRARIUM, SANCTUARY
end space	PARVIS(E)
extension beyond altar	RETROCHOIR
finial	FLECHE

gallery	TRIBUNE
—above rood-screen	ROOD-LOFT
—over aisle	TRIFORIUM
gates of temple (Indian)	GOPURA(M)
grotto-temple	SPEOS
inner chamber of temple	CELLA, NAOS
intersection of nave	
and transept	CROSSING
large church	BASILICA, CATHEDRAL
	MINSTER
lavatory in monastery	LAVABO
ledge on seat	MISERERE
	MISERICORD
little chapel	SACELLUM
magnificent church	BASILICA
monastery	CLOISTER
	CONVENT, MINSTER
—Tibetan	LAMASERY
narrow spire	FLECHE
nave	NEF
Nonconformist chapel	BETHEL, BETHESDA
north side	CANTORIAL, GOSPEL
northern apse	PROTHESIS
nuncio's office	NUNCIATURE
nunnery	CLOISTER, CONVENT
oratory	PROSEUCHE
part at right angles to nave	TRANSEPT
partition between nave	
and choir	ROOD-SCREEN
place of	
—baptism	BAPTIST(E)RY
—prayer	CHAPEL, ORATORY
—worship	TABERNACLE
platform	TRIBUNE
pointed tower	SPIRE, STEEPLE
porch	GALILEE, NARTHEX
portico	PARVIS(E)
prayer-stool	PRIE-DIEU
preacher's gallery	PULPIT
presbytery	CLASSIS
principal church of diocese	CATHEDRAL
priory church	MINSTER
pulpit in mosque	MIMBAR
rail or screen	PARCLOSE
reading desk	LECTERN, LECTURN
	LETTERN
recess	APSE, APSIS, CHEVET
—for vessels	ALMERY, A(U)MBRY
robing room	VEST(IA)RY
Roman Catholic church	
with special privileges	BASILICA
rood loft	JUBE
room for sacred objects,	
vestments etc	SACRARIUM, SACRISTY
	VEST(IA)RY
—Byzantine	PARABEMA

—Greek	DIACONICON
sacred	
—enclosure	SEKOS
—part of temple	ADYTUM
sanctuary	DELUBRUM
Scottish church	KIRK
screen	ROOD SCREEN
—or panelling	
behind altar	REREDOS(E), REREDORSE
seat	PEW
seminary (RC)	THEOLOGATE
shrine	DELUBRUM
south side	DECANAL, EPISTLE
steeple over rood-	
crossing	ROOD-STEEPLE
storey over aisle	TRIFORIUM
support for standing	MISERERE
	MISERICORD(E)
surroundings	PRECINCT
table	ALTAR
—of eucharist	PROTHESIS
temple	DELUBRUM
—Arabian	MASJED, MASJID, MESJID
—Babylonian	ZIGGURAT, ZIKKURAT
—Buddhist	CHAITYA, SANGHA
	TERA, VIHARA
—Chinese	PAGOD(A), TAA
—dedicated to hero	HEROON
—Eastern	PAGOD(A)
—Greek	NAOS, NYMPHAEUM
—Hindu	MANDIR(A)
—Indian	VIMANA
—Jain	MANDIR(A)
—Jewish	SYNAGOGUE
tent	TABERNACLE
—Mexican	TEOCALLI
—Moslem	KAABA, MOSQUE
—Sikh	GURDWARA
temple-shaped tomb	HEROON
tower	SPIRE, STEEPLE
—over church crossing	ROOD-TOWER
underground chamber	CRYPT
	UNDERCROFT, VAULT
unroofed sanctuary	SACELLUM
vestibule at front of	
—church	NARTHEX
—temple	PRONAOS
wall hanging	DOSSAL, DOSSEL, DOSSOL
washbasin	CANTHARUS
water container	FONT, STOUP
waterspout	GARGOYLE
western portico	NARTHEX

church — personnel

abbot (Greek)	ARCHIMANDRITE
	HEGUMEN
Abyssinian patriarch	ABUNA

arch-deacon (R.C.)	VICAR-GENERAL
archbishop	METROPOLITAN, PRIMATE
—Canterbury	CANTUAR
—German	ELECTOR
—York	EBOR
Armenian priest	VARTABAD
assistant	CURATE
—bishop	SUFFRAGAN
attached to military	CHAPLAIN, PADRE
attendant on cardinal	CONCLAVIST
bellringer	SEXTON
between bishop and deacon	PRESBYTER
	PRIOR
bishop	DIOCESAN
—Abyssinian	ABUNA
—Coptic	ABBA
—Eastern	ABBA
—of	
Portsmouth	CRISPIAN
Rome	POPE
—or cardinal	PRELATE
—over several dioceses	METROPOLITAN
—ranking above	
exarch	METROPOLITAN
metropolitan	PATRIARCH
—Scottish	PRIMUS
	TULCHAN-BISHOP
—Syriac	ABBA
bishop's deputy (R. C)	VICAR
bishops	EPISCOPACY, PRELACY
—itinerant	EPISCOPI VAGRANTES
Buddhist priest	BONZE
candidate for ordination	ORDINAND
canon	PREBENDARY
—other than canon regular	CANON SECULAR
—resident at cathedral	RESIDENTIARY
—who is not a member	
of cathedral chapter	MINOR CANON
—with no	
responsibilities	HONORARY CANON
caretaker	BEADLE, SEXTON
cathedral	
—administrator	DEAN
—church	MINSTER
chancellor of a diocese	VICAR-GENERAL
chief priest	PRELATE
—Roman (Syria)	SYRIARCH
clergy	CLOTH
clergyman	CAMISTER, MINISTER
	PARSON, PASTOR
	PRIEST, VICAR
—Australian	JESSER
—below priest (Episcopal)	DEACON
—in diocese	DIOCESAN
—of parish responsible	
for tithes	RECTOR

—over several parishes	RURAL DEAN
—receiving smaller tithes	
or salary	VICAR
—resident at	
cathedral	CANON RESIDENTIARY
—slang name	HOLY JOE, SKY PILOT
—who enjoys share	
of revenues	PREBENDARY
cleric who sings in	
cathedral choir	VICAR-CHORAL
Coptic bishop	ABBA
deputy	
—abbess	VICARESS
—bishop (France)	VIDAME
—church-warden	SIDESMAN
—head of abbey	PRIOR
diocesan administrator	ARCHDEACON
director of choral services	PRECENTOR
disciple	CHELA
Eastern monks	ACOEMETI
ecclesiastical	
successor (Irish)	CO(M)ARB
elder	PRESBYTER
elected representative of clergy	PROCTOR
Episcopal clergyman in	
USA or Scotland	RECTOR
exarch	METROPOLITAN
female in early Christian	
society	DEACONESS
French	
—Dominican monk	JACOBIN
—priest	ABBE, CURE
German prince-bishop	ELECTOR
gravedigger	SEXTON
head of	
—abbey	
female	ABBESS
male	ABBOT
—Abyssinian church	ABUNA
—Eastern church	PATRIARCH
—house of	
canons	PRIOR
friars	PRIOR
—priory of monks	PRIOR
—religious order	MINISTER
—Scottish church	MODERATOR
Hebrew religious teacher	RABBI
high	
—priest	PONTIFF
Roman	PONTIFEX
—ranking priest	PRELATE
itinerant	
—bishops	EPISCOPI VAGRANTES
—priest	BUCKLEBEGGAR
	HEDGE PARSON
	HEDGE PRIEST

layman who visits the sick	PARABOLANUS
leader of singers	
—female	PRECENTRESS
	PRECENTRIX
—male	PRECENTOR
legal officer	CHANCELLOR
member of an order between monks and secular clergy	CANON REGULAR
member of cathedral chapter	CANON
mendicant monk	FRIAR
metropolitan	EXARCH
minor orders	ABBE, ACOLYTE
	DOORKEEPER
	EXORCIST, LECTOR
	OSTIARY, PORTER
monk in a community	C(O)ENOBITE
next below arch-deacon	ACOLYTE, ACOLYTH
officer	
—advising pastor (Congregational)	DEACON
—dealing with secular matters (Presbyterian)	DEACON
—in charge of	
altar in convent	DEACONESS
lamps (Gr.)	LAMPADARY
robes, vessels, etc	SACRISTAN
	SEXTON
—inferior	ACOLYTE, ACOLYTH
—of	
church	BEADLE, VERGER
—Scottish	BEADLE, BED(E)RAL
ecclesiastical court	APPARITOR
—representing laity or church	CHURCH-WARDEN
—with pastoral duties (Protestant)	DEACONESS
officials of papal court	CURIA
one	
—just ordained	DEACON
—licensed to preach	PARSON
—living as	
monk without vows	BEGHARD
nun without vows	BEGUINE
—serving individual or institution	CHAPLAIN
—to whom the pope delegated a remote part of his jurisdiction	VICAR-APOSTOLIC
—using leavened bread in Holy Communion	ZYMITE
—who accepts the decrees of the Council of Trent	TRIDENTINE
—who prays for others	BEAD(S)MAN
	BEDE(S)MAN
order of bishops	EPISCOPATE

papal	
—ambassador	NUNCIO
—dignitary	MONSIGNOR
—officer	DATARY
pope	BISHOP OF ROME
	HOLY FATHER
	VICAR OF CHRIST
preacher in highly emotional sect	HOLY ROLLER
Presbyterian	ELDER, PRESBYTER
priest, religious teacher	HIEROPHANT
—Armenian	VARTABAD
—Buddhist	BONZE, LAMA
—Catholic Apostolic	PASTOR
—doing politically-committed work	LIBERATION-PRIEST
—Etruscan	HARUSPEX, LUCUMO
—French	ABBE, CURE
—Greek	PAPA
—gypsy term	PATERCOVE, PATRICO
—Hebrew	RABBI(N)
—Hindu	PUJARIA
—Italian	PRETE, SACERDOTE
—itinerant	BUCKLEBEGGAR
	HEDGE-PARSON
	HEDGE-PRIEST
—longwinded	SPINTEXT
—Moslem	AYATOLLAH, IMA(U)M
	MUEDDIN, MUEZZIN
—of Cybele	CORYBANT
—parish	PARSON, RECTOR, VICAR
—Roman	FLAMEN, PONTIFEX
Catholic	FATHER
—Scottish	MAS(S)JOHN, MES(S)JOHN
	MINISTER
with no parish	STICKIT MINISTER
—Spanish	CURA, PARROCO
	PRESTE, SACERDOTE
—Syrian (Roman)	SYRIARCH
—Tibetan	LAMA
prince of RC church	CARDINAL
priory church	MINSTER
rural dean	VICAR-FORANE
sacristan (Greek)	SCEUOPHYLAX
Scottish	
—bishop	PRIMUS, TULCHAN BISHOP
—priest	MAS(S)JOHN, MES(S)JOHN
	MINISTER
self-seeking cleric	ROME RUNNER
senior official of cathedral	PROVOST
Syriac bishop	ABBA
theologian	THEOLOGER, THEOLOGUE
—Alexandrian	ORIGEN
—American	MACKINTOSH, MATTHEWS
	RAUSCHENBURG, TILLICH
	WEIZMAN

—Austrian	BOLZANO, BUBER
—British	BEDE, CAMPBELL, INGE
	MAJOR, ROBINSON, SMITH
—Dutch	SPINOZA
—French	MALEBRANCHE
	TEILHARD DE CHARDIN
—German	BAVER, BULTMANNN
	BONHOFFER, OTTO
	SCHLEIERMACHER, SCHWEITZER
	TILLICH, TROELTSCH
—Irish	TYRELL, USSHER
—Italian	ANSELM, AQUINAS
—Swedish	SWEDENBORG
—Swiss	BARTH
title	
—given to	
certain prelates	MONSIGNOR
one in process	
of canonisation	VENERABLE
—of courtesy	ABBE
titular bishop	VICAR-APOSTOLIC
usher	BEADLE, VERGER
vicar of Chist	POPE
vicar's wife	VICARESS
Waldensian teacher	BARBE
would-be theologian	THEOLOGASTER
young deacon	ORDINEE

church — terms

administer last sacrament	ANELE
administrative	
—board	COLLEGIUM
—or legal department	CHANCERY
admission to the	
ministry by the	
laying on of hands	ORDINATION
altar-cloth	ANTEPENDIUM, FRONTAL
anointing	UNCTION
anthem	INTROIT
assembly	CONVENTICLE
	CONVOCATION, SYNOD
association of lay	
members	SODALITY
authorised doctrines	ORTHODOXY
bar sounded instead of bell	SEMANTRON
bell rung thrice daily	ANGELUS
Benedictine title	DOM
bishop's medallion of	
the Virgin	PAN(H)AGIA
bishopric	EPISCOPATE
blessing	BENEDICITE
body of cardinals	
to elect Pope	CONCLAVE
book of	
—Apocrypha	TOBIT
—hymns, prayers etc	BREVIARY
—lessons	LECTIONARY

—rules	PIE, PYE
books of the Bible	
—accepted by the Christian	
faith	CANON
—not accepted	APOCRYPHA
borderland of Hell	LIMBO, LIMBUS
calendar giving details	
of services for each	
day of the year	ORDO
canonical hours	
—dawn	MATINS
—after matins	LAUDS
—6 am	PRIME
—9 am	TIERCE
—noon	SEXT
—3 pm	NONES
—early evening	VESPERS
—late evening	COMPLINE
canopy carried	
over priest	BALDACHIN, BALDACCHINO
	BALDAQUIN
canticle of Zacharias	BENEDICTUS
Catholic title	DOM
ceremonial garments	VESTMENTS
Christ	CHR, X, XT
—appearance	CHRISTOPHANY
Christian	
—gospel	KERYGMA
—symbol	CHI RHO, FISH, ICHTHYS
code of law	CANON
	CODEX JURIS CANONICI
collection of bulls	BULLARY
college of cardinals	COLLEGIUM
confirmation	CHRIS(O)M
congregation charged	
with spreading	
the faith	PROPAGANDA (FIDE)
consecrated wafer	(EUCHARISTIC) HOST
container for	
—holy oil	CHRISMATORY
—host	MONSTRANCE, PYX
—incense	CENSER
—pyx	TABERNACLE
control by state	ERASTIANISM
court	CONSISTORY
—of papal see	CURIA
creed	APOSTLE'S, ATHANASIAN
	NICAEAN, NICENE
cross	(see separate entry)
—bearer	CRUCIFER
declaration by Pope	
—of sainthood	CANONISATION
—that a person is blessed	BEATIFICATION
degrees or grades	ORDERS
deification	APOTHEOSIS
deified ruler	THEOCRAT

deviation from authorised belief	HERESY
	HETERODOXY
devotions lasting nine days	NOVENA
digest of decrees etc	CANON LAW
discussion of the Eucharist	EUCHARISTIC THEOLOGY
divine	
—influence	GRACE
—intervention	THEURGY
doctrine	
—in which belief is obligatory	DE FIDE DOCTRINE
—of	
choice between right and wrong	TUTIORISM
infallibility	ULTRAMONTISM
last things	ESCHATOLOGY
the Holy Spirit	PNEUMATOLOGY
—that the bread and wine actually change into the body and blood of Christ	TRANSUBSTANTIATION
ecclesiastical	
—council	SYNOD
—court	CONSISTORY
—levy	ANNAT(ES)
edict of Pope under seal	BULL
endowment	BENEFICE
	PATRIMONY
eternal life	GRACE
Eucharist	HOLY COMMUNION, MASS
evening service	EVENSONG, VESPERS
exemption from ecclesiastical law	INDULGENCE
existence of Trinity each within the other	CIRCUMINCESSION
	CIRCUMINSESSION
feast of	
—Annunciation of the Virgin	LADY DAY
—birth of Christ	CHRISTMAS
—Exaltation of Cross	HOLYROOD DAY
	ROOD(MAS) DAY
—Invention of Cross	HOLYROOD DAY
	ROOD(MAS) DAY
—Resurrection	EASTER
—St Martin	MARTINMAS
—St Michael	MICHAELMAS
	(see also holidays)
feet-washing ceremony	MAUNDY, NIPTER
first	
—five books of Bible	PENTATEUCH
—seven books of Bible	HEPTATEUCH
give absolution	SHRIVE
gospel-preaching	EVANGELICALISM
governing body	CLASSIS

government by bishops	EPISCOPACY
	EPISCOPAL(IAN)ISM
grace	BENEDICITE
hand-washing ritual	LAVABO
holy	
—oil	CHRIS(O)M
—wine or vessel	AMA
home of souls of	
—those who died before the birth of Christ	LIMBUS PATRUM
—unbaptised babies	LIMBUS INFANTUM
hours set for prayers	CANONICAL HOURS
hymn	CANTICLE, CHORALE
—Holy, holy, holy	(TER)SANCTUS
—to the glory of God	DOXOLOGY
illustrated gospels	BOOK OF KELLS
	LINDISFARNE
income from benefice passed to Pope or Crown	ANNAT
indulgence given	
—for	
a	
—particular person	PERSONAL
—period	TEMPORAL
all sins	PLENARY
some sins	PARTIAL
—in a particular place	LOCAL
—until revoked	INDEFINITE
	PERPETUAL
inquisition	HOLY OFFICE
interpretation of Bible truths	HERMENEUTICS
introductory hymn etc	INTROIT
invocation of the Holy Spirit at mass	EPICLESIS
land	GLEBE
last book of the New Testament	APOCALYPSE
	REVELATIONS
Latin translation of the Bible	VULGATE
lesson	LECTION
—based on life of saint	SYNAXARION
—book	LECTIONARY
letter from	
—apostle	EPISTLE
—Pope to all bishops	ENCYCLICAL
list of	
—books banned by Church	INDEX (EXPURGATORIUS)
	INDEX LIBRORUM PROHIBITORUM
—saints	CANON
living	BENEFICE
manifestation	EPIPHANY
Mass	EUCHARIST
	HOLY COMMUNION
—for the dead	REQUIEM
--Latin	TRIDENTINE

—used from 16th c	TRIDENTINE MASS
—with music and incense	HIGH MASS
meeting	
—for worship	SYNAXIS
—of	
cardinals to elect Pope	CONCLAVE
Pope and cardinals	CONSISTORY
mercy of God	GRACE
miracle-making	THEURGY
modernisation	AGGIORNAMENTO
modernised	
Christianity	PROCESS THEOLOGY
	SECULAR CHRISTIANITY
	SOUTH BANK RELIGION
morning service	MATINS
movement involving the	
laity in worship	LITURGICAL MOVEMENT
narrative of Christ's life	GOSPEL
New Testament books	
—originally not accepted	ANTILOGOMENA
—taken as authentic	HOMOLOG(O)UMENA
non-metrical hymn	CANTICLE
office of	
—bishop	PRELACY
—deacon	DIACONATE
official	
—dress	CANONICALS
—statement by Pope	ENCYCLICAL
old hymn	(TER)SANCTUS
	TRISAGION
Old Testament (Greek)	SEPTUAGINT
origin and development of gods	THEOGONY
orthodox Roman Catholic	TRIDENTINE
papal	
—court	CURIA
—decree	BULL
settling point of	
canon law	DECRETAL
—seal	BULLA
pardonable sin	VENIAL SIN
part of	
—the Mass	CANON OF THE MASS
	DONA NOBIS
—service spoken	
in audible tones	ECPHONESIS
passage for reading	PERICOPE
place in which souls of	
the dead are purified	PURGATORY
portable shrine for relics	FERETORY
prayer	OR(A)ISON
—after a meal	GRACE
—before a meal	GRACE
--devotional	ANGELUS
—in	
ancient Greek	
church	KYRIE ELEISON

Latin church	CONFITEOR
ancient Greek in	
Latin mass	KYRIE ELEISON
—of	
belief	CREDO
confession	CONFITEOR
entreaty	LITANY
—short	COLLECT
—with responses	LITANY
prayer-book	EUCHOLOGY
	EUCHOLOGION
preliminary offering	PROTHESIS
Presbyterian church court	SYNOD
presbytery	CLASSIS
priest's handwarmer	POME
provincial synod	CONVOCATION
Psalm	CHORALE
—66	JUBILATE
—95	VENITE
—98	CANTATE
—100	JUBILATE
reading in Church	EPISTLE, GOSPEL
	LESSON
recognition as a saint	CANONISATION
release from vows	DISPENSATION
religion in relation	
to ethics	MORAL THEOLOGY
religious	
—festival	HOLY DAY
	SAINT'S DAY
—hypocrite	HOLY WILLIE
reliquary worn by Orthodox	
prelate	ENCOLPION
remission of temporal	
punishment	INDULGENCE
response	KYRIE ELEISON
revelation	EPIPHANY
rite	SACRAMENT
ritual	
—hand-washing	LAVABO
—service	LITURGY
Roman Catholic tribunal	DICASTERY
rule or custom	RUBRIC
—or law	CANON
ruling body	(GENERAL) SYNOD
—houses	BISHOPS, CLERGY, LAITY
sacrament	BAPTISM, CONFESSION
	CONFIRMATION, EXTREME UNCTION
	HOLY COMMUNION, LAST RITES
	MATRIMONY, ORDINATION
	RECONCILIATION
—at point of death	EXTREME UNCTION
	SACRAMENT OF THE SICK
	LAST RITES
—of the Lord's supper	EUCHARIST
	HOLY COMMUNION

salary	LIVING, PREBEND	—vestment	CHIMER(E), DALMATIC
	STIPEND		RATIONAL(E), ROCHET
salvation	GRACE		TUNICLE
saying(s) of Chist	AGRAPHON(AGRAPHA)	Eastern	OMOPHORION, SAKKOS
scriptures	HOLY WRIT	cape with hood	DOMINO
second		cassock	SLOP
—coming of Christ	PAROUSIA	—French	SOUTANE
—part of canon law	DECRETAL	—old	SUBUCULA
serious sin	MORTAL SIN	chorister's robe	CASSOCK
service	LITURGY	cloth covering bishop's lap	GREMIAL
short prayer	COLLECT	deacon's robe	DALMATIC
shrine carried in		Eastern	
procession	FERETORY	—bishop's vestment	OMOPHORION
song	ANTHEM, CANTICLE		SAKKOS
	HYMN, PSALM	—vestment	PH(A)ELONION
splitting of church	SCHISM	ecclesiastical	
statement of		—cape	MOZETTA
—beliefs	CREED	—scarf	TIPPET
—body of doctrines	DOGMATICS	—skullcap	ZUCHETTO
	SYSTEMATIC THEOLOGY	French cassock	SOUTANE
study of		friar's dress	HABIT
—church forms	ECCLESIOLOGY	Greek alb	STICHARION
—religion	THEOLOGY	Jewish priest's surplice	EPHOD
sudden insight	EPIPHANY	long robe	CASSOCK
supreme ecclesiastical		—Scottish	GENEVA GOWN
court	ROTA	monk's	
take confessions	SHRIVE	—dress	HABIT
teaching of Christ	GOSPEL	—hood	CAPUCHE, COWL
ten commandments	DECALOGUE	—sleeveless cloak	SCAPULAR
tenth share	TITHE	narrow shoulder vestment	STOLE
Trinity	FATHER, HOLY GHOST	nun's	
	SON	—dress	HABIT
tube for imbibing		—kerchief	BARBE
sacramental wine	FISTULA	—veil	W(H)IMPLE
Vatican department in		official dress	CANONICALS
charge of missionaries	PROPAGANDA (FIDE)	Pope's	
verse said by		—headdress	TIARA
—congregation	RESPONSE	—short cape	FANON
—leader	VERSICLE	—vestment	PALLIUM
vindication of God's		preacher's gown	GENEVA GOWN
justice	THEODICY	scarf	TIPPET
Virgin Mary's song	MAGNIFICAT	shawl worn on shoulders	HUMERAL VEIL
war against heresy or		short silk	
other religion	CRUSADE	vestment (Scot.)	CASSOCK
	HOLY WAR, JIHAD	sleeveless	
week before Easter	HOLY WEEK	—hooded vestment	COPE
church — vestments		—vestment	CHASUBLE
abbot's vestment	RO(T)CHET	square cap	BIRETTA
alb (Greek)	STICHARION	—colour for	
archbishop's vestment	PALLIUM	bishop	PURPLE
bishop's		cardinal	RED
—close-fitting surplice	RO(T)CHET	priest	BLACK
—cross	CROSIER, CROZIER	stole	TIPPET
—hat	MITRE	strip(s)	
—stockings	CALIGAE	—hanging from	
—upper robe	CHIMER(E)	neck	GENEVA BANDS

shoulders	SCAPULAR, STOLE
—worn on	
left arm	FAN(I)ON
	FANNEL(L), MANIPLE
shoulder	AMICE, HUMERAL VEIL
sub-deacon's vestment	TUNICLE
surplice	EPHOD, COTTA
	STOLA, STOLE
—Scottish	SARK
tight-sleeved vestment	ALB
white linen vestment worn	
over cassock	SURPLICE

(*see also* **belief, garments**)

cinema
actors
—American	ALLEN, ASTAIRE
	BARRYMORE, BEATTY, BOGART
	BRANDO, BRONSON, BRYNNER
	CAGNEY, CHANEY, CLIFT, COBB
	COBURN, COOPER, CROSBY, CURTIS
	DEAN, DOUGLAS, DREYFUSS
	EASTWOOD, FIELDS, FITZGERALD
	FONDA, GABLE, GOULD
	HACKMAN, HARDY, HESTON
	HOFFMAN, HOLDEN, JOLSON
	KEATON, LADD, LANCASTER
	LEMMON, LLOYD, MARCH, MARVIN
	MARX BROTHERS, MCCREA, MCQUEEN
	MITCHUM, MIX, MUNI, NEWMAN
	NICHOLSON, POWELL, POWER, QUINN
	REAGAN, REDFORD, REYNOLDS
	ROBINSON, SCOTT, SINATRA
	STALLONE, STEWART, TAYLOR, TONE
	TRACY, VALENTINO, VOIGT, WAGNER
	WALLACH, WAYNE, WEISSMULLER
	WELLES, WIDMARK
—Bahamian	POITIER
—British	ARLISS, ATTENBOROUGH
	BOGARDE, BURTON, CAINE, CHAPLIN
	COLMAN, CONNERY, CUSHING, DONAT
	FAIRBANKS, FINCH, GIELGUD
	GRAINGER, GRANT, GUINNESS
	HARDWICKE, HARRISON, HOPE
	HOWARD, KARLOFF
	LAUGHTON, LAUREL, LIVESEY, MASON
	MILLAND, MILLS, MOORE, NIVEN
	OLIVIER, PRICE, QUAYLE, REED
	RAINS, RICHARDSON, SANDERS
	SCOFIELD, SIM, SMITH
	TODD, USTINOV
—French	BARRAULT, BELMONDO, BOYR
	CHEVALIER, DELON, DEPARDIEU
	FERNANDEL, GABIN, MONTAND, TATI

(*see also* **theatre**)

—German	JANNING, SCHELL
—Hungarian	LORRE, LUGOSI
—Irish	FLYNN, HARRIS
—Italian	FABRIZI, MASTROIANNI
—Tasmanian	FLYNN

actresses
—American	BACALL, BALL, BANCROFT
	BENNETT, COLBERT, CRAWFORD
	DAVIS, DE HAVILLAND, DUNAWAY
	FONDA, FONTAINE, GARDNER
	GARLAND, GAYNOR, GISH, GRABLE
	HAYES, HAYWOOD, HAYWORTH
	HEPBURN, HOLLIDAY, KELLY
	LAMARR, LAMOUR, LOMBARD
	MCGRAW, MINELLI, MONROE
	NEAL, OBERON, PICKFORD
	ROGERS, RUSSELL, SHEARER, SHIELDS
	STANWYCK, STREISAND, STREEP
	SWANSON, TEMPLE, TREVOR, WOOD
	WOODWARD, YOUNG
—British	ANDREWS, ASHCROFT
	COLLINS, DORS, HEPBURN, HOBSON
	JACKSON, KERR, LANSBURY, LEIGH
	LOCKWOOD, SHEARER, SIMS
	TAYLOR, TODD, WELCH
—French	BARDOT, CAPUCINE
	SEYRIG, SIGNORET
—German	DIETRICH, DRESSLER
—Greek	MERCOURI
—Hungarian	GABOR
—Italian	CARDINALE, LOREN
	LOLLOBRIGIDA, MAGNANI
—Swedish	GARBO, BERGMAN

(*see also* **theatre**)

add a soundtrack	DUB
afternoon screening	MATINEE
assemblage of photographs	MONTAGE
board used to synchronise	
sound and picture	CLAPPERBOARD
biographical film	BIOPIC
brief appearance of well-	
known actor	CAMEO ROLE
cafeteria in film studio	COMMISSARY
comic	
—policeman	CLOUSEAU
—policemen	KEYSTONE COPS
	KEYSTONE KOPS
commentary by unseen	
speaker	VOICE-OVER
composite photograph	MONTAGE

directors
—American	ALLEN, ALTMAN, CAPRA
	COPPOLA, CUKOR, CURTIZ
	DE MILLE, DIETERLE, DISNEY
	FLAHERTY, FLEMING, FORD, FULLER
	GOLDWYN, GRIFFITH, HAWKS, HUSTON
	KAZAN, KUBRICK, LANG, LOSEY, LUCAS
	LUMET, LYNCH, MACK, MAMOULIAN

	MANKIEWICZ, MAYSLES, POLANSKI	some documentary	
	PORTER, PECKINPAH, PREMINGER, RAY	sequences	COMPILATION FILM
	SENNETT, SPIELBERG, VIDOR, WELLES	nude actors	SKINFLICK
	WILDER, WYLER, ZINNEMAN	filming	
—Austrian	STROHEIM	—sequence	TAKE
—British	ASQUITH, ATTENBOROUGH	—static drawings to	
	FORBES, GILLIATT, GRIERSON	simulate movement	ANIMATION
	HITCHCOCK, JORDAN, LEACOCK	first unedited print of film	RUSH
	LEAN, NEAME, POWELL	floodlight	KLEIG LIGHT
	PRESSBURGER, PUTNAM, REED		KLIEG LIGHT
	SCHLESINGER, USTINOV	French movement of 1960's	NEW WAVE
—Danish	DREYER, SIRK		NOUVELLE VAGUE
—French	AUMONT-LARA, CARNE	gaffer's assistant	BEST BOY
	CHABROL, CLAIR, COCTEAU	high-intensity lamp	KLIEG LIGHT
	DUVIVIER, FERDUR, FRANK	holes on each side	
	GODARD, MALLE, MARKER	of film	SPROCKET HOLES
	RENOIR, RESNAIS, RIVETTE	insert a shot	CROSSCUT, INTERCUT
	ROHMER, ROUCH, STRAUB	inserted shot	CUT-IN
	TATI, TRUFFAUT, VADIM, VIGO	instrument simulating	
—German	FASSBINDER, HERZOG	movement with still	
	LANG, LUBITSCH, OPHIUS	pictures	PHENAKISTOSCOPE
	VON STERNBERG, WEINE	joint in film	SPLICE
—Hungarian	CURTIZ	lighting technician	GAFFER
—Indian	RAY, ROY	list of performers and	
—Italian	ANTONIONI, BARBARO	workers	CREDITS
	BERTOLUCCI, DE SANTIS	move camera to follow action	TRACK
	DE SICA, FABRIZI, FELLINI	non-fictional	DOCUMENTARY
	GUISEPPE, LEONE, LATTUADA		DOCUDRAMA
	ROSSELLINI, VISCONTI, VITTORIO	one with artistic interest	
—Japanese	KUROSAWA, MIZOGUCHI	in films	CINEASTE
	OSHIMA, OZU	outdoor filming site	LOCATION
—Polish	POLANSKI	pornographic film	BLUE FILM
—Russian	EISENSTEIN, KOZINTZEV		SKINFLICK
	KULESHOV, TARKOVSKY	portion of film	FOOTAGE
	TRAUBERG, VERTOV	—discarded	OUTTAKE
—Spanish	BUNUEL	projection of film as	
—Swedish	BERGMAN	background for filming	
early	BIOSCOPE, NICKELODEON	other action	BACK PROJECTION
	MUTOSCOPE, ZOECHROME	quick change of image	
	ZOETROPE, ZOOPRAXISCOPE	size by use of special lens	ZOOM(ING)
electrician	GAFFER	repeated single frame	FREEZE FRAME
film	MOTION PICTURE	reversion to previous events	FLASHBACK
—library	CINEMATHEQUE	scene change by	
—dealing with		—abrupt transition	JUMP CUT
earlier events	PREQUEL	—fading one scene	
later events	SEQUEL	into another	DISSOLVE
—enthusiast	CINEASTE	—gradual change	FADE IN
—featuring cowboys and			FADE OUT
Indians	HORSE OPERA	—line moving across	
	(SPAGHETTI) WESTERN	the screen	WIPE
—making	CINEMATOGRAPHY	scenes depicting same	
—mixing fact and fiction	FACTION	event in different ways	MONTAGE
—representing life		script	
realistically	CINE VERITE	—describing camera	
—using		work and order of	
animation	CARTOON	filming	SHOOTING SCRIPT

—giving full detailed
  version of the story — TREATMENT
—used for
  acting and camera
  directions — SCENARIO
    SCREENPLAY
  ensuring consistency
  from scene to scene — CONTINUITY
sequence — FOOTAGE
single photograph
—in film — FRAME
—taken for publicity etc — STILL
small cinema — CINEMATHEQUE
studios — ELSTREE, HOLLYWOOD
superimposition of
  photographs — MONTAGE
swing camera to
  follow action — PAN
technique
—photographing at
  intervals to give
  speeded-up film — TIME-LAPSE
—using
  camera tricks — OPTICAL
  SPECIAL EFFECT
  two or more images
  on parts of one screen — SPLIT SCREEN
  ZOETROPE
toy
trolley for moving camera — DOLLY
Western — HORSE OPERA
wide screen — CINEMASCOPE
  CINEMIRACLE
  CINERAMA, IMAX
  TODD-AO, VISTAVISION

circulation
including: blood
     heart
     lymph
     veins
affecting contraction and
  dilation — VASOMOTOR
artificial regulator — PACEMAKER
artery
—blocking by
  clotted blood — THROMBOSIS
  solid fragment — EMBOLISM
—bulge in — ANEURYSM
—cutting of — ARTERIOTOMY
—deposit of cholesterol etc in — ATHEROMA
—from
  aorta to
  —abdomen — COELIAC, ILIAC
  MESENTERIC, RENAL
  —head — CAROTID
  —heart — CORONARY
  —leg — FEMORAL

—neck and arm — AXILLARY
  BRACHIAL, RADIAL
  SUBCLAVIAN, ULNAR
—upper right side — INOMINATE
heart to
—lungs — PULMONARY
—rest of body — AORTA
—hardening of — ARTERIOSCLEROSIS
—inflammation of — ARTERITIS
—narrowing of — STENOSIS
—small — ARTERIOLE
—swelling in carotid — CAROTID SINUS
blockage — CLOT, EMBOLISM
  EMBOLUS, INFARCTION
blood — GORE, PINK
—agglutination
  common to
  man and monkey — RH(ESUS) FACTOR
  of cells in same
  group — ISOAGGLUTINATION
—anti-clotting agent — HEPARIN
—antibody
  causing clumping of
  bacteria — AGGLUTININ
  in globulin — IMMUNOGLOBULIN
—antigen in red cells — RH(ESUS) FACTOR
—bacteria-destroyer — BACTERIOPHAGE
  PHAGOCYTE
—bile in the blood — CHOLAEMIA
—bleeding — HAEMORRHAGE
—bloody — SANGUINARY
—blue pigment — HAEMOCYANIN
—breaking down of leucocytes — LEUCOCYTOSIS
—bright red — ARTERIAL
—brown substance in dried
  blood — HAEMATIN
—cancer — LEUKAEMIA
—cavity containing blood — HAEMATOCELE
—cell — BLOOD CORPUSCLE
  fighting infection — LEUCOCYTE
  WHITE CORPUSCLE
  transporting oxygen — HAEMOCYTE
  RED CORPUSCLE
—checking bleeding — STYPTIC
—chemical peventing
  clotting — ANTICOAGULANT
—chloride of haematin — HAEMIN
—clotting
  agent — PLATELET, THROMBOCYTE
  enzyme — THROMBIN
—coagulating protein — FIBRIN, FIBROGEN
—cold-blooded — POIKILOTHERMIC
—colour — INCARNADINE
—compound formed by
  oxygen acting on
  haemoglobin — OXY-HAEMOGLOBIN

—constituent of haemoglobin	GLOBIN
—conversion of venous	
blood to arterial	HAEMATOSIS
—deficiency of	
blood sugar	HYPOGLYCAEMIA
red cells	(SP)ANAEMIA
—deprived of oxygen	VENOUS
—destruction of red cells	H(A)EMOLYSIS
—diffusion through membrane	
for purification	HAEMODIALYSIS
—dilation of blood vessel	ANEURISM
	ANEUYSM
—discharge of blood	HAEMORRHAGE
	STAXIS
—diseases of the blood	(see disease)
—dissolution of red	
corpuscles	HAEM(AT)OLYSIS
—dust	HAEMOCONIA
—excess of	
blood sugar	HYPERGLYCAEMIA
red cells	POLYCYTHAEMIA
—excessive bleeding	HAEMOPHILIA
—fatty	
acid in blood	TRIGLYCERIDE
deposit in vessels	ATHEROMA
	CHOLESTEROL
—fluid separated from	
coagulating blood	SERUM
—formation of	
blood	HAEMATOSIS
red cells	HAEM(AT)OPOIESIS
—granules in the blood	BLOOD-DUST
	HAEMOCONIA
—groups	A, B, AB, O
—haemoconia	BLOOD-DUST
—haemocyte	BLOOD CELL
	BLOOD CORPUSCLE
—haemoglobin in	
muscle fibre	MYOGLOBIN
—homoiothermic	WARM-BLOODED
—idiothermic	WARM-BLOODED
—immature red cell	RETICULOCYTE
—immune system cells	B-CELL, T-CELL
—immunising substance	PROPERDIN
—in combination	HAEMO-
—infection of blood	PYAEMIA
—infusion of blood from	
others	TRANSFUSION
self	AUTOLOGICAL TRANSFUSION
—in urine	H(A)EMATURIA
—large white cell	MONCYTE
—liquid constituent after	
removal of cells	PLASMA
—morbid state of blood	CACHAEMIA
—natural immuniser	
in blood	PROPERDIN

—nitrogen bubbles	
in blood	AEROEMBOLISM, BENDS
	CAISSON DISEASE
	DECOMPRESSION SICKNESS
—overproduction of white	
cells in response	
to infection	LEUCOCYTOSIS
—oxygenated haemoglobin	
	OXYHAEMOGLOBIN
—part of serum promoting	
phagocytosis	OPSONIN
—pigment	HAEM, HAEMOCYANIN
	HAEMOGLOBIN
—plasma without clotting	
agents	SERUM
—platelet	HAEMATOBLAST
	THROMBOCYTE
—poisoning	PYAEMIA, SEPTICAEMIA
	SUPRAEMIA, TOXAEMIA
—polypeptide in blood	KENIN
—pressure	BP, DISATOLIC
	RR, SYSTOLIC
high	HYPERTENSION
low	HYPOTENSION
measuring	
instrument	SPHYGMO(MANO)METER
—protective body	ALEXIN, ANTIBODY
	ANTIGEN
	GAMMA GLOBULIN
—protein	
clotting	FIBRIN
hormone	INSULIN
plasma	ALBUMEN, ALBUMIN
	FIBRINOGEN, GLOBULIN
protective	GAMMA GLOBULIN
red	HAEMOGLOBIN
—purification by	
machine	(HAEMO)DIALYSIS
—pus in blood	PYAEMIA
—red	
cell	ERYTHROCYTE
—with no	
corpuscle	ERYTHROCYTE
haemoglobin	RED CELL GHOST
pigment	HAEMOGLOBIN
—reduction of supply	ISCH(A)EMIA
—serum containing	
antibodies	ALS
	ANTI-LYMPHATIC SERUM
	GAMMA GLOBULIN
—smear on slide	BLOOD FILM
—spitting blood	EMPTYSIS
	HAEMOPTYSIS
—stimulating production	
of red cells	HAEMATINIC
—stoppage of bleeding	HAEMOSTASIS

—study of blood   HAEMATOLOGY
—substance
   preventing clotting   HEPARIN
   stimulating production
   of agglutinin   AGGLUTINOGEN
—sugar   GLUCOSE
—swelling containing blood   HAEMATOMA
—vessels   ARTERIOLE, ARTERY
     CAPILLARY, VEIN, VENULE
—vomiting blood   HAEMATEMESIS
—warm-blooded   HOMOIOTHERMIC
     IDIOTHERMIC
     IDIOTHERMOUS
—white cell   BASOPHIL, EOSINOPHIL
     LEUCOCYTE, LEUKOCYTE
     LYMPHOCYTE, NEUTROPHIL
   destroying bacteria etc   PHAGOCYTE
   with granular cytoplasm   GRANULOCYTE
   POLYMORPH(ONUCLEAR LEUCOCYTE)
development of new
   blood vessels   NEOVASCULARISATION
dilation of arteries, etc   TELANGIECTASIS
expanding of blood vessel   VASODILATION
heart
—abnormal sound   MURMUR
—cessation of
   heart-beat   CARDIAC ARREST
—chamber   ATRIUM, AURICLE
     VENTRICLE
   in some animals   SINUS VENOSUS
—contraction   SYSTOLE
—dilatation   DIASTOLE
—fast-beating   TACHYCARDIA
—fluttering of heart muscle   FIBRILLATION
—inflammation of   CARDITIS
     (*see also* **disease**)
—irregular beat   ARRHYTHMIA
—lining membrane   ENDOTHELIUM
—muscle controlling
   heart-beat   PACEMAKER
—on right side of body   DEXTROCARDIA
—opening between
   auricles   FORAMEN OVALE
—recording instrument   CARDIOGRAPH
—rhythmic pressure to
   restart heart-beat   CARDIAC MASSAGE
—sac   PERICARDIUM
—slow-beating   BRADYCARDIA
—study of   CARDIOLOGY
—valves   AORTIC, MITRAL
     PULMONARY
     TRICUSPID
heart-burn   CARDALGIA, CARDALGY
heart-failure   CARDIAC FAILURE
heart-shaped   CARDIOID
lining of blood vessels   INTIMA

lymph
—glands   ABDOMINAL, AXILLARY
     CERVICAL, INGUINAL
     MEDIASTINAL, POPLITEAL
     SUB-LINGUAL, SUB-MAXILLARY
—vessels   LACTEAL
     THORACIC DUCT
narrowing of blood
   vessel   VASOCONSTRICTION
small
—artery   ARTERIOLE
—blood vessel   CAPILLARY
—vein   VENULE
space in tissue   SINUSOID
study of
—ancient blood groups   PALAEOSEROLOGY
—blood   HAEMATOLOGY
—serums   SEROLOGY
veins
—arrangement of   VENATION
—blockage of   EMBOLISM
     THROMBOSIS
—from
   abdomen   ILIAC
   chest   (HEMI)AZYGOS
   forelimbs   ANTERIOR VENA CAVA
   head and neck   JUGULAR
   iliac veins   INFERIOR VENA CAVA
   inominate veins   SUPERIOR VENA CAVA
   intestines to liver   PORTAL
   jugular and subclavian   INNOMINATE
   kidneys   RENAL
   legs   FEMORAL
   liver   HEPATIC
   lungs   PULMONARY
   rest of body   POSTERIOR VENA CAVA
—inflammation of   PHLEBITIS
—opening of   VENESECTION
—puncturing   VENEPUNCTURE
     VENIPUNCTURE
—small   VENULE
city
Athens of the North   EDINBURGH
Auld Reekie   EDINBURGH
Big
—A   ATLANTA
—Apple   NEW YORK
—Pretzel   PHILADELPHIA
Birmingham   SECOND CITY
Brighton of the North   NAIRN
Brummagem   BIRMINGHAM
Buenos Aires   BA
City of
—100 towers   PAVIA
—angels   LOS ANGELES
—bells   BRUGES

—bridges	BRUGES	—British	AMIES, BLAIR, CONRAN
—canals	VENICE		COSTELLOE, EDELSTEIN
—kings	LIMA		EMMANUEL, FAHRI, GALLIANO
—masts	LONDON		HAMNETT, HARTNELL, HEMPEL
—monuments	BALTIMORE		JACKSON, MUIR, OLDFIELD, OSBEK
—palaces	ROME		POLLEN, QUANT, SASSOON
—plains	SODOM, GOMORRAH		TINLING, TRYON, WESTWOOD
—prophet	MEDINA	—French	BOHAN, CAROCHE
—saints	SALT LAKE CITY		CHANEL, COURREGES, DIOR
—seven hills	ROME		FATH, GAULTIER, GIVENCHY
—three kings	COLOGNE		HECHTER, LACROIX
—victory	CAIRO		LANVIN, ST LAURENT
—violet crown	ATHENS	—German	LAGERFELD
—West	GLASGOW	—Italian	ARMANI, BYBLOS, FABBRI
Crescent City	NEW ORLEANS		FENDI, FERRAGAMO, FERRE
Edinburgh	AULD REEKIE		GIGLI, MOSHINO
eternal city	ROME		SCHIAPARELLI, UNGARO
Gotham	NEW YORK		TARLAZZI, VALENTINO
granite city	ABERDEEN		VERSACE
Hollywood	TINSELTOWN	—Japanese	KAWAKUBO, KENZO
holy city	JERUSALEM, MEDINA		MIYAKE, YAMAMOTO, YUKI
	MECCA, ROME	—Russian	CASSINI, ZAITSEV
Hub of the Universe	BOSTON	—South American	HERRERA
Los Angeles	LA	—Spanish	BALENCIAGA
New York	BIG APPLE, GOTHAM, NY	—Tunisian	ALAIA
Philadelphia	BIG PRETZEL	dressmaker (odd)	MANTUA-MAKER
Quaker City	PHILADELPHIA	expensive clothing	CAPARISON, FINERY
Queen of the Riviera	NICE	guild uniform	LIVERY
Second City	BIRMINGHAM	military clothes	FATIGUES, SD
Tinseltown	HOLLYWOOD		SERVICE DRESS, UNIFORM
Venice of the north	BRUGES, LENINGRAD	model for clothes	DUMMY, MANNEQUIN
Windy City	CHICAGO	ornate clothing	FALLAL, FRIPPERY
clergy	(see church—personnel)		FROU-FROU
climate	(see meteorology)	outfit	APPAREL, ATTIRE, ENSEMBLE
clothes	DUDS, TOGS		GARB, HABILIMENTS, RAIMENT
academic clothing	SUBFUSC, SUBFUSK	plain clothes	MUFTI
baby's clothes	LAYETTE	servant's uniform	LIVERY
bride's clothes	TROUSSEAU	sports outfit	STRIP
civilian clothing	CIVVIES, MUFTI		(see also garments)
clergy's clothing	HABIT, VESTMENTS	clouds	(see meteorology)
	(see also church — vestments)	club	CUDGEL
clothes store	WARDROBE	African	KERRIE, KIERIE, KIRI
clothing	HABERDASHERY		KNOBKERRIE
—in art	DRAPERY	Australian	DOWAK, NULLA(-NULLA)
—made to order	BESPOKE		WADDIE, WADDY
—ready made	OFF THE PEG	ceremonial	MACE
—suitable for either sex	UNISEX	cudgel	ALPEEN
—worn by members of guild	LIVERY	for killing fish	PRIEST
designer of clothes	COUTURIER	golf	(see separate entry)
designers		Irish	ALPEEN, SHILLELA(G)H
—American	BEENE, BLASS, CASSINI		SHILLALY, TIPPERARY RIFLE
	DE LA RENTA, ELLIS, HALSTON	New Zealand	MERE, MERI
	JACOBS, KARAN, KELLY	policeman's	TRUNCHEON
	KORS, KLEIN, LAUREN, MACKIE	rubber	LIFE PRESERVER
	MIZRAHI, NEVILLE, ZORAN	short, heavy stick	BLUDGEON
—Australian	TRYON	spiked	ACLIDE, MACE

war-club	MAUL
weighted	COSH, SAP
clouds	(*see* **meteorology**)
Cockney rhyming slang	
Adam and Eve	BELIEVE
almond rocks	SOCKS
apple pie	SKY
apples (and pears)	STAIRS
April showers	FLOWERS
army and navy	GRAVY
army rocks	SOCKS
artful dodger	LODGER
bacon and eggs	LEGS
Baden Powell	TROWEL
bag of fruit	SUIT
baker's dozen	COUSIN
ball of chalk	WALK
Band of Hope	SOAP
Barnaby Rudge	JUDGE
bath-bun	SON
blue moon	SPOON
Bo-peep	SLEEP
butcher's (hook)	LOOK
Cain and Abel	TABLE
carving knife	WIFE
China (plate)	MATE
cut and carried	MARRIED
currant bun	SUN
Dicky Bird	WORD
Dicky Dirt	SHIRT
dinky-doo	TWENTY-TWO
Dutch (Duchess of Fife)	WIFE
four by two	JEW
frog and toad	ROAD
half-inch	PINCH, STEAL
ham and eggs	LEGS
Jack (Jones)	ALONE
Joanna	PIANO
King Dick	BRICK(LAYER), THICK
loaf (of bread)	HEAD
Mickey Mouse	HOUSE
mince pies	EYES
Mutt and Jeff	DEAF
Ned Kelly	BELLY
old Dutch	WIFE
on one's Tod (Sloan)	ALONE
penny bun	SON, SUN
pig's ear	BEER
plates/platters (of meat)	FEET
pride and joy	BOY
Richard the Third	BIRD
Rosie/Rosy Lea/Lee	TEA
skin and blister	SISTER
sky rocket	POCKET
trouble (and strife)	WIFE
tit for tat (titfer)	HAT

tit willow	PILLOW
Tod (Sloan)	ALONE
cocktails	
Advocaat and lemonade	SNOWBALL
bourbon	
—absinthe, etc	SAZERAC
—Amaretto di Saronno	
Drambuie	BARBERA
brandy with	
—Amaretto di Saronno	LEO
rum	SCORPION
—apricot brandy, lime	BACCHUS
—Chartreuse	FRENCHMAN
—cherry brandy	BRANDY FIX
—Cointreau	SIDECAR
—crème de cacao	ALEXANDER
—crème de menthe	STINGER
—dry vermouth, Calvados	KLONDIKE
—ginger ale	HORSE'S NECK
—grenadine, lemon juice	BRANDY DAISY
—peach brandy, kirsch	ROYAL WEDDING
—port, lemon juice	CREOLE PUNCH
—rum and	
Amaretto	SCORPION
Cointreau	BETWEEN THE SHEETS
—soda water, mint	BRANDY SMASH
—van der Hum, fruit juice	SUNDOWNER
Calvados	
—Benedictine	HONEYMOON
—orange juice	HARVARD COOLER
Campari, sweet vermouth	AMERICANO
champagne with	
—apricot brandy, Grand	
Marnier	PALM BEACH FIZZ
—brandy, bitters	CLASSIC
bitters, Curaçao	CHICAGO
—burgundy	COLD DUCK
—Calvados,	
bitters	CHAMPAGNE NORMANDIE
—crème de cassis	KIR ROYALE
—Curaçao	BLUE CHAMPAGNE
—Galliano, orange juice	SECRET SMILE
—gin, lemon juice	FRENCH 175
—grenadine, peach juice	BELLINI
—Guinness	BLACK VELVET
—orange juice	BUCK'S FIZZ
—Pernod	PERNOD FIZZ
—rum, crème de	
banane	CARIBBEAN CHAMPAGNE
Cointreau, Galliano	GOLDEN LINING
crème de menthe	
—crème de cacao	GRASSHOPPER
—soda	BEACHCOMBER
daiquiri with shaved ice	FROZEN DAIQUIRI
Drambuie	
—orange juice	DRAMBUIE SHRUB

—peach schnapps,	
orange juice	FUZZY NAVEL
gin with	
—apricot brandy	
Calvados	ANGEL'S FACE
orange juice	PARADISE
—bitters	PINK GIN
lemon juice	GIN SLING
—brandy, lemonade, egg white	PINK LADY
—cherry brandy,	
Cointreau	SINGAPORE SLING
—Cointreau, lemon juice	WHITE LADY
—crème de menthe	GIN FIZZ
egg white	WHITE HORSES
—Dubonnet	DUBONNET
—dry vermouth	DRY MARTINI
cherry brandy	RED KISS
Cointreau	WOODSTOCK
fruit juice	BRONX
Kirsch	COLLINSON
Mandarine	STORMY WEATHER
onion	GIBSON
--Galliano, lemon juice	MILANO
—ginger ale	HORSE'S NECK
—grenadine, egg white	PINK LADY
—Kirsch, egg white	ETON BLAZER
—lemon or lime	GIN SOUR
	TOM COLLINS
—lime juice, soda water	RICKEY
—sweet vermouth	SWEET MARTINI
Chartreuse	BIJOU
—white vermouth, orange	
juice	ORANGE BLOSSOM
in sugar-coated glass	CRUSTA
Pernod, orange juice	ORANGE CLOUD
rum with	
—Advocaat, crème de cacao	ELDORADO
—Amaretto di Saronno	SERENADE
—apricot brandy, fruit juice	ZOMBIE
—Calvados	KICKER
—cherry brandy, soda	PINK TREASURE
—coca cola, lime juice	CUBRE LIBRE
—coconut milk, fruit juice	PINA COLADA
—crème de cacao, lime	TEMPO
—dry vermouth,	
apricot brandy	ROSALIE
—fruit juice	PLANTER'S COCKTAIL
	PLANTER'S PUNCH
egg white	MAI TAI
—Galliano, apricot brandy	JOLLY ROGER
—Irish Mist, pineapple juice	EDGEMOOR
—lime	DAQUIRI
—Malibu, fruit juice	BOMBAY SMASH
—Mandarine, orange juice	WATERLOO
—orange Nassau liqueur	SUMMERTIME
—soda water, fruit juice	FLORIDA SKIES

—tequila, vodka	COCO LOCO
sherry	
—soda water	SHERRY COBBLER
—vermouth	BAMBOO
Southern Comfort,	
Amaretto di Saronno	SICILIAN KISS
spirits with ice	SWIZZLE
tequila with	
—cherry brandy,	
Galliano	BROOKLYN BOMBER
—grenadine	TEQUILA SUNRISE
—Triple Sec, fruit juice	MARGARITA
vodka with	
—Benedictine,	
grapefruit juice	RUSSIAN SECRET
—Calvados, apple	
juice	NORMAN CONQUEROR
—coffee liqueur	BLACK RUSSIAN
—Cointreau, soda water	LE MANS
—consommé	BULLSHOT
—dry vermouth, onion	GIBSON
—Galliano	
Mandarine	BEHIND THE WALL
orange juice	HARVEY WALLBANGER
—ginger beer, lime	MOSCOW MULE
—Irish Mist, orange juice	ORANGE MIST
—orange juice	SCREWDRIVER
—Parfait Amour,	
maraschino	PERFECT LOVE
—sweet vermouth, tonic	HAIR RAISER
—tequila, Curaçao	BLUE MOON
—Tia Maria, milk	WHITE RUSSIAN
—tomato juice	BLOODY MARY
whisky with	
—Amaretto di Saronno	GODFATHER
—Angostura bitters	OLD-FASHIONED
—apricot brandy	CAPRICORN
—Benedictine, dry vermouth	BRAINSTORM
—Drambuie	RUSTY NAIL
Chartreuse	ROYAL SCOT
—dry vermouth	ROB ROY
—ginger wine	WHISKY MAC
lemon juice	SUPERMAC
—Grand Marnier	RITZ OLD-FASHIONED
—grenadine	CLUB
—lemon juice	WHISKY SOUR
—lime juice	NEW YORKER
—Pernod, grenadine	WHISKY DAISY
—soda water, mint	MINT JULEP
—sweet vermouth, bitters	MANHATTAN

coffee

beans	ARABICA, ROBUSTA
Brazilian	SANTOS
drinks	CAPPUCINO, EXPRESSO, MOCHA
flavouring	CHICORY
small cup	DEMI-TASSE

very sweet	TURKISH COFFEE
with	
—brandy	FRENCH
—Cointreau	MALORCAN
—liqueur	COFFEE ROYAL
—milk	CAFE AU LAIT
—rum	CARIBBEAN
—Scotch whisky	HIGHLAND
—Tia Maria	CALYPSO
—vodka	RUSSIAN
—whiskey and cream	GAELIC COFFEE
	IRISH COFFEE
without milk	CAFE NOIR
coins	
(in ascending order)	
half-farthing	GROAT
two groats	FARTHING
farthing (old)	STICA, STYCA
½d	HA(LF)PENNY, MAG(PIE)
	MAIK, MAIL(E), MAKE
—old	OB(OLUM), OBOLUS
	PORTCULLIS
penny	COPPER, D, P
—old silver	STERLING
1½d	DANDIPRAT, DANDYPRAT
	THREE-HALFPENNY
3d	JOEY, THREEPENNY BIT
4d	GROAT, JOE(Y)
—silver	FOURPENNY
6d	SPRASI, TANNER
	TILBURY, TIZZY
—old	TESTER(N), TESTON, TESTRIL(L)
12d	SHILLING
shilling	DEANER, BOB, S
—old	TESTON, TESTER(N), TESTRIL(L)
1/6d-2/- (old)	GILDER
2 shillings	FLORIN
florin (gold)	FLORENCE
30d (old)	MANCUS
2/6d	HALF-CROWN
	SWORD-DOLLAR
5 shillings	CROWN
crown	THICKUN
6/8d	HALF-MARK, NOBLE
10 shillings	HALF-SOVEREIGN
—old	PISTOLET, RIAL, RYAL
10/6d	HALF-GUINEA
half-guinea	SMELT
13/4d (old)	MARK
15 shillings (gold)	SPUR-RIAL
	SPUR-R(O)YAL
20 shillings	POUND
—old	BROAD(-PIECE), UNITE
100p	POUND
pound	BRADBURY, NICKER, QUID
	SMACKER, SOVEREIGN

—old	CAROLUS, FLORENCE
	JACOBUS
sovereign	THICKUN
—poetic	SOVRAN
21 shillings	GEORDIE, GUINEA
22 shillings	UNITE
5 pounds	FIVER, HAWAII
10 pounds	BRITANNIA, JACK
	PLACIDO, TENNER,
25 pounds	BRITANNIA, PONY
50 pounds	BRITANNIA, HAWAII
100 pounds	BRITANNIA, TON
500 pounds	MONKEY
2,000 pounds	ARCHER
100,000 pounds	PLUM, SEYMOUR
coin issued in besieged places	SIEGE-PIECE
old gold coins	ANGEL, BRITANNIA
	ROSE NOBLE, RUDDOCK
	SCEATT, SPADE GUINEA
	SPANKER, YELLOW BOY
old silver coins	SCEATT
	THREE FARTHINGS
proposed coin	MIL(L)
small	DUMP, MAWPUS
	MOPUS, STIVER
—old silver	SILVERING
collecting	
collecting	
—birthday cards	GENETHLIADELTIOLOGY
—cards	CARTOPHILY
with similar stamps	MAXIMAPHILY
—coins	NUMISMATICS
—comics	PANEOLOGY
—labels	PHILATELY
—matchboxes	PHILLUMENY
—medals	NUMISMATICS
—pig models, etc	PORCINOLOGY
—stamps	PHILATELY, TIMBROLOGY
	TIMBROMANIA
	TIMBROPHILY
—walking sticks	RHABDOPHILY
collector of trifles	EPHEMERIST
Colombia	CO
capital	BOGOTA
coins	
—unit	CENTAVO
—100 centavos	PESO
colour	
amber	CHAMPAGNE
ashen	LIVID
black	ANTHRACITE, COAL, DWALE
	EBONY, JET, RAVEN, SABLE, SOOTY
—and	
blue	LIVID
brown	SKEWBALD
white	PIEBALD, PINTO

blackish/dark	FULIGINOUS, DUSKY
	SUBFUSC, SUBFUSK
blood-red	SANGUINE
blue	AZURE, C(A)ERULEAN
	COBALT, CYAN, GENTIAN
	INDIGO, LAPIS LAZULI
	NAVY BLUE, PERIWINKLE
	ROYAL BLUE, SAPPHIRE
	SAXE BLUE, SAXON(Y)
	SKY BLUE, SMALT
	ULTRAMARINE, WATCHET
blue/green	LOVAT
blue/grey	SLATE GREY
blue/violet	AMETHYST, AUBERGINE
	HELIOTROPE
brown	BAY, BEAVER, BISCUIT
	(BURNT) UMBER
	CAFE AU LAIT, CAMEL
	CARAMEL, CINNAMON
	COFFEE, DONKEY, DRAB, DUN
	HAZEL, MOCHA, NIGGER
	NUTMEG, SANDALWOOD
	SEPIA, TORTOISESHELL
	VANDYKE, WALNUT
brown/purple	PUCE
brownish	BEIGE, FUSCOUS
	TAN, TAUPE, TAWNY
buff	BEIGE, NANKEEN
	NANKIN
changing pattern of colour	KALEIDOSCOPE
cold colour	BLUE
colour scale	MUNSELL SCALE
	OSTWALD SCALE
dead leaves	FILEMOT
drab	QUAKER-COLOUR
dull brown	DRAB
green	APPLE, CELADON, EAU DE NIL
	EMERALD, JADE, KENDAL
	LIME, LINCOLN, MOSS, NILE
	SAGE, TEAL, TERRE-VERTE
	VIRIDIAN
green/blue	AQUAMARINE, TURQUOISE
grey	BATTLESHIP, CHARCOAL
	CLERICAL, ELEPHANT, DOVE
	DRAB, GUNMETAL, NUTRIA
grey/blue	GLAUCOUS, LOVAT
grey/brown	DUN
greyish	BEIGE
greyish-beige	GRE(I)GE
instrument for comparing	COLORIMETER
	TINTOMETER
lead coloured	LIVID
leek-green	PRASINE
light colour	PASTEL, TINT
mixture of	
—two primary colours	SECONDARY COLOUR
—two secondary colours	TERTIARY COLOUR
mouse coloured	DUN
mulberry	MURREY
multi-coloured	PRISMATIC
orange/brown	TENNE
orange/red	NACARAT
pale blue or green paint	BICE
pink	SHRIMP
primary colour	BLUE, RED, YELLOW
purple	HYACINTH, PORPHYROUS
	PUNIC
purple/red	MULBERRY, MURREY
range of colours	PALETTE, SPECTRUM
receding colour	BLUE
red	CARDINAL, CARMINE
	CHERRY, CINNABAR
	COCHINEAL, CRIMSON, LAKE
	MADDER, MODENA, RUBY
	SCARLET, SOLFERINO
	STAMMEL, VERMEIL(LE)
	VERMIL, VERMILION
red/brown	BAY, BRICK, BURNT SIENNA
	CHESTNUT, COLCOTHAR
	COROMANDEL, HENNA, MAHOGANY
	OXBLOOD, ROAN, RUBIGINOUS
	RUSSET, RUST, SIENNA, SOAR(E), SORE
	SORREL, TERRACOTTA, TITIAN
red/purple	AMARANTH, BURGUNDY
	CERISE, FUSCHIA, MAGENTA
	MAROON, MAUVE, PUCE
red/yellow	AMBER, APRICOT, CORAL
	FLAMINGO, ORANGE, PEACH
	ROSE, SALMON, TANGERINE
reddish	AUBURN, FERRUGINOUS
	GINGER, LAKE, PINK, PYRRHOUS
	RUBI(GIN)OUS, RUDDY, RUFOUS
saffron-coloured	CROCEATE, CROCEOUS
sea-green	AQUAMARINE, C(A)ERULEAN
	GLAUCOUS
shade	CAST, HUE, TINCTURE
	TINGE, TINT
shimmering colour	IRIDESCENT
	OPALESCENT
study of colours	CHROMATICS
variegated	MOTLEY, PARTI-COLOURED
	PIED, POLYCHROME
	VARICOLOURED
violet	IANTHINE
visible light	
spectrum	VIOLET, INDIGO, BLUE
	GREEN, YELLOW, ORANGE, RED
	ROYGBIV, VIBGYOR
warm colour	RED
white	ALABASTER, IVORY
whitish	BISQUE, CREAM, ECRU
	EGGSHELL, OYSTER, PUTTY

yellow/brown	CHAMOIS, CHAMPAGNE
	CITRINE, CITRON
	DAFFODIL, FALLOW, FAWN
	FLAX, GAMBOGE, GOLD
	JONQUIL, MAIZE, MUSTARD
	NANKEEN, OCHRE, RAW SIENNA
	SAFFRON, TAN, TOPAZ
yellow/green	CHARTREUSE, RESEDA
	SAP-GREEN
yellow/grey	ECRU, ISABEL(LA)
	ISABELLINE
yellow/red	APRICOT, PEACH
yellowish	FULVOUS, LUTE(OL)OUS
	SALLOW
composers	(*see* **musicians**)
computing	
ability to intercommunicate	CONNECTIVITY
access another computer	LOG ON
adapt disk to a particular machine	FORMAT
add-on parts	PERIPHERALS
alter data in file	EDIT, UPDATE
amount of storage	CAPACITY
audio signal	EARCON
basic	
—circuit	AND-GATE, GATE
	NAND-GATE, NOR-GATE
	OR-GATE
—screen unit	PIXEL
binary	B
—digit	BIT
—language	MACHINE CODE
	MACHINE LANGUAGE
bits per second	BPS
block of data	PACKET, PAGE
botched job	KLUDGE
break down	CRASH, FALL OVER
	GO DOWN
broadcast information	CEEFAX, ORACLE
	PRESTEL, TELETEXT
calculate total of stored	
data	CHECKSUM
capacity for handling	
data	CHANNEL CAPACITY
character(s)	
—per second	CPS
—used to represent	
any other character	WILDCARD
chip	
—providing	
graded choices	FUZZY CHIP
CPU	MICRO-PROCESSOR
—using superconductivity	HYBRID CHIP
circle on storage disc	TRACK
circuit board	BREADBOARD
collection of	
—data in files	DATABASE

stored	
—one after the other	SEQUENTIAL FILE
—in no particular	
order	RAM
	RANDOM ACCESS FILE
—related data	RECORD
combine files in same order	MERGE
communications	COMMS
—net with additional	
services	VAD
	VALUE-ADDED DATA
compress data	PACK, SQUEEZE
computer	
—aided	
design	CAD
typesetting	CAT
—assisted	
instruction	CAI
learning	CAL
—club	BCS
—controller	OPERATOR
—integrated	
business	CIB
manufacturing	CIM
—hypothetical	TURING MACHINE
—language	
recorder	CLR
translator	CLT
—languages	ADA, ALGOL, BASIC, C
	COBOL, FOCUS, FORTH, FORTRAN
	LISP, LOGO, LUCID, MODUL, PASCAL
	PISTOL, POWERHOUSE, PROLOG
	REPORT PROGRAM GENERATOR, RPG
	SIMULA, SMART, SNOBOL
	UNIX, ZENIX
—managed instruction	CMI
—on a chip	TRANSPUTER
—oriented language	COL
—output microfilm	COM
—providing 'intelligent'	
choices	FUZZY COMPUTER
computers	ACER, ALCATEL, ALTOS
	AMDAHL, AMDEX, AMSTRAD, AMT
	APOLLO, APPLE, APRICOT, AST, ATARI
	ATT, BULL, BURROUGHS, BUSINESSLAND
	CANON, COMMODORE
	COMPAQ, COMPUTERLAND
	COMPUTERVISION, CONTROL DATA
	CONVEX, CORDATA, CRAY, DAP
	DATA GENERAL, DATAVUE, DEC, DELL
	DG, DIGITAL EQUIPMENT, ELONEX
	EPSON, ERICSON, ESPRIT, EVEREX
	FRANKLIN, GOULD, GRID, HARRIS
	HEWLETT-PACKARD, HITACHI
	HONEYWELL (BULL), HYUNDAI, IBM
	INTERGRAPH, KAYPRO, LEADING EDGE

MITAC, MITSUBISHI, NAS, NCR, NEC
NIXDORF, NOKIA DATA, NORSK DATA
OLIVETTI, OSBORNE, PRIME, SAMSUNG
SHARP, SIEMENS, SINCLAIR, SPERRY
SUN, TANDEM, TANDON, TANDY
TATUNG, TELEVIDEO
TEXAS INSTRUMENTS, TOSHIBA
TULIP, UNISYS, VICTOR
WANG, WYSE, XIOS, ZENITH

computerised
—document store FAXBOX
—scanner CAT, CT
connection to other
 appliances CHANNEL, INTERFACE
 MODEM
continuous repetition RECURSION
control
—program for microcomputers CPM
—signal to move all bits
 one place SHIFT REGISTER
correct fault DEBUG
data
—directly read by
 computer MACHINE READABLE
—fed into computer INPUT
—of variable quantities ANALOG(UE)
—which has been processed OUTPUT
database accessible from
 several routes RELATIONAL DATABASE
delete stored data CLEAR, ERASE, ZAP
designed for a particular
 purpose DEDICATED
desk-top publishing DTP
device(s)
—attached to computer PERIPHERAL
—controlled by another SLAVE
—for
 converting one language
  to another TRANSLATOR
 drawing on screen LIGHT PEN
 giving instructions
  to computer CONSOLE, JOYSTICK
 KEYBOARD, LIGHT-PEN
 MOUSE
 handling music MIDI
 reading
  —data READ HEAD
  —and writing data READ/WRITE HEAD
 transcribing data from
  input source READER, SCANNER
 turning disks DISK DRIVE
 which work together
  without special
  adaptation COMPATIBLE HARDWARE
 writing data WRITE HEAD
—linked to computer PERIPHERAL

disk
—circle TRACK
—division SECTOR
—location marker ADDRESS MARK
—operating system DOS
doodle at keyboard NOODLE
easy to use USER-FRIENDLY
eight bits BYTE
electronic data-processing EDP
enter command by mouse CLICK
erasable program
—keyed access KEPROM
—read-only memory EPROM
error(s) BUG, VIRUS
extraction of data OUTPUT, EXPUT
fail CRASH, GO DOWN
 MALFUNCTION
fault BUG, MALFUNCTION
floating-point calculations
 per second FLOPS
garbage in, garbage out GIGO
group of
—bytes BLOCK, PACKET
—characters STRING
—interrelated units
 controlled by one CPU SYSTEM
hand-held control JOYSTICK
 LIGHT-PEN, MOUSE
hardware announced but
 not available for purchase VAPOURWARE
heart of the computer MICRO-PROCESSOR
hit keys at random NOODLE
holding area BUFFER
horizontal array of characters ROW
IBM BIG BLUE
in operation UP
Industry Standard Architecture ISA
information
—entered INPUT
—received EXPUT, OUTPUT
input/output
—device TERMINAL
—point in system (WORK)STATION
—system BIOS
instruction
—causing operation to be
 carried out OPERAND
—in a program CODE
—to a program COMMAND
interaction between user and
 computer by
 visual prompts GRAPHIC USER INTERFACE
 GUI
key
—generating a function CONTROL KEY
—to enter instructions ENTER

kilobyte (1024 bytes)	K
language	
—immediately understood	
by computer	MACHINE CODE
	MACHINE LANGUAGE
—not requiring knowledge	
of machine	
code	HIGH LEVEL LANGUAGE
	PROGRAMMING LANGUAGE
	SOURCE PROGRAM
—symbolic	LOW-LEVEL LANGUAGE
laptop computer (US)	TRASH
large computer	MAINFRAME
	SUPERCOMPUTER
light-emitting diode	LED
liquid-crystal diode	LCD
list of program options	MENU
load program(me)	(RE-)BOOT
local area network	LAN
location and presentation	
of data	RETRIEVAL
machinery	HARDWARE
main memory	PRIMARY STORAGE UNIT
maximum throughput	RATED THROUGHPUT
measure of storage	
capacity	K, KILOBYTE
(*see also* **measures** —information)	
medium-sized computer	MINI-(COMPUTER)
memory used by two CPUs	SHARED MEMORY
micro	
—channel architecture	MCA
—processing unit	MPU
million	
—bits	MEGABIT
—instructions per second	MIPS
—million bits	TERABIT
miniaturised circuit	PCB
	PRINTED CIRCUIT BOARD
modulator-demodulator	MODEM
moveable pointer	CURSOR
move blocks of data	DUMP
moving screen display	SCROLLING
musical instrument digital interface	MIDI
neither letter nor	
number	SPECIAL SYMBOL
not working	DOWN
number of bits in	
smallest stored unit	WORD
numbering system	BINARY, OCTAL
	HEXADECIMAL
one who	
—controls computer	OPERATOR
—designs programs to	
solve problems	SYSTEMS ANALYST
—plans operating	
systems	PROGRAMMER

operating system	CPM, HELIOS, MS-DOS
	TRON, UNIX, VAX
operations on	
—data	DATA PROCESSING
—script	WORD PROCESSING
operator	LIVEWARE
optical character reader	OCR
output	EXPUT
—connecting point	PORT
—device	PRINTER, SCREEN
	TURTLE
—from printer	HARD COPY
—to screen	SOFT COPY
parallel processing in units	DATAFLOW
part of	
—screen running	
separate program	WINDOW
—store used for notes	SCRATCH-PAD
people as part of the system	HUMANWARE
pertaining to data in	
—numbers	DIGITAL
—variable quantities	ANALOG(UE)
pictorial information	GRAPHICS
point in system where	
—data is input	
or received	TERMINAL
	(WORK)STATION
—different	
parts are linked	INTERFACE
portable computer	LAPTOP
printed output	HARD COPY
processed information	OUTPUT
	READOUT
processing jobs in	
sequence	BATCH PROCESSING
processor	CPU
program	SOFTWARE
—controlling	
input/output, etc	OPERATING SYSTEM
—designed to	
counteract	
bogusware	ANTIVIRUS, VACCINE
—diagram	FLOWCHART
—of general application	PACKAGE
—supplied with	
computer	SYSTEM SOFTWARE
—which	
can be used on	
different	
machines	PORTABLE PROGRAM
damages or	
destroys others	BOGUSWARE
	LOGIC BOMB
	PHANTOM BUG
	TROJAN HORSE, VIRUS, WORM
	(*see* virus *below*)

prepares data for further processing	PREPROCESSOR
translates other languages to machine code	
—before use	COMPILER
—during use	ASSEMBLER
programmable read-only memory	PROM
random access memory	RAM
rate	
—at which data can be transmitted	THROUGHPUT
—of transmission	BAUD
read-only memory	ROM
re-arrange data	EDIT
recoding to reduce number of symbols	CHUNKING
reduced instruction set computer	RISC
refuse to respond to commands	LOCK UP
representation of one system by another	SIMULATION
rules	
—governing communication between computers	PROTOCOL
—of language	SYNTAX
screen	MONITOR, VDU
—display	SOFT COPY
—drawing instrument	LIGHT PEN, MOUSE
secret code for access	PASSWORD
section of	
—disk	SECTOR, TRACK
—operating system	SYSTEMS PROGRAM
—program	SUBPROGRAM (SUB)ROUTINE
—record	FIELD
set	
—of	
commands	PROGRAM(ME)
instructions	PROGRAM(ME)
—starting values	INITIALISE
simultaneous use of facilities	(NETWORK) RESOURCE SHARING
slot-in circuit board	CARD
small	
—computer	LAPTOP, MICRO(-COMPUTER) PC, PERSONAL COMPUTER WORKSTATION
—piece of silica with etched circuits	CHIP
software	
—announced but not available for purchase	VAPOURWARE
—for a particular application	VERTICAL SOFTWARE

sorting technique	BUBBLE SORT SHELL-METZNER SORT
spacing of pixels	DOT PITCH
speed	BPS
—computer	MIPS
—printer	CPS, PPM
start of	
—message	SOM
—text	STX
start-up program	BOOT(STRAP)
storage	MEMORY
—device	BUFFER, DISKETTE FLOPPY DISK, HARD DISK MAGNETIC DISK, MAGNETIC DRUM MAGNETIC TAPE WINCHESTER DRIVE
—immediately available	ONLINE STORAGE
store	
—accessed by keywords	ASSOCIATIVE STORE
—with ferrite rings	CORE STORE
stored program that cannot be altered	MICRO-PROGRAM
suitable for learners	ENTRY-LEVEL
symbol	
—that can be processed	CHARACTER
—on screen	ICON
system	
—capable of learning	NEURAL NET(WORK)
—for building identikit pictures from stored data	E-FIT
—of linked computer and terminals	NETWORK
—operator	SYSOP
—permitting changes without disturbing existing system	OPEN-ENDED SYSTEM
several users at once	TIME SHARING
—processing several items of data at once	NEURAL NET(WORK)
—requiring operator to make adjustments	OPEN LOOP
—which is easy to operate	USER-FRIENDLY
—with decision-making ability	EXPERT SYSTEM INTELLIGENT KNOWLEDGE-BASED SYSTEM IKBS
transmission	
—between computers	PACKET SWITCHING
—of data via telephone lines	EDI ELECTRONIC DATA INTERCHANGE

temporary store	BUFFER
terminal	
—distant from CPU	REMOTE TERMINAL
—in a network	NODE
time taken	
—for complete operation	THROUGHPUT
—to act on a command	RESPONSE TIME
transfer data from	
—computer to	
another system	PORT
storage device	WRITE
—memory to screen	READ
Transient Program Area	TPA
translate machine instructions	DECODE
unauthorised user	HACKER
under the control of the CPU	ONLINE
unerasable memory	FIRMWARE
unit of	
—information	BIT
(see also **measures** -information)	
—screen area	PIXEL
unobtainable software	
or hardware	VAPOURWARE
unprocessed information	RAW DATA
use of store	
—by use of keywords	KEYED ACCESS
—in	
any order	RANDOM ACCESS
sequence	SEQUENTIAL ACCESS
using same machine	
code	SOFTWARE COMPATIBLE
vertical array of characters	COLUMN
virus	ARMAGEDDON, CASCADE
	DARK AVENGER, DATACRIME
	FISH 6, FRODO, FU MANCHU
	ISRAEL DEFENCE FORCE
	JERUSALEM, JOKER, LIBERTY
	VACCINIA, VICTOR, WHALE
viruses, etc	BOGUSWARE
visual display unit	VDU
what you see is what you get	WYSIWYG
wide area network	WAN
write once, read many	WORM
Congo	RCB
capital	BRAZZAVILLE
coin	FRANC
constellations	
Northern hemisphere	
—Arrow	SAGITTA
—Berenice's Hair	COMA BERENICE
—Big Dipper	GREAT BEAR
—Bull	TAURUS
—Charioteer	AURIGA
—Charles's wain	GREAT BEAR, PLOUGH
	URSA MAJOR
—Colt	EQUULEUS

—Crab	CANCER
—Cynosure	URSA MINOR
—Dolphin	DELPHINUS
—Dragon	DRACO
—Eagle	AQUILA
—Fishes	PISCES
—Giraffe	CAMELOPARDALIS
—Great Bear	CHARLES'S WAIN
	PLOUGH
	URSA MAJOR
—Greater Dog	CANIS MAJOR
—Hercules	HERCULES
—Herdsman	BOOTES
—Hunter	ORION
—Hunting dog	CANES VENATICI
—Lesser	
Bear	LESSER WAIN
	URSA MINOR
	WAG(G)ON
Dog	CANIS MINOR
Lion	LEO MINOR
—Lion	LEO
—Lizard	LACERTA
—Lynx	LYNX
—Lyre	LYRA
—Milky Way	VIA LACTEA
—Northern Crown	CORONA BOREALIS
—Ox-driver	BOOTES
—Plough	CHARLE'S WAIN
	GREAT BEAR
	URSA MAJOR
—Ram	ARIES
—Serpent	SERPENS CAPUT
holder	OPHIUCHUS
—Seven Stars	ORION
—Sextant	SEXTANS
—Swan	CYGNUS
—Triangle	TRIANGULUM
—Twins	GEMINI
—Virgin	VIRGO
—Wag(g)on	LESSER BEAR
	LESSER WAIN
	URSA MINOR
—Wag(g)oner	AURIGA
—Water-monster	HYDRA
—Winged horse	PEGASUS
—others	ANDROMEDA, CASSIOPEIA
	CEPHEUS, CETUS
	MONOCEROS, VULPECULUS
Southern hemisphere	
—Archer	SAGITTARIUS
—Argo's stern	PUPPIS
—Balance	LIBRA
—Bird of Paradise	APUS
—Centaur	CENTAURUS
—Chameleon	CHAMAELEON

—Clock	HOROLOGIUM
—Crane	GRUS
—Crater	CRATER
—Cross	CRUX
—Crow	CORVUS
—Dove	COLUMBA
—Eagle	AQUILA
—Easel	PICTOR
—Fishes	PISCES
—Fly	MUSCA
—Flying fish	VOLANS
—four stars	SOUTHERN CROSS
	URSA (MAJOR)
—Goat	CAPRICORNUS
—Graving-tool	CAELUM
—Hare	LEPUS
—Hunter	ORION
—Indian	INDUS
—Keel	CARINA
—Level	NORMA
—Lion	LEO
—Microscope	MICROSCOPIUM
—Net	RETICULUM
—Peacock	PAVO
—Pump	ANTLIA
—Rule	NORMA
—Sail	VELA
—Scales	LIBRA
—Scorpion	SCORPIO, SCORPIUS
—Sculptor	SCULPTOR
—Serpent	SERPENS CAUDA
—Seven Stars	ORION
—Shield	SCUTUM SOBIESKI
—Southern	
Crown	CORONA AUSTRINA
Fish	PISCIS AUSTRINUS
Triangle	TRIANGULUM AUSTRALE
—Swordfish	DORADO
—Table	MENSA
—Telescope	TELESCOPIUM
—Triangle	TRIANGULUM
—Veil	VELA
—Virgin	VIRGO
—Water	
carrier	AQUARIUS
monster	HYDRA
—Wolf	LUPUS
—others	ARA, ARGO, CETUS, ERIDANUS
	FORNAX, HYDRUS, OCTANS
	PHOENIX, PYXIS, SOUTHERN FISH

cookery

acid liquid from fermentation	VINEGAR
add	
—dash of brandy, etc	LACE, NEEDLE
—decoration	GARNISH
—dressing	DRESS

—fat to dough	SHORTEN
—flavour	SEASON
—yeast	LEAVEN, RAISE
adding liquid to dry mixture	BINDING
almond paste	MARZIPAN
appetiser	RELISH
appetisers	HORS D'OEUVRE
—Greek	MEZE
—Spanish	TAPAS
arachis oil	PEANUT OIL
aromatic seeds	ANISE(ED)
artificial sweetener	SACCHARIN
bake eggs	SHIR(R)
baked	
—in paper case	EN PAPILLOTE
—souffle	FONDUE
baking pastry without	
filling	BAKING BLIND
ball of dough, boiled	DUMPLING
batter pudding	YORKSHIRE PUDDING
bean curd	TOFU
beans, peas, etc	PULSES
	(see **pulses**)
beat	WHIP, WHISK
—to a smooth consistency	CREAM
—together fat and sugar	CREAM
—while cooking (eggs)	SCRAMBLE
become clear	FINE
blend by gently turning in	FOLD
boil	
—down	DECOCT
—gently	SIMMER
—slightly	BLANCH, CODDLE
	PARBOIL
boiled	
—fruit and sugar	CONSERVE, JAM
	PRESERVE, MARMALADE
—or stewed meat	BOUILLI
braised and served in	
brown sauce	A LA MODE
bread	(see separate entry)
break	
—into crumbs	CRUMB
—up fat in milk	HOMOGENISE
brew tea	MASH
brine solution	PICKLE
broil	GRILL
—with seasoning	DEVIL
browning meat quickly	
before grilling or roasting	SEARING
bunch or sachet of herbs	BOUQUET GARNI
	FAGGOT
buffet of various dishes	SMORGASBORD
butter substitute	MAGARINE
cake	(see separate entry)
can	PRESERVE

candied stalks	ANGELICA
cassava starch	TAPIOCA
cheese dishes	(see separate entry)
cheese vat	CHESSEL
chickpea paste	MOUM(O)US, HUMMUS
chilled	FRAPPE
chip(ped potato)	FRENCH FRY
chips, hot dogs, etc	JUNK FOOD
chocolate	
—substitute	CAROB
—used for covering	COVERTURE
chop into	
—small pieces	MINCE
—very small pieces	HASH
chopped meats, eggs, etc	SALMAGUNDI
chopped-up food	HASH
clarified butter	GHEE, GHI
coat with	
—flour	FLOUR
—sugar	CANDY, CRYSTALLISE
coated with egg and breadcrumbs	A L'ANGLAISE
coating	
—inside of mould with jelly	MASKING
—meat etc with glaze	MASKING
cold	
—dish glazed with aspic	GALANTINE
—meats	CHARCUTERIE
—mixed vegetables	SALAD
colouring	COCHINEAL, SAFFRON TURMERIC
—for gravy	BROWNING
combining ingredients so that mixture retains lightness	FOLDING IN
concentrate by boiling	DECOCT
concentrated solution of sugar and water	SYRUP
condiment	MUSTARD, PEPPER SALT, VINEGAR
container for	
—cold liquid	COOLER
—hot or cold liquid	THERMOS FLASK
conversion of sugar to alcohol	FERMENTATION
cook	
—by	
direct heat	BROIL
frying	
—gently while stirring	SCRAMBLE
—in little fat	SAUTE
—rapidly while stirring	STIR-FRY
—till crisp	FRIZZLE
grilling or frying	DEVIL
light steaming	DUM
partly boiling	PARBOIL
radiant heat	GRILL
simmering	POACH

slow simmering	BRAISE, STEW
—in	
boiling water	BOIL
closed pan	BRAISE
fat or oil in a pan	(DEEP-)FRY
front of fire	ROAST
oven	BAKE, ROAST
pressurised vessel	PRESSURE-COOK
saucepan with fat	POT-ROAST
spicy sauce	BARBECUE
stewpan	CASSEROLE
syrup	CANDY
water below boiling	POACH, SIMMER
—over	
boiling water	STEAM
hot coals	BROIL
—in the open air	BARBECUE, BBQ
—partially	BLANCH, PARBOIL PRECOOK
—slowly	
in	
—fat	SWEAT
—heatproof dish	CASSEROLE
without boiling	CODDLE
cooked	
—flour and fat	ROUX
—in	
butter and herbs (fish)	MEUNIERE
oil, garlic and tomatoes	PROVENCALE
olive oil	A LA GRECQUE
onions	LYONNAISE
red wine	BOURGUIGNONNE
white wine (fish)	MARINIERE
—on a skewer	EN BROCHETTE
—with	
breadcrumbs or cheese	AU GRATIN GRATINE
brown sugar	BRULE
cider and cream	A LA NORMANDE
potatoes	PARMENTIER
tomatoes, etc	CACCIATORE
tomatoes, onions, etc	NICOISE
cooking	
—appliance	HOTPLATE (MICROWAVE) OVEN PRIMUS, RANGE, ROTISSERIE SPIT, STOVE
—fat	BUTTER, DRIPPING, LARD (OLEO)MARGARINE, SHEA BUTTER
Indian	GHEE, GHI, VANASPATI
—high quality	HAUTE CUISINE
—method (Indian)	TANDOORI
—oil	CORN OIL, COTTONSEED OIL OLIVE OIL, PALM OIL SUNFLOWER OIL, TRAIN OIL WHALE OIL

—particular style	CUISINE
—simple style	CUISINE MINCEUR
	LEAN CUISINE
	NOUVELLE CUISINE
—very high quality	CORDON BLEU
Cornish pasty	OGGY
course following fish course	ENTREE
cover with	
—crumbs	CRUMB
—icing	ICE
—sugar	FROST
covered with breadcrumbs	
or cheese	AU GRATIN
covering breast of poultry	
with pieces of bacon	BARDING
cream	
—separating pan	CREAMER
—thick	DOUBLE CEAM
—thickened by heating	CLOTTED CREAM
—thin	POURING CREAM
	SINGLE CREAM
—treated with lactic acid	(SOUR(ED)) CREAM
crisp	
—cooked skin of meat	CRACKLING
—residue of fat	CRACKLING
crumbs from stale bread	RASPINGS
crust of crumbs or cheese	GRATIN
cube of dried meat extract	BOUILLON CUBE
cup-shaped mould	TIMBALE
cure	
—by smoking	SMOKE
—with salt and smoke	KIPPER
curry with vinegar	VINDALOO
cut	
—into small cubes	CUBE, DICE
—into slices	FILLET
—surface into chequer pattern	CUBE
decorating	
—cake	ICING, PIPING
—edge of	
glass	FROSTING
pastry	CRIMPING, SCALLOPING
—for appearance	GARNISHING, GLAZING
—with egg white etc	GLAZING
dehydrate while frozen	DRY-FREEZE
delicacy	KICKSHAW
diced meat and vegetables	
in thick sauce	SALPICON
dietary requirements	CARBOHYDRATE
	FAT, FIBRE, MINERALS
	PROTEIN, SUGAR
	TRACE ELEMENTS, VITAMIN
dilute cooking juices	
with wine, etc	DEGLAZE
dip	
—into liquid	DUNK

—made from avocado	GUAC(H)AMOLE
dish of fried food	FRY(-UP)
	MIXED GRILL
distilling apparatus	STILL
dough with fat	PASTE, PASTRY
draw off liquid	DECANT
dress meat with fat	LARD
dressing	
—for salad	MAYONNAISE
	SALAD CREAM
	SALAD OIL
—with added pickle	RUSSIAN DRESSING
	(see also sauces)
dried	
—beans, peas, etc	PULSES
—breadcrumbs	RASPINGS
—seed(s)	BACCA(E)
dry rusk	BISCOTTE
drying tray	FLAKE
dumplings (China)	WANTAN, WONTON
	WUNTUN
dye for foodstuffs	COCHINEAL
earthernware casserole	
dish	TERRINE
edible	
—entrails	(M)UMBLES
—fat	SHORTENING
—lichen	ICELAND MOSS
—seaweed	CARRAGEEN, DULSE
	IRISH MOSS, LAVER
—snail	ESCARGOT, ROMAN SNAIL
egg dishes	(see separate entry)
emulsifying agent	AGAR(-AGAR)
encased in pastry	EN CROUTE
energy-value of food	(KILO)CALORIE
enzyme for curdling	
milk	RENNET, RENNIN
evaporate by boiling	DECOCT, REDUCE
extract	
—essence	DECOCT
—of juices, etc	ESSENCE
—used for curdling milk	RENNET
extracting	
—fat by melting	RENDERING
—flavour	INFUSING
fancy dish	CONFECTION, KICKSHAW
fast food	CONVENIENCE FOOD
	TAKEAWAY FOOD
fat	
—from	
cocoa beans	CACAO BUTTER
	COCOA BUTTER
pigs	LARD
roasting meat	DRIPPING
—liquid at room	
temperature	MONO-UNSATURATED

—liquid when refrigerated	POLY-UNSATURATED	—dipped into liquid	SOP
—solid at room		—grilled on skewer	BROCHETTE, KEBAB
temperature	SATURATED	—prepared	CUISINE
fermented milk	YOG(H)URT	by expert chef	CORDON BLEU
	YOGHOURT	—ready for eating	DELICATESSEN
fermenting agent	FERMENT, YEAST	—reduced to a pulp	PUREE
fine flour or meal	FARINA	—taken to work	SNAP
finely ground		—tossed in shallow fat	SAUTE
—sugar	CASTER SUGAR	—with low nutritional	
	ICING SUGAR	value	JUNK FOOD
—wheat	FLOUR	force through nozzle	PIPE
fish dishes	(see separate entry)	forcemeat	FARCE
flat metal		forcing cream etc	
—surface for cooking	GRIDDLE	through a nozzle	PIPING
—tray	BAKING TRAY	form smooth layer	CREAM
flavouring	CONDIMENT, ZEST	firm to the teeth (pasta)	AL DENTE
—additive	MONOSODIUM GLUTAMATE	fragrance	BOUQUET
—bitter	ALMOND, JUNIPER	freshly-chopped herbs	FINES HERBES
—caffeine	COLA, KOLA	fried	
—coffee	MOCHA	—batter with filling	FRITTER
—crocus	SAFFRON	—lightly	SAUTE
—dried flowers	MELITOT	fruit	
—for tea	JASMINE	—juice	SYRUP
—from		—preserve	CONSERVE
American laurel	SASSAFRAS	fruits	(see separate entry)
Artemisia	TARRAGON	game	(see poultry)
Mexican orchid	VANILLA	game stock	FUMET
Sesamum indicum	SESAME	garnish	DRESS
Smilax	SARSAPARILLA	—for chicken dish	BONNE FEMME
Tonka beans	C(O)UMARIN	—on surface	TOPPING
Trigonella	FENUGREEK	garnished with	
—ginger	JAMAICA GINGER	—crayfish	A LA NANTUA
—lemon	LEMON THYME	—mushrooms etc	FORESTIERE
—Mexican orchid	VANILLA	—onions, mushrooms, etc	BONNE FEMME
—mint	PENNYROYAL	—potatoes	PARMENTIER
—oil	ESSENTIAL OIL	—vegetable strips	JULIENNE
—peppermint	PEPPERMINT OIL	—vegetables	JARDINIERE
—seeds	ANISEED, CARAWAY	—white grapes	VERONIQUE
—sweet	C(O)UMARIN, MELILOT	giving body to gravy etc	THICKENING
	(see also herbs, spices)	glazed	GLACE
flour		—with sugar	BRULE
—and water paste	PASTA	golden syrup	TREACLE
—eggs, milk, etc	BATTER	goose liver	FOIE GRAS
—of cassava	MANDIOC(C)A, MANIHOC	—paste	PATE DE FOIE GRAS
	MANIHOT, MANIOC(A)	gravy with ham juices	RED EYE GRAVY
—with raising		greased paper wrapper	PAPILLOTE
agent	SELF-RAISING FLOUR	grill	BROIL, DEVIL
—without raising agent	PLAIN FLOUR	grind very fine	FLOUR
food		gum used in confectionery	GUM ACACIA
—cooked			GUM ARABIC
in		hard	
—clay oven	TANDOORI	—animal fat	SUET
—cup-shaped mould	TIMBALE	—white icing	ROYAL ICING
—heatproof dish	CASSEROLE, TERRINE	heat	
on metal frame	GRILL	—sugar into caramel	CARAMELISE
		—to near boiling	SCALD

—with spices	MULL
heatproof dish	CASSEROLE
high	
—fibre food	ROUGHAGE
—standard cookery	HAUTE CUISINE
	CORDON BLEU
vegetarian	CORDON VERT
hors d'oeuvres	
—mixed	ANTIPASTO(MISTO)
—Russian	ZAKUSKI
hot	
—cake	PANCAKE
—curry	MADRAS, VINDALOO
—sandwich of cheese	
and ham	CROQUE-MONSIEUR
—seasoning	CURRY, MUSTARD
	PEPPER
ice a cake	FROST
icing	FROSTING
immerse briefly in	
boiling water	BLANCH
in pastry	EN CROUTE
Indian cooking	(*see* **Indian**)
individual Yorkshire	
pudding	POPOVER
inserting strips of fat into	
meat or poultry	LARDING
instructions for making dish	RECIPE
instrument for	
testing food	TENDEROMETER
insulated container	COOLER, HAYBOX
	THERMOS FLASK
introduce air	AERATE
jelly	GEL
—from	
cooked feet of	
—calves	CALF'S FOOT JELLY
—ox or cow	COW HEEL JELLY
cranberries	CRANBERRY JELLY
turtle	CALIPASH, CALIPEE
wild apples	CRAB APPLE JELLY
juice of	
—sugar cane	SYRUP
—unripe fruit	VERJUICE
kebab	SHASHLI(C)K
large	
—dish	TRENCHER
—prawn	KING PRAWN
—soup bowl	TUREEN
leg of cooked meat	GIGOT
liaison of flour and butter	BEURRE MANIE
light	
—dish with	
whipped cream, etc	MOUSSE
white of egg	SOUFFLE
—meal	COLLATION

liquor	
—from	
buttermaking	BUTTERMILK
meat, etc simmered in water	STOCK
thawing	DRIP
—in which meat etc	
has been cooked	STOCK
is steeped	MARINADE
—used to produce shiny coating	GLAZE
made	
—with hazel nuts	NOISETTE
—without	
meat	PAREVE
milk	PAREVE
make	
—butter by agitating milk	CHURN
—crisp	TOAST, FRIZZLE
—light	LEAVEN, RAISE
—tender by beating	TENDERISE
main dish	ENTREE
marchpane	MARZIPAN
meat	
—and vegetables cooked	
in liquid	STEW
—boiled	BOUILLI
—medium-cooked	A POINT
—set in aspic	CHAUDFROID
	GALANTINE
—underdone	AU BLEU, RARE
—well done	BIEN CUIT
	(*see also separate entry*)
meat dishes	(*see* **meat dishes**)
medium-cooked (meat)	A POINT
melted butter with	
seasoning	DRAWN BUTTER
metal frame for cooking on	GRID(IRON)
	GRILL
milk	
—dishes	CHERRICURDS, CUSTARD
	JUNKET, MACARONI PUDDING
	RICE PUDDING, SAGO PUDDING
	SEMOLINA PUDDING
—dried	POWDERED MILK
—fat content	CREAM
—fermented	YOG(H)URT, YOGHOURT
—heat-treated	PASTEURISED
	STERILISED
—partly concentrated	EVAPORATED
—powdered with malted	
cereal	MALTED MILK
—sour	CLABBER
—thick part	CURD
—thickened and sweetened	CONDENSED
—thin part	WHEY
—with little fat	SEMI-SKIMMED
—without fat	SKIMMED

minerals and trace	
elements	CALCIUM, COPPER
	FLUORINE, IODINE, IRON
	MAGNESIUM, MANGANESE
	PHOSPORUS, POTASSIUM
	SELENIUM, SODIUM, ZINC
mix	
—by tossing	TOSS
—to smooth texture	BLEND, CREAM
—with minimum liquid	BIND
mixed foods, fried	FRITTO MISTO
	MIXED GRILL
mixture of	
—cooked meat, etc used as	
filling	SALPICON
—flour and water	DOUGH
—fruits, brandy, etc	MINCEMEAT
—oil, vinegar etc for	
steeping	MARINADE
—vegetables	MIREPOIX
or fruit in jelly	MACEDOINE
moisten with fat	
during roasting	BASTE
mustard	
—hot	ENGLISH MUSTARD
—with	
vinegar	FRENCH MUSTARD
white wine	DIJON MUSTARD
oatmeal porridge	BROSE
outdoor meal	BARBECUE, PICNIC
oil from skin of citrus fruit	ZEST
open sandwich	SMORREBROD
over-brew tea	STEW
palm-tree shoots	PALM HEARTS
pancake	HOTCAKE, SLAPJACK
—mixture	BATTER
—thick	FLAPJACK
—with filling	FRENCH PANCAKE
parboil	BLANCH
partially	
—boil	BLANCH, PARBOIL
—cook	PRECOOK
—frozen	FRAPPE
—sterilise	PASTEURISE
pass through sieve	SIEVE, SIFT, STRAIN
pasta	(*see separate entry*)
paste	PATE, SPREAD
—from	
anchovies	ANCHOIADE
goose liver	PATE DE FOIE GRAS
peanuts	PEANUT BUTTER
pastry	(*see separate entry*)
peanut oil	ARACHIS OIL
peel of citrus fruit	ZEST
pertaining to	
—cooking	CULINARY

—kitchen	CULINARY
pickle	PRESERVE, SOUSE
pickled cucumber	DILL PICKLE
pickling liquid	BRAINE, SOUSE
	VINEGAR
picnic (US)	COOKOUT
piece of fruit etc cooked	
in batter	FRITTER
place fat or bacon on	
meat before cooking	BARD
plainly cooked	AU NATUREL
plunge in pickling liquid	SOUSE
poultry	(*see separate entry*)
pour	
—fat over meat while cooking	BASTE
—boiling water over to	
remove skin etc	SCALD
—water over food and leave	
to stand	STEEP
prepare food for cooking	DRESS
prepared or served with	
dressing of flaming liquor	FLAMBE
preserve	
—by	
cooling below 0°C	FREEZE
drying	CURE, DESICCATE
rapid freezing	QUICK-FREEZE
—in	
brine or salt	CORN, CURE, SALT
metal containers	CAN, TIN
strips	JERK
vinegar	PICKLE
—of fruit and sugar	CONSERVE, JAM
	JELLY, MARMALADE
preserved	
—cherry	MARAS(C)HINO
—onions etc	PICKLE
preserving liquid	PICKLE
press edged to seal	CRIMP
proteins	(*see separate entry*)
prunes on bacon,	
grilled	DEVILS ON HORSEBACK
pulp	PUREE
—by	
beating	MASH
passing through sieve	
or blender	PUREE
pure gelatine	ISINGLASS
purify	FINE
ragout of game etc	SALMI
raise	
—oven temperature before use	PREHEAT
—with yeast, etc	LEAVEN
raising agent	BAKING POWDER
	BICARBONATE OF SODA
	SALERATUS, YEAST

rare (meat)	AU BLEU
ready-prepared for consumption	CONVENIENCE FOOD
	FAST FOOD
	TAKEAWAY FOOD
real or artificial cream on food	CREME
reduce to	
—fluid consistency	LIQUIDISE
—pulp	PUREE
refined molasses	SYRUP, TREACLE
regional specialities	
—Abernethy	BISCUIT
—Aylesbury	DUCK
—Arbroath	SMOKIE
—Bakewell	TART
—Banbury	CAKE
—Bath	BUN, CHAP, OLIVER
—Cheddar	CHEESE
—Chelsea	BUN
—Cheshire	CHEESE
—Chorley	CAKE
—Cornish	CREAM, PASTY, FAIRINGS
—Cumberland	PIE
—Derby	BAKE
—Devonshire	CREAM, SPLIT
—Dundee	CAKE
—Eccles	CAKE
—Grantham	GINGERBREAD
—Irish	STEW
—Lancashire	HOTPOT
—Northumberland	SINGING HINNY
—Pontefract (Pomfret)	CAKES
—Scotch	BUN, EGG PANCAKE
—Shrewsbury	BISCUIT
—Welsh	RAREBIT
—Whitstable	OYSTERS
—Worcester	SAUCE
—Yorkshire	PUDDING, TEA-CAKE
re-heated food	RECHAUFFE
re-heating cooked vegetables after cooling with water	REFRESHING
remove	
—bones from	FILLET
—fat from surface of liquid	SKIM
—lumps	STRAIN
—pod, shell, etc	HULL, HUSK SHELL, SHUCK
—stalks, etc	TOP AND TAIL
—surface layer from liquid	SKIM
—water from	DEHYDRATE
rendered fat	DRIPPING, (LEAF)LARD
rice dishes	(see rice)
rich dish	CONFECTION

roast	
—in dry heat	PARCH
—whole	BARBECUE
roasting spit	BROACH
rod for holding meat over fire	SPIT
rolled slice of meat	ROULADE
round cake of meat or fish	RISSOLE
roughly chopped	CONCASSE
rub through sieve	PUREE
salad oil	OLIVE OIL, PEANUT OIL
salt	
—from evaporation	BAY SALT
	ROCK SALT
—solution	BRINE
—spices, etc	SEASONING
—used in baking powder	CREAM OF TARTAR
sandwich with	
—three slices of bread	CLUB SANDWICH
—two slices of bread	ROUND
sauce	DRESSING, RELISH
—for dipping	DIP
sauces	(see separate entry)
sausage in bread roll	HOT DOG
sausages	(see separate entry)
savoury	
—jelly	ASPIC
—on small piece of toast	CANAPE
—stuffing	FORCEMEAT
scald	BLANCH
score outside of meat	CRIMP
scrap of food	ORT
season highly	DEVIL
seasoned	
—filling mixture	DRESSING, STUFFING
—with sugar and lemon juice	SWEET-AND-SOUR
sedge roots	GALINGALE
sediment	GROUT, LEES
seeds of pea family	PULSES
segment of sausage chain	LINK
separate	
—fat from liquid	BREAK
—into flakes	FLAKE
—kernels from casing	HULL, HUSK, SHELL
serve on wooden board	PLANK
sesame	TIL
—seed paste	HOUM(O)US, HUMMUS TAHINA, TAHINI
setting agent	PECTIN
sift through fine mesh	BOLT
silver-coloured ball for decoration	DRAGEE
sherbet	SORBET
simmer eggs	CODDLE
skin of citrus fruit	ZEST

slash fish etc to allow heat to penetrate	CRIMP, SCORE		stew	
slice			—in	
—finely	SHRED		a closed vessel	BRAISE
—of bread	ROUND		stock	FRICASSEE
small			—with seasoning	JUG(G)
—bulb of garlic	CLOVE		stewed lentils	DA(H)L, DHAL
—bunch of herbs	BOUQUET GARNI		stews	(see separate entry)
—cake			stir	
decorations HUNDREDS AND THOUSANDS			—during cooking	SCRAMBLE
—circular piece of			—or mix	SWIZZLE
fish or meat	MEDALLION		stock	BOUILLON
—cucumber	GHERKIN		stoneware cooking pot	
—patty or pastry case	BOUCHE(E)		with heating element	CROCKPOT
—pickled onion	PEARL ONION		store in freezer	DEEP-FREEZE
—piece of			strain through fine cloth	TAMMY
food	CHIP, ORT		strip of	
—crumbed and deep-fried	CROQUETTE		—fat	
—for dipping	DUNK		for dressing	LARDO(O)N
meat	CALLOP, ESCALOPE		laid over meat	BARD(E)
crisp pork fat	SCRATCHINGS		—icing	PIPIG
—(American)	CRACKNEL		strong broth	BOUILLON
raw vegetables	CRUDITES		study of nutrition	DIETETICS
—vol-au-vent	BOUCHEE		stuff	
smear with lard	LARD		—bird with forcemeat	FARCE
smooth preparation			—with bacon or pork	LARD
for spreading	PASTE, PATE, SPREAD		stuffed	FARCI(E)
soak in blended liquid	MARINADE, MARINATE		stuffing	FARCE, FORCEMEAT
soft			style of cooking	CUISINE
—food	PAP, SOPS		substance	
—roe	MILT		—causing	
soften in liquid	MACERATE		fermentation	FERMENT, LEAVEN
soldier's emergency food	IRON RATION		gelling	GEL(L)ANT
souffle served with			—used for	
bread crumbs	FONDUE		increasing bulk of food	EXTENDER
sour cream (Russia)	SMETANA, SMETANE		raising bread, etc	LEAVEN
songbird used for food	BECCAFICO		thickening	LIAISON
soup	(see separate entry)		sugar	(see separate entry)
sour milk	CLABBER		sweet	
spiced cassava juice	CASSAREEP		—covering for cakes	ICING
split open bird and cook	SPATCHCOCK		—dish	DESSERT, PUDDING
sprinkle with	SPARGE			(see dessert)
—condiment, etc	PEPPER		—malt and water syrup	MALT EXTRACT
—flour, sugar, etc	DREDGE		sweetened jelly	GELATIN(E)
sprinkled with brandy			sweetener	SACCHARIN, SUGAR, SYRUP
and ignited	FLAMBE, FLAMED		syrup from	
squeeze juice from fruit	REAM		—cane sugar	GOLDEN SYRUP
stack milk-curd slices	CHEFFAR		—maize	CORN SYRUP
starch	FARINA		—used for sweetening	GLYCERINE
—for thickening	ARROWROOT		table with openings over	
—from			boiling water	STEAM TABLE
cassava	TAPIOCA		tasteless liquid food	SLOP
palm pith	SAGO		tasty morsel	BONNE BOUCHE
starchy root-stock	CASSAVA		test for fat content	
steep in liquor	INFUSE, MACERATE		of milk	BABCOCK TEST
	MARINATE		thick	
			—cream	DOUBLE CREAM

—dip	FONDUE
—pancake	FLAPJACK
thicken	
—by boiling	DECOCT, REDUCE
—like jelly	GEL
thickening	
—agent	LIAISON
—of fat and flour	ROUX
—starch	TAPIOCA
thin	
—cream	POURING CREAM
	SINGLE CREAM
—porridge	GRUEL
—strip of food	ALUMETTE
tie up (bird) for cooking	TRUSS
treat with	
—boiling water or steam,	SCALD
—salt or brine	CURE, SALT
uncooked	AU NATUREL
underdone	RARE, SAIGNANT
utensils	
—baking dish	
for one person	RAMAKIN, RAMEKIN
	RAMEQUIN
with close-fitting lid	CASSEROLE
—beater	BLENDER
	FOOD PROCESSOR
	MIXER, WHISK
—broad serving-knife	SLICE
—broiling frame	GRIDIRON, GRILL
—Chinese frying-pan	WO(C)K
—cooking pot	SAUCEPAN
—cup-shaped mould	TIMBALE
—cutting tool	(CARVING) KNIFE
	CLEAVER, MINCER
	SCISSORS
—double saucepan	BAIN-MARIE
—earthenware pot	TERRENE
—flat cooking surface	BAKING SHEET
	GRIDDLE
—for	
cooking fish	FISH KETTLE
deep frying in fat	FRYER
eating rice	CHOP STICKS
frying	FRYING PAN, SKILLET
grating	GRATER, ZESTER
grinding	MORTAR AND PESTLE
	PEPPER MILL, SALT MILL
holding meat together	SKEWER
icing	PIPING BAG
making stock	STOCKPOT
popcorn roasting	POPPER
steaming	STEAMER
—knife with flat blunt blade	PALETTE KNIFE
—large cooking pot	DUTCH OVEN
—lifting tool	SLICE, TONGS

—making pastry	PASTRY CUTTER
	ROLLING PIN
—mixer	BLENDER
	FOOD PROCESSOR, WHISK
—oven used with	
pre-heated bricks	
or coals	DUTCH OVEN
—ovenproof dish	CASSEROLE
—pot-stand	TRIVET
—preparing vegetables	(POTATO) PEELER
—roasting-tin used in	
front of open fire	DUTCH OVEN
—rotating bar for roasting	BROACH, SPIT
—serving	FORK, KNIFE, SLICE
	SPATULA, SPOON
—shell-shaped dish	COQUILLE
—slicer for fruit and vegetables	MANDOLIN
—small	
baking-dish	RAMEKIN
	RAMEQUIN
long-handled frying-pan	SKILLET
mould	DARIOLE
spit or skewer	BROCHETTE
—spit	BROACH
—sprinkling	CASTER, DREDGER
—stewpan	CASSEROLE
—straining	COLANDER, SALAD SHAKER
	SIEVE, STRAINER
—weighing	SCALES, (SPRING) BALANCE
vegetable	
—garnish	JARDINIERE
—salad in Russian dressing	RUSSIAN SALAD
vinegar from	
—ale	ALEGAR
—cider	CIDER VINEGAR
—solution	PICKLE
—wine	WINE VINEGAR
vitamins	(see separate entry)
warmed-up dish	RECHAUFFE
water-ice	SORBET
well done (meat)	BIEN CUIT, PERCOLT
whalemeat	MUKTUK
with wholemeal flour	
and sugar	SWEETMEAL
without raising agent	UNLEAVENED
wooden dish	TRENCHER
work dough	KNEAD, MOULD
wrapped in pastry	EN CROUTE
yeast froth	BARM
young	
—corn ears	GREEN CORN
—duck	DUCKLING
—goose	GOSLING
—hare	LEVERET
Coptic	COP(T)
bishop	ABBA

chapel	HAIKAL
dialect	SAHIDIC
Costa Rica	CR
capital	SAN JOSE
coin	COLON
measure (11 bushels)	FANEGA

counties

England	AVON, BEDFORDSHIRE
	BERKSHIRE, BUCKINGHAMSHIRE
	CAMBRIDGESHIRE, CHESHIRE
	CLEVELAND, CORNWALL, CUMBRIA
	DERBYSHIRE, DEVON, DORSET
	DURHAM, EAST SUSSEX, ESSEX
	GLOUCESTERSHIRE, GREATER LONDON
	GREATER MANCHESTER, HAMPSHIRE
	HEREFORD AND WORCESTER
	HERTFORDSHIRE, HUMBERSIDE
	ISLE OF WIGHT, KENT, LANCASHIRE
	LEICESTERSHIRE, LINCOLNSHIRE
	MERSEYSIDE, NORFOLK
	NORTHAMPTONSHIRE
	NORTHUMBERLAND
	NORTH YORKSHIRE
	NOTTINGHAMSHIRE
	OXFORDSHIRE, SHROPSHIRE
	SOMERSET, SOUTH YORKSHIRE,
	STAFFORDSHIRE, SUFFOLK, SURREY
	TYNE AND WEAR, WARWICKSHIRE
	WEST MIDLANDS, WEST SUSSEX
	WEST YORKSHIRE, WILTSHIRE
—obsolete	CUMBERLAND
	HUNTINGDONSHIRE
	MIDDLESEX
	RUTLAND, WESTMORLAND
Ireland	CARLOW, CAVAN, CLARE
	CORK, DONEGAL, DUBLIN, GALWAY
	LAOIS, LEITRIM, LIMERICK
	LONGFORD, LOUTH, KERRY
	KILDARE, KILKENNY, MAYO, MEATH
	MONAGHAN, OFFALY, ROSCOMMON
	SLIGO, TIPPERARY
	WATERFORD, WESTMEATH
	WEXFORD, WICKLOW
Northern Ireland	ANTRIM, ARMAGH, DOWN
	FERMANAGH, LONDONDERRY
	TYRONE
Scotland	BORDERS, CENTRAL SCOTLAND
	DUMFRIES AND GALLOWAY, FIFE
	GRAMPIAN REGION
	HIGHLAND REGION
	LOTHIAN, ORKNEY, SHETLAND
	STRATHCLYDE, TAYSIDE
	WESTERN ISLES
Wales	CLWYD, DYFED, GWENT
	GWYNEDD, MID-GLAMORGAN
	POWYS, WEST GLAMORGAN

cricket

3 wickets with consecutive balls	HAT-TRICK
8 consecutive balls	OVER
100 runs in an innings	CENTURY
1000 runs, 100 wickets	DOUBLE
apparent but not real catch	BUMP BALL
	SPECTATOR CATCH
appeal to umpire	HOW'S THAT, OWZAT
area	
—between stumps	PITCH, WICKET
—within 30 yards of	
wickets	FIELDING CIRCLE
ball	
—bowled	
along the ground	GRUB
at roughly head-height	BEAMER
slowly and high	DONKEY-DROP
underarm	
—fast	DAISY-CUTTER
—slow	LOB
—from which no score	
is made	DOT-BALL
—out of batsman's reach	WIDE
—that	
does not pitch between	
the wickets	FULL-PITCH
	FULL-TOSS
is	
—short-pitched and	
easy to hit	DOLLY
	HALF-VOLLEY, LONG HOP
—unlawfully	
delivered	NO-BALL
keeps low	DAISY-CUTTER, SHOOTER
moves in the air	INSWINGER
	OUTSWINGER
pitches	
—at batsman's feet	YORKER
—in or near blockhole	YORKER
turns from	
—leg to off	LEG-BREAK, LEG-CUTTER
—off to leg	OFF-BREAK
	OFF-CUTTER
batsman sent in to	
defend until close of play	NIGHTWATCHMAN
bowler who makes good	
use of seam on ball	SEAM BOWLER
bowler's	
—action	OVERARM, ROUNDARM
	UNDERARM
—aiming mark	STUMPS, WICKET
—approach	RUN-UP
children's cricket	KANGA CRICKET
	KWIK CRICKET
close innings before	
all wickets have fallen	DECLARE

continue with second innings immediately after first	FOLLOW ON	
cross-pieces on stumps	BAILS	
defend stubbornly	STONEWALL	
derisory expression when easy catch is missed	BUTTER-FINGERS	
dismissal of batsman		
—by ball striking pad	LBW	
	LEG-BEFORE-WICKET	
—caught out of his ground by wicketkeeper	STUMPED	
—deflecting ball from bat to stumps	PLAYED-ON	
—hitting ball twice	HIT BALL TWICE	
—obstructing fielder	OBSTRUCTING THE FIELD	
—running between wickets	RUN-OUT	
—touching ball	HANDLED BALL	
distance travelled by ball bowled before landing	LENGTH	
easy catch	DOLLY (CATCH)	
	SITTER	
enforced start of second innings	FOLLOW-ON	
fast		
—bowling directed at the batsman	BODYLINE	
—short-pitched ball	BOUNCER, BUMPER	
	THROAT BALL	
fielder's throw that goes beyond the wicket	OVERTHROW	
fielding positions		
—leg side	(BACKWARD) SHORT-LEG	
	(DEEP) FINE LEG	
	(DEEP) MID-WICKET	
	(DEEP) SQUARE LEG	
	FORWARD SHORT-LEG	
	LEG SLIP, LONG-ON	
	(SILLY) MID-ON	
—off side	COVER POINT	
	(DEEP) EXTRA COVER	
	(DEEP) THIRD MAN, GULL(E)Y	
	LONG-OFF, (SILLY) MID-OFF	
	SHORT EXTRA COVER	
	SHORT THIRD MAN	
	(SILLY) POINT, SLIP	
other	BAT-PAD, LONGSTOP	
	WICKETKEEPER	
grounds		
—Australia		
Adelaide	OVAL	
Brisbane	WOOLLOONGABBA GROUND	
Perth	CRICKET ASSOCIATION GROUND	
Sydney	ALBERT GROUND	

—England		
Cambridge University		FENNERS
Derbyshire		CHESTERFIELD
		QUEEN'S PARK
Essex		CHELMSFORD
Glamorgan		CARDIFF
		SOPHIA GARDENS
Gloucestershire		ASHLEY DOWN
		BRISTOL
Hampshire		HAMBLEDON
		SOUTHAMPTON
Kent		CANTERBURY
		ST LAWRENCE GROUND
Lancashire		MANCHESTER
		OLD TRAFFORD
MCC		LORDS
Middlesex		LORDS
Nottinghamshire		TRENT BRIDGE
Surrey		THE OVAL
		KENNINGTON
Sussex		EATON ROAD, HOVE
Warwickshire		EDGBASTON
Worcestershire		WORCESTER
Yorkshire		BRAMALL LANE
		HEADINGLEY
—India		
Bombay		BRABOURNE STADIUM
Calcutta		EDEN GARDENS
Delhi	FEROZ SHAH KOTLA GROUND	
Karachi		NATIONAL STADIUM
Lahore		GADDAFI GROUND
Madras	CHIDAMBARAM GROUND	
—New Zealand		
Auckland		EDEN PARK
Christchurch		LANCASTER PARK
Dunedin		CARISBROOK GROUND
Wellington		BASIN RESERVE
—South Africa		
Cape Town		NEWLANDS
Johannesburg	WANDERES GROUND	
—West Indies		
Bridgetown, Barbados		KENSINGTON GROUND
Georgetown Guyana		BOURDA GROUND
Kingston, Jamaica		SABINA PARK
Port of Spain, Trinidad		QUEEN'S PARK OVAL
inadvertent stroke		SNICK, TOUCH
left-hand side (to r-h bat)		LEG, ON
leg protectors		PADS
maiden over in which a wicket is taken		WICKET-MAIDEN
mark made by batsman in front of stumps		BLOCKHOLE

move
  —ball in the air when bowling   SWING
  —to position behind another
    fielder   BACK UP
  —up the pitch in preparation
    for run   BACK UP
no score   DUCK
  —in each innings   PAIR
obstruction of wicket
  with legs   LEG-BEFORE-WICKET
                             LBW

off-break
  —bowled by left-
    handed bowler   CHINAMAN
  —disguised as leg-break   GOOGLY
official   SCORER, UMPIRE
over from which no runs
  are scored   MAIDEN (OVER)
players
  —Australian   ARMSTRONG, BARNES
    BENAUD, BLACKHAM, BORDER
    BRADMAN, CHAPPELL, DAVIDSON
    FINGLETON, GREGORY, GRIMMETT
    HARVEY, HASSETT, IRONMONGER
    LAWRY, LILLIE, LINDWALL
    MARSH, MCCABE, MCDONALD
    MECKIFF, MILLER, OLDFIELD
    O'REILLY, PONSFORD, RITCHIE
    SIMPSON, SPOFFORTH, STODDART
    TALLON, TRUMPER, WALTERS
    WOODFULL
  —English   ALLEN, AMES, BAILEY, BARNES
    BARRINGTON, BEDSER, BOTHAM
    BOWES, BOYCOTT, CHAPMAN, CLOSE
    COMPTON, COWDREY, DE FREITAS
    DEXTER, DILLEY, EDRICH, EMBUREY
    EVANS, FENDER, FOSTER, FREEMAN
    FRY, GATTING, GOOCH, GOWER, GRACE
    HAMMOND, HENDREN, HIRST, HOBBS
    HOLLIES, ILLINGWORTH, JESSOP, KNOTT
    LAKER, LAMB, LARWOOD, LEVER
    LEYLAND, LOCK, MAY, MACLAREN
    RHODES, SHEPPARD, SMALL
    SPOONER, SNOW, STATHAM
    SUTCLIFFE, TATE, TRUEMAN
    TYSON, UNDERWOOD, VERITY, VOCE
    WARDLE, WILLIS, WOOLLEY
    WRIGHT, WYATT
  —Indian   AMARNATH, AZHARUDDIN
    BEDI, CHANDRASEKHAR
    CONTRACTOR, DEV
    DULEEPSINHJI, ENGINEER
    GAVASKAR, GUPTE, HANIF
    MANJREKAR, MANKAD, MERCHANT
    PRASANNA, RANJITSINHJI, SHASTRA
    TENDULKAR, UMRIGAR, VENGSARKAR

—New Zealand   COLLINGE, CONGDON
    COWIE, CROWE, DONNELLY
    DOWLING, HADLEE, LOWRY
    SUTCLIFFE, TURNER
—Pakistani   AKRAM, FAZAL, IMRAN
    IQBAL, JAVED, MOHSIN
    MUDASSAR, MUSHTAQ, QADIR
    QASIM, SADIQ, SARFRAZ
    WASIR, ZAHEER
—South African   BARLOW, BLAND
    CHEETHAM, FAULKNER
    NOURSE, POLLOCK, PROCTER
    RICHARDS, SCHWARTZ, TAYFIELD
    VOGLER
—Sri Lankan   MENDIS, RANATUNGA
    RANAYAKE, SILVA
    WETTIMUNY
—West Indian   BUTCHER, CONSTANTINE
    GARNER, GILCHRIST
    GREENIDGE, HALL, HAYNES
    HEADLEY, KALLICHARRAN
    KANHAI, LLOYD, MARSHALL
    RAMADHIN, RICHARDS, ROBERTS
    ROWE, SOBERS, SOLOMON
    VALENTINE, WALCOTT, WEEKES
    WORRELL
—Zimbabwean   HICK
point where bat rests on
  crease   BLOCKHOLE
position of
  —bat at rest   GUARD, LEG STUMP
    MIDDLE-AND-LEG
    MIDDLE-AND-OFF
    MIDDLE STUMP, OFF STUMP
  —batsman   STANCE
practice area   NET(S)
right-hand side (to r-h bat)   OFF
rotation of ball by bowler's
  action   SPIN
run scored from
  —ball
    pitched wide of the crease   WIDE
    that
      —is not hit   BYE
      —strikes the batsman   LEG-BYE
    unfairly delivered   NO-BALL
  —bye, leg-bye, no-ball, wide   EXTRA
                        SUNDRY
  —throw that goes beyond
    the wicket   OVERTHROW
score
  —of 100 runs or more   CENTURY
  —with prods and deflections   NURDLE
spare player   TWELFTH MAN
stop ball defensively
  with bat   BLOCK, STONEWALL

stroke	GLIDE, HOOK
	(LEG) GLANCE, OFF-DRIVE
	ON DRIVE, PULL
	(SQUARE-)CUT, SWEEP
trophy	THE ASHES
	(*see also separate entry*)
white	
—line on	
pitch	BATTING CREASE
	BOWLING CREASE
	FIELDING CIRCLE
edge of pitch	BOUNDARY
—panel set on boundary	SIGHT SCREEN
young player	COLT
cross	
archbishop's	CROSIER, CROZIER
as award	(*see* **decorations**)
Christ's cross	CRUCIFIX, ROOD(-TREE)
clerical	CARDINALS
	CONSTANTINIAN
	PASSION, ST PETER'S
crucifix	ROOD
English	ST GEORGE'S CROSS
forked	FOURCHE
having	
—arms	
bent clockwise at	
right angles	SVASTIKA
	SWASTIKA
of equal length	GREEK
with crutch heads	POTENT
—circle round point of	
intersection of limbs	CELTIC, CORNISH
	KILDALTON
—fleur-de-lis shape	FLEURY, FLORY
—pointed ends	FITCHE(E)
—three	
buds at each extremity	BOTONE, BOTTONY
	TREFLE(E), TREFLY
horizontal bars	PAPAL
—two horizontal bars	LORRAINE
	PATRIARCHAL
—two outward-curving	
branches on each limb	MOLINE
—two-pointed expanding	
limbs	MALTESE
in fretwork, as brooch etc	ROVEN CROSS
Latin cross on three steps	CALVARY
modified Greek	CAPITAL
orthodox prelate's cross	ENCOLPION
other	CROSSLET, FORME
	POMME, RUSSIAN
red on white ground	GENEVA CROSS
reverse swastika	FILFOT, FYLFOT
Scottish	ST ANDREW'S CROSS
square	QUADRATE

suspended from	
a heart	CROIX A LA JEANNETTE
swastika	GRAMMADION
	GRAMMATION
symbol of life	ANKH, ANSATE
T-shaped	ST ANTHONY'S, TAU
—with loop	ANKH, ANSATE
upright with lower limb	
the longest	LATIN
X-shaped	SALTIER, SALTIE
	ST ANDREW'S
Y-shaped	Y-CROSS
Cuba	C
capital	HAVANA
castle	MORRO
coin	CENTAVO, PESO
drum	BONGO, CONGA, ENKOMO
dance	CONGA, DANZA, DANZON
	GUAJIRA, GUARACHA
	HABANERA, HIP-HOP
	R(H)UMBA
knife	MACHETE
measure	TAREA
rattle	MARACA
secret police	PORRA
squall	BAYAMO
squash	ZAPALLO
tobacco field	VEGA
tree	CULLA, CUYA
weight	LIBRA, TERCIO
	(*see also* **West Indies**)
cycling	
leader's badge	
—Tour de France	YELLOW JERSEY
—Giro d'Italia	PINK JERSEY
races	
—Britain	MILK RACE
	TOUR OF BRITAIN
	WINCANTON CLASSIC
—France	PARIS-TOURS
	TOUR DE FRANCE
	TOUR DE PAYS BASQUE
—Germany	COLOGNE SIX DAYS
—Ireland	TOUR OF IRELAND
—Italy	GIRO D'ITALIA
	TOUR DE LOMBARDY
—Spain	TOUR DE CATALONIA
	VUELTA D'ESPANA
—types	CYCLE SPEEDWAY, PURSUIT
	SPRINT, TIME TRIAL
riders	
—American	HAMPSTEN, KNICKMAN
	LEMOND, SCHUTT
—Australian	ANDERSON, BISH, GRAY
	MOCKRIDGE, PATE, SUTTON
	VINNICOMBE, WOODS

—Belgian	CRIQUIELION, DE WILDE
	DHAENENS, HOOYDONCK
	LIBOTON, MAERTENS, MERCKX
	NOYELLE, PLANKAERT, POLLENTIER
	SERCU, STERKX, THEUNISSE
	THYS, VAARTEN
—British	ALEXANDER, BARRY
	BOARDMAN, BOOTY, CAMERON
	CAMMISH, COOK, CURRAN, DOYLE
	DREW, ELLIOTT, HARRIS, LODGE
	MCHUGH, MCLOUGHLIN, MILLAR
	PAULDING, REYNOLDS, SADLER
	SOUTHALL, STEPHENS, STURGESS
	WALLACE, WOOD, YATES
—Canadian	BAUER, SINGLETON, WALTON
—Colombian	FARFAN, PARRA
—Czech	DALER, FISERA, KUCHREK
	PENC, REHOUNEK, SIMUNTEK
	TRAK, VORBORIL
—Danish	FLACK, FREDBORG, FROST
	HANSEN, MARCUSSEN, OERSTED
—Dutch	BREUKINK, DE NIJS
	HERMANS, KUIPER, MINNEBOO
	PEETERS, ROOKS, TALEN
	THEUNISSE, VAN EGMOND, VAN IMPE
	VAN VLIET, VENIX, ZOETEMECK
—French	ANQUETIL, BAYAERT
	BEAUFRAND, BLANCHONNET
	BOBET, BONDUE, CHARPENTIER
	COLAS, DEPINE, DUPONT, FIGNON
	HINAULT, KILLY, MAGNE, MASSON
	MICHARD, MORELON, MOTTET
	REBILLARD, ROUSSEAU
	TAILLENDIER, TRENTIN
	VERNET, VIVIEN
—German	AMPLER, BRAUN, DROGAN
	GLUCKLICH, GREIL, GRUNKE
	HESSLICH, HUEBNER, KAPPES
	KLUGE, MACHA, MALCHOW
	MERKENS, PODLESCH, POEL
	RAAB, SCHEUTZ, SCHMIDTKE
	THALER, THOMS, WEBER
—Greek	KONSTANTINIDIS
—Irish	KELLY, ROCHE

—Italian	ARGENTIN, BALDINI
	BIANCHETTO, BUGNO
	CIPOLLINI, DI BASCO, DITANO
	DOTTI, FAGGIN, FONDRIEST
	GENTILI, GHELLA, GIARDONI
	GIOVANETTI, PAVESI, PETTENELLA
	SACCI, SARONNI, VIANELLI
	VICINO, ZATIN
—Japanese	HONDA, NAKANO, TAWARA
—New Zealand	BAMFORD, DAHLBERG
	RUSH
—Norwegian	KNUDSEN
—Polish	PIASECKI
—Portuguese	DA SILVA
—Russian	ECKIMOV, GANEEV
	KAPITONOV, KOPYLOV
	KOUROVTS, UMARAS
—Spanish	DELGADO, INDURAIN, OCANA
—Swedish	JOHANSSEN, STENQUIST
—Swiss	DILL-BUNDI, FREULER
	HURZELER, KURMANN
	ZIMMERMANN, ZWEIFEL
sprinter's badge	GREEN JERSEY
Cyprus	CY
capital	NICOSIA
coin	LIRA, POUND
scent	CHYPRE
Czechoslovakia	CS
capitals	PRAGUE, BRATISLAVA
castle	HRAD
coin	HALER, HELLER, KORUNA
countries	SLOVAKIA
	REPUBLIC OF CZECH STATES
	RCS
depression	KOTLINA, NIZINA
forest	LES
gate	BRANA
gymnastic club	SOKOL
measure	LATRO
mountain(s)	HORA
mountain range	HORY, POHORAI(E)
region	KRAJ
tableland	PLOSINA
town	MESTO

D

dance

acrobatic	BREAK DANCING
afternoon dance	THE DANSANT
Alpine	GAVOTTE
American	BARN DANCE, (BE)BOP
	BLACK BOTTOM, BOSTON (REEL)
	BREAK DANCE, BUNNY-HUG
	CAKEWALK, CHARLESTON
	ELECTRIC BOOGIE, GOGO, HOEDOWN
	JITTERBUG, JIVE, LINDY HOP
	PAUL JONES, RAG(TIME)
	ROCK 'N ROLL, TWIST
	TURKEY TROT, VOGUEING
Argentine	TANGO
art of dance	CHOREOGRAPHY
Austrian	LANDLER
back-to-back	DO-SI-DO
ballet	(see separate entry)
Basque	BOURREE
belly-dance (Egypt)	RAQS SARQI
Bohemian	POLKA, REDOWA
Brazilian	BATUQUE, BOSSA NOVA
	CARIOCA, LAMBADA
	MAXIXE, SAMBA
changing partners	PAUL JONES
Cockney	HOKEY-COKEY
	LAMBETH WALK
	KNEES-UP (MOTHER BROWN)
college	HOP, PROM
country	ALTHEA, AURESCA
	BARN DANCE, COTILL(I)ON
	DASHING WHITE SERGEANT
	ECOSSAISE, GAVOTTE
	HAY, HEY, HOEDOWN
	MORRIS(-DANCE), REEL
	ROUNDEL, (SIR) ROGER DE COVERLEY
	SQUARE DANCE
Cuban	CONGA, GUAJIRA
	GUARACHA, HABANERA
	HIP-HOP, R(H)UMBA
dance of death	DANSE MACABRE
disco dancing	GOGO
Dutch clog dance	MATELOT(E)
energetic	MOSHING
	SLAMDANCING
English regional dance	CLOG DANCE
	HORN DANCE
	MAYPOLE DANCE

erotic	BELLY-DANCE, DIRTY-DANCING
	HOOTCHIE-COOTCHIE
	LAMBADA, TOUCH-DANCING
fairy dance	RINGLET
fast fox-trot	QUICKSTEP
flapping arms	CHICKEN DANCING
folk-dance	(see country above)
for	
—four couples	QUADRILLE
—men only	STAG-DANCE
—opposing groups	CONTREDANSE
	COUNTERDANCE
—two persons	PAS DE DEUX, RIGADOON
fourth movement of	
quadrille	TRENISE
free-style exercise	EURYTHMICS
French	BOURREE, CANCAN, CHACONNE
	CORANTO, COURANTE, FARANDOLE
	GAVOTTE, GIGUE, RIGADOON
	RIGAUDON
—old	BRAN(S)LE, BRANTLE, BRAWL
frolicsome	CAPER
gavotte	CIBELL
German	ALLEMANDE, ALMAIN, LANDLER
gliding	COURANT(E), PALAIS GLIDE
	TWO-STEP, WALTZ
Greek	ROMAIKA, SIKINNIS
Hawaiian	HULA(-HULA)
Hebrew	HORA
hornpipe	MATELOTE
Hungarian	CSARDAS, CZARDAS
in	
—duple time	TWO-STEP
—ring	ROUND
Indian	BHANGRA, KATHAK
	NA(U)TCH
—hand movements	MUTRA
Irish	FADING, PLANXTY, REEL
	RINKAFADDA
Israeli	HORA
Italian	BERGAMASK, BERGOMASK, GIGA
	RIGOLETTO, SALTARELLO
	TARANTELLA, VOLTA
Jamaican	REGGAE
jumping	MOSHING, POGO, SLAM DANCING
leaping	ALLEMANDE, ALMAIN
like	
—minuet	PASPY, PASSEPIED
—polka	SCHOTTISCHE
lively	BOURREE, CORANTO, GALLIARD
	GALOP(ADE), GIG(UE), JIG
	RIGADOON, RIGAUDON, STOMP
—Shakespeare	CANARY, UPSPRING
Maori	HAKA
march	ONE-STEP
marching sequence	PROMENADE

Maytime	MORISCO, MORISK
	MORRIS(-DANCE)
Mexican	RASPA
modern	(BE)BOP, BODY-POPPING
	BOOGIE, BREAK-DANCE
	DISCO DANCING, FRUG, GOGO
	HIP-HOP, JITTERBUG, JIVE
	MOSHING, ROCK 'N' ROLL, SALSA
	SHUFFLE, SLAMDANCING
	TWIST, VOGUEING
	(*see also* American *above*)
Moorish	MORESCO
movement in quadrille	PANTALON
	PASTOURELLE
Neapolitan	TARANTELLA
Negro	BREAKDOWN, JUBA
	WALK-AROUND
New Zealand	HAKA
Norwegian	HALLING
obsolete (slow)	DUMP
old	BRAN(S)LE, BRANTLE
	BRAWL, CINQUE-PACE, GAILLARD
	GALLIARD, HAY-DE-GUISE
	HAY-DE-GUY(ES), HEY-DE-GUISE
	HEY-DE-GUY(ES), HUY-DE-GUY
	LAVOLT(A), LOURE, MINUET
	PASSY-MEASURE, PAVIN
	SINK-A-PACE, VOLTA
on	
—sanded surface	SAND-DANCE
—the same spot	POGO
orgiastic	SIKINNIS
originally Scottish	ECOSSAIS
Peruvian	CUECA
Polish	CRACOVIENNE, MAZURKA
	POLONAISE, VARSOVIENNE
Polynesian	HULA(-HULA), SIVA
Portuguese	FADO
Provencal	TAMBOURIN
public	RIDOTTO
quadrilles	LANCERS
quick	GALLOPADE, FOX-TROT
—movement of csardas	FRIS(KA)
—pavan(e)	PASSAMEZZO
	PASSE-MEASURE
	PASSY-MEASURE
—step	PAS REDOUBLE
ragtime	TURKEY-TROT
reel	CIRCASSIAN CIRCLE
	EIGHTSOME
ring-dance	RO(U)NDEL, ROUNDELAY
	ROUNDLE
Roman	TRIPUDIUM
round dance	ROUNDABOUT
Russian	GOPAK, KAZATZKA
	KOLO, ZIGANKA

sailor's	HORNPIPE
Scottish	ECOSSAISE, EIGHTSOME
	GAY GORDONS, HIGHLAND FLING
	HOOLACHAN, HULLACHAN
	PETRONELLA, REEL, STRATHSPEY
	SWORD-DANCE
Serbian	KOLO
shivering	SHIMMY(-SHAKE)
shuffling	FOX-TROT
Sicilian	SICILIANA, SICILIANO
	SICILIENNE
single file	CONGA
skipping	SALTARELLO
slow	CHACONNE
	(HESITATION-)WALTZ
	MINUET, PAVANE
—waltz	VALETA, VELETA
solo	VARIATION
Spanish	BOLERO, CACHUCHA, FANDANGO
	FARRUCA, FLAMENCO, JOTA
	MALAGUENA, PASO DOBLE
	PASSACAGLIA, PAVAN(E)
	PAVEN, PAVIN, SALTARELLO
	SARABAND(E), SARDANO
	SEGUIDILLA, ZAPATEADO
square	DOS-A-DOS, DO-SI-DO
	HOE-DOWN, QUADRILLE
stately	MINUET, PAVANE
under bar	LIMBO
Venetian	FORLANA, FURLANA
waltz	BOSTON, VALETA, VELETA
West Indian	BEGUINE, CHA-CHA(-CHA)
	LIMBO, MAMBO
with	
—fans	FAN-DANCE
—much jumping	LAVOLT(A)
—rigid limbs	ROBOTIC DANCING
writhing	MOSHING
decorations	
Crosses	AIR FORCE
	DISTINGUISHED FLYING
	DISTINGUISHED SERVICE
	GEORGE, MILITARY, VICTORIA
Medals	AIR FORCE MEDAL
	BURMA GALLANTRY
	CONSPICUOUS GALLANTRY
	DISTINGUISHED CONDUCT
	DISTINGUISHED FLYING
	DISTINGUISHED SERVICE
	GEORGE, MILITARY
Orders	DISTINGUISHED SERVICE
	IMPERIAL SERVICE ORDER
	INDIAN ORDER OF MERIT
	QUEEN'S SERVICE ORDER
—Order of	BATH, BRITISH EMPIRE
	BRITISH INDIA, BURMA

	COMPANION OF HONOUR
	CROWN OF INDIA, GARTER
	INDIAN EMPIRE, MERIT
	ST MICHAEL AND ST GEORGE
	STAR OF INDIA, THISTLE
—Royal	ROYAL RED CROSS ORDER
	ROYAL VICTORIAN
other	BRITISH EMPIRE MEDAL
	BRITISH EMPIRE SERVICE MEDAL
	CANADIAN FORCES DECORATION
	CANADIAN MEDAL
	COLONIAL POLICE MEDAL
	EFFICIENCY DECORATION
	EMERGENCY SERVICES DECORATION
	EMPIRE GALLANTRY MEDAL
	INDIAN DISTINGUISHED SERVICE MEDAL
	KING'S POLICE MEDAL
	MEDAL FOR MERITORIOUS SERVICE
	QUEEN'S GALLANTRY MEDAL
	QUEEN'S POLICE MEDAL
	SEA GALLANTRY MEDAL
	TERRITORIAL DECORATION
	VOLUNTEER OFFICERS DECORATION

deer

American	CARIACOU, CARIBOU, CARJACOU
	CHEVROTAIN, ELK, MOOSE
	MOUSE-DEER, VIRGINIAN DEER
Asian	MUNTJAC
European	FALLOW, RED DEER
female	DOE, HIND, ROE
knob on horn	CROCHE
male	BUCK
—in	
2nd year	BROCKETT
—(Shak.)	PRICKET
3rd year	SPAY(D), SPAD(E), SOR(R)EL
4th year (Shak.)	SOAR(E), SORE
—over	
4 years	BARE BUCK, STAG
5 years	HART
—with 12 points	ROYAL
rudimentary antler	BOSSET
small species	ROE DEER
tines	
—3rd	ROYAL
—over 3rd	SURROYAL
wax-secreting gland	CRUMEN, TEAR-PIT
	(*see also* **antelope**)

Denmark   DK

bay	BREDNING, BUGT, VIG
beach	STRAND
bog	MOSE
bread and butter	SMOR(RE)BROD
cape	NAES, ODDE
capital	COPENHAGEN, KOBENHAVN
cheese	TYBO
cliff	KLINT
coin	KR, KRONE, ORE
dunes	KLIT
fiord	ISE, LIM
harbour	HAVN
hero	HOLGER, OGIER
hill	BJERG, HOJ
hors d'oeuvres	SMOR(RE)BROD
invader	JUTE
lake	SO
Lower House	FOLKETING
measure	ALEN, ESER, LANDMILL
	MORGEN, RODE, TOMME
national flag	DANNEBROG
order	DANNEBROG
parliament	RIGSDAG
sea monster	KRAKEN
strait	BAELT
Upper House	LANDST(H)ING
valley	DAL
weight	ESER, KVINT, PUND
	QUINT, TONDE

department   DEPT, DPT
of

—Economic Affairs	DEA
—Education and Science	DES
—Employment (and Productivity)	DE, DEP
—Health and Social Security	DHSS
—the Environment	DOE
—Trade (and Industry)	DOT, DTI

desert

Africa	LIBYAN, KALAHARI
	NAMIB, SAHARA, SOMALI, TEREVE
Arabia	AN NAFUD, ARRAB'AL KHALI
	EMPTY QUARTER, SYRIAN
Asia	GOBI, TAKLAMEN
Australia	ARUNTA, GIBSON, GREAT SANDY
	GREAT VICTORIAN, NULLARBOR PLAIN
	SIMPSON, STURT, WARBURTON
Chile	ATACAMA
China	TAKLA MAKAN, ORDOS
India	INDIAN, THAR
Iran	DASHT-E LUT, IRANIAN
Middle East	SYRIAN
North America	BLACKROCK, COLORADO
	GILA, GREAT SALT LAKE
	GREAT WESTERN, MOJAVE
	PAINTED, SONORAN
Peru	DESIERTO DE SECHURA
rocky	HAM(M)ADA
Russia	KARA KUM, KYZYL KUM
	TURKESTAN
sandy	ERG
South America	PATAGONIAN
stony	REG
Sudan	BAIYUDA, NUBIAN

dessert
almond-flavoured	BAKEWELL PUDDING
	BAKEWELL TART, FRANGIPANE
	MAID OF HONOUR, PRALINE
American	APPLE PIE, BLUEBERRY PIE
	PANDOWDY, PUMPKIN PIE
apple	
—pastry	APFELSTRUDEL
—sponge	EVE'S PUDDING
Austrian	APFELSTRUDEL
baked	
—apple and spices	BROWN BETTY
—fruit in dough	DUMPLING
batter	BATTER PUDDING
	YORKSHIRE PUDDING
blancmange	FLUMMERY
boiled pudding	DUFF, ROLY-POLY
	SPONGE, SUET PUDDING
—with currants	SPOTTED DICK
	SPOTTED DOG
bread	BREAD AND BUTTER PUDDING
	BREAD PUDDING
	OSBORNE PUDDING
	SUMMER PUDDING
—crumbs	CHARLOTTE
butter, milk, sugar, etc	FUDGE
candied chestnuts	MARRONS GLACES
caramelised nuts	PRALINE
chocolate	CHOC-AU-RHUM
choux pastry roll	PROFITEROLE
cold fruit purée with cream	FOOL
cone of refined sugar	SUGARLOAF
cream	CREME BRULEE
	CREME PATISSIERE
	CUSTARD CREAM, SYLLABUB
—and eggs	PARFAIT
—cake	GATEAU
—thickened by curdling	SYLLABUB
crushed fruit etc	FOOL
custard dishes	BAVAROIS, CREME BRULEE
	FLUMMERY, FOOL
	ZABA(GL)IONE
—and egg noodles (Heb.)	LOKSHEN
—with	
caramelised sugar	CREME BRULEE
	CREME CARAMEL
floating whipped	
egg white	FLOATING ISLAND
sponge cake, jelly, etc	TRIFLE
sponge fingers	CHARLOTTE RUSSE
diced fruit salad	MACEDOINE
egg and	
—chocolate	CHOC-AU-RHUM
—cream	SOUFFLE
sugar, etc	POSSET
—flour, spirits, etc	FLUMMERY

—lemon	LEMON CHIFFON
—sugar and wine	ZABAGLIONE
egg-white	
—sugar, etc	MERINGUE, SNOW
	SOUFFLE
—water-ice	SHERBE(R)T
flat	PANCAKE, CREPE SUZETTE
	WAFFLE
frothy confection	MOUSSE, SOUFFLE, WHIP
	ZABA(GL)IONE
frozen	
—cream, etc	ICE CREAM
—dishes	BAKED ALASKA
	BOMBE, NESSELRODE
	PARFAIT
—water, flavoured	WATER ICE
fruit	
—and	
cheese	CHEESECAKE
ice cream	COUPE
sponge layers	CHARLOTTE
—baked shell side up,	
served fruit side up	UPSIDEDOWN CAKE
—candied	SUCCADE
—fried in batter	FRITTER
—in syrup	COMPOTE, SUCCADE
—layered with	
ice cream, etc	PARFAIT
sugar	AMBROSIA
—mixed	SALAD
—mixture used in frozen	
sweets	NESSELRODE
—pudding	CHRISTMAS PUDDING
	DUCHESSE PUDDING
	LAFAYETTE PUDDING
	SCOTCH PUDDING, SPOTTED DICK
	SUMMER PUDDING
—purée and cream	RODGROD
—tart	CHARLOTTE, FLAN
—topped with flour, etc	CRUMBLE
—with	
cream and sugar	FOOL, MOUSSE
custard, cream, etc	TRIFLE
ice-cream	BANANA SPLIT
	PEACH MELBA
	PEAR BELLE HELENE, SUNDAE
	TUTTI-FRUTTI
rice pudding	CONDE
fudge with eggs, sugar, etc	DIVINITY
gelatine	JELLY
Greek	BACLAVA, BAKLAVA
heavy pudding	STICKJAW
Hebrew	CHOROSET
ice-cream dishes	BOMBE, COUPE
—flavoured frozen water	WATER-ICE
—in tall glasss	KNICKERBOCKER GLORY

—Indian	KULFI
—Italian	MELA STREGATA
	SEMI-FREDDO
—with	
bananas	BANANA SPLIT
coloured layers	NEAPOLITAN
fruit, etc	CASSATA, SUNDAE
mixed fruits	TUTTI-FRUTTI
nuts and rum	TORTONI
peaches	PEACH MELBA
pears	PEAR BELLE HELENE
sponge, served hot	BAKED ALASKA
Indian	GULAB YAM
Italian	GRANITA, TIRAMISU
	ZUPPA INGLESE
jam tart (US)	CUPID
jelly from oat-husks	FLUMMERY
	SOWANS, SOWENS
light pastry with filling	PUFF
like a cake	CABINET PUDDING
made in a small mould	DARIOLE
meringue	PAVLOVA
	QUEEN OF PUDDINGS
	VACHERIN
milk dishes	(BAKED) CUSTARD
	BLANCMANGE
	CARAMEL CREAM, CORNFLOUR
	JUNKET, MACARONI
	MILK PUDDING, RENNET
	RICE PUDDING, SAGO
	SEMOLINA, TAPIOCA
mixed fruits	TUTTI-FRUTTI
molasses on pastry crumble	SHOO-FLY PIE
pancake	
—filled	FRENCH PANCAKE
—flaming	CREPE SUZETTE
—Russian	BLIN(I)
—thin	BLINTZ(E)
pastry	
—case, filled	FLAN, PIE, TART
—topping	CRUMBLE
—with	
almond-flavoured	
filling	MAID OF HONOUR
fruit	MILLE-FEUILLES
soft filling	CHEESECAKE
	(see also **pastry**)
quinces and sugar	QUIDDANY
rice and milk, etc	MILK PUDDING
	RICE PUDDING
sandwich with jam and	
jelly filling	WASHINGTON PIE
Scottish	ATHOLL BROSE
sesame seeds and honey	HALVA(H)
shaved ice, flavoured	SNOWBALL
sliced fruit with ice cream	SPLOT

small	
—confection	KISS
—tart	TARTLET
soft, spongy confection	MARSHMALLOW
sponge cake, jelly,	
custard, etc	TRIFLE
sponge pudding	EVE'S PUDDING
	JAMAICA PUDDING
	MARBLED PUDDING
	STEAMED CASTLE PUDDING
—enclosing cream	CHARLOTTE RUSSE
steamed	CHRISTMAS PUDDING
	PLUM PUDDING, SPOTTED DICK
	SPOTTED DOG, TREACLE PUDDING
suet pudding with filling	ROLY-POLY
sugar, water and flavouring	FONDANT
sweet	
—batter	PANCAKE
filled	FRENCH PANCAKE
—pancake	CREPE
flaming	CREPE SUZETTE
tart	BAKEWELL, FRUIT PIE, MINCE PIE
thin pastry with	
fruit filling	STRUDEL
Turkish	HALVA(H), HALAVAH
water-ice	FRAPPE, GRANITA
	SHERBE(R)T, SORBET
with ice-cream (US)	A LA MODE

detectives

in fiction:

African	ZONDI
American	ARCHER, EDWARDS, HAMMER
	HELM, JOHNSON, JONES
	MARLOWE, QUEEN, ROME
	SPADE, SPENSER, URTH
	VAN DUSEN, WARSHAWSKI (f)
	WOLFE
Belgian	POIROT
British	APPLETON, BLAKE, BROWN
	CAMPION, COFFIN, DALGLEISH
	DALZIEL, FORTUNE, GETHRYN, HOLMES
	LOVE, MARPLE (f), MORSE, TRENT
	WIMSEY, WEXFORD
Chinese	CHAN
Dutch	VAN DER VALK
French	DUPIN, MAIGRET
Icelandic	HJERSON
Indian	GHOTE
Irish	MINOGUE
Japanese	IMANISHI, MOKO, OTANI
Navajo	LEAPHORN
Swedish	WAHLOO
Turkish	ISKIRLAK

dialects

some dialect terms:

abide	WON

about	AWAY
accusation (N)	THREAP, THREEP
ache	WORK
active (N)	WIMBLE
adit	STULM
advancing swiftly	RAKING
affected	
—person	MIMMICK, MINNOCK
	MINNOCK
—with fear	EERIE, EERY
—with sickness	WAMBLY
afternoon snack	FOUR(SES)
aftertaste	TWANG
agitate	WHEMMLE, WHOMBLE
	WHOMMLE, WHUMMLE
agitated	HET UP
alert	SPRACK, SPRAG
all (N)	A
allow to be believed	LET ON
almost	MOST
along	ALONGST
amount carried at one journey (N)	RAKE
anemone	ENEMY
angry word	MISWORD
annual holiday	WAKE
ant	EMMET
anything shrivelled	SCRUMP, SKRIMP
	SKRUMP
apart from	OUTSIDE OF
approaching	TOWARD
apt	TOWARD
area mined (Cornwall)	SET
arouse	YERK
arrogant	COBBY
as	
—if about	LIKE
—it were	LIKE
—much as	WHAT
ass (E. Anglia)	DICK(E)Y
assertion (N)	THREAP, THREEP
astride	STRIDE-WAYS
	STRIDLING
at	
—hand	TOWARD
—least	LEAST(A)WAYS
attention	GAUM, GORM
autumn	HARVEST
awkward	UNGAIN
—girl (E. Ang)	MAUTHER
	MAWTHER
awn-removing machine	HUMMELLER
bait with dogs	SLATE
baited line for catching birds	TEAGLE
baker's peel	PALE
bar (N)	RANCE

—in chimney (N)	RANDLE-BALK
	RANDLE-PERCH, RANDLE-TREE
	RANNEL-TREE, RANNLE-TREE
	RANTLE-TREE
barge(N)	GABBARD, GABBART
bark	WAFF
barter	COPE
basket	WISKET
batter	DIALECT
be	
—off work (N)	PLAY
—over-dainty	MIMMICK, MINNICK
	MINNOCK
—painful	WORK
—peevish (N)	NATTER
—sparing	STINT
—twisted or warped	WIND
—untidy or slovenly	SLATTER
bearer of coffin	UNDERBEARER
beat	JO(U)LE, JOLL, JOWL
	POLT, YERK
—violently	WHITHER, WUTHER
because	CAUSE
bed of fireclay	THILL
bed-time	DOWN-LYING
beetle	CLOCK
behave in affected manner	MIMMICK, MINNICK
	MINNOCK
belch	YESK, YEX
belly	WAME
—band of cart-horse	WANTY
bellyful	WAMEFUL
bend	TREND
beneath	NEATH
benumb (SW)	SCRAM
besmirch	SLUR
best (N)	WALE
bewitch	BESPEAK, WISH
big man	COB
bilberry	WINE-BERRY
bind	YERK
bindweed	WITH(Y)WIND
birch	BIRK
biscuit (N)	PARKIN
bite	SNACK
blame	WITE, WYTE
blanket	WHITTLE
blast	WHITHER, WUTHER
bleat	WHICKER
blink	WAPPER
blinking	WAPPER-EYED
blow	DA(U)D, WHITHER, WUTHER
—(W)	SCAT
blustering	BLUFF
bodily build	SET

boggy	SPEWY
bogle (N)	BOGGARD, BOGGART
	BOGGLE
boisterous	RANDIE, RANDY
booby	PATCH
botch	BODGE
	MUX
bottle (with ears)	COSTREL
bounce	BANG
bound	MERE
boundary	MERE
—ridge	LINCH(ET), LYNCHET
—stone	MERESTONE
branch	GRAIN, SHROUD
brawl	FRATCH
brawling	FRATCH(ET)Y
bread soaked in gravy	BREVIS
breastbone	HEART-SPOON
breccia (N)	BROCKRAM
bring forth young	YEAN
brisk	COBBY, KEDGE, KEDGY
	KIDGE, YARE
brood	TEAM
broil (N)	BRU(I)LZE
broth	BREVIS
brushwood	RICE
bugbear (N)	BOGGARD, BOGGART
	BOGGLE
bullroarer	HUMBUZZ
bumblebee	DUMBLEDORE
bump	JO(U)LE, JOLL, JOWL
bunch	BOB
bundle of hay	WAP
burn	SCALD
burning ember	GLEED
burrow	BURY
burst (N)	BRAST
buss	SMOUCH
bustle about	WHEW
buttermilk (N)	KIRN-MILK, WHIG
cairn (N)	RAISE
candle-snuffer	SNASTE
capsize	WHEMMLE, WHOMBLE
	WHOMMLE, WHUMMLE
careful	EYEFUL
carp	YERK
carrier	TRANTER
cart with last	
harvest load	HOCKCART
cartload	FOTHER, SEAM
cat-fish (N)	WOOF
catch with a bird-line	TEAGLE
cattle	
—dung	TATH
—shed	SHIPPEN, SHIPPON
caught	CATCHED, CATCHT

caul (N)	KELL
cause to stoop (SW)	STEEP
causing sickness	WAMBLY
cavity in rock (Cornwall)	VUG
celebration drink	BEVERAGE
chaffinch	SPINK
chain	TEAM
change one's clothes	SHIFT
changeable	WANKLE
chap	SPRAY, SPREATHE, SPREETHE
	SPREAZE, SPREEZE
chapped	SPRAID, SPRAYED
charm	COMETHER
chat	COSHER
chatter	MAG
cheat	FUGLE, MUMP
cheerful	CADGY
cheese-scoop	PALE
chide	BAN
children	CHILDER
chimney	CHIMLEY, CHUMLEY
chitterlings	CHIDLINGS, CHITLINGS
choice (N)	WALE
choose/choosing (N)	WALE
chubby	CHUFF, FUBBY, FUBSY
chum	BUTTY
churn (N)	KIRN
circus tumbler	JERRY-COME-TUMBLE
clamp	HOG
clean out (ditch)	FAY, FEY
clear (N)	REMBLE
climbing plant	WITH(Y)WIND
clip	DOD
clog	CLAM
closed handful	NIEVEFUL
clot	LOPPER
clover	SUCKLING
clown	JOSKIN
club-foot	POLTFOOT
clump	TUMP
clumsy	GAUMLESS, GORMLESS
	UNHEPPEN
—person (Cornwall)	LERRUP
cluster	BOB
coal-box	DAN
coarse grass	TATH
coax	CARN(E)Y
cockchafer	BUZZARD-CLOCK
	DUMBLEDORE
	HUMBUZZ
coddle	COSHER
collapse (W)	SCAT
comb	KEMB
combed	KEMPT
comely	GAINLY, LIKELY, TIDY
comfortable (N)	CANNY

commotion	FRAISE
comrade	BUTTY
conceal	HEAL, HEEL, HELE
conceited	CONCEITY
confoundedly	GALLOWS, MORTAL
confuse	MOIDER, MOITHER
confused sound	WHOOBUB
confusion	DUDDER, WHEMMLE
	WHOMBLE
	WHOMMLE, WHUMMLE
conical hill	PAP
connecting ridge	HALSE, HAUSE, HAWSE
consort	MAKE, SORT
conspire	COLLOGUE
contemptible	CRUDDY
contend strongly with	PINGLE
contract miners	BUTTY-COLLIER(S)
	BUTTY-GANG
contrary	CONTRAIR
convenient	GAIN
coolness	COOLTH
corn	
—marigold	GOLD
—spurrey	YARR
Cornish pasty	OGGY
cough	HOAST
country bumpkin	JOSKIN
courageous	WIGHT
cover	HEAL, HEEL, HELE
—with	
dish	WHEMMLE, WHOMBLE
	WHOMMLE, WHUMMLE
soil	HELE IN
cow	
—dung	SHARN
—dung and coal cake	SHARNY PEAT
—house	SHIPPEN, SHIPPON
cow's yield	MESS
crane-fly	JENNY-SPINNER
creak	FRATCH
creature	WIGHT
creek	WICK
crisp	CRUMPY
croak	CRAKE
crook	CROMB, CROME
cross	FRANZY
crouch	DARE
crow	CRAKE
crowberry	CRAKEBERRY
crowd	MONG
crumbly	NESH
cry-baby	MARDY
cunning	VARMENT, VARMINT
—mischief (N)	PAWK
cur (N)	TYKE
curd	CRUD

curdle	LOPPER, RUN, WHIG
	(Y)EARN
currant cake (N)	SINGING-HINNY
customer	CHAPMAN
cut the hair of	DOD
dace (N)	GRAINING
dally	PINGLE
damaged piece of cloth (N)	FENT
damnably	GALLOWS
dampness	CLAM
dangerous (N)	NO'CANNY
dash	DAD, DAUD
dashing	VARMENT, VARMINT
daze	GALLY
deaf	DUNNY
decent	GRADELY, GRAITHLY
decomposed rock (Cornwall)	GOSSAN
	GOZZAN
decoy	TOLE, TOLL
defective mentally	WANTING
defile	HALSE, HAUSE, HAWSE
defilement	MOIL
deformed person	URCHIN
degree	GRE(E)CE, GRECIAN
	GRE(E)SE, GREESING, GRESSING
	GRI(E)CE, GRISE, GRIZE
demure	MIM(-MOU'D)
depression in breast	HEART-SPOON
destructive	VENGEABLE
devour	SCOFF, SKOFF
die	SWELT
dig	GRAFT
diminutive person	NIFF-NAFF
dirt	CROCK
disease of horse's hoof	FRUSH
disgusting	MAWKISH
dismayed	DARE
dispense with	WANT
dispute (N)	THREAP, THREEP
dissolute	OUTWARD
distinctive flavour	TACK
ditch	GRAFT
—(SW)	REAN, REEN, RHINE
division of county (N)	WARD
do	
—anything briskly	LILT
—without	WANT
dog (N)	TYKE
donkey	CUDDIE, CUDDY
doorpost	DURN
doze	DARE
drain	SEW, SILE
drainage canal	EA(U)
draining-shaft	STULM
dram	TIFT
draw tight (stitches)	YERK

drawl	DRA(UN)T	failure to understand	ANAN
dress up	BUCK	fair	PLAYING
drink	TIFT	fairy (SW)	PISKY
—money	BEVERAGE	faith	FAIX
drinker (N)	BIRLER	falsehood	LEASING
drone	DRA(U)NT	fantastical	CONCEITED
drop dung	TATH	farm	WICK
drudge	MOIL	farthing	FARDEN, FARDING
dwell	WON	fascinated	DARE
earliest	RATHEST	fast	
early		—horse	GANGER
—fruit or vegetables	HASTINGS	—pace	RAKER
—ripe (variety)	RATH(E)RIPE	fastidious person	QUIDDLE(R)
earwig	FORIT-TAIL, FORKY-TAIL	fat clumsy woman	HORSE-GODMOTHER
easily handled	YARE	favourable	TOWARD
eat with feeble		feeble	WEARISH
appetite	PINGLE	feeling of nausea	WAMBLE
eerie	UNKED, UNKET, UNKID	ferrule	VERREL
egg	COCKNEY	fertile	BATTLE
either	OUTHER	festival	PLAYING
elaborate flowerbed	KNOT	fibre	VIVER
embankment (N)	STAITH(E)	film (N)	KELL
embrace	HALSE, HAUSE, HAWSE	finch	SPINK
enclose	TINE	fine	GRADELY, GRAITHLY
enclosed hollow part	WAME	—Oxford	SCONCE
end	SHANK	fireside ledge	STOCK
—of season	BACK-END	fish-pond	VIVER
endearment	PIGSN(E)Y, PIGSNIE	fish-trap	WEEL
endure	ABEAR	fist	NEIF, NEIVE, NIEF, NIEVE
engage in with energy	YERK	fit	GRADELY, GRAITHLY
ensnare	SNARL	—of perversity	GEE
equal	MAKE	flap	FLACKER
escort (N)	SET	flared	FLEW, FLUE
eve	E'EN, EVEN	flat	FLEW, FLUE
everybody (N)	A'BODY	—basket	TRUG
every way (N)	A'GATE	flattery	CARN(E)Y
everywhere (N)	A'WHERE	flexible rod	WATTLE
ewe	YOW(E)	flight of steps	GRE(E)CE, GRECIAN
excavation	GRAFT		GRE(E)SE, GREESING
exceedingly	MAIN		GRESSING, GRI(E)CE
except	NOBBUT, ONLY		GRISE, GRIZE
	OUTSIDE OF, WITHOUT	floor	PLANCH
exchange	COPE, TOLSEL	—of coal-seam	THILL
	TOLSEY, TOLZEY	flounder about	TOLTER
excite loathing in	UG	fluffy	PLUFFY
exert oneself	PINGLE	flutter	FLACKER
exit (N)	OUTGATE	fly wide (hawk)	RAKE
expert	SLY	fodder	FOTHER
express yearning	YAMMER	follow scent (dog)	RAKE
expression of		fool	MUMCHANCE
—commendation	FAIR	foolish person	GUMP
courtesy	FAIR	foot-rot	HALT
extremely	MORTAL	forget	MISREMEMBER
eye	WINKER	fork	GRAIN
fade away	WALLOW	form into single file (N)	RAKE
faggot	KNITCH	forward	FORRAD

fowl	BIDDY
framework for corn-stack	HOVEL
freckle	FAIRNITIC(K)LE
	FERN(I)TIC(K)LE
	FERNYTIC(K)LE
friendly	CADGY
frightened	FRIT
frog of horse's hoof	FRUSH
frolic	GAMMOCK
frolicsome	CADGY
fuddle	FUZZLE
fuel (N)	ELDIN(G)
full cloth or yarn	WALK
fumes (SW)	SMEECH
fun	GAMMOCK, GIG
fungus for tinder	SPUNK
fuss	WORK
fusty	FROWSY, FROWZY
gable	GAVEL
gang (N)	RAKE
gap	SHARD, SHERD
garfish	HORNBEAK
gasp	CHINK
—(N)	KINK
gather windfalls	SCRUMP, SKRIMP, SKRUMP
geld	LIB
get	
—by begging	MUMP
—on well	GEE
—over	OVERGET
—together with an effort	SCAMBLE
getting on	TOWARD
ghost	GYTRASH
gid or sturdy in sheep	DUNT
gin and treacle	MAHOGANY
gird	YERK
girl	GAL
—East Anglia	MAUTHER, MAWTHER
give birth prematurely	WARP
glean	LEASE
glimpse	WHIFF
gluey material	LIME
go	GEE
—about	
idly	SAMP
noisily	CLUTTER
—astray	MISGO
—courting	WENCH
—easy (N)	CA'CANNY
—short	STINT
goad	BROD
goat (N)	GATE
goblin	
—in mine	KNOCKER
—(N)	BOGGARD, BOGGART
	BOGGLE

good	
—condition	KELTER, KILTER
—even	GOD-DEN
—number	THR(E)AVE
good-for-nothing	DONNAT, DONNOT
gooseberry	GOOSEGOG, WINE-BERRY
graceful	GAINLY
grandfather	GRANFER
grass (N)	HAVER
grating in river	HECK
grease on side of	
candle	WINDING-SHEET
great deal	MORT
greater spotted	
woodpecker	WITWALL
green woodpecker	HICKWALL, WITWALL
greyhound	GREW(HOUND)
grilse	PEAL, PEEL
grimace	MUMP
ground ivy	GILL
grumble	CHUNNER, CHUNTER
hair-net (N)	KELL
halter for hanging	WIDDY
hamper	PED
hand	DADDLE
handle	HANDFAST, STALE
	STEAL(E), STEEL
	STEIL, STELE
—on scythe shaft	NIB
handy	GEMMY, JEMMY
hanging clock (N)	WAG-AT-THE-WALL
	WAG-BY-THE-WALL
hangman's rope	WIDDY
happy chance	MERCY
harangue	SPEECH
harass	PINGLE
hard	
—blow	POLT
—work (Cornwall)	LOUSTER
hardened cutting edge	FIRE-EDGE
harmless (N)	CANNY
harsh word	MISWORD
harvest	
—home	HAWKEY, HOCKEY, HORKEY
—supper	HAWKEY, HOCKEY, HORKEY
have a mind to	MIND
having an eye	EYEFUL
hawker	TRANTER
he	A
head-pad	WASE
heap	TASS
heap (waste)	BING
heart of rotten tree	DADDOCK
hearty kiss	SMOUCH
heated	HET
heed	GAUM, GORM

help in need	BEETMISTER
helter-skelter	LIKE HEY-GO-MAD
hiccup	YESK, YEX
hidden	DE(A)RN
hide	HEAL, HEEL, HELE
hillcrest	KNAP
hillock	KNAP, TOFT, TUMP
him	UN
hither and thither	HITHER AND YON(D)
hobgoblin	BULLBEGGAR
hoist	TEAGLE
hold	HOLT
hollo	HOLLER
hollow enclosed part	WAME
homeward	UP ALONG
honey (N)	HINNY
honeysuckle	SUCKLING
hook	CROMB, CROME
hop about	LILT
horizontal mine-prop	STULL
horse	CUDDIE, CUDDY
	KEFFEL
—belly-band	WANTY
—block	JOSS-BLOCK
hot coal	GLEED
however	LEAST(A)WAYS
hubbub	WHOOBUB
hummocky	TUMPY
hunchback	URCHIN
hurdle	WATTLE
hurdy-gurdy	HUMSTRUM
hurt	NOY
husband	MASTER
hussy	HUZZY
I	A, CHE
—am	CHAM
—have	CHAVE
—will	CHILL
idler (N)	DONNAT, DONNOT
ill	QUEER
—natured person	PATCH
—tempered	STINGY
imbecile	INNOCENT
impending	TOWARD
improve	BEET, BETE
in	
—good	
condition or order	TIDY
spirits	PEART, PIERT
—order to	FOR TO
—poor health	INDIFFERENT
—the direction facing one	TOWARD
inclined	LIKE
inconvenient	UNGAIN
indict	TROUNCE
indirect	UNGAIN

infect(ion) (N)	SMIT
infectious (N)	SMITTLE
inferior asparagus (London)	SPRUE
inflate	BLAST
information	WITTING
infuse	MASH
inner door	HECK
innocent (N)	CANNY
insipid	MAWKISH
insist (N)	THREAP, THREEP
interjection of	
—excitement	HEY-GO-MAD
—surprise	LAWK(S)
inward	TOWARD
iris	GLADDON
it	A
itch(ing)	EWK, (Y)EUK, YOUK
	YUCK, YUKE
jack (bowls) (N)	KITTY
jail (N)	KITTY
jaw (N)	CHAFT
join	PIECEN
journey (N)	RAKE
jumping pole (E. Ang)	QUANT
keep from one year	
to next	OVERYEAR
keep scratching (W)	SCRATTLE
kick	WINCE, YERK
—(N)	PUNCH
kid	YEANLING
kindle	TIND
kiss	SMOUCH
knock	CON, JO(U)LE, JOLL, JOWL
—(N)	SCAT
knowledge	WITTING
known	BEKNOWN
labour	MOIL
ladder	STY
lamb	YEANLING
lame	GAMMY, MAIN
lament	YAMMER
lane between	
—houses	ENTRY
—walls or hedges	TWITTEN
lapwing	TEW(H)IT
larder	SPENCE
large beetle	CLOCKER
lark about	GAMMOCK
lash out with	YERK
last	YESTERN
late autumn	BACK-END
latter part	SHANK
lay eggs prematurely	WARP
lean from loin of pork	GRISKIN
leap(ed)	LEP
lease	SET

leash	TRASH
leave undisturbed	LET-A-BE
ledge	LINCH(ET), LYNCHET
leg	PESTLE
Lent boat races (Oxford)	TORPIDS
let	SET
letter z	IZZARD, IZZET
level a measure of grain	STRIKE
lie	LIG
—(N)	LIG(GE), LIGGEN
lies/lying	LEASING
lift	TEAGLE
light cart (N)	SHANDRY(DAN)
lightly cooked (eggs)	RARE
likely	LIKE
linger about	HANKER
liquid filth	ADDLE
litter	TEAM
little	LEET, LITE, LYTE
—pig	GRICE
—things	FEWTRILS
lively	COBBY, KEDGE
	KEDGY, KIDGE, PEART, PIERT
—(N)	KIPPER
load	FOTHER
—(N)	RAKE
loaf	MICHE
loathe	UG
loathly (N)	LAIDLY
loathsome	MAWKISH
loft (W)	TALLAT, TALLET, TALLOT
lonely	UNKED, UNKET, UNKID
long	SIDE
loose woman	MORT
lop(pings)	SHROUD
lore (N)	LARE
lounge about	HAWM
lout	LOBLOLLY
low	
—hill	HOW
—(N)	LAW
—stool	CRICKET
—whisper	PIG'S-WHISPER
lower part of door	HECK
luce	GED
lump	DAD, DAUD
	GOB, LUNCH
lunch	TIFT
lure	TOLE, TOLL
lurk	DARE
madam	MISTRESS
maggot(y)	MAWK(ISH)
maim	MAIN
maimed	GAMMY
maintain persistently (N)	THREAP
	THREEP

make	
—a	
harsh noise	FRATCH
mess of	BOSS
mound around	TUMP
sullen roaring	WHITHER, WUTHER
—an outcry	YAMMER
—progress by great effort	THRUTCH
—ready (Cornwall)	TEEL
—tea	WET
mall (N)	MELL
man	MUN
manageable	YARE
manner of doing (N)	GATE
manure	TATH
marble	MARL
marbled	MARLED, MARLY, MIRLY
mark	
—off	MERE
—with ruddle (N)	SMIT
marshy spot	SPEW, SPUE
maslin	MONGCORN, MUNGCORN
match	SPUNK
mate	MAKE
maudlin	MAWKISH
maul (N)	MELL
may (past tense)	MOUGHT
mean	FOOTY
mediator	STICKLER
mend	BEET, BETE
mentally	
—defective	WANTING
—normal	WISE
mess	MUX
mild explosion	PLUFF
militiaman	LUMP
milk-strainer	SYE
mine (Cornwall)	WHEAL
mining lease (Cornwall)	SET
mischievous	GALLOWS
missel thrush	THROSTLE-COCK
misshapen egg	COCKNEY
mixture	MONG
moderately warm	LUKE
mole	WANT
mop	MALKIN, MAWKIN
mope	MUMP
more forward	FORRADER
most convenient	EFTEST
mouch	MICHE
mould-board	PLAT
mouldy	FOUGHTY
mouthful	GOB
move	QUATCH, QUETCH
	QUITCH
—diagonally	CATER(CORNER)

—swiftly or with force	WHITHER, WUTHER
—tremulously	WAPPER
—unsteadily	WAMBLE
—with a jerk	YERK
mow	TASS
mowing	MATH
much	MORT
—(N)	MICKLE, MUCKLE
mud (N)	SLAKE
—flat (N)	SLAKE
mumble	MUMP
munch	MUMP
murderer	MURTHERER
musical instrument	HUMSTRUM
must	MAN, M(A)UN
musty	FOUGHTY
mutter	CHUNNER, CHUNTER
	MUMP
nag (horse)	KEFFEL
nail	BROD
nape of neck	NODDLE, SC(R)UFF, SCUFT
natty	VARMENT, VARMINT
near	GAIN
neat	GEMMY, JEMMY
neck	
—and spine of	
forequarter	RACK
—neck (N)	HALSE, HAUSE, HAWSE
neigh	WHICKER
neighbour	BOR
network (N)	KELL
never a ...	NARY
newt	ASK(ER)
next	NEIST
nighest	NEIST
nightjar	EVEJAR
nimble	WAN(D)LE, WANNEL, WIGHT
—(N)	WIMBLE
nipple	PAP
noise	CLUTTER
nonsense	FADDLE
normal mentally	WISE
not	
—dangerous (N)	CANNY
—one	NARY
—to be depended upon	WANKLE
—well	INDIFFERENT
notable man	COB
notice	GAUM, GORM, MIND
nourishing	BATTLE
now for	HEY FOR
nozzle	TEWEL
oak sapling	FLITTERN
oat-bread (N)	JANNOCK
oats (N)	HAVER
occasion	WHET

odd piece of cloth (N)	FENT
of	ON
—good omen	CANNY
—stone	STONERN
off we go	HEY FOR
offensive	FROWSY, FROWZY
on	
—acccount	LONG
of	ALONG
—hand	TOWARD
—the near or left side	TOWARD
one	UN
—who	
picks	PIKER
thrives	WELL-DOER
only	NOBBUT
ooze	SEW
open shed	LINHAY, LINNY
osier	
—pike-trap	KIPE
—rope	WIDDY
otter's den	HOLT
out-and-out	FAIR, TEETOTAL
outing	OUT
outlet (N)	OUTGATE
overcoat	JAMES, JEMMY
overcome	MOIDER, MOITHER
overthrow	WHEMMLE, WHOMBLE
	WHOMMLE, WHUMMLE
overturn	WHEMMLE, WHOMBLE
	WHOMMLE, WHUMBLE
oyster spawn	CUL(T)CH
pack-horse load	SEAM
pad on head	WASE
pamper	COSHER
pannier	PED
pantry	SPENCE
paralyse (SW)	SCRAM
parlour	KEEPING-ROOM
part of	
—leg of beef	MUSCLE
—spinning machine	HECK
parting gift	FOY
partition	TRAVIS, TREVIS(S)
partner	BUTTY
pass	HALSE, HAUSE, HAWSE
pasture	LEASE, LEAZE, LEASOW(E)
—(N)	RAKE
path (N)	GATE
pawky (N)	CANNY
pay attention to	GAUM, GORM
pedlar woodturner	BODGER
peel	PILL
peevish	FRANZY
peony	PINY
perch (E. Ang)	PERK

—(N)	PERK	proceed	RAKE
period of work	YOLE	profitable occupation	THRIFT
person	WIGHT	projecting under-jaw	WAPPER-JAW
pet name (cow, etc)	MOG(GY)	promptly	YARELY
petticoat	COAT	prong	GRAIN
petulant child	MARDY	pronounce	TONGUE
phosphorescence (sea)	BRIMING	prop (in mine)	STULL
physiognomy	VISNOMIE, VISNOMY	—(N)	RANCE
pick	PIKE	proper(ly)	GRADELY, GRAITHLY
—(N)	WALE	prostrate	FELL
pike	GED	protuberance	KNAP
pile (waste)	BING	protuberant part	WAME
pilfer	MICHE	public fountain (N)	PANT
pilferer	PIKER	puddle (N)	PANT
pit of stomach	HEART-SPOON	puff	PLUFF
pitch (N)	PICK	puffed up	PLUFFY
plank of oak	FLITTERN	pull	
plantain	WAYBREAD	—by the ears	SOOLE, SOWL(E)
play (N)	LAKE, LAIK	—quickly or roughly	WAP
—the beggar	MUMP	punch	POUNCE
—truant	MICHE	punt mooring-pole	RIPECK, RY(E)PECK
pleaded	PLED	punting pole (E. Ang.)	QUANT
pleasing	LIKELY	puny	WEARY
pliant	WAN(D)LE, WANNEL	—(SW)	SCRAM
plough		puppet	PUPPY
—chain	TEAM	purge	WORK
—handle	STILT	put in pickle	PUT DOWN
plump	TIDY	quake	WAMBLE
plunder	SCOFF, SKOFF	quantity	FOTHER
plunge in betting	RAKER	quarrel	FRATCH, OUTFALL, WHID
poke	PEG, POACH, POTE, PROKE	quarrelling	FRATCH(ET)Y
pole	PERCH	quick	YARE
poll	DOD	quickly	YARELY
pollard	DOD	quill	TWILL
pond	POUND	quilt	TWILT
porridge-stick (N)	THIBLE, THIVEL	quitch	QUICK(EN)
post	STOOP, STOUP	quite	FAIR
postman	POST	rack	
pot-bellied	KEDGE, KEDGY, KIDGE	—and manger	HECK AND MANGER
potato	TATER	—for fodder	HECK
pour in a stream	HUSH	ragged-Robin	WILD-WILLIAMS
powder-puff	PLUFF	raid orchards	SCRUMP, SKRIMP
practise crystal-gazing	SCRY		SKRUMP
praise	ROOSE	rail	BAN
pre-breakfast snack	MORNING	rain heavily	SILE
prepared	YARE	raised footpath	CLAPPER
preserve	PUT DOWN	ramify	SPRANGLE
press	THRUTCH	range about	RAKE
—eagerly (N)	THREAP, THREEP	rapid (SW)	STICKLE
pretend	LET ON	rat	RATTON, ROTTAN, ROTTEN
preternatural (N)	NO'CANNY	raven	CRAKE
pretty drunk	FAIRISH	readiest	EFTEST
prick	BROD	readily	GRADELY, GRAITHLY
prim	MIM(-MOU'D)	ready	YARE
prize	GREE	—to learn	TOWARD
probable	LIKE	rebuke (N)	THREAP, THREEP

recked (N)	RECKAN
recover from	OVERGET
red	
—apple (SW)	QUARANTINE
QUARENDEN, QUAR(R)ENDER	
QUARRINGTON	
—currant	WINE-BERRY
reed thicket (E. Ang.)	REED-RAND
REED-ROND	
refuge	HOLT
regard	GAUM, GORM
relating to yesterday	YESTERN
relieve	BEET, BETE
remind	REMEMBER
remnant (N)	FENT
remove (N)	REMBLE
—sprouts from	SPROUT
—stalk from (S)	STRIG
—to a distance	FAR
rend	RENT
reproach	WITE, WYTE
respectable	SPONSIBLE
responsible	SPONSIBLE
restrain	STINT
restraining hold	HANK
restraint	TRASH
rick in barn	GOAF
ricked (N)	RECKAN
ridge of land	STITCH
riot	WHOOBUB
rise	PLUFF
—with a jerk	YERK
river	EA(U)
roam	RAKE
rolling	
—in the stomach	WAMBLE
—movement	WAMBLE
roofing slab	SLAT
rootlet	VIVER
rope	WIDDY
—for securing hay	WANTY
rough	ROW
—bridge	CLAPPER
—mannered fellow (N)	TYKE
roughen	SPRAY, SPREATHE
SPREETHE, SPREAZE, SPREEZE	
roughened	SPRAID, SPRAYED
rouse	YERK
rowing-bench	THOFT
rubbish	CUL(T)CH
rump	NATCH
rung	SPELL
running water	EA(U)
rush	FEEZE, PHE(E)SE, PHEEZE
—basket	JUNKET
—of water	HUSH

sad	WO(E)
saddler	WHITTAW(ER)
sandwich	BUTTY
saucy	PEART, PIERT
scare	GALLY, SKEAR, SKEER
scarecrow	BOGGARD, BOGGART, BOGGLE
GALLYBAGGER, GALLYBEGGAR	
MALKIN, MAWKIN	
GALLICROW, GALLYCROW	
scatter	SCAMBLE
school	SCUL(L), SCULLE
scolding	HEARING
scope of choice (N)	WALE
scorch	SCALD, SCRAT
scratch	SCRAWM
screech	SHRITCH
scrimmage (Eton)	ROUGE
scuttle (W)	SCRATTLE
sea	
—bird of various kinds	TARROCK
—mist (E. coast)	HAAR
—weed	ORE, WARE
second boat or crew (Oxford)	TORPID
second-year salmon (N)	SPROD
secondary rainbow	WATER-GALL
secret	DE(A)RN
sedge	SEG
separate	SLEAVE
set	TILL
—on	SLATE
sewage	ADDLE
sewer	(COMMON-)SHORE
shaft	STALE, STEAL(E)
STEEL, STEIL, STELE	
—of vehicle	LIMBER
shake	DIDDER
shall (N)	SAL
shallot	SCALLION
shallow	FLEET, FLEW, FLUE
shamble	SCAMBLE
shank	STALE, STEAL(E)
STEEL, STEIL, STELE	
shape surface of mould	STRIKE
shapely	GAINLY, TIDY
sharp	VARMENT, VARMINT
—flavour	TWANG
she	A
sheaf of corn on end	GAIT
shed (N)	SHADE
ship's medicine	LOBLOLLY
shirt	SHIFT
shock of corn	STITCH
shoe sole	TAP
shoes	SHOON
shoot	CHIT, PLUFF
shore (N)	RANCE

short	
—and thick	PUNCH
—piece of cloth (N)	FENT
—rope	WANTY
shot	PLUFF
shove	THRUTCH
shovel	SHOOL
showy woman (N)	BOBBY DAZZLER
shrewd (N)	CANNY
shriek	SHRITCH
shrink	DARE
shrivel up	SCRUMP, SKRIMP
	SKRUMP
shrunk	WEARISH
shut	SHET, TINE
sick	QUEER
—at stomach	WAMBLE-CROPPED
sickly	MAWKISH
sieve	SYE
sigh	SITHE
sightly	EYEFUL
simpleton	GABY, ZANY
sip	TIFT
sit	SET
sitting-room	KEEPING-ROOM
skewer	SKIVER
skilful (N)	CANNY
skilfully	YARELY
skilled	
—amateur sportsman	VARMENT
	VARMINT
—in magic	WISE
skirt	COAT
skirting-board	WASH-BOARD
skulk	MICHE
slap	TWANK
slate	SLAT
slater	HELLIER
slatternly woman	BESOM
slice of meat	COLLOP
slight shower	SKIT
slime (N)	SLAKE
slimy material	LIME
slink	MICHE
slip	SLIVE
slipped	SLIVED, SLIVEN, SLOVE
slippery	GLIDDER
slop about	SLATTER
sloppy	SOZZLY
slops	SOZZLE
slow	LATE
slumber (N)	SLOOM
slush	LOPPER
slut	DRAZEL
sly (N)	CANNY
smack	SMOUCH, TACK, TWANG

small	
—branch	RICE
—enclosure (N)	PIGHTLE
—gate	HATCH
—landholder (N)	STATESMAN
—potato	CHAT
smart	GEMMY, JEMMY, SPIFF(Y)
smear	CLAM, SLUR
smoke	SMEECH
smooth	STRIKE
smothered laugh (N)	SNIRT
smut	CROCK
snack	BEVER, BUTTY
snail	DODMAN
snap	SNACK
snare	GRIN
—for fish	WEEL
snicker (N)	SNIRTLE
snigger	WHICKER
soak through	SIPE
soft	NESH
—and brittle	FROUGHY, FROWY
—sandstone (SE)	HASSOCK
soldier	SO(D)GER
something	SUMMAT
somewhat	SUMMAT
sorry	WO(E)
sound of	
—blow or blast	WHITHER, WUTHER
—rushing water	HUSH
sour	
—liquor	TIFT
—milk	WHIG
southern-wood	LAD'S LOVE
sown (N)	SAWN
spade (N)	PICK
sparing with money (N)	CANNY
spark	SPUNK
sparrow	SPUG
speaker of seditious words	LEASING-MAKER
speckled	SPRECKLED
spell (W)	SCAT
spider	ATTERCOP
spike	BROD
spill	SHED, SLATTER
—about	SWATTER
spirited person	SPUNK
spit	YESK, YEX
splash	FLOUSE, FLOUSH
	SLATTER, SOZZLE
—about	SWATTER
splayed	FLEW, FLUE
splinter	SPELL
spoil	MUX
spoilt child	MARDY
sponge	MUMP

sport	GIG
—(N)	LAKE, LAIK
spot	MOIL
spotted	GAY
sprawl	SCAMBLE, SPRANGLE
sprightly	SPRACK, SPRAG
springtime	WARE
sprout	CHIT
spruce	SPIFF(Y)
squat	FUBBY, FUBSY
squatter	SWATTER
squeamish	MAWKISH
squeeze	SCRUZE
squirrel	SKUG
squirrel's nest	CAGE
staggering movement	WAMBLE
stain (N)	SMIT
stale liquor	TIFT
stalk	STALE
—(S)	STRIG
stall	TRAVIS, TREVIS(S)
stare	DARE
statesman (N)	ESTATESMAN
steal	MAG
steep	
—narrow valley	GRIFF(E)
—(SW)	STICKLE
step	GRE(E)CE, GRECIAN, GRE(E)SE
	GREESING, GRESSING, GRI(E)CE
	GRISE, GRIZE
stern	STARN
stir	CLUTTER, QUATCH
	QUETCH, QUITCH
—up	POACH
stone or earthenware	
vessel	STEAN, STEEN
store vegetables in clamp	HOG
stout	COBBY, STUGGY
straddle	STRODDLE
straggle	SPRANGLE
straggler	STRAG
straight	GAIN
straightforward	JANNOCK
strain	SILE, SYE
strainer	SILE(R)
strange	UNKED, UNKET, UNKID
stray	STRAG
street (N)	GATE
strenuous contest	PINGLE
stretch	
—of work	YOKE
—(N)	STREEK, STREAK
strickle	STRIKE
stride	STROAM
strike	FRAP, YERK
string (N)	RAKE
strip	UNSTRIP
strive	PINGLE
stroke	JO(U)LE, JOLL, JOWL
strong	WIGHT
strop	STRAP
structure for	
shipping coal	STAITH(E)
struggle	SPRANGLE
—with difficulties	PINGLE
stubble field	AR(R)ISH
stubborn insistence (N)	THREAP, THREEP
stuffy	FROWSY, FROWZY
stupefy	MOIDER, MOITHER
stupid	GAUMLESS, GORMLESS
—person	CUDDIE, CUDDY
sudden shower (W)	SCAT
suggestion	TWANG
suit	GEE
sulk	MUMP
superiority	GREE
supple	SOUPLE, WAN(D)LE
	WANNEL
supporting pillar	
of coal	STOOP, STOUP
surly	BLUFF
surveyor of boundaries	MERESMAN
suspect	SUSPICION
sweet yellow gooseberry	HONEY-BLOB
sweetmeats	SPICE
swell	BLAST, PLIM
swift	WIGHT
taint (N)	SMIT
tainted	FOUGHTY
take the chill off	CHILL
tall awkward person	GAMMERSTANG
talon	TALENT
tap	TIT
tare	TINE
tattle	TITTLE
tease	MAG
tender	NESH
tepid	LUKE
terrace	LINCH(ET), LYNCHET
territorial division (N)	WAPENTAKE
test cheese	PALE
than	AS, NOR
that	YON
—same	THILK
(SW)	THICK
thatcher	HELLIER
the (N)	T
—one	TONE
—same	THILK
(SW)	THICK
—thing you know of	YON
they	A

thick	
—gruel	LOBLOLLY
—slice	LUNCH
thick-set	STUGGY
—man	PUNCH
thin	
—liquor	TIFT
—mud	SLUR
third finger of left hand	RINGMAN
thirty	THRETTY
this	THILK
—(SW)	THICK
those	YON
thou shalt (N)	THOUS
thrash	PAY
—(N)	RADDLE
throat	HALSE, HAUSE, HAWSE
throb	QUOP
throw	YERK
—against	DAD, DAUD
—into disorder	WHEMMLE, WHOMBLE
	WHOMMLE, WHUMMLE
—quickly or roughly	WAP
—violently	WHITHER, WUTHER
thrust	PEG, POACH, POTE
	THRUTCH, YERK
—(N)	PUT
thump	DAD, DAUD
tidy up	FETTLE
tie with a jerk	YERK
tiler	HELLIER
till next year	OVERYEAR
time	WHET
timid child	MARDY
timorous	EERIE, EERY
titter	WHICKER
to	
—bankruptcy (W)	SCAT
—some extent	LIKE
toil	MOIL
tolerate	ABEAR
toll	JO(U)LE, JOLL, JOWL
—booth	TOLSEL, TOLSEY, TOLZEY
top of hill	KNOLL
totter	DADDLE
touch-down in football (Eton)	ROUGE
towed barge	BUTTY
town	WICK
track (N)	RAKE
traditional belief (N)	THREAP, THREEP
trap	GRIN
—in knur and spell	SPELL
treat with setterwort root (N)	SETTER
tremble	WHITHER, WUTHER
trick	FUGLE
—(N)	PAWK

trifle	FADDLE, NIFF-NAFF
	PINGLE, QUIDDLE
trifles	FEWTRILS
trifling	FADDLE
trivet (Cornwall)	BRANDISAF
trouble	NOY, WORK
trouser braces	GALLUSES
trousers (N)	KECKS, KICKS
tub	DAN
tug	PUG
tun	COWL
turmoil	MOIL
turn	
—around	WAMBLE
—of string	WAP
—over and over	WAMBLE
—up to cover something	WHELM
—upside down	WAMBLE, WHEMMLE
	WHOMBLE, WHOMMLE
	WHUMMLE
turnip	TURMIT
tuyere	TEWEL
twelve-month (N)	TOWMON(D)
	TOWMONT
twig	WATTLE
twigs	RICE
twinge	TWANG
twist	WAMBLE
two	
—dozen	THR(E)AVE
stooks of sheaves	THR(E)AVE
—handled mug (Oxford)	SCONCE
uncomfortable	UNKED, UNKET, UNKID
uncouth	UNKED, UNKET, UNKID
undefiled	UNFILED
underclay	THILL
underhand throw	HAUNCH
underlip	FIPPLE, JIB
underneath	UNNEATH
undersized person	SCRUMP, SKRIMP
	SKRUMP
understanding	GAUM, GORM
unkempt	FROWSY, FROWZY
unless	WITHOUT
unpleasant	UNGAIN
unploughed strip	LINCH(ET), LYNCHET
unprepossessing	UNLIKELY
unreliable	WANKLE
unskilled	UNGAIN
unstable	WANKLE
unsteady	WAMBLY, WANKLE
—movement	WAMBLE
until (N)	WHILE
unwind	REAVE, REEVE
unyielding	STOUT
up the road	UP ALONG

uproar	WHOOBUB	wicked	WICK
urge (N)	THREAP, THREEP	widow	WIDDY
utter jerkily	YERK	widower	WIDOW-MAN
vagrant	STRAG, WALKER	wield	WELD, WIND
vegetable store	HOG	wife	WOMAN
vein of ore (N)	RAKE	wild	
veritable	FAIR	—orchis	PIONY
vermin	VARMENT, VARMINT	—vetch	TINE
very	GRADELY, GRAITHLY	will	WULL
	RIGHT	willow basket	WILL(E)Y
—much	PURELY	willowing-machine	WILL(E)Y
—small	TIDDLEY, TIDD(L)Y	wind (round, etc)	REAVE, REEVE
vexation	NOY	wisp of hay, straw etc	WASE
victory	GREE	withered	WEARISH
vigorous	SPRACK, SPRAG	—(SW)	SCRAM
village	WICK	without a mate	MAKELESS
villainous	GALLOWS	witless	GAUMLESS, GORMLESS
visit for purpose		woman	MORT, PIECE OF GOODS
of begging	MUMP	woman's head-dress	KELL
voice	STEVEN	womb	WAME
wail	YAMMER	wood	TIMBER
wait for	WAIT ON	—louse	SLATE
walk	TRAVEL	—pecker	WITWALL
—unsteadily	DADDLE	—pigeon	ZOO-ZOO
wander		woollen shawl	WHITTLE
—idly about	STROAM	word incorrectly	MISWORD
—in mind	MOIDER, MOITHER	work	
wanton	CADGY	—done at one stretch	YOKING
—girl	GAMMERSTANG	—hard	MOIDER, MOITHER
warrant	WARN	—ineffectually	PINGLE
wassail (Oxford)	SWIG	—mate	BUTTY
watch-hill (SW)	TOOT	—or roll (stomach)	WAMBLE
water-channel to mill	LEAT, LEET	worry	FRAB, PINGLE
watercourse (SW)	REAN, REEN, RHINE		WORRIT
watery-looking sky	WATER-GALL	worse (N)	WAR(RE), WAUR
wave	WAFFLE	worst (N)	WA(U)RST
way (N)	GATE	wrap (E. Anglia)	HAP
wearisome journey	JAUNCE, JAUNSE	wreck	WRACK
well		wrest (N)	WRAST
—disposed	TOWARD	wrestle (SW)	WRAXLE
—nigh	WELLY	wretched	WO(E)
wet	WEET	wriggle	WAMBLE, WIND
wharf (N)	STAITH(E)	wrinkle	FRUMPLE
whatsoever	WHATSOMEVER	writhe	WIND
wheedle	CARN(E)Y	yellow flower (N)	GOLLAN(D)
wheedling	COMETHER		GOWLAND
where are you going?	WHERE AWAY	yellow-hammer	YITE
whey	WHIG	yonder	YON
which	WHILK	young	
whine	YAMMER	—ewe	THEAVE
whisper	TITTLE	—oak	FLITTERN
wholemeal bread	RAVEL(LED) BREAD	—pig	SLIP
wholeness (N)	HALENESS	—sea-trout	PEAL, PEEL
whooping cough	CHINCOUGH	—sow	(Y)ELT
whore's baby	WOSBIRD	Yorkshireman	TYKE
wick	SNASTE	yours	YOURN

digestive system

cells in tongue	TASTE-BUD, TASTE-BULB
contractions of intestines propelling contents	PERISTALSIS
digestive fluid secreted	
—by	
liver	BILE
small intestine	SUCCIS ENTERICUS
—into mouth	SALIVA
diseases of	(*see* **disease**)
downward displacement of intestines	ENTEROPTOSIS
gland producing	
—bile etc	LIVER
—insulin etc	PANCREAS
—saliva	SALIVARY GLAND
gut	ENTERON
inflammation of	
—stomach	GASTRITIS
—intestines	ENTERITIS
internal	
—bulge(s) or pocket(s) in large intestine	DIVERTICULUM(DIVERTICULI)
—protrusion(s) in small intestine	VILLUS(VILLI)
intestines	
—in embryo	ARCHENTERON
—large	ASCENDING COLON
	CAECUM
	DESCENDING COLON
	TRANSVERSE COLON
	(VERMIFORM) APPENDIX
—small	DUODENUM
	JEJUNUM, ILEUM
lowest part of coelom	SPLANCHNOCELE
lymph vessels	LACTEALS
main digestive organ	STOMACH
membrane enclosing	PERITON(A)EUM
opening from	
—exterior to oesophagus	MOUTH
—stomach to intestines	PYLORUS
organ of taste	TONGUE
passage from	
—intestines to anus	RECTUM
—liver to small intestine	BILE DUCT
—mouth to anus	ALIMENTARY CANAL
	ENTERON
gullet	PHARYNX
stomach	GULLET
	(O)ESOPGHAGUS
—rectum to exterior	ANUS
poison causing food-poisoning	ENTEROTOXIN
protrusion of	
—intestine into top of thigh	ENTEROCELE
	HERNIA, RUPIURE
—stomach into chest cavity	DIAPHRAGM HERNIA
	HIATUS HERNIA
puncture of stomach	ENTEROCENTESIS
regurgitation of wind	BORBORYGMUS
	FLATULENCE
secondary digestive system	BOWELS, INTESTINES
slow-acting	BRADYPEPTIC
space between intestines and body-wall	COELOM
stomach	
—animals	MAW
—birds	
first	CRAW, CROP, MAW
second	GIZZARD
—ruminants	
first	PAUNCH, RUMEN
second	RETICULUM
third	MANYPLIES, OMASUM
	PSALTERIUM
fourth	ABOMASUM, MAW, RENNET
stone in stomach	ENTEROLITH
store for bile	GALL-BLADDER
surgical	
—formation of opening	COLOSTOMY
	ENTEROSTOMY
	GASTROTOMY
—incision of part	ENTEROTOMY
	GASTROTOMY
—removal of part	ENTERECTOMY
	GASTRECTOMY
upper throat	FAUCES
virus in intestines	ENTEROVIRUS
dinosaur	(*see* **lizards**)
discoveries	
including: discoverer of proposer of	
actinium	DEBIERNE
Aids virus	GALLO, MONTAGNIER
America	COLUMBUS, LEIF ERIKSON
anti	
—biotics	DUBOS
—histamines	BOVET, UNGAR
—matter	ANDERSON
—proton	LEE
—toxin	BEHRING
argon	RAMSAY, STRUTT
artificial radio-activity	JOLIOT-CURIE
astatine	CORSON, MACKENZIE
	SEGRE

asteroid	
—Bambega	PALISA
—Camilla	POGSON
—Ceres	PIAZZI
—Cybele	TEMPEL
—Davida	DUGAN
—Egeria	DE GASPARIS
—Eros	WITT
—Eugenia	GOLDSCHMIDT
—Eunomia	DE GASPARIS
—Euphrosyne	FERGUSON
—Europa	GOLDSCHMIDT
—Hidalgo	BAADE
—Hygeia	DE GASPARIS
—Icarus	BAADE
—Interamnia	CERULLI
—Juno	HARDING
—Lorelei	PETERS
—Pallas	OLBERS
—Patentia	CHARLOIS
—Psyche	DE GASPARIS
—Sylvia	POGSON
—Themis	DE GASPARIS
—Toro	HERRICK
—Vesta	OLBERS
atomic	
—mass	LAVOISIER
—theory	DALTON
atropine	BRANDES
aureomycin	DUGGAN
Australia	COOK
background radiation	PENZIAS, WILSON
bacteria	COHN, LEEUWENHOEK
benzene	FARADAY
blood	
—circulation	HARVEY
—groups	LANDSTEINER
brainwaves	BERGER
caffeine	CAVENTOU, PELLETIER
calcium	DAVY
capillaries	MALPIGHI
carbolic acid	LISTER
carbon	
—14	KAMEN, RUBEN
—dating	LIBBY
carborundum	ACHESON
cell	
—nucleus	BROWN
—theory	SCHLEIDEN
cephalosporins	BROTZU
charm(ed quark)	GLASHOW
chlorine	DAVY
chlorophyll	CAVENTOU, PELLETIER
chromatography	TSWETT
chromosomes	FLEMMING
city of Troy	SCHLIEMANN
colchicine	CAVENTOU, PELLETIER
cocaine formula	WOHLER
comet Chiron	KOWAL
conservation of energy	HELMHOLTZ
cosmic rays	HESS, MILLIKAN
cure for syphilis	EHRLICH
D° particle	GOLDHABER, PIERE
darkening of silver salts	SCHULTZE
DDT	MULLER
decipher	
—Rosetta stone	CHAMPOLLION
—Sumerian script	RAWLINSON
dendrochronology	DOUGLAS
deoxyribose	LEVENE
deuterium	UREY
diastase	PAYEN, PERSOZ
dimagnetism from superconductivity	MEISSNER
diseases caused by micro-organisms	PASTEUR
electricity in	
—muscles	GALVANI
—nerves	DU BOIS-REYMOND
electro	
—luminescence	DESTRIER
—magnetic radiation	MAXWELL
—magnetism	OERSTED
electron	THOMSON
exclusion principle	PAULI
francium	PEREY
gallium	DE BOISBAUDRAN
genetic (finger)printing	JEFFREYS
germanium	WINKLER
glycerol	SCHEELE
glycine	BRACONNOT
glycogen	BERNARD
gravity laws	NEWTON
group theory	GALOIS
hafnium	COSTER, HEVESY
helium	LOCKYER
hominids	
—Cro-Magnon man	LARTET
—Java man	DUBOIS
—Proconsul	LEAKEY
—Zinjanthropus	LEAKEY
hormones	BAYLISS, STARLING
hydrogen	
—in the sun	ANGSTROM
—radio waves	PURCELL
immunisation	PASTEUR
imprinting	LORENZ
infra-red light	HERSCHEL
inoculation against	
—anthrax	PASTEUR
—poliomyelitis	SABIN, SALK
—rabies	PASTEUR
—yellow-fever	THEILER

insulin	BANTING, BEST
interstellar gas	HARTMAN
iodine deficiency causes goitre	MARINE
isoprene	BOUCHARDAT
krypton	RAMSAY
language of bees	FRISCH
laughing gas	DAVY, PRIESTLEY
laws in inheritance	MENDEL
leucine	BRACCONOT
liposomes	BANGHAM
loss of magnetism with temperature	CURIE
LSD	HOFMAN
lutetium	URBAIN
magnesium	DAVY
magnetic induction	FARADAY
malaria carried by mosquitos	ROSS
Martian	
—canals	SCHIAPARELLI
—moons	HALL
mass of Earth	CAVENDISH
matrix mechanics	HEISENBERG
meson	YUKAWA
microsomes	CLAUDE
Minoan civilisation	EVANS
mitochondria	BENDA
morphine	SERTURNER
mutation by radiation	MULLER
Mycaenaean civilisation	SCHLIEMANN
neon	RAMSAY
Neptune	GALLE
nerves carry sensations	VON HALLER
neutrino	COWAN, REINES
neutron	CHADWICK
New Zealand	TASMAN
niridiazole	SCHMIDT
nitrogen	RUTHERFORD
nitroglycerine	SOBRERO
nitrous oxide	DAVY
North-west passage	FRANKLIN
nuclear fission	HAHN, STRASSMAN
nucleic acid	MEISCHER
—structure	CRICK, WATSON
ova in mammals	VON BAER
ovarian follicles	DE GRAAF, SCHWANN
oxygen	PRIESTLEY, SCHEELE
ozone	SCHONBEIN
ozonosphere	FABRY
penicillin	FLEMING
pepsin	SCHWANN
phenol	LISTER
photoelectric effect	LENARD
pi-meson (pion)	POWELL
piezo-electric effect	CURIE
polarised light rotated by crystals	BIOT
polio vaccine	SABIN, SALK

polonium	CURIE
positron	ANDERSON
promethium	CORYELL, GLENDENIN
	MARINSKY
proton	RUTHERFORD
protozoa	LEEUWENHOEK
pulsars	BELL, HEWISH
quantum mechanics	SCHRODINGER
quark (theory)	GELL-MANN
quasars	SCHMIDT
quinine	CAVENTOU, PELLETIER
radiation	
—belts in atmosphere	VAN ALLEN
—pressure	LEBEDEV
radio	
—activity	BECQUEREL
—emission of hydrogen	EWEN, PURCELL
—reflecting layers	APPLETON
	HEAVISIDE
—signals from space	JANSKY
—waves	HERTZ
in sun spots	HEY
radium	CURIE
radon	DORN
random movement of particles	BROWN
red blood corpuscles	SWAMMERDAM
rhenium	BERG, NODDACK
	TACKE
rh(hesus) factor	LANDSTEINER, WIENER
Rosetta stone	BOUSSARD
Saturn's moons	CASSINI
scandium	NILSON
sex hormones	ASCHEIM, ZONDEK
sickle-cell anaemia	HERRICK
silicones	KIPPING
solar	
—flares	CARRINGTON
—wind	PARKER
spermatozoa	HAM
spreading of ocean floor	VINE
static electricity	DUFAY
strangeness	GELL-MANN
streptomycin	WAKSMAN
structure of	
—atoms	RUTHERFORD
—DNA	CRICK, WATSON
—haemoglobin	PERUTZ
strychnine	CAVENTOU, PELLETIER
sulphapyridine	EVANS
superconductivity	KAMERLINGH-ONNES
Tasmania	TASMAN
technetium	LAWRENCE
tethecin	HOPPE-SEYLER
thermo-electricty	SEEBECK
thorium silicate	BREZELIUS
thyroid hormone	KENDALL

tomb of	
—Sethos	BELZONI
—Tutankhamun	CARTER
typhus carried by lice	NICOLLE
tyrosine	LIEBIG
ultra-violet light	RITTER
—as bactericide	FINSEN
uncertainty principle	HEISENBERG
vaccination	JENNER
variable star	FABRICIUS
variation in Moon's motion	TYCHO BRAHE
virus	BEIJERINCK
	IVANOVSKI
vitamins	FUNK
wave mechanics	SCHRODINGER
X-rays	RO(E)NTGEN
—from sun	FRIEDMAN
xenon	RAMSAY
yellow-fever carried by mosquitos	REED
Z particle	RUBBIA
zodiacal light	CASSINI
	(*see also* **first, inventors**)

diseases

including: complaint
　　　　　condition
　　　　　disorder
　　　　　illness
　　　　　pain

abnormal	
—behaviour	PSYCHOACTIVE
	PSYCHOTROPIC
—cartilaginous growth	ENCHONDROMA
—childhood development	AUTISM
—contraction of pupil	MYOSIS
—development affecting	
language and communication	AUTISM
—enlargement	ANEURISM, ANEURYSM
	HYPERTROPHY
of breasts in male	GYNAECOMASTIA
	GYNAECOMASTY
—elation	EUPHORIA
—functioning of organ	DYSFUNCTION
—growth of spleen	SPLENOMEGALY
—rapidity of heart beat	TACHYCARDIA
—redness of skin	ROSACEA, RUBOR
—sensation	PARAESTHESIA
—sensitivity to	
pain	HYPERALGESIA
stimuli	HYPER(A)ESTHESIA
—sound from lungs	RALE, RHONCHUS
—thickness of skin	PACHYDERMIA
abnormally	
—high	
arches	PES CAVUS
blood pressure	HYPERTENSION
body temperature	HYPERPYREXIA

—low intestines	VISCEROPTOSIS
—swollen veins	VARICOSE VEINS
—tortuous vein	VARIX
abscess	BOIL, EMPYEMA
—round tonsil	QUINSY
absorption of rays	RADIATION SICKNESS
accumulation of fat	
on buttocks	STEATOPYGIA
actinomycosis	WOODEN-TONGUE
	WOODY-TONGUE
actinobacillosis	WOODEN-TONGUE
	WOODY-TONGUE
acute toxaemia	ECLAMPSIA
affecting behaviour	PSYCHOACTIVE
	PSYCHOTROPIC
air in pleural cavity	PNEUMOTHORAX
airman's disease	AEROEMBOLISM
	AREONEUROSIS
	FLIGHT FATIGUE
alastrim	SMALLPOX, VARIOLA MINOR
allergy	HAY-FEVER
alopecia	FOX-EVIL
alternating	
—laughter and tears	DACRYGELOSIS
—muscular spasm	CLONIC SPASM
amaurosis	BLINDNESS
amnesia	FUGUE
anaemia	CHLOROSIS, GREEN SICKNESS
anthrax	SANG, WOOLSORTER'S DISEASE
anxiety about health	HYPOCHONDRIA
apoplexy	STROKE
artificial sore	JIGGER
asbestos in lungs	ASBESTOSIS
athlete's foot	EPIDERMIPHYTOSIS
back-arching spasm	OPISTHOTONOS
back pain	LUMBAGO, SCIATICA
bacterial disease	LEPTOSPIROSIS
	LISTEROSIS
—infection	SEPSIS, SEPTICAEMIA
bad state of body	CACHEXIA, CACHEXY
Banti's disease	SPLENIC ANAEMIA
bedsore	DECUBITUS ULCER
bean poisoning	FAVISM
bejel	YAWS
bilharzia	SCHISTOSOMA
	SCHISTOSOMIASIS
birthmark	MOLE
Black Death	BUBONIC PLAGUE
blackhead	COMEDO
bleeding	HAEMORRHAGE
—disease	HAEMOPHILIA
—from nose	EPITAXIS
—into	
pleural cavity	HAEMOTHORAX
tissues	HAEMATOMA
urine	HAEMATURIA

—under skin	PURPURA
blind spot	SCOTOMA
blindness	AMAUROSIS
blister	VESICLE
blockage of artery	EMBOLISM
blood	
—disease	LEUCOCYTHAEMIA
	LEOCOCYTOPENIA, LEUCOCYTOSIS
	LEUC(H)AEMIA, LEUKAEMIA
	POLYCYTHAEMIA, PY(A)EMIA
	THALASS(A)EMIA
—poisoning	PYAEMIA, SEPTICAEMIA
	SUPRAEMIA, TOXAEMIA
—spitting	HAEMOPTYSIS
bloodlessness	ANAEMIA
blueness from lack	
of oxygen	CYANOSIS
boba	BUBA, BUTTON SCURVY
	FRAMBOESIA
	VERRUGA PERUVIANA, YAWS
bodily wasting	MARASMUS
boil	ABSCESS, FURUNCLE
—on eyelid	HORDEOLUM, STYE
bone	
—and cartilage	
erosion	OSTEO-ARTHRITIS
—deformation	PAGET'S DISEASE
	PERTHES' DISEASE
—disease	OSTEOPOROSIS
—injury	FRACTURE
—marrow disease	OSTEOMYELITIS
Bornholm disease	DEVIL'S GRIP
	PLEURODYNIA
botulism	FOOD POISONING
	SAUSAGE-POISONING
bow-leggedness	VALGUS
bowel disease	CONSTIPATION, DIARRHOEA
	DUODENAL ULCER, PEPTIC ULCER
	DYSENTERY, STEATORRHEA
brain	
—disorder	DELIRIUM (TREMENS)
	DISTONIA, ENCEPHALOPATHY
	EPILEPSY
—fever	ENCEPHALITIS, MENINGITIS
	PHRENESIS, PHRENITIS
breakbone fever	DANDY FEVER, DENGUE
breakdown of	
—immune system	AIDS
—red blood cells	HAEMOLYSIS
Bright's disease	NEPHRITIS
bronchial disease	ASTHMA, BRONCHITIS
brucellosis	MALTA FEVER
bruise	ECCHYMOSIS
buba	BOBA, BUTTON SCURVY
	FRAMBOESIA, VERRUGA PERUVIANA
	YAWS

bubonic plague	BLACK DEATH
bulging eyes	EXOPHTHALMIA
	EXOPHTHALMOS
	EXOPHTHALMUS
bursitis in	
—elbow	TENNIS ELBOW
—knee	HOUSE MAID'S KNEE
—lower back	WEAVER'S BOTTOM
—shoulder	DUSTMAN'S SHOULDER
button scurvy	BOBA, BUBA, FRAMBOESIA
	VERRUGA PERUVIANA, YAWS
calenture	SHIP FEVER
callosity	TYLOSIS
cancer	(see tumour below)
caused by	
—breathing	
rarefied air	MOUNTAIN-SICKNESS
	PUNA, SAROCHE
—flies or larvae	MYIASIS
—fungus	ATHLETE'S FOOT
	CANDIDIASIS, MONILIASIS
	MYCOSIS, THRUSH, TINEA
—mould	ASPERGILLOSIS
—tea-drinking	THEISM
—treatment	IATROGENIC ILLNESS
—vegetable parasite	PHYTOSIS
cerebro-spinal fever	MENINGITIS
cessation of breathing	APNOEA
chemical disorder of joint	GOUT
chest pain	ANGINA
chickenpox	VARICELLA
chilblain	PERNIO
chlorine poisoning	FLUOROSIS
chlorosis	GREEN SICKNESS
cholesterol deposits	XANTHOMA
chorea	ST VITUS'S DANCE
cirrhosis of liver	WHISKY-LIVER
clergyman's knee	BURSITIS
clot blocking artery	MBOLUS
clotting in blood	
vessel	THROMBOSIS
club-foot	KYLLOSIS, TALIPES
—in-turned	VARUS
—out-turned	VALGUS
coal-dust in lungs	ANTHRACOSIS
cold sore	HERPES (SIMPLEX)
colour-blindness	DALTONISM
	DICHROMATISM
	MONCHROMASY
comedo	BLACKHEAD
common cold	CORYZA
compression sickness	BENDS
compulsive pulling out	
of hair	TRICHOTILLOMAN(IA
congenital idiocy	DOWN'S SYNDROME
	MONGOLISM

congestion of blood	HYPERAEMIA
conjunctivitis	PINK-EYE
connective tissue	
disease	RHEUMATOID ARTHRITIS
constriction of blood	
vessels, pores, etc	STENOSIS
consumption	TB, TUBERCULOSIS
contagious disease	ZYMOSIS
contraction of pupil	MIOSIS, MYOSIS
convulsions	EPILEPSY, FIT
	PAROXYSM
—at end of pregnancy	ECLAMPSIA
corn on foot	HELOMA
cotton workers' disease	BYSSINOSIS
cough	TUSSIS
cowpox	VACCINIA
Crohn's disease	ENTERITIS
crop of boils	FURUNCULOSIS
curvature of spine	KYPHOSIS, LORDOSIS
	SCOLIOSIS
cyst	
—in gland under tongue	RANULA
—with porridge-like	
contents	ATHEROMA
cystic fibrosis	MUSCOVISCIDOSIS
dandruff	FURFUR
dandy fever	BREAKBONE FEVER, DENGUE
day blindness	HEMERALOPIA
death of part	NECROSIS
decay	GANGRENE
defect of	
—fibrin in blood	HYPINOSIS
—red blood cells	OLIGOCYTHAEMIA
defective	
—acid-alkali balance	ACIDOSIS
	ALKALOSIS
—bone growth	OSTEOCHONDRITIS
	OSTEOCHONDROSIS
	PERTHES' DISEASE, RICKETS
	SCHEUERMANN'S DISEASE
	SCHLATTER'S DISEASE
—interpretation of writing	PARALEXIA
—reasoning	PARALOGIA
—vision	ANOPIA
deficiency	
—disease	BERI-BERI
	PELLAGRA, SCURVY
—of	
alpha-galactosidase	
	ANDERSON-FABRY DISEASE
blood	ISCH(A)EMIA
	OLIGAEMIA
blood-clotting	HAEMOPHILIA
carbon dioxide	ACAPNIA
cartilage	ACHONDROPLASIA
enzyme	PHENYLKETONURIA
essential food	MALNUTRITION
	STARVATION
haemoglobin	ANAEMIA
hydrochloric acid	ACHLORHYDRIA
insulin	DIABETES
iron	SIDEROPENIA
oxygen	ANOXIA
red blood corpuscles	SPANAEMIA
selenium	KESHAN'S DISEASE
sugar in blood	HYPOGLYCAEMIA
thyroid hormone	CRETINISM
vitamins	AVITAMINOSIS
—B	ANAEMIA, BERI-BERI
	PELLAGRA
—C	SCURVY
—D	OSTEOMALACIA, RACHITIS
	RICKETS
white blood cells	AGRANULOCYTOSIS
deformation of	
—arms and legs	PHOCOMELIA
—ear	CAULIFLOWER EAR
—fingers	DUPUYTREN'S CONTRACTURE
—foetus	TERATOMA
—foot	CLUB-FOOT, TALIPES
—head	HYDROCEPHALY, MICROCEPHALY
—hip (splayed hip)	COXA VULGA
—joints	OSTEOARTHRITIS
	OSTEOARTHROSIS
—knee (knock-knee)	GENU VALGUM
—neck muscle	TORTICOLLIS
	WRYNECK
—toe-joint	HALLUX VALGUS
degeneration of	
kidney	ADDISON'S DISEASE
	NEPHROSIS
delirium	PHRENESIS, PHRENITIS
delusion	
—man as beast	ZOANTHROPY
—seeing animals	ZOOSCOPY
—self as another	APPERSONATION
dementia praecox	SCHIZOPHRENIA
dengue	BREAKBONE FEVER
	DANDY FEVER
deposit of melanin	MELANOSIS
depression	MELANCHOLIA
	MELANCHOLY
—in winter	SAD
	SEASONAL AFFECTIVE DISORDER
deranged nutrition	TROPHESY
	TROPHONEUROSIS
dermatitis	ECZEMA
destruction of kidneys	ADDISON'S DSSEASE
devil's grip	BORNHOLM DISEASE
diarrhoea	LIENTERY, WEANING-BRASH
—from Mexican	
food	MONTEZUMA'S REVENGE

—in Middle East	GIPPY TUMMY
	GYPPY TUMMY
difficulty in	
—breathing	DYSPNOEA
—focusing on	
near objects	PRESBYOPIA
—passing urine	DYSURIA, STRANGURY
—producing sound	DYSPHONIA
—swallowing	DYSPHAGIA
—understanding thought	DYSPHASIA
dilatation of	
—arteries	TELANGIECTASIS
—artery	ANEURISM, ANEURYSM
—blood vessels	HAEMORRHOIDS, PILES
—bronchi	BRONCHIECTASIS
—pupil	MYDRIASIS
—veins in anus	HAEMORRHOIDS, PILES
dimness of sight	CALIGO
discharge	
—from	
ear	OTORRHOEA
glands	SEBORRHOEA
nose	OZAENA
—of pus	PYORRHOEA
discoloration	
—due to extravasation	
of blood	ECCHYMOSIS
—of the skin	DYSCHRO(I)A
diseased feet	TRENCH-FEET
disintegration of blood cells	LYSIS
dislocation of joint	LUXATION
disordered	
—cell growth	CANCER, CARCINOMA
—condition of body	DYSCRASIA
—hearing	PARACUSIS
—speech	PARARTHRIA
displacement of	
—eye	PROTOPSIS
—intestines	ENTEROPTOSIS
—organ	HETEROTOPIA, PROLAPSE
forward	ANTEVERSION
—parts	ECTOPIA, ECTOPY
disseminated sclerosis	DS
	MULTIPLE SCLEROSIS
distension of	
—intestines	METEORISM
—lung	EMPHYSEMA
—stomach	FLATULENCE
distrophia	
	DUCHENNE MUSCULAR DISTROPHY
diver's affliction	BENDS
	CAISSON DISEASE
	COMPRESSED AIR SICKNESS
	DECOMPRESSION SICKNESS
dizziness	SCOTODINIA, SCOTOMA
double vision	DIPLOPIA

Down's syndrome	MONGOLISM
dracontiasis	GUINEA-WORM DISEASE
drooping of upper eyelid	PTOSIS
dropsy	(O)EDEMA, HYDROPSY
—in chest	HYDROTHORAX
—of	
abdomen	ASCITES
the brain	HYDROCEPHALUS
drowsiness	NARCOSIS
dryness of	
—conjunctiva	XEROMA
	XEROPHTHALMIA, XEROSIS
—hair	XERASIA
—mouth	XEROSTOMIA
—skin	ICTHYOSIS, XERODERM(I)A
dullness of sight	AMBLYOPIA
dumdum fever	KALA-AZAR
dust in lungs	PNEUMOCONIOSIS
	PNEUMO(NO)KONIOSIS
—asbestos dust	ASBESTOSIS
	MESOTHELIOMA
—carbon dust	ANTHRACOSIS
—cotton dust	BYSSINOSIS
—fungus	FARMER'S LUNG
—iron dust	SIDEROSIS
—silica dust	SILICOSIS
dustman's shoulder	BURSITIS
dwarfism	ATELEIOSIS
dyslexia	WORD BLINDNESS
dyspepsia	INDIGESTION
ear	
—ache	OTALGIA, OTALGY
—disorder	CHOLESTEATOMA
	OSTOSCLEROSIS
	MENIERE'S DISEASE, TINNITUS
early insanity	HEBEPHRENIA
East Coast fever	TICK FEVER
ecchymosis	BRUISE
eczema	DERMATITIS
elephantiasis	BARBADOS LEG
emaciation	TABES
encephalitis lethargica	SLEEPY-SICKNESS
enlargement of	
—baby's head	HYDROCEPHALIS
—bone	EXOSTOSIS
—kidney	HYDRONEPHROSIS
—male breasts	GYNAECOMASTIA
—prostate	PROSTATISM
—spleen	SPLENOMEGALY
—thyroid	GOITRE
enteric fever	GASTRIC FEVER, TYPHOID
epidemic disease	ZYMOSIS
epilepsy	FALLING SICKNESS, PETIT MAL
	PYKNOLEPSY
eruption on	
—nose	ROSE-DROP

—palms or soles	POMPHOLYX
eruptive disease	(SHEEP-)POX
erysipelas	ROSE, ST ANTHONY'S FIRE
excess of	
—body fat	ADIPOSITY, OBESITY
—calcium	HYPERCALC(A)EMIA
—gas in stomach	FLATULENCE
—red blood cells	POLYCYTHAEMIA
—salt in blood	HYPERNATRAEMIA
—sugar in blood	DIABETES
—urea in blood	URAEMIA
—water in tissue	(HY)DROPSY, OEDEMA
—white blood cells	MONONUCLEOSIS
excessive	
—activity of	
adrenal gland	HYPERADRENALISM
sebaceous gland	SEBORRHOEA
thyroid gland	THYROTOXICOSIS
—bleeding	HAEMOPHILIA
—chyle in urine	CHYLURIA
—deposit of fat in arteries	ATHEROMA
—discharge from	
fatty glands	SEBORRHOEA
nose	RHINORRHOEA
—excitement	HYPERSTHENIA
—fibrin in blood	HYPERINOSIS
—flow of	
mucus	CATARRH
saliva	PTYALISM
—formation of	
acetone or ketone	KETOSIS
urine	POLYURIA
—frequency of	
breathing	TACHYPNOEA
—growth	ACROMEGALY, GIGANTISM
of	
—brain supporting	
tissues	GLIOMATOSIS
—fat	LIPOMATOSIS
—papillae	PAPILLOMA
—tissue	HYPERPLASIA
	HYPERTROPHY
—nose-bleeding	RHINORRHAGIA
—number of	
breasts	POLYMASTIA
	POLYMASTISM, POLYMASTY
chromosomes	POLYSOMY
—secretion of	
hormones	CUSHING'S DISEASE
mucus	BLENNORRHOEA
—sensitivity to	
pain	HYPERALGESIA
stimuli	HYPERAESTHESIA
—sweating	HIDROSIS, HYPER(H)IDROSIS
—temperature	HYPERPYREXIA
—thirst	POLYDIPSIA

—vomiting	HYPEREMESIS
—vitamins	HYPERVITAMINOSIS
—wind	FLATULENCE
exophthalmic goitre	GRAVES DISEASE
expansion of blood	
vessels	VASODILATATION
eye disease	BLEPHARISM, BLEPHARITIS
	CATARACT, CERATITIS
	CONJUNCTIVITIS, CYCLOPLEGIA
	DETACHED RETINA, DIPLOPIA
	GLAUCOMA, HYPER(METR)OPIA
	KERATITIS, MYOPIA, NYSTAGMUS
	PANNUS, TRACHOMA
	TUNNEL VISION
failure	
—of	
brain growth	ANENCEPHALY
blood circulation	SHOCK
heart to empty itself	ASYSTOLE
—to	
assimilate	
—fats, etc	COELIAC DISEASE, SPRUE
—food	MALABSORPTION
co-ordinate movements	ATAXIA
secrete	
—milk	AGALACTIA
—urine	ANURIA
faint	SYNCOPE
false	
—joint	PSEUDARTHROSIS
—pregnancy	PSEUDOCYESIS
fatty	
—degeneration	STEATOSIS
—tumour	STEATOMA
faulty	
—alignment of	
eyes	SQUINT, STRABISM(US)
teeth	MALOCCLUSION
—healing of fracture	MALUNIO
fever	PLAGUE, PYREXIA
—recurring	
daily	QUOTIDIAN
every three days	TERTIAN
fifth disease	ERYTHEMA INFECTIOSUM
	SLAPPED CHEEK SYNDROME
fit	CONVULSION, EPILEPSY
	PAROXYSM, SEIZURE
fixed delusions	PARANOIA
flat foot	PES PLANUS
flatulence	BORBORYGMUS
flatulent distension	TYMPANITIES
flea-borne	PLAGUE, TYPHUS
floating kidney	NEPHROPTOSIS
fluid in knee-joint	WATER ON THE KNEE
food-poisoning	BOTULISM, LISTERIOSIS
	PTOMAINE, SALMONELLOSIS

framboesia	BOBA, BUBA
	BUTTON SCURVY, MORULA
	VERRUGA PERUVIANA, YAWS
freckle	LENTIGO
from	
—animals	ZOONOSIS
—birds	PARROT DISEASE
	PARROT FEVER
	PSITTACOSIS
—cattle	ACTINOMYCOSIS, BRUCELLOSIS
	COWPOX, UNDULANT FEVER
—dogs	LEPTOSPIROSIS
	TOXOCARIASIS
—farm animals	ANTHRAX, LEPTOSPIROSIS
—goats	MALTA FEVER
—rabbits	RABBIT-FEVER$
	TULAR(A)EMIA
—rats	LEPTOSPIROSIS
	RAT(BITE)-FEVER
—sheep	Q-FEVER
frozen shoulder	BURSITIS
functional derangement	NEUROSIS
fungal disease	ASPERGILLOSIS
	ATHLETE'S FOOT
	BLASTOMYCOSIS
	CRYPTOCOCCOSIS
	EPIDERMIPHYTOSIS
	FARMER'S LUNG, FAVUS
	MYCOSIS, TORULOSIS
furfur	DANDRUFF, SCURF
furuncle	BOIL
fusion of	
—bones	ANCHYLOSIS, ANKYLOSIS
—legs	MERMAID SYNDROME
	SIRENOMELIA
galactose in blood	GALACTOSAEMIA
gall-stones	CHOLELITHIASIS
gangrene	PHAGED(A)ENA, THANATOSIS
gaol fever	TYPHUS
genital	
—disease	GONORRHOEA, SYPHILIS
—ulceration	CHANCROID
German measles	ROSEOLA, RUBELLA
	RUBEOLA
giddiness	VERTIGO
glanders	FARCY
glandular	
—condition	ADENOSIS
—fever	MONONUCLEOSIS
glaucoma	WALL-EYE
goitre	STRUMA
gout	PODAGRA
—in	
all joints	HAMARTHRITIS
hand	PODAGRA
head	CEPHALAGRA

gouty deposit	TOPHUS
granular deposit	SABURRA
Graves' disease	EXOPHTHALMIC GOITRE
	THYROTOXICOSIS
green sickness	ANAEMIA, CHLOROSIS
gripes	TORMINA
growth	
—disorder	ACROMEGALY
—of fibrous tissue	FIBROSIS
Guinea-worm disease	DRACONTIASIS
gumboil	PARULIS
hair disease	TRICHOSIS
hard	
—swelling	SCIRRHUS
—tumour	SCLERIASIS
hardening	
—of	SCLEROMA, SCLEROSIS
arteries	ARTERIOSCLEROSIS
	ATHEROSCLEROSIS
skin	CALLOSITY, ICTHYOSIS
	SCLERODERM(I)A
tissue	SCLEREMA, SCLERIASIS
haemorrhage	STAXIS
haemorrhoids	PILES
having	
—high blood pressure	HYPERTENSION
—low blood pressure	HYPOTENSION
headache	MIGRAINE
heart	
—burn	CARDIALGY, CARDIALGIA
	PYROSIS, WATER-BRASH
—defects (congenital)	FALLOT'S TETRALOGY
—disease	ANGINA PECTORIS
	CORONARY THROMBOSIS
	ENDOCARDITIS, PERICARDITIS
in children	KAWASAKI DISEASE
—disorder	BRADYCARDIA
	TACHYCARDIA
	TOBACCO-HEART
hepatitis	FAVISM
hereditary	
—disease	CHOREA MAJOR
	CYSTIC FIBROSIS
	HAEMOPHILIA
	HUNTINGTON'S CHOREA
—tendency to disease	DIATHESIS
hernia	RUPTURE
—of bladder	CYSTOCELE
herpes	COLD SORE, DARTRE
	SHINGLES, ZOSTER
hiccuping	SINGULTUS
high blood pressure	HYPERPIESIA
	HYPERTENSION
hip-gout	SCIATICA
hives	LARYNGITIS, NETTLE RASH
	URTICARIA

Hodgkin's disease	LYMPHADENOMA	infestation with	
hordeolum	STYE	—lice	PEDICULOSIS
hospital gangrene	PHAGED(A)ENA	—parasites	PARASITOSIS
housemaid's knee	BURSITIS	inflamed sore	FELON, MORMAL
hunchback	GIBBUS	inflammation of	
hydatid disease	TAPEWORM	—all joints	PANARTHRITIS
hydrocephalus	WATER ON THE BRAIN	—appendix	APPENDICITIS
hydrophobia	LYSSA, RABIES	—artery	ARTERITIS
	ST HUBERT'S DISEASE	—bladder	CYSTITIS
hydropsy	DROPSY, OEDEMA	—blind-gut	TYPHLITIS
hyperthyroidism	EXOPHTHALMIC GOITRE	—blood vessels	VASCULITIS
	GRAVES' DISEASE	in brain	CHOROIDITIS
	THYROTOXICOSIS	—bone	OSTEO-MYELITIS, OSTEITIS
hysterical		—brain	ENCEPHALITIS
—mania	HYSTEROMANIA		MENINGITIS
—trance	CATALEPSY		PANOPHTHALMITIS
icterus	JAUNDICE		PHRENESIS, PHRENITIS
imaginary illness	HYPOCHONDRIA	—breast	CYSTIC DISEASE, MASTITIS
immersion foot	TRENCH FOOT	—bronchi	BRONCH(IOL)ITIS
immovable joint	SYNARTHROSIS	—bursae	BURSITIS
immune system		—cerebrum	CEREBRITIS
deficiency	AIDS	—colon	COLITIS
impairment of		—conjunctiva	CONJUNCTIVITIS
—function of organ	DYSFUNCTION	—connective tissue	SYNOVITIS
—reasoning power	PARALOGIA	—cornea	CERATITIS, KERATITIS
—sensation	DYSAESTHESIA	—diverticula	DIVERTICULITIS
imperfect development of		—duodenum	DUODENITIS
—limb	DISMELIA	—ear	CONCHITIS, OTITIS
—organ or part	APLASIA	drum	MYRINGITIS
inability to		membrane	TYMPANITIS
—distinguish certain		—elbow joint	BURSITIS, TENNIS ELBOW
colours	COLOUR BLINDNESS	—eye	CONJUNCTIVITIS
—perform			OPHTHALMIA
intended motion	APRAXIA		OPHTHALMITIS
purposive movements	PARAPHRAXIA	ball	SCLER(OT)ITIS
	PARAPHRAXIS	lid	BLEPHARITIS, TYLOSIS
—swallow	HYDROPHOBIA	—Fallopian tubes	SALPINGITIS
—write	DYSGRAPHIA	—fibrous tissue	BURSITIS, FIBROSITIS
indigestion	DYSPEPSIA	—follicles	ACNE
infantile paralysis	POLIOMYELITIS	—gall-bladder	CHOLECYSTITIS
infection		—glands	ADENITIS
—after childbirth	MILK-FEVER	—gums	GINGIVITIS
	PUERPERAL MANIA	—hair follicles	SYCOSIS
—at childbirth	PUERPERAL FEVER	—head of optic nerve	PAPILLITIS
—by micro-organisms	TOXOPLASMOSIS	—heart	CARDITIS
—following disease	SEQUELA	sac	PERICARDITIS
—of		valve	VALVULITIS
fifth cranial nerve	TIC DOLOUREUX	—heel	PLANTAR FASCIITIS
lungs	(LOBAR) PNEUMONIA	—ileum	CROHN'S DISEASE, ILEITIS
mucus membranes	CANDIDIASIS	—inner ear	LABYRINTHITIS
	MONILIASIS, THRUSH	—intestines	ENTERITIS
nervous system	TORULOSIS		PERITYPHLITIS
part of lung	LOBAR PNEUMONIA	—iris	IRITIS, UVEITIS
infectious		—joints	(RHEUMATOID) ARTHRITIS
—disease	ZYMOTIC	—kidneys	BRIGHT'S DISEASE
—mononucleosis	GLANDULAR FEVER		(PYELO)NEPHRITIS, PYELITIS

226

—knee-joint	BURSITIS
	CLERGYMAN'S KNEE
	HOUSEMAID'S KNEE
—larynx	CROUP, LARYNGITIS
—lens of eye	CRYSTALLITIS
—lining of	
artery	ENDARTERITIS
heart	ENDOCARDITIS
node	RHINITIS
nose	RHINITIS
stomach	GASTRO-ENTERITIS
uterus	ENDOMETRITIS
—liver	HEPATITIS
—lymphatic glands	LYMPHANGITIS
—marrow	MYELITIS
—mastoid process	MASTOIDITIS
—mouth and throat	THRUSH
—mucous membrane of	
eyelids	TRACHOMA
mouth	STOMATITIS
nose	CATARRH, RHINITIS
—muscle	FIBROSITIS, MYOSITIS
—nail	ONYCHITIS
—nail-bed	ONYCHIA
—nerves	(POLY)NEURITIS
—nose and throat	RHINOPHARYNGITIS
—outside of stomach	PERIGASTRITIS
—ovary	OOPHORITIS, OVARITIS
—pancreas	PANCREATITIS
—parotid gland	PAROT(ID)ITIS
—part near blind-gut	PERITYPHLITIS
—pelvis of kidney	PYELITIS
—pericardium	PERICARDITIS
—peritoneum	PERITONITIS
of liver	PERIHEPATITIS
—pharynx	PHARYNGITIS
—pleura	EMPYEMA, PLEURITIS
	PLEURISY
—prostate	PROSTATITIS
—rectum	PROCTITIS
—retina	RETINITIS
—sinus	SINU(S)ITIS
—skin	DERMATITIS, INTERTRIGO
—spinal cord	(POLIO)MYELITIS
—spine	RACHITIS, SPONDYLITIS
—spleen	SPLENITIS
—stomach	GASTRITIS
and intestines	GASTRO-ENTERITIS
—subcutaneous	CELLULITIS
—tendon sheath	SYNOVITIS
—testicle	ORCHITIS
—throat	ANGINA
—tongue	GLOSSITIS
—tonsils	ANTIADITIS, TONSILLITIS
—thyroid gland	STRUMITIS, THYROIDITIS
—tongue	GLOSSITIS

—tonsils	TONSIL(L)ITIS
—trachea	TRACH(E)ITIS
—ureter	URETERITIS
—urethra	URETHRITIS
—uterus	HYSTERITIS
—uvula	STAPHYLITIS, UVULITIS
—vein	(THROMBO)PHLEBITIS
—vertebra	SPONDYLITIS
—whole eye	PANOPHTHALMIA
—womb	UTERITIS
inflammatory disease of	
the face	ERYSIPELAS
influencing brain	PSYCHOACTIVE
	PSYCHOTROPIC
influenza	GRIPPE
ingrowing toenail	ONYCHOCRYPTOSIS
insensibility	CARUS, COMA, LETHARGY
	SOPOR
intermittent fever	RELAPSING FEVER
intestinal	
—disease	CHOLERA
	C(O)ELIAC DISEASE, COLITIS
	DIARRHOEA, DIVERTICULITIS
	DUODENAL ULCER, DYSENTERY
	MEGACOLON
—displacement	ENTEROPTOSIS
intolerance of light	PHOTOPHOBIA
irregularity of heartbeat	ARRHYTHMIA
	EXTRASYSTOLE
itch	CACOETHES, PRURITIS
	PSORA, SCABIES
	SCOTCH FIDDLE
itching	PRURITIS
jail fever	TYPHUS
jaundice	ICTERUS
jelly-like tumour	MYXOMA
jet-lag	TIME-ZONE DISEASE
joint	
—disorder	GOUT, RHEUMATIC FEVER
	RHEUMATISM
—injury	FRACTURE, SPRAIN
kala-azar	DUMDUM FEVER
	LEISHMANIASIS
	LEISHMANIOSIS
kidney disease	ADDISON'S DISEASE
	BRIGHT'S DISEASE
	NEPHRITIS, NEPHROSIS
king's evil	SCROFULA, TUBERCULOSIS
knock-knees	VALGUS
kyllosis	CLUB-FOOT
lack of	
—food	MALNUTRITION, STARVATION
—hydrochloric acid	
in stomach	ACHLORHYDRIA
—muscular	
coordination	DISKINAESTH(A)ESIA

—pulsation	ACROTISM
—red cells in blood	(SP)ANAEMIA
—vitamins	AVITAMINOSIS
large boil	CARBUNCLE
laryngitis	HIVES
lateral spinal curvature	SCOLIOSIS
lead poisoning	MOLYBDOSIS
	PLUMBISM, SATURNISM
leakage of fluid	EXTRAVASATION
	EXUDATION
leprosy	LEONTIASIS
lice-borne disease	INTERMITTENT FEVER
	RELAPSING FEVER
	TRENCH-FEVER, TYPHUS
like	
—typhoid	PARATYPHOID
—typhus	TYPHOID
limited vision	TUNNEL VISION
limping	CLAUDICATION
Little's disease	CEREBRAL PALSY
	SPASTIC PARALYSIS
liver disease	CIRRHOSIS, HEPATITIS
	HODGKIN'S DISEASE
lock-jaw	TETANUS
long	
—sightedness	HYPER(METR)OPIA
—ulcer	FISTULA
looseness of bowels	DIARRH(O)EA
loss of	
—ability to	
focus eyes	PREBYOPIA
manipulate objects	APRAXIA
—all sensation	ANAESTHESIA
—appetite	ANOREXIA (NERVOSA)
	ANOREXY
—contact with reality	AUTISM
—hair	ALOPECIA, MADROSIS
	PSILOSIS
—hearing	DEAFNESS, PREBYACUSIS
—memory	AMNESIA
—menstruation	AMENORRHOEA
—mental powers	DEMENTIA
—movement in joint	ANKYLOSIS
—muscle control	PALSY
—power of	
motion	PARALYSIS
writing	AGRAPHIA
—sense of pain	ANALGESIA
—skin pigment	VITILIGO
—speech	ALALIA, APHEMIA
	DUMBNESS
—taste	AGEUSIA
—vision	AMBLYOPIA, BLINDNESS
—voice	APHONIA, APHONY
—weight	CACHEXIA
low blood pressure	HYPOTENSION

lung disease	ANTHRACOSIS, ASBESTOSIS
	BRONCHIECTASIS
	BRONCH(IOL)ITIS
	(BRONCHO)PNEUMONIA
	BYSSINOSIS, CONSUMPTION
	EMPHYSEMA, FARMER'S LUNG
	LEGIONNAIRES' DISEASE
	MESOTHELIOMA, MINER'S PHTHISIS
	PLEURISY, PNEUMONCONIOSIS
	PNEUMOTHORAX, SILICOSIS
	SIDEROSIS, TB, TUBERCULOSIS
lupus	TOUCH-ME-NOT
lymph node disease	HODGKIN'S DISEASE
	LYMPHANGITIS
lymphoid tumour	LYMPHOMA
Lyssa	HYDROPHOBIA, RABIES
maidism	PELLAGRA
malaria	MARSH-FEVER, PALUDISM
malarial fever (India)	TAP
Maltese fever	BRUCELLOSIS
matchmakers' disease	PHOSSY-JAW
measles	MORBILLI
melanin in blood	MELANAEMIA
memory disorder	PARAMNESIA
meningitis	CEREBRO-SPINAL FEVER
mental	
—derangement	PSYCHOPATHY
—disorder	ALZHEIMER'S DISEASE
	AMENTIA, AUTISM, DEMENTIA
	FOLIE A DEUX
	FRAGILE X SYNDROME
	HEBEPHRENIA, IDIOCY, IMBECILITY
	MANIA, MONGOLISM, PARANOIA
	PHOBIA, PSYCHASTHENIA
	(PSYCHO)NEUROSIS
	PSYCHOSIS, SCHIZOPHRENIA
metabolic	
—defect in	
excretion of pigment	PORPHYRIA
—disorder	PHENYLKETONURIA
mild smallpox	ALASTRIM
miner's	
—anaemia	ANCHYLOSTOMIASIS
	ANKYLOSTOMIASIS
—elbow	BURSITIS
—lung disease	PNEUMOCONIOSIS
	(*see also* dust *above*)
misshapen or incomplete	
limb	DYSMELIA
mongolism	DOWN'S SYNDROME
moniliasis	THRUSH
morbid	
—accummulation of	
bile in blood	CHOLAEMIA
—adhesion	SYNECHIA
—anxiety and despondency	DYSTHYMIA

—appetite for food	ACORIA
—condition resulting from	
anxiety about health	HYPOCHONDRIA
excess of tobacco	NICOTINISM
—contraction	STENOSIS
—enlargement of prostate	PROSTATISM
—growth of tissue	FIBROSIS
—habit of body	DYSTHESIA
—restlessness	DYSPHORIA
—state of blood	CACHAEMIA
morbilli	MEASLES
mortification	GANGRENE
morula	YAWS
mosquito-borne	FILARIASIS
	MALARIA, YELLOW FEVER
mountain sickness	PUNA, SOROCHE
mouth	
—gangrene	NOMA
—infection	APHTHA, CANDIDA
	MONILIASIS, THRUSH
	TRENCH MOUTH
	VINCENT'S DISEASE
multiple sclerosis	DS
	DISSEMINATED SCLEROSIS
mumps	PAROT(ID)ITIS
muscle	
—deterioration	MUSCULAR DYSTROPHY
—disease	MYASTHENIA
—pain	FIBROSITIS, MYALGIA
—spasm	CRAMP, OPISTHOTONOS
—tumour	MYOMA
muscular	
—atrophy	MYOPATHY
—debility	MYASTHENIA
—distrophy	MYOPATHY
—inflammation	MYOSITIS
—rheumatism	FIBROSITIS
—spasm	
contracting/relaxing	CLONIC, CLONUS
uniform	TONIC
—tension	MYOTONIA
—weakness	MYASTHENIA
	NARCOLEPSY
progressive	MYASTHENIA GRAVIS
myalgic encephalomyelitis	ME
	ROYAL FREE DISEASE
myopia	MOUSE-SIGHT
narrowing of	
—blood vessels	BUERGER'S DISEASE
	STENOSIS
	VASOCONSTRICTION
—organ	STENOSIS, STRICTURE
necrosis of jawbone	PHOSSY-JAW
	MATCHMAKER'S DISEASE
neoplasm	TUMOUR
nephritis	BRIGHT'S DISEASE

nerve pain	NEURALGIA
nervous	
—activity	NEUROSIS
—debility	NEURASTHENIA
—system	
disorder	DISSEMINATED SCLEROSIS
	EPILEPSY, LOCOMOTOR ATAXY
	MULTIPLE SCLEROSIS
	NEUROPATHY, NEUROSIS
nettle-rash	HIVES, URTICARIA
neuralgia	
—in face	FACE-ACHE, TIC DOULOUREUX
	TRIGEMINAL NEURALGIA
—of chest-wall	PLEURODYNIA
neuralgic pain in rectum	PROCTALGIA
neuritis of sciatic nerve	SCIATICA
nicotine poisoning	NICOTINISM
night-blindness	NYCTALOPIA
noise in ear	TINNITUS
nosebleed	EPITAXIS
numbness of legs	NIGHT-PALSY
nutritional disorder	TROPHESY
	TROPHONEUROSIS
obstruction of intestine	ILEAC PASSION
	ILIAC PASSION, ILEUS
oedema	(HY)DROPSY
onchocerciasis	RIVER BLINDNESS
one-eyed vision	MONOBLEPSIS
opacity of	
—cornea	LEUCOMA, ONYX
—lens	CATARACT
open sore	ULCER
ornithosis	PSITTACOSIS
over-	
—activity of thyroid	THYROTOXICOSIS
	HYPERTHYROIDISM
—excitability	HYPOMANIA
—growth of	AGROMEGALY
a part	HYPERPLASIA
skin of nose	RHINOPHYMA
—heating	HYPERTHERMIA
—nourishment	HYPERTROPHY
—production of mucus	
and fibrous tissue	CYSTIC FIBROSIS
pain in	
—foot	METATARSALGIA
—head	CEPHALALGIA
—hip	COXALGIA
—instep	TARSALGIA
—intercostal muscles	PLEURODYNIA
—joint	ARTHRALGIA
—kidneys	NEPHRALGIA, NEPHRALGY
—sciatic nerve	SCIATICA
—tongue	GLOSSODYNIA
—upper stomach	CARDIALGIA
	CARDIALGY

painful
—bodily ailment　　　　　　　PASSION
—menstruation　　　DYSMENORRH(O)EA
palsy　　　　　　　　　　　PARALYSIS
paludism　　　　　　　　　　MALARIA
papilloma　　　　　　　　　　　WART
paralysis　　　　　　　　　　　PALSY
—agitans　　　　　　PARKINSONISM
—partial　　　　　　　　　PARESIS
paralysis of
—arms and legs　　　　QUADRAPLEGIA
　　　　　　　　　　QUADRIPLEGIA
—both arms or both legs　　　DIPLEGIA
—eye muscles　　　OPHTHALMOPLEGIA
—facial nerve　　　　　BELL'S PALSY
—legs　　　　　　　　LATHYRISM
—lower body　　　　　PARAPLEGIA
—one part　　　　　　MONOPLEGIA
—part　　　　　　　　　PARESIS
—pupil　　　　　　　CYCLOPLEGIA
parasitic disease　　　BILHARZIA(SIS)
　　　　　　　　　　BILHARZIOSIS
　　　　　　　　　CHAGASS DISEASE
　　　　　　　CRYPTOSPORIDIASIS
　　　　　HOOKWORM, KALA AZAR
　　　　　　　　　LEISHMANIASIS
LEISHMANIOSIS, ONCHOCERCIASIS
　　　　　　　　SCHISTOSOMIASIS
SLEEPING SICKNESS, STRONGYLOSIS
　　　TOXOCARIASIS, TOXOPLASMOSIS
　　　TRICHINIASIS, TRICHINOSIS
TRICHOMONIASIS, TRYPANOSOMIASIS
paronychia　　　　　　　　WHITLOW
parotid gland infection　　　　　MUMPS
parot(id)itis　　　　　　　　　MUMPS
parrot-disease　　　　　　PSITTACOSIS
partial
—dislocation　　　　　SUBLUXATION
—paralysis　　　　　　　PARESIS
parulis　　　　　　　　　　GUMBOIL
pathological
—accumulation of fluid
in tissue　　　　DROPSY, (O)EDEMA
—conversion of cell walls
to gum　　　　　　　GUMMOSIS
—softening　　　　　　　MALACIA
pellagra　　　　　　　　　MAIDISM
pernio　　　　　　　　　CHILBLAIN
Perthes' disease　　　OSTEOCHONDROSIS
pertussis　　　　　WHOOPING-COUGH
perverted appetite　　　　　MALACIA
pes planus　　　　　　　FLAT FOOT
pestilence　　　　　　　　　LUES
petit mal　　　　　　　　EPILEPSY
piles　　　　　　　　HAEMORRHOIDS
pimple　　　　　　　　　LENTIGO

pink
—eye　　　　　　CONJUNCTIVITIS
—rash　　　　　　　　ROSEOLA
placental disease　　HYDATIDIFORM MOLE
pleurisy with
pneumonia　　　PLEURO-PNEUMONIA
pleurodynia　　　BORNHOLM DISEASE
plucking movements　　　CARPHOLOGY,
　　　　　　　　　FLOCCILATION
plumbism　　　　　LEAD-POISONING
poisoning by
—acetone　　　　　　KETOSIS
—antimony　　　　　STILBIALISM
—beans　　　　　　　FAVISM
—ergot　　ERGOTISM, RAPHANIA
—ketone　　　　　　　KETOSIS
—lead　　MOLYBDOSIS, PLUMBISM
　　　　　　　　SATURNISM
—mercury　　　HATTER'S SHAKES
　　　　　　　MERCURIALISM
—tobacco　　　　　NICOTINISM
poliomyelitis　　INFANTILE PARALYSIS
porous structure of bones　OSTEOPOROSIS
post-natal disease　　　　MILK-LEG
　PUERPERAL FEVER, WHITE-LEG
premature
—ageing　　　　　　PROGERIA
—greying　　　　　　POLIOSIS
—senility　　ALZHEIMER'S DISEASE
presence of
—diverticula　　　DIVERTICULOSIS
—endometrial material
in other organ　　ENDOMETRIOSIS
prickly heat　　MILIARIA, SUDAMEN
primary disease　　　　IDIOPATHY
protusion of
—eyeballs　　　　EXOPHTHALMIA
　　　　　　EXOPHTHALMOS
—meninges　　　MENINGOCELE
—organ　　　　　　HERNIA
—spinal cord　　　MYELOCELE
prunella　　QUINSY, SORE THROAT
pruritis　　　　　　　ITCH
psittacosis　　　　ORNITHOSIS
psora　　　　ITCH, SCABIES
psychosis　　　　　MANIA
—with delusions　SCHIZOPHRENIA
pus in urine　　　　PYURIA
putrefaction　SAPRAEMIA, SEPSIS
putrid fever　　　　TYPHUS
pyrexia　　　　　　FEVER
pyrosis　HEARTBURN, WATER-BRASH
quartan fever　　　　MALARIA
quinsy　　ANGINA, CYNANCHE
　　　　　　PRUNELLA
rabbit-fever　　TULAR(A)EMIA

rabies	HYDROPHOBIA, LYSSA
rachitis	RICKETS
rapid heart beat	TACHYCARDIA
rash	EXANTHEM
rat(bite)-fever	SODUKU, TULAR(A)EMIA
ravenous appetite	LIMOSIS
redness of skin	ERYTHEMA INFECTIOSUM
	FIFTH DISEASE, ROSACEA
	SLAPPED CHEEK SYNDROME
resembling typhoid	PARATYPHOID
respiratory	ASTHMA, CROUP, FLU
	INFLUENZA, PLEURISY
	PNEUMONIA
retention of	
—urine	HYDRONEPHROSIS
	STRANGURY
—waste in blood	UR(A)EMIA
rheumatism in lumbar region	LUMBAGO
rickets	RACHITIS
ringing in the ears	TINNITUS
ringworm	TINEA, TRICHOPHYTOSIS
river blindness	ONCHOCERCIASIS
Rock fever	UNDULANT FEVER
rose	ERYSIPELAS
—rash	ROSEOLA
roseola	GERMAN MEASLES
	ROSE-RASH
Royal Free disease	ME
MYALGIC ENCEPHALOMYELITIS	
rubella	GERMAN MEASLES
rubeola	(GERMAN) MEASLES
rupture	HERNIA, RHEXIS
sagging of organ	PTOSIS
sang	ANTHRAX
sausage-poisoning	BOTULISM
scabbiness	SCALL
scabies	ITCH, PSORA
	SCOTCH FIDDLE
scalp disease	FAVUS, PORRIGO
scaly scalp	DANDRUFF
scarlatina	SCARLET-FEVER
scarlet-fever	SCARLATINA
schistosomiasis	BILHARZIA
schizophrenia	DEMENTIA PRAECOX
sciatica	HIP-GOUT
scrofula	KING'S EVIL, STRUMA
	TUBERCULOSIS
scurf	FURFUR
sebaceous cyst	WEN
secretion of smelly	
sweat	OSMIDROSIS
seizure	EPILEPSY, STROKE
sensation	
—of ants on skin	FORMICATION
—without physical origin	HALLUCINATION
septic finger	FELON

severe	
—anaemia	CHLOROSIS
—anxiety neurosis	SHELL SHOCK
—depression	MELANCHOLIA
—schizophrenia	CATATONIA
shaking	TREMOR
—of brain	CONCUSSION
—palsy	PARKINSONISM
	PARKINSON'S DISEASE
shell-shock	WAR NEUROSIS
shingles	HERPES ZOSTER
ship-fever	CALENTURE, TYPHUS
shivering	AGUE, RIGOR
short-sightedness	MYOPIA
	PRESBYOPIA, PRESBYOPY
simulation of another	
disease	MIMESIS
single-minded madness	MONOMANIA
skin	
—crack	CHAP
—disease	ACNE, CHLOASMA
	CHLORACNE, DERMATITIS
	DERMATOSIS, ECZEMA
	ELEPHANTIASIS, ERYSIPELAS
	EXANTHEM(A), FAVUS, HERPES
	HIVES, ICHTHYOSIS, IMPETIGO
	INTERTRIGO, ITCH, LEPROSY
	MYXOEDEMA, NETTLE-RASH
	PEMPHIGUS, PITYRIASIS, PSORA
	PSORIASIS, ROSACEA, SCABIES
	SERPIGO, SHINGLES, THRUSH
	URTICARIA
fungal	ATHLETE'S FOOT
	CANDIDIASIS
	EPIDERMIPHYTOSIS
	MONILIASIS, RINGWORM, TINEA
old	SCALL
—eruption	EXANTHEM(A), PRURIGO
—ulcer	RUPIA
sleeping-sickness	TRYPANOSOMIASIS
sleepy-sickness	ENCEPHALITIS LETHARGICA
slow	
—digestion	BRADYPEPTIC
—heartbeat	BRADYCARDIA
small abscess	PUSTULE
smallpox	ALASTRIM, VARIOLA
soduku	RAT(BITE) FEVER
softening	MALACIA
—of bones	OSTEOMALACIA, RICKETS
sore throat	PRUNELLA
spasm	TIC
—of	
eyelids	BLEPHARISM
iris	HIPPUS
jaw muscles	TRISMUS
muscles	TETANY

spasmodic eye movement	NYSTAGMUS
speech disturbance	PARALALIA
spine	
—curvature	
backwards	KYPHOSIS
forward	LORDOSIS
sideways	SCOLIOSIS
—disease	POLIOMYELITIS
	RACHISCHISIS, RACHITIS
	SPINA BIFIDA, SPONDYLITIS
	SPONDYLOSIS, SYRINGOMELIA
spitting blood	HAEMOPTYSIS
spleen disease	HODGKIN'S DISEASE
splenic anaemia	BANTI'S DISEASE
spongy bone of ear	OTOSCLEROSIS
spontaneous bruising	PURPURA
spot on skin	PETECHIA
squint	STRABISM(US)
St Hubert's disease	HYDROPHOBIA
St Vitus's dance	CHOREA (MINOR)
stagnation of bile	CHOLESTASIS
stiff neck	MENINGISMUS
stomach	
—disease	GASTRIC ULCER
	GASTRITIS, PEPTIC ULCER
—pain	COLIC, GASTRALGIA
stone	
—gallstone	CALCULUS
—in	
body	LITHIASIS
gallbladder	CHOLELITHIASIS
kidney	NEPHROLITHIASIS
intestine	ENTEROLITH
urinary tract	UROLITH
—small stones	GRAVEL
stoppage of urine	ISCHURIA
streptococcal infection	RHEUMATIC FEVER
stroke	APOPLEXY, ICTUS
	SEIZURE
struma	GOITRE, SCROFULA
strychnine poisoning	STRYCH(NI)NISM
stye	HORDEOLUM
subnormal body	
temperature	HYPOTHERMIA
sugar in urine	GLUCOSURIA, GLYCOSURIA
summer flu	LYME DISEASE
sun-wart	ACTINIC KERATOSIS
superfluous mass	
of bone	EXOSTOSIS
suppuration in tooth	
socket	PYORRHOEA
suppurative tonsillitis	QUINSY
sweat blister	SUDAMEN
swelling	TUMOUR, TYMPANY
—composed of blood, etc	HAEMATOMA
—in nose	RHINOSCLEROMA

—of	
joints	GOUT
thyroid	GOITRE
swollen lymphatic gland	FARCY-BUD
—in groin	BUBO
syncope	FAINT
syphilis	LUES, POX
tabes dorsalis	LOCOMOTOR ATAXY
talipes	CLUB-FOOT
tapeworm	HYDATID DISEASE
tea-drunkenness	THEISM
teething rash	RED-GUM
temporary blindness	
with migraine	TEICHOPSIA
tennis elbow	BURSITIS
tetanic spasm of jaw	
muscles	TRISMUS
tetanus	LOCK-JAW
thanatosis	GANGRENE
thickening of	
—inner coat of	
arteries	ATHEROMA
—skin	ELEPHANTIASIS
thin concave fingernails	KOILONYCHIA
throat disease	CYNANCHE, DIPHTHERIA
	LARYNGITIS, PHARAYNGITIS
thrush	APHTHA, CANDIDA, MONILIASIS
thyroid	
—deficiency	MYXOEDEMA
—disease	EXOPHTHALMIC GOITRE
	GRAVES DISEASE
	THYROTOXICOSIS
thyrotoxicosis	GRAVES DISEASE
tick	
—borne disease	LYME DISEASE
	INTERMITTENT FEVER
	RELAPSING FEVER
	TYPHUS
—fever	EAST COAST FEVER
time-zone disease	JET-LAG
tinea	RINGWORM
tonsillitis	ANTIADITIS
toothache	DENTAGRA
tormina	GRIPES
torn skin beside nail	AGNAIL, HANGNAIL
torticollis	WRY-NECK
touch-me-not	LUPUS
transmitted by	
—birds	ORNITHOSIS, PSITTACOSIS
—cats	RABIES, TOXICARIASIS
	TOXOPLASMOSIS
—cattle	ACTINOBACILLOSIS
	ACTINOMYCOSIS, ANTHRAX
	BRUCELLOSIS
	FOOT AND MOUTH DISEASE
	KERATOCONJUNCTIVITIS

LEPTOSPIROSIS, MALTA FEVER
RINGWORM, SALMONELLOSIS
TUBERCULOSIS
UNDULANT FEVER
—chickens CYTOMEGALOVIRUS, CMV
—dogs TOXOCARIASIS
—flies KALA-AZAR, SANDFLY FEVER
SLEEPING SICKNESS
TRYPANOSOMIASIS
—lice INTERMITTENT FEVER
RELAPSING FEVER
TRENCH-FEVER, TYPHUS
Q-FEVER
—mites ACARIASIS, ITCH, SCABIES
SCRUB-TYPHUS
—mosquitoes DENGUE
BREAKBONE FEVER
DANDY FEVER
ENCEPHALITIS, ELEPHANTIASIS
MALARIA, YELLOW-FEVER
YELLOW-JACK
—rabbits CYTOMEGALOVIRUS, CMV
—rats TULAR(A)EMIA
—rat fleas PLAGUE
—ticks INTERMITTENT FEVER
LYME DISEASE
RELAPSING FEVER
ROCKY MOUNTAIN FEVER
TYPHUS
trembling TREMOR
trench
—fever TYPHUS
—foot IMMERSION FOOT
—mouth VINCENT'S ANGINA
trichophytosis RING-WORM
trismus LOCK-JAW
tropical diseases
—complication of
malaria BLACKWATER FEVER
—dengue BREAKBONE FEVER
DANDY FEVER
—deficiency of
protein KWASHIORKOR
vitamin B BERIBERI, PELLAGRA
—fly-borne SLEEPING SICKNESS
TRYPANOSOMIASIS
—fungal MADURA FOOT
MADUROMYCOSIS
—mouth infection NOMA
—mosquito-borne MALARIA
YELLOW-FEVER
YELLOW-JACK
—parasitic BILHARZIA(SIS)
BILHARZIOSIS, DELHI BOIL
DUMDUM FEVER, FRAMBOESIA
GUINEA WORM, HOOKWORM

KALA-AZAR, LEISHMANIASIS
LEISHMANIOSIS, LOA
ONCHOCERCIASIS
ORIENTAL SORE
RIVER BLINDNESS
YAWS
—rodent-borne LASSA FEVER
—skin disease BOBA, BUBA
BUTTON SCURVY
LEPROSY, FRAMBOESIA
PINTA, VERRUGA PERUVIANA
YAWS
—undernourishment KWASHIORKOR
—viral EBOLA DISEASE
GREEN-MONKEY DISEASE
MARBURG DISEASE
trypanosomiasis SLEEPING-SICKNESS
tuberculosis of
—lungs CONSUMPTION, PHTHISIS
—lymph nodes KING'S EVIL, SCROFULA
—skin LUPUS (VULGARIS)
—vertebrae POTT'S DISEASE
tuberculous lesion TUBERCULOMA
tular(a)emia RABBIT-FEVER
tumour
—connected with teeth ODONTOMA
—jelly-like MYXOMA
—yellow XANTHOMA
tumour of
—blood
cells MYELOMA
vessels AGIOMA, NAEVIS
—bone OSTEO(CLASTO)MA, SARCOMA
marrow MYELOMA
—connective tissue SARCOMA
of brain GLIOMA
—eyelid STY(E)
—fat LIPOMA
—fibrous tissue FIBROMA
—glands ADENOMA
—gums EPULIS
—kidney NEPHROBLASTOMA
—lungs MESOTHELIOMA
—lymph glands LYMPHOMA
—membrane CARCINOMA
—mucous membrane POLYP(E), POLYPUS
—muscle MYOMA, SARCOMA
—nerve tissue NEUROMA
—papilla PAPILLOMA
—pigmented skin MELANOMA
—sheath of tendon GANGLION
—skin RODENT ULCER
—supporting tissue of brain GLIOMA
—testicle SPERMATOCELE
—thymus THYMOMA
—uterus FIBROID

turning in of eyelashes	TRICHIASIS
twisted intestine	VOLVULUS
twitching of muscle fibre	FIBRILLATION
typhoid fever	ENTERIC FEVER
	GASTRIC FEVER
typhus	GAOL FEVER, JAIL FEVER
	PUTRID FEVER, SHIP-FEVER
	TRENCH FEVER
typist's	
—cramp	TENOSYNOVITIS
—disability REPETITIVE STRAIN INJURY, RSI	
ulceration	PHAGED(A)ENA
unconsciousness	COMA
undulant fever	BRUCELLOSIS
	MALTA FEVER
	MEDITERRANEAN FEVER
	NEAPOLITAN FEVER
	ROCK FEVER
uncontrollable sleepiness	NARCOLEPSY
uniform muscular spasm	TONIC SPASM
unnatural distension	
with air	EMPHYSEMA
unpigmented skin	LEUKODERMA, VITILIGO
unremembered automatic	
behaviour	FUGUE
urinary organ	
infection	UROSIS
urticaria	NETTLE-RASH, HIVES
vaccinia	COWPOX
varicella	CHICKENPOX, WATER-POX
variola	SMALLPOX
venereal disease	CHANCRE, GONORRHOEA
	SYPHILIS
verruca	PAPILLOMA, WART
verruga Peruviana	BOBA,BUBA
	BUTTON SCURVY
	FRAMBOESIA, YAWS
vertigo	GIDDINESS
vesicle	BLISTER
vesicular eruption	EMPHLYSIS
Vincent's angina	TRENCH MOUTH
viral disease	VIROSIS
vomiting blood	HAEMATEMESIS
vomito	YELLOW FEVER
wall-eye	GLAUCOMA
war neurosis	SHELL-SHOCK
wart	KERATOSIS, PAPILLOMA
	VERRUCA
wasting	
—away	ATROPHY, MARASMUS
—disease	HECTIC FEVER, PHTHISIS
	TABES
—of muscle tissue	DYSTROPHY
water	
—borne disease	CHOLERA
	CRYPTOSPORIDIOSIS

	LEGIONNAIRES' DISEASE
	TYPHOID
—brash	HEARTBURN, PYROSIS
—on the brain	HYDROCEPHALUS
—pox	VARICELLA
watery accumulation	(HY)DROPSY, OEDEMA
weakness of voice	PHONASTHENIA
weaning-brash	DIARRHOEA
Weil's disease	LEPTOSPIROSIS
whisky-liver	CIRRHOSIS
white	
—leg	PHLEGMASIA
—patches on	
skin	LEUKODERMA
membrane	LEUKOPLAKIS
whitlow	PANARITIUM, PARONYCHIA
whooping-cough	CHINCOUGH, PERTUSSIS
Wilm's tumour	NEPHROBLASTOMA
winter depression	SAD
	SEASONAL AFFECTIVE DISORDER
wolf-madness	LYCANTHROPY
wooden-tongue	ACTINOBACILLOSIS
woody-tongue	ACTINOBACILLOSIS
woolsorter's disease	ANTHRAX
word	
—blindness	DYSLEXIA
—substitution	PARAPHASIA
wound	TRAUMA
wrinkles caused by sun	PHOTO-AGEING
writer's cramp	SCRIVENER'S PALSY
wry-neck	TORTICOLLIS
yaws	BEJEL, BOBA, BUBA
	BUTTON SCURVY
	FRAMBOESIA, MORULA
	VERRUGA PERUVIANA
yellow	
—fever	VOMITO, YELLOW JACK
—tumour	XANTHOMA
yellowing	JAUNDICE
yuppie flu	ME
	MYALGIC ENCEPHALOMYELITIS
zoster	HERPES, SHINGLES
divination	SORTILEGE
by/from/with:	
arrows	BELINOMANCY
ashes	SPODOMANCY, TEPHROMANCY
atmospheric phenomena	AEROMANCY
augury	AURUSPICY
bible readings	BIBLIOMANCY
birds	ORNITHOMANCY
	ORNITHOSCOPY
books	BIBLIOMANCY
cards	CARTOMANCY
casting lots	SORTILEGE
Chinese book of diagrams	I CHING
crystal ball	SCRYING

divine inspiration	THEOMANCY
dreams	ONEIROMANCY
	ONEIROSCOPY
dropping of food scraps by birds	TRIPUDIUM
entrails of animals	HARUSPICATION
feet	PODOMANCY
figures on earth	GEOMANCY
fingernails	ONIMANCY
	ONYCHOMANCY
finger-rings	DACTYLIOMANCY
fire	PYROMANCY
flames	LAMPADOMANCY
flight of birds	AUGURY, AUSPICE
	ORNITHOMANCY
fortune-telling	DUKKERIPEN
ghosts	SCIOMANCY
hands	CH(E)IROMANCY
	PALMISTRY
hopping of birds while feeding	TRIPUDIUM
inspection of liver	HEPATOSCOPY
knots in umbilical cord	OMPHALOMANCY
large glasses	GASTROMANCY
lot	CIEROMANCY
lying behind waterfall on a hide	TAGHAIRM
meal strewed over victims of sacrifice	CRITHOMANCY
mirrors	CATOPTROMANCY
motions of axe	AXINOMANCY
movements of mice	MYOMANCY
numbers	NUMEROLOGY
objects used in sacrifice	HEIROMANCY
observation of animals	ZOOMANCY
oracles	THEOMANCY
patterns in dust	GEOMANCY
physical contact	PSYCHOMETRY
planets	ASTROLOGY, HOROSCOPE
plants	BOTANOMANCY
playing-cards	CARTOMANCY
rods	RHABDOMANCY
second sight	DEUTEROSCOPY
shoulder blades	SCAPULIMANCY
shoulders of beasts	ARMOMANCY
sieve and shears	COSCINOMANCY
sixth sense	ESP
	EXTRA-SENSORY PERCEPTION
smoke	CAPNOMANCY
soles of feet	PEDOMANCY
spirits of the dead	NECROMANCY
	NIGROMANCY
springs	PEGOMANCY
splits in burning shoulder-blades	OMOPLATOSCOPY
stars	ASTROMANCY

stomach noises	GASTROMANCY
stones	LITHOMANCY
transparent bodies	CRYSTALLOMANCY
visions	CLAIRVOYANCE
walking in a circle and falling from giddiness	GYROMANCY
water	HYDROMANCY
wax dropping into water	CEROMANCY
wine	OENOMANCY
Zodiac	ASTROLOGY, HOROSCOPE

Doctors of

—Canon and Civil Law	JUD, UJD
—Civil Law	DCL, JCD
—Dental Surgery	DDS
—Divinity	DD
—Education	DED
—Engineering	DENG, DING
—Law	LLD
—Letters	DLIT, LHD, LITD
—Literature	DLIT, LITD
—Medicine	MD
—Music	DMUS
—Philosophy	DPH, PHD
—Science	DSC, SCD
—Theology	DTH, THD

dogs

Abyssinian	KABERU
Afghan hound	BALKH HOUND
	BALUCHI HOUND
	BARUKZY HOUND
Afghanistan	AFGHAN HOUND
	AFGHAN SPANIEL
Africa	BAGANDA HUNTING DOG
	BASENJI, HAIRLESS DOG
	RHODESIAN RIDGEBACK
	SEALYDALE, SLUGHI
—wild	CAPE HUNTING DOG
aguara-guaza	MANED DOG, MANED WOLF
	RED WOLF
Airedale terrier	BINGLEY TERRIER
	WATERSIDE TERRIER
	WHARFEDALE TERRIER
Akita	JAPANESE DEERHOUND
	NIPPON INU
Alsatian	GERMAN SHEPHERD DOG
	SCHAFERHUND
America	AMERICAN COCKER SPANIEL
	AMERICAN (FOX)HOUND
	AMERICAN WATER SPANIEL
	CHESAPEAKE BAY RETRIEVER
	PLOTT HOUND, RACCOON DOG
	TIMBER WOLF DOG
Appenzell mountain dog	APPENZELL SENNENHUND
Arabia	SALUKI
Argentina	PILA

Arkwright pointer	BLACK POINTER
Australia	AUSTRALIAN TERRIER
	AUSTRALIAN CATTLE DOG
	BARB, KANGAROO DOG
	SIDNEY SILKY TERRIER
—Barb	BLACK KELPIE
—cattle dog	HEELER
—sheepdog	KELPIE, KELPY
—wild	DINGO
Austria	TYROLEAN SHEEPDOG
Azara's dog	AGUARACHAY, AZARA'S FOX
	BRAZILIAN DOG
Azores	FILA DA TERCEIRA
Aztec sacred dog	TEECHICHI
Balearic Islands	EIVISSENC
badgerhound	BASSET(HOUND)
	DACHSHUND
Barb	BLACK KELPIE
Barry's dog	NANA
Basenji	BELGIAN CONGO DOG
	CONGO BUSH DOG
	CONGO HUNTING TERRIER
basset	ARESIAN BASSET
	ARTOIS DOG
Bedlington terrier	NORTH COUNTIES TERRIER
	ROTHBURY TERRIER
Belgium	BICHON, BOUVIER DE FLANDRE
	BOUVIER DES ARDENNES
	BRABANCON, GRIFFON (BELGE)
	GROENENDAEL, KERTHALS GRIFFON
	LAEKENOIS, LEONBERGER
	MALINOIS, ST HUBERT HOUND
	TURVUEREN
Bergamaschi	CANE DE PASTOR BERGAMASCO
	ITALIAN BERGAMA SHEEPDOG
Bernese mountain dog	BERNESE SENNENHUND
	DURBACHLER
bird-dog	DROPPER
black and tan terrier	MANCHESTER TERRIER
bloodhound	LIME-HOUND, LYAM-HOUND
	LYME-HOUND, SLEUTH-HOUND
	SLOT HOUND
boarhound	GERMAN MASTIFF
	GREAT DANE
border terrier	REEDWATER TERRIER
borzoi	RUSSIAN GREYHOUND
	RUSSIAN WOLFHOUND
Boston terrier	ROUNDHEADED TERRIER
Bouvier	
—de Flandre	BELGIAN CATTLE DOG
—des Ardennes	ARDENNES CATTLE DOG
boxer	GERMN BULLDOG
Brabancon	SMOOTH-HAIRED GRIFFON
Branchiero	CANE DA MACELLAIO

Brazil	AZARA'S DOG
Breton spaniel	BRITTANY SPANIEL
	ESPAGNEUL BRETON
buckhound	DEERHOUND, STAGHOUND
bulldog	
—German	BOXER
—x mastiff	BULL MASTIFF
—x terrier	BOSTON TERRIER
	BULL TERRIER
bullfighter's dog	ALANO
Burns's dogs	CAESAR, LUATH
butterfly dog	PAPILLON
Cairn terrier	SHORT-HAIRED SKYE TERRIER
Canada	HARE INDIAN DOG, LANDSEER
	NEWFOUNDLAND
	NOOTKA DOG, TOGANEE
Cape hunting dog	HYENA DOG, WILDEHOND
Carisissi	BRAZILIAN FOX
	CRAB-EATING DOG
	SURINAM DOG
cartoon dog	DEPITY DAWG, LADY
	PLUTO, TRAMP
Catalan sheepdog	GOS D'ATURA
	PERRO DE PASTOR CATALAN
Chesapeake Bay retriever	AMERICAN DUCK RETRIEVER
	DUCKING DOG
chihuahua	MEXICAN DWARF DOG
	ORNAMENT DOG, PILLOW DOG
Chile	JUAN FERNANDEZ SHEEPDOG
China	ANHUI, CHINESE GREYHOUND
	CHOW-CHOW, COOLIE DOG
	HAIRLESS DOG, HAPPA DOG
	LO CHIANG, LOONG CHUA
	MANCHURIAN SNOW DOG
	MONGOLIAN MASTIFF
	PEKIN(G)ESE, PEN-LO, PUG
	SHANTUNG GREYHOUND
	SHAR PEI, SHIH TZU
—hairless dog	CRESTED DOG
chow-chow	CANTONESE BUTCHER DOG
	EDIBLE DOG, ORIENTAL SPITZ
	SHAN DOG
Clydesdale terrier	PAISLEY TERRIER
coach-dog	CARRIAGE-DOG
	DALMATIAN
coarse-haired terrier	GRIFF
cocker spaniel	COCKING SPANIEL
	WOODCOCK SPANIEL
colpeo	CHILE FOX, FOUR-TOED DOG
	MAGELLAN FOX
corgi	WELSH HEELER
coyote	NORTH AMERICAN WILD DOG
cross-bred	CUR, MONGREL, MUTT, POOCH
	TYKE, WOLF-DOG, YELLOW-DOG
Cuba	CUBAN BLOODHOUND

curly-tailed	TRENDLE-TAIL(ED)
	TRINDLE-TAIL(ED)
	TRUNDLE_TAIL(ED)
dachshund	BADGER DOG, TECKEL
Dalmatian	CARRIAGE DOG
	COACH DOG
	LESSER DANE
Dandie Dinmont	
terrier	CHARLIE'S HOPE TERRIER
	MUSTARD AND PEPPER TERRIER
Denmark	GREAT DANE
dingo	AUSTRALIAN NATIVE DOG
	AUSTRALIAN WILD DOG
	WARRIGAL
Dulux dog	OLD ENGLISH SHEEPDOG
Egypt	EGYPTIAN SHEEPDOG
	HAIRLESS DOG, MANBOUTOU
	SHILLUK DOG, TESEM
—sheepdog	ARMENT, ERMENTI, SABE
Eivissenc	BALEARIC HOUND
	CHARNEQUE, MALLORQUIN
	PODENCO IBICENCO
elkhound	GRAA DRYEHUND
	GRAHUND, GREY ELK DOG
Entlebuch mountain	
dog	ENTLEBUCHER SENNENHUND
Eskimo	HUSKY, MALAMUTE
	MALEMUTE
extinct	ANTARCTIC DOG
	BLUE PAUL, LOONG CHUA
	MANBOUTOU, NORFOLK SPANIEL
	SCOTTISH SPANIEL
	SOUTHERN HOUND, TALBOT
female	BITCH
fierce dog, tied up	BANDOG, BANN DOGE
fighting dog	BLUE PAUL
	PIT BULL TERRIER
	STAFFORDSHIRE BULL TERRIER
	TOSA
film star	LASSIE
Finland	FINNISH SPITZ, LAIKA
Finnish Spitz	BARKING BIRD DOG
	FINNISH COCK-EARED DOG
fox terrier	SMOOTH-HAIRED TERRIER
	WIRE-HAIRED TERRIER
France	CHIEN
	BEAUCERON, BOULDOGUE
	BRAQUE DE BOURBONNAIS
	BRAQUE ST GERMAIN
	BRETON SPANIEL, BRIARD
	CHIEN FAUVE DE BRETAGNE
	DOGUE DE BORDEAUX
	FRENCH BULLDOG, FRENCH POODLE
	PYRENEAN MOUNTAIN DOG
	PYRENEAN SHEEPDOG
	VENDEEN HOUND

Germany	HUND, AFFENPINSCHER
	ALSATIAN, BOXER, DACHSHUND
	DOBERMAN(N) (PINSCHER)
	HARLEQUIN PINSCHER
	JAGDTERRIER, MUNSTERLANDER
	POTSDAM GREYHOUND
	POMERANIAN (SHEEPDOG)
	POODLE, REISENSCHNAUZER
	ROTTWEILER, SCHNAUZER
	SPITZ, TECKEL, VORSTEHHUND
	WEIMARANER
Gordon setter	BLACK AND TAN SETTER
Great Dane	DANISH DOG
	(GERMAN) BOARHOUND
	TIGER DOG, ULMER MASTIFF
—coloured	HARLEQUIN
Greece	GREEK SHEEPDOG
Greenland	ANGMAGSSALIK HUSKY
greyhounds	BANJAR, CHINESE
	GRIG HOUND, HERHOUND
	ITALIAN, KANGAROO
	LEPORARIUS, LONG-DOG
	LONG-TAIL, NORTHWEST INDIAN
	PERSIAN, POTSDAM, RAMPUR
	SHANTUNG
—Afghan	BALKH
—hybrid	LURCHER
spaniel	WHIPPET
terrier	WHIPPET
—Irish	WOLFHOUND
—rough-coated	DEERHOUND
—Russian	BORZOI, TAZA
guard dogs	ALSATIAN, BANDOG
	BANN DOGE, BOXER
	BULL MASTIFF, BULL TERRIER
	CHOW-CHOW
	DOBERMAN(N) (PINSCHER)
	GREAT DANE, MALINOIS
	MASTIFF, PYRENEAN, ROTTWEILER
	STAFFORDSHIRE BULL TERRIER
—in Hades	CERBERUS
—of	
Hela	GARM
Helen	GARM
gun/sporting dogs	BRITTANY
	CHESAPEAKE BAY, CLUMBER
	COCKER, FIELD SPANIEL
	LABRADOR, POINTER
	MUNSTERLANDER
	RETRIEVER, SETTER, SPINNONE
	SPRINGER, WEIMARANER
Guyana	ARECUNA HUNTING DOG
hairless dog	NAKED DOG, PILA
Happa dog	CHINESE PUG, PEKING PUG
Hardy's dog	WESSEX
harrier	HARE HOUND

heavy-jawed dog	JOWLER	Isaac Newton's dog	DIAMOND
HMV dog	NIPPER	Japan	AKITA, CHIN (CHIN)
Holland	HERDERSHONDEN, KEESHOND		INU NUS'TO
	SCHIPPERKE, SMOUSHOND		SHIRA, SHISHI, TOSA
hounds	AFGHAN, AMERICAN, BALEARIC	John Peel's dogs	BELLMAN, RANTER, TRUE
	BALUCHI, BARUKHZY, BASSET	Kabyle dog	KABIL
	BRITTANY, HARE		NORTH AFRICAN KABYLE
	JAPANESE BEAR, LIGHTNING RAG		OULED NAIL DOG
	NORTH AFRICAN GAZELLE		SHAWIA DOG
	PLOTT, PYRENEAN, RAMPUR	kangaroo dog	KANGAROO GREYHOUND
	SLEUTH, SLOT, ST HUBERT	Keeshond	DUTCH BARGE DOG
	SWEDISH, VENDEEN, WELSH	Kerry blue terrier	IRISH BLUE TERRIER
Hungary	KOMONDOR, KUVASZ	King Charles's Spaniel	CAVALIER
	PULI, PUMI, VIZSLA		COMFORTER
hunting			ENGLISH TOY DOG
—dogs	AFGHAN, AKITA, ALAN(D)		SPANIEL GENTLE
	ALANT, ARECUNA, BASSET	kitchen dog	TURNSPIT, VERNEPATOR
	BEAGLE, BORZOI, BRACH,	kuri	MAORI DOG
	BRA(T)CHET, BUCKHOUND, COURSER		NEW ZEALAND WILD DOG
	DACHSHUND, DEERHOUND, EIVISSENC	Lakeland terrier	FELL TERRIER
	ELKHOUND, FOXHOUND, GREAT DANE		PATTERDALE TERRIER
	GREYHOUND, HARRIER	Lancashire	HEELER
	IBIZAN, IRISH WOLFHOUND	lap dog	(see toy below)
	KANGAROO DOG, KENNET, OTTERHOUND	large	GREAT DANE, MASTIFF
	PHARAOH HOUND, POCKET BEAGLE		NEWFOUNDLAND, ST BERNARD
	PODENGO, POINTER	lion-dog	LOWCHEN
	RABBIT BEAGLE, RACCOON DOG	long	
	RETRIEVER, RHODESIAN RIDGEBACK	—bodied	BEDLINGTON (TERRIER)
	SALUKI, SETTER, SLUGHI, SPITZ		BLENHEIM, DACHSHUND
	STAGHOUND, WOLFHOUND		TURNSPIT
—by scent	RACHE, RATCH	—eared	BASSET, BEAGLE
husky	ANGMAGSSALIK HUSKY		BLOODHOUND, SPANIEL
	BAFFINLAND DOG, ESKIMO DOG	loose-skinned	SHAR PEI
	MALAMUTE, MALEMUTE	Malaya	JENTERAH, SERIGALA
	MACKENZIE RIVER DOG	many-headed	CERBERUS
	OSTIAK, SLED DOG	Maremma	ABRUZZI SHEEPDOG
	TIMBER WOLF DOG, TOGANEE		CANE DE PASTOR MAREMMANO
Iceland	ICELANDIC SHEEPDOG		MAREMMES SHEEPDOG
India	BANJARA, POLIGAR	mastiff	ALAN, ALAUNT, BANDOGGE
	RAMPUR HOUND		MOLLOSSUS, TIE-DOG
—wild	DECCAN DOG, DHOLE	Mexico	CHIHUAHUA, HAIRLESS DOG
	KOLSUN, RAM-KUTTA	monkey terrier	AFFENPINSCHER
Ireland	GLEN OF IMAAL TERRIER		MONKEY PINSCHER
	IRISH SETTER, IRISH TERRIER	mountain dogs	APPENZELL, BERNESE
	IRISH WOLFHOUND, KERRY BEAGLE		ENTELBUCH, ESTRELA
	KERRY BLUE, WHEATEN TERRIER		PYRENEAN, ST BERNARD
	IRISH WATER SPANIEL	New Zealand	KURI
—setter	MODDER RHU, RED SETTER	Niam Niam	HAUTE-AGOOUE TERRIER
	RED SPANIEL		NYAM NYAM TERRIER
—wolfhound	IRISH ELKHOUND	Norway	ELKHOUND
	IRISH GREYHOUND	Nottinghamshire	CLUMBER (SPANIEL)
Italy	CANE	old	LYM, SHOUGH, SHOWGHE
	BERGAMASCHI, BOLOGNESE	Odysseus's dog	ARGOS
	ITALIAN GREYHOUND	Orient	PI(E)-DOG, PYE-DOG
	MAREMMA, NEAPOLITAN MASTIFF		PARIAH
	SEGUGIO, SPINONE, VOLPINO	Owczarek	POLISH SHEEPDOG

Pekin(g)ese	DRAGON DOG, LION DOG
	PEKING PALACE DOG
Pen-lo	PA ERH
Perdigueiro	PORTUGUESE POINTER
performing tricks	TUMBLER
Persia	SALUKI
pet	LAP-DOG, TOY-DOG, POODLE
Philippines	PHILIPPINES EDIBLE DOG
	PHILLIPINES NATIVE DOG
poacher's dog	LURCHER
Podengo	PORTUGUESE RABBIT DOG
pointers	ARKWRIGHT, BLACK, BURGOS
	GERMAN, HUNGARIAN
	PORTUGUESE, SPANISH
	YELLOW
Poland	NIZINNY, OWCZAREK
	LOWLAND SHEEPDOG
Pomeranian	SPITZ
Portugal	PODENGO
	PORTUGUESE POINTER
	PORTUGUESE CATTLE DOG
	PORTUGUESE SHEEPDOG
	PORTUGUESE WATER DOG
—Podengo	PORTUGUESE RABBIT DOG
—cattle dog	CAO DE CASTRO LABOREIRO
—pointer	PERDIGUEIRO
—sheepdog	CAO SERRA DA ESTRELA
—water dog	CAO D'AGUA
	PORTUGUESE DIVING DOG
	PORTUGUESE FISHING DOG
pug	CARLIN, LO-SZE, MOPS
Punch's dog	TOBY
Pyrenean	
—mountain dog	GREAT PYRENEES
	PYRENEAN HOUND
—sheepdog	LABRI
raccoon dog	COONHOUND
racing dog	GREYHOUND, WHIPPET
Rampur	
hound	NORTHWEST INDIAN GREYHOUND
	RAMPUR GREYHOUND
retrievers	AMERICAN DUCK
	CHESAPEAKE BAY
	CURLY-COATED, FLAT-COATED
	GOLDEN, LABRADOR
	WAVY-COATED
Rhodesian ridgeback	RHODESIAN LION DOG
Romania	CARPATHIAN SHEEPDOG
Rottweiler	ROITWEIL DOG
	ROTTWEILER METZGERHUND
rough-coated greyhound	DEERHOUND
Russia	AFTCHARKA, BORZOI
	CAUCASIAN SHEEPDOG
	SAMOYED(E), TAZA
	UKRAINIAN SHEEPDOG
	WOLFHOUND

St Bernard	ALPINE MASTIFF
saluki	GAZELLE HOUND
	PERSIAN GREYHOUND
Scandinavia	ELKHOUND
Schipperke	BELGIAN BARGE DOG
Scotland	ABERDEEN TERRIER, BLUE PAUL
	CAIRN (TERRIER)
	CLYDESDALE TERRIER
	DANDIE DINMONT, GORDON SETTER
	SCOTCH TERRIER, SCOTCH COLLY DOG
	SCOTTISH SPANIEL, SCOTTISH TERRIER
	SHETLAND SHEEPDOG, SKYE TERRIER
	WEST HIGHLAND WHITE TERRIER
—lap-dog	MESSAN
—sheepdog	COLLIE
—terrier	SCOTTIE
setters	BLACK-AND-TAN, ENGLISH
	GORDON, IRISH
	LLEWELLIN, RED
shaggy dog	ICELAND DOG
	OLD ENGLISH SHEEPDOG
	SHOCK, SHOUGH
sheep/cattle dogs	ABRUZZI, AFTCHARKA
	ANATOLIAN, ARMENT
	AUSTRALIAN CATTLE DOG
	BEAUCERON, BELGIAN, BERGAMA
	BORDER, BOUVIER DE FLANDRE
	BOUVIER DES ARDENNES
	BRANCHIERO, BRIARD, BUGEILGI
	CAO SERRA DA ESTRELA
	CARPATHIAN, CATALAN, CAUCASIAN
	COLLIE, COLLY, CUMBERLAND
	DUTCH HERDER, EGYPTIAN, ENGLISH
	GERMAN SHEPHERD, GREEK
	GROENENDAEL, HUNGARIAN
	ICELANDIC, JUAN FERNANDEZ
	KABYLE DOG, KELPIE, KELPY
	KOMONDOR, MAREMMA, MALINOIS
	NOOTKA DOG, OLD ENGLISH
	OWCZAREK, OWTCHARKA
	POLISH LOWLAND, POMERANIAN
	PORTUGUESE, PUMI, PYRENEAN
	ROMANIAN, SERRA DA ESTRELA
	SHETLAND, SIBERIAN
	TOOROOCHAN, TYROLEAN
	UKRAINIAN, VALLHUND, WELSH
Shetland Islands	SHETLAND SHEEPDOG
	SHELTIE, SHELTY
—sheepdog	PEERIE DOG, TOONIE DOG
Shiba	JAPANESE TURF DOG, KAI DOG
Shih Tzu	TIBETAN LION DOG
Shishi	AINU DOG, CHOKEN
	JAPANESE BEAR HOUND
short	
—eared dog	ALAN(D), ALANT
	SCLATER'S DOG

—legged dog	AUSTRALIAN TERRIER	Switzerland	APPENZELL MOUNTAIN DOG
	CAIRN TERRIER, CORGI		BERNESE SENNENHUND
	DANDIE DINMONT TERRIER		ENTLEBUCH MOUNTAIN DOG
	BASSET, BEAGLE, BULLDOG		ST BERNARD, SWEDISH BEAGLE
	DACHSHUND	tailless dog	SCHIPPERKE
	GLEN OF IMAAL TERRIER	Taruma hunting dog	WOYAWAI DOG
	JACK RUSSELL TERRIER	terriers	ABERDEEN, AIREDALE
	NORWICH TERRIER, SEALYHAM		AUSTRALIAN
	SIDNEY SILKY TERRIER		BEDLINGON, BINGLEY
	SKYE TERRIER, TURNSPIT		BLACK AND TAN, BORDER
	WEST HIGHLAND WHITE TERRIER		BOSTON, BULL, CAIRN, CHARLIE'S HOPE
Siberia	LAIKA, OSTIAK		CLYDESDALE, DANDY DINMONT
	SAMOYED(E)		DARJEELING, FELL, FOX
	SIBERIAN WILD DOG		GLEN OF IMAAL, HAUTE-AGOOUE
	TOOROOCHAN SHEEPDOG		IRISH (BLUE),KERRY BLUE
Sicily	BRANCHIERO		LAKELAND, MANCHESTER
silky-haired dog	MALTESE		MONKEY, MUSTARD AND PEPPER
	SIDNEY SILKY TERRIER		NORFOLK, NORTH COUNTIES
	YORKSHIRE TERRIER		NORWICH, PAISLEY
sleeve dog	(see toy below)		(PARSON) JACK RUSSELL
Slughi	NORTH AFRICAN GAZELLE HOUND		PATTERDALE, PIT BULL, POLTALLOCH
small			REEDWATER, ROSENEATH, ROTHBURY
—hunting dog	JACK RUSSELL, KENNET		ROUNDHEADED, SCOTTISH
—poodle (old)	WATER-DOG		SEALYHAM, SILKY, SKYE
Smoushond	DUTCH SMOUS		SMOOTH FOX, STAFFORDSHIRE BULL
snub-nosed dog	BULLDOG, PUG		TIBETAN, WATERSIDE
South America	BUSH DOG, SCLATER'S DOG		WELSH, WEST HIGHLAND WHITE
	TARUMA HUNTING DOG		WHARFEDALE, WHEATEN
Spain	PERRO		WIRE FOX, YORKSHIRE
	CATALAN SHEEPDOG	Tesem	EGYPTIAN HUNTING DOG
	PODENCO NAVARRO	Tibet	LHASA APSO, SHIH TZU
	PYRENEAN MOUNTAIN DOG		TIBETAN MASTIFF
	PYRENEAN SHEEPDOG		TIBETAN SPANIEL
	SPANISH POINTER		TIBETAN TERRIER
—pointer	BURGOS POINTER	—spaniel	TIBETAN PRAYER DOG
	SPANISH PEDIGUERO	—terrier	CHRYSANTHEMUM DOG
spaniels	AFGHAN, AMERICAN COCKER		DARJEELING TERRIER
	AMERICAN WATER, BRETON	Tosa	JAPANESE FIGHTING DOG
	BRITTANY, BROWN WATER		JAPANESE MASTIFF
	BUTTERFLY, CAVALIER, CLUMBER	toy/lap/sleeve dogs	AFFENPINSCHER
	COCKER, ENGLISH SPRINGER		AUSTRALIAN SILKY TERRIER
	ENGLISH TOY, ENGLISH WATER		BICHON FRISE, BOLOGNESE
	FIELD, GENTLE, IRISH WATER		BOSTON, BREVIPILIS
	KING CHARLES, NORFOLK, RED		BRUSSELS GRIFFON, CAVALIER
	RED-AND-WHITE, SCOTTISH		CHIHUAHUA, CHIN-CHIN
	SPRINGER, SUSSEX, TIBETAN		HAIRLESS DOG, HAVANA
	WELSH SPRINGER, WOODCOCK		ITALIAN GREYHOUND
Spitz	POMERANIAN		KING CHARLES'S SPANIEL
spotted dog	DALMATIAN		LHASA APSO, LOWCHEN, MALTESE
Springer spaniel	NORFOLK SPRINGER		MINIATURE PINSCHER
staghound	BUCKHOUND, DEERHOUND		MONKEY TERRIER, PAPILLON
stray dog on race-course	DERBY DOG		PEKIN(G)ESE, PEN-LO
Sudan	NIAM NIAM		POMERANIAN, POODLE, PUG
Sumatra	BATAK		ROQUET, SHIH TZU
Sweden	SWEDISH FOXHOUND		TIBETAN SPANIEL
	VALLHUND		YORKSHIRE TERRIER

tracker	BLOODHOUND, DRAGHOUND
Turkey	ANATOLIAN, HAIRLESS DOG
two-headed	ORTHOS
Vallhund	VASTGOTA SPITZ
Vizsla	HUNGARIAN POINTER
	YELLOW POINTER
Vorstehhund	GERMAN POINTER
Wales	CORGI, LLEWELLIN SETTER
	SEALYHAM, WELSH HOUND
	WELSH SHEEPDOG
	WELSH SPRINGER SPANIEL
	WELSH TERRIER
—corgi	CI SAWDL, WELSH HEELER
—hound	BYTHEUAD, WELSH FOXHOUND
—sheepdog	BUGEILGI, WELSH COLLIE
—Springer spaniel	RED-AND-WHITE SPANIEL
	STARTER, TARGI
—terrier	DAIARGI
watch-dog	(*see* guard dogs *above*)
West Highland White	
Terrier	POLTALLOCH TERRIER
	ROSENEATH TERRIER
West Indies	HAIRLESS DOG
whippet	LIGHTNING RAG HOUND
	SNAP DOG
wild	
—Abyssinia	KABERU
—Africa	SOMALI WILD DOG
	SOUTH AFRICAN WILD DOG
—America	COYOTE
—Australia	DINGO
—China	RACCOON-LIKE DOG
—India	BUANSUAH, DHOLE, PARIAH
	PI(E)-DOG, PYE-DOG
—Japan	RACCOON-LIKE DOG
—Malaya	JENTERAH, SERIGALA
—Orient	PI(E)-DOG, PYE-DOG
	PARIAH
—South America	AGUARA-GUAZA
	AZARA'S DOG, CARRISISSI
	COLPEO, ECUADOR BUSH DOG
	SANTA CATHARINA DOG
with flecked bluish	
fur	(BLUE) MERLE
worthless	CUR, HUNT-COUNTER
young dog	CUB, PUP(PY)
	SLEEVE-DOG, WHELP
young hound(s)	ENTRY
Yugoslavia	DALMATIAN
Dominica	
capital	ROSEAU
coin	CENT, DOLLAR
Dominican Republic	
capital	SAN DOMINGO
coin	CENTAVO, PESO

dramatists	
American	ALBEE, ANDERSON, ARENT
	BALDWIN, BROWN, BULLINS
	GELBER, HANSBERRY, JONES
	KOPIT, LOWELL, MCLEISH
	MILLER, ODETS, O'NEILL
	RICE, SAROYAN, WILLIAMS
Austrian	SCHNITZLER, WERFEL
Belgian	CROMMELYNCK, MAETERLINCK
British	ARDEN, AYCKBOURN, BENNETT
	BOLT, BOND, BRENTON, CLARK
	COWARD, DELANEY, DENNIS
	DRYDEN, EDGAR, ELIOT, FIELDING
	FRY, GALSWORTHY, GOLDSMITH
	GILBERT, GRANVILLE-BARKER
	GREENE, GRIFFITHS, HAMPTON
	HARE, KYD, LYLY, MARLOWE
	MCGRATH, MERCER, MIDDLETON
	MORTIMER, NICHOLLS, ORTON
	OSBORNE, PINERO, PINTER
	POLIAKOFF, POTTER, PRIESTLEY
	RATTIGAN, RUDKIN, SANDERS
	SHAFFER, SHAKESPEARE
	SHERIDAN, SIMPSON, SPENSER
	STOPPARD, STOREY, WELLAND
	WESKER, WHELAN, WHITEHEAD
	WILLIAMS, WOOD
Cuban	TRIANA
Czech	CAPEK, HAVEL
French	ANOUILH, ARRABAL, BATY
	BRIEUX, CLAUDEL, COCTEAU
	CORNEILLE, DUGARD, DURAS
	GIDE, IONESCU, JARRY
	MARTIN, MOLIERE, RACINE
	ROUSSEL, SALACROU, SARTRE
German	BALL, BRECHT, FRISCH
	GOETHE, GRASSE, HAUPTMANN
	HOCHHUTH, HOLZ, KALSER
	LARRONGE, SUDERMANN, TOLLER
	WEISS, ZUCKMEYER
Greek	AESCHYLUS, ARISTOPHANES
	EURIPIDES, SOPHOCLES
Hungarian	VON HORVATH
Irish	'BECKETT, BEHAN, GREGORY
	JOYCE, MAC LIAMMOIR, O'CASEY
	SHAW, SYNGE, WILDE, YEATS
Italian	PIRANDELLO, VERGA
Nigerian	SOYINKA
Norwegian	IBSEN
Romanian	IONESCU
Russian	ARBUZOBV, BULGAKOV
	CHEKHOV, DOSTO(Y)EVSKY
	GORKY, LUNTS, OSTROVSKY
	SUKOVO-KOBYLIN, TOLSTOY
	ZAMYATIN
South African	FUGARD

Spanish	ARRABAL, LORCA, PARMENO
	PINILLOS, SALINAS
Swedish	STRINDBERG, WEISS
Swiss	FRISCH
West Indian	HILL-JOHN, PHILLIPS
	WALCOTT, WHITE

drinks

acid drink	SOUR
African	SKOKIAAN, TOMBO
—beer	POMBE
after sunset	SUNDOWNER
aguardiente	BRANDY
alcohol flavoured or perfumed	LIQUEUR
alcoholic liquor (Scot.)	CREATURE
	THE CRATUR
ale	TIPPER
—and honey	BRAGGET
—cheap	TWOPENNY, FOUR-ALE
—new (Scots.)	SWATS
—Norfolk	NOG
—strong	MOROCCO, NAPPY
	NOG, OCTOBER
Sussex	TIPPER
—warmed and spiced	PURL
—with	
nutmeg	MACE ALE
pulped apples etc	LAMB'S-WOOL
roasted apples etc	WASSAIL
wormwood	PURL
Algerian	AGRAS
American	
—spirit, water, etc	SLING
—whisky	BOURBON, REDEYE, RYE
	TANGLEFOOT
—wine	CATAWBA, SCUPPERNONG
aniseed liqueur	OUZO
aperitif	ANIS, AMERPICON, BYRRH
	CAMPARI, CINZANO
	CREME DE CASSIS, DUBONNET
	KYR, LILLEY, MARTINI, OUZO
	PASTIS, PERNOD, PUNT E MES
	RICARD, ST RAPHAEL, SHERRY
	SUZE, VERMOUTH
bad	
—beer	SWIPES
—liquor	ROT-GUT
—whisky (US)	TARANTULA JUICE
beer	BITTER, BROWN ALE
	LIGHT ALE, MILD
	PALE ALE
—American	STEAM BEER
—Australian	AMBER, FROSTY, GROG
—Belgian	FARO
—black	GUINNESS, STOUT
—bottom-fermented	LAGER
—cheap	FOUR-ALE

—dark brown	PORTER
—drawn from cask	DRAUGHT, REALE ALE
—low in alcohol	SMALL BEER
—Egyptian	BO(U)SA, ZYTHUM
—exported	IPA, INDIA PALE ALE
—French	BIERE
—from wheat	WHEAT BEER
—German	BIER, BOCK, DORTMUNDER
	LAGER, MUNCHENER
	PILS(E)NER
—pale	BURTON
—poor (Scot.)	SWANK(E)Y
—Russian	KWASS, QUASS
—slang	GATTER, WALLOP
—stored under pressure	KEG BEER
—strong	STINGO
stout	BARLEYWINE
—top-fermented	ALE
—with	
gin	DOG'S-NOSE
ginger-beer	SHANDY(GAFF)
ground ivy	GILL-ALE, GILL BEER
lemonade	SHANDY(GAFF)
bingo	BRANDY
bitters	ANGOSTURA, FERNET BRANCA
	KHOOSH, ORANGE, PEACH
	UNDERBERG
blue ruin	GIN
bottled water	BADOIT, EVIAN, MALVERN
	PERRIER, RAMLOSA
	SPA, REINESPRING
brandy	AQUA VITAE, BINGO, EAU DE VIE
—and	
soda	PEG
water	BRANDYPAWNEE
	MAHOGANY
—Bulgarian	BRENDI
—distilled from	
cherries	KIRSCH
fruit juices (US)	MOBBIE, MOBBY
grape pomace	MARC
plums	SLIVOVITZ, TUICA
wine	FINE CHAMPAGNE
—French	ARMAGNAC, COGNAC
	EAU DE VIE, FINE
—Greek	METAXA
—Italian	GRAPPA
—Mediterranean	ROSOLIO
—obsolete	NANTZ
—Portuguese	AGUARDIENTE
—Romanian	TUICA
—South African	CAPE SMOKE
—Spanish	AGUARDIENTE
	FUNDADOR, SOBERANO
—Yugoslav	SLIVOVITZ, VINJAK
Brazilian	ASSAI

Bulgarian brandy	BRENDI
champagne	SILLERY, THE WIDOW
—and	
orange juice	BUCK'S FIZZ
stout	BLACK VELVET
—India	SIM(P)KIN
Chinese	KAOLIANG, MAO-TAI
cider	BLOODY BUTCHER
	HANDSOME MAUD
	SCRUMPY
cocktail	(see separate entry)
coffee and whiskey	IRISH COFFEE
cognac	BRANDY, FINE
cordial	PERSICO(T)
—after coffee	POUSSE-CAFE
—from	
anise	ANISETTE
berbs	LOVAGE
raisins	ROSO(G)LIO
sundew juice	ROSA-SOLIS
cups, punches, etc	APPLE POSSET
	BOATMAN'S CUP
	BUTTERED RUM
	CAIPIRINHA, CORPSE REVIVER
	EGG NOG, GLOGG, , GLUHWEIN
	HAIR OF THE DOG
	HONEYSUCKLE CUP
	HOT TODDY, MULLED ALE
	MULLED WINE
	POLISH HONEY DRINK
	PRAIRIE OYSTER, ROSE CUP
	SHERRY PUNCH, SUISSETTE
	SUMMER CUP, TEA TODDY
	WHITE WINE CUP
curdled	
—cream	SILLABUB, SYLLABUB
—milk	POSSET
demerara	RUM
different drink following	CHASER
distilled from wine	BRANDY
drink of the (Greek) gods	NECTAR
dry sherry	AMONTILLADO
	FINO, MANZANILLA
East Indies	NIPA
eastern	ARAK, ARRACK
effervescent	SHERBET
ethanol with approx	
50% alcohol	PROOF-SPIRIT
extra strong porter	STOUT
fermented	
—cow's milk	KEFIR, KEPHIR
—grape-juice	WINE
—mare's milk	K(O)UMISS
—palm juice	TODDY
—palm-sap	NIPA, SURA
—rice	RICE-BEER

fizzy	GINGER-ALE, GINGER-BEER
	LEMONADE, POP
	SHERBE(R)T, SODA-WATER
flavoured	
—milk	MILK-SHAKE
—schnapps (Tyrol)	ENZIAN
—with fruit kernels	RATAFIA
for	
—blending with spirits	MIXER
—doctoring port	GEROPIGA
—toats	WASSAIL
fortified wine	PORT
from	
—agave (Mex.)	PULQUE, TEQUIL(L)A
—almonds	ORGEAT
—anise	PERNOD
—apples	APPLEJACK, BATZI
	CALVADOS, CIDER
	EAU DE VIE DE CIDRE
	POMAGNE, TREBERN
—apricots	BARACK, PALINKA
—aromatic herbs	HERB-BEER, HERB-TEA
—barley	ORGEAT, PTISAN, TISANE
—cacao	CHOCOLATE, COCOA
—cactus	COCUI, PULQUE
—Coffea seeds	COFFEE
—cherries	KIRSCH, KIRSEBAELIKOER
—coconuts	AR(R)ACK
—corn	WHISKEY
—dandelions, sassafras	ROOT-BEER
—dates	AR(R)ACK, ZIBIB
—dough and sugar (US)	HOO(T)CH
—fruit-refuse	MARC(-BRANDY)
—ginger	GINGER WINE
—grain	AKVAVIT, AQUAVIT
	BOURBON, GENEVER
	GIN, CORN, SCHANPPS
	VODKA, WHISK(E)Y
—grape pomace	AGUARDIENTE
	BAGACEIRA
	GRAPPA, KOMOVICA
	MARC, TRESTERSCHNAPPS
—grapes	WINE
—herbs	BITTERS, LOVAGE
	PTISAN, TISANE
—honey (Welsh)	METHEGLIN
—maize	CHICHA
—milk	AWEIN, KOUMISS, SKHOU
—mint	PEPPERMINT
—molasses	AR(R)ACK, BASI, RAKEE
	RAKI, RUM
—orange flowers	ORGEAT
—Orchis	SALOOP
—palm trees	NIPA
—pears	BIRNGEIST, PERRY
	WILLIAMINE

—pepper plant	KAVA
—plums	MIRABELLE, QUETSCH
	SLIVOVITZ, TUICA
—pomegranates	GRENADINE
—potatoes	AKVAVIT, AQUAVIT
	SCHNAPPS, VODKA
—rice	AR(R)ACK, PANGASI, RAGI
	SAKE, SAKI, SHOCHU
—rose water	ZORGEAT
—spruce trees	SPRUCE BEER
—sassafras	SALOOP
—sugar cane	AGUARDIENTE, CANA
	RON, RUM
—tiger nuts	HORCHATA
—walnuts	NOCINO
—watermelons	KISLAV
fruit-juice	CRUSH, LEMONADE
	LIMEADE, ORANGEADE
	SHERBET, SQUASH
—and vinegar (Amer.)	SHRUB
fruit syrup	ROB, SUCCADE
German	
—beer	BIER, BOCK, DORTMUNDEN
	LAGER, MUNCHENER
	PILS(E)NER,
—gin	STEINHAGER
geneva	GIN
gin	BLUE RUIN, GENEVA,
	MAX, MOTHER'S RUIN
	OLD TOM, TWANKAY
—Dutch	HOLLAND, SCHNAP(P)S
	SCHIEDAM
—effervescent	GIN-FIZZ
—English	GORDON'S, LONDON DRY
	PLYMOUTH
—German	STEINHAGER
—illicit	BATHTUB(-GIN)
—with	
angostura	PINK GIN
treacle	MAHOGANY
vermouth	GIN AND IT
water	GIN-SLING
Goan	FENI, FENNY
good stuff	LIQUOR, WHISKY
grain and juniper berries	GENEVA
	GIN, HOLLANDS
grape juice	MUST
—with brandy, etc	GEROPIGA
Greek	
—spirit	MASTIKA, METAXA
	OUZO, RAKEE, RAKI
—strong drink	METHE
—wine	RETSINA, RESINATA
harsh whisky	CHAIN LIGHTNING
Hindu gods' drink	AMRITA
Holland gin	SCHNAP(P)S

honey and	
—mulberry juice	MORAT
—water	HYDROMEL, MEAD
hot	NEGUS, RUMFUSTIAN
	TODDY
—beer, spirits, etc	COBBLER'S PUNCH
—rum and eggs	TOM-AND-JERRY
—water, milk, sugar etc	CAMBRIC TEA
—wine and fruit	BISHOP, GLOGG
	GLUHWEIN
Hungarian wine	TOKAY
iced drink	COBBLER, COLLINS
	COOLER
illicit	
—gin	BATHTUB(-GEN)
—spirit (Aust., NZ)	SLY-GROG
—whisk(e)y	
America	BOOTLEG, MOONSHINE
Ireland	POT(H)EEN
imitation champagne	GOOSEBERRY(-WINE)
Indian	
—champagne	SIM(P)KIN
—spirit	SOMA
intoxicating liquor	BOOSE, BOOZE, BOUSE
—(Amer.)	TANGLEFOOT
invalid's drink	BEEF TEA, LUCOZADE
	WINCARNIS
Irish	GUINNESS
—illicit whiskey	POT(H)EEN
Italian	
—brandy	GRAPPA
—liqueur	NOCINO, SAMBUCA
—vermouth	IT
Japanese rice beer	SAKE, SAKI
late at night	NIGHTCAP
lemon juice with spirits	SHRUB
lettuce juice	THRIDACE
light beer	LAGER, PILS(E)NER
	TABLE-BEER
liqueur	
—after coffee	POUSSE-CAFE
—America	CORDIAL
	SOUTHERN COMFORT
—France	ABRICOTINE, ANISETTE
	BENEDICTINE, CHARTREUSE
	COINTREAU, GRAND MARNIER
	MANDARINE
—Germany	GOLDWASSER
—Greece	OUZO
—Holland	ADVOCAAT, KUMMEL
—Ireland	BAILEY'S IRISH CREAM
	IRISH MIST
—Italy	AMARO, AMARETTO DI SARONNO
	GALLIANO, MARASCHINO
	SAMBUCA, STREGA
—Jamaica	TIA MARIA

—made at Fécamp	BENEDICTINE	malt liquor	JOHN BARLEYCORN, STINGO
—made from		Martinique spirit	EAU DE CREOLES
almond or peach kernels	NOYAU	max	GIN
almonds	RATAFIA	medicated ale	SCURVY-GRASS
Alpine plants	GENIPI	medicinal	DILL WATER, PTISAN
aniseed			TISANE, SELTZER
—France	ANISETTE	Mediterranean spirit	RAKEE, RAKI
—Germany	GOLDWASSER		ROSOLIO
—Greece	OUZO	Mexican	PEYOTE, PULQUE, TEQUIL(L)A
apples	CALVADOS	milk	
apricots	ABRICOTINE	—and ice cream	MILK SHAKE
	APRICOT BRANDY	—curdled with wine etc	POSSET
blackberries	CREME DE MURE	—with rum or whisky	MILK-PUNCH
blackcurrants	CREME DE CASSIS	mineral water	BADOIT, EVIAN
brandy	ARMAGNAC, COGNAC		MALVERN, PERRIER, SELTZER
cherries	CHERRY BOUNCE		VICHY(WATER), VITELLOISE
	CHERRY-BRANDY		VOLVIC
	KIRSCH(WASSER)	mixed drink	TWIST
	MARASCHINO	mixer	BITTER LEMON, CANADA DRY
cumin and caraway			GINGER ALE, IT
seeds	KUMMEL		SODA WATER, TONIC WATER
herbs	BENEDICTINE, CHARTREUSE	mixture added to	
orange peel	CURACAO, CURACOA	weak beer	STUM
oranges	COINTREAU, GRAND MARNIER	molasses and water	SWITCHEL
peaches	PEACH-BRANDY	mother's ruin	GIN
peppermint	CREME DE MENTHE	muscatel	MUSCAT, MUSCADINE
plums	MIRABELLE, PRUNELLE	narcotic drink	(K)AVA
	SLIVOVITZ	negus	RUMFUSTIAN
rum and coffee	TIA MARIA	new	
sloes	SLOE-GIN	—ale (Scot.)	SWATS
tangerines		—wine	STUM
—France	MANDARINE	Norwich strong ale	NOG
—South Africa	VAN DER HUM	Old Tom	GIN
walnuts	NOCINO	on horseback	STIRRUP-CUP
whisk(e)y and			STIRRUP-DRAM
—honey	DRAMBUIE, IRISH MIST	orange juice and	
—peaches	SOUTHERN COMFORT	lemonade	HENRI, HENRY
—Scotland	DRAMBUIE	palm wine	TOMBO
—South Africa	VAN DER HUM	Paraguay tea	MATE
—Sweden	ARRACK PUNCH	peach-flavoured	PECHER
—sweet	CREME	Persian	BOSA, SHIRAZ
—West Indies	CREME DE CACAO	Philippines rice beer	PANGASI
—with		plum brandy	QUETSCH, SLIVOVIC(A)
crushed ice	FRAPPE		SLIVOVITZ
rum, lime juice, etc	SHRUB	Polynesian beer	(K)AVA
—Yugoslavia	MARASCHINO	poor beer (Scot.)	SWANK(E)Y
liquor	GOOD STUFF, MALT, TIPPLE	Portuguese brandy	AGUARDIENTE
—Scots	SKINK, STRUNT	posset made with sack	SACK-POSSET
liquorice (Scot.)	SUGARALLIE WATTER	quince-juice and sugar	QUIDDANY
Madeira	LONDON PARTICULAR	raisin wine	BASTARD
—dry	SERCIAL	Red Indian whisky	HOO(T)CH
—medium		red wine and	
dry	VERDELHO	methylated spirit	RED BIDDY
sweet	BUAL	residue from	
—sweet	MALMSEY	—brewing	DRAFF
Malay rum	TAFIA	—distilling	DUNDER

—whisky	POT ALE
—wine making	MARC
revived wine	STUM
rice spirit (China)	SAMSHOO, SAMSHU
Romanian plum brandy	TUICA
rum	DEMERARA, GROG
	NELSON'S BLOOD
—and water	GROG
—Malay	TAF(F)IA
—punch	RUMBO, TOM AND JERRY
—West Indies	TAF(F)IA
Russian	
—beer	KWASS, QUASS
—spirit	VODKA
Scandinavian spirit	AKVAVIT, AQUAVIT
Scottish	ATHOLL BROSE, HEATHER ALE
—poor beer	SWANK(E)Y
—sour, stale or thin liquor	TIFT
—spiced hot	PLOTTIE, PLOTTY
—whisky	MALT, SCOTCH
sherry with lemon, etc	SHERRY-COBBLER
sherry-type	MADEIRA
Sikh	AMRIT
small	
—beer	SWIPES
—measure	CHOTA-PEG, DRAM
	POUSSE-CAFE, SNIFTER
	SNORT(ER)
soft	BARLEY WATER, BITTER LEMON
	CREAM SODA, FLOAT, GINGER ALE
	GINGER BEER, GRENADINE
	HENRI, HENRY, JULEP
	LEMON SQUASH, LEMONADE
	LIMEADE, LUCOZADE, MILK SHAKE
	ORANGE SQUASH, ORANGEADE
	POP, PTISAN, SALOOP, SELTZER
	TISANE, TONIC WATER
—American	COCA-COLA, PEPSI-COLA
	SARSAPARILLA
sour liquor	TIFF
South African	SKOKIAAN
—beer	POMBE
—liqueur	VAN DER HUM
South American	ASSAI, AYAHUASCO
	CHICHA, DEMERARA, MATE
	PISCO, YERBA
Spanish	
—brandy	FUNDADOR, SOBERANO
—fortified wine	SHERRY
—liquor	AGUARDIENTE
—non-alcoholic	HORCHATA
—wine	ALICANT, MALAGA
	PETER-SEE-ME
	RIOJA, TARRAGONA
Shakespeare	BASTARD, SHERRIS-SACK
	(see also separate entry)

sparkling perry	BABYCHAM
spiced	
—ale	WASSAIL
—punch	TOM AND JERRY
—sherry etc	NEGUS
—sweetened wine	PIMENT
—wine	HIPPOCRAS, SANGAREE
	SANGRIA
spicy wine	MUSCADEL, MUSCATEL
spirit	
—cocktail	SWIZZLE
—from	
asclepiad	SOMA
blue plums	SLIVOVTZ
cashew nuts	FENI, FENNY
coconuts	FENI, FENNY
golden plums	MIRABELLE
pears	EAU DE VIE
purple plums	QUETSCH
raspberries	EAU DE VIE, FRAMBOISE
rice	SAMSHOO, SAMSHU
rye	RYE-WHISKY
sugar-cane	RUM
sweet-potatoes	MOBBIE, MOBBY
wormwood and aniseed	ABSINTHE
—Goan	FENI, FENNY
—Greek	MASTISKA, METAXA
	OUZO, RAKI
—Italian	CAMPARI
—Mediterranean	RAKI
—poor	ROTGUT
—Russian	VODKA
—Scandinavian	AKVAVIT, AQUAVIT
	SCHNAP(P)S
—sour or stale	TIFF
—with	
fruit juice, etc	SOUR
hot water, sugar	TODDY
water	
—and flavouring	SLING
—spice, etc	PUNCH
spoilt beer	SWIPES
spruce shoots and sugar	
or treacle	SPRUCE-BEER
stale liquor	TIFF
stimulant	BRACER
stout	GUINNESS, PORTER
strong	
—ale	MOROCCO, NAPPY, OCTOBER
Norwich	NOG
—beer	MARCH BEER, STINGO
—drink (Yiddish)	SHICKER
—liquor	HOGAN, HOGEN
Shakespeare	TICKLE-BRAIN
stum	MUST
stupefying drink	DWALE

sugar and water		Westmorland ale	MOROCCO
—Sikh	AMRIT	wheatmalt beer	MUM
—with spices	GINGER WINE	whisky	AQUA VITAE, AULD KIRK
Sussex strong ale	TIPPER		GOOD STUFF, HOO(T)CH
sweet wine	BARSAC, MALVESIE		MOUNTAIN-DEW, THE CRATUR
	MALVOISIE, MALMSEY		USQUEBAUGH
	MALVASIA, SAUTERNES	—American	BOURBON, RYE, TANGLEFOOT
sweetened		poor	REDEYE
—fruit juice	SHRUB	—from maize	BOURBON, CORN WHISKEY
—gin	OLD TOM	—harsh	CHAIN LIGHTNING
—spirits (Amer.)	SLING	—Highland	PEAT-REEK
—water (Sikh)	AMRITA	—illicit	
—wine (W. Indies)	SANGAREE	America	BOOTLEG, MOONSHINE
syrup from		Ireland	POT(H)EEN
—almonds, sugar, etc	ORGEAT	—with	
—aniseed	ANISETTE	hot water, etc	WHISKY TODDY
—apples	POMME	lemon, etc	WHISK(E)Y SOUR
—bananas	BANANE	soda	HIGHBALL, STENGAH
—blackcurrants	CASSIS		STINGER
—cherries	CERISE	white wine etc	FUSTIAN
—gooseberries	GROSEILLE	—with wormwood	VERMOUTH
—grapes	RAISIN	wine	(see separate entry)
—lemons	CITRON	with eggs added	FLIP
—mint	MENTHE	Yugoslav brandy	VINJAC
—pineapple	ANANAS	Zoroastrian ritual drink	HAOMA
—plums	PRUNE	**drugs**	
—pomegranates	GRENADINE	including: drugs of abuse	
—prunes	PRUNE	medicines	
—pure sugar	GOMME	adulterated cocaine	CRACK
—raspberries	FRAMBOISE	affecting the mind	PSYCHOTROPIC
—strawberries	FRAISE	aloes and canella bark	HICKERY-PICKERY
taken (at)			HIERA-PICRA
—after meal	DIGESTIF		HIGRY-PIGRY
—bedtime	NIGHTCAP	alpha-blocker	TOLAZOLINE
—before meal	APERITIF	amphetamine	METHEDRINE
—early evening	SUNDOWNER	anabolic steroid	ANAPOLON, ANAVAR
—mid-morning	ELEVENSES		CYPIONATE, DECA DURABOLIN
tasteless slop	WASH		DIANABOL, NOLVADEX, PARABOLON
tea	(see separate entry)		STANAZOLOL
thin liquor	GROG, TIFF	anaesthetic	BENZOCAINE, CHLOROFORM
treacle-beer	SWITCHEL		COCAINE, EPIDURAL
Turkish	AIRAN, BOZA	ETHYL CHLORIDE, EUCAIN(E), EVIPAN	
	MASTIC(H)		HALOTHANE, LAUGHING-GAS
—fruit juice	PEKMEZ		LIGNOCAINE, NITROUS OXIDE
unfermented			NOVOCAINE, PROCAINE
—grape-juice	MUST, STUM		STOVAINE, THIOPENTONE
—malt and hops	WORT	analgesic	(see painkiller below)
vinegar and honey	OXYMEL	antibiotic	ACTINOMYCIN, AMOXYCILLIN
warm alcoholic drink	CUP, MULL, PUNCH		AMPHOTERICIN, AMPICILLIN
	TODDY		AUREOMYCIN, CEPHALORIDINE
water containing salts		CEPHALOSPORIN, CHLORAMPHENICOL	
or gases	MINERAL WATER		CYCLOSERINE, ERYTHROMYCIN
Welsh fermented liquor	METHEGLIN		GRAMICIDIN, GRISEOFULVIN
West Indian			IVERMECTIN, MAGAININ
—spirit	MOBBY, MOBBIE		MITURAMYCIN, NYSTATIN
—sweetened wine	SANGAREE		OXYTETRACYCLINE, POLYMIXIN

	SEPTRIN, STREPTOMYCIN
	SULPHONAMIDE, SULPHONE
	TERRAMYCIN, TETRACYCLINE
	VIOMYCIN
anticoagulant	HEPARIN
antihistamine	CIMETEDINE, CLARITYN
	MEPYRAMINE, PRILAMINE
	TRILUDAN
anti-inflammatory	ARTRODAR, DIACERHEIN
antipyretic	ACETYSALICYLIC ACID
	ASPIRIN, FEBRIFUGE
	PHENACETIN, SALICIN
antiseptic	ACRIFLAVIN, CARBOLIC ACID
	MANDELIC ACID, PHENOL
arrow-poison	CURARE, CURARI
attacking nervous	
system	NEUROTOXIN
barbitol	DIETHYLBARBITURIC ACID
	VERONAL
barbitone	VERONAL
barbiturate	SECONAL
beta blocker	ATENOLOL, CELPROLOL
	DILEVOLOL, INDERAL
	SELECTOL, UNICARD
bhang	INDIAN HEMP
bile purgative	CHOLAGOGUE
bituminous	MUMMY
body-building	(ANABOLIC) STEROID
Brazilian	JABORANDI, PAREIRA
breaking down blood	
fibrin	FIBRINOLYSIN
calming	SEDATIVE
cannabis	BHANG, DAGGA
	(INDIAN) HEMP
	MARIJUANA, POT, PUFF
causing	
—dilation of pupil	MYDRIATIC
—flow of urine	DIURETIC
—vomiting	EMETIC
cocaine residue	BASUCO
constricting capillaries	PITRESSIN
coramine	NIKETHAMIDE
crack	FREEBASE, READY-WASH
	ROCK
dagga	BHANG, HASH, (INDIAN) HEMP
	LOVE-DRUG, MARIJUANA, POT
dilating pupil	MYDRIATIC
diuretic	ACETOZOLAMIDE, FRUSEMIDE
	MERSALYL, TROMETHAMINE
	TROMETHAMOL
East Indian	ZERUMBET
Ecstasy	E
emetic	APOMORPHINE, EMETINE
expectorant	APOMORPHINE
expelling waste matter	ECCRITIC, LAXATIVE
febrifuge	ANTIPYRETIC

for	
—contracting pupil	MIOTIC
	PILOCARPINE
—reducing	
bleeding	APROTININ
excitement	SEDATIVE
fever	ANTIPYRETIC
flatulence	CARMINATIVE
heart-rate	BETA-BLOCKER
pain	ANALGESIC
urine flow	PITRESSIN
temperature	ANTIPYRETIC, FEBRIFUGE
tension	TRANQUILLISER
—stimulating	
brain	NIKETHAMIDE
breathing	LOBELINE, PICROTOXIN
central nervous system	BEMEGRIDE
flow of urine	ACETOZOLAMIDE
	DIURETIC, MERSALYL
heart	CORAMINE, DIGITALIS
	NIKETHAMIDE
nervous system	ATROPINE, CAFFEINE
	STRYCHNINE
—treating	
abnormal cell growth	VINBLASTINE
	VINCRISTINE
Aids	ZIDOVUDINE
alcoholism	DISULFURAM
all ailments	PANACEA
allergies	ANTIHISTAMINE
	DIMOTANE
Alzheimer's	
disease	TETRAHYDROAMINO-ACRIDINE
	THA
amoebic dysentery	EMETINE
angina	ADALAT, AMYL NITRATE
	BETA BLOCKER, CARDIZEM
	VASODILATOR
anxiety	BETA BLOCKER, DIAZEPAM
	SEDATIVE, TRANQUILLISER
	VALERIAN, VALLIUM
arthritis	CORTISONE, FELDENE
	NAPROSYN, VOLTARENT
asthma	BRONCHODILATOR
	EPHEDRINE
	SALBUTAMOL, VENTOLIN
bacterial infections	ANTIBIOTIC
	ANTITOXIN
bilharzia	NIRIDAZOLE
blocked air passages	DECONGESTANT
	EXPECTORANT
blood clotting	ANTI-COAGULANT
	COUMARIN, HEPARIN
	PHENIDIONE
	TISSUE PLASMIN ACTIVATOR
	TPA, WARFARIN

burns	PICRIC ACID
cholesterol	SIMVASTIN, ZOCOR
colic	GRIPE WATER
constipation	CATHARTIC
	GLAUBER'S SALTS, LAXATIVE
	PURGATIVE
convulsions	PHENYTOIN
coughs	ANTITUSSIVE, CODEINE
depression	AMITRYPTILINE
	IMIPRAMINE, PHENELZINE
diabetes	INSULIN, TOLBUTAMIDE
diarrhoea	PAREGORIC, KAOLIN
dysentery	SULPHAGUANIDINE
epilepsy	ANTICONVULSANT
	PHENYTOIN, PRIMIDONE
fast heart-beat	PRACTOLOL
	PROPANOLOL
fever	ANTIPYRETIC
	FEBRIFUGE
fragile blood-vessels	RUTIN
fungal infections	AMPHOTERICIN
	NYSTATIN, TOLNAFTATE
glaucoma	PHYSOSTYGMINE
goitre	THIOURACIL
gout	ALLOPURINOL, CHINCHOPHEN
	COLCHICINE, PROBENECID
hay fever	CLARITYN, TRILUDAN
heart disease	CORAMINE, DIGITALIS
	DIGOXIN, EMINASE
	NIKETHAMIDE, SQUILL
herpes	ACYCLOVIR
	INOSINE, PRANOBEX
high blood	
—pressure	ANDROMEDOTOXIN
	ATENALOL, BETA BLOCKER
	CAPOTEN, CAPTOPRIL, DYAZIDE
	GUANETHEDINE, INDERAL
	METHYLDOPA, PINDOLOL
	PROPANALOL, RESERPINE
	SOTALOL, TENORMIN
	TIMOLOL, VASOTEC
—sugar level	TOLBUTAMIDE
infections	AMOXIL, CECLOR
	CLAFORAN, PRONTOSIL
	ROCEPHINT
inflammation	INDOMETHACIN
insomnia	CHLORAL HYDRATE
	HYPNOTIC, MOGADON
	NEMBUTAL, NITRAZEPAM,
	PENTOBARBITONE
	SEDATIVE, SOPORIFIC
	TRANQUILLISER
irregular heart beat	QUINIDINE
	SPARTEINE
jaundice	ICTERAL, ICTERIC
leprosy	DAPSONE
Lewis gas poisoning	BAL
	DIMERCAPROL
malaria	ARTEETHER, ATABRIN
	ATEBRIN, CHLOROQUINE
	MEPACRINE, PALUDRINE
	PRIMAQUINE, PYRIMETHAMINE
	QUINACRINE, QUININE
meningitis	CHLOROMYCETIN
	SULPHAPYRIDINE
migraine	ERGOTAMINE
mouth ulcers	DEMULCENT
muscular tension	TUBOCURARINE
nasal congestion	AMPHETAMINE
nausea	CYCLIZINE
nervous tension	NEUROLEPTIC
osteoarthritis	ARTRODAR
	DIACERHEIN
pancreatitis	APROTININ
parasitic infections	METRONIDAZOLE
	THIABENDAZOLE
Parkinson's disease	DEPRENYL
	ELDEPRYL, L-DOPA
	LEVODOPA
peptic ulcers	ATROPINE, BANTHINE
	SELEGILINE
phosphorus poisoning	PRALIDOXIME
pneumonia	SULPHAPYRIDINE
poliomyelitis	SALK VACCINE
protozoa	TRYPANOCIDE
psoriasis	CHRYSAROBIN
	DITHRANOL
rashes	ANTIHISTAMINE
respiratory problems	KEFRAL
rheumatism	CORTISONE
	IBRUPROFEN
river blindness	IVERMECTIN
schizophrenia	CLOZAPINE
	CLOZARIL
scurvy	ANTISCORBUTIC
shingles	ACYCLOVIR
shock	NORADRENALINE
skin infections	CALAMINE
	CORTISONE
	CRYSTAL VIOLET
	GENTIAN VIOLET
	METHOTREXAT
	NEOMYCIN
sleeping sickness	PENTAMIDINE
	TRYPARSAMIDE
staphylococci	SULPHATHIAZOLE
stomach disorders	ANTACID
syphilis	CALOMEL, SALVARSAN
tension	BETA BLOCKER, DIAZEPAM
	SEDATIVE, TRANQUILLISER
	VALERIAN, VALLIUM
tetanus	CURARE

travel sickness	CYCLIZINE
	DIMENHYDRINATE
	HYOSCINE
tuberculosis	CYCLOSERINE
	ETHAMBUTOL
	ISONIAZID(E), PAS
	STREPTOMYCIN
tumours	CYTOTOXIN
typhoid	CHLOROMYCETIN
ulcers	RANITIDINE, TAGAMET
	ZANTAC
virus infections	INTERFERON
water retention	DIURETIC
worms	ANTHELMITIC
	PIPERAZINE, QUASSIA
	SANTONIN, VERMIFUGE
freebase	CRACK
from	
—andromeda	ANDROMEDOTOXIN
—belladonna	ATROPINE
	HYOSC(YAM)INE
—broom	SPARTEINE
	SCOPOLAMINE
—cinchona	QUIN(ID)INE
—coal-tar	SAFFRANIN(E)
—coca leaves	COCAINE
—coffee	CAFFEINE
—cucumber	COLOCYNTH
—datura	STRAMONIUM
—ergot	ERGOMETRINE, ERGONOVINE
	ERGOTAMINE, ERGOTOXINE
	HISTAMINE, LSD
	LYSERGIC ACID
—foxgloves	DIGITALIS, DIGOXIN
—fungus	ERGOMETRINE, ERGOTAMINE
—henbane	HYOSC(YAM)INE
—jaborandi	PILOCARPINE
—lobelia	LOBELINE
—lupins	SPARTEINE
—meadow saffron	COLCHICINE
—morphine	CODEINE, HEROIN
—mould	PATULIN
—mushrooms	PSILOCYBIN
—nux vomica	STRYCHNINE
—opium	CODEINE, LAUDANUM
	MORPHIA, NARCOTINE, OPIATE
—Orchis	SALEP, SALOP
—periwinkle	VINBLASTINE, VINCRISTINE
—poppies	OPIUM, MORPHINE
	PAPAVERINE, RHOEADINE
—rauwolfia	RESERPINE
—strophanthus	OUABAIN, WABAIN
—tea	THEINE, THEOBROMINE
	THEOPHYLLINE
—thorn-apple	STRAMONIUM
—toads	BUFOTENIN
—tobacco	NICOTINE
—wood	OUABAIN
ganglion-blocker	MECAMYLAMINE
grass	MARIJUANA
hallucinatory	ACID, ANGEL-DUST
	BUFOTENIN, CANNABIS
	HALLUCINOGEN, LSD
	LYSERGIC ACID, MESCALIN(E)
	PEYOTE, PHENCYCLIDINE
	PSILOCYBIN, STP
hash(ish)	HASHEESH, INDIAN HEMP
heart stimulant	CORAMINE, NIKETHAMIDE
	NORADRENALIN
hemp	BHANG, MARIHUANA
	MARIJUANA, POT
heroin	HORSE
hormone-blocker	GOSERELIN
hypnotic	AMYTAL, BARBITOL
	BARBITONE, BARBITURATE
	DIETHYLBARBITURIC ACID
	HALCION, PARALDEHYDE
	PHENOBARBITONE, TERONAL
	VERONAL, ZIMOVANE
	ZOPICLORE
imaginary	SOMA
inactive	PLACEBO
increasing bodily activity	STIMULANT
Indian	BHANG, BIKH
inducing	
—removal of obstructions	ECPHRACTIC
—stopping of pores	EMPHRACTIC
—unconsciousness	ANAESTHETIC
—uterine contractions	ECBOLIC
killing cells	CYTOTOXIC
laxative	ECCOPROTIC, LIQUORICE
	SENNA
liquefies blood etc	VARIDASE
local anaesthetic	COCAINE, STOVAINE
lysergic acid	LSD
marijuana	BHANG, CANNABIS, DAGGA
	GRASS, HASH, INDIAN HEMP
	POT, SNOUT, TEA
mercurous chloride	CALOMEL
methylene	
dioxymethamphetamine	ADAM
	MDMA
Mexican	JALAP, MESCALIN(E)
mixture of drugs	CRACK, SPEED-BALL
muscle relaxant	CURARINE
	NARCEINE, SOMA
narcotic	MANDRAGORA, MANDRAKE
	OPIATE
—antidote	NALOXONE
opium	HOP
pain-killer	ANALGESIC, ASPIRIN
	CODEINE, INDOMETHACIN

LIDOCAINE, MORPHIA, MORPHINE
NUROFEN, OPIATE, PAMATEL
PANADOL, PARACETAMOL
PENTAZOCINE, PETHIDINE
PHENACETIN, PHENAZONE
PHENYLBUTAZONE, SALICIN, SOMA
phencyclidine   ANGEL-DUST
pot   BHANG, CANNABIS, DAGGA
HASH, INDIAN HEMP
MARIJUANA, TEA
powdered
   methamphetamine   CRYSTAL(METH)
preventing
   —blood-clotting   ANTICOAGULANT
   —coughing   ANTITUSSIVE
   —growth of micro-organisms   ANTSEPTIC
   —itching   ANTIPRURITIC
   —haemorrhage   ERGOMETRINE
ERGONOVINE
   —seizures   ANTICONVULSANT
   —sickness   ANTINAUSEANT
producing
   —symptoms imitating
     mental illness   PSYCHOSOMIMETIC
PSCYHOTOMIMETIC
   —unconsciousness   ANAESTHETIC
puff   CANNABIS
purgative   CATHARTIC, HIERA-PICRA
HICKERY-PICKERY
HIGRY-PIGRY
quack remedy   NOSTRUM
reducing
   —inflammation   ANTIHISTAMINE
   —mental activity   DEPRESSANT
relaxant   MEPROBAMATE
MILTOWN
remedy for poison   ANTIDOTE
santonin   WORM-SEED
sedative   BARBITURATE, BETEL
CODEINE, DESERPEDINE
DOWNER, GOOFBALL, LAUDANUM
MEPROBAMATE, MILTOWN
NARCEINE, NEMBUTAL, OPIATE
OPIUM, PENTOBARBITONE
PHENOBARBITONE, TETRONAL
THALIDOMIDE, THIOPENTONE
snout   MARIJUANA
sorrow-lulling   NEPENTHE
spinal anaesthetic   EPIDURAL
stimulant   ADAM, AMYL NITRATE, BENNY
BLUE, COCA(AINE), CRACK
CRYSTAL (METH), CUBEB
DOLL, E, ECSTASY, MDM, POPPER
PURPLE HEART, ROCK
READY-WASH, SNOW
SPEED(BALL), UPPER

stimulating
   —bowel movement   LAXATIVE, PURGATIVE
   —central nervous system   AMPHETAMINE
BENZEDRINE
   —expulsion of mucus   EXPECTORANT
   —heart   CORAMINE,
NIKETHAMIDE
(NOR)ADRENALIN(E), OUABAIN
   —immune system   PIROXICAM
   —ovulation   CLOMIPHENE
   —uterus   ERGOTAMINE
ERGOTOXINE
strengthening   ROBORANT
sulphonamide   PRONTOSIL
suppressing immune
   reaction   IMMUNOSUPPRESSIVE
synthetic
   —cortisone   HECOGENIN
   —sex hormone   STILBOESTROL
   —stimulant   AMPHETAMINE
BENZEDRINE
EPHEDRINE, METHADONE
PENTAZOCINE, PETHIDINE
tea   (*see* marijuana *above*)
tincture of opium   LAUDANUM, PAREGORIC
tonic   ROBORANT
tranquilliser   CHLORDIAZEPOXIDE
CHLORPROMAZINE, DIAZEPAM
HALOPERIDOL, LARGACTIL
LIBRIUM, MOGADON
MEPROBAMATE, NITAZEPAM
PHENOTHIAZINE, RESERPINE
VALIUM
treating
   —depression   ANTIDEPRESSANT
   —fast heart-beat   BETA-BLOCKER
   —infections   ANTISERUM, ANTISEPTIC
ANTITOXIN
   —muscle spasms   ANTISPASMODIC
   —respiratory problems   BRONCHIAL DILATOR
DECONGESTANT
   —snake bite   ANTIVENIN
   —worms   ANTHELMINT(H)IC
truth-drug   HYOSCINE
SCOPOLAMINE
universal antidote   MITHRIDATICUM
PANACEA, PANPHARMICON
vegetable   ANDROMEDOTOXIN
BOTANICAL
worm-seed   SANTONICA, SANTONIN
duck
domestic   AYLESBURY, BARBARY
CAMPBELL, INDIAN RUNNER
MUSCOVY, PEKIN, PERUVIAN
ROUEN, WELSH HARLEQUIN
WHALESBURY

wild	BLACK, EIDER, FERRUGINOUS
	GADWALL, GARGANEY, GOLDENEYE
	GOOSANDER, HARLEQUIN
	LONG-TAILED, MALLARD
	MANDARIN, MERGANSER, PINTAIL
	POCHARD, RING-NECKED, RUDDY
	SCAUP, SCOTER, SHELDUCK, SHOVELER
	SMEW, TEAL
	TUFTED, WI(D)GEON
Dutch	DU
administrative centre	THE HAGUE
advocate	PENSIONARY
airline	KLM
bargain	KOOP
cape (headland)	HOEK
capital	AMSTERDAM
car	DAF
channel	DIEP
cheese	EDAM, GOUDA
chief magistrate	BURGEMEESTER
	BURGOMASTER
coins	DOIT, FLORIN
—½ farthing	DODKIN, DOIT(KIN)
—penny	STIVER
—florin	GLD, GULDEN, GUILDER
—gold coin	RIDER
—silver coin	STOOTER
obsolete	RIX-DOLLAR
county	AMT
cupboard	KAS
dog	KEESHOND, SCHIPPERKE
donkey	EZEL
drink	AKVAVIT, ACQUAVIT
	ADVOCAAT, HOLLANDS
	SCHIEDAM, SCHNAP(P)S
fair	KERMESS, KERMIS, KIRMESS
former name	HOLLAND
flower	TULIP
game	KORFBALL
half-caste	GRIQUA
head of state	STAD(T)HOLDER
horse	SCHIMMEL
housewife	FROW, WROUW
island(s)	EILAND(EN)
lake	MEER
legal adviser	PENSIONARY
lock/weir	SASSE
knife	SNEE
lace	LANGET
magistrate	AMMAN, AMTMAN, SCHEPEN
man	MYNHEER
meal	MAAL
measures	
—length	DUIM, VOET
—2 acres	MORGEN
—8 gallons	ANKER

—30-35 gallons	AAM
—cask	LEAGUER
mister	(MYN)HEER
modern name	THE NETHERLANDS
municipal officer	SCHOUT
my lord	MYNHEER
news agency	ANETA
night	NACHT
path	PAD
pottery	DELFT
president	GRAND PENSIONARY
privateer	APER
provincial governor	STAD(T)HOLDER
reclaimed land	POLDER
river	MAAS
saint	SINT
sandbank	PLAAT
sand-flat	WAD
sea	MEER, ZEE
seat of government	THE HAGUE
sir	MYNHEER
States General	HOGEN-MOGEN
stream	BEEK
uncle	EME, OOM
vagrant	LANDLOOPER
viceroy	STAD(T)HOLDER
village	DORP
wife/woman	FROW, VROUW
dyes	
including: dyes	
pigments	
annatto	ROUCOU
bituminous pigment	MUMMY
coal-tar	SAFFRANIN(E)
colourless derivative	LEUCO-COMPOUND
colours	
—black	BLACK IRON OXIDE
	BONEBLACK, CARBON BLACK
	LAMPBLACK, NIGROSINE
—blue	(ANTHO)CYANIN(E), COBALT
	DYER'S WOAD, PRUSSIAN BLUE
	METHYLENE, MONASTRAL BLUE
	PHYCOCYAN(IN), ULTRAMARINE
	VERDITER
crushed glass	SMALT
—brown	BISTRE, BROWN OCHRE
	CACHOU, CATECHU, CUTCH
	(EN)MELANIN, PHYCOPHAEIN
	SEPIA, SIENNA, TANNIN, UMBER
—green	BRUNSWICK GREEN
	CHLOROCRUORIN, CHLOROPHYLL
	CHROME GREEN, CUPRIC ACETOARSENITE
	MONASTRAL GREEN, PARIS GREEN
	SCHEELE'S GREEN, SCHWEINFURT GREEN
	SUMAC(H), TERRE-VERTE
	VERDITER, VIRIDIAN

—ochre	TIVER
—orange	AN(N)ATTO, AN(N)OTTA
	ARNATTO, CAROTENE
	CAROTIN, KAMALA, KAMELA
	KAMILA, ROUCOU
—orange-red	HENNA, CHICA
—orange-yellow	SAFFRON
—purple	ANTHOCYANIN, CORKIR
	CUDBEAR, KORKIR
	LITMUS, ORCEIN
	PURPLE OF CASSIUS, TURNSOLE
	TYRIAN (PURPLE)
—purple-red	FUCHSINE, MAGENTA
—red	ALKANET, ANIL(INE)
	ANTHCYANIN, ARCHIL
	BRAZILIN, CARMINE, CAROTENE
	CHICA, CHROME RED, CINNABAR
	COCHINEAL, CONGO RED
	CORKIR, CROCEIN, CYANIN
	HAEM(ATOXYLIN), INDIAN RED
	KERMES, KORKIR, LAKE
	LOGWOOD, MADDER
	MERCURIC SULPHIDE, MINIUM
	ORCHEL(LA), ORCHIL(LA)
	ORSEILLE, PARA-RED
	PHYCOERYTHRIN, RADDLE
	RED LEAD, RED OCHRE, REDDLE
	RHODAMINE, ROSANILINE
	RUDDLE, SAFFLOWER
	TURKEY RED, TYRIAN, VERMILION
—red/yellow	CAROTENE, AROTIN
—red/violet	ANILINE VIOLET
	MAUVE, MAUV(E)IN(E)
—violet	ARCHIL, CUDBEAR
	GENTIAN (VIOLET)
	INDIGO, ORCHEL(LA)
	ORCHIL(LA), ORSEILLE
—violet-blue	ANIL, INDIGO(TIN)
—white	CHINESE WHITE
	LEAD CARBONATE
	TITANIUM WHITE
	WHITE LEAD, ZINC OXIDE
	ZINC WHITE
—yellow	ANTHIN, CADMIUM (YELLOW)
	CAROTENE, CAROTIN

	CHROME (YELLOW), CHRYSANILINE
	ETIOLIN, FLAVIN, FLAVONE, FUSTEC
	FUSTIC, GAMBOGE, INDIAN YELLOW
	LEAD ANTIMONIATE
	NAPLES YELLOW, PHYCOXANTHIN
	PICRIC ACID, UROCHROME
	YELLOW EARTH, YELLOW OCHRE
—yellow-brown	BISTE
dying technique	BATIK, KALAMKARI
	TIE-DYING
earths	OCHRE, SIENA, UMBER
eye-pigment	
—blue	IODOPSIN
—red	RHODOPSIN
found in	
—algae	FUCOXANTHIN
—blood	CHLOROCRUORIN, HAEM
	HAEMOCYANIN, HAEMOGLOBIN
—food	AMARANTH
—hair	MELANIN
—lichen	ARCHIL
—madder	TURKEY RED
—plants	
absorbing red light	PHYTOCHROME
green	CHLOROPHYLL
yellow	ANTHIN, FLAVONE
	XANTHOPHYLL
—safflower	CARTHAMINE
—seaweed	
blue	PHYCOCYAN(IN)
brown	PHYCOPHALEIN
red	PHYCOERYTHRIN
yellow	PHYCOXANTHIN
—skin	(EN)MELANIN
—trees	
Bixa	AN(N)ATTA, AN(N)ATTO
	ARNOTTO, ROUCOU
Haematoxylin	LOGWOOD
—urine	UROCHROME
roucou	AN(N)ATTA, AN(N)ATTO
	ARNOTTO
South American	CHICA, COBRES
types	ACID DYE, AZO DYE
	BASIC DYE, SYNTHETIC DYE
	VAT DYE

E

ear
bones	(*see separate entry*)
buzzing in ear	TINNITUS
cavities	CONCHA, SACCULE
	UTRICLE
ear disorders	(*see* **disease**)
eardrum	MYRINGA
	TYMPANIC MEMBRANE
external opening	(AUDITORY) MEATUS
fluid in ear	ENDOLYMPH, PERILYMPH
inner ear	MEMBRANOUS LABYRINTH
middle ear	TYMPANIC CAVITY
outer ear	PINNA
parts of ear	ANVIL, AURICLE, COCHLEA
	CONCHA, EUSTACHIAN TUBE
	FENESTRA OVALIS, HAMMER
	HELIX, INCUS, LOBE, LOBULE
	ORGAN OF CORTI, SALPINX
	STAPES, STIRRUP, TRAGUS
	TYMPANUM, UTRICLE, VESTIBULE
projection	(ANTI)TRAGUS
stone in ear	OTOLITH
testing machine	AUDIOGRAPH, AUDIOMETER
wax in ear	CERUMEN

earth (*see* **geography**)

earthquake SEISM
affected by same shock-waves	COSEISMAL
	COSEISMIC
at seabed	SEAQUAKE
line of equal earthquake shocks	COSEISMAL LINE
	HOMOSEISMAL LINE
	ISOSEISMAL LINE
location	EPICENTRE, EPICENTRUM
major earthquakes	AGADIR, ANCHORAGE
	ANDREANOL, ARMENIA, AVEZZANO
	BUCHAREST, CALCUTTA, EL ASNAM
	ERZINCAN, GANSU, GUATEMALA
	KAMCHATKA, KANSU, KWANTO PLAIN
	LEBU, LOS ANGELES, MESSINA
	NICARAGUA, NORTH YEMEN
	POTENZA, QUETTA, SAN FRANCISCO
	SHENSI, SKOPJE
	TABAS, TANGSHAN, TURKEY
recording instrument	SEISMOGRAPH
	SEISMOMETER
	TRONOMETER
record of	SEISOGRAM

scale of intensity	(GUTENBERG-)RICHTER SCALE
	KANAMORI SCALE
	MERCALLI SCALE
seismic	TERREMOTIVE
seismologist	
—American	GUTENBERG, RICHTER, REID
—British	OLDHAM
shock waves	
—after main earthquake	AFTERSHOCK
—before main earthquake	FORESHOCK
—bodily waves passing through	
Earth's core	P WAVE
	PRIMARY WAVE
stopped by Earth's core	S WAVE
	SECONDARY WAVE
—surface waves	
horizontal	LOVE WAVE
vertical	RAYLEIGH WAVE
—types	
following curve of earth	SURFACE WAVE
passing through earth	BODILY WAVE
slow movement of surface	BRADYSEISM
small	
—earthquake	TREMOR
—persistent tremor	MICROSEISM
study of earthquakes	SEISMOLOGY
subterranean origin	SEISMIC FOCUS
wave caused by earthquake	
—at sea	TSUNAMI
—in inland waters	SEICHE

East Indian
ape	ORANG(UTAN)
aromatic gum	BENZOIN, GUM BENJAMIN
	JEW'S FRANKINCENSE
—root	GALINGALE
aubergine	EGG-PLANT
berry	CUBEB
bird	CASSOWARY, JAVA SPARROW
	KORA, PADDY-BIRD, RICE-BIRD
	TAILOR-BIRD, WATER-COCK
breadfruit tree	JA(C)K (TREE)
brinjal	EGG-PLANT
civet	BINTURONG, LINSANG
	RASSE
climbing shrub	CUBEB, GAMBI(E)R
	ROSARY PEA
cloth	HUMHUM
coffee	
—flavoured plant	ABELMOST
—rat	MUSANG
coin	BONK, DUIT
condiment	CHUTNEY
currency	Y, YEN
drink	NIPA

drug	ZERUMBET	—ox	(see **ox**)
dying process	BATIK	weapon	TOMBOC
edible fat	KOKUM BUTTER	**eastern**	
egg-plant	AUBERGINE, BRINJAL	acacia	BABLAH, BABUL
fern	BAROMETZ	banker	SHROFF
fish	ANABAS, POMFRET	bedcover	PALAMPORE, PALEMPORE
flying squirrel	TAGUAN	bird	ANT-THRUSH
fruit	CARAMBOLA	bishop	ABBA
	COROMANDEL GOOSEBERRY	bishop's vestment	SAKKOS, OMOPHORION
	MANGO, MARKING-NUT	bosun	SERANG
	ROSE-APPLE, TAMPOE	camel-hair fabric	ABA
gamboge tree	TAMANU	chewing nut	BETEL(-NUT)
ginger	CASSUMUNAR	chieftain	AMEER, EMEER, EMIR
ground pigeon	GOURA	coasting vessel	GRAB
gum-resin	TACAMAHAC	coffee-cup without handle	FINGAN, FINJAN
hat	MITRE	coin	CASH
hibiscus	ROSELLE, ROZELLE	couch	DIVAN
insectivore	SQUIRREL-SHREW	cymbal	ZEL
	TREE-SHREW	dervish	SANTON
lemur	LORIS	disease	BERI-BERI
mat	TAT	dish	BEAN CURD, PILAFF
measures			PIL(L)AU, PILAW, PILOW
—dry	GANTANG	dress	CHEONG-SAM
—yard	GUZ	drink	ARAK, ARRACK
—30-35 galls	AAM	dulcimer	SANTIR, SANT(O)UR
native (New Guinea)	BOONG	dwarf goose	GOSLET
orange dye	KAMALA, KAMELA	European Time	EET
	KAMILA	eye-shadow	KOHL
palm	AT(T)AP, NIPA	fabulous bird	HUMA
parrot	LORY	folk dance	KOLO
plant yielding arrowroot	PIA	fruit	SEBESTEN
resting-frame	DUTCH WIFE	gift	BA(C)KSHEESH, BA(C)KSHISH
spice	NUTMEG		BAKHSHISH, BUCKSHISH
sqirrel-shrew	PENTAIL	gold bar	TAEL
tarsier	MALMAG	governor	MUDIR
timber	BLOODWOOD, BRAZIL(-WOOD)	governor's province	MUDIRIA, MUDIRIEH
	JELUTONG	guitar	TAMBOURA
tree	ABROMA, AGALLOCH, AGILA, BILIAN	gum	GALBANUM
	B(I)LIMBI(NG), CARAMBOLA	guide	DRAGOMAN
	CUCUMBER-TREE, EAGLEWOOD	headdress	TURBAN
	EMBLIC(A), GARJAN, GURJUN, JELUTONG	inn	(CARAVAN)SERAI
	KAMALA, KAMELA, KAMILA, KUMBUK		CARAVANSARY
	KOKUM, MANGO, MARGOSA, NUX VOMICA		CHO(UL)TRY, KHAN
	PONTIANAC, PONTIANAK	interpreter	DRAGOMAN
	POON, ROSE-APPLE, SANDAL(-WOOD)	leader	E
	SAP(P)AN, TAMANU, UPAS, SACK-TREE	magician	MAGE, MAGUS, ZENDIK
	SUNDARI, SUNDER, SUNDRA, SUNDRI	market	BAZA(A)R, SOUK
—lizard	DRAGON-LIZARD	mendicant	FAKIR
—shrew	BANGSRING, BANXRING	money-changer/lender	SHROFF
tribe	D(A)YAK, IBAN	musical instrument	PANDORA, PANDORE
turkey	TALEGALLA		PANDURA
upas tree	SACK-TREE	newcomer	GRIFFIN, GRIFFON
weasel-cat	DELUNDUNG	novice	GRIFFIN, GRIFFON
weight (3½ cwts)	BAHAR	order of monks	ACOEMETI
wild		ownerless dog	PARIAH
—hog	BABIR(O)USSA	palm	PALMYRA

paymaster	BUCKSHEE, BUKSHI
pheasant	ARGUS
plane tree	CHENAR, CHINAR
porter	HAM(M)AL
printed cambric or muslin	PERSIENNE
punishment	BASTINADE
	BASTINADO
sailor	LASCAR
saint	SANTON
salutation	SALAAM
ship	JUNK
shrub	BITTER-KING
silk-satin	ATLAS
skirt	SARONG
slipper	BABOOSH, BAB(O)UCHE
tabor	TIMBREL
tambourine	TIMBREL
temple	PAGOD(A)
tip	BA(C)KSHEESH, BA(C)KSHISH
	BAKHSHISH, BUCKSHISH
title	AG(H)A, ALI, RAS
tree	LEBBEK, SEBESTEN
unbeliever	ZENDIK
vase	POTICHE
waterwheel	SAKIA, SAKI(Y)EH
vehicle	JINRIKSHA, (JIN)RICKSHAW
	TRISHAW
vestment	PH(A)ELONION
weight	ROTL
whip	K(O)URBASH
	(*see also* **Oriental**)

eat

including: eater of	
eating	
all things	OMNIVOROUS, PANTOPHAGY
animals	ZOOPHAGOUS
ants	MYRMECOPHAGOUS
bacteria	BACTERIOPHAGOUS
bees	APIVOROUS
berries	BACCIVOROUS
blood	SANGU(IN)IVOROUS
bones	OSSIVOROUS
books (avid reader)	BIBLIOPHAGE
carrion	NECROPHAGOUS
children	P(A)EDOPHAGOUS
dead bodies	NECROPHAGOUS
decaying matter	SAPROPHAGOUS
dung	COPROPHAGOUS
	SCATOPHAGOUS
earth	GEOPHAGY
family or tribe	ENDOPHAGY
fish	ICHTHYOPHAGOUS
	PISCIVOROUS
flesh	CARNIVOROUS
	CREOPHAGOUS
	SARCOPHAGOUS

—of strangers	EXOPHAGY
frogs	RANIVOROUS
fruit	CARPOPHAGOUS
	FRUGIVOROUS
fungus	MYCOPHAGOUS
god	THEOPHAGY
grain	GRANIVOROUS
grass	GRAMINIVOROUS
	HERBIVOROUS
honey	MELLIPHAGOUS, MELLIVOROUS
horses	EQUIVOROUS, HIPPOPHAGY
insects	ENTOMOPHAGOUS
	INSECTIVOROUS
large pieces of food	MACROPHAGOUS
leaves	PHYLLOPHGOUS
lotus eaters	LOTOPHAGI
man (cannibal)	ANTHROPOPHAGOUS
many different things	POLYPHAGIA
	POLYPHAGY
nails	ONYCHOPHAGY
nuts	NUCIVOROUS
nutmegs	MYRISTICIVOROUS
one kind of food	MONOPHAGOUS
oysters	OSTREOPHAGOUS
plants	PHYTOPHAGOUS
poisons	TOXI(CO)PHAGOUS
raw flesh	OMOPHAGIA
rice	ORYZIVOROUS
roots	RADICIVOROUS
	RHIZOPHAGOUS
seeds	GRANIVOROUS
self	AUTOPHAGOUS
small pieces of food	MICROPHAGOUS
snakes	OPHIOPHAGOUS
stone	LITHOPHAGOUS
thistles	CARDOPHAGOUS
toadstools	MYCOPHAGOUS
wood	LIGNIVOROUS
	XYLOPHAGOUS
wool	MALLOPHAGOUS
worms	VERMIVOROUS

economics

accounting period	FINANCIAL YEAR
	FISCAL YEAR
acquisition of company	
to sell its assets	ASSET STRIPPING
additional security for loan	COLLATERAL
adjustment of value of	
future income to current	
monetary value	DISCOUNTED CASH FLOW
agreement on tariffs	GATT
agricultural policy (EC)	CAP
alternate restriction and	
expansion of trade	STOP-GO
amalgamation of companies	
—by acquisition	TAKEOVER

—by agreement	CONSOLIDATION
	MERGER
analysis of	
—benefit from given	
expenditure	COST-BENEFIT ANALYSIS
—economic data	ECONOMETRICS
annual percentage rate	APR
annuity which increases	
as subscribers die	TONTINE
association of persons	
buying and selling	
stocks and shares	STOCK EXCHANGE
automatic increase in inland	
revenue from increased income	FISCAL DRAG
balance in favour of	
account-holder	CREDIT
band within which	
—EC currencies are	
allowed to float	(THE) SNAKE
—world currencies float	(THE) TUNNEL
bank	
—rate	
UK MINIUMUM LENDING RATE, MLR	
USA	DISCOUNT RATE
—taking deposits and	
making short-term	
loans, etc	COMMERCIAL BANK
	JOINT STOCK BANK
—trading in	
shares, etc	MERCHANT BANK
benefit derived from	
embezzlement	BEZZLE
benefits etc	
—at no cost to recipient	ZERO-PRICE
—linked to retail	
price index	INDEX-LINKED
—paid for by tax-payer	TAX-PRICE
bills for funding	
Government debt	TREASURY BILLS
block of shares etc	TRANCHE
bond in yen issued by non-	
Japanese company	SAMURAI BOND
Bretton Woods system	IMF
INTERNATIONAL MONETARY FUND	
	WORLD BANK
British Government	
stock	CONSOLIDATED STOCK
	CONSOLS
buildings, plant, etc	CAPITAL ASSETS
buying and selling	
—against the law BLACK MARKET(EERING)	
—international debts	FORFAITING
—shares	
in one company to	
inflate the price	WASH-TRADING
not yet quoted	GREY MARKET

calculation of income	
taking account	
of time	DISCOUNTED CASH-FLOW
capital	
—needed to run	
company	WORKING CAPITAL
—of company divisible	
into shares	STOCK
—sum paid to	
new employee	GOLDEN HELLO
redundant employee	
	GOLDEN HANDSHAKE
	PLATINUM HANDSHAKE
retiring employee	GOLDEN GOODBYE
—used for wages, etc	FLOATING CAPITAL
card authorizing	
purchases by	
deferred payment	CREDIT CARD
central bank	(*see* national banks *below*)
certificate entitling exporter	
to repayment of duty	DEBENTURE
changes in	
—financial resources	FUNDS-FLOW
—working capital	CASH-FLOW
charge for delay	
—of delivery	BACKWARDATION
—in discharge or	
loading of ship	DEMURRAGE
combination of firms	
—to control prices	CARTEL
—with like interests	CONSORTIUM
	SYNDICATE
company	
—in which shareholders	
are free to transfer	
shares	JOINT STOCK COMPANY
—trading in bills, etc	DISCOUNT HOUSE
comparison of costs based	
on actual expenditure	MARGINAL COSTING
compounded annual rate	CAR
computer fraud of	
small amounts	SALAMI TECHNIQUE
contour on chart showing	
—consumer's	
objectives	INDIFFERENCE CURVE
—production	ISOQUANT
contract based on cost plus	
a percentage	COST-PLUS
control of	
—currency fluctuations	ERM
EXCHANGE RATE MECHANISM	
—money in	
circulation	MONETARY POLICY
—taxation	FISCAL POLICY
—trade by	
one company	MONOPOLY

two companies	DUOPOLOY
several companies	OLIGOPOLY
convert net figure to gross	GROSS UP
corporation made up of companies with diverse interests	CONGLOMERATE
cost of action in a perfect market	OPPORTUNITY COST
currency	
—based on a strong economy	HARD CURRENCY
—note	TREASURY NOTE
whose exchange rate is determined by supply and demand	FLOATING CURRENCY
daily average price of shares	
—Japan	NIKKEI INDEX
—UK	FINANCIAL TIMES INDEX, FT INDEX
—USA	DOW JONES INDEX
debenture	BOND
debt	DEBIT
—owed by government	NATIONAL DEBT PUBLIC DEBT
deduction from normal price	DISCOUNT
depression	RECESSION, SLUMP
difference	
—between national imports and exports	BALANCE OF TRADE
receipts and payments	BALANCE OF PAYMENTS
—in price of stock and its par value	DISCOUNT
—income and expenditure	
positive	PROFIT
negative	LOSS
discount rate (US)	BANK RATE
doctrine of macroeconomics	KEYNESIANISM
ease of exchange	LIQUIDITY
econometrics applied to economic history	CLIOMETRICS
economist	
—American	ARROW, DEBREU, DOMAR DORFMAN, DE BREU, FRIEDMAN GALBRAITH, GERARD, ISARD LEONTIET, LEWIS, MARKOWITZ MARSHALL, MEANS, ROSTOW SAMUELSON, SCOTT, SOLOW, VEBLEN
—Austrian	HAYEK
—British	BAGEHOT, CLAPHAM, DOBB DOUGLAS, HARROD, HAWTHORNE HAYEK, HICKS, HOBSON, KEYNES MALTHUS, MILL, PHILLIPS RICARDO, , ROBBINS, SHOVE SMITH, STELLARS, WALTERS
—Canadian	JOHNSON

—French	DE NEMOURS, DEBREU GERARD, WALRAS
—German	MARX, MICHELS, MORGENSTERN
—Hungarian	KALDOR
—Irish	EDGEWORTH
—Italian	PARETO, VERRI
—Norwegian	FRISCH
—Polish	DORIAR, LANGE
—Russian	LEONTIET
economy based on	
—large businesses	CORPORATISM
—private enterprise	FREE ECONOMY FREE ENTERPRISE MARKET ECONOMY
—state	
control	SOCIALISM
intervention	DIRIGISME
electronic transfer of	
—funds (at point of sale)	EFT(POS)
—shares	TAURUS
employment of more workers than necessry	OVERMANNING
entry in account on	
—creditor side	CREDIT
—debtor side	DEBIT
excessive trading to increase commission etc	CHURNING
exchange of goods for other goods	BARTER COUNTERTRADE
expenditure on assets	CAPITAL EXPENDITURE
export of capital borrowed by a country for its own development	CAPITAL FLIGHT
extreme inflation	HYPERINFLATION
face value of security	NOMINAL VALUE PAR (VALUE)
fall in value of money	INFLATION
figure summarizing statistical trends	INDEX NUMBER
finance experts	NUMERATI
Financial Times/Stock Exchange 100 share index	FOOTSIE
fixed	
—exchange rate	BRETTON WOODS SYSTEM
—interest security	DEBENTURE, LOAN STOCK
fixing limits to fluctuation of share prices	CIRCUIT-BREAKING
free trade or protection	THE FISCAL QUESTION
fund made by uniting yield of various taxes	CONSOLIDATED FUND

goods	
—bought or sold for future delivery	FUTURES
—made for production rather than consumption	CAPITAL GOODS
government stock	GILT-EDGED SECURITIES GILTS
gradual surreptitious purchase of shares	CREEPING TAKEOVER FOOTHOLD BUYING
graph of	
—balance of payments following devaluation	J-CURVE
—unemployment and inflation	PHILLIPS CURVE
group of	
—currencies	BASKET
—nations applying common customs policy	CUSTOMS UNION
guaranteed IOU issued by the Treasury	TREASURY BILL
illegal transfer of money	LAUNDERING
impose limits on expenditure	CAP
income	
—from	
business etc	EARNED INCOME
investments	UNEARNED INCOME
services	INVISIBLE EARNINGS INVISIBLES
total economy	NATIONAL INCOME
—not reported for tax purposes	BLACK MONEY
increase in	
—amount of money available in relation to its buying power	INFLATION
—economic activity	BOOM, REFLATION
—official value of currency	REVALUATION
—prices	
due to excessive demand	OVERHEATING
to cover losses from shoplifting	BUNCING
—value	APPRECIATION
index of	
—share prices	
Japan	NIKKEI INDEX
UK	FINANCIAL TIMES INDEX
US	DOW-JONES INDEX
—statistical trends	FISHER INDEX LASPEYTRES INDEX PAASCHE INDEX
inflation	
—due to rise in cost of production	COST-PUSH

—in	
expanding economy	BOOMFLATION
recession	STAGFLATION
institution for buying and selling of stocks and shares	STOCK EXCHANGE
international trade without tariffs	FREE TRADE
intersection of graph lines for 75 and 200-day share movements	GOLDEN CROSS
investigation of	
—characteristics of customers	MARKET RESEARCH
—competitors' affairs	COMPETITOR ANALYSIS
investment	
—by bank of its own funds in takeovers, etc	MERCHANT BANKING
—trust that sells units in a combined portfolio	MUTUAL FUND UNIT TRUST
issue of	
—free shares	BONUS ISSUE SCRIP ISSUE
—new shares to existing shareholders	RIGHTS ISSUE
—notes not backed by gold, etc	FIDUCIARY ISSUE
lag between public expenditure and income	FISCAL DRAG
large-scale speculation by company	ZAITECH, ZAITEKU
law relating to	
—inferior currencies	GRESHAM'S LAW
—input/output ratio	LAW OF DIMINISHING RETURNS LAW OF VARIABLE PROPORTIONS
—supply and demand	SAY'S LAW
list of securities	PORTFOLIO
loan	
—to finance purchase of one asset before sale of another	BRIDGING LOAN
—with no fixed date for repayment	FUNDED DEBT
loss of value due to wear and tear	DEPRECIATION
making debt marketable	SECURITISATION
market for short-term loans	MONEY MARKET
measures to reduce inflation	DISINFLATION
mechanism for cutting guaranteed prices	STABILISER

monetary unit not corresponding to actual currency	MONEY OF ACCOUNT UNIT OF ACCOUNT
money	
—not permanently invested	FLOATING CAPITAL
—on high interest repayable after major loans have been paid off	MEZZANINE DEBT
—order	POSTAL ORDER
national banks	
—Germany	BUNDESBANK
—international	IMF INTERNATIONAL MONETARY FUND WORLD BANK
—UK	BANK OF ENGLAND
—USA	CENTRAL BANK FEDERAL RESERVE BANK
not susceptible to a takeover bid	BID-PROOF
one	
—called in to restore a failing company	COMPANY DOCTOR
—to whom a debt is due	CREDITOR
—who	
buys and sells stocks and shares	STOCKBROKER
exchanges notes, bills, etc at a discount	DISCOUNT BROKER
buys shares in threatened company	WHITE SQUIRE
guarantees to buy all shares left over	UNDERWRITER
holds	
—in trust	FIDUCIARY, TRUSTEE
—security for a loan	LOAN-HOLDER
—shares in	
private company	SHAREHOLDER
public company	STOCKHOLDER
practises insurance business	UNDERWRITER
rescues company threatened by closure or takeover	WHITE KNIGHT
risks his own capital	ENTREPRENEUR
studies the stock market	CHARTIST
trades in shares at a profit	MARKET-MAKER
opportunity for gain provided by tax structure	TAX BREAK
ordinary shares	COMMON STOCK EQUITIES
overseas sales of	
—goods	VISIBLE EXPORTS
—services	INVISIBLE EXPORTS
paper	
—for endorsement attached to bill of exchange	ALLONGE
—money	TREASURY BILL
payment	
—for insurance cover	PREMIUM
—to individual below income tax threshold	NEGATIVE INCOME-TAX
period of	
—increased economic activity	BOOM
—reduced economic activity	DEPRESSION RECESSION, SLUMP
policy based on	
—control of	
money supply	MONETARISM
taxes	FISCAL POLICY
wages, etc	INCOMES POLICY
—decontrol, etc	ROGERNOMICS
—restraint of trade	DISINFLATION
—tax reductions and deficit spending to increase productivity	REAGANOMICS SUPPLY-SIDE
postal order	MONEY ORDER
postpone payment of debt	RESCHEDULE
practice of acquiring company to sell off assets	ASSET-STRIPPING
price	
—assumed in maximisation exercise	SHADOW PRICE
—charged by vendor	SELLING PRICE
—fixing group	CARTEL
—paid by merchant	COST PRICE
profit	
—from sale of property, etc	CAPITAL GAIN
—sharing based on gains or savings	GAIN-SHARING
promise to repay a loan	IOU NOTE OF HAND PROMISSORY NOTE
progressive increase in prices	INFLATION
property income certificate	PINC
public funds	STOCKS
—office negotiating loans	LOAN-OFFICE
—purse	FISC, FISK
purchase	
—of	
majority holding	BUY-IN

securities	INVESTMENT
shares in companies which satisfy ethical standards	CONSCIENCE INVESTMENT
surplus produce for storing	INTERVENTION
—with money borrowed from vendor	BALLOON FINANCING
raise artificially the price of a commodity	VALORISE
rate	
—at which banks can borrow	DISCOUNT RATE
—charged by central banks	BANK RATE MINIMUM LENDING RATE, MLR
ratio of borrowing to assets	GEARING
recession	DEPRESSION, SLUMP
reduced customs duty	PREFERENTIAL TARIFF
reduction	
—caused by depletion	DRAW-DOWN
—in	
amount of money available in relation to its purchasing power	DEFLATION
economic activity	DEPRESSION RECESSION, SLUMP
official value of currency	DEVALUATION
value	DEPRECIATION
risky security	JUNK-BOND
sale on trust	CREDIT
scheme of life annuity	TONTINE
school of economists	AUSTRIAN SCHOOL
sell shares one does not own	SHORT
selling	
—additional services to existing customers	CROSS-MARKETING CROSS-SELLING
—overseas at reduced prices	DUMPING
—share futures in falling market	PORTFOLIO INSURANCE
sequence of boom and depression	TRADE CYCLE
share	
—considered safe and profitable	BLUE CHIP
—on which dividends are paid before other types	PREFERENCE SHARE
—of public debt	STOCK

simultaneous trading in stocks and futures of those stocks	INDEX ARBITRAGE
slice of whole (money)	TRANCHE
slump	DEPRESSION RECESSION
speculative security	JUNK-BOND
speculator who	
—buys	
in anticipation of rising prices	BULL
to profit	
—by different prices in different markets	ARBITRAGEUR
—on newly-issued shares	STAG
—sells	
for short-term gain	PROFIT-TAKER
in anticipation of falling prices	BEAR
spending	
—equal to tax income	BALANCED BUDGET
—in excess of tax receipts	DEFICIT SPENDING
split into separate companies	DEMERGE
starting a business	FLOTATION
state	
—of the economy	CONJUNCTURE
—intervention	DIRIGISME
—treasury	FISC, FISK
statistical measure of prices etc	INDEX
—base-weighted	LASPEYRE'S INDEX
—current-weighted	PASSCHE INDEX
stock	
—certificates, bonds etc	SECURITIES
—considered safe and profitable	GILT-EDGED SECURITIES GILTS
—held with others	JOINT STOCK
—used for business	CAPITAL
study of	
—economics by statistical methods	ECONOMETRICS
—large-scale economics	MACROECONOMICS
sudden	
—attempt to buy large shareholding	DAWN RAID
—collapse of share prices	FREE FALL
sum owing	DEB(I)T
summary of accounts	BALANCE SHEET
supplementary asset such as goodwill	INTANGIBLE
surreptitious dealing in goods	BLACK MARKET

system
—based on supply and
  demand   MARKET ECONOMY
—fixing currency value
  in relation to gold   GOLD STANDARD
—generating wealth
  for individuals   CAPITALISM
—of state intervention   COLBERTISM
                                  DIRIGISME
—vesting property, etc
  in the community   SOCIALISM
  in the state   COLLECTIVISM
                                  COMMUNISM
taking excessive
interest on loan   USURY
tax
—collected by
  government agencies   DIRECT TAX
  traders   INDIRECT TAX
—on
  alcohol,
    tobacco, etc   (EXCISE) DUTY
  capital   CAPITAL LEVY
  companies   CORPORATION TAX
  estate   DEATH DUTY
                                  INHERITANCE TAX
  gains   CAPITAL GAINS TAX
  gifts   CAPITAL TRANSFER TAX
  imports   (CUSTOMS) DUTY
  income   INCOME TAX, PAYE
                                  SUPERTAX
  increased value
    of product   INPUT TAX, OUTPUT TAX
                                  VALUE-ADDED TAX, VAT
—policy   FISCAL POLICY
—rebates instead of
  social benefits   NEGATIVE INCOME TAX
                                  REVERSE INCOME TAX
temporary recovery
  of share prices   DEAD-CAT BOUNCE
theory
—of
  best strategies   NASH EQUILIBRIUM
  development of
    the economy
    over time   TURNPIKE THEOREM
  extending until marginal
    gains balance
    marginal costs   MARGINAL PRINCIPLE
—that trade cycles
  result from bank
  lending   CREDIT THEORY
total value of
—GNP less income from
  overseas investments   GDP
                                  GROSS DOMESTIC PRODUCT

—goods and services
  produced in a country
  in one year   GNP
                                  GROSS NATIONAL PRODUCT
—property of
  company   ASSETS
  deceased   ASSET
traffic in buying
  shares etc   ARBITRAGE
transfer of funds from
  account in surplus
  to one in deficit   VIREMENT
treating money as an
  article   COMMODIFICATION
unexpected profit   LUAU
unfair trading
  agreement   RESTRICTIVE PRACTICE
unfixed exchange
  rate   FLOATING EXCHANGE RATE
unfunded short-term
  loan   FLOATING DEBT
unofficial business
  evading the tax system   BLACK ECONOMY
usurer   LOAN-SHARK
value of stock
—equal to purchase price   PAR
—over par   PREMIUM
—under par   DISCOUNT
variable rate of exchange   FLOATING RATE
warrant to buy
  government securities
  at a fixed price   GILT WARRANT
workforce   MANPOWER
written
—acknowledgment of debt   DEBENTURE
—authorisation
  for credit   LETTER OF CREDIT
—IOU   NOTE OF HAND
                                  PROMISSORY NOTE
—obligation to pay
  or perform contract   BOND
yield from
—capital   INTEREST
—shares, etc   DIVIDEND
Ecuador   EC
capital   QUITO
coin   SUCRE
egg
cooked
—as light fluffy pancake   OMELETTE
—in
  baking dish   SHIRRED
  fat   FRIED
—on one side   SUNNY SIDE UP
  pan and stirred   SCRAMBLED
  water   BOILED

—lightly	CODDLED	jar	CANOPIC
without shell	POACHED	king	PHARAOH
egg dishes	ALPINE EGG, CHILLI EGGS	kings	AKHENATEN, AMASIS, AMENMESSE
	CROQUE MONSIEUR		AMENEMHET, AMENHOTEP, AMOSIS
	EGG A LA MORNAY, EGG BENEDICT		CHEOPS, HOREMHEB, KHAFRE
	EGG CUSTARD, EGG FLORENTINE		KHUFU, MENES, MENKAURE
	EGG ROLL, FRAMED EGG		MERENPTAH, PEPI, RAMESES
	MERINGUE, OMELETTE, PICKLED EGG		SESOSTRIS, SETI, SIPTAH
	PIPERADE, RAMAKIN, RAMEKIN		TUTANKHAMUN, TUTANKHATEN
	RAMEQUIN, ZABAGLIONE		TUTHMOSIS, ZOSER
in sausage meat	SCOTCH EGG	lentils and rice	MEGADARA
omelette with vegetable		life symbol	ANKH
filling	SPANISH OMELETTE	measures	
raw with seasoning	PRAIRIE OYSTER	—7½ miles	SCHENE
scrambled egg on toast		—100 sq. ft	AROURA
with anchovy paste	SCOTCH WOODCOCK	—209 sq. yds	QIRAT
white of egg	ALBUMEN, GLAIR	—1 acre	FEDDAN
—whisked till stiff	MERINGUE	—½ bushel	KELA
yellow part of egg	YOLK	—5 bushels	ARDEB
Egypt		melon	ABDALAVI
administrative district	NOME	military officer	BIMBASHI, BINBASHI
bean(s)		mongoose	ICHNEUMON
—mashed	FALAFEL	month	AHET, APAP
—puree	BISSARA	monument	OBELISK, PYRAMID, SPHINX
—stew	FOUL MADAMES	National Party	WAFD
beer	BO(U)SA, ZYTHUM	pastry	BASBOUSA
beetle	SCARAB	peasant(s)	FELLAH(IN)
boat	BARIS	picture-writing	HIEROGLYPHICS
boulevard along Nile	CORNICHE	pike	MORMYRUS
capital	CAIRO, EL QAHIRA	potsherd	OSTRACON, OSTRAKON
catfish	DOCMAC	precious alloy	ASEM
characters	ET	province	NOME
Christian	COPT	queens	CLEOPATRA, HATSHEPSUT
coin			NEFERTITI
—unit	MILLIEME	region of the dead	AMENTI
—100 milliemes	PIASTRE	religious ceremony	DOSEH
—100 piastres	POUND	river	NILE
commander	SIRDAR	royal crown	PSCHENT
cotton	MACO, PIMO, SAK(EL)	ruler	PHARAOH
cross	ANKH, TAU	ruling class	MAMELUKE
crown	ATEF, PSCHENT	secret chamber	SERDAB
dance	GHAZIYA	serpent emblem	URAEUS
dancing girl	ALMA(H), ALME(H)	ship	DAHABI(Y)EH
deities	(*see* **gods, goddesses**)		DAHABBIYEH, DAHABEEAH
department	NOME	soda	TRONA
double	KA	soldier-slave	MAMELUKE
dynasty	HYKSOS, MAMELUKE	soul	BA, KA, SAHJ
	PTOLEMAIC	soup	MELOKHIA
embalming vase	CANOPUS	sultan	MAMELUKE, SOLDAN
fish	OXYRHYNCUS, SAIDE	tambourine	RIKK
floating vegetable matter	SUDD	temporary dam	SUDD
funeral effigy	USHABTI	tomb	MASTABA
granite	STENITE	underground chamber	SERDAB
guard	GHAF(F)IR	vase (human-headed)	CANOPUS
hat	FEZ	viceroy	KHEDIVE
holy rattle	SISTRUM	viceroy's wife	KHEDIVA

water
—lift | SHADOOF, SHADUF
—lily | LOTE, LOTOS, LOTUS
weight
—variable | ROTL
—¹/₃oz | K(H)AT
—1oz | ORIEH
—3lbs | OKA
—99lbs | CANTAR, KANTAR
| QUANTAR
white slave | MAMELUKE
wire rattle | SISTRUM
eight
Biblical texts | OCTAPLA
Christmas presents | MILKMAIDS
cleft | OCTAFID
combining form | OCT-
figure of ... | SKATING
fold | OCTAPLOID, OCTOPLOID
| OCTUPL(ICAT)E
groups | EIGHTSOME, OCTAD
OCTAVE, OCTET(T), OCTETTE
OCTONARY, OCTUOR, OGDOAD
having eight
—angles | OCTAGONAL
—arms | OCTOPOD
—columns | OCTOSTYLE
—eyes | OCTONOCULAR
—faces | OCTOHEDRAL
—feet | OCTONARIAN, OCTOPOD
—leaves per sheet | OCTAVO
—parts in eights | OCTAMEROUS
—petals | OCTOPETALOUS
—pistils | OCTOGYNIAN
| OCTOGYNOUS
—rows | OCTASTICHOUS
| OCTOSTICHOUS
—segments | OCTOFID
—sepals | OCTOSEPALOUS
—sides | OCTOGONAL
—stamens | OCTANDRIAN
| OCTRANDROUS
—styles | OCTOGYNIAN
| OCTOGYNOUS
—times normal number of
chromosomes | OCTAPLOID
—tones | OCTACHORD
—year intervals | OCTENNIAL
hundred | O, OMEGA
hundred thousand | O, OMEGA
hundredth year | OCTINGEN(TEN)ARY
| OCTOCENTENARY
iron | NIBLICK
notes | OCTAVE
one over the ... | DRUNK
pieces of ... | COINS

yearly | OCTENNIAL
eighteen | MAJORITY
eighteen holes | GOLF COURSE
eighteen in team | AUSTRALIAN RULES
eighteen leaves per sheet | EIGHTEENMO
| OCTODECIMO
eighth
note | QUAVER
part of circle | OCTANT
eighty | P, PI, R
eighty-eight | PIANO
eighty thousand | P, PI, R
eighty years old | OCTOGENARIAN
| OCTOGENARY
El Salvador | ES
capital | SAN SALVADOR
coin | CENTAVO, COLON
electric
battery | CELL, VOLTAIC PILE
—terminal | ELECTRODE
cable tower | PYLON
channel for wires | CONDUIT, DUCT
circuit
—for measuring resistance | METRE BRIDGE
| WHEATSTONE BRIDGE
—producing doubled
DC voltage from AC | VOLTAGE DOUBLER
coil
—acting as magnet | SOLENOID
—in dynamo or electric
motor | ARMATURE
combination of
two waves | AM, AMPLITUDE MODULATION
| FM, FREQUENCY MODULATION
component of impedance | REACTANCE
| RESISTANCE
condenser | CAPACITOR
conducting capacity of
—circuit | CONDUCTANCE, G
—conductor | CONDUCTIVITY, K
conductor of current | ELECTRODE
connection point | SOCKET
connector for one or
more plugs | ADAPTER
current
—flowing in one
direction | DC, DIRECT CURRENT
—that changes
direction | AC, ALTERNATING CURRENT
—meter | AMMETER
—reversing commutator | RHEOTROPE
device
—based on
semiconductors | SOLID STATE
—changing voltage of
alternating current | TRANSFORMER

—monitoring large current	AMPLIDYNE
	METADYNE
—producing	
alternating current	ALTERNATOR
	GENERATOR
direct current	DYNAMO
static	
electricity	WIMSHURST MACHINE
—reducing amount of	
current passing	SHUNT
—reversing direction	
of current	COMMUTATOR
—short-circuiting unwanted	
high voltages	VARISTOR
—transferring power	
between systems	TRANSDUCER
dialectric with permanent	
polarity	ELECTRET
difference in electrical	
states at two	
points	POTENTIAL (DIFFERENCE)
eddy current	INDUCED CURRENT
	FOUCAULT CURRENT
electricity	
—at rest	STATIC ELECTRICITY
—produced by	
friction	STATIC (ELECTRICITY)
	TRIBOELECTRICITY
heat	SEEBECK EFFECT
	THERMOELECTRICITY
heated crystal	PYROELECTRICITY
light	PHOTOELECTRIC EFFECT
	PHOTOVOLTAIC EFFECT
pressure	PIEZOELECTRICITY
	PIEZOELECTRIC EFFECT
temperature gradient	
in conductor	KELVIN EFFECT
	THOMSON EFFECT
water power	HYDROELECTRICITY
electro-	
—cardiogram	ECG
—convulsive therapy	ECT
—encephalogram	ECG
—magnetic unit	EMU
—motive force	EMF
—phoresis	CATAPHORESIS
—plated	EP
—static capacitor	LEYDEN JAR
—static unit	ESU
electron	
—tube connector	ELECTRODE
with two connectors	DIODE
with three connectors	TRIODE
—volt	EV
electronic	
—component	

built on silicon chip	MICROCHIP
changing voltage	TRANSFORMER
consisting of small	
circuits in single	
structure	INTEGRATED CIRCUIT
converting	
—AC to DC	COMMUTATOR, RECTIFIER
—DC to AC	INVERTER
focussing electron beam	
on fluorescent	
screen	CATHODE-RAY TUBE
opposing flow of	
current	RESISTOR, RHEOSTAT
reacting to humidity	HYGRISTOR
reversing flow of current	COMMUTATOR
storing charge	CAPACITOR
	CONDENSER
switch based on	
special glass	OVSHINSKY DEVICE
—data processing	EDP
failure of supply	OUTAGE
filter passing only	
selected frequencies	BAND-PASS FILTER
fixed voltage across valve	GRID BIAS
frame collecting current	
from overhead line	PANTOGRAPH
frequency x 2π	PULSATANCE
generation of force by	
change in current	INDUCTANCE, L
glow seen round ship's masts etc	CORPOSANT
	ST ELMO'S FIRE
having	
—no electric charge	NEUTRAL
—same	
number of electrons	ISOELECTRONIC
potential	ISOELECTRIC
heater in water tank	IMMERSION HEATER
in living things	BIOELECTRICITY
induced current	EDDY CURRENT
	FOUCAULT CURRENT
—due to change of	
current in another	
circuit	MUTUAL INDUCTION
instruments	(see **measuring instrument**)
	(see **scientific instrument**)
intermediate electrode	DYNODE
interrupter	RHEOTOME
lamp connector	BAYONET FIXING
law governing	
—strength of induced	
magnetic field	AMPERE'S LAW
—sum of electrical	
forces	KIRCHHOFF'S LAW
—voltage and current	OHM'S LAW
loudspeaker producing	
—high notes	TWEETER

—low notes	WOOFER
measures	(*see separate entry*)
metre bridge	WHEATSTONE BRIDGE
mutual conductance in	
thermionic valve	TRANSCONDUCTANCE
negative electrode	CATHODE
non-conductor	DIELECTRIC, INSULATOR
permanently polarised	
material	ELECTRET
point of connection	TERMINAL
positive electrode	ANODE
potential difference in	
conductor in magnetic field	HALL EFFECT
prevent transfer of current	INSULATE
producer of current	ALTERNATOR
	DYNAMO, GENERATOR
	POWER STATION
property of	
—having positive or	
negative charge	POLARITY
—inducing	
force by variation	
of current in circuit	INDUCTANCE
magnetism by proximity	INDUCTION
—opposition to current flow	IMPEDANCE
	REACTANCE
	RESISTANCE
—producing current by	
proximity	INDUCTION
—storing charge	CAPACITANCE
—transferring current	
in circuit	CONDUCTANCE
	CONDUCTIVITY
protective device	CIRCUIT BREAKER, FUSE
ratio of	
—changes in current	
and voltage in	
valve	MUTUAL CONDUCTANCE
	TRANSCONDUCTANCE
—displacement of field	
strength	PERMITTIVITY
—potential at ends of	
conductor	RESISTANCE
—power to voltage and	
current	POWER FACTOR
—two electrical quantities	
as logarithm	NEPER
reciprocal	
—of capacitance	ELASTANCE
—of conductivity	RESISTIVITY
relative permittivity	DIELECTRIC CONSTANT
resistor giving	
lowered voltage	POTENTIAL DIVIDER
	POTENTIOMETER
	VOLTAGE DIVIDER
rotor of electric motor	ARMATURE

screen used to insulate	
from interference	FARADAY CAGE
semiconductor	VARISTOR
solution that conducts electricity	ELECTROLYTE
specific	
—inductive	
capacity	DIELECTRIC CONSTANT
—resistance	RESISTIVITY
substance with	
—almost no	
resistance at very low	
temperature	SUPERCONDUCTOR
—conductivity at high	
temperature or when	
impure	SEMICONDUCTOR
—no conductivity at	
low temperature or	
when pure	SEMICONDUCTOR
sudden increase in current	SURGE
superimposition of waves	MODULATION
switch in electronic circuit	
based on special glass	OVSHINSKY DEVICE
system reducing	
unwanted sound	DOLBY (SYSTEM)
transformer producing	
high voltage current	TESLA COIL
valve	
—connector	ELECTRODE
—with heated	
electrodes	THERMIONIC VALVE
variable resistor	RHEOSTAT
vibrating part of	
loudspeaker etc	ARMATURE
voltage	ELECTROMOTIVE FORCE, EMF
—divider	POTENTIOMETER
Wheatstone bridge	METER BRIDGE
	(*see also* **physics**)

elements

ancient	EARTH, AIR, FIRE, WATER
imaginary	PHLOGISTON
modern listing (*alternative or unconfirmed names in*	
brackets)	
actinium	AC
alabamine	(*see* astatine)
alucinium	(*see* beryllium)
aluminium	AL
americium	AM
antimony (regulus)	SB, STIBIUM
argon	A
arsenic	AS
astatine (alabamine, helvetium)	AT
atomic number	
—57-71	LANTHANIDE, LANTHANON
	RARE, EARTH
—above 89	ACTINIDE, ACTINOID
barium	BA

berkelium	BK
beryllium (alucinium, glucinium)	BE
bismuth	BI
boron	B
bromine	BR
cadmium	CD
caesium	CS
calcium	CA
californium	CF
carbon	C
cassiopium	(*see* lutetium)
cerium	CE
chlorine	CL
chromium	CR
cobalt	CO
columbium (niobium)	CB
copper	CU, D, P
crypton	(*see* krypton)
curium	CM
didymium (supposed element)	
dysprosium	DY
einsteinium	ES
erbium	ER
europium	EU
fermium	FM
florentium	(*see* promethium)
fluorine	F
francium (virginium)	FR
gadolinium	GD
gallium	GA
germanium	GE
glucin(i)um (beryllium)	GL
gold	AU, BULL, OR
hafnium	HF
hahnium	HA
having incomplete inner shell	TRANSITION ELEMENT
helium	HE
helvetium	(*see* astatine)
holmium	HO
hydrogen (protium, deuterium, tritium)	H
illinium	(*see* promethium)
in 7th group	HALOGEN
indium	IN
iodine	I
iridium	IR
iron	FE
kalium	(*see* potassium)
krypton	KR
kurchatovium	(*see* rutherfordium)
lanthanum	LA
lawrencium	LR, LW
lead	PB
lithium	LI
lutetium (cassiopium)	LU

magnesium	MG
manganese	MN
masurium	(*see* technetium)
mendelevium	MD, MV
mercury	AZOTH, HG
molybdenum	MO
neodymium	ND
neon	NE
neoytterbium	(*see* ytterbium)
neptunium	NP
nickel	NI
niobium	(*see* columbium)
nitrogen	AZOTE, N
nobelium	NO
osmium	OS
oxygen	O
palladium	PD
phosphorus	P
platinum	PT
plutonium	PU
polonium	PO
potassium (kalium)	K
praseodymium	PR
promethium (florentium, illinium)	PM
pro(to)tactinium	PA
radium	RA
radon	RN
regulus (antimony)	SB, STIBIUM
rhenium	RE
rhodium	RH
rubidium	RB
ruthenium	RU
rutherfordium (kurchatovium)	RF
samarium	SM
scandium	SC
selenium	SE
silicon	SI
silver	AG, ARGENTUM
sodium	NA
strontium	SR
sulphur	S
tantalum	TA
technetium (masurium)	TC
tellurium	TE
terbium	TB
thallium	TL
thorium	TH
thulium	TM
tin	SN
titanium	TI
tungsten (wolfram)	W
uranium	U
vanadium	V
virginium	(*see* francium)
wolfram	(*see* tungsten)
xenon	XE

ytterbium (neoytterbium)	YB
yttrium	Y
zinc	ZN
zirconium	ZR
eleven	SIDE, TEAM, XI
Christmas presents	PIPERS
having eleven	
—leaves	HENDECAPHYLLOUS
—notes	HENDECACHORD
—pistils	HENDECAGYNIAN
	HENDECAGYNOUS
—stamens	HENDECANDROUS
—styles	HENDECAGYNIAN
	HENDECAGYNOUS
—syllables	HENDECASYLLABIC
hundred	MC
engines of war	(*see* **weapons**)
English	
as a	
—foreign language	EFL
—second language	ESL
battles	(*see separate entry*)
capital	LONDON
Chamber Orchestra	ECO
Church Union	ECU
counties	(*see separate entry*)
Dialect Society	EDS
Golf Union	EGU
kings	(*see separate entry*)
language teaching	ELT
national emblem	ROSE
patron saint	GEORGE
river	THAMES
Speaking Union	ESU
enzymes	
action of	ZYMOLYSIS
activator	KINASE
adaptive enzyme	INDUCIBLE ENZYME
breaking down	
—acetylcholine	CHOLINESTERASE
—adrenaline	MONOAMINE OXIDASE
—amino-acids	PEPTIDASE
—asparagine	ASPARAGINASE
—ATP	ATPASE
—bacterial cells	LYSOZYME
—cane-sugar to fructose	
and glucose	INVERTASE, SUCRASE
—casein	EREPSIN
—caseinogen to casein	RENNIN
—cells	LYSOZYME
—cellulose	CYTASE
—esters	ESTERASE
—fats to alcohol and acid	LIPASE
—fibrin	FIBRINOLYSIN
—fibrinogen to fibrin	THROMBIN
—gelatine	EREPSIN

—glucose	GLUCOKINASE
—glycogen into sugar	AMYLASE
—histamines	HISTAMINASE
—hydrogen peroxide	CATALASE
—lactose to glucose	LACTASE
—maltose to glucose	MALTASE
—nucleic acids	NUCLEASE
—peptides	PEPTIDASE
—phosphates	PHOSPHATASE
—proteins	CATHEPSIN, EREPSIN
	PAPAIN, PEPSIN
	PROTE(IN)ASE
	PROTEOLYTIC ENZYME
	TRYPSIN
—rubonucleic acid	RUBONUCLEASE
—starch	
to maltose	DIASTASE
to sugar	AMYLASE, PTYALIN
—sugar to alcohol and	
carbon	ZYMASE
—trypsinogen to trypsin	ENTEROKINASE
	PEPTIDASE
—urea to ammonia and water	UREASE
catalyses oxidation	OXIDASE
—of substrate	PERIOXIDASE
—reduction	RESPIRATORY ENZYME
catalyst in	
—hydrolysis	HYDROLASE
—reduction	REDUCTASE
coagulates milk proteins	RENNIN
co-enzyme	
—acting as energy	
source	ADENOSINE TRIPHOSPHATE
	ADT
—cutting other molecules	
from RNA	RIBOZYME
—involved in energy	
transfer	ADENOSINE DIPHOSPHATE
	ADP
—reducing oxidation	DPN, FAD
	FLAVIN ADENINE DINUCLEOTIDE
	FLAVIN MONONUCLEOTIDE, NAD(P)
digestive	(CHYMO)TRYPSIN, PAPAIN
	PEPSIN, RENNIN
early stage	ZYMOGEN
emulsin	SYNAPTASE
fat-splitting	LIPOCLASTIC
ferment	ZYME
fermentation	ZYMOSIS
fermentor	ZYMOGEN
formed in response to its	
substrate	ADAPTIVE ENZYME
	INDUCIBLE ENZYME
found in	
—all living tissues	PROTE(IN)ASE
—almonds	EMULSIN, SYNAPTASE

—animal secretions	LYSOZYME
—blood	FIBRINOLYSIN
	THROMBIN
—cell nucleus	POLYMERASE
—digestive juices	LACTASE
—egg-white	LYSOZYME
—fatty tissue	ADIPSIN
—gastric juices	RENNIN
—germinating seeds	DIASTASE
—liver and kidneys	URICASE
—malt	DIASTASE
—pancreas	AMYLASE
	CHYMOTRYPSINOGEN
	RIBONUCLEASE, TRYPSIN
—pancreatic juices	DIASTASE
—papaw fruit	PAPAIN
—plants	LYSOZYME, PEROXIDASE
	(*see also* **biology**)
—prothrombin	THROMBIN
—RNA	RIBOZYME
—saliva	PTYALIN
—small intestine	ENTEROKINASE
	EREPSIN, PEPTIDASE
—stomach	PEPSIN, RENNIN
—yeast	MALTASE, ZYMASE
inactive	PROENZYME
inducible enzyme	ADAPTIVE ENZYME
inducing	
—fermentation	ZYMASE
—polymerisation of DNA	POLYMERASE
invertase	SUCRASE
inverts cane sugar	INVERTASE
no-protein part	COENZYME
not requiring inducement	
of substrate	CONSTITUTIVE ENZYME
producing	
—fructose	INULASE
—grape sugar	MALTASE
—luminosity	LUCIFERASE
—starch from sugar	DIASTASE
—sugar from starch	PTYALIN
promoting	
—alcoholic fermentation	ZYMASE
—oxidation	OXYDASE
protecting against bacteria	LYSOZYME
protein part	APOENZYME
proteolytic	CATHEPSIN
remaining inside living cell	ENDOENZYME
removes	
—amino group	DEAMINASE
—hydrogen	DEHYDROGENASE
repairs DNA	PHOTOLASE
secreted by skin	LYSOZYME
sucrase	INVERTASE
sugar-splitting	SUCROCLASTIC
synaptase	EMULSIN

used to soften meat	PAPAIN
variant type	ISO(EN)ZYME
equal	EQUI-, ISO-
agglutination of red	
cells within the same	
blood group	ISOAGGLUTINATION
antibody controlling	
isoagglutination	ISOAGGLUTININ
bilaterally symmetrical	ISOBILATERAL
day and night	EQUINOX
diagrams representing a	
particular number of instances	ISOTYPE
either of two atoms of identical mass	ISOBARE
having	
—all the teeth similar	ISODONT
—close similarity	
in crystalline form	ISOMORPHIC
—closed chain of like atoms	ISOCYCLIC
—equal	
angles	EQUIANGULAR, ISOGONIC
diameters	ISODIAMETRIC
differences	EQUIDIFFERENT
force	EQUIPOLLENT
hydrostatic equilibrium	ISOSTATIC
likelihood	EQUIPROBABLE
magnetic force	ISOMAGNETIC
meaning	EQUIVOCAL
number of electrons	ISOELECTRONIC
perimeters	ISOPERIMETRICAL
petals and stamens	ISOSTEMONOUS
political power	ISOCRACY
power	EQUIPOLLENT
	EQUIPOTENT, EQUIVALENT
pressure	ISOSTATIC
privileges	ISONOMY
rights	ISONOMY
sides	EQUILATERAL
strength	ISODYNAMIC
time units	ISORHYTHMIC
value	EQUIVALENT, EQUIVALUE
weight	EQUIPONDERANT
—gametes of equal size	ISOGAMY
—isomorphism between the	
two forms	ISODIMORPHISM
—laws	ISONOMY
—similar origins	ISOGENETIC
—spores of only one kind	ISOSPOROUS
—the same	
atomic number but different	
—energy	ISOMERIC
—mass number	ISOTOPIC
colour	ISOCHROMATIC
measure	ISOMETRIC
number of	
—atoms	ISOSTERIC
—neutrons	ISOTONE

osmotic pressure	ISOTONIC
potential	ISOELECTRIC
properties irrespective	
of direction	ISOTROPIC
tension	ISOTONIC
tone	ISOTONIC
—two	
equal sides	ISOSCELES
pairs of wings alike	ISOPTEROUS
—yolk distributed evenly	ISOLECITHAL
line	
—making equal angles	
with all meridians	LOXODROME
—of equal	
amounts of sunshine	ISOHEL
depths	ISOBATH
earthquake shock	ISOSEISMAL
frequency of auroral	
displays	ISOCHASM
magnetic dip	ISOCLINE
pressures	ISOBAR
rainfall	ISOHYET
temperatures	ISOTHERM
—in	
coldest time	ISOCRYME
summer time	ISOTHERE
—(mean winter)	ISOCHEIM, ISOCHIME
—underground	ISOGEOTHERM
time differences	ISOCHRONE
upheaval of land	ISOBASE
value with respect to	
—one variable	ISOGRAM
—two variables	ISOPLETH
—of simultaneous development	
of thunderstorms	ISOBRONT
—of variations of	
some quantity under	
conditions of	
constant volume	ISOCHOR(E)
pressure and temperature	
at constant volume	ISOMETRIC
—separating areas of	
different dialects	ISOGLOSS
masonry with courses of	
equal height	ISODOMON
multiplied by same number	EQUIMULTIPLE
performed in equal time	ISOCHRONAL
reciprocity of rights of	
citizenship	ISOPOLITY
Eskimo	HUSKY, IN(N)UIT
boat	OOMIA(C)K, UMIAK
	KAIAK, KAYAK
boot	MUCLUC, MUCKLUCK, MUCKLUK
clover	ALSIKE
conjurer	ANGEKKOK
dog	HUSKY, MALAMUTE, MALEMUTE

fur coat	ANARAK, ANORAK
house	IGLOO
language	HUSKY
skin tent	TUPAK, TUPIK
whale meat	MUKTUK
Ethiopia	ETH
	(see **Abyssinian**)
Europe	
articles	ELLA, LATHE, UNDER
Broadcasting Union	EBU
cherry	GEAN
clover	ALSIKE
Council	CE, EC
deer	ELK
Defence Community	EDC
Development Fund	EDF
dormouse	LEROT, LOIR
dwarf-cherry	GROUND-CHERRY
Economic	
—Commission	ECE
—Community	EEC
Exchange Rate Mechanism	ERM
extinct horse	TARPAN
fish (Danube)	ZINGEL
hawk	FALLER
inferior wheat	SPELT
kite	GLE(A)D, GLEDE
lily	GREEN DRAGON
Monetary Agreement	EMA
Payments Union	EPU
perennial herb	LASERPICIUM
plain	STEPPE
plant	GOLD-THREAD
Productivity Agreement	EPA
rabbit	CON(E)Y, LEPORID
rodent	ERD, LEMMING
shrub	DAPHNE, SPURGE-LAUREL
squirrel	SISEL
timber	SATIN-WOOD, ZANTE(-WOOD)
vulture	GALLINAZO, GRIFFON VULTURE,
	LAMMERGEIER, LAMMERGEYER
wildcat	CATAMOUNT
wine measure	ANKER
explorer	
American	PALMER, PEARY
Austrian	PAYER, WEYPRECHT
British	BAFFIN, BURTON, CABOT
	CONWAY, COOK, DAVIS
	GALTON, GILBERT, FITCH
	FRANKLIN, FROBISHER
	FUCHS, LIVINGSTONE, LUGARD
	MUNGO PARK, POWELL, ROSS
	SCOTT, SHACKLETON
	SMITH, SWAN, WEDDELL
Dutch	BARENTZ, TASMAN
French	CARTIER, COCTEAU

Greek	PYTHEAS	centre line	OPTIC AXIS
Italian	CABOT, COLUMBUS	coloured part of eye	IRIS
New Zealand	HILLARY	compound eye	OMMATEUM
Norwegian	AMUNDSEN, NANSEN	corner of eye	CANTHUS
Portuguese	VASCO DA GAMA	defect of lens	ASTIGMATISM
Russian	BERING	depression in retina	FOVEA CENTRALIS
Spanish	DE TORRES, MAGELLAN		MACULA
Swiss	PICCARD	dimness of vision	CALIGO
Venetian	MARCO POLO	duct from eye to nose	LAC(H)RYMAL DUCT

explosives

ammonium etc	AMATOL, AMMONAL		LACRIMAL DUCT
	AMMONITE	element(s) in	
cellulose nitrate and		compound eye	OMMATIDIUM(OMMATIDIA)
nitroglycerine	CORDITE	elementary eye	OCELLUS
crystalline compound	TNB	eye disease	(*see* **disease**)
	TRINITORBENZENE	fluid	
device used to fire		—in eyeball	VITREOUS HUMOUR
cartridges	PERCUSSION CAP	—round lens	AQEOUS HUMOUR
explosive filling in		focussing body	(CRYSTALLINE) LENS
bullets, shells, etc	PROPELLANT	fold of skin at corner	
gas — methane and air	FIRE-DAMP	of eye	EPICANTHUS
gun-cotton with		gland secreting tears	LAC(H)RYMAL GLAND
—barium nitrate	TONITE		LACRIMAL GLAND
—nitroglycerin	BLASTING GELATIN	inner lining of eyelid	CONJUNCTIVA
liquid	AZOIMIDE	insect's eye	COMPOUND
	HYDRAZOIC ACID	intersection of optic nerves	OPTIC CHIASM(A)
nitric acid on		junction of optic nerve	
—cellulose	CELLULOSE NITRATE	and retina	BLIND SPOT
	GUN-COTTON	layer of blood cells in retina	CHOROID
	NITROCELLULOSE	lens of compound eye	FACET
—starch	PYROXYLE, XYLOIDINE	ligament supporting lens	ZONULE OF ZINN
nitroglycerine		light-sensitive	
—cellulose nitrate, saltpetre etc	GELIGNITE	—layer at back of eye	RETINA
—in kieselguhr	DYNAMITE	—spot in lower animals	EYE-SPOT
—saltpetre, sawdust, etc	DUALIN		STIGMA
petroleum jelly	NAPALM	long sightedness	HYPER(METR)OPIA
picric acid	MELINITE	membrane between sclera	
—nitrobenzene and vaseline	LYDDITE	and retina	CHOROID (COAT)
plastic	SEMTEX	nerve conveying	
potassium nitrate,		sensation from eye	OPTIC NERVE
charcoal, and sulphur	GUNPOWDER	normal vision	EMMETROPIA
smokeless	AMBERITE	one-eyed	
used by Greeks in naval warfare	GREEK FIRE	—giant	CYCLOPS
yellow		—marine animal	CYCLOPS
—crystalline solid	PICRIC ACID	opening admitting light	PUPIL
—solid	TNT, TRINITROTOLUENE	outer	
		—layer of cornea	CONJUNCTIVA

eyes

abnormal		—membrane of eyeball	SCLERA, SCLEROTIC
—dryness	XEROPHTHALMIA	part of iris	AREOLA
—protusion	EXOPHTHALMIA	pigmented layer	UVEA
	EXOPHTHALMOS	point of crossing of	
	EXOPHTHALMUS	optic nerves	OPTIC CHIASM(A)
adjustable diaphragm	IRIS	protrusion of eye	EXOPHTHALMIA
angle between eyelids	CANTHUS		EXOPHTHALMOS
apple of the eye	PUPIL		EXOPHTHALMUS
blindness	AMAUROSIS	reflecting layer in retina	TAPETUM
		refracting structure	CRYSTALLINE LENS

rudimentary third eye	MEDIAN EYE	stalk supporting eye	OMMATOPHORE
	PINEAL BODY	temporary blindness	TEICHOPSIA
sensory body in retina	CONE, ROD	thickened edge of choroid	CILIARY BODY
socket for eye	ORBIT	third eye	MEDIAN EYE
spasm of iris	HIPPUS		PINEAL BODY
spasmodic movements	NYSTAGMUS	transparent front of eye	CORNEA
specialist	OCULIST	vision in poor light	SCOTOPIA
	OPHTHALM(OLOG)IST	white	
	OPTICIAN, OPTOMETRIST	—patch in angle of cornea	LEUCOMA
spots before the eyes	MUSCAE VOLITANTES	—ring round cornea	ARCUS SENILIS
squint	STRABISMUS	—ring round eye	WALL-EYE
	WALL-EYE		

F

fabric

all-wool muslin	MOUSSELINE-DE-LAINE
aluminium thread	LUREX
American cloth	LEATHER-CLOTH
Angora goat's hair	MOHAIR
artificial silk	(CUPRAMMONIUM) RAYON
Asian silk	IKAT
bark (Pacific)	PAPER-CLOTH
black dress fabric	MOURNING-STUFF
blanket material	STROUDING
blue stuff	MAZARINE, PERSE, WATCHET
bold warp twill	WHIPCORD
book muslin	ORGANDIE
bookbinding fabric	SCRIM
bright green	LINCOLN-GREEN
brocade	BALDACHIN(O)
	BALDAQUIN, BAUDEKIN
buff coloured cotton	NANKEEN, NANKIN
cambric	LAWN
camel hair	AB(B)A, ABAYA
	BAR(R)ACAN, CAMELINE
	CAMELOT, CAMLET
canvas	BINCA, BURLAP
cashmere	CIRCASSIAN, CIRCASSIENNE
	KASHMIR
checked	
—cotton	GINGHAM, MADRAS
—woollen	TARTAN
closely woven	
—cotton	PERCALE
—French	PERCALE
—nylon, etc	GLORIA
—rayon	FAILLE
—silk	GLORIA, FAILLE, SATIN
—woollen	WORSTED
cloth	
—bearing imprint of face	
of Jesus	MANDILION, MANDYLIO
—of gold	CICLATO(U)N, GOLD-CLOTH
India	SONERI
or silver	LUPPA
coarse	
—calico (Indian)	DUNGAREE
—canvas	BURLAP
—cotton	BUCKRAM, CALICO
	CANVAS, DENIM, DUCK
	FROCKING, HUCKABUCK, JEAN
	MEXICAN, OSNABURG

East Indies	HUMHUM
—hemp	
jute	HARDS, HOPSACK, HURDS
cotton	CANVAS
—homespun cloth	HODDEN, RUSSET
—jean	FROCKING
—jute	BUCKRAM, GUNNY, HESSIAN
	HOPSACK, SACKCLOTH, SACKING
—linen	BUCKRAM, DOWLAS
	DRABBET(TE)DUCK, , HARDEN
	HARN, HOLLAND, HUCKABUCK
	LOCKRAM, OSNABURG
and wool	LINSEY-WOOLSEY
Brittany	DOWLAS
—muslin	MUSLINET
—Oriental	BAFT
—printed cotton	CALICO
—silk	DUPION, FILOSELLE
and mohair	GROGRAM
India	KINCOB, TASH
—twilled cotton	CORDUROY, DENIM
	FUSTIAN, MOLESKIN
	VELVETEEN
—waved or watered silk	TABBY
—woollen	BAIZE, KELT, KERSEY, RUG
black and white	HODDEN-GREY
blanket material	STROUDING
felted	DRUGGET
Orkney	WADMA(A)L, WADMOL(L)
russet	BURREL
undyed	HODDEN
combed wool	JERSEY
corded	REP(P), REPS
—cotton and wool	RUSSEL(-CORD)
—ribbed muslin	CORTELINE
—silk	GROSGRAIN, OTTOMAN
18th c	PADUASOY
and	
—wool or cotton	BENGALINE
—worsted	POPLIN
—woollen or cotton	MOREEN
cotton	
—and	
mohair	SICILIAN
rayon	BARATHEA
silk	VELVETEEN
wool	DOMETT, LUSTRE, WOOLSEY
	WINCEY, WINSEY
worsted	ORLEANS
—Bengal	BEZAN
—checked	GINGHAM
—crinkled	SEERSUCKER
—fibre sheet	BATT(ING)
—fine	LAWN
—glossy	PERCALINE
—heavy	MONK'S CLOTH

—imitation	POPLIN
flannel	FLANNELETTE
velvet	VELVETEEN
—knitted	BALBRIGGAN
—light	JACONET, MUSLIN, NAINSOOK
—like silk	SHANTUNG
—long-stapled	LISLE
—loosely-woven	CHEESECLOTH
—mattress-fabric	TICKING
—patterned	DIAPER
—piled-fabric	TERRY(TOWELLING)
—plain, raised both sides	WINCEYETTE
—printed	CRETONNE
—shaded	JASPE
—soft	MUSLIN
—strong	COUTIL(LE)
—tufted material	CANDLEWICK
—twilled	DRILL
—white	CAMBRIC, DIMITY
—with	
coloured stripe	GALATEA, GINGHAM
deep nap	LAMBSKIN
raised nap	WINCEYETTE
silk pile	VELVERET
woven pattern	DIAPER
crape-like	CREPE(-DE-CHINE)
	CREPOLIN, CREPON
crinkled linen or cotton	SEERSUCKER
curtain fabric	NET, SCRIM
dark	
—blue or bluish-grey fabric	PERSE
—grey woollen	OXFORD MIXTURE
delicate kind of tabby	TABBINET
double twilled fustian	MOLESKIN
dress material	TOILE
durable	
—cloth	DURANCE
—silk	FLORENCE, FLORENTINE
—woollen (old)	SEMPITERNUM
elasticated	STOCKINET(TE)
	STOCKINGETTE
embossed	CLOQUE, MATEL(L)ASSE
embroidered	
—damask	DAMASSIN
—silk (Indian)	KINCOB, TASH
embroidery	CREWELLERY
fawn-coloured silk	TASAR, TUSSER
	TUSSORE, TUSSAH, TUSSEH
fibre-cloth	TAP(P)A
figured	
—cotton	MOREEN
—linen	DAMASK
Belgian	DORNICK
—muslin	TANJIB, TANZIB
—silk	BROCADE
and linen	BROCATEL(LE)
—woollen	MOREEN, PAISLEY
fine	
—cloth	SINDON
—cotton	BATISTE, CAMBRIC
	LAWN, MADRAS, MUSLIN
	ORGANDIE, PONGEE
—dress fabric	MERINO
—lace	MIGNONETTE
—linen	BYSSUS, CAMBRIC
	LAWN, SENDAL
Dutch	HOLLAND
with cotton or wool	BATISTE
—muslin	ORGANDIE
—silk	PONGEE, TULLE
and wool	EOLIENNE
transparent	CHIFFON
—twilled woollen	CASSIMERE
	KEYSEYMERE
—white linen	CAMBRIC
—wool	BATISTE, BROADCLOTH
	CASSIMERE, CARMELITE
	FOULE, KERSEYMERE
	PUKE, WORCESTER, WORSTED
with cotton	MERINO
—worsted	CUBICA
firm	
—nylon cloth	BO(U)LTING CLOTH
—silk cloth	BO(U)LTING CLOTH
flag material	BEAUFORT
for	
—aprons	BAIZE
—billiard tables	BAIZE
—blankets	STROUDING
—bookbinding etc	SCRIM
—boot linings	WIGAN
—cloaks	MANTLING
—coat linings	SHALLOON
—curtains	BROCADE, MARQUISETTE
	NET, SCRIM
—dresses	FROCKING, RATINE
	RATTEEN
—forester's clothes	KENDAL-GREEN
—hatbands	GROSGRAIN
—linings	CUBICA
—loincloths (India)	D(H)OTI, LUNGI
—mattresses	COUTIL(LE), TICKING
—mosquito nets	MARQUISETTE
—overcoats	COVERT COATING
	MELTON, PETERSHAM
—ribbons	GROSGRAIN
—sacking	DUCK, HEMP, JUTE
—sails	CANVAS, DUCK
—Scots dress	PLAID
—shirts	SARKING
—skirts (Malay)	SARONG
—smock-frocks	DRABET(TE)

—stays	COUTIL(LE)
—suits	TWEED
—tablecloths	CHENILLE
—tents	CANVAS
—trousers	TROUSERING
—umbrellas	GLORIA
—upholstery	BROCADE, DRALON
	LAMPAS, MOQUETTE
—waistcoats	TOILINETTE
	WAISTCOATING
—wound dressings	CHARPIE
forester's cloth	KENDAL-GREEN
French	
—cambric	PERCALE
—coarse cloth	BURE, DRAP
—lace	ALENCON, CLUNY
	COLBERTINE, MOUSSELINE
	TORCHON, VALENCIENNES
—muslin	MOUSSELINE
—wool	DRAP-DE-BERRY
from	
—bark fibre	BARK CLOTH
	PAPER CLOTH
—lint or flax	LINEN
—llamas	LLAMA, VICUNA
—recycled rags	MONG(E), MUNGO
	SHODDY
—sheep, goats, etc	WOOL
—vicuña	VICUNA
—waste silk	SCHAPPE
—woody fibre	GRASS CLOTH, RAMIE
fulled	
—black woollen	BROADCLOTH
—cloth (Fr.)	FOULE
furnishing	MOQUETTE, TAPESTRY
galloon	CADDI, ORRIS
gauze	
—silk-like	TIFFANY
—wool	BAREGE
gimp	ORRIS
glazed	
—cloth	CIRE
—cotton	AMERICAN CLOTH
	CHINTZ, CIRE, SATEEN
—wool	TAMMY
—worsted	TAMIN(E)
glossy	
—cotton	PERCALINE, SATIN JEAN
—linen	SATEEN
—silk	LUSTRINE, LUSTRING
	LUTESTRING, (SILK)SATIN
	TAFFETA(S), TAFFETY
—wool	CALAMANCO
goat's hair	AB(B)A, ABAYA
	ANGORA, CASHMERE, KASHMIR
	MOHAIR, THIBET, TIBET CLOTH

—leather	CORDOVAN, CORDWAIN
	MAROQUIN
—underfleece	PASH(I)M, PASHMINA
gold	
—and silver embroidered	
damask	DAMASSIN
—embroidery	ORPHREY
—or silver lace	ORRIS
green	BAIZE, KENDAL-GREEN
	LINCOLN-GREEN
grain-surfaced material	MAROCAIN
grass-cloth	RAMIE
grey	DRAB, WIGAN
—woollen	OXFORD MIXTURE
gummed stiffening	FOUNDATION-MUSLIN
	FOUNDATION-NET
haircloth	CILICE
hand-knitted woollen	TRICOT
having loops of three threads	THREE-PILE
heavy	
—cotton cloth	MONK'S CLOTH
—goat's hair fabric	THIBET
—rayon	SHARKSKIN
—silk	SAMITE
—woollen	BEAVER, FRIEZE
hemp	
—and jute	HOP-SACK
—sail-cloth	RAVEN('S)-DUCK
homespun woollen	HODDEN
—black and white	HODDEN-GREY
horsehair and linen	CRINOLINE
imitation	
—buff leather	DURANT
—cotton	POPLIN
—flannel	FLANNELETTE
—lambswool	ASTRAKHAN
—leather	DURANT, LEATHER-CLOTH
	LEATHERETTE
—poplin	POPLINETTE
—velvet	VELVETEEN
Indian silk	CABECA, CABESSE, SURAH
Indonesian silk	IKAT
inferior cloth	SHODDY
—Flemish	MOCKADO
jaconet muslin	NAINSOOK
jute	
—cotton lining	BUCKRAM
—fabric	HESSIAN, HOPSACK
	SACKCLOTH, SACKING
knitted	JERSEY
—cotton	BALBRIGGAN
—woollen	TRICOT
knotted	
—into mesh	NET
—threadwork	MACRAME, MACRAMI
lace	GALLOON

—Belgian	MECHLIN
—French	ALENCON, CLUNY
	COLBERTINE, MOUSSELINE
	TORCHON, VALENCIENNES
—machine-made	BOBBIN(N)ET
—made of	
linen	CHANTILLY LACE
silk	BLOND(E)-LACE
	CHANTILLY LACE
—patterned	TROLL(E)Y
—peasant	TORCHON
—pillow	HONITON
Flemish	DUCHESSE LACE
—with no mesh	GUIPURE
—woven with bobbins	BONE-LACE
leather-cloth	AMERICAN CLOTH
	CORDOVAN, CORDWAIN
	MAROCAIN, MAROQUIN
	MOROCCO
light	
—cashmere	CIRCASSIAN
	CIRCASSIENNE
—cotton	JEANETTE
—dress material	CREPULINE, DELAINE
—jean	JEANETTE
—mixed dress stuff	BAREGE
—silk	CRAPE, CREPE(-DE-CHINE)
	CREPOLIN, CREPON
with cotton or wool	BENGALINE
—wool	BAREGE, CASHMERE
	CIRCASSIAN, CIRCASSIENNE
	KASHMIR, SHALLOON
and cotton	DELAINE
like	
—brocade	BROCHE
—damask	TABBINET
—leather	CORDOVAN, CORDWAIN
	MAROCAIN, MAROQUIN
	MOROCCO, SUEDE CLOTH
	SUEDETTE
—satin	SATEEN
—velvet	CHENILLE, PANNE
	VELVETEEN
—wool	ALPACA, ANGORA, VICUNA
linen	
—and wool, etc	WINCEY, WINSEY
—crinkled	SEERSUCKER
—patterned	DIAPER
—shredded for dressings	CHARPIE
—twilled	DRILL, SILESIA
—unbleached	ECRU
loosely woven	CHEESECLOTH
lustrous	CRYSTALLINE, SATARA
	SATEEN
machine-made lace	BOBBIN(N)ET
Madagascar	RABANNA

Malaysian silk	IKAT
Manila	JUSSI
man-made	(see synthetic below)
military drab	KHAKI
mixed	
—colours	MOTLEY
—fabric	GRENADINE
—twill for umbrellas	ZANELLA
modified satin	SATINET(TE)
mohair and cotton	ALEPINE
mosquito net	MARQUISETTE
moth fibre	SILK
muslin	JACONET, ORGANDIE
—French	MOUSSELINE
—Indian	GURRAH, JAMDANI
	MAMMODIS, NAINSOOK
	TANJIB, TANZIB
—open	TARLATAN
needlework with raised	
design	PIQUE WORK
nylon crepe	CREPON
old upholstery cloth	PARAGON
open	
—muslin	TARLATAN
—weave	
canvas	SCRIM
cotton	BUCKRAM, NET
jute	BUCKRAM
linen	BUCKRAM
openwork embroidery	BRODERIE ANGLAISE
orange-coloured	NACARAT
ornamental	TAPESTRY
orris	GALLOON, GIMP
pale blue material	WATCHET
patterned	
—cotton	DIAPER
—lace	TROLL(E)Y
with woven figures	FACONNE
—linen	DIAPER
—wool	PAISLEY
pile with	
—three loops	THREE-PILE
—uncut loops	TERRY
pillow lace	HONITON
—Flemish	DUCHESSE LACE
pineapple leaf fibre	PINA(-CLOTH)
plain cotton raised both	
sides	WINCEYETTE
point lace	NEEDLE-POINT
Polynesian	TAP(P)A
printed	
—cambric or muslin	PERSIENNE
—cotton	CHINTZ, CRETONNE
—East Indies	BAT(T)IK
raffia (Madagascar)	RABANNA
raised embroidery	STUMP-WORK

ramie	GRASS-CLOTH
rayon	
—heavy	SHARKSKIN
—like silk	SHANTUNG
—shaded	JASPE
rep of cotton and wool	RUSSEL-CORD
ribbed	
—cotton	CORDUROY
and wool	RUSSEL
—silk	SICILIENNE
—wool	DROGUET
Indian	SATARA
rich cloth	PALL
—piled	PLUSH
rough	
—dress fabric	RATINE, RATTEEN
—napped blue cloth	PETERSHAM
—silk	SHANTUNG
—wool	(HARRIS)TWEED
satin	
—soft	CHARMEUSE
—with matt finish	SLIPPER SATIN
—wool	CALAMANCO
Scottish	
—coarse grey cloth	MALDY
—shepherd's plaid	MAUD
semi-transparent	VOILE
shiny	SATEEN
shirt material	SARKING, SHIRTING
short-corded woollen	
or cotton	MOREEN
silk	TOBINE
—Asian	IKAT
—brocade	BALDACHIN(O)
	BALDAQUIN, BAUDERKIN
	BAWDKIN
—corded	GROSGRAIN
—crape	CREPE-DE-CHINE
	CREPOLIN, CREPON
—coarse	FILOSELLE
—Ghana	KENTE CLOTH
—glossy	TAFFETA(S), TAFFETY
—heavy	SAMITE
—Indian	CABECA, CABESSE
	SURAH
—Indonesian	IKAT
—lace	CHANTILLY LACE
—muslin	MOUSSELINE-DE-SOIE
—Malaysian	IKAT
—Philippines	HUSI
—satin	ATLAS
—Shakespeare	SAY
—soft	PONGEE, SURAH
—stiff	ARMOZEEN, ARMOZINE
	TAFFETA(S), TAFFETY
—textile	FLORENCE, FLORENTINE

—thin	CHIFFON, GEORGETTE
	GRENADINE, NINON, SARCENET
	SARS(E)NET, SENDAL, TULLE
—twilled	SURAH
—undyed	PONGEE
—untwilled	FOULARD
—voile	NINON
—wild	SHANTUNG, TUSSER, TUSSORE
—with	
cotton and wool	TOILINETTE
hair	FAR(R)ANDINE
	FERRANDINE
raised pattern	MATEL(L)ASSE
short pile	VELVET
two or more threads	ORGANZINE
wool	BARATHEA, CRYSTALLINE
	FAR(R)ANDINE, FERRANDINE
	LAMPAS
worsted	CHALLI(S), SHALLI
silk-like gauze	TIFFANY
smooth-surfaced	
woollen (French)	FOULE
soft	
—cotton	MUSLIN
—muslin	MULL, MULMUL(L)
—napped	VELVET-PILE
—satin	CHARMEUSE
—silk	FOULARD, PONGEE
and worsted	CHALLIS, SHALLI
—slightly-ribbed	TRICOT
—twilled silk	SURAH
—woollen	FLANNEL, NUN'S-VEILING
	ZIBEL(L)INE
—worsted	BARATHEA
stiff	
—canvas	PETERSHAM, SCRIM, WIGAN
—cotton	BUCKRAM, PIQUE
	FOUNDATION NET
	FOUNDATION MUSLIN
—jute	BUCKRAM, SCRIM
—linen	BUCKRAM, SCRIM
—silk	ARMOZEEN, ARMOZINE
	TAFFETA(S), TAFFETY
stout white cotton	DIMITY
striped	BAYADERE, DIMITY
	DO(O)REA, DORIA
	GALATEA, GINGHAM
	MADRAS, SUSI
stretchable	ELASTICATED, LYCRA
strong	
—coarse linen	CRASH
—cotton (mattress)	COUTIL(LE)
—jute	GUNNY
—silk	PRUNELLA, PRUNELLE
	PRUNELLO
—twilled cotton or linen	DRILL

—woollen	PRUNELLA, PRUNELLE
	PRUNELLO
synthetic	ACETATE, ACRILAN
	ACRYLIC, COURTELLE
	CRIMPLENE, DACRON, DRALON
	DYNEL, LUREX, LYCRA, NYLON
	POLYESTER, RAYON, SARAN
	TERYLENE, VISCOSE
Syrian	AB(B)A, ABAYA
taffeta	ARMOZEEN, ARMOZINE
—with pile	TUFF-TAFFETA
	TUFTAFFETY, TUFT-TAFFETA
tapestry	
—Asian Minor	BERGAMA, BERGAMOT
—Belgian	BERGAMOT
—of foliage	OUDENARDE
tarred rags	HARDEN, HARDS
	HERDEN, HURDEN, HURDS
textile fabric (old)	WATERWORK
thick	
—coarse woollen	DUFFEL, DUFFLE
—strong grey cloth	DRAB
—woollen	WADMA(A)L
	WADMOL(L)
thin	
—cotton	CHEESECLOTH, LENO
	MUSLIN
—crinkly linen	
or cotton	SEERSUCKER
—glossy silk-satin	TAFFETA(S)
	TAFFETY
—linen	SENDAL, SILESIA
and wool	LINSEY-WOOLSEY
—material	GAUZE, GOSSAMER
—muslin	CHEESECLOTH, LENO
—satin	SATINET(TE)
—silk	CHIFFON, GEORGETTE
	NINON, SARCENET
	SARS(E)NET, SENDAL, TULLE
or mixed fabric	GRENADINE
twisted	CRAPE
—wool	TAMISE, ZEPHYR
—worsted	BUNTING, ZEPHYR
and cotton or silk	COBURG
transparent	GAUZE, TIFFANY
—black fabric	CYPRESS, CYPRUS
—silk	GRENADINE, OIL-SILK
	ORGANZA
trimming	GALLOON, GIMP, ORRIS
tufted	CANDLEWICK
twilled	
—cotton	CHINO, CORDUROY
	DENIM, DRILL(ING)
	FUSTIAN, JANE, JEAN
	MARCELLA, MOLESKIN
	VELVETEEN

—cotton and	
silk	SATIN-SHEETING
wool	GABARDINE, GABERDINE
worsted	BOMBASINE, BOMBAZINE
—linen	DRILL(ING), MARCELLA
	SILESIA
—silk and worsted	BOMBASINE
	BOMBAZINE
—wool	PLAIDING, WHIPCORD
—worsted	SERGE, SHARKSKIN
and cotton	GAMBROON
twisted warp	LENO
unbleached	
—cotton	BALBRIGGAN
—linen	ECRU
underfleece of goats	PASH(I)M
	PASHMINA
undyed	
—silk	PONGEE
—woollen	BEIGE
untwilled silk	FOULARD
unwoven (wool etc)	FELT
upholsterer's	
—silk	TABARET
—stiffening	BUCKRAM, SCRIM
velvety	
—cloth	CHENILLE
—corded wool	VELOUTINE
—wool	VELOUR(S)
vicuna-wool	VICUNA
wall-covering	TAPESTRY
watered	
—ribbon	PAD
—silk	MOIRE
waterproof	MAC(K)INTOSH, OILSKIN
—linen or hemp	TARPAULIN(G)
—wool	LODEN
waxed	WAX-CLOTH
Welsh	FRAIZE
white	
—cotton	CALICO, DIMITY
—woollen	BLANKET
wild silk	SHANTUNG, TUSSER
	TUSSORE
with	
—looped yarn	BOUCLE
—metal threads	LAME, LUREX
—soft nap	VELVET-PILE
—stiff pile	MOQUETTE
—woolly surface	NAP
wool	BEAVER, CHEVIOT
	DRAP DE BERRY, JAEGER
	LAMBSKIN, PAISLEY
	SAGATHY, WORCESTER
—and	
cotton	LINSEY-WOOLSEY

goat's hair	C(H)AMLET, CAMELOT
	MOHAIR
silk	ALEPINE
—embroidery	ARRASENE
—clothing fabric	MARQUISETTE
—coloured	THIBET, TIBET-CLOTH
—dark grey	OXFORD MIXTURE
—dyed red	STAMMEL
—fine	CARMELITE
—for	
coat-linings	SHALLOON
waistcoats	TOILINETTE
—French	DRAP-DE-BERRY
—homespun (Scot.)	RAPLOCH
—like	
satin	SATEEN
serge	SAY
—lustred	SATARA
—Middle Ages	BURNET
—Orkney	WADMA(A)L, WADMOL(L)
—printed	THIBET, TIBET-CLOTH
—resembling satin	SATEEN
—roughly woven	HOPSACK
—short-piled	LODEN
—smooth	FOULE
—soft	FLANNEL, NUN'S VEILING
	ZIBEL(L)INE
—speckled	HEATHER MIXTURE
—thick	WADMA(A)L, WADMOL(L)
	(HARRIS) TWEED
—thin	TAMISE, ZEPHYR
worsted	
—and	
cotton	PAR(R)AMATTA
silk	BARATHEA
—old	INKLE
—ribbon	CADDIS
—soft	BARATHEA
—thin	BUNTING, ZEPHYR
woven	TEXTILE
—coarse wool	DRUGGET
—cotton, striped	GINGHAM
—hemp	WEBBING
—like brocade	BROCHE
—on card-controlled loom	JACQUARD
—with diagonal lines	TWILL

fabulous

beast	
—Chinese	KYLIN
—human in form of wolf	WER(E)WOLF
—Spenser	ANTILOPE
bird	
—Arabian	PHOENIX
—Chinese	FUM, FUNG
—elephant-carrying	ROC, ROK, RUC
	RUKH

—part bird, part woman	HARPY
—Persian	HUMA, SIMORG
	SIMURG(H)
—restless	HUMA
—Spenser	WHISTLER
fish (Spenser)	SCOLOPENDRA
person	WEREWOLF
robber	PROCRUSTES
tree	UPAS
	(*see also* **monsters**)

Faeroe Islands	FR
capital	THORSHAVN

farewell

English	CHEERIO, GOODBYE
	SO LONG, TATA
French	ADIEU, AU REVOIR
German	AUF WIEDERSEHEN
Hawaian	ALOHA
Italian	ARRIVEDERCI, CIAO
Japanese	SAYONARA
Roman	VALE
Spanish	ADIOS, HASTA LA VISTA

fastest

animal	CHEETAH
bird	SWIFT
car	THRUST 2
liner	UNITED STATES
plane	X15
train	TGV

Fates

Greek	MOIRAE, MOIRAI
—spins thread of life	CLOTHO
—controls it	LACHESIS
—cuts it off	ATROPOS
Norse	NORNA, NORNS
—past	URD(A)
—present	VERDANDE, VERDANDI
—future	SKULD
Roman	PARCAE
	DECUMA, MORTA, NONA
	PHOBIA

fear

including: aversion to	
fear of	
hatred of	
aeroplanes	AEROPHOBIA
	PTEROPHOBIA
all things	PANTOPHOBIA
animals	ZOOPHOBIA
auroras	AUROROPHOBIA
bears	URSAPHOBIA
beards	POGONOPHOBIA
bees	API(O)PHOBIA, MELISOPHOBIA
being	
—alone	MONOPHOBIA
—buried alive	TAPHEPHOBIA
	TAPHOPHOBIA

—deformed	DISMORPHOPHOBIA
—looked at	SCOPOPHOBIA
—soiled	RYPOPHOBIA
birds	ORNITHOPHOBIA
blood	HAEM(AT)OPHOBIA
blushing	ERYTHROPHOBIA
books	BIBLIOPHOBIA
boys	ANDROPHOBIA
bridges	GEPHYROPHOBIA
cancer	CARCONOPHOBIA
cats	AIL(O)UROPHOBIA
	GATOPHOBIA
cheerfulness	CHEROPHOBIA
childbirth	TOCOPHOBIA
children	PAEDOPHOBIA
Chinese	SINOPHOBIA
choking	PNIGOPHOBIA
clouds	NEPHOPHOBIA
cold	CHEIM(AT)OPHOBIA
	CRYOPHOBIA
	PSYCHROPHOBIA
colour	CHROMOPHOBIA
computers	CYBERPHOBIA
confined spaces	CLAUSTROPHOBIA
	CLITHROPHOBIA
contamination	MYSOPHOBIA
corpses	NECROPHOBIA
criticism	RHABDOPHOBIA
crockery	CERAMOPHOBIA
crossing streets	DROMOPHOBIA
crowds	DEMOPHOBIA
	OCHLOPHOBIA
crystals	CRYSTALLOPHOBIA
dampness	HYGROPHOBIA
darkness	ACHLUOPHOBIA, LYCOPHOBIA
	NYCTOPHOBIA, SCOTOPHOBIA
dawn	EOSOPHOBIA
death	NECROPHOBIA
	THANATOPHOBIA
deep places	BATHOPHOBIA
deformity	DISMORPHOPHOBIA
demons	DEMONOPHOBIA
deserts	XEROPHOBIA
dirt	MOLYSOMOPHOBIA
	MYSOPHOBIA
	RYPOPHOBIA
disease	NOSOPHOBIA, PATHOPHOBIA
dogs	CANOPHOBIA, CYNOPHOBIA
draughts	AEROPHOBIA
dreams	ONEIROPHOBIA
drink	POTOPHOBIA
drugs	PHARMACOPHOBIA
drunkenness	DIPSOPHOBIA
dry places	XEROPHOBIA
dust	ANATHOPHOBIA, KONIPHOBIA
electrity	ELEKTROPHOBIA

elves	ALFEAR
emptiness	KENOPHOBIA
enclosed spaces	CLAUSTROPHOBIA
English	ANGLOPHOBIA
environment	ECOPHOBIA
everything	PANTOPHOBIA
eyes	OMMATAPHOBIA
excrement	COPROPHOBIA
falling from height	BATHOPHOBIA
	HYPSOPHOBIA
familiar places	NOSTOPHOBIA
fatigue	KOPOPHOBIA
fear	PHOBOPHOBIA
feathers	PTERONOPHOBIA
fire	PYROPHOBIA
fishes	ICHTHYOPHOBIA
flashes	SELAPHOBIA
flogging	MASTIGOPHOBIA
floods	ANTLOPHOBIA
flutes	AULOPHOBIA
flying	AEROPHOBIA, PTEROPHOBIA
fog	HOMICHLOPHOBIA
food	SIT(I)OPHOBIA
foreign things	XENOPHOBIA, XENOPHOBY
	ZENOPHOBIA
freedom	ELEUTHEROPHOBIA
French	GALLOPHOBIA
frogs	BATRACHOPHOBIA
fur	DORAPHOBIA
germs	BACILLIPHOBIA
	MICROPHOBIA
	SPERM(AT)OPHOBIA
Germans	GERMANOPHOBIA
ghosts	PHASMOPHOBIA
girls	GYNOPHOBIA
glass	NELOPHOBIA
god	THEOPHOBIA
going to bed	CLINOPHOBIA
grandchildren	BABUSHKAPHOBIA
gravity	BAROPHOBIA
(groundless fears)	PANOPHOBIA
hair	CHAETOPHOBIA
heart disease	CARDIOPHOBIA
heat	THERMOPHOBIA
heaven	OURANOPHOBIA
heights	ACROPHOBIA, ALTOPHOBIA
	CREMNOPHOBIA, HYPSOPHOBIA
hell	HADEOPHOBIA, STYGIOPHOBIA
heredity	PATROIOPHOBIA
home	OIKOPHOBIA
homosexuals	HOMOPHOBIA
horses	HIPPOPHOBIA
humans	ANTHROPOPHOBIA
ideas	IDEOPHOBIA
illness	NOSOPHOBIA, PATHOPHOBIA
imperfections	ATELOPHOBIA

infinity	APEIROPHOBIA
influence of the stars	ASTROPHOBIA
injections	TRYPANOPHOBIA
injury	TRAUMATOPHOBIA
insanity	LYSSOPHOBIA
	MANIAPHOBIA
insects	INSECTOPHOBIA
	ENTOMOPHOBIA
justice	DIKEPHOBIA
lakes	LIMNOPHOBIA
languages	LINGUAPHOBIA
leaves	PYHLLOPHOBIA
lice	PEDICULOPHOBIA
light	PHOTOPHOBIA
lightning	ASTRO(PO)PHOBIA
	KERAUNOPHOBIA
loneliness	AUTOPHOBIA, EREMIOPHOBIA
	MONOPHOBIA
machinery	MECHANOPHOBIA
madness	LYSSOPHOBIA, MANIAPHOBIA
marriage	GAMETOPHOBIA
men	ANDROPHOBIA
metals	METALLOPHOBIA
meteors	METEOROPHOBIA
mice	MUSOPHOBIA
mirrors	EISOPTROPHOBIA
moisture	HYGROPHOBIA
money	CHROMETOPHOBIA
monsters	TERATOPHOBIA
motion	KINESOPHOBIA
	KINETOPHOBIA
(motorway madness)	AMAXOPHOBIA
music	MUSICOPHOBIA
names	ONOMATOPHOBIA
narrowness	ANGINOPHOBIA
needles	BELONEPHOBIA
negroes	NEGROPHOBIA
new things	NEOPHOBIA
night	NYCTOPHOBIA
noise	PHONOPHOBIA
nudity	GYMNOPHOBIA
old age	GERASCOPHOBIA
one thing	MONOPHOBIA
open spaces	AGORAPHOBIA, KENOPHOBIA
pain	ALGOPHOBIA, ODYNOPHOBIA
particular	
—place	TOPOPHOBIA
—word	ONOMATOPHOBIA
pins	ENETEPHOBIA
pleasure	HEDONOPHOBIA
points	AICHUROPHOBIA
poisons	IOPHOBIA, TOXI(CO)PHOBIA
pope	PAPAPHOBIA
poverty	PENIAPHOBIA
pregnancy	MAIEUSIOPHOBIA
public speaking	GLOSSOPHOBIA

punishment	POINEPHOBIA
	RHABDOPHOBIA
rain	OMBROMOPHOBIA
reference to self	AUTOPHOBY
reptiles	BATRACHOPHOBIA
responsibility	HYPEGIAPHOBIA
returning	NOSTOPATHY
ridicule	KATAGELOPHOBIA
robbers	HARPAXOPHOBIA
ruin	ATEPHOBIA
Russians	RUSSOPHOBIA
Satan	SATANOPHOBIA
sea	THALASSOPHOBIA
sex	GENOPHOBIA
sharks	GALEOPHOBIA
shock	HORMEPHOBIA
sinning	PECCATOPHOBIA
sitting	
—down	CATHISOPHOBIA
—idle	THAASOPHOBIA
skin	DERMATOPHOBIA
sleep	HYPNOPHOBIA
slime	BLENNOPHOBIA, MYXOPHOBIA
smells	OLFACTOPHOBIA
smothering	PNIGEROPHOBIA
snakes	OPH(ID)IOPHOBIA
snow	CHIONOPHOBIA
soiling	RYPOPHOBIA
solitude	EREMITOPHOBIA
sound	AKOUSTICOPHOBIA
sourness	ACEROPHOBIA
speaking	GLOSSOPHOBIA
—aloud	PHONOPHOBIA
speech	LALOPHOBIA
speed	TACHOPHOBIA
spiders	ARACHNOPHOBIA
standing	STASOPHOBIA
stars	ASTROPHOBIA
stealing	KLEPTOPHOBIA
stings	CNIDOPHOBIA
stooping	KYPOPHOBIA
strangers	XENOPHOBIA
streets	DROMOPHOBIA
string	LINONOPHOBIA
sun	HELIOPHOBIA
surgery	ERGASIOPHOBIA
	TOMOPHOBIA
swallowing	PHAGOPHOBIA
symmetry	SYMMETROPHOBIA
syphilis	SYPHILOPHOBIA
taste	GEUMATOPHOBIA
teeth	ODONTOPHOBIA
thinking	PHRONEMOPHOBIA
thirteen	TERDEKAPHOBIA
	TRISKAIDECAPHOBIA
	TRISKAIDEKAPHOBIA

thunder	BRONTOPHOBIA
	KERAUNOPHOBIA
	TONITROPHOBIA
—and lightning	ASTRO(PO)PHOBIA
time	CHRONOPHOBIA
tiredness	KOPOPHOBIA
touch	HAPTOPHOBIA
touching	THIXOPHOBIA
trains	SIDERODROMOPHOBIA
travel	HODOPHOBIA
trees	DENDROPHOBIA
trembling	TREMOPHOBIA
venereal disease	SYPHILOPHOBIA
voids	KENOPHOBIA
walking	BATOPHOBIA
water	AQUAPHOBIA, HYDROPHOBIA
	HYGROPHOBIA
waves	CYMOPHOBIA
weakness	ASTHENOPHOBIA
wind	ANCRAOPHOBIA
	ANEMOPHOBIA
women	GYNOPHOBIA
words	LOGOPHOBIA
work	ERGOPHOBIA
worms	HELMINTHOPHOBIA
	SCOILECIPHOBIA
wounds	TRAUMATOPHOBIA
writing	GRAPHOPHOBIA
young people	PARTHENOPHOBIA
feast days	(*see* **holidays**)
feathers	
barb on shaft	VEXILLUM
bare patch on bird	APTERIUM
bastard-wing	ALULA
bird's crest	COPPLE
bunch of feathers	PLUME
—used in hawking	LURE
cause feathers to stand erect	RUFFLE
cleaning feathers	PREENING
covering quill bases	COVERTS, TECTRIX
depression holding	
feather	FEATHER FOLLICLE
develop feathers	FLEDGE
down-feather	PLUMULA, PLUMULE
expanded part of feather	VANE
eye-stripe	SUPERCILIUM
feathers	PLUMAGE
—used as plume	AIGRETTE
feather-seller	PLUMASSIER
filament	BARB
flight feather(s)	PINION
	REMEX(REMIGES)
hairlike	FILOPLUME
hollow part of feather	QUILL
large feather	PLUME, QUILL
like bristle(s) on beak	VIBRISSA(E)

mode of feathering	PTILOSIS
on back	MANTLE
—back of neck	HACKLES
—ears	AURICULAR
—neck	FRILL, RUFF
—rump of hawk	BRAIL
—shoulder	SCAPULAR
outer feathers	CONTOUR FEATHERS
plumage	PTILOSIS
projection on barb	BARBULE
shaft	RACHIS
shed feathers	MOULT
small	
—barbed projection	BARBICEL
—feather(s)	PLUMULA, PLUMULE
	TECTRIX(TECTRICES)
tail feather(s)	PENNA(E)
	RECTRIX (RECTRICES)
	SICKLE FEATHER
vane	PLUME
web	VANE
wing feather(s)	ALULA, BASTARD-WING
	PENNA(E), PRIMARY
	SECONDARY, TERTIAL
	TERTIARY
wingless	APTERAL, APTEROUS
feet	
animal with	
—2 feet	BIPED
—4 feet	QUADRUPED
—8 feet	OCTOPOD
—many feet	CENTIPEDE, MILLIPEDE
—modified feet	CEPHALOPOD
combining form	-PED(E), -PEDAL
footboard of piano	PEDAL-BOARD
	PEDAL-CLAVIER, PEDALIER
foot-operated	
—boat	PEDALO
—vehicle	MONOCYCLE, CYCLE
	PEDICAR, QUADRICYCLE
	TRICYCLE
having	
—1 foot	MONOPEDAL
—2 feet	BIPEDAL
—3 feet	TRIPEDAL
—4 feet	QUADRUPEDAL
	TETRAPODOUS
—8 feet	OCTOPODOUS
like a foot	PEDAL, PEDATE
object with	
—1 foot	MONOPOD
—2 feet	BIPOD
—3 feet	TRIPOD
—4 feet	TETRAPOD
one-footed man	MONOPODE
treatment	PEDICURE

fences
natural	HEDGE
sunken	HAHA
types	BARBED WIRE
	CHAIN-LINK, CHESTNUT PALE
	CLOSE-BOARDED, ELECTRIC
	INTERWOVEN, POST AND PANEL
	POST AND RAIL
	POST AND WIRE, RAZOR WIRE
	RING, RUSTIC

fencing
acknowledgment of hit	TOUCHE
attack after parry	RIPOSTE
backhanded stroke	REVERSO
body quilting	PLASTRON
deciding bout	BARRAGE
deflection of blade	PARADE, PARRY
downward stroke	STRAMACON
	STRAMAZON
exclamation on hit	HAY
false attack	FEINT
fencer (Shak.)	SCRIMURE
fencers	
—Belgian	ANSPACH, DELPORTE
—British (m)	CAMPBELL-GREY
(f)	SHEEN
—Cuban	DIAZ, FONST, TATHAM
—French (m)	ALIBERT, BUHAN, COSTE
	DE LA FALAISE, D'ORIOLA
	DUCRET, GAUDIN, GRAVELOTTE
	MASSARD
(f)	TRINQUET
—German (m)	HEHN, PUSCH
(f)	MEYER-SCHMID
—Greek	GEORGIADIS
—Hungarian (m)	FENYVESI, FUCHS
	KABOS, KARPATI, KOVACS
	KULCSAR, PEZSA
	PILLER, POSTA
(f)	ELEK, REJTO
—Italian (m)	CANTONE, DELFINO
	GAUDINI, MANGIAROTTI
	MARZI, NADI, PAVESE
	RICCARDI
(f)	CAMBER, LONZI
—Polish	FRANKE, WOYDA
—Romanian	DRIMBA
—Russian (m)	KORVOPUSHKOV, KRISS
	ROMANKOV, SIDIAK
	SMIRNOV, ZHDANOVICH
(f)	NOVIKOVA
—Swedish	HARMENBERG
fifth position	QUINTE
fighting area	PISTE
foot-stamping	APPEL
forward jump	BALESTA

fourth position	CARTE, QUART(E)
guard	COQUILLE
handle end of sword	FORTE
hit	HAY, VENEY
	VENEWE, VENUE
opposing movement	TRAVERSE
parry and riposte	TAC-AU-TAC
point end of sword	FOIBLE
practice	QUART(E) AND TIERCE
renewed attack	REMISE, REPRISE
running attack	FLECHE
second position	SECONDE
series of attacks	TAC-AU-TAC
sudden movement	VOLT
sword	EPEE, FOIL, SABRE
	(*see also separate entry*)
third position	TIERCE
thrust	BOTTE, FOIN, IMBROCCATA
	POTCH(E), STOCCADO, STOCCATA
	STOCK, STUCK
—into side	FLANCONADE
—with one foot forward	PASSADA
	PASSADO
upward blow	MONTANT
warning	EN GARDE
wound slightly	PINK

ferns　　　　ACROGEN, FILIC(AL)ES
	FILICINEAE
Adiantum	MAIDENHAIR FERN
aquatic	MARSILEA, MARSILIA
Asplenium	BIRD'S NEST FERN
	MOTHER SPLEENWORT
Athyrium	LADY FERN
bird's nest fern	ASPLENIUM
Boston fern	NEPHROLEPSIS
Botrychium	MOONWORT
bracken	PTERIDIUS, PTERIS
	TARA(-FERN)
button fern	PELLAEA
Christmas fern	POLYSTICHUM
cloak fern	DIDYMOCHLAENA
Cyathea	TREE-FERN
Cyrtomium	FISHTAIL FERN, HOLLY FERN
Davallia	RABBIT'S FOOT FERN
delta maidenhair	ADIANTUM
Didymochlaena	CLOAK FERN
Dryopteris	MALE FERN
feather fern	NEPHROLEPSIS
filmy fern	BRISTLE-FERN
fishtail fern	CYRTOMIUM
green brake fern	PELLAEA
hare's foot fern	PHLEBODIUM
hart's tongue fern	PHYLLITIS
holly fern	CYRTOMIUM
lace fern	NEPHROLEPIS
lady fern	ATHYRIUM

maidenhair fern	ADIANTUM
male fern	DRYOPTERIS
moonwort	BOTRYCHIUM
mother spleenwwort	ASPLENIUM
Nephrolepsis	BOSTON FERN
	FEATHER FERN
	LACE FERN, SWORD FERN
Osmunda	ROYAL FERN
peacock fern	SELAGINELLA
Pellaea	BUTTON FERN
	GREEN BRAKE FERN
Phlebodium	HARE'S FOOT FERN
Phyllitis	HART'S TONGUE FERN
Platycerium	STAG'S HORN FERN
Polystichum	CHRISTMAS FERN
	TSUSINA HOLLY FERN
Pteris	RIBBON FERN
	SILVER LACE FERN
	TABLE FERN, TREMBLING FERN
rabbit's foot fern	DAVALLIA
ribbon fern	PTERIS
rose maidenhair	ADIANTUM
royal fern	OSMUNDA
scale-fern	CETERACH
Selaginella	PEACOCK FERN
silver lace fern	PTERIS
stag's horn fern	PLATYCERIUM
sword fern	NEPHROLEPSIS
table fern	PTERIS
tara(-fern)	BRACKEN
tree-fern	CYATHEA
trembling fern	PTERIS
tropical genus	SCHIAEA
Tsusina holly fern	POLYSTICHUM
festivals	(see **holidays**)
feudal	(see **mediaeval**)
fifty	LA, L, N, NU, V
states	AMERICA, US(A)
thousand	L, N, NU, V
years old	QUINQUAGENARIAN
figures of speech	(see **rhetoric**)
Fiji	FJI
capital	SUVA
coin	CENT, DOLLAR
films	(see **cinema**)
Finland	SF
capital	HELSINGFORS, HELSINKI
coin	MARK, MARK(K)A
	MKK, PENNI
dialect	KAREL
dog	LAIKA
epic	KALEVALA
instrument	KANTELE
language	SUOMI
measure	KANNOR, TUNNA
underworld	TUONELA

first	
—first	
airship to fly round	
the world	GRAF ZEPPELIN
Astronomer Royal	FLAMSTEED
balloon to fly	
across Atlantic	DOUBLE EAGLE II
city	CATAL HUYUK
electronic computer	ENIAC
empire	AKKADIAN
English printer	CAXTON
jet airliner flight	TUPOLEV
—in service	COMET
manpowered aircraft	
to fly across the	
English Channel	GOSSAMER ALBATROSS
moving picture	BIRTH OF A NATION
non-stop flight	
round the world	
without refuelling	VOYAGER
novel written on	
a type-	
writer	THE ADVENTURES OF TOM SAWYER
postage stamp	PENNY BLACK
railway	STOCKTON-DARLINGTON
solar-powered plane to	
—fly	SOLAR CHALLENGER
over the English	
Channel	SOLAR CHALLENGER
steamboat	CHARLOTTE DUNDAS
steamship	PHOENIX
—to cross Atlantic	SAVANNAH
supersonic jet in service	CONCORD(E)
synthetic fibre	NYLON
talking picture	THE JAZZ SINGER
town	JERICHO
translation of	
gospels into	
English	LINDISFARNE GOSPELS
—first man or woman (f) to	
break sound barrier	YEAGER
build	
—computer	ECKERT
—radio telescope	REBER
—type foundry	GARAMOND
calculate mass of earth	CAVENDISH
circumnavigate the earth	MAGELLAN
—British	DRAKE
—non-stop	KNOX-JOHNSTON
—solo	SLOCUM
climb	
—Everest	HILARY, TENZING
—Matterhorn	WHYMPER
cross	
—Antarctic Circle	COOK
—Antarctica	FUCHS

crystallise
—pepsin NORTHROP
—urease SUMNER
—virus STANLEY
culture viruses GOODPASTURE
decipher
—Rosetta Stone CHAMPOLLION
—Sumerian script RAWLINSON
establish type-foundry GARAMOND
fly
—balloon over
   Atlantic ABRUZZO, ANDERSON
                      NEWMAN
   Channel BLANCHARD, JEFFRIES
—circumpolar route LONG
—hang-glider over Channel
   (m) MESSENGER
   (f) LEDEN
—in
   powered flight WRIGHT
   —in
      Europe SANTOS-DUMONT
      space GAGARIN
   —over
      Atlantic READ
      —non-stop ALCOCK, BROWN
      —solo (m) LINDBERGH
        (f) EARHART
      Channel BLERIOT
      —man-powered ALLEN
      —solar-powered PTACEK
      North Pole BYRD
      Pacific Ocean KINGSFORD SMITH
                   ULM
      South Pole BENNETT, BYRD
   —round the world WILEY POST
   non-stop without
      refuelling RUTAN, YAEGER
—supersonic YEAGER
—to Australia
   solo (m) HINKLER
      (f) JOHNSON
isolate
—ACTH OLLIP
—adrenalin TAKAMINE
—anthrax bacillus KOCH
—atropine BRANDES
—aureomycin DUGGAR
—chloramphenicol BUCKHOLDER
—chlorophyll BRANDENBERGER
—chlortetracycline DUGGAR
—cholera bacterium KOCH
—cocaine NIEMAN
—colchicine CAVENTON, PELLETIER
—diphtheria bacterium KLEBS
—ergometrine SPIRO, STOLL

—histamine VOGT, WINDUS
—hydrogen CAVENDISH
—insulin BANTING, BEST
—oestrachol MACORQUODALE
—oestrone BUTENANDT, DOISY
—parathormone CRAIG, RASMUSSEN
—progesterone ALLEN, CORNER
—secretin BAYLISS, STARLING
—testosterone GALLAGHER, KOCH, MOORE
—tuberculosis bacillus KOCH
—tubocurarine KING
—uranium 235 DUNNING
—vitamin
   A CORBET, HOLMES
   B1 WILLIAMS
   B2 KUHN
   B12 FOLKERS, SMITH
   C SZENT-GYORGI
   E EVANS, SCOTT
   K DOISY
liquefy
—helium ONNES
—hydrogen DEWAR
—oxygen PICTET
measure parallax of star BESSELL
orbit the earth
—(m) GAGARIN
—(f) TERESHKOVA
produce
—holograms LEITH, UPATNIEKS
—photograph NIEPCE
—photographic negative FOX TALBOT
—star map HIPPARCHUS
reach
—Moon ARMSTRONG
—North Pole PEARY
—South Pole AMUNDSEN
run four-minute mile BANNISTER
see
—cells through microscope HOOKE
—Jupiter's red spot
   through telescope HOOKE
swim Channel (m) WEBB
      (f) EDERLE
synthesise
—acetic acid KOLBE
—adrenalin STOLTZ
—alizarin GRAEBE, PERKIN
—aniline dye PERKIN
—chlorpromazine CHARPENTIER
—cholesterol WOODWARD
—cocaine WILLSTATER
—cortisone SARRETT
—ethyl alcohol BERTHELOT
—glucose KIRCHHOFF
—halothane SUCKLING

—impramine — HAFLIGER
—indigo — BAEYER
—magenta dye — PERKIN
—methane — BERTHELOT
—musk — RUSICKA, RUZICKA
—pethidine — EISLEB, SCHAUMANN
—quinine — WOODWARD
—riboflavin — KARRER
—strychnine — WOODWARD
—urea — WOHLER
—vitamin C — REICHSTEIN
translate Bible into English — WYCLIFFE
transplant heart — BARNARD
use
—acriflavin — EHRLICH
—aspirin — DRESSER
—ether — LONG, MORTON
—gas for illumination — MURDOCK
—nitrous oxide — WELLS
—Novocain(e) — EINHORN
—oxygen for treatment — HALDANE
—pethidine — HOECHST
—phenytoin — MERRITT, PULMAN
—procaine — EINHORN
—radioactive tracers — HEVESY, PANETH
—thyroid extract — MURRAY
—tracers — KNOOP
walk
—in space — LEONOV
—to both Poles — SWAN
(*see also* **discoveries, inventors**)

fish[1] — PISCES
including: alternative names
    descriptions
ablet — BLEAK
Acipenser — STURGEON
accompanies ships etc — PILOT-FISH
adapted to see in air
 and water — ANABLEPS
allis/allice — SHAD
Anableps — FOUR-EYES
angel-fish — MONK-FISH
angler — BRIABOT, DEVIL-FISH
FISHING-FROG, FROG-FISH
GOOSE-EGG, PEDICULATI
archer-fish — DARTER
Argonaut — NAUTILUS
Atherine — SAND-SMELT, SILVERSIDES
Atlantic — ESCOLAR
Balistes — FILE-FISH
ballan-wrasse — SEA-SWINE
banny — MINNOW
barracouta — SNOEK, SNOOK
basking-shark — SAIL-FISH, SUN-FISH
bass — ROCCUS, SEA-DACE
SEA-PERCH

bass-like
—American — GROUPER
—Australian — GROPER
bearded — BARBEL
bellows-fish — SNIPE-FISH, TRUMPET-FISH
Belone — GARFISH, SEA-PIKE
bergylt — NORWAY HADDOCK, ROSE-FISH
bib — BLAIN, BRASSY
(WHITING-)POUT
black goby — ROCK-FISH
blain — BIB, (WHITING-)POUT
bleak — ABLET, BLAY, BLEY
blenny — BUTTERFLY FISH, EEL-POUT
SHANNY
blind fish (Kentucky) — AMBYLOPSIS
blue
—fish — SKIPJACK
—roach — AZURINE
blueback salmon — SOCKEYE
Bombay duck — BUM(M)ALO(TI)
bony
—fish — ANABLEPS, COFFER-FISH
OSTEICHTHYES
OSTEOGLOSSIDAE, TELEOSTEI
TELEOSTOMI
—pike — LEPIDOSTEUS
bottom-feeder — GROUNDLING
bounce — MORGAY, SPOTTED DOGFISH
brassy — BIB, BLAIN
(WHITING-)POUT
brill — TURBOT
brisling — NORWEGIAN SPRAT
bristled head — HOG-FISH
Brosmius — CUSK, TORSK, TUSK
bull trout — SALMON-TROUT, SCURFF
SEA-TROUT
bullhead — MILLER'S-THUMB
bum(m)alo(ti) — BOMBAY-DUCK
burbot — CUSK, EEL-POUT, TORSK
burrowing fish — MUD-FISH
butter-fish — GUNNEL
Californian trout — RAINBOW-TROUT
candlefish — EULACHON, OOLAKAN
OULACHON, OULAKON
ULIC(H)ON, ULIKON
carp — CYPRINUS, ROUND-FISH
—type — BARBEL, BREAM
cartilaginous — CHIM(A)ERA
CHONDRICHTHYES
catfish — SEA-CAT, SILURE
WELS, WOLF-FISH
—(N) — WOOF
caught for sport — GAME FISH
Cestracion — SHARK
char — RED-BELLY, SAIBLING
—Welsh — TORGOCH

Chinese fish	CARP, GOLDFISH
chub	CHAVENDER, CHEVEN, CHEVIN
classes	ACTINOPTERIGYII
	CHOANYCTHYES, CHONDRICHTHYES
	OSTEOICHTHYES, DIPNEUSTI
climbing fish	ANABAS
coal-fish	BLECK, COLEY, DORSE
	GLISSAUN, SAITH(E)
	SEA-SALMON, SILLOCK
—Scottish	SILLOCK, STENLOCK
cobia	SNOOK
Cobitidae	LOACH
cod	DORSE, GADUS
	MORRHUA, TORSK
—family	HADDOCK
—like	HAKE, ROCKLING
—small	CODLING
—type	CUSK, TORSK, TUSK
American	CROAKER, TOMCOD
coffer-fish	OSTRACION
coho(e)	PACIFIC SALMON
	SILVER SALMON
coley	COALFISH, SAITHE
conger	SEA-EEL
corkwing	GOLDFINNY, GOLDSINNY
covered with bony	
plates	PLACODERM
craig-fluke	WITCH
cramp-fish	ELECTRIC RAY, TORPEDO
crayfish	CRAWFISH, SPINY LOBSTER
cross-fish	ASTERIAS
cross-mouthed	PLAGIOSTOMATA
	PLAGIOSTOMI
cured cod	DUNFISH
cusk	BURBOT, TORSK, TUSK
cuttlefish	LOLIGO, SEA-SLEEVE, SEPIA
cyclostome	ROUND-MOUTH
dab	LIMANDA, LEMON-DAB
dace	DARE, DART, GRAINING
Danube fish	ZINGEL
dealfish	RIBBON-FISH
	TRACHYPTEROUS
deep-sea	GRENADIER
demoiselle	WRASSE
devilfish	ANGLER FISH, SEA-DEVIL
Diodon	GLOBE-FISH, SEA-PORCUPINE
dog	
—fish	GREY-FISH, HOUND-FISH
	HUSS, MORGAY, NURSE
	ROUSSETTE, SEA-DOG
	SEA-HOUND
—salmon	KETA
dolphin	CORYPHAENA, CORYPHENE
	DORADO
dolphin-fish	MAHI-MAHI
dorado	GOLDEN SALMON
dory	DOREE, JOHN DORY
	ST PETER'S FISH
dragonet	DRAGON-FISH, SCULPIN
	SEA-DRAGON
drumfish	SCIAENIDAE
eagle-ray	SEA-EAGLE
eel	ANGUILLA, CONGER, GRIG
	MORAY, MURRAY
	MURR(E)Y, MURAENA
—electric	GYMNOTUS
—larval	LEPTOCEPHALUS
—like	KINGKLIP
—pout	BLENY, BURBOT
—young	ELVER
elasmobranchs	CHONDROPTERYGII
electric	RAY, TORPEDO
—catfish	RAASH
—eel	GYMNOTUS
elleck	RED GURNET
Esox	PIKE
espada	SWORDFISH
European carp	ID(E)
father-lasher	BULLHEAD
	HARD-HEAD
file-fish	OLD WIFE
finnock	HERLING, HIRLING
flat fish	BUTT, FLOUNDER, HALIBUT
	HOLIBUT, PLAICE, PSETTA
	(DOVER) SOLE, LEMON SOLE
	TURBOT
—fishes	HETEROSOMATA
flounder	FLUKE
flying	PILOT-FISH, SEA-BAT
found in lakes	LAKER
fox-shark	SEA-FOX, THRESHER
freshwater	
—carp	GUDGEON, ROACH
—fishes	LEUCISCUS
garfish	FAAP, GREEN-BONE
	HORNBEAK, MACKEREL-GUIDE
	SNOOK
garpike	NEEDLE-FISH
ged	LUCE, PIKE
giant ray	DEVIL-FISH
globe-fish	DIODON, SEA-ORB
	SEA-PORCUPINE
	SEA-HEDGEHOG, TAMBOR
goatfish	RED MULLET
goby	DRAGONET, GOBIUS
	MUD-SKIPPER
goby-like	PERIOPHTHALMUS
gold-spotted on head	GILTHEAD
golden id	ORFE
golden-yellow	DOREE, (JOHN) DORY
goldfish with double	
tail-fins	FANTAIL

goldsinny	CONNER, CORKWING
	CUNNER
goramy	GO(U)RAMI
grayling	UMBER
green fish	DERBIO
grey gurnard	KNOUD
grundel	LOACH
gudgeon	WAPPER
gunnel	BUTTER-FISH
guppy	MILLIONS
gurnard	ELLECK, GURNET
	HARD-HEAD, SEA-COCK
	SEA-ROBIN, TUBFISH .
gurnet	(*see* gurnard *above*)
Gymnotus	ELECTRIC EEL
haddock (Scot.)	HADDIE
hag-fish	MYXINE
hake	SEA-PIKE
hammerhead shark	SPHYRNA, ZYGAENIDAE
herring	CLUPEA, ELOPS
	SARDEL, SEA-RAT
—American	ALE-WIFE
—jocular	CAPON
—like	PILCHARD
—Mediterranean	ANCHOVY
—type	RABBIT-FISH, SHAD
	SPRAT, PILCHARD
—young	BRIT(T), WHITEBAIT
Hippocampus	SEA-HORSE
homelyn	SPOTTED RAY
hornyhead	JERKER
horse-mackerel	BOAR-FISH, SAUREL
	SCAD, SKIPJACK
humpback salmon	DOG-SALMON
huss	DOGFISH
inflating	BOTTLE-FISH
inkfish	SQUID
Irish trout	GILLAROO
jawless fishes	AGNATHA
jellyfish	ACALEPH(A), ACALEPHE
	ARVEL, CNIDA, MEDUSA
	QUARL, SARSIA, SCYPHOMEDUSAE
	SEA-BLUBBER, SEA-JELLY
	SEA-NETTLE
Japanese	CARP, GOLDFISH
Jew-fish	TARPON, TARPUM
kelt	LIGGER
keta	DOG-SALMON
king of herrings	RABBIT-FISH, SHAD
kingfish	MOLIDAE, OPAH, SUNFISH
Labrus	WRASSE
Lake Bala fish	GWINIAD, GWYNIAD
lamprey	CYCLOSTOME, HAG
	NINE-EYES, ROUND-MOUTH
	SAND-PRIDE, SAYNAY
Lampris	KINGFISH, OPAH, SUNFISH

langouste	(*see* shellfish)
large	
—headed	SCORPAENA
—mouthed	PELICAN-FISH
—ray	MANTA
launce	SAND-EEL
lemon-dab	SMEAR-DAB
lesser spotted dogfish	BOUNCE
ling	MOLVA
little trout	TROUTLET
	TROUTLING
lizard-fish	SAURUS
loach	GRUNDEL
lobster	(*see* shellfish)
Loch Lomond and	
Loch Eck fish	POWAN
Loligo	CUTTLEFISH, SQUID
long-tailed shark	FOX-SHARK
Lough Neagh fish	POLLAN
luce	GED, PIKE
lumpfish	LUMPSUCKER, SEA-OWL
lungfish	DIPNEUSTI, DIPNOI
	MUDFISH
—African	PROTOPTERUS
—Australian	EPICERATODUS
—South American	LEPIDOSIREN
Lutianidae	S(CH)NAPPERS
mackerel	CARANX, SCOMBER
—like	BREAM
—South Africa	ALBACORE
—type	DOREE, DORY
	JOHN DORY, WAHOO
maigre	BAR, MEAGRE, SCIAENA
Malay fish	GORAMY, GO(U)RAMI
male	MILTER
marine	
—perch	SEA-BASS
—stickleback	SEA-ADDER
Mediterranean	MEAGRE, MAIGRE
Megalops	TARPON
menhaden	HARD-HEAD, MOSSBUNKER
miller's	
—dog	PENNY-DOG
—thumb	BULLHEAD, LOGGE, POGGE
millions	GUPPY
minnow	BANNY, PINK, TIDDLER
Molidae	KINGFISH, OPAH, SUNFISH
monk-fish	ANGEL-FISH, SHARK
moonfish	OPAH
moray	MURAENA
mossbunker	MENHADEN
mud	
—fish	BOWFIN
—minnow	UMBRA
—skipper	GOBY
Mugil	MULLET

Mullis	MULLET	Prussian carp	GIBEL
mullet	ATHERINA, BOTARGO, MUGIL	Psetta	TURBOT
	MULLUS, MYXON, SARGINA	raash	CATFISH
—types	GREY, RED	rabbit-fish	KING OF THE HERRINGS
nautilus	ARGONAUT	rainbow-trout	CALIFORNIAN TROUT
needle-fish	GARPIKE, PIPE-FISH	ray	SAW-FISH, SKATE
oarfish	RIBBON-FISH		THORNBACK, TORPEDO
octopus	DEVIL-FISH	razor-fish	SOLEN
oily	MENHADEN	red	
old		—belly	CHAR
—wench	TRIGGERFISH	—eye	RUDD
—wife	TRIGGERFISH	—mullet	GOATFISH, SURMULLET
opah	KINGFISH, LAMPRIS	—northern sea fish	BERGYLT
	MOLIDAE, MOONFISH	ribbon-fish	BAND-FISH, DEALFISH
	SUNFISH		OAR-FISH, TRACHYPTEROUS
ornamental	BLACKMOOR, CARP	river	
	GOLDFISH, KOI, ORFE, RUDD	—fish	CHUB, DACE, LOACH
	SHUBUNKIN		TENCH, TROUT
Ostracion	COFFER-FISH	—lamprey	LAMPERN
oxyrhyncus	SACRED FISH	roach	ROCHET
Pacific salmon	KETA	robalo	SEA-PIKE, SNOEK, SNOOK
pandora-fish	BRAIZE	rock	
parrot-wrasse	SCAR(FISH), SCARUS	—eel	DOGFISH, ROCK SALMON
Pegasus	SEA-DRAGON	—fish	ROCK SALMON, WOLFFISH
pelican-fish	EURYPHARYNX	—goby	GRUNDEL
penny-dog	MILLER'S-DOG, TOPE	—perch	SCORPION-FISH
perch	BLACK FISH, BLACK RUFF	—salmon	DOGFISH, ROCK-EEL
	MARGOT, PERCA, ZINGEL		WOLFFISH
—like	BERYX	—turbot	WOLF-FISH
—pike	SANDER, ZANDER	rockling	MACKEREL-MIDGE
percoid	PIKE-PERCH		SEA-LOACH, WHISTLE-FISH
phosphorescent shrimps	KRILL	roker	RAY, THORNBACK
pike	ESOX, GED	rose-fish	BERGYLT
	GAR(FISH), LUCE		NORWAY HADDOCK
—perch	FOGASH	rough dab	SAND-SUCKER
—young	JACK	Royal fish	DOLPHIN, STURGEON, WHALE
pilot-fish	ROMERO, RUDDER-FISH	rudd	RED-EYE
pink	MINNOW, SAMLET	rudder-fish	PILOT-FISH
pipe		ruff(e)	POPE
—fish	NEEDLE-FISH, SEA-ADDER	Russian	GOLOMYNKA
	SUACOT	sacred fish	OXYRHYNCUS
—fishes	LOPHOBRANCH	sail	
	SYNGNATHIDAE	—fish	BASKING-SHARK, SPIKE-FISH
piranha	SERRASALMO		SWORD-FISH
plaice	PLEUONECTES	—fluke	WHIFF
Pleuronectes	PLAICE	saithe	COLEY
pogge	SEA-POACHER	Salmo	SALMON, TROUT
pollack	COAL-FISH, LYTHE	salmon	
	POLLOCK, SEA-SALMON	—1 year	BLUECAP
pope	RUFF(E)	—2 year	SPROD
porbeagle	MACKEREL-SHARK	—3 year	MORT
porgy	SCUP(PAUG)	—blueback	NERKA, SOCKEYE
Port Jackson shark	CESTRACION	—dog-salmon	KETA
pout	BIB, BLAIN, BRASSY	—female after spawning	KELT, SHEDDER
prehistoric	COELACANTH	—fry	ALEVIN
prickle-back	STICKLE-BACK	—grilse	PEAL, PEEL

—large	CHINOOK SALMON
	KING-SALMON, QUINNAT
—male after spawning	KIPPER
—old female	BAGGIT, BLACKFISH
—North Pacific	ONCORHYNCHUS
—Pacific	BLUEBACK, COHO(E), HUMP
	KETA, NERKA, SOCKEYE
—silver	COHO(E)
—sockeye	BLUEBACK, NERKA
—South America	DORADO
	GOLDEN SALMON
—spent	KELT, LIGGER
—trout	BULL-TROUT, SEA-TROUT
—type	SMELT
—young	ALEVIN, GRILSE, PAR(R)
	PINK, SALMONET, SAMLET
	SEWEN, SEWIN, SKEGGER
	SMOLT, SPRAG, SPROD
samlet	PINK
sand	
—eel	GRIG, LANCE
	LANT, (SAND) LAUNCE
—launce	SAND-EEL
—pride	LAMPREY
—sole	LEMON-SOLE
—sucker	ROUGH DAB
sander	PERCH-PIKE, ZANDER
sapphirine gurnard	TUB-FISH
sardine-type	SARDEL(LE)
Sargina	MULLET
saurel	GARANX, HORSE-MACKEREL
	SCAD, SKIPJACK
saury	SKIPPER
scad	CARANX, HORSE-MACKEREL
	SAUREL, SKIPJACK
scald-fish	MEGRIM
scaleless	EEL
scar(us)	PARROT-FISH
	PARROT-WRASSE
Sciaena	MAIGRE
Scomber	MACKEREL
scorpion-fish	ROCK-PERCH, CORPAENA
	SEA-SCORPION
sculpin	DRAGONET
	OLD WIFE, PORGY
Scyphomedusae	JELLYFISH
Scyphozoa	JELLYFISH
sea	
—adder	MARINE STICKLEBACK
	PIPEFISH
—ape	THRESHER SHARK
—bass	MARINE PERCH, ROCK-COD
—blubber	JELLYFISH
—bream	BRAISE, BRAIZE, GILT-HEAD
	PORGIE, PORGY, SAR(GO)
	SARGUS, SPARIDAE

—cat	CATFISH
—cock	GURNARD, GURNET
—dace	BASS
—devil	DEVILFISH
—dog	DOGFISH
—dragon	DRAGONET, PEGASUS
—eagle	EAGLE-RAY
—eel	CONGER
—fish with long fins	SEA-BAT
—fox	FOX-SHARK, THRESHER
—hedgehog	GLOBE-FISH
—horse	HIPPOCAMPUS
	LOPHOBRANCH
type	PIPE-FISH
—hound	DOGFISH
—jelly	JELLYFISH
—lawyer	SHARK
—loach	ROCKLING
—nettle	JELLYFISH
—owl	LUMPSUCKER
—perch	BASS(E), COMBER
	GAPER, SERRAN
—pike	BELONE, HAKE, ROBALO
—poacher	POGGE
—porcupine	DIODON, GLOBE-FISH
—robin	GURNARD
—salmon	COAL-FISH, POLLACK
—scorpion	ROCK PERCH
	SCORPAENA
	SCORPION-FISH
—sleeve	CUTTLEFISH
—snail	SNAIL-FISH
—surgeon	DOCTOR, SURGEON-FISH
—swine	BALLAN-WRASSE
—trout	BULL-TROUT, SALMOM-TROUT
young	FINNAC(K), FINNOCK
	HERLING, HIRLING, PEAL
	PEEL, PHINNOCK, PHINOC
	SEWEN, SEWIN, SMOLT
—wife	WRASSE
—wolf	WOLF-FISH
selachian	CHONDROPTERYGII, SHARK
self-inflating	GLOBE-FISH
sephen	STING-RAY
sepia	CUTTLEFISH
Serrasalmo	PIRANHA
shad	ALLIS, ALLICE
	KING OF THE HERRINGS
	TWAITE
shagreen ray	DUN-COW
shanny	SMOOTH BLENNY
shark	ANGEL-FISH, BEAGLE, CESTRACION
	GATA, HAMMERFISH, HAMMERHEAD
	MONK-FISH, MORGAY, NURSE
	PENNY-DOG, PORBEAGLE
	RHYN(E)ODON, SAW-FISH

	SEA-FOX, SEA-LAWYER, SELACHIAN	spotted	
	THRESHER, TOPE	—dogfish	BOUNCE, MORGAY
—sharks	ELASMOBRANCH, RHYNAE	—ray	HOMELYN
	SELACHII, SPHYRNA	sprat	BRISLING, CLUPEA
	ZYGAENIDAE		GARVIE, GARVOCK
sharp-beaked	SAURY	squid	LOLIGO, SLEEVE-FISH
sheat(h)-fish	CATFISH, SILURUS	star	
shrimp	MYSIS	—fish	ASTER(O)ID, FIVE FINGERS
Silurus	SHEAT(H)-FISH		SEA-PAD
silver salmon	COHO(E)	—gazers	URANOSCOPUS
skate	RAY	stenlock	COALFISH
—skates	ELASMOBRANCH	stickleback	FLUTEMOUTH
skipjack	BLUEFISH, GARANX		PRICKLE-BACK, TIDDLER
	HORSE-MACKEREL, SAUREL	sting	
	SCAD	—fish	STING-BULL, TRACHINUS
skipper	SAURY		WEEVER
sleeve-fish	SQUID	—ray	EAGLE-RAY, SEPHEN
slimy fish	BLENNY		TRYGON
small	BITTERLING, CLIONE, FRY	stockfish	LUBFISH
	KRILL, MINNOW, NEKTON	striped bass	ROCK-FISH
	SPRAT, SHRIMP, STICKLEBACK	sturgeon	ACIPENSER, BELUGA
	TIDDLER, WHITEBAIT		CHONDROSTEI, HUSO
—cod	CODLING, DORSE		OSSETER, STERLET
—herring-type	SPRAT	sucking-fish	LAMPREY, REMORA
—rockling	MACKEREL-MIDGE	sun-fish	BASKING-SHARK, OPAH
—sardine-type	SARDEL(LE)	swine-fish	WOLF-FISH
—sea-fish	WHITING	sword-fish	ESPADA, GLADUS
—shark	DOG-FISH		(H)ISTIOPHORUS, MARLIN
—sole	SLIP, SOLENETTE		SAIL-FISH, SPEAR-FISH
—sturgeon	STERLET		XIPHIAS
smear-dab	SMOOTH DAB	Syngnathidae	PIPE-FISH
smelt	ATHERINA	tarpon	ELOPS, MEGALOPS, STABALO
—Newfoundland	CAP(E)LIN	tench	TINEA
—Scottish	SPARLING, SPIRLING	Tetrapturus	SPEAR-FISH
smoked herring	BLOATER, BUCKLING	thornback	RAY, ROKER
	KIPPER	thresher	FOX-SHARK, SEA-FOX
smooth blenny	SHANNY		SEA-APE, THRASHER
snail-fish	SEA-SNAIL	Thymallus	GRAYLING
snake-fish	CEPOLA	tiddler	MINNOW, STICKLEBACK
snapper	GRUNTER	tiger-shark	DEMOISELLE
snappers	LUCIANIDAE	Tinea	TENCH
snipe-fish	BELLOWS-FISH, TRUMPET-FISH	tope	MILLER'S-DOG, PENNY-DOG
snook	COBIA, BARRACOUTA	torgoch	CHAR
	GARFISH, ROBALO, SNOEK	torpedo	(ELECTRIC) RAY
sockeye	BLUEBACK SALMON	torsk	BROSMIUS
sole	MEGRIM	Trachinus	STING-BULL, STING-FISH
Solen	RAZOR-FISH		WEEVER
southern	ESCOLAR	Trachypterous	DEALFISH, RIBBON-FISH
Sparidae	SEA-BREAM	tree-climbing fish	ANABAS
sparling	SMELT	triggerfish	OLD WENCH, OLD WIFE
spear-fish	SWORD-FISH, TETRAPTURUS	Trigla	GURNARD, GURNET
Sphyrna	HAMMER-HEADED SHARKS	trout	FINNOCK, SCUFF
spike-fish	SAIL-FISH	—American	LAKER, TOGUE
spinous loach	GROUNDLING	—Irish	GILLAROO
spiny	SCORPAENA, STICKLEBACK	—young	WHITLING
spirling	SMELT	trumpet-fish	BELLOWS-FISH, SNIPE-FISH

Trygon	STING-RAY
tubfish	GURNARD
tuna	TUNNY
tunny	ALBACORE, ALBICORE
	BONETTO, BONITO, TUNA
turbot	BRET, BRILL, PSETTA
—mouthed wrasse	ROCK-COOK
—type	SAIL-FLUKE, TOP-KNOT
	WHIFF
twaite	SHAD
Umbra	MUD-MINNOW
umber	GRAYLING
Uranoscopus	STAR-GAZER
various	LEATHER-JACKET
viviparous blenny	EEl-POUT, GREEN-BONE
weaver/weever	STING-BULL
	STING-FISH, TRACHINUS
Welsh	
—sea trout grilse	SEWEN, SEWIN
—whitefish (L. Bala)	GWINIAD, GWYNIAD
which jumps from the water	FLYING FISH
	SKIPJACK
whiff	SAIL-FLUKE
whistle-fish	ROCKLING
white fish	COREGONUS
—Lake District	VENDACE, VENDIS(S)
—Northern Ireland	POLLAN
—Scotland	VENDACE, VENDIS(S)
whiting	MIRLING
—pout	BIB, POUTING
whitish goldfish	SILVER-FISH
witch	CRAIG-FLUKE
with	
—bifocal eyes	ANABLEPS
—long under-jaw	HALF-BEAK
—lungs and gills	LUNG-FISH
—tufted gills	LOPHOBRANCH
—whiplike tail	HAIR-TAIL
wolf-fish	ROCK-TURBOT, SEA-WOLF
	SWINE-FISH
woof	CAT-FISH
wrasse	BALLAN, COMBER, CROWGER
	DEMOISELLE, GOLDFINNY
	GOLDSINNY, JULIS, LABRUS
	ROCK-FISH, SEA-WIFE
Xiphias	SWORD-FISH
young fish	BRIT
—coalfish	GREY-FISH
Scottish	PODLEY, SILLOCK
—cod	SCROD
—eel	ELVER
—herring	BRIT, SILD
—pike	JACK, PICKEREL
—pilchard	SARDINE
—salmon	(see salmon above)
—sea-trout	FINNAC(K), FINNOCK

	HERLING, HIRLING, PEAL
	PEEL, PHINNOCK, PHINOC
	SEWEN, SEWIN, SMOLT
—sprat	BRIT
—trout	WHITLING
zander	PIKE-PERCH, SANDER
Zygaenidae	HAMMER-HEADED SHARKS
	(see also fishing)

fish²

includes: general terms	
air-sac	SWIM BLADDER
arrangement of scales	PHOLIDOSIS
ascending river to spawn	ANADROMOUS
buoyancy organ	SWIM-BLADDER
descending river to spawn	CATADROMOUS
description of fishes	ICHTHYOGRAPHY
eggs	OVA, ROE, SPAWN
fins	ANAL, CAUDAL, DORSAL
	MEDIAN, PECTORAL, PELVIC
fish	
—glue	ICHTHYOCOLLA
—dish	(see separate entry)
—pond	PISCINA
fish-eating	ICHTHYOPHAGOUS
	PISCIVOROUS
fish-shaped	PISCIFORM
fishing	(see separate entry)
flap(s) covering	
gill(s)	OPERCULUM(OPERCULA)
flies	COLLIE DOG, DRURY
	HAIRWING, TUBE
	WADDINGTON, WILLIE GUNN
fossil fish	ICHTHYODORULITE
	ICHTHYODORYLITE
rearing fish	PISCICULTURE
scales like teeth	DENTICLES
	PLACOID SCALES
sound detectors along	
each side	LATERAL LINE
spawn of shellfish	SPAT
sperm	MELT, MILT
stinging organ	CNIDA, NEMATOCYST
study of	ICHTHYOLOGY
with spine	
—running into upper	
lobe of tail	HETEROCERCAL
—not running into upper	
lobe of tail	HOMOCERCAL
	(see also fishing)

fish dishes

angler fish, poached	CODA DI ROSPO
Bombay duck	BUM(M)ALO
cooked in vinegar	AU BLEU
deep-fried	GOUJON, SCAMPI, WHITEBAIT
dried	
—in open air	STOCKFISH

—salted cod	BACALAO
dumpling	QUENELLE
eels	STEWED EELS
—split and broiled	SPITCHCOCK
eggs	MILT, ROE
fishball	GEFILTE, GEFULLTE FISH
	QUENELLE, RISSOLE
French	BOUILLABAISSE, MATELOTE
Greek roe paste	TARAMASALATA
haddock	
—smoked	FINNAN
—(Scot.)	(ARBROATH) SMOKIE
herring	
—dried	KIPPER
—Dutch	MATIE, MATJE
—in vinegar	ROLLMOP
—partly dried	BLOATER
—pickled	ROLL-MOP, SOUSED
—salted and smoked	RED HERRING
—smoked	BUCKLING
in sauce with peas	WIGGLE
Indian	BOMBAY DUCK
	BUM(M)ALO, KEDGEREE
lobster	
—fat (US)	TOMALLEY
—in butter and Madeira	LOBSTER NEWBURG
—liver	TOMALLEY
Malay	OTAK OTAK
mussels	MOULES (A LA) MARINIERE
ovaries used in sauces	CORAL
oyster	
—cooked with cheese	AU GRATIN
—in the shell	AU NATUREL
paste	
—of mullet roe	TARAMASALATA
—Roman	GARUM
pie	FISHERMAN'S, RUSSIAN
	SEAMAN'S
prawns	SCAMPI
—in butter and Madeira	PRAWN NEWBURG
—with onions, peppers	PRAWN CREOLE
raw sliced fish (Jap.)	SASHIMI
relish made of roe	BOTARGO
roe of sturgeon, etc	CAVIAR(E)
Russian	COULIBIAC
salmon	SALMON TARTARE
scallops	COQUILLES
—with	
grated cheese	AU GRATIN
sauce	FRICASSEE
Scandinavian	GRAVADLAX
scored and grilled	CARBONADO
seafood and vegetables (Jap.)	TEMPURA
shark flesh	FLAKE
shellfish, etc	SEAFOOD
—stew	(CLAM) CHOWDER

slice of boneless fish	FIL(L)ET
smoked	
—haddock	FINNAN, FINDON
	SMOKIE, SMOKY
Scottish	ARBROATH SMOKIE
	FINNAN HADDIE
—herring	BLOATER, BUCKLING, KIPPER
—mackerel	BLOATER
—salmon	LOX
soft roe	MILT
sole	
—baked	
in	
—cider and cream	SOLE NORMANDIE
—herbs etc	SOLE VERONIQUE
—wine	SOLE BONNE FEMME
	SOLE DUGLERE
with	
—cheese sauce	SOLE MORNAY
—mussels etc	SOLE A LA NORMANDE
—deep-fried in	
breadcrumbs etc	SOLE COLBERT
—fried in butter	SOLE MEUNIERE
Spanish stew	ESQUEIXADA, PAELLA
split for cooking (US)	SCROD
squid	CALAMARI, CALAMARY
star	(see separate entry)
stew	(see separate entry)
stock	FUMET
strips of fish	GOUJONS
—breadcrumbed and fried	FISH FINGERS
	FISH STICKS
trout wih almonds	TRUITE AUX AMANDES
used for paté	ANCHOVY
with	
—mashed potatoes	FISH CAKE
—rice	KEDGEREE
fishing	
bait	LURE
—fixed in position	LEDGER BAIT
—thrown into water	GROUND BAIT
club for killing fish	PRIEST
compound hook	GANG-HOOK, JIG
concave lure	SPOON
connecting line	TRACE
dropping fly gently	
on surface	DAPPING
fish	
—pen	CRAWL
—tank	AQUARIUM
fisherman	ANGLER, PISCATOR
—female	PISCATRIX
fishing	
—basket	COOP, CREEL
—fly	FANCY FLY, HACKLE
—in fast-moving water	TROTTING

—with line behind a boat	TROLLING
flies	COLLIE DOG, DRURY
	HAIRWING, TUBE
	WADDINGTON, WILLIE GUNN
hand-fishing	GUDDLING, TICKLING
hooked pole	GAFF
instrument for removing	
hook	DISGORGER
line with shorter	
lines attached	PATERNOSTER
	SET LINE, TRAWL LINE
maggot	GENTLE, SQUATT
net	KEEP-NET, SEINE
	STAKE-NET, TRAMMEL
	TRAWL
ornament on fly	TAG
sea-fishing	SEINE-FISHING
	TRAWLING
skimming lure lightly	
over the water	SKITTERING
spinning bait	LURE, SPINNER
support for trace, hook etc	FLOAT
weight for line	CAPTA
weighted	
—hook	DRAIL
—line	LEDGER-TACKLE
winding back the bait	SPINNING

five

arrangement of five things	QUINCUNX
Articles	DOCTRINES
books of Old Testament	PENTATEUCH
bunch of fives	FIST
Christmas presents	GOLD RINGS
Cinque Ports	DOVER, HASTINGS
	HYTHE, ROMNEY, SANDWICH
cities	PENTAPOLIS
combining forms	PENT(A)-, QUINQU(E)-
daily interval	SEXTAN
days	PENTAD
event contest	PENTATHLON
fold	PENTAPLOID, QUINARY
	QUINQUEFARIOUS
	QUINTUPL(ICAT)E
groups	PENTAD, QUIN, QUINT
	QUINTET(T), QUINTETTE
	QUINTETTO, QUINTUPLET
having five	
—angles	PENTANGULAR
	QUINQUANGULAR
—atoms	PENTATOMIC
—bundles of stamens	PENTADELPHOUS
—electrodes	PENTODE
—faces	PENTAHEDRAL
—fingers	PENTADACTYL(E)
	PENTADACTYLIC
	PENTADACTYLOUS

—leaflets	QUINATE
	QUINQUEFOLIATE
—members	PENTAMEROUS
—parts	PENTAMEROUS
	QUINQUEPARTITE
	QUINTUPLE
—pistils	PENTAGYNIAN
	PENTAGYNOUS
—rays	PENTACT(INAL)
—rings	PENTACYCLIC
—rows	PENTASTICHOUS
	QUINQUEFARIOUS
—sets	QUINATE
—sides	PENTAGONAL
—stamens	PENTANDRIAN
	PENTANDROUS
—styles	PENTAGYNIAN
	PENTAGYNOUS
—times haploid number	PENTAPLOID
—toes	PENTADACTYL(E)
	PENTADACTYLIC
	PENTADACTYLOUS
—valencies	PENTAVALENT
—whorls	PENTACYCLIC
—xylem strands	PENTARCH
hundred	A, D
—years old	QUINCENTENARIAN
hundredth anniversary	QUINCENTENARY
	QUINGENTENARY
in	
—children's stories	FAMOUS
—government	PENTARCHY
iron	MASHIE
kings	PENTARCHY
Nations	RED INDIANS
one of five at birth	QUINTUPLET
Pentateuch	GENESIS, EXODUS
	LEVITICUS, NUMBERS
	DEUTERONOMY
Points	DOCTRINES
pound note	FIVER
rulers	PENTARCHY
senses	HEARING, SIGHT
	SMELL, TASTE, TOUCH
states	PENTARCHY
thousand	A, V
Towns	BURSLEM, HANLEY, LONGTON
	POTTERIES, STOKE, TUNSTALL
tricks	NAP
Ws	WHO, WHAT, WHERE, WHEN, WHY
years	LUSTRUM, PENTAD
	QUINQUENNIUM
—prison sentence	HANDFUL

flags

American flag	OLD GLORY
	STARS AND STRIPES

British flag	UNION JACK	cross-bred flower	HYBRID
cavalry flag	CORNET	cultivated flower	CULTIVAR
edge		cultivation of flowers	FLORICULTURE
—nearest flagpole	HOIST EDGE	drooping spike	AMENT, CATKIN
—furthest from pole	FLY EDGE	flower	
flag (flower)	IRIS, LIS	—liquid	NECTAR
flag officer	ADMIRAL, COMMODORE	—which	
flagbearer	ANCIENT, VEXILLARY	blooms continuously	PERPETUAL
flown		is pollinated by	
—on		—insects	ENTOMOPHILOUS
boats	BUNTING	—the wind	ANEMOPHILOUS
bow of ship	JACK	lives	
horizontal bar	GONFALON	—1 year	ANNUAL
mast of ship	BURGEE	—2 years	BIENNIAL
	SWALLOWTAIL	—3 years or more	PERENNIAL
—when leaving port	BLUE PETER	opens	
French flag	ORIFLAMME, TRICOLEUR	—during the day	DIURNAL
funeral flag	GUMPHION	—in the evening	VESPERINE
group of flags	HOIST	—without a stalk	SESSILE
hoisting rope	HALLIARD, HALYARD	head-dress of flowers	CHAPLET, CORONA
lance pennon	PAVON		CROWN, GARLAND
long, narrow flag	BANDEROL(E), BANDROL		WREATH
	BANNEROL, PENCEL	never-fading	AMARANTH, IMMORTELLE
	PENNANT, PENNON(CEL)	parts	ANTHER, BRACT, CALYX, CARPEL
	STREAMER		COROLLA, FILAMENT, GYNAECIUM
lower flag	STRIKE		NECTARY, OVARY, OVULE, PEDICEL
Merchant Navy flag	RED DUSTER		PERIANTH, PETAL, PISTIL
	RED ENSIGN		SEPAL, STALK, STAMEN, STIGMA
military flag	ANCIENT, BANNER		STYLE, TORUS, THALAMUS
	COLOUR, EAGLE, ENSIGN	ring of bracts	INVOLUCRE
	GUIDON, STANDARD	single flower in	
Naval Reserve flag	BLUE ENSIGN	inflorescence	FLORET
parade	TROOPING THE COLOUR	small flower	FLORET
pirate flag	JOLLY ROGER	stalk	CAULIS, PEDICEL
	SKULL AND CROSSBONES		PEDICLE, PEDUNCLE
quarantine flag	YELLOW JACK		PETIOLE
roll up flag	FURL	sun-facing flower	HELIOTROPE
Roman			(*see also* **plants**)
—standard	VEXILLIUM		
—standard-bearer	VEXILLARIUS	**football**	
	VEXILLARY	areas of pitch	CENTRE CIRCLE
Royal Navy flag	WHITE ENSIGN		GOAL AREA, PENALTY AREA
square flag	BANNER	attack opponent	TACKLE
study of flags	VEXILLOLOGY	Cup Final venue	WEMBLEY
flower		curving shot	BANANA SHOT
bell-shaped flower	CAMPANULA(TE)	grounds (British)	
bunch of flowers	BOUQUET, CORSAGE	—Aberdeen	PITTODALE
	GARLAND, LEI, NOSEGAY	—Arsenal	HIGHBURY
	POSY, SPRAY, WREATH	—Aston Villa	VILLA PARK
chain of flowers	FESTOON, GARLAND	—Birmingham	ST ANDREWS
	LEI, SWAG	—Blackburn	EWOOD PARK
cluster shapes	CAPITULUM, CORYMB	—Blackpool	BLOOMFIELD ROAD
	CYME, DICHASIUM, GLOMERULE	—Bournemouth	DEAN COURT
	INFLORESCENCE, MONOCHASIUM	—Brighton	GLADSTONE GROUND
	PANICLE, RACEME, SPADIX	—Bristol	ASHTON GATE
	SPIKE, THYRSUS, TRUSS, UMBEL	—Cambridge	ABBEY STADIUM
		—Charlton	THE VALLEY

—Chelsea	STAMFORD BRIDGE
—Coventry	HIGHFIELD ROAD
—Derby	BASEBALL GROUND
—Dundee	DENS PARK
—Everton	GOODISON PARK
—Gillingham	PRESTFIELD STADIUM
—Glasgow	
Celtic	PARKHEAD
Rangers	IBROX PARK
—Heart of Midlothian	TYNECASTLE PARK
—Hereford	EDGAR STREET
—Hibernian	EASTER ROAD
—Hull	BOOTHFERRY PARK
—Ipswich	PORTMAN ROAD
—Leeds	ELLAND ROAD
—Leicester	CUITY STADIUM
—Liverpool	ANFIELD
—Luton	KENILWORTH ROAD
—Manchester	
City	MAINE ROAD
United	OLD TRAFFORD
—Middlesborough	AYRESOME PARK
—Newcastle	ST JAMES PARK
—Norwich	CARROW LANE
—Notts County	COUNTY GROUND
—Oldham	BOUNDARY PARK
—Oxford	MANOR GROUND
—Portsmouth	FRATTON PARK
—Port Vale	VALE PARK
—Queens Park Rangers	LOFTUS ROAD
—Reading	ELM PARK
—St Mirren	LOVE STREET
—Sheffield	
United	BRAMALL LANE
Wednesday	HILLSBOROUGH
—Southampton	THE DELL
—Stoke	VICTORIA GROUND
—Sunderland	ROKER PARK
—Swansea	VETCH FIELD
—Tottenham	WHITE HART LANE
—Walsall	FELLOWS PARK
—Watford	VICARAGE ROAD
—West Bromwich	HAWTHORNS
—West Ham	UPTON PARK
—Wolverhampton	MOLINEUX
—Wrexham	RACECOURSE GROUND
illegal position	OFFSIDE
kick dropped ball	DROP-KICK, PUNT
lines on pitch	CENTRE CIRCLE
	CENTRE LINE, GOAL LINE
	TOUCH LINE
nicknames (British)	
—Aberdeen	DONS
—Arsenal	GUNNERS
—Aston Villa	VILLANS
—Birmingham City	BLUES

—Bournemouth	CHERRIES
—Bristol City	ROBINS
—Cardiff City	BLUEBIRDS
—Chelsea	PENSIONERS
—Coventry	SKY BLUES
—Crystal Palace	GLAZIERS
—Derby County	RAMS
—Everton	BLUES, TOFFEEMEN
—Glasgow	
Celtic	BHOYS, TIC
Rangers	BLUES, GERS
	TEDDY BEARS
—Heart of Midlothian	JAM TARTS
—Hibernian	HIBS
—Ipswich	TOWN
—Huddersfield Town	TERRIERS
—Hull City	TIGERS
—Leicester City	FILBERTS, FOXES
—Liverpool	POOL, REDS
—Manchester United	RED DEVILS
—Mansfield Town	STAGS
—Middlesbrough	BORO
—Newcastle United	MAGPIES
—Northampton	COBBLERS
—Norwich City	CANARIES
—Notts County	MAGPIES
—Peterborough United	POSH
—Portsmouth	POMPEY
—Sheffield	
United	BLADES
Wednesday	OWLS
—Southampton	SAINTS
—Stoke City	POTTERS
—Sunderland	ROKERITES
—Swindon	ROBINS
—Torquay United	GULLS
—Tottenham Hotspur	SPURS
—Walsall Town	SADDLERS
—West Bromwich Albion	BAGGIES
	THROSTLES
—West Ham	HAMMERS
—Wimbledon	DONS
—Wolverhampton Wanderers	WOLVES
officials	LINESMAN, REF(EREE)
old versions	
—Chinese	TSU-CHU
—Italian	CALCIO
pass ball between	
opponent's legs	NUTMEG
players	
—Argentinian	DI STEFANO, KEMPES
	MARADONA, STABILE
—Austrian	HERTZOG, KRANKL
	POLSTER, LINDENBERGER
—Belgian	CEULEMANS, DEGRYSE
	GERETS, VAN DER LINDEN

—Brazilian	BEBETO, BISMARK
	CARECA, CESAR, DIDI, EUSEBIO
	GARRINCHA, GERSON, GILMAN
	JAIRZINHO, LEONIDAS
	MOZER, PELE, RIVELINO
	ROMARIO, SANTOS, TAFFAREL
	TOSTAO, VAVA, ZICO
—Cameroon	BELL, BIYIK
—Colombian	HIGUITA, VALDERRAMA
—Czech	KOCIAN, NEJEDLY, KUIK
	STRAKA, ZIKAN
—Danish	LAUDRUP
—Dutch	CRUYFF, GULLITT, KOEMAN
	NEESKENS, RIJKAARD
	VAN BASTEN
—Egyptian	ABDEL-HAMID
	ABDEL-RASSOOL
	ABU-ZEID, EL KAS, HASSAN
—English	BALL, BANKS, BASTIN
	BLOOMER, BOWLES, BUCHAN
	CHANNON, CHARLTON, DEAN
	DOUGAN, DRAKE, FINNEY
	GREAVES, HAPGOOD, HAYNES
	HURST, JAMES, KEEGAN
	LAWTON, LINEKER, MANNION
	MATTHEWS, MILBURN, MOORE
	MORTENSEN, MORTON, ROBSON
	RUSH, SHILTON, STILES, SWIFT
	TRAUTMAN, WADDLE, WELSH
	WRIGHT
—French	FONTAINE, PLATINI
—German	BECKENBAUER, BONHOF
	HAESSLER, HOENESS, KLINSMANN
	KRAUT, MATTHAUS
	MU(E)LLER, OVERATH
	SEELER, VOLLER
—Hungarian	ALBERT, BOZSIK, CZIBOR
	GROSICS, KOCSIS, PUSKAS
	SAROSI, SZABO
—Irish	BEST, BLANCHFLOWER
	BRADY, DOHERTY, MCILROY
—Italian	BARESI, BERGOMI
	GENTO, MAZZOLA
	MEAZZA, RIVA, RIVERA
	ROSSI, VIALLI, ZOFF
—Polish	LATO
—Portuguese	COLUNA, EUSEBIO
—Romanian	BALINT, HAGI
	LACATUS, MATEUT
—Russian	ALEINIKOV, BLOKHIN
	DASAYEV, IVANOV, RATS
	YASHIN, ZAVAROV
—Scottish	BREMMER, DALGLEISH
	GALLACHER, JACKSON
	JOHNSTON, LAW, LORIMER
	MCCOIST, MCGRORY

—South Korean	SOON-HO
—Spanish	BAKERO, BUTRAGUENO
	DI STEFANO, MICHEL
	SUAREZ, VASQUEZ
—Swedish	EKSTROM, HYSEN
	MAGNUSSON
—Uruguayan	FRANCESCOLI, SOSA
—Welsh	ALLCHURCH, CHARLES
	JAMES, HUGHES
—Yugoslav	DZALJIC, JERKOVIC
	STOJKOVIC, VUJOVIC
playing positions	(CENTRE-)BACK
	CENTRE-HALF
	(CENTRE-)FORWARD, (FULL-)BACK
	GOAL-KEEPER, HALF-BACK
	INSIDE LEFT, INSIDE RIGHT
	LEFT-BACK, LEFT-HALF, LEFT WING
	RIGHT-BACK, RIGHT-HALF
	RIGHT WING, STRIKER, SWEEPER
	WINGER
result of	
—foul	FREE KICK
in penalty area	PENALTY (KICK)
—ball out of play	CORNER (KICK)
	GOAL KICK, THROW-IN
restart after	
—goal	KICK-OFF
—stoppage	DROPPED BALL
short lofted kick	CHIP
start of play	KICK-OFF
teams	
—Argentina	DEPORTIVO ESPANOL
	DEPORTIVO MANDIYA
	ESTUDIANTES DE LA PLATA
	FERRO CARRIL OESTE
	GIMNASIA ESGRIMA LA PLATA
	HURACAN, INDEPENDIENTE
	INSTITUTIO CORDOBA
	RACING CLUB, RACING CORDOBA
	RIVER PLATE, ROSARIO CENTRAL
	VELEZ SARSFIELD
—Austria	ADMIRA WACKER
	AUSTRIA SALZBURG
	AUSTRIA VIENNA, FCS TYROL
	FK AUSTRIA, GAK
	RAPID VIENNA, STURM GRAZ
	VORWAERTS STEYR
	WIENER SPORTS CLUB
—Belgium	CERCLE BRUGES
	ROYAL ANTWERP
	STANDARD LIEGE
—Brazil	FLAMENGO
—Britain	(see grounds, nicknames)
—Bulgaria	CSKA, LEVSKI, SLAVIA
—Colombia	ATLETICO NACIONAL
	MILLIONARIOS

—Czechoslovakia	BANIK OSTRAVA
	INTER BRATSILAVA
	SPARTA PRAGUE
—East Germany	CARL ZEISS JENA
	CHEMIE HALLE
	DYNAMO BERLIN
	DYNAMO DRESDEN
	ENERGIE COTTBUS
	HANSA ROSTOCK
	KARL MARX STADT
	LOKOMOTIV LEIPZIG
	ROTWEISS ERFURT
	STAHL BRANDENBERG
—Egypt	AL-AHLY, ZAMALEK
—France	PARIS ST GERMAIN
	OLYMPIQUE MARSEILLES
	RACING PARIS
—Greece	AEK, APOLLON, ARIS
	DOXA DRAMA, ETHNIKOS
	OFI CRETE, OLYMPIAKOS
	PANATHINAIKOS, PAOK
—Holland	AJAX AMSTERDAM
	FORTUNA SITTARD
	FV EINDHOVEN, WILLEM
—Hungary	BUDAPEST HONVED
	MTK VM, PECS MUNKAS
	RABO ETO GYOR
	UZPEST DOZSA
—Ireland	BOHEMIANS
—Italy	AC MILAN, ATALANTA
	INTER(NAZIONALE) MILAN
	JUVENTUS, LAZIO, NAPOLI
	ROMA, SAMPDORIA, TORINO
—Poland	GKS KATOWICE, GORNIK ZABRZE
	LECH POZNAN, LEGIA WARSZAWA
	JAGIELLONIA BIALYSTOK
	MOTOR LUBLIN, RUCH CHORZOW
	SLASK WROCLAW, STAL MIELIC
	WIDZEW LODZ, WISLA KRAKOW
	ZAGLEBIE LUBLIN
	ZAGLEBIE SOSNOWIEC
	ZAWISZA BYDGOSZCZ
—Portugal	BENFICA, GUIMARAES
	MARTITIMO
	NACIONAL, PORTO, SPORTING
—Romania	BIHOR ORADEA
	CORVINUL HUNEDOARA, CSKA
	DINAMO BUCHAREST
	FARUL CONSTANTA
	FLACARA MORENI
	INTER SIBIU, JIUL PETBOSANI
	PETROLUL PLOIESTI
	POLITEHNICA TIMISOARA
	SPORTUL STUDENTESC
	STEVA BUCHAREST, UNI CLUJ NAPOCA
	VICTORIA BUCHAREST

—Russia	DYNAMO KIEV
	MOSCOW DYNAMO
—Spain	ATLETICO BILBAO
	ATLETICO MADRID, BARCELONA
	REAL MADRID
	REAL MAJORCA, REAL SOCIEDAD
	REAL VALLECANO, REAL ZARAGOZA
	SPORTING GIJON
—Switzerland	GRASSHOPPER
	NEUCHATEL XAMAX
—Turkey	BESIKTAS, FENERBAHCE
	TRABZON
—West Germany	BAYER LEVERKUSEN
	BAYER URDINGEN
	BAYERN MUNICH
	BORUSSIA DORTMUND
	BORUSSIA MUNCHENGLADBACH
	EINTRACHT FRANKFURT
	FORTUNA DUSSELDORF
	KAISER LAUTERN
	WALDORF MANNHEIM
	WERDER BREMEN
—Yugoslavia	DINAMO, HAJDUK
	OLIMPIJA, RED STAR BELGRADE
	SPARTAK

footwear

army boots	AMMOS, AMMUNITION BOOTS
baseball boots	KICKERS
beach-wear	FLIP-FLOP
bi-coloured	CO-RESPONDENT'S SHOES
calf-length boots	RUSSIAN BOOTS
casual shoes	LOAFERS, MOCASSINS
	MOCCASINS
climber's boot	KLETTERSCHUHE
	SCARPETTO, VIBRAM
clumsy shoes	CLOD-HOPPERS
cobbler	CORDINER, CORDWAINER
	COSIER, COZIER, SNOB, SUTOR
—Scots	SOUTAR, SOUTER, SOWTAR
cobbler's paste	CLOBBER
crêpe soled shoes	BROTHEL-CREEPERS
dancing shoe	TAP-SHOE
Dutch	CLOG
elastic-sided boot	
—modern	CHELSEA BOOT
—old	JEMIMA
Elizabethan clog	HIGH CHOPIN(E)
embroidered sandal	
(Holy Roman Empire)	CALCEAMENTUM
Eskimo boot	MUC(K)LUC(K)
	MUKLUK
exercise shoes	BASEBALL BOOTS
	DAPS, GYMSHOES, KICKERS
	PLIMSOLLS, TRAINERS
felt-soled	KLETTERSCHUHE
French wooden shoe	SABOT

full-length waterproof	WADERS
half-boot	START-UP
hemp-soled	
—boot or shoe	SCARPETTO
—sandal	ALPARGATA
high boot	
—German	HESSIAN
—lumberman's	LARRIGANS
—old	BUSKIN, COTHURN(US)
—Roman	PERO
high chopin	PANTABLE, PANTOF(F)LE
	PANTOUFLE
Indian sandal	CHAPPAL
insulated boots	MOON BOOTS
Japanese sandal	GETA
jogging shoes	TRAINERS
kickers	BASEBALL BOOTS
laced boot	ALMORAL
Lancashire	CLOG
long boots	TOP-BOOTS
lumberman's boot	LARRIGAN
made from deerskin	BUCKSKIN
men's shoe	DERBY, OXFORD
—14th c	POULAINE
Mercury's winged sandals	TALARIA
metal shoe protectors	SEG, TAP, TRAMP
Norwegian boots	FINN(E)SKO, FINSKO
Oriental heel-less slipper	BABOOSH
	BAB(O)UCHE, PABOUCHE
overshoe	PANTABLE, PANTOF(F)LE
	PANTOUFLE
plastic sandals	FLIP-FLOPS
pointed	
—boot	CRACOWE
—shoe	WINKLE-PICKER
rawhide shoe	
—African	VELDSHOEN, VEL(D)SKOEN
—Scottish	RULLION
Red Indian shoe	MOCASSIN, MOCCASIN
reindeerskin boots (Norway)	FINN(E)SKO
	FINSKO
repairer	COBBLER, COSIER
	COZIER, SNOB, SUTOR
	(*see also* cobbler *above*)
Roman boot	PERO
rope-soled	
—sandal	ALPARGATA
—shoe	ESPADRILLE
rubber boot	WELLIE, WELLINGTON, WELLY
running shoes	SPIKES
Russian boots	COSSACK BOOTS
sand-shoes	SNEAKERS
shoe (Amer)	TIE
shoemaker	(*see* cobbler *above*)
slipper	PANTABLE, PANTOF(F)LE
	PANTOUFLE

—Eastern	BABOOSH, BAB(O)UCHE
—Scottish	PANTON
soft-soled shoes	SNEAKERS
sole of shoe	TAP
South African	VEL(D)SKOEN
	VELDSCHOEN
spikes	CRAMPONS
strong shoe	BROGAN, BROGUE
suede ankle-boot	CHUKKA, DESERT BOOT
—shoe	BROTHEL-CREEPER
thick-soled boot	BUSKIN
—modern	DOC MARTENS
—tragedian's	COTHURN(US)
walking boot	BALMORAL
waterproof overshoes	GALAGES, GALOSHES
	GOLOE-SHOES, GOLOSHES
—American	GUMSHOES, RUBBERS
white plimsolls	MUTTON-DUMMIES
winged sandals	TALARIA
with	
—long pointed toe	POULAINE
—rubber sole	GUMSHOE
—thick sole	PLATFORM SHOE
without laces	SLIP-ON
woman's	
—heel-less slipper	MULE
—high-heeled shoe	STILETTO
—plain shoe	COURT SHOE
—toeless shoe	PEEP-TOE
—shoe with strap at rear	SLING-BANK
wooden shoe	CLOG
—French	SABOT
—Japanese	GETA
—old	HIGH CHOPIN(E), PATTEN
Yorkshire	CLOG

fortifications

area between moat	
and castle	BERM
basket filled with earth	CORBEIL
battlement	BARTISAN, BARTIZAN
built by besiegers	CONTRAVALLATION
	SIEGEWORK
bulwark	RAMPART
central tower	DONJON, DUNGEON, KEEP
concrete bunker	BLOCKHOUSE, PILLBOX
covered passage	
across ditch	CAPONIER(E)
defensive	
—spike	CHEVAL-DE-FRISE
—stakes	TROUS-DE-LOUP
detached fieldwork	DEMI-LUNE, RAVELIN
deviating from	
general line	BRISURE
dike of piles	ESTACADE
ditch	FOSSE, MOAT
earth bank	BULWARK, RAMPART, VALLUM

earthwork	
—chest-high	BREASTWORK
—protecting	AGGER
at rear	PARADOS
from front	PARAPET
embankment	ESCARPMENT, GLACIS
enclosed area of	
fortification	ENCEINTE
fieldwork enclosed on	
all sides	REDOUBT
firing-step	BANQUETTE, BARBETTE
flat open area	ESPLANADE
flat-topped mound	RAMPART
fortified	
—area	ENCEINTE
—gatehouse	BARBICAN
—house (Scot.)	BASTEL-HOUSE
—mound	DUN
—site of dwellings	RINGFORT
fortress	FORTALICE
—in city	CITADEL
French castle	CHATEAU
German castle	SCHLOSS
grille at entrance	PORTCULLIS
hastily-constructed	
earthwork	BREASTWORK
horizontal fence	FRISE
inner	
—court(yard)	INNER BAILEY, INNER WARD
—retreat	REDOUBT, REDUIT
—side of ditch	ESCARP
inward facing fieldwork	RE-ENTRANT
keeper of castle	CASTELLAN
	CHATELAIN(E)
	CONSTABLE
look-out post	SANGAR, SUNGAR
moat	FOSSE
mound	AGGER, DUN, MOTTE
moveable	
—shield	MANT(E)LET
—siege-tower	BASTILLE
opening	
—for passage of troops	DEBOUCHE
—in parapet	CRENELLE, EMBRASURE
outer	
—court(yard)	BAILEY, OUTER WARD
—side of ditch	COUNTERSCARP
—wall	BAILEY
outside main line or wall	OUTWORK
outward facing	
—projection	SALIENT
—wall or parapet	FLECHE
outwork	
—in front of curtain	TENAIL(LE)
—protecting drawbridge	BARBICAN
	BARTISAN, BARTIZAN

—to strengthen ravelin	TENAILLON
—with two embankments	RAVELIN
overhanging turret	BARTISAN, BARTIZAN
palisade	FRISE
parapet	BARTISAN, BARTIZAN
	BATTLEMENT, TRAVERSE
—between openings	MERLON
—forming salient	FLECHE
passage into fortifications	GORGE
projecting watch-tower	BARBICAN
protection from	
enfilading fire	DEFILADE
protective	
—bank	TRAVERSE
—mound	AGGER
—wall	REVETMENT
raised	
—mound and ditch	BERM
—portion of parapet	SURTOUT
rampart	BULWARK, VALLUM
—between bastions	CURTAIN
—made of	
earth and timber	AGGER
felled trees	ABAT(T)IS
—walk	RELAIS
rough stone breastwork	SANGAR, SUNGAR
salient angle	PIEND
short trench	FOXHOLE
side of ditch nearest	
—besiegers	COUNTERSCARP
—defenders	(E)SCARP(MENT)
slope	GLACIS
—at foot of wall	TALUS
small	
—fortress	FORT
—outwork	BONNET, FORTALICE
space behind parapet	TERREPLEIN
stake barrier	STOCKADE
strengthening work at	
side of ravelin	TENAILLON
stronghold	BASTION, DONJON
	DUNGEON, FASTNESS
	KEEP, REDOUBT
talus on inner side	
of rampart	TERREPLEIN
temporary	BARRICADE
top of rampart	TERREPLEIN
tower	
—at an angle to	
fortification	BASTION, LUNETTE
—for defending fortress	BASTILLE
trench inside	
outer walls	RETRENCHMENT
two faces forming	
a salient	REDAN
underground prison	DONJON, DUNGEON

—shelter	BUNKER	—leaflets	QUADRIFOLIATE
wall of		—leaves per sheet	QUARTO
—sods	VALLUM	—letters	QUADRILITERAL
—wooden stakes	PALISADE, STOCKADE		TETRAGRAM
zigzag defensive line	CREMAILLERE	—parts	QUADRIGEMINAL
forty	F, M, MU, XL		QUADRIGEMINATE
days	QUADRAGESIMA		QUADRIGEMINOUS
	QUARANTINE		QUADRIPARTITE
Forty-five	JACOBITE REBELLION		TETRAMERAL, TETRAMEROUS
forty-niner	GOLD-SEEKER, PROSPECTOR	—petals	QUATREFOIL
in book	THIEVES	—pistils	TETRAGYNIAN
thousand	F, M, MU		TETRAGYNOUS
winks	NAP	—rays	TETRACT(INAL), TETRACTINE
year old	QUADRAGENARIAN	—rings	TETRACYCLIC
four	IV	—rows	QUADRIFARIOUS
aces etc	QUATORZE	—stamens	TETRADYNAMOUS
based	QUATERNARY		TETRANDRIAN, TETRANDROUS
branches of mathematics	QUADRIVIUM	—styles	TETRAGYNIAN, TETRAGYNOUS
Christmas presents	COLLY BIRDS	—syllables	QUADRISYLLABLE
	CALLING BIRDS		TETRASYLLABLE
cleft	QUADRIFID	—terms	QUADRINOMIAL
	QUADRIPARTITE	—times haploid number	TETRAPLOID
combining form	QUADR(I)-, QUADRU-	—toes	TETRADACTYLOUS
dramas	TETRALOGY	—valencies	QUADRIVALENT
estates	CLERGY, COMMONS		TETRAVALENT
	LORDS, PRESS	—variables	QUATERNARY
event contest	TETRATHLON	—wheels	QUADRIROTAL
feet	ELL	—whorls	TETRACYCLIC
fold	QUADRIFARIOUS, QUADRIFORM	—wings	TETRAPTERAN
	QUADRUPLEX, QUADRUPL(ICAT)E		TETRAPTEROUS
	TETR(A)-	—xylem strands	TETRARCH(ICAL)
foot	ORGAN PIPE	hundred years	QUADRICENTENNIAL
fortresses	QUADRILATERAL	hundredth anniversary	QUADRIGENARY
freedoms	FEAR, SPEECH, WANT		QUATERCENTENARY
	WORSHIP	in-hand	COACH, NECKTIE
gills	PINT	line poem	QUATRAIN
gospels	JOHN, LUKE, MARK, MATTHEW	letter word	QUADRILITERAL, TETRAGRAM
groups	QUAD, QUARTET(T), QUARTETTE	men	QUADRUMVIRATE
	QUARTETTO, QUATERNION	one of four	QUADRUPLET
	QUATERNITY, TETRAD	pence	GROAT
having four		poster	BED
—angles	QUADRANGULAR	roads meeting	QUADRIVIUM
	TETRAGONAL	times a day	QID
—cells	QUADRILOCULAR	towns	TETRAPOLIS
—columns	TETRASTYLE	years	QUADRENNIUM
—compartments	QUADRILOCULAR	**fourteen**	
—ethyl groups	TETRAETHYL	at piquet	QUATORZE
—electrodes	TETRODE	poem of fourteen lines	QUATORZAIN
—faces	TETRAHEDRAL		SONNET
—feet	QUADRUPED(AL)	pounds	STONE
	TETRAPODOUS	**fourth**	QUARTER
—fingers	TETRADACTYLOUS	dimension	TIME
—forms	QUADRIFORM, TETRAMORPHIC	man	SETH
—gills	TETRABRANCHIATE	part	QUARTER
—hands	QUADRUMANOUS	—of circle	QUADRANT
—languages	TESSARAGLOT	power of a million	QUADRILLION

France	FR, RF	**regions**	ALSACE, AQUITAINE
departments			AUVERGNE, BASSE-NORMANDIE
—Alsace	BAS-RHIN, HAUT-RHIN		BOURGOGNE, BRETAGNE, CENTRE
—Aquitaine	DORDOGNE, GIRONDE		CHAMPAGNE-ARDENNE, CORSE
	LANDES, LOT-ET-GARONNE		FRANCHE-COMTE, HAUTE-NORMANDIE
	PYRENEES-ATLANTIQUE		ILE-DE-FRANCE
—Auvergne	ALLIER, CANTAL		LANGUEDOC-ROUSSILLON
	HAUTE-LOIRE, PUY-DE-DOME		LIMOUSIN, LORRAINE, MIDI-PYRENEES
—Basse-Normandie	CALVADOS		NORD-PAS-DE-CALAIS
	MANCHE, ORNE		PAYS DE LA LOIRE, PICARDIE
—Bourgogne	COTE-D'OR, NIEVRE		POITOU-CHARENTES
	SAONE-ET-LOIRE, YONNE		PROVENCE-COTE-D'AZUR, RHONE-ALPES
—Bretagne	COTES-DU-NORD, FINISTERE	**French**	
	ILLE-ET-VILAINE, MORBIHAN	above	SUR
—Centre	CHER, EURE-ET-LOIR	abridged	ABREGE
	INDRE, INDRE-ET-LOIRE	absent-minded	DISTRAIT(E)
	LORET, LOIR-ET-CHER	about turn	VOLTE-FACE
—Champagne-Ardenne	ARDENNES, AUBE	Academician	IMMORTEL
	MARNE	accepted idea	IDEE RECUE
—Corse	HAUT-CORSE, CORSE-DU-SUD	accomplished fact	FAIT ACCOMPLI
—Franche-Comté	DOUBS, HAUTE-SAONE	according to	A LA, AUX
	JURA	—rule	DE REGLE, EN REGLE
	TERRITOIRE DE BELFORT	—the menu	A LA CARTE
—Haute-Normandie	EURE, SEINE-MARITIME	account rendered	COMPTE RENDU
—Ile-de-France	ESSONNE, PARIS	acme	COMBLE
	SEINE-ET-MARNE	across	A TRAVERS
	VAL-D'OISE, YVELINES	actor in farces	FARCEUR
—Languedoc-Roussillon	AUDE, GARD	added later	HORS SERIE
	HERAULT, LOZERE	administration	REGIME
	PYRENEES-ORIENTALES	administrative	
—Limousin	CORREZE, CREUZE	—district	PREFECTURE
	HAUTE-VIENNE	—head of department	PREFET
—Lorraine	MEURTHE-ET-MOSELLE	—law	DROIT ADMINISTRATIF
	EURE, MOSELLE, VOSGES	admission to Court	GRANDE ENTREE
—Midi-Pyrénées	ARIEGE, AVEYRON	adventurer	CHEVALIER D'INDUSTRIE
	GERS, HAUTE-GARONNE	advice	CONSEIL
	HAUTES-PYRENEES, TARN	aeroplane	AVION
	TARN-ET-GARONNE	affected (artificial)	CHICHI, RECHERCHE
—Nord-Pas-de-Calais	NORD	affecting (emotional)	FRAPPANT
	PAS-DE-CALAIS	after	APRES
—Pays de la Loire	LOIRE ATLANTIQUE	aftertaste	ARRIERE-GOUT
	MAINE-ET-LOIRE, SARTHE	again	ENCORE
	VENDEE	against the grain	A REBOURS
—Picardie	AINE, OISE, SEINE, SOMME	agent	COMMIS
—Poitou-Charentes	CHARENTE	agreed	D'ACCORD
	CHARENTE-MARITIME	ahead of the times	AVANT-GARDE
	DEUX-SEVRES, VIENNE	air	ALLURE
—Provence-Côte		alas	HELAS
d'Azur	ALPES DE HAUTE PROVENCE	Algerian infantryman	ZOUAVE
	ALPES-MARITIMES	all	TOUT(E)
	BOUCHES-DU-RHONE	—the	
	HAUTES-ALPES, VAR	same	TOUT DE MEME
	VAUCLUSE	world	TOUT LE MONDE
—Rhône-Alpes	AIN, ARDECHE, DROME	—things considered	MALGRE TOUT
	HAUTE-SAVOIE, ISERE	—together	EN MASSE
	LOIRE, RHONE, SAVOIE	alluring	AGACANT(E)

aloud	A HAUTE VOIX
already seen	DEJA VU
alternate hot and cold	DOUCHE ECOSSAISE
ambiguous	LOUCHE
ambush	EMBUSQUE
amenities	AGREMENT(S)
amongst the family	EN FAMILLE
amusement after skiing	APRES-SKI
ancient royal standard	ORIFLAMME
andiron	CHENET
angel	ANGE
annual income	RENTE
annulment of court decision	CESSATION
anthem	MARSEILLAISE
April fool	POISSON D'AVRIL
apparatus for testing strength of gunpowder	EPROUVETTE
applause	ECLAT, VIVE
apple liqueur	CALVADOS
apprentice chef	COMMIS
approval	OUI
apropos of nothing	A PROPOS DE RIEN
appropriate expression	MOT JUSTE
appropriate(ly)	APROPOS
arch	ESPIEGLE
aristocratic	
—man	GRAND SEIGNEUR
—lady	GRANDE DAME
arm(s) (body)	BRAS
armchair	FAUTEUIL
armed police force	GENDARMERIE
arrogance	HAUTEUR
arrow	FLECHE
art of	
—make-up	MAQUILLAGE
—obtaining publicity	RECLAME
artful	RUSE
article	LE, LA, LES, UN, UNE
—from magazine	TIRAGE A PART
—made of esparto	SPARTERIE
—of artistic merit	OBJET D'ART
artificially cooled	FRAPPE(E)
artistic	
—quarter of Paris	RIVE GAUCHE (LEFT BANK)
—skill	CHIC
artless	NAIF, NAIVE
as	COMME
—a friend	EN AMI
—a military man	EN MILITAIRE
—a spectacle	EN SPECTACLE
—it should be	COMME IL FAUT
—one unit	EN BLOC
ash-blond	CENDRE
assistant professor	ADJOINT
associate	CONFRERE

assumed name	NOM DE GUERRE
astonishing event	COUP DE FOUDRE
at	
—a fixed rate for board	EN PENSION
—any	
cost	A TOUT PRIX
risk	A TOUT HASARD
—bottom	AU FOND
—ease	SANS GENE
—great expense	A GRANDS FRAIS
—high speed	VENTRE A TERRE
—home	CHEZ, EN FAMILLE
—once	TOUT DE SUITE
—one's ease	EN PANTOUFLES
—random	A TORT ET A TRAVERS
—room temperature	CHAMBRE(E)
—the	
forefront	AVANT GARDE
worst	AU PIS ALLER
attitudiniser	POSEUR
attractive woman	FEMME FATALE
audacious	RISQUE
aunt	TANTE
authorised transference of surplus	VIREMENT
avenue	ALLEE
away and hang them!	A LA LANTERNE
baby's complete outfit	LAYETTE
background	FOND
back-to-back	DOS-A-DOS
bad	MAL, MAUVAIS(E)
—form	MAUVAIS TON
—luck	MAUVAISE CHANCE
—moment	MAUVAIS MOMENT
—style	MAUVAIS TON
—taste	MAUVAIS GOUT
badly groomed	MAL SOIGNE(E)
baggage	
—of army	MATERIEL
—wagon	FOURGON
bagpipe	CORNEMUSE, LOURE MUSETTE
bailiff	HUISSIER
ballet	
—company	CORPS DE BALLET
—dancer (f)	DANSEUSE
—master	MAITRE
banteringly	EN BADINANT
barley	ORGE
barracks	CASERNE
base metal	BILLON
bashfulness	MAUVAISE HONTE
basic assumption	DONNEE
basis	FOND
bath	BAIN
bay	ANSE, BAIE, GOLFE
beach	PLAGE

bean	FEVE, HARICOT	—girl	GAMINE
bearing	TENUE	brand	MARQUE
beaten track	PISTE	brandy	ARMAGNAC, COGNAC, FINE
beautiful	BEAU, BELLE	brawl	BAGARRE
bed	LIT	bread	PAIN
beef	BOEUF	—crumbs	PANURE
beer garden	BRASSERIE	—roll	PETIT PAIN
before	AVANT	breakfast	(PETIT) DEJEUNER
—this	CI-DEVANT	breeches	CULOTTE(S)
begone!	ALLEZ-VOUS-EN	bridgehead	TETE DE PONT
behind	DERRIERE, EN ARRIERE	brief outline	APERCU
being discussed	EN L'AIR	brother	FRERE
belly to the ground	VENTRE A TERRE	brotherhood	CONFRERIE
belt (clothing)	CEINTURE	brute	BETE
besides	AU RESTE	buckler	RONDACHE
best item	PIECE DE RESISTANCE	buffer zone	CORDON SANITAIRE
betrothal	FIANCAILLES	buffoon	FARCEUR
betrothed person	FIANCE(E)	bugbear	BETE NOIRE
betting-machine	PARI-MUTUEL	bulging	BOUFFANT
between		burning cloud	NUEE ARDENTE
—four	A QUATRE	business	METIER
—ourselves	ENTRE NOUS	—man	HOMME D'AFFAIRES
—two	A DEUX	butcher's shop	CHARCUTERIE
bewilderment	EGAREMENT	butler	SOMMELIER
bias	PARTI PRIS	butter	BEURRE
bill of exchange	LETTRE DE CHANGE	butterfly	PAPILLON
bitter-sweet	AIGRE-DOUX	buttocks	LE CUL
black beast	BETE NOIRE	button	BOUTON
blackmail	CHANTAGE	—hole	BOUTONNIERE
blandishments	AGREMENT(S)	by	PAR
blind alley	CUL-DE-SAC	—air	PAR AVION
blow	COUP	—all means	A TOUTE FORCE
blue		—force of arms	A MAIN ARMEE
—ribbon	CORDON BLEU	—halves	A DEMI, A MOITIE
—stocking	BASBLEU, FEMME SAVANTE	—mutual service	AU PAIR
bluish	BLEUATRE	—stealth	A LA DEROBEE
blunder	BEVUE, FAUX PAS	—the way	A PROPOS DE BOTTES
boarding-school	PENSIONNAT		EN PASSANT
boat	BATEAU	—way of ideal	PAR EXCELLENCE
bobbin lace	TORCHON(-LACE)	cab	FIACRE
boiled leather	CUIR-BOUILLI	cabaret performer	CHANSONNIER(E)
bond note	ASSIGNAT	cabbage	CHOU
bonfire	FEU DE JOIE	cabinet-maker	EBENISTE
bonnet	BONGRACE	cable-car	TELEFERIQUE
bookseller	LIBRAIRE	cafe	BISTRO
bookshop/book-trade	LIBRAIRIE	—with music	CAFE CHANTANT
bored	ENNUYE		CAFE CONCERT
boredom	ENNUI	cake	GATEAU
boring tool	AIGUILLE	calendar (Revolution)	
born	NE(E)	—January, rain	PLUVIOSE
both hands	A DEUX MAINS	—February, wind	VENTOSE
bottom of the matter	FIN MOT DE L'AFFAIRE	—March, seed	GERMINAL
bow	CONGE	—April, blossom	FLOREAL
box at theatre	LOGE	—May, pasture	PRAIRIAL
boxing with use of feet	SAVATE	—June, harvest	MESSIDOR
boyish	GAMIN(E)	—July, heat	THERMIDOR

—August, fruit	FRUCTIDOR
—September, vintage	VENDEMIAIRE
—October, fog	BRUMAIRE
—November, sleet	FRIMAIRE
—December, snow	NIVOSE
call for surrender	CHAMADE
calling	METIER
candour	FRANCHISE
cape	
—garment	MANTILLE
—headland	CAP, POINTE
capital	F, FONDS, PARIS
caprice	BOUTADE
captivated	EPRIS(E)
carat	CARAT, METRIQUE
card game	BACCARAT, BOUILLOTTE
	CHEMIN DE FER, OMBRE
carefully chosen	RECHERCHE
carriage	CARROSSE, FIACRE
	TENUE, VOITURE
—for one	DESOBLIGEANTE
—with facing seats	VIS-A-VIS
carried away	ENLEVE
case	ETUI
cask	TONNEAU
cassock	SOUTANE
castle	CHATEAU
—governor	CHATELAIN(E)
—in Spain	CHATEAUX EN ESPAGNE
casual combat	RENCONTRE
cats' concert	CHARIVARI
cattle	CHAROLLAIS, LIMOUSIN
	(see also separate entry)
cauliflower	CHOU-FLEUR
cause	RAISON
cavalier	CHEVALIER
cavalryman	CHASSEUR
ceiling	PLAFOND
censer	CASSOLETTE
challenger's loss at ombre	CODILLE
chambermaid	FILLE DE CHAMBRE
chance meeting	RENCONTRE
characteristic of the	
ideas at end of century	FIN DE SIECLE
charm carried for luck	PORTE-BONHEUR
charmingly ugly	BELLE LAIDE
	JOLIE LAIDE
charms	AGREMENT(S)
chattering	BAVARDAGE
cheap	A BON MARCHE
cheap(ly)	BON MARCHE
cheese	FROMAGE
	(see also separate entry)
—sauce	FONDUE
chestnut	MARRON
chewed	MACHE

chic	CHICHI
chicken	POULE(T)
chief	
—magistrate	AVOYER
—point of interest	CLOU
—prize	GRAND PRIX
child	ENFANT
—of	
his times	ENFANT DE SON SIECLE
the house	ENFANT DE LA MAISON
chin	MENTON
china	SEVRES
Chinese objects	CHINOISERIE
chocolate and cream cake	ECLAIR
chop	COTELETTE
choreographer	MAITRE DE BALLET
churchmen	GENS D'EGLISE
cinema enthusiast	CINEASTE
circus	CIRQUE
civil	
—officer	ADJOINT
—servant	FONCTIONNAIRE
claret glass	MOUSSELINE
classical age of France	GRAND SIECLE
clear soup	CONSOMME, JULIENNE
clearing up	ECLAIRCISSEMENT
cleric's coif	CALOTTE
cliff	ROCHER
cloak	MANTEAU
clog	SABOT
clog-wearer	SABOTIER
close-fitting coat	JUPON
closure	CLOTURE
clumsy(-iness)	GAUCHE(RIE)
coach	REPETITEUR
—driver	VOITURIER
coarseness	GROSSIERETIE
coast	COTE
coastal plain	LANDE
coffee	CAFE
—and rolls	PETIT DEJEUNER
—filtered	CAFE FILTRE
—house	CAFE
—with milk	CAFE AU LAIT
—without milk	CAFE NOIR
coin	
—unit	FRANC
—farthing (old)	LIARD
—halfpenny (old)	SOL
—5 centimes	SOU
—10 centimes	DECIME
—100 centimes	FRANC
—franc (old)	LIVRE
—20 sols	LIVRE
—5 francs	ECU, SCUTE
—20 franc piece	LOUIS(D'OR)

—20 francs (old)	NAPOLEON	—oiled paper envelope	EN PAPILLOTE
—old		cookery	CUISINE
copper coin	DENIER	—staff	BOUCHE
gold coin	ANGELOT, LOUIS(D'OR)	cooking utensils	BATTERIE DE CUISINE
silver coin	CARDECU(E)	—vessel	BAIN-MARIE
	DENIER, ECU, SCUTE	cool walk	FRESCADE
cold blood	SANG-FROID	coolness	APLOMB, FRAICHEUR
colleague	CONFRERE		SANG-FROID
collected tips	TRONC	coquetry	AGACERIE
collection of		corded silk fabric	GROS-GRAIN
—jokes	SOTTISIER	cordial relations	RAPPROCHEMENT
—songs	CHANSONNIER	corked	BOUCHE
collector of objets-d'art	GRAND AMATEUR	Corpus Christi	FETE-DIEU
collision	RENCONTRE	correct	COMME IL FAUT
colourless	FADE	cosmetics	MAQUILLAGE
come		council	CONSEIL
—in	ENTREZ	—of state	CONSEIL D'ETAT
—on	ALLONS	counterblow	CONTRECOUP
comet tail	CHEVELURE	country	PAYS
comic opera	OPERA BOUFFE	—house	BASTIDE, CHATEAU
committed to a point	ENGAGE	courtesan	LORETTE
commons	TIERS-ETAT	courtly love	AMOUR COURTOIS
communication trench	BOYAU	covered	
Communist	ROUGE	—entrance	PORTE COCHERE
company (business)	CIE, COMPAGNIE, SA	—walk	BERCEAU
competition	CONCOURS	—with crumbs or	
—based on		cheese	AU GRATIN
appearance	CONCOURS D'ELEGANCE	cradle	BERCEAU
complete change (of views)	VOLTE-FACE	—song	BERCEUSE
compromised	BRULE	cream	CREME
conciliator	PRUD'HOMME	—bun	CHOU
conclusive blow	COUP DE GRACE	creative force	ELAN VITAL
concoction of old ideas	RECHAUFFE	credulous person	GOBE-MOUCHES
concrete	BETON	crescent roll	CROISSANT
confectioner	CONFISEUR	crest of helmet	CIMIER
confectionery	CONFISERIE	crime of passion	CRIME PASSIONEL
confidential interview	TETE-A-TETE	criminal	APACHE
confidentially	ENTRE NOUS	—identification system	BERTILLONAGE
confused	DESORIENTE	—investigation	
confusion	EGAREMENT	department	SURETE
conscription	LEVEE EN MASSE	critical examination	CRITIQUE
contemptuously	DE HAUT EN BAS	crop-payment system	METAYAGE
contest	CONCOURS	cross-stitch	GROS-GRAIN
contradiction	DEMENTI	crow	CORBEAU
contribution to paper	FEUILLETON	cry from the heart	CRI DE COEUR
control by State	DIRIGISME	cunning	RUSE
controversial public		—against cunning	RUSE CONTRE RUSE
issue	CAUSE CELEBRE	cupboard	ARMOIRE
conventional		current affairs	ACTUALITES
—art	ART POMPIER	curtain	VITRAGE
—idea	IDEE RECUE	—raiser	LEVER DE RIDEAU
convict	FORCAT	curvet	COURBETTE
cook	CHEF (DE CUISINE)	custom-house	DOUANE
—shop	ROTISSERIE	customs officer	DOUANIER
cooked and served in		cutlet	COTELETTE
—brown sugar	BRULE	dainty (food)	FRIAND(E)

—served between courses	ENTREMETS
dais	HAUT PAS
daisy	MARGUERITE
damned soul	AME DAMNEE
dance	BOURREE, BRAWL, BRAN(S)LE
	BRANTLE, CAN-CAN
	CARMAGNOLE, CHACONNE
	CORANTO, COURANTE, GAVOTTE
—for two	PAS DE DEUX
—of death	DANSE MACABRE
—step	CHASSE-CROISE, CHASSEE
dandy	BEAU
dash	ELAN
daughter	FILLE
Dauphin	MONSEIGNEUR
day	JOUR
—dreamer	REVEUR, REVEUSE
—school	EXTERNAT
day's march	ETAPE
dazzling	FOUDROYANT
dead	MORT(E)
deadlock	IMPASSE
deal	DONNE
dealer in textiles	MERCIER
dear	CHER(E), CHOU,
death	MORT
debauchee	ROUE
decadent	FIN DE SIECLE
decanter	CARAFE
deception	RUSE
decision	PARTI
decorative trimming	PASSEMENT
decree	ARRET
deep red colour	SANG-DE-BOEUF
defence against cavalry	TROU-DE-LOUP
defensive	
—spike	CHEVAL DE FRISE
—stakes	TROUS-DE-LOUP
dejected	ABATTU, A LA MORT
deliberate	VOULU
delicate	FRIAND(E)
delicatessen	CHARCUTERIE
democrat	SANS-CULOTTE
denial	DEMENTI
department	
—administering monopoly	REGIE
—of	
crime detection	SURETE
Military Intelligence	DEUXIEME BUREAU
—officer	PREFET
depressed	ACCABLE
depression (emotion)	CAFARD
—about the state	
of the world	MAL DU SIECLE
deputy	COMMIS
descend rapidly	DEGRINGOLER

desk	BONHEUR DU JOUR
despatch	DEPECHE
desperate	ACHARNE
—course of action	PIS-ALLER
desperately	A CORPS PERDU
dessert	COUPE
developed	EVOLUE
diary	JOURNAL INTIME
different art	ART AUTRE
difficult	DIFFICILE
dike of piles	ESTACADE
diplomatic	DEMARCHE
—agent	CHARGE D'AFFAIRES
—Corps	CORPS DIPLOMATIQUE
—staff	CORPS DIPLOMATIQUE
disabled	HORS DE COMBAT
discomfort	MALAISE
dish	
—between main courses	ENTREE
—cloth	TORCHON
—from whipped cream	MOUSSE
—of	
fried food	FRITURE
the day	PLAT DU JOUR
	(see also cookery, menu)
disinfectant bleach	EAU DE JAVEL(LE)
dismal	MORNE
dismissal	CONGE
display of affection	MINAUDERIE
disposal of property of	
dead foreigner	AUBAINE
disposition	TALENT
distaste	DEGOUT
distinction	ECLAT
district recently included in city	FAUBOURG
ditty	CHANSONETTE
do-nothing	FAINEANT
dominant idea	CLOU
donkey	ANE
doorkeeper	HUISSIER
dormer-window	LUCARNE
dotted	CRIBLE
double meaning	DOUBLE ENTENDRE
	DOUBLE SENS
downwards	DE HAUT EN BAS
draught-horse	PERCHERON
drawing-room piece	MORCEAU DE SALON
drawing together	RAPPROCHEMENT
dream	REVE
dress	
—ball	BAL HABILLE
—maker	COUTURIER(E)
—making	COUTURE
dressing	
—case	NECESSAIRE
—gown	ROBE DE CHAMBRE

dried oranges	PETIT GRAIN
drop	GOUTTE
—by drop	GOUTTE-A-GOUTTE
drown	NOYER
drunkenness	IVRESSE
dry	BRUT, SEC
duck	CANARD
duckling	CANETON
due honour	BON ACCUEIL
duel	AFFAIRE D'HONNEUR
duenna	GOUVERNANTE
duke	DUC
dulled to pleasure	BLASE
dullness	FADEUR
dupe	BECASSE
duster	TORCHON
dynasty	BOURBON, CAPETIAN, VALOIS
early fruit	PRIMEUR
earnest man	HOMME SERIEUX
earth	TERRE
east	EST
easy	DEGAGE
eat	MANGER
eccentric person	MONSTRE SACRE
edible snail	ESCARGOT
educated savage	EVOLUE
educational quarter	
of Paris	LATIN QUARTER
	QUARTIER LATIN
eel	ANGUILLE
egg	OEUF
elder	AINE(E)
elegance	CHIC
elegant literature	BELLES-LETTRES
element	MILIEU
eleven	ONZE
Elysian Fields	CHAMPS-ELYSEES
embarrassing occurrence	CONTRETEMPS
embarrassment	GENE
—of	
choice	EMBARRAS DU CHOIX
wealth	EMBARRAS DE RICHESSES
emblem	FLEUR DE LIS
embroidered lace	FILET
embroidery	PETIT POINT
eminently	PAR EXCELLENCE
enamelled metalwork	CHAMPLEVER
encasement	EMBOITEMENT
encounter	RENCONTRE
end of	
—an era	FIN DE SIECLE
—the century	FIN DE SIECLE
endive	ESCAROLE
engaged person	FIANCE(E)
English Channel	LA MANCHE
enough	ASSEZ BIEN

entertain at a feast	FETE
enthusiasm	ENTRAINEMENT
entirely	TOUT (A FAIT)
entrance admitting carriages	PORTE-COCHERE
entry	ENTREE
environment	MILIEU
epic poem	CHANSON DE GESTE
epicure	BON VIVANT, BON VIVEUR
	FRIAND(E)
epilepsy	PETIT MAL
equal	PAREIL
equipment	MATERIEL
escapade	FREDAINE
establishment of ...	CHEZ
estuary	BOUCHE, EMBOUCHURE
estate	CHATEAU
evening party	SOIREE
event	DENOUEMENT
every	TOUT
—body	TOUT LE MONDE
—month	TOUS LES MOIS
exacting	EXIGEANT(E)
exaggerated	OUTRE
example	EXEMPLE
excellent cook(ing)	CORDON BLEU
excessive fondness	ENGOUEMENT
exchange	BOURSE
excluded from series	HORS SERIE
exotic	RECHERCHE
expected	EN L'AIR
experiment	COUP D'ESSAI
experimental balloon	BALLON D'ESSAI
explanation	ECLAIRCISSEMENT
	FIN MOT DE L'AFFAIRE
exposed to capture	EN PRISE
exposure	EXPOSE
extravagant admiration	FUREUR
face	FACADE, VISAGE
face-to-face	VIS-A-VIS
facing forward	EN FACE
faculty of knowing	SAVOIR-FAIRE
faded	PASSE(E)
fairy	FEE
—land	FEERIE
faker	TRUQUER
faking of works of art	TRUCAGE, TRUQUAGE
fall	CHUTE
false	
—modesty	MAUVAISE HONTE
—rumour	CANARD
—step	FAUX PAS
family	
—black (porcelain)	FAMILLE NOIRE
—consultation	CONSEIL DE FAMILLE
—green (porcelain)	FAMILLE VERTE
—pink (porcelain)	FAMILLE ROSE

—yellow (porcelain)	FAMILLE JAUNE	flaming torch	FLAMBEAU
famous		flash	BLUETTE
—make	GRANDE MARQUE	flask	CARAFE
—trial	CAUSE CELEBRE	flat	MAISONNETTE
fancy		—bastion	MOINEAU
—biscuit	PETIT FOUR	—cap	BERET
—cake	GATEAU	flatterer	PRONEUR
fantastic extremist	MERVEILLEUX	flayed	ECORCHE
farewell	ADIEU	fleece	TOISON
farmer who pays with crop	METAYEUR	Flemish nationalist	FLAMINGANT
fashionable	A LA MODE, CHIC	flighty	VOLAGE
—dressmaking	HAUTE COUTURE	floor	ETAGE
—society	BEAU MONDE	flower	FLEUR
father	PERE	fly-catcher	GOBE-MOUCHES
—in-law	BEAU PERE	folly	FOLIE
fat liver	FOIS GRAS	fool	BECASSE
favoured object	MAROTTE	foolish	ETOURDI(E)
favourite topic	CHEVAL DE BATAILLE	footpath	TROTTOIR
feast day	JOUR DE FETE	fop	PETIT MAITRE
feat of strength or skill	TOUR DE FORCE	for	POUR
feeler	BALLON D'ESSAI	—ever	A JAMAIS
fellow member	CONFRERE	—example	PAR EXEMPLE
fellowship	CAMARADERIE	—four hands	A QUATRE MAINS
female		—shame!	FI DONC
—attendant in regiment	VIVANDIERE	—want of better	FAUTE DE MIEUX
—dancer	DANSEUSE	forage	ETAPE
—friend	BELLE AMIE	forcemeat ball	QUENELLE
—singer	CHANTEUSE	Foreign Office	QUAI D'ORSAY
festival	FETE	foreigner	ETRANGER(E)
fickle	VOLAGE	foremast	MISAINE
film		forerunner	AVANT-COURRIER
—director	AUTEUR	foresail	MISAINE
—maker	CINEASTE	forest	BOIS, FORET
—style	NOUVELLE VAGUE	foretaste	AVANT-GOUT
finally	ENFIN	forfeiture	DECHEANCE
fine	AMENDE	forget	OUBLIER
—arts	BEAUX-ARTS	forlorn hope	ENFANTS PERDUS
—day	BEAU JOUR	former(ly)	CI-DEVANT
—deportment	BEL AIR	forward	EN AVANT
—literature	BELLES-LETTRES	foundation	FOND
—period	BELLE EPOQUE	—scholar	BOURSIER
—prospect	BELLE VUE	foundling	ENFANT TROUVE
finishing stroke	COUP DE GRACE	fountain	JET D'EAU
fipple-flute	FLUTE-A-BEC	fragment	MORCEAU
fire	FEU	frame	MONTURE
—works	FEUX D'ARTIFICE	frankness	FRANCHISE
first		free	
—attempt	COUP D'ESSAI	—thinker	ESPRIT FORT
—floor	BEL ETAGE	—verse	VERS LIBRE
—performance	PREMIERE	freedom of	
fish	POISSON	—access	ENTREE
—chowder	BOUILLABAISSE	—action	CARTE BLANCHE
fixed		freshness	FRAICHEUR
—idea	IDEE FIXE	friar	RELIGIEUX
—price	PRIX FIXE	fried	
—price meal	TABLE D'HOTE	—bread-slice	CROUTE

small piece	CROUTON
—lightly	SAUTE
—or toasted bread	CANAPE
friend	AMI(E)
—of the people	AMI DU PEUPLE
friendly agreement	ENTENTE(CORDIALE)
fringe of curls	FRISETTE
fritter	FRITURE
frogs' legs	CUISSES DE GRENOUILLES
frolicsome	ESPIEGLE
from	
—bad to worse	DE MAL EN PIS
—day to day	AU JOUR LE JOUR
—hand to mouth	AU JOUR LE JOUR
fulcrum	POINT D'APPUI
full dress	
—ladies' evening-dress	GRANDE TOILETTE
—military	GRANDE TENUE
fulled cloth	FOULE
fund	FONDS
—holder	RENTIER
fundamentally	A FOND
funeral procession	CORTEGE
furious	ACHARNE
furnishing material	MOQUETTE
fuss(y)	CHICHI
future	AVENIR
gait	ALLURE
gallant	CHEVALIER
gambling game	ROULETTE
game	JEU
—of bowls	BOULES, PETANQUE
garden	
—party	FETE CHAMPETRE
—path	ALLEE
garish	CRIANT
garlic	AIL
general	
—appearance	TOUT ENSEMBLE
—view	COUP D'OEIL
genius	BEL ESPRIT
gentleman	GENTILHOMME, M
gentlemen	MESSIEURS, MESSRS, MM
German	BOCHE
—beer	BOCK
gibe	BROCARD
giddy	VOLAGE
gift	CADEAU
gilded youth	JEUNESSE DOREE
girdle	CEINTURE
girl	FILLETTE, (JEUNE) FILLE
given	DONNE(E)
glance	OEILLADE
glass	
—dish	COUPE
—window	VITRAGE

glazed chestnuts	MARRONS GLACES
glimpse	APERCU
gloomy	MORNE
glory	GLOIRE
glued paper	PAPIER COLLE
God	DIEU
—and my right	DIEU ET MON DROIT
—with us	DIEU AVEC NOUS
godfather	COMPERE
gold	OR
golden fleece	TOISON D'OR
good	BEAU, BELLE, BON(NE)
—appearance	BONNE MINE
—bargain	BON MARCHE
—breeding	SAVOIR-VIVRE
—Christian	BON CHRETIEN
—comrade	BON CAMARADE
—day/morning	BONJOUR
—evening	BONSOIR
—faith	BONNE FOI
—friend	BON AMI
—grace	BONNE GRACE
—journey	BON VOYAGE
—luck	BONNE CHANCE
—man	HOMME DE BIEN
—nature	BONHOMIE
—reception	BON ACCEUIL
—society	BONNE COMPAGNIE
—taste	BON GOUT
—times	BEAU JOUR
goodbye	A BIENTOT, ADIEU
	AU REVOIR
good-for-nothing	VAURIEN
good-natured fellow	BON DIABLE
goose liver	FOIS GRAS
—paste	PATE DE FOIE GRAS
governess	GOUVERNANTE
	MADEMOISELLE
government	
—monopoly	REGIE
—securities	RENTE
gown	MANTEAU
gracious gesture	BEAU GESTE
grant	OCTROYER
gravy	JUS
great	GRAND(E)
—army	GRANDE ARMEE
—century	GRAND SIECLE
—luxury	GRAND LUXE
Greek	GREQUE
green earth	TERRE VERTE
grey gown	GRISETTE
grocer	EPICIER
gropingly	A TATONS
grossness	GROSSIERETE
ground	TERRE

group of	
—people	PARTI
—vineyards	CRU
guerrillero	FRANC-TIREUR
guild of clerks	BASOCHE
gulf	GOLFE
gully	COULOIR
hackney-coach	FIACRE
hairdresser	FRISEUR
hairpiece	CHIGNON
hake	COLIN
half	DEMI
—dead	A LA MORT
—dressed	DESHABILLE
—light	DEMI-JOUR
hall	SALLE
halting-place	ETAPE
ham	JAMBON
hand	MAIN
—kissing	BAISEMAIN
handkerchief	MOUCHOIR
handsome	BEAU
—man	BEAU GARCON
—medium	JUSTE MILIEU
—woman	BELLE
happy find	TROUVAILLE
hard crayon	CONTE
hardly perceptible quantity	SOUPCON
hash	HACHIS
hat	CHAPEAU
haughtiness	HAUTEUR
hauteur	MORGUE
having shirred effect	PLISSE
hazel-nut	NOISETTE
head	TETE
—of	
finger-ring	CHATON
hair	CHEVELURE
—waiter	MAITRE D'HOTEL
head-to-tail	TETE-BECHE
hearsay	ON-DI
heartbreak	CREVE-COEUR
heartfelt entreaty	CRI DE COEUR
heavenly voice	VOIX CELESTE
heedlessness	ETOURDERIE
height of fashion	BON TON
help!	AU SECOURS
helpless giggling	FOU RIRE
Her Majesty	SA MAJESTE, SM
herb mixture	FINES HERBES
here	ICI
here lies...	CI-GIT
high	HAUT(E)
—class	
cookery	HAUTE CUISINE
horsemanship	HAUTE ECOLE

prostitute	GRANDE COCOTTE
—fashion	HAUT TON
	HAUTE COUTURE
—reaches of politics	HAUTE POLITIQUE
—relief	HAUT RELIEF
—society	BEAU MONDE
	GRAND MONDE, HAUT MONDE
—spirits	JOIE DE VIVRE
highest military officer	MARECHAL
highness	ALTESSE
hill	COLLINE
His Majesty	SA MAJESTE, SM
hitch	CONTRETEMPS
holder for crayon/pencil	PORTE-CRAYON
holiday	FETE
holy water font	BENITIER
homesickness	MAL DU PAYS
honest people	GENS DE BIEN
honour with festivities	FETE
hopper	TREMIE
horse	CHEVAL
—race	GRAND PRIX DE PARIS
horse's	
—actions	MANEGE
—attempt to throw rider	ESTRAPADE
horseman in armour	GENDARME
hospital	HOTEL-DIEU
host's table	TABLE-D'HOTE
hot lava gas	NUEE ARDENTE
hotel-keeper	HOTELIER
house	MAISON
—steward	MAITRE D'HOTEL
household	MENAGE
—of three	MENAGE A TROIS
housekeeper	GOUVERNANTE
hunter	CHASSEUR
husband	MARI
I	JE
—adjust (chess)	J'ADOUBE
—don't know what	JE NE SAIS QUOI
ice cream	MOUSSE
—dessert	BOMBE
iced	FRAPPE(E)
idea	IDEE
identity card	CARTE-DE-VISITE
idling	FLANERIE
if you please	S'IL VOUS PLAIT
ill	MALADE
illustration inset	
separately into a book	HORS TEXTE
immediately	TOUT DE SUITE
immortal	IMMORTEL(LE)
impetuosity	ELAN
impish	GAMIN(E)
impishness	GAMINERIE
impulsive act	ACTE GRATUIT

in	
—a body	EN MASSE
—abundance	A GOGO
—all seriousness	AU GRAND SERIEUX
	TRES AU SERIEUX
—any case	EN TOUT CAS
—bachelor style	EN GARCON
—broad daylight	EN PLEIN JOUR
—cavalier manner	EN CAVALIER
—clear	EN CLAIR
—close touch	EN RAPPORT
—connected series	EN SUITE
—direct relation	EN RAPPORT
—due order	EN REGLE
—emulation	A L'ENVIE
—effect	EN EFFET
—festivity	EN FETE
—flattering style	EN BEAUTE
—front	EN FACE
—full court	IN BANCO
dress	EN GRANDE TENUE
—good form	EN BON POINT
—great demand	RECHERCHE
—hand	A LA MAIN
—his mother's womb	
	DANS LE VENTRE DE SA MERE
—line	EN QUEUE
—male dress (woman)	EN TRAVESTI
—my opinion	A MON AVIS
—natural state	AU NATUREL
—outlawry	HORS LA LOI
—passing	EN PASSANT
—princely style	EN PRINCE
—principle	EN PRINCIPE
—progress	EN TRAIN
—relation to	VIS-A-VIS
—requital	EN REVANCHE
—retirement	EN RETRAITE
—return	EN REVANCHE
—shelter	A L'ABRI
—slippers	EN PANTOUFLES
—spite of (everything)	MALGRE(TOUT)
—succession	EN SUITE
—sympathy	EN RAPPORT
—the	
air	EN L'AIR
country	A LA CAMPAGNE
meantime	EN ATTENDANT
open air	A LA BELLE ETOILE
	EN PLEIN AIR
rear	EN ARRIERE
way	DE TROP
—town	EN VILLE
—truth	EN VERITE
—tune	D'ACCORD
incendiary	PETROLEUR

income from government	
securities	RENTE
indefinable something	JE NE SAIS QUOI
indelicate	RISQUE
infatuated	ENTETE(E)
infatuation	ENGOUEMENT
informal conference	POURPARLER
injured majesty	LESE-MAJESTE
inlay	MARQUETER
inn	AUBERGE
inner fortified retreat	REDUIT
innkeeper	AUBERGISTE
insanity	FOLIE
insectivorous plant	GOBE-MOUCHES
insipid	FADE
instrument of capital punishment	GUILLOTINE
insurgent Huguenot	CAMISARD
intense attachment	GRANDE PASSION
interest	CHALOIR
international	
—law	DROIT DES GENS
—motor race	GRAND PRIX
—pass for car	TRIPTYQUE
intimate conversation	TETE-A-TETE
irresistible beauty	BEAUTE DU DIABLE
irridescence	REFLET
irridescent	CHATOYANT
is it not so?	N'EST-CE PAS
island	I(S)LE
issue	DENOUEMENT
item	PIECE
jacket	CARMAGNOLE
jam	CONFITURE
janitor	CONCIERGE
jargon	BARAGOUIN
jellied sauce	CHAUD-FROID
jerking of reins	EBRILLADE
jet of water	JET D'EAU
jewel	BIJOU
—on forehead	FERRONNIERE
jewelled pendant	LAVALLIERE
jewellery	BIJOUTERIE
—setting	PAVE
joiner	MENUISIER
joint	PIECE DE RESISTANCE
—stock company	COMPAGNIE ANONYME
	SOCIETE ANONYM
joker	FARCEUR
joust	PAS D'ARMES
jovial companion	BON VIVANT, BON VIVEUR
joy of living	JOIE DE VIVRE
judge's bench	BANC
jugglery	LEGER DE MAIN
juggling	ESCAMOTAGE
junior	FILS
just mean	JUSTE MILIEU

juvenile lead	JEUNE PREMIER	leading	
keeping holiday	EN FETE	—actress, dancer etc	PREMIERE
key		—film or theatre star	GRANDE VEDETTE
—novel	ROMAN A CLEF	learned woman	BAS BLEU
—chain	CHATELAINE		FEMME SAVANTE
kidnapped	ENLEVE	leather	CUIR
kind (type)	SORTE	leave to depart	CONGE
king	ROI, SM	lecturer	CONFERENCIER
—without power	ROI FAINEANT	left	GAUCHE
king's		leg of mutton	GIGOT
—eldest		legislative bill	PROJET DE LOI
son	DAUPHIN	lending	
son's wife	DAUPHINE	—against landed property	CREDIT FONCIER
—throne	LIT DE JUSTICE	—moveable property	CREDIT MOBILIER
kitchen	CUISINE	Lent	CAREME
knave	FRIPON	let	
knavery	FRIPONNERIE	—do	LAISSER-FAIRE, LAISSEZ-FAIRE
knick-knack	BIBELOT	—go	LAISSER-ALLER, LAISSEZ-ALLER
knight	CHEVALIER	—pass	LAISSEZ-PASSER
knob on top of deer's horn	CROCHE	—us go	ALLONS, EN ROUTE
know	CONNAITRE	letter	LETTRE
knowledge of		—of marque	LETTRE DE MARQUE
—polite usage	SAVOIR-VIVRE	—under royal signet	LETTRE DE CACHET
—what to do	SAVOIR FAIRE	liaison	AFFAIRE
lace	ALENCON, CLUNY	light	
	COLBERTINE, VALENCIENNES	—infantryman	CHASSEUR
—frill	JABOT	—fitting	LUMINAIRE
lack of taste	MAUVAIS GOUT	—minded	ETOURDI(E)
lady	DAME	—o'-love	COCOTTE
lady's		—verse	VERS DE SOCIETE
—maid	FEMME DE CHAMBRE	lightly armed soldier	VOLTIGEUR
—room	BOUDOIR	lightning	FOUDRE
lagoon	ETANG	like a	
lake	ETANG, LAC	—bachelor	EN GARCON
lamb	AGNEAU	—great lord	EN GRAND SEIGNEUR
lampstand	TORCHERE	—tail	EN QUEUE
land	TERRE	limited	BORNE
—jointly shared	METAIRIE	—liability	
landed property	FONDS	company	SA, SOCIETE ANONYME
landslide	EBOULEMENT	line	LIGNE
langour	ENNUI	—of	
language		sentries	CORDON SANITAIRE
—north	LANGUE D'OIL	support	POINT D'APPUI
—south	LANGUE D'OC	linen	LINGE
last	DERNIER	liqueur after coffee	POUSSE-CAFE
—resort	DERNIER RESSORT	literally	AU PIED DE LA LETTRE
—shift	PIS ALLER	little	
—word	DERNIER CRI	—box	BIJOU
latest fashion	DERNIER CRI	—song	CHANSONETTE
Latin quarter	QUARTIER LATIN	live	VIVRE
laundress	BLANCHISSEUSE	liveliness	ENTRAIN
lawyer	AVOCAT, AVOUE	lively	VIF, VIVE
lawyers	GENS DE LOI	—dance	GIGUE
layered cake	MILLE FEUILLES	liver paste	PATE DE FOIS GRAS
leader	CHEF	liveried attendant	CHASSEUR
—of Republic	CONSUL	living picture	TABLEAU VIVANT

loaf	BAGUETTE, FICELLE	manger	CRECHE
lobster	LANGOUSTE	manner of dress	TENUE
local (bar)	BISTRO	mannered	RECHERCHE
logically set out	RAISONNE	many thanks	GRAND MERCI
long live	VIVE	march	EN ROUTE
look sidelong	LORGNER	marchioness	MARQUISE
looked upon with distaste	MAL VU	marginal drawing	REMARQUE
looped yarn	BOUCLE	mark	MARQUE
loose		market-woman	DAME DE LA HALLE
—overcoat	PALETOT	marmoset	OUISTITI
—woman	COCOTTE	marriageable person	PARTI
loosely-tied bow	LAVALLIERE	marsh	MARAIS
lost		marshal	NEY
—children	ENFANTS PERDUS	marvellous	MERVEILLEUX
—one's bearings	DESORIENTE	masked ball	BAL MASQUE
—soul	AME PERDUE	masonry rubble	MOELLON
—wax	CIRE PERDUE	massive helmet	HEAUME
louvred screen	BRISE-SOLEIL	master	MAITRE
love	AMOUR	—key	PASSE-PARTOUT
—affair	AFFAIRE(D'AMOUR)	—of ceremonies	COMPERE
	AFFAIRE DE COEUR	—piece	CHEF D'OEUVRE
—at first sight	COUP DE FOUDRE	—stroke	COUP DE MAITRE
—letter	BILLET DOUX	material	MATERIEL
lover	BEAU, BELLE	matter	CHALOIR
	BON AMI	mattress	MATELAS
low	BAS	mayor	MAIRE
—minded person	AME DE BOUE	me	MOI
—vault	CUL-DE-FOUR	meal at a fixed price	TABLE D'HOTE
lower middle class	PETIT(E) BOURGEOIS(IE)	mean	MESQUIN(E)
loyalty to group	ESPRIT DE CORPS	meanness	MESQUINERIE
lunch	DEJEUNER	measure	DEMARCHE
luxurious	DE LUXE	—of watch movement	LIGNE
machine-gun	MITRAILLEUSE	measures	
madness	FOLIE	—small	MILLIMETRE
magistrate	BAILLI	—1/3 inch	CENTIMETRE
maid	BONNE	—3½ inches	DECIMETRE
—of honour	FILLE D'HONNEUR	—39 inches	METRE
	DAME D'HONNEUR	—33 feet	DECAMETRE
mail	POSTE	—2 metres	TOISE
maintain	MAINTENIR	—5/8 mile	KILOMETRE
major-domo	MAITRE D'HOTEL	—2.8 miles	LEAGUE
makeshift	PIS ALLER	—11 sq. ft.	CENTIARE
main fact	DONNEE	—12 sq. yds	DECIARE
male servant	GARCON	—120 sq. yds	ARE
malicious	NARQUOIS	—1200 sq. yds	DECARE
man	HOMME, M, MONSIEUR	—1-1½ acres (old)	ARPENT
—about town	BON VIVEUR	—2½ acres	HECTARE
—at-arms	GENDARME	—cubic metre	STERE
—in the street	HOMME MOYEN SENSUEL	—1/100 litre	CENTILITRE
—of		—1/10 litre	DECILITRE
fashion	HOMME DU MONDE	—1½ pints	LITRE
letters	HOMME DE LETTRES	—old	
wit	HOMME D'ESPRIT	capacity	MUID
worth	HOMME DE BIEN	pint	CHOPIN
management	MANEGE	—heat	THERMIE
manager of hotel	MAITRE D'HOTEL	—pressure	CENTIBAR

medal	
—civil	LEGION D'HONNEUR
—military	CROIX DE GUERRE
mediaeval	
—bishop's deputy	VIDAME
—poet	TROUVERE
medium	MILIEU
medley	MACEDOINE, MELANGE
melt	FONDRE
melted	FONDU(E)
member of	
—Académie	IMMORTEL
—literary brotherhood	FELIBRE
—majority	MAJORITAIRE
memorandum	BORDEREAU, CAHIER
men	MESSIEURS, MM
—of letters	GENS DE LETTRES
mental reservation	ARRIERE-PENSEE
menu	CARTE (DU JOUR)
merchant	MARCHAND
mere form of words	FACON DE PARLER
message	DEPECHE
metallic lustre	REFLET
method of voting	SCRUTIN-DE-LISTE
metrical tale(s)	FABLIAU(X)
middle	MILIEU
—class	BOURGEOISIE
mien	ALLURE
mild	DOUX, DOUCE
military	
—courier	ESTAFETTE
—man	HOMME D'EPEE
—men	GENS DE GUERRE
—policeman	GENDARME
—stratagem	RUSE DE GUERRE
mill	MOULIN
minor noble	VIDAME
mischievous goblin	ESPRIT FOLLET
misery	MISERE
Miss	MLLE, MADEMOISELLE
mistake	FAUX PAS
mister	MONSIEUR
mistress	BELLE AMIE, MAITRESSE
—of ceremonies	COMMERE
misunderstanding	MALENTENDU
mitten	MOUFFLE
mix	MELER
mixed face	BOIS-BRULE
mixture	MELANGE
—fruit, etc	MACEDOINE
mob	CANAILLE
mocking	NARQUOIS
mode of curling	FRISURE
model	EXEMPLE
—of sculpture	MAQUETTE
moderate Republican	GIRONDIN

moistened	MOUILLE
money	FONDS
—changing office	BUREAU DE CHANGE
monk	RELIGIEUX
monomania	IDEE FIXE
months	(see calendar above)
morale	ESPRIT DE CORPS
morsel	MORCEAU
mother	MERE
—in-law	BELLE-MERE
motionless scene by	
living persons	TABLEAU VIVANT
mottled	CHINE
mountebank	BALADIN(E), JONGLEUR
mountain	MONT
—range	CHAINE
mouth	BOUCHE
mounting	MONTURE
mournful	FUNEBRE
Mrs	MADAME
mule litter	CACOLET
museum	MUSEE
mushroom	CHAMPIGNON
musketeer	MOUSQUETAIRE
muslin	MOUSSELINE
mussels	MOULES
muzzle	MUSEROLLE
my	
—goodness!	MA FOI
—lord	MONSEIGNEUR
nail	CLOU
naive young woman	INGENUE
name	NOM
named	DIT
Napoleon's army	GRANDE ARMEE
narrow	
—braid	SOUTACHE
—entrance	GOULET
—minded	BORNE
natural	NAIF, NAIVE
naturalistic painting	BELLE PEINTURE
nave	NEF
near	PRES
nearly	A PEU PRES
neck bare	DECOLLETE
necklace of diamonds etc	RIVIERE
need	BESOIN
neglected	A L'ABANDON, NEGLIGE
neighbourhood	VOISINAGE
network	RESEAU
neutral buffer	
between states	CORDON SANITAIRE
nevertheless	MALGRE TOUT, QUAND MEME
new	NOUVEAU, NOUVELLE
—art	ART NOUVEAU
—Year's gift	ETRENNE(S)

newly rich	NOUVEAU RICHE
next friend	PROCHAIN AMI
nightclub	BOITE DE NUIT
nightmare	CAUCHEMAR
no	NON
—more bets	RIEN NE VA PLUS
—performance	RELACHE
nobility	NOBLESSE
noble	GRAND SEIGNEUR, VIDAME
—man	GENTILHOMME
non-interference	LAISSER-FAIRE
	LAISSEZ-FAIRE
nose	NEZ
nostalgia	MAL DU PAYS
not	
—at home	EN VILLE
—in	
cipher	EN CLAIR
competition	HORS-CONCOURS
notary	GREFFIER
notice	AFFICHE, AVIS(AU LECTEUR)
notoriety	ESCLANDRE, RECLAME
novel	
—about successive	
generations	ROMAN-FLEUVE
—with	
a message	ROMAN A THESE
disguised names	ROMAN A CLEF
novelty	PRIMEUR
nozzle	AJUTAGE
number	NOMBRE
—of book published in parts	LIVRAISON
nun	RELIGIEUSE
nursemaid	BONNE
nut	NOIX
object	OBJET
obligations of rank	NOBLESSE OBLIGE
obsession	IDEE FIXE
occasional verse	VERS D'OCCASION
of course	BIEN ENTENDU
off the peg	PRET-A-PORTER
officer in attendance	AIDE DE CAMP
official	FONCTIONNAIRE
offprint	TIRAGE A PART
often repeated	SANS NOMBRE
ogle	LORGNER
oil distilled from orange	PETIT GRAIN
old	
—democrat	MONTAGNARD
—game or joke	VIEUX JEU
—quilted doublet	POURPOINT
—stuff	DEJA VU
—supreme court	PARLEMENT
—fashioned	ARRIERE
nobility	ANCIENNE NOBLESSE
order	ANCIEN REGIME

on	SUR
—a	
level with	A L'HAUTEUR DE
pillion	EN CROUPE
skewer	EN BROCHETTE
—account	A COMPTE
—condition	BIEN ENTENDU
—every occasion	A TOUT PROPOS
—half-pay	EN RETRAITE
—my faith	MA FOI
—purpose	A DESSAIN
—the	
best of terms	AU MIEUX
carpet	SUR LE TAPIS
contrary	AU CONTRAIRE
crupper	EN CROUPE
first floor	AU PREMIER
road	EN ROUTE
second floor	AU SECOND
spot	SUR PLACE
one	UN(E)
—against whose decision	
there is no appeal	SANS-APPEL
—facing or opposite	VIS-A-VIS
—who	
avoids military service	EMBUSQUE
exercises power in	
the background	EMINENCE GRISE
lives on investment income	RENTIER
onion	OIGNON
open air	PLEIN AIR
opera with some spoken	
dialogue	OPERA COMIQUE
opinion-sounding	BALLON D'ESSAI
opinionative	ENTETE(E)
opposite	EN FACE
—number	VIS-A-VIS
orange colour	NACARAT
order	ORDONNER
ordinary	
—man	HOMME MOYEN SENSUEL
—rhyme	RIME SUFFISANTE
organ	ORGUE
ornamental	
—candlestick	TORCHERE
—design in book	CUL-DE-LAMPE
—stand	ETAGERE
orthodox	BIEN PENSANT
Our Lady	NOTRE DAME
out of	HORS
—action	HORS DE COMBAT
—date	PASSE(E)
—fashion	DEMODE
—season	HORS SAISON
outcast	CAGOT
outcome	DENOUEMENT

outlawed	HORS-LA-LOI	rank	GENS DE CONDITION
outline	CROQUIS, ESQUISSE	pepper	POIVRE
outside	HORS	perfect	PARFAIT
—shutter	JALOUSIE	perfectly	A MERVEILLE
outstanding feat	TOUR DE FORCE	performers of mystery plays	BASOCHE
over	SUR	perfume	MILLEFLEURS, PARFUM
overpowering attack	COUP DE MAIN	period of	
overthrow	BOULEVERSEMENT	—1795-99	DIRECTOIRE
—of government	COUP D'ETAT	—1880-1900	FIN DE SIECLE
ox		—1900-1914	BELLE EPOQUE
—blood	SANG-DE-BOEUF	—Louis XIV-XVI	HAUTE EPOQUE
—eye	OEIL-DE-BOEUF	permission to	
oysters	HUITRES	—elect	CONGE D'ELIRE
pain	MAL	—trade after quarantine	PRATIQUE
paint	PEINDRE	persecution of Prostestants	DRAGONNADE
painting		person who is deranged	DETRAQUE
—depicting figures in		pert girl	GAMINE
a pastoral setting	FETE GALANTE	pet	CHOU
—in dots	POINTILLISME	petrol	ESSENCE
pancake	CREPE	pewter	ETAIN
paper	PAPIER	pictorial representation	MISE-EN-SCENE
—trade	PAPETERIE	picture	TABLEAU
Parisian working-girl	MIDINETTE		VRAISEMBLANCE
parasol	EN TOUT CAS	piece of	
part of page used for serial story	FEUILLETON	—foil	PAILLON
particular district in town	QUARTIER	—music	MORCEAU
particularly choice	RECHERCHE	pigeon's wings	AILES DE PIGEON
parting	BOUDERIE	pithy saying	BON MOT
partition	CLOISON	placard	AFFICHE
pass		place	
—between hills	COL	—from which one cannot	
—document	LAISSEZ-PASSER	go forward	IMPASSE
passage	COULOIR	—setting	COUVERT
past one's best	PASSE(E)	—your bets!	FAITES VOS JEUX
paste	PATE	plain cooking	AU NATUREL
pastry		plainly	TOUT COURT
—case	CROUSTADE	play on words	JEU DE MOTS
—shop	PATISSERIE	pleasant	
patent	BREVET D'INVENTION	—looks	BONNE MINE
patented	BREVETE	—taste	BONNE BOUCHE
patron saint	DENIS	plebiscite	APPEL AU PEUPLE
patterned with dots	POINTILLE	plume	AIGRETTE
paved footway	TROTTOIR	pocket-book	PORTE-MONNAIE
pavement	PAVE	point of support	POINT D'APPUI
peak	AIGUILLE, CORNE	poison-pen letter writer	CORBEAU
	PIC, PUY, SOMMET	police	
pear	BLANQUET, POIRE	—man	FLIC
peas	POIS	—spy	MOUCHARD
peasant dance	BOURREE	policy reversal	VOLTE FACE
pen	PLUME	political moderate	POLITIQUE
penalty	AMENDE	popularisation of	
peninsula	PRESQU'ILE	scholarly subjects	HAUTE VULGARISATION
people	GENS	poppy	COQUELICOT
—of		popular uprising	EMEUTE
fashion	GENS DU MONDE	porcelain	SEVRES
humble condition	GENS DE PEU	pork	PORC

porter	CONCIERGE
potato	POMME DE TERRE
poultry	VOLAILLE
pout	MOUE
powdered side-curls	AILES DE PIGEON
power in the background	EMINENCE GRISE
practice of obtaining publicity	RECLAME
prank	FREDAINE
prattle	BAVARDAGE
praying-desk	PRIE-DIEU
precinct	BANLIEUE
precious	CHICHI
precocious	
—boy	GAMIN
—child	ENFANT TERRIBLE
preconceived opinion	PARTI PRIS
preface	AVANT PROPOS
pregnant	ENCEINTE
prejudice	PARTI PRIS
present	CADEAU
pretended	SOI-DISANT
pretentious	CHICHI
pretty	JOLI(E)
—well	ASSEZ BIEN
—woman	BEAUX YEUX
priest	ABBE, CURE, PERE
primogeniture	MAJORAT
prisoner	DETENU
private	
—meeting	TETE-A-TETE
—soldier	PIOUPIOU, POILU
—staircase	ESCALIER DEROBE
—talk	TETE-A-TETE
procession	CORTEGE
procurator	PROCUREUR
profession	METIER
professional male partner	GIGOLO
profligate	ROUE
prolixity	LONGUEUR
prop	POINT D'APPUI
proper	COMME IL FAUT
propriety	BIENSEANCE
prostitute	FILLE DE JOIE
protected	A COUVERT
Protestant	HUGUENOT
pseudonym	NOM DE GUERRE
public	
—confession	AMENDE HONORABLE
—dancer	BALADIN(E)
—executioner	MONSIEUR DE PARIS
—house	BISTRO
—nursery	CRECHE
—prosecutor	PROCUREUR GENERAL
—room off lobby	FOYER
publicity	RECLAME
puffed out	BOUFFANT

pulped and sieved food	PUREE
pun	JEU DE MOTS
punctured like a sieve	CRIBLE
pupil (school)	ELEVE
pure	PUR
—blood	PUR SANG
purpose of existence	RAISON D'ETRE
purr	CALEMBOUR
purse	PORTE-MONNAIE
queen	REINE, SA MAJESTE, SM
quick return	A LA VOLEE
quick(ly)	VITE
quickstep	PAS REDOUBLE
quite	TOUT
—at home	ENFANT DE LA MAISON
—brief(ly)	TOUT COURT
—the contrary	TOUT AU CONTRAIRE
rabbit	LAPIN
rabble	CANAILLE
race	LE MANS (24 HEURES)
ragout	BLANQUETTE
railway	CHEMIN DE FER, METRO
—station	GARE
rainbow	ARC EN CIEL
raise	LEVER
raised	LEVE(E)
—in relief	REPOUSSE
rake	ROUE
rammed earth or clay	PISE
rank	ETAT
—imposes obligations	NOBLESSE OBLIGE
rare	RECHERCHE
rations	ETAPE
raven	CORBEAU
ravishingly	A RAVIR
raw	BRUT
—sugar	CASSONADE
ready	A LA MAIN
—money	ARGENT COMPTANT
—to wear	PRET-A-PORTER
really	VRAIMENT
rear	ARRIERE
—part of motor car	TONNEAU
reason	RAISON
—for existence	RAISON D'ETRE
rebellious youth	BLOUSON NOIR
recommended dish of day	PLAT DU JOUR
recurring theme in music	IDEE FIXE
red tape	CHICHI
referring	RENVOI, RENVOY
refugee	EMIGRE(E)
refusal	NON
regimen	REGIME
registrar	GREFFIER
rehashed food	RECHAUFFE
relaxation	DELASSEMENT, RELACHE

—of strained relations	DETENTE
relegation	RENVOI, RENVOY
reluctantly	A CONTRECOEUR
reminder	AIDE-MEMOIRE
remove	OTER
renewal of good relations	RAPPROCHEMENT
reply	REPONDEZ
report	COMPTE RENDU, CAHIER
reproach	CRI DE COEUR
Republic	REPUBLIQUE FRANCAISE
republican	SANS-CULOTTE
reputed	DIT
required by etiquette or fashion	DE RIGUEUR
resident's permit	PERMIS DE SEJOUR
respectable people	GENS DE BIEN
rest	REPOS
restaurant	BRASSERIE
reticent	BOUTONNE
reversal of policy	VOLTE-FACE
review	CRITIQUE
revolutionary	SANS-CULOTTE
—calendar	(see calendar above)
—fighters	NATIONAL GUARD
—hymn	MARSEILLAISE
—song	CARMAGNOLE
rhymed words	BOUTS RIMES
rice	RIZ
rich	
—rhyme	RIME RICHE
—soup	BISQUE
right	DROIT
—of superior	DROIT DE SEIGNEUR
—thinking	BIEN PENSANT
—to work	DROIT AU TRAVAIL
—word	MOT JUSTE
river	FLEUVE, RIVIERE
rivers	(see separate entry)
road	CHEMIN
—along cliff face	CORNICHE
—side cafe	BUVETTE
rock	ROCHE(R)
—angle	DIEDRE
—peak	AIGUILLE
—tripe	TRIPE DE ROCHE
rocky edge	ARETE
roguish	ESPIEGLE
roguishly	EN BADINANT
roll (bread)	BRIOCHE, CROISSANT
rope	
—for gun-carriage	PROLONGE
—ladder	ETRIER
—soled shoe	ESPADRILLE
rose-coloured	COULEUR DE ROSE
rough	
—draft	EBAUCHE
—music	CHARIVARI

—paper for painting	PAPIER TORCHON
—sketch	CROQUIS
royal warrant	LETTRE DE CACHET
rudeness	GROSSIERETE
ruin	BOULEVERSEMENT
rumour	ON-DIT
running	COURANT
rural festival	FETE CHAMPETRE
sacred monster	MONSTRE SACRE
sailor	MATELOT
Saint's day	(JOUR DE) FETE
salmon	SAUMON
salt	SEL
sandbank	BANC
sandy heath	LANDE
sauce	HOLLANDAISE
saucy	RISQUE
saunterer	FLANEUR
savouries before meal	HORS D'OEUVRES
say true/truth	VOIR DIRE
scamp	FRIPON
scatterbrain	TETE FOLLE
scent	
—bottle	FLACON
—of game when high	FUMET
school	ECOLE, LYCEE
scored against	TOUCHE
scraper	GRATTOIR, RACLOIR
scuffle	BAGARRE
sea	MER
—man	MATELOT
—sickness	MAL DE MER
seaport without duties	ENTREPOT
seat of member of French Academy	FAUTEUIL
second	SECONDE
secondary school	LYCEE
see	VOIR
—you again soon	A BIENTOT
seize	GRIPPER
select group	CORPS D'ELITE
self	
—criticism	AUTO-CRITIQUE
—esteem	AMOUR PROPRE
—possession	APLOMB, SANG-FROID
—seeker	ARRIVISTE
—styled	SOI-DISANT
sending back	RENVOI, RENVOY
senior	AINE(E)
sensation of having seen something before	DEJA VU
serious	
—love affair	GRANDE PASSION
—man	HOMME SERIEUX
seriously	AU SERIEUX
servant	BONNE, VALET
served with flaming liquor	FLAMBE(E)

set of ornaments	PARURE	—cafe	ESTAMINET
setting	MILIEU, MONTURE	—country house	COTTAGE ORNE
settled matter	CHOSE JUGEE	—dish	COCOTTE
shady	LOUCHE	—house	MAISON(NETTE)
shaft		—opening in wall etc	GUICHET
—in glacier	MOULIN	—pie	BOUCHE
—of a column	TIGE	—shot	MITRAILLE
sharp-shooter	TIRAILLEUR	smart	CHIC
sheath	ETUI	smitten	EPRIS(E)
sheep	MOUTON	smooth	
shirker	EMBUSQUE	—sauce	VELOUTE
shock troops	ENFANTS PERDUS	—surfaced woollen	FOULE
shooting contest	TIR	snail	ESCARGOT
shop	BOUTIQUE	sniper	FRANC-TIREUR
—keeper	BOURGEOIS	so	
short		—called	SOI-DISANT
—and stiff (hair)	EN BROSSE	—much	TANT
—literary composition	MORCEAU	the	
—story	CONTE, NOUVELLE	—better	TANT MIEUX
—sword	ESTOC	—worse	TANT PIS
showy splendour	ECLAT	society	SOCIETE
Shrove Tuesday	MARDI GRAS	sofa for two, facing	TETE-A-TETE
shudder	FRISSON	soft	
sick	MALADE	—artificial fabric	SURAH
sickness	MAL, MALAISE	—pear	BEURRE
silk	SOIE	—rosette	CHOU
silkworm disease	PEBRINE	soldier	POILU
silly saying	FADAISE	sombre	MORNE
simply	TOUT COURT	something	
singed	FLAMBE(E)	—composed for	
sir	MONSIEUR	a special occasion	PIECE D'OCCASION
siren	FEMME FATALE	—disagreeable	DESAGREMENT
sister	SOEUR	—found	OBJET TROUVE
sketch	ESQUISSE	—that deceives the eye	TROMPE L'OEIL
ski trail	PISTE	son	FILS
skirmish	ESCARMOUCHE	song	CHANSON
skirmisher	TIRAILLEUR, VOLTIGEUR	soul	AME
skull-cap	CALOTTE	sound and light	SON ET LUMIERE
skylight	ABAT-JOUR	sounding-board	ABAT-VOIX
slacker	EMBUSQUE	soup	
slang	ARGOT	—bowl	ECUELLE
sleeping		—without solid pieces	PUREE
—berth on train	COUCHETTE	south of France	MIDI
—car	WAGON-LIT	spade	PALETTE
sleeve	MANCHE	spangle	PAILLETTE
—less jacket	JUPON	spank	BLUETTE
sleight-of-hand	LEGER DE MAIN	special passport	LAISSEZ-PASSER
slice(s) of		speculator	BOURSIER
—bread and butter	TARTINE(S)	spire	FLECHE
—veal, larded	FRICANDEAU(X)	spirit	ENTRAIN, ESPRIT
slope	COTE(AU)	spit	ROTISSERIE
small	PETIT(E)	splendid edition	EDITION DE LUXE
—and		spoilt child	ENFANT GATE(E)
cosy	INTIME	sponge cake	BRIOCHE
dainty	MIGNON(NE)	spray of jewels	AIGRETTE
elegant	BIJOU	spring	PRINTEMPS

squinting	LOUCHE	subdued light	DEMI-JOUR
S-shaped couch	VIS-A-VIS	subject	
stable	ECURIE	—lacking novelty	VIEUX JEU
staff of army, etc	ETAT-MAJOR	—of talk	SUR LE TAPIS
stag's trail	ABATURE	subscription	ABONNEMENT
stage	ETAPE	substantial course	PIECE DE RESISTANCE
—scene	MISE-EN-SCENE	suburb	BANLIEUE
stage-coach	DILIGENCE	—beyond walls	FAUBOURG
stained glass	VITRAIL	subversive stroke	COUP D'ETAT
staircase	ESCALIER	subway	METRO
star	ETOILE	success	SUCCES
state	ETAT	—of approval	SUCCES D'ESTIME
—approval	AGREMENT	—with wild enthusiasm	SUCCES FOU
—pawnshop	MONT-DE-PIETE	successful	
—prison	BASTILLE	—candidate	AGREGE
statesman	HOMME D'ETAT	—stroke	GRAND COUP
stationery	PAPETERIE	sudden	
steak	BIFTEK	—and overwhelming	FOUDROYANT
—cut from ribs	ENTRECOTE	—change (of views)	VOLTE-FACE
step	PAS, DEMARCHE	—descent	DEGRINGOLADE
stew	CASSOULET, DAUBE, RAGOUT	—outburst	BOUTADE
stewed beef	BOUILLI	—turn, as in play	COUP DE THEATRE
stirrup	ETRIER	suddenly	A L'IMPROVISTE
stocking	BAS	sufficient rhyme	RIME SUFFISANTE
Stone Age axe	COUP DE POING	suggestive	RISQUE
stonecrop	ORPIN	sulking	BOUDERIE
stop thief!	AU VOLEUR	summer	ETE
storehouse	ENTREPOT, ETAPE	summit	CIME
storey	ETAGE	sumptuous	DE LUXE
stout(ness)	EMBONPOINT	superfluous	DE TROP
straight in the face	EN FACE	superior	
strange	ETRANGER(E)	—power	FORCE MAJEURE
stratagem of war	RUSE DE GUERRE	—wine	VDQS
straw	PAILLE	supplementary race	REPECHAGE
strawberry	FRAISE	support	APPUI, APPUY
street	RUE	supporter of Bourbons	ROYALISTE
—Arab	GAMIN	surfeited	BLASE
striking	FRAPPANT	swaddling-clothes	MAILLOT
—effect	ECLAT	swamp	MARAIS
stroking massage	EFFLEURAGE	sweet	DOUX, DOUCE
stroller	FLANEUR	sweetmeat	BONBON
strong		—box	BONBONNIERE
—broth	BOUILLON	system of drill	MARTINET
—punishment	PEINE FORTE ET DURE	systematically arranged	RAISONNE
students' quarter in Paris	QUARTIER LATIN	table	
studied	VOULU	—cloth	NAPPE
studio	ATELIER	—wine	VIN ORDINAIRE
stuffed	FARCI	tact	SAVOIR-FAIRE
stupid		tactless(ness)	GAUCHE(RIE)
—blundering	ETOURDERIE	take	
—person	BETE	—leave	CONGE
stupidity	BETISE	—one's bearings	S'ORIENTER
style	CHIC	"talking drums"	ARMES PARLANTES
—of 1795-99	DIRECTOIRE	tart with tomatoes, etc	PISSALADIERE
stylish	CHICHI	tasty morsel	BONNE BOUCHE
subdivision of a Department	ARONDISSEMENT	tavern	BISTRO

tax on salt	GABELLE	title of rank	MONSEIGNEUR
tea with dancing	THE DANSANT	to	
team		—a	
—in sport	EQUIPE	certainty	A COUP SUR
—of cars	ECURIE	nicety	A POINT
technical college	GRANDE ECOLE	—arms!	AUX ARMES
tedious passage (in book)	LONGUEUR	—mere loss	EN PURE PERTE
teller of anecdotes	RACONTEUR	—no purpose	EN PURE PERTE
tempest	BOURRASQUE	—take leave	POUR PRENDRE CONGE, PPC
temporary lodging	PIED-A-TERRE	—the	
tender passion	BELLE PASSION	bitter end	A L'OUTRANCE
tenderloin	FILET	death	A L'OUTRANCE
territorial division	COMMUNE	highest degree	PAR EXCELLENCE
thanks to God	GRACE A DIEU	left	A GAUCHE
that		right	A DROITE
—is		very end	JUSQU'AU BOUT
all	VOILA TOUT	—your health!	A VOTRE SANTE
to say	C'EST A DIRE	tobacco sold by government	REGIE
—one	CELUI, CELLE	toilet-water	EAU DE COLOGNE
that's life!	C'EST LA VIE	tongue	LANGUE
the		too	
—blues	CAFARD	—late	APRES COUP
—buttocks	DERRIERE	—much	TROP
—Low Countries	LES PAYS-BAS	top	
theatre		—fashion-house	GRAND ATELIER
—box	BAIGNOIR	—to bottom	DE HAUT EN BAS
—stall	FAUTEUIL	total	PUR SANG
theatrical extravaganza	FEERIE	totalisator	PARI-MUTUEL
there is/there are	VOILA	touched	TOUCHE
thick		tourney	PAS D'ARMES
—end of undercut	FILET MIGNON	town	BOURG, VILLE
—foliage	BOCAGE	—hall	HOTEL DE VILLE
—grilled steak	CHATEAUBRIAND	—house	MAISON DE VILLE
—soup	POTAGE	toy reed-pipe	MIRLITON
thin glassware	MOUSSELINE	tradesman's stock	BOUTIQUE
thing already done	FAIT ACCOMPLI	traditional (art)	POMPIER
think	PENSER	traffic warden	PERVENCHE
third estate	TIERS-ETAT	train	MANEGE
this	CE, CET, CETTE	—of attendants	CORTEGE
thoroughbred	PUR SANG	tramp	CLOCHARD
thoroughly	A FOND	travelling	
thou	TOI, TU	companion	COMPAGNON DE VOYAGE
thoughtless	ETOURDI(E)	treachery	TRAHISON
thousand	MILLE	treason	TRAHISON
three-cornered hat	CHAPEAU BRAS	trench	CUNETTE, CUVETTE
	TRICORNE	triangular insertion in skirt	GODET
thrill	FRISSON	trickery	LEGER DE MAIN
through	A TRAVERS	triumphal arch	ARC DE TRIOMPHE
thrown	JETE	truly	VRAIMENT
thundering	FOUDROYANT	tun	TONNEAU
ticket-office window	GUICHET	turkey	DINDE, DINDON
tide-gate	ABOIDEAU, ABOITEAU	turmoil	TRACASSERIE
tilt	PAS D'ARMES	turned up	RETROUSSE
tip	POURBOIRE	turning round	VOLTE-FACE
—of toe	POINTE	tutor	REPETITEUR
titbit	BONNE BOUCHE	twaddle	FADAISE

twenty	VINGT
—one	VINGT-ET-UN
twilight	DEMI-JOUR
twin	JUMELLE
two men and two women	PARTIE CARREE
U-turn	VOLTE-FACE
unaffected	NAIF, NAIVE
unconstrained	EN PANTOUFLES
unconstraint	LAISSER-ALLER
	LAISSEZ-ALLER
uncoventional person	ENFANT TERRIBLE
under discussion	EN L'AIR, SUR LE TAPIS
undercut of beef	FILET
underground	
—chamber	SOUTERRAIN
—railway	METRO
understanding	ENTENTE
undertaker's parlour	CHAPELLE ARDENTE
undress (garment)	DESHABILLE
uneasiness	MALAISE
unembarrassed	DEGAGE
unexpectedly	A L'IMPROVISTE
unfit to fight	HORS DE COMBAT
uninspired (art)	POMPIER
unkempt	MAL SOIGNE(E)
unknown (person)	INCONNU(E)
unoriginal material	DEJA VU
unpleasant moment	MAUVAIS MOMENT
unpleasantness	ESCLANDRE
unravelling of plot	DENOUEMENT
unrestrained	DEGAGE
unsuccessful	MANQUE
unsuitable marriage	MESALLIANCE
unsweetened	BRUT
untrustworthy friend	AMI DE COUR
unwanted	DE TROP
unwilling	MALGRE
up to date	A LA PAGE
upon	SUR
upper middle class	HAUTE BOURGEOISIE
uproar	EMEUTE
upstart	NOUVEAU RICHE
	PARVENU
urchin	GAMIN
usher	HUISSIER
valiant knight	PREUX CHEVALIER
valley	VALLEE
varnishing	VERNISSAGE
vat of blended wine	CUVEE
veal	VEAU
verisimilitude	VRAISEMBLANCE
verse	VERS
very	TRES
—best	CREME DE LA CREME
—dear	AU POIDS DE L'OR
—small amount	SOUPCON

vine	
—grower	VIGNERON
—yard	CRU
violent epilepsy	GRAND MAL
visiting card	CARTE DE VISITE
visitor's permit	CARNET
vivacious young working-girl	GRISETTE
waiter	GARCON
walk	MARCHER
wall	MUR
wandering minstrel	JONGLEUR
want	BESOIN
war	GUERRE
—to the	
death	GUERRE A MORT
uttermost	GUERRE A L'OUTRANCE
warbler	FAUVETTE
warden	CONCIERGE
warehouse	ENTREPOT
warhorse	CHEVAL DE BATAILLE
warmed-up dish	RECHAUFFE
warmth of manner	EMPRESSEMENT
warning	EN GARDE
wartime guerrilla	MAQUISARD
—group	MAQUIS
watch-chain ornament	BRELOQUE
water	EAU
—bottle	CARAFE
—fall	CHUTE
—sprinkler	ASPERSOIR
wave (sea)	ONDE
way of speaking	FACON DE PARLER
weariness	ENNUI
weight	
—1 pound (old)	LIVRE
—1 cwt	QUINTAL
—small	MG, MILLIGRAMME
—10 milligrams	CENTIGRAMME, CG
—100 milligrams	DECIGRAMME, DG
—200 milligrams	(METRIC) CAR(R)AT
—10 grams	DECAGRAMME, DG
—100 grams	HECTOGRAMME, HG
—1000 grams	KG, KILOGRAMME
—1000 kilograms	MILLIER, T, TONNE
	TONNEAU
well	BIEN
—designed	BIEN ENTENDU
—done!	A LA BONNE HEURE
—groomed	SOIGNE(E)
—informed	AU COURANT, AU FAIT
—loved	BIEN-AIME
—mannered	BIEN ELEVE
—shod	BIEN CHAUSSE
—versed	BIEN ENTENDU
well-to-do classes	CLASSES AISEES
what	QUE

what's the good of it	A QUOI BON	woman	FEMME
whatever the consequences	QUAND MEME	—affecting over-refinement	PRECIEUSE
while waiting	EN ATTENDANT	—greatly involved in	
white		love affairs	GRANDE AMOUREUSE
—porcelain	BLANC DE CHINE	—of the world	FEMME DU MONDE
—wine	VIN BLANC	wonderfully	A MERVEILLE
who	QUI	woods	BOIS
—goes there?	QUI VA LA	wooden shoe	SABOT
whole	TOUT	woodland	BOCAGE
wholesale	EN BLOC	word	MOT
wholly yours	TOUT A VOUS	—fitting context	MOT JUSTE
wide road	BOULEVARD	work	
widow	VEUVE	—applied or laid on	APPLIQUE
wig	CHEVELURE, PERRUQUE	—box	NECESSAIRE
—maker	PERRUQUIER	—of artist, etc	OEUVRE
wild laughter	FOU RIRE	—shop	ATELIER
William pear	BON CHRETIEN	worker	OUVRIER(E)
willing	BON GRE	worn out	EPUISE(E)
willy-nilly	MALGRE LUI, MALGRE MOI	worse and worse	DE PIS EN PIS
wine	VIN	worst shift	PIS ALLER
	(*see separate entry*)	worthless	MAUVAIS(E)
—from famous vineyards	GRAND CRU	—fellow	MAUVAIS SUJET
	LES GRANDS VINS	would-be	SOI-DISANT
—waiter	SOMMELIER	woven	BROCHE
wing	AILE	writer of farces	FARCEUR
wink	OEILLADE	writing	
winter	HIVER	—book	CAHIER
wiping aside of ink	RETROUSSAGE	—desk	ECRITOIRE
wit	BEL ESPRIT	written statement	PROCES-VERBAL
witticism	JEU D'ESPRIRT	yesterday	HIER
with	AVEC, PAR	you	TOI, TU, VOUS
—a giant stride	A PAS DE GEANT	young	JEUNE
—air of superiority	DE HAUT EN BAS	—love	JEUNE AMOUR
—cheese	AU FROMAGE	—man kept by an older	
—child	ENCEINTE	woman	GIGOLO
—closed doors	A HUIS CLOS	**fruit**	
—justice	A BON DROIT	Actinidia	CHINESE GOOSEBERRY
—open arms	A BRAS OUVERTS		KIWI FRUIT
—pleasure	AVEC PLAISIR	African	A(C)KEE, BITO
—reference to	A PROPOS		CAPE GOOSEBERRY, DATE
—regard to	VIS-A-VIS		DIKA, HOTTENTOT FIG
within range/reach	A PORTEE		LYCHEE, MIRACLE FRUIT
without	SANS		NAARTJE, NAR(R)AS
—breeches	SANS CULOTTE		NARTJIE, PASSION FRUIT, SHEA NUT
—care	SANS SOUCI		STRAWBERRY-TOMATO, WILD MANGO
—ceremony	EN FAMILLE	aggregate fruit(s)	ACINUS(ACINI)
	SANS CEREMONIE	alligator-pear	AVOCADO
—courtesy	SANS PHRASES	American	BLUEBERRY, CHOKEBERRY
—phrases	SANS PHRASES		CRANBERRY, DEERBERRY
—preface	TOUT COURT		JUNEBERRY, HUCKLEBERRY
—reality	EN L'AIR		MARIONBERRY, MAYAPPLE
—restraint	SANS GENE		MIN(N)EOLA, SAL(L)AL-BERRY
—serifs	SANSERIF		SASKATOON, SHADBERRY
—worry	SANS SOUCI	Ananas	PINEAPPLE
witty saying	(BON) MOT	apple	POME
wolf-hole	TROU-DE-LOUP		(*see also separate entry*)

Arabian cherry	MAHALEB
Arctic	CROWBERRY
Asian	BITO, DATE
aubergine	BRINJAL, EGG PLANT
	MAD APPLE
Australian	GEEBUNG, NONDA
	NONDO, QUANDONG
avocado	ALLIGATOR-PEAR
	AQUACATE
azarole	MEDLAR
Barberry fig	INDIAN FIG
	PRICKLY PEAR
bilberry	BLAEBERRY, WHINBERRY
	WHORT(LEBERRY)
bitter orange	SEVILLE ORANGE
black	
—berry	BLACK CURRANT
	BRAMBLE-BERRY
	DEWBERRY, RUBUS
—currant	RIBES, QUINSY BERRY
—thorn	SLOE
blaeberry	(see bilberry above)
blueberry	HUCKLEBERRY
bottle gourd	DUDI
bramble	BLACKBERRY, DEWBERRY
brinjal	AUBERGINE
buckthorn	JUJUBE, RHEINBERRY
	RHINEBERRY
cactus fruit	PRICKLY-PEAR, SAGUARO
candied chestnut	MARRON GLACE
Cape gooseberry	PHYSALIS
	STRAWBERRY-TOMATO
Channel Islands	BABACO
cherry	
—bitter	MORELLO
—plum	MYROBALAN
—sweet	MAZ(Z)ARD
—wild	GEAN
Chinese	KUMQUAT, LEECHEE
	LICHEE, LI(T)CHI
	LONGAN, LOQUAT
	LUNGAN, LYCHEE
	MANDARIN(E), SATSUMA
	WAMPEE
—date	JUJUBE
—gooseberry	ACTINIDIA, CARAMBOLE
	KIWI FRUIT
—lantern	CAPE GOOSEBERRY
	PHYSALIS
—orange	MANDARIN(E), SATSUMA
—pear	TIENTSIN-YA
citrus	BERGAMOT, CITRON
	GRAPEFRUIT, LEMON
	LIME, ORANGE
Colombia	TAMARILLO
compound	SYNCARP

cowberry	IDAEAN VINE
	RED WHORTLEBERRY
crushed apples	POMACE
custard-apple	CHERIMOYA, SOURSOP
date-plum	PERSIMMON, SHARON FRUIT
dewberry	BLACKBERRY, RUBUS
dog-rose	HIP
dried grape	CURRANT, RAISIN, SULTANA
drupel	FRUITLET
dry fruit	
—containing several seeds	LEGUME
—from two carpels	
long	SILIQUA, SILIQUE
short	SILICULA, SILIC(U)LE
—indehiscent	CARYOPSIS, NUT
—not splitting	INDEHISCENT
—one-seeded	ACHENE
—part of schizocarp	MERICARP
—splitting	DEHISCENT
along one line	FOLLICLE
into	
—several parts	SCHIZOCARP
—two parts	CREMOCARP
—with hard shell	NUT
dry-fruited	BARREN STRAWBERRY
durian	JACKFRUIT
East Indian	CARAMBOLA
	COROMANDEL GOOSEBERRY
	EMBLIC (MYROBALAN)
	MANGO, MARKING-NUT
	ROSE-APPLE, STAR FRUIT
	TAMPOE
edible chestnut	MARRON
egg plant	AUBERGINE, BRINJAL
	MAD APPLE
Egyptian melon	ABDALAVI
Eurasian	SOUR CHERRY
fae-berry	FEA-BERRY, GOOSEBERRY
Ficus	FIG
fleshy fruit	POME, SARCOCARP, SOROSIS
foul-smelling	DURIAN, JACKFRUIT
fragrant	
—pear	MUSK-PEAR
—plum	MUSK-PLUM
from vines	GRAPE
fruit-eating	CARPOPHAGOUS
	FRUGIVOROUS
fruit-stone	PIT, PUTAMEN
full of seeds	FIG, POMEGRANATE
gooseberry	FAE-BERRY, FEA-BERRY
	RIBES
—US	WORCESTER-BERRY
gourd	BABACO, CALABASH, SQUASH
granadilla	GRENADILLO, PASSION-FRUIT
grape	
—dried	RAISIN

—dried, seedless	CURRANT, SULTANA
hard	
—rinded	GOURD, POMEGRANATE
—water melon	CITRON
having	
—fruit in special casing	ANGIOCARPOUS
—leathery epicarp	HESPERIDIUM
—many	
lobules	AGGREGATE FRUIT
	COLLECTIVE FRUIT
	MULTIPLE FRUIT
seeds	BERRY, CAPSULE
—in hard epicarp	PEPO
—seeds in central capsule	POME
—single hard stone	DRUPE
—stone	
easily separated	
from the flesh	FREESTONE
not easily separated	
from the flesh	CLINGSTONE
hawthorn	HAW
hedgerow	ELDERBERRY, HAW, HIP
hindberry	RASPBERRY, RUBUS
huckleberry	BLUEBERRY
hybrid	
—blackberry	JOSTABERRY
x raspberry	BOYSENBERRY
	LOGANBERRY
x dewberry	YOUNGBERRY
—boysenberry x tayberry	HILDABERRY
—citron x orange	CITRANGE
—orange x tangerine	ORTANIQUE
—tangerine	
x grapefruit	UGLI (FRUIT)
x pomelo	TANGELO
Idaean vine	COWBERRY
	RED WHORTLEBERRY
Indian	B(A)EL, BENGAL QUINCE
	BHEL, CARAMBOLA, DURIAN
	MYROBALAN
—fig	BARBARY FIG, PRICKLY PEAR
Indonesian	AMBOINA BERRY
inner layer	ENDOCARP
Israel	KUMQUAT, SHARON FRUIT
jackfruit	DURIAN
Jamaican	HOG-PLUM, KIWANO
Japanese	LOQUAT, KAKI, NASHI
juice	SYRUP
jujube	CHINESE DATE
kiwi fruit	ACTINIDIA
	CHINESE GOOSEBERRY
large damson	DAMASCENE
	DAMSON-PLUM
like	
—apple	CRAB, MEDLAR
—banana	PLANTAIN

lime (Philippines)	CALAMANSI
little drupe	DRUPEL(ET)
locust tree	CAROB
love apple	TOMATO
Malayan	DURIAN, MANGOSTEEN
	RAMBUTAN
Malaysian	TAMARILLO
medlar	AZAROLE
melon	
—African	WATER-MELON
—American	WATER-MELON
—common melon	MUSK-MELON
—Egyptian	ABDALAVI
—French	CHARENTAIS
—hard water melon	CITRON
—horned	KIWANO
—Israel	GALIA
—like	NAR(R)AS
—musk melon	CANTALOUP(E)
—New Zealand	KIWANO
—oval	HONEYDEW
—segmented	CANTALOUP(E)
—small	CHARENTAIS, OGEN
—Spanish	FUTURA, GALIA
	PIEL DA SAPO, PIEL DE SAPO
—striped	TIGER MELON
—tree-melon	PAPAYA, PAW-PAW
—winter melon	CAS(S)ABA
—yellow winter	CASABA
moorland	BILBERRY, BLAEBERRY
	CRANBERRY, CROWBERRY
	WHINBERRY, WHORT(LEBERRY)
Morus	MULBERRY
mulberry	SYCAMINE
naseberry	NEESBERRY, NISBERRY
	SAPODILLA (PLUM)
Nephelium	LONGAN, LUNGAN
New Zealand	KIWANO, KIWI FRUIT
oil-producing	BERGAMOT, OLIVE
Olea	OLIVE
orange	
—bitter	SEVILLE
—Brazilian	NAVEL ORANGE
—Chinese	MANDARIN(E), SATSUMA
—Israeli	JAFFA, SHAMOUTI, TOPAZ
—large	JAFFA, SHADDOCK
—Maltese	BLOOD ORANGE
—mandarin	CLOVE ORANGE
	NOBLE ORANGE
—North African	TANGERINE
—oval	EGG ORANGE
—Portuguese	LISBON
—red-fleshed	BLOOD ORANGE
—small	CLEMENTINE, MANDARIN(E)
	SATSUMA, TANGERINE
—South African	NAARTJE, NARTJIE

—Spanish	CLAUSELLINA, SEVILLE
—type	HESPERIDIUM
—yielding oil	BERGAMOT
orange-coloured	AMBARELLA, APRICOT
Oriental	POMEGRANATE, POMELO
	SEBESTEN, SHADDOCK
outer layer	EPICARP, HULL, HUSK
	SHELL, ZEST
ovaries of several flowers on fleshy axis	COENOCARPIUM
papaw	PAPAYA, PAW-PAW
	TREE MELON
partition(s) in pod	REPLUM(REPLA)
passion-fruit	GRANADILLA
	GRENADILLO
peach	VICTORINE
—smooth-skinned	NECTARINE
peach-plum	PUPUNHA
pear	POME
—American	SECKLE, SHAKESPEAR
	RED-GLEEK
—Chinese	TIENTSIN-YA
—early	JARGONELLE
—Italian	PASSACRASSANA
—Japanese	NASHI
—old	CARMELITE, MALAKATOONE
	MELLICOTTON, MELOCOTO(O)N
	POPRIN, POPPERING
—soft	BEURRE
—varieties	ANSON, BARTLETT
	BERGAMOT, BOSC, CATILLAC
	CLAPP'S FAVOURITE
	COLMAR, CONCORDE, CONFERENCE
	(DOYENNE DU) COMICE
	GUYOT, JOSEPHINE, KIEFFER
	LAXTON'S FAVOURITE
	PACKMAN, PASSACRANA
	SECKEL, WILLIAMS
—winter	NELI(E)S
persimmon	DATE-PLUM, SHARON FRUIT
Peruvian	CHERIMOYA, CHERIMOYER
	CHIRIMOYA
Philippines	KALUMPIT
—lime	CALAMANSI
—plantain	ABACA
Physalis	CAPE GOOSEBERRY
	CHINESE LANTERN
pineapple	ANANA(S)
pink	RASPBERRY, STRAWBERRY
pips in fleshy container	SYCOMIUM
plantain (Philippines)	ABACA
plum	
—genus	ALMOND, APRICOT, PEACH
—green	GREENGAGE
—Oriental	SEBESTEN

—purple	DAMSON, VICTORIA
—red	FRIAR, ROYSON
—variety	MYROBALAN
pome	APPLE, PEAR
pomegranate	PUNIC APPLE
pomelo	GRAPEFRUIT, SHADDOCK
prickly pear	BARBARY FIG, INDIAN FIG
	TUNA
production without fertilisation	PARTHENOCARPY
Punic apple	POMEGRANATE
purple	MULBERRY
quandong	PEACH
quince	
—Cydonia	QUINCE
—Indian	B(A)EL, BENGAL QUINCE
	BHEL
—Japonica	JAPANESE QUINCE
quinsy-berry	BLACK CURRANT, RIBES
raspberry	HINDBERRY, RUBUS
red	
—currant	
American	SALMON-BERRY
Chinese	WINEBERRY
Scottish	RIZZAR(D), RIZZART
	RIZZER
—whortleberry	IDAEAN VINE, COWBERRY
Rheinberry/Rhineberry	BUCKTHORN
Ribes	BLACK CURRANT
	GOOSEBERRY
	RED CURRANT
	WHITE CURRANT
roebuck-berry	ROE-BLACKBERRY
	STONE BRAMBLE
rose	HIP
Rubus	BLACKBERRY, BRAMBLEBERRY
	DEWBERRY, RASPBERRY
salmon-berry (US)	RASPBERRY
sapodilla	SAPOTA
—plum	NASEBERRY
	NEESBERRY, NISBERRY
saskatoon	SERVICEBERRY
Scandinavian	CLOUDBERRY
serviceberry	SASKATOON
shadbush	JUNEBERRY
shaddock	POMELO
small fruit(s) in aggregate fruit	ACINUS(ACINI)
smooth-skinned peach	NECTARINE
soft fruit	BLACKBERRY
	BOYSENBERRY
	BRAMBLE, LOGANBERRY
	RASPBERRY, STRAWBERRY
	SUNBERRY, TAYBERRY
	TUMMELBERRY
South African	(*see* African *above*)

South American	ANANAS, BABACO
	CALABASH, CARAMBOLA
	GUAVA, LUCUMA
	PINEAPPLE, STAR FRUIT
	TAMARILLO
South Sea islands	BREADFRUIT
sour cherry	MORELLO
Spanish orange	CLAUSELLINA, SEVILLE
squash	(see **vegetables**)
star fruit	CARAMBOLA
stem	RHUBARB
stewed in sugar syrup	COMPOTE
stone	PIT, PUTAMEN
—bramble	ROE-BLACKBERRY
	ROEBUCK-BERRY
—fruit	APRICOT, CHERRY
	NECTARINE, PEACH
	PLUM
—in fruit	PUTAMEN
strawberry-tomato	CAPE GOOSEBERRY
sub-tropical	AVOCADO (PEAR)
	CHINESE GOOSEBERRY
	KIWI FRUIT
sweet cherry	MAZ(Z)ARD
Thai	ROSE APPLE
tomato	LOVE APPLE
tropical	ALLIGATOR-PEAR, ANANAS
	AVOCADO, BANANA, BREADNUT
	CRAB-NUT, GRANADILLA
	GRENADILLO, GUAVA, LIME
	MANGO(STEEN), PAPAYA, PA(W)PAW
	PASSION FRUIT, PINEAPPLE
	PINGUIN, SAPETILLO
	TAMARIND, TREE MELON
types	
—dry	
in pods	LEGUME, LOMENTUM
one-seeded	ACHENE, ACH(A)ENIUM
many-seeded	ETAERIO
—fleshy, from many flowers	SOROSIS
—succulent	
one-seeded	DRUPE
many-seeded	BERRY
Vaccinium	CRANBERRY
velvet-skinned	PEACH
wall of fruit	PERICARP
—inner layer	ENDOCARP
—outer layer	EPICARP, EXOCARP
West Indian	A(C)KEE, ANANA(S)
	ANCHOVY-PEAR
	BARBADOS GOOSEBERRY
	BREADFRUIT, BULLOCK'S HEART
	CHERIMOYA, COCOPLUM, CUSTARD APPLE
	GENIPAP, GOLDEN APPLE, GRENADILLA
	GUAVA, MAMMEE (APPLE), MANGO
	NASEBERRY, PASSION FRUIT, PAW-PAW

	PENGUIN, PINGUIN, SAPODILLA (PLUM)
	SAPOTA, SOURSOP, STAR APPLE
	SWEETSOP, UGLI
	(see also tropical above)
whinberry	(see bilberry above)
whort(leberry)	(see bilberry above)
wild	
—apple	CRAB
—cherry	GEAN
—damson	BULLACE
—fig	CAPRIFIG, GOAT FIG
—plum	BULLACE
winged	SAMARA
winter melon	CAS(S)ABA
Worcester-berry (US)	GOOSEBERRY
yellow	BANANA, PLANTAIN
fungi	MYCOPHYTA
including: lichen	
mushrooms	
algal part of lichen	PHYCOBIONT
American	TUCKAHOE
attacking	
—grasses	GIBBERELLA
—maple	RHYTISMA
—skin	DERMAPHYTE
—trees	HONEY FUNGUS
bacteria, fungi and algae	THALLOPHYTA
base of stem	VOLVA
black	DEAD MAN'S FINGERS
—and brown	BACHELOR'S BUTTONS
	POPE'S BUTTONS
bluish-grey to brown	OYSTER (MUSHROOM)
brown to brick-red	BOLETUS, CEPE, CEPS
causing disease in plants	BLIGHT
	MILDEW, RUST, SMUT
classes	ASCOMYCETES, BASIDIOMYCETES
	GASTEROMYCETES
	FUNGI IMPERFECTI, MYXOMYCETES
	PHYCOMYCETES, ZYGOMYCETES
covering of cap	SCALES
division	MYCOPHYTA
dry rot	MERULIUS
edible	BEEFSTEAK FUNGUS, BLEWITS
	BOLETUS, CEPE, CEPS, CHAMPIGNON
	CHANTERELLE, JEW'S EAR
	LAWYER'S WIG, MUSHROOM
	OYSTER, PARASOL, PENNY BUN
	PUFFBALL, STINKHORN, TRUFFLE
	TUCKAHOE, WOOD BLEWITS
—lichen	LECANORA
fairy-ring mushroom	SCOTCH BONNET
fungus in symbiotic relationship with	
—algae	LICHEN
—roots of higher plants	MICOR(R)HIZA
Geaster	EARTH-STAR

genus	AMANITA, PEZIZA
	SAPROLEGNIA
gill-fungi	AGARICACEAE
greyish to pale brown	BIRCH POLYPORE
	RAZORSTROP FUNGUS
growing on elder	JEW'S EAR
head	CAP, PILEUS
higher fungi	EUMYCETES
Hydnum	JUPITER'S BEARD
knob on cap	UMBO
lichen	CETRARIA, LECANORALES
—flat	FOLIOSE
—reproductive organ	SOREDIUM
—upright	FRUTICOSE
—used for dye	CROTAL, CROTTLE
manna lichen	LECANORA
membrane joining cap to stalk	VEIL, VELUM
mildews	ASCOMYCETES
moulds	ASCOMYCETES
mushroom	CHAMPIGNON
mushroom-like	TOADSTOOL
mushrooms	AGARICACEAE
orange	ORANGE CUP
plant producing	
zygospores	ZYGOPHYTE
poisonous	DEATH CAP, FLY AGARIC
	PANTHER CAP
	DESTROYING ANGEL
Puccinia	RUST
puffballs	LYCOPERDALES
	SCLERODERMATALES
red	
—or liver-coloured	BEEFSTEAK FUNGUS
—with white spots	FLY AGARIC
reddish brown	THE DECEIVER
resting stage	SCLEROTIUM
ring on stem	ANNULUS
roots	MYCELIUM
rust(s)	PUCCINIA, URIDINALES
sac fungi	ENDOMYCETALES
seed	SPORE
skin on cap	PELLICLE
slime fungi	MYXOMYCOPHYTA
	SLIME MOULDS
spore	
—bearing area	HYMENIUM
—from union of	
adjacent buds	ZYGOSPERM
	ZYGOSPORE
spreading root system	MYCELIUM
star-shaped	EARTH-STAR, GEASTER
stink-horns	PHALLALES
thallus of fungus	MYCELIUM
thread of mycelium	HYPHA
truffles	ASCOMYCETES
underground	TRUFFLE, TUCKAHOE

vanes on underside	GILLS, LAMELLAE
weeping	WEEPING WIDOW
whitish	COMMON EARTHBALL
	MUSHROOM, SLIMY BEECHCAP
	STINKHORN, WOOD WITCH
woolly growth	MOULD
yeasts	MYCOTA
yellow	COMMON YELLOW RUSSULA
	SULPHUR TUFT
yellow-green algae	CONFERVA, HETEROCONT
	HETEROKONT
	(*see also* **biology**)

fur

American marten	SKUNK
Arctic marten	SABLE
cloak	PILCH
coypu	NUTRIA
ermine (summer)	ROSELET
garment lined with fur	PELISSE
goat (underfleece)	PASH(I)M, PASHMINA
grey	CHINCHILLA, GRIS(E)
hat of fur	BEAVER, CASTOR
hood of fur	AMICE
lamb	
—Crimea	CRIMMER, KRIMMER
—curled	ASTRAKHAN
mercury treatment	SECRETAGE
mink	KOLINSKY
musk-rat	MUSQUASH
polecat	FITCHEW, KOLINSKY
rabbit	CHINCHILLA
sable	ZIBEL(L)INE
selectively bred	MUTATION MINK
skunk	ZORINO
squirrel	VAIR
stoat	ERMINE
tippet of fur	VICTORINE
weasel	MINK
wild llama	VICUNA
Furies	ERINYES, EUMENIDES
	ALECTO, MEGAERA
	TISIPHONE

furniture

artificially aged	DISTRESSED
bedroom furniture	BEDSTEAD
	CHEVAL GLASS
	CHEST OF DRAWERS
	DIVAN, DRESSING GLASS
	DRESSING TABLE, FOUR POSTER
	LOWBOY, TALLBOY
	MIRROR, WARDROBE
bishop's	
—chair	FALDSTOOL
—seat	THRONE
within the chancel	FALDISTORY
cabinet	ALMIRA(H)

canape	SOFA	immoveable furniture	FITTINGS
cane furniture	RATTAN	inlay in wood	MARQUETRY
chair		lamp-stand	TORCHERE
—armchair	BERGERE, FAUTEUIL	leg	
—armless with low		—curved	CABRIOLE
seat	FARTHINGALE CHAIR	—square	MARLBOROUGH
—deep armchair	CLUB CHAIR	long	
—dining chair with arms	CARVER	—bench	FORM, TRESTLE
—folding	GLASTONBURY	with back	SETTLE
—old	CAQUETOIRE	—upholstered seat	CHAISE LONGUE
—other types	ABBOTSFORD CHAIR		OTTOMAN, SOFA
	DERBYSHIRE CHAIR	mirror	
	LAMBING CHAIR	—on swivels	CHEVAL GLASS
	LANCASHIRE CHAIR		DRESSING GLASS
	MENDLESHAM CHAIR	—tall and narrow	PIER GLASS
	NORFOLK CHAIR	modern style	HI-TECH
	SMOKERS' BOW (CHAIR)	moveable furniture	FITMENTS
	YORKSHIRE CHAIR	music holder	CANTERBURY
—small curved armchair	CABRIOLET	ornamental candlestick	
—sovereign's chair	THRONE	or lampholder	TORCHERE
—with		padded furniture	UPHOLSTERY
adjustable back	MORRIS CHAIR	ready-made unit	MODULE
chamberpot	COMMODE	revolving	
curved runners	ROCKER	—dessert stand	DUMB WAITER
	ROCKING CHAIR	—tray	LAZY SUSAN
legs and back fixed		scalloped edge	PIE-CRUST
into sockets		seat	
in seat	WINDSOR CHAIR	—for one	BEAN-BAG, CHAIR
semi-circular			CRICKET, MUSIC STOOL
back	CAPTAIN'S CHAIR		POUFFE, STOOL
church		—for two	DOS-A-DOS, LOVE SEAT
—desk	FALDSTOOL		TETE-A-TETE
—seat	PEW	shelves	
—table	ALTAR	—for books	BOOK CASE
combined	BED-CHAIR, BED-SETTEE	—for bric-a-brac	ETAGERE, WHATNOT
coronation		sideboard	CREDENCE, CREDENZA
—chair	THRONE		COMMODE
—stool	FALDSTOOL		(WELSH) DRESSER
cupboard	ALM(E)RY, ALMIRA(H)	sofa/couch	CANAPE, DAYBED
	A(U)MBRY	—backless	DIVAN, OTTOMAN
curved leg	CABRIOLE		POUFFE
cushion used as seat	BEAN-BAG, POUFFE	—for two	LOVE SEAT
display furniture	CHIFFONIER	back-to-back	DOS-A-DOS
	(CHINA) CABINET, ETAGERE	—large and padded	CHESTERFIELD
	(WELSH) DRESSER	—on three sides of table	TRICLINIUM
	WHATNOT	—S-shaped	TETE-A-TETE
dresser	ALM(E)RY, A(U)MBRY	—used as bed at night	SOFA-BED
fabric trimming	GIMP, GUIMP(E)		BED-SETTEE
	GUIPURE, PIPING	—with	
folding		a back	SETTEE
—bed	MURPHY BED, PUT-U-UP	one raised end	COUCH
—chair	GLASTONBURY	stool	CRICKET, TABOURET
—stool	FALDSTOOL	storage furniture	
—table	TRESTLE	—clothes	BACHELOR CHEST
furniture made from rough			(CLOTHES) PRESS, LOWBOY
branches	RUSTIC		TALLBOY, WARDROBE

—general	ARMOIRE	—for toilet	DRESSING TABLE
	BLANKET CHEST, CABINET	—on castors	DUMB WAITER, TROLLEY
	CHEST (OF DRAWERS)	—other	CARLTON HOUSE TABLE
	(CLOSE) CUPBOARD, COMMODE		CRICKET TABLE
	COURT CUPBOARD, CREDENCE		HUTCH TABLE
	CREDENZA, MULE CHEST, PRESS		LIBRARY TABLE
	SIDEBOARD, (WELSH) DRESSER		OCCASIONAL TABLE
—outdoor clothes, etc	HALL STAND		WORK TABLE
	HAT STAND	—small tea table	TEAPOY
	UMBRELLA STAND	—supported by brackets	CONSOLE TABLE
—tea	CADDY, TEAPOY	—with	
styles		central support	MONOPODIUM
—English (18th c)	ADAM, CHIPPENDALE		WINE TABLE
	HEPPLEWHITE	baize top	CARD TABLE
	QUEEN ANNE, SHERATON	flaps each end	GATE-LEG TABLE
—French			PEMBROKE TABLE
17th c	BOUL(L)E, BUHL		SOFA-TABLE
	LOUIS-QUATORZE		SUTHERLAND TABLE
18th c	LOUIS-QUINZE	folding legs	TRESTLE (TABLE)
19th c	SECOND EMPIRE	three legs	TRIPOD
—German 19th c	BIEDERMEIER	toilet	COMMODE, DRESSING TABLE
support for standing	MISERICORD(E)		TABLE, WASHSTAND
	MISERERE	wardrobe	ALMIRA(H)ARMOIRE
swivelling wheel	CASTOR	writing and books	BONHEUR-DU-JOUR
table			BOOKCASE
—beside altar	CREDENCE (TABLE)		BUREAU (ON STAND)
	CREDENZA		CANTERBURY
—between windows	PIER TABLE		DAVENPORT, DESK (BOX)
—circular	DRUM TABLE, LOO TABLE		E(S)CRITOIRE (ON STAND)
—dining	REFECTORY		LIBRARY STEPS, LIBRARY TABLE
—extendible	DRAW(-TOP) TABLE		SECRETAIRE

G

Gabon
 capital   LIBREVILLE
 coin   FRANC
Gaelic   ERSE, GAEL
 poet   OSSIAN
     (*see also* **Ireland, Scottish**)
Gambia   WAG
 capital   BANJUL, BATHURST
 coin
 —unit   BUTUT
 —100 butut   DALASI
games[1]
 including: indoor sports
          pastimes
          water sports
          winter sports
 aerial   AEROBATICS, (HANG-)GLIDING
     PARACHUTING, PARAPENTE
     PARASCENDING
     PARASAILING, SKY-DIVING
 American football   (*see separate entry*)
 athletics   (*see separate entry*)
 ball games   AMERICAN FOOTBALL
     ARENABALL
     (ASSOCIATION) FOOTBALL
     (AUSTRALIAN) RULES FOOTBALL
     BADMINTON, BALA LOCA, BANDY
     BASEBALL, BASKETBALL, BROOMBALL
     CAMOGIE, CRICKET, CROQUET
     ETON WALL GAME
     FAUSTBALL, FIVES, FLIPBALL
     (GAELIC) FOOTBALL, GOLF
     HANDBALL, HARDBALL, HOCKEY
     HORSEBALL, HURLEY, HURLING
     JAI ALAI, JAMBALL, KANGA CRICKET
     KORFBALL, KWIK CRICKET, LACROSSE
     (LAWN)TENNIS, NETBALL
     PELOTA (VASCA), POLO, PUSHBALL
     RACKETS, RACQUETS, REAL TENNIS
     ROLLERBALL, ROLLER HOCKEY
     ROUNDERS, ROYAL TENNIS
     RUGBY LEAGUE
     RUGBY UNION, SHINNY, SHINTY
     SHORT TENNIS, SOCCER, SOFTBALL
     SQUASH (RACKETS), STOOLBALL
     SUCKERBALL, TCHOUCK-BALL
     TRAP-BALL, WALLYBALL
     VOLLEYBALL

baseball   (*see separate entry*)
Basque   JAI ALIA, PELOTA (VASCA)
biathlon   SKIING, SHOOTING
bowling   BOCCIA, BOULES, BOWLS
     MARBLES, NINE HOLES
     PETANQUE, SKITTLES
     TEN-PIN BOWLING
     (*see also* **bowls**)
boxing   (*see separate entry*)
 —with use of feet   KICKBOXING, SAVATE
     THAI BOXING
card games   (*see separate entry*)
chess   (*see separate entry*)
children's
 —cricket   KANGA CRICKET
     KWIK CRICKET
 —cycling   BMX
 —games   BANDALORE, BLINDMAN'S BUFF
     CHARADES, COCKAL, CRAMBO
     DIABOLO, DIBS, HIDE-AND-SEEK
     HOOP BOWLING, HOPSCOTCH
     HOT COCKLE, HULA-HOOP
     HUNT-THE-SLIPPER
     JACKS, KNUCKLE-BONES, LEAP-FROG
     MURDER, MUSICAL CHAIRS
     PASS THE PARCEL, POGO STICK
     POSTMAN'S KNOCK, RING-O'-ROSES
     ROUNDERS, SCALECTRIX™
     SKATE-BOARDING, SKIPPING
     TIP-CAT, TOP-SPINNING, YOYO
 —races   EGG-AND-SPOON, SACK
     THREE-LEGGED, WHEELBARROW
 —tennis   SHORT TENNIS
Chinese   FAN-TAN, MAH-JONG(G), PUTZI
Christmas   LEVEL-COIL
cricket   (*see separate entry*)
cycling   (*see separate entry*)
decathlon   DISCUS
     FIFTEEN HUNDRED METRES
     FOUR HUNDRED METRES
     HIGH HUMP, HUNDRED METRES
     HURDLES, JAVELIN
     LONG JUMP, POLE VAULT
     SHOT(PUT)
dice games   CRAPS, PERUDO, POKER DICE
diving   BUNGEE ROPE DIVING
     HIGHBOARD, LAND DIVING
     SKYDIVING, SPRINGBOARD
     (*see also* **swimming**)
duathlon   CYCLING, RUNNING
Dutch   KORFBALL
equestrian   COACH-DRIVING, DRESSAGE
     EVENTING, HARNESS RACING
     PACING, POLO, RODEO
     SHOW JUMPING, TENT-PEGGING
     TROTTING

five events	PENTATHLON
fives varieties	ETON, RUGBY, WINCHESTER
football	(*see separate entry*)
four events	TETRATHLON
French	BOULES, PETANQUE, SAVATE
Gaelic	CAMOGIE, CURLING
	GAELIC FOOTBALL, HURLEY
	HURLING, SHINNY, SHINTY
golf	(*see separate entry*)
gymnastics	(*see separate entry*)
horse racing	(*see separate entry*)
hunting	BEAGLING, COURSING
	DEER HUNTING
	FOX HUNTING, OTTER HUNTING
indoor games	
—board games	BACKGAMMON, BINGO
	CHESS, CLUEDO
	CROWN AND ANCHOR
	DRAUGHTS, GO, GOBANG, GOMOKU
	HALMA, HOUSEY-HOUSEY, LEXICON
	LUDO, MAH-JONG, MONOPOLY
	PACHISI, SCRABBLE
	SNAKES AND LADDERS
	TRIC(K)-TRAC(K), TRIVIAL PURSUITS
African	MANCALA
Egyptian	SENET
Peruvian	PERUDO
—bowling	QUOITS, SKITTLES
	TEN-PIN BOWLING
—cards	(*see separate entry*)
—Chinese	FAN-TAN, MAH-JONG(G)
—Indian	PACHISI, PARCHEESI
—other	CHARADES, CONSEQUENCES
	DARTS, (DUMB) CRAMBO
	FORFEITS, HIDE AND SEEK
	HOUSEY-HOUSEY, JACK(STRAW)S
	JINGO-RING, KNUCKLEBONES
	LEVEL-COIL, MURDER
	SPILLIKINS, TOMBOLA
—table games	BAGATELLE
	BILLIARDS, BLOW FOOTBALL
	DICE, DOMINOES, NOVUM
	PINBALL, POOL, SHOVE HA(LF)PENNY
	SKITTLES, SNOOKER, SUBUTEO
	TABLE TENNIS, TIDDLEYWINKS
Irish	HURLING, HURLEY
Japanese	GO, GOBAN(G), GOMUKU, SHOGI
jumping	HIGH JUMP
	HOP, SKIP AND JUMP
	HURDLES, LONG JUMP
	STEEPLECHASE
	TRAMPOLINE, TRIPLE JUMP
—ancient Greek	HALMA
—long jump (US)	BROAD JUMP
karate styles	SHOTOKAN, WUKO
kung-fu styles	JEET-KUNE-DO, TAI CHI

martial arts	
—Chinese	KEMPO, KUNG-FU
	SHAOLIN BOXING, WU SHU
—Japanese	AIKIDO, AIKI-JITSU
	ESCRIMA, JI(U)JITSU
	JUDO(KWAN), JUJUTSA
	GOJO-RYU, KEMPO, KENDO
	KYOKUSHINKAI, NINJITSU
	SHITO-RYU, SHOTOKAI, SHOTOKAN
	TANG SOO DO, WADO-RYU
—Korean	HAPIKIDO, MU-GEN-DO
	SULKIDO, TAE KWON DO
	TANG SOO DO
—Okinawan	KARATE
—Thai	THAI BOXING
motor and motorcycle	
sports	AUTOCROSS
	CYCLO-CROSS, DRAG-RACING
	FORMULA ONE RACING
	(GO-)KARTING, GRAND PRIX RACING
	MOTOCROSS, RALLYING
	SCRAMBLING, SPEEDWAY RACING
	TOURIST TROPHY RACING
	(*see also* **motor-racing, motor-rallying**)
multi-discipline	
—2 events	BIATHLON
—3 events	TRIATHLON
—4 events	TETRATHLON
—5 events	PENTATHLON
—6 events	HEXATHLON
—7 events	HEPTATHLON
—10 events	DECATHLON
on ice	(*see* winter sports *below*)
on skates	
—blades	ICE HOCKEY
—wheels	ROLLERBALL, SUCKERBALL
outdoor activities	CAVING
	CROSS COUNTRY RUNNING
	JOGGING, MOUNTAINEERING
	ORIENTEERING, PAPER CHASE
	POT HOLING, ROCK CLIMBING
	WALKING
pentathlon	
—ancient	DISCUS THROWING, LEAPING
	RUNNING, SPEAR THROWING
	WRESTLING
—modern	
(m)	CROSS-COUNTRY RIDING
	CROSS-COUNTRY RUNNING
	FENCING, PISTOL SHOOTING
	SWIMMING
(f)	HIGH JUMP, HUNDRED METRES
	HURDLES, LONG JUMP, SHOT(PUT)
power-lifting	BENCH PRESS
	DEAD LIFT, SQUAT
	(*see also* weightlifting *below*)

pulling	TUG-O(F)-WAR
racket games	BADMINTON, BUMBLE-PUPPY
	FIVES, JAI-ALAI, LACROSSE
	SQUASH (RACKETS), TENNIS
Rugby football	(*see separate entry*)
running	CROSS COUNTRY
	FELL RUNNING
	HARE AND HOUNDS
	MARATHON, ORIENTEERING
	PAPER CHASE, RELAY
	SPARTATHLON, SPRINT
rustic game	FIVEPENNY MORRIS
	MAR(RE)LS, MEREL(L)S
	MERILS, MIRACLES, MORALS
	(NINEPENNY) MORRIS
sailing	(*see separate entry*)
'sailing' on land	LAND-SURFING
	LAND-YACHTING
	SAND-YACHTING
seven events	HEPTATHLON
shipboard	BULL, DECK QUOITS
	DECK TENNIS
shooting	
—bow and arrow	ARCHERY, TOXOPHILY
events	FIELD ARCHERY
	FLIGHT SHOOTING
	TARGET ARCHERY
—firearms	BIATHLON
	CLAY-PIGEON SHOOTING
	PISTOL, RIFLE, SKEET SHOOTING
	SMALL-BORE, TRAPSHOOTING
show-jumping	(*see separate entry*)
six events	HEXATHLON
skating	(*see separate entry*)
snooker	(*see separate entry*)
soccer	(*see* **football**)
Spanish	BALA LOCA
surfing	(*see separate entry*)
table tennis	PING-PONG
ten events	DECATHLON
terms	(*see* **games²**)
three events	TRIATHLON
throwing	CRICKET-BALL THROWING
	DARTS, HOOP-LA
	HAMMER-THROWING
	JAVELIN, QUOITS, SHOT(PUT)
	TOSSING THE CABER
trampoline	(*see* **gymnastics**)
triathlon	RUNNING, RIDING, SWIMMING
two events	BIATHLON, DUATHLON
war game	ARENABALL
water sports	NAUTICS
—ball game	WATER POLO
—boating/sailing	BOARD SAILING
	CANOEING, DINGHY SAILING
	EIGHTS, FOURS, JET SKIING

	KAYAK RACING, KNEE SKIING
	PAIRS, PEDALO, POWERBOAT RACING
	RAFTING, ROWING, SAIL BOARDING
	SCULLING, SURFING, WATER-SKIING
	WET-BIKING, WINDSURFING
	YACHTING
	(*see also* **sailing, surfing**)
—fishing	ANGLING, FLY-FISHING
—skis and paragliding	PARASAILING
—skiing without skis	BAREFOOTING
—swimming	(*see separate entry*)
—underwater	AQUAPUSH, DIVING
	SCUBA DIVING, SNORKELLING
	UNDERWATER HOCKEY
weightlifting	CLEAN AND JERK, PRESS
	SNATCH
	(*see also* powerlifting *above*)
winter sports	
—on	
ice	BANDY, BROOMBALL, CURLING
	ICE DANCING, ICE HOCKEY
	ICE POLO, ICE YACHTING
	SKATING
snow	BUMP-SKIING, DOWNHILL
	(GIANT) SLALOM
	HOT-DOGGING, LANGLAUF, LUGE
	PARAPENTE, SKI-BOB, SKIING
	SKIJORING, SKI-SURFING
	SLED-DOG RACING, SNOWBOARDING
	SNOWMOBILE, TOBOGGAN
—skiing	(*see separate entry*)
—skiing and shooting	BIATHLON
with	
—animals	BULLFIGHTING, CAMEL RACING
	CHARIOT RACING
	COACH DRIVING
	COURSING, FALCONRY, GRACING
	GREYHOUND RACING, HORSEBALL
	HORSE RACING, PIGEON RACING
	RIDE AND TIE, TRAP RACING
	TROTTING, WHIPPET RACING
—weapons	ARENABALL, JOUSTING
	FENCING
	(*see also* **fencing**)
wrestling	ALL-IN, ARM-WRESTLING
	CATCH-AS-CATCH-CAN
	CUMBERLAND STYLE
	FREESTYLE, GLIMA WRESTING
	GR(A)ECO-ROMAN STYLE
	LANCASHIRE, SAMBO, SUMO

games²

some sporting terms:

aiming mark	
—archery	BUTT, GOLD, TARGET
—baseball	PLATE
—bowls	JACK

—cricket	STUMPS, WICKET
—curling	TEE
—football	GOAL
—golf	HOLE, PIN
—hockey	GOAL
—shooting	BULL, BUTT, TARGET
aquapush	
—playing at one time	SIX
—team	TEN
Australian Rules	
—shape of pitch	OVAL
—team	EIGHTEEN
basketball	
—jumping and scoring	SLAM DUNK
—substitutes	SEVEN
—team	FIVE
billiards	
—balls	RED, WHITE
—cannon	CARAMBOLE, CAROM
—rebound	BRICOLE
—score	BREAK
—scoring shot	CANNON, IN-OFF, POT
	(see also **snooker***)*
croquet	
—aiming mark	HOOP
—implement for striking	MALLET
curling	
—aiming mark	TEE
—cannon	INWICK
Gaelic football team	FIFTEEN
handball	
—modern team,	FIVE, SEVEN
—old team	ELEVEN
high-jumping styles	FOSBURY FLOP
	STRADDLE, WESTERN ROLL
hockey	
—start of play	BULLY OFF
—team	ELEVEN
hurley team	FIFTEEN
ice-hockey	
—'ball'	PUCK
—off-ice penalty box	SIN BIN
—team	SIX
judo	
—costume	JUDOGI
—expert	BLACK BELT
—level of proficiency	DAN
—participant	JUDOKA
korfball team	TWELVE
lacrosse	
—stick	CROSSE
—team	
men	TEN
women	TWELVE
netball team	SEVEN
pelota 'bat'	CHERISTA(K)

polo	
—session	CHUKKA
—team	FOUR
—venues	CIRENCESTER, COWDRAY PARK
	GUARDS' CLUB, KIRKLINGTON PARK
	RHINEFIELD, ROYAL BERKSHIRE
	SMITH'S LAWN
shinty	CAMANACHD
—stick	CAMAN
—team	TWELVE
shooting	
—target sections	BULL, INNER
	MAGPIE, OUTER
—venue	BISLEY
softball team	SEVEN
table tennis	PING-PONG
—early	GOSSIMA
Tchouckball team	NINE
trophy	*(see separate entry)*
volleyball	
—playing positions	BLOCKER, RECEIVER
	SERVER, SETTER, SPIKER
—team	SIX
wrestling	
—hold	ARMLOCK, FULL NELSON
	HALF NELSON, HEADLOCK
	SCISSORS
—school (old)	PALAESTRA
—throw	FLYING MARE
—winning move	FALL
garments	
African	KANZU, K(H)ANGA
alb (Greek)	STICHARION
Albanian kilt	FUSTANELLA
Alpine dress or skirt	DIRNDL
ankle-length robe	TALAR
anorak	CAGOUL(E), KAGOOL
	KAGOUL(E)
apron	BARM-CLOTH, PLACKET
Austrian leather trousers	LEDERHOSEN
baby's coat	MATINEE JACKET
baggy	
—knickerbockers	PLUS-FOURS
—sweater	SLOPPY JOE
—trousers	OXFORD BAGS
ballet	
—overall garment	LEOTARD
—skirt	TUTU
—tights	MAILLOT
band embroidered	
with Agnus Dei	SUCCINCTORIUM
	SUCCINCTORY
baptismal robe	CHRIS(T)OM
	CHRISOM-CLOTH
belted coat or gown	TUNIC
bikini	TANGA

bishop's	
—scarf	ORARIUM
—stole	EPITRACHELION
—vestment	CHIMER(E), PALLIUM
	RATIONAL(E), ROTCHET
black silk cloak	DOMINO
blanket with hole for head	PONCHO
blouse	SHIRT, SHIRTWAIST
	TUNIC
—American	WAIST
—fastened at waist	BLOUSON
—Indian	CHOLI
—loose	GARIBALDI
—short	BLOUSON
blue garment	MAZARINE
bodice	CHEMISETTE
—American	WAIST
—combined with skirt	PRINCESS
—extension	BASQUE
—loose fitting	BLOUSE
—of ballet dress	GILET
—Scottish	JIRKINET
—woman's (18thc)	PIERROT
boy's suit (19th c)	SKELETON SUIT
brassière padded with foam	GAY DECEIVER
breeches	TRUSSES
—buff-coloured cotton	NANKEENS
	NANKINS
—closefitting	HOSE, TREWS, TROUSE
—footman's	PLUSHES
—full (16th c)	TRUNK BREECHES
	TRUNK HOSE
—knee	SMALL CLOTHES
—long	TROUSERS
—loose	KNICKERBOCKERS
baggy	PLUS FOURS
—man's (17th c)	PETTICOAT-BREECHES
—wide	OXFORD BAGS, SLOPS
bride's outfit	TROUSSEAU
Burmese skirt	TAMEIN
bustle	DRESS-IMPROVER
cape	
—cyclist's	PONCHO
—knitted	SONTAG
—Mexican	SERAPE, ZARAPE
—short	MOZETTA
worn by Pope	FAN(I)ON
—shoulder	TIPPET
fur	VICTORINE
—triangular	FICHU
—with hood	DOMINO
Maltese	FALDETTA
—woman's	MANTEEL, PELERINE
caped riding hood	JOSEPH
cardigan (US)	WAM(M)US, WAMPUS
cassock	SLOP, SUBUCULA

—French	SOUTANE
casual jacket	SPORTS JACKET
chemise	SHIFT, SMOCK
—Scottish	SARK
chest-protector	PECTORAL
child's	
—apron (US)	TIER
—bodice and skirt (Scot.)	POLONAISE
—coat	PELISSE
—outer garment	PILCH
—pants and shirt (US)	PANTYWAIST
—undergarment	COM(B)S, COMBINATIONS
	LIBERTY BODICE
Chinese	CHEONG-SAM, SAMFOO
	SAMFU
christening	
—robe	CHRISOM(-CLOTH)
—veil	CHRISMAL
clerical	(*see* **church—vestments**)
cloak	AMICE, AMIS, MANTEAU
	MANTLE, PALL, WRAP
—African	JELLABA
	(*see also* **African**)
—Arab	BURNOUS(E)
	(*see also* **Arabic**)
—black silk	DOMINO
—coarse leather or woollen	PILCH
—fur	PILCH
trimmed	PELISSE
—Greek	CHLAMYS, HIMATION
—lady's	CARDINAL
—Levant	GREGO
—long	CAPOTE
—loose	GABARDENE, GABARDINE
	TALMA
—man's, short	ROQUELAURE
—Mexican	SERAPE, ZERAPE
—military	PELISSE
—Moslem women	BURK(H)A, BURQA
—old	RAIL
—Roman	ABOLLA, PAENULA, PALLIUM
	SAGUM, TOGA, TOGE
—Russian	SARAFAN
—Scottish	ROCKLAY, ROKELAY
—small	MANT(E)LET
—soldier's (old)	MANTEEL
—South American	PONCHO
—theatrical	TALMA
—with cape	INVERNESS
—woman's	DOLMAN
19th c	VISITE
French	ROQUELAURE
Roman	PALLA
Russian	SARAFAN
Scottish	ROCKLAY, ROKELAY
short	CARDINAL

close-fitting	JEISTIECOR
—ballet garment	LEOTARD
—breeches	HOSE, TREWS
	TROUSE
—coat	NEWMARKET, SURTOUT
	TRUSS
French	JUPON
—jacket	MONKEY JACKET
—legless pants	BRIEFS
—surplice	ROCHET
—upper garment	DOUBLET
French	POURPOINT
—waistcoat	JERKIN
clothes of rough woollen	TWEEDS
coarse	
—leather or woollen cloak	PILCH
—linen outer garment	SMOCK-FROCK
coat	
—baby's	MATINEE COAT
—belted	TUNIC
—close fitting	NEWMARKET, SURTOUT
	TRUSS
—double-breasted	FROCKCOAT, SURTOUT
—dress	SWALLOWTAIL
	TAIL-COAT
—herald's	TABARD
—Indian	ACHKAN
—informal	SMOKING-JACKET
—Japanese raincoat	MINO
—knight's	TABARD
—loose	DUFFEL COAT, SACK-COAT
	SWAGGER COAT, WRAP RASCAL
—military	BRITISH WARM, TRENCH COAT
	TUNIC
—of	
duffel	DUFFEL COAT
twilled cotton and wool	GABARDINE
	GABERDINE
—policeman's	TUNIC
—regimental	FROCK COAT
—riding	NEWMARKET
—short	JERKIN, JUMP
	MACKINAW, SHOOTING-JACKET
—sleeveless	CAPE, JERKIN, WAISTCOAT
—small	PETTICOAT
—soldier's	TUNIC
—waterproof	MACKINTOSH, RAINCOAT
	TRENCH COAT
American	SLICKER
—with	
curved sides	CUTAWAY
hood	DUFFEL COAT
	DUFFLE COAT, PARKA
	PARKEE, PARKI
collar	
—stand-up	PICCADILLY

—woman's (17th c)	WHISK
collarless undergarment	UNDERSHIRT
cotton	
—breeches	NANKEENS, NANKINS
—suit	SAFARI SUIT
cowboy riding trousers	CHAP(ERAJO)S
	CHAPEREJOS
	CHAPS, SHAPS
cravat	
—18th c	SOUBISE
—lace	STEENKIRK
crinoline, small	CRINOLETTE
cyclist's cape	PONCHO
deacon's stole (Greek)	ORARION
denim trousers	JEANS, LEVIS
dinner-jacket (US)	TUXEDO
divided skirt	CULOTTE(S)
	HAREM SKIRT
double-breasted coat	FROCK-COAT
doublet (French)	POURPOINT
drawers	HOSE
—frilled	FRILLIES, PANTALETS
—short	PANTIES
dress	FROCK, ROBE
—18th c	TROLLOPEE
—African	K(H)ANGA
—Alpine	DIRNDL
—coat	SWALLOW-TAIL
—for riding	RIDING HABIT
—full length	MOTHER HUBBARD
—Hawaiian	MUU-MUU
—homespun	RUSSET
—improver	BUSTLE
—Japanese	KIMONO
—made from	
flowered muslin	DOLLY VARDEN
Indian silk	TASAR, TUSSAH
	TUSSEH, TUSSER
	TUSSORE
—Moslem woman's	BURKA, BURQA
—rich	ROBE
—straight	SHIRT DRESS
	SHIRTWAISTER
—tight-fitting	SHEATH, TUBE DRESS
dressing-gown	PEIGNOIR, ROBE
—woman's	NEGLIGEE, PEIGNOIR
dressing-jacket	NIGHT-RAIL
Eastern bishop's	
vestment	OMOPHORION, SAKKOS
ecclesiastical	(see church—vestments)
farm-worker's garment	SMOCK-FROCK
fawn-skin worn by	
Bacchus	NEBRIS
flannel	
—scarf with sleeves	NIGHTINGALE
—undervest (Scot.)	WYLIE-COAT

flashy type of man's suit	ZOOT SUIT
flowered muslin dress	DOLLY VARDEN
flowing gown	MOTHER HUBBARD
footman's breeches	PLUSHES
for restraint	STRAIT-JACKET
	STRAIT-WAISTCOAT
foundation	
—for skirt	UNDERSKIRT
—garment	PANTY-GIRDLE
frilled drawers	PANTALETS
frock-coat	FROCK
—19th C	SURTOUT
front part of dress	GILET
full breeches (16th c)	TRUNK-BREECHES
	TRUNK-HOSE
fur	
—cloak	PILCH
—tippet	VICTORINE
—lined	PELISSE
gaudy clothes	TRAPPINGS
goats'-hair shawl	CASHMERE, KASHMIR
gown	SLOP, STOLE
—17-18th c	MANTEAU, MANTO, MANTUA
—belted	TUNIC
—loose	MOTHER HUBBARD
old	NEGLIGEE, SLAMMAKIN
	SLAMMERKIN
—morning	PEIGNOIR
—preaching	GENEVA GOWN
—Roman	STOLA
greatcoat	PETERSHAM
—Afghan	POS(H)TEEN
—caped	ULSTER
—loose (18th c)	WRAP RASCAL
Greek	
—deacon's stole	ORARION
—kilt	FUSTANELLA
—monk's habit	SCHEMA
—one-sleeved garment	EXOMIS
—veil	CALYPTRA, KALYPTRA
—woman's	
cloak	CHLAMYS, HIMATION
robe	PEPLOS, PEPLUM
	PEPLUS
Greenlander's jacket	ANARAK, ANORAK
handkerchief	BANDAN(N)A
hats	(see **headgear**)
Hawaiian dress	MUU-MUU
herald's coat	TABARD
high	
—collar (17th c)	PICCADILL(O)
	PICCADILLY, PIKADELL
—necked garment	TURTLE NECK
homespun dress	RUSSET
hood	
—old	SURTOUT

—riding	NITHSDALE, TROT-COSEY
	TROT-COZY
—Russian	BASHLYK
—woollen	CAPELINE
hooded	
—coat	DUFFELCOAT, DUFFLE COAT
	PARKA, PARKEE, PARKI
—jacket (Levant)	GREGO
hooped skirt	CRINOLINE, FARTHINGALE
house gown	
—informal	HOUSECOAT
—loose	TEA GOWN
Hussar's jacket	DOLMAN
Indian	
—coat	ACHKAN
—dress	BANIAN, BANYAN
	SAREE, SARI
—high-collared coat	SHERWANI
—shirt	K(H)URTA
—tunic	K(H)URTA
—woman's	
blouse	CHOLI
veil	CHAD(D)AR, CHADOR
	CHUDDAH, CHUDDAR
informal	
—gown	HOUSECOAT, NEGLIGEE
—jacket	SMOKING JACKET
—shirt	TEE-SHIRT, T-SHIRT
Inquisition victim's	
garment	SANBENITO
jacket	JERKIN
—American	
loose	VAREUSE
short	ROUNDABOUT
strong	WAM(M)US, WAMPUS
—boy's	ETON JACKET
—casual	SPORTS JACKET
—Chinese	MAKWA
trousers and jacket	SAMFOO, SAMFU
—close-fitting	MESS JACKET
	MONKEY JACKET
—dinner (US)	TUXEDO
—double-breasted	REEFER(-JACKET)
—Greenlander's	ANARAK, ANORAK
—hooded (Levant)	GREGO
—Hussar's	DOLMAN
—indoor	SMOKING-JACKET
—loose	LUMBER JACKET
	NORFOLK JACKET
—mediaeval peasant's	SAYON
—military undress	MESS JACKET
	SHELL JACKET
—padded, under armour	ACTON
	HA(C)QUETON
—riding	HACKING JACKET
	NEWMARKET

—sailor's	PEA-JACKET
—Scott	RAILLY
—sleeveless (Fr.)	JUPON
—with waistband	NORFOLK JACKET
—woman's	
16th-17th c	HALF-KIRTLE
19th c	POLKA
Scottish	SHORTGOWN
short	BOLERO
skirted	BASQUE, ZOUAVE
Japanese	
—dress	(KI)MONO
—raincoat	MINO
jester's garb	MOTLEY
Jewish	TALIS
—prayer-shawl	TALLITH
—priest's surplice	EPHOD
kilt (Albanian or Greek)	FUSTANELLA
knee-breeches	SMALL-CLOTHES
knickerbockers	PLUS FOURS
knight's coat	TABARD
knitted	
—blanket or shawl	AFGHAN
—jumper and cardigan	TWIN-SET
—upper garment	CARDIGAN
	GUERNSEY, JERSEY
	JUMPER, PULLOVER, SWEATER
lace cravat	STEENKIRK
large loose sweater	SLOPPY JOE
leather	
—or quilted coat	GAMBESON
—outer garment	PILCHER
—trousers (Austria)	LEDERHOSEN
leggings	GALLIGASKINS
	PUTTEES, SPAT(T)EES
light	
—dress (17th c)	CHIMER(E), CIMAR
	CYMAR
—indoor jacket	SMOKING-JACKET
—overcoat	ULSTERETTE
—waterproof coat	RAINCOAT
little tunic	TUNICLE
loin cloth	WAISTCLOTH
—Hindu	D(H)OTI
—Indian	LUNGI
long	
—breeches	TROUSERS
—cloak	CAPOTE, DOMINO
—covering whole body	BURK(H)A
	BURQA
—dress-like coat	HOUSE-COAT
—jacket suit	DRAPE SUIT
—overcoat	CHESTERFIELD, REDINGOTE
—robe	STOLE
loose	
—blouse	GARIBALDI

—breeches	KNICKERBOCKERS
—cloak	GABARDINE, GABERDINE
	TALMA
—coat	NORFOLK JACKET
	WRAP RASCAL
—dress	SHIFT
Hawaii	MUU-MUU
—fitting bodice	BLOUSE
—garment	SLOP
—gown	MOTHER HUBBARD
17th c	MANTEAU, MANTO
18th c	NEGLIGEE
old	SLAMMAKIN, SLAMMERKIN
over armour	MANDILION, MANDYLION
—greatcoat (18th c)	WRAP-RASCAL
—house-gown	TEA-GOWN
—jacket (US)	VAREUSE
—outer garment	BLOUSE, MANTLE
	MANTUA, ROBE
—overcoat	CHESTERFIELD, PALETOT
	ULSTER
—tunic	
African	DASHIKI, KANZU
Malayan	KABAYA
—undergarment (17th c)	CHIMER(E)
	· CIMAR, CYMAR
—wrap	NIGHT-RAIL
low-necked blouse	PNEUMONIA BLOUSE
made from	
—coarse cotton	DUCKS
—corded silk	PADUASOY
—rough wool	TWEEDS
—silk with wool	
or hair	FAR(R)ANDINE
	FERRANDINE
—twilled cotton	JEANS, DENIMS
—wool with satin twill	CALAMANCO
Malayan	
—dress	SARONG
—tunic	KABAYA
man's	
—breeches (17th c)	PETTICOAT-BREECHES
—detachable shirt front	DICK(E)Y
—formal coat	TAIL-COAT
—loose coat	SACK-COAT
—neckwear	ASCOT, BOW, CRAVAT, TIE
—sash	CUMMERBUND
—short cloak (18th c)	ROQUELAURE
—suit (1940s)	ZOOT SUIT
—undergarment	BRIEFS, COMBINATIONS
	COM(B)S, JOCKEY SHORTS
	LONG JOHNS, PANTS, VEST
—undershirt (Roman)	SUBUCULA
maniple	FANON, FANNEL(L)
mantle	KIRTLE, PALL
—old	ROCHET, ROCQUET

—Roman	PALLIUM	—dialect	JAMES, JEMMY
woman's	PALLA	—German	LODEN
master's cape with hood	DOMINO	—heavy	GREATCOAT
mediaeval		—Italian	TAGLIONI
—body garment	COTE HARDIE	—Levantine	GREGO
—peasant's jacket	SAYON	—light	COVERT COAT, ULSTERETTE
Mexican cape	SERAPE, ZARAPE	—loose	CHESTERIELD, PALETOT
military			ULSTER
—cloak	PELISSE	—old	SURTOUT
—coat	BRITISH WARM	—officer's	(BRITISH) WARM
	TRENCH-COAT	—peasant's	TABARD
—undress jacket	MESS JACKET	—sailor's	PEA-COAT, PEA-JACKET
	SHELL JACKET	—short	SPENCER
monk's		—with	
—garment	FROCK, SCAPULAR	cape	INVERNESS
—habit (Gr.)	SCHEMA	sleeves in one piece	
—morning-gown	PEIGNOIR	the shoulder	RAGLAN
Moslem		overskirt	PEPLUM
—pilgrim's garb	IHRAM	peasant's overcoat	TABARD
—woman's		penitent's robe	CILICE
dress	BURK(H)A, BURQA	petticoat	PLACKET, UNDERSKIRT
veil	YASHMAK	—figured woollen	BALMORAL
narrow		—French	JUPON
—skirt	HOBBLE SKIRT	—Scottish	WYLIE-COAT
—vestment	STOLE	—stiffened	CRINOLINE
neck covering	PARTLET, RUFF		FARTHINGALE
neckerchief	BANDAN(N)A	Philippines	MALO, PAREU
—old	RAIL	pinafore	OVERALL
—woman's	WHICK	—American	TIRE
nightclothes	(see sleepwear below)	—dress (US)	JUMPER
officer's overcoat	(BRITISH) WARM	policeman's coat	TUNIC
oilskin (US)	SLICKER	Polynesian	
one-piece		—skirt	LAVA-LAVA
—ballet dress	LEOTARD	—wrap	PAREU
—bodice and skirt	POLONAISE	Pope's	
—outer garment	BOILER-SUIT	—cape	FAN(I)ON
	CAT-SUIT, JUMP-SUIT	—vestment	PALLIUM
—swim-suit	MAILLOT	preaching gown	GENEVA GOWN
—undergarment	BODY STOCKING	protective	APRON, COVERALL
	CAMIKNICKERS		DUNGAREES, OVERALL
	COMBINATIONS	—military	FATIGUES, GASCAPE
	COMBS, TEDDY		NODDY SUIT
one-sleeved garment (Gr.)	EXOMIS	pullover	
outer		—sleeveless	TANK TOP
—garment	PALL, STOLE, WRAP	—woollen	GUERNSEY, JERSEY
coarse linen	SMOCK-FROCK		SWEATER
loose	MANTLE, ROBE	raincoat	BURBERRY, GABARDENE
old	SURCOAT		GABARDINE
—petticoat	KIRTLE	—Japanese	MINO
Basque	BASQUINE	ready-made clothing	PRET A PORTER
over-jacket (old)	SPENCER		REACH-ME-DOWNS
overall	APRON, JUMPER, PINAFORE		SLOPS
overalls	DUNGAREES	religious vestment (Greek)	STICHARION
—American	COVERALL	restraining	STRAITJACKET
overcoat			STRAIT-WAISTCOAT
—19th c	TAGLIONI	rich dress	ROBE

riding		—small	TURNOVER
—breeches	JODHPURS	—triangular	FICHU
—coat	HACKING JACKET, NEWMARKET	—with shaped neck	TONNAG
—dress	RIDING-HABIT	—woollen	WHITTLE
—habit	RIDING-ROBE	sheepskin coat	AFGHAN
—hood	NITHSDALE, TROT-COSEY	—Spanish	ZAMARRA, ZAMARRO
	TROT-COZY	shepherd's plaid (Scot.)	MAUD
—neckerchief	STOCK	shift	CHEMISE, SHIRT, SMOCK
—trousers	CHAPAREJOS, CHAPEREJOS	shirt	
	CHAPS, SHAPS	—India	K(H)URTA
robe		—old	PARTLET
—Ghana	KENTE	—Scotland	SARK
—informal	HOUSECOAT, TEA-GOWN	shore clothes (Navy)	LONG-TOGS
—long	STOLE	short	
—old	PALLIAMENT, PARAMENT	—cape	MOZETTA
—penitent's	CILICE	worn by Pope	FANON
—reaching the ankles	TALAR	—coat	JERKIN, JUMP
—Roman	STOLA		SHOOTING-JACKET
Roman		—cloak (Gr.)	CHLAMYS
—cloak	TOGA, TOGE	—drawers	PANTIES
—gown	STOLA	—jacket	
—mantle	PALLIUM	boy's	ETON JACKET
woman's	PALLA	double-breasted	REEFER(-JACKET)
—military cloak	ABOLLA	military	MESS JACKET
	PALAUDAMENT(UM)		SHELL JACKET
	SAGUM	woman's	BASQUE, BOLERO
—robe	STOLA		ZOUAVE
—sleeveless garment	EXOMIS	—light overcoat	COVERT COAT
—travelling cloak	PAENULA	—loose coat	DUFFEL COAT
—undershirt	SUBUCULA		DUFFLE COAT, SACK COAT
ruff	PARTLET	—negligee	CAMISOLE
Russian		—overcoat	SPENCER
—hood	BASHLYK	—pleated skirt	RA-RA (SKIRT)
—peasant's cloak	SARAFAN	—sleeved garment (Shak.)	SEA-GOWN
sailor's		—sleeveless jacket	WAISTCOAT
—jersey	FROCK	—veil	KISS-ME
—overcoat	PEA-COAT, PEA-JACKET	at back of head	VOLET
—shore clothes	LONG-TOGS	—woollen coat	MACKINAW
—trousers	BELL-BOTTOMS	shoulder	
—upper garment	GUERNSEY	—cape	TIPPET
scarf	BANDAN(N)A	—covering	SHAWL
—bishop's	ORARIUM	shroud	WINDING-SHEET
—fur and feathers	BOA	skin-tight garment	LEOTARD
—man's	ASCOT, CRAVAT	skirt	
—rider's	STOCK	—Alpine	DIRNDL
—woman's	FICHU	—ballet	TUTU
Scottish		—Burmese	TAMEIN
—man's skirt	FILABEG, FIL(L)IBEG,	—divided	CULOTTE(S), HAREM SKIRT
	KILT, PHIL(L)ABEG	—hooped	CRINOLINE, FARTHINGALE
	PHIL(L)IBEG	small	CRINOLETTE
—nightshirt	SEMMIT	—hung from shoulders	PINAFORE DRESS
—shepherd's plaid	MAUD		PINAFORE SKIRT
—woman's jacket	SHORTGOWN	—long	MAXI
shawl	WRAP	—Malayan	SARONG
—Hebrew	TALLITH	—narrow	HOBBLE(-SKIRT)
—Scottish	MAUD	—Polynesian	PAREU

—padded at rear	BUSTLE	suit	
—short	MINI	—boy's (19th c)	SKELETON SUIT
pleated	RA-RA(SKIRT)	—cotton	SAFARI SUIT
puffy	BUBBLE SKIRT	—flashy (1940s)	ZOOT SUIT
—tight	TUBE SKIRT	—with long jacket	DRAPE SUIT
—trouser-like	CULOTTE(S)	supporting	
	DIVIDED SKIRT, HAREM SKIRT	undergarment	BRA(SSIERE), CORSET
sleepwear			CORSELET(TE), STAYS
—man's	NIGHT-SHIRT, PYJAMAS	surplice	COTTA, EPHOD, STOLA, STOLE
Scottish	SEMMIT	—Scotland	SARK
—woman's	NIGHT-DRESS, NIGHT-GOWN	swaddling cloth	PILCH
	PYJAMAS	swimsuit	
Scottish	WYLIE-COAT	—one-piece	MAILLOT
short	BABY-DOLL	—two-piece	BIKINI, TANGA
sleeveless		Syrian	AB(B)A, ABAYA
—child's garment	BARROW	tabard	CHIMER(E)
—cloak	MANTLE, PAENULA	tartan trousers	TREWS
—coat	CAPE, JERKIN, WAISTCOAT	three-cornered cape	FICHU
—dress	SUNDRESS	tights	
—jacket		—for ballet-dancer	MAILLOT
French	JUPON	—incorporating pants	PANTIHOSE
peasant's	SAYON	travelling cloak (Roman)	PAENULA
short	WAISTCOAT	triangular shawl	FICHU
—pullover	TANKTOP	trouser-like woman' garment	PANTALETS
—Roman robe	EXOMIS	trousers	BAGS, FLANNELS
—tabard	CHIMER(E)		PANTS, SLACKS
—tunic	TABARD	—Asian	SHERWAL, SHERRYVALLIES
—underbodice	CAMISOLE	—baggy	OXFORD BAGS, SLOPS
—vest	LIBERTY BODICE	—cricketer's	FLANNELS
small		—cut like skirt	CULOTTE(S)
—cloak	MANT(E)LET		DIVIDED SKIRT
—coat	PETTICOAT		HAREM SKIRT
—crinoline	CRINOLETTE	—ending	
—shawl	TURNOVER	above knee	SHORTS
—tunic	TUNICLE	below knee	BERMUDA SHORTS
smock	SHIFT, SLOP		KNEE-BREECHES
smock-frock	BLOUSE, FROCK		PLUS FOURS, PLUS TWOS
soldier's		—from the hips	HIP-HUGGERS, HIPSTERS
—cloak	MANTEEL	—made of	
—coat	TUNIC	denim	JEANS, LEVIS
—protective clothing	GASCAPE	double-twilled fustian	MOLESKINS
	NODDY SUIT	light wool	FLANNELS
—working clothes	FATIGUES	ribbed fustian	CORDUROYS
South American		—old	GALLIGASKINS
—apron	TAYO	—Pakistani	SHALWAR
—cloak	PONCHO	—Persian	SHULWAR
Spanish sheepskin coat	ZAMARRA	—tartan	TREWS
	ZAMARRO	—with	
stand-up collar	PICCADILLY	narrow	
stole	BOA	—bottoms	PEGTOPS
straight dress	SHIRT DRESS	—legs	DRAINPIPES
	SHIRTWAISTER	wide	
strip worn over shoulder		—bottoms	BELL-BOTTOMS
—by priest	SCAPULAR	—legs	OXFORD BAGS
—Scottish	PLAID	tunic	
sub-deacon's vestment	TUNICLE	—African	DASHIKI, KANZU

—Greek	CHITON
—Indian	K(H)URTA
—sleeveless	TABARD
—small	TUNICLE
Turkish robe	CAFTAN, DOLMAN, KAFTAN
underclothes	LINGERIE, SMALLS
	UNDIES
—17th c	CIMAR, CYMAR
undershirt (Roman)	SUBUCULA
underskirt	PETTICOAT
undertaker's cloak	MOURNING-CLOAK
undress	
—military jacket	MESS JACKET
	SHELL-JACKET
—regimental coat	FROCK
veil	
—christening	CHRISMAL
—covering head	MANTILLA
—draped round head etc	W(H)IMPLE
—short	KISS ME
vestments	(*see* **church—vestments**)
waistcoat	GILET
—American	VEST
—closefitting	JERKIN
waterproof	
—Australian	DRIZA-BONE
—coat	BARBOUR, BURBERRY
	RAINCOAT, TRENCH-COAT
US	SLICKER
—over-garment(s)	MAC(K)INTOSH
	OILSKIN(S)
waxed coat	BARBOUR
weatherproof anorak	CAGOUL(E), KAGOOL
	KAGOUL(E)
winding-sheet	SHROUD
windproof	ANARAK, ANORAK
	PARKA, PARKEE, PARKI
woman's	
—backless bodice	HALTER
—basque (18th c)	PIERROT
—blouse	SHIRT, SHIRTWAIST
or bodice (US)	WAIST
—cape	FICHU, MANTEEL, PELERINE
old	SURTOUT
—cloak	CARDINAL, DOLMAN
19th c	VISITE
Roman	PALLA
Russian	SARAFAN
Scottish	ROCKLAY, ROKELAY
—collar (17th c)	WHISK
—dress	FROCK, ROBE
18th c	TROLLOPEE
—dressing-gown	NEGLIGEE, PEIGNOIR
—garment with combined	
bodice and skirt	PRINCESS
India	SAREE, SARI

—informal gown	HOUSECOAT, TEA GOWN
—jacket	
16-17th c	HALF-KIRTLE
19th c	POLKA
short	BASQUE, BOLERO, ZOUAVE
—knitted cape	SONTAG
—long mantle	PELISSE
—loose jacket (Scot.)	SHORTGOWN
—morning gown	CAMISOLE, PEIGNOIR
—neckerchief (17th c)	WHISK
—outer garment	BODICE, STOLE
	TABARD
—riding	
coat	JOSEPH
hood (18th c)	NITHSDALE
—shift	SMOCK
—shirt	CHEMISE, SHIFT
—short	
cloak (Scot.)	ROK(E)LAY
jacket	BOLERO, BASQUE
	ZOUAVE
shorts	HOT-PANTS
undergarment	SPENCER
—sleeved jacket	CAMISOLE
—underclothing	LINGERIE, UNDIES
17th c	CIMAR, CYMAR
bust	BRA(SSIERE)
—and waist	BODICE, BUSTIER
	SPENCER, TEDDY
hips	GIRDLE
overall	BODYSHAPER, CAMIKNICKERS
	PETTICOAT, SLIP
pants	BLOOMERS, BRIEFS
	KNICKERS
—with stockings	PANTIHOSE, TIGHTS
stiffened	BODICE, CORSET
	CORSELET(TE)
supporting	
stockings	SUSPENDER BELT
woollen	
—coat, short	MACKINAW
—clothes, rough	TWEEDS
—knitted	(see knitted above)
—petticoat	BALMORAL
—shawl	WHITTLE
wrap	AMICE, AMIS, HAP
—loose	NIGHT-RAIL
gases	
acetylene	ETHYNE
after-damp	CHOKE-DAMP
anaesthetic	CHLOROFORM
	CYCLOPROPANE
	ETHER, NITROUS OXIDE
antimony hydride	STIBINE
argon	A
attacking nervous system	NERVE GAS

burning	MUSTARD
carbon	
—and water	WATER GAS
—dioxide	CARBONIC ACID GAS
	COO
and methane	BIOGAS
mixture	AFTER-DAMP
	BLACK DAMP, CHOKE DAMP
—monoxide	CO, WHITE DAMP
carbonyl chloride	PHOSGENE
carburetted hydrogen	ETHYLENE
causing deterioration of	
mental performance	PSYCHOCHEMICAL
	PSYCHOGAS
chlorine	CL
colourless	CARBON MONOXIDE
	ETHYLENE, HYDROGEN IODIDE
	KETEN, NITRIC OXIDE
combustible	BUTANE, FIRE-DAMP
	METHANE, PROPANE
corrosive	MUSTARD GAS, YPERITE
dichlordiethyl sulphide	MUSTARD GAS
ethyne	ACETYLENE
explosive gas	BLACK DAMP, CHOKE DAMP
	ELECTROLYTIC GAS
	EUCHLORINE
fire-damp	MARSH GAS, METHANE
fluorine	F
formed	
—by radioactive decay	EMANATION
	ACTINON, NITON
	RADON, THORON
—in incomplete	
combustion	CARBON MONOXIDE
found in coal gas	CARBON MONOXIDE
from	
—actinium	ACTINON
—boilers	FLUE GAS
—coal	COAL GAS
—coke	PRODUCER GAS, TOWN GAS
—decaying matter	EFFLUVIUM
—methanol	FORMALDEHYDE
—organic materials	BIOGAS
—steam on hot coke	WATER GAS
gas	
—burner	BUNSEN
—cooled reactor	AGR
greenish gas	EUCHLORINE, FLUORINE
helium	HE
heavy hydrogen	DEUTERIUM
hydrogen	H
—isotope	DEUTERIUM, TRITIUM
hypothetical gas	(A)ETHER
inert gas	NOBLE GAS, RARE GAS
	ARGON, HELIUM, KRYPTON
	NEON, RADON, XENON

inflammable	METHYLAMINE
irritant gas	BROMINE, CN, CS, TEAR GAS
krypton	KR
lachrymator	TEAR GAS
laughing-gas	NITROUS OXIDE
liquid	
—gas used in war	LEWISITE
—oxygen	LOX
—petroleum gas	LPG
liquefied gas	BUTANE, CALOR
marsh gas	FIRE-DAMP, METHANE
methane	FIRE-DAMP, MARSH GAS
—and carbon dioxide	BIOGAS
mustard gas	DICHLORODIETHYL SULPHIDE
	YPERITE
natural gas	FIRE DAMP, MARSH GAS
	METHANE
neon	NE
nerve gas	SARIN, TABUN
neutron	NU
niton	RADON
nitrogen	N
—and hydrogen	AMMONIA
olfiant	ETHYLENE
oxygen	O
pale yellow gas	HYDROGEN BROMIDE
phosgene	CARBONYL CHLORIDE
phosphuretted	
hydrogen	PHOSPHINE
poison gas	ANTIMONY HYDRIDE, ARSINE
	BROMINE, CARBON MONOXIDE
	CARBONYL CHLORIDE, CHLORINE
	CYANIC ACID, CYANOGEN
	MUSTARD GAS, PHOSGENE
	PHOSPHINE, PRUSSIC ACID
	STIBINE, YPERITE
propellant	FLUORINE
radon	NITON, RN
silicon hydride	SIL(IC)ANE
smelling of	
—almonds	CYANIC ACID GAS
	PRUSSIC ACID
—rotten eggs	HYDROGEN SULPHIDE
stibine	ANTIMONY HYDRIDE
tear gas	CS GAS, LACHRYMATOR
unstable oxygen	OZONE
used	
—as	
disinfectant	FORMALDEHYDE
fertiliser	AMMONIA
fuel	BUTANE, METHANE
	PROPANE
—for	
fluorescent lighting	HELIUM
	KRYPTON, NEON
illuminated signs	NEON

making
—aspirin   KETEN
—plastics   ETHYLENE
—synthetic rubber   BUTADIENE, BUTANE
riot control   CS GAS
welding   ACETYLENE, ETHYNE
    OXYGEN
—in
aerosols   CFC, CHLOROFLUOROCARBON
    PROPELLANT
fire extinguishers   CARBON DIOXIDE
    CARBONIC ACID GAS
fizzy drinks   CARBON DIOXIDE
lasers   XENON
synthesis of organic
   compounds   ETHANE
very hot gas   PLASMA
war gas   ARSINE, CHLORINE, LEWISITE
    MUSTARD GAS, NERVE GAS
    PHOSGENE, PSYCHOGAS
    PSYCHOCHEMICAL, SARIN
    TABUN, ZYKLON B
xenon   XE

gems
including: semi-precious stones
agate   SCOTCH PEBBLE
almandine   PURPLE GARNET
amber-coloured   AMBER, TOPAZ
artificial   PASTE, RHINESTONE
    STRASS
associated with birth   BIRTHSTONE
aventurine   SUNSTONE
balas ruby   SPINEL
banded   AGATE, (SARD)ONYX)
beryllium compounds   ALEXANDRITE
    AQUAMARINE, BERYL
    CHRYSOBERYL, CYMOPHANE
    EMERALD, GOSHENITE
    HELIDOR, MORGANITE
birthstones
—January   GARNET
—February   AMETHYST
—March   AQUAMARINE, BLOODSTONE
—April   DIAMOND
—May   EMERALD
—June   ALEXANDRINE, MOONSTONE
    PEARL
—July   RUBY
—August   PERIDOT, SARDONYX
—September   SAPPHIRE
—October   OPAL, TOURMALINE
—November   TOPAZ
—December   TURQUOISE, ZIRCON
black   JAD(E)ITE, JET, MELANITE
    OBSIDIAN, RUTILE
    SCHORL, TOURMALINE

bloodstone   GREEN CHALCEDONY
blue   AMETHYST, AQUAMARINE, BERYL
    EMERALD, INDICOLITE
    LAPIS LAZULI
    LAZURITE, SODALITE
    SAPPHIRE, SPINEL, TOPAZ
    TURQUOISE, ZIRCON
blue-grey   C(H)ALCEDONY, LABRADORITE
Bohemian ruby   ROSE QUARTZ
Brazilian
—emerald   TOURMALINE
—peridot   TOURMALINE
brightness of gem   LUSTRE, WATER
bronze speckled   AVENTURINE, SUNSTONE
brown   AGATE, AMBER, ANDRADITE
    CAIRNGORM, CAT'S-EYE
    CELONITE, JADE, JAD(E)ITE
    JASPER, MORGANITE
    SMOKY QUARTZ, TIGER'S-EYE
    TURQUOISE, SARDONYX
carbon   DIAMOND
carnelian   CORNELIAN, SARD
changeable   CHATOYANT
cinnamon-stone   (H)ESSONITE
    HYACINTH, JACINTH
colourless   ALEXANDRITE, DIAMOND
    JARGO(O)N, ROCK CRYSTAL
    TOPAZ, ZIRCON
corundum   RUBY, SAPPHIRE
cutter/polisher   LAPIDARY
cutting styles   BAGUETTE, BRILLIANT
    BRIOZETTE, CABOCHON
    CUSHION, MARQUISE
    NAVETTE, ROSE, STEP
    TABLE, TRAP
egeran   GARNET
emerald   SMARAGD(INE)
engraving on gems   GLYPHOGRAPHY
    LITHOGLYPH
evening emerald   PERIDOT
fabled stone from
   dragon's brain   DRACONITES
fake   DOUBLET, ICE
fel(d)spar   AMAZONITE, AVENTURINE
    LABRADORITE, MOONSTONE
    SUNSTONE
fire-opal   GIRASOL(E)
fossilised
—resin   AMBER
—wood   JET
garnet   EGERAN, (H)ESSONITE
green   ALEXANDRITE, AMAZONITE
    AQUAMARINE, BERYL, BLOODSTONE
    CHRYSOBERYL, CHRYSOPRASE
    CYMOPHANE, DELMANTOID
    GARNET, GROSSULARITE

	EMERALD, HELIOTROPE, JADE	
	JAD(E)ITE, MALACHITE, NEPHRITE	
	OBSIDIAN, OLIVINE, PERIDOT	
	SPINEL, TOPAZ, TOURMALINE	
	TURQUOISE, UVAROVITE	
	VERDITE, ZIRCON	
—chalcedony	BLOODSTONE	
—corundum	ORIENTAL EMERALD	
—fluorspar	FALSE EMERALD	
—garnet	URALIAN EMERALD	
—quartz	MOTHER OF EMERALD	
—rock crystal	CITRINE	
hydrated		
—copper carbonate	MALACHITE	
—silica	OPAL	
impure diamond	BOART	
industrial diamond	BOART	
jacinth	GARNET, QUARTZ	
	TOPAZ, ZIRCON	
jade	JAD(E)ITE, NEPHRITE	
lignite	JET	
lime-chrome garnet	UVAROVITE	
Matura diamond	ZIRCON	
magnesia-alumina	ALMANDINE, CARBUNCLE	
	DELMANTOID, GARNET	
	GROSSULARITE, MELANITE	
	PYROPE, TOPAZITE	
magnesium-iron silicate	OLIVINE, PERIDOT	
milky-white	MOONSTONE, OPAL	
multi-coloured	AGATE, (SARD)ONYX, OPAL	
opal		
—flame-coloured	FIRE-OPAL, GIRASOL(E)	
—milky	CACHALONG	
—semi-transparent	HYDROPHANE	
—transparent	HYALITE	
opaque quartz	JASP(ER), JASPIS	
orange	CARNELIAN, CHRYSOBERYL	
	CITRINE, CORNELIAN, FIRE-OPAL	
	GIRASOL(E), HESSONITE	
	JACINTH, RUBICELLE	
	SARD, TOPAZITE	
oriental		
—emerald	GREEN CORUNDUM	
—topaz	SAPPHIRE	
pink	ALMANDINE, MORGANITE	
	RHODOLITE, ROSE QUARTZ	
pointed oval shape	MARQUISE, NAVETTE	
polished uncut stone	CABOCHON	
purple	ALMANDINE (SPINEL)	
	AMETHYST, GARNET	
	RHODOLITE	
—garnet	ALMANDINE	
pyrope	RED GARNET	
quartz		
—opaque	JASP(ER), JASPIS	
—rose	BOHEMIAN RUBY	

red	ALEXANDRITE, BERYL	
	CAIRNGORM, CARBUNCLE	
	CARNELIAN, CORNELIAN	
	FIRE-OPAL, GARNET	
	GIRASOL(E), HYACINTH	
	JACINTH, JAD(E)ITE, JASPER	
	RUBASSE, RUBELLITE	
	RUBY, RUTILE, SPINEL, ZIRCON	
—garnet	PYROPE, PYROPUS	
reddish-brown	(H)ESSONITE	
rose quartz	BOHEMIAN RUBY	
sapphire	TELESIA	
sard	CARNELIAN, CORNELIAN	
silica compounds	AGATE, AMETHYST	
	CAIRNGORM (STONE)	
	CARNELIAN, C(H)ALCEDONY	
	CHRYSOPRASE, CITRINE	
	CORNELIAN, JASPER	
	ROCK CRYSTAL, ROSE QUARTZ	
	SARD, (SARD)ONYX	
	SMOKE QUARTZ	
silicate of		
—aluminium and sodium	JAD(E)ITE	
—calcium and magnesium	NEPHRITE	
—fluorine and aluminium	TOPAZ	
—sodium and iron	TIGER'S-EYE	
—zirconium	JACINTH, JARGO(O)N	
	ZIRCON	
single stone	SOLITAIRE	
smaragd(ine)	EMERALD	
smoky	CAIRNGORM (STONE)	
	SMOKE QUARTZ	
spinel	BALAS RUBY	
—blue	SPINEL SAPPHIRE	
—brown	CELONITE	
—crimson	SPINEL RUBY	
—orange	RUBICELLE	
—purple	ALMANDINE SPINEL	
—rose-red	BALSAM RUBY	
sulphide of iron	MARCASITE	
sunstone	AVENTURINE	
telesia	SAPPHIRE	
tourmaline		
—colourless	ACHROITE	
—black	SCHORL	
—blue	INDICOLITE	
—pink	RUBELLITE	
—red	RUBELLITE	
—violet	SIBERITE	
transparency of gem	LUSTRE, WATER	
transparent		
—opal	HYALITE	
—zircon	JARGO(O)N	
turquoise	TURKOIS	
twinkling like a gem	CHATOYANT	
unit of weight	CARAT	

various colours	ZIRCON	America	BOTTOM
varying composition	ACHROITE	formed by distribution of	
	INDICOLITE, RUBELLITE	moraine over wider	
	SCHORL, TOURMALINE	area	OUTWASH PLAIN, SANDIR
violet	AMETHYST, SIBERITE	—slope	BAHADA, BAHAJA
volcanic glass	OBSIDIAN	altitude above which	
white	C(H)ALCEDONY	trees do not grow	TIMBER LINE
	GOSHENITE	ancient alluvium	GEEST
	JAD(E)ITE, OPAL	angle	
with		—between horizontal and	
—incised design	INTAGLIO	direction of earth's	
—raised design	CAMEO	magnetic field	DIP
yellow	AMBER, BERYL	—between true and magnetic	
	CHRYSOBERYL, CITRINE	north	(MAGNETIC) DECLINATION
	FIRE-OPAL, GARNET		(MAGNETIC) VARIATION
	GIRASOL(E), HELIODOR	—between vertical and	
	JASPER, TOPAZ(ITE)	a fault plane	HADE
	SAPPHIRE	—horizontal	AZIMUTH
—quartz	SCOTTISH TOPAZ	—vertical	ALTITUDE
yellowish-brown	OBSIDIAN	angular distance from	
zircon		—Equator	LATITUDE
—brown	MALACON	—Greenwich meridian	LONGITUDE
—orange	HYACINTH, HYACYNTH	animal life of region	FAUNA
	JACINTH	approaching the end of a	
—yellow	JARGO(O)N	geological cycle	SENILE
geography		area	
including: geology		—adjoining sea	BEACH, COAST(AL PLAIN)
mineralogy			FORESHORE, LITTORAL
abrupt turn in course			SEABOARD, SEASIDE
of river	ELBOW CAPTURE		(SEA) SHORE, SHORELINE
absorption of one river			STRAND, TIDEWATER
by another	ABSTRACTION	—almost surrounded by	
accumulation of rock		water	PENINSULA
fragments	DEBRIS, SCREE, TALUS	—between	
aclinic line	MAGNETIC EQUATOR	low-water mark	
acquisition by one river		and edge of	
or stream of another	BEHEADING	continental shelf	SUB-LITTORAL
	RIVER CAPTURE	tides	INTERTIDAL
	RIVER PIRACY	tropics	INTERTROPICAL
action of		—bounded by watersheds (US)	WATERSHED
—climate on rocks etc	WEATHERING	—containing much soil	
—ice	GLACIATION	moisture	WETLAND(S)
ages of		—covered by	
—earth	(*see* geological ages *below*)	fresh water	BROAD, LAKE (BASIN)
—human culture	(*see* **anthropology**)		LOCH, LOUGH, MERE, TARN
agricultural system in		ice on	
hill country	TERRACE CULTIVATION	—land	ICE CAP, ICE FIELD
alignment of features	GRAIN		ICE SHEET
alkaline marsh area	ALKALINE FLAT	—water	FLOE, ICE PACK
alluvial		sand	DESERT
—deposit at mouth of river	DELTA	sand-dunes	ERG, LINKS
Scotland	CARSE	snow	SNOWFIELD
traversed by many		stones	REG
branches	BIRD'S FOOT DELTA	stunted trees or shrubs	SCRUB
—plain		trees	FOREST, JUNGLE
alongside river	FLOOD PLAIN		PLANTATION, WOOD(LAND)

—drained by river	CATCHMENT AREA
	(RIVER) BASIN, VALLEY
—encrusted with salt	SALT FLAT
	SALT PAN
—eroded by wind	DUST-BOWL
—falling to centre from	
all directions	BASIN
—frequently covered by water	WASH
—in which particular	
rocks predominate	TERRANE
—lying inland from coast	HINTERLAND
—of	
active deformation of	
Earth's crust	MOBILE BELT
arid, sandy soil	STEPPE
calms	DOLDRUMS
	HORSE LATITUDES
continent near sea	
plus the continental	
shelf	CONTINENTAL PLATFORM
dense undergrowth	THICKET
droughts and	
dust-storms	DUST BOWL
dwarf evergreen	
oaks (US)	CHAPARRAL
Earth	
—divided by Equator	
or meridian	HEMISPHERE
—covered by	
water	WATER HEMISPHERE
—just outside	
Arctic Circle	SUBARCTIC
Antarctic Circle	SUBANTARCTIC
fertile soil	
—America	BLACK EARTH
—India	BLACK COTTON EARTH
—Russia	BLACK EARTH
	CHERNOZEM
mud covered at	
high tide	MUDFLAT(S)
open water in sea ice	POLYNA
permanently frozen subsoil	TUNDRA
scrubland	
—Mediterranean	GAR(R)IGUE
	MAQUIS
—North America	CHAPARRAL
sea adjoining land	
mass	CONTINENTAL SHELF
shifting sand dunes	ERG, SAND-SEA
soft wet ground	BOG, CARR, FEN
	FLOW, MARSH, SWAMP
strong westerly	
winds	ROARING FORTIES
	SCREAMING FIFTIES
uniform climate,	
flora, etc	NATURAL REGION

unstable sand	QUICKSAND
	RUNNING SAND
untouched forest	
with undergrowth	BUSH
—reclaimed from sea	POLDER
—subject to periodic	
flooding	
by river	FLOOD PLAIN
by sea	SALTING(S), SALTMARSH
—surrounded by water	AIT, ATOLL, EYOT
	ISLAND
—underlying glacier	SUBGLACIAL
—used for crops	TILLAGE
—where asphalt or bitumen	
rises to surface	TAR PIT
—within polar circles	FRIGID ZONE
arid region of deep gullies	BAD LANDS
arrangement of	
—atoms in crystal	(SPACE) LATTICE
—grooves	STRIATION
—strata	STRATIFICATION
artificial	
—chamber in chalk	DENE-HOLE
—embankment	DIKE, DYKE
India	BUND
USA	LEVEE
—heap of stones	CAIRN
—lake	RESERVOIR
—watercourse	CANAL, DIKE, DITCH
	DYKE, RACE
—watering system	IRRIGATION
attraction of mass of bodies	GRAVITY
backwater (Austr.)	BILLABONG
bank of earth etc	DIKE, DYKE
—round area to be	
irrigated	LEVEE
bare hill	FELL
barren	
—area in North America	BADLANDS
—land	DESERT
—region of Andes	PARAMOS
—upland plateau (Scand.)	FJELD
base	
—mark for levels	BENCH MARK
	DATUM (LEVEL)
—on which organisms live	SUBSTRATE
basin	
—filling with alluvial fans	BOLSON
—forming lake after	
heavy rain	PLAYA
—shaped crater of	
volcanic origin	CALDERA
beach	SANDS
belts of high pressure on	
both sides of the Equator	HORSE LATITUDES
bend in rock	FOLD

bending etc of Earth's surface	DIASTROPHISM
blind channel from river	BILLABONG
boggy area (Scot.)	SLACK
boulder transported and deposited by glacier	ERRATIC (BLOCK)
boundary between	
—drainage areas	WATERSHED
—land and sea	COAST(LINE) SHORE(LINE)
—layers of Earth	DISCONTINUITY MOHO
MOHOROVICICIAN DISCONTINUITY	
break	
—in sequence of sedimentary rocks	DISCONFORMITY
—up of ice in spring	DEBACLE
breaking off of iceberg from a glacier	CALVING
bronze lustre in minerals	SCHILLER
building	
—of	
continents	EPEIROGENESIS
mountains	OROGENESIS
—up of surface	AGGRADATION
calcium carbonate deposit	
—from hot springs	TRAVERTINE, TUFA
—in arid regions (USA)	CALICHE
canal taking ocean-going vessels	SHIP CANAL
can(y)on	GORGE, RAVINE
capes	(see separate entry)
cardinal points	NORTH, SOUTH EAST, WEST
carrying away of surface	ABLATION
cascade pool	LIN(N)
caused by	
—flooding	DILUVIAL
—rainfall	PLUVIAL
—rotation of Earth	GEOSTROPHIC
cave	ANTRE, CAVERN
—in limestone region	GROTTO
cavity containing mineral deposit	DRUSE, DRUSY CAVITY GEODE, POCKET
central	
—mountain mass	MASSIF
—ocean or land mass	CRATON
change in	
—different rocks to become similar	CONVERGENCE
—rocks involving chemical composition	METASOMATISM
—shape of rocks	DEFORMATION
due to	
—heat	THERMAL METAMORPHISM

—pressure	DYNAMIC METAMORPHISM
—shore lines	EUSTACY, EUSTASY
—water level in lake	SEICHE
channel	
—for running water	GULL(E)Y WATERCOURSE WATERWAY
—formed by running water	GULL(E)Y, STREAMBED
circle on earth's surface	
—midway between poles	EQUATOR
—of latitude	ALMACANTAR ALMACANTUR
—passing through centre	GREAT CIRCLE
clay	
—layer left by glacier	BOULDER CLAY
—red	BOLE
—sticky	GLEY
clearing	
—in forest	GLADE
—of forest areas	DEFORESTATION
cleft	
—between hills (Scot.)	SLACK
—in rock (Scot.)	RIVA
cliff	BLUFF
—projecting into sea	HEADLAND
climate	(see **meteorology**)
coastal outline	COAST(LINE) SHORE(LINE)
—cutting across main structural lines	DISCORDANT COAST(LINE)
—parallel to main structural lines	CONCORDANT COAST(LINE) LONGITUDINAL COAST(LINE) PACIFIC COAST(LINE)
cold areas	CRYOSPHERE
collection of gas over oil deposit	GAS CAP
column of earth with boulder on top	EARTH PILLAR
combination of arable and pastoral farming	MIXED FARMING
compass direction	POINT, QUARTER
condition of soil	TILTH
containing	
—carbon	CARBONACEOUS
—clay	ARGILLACEOUS
—diatom skeletons	DIATOMACEOUS
—grains	GRANULAR, GRANULOSE GRANULOUS
—graphite	PLUMBAGINOUS
—gravel	GLAREOUS
—little silica	(ULTRA)BASIC (ULTRA)MAFIC

—platelike crystals	TABULAR	creek (Scot.)	GEO, GIO, VOE
—sand	ARENACEOUS	—small	POW
—shell-like material	TESTACEOUS	creeping of saturated	
—silica	SILICEOUS	material down slope	SOLIFLUCTION
	SILICIOUS	crescent-shaped	
continent building	EPEIROGENESIS	sand-dune	BARCHAN(E)
	EPEIROGENY		BARK(H)AN
continents		crevasse at top	
—modern	AFRICA, ANTARCTICA	of glacier	BERGSCHRUND, RIMAYE
	ASIA, AUSTRALIA	crust of dyke or vein	SALBAND
	EUROPE, NORTH AMERICA	crystal	
	SOUTH AMERICA, OCEANIA	—having	
—old	BALTIC, EURAMERICA	2 angles at right angles	MONOCLINIC
	GONDWANA(LAND)	3 unequal angles	TRICLINIC
	LAURASIA	3 angles at right angles	ORTHORHOMBIC
—old supercontinents	AMAZONIA	3 angles at right	
	BAIKALIA, KENORA	angles, two equal	TETRAGONAL
	PANGAEA	two or more parts	TWIN CRYSTAL
conversion of		—examination by	
—limestone to marble	MARMAROSIS	X-ray	X-RAY DIFFRACTION
—loose material		—showing different	
to rock	CEMENTATION	colours from	
—sediment to rock	DIAGENESIS	different angles	PLEOCHROIC
copse in boggy ground	CARR	—visible only under a	
coral reef		microscope	MICROCRYSTAL
—detached from land	CORAL ISLAND	cultivation	(see farming below)
—enclosing lagoon	ATOLL	curved	
—parallel to shore	BARRIER REEF	—delta	ARCUATE DELTA
cotton growing area (US)	COTTON BELT	—sandbar	HOOK
county	SHIRE	cut to form vertical slope	SCARP
—division	HUNDRED, LATHE	cylindrical	
covering of a region		—body of ore	PIPE
by ice	GLACIATION	—hollow concretion	INCRETION
crack in		dam in watercourse	BARRAGE
—earth	CHASM	dark spot in crystal	MACLE
—glacier	CREVASSE	debris	
—horizontal limestone	GRIKE, GRYKE	—at foot of cliff	SCREE, TALUS
—rock	FISSURE	—deposited by running	
	RIFT, SLIP	water	WASH
narrow	CHIMNEY	—from glacier	
reverse fault with		along	
small angle	THRUST FAULT	—centre	MEDIAL MORAINE
Scottish	RIVA	—sides	LATERAL MORAINE
tapering	GULL	at foot	(TERMINAL) MORAINE
where		underneath	GROUND MORAINE
—movement		—produced by weathering	
has occurred	FAULT	of rock	ELUVIUM
is		decaying organic	
—occurring	ACTIVE FAULT	matter in soil	HUMUS, LEAF MOULD
—parallel to		deep	
—strike	STRIKE FAULT	—gulf	ABYSS
—hanging wall		—hollow	CHASM
has moved upwards	REVERSE FAULT	—part of	
with no movement	JOINT	harbour, river, etc	CHANNEL
cracking off of thin layers of rock	EXFOLIATION	old meander	ENTRENCHED MEANDER
	LAMINATION	—round hollow	CIRQUE, CORRIE

deformation of Earth's		difference	
crust	DIASTROPHISM	—between latitude and 90°	COLATITUDE
dense		—in altitude	RELIEF
—evergreen shrubs	SCRUB	direction	
—forest region of Amazon	SELVA(S)	—from one point	
—scrub (America)	CHAPARRAL	to another	BEARING
—tropical forest	JUNGLE	—in which vein of ore lies	RUN
deposit		—of	
—by action of wind	AEOLIAN DEPOSIT	line at right	
	LO(E)SS, LIMON	angles to dip	STRIKE
—containing particles		stream flow	DOWNSTREAM
of gold etc	PLACER	wind	LEE, DOWNWIND
—enriched by downward		—opposite to	
filtering materials	SUPERGENE	stream flow	UPSTREAM
—from		wind	UPWIND
avalanche	AVALANCHE CONE	discontinuity in	
glacier	(GROUND) MORAINE	rock strata	UNCONFORMITY
glacier stream	KAME	disintegration of surface by	
—confined to valley	VALLEY TRAIN	—action of	
	(*see also* debris *above*)	atmospheric phenomena	WEATHERING
—of		—hot gases	PNEUMATOLYSIS
calcium carbonate		distance due	
from hot springs	TRAVERTINE, TUFA	—East	EASTING
in arid regions (US)	CALICHE	—North	NORTHING
gravel with sodium		—South	SOUTHING
(Chile)	CALICHE	—West	WESTING
	CHILE SALTPETRE	disturbance of magnetic	
minerals from upper		field	MAGNETIC STORM
layers by rainwater	ILLUVIATION	ditch	DIKE, DYKE, FOSSE
ore	LEAD, LEDGE	division of	
	LODE, MINE, REEF, VEIN	—biogeographic region	ZONE
salts	STRASSFURT DEPOSIT	—Carboniferous strata	
silt embankment		Lower	CARBONIFEROUS LIMESTONE
in river	LEVEE		MOUNTAIN LIMESTONE
—originally derived		Upper	COAL MEASURES
from land	TERRIGENOUS DEPOSIT		CULM (MEASURES)
—under prehistoric		—continent	SUB-CONTINENT
pile-dwelling (It.)	TERRAMARA	—county	HUNDRED, LATHE
depression		—Cretaceous (US)	COMANCHEAN
—caused by meteor strike	CRATER	—Devonian	OLD RED SANDSTONE
—in		—geological time	AGE, EPOCH
America	DEATH VALLEY		ERA, PERIOD
	SALTON SINK	—Lower Jurassic	LIAS(SIC)
China	TURFAN		KIM(M)ERIDGEAN
desert region	WADI, WADY	—Mesozoic	TRIAS(SIC)
Earth's surface	BASIN, BOWL, VALLEY	Africa	KAR(R)OO
Egypt	EL FAIYUM, QUATTARA	Europe	BUNTER, KEUPER
Ethiopia	DANAKIL		MUSCHELKALK
Israel	DEAD SEA	—Middle Jurassic	BATHONIAN, BAJOCIAN
ocean floor	DEEP	—Palaeozoic (US)	MISSISSIPPIAN
top of volcano	CALDERA, CRATER		PENNSYLVANIAN
—where water collects	SINK(HOLE)	—Permian strata	
description of physical		Germany	ZECHSTEIN
features of an area	TOPOGRAPHY	South Africa	KAR(R)OO
deserts	(*see separate entry*)	—rock formation	SERIES, SYSTEM
dictionary of place-names	GAZETTEER	—Upper Jurassic	RHAETIC

drainage		—boundary	
—basin (US)	WATERSHED		GUTENBERG DISCONTINUITY
—downwards from peak	RADIAL DRAINAGE	middle	MANTLE
—pattern		—boundary	MOHO
in rectangles	TRELLIS DRAINAGE		MOHOROVICIC(IAN) DISCONTINUITY
like a tree	DENDRITIC DRAINAGE	outer	CRUST, LITHOSPHERE
drowned		—higher	GRANITIC
—river estuary	FIORD, FJORD	silica and alumina	SIAL
—valley	RIA	—lower	BASALTIC
dry watercourse		silica and magnesia	SIMA
—Africa	DONGA	—model of	TERRELLA
—Arab countries	KHORA, WADI, WADY	—point at end of axis	(NORTH) POLE
—Australia	BILLABONG		SOUTH POLE
—India	NULLA(H)	—region of seas	
—Mexico/Spain	ARROYO	and oceans	HYDROSPACE
dune	DENE		HYDROSPHERE
early form of coal	LIGNITE, PEAT	—western hemisphere	NEW WORLD
Earth		earthquake	(see separate entry)
—cold areas	CRYOSPHERE	elevated area with	
—eastern hemisphere	OLD WORLD	deep valleys	DISSECTED PLATEAU
—envelope of air	ATMOSPHERE	equilibrium between	
—inhabited part of surface	ECUMENE	high and low	
—layers of atmosphere		land masses	ISOSTASY
boundaries			ISOSTATIC THEORY
—magnetosphere	MAGNETOPAUSE	erosion	(see wearing away below)
—mesosphere	MESOPAUSE	erosive action of	
—stratosphere	STRATOPAUSE	ice or water	SCOUR
—troposphere	TROPOPAUSE	excrement of sea-birds	GUANO
defining magnetic		exploration of caves	POT-HOLING
field	MAGNETOSPHERE		SPELEOLOGY
in order of height		extending across	
—lowest	TROPOSPHERE	polar region	TRANSPOLAR
	STRATOSPHERE	fall of earth,	
	CHEMOSPHERE	rocks, etc	AVALANCHE
	MESOSPHERE		BERGFALL, LANDSLIDE
	THERMOSPHERE		LANDSLIP, MUD SLIDE
—outermost	EXOSPHERE	fan-shaped	
helium	HELIOSPHERE	—area of alluvium	
hydrogen	PROTONOSPHERE	at river mouth	ALLUVIAL FAN, DELTA
hypothetical	ATHENOSPHERE	—deposit	APRON
ionised	APPLETON LAYER	farming	
	D LAYER, E LAYER	—by	
	F LAYER, IONOSPHERE	alternate strips	STRIP CROPPING
	KENNELLY-HEAVISIDE LAYER	continuous	
radiation belt	VAN ALLEN BELT	cropping	INTENSIVE CULTIVATION
where		succession of crops	ROTATION
—ozone is formed	OZONE LAYER	—raising	
	OZONOSPHERE	animals	PASTORAL
—water vapour is		—and	
broken up	HYDROXYL LAYER	crops	MIXED
—layers of Earth		trees	AGROFORESTRY
core		—in confined	
—liquid	MAGMA	areas	BATTERY FARMING
—solid (nickel and iron)	NIFE		INTENSIVE FARMING
inner	BARYSPHERE	crops	ARABLE
	CENTROSPHERE	one crop	MONOCULTURE

—using drip irrigation with nutients	FERTIGATION	different angles	ASYMMETRIC FOLD
—without		—downfold	SYNCLINE
irrigation	DRY FARMING	—overturned anticline	OVERFOLD
soil	HYDROPONICS	—parallel to	
fast-flowing part		surrounding rock	RECUMBENT
of river	RAPID(S)	—pierced by underlying	
feature remaining		material	DIAPIR
after changes in		—upfold	ANTICLINE
surrounding area	RELICT	—which is not broken	COMPETENT
fertile		—with same dip each	
—area in desert	OASIS	side	ISOCLINE
—land		force caused by	
alongside river (Scot.)	CARSE	rotation of Earth	CORIOLIS FORCE
producing two crops		forest	
per year (Spain)	HUERTA	—adjoining tundra	TAIGA
—wooded area (US)	HAMMOCK	—alongside river	GALLERY FOREST
field of granular snow	FIRN, NEVE	subject to flooding	(I)GAPO
fill with eroded material	AGGRADE	—clearance	DEFORESTATION
final stage in development			SPARTAGE
of community	CLIMAX	—clearing	GLADE
fine		—hardwood	DECIDUOUS
—grained, plastic,		—hot evergreen	EQUATORIAL
moisture-retentive soil	CLAY		TROPICAL RAIN FOREST
—material deposited		—northern coniferous	TAIGA
by river, etc	SILT	—of thorny trees in	
—mineral particles	SILT, SAND, GRAVEL	arid area	THORN FOREST
finely ground		—open (Brazil)	CAATINGA
—matter produced by		—softwood	CONIFEROUS
action of glacier	ROCK FLOUR	—swampy (Russia)	URMAN
weathering	SILT	—tropical	EQUATORIAL FOREST
—quartz	SAND		JUNGLE
flat			MONSOON FOREST
—elevated land	TABLELAND, PLATEAU		RAIN FOREST
—land alongside river	HOLM	—wet (S. Amer.)	SELVA
which floods	FLOOD PLAIN	form of landscape	MORPHOLOGY
	RIVER TERRACE	formation of	
	WATER MEADOW	—continents	EPEIOGENESIS
—limestone block or ridge	CLINT		EPEIROGENY
—plane of breakage	CLEAVAGE (PLANE)	—minerals	PARAGENESIS
—stony desert (N. Africa)	REG	—mountains	OROGENESIS
—surrounded by slopes	AMPHITHEATRE	—soil	PEDOGENESIS
—topped mountain	MESA	formed	
—treeless area	PLAIN, PRAIRIE	—after enclosing rock	EPIGENETIC
—valley (Himalayas)	D(H)OON, D(H)UN	—at base of mountains	PIEDMONT
flattish region	PENEPLAIN	fracture in Earth's	
floating mass of		surface	FAULT
vegetable matter (Sudan)	SUDD	fragment(s) of rock	CLAST, DEBRIS
flood caused by			DETRITUS, RUBBLE
overflowing river	FRESHET		SCREE, TALUS
flooded forest	(I)GAPO	frequent movement	
flow of natural water		of tribes	NOMADISM
from the ground	BOURNE, SPA, SPRING	fruit growing area (US)	FRUIT BELT
fold in rock		gap in mountains	COL, PASS
—at		gas vent in surface	MOF(F)ETTE
constant angle	MONOCLINE	general slope of land	VERSANT
		gentle slope	GLACIS

353

geographers/geologists/ mineralogists	
—American	ALVAREZ, BARGHOORN
	BERKNER, BRIGGS, CHAMBERLAIN
	DAVIS, DUTTON, EWING
	GILBERT, GUTENBERG, HESS
	ISARD, WELLS
—Australian	DAVID
—Austrian	PENCK, SEUSS, WULFEN
—British	FAWCETT, HAGGETT
	HERBERTSON, LONSDALE
	LYELL, MACKINDER, MITCHELL
	MURCHISON, ROHBY
	SEDGWICK, SMAILES
—Croatian	MOHOROVICIC
—Dutch	SLICHER, VAN BATH
—French	CHABOT, DAUBREE
	DE CHANCOURTOIS
	DEMANGEAU, GOTTMAN
	GUETTARD, MARTONNE, SIEGFRIED
	SION, VIDAL DE LA BLACKE
—German	CHRISTALLER, FUCHS
	LOSCH, MOHS, RATZEL
	WEGENER, WERNER
—Italian	MERCALLI, MONTICELLI
—Swedish	HAGERSTRAND
—Swiss	AGASSIZ, CHARPENTIER
	VENETZ
geographical regions (see zoological regions below)	
geological ages (in date order)	
—first moments	
proton era	HADRONIC ERA
electron era	LEPTONIC ERA
gamma ray era	RADIATION ERA
—earliest	HADEAN
	ARCH(A)EAN
—era	PRE-CAMBRIAN
periods	AZOIC
	ARCHAEOZOIC
	CRYPTOZOIC, PROTEROZOIC
	ALGONKIAN
—era, ancient life	PRIMARY, PALAEOZOIC
periods	CAMBRIAN
	ORDOVICIAN
	SILURIAN
	DEVONIAN
	CARBONIFEROUS
—era, middle life	SECONDARY, MESOZOIC
periods	TRIASSIC
	JURASSIC
Lower Cretaceous	NEOCOMIAN
	CRETACEOUS
—era, modern life	CAINOZOIC, CENOZOIC
	KAINOZOIC
period	TERTIARY

epochs	PALAEOCENE
	EOCENE
	OLIGOCENE
Palaeocene, Eocene and Oligocene	PALAEOGENE
	MIOCENE
	PLIOCENE
Miocene and Pliocene	NEOGENE
period	QUATERNARY
epochs	PLEISTOCENE
	POST-GLACIAL
	HOLOCENE, RECENT
—end of Mesozoic to present day	NEOZOIC
geological	
—deposit	HORIZON
—time divisions	(A)EON, AGE
	EPOCH, ERA, PERIOD
geosyncline with highly folded limbs	SYNCLORIUM
glacial	
—deposit	BOULDERCLAY, MORAINE
at	
—foot	TERMINAL MORAINE
—side	LATERAL MORAINE
during retreat of ice	RECESSIONAL MORAINE
in centre	MEDIAL MORAINE
over an area	GROUND MORAINE
—drift	TILL
—period	ICE AGE
glaciation slope (Alps)	RISS
glacier	
—at foot of mountain	PIEDMONT GLACIER
—in	
a hollow	CIRQUE GLACIER
	VALLEY GLACIER
Alaska	MALASPINA, NABESNA
Alps	ALETSCHGLETSCHER
Antarctica	BEARDMORE, DENMAN
	LAMBERT-FISHER
	NIMROD-LENNOL-KING
	RECOVERY, SLESSOR
Greenland	PETERMANS GLETSCHER
Himalayas	FEDTSCHENKO
	HISPAR-BIAFO
	KANCHENJUNGA
	SIACHEN
Iceland	VATNAVOKULL
New Zealand	TASMAN
Norway	JOSTEDALSERE
gold-bearing gravel deposit	LEAD
granular snow	FIRN, NEVE
grape growing area (US)	GRAPE BELT

graph of height against area	HYPSOGRAPHIC CURVE
grassland	
—Brazil	CAMPO
—Hungary	PUSZTAS
—North America	PRAIRIE
—regularly	
grazed	PASTURE
mown	MEADOW
—Russia	STEPPES
—South Africa	KAR(R)OO, VELD(T)
—South America	LLANOS, PAMPAS
	SAVANNA(H)
gravel	
—deposit from glacier-stream	KAME, OUTWASH
—ridge	ESKAR, ESKER, KAME OS, TOMBOLO
grazing area (US)	RANGE
groove(s) in rockface	STRIA(E)
group of islands	ARCHIPELAGO
growing	(see also **rearing**)
—in Northern areas	BOREAL
—on	
dry ground	GLARIAL
gravel	GLAREOUS
silica	SILICICOLOUS
upland slopes below treeline	SUBALPINE
Guinea coast of West Africa	WHITE MAN'S GRAVE
gully (S. Afr.)	DONGA
hardness of minerals	MOHS SCALE
1	TALC
2	GYPSUM
3	CALCITE
4	FLUORITE
5	APATITE
6	ORTHOCLASE
7	QUARTZ
8	TOPAZ
9	CORUNDUM
10	DIAMOND
having same	
—folding	ISOCLINAL
—magnetic dip	ISOCLINAL
headland	(see projection below)
heap of stones as memorial or landmark	CAIRN
heath-covered plain (France)	LANDE
high	
—area between faults	HORST
—bleak part of Andes	PUNA
—flat land	PLATEAU, TABLELAND
—land of a region	UPLAND
—plateau (S. Amer.)	ALTIPLANO, PUNA

—point from which water flows off in different directions	DIVIDE
	WATER PARTING
	WATERSHED
—tidal wave in estuary	BORE
highest point of river reached by trading vessels	HEAD OF NAVIGATION
hill	
—Arab	TEL(L)
—bare	FELL
—cliff-sided	BUTTE
—flat-topped	MESA
—formed of debris carried by glacier	DRUMLIN
ejected magma	VOLCANO
—in permafrost	PINGO
—isolated (US)	MESA
—low	HOW
—North Africa	(D)JEBEL
—old	BARROW
—pointed	KIP(P)
—rising from plain in arid region	INSELBERG
—rocky	TOR(R)
—rounded	MAMELON, MORRO
Scottish	DOD, KNOWE
—Scottish	BRAE, LAW
—South Africa	BERG, KOP(JE), KOPPIE
—volcanic (France)	PUY
—Welsh	DUN
—with one steep face	CRAG AND TAIL
	CUESTA
pointed summit	PEAK
hillocks in a valley which has been glaciated	ROCHES MOUTONNEES
hillside (Scot.)	BRAE
hilly upland region (US)	COTEAU
hole	
—in solid rock	POT HOLE
—through which water and air are forced by tides	BLOW HOLE
hollow	
—at head of valley	CIRQUE
—formed by melting of ice block	GIANT'S KETTLE KETTLE(-HOLE)
—in	
Earth's crust	BASIN
glacier containing dust	DUST WELL

hillside	COMB(E), COOMB, CWM
karst region	POLJE
limestone	
—area	DOLINA, DOLINE
—dissolved by	
rainwater	GRIKE, GRYKE
mountainside	COVE
rock face	CAVE
—into which cold air	
sinks	FROST HOLLOW
—leading to undergound	
cavern	POTHOLE, SINKHOLE
	SWALLET, SWALLOW-HOLE
—small	DELL, DIMBLE, DINGLE
—where water collects	WATERHOLE
horizontal	
—line of rock stratum	STRIKE
—mine shaft	ADIT, DRIFT
	HEAD(ING)
—sheet of igneous rock	SILL
hot water from the	
ground	GEYSER, HOT SPRING
	THERMAL SPRING
ice	
—block(s) in steep	
glacier	ICE FALL, SERAC
—cap extending into sea	BARRIER
—floating	
blocks	DRIFT ICE, PACK ICE
mass	ICEBERG
sheet	ICE FLOE
thin fragments	PAN
—forming spicules in	
fast-flowing rivers	FRAZIL ICE
—from fresh inland water	LAND ICE
—glare from light	
reflected from ice	ICEBLINK
—hanging in tapering	
column	ICICLE
—large blocks floating	
together	PACK ICE
—large sheet of ice	ICE FIELD
—mass projecting into sea	ICE FOOT
—particles in atmosphere	ICE FOG
—pillar formed by	
breaking glacier	SERAC
—refreezing after	
melting under pressure	REGELATION
—river	GLACIER
—sheet formed by	
combined glaciers	PIEDMONT GLACIER
—small iceberg	CALF
—thin plates	PANCAKE ICE
—very large area	ICE CAP, ICE SHEET
igneous	PYROGENIC
increase in land area	ACCRETION

indentation in coastline	BAY, BIGHT
	COVE, GULF
inland sheet of water	LAKE
—small	MERE, POND, POOL, TARN
	(see also lakes)
inlet, long and narrow	RIA
instrument	
—indicating direction	COMPASS
—measuring	
areas on map	PLANIMETER
distances on map	OPISOMETER
firmness of soil	PENETROMETER
hardness of rocks	SCLEROMETER
magnetic	
—dip	INCLINOMETER
—intensity	MAGNETOMETER
percolation through	
soil	LYSIMETER
slope	(IN)CLINOMETER
—recording variations	
in magnetic field	MAGNETOGRAPH
intermittent	
—hot spring	GEYSER
—stream	(WINTER)BOURNE
irregularity of surface	ACCIDENT
irrigated land giving	
one crop per annum (Spain)	VEGA
island	
—coral	ATOLL
—in river	AIT, EYOT, HOLM
—low	CAY, KEY
—Scottish	INCH
isolated	
—dune	BARCHAN(E), BARK(H)AN
—mass of rock standing above	
softer rock surfaces	MONADNOCK
—rock mass	TOR
—rural area	
Australia	OUTBACK
USA	BOONDOCKS
jointing in coal	CLEAT
junction of	
watercourses	CONFLUENCE
	CONFLUENCY
jungle of mangrove	
trees in tropical	
coastal area	MANGROVE SWAMP
lacking	
—iron	NONFERROUS
—lime	NONCALCAREOUS
lagoon at river	
mouth (Baltic)	HAFF
lakes	(see separate entry)
land	
—belonging to the	
community	COMMON

—bordering sea	BEACH, (FORE)SHORE
—entirely surrounded by water	
—in river	AIT, EYOT
—in sea	ISLAND, ISLET
—fit or used for farming	ARABLE
—forming a lake only in heavy rains	PLAYA
—mass	CONTINENT
—used for	
cultivation	ARABLE
grazing	GRASSLAND, PASTURE
large	
—anticline	GEOANTICLINE
—bay	GULF
—crystal in porphyritic rock	PHENOCRYST
—hollow in karst region	POLJE
—land mass	MAINLAND (SUB-)CONTINENT
—mass of underground igneous rock	LACCOLITH
—particle	MACROAGGREGATE
—pothole	(GIANT'S) KETTLE
—sections of Earth's crust	TECTONIC PLATES
—syncline	GEOSYNCLINE
—unbroken expanse of land	FIELD
—watercourse	RIVER
latitude	
—0°	EQUATOR
—23° N	TROPIC OF CAPRICORN
—23° S	TROPIC OF CANCER
—66° N	ARCTIC CIRCLE
—66° S	ANTARCTIC CIRCLE
law relating to deflection due to Earth's rotation	FERREL'S LAW
layer(s)	STRATUM(STRATA)
—between others	INTERBEDDED
—in geological section	HORIZON
—of	
coal	SEAM
humus	MOR
minerals	SEAM
organic materials on forest floor	LITTER
rock	STRATUM
sediment (seasonal)	VARVE
soil	
—at surface	A-HORIZON, TOPSOIL
—below surface	B-HORIZON, SUBSOIL
—overlying	SUPERSTRATUM
—underlying	SUBSTRATUM
layering	STRATIFICATION
laying down of transported material	DEPOSITION

level	
—of underground water	LEVEL OF SATURATION WATER LEVEL, WATER TABLE
—tract	
bordering river	TERRACE
cut into hillside	TERRACE
of	
—high land	PLATEAU, TABLELAND
—low land	PLAIN
limestone	
—area drained underground	KARSTLAND KARST REGION
—depression	POLJE
—needle	
hanging from ceiling	STALACTITE
rising from floor	STALAGMITE
line	
—between poles	AXIS
—bounding view of earth from a particular spot	HORIZON
—joining	
points where magnetic needle remains horizontal	ACLINIC LINE MAGNETIC EQUATOR
waterfalls in different rivers	FALL LINE
—of	
latitude	PARALLEL
longitude	MERIDIAN
—where the date changes	INTERNATIONAL DATE LINE
zero magnetic declination	AGONIC LINE
—on	
Earth's surface	
—at constant angle to meridians	LOXODROME RHUMB LINE
—of plane through centre	GREAT CIRCLE, MERIDIAN
map showing equal	
—cloudiness	ISONEPH
—depth below sea-level	ISOBATH
—earthquake shock	COSEISMIC LINE HOMOSEISMAL LINE ISOSEISMAL LINE
—height	CONTOUR
—inclination to vertical	ISOCLINIC
—magnetic	
declination	ISOGONIC LINE
intensity	ISODYNAMIC LINE ISOMAGNETIC LINE
—rainfall	EQUIPLUVE, ISOHYET
—salinity	ISOHALINE
—sunshine	ISOHEL

—temperature	ISOTHERM
below ground	ISOGEOTHERM
in coldest times	ISOCRYME
summer mean	ISOTHERE
—time difference	ISOCHRONE
—upheaval of land	ISOBASE
—separating	
areas of different dialects	ISOGLOSS
Australian from	
Oriental biogeographic	
area	WALLACE'S LINE
drainage areas	WATERSHED
—showing profile of	
valley bottom	THALWEG
	VALLEY LINE
—value of various	
features	ISOGRAM, ISOLINE
	ISOMETRIC LINE
	ISOPLETH
wind speed	ISOTACH
—where land and	
sea meet	COAST(LINE)
	SHORE(LINE)
lines representing	
slopes on map	HACHURES
living in river	
or stream	FLUVIAL, FLUVIATILE
loamy deposit laid	
down by wind	LO(E)SS
long	
—mountain range with	
jagged peaks	SIERRA
—narrow	
ridge	HOGBACK, HOG'S BACK
sea inlet	FIORD, FJORD, FIRTH
—rounded rock mound	ROCHE MOUTONNEE
—stretch of land	
almost surrounded	
by water	PENINSULA
longitude 0°	GREENWICH MERIDIAN
	PRIME MERIDIAN
loop	
—in course of river	MEANDER
—of river cut off	
forming lake	OX BOW
loose	
—pebbles	SHINGLE
—rounded rock fragments	GRAVEL
loss of	
—snow, etc, by erosion	
evaporation, etc	ABLATION
—surface by erosion	ABRASION
—water by evaporation	
and transpiration	EVAPOTRANSPIRATION
low	
—ground between hills	DALE, VALLEY

—island	CAY, KEY
—land	LOWLAND(S)
adjoining sea	BEACH, COAST
	COASTAL PLAIN
	(FORE)SHORE, LITTORAL
between	
—faults	GRABEN, RIFT VALLEY
—hills	DALE
—moist area	SLADE
—pressure equatorial belt	DOLDRUMS
—reef	CAY, KEY
—wet land	BOG, CARR, FEN, MARSH
	MORASS, SWAMP, WASH
Canada	MUSKEG
lower limit of perpetual	
snow on high ground	SNOWLINE
lowest	
—level of stream-bed	BASE-LEVEL
—part of embankment etc	TOE
lying at foot of mountain	PIEDMONT
magnetic	
—Equator	ACLINIC LINE
—property of	
earth	TERRESTRIAL MAGNETISM
main compass points	CARDINAL POINTS
maize growing	
area (US)	CORN BELT
making new forest	AFFORESTATION
man-made	(see artificial above)
map	
—drawn in outline	CHART
—making	CARTOGRAPHY
—markings showing relief	HACHURES
—projections	AITOFF'S
	BARTHOLOMEW'S NORDIC
	BARTHOLOMEW'S REGIONAL
	BARTHOLEMEW'S TIMES
	BONNE'S, CONIC(AL)
	CYLINDRICAL, EQUAL AREA
EQUIDISTANT, EQUIVALENT AZIMUTHAL
	GALL'S, GNOMIC
GOODE'S INTERRUPTED HOMOLOSINE
HAMMER(-AITOFF)HOMOLOGRAPHIC
LAMBERT'S AZIMUTHAL EQUAL-AREA
MERCATOR'S, MOLLWEIDE'S
ORTHOGRAPHIC, ORTHOMORPHIC
PETER'S, POLYCONIC
SANSON-FLAMSTEED SINUSOIDAL
	STEREOGRAPHIC
	ZENITHAL EQUAL-AREA
	ZENITHAL EQUIDISTANT
—showing	
altitude pictorially	RELIEF MAP
relief	TOPOGRAPHIC MAP
land masses in	
accurate proportions	PETERS

small area in		molten rock	
true shape	CONFORMAL	—at centre of earth	MAGMA
statistical information		—from volcano	LAVA
as diagrams	CARTOGRAM		(see also **volcano**)
mapping configuration		moorland pool (Scot.)	FLOW
of Earth's surface	TOPOGRAPHY	mountain	(see separate entry)
margin of body of water	WATERSIDE	mountainous land	HIGHLAND(S)
marshy creek or river (US)	BAYOU	mouth of river	DEBOUCHEMENT
mass of			ESTUARY
—hard rock standing		movement of	
on neck of softer		—atmosphere	ATMOSPHERIC TIDE
wind-eroded rock	ZEUGE(N)	—debris along shore	LONGSHORE DRIFT
—igneous rock formed by		—land masses	CONTINENTAL DRIFT
intrusion of magma	BATHOLITE	—rocks	
	BATHOLITH	on either side of fault	SHIFT
	BATHYLITE, BATHYLITH	producing fault	SLIP
—minerals deposited		—soil down slopes	SPOIL CREEP
from solution	CONCRETION		SOLIFLUCTION
—ore left in to support		—water or sand caused by wind	DRIFT
mine roof	PILLAR	mud flat	SLOB
—sedimentary rock		narrow	
enclosing salt deposit	SALT DOME	—canyon	CANADA
—sliding snow	AVALANCHE	—cleft in rock	CHIMNEY, CREVICE
—stone round lake-margin	LAKE RAMPART	—gorge	DEFILE, CLUSE
material			WATER GAP
—carried by river	LOAD	without water	WIND GAP
—deposited by		—headland	BILL
glacier	MORAINE	—ledge or shelf	BENCH
ice	BOULDER CLAY	—neck of land	
rain	ILLUVIUM	between rivers	DOAB
water	ALLUVIUM, SEDIMENT	joining land masses	ISTHMUS
wind	L(O)ESS	—pass	DEFILE, GORGE
—water or ice	DRIFT	—passage	GUT
—enclosing crystals, etc	MATRIX	—sea	
measure of hardness		inlet	FIORD, FIRTH, FJORD
of minerals	MOHS SCALE	passage	CHANNEL, GUT, KYLE
measurement of			SOUND, STRAIT
—angles in surveying	TRIANGULATION	—shelf on rockface	LEDGE
—area	PLANIMETRY	—tongue of sand or	
—heights above sea-level	HYPSOMETRY	gravel in sea	
—land forms	MORPHOMETRY	attached to land	SPIT
—time by decay of radio-		connecting islands	TOMBOLO
active materials	RADIOMETRICS	not attached	BAR, SANDBANK
method of survey for		—valley	COMB(E), COOMB, CWM
map-making	TRIANGULATION		DEAN, DENE, DINGLE
mineral			GLEN, GORGE
—composition of rock	MODE	—water channel in rock	VEIN
—valuable enough		natural	
to be mined	ORE	—amphitheatre	CIRQUE, CORRIE
—vein	LEDGE, LODE, REEF	—features of Earth	LANDFORM
	(see also **mineral**)	—home	HABITAT
mineralogists	(see geologists above)	navigable channel	WATERWAY
mining from surface	OPENCAST (MINING)	network of latitude	
	STRIP MINING	and longitude lines	GRATICULE, GRID
mixture of sulphides	MATTE	north as	
moat	FOSEE	—end of Earth's axis	TRUE NORTH

—indicated by compass	MAGNETIC NORTH
obstruction of stream forming lake	DAM
ocean	(*see* oceanography)
official	
—base for levels	NEWLYN DATUM
	ORDNANCE DATUM
—co-ordinates	NATIONAL GRID
—mapping authority (UK)	
	ORDNANCE SURVEY
old river affected by uplift of land	REJUVENATED RIVER
ooze	(*see* oceanography)
open	
—anchorage protected by reefs etc	ROADSTEAD
—area in woods	CLEARING, GLADE
—hilly land	DOWN
—uncultivated region	HEATH
—upland area	HEATH, MOOR
	PLATEAU, WOLD
in South Afica	KAR(R)OO
opening in ground emitting	
—carbon dioxide	MOFETTE
—gases	FUMAROLE
—hot water	GEYSER
—molten rock, etc	VOLCANO
optical illusion caused by heated layers of air	MIRAGE
ore deposit	LEAD, LEDGE, LODE
	MINE, VEIN, REEF
organic soil material	HUMUS
outcrop	BASSET
outwash plain	SANDR
overhang of snow	CORNICE
part of	
—country separated from the main part	ENCLAVE
—Earth including most of	
land areas	LAND HEMISPHERE
water areas	HYDROSPACE
	HYDROSPHERE
	WATER HEMISPHERE
partly-developed mine	PROSPECT
pass	GAP, GATE, COL
—Scottish	SLAP
—with a stream	WATER GAP
—without a stream	WIND GAP
passage	
—between land masses	INLET
—in mine	GALLERY, GANGWAY
	LEVEL
peak projecting from ice cap	NUNATAK

peat-bog	PETARY
peninsulas	ALASKA, ARABIA
	IBERIA, INDIA, LABRADOR
	SCANDINAVIA
period	
—between	
Ice Ages	INTERGLACIAL
tides	INTERTIDAL
—of	
equal night and day	EQUINOX
—in	
March	SPRING EQUINOX
September	AUTUMNAL EQUINOX
glaciation	ICE AGE
particular climatic conditions	SEASON
temporary retreat of ice	INTERSTADIAL
periodic movement of	
—Earth's crust	TIDE
—sea water	TIDE
permanent	
—area of frost	PERMAFROST
—mass of ice	GLACIER, ICECAP
	ICEFIELD
—snow	SNOWCAP, SNOWFIELD
pertaining to	
—centre of Earth	GEOCENTRIC
—Earth	CHTHONIAN, CHTHONIC
	TELLURAL, TELLURIAN
	TELLURIC, TERRENE
	TERRESTRIAL
—features of Earth	GEOMORPHIC
—form of rock masses	GEOTECTONIC
—glaciers	GLACIAL
—heat of Earth's interior	GEOTHERMAL
—Ice Ages	GLACIAL
—land	TERRENE, TERRESTRIAL
—magnetic remanence	THERMOREMANENT
—sediment on sea-floor from erosion of land	TERRIGENOUS
—soil conditions	EDAPHIC
—underground water supplies	PHREATIC
photographic representation of	
—Earth's surface	TOPOGRAPH
—model on map	PHOTO RELIEF MAP
physical features of an area	TERRAIN, TOPOGRAPHY
place showing evidence of mineral deposit	PROSPECT
places on opposite sides of Earth	ANTIPODES
plain	
—Arctic	TUNDRA

—Brazil	CAMPO
—India	MAIDAN
—North Africa	REG
—North America	PRAIRIE
—Persia	MAIDAN
—Russia	STEPPE
—South Africa	KAR(R)OO, VELD(T)
—South America	LLANO, PAMPAS
	PARAMO, SAVANNA(H)
plane	
—between strata	BEDDING PLANE
—of reverse fault	THRUST PLANE
plant	
—life of a region	FLORA
—remains	
from earlier age	FOSSIL
in coal	FUSAIN
planting of woodlands	REFORESTATION
plateau	
—Scandinavia	FJELD
—South Africa	KAR(R)OO
—Spain	MESETA
—with steep faces	TABLELAND
plates of Earth's crust	AFRICAN
	ANTARCTIC, ARABIAN
	AUSTRALIAN, CARIBBEAN
	EURASIAN, IRAN, NAZCA
	NORTH AMERICAN, PACIFIC
	PHILIPPINES, SOUTH AMERICAN
platform bordering river	RIVER TERRACE
point	
—at which slope of	
river changes	KNICK POINT
—of compass	RHUMB
pond	
—dry in summer (Ireland)	TURLOUGH
—fed by spring	WELL
—filled by condensation	DEWPOND
—formed by damming	
stream (India)	TANK
port	
—in China open to	
trade by treaty	TREATY PORT
—involved in import and	
export	ENTREPOT
precipice (S. Africa)	KRANS, KRAN(T)Z
principal compass	
points	CARDINAL POINTS
	N, NORTH, S, SOUTH
	E, EAST, W, WEST
process of deformation	
of Earth's crust	DIASTROPHISM
production of different	
rocks from common	
mother base	DIFFERENTIATION
profile of river bed	THALWEG

projecting layer of rock	LEDGE, SHELF
projection	
—from mountain or hill	OFFSET, SPUR
—into sea	BILL, CAPE
	HEADLAND, MORRO, MULL
	NAZE, NESS, POINT
	PENINSULA, PROMONTORY
	SCAW, SKAW, SPIT, TONGUE
protective barrier	
round harbour, etc	BREAKWATER, GROIN
	GROYNE, JETTY, MOLE
quicksand (Scot.)	FLOW
raised	
—area of seabed	BANK
—block between faults	HORST
—flat area(s)	PLATEAU(X)
	TABLELAND
—road or path over	
low-lying area	DIKE, DYKE, LEVEE
raising of Earth's	
surface	ELEVATION
rate of temperature	
change with altitude	LAPSE RATE
ravine	CAN(Y)ON, COULEE
	COULOIR, GAP, GORGE
	GULCH, KHOR, LIN(N)
—Scottish	CLEUCH, CLEUGH
	HEUCH, HEUGH
recession of water	DERELICTION
reclaimed land	POLDER, THWAITE
reef	CAY, KEY
reference level for altitudes	BENCHMARK
	DATUM (LEVEL)
region	
—between	
desert and temperate	
zone (Africa)	SAHELIAN
tropics and	
temperate	
region	SUB-TROPICAL REGION
tundra and cool	
temperate	
zone	COLD TEMPERATE REGION
	SUB-POLAR REGION
—inland of seaport	HINTERLAND
—of	
calms near tropics	CALMS OF CANCER
	CALMS OF CAPRICORN
intermediate rainfall	
and plant growth	GRASSLAND
seas and oceans	HYDROSPACE
	HYDROSPHERE
—south of Sahara desert	SAHELIAN
—where	
cereals are grown	
—North America	WHEAT BELT

—South America life	WHEAT CRESCENT
—exists	BIOSPHERE
—is possible	ECOSPHERE
remaining magnetism	REMANENCE
remains of plant or animal from earlier age	FOSSIL
remote country	
—Australia	OUTBACK
—USA	BOONDOCKS
removal of minerals etc from soil by rainwater	LEACHING
removing forest	DEFORESTATION
replacement of minerals by calcite and dolomite	CALCIFICATION
replanting forest	REFORESTATION
representation of Earth's curved surface on flat surface	MAP PROJECTION
resulting from deformation of Earth's crust	TECTONIC
ridge	DRUM
—carved in soft strata by wind	YARDANG
—in plain of softer rock	CUESTA
—of	
boulder clay	DRUMLIN
gravel	AS, ESKAR, ESKER KAME
—at	
foot of glacier	TERMINAL MORAINE
side of glacier	LATERAL MORAINE
—connecting island to mainland or island	TOMBOLO
—in middle of glacier	MEDIAL MORAINE
hills (S. Africa)	RAND
ice in glacier	SERAC
rocks near surface of sea	REEF
sand	DUNE
—across river mouth or harbour entrance	BAR
—extending into sea	SPIT
—wall-like	RAMPART
—with sharp summit	HOG(S)BACK
rift valley	GRABEN
rigid area of Earth's crust	CRATON
ripple on water	RIFFLE
river	(*see separate entry*)
—bank formed by deposit of silt	LEVEE
—branch joining	
—river	TRIBUTARY
—sea or lake	DISTRIBUTARY

not rejoining river	DISTRIBUTARY
rejoining	ANABRANCH
sinking into ground	ANABRANCH
—branches uniting to form network	ANASTOMOSIS
—cutting through land in its path	ANTECEDENT RIVER
—divided into network of channels	BRAIDED
—draining land which has been lifted	CONSEQUENT RIVER
—flowing opposite to consequent river	OBSEQUENT RIVER
—flowing parallel to slope	SUBSEQUENT RIVER
—landing-place	LEVEE
—mouth affected by tides	ESTUARY, FIRTH
—or stream joining larger	BRANCH TRIBUTARY
—side	
embankment	LEVEE
flat land	HOLM RIVER TERRACE
forest	GALLERY FOREST
—subject to flooding	(I)GAPO
meadow	
—Scottish	HAUGH, INCH
—subject to flooding	WATER MEADOW
plain (Scot.)	CARSE
—tributary of subsequent river	OBSEQUENT RIVER
stream	AFFLUENT
—valley	DALE
—with tributaries	DRAINAGE SYSTEM WATER SYSTEM
rock	(*see also* **rocks**)
—at sea-level composed of coral	ATOLL, BARRIER REEF CORAL REEF FRINGING REEF
—containing more than one mineral	COMPOSITE
—exposed above Earth's surface	OUTCROP
—fissure containing mineral deposit	LODE, VEIN
—formed by deposition from water, etc	SEDIMENTARY SILTSTONE
—mass forming centre of continent	SHIELD
—on ice pedestal in glacier	GLACIER TABLE
—standing above ice	NUNATAK
—through which vein of ore runs	WALL ROCK
rock-hole (Austr.)	GNAMMA HOLE

rocky	
—area in shallow water (US)	RIFFLE
—crust of Earth	LITHOSPHERE
—desert	HAM(M)ADA, REG
—edge of mountain	ARETE
—height	TOR(R)
—island	SKERRY, STACK
—mound (Scot.)	SCALP
—mountain top	KRANS, KRAN(T)Z
—peak	AIGUILLE
—place in stream (US)	RIFT
—recess	COVE
—uplands in desert region	HAM(M)ADA
—valley	RAVINE
America	GULCH
rounded	
—granule	CHONDRULE
—hillock (Scot.)	KNOWE
—hilltop (Scot.)	DOD
—lump	NODULE
formed by accretion	OOLITH
—pebbles	COBBLES, SHINGLE
route along which	
merchants regularly	
travel	TRADE ROUTE
rudaceous rock	SEDIMENTARY ROCK
rushing stream	TORRENT
salt	
—deposit left after	
evaporation of lake	SALINA, SALINE
	SALT PAN
—encrusted area	SALT-FLAT
—marsh	SALINA, SALINE
sand	
—bank formed by sea	DOLON
—dune	
crescent-shaped	BARCHAN
parallel to wind	SEIF
—hills (Scot.)	LINKS
sandy	
—desert (N. Africa)	ERG
—plains (France)	LANDES
—tract	DENE, DESERT
score marks made by	
glacial action	STRIAE
scrub	BRUSH
—Australia	MALLEE (SCRUB)
—dry, tropical	THORNBUSH
—eucalyptus	MALLEE (SCRUB)
—France	MAQUIS
—growing on poor land	GAR(R)IGUE
—Italy	MACCHIA
—Mediterranean	GAR(R)IGUE
sea	
—bed bordering	
land-mass	CONTINENTAL SHELF

—shore	BEACH, COAST
	LITTORAL
	(*see also* **oceanography**)
seasonal	
—layers of sediment	VARVE
—movement of livestock	TRANSHUMANCE
section showing slope	
of river bed	RIVER PROFILE
sedimentary	
—deposit	WARP
from river	ALLUVIAL CONE
	ALLUVIAL FAN
	ALLUVIAL PLAIN
	ALLUVIUM
—rock	RUDACEOUS ROCK
segment of Earth's	
crust	(TECTONIC) PLATE
semi-tundra (Andes)	PARAMOS
series of	
—strata	ZONE
—waterfalls	CASCADE, CATARACT
shaft in glacier	MOULIN
shallow	
—body of water	WASH
—channel worn by erosion	RILL
—lake in coastal sand dunes	ETANG
—marsh	EVERGLADE
—part of river that	
can be waded	FORD
—place in stream (US)	RIFT
—pond	
filled by dew	DEWPOND
filling with silt	ETANG
—soil over rock (US)	LITHASOL
—stretch of rough water	
in stream (US)	RIFFLE
sharp	
—point	AIGUILLE
—ridge	ARETE
sheet of	
—glacial deposit	GROUND MORAINE
—ice	
floating	(ICE) FLOE
on land	ICEFIELD
shifting sand dune area	ERG
shore raised by Earth	
movement	RAISED BEACH
showing correct	
directions from centre	ZENITHALA
side	
—exposed to wind	UPWIND, WINDWARD
—of hill or mountain	SHOULDER
—sheltered from wind	DOWNWIND
	LEEWARD
sinkhole	SWALLET
	SWALLOW-HOLE

sinking of Earth's crust	SUBSIDENCE	—farm (Scot.)	CROFT
situated		—forest	WOOD
—below		—hill	HILLOCK, HUMMOCK
Earth's crust	SUBCRUSTAL		HUMP, MOUND
glacier	SUBGLACIAL	rounded	KNOLL
ground	SUBTERRANEAN	South African	KOPIE, KOPJE
—between low and high		—hollow	DELL, DIMBLE, DINGLE
tide marks	FORESHORE	—iceberg	CALF
—beyond mountains	TRAMONTANE	—island	AIT, EYOT, HOLM
	ULTRAMONTANE	—lake	MERE, POND, POOL
—just outside		in mountains	TARN
Antarctic Circle	SUBANTARCTIC	—prominence	MONTIC(U)LE
Arctic Circle	SUBARCTIC		MONTICULUS
—north of Alps	TRAMONTANE	—ridge in sand produced	
	TRANSALPINE	by wind or water	RIPPLE (MARK)
—on		—river	RIVULET
continent(al shelf)	EPICONTINENTAL	—rocky island	SKERRY
lower slopes of Alps	SUBALPINE	near coast	STACK
or near surface		—rounded glassy stone	AUSTRALITE
of Earth	SUBAERIAL		TEKTITE
—south of Alps	CISALPINE	—spring (US)	SEEP
—under		—stream	BROOK
ocean	SUBOCEANIC	Scottish	BURN
sea	SUBMARINE	—tributary	CREEK
slide	AVALANCHE, LANDSLIDE	—valley	DELL, DENE
	MUDSLIDE		DIMBLE, DINGLE, SLADE
slope	ESCARPMENT, GRADIENT, SCARP	—village	HAMLET
—ascending	ACCLIVITY	—watercourse	BOURN(E), BROOK
—covered with			FRESHET, PIRL, PURL
rock fragments	SCREE		RILL, RIVULET
scree	BAHADA, BAJADA		RUNNEL, STREAM
—descending	DECLIVITY	America	CREEK
—formed by accumulation		Scotland	BURN
of rock fragments	TALUS	temporary	(WINTER-)BOURNE
—from		—waterfall	CASCADE
base of eroded		—wood	COPPICE, COPSE, GROVE
sea-cliff	WAVE-CUT PLATFORM		SHAW, SPINN(E)Y
continental shelf			THICKET
to ocean bed	CONTINENTAL SLOPE	smooth surface produced	
land to sea	BEACH, SHORE	by rock movement	SLICKENSIDE
—in bedrock at foot of		soft moist clay, etc	SLIME
steeper slope	PEDIMENT	soil	
—leading up to mountains	PEDIMENT	—aggregate	PED
—of		—alkaline	PEDOCAL
mountain	VERSANT	—bound by grass, etc	TURF, SOD
rock stratum	DIP	—calcareous loam	MALM
—ascending	ACCLIVITY	—chalk, etc	RENDZINA
—descending	DECLIVITY	—clay	
sluggish tributary (US)	BAYOU	and	
small		—chalk	MALM
—cavity in rock	VESICLE, VUG(G), VUGH	—lime	MARL(ITE)
—coastal inlet	BAY, COVE, CREEK, INLET	friable	BOLE
—column of rock		sand and silt	LOAN
with grooves	STYLOLITE	sticky	GLEY
—creek (Scot.)	POW	—compacted clay	CLAYPAN, HARDPAN
—elevation	MONTIC(U)LE	—containing silica	CLAY

—covering mineral deposit	OVERBURDEN
—crumbly limestone	MALM
with humus	MULL
—deposited by water	ALLUVIUM, SILT
wind	LOESS, LIMON
—earthy clay	BOLE
—formation of	PEDOGENESIS
—humus-rich	BLACK EARTH CHERNOZEM
—lacking defined layers	AZONAL
—layer A and B horizons	SOLUM
at surface	A-HORIZON, SOLUM TOPSOIL
below surface	B-HORIZON, SUBSOIL SUBSTRATUM SUBSURFACE
weathered rock	C-HORIZON
—leached by rainfall	PEDALFER
—marshy in spring, frozen in winter	GLEI SOIL
—organic	LEAF MOULD, HUMUS
—poor soil in arid or semi-arid region	
—dark	SOLONETZ
—light	SIEROZEM
—pale	SOLONCHAK
sub-polar regions	PODSOL, PODZOL
—red clayey	TERRA ROSSA
iron-bearing	LATERITE
tropical	LATOSOL
—rich in mull	BROWN EARTH BROWN FOREST SOIL
—section showing layers	SOIL PROFILE
—sequence(s) in given area	CATENA(E)
—shallow over rock (US)	LITHASOL
—sticky clay	GLEY
when wet	GUMBO
—study of	PEDOLOGY, SOIL SCIENCE
—with lime in surface layer	PEDOCAL
solar radiation on a given area	INSOLATION
solid matter transported by river	RIVER LOAD
source of —river	HEADSTREAM
—spring or stream	WELLHEAD

South African —grassland	KAR(R)OO, VELDT
—hill	KOP(J)E, KOPPIE
—mountain	BERG
—wooded grassland	BOSCHVELD(T) BUSHVELD
spot where fluid oozes from ground	SEEP
spring	FOUNTAIN, SPA, WELL
—as source of stream	FOUNTAINHEAD
—containing dissolved mineral matter	MINERAL SPRING SPA
—period of thaw (Siberia)	RASPUTITSA
steep —crevasse	CHINE
—drop in watercourse	SHOOT, WATERFALL
—headland	BLUFF
—moorland area	FELL
—ravine	CHINE
—rock	CRAG
—rockface	CLIFF, LIN(N) PRECIPICE
—sheet of rock	DIKE, DYKE
—sided hollow in glacial deposit	GIANT'S KETTLE KETTLE(-HOLE)
—slope	ESCARPMENT, SCAR(P)
—spur cut off by glacier	TRUNCATED SPUR
stepped excavation	STOPE
stony desert	REG
straight section of river	REACH
strata —dipping in the same direction	ISOCLINAL FOLDING
outwards in all directions	PERICLINAL QUAQUAVERSAL
—folded downwards	SYNCLINE
upwards	ANTICLINE
	(see also division above)
streaks in green rock	SCHLIEREN
stream that flows only after heavy rain	WINTERBOURNE
stretch of sea cut off by strip of sand	LAGOON
study of —ancient organisms	PALAEONTOLOGY
—area of Earth's surface	GEODESY
—bodies of water	HYDROLOGY
—caves	SPELEOLOGY
—centres of spatial distribution	CENTROGRAPHY

—crop production	AGRONOMY
—deposits	SEDIMENTOLOGY
—distribution of	
animals	ZOOGEOGRAPHY
—and plants	BIOGEOGRAPHY
human population	DEMOGRAPHY
plants	PHYTOGEOGRAPHY
races	ETHNOLOGY
—Earth	
measurement	GEODESY
sciences	GEOSCIENCE
	NATURAL HISTORY
—Earth's	
magnetism in past	
ages	PALAEOMAGNETISM
surface	CHOROGRAPHY
	(PHYSICAL) GEOGRAPHY
	PHYSIOGRAPHY, TOPOGRAPHY
	TOPOLOGY
—in past ages	PALAEOGEOGRAPHY
—ecology in past ages	PALAEOECOLOGY
—economic	
activity	LOCATIONAL ANALYSIS
—effects of seasons on	
flora and fauna	PHENOLOGY
—features of earth	GEOMORPHOLOGY
	PHYSIOGRAPHY
—glaciers	GLACIOLOGY
—influence of geography	
on politics	GEOPOLITICS
—past ages from	
geological data	GEOCHRONOLOGY
—physical processes	
of Earth	GEOPHYSICS
—rock strata	STRATIGRAPHY
—rocks	GEOLOGY, LIHOLOGY
	PETROLOGY
—soil	PEDOLOGY, SOIL SCIENCE
—structure of	
Earth's surface	(PLATE) TECTONICS
—succession of rock	
formation	STRATIGRAPHICAL GEOLOGY
	STRATIGRAPHY
—water in rivers, etc	HYDROLOGY
submerged valley	RIA
subterranean	
—mass of solidified rock	PLUTON
—passage	ADIT, TUNNEL
summit of hill,	
mountain, etc	CREST, CROWN
surface	
—of slip in fault	FAULT PLANE
—worn level by erosion	PENEPLAIN
	PENEPLANE
swamp	BOG, FEN, MARSH, MORASS
—Canada	MUSKEG

—in arid region	
containing much salt	SALINA, SALINE
	SALT-MARSH
swampy pine forest	URMAN
swiftly flowing part of river	RAPIDS
system of mountain	
ranges	CORDILLERA
tableland	PLATEAU
—South America	PUNA
temperate grassland	DOWNLAND, PAMPAS
	PRAIRIE, STEPPE
temporary	
—lake	PLAYA
—salt-lake (Algeria)	SHOTT
—stream	(WINTER-)BOURNE
terrace with steep	
slope on one side	MESA
territorial division	COUNTY, HUNDRED
	PROVINCE, REGION
	RIDING, STATE
territory	
—enclosed by country	
to which it does	
not belong	ENCLAVE
—governed by League	
of Nations	MANDATED TERRITORY
—jointly governed	CONDOMINIUM
—partly controlled by	
another	PROTECTORATE
—ruled by state from	
which it is detached	DEPENDENCY
—within which another	
state has freedom	
of action	SPHERE OF INFLUENCE
theory of	
—change by	
existing	
processes	UNIFORMITARIANISM
violent events	CATASTROPHISM
—continents formed	
from large	
land-mass	DISPLACEMENT THEORY
—distribution of	
land masses	TETRAHEDRAL THEORY
—rock formation by	
precipitation from sea	NEPTUNISM
subterranean heat	PLUTONISM
	VULCANISM
thicket	BRUSH(WOOD)
tidal wave in river	BORE, EAGRE
time related to a	
particular meridian	STANDARD TIME
	ZONE TIME
top of hill	BROW, CREST
tornado over the sea	WATERSPOUT
town with harbour	PORT

trading centre between countries	ENTREPOT
transformation of rock	METAMORPHISM
transportation of topsoil by rainwater	ELUVIATION
tree barrier	SHELTER BELT
treeless	
—plains of northern zones	STEPPES, TUNDRA
—upland	DOWN
tremor in Earth's crust	EARTHQUAKE
tributary	AFFLUENT
	CONFLUENT, INFLUENT
tropical coastal swamp	MANGROVE SWAMP
uncultivated	
—elevated land	MOOR(LAND)
—region	BUSH, DESERT
underground chamber	CAVE(RN)
unit of	
—ecological community	BIOME
—latitude or longitude	DEGREE
upland	
—meadow (Norway)	SAETER
—pastureland	DOWN
uplands	(see plateau above)
uplift of Earth's surface	UPTHRUST
upper	
—limit of growth in mountains	TREE LINE
—part of river	HEADWATERS
—strata pushed forward over lower	THRUST FAULT
	REVERSED FAULT
uppermost layer of forest	CANOPY
upward displacement of rock	UPTHROW
valley	VALE
—across a range	TRANSVERSE VALLEY
—American	ARROYO, CAN(Y)ON
	GULCH, RAVINE
—Arab	WADI, WADY
—between faults	GRABEN, RIFT VALLEY
—broad	STRATH
and level	VALE
—deep and narrow	GORGE, RAVINE
	GULCH
—drowned	RIA
—dry	DEAD VALLEY
—entering well above main river valley	HANGING VALLEY
—flooded as result of land subsidence	DROWNED VALLEY
	RIA, SUBMERGED VALLEY
—Indian	NULLA(H)

—long narrow	RAVINE
—narrow	COMB(E), COOMB, CWM
	DEAN, DELL, DENE, DINGLE
—parallel to range	LONGITUDINAL VALLEY
—round	CIRQUE, CORRIE
—Scottish	CLEUCH, CLEUGH
	CORRIE, GLEN, HEUCH
	HEUGH, STRATH
—side (US)	COTEAU
—small	DELL, DENE, DIMBLE
	DINGLE
—South African	DONGA
—Spanish	ARROYO
—steep	CHINE
—submerged	RIA
—transverse	CLUSE
—wide	DALE
—with	
lake in desert	BOLSON
watercourse	DALE
—without watercourse	DEAD VALLEY
	DRY VALLEY
—wooded	COMB(E), COOMB, CWM
	GHYLL
vertical	
—body of ore	SHOOT
—descent of water	WATERFALL
—displacement of fault	THROW
—distance between contours	CONTOUR INTERVAL
—height above sea level	ALTITUDE
—hole	POTHOLE
—opening to mine, etc	SHAFT
—rockface formed by erosion	RIMROCK
—shaft in	
earth	WELL
glacier	GLACIER MILL, MOULIN
rock	POTHOLE
violent	
—geological change	CATACLYSM
—stream of water	TORRENT
viscous mud	SLIME
vitrified sand fused by lightning	FULGURITE
volcano	(see separate entry)
wall of turf or stone	DIKE, DYKE
warming by trapped radiation	GREENHOUSE EFFECT
washing soil off bedrock	HUSH
water	
—bearing layer	AQUIFER
—existing below ground	GROUND WATER
	WATER TABLE

—from
  melting ice   MELTWATER
  the ground   SPA, SPRING
—hot from the ground   THERMAL SPRING
—in earth above
  water table   VADOSE
watercourses   BROOK, BURN, CANAL
           CHANNEL, DIKE, DITCH
           DYKE, RILL, RIVER, STREAM
—too small for valley
  in which it flows   MISFIT RIVER
                MISFIT STREAM
—with no outlet to
  the sea   INTERNAL DRAINAGE
          INTERIOR DRAINAGE
waterfall   FORCE, LIN(N)
—large   CATARACT
—series   CASCADE, CATARACT, RAPIDS
—small   CASCADE
          (*see also* **waterfalls**)
wearing away of land
surface   DENUDATION
—by
  breaking off of thin
    scales   EXFOLIATION
          ONION WEATHERING
       SPHEROIDAL WEATHERING
  chemical action   CORROSION
  climatic factors   WEATHERING
  loose materials in
    transport   ABRASION, ATTRITION
       CORROSION, DEGRADATION
                EROSION
  other than chemical
    action   MECHANICAL WEATHERING
  rainwater   ELUVIATION
  running water
  —in channel   GULLY EROSION
  —evenly   SHEET EROSION
  wind   DEFLATION
—producing
  channel   FRETTING
  isolated
    elevation   CIRCUMDENUDATION
  smooth surface   PLANATION
well bringing up water
by hydrostatic pressure   ARTESIAN WELL
wet
—forest (S. Amer.)   SELVA
—low-lying ground   FEN, MARSH
       MORASS, (QUAKING) BOG
       QUAGMIRE, SWAMP
—sand   QUICKSAND
winding course of stream
  or river   MEANDER
wind-ridge in snow   SASTRUGA, ZASTRUGA

yield from ore sample   PROSPECT
zone
—based on altitude (S. Amer.)
  highest   TIERRA FRIA
  middle   TIERRA TEMPLADA
  lowest   TIERRA CALIENTE
—between Capricorn
  and Cancer   TROPICS
               TORRID ZONE
—between tropics and
  polar circles   TEMPERATE ZONES
—inside Arctic and
  Antarctic Circles   FRIGID ZONES
—not affected by
  frost (US)   THERMAL BELT
—using the same time   TIME ZONE
zoological regions
—Africa below Sahara   ETHIOPIAN
—Arctic   ARCTOGAEA
—Australasia   NOTOGAEA
—Europe, North Africa
  North Asia (Old World)   PALAEARCTIC
—India, Indo-China   ORIENTAL
—Nearctic and Palaearctic   HOLOARCTIC
—Neotropical   NEOGAEA
—North America, Greenland
  (New World)   NEARCTIC
—region of the bear   ARCTOGAEA
—South and Central America   NEOGAEA
            NEOTROPICAL
—tropical America   NEOGAEA

German   D, GER
about   ETWA
aeroplane   DORNIER, FOKKER, HEINKEL
       MESSERSCHMITT, STUKA
               TAUBE
again   UBER
after   NACH
air
—force   LUFTWAFFE
—line   LUFTHANSA
alarm   STURM
Alsace-Lorraine   REICHSLAND
amiable   GEMUTLICH
ancient tribe   ALEMANNEN
and so forth   UND SO WEITER, USW
anxiety   ANGST
apple   APFEL
—cake   STRUDEL
approval   JA
aristocrat   JUNKER
armed forces   WEHRMACHT
armoured corps   PANZER
army
—reserve   LANDWEHR
—surgeon   FELDSCHER

arrangement	AUSGLEICH
art	
—school	BAUHAUS
—song	KUNSTLIED
article	DAS, DER, DIE, EIN, EINE
ass	ESEL
association	VEREIN
authentic	ECHT
bandmaster	CAPELLMEISTER
	KAPELLMEISTER
bar	BIERKELLER
baron(ess)	FREIHERR(IN)
basin	BECKEN
bay	BODDEN, BUCHT, HAFF
beach	STRAND
beef	RIND(FLEISCH)
beer	BIER, BOCK
—cellar	BIERKELLER
—mug	BIERKRUG, ENGHALSKRUG
	STEIN
biscuit rusk	ZWIEBACK
black-letter typeface	FRAKTUR
bless you!	GESUNDHEIT
blockade position (chess)	ZUGZWANG
blood	BLUT
—and	
earth	BLUT UND BODEN
honour	BLUT UD EHRE
iron	BLUT UND EISEN
—pudding	BLUTWURST
boat	BOOT
bog	MOOR, MOOS
border-crosser	GRENZGANGER
bread	BROT
broken	KAPUT(T)
brownie	KOBOLD
Brownshirts	STURMABTEILUNG
cabbage	KOHL
cake	KUCHEN
capitals	BERLIN, BONN
captain of cavalry	RITTMEISTER
carnival	FASCHING
carp	CRUCIAN, CRUSIAN
cartel	KARTELL
cast-iron	SPIEGELEISEN
castle	SCHLOSS
cattle-plague	RINDERPEST
cavalry soldier	REITER, U(H)LAN
Central European Time	MEZ
centre of diffusion of	
culture elements	KULTURKREIS
cheese	KASE
chicken	HAHN(CHEN), HUHN
chief	
—magistrate	BURGERMEISTER
	BURGOMASTER
—official	GAULEITER
child prodigy	WUNDERKIND
child(ren)	KIND(ER)
child's play	KINDERSPIEL
chocolate	SCHOKOLADE
choice	AUSLESE
civilisation	KULTUR
clamour	KATZENJAMMER
classical school	PROGYNMNASIUM
clavier	KLAVIER
cliff	WAND
climbing-boot(s)	KLETTERSCHUH(E)
clown hero	(H)OWLEGLASS, OWL-GLASS
	OWLSPIEGLE
coffee	KAFFEE
coin	
—small	PF, PFENNIG
—100 pfennigs	DEUTSCHEMARK, DM
	M, MARK
—10 marks	KRONE
—100 creutzers	FLORIN, GULDEN
—100 pfennings	GROSCHEN
—100 hellers	CROWN
—old coins	PFENNING, CROWN
	REUTZER, HELLER
	KR, KREUTZER, REICHSMARK
—gold	G(U)ILDER
—gold or silver	GULDEN
—silver	THALER
comfort	GEMUTLICHKEIT
comfortable	GEMUTLICH
commercial company	AG, GESELLSCHAFT
company	AG
complaint	MEASLES
co-ordination	GLEICHSCHALTUNG
copper	KUPFER
—ore	KUPFERSCHIEFER
count	(LAND)GRAF, LANDGRAVE
	MARGRAVE
countess	GRAFIN, LANDGRAVINE
court	HOF
courtly love	FRAUENDIENST
crevasse	BERGSCHRUND
cross-country skiing	LANGLAUF
culture	KULTUR
customs-union	ZOLLVEREIN
dachshund	TECKEL
dance	ALEMANDE, LANDLER
dance-tune	LANDLER
day	TAG
decoration	IRON CROSS
decree	DIKTAT
defector	GRENZGANGER
defence	WEHR
defile	KLAUSE
Democratic Republic	DDR, GDR

dialect	ALEMANNIC
diatonite	KIESELGUHR
dipper	DUNKER
direct perception	ANSCHAUUNG
director of orchestra	
or choir	KAPELLMEISTER
dish	SAUERKRAUT
district	GAU, GEBIET, KREIS
ditch	GRABEN
dog	HUND
	(see also dogs)
dominating principle	GEIST
don't mention it	BITTE
double(-goer)	DOPPEL-GANGER
dove	TAUBE
dramatic presentation	SINGSPIEL
drinking vessel	POKAL
dumpling	KNODEL
dynasty	CAROLINGIAN, CARLOVINGIAN
	FRANCONIAN, HANOVERIAN
	HOHENSTAUFEN, HOHENZOLLERN
	MEROVINGIAN, SALIAN
	WITTELSBACH
earth-spirit	ERDGEIST
East Germany	DDR, GDR
eastward thrust	DRANG NACH OSTEN
edition	AUFLAGE
egg	EI
elimination of all	
opposition	GLEICHSCHALTUNG
emergency	
—force	LANDSTURM
—levy	LANDSTURM
emotional distress	KATZENJAMMER
emperor	KAISER
empire	REICH
enamel	SCHMELZE
enlightenment	AUFKLARUNG
eternity	EWIGKEIT
evening	ABEND
evil spirit	RYE-WOLF
exclamation to avert	
ill-luck	UNBERUFEN
exclusion of political	
extremists from public	
office	BERUFSVERBOT
experimental task	AUFGABE
fable(s)	MARCHEN
fagging system	PENNALISM(US)
fake	ERSATZ
Fatherland	VATERLAND
Federal	
—armed forces	BUNDESWEHR
—German Republic	BRD, FRG
—lower house	BUNDESTAG
Federation of Industry	BDI

fen	MARSCH
festival writing	FESTSCHRIFT
field-grey	FELDGRAU
field-marshal	FELDMARSCHALL
fine for homicide etc	WERGILD
flame-thrower	FLAMMENWERFER
fish	FISCH
folk	
—song	VOLKSLIED
—tales	MARCHEN
foot	FUSS
for example	ZB, ZUM BEISPIEL
Foreign Office	WILHELMSTRASSE
foreigner	AUSLANDER
forest	FORST, WALD
—ranger	WALDGRAVE
form	GESTALT
free thinkers (18th c)	ILLUMINATI
freshman	PENNAL
friend	KAMERAD
frightful(ness)	SCHRECKLICH(KEIT)
fruit cake	STOLLEN
German	HUN, TEDESCO, TEUTON(IC)
gentleman	HERR
genuine	ECHT
girl	FRAULEIN
glacier	GLETSCHER
goblin	KOBOLD
goodbye	AUF WIEDERSEHEN
good luck	PROSIT
governor	BURGRAVE, GAULEITER
governess	FRAULEIN
grand piano	FLUGEL
grease	SCHMALTZ
ground	GRUND
guest	
—house	GASTHAUS, GASTHOF
—worker	GASTARBEITER
guide	FU(E)HRER
gulf	GOLF
gypsy	ZIGEUNER
hail!	HEIL
hall	SAAL
ham	SCHINKEN
hangover	KATZENJAMMER
harbour	HAFEN
having music	
specially adapted	DURCHKOMPONI(E)RT
head of university	RECTOR MAGNIFICUS
heath	HEIDE
helmet	PICKELHAUBE
heroic race	VOLSUNGS
highway	AUTOBAHN
hill	HUGEL, KOPF
hilltop	KUPPE
history of civilisation	KULTURGESCHICHTE

Hitler's bodyguard	SCHUTZSTAFFEL, SS
Hitlerite	NAZI
homesickness	HEIMWEH
host of phantoms	WILD HUNT
hotel	GASTHAUS, GASTHOF
housewife	HAUSFRAU
how are you?	WIE GEHT'S
hunter	JA(E)GER
hunting-horn	FLUGEL-HORN, WALDHORN
I	
—beg your pardon	BITTE
—serve	ICH DIEN
ice	EIS
immigrant worker	GASTARBEITER
impact radiation	BREMSSTRAHLUNG
Imperial	
—Royal	KK
—territory	REICHSLAND
industrial standards	DIN
infant school	KINDERGARTEN
inlet	FORDE
inspiring principle	GEIST
instrument	KUH-HORN
	KRUM(M)HORN
interjection	DONNERWETTER
is it not true?	NICHT WAHR
island(s)	INSEL(N)
Jew baiting	JUDENHETZE
Jews	ASHKENAZIM
joint stock company	AG
journeymanship	WANDERJAHRE
junior school	PROGYMNASIUM
juvenile delinquent	HALBSTARKER
kindness	GEMUTLICHKEIT
knight	RITTER
knowall	BESSERWISSER
lagoon	HAFF
lake	MEER, SEE, WASSER
lamb	LAMM
lancer	U(H)LAN
land bailiff	LANDAMMAN(N)
large tankard	POKAL
leader	FU(E)HRER, LEITER
—of file	FLUGELMAN, FUGLEMAN
league	BUND(E)
leap	LAUF
leather trousers	LEDERHOSEN
legend	WILD HUNT
light beer	PILS(E)NER
lightning	BLITZ
limited liability company	GMBH
liqueur	KIRSCH(WASSER)
	KUMMEL
living space	LEBENSRAUM
local governor	GAULEITER
long	LANG

lord	HERR
love	LIEB(E)
lower house of parliament	REICHSTAG
lyric(s)	LIED(ER)
—poet (12-13th c)	MINNESINGER
magistrate	AM(T)MAN
man	MANN
manor	HOF
—house	SCHLOSS
mansion	SCHLOSS
many thanks	DANKE SCHON
master	HERR, MEISTER
—of horse	STALLMEISTER
—race	HERRENVOLK
marsh	MARSCH
meat	FLEISCH
medal	
—civil	FEDERAL CROSS
—military	IRON CROSS
mediaeval court	FEHM(GERICHT)
	VEHM(GERICHT)
mercenary	LANDSKNECHT
	LANZKNECHT
	LANSQUENET
mica	GLIMMER
migrant worker	GASTARBEITER
migration	VOLKERWANDERUNG
militia	LANDWEHR
milk	MILCH
mine	GRUBE
mister	HERR
mix	MISCHEN
monoplane	TAUBE
moor	HEIDE
morals	SITTLICHKEIT
Moravian	HERRNHUTER
morning-star	MORGENSTERN
motorway	AUTOBAHN
mountain	BERG, OROS
—flour	BERGMEHL
—imp	RUBESZAHL
Mrs	FRAU
mush	SCHMALTZ
mushrooms	PILZE
musician (14-16th c)	MEISTERSINGER
mutton	HAMMEL
National Socialist	NAZI
—official	GAULEITER
necessity	ANANKE
nettle	NESSEL
new	NEUE
noble	EDEL, HERZOG, JUNKER
	MARGRAVE, WALDGRAVE
noblewoman	LANDGRAVINE
	MARGRAVINE
noodle	NUDEL

not called for	UNBERUFEN
novel about early	
development of hero	BILDUNGSROMAN
	ERZIEHUNGSROMAN
now	NUN
oath	SAPPERMENT
old	ALT
—burgher poet	MEISTERSINGER
—cornet	ZINKE
—soldiers' organisation	STAHLHELM
one	EIN
—of United Brethren	HERRNHUTER
—who thinks he knows	
better	BESSERWISSER
organised whole or unit	GESTALT
other	ANDER
outlook on the world	WELTANSCHAUUNG
over	UBER
palace	SCHLOSS
parliament	BUNDESTAG, REICHSTAG
passion for miracles	WUNDERSUCHT
pastime	ZEITVERTREIB
pattern	GESTALT
peak	GIPFEL, HORN, SPITZE
peas	URBSEN
peninsula	HALBINSEL
people	HERREN
people's car	VOLKSWAGEN, VW
philosopher	KANT, NIETZSCHE
pianoforte	HAMMERKLAVIER
pickled braised beef	SAUERBRATEN
pigeon	TAUBE
pipe	STUMMEL
pit	GRUBE
plain	PLATTE
plateau	PLATTE
please	BITTE
pleasure in others'	
misfortune	SCHADENFREUDE
polder	KOOG
pork	SCHWEIN
port	HAFEN
potato	KARTOFFEL
powdery deposit	BERGMEHL
power politics	MACHTPOLITIK
practical politics	REALPOLITIK
pretentious art	KITSCH
prince	ELECTOR
prisoner-of-war camp	OFLAG, STALAG
province	LAND
Prussian aristocrat	JUNKER
quick(ly)	SCHNELL
race	LAUF
rapid dance	WALTZ
ravine	KLAMM
reception room	KURSAAL

recurring theme	LEITMOTIF, LEITMOTIV
refusal	NEIN
region	GEBIET
relentless force	BLUT UND EISEN
religious	
—painter (19th c)	NAZARENE
—reformer (17th c)	PIETIST
revolt	PUTSCH
rice	REIS
ridge	GRAT, KAMM, RUCKEN
rifleman	JA(E)GER
rift-valley	GRABEN
river	FLUSS, RHEIN, RHINE
rock	FELS
—fall	BERGFALL
room to live	LEBENSRAUM
royal forester	WALDGRAVE
ruined	KAPUT(T)
run	LAUF
rye bread	PUMPERNICKEL
saint	SANKT
salmon	LACHS
salted biscuit	PRETZEL
sauce	SASSE
sausage	WURST
score in music	PARTITUR
sea	MEER
secondary school	GYMNASIUM
secret police	GESTAPO, STASI
selection	AUSLESE
sensation	EMPFINDUNG
sentimental enthusiasm	SCHWARMEREI
sentimentality	SCHMALTZ
Serene Highness	DURCHLAUCHT
settlement	AUSGLEICH
shape	GESTALT
sharpshooter	JA(E)GER
shell (Great War)	PIPSQUEAK
Shrovetide carnival	FASCHING
silver	ALBATA
sir	HERR
skiing	LANGLAUF
small smoked sausage	FRANKFURTER
smashed	KAPUT(T)
softly	LEISE
soldier	SOLDAT
song(s)	LIED(ER)
—without words	LIED OHNE WORTE
spa	BAD
—building	KURHAUS
space inhabited by living things	LEBENSRAUM
spirit	GEIST
—of the	
age	ZEITGEIST
mines	KOBOLD
spit	NEHRUNG

sprite	KOBOLD, NICKEL	town	STADT
squire	JUNKER	tramp about	PADDELN
star catalogue	DURCHMUSTERUNG	trash	KITSCH
state	REICH	trench	GRABEN
—bank	REICHSBANK	tribe	ANGLES, SAXONS
—legislature	LANDTAG	trombone	POSAUNE
steel	STAHL	trooper	REITER
stormtroopers	STURMABTEILUNG	trout	HUCK
stream	BACH	uncertain	MISCHEN
street	STRASSE	underground Nazi	WEREWOLF
stroke	SCHLAG	union	ANSCHLUSS, VEREIN
struggle	KAMPF	union of states	ZOLLVEREIN
student(s)	BURSCH(EN)	university	
—association	BURSCHENSCHAFT	—entrant	ARBITURIENT
—beerhouse	KNEIPE	—freshman	PENNAL
—bread	BROTSTUDIEN	—outsider	PHILISTER, PHILISTINE
—drinking party	KNEIPE	upper house	OBERHAUS
—duel	MENSUR	—of parliament	REICHSRAT(H)
—duelling sword	SCHLAGER	uproar	KATZENJAMMER
—society	CORPS	valley	GRUND, TAL, DORF
—song-book	KOMMERSBUCH	veal cutlet	(WIENER) SCHNITZEL
studies by which one		vegetables	GEMUSE
earns a living	BROTSTUDIEN	verse romance	ENGELHARD
substitute	ERSATZ	volume(s) of book	BAND(E)
superman	UBERMENSCH	war	KRIEG
superstition	ABERGLAUBE	—game	KRIEGSSPIEL
supplementary reserve	ERSATZ	—of culture	KULTURKAMPF
swarming	SCHWARMEREI	water	WASSER
swastika	HAKENKREUZ	—sprite	NIX
sweet		weight (cwt-50 kg)	CENTNER
—bread	STOLLEN	West Germany	FDR, FRG
—spiced bread toasted	ZWIEBACK	white horse	SCHIMMEL
sword	SCHLAGER	who is there?	WER DA
table	TISCH	wife	FRAU
—wine	TAFELWEIN	—of	
tank	PANZER	margrave	MARGRAVINE
tavern	KNEIPE	noble	WALDGRAVINE
teach	LEHREN	wine	(see separate entry)
teacher not member of		—cask	FUDER
salaried staff	PRIVAT DOCENT	wing	FLUGEL
	PRIVAT DOZENT	witches' revel	WALPURGIS(NACHT)
tendency	TENDENZ	with	MIT
terrier	PINSCHER	woman	FRAU
that		wooded hills	HARDT
—is to say	DAS HEISST, DH	world	WELT
—which is becoming	SITTLICHKEIT	—philosophy	WELTANSCHAUUNG
the day	DER TAG	—politics	WELTPOLITIK
thing in itself	DING AN SICH	—sorrow	WELTSCHMERZ
think	MEINEN	—spirit	WELTGEIST
thunder	DONNER	yard	HOF
—storm	DONNERWETTER	years of wandering	WANDERJAHRE
timbre	KLANGFARBE	yes	JA
title of nobility	WALDGRAVE	—indeed	JA WOHL
	WALDGRAVINE	young girl	BACKFISCH, FRAULEIN
toast	PROSIT	your health	GESUNDHEIT
tone colour	KLANGFARBE	**Ghana**	GH

capital	ACCRA
coin	
—unit	PESEWA
—100 pesewas	CEDI
former name	GOLD COAST
language	FANTEE, FANTI, TSHI, TWI
people	FANTEE, FANTI
robe	KENTE
silk cloth	KENTE CLOTH
ghosts	(*see* **spirits**)
Gibraltar	GBZ, GIB
girls	
from:	
America	BROAD, DAME
Australia	SHEILA
Egypt	BINT
France	FILLE(TTE)
Germany	FRAULEIN
Ireland	COLLEEN
Italy	RAGAZZA
Picardy	ROSE
Scotland	CUMMER, LASS
Spain	MUCHACHA, NINA
Tralee	ROSE
Troy	HELEN
Wales	MEGAN
Wessex	TESS
	(*see also* **woman**)
gland	
controlling growth	PITUITARY
discharging	
—internally	DUCTLESS GLAND
	ENDOCRINE GLAND
—through a duct	EXOCRINE GLAND
excretory gland in	
insects	MALPHIGIAN TUBULE
kidney	ADRENAL, APROCRINE
	SUPRARENAL
lymph purifying	LYMPH GLAND
	LYMPH NODE
salivary	PAROTID, PAROTIS
secreting	
—bile	LIVER
—digestive juices	PANCREAS
—disintegrated cells	HOLOCRINE
—fatty matter	SEBACEOUS
—fluid into mouth	SALIVARY
—hormone controlling	
calcium levels	PARATHYROID
metabolism and growth	THYROID
white blood cells	THYMUS
—insulin	PANCREAS
—internally	DUCTLESS
	ENDOCRINE
—milk	MAMMARY
—nectar in plants	NECTARY

—ova	OVARY
—perspiration	SWEAT GLAND
—sebum	SEBACEOUS
—seminal fluid	PROSTATE
—some disintegrated cells	APROCRINE
—sperm	SPERMARIUM
	SPERMARY
	TESTES
—tears	LACRIMAL
	LAC(H)RYMAL
—through duct	EXOCRINE
—urine	KIDNEY
—without disintegrating	MEROCRINE
situated in or near	
—abdomen	OVARY
—armpit	AXILLARY
—bladder	PROSTATE
—brain	EPIPHYSIS, HYPOPHYSIS
	PINEAL BODY, PINEAL GLAND,
	PITUITARY BODY
	PITUITARY GLAND
—chest	MEDIASTINAL, THYMUS
—eyelid	LACRIMAL, LAC(H)RYMAL
—groin	INGUINAL
—jaw	PAROTID, PAROTIS
	SUB-MAXILLARY
—kidneys	ADRENAL, SUPRARENAL
—mouth	ADENOID, TONSIL
—neck	CERVICAL, THYROID
—scrotum	TESTES
—skin	SEBACEOUS
—stomach	ABDOMINAL, PANCREAS
	PROSTATE
—thigh	POPLITEAL
—throat	(PARA)THYROID
tumour of a gland	ADENOMA
white-cell forming	LYMPH GLAND
	LYMPH NODE
glass	
blown disc	BOTTLE GLASS
	BULL'S-EYE
broken glass for re-use	CULLET
circular panes	CROWN GLASS
containing	
—alkali-lime	CROWN GLASS
—cobalt-oxide	SMALT
—lead silicate	FLINT GLASS
—sodium carbonate	SODA GLASS
convex mirror	CLAUDE LORRAINE GLASS
covering watchface	LUNETTE
dark	
—blue glass	SMALT
—spangled glass	AVANTURINE
	AVENTURINE
diamond-shaped pane	QUARREL(-PANE)
dish for cold dessert	COUPE

drinking glass	
—for	
beer	MUG, PONY, STEIN
	TANKARD
—Australian	MIDDY
champagne	BOAT, FLUTE
claret	MOUSSELINE
liqueur	PONY
rum	RUMMER
sherry	COPITA, SCHOONER
spirits	JIGGER
—large	BUMPER, STOUP, TUMBLER
sherry glass	SCHOONER
—small	PONY
—with handle	STEIN, TANKARD
flask	CARBOY, MATRASS
focussing glasses	FIELD GLASSES
	LENS, OPERA GLASSES
	PERISCOPE, TELESCOPE
fused coloured soda	MILLEFIORI
glass-fixer	GLAZIER
glasses (spectacles)	SPECS
—maker and seller	OPTICIAN
—single	MONOCLE
	QUIZZING GLASS
—with	
compound lens	BIFOCAL, TRIFOCAL
handle	LORGNETTE, LORGNON
	VARIFOCAL
—without	
frames	CONTACT LENSES, RIMLESS
side pieces	NOSE NIPPERS, PINCE-NEZ
glass-making tool	PUNTIL, PUNTY
hard glass	CROWN GLASS
	FLINT GLASS
	OPTICAL GLASS
heat resistant glass	PYREX, VITREOSIL
large tankard (German)	POKAL, STEIN
lump of glass before	
moulding	PARISON
manufacturers	
—English	BRIERLEY, STUART
	WEBB(-CORBETT)
—Irish	WATERFORD
—Scottish	EDINBURGH
multicoloured glass	AVENTURINE
	FAVRILE GLASS
	TIFFANY GLASS
	MURRHINE GLASS
ornamental	LALIQUE
potash for glass-making	POLVERINE
reacting to light	PHOTOCHROMIC
recycled glass	CULLET
reducing UV light	CROOKES GLASS
resistant to	
—chemicals	JENA GLASS

—heat	PYREX
safety glass	LAMINATED
strengthening process	ANNEALING
strong lens	MAGNIFYING GLASS
substitute for glass	PERSPEX
translucent glass	FROSTED GLASS
	OBSCURE GLASS
triangular block	PRISM
used	
—for fake jewels	PASTE, STRASS
—in decorative work	SCHMELZ
Venetian glass	AVANTURINE
	AVENTURINE
very thin glassware	MOUSSELINE
whitish glass	OPALESCENT
with bas-relief	LALIQUE
yellow-coloured	URANIUM GLASS

goats

Anatolian	ANGOLA
Asian	MARKHOR
	SERPENT-EATER
Caucasian	ATCHI, TUR
female	CAPRA, NANNY
Himalayan	GOORAL, TAHR, TEHR
	THAR, SEROW
male	BILLY, BUTTER
Pyrenean	CHAMOIS, IBEX
	IZARD, ROCK-DOE
Tibetan	TAKIN
young	KID

gods

African	
—Bushman's god	PRAYING MANTIS
—creator	NGAI
—Hottentot god	PRAYING MANTIS
—python god	ZOMBIE
—sky god	NGAI
American Indian	MANITO(U)
Anglo-Saxon	ING, SULIS
Aramaic	MAMMON
Assyrian	ASHUR
—earth	BEL
—sky	ANAT
—supreme	AS(S)HUR, AS(S)UR
—war	AS(S)HUR, AS(S)UR
Babylonian	BAAL, BEL
—atmosphere	ADDAD
—chief god	ENKI, (H)EA, MARDUK
—clouds	ADDAD
—Earth	BEL, ENLIL, KINGU
—harvest	(T)HAMMUZ
—messenger	MUMMUS
—sea	ANU
—sky	ANU
—Sun	T(H)AMMUZ
—tempest	ADDAD

—war	AS(S)HUR, AS(S)UR
	MARDUK, HERGAL
—water	APSU, (H)EA
—wisdom	MARDU, NABU, NEBO
Buddhist	BUDDHA
	GAUTAMA, SAKYAMUNI
Celtic	
—chief	DAGDA
—light	LUG(H)
—sea-god	LE(I)R
Central American rain-god	CHAC
Chaldean	NANNAR
Chinese	GOSS, JOSS, KUANYIN
	SHANGTI, SHEN-NUNG
	XANGTI
—Confucian	
supreme god	TIAN
creator of Universe	DEMIURGE
	DEMIURGUS
Egyptian	KNEPH
—air	SHU
—ape-headed	AANI
—art	THOTH
—artisans	PTAH
—artists	PTAH
—creator	KHNUM, PTAH
—darkness	SET
—dead	ANUBIS, OSIRIS
—Earth	GEB, KEB
—embalming	ANUBIS
—falcon-headed	HORUS
—fertility	AMEN, AM(M)ON
	AMUN, MIN
—harvest	OSIRIS
—hawk-headed	HORUS
—heaven	SEP
—ibis-headed	THOTH
—jackal-headed	ANUBIS
—learning	IMHOTEP
—life	AMEN, AM(M)ON, AMUN
—magic	THOTH
—medicine	IMHOTEP
—Moon	AAH, KHONS, YAH
—Nile	HAPI
—of Greeks in Egypt	SARAPIS, SERAPIS
—ram-headed	AMEN, AM(M)ON
	AMUN, BA, KHNUM
—science	THOTH
—son of Osiris	HORUS
—soul	BA
—star	SOTHIS
—Sun	HORUS, RA, RE
—supreme	AMEN, AM(M)ON
	AMUN, OSIRIS
—underworld	OSIRIS, SARAPIS
	SERAPIS, WEPWAWET

—war	SEPTU
—water	NUN
—wisdom	THOTH
—wolf-god	WEPWAWET
English war-god	TIU, TIW
Eskimo sky-god	SILA
Etruscan	MENRFA, TAGES
false	BAAL, IDOL
fish-god	EA
Germanic	(see Norse below)
Gnostic	ABRAXAS, DEMIURGE
	DEMIURGUS
Greek	
—attendant on Pan	PANISC, PANISK
—avenger	ANTEROS
—beauty	APOLLO, HELIOS
—creation	PROMETHEUS
—death	THANATOS
—destiny	NEMESIS
—divine justice	THEMIS
—dreams	MORPHEUS, ONEIROS
—earthquakes	EARTHSHAKER
	POSEIDON
—elder gods (Titans)	ATLAS, CRONUS
	HYPERION, KRONO
	IAPETUS, MNEMOSYNE
	OCEAN, PROMETHEUS
	TETHYS, THEMIS, URANUS
—fear	PHOBOS
—fire	HEPHAESTUS
—flocks	PAN
—healing	ASCLEPIOS, ASCLEPIUS
	ASKLEPIOS
—heavens	URANUS
—human justice	DIKE
—inferior	PANISC, PANISK
—light	APOLLO
—longing	HIMEROS
—love	EROS
—many-shaped	PROTEUS
—marriage	HYMEN
—medicine	APOLLO
—metal-working	HEPHAESTUS
	HEPHAISTOS
—mirth	COMUS
—mockery	MOMUS
—mountain	TMOLUS
—music	APOLLO
—north wind	BOREAS
—Olympians	APOLLO, ARES, HADES
	HEPHAESTUS, HERMES
	PLUTO, POSEIDON, ZEUS
—Poseidon	EARTHSHAKER
—rain	GANYMEDE
—re-birth	ADONIS
—reverence	AIDOS

—river	ACHELOUS, ALPHEUS
	ASOPUS, PENEUS
—sailors	CASTOR, PULLUX
—sea	GLAUCUS, NEREUS
	MELICERTES
	OCEANUS, PROTEUS
	POSEIDON, TRITON
—shepherds	PAN
—sky	ZEUS
—sleep	HYPNOS
—Sun	APOLLO, HELIOS, HYPERION
	PHOEBUS, TITAN
—supreme	CRONUS, KRONOS, ZEUS
—trade	HERMES
—travellers	HERMES
—truth	APOLLO
—tutelary god	PROMACHOS
—underworld	DIS, HADES
	PLUTO, PYTHON
—universe	URANUS
—vegetation	ADONIS, ATTIS
—vengeance	NEMESIS
—war	ARES
—wealth	PLUTUS
—wedding feasts	HYMEN
—west wind	ZEPHYRUS
—winds	(A)EOLUS
—wine	BACCHUS, DIONYSUS
—wisdom	HERMES
—woods	PAN, SILENUS, SATYR
Hebrew	ELOHIM, JAH(VEH), JAHWEH
	JEHOVAH, YAH(VEH), YAWE(H)
	YAHVIST, YAHWIST
Hindu	DEVA
—creator	BRAHMA
—demigod	GARUDA
—desire	KAMA
—destroyer	MAHADEVA, S(H)IVA
—Earth	KRISHNA
—elephant-headed	GANES(H)A
—fire	AGNI
—foresight	GANES(H)A
—good fortune	GANES(H)A
—heavens	INDRA, VARUNA
—intoxicating spirit and	
plant personified	SOMA
—love	CAMA, KAMA
	KAMADEVA
—monkey-god	HANUMAN
—Moon	SOMA
—preserver	KRISHNA, RAMA, VISHNU
—rain	INDRA
—reproducer	S(H)IVA
—storms	RUDRA
—Sun	SURYA
—supreme	BRAHMA, INDRA

—time	KALA
—war	INDRA, KARTTIKEYA
—warrior	AJUNA, BHISMA
—water	VARUNA
—wrath	MANYU
Italian (ancient)	
—son of Saturn	PICUS
—war god	QUIRINUS
Jain prophets revered	
as deities	TIRTHANKAR(A)
	TIRTHANKER
Japanese	KAMI
Knights Templar	BAPHOMET
Mexican rain god	TLALOC
Moabite	CHEMOSH
Moslem	ALLAH
mysterious infernal deity	DEMOGORGON
Norse	AS, ASA, AESIR, VANIR
—battle	TIWAZ
—blind god	HODER
—craftsmen	VOLUNDR, WAYLAND
	WE(I)LAND
—crops	THOR
—dragon-god	FAFNIR
—Earth	FREYR
—evil	LOKI
—fertility	FREYR
—fire	LOGI, LOKI
—founder-god	ING
—keeper of Bifrost	
(rainbow) bridge	HEIMDALL
—light	BALDER, BALDUR
—mischief	LOKI
—poetry	BRAGI
—sea	AEGIR, NJORD
—ships	NJORD
—sky	ALCIS
—son of Odin	BALDER, BALDUR
	HERMOD, HODER
—supreme	BALDER, BALDUR
	ODIN, WODEN, WOTAN
—thunder	DOWAR, THOR
—war	TYR
—wind	VAYU
—wisdom	KVASIR, MIMIR
Persian	(AHURA) MAZDA
	MITRA, MITHRAS(S)
	ORMAZD, ORMUZD
Philistine	DAGON
Phoenician	BAAL, BEELZEBUB
presiding deity	NUMEN
Polynesian	A'A
Red Indian	MANITO(U)
Roman	
—agriculture	LIBER PATER, MARS
	PICUS, SATURN

—boundaries	TERMINUS	—war	MARS, QUIRINUS, ROMULUS
—cattle	PALES	—wine	BACCHUS, LIBER
—dawn	JANUS	—wisdom	MERCURY
—dead	ORCUS	—woods	SILVAN, SYLVANUS
good	MANES	—working men	SATURN
wicked	LARVAE, LEMURES	—youth	JUVENTUS
—doors	JANUS	Saxon	SULIS
—eloquence	MERCURY	Semitic	ASMODAY, ASMODEUS
—farming	SILVANUS		CAB(E)IRI
—fertility	LIBER PATER, LUPERCUS		MOLECH, MOLOCH
	MARS, PICUS, PRIAPUS	South American - creator	VIRACOCHA
—fire	MULCIBER, VOLCANUS	Spanish love-god	AMADIS
	VULCAN	Sri Lankan	KOHMBA
—flocks	LUPERCUS	Syrian	RIMMON
—food and drink	PENATES	Thracian	TRIBALLUS
—forests	SYLVANUS	West Indian snake god	ZOMBI(E)
—founder of Rome	QUIRINUS	wood-god	SILVAN
—fruit trees	VERTUMNUS	Yoruba	ESHU
—gardens	PRIAPUS, VERTUMNUS	Zoroastrian	HAOMA
—gateways	JANUS	**goddesses**	
—healing	AESCULAPIUS	Australian	
—honesty	FIDES	mother-goddess	KADJERI, KUNAPIPI
—household	LAR(ES)		MUMINA
—husbands	PORTUNUS	Babylon	
—larder	PENATES	—chief	IS(H)TAR, NANAI, NINA
—light	APOLLO	—death	GULA
—love	CUPID	—dragon-goddess	TIAMAT
—manuring	STERCULIUS	—Earth	DAMKINA
—merchants	MERCURY	Celtic	(D)ANA, (D)ANU
—metalwork	MULCIBER, VOLCANUS	—fertility	BRIGIT
	VULCAN	Chaldean	NINGAL
—messenger	MERCURY	Egypt	
—Moon	JUPITER	—cat-goddess	BASH(ET), BAST(ET)
—Olympians	APOLLO, JUPITER	—cow-goddess	HATHOR
	MARS, MERCURY, NEPTUNE	—cobra-goddess	UDOT
	PLUTO, VULCAN	—creation	HEKET
—ploughmen	SYLVANUS	—destiny	SHAIT
—protection	GENIUS	—fertility	ISIS
—rain	JUPITER	—justice	MA(AT)
—ridicule	MOMUS	—lioness-headed	PASHT
—sea	NEPTUNE	—love	HATHOR
—shepherds	FAUN(US)	—maternity	APET
—sky	JUPITER	—Moon	ISIS
—sleep	SOMNUS	—queen of	
—sowing seed	CONSUS	goddesses	SATI
—spirits of the dead	MANES	heaven	ISIS
—Sun	APOLLO, JUPITER	—right	MA
—supreme	JOVE, JUPITER	—sky	NUT
—theft	MERCURY	—tombs	PASHT
—thunder	JUPITER	—truth	MA(AT)
—thunderbolts	VULCAN	—war	NEIT(H)
—travel	JANUS	Eskimo seal-goddess	SEDNA
—trees	SYLVANUS	Greek	
—two-faced	JANUS	—agriculture	ATHENA, DEMETER
—underworld	DIS (PATER), PLUTO	—barley	ALPHITO
—vines	SATURN	—beauty	APHRODITE, URANIA

—childbirth	ARTEMIS, EILEITHYIA	—rivers	SARAVATSI
	ILITHYIA	—strength	DURGA, KALI
—cities	ATHENA	Japanese (Shinto)	AMATERASU
—corn	DEMETER, PERSEPHONE	Norse	
—darkness	HECATE	—beauty	FREYA, IVERA
—dawn	EOS	—dead	HEL(A)
—discord	ERIS	—Earth	ERDA, NERTHUS
—divine justice	THEMIS	—fertility	FRIGG
—Earth	CYBELE, GE, GAEA, GAIA	—guarding golden apples	IDUNN
—female satyr	SATYRA, SATYRESS	—handmaidens, Valhalla	VALKYRIE
—fertility	ARTEMIS	—healing	EIR
—fire	HESTIA	—love	FRIGG, FRE(J)YA
—foretelling the future	CAMENAE		IVERA
—fountains	ARETHUSA	—plenty	NEHALLENIA
—good fortune	TYCHE	—receiving dead virgins	GEFION
—handicrafts	ATHENA	—sea	RAN
—harvest	DEMETER	—underworld	GERDA, HEL(A)
—health	CAMENAE, HYGEIA	—wife of	
—hearth	HESTIA	Baldur	NANNA
—hunting	ARTEMIS, CYNTHIA	Loki	SIGYN
—justice	ASTRAEA, DIKE	Thor	SIF
	THEMIS	—wisdom	FRIGGA
—law	THEMIS	—youth	FRIGG, FRE(J)YA, IVERA
—love	APHRODITE, URANIA	Peruvian	MAMA
—marriage	HERA	Phrygian	CYBELE
—memory	MNEMOSYNE	Roman	
—mischief	ATE	—beauty	VENUS
—Moon	ARTEMIS, HECATE	—cattle	BUBONA
	PHOEBE, SELENE	—chance	FORTUNA
—nature	RHEA	—chastity	DIAN(A)
—night	NOX, NYX	—childbirth	EGERIA, JUNO, LUCINA
—Olympians	APHRODITE, ARTEMIS	—corn	CERES
	ATHENA, HERA, HESTIA	—craftsmen	MINERVA
	JUNO	—crops	AN(N)ONA
—persuasion	PEITHA	—dawn	AURORA
—punishment	POENA	—Earth	TELLUS
—rainbow	IRIS	—education	MINERVA
—retribution	ARA, NEMESIS	—fate	FORTUNA
—sea	INO	—fertility	CYBELE, DIANA
—sky	HERA		FAUNA, MAIA
—springs	ARETHUSA, CAMENAE	—fields	BONA DEA, FAUNA
—underworld	PERSEPHONE	—fire	VESTA
—vengeance	NEMESIS	—flocks	PALES
—victory	NIKE	—flowers	FLORA
—war	ATHENA, ENYO	—fortune	FORTUNA
—wells	CAMENAE	—fountains	EGRERIA
—wisdom	ATHENA, ATHENE, PALLAS	—fruit	POMONA
—witchcraft	HECATE	—fruitfulness	FLORA
—youth	HEBE	—funerals	LIBITINA
Hawaiian volcano	PELE	—gardens	VENUS
Hindu		—harvest	OPS
—dawn	US(H)AS	—hearth	VESTA
—destroyer	DURGA, KALI	—herds	FAUNA
—divinity	DEVI	—horticulture	VACUNA
—mother-goddess	KAN, SHAKTA, SHAKTI	—horses	EPONA
—plenty	PURANDI	—household	VESTA

—hunting | DIAN(A), LUCINA
—light | DIAN(A), JUNO
—love | VENUS
—marriage | JUNO, LUCINA
—Moon | DIAN(A)
—morning | MATUTA
—mother-goddess | CYBELE, MAGNA MATER
—nursing mothers | RUMINA
—Olympians | DIANA, JUNO, MINERVA
VENUS, VESTA
—orchards | POMONA
—peace | IRENE
—persuasion | SUADELA
—pleasure | VOLUPTAS
—rumour | FAMA
—sea | MATER MATUTA
—spring flowers | FERONIA
—springs | CAMENAE, JUTURNA
VENUS
—underworld | LIBITINA
—victory | VICTORIA
—war | BELLONA, MINERVA
—wealth | OPS
—wells | CAMENAE, VENUS
—wisdom | MINERVA
Saxon
—spring | EASTRE, EOSTRE
Semitic
—fertility | ASTARTE
ASHTARETH, ASHTAROTH
Thracian | KOTYS, KOTYTTO

golf
courses
—America | AUGUSTA, DORAL, GLENVIEW
GRAND CYPRESS, HARBOUR TOWN
HILTON HEAD ISLAND, HOUSTON
KEMPER LAKES, KIAWAH ISLAND
LA COSTA, LAKE ORION, MEDINAH
NEWPORT, OAK HILL
OAKLAND HILLS, OAKMONT
PALM BEACH, PALM SPRINGS
PONTE VEDRA, SHINNECOCK HILLS
WILLIAMSBURG, WOODLANDS
—Australia | KINGSTON HEATH
ROYAL ADELAIDE
ROYAL MELBOURNE
—Austria | GUT ALTENTANN
—Belgium | ROYAL WATERLOO
—Canada | GLEN ABBEY
—Channel Islands | LA MOYE
—England | AINSDALE, ASHDOWN FOREST
BELFRY, BIRKDALE, BURNHAM
CAMBERLEY HEATH, DEAL, FERNDOWN
FLEMING PARK, FORMBY
FRILFORD HEATH, HOYLAKE
HUNSTANTON, HUNTERCOMBE

KNOLE PARK, LITTLE ASTON
LYTHAM, MID-SURREY, OLD THORN
PATSHULL PARK, ST GEORGES
ST MELLION, SANDWICH
SAUNTON, SEAFORD, STENEDOC
STOKE POGES, SUNNINGDALE
THORNDEN PARK, THORPE WOOD
WALTON HEATH, WENTWORTH
WOBURN, WOODHALL SPA
—France | CHANTILLY, VERSAILLES
—Germany | WORTHSEE
—Holland | KENNEKAER
—Ireland | BALLYBUNION, NEWCASTLE
PORTMARNOCK, PORTRUSH
—Jamaica | MONTEGO BAY
—Japan | TAKARAZUKA
—Monte Carlo | MONT AGEL
—Scotland | BALLATER, CARNOUSTIE
GLENEAGLES, GLENROTHES
MORAY, MUIRFIELD
MUSSELBURGH, PRESTWICK
ST ANDREWS, TROON
TURNBERRY, WESTERN GAILES
—Spain | CLUB DE CAMPO, EL BOSQUE
LA MANGA, PUERTO DI HIERRO
TRAMONTANA, VALENCIA
—Sweden | DRITTNINGHOLM
—Wales | PORTHCAWL, ST DAVIDS
ST PIERRE
players
—American (m) | ANDERSON, ARMOUR
BARNES, CALCAVECCHIA
CASPER, HAGEN, HOGAN
HUTCHINSON, JONES, LEMA
LITTLE, MILLER, NELSON
NICKLAUS, PALMER, ROGERS
SARAZEN, SHUTE, SNEAD
TREVINO, WATSON, WEISKOPF
(f) | BAUGH, BERG, CONLEY
DIDRIKSON, GEDDES, KING
LOPEZ, MOON, SHEEHAN
ZAHARIAS
—Argentinian | VINCENZO
—Australian (m) | DEVLIN, NAGLE, NORMAN
OGLE, SENIOR, THOMSON
VON NIDA
(f) | BELLOWIEN, DIBNAH
JONES, LUNN
—Belgian (m) | VAN DONCK
(f) | DESCAMPE
—Canadian (m) | BALDING, KNUDSEN
(f) | KORTGAAZO
—English (m) | ALLIS, BONALLACK, BRAID
BROWN, BURTON, COLES, COTTON
DUNCAN, FALDO, FAULKNER
HAVERS, HUNT, JACKLIN

	KING, OOSTERHUIS, PADGHAM	
	PERRY, RAY, TAYLOR, TORRANCE	
	VARDON, WARD, WEETMAN	
	WHITCOMBE	
(f)	BARTON, DAVIES	
	DOBSON, FISHWICK	
	NICHOLAS, IRVIN	
	STRUDWICK, WETHERED	
—French (f)	DE LORENZI	
—German	LANGER	
—Irish	DALY, O'CONNOR	
	RAFFERTY	
—Japanese	HOSOISHI, NAKAMURA	
	OZAKI	
—New Zealand (m)	CHARLES	
(f)	ARNOLD	
—Peruvian (f)	DIBOS	
—Scottish (m)	GALLACHER, LYLE	
(f)	WRIGHT	
— South African (m)	COLE, FROST	
	LEGRANGE, LOCKE	
	PLAYER	
(f)	MARITZ	
—Spanish (m)	BALLESTEROS, MIGUEL	
	OLAZABAL	
(f)	FIGUERAS-DOTTI	
	WUNSCH-RUIZ	
—Swedish (f)	NEUMANN	
—Welsh	REES, WOOSNAM	
terms		
—allowance		
of strokes	HANDICAP	
on putt for slope of green	BORROW	
—approach		
shot	RUN-UP	
to green	APRON	
—bonus strokes	HANDICAP	
—built-in hazard	BUNKER	
—clod of earth cut out by club	DIVOT	
—club		
carrier	CADDIE, TROLLEY	
names	BRASSIE, BRASSY, CLEEK	
	DRIVER, GOOSE, IRON	
	MASHIE, NIBLICK, PUTTER	
	(SAND-)BLASTER, SPOON	
	WEDGE, WOOD	
numbers	ONE to NINE	
—5 iron	MASHIE	
—8 iron	NIBLICK	
—distance	CARRY	
—flag placed in hole	PIN	
—game		
decided on number of holes won	MATCH PLAY	
decided on number of strokes taken	STROKE PLAY	

for		
—four	FOUR BALL, FOURSOME	
—two	TWOSOME	
with prize money for each hole	SKIN TOURNAMENT	
—handicap of nil	SCRATCH	
—hit ball		
to left	DRAW, HOOK, PULL	
right	FADE, PUSH, SLICE	
—lofted shot to green	PITCH	
—low approach shot	CHIP	
—nervous twitch when putting	YIPS	
—obstruction of ball on the green	STYMIE	
—part of course		
between tee and		
—green	FAIRWAY	
—pin	HOLE	
not mown	ROUGH	
round green	APRON	
—porter	CADDIE	
—prepare to strike ball	ADDRESS	
—putting area	GREEN	
—right to play first	HONOUR	
—score		
1 over par	BOGEY	
1 under par	BIRDIE	
2 under par	EAGLE	
3 under par	ALBATROSS	
where lead equals the number of holes left	DORMIE, DORMY	
—scoring system	STABLEFORD	
—seaside golf-course	LINKS	
—shot		
bending		
—to left	DRAW, HOOK, PULL	
—to right	FADE, PUSH, SLICE	
from		
—fairway	APPROACH SHOT	
—short distance to green	CHIP	
—tee	DRIVE	
that holes the ball		
from a bunker	GOLDEN FERRET	
on green towards hole	PUTT	
—slope on green	BORROW	
—start the game	TEE-OFF	
—starting point	TEE	
—stroke		
conceded as handicap	BISQUE	
that misses the ball	AIR-SHOT	
—strokes allowed for a hole	PAR	
—types of game	FOUR BALL, FOURSOME	
	MATCH PLAY, MEDAL PLAY	
	STROKE PLAY, TWOSOME	
—veer on drive	FADE	
—vehicle used on course	BUGGY	
—warning	FORE	

tournaments	
—American	ATLANTIC CITY CLASSIC
	BOB HOPE CLASSIC
	DOUG SANDERS CELEBRITY CLASSIC
	HERITAGE CLASSIC
	LADY KEYSTONE OPEN
	MASTERS, OPEN
	PGA CHAMPIONSHIP
	PLAYERS' CHAMPIONSHIP
	QUAD CITIES' OPEN
	ST JUDE CLASSIC
	TRADITION, VARDON TROPHY
—American/British	CURTIS CUP
	RYDER CUP, WALKER CUP
—British	BRITISH MASTERS
	BRITISH OPEN, PGA TOURNAMENT
	VARDON TROPHY
—Dubai	DESERT CLASSIC
—international	WORLD MATCH PLAY
—Japanese	FOUR TOURS
—Spanish	CATALAN OPEN

goose

domestic	BRECON BUFF, CHINESE
	EM(B)DEN, ROMAN
	TOULOUSE
wild	BARNACLE, BEAN, BRENT
	CANADA, EGYPTIAN
	GREYLAG, HAWAIIAN
	LESSER WHITE-FRONTED
	PINK-FOOTED, RED-BREASTED
	SNOW, WHITE-FRONTED

government   (*see* **power**)

governor

acting sovereign	VICEROY
Algerian	DEY
Arab	MUDIR, SHEREEF, SHERIF
Brazilian	CATAPAN
Byzantine	CATAPAN, EXARCH
castle	CASTELLAN
Chinese	TUCHUN
district	WARDEN
Dutch	STAD(T)HOLDER
eastern	MUDIR
German	BURGRAVE
—Nazi	GAULEITER
Greek	
—district	TOPARCH
—modern	EPARCH
—of the people	ETHNARCH
—province	NOMARCH
Hungarian	BAN
Indian	HAKEEM, HAKIM
	NAIK, SUBA(H)DAR
Italian	PODESTA
mediaeval	ALDERMAN, EALDORMAN
Middle East	EMEER, EMIR

Moldavian	GOSPODAR, HOSPODAR
old	GREAVE, GRIEVE, RECTOR
Pakistan	HAKEEM, HAKIM
papal	LEGATE
Persian	CHAGAN, CHAM, KHAN
	SATRAP
provincial	SATRAP
Roman	PRO-CONSUL
Serbian	ZUPAN
Spanish	ADELANTADO, ALCA(I)DE
	ALCAYDE
Spartan	HARMOST
town	WARDEN
Turkish	BASHAW, BEG, BEGLERBEG
	BEY, CAIMAC(AM), KAIMAKAM
	PACHA, PASHA, VALI, WALI
Wallachian	GOSPODAR, HOSPODAR
Yugoslav	ZUPAN

Graces   CHARITES

good cheer	THALIA
mirth	EUPHROSYNE
splendour	AGLAIA

grape   UVA

American	CATAWBA, SCUPPERNONG
	SEYVAL, ZINFANDEL
Austrian	GRUNER VELTLINER
German	RIVANDER, SCHEUREBE
	SILVANER
Hungarian	FURMINT
Italian	MOSCATO, NIEBBOLO
	SANGIOVESE
	TREBBIANO
madeira	BUAL, MALMSEY
	VERDELHO
North African	CARIGNON
Sardinian	CANNONAU
sherry	LISTAN, PALOMINO
	PEDRO XIMENEZ
South African	STEEN
Spanish	CENCIBAL, TEMPRANILLO
Swiss	FENDANT
varieties	ALIGOTE, BACCHUS, BARBERA
	CABERNET, CARINENA
	CHARDONNAY, CHASSELAS, CHENIN
	DOLCETTO, GAMAY, GARGANEGA
	GARNACHA, GRACIANO, GRENACHE
	HUXELREBE, MALBEC, MALVASIA
	MARSANNE, MERLOT, MOSCATEL
	MULLER-THURGAU, MUSCADET
	MUSCAT, ORTEGA, MUSKAT
	NEBBIOLO, PALOMINO, PINOT
	RIESLING, ROMORONTiN, SAUVIGNON
	SEMILLON, SILVANER, SYLVANER
	SYRAH, TOKAY, TRAMINER
	UGNI, VERDOT, VIOGNIER, ZINFANDEL
	(*see also* **wine**)

graph	(*see* **write**)
grass	GRAMINAE
African	(H)ALFA, PENNISETUM
	TEFF(GRASS)
agave fibre	SISAL(-GRASS)
Agrostis	BENT
Aira	HAIR-GRASS
Alopecurus	FOX-TAIL
American	PASPALUM
Ammophila	STAR(R)(-GRASS)
Anthoxanthum	VERNAL GRASS
anti-scorbutic	SCURVY-GRASS
aquatic grass	MANNA-GRASS
Australian	KANGAROO GRASS
	PORCUPINE GRASS, SPINIFEX
Avena	OAT
barley	SQUIRREL-TAIL
—type	SQUIRREL-TAIL
basket-grass	OPLISMENUS, PANICUM
bent	AGROSTIS
black salsify	VIPER'S GRASS
Bouteloua	MOSQUITO GRASS
Brazil	PARA-GRASS
Briza	QUAKING-GRASS
brome-grass	FESCUE, LOP(GRASS)
—bullrush	CAT'S-TAIL
butterwort	ROT-GRASS
canary-grass	PAINTED GRASS
cat's-tail	BULLRUSH, PHLEUM
	TIMOTHY
Ceylon grass	CITRONELLA
China grass	RAMEE, RAMI(E), RHEA
coarse grass	AIRA, AMMOPHILA
	HAIR-GRASS, LYME
	STAR(R)
cocksfoot	DACTYLIS, HARD-GRASS
cord-grass	RICE-GRASS
Cortaderia	PAMPAS-GRASS, GYNERIUM
cotton-grass	ERIOPHORUM
—Scottish	CANNA(CH)
	MOSS-CROP
couch-grass	DOG-GRASS, DOG-WHEAT
	QUICK(EN), QUITCH(-GRASS)
	(S)QUITCH, TWITCH
creeping	BUFFALO-GRASS
	CANARY-GRASS
—bent-grass	FIORIN
Cynosurus	DOG'S-TAIL GRASS
Dactylis	COCKSFOOT
darnel	LOLIUM
Digitaria	FINGER-GRASS
dog's-tail grass	CYNOSURUS
dry-stalk	BEN(N)ET
Dutch rush	SHAVE-GRASS
early-sprouting grass	VERNAL GRASS
eelgrass	GRASSWRACK, ZOSTER

esparto	(H)ALFA, SPANISH GRASS
	SPART
Falkland Islands grass	TUSSAC-GRASS
	TUSSOCK-GRASS
feather-grass	STIPA
fescue	FESTUCA, MELIC
Festuca	FESCUE, MELIC
float-grass	MANNA-GRASS
	MEADOW-GRASS
fodder-grass	RYE-GRASS
forage grass (US)	GAMA-GRASS
gardener's garters	PAINTED GRASS
	PHALARIS, RIBBON-GRASS
Gastridium	NIT-GRASS
glaucous	ELYMUS
Glyceria	FLOAT(ING)-GRASS
gold-edged	CAREX
goose-grass	CATCH-WEED, CLEAVERS
	CLIVERS
grasswrack	CLEAVERS, CLIVERS
	EELGRASS, ZOSTER
growth after hay-harvest	AFTERMATH
	FOG(GAGE)
Gynerium	CORTADERIA
	PAMPAS-GRASS
hair-grass	AIRA
Holcus	SOFT-GRASS
hybrid cereal	TRITICALE
Indian	BAJREE, DUR(R)A, JHOW
	KANS, LEMON GRASS
	RAGI, ROOSA, RUSA
Juncus	TOAD-GRASS
Kentucky	BLUE-GRASS
knot-grass	KNAWEL, PERSICARIA
	POLYGONUM, SCLERANTHUS
long-stalked varieties	WINDLESTRAW
Malayan	LALANG
manna-grass	MEADOW-GRASS
marram	MATGRASS, MATWEED
	SEA-REED
mat grass	NARDUS
meadow-grass	FLOAT(ING) GRASS, POA
mondo grass	OPHIOPOGON
moorland grass	BRIZA, MATGRASS
	MATWEED, QUAKING-GRASS
mosquito grass	BOUTELOUA
Nardus	MAT GRASS
New Zealand	TOI TOI
oat	AVENA
—type	BROME-GRASS
Ophiopogon	MONDO GRASS
Oplismenus	BASKET-GRASS, PANICUM
ornamental	PLUME-GRASS
painted grass	CANARY GRASS
	GARDENER'S GARTERS
pampas-grass	PASPALUM

Panicum	BASKET-GRASS
	OPLISMENUS, PANIC(-GRASS)
paper-reed	PAPYRUS
pasture grass	DOG'S-TAIL GRASS, RYE-GRASS
pennywort	ROT-GRASS
Persicaria	KNOT-GRASS
Phalaris	GARDENER'S GARTERS
Phleum	TIMOTHY
pinkfoot	WORMGRASS
Poa	MEADOW-GRASS, WIRE-GRASS
Polygonum	KNOT-GRASS
porcupine-grass	SPINIFEX
quitch-grass	SQUITCH
ramee/rami(e)	CHINA GRASS, RHEA
reed-mace	CAT'S-TAIL, ELEPHANT GRASS
rhea	RAMEE, RAMI(E), RHEA
ribbon-grass	GARDENER'S GARTERS
rice-grass	CORD-GRASS
rot-grass	BUTTERWORT, PENNYWORT
rush	JUNCUS
rye	DARNEL, LOLIUM, SECALE
rye-grass	LOLIUM
sand-binding	LYME-GRASS, MARRAM
	MARRUM
scurvy-grass	COCHLEARIA
sea-reed	MARRAM(-GRASS)
seaside grass	AMMOPHILA
	DOG'S-TOOTH GRASSTAR(R)
	MARRAM, MARRUM
Secale	RYE
second growth	AFTERMATH, EDDISH
	FOG(GAGE)
sedge	CAREX
sesame-grass	ZAMA GRASS
shave-grass	DUTCH RUSH
side shoot	TILLER
slow spreading	MISCANTHUS
smart-weed	WATERPEPPER
soft grass	ROT-GRASS
sorghum	SUDAN-GRASS
South American	PAMPAS GRASS
	PASPALUM, RESCUE GRASS
Spanish grass	ESPARTO, SPART
spart	ESPARTO
spartina	CORD-GRASS
stiff stalk	BENT
Stipa	FEATHER-GRASS
striped canary-grass	RIBBON-GRASS
—green/cream	MOLINIA
Sudan-grass	SORGHUM
sweet-smelling	HOLY GRASS
thin dry stalk	WINDLESTRAW
timothy	CAT'S-TAIL GRASS, PHLEUM
—America	HERD('S)GRASS
tropical	PASPALUM
Uniola	SPIKE-GRASS

variegated ribbon	GARDENER'S GARTERS
vernal grass	ANTHOXANTHUM
waterpepper	SMART-WEED
wheat/rye hybrid	TRITICALE
wire-grass	POA
woodland grass	MILLET-GRASS
wormgrass	PINKFOOT
worthless	SOFT-GRASS
Xyris (US)	YELLOW-EYED GRASS
yellow-eyed grass (US)	XYRIS
zama grass	SESAME-GRASS
Zoster	EELGRASS, GRASSWRACK
Greece	GR, HELLAS

including: classical terms
　　　　　modern words

abbot	ARCHIMANDRITE
	HEGUMEN
abode of dead	ELYSIUM
above (music)	
—Aeolian	HYPERAEOLIAN
—Dorian	HYPERDORIAN
—Lydian	HYPERLYDIAN
—Phrygian	HYPERPHRYGIAN
account	LOGOS
—of saint's life	SYNAXARION
accuser	SYCOPHANT
ace	OINE
acorn	BALANOS
additional note	PROSLAMBANOMENOS
address by	
—chorus	PARABASIS
—coryphaeus	EPIRRHEMA
admiral	NAVARCH
advocate	SYNDIC
alb	STICHARION
alcove	ZOTHECA
all	PAN
alone	MONOS
alphabet	(see letters below)
among	META
anatomist	HEROPHILUS
ancient people	PELASGI(ANS)
and	
—so forth	KAI TA LEIPOMENA, KTL
—the rest	KAI TA LOIPA, KTL
angle	GONIA
annalist	LOGOGRAPHER
ant	MURMEX
antipodes	ANTICHTHON
ape	PITHECOS
apple	MELON
architect/artist etc	HIPPODAMUS
	ICTINUS, POLYGNOTUS
	PHIDIAS, PRAXITELES
	SCOPAS, ZEUXIS
arms	HOPLA

army	
—commander	TAXIARCH
—division	TAXIS
arrogance	HUBRIS
art	TECHNE
ass	ONOS
assembly	AGYRIS, ECCLESIA
astronomer	ARISTARCHUS, ERATOSTHENES
	HIPPARCHUS, POSIDONIUS
Athenian	
—aristocrat	EUPATRID
—colony	CLERUCHIACLERUCHY
—youth	EPHEBE
athletic contest	AGON
—auditor	LOGOTHETE(S)
away, Satan!	APAGE SATANAS
Bacchic rout	THIASUS
bachelorhood	AGAMIA
back	NOTON, NOTOS, PALIN
backward	OPISO
band of soldiers	ENOMOTY
banish by vote	OSTRACISE
barricade	PHRAXIS
base	HEDRA
bathing establishment	THERM
bay	ORMOS
—leaves	DAPHNI
beak	RHYNCHOS
bear	ARKTOS
beautiful, (the)	TO KALON
—place	TEMPE
becoming	TO PREPON
bed	KLINE
bee-eater	MEROPS
behind	OPISTHEN
below (music)	
—Aeolian	HYPOAEOLIAN
—Dorian	HYPODORIAN
—Lydian	HYPOLYDIAN
—Phrygian	HYPOPHRYGIAN
beside	META
bird	ORNIS, ORNITHOS, STROUTHION
birth	TOKOS
bishop	EXARCH
bishop's stole	EPITRACHELION
black	MELAS
bladder	KYSTIS
blade	PLATE
blind	ALAOS
blood	HAIMA
—sucking witch	LAMIA
bone	OSTEON
boundary marker	HERM
boy	PAEDOS, PAIDOS
bread	PSOMI
bride	NYMPHE

brigand	KLEPHT
bristle	CHAITE
brother	ADELPHOS
bud	BLASTOS
bulk	ONCOS
business	ERGON, PRAGMATA
cake	PIT(T)A
cakes	FINIKIA
canonical hours (lauds)	ORTHROS
cape (headland)	AKRA, AKROTIRION
	MITI
captain of guards	PROTOSPATHARIUS
capital city	ATHENS
case	THEKE
cave	SPEOS
cessation	PAUSIS
chamber	THALAMOS
champion	PROMACHOS
chariot	BIGA, TRIGA, QUADRIGA
chest	LARNAX
chief	
—magician	ARCHIMAGE
—tribal officer	PHYLARCH
child	PAEDOS, PAIDOS
choral odes	STASIMA
chorus leader	CHORAGUS, CHOREGUS
church stall	STASIDION
citadel	ACROPOLIS
city	POLIS
—badge	EPISEMON
—state	POLIS
claw	ONYX
cloak	HIMATION
cloud	NEPHELE, NEPHOS
coffin	LARNAX
coins	
—small	LEPTON
—100 lepta	DRACHMA
—1½ pence	OBOL(US)
—6 oboli	DRACHMA
—2 drachmas	DIDRACHMA
—4 drachmas	TETRADRACHM
—silver tetradrachm	STATER
—100 drachmas	MINA
—6000 drachmas	TALENT
collection of sermons	PANEGYRICON
colonist in	
—Asia Minor	AEOLIAN
—Italy	ITALIOT(E)
—Sicily	SICELIOT, SIKELIOT
colonnade	STOA, XYSTOS, XYSTUS
colonnaded market-hall	STOA
colour	CHROMA
commander of	
—10	DECADARCH
—1000	CHILIARCH

—cavalry	HIPPARCH, PHYLARCH		verse	PERIOD
—division	TAXIARCH		—of people	PHYLE
—sub-division	TETRARCH		dome	THOLOS, THOLUS
—trireme	TRIERARCH		Doric magistrate	EPHOR
common informer	SYCOPHANT		down	PAPPUS
company of worshippers	THIASUS		downbeat	THESIS
container	KYTOS		dowry	PHERNE
contemptible Greek	GREEKLING		dramatist/poet	AESCHYLUS,
copper	CHALKOS			ARISTOPHANES, EURIPIDES
corn	SITOS			HEGEMON, ION, MENANDER
corslet	THORAX			SOPHOCLES
council	BOULE		dream	ONEIROS
—chamber	BOULEUTERION		dressing-room (baths)	APODYTERIUM
—division	PRYTANY		drinking	
—representing all			—cup	COTYLE, CYLIX, HOLMOS
sections	PANHELLENION			KYLIX, RHYTON, SCYPHUS
	PANHELLENIUM		—song	DITHYRAMB, SKOLION
course	DROMOS		drug	PHARMAKON
court	AREOPAGUS		dwarf	NANOS
courtesan	ASPASIA, HETAIRA		dynasty (Syria)	SELEUCID
covered portico	XYST(OS), XYSTUS		ear	OTOS, OUS
covering	SHEUE		eating in public	SYSSITIA
credit	KUDOS		egg	OION
crowd	OCHLOS		egotism	ITACISM
cupola	THOLOS, THOLUS		elliptical auditorium	SPHENDONE
custom	NOMOS		embodiment of	
cut(ting)	TOME		—justice	ARISTIDES
dagger	PARAZONIUM		—self-discipline	ARISTIPPUS
dance	ROMAIKA		epic	
dancing-girl	HETAIRA		—poem	ODYSSEY
dawn	ORTHROS		—tale	ILIAD
day	HEMERA		eucharistic fan	RHIPIDION
deacon's stole	ORARION		explorer	PYTHEAS
dead (body)	NEKROS		eye	OMMA, OPHTHALMOS
decree of Athenian assembly	PSEPHISM		fabulous robber	PROCRUSTES
defender	PROMACHOS		fame	KUDOS
defilement	MYSOS		fan	RHIPIDIUM
deities	(see gods, goddesses)		fastening of woman's girdle	VIRGIN KNOT
delegate	SYNDIC		father	PAP(P)AS
—to council	AMPHICTYON		fawn-skin	NEBRIS
department	NOME, NOMOS		fear	PHOBOS
diadem	STEPHANE		female entertainer	HETAIRA
dialects	(A)EOLIC, ATTIC		festival	
	DORIC, IONIC, KOINE		—Apollo	THARGELIA
discarded letter	SAN		—Demeter	THESMOPHORIA
discourse	LOGOS		—Dionysius	ANTHESTERIA
dish	BAKLAVA, FASOLIA		—national	PANATHENAEA
	HOUMMOUS, KEBABS		few	OLIGOS
	MOUS(S)AKA		fibre	MITOS
	PILAFE, TARAMOSALATA		field	AGROS
	TSATSIKI, TZATZIKI		fillet	MITRA
divination	MANTEIA		fitting (that which is ...)	TO PREPON
divine voice	OMPHE		flabellum	RHIPIDIUM
division	DEME		flask	AMPHORA, LAGENA, OLPE
—in			flesh	KREAS
army	TAXIS		flower	ANTHEMON

fly	MYIA
folly	MORIA
fondness	PHILIA
food	OPSON(ION), SITOS, TROPHE
—plant	LASER, SILPHIUM
foot	PODOS
forehead	METOPON
form	MORPHE
formation	GENESIS
founder of drama	THESPIS
fountain (Mt. Helicon)	AGANIPPE
fourth part of province	TETRARCHATE
	TETRARCHY
fracture	KLASIS
frankincense	LIBANOS
front portico with not more than four columns	PROSTYLE
fruit	KARPOS
galley	BIREME, TRIREME
	QUADRIREME, QUINQUEREME
gem	OPALLIOS
generals	DIADOCHI
generation	GENESIS
gift	DORON
gills	BRANCHIA
glade	NEMOS
globular oil-flask	ARYBALLOS
glue	GLOIA, KOLLA
god	THEOS
golden mean	ARISTON METRON
good genius	AGATHODAIMON
governor	EPARCH, ETHNARCH, NOMARCH
	TOPARCH, TAXIARCH
grandfather	PAPPUS
granule	CHONDROS
great	MEGA
Greece	HELLAS
Greek	ATTIC, ARGIVE, GK, GR
—in ancient Italy	ITALIOT(E)
—people	ACHAEAN, ACHIAN, ARGIVE
	ATHENIAN, SPARTAN
grief	PENTHOS
grotto	NYPHAEUM
ground	PEDON
group of verses	SYSTEM
growth	PHYSIS
guest-house	TAVERNA
gulf	KOLPOS
gymnasium at Athens	LYCEUM
hair ornament (cicada)	TETTIX
half	HEMI
hat worn by Hermes	PETASOS, PETASUS
head	KEPHALE
—dress	STEPHANE
—fillet	MITRE
healing plant	PANAX

heath	HEIDE
heavily-armed soldier	HOPLITE
hero	ACHILLES, AENEAS
	AGAMEMNON, AJAX
	ALCIDES, CADMUS, HECTOR
	HERAKLES, HERCULES, JASON
	NESTOR, ODYSSEUS, PERSEUS
	PROMETHEUS, THESEUS, ULYSSES
highest lyre string	NETE
hilltop	KUPPE
historian	AMMIANUS, HERODOTUS
	PTOLEMY, THUCYDIDES
	XENOPHON
hole	TREMA
holy meteoric stone	BAETYL
home of oracle	DELPHI
honey	MELI
hook	ONKOS
hoop	TROCHOS, TROCHUS
horn	KERAS
house	MEGARON, OIKOS
hymns	HERMOI, HERMOS
—to Bacchus	DITHYRAMB
I have found	(H)EUREKA
imitator	MIMOS
impulse	OSMOS, OTHIMOS
incline	KLINEIN
infant	NEPIOS
infantry formation	PHALANX
infantryman	EVZONE
inhabitant of part of Constantinople	FANARIOT, PHANARIOT
inlet	FORDE
inn	TAVERNA
inner chamber of temple	CELLA, NAOS
instalment of epic	RHAPSODY
instrument	BOUZOUKI, CITHARA
	KITHARA, PHORMINX
intestines	ENTERON
introduction to a play	PROLOGUE
Ionian	TEIAN
—mode (mus.)	IASTIC
irregularly divided	ALLOIOSTROPHOS
island(s)	NESOS
islander	NESIOTES
jar	AMPHORA, STAMNOS
jaw	GNATHOS
joint	ARTHRON
judge	DICAST, DIKAST, SYNDIC
—of games	AGNOTHETES
judge's court	DICASTERY
jug	OLPE
juice	OPOS
junior archon	THESMOTHETE
keynote	MESE
kidney	NEPHROS

kilt	FUSTANELLA
know thyself	GNOTHI SEAUTON
knowing	GNOSIS
lagoon	LIMNOS
lake	LIMNOS
lamb	ARNOS
lament	THRENE
lamp attendant	LAMPADARY
land	GAIA
late	OPSE
law	NOMOS
—giver	NOMOTHETE(S)
	THESMOTHETE
lead	MOLYBDOS
leader	AGOGOS
—of	
chorus	CORYPHAEUS
worshippers	THIASARCH
learning	MATHE
legislator	DRACO, NOMOTHETES
length	MEKOS
lesson on life of a saint	SYNAXARION
letter	GRAMMA
—Y	PYTHAGOREAN LETTER
	SAMIAN LETTER
letters	ALPHA, BETA, CHI, DELTA
	EPSILON, ETA, GAMMA, IOTA
	KAPPA, LA(M)BDA, MU, NU
	OMEGA, OMICRON, PHI, PI
	PSI, RHO, SIGMA, TAU, THETA
	UPSILON, XI, ZETA
	(see also obsolete letters below)
life	BIOS
—saving reward	SOSTRUM
lightly-armed soldier	PELTAST
liking for	PHILIA
line	STICHOS
liqueur	OUZO
litany	SYNAPTE
little	MIKROS, OLIGOS
lizard	SAUROS
long-jump	HALMA
lord of men	ANAXANDRON
loss of rights as citizen	ATIMY
lowest	
—note but one	PARHYPATE
—string of lyre	HYPATE
lyre	CITHARA, KITHARA
madness	MANIA
magical	
—meteoric stone	BAETYL
—stone	PANTARBE
magistrate	ARCHON, EPHOR
magnet for gold	PANTARBE
main gate of Athens	DIPYLON
man	ANDROS, ANER, ANTHROPOS

manner of life	BIOSIS
marker	STELE
market-place	AGORA
marriage	GAMOS
marrow	MYELOS
mass	ONCOS
master of feast	
or conference	SYMPOSIARCH
mathematician	ARCHIMEDES, EUCLID
	PYTHAGORAS
measure(ment)	METRON
—600 feet	STADION
—1 quart (approx)	CH(O)ENIX
measuring cup (1½ pint)	CYATHUS
meat	
—balls	KEFTEDES
—casserole	STIFADO
medallion	PERIAMMA
medical	IATRIKOS
meeting	
—for worship	SYNAXIS
—place in Athens	AGORA, PNYX
—room	ANDRON
method of investigation	ORGANON
metre	METRON
metropolitan (church leader)	EXARCH
middle	MESE
—course	ARISTON METRON
—string of lyre	MESE
military	
—commander	POLEMARCH
—formation	PHALANX
—ruler	DIADOCHI
mill	MYLE, MYLON
mind	NOUS
mine	METALLON
misanthrope (Shak.)	TIMON
mist	NEPHELE
modern	
—coin	DRACHM(A)
—Greek	DEMOTIC, ROMAIC
modesty	AIDOS
monastery	MONI
monastic	
—habit	SCHEMA
—settlement	SCETE, SKETE
monk	CALOYER, MONASTES
monster	(see separate entry)
month	MEN
Moon	MENE, SELENE
morning service	ARTHROS
mother-city of colony	METROPOLIS
mountain	OROS
mouse	MYS
mouth	STOMA
mucus	MYXA

muscle	MYS	orchestra	KONISTRA
mushroom	MYKES	outer garment	HIMATION
music hall	ODEON, ODEUM	over	HYPER
musical		oyster	OSTREON
—instrument	AULOS, BARBITOS	pain	ALGE, ALGOS, ODYNE

muscle — MYS
mushroom — MYKES
music hall — ODEON, ODEUM
musical
—instrument — AULOS, BARBITOS
BOUZOUKI, CITHARA, KITHARA
LYRE, PHORMINX, SYRINX
—interval — DITONE
—modes — AEOLIAN, IONIAN, IASTIC
(MIXO)LYDIAN, PHRYGIAN
—separation of
  chords — DIAZEUXIS
—tempo — AGOGE
mussel — MYAX
myth — MYTHOS
nail — ONYX
name — ONOMA
narrow-necked flask — LEKYTHOS
national festival — PANATHENAEA
PYTHIAN GAMES
native of Zante — ZANTIOT(E)
nature — PHYSIS
navel — OMPHALOS
necessity — ANANKE
nerve — NEURON
new — KAINOS, NEOS
night — NYKTOS, NYX
northern — ARKTIKOS
nose — RHINOS, RHIS
note above hypate — PARHYPATE
now — NYN
numberless — MYRIOS
numbness — NARKE
numeral — SAMPI
nursing — TROPHEIA
obsolete letters — EPISEMON, DIGAMMA
KOPPA, SAN, SAMPI, VAU
ode — STASIMON
office of
—exarch — EXARCHATE
—harmost — HARMOSTY
official — POLEMARCH
on — EPI
Old Testament — SEPTUAGINT
olive tree — ELATA
olives — ELIES
one
—of Greek official
  class — FANARIOT, PHANARIOT
—sleeved garment — EXOMIS
open-air auditorium — PNYX
opinion — DOXA
orator — DEMOSTHENES, GORGIAS
LYSIAS, PERICLES
order of architecture — CORINTHIAN
DORIC, IONIC

orchestra — KONISTRA
outer garment — HIMATION
over — HYPER
oyster — OSTREON
pain — ALGE, ALGOS, ODYNE
pale yellow — OCHROS
palm — PALAME
panacea — PANAX
paradise — ELYSIUM
parliament — BOULE
part of — MEROS
—Greek comedy — PARABASIS
—tetrachord — PYCNON
pass — STENON
peas — ARAKAS
penalty — POINE
peninsula — CHERSONESE, KHERSONISOS
people — DEMOS
perception — AISTHESIS
philosophers — ANAXAGORAS, ANAXIMANDER
ANAXIMENES, ANTISTHENES
ARISTIPPOS, ARISTOTLE
DEMOCRITUS, DIOGENES
EMPEDOCLES, EPICURUS
HERACLIDES, HERACLITUS, HIPPIAS
LEUCIPPUS, PARMENIDES, PLATO
PLOTINUS, PRODICUS, PROTAGORAS
PYRRHO, PYTHAGORAS, SOCRATES
STAGIRITE, THALES
THEOPHRASTUS, THRASYMACHUS
XENOPHANES, ZENO
physician — ALCMAEON, ERASISTRATUS
GALEN, HEROPHILUS
HIPPOCRATES, PRAXAGORAS
pick-axe — ORYX
plant — PHYTON
play
—first part — PROTASIS
—last part — APODOSIS
—main part — EPITASIS
poem about returning — NOSTOS
poet — (see writer below)
poetess — SAPPHO
poetic inspiration — AGANIPPE
point — AKME
political animal — ZOON POLITIKON
pollution — MIASMA
poor freeman — THETE
popular assembly — ECCLESIA
porch — STOA
portico — PTERON, STOA, XYSTOS, XYSTUS
potato — PATATA
place dedicated to a god — TEMENOS
potsherd — OSTRACON, OSTRAKON
pottery horn — RHYTON
poverty — PENIA

power	KRATOS
prayer-book	EUCHOLOGION
	EUCHOLOGY, TRIODION
precinct	TEMENOS
preliminary oblation	PROTHESIS
prestige	KUDOS
pride	HUBRIS
priest	PAPA
priest's stole	EPITRACHELION
principal hall	MEGARON
professional orator	RHETOR
prophet	MANTIS
prostitute	HETAIRA
province	NOME, NOMOS
—of	
eparch	EPARCHATE, EPARCHY
ephor	EPHORALTY
prudence	METIS
public	
—disgrace	ATIMY
—drinking-fountain	NYMPHAEUM
—eating	SYSSITIA
purchase of food	OPSONIA
purple cope	CHLAMYS
quill for string-plucking	PLECTRUM
race course	DROMOS, STADION
rabble	HOI POLLOI
rain-storm	OBROMOS
raw	·OMOS
rear-chamber in temple	OPISTHODOMOS
reason	LOGOS
renown	KUDOS
restaurant	TAVERNA
return	NOSTOS
revolving prism in theatre	PERIAKTOS
rice	RIZA
—pudding	RIZOGALO
right	ORTHOS
river encircling world	OKEANOS
rostrum	BEMA
round building	THOLOS, THOLUS
row	STICHOS
—of trees	ORCHATOS
rule	ARCHE
ruler of	
—district	TOPARCH
—people	ETHNARCH
run	DROMOS
sacred enclosure	SEKOS
sacristan	SCEUOPHYLAX
sacristy	DIACONICON, PARABEMA
	SCEUOPHYLACIUM
saddle of mountain	SELOMA
said (or written) once	HAPAX LEGOMENON
sailor	NAUTES, NAUTILOS
—in *Argo*	ARGONAUT

saint	AYIA, AYIOS
salad	HORIATIKI
sanctuary	NYMPHAEUM, SEKOS
sap	OPOS
saw	PRION
scale	CHROMA
school of philosophy	PAINTED PORCH
	(*see also* **philosophy**)
sculptor	PHIDIAS, PRAXITELES
	SCOPAS
section of psalm-book	CATHISMA
sea	THALASSA, THALATTA
—nymph	NEREID
—perch	ORPHOS
—sickness	NAUSIA
—weed	PHYKOS
second of nine archons	KING-ARCHON
secret writing	SCYTALE
sect (14th c)	HESYCHAST
seed	SPERMA
seemly	TO PREPON
seen	OPTOS
sell	POLEEIN
senate	BOULE
serf	HELOT, PENEST, THETE
service	
—book	TRIODION
—to the state	LITURGY
setting down	THESIS
seven	
—prayers	LYCHNAPSIA
—tones	HEPTACHORD
severe critic	ARISTARCH
shame	AIDOS
shape	MORPHE
sharp	OXYS
shell	OSTRAKON
shield	AEGIS
ship	ARGO, CAIQUE, HOLCAD, NAUS
	SAIC, SAIK, SAIQUE
—with 30 oars	TRIACONTER
—with 50 oars	PENTECOSTER
shoot	BLASTOS
short	
—anthem	ISODICON
—cloak	CHLAMYS
—hymn	CATHISMA, TROPARION
—sighted	MYOPS
shoulder	OMOS
shrew	MYGALE
shrine	TEMENOS
shut	MYEIN
sickness	NOSOS
side	
—scene	PARASCENIUM
—wall of temple	PTEROMA

sight	OPSIS
single	MONOS
skin	DERMA
skull	KRANION
slave	HELOT
slime	MYXA
smallest subdivision	ENOMOTY
smell	OSME
snake	OPHIS
snout	RHYNCUS
soda	NITRON
soft	MALAKOS
soldier	EVZONE, HOPLITE
solitary	MONACHOS
song	MELOS, OIDE
—sung by chorus	STROPHE
soup	AVGOLEMONO
sour	OXYS
south	NOTOS
southern hemisphere	ANTICHTHON
space in temple	PERIDROME
Spartan governor	HARMOST
speaking	PHRASIS
speech	LALIA
sphere	SPHAIRA
spice	STORAX
spirit	DAIMON
spit	OBELOS
sports-ground	STADION
squid	KALAMARAKIA
standing	STATOS
stanza	STROPHE
stationary	STASIMON
statue	KOUROS, XOANON
step	BEMA
stink	OSME
stone	LITHOS
—at Delphi	OMPHALOS
—of the Sun	PANTARBE
story	MYTHOS
straight	ORTHOS
strait	STENON
string struck with the forefinger	LICHANOS
stroke	PLEGE
strong drink	METHE
stuffed olive leaves	DOLMADAKIA
	DOLMADES, DOLMATHES
sub-division	DEME
Sun	HELIOS
sweat	HIDROS
swelling	OIDEMA, ORGASMOS
swimming	NEUSTOS
talk	MYTHOS
taper carrier	LAMPADARY
teacher	PAIDEUTES
—of rhetoric	RHETOR

temple	NAOS
—of Athene	ATHENAEUM
—slave	HIERODULE
—with one ring of columns	MONOPTERON
	MONOPTEROS
tempo	AGOGE
ten thousand	MYRIAS
tend	KOMEEIN
the	
—many	HOI POLLOI
—vulgar	HOI POLLOI
theatre	ODEON, ODEUM
thick	PACHYS
third	
—actor	TRITAGONIST
—string of lyre	TRITE
—tone of tetrachord	TRITE
thread	MITOS, NEMA
three-branched candlestick	TRICERION
tile	OSTRAKON
time	CHRONOS
tomato	DOMATA
tomb	THOLOS, THOLUS
tone	
—above the mese	PARAMESE
—below the nete	PARANETE
tongue	GLOSSA
tooth	ODOUS
torch-race	LAMPADEDROMY
	LAMPADEPHORIA
town	DEME
—hall	PYRTANEION, PRYTANEUM
—ship	DEME
toy	KLEIS, KLEIDOS
track	ICHNOS
traditional utterance of Christ	AGRAPHON
translation of Hebrew bible	SEPTUAGINT
tree-planted walk	XYST(OS), XYSTUS
tribe	PELASGI, PHYLE
tripartite building	MEGARON
troop	
—of worshippers	THIASUS
—leader	PHYLARCH
trumpet	SALPINX
tumour	ONCOS
tunic	CHITON, EXOMIUM, EXOMIS
turkey	GALAPOULA
turn(ing)	TROPOS
tusk	CEROS
tutelary god	PROMACHOS
two-handled vase	DIOTA
underground water channel	KATABOTHRON
	KAVAVOTHRON
unguent	MYRON
union	ENOSIS
unit	MONAS

unripe grape	OMPHAX
upright	ORTHOS
urn	STAMNOS
vase	DIOTA, PELIKE, PITHOS, RHYTON
veal	MOSHKARI
veil	CALYPTRA, KALYPTRA
verse style	ADONIC, ALCAIC
vespers	LYCHNIC
vessel	KYTOS
vestibule in front of temple	PRONAOS
vestment	SACCOS, SAKKOS
victory	NIKE
view	HORAMA
voice	OPS, PHONE
waist-belt	ZOSTER
war	
—cry	ALALAGMOS
—dance	PYRRHIS
watching	SKOPIA
water	HYDOR
—jar	HYDRIA, KALPIS
wax	KEROS
way	HODOS
weasel	GALEE
weight	DRACHMA
—3 pounds	OCQUE
—26-38kg (gold or silver)	TALENT
—money	MINA
well done!	EUGE
wheel	TROCHOS, TROCHUS
white	LEUKOS
—kilt for men	FUSTANELLA
wild	AGRIOS
—beast	THERION
—dance	SIKINNIS
wind	PARASCENIUM
wine	(see separate entry)
—jar	PITHOS
—throwing game	COTTABUS, KOTTABUS
wing	PTERON
—(theatre)	PARASCENIUM
wisdom	SOPHIA
with	META
woman	GYNE
woman's	
—head-band	SPHENDONE
—robe	PEPLOS, PEPLUM
womb	DELPHYS, HYSTERA
wood	HYLE
wooded pasture	NEMOS
wooden statue	ACROLITH
word	LEXIS
work	ERGON
world	KOSMOS
—city	COSMOPOLIS
worship	LATREIA

writer	AESCHYLUS, AESOP, ALCAEUS
	ANACREON, APOLLODORUS
	APOLLONIUS, ARISTOPHANES
	EURIPIDES, HERODOTUS, HESIOD
	HOMER, LUCIAN, PAUSANIAS
	PHERECRATES, PINDAR
	PLUTARCH, SIMONIDES, SOPHOCLES
	TERPANDER, TYRTAEUS
	(see also writers)
yes	OHI
young citizen	EPHEBE
youthful	NEANIKOS
	(see also mythology)
Grenada	WG
capital	ST GEORGES
coin	CENT, DOLLAR
Grenadines	WV
greyhound	
coursing event	WATERLOO CUP
famous greyhound	BEACH COMBER
	DULEEK DANDY
	GRAND CANAL, I'M SLIPPY
	JIMSUN, LACCA CHAMPION
	LAURIE'S PANTHER, LUCKY BOY
	PAGAN SWALLOW, PALME'S PRINTER
	PARKDOWN JET, TICO, TRIC-TRAC
	SARAH'S BUNNY, WHISPER WISHES
events	
—cross-country	COURSING
—track	GREYHOUND RACING
greyhound racing	GRACING, GREYCING
making a fast start	PINGING HIS LID
starting gate	TRAP
target	(ELECTRIC) HARE
venues	BIRMINGHAM, BRIGHTON
	CATFORD, EDINBURGH, OXFORD
	RAMSGATE, WALTHAMSTOW
	WEMBLEY, WIMBLEDON, WINDSOR
	WOLVERHAMPTON
group	CLASSIS
including: collection of	
group of	
mass of	
actors	CAST, COMPANY, TROUPE
ants	ARMY, COLONY
aeroplanes	FLIGHT, SQUADRON, WING
animals	FAMILY, GENUS, PHYLUM
	SPECIES
apes	SHREWDNESS
arms	STAND
artillery	BATTERY, PARK
artists	CENACLE, COTERIE
	MOVEMENT, SCHOOL
artistes	TROUPE
asses	DROVE, HERD, PACE

at cinema, theatre, etc	AUDIENCE	grass	TUFT
attendants	RETINUE, TRAIN	Greek citizens	PHYLE
badgers	CETE, COLONY	hares	DOWN, DROVE, LEASH
bards	GORSEDD		TRACE, TRIP
bears	SLOTH	harpists	MELODY
bees	HIVE, SWARM	having	
beggars	FIGHTING	—common interests	CLIQUE, COMMUNITY
beauties	BEVY, GALAXY		LOBBY, SOCIETY
birds	(see **bird²**)	—political aims	CABAL, CADRE
boars	HERD, SINGULAR, SOUNDER		CELL, JUNTA
boys	BLUSH	—same age and status	PEER GROUP
brotherhood	FELLOWSHIP, FRATERNITY	hay	BALE, TRUSS
	GUILD, SODALITY	hens	BROOD
business interests	CARTEL, CONSORTIUM	herrings	CRAN
	MONOPOLY, SYNDICATE	hermits	OBSERVANCE
butlers	DRAUGHT	hinds	PARCEL
cars	CONVOY, FLEET, MOTORCADE	horses	HARAS, HARRAS(E)
cards	HAND, SEQUENCE		HERD, REMUDA, STABLE
cats	CLOWDER, CLUSTER		TEAM, TROOP
cattle	DROVE, HERD	hounds	KENNEL, PACK
cavalrymen	TROOP	hunters	BLAST
church representatives	CONVOCATION	in	
clans	GATHERING	—Air Force	FLIGHT, SQUADRON, WING
cobblers	DRUNKENNESS	—Army	BATTALION, BRIGADE, COMPANY
	DRUNKENSHIP		CORPS, DIVISION, MESS, PLATOON
colts	RAG, RAKE		REGIMENT, SECTION
co-operating with			SQUAD(RON), TROOP
each other	ALLIANCE, ALIGNMENT	—Navy	CREW, FLEET, MESS
	BLOC, COALITION		SQUADRON, WATCH
	CONFEDERACY, FEDERATION	intellectuals	COTERIE, MOVEMENT
	LEAGUE	items	AGGREGATE, ASSEMBLAGE
corn	SHEAF		CONGERIES
cotton	HANK, SKEIN		CONGLOMERATION
cuckolds	INCREDIBILITY	jazz musicians	BAND, COMBO, GROUP
curs	COWARDICE	kangaroos	HERD, MOB, TROOP
dancers	CORPS DE BALLET, TROUPE	kine	DROVE
deer	HERD, LEASH	kittens	KINDLE, LITTER
directors	BOARD	knaves	RAYFUL
dogs	KENNEL, PACK	lawmen	POSSE
dolphins	POD	leopards	LEAP, LEPE
donkeys	DROVE, HERD, PACE	lions	PRIDE, TROOP
druids	GORSEDD	living in same area	COMMUNITY
eggs	CLUTCH	majors	MORBIDITY
elephants	HERD	machine-guns	NEST
elks	GANG	mares	STUD
famous people	GALAXY	martens	RICHESSE
ferrets	CAST, FESNYING	moles	COMPANY, LABOUR
firemen	BRIGADE, WATCH		MOVEMENT
fish	SHOAL	monkeys	CARTLOAD, TRIBE, TROOP
flower pots	CASTE	monopolising trade	CARTEL
foresters	STALK	Moslem theologians	ULEMA
foxes	LEAD, SKULK	mules	BARREN, PACK, RAKE, SPAN
friars	SKULK	musicians	BAND, COMBO, GROUP
frogs	ARMY, COLONY		OCTET, NONET, ORCHESTRA
funeral attendants	CORTEGE		QUARTET, QUINTET, SEPTET
goats	FLOCK, HERD, TRIBE		SEXTET, TRIO

nuns	SUPERFLUITY	similar items	COMPENDIUM, ENSEMBLE
officers	MESS		SUITE
ornaments	GARNITURE, PARURE	singers	CHOIR
otters	BEVY, FAMILY	small group	COVEY
oxen	SPAN, TEAM, YOKE	snakes	DEN, NEST, PIT
papers	BUDGET, QUIRE, REAM	soldiers	(see in Army above)
pardoners	LYING	songs, plays, etc	REPERTOIRE
pearls	ROPE	sportsmen	SIDE, TEAM
pedlars	MALAPERTNESS	stars	CLUSTER, CONSTELLATION
people	CONCOURSE, CONFLUENCE		GALAXY
	CROWD, DROVE, HORDE	strawberries	PUNNET
	HOST, MOB, MULTITUDE	subalterns	MESS, SIMPLICITY
	PHALANX, RUCK, THRONG	swine	DROYLT, SOUNDER
performers	TROUPE	tailors	DISGUISING
pigs	HERD, SOUNDER	tame swine	DROYLT
piglets	FARROW, LITTER	teams	LEAGUE
pipers	POVERTY	thieves	GANG
players	CAST, SIDE, TEAM	thread	HANK
playing		tigers	AMBUSH
—cricket	ELEVEN	tinkers	WANDERING
—football	ELEVEN	trees	CLUMP, COPPICE, COPSE, FOREST
—games	SIDE, TEAM		GROVE, SPINNEY, WOOD
—Rugby League	THIRTEEN	turtles	DULE
—Rugby Union	FIFTEEN	undesirables	GALERE, ROGUES' GALLERY
polecats	CHINE	vehicles	CONVOY
political	BLOC, CADRE, CAUCUS	vigilantes	POSSE
	ENCLAVE, FACTION, PARTY	voters	CONSTITUENCY
porpoises	SCHOOL	walruses	HERD, POD
porters	SAFEGUARD	whales	GAM, HERD, POD, SCHOOL
princes	STATE	whelps	LITTER
puppies	LITTER	wolves	HERD, PACK, ROUT
rabbits	BURY, COLONY	women	SORORITY
—young	NEST	wool	BALL, HANK
raches	KENNEL	workers	BEE, GUILD, UNION
rats	COLONY	worshippers	CONGREGATION
religious	CHURCH, FACTION, SECT	—Greek	THIASUS
representatives	DELEGATION, DEPUTATION	writers	COTERIE
rhinoceroses	CRASH	zebras	HERD
rifles	STAND	**Guatemala**	GCA
rowers	EIGHT, FOUR, PAIR	capital	GUATEMALA CITY
sailors	(see in Navy above)	coin	CENTAVO, QUETZAL
saints	COMMUNITY	**Guernsey**	GBG
savages	HORDE, POSSE	**gum**	
schoolchildren	CLASS, FORM	including: balsam	
seals	BOB, COLONY, CRASH	resin	
	HERD, POD, TEAM	amber	SUCCINIE
secret intriguers	CABAL, JUNTA	balsam fir	CANADA BALSAM
sergeants	MESS, SUBTILNE	British gum	DEXTRIN(E), STARCH GUM
		colophony	ROSIN
sharing property	COMMUNE	ester gum	ROSIN ESTER
sheaves	STOOK	dark red	SHELLAC, SHELL-LAC
sheep	DROVE, FLOCK, FOLD, TRIP	fossil resin	AMBER, SUCCINITE
ships	CONVOY, FLEET	from	
	FLOTILLA, NAVY	—acacia	GUM ACACIA, GUM ARABIC
	SQUADRON	—barberry	PODOPHYLLIN
silk	SKEIN	—bullet (bully) tree	BALATA

—Canarium	ELEMI
—Commiphora tree	BDELLIUM
—fennel	AS(S)AF(O)ETIDA
—Garcinia	GAMBOGE
—hemp	CHARAS, CHURRUS
—lentisk	MASTIC(H)
—locust tree	ANIME, COURBARIL
—shrubs	TRAGACANTH
—trees	COPAL, DAMMAR, DAMMER
—turpentine	COLOPHONY, ROSIN
gamboge	CAMBOGIA GUM
Indian	DHOONA
liquid resin	BALSAM
Moroccan	SANDARAC(H)
natural resin from trees	COPAL
plum gum	CERASIN
South American	ANGICO, BALATA
	CARRANA, CARAUNA
synthetic	FURAN RESIN
	FURFURAL RESIN
thermosetting	UREA FORMALDEHYDE
tropical	CONIMA
used in	
—foam	URETHANE RESIN
—food	GUM ACACIA, GUM ARABIC
—lacquers	URETHANE RESIN
—metal coatings	FURAN RESIN
—varnish	COPAL, URETHANE RESIN
West Indian	ANIME, COURBARIL
yellow	GAMBOGE, MASTIC(A)

gun

Afghan rifle	JEZAIL
air-gun	WIND-GUN
anti-aircraft	BOFORS, OERLIKON
	POMPOM
—submarine mortar	SQUID
—tank weapon	PIAT, BAZOOKA
arquebus	HACKBUT, HAGBUT
automatic	
—pistol	
American	AUTO-MAG, BROWNING, COLT
	DARDICK, GYROJET
	SMITH AND WESSON
Austrian	LAUMANN, MANNLICHER
	ROTH-STEYR, SCHONBERGER
Belgian	BROWNING
British	PAULSON-MARS
	WEBLEY(-FOSBERY)
German	BEHOLLA
	BERGMAN(-BAYARD)
	BORCHARDT, HECKLER AND KOCH
	LUGER, MANNLICHER, MAUSER
	WALTHER
Hungarian	FEGYVERGYAL
Italian	BERETTA, GLISENTI
Japanese	NAMBU

Russian	STECHKIN
—rifle	
American	ARMALITE, BANG, BAR
	BROWNING, COLT COMMANDO
	GARAND, M-16, PEDERSEN
Belgian	FAL, FN BROWNING
British	FARQUHAR-HILL
Danish	BANG
French	RSC, ST ETIENNE
German	STURMGEWEHR
Italian	CEI-RIGOTTI
Mexican	MONDRAGON
Russian	AK-47, FEDEROV
	KALASHNIKOV
bell-mouthed	BLUNDERBUSS
big gun	BIG BERTHA
camel-mounted	ZOMBORUK
	ZUMBOORU(C)K
cannon	FALCON
—9-10 pounder	DEMI-CULVERIN
—18 pounder	CULVERIN
—30-36 pounder	DEMI-CANNON
—dummy	QUAKER-GUN
—long	CULVERIN, LONG TOM
—modern naval	TURRET-GUN
—old	BASILISK, SERPENTINE
American	COLUMBIAD, DAHLGREN GUN
	SODA WATER BOTTLE
British	ARMSTRONG
—short	CARRONADE, HOWITZER
—small	CHAMBER, FALCONET
	MURDERER, MURDERING-PIECE
	SAKER
—stone-firing	PERRIER
—very large	BIG BERTHA, DUILLE GRETE
	HOCHDRUCKPUMPE
	MAD MARGARET
	MONS MEG, SCHLANKE EMMA
	SLENDER EMMA, SUPER GUN
carbine	ESCOPETTE
cowboy's	
—revolver	COLT (45)
—rifle	WINCHESTER
Dahlgren gun	SODA WATER BOTTLE
dummy cannon	QUAKER(GUN)
elephant gun	ROER
field-gun	FOUR-POUNDER
fired with spike	NEEDLE-GUN
firing stones, etc	PADERERO, PATERERO
	PED(E)RERO, PERRIER
flintlock	SNAPHA(U)NCE, SNAPHAUNCH
—British	BROWN BESS
—musket	FUSEE, FUSIL
for firing	
—salutes	PADERERO, PATERERO
	PED(E)RERO

—stones	PERRIER
fowling-piece	SHOTGUN
grenade-thrower	CO(E)HORN
hand-gun	GAT, IRON, PIECE
	PISTOL, REVOLVER
high angle	HOWITZER
	(TRENCH) MORTAR
horse-pistol	PETRONEL
large pistol	HORSE PISTOL
light	
—field-gun	AMUSETTE
—machine-gun	BREN, SUBMACHINE-GUN
—musket	CALIVER, CAR(A)BINE
—shotgun	FOWLING-PIECE
loaded from	
—front end	MUZZLE-LOADER
—rear end	BREECH-LOADER
long-barrelled	
—cannon	CULVERIN, LONG TOM
—revolver	BUNTLINE SPECIAL
machine gun	
—American	BENET-MERCIE, BROWNING
	GATLING, MARLIN
	MAXIM, VULCAN
—Austrian	SALVATOR-DORMUS, SKODA
	SCHWARZLOSE
—British	BETHEL-BURTON, BREN,
	DAVIS, ROBEY-PETERS
	LEWIS, VICKERS
—Czech	BREN
—Danish	MADSEN
—French	CHATELLERAULT, CHAUCHAT
	HOTCHKISS, MITRAILLEUSE
	ST ETIENNE, VICKERS-BETHIER
—German	BECKER, BERGMAN, DREYSE
	GAST, MACHINENGEWEHR
	PARABELLUM, RHEINMETALL
	SEMAG, SPANDAU, SZAKATS
—Italian	AGNELLI, BREDA, FIAT-REVELLI
—Russian	BERESIN, PULEMYOT MAXIMA
mortar	HOBIT
—anti-submarine	SQUID
—German (WW2)	MOANING MINNIE
	TOTENORGEL
—trench mortar	TOC EMMA
—types	ROCKET MORTAR
	SPIGOT MORTAR
	STOKES MORTAR
	TRENCH MORTAR
multi-barrelled	
—American	BILLINGHURST, GARDNER
	MARSTON PISTOL
	REFORM PISTOL
	REQUA BATTERY
	VANDENBURG, VOLLEY GUN
—Belgian	MARIETTE

—British	ALLEN, BOND, BUDDING
	KNOBLEY, NOCK, PROBIN
—cannon	MOB GUN, ORGAN
	ORGUE, POMPOM
—Danish	(ORGEL) ESPINGOLE
—French	MITRAILLEUSE
—German	MOANING MINNIE
	TOTENORGEL
—machine-gun	MAXIM, MITRAILLEUSE
—musket	RIBAULD(EQUIN)
—pistol	DUCKSFOOT, PEPPERPOT
—Russian	GORLOFF
—Swedish	NORFDENFELT
naval blunderbuss	MUSKETOON
old	
—cannon	BASILISK, SERPENTINE
—gun	RABINET
—mortar	CO(E)HORN
—musket	BISCAYAN, CALIVER, DOGLOCK
	DRAGOON, FLINTLOCK, FUSIL
	HACKBUT, HAKBUCHSE
	HACKENBUCHSE, (H)ARQUEBUS
	HARQUEBUSS, MATCHLOCK
	SNAPHAUNCE, WHEEL-LOCK
American	HUDSON'S BAY FUKE
	INDIAN MUSKET
	MACKINAW GUN
	NORTHWEST GUN
British	BROWN BESS
Chinese	GINGAL(L), JINGAL
French	CHARLEVILLE
German	SCHINKE
Indian	GINGAL(L), JINGAL
—pistol	DAG
cavalry	PETRONEL
German	PISTALA
—revolver	
American	ALLEN, (COLT) PEACEMAKER
	DERRINGER, LE MAT
	MANHATTAN, PATERSON
	READ, REMINGTON
	SCHOFIELD, WHEELER
British	(BEAUMONT-)ADAMS, COLLIER
	KERR, TRANTER, WEBLEY
Danish	RASMUSSEN
European	DREYSE
French	APACHE PISTOL, HOULLIER
	LEBEL, LEFAUCHEUX, MARCOU
	RAPHAEL, PERRIN
Italian	BODEO
long-barrelled	BUNTLINE SPECIAL
Russian	NAGANT
short-barrelled	BULLDOG, DERRINGER
Swedish	OFFRELL
—revolving gun	AGER, MAXIM, PUCKLE
—rifle	MINIE, MUZZLE-LOADER

American	CHAMBERS, HALL
	HARPER'S FERRY RIFLE, HAWKEN
	KENTUCKY RIFLE, KRAG-JORGENSEN
	LINDSAY, MAYNARD, PEABODY
	PLAINS RIFLE, REMINGTON
	SHARPS(-BORCHARDT), SPRINGFIELD
Austrian	WERDER
British	BAKER, (LEE-)ENFIELD
	FERGUSON, LANCASTER
	MARTINI(-HENRY), SNIDER
	WHITWORTH
Canadian	ROSS
Danish	KRAG-JORGENSEN
European	DREYSE, J(A)EGER
	NEEDLE-GUN
	SCHEUTZEN RIFLE
French	BERTHIER, CHASSEPOT
	LEBEL, PAULY
Israeli	GALIL
Japanese	ARISAKA
Russian	BERDAN, MOSIN-NAGANT
Scandinavian	SNAPLOCK RIFLE
short	CARBINE
slang	BANDOOK, BUNDOOK
Spanish	MIQUELET
Swiss	SCHMIDT-RUBIN
on	
—one side of ship	BROADSIDE
—pivot	SWIVEL-GUN
plastic	STEYR
queen's-arm	MUSKET
repeating rifle	
—American	CHAFFEE-REESE, HENRY
	PIM, SPENCER, VOLCANIC
	VOLITIONAL REPEATER
	WINCHESTER
—Austrian	FRUWIRTH, MANNLICHER
—British	COOKSON
—German	MAUSER
—Swiss	VETTERLI
revolver	GAT, HEATER, IRON, PIECE
	ROD, ROSCOE
	SHOOTING-IRON, SIX-SHOOTER
rifle	
—Afghan	JEZAIL
—African	ROER
—American	ARMALITE, GARAND
	WINCHESTER
—British	LEE-ENFIELD
—Davy Crockett's	OLD BETSY
—German	MANNLICHER, MAUSER
—Russian	KALASHNIKOV
—Sam's	MUSKET
set as a trap	SPRING-GUN
short	
—cannon	CARRONADE, HOWITZER
—gun	HOBIT
—musket	MUSQUETOON, MUSKETOON
—pistol	DAG
—revolver	BULLDOG
—rifle	CARBINE
shot-gun	CHOKE-BORE, SCATTER-GUN
siege-gun	HOWITZER
small	
—bore rifle	PEA-RIFLE
—cannon	CHAMBER, MURDERER
	MURDERING-PIECE
	FALCONET, SAKER
—hand-gun	DER(R)INGER, PISTOLET
—mortar	CO(E)HORN
smooth-bore	MUSKET, SHOTGUN
sporting	CHOKE BORE, FOWLING PIECE
	PUNT GUN, SHOT GUN
stone-firing cannon	PERRIER
sub-machine gun	
—American	THOMPSON, TOMMY GUN
—Australian	OWEN GUN
—British	LANCHESTER, STEN
	STERLING
—Czech	SKORPION
—fast-firing	BURP-GUN, ZIPGUN
—Finnish	LAHTI, SUOMI
—German	BERGMAN, SCHMEISSER
—Israeli	UZI
—Italian	BERETTA, VILLAR PEROSA
—Russian	STECHKIN
—Swiss	STEYR-SOLOTHURN
swivel	
—gun	LONG TOM
—musket	GINGAL(L), JINGAL
Tommy gun	CHICAGO PIANO
used in	
—police actions	RIOT GUN
—shooting gallery	SALOON-PISTOL
	SALOON-RIFLE
—war games	PAINTBALL GUN
wind-gun	AIR-GUN
Guyana	GUY
capital	GEORGETOWN
coin	CENT, DOLLAR
gymnastics	
asymmetric bar	
exercises	DISLOCATION CATCH
	HECHT DISMOUNT, HIP CIRCLE
	LONG HANG, MILL CIRCLE
	PIKED HANG, RADOCHLA SOMERSAULT
	SEAT CIRCLE, SOMERSAULT
	TUMBLE TURN, UNDERSWING
	UPSTART, WRAP
attendant	SPOTTER
backflip	FLIC-FLAC
backward body-arch	BRIDGE

beam exercises	BACKFLIP, CARTWHEEL
	(FREE)WALKOVER, JUMP, ROLL
	SCISSORS MOUNT
	SINGLE-LEG SQUAT
	SPLITS BRIDGE, SQUAT
	STRADDLE, TINSICA
extended legs raised	PIKE
floor exercises	BACKFLIP
	BACKWARD ROLL, CARTWHEEL
	FORWARD ROLL, FREEWHEEL
	HAND BALANCE, HANDSPRING
	HANDSTAND, HEADSPRING
	HEADSTAND, LEVER, NECKSPRING
	ROUND-OFF, SCALE, SOMERSAULT
	SUPPORT SEAT, TINSICA
	WALKOVER
full body extension	LAYOUT
gymnasts	
—American (m)	GLASS, HEIDA, HENNIG
	KORMANN, KRIZMERZ
(f)	DUNBAR
—British (m)	STUART, THOMAS
	WILD, WILSON
(f)	LENNOX, MUGRIDGE
	SLATER, WILLETT
—Czech (m)	PRAZAK, TABAK, VACHA
(f)	BOSAKOVA, CASLAVSKA
—French	BLONDIN, GRAVELET, LEOTARD
—German (m)	BRUCKNER, GIENGER
	KOESTE, SCHWARTZMANN
	WEINGARTNER
(f)	BURDA, GERSCHAU
	GITTA, GNAUCK, HELLMAN
	HINDORF, JANZ, KISCHE
	KRAKER, ZUCHOLD
—Hungarian (m)	MAGYAR, PELLE
(f)	CSASZAR, KELETI
	KORONDI
—Italian (m)	BRAGLIA, MENICHELLI
—Japanese (m)	ENDO, KAJIYAMA
	KASAMATSU, KENMOTSU
	NAKAYAMA, OKAMURA, ONO
	KATO, TAEKEMOTO
	TSUKAHARA, YAMASHITA
—Romanian (m)	GRECO
(f)	COMANECI, CONSTANTIN
	EDERLE, GABOR, TRUSCA
	UNGURREANU
—Russian (m)	ANDRIANOV, AZARIAN
	CHUKARIN, DETYATIN
	KLIMENKO, SHAKHLIN
	TITOV, VORONIN
(f)	ASTAKHOVA, FILATOVA
	GOROKHOVSKAYA, GROSDOVA
	KALINCHUK, KIM, KORBUT
	KOVAL, KUCHINSKAYA, LATYNIVA
	LAZAKOVITCH, SAADI
	T(O)URISCHEVA, VORONINA
—Swiss (m)	MACK, MIEZ, STALDER
horizontal bar	
exercises	BACK HIP CIRCLE, CIRCLE
	ENDO, FRONT HIP CIRCLE
	GIANT CIRCLE, GIANT SWING
	HALF GIANT SWING, SEAT CIRCLE
	SOLE CIRCLE, STALDER
	SWING, WHEEL
legs raised to chest	TUCK
one-legged pose	SCALE
parallel-bar	
exercises	CAST, DLOMIDOV
	HANDSTAND, HANG SWING
	KIP, ROLL, SHOULDER STAND
	STRELLI, STUTZE
	SUPPORT SWING, UPRISE
parts of vaulting horse	CROUP, NECK
	POMMEL, SADDLE
pommel-horse	
exercises	DOUBLE LEG CIRCLE
	FORWARD SCISSORS
	SINGLE LEG CIRCLE
	SINGLE LEG HALF-CIRCLE, TRAVEL
ring exercises	BACK LEVER, BODY CROSS
	CRUCIFIX, DISLOCATE
	HANDSTAND, KIP, L-SUPPORT
	(PIKED)HANG, PLANCHE
	STRADDLE LEVER, SWING
	UNDERSWING, UPRISE
routines	
—for men	FLOOR, HORIZONTAL BAR
	PARALLEL BARS, POMMEL HORSE
	RINGS, TRAMPOLINE, VAULT
—for women	ASYMMETRICAL BARS, BEAM
	FLOOR, TRAMPOLINE, VAULT
springboard	REUTHER BOARD, SKI RUN
tower of athletes	PYRAMID
trampoline exercises	BACK DROP
	BOUNCE, FACE DROP
	HALF TURNTABLE
	HALF TWIST DROP
	HALF TWIST JUMP
	HANDS AND KNEES DROP
	KNEE DROP, (PIKED)STRADDLE
	SEAT DROP, SWIVEL HIPS
	TWIST DROP, TWIST JUMP
vaults	FLANK, (GIANT)HECHT
	HANDSPRING, SQUAT, STOOP
	STRADDLE, THIEF, TSUKAHARA
	YAMASHITA
gypsy	CHAL, ROM
gentleman	RYE
priest	PATERCOVE, PATRICO
woman	CH(A)I

H

hair	PILUS
animal's hair	PELAGE
arrangement	COIFFURE
artificial hair	CHEVELURE, CHIGNON
	CREPE HAIR, DALMAHOY
	(PERI)WIG, PERUKE
	PERRUQUE, RUG
	SWITCH, TOUPEE
beard	BARBEL
—short pointed	VAN DYKE
—small triangular	CHARLEY, CHARLIE
—square	SPADE
bearded	BARBATED
braid	TRESS
—at back of head	PIGTAIL, QUEUE
braided queue	PLAIT
bristle	SETA, STRIGA
—on worm segment	CHAETA
bristling of hair on body	GOOSEFLESH
	HORRIPILATION
bushy wig (18th c)	DALMAHOY
clip (bar-shaped)	BARRETTE
coat of hair	PELAGE
coiffure (Scot.)	COCKERNONY
colour	ASH BLONDE, BROWN(ETTE)
	BRUNETTE, FLAXEN, REDHEAD
	(STRAWBERRY) BLONDE, TITIAN
comb (Scot.)	REDDING-COMB
	REDDING-KAME
court wig	TIE-WIG
curl on forehead	KISS-CURL
curly fringe	FRISETTE
downy hair of	
—beard	PAPPUS
—embryo	LANUGO
dress hair	COIF, SET
dressing	
—cleanser	SHAMPOO
—cream or oil	BRILLIANTINE
—gummy	BANDOLINE
—oil	(MACASSAR) OIL
—ointment	POMADE, POMATUM
dye	HENNA, PEROXIDE
embryonic hair	LANUGO
false hair	(see artificial (above) and wig (below))
false hair piece	COCKERNONY
fillet of hair	COCKERNONY, SNOOD
goat's hair	MOHAIR

hairband	BANDEAU
hairdresser	BARBER, COIFFEUR
	COIFFEUSE, FRISEUR
	TONSOR
hairdressing	
establishment	SALON
hairless	GLABRATE, GLABROUS
hairlike	PILLARY
—process	VILLUS
—thread(s))	CILIUM(CILIA)
hairnet	CAUL, SNOOD
—Northern	KELL
hairpiece	CHIGNON, MERKIN
	SWITCH, TOUPEE
—Scottish	COCKERNONY
hairpowder	M(O)UST, MUIST
hairy	CRINIGEROUS, CRINITE
	CRINOUS, HIRSUTE, PILAR
	PILOSE, PILOUS
having	
—grey hair	GRIZZLED
—hair	CRINATE(D), CRINOSE
	CRINITE, HIRSUTE
	PILIFEROUS, PILOSE
	PILEOUS, VILLOUS
—hairy tufts	BARBATE
—short hair	CILIOLATE
—smooth hair	LISOTRICHOUS
—straight hair	LEIOTRICHOUS
—wavy hair	CYMOTRICHOUS
—woolly hair	LANATE, ULOTRICHOUS
head of hair	CHEVELURE, MANE
in nostrils	VIBRISSA(E)
light streak in hair	HIGHLIGHT
liquid for	
—colouring	BLEACH, TONER
—fixing	SETTING LOTION
—washing	SHAMPOO
lock across forehead	COWLICK
	LOVELOCK, QUIFF
long	
—curl	RINGLET
—flowing hair	TRESS(ES)
—hair	MANE
—lasting set	PERM(ANENT WAVE)
—lock	DREADLOCK
	RAT('S)-TAIL, TRESS
—soft hair	VILLUS
loss of hair	ALOPECIA, BALDNESS
	MADAROSIS, PSILOSIS
matted condition	PLICA (POLONICA)
method of curling	FRISURE
moustache	
—bushy	HANDLEBAR
—small	CHARLEY, CHARLIE
old slang	STRAMMEL, STRUMMEL

on
  —animal's neck   FRILL, HACKLES
                               MANE, RUFF
  —genital areas   PUBES
  —horse's
    hoof   CRONET
    neck   MANE
  —man's
    cheek   SIDEBOARD, SIDEBURN
            (MUTTONCHOP)WHISKERS
    chin   BEARD
    upper lip   MOUSTACHE
  ornament   POMPOON
  —Greek   TETTIX
pad   TOQUE
periwig   CHEVELURE
pigment in hair   MELANIN
pigtail   QUEUE
plait   TRESS
powder for hair   M(O)UST, MUIST
protein in hair   KERATIN
removal of hair   (D)EPILATION
ringlet   LOCK
root sac of hair   FOLLICLE
shampooing   TRIPSIS
shaven head   TONSURE
shaving   POGONOTOMY
shed hair   MOULT
short soft hair DOWN, LANUGO, PILE
single curl of hair   RINGLET
specialist   TRICHOLOGIST
stiff hair   BRISTLE, WHISKER
study of hair   TRICHOLOGY
style   COIFFURE, TONSURE
  —men   BRUTUS, CREW CUT, DA
     DUCK'S-TAIL, EN BROSSE
    African   AFRO
    Red Indian   MOHICAN
    West Indian DREADLOCKS
  —women BANG, BEEHIVE, BOB
                 BOUFFANT
     CRIMP, ETON CROP
 FRENCH PLEAT, FRENCH ROLL
 FRIZETTE, MARCEL WAVE
 PAGEBOY, PERM(ANENT WAVE)
POMPADOUR, PONY-TAIL, POUFFE
  SHINGLE, URCHIN CUT
    African   AFRO, CORN-ROWS
tactile hair(s)   VIBRISSA(E)
  —in insects   SCOP(UL)A(E)
thick mass of hair   SHAG, SHOCK
tuft of hair FEATHER, FLOCCUS, LOCK
  —small   FLOCCULUS
used for propulsion CILIUM(CILIA)
    FLAGELLUM(FLAGELLA)
wash with cleaning liquid SHAMPOO

wave with hot iron MARCEL (WAVE)
whiteness of hair   CANITIES
wig   BRUTUS, CAXON
                CHEVELURE
DALMAHOY, JAS(E)Y, JAZY
     PERIWIG, PERUKE
    PERRUQUE, SPENCER
    TRANSFORMATION
  —maker   PERRUQUIER
  —partly covering head SCRATCH(-WIG)
  —Scottish   GIZZ, JIZ
Haiti   RH
  capital   PORT AU PRINCE
  coin   CENTIME, GOURDE
harness   (*see* **horse**)
Harpies   AELLO, CELAENO
 (or PODARGE), OCYPETE
hat   (*see* **headgear**)
having
  additional syllable PERISSOSYLLABIC
  alimentary canal   ENTERATE
  all
    —knowledge   OMNISCIENT
    —power   OMNIPOTENT
    —sides equal   EQUILATERAL
    —stamens united MONADELPHOUS
  alternation of
    generations HETEROGONOUS
  anthers formed into tube SYNANTHEROUS
      SYNGENESIOUS
  armoured plates or scales LORICATE
  backbone VERTEBRATE(D)
  backward-pointing lobes RUNCINATE
  bad breath   HALITOTIC
  bag   UTRICULAR
  base joined round stem PERFOLIATE
  barbs   BARBATE(D)
  battlements   CASTELLATED
      CRENELLATED
  beak   NASUTE
  —and keel ROSTROCARINATE
  beams or lintels TRABEATE(D)
  beard   BARB(ELL)ATE
  belts   ZONATE(D)
  bilateral symmetry ISOBILATERAL
  bill curved downwards CURVIROSTRAL
  bladder   UTRICULAR
  blisters   BULLATE
  blood   SANGUINEOUS
  bones of palate
    separate SCHIZOGNATHOUS
  bony scales   PLACOID
  bracteoles BRACTEOLATE
  bracts   BRACTEATE
  breasts   MAMMATE
    MAMMIFEROUS

bristles	STRIGATE, STRIGOSE
	STYLAR, STYLATE
—with barbs	BARBELLATE
broad	
—bill	LATIROSTRAL
—nose	PLATYRRHINE
—partition	LATISEPTATE
bulges	TOROSE
bulging eyeballs	EXOPHTHALMIC
bushy habit of growth	DUMOSE, DUMOUS
calyx and corolla	
different	HETEROCHLAMYDEOUS
carpels and stamens on	
same flower	ASEXUAL
	HERMAPHRODITE
case	THECATE
cavities	LACUNOSE
cell	UTRICULAR
central spot of	
another colour	PUPILLATE
chain of segments	STROBILACEOUS
chinks	FATISCENT
circumflex accent on last	
syllable	PERISPOMENON
claws	UNGUAL, UNGUICULATE(D)
closed chain of	
—different atoms	HOMOCYCLIC
—similar atoms	HETEROCYCLIC
cloven	
—feet	BISULCATE
—tongue	FISSILINGUAL
club-shaped antennae	CLAVICORN
column	SCAPIGEROUS
comb-like gills	PECTINIBRANCHIATE
conical beak	CONIROSTRAL
cracks	FATISCENT, RIMOUS
crescent-shaped ridges	
on teeth	SELENODONT
crest	CRISTATE
crooked tail	CURVICAUDATE
crossed mandibles	METAGNATHOUS
curved	
—leaves	CURVIFOLIATE
—ribs	CURVICOSTATE
curves	CURVATE(D), CURVILINEAL
	CURVILINEAR
cutting back teeth	SECODONT
daily rest	MONOPHASIC
deep grooves (round disc)	CONTORNIATE
definite shape	EFFIGURATE
depression	FOSSULATE
—like a navel	UMBILICATE
different	
—areas of distribution	ALLOPATRIC
—kinds of	
leaf	HETEROPHYLLOUS

spores	HETEROSPOROUS
—names	DISQUIPARANT
—numbers of parts	
in different whorls	HETEROCYCLIC
	HETEROMEROUS
—sets of teeth	HETERODONT
—types of mycelium	HETEROTHALLIC
divided ribs	FISSICOSTATE
double	
—beak	BIROSTRATE
—nature	TWO-NATURED
—womb	DIDELPHIC
down	PLUMULATE
downy covering	PUBESCENT, TOMENTOSE
drops	GUTTATE(D)
ears	AURATE
Earth as centre	GEOCENRIC
energy higher than that of	
thermal agitation	EPITHERMAL
equal	
—diameters	ISODIAMETRIC
—enthalpy	ISENTHALPIC
—entropy	ISENTROPIC
—power	EQUIPOLLENT
erect branches	FASTIGIATE
eyelike spots	OCELLATE(D)
eyes	OCULATE(D)
—meeting in front	HOLOPTIC
—on stalks	PODOPHTHALMUS
—without stalks	EDRIOPHTHALMIC
faces of crystalline form	IDIOMORPHIC
fat buttocks	STEATOPYGOUS
feathers	PENNATE, PINNATE(D)
—on	
feet	PLUMIPED
legs or feet	BRACCATE
shoulders	SCAPULATED
feet or legs used as oars	REMIPED
few parts	OLIGOMEROUS
fine	
—notches	CREN(UL)ATE(D)
—wrinkles	RUGULOSE
fins	PENNATE, PINNATE(D)
first and second toes	
turned backwards	HETERODACTYLOUS
fissure	SULCATE(D)
flat nose	CAMUS
flavour	SAPOROUS
flowers	
—in spathe	SPADICIFLORAL
—of both sexes	MONOECIOUS
foot	PEDATE
forms belonging to	
different declensions	HETEROCLITE
freckles	LENTIGINOSE
	LENTIGINOUS

fringe	FIMBRIATE
fruit enclosed in	
special casing	ANGIOCARPOUS
full powers	PLENIPOTENTIARY
furrow	SULCATE(D)
fused digits	SYNDACTYL(OUS)
gaping beak	FISSIROSTRAL
gaps	LACUNOSE
gills and lungs	DIPNOUS
glistening outer scales	GANOID
great	
—appetite	VETRIPOTENT
—diversity	MULTIFARIOUS
grey hair	GRIZZLED
groove	SULCATE(D)
groups of four spores	TETRASPORIC
	TETRASPOROUS
gynaecium with flower	
parts	
—around	PERIGYNOUS
—below	HYPOGYNOUS
—enclosing	EPIGYNOUS
hair	CILIATE(D), CRINATE(D)
	CRINITE, CRINOSE
	PILIGINOUS, VILLOUS
hairy	
—buttocks	DASYPYGAL
—leaves	DASYPHYLLOUS
—tufts	BARBATE
handle	ANSATE
hard	
—dry stem	SCLEROCAULY
—shell	LORICATE
—skeleton tissue	SCLERENCHYMATOUS
—skin	SCLERODERMIC
	SCLERODERMOUS
—tissue cells	SCLERENCHYMATOUS
heather-like leaves	ERICOID
hermaphrodite and	
female flowers	GYNOMONOECIOUS
hoof divided into	
more than two parts	MULTUNGULATE
hoofs	UNGULATE
hooks	HAMATE, HAMOSE
	HAMOUS, UNCATE
	UNCINATE(D)
—at the end	CORNICULATE
horns	KERATOSE
horny skeleton	BISSEXTILE
intercalary day	PSOR(AT)IC
itch	CARINATE
keel	RATITE
keelless breastbone	NODOSE, NODOUS
knots	LACUNOSE
lacunae	
large	
—buttocks	STEATOPYGOUS

—head	MACROCEPHALIC
	MEGACEPHALOUS
layers	STRATIFORM, STRATOSE
leaf-margin overlapping	INCUBOUS
leafless stem	NUDICAUL(OUS)
leaflets each side	PINNATE
lips	LABIATE
long	
—feathers	LONGIPENNATE
—fingers	MACRODACTYLOUS
—fins	MACROPTEROUS
—nose	LEPTORRHINE
—shoots	VIMINEOUS
—tail	LONGICAUDATE, MACRURAL
	MACRUROUS
—toes	MACRODACTYLOUS
—wings	LONGIPENNATE
	MACROPTEROUS
lower jaw projecting	HYPOGNATHOUS
lungs	PULMONARY
made a will	TESTATE
male	
—and female	
characteristics	ANDROGYNOUS
	HERMAPHRODITE
flowers	MONOECIOUS
reproductive organs	
near each other	PAROICOUS
—and hermaphrodite	
flowers	ANROMONOECIOUS
mane	JUBATE
mantle	CHLAMYDATE, PALLIATE
many...	(see separate entry)
medium-sized head	MESATICEPHALOUS
membrane	VELATE(D)
minute serrations	SERRATULATE
more than	
—one	
embryo	POLYEMBRYONATE
	POLYEMBRYONIC
spouse	POLYGAMOUS
—two	
dentitions	POLYPHYDONT
dimensions	MULTIDIMENSIONAL
cusps	MULTICUSPID(ATE)
terms	MULTINOMIAL
—three wheels	MULTICYCLE
—five foils	MULTIFOIL
—usual number of	
fingers or toes	POLYDACTYL
mouth-like opening	OSTIATE
multiple origins	POLYPHYLETIC
narrow	
—bill	ANGUSTIROSTRATE
—leaves	ANGUSTIFOLIATE
—mouth	ANGIOSTOM(AT)OUS

—nose	LEPTORRHINE
—opening	STENOPA(E)IC
neck	TRACHELATE
needles	SPICULATE
needle points	ACESOSE
nipples	MAMILLATE(D), PAPILLATE(D)
nodes	NODOSE
nodules	NODULATED, NODULOSE
	NODULOUS
notched beak	DENTIROSTRAL
notches	CRENATE(D)
nucleus	NUCLEOLATE
odd number of toes	PERISSODACTYL(ATE)
	PERISSODACTYLIC
	PERISSODACTYLOUS
opening	OSTIOLATE
ossified septum	TICHORRINE
other floral parts	
below the ovary	HYPOGYNOUS
overlapping scales	IMBRICATE
paired	
—chromosomes	DIPLOID
—gills	ZYGOBRANCHIATE
—leaves	JUGATE
panicles	PANICLED, PANICULATE
partitions	SEPTIFEROUS, SEPTIFORM
parts in eights	OCTAMEROUS
pearly lustre	MARGAR(IT)IC
perianth	CHLAMYDEOUS
—leaves free	POLYPHYLLOUS
petals united	SYMPETALOUS
phosphorescence	NOTILUCOUS
pistils	PISTILLATE
pits	FOSSULATE
plate-like scales	PLACOID
point	COSTATE
pouch	SACCATE
power to	
—strike	PERCUTIENT
—combine with	
hydrogen atoms	(*see* valency *below*)
prickles	ECHINATE(D)
proboscis	PROMUSCULATE
protecting plates	SCUTATE
protective shell	LORICATE
pupa-case	PUPIGEROUS
pupae within body of mother	PUPIPAROUS
rank smell	OLID
reduced wings	MICROPTEROUS
resistance to disease	KLENDUSIC
retreating jaws	OPISTHOGNATHOUS
rhizoids	RADICULOSE
rootlets	RADICULOSE
rough scales	SQUARROSE
rows of leaflets	PINNATE(D)
royal privileges	PALATINE

ruddy glow	RUTILANT
runners	SARMENTOSE
	SARMENTOUS
S-shaped curves	OGEE
same	
—areas of distribution	SYMPATRIC
—colour	ISOCHROM(AT)IC
—constituents throughout	HOMOGENEOUS
—curvature in all	
directions	SYNCLASTIC
—essence	HOMO(O)USIAN
—form, different	
composition	HOMEOMORPHOUS
—fundamental structure	HOMOTYPIC
—magnetic force	ISOMAGNETIC
—measures	ISOMETRIC
—number of	
atoms	ISOTERIC
leaves	EUCYCLIC
petals and stamens	ISOSTEMONOUS
—potential	ISOELECTRIC
—tenor or tone	HOMOTONOUS
saw-bill	SERRATIROSTRAL
scales	LEPIDATE, SQUAMATE
	SQUAMOSE, SQUAMOUS
scattered	
—hairs	PILOSE
—perforations	TEREBRATE
schizophrenic characteristics	SCHIZOID
seal	SIGILLATE
separate	
—carpels	APOCARPOUS
—digits	FISSIPED(E)
—petals	POLYPETALOUS
—sepals	POLYSEPALOUS
serrated	
—antennae	SERRICORN
—beak	SERRATIROSTRAL
—feet	SERRIPED
several	
—alternating currents	POLYPHASE
—at one birth	POLYTOCOUS
—axons	MULTIPOLAR
—beats	POLYCROTIC
—broods	MULTIVOLTINE
—bundles of stamens	POLYADELPHOUS
—cells	POLYTHALAMOUS
—chambers	POLYTHALAMOUS
—cotyledons	POLYCOTYLEDONOUS
—hydrogen atoms	POLYACID
—hydroxyl groups	POLYHYDRIC
—mates	POLYANDROUS
—meanings	POLYSEM(ANT)IC
—musical keys	POLYTONAL
—nuclei	MULTINUCLEAR
	MULTINUCLEATE

—nucleoli	MULTINUCLEOLATE	—spines	SPINULATE
—phases of activity	POLYPHASIC		SPINULIFEROUS
—poles	MULTIPOLAR		SPINULOSE, SPINULOUS
—words	POLYONYMIC	—swellings	TORULOSE
	(*see also* **many**)	—wings	MICROPTEROUS
shaft	SCAPIGEROUS	smell	OLENT
shapely curves	CURVACEOUS	smooth hair	LISSOTRICHOUS
sharp points	ACEROSE, EPICULATE	spaces	LACUNOSE
	MURICATE(D), PUNGENT	specific gravity greater	
sheath	THECATE	than cerebro-spinal fluid	HYPERBARIC
short		spicules	SPICULATE
—hairs	CILIOLATE	spike	SPICATE(D)
—wings	BREVIPENNATE	spines	SPINATE(D), SPINIFEROUS
shoulder feathers	SCAPULATED	spore-case	THECATE
single chromosomes	HAPLOID	spots	GUTTATE(D)
similar		—eyes	OCULATE(D)
—calyx and corolla	HOMOCHLAMYDEOUS	stalk	PEDICELLATE
—essence	HOMOIOUSIAN		PEDICLED, PEDICULATE(D)
—parts	HOM(O)EOMEROUS		PETIOLATE(D)
	HOMOIOMEROUS	—near middle of leaf	PELTATE
single		stalkless eyes	EDRIOPHTHALMIC
—chromosomes	HAPLOID	stamens	STAMINATE
—nucleus	MONONUCLEAR	—fused with carpels	GYNANDROUS
—opening	MONOTREMATOUS	—in two bundles	DIADELPHOUS
	MONOTREME	stem	CAULESCENT
siphon	SIPHONATE	stiff leaves	SCLEROPHYLLOUS
slender		stipes	STIPITATE
—bill	TENUIROSTRAL	straight	
—build	LEPTOSOM(AT)IC	—bill	RECTIROSTRAL
—leaves	LEPTOPHYLLOUS	—hair	LEIOTRICHOUS
—nose	LEPTORRHINE	styles	STYLAR, STYLATE
—tail	LEPTOCERCAL	—of different lengths	HETEROSTYLOUS
—toes	LEPTODACTYLOUS	Sun as centre	HELIOCENTRIC
small		supernumary	
—bags	UTRICULAR	—breasts	POLYMASTIC
—bladders	UTRICULAR	—chromosomes	POLYPLOID
	VESICULATE(D)	swellings	NODOUS, TOROSE
	VESICULOSE	—in middle	VENTRICOSE
—blisters	VESICULATE(D)		VENTRICOUS
	VESICULOSE	sword-shaped leaves	XIPHOPHYLLOUS
—branches	RAMULOSE, RAMULOUS	tail	CAUDATE(D)
—bulges	TORULOSE	—used for propulsion	UROSTHENIC
—cavities	VACUOLATE(D)	taste	SAPOROUS
—compartments	LOCELLATE, LOCULATE	teeth	DENTATE(D)
—feathers	PLUMULATE	—all alike	HOMODONT, ISODONT
—fibres	FIBRILLOSE	—like comb	PECTINAL, PECTINATE(D)
	FIBRILLOUS	—with	
—head	MICROCEPHALOUS	crescent-shaped ridges	SELENODONT
—holes	FORAMINATED	paired cusps	ZYGODONT
	FORAMINOUS	transverse ridges	LOPHODONT
—hooks	HAMULATE	v-shaped ridges	ZALAMBDODONT
—projections	MONTICULATE	temperature of one's own	IDIOTHERMOUS
	MONTICULOUS	thick	
—sac	UTRICULAR	—digits	PACHYDACTYL(OUS)
—scales	SQUAMULOSE	—lips	LABROSE
—scattered crystals	POIKILITIC	—pericarp	PACHYCARPOUS

—skin	PACHYDERMIC
	PACHYDERM(AT)OUS
—woolly leaves	DASYPHYLLOUS
threads	FILAR
tongue attached	
in front	OPISTHOGLOSSAL
toothed	
—beak	RHYNCHODONT
—jaws	ODONTOSTOMATOUS
transverse	
—bars	TRABECULATE(D)
—lamellae on edge	
of bill	LAMELLIROSTRAL
triple form	TRIFORM(ED)
tubercles	TUBERCLED, TUBERCULAR
	TUBERCULATE(D)
tuberculosis	TUBERCULOSE(D)
	TUBERCULOUS
tubers	TUBEROSE, TUBEROUS
tufted gills	LOPHOBRANCHIATE
tufts	C(A)ESPITOSE
	PENICILLATE, SCOPATE
tunic	TUNICATE(D)
turrets	CASTELLATED
	TURRICULATED
twenty or more stamens	ICOSANDRIAN
	ICOSANDROUS
twigs	SARMENTOSE
	SARMENTOUS
uncloven hoofs	SOLIDUNGULATE
	SOLIPED(OUS)
undivided heart	MONOCARDIAN
unequal convex sides	GIBBOUS
unfeathered nostrils	GYMNORHINAL
united sepals	MONOSEPALOUS
unlimited power	OMNIPOTENT
unpaired chromosomes	HAPLOID
up-bent bill	RECURVIROSTRAL
upper and lower lobes	
of tail-fin alike	HOMOCERCAL
valency	
—above one	MULTIVALENT
—of	
one	UNIVALENT
two	DIVALENT
three	TERVALENT, TRIVALENT
four	QUADRIVALENT, TETRAVALENT
five	PENTAVALENT, QUINQUEVALENT
six	SEX(I)VALENT
valve	VALVATE, VALVULAR
variable blood-	
temperature	POIKILOTHERMIC
veil	VELATE(D)
veins	NERVATE, VENOSE
walls of carpels separate	
from septa	SEPTIFRAGAL

warts	VERRUCOSE, VERRUCOUS
water-storing tissue	PERICHYLOUS
waves	CRISPATE
wavy edges	CREN(UL)ATE(D)
	REPAND, SINUATE
webbed feet	PALMATE, PALMIPED(E)
	STEGANOPODOUS
whorls	VERTICILLATE(D)
wind-pipe	TRACHEATE(D)
winged feet	ALIPED
wings	ALARY, PENNATE
	PINNATE(D)
wires	FILAR
woody stem-base	SUFFRUTICOSE
woolly hair	LANATE, ULOTRICHOUS
wrinkles	RUGOSE, RUGOUS
zones	ZONATE(D)

Hawaii

acacia	KOA
dance	HULA(-HULA)
dish	POI
dolphin-fish	MAHI-MAHI
dress	MUU-MUU
drink	(K)AVA
fibre	PULU
garland	LEI
goddess	PELE
goose	NENE
greeting	ALOHA
group marriage	PUNALUA
ropy lava	PAHOEHOE
rough lava	AA
wreath	LEI

head

2-headed	BICEPS, BICIPITAL
	DICEPHALOUS
3-headed	TRICEPHALOUS, TRICEPS
4-headed	QUADRACEPS, QUADRICEPS
	QUADRICIPITAL
boat-shaped	SCAPHOCEPHALOUS
bony-plated	STEGOCEPHALOUS
flat-headed	PLATYCEPHALOUS
having	
—a head	CEPHALATE, CEPHALOUS
—own head	AUTOCEPHALOUS
large-headed	MACROCEPHALIC
	MACROCEPHALOUS
long-headed	DOLICOCEPHALOUS
man-headed	ANDROCEPHALOUS
many-headed	MULTICAPITATE
	MULTICIPITAL
medium-sized head	MESATICEPHALIC
	MESATICEPHALOUS
	MESOCEPHALIC
	MESOCEPHALOUS
pain in the head	CEPHALALGIA

pertaining to the head	CEPHALIC	—old	CASK
ratio of length to		derby	BOWLER
breadth	CEPHALIC INDEX	Dervish's hat	TAJ
short-headed	BRACHYCEPHALIC	ecclesiastical skull-cap	ZUCHETTA
	BRACHYCEPHALOUS		ZUCHETTO
small-headed	MICROCEPHALIC	Egyptian	FEZ, TARBOOSH
	MICROCEPHALOUS		TARB(O)USH
headgear	COIF	Etonian cap	SCOG(GER)
academic	MORTARBOARD	fanciful (Shak.)	TIRE-VALIANT
	TRENCHER	felt	
African	TURBAN	—cap	
—French soldier's	CHECHIA	Roman	PILEUS
American		Turkish	CALPA(C)K, KALPAK
—bowler	DERBY	—used in hats	BAT(TING)
—cowboy's hat	STETSON	flat	
	TEN-GALLON (HAT)	—cap	BARRET(-CAP), SCOTCH BONNET
—trilby	FEDORA		TAM-O'SHANTER, TAMMY
—woman's widebrimmed		—round hat	BER(R)ET
hat	SUNDOWN	for night-time wear	NIGHTCAP
Arab	CHECHIA, FEZ	fur	
	KAFFIYEH, KEFFIYEH	—hat	BEAVER, CASTOR
	KUFIAH, KUFIYA(H)	—hood	AMICE
	TARBOOSH, TARB(O)USH	hair	
awarded to		—band	BANDEAU
—champion	LAUREL WREATH	—net	KELL, SNOOD
—sportsman	CAP	hard round hat	BOWLER, CRASH HELMET
Basque hat	BER(R)ET		SAFETY HELMET
beaver fur hat	CASTOR	hat	
bishop's hat	MITRE	—feather	COCKADE
brimless	CAP	—maker	MILLINER
—fur	COSSACK HAT	hats for women	MILLINERY
bullfighter's hat	MONTERA	headcloth	ROMAL, RUMAL
Canadian cap	TUQUE	headdress	HEAD-TIRE, TIRE
cap		—with flaps	LAPPET-HEAD
—flat	BARRET(-CAP)	headscarf	CURCH, KERCHIEF
	SCOTCH BONNET	—Moslem	HIJAB
—military	CHEESE CUTTER, FORAGE CAP	Hebrew	
—Roman	PILEUS	—prayer	
—Scottish	TAM-O'SHANTER, TAMMY	cap	YARMULKA, YARMULKE
flat cap	BLUE BONNET	shawl	TALLITH
starched	COCKERNORY	—priest's hat	TIARA
woman's	MUTCH	Hermes's hat	PETASUS
—soft	BONNET	Holmes's hat	DEERSTALKER
—with		hood	CAPUCHE, COWL
side flaps	HUMMEL BONNET, TOY	huntsman's hat	MONTERO
square peak	CHEESECUTTER	Indian	
—worn		—headcloth	ROMAL, RUMAL
inside coronet	BONNET	—headdress	TAJ, TURBAN
on Sundays	STATUTE CAP	—sun-hat	(see pith helmet below)
ceremonial	CORONET, CROWN, TIARA	—turban	LUNGI, PAGRI, PUGG(A)REE
child's cap	BIGGIN		PUGGERY, PUGRI
clergyman's hat	BIRETTA	—ventilated hat	TERAI
college hood	AMICE	indoor cap	MOB-CAP
cord trimming	TORSADE	jewelled	CIRCLET, CORONET
cover for head	CASQUE, COIF		CROWN, DIADEM, TIARA
	CURCH, HEADSCARF	light sunhat	PANAMA

man's hat (18th c)	RAMIL(L)IE(S)
Mexican	SOMBRERO
military headgear	
—cylindrical	SHAKO
—French	KEPI
—fur hat	BEARSKIN, BUSBY
—Guards	BEARSKIN
—helmet	
German	COALSCUTTLE
	PICKELHAUBE
modern	BATTLE BOWLER, TIN HAT
old	(*see* **armour**)
—Highland Regiment	HUMMEL BONNET
—Highlander's cap	GLENGARRY
—Hungarian	SHAKO
—hussars	BUSBY
—Polish	CHAPKA, CZAPKA
	SCHAPSKA
—undress cap	BERET, FORAGE-CAP
—woollen	STOCKING-CAP
monk's hood	CAPUCHE, COWL
motorcyclist's hat	CRASH HELMET
	SKID LID
narrow-brimmed felt hat	HOMBURG
nightcap	BIGGIN
nun's headdress	WIMPLE
official headgear	CAP
peaked cap, 15th c	BYCOKET
Persian	CIDARIS, TIARA
pilgrim's hat	COCKLE-HAT
pith-helmet	SOLA(R) HAT
	SOLA(R) HELMET, SOLAH HAT
	SOLAH HELMET
	TOPEE, TOPI
Polish peasant's cap	CHAPKA, CZAPKA
	SCHAPSKA
Pope's crown	TIARA
protective	HARD HAT, CRASH HELMET
Roman	
—felt cap	PILEUS
—God's headdress	MODIUS
—headband	VITTA
sailor's hat	TARPAULIN
Scottish	
—broad cap	KILMARNOCK
—flat cap	BLUE BONNET
	TAM-O'-SHANTER
	TAMMY
—Highlander's cap	GLENGARRY
—night cap	KILMARNOCK COWL
	PIRNIE
—with side flaps	HUMMEL BONNET, TOY
—woman's cap	MUTCH
serjeant-at-law's cap	COIF
slang	LID, TILE, TITFER
small bonnet	KISS ME QUICK

soft	
—broad-brimmed hat	SHOVEL
	SLOUCH (HAT), TRILBY
	WIDEAWAKE
—cap	BONNET
Spanish	
—horseman's	MONTERO(-CAP)
—lady's	MANTILLA
sportsman's hat	DEERSTALKER
square-peaked cap	CHEESE-CUTTER
squirrel-skin hat	SQUIRREL-TAIL
starched cap (Scot.)	COCKERNONY
straw hat	BALIBUNTAL, BOATER
	HIVE
sun-helmet	PITH HELMET, TERAI
	TOPI
symbolic head-dress	CAP
tall	
—17th/18th c	FONTANGE
—cylindrical hat	STOVEPIPE (HAT)
	TOP HAT
Tatar	CALPAC(K), KALPAK
top hat	OPERA HAT
—American	PLUG-HAT
three-cornered	CHAPEAU-BRAS
	TRICORN(E)
trimmed with flowers	DOLLY VARDEN
turban	LUNGI, PAGRI, PUGG(A)RE
	PUGGERY, PUGRI
Turkish	FEZ, MARTAGAN
—felt cap	CALPAC(K), KALPAK
two-cornered	BICORN
veil round head and neck	WIMPLE
ventilated sun-helmet	TERAI
waterproof	SOU'WESTER, TARPAULIN
with ear-flaps	DEERSTALKER
	HUMMEL BONNET, TOY
women's hats	
—16th c cap or turban	TOQUE
—bell-shaped	CLOCHE
—brimless hat	PAGE-BOY HAT
	PILL-BOX, TOQUE
—broad-brimmed	BONGRACE
—cap (Scot.)	MUTCH
with side pieces	TOY
—close-fitting	CLOCHE
—frilly indoor hat	MOB-CAP
—head cover	COIF
—headdress	KELL
—headwrap (fleecy)	NUBILIA
—hood	
and cape (Malta)	FALDETTA
with hoops	CALASH
—large	
hat trimmed with	
flowers	DOLLY VARDEN

high hat	COMMODE
—light head-dress	CAP
—soft broad-brimmed hat	SLOUCH (HAT)
—tall conical hat	CORNET
—very tall	FONTANGE
—with	
projecting front	POKE BONNET
strings	BONNET
heart	(*see* **circulation**)
Hebrew	HEB(R)
including: Israeli	
Jewish	
Yiddish	
acacia wood	SHITTIM(WOOD)
agricultural settlement	KIBBUTZ, MOSHAV
airline	EL AL
almond cake	MANDELBROT
alphabet	(*see* letters *below*)
ancient incense	ONYX
annual feast	PASSOVER
armies	SABAOTH
ascetic	ESSENE, NAZARITE, NAZIRITE
assassins (Biblical)	SICARII
assembly	SANHEDRIM, SANHEDRIN
—for worship	SYNAGOGUE
avenger	GOEL
beef sausage	VIENNA
beg(gar)	SCHNORR(ER)
Bible	TANAKH, T(H)ORAH
bitterness	MARAH
book of law	TALMUD, T(H)ORAH
bond	STARR
boring person	SCHMO(E)
bread	HALLAH, MATZO
—offering	SHEW-BREAD
cabbalistic method of	
interpreting Scriptures	GEMATRIA
candelabrum	MENORAH
cantor	CHAZAN
cape	ROSH
casserole	CHOLENT, TZIMMES
ceremonial meal	SEDER
cheek	CHUTZPAH
chicken-pea snack	FALAFEL
chief singer	CHAZAN
Christian	EBIONITE, GOY, MARRANO
circumciser	MOHEL
clean	KOSHER
cloak	GABARDINE, GABERDINE
clumsy person	KLUTZ, S(C)HLEMIEL
	SCHLEMIHL, SCHLEP
coins	
—small	GERAH
—10 gerahs	BEKA(H)
—12 gerahs	(GOLDEN) DADIC
—2 bekahs	SHEKEL
—50 shekels	MANEH, MINA
—3000 shekels	TALENT
—Israeli	AGORA, SHEKEL
—old	ZUZ
commandment	MITZVAH
commentaries on OT	AGADAH, HAGGADA(H)
	HALACHA(H), HALAKAH
	MIDRASHIM
commune	KIBBUTZ
complaint	KVETCH
compulsory marriage	LEVIRATE
container for Torah scrolls	ARK
council	SANHEDRIM, SANHEDRIN
	SYNEDRION, SYNEDRIUM
court	SANHEDRIM, SANHEDRIN
	SYNEDRION, SYNEDRIUM
crazy	MESHUG(G)A, MESHUGGE
—person	MESHUGGENAH
	MESSHUGENEH
critical OT notes	MASORA(H)
	MASORETH, MASSORAH
dagger	SICA
dance	HORA
devotional offering	CORBAN
dietary laws	KASHRUT(H), KOSHER
dirge	KINNAH
dish of bitter herbs	MAROR
dispersion	DIASPORA, GOLAH
divine presence	S(H)ECHINAH
	S(H)EKINAH
divorce	GET
doctor of law	RABBI, RABIN
dolt	GOLEM
drag	SCHLEP
drum	TOPH
dumpling filled with	
meat etc	KREPLACH
dunes	HOLOT
early Christian Jew	NAZARENE
Easter	PASCH
ecclesiastical court	BETH DIN
effrontery	CHUTZPAH
egg custard	LOKSHEN
eve of Sabbath	PARASCEVE
evening prayer	SHEMA
evil spirit	DYBBUK
exposition of OT	AGADAH, HAGGADA(H)
	HALACHA(H), HALAKAH
	MIDRASH
expounder of law	RABBI, RABIN
expounders of law	SOPHERIM
fallow year	SABBATICAL YEAR
feasts	HANUKAH, ISODIA, PASSOVER
	PURIM, YOM KIPPUR
	YOM TERUAH, YOM TOB, YOM TOV
	(*see* **holidays**)

field of blood	ACELDEMA		manna	GEN
fiftieth year festival	JUBILEE		marginal note	K'RI, KTHIBH
fish-balls	GEFILTE FISH		marriage	
fool	SCHLEP, SCHMO(E)		—broker	SHADCHEN
	SCHMOCK, SCHMUCK		—custom	LEVIRATE
	SCHNOOK		measures	
forceful woman	BERRIEH		—18 inches	CUBIT
formalist	PHARISEE		—52 inches	REED
Friday	PARASCEVE		—6 cubits	CANEH, KANEH
funeral prayer	KADDISH		—3/4 pint	LOG
fuss	TZIMMES		—3 pints	CAB
garment	TALIS		—12 pints	HIN
Gentile	GOY		—14 pints	SEAH
German and Polish Jews	ASKENAZIM		—6 galls	BATH
giant	ANAK		—1/10 ephah	OMER
God	ELOHIM, JEHOVAH		—bushel	EPHA(H)
good deed	MITZVAH		—11 bushels	COR, HOMER
gossip	SCHMOOSE, SCHMOOZE		mercy seat	PROPITIATORY
harp	NEBEL		militia	HAGANAH
hellenising Jew	GREEK		miraculously provided food	GEN, MANNA
high priest's			months	

Civil   Ecclesiastic,

—breastplate	RATIONALE		1. Sep-Oct 7	ETHANIM, TIS(H)RI
—mitre	TIARA		2. Oct-Nov 8	BUL, (C)HES(H)VAN
Holocaust	SHOAH			MARCHES(H)VAN
homeland	ZION		3. Nov-Dec 9	CHISLEV, KISLEU, KISLEV
human image	GOLEM		4. Dec-Jan 10	TEBET(H), TEVET, THEBET
idol	REMPHAN		5. Jan-Feb 11	S(H)EBAT, SHEVET
image(s)	TERAPH(IM)		6. Feb-Mar 12	ADAR
incompetent person	SCHLEP		7. Mar-Apr 1	ABIB, NISAN
inferior priest	LEVITE		7. Apr-May 2	(I)YAR, YAVAR, ZIF
Jehovah	LORD OF HOSTS		9. May-Jun 3	SIVAN
Jew-baiting (German)	JUDENHETZE		10. Jun-Jul 4	TAMMUS, T(H)AMMUZ
Jewish quarter	GHETTO		11. Jul-Aug 5	AB, AV
knife	SICA		12. Aug-Sep 6	ELIL, ELUL
lake	YAM		intercalary	ADAR SHENI, VEADAR
land of rest	BEULAH		morning prayer	SHEMA
language	IVRIT, YIDDISH		Moslem	DEUNME
law	T(H)ORAH		mountain	HAR, SHELUHAT
lawyers	SOPHERIM		mush	SCHMALTZ
leader	H, MOSES		musical instrument	ASOR, SHOFAR
letters	AIN, ALEPH, AYIN			SHOPHAR, TIMBREL
	BETH, CAPH, CHETH, DALETH			TOPH
	GIMEL, HE, HETH, JOD, KAPH		my great master	RABBONI
	KOPH, LAMED, LOD, MEM, NUN		native-born Israeli	SABRA
	PE, RESH, SAMECH, SAMEKH		New Year	ROSH HASHANAH
	SCHIN, SHIN, TAU, TETH, TZADDI		non-Jew	GENTILE, GOY
	VAU, ZADE, ZAIN, ZAYIN		—woman	SHIKSA
liquid myrrh	STACTE		nose	SCHNOZZLE
literary collection of laws			not Kosher	TEREFA(H), TREF(A)
and practices	TALMUD		nothing	BUBKES
lord	ADONAI, ELOHIM		of inferior quality	SCHLOCK
lost book	JASHAR, JASHER		old-fashioned	SCHMALTZY
lyre	ASOR		oral law	GEMARA, MISHA(H)
mad	MESSHUG(G)A, MESSHUGGE			MISHN(AY)OTH
manhood ceremony	BAR MI(T)SVAH		orthodox Jews	(C)HAS(S)IDIM
	BAR MI(T)ZVAH			

OT commentary	AGADAH, HAGGADA(H)	roll (bread)	BAGEL
	HALACHA(H), HALAKAH	room for safe-keeping	
	MIDRASH, MASORA(H)	of documents	GENIZAH
	MASSORA(H), MASORETH	ruins	HORVOT
pancake	BLINTZ(E)	Sabbath	SATURDAY, SHABBOS
—cheese	BLIN(I)	—eve	PARAS(C)EVE
—potato	LATKES	sacred objects	URIM
parchment scroll	MEZUZA(H)	sage	HAKAM
parliament	KENESET, KNES(S)ET	Sanhedrin	SYNEDRION, THE SEVENTY
	SANHEDRM, SANHEDRIN	school for religious	
	SYNEDRION, SYNEDRIUM	studies	YESHIVA
part of		scribes	SOPHERIM
—Midrash	AGADAH, HAGGAD(H)	sea	YAM
	HALACHA(H), HALAKAH	secret lore	CAB(B)ALA, KAB(B)ALA
—Talmud	GEMARA, MISHNA(H)	sect	(C)HAS(S)IDIM, ESSENE
Passover ritual	HAGGADA, SEDER		HEMEROBAPTIST, KARAITE
pasta	FARFAL, FARFEL		MANDAEAN, MARONITE
pastry roll	FIGUELA	seventh year	SABBATICAL YEAR
—filled	KNISHES	strip of parchment	
pause (in Psalms)	SELAH	with passage from	
peak	SHELUHAT	Scripture	PHYLACTERY
Pentateuch	T(H)ORAH	skullcap	YARMULKA, YARMULKE
phylacteries containing		something trivial	BUBKES
sacred texts	TEFILLIN	song	HAT(T)IKVAH
place of		Spanish Jews	SEPHARDIM
—departed spirits	SHE'OL	—converted to	
—torment	TOPHET	Christianity	MARRANOS
—worship	SYNAGOGUE	spice	STACTE
plain	EMEQ	spleen	MILTZ
point	ROSH	sponge cake	PLAVA
Portuguese Jews	SEPHARDIM	sponger	SCHNORRER
potato pancake	LATKE	star of David	MAGEN DAVID, MOGEN DAVID
prayer	KADDISH, SHEMA	stew	TZIMMES
—book	MA(C)HZOR, SIDDUR, SUDDUR	strong drink	SHICKER
—shawl	TALLIT(H)	studies	YESHIVA
priest	AARONITE, RABBI	stupid person	SCHLEP, SCHMO(E)
	RABIN, SAGAN		SCHMOCK, SCHMUCK
priest's breastplate	PECTORAL		SCHNOOK
	RATIONAL(E)	sugary sentiment	SCHMALTZ
Portuguese Jews	SEPHARDIM	Supreme Council	SANHEDRIM, SANHEDRIN
—converted to			SYNEDRION, SYNEDRIUM
Christianity	MARRANOS	surplice	EPHOD
pull	SCHLEP	synagogue	S(C)HUL
pure	KOSHER	teacher	RABBI, RABIN
quarter	GHETTO	temple	SYNAGOGUE, TABERNACLE
rabbinical commentator	HAKAM	—servants	NETHINIM
ram's horn trumpet	SHOFAR, SHOPHAR	thanksgiving	KADDISH
received tradition	QUBALLAH	The Seventy	SANHEDRIN
religious		theological college	YESHIVAH
—service	MINYAN	title	RABBONI
—symbol	STAR OF DAVID	town	QIRYAT
ridge	REKHES	traditional oracle	URIM, THUMMIM
ritual		tree	SHITTAH
—candlestick	MENORAH	tribe	DAN, GAD, LEVITE
—food preparation	KASHRUT(H), KOSHER	unclean	TEREFA(H)
robot	GOLEM	unleavened bread	MATZA(H), MATZO(H)

unlucky person	S(C)HLIMAZEL
unquiet spirit	DYBBUK
veil	HUMERAL
village	KEFAR
vowel point	SCHWA, SEG(H)OL, SHEVA
wafer of bread	MATZA(H), MATZO(H)
weight	
—14 grams	SHEKEL
—20 gerahs	SHEKEL
well(s)	BE'ER(OT)
whine	KVETCH
wise man	HAKAM
womanhood ceremony	BAS MI(T)SVAH
	BAS MI(T)ZVAH
	BAT(H) MI(T)SVAH
	BAT(H) MI(T)ZVAH
Hell	ABADDON, AVERNUS
	DIS, EREBUS, HADES
	PIT, SHE'OL, TARTARUS
hens	ANDALUSIAN
	CUCKOO MARAN, DORKING
	GOLDEN SEABRIGHT
	MARENNES, MINORCA, LIGHT SUSSEX
	NORTH HOLLAND BLUE
	ORPINGTON, NEW HAMPSHIRE RED
	PARTRIDGE PEKIN, PLYMOUTH ROCK
	RHODE ISLAND RED, SPANISH
	SEBRIGHT BANTAM
	(SPECKLED)SUSSEX
	WHITE LEGHORN, WYANDOTTE
Australian	AUSTRALORP
Chinese	LANGSHAN
Indian	CHITTAGONG, MALAY
male	COCK(EREL), ROOSTER
small	BANTAM
tailless	RUMKIN
Turkish	SULTAN
Her	
Her (Britannic) Majesty	H(B)M
Her Catholic Majesty	HCM
Her Exalted Highness	HEH
Her Grace	HG
Her Imperial Highness	HIH
Her Imperial Majesty	HIM
Her Majesty's Customs	HMC
Her Majesty's Government	HMG
Her Majesty's Inspectorate	HMI
Herr Majesty's Service	HMS
Her Majesty's Ship	HMS
Her (Royal) Highness	H(R)H
Her Serene Highness	HSH
	(see also **His**)
heraldry	BLAZONRY, HER
about to take wing	RISING, ROUSANT
additional charge	AUGMENTATION
antelope	ARGASILL

antelope/horse	BAGWYN
antlers	ATTIRES
arched	ENARCHED, INVEXED
arms of deceased	HATCHMENT
arrowhead	PHEON
art of drawing coats-of-arms	(EM)BLAZONRY
back to back	ADDORSED
badge	COGNISANCE
ball of gold	MOUND
barbed head of arrow	PHEON
barrel-shaped metal	
cage	HERSE
barrulet	COTICE, COT(T)ISE
baton	BASTON, WARDER
bear quarterly	QUARTER
bearing	FLEUR-DE-LIS
	FLEUR-DE-LYS
—arms	ARMIGEROUS
—fruit	FRUCTED
—like a fish-trap	WEEL
—like a pallium	PALL
beasts	(see **monsters**)
beast's leg	GAMB, JAMB
bendlets interlaced	
with a mascle	FRET
bent	FLEXED
—round, striking side	PERCUSSANT
bird's leg cut off at thigh	A LA QUISE
black	DWALE, SABLE
blue	AZURE
border	
—near edge of shield	ORLE
—of shield	BORDURE
—with	
cotises	COT(T)IS
semi-circular indents	ENGRAIL
bowed	FLEXED
branch	SCROG
broad vertical stripe	PALE
broken	ROMPU
cadency mark of	
—eldest son	LABEL
—fourth son	MARTLET
—son	MULLET
cap	CHAPEAU
centre of escutcheon	FESSE-POINT
charge borne upon	
an ordinary	SUPERCHARGE
charged with	
—flowers etc	VERDOY
—squirrel fur	VERR(E)Y
—vair	VAIRE, VAIRY
charges used as border	ORLE
chequered	CHECKY
chief herald	GARTER KING-OF-ARMS
—of Scotland	(LORD)LYON

circular	
—shield (Scot.)	TARGE(T)
—symbol	ROUNDEL
—wreath	CHAPLET, GARLAND
clover-leaf	TREFOIL
coat of arms	BLAZON
colour	TINCTURE
—black	SA, SABLE
—blood red	SANGUINE
—blue	AZURE
—flesh colour	CARNATION
—gold	OR
—green	VT, VERT
—mulberry	MU, MURREY
—orange	TENNE
—purple	PURP, PURPURE
—scarlet	GU, GULES
—sky-blue	BLEU CELESTE
—tawny	TENNE
—yellow	OR
column with bifurcated	
capital and base	ZULE
combine palewise	IMPALE
coming	
—forth	NAISSANT
—up from another	ISSUANT
concave	CHAMPAGNE, CHAMPAINE
	INVEXED
—indentation	FLA(U)NCH
conventional figure	ORDINARY
conventionalised flower	PRIMROSE
cormorant	LIVER BIRD
cotice	BARRULET
covered with shells	ESCALLOPED
covering the field	SANS NOMBRE
crest	COGNISANCE, TIMBRE
cross	QUADRATE
—of filberts	AVELLANE
—with	
curved ends	MOLINE
three claw-like	
divisions	PATTE(E)
crutch-shaped	POTENT
curved backwards	REFLEXED
cushion tied at corners	WOOL PACK
cut off evenly	COUPE(D)
—to a point	FITCHE(E), FITCHY
death's head	MORTHEAD
depict	EMBLAZON
—in heraldic terms	BLAZON
device on a shield	CHARGE
devouring	VORANT
—prey	TRUSSING
diagonal cross	SALTIRE
diagonally	BENDWISE
diamond-shaped panel	HATCHMENT

diminish	REBATE
diminutive of	
—bend	COT(T)ISE
—bend sinister	SCARP
—fess	TRANGLE
—orle	TRESSURE
displaced	ROMPU
distinguishing arms of	
branch from main line	DIFFERENCE
divide quarterly	QUARTER
divided into	PARTY
—bends	BENDY
—quarters	QUARTERLY
—three	TIERCED, TRIPARTED
—vertically	PALY
diving	URINANT
division of	
—coat	QUARTERING
—shield for two coats	IMPALEMENT
double-bodied	BICORPORATE
drapery of coat-of-arms	MANTLING
drop	GOUTTE
eagle	AL(L)ERION
eight	
—leaved flower	EIGHTFOIL
—spoked charge	(ES)CARBUNCLE
elongated rhomboid	FUSIL
emblem	BEARING, CHARGE
	DEVICE
emerging from	
—behind	ISSUANT
—middle	NAISSANT
encircled	ENVIRONED, INVOLVED
—by sun's rays	EN SOLEIL
end-to-end	ABOUTE
entwined	ENVELOPED
escutcheon or shield	
—granted to commemorate	
a deed	ACHIEVEMENT
—hung over a tomb	ACHIEVEMENT
facing	
—each other	RESPECTANT
—the	
beholder	G(U)ARDANT
sinister	TRAVERSED
family shield	ESCUTCHEON
fan of feathers	PANACHE
fettered	SPANCELLED
field	CHAMP
figure surmounting helmet	CREST
fillet with pendants	LABEL
fire-bucket on pole	BEACON, CRESSET
five	
—petalled flower	CINQUEFOIL
—pointed star	MULLET
flame-shaped	RAYONNE

fleur-de-lis	LIS
floating in air or water	FLOTANT
flower with	
—four petals	QUATREFOIL
—five petals	CINQUEFOIL
—eight petals	OCTOFOIL
flying	
—horizontally	VOLANT
—tail down	CABRE
—upwards	SOARING
formed of crutch-heads	POTENT
full-face	CABOCHED, CABOSHED
fullness (of Moon)	COMPLEMENT
fully armed	CAP-A-PIE
funeral banner	GUMPHION
fur	ERMINE(S), ERMINOIS
	PEAN, TINCTURE, VAIR
gliding	GLISSANT
goat rampant	CLIMANT
gold	OR
—circle	BESA(U)NT, BEZANT
	TALENT
—or silver as tincture	METAL
green	VERT
grenade	PETARDIER
half a quarter	ESQUIRE, GYRON
halo	GLORY
hanging	PENDENT
having	
—a	
pommel	POMMELE
square opening	SQUARE-PIERCED
tongue	LANGUED
—another figure laid over	SURMOUNTED
—battlements	EMBATTLED
—border of convex curves	INVECTED
—branch stubs	RAGULY
—convex curvature	NOWY
—crown or coronet	
about the neck	GORGED
—empty centre	VOIDED
—endorse each side	ENDORSED
—ends entering mouth	
of animal	ENGOULED
—fesses	FESSE(E)-WISE
—fleurs de lis	FLEUR(ETT)Y
	FLOR(ETT)Y
—gyrons	GYRONNY
—head	
bowed	URINANT
facing up	HAURIENT
—horns etc a different	
colour from body	ENARMED
—inner part cut away	VOIDED
—narrow border	FIMBRIATE
—official headgear	ENSIGNED

—overlapping	
feathers	PLUMET(T)E, PLUMETTY
scales	PAPELLONE, PAPILLONE
—part displaced	FRACTED
—points	URDE(E), URDY
—raised wings	SEGREANT
—right foot raised	TRIPPANT
—small squares	CHECKY
—steps	GRIECED
—tail hanging down	DECLINANT
—trellis pattern	FRETTY
—wings	
expanded	DISPLAYED
folded	TRUSSED
joined	A VOL, IN LURE
open	OVERT
thrown back	ENDORSED
—water flowing through	TRANSFLUENT
hatchment	ACHIEVEMENT
hedgehog	HERISSON, HERIZON
	URCHIN
helmet	MANTLING
herald	BLAZONER
Herald of Arms	
—England	ARUNDEL, CHESTER
	NORFOLK, SOMERSET
	SURREY, YORK
—Scotland	ALBANY, DINGWALL
	MARMONT
	RICHMOND, SNOWDOUN
heraldic bearings	BLAZON
hollowed with narrow	
border	CLECHE
horizontal band	BAR, FESS(E)
horseman	CHEVALIER
in	
—sleeping posture	DORMANT
—the	
direction of	PER
manner of	PER
—upper part of shield	IN CHIEF
indentation in curved lines	ENGRAILMENT
indented	WAVED
interlaced	BRACED
inverted pyramidal	
figure	PILE
iron hat	CHAPEL-DE-FER
issuing from another	ISSUANT
jumping	SALIENT
King of Arms	
—England	CLARENC(I)EUX
	GARTER, NORROY AND ULSTER
—Scotland	LYON
knight	MILES
knotted	NOWED
—gold or silver cord	CORDELIERE

leaping	SALIENT
left hand side from front	DEXTER
less honourable armorial charge	SUBORDINARY
like	
—a dragon in rear parts	DRAGONNE
—an arch	ENARCHED
—millstone rind	MOLINE
lily	FLEUR-DE-LIS
	FLEUR-DE-LYS
line	DOUBLE
lines from edge of escutcheon to fesse-point	GIRON, GYRON
lion passant gardant	LEOPARD(ESS)
lizard	AMPHISBAENA
long flag	STANDARD
looking backward	REG(U)ARDANT
lower part of shield	BASE
lozenge	FUSIL
—pierced with circle	RUSTRE
—shaped bearing	MASCLE
lying down	
—head on paws	DORMANT
—head up	COUCHANT
mark of dishonour	ABATEMENT
—with badge or sign	ENSIGN
mastiff	ALANT
merman	NEPTUNE
metal	ARGENT, OR, TINCTURE
monster	(see separate entry)
most ancient	PREMIER
narrow	
—band of colour	FIMBRIATION
—bendlet	RIBAND
negro	BLACKAMOOR
of a cross with flower-decorated ends	PATONCE
officer below herald	PURSUIVANT
often repeated	SANS NOMBRE
one of nine fixed positions	POINT
open lozenge	MASCLE
orb of gold	MOUND
ordinary	
—from	
dexter chief to sinister base	BEND
sinister chief to dexter base	BEND SINISTER
—horizontal	FESS(E)
—occupying	
fourth of shield	QUARTER
upper part of shield	CHIEF
—of shield	CANTON
outline sketch	TRICK
overlaid	OPPRESSED, SUPPRESSED
overlying	JESSANT
painted in	TRICK
pair of bars	GEMMAL
parrot	POPINJAY
part of quartered shield	QUARTER
parted	PARTY
pass through	ENFILE
passing in opposite directions	COUNTER-PASSANT
personal flag on horizontal pole	GONFALLON
	GONFANNON
pierced	TRANSFIXED
place bearing on	CHARGE
—quarterly	QUARTER
point	
—at centre of shield	FESSE-POINT
—below centre of shield	NAVEL, NOMBRIL
—just above fesse-point	HONOUR-POINT
pointed	URDE(E), URDY
—at the foot	FITCHE(D), FITCHY
pole battle-axe	DOLOIRE, HALBERD
potent	POTENCE
powdered	SEME(E)
punning shield or emblem	ARMES PARLANTES
	CANTING ARMS
Pursuivant	
—English	FITZALAN, BLUE MANTLE
	PORTCULLIS, ROUGE CROIX
	ROUGE DRAGON
—Scottish	BUTE, CARRICK, KINTYRE
	MARCH, ORMONDE
rabbit	CONEY
ragged	RAGULY
raguly	RAGGED
raised on steps	MOUNTED
rampant	
—goat	CLIMANT
—griffin	SEGREANT
raven	CORBIE
rearguard	ARRIERE-GARDE
rearing	CABRE
—horse	FORCENE
red	GULES
reference book	ORDINARY
relative status of sons	CADENCY
represent half of	DIMIDIATE
representation of two rafters	CHEVRON
represented as flying	VOLANT
right-hand side from front	SINISTER
ring	ANNULET
rising	NAISSANT
—as	
a bird	ROUSANT

if to breathe	HAURIANT
	HAURIENT
—from the sea	ASSURGENT
rosette	COCKADE
roundel	
—azure	HURT
—black	GUNSTONE, OGRESS, PELLET
—blue	H(E)UT, HEURTE
—blue/silver	FOUNTAIN
—gold	BEZANT
—green	POMEIS, POMEY, POMME
—gules	TORTEAU
—murrey	MULBERRY
—purpure	GOLP(E)
—sable	GUNSTONE, OGRESS
	PELLET
—sanguine	GUZE
—silver	PLATE
—tenne	ORANGE
rows of squares of	
alternate tinctures	COMPONE
	COMPONY, GOBONY
ruling body	COLLEGE OF ARMS
—Scotland	COURT OF THE LORD LYON
running	COURANT
salient in opposite	
directions	COUNTER-SALIENT
scarf over helmet	LAMBREQUIN
science of coats-of-arms	BLAZON
Scottish	
—Herald	ALBANY
—King of Arms	(LORD) LYON
—pursuivant	UNICORN
scroll	ESCROL(L)
sea-horse	HIPPOCAMPUS
segment of circle	FLANCH
segmented cross	ARRONDEE
shackle for horse	FETTERLOCK
sheaf	GARB(E)
shedding drops of ...	DISTILLING
shield	BUCKLER
	(E)SCUTCHEON, SCOTCHEON
ship (Scot.)	LYMPHAD
shoulder guard	AILETTE
showing tincture	
of field	VOIDED
sign of illegitimacy	BAR-SINISTER
	BATON-SINISTER
silver	ARGENT
simple figure	ORDINARY
single shield borne	
as a charge	INESCUTCHEON
sitting	SEJANT
—on nest	EYRANT
six-rayed star	ESTOIL
skull	MORTHEAD
sleeve	MANCH(E), MAUNCH
small	
—banner	BANNERET, BANNEROLE
	BANNEROLL
—bend	BENDLET
—chevron	CHEVRONEL
—fesse	TRANGLE
—lion	LIONCEL
—pale	PALLET
—pennon	PENCELL, PENSELL
	PENNONCELLE
—shield at fesse	INESCUTCHEON
smeared	TRICK
spool of golden thread	TRUNDLE
spreading towards the ends	PATTE(E)
spur rowel	MOLET, MULLET
square	
—charge	CANTON
—sod	DELF, DELPH
squares of alternate	
tinctures	COMPONE, COMPONY
	GOBONY
squirrel fur	VAIR
St Andrew's cross	SALTIER, SALTIRE
standing	
—in profile	RAMPANT
—on four feet	STATANT
—shield for archer	PAVISE TALLEVAS
—still	POSE
star with wavy points	ESTOILE
stepped	GRIECED
stick with branch	
stubs	RAGGED STAFF
strawberry flower	FAISE
streamer	BANDEROLLE
strewn with small bearings	SEME(E)
subordinary	TRESSURE
sun with human face	SPLENDOUR
surcoat	CYCLAS
surface of shield	FIELD
surrounded by	ENVIRONED
	ENTOURED
swallow without feet	MARTLET
swimming horizontally	NAIANT
T-shaped mark	POTENCE
tail between the legs	COWARD
tearing prey	RAPING
tent	PAVILION, TABERNACLE
three-lobed	TREFOIL
tinctures	(see colour above)
—reversed	COUNTER-CHANGED
triangular	
—flag	PINSEL, PINSIL
—wedge	PILE
tripping	TRIPPANT
trumpet	CLARION

two parallel lines	
bounding an ordinary	BEND (SINISTER)
unde	OUNDY
upright rectangle	BILLET
variation of coat of arms	BRISURE
vertical band on shield	ENDORSE
vertically	PALEWISE
visit of herald	VISITATION
walking	AMBULANT
—stag	TRIPPANT
—to right	PASSANT
warhorse	DESTRIER
wavy	NEBULE, NEBULY, UNDE(E)
waxing (of Moon)	INCRESCENT
wheat-sheaf	GARBGERBE
wheel set with teeth	CATHERINE-WHEEL
whirlpool	GORGE, GURGES
white	ARGENT
wild boar	SANGLIER
wound	GOLPE, VULN
wreath	TORSE
Y-shaped ordinary	PALL
—with fringed bottom	PALLIUM
yellow circle	BEZANT
yoke on water-bags	BOUGET
zigzag or indented	
line	DANCETTE, DANCETTY
	RAGULY
	SIMPLE
herb	(WOOD-)AVENS
bennet	
burnt in medical treatment	MOXA
Christopher	BANEBERRY
for seasoning	POTHERB
mixture of fresh herbs	FINES HERBES
of	
—grace	RUE
—repentance	RUE
others	AGRIMONY, ALOE, AMARACUS
	ANGELICA, ANISE, AVENS, BALM
	BANEBERRY, BASIL, BAY, BENNET
	BERGAMOT, BETONY, BLITE, BORAGE
	BURDOCK, CALAMINT, CAPER, CARAWAY
	CATMINT, CATNIP, C(H)AMOMILE, CHERVIL
	CHICORY, CLARY, COMFREY, CORIANDER
	CORNEL, COSTMARY, COVENS, CRESS
	DILL, DITTANY, ELECAMPANE, ENDIVE
	FENNEL, FENUGREEK, FINOC(C)HIO
	FINNOCHIO, GENTIAN, GINSENG
	HAMBURG PARSLEY, HELLEBORE
	HENBANE, HOREHOUND, HORSERADISH
	HYSSOP, ISATIS, LAD'S LOVE
	LADY'S MANTLE, LEMON BALM
	LEMON VERBENA, LICORICE, LIQUORICE
	LOVAGE, MARJORAM, MEDIC, MILFOIL
	MINT, MUGWORT, MUSTARD, MYRRH
	OREGANO, ORIGAN(E), ORIGANUM,

	ORPIN(E), PANICUM, PARSLEY
	PENNY ROYAL, PEPPERMINT
	PURSLANE, PURSLAIN, QUINOA
	RAMPION, ROSEMARY, RUE, SAFFRON
	SAGE, SALAD BURNET, SAMPHIRE
	SAVORY, SEDUM, SENNA, SESAME
	SORREL, SOUTHERNWOOD
	SPICKNEL, SUMMER SAVORY
	SUCCORY, SWEET CHERVIL
	SWEET CICELY, TANSY, TARRAGON
	TORMENTIL, THYME, VERVAIN
	WAYBREAD, WOAD, WOODRUFF
	WORMWOOD, YARROW
Paris	TRUE-LOVE
Peter	COWSLIP
Robert	STINKING CRANE'S-BILL
trinity	PANSY
wood sorrel	OXALIS
Hindu	
Absolute	OM
adherent of Siva	S(H)AIVA
an age of the world	KALPA, KALIYUGA
	YUG(A)
ancient	
—language	SANSKRIT
—way of life	SANATAN-DHARMA
aphorism	SUTRA
Aryan way of life	ARYA-DHARMA
ascetic	SAD(D)HU, YOGI(N)
	GYMNOSOPH(IST), SIDDHU
aurora	USHAS
banker	SOUCAR
barge	BUDGERO(W)
bathing in Ganges	KUMBHA MELA
beauty spot	TIK(K)A
being	SAT
blackmail	CHOUT
bliss	ANANDA
book of	
—erotic love	KAMASUTRA
—ritual	SUTRA
Brahman beggar	SANNYASI(N)
caste	JATI, VARNA
(highest first)	
—priests	BRAHMANS, BRAHMINS
—barons/warriors	KSHATRIYAS
—commoners/merchants	VAISYAS
—artisans/labourers	SOODRA, S(H)UDRA
—untouchables	HARIJAN
—mark	TI(K)KA
chant	HARE KRISHNA
circle	MANDOLA
concentration	SAMADHI
convert to Islam	SHEIK(H)
cosmic age	YUGA
cycle of birth and death	SAMSARA

dancing-girl	BAYADERE	home of gods	MERU
dark planet	RAHU	idol	SWAMI
day (of Brahma)	CALPA, KALPA	ignorance	AVIDYA
deities	(*see* **gods, goddesses**)	illusion	MAYA
demigod	GARUDA	immortality	AMRITATTVA
demon that swallows		Indian Republic	BHARAT
the Sun and Moon		incarnation	AVATAR
at eclipses	RAHU	—of Vishnu	JAGANNATH, JUGGERNAUT
desire	KAMA		KRISHNA, RAMA
devotion	BHAKTI	instrument	SIT(T)AR
devotional		interpreter	DHOBASH
—offering	S(H)RADDHA	knowledge	GYAN, JNANA
—song	BHAJAN	land revenues	JAGHIRE
divine		law of causation	KARMA
—in self	ATMAN	liberation (from circle	
—power	MAYA	of re-births)	MOKS(H)A
divinity	DEVA	library	BHANDAR
dramatic performance		life	
of Ramayana	RAMLILA	—cycle rites	SAMSKARAS
drink of the gods	AMRITA	—principle	ATMAN, JIVA
drug	BIKH	loin-cloth	DHO(O)TI
epic	BHAGAVADGITA	love	KAMA
	MAHABHARATA	low caste	HARIJAN, UNTOUCHABLE
	RAMAYANA	man/bird	GARUDA
errand boy	HURKARU	manifestation	DARSHANA
European	FARINGEE, FERINGHEE	material gain	ARTHA
	FERINGHI	mediaeval texts	PURANAS
evil spirit	RAKSHAS(A)	mendicant	SAD(D)HU
extortion	CHOUT	merchant	BUN(N)IA
fairy	GLENDOVEER	metal worker	KOFTGAR
fate	KARMA	moral order	RITA
female principle	S(H)AKTI	musical form	RAGA
festival	DEWALI, DI(PI)VALI	mythical planet	RAHU
	DIWALI, DURGA PUJA, HOLI	mythological age	KALIYUGA
	KUMBHA MELA, NAVARATRA	non-violence	AHIMSA
	NAVARATRI, ONAM, PONGAL	of high caste	TWICE-BORN
	RSI-PANCAMI	official script	DEVANAGARI
first		paradise	SVARGA, SWARGA
—mortal	YAMA	period (4320 million	
—of Vedas	RIGVEDA	years)	CALPA, KALPA
forehead mark	TI(K)KA	philosopher	GYMNOSOPH(IST)
gate tower	GOPURAM	philosophical	
gentleman	BABOO, BABU	treatise	UPANIS(H)AD
gesture	MUDRA	philosophy	NYAYA, PURVA-MIMAMSA
ghost	BHUT		SAMKYHA, SANKHYA
gnome	YAKSKA		VAISESIKA, VEDANTA, YOGA
god in three forms	TRIMURTI	poison	BIKH
gold ornament	TAHLI	police officer	TANADAR
good spirit	DEVA	present age of the world	KALIYUGA
heaven	SVARGA, SWARGA	priest	PUJARI
hermitage	ASHRAM	priestly caste	BRAHMAN, BRAHMIN
hero	ARJUNA, RAMA	Rajput prince	RANA
holy		religious	
—book	VEDA	—commentary	VEDANGA
—man	SAD(D)HU	—instructor	GOOROO, GURU
—writing	SHASTER, S(H)ASTRA		MAHARISHI, SWAMI

—instruction	SIDDHU
—retreat	ASHRAM
—school	ARYA SAMAJ
—treatise	UPANIS(H)AD
—writing	SMRITI, TANTRA, VEDA
righteousness	DHARMA
ritual	PUJA
—texts	BRAHMANAS
ruling class	RAJPOOT, RAJPUT
rural districts	MOFUSSIL
sacred	
—books	MANTRA(M), PURANA
	SHASTER, S(H)ASTRA
—snake	NAGA
—scriptures	SHRUTI
—text	MANTRA(M)
—writings	TANTRA, VEDA
sage	MUNI, RISHI
salvation	MOKSA
self-immolation by widow	SATI, SUTTEE
serpent-king	SESHA
short verse	SUTRA
Siva's trident	TRISUL(A)
slave	DASI
society	SOMAJ
soul	ATMAN
spirit	PURUSHA
spring festival	HOLI
statues of gods	MURTI
store	BHANDAR
strands	GUNAS
supreme	
—glorification	AVATAR
—principle of life	ATMAN
symbol of	
—Siva	LINGAM
—the universe	MANDALA
temple	MANDIR(A)
—attendant	PUJARI
theistic society	BRAHMA SAMAJ
	BRAHMO SOMAJ
title	MAHATMA, PANDIT, PUNDIT
trader	BANIAN, BANYAN
tradition	SRUTI
transmigration of soul	SAMSARA
trident of Siva	TRISULA
trinity of gods	TRIMURTI
truth	SAT
twice-born	DVIJA
untouchables	HARIJAN
usher	SOUCAR
Veda	ATHARVAVEDA, RIGVEDA
	SAMAVEDA, YAJURVEDA
—commentary	VEDANGA
Vedic	
—hymn	MANTRA(M)

—philosophical texts	UPANISHADS
veil	CHAD(D)AR, CHADOR
	CHUDDAH, CHUDDAR
Vishnu's consort	S(H)AIVA
vision	DARSHANA
wealth	ARTHA
wife of Siva	S(H)AKTI
wisdom	JNANA
wise man	MAHATMA, PANDIT
	PUNDIT
woman's garment	SAREE, SARI
worship	BHAKTI, POOJA(H), PUJA
worshipper	
—of Sakti	S(H)AKTA
—of Vishnu	VAISHNAVA
yoga	BHAKTI, HATHA, JNANA
	KARMA, KUNDALINI, LAYA
	MAHA, MANTRA, RAJA, SIDDHU
	(*see also* **Indian**)

His

His (Britannic) Majesty	H(B)M
His Catholic Majesty	HCM
His Eminence	HE
His Exalted Highness	HEH
His Excellency	HE
His Grace	HG
His Imperial Highness	HIH
His Imperial Majesty	HIM
His Majesty's Customs	HMC
His Majesty's Government	HMG
His Majesty's Inspectorate	HMI
His Majesty's Service	HMS
His Majesty's Ship	HMS
His (Royal) Highness	H(R)H
His Serene Highness	HSH
	(*see also* **Her**)

historians

American	FOGEL, KENNAN, SCHLESINGER
	TURNER, VANTINA, WITT,
Australian	CHILDE
British	ACTON, BRIGGS, BUTTERFIELD
	CLAPHAM, CLARENDON
	COHN, COLLINGWOOD
	GIBBON, HILL, HOBSBAWM
	HOLINSHED, KIER, MACAULAY
	MORRIS, NAPIER, NEEDHAM
	TAWNEY, TAYLOR
	TOYNBEE, TREVOR-ROPER
	SYME, (VENERABLE) BEDE
	WEDGWOOD, WOOLF
Dutch	HUIZINGA
French	BAIVILLE, BLOCH, BRAUDEL
	CHAUNU, DE TOCQUEVILLE
	GOUBERT, HALEVY, LADURIC
	LE FEBVRE, LE POPELINIERE
	LE ROY LADURIE

German	BAUER, FLECHTHEIM
	HARNACK, UHDE, WITTFOGEL
Greek	AMMIANUS, HERODOTUS
	PTOLEMY, THUCYDIDES
	XENOPHON
Indian	PANIKKAR
Roman	LIVY, TACITUS
Swiss	BLEULER

holidays
including: fast
        feast
        festival
        saint's day

American	
—July 4th	INDEPENDENCE DAY
—September	LABOR DAY
—October	COLUMBUS DAY
—November	THANKSGIVING (DAY)
Australian	
—April 25th	ANZAC DAY
Buddhist	
—July	BON, FEAST OF LANTERNS
—August	KUAN-YIN
—November	FESTIVAL OF LIGHTS
	KATHINA CEREMONY
Burmese	KATHINA CEREMONY
Canadian	
—July 1st	CANADA DAY, DOMINION DAY
—September	LABOR DAY
Chinese	
—Jan/Feb	NEW YEAR
—Feb/Mar	LANTERN FESTIVAL
—Mar/Apr	FESTIVAL OF BRIGHTNESS
—May/Jun	DRAGON-BOAT FESTIVAL
—Aug	ALL SOULS, KUAN-YIN
—Sep	MIDSUMMER
—Sep/Oct	DOUBLE NINTH FESTIVAL
—Nov/Dec	WINTER SOLSTICE
Christian	
—7 weeks before Easter	ASH WEDNESDAY
	SHROVE TUESDAY
—7th Sunday after Easter	PENTECOST
	WHITSUN(DAY)
—10-14 days after	
Pentecost	CORPUS CHRISTI
—40th day after Easter	ASCENSION DAY
—January 6th	EPIPHANY
	TWELFTH NIGHT
20th	ST AGNES'S EVE
—February 2nd	CANDLEMAS
	HYPAPANTE
—March 25th	LADY DAY
—March/April	EASTER, HOLY WEEK
	LENT
—May	ASCENSION DAY
—May/June	TRINITY SUNDAY

—June 11th	ST BARNABY'S DAY
23rd	ST JOHN'S EVE
—August 1st	LAMMAS
15th	ASSUMPTION DAY
—November 1st	ALL HALLOWS
	ALL SAINTS, HALLOWMAS
11th	MARTINMAS
—November/December	ADVENT
—December 24th	CHRISTMAS EVE
25th	CHRISTMAS (DAY)
27th	ST JOHN'S DAY
—All Hallows	HALLOWMAS
—All Saints	HALLOWMAS
—first fruits	LAMMAS
—Friday before Easter	BLACK FRIDAY
	GOLDEN FRIDAY
	GOOD FRIDAY
—harvest	HARVEST FESTIVAL
—love feast	AGAPE
—Resurrection	EASTER (DAY)
—Saturday before	
Easter	HOLY SATURDAY
—Sunday before Easter	PALM SUNDAY
—Thursday before	
Easter	MAUNDY THURSDAY
English	
—January 1st	NEW YEAR'S DAY
—February 14th	ST VALENTINE'S DAY
—April 23rd	ST GEORGE'S DAY
—July 15th	ST SWITHIN'S DAY
—September 29th	MICHAELMAS
—October 31st	HALLOWE'EN
25th	ST CRISPIN'S DAY
—Nov 5th	GUY FAWKES'S DAY
11th	ARMISTICE DAY
—December 26th	BOXING DAY
31st	NEW YEAR'S EVE
—beer festival	ALE
—shoemakers' festival	ST CRISPIN'S DAY
Epiphany	TWELFTH NIGHT
French	
—July 14th	BASTILLE DAY
—Shrove Tuesday	MARDI GRAS
German	
—April 30th	WALPURGISNACHT
	WALPURGIS NIGHT
—Shrovetide	FASCHING
Greek	
—festival of	
Adonis	ADONIA
Apollo	THARGELIA
Demeter	THESMOPHORIA
Dionysius	ANTHESTERIA
—national festival	PANATHENAEA
Hebrew	
—Jan/Feb	FESTIVAL OF LOTS, PURIM

—Feb/Mar	FAST OF ESTER	23rd	LABOUR DAY
	TAANIT ESTER	Moslem	
—March 1st	FEAST OF LOTS, PURIM	—after Ramadan	BAIRAM, BAYRAM
—Mar/Apr	FAST OF THE FIRSTBORN	—Mar/Apr	RAMADAN
	TAANIT BEHORIM	—April 16th	ID-UL-FITR
	PASSOVER, PESAC(H)	—June 23rd	ID-UL-ADHA
	HOLOCAUST DAY	—July 13th	NEW YEAR
	YOM HASHOAH	—Jul/Aug	MOHARRAM, MUHARRAM
—Apr/May	INDEPENDENCE DAY		MUHARREM
	YOM HAATZMAUT	—other	SAUM, SAWM
	JERUSALEM DAY	New Orleans	MARDI GRAS
	YOM YER SHALAYIM	New Zealand	
	REMEMBRANCE DAY	—February 6th	WAITANGI DAY
	YOM HAZIKHARON	—April 25th	ANZAC DAY
—May/Jun	FESTIVAL OF THE WEEKS	Northern Ireland	
	PENTECOST, SHABUOTH	—July 12th	GLORIOUS TWELFTH
—Sep/Oct	DAY OF ATONEMENT		ORANGEMAN'S DAY
	SUCCOT(H), SUKKOT(H)	pancake day	SHROVE TUESDAY
	YOM KIPPUR	Pentecost	WHITSUN(DAY)
	EIGHTH DAY OF CONCLUSION	Peru	INTI RAYIMA
	SHEMINI ATZERET	Red Indian	POTLA(T)CH
	FAST OF GEDALIAH	Roman	
	TSOM GEDALIAH	—February 17th	QUIRINALIA
	FEAST OF TABERNACLES	—April 21st	PALILIA
	SUCCOTH, SUKKOT()H	23rd	VINALIA
	REJOICING IN THE TORAH	—May 9-13th	LEMURIA
	SIMHAT TORAH	—August 23rd	VULCANALIA
—Sep 20th	ROSH HASHANAH	—Bacchus	BACCHANALIA
—Nov/Dec	(C)HANUKKAH	—boundaries	TERMINALIA
	FESTIVAL OF LIGHTS	—crops	AMBARVALIA
	HANUKAH	—expiation	LUPERCALIA, QUIRINALIA
—New Moon	ROSH HODESH	—fertility	LUPERCALIA
—New Year	ROSH HASHANAH	—flocks	PALILIA
—other	YOM TERUAH	—shepherds	PALILIA
	YOM TOB, YOM TOV	—the dead	LEMURIA
—presentation of the virgin	ISODIA	—Vulcan	VULCANALIA
—sabbath	SHABAT	—wine	VINALIA
Hindu		Roman Catholic festival	CARNIVAL
—January	KUMBHA MELA, PONGALA	Scottish	
—Feb/Mar	HOLI	—January 25th	BURNS NIGHT
—Aug/Sep	KRISHNA JAYANTI, ONAM	—November 30th	ST ANDREW'S DAY
—Sep/Oct	DURGA PUJA	—December 31st	HOGMANAY
—October	GANDHI JAYANTI	Shinto	
—Oct/Nov	FESTIVAL OF LAMPS	—Jan 1st	NEW YEAR'S DAY
—Festival of Lamps	DEEPAVALI, DEWALI	—equinoxes	IMPERIAL SPIRIT DAY
	DI(PI)VALI, DIWALI	—February 11th	EMPIRE FOUNDATION DAY
—other	NAVARATRA, NAVARATRI	—April 3rd	DEATH OF JIMMU
	PONGAL, RSI-PANCAMI	—October 17th	PRESENTATION OF RICE
—twelve-yearly	KUMBHA MELA	—November 23rd	THANKSGIVING
—wife of Siva	DURGA PUJA	Sikh	
Irish	FEIS(ANNA)	—Festival of Lamps	DEEPAVALI
—March 17th	ST PATRICK'S DAY		DEWALI, DI(PI)VALI
—December 26th	ST STEPHEN'S DAY		DIWALI
Jain	PAJJUSANA, PARYUSANA	—Oct/Nov	FESTIVAL OF LAMPS
Japanese		South African	
—November 3rd	ARTS AND CULTURE DAY	—December 16th	DAY OF THE VOW

Twelfth Night	EPIPHANY
Vietnamese New Year	TET
Whit Sunday	PENTECOST
Welsh	
—March 1st	ST DAVID'S DAY
Holland	(*see* **Dutch**)
holy	
Holy City	JERUSALEM, MECCA
	MEDINA, ROME
Holy Communion	EUCHARIST, HC
holy man	S, SAINT, ST
Holy Mother Mary	SMM
holy river	GANGES
Holy Roman Empire	SRI
Holy Virgin	HV
Holy Writ	BIBLE, NT, OT
hominids	(*see* **anthropology**)
Honduras	
capital	TEGUCIGALPA
coin	CENTAVO, LEMPIRA
Hong Kong	HK
hormone	AUTACOID
adrenaline	EPINEPHRINE
anti-diuretic	ADH, VASOPRESSIN
breaking glycogen down	
to glucose	GLUCAGON
causing moulting (insects)	ECDYSONE
controlling	
—adrenals	ACTH
—calcium in blood	(THYRO)CALCITONIN
—sugar metabolism	INSULIN
—synthesis of	
protein	INSULIN
female sex	(O)ESTRADIOL, (O)ESTRIOL
	(O)ESTROGEN, (O)ESTRONE
	PROGESTERONE, PROGESTOGEN
from	
—adrenal glands/kidneys	ACTH
	(AD)RENIN, ALDEROSTERONE
	CORTICOSTEROID
	CORTISOL, CORTISONE
	(NOR)ADRENALIN(E)
	(NOR)EPINEPHRINE
	ERYTHROPOIETIN
—pancreas	GLUCAGON, INSULIN
	PANCREATIN, SECRETIN
—parathyroid gland	CALCITONIN
	PARATHORMONE
—pineal gland	MELATONIN
—pituitary gland	ACTH
	ANTIDIURETIC HORMONE, ADCH
	CORTICOTROP(H)IN
FOLLICLE-STIMULATING HORMONE, FSH	
GONADOTROP(H)IC HORMONE	
	GONADOTROP(H)IN
	LACTOGENIC HORMONE, LTH
	LUTEOTROPIC HORMONE
	OXYTOCIN, OXYTONE
	PITUITRIN, PROLACTIN
THYROTROP(H)IC HORMONE, TSH	
SOMATOTROP(H)IC HORMONE, STH	
	VASOPRESSIN
—stomach	GASTRIN
—thyroid	CALCITONIN
	LUTEINIZING HORMONE
	THYROCALCITONIN
	THYROXIN
inducing sleep	MELATONIN
lactogenic	PROLACTIN
loosening pelvic ligaments	RELAXIN
male sex	ANDROGEN
	ANDROSTERONE
	TESTOSTERONE
plant	KINETIN, KININ
	PHYTAMIN
—affected by vernalisation	VERNALIN
—cytokinin	ZEATIN
—hypothetical	FLORIGEN
—inhibiting	
action of auxin	ANTIAUXIN
growth	ABSCISIC ACID
	ABSCISIN, DORMIN
—regulating growth	AUXIN
—stimulating	
cell division	CYTOKININ, PHYTOKININ
stem growth	GIBBERELLIN
preparing organs for	
pregnancy	PROGESTERONE
protects embryo	PROGESTERONE
reducing inflammation	CORTISONE
stimulating	
—growth	SOMATOTROPIC HORMONE
	STH
—production of	
milk	LACTOGENIC HORMONE, LTH
	LUTEOTROPIC HORMONE
	PROLACTIN
pancreatic juices	SECRETIN
progesterone	LACTOGENIC HORMONE
	LTH, LUTEOTROPIC HORMONE
	PROLACTIN
red blood cells	ERYTHROPOIETIN
sperm and	
ova	
FOLLICLE-STIMULATING HORMONE	
	FSH
—uterine contraction	OXYTOCIN
—sexual	
impulses	GONADOTROP(H)IC HORMONE
	GONADOTROPIN
—thyroid	
THYROTROP(H)IC HORMONE, TSH	

—water		fossil horse	HIPPARION
reabsorption	ANTIDIURETIC HORMONE	French	ARDENNES, PERCHERON
	ADH	from Medusa's blood	CHRYSAOR
synthetic oestrogen	STILB(O)ESTROL	general use	HACK(NEY)
horse[1]	CAPLE, CAPUL	genus	EQUUS
including: breeds		golden coloured	PALOMINO
colours		grey-brown	DUN
descriptions		heavy horse	(see workhorse below)
American		highly bred	ARAB, THOROUGHBRED
—Indian	CAYUSE	Himalayan pony	GOONT
—piebald	APPALOOSA, PINTO	hybrid	(see separate entry)
—poor	TACKY	Indian	TAT(TOO)
—riding	MORGAN	Irish	CONNEMARA
—wild	DUN, MUSTANG	Jerusalem pony	ASS
Arabian	ARAB	loser	STUMER
Argentinian	FALABELLA	light workhorse	HALF-LEG
Asian	PRZEWALSKI'S HORSE	male	COLT, GELDING, STALLION
ass	BURRO, DONKEY		STEED, STUD
Australian	WALER	mare (Scot.)	YAUD
Austrian	HAFLINGER, LIPPIZ(Z)ANA	miniature	FALABELLA
	LIP(P)IZ(Z)ANER	mixed colour	ROAN
bay	BAYARD	moderate racehorse	PLATER
black and white	PIEBALD	Mohammed's flying horse	BORAK
broken-winded horse	WHISTLER	mythological	
Brunnhilde's horse	GRANE	—horse	PEGASUS, UNICORN
burro	ASS, DONKEY	—horse/man	(HIPPO)CENTAUR
Caligula's horse	INCITATUS	Napoleon's horse	MARENGO
carthorse	CLYDESDALE, SHIRE	Odin's horse	SLEIPNIR
chaser	HUNTER	pacer	HOBBY
circus	LIBERTY HORSE	pack-horse	BATHORSE
colt	STAG	pony	GRIFEN, GRIFFON
—Scottish	STAIG		GRIPE, GRYPHON
competition horse	EVENTER	poor specimen	CROCK, HACK, JADE, PLUG
cowboy's mount	BRONC(H)O		NAG, RIP, ROSINANTE
dark-coloured horse	MOREL		ROZINANTE, SCREW
Dick Turpin's horse	BLACK BESS	racehorse	CHASER, PLATER
display horse	LIPPIZ(Z)ANA	reddish-brown colour	SORREL
	LIP(P)IZ(Z)ANER	reliable horse	STAYER
docked	CURTAIL	riding-horse	NAG, HACK(NEY)
—Shakespeare	CUT		ROUNCY
donkey	ASS, BURRO	Rinaldo's horse	BAYARD
Don Quixote's horse	ROSINANTE	roan horse	SCHIMMEL
	ROZINANTE	saddle horse	PALFREY
draught-horse	PERCHERON, SHIRE	Scottish	CUDDIE, CUDDY
	SUFFOLK PUNCH		GALLOWAY, SHELTIE
eight-legged	SLEIPNIR		SHETLAND
El Cid's horse	BABIECA	—mare	YAUD
entire	STALLION	—old	AVER, YAUD
extinct		—spirit horse	KELPIE
—breed	TARPAN	—stallion	STAIG
—type	EOHIPPUS	shaft-horse	FILLHORSE, THILLHORSE
family	EQUIDAE	short-legged breed	COB
fast horse	DAISY-CUTTER	slang name	PRAD
female	DAM, MARE	small horse	NAG, CANUCK, KANUCK
fine horse	BAYARD		GARRAN, GARRON, HOBBY
first horse (myth)	ARION		PONY, SHETLAND

—Spanish	JENNET, GEN(N)ET
Spanish	ANDALUCIAN
	ANDALUSIAN
spirit horse (Scot.)	KELPIE
spirited horse	STEED
sprinter (US)	QUARTER-HORSE
stallion	ENTIRE, STAG
	STONE-HORSE
—Scottish	STAIG
—x she-ass	HINNY
Stevenson's donkey	MODESTINE
Suffolk	PUNCH
swift horse	BARB, CHARGER, COURSER
Swift horse	HOUYHNHNM
tan with white mane	PALOMINO
thoroughbred	BLOODSTOCK
trained horse	EVENTER
warhorse	DESTRIER
Wellington's horse	COPENHAGEN
white and	
—black	PIEBALD
—another colour	SKEWBALD
wild	
—ass	DZIGGETAI, HEMIONE, HULAN
	KIANG, K(O)ULAN, KYANG
	ONAGER
—horse	BRONC(H)O
	PRZEWALSKI'S HORSE, TARPAN
—ponies	DARTMOOR, NEW FOREST
	WELSH
workhorse	CARTHORSE, DOBBIN
	DRAYHORSE, MALT-HORSE
	PERCHERON, SHIRE(HORSE)
—Shakespeare	CUT
young	
—horse	FOAL
—mare	FILLY
—stallion	COLT

horse²

including: tackle	
terms	
art of horsemanship	EQUITATION, MENAGE
attendant	GROOM, (H)OSTLER
	STABLEMAN
bitless bridle	HACKAMORE
bits	BRIDOON, DOUBLE-BRIDLE
	DOCTOR BRISTOL
	DOUBLE-JOINTED SNAFFLE
	EGGBUTT SNAFFLE
	FULMER SNAFFLE
	KIMBLEWICK, PELHAM
	SCRATCH, SNAFFLE
brush	COMB, CURRY, DANDY BRUSH
canine tooth	TUSH
caper	TITTUP
change of pace	TRANSITION

classical style of riding	HAUTE ECOLE
conveyance	HORSE-BOX
dealer	COPER
enclosure	CORRAL, LIVERY
	LOOSE-BOX, PADDOCK
	STABLE
exercises	RENVERS, TRAVERS
goad on heel of boot	SPUR
go lame	FOUNDER
harness	CAPARISON, TACK
	TRAPPINGS
—maker	
leather	SADDLER
metal	LORIMER, LORINER
spurs	SPURRIER
—parts	BARNACLE, BELLY BAND
	BLINDER, BLINKER
	BREECHING(LUG), BREECHING SEAT
	BRIDLE, BROW BAND, CHEEK BAND
	CHEEK PIECE, CINCH, COLLAR
	CROWN PIECE, CRUPPER, DRAGHOOK
	FRONT BAND, GIRTH-CINCH, HALTER
	HAME, HAME HASP, HAME TUG
	HIP STRAP, LOIN STRAP, MARTINGALE
	MUSROL, NOSEBAND, NOSE PIECE
	POMMEL, REIN, SADDLE
	SADDLE GIRTH, SADDLE PAD
	SHAFT TUG, SURCINGLE, TERRET
	THROAT STRAP, TRACE, WINKER
holding-rope	HACKAMORE, HALTER
horsemanship of the	
highest standard	HAUTE ECOLE
horse's actions and paces	MANEGE
horse-shoe	PANTON
horse show	GYMKHANA
jerking of rein	EBRILLADE
jumping competition	SHOW-JUMPING
—with very high jumps	PUISSANCE
long training rein	LUNGING REIN
measure of height (4")	HAND
meeting for equestrian	
sports	GYMKHANA
movements	
—in dressage	(*see* **show jumping**)
—responding to rider's	
indications	DRESSAGE
noseband	CAVESSON, GRACKLE
obstacle with hedge	
and rail	OXER
paces	CANTER, GALLOP, FOXTROT
	TROT, WALK
pad under saddle	NUMNAH, PANEL
parts	
—back	COUPLING
—foot	COFFIN, FROG, HOOF
—head	FORELOCK, FORETOP, POLL

—leg	CANNON, CASTOR, CHESTNUT
	FETLOCK, GAMBREL, GASKIN
	HOCK, PASTERN, STIFLE
—mane	ENCOLURE
—rear	CROUP(E), CROUPON
	CRUPPER, RUMP
—shoulders	WITHERS
performer on horseback	EQUESTRIAN
	EQUESTRIENNE
prance	TITTUP
racing	(see separate entry)
rail for training	CAVALETTO
rider	CAVALIER, EQUESTRIAN
	JOCKEY, POSTIL(L)ION
riding	
—for pleasure	HACKING
—school	MANEGE
saddle	
—blanket	PANEL
—cloth (military)	SHABRACK
shoer of horses	BLACKSMITH, FARRIER
show jumping	(see separate entry)
shy or refuse at a jump	BAULK, JIB
slaughterer	KNACKER
spur with one spike	PRICK-SPUR
stirrup-guard	TAPADERA
stud	HARAS, HARRAS(E)
training	
—of horses and riders	MANEGE
—in deportment	DRESSAGE
urine	STALE
wheel on spur	ROWEL
wound with spur	SPUR-GALL
horse diseases	
African	HORSE SICKNESS, NAGANA
Asian	SURRA
atrophy of shoulder muscles	SWEENY
blindness	GLASS-EYE
broken wind	HEAVES
contagious disease	DOURINE, STRANGLES
crack in hoof	SAND-CRACK
distemper	FIVES
eye diseases	MOON-EYE, PINK-EYE
farcy	GLANDERS
fever (Scot.)	WEED, WEID
foot disease	FRUSH, SEEDY-TOE
	WIRE-HEEL
glanders	FARCY
growth on leg	OSSELET, RAT(S)-TAIL
indigestion	GRASS-STAGGERS
	STOMACH-STAGGERS
inflammation of	
—bones	LAMINITIS
—brain	MAD STAGGERS
	SLEEPY STAGGERS
—frog	THRUSH

—hoof	FOUNDER, LAMINITIS
—scaphoid bone	NAVICULAR DISEASE
jaundice	YELLOWS
lameness	SPRING-HALT
leg tumour	GRAPE
lump in skin	SITFAST
lumpy jaw	ACTINOMYCOSIS
parasitic infection	DOURINE, NAGANA
respiratory	SCALMA
skin	
—disease of	
hock	SALLENDERS
pastern	SCRATCHES
—eruption	MAL(L)ANDER, MALLENDER
sore hoof	QUITTER, QUITTOR
spread by tsetse fly	NAGANA
study of horse diseases	HIPPIATRICS
swelling	GALL
—in mouth	LAMPAS(SE)
—on	
hock	BONE-SPAVIN
leg	CURB, GOURDINESS
pastern	CRATCHES
swollen	
—glands	VIVES
—hoof	QUITTER, QUITTOR
	TWITTER(BONE)
—vein on hock	BLOOD-SPAVIN
	BOG-SPAVIN
various diseases	STAGGERS
wart	ANBURY
wound in hind ankle	CREPANCE
horse racing	
be placed third or fourth	SHOW
bet	
—11 bets on four horses	YANKEE
—by bookmaker to divert	
attention from favourite	BLIND BET
—cumulative	ACCUMULATOR
	PARLAY
—first and second	EXACTA, FORECAST
	PERFECTA
—on	
win or place	EACH WAY
winners of two races	DOUBLE
—placed up to day	
before race	ANTEPOST BET
betting system in which	
all bets are pooled	PARI-MUTUEL
	TOTALISATOR, TOTE
bookmaker's system	
of hand-signals	TICKTACK
certain winner	CERT, NAP
Classics	DERBY, GRAND NATIONAL
	OAKS, THOUSAND GUINEAS
	TWO THOUSAND GUINEAS

cross-country race	POINT-TO-POINT
famous	
—fences	BECHER'S BROOK
	FOINAVON
	VALENTINE'S BROOK
—horses	
American	EASY GOER, SUNDAY SILENCE
British	ARKLE, BAHRAM
	DANCING BRAVE, DESERT ORCHID
	ECLIPSE, FREEBOOTER
	GOLDEN MILLER, HYPERION
	MARCH TOR, MILL REEF, NASHWAN
	NIJINSKY, NORTHERN DANCER
	OLD VIC, PHAR LAP
	RED RUM, REYNOLDSTOWN
	ROIMOND, SIR KEN, WINDSOR LAD
French	L'ESCARGOT, MA BICHE
	MIESQUE, RAVINELLA
Irish	DAWN RUN, PERSIAN WAR
	SEA PIGEON, SHERGAR
finishing position	PLACE
group of horses belonging	
to one owner	STRING
holding back by jockey	PULLING
horse entered under the	
name of another	RINGER
jockey's cap and shirt	SILKS
jockeys	
—American	ASMUSSEN, CAUTHEN
	CORDERO, LONGDEN, PINCAY
	SANTOS, SHOEMAKER
	VELASQUEZ
(f)	KRONE
—British	ARCHER, BRABAZON, CARSON
	CHAMPION, COCHRANE, EDDERY
	FRANCIS, FRANCOME, GILBERT
	MARSHALL, PIGGOTT, RICHARDS
	ROBERTS, SAUNDERS, SCUDAMORE
	SMIRKE, SWINBURN, WINTER
—Irish	MOLONY
—Italian	DETTORI
—French	ST MARTIN
—Peruvian	JACINTO
—Russian	NASIBOV
—South African	ROBERTS
jumping race	HURDLES, STEEPLECHASE
likely winner	FAVOURITE
odds offered	
—at start of race	SP, STARTING PRICE
—on	
likely winner	SHORT ODDS
unlikely winner	LONG ODDS
not subject to Jockey	
Club or National	
Hunt rules	FLAPPING
parade area	PADDOCK

place of bets to reduce	
possible losses	HEDGE, LAY OFF
race	
—for two-year olds	NURSERY STAKES
—in which	
extra weight is carried	
by some horses	HANDICAP
whole prize is awarded	
to the winner	SWEEPSTAKE
winner must be put	
up for sale	SELLING PLATE
	SELLING RACE
—with one starter	WALKOVER
races	
—America	ARLINGTON MILLION
	BELMONT STAKES
	BREEDER'S CUP MILE
	FLORIDA OAKS
	KENTUCKY DERBY
	PREAKNESS STAKES
—Australia	DALGETY CUP
	MACKINNON STAKES
	MELBOURNE CUP
	VICTORIA CUP
—England	CAMBRIDGESHIRE
	CESAREWITCH
	CHAMPAGNE STAKES
	CHAMPION STAKES
	CHELTENHAM GOLD CUP
	CORONATION STAKES, DERBY
	ECLIPSE STAKES, GIMCRACK STAKES
	GOLDEN MILE, GRAND NATIONAL
	GRAND SEFTON, KING GEORGE VI CHASE
	NASSAU STAKES, NELL GWYN STAKES
	OAKS, , PRINCESS OF WALES STAKES
	ST JAMES PALACE STAKES
	ST LEGER, STANLEY CHASE
	TOTE GOLD CUP
	(TWO) THOUSAND GUINEAS
	WHITBREAD GOLD CUP
—France	FRENCH DERBY, FRENCH OAKS
	FRENCH ST LEGER
	FRENCH (TWO) THOUSAND GUINEAS
	PRIX DE JACQUES LE MAROIS
	PRIX DE L'ARC DE TRIOMPHE
—Ireland	GALWAY HURDLE
	GALWAY PLATE, IRISH DERBY
	IRISH OAKS, IRISH GRAND NATIONAL
	IRISH ST LEGER
	IRISH (TWO) THOUSAND GUINEAS
	MILLION STAKES
—Italy	PALIO
—Japan	JAPAN CUP
—Scotland	AYR GOLD CUP
	SCOTTISH GRAND NATIONAL
racecourse official	STEWARD

racecourses
—America ARLINGTON, BELMONT PARK
CHURCHILL DOWNS
HOLLYWOOD PARK
TAMPA BAY DOWNS
—Australia (Sydney) WARDEN'S FARM
—Czechoslovakia VELKA PARDUBICKA
—England AINTREE, ASCOT, BATH
BEVERLEY, BRIGHTON, CARLISLE
CARTMEL, CATTERICK BRIDGE
CHELTENHAM, CHEPSTOW, CHESTER
DONCASTER, EPSOM, EXETER
FAKENHAM, FOLKESTONE
FONTWELL PARK
GOODWOOD, HAYDOCK, HEREFORD
HEXHAM, HOYLAKE, HUNTINGDON
KELSO, KEMPTON PARK, LEICESTER
LINGFIELD PARK, LIVERPOOL
LUDLOW, MARKET RASEN, NEWBURY
NEWCASTLE, NEWMARKET
NEWTON ABBOT, NOTTINGHAM
PLUMPTON, PONTEFRACT
REDCAR, RIPON, SALISBURY
SANDOWN PARK, SEDGEFIELD
SOUTHWELL, STRATFORD, TAUNTON
THIRSK, TOWCESTER, UTTOXETER
WARWICK, WETHERBY, WINCANTON
WINDSOR, WOLVERHAMPTON
WORCESTER, YARMOUTH, YORK
—France CHANTILLY, CLAREFONTAINE
DEAUVILLE, LA TOQUES
LONGCHAMPS
—Ireland FAIRYHOUSE
PHOENIX PARK, (THE) CURRAGH
—Japan TOKYO
—Scotland AYR, EDINBURGH
HAMILTON PARK, PERTH
—Wales BANGOR
racetrack HIPPODROME
ruling bodies JOCKEY CLUB
NATIONAL HUNT COMMITTEE
second, third or fourth PLACE
starting line GATE, STALLS
weight penalty HANDICAP, IMPOST
winning margin NOSE, LENGTH
(SHORT) HEAD

house
House of Keys HK
housemaid WENDY
housemaid's knee BURSITIS
Royal house ANJOU, BLOIS
BRUNSWICK-LUNEBERG, GOTHA
GREY, HANOVER, HABSBURG
LANCASTER, NORMANDY, ORANGE
PLANTAGENET, SAXE-COBURG
STUART, TUDOR, WINDSOR, YORK

hundred CENTURY, TON
100th anniversary CENTENARY
150th anniversary SESQUICENTENNIAL
hundred
—(number) C, CENTUM, CENTURY
P, R, RHO, TON
—(county division) CANTRED, CANTREF
CENTUM, CHILTERN
—and
one CI
four CIV
twenty GREAT HUNDRED
LONG HUNDRED
fifty CL, Y
sixty T
thousand LAC, LAKH, P, R, RHO
—pounds SEYMOUR
fifty thousand Y
sixty thousand T
hundredth CENTI-
Old Hundred PSALM
pounds
—sterling TON
—weight CENTAL
weight CWT
years CENTENARY
CENTENNIAL, CENTURY

Hungary H, HUNG
brigand HAIDUK, HEYDUCK
capital BUDAPEST
coin FILLER, FORINT
dance CSARDAS, CZARDAS
division BAN(N)AT, BANATE
dog VIZSLA
dynasty ARPAD
governor BAN
guerrilla HAIDUK, HEYDUCK
gypsy TZIGANE, TZIGANY
ZIGAN
Hungarian MAGYAR, TRANSLETHIAN
musical instrument CIMBALON, CIMBELON
pepper PAPRIKA
quick movement
of csardas FRIS(KA)
servant HAIDUK, HEWYDUCK
soldier PAND(O)UR
wine TOKAY

hybrid
American x Asian AMERASIAN
x Mexican CHICANO
American-Indian
x mulatto SAMBO
x Negro SAMBO
ass x mare MULE
canary x finch MULE
Caribbean CREOLE

cattle		x Indian	(BOIS-)BRULE
x bison	CAT(T)ALO		METIS(SE)
x zebu	CATEBU	fruit	(*see separate entry*)
cow		half-caste	MESTINO, MESTIZO
x bison	BEEFALO	—Negro redhead	BRIQUE
x yak	DHOMO, DSOBO, DSO(MO)	he-ass x mare	MULE
	(D)ZO, JOMO, Z(H)O	lion x tigress	LIGER
	ZHOMO, ZOBO, ZOBU	mixed race, southern USA	CREOLE
dog	MONGREL	native but of mixed-blood	CREOLE
	(*see also* **dogs**)	one with	
European		—eighth negro blood	OCTAROON
x African	EURAFRICAN		OCTOROON
x Asian	EURASIAN	—quarter negro blood	QUADROON
x coloured	HALF-BREED	partridge x quail	PERCOLIN
	HALF-CASTE	sheep x goat	GEEP
x half-caste	QUADROON	South African	(CAPE) COLOURED
x Latin American	CRIOLLO	Spaniard x American	GREASER
x mulatto	QUADROON	x South American	
x Negro	MULATTO	x Indian	MESTINO, MESTIZO
x quadroon	MESTEE, METIF, MUSTEE	stallion x female ass	HINNY
	OCTAROON, OCTOROON	x female zebra	ZEBRINNY
x South American		tiger x lioness	TIGON
Indian	LADINO, MAMELUCO	wheat x rye	TRITICALE
French x American Negro	CREOLE	zebra x female ass	ZEBRASS
French-Canadian	CANUCK	x female horse	ZEBRULA, ZEBRULE
			(*see also* **monsters**)

I

Iceland	IS
bay	FLOI
beach	FJARA
cape (headland)	NES
capital	REYKJAVIK
cave	HELLIR
cliffs	HAMRAR
coin	AURA, EYRIR, KRONA
fiord	DJUP
glacier	JOKULL
hill	FELL, FJOLL, KULUR, NUPUR
island	DRANGAR, DRANGUR
lake	VATN
lava-field	HRAUN
lignite	SURTARBAND
	SURTURBAND
mountain	BUNGA, DYNGJA, FELL, FJOLL
	HAMAR, HOFOI, HRYGGUR
	HYRNA, KULUR
—range	FJALLGAROUR
peak	HORN, HYRNA
river	FLJOT
sandbank	EYRI
stream	FLJOT
valley	DALUR
waterfall	FOSS
India	BHARAT, IDN, IND
aconitine	BIKH
acrobat	,NAT
adept	MAHATMA
adjutant stork	ARGALA
administrative	
—district	ZILA, ZILLAH
—service	IAS
affected speech	CHEE-CHEE
Afghan	PATHAN
agent	VAKEEL, VAKIL
agricultural society	SANTALS
allowance	BATTA
ancient	
—alphabet	BRAHMI
—language	SANSKRIT
—throne	PEACOCK-THRONE
antelope	ANTILOPE
	(*see also* **antelope**)
arboreal mammal	COLUGA
arched gateway	TORAN(A)
armed tribal force	LASHKAR

army officer	JAMADAR, JEMADAR
	JEMIDAR
arrangement	BANDOBAST, BUNDOBUST
ascetic	FAKEER, FAKIR
at once	EK DUM
attorney	VAKEEL, VAKIL
aubergine	BRINJAL
authority on law etc	PANDIT, PUNDIT
backgammon	PACHESI, PACHISI
bailiff	NAZIR
baking in clay oven	TANDOORI
balsam	GURJUN
Baluchi chief	TOMUNDAR
bamboo mat	TATTY
banana	PLANTAIN
bandicoot rat	PIG-RAT
bean	MUNG, URD
bear	BALOO, BALU
	HIMALAYAN BEAR
	SUN-BEAR
beast-fables	PANCHATANTRA
bedstead	CHARPOY
beggar	FAKEER, FAKIR
Bengal quince	BHEL
best quality	FIRST CHOP
betel	ARECA, PA(W)N, SIRI(H)
bird	AMADAVAT, AVADAVAT, BULBUL
	COUCAL, LARK-HEELED CUCKOO
	MINIVET, PRINIA, SHAMA
bitter gourd	KARELA
black	
—bear	SLOTH-BEAR
—mail	CHOUT
—soil	REGAR, REGUR
blessing (seeing or	
touching holy person)	DARSHAN
blouse	CHOLI
bo-tree	PEEPUL, PIPAL, PIPUL
board game	PACHISI
boat	BUDGERO(W), LANCHA
	PULWAR, PUTELI
book of aphorisms	SUTRA
bosun	SERANG
bottle	DUPPER
boycott	HARTAL, SWADESHI
braised meat	KORMA
brand	CHOP
brandy-and-water	BRANDY-PAWNEE
brass pot	LOTA(H)
bread	CHAPAT(T)I, CHAPATTY
	CHUPAT(T)I, NAN, PARATHA
	POP(P)ADOM, POP(P)ADUM
	PURI, ROTI
breakfast	(CHOTA-)HAZRI
bribe	DUSTOORY
British monarch	KAISAR-I-HIND

buffalo	ARNA, ARNEE, ARNI	—16 annas	R, RUPEE
	BUBALUS, WATER-BUFFALO	—100 new pice	R, RUPEE
bullock-cart	BANDY, HACKERY	—15 rupees	MOHUR
burial site (holy person)	DARGA	—100,000 rupees	LAC, LAKH
bum(m)alo	BOMBAY DUCK	—100 lac	CRORE
bustard	FLORICAN	—gold coin	PAGODA
butter	GHEE, GHI	—silver coin (Goa)	XERAFIN, XERAPHIN
—tree	MAHUA, MAHWA, MOW(R)A	collection of fables	HITOPADESA
calico	DUNGAREE	collectorate	TALUK
calling attention to		commander	SIRDAR
injustice etc	DHARNA	—of garrison	KILLADAR
camel	OONT	compliment	TASHRIF
camp		cooked	
—of soldiers	LASHKAR	—by steaming	DUM
—servant	BILDAR	—in	
cane sugar	GOOR, GUR	clay oven	TANDOORI
canopy	SHAMIANA(H)	curd etc	KHORMA
capital	DELHI	curry sauce	VINDALOO
captain	SUBA(H)DAR	copper pot	LOTA(H)
carpet fabric	D(H)URRIE	corporal	NAIK
carriage	BANDY, BUGGY	corruption	KHUTPUT
cart	G(H)ARRI, G(H)ARRY, TONGA	costus-root	PACHAK, PUTCHOCK
cattle food	BHOOSA		PUTCHUK
cavalry commander	RESSALDAR, RISALDAR	cotton cloth	BEZAN, SHALLI, SURAT
central shrine	VIMANA	coucal	SWAMP-PHEASANT
champagne	SIM(P)KIN	court	DURBAR
charging before		courthouse	CUTCHER(R)Y
magistrate	CHAL(L)AN		KACHAHRI, KACHERI
cheese	PANEER	crab's-eye plant	INDIAN LIQUORICE
chickpea flour	BESSAN	crane	SARUS
chief	SUDDER	cremation site	GHA(U)T
—minister of Mahrattas	PESWA	—of holy person	DARGA
	PEISHWA(H)	crocodile	MAGAR, MUGGER, NUGGAR
chintz	KALAMKARI		G(H)ARIAL, GAVIAL
cigarette	BEEDI	crop	KHARIF
civet	LINSANG, MONGOOSE	crown	RAJ
civil disobedience	SATYAGRAHA	cuckoo	BRAIN-FEVER BIRD, KOEL
Civil Service	CIS	cupboard	ALMIRA(H)
claret	LOLL-SHRAUB, LOLL-SHRUB	curry	
clay oven	TANDOOR	—dry	BHUNA
clerk	BABOO, BABU	—hot	MADRAS, VINDALOO
	CIRCAR, SIRCAR, SIRKAR	—lamb	ROGAN JOSH, ROGHAN GOSHT
cloak	CHUDDAH, CHUDDAR	—mild	DOPIAZI, DUPIAZI
cloth	KHADDAR, KHADI, SATARA	—rice and lentil	BIR(I)YANI
—of gold	SONERI	—with coconut milk	MOLEE
coarse		curtain to conceal women	PURDAH
—calico	DUNGAREE	cushion	GADI
—sugar	JAGGERY	cutlet	TIKKA
coat	ACHKAN	cymbals	DIN-DIN
coconut oilcake	POONAC	dagger	KUTTAR
coins		dal	PIGEON-PEA
—1/100 rupee	(NAYA)PAISA	dam	BAND(H), BUND
—1/40 rupee	DA(W)M	dance	KATHAK, NACH, NA(U)TCH
—1/12 anna	PIE	—drama	KATH(A)KALI
—3 pie	PICE	dancing	
—4 pice	ANNA	—girl	NA(U)TCH(-GIRL)

—hand movements	MUDRA	—office of	DEWANI, DEWANNY
—performance	NACH, NA(U)TCH	financier	BANIAN, BANYAN
development of vowel	SVARABHAKTI	fine flour	SOOJEE, S(O)UJEE
dhak tree	PALAS	fish	BOMBAY DUCK, BUM(M)ALO
diamond mine	GOLCONDA		DORAB, HILSAH, MAHSEER
diet supplement	AMRIT KALASH		MAHSIR
district	CIRCAR, SIRCAR, SIRKAR	flowers	BASTARD SAFFRON
division	TAHSIL		SAFFLOWER
door-screen	CHI(C)K	fly-whisk	CHOWRY
dress	BANIAN, BANYAN, SAREE, SARI	foot-soldier	PEON
dried		forced labourer	BEGAR
—fish	BOMBAY DUCK	form for money payment	CHAL(L)AN
—mud	CUTCHA, KACH(CH)A, KUTCHA	fort commander	KILLADAR
drink	ARRACK, SOMA	fortress	GURRY
—after sunset	SUNDOWNER	fowl	CHITTAGONG
drug	BHANG, BENJ, CUBSHA	freebooter	PINDAR(EE), PINDARI
	GANJA, MAJOON, SOMA	fried dough	PAPPADOM, POP(P))ADUM
drums	TABLA	fruit	BAEL(-FRUIT)
dry curry	BHUNA		BENGAL QUINCE
durra	GUINEA-CORN, JAWARI, JOWAR	—tree	DURIAN, DURION
dye tree	DHAK	fuss	TAMASHA
dyeing process	KALAMKARI	game	PACHISI
dynasty	MOG(H)UL, MUGHAL	gardener class	MALLEE, MALI
edible plant	SWORD-BEAN	garland hung between	
elephant		two points	TORAN(A)
—driver	MAHOUT	gentleman	PUKKA SAHIB
—enclosure	KEDDAH, KHEDDA	gift	NUZZER
—goad	ANKUS	ginger	CURCUMA, ZEDOARY
embankment	BAND(H), BUND	good	PAKKA, PUCKA, PUKKA
embroidered fabric	KINGCOB	government	CIRCAR, SIRCAR, SIRKAR
emperor	GREAT MOGUL, NAWAB	governor	HAKEEM, HAKIM
Englishman	QUI-HI, QUI-HYE		NAIK, SUBA(H)DAR
entertainment	TAMASHA	—of province	SUBA(H)DAR
epic tale	MAHABHARATA	grain harvest	RABI
Eurasian	CHEE-CHEE	grass	BAJREE, DUR(R)A, JHOW
European	SAHIB, TOPI-WALLAH		KANS, ROOSA, RAGA, RUSA
—lady	MEMSAHIB, SAHIBA(H)	—mat	TATTY
—(plural)	SAHIB-LOG	groom	MEHTAR, S(A)ICE, SYCE
evil-doer	BADMASH, BUDMASH	guide	DUBASH
exclamation of surprise	BOBBERY	guitar	SAROH
extortion	CHOUT	Gurkha knife	KUKRI
eyeshadow	SURMA	gypsy	BAZIGAR
factor	AMILDAR, AUMIL	handkerchief	BANDAN(N)A, ROMAL
factotum	CIRCAR, SIRCAR, SIRKAR		RUMAL
fan	PUNKA(H)	hat	TERAI, TOPEE, TOPI
fasting on offender' doorstep	DHARMA	head	
felt rug	NUMDAH	—cloth	ROMAL, RUMAL
festival	POOJA(H), PUJA	—of state	RAJPRAMUKH
fibre	CUSCUS, CUSKUS, DA, JUTE	headdress	TAJ, TURBAN
	K(H)USK(H)US, MADRAS, OADAL	heavy stick	LATHEE, LATHI
	SUNN (HEMP)	hemp	BHANG, DAGGA, KIF
fiddle	SARANGI	—matting	TAT
fig	OPUNTIA	—resin	CHARAS, CHURRUS
—tree	BANIAN, BANYAN, OPUNTIA	herb	PIA, REA, SESAME, SOLA
figured muslin	TANJIB, TANZIB	hermitage	ASHRAM(A)
finance minister	DEWAN, DIWAN	high-collared coat	SHERWANI

Himalayan	
—animal	PANDA, YETI
—cedar	DEODAR
—pheasant	MONA(U)L
Hindu	BABOO, BABU, GENTOO
hired	TICCA
holder of a taluk	TALUKDAR
holy leader	MAHATMA
home rule	SWARAJ(I)
honey-badger	RATEL
honorary title	NAWAB
horse from Australia	WALER
hour	GHURRY
house for travellers	DAK(-BUNGALOW)
household attendant	CHAPRASSI
	CHUPRASSY
hundred thousand	LAC, LAKH
hunter	SHIKAREE, SHIKARI
hunting	SHIKAR
ice-cream	KULFI
illusion	MAYA
infantry regiment	PULTAN, PULTO(O)N
	PULTUN
inlaid metal	KOFTGARI, KOFTWORK
—worker	KOFTGAR
interpreter	DOBHASH, MOONSHEE
	MUNSHI
intrigue	KHUTPUT
irregular	
—cavalryman	SILLADAR
—soldier	SEBUNDEE, SEBUNDY
isolated pillar	LAT
jacket	BANIAN, BANYAN
jaggery palm	KITTUL
judge	HAKEEM, HAKIM
labourer	COOLIE, COOLY
ladies's fingers	BHINDI, OKRA
lake	SAGAR(A)
land	
—division	PARGANA, PERGUNNAH
—owner	ZAMINDAR
—revenue	JAG(H)IR, JAGHIRE
holder of	JAGHIRDAR
—tenure	RAIYATWARI, RYOTWARI
language	ASSAMESE, BENGALI
	CANARESE, DRAVIDIAN
	GUJARAT(H)I, GUJERAT(H)I
	GURKHALI, HINDEE, HINDI
	HINDOOSTANEE, HINDUSTANI
	KANARESE, KANNADA
	KAS(H)MIRI, KOLARIAN
	MALAYALAM, MARATHI, MUNDA
	ORIYA, PALI, PANJABI, PUNJABI
	PUNJA(U)BEE, SANSKRIT
	SINDHI, TAMIL, TELEGU, URDU
—group	INDIC

—or dialect	PRAKRIT
law officer	NAIB
lawyer	MOOKTAR, MUKTAR
learned man	PANDIT, PUNDIT
lease	POTTAH
leggings	PUTTEE, PUTTIE
lentil	ARRAH, D(H)AL
—flour	BESAN
letter	DA(W)K
light	
—breakfast	CHOTA-HAZRI
—meal	TIFFIN
—scarf	PAGRI, PUGG(A)REE, PUGGERY
limestone	KUNKAR, KUNKUR
liquorice	JEQUIRTY
liquorice-tree seeds	
(prayer-beads)	CRABS-EYES
	CRAB-STONES
	JEQUIRITY (BEANS)
litter	DHOOLIE, DHOOLY, DOOLIE
loin-cloth	LUNGI
loom	TANTY
low caste	PARIAH
lunch	TIFFIN
Kashmiri	PUNCHI
magic	MAYA
magistrate	COTWAL, KOTWAL
magistrate's office	CUTCHERY
	KACHAHRI, KACHERI
Mahratta ruler	PE(I)SHWA(H)
mail	DA(W)K
—carrier	DAK-RUNNER
makeshift	CUTCHA, KACH(CH)A
malarial fever	TAP
mallow	URENA
manager	AMILDAR, AUMIL
manual of statecraft	ARTHSHASTRA
margosa	NIM
measures	
—1"	UNGUL
—1¾ miles	COSS, KOS(S)
—5 miles	YOJAN(A)
—½ acre	BEEGAH, BIGHA
—1 acre	CAWNY
—24 minutes	GHURRY
—hour	GHURRY
meat-ball	KHEEMA, KOFFA
messenger	PEON
metal ware	BIDRI
Melia	NIM
military head	SIRDAR
millet	BAJRA, BAJREE, BAJRI
	DARI, D(O)URA, D(H)URRA
	RAGGEE, RAGGY, RAGI
Miss	KUMARI
money of account	FANAM

Mongol	MOGUL
mongoose	URVU
Moslem	COSSA
—shrine	DURGAH
mountain pass	GHA(U)T
mounted attendant	SOWAR
murder	THAGI, THUGGEE
	THUGGERY
murderer	THUG
musical	
—form	RAGA
—instrument	CHIKARA, SARANGI, SAROD
	SERINGHI, SITAR, TABLA
	TAMBOURA, VINA
—rhythm	TALA
musk	
—rat	SONDELI
—shrew	SONDELI
musket	GINGAL(L), JINGAL
muslin	GURRAH, JAMDANI
	MAMMODIS
nationalist movement	SWADESHI
nafive tribe	GOND
needlewoman	DIRZEE
ne'er-do-well	BUDZAT
nim tree	MELIA
no good	NO CHOP
noisy row	BOBBERY
non-violent campaign	SATYAGRAHA
noodle	PHALUDA
nose flute	POOGYE
nursemaid	AMAH, AYAH
nut	ILLIPE, ILLUPI
office	
—boy	CHOKRA
—messenger	CHAPRASSI, CHUPRASSY
official residence	STATION
okra	BHINDI
	LADIES' FINGERS
one-horse carriage	EKKA
open space	MAIDAN
orchid	FAHAM
orderly	CHAPRASSI, CHUPRASSY
ornamental	
metalwork	BENARES WARE
ox	BHYLE, BRAHMIN-BULL, GAUR
	G(A)YAL, MITHAN
	S(E)LADANG, ZEBU
—cart	HACKERY
pagan	GENTOO
palanquin	DHOOLIE, DHOOLY, DOOLIE
	PALKEE, PALKI
palm-cat	MUSANG, PALM-CIVET
	PARADOXURE, TODDY-CAT
panther	BAGHEERA
parade ground	MAIDAN
paradoxure	MUSANG, PALM-CAT
	PALM-CIVET, TODDY-CAT
parcel	DA(W)K
pariah-dog	PI(E)-DOG, PYE-DOG
parliament	
—Lower House	LOK SABHA
—Upper House	RAJYA SABHA
parrot	ZATI
partridge	CHIK(H)OR, CHUKAR
	CHUKOR
pass	CHAL(L)AN
passive resistance	SATYAGRAHA
paymaster	BUKSHEE, BUKSHI
pea	D(H)AL, DHOLL
peasant	KISAN, RAIYAT, RYOT
percussion instrument	TABLA
perennial grass	LEMON-GRASS
pheasant	IMPEYAN
pigeon-pea	D(H)AL, DHOLL
pig-rat	BANDICOOT
pilaw	BIRYANI
pith-helmet	TOPEE, TOPI
plain	MAIDAN
planned effort against	
corruption	VIGILANCE
plant	AMIL, CHAY(A), DAL
	DHOOP, GOA BEAN
	HAT-PLANT, JUTE, MUDAR
	RAMIE, SHAYA, SOLA
	SPONGEWOOD, SPIKENARD
	TELEGRAPH-PLANT
—extract (tannin)	CATECHU, CUTCH
pleader	VAKEEL, VAKIL
pods (tanning)	BABLAH, BABUL
poet	RISHI
policeman	PEON, SEPOY, SIPAHI
police	
—officer	JAMADAR, JEMADAR
	JEMIDAR, TANNADAR
	T(H)ANADAR
—station	TANA, TANNA(H)
	THANA(H), THANNA(H)
political prisoner	DETENU
pond	TANK
pony	TAT(TOO)
—Himalayan	GOONT
poor quality	NO CHOP
prayer beads	INDIAN LIQUORICE
prince	NIZAM, (MAHA)RAJA(H)
princess	BEGUM, (MAHA)RANEE
	(MAHA)RANI
prison	CHOKEY
product made in India	SWADESHI
province	CIRCAR, SIRCAR
	SIRKAR, SUBAH
provinces	MOFUSSIL

pulses	D(H)AL, DHOLL
quince	BHEL
races	BHIL, CANARESE, GOORKHA
	GURKHA, HINDOO, HINDU, KANARESE
	LEPCHA, MAHRATTA, MARATHA
	MUNDA, PUNJABI, TELUGU, SIKH
raft	ZAK
Rajput chief	RANA
representative	VAKEEL, VAKIL
rat	BANDICOOT
ratel	HONEY-BADGER
ravine	KHUD, NAL(L)A
	NALLAH, NULLA(H)
rebel sepoy	PANDT
reception	DURBAR
red dye	CHAY(A)-ROOT
religious hostel	DHARMS(H)ALA
reservoir	TANK
resin	DHOONA
respect	TASHRIF
revenue	
—division	TAHSIL
—officer	TAHSILDAR
reverential observance	
of festival	POOJA(H), PUJA
revolution	INQILAB
rhythmic pattern	TALA
ribbed woollen cloth	SATARA
rice	
—and lentil curry	BIR(I)YANI
—dish	PILAFF, PIL(L)AU
	PILAW, PILOW, PULAO
—water	CONGEE, CONJEE
rich	
—European	NABOB
—soil	REGAR, REGUR
river	GANGES
robber	DACOIT, DAKOIT
robbery	DACOITAGE
	DACOITY, DAKOITI
robe of honour	KELLAUT, KHALAT
	KHILAT, KILLUT
rosewood	BITI
ruler of	
—Baroda	GAEKWAR, GAIKWAR
	GUICOWAR
—Hyderabad	NIZAM
sabre	TULWAR
sacking	GUNNY
sacred	
—book	PURANA
—lotus	PADMA
saddlecloth	NUMNAH
sailor	CLASHEE, LASCAR
salt efflorescence	REH
sash	LUNGI

savoury snack in batter	PAKORA
scarf	PAGRI, PUGG(A)REE
	PUGGERY
scholar	INDIANIST
seal (impression)	CHOP
seclusion of women	PURDAH
secretary	MOONSHEE, MUNSHI
sect	JAIN(A), GHEBER, GHEBRE
	GUEBER, GUEBRE, ORIYA
	PARSEE, PARSI, SIKH
sedan-chair	JAMPAN
—bearer	JAMPANEE, JAMPANI
self-government	SWARAJ(I)
sergeant	HAVILDAR
servant	MEHTAR, FERASH
—of rajah	CHOBDAR
sesame (oil)	GINGELLY, GINGILI
	JINJILI, TEEL (OIL), TIL (OIL)
settlement	BANDOBAST, BUNDOBUST
	BUSTEE
shawl	CHUDDAH, CHUDDAR
	ROMAL, RUMAL
ship	PATAMAR
shirt	K(H)URTA
shooting platform	MACHAN
shot (plant)	CANNA
show	TAMASHA
shrine	VIMANA
side dish	SAMBUL, SUMBOL
silk	CABECA, CABESSE, SURAH
—fabric	KINGCOB, TASH
small	
—brass or copper pot	LOTA(H)
—piece of meat	
for cooking	TIKKA
solar hat	TOPEE, TOPI
soldier	JAWAN, PEON, SEPOY
	SIKH, SIPAHI
sovereignty	RAJ
spinach	SAG
spinning wheel	CHARKHA
spirit of place	BONGA
spiritual	
—father	BAPU
—teacher	GOOROO, GURU
spoken language	BAT
spotted wild-cat	LEOPARD-CAT
staff officers	OMLAH
starling	MINA, MYNA(H)
state	PRADESH
states	ANDHRA PRADESH, BIHAR
	GUJARAT, HARYANA, HIMCHA
	JAMMU, KARNATAKA, KASHMIR
	KERALIA, MADHYA PRADESH
	MAHARASHTRA, NORTHERN AREAS
	ORISSA, PUNJAB, RAJASTHAN

	TAMIL NADU, UTTAR PRADESH
	WEST BENGAL
steel	WOOTZ
steep in oil	TARKKA
stew	CURRY, CURRIE, DHANSAK
stoppage	BAND(H), BUND, HARTAL
stork	ADJUTANT, ARGALA
strangler	THUG
sub-division	
—of district	TALUK
—officer	TALUKDAR
sugar	RAAB
sun-blind	CHI(C)K
supreme court	SUDDER
surf-boat	MASOOLAH, MASSOOLA
	MASULA
sweet dish	BARFI, GULAB JAM
	JALEBIS, JELLABIES
table servant	K(H)IDMUTGAR
	K(H)ITMUTGAR
tailor	DARZI
tamarind	ABLI
tannin extract	CATECHU
tax collector	AMILDAR, AUMIL
	ZAMINDAR, ZEMINDAR
Telugu-speaker	GENTOO
temple gate	VIMANA
—tower	GOPURA(M)
ten million	CRORE
tent	SHAMIANA(H)
thicket	SHOLA
thin cotton fabric	SEERSUCKER
throne	GADI
timber	(see separate entry)
tip	BA(C)KSHEESH, BA(C)KSHISH
	BUCKSHISH, DUSTOORY
title of respect	BAHADUR, HUZOOR
	MIAN, SAHIB, S(H)RI
toll station	CHOKRY
tongue disease	AGROM
torch	MUSSAL
tract of land	TALUK
traditional theatre	TAMASHA
travelling	
—box for clothes	PETARA
—dealer (grain or salt)	BRINJARRY
tree	AMLI, AMPAC, BANYAN
	BASTARD TEAK, BHEL, BO, BUTEA
	CHAMPAC, CHAMPAK, CHAULMOOGRA
	CHAULMUGRA, COTTON-TREE
	DAR, DHAK, DITA, HYDNOCARPUS
	ILLIPE, ILLUPI, IVORY-TREE
	JAMBOOL, JAMBU(L)
	JAMBOLAN(A), JAROOL, JARUL, KHAIR,
	KOKRA, MARGOSA, MELIA
	MYROBALAN, NEEM, NIEPA, NIM

	PALAY, POON, SA(U)L, SIRIS, SISSOO
	TEAK, TIKUL, TOON
—snake	DENDROPHIS
trellis	TATTA, TATTIE
triangular pastry case	
filled and fried	SAMOSA
tribe	JAT, TAMIL, TELUGU
trooper	SOWAR
tunic	K(H)URTA
turban	LUNGI, PAGRI
	PUGG(A)REE, PUGGERY
two-wheeled vehicle	TONGA
umbrella	CHATTA(H)
usher	CHOBDAR
viceroy	NAWAB
village	BUSTEE
—chieftain	POLIGAR
—council	PANCHAYAT
washerman	DHOBI(E)
watchman	CHOKY, CHO(W)KIDAR
water	
—carrier	BHEESTIE, BHEESTY
	BHISTI(E)
—course	NULLA(H)
—lift	JANTU
—lily	LOTE, LOTOS, LOTUS, PADMA
—pot	CHATTY
waybill	CHAL(L)AN
weapon	PATA
weights	
—180 grains	TOLA
—2lbs	SEER
—3lbs	VISHAM
—25-80lbs	MAUND
—20 maunds	CANDIE, CANDY, KANDY
whisky and soda	STENGAH, STINGER
widow's suicide	SATI, SUTTEE
wild	
—cat	CHAUS, CIVET
—dog	DHOLE
—elephants	HATHI
wise man	GURU, MAHATMA
	PANDIT, RISHI
woman's	
—garment	SAREE, SARI
—quarters	ZENANA
wood for flutes	KOKRA
woollen rug	RABJIK
worship	POOJA(H), PUJA
young prince	UPPER ROGER
zinc alloy	TUTENAG
	(see also **Hindu, Sikh**)

Indonesia

	RI
bay	TELUK
bread	ROTI
cape (headland)	TANJONG, UJUNG

capital	(D)JAKARTA	bark-beetles	SCOLYTUS
channel	SELAT	bedbug	CIMEX, CINCH
chicken	AJAM	bee-moth	WAX-MOTH
coin		bees	
—unit	SEN	—bumble	BOMBIDAE
—100 sen	RUPIAH	—hive	APIDAE
cooperation in work	ROJONG	—homeless	NOMADIDAE
curry	GULE	—humble	BOMBIDAE
estuary	MUARA	—leafcutter	MEGACHILIDAE
fish	IKAN	—mining	ADRENIDAE
—paste	BLACHAN, BLAKHAN	—potterflower	ANTHROPHORIDAE
fried noodles	BAMI(E) GORENG	beetle	BUPRESTIS, CHAFER
island	NUSA, PULAU		CLAVICORNIA, WEEVIL
kebab	SATAY, SATE	—with long antennae	LONGICORN
lake	DANAO	beetle	
lizard	KOMODO DRAGON	—ambrosia beetle	SCOLYTUS
measure (1½m)	PAAL	—rose beetle	CETONIA, ROSE CHAFER
meat	DAGING	—rove beetle	DEVIL'S COACH-HORSE
mixed cooked vegetables	GADO-GADO	—sacred (Egyptian)	SCARAB
mountain	GUNUNG	beetles	COLEOPTERA
—range	PEGUNUNGAN		LAMELLIFORMES
omelette	DADAR	—sub-orders	
ox	ANOA, SAPI-(O)UTAN	carnivorous	ADEPHAGA
rice	NASI	omnivorous	POLYPHAGA
—dishes	RIJSTAF(F)EL	—families	
river	KALI, SUNGAI	bark beetles	SCOLYTIDAE
sea	LAUT	blister beetles	MELOIDAE
strait	SELAT	burying beetles	SILPHIDAE
stream	AIR, CI	cardinal beetles	PYROCHROIDAE
village	KAMPUNG	carrion beetles	SILPHIDAE
witchdoctor	PAWANG	chafers	SCARABAEIDAE
wood	SAPUR	click beetles	ELATERIDAE
insects[1]	HEXAPODA, INSECTA	dung beetles	SCARABAEIDAE
including: mites		glow-worms	CANTHARIDAE
spiders		ladybirds	COCCINELLIDAE
types		leaf beetles	CHRYSOMELIDAE
ambrosia beetle	SCOLYTUS	longhorn beetles	CERAMBYCIDAE
ant	EMMET, PISMIRE	nocturnal beetles	TENEBRIONIDAE
ants	FORMICIDAE	oil beetles	MELOIDAE
—male	ANER	rove beetles	STAPHYLINIDAE
—male/worker	ERGATANDROMORPH	soldier beetles	CANTHARIDAE
—undeveloped female	ERGATE(S)	stag beetles	LUCANIDAE
—wingless	ERGATOMORPH	water scavengers	HYDROPHILIDAE
female	ERGATOGYNE	weevils	CURCULIONIDAE
male	ERGATANER	bird	
—worker	ERGATE(S)	—eating spider	AVICULARIA
aphis	GREENFLY, PLANT-LOUSE	—lice	MALLOPHAGA
	SMOTHER-FLY	biting	
apple pest	APPLE SAWFLY	—lice	MALLOPHAGA
	CODLIN(G)-MOTH	—midge	SAND-FLY
	RED SPIDER MITE	black	
	ROSY APPLE APHID	—aphis	DOLPHIN-FLY
	TORTRIX MOTH, WINTER MOTH	—beetle	COCKROACH
arachnids	SOLIFUGAE	—currant pest	BIG BUD MITE
Arctiidae	TIGER-MOTHS	blister-beetle	CANTHARID, SPANISH-FLY
Athalia	SAWFLY	blood-sucker	FLEA, LOUSE, TICK

blowfly	MEAT-FLY
Bombyx	SILKWORM
book	
—lice	CORRODENTIA, PSOCOPTERA
—scorpion	CHELIFER
boring flies	TRYPETA
bot-fly	BREESE, BREEZE, BRISE
	GAD-FLY, WARBLE-FLY
bristle-tail	THYSANURA
bumble-bee	HUMBLE-BEE
burnet-moth	ZYGAENA
burrowing	
—insect	DIGGER-WASP
	FEN-CRICKET, MOLE-CRICKET
	SAND-WASP
—mite	ITCH-MITE
burying-beetle	SEXTON(-BEETLE)
butterfly	(see separate entry)
cabbage pest	CABBAGE-APHID
	CABBAGE MOTH
	CABBAGE ROOT FLY
	TURNIP-FLEA
caddis-flies	TRICHOPTERA
caddis-fly	MAY-FLY, SEDGE-FLY
cantharid	BLISTER-BEETLE
	SPANISH-FLY
Carabidae	GROUND-BEETLES
carnivorous water-	
beetle	DYTI(S)CUS
carrot pest	CARROT FLY
caterpillar	CUT-WORM
cattle-fly	GAD-FLY, OX-WARBLE
centipede	THOUSAND-LEGS
centipedes	DIPLOPODA
—and millipedes	MYRIAPODA
cereal pest	HESSIAN FLY, WHEAT-FLY
	WHEAT-MIDGE, WHEAT-MOTH
Cetonia	ROSE-BEETLE, ROSE-CHAFER
cheese mite	TYROGLYPHID
cheese pest	CHEESE-HOPPER
	CHEESE-MITE
chigoe	JIGGER, SAND-FLEA
	SAND-HOPPER
cicada	TETTIX
Cicindelidae	TIGER-BEETLES
classification	
—class	INSECTA
—sub-classes	
wingless	AMETABOLA
	APTERYGOTA
winged forms	METABOLA
	PTERYGOTA
—divisions	
wings develop	
—externally	EXOPTERYGOTA
—internally	ENDOPTERYGOTA

—orders	
Apterygota	PROTURA
—bristletails	DIPLURA, THYSANURA
—springtails	COLLEMBOLA
Exopterygota	
—booklice	PSOCOPTERA
—bugs	HEMIPTERA
	RHYNCOTA
—cockroaches	ORTHOPTERA
—crickets	ORTHOPTERA
—demoiselle-flies	ODONATA
—dragonflies	ODONATA
—earwigs	DERMAPTERA
—grasshoppers	ORTHOPTERA
—lice	ANOPLURA
—mayflies	EPHEMEROPTERA
—stoneflies	PLECOPTERA
—thrips	THYSANOPTERA
Endopterygota	
—alderflies	NEUROPTERA
—ants	APOCRITA, HYMENOPETRA
—bees	HYMENOPTERA
—beetles	COLEOPTERA
—butterflies	LEPIDOPTERA
—caddis flies	TRICHOPTERA
—fleas	APHANIPTERA
	SIPHONAPTERA
—gall wasps	APOCRITA
	HYMENOPTERA
—horntails	HYMENOPTERA
	SYMPHYTA
—ichneumons	APOCRITA
	HYMENOPTERA
—lacewings	NEUROPTERA
—moths	LEPIDOPTERA
—sawflies	HYMENOPTERA
—scorpion-flies	MECOPTERA
—snakeflies	NEUROPTERA
—stylops	STREPSIPTERA
—termites	ISOPTERA
—thrips	THYSANOPTERA
—two-winged flies	DIPTERA
—wasps	APOCRITA
	HYMENOPTERA
—wood wasps	HYMENOPTERA
	SYMPHYTA
—white ants	ISOPTERA
click beetles	ELERATIDAE
clothes-moth	TINEA
Coccidae	WAX-BEETLES
cockchafer	BUZZARD-CLOCK
	MAY-BEETLE, MAY-BUG
coffee-tree pest	COFFEE-BUG
collector's name for	
some moths	MUSLIN, WAINSCOT
Collembola	SPRINGTAILS

crane-fly	(DADDY-)LONG-LEGS, TIPULA
—larva	LEATHER-JACKET
cricket	CICADA, CICALA
	GRASS-HOPPER, GRIG
cuckoo-fly	GOLD-WASP, RUBY-TAIL
Curculio	WEEVIL
cutworm-moth	DART-MOTH
daddy-long-legs	CRANE-FLY, TIPULA
death-watch beetle	ANOBIUM
destructive insect	LOCUST
devil's coach-horse	OCYPUS
	ROVE-BEETLE
dog-bee	DRONE
dor-beetle	DUNG-BEETLE
	SHARD-BEETLE
dragon-fly	DEMOISELLE, ODONATA
drone	DOG-BEE
Drosophila	FRUIT-FLY, POMACE-FLY
dung-beetle	COPROPHAGAN, SCARAB
earwig	FORFICULA
Egyptian scarab	SACRED BEETLE
Ephemera	DRAKE, MAY-FLY
flea	PULEX
fleas	SIPHONAPTERA
flesh-flies	SARCOPHAGA
flies	DIPTERA
—bat lice	NYCTERIBIDAE
—bee flies	BOMBYLIDAE
—bee lice	BRAULIDAE
—bluebottles	CALLIPHORIDAE
—blow-flies	CALLIPHORIDAE
—bot-flies	OESTRIDAE
—clegs	TABANIDAE
—crane-flies	TULIPIDAE
—Daddy-long-legs	TULIPIDAE
—forest flies	HIPPOBOSCIDAE
—fungus gnats	MYCETOPHILIDAE
—gad flies	TABANIDAE
—gall midges	CECIDOMYIDAE
—gnats	CULICIDAE
—green-bottles	CALLIPHORIDAE
—horse flies	ABANIDAE
—house flies	MUSCIDAE
—hover-flies	SYRPHIDAE
—midges	CHIRONOMIDAE
—mosquitoes	CULICIDAE
—parasitic flies	LARVAEVORIDAE
	TACHINIDAE
—robber flies	ASILIDAE
—sheep keds	HIPPOBOSCIDAE
—soldier flies	STRATIOMYIDAE
—stable flies	MUSCIDAE
—thick-headed flies	CONOPIDAE
—warble-flies	OESTRIDAE
flour mite	TYROGLYPHID
flying beetle	COCKCHAFER

forest	
—ant	WOOD-ANT
—fly	HORSEFLY
frog-hopper	FROTH-FLY
	FROTH-HOPPER
froth-fly	FROG-HOPPER
fruit pest	DROSOPHILA, POMACE-FLY
	RASPBERRY BEETLE
	RED SPIDER MITE
	VINEGAR-FLY
Fulgoridae	LANTERN-FLIES
gadfly	BREEZE, BREESE
	BRISE, TABANUS
gall	
—fly	RHODITES
—midge	CECIDOMYA
—wasp	CYNIPS
gallinipper	MOSQUITO
garden-spider	ARANEA, EPEIRA
Glossina	TSETSE
gnat	CULEX
gold-wasp	CUCKOO-FLY, RUBY-TAIL
golden-eye	LACE-WING
gooseberry moth	MAGPIE MOTH
gout fly	CORN FLY
grain pest	CORN-THRIP, CORN-WEEVIL
	CORN-WORM
grass-moth	VENEER-MOTH
grasshopper	CRICKET, CICADA
	CICALA, GRIG
greenfly	APHIS, PLANT-LOUSE
ground beetle	CARABUS
harvestmen	OPILIONES, PHALANGIDAE
hawk-moth	DEATH'S-HEAD MOTH, HAWK
	SPHINX
hive-bee	HONEY-BEE
hop pest	HOP-FLEA, HOP-FLY
horse-fly	FOREST-FLY
horse-pest	BOT-FLY, FOREST-FLY
	HORSE-FLY, WARBLE-FLY
hothouse pest	MEALY-BUG
house-fly	MUSCA
hunting-spider	LYCOSA
imagined to live in fire	PYRALIS
insect-eating fly	ROBBER-FLY
itch mites	SARCOPTES
Ixodidae	WOOD-TICKS
jigger	CHIGOE, SAND-FLEA
	SAND-HOPPER
jumping spiders	SALTIGRADE
ladybird	LADYBUG, LADYCOW
	LADYFLY, VEDDA
large	
—beetle	RHINOCEROS-BEETLE
—centipede	SCOLOPENDRA
—moths	SATURNIA, THRIPS

leaf pest	LEAF-HOPPER, RED SPIDER
leaf-insect	PHASMID, SPECTRE
	WALKING-LEAF
Lepisma	SILVER-FISH, SPRINGTAIL
library pest	BOOK SCORPION
like leaves	LEAF-INSECT
long-legged spider	HARVESTER
longicorn beetle	LONGHORN
lowest order	AMETABOLA
Lucilia	GREENBOTTLE
Lycosa	HUNTING-SPIDERS
	TARANTULA
	WOLF_SPIDER
Lymantriidae	TUSSOCK-MOTHS
magpie moth	GOOSEBERRY-MOTH
male	
—ant	ANER
—honey-bee	DRONE
may-flies	PLECTOPTERA
mayfly	GREEN-DRAKE, SEDGE-FLY
meal-worm	TENEBRIO
Mecoptera	SCORPION-FLY
Meloe	OIL-BEETLE
metallic-coloured	
—fly	BLUEBOTTLE
	GREENBOTTLE
—wasp	GOLD-WASP
midge	CHIRONOMID
millipede	PILL-WORM
	THOUSAND-LEGS
—millipedes	HILPODA
mite(s)	ACARID, ACARIDA(E)
	ACARUS(ACARI), (ACARINA)
	TYROGLYPHID
money-spider	MONEY-SPINNER
mosquito	AEDES, ANOPHELES
	STEGOMYIA
—America	GALLINIPPER
moth-like midge	SAND-FLY
moths	(*see separate entry*)
Ocypus	DEVIL'S COACH-HORSE
oil-beetle	MELOE
Oniscus	WOODLICE
owlet-moths	NOCTUID(AE)
parasitic insect	ICHNEUMON(-FLY)
	MALLOPHAGA
—on others	STREPSIPTERA
pear pest	CODLIN(G) MOTH
	PEAR SUCKER
	PEAR BEDSTRAW APHID
	TORTRIX MOTH
Perla	STONE-FLY
phalangid	HARVESTMAN
phasmid	LEAF-INSECT, STICK-INSECT
	SPECTRE
pill-bugs	ISOPODA

pine-beetle	PINE-CHAFER
plant pest	APHIS, CAPSID(-BUG)
	DOLPHIN-FLY, GALL-MIDGE
	GALL-WASP, GREENFLY
	LEAF-HOPPER
Podura	MYRIENTOMATA
potato pest	CLICK BEETLE
	COLORADO-BEETLE
	PEACH POTATO APHID
	WIREWORM
praying mantis	HOTTENTOT'S GOD
pubic louse	CRAB-LOUSE
Pulex	FLEA
puss-moth	SALLOW-KITTEN
rat pest	RAT-FLEA
red moth	CINNABAR
Rhaphidia	SNAKE-FLY
Rhopalocera	BUTTERFLIES
riverside insect	ALDER-FLY
rose	
—beetle	CETONIA, ROSE-CHAFER
—chafer	CETONIA, ROSE-BEETLE
—pest	RHODITES
rove-beetle	DEVIL'S COACH-HORSE
ruby	
—tail	CUCKOO-FLY, GOLD-WASP
—wasp	GOLD-WASP
sacred beetle	(EGYPTIAN) SCARAB
sand	
—flea	CHIGOE, JIGGER
	SAND-HOPPER, SAND-SKIPPER
—wasp	BEMBEX
sawfly	ATHALIA
scarab	DUNG-BEETLE
	SACRED BEETLE
Scolytus	AMBROSIA BEETLES
	BARK-BEETLES
scorpion	
—flies	MECOPTERA
—spider	WHIP-SCORPION
sea-spider	PYCNOGONID
sedge-fly	CADDIS FLY, MAYFLY
shard-beetle	DOR-BEETLE
sheep pest	SHEEP-LOUSE, SHEEP-KED
	SHEEP-TICK
short-lived insect	DRAGON-FLY
	EPHEMERA, MAY-FLY
silkworm	BOMBYX
silver-fish	LEPISMA, SPRINGTAIL
Sirex	WOOD-WASP
skipjack beetle	ELATER
skipper butterfly	HESPERID
small	
—fly	GNAT, SCIARID
—gnat	GNATLING
—gnat-like fly	MIDGE

—male ant	MICRANER
—puss-moth	KITTEN-MOTH
—spider	MONEY-SPIDER
smother-fly	APHIS
snake-fly	RAPHIDIA
snow-flea	SPRINGTAIL
soldier ant	WHITE ANT
Solifugae	ARACHNIDS
sow-bug	WOOD-LOUSE
Spanish-beetle	BLISTER-BEETLE
	CANTHARID
spectre	LEAF-INSECT, PHASMID
	STICK-INSECT
	WALKING-LEAF
	WALKING-STICK
	WALKING-STRAW
Sphinx	HAWK-MOTH
spider	ARACHNID, ARANEID
	EPEIRA
springtail	SILVER-FISH, SNOW-FLEA
—springtails	COLLEMBOLA, LEPISMA
	PODURA
stick-insect	LEAF-INSECT, PHASMID
	SPECTRE, WALKING-LEAF
	WALKING-STICK
	WALKING-STRAW
stinging insect	BEE, HORSE-FLY
	MOSQUITO, WASP
stone-fly	PERLA, PLECOPTERA
Stratiotes	WATER-SOLDIER
Strepsiptera	RHIPODOPTERA
	RHIPIPTERA
sugar pest	SUGAR-MITE
swallow-tailed butterfly	PAPILIO
Syrphus	HOVER-FLY
Tabanus	GAD-FLY
tarantula	HUNTING-SPIDER, LYCOSA
	WOLF-SPIDER
Tenebrio	MEAL-WORM
termite	WHITE ANT, WOOD-ANT
tettix	CICADA
Thrips	LEAF-HOPPER
Thysanura	BRISTLE-TAILS
tick	ACARID, ACARUS
	SHEEP-KED
tiger	
—beetles	CICINDELIDAE
—moths	ARCTIIDAE
tinea	CLOTHES-MOTH
Tipula	CRANE-FLY
	DADDY-LONG-LEGS
Tortrix	MOTH
tree pest	PINE-BEETLE, PINE-CHAFER
Tricoptera	CADDIS-FLIES
Troglyphid	CHEESE MITE, FLOUR MITE

Trombidium	HARVEST-BUG
	HARVEST-LOUSE
	HARVEST-MITE, HARVEST-TICK
Trypeta	BORING FLIES
tsetse flies	GLOSSINA
turnip pest	CUTWORM, TURNIP-FLEA
	TURNIP-FLY
tussock-moth	GYPSY MOTH, NUN
—tussock-moths	LYMANTRIIDAE
two-winged	DIPTERAN
Tyroglyphid	CHEESE MITE, FLOUR MITE
undergoing metamorphosis	METABOLA
various insects	SAW-FLY
vegetable pest	WHITE-FLY
veneer-moth	GRASS-MOTH
venomous spider	SOLPUGA
very small insect	MITE
Vespa	WASP
vine pest	GRAPE-LOUSE
	VINE-FRETTER
	PHYLLOXERA
vinegar-fly	FRUIT-FLY
warble fly	BOTFLY
wasp	SPHEX, VESPA
—digger	SPHECIDAE
—gall	CYNIPDAE
—ichneumon	BRACONIDAE
—mason	EUMENIDAE
—potter	EUMENIDAE
—solitary	EUMENIDAE
—spider	POMPILIDAE
wasps	VESPIDAE
wasp-like flies	SYRPHUS
water	
—beetle	GYRINUS, WHIRLIGIG
—boatman	NOTONECTA
—fleas	CLADOCERA
—insect	WATER-BEETLE
	WATER-BOATMAN
	WATER-BUG, WATER-FLEA
	WATER-FLY, WATER-STRIDER
—skaters	GYMNOCERATA
—soldier	STRATIOTES
wax	
—insects	COCCIDAE
—moth	BEE-MOTH
weevil	CURCULIO
wheat-pest	GOUTFLY
whip-scorpion	SCORPION-SPIDER
whirligig	GYRINUS, WATER-BEETLE
white	
—ant	SOLDIER, TERMITE
—moth	GHOST-MOTH
wingless	AMETABOLA, APTERYGOTA
—male ant	ERGATANER
—parasite	LOUSE

wolf-spider	LYCOSA, TARANTULA
wood	
—ant	TERMITE
—beetle	WOOD-ENGRAVER
—boring insect	DEATH-WATCH BEETLE
	FURNITURE BEETLE
	SIREX, WOOD-WASP
—eating insect	CARPENTER-BEE
—engraver	BEETLE
—lice	ONISCUS
—louse	MILLIPED(E)
	PILL-BUG, SOW-BUG
—ticks	IXODIDAE
—wasp	SIREX
worker ant	ERGATE(S)
yellow-fever fly	STEGOMYIA
Zygaena	BURNET-MOTH

insects[2]

including: terms	
air tube(s)	TRACHEA(E)
appendage on antenna	ARISTA
back-plate	TERGUM
—of rear section	PYGIDIUM
breathing hole(s)	SPIRACLE(S)
	STIGMA(TA)
edge of wing	COSTA
eyes	COMPOUND, SIMPLE
—simple eye(s)	OCELLUS (OCELLI)
feeler(s) on	
—head	ANTENNA(E)
—mouth	PALP, PALPUS (PALPI)
—rear	CERCUS (CERCI)
forewing(s)	TEGMEN (TEGMINA)
having larvae with biting	
jaws	METAGNATHOUS
insect-eater	INSECTIVORE
insecticides	CARBENDAZIM, DDT
	FENARIMOL, MALATHION
	PEMETHRIN
moult of larva	ECDYSIS
outer shell	EXOSKELETON
piercing instrument	STILET, STYLET
rear wings (rudimentary)	HALTERES
scale on wing	TEGULA
segment of	
—abdomen	VRITE
—body	ABDOMEN, HEAD, THORAX
—leg	COXA, TROCHANTER
—thorax	
front	PROTHORAX
middle	MESOTHORAX
rear	METATHORAX
sidewall of thorax	PLEURON
sound made by rubbing	STRIDULATION
stage	
—adult(s)	IMAGO (IMAGINES)

—between moults	INSTAR
—change	ECDYSIS
—early	CATERPILLAR, GENTLE
	GRUB, LARVA, MAGGOT
—immature adult	NYMPH
—passive	CHRYSALIS, PUPA
sucking proboscis	HAUSTELLUM
upper lip(s)	LABRUM(LABRA)
wax-producing tube	CORNICLE
	CORNICULUM
wingcase(s)	ELYTRUM(ELYTRA)

institute/institution

of:	
Actuaries	IA
Advanced Motorists	IAM
Bankers	IB
Building	IOB
Civil Engineers	ICE
Contemporary Artists	ICA
Journalists	IOJ
Linguists	IL
Mining and Metallurgy	IMM
Municipal Engineers	IMUNE
Physics	IP
Practitioners in Advertising	IPA

instrument	(*see* **instrument of torture,**
	measuring instrument,
	musical instrument)

instrument of torture

beating soles of feet	BASTINADE
	BASTINADO
body	
—crushing machine	
	SCAVENGER'S DAUGHTER
	SKEFFINGTON'S DAUGHTER
	SKEVINGTON'S DAUGHTER
—stretching machine	RACK
cucking-stool	TUMBREL, TUMBRIL
dropping from height tied	
to rope	STRAPPADO
finger-crushing instrument	PILLIWINKS
flogging	CAT-O'-NINE-TAILS
frame for	
—flogging	TRIANGLE
—head and hands	PILLORY
—head, hands and legs	STOCKS
iron	
—'coffin' with spikes	
internally	IRON MAIDEN
—ring round neck	JOUGS
pillory	TUMBREL, TUMBREL
—Scottish	JOUGS
stocks	CIPPUS
stool on which	
—scolds were tied	
and pelted	CUCKING-STOOL

—offenders were ducked in pond	DUCKING-STOOL
thumb-crushing instrument	THUMB-SCREW
torturing feet	SARPINES
yoke	DEVIL-ON-THE-NECK

international

bank	BIS
Development Association	IDA
Electrotechnical Commission	IEC
Finance Corporation	IFC
honour	CAP
Labour Organisation	ILO
Monetary Fund	IMF
Olympic Committee	IOC
organisation	UNO
Organisation for Standardisation	ISO
Phonetic Alphabet	IPA
Publishers' Association	IPA
Publishing Corporation	IPC
Rail Transport	TIF
Road Transport	TIR
Social Services	ISS
subscriber dialling	ISD
Telecommunications Union	ITU
Trade Organisation	ITO
unit	IU
Vehicle Registration	IVR

inventors

inventor of:

achromatic microscope	LISTER
actuarial tables	HALLEY
adding machine	PASCAL, SCHICKARD
aeroplane	WRIGHT
air-conditioning unit	CARRIER
airship	ZEPPELIN
—non-rigid	GIFFARD
alphabet for blind	BRAILLE
amplitude modulation	FESSENDEN
amusette	SAXE
anastigmatic lens	AIRY
antiseptic surgery	LISTER
artificial heart	JARVIK
artificial languages	
—Esperanto	ZAMENHOF
—Interglossa	HOGBEN
—Neo	ALFANDARI
—Novial	JESPERSON
—Volapük	SCHLEYER
bakelite	BAEKELAND
ball-point pen	BIRO, LOUD
bandore	ROSE
barbed wire	SMITH
barometer	TORRICELLI
bath glaze	BUICK
bathyscaphe	PICCARD

bathysphere	BEEBE
bicycle	MACMILLAN
—small-wheeled	MOULTON
bifocal lens	FRANKLIN
binary system	LIEBNITZ
blast furnace	BESSEMER
blind language	BRAILLE
bubble chamber	GLASER
bunsen burner	BUNSEN
burglar alarm	HOLMES
cable-suspended bridge	SEGUIN
calculating machine	LIEBNITZ
calculus	NEWTON
camera	
—folding	EASTMAN
—Leica	BERNAK
—pinhole	DELLA PORTA
—Polaroid	LAND
—roll-film	EASTMAN
—single-lens reflex	SUTTON
—twin-lens reflex	BECK
car	BENZ
carbon dating	LIBBY
carburettor	DAIMLER
carpet sweeper	BISSELL
cash register	RITTY, PARMALEE
cellophane	BRANDENBERGER
celluloid	HYATT, PARKES
cherista(k) (pelota)	CURUCHAGE DITHURBIDE
Christmas cracker	SMITH
chronometer	HARRISON
cinema	LUMIERE
Cinemascope	CHRETIEN
clinical thermometer	ALLBUTT
clock - pendulum	HUYGENS
Coca-Cola	PEMBERTON
collapsible boat	BERTHON
colour photography	LIPPMANN
compass	GIOIA
computer	ECKERT, MAUCHLY TURING
—language (Forth)	MOORE
computing machine	BABBAGE
concrete music	SCHAEFFER
cordite	ABEL, DEWAR
cotton gin	WHITNEY
cryostat	COLLINS
cybernetics	WIENER
cyclotron	LAWRENCE
dental plate (rubber)	GOODYEAR
dentures	PLANTSON
diesel engine	DIESEL
diffusion cloud chamber	LANGSDORF
diode valve	FLEMING
disc brakes	LANCHESTER

diving suit	SIEBE
double sleeve-valve engine	KNIGHT
dry photographic plates	EASTMAN
dynamite	NOBEL
dynamo	FARADAY, PIXII
electric	
—battery	TORRICELLI, VOLTA
—iron	SEELEY
—lamp	EDISON, SWAN
—motor	GRAMME, HENRY, TESLA
—razor	SCHICK
—telegraph	HENRY, MORSE
—welder	THOMSON
electrocardiograph	EINTHOVEN
electromagnet	STURGEON
electron microscope	KNOLL, RUSKA
electrophoresis	TISELIUS
electrostatic generator	VAN DE GRAAF
embossed letters for the blind	BRAILLE, MOON
Esperanto	ZAMENHOF
field ion microscope	MUELLER
film	
—moving	LE PRINCE
—musical	DE FOREST
—negative	FOX TALBOT
—talking	ENGL, MUSSOLLE, VOGT
folding bed	MURPHY
food processor	VERDUN
fountain pen	WATERMAN
four-stroke engine	OTTO
fuel cell	GROVE
Gaia hypothesis	LOVELOCK
galvanometer	AMPERE, SCHWEIGGER
game of life	CONWAY
gas lighting	MURDOCK
Glossic alphabet	ELLIS
governor	WATT
gramophone	EDISON
—disc	BERLINER
long-playing	GOLDMARK
guncotton	SCHONBEIN
gyroscope	FOUCAULT
gyroscopic compass	SPERRY
helicopter	OEHMICHEN
	SIKORSKY
hot-air balloon	MONTGOLFIER
hovercraft	COCKERELL
hydraulic lift	OTIS
iconoscope	ZWORYKIN
inflatable tyre	THOMSON
inoculation	PASTEUR
intelligence tests	BINET, SIMON
interferometer	MICHELSON
Interglossa	HOGBEN
internal combustion engine	LENOIR
invar	GUILLAUME

iris chart	JENSEN
italic type	MANUTIUS
jet engine	WHITTLE
katathermometer	HILL
laser	MAIMAN, TOWNES
—card	DREXLER
launderette	CANTRELL
lead/acid battery	PLANTE
Lego	CHRISTIANSEN
Leyden jar	VON KLEIST
lie detector	KEELER, LARSEN
lifeboat	GREATHEAD
	WOULDHAVE
light field gun	SAXE
lightning conductor	FRANKLIN
linoleum	WALTON
locomotive	TREVITHICK
logarithms	NAPIER
long-playing record	BACHMAN, GOLDMARK
loom	CARTWRIGHT
loudspeaker	SHORT
machine-gun	GATLING, PUCKLE
man-carrying glider	CAYLEY
map of magnetic	
declination	NORMAN
margarine	MEGE-MOURIES
mass	
—production	WHITNEY
—spectrograph	ASTON
matches	WALKER
method acting	STANISLAVSKI
microchip	KILBY, NOYCE
microphone	BELL
microscope	GALILEO, JANSSEN
	LEUUWENHOEK
miner's lamp	DAVY, STEPHENSON
minnonette (volleyball)	MORGAN
mobiles	CALDER
motion pictures	LE PRINCE
motor-cycle	DAIMLER
movable type	GUTENBERG
moving film equipment	EDISON
Neo	ALFANDARI
neon lamp	CLAUDE
nitro	
—cellulose	SCHONBEIN
—glycerine	SOBRERO
Novial	JESPERSON
nylon	CAROTHERS
open-hearth steel	SIEMENS
Oxford bags	ACTON
paper	CAI LUN, TS'AI LUN
—clip	VAALER
parachute	BLANCHARD, LENORMAND
parking meter	MAGEE
particle counter	GEIGER

pasteurisation	PASTEUR
pendulum clock	HUYG(H)ENS
perforated card control	
of machines	JACQUARD
period/luminosity curve	
for Cepheid variables	LEAVITT
periodic table	MENDELEEV
phonograph	EDISON
photography	
—calotype	FOX TAKBOT
—dry plate process	MADDOX
—on	
film	CARBUTT
metal	NIEPCE
paper	FOX TALBOT
—wet plate process	ARCHER
—with strobe lights	EDGERTON
pig-iron boiling process	HALL
pinhole camera	DELLA PORTA
plastic film	EASTMAN
plastics	PARKS
pneumatic tyres	DUNLOP
Polaroid camera	LAND
polygraph	KEELER, LARSEN
Portland cement	ASPDIN
pressure cooker	PAPIN
printing	
—machine (rotary)	HOE
—press	GENSFLEISCH
	GUTENBERG
propellor (ship)	SMITH
radar	TAYLOR, WATSON-WATT
	YOUNG
radio	MARCONI
—astronomy	JANSKY
—telegraphy	LOOMIS
transatlantic	MARCONI
rayon	CHARDONNET, SWAN
razor	
—electric	SCHICK
—safety	GILLETTE
refrigerator	HARRISON, TWINING
revolver	COLT
rifling	BESSEMER
roller skating	MERLIN, PLIMPTON
rubber tyres	HANCOCK
rubberised cloth	MACINTOSH
Rubik's cube	RUBIK
safety	
—lamp	DAVY, STEPHENSON
—pin	HUNT
—razor	GILLETTE
sailboard	CHILVERS
saxophone	SAX
Scotch tape	DREW
seismograph	PALMIERI

self-starter	KETTERING
servo-mechanism	FARCOT
sewing-machine	THIMMONNIER
silicon chip	KIRBY
skyscraper	JENNY
slide rule	OUGHTRED
smear test	PAPANICOLAOU
snooker	CHAMBERLAIN
softball	HANCOCK
sousaphone	SOUSA
spark chamber	FUKUI, MIYAMOTO
spectrohelioscope	HALE
spectroscope	BUNSEN, KIRCHHOFF
sphygmo(mano)meter	RIVA-ROCCI
spinning	
—frame	ARKWRIGHT
—jenny	HARGREAVES
—mule	CROMPTON
staining bacteria	GRAM
stainless steel	BREARLEY
standardisation of wine	GALL
steam	
—boat	FITCH
—car	CUGNOT
—engine	SAVERY
low-pressure	NEWCOMEN, WATT
—hammer	NASMYTH
—horseless carriage	MURDOCK
—locomotive	STEPHENSON
—ship	PERRIER
—turbine	PARSONS
steel process	BESSEMER
stethoscope	LAENNAC
strobe photography	EDGERTON
submarine	BUSHNELL
superheterodyne receiver	ARMSTRONG
tank	SWINTON
tape recording	POULSEN
telegraph	LAMMOND
—code	MORSE
telephone	BELL, MEUCCI
telescope	
—reflecting	GREGORY
—refracting	LIPPERSHEIM
	LIPPERSHEY
television	
—electronic	FARNSWORTH
—mechanical	BAIRD
television camera	ZWORYKIN
temporary bridge	BAILEY
Terylene	DICKSON, WINFIELD
test for diphtheria	SCHICK
thermometer	GALILEO
thermostat	DREBBLE
torsion balance	COULOMB, MICHELL
transformer	FARADAY

transistor	BARDEEN, BRATTEN	boat	CURRACH, CURRAGH
	SHOCKLEY	booth	BOTHAN
triode valve	DE FOREST	boy	GORSOON, GOSSOON
turbine	PARSONS		SPALPEEN
tutania	TUTIN	bridge	FORD, WATERSPLASH
typewriter	TARRI	brownie	LEPRECHAUN, LEPRECHAWN
ultra-centrifuge	SVEDBERG	bustling person	STIR-ABOUT
vaccination	JENNER	cajoling talk	BLARNEY
vacuum		capital	DUBLIN
—cleaner	SPANGLER	carriage	BIANCONI, GINGLE
—flask	DEWAR		JAUNTING-CAR, JAUNTY
Velcro	MESTRAL	Celtic noble	TAOISE(A)CH
viscose	CROSS	chief's heir elect	TANIST
Volapük	SCHLEYER	clan	SEPT
volleyball	MORGAN	clay pipe	DUDEEN
voltage multiplier	COCKCROFT, WALTON	clotted milk	BONNY-CLABBER
vulcanising	GOODYEAR	close-fitting breeches	TROUSE
watch	MANFREDI	club	SHILLALY
water			SHILLELA(G)H
—closet	HARINGTON	coins	
—skiing	SAMUELSON	—counterfeit halfpenny	RAP
waterproof fabric	MACINTOSH	—old halfpenny	PATRICK
wax cylinder	TAINTER	—pound	PUNT
wireless telegraphy	MARCONI	compulsory billeting	COSHERY, SOREHON
Xerography	CARSON	corn	OATS
zip fastener	JUDSON	counterfeit coin	RAP
	(see also **discoveries, first**)	creature	CRATUR
Iran	IR	cudgel	SHILLALY, SHILLELAGH
	(see also **Persia**)	currant bun	BARMBRACK
Iraq	IRQ	dance	FADING, PLANXTY
capital	BAGHDAD		RINKAFADDA
coin		Danish settlers	OSTMEN
—unit	FIL	darling	ACUSHLA, ASTHORE
—50 fils	DIRHAM		MAVOURNEEN
—4 dirhams	RIYAI	death omen	BANSHEE
—5 riyals	DINAR	deer (extinct)	IRISH ELK
Ireland	EIRE, ERIN, EMERALD ISLE	deputy Prime Minister	TANAISTE
	GREEN ISLE, IR, IR(E)L	devotee	VOTEEN
accent	BROGUE	dirge	CORONACH
active person	STIR-ABOUT	dish	CHAMP, COLCANNON
again	AGIN	district where the	
agrarian rebel		English had power	ENGLISH PALE
—18th c	WHITEBOY	division of	
—19th c	MOONLIGHTER	—county	BARONY
alphabet	OG(H)AM	—tribe	SEPT
ancient		doctor	OLLAM(H), OLLAV
—assembly(-blies)	FEIS(EANNA)	driver of carriage	JARVEY
—people	TUATH	drunk	STOTIOUS
—soldier	FIANN	Dublin Society	RDS
	GALLO(W)GLASS	dynasty	O'NEILL
—territorial division	TUATH	elf	LEPRECHAUN
anti-British association	FENIAN		LEPRECHAWN
basket	SKEOUGH	Elysium	TIR NAN-OG
black magic	PISHOGLE	emblem	SHAMROCK
blandish	SOOTHE	evening of song and story	CEILIDH
blood-fine	EIRIACH, ERIC	expression of emotion	ARRAH

fairy	BANSHEE, BENSHI
favourite	WHITE-HEADED BOY
female fairy	BANSHEE
festival	FEIS(EANNA)
field	PARK
flatter	SOOTHE
flattery	BLARNEY
flowers	SHAMROCK
fool	OMADHAUN
foot soldier	KERN(E)
fort	RATH
fortified island	CRANNOG
free accommodation	
of lord by tenant	SORREN
Free State	IFS
funeral dirge	CORONACH
Gael	GADHEL, GOIDEL
Gaelic	ERSE
game	HURLEY, HURLING, SHINTY
genealogist	SE(A)NNACHIE, SEANNACHY
	SHANACHIE
gentleman without money	STALKO
girl	COLLEEN
good	
—fellow	BROTH OF A BOY
—health!	SLAINTE
guard(s)	GARDA(I)
head	
—king	ARDRI(GH)
—of family	CO(M)ARB
heath	ST DABEOC'S HEATH
hero	NAOISE
hockey	HURLEY, HURLING
house	DAIL
hut	BOTHAN
ill luck	BAD CESS
illegal drinking-den	BOTHAN
illicit	
—liquor-shop	SHEBEEN
—whiskey	POT(H)EEN
indeed	AROO, ARU
injure seriously	KILL
interjection of	
—lament	O(C)HONE
—surprise	MUSHA
invite a quarrel	TRAIL ONE'S COAT
Ireland forever	ERIN GO BRAGH
Irishman	BOG-TROTTER, GREEK
	MICK(E)Y, PADDY, PAT
Irish-speaking area	GAELTACHT
Jacobites who migrated	
to the Continent	WILD-GEESE
jaunting-car	INSIDE-CAR
	OUTSIDE-CAR
—driver	JARVEY
jocose	JOCOROUS
judge	BREHON
killed	KILT
labourer newly arrived	
in England	GRECIAN
lake	LOUGH
—dwelling	CRANNOG
land	
—of the young	TIR NAN-OG
—reform association	LAND LEAGUE
language	CELTIC, ERSE
	GAELIC, KELTIC
lament	ULLALOO
lane	BOREEN
legislature	OIREACHTAS
limestone	CALP
madman	OMADHAUN
master	OLLAM(H), OLLAV
measures	
—2 feet	BANDLE
—2240 feet	MILE
—7840 sq. yd (old)	ACRE
member of	
—Dail	TD, TEACHTA (DALA)
—peasant's	
association	WHITEBOY
Methodist	SWADDLER
mischievous fellow	SPALPEEN
mocking ballad	LILLIBULLERO
moderate party	FINE GAEL
money-lender	GOMBEEN-MAN
mud	CLABBER
my	
—child	ALANNAH
—dear	MACHREE, MOCHREE
—love	MACHREE, MOCHREE
national emblem	SHAMROCK
never	SORRA
nickname	PAT, TEAGUE
no!	SORRA
not	SORRA
oath	BEDAD, BEGORRA(H)
	BEJABERS
old	
—laws	BREHON LAWS
—mayor	SOVRAN
—Protestants	PEEP-O'-DAY BOYS
outlaw	WOODKERN
parliament	
—lower house	DAIL (EIREANN)
—upper house	SEANAD (EIREANN)
penniless gentleman	BUCKEEN
people	TUATH
pet	WHITE-HEADED BOY
petty squire	SQUIREEN
plunderer	RAPPAREE
police	GARDA(I), RIC, RUC

—force	GARDA SIOCHANA
—man	GARDA
—men	GARDAI
political movement	SINN FEIN
politician	TD, TEACHTA (DALA)
pond dry in summer	TURLOUGH
poor Southerner	BUCKEEN
porridge	STIR-ABOUT
potato	MURPHY, PRATIE, PRATY
prehistoric fort	RATH
Prime Minister	TAOISEACH
Protestant	SWADDLER
rascal	SPALPEEN
rebel	CROPPY
region where Gaelic is spoken	GAELTACHT
Republican	
—Army	IRA
—Brotherhood	IRB
—Party	FIANNA FAIL
Republicans	SINN FEIN
river	LIFFEY, SHANNON
road	TOBY
robber	RAPPAREE, TORY
robbery on the road	TOBY
salt marsh	CORCASS
script	OG(H)AMIC, OGMIC
secret jargon	SHELTA
shale bed	CALP
shield of wickerwork	SKIATH
shinty	CAMANACHD
—stick	CAMAN
short clay pipe	DUDEEN
social gathering	CEILIDH
sod	SCRAW
sorcery	PISHOGUE
sorrow	SORRA
stew	COLCANNON
stream	STREEL
stringed instrument	TYMPAN
sublet	CO(R)NACRE
sub-tenant	WELDER
sweetheart	GRA
system of succession	TANISTRY
television service	RADIO TELEFIS EIREANN
	RTE
tenant	COTTIER
tenure	SOREHON, TANISTRY
term of abuse	SORRA
—to woman	STRAP
terrorists	IRA
tinker's jargon	SHELTA
trail	STREEL
transmitter of	
family lore	SE(A)NNACHIE, SEANNACHY
	SHANACHIE
transport organisation	CIE

tribal law	CINEL
Trinity College	TCD
trout	GILLAROO
turf	SCRAW
United Ireland	FINE GAEL
upper house	SEANAD
usurper	GOMBEEN-MAN
usury	GOMBEEN
vagrant's jargon	SHELTA
verse	RANN
wander	STREEL
water-plant	PIPEWORT
whiskey	POT(H)EEN, THE CRATUR
	USQUEBAUGH
witchcraft	PISHOGLE
young lad	BUCKO
Islam	(*see* **Moslem**)
Isle of Man	GBM, IOM
Isle of Wight	IOW, IW
Israel	
capital	JERUSALEM, YERUSHALAYIM
coin	
—unit	AGORA
—100 agorot	SHEKEL
	(*see also* **Hebrew**)
Italy	I
à la carte	AL CONTO
again	ANCORA
almond cakes	AMARETTI
anchovies	ALICI
ancient	ANTICO
—language	LATIN, OSCAN
	SAMNITE, UMBRIAN
—people	ACQUI, ETRUSCANS
	HERNICI, LATINS, OSCAN
	SABINES, SAMNITE, VOLSCI
applause	VIVA
approval	SI
aptly invented	BEN TROVATO
armed policeman	CARABINIERE
articles	IL, LA, LE, LO, UNA, UNO
artist's studio	BOTTEGA
aside	SOTTO VOCE
at	
—first sight	A PRIMA VISTA
—most	AL PIU
—pleasure	A PIACERE
bagpipes	PIFFERO, ZAMPOGNA
bakery	PANIFICIO
balcony	TERRAZZO
ball	PALLA
—game	PALLONE
barge	BARCA
bas relief	BASSO-RILIEVO
bay	GOLFO
bean purée	MACCO

beaten	BATTUTA	congenial	SIMPATICO
beef	MANZO	connoisseur	COGNOSCENTO
—casserole	STUFATO	contour	CONTORNA
beggar	BESOGNIO, LAZZARONE	contract	APPALTO
bird	BECCAFICO	council meeting	CONSULTA
biscuits	AMARETTI	councillors	ANZIANI
black	NERO	country retirement	VILLEGGIATURA
—pudding	SANGUINACCIO	courage!	CORAGGIO
boat	BARCA, GONDOLA	courgette	ZUCCHINI
—song	BARCAROLA	course	CORSO
borough	BORGO	criminal society	COSA NOSTRA, MAF(F)IA
boys	RAGAZZI	cup	TAZZA
bound	LEGATO	cured goat's meat	VIOLINI
brazier	SCALDINO	dance	BERGAMASK, BERGOMASK
bread	PANE		RIGOLETTO, TARANTELLA
—rolls	PANINAROS		VOLTA
brother	FRA(TELLO)	dancing party	RIDOTTO
burial ground	CAMPO SANTO	dash	BRAVURA
butter	BURRO	dear	CARA, CARO
by		device	IMPRESA
—fits and starts	A SALTI	dictator	DUCE
—your leave	BENE PLACITO	discussion group	CONVERSAZIONE
cab	VETTURA	dish	ANTIPASTO, GNOCCHI
—driver	VETTURINO		LASAGNE, OS(S)O BUCCO
camomile	MANZANILLA		PASTA, PEPERONATA, PIZZA
cape (headland)	CAPO, PUNTA		PROSCIUTTO, RAVIOLI
capital	ROMA, ROME		RISOTTO, SALTIMBOCCA
car	VETTURA		TOURNEDOS ROSSINI
carriage	VETTURA		(*see also* **pasta**)
—procession	CORSO	do nothing	FAR NIENTE
carved chest	CASSONE	doctor	MEDICO
cathedral	DUOMO	dog	CANE, VOLPINO
cheese	FORMAGGIO	double speed	DOPPIO MOVIMENTO
	(*see also separate entry*)	drinking song	BRINDISI
chicken	POLLO	driver of carriage	VETTURINO
chief magistrate	GONFALONIERE	duck	ANITRA
	PODESTA	duel	DUELLO
child	BAMBINA, BAMBINO	dumplings	GNOCCHI
circuit	CONTORNO	dynasty	SAVOY
city	CITTA	Earth	TERRA
clerk	SCRIVANO	Easter cake	PASTIERA
coins		egg	UOVO
—unit	CENTESIMO	employer	PADRONE
—100 centesimi	L, LIRA	enclosed courtyard	CORTILE
—Florentine	FLORIN	encore	ANCORA
—silver	DUCAT, SCUDO	enough	BASTA
—old	AMBROSIN	enthusiasm	ESTRO, GUSTO
	SOLDO, TESTOON	essence	ALMA
—old Papal	PAOLO	estuary	BOCCHE
coloured glass or enamel	ZMALTO	evening	SERA
comic opera	BURLETTA	evil eye	JETTATURA
	OPERA BUFFA	extra day off	PONTE
company	GIA, COMPAGNIA	face to face	A QUATTR'OCHI
comparative value of		farm	PODERE
currency	VALUTA	father	PADRONE
confused mass	IMBROGLIO	fencing thrust	IMBROCCATA

festival	FESTA	harbour	PORTO
field	CAMPO	hare	LEPRE
fifteenth century	QUATTROCENTO	headland	CAPO
fig-pecker	BECCAFICO	headman	CAPITANO
firm to the teeth	AL DENTE	hell	INFERNO
first	PRIMA, PRIMO	here is	ECCO
fish	PESCE, TONETTO	hero	GARIBALDI
—soup	BRODETTO	high fashion	ALTA MODA
—stew	BRODETTO, BURIDDA	highness	ALTEZZA
	CACCIUCCO	hill	COLLINA
fixed rate	AL PASTO	holiday	FESTA
fizzy	FRIZZANTE	hollow	CONCA
flour	FARINA	hors d'oeuvre	ANTIPASTO
—dough	PASTA	house	CASA
flowering	FIORITURA	ice cream	GELATO
flute	ZUF(F)OLO	image of child Jesus	BAMBINO
folk-tales	PENTAMERON	imitation stone	SCAGLIOLA
follows	SEGUE	in	
fool	CAPOCCHIA	—a low voice	SOTTO VOCE
football (old)	CALCIO	—an undertone	SOTTO VOCE
forward!	AVANTI	—blank	IN BIANCO
four hundred	QUATTROCENTO	—devotional manner	RELIGIOSO
fourteenth century	TRECENTO	—French style	ALLA FRANCA
franked	FRANCO	—German style	ALLA TEDESCA
free	SCIOLTO	—marching style	ALLA MARCIA
fresh	FRESCO	—one's own mind	IN PETTO
friar	FRATE	—strict time	A BATTUTA
fried savouries	FRITTO MISTO	—the	
furious person	FURIOSO	breast	IN PETTO
gallant	CAVALIERE SERVENTE	manner of fugue	FUGATO
game (old)	LONGUE PAUME, PALLONE	—time	A TEMPO
garden warbler	BECCAFICO	—white	IN BIANCO
garlic	AGLIO	indifferent	POCOCURANTE
gentle blood	BEL SANGUE	informal greeting	CIAO
girl	RAGAZZA	inn	ALBERGO
glazing by hand-rubbing	VELATURA	—keeper	PADRONE
good	BENE	instrument	CHITARRONE
—bye	ADDIO, A(R)RIVEDERCI	island(s)	ISOLA(ISOLE)
	CIAO	isolation hospital	LAZARET(TO)
—day	BUON GIORNO	Italian	AUSONIAN, EYETI(E), EYTIE
—evening	BUONA SERA	judge	PODESTA
—life	DOLCE VITA	king	RE
—night	BUONA NOTTE	lady	DONNA, SIGNORA
goose	OCA	lake	LAGO
government	QUIRINAL	lamb	AGNELLO
governor	PODESTA	landlord	PADRONE
granite	MIAROLO	language	TUSCAN
grape stalk	GRAPPA	large village	BORGHETTO
great	GRAN	leader	DUCE
guide	CICERONE	leading	
guild comedy	COMMEDIA DELL'ARTE	—dancer	PRIMA BALLERINA (ASSOLUTA)
gulf	GOLFO	—singer	PRIMA DONNA (ASSOLUTA)
gypsy (gipsies)		liberation and	
—man	ZINGARO(ZINGARI)	unification	RISORGIMENTO
—woman	ZINGARA(ZINGARE)	life of pleasure	LA DOLCE VITA
hand	MANO	limestone	SCAGLIA

little	POCO
—by little	POCO A POCO
liveliness	BRIO
look there	ECCO
Madam	DONNA, SIGNORA
madman	FURIOSO
mafia	COSA NOSTRA
magistrate	PODESTA
male	
—exhibitionist	FUSTO
—soprano	CASTRATO
mansion	PALAZZO
marchioness	MARCHESA
mark	MARCARE
marquis	MARCHESE
master	MAESTRO
meal	PRANZO
measure (cubit)	BRACCIO
meat	CARNE
—balls	POLPETTE
—rolls	INVOLTINI
medieval drama	LAUDA
medium relief	MEZZO-RILIEVO
melancholy	PENS(I)EROSO
member of Florentine	
Academia	DELLA-CRUSCAN
mendicant Franciscan	FRATE
mercenary leader	CONDOTTIERE
merry cheerful man	L'ALLEGRO
middle	MEZZO
Milanese opposed to	
marriage of priests	PATARIN(E)
Miss	SIGNORINA
Mister	SIGNOR
mixed dish of	
fried food	FRITTO MISTO
mizzen-sail	MEZZANA
model sculpture	BOZETTO
modernising	AGGIORNAMENTO
monopoly	APPALTO
more	PIU
most illustrious	ILLUSTRISSIMO
mother	MADRE
—of God	MADONNA
motor-boat	MOTOSCAFO
motorway	AUTOSTRADA
motto	IMPRESA
mountain	MONTE
—troops	ALPINI
mouth	BOCCA
much	MOLTO
mushrooms	FUNGHI
nationalist	FASCIST(O)
Neapolitan	
—dance	TARANTELLA
—secret society	CAMORRA

night	NOTTE
nonchalant	POCOCURANTE
not so quick	MENO MOSSE
official prosecutor	AVVOGADORE
open pie of tomatoes etc	PIZZA
or	O, OSSIA
orange	ARANCIA
ornamental glass	MILLEFIORI
overcoat (19th c)	TAGLIONI
palace	PALAZZO
papal treasurer	CAMERLENGO
	CAMERLINGO
party (19th c)	IRREDENTISTS
pass	COLLE, PASSO
pasta	(see separate entry)
peak	PIZZO
peasant	CONTADINO
peninsula	PENISOLA
pensive man	IL PENSEROSO
perpetual motion	MOTO PERPETUO
pheasant	FAGGIANO
pie	TORTA, PASTICCIO, PIZZA
pleasant idleness	DOLCE FAR NIENTE
poem	POEMA, POESIA
poet	ARIOSTO, DANTE
	MARINI, TASSO
poetic inspiration	ESTRO
policeman	SBIRRO
porridge	POLENTA
port	PORTO
post-free	FRANCO
pottery	MAIOLICA, MAJOLICA
poultry	POLLAME
prawns	SCAMPI
proprietor of inn	PADRONE
puppets	FANTOCCINI
quicker	PIU MOSSO
quickly!	PRESTO
rabbit	CONIGLIO
race	CORSO
rebirth	RISORGIMENTO
recasting of literary	
or musical work	RIFACIMENTO
reef	SCOGLIO
refusal	NON
relief	RILIEVO
relish (roe)	BOTARGO
restaurant	RISTORANTE, TRATTORIA
revival	RISORGIMENTO
rice	RISO
rifleman	BERSAGLIERE
river	FIUME
—mouth	FOCE
roast piglet	PORCHETTA
rock	SCOGLIO
run	CORSO

sad	MESTO	terrace	TERRAZZO
Saint's day	FESTA	there!	ECCO
score in music	PARTITURA	thick laying on of paint	IMPASTO
sea	MARE	three strings	TRE CORDE
second	SECONDO	thrusting	ALLA STOCCATA
secret society	CAMORRA	time	TEMPO
	CASA NOSTRA	tip	B(U)ONAMANA
	COMORRA, MAF(F)IA	title of rank	MONSIGNOR(E)
serious opera	OPERA SERIA	toast	BRINDISI
sharpshooter	BERSAGLIERE	too much	TROPPO
short verse-form	STORNELLO	touchstone	PARAGONE
simple	GONZO	touring car	GRAN TURISMO
singing style	BEL CANTO	town	CITTA
sixteenth century	CINQUECENTO	trade jargon	LINGUA FRANCA
skull-cap	ZUCHETTA, ZUCHETTO	trio	TERZETTO
sliding	GLISSANDO	turkey	TACCHINO
slow	LENTO	turn	VOLTA
small group	GRUPPETTO	type of carving	CAVO-RILIEVO
snails	LUMACHE	uninterested	POCOCURANTE
soldier	BERSAGLIERE, SOLDATO	unknown	INCOGNITO
songbird	BECCAFICO	veal	VITELLO
soul	ALMA, ANIMA, SPIRITO	vendetta	FAIDA
soup	MINISTRE, MINESTRA	venison	CERVA
	MINESTRONE, ZUPPA	vermicelli	FEDELINI
sour cherry	(A)MARASCA	vermouth	IT
spade	PALETTA	verse form in triplets	TERZA-RIMA
sparkling	FRIZZANTE	very	MOLTO
spiced sausage(s)	SALAME (SALAMI)	—earnestly	CON AMORE
spirit	BRAVURA, BRIO	vivacity	BRIO
square	PIAZZA	warbler	BECCAFICO
squid	CALAMARI	weight (variable)	ROTOLO
standard of money	VALUTA	well	BENE
state pawnshop	MONTE DI PIETA	what	CHE
stew	OSSOBUCO	wine	VINO
storm	BORASCO		(see also **wine**)
strait	STRETTO	with	CON
street	CALLE, STRADA, VIA	—fire	CON FUOCO
—where processions		—grief	CON DOLORE
are held	CORSO	—love	CON AMORE
stringed instrument	PANDURA	—movement	CON MOTO
sucking pig	PORCHETTA	—resolution	RISOLUTO
summit	CIMA	—spirit	SPIRITOSO
supreme commander	GENERALISSIMO	wood inlay	INTARSIA, INTARSIO
sweet dish	ZABAGLIONE	woodcock	BECCACCIA
taste	GUSTO	workshop	BOTTEGA
tangle	IMBROGLIO	zest	GUSTO
tear	LACRIMA	**Ivory Coast**	CI

J

Jamaica	JA
bark	CARIBBEE BARK
birthwort	CONTRAYERVA
capital	KINGSTON
cedar	BARBADOS CEDAR
coin	CENT, DOLLAR
drink	RUM
ebony	COCUS-WOOD
pepper	ALLSPICE
plum	HOG-PLUM
Japan	J, NIPPON
abacus	SOROBAN
aboriginal race	AINO, AINU
acupressure	SHIATSU
administrative district	PREFECTURE
aeroplane	ZERO
airline	JAL
alcove	TOKONOMA
alphabet	KATAKANA
armorial device	MON
bamboo shoots	TAKENOKO
barehanded fighting	J(I)-JITSU
baron	DAIMIO
bay	KAI, WAN
bean	ADZUKI
beauty of age	SHIBUI
bed-roll	FUTON
beef	GYUNIKU
—dish	SHABU-SHABU
body-language	HARAGEI
box	INRO
boxing	KEMPO
bread	PAN
Buddhist sect	SOKA GAKKAI, ZEN
cake	MANJU
calligraphy	SHODO
cane	WHANGEE
cape (headland)	BANA, MISAKI, ZAKI
capital	TOKYO
carriage	JINRICKISHA
	(JIN)RICKSHA(W)
carved ornament	NETSUKE
cedar	SUGI
champion wrestler (sumo)	OZEKI
channel	SETO, SUIDO
cherry	FUJI
cherry-blossom time	SAKURA
chess	SHOGI

chicken	NIWATORI
chopsticks	WARIBASHI
chrysanthemum badge	KIKUMON
church	TERA
cloisonné ware	SHIPPO
code of chivalry	BUSHIDO
coins	
—unit	SEN
—100 sen	Y, YEN, YN
—old gold coins	COPANG
	KOBAN(G), OBANG
commander-in-chief	SHOGUN(AL)
	TYCOON
conifer	UMBRELLA-FIR
court	DAIRO, DARI
current	KUROSHIO
dancing girl	GEISHA
deep-fried seafood or vegetables	TEMPURA
deer	SIKA
deities	(*see* **gods, goddesses**)
demi-god	KAMI
dish	SUKIYAKI, SUSHI
	TEMPURA, TERIYAKI
drama	KABUKI, NOGAKU, NO(H)
drink	SAKE, SAKI
dumpling	DANGO
dwarf tree	BONSAI
early civilisation	EDO
edible shoots (Aralia)	UDO
elder statesmen	GENRO
emigrant to US	ISSEI
emperor	MIKADO, TENNO
enamel ware	SHIPPO
exalted gate	MIKADO
fan	OGI
fast food	TONK-ATSU
fastener	NETSUKE
female entertainer	GEISHA
fencing	IAIDO
firing process for	
porcelain	RAKU
fish	AYU, FUGU, CARP
	GOLDFISH
—in batter	TEMPURA
—raw	SASHIMI
with vegetables	CHIRINABE, NUTA
floor covering	TATAMI
flower arranging	IKEBANA
flowering tree	CATALPA, CHERRY
forever	BANZAI
fried pork	TONK-ATSU
fruit	LOQUAT, KAKI
game	GO, GOBAN(G), GOMUKU
	SHOGI
garment	(KI)MONO
gentle way	JUDO

gentry	SHIZOKU	—ruler	SHOGUN
girdle	OBI	mountain	SEN, ZAN
girl	MOUSME(E)	mountain(s)	YAMA
god	KAMI	mushroom	KINOKO
gold foil work	KIRIKANE	musical	
goodbye	SAYONARA	—drama	KABUKI
grass	WHANGEE	—instrument	KOTO, S(H)AMISEN
grotesque figure	MAGOT	narrow print	HASHIRA
guest-house	MINSHUKU	noble	DAIMIO, KUGE
guitar	S(H)AMISEN	noodles	MENRUI
gulf	NADA	orange	SATSUMA
healing art	SHIATSU	ornament	NETSUKE
helmet	JINGASA	outcast	RONIN
horse-radish	WASABI	outsider	GAIJIN
image	ZO	painting style	UKIYO-E
informal feeling out	NEMAWASHI	palanquin	KAGO, NORIMON
inlay work	ZOGAN	paper	FUSAMI
inlet	GATA, KO	—folding art	ORIGAMI
island	JIMA, KO, SHIMA, TO	—screen	SHOJI
ivy	UDO	pass	TOGE
jacket	TANZEN	patina	SABI
jelly	KANTEN	peak	DAKE, TAKE
judo		peninsula	HANTO
—costume	JUDOGI	persimmon	KAKI
—expert	JUDOKA	pinball game	PACHINKO
kimono	YUKATA	plant	HOSTA, KUDZU
knife	KOZUKA	play	NO(H)
lacquer	URUSHI	plum	UMEBOSHI
—ware	NURIMONO	poem	HAIKAI, HAIKU, HOKKO
—work	KANAGAI	—with 5 lines	LINKED VERSE
lagoon	GATA		RENGA, TANKA
language	AINU	pork	BUTANIKU
laurel	AUCUBA JAPONICA	pottery	KYOTO, SATSUMA WARE
lord	KAMI	province	SATSUMA
low caste	ETA, HEIMIN	puppet theatre	BUNRAKU
martial art	AIKIDO, AIKI-JITSU	quince	CYDONIA JAPONICA
	JUDO, J(I)U-JITSU		PYRUS JAPONICA
	JUJUTSA, KARATE, KENDO	radish	DAIKON
mat	TATAMI	raincoat	MINO
measures		raspberry	WINE-BERRY
—1"	SUN	raw fish dish	SASHIMI
—12"	SHAKU	religion	BUDDHISM, SHINTO(ISM)
—2 yards	KEN	rice	GO-HAN, RAISU
—120 yards	CHO	—beer	SAKE, SAKI
—2½ miles	RI	river	GAWA, KAWA
—4sq. yds	TSUBO	robe	KIMONO
—¼ peck	SHO	root binding	NEMAWASHI
—5 bushels	KOKU	rose	KERRIA
—4 galls	TO	royal badge	KIKUMON, KIRIMON
—10,000 years	BANZAI	ruler	MIKADO
meat cooked in soy sauce	SUKIYAKI	salmon	MASU
medicine chest	INRO	salutation	BANZAI
medlar	LOQUAT	sash	OBI
Mikado's palace	DAIRI	script	KAKEMONO, KANA
military		scroll	MAKIMONO
—caste	SAMURAI	sea	KAI, NADA

—bream	TAI	Jersey	GBJ
—weed	KO(M)BU	Jesus	IHC, IHS, JC, JHC
secret society	YAKUZA	jewellery	
set meal	TEISHOKU	assortment of small	
ship	MARO, MARU	diamonds	MELEE
shrub	KERRIA	artificial	LOGIE, PASTE
sliding partition	SHOJI	—with glass under real	
sport	SUMO	jewels	DOUBLET
strait	SETO, SUIDO	beetle-shaped	SCARAB
street	GINZA	bone-shaped	SEVIGNE
sudden enlightenment	SATORI	brooch	FIBULA
suicide	HARAKARI, HARAKIRI	—clasp	OUCH
	SEPPUKU	—in hat	ENSEIGNE
—attack	KAMIKAZE	cameo sewn to clothes	OUCH
sword		clasped ornament	OUCH
—fighting	KENDO	cheap jewellery	BAUBLES
—hilt	TSUBA		BRUMMAGEN
syllabary	HIRAGANA, KATAKANA		GEEGAWS, PASTE
tea	O-CHA		TRINKETS
—ceremony	CHANOYU, SADO	clasp for cloak	FIBULA
temple gateway	TORII	clasped ornament	OUCH
tidal wave	TSUNAMI	close-fitting necklace	CHOKER
title	KAMI	compartment in gold work	CLOISON
tree	GINGKO, GINKGO, HONOKI	corsage	STOMACHER
	LOQUAT, MAIDENHAIR-TREE	cross suspended	
	PAULOWNIA, RED-LAC, TSUGA	from a heart	CROIX A LA JEANNETTE
tuna	MAGURO	cut	
waitress	MOUSME(E)	—4 facets	MAZARIN CUT, ROSE CUT
wall-hanging	KAKEMONO	—11 facets	EMERALD CUT, STEP CUT
war-cry	BANZAI	—56 facets	DIAMOND CUT
warm current	KUROSHIO	—chamfered	BAGUETTE
warrior class	SAMURAI	—domed	CABOCHON
weights		—flat plane	FACET
—1oz	RIO	—pointed oval	NAVETTE
—1½lbs	CATTY, KIN	decorative plaque	
—8lbs	KWAN	on belt	CHATELAINE
wood block	YOKO	delicate jewellery	BIJOUTERIE
wooden		ear	
—chopsticks	HASHI	—ornament	DROPPER, EAR-RING
—shoes	GETA	temporary	SLEEPER
wrestling	SUMO	—ring	
—champion	OZEKI	cone hung from	
—tournament	SASHO	crescent	PELTA
writing system	KANA	long pendants	POISSOIDES
Javanese	JAV		FISHWIVES
badger	STINKARD, TELEDU	enamelling	
bird	JAVA SPARROW	—between wires	
capital	DJAKARTA	soldered to plate	FILIGREE
civet	RASSE	—carved and enamelled	BASSE TAILLE
man	PITHECANTHROPUS		CHAMPLEVE
orchestra	GAMELAN(G), GAMELIN	—engraved and	
plum	JAMBOLANA	enamelled	TAILLE D'EPERGNE
tree	ANTIAR, UPAS	—in	
—shrew	BANGSRING, BANXRING	cells	CLOISONNE
weapon	TOMBOC	openwork	PLIQUE A JOUR
weasel-cat	DELUNDUNG	—modelled on surface	EN RONDE BOSSE
		expert	LAPIDARIST

flange holding stone	BEZEL	ring	
Greek medallion	PERIAMMA	—cheap	GYPSY RING
head		—of metal holding stone	COLLET
—band	CIRCLET, CORONET	—with	
	CROWN, DIADEM, TIARA	interlocking loops	GIMMAL RING
—ornament	TRESSON		GIMMEL RING
heart-shaped	CARDIACE	monogram	SIGNET RING
hinged case	LOCKET	single stone	SOLITAIRE
imitation		stones all round	ETERNITY RING
—diamonds	DIAMANTE, PASTE	scroll-shaped	CARTOUCHE
—pearl	OLIVET	setting with stones	
inlaid with hard stones	PIETRA-DURA	butted together	PAVE
jewel-box	CASKET	sham	LOGIE, PASTE
lentil-shaped pendant	BULLA	sheen of	
lustre of pearl	ORIENT	—diamond	WATER
matching set		—moonstone	SCHILLER
—2 or 3 pieces	DEMI-PARURE	—pearl	LUSTRE, ORIENT
—3 or more pieces	PARURE	—ruby	SILK
matt gold	CANNETILLE	—sapphire	SILK
misshapen pearl	BAROQUE PEARL	ship-shaped	NEF
mourning jewellery	MEMENTO MORI	socket for stone	OUCH
neck ornament	GORGET, TORC	spray of feathers	AIGRETTE
	TORQUE	stone	
necklace		—cutter	LAPIDARY
—or collar	CARCANET, TORQUE	—used to test gold or	
—with several strands	RIVIERE	silver	TOUCHSTONE
ornament worn		—with	
—as charm	AMULET	incised carving	INTAGLIO
—on		relief carving	CAMEO
ankle	ANKLET, SLAVE BRACELET	twisted necklace	TORC, TORQUE
arm	BANGLE, BRACELET	used for religious	
chain	LAVALIERE, PENDANT	purposes	VOTIVE JEWELS
chest	PECTORAL	worn to ward off evil	AMULET, TALISMAN
ear	DROPPER, EAR-RING	yellow-coloured diamond	CAPE
forehead	FERRON(N)IERE		(*see also* **gems**)
head	TRESSON	**Jewish**	(*see* **Hebrew**)
lip	LABRET	**Jordan**	HKJ
pendant with		capital	AMMAN
—singly mounted stones	LAVALLIERE	coin	DINAR, FIL
	NEGLIGE	**June**	
—smaller jewels attached	GIRANDOLE	June 6th	D-DAY
perfume container	POMANDER	June 25th	LONGEST DAY
polished but uncut stone	CABOCHON		MIDSUMMER, SOLSTICE

K

Kampuchea	(see Cambodia)
Kenya	EAK
capital	NAIROBI
coin	CENT, POUND, SHILLING
kill	
algae	ALGICIDE
babies	INFANTICIDE
bacteria	BACTERICIDE, GERMICIDE
bears	URSICIDE
birds	AVICIDE
brother	FRATRICIDE
children	FILICIDE, INFANTICIDE
	PROLICIDE
environment	ECOCIDE
father	PATRICIDE
f(o)etus	ABORTION, F(O)ETICIDE
fox	VULPICIDE
fungus	FUNGICIDE
giant	GIGANTICIDE
god	DEICIDE
human race	PROLICIDE
insects	INSECTICIDE
king	REGICIDE
larvae	LARVICIDE
living things	BIOCIDE
man	HOMICIDE
mind (brainwashing)	MENTICIDE
mites	ACARICIDE
mother	MATRICIDE
offspring	PROLICIDE
one's own children	FILICIDE
parasites	PARASITICIDE
parents	PARRICIDE
pest	PESTICIDE
plants	HERBICIDE
poet	VATICIDE
prophet	VATICIDE
protozoa	TRYPANOCIDE
race	ETHNOCIDE, GENOCIDE
rats	RODENTICIDE
reputation	FAMICIDE
rodents	RODENTICIDE
seaweed	ALGICIDE
self	SUICIDE
sheep	OVICIDE
sister	SORORICIDE
social group	ETHNOCIDE
sperm	SPERMICIDE

tyrant	TYRANNICIDE
vine	VITICIDE
virus	VIRICIDE
weeds	HERBICIDE, WEEDICIDE
wife	UXORICIDE
women	GYNOCIDE
worms	VERMICIDE
king	
including: general	
Cockney king	PEARLIE, PEARLY
King Charles	CR
King Edward	ER
king-emperor	RI
King George	GR
king of Basham	OG
king of France	ROI, SM
King William	WR
King's Bench	KB
King's College	KC
King's Counsel	KC
Sun King	LOUIS XIV
kings	
including: British	
pre-Conquest	ALFRED
	ATHELSTAN
	CANUTE, CNUT
	EDGAR ETHELING
	EDMUND IRONSIDE
	EDRED
	EDWARD THE CONFESSOR
	EDWARD THE ELDER
	EDWARD THE MARTYR
	EDWY
	ETHELRED
	EGBERT
	HAROLD GODWINSON
	HAROLD HAREFOOT
	HARTHACNUT
	SWEGN
English	CHARLES I-II
	EDWARD I-VIII
	GEORGE I-VI
	HENRY I-VIII
	JAMES I-II
	JOHN
	RICHARD I-III
	STEPHEN
	WILLIAM I-IV
Scottish	ALEXANDER I-III
	DAVID I-II
	DONALD
	DUNCAN I-II
	EDGAR
	JAMES I-VI
	JOHN
	LULACH

	MACBETH
	MALCOLM I-IV
	ROBERT I-III
	WILLIAM
knife	
African	PANGA
American	BOWIE KNIFE, TOOTH-PICK
Arab dagger	JAMBIA, KHANJAR
artist's knife	PALETTE KNIFE
Burmese	DA(H), DHAR, DOUT, DOW
carpenter's/cooper's	
knife	DRAW(ING)-KNIFE
Cuban	MACHETE
dagger	
—curved	JAMBIYA(H)
—Greek	PARAZONIUM
—Hebrew	SICA
—narrow-bladed	MISERICORD(E)
	STILET(TO), STYLET
—old	BAS(E)LARD, PUNCHEON
—Roman	SICA
—short	AN(E)LACE
—small	BODKIN, DIRK, DUDGEON
	PONIARD, WHINGER
	WINIARD, WINYARD
Dutch	SNEE
fighting knife	SNICKERSNEE
folding knife	CLASP-KNIFE, JACK-KNIFE
—Scots	JOCKTELEG
French	COUTEAU
general purpose knife	STANLEY KNIFE
	SWISS ARMY KNIFE
German	MESSER
glazier's tool	PUTTY KNIFE
Gurkha	KUKRI
heavy knife	DA
Highland	DIRK
Inca ceremonial knife	TUMI
Indian	KUTTAR
Italian	COLTELLO
Japanese	KOZUKA
large	CUTTO(E)
leatherworker's knife	MOON-KNIFE
Malay	CREASE, CREESE, KRIS
	KREESE, PARANG
midshipman's knife	DIRK
Middle East	JAMBIYA(H)
military knife	BAYONET
	SWISS ARMY KNIFE
	TRENCH KNIFE
painter's knife	PALETTE KNIFE
Persian	HAN(D)JAR
Philippines	BOLO
Scottish	DIRK, GULLEY
	SKEAN(DHU), SKENE(DHU)
	SKEAN(OCCLE), SKENE(OCCLE)

—clasp knife	JOCKTELEG
Sikh	KIRPAN
slang	CHIV, SHIV
Spanish	CUCHILLO
spring-loaded	FLICK KNIFE
	SWITCH-BLADE (KNIFE)
surgical	BISTOURY, LANCET
	SCALPEL
Turkish	ATAGHAN, HAN(D)JAR
	YATAG(H)AN
knight	K, KT, N, SIR
Knight Bachelor	KB
Knight Commander of the	
—Bath	KCB
—British Empire	KBE
Knight Grand Cross of	
—Hanover	GCH
—the	
Bath	(K)GCB
British Empire	GBE
Knight of	
—Labour	KL
—Malta	KM
—the	
Bath	KB
Legion of Honour	KLH
Order of the Garter	KG
Thistle	KT
knot	BLACKWALL HITCH, BOWLINE
	CARRICK BEND, CAT'S-PAW
	CLOVE HITCH, COMMON BEND
	COW HITCH, GRANNY KNOT
	FIGURE-OF-EIGHT
	FISHERMAN'S BEND
	FISHERMAN'S KNOT
	HALF HITCH, JURY-MAST KNOT
	OVERHAND KNOT, REEF KNOT
	ROLLING HITCH, SHEET BEND
	SHEEPSHANK, SLIP-KNOT
	SQUARE KNOT
	STEVEDORE'S KNOT
	SWAB HITCH, THUMB KNOT
	TIMBER HITCH, TURK'S HEAD
Korea	ROK
airline	KAL
capital	
—North	PYONGYANG
—South	S(E)OUL
coin	CHON, HWAN, JEON
	JUN, WON
house	WON
martial art	HAPKIDO, TAEKWONDO
	TANG SOO DO
trance	KUT
Kuala Lumpur	KL
Kuwait	KWT

L

lake
Africa	NYANZA
—lakes	ALBERT, BANGWEULU
	EDWARD, EYASI, KARIBA
	KIVU, MAI NDOMBE, MALAWI
	MOBUTU SESE SEKO, MWERU
	NYASA, RUDOLF, TANGANYIKA
	(T)CHAD, TURKANA, VICTORIA
America (N)	CHAMPLAIN LAKE
	GREAT LAKES
	GREAT SALT LAKE
	OKEECHOBEE, PEPIN
—Great Lakes	ERIE, HURON, MICHIGAN
	ONTARIO, SUPERIOR
artificial	RESERVOIR
Australia	AMADEUS, ERYE
	DISAPPOINTMENT, EVERARD
	FROME, GARDNER, MOORE
	TORRANCE, TORRENS
Bolivia	POOPO, TITICACA
Brazil	DOS PATOS, MIRIM
Cambodia	GREAT LAKE, TONLE SAP
Canada	ATHABASCA, GARRY
	GREAT BEAR LAKE
	GREAT SLAVE LAKE
	REINDEER LAKE, ST JOHN
	WINNIPEG, WINNEPEGOSIS
	(*see also* Great Lakes *above*)
China	BAGRASH KOL, LOP NOR
	KOKO NOR, POYANGHU, TAI HU
	TUNG TING HU
connecting with sea	SEA LOCH
dries up in hot conditions	PLAYA, SHOTT
England	BASSENTHWAITE LAKE
	BUTTERMERE, CONISTON
	CRUMMOCK WATER
	DERWENTWATER
	ENNERDALE WATER
	GRASMERE, HAWES WATER
	RYDAL WATER, THIRLMERE
	ULLSWATER, WASTWATER
	WINDERMERE
Estonia	LAKE PEIPUS
Ethiopia	LAKE TANA
Finland	INARI
formed by	
—blocking of valley	BARRIER LAKE
—meandering river	OXBOW, MORTLAKE

France	LAC
Germany	SEE
—lake	BODEN SEE
Guatemala	ATITLAN
having	
—deficiency of nutrients	OLIGOTROPHIC
—excess of nutrients	EUTROPHIC
Hungary	LAKE BALATON
	LAKE HEVIS
in	
—extinct volcano	CRATER LAKE
—mountains	TARN
Iran	LAKE URMIA
Ireland	LOUGH
—loughs	ALLEN, CONN, CORRIB, DERG
	ERNE, MASK, NEAGH, REE
Israel	LAKE TIBERIAS
Italy	LAGO
—lakes	BOLSENA, BRACCIANO, COMO
	ISEO, GARDA, MAGGIORE
	ORTA, TRASIMENO
Kashmir	DAL
made salty by evaporation	SALT LAKE
Mexico	LAKE CHAPALA
mountain lake	TARN
New Zealand	PUKAKI, TAUPO
	TE ANAU, TEKAPO
Nicaragua	LAGO DA NICARAGUA
North Africa - shallow lake	SHOTT
Peru	LAKE TITICACA
ridge of stones round margins	LAKE RAMPART
Russia	OZERO
—lakes	ALAK, BAIKAL, BALKHASH
	BAYKAL, HOVSGOL NOUR, ISSYK KUL
	KHANKA, KUYBYSHEVSKOYE
	LADOGA, LADOZHSKOYE
	ONEGA, ONEZHSKOYE, SEVAN
	STALINGRADSKOYE
	TENGIZ, ZAYSAN
salt	SALINA
Scotland	LOCH
—lochs	ARKAIG, AWE, FYNE, EARN
	ERICHT, LAGGAN, LINNHE
	LOCHY, LOMOND, LONG, MAREE
	MORAR, NEVIS, NESS
	RANNOCH, SHIEL, SHIN, TAY
—moorland pool	FLOW
sea-lake	FIORD
seasonal lake	PLAYA
shallow lake	
—in coastal sand dunes	ETANG
—large	EVERGLADE

—North Africa	SHOTT
small	MERE, TARN
Spain	LAGO
submerged river valley	RIA
Sweden	MALAR, VANERN
	VATTERN
Switzerland	LAC, SEE
—lakes	BODENSEE, BRIENZER SEE
	LAKE CONSTANCE, LAKE GENEVA
	HALLWILER SEE, LAC LEMAN
	LAC NEUCHATEL, SEMPACHER SEE
	THUNER SEE, URNER SEE
	VIERWALDSTATTER SEE
	WALENSEE, ZUGER SEE, ZURICH SEE
Turkey	AMIK, BATAKUK, BEYSEHID
	BURDUR, HOYRAN, IZNIK
	KUS, SUGLA, TUZ, ULLBAT, VAN
Uruguay	LAGO DA MANGUIERA
	LAKE MIRIM
valley	(see geology)
Venezuela	LAGO DE MARACAIBO
	LAGO VICTORIA
Wales	L(L)YN
—lakes	BALA LAKE, LAKE VYRNWY
	LYN CELIN, LYN TEGID
	TRAWSFYNYDD LAKE
water	
—higher level (warm)	HYPOLIMNIUM
—layer in between	THERMOCLINE
—lower level (cold)	EPILIMNIUM
—receiving sufficient	
sunlight for	
photosynthesis	PHOTIC ZONE
Yugoslavia	LAKE BOHINJ
Lamb (Charles)	ELIA
language	LINGO
1984 language	NEWSPEAK
ability to	
—read	LITERACY
—use	
language	ORACY
numbers	NUMERACY
Abyssinia	AMHARIC, GALLA, GEEZ
	GIZ, SOMALI
accent	BROGUE, DIALECT, TWANG
	(see also **punctuation**)
accidental omission	
of letters	LIPOGRAPHY
adage	PAROEMIA
addition	
—to word	EPITHESIS, PARAGOG(U)E
—of	
final r	NUNNATION
prefix	PROTHESIS
words to clarify	EPEXEGESIS
affected talk	CANT

Afghanistan	DARI, PAK(H)TO, PAK(H)TU
	PASHTO, PASHTU
	PUSHTO(O), PUSHTU
Afrasian	ARABIC
Africa	(see **Africa**)
Alfandari's language	NEO
Algeria	ARABIC, BERBER
	FRENCH
alteration of word from another	
language to fit familiar	
sound	FOLK ETYMOLOGY
	HOBSON-JOBSON
alternative form of phoneme	ALLOPHONE
alphabet	(see separate entry)
ambiguous	DOUBLETALK, NEWSPEAK
—phrase	AMPHIBOLOGY
American sign language	AMESLAN
Amerindian	MAYA, TUPI
analysis of	
—sentences	CONSTITUENT ANALYSIS
	PARSING
—sounds	PHONEMICISATION
—word	
meanings	COMPONENTIAL ANALYSIS
Andorra	CATALAN
Angola	BAKONGO, CHOKWE
	KIMBUNDU, OVIMBUNDU
apparently contradictory	
statement	PARADOX
appropriate word	MOT JUSTE
Aramaic dialect	SYRIAC
argument	LEMMA
arrangement of	
connections	PARATAXIS
articulated	
—weakly	LENIS
—strongly	FORTIS
artificial	INTERLINGUA, SPELIN
—by	
Alfandari	NEO
Hogben	INTERGLOSSA
Jesperson	NOVIAL
Schleyer	VOLAPUK
Zamenhof	ESPERANTO
—from Esperanto	IDO
as used	PAROLE
attack made verbally	INVECTIVE
Australia	STRINE
—aborigine	NYUNGAR
Austronesia	INDONESIAN, POLYNESIAN
	TAGALOG
Avestan	AVESTIC, ZEND
bad language	OBSCENITY, SWEARING
Bangaladesh	BENGALI
based on	
—analysis	DESCRIPTIVISM

—ideas of		internal letters	METATHESIS
correctness	NORMATIVE GRAMMAR	vowel	ABLAUT, DIPHTHONG
	PRESCRIPTIVISM		GRADATION, MUTATION
—inflection	SYNTHETIC	—to	
—Latin	ROMANCE	less favourable	
—word order	ANALYTICAL, ISOLATING	sense	DETERIORATION
basic unit			PEJORATION
—in lexicology	LEXEME	more favourable	
—of		sense	(A)MELIORATION
language	MORPHEME		ELEVATION
meaning	GLOSSEME, SEMANTEME	character representing	
	SEMEME	sound	PHONOGRAM
sound	PHONEME	characteristic	
Basque	EUSKARA	expression	IDIOM
Belgium	FLEMISH, FRENCH, GERMAN	Chile	SPANISH
Bhutan	BUMTHANGKHA, DZONGKHA	China	CANTONESE, KUO-YO
	SARCHAPPKHA		MANCHOO, MANCHU
blind language	BRAILLE		MANDARIN, PEKIN(G)ESE
Bolivia	AMYARA, QUECHUA		SHAN
bookmaker's sign language	TICK TACK	—dialect	AMOY, HAKKA, WU
Botswana	SETSWANA	Chinese Turkestan	TOCHARIAN
Brazil	PORTUGUESE		TOCHARISH, TOKARIAN
Breton dialect	ARMORIC		TOKARISH
Brunei	MALAY	choice of words	DICTION, PARLANCE
Buddhist sacred			PHRASEOLOGY
language	PALI	circumlocution	PERIPHRASIS
bureaucratic language	GOBBLEDEGOOK	clarity of speech	ARTICULACY
	JARGON, OFFICIALESE		ARTICULATION, DICTION
Burkina Faso	FRENCH, MOSSI		ELOCUTION, ENNUNCIATION
Burma	SHAN	class of	
Burundi	FRENCH, KIRUNDI	—nouns	DECLENSION,
	KISWAHILI	—verbs	CONJUGATION
Cape Verde Islands	CRIOULO, PORTUGUESE	classroom with tape	
Carthage	PUNIC	recorders, etc	LANGUAGE LABORATORY
case (of noun)		clause	
—direct object	ACCUSATIVE	—conditional	PROTASIS
—direction from, etc	ABLATIVE	—consequent	APODOSIS
—indirect object	DATIVE	—starting with	
—origin or possession	GENITIVE	(al)though	CONCESSIVE
—personal address	VOCATIVE	if	CONDITIONAL
—subject	NOMINATIVE	clever turn of phrase	CONCETTO
Caucasus	ANDO, ARMENIAN, AVAR	coincidence of vowels	ASSONANCE
	DAGESTANIAN, DARGWA, DIDO	collection of utterances	CORPUS
	GEORGIAN, LAKK, LEZGIAN, NAKH	Colombia	SPANISH
Celtic	BRETON, CORNISH, GAELIC	colonial patois	CREOLE
	GAULISH, IRISH, MANX, WELSH	combination and distortion	
Central African Republic	SANGHO	of two languages into one	PIDGIN
Chad	ARABIC, FRENCH	Comoros	ARABIC, COMORAN
change			SWAHILI
—in		composition of	
form showing		unconnected pieces	CENTO
—function	CASE	compound word where	
—tense, gender	ACCIDENCE	—each part has equal status	DVANDVA
	INFLECTION	—first part modifies the second	BAHUVRIHI
sound of			TATPURUSHA
consonant	ASSIMILATION	conditional clause	PROTASIS

confused language	BABBLE, BABEL	—Romance	FRIULIAN, LADIN(O)
	GALIMATIAS		RHAETO-ROMANIC
	GIBBERISH		ROMANSCH
confusion of meaning	SYNCHYSIS	—Scottish	LALLANS
Congo	BANTU, FRENCH	—which becomes common	
consequential clause	APODOSIS	language	CREOLE, KOINE
context			(*see also* **dialect**)
—bound	RESTRICTED CODE	difficulty in speaking	PHONASTHENIA
—free	ELABORATED CODE	dirty talk	COPROLALIA
Coptic dialect	SAHIDIC	distinguished by pitch	TONE LANGUAGE
core of word	STEM	Djibouti	AFAR, ARABIC
correct			FRENCH, SOMALI
—expression which ousts		Dominican Republic	SPANISH
wrong one	SUMPSIMUS	doubling for emphasis	EPIZEUXIS
—pronunciation	ORTHOEPY	Dravidian	CANARESE, KANARESE
—use of language	GRAMMAR		KANNADA, MALAYALA(A)M
correspondence in sound	ASSONANCE		TAMIL, TELUGU
Costa Rica	SPANISH	earliest known form	
Creolised English	GULLAH	of word	ETYMON
current use	USUS LOQUENDI	ease of conversation	EUTRAPELIA
Cyprus	GREEK, TURKISH		EUTRAPELY
deaf language	AMESLAN, SIGNING	East Iranian	AVESTAN, AVESTIC, ZEND
defect in		Ecuador	SPANISH
—articulation	PSELLISM(US)	effective speaking	ELOCUTION
—speech	IMPEDIMENT	Egypt	ARABIC
	STAMMER, STUTTER	El Salvador	SPANISH
definition relating		emphasis	ARSIS
words to objects	OSTENSIVE	Equatorial Guinea	BUBI, FANG, SPANISH
deliberately distorted	DOUBLETALK	error of mixing	
	NEWSPEAK	categories	CATEGORY ERROR
derivation of rules		Ethiopia	(*see* Abyssinia *above*)
of grammar	DISCOVERY PROCEDURE	evasive talk	CIRCUMLOCUTION
derived from Latin	ROMANCE	everyday speech	COLLOQUIAL, DEMOTIC
describe grammar of word	PARSE		VERNACULAR, VULGATE
description of		example of inflection	PARADIGM
—functional relationships	EMIC	exclusive to group	ARGOT, CANT, JARGON
—physical patterns	ETIC	expert	LINGUIST
development of		expressing negation	PRIVATIVE
—initial sound	PROTHESIS	expression	PHRASE
—vowel		familiar combination	
between consonants	ANAPTYXIS	of words	COLLOCATION
India	SVARABHAKTI	family	
dialect	IDIOM, LINGO	—European	INDO-EUROPEAN
—Aramaic	MANDAEAN, SYRIAC	—from Latin	ROMANCE
—Berber	KABYLE	fashionable word	BUZZ WORD
—Chinese	AMOY, HAKKU, WU	faulty vocabulary or spelling	CACOLOGY
—Coptic	SAHIDIC	feeling for correct use	SPRACHGEFUHL
—French	LANGUEDOC	figurative	TROPOLOGY
	LANGUE D'OUI	Fiji	FIJIAN, HINDI
—illiterate	PATOIS	final word sound	AUSLAUT
—London	COCKNEY	Finland	FINNISH, SWEDISH
—Liverpool	SCOUSE	Finno-Ugrian	
—Louisiana	GUMBO	—Permic	PERMIAN, PERMYAK
—Newcastle	GEORDIE		UDMURT-KOMI, VOYTAK
—Persian	DARI		ZYRYAN
—provincial	PATOIS	—Ugrian	MAGYAR, OSTIAK, VOGUL

flippant speech	BANTER, PERSIFLAGE
for the blind	BRAILLE
form(s) of	
—expression	IDIOM, USAGE
—language	IDIOM, DIALECT
—noun	CASE
—verb	CONJUGATION
	MOOD, VOICE
indicating	
—action turned back	
on the subject	REFLEXIVE
—mode of action	MOOD
—whether subject acts	
or is acted upon	VOICE
used in forming tenses or	
as an adjective	PARTICIPLE
France	BASQUE, PROVENCAL
	ROMANCE
—Brittany	BRETON
—Languedoc	OCCITAN
—North	LANGUE D'OUI
	LANGUE D'OIL
—South	LANGUE D'OC, PROVENCAL
French/Louisiana	CREOLE
Gabon	ESHIRA, FANG
	MBETE, FRENCH
Gambia	FULA, MANDIKA, WOLLOF
genuine or literal	
sense of a word	ETONYM
German Hebrew	YIDDISH
Germanic dialects	ANGLIAN, JUTISH
	SAXON
Ghana	ASANTI, DAGBANI
	EWE, FANTE, GA
gibberish	BABBLE, BABEL
	GALIMATIAS
glib speech	PATTER, SPIEL
graceful use of language	ELOQUENCE
gradation of linguistic	
features	CLINE
grammarians	
—American	CHOMSKY
—English	ORM, FOWLER
	PARTRIDGE
—Greek	ARISTARCHUS
grammatical	
—rules	RECTION
which can produce	
sentences	GENERATIVE GRAMMAR
—structure	SYNTAX
Greek dialect	(A)EOLIC, ATTIC
	DORIC, IONIC, KOINE
group of speech sounds	PHONEME
groups	AFRASIAN, ALENT
	ALTAIC, AMERINDIAN
	AUSTRALIAN ABORIGINE

	AUSTRONESIAN, CHINESE
	DRAVIDIAN, ESKIMO
	HAMITO-SEMITIC
	INDO-EUROPEAN, INDO-IRANIAN
	JAPANESE, KHOISAN, KOREAN
	MALAYO-POLYNESIAN, MON KHMER
	NIGER-CONGO, NILO-SAHARAN
	PALEO-SIBERIAN, SINO-TIBETAN
	TURKIC, URALIC
Guinea	FRENCH, FULANI
	MALINKE, PULAR, SUSU
Guinea-Bissau	BALANTE, FULANI
	MALINKE, PORTUGUESE
Guyana	HINDI, URDU
gypsy	
—jargon	ARGOT, CANT
—language	ROMANES, ROMANI
	ROMANY, SHELDRU
Haiti	CREOLE, FRENCH
Hamito-Semitic	ARABIC
having same syllable	
arrangement	TAUTOMETRIC(AL)
heading	LEMMA
Hebrew - modern	IVRIT
Holland	DUTCH
Honduras	SPANISH
Hungary	MAGYAR
hypothetical language	PROTOLANGUAGE
illiterate dialect	PATOIS
in the abstract	LANGUE
incorrect pronunciation	CACOEPY
increased vocal pitch	ARSIS
index of all words in text	CONCORDANCE
Indian	(*see* **India**)
individual speech habits	IDIOLECT
Indo-European languages	BENGALI
	(CLASSIC) GREEK
	CELTIC, ENGLISH, FRENCH
	GERMAN(IC), HINDUSTANI
	HITTITE, ITALIAN, JAPHETIC
	KELTIC, LATIN, MARATHI
	MYCAENEAN, POLISH, PORTUGUESE
	PUNJABI, ROMANCE, RUSSIAN
	SPANISH, UKRAINIAN, URDU
Indo-Iranian	DARD(IC), KAFIRI
	KASHMIRI, KHOWARI, PERSIAN
	PISAC(H)E, SANSKRIT, SHIHA
	VEDIC
Indonesia	BAHASI, BATAK, BUGIS
	JAVANESE, MACASSAR
	MADURESE, SUDANESE
inflections of	
—noun, pronoun or	
adjective	DECLENSION
—verb	CONJUGATION, MOOD
	VOICE

informal speech	COLLOQUIALISM
	DEMOTIC, SLANG
	VERNACULAR, VULGATE
ingenious use of words	CONCETTO
international at sea	SEASPEAK
interpreter (US)	LINGUISTER
insertion of extra sound	EPENTHESIS
invent a new word	COIN
Iran	ARABIC, AZERBAIJANI
	AZERBAIZHANI, DARI
	FARSI, KURDISH, IRANIAN
	PAHLAVI, PARSEE, PARSI
	PEHLEVI, ZEND
Iraq	ARABIC, KURDISH
	TURKOMAN
Ireland	ERSE, GAELIC
—accent	BROGUE
Israel	ARABIC, HEBREW
	IVRIT, YIDDISH
Italian	
—ancient	OSCAN, LATIN
	SAMNITE, UMBRIAN
—classical	TUSCAN
—dialect	LADIN(O)
Japan	AINU
jargon	BARAGOUIN, LINGO
—American Indian	
traders	CHINOOK
—Brazil	GERAL, LINGUA GERIL
—bureaucratic	GOBBLEDEGOOK
	OFFICIALESE
—combining English with	
another language	PIDGIN
—gypsy	ARGOT, CANT, SHELTA
—index	FOG INDEX
—Irish	SHELTA
—jazz	HIP, RAP, SCAT, VOUT
—lawyers	LEGALESE
—newspapers	JOURNALESE
—psychologists	PSYCHOBABBLE
—sect	CANT
—sociologists	SOCIOBABBLE
—Spanish Jews	LADINO
—technologists	TECHNOBABBLE
—thieves	ARGOT
—tinkers	SHELTA
—trade	
American Indian	CHINOOK
Brazil	LINGOA GERAL
English/Chinese	PIDGIN
Italy/Levant	LINGUA FRANCA
—vagrants	SHELTA
Jordan	ARABIC
Kampuchea	FRENCH, KHMER
Kenya	LUO, KIKUYU, SWAHILI
Kerala	MALAYALA(A)M

Khoisan	BUSHMAN
Kiribati	GILBERTESE, KIRIBATI
Kuwait	ARABIC
Laos	FRENCH, LAO
law governing	
—length of conjunct	
words	BEHAGEL'S LAW
—sound variations	
over a period	SOUND LAW
Lebanon	ARABIC, ARMENIAN
	FRENCH
lengthening of	
short syllables	ECTASIS
Lesotho	SETHOSO
letter with several	
sounds	POLYPHONE
Libya	ARABIC, BERBER
Liechtenstein	GERMAN
light-hearted style	BADINAGE, BANTER
	PERSIFLAGE, RAILLERY
limiting adjective	DETERMINER
line on language map	ISOGLOSS
linguists/philologists	
—American	BLOOMFIELD, CHOMSKY
	FILLMORE, HOCKETT, LAMB
	PIKE, SAPIR, WHORF
—British	BERNSTEIN, FIRTH
	HALLIDAY, HOGBEN
	LYONS, MULLER, OGDEN
—Danish	HJELMSLEV, JESPERSON
—French	LOISY
—German	AUERBACH, MULLER
	SCHLEYER
—Italian	ALFANDARI
—Polish	ZAMENHOF
—Russian	JAKOBSEN, TRUBETSKOY
—Swiss	SAUSSURE
linguistic	
—branches	BLOOMFIELDIANISM
	CASE GRAMMAR
	COMPUTATIONAL LINGUISTICS
—classification	CATEGORY
—unit	MORPHEME
literal translation of	
foreign expression	CALQUE
	LOAN TRANSLATION
literary or	
oratorical	RHETORIC, PERIODS
long-windedness	CIRCUMLOCUTION
	PERIPHRASIS, PROLIXITY
	SESQUIPEDALIANISM
Louisiana negro	
patois	GUMBO
Luxemburg	FRENCH, GERMAN
	LETZEBURGESCH
	LUXEMBOURGOIS

Madagascar	FRENCH, MALAGASY	Nilo-Saharan	LUO
make a vocal sound	PHONATE	Norway	LANDSMA(A)L
Malawi	CHICHEWA		NEW NORSE, NYNORSK
Malayo-Polynesian	BAHASA, INDONESIAN	noun	SUBSTANTIVE
	JAVANESE, MALAY	—indeclinable	APTOTE
Malaysia	CHINESE, IBAN, MALAY	—with four cases	TETRAPTOTE
	TAMIL	object of meaning	REFERENT
Maldives	DHIVEHI, MALDIVIAN	obscene speech	BAWDRY, COPROLALIA
Mali	BAMBARA, FULANI, FRENCH		SMUT
Marrowsky	SPOONERISM	obsolete word	FOSSIL
Mauritania	ARABIC, FRENCH	of	
	HASSANIYA	—an idividual	IDIOLECT
Mauritius	BHOJPURI, CREOLE	—local area	DIALECT, VERNACULAR
	HINDI, URDU	Oman	ARABIC
meaning		omission of	
—by implication	CONNOTATION	—conjunctions	ASYNDETON
—in normal use	ACCEPTATION	—sound or syllable from	
—on explicit reference	DENOTATION	middle of word	HAPLOLOGY
meaningless	GIBBERISH		SYNCOPATION, SYNCOPE
Melanesian/English	NEO-MELANESIAN	—word(s)	ELLIPSIS
mental images of		one	
language forms	LANGUE	—clever with words	LOGODAEDALUS
method of specifying		—converting one language	
meanings of		to another	
words	COMPONENTIAL ANALYSIS	spoken	INTERPRETER
Mexico	MAYAN, SPANISH	written	TRANSLATOR
Middle Persian	PAHLAVI, PEHLEVI	origin of words	DERIVATION
mixed, witty language	MACARONIC		ETYMOLOGY
mode of expression	IDIOM	original	
modifying word	DETERMINER	—root of word	ETONYM
Monaco	FRENCH	—speech	URSPRACHE
Mongolia	KHALKH, MONGOLIAN	Orwell's language	NEWSPEAK
Mon Khmer	KHMER, VIETNAMESE	out of date	ARCHAISM
mood (of verb)		pair of words	DOUBLET
—calling for action	IMPERATIVE	Paleo-Siberian	KET
—expressing		Panama	SPANISH
condition or supposition	SUBJUNCTIVE	Papua New Guinea	MORU, PIDGIN
idea without		Paraguay	GUARANI, SPANISH
number or person	INFINITIVE	part of	
query	INTERROGATIVE	—grammar dealing	
—indicating matter		with inflections	ACCIDENCE
of fact	INDICATIVE	—sentence	PHRASE
Morocco	ARABIC, BERBER	which follows verb	
Mozambique	PORTUGUESE	to complete predicate	COMPLEMENT
nasal speech	RHINOLALIA	which says something	
needing other words to		about something	PREDICATE
form a term	SYNCATEGOREMATIC	participle that has	
negro (south-east USA)	GULLAH	no clear connection	
Nepal	NEPALI, METHIR	with the word	
	TAMANG	it modifies	DANGLING PARTICIPLE
Netherlands	DUTCH		MISRELATED PARTICIPLE
new word or phrase	NEOLOGISM, NEOLOGY	parts of speech	ADJECTIVE, ADVERB
New Zealand	ENGLISH, MAORI		CONJUNCTION, INTERJECTION
Nicaragua	MISKITO, SPANISH		NOUN, PREPOSITION
Niger	DIERMA, FULANI, FRENCH		PRONOUN, VERB
	HAUSA, TUAREG	peculiar talk	CANT

Persia	(see Iran above)	—vowels together	SYN(A)ERESIS
personal style	IDIOLECT, IDIOM	—words together	SLUR
	PARLANCE	Rwanda	KINYARWANDA, KISWAHILI
persuasive style	RHETORIC		FRENCH
pert speech	DICACITY	sacred language	PALI
Peru	AYMARA, QUECHUA	San Marino	ITALIAN
	QUICHUA, SPANISH	Sao Tome	PORTUGUESE
Philippines	AT(T)A, BIKOL, CHEBUANO	Scotland	GADHELIC, GAELIC, LALLANS
	FILIPINO, ILOCANO, MORO	script	(see alphabet)
	TAGAL(OG), TINO	secret language	CIPHER, CODE
pictorial			CRYPTOLOGY
representation of		Semitic	ARAMAIC, ARABIC, HEBREW
—letter	PICTOGRAM	Senegal	FRENCH, FULANI, SERER
—object described	IDEOGRAM		TOUCOULEUR, WOLOF
—sound	PHONOGRAM	sentence	CLAUSE
—word	REBUS	Seychelles	CREOLE, FRENCH
pithy saying	ADAGE, APHORISM	short statement of a	
	APO(PH)THEGM, EPIGRAM	general truth	AXIOM, MAXIM
	GNOME, LACON(IC)ISM	single voice-sound	SYLLABLE
	MAXIM, PROVERB, SAW	Siberia	OSTIAK, OSTYAK
play on words	JEU DE MOTS, PUN	Sierra Leone	KRIO, MENDE, TEMNE
pleasant pronunciation	EUPHONY	sign	
pompous language	BOMBAST, EUPHUISM	—language	AMESLAN, SIGNING
	FUSTIAN, GRANDILOQUENCE		TICK TACK
	RHODOMONTADE	—representing	
popular phrase	CATCHPHRASE	diphthong	DIPHONE
	CATCHWORD	word	LOGOGRAM
possessive case	(SAXON) GENITIVE	—system	SEMIOLOGY, SEMIOTICS
primitive language	URSPRACHE		(see also pictorial above)
pronounce unclearly	SLUR	simple vowel sound	MONOPHTHONG
proverb	PAROEMIA	Singapore	MALAY, MANDARIN
provincial dialect	PATOIS		TAMIL, SINGLISH
Qatar	ARABIC	Sino-Tibetan	BEIFANGHUA, CANTONESE
raillery	DICACITY		CHINESE, FUKIEN, GUOYU
related to Sanskrit	PAKRIT		MANDARIN, MIN, WU
repetition of		slang	ARGOT, CANT
—initial letters	ALLITERATION		JARGON, LINGO
—'s' sound	SIGMATISM	sleep-talking	SOMNILOQUENCE
—sound	TAUTOPHONY	slurring of sounds	ELISION
—sounds	ASSONANCE	soft manner	
representation of sound	PHONETICISM	of speaking	DULCILOQUY
Romance		Somalia	ARABIC, ITALIAN, SOMALI
—dialects	FRIULIAN, LADIN(O)	sound	
	LANGUE D'OC, LANGUE D'OIL	—quality	ACOUSTICS, TIMBRE
	LANGUE D'OUI	—system	PHONEMICS, PHONETICS
	RHAETO-ROMANIC, ROMANSCH		PHONOLOGY
—languages	FRENCH, ITALIAN	sounding	
	PORTUGUESE, PROVENCAL	—of	
	ROMANIAN, ROMANSCH	final consonant	LIAISON
	SPANISH	'r' after vowel	RHOTACISM
rough 'r' sound	BUR(R)	—pleasant	EUPHONIOUS
roundabout speech	CIRCUMABAGES	—rich	RESONANT, SONOROUS
	CIRCUMLOCUTION	South Africa	AFRIKAANS, SEPEDI
running			SESOTHO, SESUTO, SETSWANA
—final vowel into			TSWANA, XHOSA, ZULU
next word	SYNALOEPHA	South American	TUPI

South Seas	BEACH-LA-MAR
	BECHE-DE-MER
Spanish	BASQUE, CASTILIAN, CATALAN
	LADRINO, GALICIAN
speaking	DIALOGUE
—between	
three people	TRIALOGUE
two people	DUOLOGUE
—by one person	MONOLOGUE
—in	
sleep	SOMNILOQUENCE
tongues	GLOSSOLALIA
—one language	MONOGLOT
	MONOLINGUAL
—to oneself	SOLILOQUY
—together	COLLOQUY
—two languages	BILINGUAL, DIGLOT
—many languages	MULTILINGUAL
	POLYGLOT
speech	
—longer than sentence	DISCOURSE
—of	
characters in story	DIALOGUE
individual	IDIOLECT
particular	
—area	BROGUE, DIALECT, PATOIS
	VERNACULAR
—group	ARGOT, CANT
	JARGON, SLANG
—sound	PHONE
—sounds	
breathy	ASPIRATE
briefly blocking breath	PLOSIVE
explosive	PLOSIVE
hissing	SIBILANT
partially blocking	
breath	FRICATIVE
	SPIRANT
releasing breath	AFFRICATE
throaty	GUTTURAL, UVULAR
unstressed vowel	SCHWA
using	
—glottis	GLOTTAL STOP
—gums	DENTAL
—lips	LABIAL
and teeth	LABIODENTAL
—teeth	DENTAL
—tip of tongue	APICAL
—tongue and teeth	DENTILINGUAL
with tongue	
—behind teeth	ALVEOLAR
—on soft palate	VELAR
—which is	
capable of two	
explanations	AMBIGUITY
	EQUIVOCATION

charming but deceitful	BLARNEY
emotional	DECLAMATION
	ORATORY
empty of meaning	RHETORIC
ecstatic	GLOSSOLALIA
hypocritical	CANT
long-winded	CIRCUMLOCUTION
	PERIPHRASIS, PROLIXITY
pleasant in sound	EUPHONY
pompous	BOMBAST, EUPHUISM
	FUSTIAN, FLATULENCE
	GRANDILOQUENCE
ugly in sound	CACOPHONY
splitting of word by	
insertion of another	TMESIS
spoken language	PAROLE
Spoonerism	MARROWSKY
Sri Lanka	SINHALI, TAMIL
string of clichés, etc	CENTO
study of	
—comparative philology	GLOSSOLOGY
	GLOTTOLOGY
—conversational pauses	CHRONEMICS
—correct pronunciation	ORTHOEPY
—derivation of words	ETYMOLOGY
—form of words	MORPHOLOGY
—grammar	SYNTAX
—internal structure	
of language	STRUCTURALISM
—language	LINGUISTICS
	PHILOLOGY
at any one time	SYNCHRONIC
in relation to	
—behaviour, etc	METALINGUISTICS
—location	STYLISTICS
—thought	PSYCHOLINGUISTICS
through historical	
development	DIACHRONIC
—local variations	DIALECTOLOGY
—mathematics of	
language	MATHEMATICAL LINGUISTICS
—meaning	SEMANTICS
as depending on user	PRAGMATICS
—neurological preconditions	
for development of	
language	NEUROLINGUISTICS
—orthography of language	GRAPHOLOGY
—pronunciation	PHONETICS
—relationship of	
basic units	STRUCTURAL LINGUISTICS
language patterns to	
psychological	
ideas	PSYCHOLINGUISTICS
languages over	
time	GLOTTOCHRONOLOGY
	LEXICOSTATISTICS

phonological shapes	MORPHOPHONEMICS
	MORPHO(PHO)NOLOGY
structure to meaning	
and gesture	METALINGUISTICS
—signs or signals	SEMIOLOGY, SEMIOTICS
—sound	PHONICS
in relation to words	PHONOTATICS
—speech sounds	PHONEMICS, PHONETICS
	PHONOLOGY
—spoken sounds	PHONICS
—use of	
language	GRAMMAR
words by a particular	
author	STYLOMETRY
—variations in language	STYLISTICS
style	
—appropriate to setting	REGISTER
—of expressing	DICTION
	PHRASEOLOGY
subtle argument	QUILLET
Sudan	ARABIC, NILOTIC
suppression of	
—sound	ECTHLIPSIS
—vowel or syllable	ELISION
Suriname	CREOLE, DUTCH
	HINDUSTANI, JAVANESE
Swaziland	SISWATI
Switzerland	FRENCH, GERMAN
	ITALIAN, ROMANSCH
syllable	
—character set	SYLLABARY
—writing (Jap.)	HIRAGANA, KATAKANA
symbol	CATCHWORD, WATCHWORD
	(see pictorial representation, sign above)
syntactic	SYNTAGMA
syntax	SYNESIS
Syria	ARABIC, ARAMAEAN, ARAMAIC
	ARMENIAN, CIRCASSIAN
	KURDISH, SYRIAC, TURKISH
Taiwan	AMOY, CHINESE
Tanzania	SWAHILI
teaching by formal	
grammar	DIRECT METHOD
tense (of verb)	AORIST, FUTURE (PERFECT)
	(HISTORIC) PAST
	IMPERFECT, INFINITIVE
	(PLU)PERFECT, PRESENT
	PRETERIT(E)(-PRESENT)
	PRETERITO-PRESENT(IAL)
Thailand	THAI, SHAN
theme	LEMMA
theory of language and	
mathematics	GLOSSEMATICS
thieves' jargon	ARGOT
three vowels in one syllable	TRIPHTHONG
tinkers' jargon	SHELTA

Tobago	FRENCH, HINDI, SPANISH
Togo	EWE, FRENCH, KABIYE
trade jargon	(see jargon above)
transposition of	
—initial letters	MARROWSKY
	SPOONERISM
—letters or sounds	METATHESIS
—words	HYPERBATON
Trinidad	HINDI, FRENCH, SPANISH
troubadours' language	LANGUE D'OC
trouvères' language	LANGUE D'OIL
	LANGUE D'OUI
Tunisia	ARABIC, FRENCH
Turanian	URAL-ALTAIC
Turkey	ARABIC, KURDISH
	TURKISH, ZAZA
Turkic	OGHUZ, TURKISH
two	
—letters printed as one	AESC
	DIPHTHONG
	LIGATURE
—nouns joined by 'and' to	
replace adjective and noun	HENDIADYS
—vowels in one syllable	DIPHTHONG
Uganda	ATESO, LUGANDA
	RUNYANKOGE
ugly sound	CACOPHONY, DISCORDANCE
	DISSONANCE
unaspirated consonant	TENUIS
uninflected verb	INFINITIVE
unintelligible	DOUBLE-DUTCH
	DOUBLE-TALK
—jargon	BARAGOUIN
—pronunciation	IDIOGLOSSIA
union of two vowels	SYN(A)ERESIS
	SYNECPHONESIS
	SYNIZESIS
Ural-Altaic	FINNO-UGRIAN, MANCHOO
	MANCHU, MONGOLIAN
	TUNGUS, TURKO-TATAR
Uralic	FINNO-UGRIC, HUNGARIAN
	SAMOYED
Uruguay	SPANISH
use of	
—complex words formed	
from component units	AGGLUTINATION
—descriptive words	
(time and place)	DEIXIS
—language to communicate	
feelings rather than ideas	PHASIS
—symbol	
for sound	PHONETIC SPELLING
to represent initial	
sound only	ACROPHONY
—words having same	
meaning	TAUTOLOGY

used	
—between speakers of	
different languages	LINGUA FRANCA
—to	
discuss another	
language	METALANGUAGE
establish	
relationships	PHATIC LANGUAGE
utter	
—childish sounds	PRATTLE
—meaningless sounds	GIBBER
Vanuatu	BISLAMA
variation of	
—tone carrying different	
meaning	PROSODIC FEATURE
—voice pitch	INTONATION
—word endings	INFLECTION
Venezuela	SPANISH
verb	
—accompanying main verb	
to indicate tense etc	AUXILIARY
—acting on the subject	REFLEXIVE
—expressing command	JUSSIVE
—that takes	
a direct object	TRANSITIVE
an indirect object	INTRANSITIVE
verbal	
—adjective	GERUNDIVE
—attack	INVECTIVE
—dexterity	LOGODAEDALY
—noun	GERUND
vocal sounds affecting	
tones of voice	PARALANGUAGE
voice (of verb)	ACTIVE, MIDDLE, PASSIVE
vowel-rhyme	ASSONANCE
witticism	BON MOT, JEU D'ESPRIT
word(s)	
—a, an or the	ARTICLE
—as expression of style	LOCUTION
—blindness	DYSLEXIA
—borrowed from another	
language	LOAN WORD
—coined for one	
occasion	NONCE WORD
—commonly used	COLLOQUIALISM
—comprising	
all letters of other	
word(s)	ANAGRAM
	TRANSPOSITION
first letters of	
other words	ACRONYM, ACROSTIC
syntactic unit	SYNTAGMA
—conveying a particular	
meaning	SEMANTEME
	SEMEME
—difficult for stutterers	JONAH WORD

—element used at	
either end	AFFIX
the beginning	PREFIX
the end	SUFFIX
—expressing emotion	INTERJECTION
—formed from supposed	
derivative	BACK FORMATION
—having	
opposite meaning	ANTONYM
same	
—meaning	SYNONYM
—pronunciation	
but different meaning	HOMOPHONE
with	
—same spelling	HOMOGRAPH
—perhaps the same	
spelling	HOMONYM
second meaning	DOUBLE ENTENDRE
two opposite	
meanings	ANTILOGY
—imitating sound	ONOMATOPOEIA
—indicating	
contrast	DISJUNCTIVE
equality	CONJUNCTIVE
increased size	AUGMENTATIVE
relationship	PREPOSITION
smallness	DIMINUTIVE
—list	DICTIONARY, GLOSSARY
	LEXICON, LEXIS
	VOCABULARY
—modifying,	
adjective, verb, etc	ADVERB
noun	ADJECTIVE
—newly invented	COINAGE, NEOLOGISM
—of action	VERB
—out of date	ARCHAISM
—overused	CLICHE
—placed before noun, etc	PREPOSITION
—regarded as a series of	
sounds	VOCABLE
—related in origin	COGNATE, PARONYM
—repeated in meditation	MANTRA
—standing for a noun	PRONOUN
—structure	MORPHOLOGY
—substituted for	
less offensive word	DYSPHEMISM
more offensive word	EUPHEMISM
noun	PRONOUN
—suggesting but evading	
promise	WEASEL WORD
—used	
as actor's cue	CATCHWORD
at top of page in	
dictionary, etc	CATCHWORD
for	
—description	ADJECTIVE

—identification	PASSWORD
	SHIBBOLETH, WATCHWORD
in headlines	CATCHWORD
	HEADWORD, LEMMA
incorrectly	BARBARISM, MALAPROPISM
	SOLECISM, SPOONERISM
to join phrases	CONJUNCTION
—using parts of two or	
more words	BLEND
	PORTMANTEAU WORD
—with	
circumflex accent on last	
—syllable	PERISPOMENON
—but one syllable	PROPERISPOMENON
acute accent on	
last	
—syllable	OXTYONE
—but one syllable	PAROXYTONE
—third last syllable	PROPAROXYTONE
—without accent	ENCLITIC
—worship	EPEOLATRY
word or phrase	
—serving as noun	SUBSTANTIVE
—with two meanings	DOUBLE ENTENDRE
word(-unit) that	
cannot be divided	MORPHEME
writing alternately from	
L to R and R to L	BOUSTROPHEDON
Yugoslavia	MACEDONIAN, SERBIAN
	SERBO-CROAT(IAN)
	SLOVENE, SLOVENIAN
Zaire	FRENCH, KIKONGO, KISWAHILI
	LINGALA, TSHILUBA
Zambia	BEMBA, LOZI, LUNDA
	LUVALE, NYANJA, TONGA
Zimbabwe	CHISHON, SINDEBELE
	(see also **rhetoric***)*
Laos	LAO
capital	VIENGCHANE, VIENTIANE
coin	
—unit	AT
—100 at	KIP
Latin	
abandoned suit	NOLI PROSEQUI
about	CIRCA
absolute sovereignty	IMPERIUM
abyss	BARATHRUM
acceptable person	PERSONA GRATA
accidentally	EX ACCIDENTI
according to	SECUNDUM
—circumstances	PRO RE NATA
—one's prayer	EX VOTO
—the exigencies of the case	E(X) RE NATA
acquittance	QUIETUS
action	SUIT
—by informer	QUI TAM

actual	DE FACTO
administrative board	COLLEGIUM
adorn	ORNARE
after the manner	AD MODUM
—of our ancestors	MORE MAJORUM
against	CONTRA, V, VS, VERSUS
—the world	CONTRA MUNDUM
agreeable	GRATUM
alcohol	AQUA VITAE
all	OMNIS
—go out	EXEUNT OMNES
—that sort	HOC GENUS OMNE
—the more so	A FORTIORI
alternately	ALTERNIS VICIBUS
always	SEMPER
—faithful	SEMPER FIDELIS
—ready	SEMPER PARATUS
—the same	SEMPER IDEM
amateur musicians	COLLEGIUM MUSICUM
amazingly	MIRABILE DICTU
amicable arrangement	MODUS VIVENDI
among other	
—persons	INTER ALIOS
—things	INTER ALIA
amongst themselves	INTER SE
and	AC, ATQUE, ET
—all that sort of	
thing	ET HOC GENUS OMNE
—other	
people	ET AL, ET ALII
things	ET AL, ET ALIA
—so on	ETC, ET CETERA
—that which follows	ET SEQUENS
—the rest	ETC, ET CETERA
—those that follow	ET SEQUENTES
	ET SEQUENTIA
anew	DE NOVO
animal able to laugh	ANIMAL RISIBILE
annual average	COMMUNIBUS ANNIS
any	ULLUS
appealing to pity	AD MISERICORDIAM
appease	PACARE
applaud	PLAUDITE
apple	MALUM
argument	ARGUMENTUM
—for the sake of it	ARGUMENTI CAUSA
—from absurdity of	
the contrary	PER IMPOSSIBILE
—of the stick	AD BACULINUM
—to	
common sense	AD JUDICIUM
cupidity	AD CRUMENAM
opponent's	
—ignorance	AD IGNORANTIAM
—previous admissions	AD HOMINEM
prejudices	AD INVIDIAM

the point/purpose	AD REM
around	CIRCA
artificial memory	MEMORIA TECHNICA
as	QUA, UT
—a	
consequence	IPSO FACTO
favour	EX GRATIA
matter of form	PRO FORMA
poor man	IN FORMA PAUPERIS
present from	EX DONO
warning	IN TERROREM
whole	IN TOTO
—above	UT SUPRA
—an	
act of	
contumacy	IN CONTUMACIUM
grace	EX GRATIA
honour	HONORIS CAUSA
	HONORIS GRATIA
—below	UT INFRA
—far as	
concerns	
sacred matters	QUOAD SACRA
(this)	QUOAD (HOC)
—from the beginning	QUALIS AB INCEPTO
—if	QUASI
—it were	QUASI
—much	
as he deserved	QUANTUM MERUIT
more	ALTERUM TANTUM
—often as	TOTIES QUOTIES
—such	PER SE
—undivided	PRO INDIVISO
asses' bridge	PONS ASINORUM
at	
—a lucky moment	DEXTRO TEMPORE
—first sight	PRIMA FACIE
—full length	IN EXTENSO
—hand	AD MANUM
—my own risk	MEO PERICULO
—pleasure	AD LIB(ITUM)
—the	
last gasp	IN EXTREMIS
point of death	IN ARTICULO MORTIS
	IN EXTREMIS
—this time	HOC TEMPORE
Attic salt/wit	MERUM SAL, SAL ATTICUM
attendant	MINISTER
attested copy	VIDIMUS
author	AUCTOR
authoritatively	EX CATHEDRA
avowedly	EX PROFESSO
awnless	MUTICUS
back	DORSUM
bad	MALUS
badly	MALE

baggage	IMPEDIMENTA
bain-marie	BALNEUM MARIAE
bankruptcy process	CESSIO BONORUM
barley	HORDEUM
bastard	FILIUS NULLIUS
be	
—bent, not broken	FLECTI NON FRANGI
—born	NASCI
—silent!	TACE
beak	MUSUS
beaten path	VIA TRUTA
before	
—noon	ANTE MERIDIEM
—the	
light	ANTE LUCEM
war	ANTE BELLUM
begging the question	PETITIO PRINCIPII
behold the	
—man	ECCE HOMO
—proof	ECCE SIGNUM
—sign	ECCE SIGNUM
below	INFRA
—one's dignity	INFRA DIG(NITATEM)
benign mother	ALMA MATER
bereaved	ORBUS
besiege	OBSIDERE
best	OPTIMUS
better	MELIOR
between	
—parties	INTER PARTES
—themselves	INTER SE
beware	CAVE
—buyer	CAVEAT EMPTOR
—doer	CAVEAT ACTOR
—of the dog	CAVEAT CANEM
beyond	ULTRA
—measure	EXTRA MODUM
—one's power	ULTRA VIRES
—the walls	EXTRA MUROS
biographical sketch	CURRICULUM VITAE
bird	AVIS
bite	MORDERE, MORSUS
black	NIGER
blank tablet	TABULA RASA
bless you	BENEDICITE
blessed are the	
peace makers	BEATI PACIFICI
bold and cautious	AUDAX ET CAUTUS
bone	OS
book	LIBER
—plate	EX LIBRIS
bottom	FUNDUS
boxing glove	C(A)ESTUS
branch	RAMUS
brandy	AQUA VITAE
bravely	FORTITER

bread	PANIS
bread-basket	PANARIUM
breast	MAMMA, PECTUS
breathe upon	INHALARE
breathing	SPIRITUS
breeding animal	MATRIX
breeze of popularity	AURA POPULARIS
bride	NYMPHA
bridge of asses	PONS ASINORUM
bridle	FRENUM
bright	NITIDUS
brine	MURIA
bronze	AER
brother	FRATER
burden	ONUS
butterfly	PAPILIO
buttocks	NATES
by	PER
—common consent	COMMUNI CONSENSU
—courage and faith	ANIMO ET FIDE
—divine law	JURE DIVINO
—faith and	
confidence	FIDE ET FIDUCIA
fortitude	FIDE ET FORTUDINE
love	FIDE ET AMORE
—faith, not arms	FIDE NON ARMIS
—gift	EX DONO
—hand	MANU
—head of population	PER CAPITA
—heart	MEMORITER
—himself	PER SE
—human law	JURE HUMANO
—labour and honour	LABORE ET HONORE
—law	JURE
—leave of	PACE
—logical conversion	E CONVERSO
—my own fault	MEA CULPA
—oral testimony	VIVA VOCE
—reason of a vow	EX VOTO
—right	DE JURE
—that	
fact	IPSO FACTO
name	EO NOMINE
—the	
grace of God	DEI GRATIA
living voice	VIVA VOCE
very fact	IPSO FACTO
way	OBITER
whole heavens	TOTO CAELO
—virtue of office	EX OFFICIO
	VIRTUTE OFFICII
—way of	VIA
consequence	EX CONSEQUENTI
example	EG, EXEMPLI GRATIA
—what	
right	QUO JURE

warrant	QUO WARRANTO
—your leave	PACE TUA
canonical hours	HORAE CANONICAE
case	
—already decided	RES JUDICATA
—of conscience	CASUS CONSCIENTIAE
cast	DRAMATIS PERSONAE
catch	MORSUS
cattle	PECORA
cause	
—of war	CASUS BELLI
—to be done	FIERI FACIAS
celebration of sacrament	OPUS OPERATUM
censor of morals	CENSOR MORUM
certain person	QUIDAM
chaff	PALEA
chamber	CAMERA
characters in play	DRAMATIS PERSONAE
charity	CARITAS
chide	JUGARE
chief good	SUMMUM BONUM
chin	MENTUM
church with a font	DELUBRUM
circle	ORBIS
—of lands	ORBIS TERRARUM
circumlocution	CIRCUITUS VERBORUM
civil	
—arm	BRACHIUM CIVILE
—law	JUS CIVILE
clamour of forum	FORENSIS STREPITUM
clap your hands	PLAUDITE
classical passage	LOCUS CLASSICUS
clean	MUNDUS
cloak	PALLIUM
closed sea	MARE CLAUSUM
cloth	PANNUS
cloud	NUBES
collection of dried	
plants	HORTUS SICCUS
college of cardinals	COLLEGIUM
combined with	CUM
comic power	VIS COMICA
command	IMPERIUM
commander	IMPERATOR
common	COMMUNIS
—good	COMMUNE BONUM
—people	VULGUS
commonly	VULGO
completely	IN TOTO
compliance	OBSEQUIUM
compromise between	
people of different	
views	MODUS VIVENDI
compulsion from behind	VIS A TERGO
conclusion	FINIS
confidential	A LATERE

confidentially	SUB ROSA	divided	PARTITUS
conscript fathers	PATRES CONSCRIPTI	divine right	JUS DIVINUM
consider the end	FINEM RESPICE	divinity	NUMEN
contract	PACISCERE	do not	
contrariwise	E CONTRA	—despair	NIL DESPERANDUM
contrived solution	DEUS EX MACHINA	—touch me	NOLI ME TANGERE
conversely	E CONTRA, E CONVERSO	dogged labour	LABOR IMPROBUS
council representing		dogmatic pronouncement	IPSE DIXIT
all sections of Greeks	PANHELLENIUM	dregs of the people	FAEX POPULI
country in town	RUS IN URBE	dried dung	ALBUM GRAECUM
course of life	CURRICULUM VITAE, CV	drink	
created nature	NATURA NATURATA	—up!	BIBITE
creative nature	NATURA NATURANS	—distilled from	
crime	NEFAS	spices and wine	AQUA MIRABILIS
—of forgery	FALSI CRIMEN	drudge	MEDIASTINUS
crucial test	EXPERIMENTUM CRUCIS	dry wit	MERUM SAL, SAL ATTICUM
crumb	MICA	dumb	MUTUS
cup	CALYX	during life	DURANTE VITA
current usage of speech	USUS LOQUENDI	duty	OFFICIUM
cursorily	OBITER	dwelling	MANSIO
cursory remark	OBITER DICTUM	earnestly	EX ANIMO
customs	MORES	earth	TERRA
darnel	LOLIUM	easy first	FACILE PRINCEPS
day	DIES	eat and drink	EDITE BIBITE
—of		egg	OVUM
judgment	DIES IRAE	eighth	OCTAVUS
wrath	DIES IRAE	either	UTER
days		emperor	IMPERATOR
—of		emperor's decree	NOVELLA
festival	DIES FERIAE, DIES FESTI	empirical	A POSTERIORI
wrath	DIES IRAE	enclosing wall	PERIBOLUS
—when		encumbrances	IMPEDIMENTA
judges do not sit	DIES NON	end	FINIS, TERMINUS
judgment could		enjoy the present	CARPE DIEM
—be pronounced	DIES FASTI	enlightened	ILLUMINATI
—not be pronounced	DIES NEFASTI	enough	
dead force	VIS MORTUA	—for the wise	SAT SAPIENTI
death	MORS	—of words	SATIS VERBORUM
defender of the faith	FID DEF	enthusiasm	FUROR
	FIDEI DEFENSOR	entirely	IN TOTO
deity	DEUS	entity	ENS
deliver formally	SERVE	—actually existing	ENS REALE
delusive idea	IGNIS-FATUUS	—existing	
deputy	LOCUM(TENENS)	as accident	ENS PAR SE
destination	TERMINUS AD QUEM		ENS PER ACCIDENS
diametrically opposite	TOTO CAELO	in the mind	ENS RATIONIS
disc-thrower	DISCOBOLUS	equal	PAR
discharge	QUIETUS	equally	EX AEQUO
disease	MORBUS	equitably	EX AEQUO
disgustingly	AD NAUSEAM	essentially	PER SE
disinterested adviser	AMICUS CURIAE	everywhere	PASSIM, UBIQUE
dispersedly	PASSIM	evil omen	MONSTRUM
disputed question	VEXATA QUAESTIO	examine orally	VIVA (VOCE)
distinguishing		example of all the rest	INSTAR OMNIUM
properties	DIFFERENTIA	examples	EXEMPLA
divide and rule	DIVIDE ET IMPERA	except	NISI

excess	LUXUS	—this turn or occasion	PRO HAC VICE
excitement	FUROR	force	VIS
existing condition	STATUS QUO	forename	PRAENOMEN
exploits	RES GESTAE	formal or solemn command	FIAT
extinction	QUIETUS	former	QUONDAM
extortioner	BARATHRUM	—pupil	ALUMNUS
extracts	EXERPTA	formerly	FORMALITER
extravagant	EXTRA MODUM	foster-son	ALUMNUS
extreme perfection	NE PLUS ULTRA	freak of nature	LUSUS NATURAE
exult	OVARE	freely	AD LIB(ITUM)
eye	OCULUS	French disease	MORBUS GALLICUS
eyelid	PALPEBRA	frenzy	FUROR
facts relevant to case	RES GESTAE	from	EX
fair reward	QUANTUM MERUIT	—cause to effect	A PRIORI
faith	FIDES	—effect to cause	A POSTERIORI
faithful and bold	FIDUS ET AUDAX	—excess caution	EX ABUNDANTI CAUTELA
father	PATER	—his own impulse	EX MERO MOTU
—of his country	PATER PATRIAE	—inside	AB INTRO
favour	MERCES, OFFICIUM	—memory	MEMORITER
—in return	QUID PRO QUO	—office	AB OFFICIO
fear	METUS	—one living person	INTER VIVOS
fearful	TIMIDUS	—one's own resources	EX PROPRIIS
feather	PENNA	—outside	AB EXTRA
featherless animal	ANIMAL IMPLUME	—the	
fidelity and justice	FIDES ET JUSTITIA	beginning	AB INITIO, AB OVO
field of Mars	CAMPUS MARTIUS	books	EX LIBRIS
finger	DIGITUS	chair of office	EX CATHEDRA
first	PRIMUS	circumstances	E(X) RE NATA
—among equals	PRIMUS INTER PARES	converse	E(X) CONVERSO
fish's bladder	VESICA PISCIS	depths	DE PROFUNDIS
flame	FLAMMA	first	AB ORIGINE
flax	LINUM	founding of the city	
flourished	FLORUIT	(Rome)	AB URBE CONDITA
fluency	COPIA VERBORUM	greater	A MAJORI
fly	MUSCA	hypothesis	EX HYPOTHESI
focal chord	LATUS RECTUM	less	A MINORI
following	SECUNDUM	mind	EX ANIMO
font	DELUBRUM	nature of things	A NATURA REI
food	PABULUM		EX NATURA REI
foot	PES		EX NATURA RERUM
for	PRO	side	A LATERE
—a		—what	
memorial	PRO MEMORIAM	has been conceded	EX CONCESSIS
pledge	IN DEPOSITO	is prior	A PRIORI
special emergency	PRO RE NATA		EX CONCESSO
—altars and		furrow	SULCUS
firesides	PRO ARIS ET FOCIS	further on in book	INFRA
—instance	EG, EXEMPLI GRATIA	gain	LUCRUM
—making inquiry	AD INQUIRENDUM	garden	HORTUS
—nothing	GRATIS	gardener	(H)OLITOR, HORTULANUS
—one's country	PRO PATRIA	gem	OPALUS
—so much	PRO TANTO	generalisation	
—special purposes	AD HOC	from experience	AXIOMA MEDIUM
—the		genuine	BONA FIDE(S)
public good	PRO BONO PUBLICO	gift of the king	REGIUM DONUM
time being	PRO TEMPORE	girdle	C(A)ESTUS

—of Venus	CINGULUM VENERIS		—had it made	FF, FIERI FECIT
give us peace	DONA NOBIS PACEM		—hammered (this)	EXCUDIT
glove	MANICA		—has left well	BENE DECESSIT
glory	GLORIA		—invented (this)	INV(ENIT)
—(to God) on high	GLORIA IN EXCELSIS		—is ill	AEGROTAT
glowing language	ARDENTIA VERBA		—made (this)	F, FEC(IT)
go			—painted (this)	P, PINX(IT)
—in peace	VADE IN PACE		—printed (this)	EXCUDIT
—out	EXEUNT		—said (this)	IPSE DIXIT
—with me	VADE MECUM		—sculpted (this)	SCULP(SIT)
God	DEUS		—struck (this)	EXCUDIT
—be with you	DEUS VOBISCUM		head	CAPUT
—forbid	DEUS AVERTAT		—of family	PATERFAMILIAS
—grant	DEUS DET		heavenly voice	VOX ANGELICA
—out of the machine	DEUS EX MACHINA			VOX CAELESTIS
—willing	DEO VOLENTE		held of the Crown	IN CAPITE
	VOLENTE DEO		herbarium	HORTUS SICCUS
—wills it	DEUS VULT		herd of hirelings	GREX VENALIUM
goddess	DEA		here	
gold	AURUM		—and everywhere	HIC ET UBIQUE
golden	AUREUS		—buried	HIC SEPULTUS
—mean	AUREA MEDIOCRITAS		—lies	HIC JACET
good	BONUM		high Mass	MISSA SOLEMNIS
—faith	BONA FIDE(S)		highest	SUMMA
—health!	BENE VOBIS		his mere word	IPSE DIXIT
—manners	BONOS MORES		Holy	
goods	BONA		—of Holies	SANCTUM SANCTORUM
goose	ANSER		—water vessel	ASPERSORIUM
Graeco-Roman brickwork	OPUS LATERICUM		honey	MELL
grand			hoof	UNGULA
—father	AVUS		horn	CORNU
—son	NEPOS		hot bath	CALDARIUM
great work	MAGNUM OPUS		household gods	DI PENATES
greater gods	DI MAJORUM GENTIUM			LARES ET PENATES
grin	RISUS		humanities	LIT(T)ERAE HUMANIORES
grove	NEMUS		husband	MARITUS
hail and farewell	AVE ATQUE VALE		I	
halo of two circles	VESICA PISCIS		—am present	ADSUM
hammer	MALLEUS, MARCUS		—being judge	ME JUDICE
hand	MANUS		—distinguish	DISTINGUO
—book	VADE MECUM		—give that you may give	DO UT DES
—cuff	MANICA		—have spoken	DIXI
happily	FELICITER		if anybody (wants to	
harbour	PORTUS		know etc)	SI QUIS
harlot	MERETRIX		ignorant	NESCIUS
harvest	MESSIS		ignoring the point	IGNORATIO ELENCHI
hasten slowly	FESTINA LENTE		illegal compact	PACTUM ILLICITUM
have the body	HABEAS CORPUS		illogical conclusion	NON SEQUITUR
having			immediately	INSTANTER
—held an office	FUNCTUS OFFICIO		improvised	AD LIB(ITUM)
—legal right to act	SUI JURIS		in	
he			—a vacuum	IN VACUO
—cut (this)	INC(IDIT)		—absence	IN ABSENTIA
—devised (this)	INV(ENIT)		—accordance with the law	DE JURE
—executed (this)	F, FEC(IT)		—appearance	QUASI
—forged (this)	EXCUDIT		—bad faith	MALE FIDE

—capacity of	QUA
—characteristic fashion	MORE SUO
—chief	IN CAPITE
—deep despair	DE PROFUNDIS
—desperate circumstances	IN EXTREMIS
—English	ANGLICE
—equal quantities	ANA, AA, A
—express terms	EXPRESSIS VERBIS
—fact	DE FACTO
—flocks	GREGATIM
—former state	IN STATU QUO
—German	GERMANICE
—glass	IN VITRO
—his own way	MORE SUO
—ill condition	MALE HABITUS
—itself	PER SE
—just so many words	TOTIDEM VERBIS
—living organism	IN VIVO
—my opinion	ME JUDICE
—nature	IN RERUM NATURA
—order	SECUNDUM ORDINEM
—original situation	IN SITU
—part	PARTIM
—passage	IN TRANSITU
—peace	IN PACE
—person	IN PROPRIA PERSONA
—place of parent	IN LOCO PARENTIS
—presence of	
the king	CORAM DOMINO REGE
the people	CORAM POPULO
us	CORAM NOBIS
—private room	IN CAMERA
—proportion	AD VALOREM, PRO RATA
—reality	DE FACTO
—respect of	
all things	QUOAD OMNIA
formal element	FORMALITER
—secret	IN CAMERA
—self-defence	SE DEFENDENDO
—so far	QUA
—some respects only	SECUNDUM QUID
—the	
absence of the	
accused	ABSENTE REO
abstract	IN ABSTRACTO
beginning	I PRINCIPIO
bosom	IN GREMIO
father's lifetime	VITA PATRIS
first place	IMPRIMIS
highest degree	IN EXCELSIS
Lord	IN DOMINO
manner	MORE
matter (of)	IN RE
meantime	AD INTERIM
middle of things	IN MEDIAS RES
natural world	IN RERUM NATURAE

open air	SUB DIVO
order of nature	IN RERUM NATURAE
passage cited	LOC CIT
	LOCO CITATO
place of a parent	IN LOCO PARENTIS
same place	IB, IBID(EM)
test-tube	IN VITRO
time of	TEMPORE
very act	FLAGRANTE DELICTO
work cited	OP CIT, OPERE CITATO
—this	
place	HOC LOCO
year	HOC ANNO
—of	
Christ	ANNO CHRISTI
foundation of	
city (Rome)	AB URBE CONDITA
	ANNO URBIS CONDITAE
our Lord	ANNO DOMINI
redemption	ANNO SALUTIS
the	
—reign	ANNO REGNI
—world	ANNO MUNDI
—transit	IN TRANSITU
—unfavourable manner	IN MALAM PARTEM
—wine is truth	IN VINO VERITAS
incidental remark	OBITER DICTUM
index of	
—authors	INDEX AUCTORUM
—places	INDEX LOCORUM
—things	INDEX RERUM
—words	INDEX VERBORUM
indispensable condition	SINE QUA NON
ineffectual	BRUTUM
ingenuity	INGENIUM
inhabit	COLERE
injured majesty	LAESA MAJESTAS
inspection (accounts)	VIDIMUS
intermediate object	TERTIUM QUID
into the midst of things	IN MEDIAS RES
is silent	TACET
it is	
—denied	NEGATUR
—does not follow	NON SEQUITUR
—not	
allowed	NON LICET
clear	NON LIQUET
Italian millet	PANICUM
itch for	
—speaking	CACOETHES LOQUENDI
—writing	CACOETHES SCRIBENDI
jar	OLLA
joy of combat	GAUDIUM CERTAMINIS
journey	ITER
judge of taste	ARBITER ELEGANTIARUM
judicially	EX CATHEDRA

juice of grapes	MUSTUM
just now	MODO
keeper of the rolls	CUSTOS ROTULORUM
kind reader	LECTOR BENEVOLE
kiss	OSCULUM
knee	GENU
knotted	NODATUS
know thyself	NOSCE TEIPSUM
lamb of God	AGNUS DEI
land	AGER
landed estate	LATIFUNDIUM
lantern	NOCTILUCA
large	MAGNUS
—pearl	UNIO
larger	MAJOR
last argument	ULTIMA RATIO
law of	JUS, LEX
—nations	JUS GENTIUM
—nature	JUS NATURALE
—the talion	LEX TALIONIS
lawful days	DIES FASTI
	DIES PROFESTI
leader	DUX
leaf	FOLIUM
learned men	LITERATI
leave	
—of absence	ABSIT
—the stage	EXEUNT
—to appeal	AUDITA QUERELA
leaving certificate	BENE DECESSIT
legal right	JUS
leisure	OTIUM
less	MINOR
let	
—him	
go out	EXEAT
not depart	NE EXEAT
—it	
be	
—done	FIAT
—printed	IMPRIMATUR
flourish	FLOREAT
—sleeping dogs lie	QUIETA NON MOVERE
—there be light	FIAT LUX
—us	
be glad	GAUDEAMUS
therefore rejoice	GAUDEAMUS IGITUR
letter	LIT(T)ERA
—for letter	LIT(T)ERATIM
life	VITA
—like	AD VIVUM
light	LUX
—bringer	LUCIFER
—of the world	LUX MUNDI
lily	LILIUM
limit	TERMINUS

—from which	TERMINUS A QUO
—to which	TERMINUS AD QUEM
lion	LEO
list of prohibited	
books	INDEX EXPURGATORIUS
little	PARVUS, PAUL(L)US, PAUCUS
—mouth	OSCULUM
living	VIVUS
—force	VIS VIVA
lobster	LOCUSTA
long	LONGUS
—live	VIVAT
look out!	CAVE
love of country	AMOR PATRIAE
lower down the page	INFRA
lowest species	INFIMA SPECIES
lucky day	DIES FAUSTUS
male	MASCULUS
man	ANIMAL BIPES, HOMO
manner	MODUS
manners	MORES
marble	MARMOR
mark	NOTA
—well	NB, NOTA BENE
marks	INDICIA
mass	MISSA, MOLES
master	MAGISTER
Master of Arts	MAGISTER ARTIUM
measure	MENSURARE
measuring rod	GROMA
medical certificate	AEGROTAT
medicine (with gold)	AURUM POTABILE
medlar	MESPILUS
men of letters	LITERATI
mere assertion	GRATIS DICTUM
merrymaking	GAUDEAMUS
mesh	MACULA
messenger	NUNTIUS
metal	METALLUM
method of investigation	ORGANUM
middle	MEDIUS
—coat	MEDIA TUNICA
—course	VIA MEDIA
—letter	MEDIA LITTERA
—vein	MEDIA NENA
midwife	OBSTETRIX
mild	MITIS
military service or force	MILITIA
Milky Way	VIA LACTEA
mill	MOLA
mind	ANIMUS, MENS
mine and thine	MEUM ET TUUM
mint	MONETA
mist	NEBULA
mixed	MIXTUS
mnemonic device	MEMORIA TECHNICA

mob	FAEX POPULI
mode of operations	MODUS OPERANDI
modillion	MUTULUS
money	MONETA
monster	MONSTRUM
month	MENSIS
moon	LUNA, NOCTILUCA
more	PLUS
—haste, less speed	FESTINA LENTE
mosaic work	OPUS MOSIVUM
moss	MUSCUS
mother	MATER
—of family	MATERFAMILIAS
—stood	STABAT MATER
mountain	MONS
mourn	LUGERE
mouse	MUS
mouth	ORIS, OSTIUM
moveable goods	BONA MOBILIA
much	MULTUS
—in little	MULTUM IN PARVO
—not many things	MULTUM NON MULTA
mud	LUTUM
mulberry	MORUM
murmur	MUTTUM
muscle	MUS
musk	MUSCUS
must be believed	DE FIDE
mutual consent	MUTUUS CONSENSUS
my fault	MEA CULPA
myth	MYTHUS
naked	NUDUS
name	NOMEN
—being changed	MUTATO NOMINE
namely	SC, SCILICET
	VIDELICET, VIZ
native soil	NATALE SOLUM
natural law	JUS NATURALE
nature	NATURA
necessity	SINE QUA NON
necklace	MONILE
neither	NEUTER
nest	NIDUS
never say die	NIL DESPERANDUM
new	DE INTEGRO, NOVUS
—wine	MUSTUM
newsmonger	QUIDNUNC
night	NOX
nine	NOVEM
ninety	NONAGINTA
ninth	NONUS
nitric acid	AQUA-FORTIS
—and hydrochloric	AQUA-REGIA
no	
—ill omen	ABSIT OMEN
—more beyond	NE PLUS ULTRA

—offence	ABSIT INVIDIA
nobody	NEMO
nod to the wise	SAT SAPIENTI
non-speaking character	PERSONA MUTA
none	NULLUS
nose	NASUS
nostrils	NARES
not	NE, NON
—allowed	NON LICET
—any	NULLUS
—clear	NON LIQUET
—hindering	NON OBSTANTE
note	NOTARE
noteworthy sayings	NOTABILIA
nothing	NIHIL
—further	NE PLUS ULTRA
—to	
be despaired of	NIL DESPERANDUM
the point	NIHIL AD REM
notwithstanding	NON OBSTANTE
now	NUNC
number	NUMERUS
nut	NUX
nutlike	NUCALIS
obviously pre-eminent	FACILE PRINCEPS
occupy	OBTINERE
of	
—blessed memory	BEATAE MEMORIAE
—himself,herself,itself	SUI
—his own accord	EX MERO MOTU
	EX PROPRIO MOTU
	MOTU PROPRIO
—his/her age	AETATIS SUAE
—its own kind	SUI GENERIS
—one's own accord	SPONTE SUA
—sound mind	COMPOS MENTIS
—the	
morning	MATUTINUS
same kind	EJUSDEM GENERIS
offered up	OBLATUS
off-hand	BREVI MANU
	CURRENTE CALAMO
oil	OLEUM
old	
—boy	ALUMNUS
—school	ALMA MATER
—verse metre	SATURNIAN
on	
—either side	EX UTRAQUE PARTE
—high	IN EXCELSIS
—one side only	EX PARTE
—that claim	EO NOMINE
—the	
contrary	E CONTRARIO
face of it	PRIMA FACIE
first view	PRIMA FACIE

heights	IN EXCELSIS	—regrets	PIA DESIDERIA
threshold	IN LIMINE	place	LOCUS
one	UNUS	—for standing	LOCUS STANDI
—of low birth	FILIUS TERRAE	plant	HERBA
onion	UNIO	plate	LANX
only one of its kind	SUI GENERIS	pledge	PIGNUS
opaque	OPACUS	plummet	LIBELLA
open	PATERE	pocket-companion	VADE MECUM
opportunity	OCCASIO	poetic	
or	AUT	—frenzy	FUROR POETICUS
oral examination	VIVA (VOCE)	—licence	LICENTIA VATUM
order	ORDINARE	polite letters	LIT(T)ERAE HUMANIORES
original edition	EDITIO PRINCEPS	pot-herb	(H)OLUS
other	ALTER	pouch	SACCUS
—things being equal	CETERIS PARIBUS	power of	VIS
out of	EX	—decision	ARBITRIUM
—abundance	EX ABUNDANTIA	—inertia	VIS INERTIAE
—court	EX CURIA	powerful	POTENS
—goodness	EX GRATIA	praise	LAUS
—office	FUNCTUS OFFICIO	—to God	LAUS DEO
—the depths	DE PROFUNDIS	pray	ORARE
outside	EXTRA	—and work	ORA ET LABORA
oval window (ear)	FENESTRA OVALIS	—for us	ORA PRO NOBIS
over	SUPER	prayer for the dead	REQUIESCAT
—one's cups	INTER POCULA	precinct	PERIBOLUS
owing to a crime	EX DELICTO	prejudiced	EX PARTE
ox	BOVIS	present position	STATUS QUO
Oxford		privately	SUB ROSA
examination	LII(T)ERAE HUMANIORES	professionally	SECUNDUM ARTEM
oyster	OSTREA	profound silence	ALTUM SILENTIUM
pact	PACTUM	proof texts	DICTA PROBANTIA
—without consideration	PACTUM NUDUM	property	BONA
paint	PIGMENTUM	Psalm	
painted	PINXIT	—95	VENITE
pale	PALLIDUS	—98	CANTATE
pan	PATELLA	public opinion	VOX POPULI
pardon	VENIA	Punic faith	FIDES PUNICA
partial	EX PARTE		PUNICA FIDES
partially	PARTIM	public intimation	SI QUIS
passage	PORUS	pure salt	MERUM SAL
passive resistance	VIS INERTIAE	puzzle for critics	CRUX CRITICORUM
patron	PATRONUS	question is asked	QUAERITUR
peace	PAX	quickly	CITO
—be with you	PAX VOBISCUM	quite naked	IN PURIS NATURALIBUS
pending the suit	LITE PENDENTE	race	GENUS
perishable goods	BONA PERITURA	rag	PANNUS
perjury	CRIMEN FALSI	rage	FUROR
perpetual motion	PERPETUUM MOBILE	—for	
persistent labour	LABOR IMPROBUS	speaking	FUROR LOQUENDI
person	PERSONA	writing	FUROR SCRIBENDI
—not acceptable	PERSONA NON GRATA	rain-water	AQUA CAELESTIS
—of humble birth	TERRAE FILIUS	rare bird, person or thing	RARA AVIS
personally	IN PROPRIA PERSONA	razor	NOVACULA
physician	MEDICUS	reader	LECTOR
pious	PIA	reasoning animal	ANIMAL RATIONALE
—fraud	FRAUS PIA, PIA FRAUS	received text	TEXTUS RECEPTUS

refusal to accept	
responsible post	NOLO EPISCOPARI
refuse matter	EXCREMENTA
rejoicing	GAUDEAMUS
remains (on stage)	MANET, MANENT
reproach	PROBRUM
rest	
—in peace	REQUIESCAT IN PACE
	RIP
—is missing	CETERA DESUNT
résumé of career	CURRICULUM VITAE
retaliation	QUID PRO QUO
reticulated work	OPUS RETICULATUM
retrospective(ly)	EX POST FACTO
rib	COSTA
right	
—being saved	SALVO JURE
—of	
feudal superior	JUS PRIMAE NOCTIS
husband	JUS MARITI
—side	LATUS RECTUM
—to interfere	LOCUS STANDI
rightful	DE JURE
rise	ORIRI
road	VIA
roll	VOLVERE
room for penitence	LOCUS PAENITENTIAE
rotten	PUTER
rough breathing	SPIRITUS ASPER
round	ROTUNDUS
—window (ear)	FENESTRA ROTUNDA
rule	NORMA
ruler	IMPERATOR
sacred	SACER
safe	
—path	VIA TUTA
—through taking care	CAVENDO TUTUS
sailor	NAUTA, NAVITA
salmon	SALMO
same	IDEM
sanctuary	DELUBRUM
sane	COMPOS MENTIS
sardonic grin	RISUS SARDONICUS
satisfaction	POENA
saving the right	SALVO JURE
saw	SERRA
saying	DICTUM
scale of balance	LANX
sea	MARE
—carp	MERULA
—monster	ORCA
—nymph	NERINE
seat	SEDES
second	SECUMDUM
—to none	NULLI SECUNDUS
secret poison	AQUA TOFANA
secretly	SUB ROSA
secular arm	BRACHIUM SECULARE
see	VIDE
—above	VIDE SUPRA
—below	VIDE INFRA
selections	EXCERPTA
self-evident	A PRIORI
service	OFFICIUM
severe test for beginner	PONS ASINORUM
shadow	UMBRA
shape	FORMA
sheep	OVIS
shield	SCUTUM
shining	NITIDUS
ship	NAVIS
shore	ORA
shrine	DELUBRUM
sickness certificate	AEGROTAT
side	LATUS
siege	OBSIDIO
signs	INDICIA
silencing	QUIETUS
silently	EX TACITO
sinew	NERVUS
skilfully	SECUNDUM ARTEM
slanting	LIQUIS
slave-dealer	MANGO
sleeve	MANICA
slight fault	CULPA LEVIS
slip	LAPSUS
—of the	
memory	LAPSUS MEMORIAE
pen	LAPSUS CALAMI
tongue	LAPSUS LINGUAE
slippery	LUBRICUS
small	MINUTUS
smallest	MINIMUS
smallness	MINUTIA
smooth	
—breathing	SPIRITUS LENIS
—tablet	TABULA RASA
snow	NIX
so	SIC
—much the richer	TANTO UBERIOR
—throughout	SIC PASSIM
soft	MOLLIS
softening	MOLLITIES
soldier	MILES
some	ULLUS
somebody	QUIDAM
something	
—for something	QUID PRO QUO
—in addition	ETC, ET CETERA
—said	DICTUM
by the way	OBITER DICTUM
—sought for	QUAESITUM

son of		thee therefore	TE IGITUR
—nobody	FILIUS NULLIUS	there sat	SEDERUNT
—the		thereby	IPSO FACTO
people	FILIUS POPULI	thin plate	LAMELLA, LAMINA
soil	FILIUS TERRAE	thing	RES
	TERRAE FILIUS	things	
soul	ANIMA	—to be seen	VIDENDA
—of the world	ANIMA MUNDI	—worthy of notice	NOTABILIA
sounding the same	IDEM SONANS	third	TERTIUS
source and origin	FONS ET ORIGO	—person in triangle	TERTIUM QUID
spade	PALA	—something	TERTIUM QUID
spirit	SPIRITUS	this	HIC, HOC
—of the place	GENIUS LOCI	—do	HOC AGE
spit	OBELUS	thousand	MILLE
sport	LUSUS NATURAE	thread	FILUM
sports champion	VICTOR LUDORUM	threats	MINAE
spot	MACULA	throughout	A, AA, ANA, PASSIM
spring-water	AQUA FONTANA	thunderbolt	FULMEN
stake	PALUS	thus	SIC
star	STELLA	time	
starting-point	TERMINUS A QUO	—flies	TEMPUS FUGIT
state in which	STATUS QUO	—for penitence	LOCUS PAENITENTIAE
statute law	LEX SCRIPTA	to	
stem	CAULIS	—a nicety	AD UNGUEM
step	PASSUS	—be	ESSE
—mother	NOVERCA	further considered	AD REFERENDUM
stock quotation	LOCUS CLASSICUS	—each his own	SUUM CUIQUE
strong		—everyone	URBI ET ORBI
—defence	AES TRIPLEX	—for or with God	DEO
—smell	NIDOR	—infinity	AD INFINITUM
substance	QUID	—the	
substances used in		city and the world	URBI ET ORBI
medicine	MATERIA MEDICA	clergy	AD CLERUM
successfully	FELICITER	end	AD FINEM
sufficient quantity	QUANTUM SUFFICIT	greater	AD MAJUS
suicide	FELO DE SE	highest point	AD SUMMUM
Sun	SOL	less	AD MINUS
superior force	VIS MAJOR	man	AD HOMINEM
surveying pole	GROMA	nail	AD UNGUEM
sweet	DULCIS	point	AD REM
table	MENSA	—of disgust	AD NAUSEAM
tail	CAUDA	purpose	AD REM
take note	NB, NOTA BENE	purse	AD CRUMENAM
tear	LACRIMA	stars	AD ASTRA
temple	DELUBRUM	—this extent	QUOAD
test for beginner	PONS ASINORUM	—wit	SC, SCILICET, VIDELICET, VIZ
thanks to God	DEO GRATIAS	toga-wearing nation	GENS TOGATA
that		together	PARI PASSU
—is	ID EST, IE	token of respect	HONORIS CAUSA
—which a thing is	QUID		HONORIS GRATIA
the		tongue	LINGUA
—Fates oppose	FATA OBSTANT	tooth	DENS
—hour flies	HORA FUGIT	totally	IN TOTO
—King's Bench	IN BANCO REGIS	town	OPPIDUM
—same	ID, IDEM	traveller	VIATOR
—very words	IPSISSIMA VERBA	treacherously	MALA FIDE

treachery	FIDES PUNICA
tree	ARBOR
—of life	ARBOR VITAE
trifles	NUGAE
true value	QUAESITUM
turned against	OBVERSUS
turnip	NAPUS
twice	BIS
two-footed animal	ANIMAL BIPES
unacceptable person	PERSONA NON GRATA
unclaimed goods	BONA VACANTIA
under	
—consideration	SUB JUDICE
—penalty	SUB POENA
—that heading	SUB VOCE
—the	
appearance or aspect	SUB SPECIE
rose	SUB ROSA
sky	SUB DIVO
—this condition	HAC LEGE
unexpectedly	EX IMPROVISO
unformed mind	TABULA RASA
union	UNIO
unique	SUI GENERIS
university	ALMA MATER
unknown country	TERRA INCOGNITA
unlawful days	DIES NON
unless	NISI
unlucky days	DIES INFAUSTUS
unmixed	MERUS
unowned property	RES NULLUS
unspeakable	NEFANDUS
unusual person or	
thing	RARA AVIS
unwelcome person	PERSONA NON GRATA
unwritten law	LEX NON SCRIPTA
uprightly	RECTE
urn	OLLA
uttermost point	NE PLUS ULTRA
vacant see	SEDES VACANS
	SEDE VACANTE
valued possessions	LARES ET PENATES
various readings	VARIAE LECTIONES
vegetable	(H)OLUS
voice	VOX
—of	
God	VOX DEI
the people	VOX POPULI
votive (offering)	EX VOTO
wages	MERCES
wall	MURUS
war of	
extermination	BELLUM INTERNECINUM
was	ERAT
wash	LUERE
water	AQUA, LYMPHA

wave	UNDA
way	VIA
—of	
life	MODUS VIVENDI
the Cross	VIA DOLOROSA
working	MODUS OPERANDI
wayfarer	VIATOR
we	NOS
—command	MANDAMUS
—learn by	
teaching	DOCENDO DISCIMUS
weariness of life	TAEDIUM VITAE
weasel	MUSTELA
well-deserved	BENE MERENTIBUSHVX
what now?	QUID NUNC
wheel	ORBIS
—track	ORBITA
where	UBI
—are you going?	QUO VADIS
—mentioned above	UBI SUPRA
which	
—see	QUOD VIDE, QV
—was to be	
demonstrated	QED
	QUOD ERAT DEMONSTRANDUM
while	
—(she is) chaste	DUM CASTA
—war rages	FLAGRANTE BELLO
whisky	AQUA VITAE
whither	QUO
—goest thou?	QUO VADIS
who	QUI
—as much?	QUI TAM
—gains?	CUI BONO
whole world	ORBIS TERRARUM
why does he hinder?	QUARE IMPEDIT
wild animals	FERAE NATURAE
Will-o'-the wisp	IGNIS FATUUS
willy-nilly	NOLENS VOLENS
wing	PENNA
winner of the games	VICTOR LUDORUM
with	
—a grain of salt	CUM GRANUM SALIS
—distinction	MAXIMA CUM LAUDE
—easy mind	AEQUO ANIMO
—equal pace	PARI PASSU
—full authority	PLENO JURE
—God's favour	DEO FAVENTE
—greatest	
distinction	SUMMA CUM LAUDE
—many other things	CUM MULTIS ALIIS
—necessary changes	MUTATIS MUTANDIS
—notes of various	
(critics)	CUM NOTIS VARIORUM
—one	
mind	UNO ANIMO

voice	UNA VOCE	yoke	JUGUM
—praise	CUM LAUDE	you too	TU QUOQUE
—privilege	CUM PRIVILEGIO	you're another	TU QUOQUE
—proper			(*see also* **Roman**)
exceptions	EXCEPTIS EXCIPIENDIS	**law**[1]	
—running pen	CURRENTE CALAMO	some legal terms:	
—stronger reason	A FORTIORI	abandoned suit	NOLI PROSEQUI
—this law	HAC LEGE	abandonment of	
—thumb turned up	POLLICE VERSO	—claim	ABATEMENT
within	INTRA	—prosecution	NOLLE PROSEQUI
—legal powers	INTRA VIRES	absorption of estate	MERGER
—the		acknowledgment of justice	COGNOVIT
treaty	CASUS FOEDERIS	act backward	RETROACT
wall	INTRA MUROS	act of annulling	VACATUR
without	SINE	addition to will	CODICIL
—a day appointed	SINE DIE	against	V, VS, VERSUS
—changing letter	LITERATIM	alienate	DEVEST
—doubt	SINE DUBIO	annul	OVERRULE
—finishing the business	RE INFECTA	annulment	CASSATION
—issue	SINE PROLE	answer to charge	PLEA
—opposition	NEM CON	apply to the past	RETROACT
	NEMINE CONTRADICENTES	as near as possible	CY PRES
—payment or recompense	GRATIS	assize	OYER
—which not	SINE QUA NON	assumption from	
witness	TESTIS	known fact	PRESUMPTION
woe to the conquered	VAE VICTIS	at first sight	PRIMA FACIE
wolf	LUPUS	attested copy	VIDIMUS
womb	ALVUS, MATRIX, UTERUS	authority to act	
wonderful	MIRABILIS	for another	POWER OF ATTORNEY
—to		awareness of wrong act	MENS REA
see	MIRABILE VISU	be sustainable	LIE
tell	MIRABILE DICTU	being aware	SCIENTER
wonders	MIRABILIA	betray client by collusion	PREVARICATE
word		between parties	INTER PARTES
—for word	AD VERBUM, VERBATIM	beyond one's power	
—to the wise	VERB(UM) SAP(IENTES)	or authority	ULTRA VIRES
work	OPUS	bill of equity	INTERPLEADER
—is prayer	LABORARE EST ORARE	body of	
works	OPERA	—canon law	CORPUS JURIS CANONICI
workshop	OFFICINA	—civil law	CORPUS JURIS CIVILIS
world	MUNDUS	breach of	
worthwhile	TANTI	—civil law	TORT
worthless residue	CAPUT MORTUUM	—statute law	CRIME
wretched	MISER	bringing legal action	LITIGATION
writ			PROSECUTING, SUING
—in disputed		call for evidence	INVOCATION
presentation		cancel bequest	ADEEM
to benefice	QUARE IMPEDIT	case-law	PRACTIC
—requiring appearance	SCIRE FACIAS	claim	PLEA
—removing case		clause in deed defining	
to High Court	CERTIORARI	—tenure	TENENDUM
wrong	NEFAS	—terms	TESTATUM
yawn	OSCITARE	clearing from suspicion	PURGATION
year	ANNUS	codicil	LABEL
—of wonders	ANNUS MIRABILIS	come	
yellow	LUTEUS	—into effect	ENURE

—to a point or fact	ISSUE	equal law, rights, etc	ISONOMY
commit waste as tenant	ESTREPE	equality	OWELTY, PARAGE
compounding of		essential facts	
theft	THEFTBOOT, THEFTBOTE	of the crime	CORPUS DELICTI
conveyance of property	GRANT	establishing validity	
conditional release	PAROLE	of will	PROBATE
copy of legal writing	TRANSUMPT	exact copy of record	ESTREAT
corroboratory evidence	ADMINICLE	excessive	RANK
court		exchange of lands	EXCAMBION
—hearing	OYER		EXCAMBIUM
—sitting (Scot.)	SEDERUNT	excuse for not	
crime		appearing in court	ESSOIN, ESSOYNE
—minor	MISDEMEANOUR	exemption from penalties	
—serious	FELONY	or liabilities	INDEMNITY
criminal intent	MENS REA	fire-raising	ARSON
date back in application	RELATE	forbid	ENJOIN
decision of court	PLACITUM	forgery	FALSI CRIMEN
declare		formal document	DEED, WRIT
—heir (Scot.)	SERVE	fraud	STELLIONATE
—invalid	OVERRULE	—by mariners	BARRATRY
—will orally	NUNCIATE	free transfer of title	DONATION
deed		from	
—in hands of third		—another source	ALIUNDE
party	ESCROL(L), ESCROW	—one living person	
—under seal	SPECIALTY	to another	INTER VIVOS
defamation by spoken words	SLANDER	general pardon	AMNESTY
defendant's answer	REJOINDER	give	
definitely fixed	PEREMPTORY	—effect to	SERVE
delay	MORA	—up voluntarily	WAIVE
deliver formally	SERVE	handing over	TRADITION
denial of		hanging first, trying	
—part of allegation	SPECIAL ISSUE	afterwards	JEDDART JUSTICE
—whole of allegation	GENERAL ISSUE		JETHART JUSTICE
deprive of possession	DISSEISE		LYDFORD LAW, LYNCH LAW
	DISSEIZE	harsh	DRACONIAN
discuss adverse		having knowledge of	SCIENTER
claims	INTERPLEAD	hinder	ESTOP
dispossess	DISSEISE, DISSEIZE	holding what belongs	
dispossession	OUSTER	to another	DETAINER
distraint	NA(A)M, STRESS	illegal	
divine right	JUS DIVINUM	—bargain	CHAMPERTY
document	DEED	—deed	MALFEASANCE
—transferring		immovable property	REALTY
property	CONVEYANCE, DEED	in	
—certifying validity		—judge's chambers	IN CAMERA
of will	PROBATE	—secret	IN CAMERA
during litigation	PENDENTE LITE	—the act	IN FLAGRANTE DELICTO
ejection	OUSTER	incorrect union	MISJOINDER
emancipate from		information without oath	SUGGESTION
paternal authority	FORISFAMILIATE	infraction of law	OFFENCE
encroachment on		instigator of suit	PLAINTIFF
public property	PURPRESTURE	instructions to barrister	BRIEF
endow	VEST	intermediate	MESNE
enter		international law	JUS GENTIUM
—an action in court	LAY INFORMATION	interpose an action	INTERVENE
—unlawfully	TRESPASS	intrude on freehold	ABATE

issue for trial by agreement of parties	FEIGNED ISSUE
judge's	
—commission	DEDIMUS
—order or warrant	FIAT
keep out by force	DEFORCE
kidnapping	PLAGIUM
killing	HOMICIDE
	MANSLAUGHTER
	MURDER
	(*see also* **kill**)
know	WIT
land	REALTY
—tenure with only religious obligations	FRANKALMOIGN
lapse	RESOLVE
law-breaking	
—civil	TORT
—statute	CRIME, FELONY
	MISDEMEANOUR
lawyer	ADVOCATE, BARRISTER
	SOLICITOR
—American	ATTORNEY
—as paid magistrate	STIPENDIARY
—giving legal advice	COUNSEL
—government	ATTORNEY-GENERAL
	DIRECTOR OF PUBLIC PROSECUTIONS
	DPP, PUBLIC PROSECUTOR
	SOLICITOR-GENERAL
—in training	ARTICLED CLERK
	BARRISTER, SOLICITOR
—paltry	PETTIFOGGER
—Scottish	LAW-AGENT
	(PROCURATOR-)FISCAL
—using dubious methods	PETTIFOGGER
laws of natural justice	EQUITY
leasing on rent	LOCATION
legal	
—authorisation	POWER OF ATTORNEY
	PROCURATION
—case of great public interest	CAUSE CELEBRE
—claim	DROIT
—document	DEED, WRIT
—investigation	FORENSIC
—means of redress	REMEDY
—philosophy	JURISPRUDENCE
—right(s)	JUS(JURA)
—usage	PRACTIC
legally	
—acceptable	ADMISSIBLE, VALID
—qualified	COMPETENT, ELIGIBLE
—required	LIABLE
limitation of inheritance	TAIL
—to male heirs	TAIL MALE
list of court rulings	DIGEST

loss of rights after conviction for treason	ATTAINDER
magistrate's warrant	PRECEPT
maker of conveyance	GRANTER, GRANTOR
malicious	
—and defamatory publication	LIBEL
statement	SLANDER
—damage	MAYHEM
married woman	FEME COVERT
material evidence	CORPUS DELICTI
misdemeanour	DELICT
misspelt word accepted	IDEM SONANS
mother	VENTER
moveable effects	CHATTELS, FUNGIBLES
nationality dependent on	
—country of birth	JUS SOLI
—parentage	JUS SANGUINIS
natural	
—justice	EQUITY
—law	JUS NATURALE
negligence	LACHES
not	
—admitting	NOLO CONTENDERE
—enforced	DEAD LETTER
—proceeded with	NOLLE PROSEQUI
—under bonds of matrimony	DISCOVERT
note of transaction	MEMORANDUM
number of words taken as length of document	FOLIO
oath administered to witness	VOIR DIRE
obtain	
—a judgment	RECOVER
—other than by inheritance	PURCHASE
offer to make oath	WAGE
officer who filed writs	FILACER
	FILAZER
old distress warrant	DISTRINGAS
on	
—behalf of	EX PARTE
—one side only	EX PARTE
—the first view	PRIMA FACIE
one	
—acting as surety	MAINPERNOR
—for whom another becomes surety	PRINCIPAL
—who	
abets a crime	PRINCIPAL
commits a crime	PRINCIPAL
employs another	PRINCIPAL
holds property	
—at owner's discretion	TENANT-AT-WILL
—from sovereign	TENANT-IN-CHIEF

is sued	DEFENDANT
lays information	RELATOR
receives property	ALIENEE
refuses to plead	MUTE
sues	PLAINTIFF
transfers property	ALIENOR
oral defamation	SLANDER
order	
—to keep the peace	BIND OVER
—putting receiver in possession	RECEIVING-ORDER
—requiring person not to pay another	GARNISH(EE)MENT
original document	SCRIPT
paper attached to will	LABEL
partial remission	RELAXATION
penalty	SANCTION
person	
—having interest	PRIVY
—sued	DEFENDANT
personal property	CHOSE, PERSONALTY
pertaining to	
—an agent or factor	INSTITORIAL
—fixed things	REAL
—property	REAL
plea(ding)	PLACITUM
—that facts do not support the case	DEMURRER
poor lawyer	PETTIFOGGER
possession	SASINE, SEISIN
postponed case	REMANET
preclude	ESTOP
premeditation	MALICE AFORETHOUGHT MALICE PREPENSE
privately	SUB ROSA
process	INSTANCE
procuring advantage by	
—concealing the truth	SUBREPTION
—false statement	OBREPTION
produce for probate	PROPOUND
prohibit by injunction	ENJOIN
proof of will	PROBATE
property	REALTY
—acquired otherwise than by inheritance	PERQUISITE
—that can be passed to an heir	HEREDITAMENT
—right	APPURTENANCE
protection of intellectual rights, etc	COPYRIGHT
public prosecutor	DPP
—Scotland	PROCURATOR FISCAL
put in possession	SEISE, VEST
—of whole of father's land	FORISFAMILIATE
putting an end to a right	EXTINGUISHMENT

receiver of	
—conveyance	GRANTEE
—wrecks	ABANDONEE
receiving	PERNANCY
reciprocal rights of citizenship	ISOPOLITY
recover good distrained upon	REPLEVY
red-handed	IN FLAGRANTE DELICTO
reduction of legacy	ABATEMENT
reference of a case to another	REMIT
refusing to plead	MUTE (OF MALICE)
relevant facts	RES GESTAE
rendering void	DEFEASANCE
renounce title to a further share	FORISFAMILIATE
reply to defendant's	
—rebuttal	SURREBUT(TAL)
—rejoinder	SURREJOIN(DER)
reserving clause in lease	REDDENDUM
return an answer	REBUT
right(s)	DROIT, JUS(JURA), LIEN
—of	
husband	JUS MARITI
property	APPURTENANCE
—over another's land	EASEMENT
—to	
claim free lodgings	COR(R)ODY
cut	
—green trees	VERT
—wood	HAY-BOTE, HEDGE-BOTE
deal with thief taken outside one's jurisdiction	OUTFANGTHIEF
drop roof water	STILLICIDE
fish	PISCARY
fold sheep for manure	FALDAGE
graze the aftermath	FOGGAGE
hold a court	LEET, SAC, SOC
hunt game	WARREN
keep game	WARREN
necessaries allowed by law	ESTOVER
resume earlier status	POSTLIMINY
retain tenure on reasonable terms	TENANT RIGHT
search for food in forest	PU(L)TURE
seize property in war	ANGARY
take peat	TURBARY
unobstructed light	ANCIENT LIGHTS
use	
—another's property	USUFRUCT
—something not one's own	EASEMENT

rights held in common	PRO INDIVISO	unit of land	HIDE
royal commission to determine criminal charges	OYER AND TERMINER	unlawful	ILLEGAL, ILLEGITIMATE ILLICIT
science of law	JURISPRUDENCE NOMOLOGY	unowned property	RES NULLIUS
		unspecified fraud	STELLIONATE
		use and profit	USUFRUCT
second trial for same offence	DOUBLE JEOPARDY	venue	VISNE
		verdict giving right of recovery of debts	RECOVERY
secure	VEST	void	INEPT
seize	DISTRAIN, EXTEND	warrant of imprisonment	MITTIMUS
seizure	DISTRAINT SEQUESTRATION	widow	FEME SOLE
		wilfully	SCIENTER
session of court	ASSIZES	withdrawal of action	NONSUIT
settle	ENTAIL, VEST	without consideration	NUDE
settlement on series of heirs	ENTAILMENT	witness's oath	VOIR DIRE
spinster	FEME SOLE	woman	FEME
statement of grievance	PLAINT	womb	VENTER
sub-tenant	VALVASSOR VAVASOUR	word of honour	PAROLE
		writ	NOVERINT, PROCESS
submission		—authorising	
—by one not party to a case	AMICUS BRIEF	arrest one other than a judge	CAPIAS
—submission of dispute for decision	REFERENCE	to act as judge	DEDIMUS
suit	INSTANCE	—commanding appearance	SUBPOENA
summons	MONITION, SUBPOENA WRIT	—for person in hiding	LATITAT
supplement to will	CODICIL	recovery of goods distrained upon	REPLEVIN
surety	MAINPRISE	—moving case to	
surrender of claim	REMISE	county court	TOLT
sworn statement	AFFADAVIT, DEPOSITION	High Court	CERTIORARI
taking		—of	
—back	RECAPTION	distraint	DETINUE, DISTRINGAS FIERI FACIAS
—effect from a date in the past	EX POST FACTO RETROACTIVE RETROSPECTIVE	execution	FIFA
		higher court	MANDAMUS
		Richard II	PRAEMUNIRE
—possession	ENTRY	—requiring	
temporary suspension of law	RESPITE	appearance to show cause	SCIRE FACIAS
theft	LARCENY	attendance at court	SUBPOENA
temporary owner	TERMOR	reasons for hindering presentation to benefice	QUARE IMPEDIT
tenure by service	BURGAGE, SERGEANTRY SERJEANTRY, SOC(C)AGE SOKEMANRY		
token of possession	SASINE, SEISIN	—to	
transfer of property to		produce prisoner	HABEAS CORPUS
—a corporation	MORTMAIN	seize property of debtor	EXTENT
—another	ATTORN	show by what warrant one holds office	QUO WARRANTO
transgression	DELICT, OFFENCE		
under		stay proceedings	INHIBITION
—consideration	SUB JUDICE	written	
—legal age of maturity	INFANT	—accusation	INDICTMENT, LIBEL
undertaking	RECOGNISANCE	—declaration on oath	AFFADAVIT DEPOSITION
undue delay	LACHES		
union	JOINDER		

—defamation	LIBEL
—purpose	MENS REA
wrong	TORT
wrongful	
—act	DELICT, TORT
—detention of goods	DETINUE
—purpose	MENS REA

law²

law: describing governing stating that anything that can go wrong will do so	MURPHY'S LAW SOD'S LAW
bad money drives out good money	GRESHAM'S LAW
changes in stopped consonants	GRIMM'S LAW
displacement of island species	SETON'S LAW
effect of accent	VERNER'S LAW
expansion of work	PARKINSON'S LAW
flow of groundwater	DARCY'S LAW
help the less fortunate	CUTTER'S LAW
history of race repeated in individuals	BIOGENETIC LAW
inheritance	MENDEL'S LAWS
length of conjunct words	BEHAGHEL'S LAW
mathematical operations	ASSOCIATIVE LAW COMMUTATIVE LAW
movement of	
—planets	KEPLER'S LAWS
—winds	BUYS BALLOT'S LAW
only the impossible happens	MURPHY'S SECOND LAW
promotion	PETER PRINCIPLE
requisite variety	ASHBY'S LAW
supply creates demand	SAY'S LAW
	(see also **electric, physics**)

leader

including: commander potentate prince religious leader ruler	
general terms:	BELLWETHER GROUNDBREAKER, GUIDE INNOVATOR, PACEMAKER SCOUT, TRAILBREAKER TRENDSETTER, VANGUARD
acting sovereign	(VICE)REGENT, VICEROY
African	
—Ashanti chief	ASANTEHENE
—headman	CABOCEER

—ruler of Uganda	KABAKA
Albanian ruler	MPRET
American	PRESIDENT
—Indian	
North America	SACHEM, SAGAMORE
South America	CACIQUE
Arab	
—chief	AMEER, AMIR, CAID, EMEER EMIR, KAID, RAIS, SA(Y)ID SAYYID, SCHIEK, SHEIK(H)
—headman	MOCUDDUM, MOKADDAM MOQADDAM
Asian prince or chief	CHAM, KHAN
Austro-Hungarian emperor	KAISER
Baluchi chief	TOMUNDAR
borough	MAYOR
British	KING, QUEEN
—ancient chief	PENDRAGON
Chinese	
—military governor	TUCHUN
—senior official	MANDARIN
chorus	CORYPHAEUS
city council	LORD MAYOR
company	MANAGER MANAGING DIRECTOR
corporation	CHAIRMAN MANAGING DIRECTOR MAYOR
Cossack	ATAMAN, HETMAN
council	CHAIRMAN, MAYOR
deified ruler	THEOCRAT
Dutch viceroy	STAD(T)HOLDER
empire	EMPEROR, EMPRESS
English	KING, QUEEN
Egyptian	
—commander	SIRDAR
—ruler	PHARAOH
—sultan	MAMELUKE, SOLDAN
—viceroy	KHEDIVE
feudal lord	SEIGNEUR, SEIGNIOR SUZERAIN
French	PRESIDENT
—one of three heads of the Republic	CONSUL
German	LEITER
—archbishop	ELECTOR
—district official	GAULEITER
—emperor	KAISER
—leader in military drill	FUGELMAN, FUGLEMAN
—national leader	CHANCELLOR FU(E)HRER
—political leader	FUGELMAN, FUGLEMAN
—prince	ELECTOR
Greek	AGOGOS

—commamnder of	
10 men	DECADARCH
1000 men	CHILIARCH
division	TAXIARCH
subdivision	TETRARCH
trireme	TRIERARCH
—leader of worshippers	THIASARCH
—military rulers	DIADOCHI
—ruler of	
district	TOPARCH
the people	ETHNARCH
governor	(see separate entry)
head of Commonwealth	PROTECTOR
Holy Roman Emperor	KAISER
Indian	
—administrative officer	COLLECTOR
—British monarch	KAISAR-I-HIND
—chief	SUDDER
—head of state	RAJPRAMUKH
—Hindu	MAHATMA
—king	RAJAH
—military leader	SIRDAR
—Moslem prince	NAWAB
—potentate	HUZOOR
—prince	RAJAH
—Rajput chief	RANA
—ruler of	
Baroda	GAEKWAR, GAIKWAR
	GUICOWAR
Hyderabad	NIZAM
Sikkim	CHOGYAL
—viceroy of Mogul empire	NAWAB
—village chieftain	POLIGAR
Irish	
—head of family	CO(M)ARB
—king	(ARD)RI(GH)
—prime minister	TAOISEACH
Italian	
—chief official in	
Genoa and Venice	DOGE
—leader of mercenaries	CONDOTTIERE
—national leader	DUCE
Japanese	
—emperor	MIKADO, TENNO
—military commander	SHOGUN, TYCOON
Mafia leader	CAPO, DON
Malay chief	RAJAH
mediaeval lord	SUZERAIN
Moldavian prince	GOSPODAR, HOSPODAR
Moroccan prince	SHEREEF, SHERIF
Moslem	
—appearing in last days	MAHDI
—chief	DATTO
—high official	VEZIR, VISIER
	VIZI(E)R, WIZIER
—Ismaili leader	AGA KHAN

—prince	AMEER, AMIR, EMEER
	EMIR, NAWAB, SHEREEF
	SHERIF
—religious leader	AYATOLLAH, IMA(U)M
	MAHDI, MUFTI, SHEIK(H)
—revolutionary	MAHDI
—ruler	CALIF, CALIPH
	KHALIF(A)(H), SULTAN
—Shiite leader	AYATOLLAH
New Zealand	RANGATIRA
noble	(see separate entry)
Norse chieftain	JARL, YARL
North African prince	CHAM, KHAN
paramount ruler	SUZERAIN
Persian	
—ruler	CALIF, CALIPH, K(H)ALIF
	(PADI)SHAH, SOPHI, SOPHY
—viceroy	SATRAP
Red Indian chief	MUGWUMP, SACHEM
	SAGAMORE
republic	PRESIDENT
Roman	
—absolute ruler	CAESAR
—commander of	
10 soldiers	DECURION
100 soldiers	CENTURION
—emperor	CAESAR, IMPERATOR
—head of state	PRINCEPS POPULI
—leader	DUX
—lord	DOMINUS
—noble	PATRICIAN
—one of	
2	
—chief officials	CONSUL
—sharing power	DUUMVIR
3 sharing power	TRIUMVIR
—ruler of part of	
province	TETRARCH
ruler	DYNAST, PROTECTOR
	REGENT
—of the world	COSMOCRAT
—with absolute power	DESPOT, DICTATOR
	TYRANT
Russian	
—Cossack chief	ATAMAN, HETMAN
—emperor	CZAR, TSAR
Spanish	
—headman	CAPITANO
—leader	CAUDILLO, CID
subordinate prince	TETRARCH
supreme ruler	SUZERAIN
Tibetan Buddhists	
—deputy leader	PANCHEN LAMA
—leader	DALAI LAMA
Turkish	
—commander	AG(H)A, SERASKIER

—head of division	MUTESARRIF	like heather	ERICOID
—high official	(ATA)BEG, ATABEK	which fall each year	DECIDUOUS
	BEY, VEZIR, VISIER	—megasporangia	MACROSPOROPHYLL
	VIZI(E)R, WIZIER		MEGASPOROPHYLL
—military leader	BASHAW, DEY, PACHA	—same structures on	
	PASHA, ZAIM	each side	ISOBILATERAL
—prime minister	GRAND VIZIER	—slender leaves	LEPTOPHYLLOUS
—religious	CALIF, CALIPH	—sporangia	SPOROPHYLL
	KHALIF(A)(H)	—stiff leaves	SCLEROPHYLLOUS
	PADISHAH, SULTAN	—unbranched vein system	MICROPHYLL
—ruler	ATABEG, ATABEK	—woolly leaves	DASYPHYLLOUS
	CALIPH, KHAN	in carving	ACANTHUS
	PADISHAH, SULTAN	leaf	
visionary (leader)	GURU, MESSIANIC	—rosette	ROSULA
Wallachian prince	GOSPODAR, HOSPODAR	—scale	LIGULE
West Indian chief	CACIQUE, CAZIQUE	leaf-eating	PHYLLOPHAGOUS
	(*see also* **nobles, power**)	leaflet	PINNA, PINNULE
leaf	PHYLLOME	leaflike	
angle between leaf		—plant	STIPULE
and stem,	AXIL	—sheath	SPATHE
appendage at base of		leaves	FOLIAGE
—leaf	STIPULE	notch in edge of leaf	SINUS
—leaflet	STIPEL	overlapping	IMBRICATE
arrangement of		palm leaf	FROND
—leaves	PHYLLLOTAXIS	part of corolla	PETAL
	PHYLLOTAXY, VERNATION	petiole acting	
—veins	VENATION	like a leaf	PHYLLODE
axis of leaf	RACHIS	pigment in leaves	CHLOROPHYLL
blade of leaf	LAMINA	pinnate	
branch acting like		—leaf	RACHIS
a leaf	CLADODE, PHYLLOCLADE	—without leaflet at the end	PARIPINNATE
bud	GEMMA	pore	STOMA
cluster of leaves	FASCIC(U)LE	projecting part of leaf	LOBE
conversion of sunlight		projection on base	AURICLE
by leaves	PHOTOSYNTHESIS	radiating leaves	WHORL
division of		recess between lobes	SINUS
—leaf	PINNA	rib or vein	NERVURE
—pinna	PINNULE	rudimentary leaf	CATAPHYLL
excessive leaf		scale-like	AMPHIGASTRIUM
production	PHYLLOMANIA	seed-leaf	COTYLEDON
extension along stem	ALA	shapes	
fern leaf	FROND, STIPE	—arrowhead	SAGITTATE
having		—blade	SPATULATE
—2 or more leaf types	HETEROPHYLLOUS	—circular	ORBICULAR
—3 leaflets	TREFOIL, TRIFOLIATE	—feather	PINNATE, PINNATIFID
—4 leaflets	QUADRIFOIL	—finger	DIGITATE
	QUADRIFOLIATE	—hand	PALMATE
	QUATREFOIL	—heart	CORDATE
—5 leaflets	CINQUEFOIL	—irregularly notched	EROSE
—branched vein system	MEGAPHYLL	—kidney	RENIFORM
—different structures		—lance	LANCEOLATE
on each side	DORSIVENTRAL	—long and narrow	LINEAR
—flower in axil	BRACT	—lyre	LYRATE
—leaves		—needle-pointed	ACEROSE, ACIFORM
folded over		—oval	ELLIPTIC, O(BO)VATE
succeeding leaves	EQUITANT	—round-toothed	CRENATE

—saw-toothed	DENTATE
—scimitar	ACINACIFORM
—sharp-toothed	SERRATE
—shield	PELTATE
—shovel	SPATULATE
—sickle	FALC(UL)ATE
—spade	SPATULATE
—spear	HASTATE
—tapering to a point	ACUMINATE
	APICULATE, CUSPIDATE
—wavy-edged	CREN(UL)ATE, REPAND
	SINUATE
small leaf on	
flower-axis	BRACTEOLE, PROPHYLL
stalk	PETIOLE, STIPE(S)
stem acting as leaf	CLADODE
	PHYLLOCLADE
stiff leaf	SCLEROPHYLL
strip leaves	DEFOLIATE
swelling at base	PULVINULE, PULVINUS
transformation	
into leaves	PHYLLODY
vein	NERVURE
without a stalk	SESSILE
leather	
armour (Roman)	LORICA
bottle	JACK
calfskin, chrome tanned	BOX CALF
coat	GAMBESON, JACK
corslet(s)	LORICA(E)
doublet	PLACCAT(E), PLACKET
dress leather	DUB, CURRY, TAN, TAW
dresser	CURRIER
fawn-skin (Bacchus)	NEBRIS
flask (Greek)	OLPE
from	
—antelope	CHAMOIS
—buffalo	BUFF, PARFLECHE
—calves	BOX CALF(SKIN), SLINK
—deer	CHAMOIS
—elk	BUFF
—goat	CHEVEREL, CHEVERIL
	CHEVRETTE, CORDOVAN
	CORDWAIN, LEVANT
	MOCHA, MOROCCO
—kid	NAPPA, SUEDE
—lamb	NAPPA
—ox	BUFF
—reptiles	CROCODILE-SKIN
	SNAKESKIN
—sharks	SHAGREEN
—sheep	CABRETTA, CAPESKIN
	MOCHA, ROAN, SKIVER
—swine	HOGSKIN, PIGSKIN
—young ox or cow	KIPSKIN, KIP-LEATHER
glossy leather	GLACE (KID), PATENT

grained leather	ROAN
knife	MOON-KNIFE
leather-	
—dresser	CURRIER
—worker	CORDINER, CORDWAINER
morocco	LEVANT
outer garment	PILCHER
protective coat	JACK
rawhide	
—shoe (Scot.)	RULLION
—thong	RIEM
narrow	RIEMPIE
red-brown	RUSSIA LEATHER, YUFT
riding-leggings	CHAP(ARAJO)S
	CHAPAREJOS
Russia leather	YUFT
shavings from skins	MOSLINGS
shorts	LEDERHOSEN
sleeveless coat	JERKIN
stirrup guard	TAPADERA, TAPADERO
strap	BELT, STROP, TAWSE
	THONG
tanned with	
—chrome	CHROME-LEATHER
—sumach and dyed	SAFFIAN
treated for writing	PARCHMENT
trousers (Ger.)	LEDERHOSEN
undressed kid	SUEDE
untanned leather	RAWHIDE
water bottle	WATER-BOUGET
worker	LEATHERSMITH, SADDLER
yuft	RUSSIA LEATHER
Lebanon	
capital	BEIRUT
coin	
—unit	PIASTRE
—100 piastres	POUND
Lesotho	LS
capital	MASERU
coin	LISENTE, (MA)LOTI
language	SESOTHO
Liberia	LB
capital	MONROVIA
coin	DIRHAM, DINAR
library	
copyright libraries	BODLEIAN, OXFORD
	BRITISH NATIONAL
	CAMBRIDGE UNIVERSITY
	SCOTTISH NATIONAL
	TRINITY COLLEGE, DUBLIN
	WELSH NATIONAL
Libya	LAR
capital	TARABULUS, TRIPOLI
coin	DIRHAM, DINAR
newsagency	JANA
	(*see also* **Arab**)

Licentiate	
of	
—Apothecaries' Company	LAC
—College of Preceptors	LCP
—Society of Apothecaries	LSA
in	
—Dental Surgery	LDS
—Surgery	LCH
—Theology	LTH, THL
lichen	(*see* **fungus**)
Liechtenstein	FL
capital	VADUZ
coin	
—unit	CENTIME, RAPPEN
—100 rappen	FRANC
life symbol	ANKH
lifestyle	
affecting	
—a working-class image	MOCKNEY
—style of earlier	
generation	YOUNG FOGEY
black yuppie	BUPPIE, BUPPY
devoted to yacht-racing	CUPPIE, YOTTIE
double income, no kids	DINKY
drop-out	BEATNIK, HIPPIE
greying, leisured, affluent	
and married	GLAM
Japanese yuppie	JUPPIE, JUPPY
living in redeveloped	
docklands	DOCKN(E)Y
lots of money but a real	
dickhead	LOMBARD
no income, lots of kids	NILKY
old person	CRINKLY, CRUMBLY
	WRINKLY
person inheriting	
parents' property	PIPPIE, PIPPY
recently-acquired income	
deficiency syndrome	RAIDS
rich urban biker	RUB
success with peace of mind	SPOM
upper class, resident	
—in Sloane Square area	SLOANE RANGER
—near Sloane Square	SOANLY RANGER
wanting to be like someone else	WANNABEE
we have a nanny	WHANNY
well-off older person	WOOPIE
young	
—upwardly mobile	YUPPIE, YUPPY
—working-class male	PRINGLE
Youth International Party	YIPPIE
youthful, energetic,	
elderly person	YEEPIE
literature	LIT
addition	ADDENDUM
—at end	APPENDIX

affected style	GONGORISM
anonymous works	ADEPOTA
bombastic style	EUPHUISM
books	(*see separate entry*)
brief	
—account	ANECDOTE
—description	BLURB, PRECIS
	SUMMARY
category	GENRE
central idea	THEME
collected fragments	ANALECTA, ANALECTS
collection	ANTHOLOGY, CANON
composition	ESSAY
—of unconnected fragments	CENTO
controversial piece	POLEMIC
copies produced at one	
printing	EDITION
critical comment	ANNOTATION, GLOSS
delete offensive words etc	BOWDLERISE
	CENSOR
depicting	
—character's	
thoughts	INTERIOR MONOLOGUE
	STREAM OF CONSCIOUSNESS
—reality as	
representing	
underlying existence	SYMBOLISM
—section of society	SLICE OF LIFE
	TRANCHE DE VIE
double meaning	ALLEGORY
	DOUBLE ENTENDRE, PUN
dramatists	(*see separate entry*)
elegant	AUGUSTAN
excessively detailed	
description of trivia	CHOSISM
expression	PHRASE
extremism	ULTRAISM
factual	DOCUMENTARY
first part of work	PROLOGUE
florid style	EUPHUISM, GONGORISM
formal study	TREATISE
French movement (20th c)	LETTRISM
from the sublime to the	
ridiculous	BATHOS
fulsome comment	BLURB
German literary	
movement (18th c)	STURM UND DRANG
group of sentences	
on same subject	PARAGRAPH
handwritten	MANUSCRIPT
historians	(*see separate entry*)
homily	POSTIL
imaginative	FICTION
—set in the future	SCIENCE FICTION
imitation	
—based on ridicule	PARODY

—of another's style	PASTICHE
index of all words	CONCORDANCE
law protecting writers against plagiarism	COPYRIGHT
letter	EPISTLE
life-story by	
—others	BIOGRAPHY
—self	AUTOBIOGRAPHY
light-hearted work	JEU D'ESPRIT
list of	
—books	BIBLIOGRAPHY
	BIBLIOTHECA
—words	GLOSSARY
literary	
—characters	PERSONAE
—circle	BLOOMSBURY GROUP
	CLIQUE, COTERIE
	CENACLE
—essays	BELLES LETTRES
—theft	PLAGIARISM
literature as art	BELLES-LETTRES
long	
—essay	THESIS
—narrative	EPIC, SAGA
marginal note	POSTIL
materials for critical study of document	APPARATUS CRITICUS
novel	
—about wandering rogue	PICARESQUE NOVEL
—in form of letters	EPISTOLARY
—involving macabre incidents	GOTHIC NOVEL
—of	
early development of hero	BILDUNGSROMAN
family saga	ROMAN-FLEUVE
—representing real people	ROMAN A CLEF
—with no discernible plot	ANTI-NOVEL
one who	
—disputes authorship	CHORIZONT(IST)
—writes for another	GHOST WRITER
overused expression	CLICHE
part of sentence	PHRASE
pedantic style	EUPHUISM, GONGORISM
pen-name	NOM-DE-PLUME
	PSEUDONYM
persuasive style	RHETORIC
playwrights	(see dramatists)
poetry	(see verse)
poets	(see separate entry)
publishing another's work as one's own	PLAGIARISM
recasting	RIFACIMENTO

recurring theme	LEITMOTIF
rhetorical	
—style	EUPHUISM
—use of hypothetical works of another	MIMESIS
Russian literary	
—group	SERAPION BROTHERS
—movement	SOCIALIST REALISM
section of story	PASSUS
set of three works	TRILOGY
selection of works	ANTHOLOGY, ANALECTS
	CHRESTOMATHY, DIGEST
sentence	PHRASE
serious dramatic work	TRAGEDY
short	
—description	CAPTION
—introduction	FOREWORD
	PREFACE
—narrative with moral	FABLE
—novel	NOVELLA
—pithy saying	APHORISM
	APO(PH)THEGM
	EPIGRAM, WISECRACK
—statement of general truth	AXIOM, MAXIM
—summary	PRECIS
—version of book	ABRIDGED EDITION
	DIGEST
showy style	INKHORN
Spanish movement	ULTRAISM(O)
spoken or written narrative	STORY, TALE, YARN
stock theme	TOPOS
story	NARRATIVE
—based on	
fact	FACTION
imagination	FICTION
ridicule	PARODY, SATIRE
—containing facts and myths	LEGEND
—fictional	NOVEL
—in verse	FABLIAU
—of superhuman or supernatural events	MYTH
—with double meaning	ALLEGORY
summary	PRECIS, SYNOPSIS
—at start of play, etc	EXPOSITION
symbolic reference	ALLEGORY
textural comments	ANNOTATION
trite expression	CLICHE
true-to-life style	NATURALISM
twentieth-century style of novel	ANTI-NOVEL
valediction to the dead	EPITAPH
	OBIT(UARY)
verse	(see separate entry)

word indicating literal quotation	SIC
words	
—in common use	COLLOQUIALISM
—of	
oper(ett)a	LIBRETTO
song	LYRICS
work published in author's real name	AUTONYM
writers	*(see separate entry)*
lizards	AGAMA, AGAMID(AE)
	GECKO(NES), LACERTA
African	GECKO, (I)GUANA
	MONITOR, SKINK
American	ANOLIS, FENCE-LIZARD
	GILA MONSTER, UTA
Asian	FRILLED LIZARD, MONITOR
Australian	BLUE TONGUE
	CHLAMYDOSAURUS
	FRILLED LIZARD, GO(H)ANNA
	MOLOCH, MONITOR, PERENTIE
	THORN-DEVIL
barking gecko	TOKAY
colour-changing	CHAM(A)ELEON
duck-billed	HADROSAUR
Egyptian	ADDA, WORRAL, WORREL
European	MAGYAROSAURUS
fish-like	ICHTHYOPTERYGIA
	ICHTHYOSAURUS
Indonesian	KOMODO DRAGON
	KOMODO LIZARD
monitor	VARANUS
Philippines	IBID, IBIT
prehistoric	ALLOSAURUS, ANATOSAURUS
	BRACHIOSAURUS, CARNOSAURUS
	CERATOSAURUS, COELUROSAURUS
	CORYTHOSAURUS, DEINOSAUR
	DINOSAUR, ELASMOSAURUS
	GORGOSAURUS, HYPSELOSAURUS
	HYPSILOPHODON(T), KRONOSAURUS
	LABYRINTHODONT, MELANOSAURUS
	MAMENCHISAURUS, MOSASAURUS
	ORNITHOSUCHUS, PANOPLOSAURUS
	PACHYCEPHALOSAURUS
	PARASAUROLOPHUS
	PELYCOSAURUS
	PLIOSAURUS, POLACANTHUS
	SAURIOPSIDA, SAURISCHIA
	STRETOSAURUS, THERAPODA
	TYLOSAURUS,
—Colorado/Wyoming	APATOSAURUS
	ATLANTOSAURUS
	BRONTOSAURUS
—Cretaceous	ANKYLOSAURUS
	HADROSAURUS
	IGUANODON, MEGALOSAURUS

	(PA)RHABDODON
	TITANOSAURUS, TRICERATOPS
	TYRANNOSAURUS (REX)
—flying	ARCHAEOPTERYX
	ORNITHOSAURUS
	PTERODACTYL(E)
	PTERANODON
	PTEROSAURUS, SAURURAE
—giant dinosaur	SAUROPOD, THERAPOD
—Jurassic	ATLANTOSAURUS
	CETEOSAURUS
	COMPSOGNATHUS
	DIPLODOCUS, EPANTERIAS
	IGUANADON, CETEOSAURUS
	STEGOSAURUS
—medium-sized dinosaur	LUFENGOSAURUS
	PROTOSAUROPOD
—Mesozoic	D(E)INOSAUR
	ICHTHYOSAURUS
	PLESIOSAURUS
—Tertiary	D(E)INOTHERIUM
South American	AMPHISBAENA, BASILISK
	(I)GUANA, TEGUEXIN
Varanus	MONITOR
venomous	GILA MONSTER
West Indian	GALLIWASP
logic	
apparently genuine but illogical argument	FALLACY
argument of probability	ENTHYMEME
based on	
—deductions	ARISTOTELIAN LOGIC
—mathematical relationships	BOOLEAN ALGEBRA
classification of propositions	MODAL LOGIC
	MODALITY
conclusion from premise	INFERENCE
converse of logical consequence	ENTAILMENT
deduction of body of laws	LOGICAL CALCULUS
diagram of relationships	VENN DIAGRAM
drawing	
—general from particular	INDUCTION
—particular from general	DEDUCTION
from	
—cause to effect	A PRIORI
—effect to cause	A POSTERIORI
illogical conclusion	NON SEQUITUR
imaginative rather than logical thinking	LATERAL THINKING
jump in argument	SALTUS
logical	RATIONAL

—argument in three propositions	SYLLOGISM
—disproof	REDUCTIO AD ABSURDUM
—element	CONSTRUCT
—error	FALLACY
—reasoning	DEDUCTION, SYNTHESIS
	RATIOCINATION
by inference	INDUCTION
logically	
—consistent	COHERENT
	LEGITIMATE, VALID
—inconsistent	INVALID, INCOMPATIBLE
—self-evident	APODITIC, TAUTOLOGOUS
meaning of expression	CONNOTATION
particular	SUBALTERN
preliminary proposition	LEMMA
premise taken for granted	LEMMA
proposition(s)	
—both of which	
are true	CONSISTENT
—stated or assumed	PREMISE, PREMISS
refutation	ELENCH(US)
relating to part of class	PARTICULAR
sophism	ELENCH(US)
sophistical puzzle	SORITES
species comprising lower genus	SUBALTERN
specious fallacy	SOPHISM
state as a property	PREDICATE
string of propositions	SORITES
study of	
—given truths	AXIOMATICS
—necessity	MODAL LOGIC
syllogism	
—confirmed by	
incidental proposition	EPICHEIREMA
—in which	
conclusion becomes	
major premise	PROSYLLOGISM
one premise is suppressed	ENTHYMEME
the minor premise	
is only probable	ABDUCTION
syllogistic argument	SORITES
technique for testing	
truth of a proposition	DECISION PROCEDURE
theory	
—about explanations	
of events	COVERING LAW THEORY
—referred to in	
expression	DENOTATION
(*see also* **mathematics, philosophy**)	
using symbols	MATHEMATICAL LOGIC
	SYMBOLIC LOGIC
word which	
—can be predicted of itself	AUTOLOGICAL
—cannot be predicted	
of itself	HETEROLOGICAL

London

and North-Eastern Railway	LNER
County Council	LCC
Midland and Scottish	LMS
Missionary Society	LMS
Philharmonic Orchestra	LPO
School of Economics	LSE
Symphony Orchestra	LSO

lord

Lord (Chief) Justice	L(C)J
Lord Provost	LP
lordship	LD, LP
(*see also* **leaders, nobles**)	

Louis XIV	SUN KING

love

including: addiction to
          excessive love for
          love of
          lover of
          loving
          mania for
          obsession with

alcohol	DIPSOMANIA, METHOMANIA
animals	ZOOPHILIA, ZOOPHILISM
	ZOOPHILY
archery	TOXOPHILY
ballet	BALLETOMANIA
birds	ORNITHOPHILY
bonds	SCRIPOPHILY
books	BIBLIOMANIA
	BIBLIOPHILY
bridges	GEPHYRMANIA
cats	AIL(O)UROPHILIA
Celts	CELTOMANIA
	KELTOMANIA
China	SINOPHILISM, SINOPHILY
cigarette-cards	CARTOPHILY
climbing buildings	STEGOPHILY
cold	PSYCHROPHILIA
combs	CTENOPHILY
corpses	NECROMANIA, NECROPHILIA
	NECROPHILISM, NECROPHILY
crowds	DEMOMANIA, OCHLOMANIA
Dante	DANTOPHILY
darkness	SCOTOPHILIA
	SKOTOPHILIA
death	THANATOMANIA
decaying matter	SAPROPHILIA
devils	DEMONOMANIA
dogs	CANOPHILIST, CYNOMANIA
dry conditions	XEROPHILY
drugs	NARCOMANIA
dung	COPROPHILIA
eating	PHAGOMANIA, SITOMANIA
English	ANGLOPHILY
ether	ETHEROMANIA

exaggerating	MYTHOMANIA
familiar places	NOSTOMANIA
ferns	PTERIDOMANIA
	PTERIDOPHILIA
filth	COPROPHILIA
fire	PYROMANIA
flowers	ANTHOMANIA
	ANTHOPHILOUS
foreign things	XENOMANIA
French	FRANCOPHILY
	GALLOMANIA, GALLOPHILY
Germans	GERMANOPHILY
god	THEOMANIA
—and man	THEOPHILANTHROPY
gold	CHRYSOPHILY
	GOLD FEVER
gramophone records	DISCOPHILY
Greece	PHILHELLENISM
heat	THERMOPHILY
horses	HIPPOMANIA, HIPPOPHILY
imitating Oriental	POTICHOMANIA
insects	ENTOMORPHILY
knowledge	PHILOSOPHY
lakes	LIMNOPHILOUS
language	LINGUAPHILY
leaf production	PHYLLOMANIA
learning	PHILOMATHY
light	PHOTOPHILY
low temperatures	PSYCHROPHILY
lying	MYTHOMANIA
mankind	PHILANTHROPY
moisture	HYGROPHILY
mushrooms	MYCOPHILIA
music	MELOMANIA, PHILHARMONY
negroes	NEGROPHIL(Y)
new things	NEOPHILIA
offspring	PHILOPROGENITIVENESS
oils	OLEOPHILIC
old people	GERONTOPHILY
personal cleanliness	ABLUTOMANIA
pictures	ICONOPHILIA
play-going	THEATROMANIA
pleasure	HEDONOMANIA
poisons	TOXICOMANIA
power	MEGALOMANIA
printing	TYPOMANIA

pulling out hair	TRICHOTILLOMANIA
rain	OMBROPHILE
religion	(EN)THEOMANIA
riches	CHREMATOMANIA
	PLUTOMANIA
Russians	RUSSOPHILE
salt	HALOPHILE
sand	AMMOPHILY
—(plants)	PSAMMOPHIL(Y)
seeds	SPERMOPHILY
self	EGOMANIA
sexual passion	EROTOMANIA
	NYMPHOMANIA
	SATYROMANIA
—pleasure	SCOP(T)OPHILIA
single idea	MONOMANIA
snakes	OPHIOPHILISM
special food	OPSOMANIA
stamps	TIMBROMANIA
	TIMBROPHILY
stealing	KLEPTOMANIA
stone	LITHOPHILY
sun	HELIOPHILY
surgery	TOMOMANIA
talking	LOGOMANIA, VERBOMANIA
travelling	DROMOMANIA, HODOMANIA
	PORIOMANIA
tulip-growing	TULIPOMANIA
Turks	TURCOPHILY
types in the Old Testament	YPOMANIA
washing	ABLUTOMANIA
water	HYDROPHILY
wine	OENOMANIA
	OENOPHILY
wisdom	PHILOSOPHY
women	PHILOGYNY
wood	XYLOPHILY
low	
low frequency	LF
Low German	LG
Low Latin	LL
low pressure	LP
low tension	LT
lower case	LC
Luxembourg	L

M

Madagascar   MALAGASH, MALAGASY, RM
bird   DRONGO-CUCKOO
brush turkey   TALEGALLA
capital   ANTANANARIVO, TANANARIVE
civet   FO(U)SSA
climbing plant   WAX-FLOWER
flower   STEPHANOTIS
hedgehog   TANREC, TENREC
insectivore   TENREC
language   MALAGASH, MALAGASY
lattice-leaf   WATER-YAM
lemur   MONGOOSE
poison   TANGHIN
race   HOVA
raffia fabric   RABANNA
snake   LANGAHA
tree   TANGHIN, TRAVELLER'S-TREE
water-plant   LATTICE-LEAF, OUVIRANDRA
wingless bird   AEPYORNIS
magistrate   JURAT, SYNDIC
including: chief magistrate
         judge
English
—old   REEVE
—paid   STIPENDIARY
—quarter-sessions   RECORDER
French   BAILLI
—chief   AVOYER
German   AM(T)MAN
Greek   ARCHON, EPHOR, SYNDIC
Indian   COLLECTOR, COTWAL, KOTWAL
Irish   BREHON
Italian   GIUDUCE, GONFALONIERE
       MAGISTRATO, PODESTA
—old   PRIOR
mediaeval   REEVE
Moslem   CADI, KADI, SHEREEF, SHERIF
Netherlands   AM(T)MAN, STAD(T)HOLDER
Orkney   FOUD
Pakistan   HAKEEM, HAKIM
Roman   AEDILE, CONSUL
Scandinavian   AM(T)MAN
Scottish   BAIL(L)IE, PROVOST
Shetland   FOUD
South African   FIELD-CORNET
       LANDDROS(T)
Spanish   ALCALDE, CORREGIDOR
Swiss   AM(T)MAN, LANDAMMAN(N)

Venetian   DOGE, PODESTA
Malagasy   (*see* Madagascar)
Malawi   MW
capital   LILONGWE
coin
—unit   TAMBALE
—100 tambale   KWA(T)CHA
Malaya
apple   OTAHEITE
aromatic oil   CAJEPUT, CAJUPUT
badger   TELEDU
bear   BRUANG, HONEY-BEAR
       SUN-BEAR
betel   ARECA, SIRI(H)
blow-pipe   SUMPIT(AN)
boat   COROCORE, COROCORO
       PRA(H)U, PROA
bosun   SERANG
cape (headland)   TANJONG
capital   KUALA LUMPUR
civet   HEMIGALE, PARADOXURE
courtyard   KAMPONG
dish   OTAK-OTAK
estuary   KUALA
field   PADANG
fish   GORAMY, GO(U)RAMI
fruit   RAMBUTAN
—bat   KALONG
—tree   DURIAN, DURION
garment   SARONG
grass   (L)ALANG(ALANG)
harbour   BANDAR, PELABOHAN
hill   BUKIT
inlet   BANDAR
island   PULAU
knife   CREASE, CREESE
       KREESE, KRIS, PARANG
lake   TASEK
language   SAKAI
lord   TUAN
mountain   GUNUNG
nut   ARECA-NUT, BETEL-NUT
petty-officer   TINDAL
phalanger   CUS-CUS
port   BANDAR
river   SUNGAI
sailor   LASCAR
rum   TAFIA
sir   TUAN
skirt   SARONG
timber   TEAK
title of respect   TUAN
tree   ILANG-ILANG, RAMBUTAN
       SAP(P)AN, TEAK
       YLANG-YLANG
tribe   SAKAI

tunic	KABAYA	—feet	MULTIPED
verse form	PANTO(U)M	—fine teeth	MULTIDENTICULATE
village	KAMPUNG, KAMPONG	—fingers	MULTIDIGITATE
whisky and soda	STENGAH, STINGER	—flowers	MULTIFLOROUS
Malaysia	MAL	—forms	PLEOMORPHIC
capital	KUALA LUMPUR		POLYMORPHIC
chicken	AYAM	—fruiting periods	POLYCARPIC
coin			POLYCARPOUS
—unit	SEN	—furrows	MULTISULCATE
—100 sen	RINGGIT	—heads	MULTICAPITATE
curry	GULAI, GULE		MULTICIPITAL
fish	IKAN	—husbands	POLYANDROUS
kebab	SATAY, SATE		POLYGAMOUS
Maldives		—hydroxyl groups	POLYHYDRIC
capital	MALE	—individuals in colony	POLYZOIC
coin		—joints	MULT(I)ARTICULATE
—unit	LAARI	—languages	MULTILINGUAL
—100 laaris	RUFIYAA, RUPEE	—leaflets	MULTIFOLIOLATE
Mali	RMM	—leaves	MULTIFOLIATE
capital	BANAKO	—lines	MULTILINEAL, MULTILINEAR
coin	FRANC	—lobes	MULTIFID(OUS)
Malta	M		MULTILOBATE, MULTILOBED
boat	DGHAJSA	—lobules	MULTILOBULAR
capital	VALLETTA		MULTILOBULATE
coins		—meanings	MULTIVOCAL
—unit	MIL	—names	POLYONYMOUS
—10 mils	CENT	—pairs of leaflets	MULTIJUGATE
—100 cents	LIRA		MULTIJUGOUS
hood	FALDETTA	—parents	POLYHYBRID
measure	CANNA, PIEDE	—partitions	MULTISEPTATE
weight	ROTOLO	—parts	MULTIPARTITE
Manx			MULTI-STAGE
parliament	TYNWALD		POLYMEROUS
—lower house	HOUSE OF KEYS	—pips	ACINACEOUS
many		—pistils	POLYGYNIAN
combining form	MULT(I)-, POLY-		POLYGYNOUS
having many		—rays	POLYACT(INAL)
—amino-acids	POLYPEPTIDE		POLYACTINE
—atoms	POLYATOMIC	—ribs	MULTICOSTATE
—axes	POLYAXIAL, POLYAXON	—rings	POLYCYCLIC
—branches	MULTIRAMIFIED	—sepals	POLYSEPALOUS
—cells	MULTICAMERATE	—shapes	MULTIFORM, POLYMORPHIC
	MULTICELLULAR	—sides	MULTILATERAL
	POLYTHALAMOUS	—small teeth	POLYPROTODONT
—centres	MULTICENTRAL	—sounds	MULTISONANT
—chambers	MULTICAMERATE	—stems	MULTICAULINE
	MULTILOCULATE	—styles	POLYGYNIAN, POLYGYNOUS
	POLYTHALAMOUS	—syllables	POLYSYLLABIC
—circles	POLYCYCLIC	—teeth	MULTIDENTATE
—coils	MULTISPIRAL	—times normal number	
—colours	MULTICOLOURED	of chromosomes	POLYPLOID
	POLYCHROM(AT)IC	—toes	POLYDACTYLOUS
—columns	POLYSTYLAR, POLYSTYLE	—tones	POLYTONAL
—components	MULTIPLE	—tubercles	MULTITUBERCULATE
—elements	MULTIPLE, POLYSYNTHETIC	—turns	POLYCYCLIC
—faces	MULTIFACED	—types	POLYTYPIC

—variables	MULTIVARIATE
—voices	POLYPHONIC
—ways	MULTIVIOUS
—whorls	POLYCYCLIC
—wives	POLYGYNOUS
—xylem strands	POLYARCH
—zones or belts	POLYZONAL
Maori	(*see* **New Zealand**)
martial arts	(*see* **games**)
masonry	(*see* **architectural features**)
master	
Master of	
—Arts	MA
—Dental Surgery	MDS
—Foxhounds	MOF
—Laws	LLM
—Science	MSC
—Surgery	MCH, MS, CHM, CM
—the Rolls	MR, CHAUFFEUR
—Theology	MTH
material	(*see* **fabrics**)
mathematics	
1 - cosine	VERSED SINE, VERSIN(E)
1 - sin	COSEC(ANT)
2,8,20,28,50,82,126	MAGIC NUMBERS
25% percentile	QUARTILE
50% percentile	MEDIAN
75% percentile	QUARTILE
addition	SUMMATION
aggregate	MANIFOLD
—of variables	(CO)DOMAIN
all elements	UNIVERSAL SET
analysis of	
mathematics	METAMATHEMATICS
analytical	
geometry	CO-ORDINATE GEOMETRY
angle	
—less than (<)90°	ACUTE
—90°	QUADRANT
	RIGHT ANGLE
—greater than (>)90°	OBTUSE
—180°	STRAIGHT ANGLE
—greater than (>)180°	REFLEX
—360°	PERIGON
	ROUND ANGLE
—and distance fixing	
position	POLAR COORDINATE
—between axis and vector	ARGUMENT
—measurement	DEGREE, MINUTE
	RADIAN, SECOND
—subtended by arc equal	
to radius	RADIAN
angles	
—on opposite sides of	
two intersecting	
lines	ALTERNATE ANGLES

—which total	
90°	COMPLEMENTARY ANGLES
180°	SUPPLEMENTARY ANGLES
apex of cone	VERTEX
Arabic notation	ALGORISM, ALGORITHM
area bounded by two	
concentric circles	ANNULUS
arithmetic average	MEAN
arrangement into	
—a possible order	COMBINATION
—every possible order	PERMUTATION
—groups	PERMUTATION
array of coefficients	
in a grid	MATRIX
assumption for proof of	
proposition in set	
theory	AXIOM OF CHOICE
	MULTIPLICATIVE AXIOM
at right angles	PERPENDICULAR
—to	
horizontal	PERPENDICULAR
vertical	HORIZONTAL
average	ARITHMETIC MEAN
—of	
number of errors	
or deviations	STANDARD DEVIATION
squares of	
deviation	VARIANCE
based on triangles	TRIGONOMETRY
branches	ALGEBRA, ARITHMETIC
	CALCULUS, GEOMETRY
	SETS, TOPOLOGY
	TRIGONOMETRY
—modern concepts	FRACTAL GEOMETRY
	MANDELBROT SET
	MENGER SPONGE
	STERPINSKI CARPET
	STRANGE ATTRACTORS
calculating device	ABACUS
	(ELECTRONIC) CALCULATOR
	NAPIER'S BONES, NAPIER'S RODS
	SLIDE RULE
calculation of continuously	
changing variables	CALCULUS
capable of coincident	
superimposition	CONGRUENT
chart giving values	
of variables	NOMOGRAM
	NOMOGRAPH
circular band	
incorporating	
180°twist	MOBIUS STRIP
class	SET
collection of	
defined elements	SET
co-ordinate geometry	ANALYTIC GEOMETRY

combination of
  —elements in set — OPERATION
  —real and imaginary
    numbers — COMPLEX NUMBER
common fraction — VULGAR FRACTION
comparison of two
  similar quantities — RATIO
cone with axis not
  perpendicular to base — SCALENE
conic section
  —not parallel to side — HYPERBOLA
  —oblique to
    axis — ELLIPSE
    base — UNGULA
  —parallel to
    base — CIRCLE
    side — PARABOLA
consisting of
  —straight lines — RECTILINEAR
  —whole numbers — INTEGRAL
constant
  —describing a conic section — ECCENTRICITY
  —factor in conversion — MODULUS
correspondence of
  —all points of image
    with object in a
    transformation — ROTATIONAL SYMMETRY
  —parts about an axis — SYMMETRY
corresponding
  —ratios of two pairs
    of quantities — PROPORTION
  —variables — FUNCTION
counting frame — ABACUS
corner of figure or solid — VERTEX
covering area with
  polygons to form
  regular pattern — TESSELLATION
curve
  —by which a curved figure
    may be squared — QUADRATRIX
  —conic section — HYPERBOLA
    — PARABOLA
  —drawn without retracing
    any part of path — UNICURSAL
  —expressed by
    exponential
    equation — EXPONENTIAL CURVE
  —generated by
    2 points for which the
    difference of their
    distances from two fixed
    points is constant — HYPERBOLA
    centres of curvature
    of involute curve — EVOLUTE
    chain suspended at
    each end — CATENARY

intersection of
  plane and cone — CONIC SECTION
point
  —equidistant from a
    fixed point and a
    fixed straight line — PARABOLA
  —revolving about a
    moving axis — AXOID
$r = a \sin m\theta$ — ROSETTE
sine wave — SINUSOID(AL)
string wound off or
  on to another curve — INVOLUTE
$y^2 = 4ax$ — PARABOLA
$y^n = px^m$ — PARABOLA
    (*see also* figure *below*)
    (*see also* solid *below*)
  —inward — CONCAVE
  —like shell — CONCHOID
  —of variable quantities
    under fixed volume — ISOCHOR(E)
  —outward — CONVEX
dealing with variable
  quantities — DIFFERENTIAL CALCULUS
    — INTEGRAL CALCULUS
decimal
  —fraction repeating
    indefinitely — RECURRING DECIMAL
  —portion of logarithm — MANTISSA
decision-making based
  on probabilities
  and odds — GAME THEORY
    — THEORY OF GAMES
definition of dimensions
  for intricate shapes — MEASURE THEORY
derived function — DERIVATIVE
determinant derived from variables
    — JACOBIAN (DETERMINANT)
determination of
  —intermediate values — INTERPOLATION
  —length of curve — RECTIFICATION
  —values beyond range of
    given data — EXTRAPOLATION
deviation from mean — VARIATION
diagram
  —for reckoning
    probabilities — PASCAL'S TRIANGLE
  —from which data
    can be scaled — ABAC, ISOPLETH
    — NOMOGRAM, NOMOGRAPH
  —of lines — NETWORK
  —showing
    information using a motif — PICTOGRAM
    relationship
    between sets — ARROW DIAGRAM
    of variables — GRAPH
  —used in set theory — VENN DIAGRAM

difference from the mean	DEVIATION	chord and arc	SEGMENT
differential		diameter and arc	SEMI-CIRCLE
—coefficient	DERIVATIVE	straight lines	POLYGON
—operator	LAPLACE OPERATOR	—derived from another	TRANSFORMATION
distance		—generated by	
—across circle		centre of circle rolling	
through centre	DIAMETER	round another	EPICYCLE
—along		conic section round	
x-axis	ABSCISSA	a straight line	TORUS
y-axis	ORDINATE	point	
—from centre of circle		—on circle rotating	
to circumference	RADIUS	inside larger circle	HYPOCYCLOID
—round		—on circumference	
circle	CIRCUMFERENCE	of revolving circle	CYCLOID
sides of figure	PERIMETER	—rotating about	
distribution of		another point	CIRCLE
rare events	POISSON DISTRIBUTION	rotating	
eight-sided figure	OCTAGON	—ellipse	ELLIPSOID
eighth of circle	OCTANT	—rectangle	CYLINDER
element of set	MEMBER	—having	
equal in all respects	CONGRUENT	1 pair of sides parallel	TRAPEZIUM
equality of two ratios	PROPORTION	2 dimensions	PlANE FIGURE
equation(s)		2 pairs of sides parallel	
—in which the variable		—at right angles	RECTANGLE
occurs in the		—not at right angles	PARALLELOGRAM
exponent	EXPONENTIAL	3 dimensions	SOLID
—having same solutions	SIMULTANEOUS	3 sides	TRIANGLE
—involving derived		—all sides	
functions	DIFFERENTIAL	equal	EQUILATERAL
—of		unequal	SCALENE
first degree	LINEAR	—two sides equal	ISOSCELES
second degree	QUADRATIC	4 sides	QUADRILATERAL
—requiring integers		—all sides equal	
as solution	DIOPHANTINE EQUATION	at right-angles	SQUARE
—showing connection		not at right angles	RHOMBUS
between equalities	FORMULA	—2 pairs of sides equal	
Euclidean space	HOMALOID	at right angles	SQUARE
exact divisor	ALIQUOT PART	not at right	
exponent	INDEX	angles	PARALLELOGRAM
expression		all sides of equal	
—consisting of		length	EQUILATERAL FIGURE
2 terms	BINOMIAL	no sides parallel	TRAPEZOID
3 terms	TRINOMIAL	several sides	POLYGON
several terms	POLYNOMIAL	—kite-shaped	DELTOID
—derived from another	TRANSFORMATION	—polygon	
external		with 1 reflex angle	RE-ENTRANT
—edge of plane figure	PERIMETER	with all sides and angles	
—surface of solid	PERIPHERY	the same	REGULAR POLYGON
factor		—representing a number	DIGIT
—of a quantity which, taken		—which can be inscribed	
a number of times, produces		in a circle	CYCLIC FIGURE
that quantity	ROOT		(*see also* **shape**)
—which is a prime number	PRIME FACTOR	find total value	INTEGRATE
figure(s)		finding a square equal to	
—bounded by		a given figure	QUADRATURE
2 radii and an arc	SECTOR	fixed value	CONSTANT

flat surface	PLANE
formulae for faces etc of polyhedra	EULER'S FORMULAE
fraction(s)	
—expressed as negative power of ten	DECIMAL FRACTION
in binary	BICIMAL
—into which a fraction can be separated	PARTIAL FRACTIONS
—less than unity	PROPER FRACTION
—not less than unity	IMPROPER FRACTION
—that cancel to the same fraction	EQUIVALENT FRACTIONS
—with denominator of 100	PERCENTAGE
numerator greater than denominator	IMPROPER FRACTION
numerator less than denominator	PROPER FRACTION
—written with one number above and one below a line	COMMON FRACTION
	VULGAR FRACTION
fractional part of logarithm	MANTISSA
frequency distribution diagram	HISTOGRAM
function	OPERATOR
—analogous to trigonometrical ratios	HYPERBOLIC FUNCTION
—moving inversely against a variable	TRANSIENT
—obtained by fitting polynomials together	SPLINE FUNCTION
integration	INTEGRAL
—symbol	NABLA
—of function	FUNCTIONAL OPERATOR
geometry of	
—curved space	RIEMANNIAN GEOMETRY
—three-dimensional space	EUCLIDEAN GEOMETRY
graph	
—showing distribution of events	FREQUENCY CURVE
frequency by area of bars	HISTOGRAM
—using columns	BAR CHART
sectors of circle	PIE CHART
greater than any real quantity	INFINITY
group with at least one common characteristic	SET

half of	
—circle	SEMICIRCLE
—diameter of circle	RADIUS
—sphere	HEMISPHERE
—versine	HAVERSINE
having	
—1 dimension	LINEAR
—2 intersecting planes	DIHEDRAL
terms	BINOMIAL
or more terms	MULTINOMIAL
	POLYNOMIAL
—equal diameters	ISODIAMETRIC
perimeters	ISOPERIMETER
—same centre	CONCENTRIC
shape	SIMILAR
—and size	CONGRUENT, IDENTICAL
higher arithmetic	NUMBER THEORY
highest	
—derivative in differential equation	ORDER
—value of a variable	MAXIMUM
horizontal	
—and vertical lines in graph	CARTESIAN COORDINATES
—measurement in graph	ABSCISSA
hyperbolic functions	COSECH, COSH
	COTH, SECH, SINH, TANH
in the same plane	COPLANAR
ideal proportions	GOLDEN MEAN
	GOLDEN SECTION
independent variable	ARGUMENT
indirect relationship of variables	IMPLICIT FUNCTION
intersection of curve and axis	VERTEX
invariable quantity	CONSTANT
inverse of	
—differentiation	INTEGRATION
—number	RECIPROCAL
—power	LOGARITHM
inverted delta symbol	NABLA
involving right angles	ORTHOGONAL
irrational quantity	SURD
largest number which is a factor of two other numbers	HIGHEST COMMON FACTOR
law	
—governing relationship of addition and multiplication	DISTRIBUTIVE
—stating irrelevance of order of operations	ASSOCIATIVE
	COMMUTATIVE

likelihood of happening	PROBABILITY
line(s)	
—at right angles to	
horizontal	VERTICAL
vertical	HORIZONTAL
—between two points	
on a curve	CHORD
—by reference to which a	
curve can be defined	DIRECTRIX
—cutting	
circle in half	DIAMETER
line, etc, in half	BISECTOR
off part of a circle	CHORD
—from centre	
to circumference	
of circle	RADIUS
perpendicular to side	
of polygon	APOTHEM
—from corner of triangle to	
centre of side opposite	MEDIAN
—in same plane which	
never meet	PARALLEL LINES
—joining	
corners of figure	DIAGONAL
two points on a curve	CHORD
—not parallel nor intersecting	SKEW
—on surface of sphere	
which cuts all meridians	
at the same angle	LOXODROME
—parallel to horizon	HORIZONTAL
—passing through centre	
of Earth	VERTICAL
—perpendicular to another	CATHETUS
—which	
approaches but never	
reaches curve	ASYMPTOTE
cuts a curve at two or	
more places	SECANT
touches a circle at	
a point	TANGENT
logarithm	
—to base 10	COMMON LOGARITHM
—to base e	NAPERIAN LOGARITHM
	NATURAL LOGARITHM
longer axis of ellipse	MAJOR AXIS
longest side in	
right-angled triangle	HYPOTENEUSE
lowest value of a variable	MINIMUM
mapping back from	
an image	INVERSE FUNCTION
	INVERSE MAPPING
mathematicians	
—Alexandrian	DIOPHANTOS, EUCLID
—American	BOWDITCH, CHURCH, DANZIG
	ELO, FULLER, GODEL
	MINSKY, MOULTON, SHANNON

	TARSKI, VON NEUMANN
	WHITEHEAD, WIENER
—Australian	BULLEN
—Austrian	EULER, HAHN, MENGER
—Belgian	LEMAITRE
—British	BABBAGE, BONDI
	BOULE, CLIFFORD, DE MORGAN
	FLETCHER, HAMILTON, HOYLE
	KEMP, MAXWELL, NAPIER
	NEWTON, POWELL, RUSSELL
	TURING, WHITEHEAD
—Czech	GOBEWL
—Dutch	SNEL VAN ROYEN, SNELLIUS
—French	CAUCHY, CLAIRAULT
	CORIOLIS, DESCARTES
	FERMAT, GALOIS, JORDAN
	LAPLACE, LISSAJOUS
	MERCENNE, PASCAL
	POINCARE
—German	BESSEL, CANTOR, FREGE
	GAUSS, HILBERT, KRONECKER
	LEIBNITZ, MINKOWSKI, OHM
	RIEMANN, WEIERSTRASS
	ZERMEL
—Greek	ARCHIMEDES, EUCLID
	PYTHAGORAS
—Hungarian	VON NEUMANN
—Irish	FITZGERALD, HAMILTON
—Italian	CARDANO, FIBONACCI
	GALILEO, LEONARDO
	PEANO, TARTAGLIA
—Paris group	BOURBAKI
—Polish	TARSKI
—Romanian	OBERTH
—Russian	CANTOR, KOLMOGOROV
	MARKOV, MINKOWSKI
—Swiss	BERNOULLI
matrix used in probability	
theory and binomial	
distribution	PASCAL'S TRIANGLE
measurement of	
—likelihood	PROBABILITY
—lines and figures	MENSURATION
measurements which fix a	
point in a frame of	
reference	COORDINATES
meeting point of	
straight lines	VERTEX
method of	
—dealing with continuously	
varying	
quantities	DIFFERENTIAL CALCULUS
—solving simultaneous	
equations	DETERMINANTS
—statistical	
reasoning	BAYESIAN STATISTICS

moment of inertia about axis	RADIUS OF GYRATION
most frequently occurring number in a set	MODE
movement by rotating, reflecting, translating or dilating an object	TRANSFORMATION
multiplier	
—$\frac{1}{2}$	HEMI-, SEMI-
—1	MONO-, UNI-
—1$\frac{1}{2}$	SESQUI-
—2	BI-, DI-
—3	TER-, TRI-
—4	QUADR(I)-, TETR(A)-
—5	CINQ-, PENT-, QUIN-
—6	HEX(A)-, SEX(I)-
—7	HEPTA-, SEPT(I)-
—8	OCTA-, OCTO-
—9	ENNEA-, NONA-
—10	DECA-
—11	UNDECA-
—12	DODECA-, DUODECI-
—of algebraic expression	COEFFICIENT
	FACTOR
—that results in unity	RECIPROCAL
nth root of product of n numbers	GEOMETRIC MEAN
number	
—0	CIPHER, NIL, NOUGHT
—above the line in a fraction	NUMERATOR
—added	ADDEND
—average	MAN
—below the line in a fraction	DENOMINATOR
—expressing cube root	SUBTRIPLICATE
irrational quantity	SURD
—from which another is subtracted	MINUEND
—giving power of another	EXPONENT
—greater than 0	POSITIVE NUMBER
—indicating power	EXPONENT, INDEX
quality	CARDINAL
sequence	ORDINAL
—involving square-root of negative number	IMAGINARY NUMBER
—large	ARMY, HOST
	MULTITUDE, MYRIAD
10^6	MEGA-, MILLION
—USA	BILLION
10^9	GIGA
10^{12}	BILLION, TERA-
10^{15}	PETA-

10^{18}	TRILLION
10^{24}	EXA-, QUADRILLION
10^{30}	QUINTILLION
10^{36}	SEXTILLION
10^{42}	SEPTILLION
10^{48}	OCTILLION
10^{54}	NONILLION
10^{60}	DECILLION
10^{100}	GOOGOL
10^{120}	VIGINTILLION
10^{140}	ASANKHYEYA
10^{600}	CENTILLION
10^{googol}	GOOGOLPLEX
$((((10^{10})^{10})^{10})^{10})^3$	SKEWES' NUMBER
Buddhist	ASANKHYEYA
hypothetical	MEGISTON
unspecified	ZILLION
—less than 0	FRACTION
	NEGATIVE NUMBER
—making a whole	COMPLEMENT
—most frequent in a list	MODE
—non-existent quantities	IMAGINARY NUMBERS
—not commensurable with natural number	IRRATIONAL NUMBER
expressible in rational numbers	SURD
—of arcs meeting at a node	ORDER
times a function has been differentiated	ORDER
—ratio of two integers	RATIONAL NUMBER
—rational or irrational	REAL NUMBER
—represented by a logarithm	ANTILOG(ARITHM)
—resulting from addition	SUM, TOTAL
—of real and imaginary numbers	COMPLEX NUMBER
division	QUOTIENT
—of sum of numbers in set by size of set	AVERAGE, MEAN
—into 1	INVERSE
	RECIPROCAL
multiplication	PRODUCT
—small	
10^{-6}	MICRO-
10^{-9}	NANO-
10^{-12}	PICO-
10^{-15}	FEMTO-
10^{-18}	ATTO-
—subtracted	SUBTRAHEND
—system based on 2	BINARY

8	OCTAL
10	DECIMAL
16	HEX(ADECIMAL)
—the square root of which is an integer	SQUARE NUMBER
—to be subtracted	SUBTRAHEND
—used as base of number system	RADIX
—which can be	
—divided by 2	EVEN NUMBER
exactly into another	ALIQUOT, FACTOR
—written as a fraction	RATIONAL NUMBER
cannot be	
—divided by 2	ODD NUMBER
—written as a fraction	IRRATIONAL NUMBER
contains an exact number of another	MULTIPLE
equals the sum of its factors	PERFECT NUMBER
has a negative square	IMAGINARY NUMBER
is	
—added to another	SUMMAND
—divided	
by another	DIVIDEND, NUMERATOR
into another	DIVISOR
	DENOMINATOR
—not a fraction	WHOLE NUMBER
—the sum of the two preceding numbers	FIBONACCI NUMBER
—multiplied by itself produces the number in question	SQUARE ROOT
—whole number (+ and —) and zero	INTEGER
with fraction	MIXED NUMBER
—with	
associated direction	VECTOR
equal number of numbers greater and less than itself	MEDIAN
no	
—associated direction	SCALAR
—factors	PRIME NUMBER
variable exponent	EXPONENTIAL FUNCTION
—written	DIGIT, FIGURE
above another	SUPERSCRIPT
below another	SUBSCRIPT
	(*see also* quantity *below*)

numbers	
—in which the order of a pair is significant	ORDERED PAIR
—intermediate between Hindu and Arabic	GOBAR NUMERALS
—used to	
count in different directions	DIRECTED NUMBERS
fix points	COORDINATES
—which have the same remainder when divided by a third number	CONGRUENT
numerical expression of factor in a term	COEFFICIENT
omission of some digits in decimal fraction	ROUNDING
one of equal factors	ROOT
operation of	
—combining functions	COMPOSITION
—converting vectors	QUATERNION
—deducting one number from another	SUBTRACTION
—splitting number into equal parts	DIVISION
operator	FUNCTION
parameter	COEFFICIENT
part of	
—circle bounded by	
chord and arc	SEGMENT
two radii and an arc	SECTOR
—circumference of circle	ARC
—whole number	FRACTION
partially ordered set	LATTICE
path generated by point in space	LOCUS
pattern of rays	
—reflected from curved surface	CATACAUSTIC
—refracted by curve	DIACAUSTIC
peculiarity of argument of some functions	SINGULARITY
perimeter of circle	CIRCUMFERENCE
perpendicular	NORMAL
—to side from centre	APOTHEM
pertaining to	
—cube roots	SUBTRIPLICATE
—square roots of cubes	SESQUIPLICATE
plane	HOMALOID
—dividing solid into two mirror images	PLANE OF SYMMETRY
—figure bounded by straight lines	POLYGON
—figures	(*see* **shape**)
—shape which folds to produce a solid	NET

point	
—at which	
axes of graph cross	ORIGIN
concave curve changes	
to convex	INFLEXION
—being transformed	OBJECT
—defining curve	FOCUS
—line or plane which	
generates a line,	
plane or solid	GENERATRIX
—of	
common tangent of	
two curves	TACNODE
intersection	NODE, ORIGIN
—of medians	CENTROID
—on curve with more than	
one tangent	NODE
—transformed	IMAGE
potency of point with	
respect to circle	POWER
power of number to given	
base	LOG(ARITHM)
preliminary proposition	LEMMA
procedure for solving	
problems	ALGORITHM, ALGORISM
process	
—of determining	
differential	
coefficients	DIFFERENTIATION
—used in calculus	INTEGRATION
—using integration	INTEGRAL CALCULUS
—with some element	
of probability	STOCHASTIC PROCESS
product of	
—a number	
and all numbers below it	
down to 1	FACTORIAL
of equal factors	POWER
properties of	
—figures unchanged	
in deformation	TOPOLOGY
—lines, surfaces and	
solids	GEOMETRY
proportion where ratio of	
larger section to whole	
equals that of larger	
section to smaller	GOLDEN MEAN
	GOLDEN SECTION
proposition	
—proved by negation	
of the opposite	INDIRECT PROOF
—without proof	AXIOM
putting calculated values	
—between known values	INTERPOLATION
—on each side of	
known values	EXTRAPOLATION

quantity	
—defined by magnitude	
alone	SCALAR QUANTITY
and angle	VECTOR
—given by multiplying a	
number by itself	SQUARE
—on which	
a system of numeration	
is based	RADIX
another depends	ARGUMENT
—relating	
face to effect	MODULUS
force to effect	MODULUS
—used to transform systems	
of coordinates	TENSOR
—which	
can assume any value	VARIABLE
cannot be expressed	
algebraically	TRANSCENDENTAL
does not change when	
multiplied by itself	IDEMPOTENT
gives specified number	
when raised to	
third power	CUBE ROOT
—with variable	
exponent	EXPONENTIAL FUNCTION
	(*see also* number *above*)
quarter of a circle	QUADRANT
quotient of two vectors	QUATERNION
ratio of	
—angle and its sine	SINE CURVE
	SINUSOID(AL) CURVE
—circumference to	
diameter	PI
—sides of right-angled	
triangle	TRIGONOMETRICAL RATIO
height to base	TAN(GENT)
hypotenuse to	
—base	SECANT
—side opposite given	
angle	COSEC(ANT)
side	
—adjacent to side	
opposite	COT(ANGENT)
—opposite given angle	
to hypotenuse	SIN(E)
—two whole numbers	RATIONAL NUMBER
—vertical to horizontal	
distance	GRADIENT
rational	
—integral function of	
two or more variables	QUANTIC
—or irrational number	REAL NUMBER
rectangle between	
segments of chord	
or circle	POTENCY

rectangular	ORTHOGONAL		sequence of numbers	
—arrangement of quantities	MATRIX		—in general form	SERIES
reference line	AXIS		—limited by zero	NULL SEQUENCE
regular			—tending	
—six-sided figure	CUBE		to move up and down	OSCILLATING
—solid	PLATONIC SOLID		towards	
relationship			—infinity	DIVERGING
—between			—given number	CONVERGING
similar quantities	RATION		series	
variables	FUNCTION		—based on	
—in which each object has			constant increment	ARITHMETIC
an image	MAPPING		constant multiplier	GEOMETRIC
resolve into factors	FACTORISE		powers	EXPONENTIAL
result of			—of	
—addition	SUM		numbers each of	
—differentiation	DERIVED FUNCTION		which is the sum of	
	DERIVATIVE		the preceding	
—division	QUOTIENT		two	FIBONACCI SEQUENCE
into 1	INVERSE, RECIPROCAL		reciprocals in	
—multiplication	PRODUCT		arithmetic	
—transformation	IMAGE		progression	HARMONIC SERIES
root			—with	
—number	RADIX		constant common	
—which cannot be			difference	
enumerated exactly	SURD			ARITHMETICAL PROGRESSION
rule			common multiplier	
—for				GEOMETRICAL PROGRESSION
calculating irregular			set	CLASS
areas	SIMPSON'S RULE		—of	
	TRAPEZOIDAL RULE		computational	
solving problems	ALGORISM		procedures	ALGORISM, ALGORITHM
	ALGORITHM		elements	
—of proportions	CHAIN-RULE		—common to two sets	INTERSECTION
—relating sides and angles			—on which binary	
of triangle	SINE RULE		operations can be	
scalar quantity which changes			carried out	FIELD
sign in transition of			equations with	
co-ordinates	PSEUDO-SCALAR		common	
scale			variables	SIMULTANEOUS EQUATIONS
—representing			four	QUATERNION
tenfold			numbers mapped by a	
increase	LOGARITHMIC SCALE		function	DOMAIN
—showing relative			real numbers	CONTINUUM
change	INDEX		transformations	GROUP
scatter of numbers			—in every possible order	PERMUTATION
about their			—selected without	
mean value	STANDARD DEVIATION		regard to order	COMBINATION
section of			—which is part of	
—circle			larger set	SUB-SET
between two radii	SECTOR		—with no elements	EMPTY SET
cut off by chord	SEGMENT			NULL SET
—solid cut off by plane			shape	
parallel to the base	FRUSTUM		—being transformed	OBJECT
selection of specified			—transformed to	IMAGE
number from larger			—with all parts in	
number	COMBINATION		one plane	PLANE FIGURE

three dimensions	SOLID
	(*see* figure *above*)
	(*see also* **shape**)
sheet	NAPPE
shorter axis of ellipse	MINOR AXIS
side	
—of polyhedron	FACE
—opposite right-angle	HYPOTENUSE
single numeral	DIGIT
size of	
—matrix	ORDER
—solid	VOLUME
—surface	AREA
slope of line or plane	GRADIENT
smaller than any real quantity	INFINITESIMAL
smallest number which	
contains two or more	
numbers	LCM
	LOWEST COMMON MULTIPLE
solid	
—angle	STERADIAN
enclosing surface area	
equal to square of	
radius of sphere	STERADIAN
—bounded by plane	
surfaces	POLYHEDRON
—catenary shape	CATENOID
—cut off by plane not	
parallel to base of cone	
or cylinder	UNGULA
—generated by	
line through a point	
moving round a circle	CONE
rotation of	
—circle on axis	SPHERE
—ellipse on axis	ELLIPSOID
	SPHEROID
—rectangle on axis	CYLINDER
—with	
equal square faces	CUBE
one polygonal face	
and several	
triangular faces	PYRAMID
polygonal faces	POLYHEDRON
rectangular faces	CUBOID
two congruent	
parallel faces	PRISM
	(*see also* **shapes**)
space	
—enclosed by surfaces	SOLID
—occupied by a body	VOLUME
speed in a given direction	VELOCITY
spiral	HELIX
square	
—of	
mean deviation	VARIANCE

natural number	SQUARE NUMBER
—inscribed in	
circle	CYCLIC QUADRILATERAL
statement	
—of equality between	
quantities	EQUATION, IDENTITY
—proved by logical	
deduction	THEOREM
—that one quantity is not	
equal to another	INEQUALITY
statistical	
—analysis of several	
types of	
measurement	MULTIVARIATE ANALYSIS
—procedure with	
random numbers	MONTE CARLO METHOD
—spread	VARIANCE
strip of paper twisted	
and formed into loop	MO(E)BIUS STRIP
study of	
—boundaries	HOMOLOGY (THEORY)
—natural numbers	NUMBER THEORY
—numerical data	STATISTICS
—shapes when	
stretched	HOMOTOPY (THEORY)
	TOPOLOGY
—triangles	TRIGONOMETRY
sum of	
—exponents of variables	DEGREE
—sequence of terms	SERIES
surface of sphere cut	
off by two parallel planes	ZONE OF SPHERE
symbol	
—representing	
negative	MINUS
nil	NOUGHT, ZERO
number	NUMERAL
positive	PLUS
—or negative	SIGN
value or relationship	EXPRESSION
zero	NOUGHT
—showing power to which	
a number is raised	EXPONENT
—which can take	
any value	VARIABLE
symbolic logic	BOOLEAN ALGEBRA
symmetry about axis	AXIAL SYMMETRY
system for finding values	
—for allocating variables	
to different	
sources	VARIANCE ANALYSIS
—for general	
expressions	DIOPHANTINE ANALYSIS
—involving random	
occurrences which	
are time-dependent	STOCHASTIC PROCESS

term subjected to integration	INTEGRAND
theorem	
—giving any power of a binomial	BINOMIAL THEOREM
value of number in terms of logarithm	EXPONENTIAL THEOREM
—of properties of right-angled triangle	PYTHAGORAS' THEOREM
theory of	
—conflict between two rational people	GAMES THEORY
—even numbers as sum of 2 prime numbers	GOLDBACH'S CONJECTURE
third power of number	CUBE
three-dimensional co-ordinates	SPHERICAL COORDINATES
transformation in which	
—all points coincide with the image	IDENTICAL TRANSFORMATION
slide parallel to a line or plane	SHEAR
turn through the same angle	ROTATION
—figure slides without turning	TRANSLATION
—lengths remain the same	ISOMETRY
treating	
—calculation by symbols	ALGEBRA
not representing arithmetical quantities	BOOLEAN ALGEBRA
—points, lines, surfaces, etc	GEOMETRY
—properties of figures which remain unchanged after distortion	TOPOLOGY
—triangles	TRIGONOMETRY
triangle on surface of sphere	SPHERICAL TRIANGLE
trigonometrical	
—ratio	COSECANT, COSINE COTANGENT, SECANT SINE, TANGENT
—series expanded from function or curve	FOURIER ANALYSIS
trigonometry of spherical triangles	SPHERICAL TRIGONOMETRY

unvarying quantity	CONSTANT
using symbols for numbers, etc	ALGEBRA
value of	
—angle and distance fixing position of a point	RADIUS VECTOR
vector fixing position of point	POLAR COORDINATE
—function of variable whose differential coefficient is known	INTEGRAL
—limiting specified percentage of large sample	PERCENTILE
—number given by one divided by that number	RECIPROCAL
—variable and associated probabilities	DISTRIBUTION
which satisfies an equation	ROOT
variable	PARAMETER
—defined in terms of another	EXPLICIT FUNCTION
—which produces change in another	FUNCTION
—within a given range of values	VARIATE
variation as result of error term affecting fixed values	REGRESSION
vector	
—operator symbol	NABLA
—quantity which changes sign in transition of coordinates	PSEUDO-VECTOR
—representing relationship of vectors	TENSOR
versed sine	SAGITTA
vertical measurement in graph	ORDINATE
vulgar fraction	COMMON FRACTION
weighted mean	EXPECTATION
whole number	INTEGER, NATURAL NUMBER RATIONAL NUMBER
—or fraction	RATIONAL NUMBER
whole-number	
—part of logarithm	CHARACTERISTIC INTEGRAL
—sets which fit Pythagoras' theorem	PYTHAGOREAN TRIPLES
written number	DIGIT, FIGURE
Mauritania	RIM

capital	NOUAKCHOTT
coin	
—unit	KHOUM
—5 khoums	OUGUIYA
Mauritius	MS
extinct bird	DODO
May	
May 8th	V-DAY
Mayday	SOS
measures	
angle	
—unit	SECOND
—60 seconds	MINUTE
—60 minutes	DEGREE
—15 degrees	HOUR
—57.3 degrees	RADIAN
—90 degrees	QUADRANT, RIGHT ANGLE
—360 degrees	CIRCLE, PERIGON
	ROUND ANGLE
—1/8 circle	OCTANT
—1/6 circle	SEXTANT
—1/4 circle	QUADRANT
—1/100 right angle	GRADE
—angular distance of 90°	QUADRATURE
—division of	
arc	SCRUPLE
compass	POINT
—solid angle	STERADIAN
area	
—272 sq. ft	ROD, PERCH, POLE
—4840 sq. yds	ACRE
—1/4 acre	ROOD
—2.48 acres	HECTARE
—13 acres	BOVATE, OXGATE, OXGANG
—26 acres	HUSBANDLAND
—30 acres	YARDLAND, VIRGATE
—100 acres	CARUCATE
—120 acres	HIDE
—circle	CIRCULAR MIL
—cross-section of nucleus	BARN
atmospheric pressure	BAR
—1mm of mercury	TORR
—1000 bars	KILOBAR
—low pressure unit	TORR
—normal pressure	STANDARD ATMOSPHERE
capacity	
—577 cc	PINT
—277 cubic inches	GALLON
—60 minims	FLUID DRACHM
—8 fluid drachms	FLUID OUNCE
—16 fluid ounces (US)	PINT
—20 fluid ounces	PINT
—1/3-1/6 gill (spirits)	TOT
—1 gill (spirits)	NOGGIN
—4 gills	PINT
—1/4 pint	GILL, NOGGIN, QUARTERN
—1/4 pint (beer)	NIP, SMALL
—1 1/3 pints	BOTTLE
—2 pints	QUART
—2 pints (beer)	FLAGON
—2 1/2 pints	YARD OF ALE
—4 pints (wine)	MAGNUM
—1/3 bottle	DOP
—2 bottles	MAGNUM
—3 bottles	FLAGON, TREGNUM
—4 bottles	JEROBOAM
—6 bottles	REHOBOAM
—8 bottles	IMPERIALE
	METHUSELAH
—12 bottles	SALMANAZAR
—16 bottles	BALTHAZAR
—20 bottles	NEBUCHADNEZZAR
—1, 3 or 6 quarts (liquor)	TAPPIT
—2 quarts	POTTLE
—4 quarts	GALLON
—1/2 gallon	STOUP
—2 galls	PECK
—4 1/2 galls	PIN
—8 galls	BUSHEL
—9 galls	FIRKIN
—10 gallons (beer)	ANKER
—18 galls	KILDERKIN
—36 galls	BARREL
—42 galls	TIERCE
—46 gallons (petrol, USA)	BARREL
—46 galls (claret)	HOGSHEAD
—52 1/2 galls	HOGSHEAD
—54 galls (beer)	HOGSHEAD
—63 galls (wine)	HOGSHEAD
—70-120 galls	PUNCHEON
—108 galls (beer, sherry)	BUTT
—126 galls (wine)	BUTT
—200 gallons (wine)	TONNEAU
—216 galls (ale)	TUN
—252 galls (wine)	TUN
—9 pecks (apples)	SEAM
—2 bushels	CO(O)MB
—4 bushels	CO(O)MB, COMBE
—6 bushels	BOLL
—8 bushels	QUARTER
—8 bushels (grain)	SEAM
—9 bushels	FAT
—40 bushels (corn or salt)	WEY
—96 bushels	CHALDER
—1 hogshead	MUID
—1/6 pipe	OCTAVE
—3 tierces	PIPE
—2 hogsheads	PIPE
—corn, etc	MUID
—mouthful (liquor)	SLUG
—small	MINIM
handful or pinch	PUGIL

cloth
—1½ yards	ELL
—20 hanks (linen yarn)	BUNDLE
—80 yards (worsted yarn)	LEA
—120 yards (cotton yarn)	LEA
—300 yards (linen yarn)	LEA
—180,000 yds (linen yarn)	BUNCH

distance
—2.25 mm	LIGNE
—1^{-23328}cm	PLANCK LENGTH
—10^{-13} cm	FERMI
—$^1/_{1000}$"	MIL
—$^1/_{72}$"	POINT
—$^1/_{16}$"	LINE
—$^1/_3$"	BARLEYCORN
—$^3/_4$"	DIGIT
—2½"	NAIL
—3-4"	PALM
—4"	HAND
—8"	LINK
—9"	SPAN
—12"	FOOT, LAST
—18"-22"	CUBIT(US)
—30"	PACE
—33" (approx)	METRE
—36"	YARD
—37"	CLOTH-YARD
—45"	ELL
—58"	ROMAN PACE
—63,360"	MILE
—6 feet	FATHOM
—6,395 feet (Fr.)	TOISE
—20 feet	ROPE
—600 feet	CABLE
—600 feet (Greek)	STADION, STADIUM
—5280 feet	MILE
—6082 feet	KNOT, NAUTICAL MILE
—5½ yards	PERCH, POLE, ROD
—22 yards	CHAIN
—1760 yards	MILE
—1976 yards	SCOTIISH MILE
—2240 yards	IRISH MILE
—1000 double paces	ROMAN MILE
—10 chains	FURLONG
—8 furlongs	MILE
—1 minute of latitude	GEOGRAPHICAL MILE
—$^5/_8$ mile (approx)	KILOMETRE
—1.4 miles	ROMAN MILE
—2.8 miles	FRENCH LEAGUE
—3 miles	LEAGUE
—4.2 miles	SPANISH LEAGUE
—60 miles	DEGREE
—93 million miles	ASTRONOMICAL UNIT, AU
—6 billion miles	LIGHT-YEAR
—19 billion miles	PARSEC

—fathom (old)	FEDDON
—handsbreadth	PALM
—length of forearm	CUBIT
—parallax of 1 second of arc	PARSEC
—small	BARLEYCORN
	EL, EM, EN, MM
—stretch of arms	FATHOM
—very small	ANGSTROM, FERMI
	MICROMILLIMETRE, MICRON

electrical
—1000 electron-volts	KeV
—1,000,000 electron-volts	MeV
—96,500 coulombs	FARADAY
—amplitude	IMPEDANCE, Z
—capacitance	C, FARAD
—charge	COULOMB, Q
—charging unit	KILOWATT HOUR
—conductance	G, MHO, SIEMENS
—current	A, AMPERE, J
—dipole moment	DEBYE
—elastance	DARAF
—electrostatic charge	STATCOULOMB
—electromotive force	VOLT
—energy	ELECTRON-VOLT
	ELECTROMOTIVE FORCE
	EMF, VOLT
—impedance	Z
—inductance	HENRY
—power	WATT
—quantity	AMPERE-HOUR
—ratio of currents or voltages	NEPER
—reciprocal	
farad	DARAF
henry	YRNEH
ohm	MHO
—resistance	OHM
—signalling speed	BAUD
—transconductance	MHO, RECIPROCAL OHM

energy, work and heat
	BTU, ERG, DYNAM
	DYNE, ERG
	JOULE, POUNDAL
—10^7 ergs	JOULE
—10^9 ergs	ERG-NINE
—100,000 BTUs	THERM
—746 watts	HORSEPOWER
—1000 lbs force	KIP
—1055 joules	HEAT UNIT
—1400 joules/second/square metre	SOLAR CONSTANT
—1,000,000 joules	MEGAJOULE
—British Thermal Unit	BT(H)U, HEAT UNIT
—energy content (food)	KCAL(ORIE)
	(LARGE)CALORIE
—force	DYNE, N, NEWTON, STHENE
—heat	BTU, CALORIE, JOULE, THERM
value	CALORIFIC VALUE

—kilowatt-hour	KELVIN, KWH
—large unit	MEGAWATT-DAY
—power	HORSEPOWER, WATT
—pressure	BARYE, PASCAL
—quantum of energy	PLANCK'S CONSTANT
—rate of flow	FLUX
—thermal efficiency	CARNOT
frequency	CYCLES PER SECOND
	HERTZ
—10^{12} hertz	FRESNEL
—transmission rate	BAUD
herrings	
—4 herrings	WARP
—33 warps	LONG-HUNDRED
—37½ gallons	CRAN
—5 long hundreds	MA(I)SE, MA(I)ZE, MEASE
information	
—binary digit	BIT
—1.44 bits	NEPIT, NIT
—4 bits	NIBBLE
—8 bits	BYTE
—2 bytes	WORD
—4 bytes	LONGWORD
—1024 bytes	K, KILOBYTE
—million instructions per second	MIPS
—transmission rate	BAUD
light	
—brightness	LAMBERT, STILB
of star	MAGNITUDE
—colour temperature	KELVIN, MIRED
—energy	LAMP-HOUR, TALBOT
—flux	LUMEN
—illumination	FOOT-CANDLE
	LUX, METRE-CANDLE
	PHOT, THORLAND
—light-bending power	REFRACTIVE INDEX
—low intensity	SKOT
—luminance	FOOT-LAMBERT, NIT
—luminous intensity	CANDELA
	(NEW) CANDLE
—reflectivity	ALBEDO
—refractive power	ABBE NUMBER
—wavelength	ANGSTROM (UNIT), AU
	NANOMETER
magnetism	
—10^{-8} webers	MAXWELL
—field strength	OERSTED
—flux	GAUSS, MAXWELL
	TESLA, WEBER
—magnetomotive force	AMPERE-TURN
	GILBERT, RELUCTANCE
—ratio of flux density to magnetising force	MAGNETIC PERMEABILITY
—reciprocal of reluctance	PERMEANCE

—strength	MAGNETIC POLE UNIT
metric	
—area	ARE
—capacity	LITRE
—length	METRE
—volume	STERE
—increments	
—million-million-millionth	ATTO-
—thousand-million-millionth	FEMTO-
—million-millionth	MICROMICR(O)-
	PICO-
—thousand-millionth	NANO-
—millionth	MICRO-
—thousandth	MILLI-
—hundredth	CENTI-
—tenth	DECI-
—ten	DECA-
—hundred	HECTO-
—thousand	KILO-
—million	MEGA-
—thousand million	GIGA-
—million million	TERA-
—thousand million million	PETA-
—million million million	EXA-
miscellaneous	
—¹/₁₂ of carbon 12 atom	ATOMIC MASS UNIT
—12 items	DOZEN
—12 dozen	GROSS
—24 arrows	SHEAF
—20-26 tubs (coal)	SCORE
—100 cu. ft (ship)	TON
—100 runs	TON
—100 miles per hour	TON
—250 pulls (handpress work)	TOKEN
—1000 tons (explosives)	KILOTON
—acceleration	G, GAL
—area of nucleus	BARN
—bundle of hay	BOTTLE
—cloud cover ¹/₈ of sky area	OKTA
—distance/velocity of galaxy	HUBBLE CONSTANT
—dried fruit in basket	CAROTEEL
—earthquakes	(GUTENBERG-)RICHTER SCALE
	KANAMORI SCALE
	MERCALLI SCALE
—flow of liquid in tube	REYNOLDS NUMBER
—fluidity	RHE
—fourth part of	FARDEL
circle	QUADRANT
hour	QUARTER
moon period	QUARTER
year	QUARTER

—genetic information	CISTRON	paper		
—gold	CAR(R)AT	—4 sheets		QUIRE
—gravitational unit	SLUG	—216 sheets		PRINTER'S REAM
—hardness	BRINELL NUMBER, MOH	—20 quires		REAM
—hotness of		—2 reams		BUNDLE
chillies	SCOVILLE HEAT UNIT	—10 reams		BALE
—ignition measurement	CETANE NUMBER	—leaves per sheet		
—insulation value	U-VALUE	2		FOLIO
of fabric	TOG	4		QUARTO
—lens power	DIOPTER, DIOPTRE	6		SEXTO
—mass	CRITH, GRAM	8		OCTAVO
	MOL(E), POUND, SLUG	12		DUODECIMO
of isotope	ATOMIC MASS UNIT	16		DECIMO-SEXTO
—metre/kilogram/second	MKS			SEXTODECIMO
—molecular				SIXTEENMO
volume	PARACHOR	18		EIGHTEENMO
weight of compound	MOL(E)			OCTODECIMO
—number of		—sizes (inches)		
atoms per mole	AVOGADRO'S CONSTANT	9" x 11½"		QUARTO
	AVOGADRO'S NUMBER, L, N	13½" x 17"		FOOLSCAP
molecules of gas		15" x 19"		POST
per cc	LOSCHMIDT'S CONSTANT	15" x 20"		CROWN
neutrons/second/sq cm	NEUTRON FLUX	16½" x 21"		LARGE POST
protons in nucleus	ATOMIC NUMBER	17½" x 22"		DEMY
—print measure	EL, EM, EN	18" x 23"		MEDIUM
—purchaser's allowance	TRET	20" x 25"		ROYAL
—rate of flow (liquid)	CUMIN, CUSEC	20" x 30"		DOUBLE CROWN
—ratio of circumference		22" x 30"		IMPERIAL
to diameter	PI	23" x 28"		ELEPHANT
—skins		26" x 34"		ATLAS
30 chamois skins	KIP	27" x 40"		DOUBLE ELEPHANT
50 goat skins	KIP	30" x 53"		ANTIQUARIAN
—sound	(DECI)BEL, PHON, SOME	36" x 45"		SADDLEBACK
—specific gravity	TWADDELL SCALE	48" x 72"		EMPEROR
—speed	KNOT, MPH	imperial		GRAND JESUS
of sound ratio	MACH (NUMBER)	larger than royal		JESUS, SUPER ROYAL
—strength of radio		precious stones		POINT
emission	JANSKY	—100 points		CARAT
—temperature	CELSIUS, CENTIGRADE	—200 grams		METRIC CARAT
	FAHRENHEIT, KELVIN	—205 grams		CARAT
	REAUMUR	radiation		
—tenth part	TITHE	—concentration of		
—turning force	TORQUE	strontium 90		STRONTIUM UNIT
—type (¹/₇₂")	POINT	—disintegration rate		CURIE
—unit of		—dosage		BECQUEREL, GRAY
meaning	SEMANTEME			RAD, REM, REP
sound	PHONEME			R(ONTGEN), SIEVERT
substance	GRAM-ATOM	—period over which		
	GRAM-EQUIVALENT	half the radioactive		
	GRAM-ION, GRAM-MOLECULE	atoms decay		HALF-LIFE
	MOL(E)	—radioactive decay		RD, RUTHERFORD
—viscosity	POISE, STOKES	—X-ray wavelength		XU, X UNIT
—watch movement	LIGNE	timber		
—water flow in 24 hours	MINER'S INCH	—35 cu. ft		STERE
—windspeed	BEAUFORT SCALE	—128 cu. ft		CORD
—wool (½ sack)	POCKET	—216 cu. ft		FATHOM

—100 sq. ft flooring	SQUARE
—round timber	HOPPUS (CUBIC) FOOT

time

—10⁻⁴² second	PLANCK TIME
—60 seconds	MIN(UTE)
—60 minutes	H, HOUR, HR
—24 hours	D, DAY
—7 days	WK, WEEK
—14 days	FORTNIGHT
—27.32 days	PERIODIC MONTH
	SIDEREAL MONTH
	TROPICAL MONTH
	STELLAR MONTH
—27.55 days	ANOMALISTIC MONTH
—28-31 days	M, MONTH, MTH
—29.53 days	SYNODIC MONTH
—354 days	LUNAR YEAR
—364 days	EMBOLISMIC YEAR
—365 days	Y, YEAR, YR
—365 days 5h	ASTRONOMICAL YEAR
—365¼ days	JULIAN YEAR
—365 days 6h 9m	SIDEREAL YEAR
—365 days 6h 13m	ANOMALISTIC YEAR
—366 days	LEAP-YEAR
—6585 days	SAROS
—12/13 months	HEBREW YEAR
	LUNISOLAR YEAR
—5 years	LUSTRUM
—10 years	DECADE
—19 years	METONIC CYCLE
—76 years	CAL(L)IPPIC CYCLE
—100 years	CENTENARY, CENTENNIAL
	CENTURY
—400 years (Maya)	BAKTUN
—1000 years	MILLENARY, MILLENNIUM
—1460 years	SOTHIC CYCLE
	SOTHIC PERIOD
—3600 years	SAROS
—225 million years	COSMIC YEAR
—1000 million years	(A)EON
—4320 million years	
(Hindu)	KALPA
—accounting period	FINANCIAL YEAR
	FISCAL YEAR
—between successive	
returns of Sun	
to meridian	SOLAR DAY
—Canicular year	SOTHIC YEAR
—complete cycle of	
heavens	PLATONIC YEAR
—division of time	SCRUPLE
—in which	
half of radioactive	
atoms decay	HALF-LIFE
photon travels	
diameter of electron	CHRONON

—short period	MIN, MO, SEC, TICK
—Sothic year	CANICULAR YEAR
—very short period	MILLISECOND
	NANO-SECOND
	PICOSEC

volume

—144 cu. in	CUBIC FOOT
—27 cu. ft	CUBIC YARD
—306 cu. ft	ROD
—occupied by	
mole	GRAM-MOLECULAR VOLUME
	(for metric measures *see* **French**)

measuring instrument

for:

air breathed	PNEUMATOMETER
alcohol in wine	VINOMETER
altitude	
—from boiling point	HYPSOMETER
—of heavenly bodies	ALTAZIMUTH
	ASTROLABE
angles	ALAIDAD(E), DIOPTER
	OCTANT, OPTICAL SQUARE
	QUADRANT, PLANE TABLE
	PROTRACTOR, SEXTANT
	TACHEOMETER, THEODOLITE
—of crystals	GONIOMETER
angular distance of Sun	HELIOMETER
area	PLANIMETER
atmospheric pressure	BAROGRAPH
	(FORTIN)BAROMETER
	SYMPIESOMETER
—and temperature	THERMOBAROGRAPH
atomic weights	MASS SPECTROGRAPH
bearing of heavenly	
bodies	ALMUCANTAR
	OCTANT, SEXTANT
blood pressure	SPHYGMO(MANO)METER
	TONOMETER
blueness of sky	CYANOMETER
bodily organs	ONCOMETER
boiling-points	EBULLIOSCOPE
	HYPSOMETER
brain waves	ELECTROENCEPHALOGRAPH
breathing movement	SPIROGRAPH
calculating	ABACUS, ARITHMOMETER
	CALCULATOR, COMPTOMETER
	COMPUTER, SLIDE RULE
changes in pressure	TASIMETER
chlorine	CHLORIMETER
	CHLOROMETER
circuit power	WATTMETER
cloud speed and	
direction	NEPHOSCOPE
cloudiness of liquids	NEPHELOMETER
colour concentration	COLORIMETER
colours	IRISCOPE

comparing	
—colour	
densities	(LOVIBOND) TINTOMETER
—wavelengths	SPECTROPHOTOMETER
compressibility	PIEZOMETER
consistency of soil	PENETROMETER
cooling power of air	KATATHERMOMETER
cornea	AUTOREFRACTOR
	KARATOMETER
	KERATOMETER
	PHOROPTER, RETINOSCOPE
counting paces	PEDOMETER
current of fluid	RHEOMETER
—pressure	SYMPIESOMETER
curvature	SPHEROMETER
density of	DENSIMETER
—air	AEROMETER
—gas	AEROMETER, DASYMETER
—liquid	HYDROMETER
	PYKNOMETER
—photographic	
image	DENSITOMETER
depth of water	BATHOMETER
	FATHOMETER
dew	DROSOMETER
diameter of	
—circular object	CAL(L)IPERS
	MICROMETER
—star	INTERFEROMETER
dichroism of crystals	DICHRO(O)SCOPE
diffracted X-rays	DIFFRACTOMETER
dip circle	INCLINOMETER
distance	DISTOMAT, (H)ODOMETER
	ODOGRAPH, TACHEOMETER
	TACHYMETER, TELEMETER
	TELLUROMETER, TROCHEAMETER
	TROCHOMETER
—between fluid levels	CATHETOMETER
—by	
vehicle	(H)ODOMETER, TACHOGRAPH
	TAXIMETER
wheel	CYCLOMETER, VIAMETER
—from size of image	ICONOMETER
—on maps	OPISOMETER
—using light beams	MEKOMETER
—walked	PEDOMETER
drops	STACTOMETER
dust in air	KONIMETER
earthquakes	SEISMOGRAPH, SEISMOMETER
elastic properties	
of wood	XYLOPHONE
elasticity	TENSIOMETER
electrical	
—charge	ELECTROSCOPE
	GALVANOMETER
—conductivity	DIAGOMETER, TASIMETER

—current	AMMETER
	ELECTRODYNAMOMETER
	ELECTROGRAPH, MILLIAMETER
	(TANGENT) GALVANOMETER
	VOLT(A)METER
—electrostatic	
voltage	ELECTROMETER
—inductance	INDUCTOMETER
	VARIOMETER
—potential	ELECTROMETER
	POTENTIOMETER
	VOLTMETER
—resistance	METRE BRIDGE, OHMMETER
	WHEATSTONE BRIDGE
electricity in body	ELECTROSCOPE
elements in sample	QUANTOMETER
endosmotic action	ENDOSMOMETER
energy distribution of	
radiation	(SCINTILLAION) SPECTROMETER
evaporation	EVAPORIMETER
exposure (film)	ACTINOMETER
eyes	AUTOREFRACTOR
	KARATOMETER, OPHTHALMOMETER
	OPTOMETER, PHOROPTER
	RETINOSCOPE
fare due	TAXIMETER
fermentation	ZYMO(SIM)METER
field of vision	PERIMETER
fluid	
—flow	FLOWMETER
—pressure	KYMOGRAPH
in eyeball	TONOMETER
fluorescence	FLUORIMETER
	FLUOROMETER
force	DYNAMOGRAPH
	DYNAMOMETER
—of breathing	PNEUMATOMETER
frequency of	
—radio waves	ONDOMETER
—tones	TONOMETER
gas	
—consumed	GAS-METER
—pressure	MANOMETER
gases	EUDIOMETER
gradient of magnetic	
field	GRADIOMETER
gradients	GRADIENTER
grain of film	DENSIMETER
gravitational field	GRAVIMETER
hardness of minerals	SCLEROMETER
hearing	AUDIOGRAPH
	AUDIOMETER
heart beats	ELECTROCARDIOGRAPH
heat	CALORIMETER
—based on electrical	
resistance	RESISTANCE THERMOMETER

—from Sun	PYRHELIOMETER	—work	ERGOGRAPH, ERGOMETER
—of		musical beat	METRONOME
light	ACTINOMETER		RHYTHMMOMETER
radiation	BOLOMETER, RADIOMETER	nitrogen	NITROMETER
	PYROSCOPE	optical transmission	DENSITOMETER
reaction	BOMB CALORIMETER	osmotic pressure	OSMOMETER
	THERMOPILE	oxygen in blood	OXIMETER
height	(RADIO) ALTIMETER	pelvis	PELVIMETER
—above sea-level	HYPSOMETER	percolation	LYSIMETER
	OROMETER	permeability	PERMEAMETER
—of		plane surfaces	PLANOMETER
cloud base	CEILOMETER	plant growth	AUXANOMETER
	CLOUD-BASE RECORDER	porosity	POROSCOPE
Nile	NILOMETER	power	DYNAMOGRAPH
water	WATER-GAUGE		DYNAMOMETER
high temperatures	PYROMETER		WATTMETER
	RESISTANCE THERMOMETER	pressure	PIEZOMETER
hours	CLOCK, CHRONOMETER	—by electrical charges	TASIMETER
	HOROLOGE, SUNDIAL	—in	
humidity	GRAVIMETER, HYGRODEIK	baby's skull	FONTANOMETER
	HYGROGRAPH, HYGROSCOPE	eyeball	TONOMETER
	HYGROMETER, PSYCHROMETER	—of	
	TENSIOMETER	current	SYMPIESOMETER
intensity of		fluids	MANOMETER
—colour	SPECTROPHOTOMETER	pulse	PULSIMETER, SPHYMOGRAPH
—light	EXPOSURE METER	radiant	
	LIGHT METER, PHOTOMETER	—energy	BOLOMETER, LIGHT-MILL
—radiated light	CROOKES RADIOMETER		RADIOMETER
—radiation	ACTINOMETER	—heat	PYROSCOPE
—sunlight	HELIOGRAPH	radiation	DOSIMETER, RADIOGRAPH
light	PHOTO(-ELECTRIC) CELL	radio waves	RADIO TELESCOPE
loudness	PHON(O)METER	radioactivity	GEIGER(-MULLER) COUNTER
low temperatures	CRYOMETER		OBROMETER
luminous intensity	PHOTOMETER		SCINTILLATION COUNTER
lung capacity	SPIROMETER		SCINTILLATOR
magnetic			SCINTILLOMETER
—declination	DECLINATOR		OBROMETER
	DECLINOMETER	rainfall	HYETOGRAPH, HYETOMETER
—dip	INCLINOMETER		HYETOMETROGRAPH, OBROMETER
—field	MAGNETOMETER		RAIN-GAUGE, PLUVIOMETER
—flux	FLUXMETER		UDOMETER
density	GAUSSMETER	rate of	
moment	BOHR MAGNETON	—climb or descent	VARIOMETER
	NUCLEAR MAGNETON	—evaporaion	ATMOMETER
—forces	VARIOMETER		EVAPORIMETER
—variations	MAGNETOGRAPH	—flow	PITOT TUBE, ROTAMETER
magnitude of stars	ASTRO(PHANO)METER		VENTURI TUBE
meridian passage	DIPLEIDOSCOPE	—increase of speed	ACCELEROMETER
metronome	RHYTHMMOMETER	reaction times	PSYCHOMETER
mileage, speed etc	TACHOGRAPH	recording over	
molecular weight		a distance	TELEMETER
of gases	EFFUSIOMETER	reflected light	PHOTOMETER
movement of clouds	NEPHOGRAPH	reflective properties	DENSITOMETER
	NEPHOSCOPE	refraction of eye	OPTOMETER
muscular		refractive indices	REFRACTOMETER
—contraction	ELECTROMYOGRAPH		SPECTROMETER

relations of sounds	HARMONOMETER
relative	
—density of	
liquids	HYDROMETER
milk	LACTOSCOPE
—humidity	HYGRODEIK, HYGROMETER
	HYGROSCOPE
—number of	
particles	MASS SPECTROMETER
revolutions	TACHOMETER
richness of milk	LACTOSCOPE
rotation of plane of	
polarisation of light	POLARIMETER
saltness of water	SALI(NO)METER
sensitivity of film	SENSITOMETER
sight	OPSIOMETER
	OPTOMETER
size derived from image	ICONOMETER
sliding friction	TRIBOMETER
slopes	INCLINOMETER
small	
—angles	MICROMETER
—diameters	ERIOMETER
—differences in levels	
of liquids	CATHETOMETER
—distances	MICROMETER
—earthquakes	TRONOMETER
—forces	TORSION BALANCE
—sound intensities	AUDIOMETER
—strains	EXTENSOMETER
—temperature	
changes	AETHERIOSCOPE
	BECKMAN THERMOMETER
—thicknesses	PACHYMETER
	SPHEROMETER
—time intervals	CHRONOSCOPE
	CHRONOTRON
—variations in	
density of image	MICROPHOTOMETER
solar radiation	PYRHELIOMETER
solids	STEREOMETER
sound	
—pitch	TONOMETER
—vibration	PHONAUTOGRAPH
specific gravity	AR(A)EOMETER
	HYDROMETER, PYCNOMETER
	PYKNOMETER
—of	
milk	GALACTOMETER
solids	STEREOMETER
wood	XYLOMETER
speed	SPEEDOMETER
—in relation to sound	MACHMETER
—of	
celestial objects	NEPHOSCOPE
clouds	NEPHOSCOPE

rotation	TACHOGRAPH, TACHOMETER
wind	ANEMOMETER
squint	STRABOMETER
strains in structures	TASEOMETER
strength of	
—acid	ACIDIMETER
—wine	OENOMETER
subterranean	
temperature	GEOTHERMOMETER
sugar solution	SACCHARIMETER
	SACCHAROMETER
surface tension	STALAGMOMETER
	TENSIOMETER
surveying	TACHEOMETER, TACHYMETER
	THEODOLITE
swing of voting	SWINGOMETER
temperature	THERMO(METRO)GRAPH
	THERMOMETER
—bodily	CLINICAL THERMOMETER
—from	
bimetallic junction	THERMOCOUPLE
	THERMO-ELECTRIC
	THERMOMETER
electrical resistance	
	PLATINUM RESISTANCE
	THERMOMETER
light intensity	OPTICAL PYROMETER
pressure of gas	GAS THERMOMETER
—low	CRYOMETER
tensile strength	TENSIOMETER
testing food	TENDEROMETER
ticket-issuing	PASSIMETER
tides	MARIGRAPH
tilt of aeroplane	INCLINOMETER
time	CLOCK, CHRONOMETER
	SUN-DIAL, WATCH
—by	
sand	EGG-TIMER, HOUR-GLASS
water	HYDROSCOPE
transmitting measurements	TELEMETER
transparency	DENSIOMETER
trees	DENDROMETER
uptake of oxygen	WARBURG MANOMETER
vapour pressure	TONOMETER
variations in	
body size	PLETHYSMOGRAPH
vertical angles	ALIDAD(E), DIP CIRCLE
	(IN)CLINOMETER, OCTANT
	SEXTANT, TACHEOMETER
vibrations	VIBROGRAPH, VIBROMETER
—in rotating shaft	TORSIOGRAPH
viscosity	VISCOMETER
vision	OPTOMETER, OPSIOMETER
volume	
—changes in chemical	
reaction	EUDIOMETER

—expansion	DILATOMETER
—of	
gas	VOLUMETER
solid bodies	VOLUMOMETER
voting changes	SWINGOMETER
water	
—absorption by plant	POTOMETER
—in ship's hold	SOUNDING-ROD
wave-forms	OSCILLOSCOPE
wavelengths	ETALON, INTERFEROMETER
	SPECTROMETER, WAVEMETER
weight of air or gas	AEROMETER
windspeed	ANEMOMETER
X-ray	
—diffraction	DIFFRACTOMETER
—examination	FLUOROSCOPE
zenith distance	ZENITH-SECTOR

(*see also* **scientific instruments**)

meat

bacon	
—cuts	BACK, BUTT, COLLAR
	(CORNER) GAMMON, GAMBREL
	GRISKIN, FLANK, FOREHOCK
	FORE SLIPPER, HOCK, MIDDLE CUT
	MIDDLE GAMMON, OYSTER BACK
	STREAKY
—side	FLITCH
—slice	RASHER
—uncured	GREEN BACON
braised	POT ROAST
brawn (US)	HEADCHEESE
calf	VEAL
—cuts	BREAST, CHOP, CUTLET
	ESCALOPE, FILLET, KNUCKLE
	LEG, LOIN, NECK, SCRAG
	SHIN, SHOULDER
—sweetbreads	RIS DE VEAU
cold meats	CHARCUTERIE
—set in jelly	GALANTINE
cooked, dried, salted	
or smoked meat	CHARCUTERIE
—cured	
ham	PARMA HAM, PROSCIUTTO
pig fat	FATBACK
—dried	
beef, sliced	CHIPPED BEEF
meat	BILTONG, CHARQUI
	JERKED MEAT, JERK(Y)
	PEM(M)ICAN
—salted	
beef	JUNK
pig	BACON
pork	SOWBELLY
sausage	SALAMI
—smoked	
beef	PASTRAMI

ham	VIRGINIA HAM
	WESTPHALIAN HAM, YORK HAM
pig	BACON
—tinned beef	BULLY BEEF, CORNED BEEF
cow	BEDPIECE, BEEF, STEAK
—cuts, beef	BARON, BLADE BONE, BRISKET
	CHUCK, CLOD, FLANK
	FLESHEND, FORERIB, GULLET
	LEG, LOIN, MOUSE, NECK, OXTAIL
	RIB, ROUND(END), SHIN, SHOULDER
	SKIRT, SILVERSIDE, SIRLOIN
	SLOAT, STICKING, TOPRIB
	TOPSIDE, VEIN, WING RIB
—cuts, steak	ENTRECOTE
	FILET MIGNON, FILLET
	PORTERHOUSE, RUMP, T-BONE
	TENDERLOIN, TOURNEDOS
	UNDERCUT
cube for grilling	KEBAB
cut	
—boneless	FIL(L)ET
—crossways for broiling	CARBONADO
—embedded in fat	EYE
—hindquarters	HAUNCH
—including	
both forequarters	FORESADDLE
the backbone	CHINE
—from neck	CUTLET
—front	
leg	FORELEG
—of pig	FOREHOCK
of side with leg	FOREQUARTER
—large piece for	
roasting	JOINT
—neck and spine	RACK
—rear of side with leg	HINDQUARTER
—small round piece	MEDALLION
	NOISETTE
—thin slice	ESCALOPE
—triangular thigh piece	EYE
—underpart of forequarter	PLATE
cutlet (Ind.)	TIKKA
crisply cooked skin	CRACKLING
deer meat	VENISON
edible	
—entrails	(M)UMBLES
cooked	CHITTERLING, TRIPE
—parts, not flesh (US)	VARIETY MEAT
forcemeat ball	QUENELLE
grilled on skewer	
—Greek	SOUVLAKIA
—Turkish	SHISH KEBAB
heart, liver and lungs	PLUCK
lamb	
—cuts	BEST END NECK, BREAST
	CHUMP, FILLET, LEG, LOIN

	MIDDLE NECK, NOISETTE
	RACK, SADDLE, SCRAG (END)
	SHOULDER
layer of fat lining	
abdomen	LEAF FAT, MESENTERY
leg	SHANK
lungs	LIGHTS
meat products	BEEFBURG(H)ER
	BLACK PUDDING, BRAWN
	CORNED BEEF, CROQUETTE
	FAGGOT, HAM, HAMBURGER, HASLET
	LUNCHEON MEAT, QUENELLE
	PATE, PASTE, RISSOLE, SAUSAGE
	SPAM, TONGUE, VIENNA STEAK
	(see also **sausage**)
meat substitute	KESP
	TEXTURED VEGETABLE PROTEIN
	TVP
meatball (Ind.)	KHEMA, KOFTA
minced meat	MINCE
offal	BRAIN, FEET, HEAD, KIDNEY
	LIVER, HEART, INTESTINES
	OXTAIL, STOMACH, SWEETBREAD
	TONGUE, TRIPE
pancreas	SWEETBREAD
pig	BACON, HAM, PIG-MEAT, PORK
—cuts	BARON, BATH CHAP, BELLY
	BLADE, BUFF, (CHUMP) CHOP
	COLLAR, FILLET, FLANK
	FOREHOCK, GAMMON, HAM
	HAND, HOCK, JOWL, KNUCKLE
	SLIPPER, SPARE RIB, SPRING
	TROTTER, (TENDER)LOIN
—feet	CRUBEENS, PETTITOES, TROTTERS
sheep	LAMB, MUTTON
—cuts	BREAST, CHOP, CROWN, CUTLET
	FILLET, GIGOT, KNUCKLE
	LEG, LOIN, NOISETTE, RIB
	SADDLE, SCRAG(-END)
	SHOULDER
sliced and rolled	ROULADE
small round piece	NOISETTE
strip of fat for dressing	LARDO(O)N
thin slice with	
savoury filling	PAUPIETTE, ROULADE
thymus gland	SWEETBREAD
unfit for food	CAGMAG
young goat	KID
	(see also **cookery, menu**)
meat dishes	
bacon	BACON-BURGER, BACON JACK
	(CARAMELLED) GAMMON
	DERBY BAKE
braised meat (Ind.)	KORMA
beef	BEEF OLIVE, BEEFBURGER
	BOURGUIGNONNNE, CARBON(N)ADE

	CORNED BEEF, DIANE
	EN CROUTE, EN DAUBE
	GOULASH, STIFADO, STROGANOFF
	STROGANOV, STUFATO
ham	CHARLOTTE, MONTMORENCY
—and veal in	
butter	SALTIMBOCA
lamb	BLANQUETTE D'AGNEAU
	CROWN OF LAMB, (DONER) KEBAB
	GIGOT, NAVARIN, NOISETTE
	YIOUVETSI
meatball	QUENELLE, RISSOLE
medallion	PICATA
mince	CHILLI CON CARNE
	COTTAGE PIE, CUMBERLAND PIE
	KROMESKY, MOUS(S)AKA
	SALMAGUNDI
	SCOTCH(ED) COLLOPS
	SHEPHERD'S PIE, TAMALE
—set in mould	SCRAPPLE
offal	CHITTERLING, HAGGIS, TRIPE
pies	BRIDIE, CORNISH PASTY
	FLORENCE, PORK PIE
	SAUSAGE ROLL, SQUAB PIE
pork	CROWN, FRIKADELLER
	NORMANDY, SPANISH
	SPARERIB, SWEET-AND-SOUR
several meats	MIXED GRILL
steak	DIANE, CARPETBAG
	CHATEAUBRIAND, HAMBURG(H)ER
	SAUTERNES, SWISS, TAGALOG
	TARTARE, TOURNEDOS (ROSSINI)
veal	ESCALOPE, FRICANDEAU
	OSSO BUC(C)O, VIENNA STEAK
	WIENER SCHNITZEL
white meat in sauce	BANQUETTE
medal	(see **decorations**)
medi(a)eval	
including feudal terms:	
acknowledgment of	
allegiance	HOMAGE
allegiance owed to	
feudal lord	FEALTY
amount of land adequate	
to support a household	HIDE
armour-bearer	ARMIGER
assembly	GEMOT, MOOT
attendant on knight	ARMIGER, (E)SQUIRE
	SCUTIGER
building for storage of	
grain paid as tithes	GRANGE
	TITHE-BARN
chief magistrate	REEVE
collector of tithes	TITHE-PROCTOR
copyholder	VILLEIN
council chamber	MOOT-HALL, MOOT-HOUSE

court	GEMOT, MOOT
district under particular jurisdiction	SOKE(N)
division of county	CANTRED, CANTREF HUNDRED
domestic slave	ESNE
eorl	EARL
estate not subject to feudal superior	AL(L)OD(IUM)
feudal lord	LORD SUPERIOR SEIGNEUR, SEIGNIOR SUZERAIN
fine when tenant died	HERIOT
forced loan or contribution	BENEVOLENCE
foreign service due to overlord	FORINSEC
free villager	VILLEIN
freehold	FRANK-TENEMENT
freeholder	FRANKLIN
freeman not of noble birth	CEORL, CHURL
governor of a district	ALDERMAN EALDORMAN
group of ten householders bound by mutual responsibility for good behaviour	TITHING
holding land by feudal tenure	FEODARY, FEUDA(TO)RY
house and land kept by lord for his own use	DEMESNE
king's	
—companion	THANE, THEGN
—farrier	MARSHAL
land	
—endowed to parish church	GLEBE
—for which knight-service was required	KNIGHT'S-FEE
—held in return for military service	FEE, FEOFF FEUD, FIEF
—tenanted with only religious obligations	FRANKALMOIGN
landed proprietor	(E)SQUIRE
licensed seller of Papal indulgences	PARDONER
lord	LIEGE
—holding land from a superior	MESNE LORD
—of manor	SEIGNEUR, SEIGNIOR SUZERAIN
—to whom feudal service is due	LIEGE (LORD)
lowest (of tenant)_	PARAVAIL
loyal vassal	LIEGE

major-domo	SENESCHAL
meeting	GEMOT, MOOT
militia	FYRD
mutual security of a tithing	FRANKPLEDGE
noble	
—below eorl	THANE, THEGN
—next below knight	(E)SQUIRE
—of highest rank	ALDERMAN EALDORMAN
—royal prince	A(E)THELING
obligation to perform unpaid labour	CORVEE
officer dealing with	
—ceremonies etc	MARSHAL
—domestic matters	SENESCHAL
—military matters	CONSTABLE
—offences within twelve miles of the King's abode	KNIGHT-MARSHAL
one	
—holding land from a tenant-in-chief	VALVASSOR VAVASO(U)R
and owing allegiance to a superior	VASSAL
—owing service to his lord but not in bondage	VILLEIN
—under feudal tenure	LIEGE
peasant bound to land	SERF
pig paid as tithe	TITHE-PIG
property that returns to feudal lord for want of heir or by forfeiture	ESCHEAT
pursuit of a felon	HUE AND CRY
rent	
—based on number of horned cattle	CORNAGE, HORNGELD
—paid in lieu of services	QUITRENT
right	
—of	
feudal lord over vassals	DROIT DE SEIGNEUR
to entertainment	CUDDY
king to share of imported wine	PRISAGE
—to	
claim free lodgings	COR(R)ODY
cut green trees	VERT
cut peat	TURBARY
deal with thief taken outside one's jurisdiction	OUTFANGTHIEF
drop roof water	STILLICIDE
fish	PISCARY
fold tenant's sheep for manure	FOLDAGE

hold local court	SOC
necessaries allowed	
by law	ESTOVER
pasture	
—on a common	COMMONAGE
—swine in forest	PANNAGE
use another's property	USUFRUCT
shield-bearer	(E)SQUIRE, SCUTIGER
steward	SENESCHAL
sub-division of cantred	
or hundred	COMMOT
superior	PARAMOUNT
supreme council	WITAN, WITENAGEMOT
tax	GELD
—for building and	
maintaining city walls	MURAGE
—in lieu of military	
service	SCUTAGE
—of one-tenth paid	
to church	TITHE
—on land	HIDAGE
tenant by socage	SOCAGER, SOCMAN
	SOKEMAN
tenure	
—by	
knight on condition	
of military service	KNIGHT-SERVICE
service	SOC(C)AGE
socage	SOKEMANRY
—in fee simple	FRANK-FEE
town-hall	MOOT-HALL, MOOT-HOUSE
vassal	LIEGE
vassals	MANRED
villein granted cottage	
in return for work	BORDAR, COTTAR
	COTTER

medical

medical instruments	(*see* **surgery**)
Medical Officer (of Health)	MO(H)
medical social worker	MSW
medicine	(*see* **drugs**)

Mediterranean

	MED
artichoke	CARDOON
borage	ALKANET
buckthorn	CHRIST'S THORN
	JEW'S THORN
captain of ship	PATRON
edible gall	SAGE-APPLE
fever	BRUCELLOSIS
fish	ANCHOVY, BAND-FISH
	DENTEX, GILTHEAD, MEAGRE
	MAIGRE, PARROT-WRASSE
	PEACOCK-FISH
hen	ANCONA, ANDALUSIAN, MINORCA
Jew(s)	SEPHARDI(M)
lizard	STELLION, STELLIO LIZARD

mock privet	PHYLLYREA
plant	CUM(M)IN, ISATIS, LENTIL
	PLUMBAGO, RUE
	ROSEMARY, WOAD
salad-plant	ROCKET
scrubland	GAR(R)IGUE
shark	PORBEAGLE
ship	(*see separate entry*)
shrub	CHRIST'S THORN
	LAVENDER-COTTON
	NABK, NEBBUK, NEBE(C)K
	ANTOLINA
spirit	RAKE, RAKI
thicket	MAQUIS
tree	ALGARROBA, CAROB, LOCUST
	NUT-PINE, STONE-PINE
	TURKEY-OAK
wind	LEVANT(ER), GREGALE
wrasse	PEACOCK-FISH

member

Member of	
—Congress	MC
—Council	MC
—County Council	MCC
—House of Representatives	MHR
—Institute of Journalists	MJI
—Legislative	
Assembly	MLA
Council	MLC
—Order of the British Empire	MBE
—Parliament	MP
—Pharmaceutical Society	MPS
—Philological Society	MPS
—Royal Victorian Order	MVO

menu

additional charge	COVER CHARGE
	SERVICE CHARGE
appetiser	ENTREMES(SE), ENTREMETS
	HORS D'OEUVRES
bread, cheese,	
pickles, etc	PLOUGHMAN'S LUNCH
breakfast	
—cooked	ENGLISH BREAKFAST
—rolls and butter	FRENCH BREAKFAST
charge for drinks	
brought in	CORKAGE
chef	
—assistant	SOUS CHEF
—cold meats	GARDE-MANGER
set in jelly	GALANTINE
—deputy	COMMIS-CHEF
—pastry cook	PATISSIER
chilled	FRAPPE
choice of dishes	A LA CARTE
coated with	
—breadcumbs	AU GRATIN

519

—cheese	AU GRATIN, GRATINE		—served on platter	PLATE
—egg and breadcrumbs	(A LA) MILANESE		—US	PLATE
	A L'ANGLAISE		meal	
cold dish glazed with aspic	GALANTINE		—afternoon	TEA
complete			—early	
—leg (lamb)	GIGOT		evening	HIGH TEA
—rib section (lamb, pork)	CROWN		morning	BREAKFAST
—sirloin (beef)	BARON		—evening	DINNER
	(see also **meat**)		—late	
cooked			evening	SUPPER
—at the table	NABE-MONO		morning	BRUNCH
—in			—light	SNACK
brown sauce	A LA MODE		—midday	LUNCH(EON)
butter and			—of the day	PLAT DU JOUR
—herbs (fish)	MEUNIERE		medium cooked	A POINT
—parsley	MAITRE D'HOTEL		mixed herbs	FINES HERBES
cider	NORMANDE		partly frozen	FRAPPE
oil, garlic, tomatoes	PROVENCALE		pastry cook	PATISSIER
olive oil	A LA GRECQUE		place setting	COVER
paper case	EN PAPILLOTE		plainly cooked	AU NATUREL
pastry case	EN CROUTE		separately priced	A LA CARTE
red wine	BOURGUIGNON		set price	PRIX FIXE
white wine (fish)	MARINIERE		small green peas	PETIT POIS
—on a skewer	EN BROCHETTE		steak	
—slightly	AL DENTE		—centre of fillet	FILET MIGNON
—with				TOURNEDOS
apples	NORMANDE		—flambé	DIANE
brown sugar	BRULE		—hindquarter	RUMP STEAK
cider and cream	A LA NORMANDE		—large fillet	CHATEAUBRIAND
garlic, tomatoes	NICOISE		—raw, minced	TARTARE
potatoes	PARMENTIER		—sirloin	ENTRECOTE, T-BONE
rice and tomatoes	CREOLE		large	PORTERHOUSE
spinach	FLORENTINE		—small	CLUB STEAK
dish of the day	PLAT DU JOUR		—stuffed with oysters	CARPETBAG STEAK
firm to the teeth	AL DENTE		—thin	MINUTE STEAK
first course	STARTER		—top of sirloin	CONTRE-FILET
fish in vinegar	AU BLEU			FAUX-FILET
fixed			stuffed	FARCI(E)
—meal	TABLE D'HOTE		sweet course	DESSERT
—price	AL PASTO, PRIX FIXE		underdone	EN BLEU, RARE
flamed in brandy	FLAMBE		veal stuffed and roasted	FRICANDEAU
frogs	GRENOUILLES		very thin toast	MELBA TOAST
garnished with			well done	BIEN CUIT
—crayfish	A LA NANTUA		wine waiter	SOMMELIER
—mushrooms etc	FORESTIERE		with milk	AU LAIT
—onions, mushrooms, etc	BONNE FEMME		**merchant**	
—potatoes	PARMENTIER		Merchant Navy	MV
—vegetable strips	JULIENNE		merchant vessel	MV
—vegetables	JARDINIERE		**meteor**	(see **astronomy**)
—white grapes	VERONIQUE		**meteorology**	AEROGRAPHY
head waiter	MAITRE D'HOTEL			AEROLOGY
in cooking juices	AU JUS		absolute humidity	VAPOUR CONCENTRATION
including service charge	COMPRIS		amount of water	
fixed menu	TABLE D'HOTE		vapour in the	
leg (of lamb)	GIGOT		atmosphere	ABSOLUTE HUMIDITY
main course	ENTREE		analysis of clouds, etc	NEPHANALYSIS

anticlockwise movement of wind	BACKING
arc of colours	
—caused by sun on	
mist	SUNBOW
raindrops	RAINBOW
—seen in fog	FOG-BOW, (SEA-)DOG
area	
—between two areas	
of high or low pressure	COL
—of	
calms	DOLDRUMS
	HORSE LATITUDES
earth based on	
climate	CLIMATIC REGION
high atmospheric	
pressure	CYCLONE, HIGH, RIDGE
light rainfall in	
lee of high ground	RAIN SHADOW
low atmospheric	
pressure	CYCLONE
	DEPRESSION, LOW
warm air between	
fronts	WARM SECTOR
—permanently covered	
with snow	ICECAP, ICEFIELD
	SNOWFIELD
atmospheric	
—conditions	
averaged over long	
period	CLIMATE
over a period	WEATHER
—disturbance	ELECTRIC STORM
—layers	(*see* **geology**-Earth)
balloon carrying	
meteorological	
instruments	BALLON SONDE
	RAWINSONDE, RADIOSONDE
	SOUNDING BALLOON
bank of wind-blown snow	SNOWDRIFT
boundary	
—between	
air masses	DISCONTINUITY, FRONT
cold and warm air	POLAR FRONT
—of	
advancing	
—cold air	COLD FRONT
—warm air	WARM FRONT
air which is	
not moving	STATIONARY FRONT
brief flood after	
heavy rains	FLASH FLOOD
broad expanse of	
—ice	ICEFIELD
—snow	SNOWFIELD
caused by	
—action of hot water	HYDROTHERMAL

—floods	DILUVIAL
—rain	PLUVIAL
centre of cyclone	EYE
change(s)	
—caused by heat	
	THERMAL METAMORPHISM
—from	
liquid to vapour	EVAPORATION
vapour to liquid	CONDENSATION
—in	
atmospheric pressure	
over specified	
periods	PRESSURE TENDENCY
colour of moon from	
dust in atmosphere	BLUE MOON
temperature with	
height	LAPSE RATE
chart	(*see* map *below*)
clearness of atmosphere	VISIBILITY
climate	
—cooler than	
temperate	SUBTEMPERATE CLIMATE
—dependent upon	
altitude	MOUNTAIN CLIMATE
—hot	
and humid	EQUATORIAL, TROPICAL
dry season, cooler	
wet season	MONSOON CLIMATE
dry summer, mild	
winter	
	MEDITERRANEAN CLIMATE
—in	
cereal-growing	
areas	CORN BELT CLIMATE
cotton-growing	
area	COTTON BELT CLIMATE
equatorial region	EQUINOCTIAL
islands or coastal	
regions	INSULAR
large land masses	CONTINENTAL
polar regions	ICE-CAP CLIMATE
small habitat	MICROCLIMATE
warm temperate area	MEDITERRANEAN
—influenced by sea	MARITIME
—lacking regular	
rainfall	DESERT CLIMATE
—low rainfall	
hot days, cold	
nights	DESERT CLIMATE
very cold	POLAR CLIMATE
wide temperature	
variation	CONTINENTAL CLIMATE
—short summer, very	
cold winter	SUB-POLAR CLIMATE
—warm damp summer,	
mild wet winter	TEMPERATE CLIMATE

climatic zones		—sheet	ALTOSTRATUS
—between		rain cloud	NIMBOSTRATUS
pole and polar circle	FRIGID	—mother-of-pearl	MACREOUS CLOUD
polar circle and		—on lee side of peak	ANNER CLOUD
tropics	TEMPERATE	—pertaining to	NUBIFORM
tropics	TORRID	—rounded	
clockwise movement of wind	VEERING	cumulus with	
closing of cold front		horizontal base	WOOLPACK
to warm front	OCCLUDED FRONT	heaps of cloud	CUMULUS
	OCCLUSION	mass of cumulus	THUNDERHEAD
cloud		—small	
—bearing	NUBIFEROUS	flakes or ripples	CIRROCUMULUS
—born	NUBIGENOUS	rain cloud	WATER-DOG
—flying	RACK	—thin streaks of cirrus	MARE'S-TAILS
—map	ISONETH	—very dark coloured	THUNDERCLOUD
cloudiness	NUBECULA	—with rounded projection	CASTELLANUS
clouds		cloudy	NUBILOUS
—anvil-like	CUMULONIMBUS	cold sea-mist	HA(A)R
—at centre of tornado		cooling factor combining	
or waterspout	FUNNEL CLOUD	wind and temperature	CHILL FACTOR
—bluish	NOCTILUCENT		WINDCHILL
—breaking off from top		covering of ice	
of cumulo-nimbus	FALSE CIRRUS	crystals	FROST, HOAR, RIME
—cauliflower-like	CUMULUS	current affecting climate in	
—charged with static	THUNDERCLOUD	—Atlantic	GULF STREAM
—cirro-cumulus	WOOL-PACK	—Pacific	EL NINO
—cirrus	GOAT'S-HAIR	cycle of climatic	
—covering		conditions	BRUCKNER CYCLE
high ground	HILL FOG	cyclone in China Sea	TYPHOON
of alto- or cirro-		dark appearance of sky	
cumulus clouds	MACKEREL SKY	due to reflection	
—deep	CUMULONIMBUS	from water	WATER SKY
—delicate cirrus	CUMULOCIRRUS	descent of air mass	
—discharging showers	NIMBUS	towards earth's surface	SUBSIDENCE
—flying	RACK	description of atmosphere	AEROGRAPHY
—fragmented low cloud	SCUD	development of	
—globular masses	STRATOCUMULUS	—cyclone	CYCLOGENESIS
—height of lowest	CEILING	—weather front	FRONTOGENESIS
—high	CIRRUS	diagram of	
detached	CIRRUS	—weather data	TEPHIGRAM
fleecy	ALTOCIRRUS	—wind direction	WIND ROSE
sheet	CIRROSTRATUS	difference between	
thin layer	CIRROSTRATUS	highest and lowest	
transparent veil	CIRROCUMULUS	temperature	
—horizontal sheet	STRATUS	—for each day	MEAN DIURNAL RANGE
—lens shaped	LENTICULAR CLOUD	—in given period	TEMPERATURE RANGE
—loose wind-driven		distance at which	
clouds	SCUD	objects can be seen	VISIBILITY
—low		disturbance in magnetic	
narrow masses	MACKEREL SKY	field of earth	(GEO)MAGNETIC STORM
rain	NIMBOSTRATUS	driving mist	RACK
rounded masses	STRATOCUMULUS	drizzly mist	ROKE
—mackerel sky	CIRROCUMULUS	—Scottish	DROW
—middle		dust etc causing reduced visibility	HAZE
grey		electrical discharge	
—cloud layer	STRATUS	—from cloud	LIGHTNING

—in	
northern region	AURORA BOREALIS
	NORTHERN LIGHTS
southern region	AURORA AUSTRALIS
—round masts, etc	ST ELMO'S FIRE
end of frost	THAW
envelope of air round the	
earth	ATMOSPHERE
	(*see also* **geography**)
extent of clouds	CLOUD COVER
faint light before dawn	
and after sunset	TWILIGHT
falling ice crystals	HAIL, SNOW
fine	
—dry snow	POWDER
—rain	DRIZZLE
fog	
—bow	SEA-DOG
—caused by	
damp air over cool	
surface	ADVECTION FOG
loss of heat radiated	
on clear night	RADIATION FOG
—with suspended dust, etc	SMOG
front formed when cold	
front overtakes	
warm front	OCCLUDED FRONT
	OCCLUSION
frost	
—from frozen	
dew	HOAR, RIME
fog	RIME
—smooth ice from	
frozen rain	GLAZED FROST
frozen	
—dew	HOAR FROST
—moisture	FROST
—rain	GRAUPEL, HAIL, SLEET, SNOW
—snowflakes	GRAUPEL
glow	(*see light below*)
graph of various types	
of climate	CLIMATOGRAPH
granular ice crystals	RIME FROST
	FROST FEATHERS
grass temperature of	
below 30°F	GROUND FROST
halo round tall objects	
caused by electrical	
discharge	ST ELMO'S FIRE
haze (Mediterranean)	CALINA
heating due to increase	
of carbon dioxide in	
atmosphere	GREENHOUSE EFFECT
heavy mists (W. Africa)	CACIMBO
high pressure area	ANTICYCLONE, HIGH
	RIDGE

ice-film on rock, etc	VERGLAS
illusion caused by	
heated air layers	MIRAGE
increase in temperature	
with altitude	INVERSION
instrument for	
—measuring	
atmospheric	
pressure	(ANEROID) BAROMETER
	WEATHER GLASS
height of cloud base	CEILOMETER
	CLOUDBASE RECORDER
moisture in soil	TENSIOMETER
rainfall	RAIN GAUGE
relative humidity	HYGROMETER
	PSYCHROMETER
snowfall	SNOW GAUGE
temperature	THERMOMETER
windspeed	ANEMOMETER
—observing clouds	NEPHOSCOPE
—recording	
atmospheric pressure	BAROGRAPH
clouds	NEPHOGRAPH
rainfall	HYETOGRAPH
relative humidity	HYGROGRAPH
temperature	THERMOGRAPH
—highest	MAXIMUM THERMOMETER
—lowest	MINIMUM THERMOMETER
windspeed	ANEMOGRAPH
—showing	
changes in humidity	HYGROSCOPE
direction of wind	WEATHER VANE
	WIND VANE
intermediate pressure	
area	COL
law relating to	
deflection due to	
Earth's rotation	FERREL'S LAW
light	
—above low Sun	SUN PILLAR
—in sky	
after twilight in	
east or before dawn	
in west	ZODIACAL LIGHT
caused by ice	
crystals	PARAHELIC CIRCLE
over	
—expanse of snow	SNOW-BLINK
—North Pole	AURORA BOREALIS
	NORTHERN LIGHTS
—South Pole	AURORA AUSTRALIS
after sunset in	
mountainous regions	AFTERGLOW
	ALPENGLOW
—over marsh	IGNIS FATUUS
	WILL-O'-THE-WISP

—round

Brocken spectre	GLORY
light source	CORONA
masts, etc	ST ELMO'S FIRE
Moon or Sun	HALO

—snowfall FLURRY

lightning

—striking upward	FLACHENBLITZ
—types	BALL, CHAIN, FORKED
	SHEET, THUNDERBOLT

line

—drawn through places with highest mean temperatures	THERMAL EQUATOR
—marking	
boundary between cold and warm air masses	FRONT
simultaneous thunderstorms	ISOBRONT
—showing places of equal	
cloudiness	ISONEPH
duration of sunshine	ISOHEL
frequency of auroral phenomena	ISOCHASM
pressure	ISOBAR
—change	ISALLOBAR
rainfall	EQUIPLUVE, ISOHYET
sunshine	ISOHEL
temperature	ISOTHERM
—below ground	ISOGEOTHERM
—in coldest time	ISOCHEIM
	ISOCRYME
—summer mean	ISOTHERE
value of specific climatic elements	ISOGRAM
	ISOLINE, ISOMETRIC LINE
	ISOPLETH
variation from normal climatic standards	ISANOMALOUS LINE
wind speed	ISOTACH

long

—area of	
high pressure	RIDGE, WEDGE
low pressure	TROUGH
—period of	
drought	BIG DRY
rain	BIG WET
longest day	SUMMER SOLSTICE
low-pressure area	CYCLONE, DEPRESSION
lower limit of perpetual snow on high ground	SNOWLINE
luminous ring opposite sun	ANTHELION
map showing	
—clouds, etc	NEPHANALYSIS

—weather conditions for particular area	SYNOPTIC CHART
	WEATHER CHART
	WEATHER MAP
mass of condensed vapour	
—at ground level	FOG, MIST
—in atmosphere	CLOUD
maximum humidity at a given temperature	SATURATION
measure of cloud cover	OKTA
measurement of	
—atmospheric conditions	SOUNDING
—heat	TEMPERATURE
—moisture	HUMIDITY
melting of ice and snow	THAW
meteorologists	
—British	CHAPMAN
—French	DE BORT
mirage with vertical distortion	FATA MORGANA
mixture of snow and rain	SLEET
moisture	
—caused by condensation in atmosphere	FOG, MIST
on the ground	DEW
—in atmosphere from cloud near ground	MIZZLE
	SCOTCH MIST
more than 6/10 covered	CLOUDY
morning and evening mists (Guinea)	SMOKES
movement	
—caused by freezing of ground	FROST HEAVE
—of	
air	WIND
atmosphere	
—downward	DOWNDRAUGHT
—irregular	TURBULENCE
—upward	UPDRAUGHT
heat in atmosphere	
—horizontal	ADVECTION
—vertical	CONVECTION
high-pressure area	CLOCKWISE
low-pressure area	ANTICLOCKWISE
wind	
—anticlockwise	BACKING
—clockwise	VEERING
partly	
—frozen rain	SLEET
—melted snow	SLUSH
period of	
—15 days	
with	
—little rain	DRY SPELL
—some rain	RAINY SPELL, WET SPELL

without rain	ABSOLUTE DROUGHT
—29 days with little rain	PARTIAL DROUGHT
—dry weather	DROUGHT
—thaw (Siberia)	RASPUTITSA
—weather warm enough to melt ice and snow	THAW
phenomenon produced by moisture in atmosphere	HYDROMETEOR
photograph of cloud	NEPHOGRAM
place (in Siberia) which experiences excessively low temperatures	COLD POLE
powdery ice crystals	HOAR FROST
precipitation	
—liquid	DRIZZLE, RAIN
—semi-solid	SLEET
—solid	HAIL, SNOW
prehistoric climate (earliest first)	FEMIAN, SANGAMONIAN
	ST GERMAN
	PRE-BRORUP
	MOERSHOOFD
	HENGELO
	DENEKAMP
	OLDEST DRYAS
	BOLLING
	ALLEROD
	YOUNGER DRYAS
	PREBOREAL
	BOREAL
	ATLANTIC
	EARLY SUB-BOREAL
	LATE SUB-BOREAL
	SUBATLANTIC
	SCANDIC
	NEOATLANTIC
	PACIFIC
	LITTLE ICE AGE
	MODERN
pressure due to weight of air	ATMOSPHERIC PRESSURE
process of freezing	FROST
protective shelter for instruments	STEVENSON SCREEN
radiant heat from sun distributed over earth's surface	INSOLATION
rain	
—caused by cooling of rising air	CONVECTION RAIN
cyclonic conditions	CYCLONIC RAIN
moisture-laden air	
—filling low-pressure area over land mass	MONSOON

—rising over mountains	OROGRAPHIC RAIN RELIEF RAINFALL
—coloured red by desert sand	BLOOD-RAIN
—fine	DRIZZLE
Scotland	SMIR(R), SMUR
—frozen	HAIL, SNOW
—hail, sleet, snow	PRECIPITATION
—heavy downpour	CLOUDBURST
—measuring instrument	RAIN GAUGE
—short fall	SHOWER
—total on given area in given time	RAINFALL
—which eventually reaches streams	RUN-OFF
—with	
high acidity	ACID RAIN
snow	SLEET
thunder and lightning	THUNDERSTORM
rains	
—Australia	THE WET
—autumn (E. Africa)	MILLET RAINS
—periodic (India)	MONSOON
—spring (E. Afica)	MAIZE RAINS
(S. E. Asia)	BLOSSOM SHOWERS
	MANGO RAINS
—summer (Jap.)	BAI U, PLUM RAINS
rate of change of	
—atmospheric pressure	PRESSURE GRADIENT
—temperature	TEMPERATURE GRADIENT
ratio of actual to	
—maximum water vapour in air	RELATIVE HUMIDITY
—normal rainfall	
	PLUVIOMETRIC COEFFICIENT
record of	
—air temperature	THERMOGRAM
—relative humidity	HYGROGRAM
—vertical variation of atmospheric conditions	TEPHIGRAM
reduction of vision by	
—dust, etc	HAZE
—ice-particles	ICE-FOG
—moisture in atmosphere	FOG, MIST
—smoke and fog	SMOG
haze (US)	SMAZE
—snow	WHITEOUT
—wind-borne particles	DUST-STORM SAND-STORM
reversal of temperature gradient	INVERSION

ring of light round sun or moon	HALO
rising air current	CONVECTION CURRENT
	THERMAL
rocket carrying meteorological instruments	SOUNDING ROCKET
route of depressions crossing North America	NORTHERN CIRCUIT
	SOUTHERN CIRCUIT
satellite relaying meteorological data	WEATHER SATELLITE
sea	
—dog	FOGBOW
—fog	HAAR
—mist	FRET
shadow of observer on cloud or fog	BROCKEN SPECTRE
sheltered lee of mountain receiving little rain	RAIN SHADOW
ship making meteorological observations	WEATHER SHIP
short dry season (S. America)	VERANO
shortest day	WINTER SOLSTICE
small	
—area of low pressure associated with larger	SECONDARY DEPRESSION
—intense depression in tropics	TROPICAL CYCLONE
	TROPICAL REVOLVING STORM
snow	
—fine, dry	POWDER
—granular	FIRN
—soft	GRAUPEL
soft hail or snow	GRAUPEL
solar radiation on given area	INSOLATION
sound produced after lightning flash	THUNDER
spell of fine weather	
—in	
autumn	INDIAN SUMMER
October	ST LUKE'S SUMMER
November	ST MARTIN'S SUMMER
—very hot weather	HEAT WAVE
spring thaw (Siberia)	RASPUTITSA
squall (Scot.)	DROW
station making meteorological observations	WEATHER STATION

statistical description of velocity of molecules	MAXWELL-BOLTZMANN DISTRIBUTION LAW
storm with	
—snow	SNOWSTORM
and wind	BLIZZARD
—thunder and lightning	THUNDERSTORM
study of	
—atmosphere	AEROLOGY
—climate	CLIMATOLOGY
	METEOROLOGY
in	
—past ages	PALAEOMETEOROLOGY
—small systems	MICROCLIMATOLOGY
	MICROMETEOROLOGY
—clouds	NEPHOLOGY
—water in atmosphere	HYDROMETEOROLOGY
sudden	
—inrush of cold air from interior of land mass	COLD WAVE
—shower	SCAT
—storm	SQUALL
swirling dust column	DUST DEVIL
temperature	
—0°C or 32°F	FREEZING POINT, FROST
—100°C or 212°F	BOILING POINT
—at which moisture condenses	DEW-POINT
—change with altitude	LAPSE RATE
—increase caused by warm air from lower latitudes	WARM WAVE
—recorded by hygrometer	WET BULB TEMPERATURE
thick mist (Peru)	GARUA
thin transparent ice	BLACK ICE
	GLAZED FROST
treat clouds to produce rain	SEED
treatment of disease by climatic environment	CLIMATOTHERAPY
tropical storm	CYCLONE, HURRICANE
	MONSOON, TORNADO
	TYPHOON
turbulence in cloudless conditions	CLEAR AIR TURBULENCE
unit of atmospheric pressure	BAR, INCH OF MERCURY
	MILLIBAR, TORR
upper atmosphere as seen from Earth	SKY
variation in daily extremes of temperature, etc	DIURNAL RANGE

violent		floating garden	CHINAMPA
—rainstorm	CLOUDBURST	flower	BELLE-DE-NUIT
—snowstorm	BLIZZARD		MARVEL OF PERU
—thunderstorm	ELECTRIC STORM		TAGETES, TIGER-FLOWER
—wind	GALE, HURRICANE	grass	OTATE, TEOSINTE
	SQUALL	ground-cuckoo	CHAPARRAL-COCK
visible light from sun	SUNSHINE	hat	SOMBRERO
warm air between cold		hog	PECCARY
and warm fronts	WARM SECTOR	hors d'oeuvres	GUAC(H)AMOLE, TAPAS
warning of bad weather	STORM CONE	Indian market	TIAGUI
water		Indians	OMATIA, ZUNI
—droplets suspended		language	NAHUATL
in atmosphere	FOG, MIST	leaf fibre	HENEQUEN, HENEQUIN
—spout (US)	TWISTER		HENIQUIN
—vapour content of		leather riding leggings	CHAPARAJOS
atmosphere	HUMIDITY		CHAPAREJOS
given volume		maize	
of air	ABSOLUTE HUMIDITY	—cake	TORTILLA
watery snow	SLEET, SLUSH	—dish	TAMAL(E)
weather phenomenon	METEOR	minced-meat dish	TAMALE, TOMALLEY
—from 1-100Km	MESOSCALE	mushroom drug	PSILOCYBIN
wind-formed bank of snow	(SNOW)DRIFT	musical instrument	CLARIN
winds	(*see separate entry*)	pancake	ENCHILADA, TACO
Mexico	MEX		TORTILLA
agave	HENEQUEN, HENEQUIN	peasant	PEON
	HENIQUIN	peyote cactus	MESCAL
aloe	AGAVE, CENTURY PLANT	pepper sauce	TABASCO
	MAGUEY	persimmon	CHAPOTE
ancient		plums	ZAPOTE
—language	NAHUATL	pyramid temple	TEOCALLI
—race	AZTEC, MAYA, MIXTEC	rat	TUCAN, TUZA
	OLMEC, TOLTEC, ZAPOTEC	ranch	HACIENDA, RANCHO
avocado	CHININ, COYO	riding blanket	SERAPE, ZARAPE
Aztec emperor	MOCTEZUMA, MONTEZUMA	ringtail (cat)	CACOMISTLE, CACOMIXL
bean	FRIJOL(E)	river	RIO GRANDE
bird	CHAPARRAL-COCK	rodent	TUCAN
	ROAD-RUNNER	rubber-plant	GUYALE
blanket	SERAPE, ZARAPE	settlement	PUEBLO
brushwood thicket	CHAPARRAL	shirt	GUYAVERA
bulbous plant	JACOBEAN LILY	shrub	MESQUIT(E), JOJOBA
cactus	MESCAL, NOPAL, PEYOTE		POINSETTIA
capital	MEXICO CITY	spear-thrower	ATLATL
cape	SERAPE, ZARAPE	spiny tree	RETAMO
cherry	CAPULIN	spurge(wax)	CANDELILLA
coarse sugar	PANOCHA	stewed pork	CARNITAS
coin	DOLLAR, PESO	stirrup-guard	TAPADERA, TAPADERO
corn mush	ATOLE	street musicians	MARIACHI
cross of twigs	GOD'S EYE	sugar	PANOCHA
day-labourer	PEON	symbol of luck	GOD'S EYE
dog	CHIHUAHUA	tea	GOOSEFOOT
drink	MESCALI, PEYOTE	temple	TEOCALLI
	PULQUE, TEQUILA	timber	CANDLE-WOOD
drug	JALAP, MESCALINE	tortilla chip	FRITO
	PSILOCYBIN	town	PUEBLO, TULA
early civilisation	OLMEC, TOLTEC	trader with Indians	COMANCHERO
feathered serpent	QUETZALCOATL	tree	JOJOBA, MESQUITE

water gardens	CHALCHIHUITLICUE
wild pig	PECCARY, TAJACU
military	
advance	ANABASIS
assign accommodation	BILLET, CANTON
	QUARTER
attack or raid	INCURSION
auxiliary unit	RESERVE, PARAMILITARY
	TA, TERRITORIALS
bag on sword-belt	SABRETACHE
barracks or quarters	CASERN
base or camp	INSTALLATION
cane	SWAGGER-STICK
canteen or shop	NAAFI
cartridge belt	BANDOLEER, BANDOLIER
cleaning	
—material	SOLDIER'S FRIEND
for	
—buckles, etc	BRASSO
—rifle barrels	FOUR-BY-TWO
—webbing	BLANCO
—tool for rifle-barrel	PULL-THROUGH
commission for higher rank	BREVET
cord on left shoulder	FOURRAGERE
courier	ESTAFETTE
demand for supplies	REQUISITION
device used when	
polishing brass	
buttons, etc	BUTTON STICK
department in charge of	
food supplies etc	COMMISSARIAT
detachment	
—protecting	
front	VANGUARD
rear	REARGUARD
—sent in to support	REINFORCEMENTS
discharge	
—from service	DEMOB(ILISE)
—with	
dishonour	CASHIER, DRUM OUT
illness or wounds	INVALID
disciplinarian	MARTINET
disorderly retreat	ROUT
display outdoors	TATTOO
dress	BATTLE DRESS, FATIGUES
	UNIFORM, SD, SERVICE DRESS
drill	
—on barrack-square	SQUARE-BASHING
—sergeant's folding stick	PACE-STICK
emergency rations	C RATION, K RATION
	IRON RATIONS
encampment	BIVOUAC
engines of war	(*see* **weapons**)
equipment	MATERIEL
establishment	
—American	PENTAGON

—British	WAR OFFICE, WO
express	ESTAFETTE
force into service	COMMANDEER
	CONSCRIPT, CRIMP, DRAFT
	(IM)PRESS), LEVY
	PRESS(GANG)
formation	PHALANX, TESTUDO
government by military	STRATOCRACY
heavy concentration of	
bombing or shelling	BARRAGE
	SATURATION, STONK
join services	ENLIST, ENROLL
—of own free will	VOLUNTEER
leaders	(*see separate entry*)
leave	FURLOUGH
lightning attack	BLITZKRIEG
manoeuvre	
—attacking on both	
flanks	PINCER MOVEMENT
—drawing enemy away from	
planned attack	DIVERSION
—using surprise	STRATAGEM
medal	(*see* **decorations**)
menial work in barracks	FATIGUE
Military	
—Intelligence	MI
—Police	(R)MP
minor encounter	SKIRMISH
move forces to new area	REDEPLOY
mule litter	CACOLET
official commendation	CITATION
	MENTION IN DESPATCHES
operation to achieve	
—immediate objective	TACTIC
—long-term objective	STRATEGY
organisation and transport	
of men and equipment	LOGISTICS
persecution by military	DRAGONNADE
	DRAGOONING
planning as an art	
or science	STRATEGY
policy of destroying	
anything useful to	
an enemy	SCORCHED-EARTH
position established	
—in enemy	
territory	BRIDGEHEAD, SALIENT
—on enemy shore	BEACHHEAD
post of soldiers	
stationed there	GARRISON
protective clothing	GAS CAPE
	NODDY SUIT
punishment	DETENTION, FATIGUES
	JANKERS, PACK DRILL
	REPRIMAND
ranks	(*see* **soldier**)

removal of	
—military presence	DEMILITARISATION
—weapons	DISARMAMENT
rifle-cleaning tool	PULL-THROUGH
ruling group of officers	JUNTA
saddle-cloth	SHABRACK
seize for military use	COMMANDEER
	REQUISITION
shop	
—American	POST EXCHANGE, PX
—British	NAAFI
sign up new members	ENLIST, ENROL
	RECRUIT
soldier	(*see separate entry*)
soldier's	
—belt	BALDRIC(K)
—equipment	ACOUTREMENTS
—mattress section	BISCUIT
straps, pack, etc	WEBBING
subdivision	ECHELON
tent	BIVOUAC
trial	COURT MARTIAL
unit	
—detached from main body	OUTPOST
—forming core of larger unit	CADRE
—of Army (in increasing	
size)	SECTION, PLATOON
	COMPANY, BATTALION
	REGIMENT, BRIGADE
	CORPS, ARMY, ARMY GROUP
—selected for	
special mission	DETACHMENT, PATROL
	STRIKE FORCE, TASK FORCE
—specialising in quick	
destructive raids	COMMANDO
	LONG RANGE DESERT GROUP
	SPECIAL BOAT FORCE
—within a military force	CONTINGENT
unofficial units	PARAMILITARY
volunteer for service	ENLIST, ENROL
weapons, ammunition etc	ORDNANCE
withdraw from action	DISENGAGE
	(*see also* **soldier**)
million	M, MEGA-
million cycles per second	MPS
million electron-volts	MEV
million joules	MJ
million to power of	
—two	BILLION
—three	TRILLION
—four	QUADRILLION
—five	QUINTILLION
—six	SEXTILLION
—seven	SEPTILLION
—eight	OCTILLION
—nine	NONILLION

—ten	DECILLION
—hundred	CENTILLION
thousand million	BILLION, GIGA-
	MILLIARD
million million	TERA-
million million million	EXA-
Milton	
some words found in	
Milton's works:	
able to speak	SPEAKABLE
abstruse	SUTTLE
act	
—as bishop	EPISCOPATE
—of planting	PLANTATION
adverse	PERVERSE
allow oneself	SPARE
amaurosis	DROP SERENE
archangel	HIERARCH
armour for forearm	VANTBRASS
arouse	UPRAISE
assail with din	PEAL
assembly	FREQUENCE
assuage	SWAGE
atmosphere	REGION
await	REMAIN
awakening	WAKEFUL
base wretch	RAKESHAME
battle	HOSTING
be	
—bent on	RAGE
—called	HEAR
—in excess	REDOUND
—subordinate	SUBSERVE
beat	SWINDGE
believe to exist	THINK
beloved	LIKING
beyond description	INEXPRESSIVE
blameless	UNREPROVED
blindness	DROP SERENE
blowing back	REBUFF
boisterous brawler	TURMAGANT
bottomless	UNFOUNDED
bragging	TONGUE-DOUGHTIE
bridesmaid	PARANYMPH
bridge(-work)	PONTIFICE
bring	
—back	
again	RECOLLECT
to better state	RECURE
—to perfection	SUM
bully	TURMAGANT
by the influence of heaven	HEAVENLY
call to witness	PROTEST
called	YCLEAP'D
canopy	STATE
capacity for receiving	RECEPTION

captive led in triumph	TRIUMPH	dye red	ENVERMEIL
cast	FUSIL(E)	early	RATHE
cause to degenerate	DEGENERATE	earn	ERN
chastise	SWINDGE	Earth's axis	HINGE
celebrate	REPEAT	easy to roll	VOLUBIL
claim	EXPOSTULATE	elusive	SUTTLE
close	STRAIT	encircle	WHEEL
compassionate feeling	REMORSE	encouraging	INCENTIVE
complete development of	SUM	ethereal	ETHEREOUS
concede to oneself	SPARE	even	EEV(E)N
confine	IMMANACLE	evening	EEVNING
confirm	STABLISH	evil	SHREWD
confusion	LURRY	exalted	HAUGHT, HAU(L)T
conjunction	INJUNCTION	exceed	EXCEL
constant	SAD	excessively exact	OVER-EXQUISITE
construct	FABRIC	excite	UPRAISE
contrive	PRACTISE	excommunication	EXCOMMUNION
coy	NICE	exhausted	FAINTED
crafty	SUTTLE	expand	INTEND
crash	RACK	expect	SUPPOSE
crowd	FREQUENCE	experience	TRY
cunning	SUTTLE	explode	DISPLODE
cure	RECURE	fabricate	FANGLE
defeat	DISCOMFIT	fallen	
delicate	SUTTLE	—angel	BELIAL
democracy	DEMOCRATY	—from heaven	HEAVEN-FALLEN
deprive of commission	DISCOMMISSION	false notion	IDOLISM
designate in print	PRINT	fancy	FANGLE
determine the value of	STATE	farmyard	VILLATIC
dethrone	DISENTHRONE	fatigued	SWINK'T
differentiated	DISTINCT	feed voraciously	ENGORGE
digression	EXTRAVAGANCE	female	FEMAL
dim-eyed	PALE-EYED	fetter	IMMANACLE
diminutive creature	MINIM	fiend	FEND
direct	INFORM	fine	QUAINT, SUTTLE
discharge	DISPLODE	fish route	SEA-PATH
discomposed	INCOMPOSED	flavoured by steam of	
disdain	SDAINE, SDAYN	melted ambergris	GRIS-AMBER-STEAM'D
	SDEIGNE, SDEIN	flourish	SWINDGE
disfavour	DISGUST	flow	FLOAT
disgrace	DISWORSHIP	flowed	FLOWN
dishonour	DISWORSHIP	flowering in spring	VERNANT
dispensation	DISPENSE	flowing forth	PROFLUENT
displeasure	DISGUST	fluency	FLUENCE
dissolute wretch	RAKESHAME	flying	FLIGHTED
distaste	DISGUST	forbid	RESTRAIN
distinguished	DISTINCT	foreign	FORREN
distracted	DISTRACT	form a sphere	INGLOBE
divided into groups		friar	FRIER
of four	QUATERNION'D	frightful	GREISLY
division of atmosphere	REGION	from	ON
Dog-star	SWART STAR	fulminate	FULMINE
double the darkness of	DOUBLE-SHADE	further	FURDER
drawn up again		fusible	FUSIL(E)
in battle	REIMBATTELL'D	gabbled formula	LURRY
dressed with flowers	FLOWERY-KIRTLED	gaping apart	INTERRUPT

ghastly	GREISLY	landing-place	STRAND
give		landscape	LANTSKIP
—red colour to	ENVERMEIL	lash	SWINDGE
—way	RELENT, SWERVE	lay low	SUPPLANT
glassy transparent surface	HYALINE	layer	LOFT
grating	SCRANNEL	lewdness	SENSUALITY
goal	GOLE	libration of celestial	
gory	GOARY	sphere	TREPIDATION
granary	GRANGE	like a devil	DEMONIAN
great expanse	MAIN	limit	MEASURE
grieve for	PINE, PYNE	look-out	PROSPECT
grisly	GREISLY	lost	UNOWNED
groomsman	PARANYMPH	lustful	LUSTY
guide	LAND-PILOT	luxuriant	LUXURIOUS
halt	ALT	make	
hard-pressed	STRAIT	—a paradise of	IMPARADISE
haughty	HAUGHT, HAU(L)T	—stable	STABLISH
having		mark out	REMARK
—forebodings	DIVINE	marked	DISTINCT
—perches	PERCHED	marry	SPOUSE
heal	RECURE	means of sustenance	SUSTAIN
heathen(dom)	PANIM	mind	NOTION
held back	SUSPENS, SUSPENCE	mischievous	SHREWD
hesitate	DEMUR	mix in	IMMIX
hideous	DEFORM	moisten	DIP
hold out	SUBSIST	molestation	INFESTATION
holder of bishopric	EPISCOPANT	molten	FUSIL(E)
honesty	REALTIE	monarch	SOVRAN
honeysuckle	EGLANTINE	Moon not yet visible	SILENT
hot-tempered	HOT-LIVERED	morning song	MATIN
huddle	PESTER	motive power	PRINCIPLE
hurtful	SHREWD	move nimbly	TROULE
idolater	IDOLIST	moving	
igniting	INCENTIVE	—aslope	SLOPE
ill-conditioned	SHREWD	—slowly	LEADEN-STEPPING
ill-natured	SHREWD	murmuring	MUTTER
immaterial	UNESSENTIAL	mutiny	MUTINE
impalpable	SUTTLE	named	YCLEAP'D
impervious to starlight	STAR-PROOF	narrow	STRAIT
impossible to		needy	STRAIT
—be formed	UNCONJUCTIVE	nice	SUTTLE
—undo	UNRECALLING	non-Christian	PANIM
impregnable in virtue	VERTUE-PROOF	northern	SEPTENTRION(AL)
impregnate	IMPREGN	not	
in due time	MATURE	—discordant	UNDISCORDING
inciting	INCENTIVE	—having skin	UNHIDEBOUND
inhabited world	INHABITATION	—in liquor	UNLIQUORED
inlaid ornament	EMBLEM	—subject to suspicion	UNSUSPECT
innocent	OFFENCELESS	—suited to marriage	UNCONJUGAL
inordinate	DISORDINATE	—to be recalled	UNRECALLING
inseparable	INDIVIDUAL	object of favour	FAVOUR
involve in mixture	IMMIX	obsequy	OBSEQUIE
jasmine	GESSAMINE	opposition	RELUCTANCE
keep evenly outspread	WEIGH	original elements	ORIGINS
kerchiefed	CHERCHEF'T	outnumber	OVERMULTITUDE
kindle	TINE	overrefined	SUTTLE

pagan	PANIM
paltry	PITEOUS
partisan	SIDESMAN
paynim	PANIM
penetrating	SUTTLE
perfect	PERFET
permissible	VENIAL
persevere	INSIST
persuasion	INDUCEMENT
pertaining to numbness	NUMB
pestilence	MURREN
petty politician	POLITICASTER
pick out challengingly	SINGLE
pinion	PENNON
pity	REMORSE
place of rest	REPOSE
plant with magic properties	HAEMONY
planting	PLANTATION
pointing to stars	STAR-YPOINTING
precedent	PRESIDENT
preface	EPISTLE
preparedness	PROCINCT
prescient	DIVINE
president	PRESIDENT
prey	RAVEN, RAVIN(E)
private person	PRIVATE
product	PRODUCEMENT
prompt	PERNICIOUS
prune	REFORM
punishment	PENANCE
purpose	MIND
put	
—in	
a vial	VIOLD
chains	IMMANACLE
paradise	IMPARADISE
—into operation	ENURE
—under embargo	IMBAR
quash	REPEAL
quicksand	SYRTIS
raiment	WARDROP
rarefied	SUTTLE
ravishment	RAPINE
ready	PERNICIOUS
rebel	MUTINE
rebuild	REFORM
reck	WRECK
refusing indulgence	UNCONNIVING
remedy	RECURE
render	INFER
—unfamiliar	DISINURE
repress	REPEAL
resistance	RELUCTANCE
resort	SEEK
rest	ALT
restore	REFORM

revoke what has	
been predicted	UNPREDICT
revolving easily	VOLUBIL
rigorous	STRAIT
rise aloft	TOWER
river Oceanus	OCEAN-STREAM
rough	ROBUSTIOUS
round	GLOBY
rousing	WAKEFUL
route taken by fish	SEA-PATH
ruffled up	TO RUFFL'D
said	SED
sayest	SAIST
scaling-ladder	SCALE
scare	SCAR(RE)
scatter	SHATTER
scent	SENT
school	SCUL(L), SCULLE
scratchy	SCRANNEL
scythe	SITHE
second	VOUCH
seize	CEAZE, SEASE, SEAZE
sense	SENT
separable	DIVIDUAL
separate after bethrothal	DISESPOUSE
serenade	SERENATE
set	
—apart	EXEMPT
—as a plume	PLUME
—aside	REPEAL
—in	
a border	EMBORDER, IMBORDER
motion	WINNOW
—to words that smoothly	
fit the tune	SMOOTH-DITTIED
—up	STABLISH
shaft of light	RULE
shared in common	DIVIDUAL
sharpness	SHARP
showing fine discrimination	SUTTLE
shriek	SHREIK
shrink	SWERVE
sincerity	REALTIE
sluice	SLUSE
smell	SENT
snake	ELLOPS
snare	FRAUD
sober	UNLIQUORED
soft	DOUGH-KNEADED
soldier wearing armour	CATAPHRACT
source of motive power	PRINCIPLE
south-west wind	LIBECCHIO
sovereign	SOVRAN
span	OVERLAY
spareness	SPARE
sparing in giving	STRAIT

sphere	SPHEAR(E)
spot	FREAK
spreading like a sail	SAIL-BROAD
sprouting in spring	VERNANT
square space	QUADRATURE
stand fast	SUBSIST
steadfast	SAD, STEDFAST
steer	STEAR(E)
steerage	STEARAGE
steersman	STEARSMATE
stir violently	TEMPEST
stolen	STOLN
strait	STREIGHT
streak	FREAK
strict	STRAIT
strong	MAIN, ROBUSTIOUS
struggling	RELUCTANT
studded with ice spangles	ICY-PEARLED
stupendous	STUPENDIOUS
stupidity	INSULSITY
subjacent	SUBJECT
subtle	SUTTLE
sublety	SUTTLETIE
suffuse	DIP
sung to the timbrel	TIMBREL'D
superintendence	EPISCOPY
superintending	PRESIDENT
support	VOUCH
supremely happy or blessed	HIGH-BLEST
surging	REDUNDANT
survey	EPISCOPY
suspended	SUSPENS, SUSPENCE
sward	SORD
swashbuckler	SWIN(D)GE-BUCKLER
sway	SWINDGE
swift	DISPATCHFUL, PERNICIOUS
tapestry	TAPSTRY
tenuous	SUTTLE
thin	SUTTLE
things stolen	STEALTH
time of shutting	SHUT
toil-worn	SWINK'T
token of victory	TRIUMPH
transparent	TRANSPICIOUS
transport	RAPINE
trick out	FANGLE
troop	TURME
turban	TURBANT
turf	TERF(E)
turquoise	TURKIS
ugly	OUGHLY-HEADED
unchristianise	UNCHRISTEN
undergo	TRY
undeserving	IMMERITOUS
undistilled	UNFUME
uninstructed	UNPRINCIPLED

unknown insect	GRAYFLY
unless	LESS
unlike	UNCONFORM
unnaturally	UNKINDLY
unobserved	UNSP'D
unoffending	OFFENCELESS
unshapely	DEFORM
upper air	REGION
vapid	FLASHY
variegate	FREAK
variegated	DISTINCT
venture	VENTER
venturous	VENTROUS
verdict	VERDIT
view-point	PROSPECT
village	VILLATIC
voluble	VOLUBIL
vouchsafe	VOUTSAFE
wag the tongue	TROULE
want of distinct utterance	INFANCY
wardrobe	WARDROP
watch	VIGILANCE
western	PONENT
wheel of night and day	RHOMB(US)
whirlpool	GURGE
wild musical note	WOOD-NOTE
wing	PENNON
with	
—difficulty	SCARCE
—hands joined	HANDED
withholding the gospel	DISGOSPELLING
without	
—being	UNESSENTIAL
—bottom	UNFOUNDED
—knowing	UNWARE
—light	UNLIGHTSOME
—origin or birth	UNORIGINAL
—pause	UNRESPITED
womb	SIDE
worm injuring flocks	TAINT-WORM

mineral

acid	
—igneous rock	LIPARITE, RHYOLITE
—magnesium silicate	TALC
agate	MURRINESCOTCH PEBBLE
—with layers	ONYX
albite feldspar	PERICLINE
	PERISTERITE
Alpine	
—granite	PROTOGINE
—sandstone	FLYSCH
altered	
—andesite	PORPHYRITE, PROPYLITE
—basalt	MELAPHYRE
—biotite	RUBELLAN
—dolerite or basalt	DIABASE

—feldspar	SAUSSURITE
—mica	VERMICULITE
alum-stone	ALUNITE
alumina	ARGIL, CORUNDUM
aluminate of iron	HERCYNITE
aluminium	
—hydroxide	DIASPORE
—ore	B(E)AUXITE
—oxide	CORUNDUM
—phosphate	SPHAERITE, TURQUOISE
	VARISCITE
—silicate	CYANITE, FIBROLITE
	FULLER'S EARTH, HALLOYSITE
	KAOLINITE, KYANITE
	SILLIMANITE
—sodium silicate	NOSEAN
—magnesium silicate	SAPPHIRINE
alumino-silicate	ZEOLITE
amorphous silica	OPAL
anatase	OCTAHEDRITE
andalusite	CHIASTOLITE
antimonite	STIBNITE
antimony	
—oxysulphide	KERMES(ITE)
—trisulphide	STIBNITE
aquamarine	BERYL
aragonite	SATIN-SPAR
arborescent agate	DENDRACHATE
argentite	SILVER-GLANCE
argillaceous rock	MUDSTONE
arsenate of	
—cobalt	COBALT BLOOM, ERYTHRITE
—copper	ERINITE
arsenic	
—monosulphide	REALGAR, SANDARAC(H)
—trisulphide	ORPIMENT
arsenical pyrites	MISPICKEL
arsenide of	
—nickel	COPPER-NICKEL, NICCOLITE
—platinum	SPERRYLITE
asphalt	UINTA(H)ITE
augite	DIALLAGE
auriferous conglomerate	BANKET
autunite	TORBERNITE, URANITE
aventurine feldspar	SUNSTONE
banded	
—chalcedony	AGATE
—silica	CHALCEDONY
barium	
—carbonate	WITHERITE
—sulphate	BARITE, BARYTES
	CAULK
barytes with sulphur smell	HEPATITE
basalt	OCEANITE, WHIN(STONE)
—black	TACHYLITE, TACHYLYTE
	TOUCHSTONE

—lava	TOAD-STONE
—rich in aluminium	THOLEITE
—with nepheline	NEPHELINE-BASALT
basaltic rock	TEPHRITE
basic igneous rock	DOLERITE
beryllium	
—aluminate	CHRYSOBERYL
—aluminium silicate	EUCLASE
—silicate	PHENACITE
	PHENAKITE
between clay-slate and	
mica-schist	PHYLLITE
bituminous	ASPHALT(UM)
black	COAL
—basalt	TOUCHSTONE
—bitumen	ALBERTITE
—copper ore	MELACONITE, TENORITE
—diamond	CARBONADO
—garnet	MELANITE
—glassy igneous rock	TACHYLITE
	TACHYLYTE
—iron mineral	ILMENITE
—jasper	BASANITE
—lead	GRAPHITE
—marble	NERO-ANTICO, TOUCH
—mica	BIOTITE, LEPIDOMELANE
and plagiocite	KERSANITE
—spinel	HERCYNITE
—tourmaline	SCHORL
blackjack	ZINCBLENDE
bloodstone	HELIOTROPE
blue	
—asbestos	CROCIDOLIE
—cordierite	WATER-SAPPHIRE
—corundum	SAPPHIRE
—mineral like nosean	HAUYNE
—quartz	SAPPHIRE-QUARTZ
—stone	HYACINTH
—violet quartz	AMETHYST
boric acid	SASSOLITE
bornite	HORSEFLESH ORE
	PEACOCK-ORE
botryoidal graphite	PENCIL-ORE
brassy yellow	IRON PYRITE(S)
brick-earth	GAULT
bright non-metallic mineral	SPAR
brilliant pale zircon	JARGO(O)N
brown	
—coal	LIGNITE
—iron ore	LIMONITE
—or yellow quartz	CAIRNGORM-STONE
—tin dioxide	CASSITERITE
—with axe-shaped crystals	AXINITE
cadmium sulphide	GREENOCKITE
Cairngorm stone	SMOKY QUARTZ
calc-sinter	TUFA, TUFF

calcite-coloured ultramarine	LAPIS-LAZULI
calcium	
—aluminium	
silicate	ANORTHITE
	CHABAZITE, PREHNITE
magnesium	MELILITE
—carbonate	AR(R)AGONITE, CALCITE
	CALCSPAR, CARBONATITE
	ICELAND SPAR, LIMESTONE
—carbonate, etc	RENDZINA
—chloride	HYDROPHILITE
—fluoride	FLUORITE, FLUORSPAR
—in toothlike form	DOG-TOOTH SPAR
—magnesium	
amphibole	TREMOLITE
carbonate	DOLOMITE
pyroxene	DIOPSIDE
silicate	MONTICELLITE
—molybdate	POWELLITE
—oxalate	WHEWELLITE
—phosphate	
and fluoride	APATITE
etc	PHOSPHORITE
—potassium silicate	APOPHYLLITE
—salts in peat	DOPPLERITE
—silicate and titanate	SPHENE
	TITANITE
—sodium silicate	PECTOLITE
—sulphate	GYPSUM
anhydrous	ANHYDRITE
—tantalum, oxygen	MICROLITE
—titanium antimonate	LEWISITE
—tungstate	SCHEELITE
carbon	GRAPHITE
carbonaceous rock	COAL
carbonate of	
—calcium etc	ANKERITE
—copper	AZURITE, CHESSYLITE
	MOUNTAIN-BLUE
—iron	IRON-STONE
—nickel	ZARATITE
—sodium	NATRON, URAO
—strontium	STRONTIANITE
cassiterite	NEEDLE-TIN
cat's-eye	CHRYSOBERYL
	CYMOPHANE
cavity containing	
crystals	DRUSE, DRUSY CAVITY
	GEODE
cerium ore	CERITE
chalcedony	CHERT, MOSS AGATE
	SILICA
chalcopyrite	COPPER PYRITES
chalybite	SIDERITE
chiastolite	CROSS-STONE, MACLE

china-clay	KAOLIN, LITHOMARGE
chloride and phosphate of	
—lead	PYROMORPHITE
—potassium	CARNALLITE
chlorite with quartz	CHLORITE-SCHIST
chrome with iron oxide	CHROMITE
cinnamon-stone	(H)ESSONITE
	HYACINTH
clay	
—and	
alumina	B(E)AUXITE
sand	LOAM
—dark blue or grey	OXFORD CLAY
—formed by weathering	LATERITE
—from	
decomposed silicate	ILLITE
Lemnos	LEMNIAN EARTH
—ironstone	IRON-CLAY
	SPHAEROSIDERITE
—like kaolinite	NACRITE
—marble	(K)NICKER
—mineral	BENTONITE, FULLER'S EARTH
	JARGILLITE
	MONTMORILLIONITE
—rock	SHALE
—slate	OTTRELITE-SLATE
—splitting easily	
into layers	SHALE
—used for	
refractory bricks, etc	FIRE-CLAY
sun-dried bricks	ADOBE
—white	MEERSCHAUM, SEPIOLITE
—with little lime	FIRE-CLAY
—yellow	LONDON CLAY
clayey alum ore	ALUM-SHALE, ALUM-SLATE
	HALLOYSITE
clinkstone	PHONOLITE
clinochlore	RIPIDOLITE
coal	WALLSEND
—and iron	
carbonate	BLACK-BAND IRONSTONE
—early form	LIGNITE, PEAT
—from	
algae, etc	BOGHEAD COAL
sediment on	
sea bottom	SAPROPELITE
—glance	ANTHRACITE
coarse	
—grained igneous rock	GABBRO
	MONZONITE, PEGMATITE
	PERIDOTITE, SYENITE
—metamorphic rock	GNEISS
—nephaline syenite	LA(U)RDALITE
—oolite	PISOLITE
cobalt	
—arsenide	SKUTTERUDITE, SMALTITE

—carbonate	SPHAEROCOBALTITE		—porphyritic rock	MELAPHYRE
cockscomb pyrites	MARCASITE		—tuff with crystals	PEPERINO
coloured corundum	ORIENTAL AMETHYST		decomposed	
	ORIENTAL EMERALD		—basalt	WACKE
	ORIENTAL TOPAZ		—ironstone	ROTTENSTONE
	ORIENTAL RUBY		—rock	GOSSAN
colourless			devitrified igneous rock	FELSITE
—opal	HYALITE		diabase	OPHITE
—quartz	ROCK-CRYSTAL		diamond	
common feldspar	ORTHOCLASE		—coarse	BO(A)RT
compact flinty chalcedony	CHERT		—fragments or dust	BO(A)RT
compacted sand	SANDSTONE		—matrix	KIMBERITE
composed of			—ore	BLUEGROUND
—pebbles	PSEPHITE		—used as abrasive	CARBONADO
—sand-grains	PSAMMITE		diatomite	KIESELGUHR, TRIPOLI
concretion of silica	FLINT		dichroite	CORDIERITE, IOLITE
conglomerate	PUDDINGSTONE		dioptase	EMERALD-COPPER
—of quartz	BANKET		diorite	DIABASE
containing			—etc	GREENSTONE
—olivine	CIMINITE		—with quartz	GRANODIORITE
—quartz	GRANODIORITE		doggar	IRONSTONE
copper			dolomite	BITTERSPAR, BROWNSPAR
—arsenate	OLIVENITE		—rock	MAGNESIAN LIMESTONE
—carbonate	MALACHITE		dome of igneous rock	LACCOLITE
—glance	REDRUTHITE			LACCOLITH
—hydrogen arsenite	SCHEELE'S GREEN		double	
—lead selenite	ZORGITE		—carbonate of calcium	
—oxide	BORNITE		and magnesium	DOLOMITE
—pyrites	CHALCOPYRITE		—sulphate of aluminium	
	PEACOCK-COPPER		and potassium	ALUM
	PEACOCK-ORE		dunite	OLIVINE
—silicate	DIOPTASE		dyke rock	ELVAN
—sulphide	CHALCOCITE		elastic bitumen	ELATERITE
copperas	MELANTERITE		electric calamine	HEMIMORPHITE
cordierite	DICHROITE, IOLITE		emerald	BERYL, SMARAGD
corundum	EMERY		enclosed in another	ENDOMORPH
cryoloite	ICE-STONE		enclosing another	PERIMORPH
crystal enclosed in a			epidote and quartz	EPIDOSITE
different mineral	ENDOMORPH		erubescite	HORSEFLESH ORE
crystalline	SCHIST		exfoliating clay	PYROPHYLLITE
—fibre in rock	SPHERULITE		feldspar	ANDESINE
—igneous rock	GABBRO		—bluish	ANORTHOCLASE
—limestone	MARBLE		—from Labrador	LABRADORITE
—olivine	DUNITE		—greyish	ANORTHITE
crystallised			—intermediate	BYTOWNITE
—calcite	NAIL-HEAD-SPAR		—opalescent	MOONSTONE
—haematite	OLIGIST		—reddish	ANORTHITE
cubic			—with	
—carbon	DIAMOND		aluminium silicate	ANDESINE
—zeolite	ANALCIME, ANALCITE		barium	HYALOPHONE
cupreous oxide	CUPRITE		cleavage not at	
cupric sulphide	COVELLITE		right angles	ANORTHITE
dark blue or grey				PLAGIOCLASE
—clay	OXFORD CLAY		nepheline and aegirine	TINGUAITE
—fine-grained igneous rock	TRAP		olivine	TROCTOLITE
—green silicates	CHLORITE			TROUTSTONE

potassium	TRACHYTE	
feldspathic rock	PETUNTSE, PETUNTZE	
feldspathoid	ULTRAMARINE	
felstone	FELSITE	
ferric		
—arsenite	SCORODITE	
—oxide	GO(E)THITE, LIMONITE	
—sedimentary rock	RED BED	
ferro-magnesian mica	BIOTITE	
ferrous		
—carbonate	CHALYBITE, SIDERITE	
—phosphate	VIVIANITE	
—sulphide	TROILITE	
ferruginous red earth	TERRA-ROSSA	
fibrolite	SILLIMANITE	
fibrous		
—amphibole	ASBESTOS, CROCIDOLITE	
	MOUNTAIN-LEATHER	
—asbestos	AMIANT(H)US	
—barytes	BOLOGNA STONE	
—calcite	SATIN-SPAR	
—serpentine	CHRYSOTILE	
—sillimanite	FRIBROLITE	
fiery red gem	PYROPE, PYROPUS	
fine asbestos	AMIANT(H)US	
fine-grained		
—basalt	TEPHRITE, TOUCHSTONE	
—diorite	PORPHYRITE	
—igneous rock	APHANITE	
	KERATOPHYRE	
	PHONOLITE, SPILITE	
	TRACHYTE, TRAP	
—lamprophyric rock	MONCHIQUITE	
—metamorphic rock	SLATE	
—quartz, etc	GAN(N)ISTER	
—sedimentary	SHALE	
—silicious rock	NOVACULITE	
—syenitic rock	ORTHOPHYRE	
finer portions of		
crushed ore	SCHLICH	
fissile		
—greywacke	GREYWACKE-SLATE	
—limestone	FOREST MARBLE	
flinty		
—chalcedony	CHERT, HORNSTONE	
—quartz	CHERT	
fluoride of yttrium etc	YTTRO-CERITE	
fluorspar	BLUE JOHN	
formed of thin layers	FOLIACEOUS	
	FOLIATED	
found in Cornwall	REDRUTHITE	
French		
—chalk	SOAPSTONE	
	SPANISH CHALK	
—limestone	CAEN-STONE	
fuller's earth	CIMOLITE	

gabbro		
—of hornblende and		
magnetite	GARNET-ROCK	
—with pyroxene	NORITE	
and		
—omphacite	ECLOGITE, EKLOGITE	
—smaragdite	ECLOGITE, EKLOGITE	
garnet with calcium		
and iron	ANDRADITE	
geyserite	SINTER	
glassy		
—lava	PUMICE	
—orthoclase	ICE-SPAR	
—stone	AUSTRALITE, TEKTITE	
glimmer	MICA	
gneiss	MIGMATITE	
gneissose granite	PROTOGINE	
gold ore	BANKET	
gooseberry-stone	GROSSULAR(ITE)	
granite, decomposed	CHIN-STONE	
—with markings like		
Hebrew characters	GRAPHIC GRANITE	
granular anhydrite	VULPINITE	
graphic granite	PEGMATITE	
graphite	PLUMBAGO	
greasy nepheline	ELAEOLITE	
green		
—amphibole	ACTINOLITE, PARGASITE	
	SMARAGDITE	
—banded marble	CIPOLLINO	
—beryl	AQUAMARINE, EMERALD	
—chalcedony	CHRYSOPRASE	
—chlorite	CLINOCHLORE	
—chromium mica	FUCHSITE	
—chryso-beryl	ALEXANDRITE	
—hornblende	AUGITE	
—microcline	AMAZON-STONE	
—mottled	OPHITE	
—nickel magnesium silicate	GARNIERITE	
—nickel-arsenate	ANNABERGITE	
—porphyry	ORIENTAL VERD-ANTIQURE	
—potassium, iron and		
aluminium silicate	GLAUCONITE	
—pyroxene	AEGIRINE, AUGITE	
	OMPHACITE	
—quartz	PRASE	
—spodumene	HIDDENITE	
greenish beryllium	CHRYSOBERYL	
Greenland spar	CRYOLITE	
grey		
—igneous rock	GRANODIORITE	
—or black mineral		
with metallic lustre	GLANCE	
—sandstone	GREYWACKE	
gypsum	ALABASTER, PLASTER-STONE	
	SATIN-SPAR, SELENITE	

haematite	SPECULAR IRON	—disulphide	PYRITE(S)
halite	ROCK-SALT	—olivine	FAYALITE
halloysite	MOUNTAIN-SOAP	—ore	BABINGTONITE, CHALYBITE
hard			HAEMATITE, SIDERITE
—chlorite	OTTRELITE		TACONITE
—coal	ANTHRACITE, SPLINT-COAL	with coal	BLACKBAND
—green stone	JADE	—pyrites	FOOL'S GOLD, MUNDIC
—quartz	FLINT	—tantalate	TANTALITE
—sandstone	MILLSTONE-GRIT	—titanium and oxygen	ILMENITE
	QUARTZITE	ironstone	DOGGAR
—siliceous stone	GAN(N)ISTER	jacinth	HYACINTH
—stone	RAG(G)	jade	NEPHRITE, SPLEEN-STONE
hardest mineral	DIAMOND		YU-STONE
hardness	(see geography)	kaolin	CHINA CLAY
harmotome	CROSS-STONE	kyanite	DISTHENE
hatchettite	MOUNTAIN-TALLOW	lake deposit	SHELL-MARL
having		laminar lignite	PAPER-COAL
—crystal form of		laminated	
another mineral	PSEUDOMORPH	—bituminous mineral	DYSODIL
—crystals arranged like			DYSODILE, DYSODYLE
lettering	GRAPHIC	—clay	SHALE
—metallic lustre	GLANCE	lead	
heavy spar	BARYTES	—antimony and sulphur	JAMESONITE
hemimorphite	ELECTRIC CALAMINE	—arsenate	MIMETITE
hone-stone	NOVACULITE	—chromate	CROCOISITE
horn-silver	CERARGYRITE	—glance	GALENA
hornblende	SYNTAGMATITE	—monoxide	LITHARGE
hyacinth	JACINTH	—sulphate	ANGLESITE
hydrogen calcium borate	PANDERMITE	—sulphide	GALENA
hydrous		—vanadate and chloride	VANADINITE
—aluminium silicate	ALLOPHANE	Lemnian earth	TERRA SIGILLATA
—zinc silicate	HEMIMORPHITE	leucite	FEL(D)SPATHOID
ice-stone	CRYOLITE	lignite	COLOGNE-EARTH, JET
idocrase	VESUVIANITE	—Iceland	SURTARBAND, SURTURBAND
igneous rock	AMYGDALOID, BASALT	lime	
	BASANITE, BATHOLITE	—alumina	
—of labradorite etc,	GABBRO	garnet	GROSSULAR(ITE)
—with feldspar	VARIOLITE	mica	MARGARITE
ilmenite	TITANIC IRON	—chrome garnet	UVAROVITE
impure		—feldspar etc	EUCRITE
—apatite	PHOSPHORITE	—silicate	HORNFELS
—talc or steatite	POTSTONE	—zeolite	SCOLECITE
—zinc	SPELTER	limestone	OOLITE
in Chinese porcelain	PETUNTSE	—composed of	
	PETUNTZE	shells, etc	CHALK, COQUINA
intergrowth of albite		—decomposed	ROTTENSTONE
and orthoclase	PERTHITE	—deposited from	
intrusive quartz sheet	WHIN-SILL	solution	TRAVERTIN(E)
—with black mica etc	LAMPROPHYRE	—fetid	STINK-STONE
iolite	CORDIERITE	—used for coffins	SARCOPHAGUS
	DICHROITE	—white	CHALK, COQUINA
iridium and osmium	IRIDOSMINE	—with dendritic	
	IRIDOSMIUM, OSMIRIDIUM	markings	LANDSCAPE-MARBLE
iron	FERRITE	limonite	BOG-IRON, BOG-ORE
—arsenic and sulphur	ARSENO-PYRITES		PEA-IRON, STILPNOSIDERITE
	MISPICKEL	limy clay	MARL

linite	WOOD-COAL
liparite	RHYOLITE
lithia mica	LEPIDOLITE
lithium aluminium silicate	SPODUMENE
loadstone	MAGNETITE
loamy deposit	LO(E)SS
loose rock at surface	MANTLE ROCK
Lydian stone	TOUCHSTONE
magnesia	PERICLASE
—alumina garnet	PYROPE, PYROPUS
—iron spinel	CEYLANITE, CEYLONITE
	PLEONASTE
—mica	PHLOGOPITE
magnesian limestone	DOLOMITE
magnesium	
—aluminate	SPINEL
—and iron	MAFIC
—borate and chloride	BORACITE
—carbonate	DIALOGITE, MAGNESITE
—hydroxide	BRUCITE
—orthosilicate	HUMITE
—oxide	BRAUNITE, PERICLASE
—silicate	ENSTATITE, FORSTERITE
	MEERSCHAUM, SERPENTINE
	TALC
—sulphate	KIESERITE, KAINITE
magnetic	
—iron ore	MAGNETITE
—oxide of iron and	
chromium	CHROMITE
—pyrites	PYRRHOTITE
manganese	
—alumina garnet	SPESSARTITE
—aluminium arsenate	SYNADELPHITE
—dioxide	PYROLUSITE
—ore	WAD(D)
—oxide	POLIANITE
—silicate	RHODONITE
—spar	RHODOCHROSITE
—sulphide	ALABANDITE
marble with green	
serpentine	OPHICALCITE
marcasite	COCKSCOMB PYRITES
	SPEAR PYRITES, WHITE PYRITES
meerschaum	SEPIOLITE
melaconite	TENORITE
melanterite	COPPERAS
mellite	HONEY-STONE
mercuric	
—sulphate	QUEEN'S YELLOW
	TURPETH MINERAL
—sulphide	CINNABAR
mercurous chloride	CALOMEL
	HORN-MERCURY
metamorphosed	
—diorite	EPIDIORITE

—gabbroite	EPIDIORITE
—sandstone	QUARTZITE
mica	GLIMMER
—and quartz	MICA-SCHIST, MICA-SLATE
—ferro-magnesian	BIOTITE
—peridotite	KIMBERLITE
milky quartz or opal	CACHOLONG
mineral	
—coal	STONE-COAL
—pitch	MALTHA
mispickel	ARSENICAL PYRITES
	ARSENO-PYRITES
molten rock	MAGMA
molybdate of lead	WOLFENITE
molybdenum disulphide	MOLYBDENITE
moss agate	MOCHA STONE
mostly hypersthene	HYPERSTHENITE
mountain	
—soap	HALLOYSITE
—tallow	HATCHETTITE
muscovite granite	GRANITITE
nepheline	FEL(D)SPATHOID
—and pyroxene	NEPHELINITE
—syenite	LA(U)RDALITE
nephrite	GREENSTONE, JADE
nickel	
—and iron	NIFE
—arsenide	COPPER-NICKEL
	KUPFERNICKEL, NICCOLITE
niobate and titanate	
of yttrium etc	EUXENITE
nodular rhyolite	PYROMERIDE
nodule of oxide	
of iron	EAGLE-STONE
novaculite	TURKEY HONE, TURKEY STONE
oil-shale	TORBANITE
olivine	CHRYSOLITE, DUNITE
	PERIDOT(E)
—and	
augite	LIMBURGITE, MONCHIQUITE
iron oxides	MUGEARITE
—with	
ferromagnesium	PICRITE
pyroxenes	LHERZOLITE
onyx	
—marble	ONYCHITE
—with cornelian or sard	SARDONYX
	ORIENTAL ALABASTER
oolitic limestone	PORTLAND STONE
opal	SILICA
opalescent	
—chrysoberyl	CYMOPHANE
—feldspar	MOONSTONE
opaque	
—quartz	JASPER, JASPIS
—white mineral	ALBIN

orange-coloured spinel	RUBICELLE
orbicular diorite	NAPOLEONITE
ore yielding profit	PAY DIRT
oriental alabaster	ONYX-MARBLE
orthoclase and	
—biotite	MINETTE
—hornblende	SYENITE
orthorhombic pyroxene	HYPERSTHENE
oxide of	
—aluminium	ALUMINA
—lead and molybdenum	WULFENITE
—lithium	LITHIA
—manganese	MANGANITE
	PSILOMELANE, WAD
—sodium and boron	KERNITE
—tellurium	TELLURITE
—tungsten	TUNGSTITE
—uranium	URANITE
—zinc	ZINCITE
pea	
—iron	LIMONITE
—stone	PISOLITE
peacock-ore	BORNITE
pearly	
—lustred mineral	MARGARITE
—zeolite	STILBITE
peridotite	SAXONITE
philosopher's	
stone	LAPIS PHILOSOPHICUS
phonolite	CLINKSTONE
phospate of	
—aluminium	LAZULITE
	WAVELLITE
—copper and uranium	TORBERNITE
—thorium etc	MONAZITE
—uranium and calcium	AUTUNITE
picolite	CHROME-SPINEL
pink	
—garnet	RHODOLITE
—topaz	ROSE-TOPAZ
pinkish quartz	ROSE-QUARTZ
pisolite	PEA-STONE
pissasphalt	MINERAL TAR
pitchblende	CLEVEITE
	URANINITE
plagioclase and	
—augite	TESCHENITE
—hornblende	CAMPTONITE
	DIORITE
—feldspar	ANORTHITE
—nepheline and augite	THERALITE
pleochroic pyroxene	AEGIRINE
plumbago	GRAPHITE
plutonic rock	GRANITE, SYENITE
porous rock	CALC-SINTER
	TUFA, TUFF

porphyry with embedded	
crystals	GROUNDMASS
potash	
—feldspar	MICROCLINE
	ORTHOCLASE, SANIDINE
—mica	SERICITE
potassium chloride	SYLVINE
potstone	LAPIS OLLARIS
potter's clay	ARGIL
powdery constituent	
of coal	FUSAIN
precious spinel	RUBY-SPINEL
	SPINEL-RUBY
pseudomorph of quartz	TIGER('S)-EYE
purple and white	
—garnet	RHODOLITE
—hard rock	PORPHYRY
pyromeride	RHYOLITE
pyrophyllite	PENCIL-STONE
pyroxene	AEGRINE, AUGITE
	COCCOLITE, OMPHACITE
pyrrhotite	MAGNETIC PYRITES
quartz	SILICA
—and	
feldspar	HALLEFLINTA
	QUARTZ-PORPHYRY
mica, etc	GREISEN
orthoclase	ELVAN, FELSITE
—biotite diorite	TONALITE
—clear	ROCK CRYSTAL
—containing topaz	GREISEN
—crystal	BRISTOL-DIAMOND
—feldspar	
and	
—mica	GRANITE, GNEISS
—hypersthene	CHARNOCKITE
etc	GRAYWACKE
	GREYWACKE
with garnets	GRANULITE
—flinty	CHERT
—leek-green	PRASE
—like diorite	GRANDIORITE
—milky	CACHALONG
—opaque	JASP(ER), JASPIS
—plagioclase	DACITE
—porphyry	GRANOPHYRE
—rock	QUARTZITE
—rough	BUHRSTONE, BURRSTONE
—transparent	ROCK CRYSTAL
—with mica	AVANTURINE, AVENTURINE
quartzite	ITACOLUMITE
quicksand	SYRTIS
realgar	SANDARAC(H)
red	
—chalcedony	CARNELIAN, CORNELIAN
	SARD(IUS), SARDINE

—clay	BOLE	shelly limestone	PURBECK MARBLE
—copper ore	CUPRITE		PURBECK STONE
—corundum	RUBY	siderite	CHALYBITE
—garnet	ALABANDINE	silver-glance	ARGENTITE
	ALMANDINE	silica	CHALCEDONY, QUARTZ
—mercuric sulphide	CINNABAR	—and alumina	SIAL
—ochre from Lemnos	LEMNIAN RUDDLE	—in hexagonal scales	TRIDYMITE
—orthosilicate	GARNET	silicate minerals	AMPHIBOLES
—precious stone	CARBUNCLE	silicate of	
—spinel	BALAS(RUBY)	—alumina	CHLORITE
—tourmaline	RUBELLITE	—aluminium	ANDALUSITE, BENTONITE
—brown or yellow zircon	HYACINTH		CHIASTOLITE, CORDIERITE
redruthite	COPPER-GLANCE		DICHROITE, FULLER'S EARTH
repidolite	CLINOCHLORE		HAROMTOME, IDOCRASE
resembling spar	SPATHIC		IOLITE, JADEITE, LEUCITE
reworked china clay	BALL CLAY		MONTMORILLONITE, MUSCOVITE
rhodochrosite	MANGANESE SPAR		PENNINE, SCAPOLITE, SPODUMENE
rhodonite	MANGANESE SILICATE		STAUROLITE, TOPAZ, VESUVIANITE
rhyolite	LIPARITE	—beryllium	AQUAMARINE, BERYL
rock			EMERALD
—containing ores	GANG(UE), LODE	—boron and calcium	DATOLITE
—crystal	RHINESTONE	—calcium	TABULAR SPAR
—derived from clay or mud	PELITE		THAUMASITE, WOLLASTONITE
—forming	FEL(D)SPAR, MICA	and aluminium	ZOISITE
—of angular fragments	BRECCIA	etc	EPIDOTE, HORNBLENDE
—salt	HALITE		IDOCRASE, VESUVIANITE
	(see also **rock**)	—complex	TOURMALINE
rose-red pyroxene	RHODONITE	—copper	CHRYSOCOLLA
ruby	STAR-STONE	—iron	CHLORITE, FAYALITE
—copper	CUPRITE		GREEN EARTH
—silver	PROUSTITE, PYRARGYRITE	and magnesium	OLIVINE
sandarac(h)	REALGAR	—magnesia	CHLORITE
sandstone	HOLYSTONE	—magnesium and	
—formed from granite	ARKOSE	aluminium	SAPONITE
—grey	GREYWACKE	iron	HYPERSTHENE
—rough	GRIT(STONE)	—manganese	TEPHRITE
—with		—mineral	PYROXENE, PYROXENITE
feldspar	ARKOSE	—potassium etc	PHILLIPSITE
glauconite	GREENSAND	—sodium	
limonite	CARSTONE	and	
sandy shale	FA(I)KES	—aluminium	JADEITE
sapphire	STAR-STONE	—iron	CROCIDOLITE, RIEBECKITE
scapolite	MARIALITE, MEIONITE	etc	NEPHELINE NEPHELITE
	MIZZONITE	—thorium	THORITE
schistose quartzite	QUARTZ-SCHIST	—yttrium etc	GADOLINITE
schorl	TOURMALINE	—zirconium etc	EUDIALYTE
—and quartz	SCHORL-ROCK	silicon	
scoriaceous lava	SLAG	—and magnesium	SIMA
selenite	MOONSTONE, PHENGITE	—compound	SILICATE
sepiolite	MEERSCHAUM	—dioxide	CHALCEDONY, OPAL
serpentine			QUARTZ, SILICA
—and calcite	VERDE-ANTICO	sillimanite	FIBROLITE
	VERD-ANTIQUE	silver and	
—rock	OPHITE	—antimony	DYSCRASITE
shale (Scotland)	TORBANITE	—chloride	CERARGYRITE
sheet of rock	NAPPE	—glance	ARGENTITE

—iodide	IODYRITE	
—mica	CAT-SILVER	
—ore	STEPHANITE	
red	PROUSTITE	
silvery metal	ALUMINIUM	
sinter	GEYSERITE	
skeleton crystal	DENDRITE	
slaty diabase tuff	SCHALSTEIN	
smaltite	SPEISS-COBALT	
smaragd	EMERALD	
smoky quartz	CAIRNGORM (STONE)	
soapstone	FRENCH CHALK	
	SPANISH CHALK, STEARITE	
soda		
—amphibole	ARFVEDSONITE	
—lime feldspar	ANORTHOSITE	
	OLIGOCLASE	
—mica	PARAGONITE	
—syenite	LA(U)RVIKITE	
—trachyte	KERATOPHYRE	
sodalite	FEL(D)SPATHOID	
sodium		
—aluminium		
fluoride	CRYOLITE	
silicate	ANALCIME, ANALCITE	
	LAZURITE, SODALITE	
zeolite	GMELINITE	
—calcium sulphate	GLAUBERITE	
—carbonates	TRONA	
—chloride	(ROCK) SALT	
—nitrate	CHILE NITRE	
	CHILE SALTPETRE	
softest mineral	TALC	
South African quartz	CROCIDOLIE	
Spanish chalk	FRENCH CHALK	
	SOAPSTONE	
spear pyrites	MARCASITE	
specular iron	HAEMATITE	
speiss-cobalt	SMALTITE	
spelter	ZINC	
sphalerite	ZINC BLENDE	
sphene	TITANITE	
spheroidal crystallite	GLOBULITE	
spinel containing iron etc	PICOTITE	
spleen-stone	JADE	
splitting into flakes	SPATHIC	
spotted		
—schist	KNOTENSCHIEFER	
—slate	KNOTENSCHIEFER	
	SPILOSITE	
stalactitic calcite	DROP-STONE	
star-stone	RUBY, SAPPHIRE	
staurolite	CROSS-STONE	
stearite	SOAPSTONE	
steatite	FRENCH CHALK, SOAPSTONE	
	VENICE TALC	

stibnite	ANTIMONITE	
stilbite	DESMINE	
stilpnosiderite	LIMONOITE	
stinkstone	SWINESTONE	
streaks in igneous rock	SCHLIEREN	
streaky granular rock	MYLONITE	
stretching of rock into		
sausage shape	BONDINAGE	
strontium sulphate	CELESTINE	
sulph-arsenide		
of cobalt	COBALTITE	
	COBALT GLANCE	
sulphate of		
—aluminium	ALUNITE	
—iron	COQUIMBITE	
and potassium	JAROSITE	
—magnesium etc	POLYHALITE	
sulphide		
—minerals	PYRITES	
—of		
antimony	STIBNITE	
arsenic	REALGAR, ZARNEC, ZARNICH	
—and silver	PROUSTITE	
copper		
—and		
iron	COPPER PYRITES	
antimony	TETRAHEDRITE	
—etc	STANNITE	
iron	IRON PYRITES, MARCASITE	
—and nickel	PENTLANDITE	
lead	GALENA	
—and antimony	ZINKENITE	
mercury	CINNABAR	
silver	ARGENTITE	
—and antimony	PYRARGYRITE	
zinc	ZINCBLENDE	
sulphur, arsenic etc	TENNANTITE	
sylvine and rock-salt	SYLVINITE	
tabular spar	WOLLASTONITE	
tachylite	HYALOMELAN(E)	
talc		
—soapy	FRENCH CHALK	
	SOAPSTONE, STEATITE	
—with other minerals	TALC-SCHIST	
tantalate of		
yttrium etc	YTTRO-COLUMBITE	
	YTTRO-TANTALITE	
telluride of gold		
or silver	SYLVANITE	
tennantite	FAHLERZ, FAHLORE	
tenorite	MELACONITE	
tetrahedrite	FAHLERZ, FAHLORE	
titanic iron	ILMENITE	
thin-bedded sandstone	FA(I)KES	
thorium		
—and uranium ore	CHERALITE	

—silicate	THORITE
thulite	ZOISITE
tin	
—copper etc	STANNITE
—dioxide	CASSITERITE, TINSTONE
titanite	SPHENE
titanium oxide	ANATASE, BROOKITE
	RUTILE
toad-stone	BASALT LAVA, TUFF
topaz	PYCNITE
torbernite	AUTUNITE, URANITE
touchstone	LYDIAN STONE
tourmaline	SCHORL
—granite	LUXUL(L)IANITE
	LUXULYANITE
translucent opal	HYDROPHANE
transparent	
—calcite	ICELAND SPAR
—feldspar	ADULARIA
—gypsum	SELENITE
—mineral	SPECULAR STONE
—non-metallic	SPAR
—quartz	ROCK CRYSTAL
—silicate	TOURMALINE
—stone	PHENGITE
—zircon	JACINTH
travertine	CALC-SINTER, CALC-TUFF
	ONYX-MARBLE
treelike crystal	DENDRITE
tripoli	DIATOMITE
trisulphide of arsenic	ORPIMENT
troctolite	TROUTSTONE
troutstone	TROCTOLIE
tufa	CALC-SINTER, TUFF
tuff	CALC-SINTER
	TOAD-STONE, TUFA
tungstate of iron, etc	WOLFRAMITE
tungsten	WOLFRAM
Turkey stone	TURQUOISE
turquoise	TURKEY-STONE
under-clay	WARRANT
uraninite	PITCH-BLENDE
uranite	AUTUNITE, TORBERNITE
uranium	
—ore	COFFINITE, SAMARSKITE
—oxides	PITCHBLENDE
useless	GANGUE
vanadate of uranium	CORNOTITE
variety of garnet etc	JACINTH
veinstone	GANG(UE)
Venice talc	STEATITE
vesuvianite	IDOCRASE
vitreous lava	PALAGONITE
volcanic	
—dust	POZZ(U)OLANA, PUZZOLANA
—glass	PE(A)RLITE, PITCHSTONE
—rock	ANDESITE, OBSIDIAN
	PALAGONITE-TUFF
banded	EUTAXITE
—tuff	TARRAS, TERRAS, TRASS
	(*see also* **volcano**)
Wallsend	COAL
warrant	UNDER-CLAY
water-sapphire	CORDIERITE
waxy hydrocarbon	HATCHETTITE
	OZOCERITE, OZOKERITE
whin(stone)	BASALT
white	
—and grey chalcedony	CHALCEDONYX
—clay	KAOLIN(E)
	MEERSCHAUM, SEPIOLITE
—earthy mineral	TERRA ALBA
—feldspar	ALBITE
—lead ore etc	HEDYPHANE
—limestone	CHALK, COQUINA
—marble	PARIAN
—metal	ANTIMONY, NICKEL
	SILVER
—mica	MUSCOVITE
—pyrites	MARCASITE
Wollastonite	TABULAR SPAR
wood-coal	LIGNITE
worthless	GANGUE
yellow	
—beryl	HELIODOR
—clay	LONDON CLAY
—corundum	ORIENTAL TOPAZ
—garnet	TOPAZOLITE
—metal	COPPER, GOLD
—rock crystal	CITRINE
yellowish garnet	CINNAMON-STONE
yu(-stone)	JADE
zeolite	ANALCINE, ANALCITE
	CHABAZITE, HEULANDITE
	PHACOLITE, STILBITE
zinc	SPELTER
—blende	SPHALERITE
—carbonate	CALAMINE, HYDROZINCITE
	SMITHSONITE
—manganese spinel	FRANKLINITE
—oxide	ZINCITE
—silicate	HEMIMORPHITE
—spinel	GAHNITE
—sulphide	SPHALERITE
zirconium	
—dioxide	BADDELEYITE
—silicate	JACINTH, JARGOON, ZIRCON
—sulphate	GOSLARITE
zoisite	THULITE
Miss	
Atwell	MABEL (LUCY)
Austen	JANE

Barrett	ELIZABETH
Bell	DAISY
Brontë	CHARLOTTE, EMILY, ANN
Darling	GRACE
Doone	LORNA
Durbeyfield	TESS
Eyre	JANE
Gabler	HEDDA
Garbo	GRETA
Gardner	AVA
Hayworth	RITA
Laurie	ANNIE
Liddell	ALICE
Lind	JENNY
Lloyd	MARIE
Locket	LUCY
MacDonald	FLORA, JEANETTE
Monroe	MARILYN
Oberon	MERLE
Piggy	GILT
Scoley	AMELIA
Spenlow	DORA
Tilley	VESTA
Wickfield	AGNES
Wilfer	(ISA)BELLA
Woodhouse	EMMA

missile

American	ARROW, CRUISE, HAWK
	LANCE, MINUTEMAN
	PATRIOT, PERSHING, POLARIS
	STINGER, TRIDENT
British	BLOWPIPE, BLUE STEEL
	BLUESTREAK, LANCE, THOR
German	V1, V2
Indian	AGNI, PRITHVI
Israeli	JERICHO
Russian	SAM, SCUD
South African	SKERPION
	(*see also* **space**)

Mongolia

capital	ULAAN BAATAR, ULAN BATOR
coin	
—unit	MONGO
—100 mongo	TUGRIK

monkeys

African	
—ape	CHIMPANZEE, GORILLA
—baboon	CHACMA, DRILL
	MANDRILL
—black and white	GUEREZA
—lemur	ANGWANTIBO, BUSH-BABY
	GALAGO, NIGHT-APE, POTTO
—long-tailed	COLOBUS
	CERCOPITHECUS
	DIANA MONKEY, GRIVET
	GUENON, MONA, VERVET

—guenon	TALAPOIN
—white-eyelid	MANGAB(E)Y
American	MARMOSET, SPIDER MONKEY
anthropoid ape	TROGLODYTE
Assam gibbon	HOOLOCK
Ateles	SPIDER-MONKEY
Barbary ape	INUUS, MAGOT, MACAQUE
black	
—crested langur	SIMPAI
—tailed marmoset	MICO
broad-nosed	PLATYRRHINE
Borneo	PROBOSCIS MONKEY
Brazil	BELZEBUTH, GUARIBA
	MIKRIKI, SAI, TAMARIN
Burma gibbon	HOOLOCK, LAR
capuchin	CEBUS, SAI, SA(PA)JOU
Ceylon	
—langur	WANDEROO
—lemur	LORIS
—macaque	TOQUE
chimpanzee	ANTHROPOPITHECUS
Cochin-China	DOUC
dog-ape	BABOON
dog-faced baboon	CYNOCEPHALUS
East Indian	
—ape	ORANG(-UTAN)
	ORANG-OUTANG, GIBBON
—lemur	LORIS, MALMAG, TARSIER
—tarsier	MALMAG
Ethiopian baboon	GELADA
flying lemur	COLUGO, CYNOCEPHALUS
	DERMOPTERA
	GALEOPITHECUS
gibbon	HYLOBATE
gorilla	PONGO
Guinea baboon	SPHINX
Indian	
—bonnet monkey	MACAQUE, ZATI
—lion-tailed	
macaque	SILENUS, WANDEROO
—monkeys	BANDAR, BOONDER, LORIS
	RHESUS, TARSIER, TOGUE
—sacred monkey	ENTELLUS
	HANUMAN, LANGUR,
Java gibbon	WOU-WOU, WOW-WOW
lemur	HALFAPE, MACACO
	MEERCAT, MEERKAT
macaque	TOQUE
Madagascar	
—lemur	AYE-AYE, BABACOOTE
	BABAKOTO, INDRI(S)
	MONGOOSE
—monkey	VARI
Malay lemur	KUKANG
mangabey	WHITE-EYED MONKEY
marmoset	MIDAS, WISTITI

New World	PLATYRRHINE
(of pile-driver)	RAM
Old World	CATAR(R)HINE
orang-utan	PONGO, SATYR
Philippines - tarsier	MALMAG
rhesus	MACAQUE
Satan monkey	BLACK SAKI
South American	
—black saki	SATAN MONKEY
—broad-nosed	PLATYRRHINE
—cowled monkey	CAPUCHIN
—golden	SQUIRREL-MONKEY
—grey	GRISON
—howler	MYCETES, MYCETIS
—long-tailed	SAKI, UAKARI
—marmoset	JACCHUS
—monkeys	TEE-TEE, TITI
	SAGOIN, SAG(O)UIN
—night-ape	DOUROUCOULI, DURUKULI
—spider-monkey	COAITA, SAPAJOU
—squirrel-monkey	SAIMIRI, TAMARIN
spider-monkey	ATELES
Sumatra	
—gibbon	SIAMANG, WOU-WOU
	WOW-WOW
—langur	SIMPAI
proboscis genus	NASALIS
tarsier	MALMAG, SPECTRE-LEMUR
toque	MACAQUE
tufted monkey	MUSTAC
white-eyed monkey	MANGABEY
with divided nostril	CATAR(R)HINE

monsters

including: heraldic beasts	
mythical beasts	
American	BIGFOOT, SUSQUATCH
amphibious	WATER-BULL
antelope	ARGASILL, IBEX
—horse	BAGWYN
—with swivelling horns	YALE
Arab demon	AFREET
Australian	BUNYIP
Bantu	PALATYI
biblical	BEHEMOTH, LEVIATHAN
	LILITH
bird	ROC, ROK, RUC, RUKH
—Arabian	PHOENIX
—Persian	SIMORG, SIMURG(H)
—restless	HUMA
—rising from ashes/flames	PHOENIX
—whose whistle was fatal	WHISTLER
bird/woman	HARPY
blood-sucking witch	LAMIA
bull	
—fish	BULL MARINE, SEA-BULL
—horse	BON(N)ACPON

—mare	JUMART
—with flames from	
mouth	CARETYNE
bull-headed	BONNACON, MINOTAUR
Carroll	BANDERSNATCH
	JABBERWOCK(Y)
cat with horns	CALYGREYHOUND
camel/goat	YPOTRILL
centaur	HIPPOCENTAUR
—with bow and arrow	SAGITTARIUS
	SAGITTARY
chaste-wife eater	CHICHEVACHE
cock/serpent	COCKATRICE
cockatrice/dragon	BASILISK
cow/stallion	JUMART
Cretan	MINOTAUR
cruel	OGRE
decorative (China)	KYLIN
dog	
—2 headed	ORTHOS
—3 headed	CERBERUS
—fish	HOUND MARINE, SEA-DOG
dragon	BASILISK
—fish	SEA-DRAGON
—Norse	FAFNIR, NIDHOGG
—wingless	LINDWORM
—with	
two legs	WIVERN, WYVERN
wings	GORGON
eagle with horns	TRAGOPAN
female	EURYALE, GORGON
	MEDUSA, STHENO
firebreathing	CHIM(A)ERA, DRAGON
fish	SCOLOPENDRA
fish-tailed, horselike	HIPPOCAMPUS
fox/greyhound/wolf	ENFIELD
Furies	(see separate entry)
giraffe	CAMELOPARD
—with horns	CAMELOPARDEL
goat/stag	HIRCOCERVUS, TRAGALEPH
Greek	LAMIA, TYPHOEUS
green-eyed	ENVY
griffin-headed winged	
horse	HIPPOGRIFF
	HIPPOGRYPH
hairy tyger	NEBEK
Himalayas	ABOMINABLE SNOWMAN, YETI
Hindu	GARUDA
horned beast (Spenser)	ANTELOPE
horse	
—cow	JUMART
—fish	HIPPOCAMPUS
—goat	SILENUS
—griffin	HIPPOGRIFF, HIPPOGRYPH
—with	
single horn	UNICORN

tusks, horns, etc	YALE	reindeer with forward	
wings	HIPPOGRIFF, HIPPOGRYPH	curving horns	TROGODICE
	PEGASUS	Rocky Mountains	BIGFOOT, SUSQUATCH
human wolf	WEREWOLF	Roman	LAMIA, TYPHON
hundred		Scandinavian	TROLL
—handed	AEGEON, BRIARAEUS	Scottish water-horse	KELPIE
	CENTIMANUS, COTTUS	sea	
	GY(G)ES, HECATONCHIRES	—horse	HIPPOCAMPUS
—headed	TYPHAEUS, TYPHON	—monster	LEVIATHAN, ORC
Jewish	GOLEM	German	WASSERMAN
Lewis Carroll's		Norwegian	KRAKEN
invention	BANDERSNATCH	man-shaped	WASSERMAN
	JABBERWOCK(Y)	scaly	PHOCA
lion		—swallower	CHARYBDIS
—dragon	OPINICUS	six-headed	SCYLLA
—eagle	BOREYNE, GRIFFIN, GRIFFON	snake-haired	EURYALE, GORGON
	GRIPE, GRYPHON		MEDUSA, STHENO
—fish	SEA-LION	Spenser	ANTELOPE, PHOCA
—goat	CHIM(A)ERA		ROSMARINE, SEASATYRE
—leopard/serpent	QUESTING BEAST		ZIFFIUS
—scorpion	MANTICORE, MANTICORA	stag/goat	HIRCOCERVUS, TRAGLEPH
—with helmet	BOTRAGER	star-spangled hind	PANTHEON
—wolf	TYGER	three	
lizard	AMPHISBAENA	—bodied	GERYON
—in flames	SALAMANDER	—headed	CERBERUS
man		Tibetan	YETI
—ass	ONOCENTAUR	two	
—bird	GARUDA	—headed	JANICEPS
—bull	MINOTAUR	dog	ORTHOS
—covered with green hair	WODEHOUSE	snake	AMPHISBAENA
—dragon	CECROPS	—tailed mermaid	MELUSINE
—eating	OGRE	under	
—fish	MERMAN	—Etna	TYPHOEUS
—goat	FAUN, SATYR	—rock	CHARYBDIS
—horse	(HIPPO)CENTAUR	unicorn/fish	SEA-UNICORN
	SAGITTARIIUS	water	
	SAGITTARY, SILENII	—demon	NICKER
—lion/antelope	SATYRAL	—snake	HYDRA
—lion/scorpion	MANTICORA	whale-like	WHIRLPOOL
	MANTICORE, MANTYGRE	whirlpool	CHARYBDIS
—with legs in form		wildcat	CAT-A-MOUNTAIN
of serpents	GIGANTES	winged	
—wolf	WEREWOLF	—dragon	WIVERN, WYVERN
man's head with ears		—female	GORGON
of ass	MIDAS'S HEAD	—horse	HIPPOGRIFF, HIPPOGRYPH
many-headed	HYDRA, PEOPLE		PEGASUS
	TYPHAEUS, TYPHON	—serpent	PYTHON
mastiff/bloodhound	TALBOT	wingless dragon	LINDWORM
(monstrous regiment)	WOMEN	with knotted tail	ALPHYN
Norse		wolf	
—dragon	FAFNIR, NIDHOGG	—cat/goat	CHATLOUP
—serpent	MIDGARD	—fish	SEA-WOLF
Norwegian	KRAKEN	—fox/greyhound	ENFIELD
one-eyed	CYCLOPS	—with cloven feet	THEOW, THOS
Persian bird	SIMORG, SIMURG(H)	woman	
prehistoric	DINOSAUR	—fish	MERMAID

—lioness	SPHINX	cloak	BURK(HA), BURQA
—seabird	SIREN		(D)JIBBAH, (D)JUBBAH
—serpent	ECHIDNA, LAMIA	cloth cover for Kaaba	KASWA
—vulture	HARPY	college	MADRAS(S)A(H)
moons	(*see* **astronomy**)		MEDRESSAH
Moor	SARACEN	confession of faith	SHAHADA
carpet	SOFRA, ZOFRA	convert (Hindu)	SHEIK(H)
dance	MORESCO	court official	HAJIB
dynasty (Spain)	NASRID	dancing fanatic	WHIRLING DERVISH
drum	ATABAL	date (after Hegira)	AH
pirate	SALLEE-MAN, SALLEE-MAN	demon	DJINN(I), GENIE, GINN
ship	GALLIVAY, XEBEC(K), ZEBEC(K)		JANN, JINN(EE), JINNI
violin	REBEC(K)	dervish	CALENDER, SADITE
	(*see also* **Morocco**)	dervish's cap	TAJ
Morocco		descendant of	
capital	RABAT	—Fatima	FATIMID, SAID
chicken dish	DJEJ MATISHA		SAY(Y)ID
	DJEJ MQUALLI, MESLA	—Mohammed	EMIR, SEID
coin	CENTIME, DERHAM, DIRHAM		SHEREEF, SHERIF
	DIRHEM, FRANC	disciple	MURID
dancer	CHIKHAT	emblem	CRESCENT
filled pancakes	BRIOUATES	empty litter in pilgrimage	
marzipan pastries	KAAB EL GHZAL	to Mecca	MAHMAL
measure		evil spirit	MAHOUN(D)
—22 inches	DRAH	examiner of the dead	NAKIR
—bushel	MUDD	example of Mohammed	SUNNA
pigeon pie	BISTEEYA	expert on law of Koran	MUFTI
ruler	SULTAN	faith	CRESCENT
spice sauce	CHERMOULA	fallen angel	EBLIS, IBLIS
tree	ARAR, ARGAN	fanatic	ABDELS, GHAZI, MOOLA(H)
	SANDARAC(H), THYINE		MOLLA(H), MULLA(H)
tribe	RIFF, MOOR	fast	MOHARRAM, MUHARRAM
Moslem	MUSLIM, MUS(S)ULMAN		MUHARREM, RAMAD(H)AN
	SARACEN		SAUM, SAWM
ablution	WUDU, WUZU	festival	BAIRAM, BAYRAM
alluring woman	HOURI	flight of Mohammed	HEJ(I)RA
almsgiving	ZAKAT		HEGIRA, HIJRA
angel of death	AZRAEL	god	ALLAH
animal slaughter	HAL(L)AL	great leader	MAHDI
ascetic	DERVISH, FAKIR	greeting	SALAAM
	FAQUIR	headscarf	HIJAR
ascribing partners		hermit	MARABOUT
to God	SHIRK	holy	
become Moslem	TURN TURK	—building in Mecca	KAABA(H)
Bulgarian	POMAK	—city	MECCA, MEDINA
caliphate	KHILIFAT	—man	IMA(U)M
call to prayer	ADAN, AZAN	—state of pilgrim	IHRAM
canon law	SHARIA	—war	CRESCENTADE
chapter of Koran	SURA(H)		JEHAD, JIHAD
chief	AMEER, AMIR, DATTO	home of spirits	KAF
	EMEER, EMIR	if God wills	INSHALLAH
—magistrate	SHEREEF, SHERIF	in India	COSSA
chieftain	AMIR, AMEER	infidel	GIAOUR, KAFIR
	EMEER, EMIR	interpretation of Koran	TAFSIR
Christian turned Moslem	RENEGADE	Jesus	NABI ISA
	RENEGADO	knowledge of Koran	HAFIZ

law	SHARIA(T), SHERIA(T)
lawyer	ALFAQUI, MOOLVEE, MOOLVI(E)
	MOOLWEE, MUFTI
leader	AG(H)A, IMA(U)M, MAHDI
legal decision	FATWA(H), FETWA
magistrate	CADI, KADI
member of dynasty	ABBASID(E)
mendicant	FAKIR, FAQUIR
minister	VEZIR, VISIER
	VIZI(ER), WAZIR, WIZIER
monk	DERVISH
months	
1	MOHARRAM, MUHARRAM
	MUHARREM
2	SAFAR
3	RABIA I
4	RABIA II
5	JUMADA I
6	JUMADA II
7	RAJAB
8	SHABA(A)N
9	RAMADAN
10	SHAWWAL
11	ZU'LKADAH
12	ZU'LHIJJAH
mosque	MASJED, MASJID
—school	MADRAS(S)A(H), MEDRESSEH
mystic	SOFI, SUFI
niche in mosque	
pointing to Mecca	KEBLAH, KIBLAB
	MIHRAB, QIBLA
North African	SENUSSI
nymph of paradise	HOURI
one who calls to prayer	MUEZZIN
orthodox Moslem	HANIF, SHAFI(ITE)
	SUNNI
pilgrim	HADJI, HAJ(J)I
—garb	IHRAM
pilgrimage	HADJ, HAJ(J)
prayer	KHOTBAH, KHOTBEH
	KHUTBAH, SALAT
preacher	AYATOLLAH, MOLLA(H)
	MOOLA(H), MULLA(H)
priest	IMA(U)M, MUEDDIN, MUEZZIN
prince	AMEER, AMIR, EMEER, EMIR
	SHEREEF, SHERIF
princess	BEGUM
prophet	MAHDI, MAHOMET
	MOHAMMED
public procession	MOHARRAM, MUHARRAM
	MUHARREM
pulpit in mosque	MIMBAR, MINBAR
purgatory	ARAF
religion	ISLAM, MOHAMMEDANISM
	MAMMETRY, MAUMETRY
	MAWMETRY, MOMMETRY

religious	
—leader	AYATOLLAH
—war	(*see* holy war *above*)
revealed law	SHARIA
rites	ABDEST, MADHAHIB
ritual animal	
slaughter	HAL(L)AL
ruler	CALIPH, SULTAN
Sabbath	JUMA
sacred	
—book	ALCORAN, (AL)KORAN
—fountain	ZEMZEM
—stone	BLACK STONE
saint's shrine	DURGAH
schoolmaster	MOLLA(H), MOOLA(H)
	MULLA(H)
scriptures	ALCORAN, (AL)KORAN
	QORAN, QURAN
sect	DRUSE, DRUZ(E)
	KHARIVISM, ISMAILI
	KARMATHIAN, MUTAZILAH
	SEN(O)USSI, SHIA(H), SHIITE, SOFI
	SUFI, SONNA, SONNI, SUNNI
	WAHABEE, WAH(H)ABI
Shiite	ISMAILI
shrine	MARABOUT, ZIARA
slab in mosque	MIHRAB
slave	DURGAH
spirit	GENIE, JINNEE, (D)JINNI
	GINN, DJINN
spiritual leader	CALIF, CALIPH
	KALIF(A)(H)
student	SOFTA
sultan's	
—lady	SULTANA
—standard bearer	ALEMBDAR
teacher	MOLLA(H), MOOLA(H)
	MOLLA(H), MULLA(H)
temple	KAABA, MOSQUE
theologians	ULEMA
title of respect	SIDI
tomb cloth	CHAD(D)AR, CHADOR
	CHUDDAH, CHUDDAR
towards Mecca	KEBLAH, KIBLAH
tower of mosque	MINARET
traditional lore	HADITH, SUNNA
tribune	DIKKAH
Turkish sect	KARMATHIAN
unbeliever	KAFIR
voluptuous woman	HOURI
warrior	GHAZI
what God wills	MASHALLAH
whole Moslem world	ISLAM
witness	SHAHADA
woman's	
—loose garment	BURK(H)A, BURQA

—headscarf	HIJAB
—veil	CHAD(D)AR, CHADOR
	CHUDDAH, CHUDDAR, YASHMAK
—wrap	IZAR
women's quarters	HARAM, HAREM, HARIM
	SERAGLIO, SERAIL
wonder-worker	FAKIR, FAQUIR
worship	SALAT
moths	HETEROCERA
Abraxas	GOOSEBERRY MOTH
	MAGPIE MOTH
clothes moth	TENEID
Crethocampus	PROCESSIONARY MOTH
day-flying	CINNABAR
	CURRANT CLEARWING, EMPEROR
	FIVE-SPOT BURNET, FOX
	HORNET CLEARWING
	KENTISH GLORY, OAK EGGAR
	ORANGE UNDERWING, SILVER-Y
	SIX-SPOT BURNET, VAPOURER
Geometers	BEAUTY, CARPET, EMERALD
	MAGPIE, MOTTLED UMBER
	PALE BRINDLED BEAUTY
	PEPPERED, PUG, SWALLOWTAIL
	THORN, WINTER
gooseberry moth	ABRAXAS
Hawk moths	BEE HAWK
	CONVOLVULUS HAWK
	DEATH'S HEAD HAWK, EMPEROR
	EYED HAWK, HUMMING-BIRD HAWK
	LIME HAWK, PINE HAWK
	POPLAR HAWK
	(SMALL) ELEPHANT HAWK
magpie moth	ABRAXAS
night-flying	BUFF-TIP
	BULRUSH WAINSCOT
	BURNISHED BRASS
	COMMON SWIFT, DRINKER
	GHOST SWIFT, GOAT
	GOLDEN PLUSIA, GOLDEN-Y
	GOLD SPANGLE, GOLD SPOT
	GOLD SWIFT, HERALD, KITTEN
	LACKEY, LAPPET
	LARGE YELLOW UNDERWING
	LEOPARD, LOBSTER
	MAP-WINGED SWIFT
	NOCTUID, NORTHERN SWIFT
	OLD LADY, ORANGE SWIFT, OWLET
	PUSS, RED-NECKED FOOTMAN
	RED UNDERWING, SHARK
	TUSSOCK
plant pests	ABRAXAS, BRINDLED BEAUTY
	BROWN-TAIL, BUFF-TIP
	CABBAGE-WHITE, CLEAR-WING, CHERRY
	CODLING, DIAMOND BLACK, GOAT
	GOOSEBERRY, LACKEY, LEAFROLLER

	MAGPIE, MARCH, MOTTLED UMBER
	PALE TUSSOCK, PINE BEAUTY, PITH
	RASPBERRY
	SMALL ERMINE, SWIFT, TORTRIX
	TURNIP, VAPOURER, WINTER
	WOOD LEOPARD
	YELLOW UNDERWING
silkworm	BOMBYCID, PSYCHE
small moths	TENEIDAE
tiger moths	BUFF ERMINE TIGER
	CREAM-SPOT TIGER
	GARDEN TIGER, RUBY TIGER
	WHITE ERMINE TIGER
	WOOD TIGER
motor car	GT, MINI, RR
air deflector	AIR-DAM, SPOILER
automatically synchronised	
gears	SYNCHROMESH
axle	
—containing revolving axle	LIVE AXLE
—dead with independent	
half-shafts	DE DION
—not revolving	DEAD AXLE
—with	
half-shafts revolving with	
the wheels	FLOATING AXLE
pivoting axle casing	SWING AXLE
bar on front and rear	BUMPER
body	SHELL
—in one piece	MONOCOQUE
booster	SUPERCHARGER
	TURBOCHARGER
brake types	BAND, DISC, DRUM
braking system	
—front	FWB
—self-correcting	ABS
—using	
cables or rods	MECHANICAL
oil in pipes	HYDRAULIC
car with enclosed rear	
compartment	TOWN CAR
clutch types	CONE, PLATE, SCROLL
computerised	
suspension	(RE)ACTIVE SUSPENSION
cooling system	FAN, RADIATOR
decorative line	COACH-LINE
designer	
—British	CHAPMAN, HELPERT
	ISSIGONIS
—Italian	BERTONI, (PININ)FARINA
	GANDINI, GHIA, GUIGIARO
dilapidated	BANGER, BONE-SHAKER
	CRATE, HEAP
	JALOP(P)Y, RATTLETRAP
direction indicator	TRAFFICATOR
double overhead camshaft	DOHC

drive-shaft/axle	
connection	DIFFERENTIAL (GEAR)
early car	VOITURETTE
eccentric revolving part	CAM
electrical system	ALTERNATOR
	BATTERY, COIL, DISTRIBUTOR
	DYNAMO, FUSE, GENERATOR
	MAGNETO, (SPARK(ING)) PLUG
	WIRING HARNESS
engine	
—cycle	OTTO CYCLE
—double sleeve-valve	KNIGHT ENGINE
—four-stroke	COMPRESSION, EXHAUST
	IGNITION, INDUCTION
—igniting fuel by	
compression	DIESEL
—types	AIR-COOLED, WATER COOLED
	FOUR-STROKE, TWO-STROKE
—with	
all cylinders cast	
in one piece	MONOBLOC
cylinders cast in	
blocks of two	PAIR-CAST
opposed cylinders	FLAT-FOUR
	FLAT-TWIN
overhead inlet and	
side outlet valves	F-HEAD
rotating piston	ROTARY, WANKEL
side valves	L-HEAD
—on each side	T-HEAD
two blocks of cylinders	BI-BLOCK
epicyclic gear	PLANETARY GEAR
film car	GENEVIEVE
folding rear seat	DICKEY SEAT
	RUMBLE SEAT
footboard	RUNNING BOARD
framework	CHASSIS
gear	
—types	AUTOMATIC
	CONTINUOUSLY VARIABLE
	CRYPTO, EPICYCLIC, MANUAL
	PLANETARY
—wheel	
used for final drive	BEVEL GEAR
	WORM DRIVE
with teeth on internal	
circumference	ANNULAR GEAR
gears etc	TRANSMISSION
having	
—2 doors	COUPE
—2 rows of seats	SALOON, SEDAN
—folding hood	CABRIOLET, CONVERTIBLE
	DROPHEAD COUPE,
	LANDAULET(TE), RAGTOP
	SOFT-TOP, SPYDER, TOURER
—removable top	HARDTOP

—sloping rear	FASTBACK
—upward opening	
rear door	ESTATE CAR
	HATCHBACK, STATION WAGON
high-speed car	DRAGSTER, GT
	GRAN TURISMO, HOT ROD
ignition system	ELECTRIC IGNITION
	HOT-TUBE IGNITION
indicator	TRAFFICATOR
inlet valve over	
exhaust valve	IOE
instruments	AMMETER
	(H)ODOMETER
	OIL PRESSURE GAUGE
	PETROL GAUGE
	REV(OLUTION) COUNTER
	SPEEDOMETER
	WATER TEMPERATURE GAUGE
interior light	COURTESY LIGHT
large car	TOURER, TOURING CAR
—American	GAS-GUZZLER
lubrication system	DRIP FEED, DRY SUMP
	SPLASH LUBRICATION
luxurious car	LIMO(USINE)
jointed shaft driving	
rear axles	CARDAN
joint in drive-shaft	UNIVERSAL JOINT
makes	
—American	AUBURN, BUICK, CADILLAC
	CHEVROLET, CHRYSLER, CORD
	DODGE, DUESENBERG, EDSEL, ESSEX
	FORD, GENERAL MOTORS, GM, HUDSON
	KAISER, LA SALLE, LENOX
	LINCOLN, MARMON, MCFARLAN
	MERCER, NASH, OAKLAND, OLDSMOBILE
	OVERLAND, PACKARD, PIERCE-ARROW
	PONTIAC, SIMPLEX, STUDEBAKER
	STUTZ, TUCKER, WELCH
—Austrian	STEYR-PUCH
—Australian	HOLDEN
—Belgian	MINERVA
—British	AC, ALLARD, ALVIS
	ARMSTRONG-SIDDELEY
	ASTON MARTIN
	AUSTIN(-HEALEY), BEAN, BENTLEY
	BOND, BRISTOL, CLYNO, CONNAUGHT
	CROSSLEY, DAIMLER, FORD
	FRAZER-NASH, GILBERN, GUY
	HEALEY, HILLMAN, HRG, HUMBER
	INVICTA, JAGUAR, JENSEN, JOWETT
	LAGONDA, LANCHESTER, LEA-FRANCIS
	LEYLAND, LOTUS, MARCOS, MG
	MINI(JEM), MORGAN, MORRIS
	PANTHER, PIPER, RELIANT, RILEY
	ROLLS-ROYCE, ROVER, SINGER
	STANDARD, SUNBEAM(-TALBOT),

	SWALLOW, TRIUMPH, TVR
	VANDEN PLAS, VAUXHALL
	WESTFIELD, WOLSELEY
—Czech	SKODA, TATRA
—Dutch	DAF
—French	AMILCAR, BEDELIA, BOLLEE
	BUGATTI, CITROEN, DE DIETRICH
	DE DION, DECAUVILLE, DELAGE
	DELAHAYE, DELAUNEY, FACEL VEGA
	HISPANO-SUIZA, HOTCHKISS
	PANHARD(-LEVASSOR), PEUGEOT
	RENAULT, SIMCA, TALBOT-LAGO
	VESPA, VOISIN
—German	AMPHICAR, AUDI, AUTO-UNION
	BMW, BORGWARD, DKW
	EUROCAR, GLAS, HEINKEL
	MAYBACH, MERCEDES(-BENZ)
	MESSERSCHMITT, NOBEL, NSU, OPEL
	PORSCHE, TRABANT, VOLKSWAGEN
	WARTBURG
—Italian	ABARTH, ALFA ROMEO
	CISITALIA, CIZETA MORODER
	DE TOMASO, ERMINA, FERRARI
	FIAT, ISO, ISOTTA-FRASCHINI
	ITALA, LAMBORGHINI, LANCIA
	MASERATI, SIATA
—Japanese	COLT, DAIHATSU, DATSUN
	HONDA, ISUZU, MAZDA
	MITSUBISHI, SUBARU, SUZUKI
	TOYOTA
—Korean	HYUNDAI
—Malaysian	PROTON
—Russian	GAZ, LADA, MOSKVITCH
	SPARTAK, TCHAIKA, VOLGA
	ZAPOROZHETS, ZAZ, ZIL, ZIM
—Spanish	HISPANO-SUIZA
	PEGASO, SEAT
—Swedish	SAAB, VOLVO
—Swiss	MONTEVERDI
—Yugoslav	SANA, YUGO
	(*see also* **motor racing**)
manufacturer's name	MARQUE
old	
—car	MODEL T (FORD)
	TIN LIZZIE
with	
—back-to-back seating	DOS-A-DOS
—face-to-face seating	VIS-A-VIS
—carburettor	SURFACE CARBURETTOR
—clutch	SCROLL CLUTCH
—ignition coil	TREMBLER COIL
—lubrication system	DRIP FEED
	SPLASH LUBRICATION
—open touring car	PHAETON
—tyred	CLINCHER
offset cylinder	DESAXE

open car	TOURER
panel housing instruments	CONSOLE
	DASHBOARD
pioneers	
—American	APPERSON, BRISCOE, BUICK
	CHADWICK, CHAPIN, CHRISTIE
	CHRYSLER, CORD, DOBLE
	DODGE, DUESENBERG, DURANT
	DURYEA, EARL, FLANDERS
	FORD, FRAZER, KETTERING, KING
	MAXWELL, METZ, NASH, OLDS
	PENNINGTON, PORTER, SLOAN
	STANLEY, STUTZ, THOMAS, WHITE
	WILLS, WILLYS, WINTON
—Austrian	LEDWINKA, MARKUS, PORSCHE
—Belgian	LENOIR
—British	AUSTIN, BENTLEY, CHAPMAN
	HAYNES, ISSIGONIS, LANCHESTER
	LAWSON, MORRIS, ROLLS, ROYCE
	SIMMS
—French	BOLLEE, CHARRON, CITROEN
	CLEMENT, COATALEN, DARRACQ
	DE DION, DELAGE, LAVASSOR
	PEUGEOT, RENAULT, SERPOLLET
	VOISIN
—German	BENZ, DAIMLER, HORSCH
—Italian	BUGATTI, FERRARI, JANO
—Swiss	BIRKIGT, CHEVROLET
	ROESCH
planetary gear	EPICYCLIC GEAR
police car	BLACK MARIA, PANDA
	PROWL CAR
power rating	ALAM RATING
	BHP, BRAKE HORSEPOWER
—French	CV, CHEVAL-VAPEUR
—German	PFERDE STARKE, PS
pre-1905	VETERAN
1905-1919	EDWARDIAN
1919-1930	VINTAGE
procession	MOTORCADE
rear of body	TONNEAU
revolutions per minute	REVS, RPM
ring sealing piston	JUNK RING
	PISTON RING
rod	
—carrying cams which operate (overhead) valves	(OVERHEAD)CAMSHAFT
—connecting piston to crankshaft	CON(NECTING) ROD
—engine to rear wheels	TRANSMISSION SHAFT
—moving overhead valve	PUSHROD
—operating pushrod	ROCKER(-ARM)
—long rocker-arm	WALKING BEAM
—securing road wheels	KING-PIN

safety belt	SEAT BELT
—light	BRAKE LIGHT
	HAZARD WARNING LIGHT
saloon car (American)	SEDAN
small two-seater	RUNABOUT
specially made	CUSTOM-BUILT
sports car	ROADSTER
steam car	DOBLE, SERPOLLET
	STANLEY, WHITE
steering	STEERING COLUMN
	STEERING WHEEL, TRACK ROD
	WHEELS
strengthening bar	ROLL-BAR, ROLL-CAGE
suspension	
—independent	
front wheel	IFS
rear wheel	IRS
—system parts	SHOCK ABSORBER
	SPRING
supercharger	BLOWER
taxation class	RAC RATING
transmission	
—connection	UNIVERSAL (JOINT)
—disconnecting system	CLUTCH
—gears	CROWN WHEEL, PINION
—shaft	JACK SHAFT, HALF-SHAFT
	PROP(ELLOR) SHAFT
—system using	
leather or rubber	
belts	BELT DRIVE
petrol engine to drive	
a dynamo	PETROL-ELECTRIC
wheel rubbing on	
flywheel	FRICTION DRIVE
valve	
—chain-driven	ROTARY VALVE
—in four-stroke engine	POPPET VALVE
—opened and closed	
mechanically	DESMODROMIC VALVES
—overhead	OHV
—side	SV
—sliding	SLEEVE VALVE
wheel	
—maintaining momentum	FLYWHEEL
—with	
fine steel spokes	WIRE WHEEL
wooden or steel	
spokes	ARTILLERY WHEEL
wooden frame with steel	
plates	ARMOURED CHASSIS
motorcycle	
circuits	
—Australia	SYDNEY
—Austria	SALZBURG
—Belgium	SPA FRANCORCHAMPS
—Brazil	RIO DE JANEIRO

—Britain	BRANDS HATCH
	CADWELL PARK
	DONINGTON, DOUGLAS
	SILVERSTONE, SNETTERTON
—Czechoslovakia	BRNO
—Finland	KOUVOLA
—France	LE CASTELLE, LE MANS
	MONTL(H)ERY
—Germany	NURBURGRING
—Holland	ASSO
—Hungary	HUNGARORING
—Italy	MISANO ADRIATICO
—Japan	SUGO, SUZUKO
—Netherlands	ASSEN
—Portugal	VILA REAL
—Spain	JARAMA
—Sweden	ANDERSTOP
—USA	MONTEREY
—Yugoslavia	RIJEKA
luggage carrier	PANNIER
make	
—American	ACE, HARLEY-DAVIDSON
	HENDERSON, INDIAN
	PIERCE ARROW
—Belgian	FN, GILLET-HERSTAL
	MINERVA, SAROLEA
—British	ABC, AJS, ARIEL
	BROUGH (SUPERIOR), BSA
	CHATER-LEA, COTTON
	COVENTRY EAGLE, DOT, DOUGLAS
	EXCELSIOR, FRANCIS-BARNETT
	GRINDLEY-PEERLESS, HRD
	JAMES, MATCHLESS
	MONTGOMERY, NEW IMPERIAL
	NORTON, PANTHER, REX-ACME
	RALEIGH, ROYAL RUBY
	RUDGE-WHITWORTH, SCOTT
	SUNBEAM, TRIUMPH
	VAUXHALL, VELOCETTE
	VICTORIA, VINCENT, ZENITH
—Czech	CZ, JAWA
—Danish	NUMBUS
—Dutch	EYSINK
—French	DAX, PEUGEOT
	RATIER, SUBLIME
—German	ARDIE, BMW, DKW
	IMPERIA, MABECO, MAICO
	MZ, NSU, PATRIA
	SCHUTTOFF, SIMSON
	SPERBER, VICTORIA, ZUNDAPP
—Italian	AERMACCHI, APRILIA
	AZZARIA, BENELLI, BIANCHI
	DUCATI, GILERA, LAVERDI
	MORINO, MOTO GUZZI
	MV AGUSTA, PARILLA
	RONDINE

—Japanese	HONDA, KAWASAKI
	SUZUKI, YAMAHA
—Spanish	BULTACO, MONTESA
—Swedish	HUSQVARNA
—Swiss	CONDOR, MOTOSACOCHE
	UNIVERSAL
passenger	
—compartment	SIDECAR
—seat	PILLION
races	DIRT-TRACK, GRASS-TRACK
	ROAD, SPEEDWAY, TRACK
riders (motocross)	
—Australian	LEISK
—Belgian	GEBOERS
—British	THORPE
riders (track)	
—American	GARDNER, LAWSON
	MAMMOLA, RAINEY
	SCHWANTZ
—Australian	DOOHAN, MAGEE
	GARDNER, GODDARD
—Belgian	DE COSTER, ROBERT
—British	ARMSTRONG, DUKE
	FRITH, GUTHRIE, HAILWORTH
	HASLAM, KAVANAGH, MACKENZIE
	REDMAN, RYMER, SHEENE, SPENCER
	SURTEES, WALKINSHAW, WOODMAN
—Czech	FRIEDRICHS
—Dutch	SPANN
—French	RUGGIA, SARRON, VIEIRA
—German	PREIN, ROTH
—Irish	WOODS
—Italian	AGOSTINI, CALDALORA
	GIANOLA, GRESINI, LORENZETTI
	MASETTI, MILLANI
	PASOLINI, PROVINI
	REGGIANI, UBBIALI
—Japanese	KATOH, MIYAZAKI, OHSHIMA
—Spanish	JARRICA, MARTINEZ, PONS
—Swedish	ABERG, CORNU, LUNDIN
	NILSONN, TRIBBLIN
trophy	EUROLANTIC TROPHY
	ULSTER TOURIST TROPHY

motor racing

assembly area	PADDOCK
body shell	MONOCOQUE
cars	
—American	CHEVROLET, CUNNINGHAM
	DE SOTO, DUESENBERG, KISSEL
	MARMON, MILLER, THOMAS FLYER
—British	ALVIS, ARROWS, BENETTON
	BENTLEY, BRABHAM, BRM
	COOPER, ERA, FRAZER-NASH
	HESKETH, JAGUAR, LOLA, LOTUS
	MARCH, MCLAREN
	(TALBOT-)SUNBEAM

	THOMAS, TYRELL, VANWALL
	SHADOW, WILLIAMS
—French	BALLOT, BUGATTI, CHARRON
	DE DIETRICH, DELAGE, GORDINI
	HISPANO-SUIZA, LIGIER
	MATRA, MORS, RENAULT
	SALMSON, (TALBOT-)DARRACQ
	VOISIN
—German	AUTO-UNION, DAIMLER-BENZ
	MERCEDES, PORSCHE
	ZAKSPEED
—Italian	ALFA-ROMEO, FERRARI
	FIAT, ITALA, LANCIA, MASERATI
	MINARDI, OSELLA
—Japanese	HONDA
circuits	
—America	BROOKLYN, DETROIT
	INDIANAPOLIS
	LONG BEACH, MEADOWLANDS
	PEBBLE BEACH, PHOENIX
	RIVERSIDE, SEBRING
	WATKINS GLEN
—Argentina	BUENOS AIRES
—Australia	ADELAIDE
—Austria	OSTERREICHRING
—Belgium	SPA (FRANCORCHAMPS)
	ZOLDER
—Brazil	INTERLAGOS, JACAREPAGUA
	RIO DE JANEIRO, SAO PAULO
—Britain	AINTREE, BRANDS HATCH
	BROOKLANDS, DONINGTON
	MALLORY PARK, SANTA POD
	SILVERSTONE, THRUXTON
—Canada	MONTREAL, MOSSPORT
—France	CLERMONT-FERRAND
	DIJON, LE CASTELLET
	MONTLHERY, PAU, PAU
	RICARD, REIMS, ROUEN
—Germany	HOCKENHEIM
	NURBURGRING
—Holland	ZANDVOORT
—Hungary	BUDAPEST, HUNGARORING
—Ireland	DUNDROD
—Italy	MODENA, MONZA, PESCARA
—Japan	SUZUKA
—Mexico	MEXICO CITY
—Monaco	MONTE CARLO
—Morocco	CASABLANCA
—Portugal	OPORTO
—San Marino	IMOLA
—Sicily	SYRACUSE
—South Africa	KYALAMI
—Spain	BARCELONA, JARAMA
	JEREZ
—Sweden	ANDERSTORP
—Switzerland	BERNE

drivers
—American ANDRETTI, CHEEVER
FOYT, GINTHER, JONES
MEARS, OLDFIELD, RAHAL
RUTHERFORD, UNSER
—Argentinian FANGIO, GONZALES
REUTEMAN
—Australian BRABHAM, JONES
—Austrian BERGER, LAUDA, RINDT
—Belgian BOUTSEN, ICKX
—Brazilian FITTIPALDI, PIQUET, SENNA
—British AMON, BARNATO, BIRKIN
BROOKS, BRUNDLE, CAMPBELL
CLARK, COBB, COLLINS, DON
FAIRMAN, GERARD, HAWTHORN
HERBERT, HILL, HUNT, IRELAND
MANSELL, MOSS, SALVATORI
SEAMAN, SEAGRAVE, STEWART
THOMAS, TYRELL, WARWICK
WATSON
—Canadian VILLENEUVE
—Dutch LUYENDYK, SPYKER
—Finnish ROSBERG
—French ARNOUX, BEHRA
CHIRON, LAFITTE, PROST
TAMBAY, TRINTIGNANT
—German MASS, STUCK
VON BRAUCHITSCH
—Italian ALBORETO, ASCARI
CARACCIOLA, DE ANGELIS
DE CESARIS, ETANCELIN
FARINA, NUVOLARI, PATRESE
—Japanese NAKAJIMO, SUZUKI
—New Zealand AMON, HULME, MCLAREN
—South African SCHECKTER
—Siamese BIRA(BONGSE)
—Swedish JOHANNSON, NILSSON
PETERSEN
—Swiss REGAZZONI
end-of-race signal CHEQUERED FLAG
famous cars
—Campbell BLUEBIRD
—Eldridge MEPHISTOPHELES
—Jenatzy LA JAMAIS CONTENTE
—Noble THRUST 2
—Seagrave GOLDEN ARROW
SUNBEAM TIGER
—Zborowski CHITTY-CHITTY-BANG-BANG
HIGHAM SPECIAL
first at start POLE POSITION
ground-hugging design GROUND EFFECT
jet-powered THRUST 2
maintenance bay PIT
race DAYTONA 24 HOURS
FORMULA 1,2,3,3000
FORMULA FORD

GRAND PRIX, INDIANAPOLIS
KAISERPREIS, LE MANS
MILLE MIGLIA, SEBRING
TARGA FLORIO
safety barrier ARMCO, STRAW BALE
sharp bend CHICANE
smooth tyres SLICKS
starting area GRID
team ECURIE
trophy (*see separate entry*)
motor rallying
drivers
—Belgian ICKX, DELFERRIER, TARIN
—British ARTHUR, BROOKES, COWAN
HOPKIRK, LLEWELLIN, LOVELL
MCRAE, POND, SHORT, WILSON
—Finnish ALEN, ARIKKALA
KANK(K)UNEN, MIKKOLA
SALONEN, SILANDER, VATANEN
—French AURIOL, FONTENAY, LAFITTE
MUSMARRA, SABY, TAMBAY
WAMBERGUE
—German SCHWARZ
—Italian BIASSION, CERRATO
—Spanish JUNCOSA, MOYA
PRIETO-PEREZ, REPO, SAINZ
—Swedish BERGLUND, CARLSSON
CEDERBERG, EKLUND
ERIKSSON, PARMANDER
SUNDSTROM, WALDEGAARD
—New Zealand MILLEN
rallies
—Africa EAST AFRICA SAFARI
IVORY COAST, KENYA SAFARI
PARIS-DAKAR
—America PIKE'S PEAK
—Britain (LOMBARD)RAC, SCOTTISH
ULSTER
—Corsica TOUR OF CORSICA
—Europe PIRELLI CLASSIC
—Finland THOUSAND LAKES
—France MONTE CARLO
—Greece ACROPOLIS
—Ireland CIRCUIT OF IRELAND
—Italy SAN REMO
mountain ALP, BEN, FELL, SIERRA, TOR
including: equipment
mountaineers
some hill ranges
boots KLETTERSCHUHE, VIBRAM
central mass MASSIF
climbing equipment ALPENSTOCK
CRAMPON, ETRIER
EVEREST PACK, ICE-AXE
JUMAR, KARABINER
PIOLET, PITON, ROPE

clip for rope	JUMAR, KARABINER
crack in	
—glacier	BERGSCHRUND, CREVASSE
—rock	CHIMNEY
descend by double ropes	ABSEIL, RAPPEL
description	OROGRAPHY
dividing ridge	DIVIDE, WATERSHED
facing	
—away from	
Equator	OPACO, SCHATTENSEITE
—towards	
Equator	ADRET(TO), SONNENSEITE
flat-topped	MESA
—in plain	BUTTE
formed by	
—cracking	MASSIF
—deposit on	
surface	MOUNTAIN OF ACCUMULATION
—earth movement	FOLDED MOUNTAIN
—erosion of surrounding	
rock	
	MOUNTAIN OF CIRCUMDENUDATION
	MOUNTAIN OF CIRCUMEROSION
	RELICT MOUNTAIN
—lowering of land around	HORST
—raising between faults	BLOCK
from which Moses	
—descended with	
the tablets	SINAI
—saw the Promised Land	PISGAH
group of mountain systems	CORDILLERA
high mountain	ALP
hill with one steep and	
one gentle slope	CRAG-AND-TAIL
—France	PUY
hills	
—England	BERKSHIRE DOWNS
	CHEVIOTS, CHILTERNS
	CLENT, CLEVELAND HILLS
	COTSWOLDS, DARTMOOR, EXMOOR
	GOG MAGOG HILLS, HAMPSHIRE DOWNS
	LINCOLN WOLDS, MALVERN, MENDIPS
	NORTH DOWNS, PURBECK DOWNS
	SOUTH DOWNS, THE WEALD
	WHITE HORSE HILLS
	YORKSHIRE MOORS
	YORKSHIRE WOLDS
—Scotland	CAMPSIE FELLS
	LAMMERMUIR, MOORFOOT
	OCHIL, PENTLAND
	SIDLAW, TWEEDSMUIR
ice-axe	PIOLET
in mythology	OSSA, PELION
metal peg	PITON
mountain	
—building	OROGENESIS, OROGENY

—dwelling	MONTICOLOUS
mountain in	
—Afghanistan	GUL KOH, NOSHAQ
—Africa	BERG
	BATIAN, DUWONI, EDWARD PEAK
	HAKANNSON, HUMPHREY'S PEAK
	IOLANDA PEAK, KARISIMBI
	KIBARA, KILIMANJARO, KULAL
	KUNDELUNGU, MARGHERITA PEAK
	MARUNGU, MOUNT BAKER
	MOUNT ELGON, MOUNT EMIN
	MOUNT GESSI, MOUNT KENYA
	MOUNT STANLEY, NGALIEMMA
	NYIRU, RUNGWE, RUWENZORI
	SELLA PEAK, TABLE MOUNTAIN
	THABANA NTLENYANA
	UHURU POINT, UMBEATO PEAK
—Alaska	BLACKBURN, BONA
	FAIRWEATHER, FORAKER
	LUCANIA, KING PEAK
	MCKINLEY, ST ELIAS, SANFORD
	SHISHALOIN, STEELE
—Albania	GRIBA, KORABI
—Algeria	ATAKOR
—Alps	EIGER, MATTERHORN
—Andorra	PLA DEL ESTANY
—Angola	SERRA VIGO
—Antarctica	ELIZABETH, EPPERLEY
	FALLA, FISHER, GARDNER
	GIOVINETTO, KAPLAN, KIRKPATRICK
	LISTER, LONG GABLES, MACKELLAR
	MARKHAM, MINTO, NANSEN
	OSTENSO, SHINN, SIDLEY
	TYREE, VINSON MASSIF, WADE
—Arabia	(D)JEBEL
	JEBEL HADHAR, JEBEL RAZIKH
—Argentina	ACONCAGUA, AMEGHINO
	ANTOFALLA, BONETE
	CERRO MANSO, EL MUERTO
	GONZALEZ, INCAHUASI
	LLULLAILLACO, MERCEDARIO
	NACIMIENTO, OJOS DE SALADO
	PISSIS, POQUIS, RAMADA
	TRES CRUCES, TUPUNGATO
—Assam	HKAKABO RAZI
—Australia	AUGUSTUS, BARRINGTON
	BARTLE FRERE, BEN LOMOND
	BLACK SUGARLOAF, BOGONG
	HEUGHLIN, KOSCIUSKO
	LINDESAY, MAGNET
	MOUNT MEHARRY, MOUNT ZIEL
	OXLEY'S PEAK, ROUND MOUNTAIN
—Austria	GROSSGLOCKNER
—Bahamas	MOUNT ALVERNIA
—Barbados	MOUNT HILLABY
—Belgium	BOTRANGE

—Belize	VICTORIA PEAK
—Bhutan	KHULA KANGRI
—Bolivia	ANCOHUMA, ILLAMPU
	ILLIMANI, NEVADA SAJAMA
	OLLAGUE, PALOMANI
	PUPAYA, SONEQUERA, SORATA
	TOCORPURI, TUNARI, UBINA
—Bulgaria	MUSALA, SYUTKYA
—Burkina Faso	MOUNT TEMA
—Burma	HKAKADO RAZI
	MOUNT VICTORIA
—Brazil	MOUNT RORAIMA
	PICO DE BANDIERA
—Cambodia	(*see* Kampuchea *below*)
—Cameroon	CAMEROON MOUNTAIN
—Canada	KEEL PEAK, ALBERTA
	ASSINIBOINE, CAMPBELL, CHRISTIE
	COLUMBIA, EDITH CAVELL
	EDUNI, FORBES, KING GEORGE
	LOGAN, LYELL, MITCHELL
	NELSON, ST ELIAS, SELOUS
	SIR DOUGLAS, RAINIER
	ROBSON, VANCOUVER, WOOD
—Canary Islands	MOUNT TEIDE
—Central African	
Republic	MOUNT GAOU
—Chad	EMI KOUSSI
—Chile	ARENALES, AZUFRE
	CAMPANARIO, CASTILLO, COPAHUE
	COPIAPO, CORCOVADO, CUMBRERA
	EL MUERTO, HORNIPIREN
	HUDSON, ILIAMA, ISLUGA
	LLULLAILLACO, LONGAVI, MACA
	MAINO, MELIMOYU, MERCADARIO
	O'HIGGINS, OJOS DE SALADO
	OSORNO, PETEROA, PIRAMIDE
	PISSIS, SAN LORENZO
	SILLAJHUAY, SOCAMPA
	TINGUIRIRICA, TRES CRUCES
	TRONADOR, TUPUNGATO
	VALENTIN, VILLARRICA
—China	AMNE MACHIN, DULAN KARA
	ILISU, KONGUR, MINYA KONKA
	MUNKU SARDYK, MUZTAGH ATA
	PEAK POPEDY, TUGADIR
	TURGEN ULA
—Colombo	COLON, HUILA
	PICO CRISTOBAL, SOTARA
	TOLIMA
—Comoros	MOUNT KARTALA
—Corsica	L'INCUDINE, MONTE CINTO
	MONTE ROTONDO
—Costa Rica	BLANCO, CHIRRIPO
—Crete	IDHI
—Cuba	PICO TURQUINO
—Cyprus	MOUNT OLYMPUS

—Dominica	IMRAY'S VIEW
—Dominican Republic	PICO DUARTE
	TRUJILLO
—East Indies	ENGGEA, IDENBERG TOP
	KERINTJE, KINABALU
	MOUNT BANGETA
	MOUNT ALBERT EDWARD
	MOUNT GILUWE, MOUNT HERBERT
	MOUNT HOGAN, MOUNT KINABALU
	MOUNT KUBOR
	MOUNT LEONARD DARWIN
	MOUNT SARAWAKET
	MOUNT VICTORIA
	MOUNT WILHELM, NGGA PULU
	PEAK JULIANA, PEAK MANDALA
	PEAK SUKARNO, PEAK TRICORA
	PEAK WILHELMINA
	PEAK WISNUMURTI
	PUNCAK JAYAKUSUMU
	SUNDAY PEAK
—Ecuador	ANTISANA, CHIMBORAZO
	COTOPAXI, PICHINCHA
	SANGAY
—Egypt	JEBEL KATHERINA
—England	BOWFELL, CONISTON OLD MAN
	COOMBE HILL, CROSS FELL
	DUNKERY BEACON, ESK PIKE
	FAIRFIELD, GARROWBY HILL
	GREAT GABLE, HELVELLYN
	LEITH HILL, PILLAR FELL
	PILOT HILL, SCAFELL(PIKE)
	SKIDDAW, THE CHEVIOT
	THE PEAK, THE WREKIN
	URRA MOOR, WALBURY HILL
—Equatorial Guinea	MOCA, MOKA
—Ethiopia	AMARA, AMEDAMIT
	BADDA, BIRHAN, DENDI
	GITCH, GARA GORFU
	GUNA, RAS DAJAN, RAS DASHAN
	SARENGA
—Europe/Asia	DYKH TAU, DZHANGI TAU
	EL BRUS, GESTOLA, JANGA
	JANGI TAU, KAZBEK, KATYJNH TAU
	KOSHTANTAU, KUNJUM MISHURGI
	MISHIRGI, PIK PUSHKIN
	PIK RUSTAVELI, SHKHARA, TETNULD
—Fiji	MOUNT TOMANIIVI
	MOUNT VICTORIA
—Finland	HALTIATUNTURI
—France	MONTAGNE
	AIGUILLE DU MIDI
	DENT DU GEANT, L'INDEX
	MONT BLANC, MONT VALLIER
	POINTE MONTCALM
	TETE BLANCHE, TOUR RONDE
—Gabon	MONT IBOUNDJI

—Germany	BERG
	FICHTELBERG, ZUGSPITZE
—Greece	ELIKON, ERIMANTHOS
	IMITTOS, LIKODHIMOS
	MAVROVOUNI, OITI, OXIA
	OLIMBOS, OLYMPUS
	PANAKHAIKON, PARNASSOS
	PARNASSUS, PARNIS
	PARNON, PERISTERI, PILION
	SMOLIKAS, TIMFRISTOS, TRINGIA
	TZOUMERKA, YERAKOVOUNI
—Guatemala	TAJUMULCO
—Guinea	MOUNT NIMBA
—Guyana	MOUNT RORAIMA
—Haiti	PIC LA SELLE
—Hawaii	MAUNA KEA, MAUNA LOA
—Himalayas	ANNAPURNA, CHANGTSE
	CHO OYU, CHOMO LONZO
	CHUMALHARI, DHAULAGIRI
	EVEREST, FANG, GOSAINTHAN
	GUARI SANKAR, GURLA MANDHATA
	GYACHUNG KANG, HIMALCHULI
	JANNU, K2, KAILAS, KAMET
	KANGBACHEN, KANCHENJUNGA
	KHINYANG, KULAKHANGRI, LANGPHU
	LHOTSE, MAKALU, MANASLU
	MOLAMENQING, NAMONA BARWA
	NANDA DEVI, NANGA PARBAT
	NGOJUMBA RI, NUPTSE
	PHOLA GANGCHEN, SAGARMATHA
	SHARTSE, SHISHMA PANGMA
	YALUNG KANG, ZEMU GAP
—Honduras	CERRO LAS MINAS
—Hungary	KEKES
—Iceland	HVANNADALSHNUKUR
—India	ANAI MADI, NANDA DEVI
—Indonesia	MOUNT SUKARNO
	NGGA PULA, PUNCAK JAYA
—Iran	GUH KUH, KUH-E-BUL
	KUH-E-HAZARAN, KUH-E-KHAIZ
	KUH-E-KONJ, KUHRAN
	MOUNT DEMAVENDZARD KHU
—Ireland	BAURTREGAUM, BEENKERAGH
	BRANDON, CAHER
	CARRANTUOHILL, CARRAUNTUAL
	ERRIGAL, GALTYMORE
	KIPPURE, LUGNAQUILLIA
	MULLACLEEVAUN, MWEELREA
	NEPHIN, SAWEL, SLIEVE DONARD
	TROSTRAN
—Isle of Man	SNAEFELL
—Italy	CORNO GRANDE, LA META
	MONTE ALBURNO, MONTE AMIATA
	MONTE BIANCO, MONTE CASSINO
	MONTE CATRIA, MONTE CERVATI
	MONTE CIMONE, MONTE CORNO
	MONTE EBRO, MONTE PAPA
	MONTE POLLINO, MONTE VELINO
—Ivory Coast	MONT TOUKUI
—Jamaica	BLUE MOUNTAIN
—Japan	FUJI(YAMA)
—Jordan	JABAL RAMM, HAR MERON
	MOUNT ATZMON
—Kampuchea	MOUNT KA KUP
—Kashmir/Nepal	BATURA MUZTAGH
	BILAPHOND, CHOGOLISA, DASPAR
	DIAMIR, , DISTEGHIL SAR
	GASHERBRUM, GOLDEN THRONE
	KANJUT SAR, KHULA KANGRI
	KUN, MAMOSTONG KANGRI
	MASHARBRUM, MOUNT SER
	MUZTAGH ATA, NANGA PARBAT
	NUN, QUNGUR, RAKAPOSHI
	SALTORO KANGRI, SASER KANGRI
	SHINGSHAL, SHISHPARE
	SKYANG KANGRI, TERAM KANGRI
	TIRICH MIR, TRIVOR
	ULUGH MUZTAGH, WHITE NEEDLE
	YUKSHIN GARDAS SAR, ZASKA
	(see also Himalayas above)
—Kenya	MOUNT KENYA
—Korea	HALLA SAN, PAITOUSHAN
	PEKTU SAN
—Laos	PHOU BIA, PHOU LEI LENG
	PHOU SAN
—Lebanon	ARUBA, JEBEL SANNIN
	QURNET ES SAUDA
—Lesotho	THABANA NTLENYANA
	THADENTSONYANE
—Liberia	MOUNT NIMBA
—Libya	PICO BETTE
—Liechtenstein	GRAUSPITZE
—Luxemburg	BOURGPLATZ
—Madagascar	ANKARATRA
	MAROMOKOTRO
—Malaysia	MOUNT KINABALU
—Malawi	MOUNT SAPITWA
—Mali	HOMBORI TONDO
—Mauritius	BLACK RIVER MOUNTAIN
—Mexico	CITLALTEPETL, COLIMA
	IXTACCIHUATL
	POPOCATEPETL, TANOITARO
	TOLUCA, YEOTEPEC
	ZEMPOALTEPEC
—Mongolia	MONH HAYRHAN
—Morocco	TOUBKAL
—Mozambique	MONTE BINGA
—Namibia	SPITZKOPPIE
—New Zealand	ASPIRING, COBB, COOK
	EGMONT, HECTOR, POLLUX
	RUAPEHU, SEFTON, TAPUAENUKU
	TASMAN, THE TWINS, TYNDALL

—Nicaragua　　　　　　　　PICO MOGOTON
—Niger　　　　　　　　　　MONT GREBOUN
—Nigeria　　　　　　　　　　DIMLANG
—North Africa　　　　　　　　(D)JEBEL
　　　　　　　　　　DJEBEL TOUBKAL
—North America　　ADAMS, BALDY, BAKER
　　CHARLESTON, CLOUD, COWEN
　　DELANO, ELBERT, FREMONT
　　GANNET PEAK, GRAND TETON
　　HARVARD, HOLY CROSS, HOOD
　　LASSEN, LONGS PEAK, MANSFIELD
　　MARCY, MEDICINE BOW PEAK
　　MITCHELL, MONARCH, PIKES PEAK
　　RAINIER, SIERRA BLANCA
　　SAN FRANCISCO, SCOTT, SHASTA
　　WASHAKIE NEEDLES, WHITNEY
　　WIND RIVER, WYOMING
—Norway　　　　　　　GALDHOPIGGEN
—Oman　　　　　　　JEBEL ASH SHAM
—Pakistan　　SAD ISTRAGH, TIRICH MIR
—Papua New Guinea　　MOUNT WILHELM
—Paraguay　　　　　　　CERRO TATUG
—Peru　　　AUSANGATE, CHACHANI
　　　　　　　　　　COROPUNA
　　HUAMINA, HUASCARAN, MISTI
　　PISCO, TOCLARRAJU, YERUPAJA
　　YUCAMANI, WALLANARAJU SUR
—Philippines　　　　　　MOUNT APO
—Poland　　　　　　　　RYSY
—Romania　　　　　　MOLDOVEANU
—Russia　　BELUKHA, GORA BELUKHA
　　GORA MAS KHAYA, GORA NARODNAYA
　　KLYUCHEVSKAYA SOPKA
　　PIK KOMMUNIZMA, PIK LENINA
　　PIK POBEDA, STALINA PIK
—Rwanda　　　　　MOUNT KARISIMBA
—Sardinia　　MONTE DEL GENNARGENTU
　　MONTE DI SAN VITTORIA
　　MONTE LINAS, MONTE RASU
—Scotland　　　　　　　　BEN
　　AN TEALLACH, AONACH BEAG
　　AONACH MOR, BEINN AIBHUIRD
　　BEN ALDER, BEN CRUACHAN
　　BEN DEARG, BEN EIGHE, BEN HOPE
　　BEN LAWERS, BEN LOYAL, BEN MACDHUI
　　BEN MORE, BEN NEVIS, BEN VORLICH
　　BEN-Y-GLOE, BRAERIACH
　　BROAD LAW, CAIRN EIGE
　　CAIRN GORM, CAIRN MOR DEARG
　　CAIRN TOUL, CREAG MEAGAIDH
　　GLAS MAOL, GREAT FELL, HART FELL
　　LADHAR BHEINN, LIATHACH, LOCHNAGAR
　　MERRICK, SGURR MOR
　　SCHIEHALLION, SLIOCH
　　THE STORR, SUILVEN
—Senegal　　　　　　　GOUNOU

—Sicily　　　　ETNA, LE MADONIE
　　　　　　　MONTE LAURA
—Sierra Leone　BINTIMANII, KUNDUKONKO
—Somalia　　　MAKARAKOMBOU
—South Africa　　　　INJASUTI
　　　　　TABLE MOUNTAIN
—Spain　　　　MONTE PERDIDO
　　　　　MONTES MALDIDOS
　　　　MULHACEN, POSETS
—Sri Lanka　　　ADAM'S PEAK
　　　　PIDURUTALAGALA
—Sudan　　　MOUNT KINYETI
—Suriname　　　JULIANA TOP
—Swaziland　　　EMLEMBE
—Sweden　　　KEBNEKALSE
—Switzerland　BREITHORN, DOM
　　DUFOURSPITZE, EGGINER
　　EIGER, FINSTERAARHORN
　　JAGIHORN, JUNGFRAU
　　LA DENT BLANCHE, LA LUETTE
　　LENZSPITZE, L'EVEQUE
　　MATTERHORN, MONCH
　　MONTE ROSA, NADELHORN
　　POINTE KURTZ, TASCHHORN
　　WELLENKUPPE
—Syria　　　JABAL ASH-SHAIKH
　　　　MOUNT HERMON
—Tanzania　　KILIMANJARO
—Tasmania　CRADLE MOUNTAIN
　　　　　LEGGES TOR
—Taiwan　MOUNT MORRISON, YU SHAN
—Thailand　　DOI INTHANON
—Tibet　JOMA, MINYA KONKA
　　　NAMCHA BARWA
　　(*see also* Himalayas *above*)
—Tonga　　　　　KAO
—Tunisia　　DJEBEL CHAMBI
—Turkey　BOZ, BUYUK AGRIDAGA
—Uganda　　MOUNT STANLEY
—Uruguay　CERRO DE LAS ANIMAS
—Venezuela　MOUNT RORAIMA
　　　　PICO BOLIVAR
—Vietnam　　　FAN SI PAN
—Wales　ARAN FAWDDWY, CADER IDRIS
　　CARNEDD DAFYDD
　　CARNEDD LLEWELYN
　　ELIDIR FAWR, FOEL TRAS
　　GLYDER FACH, GLYDER FAWR
　　MYNYDD, PLYNLIMON
　　SNOWDON, TRYFAN, Y GARN
—Western Samoa　MAUGA SILISLI
—Yemen　　JEBEL HADHAR
　　QUARED AUDILLA
—Yugoslavia　DURMITOR, MAGANIK
　　MAGLIC, RAVNO, TRIGLAV
—Zaire　MOUNT STANLEY, NGALIEMA

—Zimbabwe	INYANGANI		TOMKINSON RANGE
mountain over 3000 feet	MUNRO		TRUER RANGE, SELWYN RANGE
mountaineers			STIRLING RANGE, SNOWY MOUNTAINS
—Austrian	JOCHLER, TICHY	—Austria	ALPS, DOLOMITES
—British	BONINGTON, BROWN	—Belgium	ARDENNES
	CROUCHER, HUNT, IRVINE	—Belize	MAYA MOUNTAINS
	MALLORY, MUMMERY	—Bhutan	HIMALAYAS
	SHIPTON, VENABLES	—Bolivia	CORDILLERA DE LOS ANDES
—Italian	COMPAGNON, LACEDELLI		CORDILLERA CENTRAL
—Nepali	TENZING		CORDILLERA ORIENTAL
—New Zealand	HILLARY		CORDILLERA REAL
—Swiss	EGGLER, EISELIN	—Brazil	ATLANTIC COAST RANGE
	LUCHSINGER, REISS		CORCOVADO
—US	DYHRENFURTH, HOUSTON		SIERRA DE MANTIQUEIRA
overhang of snow	CORNICE		SIERRA DO MAR, SIERRA GERAL
pass	COL		SIERRA GRANDE
piolet	ICE-AXE		SIERRA TAGUANTINGA
projecting part	BUTTRESS	—Bulgaria	STARA PLANINA
pyramid-shaped	HORN	—Burma	ARAKAN YOMA, CHIN HILLS
range	CORDILLERA, SIERRA		NAGA HILLS, PEGU YOMA
range in		—Canada	CASCADES, CASSIAR, COAST
—Afghanistan	BAND-I-BABAO		COLUMBUS, DAWSON RANGE
	BAND-I-BAIAN, KOH-I-BABA		MACKENZIE, OGILVIE, PELLY
	HINDU KUSH, PAGHMAN		ROCKIES, ROCKY MOUNTAINS
	PAROPAMBUS		SELWYN, ST ELIAS
—Africa	DRAKENSBERG, MITUMBA	—Central African	
	MUCHINGA	Republic	CHAINE DE MONGOS
—Alaska	ALASKA RANGE	—Chad	ENNEDI, TIBESTI
	ALEUTIAN RANGE	—Chile	CORDILLERA DE LOS ANDES
—Albania	ALPS	—China	ASTIN TAGH, BAYAN KARA SHAN
—Algeria	AHAGGAR, ATLAS, HOGGAR		HIMALAYAS, KUNLUN SHAN
	MASSIF DE L'OUARSENIS		NAIN SINGH RANGE
—Andorra	PYRENEES		NAN (LING) SHAN
—Angola	BENGUELA PLATEAU, CHELA		TANGLIA RANGE, TIEN SHAN
	HUMPATO, RAND PLATEAU	—Colombia	CORDILLERA CENTRAL
—Antarctica			CORDILLERA DE LOS ANDES
	TRANS-ANTARCTIC MOUNTAINS		CORDILLERA OCCIDENTAL
—Arabia	TIHAMAT ASH SHAM		CORDILLERA ORIENTAL
—Argentina	CORDILLERA DE LOS ANDES	—Congo	SERRO DO CRYSTAL
	SIERRA DE CORDOBA	—Costa	
—Asia	HIMALAYAS, HINDU KUSH	Rica	CORDILLERA DEL GUANTACASTE
	KARAKORAM, PAMIR		CORDILLERA DE TALAMANCA
	TIEN SHAN	—Cuba	SIERRA MAESTRA
—Australia	AUSTRALIAN ALPS	—Cyprus	KYRENIAN MOUNTAINS
	BLUE MOUNTAINS,		TROODOS
DARLING RANGE, DAVENPORT RANGE		—Czechoslovakia	BOHEMIAN HIGHLANDS
FLINDERS RANGE, GAWLER RANGE			GIANT MOUNTAINS, KRKONOSE
GREAT DIVIDING RANGE			MORAVIAN HIGHLANDS, TATRAS
GREGORY RANGE, GREY RANGE		—Dominican	
HAMERSLEY RANGE, KIRBY RANGE		Republic	CORDILLERA CENTRAL
LIVERPOOL RANGE		—East Indies	CENTRAL BORNEO RANGE
MACDONNELL RANGES			EAST SUMATRAN RANGE
MIDDLEBACK, MOUNT LOFTY RANGE			JAVANESE RANGE
MUSGRAVE RANGES		—Ecuador	CORDILLERA DE LOS ANDES
NEW ENGLAND RANGE		—Egypt	EASTERN COASTAL RANGE
PETERMAN RANGES			SINAI

—England	CUMBRIAN MOUNTAINS
	PENNINES
—Ethiopia	CHOKE, EASTERN HIGHLANDS
	ERITREAN HIGHLANDS
	ETHIOPIAN HIGHLANDS, MENDEBO
	SEMIEN MOUNTAINS
	TIGRAY PLATEAU, TIGRE PLATEAU
—Finland	MAANSELKA, SUOMENSELKA
—France	ALPS, BLACK MOUNTAINS
	CEVENNES, JURA
	MASSIF CENTRAL
	PYRENEES, VOSGES
—Germany	ALPS, BLACK FOREST
	ERZ GEBIRGE, SCHWARZWALD
	THURINGER WALD
—Ghana	AFADIATO
—Greece	PINDUS
—Guatemala	SIERRA DE CUACHUS
	SIERRA DE LAS MINAS
	SIERRA DE LOS CUCHUMANTANES
	SIERRA MADRE
—Guinea	FOUTA DJALON
—Guyana	KAMOA, KANUKU, PAKARAIMA
	SIERRA ACARAI
—Haiti	MASSIF DE LA HOTTE
—Hungary	BAKONY, BUKK,
	CSERHAT, MATRA
—India	ARAVALLI RANGE
	CHOTA NAGPUR, EASTERN GHATS
	GRAVALLI, GRAVALTI
	HAZARIBAGH RANGE
	HIMALAYAS, MAHADEO HILLS
	MAIKAL RANGE, SATPURA RANGE
	WESTERN GHATS, VINDHYA RANGE
—Indonesia	BARISAN, BUKIT
	PEQUNUNGAN JAYAWIJAYA
—Iran	ELBURZ MOUNTAINS
	KUHHA-YE-ZAGROS
—Iraq	KURDISTAN MOUNTAINS
—Ireland	ANTRIM, CAHA, COMERAGH
	CONNEMARA, DONEGAL
	GALTEE, KNOCKMEALDOWN
	MACGILLYCUDDYS REEKS
	MAYO, MOURNE, SILVERMINE
	SPERRIN, WICKLOW
—Italy	ALPS, APENNINES, DOLOMITES
—Ivory Coast	GUINEA HIGHLANDS
	MAN MOUNTAINS
—Jamaica	BLUE MOUNTAINS
—Japan	HIDA
—Jordan	JUDEA MOUNTAINS
—Kampuchea	CHAINE DES CARDAMOMES
—Kashmir	KARAKORAM RANGE
—Kenya	ABERDARE
—Korea	NAGNIM SANMAEK
—Laos	ANNAMITIC RANGE

—Lebanon	ANTI-LEBANON
—Lesotho	DRAKENSBERG
—Liberia	GUINEA HIGHLANDS
—Libya	AL ASWAD, AL KUFRAH
	AL HARUN, JABAL ASSAWDA
—Liechtenstein	ALPS
—Luxemburg	ARDENNES
—Madagascar	ANKARATRA
	MALAGASY RANGE
	MASSIF DU TSARATANANA
—Malaysia	TRENGGANU HIGHLANDS
—Mali	ADRAR DES IFORAS
	MANDIGUE PLATEAU
—Mexico	SIERRA MADRE
	SIERRA TARAHUMARE
—Mongolia	ALTAI MOUNTAINS
	HANGAYN NURUU
—Morocco	ANTI-ATLAS, ATLAS
—Mozambique	LEBOMBO RANGE
—Nepal	HIMALAYAS
	MAHABHARAT RANGE
—New Guinea	CENTRAL RANGE
	OWEN STANLEY RANGE
—New Zealand	CAMERON
	COROMANDEL RANGE, DUNSTAN
	HUIARAU RANGE, KAIKOURA RANGE
	KAIMANAWA, KEPLER, LYELL RANGE
	MURCHISON, PUKETERAKI RANGE
	RAUKUMARA RANGE, RICHARDSON
	RICHMOND RANGE, SOUTHERN ALPS
	SPENSER, STUART, TARARUA RANGE
	YOUNG RANGE
—Nicaragua	CORDILLERA DE DARIEN
	CORDILLERA ISABELLA
—Niger	AIR, AZBINE
	PLATEAU DU DJADO
—Nigeria	JOS PLATEAU
—North Africa	ATLAS, DES KSOURS
	NOULED NAIL
—North America	ADIRONDACKS
	ALLEGHENY
	APPALACHIAN, BIGHORN
	BLUE RIDGE, BOSTON
	CASCADES, COAST RANGE
	NOTRE DAME, ROCKIES
	ROCKY MOUNTAINS
	SAN BERNARDINO
	SANGRE DE CRISTO
	SIERRA NEVADA, ST JUAN
	WHITE, WIND RIVER RANGE
—Norway	LANGFJELLENE
	SCANDINAVIAN RANGE
—Oman	GREEN MOUNTAINS
	JABAL AKHDAS
—Pakistan	SALT RANGE
	SULAIMAN RANGE

—Panama	SERRANIA DE SAN BLAS
	SERRANIA DE TABASARA
—Papua New Guinea	BISMARCK
—Paraguay	CORDILLERA AMAMBAY
	SIERRA DE MARACAJU
—Peru	CORDILLERA DE LOS ANDES
—Philippines	CORDILLERA CENTRAL
	DIUATA RANGE
—Poland	BESKIDS, CARPATHIANS
	TATRA RANGE
—Portugal	SIERRA DA ESTRELA
—Romania	CARPATHIANS
—Russia	ALTAI, CAUCASUS
	KORYAKSKIY KREBET
KREBET CHERSKOGO, KOLYMSKIY	
	PAMIR, SREDINNIY KREBET
	TIEN SHAN, URALS
	VERKHOYANSKIY KREBET
—Rwanda	CHAINE DE MITUMBA
—Scotland	CUILLINS, GRAMPIANS, LIATH
	NORTHWEST HIGHLANDS
	SOUTHERN UPLANDS
	TROSSACHS
—Senegal	FOUTA DJALON
—Sierra Leone	LOMA
—Somalia	GUBAN
—South Africa	DRAKENSBERG
—South	
America	(CORDILLERA DE LOS) ANDES
—Spain	CORDILLERA CANTABRICA
	PICOS DE EUROPA
	PYRENEES, SIERRA MORENA
	SIERRA NEVADA
—Sudan	DARFUR HIGHLANDS
	NUBIAN MOUNTAINS
—Suriname	KAYSER GEBERGTE
	WILHEMINA GEBERGTE
—Swaziland	LUBOMBO
—Sweden	NORRLAND MOUNTAINS
	SMALANH HIGHLANDS
—Switzerland	ALPS
—Syria	ANSARIYAH RANGE
	JABAL AD DURUZ
	JABAL MALULA
—Taiwan	CHU NYANG SHANMO
—Tanzania	SOUTHERN HIGHLANDS
—Tasmania	HIGHLANDS
—Tibet	ARKA TAGH, HIMALAYAS
	KARAKORAM RANGE
—Turkey	ARMENIAN PLATEAU
	TAURUS MOUNTAINS
	TOROS DAGLARI
—Uganda	RUWENZORI
—Venezuela	CORDILLERA DO MERIDA
	LA GRAN SABANA
	SIERRA DE PERIJA

—Wales	BERWYN, BLACK
	BRECON BEACONS
	CAMBRIAN
—Yemen	YEMEN HIGHLANDS
—Yugoslavia	BALKAN MOUNTAINS
	CARPATHIANS
	RHODOPE RANGE
	SAR-PINDUS RANGE
	SLOVENE ALPS
—Zaire	MITUMBA, RUWENZORI
—Zambia	MUCHINGA MOUNTAINS
—Zimbabwe	ENYANGA, MELSETTER
region above treeline,	
below snowline	ALPINE
—on east slope of Andes	MONTANA
ridge of hills formed	
by erosion	CUESTA
rope ladder	ETRIER
rubble at foot of	
—cliff	SCREE, TALUS
—glacier	MORAINE
sacred mountain	OMEI
series of	
—parallel ranges	CORDILLERA
—ridges	RANGE
sharp	
—peak	AIGUILLE
—ridge	ARRETE
sickness	PUNA, SOROCHE
slope of	
—loose stones	SCREE
—mountains	VERSANT
spiked staff	ALPENSTOCK
steep rock	CRAG
study of mountains	OROLOGY
submarine mountain	GUYOT
system of	
—parallel ranges	CHAIN
—ranges	CORDILLERA
top of mountain	PEAK
where Noah's ark landed	MOUNT ARARAT
with	
—pointed summit	PIKE
—pyramidal peak	HORN

Mozambique

capital	LM, LOURENCO MARQUES
	MAPUTO
coin	
—unit	CENTAVO
—100 centavos	METICAL

Mrs

Boaz	RUTH
Copperfield	DORA
de Winter	REBECCA
Dombey	EDITH
Mopp	CHAR(WOMAN)

Partlett	HEN
Punch	JUDY
muscle	
albumin in muscle	MYOGEN
cell	
—developing from	
myoblast	MYOTUBE
—which produces muscle	MYOBLAST
circular	CONSTRICTOR
	SPHINCTER
contraction	CONVULSION
—of intestines	PERISTALSIS
—spontaneous	MYOGENIC
diseases affecting	
muscles	(*see* **disease**)
fibres attaching	
muscle to bone	TENDON
haemoglobin in muscle	MYOGLOBIN
having two adductor	
muscles	DIMYARIAN
in	
—buttock	GLUTEUS MAXIUMUS
	SUPINATOR
—chest	PECTORAL(IS MAJOR)
	SERRATUS ANTERIOR
—ear	STAPEDIUS
—eye	CILIARY, OBLIQUE, RECTUS
—forearm	EXTENSOR, FLEXOR
	PRONATOR
—head	ZYGOMATIC
—heart	MYOCARDIUM, PACEMAKER
—jaw	MASSETER, MYLOHYOID
—larynx	ARYT(A)ENDID
—loins	PSOAS
—lower leg	EXTENSOR, GASTROCNEMIUS
	SOLEUS
—neck	PLATSUMA, SPLENIUS
	STERNO-MASTOID
—pelvis	PSOAS
—shoulder	DELTOID, TRAPEZIUS
—spermatic cord	CREMASTER
—stomach	DIAPHRAGM
	RECTUS ABDOMINUS
—thigh	HAMSTRING, QUADRICEPS
	SARTORIUS, VASTUS
—thorax	SERRATUS
—upper arm	BICEPS, DELTOID
	TRICEPS
instrument recording	
contractions	MYOGRAPH
muscle sense	KINAESTHESIA
partial contraction	TONE
protein in muscle	MYOSIN
sheath	FASCIA, SARCOLEMMA
straight muscle	RECTUS
study of muscles	MYOLOGY

tissue binding muscles	PERIMYSIUM
tumour	MYOMA
twitching of muscle	FIBRILLATION
types	CARDIAC, SMOOTH
	STRIATED
—smooth	INVOLUNTARY, PLAIN
	VISCERAL
—striated	SKELETAL, STRIPED
	VOLUNTARY
which	
—cannot be	
consciously	
controlled	INVOLUNTARY MUSCLE
	REFLEX MUSCLE
—draws	
away	ABDUCTOR
down	DEPRESSOR
together	ADDUCTOR
—tightens	TENSOR
—turns hand	PRONATOR, SUPINATOR
Muses	PIERIDES
astronomy	URANIA
comedy	THALIA
dance	TERPSICHORE
erotic poetry	ERATO
epic poetry	CALLIOPE
festivals	THALIA
history	CLIO
lyric poetry	EUTERPE
music	EUTERPE
sacred song	POLY(HY)MNIA
tragedy	MELPOMENE
mushroom	(*see* **fungi**)
music	
above	SOPRA
accented	FORZATO, FZ
accidental	FLAT, NATURAL, SHARP
accompaniment	OBBLIGATO
additional bottom	
note	PROSLAMBANOMENOS
agitated	AGITATO
African	KWELA
all performers	TUTTI
allowing freedom of	
interpretation	ALEATORIC
	ALEATORY MUSIC
altered rhythm	SYNCOPATION
alternation of two notes	SHAKE, TRILL
alternative	OSSIA
always	SEMPRE
American	ARISTO-POP, BEACH MUSIC
	(BE)BOP, BLUES, (CHICAGO)HOUSE
	COUNTRY (AND WESTERN)
	COUNTRY ROCK, FUNK, GLAM ROCK
	GOSPEL, HEAVY METAL
	HILLBILLY, HIP-HOP, JAZZ

	POMP ROCK, POP, PSYCHOBILLY	4 notes	TETRACHORD
	PUNK (METAL), PUNK ROCK	5 notes	PENTACHORD
	RAG(TIME), RAP, ROCK (AND ROLL)	6 notes	HEXACHORD
	RHYTHM AND BLUES, SOUL	7 notes	HEPTACHORD
	SPEED METAL, THRASH(CORE)	8 notes	OCTACHORD
	TRASH METAL	church cantata	MOTET(T)
animatedly	ANIM(ATO)	clef	ALTO, BASS, C, F, G
answer in fugue	REPLY		SOPRANO, TENOR
anthem	MOTET(T)		TREBLE
Arabian	MAQAM	collection of songs	CANCIONERO
arrange	ORCHESTRATE	combined melodies	CHANSONNIER
augmented fourth	TRITONE		COUNTERPOINT
background music	MUSAK	complex tone	KLANG
	WALLPAPER MUSIC	composition	OPUS
bagpipe music	CEOL MOR, PIBROCH, PORT	—18th century	CASSATION
ballad	CANTILENA, SINGSONG	—for	
ballet interlude	DIVERTIMENTO	1	SOLO
	DIVERTISSEMENT	2	DUET, DUO
barely audible	SOTTO VOCE	3	TRIO
based on		4	QUARTET(T), QUARTETTE
—12 tone scale	DODECOPHONY		QUARTETTO
	SERIAL MUSIC	5	QUINTET(T), QUINTETTE
—set of notes rather			QUINTETTO
than a scale	SERIAL MUSIC	6	SESTET(T), SESTETTE
basic			SEXTET(T), SEXTETTE
—set of notes	TONE ROW	7	SEPTET(T), SEPTETTE
—tune or motif	THEME	8	OCTET(T), OCTETTE
bass octave	GREAT OCTAVE	9	NONET(TE), NONETTO
becoming		solo and orchestra	CONCERTO
—quicker	ACCELERANDO, STRINGENDO	voices and orchestra	ORATORIO
—slower	ALLARGANDO, CALANDO	—light symphony	SERENADE, SERENATA
	RALL(ENTANDO)	—polyphonic	FUGUE
—softer	DIM(INUENDO)	—using	
boating-song	BARCAROL(L)E	all notes equally	SERIAL MUSIC
bold style	DIASTALTIC	natural sounds	CONCRETE MUSIC
briskly	ALLEGRETTO		MUSIQUE CONCRETE
	ALLEGRO, CON MOTO	—with	
	VIVACE	much repetition	CANON, RONDO
broad and slow	LARGO		ROTA, ROUND
cacophonous music	CHARIVARI	several movements	SUITE
cadence	MODULATION		SYMPHONY
canon sung in unison	ROUND	concluding passage	CODA, POSTLUDE
cats' concert	CHARIVARI		VOLUNTARY
change key	TRANSPOSE	confusion	IMBROGLIO
cheerful song	LILT	continue	
choral		—in like manner	SIMILE
—composition	ANTHEM, CANON	—to next movement without	
	CANTATA, MOTET(T)	pause	SEGUE
	ORATORIO	continuous	
—ode(s)	STASIMUS(STASIMA)	—bass part	CONTINUO, THROUGH-BASS
chord	ITALIAN SIXTH	—glide	PORTAMENTO
	NEAPOLITAN SIXTH	country music	PASTORALE
—closing work or part	CADENCE	cradle song	BERCEUSE
—etc, on woodwind	BARTOLOZZI SOUNDS	crisply	STACCATO
—of		Cuban	SALSA
3 notes	TRIAD, TRICHORD	damped	SORDO

dance music	GAVOTTE, HORNPIPE, PASPY	eighth	OCTAVE
	PASSEPIED, RIGADOON	elaborate	
	TWO-STEP	—composition	ARABESQUE
—16/17th c	GAILLARD, GALLIARD	—fugue	RICERCAR(E), RICERCATA
—17th c	MINUET	embellishment	FIORITURA, MELISMA
—Argentinian	TANGO		ROULADE
—Bohemian	POLKA, REDOWA	end	FINE
—Brazilian	MAXIXE, SAMBA	ending	CODA
—French	CHACONNE	entr'acte	INTERMEZZO
—German	ALLEMANDE, LANDLER	essential part	OBBLIGATO
—hillbilly	HOE-DOWN	evening open-air performance	SERENADE
—Irish	PLANXTY		SERENATA
—Italian	SALTARELLO	excessively	TROPPO
—like polka	SCHOTTISCHE	exercise	
—Neapolitan	TARANTELLA	—in sol-fa	SOLFEGGIO
—Negro	WALK-AROUND	—piece	ETUDE, STUDY
—Norwegian	HALLING, SPRING	extended intervals	DIASTALTIC
—Polish	CRACOVIENNE, KRAKOWIAK	fading away	MANCANDO, MANCANTE
	MAZURKA, POLONAISE	falling volume	DECRESCENDO, DIMINUENDO
	VARSOVIENNE	fantasia	TOCCATA
—Provençal	TAMBOURIN	fast	PRESTO
—Scottish	REEL, SPRING, STRATHSPEY	fifth	QUINT
—slow	CHACONNE, WALTZ	—above tonic	DOMINANT
	PASSACAGLIA	figured bass	TASTO SOLO, TS
—Spanish	FLAMENCO, PASSACAGLIA	final theme	CODA
	PAVANE, SEGUIDILLA	first or principal part	PRIMO
—square	HOE-DOWN, QUADRILLE	five	
—West Indian	REGGAE	—lines on which music	
	(*see also* **dance**)	is written	STAVE
death of Christ	PASSION-MUSIC	—note octave	PENTATONIC SCALE
decrease in volume	DECRESC(ENDO)	florid	
decreasing	CAL(ANDO)	—embellisment	FIORITURA
depress soft pedal	UNA CORDA, UC	—in melody	MELISMATIC
detached	STACCATO	—treatment	FIGURATION
diapason	OCTAVE	—vocal passages	COLORATURA
difference in pitch	INTERVAL	flourish	CADENZA, FANFARE
direction to pianist	TRE CORDE	follow the	
dissonance in keyed		—singer	COLLA VOCE
instrument	WOLF(-NOTE)	—solo part	SUIVEZ
distorted rhythm	RUBATO	following	SEGUE
division of long work	MOVEMENT	for dancing in a ring	ROUND
double		forced	SF(Z), SFORZANDO
—speed	DOPPIO MOVIMENTO		SFORZATO
—tempo	ALLA BREVE	forerunner of fugue	RICERCAR(E)
dramatic oratorio	AZIONE(SACRA)		RICERCATA
draw out slightly	TEN(UTO)	form of first movement	SONATA FORM
drinking-song (Greek)	DITHYRAMB, SKOLION	four notes against three	SEQUITERTIA
dying away	MANCANDO, MANCANTE	fourth	QUART
	MORENDO, PERDENDO	—fifth or octave	PERFECT INTERVAL
each note		fraction of note	MICROTONE
—emphasised	MARC(ATO)	free	SCIOLTO
—shortened	STACCATO	—choice of time etc	AD LIB(ITUM)
early counterpoint	FA(UX)BURDEN	—style composition	CAPRICCIO
easy and flowing	CANTABILE		FANTASIA
eccentric piece	EXTRAVAGANZA	freedom of tempo	RUBATO
ecclesiastical melody	CANTUS	French Antilles	ZOUK

full range of	
—sound	DIAPASON
—voice	GAMUT
fundamental	
—and harmonics	KLANG
—note of chord	ROOT
funeral piece	CORONACH, DIRGE
	REQUIEM
Gaelic boating-song	JORRAM
gavotte trio	MUSETTE
gently	SORDAMENTE
German	
—song(s)	LIED(ER)
—style of opera	SINGSPIEL
grace note	ACCIACCATURA
	APPOGGIATURA
	MORDENT, NACHSCHLAG
	ORNAMENT, PRALLTRILLER
gracefully	GRAZIOSO
gradually	
—becoming	
quicker	ACCELERANDO, STRIGENDO
slower	CALANDO
—and softer	SMORZ(ANDO)
—decreasing speed	RIT(ARDANDO)
—fading	SMORZ(ANDO)
Gregorian cadence	EUOUAE, EVOVAE
ground-bass	OSTINATO
group of	
—2 notes	DUOLE, DUPLET
—3 notes	TRIAD, TRICHORD, TRIPLET
—4 notes	QUADRUPLET, TETRACHORD
—5 notes	PENTACHORD, QUINTUPLET
—6 notes	HEXACHORD, SEXTOLET
	SEXTUPLET
—7 notes	HEPTACHORD, SEPTIMOLE
	SEPTUPLET
—8 notes	OCTACHORD, OCTUPLET
—9 notes	NONUPLET
—10 notes	DECUPLET
—11 notes	UNDECIMOLE
—12 half-tones	OCTAVE
—notes played	
as one phrase	LIGATURE
at once	CHORD, TONE-CLUSTER
in different beat	TURLET
half staccato	SPICCATO
harmony in 3rds and 6ths	FAUXBOURDON
	FA(UX)BURDEN
hastening the time	STRINGENDO
having	
—5 notes	PENTATONIC
—7 notes	HEPTATONIC
—12 tones	DODECAPHONIC
—final in middle	PLAGAL
—several melodic lines	POLYPHONIC

heavy	PESANTE
height of note	PITCH
high soprano	COLORATURA
highest voice	SOPRANO, TREBLE
hold for full value	TEN(UTO)
humorous	
—medley of tunes	QUODLIBET
—piece	FANTASIA, HUMORESQUE
hymn	CANTICLE, CHORALE
idyllic opera	PASTORALE
immediately following	SEGUE
in	
—a	
marked manner	MARC(ATO)
melodious manner	ARIOSO
singing manner	CANTABILE
—declamatory style	PARLANDO
—devotional manner	RELIGIOSO
—free style	CAPRICCIOSO
—the	
manner of fugue	FUGATO
usual manner	SOLITO
increase volume	CRES(CENDO)
increasing in speed	ACCEL(ERANDO)
	STRINGENDO
Indian	BHANGRA, RAGA
—rhythmic pattern	TALA
informal evening	
of music (Gaelic)	CEILI(DH)
instantaneous	
composition	HEAD ARRANGEMENT
	IMPROVISATION
instrumental	
—composition	SONATA
—melody	CANTILENA
—passage in vocal	
work	RITORNEL(LO)
	RITORNELL(E)
	RITOURNELLE
—piece like a madrigal	CANZONE
—prelude	OVERTURE
intermediate	
—movement	INTERMEZZO
—part	MEAN
interpreting	
non-musical subject	TONE POEM
interval of	
—3 tones	TRITONE
—3rd	TIERCE
—4th	DIATESSARON
—5th	QUINT
—6th	SEXT
—7th	HEPTACHORD, SETTIMA
	SETTIMO
—8th	OCTAVE
—12th	DUODECIMO

—12 semitones	OCTAVE	medley of popular tunes	POTPOURRI
	SESQUITERTIA		QUODLIBET
—small	LIMMA	melodiously	ARIOSO
—with vibrations as		melody	
2 to 3	PERFECT FIFTH	—added to another	COUNTERPOINT
3 to 4	PERFECT FOURTH	—with no second part	CAVATINA
introduction	ENTREE, PRELUDE	mixing of two keys	BITONALITY
—to opera	OVERTURE	mock serenade	CHARIVARI
inverted mordent	PRALLTRILLER	moderate speed	ANDANTE, ANDANTINO
Irish	CEILI(DH)		MODERATO
irregular	RHAPSODY	moderately	
is silent	TACET	—loud	MEZZO-FORTE, MF
Italian folk song	RISPETTO	—slow	LARGHETTO
jazz	BEBOP, BLUES	—soft	MEZZO-PIANO, MP
	BOOGIE-WOOGIE, BOP, CHICAGO	modern	(*see also* American, jazz *above*)
	COOL, DIXIELAND, GUTBUCKET	modified rhythm	RUBATO
	HONKY-TONK, HOT MUSIC	modulation	CADENCE
	MAINSTREAM, RAGTIME, STRIDE	morning music	AUBADE
	SWING, TAILGATE, TRAD(ITIONAL)	most lively	VIVACISSIMO
	WEST COAST	mouth-music	PORT A BEUL
—type of folk-music	SKIFFLE	moving lightly and	
key	BASS, CLEF, MAJOR	rapidly	VOLANTE
	MINOR, TREBLE	much	MOLTO
—note	TONIC	music-loving	PHILHARMONIC
—of C major	PROPER CHANT	musical	
lament	DUMKA	—accompaniment to	
light		improvised poetry	RAP(PING)
—musical drama	OPERETTA	—drama	OPERA
—piece	DIVERTIMENTO	—instruments	(*see separate entry*)
	DIVERTISSEMENT	—shows	(*see* **musicals**)
little aria	ARIETTA	—stock-in-trade	REPERTOIRE
liturgical music	MASS, REQUIEM	—story, usually Biblical	ORATORIO
lively	SPIRITOSO, VIVACE	—training based on	
—dance tune	GIGUE	dancing	EURYTHMICS
—movement	SCHERZO	musicians	(*see separate entry*)
—tune	RANT	mute	SORDINO, SOURDINE
loud	F, FORTE	muted	SORDO
—as possible	FFF, FORTISSISSIMO	natural scale	DIATONIC
—then soft	FORTE-PIANO, FP	naturalism	VERISM(E)
love song	AMORET, TORCH-SONG	neither sharp nor flat	NATURAL
lovingly	AMOROSO	night music	NOCTURNE, SERENADE
low		non-stop piece	MOTO PERPETUO
—drum-beat	RUFF	normal range of voice	TESSITURA
—soprano	MEZZO-SOPRANO	not	
lower part of duet	SECONDO	—governed by rules	
lowest note of chord	FUNDAMENTAL	of form	FANTASIA
lyrical recitative	ARIOSO	—too much	NON TROPPO
madrigal	FA-LA	note(s)	BREVE, CROCHET
majestically	MAESTOSO		DEMI-SEMIQUAVER, MINIM
major third	PICARDY THIRD		QUAVER, SEMIBREVE
	TIERCE DE PICARDIE		SEMIQUAVER
march in procession	WALK-AROUND	—bass G	GAMUT
Martinique	ZOUK	—effecting smooth	
mass for dead	REQUIEM	transition	PASSING-NOTE
medium slow	ANDANTE	—forming unprepared	
	ANDANTINO	discord	PASSING-NOTE

—of	
chord played in	
rapid succession	ARPEGGIO
scale	DO(H), FA(H), LA(H)
	ME, MI, RE, SI, SO(H)
	SOL, TE, TI
—old	E-LA(-MI)
—played	
in progression	CHROMATIC
together	CHORD
—two octaves and a third	
above	TIERCE
obsolete ornament	BACKFALL
octave	DIAPASON
on the	
—bridge	SUL PONTICELLO
—key	SUL TASTO
one string	UNA CORDA, UC
opera	(*see separate entry*)
operatic air	CAVATINA
orchestral composition	SYMPHONY
original tempo	TEMPO PRIMO
ornament	ACCIACCATURA
	APPOGGIATURA
	GRACE NOTE, REL(L)ISH
—of four notes	TURN
out of tune	SCORDATO
overture	TOCCATA
part	
—in parallel motion	ORGANUM
—of	
aria	CABALETTA
fugue	STRETTO
larger work	MOVEMENT
—song	CATCH, GLEE
	MADRIGAL, ROUND
parts with independent	
melody	POLYPHONY
passage	
—for whole orchestra	TUTTI
—in quicker time	STRETTA, STRETTO
passionately	AFFETTUOSO
	APPASSIONATO
pastoral melody	MUSETTE
pause	FERMATA
percussion	TRIANGLE
perfect	
—fifth	HEMIOLIA, SESQUIALTERA
—fourth	SESQUITERTIA
Persian	DASTGAH
piano styles (jazz)	BOOGIE-WOOGIE
	HONKY-TONK, STRIDE
	WALKING BASS
piped music	MUSAK, MUZAK™
pitch standard	DIAPASON
plain	SECCO

—song	CANTO FERMO, CANTUS FERMUS
plaintively	LAGRIMOSO
play as desired	AD LIB(ITUM)
played by plucking	PIZZICATO
playful	PIACEVOLE
—piece	HUMORESQUE
playfully	SCHERZANDO
pleasant	PIACEVOLE
pluck the strings	PIZZ(ICATO)
polyphonic composition	FUGUE
preliminary passage	ENTREE
	PRAELUDIO, PRAELUDIUM
	PRAELUSION, PRELUDE
prelude	ENTREE, RITORNEL(LO)
	RITORNELL(E), RITOURNELLE
pretentious pop-music	POMP ROCK
progression of part	MOTION
quality of sound	KLANG, TIMBRE
quick	PRESTO
—dance	GALLOPADE
—staccato	SALTANDO, SALTATO
quicker	PIU MOSSO
quickly	PRESTO, VELOCE
quivering	TREMOLO, TREMOLANDO
rapidly	VELOCE
raising of a tone	ECBOLIC
random selection of notes	ALEATORIC MUSIC
rather loud	MEZZO-FORTE
recasting of composition	RIFACIMENTO
recurring theme	LEITMOTIV
refrain	EPISTROPHE, FA(UX)BURDEN
	RITORNEL(LO), RITORNELL(E)
	RITOURNELLE
recitative	PARLANDO
regular	GIUSTO
reinforced	RF(Z), RINF(ORZATO)
release soft pedal	TRE CORDE
religious story set to music	ORATORIO
remove mute	SENZA SORDINO
repeat	REPLICA
repeated figure	OSTINATO
—in jazz	RIFF
repetition	REPRISE
repetitions in higher tone	ROSALIA
resumption of first subject	REPRISE
retrained	RITENUTO
return to	
—pitch	LOCO
—sign	DAL SEGNO, DS
—the beginning	DA CAPO, DC
reverting to original speed	A TEM(PO)
rhythm	TEMPO
run	
—between two notes	TIRADE
—sung to one syllable	ROULADE
sad	MESTO

sadly	DOLOROSO	CONTRALTO, COUNTER-TENOR	
sailors' song	CHANT(E)Y, CHANTIE	LYRIC SOPRANO	
	SHANTY	MEZZO-SOPRANO, TENOR	
score	PARTITUR(A)	TREBLE	
scale	MAJOR, MINOR	singsong	BALLAD
—5 notes	PENTATONIC	sixth	SEXT
—5 whole, 2 semi-tones	DIATONIC	—above tonic	SUBMEDIANT
—6 hexachords	DITHYRAMB	sliding effect	GLISSANDO
—12 semitones	CHROMATIC	slow	ADAGIO, LENTO
—without sharps or flats	NATURAL	—and luxurious	LYDIAN
scene	SCENA	—beginning of trill	RIBATTUTA
school of music	CONSERVATOIRE	—movement	DUMKA
Scottish	CEILI(DH)	of csardas	LASSU
second movement	TRIO	—solemn dance style	PASSACAGLIA
semitone	FLAT, LIMMA, SHARP	—vocal composition	CHORALE
set of variations	PARTITA	—waltz	VALETA, VELETA
sharpening of a tone	ECBOLE	slowing	LENTANDO, RALLENTANDO
sharply	STACCATO		RITARDANDO
short			SLARGANDO(SI)
—aria	CAVATINA	slowly	LENTAMENTE
—cadence	TROPE	small interval	MICROTONE
—concerto	CONCERTINO	smoothly	LEG(ATO)
—fugue	FUGHETTA	soft	P, PIANO
—hymn or anthem	CATHISMA	—pedal	UNA CORDA
	ISODICON, TROPARION	softly	PIANO, SORDAMENTE
—instrumental piece	CAVATINA	—and sweetly	DOLCEMENTE
—opera or oratorio	CANTATA	solfeggio	CANTILENA
—rondo	RONDINO	solo narrative with music	CANTATA
—sonata	SONATINA	somewhat slow	LARGHETTO
—stressed note with		sonata movement	MINUET
longer note after	SCOTCH CATCH	song	CHANSON, LAY, MELISMA
	SCOTCH SNAP	—German	LIED
—toccata	TOCCATELLA, TOCCATINA	—in spoken style	RECITATIVE
show-piece	TOCCATA	—like a madrigal	CANZONE
sign		—little	CHANSONETTE
—at beginning or end		—of	
of repetitions	SEGNO	lamentation	THRENE, THRENODY
—of		praise	ANTHEM
change in pitch of note	NEUME	thanksgiving	P(A)EAN
pitch of		the dawn	AUBADE
—piece	CLEF, KEY SIGNATURE	—solo in opera, etc	ARIA
—note	ACCIDENTAL, FLAT	—unaccompanied	MADRIGAL, MOTET(T)
	NATURAL, SHARP	—West Indies	CALYPSO
tempo	TIME SIGNATURE	—with refrain	ROUNDELAY
silent	TACET	soprano	TREBLE
simple	SEMPLICE	Spanish	
simultaneous notes	DOUBLE STOP	—dance music	PASSCAGLIA
singing		—gypsy music or song	FLAMENCO
—exercise	CANTILENA, SOLFEGGIO	—serenade	RONDENA
—nonsense words (jazz)	SCAT(SINGING)	speed	TEMPO
—operatic style	BEL CANTO	spirited	SPIRITOSO
—unaccompanied	A(LLA) CAPPELLA	square dance	QUADRILLE
	ALLA BREVE	story set to music	OPERA
—voices	ALTO, BARITONE	—religious	ORATORIO
	BARYTON(E), BASS	strike strings with bow	COL LEGNO
	COLORATURA SOPRANO	strong tenor	HELDENTENOR

strongly accented	SFORZATO-PIANO, SFP
	SF(Z), SFORZANDO
	SFORZATO
study	ETUDE
—of properties of music	HARMONICS
succession of	
—chords at end	CADENZA
—notes sung to one	
syllable	NEUM(E)
sudden slowing	RITENUTO
suddenly accented	RF(Z), RINF(ORZATO)
suitable	GIUSTO
suite (18th c)	PARTITA
sung	
—common service	MASS
—mass for the dead	REQUIEM
—narrative	RECITATIVE
sunrise song	AUBADE
supplementary	RIPIENO
sustained	SOS(TENUTO), TENUTO
sweet	DOLCE
symphony	SINFONIA
syncopated music	JAZZ, RAG(TIME)
system of notation	SOLFEGGIO
	SOLMISATION
	TONIC SOL-FA
temporarily out of tune	SCORDATURA
temporary key signature	ACCIDENTAL
tender	AMOROSO
tenderly	AFFETTUOSO
tenor octave	SMALL OCTAVE
test piece	ETUDE
text of opera	LIBRETTO
third	
—above tonic	MEDIANT
—tone of tetrachord	TRITE
three	
—part structure	TERTIARY FORM
—strings	TRE CORDE
throbbing effect	VIBRATO
throughout	SEMPRE
timbre	KLANG
time	TEMPO, VOLTA
—division	BAR, BEAT, MODE
tone	
—colour	KLANG, TIMBRE
—one or more octaves	
from given tone	REPLICATE
too much	TROPPO
training piece	ETUDE
transformation of theme	VARIATION
treble	SOPRANO, TRIPLE
trembling	TREMANDO, TREMOLO
	TREMOLANDO
tremulous effect	TREMOLO
—on clavichord	BEBUNG

triplet	HEMIOLIA
trivial dance-tune	TOY
troubadour's lay	SIRVENTE
tune	MELISMA
turn	GRUPETTO, VOLTA
—over quickly	VOLTE SUBITO, VS
twelve semitones	OCTAVE
two	
—beats per bar	DUPLE
—crotchets per bar	TWO-FOUR
—or more tunes	
together	COUNTERPOINT
unaccompanied	A CAPELLA, ALLA BREVE
	SECCO
—song	GLEE, MOTET(T)
under the breath	SOTTO VOCE
undersong	FA(UX)BURDEN
unmeasured music	PLAINSONG
unpretentious composition	BAGATELLE
using several keys	POLYTONAL(ITY)
varying tempo	RUBATO
very	ASSAI, MOLTO
—loud	FF, FORTISSIMO
—quick	PRESTISSIMO
—slow(ly)	LENTISSIMO
—soft	PIANISSIMO, PP
vigorously	CON BRIO, VIGOROSO
violin strings	A. D. E. G
virtuoso passage	CADENZA
vocal	
—composition	CHORALE
—melody	CANTILENA
wallpaper music	MUSAK, MUZAK™
wavering of pitch	VIBRATO
weighty	PESANTE
West Indies	REGGAE, SKA
with	
—alternating subjects	RONDO
—bow close to	
bridge	SUL PONTICELLO
fingerboard	SUL TASTO
—dignity or majesty	MAESTOSO
—diminishing speed	RITARDANDO
—each note detached	STACCATO
—fervour	ZELOSO
—fire	CON FUOCO
—full time allowed for	
each note	SOS(TENUTO)
—fury	FURIOSO
—great rapidity	VELOCE
—hammering touch	MARTELLATO
—medium volume	MEZZA VOCE
—movement	CON MOTO
—mute	CON SORDINO
—parts each having	
separate melody	POLYPHONY

—rebounding bow	(ARCO)SALTANDO
	(ARCO)SALTATO
—spirit	CON SPIRITO, SPIRITOSO
—sudden	
accent	RINFORZANDO
emphasis	(S)FORZANDO, (S)FORZATO
—syncopation	(ALLO)ZOPPO
—the	
bow	(COLL')ARCO
voice	COLLA VOCE
wood	COL LEGNO
—tremulous effect	TREMOLANDO
without	SENZA
—a	
break	LEG(ATO)
mute	SENZA SORDINO
pause	SEGUE
—embellishments	SEMPLICE
write parts for	
instruments	ORCHESTRATE

musical instruments

accordion	MELODEON
African	BALTON, HARP-LUTE
	GORA(H), GOURA, KONA
	KORA, ZANZE
—one-stringed	GURKEL
ancient	
—flute or pipe	TIBIA
—lute	DICHORD
Argentinian accordion	BANDOEON
Australian	DIDGERIDOO, WOBBLE BOARD
bagpipe	
—French	CORNEMUSE, MUSETTE
	SOURDELINE
—Italian	PIFFERO, ZAMPOGNA
—old	CHORUS
bandore	PANDORA, PANDORE
	PANDURA
barrel-organ for training	
song-birds	SERINETTE
bass	
—drum	TAMBOUR
—fiddle	(VIOLON)CELLO
—lute	THEORBO
—saxhorn	EUPHON(IUM)
—tuba	BOMBARDON
—viol	VIOLA DA GAMBA, VIOLONE
bassoon	FAGOTTO
bassoon-like (old)	RACKET(T)
bell and bars	GLOCKENSPIEL
bellows	ACCORDION, CONCERTINA
	MELODEON
bells	CARILLON
bird	
—call	QUAIL-CALL, QUAIL-PIPE
—shaped	OCARINA

boatswain's whistle	PIPE
Bolivian	CHARANGA
bombardon	BASS TUBA
brass	
—bass	BOMBARDON, HELICON, SAXHORN
	SOUSAPHONE, TUBA
—reed	SARRUSOPHONE
	SAXOPHONE, STRITCH
—slide	BAZOOKA, TROMBONE
—valved	CLARION, CORNET(-A-PISTONS)
	CORNOPEAN, ENGLISH HORN
	EUPHONIUM, FLUGEL-HORN
	FRENCH-HORN, MELLOPHONE
	OPHICLEIDE
	TRUMP(ET), (WAGNER) TUBA
—valveless	BUGLE
Bronze Age trumpet	LUR(E)
Burmese	TURR
Chinese	CHENG, KIN, SANG
cithern	GITTERN
—Shetland	LANGSP(I)EL
clavichord	CZLARICHORD, MONOCHORD
concertina	SQUEEZE-BOX, SQUIFFER
cornet-type (German)	ZINKE
crude oboe	PIFFERO
cymbal (Oriental)	ZEL
double	
—bass	VIOL
—necked lute	THEORBO
—reeded	BASSOON, COR ANGLAIS
	CRUMHORN, ENGLISH HORN
	KRUM(M)HORN, OBOE
	SHALM, SHAWM
drum	(*see also* percussion *below*)
dulcimer	CEMBALO, CIMBALON
	CIMBELON, ZIMBALOM
	PANTALEON
early	
—clarinet	CHALUMEAU
—piano	FORTEPIANO
Eastern	PANDORA, PANDORE, PANDURA
	SANTIR, SANT(O)UR
Egyptian tambourine	RIZZ
electronic	CLAVINOVA, MARTENOT
	MOOG, (ONDES) MARTINET
	MELLOTRON, SYNTHESISER
	THEREMIN
Elizabethan	BANDORE
English	
—flute	RECORDER
—horn	COR ANGLAIS, CORNO INGLESE
fiddle	
—Shetland	GJU, GU(E)
—Welsh	CROUTH, CROWD
—with strings in pairs	SULTANA
fife	PIFFERO

Finnish	KANTELE
fipple-flute	FLAGEOLET, FLUTE-A-BEC
	RECORDER
flageolet	FIPPLE-FLUTE
	PENNY-WHISTLE
French	
—bagpipe	CORNEMUSE, MUSETTE
	SOURDELINE
—horn	CORNO
without valves	WALDHORN
—viol	VIELLE
—woodwind	COUTAUT
German	
—trombone	POSAUNE
—woodwind	DULZIAN
glass harmonica	EUPHON
gong	TAM-TAM
gourd rattle	MARACA
graduated tuning forks	DULCITONE
grand piano	PIANO(FORTE)
Greek	AULOS, BARBITOS, BOUZOUKI
	CITHARA, KITHARA, LYRE
	PHORMINX, SALPINX, SYRINX
guitar	GITTERN
—Eastern	TAMBOURA
—Indian	SITAR
—Japanese	S(H)AMISEN
guitar-like	BANJO, MANDOLIN(E)
hand organ	HARMONICON, HURDY-GURDY
harmonica	MOUTH-ORGAN
	MUSICAL GLASSES
harmonium	REED-ORGAN
—early	PHYSHARMONICA
harp-like (old)	SACKBUT, SAMBUCA
	SAMBUKE
harpsichord	CLAVERIN
Hebrew	ASOR, SHOFAR, SHOPHAR
	TIMBREL, TOPH
—harp	NEBEL
highest-toned instrument	SOPRANINO
horn without valves	COACH HORN
	COR DE CHASSE, POST HORN
Hungarian	CIMBALON, CIMBELON
	ZIMBALOM
hunting-horn	FLUGEL-HORN, WALDHORN
hurdy-gurdy	VIELLE
Indian	CHIKARI, SAROD, SARANGI
	SERINGHI, SITAR, TABLA
	TAMBOURA
Irish	TYMPAN
Italian	CHITARRONE, FAGOTTO
Japanese	KOTO, S(H)AMISEN
Jew's harp	GUIMBARD, TRUMP
juke-box	NICKELODEON
kettledrum	NAKER, TIMBAL, TYMBAL
	TIMPANO, TYMPANO

key-bugle	FLUGEL-HORN, KENT-BUGLE
	OPHICLEIDE
keyboard	ACCORDION, BANDONEON
	CALLIOPE, CELESTA, CELESTE
	CLAVICEMBALO, CLAVECIN
	CLARICHORD, CLAVECIN
	CLAVICHORD, CLAVICYTHERIUM
	CLAVIER, DULCITONE
	HAMMOND ORGAN, HARMONICHORD
	HARMONIPHON(E), HARMONIUM
	HARPSICHORD, KLAVIER
	MELODEON, MELLOTRON
	(MOOG)SYNTHESISER
	(ONDES)MARTINET, ORGAN
	ORGANO, PIANO ACCORDION
	PIANOFORTE, (PLAYER) PIANO
	PORTATIVE ORGAN, REGAL
	SPINET(T), SPINETTE
	VIRGINAL, WURLITZER
—reed	SERAPHINE, VOCALION
—soundless	DUMB-PIAN
large	
—dulcimer (18th c)	PANTELEON
—lute	CHITARRONE, OPHARION
	OPHEOREON
—mandoline	MANDOLA, MANDORA
—serpent	ANACONDA
light-operated	LIGHT-ORGAN
like a lute	POLYPHONE
lute played by wheel	VIELLE
mechanical	GRAMOPHONE, JUKEBOX
	MUSIC BOX, MUSIC CENTRE
	PANHARMONICUM, PIANOLA
	PLAYER PIANO, POLYPHON
	RECORD PLAYER
mediaeval	CITOLE, ROTE
Mexican	CLARIN
mouth-organ	HARMONICA, HARMONICON
—Chinese	SANG
musical	
—box	POLYPHONE
—glasses	HARMONICA
Neapolitan	PANDURA
nickelodeon	JUKE-BOX
Northumberland bagpipes	SMALL-PIPES
oboe type	HECKELPHONE
old	
—fiddle	GJU, GU(E), SULTAN
—harplike	LYRE
—Scottish	STOCK-AND-HORN
—trumpet (Scand.)	LUR(E)
—viol	VIELLE
—viola	LYREA-VIOL
—zither-like	PSALTERY
orchestral	
—horn	FRENCH HORN

—kettledrum	TIMPANO
orchestrion	HARMONICON
panharmonicon	ORPHEUS HARMONICA
Pan('s) pipes	OATS, SYRINX
percussion	CYMBAL, DRUM, GONG
	IDIOPHONE, TAMBOURINE
	TRIANGLE, TUBULAR BELLS
—corrugated board	WASHBOARD
—Cuban	BONGO, CONGA, ENKOMO
—drum(s)	BASS DRUM, KETTLE DRUM
	PEDAL DRUM, SIDE DRUM
	SNARE DRUM, TABOR
	TAMBOUR, TAM-TAM
	TENOR DRUM, TIMBAL
	TOMTOM, TRAPS, TYMPAN
	TYMPANUM(TYMPANA)
	TYMPANY
—dulcimer	CEMBALO, CYMBALO
—Eastern	GAMELAN
—gourd	MARACA
—Indian	TABLA
—jazz	TRAP
—metal bars	DULCIMER, GLOCKENSPIEL
	TUBULAR BELLS
	VIBRAHARP, VIBRAPHONE
—Spanish	CASTANETS
—stones	LITHOPHONE
—wooden	
bars	MARIMBA, XYLOPHONE
block	CHINESE BLOCK
sticks	CLAVES
piano	PIANOFORTE
piano-like barrel-organ	PIANO-ORGAN
piccolo	OCTAVE-FLUTE
pipe made from reed	QUILL
player-piano	PIANOLA
pocket violin	KIT
portable organ	REGAL
practice instrument	DUMB-PIANO
primitive drum	TOM-TOM
rackett	SAUSAGE-BASSOON
recorder	FIPPLE-FLUTE
reed	
—organ	HARMONIUM, MELODEON
—pipes	OATS, PAN('S)-PIPES, SYRINX
Russian	BALALAIKA, DOMRA
	GUSLA, GUSLE, GUSLI
San Domingo	TUMBA
sausage-bassoon	RACKETT
Scottish	BAGPIPES, STOCK-AND-HORN
shallow drum	TAMBOURINE
shepherd's pipe	OAT
Shetland	GU(E), LANGSP(I)EL
small	
—bagpipe (French)	SORDELINE
—banjo	BANJULELE

—drum	TABO(U)R(IN), TABRET
—flute	FIFE, FLAGEOLET
	PICCOLO
—tabor	TABRET
sound-box and metal	
strips	HARMONICA
Spanish	CASTENETS, TENORA
	VIHUELA, ZAMBOMBA
squeeze-box	CONCERTINA, SQUIFFER
steam whistles with	
keyboard	CALLIOPE
straight trumpet (Roman)	TUBA
straw pipe	OAT
stringed	BASS FIDDLE, CELLO
	CONTRABASS(O), COUNTERBASS
	DOUBLE BASS, GUITAR, HARP
	MANDOLIN(E), UKELELE, UKULELE
	VIOLA, VIOLIN, VIOLONCELLO
—African	GURKEL, OUD
—Asian	OUD
—Celtic	CROUTH, CROWD
—early	CITHERN, GITTERN, LUTE
	PSALTERY, REBEC(K)
	REBIB(L)E, VIOL
—eastern	BANDORE, PANDORA
	PANDORE
—French	VIELLE
—Greek	BOUZOUKI, CITHARA
	KITHARA, LYRE
—Hawaiian	UKELELE, UKULELE
—Hungarian	CIMBALON
—Indian	SARANGI, SAROD, SITAR
—Irish	CLAIRSCHACH, TYMPAN
—Japanese	KOTO, S(H)AMISEN
—mediaeval	BANDORE, GITTERN
	ROTE
—Russian	BALALAIKA
	GUSLA, GUSLE, GUSLI
—Shetland	GJU, GU(E)
—Tirolese	CITHER(N), CITTERN
—viol	VIELLE
—Welsh	CROUTH, CROWD
—wind harp	AEOLIAN HARP
—with	
1 string	MONOCHORD
—African	GURKEL
—Balkan	GUSLA, GUSLE, GUSLI
3 strings	TRICHORD
4 strings	TETRACHORD
5 strings	BANJO, PENTACHORD
6 strings	GUITAR
7 strings	HEPTACHORD
8 strings	OCTACHORD
10 strings	TETRACHORD
29-42 strings	ZITHER(N)
Swiss	ALPENHORN

syrinx	PAN('S)PIPES		HAUTBOIS, HAUTBOY
tabor (Eastern)	TIMBREL		HOBOY, KRUM(M)HORN
tambourine (Eastern)	TIMBREL		OBOE D'AMORE, OBOE DI CACCIA
tenor			SERPENT, SHALM, SHAWM
—fiddle	VIOLA	xylophone	GAMELAN, MARIMBA
—oboe	TENOROON		METALLOPHONE
—saxhorn	ALTHORN		STICCADO, STICCATO
—viol	VIOLA D'AMORE	zither-type	AUTOHARP
	VIOLA DA BRACCIO	**musicals**	42ND STREET
	VIOLA DA SPALLA		A CHORUS LINE, A LITTLE NIGHT MUSIC
tin whistle	PENNY-WHISTLE		ANNIE GET YOUR GUN, ANYTHING GOES
Tirolese zither	CITHER(N), CITTERN		ASPECTS OF LOVE, BARNUM, BITTER SWEET
toy	KAZOO, MUSICAL BOX		BRIGADOON, BROADWAY MELODY
	OCARINA		CALL ME MADAM, CAMELOT
—reed-pipe	MIRLITON		CANCAN, CAROUSEL
tromba marina	MONOCHORD, NUN'S-FIDDLE		CATS, CHARLIE GIRL, COMPANY
	TRUMP MARINE		DESERT SONG, EVITA, FOLLIES
trombone (German)	POSAUNE		GIGI, GUYS AND DOLLS, GYPSY, HAIR
trumpet	CLARION		JESUS CHRIST SUPERSTAR
—Bronze Age	LUR(E)		KING'S RHAPSODY, KISS ME KATE
—Greek	SALPINX		LADY BE GOOD, LAND OF SMILES
—Roman	TUBA		LAND OF SONG, MAID OF THE MOUNTAINS
tuning forks	DULCITONE		MAME, MISS SAIGON, MY FAIR LADY
Turkish	SAZ		NAUGHTY MARIETTA
upright			NEW MOON, OKLAHOMA
—piano	PIANO(FORTE)		ON THE TOWN, ONE TOUCH OF VENUS
—spinet	CLAVICYTHERIUM		PAINT YOUR WAGON, PAL JOEY
using flames	PYROPHONE		PHANTOM OF THE OPERA
viol			PORGY AND BESS, PYJAMA GAME
—medieval	REBEC(K)		ROSE MARIE, SAIL AWAY
—obsolete	TROMBA MARINA		SHOWBOAT, SINGING IN THE RAIN
—tenor	QUINT(E)		SOUTH PACIFIC, STARLIGHT EXPRESS
viola da gamba	GAMBA		SWINGTIME, THE BOHEMIAN GIRL
violin	AMATI, CREMONA, FIDDLE,		THE BOY FRIEND, THE DANCING YEARS
	STRAD(IVARIUS)		THE FIREBIRD, THE KING AND I
Welsh	HORNPIPE, WELSH-HARP		THE VAGABOND KING
—fiddle	CROUTH, CROWD		THREEPENNY OPERA
wind instrument	AEROPHONE		TOMMY, WEST SIDE STORY
—like cornet (old)	ZINKE	D'Oyly Carte	BUNTHORNE'S BRIDE
—with			CASTLE ADAMANT, FALLEN FAIRIES
loudspeaker	PIPELESS ORGAN		HMS PINAFORE, IOLANTHE
slide	SACKBUT, TROMBONE		PATIENCE, PIRATES OF PENZANCE
woodwind	BASSET HORN, BASSOON		PRINCESS IDA, RUDDIGORE
	CLARI(O)NET, CONTRABASSOON		THE GODS GROW OLD
	CONTRAFAGOTTO, COR ANGLAIS		THE GONDOLIERS, THE GRAND DUKE
	CORNO DI BASSETTO, CORNO INGLESE		THE LASS THAT LOVED A SAILOR
	FIFE, FLAGEOLET, FLUTE		THE MIKADO, THE PEER AND THE PERI
	HECKELPHONE, OBOE, PICCOLO		THE SLAVE OF DUTY, THE SORCERER
	RECORDER		THE TOWN OF TITIPU, THE WITCH'S CURSE
—old	ANACONDA, BASS HORN		THE YEOMEN OF THE GUARD, THESPIS
	CHALUMEAU		TRIAL BY JURY, UTOPIA LTD,
	CHORISTFAGOTT, CORNET(T)	**musicians**	
	CREMONA, CREMORNE, CROMORNA	classical	
	CROMORNE, CRUMHORN	—composers	
	CURTAL(L), COURTANT	American	BABBITT
	DULZIAN, FAGOTTO		BERNSTEIN, CAGE, CARTER

	COPLAND, COWELL, GERSHWIN
	IVES, SONDHEIM
	VARESE, WEILL
Argentinian	KAGEL
Austrian	BERG, BRUCKNER, HAYDN
	MAHLER, SCHO(E)NBERG
	SCHUBERT, J. STRAUSS, SUPPE
	WEBERN, WELLESZ, WOLF
British	BAX, BYRD, BRITTEN
	CAGE, COWARD, DAVIES, DELIUS
	ELGAR, FRICKER, GIBBONS, GRAINGER
	HANDEL, HESELTINE, HOLST
	LLOYD-WEBBER, NOVELLO
	PARRY, PURCELL, RAWSTHORNE
	SEARLE, SMALLEY, SULLIVAN
	TIPPETT, WALTON, WARLOCK
	WILLIAMS
Canadian	ELSLER
Czech	DUSSEK, DVORAK, HABA
	JANACEK, SMETANA
Danish	NIELSEN
Dutch	ARCADELT, DE MONTE
	LASSUS, WILLAERT
Finnish	SIBELIUS
French	AURIC, BERLIOZ, BIZET
	BOULEZ, CHOPIN, COUPERIN
	DEBUSSY, DELIBES, DUPARC
	DUREY, FAURE, FRANCK
	GOUNOD, HALEVY, LULLY, MASSENET
	MESSIAEN, MILHAUD, POULENC
	POUPARD, POUSSEUR, RAMEAU
	RAVEL, SAINT-SAENS, SATIE
	SAUGES, SCHAEFFER, SPONTINI
	TAILLEFERRE, VARESE
German	BACH, BEETHOVEN, BRAHMS
	GLUCK, HANDEL, HENZE, HINDEMITH
	HOFFMAN, HUMMEL, MENDELSSOHN
	MEYERBEER, MOZART, PFIZNER
	REGER, SCHEIDT, SCHEIN
	SCHUMANN, SCHUTZ
	STOCKHAUSEN, R. STRAUSS
	WAGNER, WEBER, WEILL
Greek	XENAKIS
Hungarian	BARTOK, DOHNANYI
	KODALY, LISZT, SOLTI
Italian	ALBINONI, BELLINI
	BERIO, BOCCCHERINI, BUSONI
	CASELLA, CAVALIERI, CAVALLI, CESTI
	CIMAROSO, CORELLI, DONIZETTI
	GABRIELLI, GEMINIANI
	MADERNA, MALIPIERO, MASCAGNI
	MONTEVERDI, PALESTRINA
	PRATELLA, PUCCINI, RESPIGHI
	ROSSINI, SCARLATTI, STRADELIA
	TORELLI, VERDI, VIVALDI
Japanese	TAKEMITSU

Norwegian	GRIEG
Polish	CHOPIN
Russian	BALAKIROFF, BORODIN
	GLINKA, MUSSORGSKY
	RIMSKY-KORSAKOV, SCRIABIN
	SHOSTAKOVITCH, STRAVINSKY
	TCHAIKOVSKY
Spanish	ALBENIZ, DE FALLA
	GRANADOS, TURINA, VICTORIA
Swedish	BLOMDAHL
Swiss	HONEGGER, MARTIN
—conductors	
American	BERNSTEIN, PREVIN
	STOKOWSKI
Austrian	BOHN, BRENDEL, MAHLER
	STRAUSS, WELSER-MOST
British	BARBIROLLI, BEECHAM
	BOULT, CAMERON
	DAVIS, LAMBERT, MACKERRAS
	PRITCHARD, RATTLE, SARGENT
	SOLTI, STOKOWSKI, WOOD
Dutch	HAITINK
Estonian	JARVI
French	BOULEZ
German	FURTWANGLER
	KNAPPERTSBUSCH, MASUR
	VON KARAJAN
	WALTER, WEINGARTEN
Hungarian	DOHNANYI, SOLTI
Indian	MEHTA
Italian	ABBADO, DE SABATA
	MUTI, TOSCANINI
Japanese	OZAWA
Latvian	JANSONS
Russian	ASHKENAZY, ROSTROPOVICH
—instrumentalists	
cello	CASALS, DU PRE, GENDRON
	HORNOY, MAISKY, OFFENBACH
	ROSTROPOVICH, TORTELIER
clarinet	BRYMER, DE PEYER, KELL
	THURSTON
flute	GALWAY
French horn	BRAIN, TUCKWELL
guitar	BREAM, SEGOVIA
oboe	GOOSENS
piano	ABBADO, ARRAU, ASHKENAZY
	BACKHAUS, BARENBOIM, BRENDEL
	BUSONI, CABEZON, CHOPIN, COWELL
	DOHNANYI, GIESEKING, HOROWITZ
	LIPATI, LISZT, LYMPANY, MEHTA
	MENDELSSOHN, MICHELANGELI, OGDON
	PADEREWSKI, PERAHIA, RICHTER
	RUBINSTEIN, SCHIFF, SCHNABEL
	ZIMMERMAN
trumpet	ANDRE
viola	BASHMET

violin	CHUNG, HEIFETZ, KREISLER	
	KYUNG-WHA, MENUHIN, MUTTER (f)	
	OISTRAKH, PAGANINI, PERLMAN	
	STERN, ZUKERMAN	

jazz
—composers BERLIN, BLEY(f),
CARMICHAEL, CARTER, COREA
ELLINGTON, EVANS, GERSHWIN
HEFTI, HENDERSON, JARRETT
JOPLIN, LUNCEFORD, MERCER
MONK, POWELL, STRAYHORN
TAYLOR, WESTBROOK

—instrumentalists
bass BLANTON, BRAUD, BROWN
CROSBY, HEATH, MINGUS
PAGE, PEDERSON
clarinet BECHET, BIGARD, COE
DAVERN, DE FRANCO, DODDS,
GOODMAN, HAMILTON, HERMAN
HUCKO, LEWIS, MATLOCK
NOONE, RUSSELL, SHAW
WASHINGTON
drums BLAKEY, CALLOWAY, CATLETT
CLARKE, COLE, HAMPTON, JONES
KRUPA, PARNELL, RICH, ROACH
TOUGH, WEBB
guitar BENSON, BUNN, CHRISTIAN
CONDON, ELLIS, FARLOW
GAILLARD, GREEN, KESSEL
KING, LANG, MCLAUGHLIN
METHANY, MONTGOMERY
PASS, REINHARDT
WALKER, WATERS
piano AMMONS, BASIE, BLAKE
BLEY(f), BRUBECK, COLE, COREA
CHARLES, ELLINGTON, EVANS
GARNER, HANCOCK, HINES, JARRETT
JOHNSON, KENTON, LEWIS, MONK
MORTON, MOTEN, PETERSON
POWELL, RUSSELL, SHEARING
SILVER, STRAYHORN, SUTTON
TATUM, TAYLOR, TRACY, TYNER
WALLER, WESTBROOK
WILLIAMS(f), WILSON
saxophone
—alto ADDERLEY, CARTER
COLEMAN, DESMOND
DOLPHY, DORSEY, HODGES
JORDAN, KONITZ, MCLEAN
PARKER, PEPPER, STITT
WOODS
—tenor AYLER, BARBIERI, BYAS, COE
COHN, COLEMAN, COLTRANE
DASH, DAVIS, FREEMAN, GETZ
GONSALVES, GORDON, GRAY
GRIFFIN, HAMILTON, HAWKINS

HAYES, JACQUET, KIRK
MILLER, PHILLIPS, PINE
QUEBEC, RIVERS, ROLLINS
RUSSELL, SANDERS, SCOTT
SHEPP, SHORTER, SIMS, STITT
STOBART(f), TATE, TURRENTINE
VENTURA, WASHINGTON
WEBSTER, YOUNG
—baritone CARNEY, MULLIGAN
SURMAN, TEMPERLEY
—bass ROLLINI
trumpet/cornet ALLEN, ANDERSON
ARMSTRONG, BAKER
BEIDERBECKE
BERIGAN, BOLDEN, BRAFF
BROWN, CANDOLI, CARTER
CHERRY, CLAYTON, DAVIS
DAVISON, EDISON, ELDRIDGE
ELMAN, FAIRWEATHER, FERGUSON
GILLESPIE, GONELLA, HACKETT
HUBBARD, JAMES, JOHNSON
LITTLETON, MARSALIS
MASKELA, MCGHEE, MILEY
MORGAN, NAVARRO, OLIVER
PAGE, ROGERS, SHAVERS
SANDOVAL, SPANIER, STEWART
TERRY, WHEELER
trombone BARBER, BROOKMEYER
DICKENSON, DORSEY, GRAY
GREEN, JOHNSON, LUSHER
MILLER, NANCE, NANTON, ORY
ROSSOLINI, TEAGARDEN, TIZOL
WELLS, WINDING
vibraphone BURTON, HAMPTON
HUTCHERSON, JACKSON
NORVO
violin GRAPELLI, JENKINS, NANCE
PONTY, SMITH, VENUTI
—leaders ANTHONY, BARNET, BASIE
BROWN, CROSBY, DORSEY
ELLINGTON, GOODMAN, GRAY
HEATH, HEFTI, HENDERSON
HERMAN, KENTON, KIRK
LUNCEFORD, MILLER, SHAW
—singers
(f) FITZGERALD, LAINE, HOLIDAY
LEE, MCCRAE, O'DAY
RAINEY, ROSS, SIMONE
SMITH, STAFFORD, VAUGHAN
WASHINGTON, WILSON
(m) ARMSTRONG, CALLOWAY, COLE
GAILLARD, MELLY, RUSHING
TURNER, WALLER
WITHERSPOON
Muslim (see Moslem)
Myanmar (see Burma)

mythology
—**Greek and Roman**

abandoned by	
—Aeneas	DIDO
—Neoptolemus	ANDROMACHE
—Paris	OENONE
—Theseus	ARIADNE
Achilles	AEACIDES
Aeacides	ACHILLES
Aero	MEROPE
Aesculapius	PAEAN
Alcides	HERCULES
Alexander	PARIS
Aloadae	EPHIALTES, OTUS
Anadyomene	APHRODITE
animal of	
—Ares	DOG
—Artemis	DEER
—Hera	COW
Antiope	HIPPOLYTA
Aphrodite	ANADYOMENE
	CYPRIAN, CYTHEREA
Aphrodite's girdle	CESTUS
Apollo	DELIAN, PAEAN, PYTHIAN
	SMINTHIAN
Arges	CYCLOPS
Argonauts	MINYAE
armour-bearer to Hercules	HYLAS
Artemis	CYNTHIA, HECATE
	ORTHIA, PHOEBE
	SELENE
Ascanius	IULUS
ate himself	ERYSICHTHON
Bacchantes	MAENADS
Bacchus	DIONYSIUS
battles with	
—Centaurs	LAPITHAE, THESEUS
—Lapithae	CENTAURS
bearer of magic wand	HERMES
beautiful valley	TEMPE
beekeeper	ARISTAEUS
betrayed Zeus's secret	SISYPHUS
bird of	
—Aphrodite	DOVE, SPARROW, SWAN
—Apollo	RAVEN
—Ares	VULTURE
—Athena	OWL
—Hera	PEACOCK
—Zeus	EAGLE
birthplace of	
—Aphrodite	CYTHERA
—Apollo	DELOS
—Artemis	DELOS
bitten by serpent and abandoned	PHILOCTETES
blind prophet	TEIRESIAS

blinded	
—Lycurgus	ZEUS
—Orion	OENOPION
—Polyphemus	ODYSSEUS
—Thamyris	MUSES
blinded by	
—a dryad	RHOECUS
—himself	OEDIPUS
—Muses	THAMYRIS
—Odysseus	POLYPHEMUS
—Oenopion	ORION
—Zeus	LYCURGUS
Bona Dea	MAIA
breastplate of Zeus	AEGIS
brother of	
—Aegyptus	DANAUS
—Agamemnon	MENELAUS
—Amphion	ZETHUS
—Antigone	ETEOCLES, POLYNEICES
—Ares	HEPHAESTUS
—Artemis	APOLLO
—Atlas	EPIMETHEUS, PROMETHEUS
—Atreus	THYESTES
—Biton	CLEOBIS
—Cleobis	BITON
—Danaus	AEGYPTUS
—Deiphobus	HECTOR, PARIS
—Dictys	POLYDECTES
—Dido	PYGMALION
—Electra	ORESTES
—Ephialtes	OTUS
—Epimetheus	ATLAS, PROMETHEUS
—Eris	ARES
—Eteocles	POLYNEICES
—Europa	CADMUS
—Hebe	ARES, HEPHAESTUS
—Hector	DEIPHOBUS, PARIS
—Helen	CASTOR, POLLUX
—Heliades	PHAETON
—Helle	PHRIXUS
—Hephaestus	ARES
—Hera	ZEUS
—Hestia	PLUTO, POSEIDON, ZEUS
—Iphigenia	ORESTES
—Ismene	ETEOCLES, POLYNEICES
—Jocasta	CREON
—Medea	APSYRTUS
—Menelaus	AGAMEMNON
—Neleus	PELIAS
—Niobe	PELOPS
—Otus	EPHIALTES
—Paris	DEIPHOBUS, HECTOR
—Pelias	NELEUS
—Philomena	ERECHTHEUS
—Pluto	POSEIDON, ZEUS
—Polydectes	DICTYS

—Polyneices	ETEOCLES
—Poseidon	HADES, ZEUS
—Procne	ERECHTHEUS
—Prometheus	ATLAS, EPIMETHEUS
—Selene	HELIOS
—Thyestes	ATREUS
—Zethus	AMPHION
—Zeus	PLUTO, POSEIDON
brought	
—back	
bull from Crete	HERCULES
cattle of Geryon	HERCULES
Golden Apples	HERCULES
stag with golden horns	HERCULES
to life by	
—Aesculapius	HIPPOLYTUS
—Calypso	PROTESILAUS
—Cerberus from Hades	HERCULES
—from Hades by	
Hercules	CERBERUS, THESEUS
Hermes	PERSEPHONE
—Hippolytus back to life	AESCULAPIUS
—Persephone from underworld	HERMES
—Protesilaus from dead	CALYPSO
built	
—Argo	ARGUS
—labyrinth	DAEDALUS
—walls of Thebes	AMPHION, ZETHUS
captor of	
—Amazon	THESEUS
—boar on Mt Erymanthus	HERCULES
—Cerberus	HERCULES
—Odysseus	CALYPSO
—Proteus	MENELAUS
captured by	
—Greeks	ANDROMACHE
—Hercules	ANTIOPE, CERBERUS
	HIPPOLYTA
—Menelaus	PROTEUS
cared for	
—Aesculapius	CHIRON
—Zeus	IDA
—by	
Chiron	AESCULAPIUS
Ida	ZEUS
carried away by	
—Apollo	CREUSA
—Aurora	CEPHALUS
—Boreas	OREITHYIA
—bull	EUROPA
—Dionysius	SEMELE
—dragons	MEDEA
—eagle	GANYMEDE
—golden ram	HELLE, PHRIXUS
—Idas	MARPESSA
—Zeus	AEGINA

carried world on his shoulders	ATLAS
Castor and Pollux	DIOSCURI
centaur	CHIRON, NESSUS
—friend of Achilles	PHOLUS
challenged	
—Apollo at flute-playing	MARSYAS
—Minerva at weaving	ARACHNE
—Muses at poetry	THAMYRIS
changed	
—Actaeon into stag	ARTEMIS
—Callisto into bear	HERA
—Perdix into partridge	MINERVA
—Scylla into monster	CIRCE
—Tithonus into grasshopper	AURORA
changed into	
—bear by Hera	CALLISTO
—bird	ALCYONE, CEYX, SCYLLA
—cow	IO
—eagle	NISUS
—grasshopper by Aurora	TITHONUS
—hawk	TEREUS
—laurel tree	DAPHNE
—linden tree	BAUCIS
—monster by Circe	SCYLLA
—myrtle	MYRRHA
—nightingale	PROCNE
—oak tree	PHILEMON
—partridge	PERDIX
—poplar trees	HELIADES
—sea	
god	GLAUCUS, MELICERTES
goddess	INO
—spider	ARACHNE
—spring by Artemis	ARETHUSA
—stag by Artemis	ACTAEON
—stone	NIOBE
—sunflower	CLYTIE
—swallow	PHILOMENA
—tree	DRYOPE
—tuft of reeds	SYRINX
—wolf	LYCAON
changing shape at will	PROTEUS
charioteer	MYRTILUS
Charites	GRACES
	(*see also* **Graces**)
Clashing Rocks	SYMPLEGADES
cleaned Augean stables	HERCULES
cliff	SCYLLA
cloud-gatherer	ZEUS
conquered by	
—Atalanta	PELEUS
—Bellerophon	AMAZONS, SOLYMI
—Theseus	AMAAZONS
conqueror of	
—Amazons	BELLEROPHON, THESEUS
—Peleus	ATALANTA

—Solymi	BELLEROPHON
Corybantes	CURETES
cousin of	
—Hercules	THESEUS
—Orestes	PYLADES
—Pylades	ORESTES
—Theseus	HERCULES
created from ants	MYRMIDONS
creator of mankind	PROMETHEUS
Cronus	KRONUS
cup-bearer to gods	GANYMEDE, HEBE
Curetes	CORYBANTES
cut	
—down tree in Ceres'	
grove	ERYSICHTHON
—off Nisus's hair	SCYLLA
—out tongue of Philomena	TEREUS
—the Gordian knot	ALEXANDER
—to pieces by his daughters	PELIAS
Cyclops	ARGES, POLYPHEMUS
	STEROPES
Cynthia	ARTEMIS
Cyprian	APHRODITE
Cytherea	APHRODITE
Danaid	AMYMONE
daughter of	
—Acrisius	DANAE
—Aeolus	ALCYONE, ARNE
—Aesculapius	HYG(I)EIA, OCYRRHOE
—Aetes	MEDEA
—Agamemnon	CHRYSOTHEMIA
	ELECTRA, IPHIGENIA
—Alcinous	NAUSICAA
—Amata	LAVINIA
—Aphrodite	HARMONIA
—Apollo	HILARA
—Ares	AMAZONS, HARMONIA
—Arete	NAUSICAA
—Asopus	AEGINA
—Athamas	HELLE
—Atlas	HESPERIDES
	HYADES, MAIA
—Cadmus	AGAVE, AUTONOE
	INO, SEMELE
—Cassiopeia	ANDROMEDA
—Cecrops	AGLAUROS, HERSE
	PANDROSOS
—Cepheus	ANDROMEDA
—Clytemnestra	ELECTRA, IPHIGENIA
—Coeus	LETO
—Cronus	DEMETER, HESTIA
—Danaus	DANAIDS
—Demeter	PERSEPHONE
—Dione	APHRODITE
—Doris	NEREIDS
—Erectheus	CREUSA, ORITHYIA, PROCRIS

—Eurynome	AGLAIA, EUPHROSYNE
	GRACES, THALIA
—Eurystheus	ADMETA
—Eurytus	IOLE
—Graiae	EURYALE, MEDUSA, STHENO
—Harmonia	AGAVE, AUTONOE
	INO, SEMELE
—Harmony	AMAZONS
—Hecuba	POLYXENA
—Helen	HERMIONE
—Hera	HEBE, ILITHYIA
—Iasus	ATALANTA
—Icarius	PENELOPE
—Inachus	IO
—Jocasta	ANTIGONE, ISMENE
—king of	
Lemnos	HYPSIPYLE
Sidon	EUROPA
—Laomedon	HESIONE
—Latinus	LAVINIA
—Leda	CLYTEMNESTRA, HELEN
—Leto	ARTEMIS
—Leucippus	HILARA
—Lycaon	CALLISTO
—Menelaus	HERMIONE
—Minos	ARIADNE
—Nephele	HELLE
—Nereus	NEREIDS
—Nisus	SCYLLA
—Ocean	DORIS, EURYNOME
	OCEANIDS
—Oedipus	ANTIGONE, ISMENE
—Oenopion	AERO
—Pelias	ALCESTIS
—Phoebe	LETO
—Phorcys	GORGONS
—Priam	CASSANDRA
—Rhea	DEMETER, HESTIA
—Salmoneus	TYRO
—Schoeneus	ATALANTA
—Tantalus	NIOBE
—Themis	ASTRAEA
—Thestius	ALTHEA, LEDA
—Tyndareus	CLYTEMNESTRA
	TYNDARIS
—Zeus	AGLAIA, APHRODITE
	ARTEMIS, ASTREA, ATHENA
	EUPHROSYNE, GRACES, HEBE
	HELEN, MUSES, THALIA
death	
—Greek	THANATOS
—Roman	MORS
deified Romulus	QUIRINUS
Diomedes	TYDIDES
Dionysius	BACCHUS, IACCHUS
discoverers of iron	DACTYLA

divisions of underworld	EREBUS
	TARTARUS
dog guarding entrance to	
Hades	CERBERUS
drowned	
—by water nymph	HYLAS
—in Hellespont	HELLE, LEANDER
Earth	GAEA
earthshaker	POSEIDON
east wind	EURUS
eaten by his horses	GLAUCUS
Erechtheus	ERICTHONIUS
Ericthonius	ERECHTHEUS
Erinyes	EUMENIDES, FURIES
Fate(s)	
—Greek	MOIRA(E)
—Roman	PARCAE
	(see separate entry)
father of	
—Abas	LYNCEUS
—Achilles	PELEUS
—Admeta	EURYSTHEUS
—Adonis	CINYRAS
—Aeacus	ZEUS
—Aegina	ASOPUS
—Aegisthus	THYESTES
—Aeneas	ANCHISES
—Aeolus	HELLEN
—Aepytus	CRESPHONTES
—Aero	OENOPION
—Aesculapius	APOLLO
—Aetolus	ENDYMION
—Agamemnon	ATREUS
—Agave	CADMUS
—Agenor	PRIAM
—Aglaia	ZEUS
—Aglauros	CECROPS
—Ajax	OILEUS, TELAMON
—Alcestis	PELIAS
—Alcyone	AEOLUS
—Althea	THESTIUS
—Amazons	ARES
—Amphion	ZEUS
—Amphitryon	ALCAEUS
—Androgeus	MINOS
—Andromeda	CEPHEUS
—Antigone	OEDIPUS
—Antilochus	NESTOR
—Aphrodite	ZEUS
—Apollo	ZEUS
—Apsyrtus	AETES
—Arcas	ZEUS
—Ares	ZEUS
—Aristaeus	APOLLO
—Arne	AEOLUS
—Artemis	ZEUS

—Ascanius	AENEAS
—Astraea	ZEUS
—Astyanax	HECTOR
—Atalanta	IASUS, SCHOENIUS
—Athena	ZEUS
—Atlas	IAPETUS
—Atreus	PELOPS
—Autonoe	CADMUS
—Bellerophon	GLAUCUS, POSEIDON
—Calais	BOREAS
—Callisto	LYCAON
—Cassandra	PRIAM
—Ceyx	LUCIFER
—Chrysothemia	AGAMEMNON
—Clytemnestra	TYNDAREUS
—Cresphontes	HERCULES
—Creusa	ERECHTHEUS
—Cronus	HEAVEN, URANUS
—Danae	ACRISIUS
—Daphne	PENEUS
—dawn	HYPERION
—Deiphobus	PRIAM
—Demeter	CRONUS
—Deucalion	PROMETHEUS
—Diomedes	TYDEUS
—Dionysius	ZEUS
—Doris	OCEAN
—Electra	AGAMEMNON
—Electryon	PERSEUS
—Epaphus	ZEUS
—Ephialtes	POSEIDON
—Epimetheus	IAPETUS
—Eteocles	OEDIPUS
—Euphrosyne	ZEUS
—Eurynome	OCEAN
—Glaucus	SISYPHUS
—Gorgons	PHORCYS
—Graces	ZEUS
—Harmonia	ARES
—Hebe	ZEUS
—Hector	PRIAM
—Helen	ZEUS
—Helle	ATHAMAS
—Hellen	DEUCALION
—Hercules	ZEUS
—Hermes	ZEUS
—Hermione	MENELAUS
—Herse	CECROPS
—Hesione	LAOMEDON
—Hesperides	ATLAS
—Hestia	CRONOS
—Hilara	APOLLO, LEUCIPPUS
—Hippolytus	THESEUS
—Hyades	ATLAS
—Icarus	DAEDALUS
—Icelus	HYPNOS

—Ino	CADMUS	—Polydorus	CADMUS, PRIAM
—Io	INACHUS	—Polyneices	OEDIPUS
—Iole	EURYTUS	—Polyphemus	POSEIDON
—Ion	APOLLO	—Pontus	NEREUS
—Iphicles	AMPHITRYON	—Procris	ERECHTHEUS
—Iphigenia	AGAMEMNON	—Prometheus	IAPETUS
—Ismene	OEDIPUS	—Proteus	PSODEIDON
—Itys	TEREUS	—Pyrrha	EPIMETHEUS
—Jason	AESON	—Rhadamanthus	ZEUS
—Jupiter	SATURN	—Sarpedon	ZEUS
—Latinus	FAUNUS	—Scylla	NISUS
—Lausus	MEZENTIUS	—Semele	CADMUS
—Lavinia	LATINUS	—Silenus	PAN
—Leda	THESTIUS	—Sun	HYPERION
—Leto	COEUS	—Tantalus	ZEUS
—Linus	APOLLOA	—Telamon	AEACUS
—Machaon	AESCULAPIUS	—Telemachus	ODYSSEUS
—Maia	ATLAS	—Telephus	HERCULES
—Medea	AETES	—Tereus	ARES
—Meleager	OENEUS	—Teucer	SCAMANDER, TELAMON
—Memnon	TITHONUS	—Thalis	ZEUS
—Menelaus	ATREUS	—Theseus	AEGEUS
—Menoeceus	CREON	—Thyestes	PELOPS
—Midas	GORDUS	—Triton	POSEIDON
—Minos	ZEUS	—Troilus	PRIAM
—Moon	HYPERION	—Tydides	TYDEUS
—Morpheus	HYPNOS	—Tyndaris	TYNDAREUS
—Muses	ZEUS	—Tyro	SALMONEUS
—Nausicaa	ALCINOUS	—Zetes	BOREAS
—Neleus	POSEIDON	—Zethus	ZEUS
—Neoptolemus	ACHILLES	—Zeus	CRONOS
—Nereids	NEREUS	favourite	
—Nestor	NELEUS	—child of Zeus	ATHENA
—Niobe	TANTALUS	—Jupiter	MERCURY
—Oceanids	OCEAN	—Zeus	CYCLOPES
—Ocyrrhoe	AESCULAPIUS	ferryman	CHARON, NESSUS
—Odysseus	LAERTES	first	
—Oedipus	POLYBUS	—horse	ARION
—Orestes	AGAMEMNON	—man ashore at Troy	PROTESILAUS
—Orithyia	ERECHTHEUS	—woman	PANDORA
—Otus	POSEIDON	fisherman	DICTYS, GLAUCUS
—Pallas	EVANDER	flayed by Apollo	MARSYAS
—Pan	HERMES	flew too near the sun	ICARUS
—Pandrosos	CECROPS	flower of Adonis	ANEMONE, WINDFLOWER
—Paphos	PYGMALION	followers of	
—Paris	PRIAM	—Achilles	MYRMIDONS
—Parthenopaeus	MELANION	—Bacchus	BACCHANTES, MAENADS
—Pelias	POSEIDON		THYIADES
—Pelops	TANTALUS	foretelling the future	PROTEUS
—Penelope	ICARIUS	founder of	
—Perseus	ZEUS	—Carthage	DIDO
—Phaeton	HELIOS	—Rome	REMUS, ROMULUS
—Phantasus	HYPNOS	—Trojans	DARDANUS
—Philoctetes	POEAS	fountain (Parnassus)	CASTALIA
—Phrixus	ATHAMAS	freed by	
—Pollux	ZEUS	—Circe	ODYSSEUS

—Hercules	PROMETHEUS
—Hermes	ARES
friend of	
—Achilles	PATROCLUS
—Aeneas	ACHATES
Friendly Sea	EUXINE
Furies	ERINYES. EUMENIDES
	(*see also separate entry*)
gave	
—asses's ears to Midas	APOLLO
—golden apple to Aphrodite	PARIS
—necklace to Harmonia	APHRODITE
—shield to Perseus	ATHENA
giant	ANTAEUS, CACUS
	EPHIALTES, OTUS
	POLYBOTES, PORPHYRION
	RHOETUS, TITYUS
girdle of Amazons got by	HERCULES
given	
—ivory shoulder by gods	PELOPS
—necklace by Aphrodite	HARMONIA
—skin of Calydonian boar	ATALANTA
giver of	
—Golden Fleece to Aetes	PHRIXUS
—horse to mankind	POSEIDON
gnomes	CERCOPES
goat whose milk fed Zeus	AMALTHEA
Golden Fleece given by	
Phrixus to	AETES
good Centaur	CHIRON
Gorgons	EURYALE, MEDUSA, STHENO
Graces	CHARITES
	(*see separate entry*)
greatest musician	ORPHEUS
Greek equivalents	
—Aesculapius	ASKLEPIOS
—Ammon	ZEUS
—Bellona	ENYO
—Ceres	DEMETER
—Cupid	EROS
—Diana	ARTEMIS, LUCINA
—Dis	HADES, PLUTO
—Eileithyia	LUCINA
—Juno	HERA, LUCINA
—Jupiter	AMMON, ZEUS
—Latona	LETO
—Liber	BACCHUS, DIONYSIUS, LYAEUS
—Liberia	PERSEPHONE
—Lucina	DIANA, JUNO
—Maia	BONA DEA
—Mars	ARES
—Mater	
Matuta	AURORA, INO
Turrita	CYBELE, RHEA
—Mercury	HERMES
—Minerva	ATHENA

—Mors	THANATOS
—Mulciber	HEPHAESTUS
—Neptune	POSEIDON
—Proserpine	PERSEPHONE
—Saturn	CRONUS
—Sol	HELIOS
—Somnus	HYPNOS, HYPNUS
—Ulysses	ODYSSEUS
—Venus	APHRODITE
—Vesta	HESTIA
—Victoria	NIKE
—Vulcan	HEPHAESTUS
guardian(s) of	
—golden apples	HESPERIDES, LADON
—Hades	CERBERUS
—infant Zeus	CORYBANTES
	CURETES
—stream flowing with gold	GRIFFINS
guide of the dead	HERMES
Hades	PLUTO, POLYDECTES
hanged herself	ARACHNE
healer	APOLLO
Hecabe	HECUBA
Hecate	ARTEMIS, TRIVIA
Hecuba	HECABE
Helen	TYNDARIS
helped Theseus to escape	DAEDALUS
herald	HERMES
Hercules	ALCIDES
Hermes	PSYCHOPOMPUS
heroine of Troy	HELEN
Hesper	VESPER
Hesperia	ITALY
Hippolyta	ANTIOPE
Hippomenes	MELANION, MILANION
home of	
—the gods	OLYMPUS
—Hydra	LERNA, LERNE
—Titans	OTHRYS
horse from Medusa's blood	CHRYSAOR
hounds of Zeus	HARPIES
huntress	ARETHUSA, ARTEMIS
husband of	
—Aerope	ATREUS
—Aethra	AEGEUS
—Aglaia	HEPHAESTUS
—Alcestis	ADMETUS
—Amata	LATINUS
—Amphitrite	POSEIDON
—Andromache	HECTOR, HELENUS
—Andromeda	PERSEUS
—Anteia	PROETUS
—Aphrodite	HEPHAESTUS
—Arete	ALCINOUS
—Atalanta	MELANION
—Aurora	TITHONUS

—Baucis	PHILEMON
—Cassiopeia	CEPHEUS
—Clytemnestra	AGAMEMNON
—Creusa	XUTHUS
—Deianira	HERCULES
—Dido	SICHAEUS
—Dirce	LYCUS
—Doris	NEREUS
—Electra	PYLADES
—Eriphyle	ADRASTUS
—Eurydice	ORPHEUS
—Eurynome	GLAUCUS
—Evadne	CAPANEUS
—Gaea	URANUS
—Galatea	PYGMALION
—Harmonia	CADMUS
—Hebe	HERCULES
—Hecuba	PRIAM
—Helen	MENELAUS
—Hera	ZEUS
—Hermione	NEOPTOLEMUS
—Hesione	PROMETHEUS
—Hippodamia	PELOPS, PIRITHOUA
—Hippolyta	THESEUS
—Hypermnestra	LYNCEUS
—Ino	ATHAMAS
—Jocasta	LAIUS, OEDIPUS
—Laodamia	PROTESILAUS
—Lavinia	AENEAS
—Leda	TYNDAREUS
—Lybia	POSEIDON
—Maia	VULCAN
—Megara	HERCULES
—Merope	CRESPHONTES, POLYPHONTES
—Nephele	ATHAMAS
—Niobe	AMPHION
—Ops	SATURN
—Penelope	ODYSSEUS
—Persephone	HADES
—Phaedra	THESEUS
—Procne	TEREUS
—Procris	CEPHALUS
—Psyche	CUPID
—Pyrrha	DEUCALION
—Rhea	CRONOS
—Sidero	CRETHEUS
—Tethys	OCEAN
—Thetis	PELEUS
—Tyro	CRETHEUS
Hyades	NYSAEAN NYMPHS
Hypnos	HYPNUS
Iacchus	DIONYSIUS
immortal who grew older	TITHONUS
imprisoned	
—by	
Calypso	ODYSSEUS

Minos	DAEDALUS, ICARUS
—Daedalus	MINOS
—Icarus	MINOS
—in Labyrinth	DAEDALUS, ICARUS
inhabitant(s) of	
—Dodona	SELLI
—far bank of Ocean	CIMMERIANS
—Labyrinth	MINOTAUR
—north	HYPERBOREANS
—swamp at Lerna	HYDRA
Ino	LEUCOTHEA
inventor of	
—compass	PERDIX
—flute	ATHENA
—horse bridle	ATHENA
—lyre	HERMES
—saw	PERDIX
island sacred to Aphrodite	CYPRUS
Italy	HESPERIA
Iulus	ASCANIUS
judge in underworld	AEACUS, MINOS
	RHADAMANTHUS
kept snakes as pets	MELAMPUS
kidnapped by Theseus	HELEN
kidnapper of Helen	THESEUS
killed	
—and boiled	
by	
—Procne	ITYS
—his father	PELOPS
son	TANTALUS
—by	
Achilles	HECTOR, CHIRON
	MEMNON, PENTHESILEA
	TROILUS
Aegisthus	AGAMEMNON
Aeneas	TURNUS
Agave	PENTHEUS, CORONIS
	CYCLOPES, HYACINTH(US)
Apollo	TITYUS
Artemis	CORONIS, ORION
Bellerophon	CHIMAERA
boar	ADONIS
bull	ANDROGEUS
Cephalus	PROCRIS
Clytemnestra	AGAMEMNON
	CASSANDRA
Daedalus	PERDIX
Ephialtes	OTUS
Eteocles	POLYNEICES
Hercules	ANTAEUS, DIOMEDES
	EURYTUS, HYDRA, LAOMEDON
	LINUS, LITYERSES, MEGARA
	NEMEAN LION, NESSUS
Hermes	ARGUS
Idas	CASTOR

Ino	MELICERTES
Jason	APSYRTUS
Lycomides	THESEUS
Lycus	DIRCE
Maenads	ORPHEUS, PENTHEUS
Medea	APSYRTUS
Neoptolemus	PRIAM
Oedipus	LAIUS
Orestes	AEGISTHUS
	CLYTEMNESTRA, EPHIALTES
Paris	ACHILLES
Pelias	SIDERO
Pelops	MYRTILUS
Perseus	ACRISIUS, GORGONS
Philoctetes	PARIS
Polyneices	ETEOCLES
Polyphemus	ACIS
Theseus	MINOTAUR, PROCRUSTES
	SINIS, SCIRON
Zeus	ASKLEPIOS, SALMONEUS

killer of

—Achilles	PARIS
—Acis	POLYPHEMUS
—Acrisius	PERSEUS
—Aegisthus	ORESTES
—Agamemnon	AEGISTHUS
	CLYTEMNESTRA
—Antaeus	HERCULES
—Apsyrtus	JASON, MEDEA
—Argus	HERMES
—Asklepios	ZEUS
—Calydonian boar	MELEAGER
—Cassandra	CLYTEMNESTRA
—Castor	IDAS
—Chimaera	BELLEROPHON
—Chiron	ACHILLES
—Clytemnestra	ORESTES
—Cornis	ARTEMIS, APOLLO
—Cyclopes	APOLLO
—Diomedes	HERCULES
—Dirce	LYCUS
—dragon guarding spring	CADMUS
—eagle attacking Prometheus	HERCULES
—Ephialtes	OTUS
—Eteocles	POLYNEICES
—Eurytus	HERCULES
—Gorgons	PERSEUS
—Hector	ACHILLES
—Hyacinth(us)	APOLLO
—Hydra	HERCULES
—Itys	PROCNE
—Jason's bride	MEDEA
—Lalus	OEDIPUS
—Laomedon	HERCULES
—Linus	HERCULES
—Lityerses	HERCULES

—Megara	HERCULES
—Melicertes	INO
—Memnon	ACHILLES
—Minotaur	THESEUS
—Myrtilus	PELOPS
—Nemean lion	HERCULES
—Nessus	HERCULES
—Niobe's children	APOLLO, ARTEMIS
—Orion	ARTEMIS
—Orpheus	MAENADS
—Otus	EPHIALTES
—Paris	PHILOCTETES
—Penelope's suitors	ODYSSEUS
—Penthesilea	ACHILLES
—Pentheus	AGAVE, MAENADS
—Perdix	DAEDALUS
—Polyneices	ETEOCLES
—Priam	NEOPTOLEMUS
—Procris	CEPHALUS
—Salmoneus	ZEUS
—Sidero	PELIAS
—Stymphalian birds	HERCULES
—Theseus	LYCOMIDES
—Thespian Lion	HERCULES
—Tityus	APOLLO
—Troilus	ACHILLES
—Turnus	AENEAS

killers of husbands   DANAIDS

king of

—Aegina	AEACUS
—Alba Longa	AENEAS SYLVIUS
—Arcadia	LYCAON
—Argos	ACRISIUS, ADRASTUS
	PROETUS
—Athens	AEGEUS, ERECHTHEUS
—Attica	CECROPS
—Calydon	OENEUS, THESTIUS
—Chios	OENOPION
—Colchis	AEETES
—Corinth	GLAUCUS, POLYBUS
	SISYPHUS
—Crete	MINOS
—Greece	ATHAMAS
—Ithaca	ODYSSEUS
—Lapithae	PEIRITHEOS
—Latium	LATINUS
—Lydia	TANTALUS
—Megara	NISUS
—Mycenae	EURYSTHEUS
—Phaeacians	ALCINOUS
—Phocis	STROPHIUS
—Phrygia	MIDAS
—Rutulians	TURNUS
—Sparta	MENELAUS
—Thebes	CADMUS, LAIUS, LYCUS
	OEDIPUS, PENTHEUS

—Thessaly	ADMETUS, AEOLUS	—Selene	ENDYMION
	CEYX,MINYAS	—Theseus	ARIADNE
—Thrace	DIOMEDES	—Thisbe	PYRAMUS
—Troezen	PITTHEUS	—Vertumnus	POMONA
—Troy	LAOMEDON, PRIAM	—Zeus	AEGINA, CALLISTO
	TEUCER		IO, LETO, SEMELE
—Tyre	PYGMALION	Lyaeus	BACCHUS
—winds	AEOLUS	lyre given by Hermes to	APOLLO
Kora	PERSEPHONE	made	
Kronus	CRONUS	—Psyche immortal	JUPITER
lame god	HEPHAESTUS	—Tithonus immortal	ZEUS
land of oak trees	DODONA	Maenads	BACCHANTES
leader of Cretans	IDOMENEUS	magic	
Leucothea	INO	—herb given to Odysseus	MOLY
liberator of		—wand of Hermes	CADUCEUS
—Ares	HERMES	magical beings of Lemnos	CABEIRI
—Odysseus	CIRCE	maid of Tyro	SIDERO
—Prometheus	HERCULES	maker of	
loved by		—Labyrinth	DAEDALUS
—Adonis	PERSEPHONE	—lyre	CALYPSO
—Aegisthus	CLYTEMNESTRA	—reed pipe	PAN
—Anteia	BELLEROPHON	—shepherd-pipe	CALYPSO
—Aphrodite	ADONIS	—Wooden Horse	EPEUS
—Apollo	CORONIS, DAPHNE	Melanion	MILANION, HIPPOMENES
	MARPESSA	Melicertes	PALAEMON
—Ariadne	THESEUS	Merope	AERO
—Aurora	CEPHALUS, ORION	messenger of Gods	CALYPSO, HERMES
—Boreas	ORITHYIA		MERCURY
—Circe	GLAUCUS	Minyae	ARGONAUTS
—Clytemnestra	AEGISTHUS	mother of	
—Dido	AENEAS	—Abas	HYPERMNESTRA
—Echo	NARCISSUS	—Achilles	THETIS
—Ephialtes	ARTEMIS	—Actaeon	AUTONOE
—Eurydice	ORPHEUS	—Adonis	MYRRHA
—Galatea	ACS	—Aeacus	AEGINA
—Glaucus	SCYLLA	—Aeneas	APHRODITE
—Hades	PERSEPHONE	—Aepytus	MEROPE
—Hercules	IOLE	—Aesculapius	ARSINOE, CORONIS
—Hero	LEANDER	—Agamemnon	AEROPE
—Jason	MEDEA	—Agave	HARMONIA
—Leander	HERO	—Aglaia	EURYNOME
—Medea	JASON	—Aloadae	IPHIMEDEA
—Meleager	ATALANTA	—Amazons	HARMONY
—Minos	SCYLLA	—Amphion	ANTIOPE
—Oenone	PARIS	—Andromeda	CASSIOPEIA
—Orpheus	EURYDICE	—Antigone	JOCASTA
—Orion	AERO, AURORA, MEROPE	—Aphrodite	DIONE
—Paris	OENONE	—Apollo	LETO
—Pasiphae	BULL	—Arcas	CALLISTO
—Persephone	ADONIS	—Ares	HERA
—Phaedra	HIPPOLYTUS	—Aristaeus	CYRENE
—Polyphemus	GALATEA	—Artemis	LETO
—Pomona	VERTUMNUS	—Astraea	THEMIS
—Pyramus	THISBE	—Astyanax	ANDROMACHE
—Sappho	PHAON	—Atreus	HIPPODAMIA
—Scylla	MINOS	—Autonoe	HARMONIA

—Bellerophon	EURYNOME
—Biton	CYDIPPE
—Calais	ORITHYIA
—Castor	LEDA
—Cerberus	ECHIDNA
—Cleobis	CYDIPPE
—Clytemnestra	LEDA
—Cupid	APHRODITE
—Dardanus	ELECTRA
—Deiphobus	HECUBA
—Demeter	RHEA
—Dionysius	SEMELE
—Electra	CLYTEMNESTRA
—Electryon	ANDROMEDA
—Epaphus	IO
—Ephialtes	EPHIMEDIA
—Eros	APHRODITE
—Euphrosyne	EURYNOME
—Graces	EURYNOME
—Harmonia	APHRODITE
—Hebe	HERA
—Hector	HECUBA
—Helen	LEDA
—Helle	NEPHELE
—Hellen	PYRRHA
—Hercules	ALCMENA
—Hermes	MAIA
—Hermione	HELEN
—Hestia	RHEA
—Hippolytus	HIPPOLYTA
—Hydra of Lerna	ECHIDNA
—Ilithyia	HERA
—Ino	HARMONIA
—Ion	CREUSA
—Iphigenia	CLYTEMNESTRA
—Itys	PROCNE
—Lavinia	AMATA
—Leto	PHOEBE
—Linus	PSAMATHE
—Meleager	ALTHEA
—Melicertes	INO
—Memnon	AURORA
—Minos	EUROPA
—Minotaur	PASIPHAE
—Muses	MNEMOSYNE
—Nausicaa	ARETE
—Neleus	TYRO
—Nemean Lion	ECHIDNA
—Neoptolemus	DEIDAMIA
—Nereids	DORIS
—Oceanids	TETHYS
—Orestes	CLYTEMNESTRA
—Otus	EPHIMEDIA
—Palaemon	LEUCOTHEA
—Paphos	GALATEA
—Paris	HECUBA
—Parthenopaeus	ATALANTA
—Pelias	TYRO
—Pentheus	AGAVE
—Persephone	DEMETER
—Perseus	DANAE
—Phrixus	NEPHELE
—Pollux	LEDA
—Polyxena	HECUBA
—Pontus	MOTHER EARTH
—Pyrrhus	DEIDAMIA
—Rhadamanthus	EUROPA
—Sarpedon	DEIDAMIA, EUROPA
—Semele	HARMONIA
—Telemachus	PENELOPE
—Thalia	EURYNOME
—Theseus	AETHRA
—Thyestes	HIPPODAMIA
—Triton	AMPHITRITE
—Xuthus	HELEN
—Zetes	ORITHYIA
—Zethus	ANTIOPE
Moira(e)	FATE(S)
mountain of	
—Apollo	PARNASSUS
—the	
gods	OLYMPUS
Muses	HELICON
Muses	PIERIDES
	(see also separate entry)
musician of gods	APOLLO
Neoptolemus	PYRRHUS
Nereid	AMPHITRITE, PANOPE
	THETIS
north wind	AQUILO, BOREAS
nursed by	
—Adrastea	ZEUS
—Eurycleia	ODYSSEUS
—Hyades	BACCHUS
nurse(s) of	
—Bacchus	HYADES, NYSAEAN NYMPHS
—Odysseus	EURYCLEIA
—Zeus	ADASTREA, IDA
nymph	ADASTREA, IDA
	LOTI, SYRINX
nymphs	(see separate entry)
Nysaean Nymphs	HYADES
obtained girdle of Hippolyta	HERCULES
Old Man of the Sea	NEREUS
Olympians	(see also gods, goddesses)
one-eyed horseman	ARIMASPI
oracle of	
—Apollo	DELPHI
—Zeus	DODNA
Orthia	ARTEMIS
outran Atalanta with	
golden apples	MELANION

owner of
—horn of plenty   AMALTHEA
—man-eating horses   DIOMEDES
Paean   AESCULAPIUS, APOLLO
painkilling drug given
  to Helen   NEPENTHE
Palaemon   MELICERTES
Paris   ALEXANDER
perpetually weeping   NIOBE
Persephone   KORA
Phoebe   ARTEMIS, SELENE
physician   AESCULAPIUS
—of the gods   PAEAN
—to Greek army at Troy   MACHAON
Pierides   MUSES
Pillars of Hercules   ABYLA, CALPE
Pleiades   ALCYONE, CELAENO
ELECTRA, MAIA, MEROPE
STEROPE, TAYGETE
Pluto   HADES
Polydectes   HADES
Polydeuces   POLLUX
priestess of
—Aphrodite   HERO
—Hera   CYDIPPE
priests of Mars   SALII
prince of
—Athens   THESEUS
—Ethiopia   MEMNON
princess of
—Crete   ARIADNE
—Thebes   ANTIOPE, MEGARA, SEMELE
prophet   PHINEUS
—of Troy   HELENUS
protectress of youth   ARTEMIS
Psychopompus   HERMES
punished by
—Hera   ECHO, IXION
—Olympians   TANTALUS
—Zeus   HERCULES, LYCAON
SISYPHUS
pupil of
—Athena   EURYNOME
—Chiron   ACHILLES, ACTAEON
AESCULAPIUS
—Daedalus   PERDIX
purple-haired king   NISUS
pursued by Orion   PLEIADES
put eyes into peacock's tail   HERA
Pyrrhus   NEOPTOLEMUS
queen of
—Amazons   HIPPOLYTA, PENTHESILEA
—Babylon   SEMIRAMIS
—Ethiopia   CASSIOPEIA
—Lydia   OMPHALE
—universe   RHEA

raised by
—she-bear   ATALANTA
—she-wolf   REMUS, ROMULUS
received
—asses's ears from Apollo   MIDAS
—golden apple from Paris   APHRODITE
—necklace from Aphrodite   MARMONIA
recovered
—by Menelaus   HELEN
—Helen   MENELAUS
—sight at Lemnos   ORION
rescued by
—Artemis   ARETHUSA, IPHIGENIA
—Athena   IPHIGENIA, ORESTES
PYLADES
—Calypso   ODYSSEUS, PHRYXUS
—Castor and Pollux   HELEN
—Dionysius   ARIADNE
—Hercules   HESIONE
—Ino   ODYSSEUS
—Iris   HARPIES
—Nausicaa   ODYSSEUS
—Perseus   ANDROMEDA
—Poseidon   AMYMONE
—Zephyr   PSYCHE
—Zeus   ODYSSEUS
rescued from Hades
by Hercules   ALCESTIS, THESEUS
rescuer of
—Alcestis from Hades   HERCULES
—Amymone   POSEIDON
—Andromeda   PERSEUS
—Arethusa   ARTEMIS
—Ariadne   DIONYSIUS
—Harpies   IRIS
—Helen   CASTOR, POLLUX
—Hesione   HERCULES
—Iphigenia   ARTEMIS, ATHENA
—Odysseus   CALYPSO, INO
NAUSICAA, ZEUS
—Orestes   ATHENA
—Phryxus   CALYPSO
—Prometheus   HERCULES
—Psyche   ZEPHYR
—Pylades   ATHENA
—Theseus from Hades   HERCULES
restored to life by gods   PELOPS
Rhea   CYBELE
rider of Pegasus   BELLEROPHON
river
—encircling Earth   OCEAN
—in
  Delphi   CEPHISSUS
  Hades   ACHERON, COCYTUS
LETHE, PHLEGETHON, STYX
  Phrygia   MEANDER

Tempe	PENEUS
Thrace	HEBRUS
—not seen by mortals	ERIDANUS
—of Troy	SCAMANDER, SIMOIS
	XANTHUS
Roman equivalents	
—Aphrodite	VENUS
—Ares	MARS
—Artemis	DIANA
—Asklepios	AESCULAPIUS
—Athena	MINERVA
—Aurora	MATER MATUTA
—Cronus	SATURN
—Demeter	CERES
—Dionysius	BACCHUS, LIBER, LYAEUS
—Enyo	BELLONA
—Eros	CUPID
—Hades	DIS
—Helios	SOL
—Hephaestus	MULCIBER, VULCAN
—Hera	JUNO
—Hermes	MERCURY
—Hestia	VESTA
—Hypnos	SOMNUS
—Ino	MATER MATUTA
—Leto	LATONA
—Eileithyia	JUNO, LUCINA
—Lyaeus	LIBER
—Nike	VICTORIA
—Odysseus	ULYSSES
—Persephone	LIBERIA, PROSERPINE
—Pluto	DIS
—Poseidon	NEPTUNE
—Thanatos	MORS
—Zeus	JOVE, JUPITER
ruler of Titans	CRONUS, EURYNOME
	OPHION
sacrificed before Troy	IPHIGENIA
satyr	FAUN, MARSYAS
saved	
—Amymone from satyr	POSEIDON
—Argonauts from Talus	MEDEA
—by	
Ariadne	THESEUS
dolphins	ARION
Medea from Talus	ARGONAUTS
Theseus	PIRITHOUS
Poseidon from satyr	AMYMONE
—Pirithous	THESEUS
—Theseus	ARIADNE
saviour of mankind	PROMETHEUS
sculptor	PYGMALION
sea nymph	DORIS, GALATEA
	HESIONE, THETIS
seer of Corinth	POLYIDUS
Selene	ARTEMIS, PHOEBE

serpent guarding golden apples	LADON
seven sisters	PLEIADES
shepherd	ENDYMION
—in Sicily	DAPHNIS
shield-carrier for Zeus	ATHENA
ship's pilot	ACETES, PALURINUS
shot Centaurs	ATALANTA
Sicily	TRINACRIA
Siren	PARTHENOPE
sister of	
—Agave	AUTONOE, INO, SEMELE
—Aglauros	HERSE, PANDROSUS
—Antigone	ISMENE
—Apollo	ARTEMIS
—Apsyrtus	MEDEA
—Ares	ERIS, HEBE
—Ariadne	PHAEDRA
—Autonoe	AGAVE, INO, SEMELE
—Cadmus	EUROPA
—Castor	HELEN
—Creon	JOCASTA
—Creusa	ORITHYIA, PROCRIS
—Doris	GALATEA
—Dryope	IOLE
—Erechtheus	PROCNE, PHILOMENA
—Eteocles	ANTIGONE, ISMENE
—Galatea	DORIS
—Gorgons	GRAIAE
—Graiae	GORGONS
—Helios	SELENE
—Herse	AGLAUROS, PANDROSUS
—Ino	AGAVE, AUTONOE, SEMELE
—Iole	DRYOPE
—Ismene	ANTIGONE
—Orestes	ELECTRA, IPHIGENIA
—Orithyia	CREUSA, PROCRIS
—Pandrosus	AGLAUROS, HERSE
—Pelops	NIOBE
—Phaedra	ARIADNE
—Phaeton	HELIADES
—Philomena	PROCNE
—Phrixus	HELLE
—Pluto	HESTIA
—Polyneices	ANTIGONE, ISMENE
—Poseidon	HESTIA
—Procne	PHILOMENA
—Procris	CREUSA, ORITHYIA
—Pygmalion	DIDO
—Semele	AGAVE, AUTONOE, INO
site of Orpheus' burial	LIBETHRA
slave of	
—Admetus	APOLLO
—Omphale	HERCULES
slept for 57 years	EPIMENIDES
Sminthian	APOLLO
snake-haired monsters	GORGONS

son of

—Achilles	NEOPTOLEMUS
—Aeacus	TELAMON
—Aegeus	THESEUS
—Aegina	AEACUS
—Aeneas	ASCANIUS
—Aerope	AGAMEMNON
—Aesculapius	MACHAON
—Aeson	JASON
—Aetes	APSYRTUS
—Aethra	THESEUS
—Agamemnon	ORESTES
—Agave	PENTHEUS
—Alcaeus	AMPHITRYON
—Alcmena	HERCULES, IPHICLES
—Althea	MELEAGER
—Amphitrite	TRITON
—Amphitryon	IPHICLES
—Anchises	AENEAS
—Andromache	ASTYANAX
—Andromeda	ELECTRYON
—Antiope	AMPHION, ZETHUS
—Aphrodite	AENEAS, CUPID, EROS
—Apollo	AESCULAPIUS, ARISTAEUS
	ION, LINUS
—Ares	TEREUS
—Arsinoe	AESCULAPIUS
—Atalanta	PARTHENOPAEUS
—Athamas	PHRIXUS
—Atreus	AGAMEMNON, MENELAUS
—Aurora	MEMNON
—Autonoe	ACTAEON
—Boreas	CALAIS, ZETES
—Cadmus	POLYDORUS
—Callisto	ARCAS
—Calypso	PAN, SILENUS
—Cinyras	ADONIS
—Clytemnestra	ORESTES
—Coronis	AESCULAPIUS
—Creon	MENOECEUS
—Cresphontes	AEPYTUS
—Creusa	ION
—Cronos	ZEUS
—Cydippe	BITON, CLEOBIS
—Cyrene	ARISTAEUS
—Daedalus	ICARUS
—Danae	PERSEUS
—Deucalion	HELLEN
—Electra	DARDANUS
—Endymion	AETOLUS
—Europa	MINOS, RHADAMANTHUS
	SARPEDON
—Eurynome	BELLEROPHON
—Evander	PALLAS
—Faunus	LATINUS
—Galatea	PAPHOS

—Glaucus	BELLEROPHON
—Gordus	MIDAS
—Heaven	CRONUS
—Hector	ASTYANAX
—Hecuba	DEIPHOBUS, HECTOR
	PARIS
—Helen	XUTHUS
—Hellen	AEOLUS
—Hera	ARES, HEPHAESTUS
—Hercules	CRESPHONTES, TELEPHUS
—Hermes	PAN
—Hippodamia	ATREUS, THYESTES
—Hypermnestra	ABAS
—Hypnos	ICELUS, MORPHEUS
	PHANTASUS
—Iapetus	ATLAS, PROMETHEUS
	EPIMETHEUS
—Ino	MELICERTES
—Io	EPAPHUS
—Iphimedia	EPHIALTES, OTUS
—Laertes	ODYSSEUS
—Leda	CASTOR, POLLUX
—Leto	APOLLO
—Lucifer	CEYX
—Lucothea	PALAEMON
—Lynceus	ABAS
—Maia	HERMES
—Merope	AEPYTUS
—Mezentius	LAUSUS
—Minos	ANDROGEUS
—Mother Earth	PONTUS
—Myrrha	ADONIS
—Neleus	NESTOR
—Nepele	PHRIXUS
—Nereus	PONTUS
—Nestor	ANTILOCHUS
—Odysseus	TELEMACHUS
—Oedipus	ETEOCLES, POLYNEICES
—Oeneus	MELEAGER
—Oileus	AJAX
—Orithyia	CALAIS, ZETES
—Pan	SILENUS
—Peleus	ACHILLES
—Pelops	ATREUS, THYESTES
—Penelope	TELEMACHUS
—Perseus	ELECTYRON
—Poeas	PHILOCTETES
—Polybus	OEDIPUS
—Poseidon	EPHIALTES, NELEUS, OTUS
	PELIAS, POLYPHEMUS
	PROTEUS, TRITON
—Priam	AGENOR, DEIPHOBUS, HECTOR
	PARIS, POLYDORUS, TROILUS
—Procne	ITYS
—Prometheus	DEUCALION
—Psamathe	LINUS

—Pygmalion	PAPHOS
—Pyrrha	HELLEN
—Saturn	JUPITER
—Scamander	TEUCER
—Semele	DIONYSIUS
—Sisyphus	GLAUCUS
—Sun	PHAETON
—Tantalus	PELOPS
—Telamon	AJAX, TEUCER
—Tereus	ITYS
—Theseus	HIPPOLYTUS
—Thetis	ACHILLES
—Thyestes	AEGISTHUS
—Tithonus	MEMNON
—Tydeus	DIOMEDES, TYDIDES
—Tyro	NELEUS, PELIAS
—Uranus	CRONUS
—Venus	AENEAS
—Zeus	AEACUS, AMPHION, APOLLO
	ARCAS, ARES, DIONYSIUS
	EPAPHUS, HEPHAESTUS, HERCULES
	HERMES, PERSEUS, POLLUX
	SARPEDON, TANTALUS, ZETHUS
soothsayer to Argonauts	MOPSUS
south wind	AUSTER, NOTUS
sowed dragon's teeth from which soldiers sprang	CADMUS
spear of Poseidon	TRIDENT
spirit in all things	GENIUS
spoke the language of animals	MELAMPUS
sprang from	
—foam of sea	APHRODITE
—head of Zeus	ATHENA
—Heaven's blood	GIANTS, ERINYES
	EUMENIDES, FURIES
spring	
—in	
Corinth	PIRENE
Delphi	CASTALIA
—on Mount Helicon	HIPPOCRENE
star-maiden	ASTRAEA
stole	
—Apollo's herds	HERMES
—cattle from Hercules	CACUS
—weapons from Hercules	CERCOPES
subdued Aetean bulls	JASON
suitor of Penelope	ANTINOUS
swallowed by Zeus	METIS
swam Hellespont nightly	LEANDER
swineherd	EUMAEUS
temple of Athena	PARTHENON
three women with one eye between them	GRAIAE
three-bodied monster	GERYON
thrown from walls of Troy	ASTYANAX

thunderer	ZEUS
tied to	
—bull by her hair	DIRCE
—wheel for ever	IXION
Titans	(see **gods**—Greek)
tongue cut out by Tereus	PROCNE
torn to pieces by his dogs	LINUS
tree of	
—Aphrodite	MYRTLE
—Artemis	CYPRESS
—Athena	OLIVE
—Zeus	OAK
Trinacria	SICILY
Trivia	HECATE
trumpeter of the sea	TRITON
turned	
—Anaraxete to stone	VENUS
—men into beasts	CIRCE
tutor of	
—Achilles	CHIRON
—Aesculapius	CHIRON
—Eurynome	ATHENA
—Perdix	DAEDALUS
twin brothers	AMPHION, ZETHUS
	CASTOR, POLLUX
	NELEUS, PELIAS
twins	APOLLO, ARTEMIS
Tydides	DIOMEDES
Tyndaris	CLYTEMNESTRA, HELEN
Typhoeus	TYPHON
Typhon	TYPHOEUS
ugly god	HEPHAESTUS
Unfriendly Sea	AXINE
usurper of Greek throne	PELIAS
valley in Thessaly	TEMPE
Vesper	HESPER
virgin goddess	ATHENA, ARTEMIS
	HESTIA
watchman with 100 eyes	ARGUS
wearer of winged	
—headgear	HERMES
—sandals	HERMES
weaver	ARACHNE
west wind	FAVONIUS, ZEPHYR
whirlpool	CHARYBDIS
winged horse	PEGASUS
witch	CIRCE
wife of	
—Admetus	ALCESTIS
—Adrastus	ERIPHYLE
—Aegeus	AETHRA
—Aeneas	LAVINIA
—Agamemnon	CLYTEMNESTRA
—Alcinous	ARETE
—Amphion	NIOBE
—Amphitryon	ALCMENA

—Athamas	INO, NEPHELE	wounded by	
—Atreus	AEROPE	—Cronus	HEAVEN
—Cadmus	HARMONIA	—Diomedes	AENEAS
—Capaneus	EVADNE	—Hercules	CHIRON, TELEPHUS
—Cephalus	PROCRIS	**—Norse**	
—Cepheus	CASSIOPEIA	Asgarth	ASGARD
—Ceyx	ALCYONE	ash tree	YG(G)DRASIL(L)
—Cresphontes	MEROPE	Attila	ATLI
—Cretheus	SIDERO, TYRO	Balder	BALDUR
—Cronus	RHEA	battlefield of gods' defeat	VIGRID
—Cupid	PSYCHE	blind god	HODER, HODUR
—Deucalion	PYRRHA	boar	
—Glaucus	EURYNOME	—providing food in Valhalla	SERIMNIR
—Hades	PERSEPHONE	—pulling Freyr's car	GULLINBURSTI
—Hector	ANDROMACHE	—with golden pelt	GULLINBURSTI
—Helenus	ANDROMACHE	brother of	
—Hephaestus	AGLAIA, APHRODITE	—Balder	HODER
—Hercules	DEIANIRA, HEBE	—Fafnir	REGIN, OTTER
	MEGARA	—Gudrun	GUNNAR
—King Tyndareus	LEDA	—Hoder	BALDER
—Laius	JOCASTA	—Otter	FAFNIR, REGIN
—Latinus	AMATA	—Regin	FAFNIR, OTTER
—Lycus	DIRCE	—Signy	SIGMUND
—Lynceus	HYPERMNESTRA	bound with magic chain	FENRIS
—Melanion	ATALANTA	bridge to Asgard	BIFROST
—Menelaus	HELEN	changed into dragon	FAFNIR
—Minos	PASIPHAE	chasm before the creation	GINUNGAGAP
—Neoptolemus	HERMIONE	choosers of the slain	FREYA, VALKYRIES
—Nereus	DORIS	city of giants	JOTUNHEIM
—Ocean	TETHYS	cow whose milk fed Ymir	AUDHUMBLA
—Odysseus	PENELOPE	daughter of	
—Oedipus	JOCASTA	—Angerbode	HELA
—Orpheus	EURYDICE	—Griemhild	GUDRUN
—Peleus	THETIS	—Sigurd	SWANHILD
—Pelops	HIPPODAMIA	—Volsung	SIGNY
—Perseus	ANDROMEDA	day of doom	RAGNAROK
—Philemon	BAUCIS	died	
—Pirithous	HIPPODAMIA	—in burning house	SIGNY
—Polyphontes	MEROPE	—of broken heart	NANNA
—Poseidon	AMPHITRITE, LYBIA	dog guarding Hela's gate	GARM
—Priam	HECUBA	dragon	FAFNIR, NIDHOGG
—Proetus	ANTEIA	dwarf	ANDVARI
—Prometheus	HESIONE	enemies of gods	GIANTS
—Protesilaus	LAODAMIA	end of world	RAGNAROK
—Pygmalion	GALATEA	father of	
—Pylades	ELECTRA	—Gunnar	GIUKI
—Rhadamanthus	EUROPA	—Odin	BOR
—Saturn	OPS	—Signy	VOLSUNG
—Sichaeus	DIDO	—Sigurd	SIGMUND
—Tereus	PROCNE	—Sinfiotli	SIGMUND
—Theseus	PHAEDRA	—Swanhild	SIGURD
	HIPPOLYTA	—Vidar	ODIN
—Tithonus	AURORA	fates	(*see separate entry*)
—Uranus	GAEA	first	
—Xuthus	CREUSA	—giant	YMIR
—Zeus	HERA	—man	ASK

—woman	EMBLA
follower(s) of Siegfried	NIBELUNG(EN)
gave up an eye for wisdom	ODIN
giant	FAFNER, FAFNIR
	FASOLT, JOTUM, MIMIR
	TAROLL, THRYM, YMER
	YMIR
giantess	GERDA, GROA, NATT
goblin	NIS, TROLL
gods	AESIR
guardian(s) of	
—treasure	NIBELUNG(EN)
—Urda's well	NORNA, NORNS
—Well of Knowledge	MIMIR
half-brother of	
—Gunnar	GUTTORM
—Guttorm	GUNNAR
hall	
—in Asgard	VALHALLA, WALHALLA
—for the slain	VALHALLA, WALHALLA
heaven	ASGARD, ASGARTH
	VALHALLA, WALHALLA
heroic race	VOLUSPA
holy well	URDA'S WELL
home of	
—elves	ELFHEIM
—goddesses	VINGOLF
—gods	ASGARD, ASGARTH
	VALHALLA, WALHALLA
horn of Heimdall	GIALLAR
horse of Odin	SLEIPNIR
husband of	
—Brynhild	GUNNAR
—Frigga	ODIN
—Gerda	FREYR
—Gudrun	ATLI, SIGURD
—Iduna	BRAGI
—Nanna	BALDER
—Signy	SIGGEIR
—Sigyn	LOKI
—Swanhild	JOMUNREK
inhabitants	
—of	
Jotunheim	FROST GIANTS
	MOUNTAIN GIANTS
Midgard	MANKIND
Utgard	GIANTS
—under Midgard	DWARFS
keeper of	
—apples of youth	IDUNA
—rainbow bridge	HEIMDALL
—flowers and streams	ELVES
killed by	
—Gudrun	ATLI
—Guttorm	SIGURD
—horses	SWANHILD

—Jomunrek	SWANHILD
—Loki	OTTER
—mistletoe bough	BALDER
—Odin	YMIR
—Sigurd	FAFNIR, REGIN
killer of	
—Atli	GUDRUN
—Fafnir	SIGURD
—Otter	LOKI
—Regin	SIGURD
—Sigurd	GUTTORM
—Swanhild	JOMUNREK
—Ymir	ODIN
king	ATU
—of Giukungs	GUNNAR
land of	
—fire	MUSPELHEIM
—giants	UTGARD
—mankind	MIDGARD
magic(al)	
—chain	GLEIPNIR
—inscriptions	RUNES
—ship	SKIDBLADNIR
maidens	VALKYRIE, WALKYRIE
man made from	ASH
memory	MUNIN
middle earth	MIDGARD
most loved god	BALDER
mother of	
—Balder	FRIGGA
—Fenris	ANGERBODE
—Gudrun	GRIEMHILD
—Gunnar	GRIEMHILD
—Hela	ANGERBODE
—Hermod	FRIGGA
—Midgard serpent	ANGERBODE
—Sinfiotli	SIGNY
Odin	WODEN
palace of	
—dead	VALHALLA, WALHALLA
—Frigga	FENSALIR
—Odin	GLADSHEIM
paradise	ASGARD, ASGARTH
	VALHALLA, WALHALLA
put to sleep by Odin	BRYNHILD
rainbow bridge	BIFROST
ravens of Odin	HUGIN, MUNIN
region of mist	NIFLHEIM
ruler of	
—Jotunheim	UTGARD-LOKI
—Muspelheim	SURTR
serpent	MITGARD
servant of	
—Freyr	SKIRNIR
—Loki	THIALFI
served by Thialfi	LOKI

ship built by dwarfs	SKIDBLADNIR
sister of	
—Gunnar	GUDRUN
—Sigmund	SIGNY
son of	
—Bor	ODIN
—Frigga	BALDER, HERMOD
	HODER, VIDAR
—giant	LOKI
—Giuki	GUNNAR
—Griemhild	GUNNAR
—Odin	BALDER, HERMOD
	HODER, VIDAR
—Sigmund	SIGURD, SINFIOTLI
—Signy	SINFIOTLI
sprang from ice	BOR
stole Thor's hammer	THRYM
supernatural	
—dwarf	TROLL
—race	NIBELUNG(EN)
swiftest of gods	HERMOD
thought	HUGI(N)
threw mistletoe at Balder	HODER

tied up in cavern	LOKI
trampled by horses	SWANHILD
underworld	NIFLHEIM
Valkyrie	BRYNHILD
wakens Brynhild	SIGURD
Walhalla	VALHALLA
Woden	ODIN
wife of	
—Atli	GUDRUN
—Balder	NANNA
—Bragi	IDUNA
—Freyr	GERDA
—Gunnar	BRYNHILD
—Jomunrek	SWANHILD
—Loki	SIGYN
—Odin	FRIGGA
—Siggeir	SIGNY
—Sigurd	GUDRUN
wolf	FENRIS
—of Odin	FREKI, GERI
world ash-tree	YG(G)DRASIL(L)
Ymer	YMIR

(see also **gods, goddesses***)*

N

names
added name	AGNOMEN
assumed name	ALIAS, PSEUDONYM
code name	NOM DE GUERRE
distinguished name	EPONYM
false	ALIAS, ANONYM, PSEUDONYM
familiar name	COGNOMEN, NICKNAME
first name	CHRISTIAN NAME, FORENAME
giver of names	NOMENCLATOR
having	
—many names	MULTINOMIAL
	POLYNOMIAL
	POLYNOMIC
	POLYNYMOUS
—similar name	COGNOMINAL
last name (Roman)	COGNOMEN
name	
—taken from ancestor	PATRONYMIC
—with	
two words	BINOMIAL
three words	TRINOMIAL, TRIONYM
several words	POLYNYM
—without description	NOMEN NUDUM
nameless	ANONYMOUS
namesake	HOMONYM
naming	
—by	
2 attributes	BINOMIAL
3 attributes	TRINOMIAL
—parents from child	TEKNONYMY
—the subject	NOMINATIVE
nickname	COGNOMEN, SOBRIQUET
nicknames	(see separate entry)
one	
—named	NOMINEE
—whose name is used for	
some object	EPONYM
opposite	ANTONYM
pen name	NOM DE PLUME
	PSEUDONYM
pertaining to names	NOMINAL
place name	TOPONYM
propose by name	NOMINATE
pseudonym	TELONISM
real name (of author)	AUTONYM
rejected name in biology	HOMONYM
same name	HOMONYM, SYNONYM
second name (Roman)	NOMEN

surname	COGNOMEN
system of names	NOMENCLATURE
systematic name	SYNONYM
with author's name	ONYMOUS
written backwards	ANANYM
Namibia	SWAZA
capital	WINDHOEK
national	
National Board for Prices and Incomes	PIB
National Book League	NBL
National Broadcasting Company	NBC
National Bureau of Standards	NBS
National Cash Register Company	NCR
National Coal Board	NCB
National Enterprise Board	NEB
National Exhibition Centre	NEC
National Farmers' Union	NFU
National Fire Service	NFS
National Front	NF
National Graphical Association	NGA
National Health	
—Insurance	NHI
—Service	NHS
National Incomes Commission	NIC, NICKY
National Insurance	NI
National Opinion Poll	NOP
National Physical Laboratory	NPL
National Portrait Gallery	NPG
National Rifle Association	NRA
National Trust (for Scotland)	NT(S)
National Union of	
—Journalists	NUJ
—Mineworkers	NUM
—Railwaymen	NUR
—Seamen	NUS
—Students	NUS
—Teachers	NUT
National University of Ireland	NUI
National Youth Orchestra	NYO
naturalists	(see **biology**)
Navy	RN
Naval Reserve Decoration	NRD
	(see also **sailor**)
Nepal	
capital	KAT(H)MANDU
coin	
—unit	PAISA
—100 paisa	RUPEE
nerve	
acting automatically	AUTONOMOUS
	REFLEX
all nerves except	
central nervous	
system	
PERIPHERAL NERVOUS SYSTEM	
axon of nerve-cell	NERVE-FIBRE

brain and spinal cord	CENTRAL NERVOUS SYSTEM CNS	dorsal root	POSTERIOR ROOT
		external sheath	NEURILEMMA NEUROLEMMA
branching process	DENDRITE, DENDRON	fibre carrying impulse	AXON
bundle of		flat area of nerve	
—nerve fibres	TRACT	tissue	NEURAL PLATE
connecting centres	COMMISSURE	gap in nerve sheath	NODE OF RANVIER
—nerves	FASCIC(U)LE, FINICULUS	group of nerve cells	GANGLION
	GIANT FIBRE	in or controlling	
carrying		—arm	BRACHIAL, MEDIAN
—instructions for			RADIAL, ULNAR
movement	MOTOR	—arterioles	VASOMOTORA
—sensations		—back	COCCYGEAL, LUMBAR
from brain	DEFERENT, EFFERENT		SACRAL
to		—balance	VESTIBULAR
—brain	AFFERENT	—blood vessels	CONSTRICTOR, DILATOR
—central nervous		—breathing	PNEUMOGASTRIC, VAGUS
system	SENSORY	—calf	SURAL
cell	NEURON(E)	—chest	INTERCOSTAL, THORACIC
—body	CYTON	—digestive organs	PNEUMOGASTRIC
—connected with			VAGUS
receptor	SENSORY NERVE-CELL	—ear	AUDITORY, ACOUSTIC, OTIC
	SENSORY NEURON(E)	—eye	OPTIC, OPHTHALMIC
—connection	SYNAPSE	—eye muscles	ABDUCENT, OCULOMOTOR
—in retina	CONE, ROD		TROCHLEAR
—which		—face	(TRI)FACIAL, TRIGEMINAL
becomes nerve-cell	NEUROBLAST	—hearing	AUDITORY
sheathes nerve-fibres	SCHWANN CELL	—heart-beat	VAGUS
central nervous system	CNS	—jaw	MANDIBULAR, MAXILLARY
centre	GANGLION		TRIFACIAL, TRIGEMINAL
—controlling appetite	APPESTAT	—leg	FEMORAL, PERONEAL
channel holding spinal			SCIATIC, TIBIAL
cord	NEURAL CHANNEL	—lungs	PNEUMOGASTRIC, VAGUS
chemical messenger	NEUROTRANSMITTER	—neck	ACCESSORY, CERVICAL
	NEUROHUMOUR	—pharynx	GLOSSOPHARYNGEAL
connection	SYNAPSE	—shoulder	ACCESSORY
constriction in		—scalp	TRIFACIAL, TRIGEMINAL
nerve-fibre	NODE OF RANVIER	—skull	CRANIAL NERVE
core of nerve fibre	AXIS CYLINDER	—smell	OLFACTORY
cranial nerves		—spinal cord	SPINAL NERVE
—1. smell	OLFACTORY	—stomach	PNEUMOGASTRIC
—2. vision	OPTIC		SOLAR PLEXUS, VAGUS
—3. eye movements	OCULOMOTOR	—thigh	SCIATIC
—4. eye movements	TROCHLEAR	—tongue	HYPOGLOSSAL
—5. eye movements	ABDUCENT	inflammation	NEURITIS
—6. face and scalp, jaw	TRIFACIAL	intersection of nerves	CHIASM(A)
	TRIGEMINAL	large-diameter nerve	GIANT FIBRE
—7. face movements	FACIAL	mass of axons and dendrites	NEUROPIL
—8. acoustic		membranes covering	
balance	VESTIBULAR	central nervous system	
hearing	COCHLEAR		PIA-ARACHNOID MEMBRANES
—9. back of mouth	GLOSSOPHARYNGEAL	—inner	PIA MATER
—10. digestion, heart, etc	VAGUS	—outer	ARACHNOID
—11. neck and shoulder		motor	
muscles	ACCESSORY	—nerve root	ANTERIOR ROOT
—12. tongue	HYPOGLOSSAL		MOTOR ROOT, VENTRAL ROOT

—nerves to smooth muscles	AUTONOMIC NERVOUS SYSTEM
nerve-ending	EFFECTOR, RECEPTOR
nerve-fibre bundle uniting nerve centres	COMMISSURE
nervous	
—illnesses	NEURASTHENIA NEOROPATHY, NEUROSIS
—tissue in embryo	NEURAL TISSUE
network of cells	PLEXUS
neuro-transmitter	ACETYL CHOLINE
organ at end of motor nerve	MOTOR ENDPLATE
pain in nerve	NEURALGIA
part of system producing immediate response	REFLEX ARC
parts of nerve	AXON, DENDRITE DENDRON MEDULLARY SHEATH MYELIN, (NEUR)AXON NEURILEMMA, NODE SYNAPSE, TERMINAL
peripheral nerve	SENSORY NERVE
raised edge of neural plate	NEURAL FOLD
ridge in neural plate	NEURAL CREST
reacting to	
—coarse stimuli	PROTOPATHIC
—small stimuli	EPICRITIC
region with special function	NERVE CENTRE
root	
—animal	DORSAL, VENTRAL
—human	ANTERIOR, POSTERIOR
—in spinal cord	NERVE ROOT
—motor nerve	MOTOR ROOT
—with sensory fibres	SENSORY ROOT
secreting	
—adrenalin	ADRENERGIC
—acetylcholine	CHOLINERGIC
serving	
—automatic muscles	AUTONOMIC SYSTEM
—involuntary muscles	SYMPATHETIC SYSTEM
sheath round nerve fibres	MYELIN SHEATH
study of origins of nervous system	NEUROGENETICS
strand of nerve tissue	NERVE CORD
substance	
—forming nerve-sheaths	MYALIN
—secreted at nerve-ends	ACETYLCHOLINE, ACH ADRENALIN(E)
supporting tissue	(NEURO)GLIA

system	AUTONOMIC, CENTRAL (ORTHO)SYMPATHETIC PARASYMPATHETIC PERIPHERAL
—controlling movement	MOTARIUM
—in invertebrates	NERVE NET
—sensory	SENSORIUM
theory of discrete nerve-cells	NEURONE THEORY
tissue	
—binding nerves	PERINEURIUM
—carrying impulses	NERVE FIBRE
trifacial	TRIGEMINAL
tumour of nerve tissue	NEUROMA
vagus	PNEUMOGASTRIC NERVE
Netherlands	NL
Netherlands Antilles	NT
	(*see also* **Dutch**)
New	
New Church	NC
New England	NE
New English	
—Bible	NEB
—Dictionary	NED
New Jersey	CALF, NJ
New Orleans	NO
New Providence	NP
New Smoking Material	NSM
New South Wales	NSW
New Testament	NT
New York	BIG APPLE, GOTHAM, NY
—City	NYC
district	BOWERY, BRONX HARLEM, MANHATTAN QUEENS
opera	MET
New Version	NV
New Zealand	NZ
including: Maori	
abalone	PAUA, PAWA
aborigine	MAORI
ancestral ornament	(HEI) TIKI
animal	TAEPO, TAIPO
basket	KIT(E)
biological region	ORNITHOGAEA
bird	APTERYX, BELL-BIRD, BUSH-WREN HONEY-BIRD, HUIA, KABOB, KIWI KOKAKO, MAKO, MAORI-HEN NOTORNIS, OWL-PARROT PARSON-BIRD, POAKA RIFLE(MAN)-BIRD TAKAHE(A), WEKA, WRY-BILL
blood-money	UTU
boy	TAMA
canoe	WAKA

capital	WELLINGTON	—bill	GLORY-PEA
chief	RANGATIRA	parson-bird	POE(-BIRD)
cloth	PAR(R)AMATTA		POY(-BIRD), TUI
club	MERE, MERI	penguin	KORORA
currant bread	BROWNIE	plant	FLAX-BUSH, FLAX-LILY
dock labourer	SEAGULL		VEGETABLE SHEEP
eel	TUNA	political union	ANZUS
emblem	KOWHIA	requital	UTU
extinct bird	MOA	resin	KAURI-GUM
feast	KAIKAI	Rugby team	ALL BLACKS
fertility symbol	HEI TIKI	settlement	PA(H)
fish	HIKU, MORWONG	settler	SHAGROON
	PAGROSOMUS	shellfish	PAUA, PAWA
	SNAPPER, TRUMPETER		TOHEROA
flax	PHORMIUM	shrub	HOHERIA, KARO, KIEKIE
food	KAI(-KAI)		KOWHAI, MANOAO
fort	PA(H)		PLAGIANTHUS, TUTU
funeral	TANGI	soldier	ANZAC
glory pea	KOWHAI, PARROT-BEAK	spear	TAIAHA
	PARROT-BILL, PARROT-JAW	spider	KATIPO, NIGHT-STINGER
good health!	KIA-ORA	stockade	PA(H)
grass	TOI TOI	stone figurine	(HEI) TIKI
hedge	KARO, KOHUHU	storage pit	RUA
house	WHARE	sweet potato	KUMARA
husband	TANGATA	tattooing	MOKO
hut	WHARE	tea	MANUKA
image	(HEI) TIKI	thrush	TURNAGRA
Indian corn	KANGA	thylacine	TIGER-WOLF
laburnum	KOWHIA	tree	HINAU, HINO, HINOU, KARAKA
Land of Long White Cloud	AOTEAROA		KAURI(-PINE), MANUKA, MAKOMAKO
language	MAORI		MIRO, NGAIO, PELU, RATA, RIMU, TAWA
lavatory	DUNNY		TITOKI, TOTARA, TUTU, WINE-BERRY
leaves used for tea	MANUKA	war-dance	HAKA
lily	PHORMIUM	welcome!	HAERE MAI
lizard	HATTERIA, SPHENODON	white man	PAKEHA
	TUATARA, TUATERA	wife	WAHINE
locust	WETA	woman	WAHINE
man	TANGATA	work	MAHI
Maori greeting	HONGI	youth	TAMA
measure of beer	HANDLE	zoological realm	NOTOGAEA
meeting-place	MARAE	**newspaper**	
mourning	TANGI	Australia	THE AUSTRALIAN
mysterious power	MANA		SUN NEWS HERALD
native	MAORI	Canada	TORONTO GLOBE AND MAIL
neck pendant	HEI TIKI	China	PEOPLE'S DAILY
New Zealand	AOTEAROA	Egypt	AL NOOR, EL AKHBAR
New Zealander	DIGGER, KIWI	France	LE FIGARO, LE MONDE
noble	RANGATIRA		LE PARISIEN, LIBERATION
nose-rubbing as greeting	HONGI	Germany	BERLINER ZEITUNG
original settler	SHAGROON		BILD AM SONNTAG, BILD ZEITUNG
oven	HA(A)NGI		DIE WELT
owl	MOPEHAWK, MOPOKE		FRANKFURTER ALLEGEMEINE ZEITUNG
	MOREPORK, PEHO, RURU	Great Britain	
owl-parrot	KAKAPO, STRI(N)GOPS	—national	DAILY EXPRESS, DAILY MAIL
palm	NIKAU		DAILY MIRROR, DAILY TELEGRAPH
parrot	KAKA(-BEAK), KAKA-BILL, KEA		FINANCIAL TIMES, GUARDIAN

	INDEPENDENT, MORNING STAR
	SPORTING LIFE, STAR, SUN
	TIMES, TODAY
Sunday	INDEPENDENT ON SUNDAY
	MAIL ON SUNDAY
	MIRROR, NEWS OF THE WORLD
	OBSERVER, PEOPLE
	SUNDAY EXPRESS, SUNDAY SPORT
	SUNDAY TELEGRAPH
	SUNDAY TIMES
—provincial	BIRMINGHAM POST
	BIRMINGHAM EVENING MAIL
	DAILY POST, EAST ANGLIAN DAILY
	EASTERN DAILY PRESS
	EASTERN MORNING NEWS
	EVENING CHRONICLE
	EXPRESS AND STAR, LIVERPOOL ECHO
	LONDON EVENING STANDARD
	MANCHESTER EVENING NEWS
	NORTHERN ECHO, STAR
	THE JOURNAL
	WESTERN DAILY PRESS
	WESTERN MAIL, YORKSHIRE POST
Finland	ILTALEHTI
Germany	BERLINER ZEITUNG
	BILD AM SONNTAG, BILD ZEITUNG
	DIE WELT
	FRANKFURTER ALLGEMEINE ZEITUNG
India	TIMES OF INDIA
Iran	ABRAR
Iraq	BAGHDAD OBSERVER, EL QADISIYAH
Ireland	BELFAST TELEGRAPH
	IRISH NEWS, IRISH TIMES
Italy	CORRIERE DELLA SERA
	LA REPUBBLICA, LA STAMPA
Japan	ASAHI SHIMBUN
	MAINICHI SHIMBUN
	YOMIURI SHIMBUN
Pakistan	THE NATION
Russia	IZVESTIA, MOSCOW NEWS
	PRAVDA
Scotland	DAILY RECORD
	EVENING TIMES
	GLASGOW HERALD
	PRESS AND JOURNAL, SCOTSMAN
South Africa	BEEL, DAILY MAIL
Spain	EL PAIS
Syria	AL-THAWRA
Switzerland	DER BUND
USA	CHICAGO SUN-TIMES
	CHICAGO TRIBUNE, HERALD-TRIBUNE
	LOS ANGELES TIMES
	NEW YORK DAILY NEWS
	NEW YORK TIMES
	WALL STREET JOURNAL
	WASHINGTON POST

Nicaragua	NIC
capital	MANAGUA
coin	CENTAVO, CORDOBA
nickname	COGNOMEN, SOBRIQUET
Allen, G O	GUBBY
Armstrong, Louis	SATCHMO
Basie, William	COUNT, THE CHIEF
	THE KID FROM RED BANK
Bonaparte, Napoleon	BONEY, NAP
Cole, Nat(haniel)	KING
Cromwell, Oliver	NOLL
Durante, Jimmy	SCHNOZZLE
Eisenhower, Dwight	IKE
Elizabeth I	CYNTHIA, DARK LADY
	GLORIANA, GOOD QUEEN BESS
	VIRGIN QUEEN
Ellington, Edward K	DUKE
Gladstone, William	GOM, GRAND OLD MAN
Great Britain	JOHN BULL
	PERFIDIOUS ALBION
Hawkins, Coleman	THE BEAN, HAWK
Heseltine, Michael	TARZAN
Higgins, Alex	HURRICANE
Hines, Earl	FATHA
Holiday, Billie	LADY DAY
Howe, Sir Geoffrey	MOGADON MAN
IBM	BIG BLUE
Kinnock, Neil	WELSH WINDBAG
Laye, Evelyn	BOO
Lloyd George, David	WELSH WIZARD
Macmillan, Harold	SUPERMAC
McCartney, Paul	MACCA
McEnroe, John	SUPERBRAT
Morton, Ferdinand	JELLY ROLL
Nicklaus, Jack	GOLDEN BEAR
Nixon, Richard	TRICKY DICKY
Norman, Greg	GREAT WHITE SHARK
Parker, Charlie	BIRD
Skinner, Dennis	BEAST OF BOLSOVER
Smith, Willie	THE LION
Stalin	UNCLE JOE
Sutherland, Joan	LA STUPENDA
Thatcher, Mrs M	IRON LADY
Tormé, Mel	VELVET FOG
Trevino, Lee	SUPERMEX
United States	UNCLE SAM
Vaughan, Sarah	DIVINE SARAH, SASSY
Wellington, Duke of	IRON DUKE
Wilberforce, Samuel	SOAPY SAM
Wodehouse, P G	PLUM
	(*see also* **boxing, football**)
Niger	RN
capital	NIAMEY
coin	FRANC
Nigeria	WAN
capital	LAGOS

coin	
—unit	KOBO
—100 kobo	NAIRA
nine	IX, THETA
based	NONARY
Christmas presents	LADIES
combining form	ENNEA-, NON-
dancers	MORRIS MEN
days	ENNEATIC
—of devotion	NOVENA
days'...	WONDER
eyes	LAMPREY
groups	ENNEAD, NON-, NONET(TE)
	NONETTO, NONUPLET
	NOVENARY
having 9	
—angles	ENNEAGONAL, NONAGONAL
—columns	ENNEASTYLE
—faces	ENNEAHEDRON
—petals	ENNEAPETALOUS
—pistils	ENNEAGYNIAN
	ENNEAGYNOUS
—sides	ENNEAGONAL
	NONAGONAL
—stamens	ENNEANDRIAN
	ENNEANDROUS
—styles	ENNEAGYNIAN, ENNEAGYNOUS
hundred	CM, SAMPI
inches	SPAN
iron	NIBLICK
lives	CAT
magistrates of Athens	ARCHON
Muses	(see **Muses**)
ninth	ENNEATIC
orders of angels	ARCHANGELS, ANGELS
	CHERUBIM, DOMINIONS
	POWERS, PRINCIPALITIES
	SERAPHIM, THRONES, VIRTUES
pins	SKITTLES
points of...	LAW
times	ENNEATIC
worthies	ALEXANDER, ARTHUR
	CHARLEMAGNE, DAVID
	GODFREY, HECTOR, JUDAS
	JULIUS, JOSHUA
yearly	NOVENNIAL
nineteenth	
hole	BAR, CLUBHOUSE
pertaining to nineteen	DECENNOVAL
ninety	N, Q, XC
having ninety faces	ENNEACONTAHEDRAL
ninetieth	NONAGESIMAL
ninety-nine	IC
—beautiful names	ALLAH
ninety thousand	N, Q
ninety years old	NONAGENARIAN

nobles	
Anglo-Saxon	A(E)THELING, ALDERMAN
	EALDORMAN, EORL
	(E)SQUIRE, THEGN, THANE
	VAVASOUR, VALVASOOR
Athenian	EUPATRID
Austrian	HERZOG
—count(ess)	GRAF(IN)
Celtic	TAOISEACH
continental	COUNT
count palatine	PALSGRAVE
eldest son of earl	LORD
English	BARON(ESS), BARONET
	COUNTESS, DUCHESS, DUKE, EARL
	KNIGHT, LORD, MARCHIONESS
	MARQUESS, MARQUIS
	VISCOUNT(ESS)
Etruscan prince	LUCOMO
French	
—dauphin's wife	DAUPHINE(SS)
—king's eldest son	DAUPHIN
—knight	CHEVALIER
—marchioness	MARQUISE
—mediaeval	VIDAME
feudal lord	SUZERAIN
German	BURGRAVE, BURGRAVINE
	EDEL, HERTZOG, (LAND)GRAF
	LANDGRAVE, LANDGRAVINE
	MARGRAVE, MARGRAVINE
—count(ess)	GRAF(IN)
—prince	ELECTOR
—young	JUNKER
Indian prince	GAEKWAR, (MAHA)RAJAH
	NAWAB, NIZAM
Irish	TAOISE(A)CH
Italian	
—marchioness	MARCHESA
—marquis	MARCHESE
Japanese	DAIMIO, KUGE
knight leading into	
battle	BANNERET
Moldavian prince	GOSPODAR, HOSPODAR
Moroccan prince	SHEREEF, SHERIF
Moslem	
—lord	OMRAH
—prince	AMEER, AMIR, EMEER
	EMIR, NAWAB
—princess	BEGUM
New Zealand	RANGATIRA
noble man	GALAHAD, KNIGHT
	MAGNATE
Norse	JARL
Persian prince	MIRZA
Polish	SAROSTA
Portuguese	FIDALGO, DOM
—prince	INFANTE

—princess	INFANTA	island	HOLMEN
Prussian	JUNKER	lake	S(J)O, VANN, VATN
Roman	PATRICIAN	language	LANDSMA(A)L, NORSE
Russian	BOYAR(D)		NYNORSK
son of duke or		measure (²/₃ acre)	MORGEN
marquis	LORD	mountain	BERG, FJELL(ET), VARRE
Scottish	BARONETESS	—hut	S(A)ETER
Spanish	ADELANTADO, HIDALGA	—pasture	S(A)ETER
	HIDALGO, DON, DONA	parliament	STORT(H)ING
	GRANDEE	peak	HO
—prince	INFANTE	reindeer skin boots	FINN(E)SKO, FINSKO
—princess	INFANTA	river	ELV(A)
Swedish count(ess)	GRAF(IN)	sea	
Venetian	DOGE, MAGNIFICO	—loch	FIORD, FJORD
Wallachian prince	GOSPODAR, HOSPODAR	—monster	KRAKEN
	VOIVODE	toast	SKOAL
wife of		upland meadow	SAETER
—earl	COUNTESS	Upper House	LAGT(H)ING
—marquis	MARQUISE, MARCHIONESS	valley	DAL
	(*see also* **leader**)	waterfall	FOSS
		whirlpool	MAELSTROM
Norse		wooden church	STAVE-CHURCH
chieftain	JARL, YARL		(*see also* **Norse, Scandinavian**)
minstrel	SKALD		
myths	EDDAS, VOLUSPAS	**nose**	
pirate	VIKING	membrane	SCHNEIDERIAN MEMBRANE
ship	LONGSHIP	parts of nose	ALA, DORSUM
warrior	BERSERK(ER)		NARES, SEPTUM
	(*see also* **mythology**)	passage to	
north	N	—mouth	INTERNAL NARES
North Africa	MAGHREB, NA	—surface	EXTERNAL NARES
	(*see also* **Africa**)	shape of nose	
North America	NA, US, USA	—curved	AQUILINE
	(*see also* **America**)	—high-bridged	ROMAN
North British	NB	—hooked	AQUILINE
North Pole	NP	—long and straight	GRECIAN
Northern French	NF	—short and flat	PUG (NOSE)
Northern Ireland	NI	—turned up	RETROUSSE, SNUB
Northern Territory	NT	slang	CONK, HOOTER
Norway	N		PROBOSCIS, SCHNOZZLE
airline	NAL	**Nova Scotia**	ACADIA, NS
bay	BOGEN, BUKT(EN)	capital	HALIFAX
	VAG, VIK	island	CAPE BRETON
bread and butter	SMOR(RE)BORD	**nuclear reactors**	ADVANCED GAS-COOLED
cape (headland)	KAPP, NES, ODDE		AGR
capital	OSLO		BOILING WATER, BWR
coins	KR, KRONE, ORE		GRAPHITE-MODERATED
country dance	HALLING		(FAST) BREEDER
dance tune	SPRING		MAGNOX, POWER REACTOR
dog	ELKHOUND		PRESSURISED WATER
forest cat	SKOGCATT		PRODUCTION REACTOR
glacier	BRE(EN), FONN, JOKULEN		PROPULSION REACTOR
harbour	HAMN, HAVN		THERMAL REACTOR
herring	SILD	**numbers**	(*see* **mathematics**)
hill	HAUG	**nut**	
hors d'oeuvres	SMOR(RE)BORD	acajou	CASHEW
hut	SAETER	African	COLA, KOLA

American	PECAN	monkey-nut	PEA-NUT
—horse chestnut	BUCK-EYE	nicker	BONDUC, MOLUCCA BEAN
—tiger-nut	CHUFA	palm	BETEL, COCONUT, COHUNE-NUT
—white walnut	BUTTERNUT		COQUILLA, COROZO-NUT
Anacard	CASHEW		IVORY-NUT
Arachis	(*see* pea-nut *below*)	pea-nut	ARACHIS, MONKEY-NUT
areca	BETEL		EARTH-NUT, EARTH-PEA
Asiatic	PISTACHIO		PIG-NUT
Australian	QUANDONG-NUT	pecan	HICKORY
	QUEENSLAND-NUT	Philippines	PILI(-NUT)
beechnuts	MAST	sumach	PISTACHIO
betel	ARECA	tropical	BEN(-NUT), CARAP-NUT
bonduc	MOLUCCA BEAN, NICKER BEAN		CASHEW(-NUT), CRAB-NUT
Brazil	BERTHOLETTIA	true chestnut	SPANISH CHESTNUT
	BRAZIL-NUT, COQUILLA	used in game	PHILOPOENA, PHILIPPINA
	PARA-NUT, SAPUCAIA		PHILIPPINE
calthrop	WATER CHESTNUT	water chestnut	CALTHROP
cashew	ACAJOU, ANACARD	West Indian peanut	PINDA
Castanea	CHESTNUT	**nymph(s)**	
conker	HORSE-CHESTNUT	apple	MAELID
crab-nut	CAROB	ash	MELIC NYMPHS
cream-nut	BRAZIL	Buddhist	YAKSHI
double	COCO-DE-MER	Milton's	LIBERTY
earthnut (tuber)	ARNUT, PIGNUT	Mohammedan	HOURI
	EARTH CHESTNUT	mountain	EGERIA, OREAD(S)
earth-nut	(*see* pea-nut *below*)		OREAD(ES)
East Indian	KOKUM, MARKING-NUT	Nysaean	HYADES
European sedge root	CHUFA, TIGER-NUT	ocean	OCEANID(ES)
ground-nut	(*see* pea-nut *below*)	river	NAIAD(ES)
Guiana	BUTTERNUT, SOUARI	Russian (water)	RUSALKA
hard-shelled	ALMOND, BRAZIL	sea	AMPHITRITE, CALYPSO
hazel	COB, FILBERT		DORIS, GALATEA, HESIONE
hickory	PECAN		NEREID(S), SCYLLA, TETHYS, THETIS
Indian	ILLIPE, ILLUPI	spring	ARETHUSA
Juglans	WALNUT	water	ARETHUSA, CYRENE, HYDRIAD(ES)
large almond	JORDAN ALMOND		ONDINE, UNDINE(S)
	SPANISH ALMOND	wood	DRYAD(S)(ES), HAMADRYAD, LOTIS

O

observatory
including: optical telescopes
radio telescopes
lens
—nearest eye | EYEPIECE
—nearest object | OBJECTIVE
network of
—linked radio telescopes | MERLIN
—wires in eyepiece | GRATICULE
radio telescope | PARABOLIC REFLECTOR
RADIO INTERFEROMETER
sites
—America | ALLEGHENY, FORT DAVIS
GREENBANK, KITT PEAK
LICK, MOUNT HOPKINS
MOUNT PALOMAR, MOUNT WILSON
NEW MEXICO, YERKES
—Australia | MOUNT STROMLO
SIDING SPRINGS
—Canada | RICHMOND HILL
—Canary Islands | LA PALMA
—Chile | CERRO TOLOLO, LA CILLA
—England | CAMBRIDGE, HERSTMONCEUX
JODRELL BANK, KEW
—France | HAUTE PROVENCE
MEUDON, NICE
—Germany | POTSDAM
—Hawaii | MAUNA KEA
—in space | HUBBLE
—Puerto Rico | ARECIBO
—Russia | NAUCHNY
—Sweden | STJAERNEBERG
telescope
—radio | ARECIBO, CAMBRIDGE
—reflecting
100" | HOOKER
120" | LICK
158" | CERRO TOLOLO
200" | HALE
—refracting
33" | MEUDON
36" | LICK
40" | YERKES
—types | CASSEGRAIN(IAN)
CATHETOMETER, COLLIMATOR
COUDE SYSTEM, FINDER
GALILEAN, GREGORIAN
MAKSUTOV, NEW TECHNOLOGY, NTT

NEWTONIAN, OPTICAL, RADIO
REFLECTING, REFRACTING
oceanography
area of
—Earth covered by
oceans etc | HYDROSPACE, HYDROSPHERE
WATER HEMISPHERE
—open water in ice | POLYNA
—sandbanks | SHOAL
—sea adjoining land
mass | CONTINENTAL SHELF
average level of sea
over a period | MEAN SEA LEVEL
backward flow of waves | BACKWASH
bay | BIGHT, COVE
—Africa | BIGHT OF BENIN
BIGHT OF BIAFRA, FALSE BAY
GULF OF ADEN, GULF OF GUINEA
—Alaska | BRISTOL BAY, COOK INLET
GULF OF ALASKA
NORTON SOUND
—Argentina | BAHIA BIANCA
BAHIA GRANDE
GULF OF SAN JORGE
GULF OF SAN MATIAS
—Australia | EXMOUTH GULF
GREAT AUSTRALIAN BIGHT
GULF OF CARPENTARIA
JOSEPH BONAPARTE GULF
KING SOUND, MORETON BAY
SHARK BAY, SPENCER GULF
VAN DIEMEN GULF, VINCENT GULF
—Burma | GULF OF MARTABAN
—Canada | AMUNDSEN GULF
BAY OF FUNDY, CHALEUR BAY
CORONATION GULF, FOXE BASIN
GULF OF BOOTHIA
GULF OF ST LAWRENCE
HAMILTON INLET, HUDSON BAY
JAMES BAY, PLACENTIA BAY
UNGAVA BAY
VISCOUNT MELVILLE SOUND
—Central America | GULF OF CAMPECHE
GULF OF HONDURAS
GULF OF MEXICO
GULF OF PANAMA
—Chile | GULF OF GUAFO
GULF OF PENAS
—China | GULF OF TONKING
—Colombia | GULF OF DARIEN
—Ecuador | GULF OF GUAYAQUIL
—England | LYME BAY, THE WASH
—France/Spain | BAY OF BISCAY
—Greenland | BAFFIN BAY
—Indonesia | GULF OF CAMBAY
GULF OF KUTCH

	GULF OF MANNAR
	GULF OF PAPUA
—Iran	PERSIAN GULF
—Ireland	BANTRY BAY, DONEGAL BAY
	DUNDALK BAY
—Libya	GULF OF SIRTE
—New Zealand	BAY OF PLENTY
	HAURAKI GULF
—North America	CHESAPEAKE BAY,
	GOLDEN GATE
	GULF OF CALIFORNIA
—Peru	BAY OF SECHURA
—Scandinavia	GULF OF BOTHNIA
	GULF OF FINLAND
—Siberia	GULF OF TARTARY
—Thailand	GULF OF SIAM
—Venezuela	GULF OF MARACAIBO
	GULF OF PARIA
	GULF OF VENEZUELA
—Wales	CARDIGAN BAY

between low-water
mark and edge of
continental shelf SUBLITTORAL
bight (*see* bay *above*)
broad sea inlet SOUND
calcareous mud on
bottom GLOBIGERINA OOZE
calendar of tidal
movements TIDE TABLE
changes in coastline
as a result of changes
in sea-level EUSTACY, EUSTASY
channel
—Africa MOCAMBIQUE CHANNEL
—Alaska BERING STRAIT
KOTZEBUE STRAIT
—Antarctica DRAKE PASSAGE
—between reef and
mainland LAGOON
—Britain BRISTOL CHANNEL
ENGLISH CHANNEL, FIRTH OF CLYDE
FIRTH OF FORTH, IRISH CHANNEL
LITTLE MINCH, MORAY FIRTH
NORTH CHANNEL, PENTLAND FIRTH
ST GEORGE'S CHANNEL, SOLENT
SOLWAY FIRTH, SOUTH MINCH
SPITHEAD, STRAITS OF DOVER
—Canada CUMBERLAND SOUND
DIXON ENTRANCE, FOXE CHANNEL
LANCASTER SOUND, HECATE STRAIT
HUDSON STRAIT
NORTHUMBERLAND CHANNEL
PRINCE REGENT INLET
STRAIT OF BELLE ISLE
STRAIT OF GEORGIA
—Central America YUCATAN CHANNEL

—Chile	STRAITS OF MAGELLAN
—China	STRAIT OF FORMOSA
—Falkland Islands	FALKLAND SOUND
—Greenland	DAVIS STRAIT
	DENMARK STRAIT
—in which tide runs	TIDEWAY
—India	EIGHT DEGREE CHANNEL
	NINE DEGREE CHANNEL
	PALK STRAIT
—Indonesia	TORRES STRAIT
—New Zealand	COOK STRAIT
	FOVEAUX STRAIT
—North America	FLORIDA STRAIT
	JUAN DE FUCA STRAIT
—Scandinavia	KATEGAT, SKAGERRAK
—Siberia	BERING STRAIT
—Spain	STRAITS OF GIBRALTAR
—Tasmania	BANKS STRAIT, BASS STRAIT
—Wales	MENAI STRAIT
—West Indies	WINDWARD PASSAGE

circular flow EDDY, WHIRLPOOL
coal from sediment on bottom SAPROPELITE
coastline
—cutting across general
structural
features DISCORDANT COAST(LINE)
—parallel to structural
features CONCORDANT COAST(LINE)
LONGITUDINAL COAST(LINE)
PACIFIC COAST(LINE)
cold sea-fog HAAR
coral reef separated
from land by lagoon FRINGING REEF
current
—equatorial CROMWELL CURRENT
EQUATORIAL COUNTER CURRENT
INDIAN COUNTER CURRENT
MONSOON DRIFT
NORTH EQUATORIAL CURRENT
SOUTH EQUATORIAL CURRENT
—flowing
across another CROSSCURRENT
in opposite direction to
—another COUNTERCURRENT
—surface current EDDY, UNDERTOW
out from shore from
return of waves RIPTIDE
—in channel TIDEWAY
—northern ALASKA CURRENT
CALIFORNIA CURRENT
CANARIES CURRENT
GULF STREAM, KURO SHIO
LABRADOR CURRENT
NORTH ATLANTIC DRIFT
NORTH PACIFIC DRIFT
OYA SHIO

—slow-moving	DRIFT
—southern	AGULHAS CURRENT
	BENGUELA CURRENT
	BRAZIL CURRENT
	CAPE HORN CURRENT
	EAST AUSTRALIAN CURRENT
	EL NINO, MOZAMBIQUE CURRENT
	PERU CURRENT
	WEST AUSTRALIAN CURRENT
	WEST WIND DRIFT
deep	
—channel in sea floor	TRENCH
—part of	
harbour, river, etc	CHANNEL
	ROADS(TEAD)
sea	ABYSS, GULF
—sea vehicles	(*see* undersea *below*)
deposits	
—inorganic	RED CLAY
—mud with	
iron	
—oxide	RED MUD
—sulphide	BLUE MUD
potassium	GREEN MUD, GREENSAND
—ooze	
shells	
—foraminifera	GLOBIGERINA OOZE
—molluscs	PTEROPOD OOZE
—radiolaria	RADIOLARIAN OOZE
—diatoms	DIATOMIC OOZE
—sediment	SAPROPEL
depression between waves	TROUGH
depth-sounder	SONAR
depths	SOUNDING
—highest level	LITTORAL
—intermediate	PELAGIC
—deepest	ABYSSAL
—less than 200m	NERITIC
—over 200m	OCEANIC
—200-1800m	BATHYAL
—below 6000m	HADAL
difference between	
high and low tides	TIDAL RANGE
direction of flow	SET
distance travelled by	
waves without	
obstruction	FETCH
drifting organisms	PLANKTON, SESTON
earthquake at sea-bed	SEAQUAKE
excrement of sea-birds	GUANO
fast tidal current	RACE
flat-topped submarine	
mountain	GUYOT
floating	
—block of ice	GROWLER, ICEBERG
—organisms	PLANKTON, SESTON

—sheet of ice	DRIFT ICE, FLOE
	PACK ICE
flora and fauna on	
sea bed	BENTHOS
formation of lake or bay	EMBAYMENT
frothing water	WHITE-WATER
gulf	(*see* **bay**)
having equal tide	
movements	COTIDAL
highest	
—level of tide	HIGH-WATER MARK
—tide	SPRING TIDE
hole through which tide	
forces air and water	BLOW-HOLE
ice	
—cap extending into sea	BARRIER
—floating	FLOE, GROWLER
	DRIFT ICE, ICEBERG
	PACK ICE
inflow of tide	FLOOD
instrument	
—measuring depth	ECHO-SOUNDER
	FATHOMETER, SONAR
—recording tides	MARIGRAPH
island	
—coral	ATOLL
—in river	AIT, AYOT
—low	CAY, KEY
—rocky	SKERRY
—Scottish	INCH
islet near coast	STACK
lagoon	HAFF
land adjoining sea	BEACH, COAST
	LITTORAL, SHORE
	STRAND
—US	TIDEWATER
large	
—bay	BIGHT, GULF
—surge of water	SWELL
layer(s) of	
—sediment with bands	
of clay or silt	VARVE
—water	STRATUM(STRATA)
lines on map of	
equal depth	ISOBATH
living	
—at moderate depths	PELAGIC
—near sea bottom	DEMERSAL
long	
—narrow trench in	
sea-floor	DEEP
—surge of water	SWELL
lowest	
—level of tides	LOW-WATER MARK
—tide	NEAP TIDE
mark left by highest tide	TIDEMARK

mean level between high and low tides	SEA LEVEL
measurement of depth	BATHYMETRY SOUNDING
mouth of river	ESTUARY
movement of	
—debris along coast by tidal action	LONGSHORE DRIFT
—surface water	(OCEAN) CURRENT SWELL, TIDE
caused by	
—earthquake	TSUNAMI
—ground tremor	GROUNDSWELL
—wind	GROUNDSWELL
mud-flat	SLOB
narrow	
—area with strong tides	EURIPUS
—bay (Orkney)	VOE
—channel in sandbank	SWASH (CHANNEL)
—neck of land	ISTHMUS
—passage of water	
between land areas	INLET
through pack-ice	LEAD
—sea	
inlet	CREEK, FIORD, FIRTH FJORD, GEO, VOE
passage	CHANNEL, GUT, KYLE SOUND, STRAIT
—tongue of sand or gravel	
attached to land	SPIT
connecting islands	TOMBOLO
not attached to land	BAR, SANDBANK
ocean floor (3500-5500m)	DEEP-SEA PLAIN
oceanographer	
—American	CROMWELL, EWING, HEEZEN HESS, MAURY, VOORHIS
—British	SWALLOW
oceans	
—modern	ARCTIC, ANTARCTIC NORTH ATLANTIC, NORTH PACIFIC SOUTH ATLANTIC, SOUTH PACIFIC INDIAN
—old	IAPETUS, TETHYS
open water in sea-ice	POLYNA
organisms in sea	
—floating	PLANKTON, SESTON
in Polar regions	PARMALES
—in reach of sunlight	PHOTOBENTHOS
—on the	
bottom	BENTHOS
surface	NEUSTON
—swimming	NEKTON
outflow of tide	EBB
passage	
—connecting two bodies of water	SOUND
—separating island from mainland	SOUND
period of no tidal movement	SLACK WATER
periodic rise and fall of sea	TIDE
pertaining to temperature and salinity	THERMOHALINE
pillar of rock in sea	STACK
plants living on sea-bottom	PHYTOBENTHOS
reclaimed land	POLDER
regular movement of sea surface	SWELL
ridge of	
—rocks	
just below the surface	LEDGE, SHELF, SHOAL
on seabed	REEF
—sand	
extending into sea	SPIT
in sea or river	SANDBANK, SANDBAR
rise and fall of sea	TIDE
rough sea caused by opposing tides or winds	RIPTIDE
rush of water up beach from breaking wave	SWASH
salt gradient	HALOCLINE
saltiness	SALINITY
sandbank formed by sea	DOWN
—under surface	BAR
sea	
—abounding in islands	ARCHIPELAGO
—adjoining coast (3 miles)	TERRITORIAL WATERS
—Africa	ARABIAN, RED
—Antarctic	ROSS, WEDDELL
—Arctic	BARENTS, BEAUFORT CHUKCHI, EAST SIBERIAN GREENLAND, KARA, LAPTEV LINCOLN, WHITE
—Asia	BERING, EAST CHINA SEA OF JAPAN, SEA OF OKHOTSK SOUTH CHINA, YELLOW
—Australia	TASMAN
—basin (Scot.)	FLOW
—deep	THALASSIC
—Europe	ADRIATIC, AEGEAN BALTIC, IONIAN, IRISH LIGURIAN, MEDITERRANEAN NORTH, NORWEGIAN SEA OF CRETE, TYRRHENIAN
—fog	HAAR
—Indonesia	ARAFULA, BANDA FLORES, CELEBES, CORAL SAVU, SOLOMOM, SULU, TIMOR

—inland	ARAL, BLACK, CASPIAN
	DEAD, SEA OF AZOV
	SEA OF GALILEE
	SEA OF MARMARA
—main body of water	PELAGIC
—Malaysia	ANDAMAN
—mist	FRET
—monsters	(*see* **monsters**)
—over Continental Shelf	NERITIC
—visible from shore	OFFING
—West Indies	CARIBBEAN
sediment	
—deposited by turbidity	
current	TURBIDITE
—on bottom	SAPROPEL
series of waves	SURGE
ships	CHALLENGER, METEOR
slope from continental	
shelf to ocean	
floor	CONTINENTAL SLOPE
small	
—bay	COVE
—iceberg	GROWLER, CALF
—inlet	CREEK
—plankton	SESTON
—ridge on sand produced	
by wind or wave	RIPPLE MARK
—wave	RIPPLE
US	RIFFLE
—whirlpool	EDDY
spread of sea over land	TRANSGRESSION
strait	SOUND
—connecting two	
bodies of water	NARROW(S)
—Scotland	KYLE
	(*see also* channel *above*)
structure built to	
protect coast	BREAKWATER, GROIN
	GROYNE, JETTY, MOLE
	PIER, SEAWALL
strong current	RACE, RIPTIDE
study of	
—bodies of water	HYDROGRAPHY
—distribution of water	HYDROLOGY
swimming organisms	NEKTON, NEUSTON
tidal	
—eddy	MAELSTROM
—estuary	CREEK
—flood	BORE, EAGRE
—movement affected by	
moon	LUNITIDAL
—race (Scot.)	ROOST, SWELCHIE
—wave	
caused by earthquake	TSUNAMI
in estuary	BORE, EAGRE
tornado at sea	WATERSPOUT

undercurrent	
—carrying sediment	TURBIDITY CURRENT
—of returning wave	UNDERTOW
undersea	
—area bordering land	
mass	CONTINENTAL SHELF
—craft	BATHYSCAPHE, BATHYSPHERE
	BARYSPHERE, BENTHOSCOPE
	CENTROSPHERE, DIVING BELL
	MESOSCAPHE, SUBMARINE
—deep points in sea floor	
Java Trench	PLANET DEEP
Mariana(s) Trench	CHALLENGER DEEP
Peru-Chile Trench	BARTHOLOMEW DEEP
Philippines Trench	GALATHEA DEEP
Puerto Rico Trench	MILWAUKEE DEEP
South Sandwich Trench	METEOR DEEP
Tonga-Kermadec Trench	VITYAZ
—explorer	BARTON, BEEBE
	COUSTEAU, PICCARD
—mountain	GUYOT, SEAMOUNT
—ridge or reef	LEDGE, SHELF, SKERRY
—ridges	ALBATROSS PLATEAU
	AZORES-CAPE ST VINCENT RIDGE
	BROMLEY PLATEAU, COCOS RIDGE
	FAEROE RISE
	GRAND NEWFOUNDLAND BANKS
	HAWAIIAN RIDGE
	INDIAN-ANTARCTIC RIDGE
	KERGUELEN-GAUSSBERG RIDGE
	LACCADIVE-CHAGOS RIDGE
	MACQUARIE-BALLENY RIDGE
	MID-ATLANTIC RIDGE
	MID-INDIAN RISE
	PACIFIC-ANTARCTIC RIDGE
	PRINCE EDWARD-CROZET RIDGE
	WALVIS RIDGE
	WYVILL-THOMPSON RIDGE
—valley	BASIN, DEEP, TRENCH
—valleys	AGULHAS BASIN
	ALEUTIAN TRENCH, ARGENTINE BASIN
	BANDA TRENCH, BRAZILIAN BASIN
	CAPE BASIN, CAPE VERDE BASIN
	CAYMAN TRENCH
	CENTRAL PACIFIC BASIN
	EAST PACIFIC BASIN
	GREAT GLOBAL RIFT
	GUATEMALA TRENCH, GUINEA BASIN
	IDZU-BONIN TRENCH
	JAVA TRENCH, JAPAN TRENCH
	KERMODEC TRENCH, KURIL TRENCH
	MARIANA(S) TRENCH
	NEW BRITAIN TRENCH
	NEW HEBRIDES TRENCH
	NANSEI-SHOTO TRENCH
	NORTH PACIFIC BASIN

NORTH TRENCH
NORTH-EASTERN ATLANTIC BASIN
NORTH-WEST ATLANTIC BASIN
PALAU TRENCH, PUERTO RICO TRENCH
PERU-CHILE TRENCH
PHILIPPINE TRENCH, ROMANCHE TRENCH
RYUKYU TRENCH, SOLOMON TRENCH
SOUTH SANDWICH TRENCH
SOUTH-EASTERN ATLANTIC BASIN
SOUTH-EASTERN PACIFIC BASIN
SOUTH-WESTERN PACIFIC BASIN
SUNDA TRENCH
TONGA-KERMADEC TRENCH
YAP TRENCH

water
—content of Earth   HYDROSPACE
                   HYDROSPHERE
—overflowing on land
   at flood tide   TIDEWATER
wave
—broken on rock or shore   BREAKER
—following earthquake   TSUNAMI
—large   PURLER, SURGE
—long
   foaming   COMBER
   heavy   ROLLER
—very high   TIDAL WAVE
   in estuary   BORE, EAGRE
—white-topped   WHITE HORSE
whirlpool
—Scottish   ROOST, SWELCHIE
—small   EDDY
—strong   MAELSTROM
wide bay   BIGHT, GULF

old[1]
meaning: ancient
        archaic
        Biblical
        historical
        obsolete
'a' as a word   A-PER-SE
a little while ago   WHILE-ERE
abandon (stolen goods)   WAIVE
abate   VAIL
abdomen   WOMB
abide   WON
ability   ENGINE, INGINE
abjure   REN(A)Y, RENEY
able to
—be seen   VISIVE
—see   VISIVE
abode   INN, MANSION, WON
abounding   ENORMOUS
about 9 a.m.   UNDERN
abrupt   SQUAB
abscess   IMPOST(H)UME

absolute   MERE
absolve   ASSOIL
abstruse   EXQUISITE
abundance   COPY
abut   CONFINE
abyss   ABYSM
accept   ALLOW
acceptable   PLAUSIBLE
acclaim   VOICE
accomplice   COMPLICE, FEDDARY
accost   ABORD
account   ACCOMPT, NOTE
   —of daily transactions   EPHEMERIS
accumulate possessions   PURCHASE
accusation   TAX
accuse   ARGUE, REPROVE
accustom   OCCASION
ace of trumps in gleek   TIB
ache   AKE
achievement   CHEVISANCE
acid   EAGER
acknowledge   AGNISE, AGNIZE
                   KNOWLEDGE
acknowledgment
 of mistake   JEOFAIL
acolyte   ACOLUTHITE
acquaintance   COAST
acquired by unjust methods   PURCHASED
acquisitiveness   COVETIVENESS
acquit   ACQUITE, ACQUIGHT
                   ASSOIL
across   YOND
act   FACT, PRESENT
   —as
      husband   HUSBAND
      paid dance partner   HOSTESS
   —carnally   CARNAL
   —earlier than   PREVENT
   —foolishly   FOLLY
   —of
      guaranteeing   WARRANTISE
      putting together   STRUCTURE
      theft   MAINO(U)R, MANNER
      touching   ATTAINT
   —the master   MASTER
action at law   QUARREL
active   WIELDY
activity   FUNCTION
actor   STAGER
adapt   APPLY
adaptation   CONTEMPERATION
adapted for viewing   SPECULATORY
address in conciliatory tone   SPEAK FAIR
adduce   OBJECT
adjudge   AREAD, AREDE
                 ARREEDE, ARET(T)

adjustment of dispute	MISE	alkali	KALI
administration of remedy	EXHIBITION	allay	ALAY
administrative division	GOVERNMENT	allayment	ALAIMENT
admiration	WONDER	allegation	SURMISE
adorn	BEDIGHT, BESEE	allege	ALLEDGE, PRETEND, TRUMP
	ILLUSTRATE	allow to escape	LET
adorn(ed)	DIGHT	allowance	SIZE
adroit	PERT	—of food etc to servants	LIVERY
adulterate	VITIATE	—to public officers	APPOINTMENT
adulterer	AVOUTERER	allure	TRAIN, TROLL
adultery	AVOUTRY	alluring grace	VENUS
advance	VAUNCE	ally	COLLEAGUE
—towards	COAST	almond	AMYGDAL
advanced	FAR	almost	NIGHLY
adventure	AUNTER, AVENTURE	—always	MOST AN END
advice	REDE	alms	DEVOTION
advise	AVISE, AVIZE, AVYZE	aloes-wood	LIGN(-)ALOES
	REDE, VISE	along	ALONGST, ENDLONG
—against	DISSUADE	always	ALGATE
affability	FACILITY	ambassador	EMBASSADOR, LEAGUER
affable	FACILE		LE(I)DGER, LEIGER, LIEGER
affect	AMOVE	amber	LIGURE
—coyness	COY	ambergris	GRIS-AMBER
—with regret	RUE	amends	MENDS
affected by rheum	RHEUMATIC	ammonia	VOLATILE ALKALI
affectedly fanciful	QUAINT	among	EMONG(ES)
affection	AFFECT	amongst	EMONG(E)ST
affianced	ASSURED	amorous	WANTON
affinity	AFFIANCE	—sport	TOY
afflict	VISIT	amuse	PLAY, SPORT
affliction	LANGUOR, TEEN(E), TENE	ancestor	GRANDSIRE
affray	EFFRAY	ancestry	OFFSPRING
affright	DREAD, GRISE	ancient	ANTIENT
afraid	EFFRAIDE, FEARED	and	AN
afternoon	UNDERN	anew	OF NEW
afterwards	EFT	anger	GRAM(E), TEEN(E), TENE
again	AGEN, EFT	Anglican bishop	MAGPIE
against the grain	AGAINST THE HAIR	angling fly	WATCHET
agate	MURRINE	angry	CURST
age	ELD	aniline	CRYSTALLINE
aged	WINTERED	animal with docked tail	CURTAL
aghast	AGAST	ankle	ANCLE
agree	FADGE, CONDESCEND	—boot	HIGH-SHOE
ailment supposed to be		—high shoe	HIGH-LOW
caused by a worm	WORM	announce	DENOUNCE, MELD
alas	ALS, HARO, HARROW	annoy	HATTER
albeit	AL(L)BE, ALBEE	annul	VACUATE
alchemical	CHEMIC	anoint	ANELE
alderman	EALDORMAN	answer	RESOLVE
ale		ant	EMMET
—house	MUG-HOUSE	anthropoid ape	PIGMY, PYGMY
—sold at 4d per quart	FOUR-ALE		TROGLODYTE
—with wormwood	PURL	antic	ANTICK
alien	FORINSECAL	anticipate	PREVENT
aligning	LIN(E)AGE	antiphon	ANTHEM
alive	QUICK	antique	ANTICKE

anxiety	CARK	arsenic monosulphide	RESALGAR, ROSAKER
anything		art	MISTERY, MYSTERY
—done	FACT	—of	
—hackneyed	HACK	engraving	ENGRAVERY
—prepared after a recipe	RECEIPT	medicine	LEECHCRAFT
—that whirls	RHOMB(US)	pastry-making	PASTRY
apartment	MANSION	artful trick	SLIGHT
ape	JACKANAPES, PIGMY	artifice	CRAFT, CROOK, REACH
	PYGMY, TROGLODYTE	artificial penis	DILDO
aperture	OVERTURE	as	ALS
apology	SIR-REVERENCE	ascribe	APPLY
Apostle's Creed	THE BELIEF	ash of saltwort	KALI
apparatus	EQUIPAGE	Ash Wednesday	PULVER WEDNESDAY
apparel	TIRE		PULVERING DAY
appeal to pity	FOR MERCY	ask	
appearance	FAVOUR, VISIBILITY	—back	REPEAT
appease	ASLAKE	—for	BID, YEARN
appendage to shoe	FORETOP	—price of	CHEAPEN
appertain	EFFEIR, EFFERE	askance	ASCONCE
apple	POME	aspect	RESPECT, VISOR, VIZOR
application of kind	INTENTION	aspirant to knighthood	DONZEL
apply, as embroidery	LAY DOWN	aspire to	AFFECT
appoint	VOICE	assail	INSULT
apprise	ASCERTAIN	assailant	ONSETTER
approach	APPROPINQUATE	assay	SAY
	APPROPINQUE, COAST	assayer	SAY-MASTER
approaching	TOWARD	assembly	GEMOT, MOOT, THING
approbation	WELL-LIKING	assert	VOUCH
apricot	ABRICOCK, APRICOCK	assess	CENSE
apron	BRAT, PLACARD	assign	ARET(T)
apt	TOWARD	assigned place	ROOM
arbitrator	STICKLER	assistance	EASEMENT
arboretum	ARBORET	assistant	
arch	EMBOW	—clown or buffoon	ZANY
archery target	GOAL	—minister	HELPER
ardent desire	COVETISE	assize	SIZE
area near capital	INLAND	assuage	ASSWAGE, LENIFY
argue	WRANGLE	assure	ASCERTAIN, RESOLVE
aristocratic ruffian	MOHOCK	astonish	ASTONE, ASTONY, ASTUN
arithmetic	ARSMETRICK	astonishment	MARVEL
arm	ENARM	asunder	ATWAIN
armed citizens	TRAIN-BAND	asylum	FRITHSOKEN, GIRTH
armistice	STILL-STAND		GRITH
armour	WEED	—for prostitutes	PENITENTIARY
—for man or horse	HARNESS	at	
armoury	GARDEROBE	—a loss to know	SEEK
army	HOST, WAR	—hand	TOWARD
—clothing account	OFF-RECKONING	—home	WITHIN
arrange	ADDRESS	—once	PRESENTLY, SWITH
arranged	ADDRESSED, ADDREST		TIGHT, TIT, TITE(LY), TYTE
—in harrow form	HERSED	—present	PRESENTLY
array	BEDIGHT, RAY	—the	
arresting officer	SERGEANT, SERJEANT	door	ADOORS
arrive	BECOME	same time that	WHILES
arrogance	SURQUEDY	athletic contest	PRIZE
arrogant	STOUT, WANTON	atone	ABY(E), ABIDE

atrocious	ENORMOUS
attached band or strip	LABEL
attack	ATTEMPT, BRASH
	STAND UPON
attaint	TAINT
attempt	FAND, FOND
attend	INTEND
attendant	VARLET, WAITING-VASSAL
attending servant	WAITER
attentive	ADVICEFUL, LISTFUL
	WHIST
attire	SUIT, TIRE
attired	READY
attribute importance to	FORCE
auction sale	OUTROOP
auctioneer	OUTROOPER
audacity	HARDIHEAD
augury	SOOTH
aunt	NAUNT
aurochs	URE
austere	STOOR, STOUR, STOWRE
	STURE
authorisation	WARRANTISE
autumn	HARVEST
avail	DOW, STEAD, VAIL
avenge	WREAK
average	MEDIUM
avert	FORFEND
avoid	VOID, WAIVE
await	BIDE, EXPECT, STAY, TARRY
award	ADEEM, ARET(T)
aware	KNOWING TO, WARE
away from	FROWARD(S)
awkward	UNGAIN
axiom	PETITION
axle	AXIS
babble	BRABBLE
back	RIDGE
—board	MONITOR
—bone	CHINE
—handed	AWKWARD
—of head	NODDLE
—side	BREECH
—to-back	DOS-A-DOS
—up	SOOTHE
backer	STICKLER
backgammon	GAMMON, TABLES
	VERQUERE
bad	LEWD, LITHER, NAUGHT
—lot	NAUGHTY PACK
—luck to	FOUL (BE)FALL
badger	GRAY, GREY
baffle	MATE
bag	COD
bagpipes	SYMPHONY
bail	REPLEVY

bailiff	HUNDREDER, REEVE
baker	BAXTER
balance	PEASE, PEAZE, PEISE
	PEIZE, PEYSE
—beam	BA(U)LK
baldmoney	SPICKNEL
bale in hide wrapper	SERO(O)N
ball	BOWL
ballast	POISE
band	FASCIA
—of musicians	MUSIC, NOISE
bandalore	QUIZ
bandy words	BA(U)LK
—in emulation	REVIE
bandying about	JACTITATION
banishment	EXPULSION
bank	CONTINENT, LINK
—of river	CONTINENT
banker	EXCHANGER
banquet	ENTERTAINMENT
bar	ESTOP
barded	BARD
bare	LEWD
—place	GALL
barefoot Highlander	GILLIE-WHITE-FOOT
	GILLIE-WET-FOOT
barely	SCRIMP
bargain	INDENT, PURCHASE
barred	BARD
barrel-organ	MUSIC-BOX
barter	PERMUTATION
base	HARLOTRY
basin	BASON
bass	BURTHEN
bath-house	BAGNIO
baton	BATOON
—of authority	WARDER
battalion	BATTLE
battle	
—array	HERSE
—axe	GISARME, SPARTH(E)
—field	PLACE
battlement	BARMKIN
bauble	GAUD
bay	REACH
—of library	CLASSIS
be	
—a	
claimant	PRETEND
schoolmaster	MASTER
—able	DOW
—anxious about	FEAR
—apprehensive	DOUBT
—associated and in concord	WALK
—aware of	WIT
—commonly stated	VOICE

—consequence of	IMPORT
—defeated	GO BY THE WORST
	GO WITH THE WORST
—earlier than	PREVENT
—equal to	FILE WITH
—extended at full length	LIE ALONG
—false to	FALSE, FALSIFY
—fitting	LONG
—foolish	DOAT, DOTE, FON
—frivolous	FLUTTER
—good for a purpose	DOW
—impatient	BATE
—in	
attendance	INTEND
expectation of	WAIT
motion	WALK
the habit	USE
—intemperate	EXCEED
—like	SEMBLE
—likely	LIKE
—off	VIA, WAG
—on watch	WAIT
—prominent	TOOT
—renewed	NEW
—rife	WALK
—rumoured	VOICE
—spent (time)	WASTE
—stupid	DOAT, DOTE
—sulky	GLOUT
—troublesome	IMPORTUNE
—whimsical	WHIM
become accustomed	WON
beacon	FANAL
beadle	BEDEL(L)
bear	EAN
beat	BOUNCE, FEEZE, PHE(E)SE
	PHEEZE, TUND
—back	REBUKE
—down	FOIL
—everything	PASS
—soundly	RIB-ROAST
—to windward	LAVEER
beaten	YBET
beautiful	BRIGHT, SMICKER, SPECIOUS
beautifully	FAIRISH, LOVELY
beauty	FEATURE, FORM
beaver	BEVER
becalm	ENCALM
because	FORWHY
—of	IN RESPECT OF
become	BESIT, PROVE, WEAR
—angry	WRATH
—feeble	FAINT
—hairless	PILL
—husband	HUSBAND
—neglectful	FOR(E)SLACK

—scant	SCANTLE
—slack	FOR(E)SLACK
—surety	STIPULATE
—unveiled	UNVAIL(E)
—weak	FAINT
becoming	HANDSOME
—stone	LAPIDECENT
bed	DOWNY
bedaub	MOIL
bedraggle	DAG
bedroom	DORMER
been	BENE
beer flavoured with	
ground ivy	GILL(ALE), GILL BEER
befall	FORTUNE
—unluckily	OSFALL
befit	SORT
befool	ASSOT, BOB, FON, POOP, POUPE
before	OR, TOFORE
befoul	BE(W)RAY
befriend	FRIEND
beg	MAUND
began	GAN
beget	KIND
begetting	GET
beggar	MAUNDER, MUMPER
—hawking glass	GLASSMAN
—posing as maimed	
soldier	RUFFLER
begging friar	MENDICANT
begin	GIN, INCEPT, INCHOATE
beginning	ENTRANCE, PRINCIPLE
	TO-FALL
begone	AVAUNT
begrime with coal dust	COLLY
beguile	AMUSE, GLEEK
behave	USE
—lewdly	PLAY THE WANTON
—riotously or noisily	ROAR
—towards	ENTREAT
—with boastful	
insolence	INSULT
behaviour	CARRIAGE, GOVERNANCE
behead	HEAD
behove	IMPORT
belabour	SAUCE
belching	RUCTATION
beleaguer	LEAGUER
believe	GUESS, TROW, WEEN
	WIS(H), WIST
believer in medical	
use of mercury	MERCURIALIST
bellows of organ	WIND-BAG
belly	WEM(B), WEAMB
belong	LONG
beloved	L(I)EVE, LIEF

bend	EMBOW
benign	BENEDICT
bent	WRONG
benumb	DEAD
bereaved	ORB
bereavement	ORBITY
beset	IMPEACH, OBSESS
besiege	BESIT, OBSESS
besot	ASSOT
bestow part of	IMPART
bestrew	STROW
bet	HOLD
betray	BEWRAY
betrayer	TREACHER(ER), TREACHOUR
betroth	ENSURE, HANDFAST
	TROTH-PLIGHT
betrothal	HANDFAST(ING)
—by giving ring	
or gift	SUBARR(H)ATION
betrothed	AFFIED
bewilder(ment)	AMAZE
bewitch	BESPEAK, FASCINATE
	OVERLOOK
bicycle	BONESHAKER, VELOCIPEDE
bid	VIE
bier	HEARSE
bill	NOTE
bind	WAP
binding together	CONNEXIVE
bird's crest	COPPLE
birthmark	NAEVE
bishop's throne	SEE
bite	PINCH
—back	CROSSBITE
bitter	EAGER
black	
—bile	MELANCHOLY
—bird	OUSEL, OUZEL
—leg	SNOB
—marble	PARAGON, TOUCH
blame	WITE, WYTE
—for	GUILTY OF
blank panel	ORB
bleaching powder	CHEMIC
blended	(Y)BLENT
blending together	CONTEMPERATION
blessed	BENEDICT
blind	BLEND
—window	ORB
blinded	YBLENT
blindfold	MUFFLE
blinking	TWINKLING
blister	BLAD, MEASLES
blockhead	MOME
blow	BUFF, HUFF, PLAGUE
	WHERRET, WHIRRET

—into	INSPIRE
—on the	
neck	NECK-HERRING
ribs	RIB-ROASTER
blue	
—grey	GRISEOUS
—pigment	VERDITER
bluster(er)	HUFF
blustering	BULLY
board	COMMON
boast	AVAUNT, CRACK, GLORY
	YELP
boastful	THRASONICAL
—spirit	GLORY
bob	DOP, S, SHILLING
bobby	QUEACHY, QUEECHY
bodies	BODICE
body	BULK
—living or dead	LICH
—of	
forces	HEAD
soldiers in square	SQUADRON
vassals	MANRED
watchmen	WATCH
boggy	QUEACHY, QUEECHY
boiled	SODDEN
—vegetables	POTTAGE
bold	HAUGHTY
—faced person	FACER
boldness	HARDIHEAD
bombastic	GRANDILOQUOUS
bond	BAND
book	
—always in the	
same place	LEDGER, LIDGER
—of	
Bible readings	LEGEND
rules	ORDINAL
—seller	STATIONER
boon-companion	FRANION
boorish	SWAINISH
—fellow	JACK
booty	PURCHASE
border	COAST, CONFINE
—of false hair	TOUR
bore	BARE
boredom	SPLEEN
born a thrall	NATIVE
borne	YBORE
borough	BURGH, PORT
bosses of gold set with	
diamonds	OWCHES
bottom	GROUND
bought	BOUGHTEN
—provisions	ACATES
bound	BAND, HANDFAST

—by religious vows	VOWED
boundary	BOURN, GOAL, LIST, MARK
—fence	MOUND
bourdon	BURTHEN
bout	BRASH
bow	CROOK, LOUT, LOWT, MOVE
	MAKE ONE'S MANNERS
Bow Street officer	RUNNER
bowels	WOMB
box	BRUISE
boxer	PUGIL
boxing-glove	MUFFLE
boy	KINCHIN-COVE, GROOM
braggart	PUCKFIST
bragging	THRASONICAL
braid	BREDE
branch	BRAUNCH, GRAFT
brandish	WAG
brandy	NANTZ
—and water	MAHOGANY
brass	ALCHEMY, ALCHYMY
bravado	BRAVERY
brave person	VALIANT
bravo	BRAVE
brawl	BRABBLE
brawler	NICKER, ROARER
	ROARING-BOY
breach of law	UNLAW
bread	LOAF
—from finest flour	MANCHET
	WASTEL(-BREAD)
—soaked in gravy	BREWIS
break	
—in pieces	TO-BREAK
—up	REFORM, TO-BRUISE
breakfast	DEJEUNE
breaking of the sea	BREACH
breastplate	PLACARD
breath	SPIRIT
breathe into	INSPIRE
breed of sheep	HERDWICK
bribe	GIFT, GRATIFICATION
	TOUCH, VALES, VAILS, WAGE
bridesmaid	PARANYMPH
bright	NET(T), SHEER
—red	COCCINEOUS
brightly shining	SPLENDIDIOUS
bring	
—about	PURCHASE
—back	REDUCE
—forth young	YEAN
—forward	OBJECT
—in	INBRING, INDUCE
—success	SPEED
—to	
an end	DEFINE, SPEED

court	INBRING
finished state	SPEED
sorry plight	SPEED
—vessel close to wind	LOOF
bringing	
—back	REDUCTIVE
—intelligence	INTELLIGENT
—up	NOUR(R)ITURE
brisk	GAILLARD, GALLIARD, YARE
briskly	TIGHTLY
British soldier	LOBSTER
broach	BROCH
broiling-meat	CARBONADO
broke	BRAKE
broken	INFRACT
—pottery	POTSHARD
—tree	RAMPICK, RAMPIKE
brokerage	BROKERY
bronze	BRASS
brooch	BROCH
brood	TEAM
—(pheasants)	EYE
broth	BREVWS
brothel	BORDEL(L)O, CORINTH
	VAULTING-HOUSE
brought from a	
remote place	FAR-FETCHED
browned by sun	ADUST
bruise severely	TO-BRUISE
brushwood	BAVIN, RICE
bucket	SITULA, STOOP, STOUP
buffoon	ANTIC, INIQUITY
	JACK-PUDDING, MOME
build	EDIFY, TIMBER
building where salt	
is made	SALT-COTE
bulk	GREAT
bully	HUFF
bumper	ROUSE
bumpkin	PUT(T)
bunch of flowers	BOUGHPOT, BOWPOT
bundle	TROUSSEAU
burden	BURTHEN
burdensome	IMPORTUNATE, IMPORTUNE
burgess	PORTMAN
burial-place	CHARNEL
burly	BRAVE
burn	BREN(NE)
—in	INURE
burned	YBRENT
—in	INUST
burnet(-saxifrage)	PIMPERNEL
burning	UST(ULA)ION
—in	INUSTION
burnt	YBRENT
—up	ADUST

bury	EARTH, GRAVE	cart	
	INEARTH	—for removal of night-soil	NIGHT-CART
bus conductor	CAD	—load	SEAM
bustle	COIL	carve	ENTAIL, ENTAYLE
butt	PUSH		INSCULP
buttocks	CROUPON	—birds	DISMEMBER
buy and re-sell to		casque	CASK
raise price	REGRATE	cast	KEST, WARP
by	FORBY	—as obstruction	TRUMP
—day	ADAYS	—evil eye on	FASCINATE
—my faith!	PERFAY	—off clothes	FRIPPERY
—Our Lady(kin)	BYRLADY, BYRLAKIN	—spell on	ENCHARM
—way of love	PARAMOUR	castor	TRUCKLE
byword	NAY-WORD	casualty	CADUAC
cabbage	WORT	catalogue	CATELOG, RAGMAN
cake of soap	BALL		RAGMENT
calamity	BALE, RUTH	catamite	GANYMEDE, INGLE
calf	VEAL	catch	DEPREHEND, FANG
call	CLEEP, CLEPE, ENSTYLE	caterer	ACATER, ACATOUR, CATER
	HETE, HIGHT	cattle	AVER, FEE, NEAT
—back	REVOKE	—herder	HAYWARD
—in question	QUARREL	caught	IN BY THE WEEK
—out	PROVOKE	—at fault	TARDY
—to witness	ATTEST	cause	OCCASION
—to-arms	ALARM	—not to be	UNBE
called	HIGHT, HOTEN, NEMPT	—to	
	YCLEPED, YCLEPT	fall	FALL
camp	LEAGUER	fear	DREAD
campaign	JOURNEY	feel scruples	SCRUPLE
camphor	CAMPHIRE	glance	GLANCE
canal without locks	WATER-PLANE	know	KEN
cancerous growth	WOLF	sin	OFFEND
candied fruit	SUCKET	swear	ADJURE
cannon	BASILISK	causing	
—balls	GUN-STONES	—devastation	WASTEFUL
canopy	PAVILION	—uneasiness	IRKSOME
canto	FIT(T), FITTE, FYTTE	—wasting	WASTEFUL
cap	BIGGIN(G)	cauterisation	INUSTION, USTION
capable of	NOTABLE	caution	CAUTEL
—erring	ERRABLE	cautious	CAUTELOUS, WARE
—living	VITAL	Cavalier	MALIGNANT
capitalist	MONEYER	cavalry	
caprice	SPLEEN	—man	PLUNGER
capricious	HUMOUROUS, WANTON	fatigue cap	WATERING-CAP
captious arguing	CROCODILITE	—officer	CORNET
captivity	ENDURANCE	—standard	CORNET
care	CARK, FORCE, PASS	caviar	CAVIARIE
—for	KEEP, RECK	cavity	
career	CARIERE	—in the earth	MINE
careful	CHARY	—of a raised pie	COFFIN
carelessness	SECURITY	cease	STINT
carousal	ROUSE, UPSEE, UPS(E)Y	—from	RESPITE
carper	MOME	celebrate	MEMORISE, MEMORIZE
carry		—in song	BESING
—off	HENT, TRUSS	—Whitsun	SHROVE
—out the duties of	WAIT (UP)ON	celestial sphere	WHEEL

censure	TAXATION
centering	CENTRY
certain	SICCAR, SICKER
certainly	IWIS, YWIS
cessation	STINT
chafing-dish	CHAFER
chair	
—of sanctuary	FRITHSTOOL
—or canopy of state	ESTATE
chalaza	SPERM
challenge	APPEAL, CHAMPION
	DARRAIGN(E), DARRAIN(E)
	DARRAYN, DERAIGN
	DEFY, PROVOKE, VIE
challenger	APPELLANT
chambermaid	BOWERY WOMAN
champion	KEMP
chance	CHAUNCE, VENTURE
change	EXCHANGE, WEND
—colour	BRAID
—one's clothes	SHIFT
—the course of	WIND
changeable	HUMOROUS, VOLUBLE
chaplet	ROSARY
character	HAIR, PROPRIETY
—of a blackleg	LEGGISM
charcoal-burner	COLLIER
charge	QUARREL, TAX
chariot	WAG(G)ON, WAIN
charioteer	WAG(G)ONER
charm	ENCHARM, WEIRD
chase	CHACE
chaste	HONEST
chattel forfeited to Crown	DEODAND
cheap	GOOD-CHEAP
cheat	BAFFLE, BITE, CONY-CATCHER
	FOB, SLUR
—in return	CROSSBITE
check	BAFFLE, FOIL, REBUKE, SNEAP
—mated	MATE
cheek	WANG
cheer	ENCHEER
cheerful	LUSTICK
chemise	SMOCK
chemist	APOTHECARY, CHEMIC
chemistry	CHYMISTRY
cherish	REFOCILLATE
—with heat	FOMENT
chess board or piece	CHEQUER
chest	CAP-CASE
chicken	CHUCK
chided	CHOSE
chief	DUKE
—fifer	FIFE-MAJOR
—magistrate	(PORT)REEVE
—place in popular esteem	VOGUE

chignon	WATERFALL
child	WENCH
—left to be minded	MINDER
children	CHILDER
child's cap	BIGGIN
chimney-sweeper's boy	CHUMMY
chintz	PINTADO
chloride	MURIATE
choir	QUIRE
—stall with back	
to screen	HEADSTALL
choose	CHUSE
chorister	QUIRISTER
chough	CHEWET
Christ's cross	ROOD-TREE
christening robe	BEARING-CLOTH
Christmas game	LEVEL-COIL
church building	STEEPLE-HOUSE
churl	CARL
churlish	CARLISH
cider and water	BEVERAGE
cinnamon	CANELLA
circuitous movement	WINDLASS
circulate	TROLL, WALK
circumstanced	STATED
cite	ALLEGE
city	TROY, UR
clad	YCLAD, YCLED
—in satin	SATIN
claim	DARRAIGN(E), DARRAIN(E)
	DARRAYN, DERAIGN, PRETEND
—as one's own	OWN
—equality	MATE
claimant	TITLER
clamour	BRABBLE
clary	ORVAL
clash	HURTLE
clasp	SPANG, TACH(E)
class	SIEGE
—of	
inferior persons	VULGAR
thief	WASTER
claw	FANG, SERE
clean	EMUNGE, NEAT, NET(T)
—cut	TERSE
cleanse	GARBLE
clear	SHEER
—away	VOID
—space	HALL
—up	SALVE
cleared for action	PREDY
clever	ARTFUL, CONCEITED
	NOTABLE
climate	TEMPERAMENT
climb	STY
climbed	CLOMB

clip	DOD	commemorate	REMEMBER
cloak	CLOKE, PALLIATE	commendable	WELL-FOUND
clock-weight	POISE	comment	GLOZE
clod	GLEBE	commercial	
cloddy	GLEBOUS, GLEBY	—privilege	OCTROI, OCTROY
clog	PESTER	—traveller	RIDER
close	STRICT, CONSTIPATE	commit adultery	ADULTERATE
—fitting	JUST, SUCCINCT	commodities	TRAFFIC
breeches or drawers	HOSE	common	
closed handful	NIEVEFUL	—kite	GLED(E)
closely	NIGHLY, STRAIT	—land	MARK
—united	CONTINUATE	—man	JACK
cloth		—topic	COMMONPLACE
—covering Eucharist	CORPORAS	commons	FOLK
—of		commonwealth	(COMMON)WEAL
gold	CICLATO(U)N	compact	COVIN, COVYNE, MATCH
mixed colours	MOTLEY	companion	COPESMATE, FE(A)RE, FEER
—pieced together	PANE		FIERE, PHEERE, MARROW
—separated by slashing	PANE	company	GING, SORT
clothes	SHROUD, WEARING	—taking meal at	
clothing	WEED	fixed price	ORDINARY
clove-pink	SOPS-IN-WINE	compare	CONFER, PARAGON
clown	ANTIC		RESEMBLE
clownish	BOR(R)EL(L), CARLISH	compartment in chest	TILL
club	BOURDON, HETAIRIA, POLT	compass	PRACTISE
clumsy	UNHANDSOME	compassionate	PITEOUS, REMORSEFUL
co-exist	CONSIST	compel	COMPULSE
coal dealer	COLLIER	compelled	FAIN
coarse		competition	CONCURRENCE, GOAL
—flour/meal	CRIBBLE	competitor	CONCURRENT
—woollen fabric	RUG	compiler	UNDERTAKER
Orkney	WADMA(A)L, WADMALL	complain	PLAIN
cobblestone	COPPLESTONE	complaint	PLAIN, QUARREL
coddled child	COCKNEY	complaisance	PLEASANCE
codlin	QUODLIN	complete	COMPLEAT
cohabit with	OCCUPY	complexion	BLEE
coin	CROSS	compliment	DOUCEUR
	(see also **coins**)	comply	CONDESCEND
coiner	MONEYER	comport oneself	USE
cold in the head	RHEUM	compose	DITE, STICKLE
collection of things said	RHAPSODY	composition	DITE
colonial governor	PRESIDENT	—of drugs	CONFECTION
colonist	INHABITOR	compound	ETHIOPS
comb	KEMB	compromise	TEMPERAMENT
combed	KEMPT	compulsion	DISTRESS
come	VIA	conceal	VIZARD
—about	SORT	concede	CONDESCEND
—forth	FORTHCOME	conceit	DEVICE
—near	LIKE	conceive	CONCEIT
—to		concern	
grief or ruin	SPILL	—closely	NIP
near an end	GROW TO WASTE	—oneself with	MEDDLE
comfit	CONFIT	concerned with fate	WEIRD
comfort	ENCHEER	concert of voices	CONCENT
coming from the eye	VISUAL	conciliatory	COASTING
command	HETE, WILL	—words	FAIR WORDS

conclusion	FINE
concord	CONCENT
concubine	MADAM
condemn	CAST
condescend to	
—allow	VOUCHSAFE, VOUTSAFE
—grant	VOUCH(SAFE), VOUTSAFE
condition	CENSE, LIKING
condole with	MOAN
conduct	RULE
—on a journey	TRAVEL
confectioner	SUGAR-BAKER
confess	AGNISE, AGNIZE
confidential	INWARD
confine	STRAITEN
confinement	CONFINE
confirm	SOOTHE, STABLISH
—correctness of	RATIFY
conflict	CAMP
confound	MATE
confounded	POCKY
confront	CROSS
confused mass	FARRAGO
confusion	BAFFLE
confute	REDARGUE, REFEL
congratulate	GRATULATE, GREET
congratulatory	GRATULANT
conjectural	STOCHASTIC
connecting ridge	HALSE
conned	YCOND
conscience	INWIT
consecrate	HALLOW
consecration	SACRING
consent	CONDESCEND
conserve	CONFITURE
consider	ADVISE, CAST, VISE
considerable	NOTABLE
considered	CONSIDERATE
consort	LADY, MAKE, MATE
conspiracy	COVIN, COVYNE
conspire	COLLEAGUE, CONJURE
constable	BOW STREET RUNNER
	HARMAN(-BECK)
constable's district	CONSTABLEWICK
constant	UNREMOVABLE
constrain	OBLIGATE, PERSTRINGE
construe	CONSTER
consume	BEZZLE
consuming	WASTEFUL
contact	CONTINGENCY
contend	DEBATE
—with weapons	PLAY
content for want of	
something better	FAIN
contention	TOIL
contents of wardrobe	GARDEROBE

contest for prize	WAGE
continuance	DURANCE
continue	DURE, PERSEVERE
continuity of state	TENOUR
contradict	OUTFACE, UNDERSAY
contrary	CONTRAIR
contrivance	ENGINE
—for holding up	
skirt	PAGE
contrive	ENGINE, FRAME, WORK
control	WIND
controller	RECTOR
controlling fate	WEIRD
convenience	COMMODITY
convenient	HANDSOME, HEND
conversation	PARLANCE
convey to a distance	ELOI(G)N
	ESLOIN, ESLOYNE
conveying no idea	UNIDEAL
convict of	REPROVE
convince	RESOLVE
copious	FULSOME
copiousness	COPY
copper	AS, D, P
copse	SPRING
copy of legal writing	TRANSUMPT
copyholder	VILLEIN
cordial	ROSA-SOLIS
cornage	HORNGELD
corner	CANTON
corporate body	UNIVERSITY
correct	CHASTISE, CHASTIZE
—thing	CHEESE
correspondent	RESPONSIBLE
corroded	CANKERED
corrosive	CORSIVE
cosmetic	FUCUS
coupled	ME(I)NT, MENGED
	MEYNT, MINGED
couch	DAY-BED
could	COUTH
council	THING
counsel	ADVISEMENT, REDE
count	NICK
countable	COMPTIBLE
countenance	CHEER, FAVOUR
count(er)	COMPT(ER)
counter	COMPTER
counterbalance	POISE
counterfeit coin	SLIP
counterfeiter	FALSER
counterpoint	DESCANT, FA(UX)BURDEN
country	
—dweller	RURAL
—house	GRANGE
count(ship)	COUNTY

county division	WAPENTAKE	crossed by streams	WATER-SHOT
couple	MARROW, TWAIN	crown	GARLAND
—up	MENG(E), MING	cruel	FELON
courageous	WIGHT	crupper	CROPPER
course	LOOSE, MESS, TRADE	crush	OPPRESS
court	MOOT, SUE, THING	crutch	POTENT
—held in fairs		crwth	CROWD
and markets	COURT OF PIEPOWDERS	cry	
—messenger	BEADLE	—at masque	A HALL, A HALL
—of		—in fencing	HAY
guild	HALL-MOOT	—of	
lord of manor	HALL-MOOT	impatience	CRIMINE
the manor	LEET	surprise	CRIMINE
—official	CH(E)IROGRAPHER	—out	DISCLAIM
	APPARITOR	—up	SELL
courteous	HEND	cucking-stool	TUMBREL, TUMBRIL
courtesan	STALLION	cuckold	CORNUTE, CORNUTO
courtesy	GENTILESSE, GENTLENESSE		ENGRAFT
cousin	COOSEN	—maker	HORNER
coven	COVEN, COVYNE	cuckoldise	GRAFT
cover	COUR, OVERCOME	cuckoldry	HORNWORK
—completely	WHELM	cudgel	WASTER
—dispersedly	STROW	cultivate	HUSBAND, MANURE
—with		cultivated	SATIVE
earthwork	ENSCONCE	cultivation	MANURANCE
sconce	ENSCONCE	cunning	QUAINT, SLIGHT
covering	TAPIS	—rogue	GREEK
covetousness	COVETISE	cunningly made	SLY
coward(ly)	HILDING, NITHING	curb	REFRAIN
cower	COURE	curd	CRUD
coxcomb	PRIG	curdle	CRUDDLE, YEARN
cozen	COOSIN, POOP, POUPE	cure	RECURE, REMEDY
craft	MISTER(Y), MYSTERY	curled	CRISP
craftsman	ARTSMAN	curling	CRISP
crafty	SUBDOLOUS	currency	PASS
—action	WINDLASS	curse	BAN
cram	STOP	cursory	CURSORARY
crate	SERO(O)N	curt	SQUAB
create		curtsy	DOP, MAKE ONE'S MANNERS
—at same time	CONCREATE	curved	WRONG
—with	CONCREATE	custard	FLAM(M), FLAUNE, FLAWN
creature	WIGHT	custody	HANDFAST
creeping or crawling animal	WORM	custom	WON
crime committed	FACT	—house seal	COCKET
crimp with poting-stick	POTE	customer	CHAPMAN
crimping	PRINT	customs officer	WAITER
—stick for ruffs	POTING-STICK	cut	ENTAIL, ENTAYLE
crimson	PURPLE	—short	CURTAL
crippled	HALT	—the hair of	DOD
crisis	ACME, FIT	cutting	SARMENT
critic	OVERSEER	—back	RECISION
critical	NICE	—off	RESCISSION
—moment	ARTICLE	—short	SYNCOPE
crooked	CRABBED, WRONG	cylindrical plait	QUILL
Cross	WOOD	cymbal	SYMBOLE
cross-grained	FRAMPOLD	cypress	GOPHER

dagger	BASELARD, PUNCHEON
dainties	CATES
dais	ESTATE
dally	TICK AND TOY
damage	WORST, WREAK
damned beforehand	FORE-DAMNED
dandy	FANTASTIC, JESSAMY
	MASHER, MUSCADIN
	PUSS-GENTLEMAN
dangerous	PERICULOUS
Danish underking	EORL
dark	WAN
—brown	BURNET
—colour	PUKE
—coloured horse	MOREL
darnel	TARE
dart	LANCE
dash	RASH
dastard	HILDING
dastardly	NITHING
daunt	AMATE, DANT, PALL, QUAIL
dawdle	DRAWL
dawn	DAW, SPRING
day	
—for begging	MUMPING-DAY
day's work or travel	JOURNEY
days of makeshift meals	SCAMBLING-DAYS
daze	AMAZE
dazzle	BLEND
dead tree	RAMPICK, RAMPIKE
deaden	DEAD
deaf	SURD
deal	ENTREAT
—with	TRANSACT
dealer	CHAPMAN, OCCUPIER
—in	
horses	HORSE-COURSER
second-hand goods	UPHOLDER
dealing	MERCHANDISE
dear	L(I)EVE, LIEF
death	EXPIRATION, MORT
debar	CONCLUDE
debased by commonness	PROSTITUTE
debate	WRANGLE
debauch	DEBOSH
decamp	SCAMPER
decay	FAINT, FORFAIR
decayed tree	RAMPICK, RAMPIKE
deceit	BARRAT, FORGERY
deceitfulness	FALLACY, FALSEHOOD
deceive	CHICANE, FALSE, TRUMP
—with smooth words	GLOZE
deceiver	TREACHER(ER)
	TREACHOUR
December 21st	MUMPING-DAY
deception	FALLACY, FUBBERY, GULLERY

decide	AREAD, AREDE, ARREEDE
	DARRAIGN(E), DARRAIN(E)
	DARRAYN, DERAIGN, DISCUSS
—against	CAST
decision of council	REBOUND
declare	AREAD, AREDE, ARREEDE
	MELD, VIE, VOUCH
—on oath	ALLEGE
—to be true	SOOTHE
decline	DEVALL, QUAIL, WELK
decoration	FLOURISH, PARAMENT
decorum	HONESTY
decoy for birds	STALE
decrease	WANZE
—in volume	WANE
dedicate to church	IMMOLATE
deduce	DEDUCT
deduct part of	DEFALLATE
deed	ASSURANCE, FACT
deeds	WORKINGS
—of prowess	VASSALAGE
deep metal plate	MAZARINE
deer's	
—entrails	QUARRY
—sweetbread	INCHPIN
defeat	PUT TO THE WORSE
defeated	PROFLIGATE
defenceless	SILLY
defend	WARRANT
—by flankers	FLANKER
defender	WARRANT
defiant protest	MARRY COME UP
deficient in interest	INCURIOUS
defile	HALSE, MOIL
defilement	CONSPURCATION, MOIL
deflect	WIND
deformed person	URCHIN
defraud	COG, LURCH
degree	GRE(E)CE, GRECIAN, GRE(E)SE
	GREE, GREESING, GRESSING
	GRI(E)CE, GRISE, GRIZE
dejected	AMORT
delay	FRIST, LET, TARRY
	TARRIANCE
—in action	RESPITE
deleterious	PREDATORY
deliberate	CONSIDERATE
deliberative	
assembly	MOOT
delicacy	CATE, TRINKET, JUNKET
delighting	RAPING
delineate	STELL
delirium	PHRENITIS
deliver	TAKE
—of a child	LAY
delivered of a child	LIGHT

delivery	LIVERY
demonstrate	REMONSTRATE
demonstration	MUSTER
deny	DENAY, REN(A)Y, RENEY
denial	DENAY
depart	AVAUNT, VADE, WALK, WEND
depict	DEVISE, RESEMBLE
depraved	FELONIOUS, GRACELESS
deprive	TWIN(E)
—of	
colour	STAIN
provisions	DISPURVEY
deputy to earl	VISCOUNT
derived	EXTRACT
describe	DESCRIVE, DEVISE, SPEAK
desert	DEMERIT
deserving of	GUILTY OF
—reproach	REPROACHFUL
design	MODEL
desirable	WISHFUL
desire	COURAGE, RECK
	RETCH, WILL
—strongly	EARN
desired	WISHFUL
despair	WANHOPE
despicable fellow	CULLION
despise	FORHOW
despite	DESPIGHT
destinate	DESTINE
destitute	VOID
—of	HELPLESS
destroy	FORDO, SPILL, UNBE
destructive	WASTEFUL
detached	DISCREET
detailed narration	ENARRATION
deteriorate	STARVE
determine	ASSOIL, PITCH
devastate	POPULATE
devastated	WASTE
devastation	WASTENESS
deviate	PREVARICATE
deviation from right way	ERROR
device	ENGINE
devoid	VAIN, VOID
dexterity	SLIGHT
dexterous	FEAT(E)OUS, FEATUOUS
	WIELDY
diagram	PLAT
dial of clock	WATCH
diamond	ADAMANT
dice	GOURDS
dictate	DITE
diction	PARLANCE
did	COUTH, GAN
die	GO UNDER, STERVE, SWELT
—impenitent	DIE HARD
—of hunger or thirst	FAMISH
difference	DIFFERENCY
	DIFFICILE
difficult	UNEASY, UNEATH
difficulty	HOBBLE
diffuse	LARGE
dig	GIRD, GRAVE
digest	ENDUE, INDUE
digest(ion)	DISGEST(ION)
dignity	WORSHIP
dilute	LOWER
dinner	DINE
—time	DINE, PUDDING-TIME
dip	MERGE
direct one's course	WEND
direction of mind	INTENTION
dirty drab	PUCELLE, PUZZLE
disadvantageous	DISADVANTAGEABLE
disaffected	MALIGNANT
disapprobation	MISLIKE
disapprove	DISPROVE, MISLIKE
disband	REFORM
disbanded soldier	REFORMADO
discard	DEFY
discern	WIT
discharge	ASSOIL
disclose	UNVAIL(E)
discomfit	SHEND
discontent	MISCONTENT
discourse	PARABLE, SPELL
discover	BEWRAY
discreet	WITTY
—man	PRUD'HOMME
discrete	DISCREET
discrimination	SKILL
disease of trees	MEASLES
disgrace	SCANDAL, SHEND
	VILLA(I)NY
—publicly	BAFFLE
—with inadequate	
praise	INDIGNIFY
disgraceful	INDIGN, OPPROBRIOUS
	REPROACHFUL
disguise	PALLIATE, VIZARD
dish	
—of food	MESS
cooked in cup-shaped	
mould	TIMBALE
—used in the Eucharist	PATINE
dishonest	UNHONEST
dishonourable	UNHONEST
dislike	DEFY, DISTASTE, MISLIKE
dismal	TRIST
dismay	AMATE
dismayed	MATED
dismiss	REFORM, VOID

dismissed soldier	REFORMADO
disobliging	INOFFICIOUS
disorder	MISTEMPER
disown	REPROBATE
dispel	ASSOIL
dispenser of hospitality	HOUSEKEEPER
disperse	SPERSE
dispirited	SACKLESS
display	MUSTER, SPLAY
displease	MISLIKE
dispose	DISPONE
disposed	DIGHT
disproof	REPROOF
disprove	REFEL
dispute	REPROVE, WRANGLE
disregard	WAIVE
disreputable fellow	SHAKE-RAG
dissension	SQUARE
dissolute behaviour	DISSOLUTION
distillate	ALCOHOL
distillery receiver	BOLT
distinctness	DISTINCTION
distinguished	EGREGIOUS, EXIMIOUS
distort	WRITHE
distortion	WRY
distracted	BESTRAUGHT
distraint	NA(A)M
distraught	BESTRAUGHT
distress	MISEASE
—warrant	DISTRINGAS
distressing	UNEATH
district of	
—court	SOKE
of lord	MANOR
—warden	WARDENRY
disturb	BRASH
disuse	INUSITATION
divest oneself of	VOID
divide	DEPART
—into chapters, etc	QUOTE
divinely	HEAVENLY
division	CANTON
—of	
a song	FIT
county	CANTRED, CANTREF
the night	WATCH
time or arc	SCRUPLE
do	EXERT
—for	POOP, POUPE, SPEED
—homage	VAIL
—one's utmost	DO ONE'S ENDEAVOUR
docked	CURTAL
doctrine	LORE
document with	
pendant seals	RAGMAN, RAGMENT
doe	TEG(G)

doff	AVAIL(E), AVALE, VAIL
dole	DOOL(E), VALES, VAILS
doll	BABY
dolphin	MEERSWINE
dolt	MOME
domain	REAME, REIGN
domestic	DOMESTICAL
—slave	ESNE
don	ADDRESS
dormitory	DORMER, DORTER, DORTOUR
dot	PRICK
double Dutch	HIGH DUTCH
doubt	SCRUPLE
doughty	TALL
dovecote	LOUVER, LOUVRE
downward cut in	
fencing	STRAMACON, STRAMAZON
drag	RASH
dragon	WORM
drain out	EMULGE
dram-shop	GILL-HOUSE
dramatic	
—action	SCENERY
—performance	PAGEANT
draw	LIMN
—along or on	TRAIN
—together	ENTRAIN
drawer in chest	TILL
dread	GASTINESSE
dreaded	YDRAD, YDRED
dream	SWEVEN
dress	GUISE, RAY, TIFF
—distaff with flax	DIZEN
—of puppets	PUPPETRY
—ostentatiously	PRANK
—up	DIZEN
dressed	READY
dressing	
—for the head	HEAD
—gown	NIGHT-GOWN
—jacket	NIGHT-RAIL
drink	
—copiously	WASH ONE'S BRAINS
—deeply	BOUSE
—hard	BEZZLE
drinking	
—party	SYMPOSIUM
—vessel	RUMKIN, STOOP, STOUP
drive	DRAVE
—off	FEEZE, PHE(E)SE, PHEEZE
—out	EXTERMINATE, WREAK
drop	DRIB, GOUT
dropped	KEST
drove	DRAVE, DRIFT
drown	DRENH
druggist	APOTHECARY, DRUGGER

drum	SYMPHONY	—on	EDGE
drunk	CONCERNED, GROGGY	eglantine	EGLATERE
	OVERSEEN	egregious	PASSING
drying	AREFACTION	eightieth	FOUR-SCORTH
—room	HOT-FLUE	either	OUTHER
due	DEW, LOT	eject	EXPULSE
duenna	GRIFFIN, GRIFFON	elation	RUFF(E)
	GRIPE, GRYPHON	eldest daughter's right	
dull	DEAD, PERSTRINGE	of first choice	ESNECY
dumpy person	HODDY-DODDY	elect	VOICE
dung of deer, hare, etc	FEWMET(S)	elevation of gun	RANDOM
	FUMET(S)	elf	URCHIN
dunnage	FARDAGE	eloquence	ELOCUTION
dupe	PLOVER	elude	DELUDE
duped husband	HODDY-DODDY	embalm	BALM
durability	DURANCE	emblematic device	IMPRESA
durable		embrace	CLIP, COLL, COMPRESS
—cloth	DURANCE	embroidery frame	TENT
—woollen cloth	SEMPITERNUM	embryo	EMBRION
duration	ENDURANCE	emetic	PUKE
—of existence	DATE	eminence where	
duty	MISTERY, MYSTERY	idol stands	HIGH-PLACE
—of sentinel	WATCH	eminent	PASSING
dwell	STALL, WON	emit with force	UTTER
dwelling	MANSION, WONING	emollient	LENIENT
dye	TINCT	emotional activity	WORKING
each other	OTHER	employment of waiter	WAITERHOOD
eager	RATH(E)		WAITERING
—to	FAIN	empty	AVOID, VACUATE, VAIN
earl	COUNTY, EORL	encage	INCAGE
earliest	RATHEST	enchant	FASCINATE
early	RARE(LY), REAR, SOON	enchantment	GRAMMARY(E), MALEFICE
—evening	UNDERN	encircle	EMBAIL
—ripe	RARE-RIPE	enclose	EMBOWEL, ENCHASE
variety	RATH(E)RIPE	—in the bowels	EMBOWEL
earn	YEARN	—to prevent accidents	WARD
earnest	EAGER, FORWARD, WISTFUL	enclosed	
—desire	VOTE	—hollow part	WEM(B), WEAMB
earth	MOULD	—space	IMPALEMENT
easily		enclosure	HAW, TOWN
—handled	YARE	end	FINE, UPSHOT
—injured	NICE	—of existence	DATE
East	LEVANT	endanger	PERICLITATE
Easter	PASCH	endearment	PEAT, PIGGESNYE
easy	EATH, ETHE		PIGSN(E)Y, PIGSNIE
—to roll	VOLUBLE	endeavour	WORKING
ecclesiastical scarf	TIPPET	endorse	CONCLUDE
eclipse	DELIQUIUM	endue	ENDEW
eclogue	AEGLOGUE	endure	DURE, ENDEW
eddish	EADISH	enfold	PLIGHT
editor	OVERSEER, UNDERTAKER	enforced	NECESSARY
educate	INSTITUTE	engage in	VOUCHSAFE, VOUTSAFE
educational	INSTITUTIONARY	engine	GIMMAL
efficient action	EFFICIENCE	engraft	ENGRAFF, IMP
egg	COCKNEY	engulf	ENGULPH, INGULPH
—fried with bacon	COLLOP	enjoy	TASTE, WIELD

enjoyable	GUSTFUL
enjoyment	PLEASANCE, SUFFISANCE
ennoble	GENTLE
enormous	ENORM
enough	ENOW
—of that	VIA
enraged like a cuckold	HORN-MAD
enshrine (in verse)	ENCHASE
ensign	ANCIENT, PAVILION
ensphere	EMBOW
entangle	ENGAGE
enterprise	EMPRISE, VOYAGE
entertainment for benefit of one in need	FRIENDLY LEAD
entice	ATTEMPT
entire	INTIRE
entirely	MERELY
entomb	GRAVE
entrance	INFARE
entrap	CROSSBITE
entreating	ENTREATIVE
entreaty	EXORATION
entremets	ENTREMES(SE)
epic poet	EPIC
epistolatory	LITERARY
epoch	EPOCHA
equal	FE(A)RE, FEER, FIERE, PHEERE MAKE, MARROW, MATE PARAGON, PEREGAL
equip	APPAREL, BEDIGHT DIGHT, EQUIPAGE
equipment	ORDINANCE, TIRE
equipped	ADDRESSED, ADDREST
—for fighting	WARLIKE
ermine	ERMELIN
errand-runner	CAD
error in pleading	JEOFAIL
erst	EARST
escape	ESCAPADE
especially	IN SPECIAL
espial	SPIAL
espoused	HANDFAST
establish	EDIFY, STABLISH
estate	HAVING
esteem	PASS
eternal	ETERNE
eulogistic	EPAENETIC, EPAINETIC
eulogy	LAUD
euphony	EUPHONIA
evade	SHIFT, WAIVE
eve	E'EN, EVEN
—of Jewish Sabbath	PARASCEVE
even	EEV(E)N
evening	EEVNING
evil	BALE, NAUGHT
—being	SHREW
—deed	MALEFICE, PRANK
ewer	AQUAMANALE, AQUAMANILE
exact transcript	TENOUR
exactitude	PRINT
examination by torture	QUESTION
example	ENSAMPLE
—for warning	SAMPLE
exceeding the normal	ENORMOUS
exceedingly	EXCEEDING, HEAVENLY MONSTROUS, PASSING
—great	STRANGE
excellent	EXIMIOUS, PURE
except	OUTTAKEN, WITHOUT
exceptional	STRANGE
excess	NIMIETY
excessive	UNEQUAL
excessively	WOUND(IL)Y
excite	URGE
—loathing in	UG
excitement	RUFF(E)
exclamation of	
—astonishment	ZOUNDS
—defiance	MARRY COME UP
—failure to understand	ANAN
—surprise	HOOKEY WALKER MARRY
exemplar	SAMPLER
exercise	INURE
exertion of influence	LABOUR
exhaust	FORDO
exhausted	FOREDONE FORFAUGHTEN
exile	WRETCH
expect	HOPE, WEEN
expeditate	LAW
expeditation	LAWING
expel forcibly	EXPULSE
expend	DISPEND
expenditure	GOINGS-OUT, MISE
experience	GUST, PROOF, RELISH
experienced	WELL-SENN
experiment	CONCLUSION, EXPERIENCE
expert	SLY
—in gems	LAPIDARY
explain	AREAD, AREDE, ARREEDE GLOZE, SALVE
—by hypothesis	SALVE
explanation	GLOZE
expose	DETECT
exposed	OBNOXIOUS
exposition	ENARRATION
expound	GLOZE, REDE
—scriptures	PROPHESY
express	
—desire for	YEARN

—in words	LANGUAGE
—joy at expressing	GRATULATE
—freely	LAXATIVE
—love	ENDEARING
expression of face	MIEN
exquisite	PINK
exterminate	EXTIRP
external appearance	GARB
extinguish hope	QUENCH
extol	ADVANCE
extract gently	SOLICIT
extraction	BROOD
extraordinarily great	VENGEABLE
extremely	PARLOUS
extremity	EXIGENT
extricate oneself	WIND OUT
extrinsic	FORINSECAL
eye	LIGHT, PIGGESNYE
	PIGSN(E)Y, PIGSNIE
eyelet	OILLET
eyes	EINE, EYNE
face	CHEER, FAVOUR
	VISOR, VIZOR
facetious	FACETE
fade	FAINT
faded	BRAID, FADE
failing to pass a test	REPROBATE
fainting fit	SOUND, SWOUN
fair where servants were hired	HIRING
fairy	FAERIE, FAERY
fairyland	FAERIE, FAERY
faith	TROTH
falchion (sword)	FAULCHI(O)N
fall	
—back	RECOIL
—short	FAULT
falling of jaw	JAWFALL
false	
—appearance	FALSEHOOD
—representation	SUGGESTION
falsehood	FALSE
falsification	ADULTERY
falsifier	FALSER
familiar	PRIVY
—acquaintance	HABITUDE
—friend	GOSSIP
—to all	GENERAL
fan	FLABELLUM
fanciful notion	REVERIE
fancy	FANTASY, PHANTASY, WEEN
fang	PHANG
fantastic creation	WHIM
far	
—fetched	FAR-FET

—from choice	PROMISCUOUS
—through	THROUGHLY
farcical afterpiece or interlude	JIG
farcy (glanders)	FARCIN
farm	
—worker	HIND
—yard	HOMESTALL
farthing	FARDEN, FARDING
fashion	FEIGN, ENTAIL, ENTAYLE
fashionable	FLASH
fast ship	ADVICE-BOAT
fastening	TACH(E)
fastidiously exact	POINT-DEVICE
	POINT-DEVISE
fate	EVENT, WEIRD
fathom	FEDDON
fatigue	FATIGATE
fatigued	SWINKED
fatten	BATTEN
fault	DEFAULT, GALL
favourable	GRACIOUS, TOWARD(LY)
favoured advocate	PEAT
favourite	GRACIOSO
fear	ADREAD, DOUBT, HOPE
	REDOUBT
feat	POINT
feathery structure	PLUME
features	FAVOUR
feeble	SACKLESS
feed	BATTLE
—with fine food	PAMPER
feeding	PASTURE, RELIEF
	CIBATION
feel	
—joy or sorrow because of	RESENT
—vexation at	ENVY
feign	DISSEMBLE, FALSIFY
feigned	PERSONATE
fel(d)spar	FELSPATH
fellow	JACK, WAG
—Christian	EVEN-CHRISTIAN
—lodger	INMATE
felsite	FELSTONE
female	
—camp-follower	LEAGUER-LADY
	LEAGUER-LASS
—child	MAID-CHILD
—ruler	GOUVERNANTE
fence	HAY
—in with stakes	IMPALE
ferment (liquid)	FRET
ferrule	VERREL
festival day	GAUDY
festivity	GAUD, TRIUMPH

fetch	FET(T)
fetched	FET
—from remote place	FAR-FETCHED
fetter	BILBOES
feudal	
—land division	VILL
—right to dispose of vassal's heir in marriage	MARITAGE
—tax	TALLAGE
few	WHEEN
fictitious suit	FINE
fiddle	GU(E)
fiddler	CROWDER
fidelity	TROTH
field	GLEBE
—glass	PROSPECT
fierce	STOUT
fiery	FRAMPOLD
fight	CAMP
—for	DEBATE
—with knives	SNICK AND SNEE
	SNICK-A-SNEE, SNICKERSNEE
	SNICK OR SNEE, STICK OR SNEE
fighter	GLADIATOR
fighting spirit	GAME
figure	IDOL
—planted in box	KNOT
filbert	FILBERD
filch	DRIP, LURCH
fill	
—full	FULFIL
—up a deficiency in	SUPPLY
—with people	EMPEOPLE
fillet	FASCIA
filling completely	FULFILLING
film over the eye	WEB
filth	GORE
final settlement	FINE
find fault with	PINCH
fine	ISSUE, PURE, UNLAW
—cloth	SINDON
—paid	
by tenant's heir on marriage of daughter	RELIEFAF
	MERCHET
—woollen cloth	PUKE
finger-bowl	WATER-GLASS
fire	
—engine	WATER-ENGINE
—work	WATERLOO CRACKER
firm	SICCAR, SICKER
—grip	HANDFAST
first	
—born	PRIMOGENIT
—experience	MAIDENHEAD
—use	MAIDENHEAD
firstly	ONCE
fish	
—carrier	RIPP(I)ER
—hook	ANGLE
—pond	VIVER
fist	NEIF, NEIVE, NIEF, NIEVE
fitness	PROPERTY
fix	PITCH
fixed	UNREMOVABLE
—payment	FARM
—quantity	RATE
flag	ANCIENT, PAVILION
flat	
—part	PLAT
—thing	PLAT
flatter	CLAW, GLOZE, STROKE
flatterer	COURT-DRESSER
flattery	COURT HOLY WATER
flavour	GUST
flax fibre or seed	LINE
flay	UNCASE
flee from	ESCHEW
fleet	FLIT(T)
fleeting	FLIT(T)
flesh-colour	CARNATION
fleur-de-lis	FLOWER-DELICE
	FLOWER-DE-LUCE
flight of	
—larks	EXALT
—steps	GRE(E)CE, GRECIAN
	GRE(E)SE, GREESING
	GRESSING, GRI(E)CE
	GRISE, GRIZE, SCALE
flighty girl	GIG
fling (oneself)	LANCE
flintlock	SHAPHA(U)NCE, SNAPHAUNCH
flirt	MASH, PICKEER
—with	COQUETTE
float	FLEET, WAVE
flogging	WHIPPING-CHEER
floor	PLANCH
flout	FRUMP
flow	RAIL
flower-pot	BOUGHPOT, BOWPOT
flue	TEWEL
fluoride	FLUATE
flush	GILD
flute	TIBIA
flying about	VOLATIC
foiled	NAUGHT
fold	PLIGHT, PRAN(C)K(E)
follow	USE
—after	ENSUE
followers	SEQUEL
fondness	WELL-LIKING

fool	ANTICK, FON, PATCH	—town	PLACE
	SOT, ZANY	fortify	INSCONCE
foolish	FOND, PEEVISH	fortress	PLACE
foolishly simple	NICE	fortunate	SEELY
football	CAMP	fortune	EVENT
footing	TROD	forty	QUADRAGESIMAL
fop	FANTASTIC, MUSCADIN	—days of Lent	QUADRAGESIMA
foppish	FALLAL, FANTASTIC(AL)	fought	FOUGHTEN
for		foul	HARLOTRY, PAW(PAW)
—love's sake	PARAMOUR	foulness	SOILINESS
—the time being	PRESENTLY	founder (of colony)	OECIST, OIKIST
forage	PICKEER	four branches of	
forbid	DEFEND, DISCHARGE	mathematics	QUADRIVIUM
	FOR(E)SAY, FOR(E)SPEAK, WARN	fourth part	FARDEL, FARTHING
force	VIOLENT	framework boarding	CONTIGNATION
—again	RENFORCE	frankpledge	FRITHBOHR
—back	RECOIL	frantic	PHRENTICK
—open	SPORT	fraud	CONVEYANCE
forcible	VIVE	fraudulent	COVINOUS
forecourt	VESTIBULE	freckle	FERN(I)TIC(K)LE
foreign	FORINSECAL		FAIRNITIC(K)LE
	OUTLANDISH		FERNYTIC(K)LE
—coin bearing head	POLL	free	VINDICATE, VOID
forenoon	UNDERN	—booter	SNAPHA(U)NCE
foreshow	FIGUE		SNAPHAUNCH
forestall	LURCH, PREVENT	—from	
forester	WALKER	impediment	EXPEDITE
forester's rights	PU(L)TURE	superfluous fat	ENSEAM
foretaste	ANTEPAST	—passenger	CAD
foretokening	SOOTH	—villager	VILLEIN
forfeit	CHEAT, FOR(E)GO	freeze	FRIZE
forgot	FORGAT	freight	FRAUGHT
forgotten	FORGOT	freighted	FREIGHT
fork of the body	TWIST	frenzical	PHRENSICAL
form		frenzy	PHRENITIS, PHRENSY
—a scum	MANTLE	frequent	HABITUATE, PRACTISE
—by carving	INSCULP	fret	VEX
—into		—into anger or sorrow	GRATE
community	EMPEOPLE	fretful	FRAMPOLD
knot	KNIT	friar licensed to beg	LIMITER
forming a thicket	QUEACHY, QUEECHY	Friday	PARASCEVE
formally set, crimped		friend	INGLE
or plaited	IN PRINT	frieze	FRIZE
former	FORE	frightful	UGLY
former(ly)	WHILE-ERE, WHILOM	frill	CHITTERLING
formidable	STOOR, STOUR	fringe	GUARD
	STOWRE, STURE	frisk	FISK
forming a thicket	QUEACHY, QUEECHY	frock-coat	SURTOUT
forsake	DESTITUTE, FORLESE	frog	PADDOCK
	WAIVE	from	FRO
forsaken	LORN	—the east	EOTHEN
forsooth	QUOTHA, MARRY	front of top of head	FORETOP
forswear	REN(A)Y, RENEY	froth on beer	YEAST
forthwith	EFT	froward	AWKWARD
fortified		fruit	
—dwelling	PEEL-HOUSE, PEEL-TOWER	—pip	PIPPIN

—preserved in syrup	SUCKET
fruits of own actions	BRINGINGS FORTH
frustration	FOIL
full	
—of moans	GROANFUL
—speed	RANDOM
fully equal	PEREGAL
funeral	
—pyre	BALE-FIRE
—undertaker	UPHOLDER
furnish	BEDIGHT, BESEE, PREPARE
—with a loft	LOFT
furniture	TIRE
further	FURDER
fuse	COLLIQUATE
fustet	FUSTIC, FUSTOC
gabble prayers	PATTER
gad	FISK
gadfly	BRIZE
gage	WAGE
gain	ESCHEAT, THRIFT, WIELD
—anew	REPRISE
gallery	ALURE
gallop	WALLOP
gallows	GALLUS, NUB
	NUBBING-CHEAT
game	NINE MEN'S MORRIS, PARTY
—with	
cherry stones	CHERRY-PIT
pins of wood	LOGGATS
gang	GING
garb	VESTIMENT
garden	ARBOUR
gargle	GARGARISE, GARGARISM
	GARGARIZE
garland	GIRLOND, SHROUD, WEED
garment	VESTIMENT
garrison	STUFF
gatekeeper	WARDEN
gauge	SCANTLING
gay	BONNY, BONNIE
—fellow	GAILLARD, GALLIARD
gaze at	WAIT (UP)ON
geld	GELT
general run or course	TENOUR
genius	ENGINE, INGINE
gentile	ETHNIC
gentle	MANSUETTE
gentleman-at-arms	PENSIONARY
gentlemanly	JA(UN)TEE
gentlemen	LORDINGS
gently	FAIRISH
genuine	ENTIRE
German	ALMAIN, DUTCH
get	FALL
—along somehow	SCAMBLE
—at	AREACH
—by heart	RECORD
—goods on credit	FINEER
—over	OVERGET
—the	
better of	WIN OF
start of	LURCH
—well	RECURE
getting	
—on	TOWARD
—out of bed	LEVEE
giant	ETEN, ETTIN, ROUNCEVAL
gibbet	POTENCE
gibe	GLEEK
gimbal	GIMMAL
gin	MAX
—and treacle	MAHOGANY
gipsy	EGYPT
girded up	SUCCINCT
girdle	WAIST
girl	GILL, JILL
	KINCHIN-MORT, PIGEON
give	TAKE
—a sharp blow to	WHERRET, WHIRRET
—an example of	ENSAMPLE
—as a remedy	EXHIBIT
—distinction or honour to	ILLUSTRATE
—form to	INFORM
—in	KNOCK UNDER
—one satisfaction	DO ONE REASON
—pleasure to	PLEASURE
—success	SPEED
—up	FORBEAR, RESPITE
—vogue to	VOGUE
giving freedom	LAXATIVE
glad	FAIN
glance	EY(E)LIAD, TWEER, TWIRE
glassy	GLAZEN
glazed	GLAZEN
gleam	SHEEN
—of light	LEAM, LEME
gliding	LAPSE
—movement in dancing	SLUR
glint	GLENT
glisten	GLISTER
glittering ornament	SPANG
gloomy	WAN
glorify	GLORY
gloss over	SOOTHE
glossy	POLITE
glow	LEAM, LEME
glum	GLUMPISH
glutton	LURCHER
go	BING, TRADE, WIND
—astray	MISGO

—away from	VOID
—before	PREVENT
—down	VAIL
—faster than	PREVENT
—forward	PRETEND
—little by little	DRIB
—on wooden shoes	PATTEN
—swiftly	STRIP
—to	
law	LAW
unfashionable part	MOB IT
—wrong	MISS
goat	GATE
goblin	PUG
God	GOG
—like	GODLILY
—save	UDS
God's	UDS
—eyelid	'SLID
—heart	'SHEART
—life	'SLIFE
—light	'SLIGHT
—nails	'SNAILS
—wounds	'OONS, ZOUNDS
gold	SOL
golf	GOFF
good	RUM, SEELY
—bargain	GOOD-CHEAP
—condition	PLIGHT
—evening	GOOD-DEN
—for nothing	NAUGHT
—fortune	SPEED
—luck to	FAIR (BE)FALL
—many	WHEEN
—morning	GOOD-MORROW
gossip	AUNT
gourmand	GORMAND
governed by humour	HUMOUROUS
government	REGENCE
governor	GREAVE, GRIEVE, RECTOR
—of	
Papal province	LEGATE
town or district	WARDEN
Moldavia	GOSPODAR, HOSPODAR
	VOIVODE
Wallachia	GOSPODAR, HOSPODAR
	VOIVODE
gracious	HANDSOME, HEND
graft	GRAFF, IMP
granary	GIRNEL
grand	
—father	GRANDSIRE
—mercy	GRAMERCY
—ship	ARGOSY
—son	NEPHEW
—thanks	GRAMERCY

grant	CONDESCEND, PAY
—of money to king	SUBSIDY
—religious liberty	INDULGE
—time	FRIST
—to ministers	REGIUM DONUM
grantor's warranty	WARRANDICE
grape	WINE-BERRY
grasp	HENT
grassy plot or seat	ARBOUR
gratification	EASEMENT, GUST
gratuity to servants	
or officers of court	GLOVE-MONEY
gravel	GRIT
grazing ground	HERDWICK
grease	ENSEAM, SMEAR
great	MUCH, STOOR, STOUR
	STOWRE, STURE
—auk	PENGUIN, PINGUIN
—bouncing woman	ROUNCEVAL
—quantity	MICKLE
—Roll of the Exchequer	PIPE ROLL
—thanks	GRAMERCY
greater part	HEFT
green pigment	VERDITER
greenhorn	PUT(T)
greet	HALSE
grey	GRIS(E), GRISEOUS
—fur	GRIS(E)
grief	GRAM(E), TEEN(E), TENE
grieve	RUE, VEX
grim	GRISY
grin	SNEER
grisly	GRISY
grocer	PEPPERER
groom	COISTREL, COISTRIL
	COYSTREL, COYSTRIL
groomsman	PARANYMPH
grooved border	SWAGE
gross	
—in language	LIBERAL
—overgrown person	FUSTILUGS
ground-plan	PLATFORM
grounds	WALK
group	GLOBE, SORT
grow	
—in wealth	INCREASE
—rich	RICH
—worse	WORST
growing	
—beneath	SUBNASCENT
—under water	DEMERSED
growl	GROIN
grown	WAXEN
grudge	ENVY, MALIGN
grumble	GROIN
grunt	GROIN

guarantee	VOUCHSAFE, VOUTSAFE
	WARRANDICE, WARRANTISE
guard	WARD
guardianship	TUITION
guardship	ARMOUR
guess	AREAD, AREDE, ARREEDE
guile	DOLE
guileless	SACKLESS
guinea-fowl	TURKEY
—hen	TURKEY-HEN
gullet	WEAZAND
gullible person	CHIAUS, CHOUSE
gunner's assistant	MATROSS
gunwale	PORTLAST, PORTOISE
gush	RAIL
habit	WON
hackneyed	PROSTITUTE
hail from a distance	WHOA-HO-HO(A)
hair	STRAMMEL, STRUMMEL
—on horse's hoof	CRONET
—ornament	POMPOON
—pad	TOQUE
half	
—boot	START-UP
—guinea	SMELT
—penny	MAG, MAIK, MAKE
	MAGPIE, MAIL(E)
	PORTCULLIS
halter	WITHE
hamper	SERO(O)N
hand	HOND
handing over	LIVERY
handkerchief	MUCKENDER, ORARIUM
handle	HAND
—clumsily	GAUM, GORM
—of dagger	DUDGEON
handsome	FEAT(E)OUS, FEATUOUS
	FEATURELY
handy	HANDSOME
hang	HONG, JUSTIFY, KILT
	NUB, TRUSS
hanger	BASELARD
—on	CAD
hanging	TAPIS
hangman	NUBBING-COVE
hangman's rope	TIPPET
haphazard meal	SCAMBLING
happen	TIDE
happening	WEIRD
happy	SEELY
harangue	SPEECH
harass	TROUNCE
hard	
—drinking	CAROUSE
—plight	QUANDARY
hardihood	HARDIMENT

hardly	UNE(A)TH, UNEATHES
	UNNETHES
hardship	STRESS
hare	WAT
harlot	PUG, WAGTAIL
harm	BANE, WREAK
harmonise	ATONE, SALVE
harmony	CONCENT
—in thirds and sixths	FA(UX)BURDEN
harm physically	WRONG
harrow	HERSE
harsh	ASPER, STOOR, STOUR
	STOWRE, STURE
hart in third year	SPADE
	SPAY(AD), SPAYD
hasten	URGE
hasty and abridged Mass	HUNTING-MASS
hateful	LO(A)TH
haughtiness	HOGEN-MOGEN
haughty	SUPERB
haunch	HANCH
have	
—a liking for	AFFECT
—an inkling	SMOKE
—as essence	CONSIST-IN
—lustre	SHEEN
—sex with	KNOW
—traffickings	TRINKET
—underhand dealings	TRINKET
having	
—friends	FRIENDED
—good constitution	WELL-TEMPERED
—memory	MINDFUL
—natural ability	INGENIOUS
—seen many winters	WINTERED
—virtue or efficacy	VIRTUAL
hawk in first year	SOAR(E), SORE
hawk's	
—nostril	NARE
—quarry	MARK
hawker of	
broadsheets	SPEECH-CRIER
hawthorn	ALBESPINE, ALBESPYNE
hazard	VENTURE, WAGE
hazardous	NICE
—undertaking	EMPRISE
head	COSTARD
—and shoulders	
of a ling	POLL
—dress	HEAD, HEAD-TIRE, TIRE
with flaps	LAPPET-HEAD
—of frankpledge, tithing	
or decennary	HEADBOROUGH
—wind	DEAD WIND
headlong	PROCLIVE
—fall	PRECIPICE

heal	SAIN
health	HAIL, HEAL
healthy	SANE, WELL-DISPOSED
heap of slain	CARNAGE
hearse	HERSE
hearten	HEART
heartstricken	HEART-STROOK
heat	CALORIC, FLUSTER
heathen	ETHNIC, PA(I)NIM, PAYNIM
heathenism	HEATHENDOM, HEATHENESSE
	PA(I)NIM, PAYNIM
heavens	REGION
heavily armed soldier	GALLO(W)GLASS
heaving	HEFT
hedge	HAW, HAY, MOUND
heel	HEALD
—over suddenly	SEEL
height	HIGHT(H)
—of exaltation	RUFF(E)
heiress	FORTUNE
hele	HELL
heliotrope	GIRASOL(E)
hellenising Jew	GREEK
helm	STERN, TIMON
helmsman	TIMONEER
help	STEAD, SUPPLY
—in need	BEETMISTER
—to success	SPEED
helped	HOLP(EN)
hemp	NECK-WEED
henna	CAMPHIRE
herb	WORT
herdsman	HERD-GROOM
hereditary	SUCCESSIVE
hero	EORL
herring's head	COB
hest	COMMAND
hidden	ABSTRUSE, DE(A)RN
hide	PELL
hideous	LOATHLY
high	
—birth	GENEROSITY
—chopin	PANTOF(F)LE, PANTOUFLE
—Churchman	HIGH-FLIER, HIGH-FLYER
—Church Tory	TANTIVY
—minded	GENTLE
—official	REEVE
—pasture-ground	WALK
—spirits	HEYDAY, SPLEEN
—standing	WORSHIP
Highland chief's attendant	G(H)ILLIE
highway	
—man	HI(GH)JACKER, SCAMP
—robbery	LATROCINIUM, LATROCINY
hill	LOW
—crest	KNAP
hillock	KNAP
hinder	EMBAR, IMPEACH, LET
hindrance	LET
hinge	GEMMAL
hired	
—assassin	BRAVE
—drudge	HACKNEY
—thug	BULLY
hire for pay	WAGE
hit	HAY
—in tilting	TAINT
—it off	FADGE
hoard	HOORD, MUCKER, SPARE
hoax	FUN, GULL, SHAM
hobble for horse	PASTERN
hoist	HOISE
hoisted	HOISED, HOIST
hold	HOLT
—a late revel	WAKE
—together	CONSIST
holding of land	ROOM
hole in wall	
for light	DREAM-HOLE
holiness	HALIDON, SANCTIMONY
hollow enclosed part	WEM(B), WEAMB
holy	SANCTIMONIOUS
—place or thing	HALIDOM
homage	MANRED
homely	RUSSET
homespun	RUSSET
home-thrust	HAY
homestead	HOMESTALL, TOFT
homily	PRONE
honey	
—dew	MILDEW
—moon	HONEYMONTH
—suckle	CAPRIFOLE
hoot	WHOOT
hornbook	BATTLEDOOR, BATTLEDORE
horologe	HOROLOGIUM
horrible	GRISY, UGLY
horse	
—cloth	TRAP
—covering	FOOT-CLOTH
—doctor	HORSE-LEECH
—fly	BRIZE
horseman used for light work	HOBBLER
horse's pack strap	WANTY
hospital	SPITAL
	SPITTLE(-HOUSE)
hospitaller	HOSTEL(L)ER
host	HARBINGER
hostage	PLEDGE
hostel	ENTRY
—for travellers	HOSPITAL
hostess	LANDLADY

hostile	INFEST	—natured person	ATTERCOP
hostility	ENVY	—will	ENVY, MAU(L)GRE
hot	WHOT	imagination	WIT
—bathing establishment	HOTHOUSE	imagine falsely	FEIGN
hound	BRACH	imagined	FEIGNED
hour	HOWRE	—substance	MAGNESIA
house for receipt of		imbue	TINCT
stolen goods	STALLING-KEN	immature	UNSIZ(E)ABLE
household management	ECONOMICS	immediately	INCESSANTLY
housewife	HUSSY, HUSWIFE	immerse	DEMERSE
hover	WAVE	immoral	NAUGHT, UNHONEST
howsoever	HOWSO	immure	ENCLOISTER
hubbub	LEVEL-COIL	imp	URCHIN
huge	HIDEOUS	impair	APPAIR, EMPERISH
humble	SILLY, PLUCK, DEMISSIVE		IMPEACH, WRONG
humbug	HOOKEY WALKER	impart	IMPUTE
humility	LOWLIHEAD	impassable	INVIOUS
humorous	LUDICROUS	impede	IMPEACH, PESTER
hunchback	URCHIN	impending	TOWARD
hundred	CANTRED, CANTREF	imperceptibly	UNSENSIBLY
—weight	QUINTAL	impetuous	STURDY
hung	HONG	implement	LOOM
hunter's horn-call	MOT	imply more than is said	EMPHASIS
hunting-ground	WALK	import	CARRIAGE
hurdy-gurdy	SYMPHONY	importance	ESTIMATION
hurricane	HURRICANO	importunately	INSTANTLY
hurt	GRIEVE, NOY, NUISANCE	impose upon	SHAM
hurtful	NAUGHT	impostor	FAITOR, FAITOUR
husband	FEARE, FEER, FE(E)RE		PHANTASM
	LORD, PHEERE	impoverish	EMPOVERISH, WASTE
husbandman	CARL, HUSBAND	impregnated	IMPREGNANT
hush up	HUDDLE	impression	DINT
hushed	WHIST	imprison	LUMBER
hussif	HUSSY	improve	BEET, BETE
hustle out of sight	HUDDLE	impudence	BRONZE
hypnotism	BRAIDISM	impudent person	SAUCE
hypochondria	HIP, HYP	impulse	SPLEEN
hysteria	MOTHER	in	ON
I am ready to go		—another way	OTHERGATES
with you	HAVE WITH YOU		OTHERGUESS
iatrochemical	CHEMIC	—as much as	WHENAS
idiot	NATURAL, NIDGET	—company	IN FERE, YFERE
idle		—comparison with	IN RESPECT OF
—fancy	FLAM	—dishabille	MOBBED
—report	TOY	—exact order	IN PRINT
—tale	TOY	—extreme danger	PERDU(E)
idols	HIGH-PLACE	—front	AFRONT
if	AN, GIF	—good condition	TAUGHT, WELL-LIKING
ignorant	INGRAM, INGRUM, LEWD	—great excitement	IN HIGH LEG
—priest	HEDGE-PRIEST, LACK-LATIN	—hardship	UNE(A)TH, UNEATHES
ilk	YLKE		UNNETHES
ill		—inner room	WITHIN
—advised	OVERSEEN	—order to	FOR TO
—conduct	MISCARRIAGE	—part	PARCEL
—humour	RHEUM, SPLEEN	—particular	IN SPECIAL
—mannered fellow	JACK	—practice	PRACTIC

—ruins	RUINATE
—short	AT A WORD, ONCE
—some degree	SOMEDEAL
—spite of	MALGRADO, MAU(L)GRE
—the	
direction facing	
one	TOWARD
manner of	UPSEE, UPS(E)Y
—times past	OF YORE
—vain	IN WASTE
—want	PENURIOUS
inadequate	UNEQUAL
incapable of being	
fashioned	UNFASHIONABLE
incautious	WARELESS
incidence	TO-FALL
incidental occurrence	OBVENTION
incite	WHET
inclined	PROCLIVE
include	CONCLUDE
incommode	DISCOMMODE
inconvenience	DISCOMMODITY
inconvenient	UNGAIN, UNHANDSOME
increase	ENCREASE, IMPROVE
—of wealth	THRIFT
incubus	EPHIALTES
incurable	RECURELESS
indecent	UNHONEST
—matter	STUFF
indecently opprobious	SCURRIL(E)
indeed	INSOOTH, IN GOOD TIME
indeed!	MARRY
indicate	PRETEND
indict	(EN)DITE
indifferent actor	JAY
indignation	INDIGNANCE
indirect	UNGAI
—action	WINDLASS
indite	(EN)DITE
individually	IN PARTICULAR
induce	ENTREAT
industrious	NOTABLE
indwelling	INEXISTENT
inelegant	UNPOLITE
inexperienced	UNSEEN
inexpressible	INEXPRESSIVE
infamous	OPPROBRIOUS
—person	NITHING
infantile thrush	SPRUE
infantry regiment	TERCIO
infatuate	ASSOT
infect with measles	MEASLES
inferior	
—assistant	CAD
—Flemish cloth	MOCKADO
infest	PESTER

inflict bodily pain on	GRIEVE
inflow	INFLUENCE
infold	CLIP
inform	RESOLVE
information	WIT(TING)
informed of	KNOWING TO
informer	DISCOVERER
ingenious	ARTIFICIAL, QUAINT, WITTY
ingenuity	ENGINE
ingoing	INFARE
ingot of gold or silver	WEDGE
inhabit	HABIT
inhabitant	INHABITOR
—of	
garret	GARRETEER
hundred	HUNDREDER
inhere in	CONSIST IN
inherence	INEXISTENCE
inheritance	FEE
injure	DE(A)RE, MISDO
injury	BALE, DISGRACE, GRIEVANCE
	NUISANCE, TEEN(E), TENE
injustice	UNREASON
ink-holder	INK-HORN
inland	WITHIN LAND
inn	WATERING-HOUSE
—keeper	ALE-DRAPER
innate character	KIND
innocent	SACKLESS
innovation	NOVITY
inopportune	IMPORTUNATE
inordinately big	UNSIZ(E)ABLE
inscribed with book	
titles	RUBRIC
insect	
—imagined to live in fire	PYRALIS
—pupa	NYMPH
—vermin	MOTH
insert between	INTERSERT
insignificant person	DANDIPRAT
	DANDYPRAT
insolent	WANTON
inspect urine	CAST-WATER
inspection	PERSPECTIVE, INSPECT
installation	INSTALLMENT
instantly	INSTANTIAL
instrument	
—for winding spring	SPANNER
—of	
punishment	TUMBREL, TUMBRIL
torture	ENGINE
insult	INJURY
insure	ENSURE
insurrectionary force	HEAD
intellect	INTELLECTUAL
intended for use in war	WARLIKE

intensify	INTEND	jester	PATCH
intent	WISTFUL	jester's garb	MOTLEY
intentness	INTENT	jetsam	JETSOM, JETSON
inter	EARTH, INEARTH	jettison	JETSAM
intercept	WAYLAY	Jew	SMOUCH, SMOUS(E)
intercepting	INTERCIPIENT	jewelled head ornament	CARCANET
intercession	INTERPELLATION	jibe	BOB, GIRD
intercessor	MEAN	jingle	JIG
interchange	ENTERCHAUNGE	Joan of Arc	PUCELLE
intercourse	INTERDEAL	job	SPOT
interest	USURY	joining timber	CONTIGNATION
—on money	USAGE, USE	joint	ARTICLE
interfere with	MAR	joke	GLEEK
interjection		journey	VOYAGE
—of		jovial	WANTON
dismissal	VIA	joy	LIST
impatience	'SDEATH	judge	CENSURE, SCAN, STICKLER
surprise	MARRY	jug	NEWGATE
thanks or surprise	MERCY	juggle	PALTER
—pledging health	TOPE	juggler	TREGETOUR
intermediate	MIDDLING	juggling trick	SLIGHT
internal government		jumping-jack	PANTINE
of state	POLICE	jury-writ	VENIRE(FACIAS)
interpose	STICKLE	justify	DARRAIGN(E), DARRAIN(E)
interpret	AREAD, AREDE, ARREEDE		DARRAYN, DERAIGN
interpreter	TRUCHMAN	jut	JET
intimate	PRIVY, STRICT	keep	WARRANT
intriguer	CHAMBERER, TRINETER	—away from	REFRAIN
invention	WIT	—company	ASSORT
inverted	AWKWARD	—in bondage or custody	WITHHOLD
invite	BID	—into later year	OVERYEAR
inviting	COASTING	—out of the way	BE NAUGHT
involve	WIND(UP)	—under observation	WAIT (UP)ON
invulnerable	WOUNDLESS	—watch	WAKEN
inward	TOWARD	keeper of a warren	WARRENER
iris	FLOWER-DELICE	kettledrum	TIMBAL, TYMBAL
	FLOWER-DE-LUCE	key	KAIE
Irish		—of C major	PROPER CHANT
—labourer newly		keynote	KEY
arrived	GRECIAN	khan	CHAGAN, CHAM
—magistrate	RESIDENT MAGISTRATE, RM	kick	WINCE
irregular	HUMOUROUS	—about the limbs	SPRAWL
issue	PROOF	kid	YEANLING
item	PARCEL	—glove	CHEV(E)RON
—of news	OCCURRENT	kidney	REIN
itinerant	PIEPOWDER	kill	QUELL, MISDO, MORTIFY
jack-maker	JACKSMITH		SPILL, STRANGLE
jackdaw	CHOUGH, DAW-COCK	kind treatment	CHEER
jade	SPLEEN-STONE	kindness	CANDOUR
jargon	PARLANCE	king	COLE, LUD, OFFA, PRINCE
jasmine	JESSAMY	king's	
jealousy	YELLOWNESS	—bodyguard	HOUSE-CARL
jemmy	BETTY	—companion	THANE
jerk	BRAID, YERK	kingdom	REAME, REIGN
jerking movement	JUT	kinship	SIB
jest	BOURD, JIG, TOY	knave	BOY, VARLET

—in cards	MAKER, PUR
knell	KNOLL
knew	COUTH
knife	CUTTLE
knob	POMMEL
know	CAN, WIS(H), WIST, WIT, WOT
knowledge	CUNNING, WITTING
known	BEKNOWN, COUTH
labour	MOIL
labours of thought	WORKINGS
lace	GUARD
—head-covering	SHADE
—up	TRUSS
laciniation	DAG
lackey	SKIP-KENNEL
ladder	SCALE, STY
lady	BURD
lady's	
—cape	MANTEEL
—hood	SURTOUT
—maid	TIRE-WOMAN
lamb	YEANLING
lament	PLAIN
lance-corporal	LANCE PESADE, PRISADE
	PRISADD, SPEISADE
land	MOULD
—holding	ROOM
—tax	TALLAGE
—tenure based on	
military service	KNIGHT SERVICE
—valued at a penny	
a year	PENNYLAND
languish	QUAIL
lap-dog	PUPPY
last	YESTERN
—night	TONIGHT
late	LOW
lately	ALATE, NOW OF LATE
later spring	MARTLEMAS
lavish	WASTEFUL
law-officer's coif	BIGGIN
lawsuit	PLEA
lay	
—aside	VOID
—blame on	WITE, WYTE
—down	SUBMIT
—hold of	LATCH
—out in trade	OCCUPY
—table	COVER
lazar-house	SPITAL, SPITTLE(-HOUSE)
laziness	IDLEHOOD
lazy	LITHER
—fellow	LUSK
lead astray	BEWILDER
leading idea	BURTHEN
leap	SA(U)LT

leather	
—doublet	PLACCATE, PLACARD
—water-bottle	WATER-BOUGET
leave out of	
consideration	WAIVE
leer	TWEER, TWIRE
leg armour	JAMBEAU, JAMB(I)ER
legging	START-UP
legislative assembly	MOOT
legislature	STATES
leisure	RESPITE
lengthen out	REACH
—in utterance	PROLATE
Lent	SCAMBLING-DAYS
leopard	LIBBARD, LUBBAR
leper	MEAZEL, MESEL
lesson memorised	LIRIPIPE, LIRIPOOP
let down	VAIL
level to the ground	SLIGHT
liable to censure	OBNOXIOUS
liberal	FRANK
libration of celestial	
sphere	TREPIDATION
lie	
—about	LUSK
—in ambush	WAIT
life	LIVELIHEAD, QUICK
lift one's hat	VAIL
light	
—blow	BOB
—evening meal	VOIDE
—meal	UNDERN
lighting up	ILLUSTRATION
lightly cooked (eggs)	RARE
like	MARROW
limit	COAST, STINT, MARK
lineage	PARAGE
lineal descendant	NEPHEW
liquid measure	WINE-MEASURE
listen	LIST
listening	ATTENT
literary composition	STYLE
litter	TEAM
little	LITE, LYTE, WHEEN
—ball	BULLET
—boat	NACELLE
—boy	DANDIPRAT, DANDYPRAT
—gentleman	FRANKLIN
—hut	CABINET
—star	STARNIE
livelihood	LIVELIHEAD
liveliness	LIVELIHEAD
lively	VIVE
liver, brain and heart	PERFECTIONS
living	
—flesh	QUICK

—form	LIVELIHEAD	lying in ambush	WATCH
load	BURTHEN	mace	MAUL
loaded	LOADEN	mad	LYMPHATIC
loaf from finest flour	MANCHET	madam	MISTRESS
loathe	UG	magic	GRAMMARY(E)
loathsome	LOATHLY	magnetic attraction	ADAMANTINE
lock	SASSE	magnify	MULTIPLY
lock-up	ROUND-HOUSE	maid (of Orleans)	PUCELLE
lodestone	MAGNES	maiden	BURD
lodge	BESTOW, KEEP	main body	CONTINENT
lodgings for debtors	SPUNGING-HOUSE	—body of army	BATTALIA
lofty	STEEP	make	
log-throwing game	LOGGAT	—a	
logic	REDECRAFT	difference	SKILL
lollipop	LULIBUB	lord	LORD
long	PROLIX	mouth	MOE
—ago	YORE	—angry	WRATH
—baby-clothes	LONG-COATS	—away with	RID
—for	EARN	—bold	BOLDEN
longer	LENGER	—bright	ILLUSTRATE
longest	LENGEST	—clear to the mind	ILLUSTRATE
look		—hairless	PILL
—at	VISE	—ready	ADDRESS, PRED
again	REVISE	—safe	SAFE
—to	BESEE	—scant	SCANTLE
lookout	SPECULATOR	—stable	POISE, STABLISH
—place	TOOT	—the sign of the	
loom	FRAME	cross over	SAIN
loose		—ugly	UGLY
—character	RIBALD	—up	
—cloak	GABARDINE	hastily	JUMP
—gown	SLAMMAKIN, SLAMMERKIN	with cosmetics	PRIME
—greatcoat	WRAP-RASCAL	—war upon	WARRAY, WARREY
—woman	MOB, NAUGHTY PACK	—wheel-shaped	WHEEL
—wrap	NIGHT-RAIL	—worse	WORST
lord	SIRE	male guinea-fowl	TURKEY-COCK
lose	GO BY THE WORST	malice	SPLEEN
	GO WITH THE WORST	maliciously	UNHAPPILY
—strength	PALL	manage	MANURE
—vitality	DEAD	manageable	YARE
lost	BEWILDERED, LORN	manganese	MAGNESIA, MAGNESIUM
lot	WEIRD	manner	WISE
lotion	LAVATORY	manor	VILL
louvre	LOVER	manorial holding	HUSBANDLAND
love	AFFECT	mantle	ROCHET, ROCQUET
—making	SWAINING	manual	MECHANICAL
lover	PARAMOUR, SWAIN	map of the world	MAPPEMOND
low-born		marked attention	PARTICULARITY
—character	RIBALD	market	VENT
—churchman	LOW-BOY	marriage	HYMEN
—fellow	LOON	married woman	WOMAN OF THE WORLD
lower	SUBMIT, VAIL	Martinmas	MARTLEMAS
luck	VENTURE	marvel	MARL(E)
lump	LOAF	marvellous	WOND(E)RED
lusty	RANK	mask	VIZARD
luxurious	WANTON	masked sword-dance(r)	MATACHIN

mass	MESS, SAL(A)MON	military	
—of rock or stone	QUARRY	—engine	TREBUCHET
master	MAISTER, MAS(S)	—expedition	VOYAGE
	MES(S), SIRE	militia	FYRD
match	COPE, MARROW	milk	MANSUETTE
	PARAGON, SAMPLE	mind	WIT
mate	MAKE, MARROW	mineral dug from earth	FOSSIL
material	MASS	mirth	SPLEEN
—universe	KIND	misshapen egg	COCKNEY
matter	MASS, SENTENCE, SKILL	mischief	BALE
—of discourse	PLACE	misery	BALE
may	MOTE, MOUGHT	misfortune	CHANCE, DECAY, RUTH
mayor	PORTREEVE	misleading	SINISTER
mead	MEATH(E)	missile	MISSIVE
meadow-sweet	MEAD-SWEET, MEADWORT	missiles	ARTILLERY
meal	MEAT, MESS	mistaken	OVERSEEN
—time	MEAL-TIDE	mistletoe	MISLETOE, MISSEL
mean	MEDIUM, MENE, SOUND	mistress	WENCH
meaning	SENTENCE	mitigate	ASLAKE
measure	BE METE, MEED	mix	(CO-)MEDDLE, , MENG(E)
meatless days	BANIAN-DAYS		MING, MOULD
medal	MODEL	mixed	ME(I)NT, MENGED
mediate	STICKLE		MEYNT, MINGED
mediator	MEAN	mixing	CONTEMPERATION
medical	PHYSIC	mixture	MIXTION
medicinal	PHYSICAL	—of liquids	BALDERDASH
meet	OCCUR	mock orange	PIPE-TREE
—in advance	PREVENT	mockery	MOCKAGE
—on the way	OBVIATE	mocking ballad	JIG
melancholy	SPLEEN	model	PRECEDENT
melt	COLLIQUATE, RELENT	—of fashion	MODE
melting	COLLIQUABLE, COLLIQUANT	moderate	CHASTISE, CHASTIZE, MEAN
	COLLIQUATION	modest	PUDENT, PUDIC
mend	BEET, BETE	moisture	HUMOUR
menial of lowest grade	RIBALD	molar	WANG(-TOOTH)
menstrual discharge	FLOWER	moment	PUN(C)TO
mental activity	WORKING	monastery	MINSTER
mention	MIND, REMEMBER	money	CRAP, ROWDY
mercenary horse-soldier	RUTTER	—grubber	MUCKER
merciless	WANTON	monkey	JACKANAPES, MEERKAT
mercurial character	MERCURY	monstrosity	MONSTRUOSITY
mere	MEER	monstrous	MONSTRUOUS
merry		monumental stone	TOUCH
—andrew	JACK-PUDDING	mope	PEAK
	PICKLE-HERRING	more	MO(E)
—mood	MERRY PIN	mortal	WORLDLING, WORLDLY
metal that is not		motto	MOT, POESY
malleable	SEMI-METAL	moulded border	SWAGE
metaphor	TRANSUMPTION	mound	MOT(T)E, MOTE-HILL
Meum	SPICKNEL	mount	STY
mica	DAZE	mountebank	ANTIC, SALTIMBANCO
middle		mousetrap	SAMSON('S) POST
—class revolutionary	MUSCADIN	mouth	NEB
—of day or night	WAIST	move	MEVE, MOOVE, QUATCH
midwife	LUCINA		QUETCH, QUITCH, TROLL
migraine	MEGRIM	—faster	PUT ON

—off	WALK
—on	WAG
moveable	
—shed for besiegers	SOW
—stage	PAGEANT
moving	MOTIVE
much	MICKLE, MUCHEL
muddy	LIMOUS
muffle	MOB(B)LE
—the head	MOB
muffler	MUFFETTEE
mugger	SCOWRER
mulberry-tree	SYCAMINE
mule	MOYL(E)
multitude	NUMBER
mummy	ANATOMY
municipal officer	VARLET
murder	MURTHER, QUELL
murderer	MURTHERER
muscatel	MUSCADINE
muscle	MOUSE
musical	
—composition	MUSIC
—instrument	ORGAN
—instruments	MUSIC
various	SYMPHONY
musicians at municipal	
ceremonies	WAITS
must	MOTE
mutiny	MUTINE
mutual dealings	INTERDEAL
nag	ROUNCY
name	CLEEP, CLEPE, HETE
	HIGHT, NEMN
—in a list or	
document	ENGROSS
named	BENEMPT, BYNEMPT, HIGHT
	NEMPT, YCLEPED, YCLEPT
narcissus	ROSE OF SHARON
narrate	RECORD
narrative	PROSE
narrow	STRAIT, STRICT
narrowing	REBATEMENT
narrowly	STRAIT
native-born	KINDLY
natural	KINDLY
naturally able	INGENIOUS
nature	KIND
naval camouflage	WAISTCLOTH
nave	NEF
navigation manual	PORTOLAN(O)(CHART)
near	FORBY, NIE
neat	FEAT(E)OUS, FEATUOUS
	NET(T)
neck	HALSE, SWIRE
—covering	PARTLET
—tie	WATERFALL
neckerchief	NECKATEE
needle	NEELD, NEELE
needy	WANTING
négligé	MOB
negotiation	PRACTICE
negotiations	INTERDEAL
negro	NIGER
neighbourhood	VOISINAGE
neighbouring	NEIGHBOUR
neither Christian nor Jew	HEATHEN
nevertheless	ALGATE
news	ADVERTISEMENT
newness	NOVITY
nick of time	ARTICLE
niggard	PUCKFIST
niggardly	NITHING
nigh	NY
night	
—cap	BIGGIN
—dress	NIGHT-SHIFT
—mare	EPHIALTES
nimble	FLIPPANT, WIGHT
nimbly	YARELY
no matter what	
may happen	FALL BACK, FALL EDGE
noble	GENEROUS, GENTLE, THANE
—youth	CHILD(E), CHYLDE
nobleman's bodyguard	HOUSE-CARL
noise	BRUIT
noisy	STREPENT
nominate	VOICE
non-Christian	SARACEN
noodle	DAW-COCK, HODDY-DODDY
normal	JUST
Norwich strong ale	NOG
nose	
—band for horse	MUSROL
—bleed	YARROW
nostril	NARE
nostrum	SECRET
not	NE
—bated	BATELESS
—burdened	UNBURTHENED
—customary	UNCUSTOMED
—described	NONDESCRIPT
—discovered with test	OCCULT
—easily	UNEATH
—exquisite	INCURIOUS
—facetious	INFECITE
—fastidious	INCURIOUS
—fitting	UNDECENT
—handsome	UNDECENT
—helped	UNHOLPEN
—improbably	LIGHTLY
—known	UNWIST

—made polished	UNFASHIONED
—provided with	UNPURVEYED
—to respect	DISRESPECT
—used up	INEXHAUSTED
—well up	UNSEEN
note	COMMON-PLACE
—G	GAMUT
—in written music	PRICK
notice	MIND
notion	NOTICE
notwithstanding	MAU(L)GRE
	NATH(E)LESS(E)
	NAYTHLES
now	PRESENTLY
number of people	CONSORT
nun	VOWESS
nuptials	HYMENALS
nurse	NOURICE
nurture	NOUR(R)ITURE
oaths	SBLOOD, SBODIKINS
	SBUDDIKINS, ZBUD
oatmeal porridge	POTTAGE
obedience	OBEISANCE
obedient	BUXOM
obeisance	OBEDIENCE
object	
—of	
taunts	TAUNT
terror	BUG
—to	QUARREL
objection	QUARREL
objectionable	PERT
obliging	OFFICIOUS
oblique	AWKWARD
obscene	PAW(PAW)
obscure	BLEND
obsequious person	WAGTAIL
observance	TRIUMPH
observation	SPIAL
observe	SMOKE, SPECULATE, USE
obstinate	STIFF-HEARTED
obstruct	WAYLAY
obstructed	LET
obstruction	LET, TRUMP
obverse of coin	CROSS
occupy	MANURE
—oneself	TRADE
occur to	REMEMBER
occurrence	OCCURRENT
octave of festival	UTAS
oddness	IMPARITY
oeillade	EY(E)LIAD
of	ON
—another kind	OTHERGATES
	OTHERGUESS
—good disposition	WELL-THEWED

—high social position	WORTHY
—no	
avail	UNAVAILABLE
effect	IN WASTE
—silver	LUNAR
—stone	STONERN
—things of the	
same species	UNIVOCAL
—whatever kind	WHATSO
offal	INCHPIN, QUARRY
offence	DEFAULT, DISTASTE
	INJURY
offend	DISTASTE
offer	PREFER, PRETEND
—as a pledge	WAGE
—for sale	UTTER
—greeting of	PRESENT
office	MISTERY, MYSTERY
—in Court of Exchequer	PIPE OFFICE
—of	
Chancellor	CHANCERY
warden	WARDENRY
officer	
—who rounded up	
stray pigs	HOG-REEVE
	HOG-CONSTABLE
—without command	REFORMADO
official	
—in lists	MARSHAL
—permit	PLACARD
—who clears the way	WHIFFLER
offspring	SPERM, STRAIN
old	
—clothes	ELD, YORE
dealer	FRIPPER(ER)
shop	FRIPPERY
trade	FRIPPERY
—person	ELD
—time	ELD, YORE
—woman	AUNT, GRANDAM, GRANNAM
omission	BA(U)LK
on	AN
—a	
desperate enterprise	PERDU(E)
forlorn hope	PERDU(E)
—account of	ALONG
—approval	ON LIKING
—hand	TOWARD
—purpose	NONCE
—the	
near or left side	TOWARD
table	ON THE TAPIS
—wheels	AWHEELS
once	WHILOM
one	
—acting as surety	MAINPERNOR

—after the other	A-ROW	oral	LIVELY
—apt to change	CHANGELING	orchard	ARBOUR, ORCHAT
—born under Mercury	MERCURIAL	order	INSTITUTE, WILL
—bound to keep horse		—of battle	BATTALIA
for military service	HOBBLER	orderless composition	RHAPSODY
—given to sensual		organ-bellows	WIND-BAG
enjoyment	EPICURE	organised for	
—granting indulgencies	QUESTOR	rapid movement	VOLANT
—in charge of fences	HAYWARD	ornamental rosary bead	GAUD
—of		ostentatious vulgarian	SNOB
a pair	MARROW	ostrich	ESTRICH, ESTRIDGE
low rank	SNOB	otter	WATER-DOG
the rabble	RASCAL	out	
worthless character	PACK	—of	
—sent before to		kindness	PARAMOUR
provide lodgings	HARBINGER	the way	GEASON
—who		—upon it	HARO, HARROW
barters	SCORSE	outcast	WRETCH
becomes surety	PLEDGE	outcome	PROOF
clears the table	VOIDER	—of toil	LABOUR
complains	PLAINANT	outdo	SUPERATE
constructs		outer	UTTER
—fortifications	ENGINEER	—garment	SURCOAT
—military engines	ENGINEER	outermost sphere	PRIMUM MOBILE
deposited money on		outflank	OVERWING
going abroad	PUTTER-OUT	outlast	OUTDURE
deserves hanging	WAGHALTER	outlaw a woman	WAIVE
dwells in fancied		outlawed	BROKEN
security	SECURITAN	outlay	MISE
haunts draper's shops	SILKWORM	output	GET
is		outrageous	ENORMOUS
—disliked	WARLING	outride	OVERRIDE
—fantastical	FANTASTIC	outstrip	COTE, STRIP
—good for nothing but		outward appearance	SPECIES
paying the bill	SHOT-CLOG	—of promise	UPCOME
leads astray	SEDUCTOR	outwit	CROSSBITE
plots	ENGINEER	over	ORE
practises	OCCUPIER	overbearing	SUPERCILIOUS
puts on a false show	FACER	overcoat	SURTOUT
sells short weight	LEGER	overcome	EVINCE, FORDO, SUPERATE
serves in war	SERVITOR	overflow	SURROUND
talks nonsense	TWADDLE	overflowing	REDUNDANT
with coat of arms	GENTLEMAN	overgarment	BRAT
within confines	CONFINER	overhang	OVERWHELM
onward rush	RACE	overhanging	INCUMBENT
open	(A)PERT	overpower	EVINCE
—space between woods	LAWN	overpowering lustre	GLARE
—to view	UNVAIL(E)	overreach	LURCH, OUTGO
opening	OVERTURE	overrun	OVERREN
operate	PLAY	overshoe	PANTOF(F)LE, PANTOUFLE
operation	URE	overspread	OVERCOME
oppress	OVERSET	overtake	OVERCATCH, OVERGET
oppressed with hunger	A(N)HUNG(E)RED		OVERRIDE
	(A)HUNGRY	overthrown	PROFLIGATE
oppressive	FAINT	owner	LORD
optical/optics	PERSPECTIVE	ownership	FEE, PROPRIETY

oxygen	VITAL AIR
pack	
—horse	SUMMER
—load	SEAM
—of cards	PAIR
packet-boat	POST
paeony	PION(E)Y
pah	PAW
pain	WO(E)
painful	BALE
pains	TEEN(E), TENE
paint	LIMN, PEINCT
—for face	FUCUS
painter	BRUSH, LIMNER
pair	TWAIN, TWIN
pale	PALL, WHITELY
—blue	WATCHET
—by comparison	STAIN
palisade	STACKET
palisaded enclosure	PEEL
paltry	BALD
pampered effeminate	
person	WANTON
pan	WORK
panacea	DIACATHOLICON
pancake	FLAM(M), FLAUNE, FLAWN
pander	BROKER
panegyric	ELOGE, ELOGY, ELOGIUM
panic	AMAZE
pansy	PA(U)NCE, PAWNCE
Papal province	LEGATION
paramour	FRANION, LEMAN
parcel	SORT
pardon	GRACE
parentage	BROOD
parish	TOWNSHIP
park	WALK
parliament	THING
parliamentary bill	PETITION
parsimony	PARCIMONY
part	PARTY, TWIN(E)
partake	PERTAKE
partition	TRAVIS, TREVIS(S)
partly	PARCEL
—burned tree	RAMPICK, RAMPIKE
partner	COMPANION
pass	HALSE, PACE
—round the table	TROLL
—the night	LIE
passage	ALURE, PACE
—in a book	PLACE
passionate person	FUME
password	WATCHWORD
past	FORBY
pastime	PASTANCE
patch up	JUMP

patchwork	MOTLEY
path	STY, TROD
pattern	SAMPLER, SPOT
pause	ALLOW
pawn	OPPIGNERATE, OPPIGNORATE
—broker	LUMBERER
—shop	LUMBER
pay	YIELD
—out	DISPEND
—retribution for	ABY
—wages to	WAGE
payment	
—for nurse	NOURICE-FEE
—in	
goods	TRUCK SYSTEM
lieu of military	
service	WARD-CORN
pea	
—plants	PEASON
—shooter	TRUNK
peace	FRITH
peach	MALAKATOONE
	MELICOTO(O)N, MELLICOTTON
pearl-grey	GRISEOUS
peas	PEASON
peasant	PESA(U)NT, PEZANT, SWAIN
peep-show	PERSPECTIVE
peevish	FRAMPOLD
pellucid	SHEER
pelt with stones	LAPIDATE
pen-case	PENNER
penalty	UNLAW
pendant	BOB
penned	PEND
penny	D
peony	PINY, PION(E)Y
people	FOLK, ICENI
peopled part of country	INLAND
perceiving together	CO-SENTIENT
perchance	PERCASE
perfect	PERFET
perform	EXERT, JUGGLE
performance	FUNCTION
—of music	LESSON
perhaps	BELIKE, PERCASE
periodical	
—gathering to check	
weaponry	WAPINS(C)HAW
	WEAPON-S(C)HAW
	WAP(P)ENS(C)HAW
—payment	PENSION
perish	FORFAIR, STARVE
perjured	MANSWORN
perquisite	VALES, VAILS
persistent attack	OBSESSION
person	WIGHT

—blindfolded in blindman's buff	HOODMAN
—used as tool	ENGINE
—with a tail	TAILARD
personal	
—appearance	CHARACTER
—attendant	GENTLEWOMAN
personate	PRESENT
pert	BRISK
—person	SAUCE, WAGTAIL
pertain	LONG
pertaining to	
—carrying in the womb	GESTATORIAL
	GESTATORY
—eggs	OVAL
—generation	GENIAL
—letters of the alphabet	LITERARY
—marriage	GENIAL
—sight	VISIVE
—whirlpool	VORAGINOUS
perturbation	DISTEMPERATURE
perverse	FROWARD
pestilence	MURRAIN
pet	PEAT
Peter's penny	ROME-PENNY, ROME-SCOT
petitioner	ORATOR
petticoat	PLACARD, PLACKET
petty	PELTING
phantom	FEATURE
philosopher's stone	TINCTURE
philtre from mare	HIPPOMANES
phraseology	PARLANCE
phrenetic	PHRENTICK
physical pain	WO(E)
physician	LEECH, MEDIC, MEDICINER
physiognomy	VISNOMIE, VISNOMY
pickpocket	FILE
pie	
—crust	COFFIN
—of meat and eggs	LUMBER-PIE
piece	PEECE
—of	
cloth	PANE
doggerel	JIG
excrement	SIR-REVERENCE
music	LESSON
needlework	SPOT
news	NOVEL
plunder	CHEAT
work	SPOT
—together	RHAPSODISE
	RHAPSODISE
pieces of old cordage	JUNK
pierce	ENGORE, RIVE
pike	PARTISAN
pilchard	PILCHER

piles	FIG
pile up	BALK
pilfer	NIM
pilfered	NAM, NIMMED
pilgrim's staff	BOURDON
pill	PEEL
pillage	PEEL
pillory	TUMBREL, TUMBRIL
pimp	BROKER, BULLY
pinafore	BRAT
pineapple	PINA, PINE-CONE
pink	POUNCE
pip	PEEP
pipe	TIBIA
pippin	PIP
piratical publisher	LAND-PIRATE
pistil	POINTEL
pitch reached by bird of prey	PLACE
pitched	(Y)PIGHT
pith of plants	MARROW
pity	PIETY
placcate	PLACARD
place	DO
—for	
hawking	RIVER
performance of penance	PENITENTIARY
—in favourable position	STATE
—of	
abode	LIBKEN
retirement	RETIRE
—underneath	SUPPOSE
placed	YPLAST
placket	PLACARD
plague-spot	TOKEN
plaintiff	PLAINANT
plait	PLIGHT
plan	MODEL, PLAT, PLATFORM
plane	
—figure or surface	PLATFORM
—tree	PLANTAIN
plank	PLANCH
plant	GRAFT
—resembling animal	ZOOPHYTE
platane	PLANTAIN
plate for tableware	NEF
platter	LANX
play	
—the	
epicure	EPICURISE, EPICURIZE
fool	FON
—trick on	GLEEK
—with	DELUDE
fingers	PADDLE
wooden sword	WASTER

playful	FLIPPANT
plead	PERSUADE
pleasant	AMENE, LUSTY, MERRY
—behaviour	PLEASANCE
—sound	EUPHONIA
—words	FAIR WORDS
pleasantness	PLEASANCE
please	AGGRATE, LIKE, LIST
pleasing	LIKING, LUSTY
pleasure	PLEASANCE
—of taste	GUST
—seeking	PLEASURABLE
pleat	PINCH, PRAN(C)K(E)
pledge	BORROW, ENGAGE, SECURE
	WAGE, WED
—oneself to	BETROTH
plentiful (yield)	FOISON
plight	LIKING, SECURE
plighted	YPLIGHT
plot	PLOD
—of ground	PLAT
plough	EAR, ERE
plucked	PLUMED
plump	WELL-LIKING
plunder	ESCHEAT, PEEL, PILL, RAPE
plunge	MERGE
pocket	PLACARD
pod (pea)	PEA(S)(E)COD
poem	DIT(T), POESY
poet	MAKER
—laureate	ARCH-POET
poetry	POESY
point	PIQUE, POYNT, PUN(C)TO
—at whist	CORNER
—of	
perfection	POINT-DEVICE
	POINT-DEVISE
weapon	ORD
pointed bar	GAD
poise	POYSE
poison	POYSON
poke	POTE
pole	PERCH
policeman	RUNNER
polished	POLITE
political	STATIST
poll	DOD
pollard	DOD
polluted	CANKERED
pomegranate	PUNIC APPLE
pomp	TRIUMPH
ponder	POISE
poniard	POI(G)NADO
pooh	PUGH, TUSH
poor	SEELY, WANTING
—author	GARRETEER

pope	PAPA
porpoise	MEERSWINE
port	LARBOARD
portable	
—inkwell	INK-HORN
—organ	PORTATIVE
portcullis	CATARACT
portent	PRODIGY
portion	MEED, PIECE
—of food and drink	SIZE
portrait	POURTRAICT
portray	PORTRAIT, POUTRAY
portrayed	POURTRAYD, PURTRAID
	PURTRAYD
position of honour	WORSHIP
positive	POZ(Z)
possess	WIELD
possession	FEE, HAVEOUR, HAVIOUR
possessions	AVER, WORTH
possibility of recovery	RECOVER
post for various	
exercises	QUINTAIN
postman	POST
postpone	FRIST, REFER
postponed	PROTRACTED
postulate	PETITION
posture	GESTURE
posy	POESY, TUZZI-MUZZY
potash	KALI
potsherd	POTSHARD
pottage	PORRIDGE
powder	POULDER, POULDRE, POUNCE
power	DANGER
—of	
explaining	INTERPRETATION
seeing	VISIBILITY
powerless	IMPUISSANT
practic	PRACTICK, PRACTIQUE
practice	URE
—of pastry-making	PASTRY
practise	USE
—crystal-gazing	SCRY
—extortion on	POLL
—with waster	WASTER
practising	PRACTIC
praise	LO(O)S
prank	ESCAPE, GAUD, REAK, REIK
pranks	REAKS, REX
pranky	FROLIC
pray	BID
—thee	PRITHEE, PRYTHEE
prayer	BEAD
preach	PROPHESY
precede	PREVENT
precious	CHARY
—metal	PLATE

—stone	JASPER
preciousness	PRICE
pre-eminence	PREHEMINENCE
pre-eminently	ONLY
preen	PROIN(E), PROYN(E)
	PROIGN, WHET
preference	PRE-ELECTION
—for	MARK ON
prefix	PREPOSITION
pregnant	GREAT, QUICK
prejudge	PREJUDICE
prejudgment	PREJUDICE
preparation	ORDINANCE, PARASCEVE
prepare	ADDRESS, INSTRUCT
prepared	YARE, BOUND
presbytery	CLASSIS
prescription	LEECHDOM
present	PREFER
—to mind	OBJECT
preserve	
—in sugar	CONSERVE
—unhurt	SALVE
press	STRIP
—hard	OVERSET
—together	CONSTIPATE
pretended friend	BACK-FRIEND
pretext	SALVO
prevail	PERSUADE
prevent	LET, SECURE
previous	FORE
price	PURCHASE
prick with nail	ACCLOY
priests	MAGI
prince's friend	PRIVADO
princely stables	EQUERRY
principle extracted	TINCTURE
printed	PRINT
prison	LUMBER, NEWGATE
—chaplain	ORDINARY
privacy	PRIVITY
private	INWARD
—apartment	PARADISE
—end	SELF-END
—friend	PRIVADO
—marriage	HANDFASTING
—parts	SHAME
—property or right	PECULIAR
—room	CONCLAVE, GARDEROBE
privy	GARDEROBE, PRIVATE, SIEGE
prize	PURCHASE
probably	BELIKE
probationary marriage	HANDFASTING
probe	TENT
proceed	FAND, FOND, TRACE
proceeding from	
divine favour	GRACIOUS

proceeds	AVAIL
proclamation	PLACARD
procuress	AUNT, BROKER
procuring	BROK(ER)AGE
profession	FUNCTION, MISTER
profile	PURFLE
profit	(A)VAIL, UTILITY
profitable	BEHOVEFUL, BEHOVELY
profitless	WASTEFUL
profuse inflow	COLLIQUATIVE
profusion	LAVISH, WASTE
progeny	IMP, INCREASE
prohibit	DEFEND
projectile	FIREWORK
projecting window	SHOT-WINDOW
projector	SCHEMATIST
prolong	PROROGUE
prominent	EGREGIOUS
promise	BANK, BEHIGHT, BEHOTE
promising	TOWARDLY
prompt	EXPEDITE
promptly	BELIVE, TIGHT(LY), TIT
	TITE(LY), TYTE, YARELY
prone	PROCLIVE
proof	PREEVE, PREIF(E)
property	FEE, PROPRIETY
propitiation	PROPITIATORY
propagate	TRADUCE
proposal	SUPPOSAL, PROPOSE
propriety	PROPERTY
prospect-glass	PROSPECT
prosperity	THRIFT, WEALTH
prostitute	COCKATRICE, MUTTON
	PLOVER, PUBLIC WOMAN
	PUNK, STEW, TRULL
protect	WARRANT
—with	
earthwork	ENSCONCE
sconce	ENSCONCE
protective covering	BARD
Protestant	RELIGIONER
Protestantism	RELIGION
protuberance	KNAP
protuberant part	WEM(B), WEAMB
proud	STIFF-RUMPT, STOUT, SUPERB
prove	ASCERTAIN, DARRAIGN(E)
	DARRAIN(E), DARRAYN
	DERAIGN, PREEVE
—to be true	SOOTHE
proved/proven	PREVE
proverb	PARABLE
provide	PREPARE
—battlements	BATTLE
—for	BESEE
in advance	PREVENT
province	REAME

provision	STUFF
—of things for use in rotation	SHIFT
provisions	BELLY-TIMBER
—of the table	ENTERTAINMENT
prowess	VASSALAGE
prowl	PROLL
prowler	PROLER
prudent	CONSIDERATIVE, WARE
prune	PROIGN, PROIN(E) PROIN(E), PROYN(E) PRUINE, PREWYN, SHRED
Prussia	(S)PRUCE
pshaw	TUSH
psychosis	DERANGE
public	APERT
—report or rumour	FAME
publication of book	EDITION
publisher	STATIONER, UNDERTAKER
puck	PUG
puddle	FLUSH
puff	
—of wind	HUFF
—up	HUFF
pulley	TRICE
pulp of plants	MARROW
pulpit	CHAIR
pun	PUNDIGRION
punctilio	PIQUE, PUN(C)TO
puncture	POUNCE
punish	JUSTIFY, SHEND VISIT, WREAK
punishment	PINE, PYNE, WAR(R)ISON WRACK, WREAK
puny	PUISNE
puppet show(man)	MOTION(-MAN)
purchaser	CHAPMAN
pure	MERE, NET(T)
purely	MERELY
purgative electuary	DIACATHOLICON
purify	CHASTISE, CHASTIZE
purity	CANDOUR
purple	PUNIC
purplish/black	PUKE
purport	TENOUR
purpose	CAST, PRETEND PURPORT, SHAPE
purse	BUNG
purser	NIP-CHEESE
pursue	PERSUE
put	DO
—an end to	WASTE
—away	WAIVE
—down	DO DOWN
—forth	EXERT
—forward	PREFER

—in difficulty	STRAIT
front of	OBJECT
—off	FUB
in time	PROTRACT
—one's seal to	ENSEAL
—or keep in loft	LOFT
—out	UTTER
of countenance	DOR
—to	
shame	REBUKE, SHEND
trouble	PAIN
puzzle	PUSLE
quack	SALTIMBANCO
quadrate	QUARTILE
qualify	CONDITIONATE
quality	PROPRIETY
quarrel	SQUARE
quarry	CURRIE, CURRY
quay	KAY, KEY
queen	PRINCE
—bee	KING
question	SCRUPLE
quick	EXPEDITE, RATH(E), YARE
quickly	BELIVE, SWITH, YARELY
quiet	HUSH
quinsy	SQUINANCY
quire	QUAIR
quit	QUITE, VOID
quiz	SMOKE
quoth	QUOD
rabbit-hole	CLAPPER
rabble	RASCAILLE, RASCAL
race	GOAL, ROD
—course	HIPPODROME
rack	TOUSE, TOUZE, TOWSE, TOWZE
rag	ROW
rail	RAYLE
railway	GWR, LMS, LNER, SR
rain	RAYNE
raised edge	LEDGE
rake	SWINGE-BUCKLER
rally	REALLY, RELY
ramble	TROLL
rampart	RAMPIRE
range	RAUNGE
rank	CENSE, GREE, SIEGE
—of captain	CAPTAINRY
—with	FILE WITH
rant	TEAR A CAT, TEAR THE CAT
rapine	RAPE
rarely	SELD
rascal	RASCAILLE
rash	HASTY-WITTED
rate	ROW
—of tax	CENSE, CESS

rather	LIEFER, LIEVER	—from	OVERGET
rational	SOBER	recovery	RECOVER, RECURE
ravages	WASTES	red	
ravish	CONSTUPRATE, OPPRESS	—ochre	RUBRIC
	VITIATE	—pimple	BUBUKLE
—with delight	RAPE	reddish-brown	SOAR(E), SORE
raze	SLIGHT	redoubtable	REDOUBTED
reach	AREACH, HENT	reduce to hardship	STRAIT
—forward	PRETEND	reduction	BATEMENT
reached	RAUGHT, ROUGHT	reed	
read	REDE	—bunting	JUNCO
readily	YARELY	—grass	FLAG
reading	LECTURE	refinement	EXILITY
ready	YARE, BOUND	reflect	ADVISE
—for action	PREDY	reflection of self in eye	BABY
—to		reformed person	REFORMADO
learn	TOWARD	reformer	REFORMADO
make advances	COMING	refract	REFRINGE
take offence	MIFTY	refrain	BURTHEN, FA(UX)BURDEN
wither away	MIFTY		WITHHOLD
realgar	RESALGAR, ROSAKER	—of song	BOB
realm	REAME, REIGN	refresh	REFOCILLATE
rebellious	MALIGNANT	refreshment on journey	BAIT
rebound	RESULT	refuge	SUBTERFUGE
rebuked	SHENT	refutation	CONVINCEMENT, ELENCH
rebut	ELIDE	refute	CONVINCE, REDARGUE
recall	REVOKE		REFEL(L), REPROVE
—from banishment	REPEAL	regard with malice	MALIGN
recapture	REPRISE	regent	WARDEN
receive	ENTERTAIN, LATCH	registrar	REGISTER
	UNDERTAKE	regulate a contest	STICKLE
—a		reign	RAYNE
part of	PARTICIPATE	reinforce	RENFORCE, SUPPLY
person well or ill	RESENT	reinforcement	RECRUIT
recent (dates)	LOW	reject	CAST, WAIVE
receptacle	RESERVATORY	rejoicing	OVATION
reception		relate	REDE
—after childbirth	UPSITTING	relating to	
—of visitors while		—passions	PATHETIC
dressing	TOILET	—time	CHRONIC
reciter of romances	JESTER	—yesterday	YESTERN
reck	PASS, RETCH	relation	AFFINE, HABITUDE
—of	KEEP	release	ASSOIL
recked	RAUGHT	relic	RELICT
reckless	RECHLESS	relieve	BEET, BETE
reckon	IMPUTE, VOGUE	—by a pause	RESPITE
reckoning	NICK	religious	
recognise	ACKNOW, WIT	—direction	CAUTEL
—at a distance	KEN	—faith	LAY
recommend	WISH	—offerings	DEVOTION
recompense	GRATIFICATION	relish	GUST, TASTE
reconcile	ATONE	relishingly	SAVOURLY
record	MEMORISE, MEMORIZE	remain	
	MIND, REMEMBER	—awake	WAKEN
recount	REFER	—in expectation of	WAIT
recover	RECURE	remarkably	UNCOMMON

remedial	WHOLESOME
remedy	LEECHDOM, REMEAD
	REMEDE, REMEID
remember	PRESENT, RECONNOITRE
remind	MIND, REMEMBER
remorse	AYENBITE, HAD-I-WIST
remove	SUBLATE, VOID
—a veil from	UNVAIL(E)
—wrongfully	MISTAKE
rend	RENT
—in pieces	TO-REND
render as due or fitting	YIELD
renew efforts	RENFORCE
renounce	REN(A)Y, RENEY
rent	GAVEL, YRENT
repay	AP(P)AY, QUIT, YIELD
repeat the Lord's Prayer	PATTER
repentance	PENANCE
report with clamour	BRUIT
reprehend sharply	NIP
represent	PRESENT, REFER
—as bad	DEPRAVE
representative of King of Spain	VISITOR GENERAL
reprisals	MARQUE
reproach	SHEND
—with	EXPROBATE
reproduce	REFER
reproof	CORREPTION
republic	STATE
repulse	FOIL, REFEL
repulsive	LO(A)TH
reputation	LO(O)S, VOICE, WORSHIP
repute	SAVOUR, VOGUE
request	REQUIRE
require	WILL
requite	REQUIT
reservation	SALVO
reservoir	RESERVATORY
resident	LE(I)DGER, LEIGER, LIEGER
resign	WAIVE
resist	GAINSTRIVE
resolution	POINT
resort	FREQUENCY, USE
respect	WORSHIP
respectful	RESPECTIVE
respite	FRIST
rest	REQUIEM
resting-place	GITE
—on journey	MANSION
restive	RESTIFF, HOT-MOUTHED
restless	DISQUIET
restrain	CHASTISE, CHASTIZE, CONCLUDE
	REBUKE, REFRAIN, STINT
restrict	STINT

resulting from accident	OCCASIONAL
retain in service	ENTERTAIN
retreat	RECOIL, RETIRE
	RETRAI(C)T, RETRAITE
retrograde	REGREDE
return	RETIRE, REVOLVE
reveal	BEWRAY, UNVAIL(E)
reveller	ROARER, ROARING-BOY
reverse of coin	PILE
revert	RECOIL, RESORT
revile	MISSAY
revolving easily	VOLUBLE
reward	MEED, WAR(R)ISON, YIELD
rhetorical figure	SCHEME
rhinoceros	RHINOCEROT(E)
rhyme	RHIME, RHYTHM, RYTHME
ribaldry	RIBAUDRY
rich	
—cloth	PALL
—decoration	PARAMENT
rid	QUIT
riddle	CRIBBLE
ridge	BA(U)LK
ridicule	SMOKE
riding-horse	ROUNCY
right	
—moment	PUDDING-TIME
—to	
cut wood	HAY-BOTE, HEDGE-BOTE
food in forest	PU(L)TURE
hold court	LEET
hunt or keep game	WARREN
rigorously	STRAIT
rim	RYMME
rime	RHIME
ring-dance	CAROL
rioter	SWINGE-BUCKLER
rise	STY(E)
risk	PLIGHT
risque	RISK
rival	MATE, PARAGON
rive	RYVE
riven	YRIVD
river-mouth	OSTIUM
roast	ROST
roasting	USTULATION
robbed	RAFT
robe	PARAMENT
robustness	HARDIHEAD
rock dug from earth	FOSSIL
rod	GAD
rode	RID
rogue	LIMMER
roguish	ROGUY
—child or animal	WANTON
roll	TROLL, WALK

—back	REVOLVE
—in	
blood	WELTER
the grass	GREEN GOWN
—of parchment	PELL
rolling	VOLUTATION
—gait	WALLOW
Roman	ROMISH
romance	ROMAUNT
room	ROUM
—beside stage for	
musicians	MUSIC-ROOM
—mate	CHAMBER-FELLOW
root	WROOT
rote	ROATE
rough	ASPER, CRABBED, ROW, STURDY
round	ROWND
rout	HURRICANE
row of	
—stakes	ORGUE
—trees trained on stakes	ESPALIER
royal	REAL
Royalist	MALIGNANT
royalty	REALTY
rub	FEEZE, PHE(E)SE, PHEEZE
rudely jesting	INFECITE
ruff	PARTLET
ruffle	ROUSE
—feathers	FRILL
ruin	FORDO, HEAP
ruined	NAUGHT, RUINATE
ruinous	WASTE
rule	WIELD
—over	OVERRULE
ruler	RECTOR
rum	RUMBULLION
rumour	NOISE, SPEECH, TOY, VOICE
rump of horse	CROUPON
run	COURSE, RACE
—about	TROLL
—aground	GRAVEL
rush	LANCE, LOOSE, RANDOM, RASH
rustic	BOR(R)EL(L), RUSSET, SWAIN
	UPLANDISH, WOOLLEN
sack	BUDGET
—contents	BUDGET
sacrifice	SCARIFY
—of animal's shoulder	HEAVE-SHOULDER
sacrificial victim	HOST
sad	WO(E)
sadden	ATTRIST, CONTRIST
saddle	
—bow	ARSON
—cloth	PANEL
saddler	HORSE-MILLINER
sailor	SHIPMAN

saint	HALLOW
salad	SALLAD, SALLET
sale	VENT
salt	IODURET
—of uric acid	LITHATE
salutation in	
drinking	WASSAIL
salute	HALSE, MAKE ONE'S MANNERS
	MOVE, SALUE
—by raising hat	HAT
sanctuary	FRITH(SOKEN)
	GIRTH, GRITH
sane	SOBER
sarcasm	GIRD
sat	SATE
Satan	LEVIATHAN
satisfaction	CONTENTATION, SUFFISANCE
satisfied	PAID
satisfy	AP(P)AY, PAY
—in advance	PREVENT
saucepan	CHAFER
savage	SALVAGE
save	SA, SPARE
—from objection	SALVE
—your-reverence	SIR-REVERENCE
savings	THRIFT
savour	RESENT
savourless	WEARISH
savoury	GUSTFUL
say	
—in answer	UNDERSAY
—wrongly	MISSAY
saying	SPEECH
says	SAITH
scabbiness	SCALL
scantily	SCARCELY
scanty	PENURIOUS
scarcely	UNE(A)TH, UNEATHES
	UNNETHES
scarlet pimpernel	WINCOPIPE
scatter	STROW
scattered	BESPRENT
scent out	SMOKE
scheme	PLAT
scholar	ARTSMAN
school-teacher	SCHOOL-DOCTOR
scimitar	SEMITA(U)R, SYMITAR(E)
scion	IMP
scoff	DOR, GLEEK
scorched	ADUST
score	LAW
—for keeping account	NICK
Scottish	SCOTIAN
scout	SCURRIER, SCURRIOUR
	SPIAL
scrape	HOBBLE

scratch	SCRAT
screech	SHRITCH
screw	VICE, WREST
scribe	SCRIVENER
scrub	SHRUB
scrupulous	CURIOUS
scrupulousness	CURIOSITY
scum	MANTLE
sea	
—bird	PINK
—bottom	GROUND
—bred officer	TARPAULIN(G)
—monster	WASSERMAN
—serpent	ELLOPS
—wolf	SEA-ELEPHANT
seal up	ENSEAL
search	INQUEST
—out	INDIGATE
seasonable	TIDY
seasoning	SEASON
seat	ROOM, SEL(LE), SIEGE
—of	
authority	SEE
dignity	SEE, SIEGE
emotions	ENTRAILS
sanctuary	GRITH-STOOL
seclude oneself	SEQUESTER
second	STICKLER
secondary rainbow	WATER-GALL
secret	DE(A)RN
—arrangement	PACK
secure	RUG
security	BANK, WED
sedge	SEG
seduce	JAPE
seek	ENQUIRE, INQUIRE
—again	REPEAT
—by enquiry	HEARKEN
—to	
bring about	PURCHASE
induce	PERSUADE
seeking food	RELIEF
seem	BESEEM, SEMBLE
—likely	LIKE
segment	ARTICLE
seize	DEPREHEND, AREACH, LATCH
	REACH, SEIS, SURPRISE
—and carry off	RAPE
—upon	FANG
seized	HENT
seizure	PRIZE, PURCHASE, RAPE
seldom	SELD
select what serves	
one's purpose	GARBLE
self	
—congratulatory spirit	GLORY
—indulgent	WANTON
—seeking cleric	ROME-RUNNER
—willed	FROWARD
selfish end	SELF-END
seller of indulgences	PARDONER
semblance	LIKELIHOOD
send	
—away	VOID
—on a journey	TRAVEL
sense	SENTENCE
—of shame	PUDOR
senseless	SURD
sensible	WITTY
sentinel	CENTINEL(L), WAIT, WARDEN
sentry	CENTRY
separate	DISCREET, INTERVENE
	TWIN(E)
—and remove	ESLOIN, ESLOYNE
	ELOI(G)N
—from one another	DEPART
—lodging	MANSION
serf	HELOT, VILLEIN
serge	SURGE
sermon	SPELL
serpent	WORM
servant	FEEDER, (KITCHEN-)KNAVE
	SCULLION
serve	KA(E), STEAD
—as a soldier	MILITATE, TRAIL A PIKE
service	FEE, MISTERY
	MYSTERY, WAITERAGE
set	STEAD, TILL
—aside a veil	UNVAIL(E)
—forth	RECORD
—hand to	HAND
—in	
array	PITCH
front	PREFER
order	DISPONE, PRAN(C)K(E)
—of	
dice	BALE
persons eating together	MESS
—on edge	SURBED
—rolling off the tongue	TROLL
—up	ROUSE, STABLISH
—with stars	STELLIFY
setting	PRINT
settle	DISCUSS
—in	HABITUATE
settled	SPED
settler	INHABITOR
seven years	PROPHETIC WEEK
severally	IN PARTICULAR
sewer	(COMMON-)SHORE, SURE
sex	KIND, RACE
sexual intimacy	KNOWLEDGE

shake the feathers of	ROUSE
shaken	SHAKED, SHAKT, SHOOK
shameful	PUDENDOUS
shape	FEATURE
shaped	SHAPEN
shapely	FEAT(E)OUS, FEATUOUS
share	SNACK
—a dwelling	STALL
—of expense	LAW
—out	IMPART
sharpened	GROUNDEN
sharper	CONEY-CATCHER
shed light on	ENLIGHT(EN)
sheep	MUTTON
shelter from	WEATHER
shepherd	FEEDER
—boy	HERD-GROOM
sheriff	GREAVE, GRIEVE, VISCOUNT
shield worn on left arm	GLOVE-SHIELD
shine	LEAM, LEME, SHEEN
ship	ARGO, WOODEN HORSE
ship's decoration	WAISTCLOTH
shirt	PARTLET
shock	SCANDAL
shoes	SHOON
shoot	IMP, SPRNG
—arrow short or wide	DRIB
—out	LANCE
shore	CONTINENT, RIVAGE
short	
—burst of bird song	JERK
—musical phrase	POINT
—spear	DEMI-LANCE
—time ago	EVEN NOW
—veil at back of head	VOLET
shorten (sail)	SCANTLE
shortened	DAG
shortening in pronunciation	CORREPTION
shortly	AT A WORD
shot	SHOTTEN
—out into nooks	NOOK-SHOTTEN
shoulder-cloth while hair-dressing	TOILET
show	CON
—a (bold) face	FACADE
—forth	DETECT
—in favourable light	ILLUSTRATE
—place	VISIBILITY
showing care or nicety	CURIOUS
showy dress	BRAVERY
shrew	SHROW
shrewish	CURST
shrewd	SHROWD
shriek	SCRIKE, SHRITCH
shrivel	WELK
shrivelled	WRITHLED
shrubbery	ARBORET
shudder	GRISE
shuffle cards (dishonestly)	PACK
shut	SHET
—in	IMPALE
—the eyes	WINK
sickly	QUEACHY, QUEECHY
—smelling	FAINT
side	COAST, PLAT
sideboard	CREDENCE
siege	LEAGUER, OBSESSION
—engine	WAR-WOLF
sift	CRIBBLE, GARBLE
sigh	SITHE
sighed	SIGHT
sight	VISIBILITY
signify	BEMEAN, MAGNIFY, SKILL
silent	HUSH, WHIST
—game of cards or dice	MUMCHANCE
silly person	LIRIPIPE, LIRIPOOP
silver 1½d piece	DANDIPRAT, DANDYPRAT
similitude	LIKELIHOOD
simple	SILLY
simpleton	COKES, ROOK WOODCOCK, DAW
simulate belief	COLLOGUE
sin	FOLLY
since	SIN, SITHEN
sincerely	ENTIRE
sing	RECORD
singly	ONLY
sink	DEVALL
sip	DELIBATE
sir	LORDING
sit	SET
—well on	BESIT
sixpence	BENDER, TESTER(N)
skein	SKENE
ski	SNOW-SHOE
skilful	HEND, WELL-SEEN
skilfulness	WISDOM
skilfully	YARELY
skilled workman	PRUD'HOMME
skin	PELL
skirmish	ESCARMOUCHE
skirt	GORE
skulk	LUSK
slack	LASH
slake	ASLAKE
slander	MISSAY
slash	CARBONADO
slattern	SLAMMAKIN, SLAMMERKIN
slave	NATIVE, THEOW

sledge taking criminals to the gallows	HURDLE
slenderness	EXILITY
slid	SLIDED
slighting	SLIGHT
slimy	LIMOUS
slip glidingly	SLUR
slipper	SLIP-SHOE
slippery	GLIB(BERY)
slogan	SLUGHORN(E)
slovenly-dressed woman	SLAMMAKIN
	SLAMMERKIN
slow	LASH
sluggish	LENTOUS
sluggishness	LENTOR
sluice	SASSE
slut	PUCELLE, PUZZLE
small	
—articles of wood	TREEN
—branch	RICE
—bulb	CHIVE
—freeholder	FRANKLIN
—horse	PONEY
—hunting dog	KENNET
—quantity	DRIB
—river	RIVERET
—silver coin	SILVERLING
—stone implement	MICROLITH
smallness	EXILITY
smear with blood	GILD
smile	SMOILE, SMOYLE
smiling	BONNIE, BONNY
smock	SHIFT
smoke (tobacco)	DRINK
smoker	TOBACCONIST
smooth	GLIB, SLIGHT, TERSE
smote	SMIT
smother	OPPRESS
smuggle	OWL
smuggler	OWLER
snake	ELLOPS, WORM
snap	SNIP
snare	ENGINE
snatch	REACH
—away	HENT
sneaking	SHEEP-BITING
snub	FRUMP
snug	RUG
soaked in blood	BEWELTERED
sob	SINGULT
sociable	COMPANIABLE
social party	HURRICANE
socially accessible	GENERAL
society	HETAIRIA
sod	SCRAW

sofa	DAY-BED
softening	LENIENT
spiked barrier	TURNPIKE
soil	GLEBE
sojourn	TARRY
soldier	CENTINEL(L), MAN-OF-WAR MILITARY, SOULDIER
soldier's	
—bastard	SON OF A GUN
—cloak	MANTEEL
sole of foot	PALM
solicitude	CARK
solitary	DEARN
solve	ASSOIL
something	
—preparatory to	INDEX
—that surrounds	WAIST
somewhat	SOMEDEAL
son	SONNE
song	FIT(T), FITTE, FYTTE
soothe	BALM, STROKE
soothing	LENIENT
sophism	ELENCH
soreness of eyes	LIPPITUDE
sorrel	SOAR(E), SORE
sorrow	CONDOLEMENT, TEEN
sorrowful	BALE, TRIST
sorry	WP(E)
sou	SOUS(E)
sound	SANE
—in health	WHOLE
sounding dreadfully	HORRISONOUS
soundness	HEAL
sour	EAGER
source	OFFSPRING
—of	
hangman's rope	NECK-WEED
motion	PRIMUM MOBILE
souse	SOUCE, SOWCE, SOWS(S)E
soused	SOUCT
spa	SPAW
space	CANTON
Spanish broom	SPART
sparing	SCARCE
sparkle	GLISTER
spawn	SPERM
speak	BESPEAK
—fair	PALP
—of	VOICE
—to or of	WORD
—wrongly	MISSAY
speaking	WORDING, PARLANCE
—freely	LAXATIVE
spear	GAD(E), GAID, GLAIVE LA(U)NCEGAY(E)
—rest	FEUTRE, FEWTER

spectacles	GLASS EYES
speculation	WISDOM
speculative imagination	PROJECT
speech	PARLANCE, PARLE, SPELL
spell	WEIRD
spend labour on	LABOUR
spew	SPUE
spiced sweetened wine	PIMENT
spider	ATTERCOP
spied	SPIDE
spignel	SPICKNEL
spiked portcullis	HERSE
spin	TROLL
spine	CHINE
spinner	SPINSTER
spinning top	NUN
spiritless	AMORT, HILDING
	SPRIGHTLESS
spiritual perception	WISDOM
spit on	BESPIT
spite	MAU(L)GRE, SPLEEN
splendent	SPLENDIDIOUS
splint	SPLINTER
spoil	BRIBE, WRONG
spoilt child	WANTON
spokesman	ORATOR
sponge	SPUNGE
sponsor	SUSCEPTOR, UNDERTAKER
—at baptism	GOSSIP
sport	BOURD
sportive	LUDICROUS
—child or animal	WANTON
spot	GOUT, MOIL
—of iron-mould	MOLE
spotted as with plague	TOKENED
spouse	COMPANION, FE(A)RE
	FEER, FIERE, PHEERE
spread	SPRED(D), SPREDDE(N)
	STROW, WALK
—out	POUR
spring	LENT
—catch or trap	SNAPHA(U)NCE
	SNAPHAUNCH
sprinkle	POUNCE
—with ornaments	SPANG
sprinkled	SPRENT
—over	BESPRENT
spruce	BRISK
spy	SPIAL, WAIT
squander	BEZZLE, LASH, SPORT
squire	DONZEL
St Thomas's Day	MUMPING-DAY
staff of authority	WARDER
stag's brow	RIGHTS
stage	
—machine	PAGEANT
—performance	SCENE
—producer	UNDERTAKER
stain	SMIT, SOILINESS, STAYNE
stair	STAYRE
stake	PEEL, VIE
—higher	REVIE
stalemate	STALE
stall	TRAVIS, TREVIS(S)
—keeper	STALLENGER, STALLINGER
stalwart	PRETTY
standard bearer	ANCIENT
standing out	EXTANT
stanza	STANCE
star	ASTER, STARN, STERN
start	BRAID
starting-post	GOAL
starvation	FAMISHMENT
starve	STERVE
state	ESTATE, REPUBLIC
state	
—barge	GALLEY-FOIST
—governor	PRESIDENT
—of being	
awake	WATCH
well	WEAL
static	
electricity	VITREOUS ELECTRICITY
statue	STATUA
stay	MANSION
stayed	STAID
steadfast	STEDFAST
steady	STEDDY, STEEDY
steal	BRIBE, NIM
steer	STEAR(E)
steerage	STEARAGE
steered	STEARD
steering-gear	STERN
steersman	PILOT, STEARSMATE
steersman's place	STERN
step	GREE, GRE(E)CE, GRECIAN
	GRE(E)SE, GREESING
	GRESSIN, GRI(E)CE
	GRISE, GRIZE
—mother	STEP-DAME
steward	REEVE
stick	GAD
stiff	STOOR, STOUR
	STOWRE, STURE
stimulate	URGE
stint	SCANTLE
stir	QUATCH, QUETCH, QUITCH
—up	AMOVE
stirring the emotions	WORKIN
stocks	HARMANS
stocking	NETHERSTOCK
stole	NAM, NIMMED, STALE

stolen	STOLE	struck	STRAKE, STOKE, STROOK(E)
—article	CHEAT		STRICKEN, STRO(O)KEN
—goods	PURCHASE		STRUCKEN
abandoned	WAIF	structure erected	
stomach	HEART, WOMB	at conduit	STANDARD
stoop	LOUT, LOWT	struggle	CAMP
stop	EMBAR, ESTOP, STAP, STINT	strumpet	BULKER, PUNK
—contention	STICKLE		WAISTCOATEER
—for refreshment	BAIT	strut(ting movement)	JET
—up	CONSTIPATE	stubborn	STOUT
stout	TALL	stumbling	OFFENCE
—robber	ROBERDSMAN	stun	AMAZE, STON(NE)
	ROBERTSMAN	stung	STONG
straddle	STRODDLE	stupendous	STUPENDIOUS
straight	STRAIT	stupid person	WOODCOCK
—on	ENDLONG	sturdy beggar	ABRA(HA)M-MAN
straightness	RECTITUDE	style	ENSTYLE
straightway	INCONTINENT	subaqueous	DEMERSAL
strain	FIT(T), FITTE, FYTTE	sub-division of	
	INTEND, STREIGNE	cantred or hundred	CAMMOT
straits	STRESS	subdue	DO DOWN, MATE, QUAIL
strap for horse's load	WANTY	subject	
straw	STRAMMEL, STRUMMEL	—for dissection	ANATOMY
—hat	HIVE	—to	
streaked in rings	RING-STRAKED	authority	OBNOXIOUS
stream	LAKE	transmutation	TINCT
street		sublet	UNDERSET
—bully	SCOWRER	submissive	SUBMISS, SUBORDINATE
—cleaner	SCAVAGER	submissively	SUBMISSLY
—refuse	SCAVAGE	submit	PREFER
—thief	BULKER	substance	SUBJECT
strength	HEAD	substitute fraudulently	SUPPOSE
strengthen	COMFORT	subtenant	VALVASSOR
stretch	REACH		VAVASOUR
stretched	INTENDED	subtle	SUBTIL(E)
strew	STRAW, STROW	succeed	FADGE
strewed	STRAWED, STRAWN, STROWED	success	SPEED
	STROWN, STRAWED, STRAWN	successors	SEQUEL
strife	BARGAIN, BARRAT	sucker	GRAFT
strike		sudden	
—to the heart	HEART-STRIKE	—heeling	SEEL
—with fear	AMAZE	—inflow	ANCOME
string up	KILT, TRUSS	—movement	BRAID
stringing together		suddenly	UNWARES
of poems	RHAPSODY	sue	IMPLEAD
striped	GUARDED	—for	PLEAD
strive	FORCE	suffer injustice	
—against	GAINSTRIVE	or injury	HAVE WRONG
strode	STRID	suffering	PASSIVE, PINE, PYNE
stroke	BUFF, JERK, STRIKE	sufficiency	SUFFISANCE
stroll	TROLL	sugar-refiner	SUGAR-BAKER
strong	RANK, VALIANT, VALID	suit	EFFEIR, EFFERE, FADGE, HIT
	WIGHT	suitable	HANDSOME
—drink	BUB	suite	SUIT
—tobacco	MUNDUNGUS	sulks	GLOUT, GLUMPS
strop	STRAP	sulky look	GLOUT

sullen	SOLEIN
sultan	SOLDAN
sum and substance	CONTINENT
summon	PROVOKE
summons	INTERPELLATION
sun	SONNE
—dew	ROSA-SOLIS
—flower	GIRASOL(E)
sunk and dispirited	AMORT
supercargo	MERCHANT
supercilious(ly)	OVERLY
superintend	INTEND
superior	OVERLY
supernatural being	WIGHT
supine	BOLT UPRIGHT
supplement	MEND, SUPPLY
supply with husband	HUSBAND
support	EASEMENT, SOOTHE
suppose	GUESS
supposititious	SUPPOSED
supreme	
—chief	PENDRAGON
—council in Anglo-	
Saxon times	WITENAGEMOT
sure	SICCAR, SICKER
surety	BORROW, MAINPRISE
	UNDERTAKER
—for keeping the peace	FRITHBOHR
surgeon	CHIRURGEON
surgery	CHIRURGERY
surgical	CHIRURGICAL
surliness	MELANCHOLY
surpass everything	PASS
surpassing	PASSING
surplus	SUPERPLUS
surprising by stealth	OBREPTION
surrender	SURRENDRY
surveyor's staff	JACOB'S STAFF
surviving trace	RELICT
survivor	RELICT
suspect	DOUBT, SMOKE
suspicion	AIM
swagger	SQUARER
swaggerer	BRAVADO, ROARER
	ROARING-BOY
sweat-bath	POWDERING-TUB
sweating-sickness	STOOP-GALLANT
sweep over	ENSWEEP
sweet	DOUCE, SOOT(E)
—food	SWEETMEAT
—heart	AMORET, JUNKET, LEMAN
—meat	MARCHPANE
tray	VOIDER
sweeten	EDULCORATE
sweetness of manner	DOUCEUR
swell	HUFF

swerve	WRY
swift	WIGHT
swim (head)	WHIM
swindle	BUNCKET
swindler	LEGER
swine	PORK
swoon	DELIQUIUM
sword	FOX, GLADIUS, GLAIVE
swordplay	SPADROON
sycophant	PLACEBO
symbolic meaning	MYTHOLOGY
symbolise	BETOKEN, FIGURE
syncopation	SYNCOPE
system of	
—drill	MARTINET
—principles	INSTITUTION
table	
—implement	SUCKET-FORK
	SUCKET-SPOON
—linen	NAPERY
—of contents	INDEX
tag	DAG
tail of graduate's hood	LIRIPIPE
	LIRIPOOP
take	HENT, LATCH
	NIM, REACH
—a	
little	DRIB
roundabout course	WINDLASS
—across	TRAJECT
—by surprise	OPPRESS
—care of	BEWARE
—comfort	CHEER
—into stomach	ENDUE, INDUE
—on (as servant)	ENTERTAIN
—out	OUTTAKE
—pleasure in	PLEASURE
—possession of	HENT
—purses	PURSE
—to the highway (as robber)	SCAMP
taken	TANE
taking food	CIBATION
tale of fate	WEIRD
talk	DEVISE, PARLE, SPELL
talkative	DISCOURSIVE
talker of twaddle	TWADDLE
talon	FANG
tame	MANSUETTE
tapestry	TAPIS
—frame	TENT
tarnished	BRAID
tarragon	STARAGEN
tarry	LENG
tarrying	TARRIANCE
taste	ASSAY, GUST, RELISH
tasteless	WEARISH

taunt	GIRD	thane	THEGN
taut	TAUGHT	thank	REMERCY
tavern open at night	NIGHT-HOUSE	—God	GOD-A-MERCY
tax	CESS, GELD, LOT	that	
—farmer	UNDERTAKER	—may be	
—on		applauded	PLAUSIBLE
land	CARUCAGE, HIDAGE	shown	OSTENSIBLE
wine	PRISAGE	—which	
teach	CON, LEAR(E), LEIR, LERE	comes into contact	OCCURRENT
teacher	DOCTOR	contains	CONTINENT
teaching	DOCTRINE, LORE	humbles gallants	STOOP-GALLANT
team	TEME	institutes	INSTITUTION
tear	RASH	instructs	INSTITUTION
tearful	MAUDLIN	is	
tease out	TOUSE, TOUZE, TOWSE, TOWZE	—got	GET
technical	MECHANICAL	—laid waste	WASTE
teeming	GREAT	—preserved from loss	
telescope	OPTIC TUBE	in battle	PREY
	PROSPECT, TRUNK	—worn	WEARING
tell falsehood	FABLE	softens	LENIENT
temper	CONDITION, TAMPER	—with which one	
	TEMPERATE	is equipped	EQUIPAGE
tempering	TEMPERAMENT	the	YE
temporal	TIMELY	—one	TONE
tempt	ASSAY, ATTEMPT	theatre	
temptation	TENTATION	—dressing-room	TIRING-HOUSE
tenant			TIRING-ROOM
—by service	SOCAGER, SOCMAN	—seat	ROOM
	SOKEMAN	them	HEM
—farmer	GEBUR	thick woollen cloth	WADMA(A)L
tend	SOUND		WADMOL(L)
tenor	TENOUR	thicken	INCRASSATE
tense	TAUGHT	thicket	QUEACH
tenure		thief	LIMMER, WASTER
—by service	SOC(C)AGE, SOKEMANRY	thieves' decoy	STALE
—in Kent	GAVELKIND	thieving	SHEEP-BITING
terce	UNDERN	thing	RES
terebinth-tree	TEIL	—doubtful or questioned	DOUBT
term of		—stolen	MAINO(U)R, MANNER
—abuse	SCARAB	—to lean on	LEAN
—address to king	SIRE	—which contains	CONTINENT
—contempt	JACK, MECHANIC	things of the	
	WHIPSTER	intellect	INTELLECTUALS
—endearment	FOOL, MOUSE	think	CENSE, GUESS, WEEN
—exultation	VIA	third	TIERCE
—familiarity	BULLY	—finger of left hand	RINGMAN
—opprobium	HARLOT	—hour	UNDERN
—reproach	TRUANT	thirst	THRIST
terrace	TERRAS	thirsty	ADRY
terrify	FEAR	thong	LATCHET, LORE
terrifying word	BUGWORD	thoroughly	THROUGHLY
territory	GOVERNMENT, MARK	thought	CONCEIT
—of lord	LORDSHIP	thoughtful	CONSIDERATIVE
terror	BUG	thrash	JERK, SMOKE, SWADDLE
test	EXPERIENCE, TASTE	thread	FILE
—fatness	ASSAY	throat	HALSE, QUAIL-PIPE, WEAZAND

throb	QUOP	together	IN COMMON, INFERE, YFERE
throne	SEE, STOOL	toil	SWINK
through	THOROUGH, YOND	—worn	SWINKED
throw	WARP	token	RECOGNISANCE
—away	ABJECT	tomb	BURIAL
—in or on	INJECT	ton	TUN
—stones at	LAPIDATE	too	
thrust	POTE, PUT, STOP	—drunk to whistle	WHISTLE(D)-DRUNK
—out	ELIMINATE	—early	OVERTIMELY
thump	TUND	—little	UNSIZ(E)ABLE
thunder	INTONATE	took	NAM, NIMMED
tie		tool	LOOM
—the points of	TRUSS	toothache	WORM
—together	KNIT	top	SUPERATE
tight	STRAIT	—of anything	CROP
—gripping	HANDFAST	topic	PLACE
tighten	STRAIT(EN)	torch-bearer	LINKBOY, LINKMAN
tightly	STRAIT	tore	TARE
till	EAR	torment	PINE, PYNE
tilt	JOSTLE, JUSTLE	torture	PINE, PYNE
time		—with heat	FRY
—observer	TIMIST	torturer	TORMENTOR
—of		Tory High Churchman	TANTIVY
currency	TENOUR	toss	
midday meal	UNDERNTIME	—a coin	FLUTTER
tinder	SPUNK	—about	WALK
tinge	TAINT, TINCT	the limbs	SPRAWL
tinker	PRIG	tossing about	JACTITATION
tinner's poll-tax	WHITE-RENT	touch on	PERSTRINGE
tint	TAINT, TINCT	touchwood	SPUNK
tip	GRATIFICATION, VALES, VAILS	touchy	MIFTY
titled person	PERSON OF HONOUR	tournament	TOURNEY
to		—lists	BARRACE
—a great degree	OUT OF MEASURE	tout	PLIER
—an inner room	WITHIN	town with market	
—ask a question	REQUIRE	privileges	PORT
—be		township	VILL
brief	AT A WORD	townsman	CIT
pitied	SEELY, SILLY	toy	BANDALORE
—cause to burn with anger	EMBOIL	—dog	PUPPY
—conceive mentally	FANTASY, PHANTASY	—with	FON
—coop in	EMBAIL	fingers	PADDLE
—make famous	FAMOUS	track	TROD
—put under embargo	EMBAR	trackless	BEWILDERED, INVIOUS
—sing for money		tractable	TOWARDLY
at Whitsun	SHROVE	trade	MISTER, MISTERY
—the smallest detail	POINT-DEVICE		MYSTERY, OCCUPY
	POINT-DEVISE	—guild	MISTERY, MYSTERY
—them	HEM	trader	PLIER
—windward	ALOOF	trading voyage	TRAFFIC
toad	PADDOCK	traitor	NITHING, TREACHER(ER)
toadstool	PADDOCK-STOOL		TREACHOUR
toady	ZANY	trample with feet	FOIL
toast	DRINK-HAIL, WASSAIL	tranquillity	LEE
tobacco-pipe	WOODCOCK'S-HEAD	transcribe officially	TRANSUME
toffee	TAFFY	transcription	TRANSUMPTION

transept	CROSS-AISLE
transference	TRAJECT, TRANSUMPTION
transgression	ESCAPE
translate	TRADUCE
translator	INTERPRETER
transmission	TRAJECT
transmit	TRADUCE
transmuting element	TINCTURE
transport with delight	RAPE
trapped	IN BY THE WEEK
travail	TRAVEL
travel	TRAVAIL, VOYAGE
—on foot	WAYFARE
—with post-horses	POSTAGE
travelling	
—bag	MAIL
—case	CAP-CASE
tray for dirty dishes	VOIDER
treacherous person	TREACHER, TREACHOUR
tread	TRADE
—a measure	TRACE
treasure ships	PLATE-FLEET
treasurer	FISCAL
treat	BESEE, ENTERTAIN, ENTREAT
—with signs	
of honour	WORSHIP
treatise on gems	LAPIDARY
treatment	ENTREATMENT
tree	BEAM, WOOD
triad	TERN
trial	EXPERIENCE
tribe	ROD
tribute	GAVEL
trick	BANTER, CROOK, FOB
	FUN, GLEEK
—out	TIFF
trickery	SLIGHT
trickle	DRIB
tried	TRIDE
trifing	FALLAL
trifle	PADDLE
trim	NET(T)
trimmed	GUARDED
trimming on gown	ROBIN
trip	SPURN
tripod	TRIPOS
triumvirate	TRIUMVIRY
trivial	BALD
—dance-tune	TOY
trouble	BARRAT, GRAM(E)
	HATTER, NOY, VISIT
—taken	LABOUR
troublesome	INCOMMODIOUS, INFEST
trousers	TROSSERS, TROWSERS
truant	MICHER
truck	TRUNDLE

true	TREW
trump	TRIUMPH
trumpery	MOCKADO
trumpet of brass	ALCHEMY, ALCHYMY
trundle	TROLL
truss up	KILT
trust	AFFY, LET ALONE, TROW
truth	TROTH
try	FAND, FOND, TASTE, TRIE
tub	COWL
—for treatment of	
veneral disease	POWDERING-TUB
tuberculous	
excrescence	WOLF
tumulus	LOW, MOT(T)E, MOTE-HILL
tune	DUMP, NOTE
tunnel	TONNEL
turban	TULBAN, TULIPANT
tureen	TERREEN
turf	SCRAW
turfy	GLEBOUS, GLEBY
turkey	GUINEA-HEN
turmoil	MOIL
turn	CHAR(E)
turn	LOT, WEND
—about	CONVERT
—aside by caprice	WHIM
—from	
straight line	CROOK
what is right	CROOK
—of mind	ENGINE
—out	FADGE, SORT
well	PROVE
—over	VOLVE
—round (head)	WHIM
—the leaves of	TOSS
—to stone	LAPIDIFY
turned away	FROWARD
turning	VOLUTATION
—over in the mind	REVOLUTION
turnstile	TURNPIKE
turquoise	LIGURE, TURKIS
turret	GARRET
tutelage	TUTORAGE
tutor	GOVERNOR
twig	SARMENT, TWIST
twigs	RICE
twin	GEMMEL
twisted	WRONG
two	TWAIN
—tables of the law	TESTIMONY
type	HAIR, SAMPLER
tyrant	TYRAN(NE)
ugly	LO(A)TH, OUGHLY, OUGLIE
umbrella	OMBRELLA, UMBRELLO
unable	UNHABLE

—to	
take in	INCAPABLE
visit	UNVISITABLE
unaccustomed	UNCUSTOMED, UNWONT
	WONTLESS
unafraid	UNFEARED
unaware	WARELESS, UNWARES
unbending	STIFF-RUMPT
unborn child	BURDEN
unburdened	UNBURTHENED
uncanny	WEIRD
unchaste	LIGHT-HEELED
uncle	EME
unconnected composition	
or collection of things	RHAPSODY
uncover	DETECT
uncreated	INCREATE
uncritical	INCURIOUS
uncultivated	INCULT
under	
—consideration	ON THE TAPIS
—constable	THIRDBOROUGH
—iron for striking coins	PILE
—the control of	UNDERNEATH
underhand arrangement	PACK
—representation	SUGGESTION
undersong	FA(UX)BURDEN
understanding	WIT
undertake with intention	
of defeating	PREVARICATE
undisciplined	WANTON
undo	FOREDO, POOP, POUPE
undoing	DEFEASANCE
undress	MAKE UNREADY
unearthly	WEIRD
uneasiness	DISEASE, MISEASE
uneasy	DISQUIET
unencumbered	EXPEDITE
unexpected	INOPINATE, UNHOPED
unexpectedly	UNWARES
unfamiliar	UNCOUTH
unfitting	UNDECENT
unfledged	EYAS, NYAS
unfortunate	MISFORTUNED
unfriendliness	UNFRIENDSHIP
ungodly	WORLD
ungrateful	INGRATE
unhandsome	UNDECENT
unintelligent	INCAPABLE
union of neighbours	FRITHGILD
unite	ME(I)NT, MENG(E)
	MEYNT, MING
unite(d) in one body	CONCORPORATE
unjust	UNEQUAL
unknown	IGNORANT, UNCOUTH
—precious stone	LIGIURE

unless	EXCEPT, WITHOUT
unlucky days	DISMAL
unmanageable	WANTON
unmixed	MERE, NET(T)
unpleasant	DISPLEASANT, UNGAIN
—experience	DISTASTE
unpleasing	INGRATE
unpolished	UNPOLITE
unprepared	UNPURVEYED
unprepossessing	UNLIKELY
unproductive consumer	CATERPILLAR
unpromising	UNLIKELY
unprovided	UNPURVEYED
unquiet	DISQUIET
unreasonable	FROWARD
unrestrained	FRANK
unruly	WANTON
unseemly	UNHONEST
unsettled	UNDISCUSSED
unshaken	UNREMOVABLE
unskilful in action	UNHANDSOME
unskilled	UNGAIN, UNPERFECT
unstock	LAUNCH
unsuitable	UNLIKELY
—for	INCOMMODIOUS
until	WHILE
untimely	IMPORTUNE, OVERTIMELY
unwanted	INUSITATE
unwarily	UNWARELY
unworthiness	INDIGNITY
unworthy	INDIGN, WORTHLESS
unyielding	STOUT
up to	UP-TILL
upbraid	EXPROBATE
upholsterer	UPHOLDER
upholstery cloth	PARAGON
upper servant	PUG
upshot	PROOF
upside down	UP SO DOWN
upward curl of hat brim	PINCH
urate	LITHATE
urge on	EDGE
urgency	INSTANCE
urgent	INSTANT
urus	URE
use	INURE, URE
—tricks	CHICANE
used in oaths for God	DOG
useful	BEHOVEFUL, BEHOVELY
useless	WASTE
usual	WONTED
—fare	ORDINARY
utmost degree	UTTERANCE
—effort or force	UTTERANCE
utter	PEREMPTORY, WIELD
—fluently	TROLL

utterance	WORDING
utterly damned	FORE-DAMNED
vacate	WAIVE
vacillate	WAVE
vagabond	GADLING
vagrant	CURSITOR, TRUANT
vain	WASTE, WASTEFUL
—regret	HAD-I-WIST
valiant	PROW
valour	VIRTUE
—proved in war	WAR-PROOF
value	PRICE, VALOUR
vanish	FAINT
variable	FLUXIONARY
various musical	
instruments	SYMPHONY
vault	EMBOW, VAUT(E)
	VAWTE
vaunt	GAB
vegetable	WORT
veil	VAIL
velocipede	MULTICYCLE
veneer	FINEER
venery	VENUS
vengeance	WRACK, WREAK
venial offence	ESCAPE
venture	VENTER, VENTRE
venturous	VENTROUS
veranda(h)	VIRANDA, VIRANDO
verbal message	ERRAND
verbose	WORDISH
verdict	VARDY, VERDIT
verse of retraction	PALINODY
versed (in)	OVERSEEN
versify	MAKE
vertebra	RACK
very	RIGHT, UNCOMMON
—attentive	PARTICULAR
vestment	VESTIMENT
vexation	NOY
vexatious	PEEVISH
viands	CATES
vice	INIQUITY
view	ADVISE
—in a mirror	SPECULATE
viewing	SPECULATION
vigorous	RANK
vile	VILD(E)
vindicate	DARRAIGN(E), DARRAIN(E)
	DARRAYN, DERAIGN, SALVE
vinegar	EISEL(L), ESIL(E)
violate	VITIATE
violent	RANK, STURDY
violently	HEAD AND SHOULDERS
—angry	WRATH
violin	ROCTA

virgin	PUCELLE
virginal	SYMPHONY
virginity	PUCELAGE
virtue	VERTU(E)
virtuous	VIRTUAL
viscid	LENTOUS
viscidity	LENTOR
visible form	SPECIES
vision	SPECULATION
visit of herald	VISITATION
visiting-card	TICKET
visual	VISIVE
—image	SPECIES
vital	LIVELY
—power	NATURE
vitality	VIVACIOUSNESS
	VIVACITY, VIVENCY
vitiate	VICIATE
vivid	VIVE
vocabulary	NOMENCLATURE
voice	BREAST
voiceless	SHARP
void of shame	FRONTLESS
volunteer	VOLUNTARY
—serving as officer	REFORMADO
vomit	PARBREAK
voracious	VORAGINOUS
vouchsafe	VOUCH, VOUTSAFE
vow	BEHIGHT, BEHOTE
vulgar	SCURRIL(E)
vulture	GIER-EAGLE
wag the tongue	WALK
wage war	WARFARE
wager	WAGE, WED
wages	MEED
waggish	UNHAPPY
waist	GIRDLESTEAD, WAST
wait	EXPECT
—for	WATCH
waiting	TARRIANCE
wakeful	WATCHFUL
waldgrave	WILDGRAVE
walk	GO, TRACE
—behind battlements	ALURE
walking cane	WAND
wall	
—in	INTERMURE
—plant	HYSSOP
wallow in mud	MUDDLE
wallowing	VOLUTATION
wander	
—from right way	ERR
—till wearied	FORWANDER
wandering	EXTRAVAGANT
—course	ERROR
wane	WELK

want of	
—equity	INIQUITY
—fairness	INIQUITY
wanting in strength	FAINT
wanton	GIGLET, GIGLOT
—woman	JAY
war	
—club	MAUL
—equipment	WAR
—horse	DESTRIER
ward off	FORFEND
wardrobe	GARDEROBE
wariness	CAUTEL
warrant	WARRAN(D)
—safe	VOUCHSAFE, VOUTSAFE
warrior	EORL, WARMAN
wary	WARE
washed	WASHEN
waste	WAST
—away	WANZE
—place	WASTENESS
wasting	COLLIQUATION, COLLIQUATIVE
	COLLIQUABLE, COLLIQUANT
watch	AWAIT
—for	WAIT
—over	WARD
watchdog	HOUSEKEEPER
watchman	SPECULATOR
	WAIT(ER), WAKEMN
watchtower	GARRET, SENTRY-GO
watchful guardian	GRIPE, GRYPHON
	GRIFFIN, GRIFFON
watchman's cry	WATCH
water-channel	LAKE
water monster	NICKER
waterfall	OVERFALL
waterproof leggings	ANTIGROPILO(E)S
watery	
—looking sky	WATER-GALL
—place	FLUSH
wave	FLOTE
waver	WAVE
wax	WEX(E)
—candle	TAPER
—pale	APPAL
way	TRADE, VIA, WISE
wayfarer	DUSTY-FOOT, PIEPOWDER
wayside shrine	WEEPING-CROSS
weak	FADE
—in spirit	FAINT
—or effeminate man	DILDO
weaken	ENTENDER
	INTENDER, PALL
weald	WILD
wealth	WAR(R)ISON
weapon	WELSH-HOOK, VOU(L)GE

—with several barrels	ORGUE
wear before (others)	PREOCCUPY
wearer of	
—frock	FROCK
—silk	SILKWORM
weather	WELK
—conditions	WEATHERING
weave	PLIGHT
weaver	WEBSTER
wedding-feast	BRIDE-ALE
week	SENNIGHT
weigh	
—anchor	LOOSE
—down	POISE
—in the mind	POISE
weighed	WAID(E)
weight	BURTHEN, PEASE, PEAZE
	PEISE, PEIZE, PEYSE, POISE
welcome	GRATULATE
welfare	HEAL
well	
—being	WEALTH
—born	GENTLE
—disposed	TOWARD(LY)
	WELL-GIVEN
—judged liberality	MAGNIFICENCE
—made	FEAT(E)OUS, FEATUOUS
—mannered	WELL-THEWED
werewolf	TURNSKIN
wet	MOIL
whale-like sea-monster	WHIRLPOOL
what kind of	WHAT FOR A
whatever	WHATSO
—one can do for	
oneself	PURCHASE
whatsoever	WHATSO
when	WHENAS
where	WHEAR(E)
whereas	WHENAS
which	WHILK
while	THE WHILST
whim	FLAM
whimsical	
—person	WHIM
—tune or impromptu	MAGGOT
whip	
—out	BRAID
—top	GIG
whisper	ROUND
whist	WHISK
white	CANDID
—and viscous	GLA(I)REOUS
whiteness	CANDOUR
whitewash	WHITE-LIME
whiting	MIRLING
whitish	WHITELY

whitlow	ANCOME
who	WHAT
whoever	WHATSO
whole body	CONTINENT
whole(sale)	GREAT
wholemeal bread	RAVEL(LED) BREAD
whore (verb)	WENCH
why	FOR WHY
wicked	FACINOROUS, FELON
	FELONIOUS, GOAT
	SCELERAT(E), WICK
—person	FELON
wickedness	NAUGHT
widow	RELICT
widow's share of	
husband's estate	WIDOW'S-BENCH
wield	WELD, WILD, WIND
wife	LADY
wig	MAJOR
wile	ENGINE
will not	NILL
willing	VOLITIENT
willingly	L(I)EVE, LIEF
wind up	SPAN
windfall	CADUAC
winding	MEANDRIAN
—course	ERROR
windlass	WINDAS
window with hinged	
shutter	SHOT-WINDOW
windpipe	WEAZAND
wine	
—cup	PIECE
—mixing bowl	CRATER
wink	EY(E)LIAD
winter	WINTER-TIDE
wipeout	NULL
wise	WITTY
—man	WIZARD
wish	WISE
—for	WILL
wit	WEET
witch	WEIRD
witchery	GLAMOUR
with	
—difficulty	UNE(A)TH
	UNEATHES, UNNETHES
—exactitude	POINT-DEVICE
	POINT-DEVISE
—hardship	STRAIT
—wool next to skin	WOOLWARD
withdraw	WALK
—from	VOID
wither	BLAST
withheld	WITHHAULT
within	ENTIRE

without	WITHOUTEN
—a mate	MAKELESS
—counsel or wisdom	REDELESS
—favour	GRACELESS
—ideas	UNIDEAL
—mercy	GRACELESS
—modesty	FRONTLESS
—self-control	IMPOTENT
—using flesh	MAIGRE
witty	CONCEITED
woe	BALE
woman	FAIR, WOMANKIND
—fit for spinning-	
house	SPINSTER
—friend who comes	
at a birth	GOSSIP
—of fashion	GALLANT
—who has taken vows	VOWESS
woman's	
—morning cap	MOB(-CAP)
—shift	SMOCK
—silk necktie	TAWDRY-LACE
womb	MOTHER, WEM(B), WEAMB
won	WAN
wonder at	ADMIRE, MARVEL
wonderful	GEASON
woo	ADDRESS
wooden	
—post	STUD
—shoe	PATTEN
—sole on iron ring	PATTEN
—sword	WASTER
woodlouse	MULTIPED(E)
woodruff	WOOD-ROOF
woolsack	WOOL-PACK
words of	
—a villain	VILLA(I)NY
—song	DIT(T)
wore	WARE
work	
—liquid	FRET
—secretly against	UNDERWORK
workaday	WORKY-DAY
workmanship	ARTIFICE
workshop	WORKING-HOUSE
world	MAPPEMOND, MOULD
—of fairies	FAERIE, FAERY
worship	SERVE
worst	WORSE
—state	PESSIMISM
worth	PRICE, VALOUR
worthless	NAUGHT(Y), RACA, VOID
—beast	HILDING
would be willing	HAD AS LIEF
would-be wit	HALF-WIT
wound	ENGORE, PLAGUE

—by reproach	BITE
wrangle	BRANGLE, CAMPLE
wrap	WAP
wreaked	WROKE(N), WROKEN
wrestling school	PALAESTRA
wretched	WO(E)
wriggle	WIND
wrinkled	WRITHLED
writ	
—issued by sheriff	VENIRE (FACIAS)
—moving case to	
county court	TOLT
—of Richard II	PRAEMUNIRE
write	
—between	INTERSCRIBE
—out in musical notation	PRICK
writhe	WIND
writing	DITE, WRIT
written	WRATE, WRIT
wrong	UNRIGHT
wrongfully	UNDULY
wrote	WRIT, WROOT
yarrow	NOSE-BLEED
yearn	EARN
yeast	YEST
yellowish-green	GAUDY-GREEN
yeoman	GOODMAN
yew	EUGH
yewen	EUGHEN, EWGHEN
yield	KNOCK UNDER, VAIL
young	
—girl	DELL
—lady	DEMOISELLE
—man	IMP, SWAIN
—manservant	GROOM
—person	YONKER
your	THY
youth	YOUTHHOOD
—training for knighthood	PAGE
zealot	ZEAL
zealously	INSTANTLY
zedoary	CETYWALL, SETUALE
	SETWALL
	(*see also* **medi(a)eval**)
old²	
including: former	
old age pension(er)	OAP
old boy	ALUMNUS, OB
Old English	OE
old Dutch	WIFE
old Etonian	OE
Old French	OF(R)
old girl	ALUMNA, WIFE
Old Irish	OIR
old lady	WIFE
Old Measurement	OM

Old Norse	ON
Old Style	OS
Old Testment	OT
old woman	BETTER HALF
Olympians	(*see* **gods, goddesses**)
Oman	
capital	MASQAT, MUSCAT
coin	
—unit	BAIZA
—1000 baiza	RIAL
one	A, ACE, AN, MONAD, SINGELTON
	SINGULAR, SOLO, UNIT
and a half	SESQUI-
Christmas present	PARTRIDGE, PEAR-TREE
combining form	MON(O)-, UNI-
each	PER
having one	
—adductor muscle	MONOMYARIAN
—amino group	MONOAMINE
—ancestral group	MONOPHYLETIC
—atom	MONATOMIC
—axis	MONAXIAL, MONAXON(IC)
	UNIAXIAL
—brood per annum	UNIVOLTINE
—bundle of stamens	MONODELPHOUS
—buttock	HEMIPYGIC
—carpel	MONOCARPELLARY
—case	MONOTHECAL
—cavity	UNILOCULAR
—cell	MONOTHALAMOUS
	UNICAMERAL
	UNICELLULAR, UNILOCULAR
—centre	UNICENTRAL
—chamber	MONOTHALAMOUS
	UNICAMERAL
—colour	MONOCHRO(MAT)IC
	UNICOLORATE
	UNICOLOROUS, UNICOLOUR
—column	MONSTYLAR
—cotyledon	MONOCOTYLEDONOUS
—degree of freedom	UNIVARIANT
—dimension	LINEAR
—ear	MONAURAL, MONOPHONIC
—eye	MONOCULAR
—finger	MONODACTYLOUS
—flower	UNIFLOROUS
—foot	MONOPODE, MONOPOD(IAL)
	UNIPED
—fruiting period	MONOCARPIC
	MONOTOCOUS
—god	MONOTHEISTIC
—heart	MONOCARDIAN
—horn	MONOCEROUS, UNICORN
—husband	MONOGAMIC
	MONOGAMOUS
—hydrogen atom	MONACID, MONOBASIC

—hydroxyl group   MONOHYDRIC
—key   MONOTONAL
—leg   MONOPODE, MONPOD(IAL)
       UNIPOD
—language   MONOGLOT, MONOLINGUAL
       UNILINGUAL
—leaf   UNIFOLIATE
—letter   UNILITERAL
—line   MONOSTICHOUS
—lip   UNILABIATE
—lobe   MONOTHECAL, UNILOBAR
       UNILOBED
—lobule   UNILOBULAR
—loculus   MONOTHECAL, UNILOCULAR
—marriage   MONOGAMOUS
—meaning   UNIVOCAL
—measure   MONOMETER
—metal   MONOMETALLIC
—nostril   MONORHINE, MONORHINAL
—nucleus   MONONUCLEAR, UNINUCLEAR
       UNINUCLEATE
—offspring at one birth   MONOTOCOUS
       UNIPAROUS
—ovary   MONOCARPIC
       MONOCARPOUS
—oxygen atom   MONOXIDE
—part   UNIPARTITE
—perianth whorl   HAPLOCHLAMYDEOUS
       HOMOCHLAMYDEOUS
       MONOCHLAMYDEOUS
—person ruling   DICTATORSHIP
       DESPOTISM, MONARCHY
—petal   MONOPETALOUS
—phase   MONOPHASE, MONOPHASIC
—plane of symmetry   MONOSYMMETRIC(AL)
—pole   UNIPOLAR
—rail   MONORAIL
—ray   MONACT(INAL), MONACTINE
—rib   UNICOSTATE
—ring   MONOCYCLIC
   of columns   MONOPTERAL
—row   MONOSERIAL
       MONOSTICHOUS
       UNISERIAL, UNISERIATE
—ruler   MONARCHY
—sac   MONOTHECAL
—sepal   MONOSEPALOUS
—series   MONOSERIAL
—serrated edge   MONOPRIONIDIAN
—set of
   chromosomes   HAPLOID
   teeth   MONOPHYDONT
—sex   MONOECIOUS, UNISEX(UAL)
—sheath   MONOTHECAL
—side   UNILATERAL
   developed   DIMIDIATE

—stamen   MONANDROUS
—term   MONOMIAL
—thread   UNFILAR
—toe   MONODACTYLOUS
—tone   MONOTONAL
—turn   MONOCYCLIC, UNICYCLIC
—tusk   MONODONT
—type of mycelium   HOMOTHALLIC
—valency   MONATOMIC
       MONOVALENT
       UNIVALENT
—valve   UNIVALVE, UNIVALVULAR
—variant quantity   UNIVARIATE
—wavelength   MONOCHROMATIC
—wheel   MONOCYCLE, UNICYCLE
—whorl   MONOCYCLIC
—whorled perianth   MONOCHLAMYDEOUS
—wife   MONOGAMIC
       MONOGAMOUS
       MONOGYNIAN
       MONOGYNOUS
—wing   MONOPLANE
—word   MONOMIAL
xylem strand   MONARCH
yearly occurrence   ANNUAL
thousand   IM, LAC
—pounds   GRAND
under par   BIRDIE

opera
operas
—Balfe   THE BOHEMIAN GIRL
—Beethoven   FIDELIO
—Bellini   NORMA, THE FOREIGNER
       THE PIRATE, THE PURITANS
       THE SLEEPWALKER
—Berg   WOZZECK
—Berlioz   THE DAMNATION OF FAUST
—Bizet   CARMEN
       THE PEARL-FISHERS
—Britten   ALBERT HERRING
       BILLY BUDD, GLORIANA
       MIDSUMMER NIGHT'S DREAM
       PETER GRIMES
       THE RAPE OF LUCRETIA
       THE TURN OF THE SCREW
—Charpentier   LOUISE
—Cilea   THE ARLESIAN GIRL
—Debussy   PELLEAS AND MELISANDE
—Delibes   LAKME
—Donizetti   DON PASQUALE
       THE LOVE POTION
       LUCIA DI LAMMERMOOR
       LUCREZIA BORGIA
       THE DAUGHTER OF THE REGIMENT
—Flotow   MARTHA
—Gershwin   PORGY AND BESS

—Giordano	ANDREA CHENIER, FEDORA	—A Masked Ball	AMELIA
—Gluck	ORPHEUS AND EURYDICE	(Un Ballo in Maschera)	RICCARDO, SAM
—Gounod	FAUST		TOM, ULRICA
—Handel	ACIS AND GALATEA	—Andrea Chenier	ANDREA, GERARD
	BERENICE, XERXES		MADELEINE, ROUCHER
—Humperdinck	HANSEL AND GRETEL	—Billy Budd	BILLY, CLAGGART, VERE
—Leoncavallo	PAGLIACCI	—Boris Godunov	BORIS, GRIGORY
—Mascagni	RUSTIC CHIVALRY		MISSAIL, PIMEN
—Massenet	MANON, THAIS		VARLAAM
—Menotti	AMAHL AND THE NIGHT	—Carmen	CARMEN, DON JOSE
	VISITORS		ESCAMILLO, MICAELA
—Meyerbeer	THE AFRICAN GIRL		ZUNIGA
	THE HUGUENOTS	—Cosí fan tutte	DON ALFONSO
—Mozart	COSI FAN TUTTE		DORABELLA, FERRANDO
	DON GIOVANNI		FIORDILIGI, GUGLIELMO
	THE MAGIC FLUTE	—Don Carlos	PRINCESS EBOLI, RODRIGO
	THE MARRIAGE OF FIGARO	—Don Giovanni	DON GIOVANNI
—Mussorgsky	BORIS GODUNOV		DONNA ANNA, ELVIRA
—Offenbach	BEAUTIFUL HELEN		LEPORELLO, MASETO
	ORPHEUS IN THE UNDERWORLD		ZERLINA
	THE TALES OF HOFFMAN	—Don Pasquale	DON PASQUALE
—Ponchielli	THE JOYFUL GIRL		ERNESTO, MALATESTA
—Puccini	GIANNI SCHICCHI		NORINA
	LA BOHEME	—Elektra	CHRYSOTHEMIS, ELEKTRA
	MADAME BUTTERFLY		KLYTEMNESTRA, OREST
	MANON LESCAUT, THE CLOAK	—Ernani	DE SILVA, DON JUAN
	THE GIRL OF THE GOLDEN WEST		ELVIRA, ERNANI
	TOSCA, TURANDOT	—Eugene Onegin	LARINA, ONEGIN
—Rossini	SEMIRAMIDE		LENSKY, TATIANA
	THE BARBER OF SEVILLE	—Falstaff	ANNE, BARDOLPH
	THE ITALIAN GIRL IN ALGIERS		FALSTAFF, FENTON, FORD
—Saint-Saëns	SAMSON AND DELILAH		PAGE, PISTOL, QUICKLY
—Smetana	THE BARTERED BRIDE	—Faust	FAUST, MARGUERITE
—Strauss	ELEKTRA, THE BAT		MEPHISTOPHELES
	THE KNIGHT OF THE ROSE		SIEBEL, VALENTIN
—Tchaikovsky	EUGENE ONEGIN	—Fidelio	FLORESTAN, LEONORE
—Verdi	AIDA, DON CARLOS, ERNANI		MARZELLINE, PIZARRO, ROCCO
	FALSTAFF, , LUISA MILLER	—Gianni Schicchi	LAURETTA
	MACBETH, A MASKED BALL		RINUCCIO, SCHICCHI
	NEBUCHADNEZZAR, OTHELLO	—Hänsel und Gretel	GERTRUDE, GRETEL
	RIGOLETTO, SIMON BOCCANEGRA		HANSEL, WITCH
	THE FORCE OF DESTINY	—Rustic Chivalry	ALFIO, LOLA
	THE TROUBADOUR	(Cavalleria Rusticana)	SANTUZZA, TURIDDU
	THE WAYWARD ONE	—La Bohème	ALCINDORO, MARCELLO
—Wagner	PARSIFAL		MIMI, MUSETTA
	SIEGFRIED, TANNHAUSER		RODOLFO, SCHAUNARD
	THE FLYING DUTCHMAN	—Lakmé	GERALD, LAKME, NILAKANTHA
	THE RHINE GOLD	—Lohengrin	ELSA, KING HENRY
	THE TWILIGHT OF THE GODS		HERALD, LOHENGRIN
	THE VALKYRIES		ORTRUD
	TRISTAN AND ISOLDE	—Louise	JULIEN, LOUISE
—Wolf-Ferrari	CINDERELLA	—Lucia di Lammermoor	ALICE, EDGAR
	THE JEWELS OF THE MADONNA		HENRY, LUCY
principal characters			NORMAN
—Aida	AIDA, AMNERIS, AMONASRO	—Luisa Miller	FREDERICA, LUISA
	RADAMES, RAMFIS		MILLER, RODOLFO, WURM

—Madame Butterfly	CIO-CIO-SAN, GORO
	KATE, PINKERTON
	SHARPLESS, SUZUKI
	YAMADORI
—Manon	DE BRETIGNY, DES GRIEUX
	LESCAUT, MANON
—Manon Lescaut	DES GRIEUX, GERONTE
	LESCAUT, MANON
—Martha	HARRIET, LIONEL, NANCY
	PLUNKETT, SHERIFF
	TRISTAN
—Nebuchadnezzar	ABIGAILLE
(Nabucco)	NABUCCO
—Norma	ADALGISA, CLOTILDA
	FLAVIO, NORMA
	OROVESO
—Othello	CASSIO, DESDEMONA
(Otello)	EMILIA, IAGO
	LODOVICO
	MONTANA, OTELLO
—Pagliacci	BEPPE, CANIO
	NEDDA, TONIO
—Parsifal	AMFORTAS, GURNEMANZ
	KLINGSOR, KUNDRY
	PARSIFAL
—Pelléas and Mélisande	KING ARKEL
(Pelléas et Mélisande)	GENEVIEVE,
	GOLAUD, MELISANDE
	PELLEAS, YNIOLD
—Peter Grimes	ELLEN, PETER
—Porgy and Bess	BESS, CROWN, PORGY
	SERENA, SPORTIN' LIFE
—Rigoletto	BORSA, DUKE, GILDA
	GIOVANNA, MADDALENA
	RIGOLETTO, SPARAFUCILE
—Siegfried	BRUNNHILDE, FAFNER
	MIME, SIEGFRIED
	WOTAN
—Simone Boccanegra	AMELIA
	BOCCANEGRA, FIESCO
	GABRIELE, MARIA
	PAOLO, PIETRO
—Tännhauser	ELISABETH, HERMANN
	TANNHAUSER, VENUS
	WOLFRAM
—Thaïs	ATHANAEL, THAIS
—The African Girl	INEZ, NELUSKO
(L'Africaine)	SELIKA
	VASCO DA GAMA
—The Barber of Seville	ALMAVIVA
(Il Barbiere di Siviglia)	BARTOLO
	DON ALONSO
	DON BASILIO, FIGARO
	LINDORO, ROSINA
—The Bartered Bride	JENIK, KECAL
	MARENKA, VASEK

—The Bat	ADELE, ALFRED, BLIN0D
(Die Fledermaus)	EISENSTEIN, FALKE
	FRANK, ORLOFSKY
	ROSALINDE
—The Bohemian Girl	ARLINE, ARNHEIM
	THADDEUS
—The Flying Dutchman	DALAND
(Der Fliegende Höllander)	ERIK, SENTA
—The Force of Destiny	CALATRAVA
(La Forza del Destino)	DON ALVARO
	DON CARLO
	GUARDIANO
	LEONORA
—The Girl of the Golden West	JOHNSON
(La Fanciulla del West)	MINNIE
	RANCE
—The Italian Girl in Algiers	ISABELLA
(L'Italiana in Algeri)	ELVIRA
	LINDORO
	MUSTAPHA
—The Jewels of the Madonna	GENNARO
(I Gioielli della Madonna)	MALIELLA
	RAFAELE
—The Joyful Girl	BADOERO, BARNABA
(La Giaconda)	GRIMALDI, LA CIECA
	LA GIACONDA, LAURA
—The Knight of the Rose	ANNINA
(Der Rosenkavalier)	FANINAL, OCTAVIAN
	PRINCESS, SOPHIE
	VALZACCHI
	VON LERCHENAU
—The Love Potion	BELCORE
(L'Elisir d'amore)	DULCAMARA
	NEMORINO
—The Magic Flute	MONOSTATOS
(Die Zauberflöte)	PAMINA, PAPAGENO
	QUEEN OF THE NIGHT
	SARASTRO, TAMINO
—The Marriage of Figaro	BARTOLO
(Le Nozze di Figaro)	CHERUBINO
	COUNT ALMAVIVA
	COUNTESS
	FIGARO, SUSANNA
—The Mastersingers	BECKMESSER
(Die Meistersinger)	DAVID, EVA
	KOTHNER, MAGDALENE
	POGNER, SACHS
	WALTHER
—The Pearlfishers	LEILA, NADIR
(Les Pêcheurs de Perles)	NOURABAD
	ZURKA
—The Puritans	ELVIRA, HENRIETTA
(I Puritani)	TALBOT, WALTON
—The Rape of Lucretia	COLLATINUS
	LUCRETIA
	TARQUINIUS

—The Rhinegold	ALBERICH, ERDA
(Das Rheingold)	FASOLT, FAFNER, FREIA
	FRICKA, HUNDING, LOGE
	SIEGLINDE, SIEGMUND
	WOTAN
—The Sleepwalker	AMINA, ELVINO
(La Sonnambula)	LISA, RODOLFO
—The Tales of Hoffman	ANDRES, ANTONIA
	COPPELIUS, CRESPEL
	DAPERTUTTO, GIULIETTA
	HOFFMAN, LINDORF
	NICKLAUSSE, SCHEMIL
	SPALANZANI, STELLA
—The Troubadour	AZUCENA, DI LUNA
(Il Trovatore)	INEZ, LEONORA
	MANRICO, RUIZ
—The Valkyries	BRUNNHILDE
(Die Walküre)	SIEGLINDE
	SIEGMUND, WOTAN
—The Wayward One	ALFREDO, FLORA
(La Traviata)	GIORGIO, VIOLETTA
—Tosca	ANGELOTTI, ATTAVANTI
	CAVARADOSSI, SCARPIA
	SPOLETTA, TOSCA
—Tristan and Isolde	ISOLDE
(Tristan und Isolde)	KING MARK
	KURWENAL, MELOT
	TRISTAN
—Turandot	CALAF, LIU, PANG
	PING, PONG, TIMUR
	TURANDOT
—Twilight of the Gods	BRUNNHILDE, HAGEN
(Götterdammerung)	GUNTHER
	GUTRUNE, NORNS
	SIEGFRIED, WALTRAUTE
—Wozzeck	ANDRES, DRUM MAJOR
	MARIE, WOZZECK
singers	
—American (m)	MELCHIOR, MERRILL
	MILNES, TIBBETT
(f)	ANDERSON, DUNN, HORNE
	KIRSTEN, MILLO, NORMAN
	PONCELLE, PRYCE
	VAMNESS
—Australian (m)	DOWD
(f)	MELBA, SUTHERLAND
—Austrian (m)	TAUBER
(f)	LEHMANN
—Bulgarian (m)	CHIAUROV, CHRISTOFF
(f)	TORNOVA-SINTON
—Brazilian (f)	SUPERVIA
—Czech (m)	DVORSKY
(f)	DESTINN
—Danish (m)	MELCHIOR
—English (m)	NASH, PEARS, VICKERS
(f)	BAKER, BUTT, CROSS

	FERRIER, GERHARDT
	SHUARD, TEYTE, TURNER
—Finnish	TALVELA
—French (f)	PONS
—German (m)	ERB, FISCHER-DIESKAU
	HOTTER
(f)	BERGER, GERHARDT
	SCHUMANN, SCHWARZKOPF
—Greek (f)	CALLAS
—Irish	MCCORMACK
—Italian (m)	BATISTINI, BERGONZI
	CARUSO, CORELLI
	DE MONACO, DE STEFANO
	GIGLI, GOBBI
	MARTINELLI, PAVAROTTI
	PERTILE, PINZA, RUFFO
	SCHIPA, TAMAGNO
(f)	FRENI, GALLI-CURCI
	PATTI, PIRELLI, SCOTTO
	STIGNANI, TEBALDI
	TETRAZZINI
—New Zealand (f)	HAMMOND, TE KANAWA
—Norwegian (f)	FLAGSTAD, NILSSON
—Polish (m)	DE RESZKE
(f)	SEMBRICH
—Romanian (f)	COTRUBAS
—Russian (m)	CHALIAPIN
(f)	DIMITROVA, GRUBEROVA
	SLOBODSKAYA
	VISHNEVSHKAYA
—Spanish (m)	CARRERAS, DOMINGO
(f)	BERGANZA, CABALLE
	DE LOS ANGELES
—Swedish (m)	BJORLING
(f)	GULBRANSON, LIND
—Welsh (m)	EVANS, GLYNNE
(f)	JONES
—Yugoslav (m)	DERMOTA
song	
—in speaking voice	RECITATIVE
—solo	ARIA
theatres	
—Barcelona	GRAN TEATRO LICEU
—Bayreuth	FESTSPIELHAUS
—Berlin	DEUTSCHE OPER
	KOMISCHE OPER
	STAATSOPER
—Brussels	THEATRE DE LA MONNAIE
—Buenos Aires	TEATRO COLON
—Florence	TEATRO COMMUNALE
—Genoa	TEATRO CARLO FELICE
—Leningrad	KIROV THEATRE
—London	COVENT GARDEN
	DRURY LANE, LYCEUM THEATRE
	ROYAL FESTIVAL HALL
	SADLER'S WELLS THEATRE

—Manaus	TEATRO AMAZONAS
—Milan	LA SCALA
	TEATRO ALLA SCALA
—Monte Carlo	L'OPERA DE MONTE CARLO
—Moscow	BOLSHOY TEATR
—Munich	HOF-UND NAZIONALTHEATER
—Naples	TEATRO SAN CARLO
—New York	METROPOLITAN OPERA HOUSE
	PALMO'S OPERA HOUSE
—Paris	L'ACADEMIE DE MUSIQUE
	PARIS OPERA
	THEATRE DES CHAMPS-ELYSEES
	THEATRE-LYRIQUE
—Prague	CZECH THEATRE
	NARODNI DIVADLO
	NATIONAL THEATRE
—Rome	TEATRO APOLLO
	TEATRO DELL'OPERA
	TEATRO REALE
—Sydney	OPERA HOUSE
—Turin	TEATRO REGIO
	TEATRO VITTORIO EMANUELE
—Venice	TEATRO LA FENICE
	TEATRO SAN SAMUELE
—Vienna	BURGTHEATER
	STAATSOPER, VOLKSOPER
operetta	(*see* **musicals**)
Order	
Order of	
—British Empire	OBE
—Merit	OM
—St	
Augustine	OSA
Benedict	OSB
Francis	OSF
	(*see also* **decorations**)
Ordinary	
Ordinary National	
—Certificate	ONC
—Diploma	OND
ordinary seaman	OS
Ordnance	
Datum	OD
Survey	OS
organ stops	CLARABELLA
	CORNET, CORNO DI BASSETTO
	CROMORNA, CROMORNE, DOLCE
	DULCIANA, FLUTE, KRUM(M)HORN
	MUTATION-STOP, NASARD, OCTAVE
	PICCOLO, PRINCIPAL, PYRAMIDON
	QUINT, SALICET, SALICIONAL
	SESQUIALTERA, SEXT
	SUPEROCTAVE, TRUMPET

	TUBA, VOIX CELESTE, VOX HUMANA
	WALDFLUTE, WALHHORN
Organisation	
of	
—African Unity	OAU
—American States	OAS
oriental	
bathing establishment	HAMMAM
	HUMM(A)UM
bosun	SERANG
coin	DERHAM, DIRHAM
	DIRHEM
fruit	SHADDOCK
heel-less slipper	BABOOSH, BAB(O)UCHE
	PABOUCHE
javelin	JEREED, JERID
petty officer	TINDAL
plant	TURBITH, TURPETH
prison	BAGNIO
sailor	LASCAR
shrub	HENNA
tree	SEBESTEN
weight	DERHAM, DIRHAM, DIRHEM
	(*see also* **Eastern**)
ox	KINE, NEAT
Abyssinian	GALLA, SANGA
	SANGU, SUNGA
African	CAPE BUFFALO
	CONGO BUFFALO
	ZAMOUSE
American	BISON, BUFFALO
bison	BONAS(S)US
buffalo	BUBALUS
castrated	STEER
cattle/bison hybrid	CAT(T)ALO
cattle/zebu hybrid	CATTABU
Celebes (Sulawesi)	ANOA, SAPI-(O)UTAN
cow/yak	(*see* Himalayan *below*)
East Indian	BANTENG, BANTING
	TAMAROU
European	AUROCHS, BISON, URUS
extinct	AUROCHS
Himalayan	DSOMO, DSOBO, JOMO
	Z(H)O, ZHOMO, ZOBO, ZOBU
Indian	BHYLE, BRAHMIN BULL
	G(A)YAL, GAUR, MITHAN
	S(E)LADANG, ZEBU
Indonesian	DWARF BUFFALO
musk-ox	OVIBOS
old	ROTHER
Tibetan	SARLAC, SARLAK, YAK
wild ox	BUGLE, OWRE
young	CALF, STEERLING, STIRK

P

abstract art	ABC ART, CONCRETE ART
	MINIMALISM
	NON-FIGURATIVE ART
	NON-REPRESENTATIONAL ART
actual colour uninfluenced by reflected colour	LOCAL COLOUR
aesthetic element in picture	SIGNIFICANT FORM
altar	
—frontal	ANTEPENDIUM, PALIOTTO
—piece	
two panels	DIPTYCH
three panels	TRIPTYCH
several panels	POLYPTYCH
apply monochrome base to detailed drawing	LAY-IN
appreciation of form in terms of light and shade	MALERISCH
areas of colour separated by blue or black lines	CLOISONNISME
arrangement	COMPOSITION
art of the real	MINIMALISM
austere and tragic quality	TERRIBILITA
backing plaster coat in fresco work	ARRICCI(AT)O
based on	
—antique exemplars	(NEO-)CLASSIC(AL)
—ink blobs	BLOT DRAWING
—light and movement	KINETIC ART
—living organisms	BIOMORPHIC ART
—passions	ROMANTIC
—use of the products of modern life	POP ART
binder for pigment	OIL, TEMPERA
black, red or brown chalk	CONTE
blot painting	TACHISM(E)
blue colours	COLD COLOUR
	COOL COLOUR
book of Claude drawings	LIBER VERITATIS
brown pigment	BISTRE, SEPIA
built up from various materials	COLLAGE
canvas prepared with dark brown earth and binder	BOLUS GROUND

carbon twigs	CHARCOAL
chalk on canvas	ABSORBENT GROUND
circular picture	TONDO
Cloisonnisme	SYMBOLISM, SYNTHETISM
collage	ASSEMBLAGE
	COMBINE-PAINTING
	TABLEAU-PIECE
colouring	PIGMENT
—blue	SMALT
—earths	BOLE, OCHRE, SIENA, UMBER
combination	
—into satisfactory visual whole	COMPOSITION
—of painting with objects	COLLAGE
combining human, animal and plant forms	GROTESQUE
contrasting light and shade	CHIAROSCURO
controlled by	
—subconscious mind	AUTOMATIC PAINTING
	AUTOMATISM
—unconscious mind	ACTION PAINTING
creating	
—three-dimensional effect	MODELLING
	PERSPECTIVE
	TROMPE L'OEIL
—visual illusions	OP(TICAL) ART
	TROMPE L'OEIL
critic	
—English	RUSKIN
—French	DIDEROT
dabs of primary colour	DIVISIONISM
dark brown or reddish earth	BOLE
depending on patterns of outlines	LINEAR COMPOSITION
depicting	
—a particular moment in a story	NARRATIVE PAINTING
—contemporary scene	SOCIAL REALISM
—the squalid and depressing	REALISM
—Virgin Mary with dead Christ	PIETA
design made by scratching through top layer	SGRAFFITO
detailed drawing for painting	CARTOON
doodling	AUTOMATIC PAINTING
	AUTOMATISM
dots of primary colours	POINTILLISM(E)
—in place of secondaries	OPTICAL MIXTURES
drying substance	SICCATIVE

dull finish	MAT, MATT(E)	ideal proportion	GOLDEN MEAN
easel painting inserted			GOLDEN SECTION
into ceiling		imaginary view	VEDUTA IDEATA
decoration	CARRIED PICTURE	imitation using motifs	
	QUADRO RIPORTATO	from several genuine	
elaborate ornament	GROTESQUE	works	PASTICCIO, PASTICHE
engraving		impression of the	
—technique	AQUATINT, CAMEO, CRAYON	open air	PLEIN AIR
	DRY-POINT, ETCHING	Impressionist views of	
	INTAGLIO, LINE, MEZZOTINT	everyday life	INTIMISME
	NIELLO, PLANAR, RELIEF	in	
	STIPPLE, SURFACE	—dots of colour	POINTILLISM(E)
—tool	BURIN, GRAVER	—one colour	MONOCHROME, GRISAILLE
—with punched dots	DOTTED PRINT	Japanese style	UKIYO-E
etching technique	AQUATINT, DRY-POINT	jelly-like paint	THIXOTROPIC
exaggerated		landscape	PAYSAGE
characterisation	CARICATURE	large altarpiece	ANCONA
exhibition (French)	SALON (D'APOLLON)	layer of paint not	
fantasy painting	CAPRICCIO	entirely covering	
figure or object in the		paint beneath	SCUMBLE
extreme foreground	REPOUSSOIR	Les Fauves	DERAIN, MANGUIN, MARQUET
figures and animals in			MATISSE, PUY, VALTAT
landscapes	STAFFAGE		VLAMINCK
film caused by aging	PATINA	lifelike flesh painting	MORBIDEZZA
first		line engraving	TAILLE-DOUCE
—coat	GESSO, GROUND	low-key painting	TENEBRISM
	PRIMER, PRIMING	made from fragments	COLLAGE
—print of engraving	PROOF	medium	ACRYLIC, DISTEMPER
Florentine engravings	BROAD MANNER		GOUACHE, INK, MAGILP
	FINE MANNER		MEGILP, OILS, PASTEL
			TEMPERA, VEHICLE
flowing linear			WATER COLOUR
decoration	ARABESQUE		
form showing through		mirror-image	
overpainting	PENTIMENTO	reproduction	COUNTERPROOF
frigid Neo-Classicism	L'ART POMPIER		OFFSET
front edge of imaginary		misty effect	SFUMATO
space in a picture	PICTURE PLANE	mixing-board	PALETTE
geometrical abstract		modelled by	
style	SUPREMATISM	—dots and flecks	STIPPLING
German school of design	BAUHAUS	—rubbing	STUMPED
glazing by rubbing		monochrome painting	GRISAILLE
by hand	VELATURA	naive art	PRIMITIVE ART
gradations of tone	VALUES	natural object as art	FOUND OBJECT
gradual transition			OBJET TROUVE
of colour	SFUMATO	network of small cracks	CRAQUELURE
ground	IMPRIMATURA	night-piece	NOCTURNE
gypsum or chalk used		not representing	
as ground	GESSO	any object	ABSTRACT
halo		of	
—enclosing whole figure	MANDORLA	—a	
—round heads	AUREOLE	detail	STUDY
	VESICA PISCIS	place	VEDUTA
hard glossy paint	ENAMEL	—angel	AMORINO, PUTTO
horizontal band	FRIEZE	—buildings	TOWNSCAPE
humorous or satirical		—Christ	
drawing	CARTOON	as child	BAMBINO

Mary and St John	DEESIS
or saint on a panel	ICON
standing in tomb	IMAGO PIETATIS
—Cupid	AMORINO, PUTTO
—everyday life	GENRE
—figures with heads on same level	ISOCEPHALY
—guard-room scenes	CORPS DE GARDE KORTEGAARDJES
—inanimate objects	STILL LIFE
—low-life and peasant subjects	BAMBOCCIATA GENRE
—Madonna and Child	
in rose garden	HORTUS CONCLUSUS
surrounded by angels	MAESTA
with saints	SACRA CONVERSAZIONE
—Mary mourning Jesus	PIETA
—person	EFFIGY, PORTRAIT
—rural	
life	PASTORAL, PAYSAGE
setting (Fr.)	FETE CHAMPETRE FETE GALANTE
—saint	ICON, IKON
—sea	SEASCAPE
—small boy	AMORINO, PUTTO
oil over tempera	MIXED METHOD
on	
—circular panel	TONDO
—dry plaster	FRESCO SECCO
—fresh plaster	BUON FRESCO
—oval panel	MANDORLA
—wall or ceiling	FRESCO, MURAL
opaque watercolour	BODY COLOUR, GOUACHE
outdoor work	PLEIN AIR
outline forming boundary of shape	CONTOUR
over-sentimental religious art	BONDIEUSERIE
paint	
—containing rubber	LATEX PAINT
—diluter	EXTENDER, LINSEED OIL TURPENTINE, WHITE SPIRIT
—thinned with turpentine	LEAN PAINT
painted	
—crucifix	CHRISTUS PATIENS CHRISTUS TRIUMPHANS
—out of doors	PLEIN AIR
—scroll	CARTELLINO
painter	
—before c 1500	PRIMITIVE
—having completed apprenticeship	JOURNEYMAN
—naive and untrained	PRIMITIVE
—of devotional Madonnas	MADONNIERI

—outside main tradition	PRIMITIVE
painter's	
—hand-rest	MAHLSTICK, MAULSTICK
—studio	ATELIER, BOTTEGA
painters	
—American	AUDUBON, BELLOWS, CASSATT COPLEY, DE KOONING, DEMUTH DICKINSON, DINE, EAKINS GORKY, GOTTLIEB, HENRI, HICKS HOFFMANN, HOMER, JOHNS, KAPROW KELLY, KIENHOLZ, KLINE LICHTENSTEIN, LUKS, MACLUNUS MAN RAY, MCLAUGHLIN, MOHOLY-NAGY MOSES, MOTHERWELL, NEWMAN O'KEEFE, POLLOCK, RAUSCHENBERG REINHARDT, RICHTER, ROTHKO SARGENT, SHEELER, SLOAN WARHOL, WEST, WHISTLER
—Argentinian	LE PARC
—Australian	DRYSDALE, NOLAN
—Austrian	HAUSMANN, KLIMT, KOCH KOKOSCHKA, MOSER SCHIELE
—Belgian/Flemish	ALECHINSKY, BREUGHEL CORNEILLE, DELVAUX DOTREMONT, ENSOR, GOES GOSSAERT, JORDAENS, LEMMEN MAGRITTE, MEMLING, RUBENS TENIERS, VAN DER WEYDEN VAN DYCK, VAN EYCK VAN RYSSELBERGHE
—British	AUERBACH, BACON BELL, BEVAN BLAKE, BONINGTON, BOMBERG BRATBY, BROWN, BURNE-JONES COLDSTREAM, CONSTABLE COOPER, COTMAN, CROME, DEMUTH DOBSON, DRUMMOND, ETTY, FLINT FORBES, FREUD, FRY, FUSELI GAINSBOROUGH, GILLMAN GIRTON, GORE, HAMILTON HEDLEY, HERRING, HILLIARD HOCKNEY, HOGARTH, HUNT, JOHN KNELLER, KNIGHT, LANDSEER LELY, LEWIS LONG, MILLAIS, MORRIS, MUNNINGS NASH, NEVINSON, NICHOLSON PALMER, PASMORE PIPER, PRITCHARD RATCLIFFE, REYNOLDS, RILEY(f) ROBERTS, ROMNEY, ROSSETTI ROWLANDSON, SICKERT, SISLEY SMITH, SPENCER, STEER STUBBS, SUTHERLAND, TURNER WADSWORTH, WALTON, WATTS WILSON

—Czech	COUBINE, KUPKA
—Danish	JORN
—Dutch	APPEL, BOSCH, DE HOOCH, HALS
	KOONING, LEYDEN, MONDRIAN
	NEUWENHUYS, REMBRANDT
	RUISDAEL, VAN DOESBURG
	VAN DONGEN, VAN GOGH
	VERKADE, VERMEER
—French	ARMAN, ARNATT, ARP, BERNARD
	BONNARD, BOUCHER, BOUDIN
	BRAQUE, BRIANCHON, CAMOIN
	CASSANDRE, CEZANNE, CHAGALL
	CHANTREUIL, CHARDIN, CLAUDE
	COROT, COURBET, CROSS, DAUMIER
	DAVID, DEGAS, DELACROIX
	DELAUNAY, DENIS, DERAIN
	DE STAEL, DES VALLIERES, DUBUFFET
	DUCHAMP, DUFY, FANTIN-LATOUR
	FOUQUET, FRAGONARD, GAUGUIN
	GELLEE, GERICAULT, GLEIZES
	GREUZE, GRIS, GUILLAUMIN
	INGRES, KLEIN, KISLING
	KUPKA, LACOMBE, LAURENS, LATOUR
	LE FAUCONNIER, LE PAGE, LEGER
	LORRAIN, LUCE
	MANET, MANGUIN, MARQUET, MASSON
	MATISSE, METZINGER, MILLET, MIRO
	MONET, MOREAU, MORISOT (f), OZENFANT
	PASCIN, PEVSNER, PICABIA
	PISSARRO, POUSSIN, PUNI, PUY
	RAISSE, REDON, REDOUTE
	RENOIR, RIBOT, ROUAULT, ROUSSEAU
	SCHOFFER, SEURAT, SIGNAC
	SOUTINE, SURVAGE
	TANGUY, TOULOUSE-LAUTREC
	UTRILLO, VALADON(f), VALTAT
	VAN DONGEN, VASARELY, VLAMINCK
	VUILLARD, WATTEAU
—German	ALBERS, ALTDORFER, BECKMAN
	BEUYS, CAMPENDONK, CRANACH
	DIX, DURER, ENDE, ERBSLOH, ERNST
	FRIEDRICH, GROSZ, HEARTFIELD
	HECKEL, HOCH, HOFFMANN
	HOLBEIN, KIRCHNER, KNELLER
	KRANOLDT, MACKE, MARC, NOLDE
	NEUMANN, OVERBECK, PECHSTEIN
	RICHTER, SCHAD, SCHLEMMER
	SCHLICHTER, SCHWITTERS, VOGELER
	WEISS, ZEIGLER, ZIMMERMAN
—Greek	EL GRECO
—Hungarian	MOHOLY-NAGY, VASARELY
—Italian	AGOSTINO, BALLO, BELLINI
	BOCCIONI, BOTTICELLI, CARRA
	CARAVAGGIO, CASORATI,
	CHIRICO, DA MESSINA
	DEL CASTAGNO, DEL SARTO

	DUCCIO, FRA ANGELICO
	FRA FILIPPO LIPPI, FRANCESCA
	GENTILE, GIOTTO, GIOVANNI
	LEONARDO, LORENZETTI, LORENZO
	MANTEGNA, MARTINI, MASACCIO
	MICHELANGELO, MODIGLIANI
	MORANDI, ORCAGNA, PARMIGIANINO
	PERUGINO, PIERO, PREVIATI
	RAPHAEL, ROMANO, RUSSOLO
	SEGANTINI, SIGNORELLI
	TINTORETTO, UCCELLO
	(see also Venetian below)
—Japanese	FOUJITA, HIROSHIGE
	HOKUSAI, MOTONUBU
	UTAMARO
—Lithuanian	CIURLIONIS
—Mexican	OROZCO, RIVERA, SIQUEROS
—Norwegian	MUNCH
—Polish	KISLING, MULLER
—Russian	BURLIUK, CHAGALL
	DELAUNAY-TERK (f), EXTER, FALK
	GABO, GONCHAROVA(f), JAWLENSKY
	KANDINSKY, KONCHALOVSKY
	LARIONOV, LENTULOV, LISSITSKY
	MALEVICH, MASHKOV, NUSBERG
	PEVSNER, POPOVA(f), PUNI
	REPIN, RODCHENKO, SOUTINE
	STEPANOVA(f), SURVAGE
	TATLIN, UDALTSOVA(f)
—Scottish	CAMERON, CRAWHALL
	HORNEL, MACGREGOR, MELVILLE
	PATERSON, RAEBURN
	RAMSAY, WALTON
—Spanish	CANO, DALI, EL GRECO
	GOYA, GRIS, MASIP, MIRO
	MURILLO, PICASSO, RIBERA
	TAPIES, VELASQUEZ
—Swedish	DAHL, EGGLING, WEISS
—Swiss	BILL, DAW, ITTEN
	KAUFMANN, KLEE
—Venetian	BELLINI, CANALETTO
	CORREGGIO, GIORGIONE, GUARDI
	MONTAGNA, PIRANESI, TIEPOLO
	TINTORETTO, TITIAN, VERONESE
—West Indian	PISSARRO
painting	
—complete picture at	
one session	ALLA PRIMA
	AU PREMIER
—medium	BASE, VEHICLE
—miniatures	LIMNING
—on stone	LITHOCHROMATICS
	LITHOCHROMY
—surface	GROUND
—used for instruction	ACADEMY FIGURE
pair of paintings	DIPTYCH

paper	
—collage	PAPIER COLLE
—for water colours	TORCHON PAPER
patron saint	ST LUKE
pedigree of painting	PROVENANCE
pencil(ling) (18th c)	BRUSH(WORK)
perspective	
—obtained by	
overlapping features	COULISSE
—of single object	FORESHORTENING
pigment	
—brown	BISTRE
—reddish	BOLE
—with hot glue-size	SIZE COLOUR
	(see also **dye**)
pose with body twisted	CONTRAPPOSTO
preliminary	
—lay-in	UNDERPAINTING
—sketch	CARTOON, EBAUCHE
primacy of colour	
over form	ORPHIC CUBISM
	ORPHISM(E)
priming on	
—canvas or panel	IMPRIMATURA
—plaster	CLEARCOLLE
	GESSO, SIZE
print from	
—copper	
engraving	MEZZOTINT(O)
etching	AQUATINT
proof with annotated	
margins	REMARQUE PROOF
quasi-topographical	
subject	CAPRICCIO
quick-drying paint	ACRYLIC PAINT
range of colours	PALETTE
realism	VERISMO
red	
—colours	HOT COLOUR
	WARM COLSUR
—blue and yellow	PRIMARY COLOUR
reddish-brown	
—chalk	SANGUINE
—earth colour	SINOPIA
representing	
—mental concept	IDEAL ART
—objects	FIGURATIVE
roll of paper used to rub	
charcoal drawings	STUMP
rough sketch	BOZZETTO, MAQUETTE
rubbing technique	FROTTAGE
school	(see styles below)
scratched through	
surface to reveal	
colour	SGRAFFITO
sealing liquid	GESSO, SIZE

shading with parallel	
lines	HATCHING
silk-screen printing	SERIGRAPHY
single print	MONOTYPE
small	
—canvas used for	
portraits	KIT CAT, KITKAT
—easel painting	CABINET PICTURE
—painting	MINIATURE
—sketch for larger	
landscape	POCHADE
—version of larger	
picture	MODELL(ETT)O
smearing of ink on	
printing plate	RETROUSSAGE
Spanish kitchen scenes	BODEGON
stage of development	STATE
stand for painting	EASEL
still life	
—intimating brevity	
of life	VANITAS
—of solid subjects	RHYPAROGRAPHY
strip of paintings	
below altarpiece	PREDELLA
styles and schools	
—12th/13th c	GOTHIC
—14th c	INTERNATIONAL GOTHIC
—14th-15th c German	SOFT STYLE
—15th-16th c	
drawing technique	SILVERPOINT
—16th c	MANNERISM
French style	FONTAINEBLEAU
—17th c	
Dutch	UTRECHT SCHOOL
French movement	RUBENISME
painters	ITALIANISERS
—17th-18th c	BAROQUE
—17th-19th c Japanese	UKIYO-E
—18th c	NEO-CLASSICISM, ROCOCO
—18th-19th c	ROMANTICISM
—19th c	ART NOUVEAU
	ARTS AND CRAFTS MOVEMENT
	DIVISIONISM
	(NEO-)IMPRESSIONISM
	POINTILLISM
	POST-IMPRESSIONISM
	REALISM, ROMANTICISM
	SYMBOLISM
domestic scenes	INTIMISME
English	
painters	NEW ENGLISH ART CLUB
	PRB
	PRE-RAPHAELITE BROTHERHOOD
European	LES VINGT
French	
—Breton school	PONT-AVEN

—group	IMPRESSIONISTS
	LES NABIS
—landscape	
painters	BARBIZON SCHOOL
—symbolism	SYNTHETISM
German	
—movement	BAUHAUS, SEZESSIONEN
—religious school	BEURON SCHOOL
—style	BIEDERMEIERSTIL
Italian	
—group	I MACCHIAIOLI
—style	METAPHYSICAL PAINTING
	PITTURA METAFISICA
Scottish	GLASGOW SCHOOL
Viennese school	LUKASBRUDER
	NAZARENES
—19th/20th c	
American realist	ASHCAN SCHOOL
—20th c	ABC ART
	(ABSTRACT) EXPRESSIONISM
	ABSTRACT IMPRESSIONISM
	ACTION PAINTING, ART DECO
	ART OF THE REAL, BODY ART
	CONCEPTUAL ART, CUBISM, DADAISM
	EARTH ART, FIGURATIVE ART
	LAND ART, MINIMALISM
	NON-REPRESENTATIONAL ART
	SITUATIONISM, SURREALISM
American	NEW YORK SCHOOL
	PRECISIONISM
based on	
—everyday objects	POP ART
—movement	KINETIC ART
—optical effects	OP ART
Dresden painters	DIE BRUCKE
	THE BRIDGE
English	
—cubism	VORTICISM
—painters	BOROUGH GROUP
	CAMDEN TOWN GROUP
	EUSTON ROAD GROUP
	LONDON GROUP, NEWLYN SCHOOL
European group	COBRA
French	
—group	LES FAUVES
—movement	FAUVISM
	SCHOOL OF PARIS
German	
—group	FLUXUS
—movement	MAGIC REALISM
	MAGISCHER REALISMUS
	NEUE SACHLICHKEIT
	NEW OBJECTIVITY
—painters	BLUE FOUR
	DER BLAUE REITER
	THE BLUE RIDER

Italian movement	FUTURISM
	METAPHYSICAL PAINTING
	PITTURA METAFISICA
return to formal	
style of art	POST-IMPRESSIONISM
Russian movement	CONSTRUCTIVISM
	CUBO-FUTURISM
	RAYONISM, SUPREMATISM
suggestion implied in	
unfinished work	NONFINITO
sweetly sentimental	SOFT STYLE
system for representing	
three-dimensional space	PERSPECTIVE
technique using colour	
mixed with wax	ENCAUSTIC WAX
texture-rubbing	FROTTAGE
thickly applied paint	IMPASTO
thinner	WHITE SPIRIT
	TURPENTINE
three-dimensional	
—effect	MODELLING
	TROMPE-L'OEIL
—quality	PLASTICITY
three paintings	
created as unity	TRIPTYCH
top	
—layers of gesso	GESSO SOTTILE
—plaster coat in	
fresco work	INTONACO
total output of painter	OEUVRE
townscape	VEDUTA
traces of earlier	
painting showing	
through	PENTIMENTO
transparent layer of	
oil paint	GLAZE
travelling apprenticeship	WANDERJAHRE
two	
—or more portraits	
in one painting	CONVERSATION PIECE
—paintings created	
as a pair	DIPTYCH
—primary colours	
mixed	COMPLEMENTARY COLOUR
undercoat of gesso	GESSO GROSSO
unsophisticated painter	PRIMITIVE
using	
—abstract shape	
and primary colours	MINIMAL ART
—chalk or crayon	PASTEL
—dots	STIPPLING
of primary colours	POINTILLISM
—grey tones	GRISAILLE
—optical illusions	OP ART
	TROMPE L'OEIL
—several pictures	MONTAGE

—single colour	MONOCHROME	Cordyline	GRASS PALM
	MONOTINT	corn palm	DRACAENA
—transparent colours	AQUARELLE	cycad	ZAMIA
—variety of materials	COLLAGE	Dracaena	CORN PALM
	LAND ART	East Indian	AT(T)AP, NIPA
varnish sprayed on		Elaeus	OIL-PALM
drawings	FIXATIVE	European	CHAMAEROPS, PALMETTO
vehicle	MEDIUM	fan-palm	TALIPAT, TALIPOT, TALIPUT
very small painting	MINIATURE		WASHINGTONIA
view of head that		grass palm	CORDYLINE
is turned away	PROFIL PERDU	Indian	JAGGERY PALM, KITTUL
visual		Leopoldinia	PIASSABA, PIASSAVA
—deception	ILLUSIONISM	Malagasy	RAPHIA
	QUADRATURE, TROMPE-L'OEIL	Malay	GOMUTI, GOMUTO
—theme	MOTIF	Mexican	WASHINGTONIA
voluptuous nude	ODALISQUE	miriti	ITA, MORICHE
wall-painting	FRESCO, MURAL	New Zealand	NIKAU
—method	FRESCO, SECCO	oil-palm	ELAEUS
water		palmetto	FAM-PALM, HEMP-PALM
—based paint	DISTEMPER, EMULSION		SABAL
—colour with gum	GOUACHE	peach-palm	PUPUHHA
white		Philippine	NIPA
—ground	GESSO	piassava	CHIQUICHIQUI
—line of canvas between		producing	
areas of colour	ANTI-CERNE	—black fibre	GOMUTI, GOMUTO
wooden model	LAY FIGURE	—canes	CALAMUS
Pakistan	PAK	—edible pith	SAGO PALM
airline	PIA	raphia	JUPATI, RAFFIA, WINE-PALM
capital	ISLAMABAD	royal palm	CABBAGE-PALM
coins	PAISA, RUPEE	sago-palm	ARENG, EJOO
governor	HAKEEM, HAKIM		GOMUTI, GOMUTO
judge	HAKEEM, HAKIM	South American	ACCROCOMIA, ASSAI
palaeontology	(see **archaeology**)		BURITI, BUSSO, COHUNE, COROZO
Palestine	PAL		GROO-GROO, GRU-GRU, JUPATI
Liberation Organisation	PLO		MACAHUBA, MACAW-TREE, MACOYA
palm	EUTERPE		MIRITI, PEACH-PALM, PUPUNHA
African	DATE-PALM, DOOM PALM		TUCUM, WAX-PALM
	D(O)UM PALM, PALMYRA	toddy palm	COCONUT PALM, PALMYRA
Arenga	GEMUTI, GEMUTO	Trachycarpus	CHUSAN PALM
Asian	DATE-PALM, PALMYRA	tropical seaside	COCO-PALM, COCO-TREE
	TALIPAT, TALIPOT, TALIPUT		COCONUT-PALM
betel nut	ARECA		DHANI, DUNNY
Borassus	WINE-PALM	wine-palm	BORASSUS, RAPHIA
Brazilian	ATTALEA, BABASSU	**Panama**	PA(N)
	CARNA(H)UBA, CHIQUICHIQUI	capital	PANAMA CITY
	COQUILLA, INAJA, LEOPOLDINIA	coin	BALBOA, CENTESIMO
	PIASSABA, PIASSAVA, PAXIUBA	**Papal**	
bussu	TROELIE, TROELY, TROOLIE	ambassador	NUNCIO
Californian	WASHINGTONIA	court	CURIA
cane	CALAMUS	delegate	EMISSARY, LEGATE
Ceylonese	CORYPHA, JAGGERY PALM	document	BULL
	KITTUL, TALIPAT	edict	DECRETAL
	TALIPOT, TALIPUT	inability to err	INFALLIBILITY
Chilean	COQUITO	letter	BULL
Chusan palm	TRACHYCARPUS	—of instructions	BRIEF
climbing	RAT(T)AN	—to all bishops	ENCYCLICAL

licence	INDULT
officer who registers bulls	DATARY
representative	EMISSARY, LEGATE
treasurer	CAMERLENGO
	CAMERLINGO
Papua New Guinea	PNG
capital	PORT MORESBY
coin	
—unit	TOEA
—100 toea	KINA
Paraguay	PY
capital	ASUNCION
coin	CENTIMO, GUARANI
tea	YERBA, YERBA(DE)MATE
parliament	
Abyssinian	SHENGO
Andorra	GENERAL COUNCIL OF THE VALLEY
Anglo-Saxon	WITENAGEMOT
Antigua	
—lower house	HOUSE OF REPRESENTATIVES
—upper house	SENATE
Austria	BUNDESRAT
	BUNDESVERSAMMLUNG
	FEDERAL ASSEMBLY
	NATIONALRAT
Australia	
—lower house	HOUSE OF REPRESENTATIVES
—upper house	SENATE
Bahamas	
—lower house	HOUSE OF REPRESENTATIVES
—upper house	SENATE
Bangladesh	JATIYA SANGSAD
Barbados	
—lower house	HOUSE OF REPRESENTATIVES
—upper house	SENATE
Belize	
—lower house	HOUSE OF REPRESENTATIVES
—upper house	SENATE
Bohemia	LANDTAG
Bolivia	
—lower house	HOUSE OF DEPUTIES
—upper house	SENATE
Brazil	NATIONAL CONGRESS
—lower house	HOUSE OF DEPUTIES
—upper house	SENATE
Bulgaria	NARODNA SUBRANIE
Canada	FEDERAL PARLIAMENT
—lower house	HOUSE OF COMMONS
—upper house	SENATE
Channel Islands	
—Alderney	STATES OF ALDERNEY
—Guernsey	STATES OF DELIBERATION
—Jersey	STATES OF JERSEY
—Sark	COURT OF CHIEF PLEAS
Colombia	
—lower house	HOUSE OF REPRESENTATIVES

—upper house	SENATE
Cornwall	STANNARY
Denmark	FOLKETING, RIGSDAG
—Upper House	LANDST(H)ING
Dominica	HOUSE OF ASSEMBLY
Dominican Republic	
—lower house	HOUSE OF REPRESENTATIVES
—upper house	SENATE
Ethiopia	SHERGO
Fiji	
—lower house	HOUSE OF REPRESENTATIVES
—upper house	SENATE
Finland	EDUSKUNTA
France	
—lower	NATIONAL ASSEMBLY
—upper	SENATE
Gambia	HOUSE OF REPRESENTATIVES
Germany	DEUTSCHES-BUNDESTAG
	REICHSTAG
—upper house	BUNDESRAT(H)
	REICHSRAT(H)
—State	LANDTAG
Greece	VOULI
Greenland	LANDSTRAAD
	NATIONAL CONGRESS
Holy Roman Empire	LANDTAG
Iceland	ALTHING
India	
—Lower House	LOK SABHA
—Upper House	RAJYA SABHA
Iran	MAJLIS, MEJLIS
Ireland	OIREACHTAS
—lower house	DAIL(EIREANN)
—upper house	SEANAD(EIREANN)
Isle of Man	TYNWALD(COURT)
—lower house	HOUSE OF KEYS
Israel	KENESET, KNES(S)ET
Italy	
—lower house	HOUSE OF DEPUTIES
—upper house	SENATE
Jamaica	
—lower house	HOUSE OF REPRESENTATIVES
—upper house	SENATE
Japan	DIET, KOKKAI
—lower house	SHUGIIN
—upper house	SANGIIN
Jordan	NATIONAL ASSEMBLY
—lower house	CHAMBER OF DEPUTIES
—upper house	CHAMBER OF NOTABLES
Liechtenstein	DIET, LANDTAG
Malaysia	
—lower house	DEWAN RAKYAT
—upper house	DEWAN NEGARA
Mexico	
—lower house	HOUSE OF DEPUTIES
—upper house	SENATE

Mongolia	KHURAL
Moravia	LANDTAG
Morocco	CHAMBER OF REPRESENTATIVES
Nepal	NATIONAL PANCHAYAT
Netherlands	STATEN-GENERAAL
	STATES GENERAL
New Zealand	HOUSE OF REPRESENTATIVES
Norway	STORT(H)ING
—lower house	ODELST(H)ING
—upper house	LAGT(H)ING
Paraguay	NATIONAL CONGRESS
—lower house	HOUSE OF DEPUTIES
—upper house	SENATE
Persia	MAJLIS, MEJLIS
Portugal	CORTES
Russia	D(O)UMA
South Africa	HOUSE OF ASSEMBLY
	(VOLKS)RAAD
Spain	CORTES
—lower house	CONGRESS OF DEPUTIES
—upper house	SENATE
Sweden	RIKSDAG
—provincial	LANDST(H)ING
Switzerland	BUNDESVERSAMMLUNG
	COUNCIL OF STATES
	FEDERAL ASSEMBLY
United States	CONGRESS
—lower house	HOUSE OF REPRESENTATIVES
—upper house	SENATE
Venezuela	NATIONAL CONGRESS
—lower house	COUNCIL OF DEPUTIES
—upper house	SENATE
West Germany	DEUTSCHES-BUNDESTAG
Yugoslavia	SKUPSHTINA
Zambia	NATIONAL ASSEMBLY
Zimbabwe	
—lower house	HOUSE OF REPRESENTATIVES
—upper house	SENATE

Parliamentary

Labour Party	PLP
Private Secretary	PPS

particle

baryons	LAMBDA PARTICLE
	NEUTRON, NUCLEON
	OMEGA (MINUS) PARTICLE
	PROTON, SIGMA PARTICLE
	XI PARTICLE
—and mesons	HADRONS
basic particles	QUARKS
charged particle	ION
—negative	ANION, ANTI-PROTON
	ELECTRON, HYDROXYLION
—neutral	NEUTRON
—positive	CATION, POSITRON
	PROTON
and negative	ZWITTERION

circling nucleus	ELECTRON
curved path	BRACHISTOCHRONE
electrons, muons	
and neutrinos	LEPTONS
emitted by hot body	THERMION
force-carrying	
—colour force	GLUON
—electromagnetic force	PHOTON
—gravity	GRAVITON
—strong force	MESON
—weak force	W-MESON
gravity particle	GRAVITON
hadrons	BARYON, MESON
having spin	
—= ½	FERMION
—= 1	BOSON
heavy particle	BARYON, HYPERON, MESON
helium nucleus from	
radioactive source	ALPHA PARTICLE
	BETA PARTICLE
	GAMMA PARTICLE
hyperons	LAMBDA PARTICLE
	OMEGA PARTICLE
	SIGMA PARTICLE, XI PARTICLE
in nucleus	NEUTRON, PROTON
interacting	
—strongly	ELECTRON, LEPTON
	MUON, NEUTRINO, TAU
—weakly	BARYON, KAON, MESON
	NEUTRON, PION, PROTON
leptons	ELECTRON (NEUTRINO)
	MUON (NEUTRINO)
light particle	LEPTON
massless particle	GRAVITON, NEUTRINO
	PHOTON
meson	
μ-meson	LEPTON, MESOTRON, MUON
π-meson	PION
χ-meson	KAON
ψ-meson	PSION
mesons	CHARGED PION
	NEUTRAL PION
	NEUTRAL D PARTICLE
	NEUTRAL PSI PARTICLE
negative proton	ANTI-PROTON
nucleon	NEUTRON, PROTON
nucleus of heavy hydrogen	DEUT(ER)ON
	DIPLON
particle accelerator	(*see* **scientific instruments**)
positive electron	POSITRON
produced from nothing	VIRTUAL PARTICLE
properties of quarks	BEAUTY, BOTTOM
	CHARM, COLOUR
	SPIN, STRANGENESS
	TOP, TRUTH
protons and neutrons	BARYON

quantum of	
—gravity	GRAVITON
—light	PHOTON
quarks	CHARMED, DOWN
	STRANGE, UP
rules of spin	BOSE-EINSTEIN STATISTICS
	FERMI-DIRAC STATISTICS
study of charged	
particles	THERMIONICS
suggested particle	AXION, NUTRETTO
	PARTON, PREON
travelling	
—at speed of light	LUXON
—faster than light	TACHYON
—slower than light	TAROYON
uncharged particle	GRAVITON, NEUTRINO
	NEUTRON, PHOTON
unknown particle	GRAVIPHOTON
	GRAVISCALAR
	INTERMEDIATE BOSON
	W PARTICLE, Z PARTICLE
weakly-interactive	
massive particle	WIMP
pasta	
bows	FIOCHETTI
butterflies	FARFALLE
cartwheels	RUOTI
cocoons	BOZZOLI
coin-shaped	CORZETTI
corkscrews	FUSILLI
corrugated strips	MAFALDE
curls	CASARECCI
dumplings	GNOCCHI
elbows	TUBETTI LUNGHI
flat strips	LINGUINI
narrow strip	NOODLE
pipes	CANELLONI, MACARONI
quills	PENNE
ribbed tubes	RIGATONI
ribbons	FETTUCINI, TAGLIATELLE
rings	ANELLI
—small	ANELLINI
rods	SPAGHETTI
ruffled ribbons	LASAGNETTE
sheets	LASAGNE
shells	CONCHIGLIE
small	BUCATINI
—butterflies	FARFALLINI
—rings	ANELLINI
spinsters	ZITE
spirals	TROFIE
stars	STELLINE
strings	SPAGHETTI
thin	ANGEL'S HAIR, CAPELLINI
	VERMICELLI
—ribbons	TAGLIARINI

tubes	MANICOTTI, MILLERIGHI
—ridged	RIGATONI
twists	SPIRALE
wheels	ROUT(IN)E
pasta dishes	CANELLONI, FARFELLE
	LASAGNA, LASAGNE, MACARONI
	MACHERONI, TAGLIATELLE
	PANSOTTI, PAPARDELLE, RAVIOLI
	SPAGHETTI (BOLOGNESE)
	TORTELLI, TORTELLINI
—Hebrew	FARFAL, FARFEL
pastry	
boiled	
—ball of dough	DUMPLING
—pudding with	
bacon	BACON JACK
currants	SPOTTED DICK
	SPOTTED DOG
meat etc	STEAK AND
	KIDNEY PUDDING
choux pastry	
—filled with cream	PROFITEROLE
—with cheese	GOUGERE
Christmas confection	MINCE PIE
circle of pastry filled and	
folded in half	TURNOVER
covering for pie	PIECRUST
crisp pastry	SHORT(CRUST)
decoration from scraps of	
pastry	FLEURON
deep-fried	
—ball of	
choux	BEIGNET
dough (US)	HUSH PUPPY
—choux pastry	AIGRETTE
encased in pastry	EN CROUTE
flaky with apples	APFELSTRUDEL
Italian	PASTA
	(see separate entry)
light pastry	FLAKY, HUFF, PUFF
open case with filling	FLAN
pastry case filled with	
—almond paste	MAID OF HONOUR
—cream cheese	CHEESECAKE
—egg custard, etc	QUICHE(LORRAINE)
—meat	PATTIE, PATTY, PORK PIE
—mincemeat	MINCE PIE
—sausage meat	SAUSAGE ROLL
—sweet	
filling	FLAN, PASTRY, PIE, TART
or savoury filling	BOUCHE(E)
	PATTY, VOL-AU-VENT
—various fillings	QUICHE
Hebrew	KNISHES
Indian	SAMOSA
—vegetables	CORNISH PASTY

pastry cook	PATISSIER
shell	DARIOLE
short, with spices	VIENNA PASTRY
slices	VANILLA SLICES
small tart	TARTLET
strip with icing	ALLUMETTE
sweet pastry items	PATISSERIE
thin pastry	
—German	STRUDEL
—Greek	FILO
types of pastry	CHEESE, CHOUX, FILO
	FLAKY, FLAN, FORK-MIX
	HOT-WATER CRUST, QUICHE
	(ROUGH) PUFF, SHORT(CRUST)
	SUET CRUST, VIENNA
with fat	PASTE, SUET PASTRY
perfume	
from	
—Asian tree	PATCHOULI
—beaver	CASTOR
—citrus fruit	BERGAMOT
—flower petals	ATTAR
—iris	ORRIS
—tropical grass	CITRONELLA
—various animals	CIVET, MUSK
gum used in perfumes	MYRRH
mixed dried flower petals	POMANDER
	POTPOURRI
oil used in perfume	SAFROLE
perfumed	
—oil or cream	MACASSAR OIL
	POMADE, POMANDER
—smoke	INCENSE
—stick	JOSS STICK
—toilet water	EAU DE COLOGNE
Persian	
ancient people	ELAMITES, MEDES
bad principle	AHRIMAN
bosun	SERANG
bravo!	SHABASH
camel litter	KAJAWAH
canopy	SHAMIANA(H)
capital	TEH(E)RAN
carpet	KALI
chief ruler	PADISHA(H)
chintz	KALAMKARI
coins	
—unit	DINAR
—100 dinars	RIAL
—10,000 dinars	TOMA(U)N
—old	
copper	KRAN, SHAHI
gold	DINAR, MOHUR
—or silver	DARIC
council chamber	DIVAN
dagger	HAN(D)JAR

decree	FIRMAN
deities	(*see* **gods, goddesses**)
demi-god	YIMA
desert	DASHT
dog	SALUKI
drink	BOSA, SHIRAZ
dulcimer	SANTIR, SANTO(U)R
dyeing process	KALAMKARI
dynasty	ACHAEMENID, PAHLAVI
	QUAJAR, SAFAVID
	SASSANID, SELEUCID, ZAND
evil spirit	AHRIMAN, DEEV, DIV
excise duty	ABKARI
fabulous bird	SIMORG, SIMURG(H)
fairy	PERI
gateway	DAR
good principle	ORMAZD, ORMUZD
governor	CHAGAN, CHAM
	KHAN, SATRAP
gum-resin	OPOPANAX, SARCOCOLLA
hall	APADANA
harbour	BANDAR
headdress	CIDARIS, TIARA
headscarf	ROMAL, RUMAL
hookah	KALIAN, NARG(H)ILE
	NARGILEH, NARG(H)IL(L)Y
inn	CARAVANSARAI
	CARAVANSARY, CARAVANSERAI
	KHAN, SERAI
irrigation pipe	QANAT
lady	KHANUM
lake	DARYACHEH
language	FARSI, IRANIAN, PAHLAVI
	PARSEE, PARSI, PEHLEVI, ZEND
loincloth	LUNGI
lynx	CARACAL
king	CYRUS, SHAH, XERXES
magician	MAGE, MAGUS
measure (4 miles)	FARSANG, PARASANG
mineral	TURQUOISE
modern name	IRAN
Moslem fanatics	ABDALS
mountain	DAGH, KUH
—range	RESHTEH
musical form	DASTGAH
nightingale	BULBUL
open-vaulted hall	DIVAN
parade ground	MAIDAN
parliament	MAJLIS, MEJLIS
pass	GARDANEH, KUTAL, TANG
paymaster	BUCKSHEE, BUKSHI
philosophy	MAGISM, MAGIANISM
phoenix	HUMA
pickles	ACHAR
pleasure-ground	PARADISE
plain	MAIDAN

prayer-book	YASHT
priest	MAGE, MAGUS
prince	MIRZA
province	KHANATE, OSTAN, SATRAPY
religion	BAB(I)ISM, BABEEISM
	BAHAI(M), MITHRAISM, PARS(I)ISM
	PARSEEISM, ZOROASTRIANISM
river	AB, RUD(KHANEH)
robe	CAFTAN, KAFTAN
rug	HAMADAN, ISFAHN, KALI
	NAMMAD, SENNA
ruler	CALIF, CALIPH, K(H)ALIF
	SASSANID, SHAH, SOPHI, SOPHY
sailor	LASCAR
salt-desert	NAMAKZAR
sand	QUM
sash	LUNGI
script	NASTALIK, NASTALIQ
scriptures	(ZEND)-AVESTA
shawl	ROMAL, RUMAL
sovereign's seat	PEACOCK THRONE
stream	CHAI
tent	SHAMIANA(H)
throne	MUSNUD
tiara	CIDARIS
title	MIRZA
—of respect	(K)HODJA, KHOJA
tobacco	TUMBUK
torture	SCAPHISM
town	SHAHR
tribe	KURD
trousers	SHULWAR
turban	LUNGI
underground water channel	QANAT
verse	G(H)AZAL, GHAZEL
water	
—bag	MASHAQ
—pipe	HOOKA(H), KALIAN
—wheel	NORIA, SAKIA, SAKI(Y)EH
whip	CHABOUK
women's quarters	ZENANA
writing-case	KALAMDAN

pertaining
meaning: concerning	
like	
of	
of the nature of	
pertaining to	
relating to	
abdomen	COELIAC
abdominal organs	SPLANCHNIC, VISCERAL
abundance of moisture	HYDRIC
action	PRACTIC
—of heated water	HYDROTHERMAL
adjectives	EPITHETIC
adolescence	NEANIC

adult period	EPHEBIC
after-image	ACOL(O)UTHIC
agents	INSTITORIAL
ageing (period)	GERONTIC
agricultural	GEOPONIC, GEORGIC
air	PNEUMATIC
albumen	ALBUMINOID
alchemy	ALCHEMICAL, SPAGYRIC
algae	CONFERIOID
all-heal	VALERIANACEOUS
almonds	AMYGDALOID
almsgiving	ELEEMOSYNARY
amber	SUCCINIC
angels	HIERARCHAL, HIERARCHIC
animal	
—behaviour	EPIMELETIC, ETEPIMELETIC
—diseases	VETERINARY
—that lives on surface	
of another animal	EPIZOOTIC
animals	ZOIC
ankles	TARSAL
antelopes	ANTILOPINE
anthrax	ANTHRACOID
antimony	ANTIMONIAL, STIBIAL
ants	FORMIC, MYRMECOID
apes	PITHECOID, SIMIAL, SIMIAN
	SIMIOUS
apples	POMACEOUS
arches	FORNICATE
argument	ELENCTIC
armies	MILITARY
armpits	AXILLAR(Y)
arms	BRACHIAL
arrangement of five	
things	QUINCUNCIAL
arrows	SAGITTAL
artisans	BANAUSIC
asbestos	ASBESTIFORM, ASBESTOUS
ashes	CINERARY
athletic exercises	GYMNASTIC
atmospheric conditions	EPEDAPHIC
authors	AUCTORIAL
back	DORSAL, LUMBAR
—consonant	VELARIC
—of knee	POPLITEAL
—sides	PYGAL
badgers	MELINE, MUSTELINE
bags	UTRICULAR
ball of thumb	THENAR
baptism	CHRISMAL
Basques	EUSKARIAN
bathing/baths	BALNEAL
beans	FABACEOUS, LEGUMINOUS
bears	ARCTOID, URSINE
beasts	THERIOMORPHIC
	THERIOMORPHOUS, THEROID

beer	CERVISIAL
bees	APIAN
beetles	SCARABOID
belly	ALVINE, C(O)ELIAC
beans	LEGUMINOUS
berries	ACINACEOUS, ACINIFORM
biological cycle	CIRCADIAN
birds	AVIAN, AVINE, ORNITHIC
	ORNITHOID, VOLUCRINE
—of prey	RAP(TA)TORIAL
birth	NATAL
birthday	GENETHLIAC, NATALITIAL
birthmarks	NAEVOID
bishops	EPISCOPAL, PONTIFIC(AL)
bite	MORSAL
black tourmaline	SCHORLACEOUS
bladders	UTRICULAR, VESICAL
bladderwrack	FUCOID(AL)
blisters	VESICAL, VESIC(ULAR)
blood	HAEM(AT)IC, HAEMATOID
	SANGUINEOUS
—vessel	ANGIOID, VASCULAR
boars	PORCINE, SUIDIAN, SUILLINE
body	CORPOREAL, SOMATIC
body-segments	STROBILATE, STROBILIFORM
	STROBILINE, STROBILOID
bones	OSSEOUS, OSTEAL, OSTEOID
—marrow	MYELOID
—of forearm	RADIAL, ULNAR
boroughs	BURGHAL
bosom	GREMIAL
boundary	PERIMETRIC, PERIPHERAL
bowels	ENTERIC
bracelets	ARMILLARY
bracts	BRACTEAL, GLUMACEOUS
brain	CEREBRAL, CEREBRIC
—and spine	CEREBRO-SPINAL
bran	FURFURACEOUS, PITYROID
branch	RAM(E)AL, RAM(E)OUS
	RAMULAR
brass	ORICHALCEOUS
bread	PANARY
breaking up of red	
corpuscles	HAEMOLYTIC
bream	SPAROID
breast	MAM(M)ILLAR(Y), MAMMARY
	MASTOID, PECTORAL
—bone	STRENAL
breathing-holes	SPIRACULAR
	SPIRACULATE
bristles	STRIGATE, STRIGOSE
	STRIGOUS, STYLOID
brother	FRATERNAL
building	TECTONIC
bullheads	COTTOID
bulls	BOVINE, TAURIC, TAURINE

bunch of grapes	BOTRYOID, RACEMOSE
	STAPHYLINE
butter	BUTYRACEOUS
butterflies	PAPILIONACEOUS
	RHOPALOCERAL
	RHOPALOCEROUS
buttocks	PYGAL
calculation	LOGISTIC(AL)
calf	VITULAR, VITULINE
—of leg	SURAL
calling	VOCATIVE
calving	VITULAR
calyx	CALYCINAL, CALYCINE
	CALYCOIDEOUS
camel	CAMELOID
camp	CASTRAL
camphor	CAMPHORACEOUS
	CAMPHORIC
canal	CANALICULAR, MEATAL
cane	BACULINE, FERRULACEOUS
canton	CANTONAL
carbuncle	CARBUNCULAR
care of children by	
parents	EPIMELETIC
carp	CYPRINE, CYPRINOID
carriage in womb	GESTATORIAL
	GESTATORY
cartilage	CHONDROID
carving	GLYPTIC
case	THECAL
—expressing origin	GENITIVE
casting of nativities	GENETHLIAC
castor-oil	RICINOLEIC
cat	FELINE
—fishes	SILUROID
catechism	CATECHISMAL
	CATECHISTICAL
caterpillar	ERUCIFORM
catkins	AMENTAL, AMENTACEOUS
cattle	BOVINE, BUCOLIC
—tending	BUCOLIC
cave-dwellers	TROGLODYTIC(AL)
caves	SPELEOLOGICAL
cavities	LACUNARY, LACUNATE
cedars	CEDRINE
cell	CYTOID, UTRICULAR
centre of gravity	BARYCENTRIC
cereals	FARINACEOUS
chaff	PALEOUS
chain of segments	STROBILIFORM
	STROBILINE, STROBILOID
chains	CATENARY, CATENATE
chalk	CRETACEOUS
charity	ELEEMOSYNARY
chased metalwork	TOREUTIC
cheek	BUCCAL, MALAR

cheese	CASEOUS	connecting bars	ZYGAL
chest	PECTORAL, THORACIC	consent	CONSENSUAL
chickenpox	VARICELLAR, VARICELLOID	contraction	STENOTIC
chief		controversy	ERISTIC
—clerk of court	PROT(H)ONOTARIAL	cooking	CULINARY
—priests	PRELATIC	copper-rust	AERUGINOUS
child		coral	CORALLACEOUS
—birth	PUERPERAL	cords	FUNICULAR, FUNICULATE
—talk	HYPOCORISTIC(AL)		RESTIFORM
children	INFANTILE	cork	PHELLOID, SUBEROSE
	P(A)EDOMORPHIC, PUERILE		SUBEROUS
children's teeth	PAEDODONTIC	corn	FRUMENTARIOUS
chin	GENIAL	council	CONCILIAR(Y), CONSISTORIAL
China	SINAEAN, SINIC		CONSITORIAN
choliamb	SCAZONTIC	count	COMITAL
church	ECCLESIASTIC(AL)	country	RURAL
chrysalis	PUPAL	county	COMITAL
circle	CYCLOID	cows	BOVINE, BUCOLIC
cirrus	CIRRATE		VACCINE
city	URBAN(E)	crabs	CANCRINE, CANCROID
civet	VIVERRINE	cretin	CRETINOID
civil matters	SECULAR	crickets	GRILLID
clauses	CLAUSULAR	cross	CRUCIAL
claustrum	CLAUSTRAL	—examination	ELENCTIC
claws	UNGUAL	—roads	COMPITAL
clay	ARGILLACEOUS, BOLAR	crow	CORVINE
clergy	CLERICAL, PRELATIC	crow's beak	CORONOID
clothes	HABILATORY, SARTORIAL	crown	CORONAL, CORONARY
	VESTIARY	crustacean larvae	NAUPLOID
cloud	NUBIFORM	crypt	CRYPTAL
clypeus	CLYPEAL	crystal	CRYSTALLOID
coast	ORARIAN	cultivation	MANURIAL
cobblers	CREPIDARIAN	cups	CUPULAR, CUPULATE
cobbling	SUTORIAL, SUTORIAN	curves in rays	
cobra	COBRIFORM	of light	DIACAUSTIC
cobwebs	ARACHNOID, ARANEOSE	cushion	PULVILLAR, PULVINAR
	ARANEOUS		PULVINATE
coccyx	COCCYGEAL, COCCYGIAN	customs of city	CUSTUMAL
cochlea	COCHLEAR	cutting edge	MORSAL
cod	GADOID	cuttlefish	SEPIARY
coins	NUMISMATIC	cyanogen	CYANIC
	NUMM(UL)ARY	dancing	ORCHEST(R)IC
college	COLLEGIATE		TERPSICHOREAN
colours	CHROMATIC	daughter	FILIAL
columns	COLUMNAL, COLUMNAR	dauphin	DELPHIN
comb	PECTIN(E)AL	dawn	AURORAL, AUROREAN
common		day	DIURNAL, EOAN
—people	PLEBEIAN, VULGAR	deacons	DIACONAL
—rank	GREGARIAN	decree	DECRETAL
community	CIVIL	deep sea	BATHYAL, THALASSIC
companionship	CONTUBERNAL	deer	CERVINE, DAMINE
conducting vessels	VASCULAR	descent	PHYLETIC
condyle	CONDYLAR, CONDYLOID	desert	EREMIC
cone	CONOID(AL)	desire	EPITHYMETIC
confirmation	CHRISMAL	devil	LUCIFER(I)AN, LUCIFERINE
conjunction	SYZYGIAL	dew	RORAL, RORIC, RORID, ROSCID

dialect	DIALECTIC
diaphragm	PHRENIC
digging	ORYCTIC
dinner	PRANDIAL
discourse	DIALECTIC
diseases of animals	VETERINARY
disputatious reasoning	ERISTIC
dissection	PROSECTORIAL
distribution of justice	JURIDICAL
divination	MANTIC
docks (weeds)	POLYGONACEOUS
Dog Star	CANICULAR
dogs	CANICULAR, CANINE
donkeys	ASININE
double womb	DIDELPHIC
doves	COLUMBINE
down	PAPPOSE, PAPPOUS
dragons	DRACONIC
dreams	ON(E)IRIC, SOMNIAL
dress	SARTORIAL
dressing	HABILATORY
dropsy	(O)EDEMATOUS
dross	SCORIAC(EOUS)
drum	TYMPANIC
dryness of skin	XERODERM(AT)IC
	XERODERMATOUS
duke	DUCAL
dung	STERCORACEOUS, STERCORAL
dyeing	TINCTORIAL
eagles	AQUILINE
ear	AURAL, AURICULAR, OTIC
—drum	TYMPANIC
earl	COMITAL
earliest times	PRISTINE
earth	CHTHONIAN, CHTHONIC
	TELLURAL, TELLURIAN
	TELLURIC, TERRENE
	TERRESTRIAL
earthquakes	SEISMAL, SEISMIC
	TERREMOTIVE
ecclesiastical council	CONCILIAR
echoes	PHONOCAMPTIC
edentates	EDENTAL
eels	ANGUILLIFORM
egg-yolk	VITELLARY
eggs (obsolete)	OVAL
Egyptian	
—king	PHARAONIC
—writing	HIERATIC
eight	OCTAL
electric current	GALVANIC, VOLTAIC
electricity and heat	ELECTROTHERMIC
elegy	EPICEDIAL, EPICEDIAN
elephant	ELEPHANTINE
	ELEPHANTOID
elf	ELFIN, ELFISH, ELVAN, ELVISH

ellipse	ELLIPTIC(AL)
elms	ULMACEOUS
embossed metalwork	TOREUTIC
embossing	EMPAESTIC
embryonic period	NEPIONIC
emeralds	SMARAGDINE
emotional forces	PSYCHODYNAMIC
emperor/empire	IMPERIAL
endosmosis	ENDOSMOTIC
enlarged veins	VARICOSE
entire Christian Church	ECUMENIC
episode	EPISODICAL
equinoxes	EQUINOCTIAL
erotic dreams	ON(E)IROTIC
examination of drugs	DOCIMASTIC
exchange	CATALLACTIC
excrement	EXCREMENTITIOUS
expenses	SUMPTUARY
experiment	PEIRASTIC
explanations	EXEGETIC(AL)
eye(s)	OCULAR, OPHTHALMIC
	OPTIC
—brows	SUPERCILIARY
—lids	PALPEBRAL
—like spots	OCELLAR
face	FACIAL
factor	INSTITORIAL
fairs	NUNDINAL
Fallopian tubes	SALPINGIAN
fat	ADIPOSE, LIPOID
	SEBACEOUS
father	PATERNAL
fathers of Church	PATRISTIC(AL)
fatty tumours	STEATOMATOUS
feast	FESTAL
feathered feet or legs	BRACCATE
feathers	PENNACEOUS
	PLUMOSE, PLUMOUS
federated state	STATAL
feet	PODAL(IC)
felony	FELONIOUS
felt	PANNOSE
fermentation	ZYMOGENIC, ZYMOID
	ZYM(OT)IC
ferns	CRYPTOGAMIAN, CRYPTOGAMIC
	CRYPTOGAMOUS
ferrets	MUSTELINE, VIVERRINE
fibrin	FIBRINOID, FIBRINOUS
fibrous structure	FIBRILLAR(Y)
	FIBRILLATE(D)
fibula	PERONEAL
field of vision	PERIMETRIC
fields	AGRESTIC, CAMPESTRAL
	CAMPESTRIAN
fifth degree	QUINTIC
fifty	QUINQUAGESIMAL

filament	FILAMENTARY	germs	GERMINAL
finches	FRINGILLACEOUS, FRINGILLINE	giant fennel	FERRULACEOUS
first		giants	CYCLOPEAN, CYCLOPIAN
—ages	PRIM(A)EVAL		CYCLOPIC
—born	PRIMOGENITAL	gibbets	PATIBULARY
	PRIMOGENITARY	giddiness	DINIC
	PRIMOGENITIVE	gills	BRANCHIAL, BRANCHIATE
—fruits	PRIMITIAL	ginger	ZINGIBERACEOUS
fish	ICHTHYOID(AL), PISCINE		ZINZIBERACEOUS
—ascending rivers		glacial rivers	FLUVIO-GLACIAL
to spawn	ANADROMOUS	gland	ADENOID, GLANDULAR
—descending rivers			GLANDULOUS
to spawn	CATADROMOUS	glass	HYALINE, VITREOUS
fishing	HALIEUTIC, PISCATORIAL		VITRIFORM
	PISCATORY	glumes	GLUMACEOUS
fissure	SULCAL	gnats	CULICIFORM, CULICINE
flags	IRIDEAL, VEXILLARY	gneiss	GNEISS(IT)IC, GNEISSOID
flesh	CARNEOUS, CARNOSE		GNEISSOSE
flour	FARINACEOUS	goats	CAPRIC, CAPRIFORM
flowers	FLORAL		CAPRINE, HIRCINE
foam	SPUMOUS, SPUMY	god	MERCURIAL
f(o)etal envelope	CHOR(I)OID	—of war	MARTIAL, MARTIAN
f(o)etus	F(O)ETAL	goitre	STRUMATIC, STRUMOSE
foliage	FOLIACEOUS, FOLIAR, FOLIOSE		STRUMOUS
foot	PEDAL, PEDATE	gold	AURAL, AURIC
—of two syllables	PYRRHIC	goldcrests	REGULINE
formation of earth	GEOGONIC	good digestion	EUPEPTIC
fowl	GALLINACEOUS	gorillas	GORILLINE
foxes	ALOPECOID, VULPINE	gourds	CUCURBITACEOUS
Franks	SALIAN		CUCURBITAL
frogs	ANURAN, BATRACHIAN	gout	PODAGRAL, PODRAGRIC(AL)
	RANARIAN, RANIFORM		PODAGROUS
	RANINE, SALIENTIAN	government	POLITIC
froth	SPUMOUS, SPUMY	—by	
funeral	FERAL, FUNERARY	elders	PRESBYTERIAN
	FUNEREAL, FUNEBR(I)AL	priests	HIERARCHICAL, HIERARCHIC
fungus	FUNGOUS		HIEROCRATIC
furrow	SULCAL	governors	GUBERNATORIAL
gabbro	GABBROID	grain	CEREAL
gall-nuts	ELLAGIC	grandfather	AVITAL
Gal(lo)way	GALLOVIDIAN	grandparents	AVAL
	GAL(LO)WEGIAN	granite	GRANITIFORM
gallows	PATIBULARY	graphite	PLUMBAGINOUS
gametes	GAMETAL	grass	GRAMIN(AC)EOUS
gaps	LACUNARY, LACUNATE	gravel	GLAREOUS
garlic	ALLIACEOUS	Greece	ACHAEAN, ACHIAN, HELLENIC
garrison	PRESIDIAL	gripes	TORMINAL, TORMINOUS
gas	PNEUMATIC	grit	SABULOUS
geese	ANSERINE	groin	INGUINAL
gem-carving	GLYPTIC	groove	SULCAL
generation	GENITIVE	group or radical of	
Gentile	ETHNIC	different nature	PROSTHETIC
geometry of curved		grove	NEMORAL
surfaces	GEODESIC	gull	LAROID
Germans	ALEMANNIC, TEUTONIC	gullet	OESOPHAGEAL
germ-plasm	BLASTOGENIC	gum	MUCILAGINOUS

gums	GINGIVAL
guts	ENTERAL, ENTERIC
	SPLANCHNIC
H-shaped fissure of	
brain	ZYGAL
hair	CAPILLACEOUS
	CRINAL, TRICHOID
—cutting	TONSORIAL
halls	AULARIAN
hammerheaded-sharks	ZYGAEN(O)ID
	ZYGAENINE
hands	CH(E)IRAL, MANUAL
	PODIAL
handle	MANUBRIAL
hard skin	SCLERODERMIC
	SCLERODERMOUS
hares	LEPORINE
harlotry	MERETRICIOUS
hawks	ACCIPITRINE
head	(EN)CEPHALIC
—of tree or comet	COMAL, COMATE
	COMOSE, COMOUS
healing	AESCULAPIAN
healthy nutrition	EUTROPHIC
heart	CARDIAC(AL)
—and blood vessels	CARDIOVASCULAR
—sac	PERICARDIAC
	PERICARDIAL
	PERICARDIAN
heat	THERMAL, THERMIC(AL)
	THERMOTIC(AL)
—of the earth	GEOTHERMAL
	GEOTHERMIC
heath	ERICACEOUS
heathen	ETHNIC
heavens	URANIAN
hedgehog	ECHINATE(D)
heightened state	
of perception	PSYCHEDELIC
	PSYCHODELIC
hemp	CANNABIC
hens	GALLINACEOUS
herald(ry)	HERALDIC
herbs	HERBACEOUS, HERBY
high	
—atmospheric pressure	HYPERBARIC
—priest	PONTIFIC(AL)
highest heaven	EMPYREAL, EMPYREAN
holidays	FERIAL, FESTAL
horn	KERATOID
horns	CORNUAL, CORNY
horse	CABALLINE, EQUINAL
	EQUINE, HIPPIC
horsemanship	EQUESTRIAN
hospital	NOSOCOMIAL
hospitality	XENIAL

hours	HORAL, HORARY
houses	DOMAL, DOMESTIC
hunting	CYNEGETIC, VENATIC(AL)
husband	MARITAL
hyacinth	HYACINTHINE
hyenas	THOOID
hypersthenia	HYPERSTHENIC
iambic trimeter	SCAZONTIC
icicles	STALACTIC(AL)
	STALACTICIOUS
ideas	NOTIONAL
ideology	IDEOLOGIC
idylls	IDYLLIAN, IDYLLIC
ileum	ILEAC, ILIAC
ill-health	VALETUDINARIAN
	VALETUDINARY
inch	UNCIAL
infants	INFANTILE
infectious disease	ZYMOTIC
inhabitants of Earth	TERRESTRIAL
insects	ENTOMIC
	INSECTIFORM, INSECTILE
interior of the ear	ENTOTIC
internal organs	SPLANCHNIC
interpretation	EXEGETIC(AL)
intestines	ENTERAL, ENTERIC
	SPLANCHNIC
introductions	ISAGOGIC, PROEMIAL
	PROLEGOMENARY
	PROLEGOMENOUS
—to discourse	EXORDIAL
introductory treatise	PRODROMAL
	PRODROMIC
irises	IRID(I)AL, IRIDIAN, IRIDIC
iron	FERREOUS
itching	PRURITIC
ivory	EBURNEAN
ivy	ARALIACEOUS, HEDERAL
jaundice	ICTERAL, ICTERIC
jaw	MAXILLARY
jawbone and hyoid	
bone	MYLOHYOID
jellyfish	MEDUSIFORM, MEDUSOID
Jews	JUDAIC
judge	JUDICIAL, JURIDICAL
judgements	JUDICIARY
kangaroos	MACROPINE
kidneys	NEPHRIC, NEPHRI)IC(AL)
	RENAL
kings	REGAL
kissing	OSCULAR, OSCULATORY
kitchen	CULINARY
—vegetables	OLITORY
knee	GENUAL
kneecap	PATELLAR
knot-grass	POLYGONACEOUS

knowledge of	
medicines	PHARMACEUTIC(AL)
labour	FABRILE
labyrinths	LABYRINTHAL, LABYRINTHINE
	LABYRINTHIAN
lacunae	LACUNARY, LACUNATE
ladders	SCALAR(IFORM)
lakes	LACUSTRINE
land	PR(A)EDIAL, TERRENE
	TERRESTRIAL
—and water	TERRAQUEOUS
—register	CADASTRAL
languages	LINGUISTIC(AL)
—spoken	PHONETIC
lap	GREMIAL
larch	LARCHEN
laughter	GELASTIC
law	EDICTAL, LEGAL
lay matters	SECULAR
lead	PLUMBAGINOUS
leaflets	FOLIOLATE, FOLIOLOSE
leather	CORI(ACE)OUS
leaves	FOLIACEOUS, FOLIAR
	FOLIATE, FOLIOSE
	FRONDESCENT, FRONDOSE
leeks	PRASINE
legal investigation	FORENSIC
legislation/legislators	LEGISLATORIAL
legs	CRURAL
lemurs	LIMURIAN, LIMURINE
	LIMUROID, TARSIOID
lenses	LENTICULAR, LENTOID
lentil-seed	LENTICELLATE
leopards	PARDINE
letters of alphabet	LITERAL, LITERARY
libido	LIBIDINAL
lice	PEDICULAR
life	ZOETIC
light	PHOTIC
lightning	FULGURAL, FULGUROUS
lilies	ARACEOUS, AROID
	LILIACEOUS
limbs	MEMBRAL
lime	CALCAREOUS
lines of verse	STICHIC
lips	LABIAL
lithium	LITHIC
liver	HEPATIC
liverworts	HEPATIC
living in slimy	
sediment	SAPROPELIC
lizards	AGAMOID, LACERT(IL)IAN
	LACERTINE
lobes	LOBAR
loins	ILIAC, LUMBAR
loss of hair	PSILOTIC

love	AMATORY
—of offspring	PHILOPROGENITIVE
low cloud	STRATOUS
lower leg	PERONEAL
lunch	CENAL
lungs	PNEUMONIC, PULMONARY
	PULMONIC
—and stomach	PNEUMO-GASTRIC
lymph	LYMPHATIC
—vessels	ANGIOID, LYMPHANGIAL
lynx	LYNCEAN
lyres	LYRICAL
mackerel	SCOMBROID
magic by good spirits	THEURGIC(AL)
magistrates	MAGISTERIAL
magnetic remanence	THERMOREMANENT
maigre (fish)	SCIAENOID
mail-service	POSTAL
mammals	THERIOMORPHOUS, THEROID
man	ANTHROPOID
	ANTHROPOMORPHOUS
manor	MANORIAL
mantles	PALLIAL
many arts or subjects	POLYTECHNIC(AL)
marble	MARMOREAL
markets	NUNDINAL
marks	STIGMATIC
marriage	CONNUBIAL, CONJUGAL
	HYMENAL, JUGAL, MARITAL
	MATRIMONIAL, NUPTIAL
	SPONSAL
—of unequals	MORGANATIC
marrow	MYELOID
Mars	MARTIAL, MARTIAN
marshes	PALUD(IN)AL, PALUDINE
	PALUDINOUS, PALUDOSE
	PALUDOUS, PALUSTRAL
	PALUSTRIAN, PALUSTRINE
martens	MELINE, MUSTELINE
master artist	MAGISTERIAL
meal	FARINACEOUS
meanings	SEMANTIC
measles	MORBILLIFORM, MORBILLOUS
measurement	MENSURAL, METRICAL
—by	
weight	GRAVIMETRIC
gas	GASOMETRIC
—of time	HOROMETRICAL
medical treatment	
of children	PAEDIATRIC
medicine	IATRIC(AL), OFFICINAL
	PHYSICKY
melody	CHROMATIC
membrane	MEMBRAN(AC)(E)OUS
meninx/meninges	MENINGEAL
mental forces	PSYCHODYNAMIC

merchants	MERCANTILE	natural right	JURAL
messengers	INTERNUNCIAL	navels	OMPHALOID, UMBILICATE
metalloid	METALLOIDAL	navigation	NAUTICAL
metals	METALLIC, METALLINE	neck	CERVICAL, JUGULAR
metonymy	METALEPTIC(AL)	nectar	NECTAREAL, NECTAREAN
mice	MURINE		NECTAR(E)OUS
mid-brain	MESENCEPHALIC	—gland	NECTARIAL
midday	MERIDIAN	needles	SPICULAR
midline	MEDIAL	Negroes	NEGROID(AL)
midwifery	OBSTETRIC	Nero	NEROTIC
milk	LACTEAL, LACTIC	nerves	NERVAL, NEURAL
mill(er)s	MOLENDINAR(Y)	nests	NIDAL
millet-seed	MILIARY	nets	RETIARY, RETICULAR
millions	MILLIONARY		RETICULATE(D)
mimicry	MIMETIC(AL)	nettle	URTICACEOUS
mind	INTELLECTUAL, PSYCHIC	network	RETIAL
mining	ORYCTIC	newly born	NEONATAL
minister/ministry	MINISTERIAL	night	NOCTURNAL
mirrors	SPECULAR	night-shade	SOLANACEOUS
mites	ACAROID	night-wandering	NOCTIVAGANT
mitres	MITRAL	Nile	NILOTIC
moderate water-supply	MESIC	nine	NOVENARY
modulus	MODULO	nineteen	DECENNOVAL
moles	TALPINE	nipple	MASTOID
monads	MONADIC(AL), MONADIFORM	Noah	NOACHIAN
monasteries	MONASTERIAL, MONASTIC	nodes	NODICAL, NODULAR
money	NUMISMATIC, PECUNIARY	north	SEPTENTRIONAL
mongooses	HERPESTINE	—wind	BOREAL
monkeys	SIMIAN	nose	NASAL, RHINAL
monks	MONASTERIAL, MONASTIC	—and	
months	MENSAL	frontal bone	NASOFRONTAL
Moon	LUNAR, SELENIAN	tears	NASOLACRYMAL
—and Sun	LUNISOLAR	nostrils	NARIAL, NARINE
morning	MATUTINAL, MATUTINE	nucleus of cell	KARYOLOGICAL
mosses	SPHAGNOUS	nuns	MONASTERIAL, MONASTIC
mother	MATERNAL	nutrition	TROPHIC
—of-pearl	NACREOUS	nymphs	NYMPHAL
motion	KINETIC	oak	QUERCINE
—of electricity	ELECTROMOTIVE	oats	AVENACEOUS
mountain-building	OROGEN(ET)IC	oblivion	LETHEAN
mouse	MURINE	oceans	PELAGIC
mouth	BUCCAL, ORAL, OSTIAL	octaves	OCTAVAL
	STOMATIC	ode of lamentation	THRENODIAL
—and stomach	STOMATOGASTRIC		THRENODIC
mucilage	MUCILAGINOUS		THRENETIC(AL)
mucus	MUCOID, MUCOUS	old age	GERIATRIC
	MUCULENT, PITUITARY	omens	OMINOUS
multiple origins	POLYPHYLETIC	once in a lifetime	SECULAR
muscles	MYOID	one	
muses	AONIAN	—eye	MONOCULAR
mysteries	TELESTIC	—person	PRIVY
names	ONOMASTIC	opals	OPALINE
nasal partition	VOMERINE	opposition	SYZYGIAL
—and cavity	VOMERONASAL	oracles	ORACULAR
nations	ETHNIC	order	ORDINAL
native land	PATRIAL	ordinary life	CIVIL

organic matter in soil	HUMIC, HUMOUS
origin	GENETIC
origins	FONTAL
orioles, etc	ICTERINE
oryx	ORYGINE
ostriches	STRUTHIOID, STROUTHIOUS
otters	LUTRINE, MUSTELINE
ounce	UNCIAL
ovary	OVARIAN
ovules	OVULAR
owls	STRIGIFORM, STRIGINE
own sex	HOMOSEXUAL
oxide of yttrium	YTTRIC, YTTRIOUS
oyster	OSTRACEAN, OSTRACEOUS
painters	PICTORIAL
palate	PALATINE
palm	
—(hand)	PALMAR, THENAR, VOLAR
—(tree)	PALMACEOUS
paper	CARTACEOUS
	PAPYRACEOUS
parabolas	PARABOLIC
parab(o)le	PARABOLIC
parasitic disease	TRICHINOTIC
	TRICHINOUS
parchment	PERGAMENEOUS
parish	PAROCHIAL
parrots	PSITTACINE
partition	SEPTIFORM
parturition	PARTURIENT
passage	MEATAL
pastors	PASTORAL
pastures	PASTORAL
peacocks	PAVONIAN, PAVONINE
pears	POMACEOUS
peas	LEGUMINOUS
pellagra	PELLAGROUS
penal settlement	PRESIDIAL
penance	PENITENTIARY
people	DEMOTIC, LAY, POPULAR
perch	PERCIFORM, PERCINE
	PERCOID
perching birds	PASSERINE
perineum	PERINEAL
pestilence	LUETIC
phalanx	PHALANG(E)AL
Pharisee	PHARISAIC(AL)
pharmacy	PHARMACEUTICAL
pharynx	PHARYNG(E)AL
phlegm	PITUITARY
phlox	POLEMONIACEOUS
phyla	PHYLETIC
physicians	IATRIC(AL)
pictures	PICTORIAL
	PICTURAL, PICTURESQUE
pigeons	PERISTERONIC

pigs	PORCINE, SUIDIAN
	SUILLINE
pile	VILLOSE, VILLOUS
pillars	STYLAR
pimple	PAPULOSE, PAPULOUS
pineal gland	CONARIAL
pineapples	BROMELIACEOUS
pitch	PICEOUS
plane-trees	PLATANACEOUS
planes	HOMALOIDAL
planet	JOVIAN, MARTIAL, MARTIAN
	MERCURIAL, NEPTUNIAN, PLUTONIAN
	SATURNIAN, URANIAN, VENUSIAN
planets	PLANETARY
planning of towns	URBANISTIC
plantain	PLANTAGINACEOUS
plants	BOTANICAL, HERBACEOUS
plates	PLACOID
plea(ding)s	PLACITORY
pleasure	APOLAUSTIC
ploughed land	ARVAL
plums	PLUMY
plunder	PREDATORY
polecats	MUSTELID, MUSTELINE
policy	POLITIC
pollen	POLLINIC
—baskets	CORBICULATE
polyp	POLYPOUS
polypus	POLYPOID
polyzoa	POLYZOOID
poor classes	LUMPEN
Pope	PONTIFIC(AL)
Pope's representative	INTERNUNCIAL
poppies	PAPAVEROUS
pores	POROSE
porphyry	PORPHYRITIC
position	STATIONAL
—in space	LOCAL
posterior	PYGAL
—part of iris	UVEAL
pot-herbs	OLERACEOUS
potassium	POTASSIC
potatoes	SOLANACEOUS
pouch	MARSUPIAL, SACCATE
	SACCIFORM, SACCULAR
practices	PRACTIC
preaching	HOMILETIC
preface	PREFATORY, PROEMIAL
prehistoric masonry	CYCLOPEAN
	CYCLOPIAN, CYCLOPIC
prelates	PRELATIC
preliminary deliberation	PROBOULEUTIC
preludes	PRELUDIAL, PRELUDIOUS
	PRELUSIVE, PROEMIAL
premonitions	PRODROMAL, PRODROMIC
present day	HODIERNAL

—world	SECULAR
presidents	PRESIDIAL
presidio	PRESIDIAL
priests	HIERATIC, SACERDOTAL
—of Mars	SALIAN
prisms	PRISMATIC(AL)
probability of recurrence of a particular state	ERGODIC
proboscis	PROMUSCULATE
processions in honour of Dionysos	ITHYPHALLIC
producing	GENITIVE
prophecy	VATIC
proverbs	PAROEMIAL
prudence	PRUDENTIAL
psyche	PSYCHIC
pubic bone	PECTINEAL
public	
—revenues	FISCAL
—treasury	FISCAL
pulse	SPHYGMOID
pulses (peas, etc)	LEGUMINOUS
punishment	PENAL
pyrites	PYRITIC(AL), PYRITOUS
quartz	QUARTOSE
quartzite	QUARTZITIC
questioning	PYSMATIC
rabbis	RABBINIC(AL)
rabbits	LEPORINE, ORYCTOLAGINE
race	ETHNIC
—course	CURSAL
—improvement	EUGENIC
racemes	RACEMOSE
radicles	RADICULAR
rain	HYETAL, PLUVIAL
—bow	IRID(I)AL, IRIDIAN
rattlesnakes	CROTALINE
ravens	CORVINE
reasoning	LOGISTIC(AL)
receptors	SENSORY
red deer	ELAPHINE
reeds	ARUNDINACEOUS
	FERRULACEOUS
reflected light	CATOPTRIC
reflection and refraction	CATADIOPTRIC
refraction of sound	DIACOUSTIC
refutation	ELENCTIC
region beyond the moon	TRANSLUNAR
registers	MATRICULAR
registrar of court	PROT(H)ONOTARIAL
regular pattern	QUOTIDIAN
relations with guests	XENIAL
religious art	HIERATIC
reports	REPORTORIAL

reproduction	GENITAL
—in larval state	PAEDOGENETIC
reptiles	HERPETINE, HERPETOID
rhinoceroses	RHINOCEROTIC
rhombus	RHOMBIC, RHOMBOID(AL)
ribbon	TAENIATE, TAENIOID
ribs	COSTAL, COSTATE
river-banks	RIPARIAN
rivers	FLUVIAL, FLUVIATIC
	FLUVIATILE, POTAMIC
roads	VIATIC
rock masses	GEOTECTONIC
rodents	GLIRINEAL
rods	RHABDOID
Roman	
—dance	TRIPUDIARY
—heralds	FECIAL, FETIAL
—mile	MILIARY
—standards	VEXILLARY
roofs	TECTIFORM
rootlets	RADICULAR
roots	RADICAL, RADICIFORM
	RHIZOIDAL, RHIZOMATOUS
rope	FUNICULAR, FUNICULATE
roses	ROSACEOUS, ROSEAL
	ROSEATE
rotary motion	TROCHILIC
royal palaces	BASILICAN
ruby	RUBINEOUS
rudiments	GERMINAL
rump of animal	PYGAL
runners	SARMENTACEOUS
running	CURSORIAL
rural dean(ery)	RURIDECANAL
sable	ZIBEL(L)INE
sacs	THECAL
sacred writing	HIEROGRAPHIC(AL)
sacrum	SACRAL
sailors	NAUTICAL
saints	PATRONAL
saliva	SIALOID
saltwort	SALSOLACEOUS
salvation	SOTERIAL
sand	ARENACEOUS, SABULOUS
sandalwood	SANTALACEOUS
sapphires	SAPPHIRINE
Satan	LUCIFERAN
Saturday	SABBATINE
Saturn	SATURNIAN
scad	CARNGOID
scales	FURFURACEOUS
	SQUAMIFORM, SQUAMOSE
	SQUAMOUS
scallops	PECTINACEOUS
scapula	SCAPULAR
scarab	SCARABOID

scazon	SCAZONTIC
scissors	FORFICULATE
screw	HELICOID(AL)
scurf	FURFURACEOUS
scurvy	SCORBUTIC(AL)
sea	MARINE, MARITIME
	PELAGIC, THALASSIC
—lions	OTARINE
—sediment	TERRIGENOUS
—shore	LITTORAL
—trade	MARITIME
—urchin	ECHINOID
—weed	ALGOID, FUCOID
seals	
—(mammals)	PHOCID, PHOCINE
—(signets)	SIGILLARY, SPHRAGISTIC
second	
—skin	HYPODERMIC
—year student	SOPHOMORIC(AL)
sedge	CYPERACEOUS
sediment on sea floor	TERRIGENOUS
seed	SEMINAL
senescent period	GERONTIC
sensation after	
stimulus	ACOL(O)UTHIC
sense of smell	OLFACTORY
septum	SEPTIFORM, VOMERINE
serums (sera)	SEROUS
servants	MENIAL, SERVILE
servile work	MENIAL
seven	SEPTIMAL
seventy	SEPTUAGENARY
sewers	CLOACAL
sewing	SUTORIAL, SUTORIAN
sex organs	GENITAL
sexual	
—attraction towards	
opposite sex	HETEROSEXUAL
same sex	HOMOSEXUAL
—love	EROTIC
sheaths	THECAL
sheep	OVIFORM, OVINE, VERVECINE
shells	CONCHOIDAL
shepherds	PASTORAL
sheriff	SHRIEVAL
ships	NAUTICAL
shoemaker	CREPIDARIAN
shops	OFFICINAL
shoulder	HUMERAL
—blade	SCAPULAR
—and hyoid	OMOHYOID
side	LATERAL
—of cranium	TEMPORAL
sieges	OBSIDIONAL
sieves	CRIBRATE, CRIBRIFORM
	CRIBROSE, ETHMOID(AL)

sight	VISIVE, VISUAL
signature	ONOMASTIC
signets	SPHRAGISTIC
silica	SILICEOUS, SILICIOUS
silk	SERIC(EOUS)
silver	ARGENTINE
simultaneous	
sister	SORORAL
transmission of messages	
over same wire	DIPLEX
sine waves	SINUSOID(AL)
single eye	CYCLOPEAN, CYCLOPIAN
	CYCLOPIC
Sirius	CANICULAR
sixty	SEXAGESIMAL
skin	CUTANEOUS, DERMATIC
	DERMATOID
skinks	SCINCOID
skull	CRANIAL
skunks	MUSTELINE
slag	SCORIAC(EOUS)
slaves	SERVILE
sleep	HYPNIC, HYPNOID(AL)
slug	LIMACEOUS
small	
—bag, bladder	UTRICULAR, VESICULAR
—blisters	VESICULAR
—cavities	VACUOLAR
—cushions	PULVILLAR
—feathers	PLUMULACEOUS, PLUMULAR
—fibres	FIBRILLAR(Y), FIBRILLATE
	FIBRILLOUS
—hooks	HAMULAR
—matter	ATOMIC
—passage	POROSE
—sac	UTRICULAR, VESICULAR
—stars	STELLULAR, STELLULATE
—valves	VALVULAR
—worlds	MICROCOSMIC
smallpox	VARIOLOUS
smells	OLFACTORY
snakes	ANGUINE, COLUBRIFORM
	COLUBRINE, HERPETINE, HERPETOID
	OPHIDIAN, OPHIURAN
	OPHIUR(O)ID, SERPENTINE
snow	NIVEOUS
soap	SAPONACEOUS
soda	SODAIC
soft hair	VILLOSE, VILLOUS
soil	EDAPHIC
soldiers	MILITARY
sole (foot)	PLANTAR, THENAR
	VOLAR
son	FILIAL
song of mourning	THRENODIAL, THRENODIC
	THRENETIC(AL)

songbirds	OSC(IN)INE
sorcerer	MAGIAN
soul	PSYCHIC
sound	SONIC
—of speaking into bottle	AMPHORIC
—reproduction	ACOUSTIC
south of Sahara desert	SAHELIAN
space	LACUNARY, LACUNATE
	SPATIAL
spar	SPATHIC, SPATHOSE
speech sound	PHONETIC
spicule	SPICULAR
spinage	SPINACEOUS
spindles	CLOSTRIDIAL
spinster	SPINSTERIAL, SPINSTERIAN
spiral	HELICAL, HELICOID(AL)
spirit	ETHEREAL, ETHERIAL
spleen	LIENAL
splints	SPLENIAL
sponge	SPONGIFORM, SPONGOID
spore(s)	SPORIDIAL
—cases	THECAL
spring	VERNAL
squint	STRABISMAL, STRABISMIC(AL)
squirrels	SCIURINE, SCIUROID
stalactites	STALACTITAL
	STALACTIC(AL)
	STALACTIFORM
	STALACTITIOUS
stalagmites	STALAGMITIC
stalks	PEDUNCULAR, PETIOLAR
	STIPITATE
standing water	LENTIC
starlings	STURNINE, STURNOID
stars	ASTEROID, ASTRAL
	SIDEREAL, STELLAR
statue	STATUESQUE
stems	CAULINE, CAULINARY
stepmother	NOVERCAL
sticks	BACULINE
stimuli from movement	PROPRIOCEPTIVE
stomach	GASTRIC
stone	LAPIDARIAN, LAPIDARY
	LITHIC, LITHOID(AL)
	PETROSAL
—fruits	DRUPACEOUS
storms	ORAGIOUS
strap	LIGULATE, LORATE
straw	STRAMINEOUS
striking	PERCUTIENT
style	STYLIFORM, STYLOID
suffragan bishop	CHOREPISCOPAL
sugar	SACCHARINE
summer	AESTIVAL
Sun	HELIAC, SOLAR

surrounding region	PERIPHERAL
	PERIPHERIC
swallows	HIRUNDINE
sweat	HIDROTIC, SUDATORY
swimming	NATATORIAL, NATATORY
swine	PORCINE
swineherds	SYBOTIC
symptoms	SEM(E)IOTIC
syphilis	LUETIC
table	MENSAL
tailless amphibia	BATRACHIAN
tailors	SARTORIAL
tails	CAUDAL, CERCAL
tallow	SEBACEOUS
tapeworms	CESTOID, SCOLECIFORM
	TAENIATE, TAENIOID
taste	GUSTATIVE, GUSTATORY
taxation	FISCAL
teacher	MAGISTERIAL
teaching	DOCTRINAL
tears	LAC(H)RYMAL, LAC(H)RYMARY
	LAC(H)RYMATORY
	LACRIMAL, LACRIMA(TO)RY
teeth	DENTAL, ODONTIC
	ODONTOID
—with paired cusps	ZYGODONT
temperature and salinity	THERMOHALINE
tempered steel	CHALYBEOUS
temples	TEMPORAL
temporal bone	PETROSAL
tendon sheaths	SYNOVIAL
tendrils	CAPREOLATE
terminate variations	ORTHOGENETIC
testing minerals by flame	PYROGNOSTIC
thigh (bone)	FEMORAL
thin plate	LAMELLAR, LAMELLATE
	LAMELLIFORM, LAMELLOID
	LAMELLOSE, LAMINAR(Y)
things	
—not spiritual	SECULAR
—similar in form	HOM(O)EOMORPHIC
thorn	SPINIFORM
thought	DIANOETIC
thread	FILOSE
three	TERNAL
—parties	TRIPARTITE
—vowel sounds	TRIPHTHONGAL
throat	GUTTURAL
thrushes	TURDINE
thunder and lightning	FULMIN(E)OUS
tides controlled by moon	LUNITIDAL
tigers	TIGERY, TIGRINE, TIGROID
tin	STANNOUS

tissues	HIST(I)OID	veins	VENOUS
—round teeth	PERIODONTAL	verbs	RHEMATIC
title	TITULAR	verdigris	AERUGINOUS
toads	BATRACHIAN, SALIENTIAN	vertigo	DINIC
tobacco	NICOTINA	vervain	VERBENACEOUS
tombs	SEPULCHRAL	very young	F(O)ETAL
tone	TONAL, TONEMIC, TONETIC	vessels	VASCULAR
tongue	GLOTTAL, GLOTTIC, LINGUAL	views	VISTAL
tonsils	TONSILLAR	vintage	VINDEMIAL
top	CACUMINAL	viscera	SPLANCHNIC
touch	HAPTIC	visibility of objects	
trachea	TRACHEAL	within the eye	ENTOPTIC
trade	MERCANTILE	vision	OCULAR
travel(ling)	VIATIC	vital urge	LIBIDINAL
treatment of		voice	PHONAL, PHONIC
—disturbed children	ORTHOGENIC	—training	VOCICULTURAL
—horse diseases	HIPPIATRIC	volcanoes	VOLCANIC, VULCANIC
trees	ARBOREAL, ARBOREOUS		VULCANIAN
	DENDRITIC(AL)	vultures	VULTURINE, VULTURISH
	DENDRIFORM, DENDROID(AL)		VULTUROUS
Troy	ILIAC, ILIAN	wading birds	GRALLATORIAL
trunk	TRUNCAL	walking	PEDESTRIAN
trust	FIDUCIARY	walls	MURAL, MURIFORM, PARIETAL
tubers	TUBERACEOUS	walruses	ODOBENID, PHOCINE
tumours of teeth	ODONTOMATOUS	war	MARTIAL
turf	C(A)ESPITOSE	—dance	PYRRHIC
twelve	DUODENARY	warfare	MILITARY
twenty	ICOSIAN	wart	VERRUCIFORM
twigs	SARMENTACEOUS	washing	LAVATORIAL
twilight	CREPUSCULAR	water	
	CREPUSCULOUS		
two supreme gods	DITHEISTIC(AL)	—cysts	HYDATIFORM
tympanum	TYMPANIC, TYMPANAL	—ferns	SALVINIACEOUS
typhoid	TYPHOIDAL	—rails	RALLINE
typhus	TYPHOID, TYPHOUS	waves/waving	UNDULATORY
ulcer	HELCOID	wax modelling	CEROPLASTIC
unborn baby	F(O)ETAL	weasels	MUSTELINE
uncle	AVUNCULAR	weddings	MATRIMONIAL, NUPTIAL
underground water		week	HEBDOMADAL
supplies	PHREATIC	west wind	FAVONIAN
underside of tongue	RANINE	whales	CETACEAN
underworld	CHTHONIAN, CHTHONIC	wheat	TRITICEOUS
	HADEAN	wheel	TROCHAL, TROCHOID
undifferentiated		whetstone	COTICULAR
plant body	THALLINE, THALLOID	whirlpool	VORAGINOUS
upper		whirlwinds	TYPHONIC
—alimentary tract	STOMATOGASTRIC	whole world	MONDIAL
—stomach	CARDIAC(AL)	wife	UXORIAL
urine	URETIC, URINARY, URINOUS	wild beasts	FERINE
use in a country	ENCHORIAL	wills	TESTAMENTAL, TESTAMENTARY
valve	VALVAL, VALVAR, VALVATE	wind	AEOLIAN
varied learning	POLYHISTORIC	wine	VINOUS
	POLYMATHIC	wings	ALARY, PENNATE
veal	VITULINE		PINNATE(D), PTERYGOID
vegetable matter	VEGANIC	winter	BRUMAL, BRUMOUS
vegetables	OLITORY		HIBERNAL, HIEMAL

wolves	LUPINE, THOOID	pepper	MATICO
woman who has more		plant	INDIAN CRESS
than one child	MULTIPAROUS	shrub	COCA, MATICO, RATANY
	POLYTOKOUS	skunk	ATOC, ATOK
womb	UTERINE	**Pharmaceutical Society**	PS
women	GYNAECOID	**Pharmacopoeia Britannica**	PB
wood	LIGNEOUS, NEMORAL	**Philippines**	
	XYLOID	aborigines	AT(T)A, ITA, TAGAL
woodcock	SCOLOPACEOUS	barge/lighter	CASCO
woodlice	ONISCOID	beef dish	STEAK TAGALOG
woodpeckers	PICARIAN	braised stew	ADOBO
woods	SILVAN, SILVATIC	candle-nut tree	LUMBANG
	SILVESTRIAN	capital	MANILA
wool	LANATE	coin	PISO
words	RHEMATIC	dumpling soup	PANCIT MOLO
worker	ERGATOID	fibre (Manila hemp)	ABACA
working classes	PROLETARIAN	fish	TANGUINGUE
	PROLETARY	knife	BOLO
world	MONDIAL	language	AT(T)A, BIKOL, MORO
worms	LUMBRICAL, VERMICULAR		TAGAL(OG), TINO
wrasse	LABROID	lime (fruit)	CALAMANSI
wrist	CARPAL	lizard	IBID, IBIT
writers	AUCTORIAL, AUTHORIAL	measure	APATAN, CHUPA, GANTA
writing	LITERARY	native	FILIPINO
—desk	ESCRITORIAL	nut	PILI(-NUT)
wrong	TORTIOUS	parrot	ABACAY, CAGIT, CALANGAY
wrongful injury	NOXAL	peasant	TAO
yesterday	HESTERNAL, PRIDIAN	plantain	ABACA, MANIL(L)A-HEMP
yokes	JUGAL	plum	DUHAT, LANSEH
yolk of egg	VITELLARY	public service vehicle	JEEPNEY
young	F(O)ETAL	race	TAGALOG
zebras	ZEBRINE, ZEBROID	rice beer	PANGASI
zeolite	ZEOLITIC, ZEOLITIFORM	servant	ALILA
zone	ZONOID	silk	HUSI
Peru	PE	straw	BAKU
bark	CALISAYA, CINCHONA	tree	DITA, ILANG-ILANG, KALUMPIT
bird	YUTA, YUTU		LIGAS, MABOLA, YLANG-YLANG
capital	LIMA	white man	CACHIL
civilisation	CHAVIN, INCA	**Philological Society**	PS
coins		**philosophy**	
—unit	CENTIMO	absolute authority	
—100 centimos	INTI	of moral law	CATEGORICAL IMPERATIVE
—old	LIBRA, SOL	abstract properties	UNIVERSALS
counting device	QUIPO, QUIPU	act performed by	
dance	CUECA	utterance	ILLOCUTION
dice game	PERUDO	actuality	ENTELECHY
dried beef	CHARQUI	all things determined by	
emperor	INCA	—causes	DETERMINISM
fever	VERRUGA	—exercise of choice	FREE-WILL
fruit	CHERIMOYA, CHERIMOYER	analysis	REDUCTIONISM
	CHIRIMOYA	apparently ridiculous	
Indian	QUECHUA, QUICHUA, INCA	but logical statement	(LOGICAL)PARADOX
king	INCA	apriorism	RATIONALISM
knotted cord	QUIPO, QUIPU	argument	THESIS
language	AYMARA, QUECHIA	assertion	
	QUECHUA	—based on aesthetics	VALUE-JUDGMENT

—of unsupported facts	DOGMATISM	doctrine that	
atomic materialism	EPICUREANISM	—abstract entities	
attribution to		do exist	PLATONISM
—abstract things of		—all that exists is material	MATERIALISM
real existence	HYPOSTATISATION	—faith and reason agree	THOMISM
—objects of a soul	ANIMISM	—Gods are men writ large	EUHEMERISM
based on first		—highest good is	
principle of		happiness from	
—beauty	AESTHETICISM	—pleasure	HEDONISM
—behaviour	BEHAVIOURISM	—reason	EUD(A)EMONISM
—chief good	HEDONISM	mankind's interests	HUMANISM
—pleasure	HEDONISM		NATURISM
—well-being of man	HUMANISM	pleasure	HEDONISM
basis of morality		practical consequences	PRAGMATISM
lies in utility		serving	
of actions	UTILITARIANISM	—others	ALTRUISM
being	ONTOLOGY	—self	EGOTISM
belief		the world of the	
—governed by reason	RATIONALISM	spirit	ASCETICISM
—in		—individuals have	
concept of God	DEISM, THEISM	freedom and	
development of		responsibility	EXISTENTIALISM
—discrete units	ATOMISM		PERSONALISM
—independent		—knowledge	
phenomena	EVOLUTIONISM	comes from direct	
mind and matter	DUALISM	perception	REPRESENTATIONALISM
nothing	NIHILISM	depends on an	
ultimate reality beyond		individual	
experience	TRANSCENDENTALISM	viewpoint	PERSPECTIVISM
unconscious patterns		is relative	POSITIVISM
of thought	STRUCTURALISM	—mental states exist	SOLIPSISM
—regulated by reason	RATIONALISM	independently	MENTALISM
—that		—moral truth is known	
all events are determined		directly	INTUITIONISM
beforehand	FATALISM	—nothing can be known	
	(PRE)DETERMINISM	for certain	SCEPTICISM
	PREDESTINATION	—only	
the universe is		matter exists	MATERIALISM
—the		one (kind of) thing	
best possible	OPTIMISM	exists	MONISM
worst possible	PESSIMISM	sensations are real	SENSATIONALISM
the world can be		—phenomena	
improved	MELIORISM	are result of	
class of terms	CATEGORY	mechanical causes	MECHANISM
consequentialism	TELEOLOGY	can be explained in	
creative evolution	BERGSONISM	physical terms	PHYSICALISM
denial of			POSITIVISM
—absolute values	EXISTENTIALISM	—pleasure is the highest good	HEDONISM
—existence of abstract		—soul is the vital principle	ANIMISM
entities	NOMINALISM	—the world is a	
—traditional values	NIHILISM	collection of	
direct experience(s)	SENSE DATUM(DATA)	experiences	NEUTRAL MONISM
doctrine of		—things perceived have	
—final causes	TELEOLOGY	a real existence	REALISM
—personal experiences	PHENOMENOLOGY	—truth depends on time	
—pleasure	APOLAUSTIC	and the observer	RELATIVISM

—vital principle invests all living things	VITALISM
—we	
can know only phenomena	POSITIVISM
cannot know things outside experience	CRITICAL IDEALISM
do not know	AGNOSTICISM
doctrines of	
—Adam Smith	POLITICAL ECONOMY
—Alfred Ayer	LOGICAL POSITIVISM
—Alfred Whitehead	EVOLUTIONISM
—Arthur Schopenhauer	IDEALISM
—Aristippos	HEDONISM
—Aristotle	IDEALISM
—Auguste Comte	POSITIVISM
—Averroes	NEO-PLATONISM
—Benedetto Croce	REALISM
—Benedict de Spinoza	RATIONALISM
—Bertrand Russell	LOGICAL ATOMISM
	SCIENTISM
—Blaise Pascal	CRITICISM
—Boethius	NEO-PLATONISM
—Charles Pierce	PRAGMATISM
—David Hume	EMPIRICISM
—Edmund Husserl	PHENOMENOLOGY
—Emmanuel Mournier	PERSONALISM
—Emanuel Swedenborg	MYSTICISM
	SWEDENBORGIANISM
—Epicurus	ATOMISM, EPICUREANISM
	HEDONISM
—Erasmus	HUMANISM
—Erich Engels	DIALECTICAL MATERIALISM
—Francis Bacon	INDUCTIVE REASONING
—Friedrich Nietszche	EVOLUTIONISM
—Georg Hegel	ABSOLUTISM
—George Moore	IDEAL UTILITARIANISM
	LINGUISTIC PHILOSOPHY
—George Santayana	CRITICAL REALISM
—Georgy	
Plekhanov	DIALECTICAL MATERIALISM
—G E Stahl	ANIMISM
—Gottfried von Liebnitz	ABSOLUTISM
	IDEALISM, OPTIMISM
—Henri Bergson	EVOLUTIONISM
—Herbert	
Spencer	EVOLUTIONARY COSMOLOGY
—Immanuel Kant	CRITICAL PHILOSOPHY
—Jean-Paul Sartre	EXISTENTIALISM
—Jeremy Bentham	UTILITARIANISM
—Johann Fichte	ABSOLUTE IDEALISM
—John Dewey	INSTRUMENTALISM
	PRAGMATISM
—John Locke	DUALISM, EMPIRICISM
—John Stuart Mill	PHENOMENALISM
	UTILITARIANISM

—Karl Jaspers	EXISTENTIALISM
—Karl Marx	COMMUNISM
—Karl Popper	CRITICAL RATIONALISM
—Ludwig	
Wittgenstein	LINGUISTIC PHILOSOPHY
	LOGICAL ATOMISM
—Martin Heidegger	PHENOMENOLOGY
—mediaeval schoolmen	SCHOLASTICISM
—Nicolò Machiavelli	REALISM
—Parmenides	IDEALISM
—Peter Abelard	NOMINALISM
—Peter Ramus	RAMISM
—Plato	IDEALISM
—Plotinus	NEO-PLATONISM
—Protagoras	HUMANISM, RELATIVISM
—Pyrrho	SCEPTICISM
—Pythagoras	DUALISM
—René Descartes	DUALISM
—Roger Bacon	EMPIRICISM
—R W Emerson	TRANSCENDENTALISM
—St Anselm	REALISM
—St Augustine	ABSOLUTISM, OPTIMISM
—St Bonaventure	MYSTICAL ASCETICISM
—St Thomas Aquinas	THOMISM
—Socrates	IDEALISM
—Søren Kierkegaard	EXISTENTIALISM
—Thales	MONISM
—Thomas Hobbes	MATERIALISM
—Thomas More	UTOPIANISM
—Vienna Circle	LOGICAL POSITIVISM
	LOGICAL EMPIRICISM
—William James	PRAGMATISM
—William of Occam	NOMINALISM
—Zeno	EVOLUTIONISM
	PANTHEISM
	STOICISM
enquiry after truth	ZETETIC PHILOSOPHY
example of a concept	PARADIGM CASE
existence	ONTOLOGY
experiences of self	PHENOMENOLOGY
explanation of phenomena	
—by	
natural means	NATURALISM
reason alone	RATIONALISM
—requiring extra- material concept	NEO-VITALISM
—without reference to other things	ABSOLUTISM
fallacious argument	SOPHISTRY
fallacy	IDOLON, IDOLUM
fictitious school	RESISTENTIALISM
fine arts	AESTHETICS
forces of Empedocles	HATE, LOVE
from	
—cause to effect	A PRIORI
—effect to cause	A POSTERIORI

general terms have no
  reality — NOMINALISM
gradual introduction
  of Socialism — FABIANISM
hedonism — EPICUREANISM
ideas are not created
  by human minds alone — CONCEPTUALISM
indifference to
  pleasure or pain — STOICISM
indivisible constituents
  of all things — MONADS
inevitability — HISTORICISM
interpretation of
philosophical problems
  in psychological terms — PSYCHOLOGISM
investigation of a
priori knowledge — TRANSCENDENTALISM
knowledge
  —can only comprehend
    phenomena — PHENOMENALISM
  —from
    direct
      perception — REPRESENTATIONALISM
      experience — A POSTERIORI
      induction — SCIENTISM
      reason — A PRIORI
  —lies between scepticism
    and dogmatism — CRITICISM
  —of
    man's nature — ANTHROPOSOPHY
    phenomena is relative — COMTISM
    (LOGICAL) POSITIVISM
  —only
    from
      —experience and
        induction — EMPIRICISM
        RATIONALISM
    —scientific method — SCIENTISM
of
  —phenomena — COMTISM
  (LOGICAL) POSITIVISM
  —practical
    consquences — PRAGMATISM
law — JURISPRUDENCE
life ruled by reason — EUD(A)EMONIA
  EUD(A)EMONY
linguistic
  classification — CATEGORY
living each moment to
  the full — EXISTENTIALISM
meaning of
  —expression — CONNOTATION
  —term — CONCEPT
mental sphere — NOOSPHERE
morals — ETHICS
necessitarianism — DETERMINISM

non-physical love — PLATONISM
nothingness
  —Heidegger — DAS NICHTS
  —Sartre — LE NEANT
objects are really ideas — IDEALISM
only matter exists — MATERIALISM
outcome of opposing
  arguments — SYNTHESIS
perfect future — MILLENIARISM
phenomena are the only
  realities — PHENOMENALISM
philosophers
  —Arabic — AVICENNA
  MAIMONIDES
  —American — BURKE, BURNHAM, CARNAP
  CHOMSKY, CHURCH, DEWEY, EMERSON
  FIEGL, JAMES, LEWIS, LOVEJOY
  MARCUSE, PIERCE, QUINE, SANTAYANA
  SCHUTZ, SCRIVEN, STEVENSON
  WATTS, WHITEHEAD
  —Australian — SMART
  —Austrian — FIEGL, HAYEK, KELSEN
  KLAGES, MACH, POPPER, SCHLICK
  SCHUTZ, WAISMANN, WITTGENSTEIN
  —Chinese — LAO-TSE, LAO-TZE, LAO-TZU
  —Cretan — EPIMENIDES
  —Danish — KIERKEGAARD
  —Dutch — ERASMUS, SPINOZA
  —English — ADAMSON, AYER, BACON
  BENTHAM, BERLIN, BRADLEY
  BUTLER, CHAMBERLAIN, CLIFFORD
  COLERIDGE, COLLINGWOOD, GREEN
  HARE, HICKS, HOBBES, HOBHOUSE
  HULME, LOCKE, MCTAGGART, MILL
  MOORE, MORE, OCCAM, OCKHAM
  PEARSON, POLANYI, POPPER
  RASHDALL, RUSSELL, RYLE
  SCRIVEN, SMART, SPENCER
  STRAWSON, WAISAMANN
  WHITEHEAD
  —French — ABELARD, ALTHUSSER
  BACHELARD, BENDA, BERGSON
  BONALD, BRENTANO, BRUNSCHVIG
  COMTE, CONDORCET, DESCARTES
  GASSENDI, MARRITAIN, MERLEAU-PONTY
  MONTESQUIEU, PASCAL, POINCARE
  RENOUVIER, ROUSSEAU, SARTRE
  SOREL, TEILHARD DE CHARDIN
  VOLTAIRE
  —German — CARNAP, CASSIRER, COHEN
  DILTHEY, ENGELS, FEVERBACH
  FICHTE, FREGE, JASPERS, HEGEL
  HEIDEGGER, HERBART, HORKHEIMER
  HUSSERL, KANT, KLAGES, KRAFT-EBBING
  KRAUSE, LANGE, LIEBNI(T)Z, MARCUSE
  MARX, NATORP, NEURATH, NIETSZCHE

REICHENBACH, RICKERT, SCHELER
SCHELLING, SCHLEIERMACHER
SCHOPENHAUER, TIEDEMAN
TONNIES, TROELTSCH
—Greek ANAXAGORAS, ANAXIMANDER
ANAXIMENES, ANTISTHENES
ARISTIPPOS, ARISTOTLE
DEMOCRITUS, DIOGENES
EMPEDOCLES, EPICURUS, HERACLIDES
HERACLITUS, HIPPIAS, LEUCIPPUS
PARMENIDES, PLATO, PLOTINUS
PRODICUS, PROTAGORAS, PYRRHO
PYTHAGORAS, SOCRATES
STAGIRITE, THALES, THEOPHRASTUS
THRASYMACHUS
XENOPHANES, ZENO
—Hungarian LUKACS
—Irish BERKELEY, BURKE, TOLLAND
—Italian ANSELM, BRUNO, CROCE
JOHN OF FIDANZA, MACHIAVELLI
ST BONAVENTURE
ST THOMAS AQUINAS, SOFFICI
—Polish ZAK
—Roman AUGUSTINE, BOETHIUS
LUCRETIUS, SENECA
—Russian IVANOV, LAVROV
TRUBETSKOY
—Scottish ADAMSON, HUME, REID, SMITH
—Sicilian EUHEMERUS
—Spanish AVERROES
MAIMONIDES, ORTEGA
SANTAYANA
—Swedish SWEDENBORG
Platonism with Oriental
elements NEO-PLATONISM
positivism COMTISM
pragmatism INSTRUMENTALISM
predestination FATALISM
proof of truth VERIFICATION
proposition which is
—not necessarily true CONTINGENT
—self-evident AXIOM
rationalism APRIORISM
real, not abstract PARTICULAR
reality
—has
more than two
components PLURALISM
two components DUALISM
—is
beyond normal
experience
TRANSCENDENTAL METAPHYSICS
combination of
—mental
and physical DUALISM

physical
and essences CRITICAL REALISM
direct contact
with God MYSTICISM
material and based on
strife DIALECTICAL MATERIALISM
neither physical
nor spiritual NEUTRAL MONISM
only appearance PHENOMENALISM
psychical IDEALISM
what we
experience IMMANENT METAPHYSICS
reasoning from
—cause to effect A PRIORISM
—thesis and antithesis DIALECTIC
rejection of
—a priori knowledge EMPIRICISM
—absolute values RELATIVISM
—conventional mores ANTINOMIANISM
—existence of spirit MATERIALISM
—God ATHEISM
—idealism REALISM
—objective universal
values EXISTENTIALISM
—orthodoxy TRANSCENDENTALISM
—positivism PHENOMENOLOGY
—realism IDEALISM
—reality NIHILISM
—supernatural HUMANISM, MATERIALISM
RATIONALISM
relationship of
—bodily and mental
events EPIPHENOMENALISM
—cause and effect CAUSALITY, CAUSATION
scepticism PYRRHONISM
search for the best IDEALISM
self
—evident statement AXIOM
—is the only certainty SOLIPSISM
—origination ASEITY
statements about good
or evil merely prescribe
moral attitudes PRESCRIPTIVISM
study of
—analysis and reason LOGIC
—assessment of
pleasure or pain FELICIFIC CALCULUS
—conduct and morals ETHICS
—duty DEONTOLOGY
—ends TELEOLOGY
—ethics DEONTOLOGY
—feelings and sensations AESTHETICS
—first principles METAPHYSICS
ONTOLOGY
—nature
and reality METAPHYSICS

of knowledge	EPISTEMOLOGY
—pure being	METAPHYSICS, ONTOLOGY
—purposes	TELEOLOGY
—reality	AXIOLOGY
—relationship of words	
to objects	SEMANTICS
—things	ONTOLOGY
—unconscious patterns	
of thought etc	STRUCTURALISM
—values	AXIOLOGY
system of logic	RAMISM
teleology	CONSEQUENTIALISM
terms have	
—a corresponding reality	REALISM
—no corresponding reality	NOMINALISM
theory	
—of	
all existence as	
an organism	ORGANICISM
knowledge	EPISTEMOLOGY
—that essences exist	ESSENTIALISM
thing	
—in itself	DING-AN-SICH, NOUMENON
—referred to in	
experience	DENOTATION
thought as	
—basis of reality	IDEALISM
—instrument	INSTRUMENTALISM
truth	
—from practical	
consequences	PRACTICALISM
	PRAGMATISM
—is	
found in consideration	
of ends	TELEOLOGY
known by intuition	INTUITIONISM
not absolute	RELATIVISM
underlying principles	METAPHYSICS
unit of discourse	
—combined	PROPOSITION
—smallest	CONCEPT
unknowableness	ACATALEPSY
value-judgements are	
—expressions of emotion	EMOTIVISM
—only personal	SUBJECTIVISM
wholes are greater	
than the sum of	
the parts	HOLISM, ORGANICISM
will is the determining	
factor	VOLUNTARISM
	(*see also* **belief**)

Philosophy, Politics
and Economics — PPE
phobias — (*see* **fear**)
photography
3-D camera — NIMSLO, STEREOSCOPE

abstract photograph with	
kaleidoscope	VORTOGRAPH
accessory holder	HOT SHOE
adjustable part of shutter	DIAPHRAGM
amount of light falling	
on film	EXPOSURE
aperture size	F NUMBER
	STOP (NUMBER)
automatic exposure system	
—aperture	
automatic,	
speed manual	SHUTTER PRIORITY
manual,	
speed automatic	APERTURE PRIORITY
auto-winder delay	INTERVALOMETER
back-lighting	CONTRE-JOUR
bar-code on film cassette	DX CODE
border effect	EBERHARD EFFECT
borders of image	FRAME
camera	
—makes	ALPHA ROTO, ASAHI
	(BOX) BROWNIE, BRONICA
	CALUMET, CANON, CHINON
	CONTAX, CROWN GRAPHIC, DEARDORFF
	ERMANOX, FUJI, HANIMEX, HASSELBLAD
	HORSEMAN, HULCHER, JOS-PE,
	KI-MONOBAR, KODAK, KONICA, LEICA
	LEITZ, LINHOF, LUBITEL
	MAMIYA, MAREY, MARIONS, MINOLTA
	MINOX, NIKON, NIMSLO, OLYMPUS
	OMEGA, PENTAX, POLAROID
	PRAKTICA, PRAKTINA, RICOH
	ROBOT, ROLLEI(FLEX)
	SINAR, SOHO, SPEED GRAPHIC
	THORNTON-PICKARD
—types	3D, BASEBOARD, BRIDGE, BOX
	CHRONOGRAPHIC, CINE,
	COMPACT, DETECTIVE, DISC
	DOLLY, FIELD, FLAT-BED
	HALF-FRAME, HALF-PLATE
	INSTAMATIC, MIRROR
	MONORAIL, NODARK, ONE-SHOT
	PANORAMIC, PERIPHERY, PINHOLE
	PLATE, POLAROID (LAND)
	QUARTER-PLATE, REFLEX
	SINGLE-LENS REFLEX, SLR
	STAND, STEREOSCOPIC, STUDIO
	(SUB-)MINIATURE, SWING, TECHNICAL
	TELEVISION, THREE DIMENSIONAL
	TLR, TWIN-LENS REFLEX
	TV, VIDEO, VIEW
colour classification	MUNSELL SYSTEM
	OSTWALD SYSTEM
—temperature scale	KELVIN, MIRED
coloured fringe	
round image	CHROMATIC ABERRATION

combination of photographs of different colours	CHROMOGRAM
composite photograph	MONTAGE, MOSAIC
defect in	
—flash photograph where subject looks at camera	RED-EYE
—lens	ASTIGMATISM CHROMATIC ABERRATION
delayed exposure	B, BULB, T, TIME, Z, ZEIT
deliberate under-exposure by using high film-speed number	PUSHING FILM
destruction of image by infra-red rays	HERSCHEL EFFECT
developing chemicals	
—groups	ACCELERATOR, ANTIOXIDANT BLIX, FIXER, MORDANT NEUTRALISER (PRE-)HARDENER, REDUCER RESTRAINER, STABILISER, TONER
—types	ACETIC ACID, ACETONE, ALUM AMIDOL, AMMONIA AMMONIUM CHLORIDE BICHROMATE, BORAX, CAUSTIC POTASH CHLORHYDROQUINONE, CHLORQUINOL CHROME ALUM, COPPER CHLORIDE COPPER SULPHATE, ELON FARMER'S REDUCER, FERRIC CHLORIDE HYDROCHLORIC ACID HYDROGEN PEROXIDE HYDROQUINONE, HYPO, IODINE LEAD ACETATE, MERCURIC CHLORIDE METOL, METOQUINONE, OXALIC ACID PHENIDONE, PINCRYPTOL POTASSIUM BROMIDE/CHLORIDE/CITRATE POTASSIUM DICHROMATE/FERROCYANIDE POTASSIUM HYDROXIDE/METABISULPHITE POTASSIUM PERMANGANATE/ THIOCYANATE POTASSIUM SULPHIDE, QUINOL QUININE, RODINAL SAL AMMONIAC, SILVER NITRATE SODIUM BICHROMATE/BISULPHITE SODIUM CARBONATE/CHLORIDE SODIUM HYPOSULPHITE/HYDROXIDE SODIUM METABISULPHITE/SULPHIDE SODIUM SULPHITE/THIOCYANATE SODIUM THIOSULPHATE SULPHURIC ACID, URANIUM NITRATE
developing, printing, etc	PROCESSING
device for	
—controlling exposure time	SHUTTER
—correcting chromatic aberration	TEINOSCOPE

—firing flash-gun	HOT-SHOE MICROPHOTOMETER
—increasing magnification	EXTENSION TUBE
—measuring light	EXPOSURE METER LIGHT METER
time-lapse photography	INTERVALOMETER
variations in reflectivity	DENSITOMETER
—transporting film automatically	AUTOWINDER MOTOR-DRIVE
—viewing negatives	VERTOSCOPE
discs of light	CIRCLES OF CONFUSION
distance from lens to focal point	FOCAL LENGTH
distortion caused by lens	SPHERICAL ABERRATION
existing light, natural or artificial	AVAILABLE LIGHT
exposure	
—calculator	ACTINOMETER
—value	EV, T STOP
extending development time to compensate for under-exposure	PUSH-PROCESSING
feature which adjusts amount of light admitted	AUTOMATIC EXPOSURE
film	
—container	CASSETTE
—for	
colour	
—prints	COLOUR NEGATIVE FILM
—slides	COLOUR REVERSAL FILM
sunlight or flash	DAYLIGHT FILM
—giving correct colour rendering	ISOCHROMATIC ORTHOCHROMATIC
—on iron plate	FERROTYPE
—sensitive to all colours	PANCHROMATIC
—sensitivity	SPEED
—speed scale	ANSI, ASA, BSI GOST, ISO, SCHEINER
filters	
—absorbing blue cast	SKYLIGHT
infra-red	HEAT FILTER
reflections	POLARISING, POLA-SCREEN
—colour conversion	CC
printing	CP
rendition	CORRECTION FILTER

—coloured sheet	GELATIN
—colourless	HAZE, ULTRA-VIOLET, UV
—grey	NEUTRAL DENSITY
—metallic-coated	DICHROIC
—monochrome	PANCHROMATIC VISION
—partly-coloured	GRADUATED
—primary colours	TRI-COLOUR
flash gun	
—control	THYRISTOR
—photography	SPARK PHOTOGRAPHY
—with daylight	SYNCHRO-SUN(LIGHT)
flexible lead to	
shutter	CABLE RELEASE
granular texture in	
photograph	GRAIN
hole in shutter	APERTURE, STOP
image	
—composed of many	
identical elements	MANDALA
—produced without	
a camera	PHOTOGRAM, RAYOGRAPH
	SCHADOGRAPH
intensification of	
latent image	LATENSIFICATION
interference rings	NEWTON'S RINGS
intrusive	
photographer(s)	PAPARAZZO(PAPARAZZI)
lamp attachment	BARN DOORS, DIFFUSER
	EVENLITE, HONEYCOMB
	KEYLITE, SLATS, SNOOT
	SOFTLITE,
lens	
—attachment	AFOCAL LENS, AUXILIARY
	EXTENSION TUBE
	LENS HOOD, LENS SHIELD
	MACRO, SUPPLEMENTARY
—distortion	ABERRATION
asymmetrical	COMA
causing	
curvature	PINCUSHION DISTORTION
due to	
—colour	CHROMATIC ABERRATION
—lens	BARREL DISTORTION
	SPHERICAL ABERRATION
of points	ASTIGMATISM
—treatment to	
cut out reflections	BLOOMING
	COATING
offset diffraction	APODISATION
—types	
1 element	SIMPLE
2 elements	DOUBLET
2 doublets	RAPID RECTILINEAR
2+ elements	COMPOUND
3 elements	TRIPLET
180°	FISHEYE, HILL CLOUD LENS

close-up	MACRO, SUPPLEMENTARY
compressing in one	
direction	ANAMORPHIC
concave/convex	MENISCUS
condenser with	
concentric rings	FRESNEL
continuously variable	ZOOM
converging	CONVEX, POSITIVE
diverging	CONVEX, NEGATIVE
double curvature	BI-SPHERICAL
highly corrected	PROCESS
increasing focal	
length	TELECONVERTER
	TELE-EXTENDER
long focal length	LONG TOM
	TELEPHOTO
moveable	SHIFT AND TILT
non-spherical	ASPHERICAL
non-symmetrical triplet	TESSAR
normal focal length	STANDARD
producing diffused	
image	SOFT FOCUS
protector	GOBO, LENS CAP
short focal	
length	INVERTED TELEPHOTO
	WIDE ANGLE
small aperture	SLOW
telephoto in short barrel	MIRROR
variable focus	ZOOM
wide	
—angle, curved field	PETZVAL
—wide aperture	FAST
with mirrors and lens	CATADIOPTRIC
without	
—astigmatism	ANASTIGMAT(IC)
—chromatic aberration	ACHROMATIC
—chromatic or spherical	
aberration	APOCHROMATIC
—spherical aberration	APLANAT(IC)
light	
—falling directly	
on subject	INCIDENT LIGHT
—line round dark area	MACKIE EFFECT
—outlining subject	
against a dark	
background	RIM LIGHTING
light-meter built	
into camera	THROUGH-THE-LENS METER
	TTL METER
light-sensitive	
layer of film	EMULSION
measure of	
—colour temperature	KELVIN, MIRED
—image sharpness	ACUTANCE
—light source	FLASH FACTOR
	GUIDE NUMBER

—refractive power	ABBE NUMBER
movement of parts of	
image in development	KOTINSKY EFFECT
opacity of	
negative	PHOTOGRAPHIC DENSITY
opening in front	
of lens	APERTURE
panoramic camera	PANTOSCOPE
paper	ALBUMEN, BROMIDE, CHLORIDE
	CHLOROBROMIDE, CHROMATYPE
	CONTACT, MULTI-GRADE
	PHOTOLINEN, PLATINUM, POP, RC
	RESIN-COATED, SELF-TONING
part positive, part	
negative effect	SABATTIER EFFECT
photograph	
—in natural colours	HELIOCHROME
—of manuscript	ROTOGRAPH
—produced without a camera	PHOTOGRAM
	PICTOGRAM
	RAYOGRAM
photographers	
—American	ARBUS, ANSEL ADAMS
	ARNOLD(f), AVEDON, FEININGER
	KLEIN, MAN RAY
	MAPPLETHORPE, PENN
	SHEELER, WINDGRAND
—Brazilian	SALGADO
—British	BAILEY, BEATON
	BOWN, BRANDT, CAMERON, FRESON
	HASKINS, IVES, LICHFIELD
	MCCULLIN, PARKINSON, RODGER
	SNOWDON
—Canadian	KARSH
—French	CARTIER-BRESSON
	DOISNEAU, LARTIGUE
—German	JACOBI(f), SCHAD
—Hungarian	CAPA
—intrusive (Italian)	PAPARAZZO
—Polish	SEYMOUR, SZYMIN
photography	
—by	
infra-red rays	THERMOGRAPHY
split laser beam	HOLOGRAPHY
X-rays	RADIOGRAPHY
	TOMOGRAPHY
—of	
cyclic movement	CHRONOCYCLOGRAPHY
moving objects	CHRONOPHOTOGRAPHY
small, inaccessible	
areas	ENDOSCOPY
—producing	
extreme close-ups	MACROPHOTOGRAPHY
larger-than-life	
images	PHOTOMICROGRAPHY
very small images	MICROPHOTOGRAPHY

—recording differences	
in refractive	
index	SCHLIEREN PHOTOGRAPHY
—three-dimensional	ANAGLYPH SYSTEM
	(FRAME SEQUENTIAL) STEREOSCOPY
	NIMSLO SYSTEM, NUOPTIC
	TACHISTOSCOPY, XOGRAPHY
pioneers	BARNACK, BAYARD
	BOLTON, BRADY, BREWSTER
	CAMERON, CAPA, CROS
	DAGUERRE, DAVY, DRIFFIELD
	DU HAURON, EASTMAN, ENGLAND
	FARMER, FENTON, FISHER
	FOX-TALBOT, GABOR, HERSCHEL
	HURTER, JOLY, KENNETT
	LANCHESTER, LAND, LIPPMAN
	LUMIERE, MADDOX, MAREY
	MAXWELL, MUYBRIDGE, NIEPCE
	READE, RUSSELL, SANGER, SAYCE
	STURM, VOGEL, WAINWRIGHT
	WEDGWOOD, WRATTEN, ZAHN, ZEISS
process	AGFACOLOUR, AMBROTYPE
	AMPHITYPE, ARISTOTYPE
	ARGENTOTYPE, AUTOCHROME
	BLUE PRINT, BROMETCHING
	BROMOIL, BROTYPE, CALOTYPE
	CARBRO, CIBACHROME
	CLICHE-VERRE, COLLAGE
	CYANOTYPE, DAGUERROTYPE
	DRY PLATE, DUFAY, EKTACHROME
	ELECTROPHOTOGRAPHY
	FERROTYPE, FINLAY, FUJI
	GALVANOGRAPHY, GELATIN SUGAR
	GUM BICHROMATE, GUM PLATINOTYPE
	HELIOTYPE, IVORYTYPE, JOLY
	JOS-PE, KALLITYPE, KODACHROME
	LIPPMAN, MONTAGE, OPALOTYPE
	OZOBROME, PAGET, PARAPHOTOGRAPHY
	PHOSPHOROPHOTOGRAPHY
	PHOTO-ENGRAVING, PHOTO-ETCHING
	PHOTOGRAVURE, PHOTOLITHOGRAPHY
	PHOTO SILK-SCREENING
	PLATINOTYPE, POSTERISATION
	SILK PRINT, SILK SCREEN
	SOLARISATION, STANNOTYPE
	TRICHROME CARBRO
	VIGNETTING, (WET) COLLODION
	WET PLATE, WOODBURYTYPE
	XEROGRAPHY
positive image viewed by	
transmitted light	DIAPOSITIVE, SLIDE
	TRANSPARENCY
rapid flash	STROBE
	STROBOSCOPIC FLASH
reflected light	
from flash-gun	BOUNCE FLASH

retouching	AIR BRUSHING, SPOTTING
reversal of tones	SOLARISATION
reversed image	ALBERT EFFECT
scattering of light	
in condenser	CALLIER EFFECT
shape and size of	
negative	FORMAT
shutter types	BETWEEN-THE-LENS, BTL
	CAPPING, COMPUR
	DIAPHRAGM, ELECTRONIC
	EVERSET, FARRADAY
	FOCAL PLANE
	KERR CELL, LEAF, SLIT
swing camera to	
follow subject	PAN
transparency	DIAPOSITIVE, SLIDE
unsharp image	BLUR
unwanted light on film	FLARE
wide-angle lens	PANTOSCOPE
zone of sharpness	DEPTH OF FIELD

physician

including: anatomist
            physiologist
            surgeon

American	AXELROD, BAILEY, BALTIMORE
	BEADLE, BEAUMONT, BEIDLER
	BEKESY, BENACERRAF
	BEST, BLOCH, BLUMBERG
	BROWN, CANNON, CASTLE
	COOLEY, CROHN, CUSHING
	DE BAKEY, DELBRUCK
	DELGADO, DEMENT, EDELMAN
	ENDERS, ERLANGER, FRIDERICIA
	GAJDUSEK, GASSER, GOLDBERGER
	GOLDSTEIN, GOODPASTURE
	GOURNAND, GUILLEMIN, HALSTEAD
	HARARY, HARTZINE, HENCH, HERRICK
	HERSHEY, HOLLEY, HOLM, HOLMES
	HUBEL, HUGGINS, JARVIK, JENSEN
	KENDAL, KHORANA, KOLLER
	KORNBERG, LANDSTEINER
	LINDSLEY, LIPMANN
	LURIA, MARINE, MCCLINTOCK
	MINOT, MURPHY, NATHANS
	NIRENBERG, OCHOA, OLDS
	PAPANICOLAOU, PENFIELD
	REED, RICHARDS, ROBBINS
	ROUS, SABIN, SALK, SCHALLY
	SHUMWAY, SIMS, SMITH, SNELL
	SPERRY, STEINER, SUTHERLAND
	TAUSSIG(f), TEMIN, THEILER
	WAKSMAN, WALD, WATSON
	WEDERBERG, WELLER, WHIPPLE
	WIESEL, YALON
Argentinian	MILSTEIN
Australian	BURNET, ECCLES, SMITH

Austrian	ADLER, BREUER, GALL
	LANDSTEINER, LOEWI, LORENZ
	MESMER, SEMMELWEISS
	VON FRISCH
Belgian	DE DUVE, VESALIUS
British	ADDISON, ADRIAN, ANDERSON(f)
	ASHBY, BAYLISS, BELL
	BOWMAN, BRAID, BRIGHT, BUIST
	CHRISTISON, CORMACK, CRICK
	DALE, DART, DOWN, FINDLAY
	GARROD, GILBERT, HALDANE
	HALES, HALL, HARVEY
	HENSON, HILL, HODGKIN
	HOUNSFIELD, HUNTER, HUXLEY
	JACOUB, JENNER, JERNE, KATZ
	KEITH, KREBS, LIND, LISTER
	LISTON, MACINDOE, MCLEOD
	MEDAWAR, MILSTEIN
	MANSON, PAGET, PITT
	PORTER, POTTS, PROUT, RINGER
	ROSS, SHARPET-SCHAFER
	SHERRINGTON, SIMPSON, SMITH
	SNOW, STARLING, STENHOUSE
	STEVENS, SYDENHAM, TINBERGEN
	VANE, WALTER, WILKINS
	WILLIS
Canadian	BANTING, BEST
	HUGGINS, OSLER
Czech	PURKINJE
Danish	BANG, ELLERMAN
	FINSEN, GRAM, JERNE, WORM
Dutch	DE GRAAF, EIJKMAN
	EINTHOVEN, INGEN-HOUSZ
	ONNES, PEKELHARIN
	SWAMMERDAM
French	BABINSKI, BERNARD, BERT
	BICHAT, BORREL, BROCA
	CARREL, CHARGOT, CHRETIEN
	DAUSSET, DAVAINE, D'AZYR
	DUBOIS, DUCHENNE, DUPUYTREN
	DUTROCHET, FERNEL, FLOURENS
	GAUTIER, JACOB, LAENNAC
	LEJEUNE, LWOFF
	MAGENDIE, MONOD, OUDIN
	PARE, RICHET, TURPIN
German	BEHRING, BILLROTH
	DU BOIS-REYMOND
	EHRLICH, FORSSMANN, FRI(T)SCH
	HERING, HITZIG, KLEBS, KOCH
	KOHLER, KUHNE
	LANGERHANS, LOEWI, LORENZ
	LINEN, MINKOWSKI, MULLER
	SCHNEIDER, SCHULZE, SCHWANN
	SPEMANN, THAL, VIRCHOW, VON BAER
	VON MERING, VON WALDEYER
	WESTPHAL, WOLFF, WUNDT, ZINN

German/Swiss	PARACELSUS
	VON HOHENHEIM
Greek	ALCMAEON, ERASISTRATUS
	GALEN, HEROPHILUS
	HIPPOCRATES, PAPANICOLAOU
	PRAXAGORAS
Homeric	P(A)EAN
Hungarian	BEKESY
Irish	BENNETT, GRAVES
Italian	BOVET, CORTI, DE LUZZI, DULBECCO
	FABRICIUS, FABRIZZI
	FALLOPIO, FRASCATORO
	LEVI-MONTALCINI, MALPIGHI
	MONTESSOIR(f), REDI
Japanese	TONEGAWA
Mexican	CLAUDE, ROSENBLEUTH
of the Gods	P(A)EAN
Polish	LISTER
Portuguese	MONIZ
Roman	CELSUS, GALEN
Romanian	PALADE
Russian	PAVLOV
South African	BARNARD
Spanish	DELGADO, RAMON Y CAJAL
Swedish	BERGSTROM, HYDEN, RETZIUS
	EULER, GRANIT
	SAMUELSSON, THEGRELL
Swiss	ARBER, ERASTUS, HESS, KOCHER
	REICHSTEIN, RORSCHACH
	VON HALLER
	(*see also* **surgery**)

physics

ability	
—of lens system to	
separate small objects	RESOLVING POWER
—to transmit heat	DIATHERMANCY
absolute Fahrenheit	
scale	RANKINE SCALE
absorption	
—and re-emission of light	
using different	
wavelengths	FLUORESCENCE
—lines in Sun's	
spectrum	FRAUNHOFER LINES
—of neutron	PARASITE CAPTURE
accumulator	SECONDARY CELL
acting without gaining	
or losing heat	ADIABATIC
actinides (elements)	ACTINONS
	LANTHANIDES
action of forces	MECHANICS
—on body	
at rest	STATICS
in motion	DYNAMICS
addition of impurity	
to semiconductor	DOPING

aerial with two rods	DIPOLE
alternate speeding and	
slowing of electron	
stream	VELOCITY MODULATION
alternative form	
of element	ALLOTROPE
amount of	
—light	
emitted per	
second	LUMINOUS INTENSITY
passing through an area	
in one second	LUMINOUS FLUX
—material needed to start nuclear	
chain-reaction	CRITICAL MASS
analysis of mixtures by	
electrical conductivity	
of gases	GAS CHROMATOGRAPHY
angle	
—between	
Earth's magnetic field	
and horizontal	INCLINATION
	MAGNETIC DIP
geographical and magnetic	
north	MAGNETIC DECLINATION
	MAGNETIC VARIATION
vectors of	
quantities having the	
same frequency	PHASE ANGLE
—from geographical	
meridian	LONGITUDE
—subtended by radius of	
Earth at one astronomical	
unit	SOLAR PARALLAX
angular distance from	
Equator	LATITUDE
apparent	
—change in frequency	
due to motion	DOPPLER EFFECT
	DOPPLER SHIFT
—loss of weight of	
body in liquid	ARCHIMEDES PRINCIPLE
—movement of object	
resulting from movement	
of observer	PARALLAX
area	
—of high mass on Moon	MASCON
—within which a body	
exercises force	FIELD
arrangement of elements	
by atomic weight	PERIODIC TABLE
assembly used to study	
moderators in nuclear	
reactions	SIGMA PILE
atomic	
—energy	NUCLEAR ENERGY
—nucleus of isotope	NUCL(E)IDE

—number	PROTON NUMBER, Z
—pile	NUCLEAR REACTOR
—weight of	
element in grams	GRAM-ATOM
isotope	ISOPIC WEIGHT
	MASS NUMBER
atoms	
—of same element but	
different mass numbers	ISOTOPE
—with same number of	
neutrons but different	
atomic weights	ISOTONES
attraction	
—between	
bodies	GRAVITY
protons and neutrons in	
nucleus	NUCLEAR FORCE
—or repulsion due	
to magnetism	MAGNETIC FORCE
average	
—distance travelled by	
particle between	
collisions	MEAN FREE PATH
—time between two	
collisions of	
particle	MEAN FREE TIME
battery	(see cell below)
beat produced by	
superimposed waves	HETERODYNE
becoming liquid	DELIQUESCENT
bent tube which	
transfers liquids	
from high to low level	SIPHON
Big Bang theory	SUPERDENSE THEORY
blocking of light from	
one body by another	OCCULTATION
bluish light radiated	
by particles at	
high speed	C(H)ERENKOV RADIATION
body absorbing all	
radiation	BLACK BODY
brake radiation	BREMSSTRAHLUNG
break-up of nucleus	
into three parts	TERNARY FISSION
breakdown of	
—radioactive material	DECAY
—water molecules	
by uv radiation	PHOTO-DISSOCIATION
cable carrying signals	
as light	OPTICAL FIBRE
cadmium cell	WESTON CELL
cataphoresis	ELECTROPHORESIS
cathode ray tube with	
—four screens	CHROMATRON
	CHROMOSCOPE
—three electron guns	COLOURTRON

cell	
—producing energy	
from sunlight	SOLAR BATTERY
	SOLAR CELL
—secondary	GRAVITY CELL
(NICKEL-IRON) ACCUMULATOR	
—using photoconductive	
or photovoltaic	
effect	SELENIUM CELL
centre	
—line of lens	OPTICAL AXIS
—of	
atom	NUCLEUS
mass	BARYCENTRE
chamber with thermostatic	
control	INCUBATOR
change	
—in	
direction of light	
—bouncing off surface	REFLECTION
—passing through	
medium	REFRACTION
frequency of light passing	
through transparent	
medium	RAMAN EFFECT
optical rotation	MUTAROTATION
shape due to applied	
force	STRAIN
size due to	
magnetisation	MAGNETOSTRICTION
volume	DILAT(AT)ION
—from liquid to solid	FUSION
charge-to-mass ratio	
of a particle	SPECIFIC CHARGE
charged central part	
of atom	(ATOMIC) NUCLEUS
circle of plane through	
centre of sphere	GREAT CIRCLE
circuit	
—in	
single chip	
or package	INTEGRATED CIRCUIT
which there are	
several voltages	PHASE
—with several inputs	
and one output	GATE
circular laboratory dish	PETRI DISH
classification of	
particles by	
properties	UNITARY SYMMETRY
coagulation of fine	
particles into	
larger	FLOCCULATION
coherent beam of light	
of single wavelength	LASER
coil of electromagnet	FIELD COIL

cold flame	CHEMOLUMINESCENCE
combination of heavy atomic nuclei from lighter, releasing energy	NUCLEAR FUSION
communication by electro-magnetic radiation without wires	RADIO
composite photograph of particle track	MOSAIC
compressing metal particles into solid	SINTERING
concavo-convex lens	MENISCUS (LENS)
concentration of magnetic flux	FLUXOID
concept	
—of work done by magnetic force	MAGNETIC POTENTIAL
—that any situation should be reversible in time	TIME REFLECTION SYMMETRY
conductivity caused by	
—electrons	N-TYPE CONDUCTIVITY
—holes	P-TYPE CONDUCTIVITY
conductor	
—for microwaves	WAVE GUIDE
—where resistance varies inversely with temperature	SEMI-CONDUCTOR
constant	
—factor in conversion	MODULUS
—of proportionality of acceleration	MASS
—in gas equation $R=1,9858$ cal/°C/mole	GAS CONSTANT, R
—relating frequency to energy	PLANCK'S CONSTANT
to spectra similar to hydrogen	RYDBERG CONSTANT
constriction of	
—liquid conductor by large current	PINCH EFFECT
—plasma by strong magnetic field	PINCH EFFECT
containing bivalent iron	FERROUS
control of particles by magnetic field	PINCH EFFECT
controlled heating and cooling	ANNEALING
converse of particle with opposite charge	ANTI-PARTICLE
conversion of	
—alternating to direct current	RECTIFICATION
—kinetic energy to radiation	BRAKE RADIATION BREMSTRAHLUNG

—light to radiant heat	CALORESCENCE
—liquid to vapour	EVAPORATION
—metals to oxides by heat	CALCINATION
—vapour to liquid	CONDENSATION
cooling below freezing-point without freezing	SUPERCOOLING
cross-magnetism	DIAMAGNETISM
curved	
—path of particle	BRACHISTOCHRONE
—liquid surface	MENISCUS
cycles per unit of time	FREQUENCY
damping device	DASH-POT
dark lines in spectrum	ABSORPTION SPECTRUM FRAUNHOFER'S LINES
defect	
—caused by removal of atom from its normal lattice position	FRENKEL DEFECT
—of lens	ASTIGMATISM
deflection by fine particles	SCATTERING
delay between cause and effect	HYSTERESIS
demagnetisation	DEGAUSSING
descent in gravitational field	FREE-FALL
description of process of electrolysis	IONIC HYPOTHESIS
deuterium	HEAVY WATER
—oxide	HEAVY WATER
device	
—amplifying microwaves	MASER
—causing light beam to converge or diverge	LENS
—controlling large current by smaller	TRANSISTOR
—converging light rays	CONVEX LENS OPTICAL CONDENSER
—converting alternating to direct current	RECTIFIER
direct to alternating current	TRANSFORMER
electrical energy to mechanical	ELECTRIC MOTOR SOLENOID
mechanical work to electricity	DYNAMOGENERATOR
—correcting chromatic aberration	TEINOSCOPE
—detecting and measuring light	PHOTOCELL PHOTO-ELECTRIC CELL
radiation	GEIGER COUNTER

—extracting heat from a fluid	HEAT PUMP
—firing electrons in cathode ray tube	ELECTRON GUN
—in which electrons flow from heated cathode to anode	THERMIONIC TUBE THERMIONIC VALVE
heat measurements can be made	CALORIMETER
—increasing signal strength	AMPLIFIER
—measuring radiation	IONISATION CHAMBER
—polarising light	NICOL PRISM
—producing electricity from chemical reaction	ACCUMULATOR BATTERY, FUEL CELL PRIMARY CELL VOLTAIC CELL
enlarged image	MICROSCOPE
images on screen from projected electrons	CATHODE RAY TUBE, CRT
—selecting parts of a wave	GATE
—splitting light into its constituent colours	PRISM
—storing electric charge	CAPACITOR
optical image electrically	MOSAIC
—transferring heat from one fluid to another	HEAT EXCHANGER
power from one system to another	TRANSDUCER
—transforming one type of signal to another	TRANSDUCER
—using magnetism to contain plasma	MAGNETIC BOTTLE
—which alters frequency distribution	FILTER
amplifies —light input to intense narrow beam	LASER
—radiation by velocity modulation	KLYSTRON
dewpoint	SATURATION POINT
diamagnetism as a result of superconductivity	MEISSNER EFFECT
dielectric material with some electrical properties	FERROELECTRIC

difference between —isotopic weight and mass number	MASS DECREMENT
—mass of nucleus and total mass of nucleons	MASS DEFECT
—number of neutrons and protons	ISOTOPIC NUMBER NEUTRON EXCESS
different elements with same atomic number	ISOBARE
diffraction when light source is at —finite distance	FRESNEL DIFFRACTION
—infinite distance	FRAUNHOFER DIFFRACTION
diffusion through membrane	OSMOSIS
dimensional change of dielectric in electric field	ELECTROSTRICTION
direction of propagation of light without double refraction	OPTIC AXIS
directional aerial used in TV and radio astronomy	YAGI AERIAL
disappearing mass	MASS DEFECT
discharge of particles from metal plate struck by uv radiation	PHOTOELECTRIC EFFECT
displacement —of atoms in crystal	DISORDERING
—towards red end of spectrum	EINSTEIN SHIFT RED SHIFT
distance between crests in wave motion	WAVELENGTH
distillation at reduced pressure	VACUUM DISTILLATION
distortion —caused by lens	SPHERICAL ABERRATION
—of crystal lattice by radiation	WIGNER EFFECT
distribution of —electromagnetic radiation	SPECTRUM
—electrons in shells	EXCLUSION PRINCIPLE
disturbance at intersection of waves of same length	INTERFERENCE
drift due to rotation of earth	CORIOLIS EFFECT
efficiency of electric circuit	GAIN
eight electrons in outer shell of atom	OCTET

Einstein's theory	RELATIVITY	
electrically		
—charged particle	ION	
—induced distortion of		
lattice	PHONON	
electricity	(see **electric**)	
electrode in transistor	EMITTER	
electromagnetic radiation		
(shortest first)	COSMIC RAYS	
	GAMMA RAYS, X-RAYS	
	ULTRA-VIOLET RAYS	
	VISIBLE LIGHT, INFRARED RAYS	
	HEAT, RADIO WAVES	
—comes in packets	QUANTUM THEORY	
electron		
—emission resulting from		
change to lower-energy		
state	AUGER EFFECT	
—emitted by		
heated plate		
in valve	THERMIONIC EMISSION	
radio-isotope	BETA PARTICLE	
—in outer shell	VALENCE ELECTRON	
	VALENCY ELECTRON	
—revolving round		
atomic nucleus	ORBITAL ELECTRON	
	PLANETARY ELECTRON	
—shells	K-SHELL to P-SHELL	
—stream escaping from		
valency band in		
magnetic field	ZENER CURRENT	
electrovalent bond	IONIC BOND	
element with some		
properties of both		
metals and non-metals	METALLOID	
emanation of actinium	ACTINON	
emission		
—by radioactive		
material	ALPHA RAY, BETA RAY	
	GAMMA RAY	
—of		
electrons caused by		
—electric field	FIELD EMISSION	
—incident light	PHOTOEMISSION	
flashes from incident		
radiation	SCINTILLATION	
gamma rays by		
nuclei	MOSSBAUER EFFECT	
light by crystals		
when crushed	TRIBOLUMINESCENCE	
nuclear particles		
caused by incident		
particle	SPALLATION	
particles from nucleus	DISINTEGRATION	
wavelengths longer than		
incident waves	FLUORESCENCE	

energy	
—absorbed or emitted	
during a reversible	
process	FREE ENERGY, G
	GIBBS FUNCTION
—as electromagnetic	
radiation	RADIANT ENERGY
—cycle	CARNOT CYCLE
—from	
conversion of mass	ATOMIC ENERGY
	NUCLEAR ENERGY
temperature difference	HEAT
—needed to move nucleon	
from nucleus	BINDING ENERGY
	SEPARATION ENERGY
—of	
motion	KINETIC ENERGY
neutrons expressed as	
temperature	NEUTRON TEMPERATURE
particles due to rotation	SPIN
substance at	
absolute zero	ZERO POINT ENERGY
—possessed by virtue	
of position	POTENTIAL ENERGY
—region round nucleus	NUCLEAR BARRIER
—released in nuclear	
reaction	Q-VALUE
—required to separate	
crystal ions	LATTICE ENERGY
—state of atom	SHELL
—stored in crystal	
after irradiation	WIGNER ENERGY
entrapment of charged	
particles in the	
atmosphere	CHRISTOFILOS EFFECT
equal	
—and opposite forces	COUPLE
—numbers of atoms and	
electrons	ISOSTERISM
—volumes of gas	
contain equal numbers of	
moles	AVOGADRO'S LAW
have equal number	
of particles	AVOGADRO'S PRINCIPLE
equation	
—governing	
distribution of	
molecules in	
gas	
MAXWELL-BOLTZMANN DISTRIBUTION	
flow of liquid	
through tube	POISEUILLE'S EQUATION
particles moving	
in a force	
field	
SCHRODINGER'S WAVE EQUATION	

—of
  physical laws for right-
   and left-hand
   systems   PARITY
   time and speed   KINEMATIC EQUATION
—relating space
  and time
        LORENTZ TRANSFORMATION
excitation in polar
 molecules   POLARON
excited state
 —in semiconductor   EXCITON
 —state of particle   METASTABLE STATE
existence in
 —one form   MONOTROPY
 —several forms   ALLOTROPY
             POLYMORPHISM
experiment to test directional
 speed of light
   MICHELSON-MORLEY EXPERIMENT
expression of strength
 of solution   MOLALITY, MOLARITY
factor
 —defining Earth's
   magnetic field   MAGNETIC ELEMENT
 —which measures
   specific property   COEFFICIENT
false line in spectrum   GHOST
faster than
 —Mach 1   SUPERSONIC
 —Mach 5   HYPERSONIC
figure representing
 —three forces
   acting at a point   TRIANGLE OF FORCES
 —velocities acting
   on a body   TRIANGLE OF VELOCITIES
fixed
 —part of electric
   generator or motor   STATOR
 —time curve   TAUTOCHRONE
flow of
 —electrons across gap   EDISON EFFECT
 —fluid over streamlined
   surface   LAMINAR FLOW
 —solids   CREEP
fluid
 —closest to surface
   below   BOUNDARY LAYER
 —used for cooling   COOLANT
 —which flows without
   friction   SUPERFLUID
force
 —acting
  between
   —atoms and
    molecules   VAN DER WAALS' FORCE

—basic particles   WEAK FORCE
—quarks   COLOUR FORCE
on
 —a surface   PRESSURE
 —all
  charged particles
    ELECTROMAGNETIC FORCE
  matter   GRAVITY
 —within the nucleus   STRONG FORCE
—field round magnet or
 electrical conductor   MAGNETIC FIELD
—including gravity and
 antigravity   SUPERGRAVITY
—of rotation   TORQUE
 towards
  —centre   CENTRIPETAL FORCE
  —rim   CENTRIFUGAL
—per unit area   PRESSURE, STRESS
—producing
 rotation   TORQUE
 same effect as several
  forces acting together   RESULTANT
formation of
 —closed ring of atoms   CHELATION
 —ions   IONISATION
formula
 —connecting pressure,
  volume, quantity and
  temperature
  of gas   GAS EQUATION
 —connecting pressure,
  volume, and temperature
  of gas   VAN DER WAALS' EQUATION
four
 —forces   ELECTROMAGNETIC
   GRAVITY, STRONG (NUCLEAR)
       WEAK (NUCLEAR)
 —states of matter   GAS, LIQUID
      PLASMA, SOLID
freezing   GELATION
frequencies in a group
 of emission spectra   SPECTRAL SERIES
frequency
 —at which light causes
  emission of electrons
  from metal   THRESHOLD FREQUENCY
 —of sound   PITCH
 —response   FIDELITY
gamma rays unaffected
 by nuclear recoil   MOSSBAUER EFFECT
gas
 —below critical temperature   VAPOUR
 —constant divided by
  Avogadro's
  constant   BOLTZMANN'S CONSTANT, K
 —ionised   PLASMA

gases	(*see separate entry*)
grand unified theory	GUT
gravitational attraction	
—determining inertial frames	MACH('S) PRINCIPLE
—of Earth on mass	WEIGHT
great circle through geographical poles	(TERRESTRIAL) MERIDIAN
grouping of spectral lines in magnetic field	ZEEMAN EFFECT
half-shadow	PENUMBRA
handedness	PARITY
hardness test	BRINELL TEST
having	
—all waves in same phase	COHERENT
—equal	
enthalpy	ISENTHALPIC
entropy	ISENTROPIC
osmotic pressure	ISOTONIC
—little or no reverberation	ANECHOIC
—no electric charge	NEUTRAL
—only one stable form	MONOTROPIC
—two axes at right-angles to third axis	MONOCLINIC
heat	
—content per unit	ENTHALPY, H
—required to raise unit mass 1 degree	SPECIFIC HEAT
—taken up or released in change of state	LATENT HEAT
—transference	
across intervening space	RADIATION
by movement of fluid	CONVECTION
through a solid	CONDUCTION
—waves longer than red light	INFRARED RAYS
heating	
—chamber	AUTOCLAVE, FURNACE
—vessel	CRUCIBLE
heavy	
—hydrogen	DEUTERIUM
—water	DEUTERIUM (OXIDE)
helium	
—making	NUCLEOSYNTHESIS
—nucleus	ALPHA PARTICLE
Helmholtz free energy	F, WORK FUNCTION
high-temperature zone where particle passes through a substance	THERMAL SPIKE
highest temperature at which liquid and vapour can exist together	CRITICAL TEMPERATURE

hot ionised gas	PLASMA
hotness of body	TEMPERATURE
hydrogen	
—atom spectrum theory	BOHR THEORY
—manufacturing process	SILICOL PROCESS
hydrolysis by an acid	ACIDOLYSIS
hydroxide of metal	ALKALI
hypothetical	
—force	SUPERGRAVITY
—one-dimensional constituent of matter	(SUPER)STRING
—particle	(*see* **particles**)
—two-dimensional constituent of matter	SUPERMEMBRANE
ignition measurement	CETANE NUMBER
image with coloured fringes	CHROMATIC ABERRATION
imperfection in semiconductor	ACCEPTOR, DONOR
increase in	
—conductivity due to absence of resistance at very low temperature	SUPERCONDUCTIVITY
increased light intensity	PHOTOCONDUCTIVE EFFECT
—energy of particle due to change of state	EXCITATION
—size due to heat	COEFFICIENT OF EXPANSION
—vibration caused by small vibration of same frequency	RESONANCE
indeterminancy principle	UNCERTAINTY PRINCIPLE
induction	
—due to change of current in another circuit	MUTUAL INDUCTION
—of	
magnetism by another magnetic field	MAGNETIC INDUCTION
radioactivity	ACTIVATION
interference	
—effect of lenses	NEWTON'S RINGS
—patterns due to wave motion of light	DIFFRACTION
insulator	DIELECTRIC
interval when ratio of frequencies is two to one	OCTAVE
invisible heat radiation	INFRARED RADIATION RADIANT HEAT

ion having
—negative charge ANION
HYDROXYL ION
—positive
and negative
charges ZWITTERION
charge CATION
ionic bond ELECTROVALENT BOND
ionised layers of
atmosphere APPLETON
HEAVISIDE(-KENNELLY)
ionising radiation
—of
high penetrating
power HARD RADIATION
low penetrating
power SOFT RADIATION
isobaric spin ISOTOPIC SPIN, T
isotope of element ISOBAR
isotopic
—number NEUTRON EXCESS
—spin ISOBARIC SPIN, T
lagging of effect
behind cause HYSTERESIS
lanthanides (elements) ACTINIDES
ACTINONS
large
—particles in solution COLLOID
—vibration caused by
smaller RESONANCE
law governing
—angle of polarisation BREWSTER'S LAW
—atomic weights PERIODIC LAW
—attraction between
charged bodies COULOMB'S LAW
—combination of
gases GAY-LUSSAC'S LAW
—conductivity of
electrolyte KOHLRAUSCH'S LAW
—deflection by rotation
of Earth FERRELL'S LAW
—diffusion of gases GRAHAM'S LAW
—dissociation OSTWALD'S DILUTION LAW
—dissolved gases HENRY'S LAW
—electrolysis FARADAY'S LAWS
—energy of gas JOULE'S LAW
—equivalence of
mass and energy EINSTEIN'S LAW
—formation of valency
bonds RULES OF FAJANS
—frequency and
energy PLANCK'S LAW OF RADIATION
—gravitational
attraction NEWTON'S LAW
—heat produced by
electric current JOULE'S LAW

—magnetic susceptibility CURIE'S LAW
—movement of planets KEPLER'S LAWS
—number of molecules
in quantity of gas AVOGADRO'S LAW
AVOGADRO'S HYPOTHESIS
—osmotic pressure VAN'T HOFF'S LAW
—partial pressures DALTON'S LAW
—periodic law MENDELEEV'S LAW
of Newlands LAW OF OCTAVES
—planetary motion KEPLER'S LAWS
—pressure of
fluid PASCAL'S LAW
gas BOYLE'S LAW, CHARLES' LAW
MARIOTTE'S LAW
—quantum properties of
electrons
PAULI EXCLUSION PRINCIPLE
—radiant heat from
black body STEFAN-BOLTZMANN LAW
STEFAN'S LAW
—ratio of
expansion coefficient
to specific heat GRUNEISEN'S LAW
latent heat to
boiling point TROUTON'S RULE
thermal to electrical
conductivity
WIEDEMANN-FRANZ LAW
—reflected X-rays BRAGG'S LAW
—refractive indices SNELL'S LAW
—relationship of
induced current to moving
magnetic field LENZ'S LAW
strain and stress HOOKE'S LAW
—sines of angles of
incidence and
refraction SNELL'S LAW
—sparking potential of
electrodes PASCHEN'S LAW
—speed of chemical
change MASS ACTION LAW
—strength of induced
magnetic field AMPERE'S LAW
—sum of electric
forces KIRCHHOFF'S LAW
—thermodynamics NEWTON'S LAWS
—vapour pressure
in solutions RAOULT'S LAW
of solvent BABO'S LAW
—velocity
of air
molecules
MAXWELL-BOLTZMANN LAW
in viscous media STOKES' LAW
—voltage and current OHM'S LAW
(*see also* principle *below*)

layers of charged
particles in
atmosphere
    VAN ALLEN (RADIATION) BELTS
left-right symmetry   PARITY
lens
—causing
  parallel beam to
  —focus   CONVERGING LENS
  —spread   DIVERGING LENS
—nearest the object   OBJECTIVE
—types   BI-CONCAVE, BI-CONVEX
    CONCAVO-CONVEX, MENISCUS
    PLANO-CONCAVE, PLANO-CONVEX
—with no
  —chromatic aberration
    ACHROMATIC LENS
  —astigmatism   ANASTIGMATIC LENS
    (*see also* **photography**)
light
—caused by high
  temperature   INCANDESCENCE
—emission not caused
  by temperature   LUMINESCENCE
—emitted when
  charged particles pass
  through transparent
  medium
    C(H)ERENKOV RADIATION
  ultrasound passes
  through fluid   SONOLUMINESCENCE
—emitting property   LUMINOSITY
—from chemical
  reaction   CHEMOLUMINESCENCE
    COLD FLAME
—quantum   PHOTON
line
—defect in crystal   DISLOCATION
—giving relationship between
  pressure and temperature
  of liquid   ISOCHORE
—of
  equal
  —magnetic
    declination   ISOGONAL LINE
    dip   ISOCLINAL
    intensity   ISODYNAMIC LINE
  —pressure   ISOBAR
  —temperature   ISOTHERM(AL LINE)
  magnetic declination   AGONIC LINE
  zero magnetic dip   ACLINIC LINE
    MAGNETIC EQUATOR
—on curved surface   GEODESIC (LINE)
—pattern of X-rays
  emitted by an
  element   X-RAY SPECTRUM

—showing temperature
  change with pressure   ISOMETRIC LINE
lines in visible
  spectrum of hydrogen   BALMER SERIES
link binding atoms
  in molecule   VALENCY BOND
linking of output
  to input   FEEDBACK
liquid of condensation   DISTILLATE
locating system using
  microwaves   RADAR
loss of
—electrical resistance at
  low temperatures   SUPERCONDUCTIVITY
—energy of
  X-rays striking
  matter   COMPTON EFFECT
  light passing
  through medium   RAMAN EFFECT
low-temperature
  microwaves   BACKGROUND RADIATION
lowest
—freezing point of
  mixture of solids   EUTECTIC POINT
—possible temperature   ABSOLUTE ZERO
    ZERO KELVIN
—value producing
  specific effect   THRESHOLD
luminescence when emitted
  wavelength is different
  from that absorbed   FLUORESCENCE
    PHOSPORESCENCE
luminosity from
  electrical discharge
  through gas   GLOW DISCHARGE
luminous
—discharge round
  conductor   CORONA DISCHARGE
—intensity   LUMINANCE
—region near positive
  electrode   POSITIVE COLUMN
machine
—for producing electrical
  energy   ALTERNATOR, DYNAMO
    GENERATOR
—speed regulator   GOVERNOR
magnetic
—equator   ACLINIC LINE
—field focusing
  electron beam   ELECTRON LENS
—fields used to
  contain plasma   MAGNETIC BOTTLE
—flux
  density   B, MAGNETIC INDUCTION
  through unit area
    MAGNETIC FLUX DENSITY

—induction   B, MAGNETIC FLUX DENSITY
magnetism
  —across a force field   DIAMAGNETISM
  —increases in steps   BARKHAUSEN EFFECT
  —induced
    by electric coils   ELECTROMAGNETISM
    in ceramics   FERRIMAGNETISM
  —parallel to force
    field   PARAMAGNETISM
  —strong   FERROMAGNETISM
              PARAMAGNETISM
maser using gas
molecules   GAS MASER
mass
  —defect divided by
    mass number   PACKING FRACTION
  —determined by
    gravitational
    attraction   GRAVITATIONAL MASS
    momentum   INERTIAL MASS
  —number   A, NUCLEON NUMBER
  —of
    body
      —at speed
      approaching the
      speed of light   RELATIVISTIC MASS
      —not in motion   REST MASS
    isotope   ATOMIC MASS
    unit volume   DENSITY
material which will return
to original length after
stretching   ELASTOMER
mathematical expression
of wave motion   WAVE EQUATION
maximum
  —oscillation   AMPLITUDE
  —velocity produced
    by given force   TERMINAL VELOCITY
measure of
  —capacity for work   E, ENERGY
  —disorder   ENTROPY, S
  —efficiency of fuel
    and oxidiser   SPECIFIC IMPULSE
  —heat content   ENTROPY, S
  —light absorbed by
    dissolved substance
      EXTINCTION COEFFICIENT
  —light-bending power
    of transparent
    medium   REFRACTIVE INDEX
  —radiant energy related
    to solar energy   SOLAR CONSTANT
  —radiation-reflecting
    capacity   REFLECTANCE
  —radioactive decay   HALF-LIFE
  —refraction   OPTICAL DENSITY

—resistance to
  shearing   RIGIDITY MODULUS
—rotating tendency
  of a force   MOMENT OF FORCE
—vibration in crystal   PHONON
measurement
  —of atmospheric
    humidity   PSYCHROMETRY
  —system   CGS SYSTEM, FPS SYSTEM
          SI SYSTEM
mechanics of
  —liquids   FLUID MECHANICS
  —motion   KINETICS
  —very small
    systems   QUANTUM MECHANICS
          WAVE MECHANICS
metal which
  —corrodes   BASE METAL
  —does not corrode   NOBLE METAL
metallic elements similar
in properties and
difficult to separate   RARE EARTHS
microscope with
  —one lens   SIMPLE MICROSCOPE
  —two lenses   COMPOUND MICROSCOPE
  —using electron
    beams instead
    of light   ELECTRON MICROSCOPE
microwave-producing
valve   MAGNETRON
migration of particles
in electric field   CATAPHORESIS
      ELECTROPHORESIS
minimum
  —distance for receipt
    of sky wave   SKIP DISTANCE
  —quantity of radioactive
    material for chain
    reaction   CRITICAL MASS
mixture of
  —fluids due to movement
    of particles   DIFFUSION
  —two
    primary colours   SECONDARY COLOUR
    secondary colours   TERTIARY COLOUR
mnemonics for electric
machines   FLEMING'S RULES
modulation types   AMPLITUDE
    FREQUENCY, PHASE
    VELOCITY
Mohs scale 1   TALC
          2   GYPSUM
          3   CALCITE
          4   FLUORITE
          5   APATITE
          6   ORTHOCLASE

7	QUARTZ
8	TOPAZ
9	CORUNDUM
10	DIAMOND

molecular
  weight   RELATIVE MOLECULAR MASS
molecule
  —constituting electric
    dipole   POLAR MOLECULE
  —weight of compound   GRAM-MOLECULE
                           MOL(E)
moment of inertia   I
  —about axis   RADIUS OF GYRATION
motion
  —of fluids in
    parallel layers   LAMINAR FLOW
  —round fixed point
    or axis   GYRATION
movement of
  —liquid
    in narrow tube   CAPILLARITY
                CAPILLARY ACTION
    through semipermeable
    membrane   OSMOSIS
  —particles in colloid
         BROWNIAN MOVEMENT
                   PEDESIS
  —polarised particles
    in electric field   DIELECTROPHORESIS
multiple of fundamental
  frequency   HARMONIC
mutual conductance   TRANSCONDUCTANCE
narrow tube   CAPILLARY TUBE
natural course
  followed by fluid   STREAMLINE
negative
  —acceleration   DECELERATION
                   RETARDATION
  —entropy   NEGENTROPY
  —magnetism   DIAMAGNETISM
network of points
  in crystal   LATTICE
neutron
  —excess   ISOTOPIC NUMBER
  —number   N
nickel-iron
  accumulator   EDISON ACCUMULATOR
no entropy change
  at absolute zero   NERNST HEAT THEOREM
noises produced during
  remagnetisation   BARKHAUSEN EFFECT
non-conductor   INSULATOR
  —of electricity   DIELECTRIC
non-magnetic form of iron   GAMMA-IRON
normal energy state of atom   GROUND STATE
north-seeking pole   POSITIVE POLE

note of higher frequency
  than the fundamental   OVERTONE
nuclear
  —emission caused
    by photon   PHOTODISINTEGRATION
              PHOTODISSOCIATION
  —energy   ATOMIC ENERGY
    change   Q-VALUE
  —fission caused by
    photons   PHOTOFISSION
  —heat of reaction   Q-VALUE
  —reactor   ATOMIC PILE
nucleon number   A, MASS NUMBER
nucleus
  —of
    deuterium atom   DEUTERON
    tritium atom   TRITON
  —with
    odd number of protons
    —and neutrons   ODD-ODD NUCLEUS
    —even number of
      neutrons   ODD-EVEN NUCLEUS
nuclides with equal
  —mass numbers   ISOBARES
  —number of protons   ISOTOPES
number
  —defining state of
    small system   QUANTUM NUMBER
  —describing type of
    flow of liquid
    in tubes   REYNOLDS NUMBER
  —of
    atoms in mole   AVOGADRO CONSTANT
       AVOGADRO NUMBER, L, N
    molecules of
    gas per cubic
    centimetre   LOSCHMIDT'S CONSTANT
    nucleons in nucleus   MASS NUMBER
    units of protons in
    nucleus   ATOMIC NUMBER
    waves per unit length   WAVE NUMBER
occurrence of mirror-
  image cystalline
  forms   ENANTIOMORPHISM
opacity to radiant heat   ATHERMANCY
opaque to radiation   RADIO-OPAQUE
opening admitting light   APERTURE
opposite
  —ends of magnet   MAGNETIC POLES
  —of centrifugal
    force   CENTRIPETAL FORCE
optical
  —maser   LASER
  —transistor   TRANSPHASOR
orbit of electrons
  round nucleus   ELECTRON SHELL

orbital electron	PLANETARY ELECTRON
oscillation caused by surge in voltage etc	TRANSIENT
outward force of rotation	CENTRIFUGAL FORCE
pairs of isobares with difference of one between atomic and neutron numbers	WIGNER NUCLIDES
partial sterilisation	PASTEURISATION
particle(s)	
—accelerator	(*see* **scientific instruments**)
—considered as waves	WAVE MECHANICS
—imagined to be exchanged by interacting bodies	VIRTUAL PARTICLE
—which cannot be sub-divided	ELEMENTARY PARTICLE
	(*see also* **particles**)
partly transparent to radiation	RADIOLUCENT
passage of electron energy barrier in semiconductor	TUNNEL EFFECT
path of	
—electron round nucleus	ORBIT
—projectile	TRAJECTORY
pattern	
—of scanning lines in cathode ray tube	RASTER
—showing wavelengths of electromagnetic radiation	SPECTRUM
periodic law	MENDELEEV'S LAW
—of Newlands	LAW OF OCTAVES
physicists	
—American	ALBURGER, ALVAREZ

ANDERSON, BAKER, BARDEEN
BETHE, BLOCH
BLOEMBERGEN, BRATTAIN
BRIDGMAN, CHAMBERLAIN, CHANCE
CHANDRASEKHAR, CHIU, CHRISTOFILOS
COBLENZ, COMPTON, COOPER, COTTON
COWAN, CREWE, CRONIN, DAVIS, DEUTSCH
DEMPSTER, DICKE, DUNNING, FERMI
FESSENDEN, FEYNMAN, FITCH, FOWLER
FRANK, FRANKLIN, FRIEDMAN, GAMOW
GELL-MANN, GEORGI, GIBBS, GIAEVER
GLASER, GLASHOW, GROEPPART-MAYER
HAFELE, HENRY, HEYL, HOLLOWAY
HOFSTADTER, HUGHES, KASPER
KEATING, KENNELLY, KERST, KUSCH
LAMB, LAND, LANGLEY, LAWRENCE, LEE
LYONS, MAIMON, MAYER, MCMILLAN
MICHELSON, MILLIKAN, MOTTELSON
MOULTON, NEUMANN, NEWELL

OPPENHEIMER, PARKER, PENZIAS
PLASS, PUNCELL, RABI, RAINWATER
REINES, RICHTER, ROWLAND, RUARK
RUMFORD, SCHLAWLOW, SCHRIEFFER
SCHRODINGER, SCHWINGER, SEGRE
SHOCKLEY, SZILARD, TELLER, THOMPSON
TING, TOWNES, VAN ALLEN
VAN DER GRAAF, VAN VLECK
WEINBERG, WIGNER, WILLIAMS
WILSON, YANGZINN

—Australian	BOWEN, ELWIN
—Austrian	BOLTZMANN, DEUTSCH

DOPPLER, FRANK, HESS
MACH, MEITNER, PAULI
SCHRODINGER, STEFAN

—Belgian	NICOLET
—British	APPLETON, ASTBURY

BACON, BARKLA
BLACKETT, BOYLE, BRAGG, CANTON
CAVENDISH, CHADWICK, COCKCROFT
CRANSTON, CRICK, CROOKES, DALTON
DIRAC, EDDINGTON, FARADAY, FOWLER
GABOR, GALTON, GILBERT, GROVE
HAUKSBEE, HAWKING, HEAVISIDE
HEWISH, HOOKE, JEANS
JOSEPHSON, JOULE, KELVIN, KURTI
LODGE, LONDON, MAXWELL, MOSELEY
MOTT, NEWTON, NICOL, POWELL, RANKIN
RAYLEIGH, RICHARDSON, RUTHERFORD
RYLE, SODDY, STOKES, STRUTT
THOMSON, WALTON, WILSON
WATSON-WATT, WHEATSTONE
WYNN-WILLIAMS, YOUNG

—Canadian	DEMPSTER, PONTECORVO
	ZINN
-Chinese	CHIU, LEE, YANG
-Danish	BOHR, COSTER, MOTTELSON
	OERSTED, MOLLER
-Dutch	BLOEMBERGER, DEBYE, GOUDSMIT

HUYGHENS, KEESOM, LORENTZ
ONNES, UHLENBECK
VAN DER MEER, VAN DER WAALS
ZERNICKE

-French	AMONTONS, AMPERE, BABINET

BECQUEREL, BIOT, CARNOT
CHARLES, COULOMB, CURIE
DE BROGLIE, DE LATOUR, DEBIERNE
DESTRIER, FABRY, FIZEAU, FOUCAULT
FOURIER, GAY-LUSSAC, GUILLAUME
JOLIOT-CURIE, KASTLER, KOWARSKI
LAPLACE, LAVOISIER, LIPMAN
MALUS, NEEL, PASCAL, PERRIN
PLANTE, REAUMUR, WEISS

-German	ABBE, BALMER, BARKHAUSEN

BECKER, BEDNORZ, BERG, BETHE
BINNIG, BORN, BOTHE

BRILL, BYERMAN, CLAUSIUS, DORN
EINSTEIN, FAHRENHEIT, FRANCK
FRAUNHOFER, GEIGER, GOLDSTEIN
GUERICKE, HAHN, HEISENBERG
HELMHOLTZ, HERTZ, HERZOG, JENSEN
KIRCHER, KIRCHHOFF, KLITZING
LAVE, LENARD, LINDE, LONDON, MEITNER
MEYER, MICHELSON, MOSSBAUER
NERNST, NIEN, NODDACK, PLANCK
PENZIAS, RITTER, ROENTGEN, ROHRER
RUSKA, SCHWEIGGER, SEEBECK
STARKE, STERN, STRASSMAN
TACKE, VON LAUE, WUNDERLICH,
—Greek   CHRISTOFILOS
—Hungarian   GABOR, KURTI, NEUMANN
NORDAU, SZILARD, TELLER
WIGNER
—Indian   BOSE, RAMAN
—Iranian   JAVAN
—Irish   ANDREWS, FITZGERALD
STONEY, TYNDALL, WALTON
—Israeli   NE'EMEN, PERKERIS
—Italian   FERMI, MARCONI, PALMIERI
PONTECORVO, RUBBIA
TORRICELLI, VIVIANI
—Japanese   ESAKI, TOMONAGA, YUKAWA
—Norwegian   BIRKELAND
—Pakistani   SALAM
—Polish   DANYSZ, PNIEWSKI
—Russian AMBARTSUMIAN, ARTSIMOVICH
BASOV, C(H)ERENKOV, DERYAGIN
FLEROV, FRANK, GAMOW, KAPITZA
LANDAU, LEBEDEV, PETRJAK
POMERANCHUK, PROCHOROV
SAKHAROV, TAMM, VEKSLER
—Serbian   MILANKOWICH
—Swedish   ALFVEN, ANGSTROM, KLEIN
MULLER, SIEGBAHN, SIEVERT
—Swiss   BLOCH, GUILLAUME
PICCARD, PICTET
—Yugoslav   MILANKOVICH
Planck's constant   H
planetary electron   ORBITAL ELECTRON
point
—at
geometrical centre
of lens   OPTICAL CENTRE
which mass is
concentrated   CENTRE OF MASS
—in lens system   NODAL POINT
—of
convergence of rays   FOCUS
zero wave displacement   NODE
—through which resultant
force of gravity
passes   CENTRE OF GRAVITY

positive
—charge on nucleus   NUCLEAR CHARGE
—ion   CATION
—particle   PROTON
potential
—gradient in conductor
due to temperature
gradient   KELVIN EFFECT
THOMSON EFFECT
—produced by temperature
gradient in magnetic
field   NERNST EFFECT
practical application
of hydrodynamics   HYDRAULICS
preparation of metals
from oxides   GOLDSCHMIDT PROCESS
pressure
—applied to any part of fluid
is transferred to
all points   PASCAL'S PRINCIPLE
—needed to prevent
osmotic flow   OSMOTIC PRESSURE
primary cell   BUNSEN CELL
CADMIUM CELL, CLARK CELL
DANIELL CELL, LECLANCHE CELL
MERCURY CELL, VOLTAIC CELL
WESTON CELL
—with constant voltage   STANDARD CELL
primary colours
—light   BLUE, GREEN, RED
—pigment   BLUE, RED, YELLOW
primordial matter   YLEM
principle governing
—identical quantum
states
PAULI'S EXCLUSION PRINCIPLE
—position and
momentum   UNCERTAINTY PRINCIPLE
—transfer of pressure
in fluids   PASCAL'S PRINCIPLE
—weight of floating
body   ARCHIMEDES' PRINCIPLE
probability of particle
passing through
nuclear barrier   PENETRATION FACTOR
process
—for fixing atmospheric
nitrogen   SERPEK PROCESS
—releasing heat   EXOERGIC PROCESS
EXOTHERMIC PROCESS
product of
—area and magnetic
field strength   MAGNETIC FLUX
—area and vector   FLUX
—magnetic pole strength
and length of magnet MAGNETIC MOMENT

—mass and velocity	MOMENTUM
production of	
—current in	
bimetallic circuit	
by heat	SEEBECK EFFECT
one circuit by	
current in another	INDUCTION
—electricity by electro-	
magnetic radiation	PHOTO-EMISSION
—electron and positron	
when particle interacts	
with nucleus	PAIR PRODUCTION
—heat at bimetallic	
junction	PELTIER EFFECT
property of	
—extreme	
stretchability	SUPERPLASTICITY
—liquid surface	SURFACE TENSION
proportion of solute	
to solvent	MOLALITY, MOLARITY
protons and neutrons	NUCLEONS
pull of gravity on	
a body	WEIGHT
pulse height analyser	KICKSORTER
quantity of	
—direction and magnitude	VECTOR
—matter	M, MASS
—substance	MOL(E)
quantum of	
—electromagnetic energy	PHOTON
—energy in vibrating	
crystal	PHONON
—gravity	GRAVITON
—radiation	PHOTON
radar screen	CATHODE RAY OSCILLOSCOPE
	CRO
radiation	
—from	
accelerating	
particle	BRAKING RADIATION
	BREMSSTRAHLUNG
Big Bang	BACKGROUND RADIATION
space	COSMIC RAYS
surroundings	BACKGROUND RADIATION
—of one wavelength	MONOCHROMATIC
—power loss	ATTENUATION
—spectrum (shortest first)	
	COSMIC RAYS
	GAMMA RAYS
	X-RAYS
	ULTRAVIOLET RAYS
	VISIBLE LIGHT
	INFRARED RAYS
	RADIO WAVES
—visible to human	
eye	VISIBLE SPECTRUM

radio wave(s)	HERTZIAN WAVES
—of constant amplitude	
and frequency	CARRIER WAVE
—received without	
reflection	DIRECT WAVES
	GROUND WAVES
radioactive	
—elements	ACTINIDES
—emissions	ALPHA RAY, BETA RAY
	GAMMA RAY
	KANALSTRAHLEN RAYS
	CHANNEL RAYS
—material from nuclear	
explosion	FALLOUT
random motion of	
small particles	BROWNIAN MOTION
	BROWNIAN MOVEMENT
range of energy states	
which can be occupied by	
valency electrons	VALENCY BAND
rare-earth metals	ACTINIDES
	LANTHANIDES
rate of	
—doing work	POWER
—heat transfer	THERMAL CONDUCTIVITY
—increase of speed	ACCELERATION
—loss of information	
due to noise	EQUIVOCATION
—motion	VELOCITY
ratio of	
—changes in current	
and voltage in	
valve	MUTUAL CONDUCTANCE
	TRANSCONDUCTANCE
—density of substance	
to that of water	RELATIVE DENSITY
	SPECIFIC GRAVITY, SG
—dimensions under stress	
to original dimensions	STRAIN
—energy output to input	EFFICIENCY
—intensity of beam after	
passing through medium	
to its original	
intensity	TRANSMISSION COEFFICIENT
—latent heat to	
boiling point	TROUTON'S RULE
—lateral and	
longitudinal	
strains	POISSON'S RATIO
—magnetomotive force	
to magnetic flux	RELUCTANCE
—magnetic flux density	
to external field	PERMEABILITY
—maximum load to	
sectional area	TENACITY
	ULTIMATE STRESS

—moles in substances in mixture	MOLE FRACTION
—potential difference to current	RESISTANCE
—sines of incident and refracted angles	REFRACTIVE INDEX
—size of image to object	MAGNIFICATION
	MAGNIFYING POWER
—stress to strain	ELASTIC MODULUS
	YOUNG'S MODULUS
—velocity of body to that of sound	MACH NUMBER
—viscosity to density	KINEMATIC VISCOSITY
—weight of	
atom of substance to that of oxygen	ATOMIC WEIGHT
substance to weight of water	SPECIFIC GRAVITY
rays from uranium compounds	BECQUEREL RAYS
reaction against stress	LE CHATELIER PRINCIPLE
reciprocal of	
—fluidity	VISCOCITY
—magnetic permeability	RELUCTIVITY
—poise	RHE
—rhe	POISE
—transmittance	OPACITY
—viscosity	FLUIDITY
—wavelength	WAVE NUMBER
reduction of energy when photon collides with electron	COMPTON EFFECT
refractive index - 1	REFRACTIVITY
region of gas where positive and negative ions are approximately equal	PLASMA
regular	
—array of atoms in crystal	LATTICE
—displacement either side of a mean	WAVE MOTION
relationship of	
—heat to other forms of energy	THERMODYNAMICS
—stress and strain	HOOKE'S LAW
—temperature to	
surface tension	PARACHOR
volume	CHARLES' LAW
—volume and pressure	BOYLE'S LAW
relative	
—atomic mass	ATOMIC WEIGHT
—density	SPECIFIC GRAVITY, SG
of gas or vapour	VAPOUR DENSITY
—molecular mass	MOLECULAR WEIGHT

—pressure of water vapour in atmosphere	RELATIVE HUMIDITY
remaining magnetism	REMANENCE
removal	
—by dissolving in liquid	ELUTION
—of	
moisture	DESICCATION
salt	DESALINATION
residual magnetism	REMANENCE
resistance	
—per unit length	RESISTIVITY
—to flow	VISCOSITY
restriction of vibration to single plane	POLARISATION
Röntgen	
—equivalent man	REM
—ray	X-RAY
rotating	
—part of machine	ROTOR
—polarised light to	
left	LAEVOROTATORY
right	DEXTROROTATORY
rotation of	
—atom caused by motion of electrons	LARMOR PRECESSION
—light related to wavelength	ROTARY DISPERSION
—particle on its axis	SPIN
—plane of	
polarisation by magnetism	FARADAY EFFECT
polarised light	OPTICAL ACTIVITY
	OPTICAL ROTATION
—polarised light by current	KERR EFFECT
rules	
—governing mass and length as affected by speed	LORENTZ-FITZGERALD EQUATIONS
—of spin of particles	BOSE-EINSTEIN STATISTICS
	FERMI-DIRAC STATISTICS
saturation point	DEWPOINT
scale of	
—hardness	MOHS SCALE
—specific gravity	BAUME SCALE
—temperature	CELSIUS, CENTIGRADE
	FAHRENHEIT, KELVIN
	RANKINE, REAUMUR
scattering of	
—light by particles	TYNDALL EFFECT
—photons by electrons	THOMSON SCATTERING
secondary cell	(see cell above)

semiconductor used for amplification, etc	TRANSISTOR
sensitive photo-electric cell	ELECTRON MULTIPLIER PHOTOMULTIPLIER
separately magnetised part of ferromagnetic substance	MAGNETIC DOMAIN
separating dish	CUPEL
separation of	
—gases	ATMOLYSIS
—insoluble matter from liquid by settlement	SEDIMENTATION
—isotopes	CASCADE PROCESS
—metals by hot-air process	CUPELLATION
—mixture into parts with different properties	FRACTIONATION
—particles by size by suspension	ELUTRIATION
—solids by melting	LIQUATION
sequence of energy transfer	CARNOT CYCLE
short focal lens with smaller lens in surface	FRESNEL LENS
short-wave electromagnetic radiation	MICROWAVES
shortening due to speed	FITZGERALD CONTRACTION
SI unit	
—distance	METRE, M
—electric current	AMPERE, A
—luminous intensity	CANDELA, CD
—mass	KILOGRAM, KG
—quantity	MOLE, MOL,
—temperature	KELVIN, K
—time	SECOND, S
slowing of atom vibrations by gravity	EINSTEIN SHIFT
small dynamo with spark-coil	MAGNETO
smallest portion retaining characteristics of the original substance	MOLECULE
solid carbon dioxide	DRY ICE
solution	
—carrying current which decomposes it	ELECTROLYTE
—from which substances have been crystallised	MOTHER-LIQUID MOTHER-LYE
south-seeking pole	NEGATIVE POLE
space	
—above inverted tube of mercury	TORRICELLIAN VACUUM

—within which one body attracts another	GRAVITATIONAL FIELD
—without matter	VACUUM
specific gravity	RELATIVE DENSITY
spectrum	
—lines in ultraviolet region	LYMAN SERIES
—of	
hydrogen	BALMER SERIES
increasing electric charge of ion beam	MASS SPECTRUM
—white light	VISIBLE SPECTRUM *(see also* radiation *above)*
speed	
—approaching the speed of light	RELATIVISTIC VELOCITY
—limit imposed by overheating	THERMAL BARRIER
—of	
light	C
sound	MACH NUMBER
spherical aberration in lens or mirror	COMA
spinning wheel maintaining position in space	GYROSCOPE
splitting of nucleus of atom, releasing energy	NUCLEAR FISSION
spontaneous disintegration of unstable nuclei	RADIOACTIVITY
spreading of light to produce spectrum	DISPERSION
state of particle imagined to be exchanged by interacting bodies	VIRTUAL STATE
statement of impossibility of determining both position and speed	INDETERMINANCY PRINCIPLE UNCERTAINTY PRINCIPLE
steam above normal boiling-point	SUPERHEATED STEAM
storage battery	ACCUMULATOR
strength of field through given area	FLUX
stress acting along the plane of a face	SHEAR
strong	
—heating	CALCINATION
—magnet reversing plasma flow	MAGNETIC MIRROR
strongly magnetic	FERROMAGNETIC
study of	
—charged particles	THERMIONICS
—deformation of matter	RHEOLOGY

—dynamics of gases	PNEUMATICS
—electricity	ELECTROLOGY
—electrodynamics of	
electrons in	
fluids	MAGNETOHYDRODYNAMICS
—fluids	HYDRAULICS
in	
—equilibrium	HYDROSTATICS
and in motion	HYDRODYNAMICS
motion	HYDROKINETICS
—friction and lubrication	TRIBOLOGY
—heat and energy	THERMODYNAMICS
—ions in solution	POLAROGRAPHY
—jets of fluid in	
circuits	FLUID LOGIC, FLUIDICS
—light	OPTICS
—measurements	METROLOGY
—sound	ACOUSTICS, SONICS
beyond human hearing	ULTRASONICS
—very low temperatures	CRYOGENICS
	(*see also* **study**)
substance	
—between conductor and	
insulator	SEMICONDUCTOR
—in gaseous state	VAPOUR
—producing luminescence	PHOSPHOR
—providing energy in	
nuclear reaction	NUCLEAR FUEL
—which	
loses plasticity when	
cooled after being	
heated	THERMOSETTING PLASTIC
reduces surface	
tension	WETTING AGENT
slows neutrons	MODERATOR
softens with heat	THERMOPLASTIC
turns litmus	
—blue	ALKALI
—red	ACID
varies its resistance with	
temperature change	THERMISTOR
—with atoms all of the	
same atomic number	ELEMENT
sum of atomic weights	
in ion	GRAM-ION
super-heavy hydrogen	TRITIUM
superdense theory	BIG BANG THEORY
supposed unit of	
magnetic charge	MAGNETIC MONOPOLE
suspended weight free	
to swing in all	
directions	FOUCAULT PENDULUM
system of	
measurement	FOOT-POUND-SECOND SYSTEM
	FPS SYSTEM
	CGS SYSTEM, SI UNITS

taking up moisture	
from the air	DELIQUESCENT
temperature	
—above which ferromagnets	
become paramagnetic	CURIE POINT
—at which	
all three states are	
in equilibrium	TRIPLE POINT
condensation occurs	DEWPOINT
	SATURATION POINT
element changes	
state	TRANSITION POINT
	TRANSITION TEMPERATURE
enough inflammable	
vapour is produced to	
cause a flash	FLASH POINT
ice and water are in	
equilibrium	ICE POINT
liquid	
—and vapour are	
in equilibrium	STEAM POINT
—changes to	
gas	BOILING POINT
solid	FREEZING POINT
magnetism is	
lost	CURIE TEMPERATURE
saturation vapour pressure	
of liquid equals	
external pressure	BOILING POINT
—calculated from	
light mission	OPTICAL TEMPERATURE
—change from pressure	
differential	JOULE-KELVIN EFFECT
	JOULE-THOMSON EFFECT
—scale	CELSIUS, CENTIGRADE,
	FAHRENHEIT, KELVIN
	RANKINE, REAUMUR
temporary magnet using	
electric current	ELECTROMAGNET
tendency to preserve existing	
state of rest or motion	INERTIA
theory	
—denying absolute	
motion	THEORY OF RELATIVITY
—of	
combustion	PHLOGISTON THEORY
energy as discrete	
units	QUANTUM THEORY
light	
—as packets of	
energy	CORPUSCULAR THEORY
—as waves	WAVE THEORY
motion of particles	
based on quantum	
theory	QUANTUM MECHANICS
	WAVE MECHANICS

origin of universe	BIG BANG THEORY
	STEADY STATE THEORY
	SUPERDENSE THEORY
—to cover all four known forces	UNIFIED FIELD THEORY
thermal permeability	DIATHERMANCY
thermionic valve	VACUUM TUBE
time	
—between successive fissions in nuclear reaction	GENERATION TIME
—in which half the radioactive atoms decay	HALF-LIFE
—of one complete oscillation	PERIOD
toroidal container holding plasma in magnetic field	TOKAMAK
total pressure in liquid in tube is constant	BERNOULLI'S THEOREM
transconductance	MUTUAL CONDUCTANCE
transfer of	
—energy or matter by gas stream	ADVECTION
—heat	
by	
—air current	CONVECTION
—solid objects	CONDUCTION
through space	RADIATION
—light through fine glass rods	FIBRE OPTICS
transition from one energy level to another	QUANTUM LEAP
transparency to radiant heat	DIATHERMANCY
transparent cell with two electrodes	KERR CELL
travelling faster than	
—Mach 1	SUPERSONIC
—Mach 5	HYPERSONIC
triangular transparent prism	OPTICAL PRISM
turning effect	MOMENT, TORQUE
two equal but opposite charges	DIPOLE
ultra-violet from sun	ACTINIC RAYS
uncertainty principle	INDETERMINANCY PRINCIPLE
unit of	
—absorbed radiation	RAD
—energy	QUANTUM
—light	PHOTON
	(*see also* **measures**)
universal constant of energy	PLANCK'S CONSTANT

unoccupied site in crystal lattice	SCHOTTKY DEFECT
	VACANCY
unpredictable behaviour in systems	CHAOS
vacuum	
—in a barometer	TORRICELLIAN VACUUM
—tube	(THERMIONIC) VALVE
displaying cathode rays	CATHODE RAY TUBE, CRT
valve	
—carrying very high current	THYRATRON
—with	
2 electrodes	DIODE
3 electrodes	TRIODE
4 electrodes	TETRODE
5 electrodes	PENTODE
many electrodes	TROCHOTRON
vaporisation of liquid and condensation of vapour	DISTILLATION
vapour existing in equilibrium with the liquid form	SATURATED VAPOUR
variation of	
—carrier wave	AMPLITUDE MODULATION
	FREQUENCY MODULATION
—some characteristic of wave motion	MODULATION
—time shown by stationary and moving clocks	CLOCK PARADOX
—wavelength of radiation	DOPPLER-FIZEAU EFFECT
sound	DOPPLER EFFECT
velocity	
—of ion	ION MOBILITY
—required to overcome gravity	ESCAPE VELOCITY
sustain body in orbit	ORBITAL VELOCITY
very hot ionised gas	PLASMA
vibration at regular frequency	OSCILLATION
visible	
—display of colours in light	SPECTRUM
—electromagnetic waves	LIGHT
Voltaic pile	ELECTRIC BATTERY
voltage needed to cause spark to jump gap	SPARKING POTENTIAL
	SPARKING VOLTAGE
volume	
—of	
one mol	MOLECULAR VOLUME
unit mass	SPECIFIC VOLUME

—related to temperature   CHARLES' LAW
wave
  —form whose oscillation
    is represented by a
    sinusoidal curve   SINE WAVE
  —produced by two opposing
    waves   STANDING WAVE
      STATIONARY WAVE
  —which alternates between
    two values for equal
    times   SQUARE WAVE
  —with displacement
    across line of
     travel   TRANSVERSE WAVE
    in direction of
     travel   LONGITUDINAL WAVE
Weston cell   CADMIUM CELL
white heat   INCANDESCENCE
wireless waves   HERTZIAN WAVES
work
  —function   F, HELMHOLTZ FREE ENERGY
  —per unit of time   POWER
X-ray   ROENTGEN RAY
zone of wave differing from
  adjacent zone by half
  a period   FRESNEL ZONE
     HALF-PERIOD ZONE

pigs
Biblical   GADARENE SWINE
British   ESSEX, GLOUCESTER OLD SPOT
   HAMPSHIRE, LARGE BLACK
LARGE WHITE, LONG WHITE LOP-EARED
   SADDLEBACK, TAMWORTH
   WELSH, WESSEX
Belgian   PIETRAIN
female   SOW
foot   TROTTER
herd of swine   SOUNDER
in novel   NAPOLEON, SNOWBALL
   SQUEALER
male   BOAR
smallest in litter   RECKLING, RUNT
   ST ANTHONY (PIG)
   TANTONY (PIG)
Swedish   LANDRACE
wild boar   SANGLIER
young   SHOAT, SHOTE, SHOT(T)
  —at one birth   FARROW, LITTER
  —boar   SOUNDER
  —sow   ELT, GILT

pigeon
including: dove
domestic   AFRICAN OWL
   AMERICAN DOMESTIC FLIGHT
   ARCHANGEL, BARRED STARLING
   BRUNETTE FRILL, CARRIER

CHECKERED ICE, CRESTED HELMET
DUN-FACED BLONDINETTE
ENGLISH POUTER, FANTAIL
FRANCONIAN, FRILLBACK
FLYING POUTER, GAZZI
GERMAN TOY, GIANT HOMER
GIANT RUNT, GIMPEL, HELMET
HIGHFLIER, ICE PIGEON, LARK
LAHORE, MAGPIE, MALTESE
MODENA, NORWICH CROPPER
ORIENTAL FRILL, ORIENTAL ROLLER
OWL PIGEON, PARLOUR TUMBLER
PEKIN NASAL-TUFTED
PIGMY POUTER, RACING HOMER
ROLLER, SATINETTE FRILL
SCANDAROON, SCHIETTI
SCHOENEBERG TUMBLER
SHIELD, SHOW HOMER, SHOW TIPPLER
SHORT-FACED TUMBLER
SILVERETTE FRILL, STARLING
SWALLOW, SWING POUTER
TIPPLER, TRUMPETER, TUMBLER
VELVET-SHIELD, WHITE DANZIG
   WHITE KING
extinct (USA)   PASSENGER PIGEON
wild   BARBARY DOVE, COLLARED DOVE
   FERAL PIGEON, ROCK DOVE
   STOCK DOVE, TURTLE DOVE
   WOOD PIGEON

pilot
automatic pilot   GEORGE
Pilot-Officer   PO
   (*see also* **aircraft**)
pirate   BLACKBEARD, CORSAIR
   FLINT, MORGAN
   PRIVATEER, SILVER
pirate flag   JOLLY ROGER
   SKULL AND CROSSBONES

Planck's constant   H
planets   (*see* **astronomy**)
plants
Abrus   INDIAN LIQUORICE
   LIQUORICE-VINE
Acacia   MIMOSA
Acalypha   CHENILLE PLANT
   RED-HOT CATSTAIL
acanthus   BEAR'S-BREECH
   BRANKURSINE, RUELLIA
Aceras   MAN ORCHIS
Achimenes   CUPID'S BOWER
   HOT WATER PLANT
Achillea   MILFOIL, YARROW
Acidanthera   ETHIOPIAN GLADIOLUS
aconite   MONKSHOOD, WOLF'S-BANE
   WOLFSBANE
Acorus   SWEET-FLAG

Adam's	
—flannel	MULLEIN
—needle	CASSAVA, YUC(C)A
adder's-tongue	OPHIOGLOSSUM
adderweed	BISTORT
Adoxa	MOSCHATEL
Aechmea	URN PLANT, VASE PLANT
Aeschynanthus	LIPSTICK VINE
African	
—corn lily	IXIA
—lily	AGAPANTHUS
—marigold	TAGETES
—rue	HARMALA, HARMEL
—violet	SAINTPAULIA
Agapanthus	AFRICAN LILY
	LILY OF THE NILE
agave	SILK-GRASS
Alchemilla	LADY'S-MANTLE
ale-cost	COSTMARY
Alisma	WATER-PLANTAIN
all-heal	VALERIAN
Allium	ESCHALOT, GOLDEN GARLIC
	SHAL(L)OT
	GARLIC, LEEK
Alpine	
—flower	EDELWEISS, GENTIAN
—herb	CORNEL
—rose	RHODODENDRON
alsike	CLOVER
Alstro(e)meria	AMARYLLIS, HERB LILY
Althaea	HOLLYHOCK
	MARSH-MALLOW
aluminium plant	PILEA
Alyssum	GOLD DUST, MADWORT
Amaracus	MARJORAM
Amarant(h)us	LONDON PRIDE
	LOVE-LIES-BLEEDING, PIGWEED
	PRINCE'S FEATHER
Amaryllis	ALSTRO(E)MERIA
	BELLADONA LILY
	HIPPEASTRUM, LILY
	POLIANTHES
Ampelopsis	VIRGINIA CREEPER
ammoniac	OSHAC
Anacharis	CANADIAN PONDWEED
	WATER-WEED
Anagallis	BOG PIMPERNEL
Anana(s)	PINEAPPLE
	PAINTER'S PALETTE
Anatolian convolvulus	SCAMMONY
anemone	CORONARIA
	PASCHAL-FLOWER
	PASQUE-FLOWER, WIND-FLOWER
Angelica	AIT-SKEITER, OAT-SHOOTER
angel's wings	CALADIUM
anise	PIMPINELLA

Antennaria	EVERLASTING(-FLOWER)
Anthyllis	KIDNEY VETCH
Anthurium	FLAMINGO FLOWER
antirrhinum	FROG'S-MOUTH, SNAPDRAGON
Aphelandra	ZEBRA PLANT
aquatic plant	FONTINALIS, FROG-BIT
Aquilegia	COLUMBINE
Arabis	ROCK-CRESS, WALL-CRESS
Aralia	CASTOR-OIL PLANT
	FATSIA, PANAX
Ardisia	CORAL BERRY
Arenaria	SANDWORT
Argemone	PRICKLY-POPPY
Aristolochia	DUTCHMAN'S PIPE
	GOOSE-FLOWER, SNAKEROOT
Armeria	SEA-PINK, THRIFT
Arnoseris	SWINE'S-SUCCORY
aromatic plant	HYSSOP, PEPPERMINT
	SPEARMINT, SPIKENARD
arrow	
—head	SAGITTARIA
—root	MARANTA
—vine	SYNGONIUM
Artemisia	WORM-SEED, WORMWOOD
artillery plant	PILEA
arum	ACORUS, COLOCASIA
	ZANTEDESCHIA
Asclepias	MILK-WEED
asparagus	ASPIDISTRA
Asperugo	MADWORT
Asplenium	SPLEEN-WORT
aster	ALYCOMPAINE, ELECAMPANE
	STARWORT, STITCHWORT
Astilbe	GOAT'S BEARD, SPIRAEA
Astragalus	GOAT'S-THORN
	LIQUORICE-VETCH
	MILK VETCH
Astrantia	MASTERWORT
astrophel	PENTHIA, STARLIGHT
Aubrietia	BLUE ROCK CRESS
auricula	BEAR'S-EAR, DUSTY-MILLER
autumn-crocus	MEADOW-SAFFRON
avens	GEUM, HERB-BENNET
baby's tears	HELXINE
bacon and eggs	LINARIA, TOADFLAX
baldmoney	MEUM, SPICKNEL, SPIGNEL
balloon-vine	HEARTPEA, HEARTSEED
Ballota	BLACK HOREHOUND
	STINKING HOREHOUND
balsam	IMPATIENS, NOLI-ME-TANGERE
	TOUCH-ME-NOT
baneberry	BUGBANE, BUGWORT
	HERB-CHRISTOPHER
Barbarea	WINTER-CRESS
	YELLOW-ROCKET
barley	HORDEUM

basil(-thyme)	CALAMINT	Blechnum	HARD-FERN
bastard		bleeding-heart	DICENTRA, DIELYTRA
—pimpernel	CENTUNCULUS	—vine	CLERODENDRUM
—saffron	SAFFLOWER	blood	
bayberry	CANDLEBERRY	—leaf	IRESINE
bead plant	NERTERA	—lily	HAEMANTHUS
beans, peas, etc	PULSE	—root	POPPY
bearberry	FOXBERRY, UVA-URSI	blue	
bearded tongue	PENTSTEMON	—alpine flower	GENTIAN
bedwort	CROSSWORT	—bell	SCILLA, WOOD-HYACINTH
beefsteak plant	IRESINE		WILD HYACINTH
beet	GOOSEFOOT		WOOD HYACINTH
begonia	ANGEL'S WINGS	—bottle	CORNFLOWER
	ELEPHANT'S EARS	—rocket	LARKSPUR, MONKSHOOD
—vine	CISSUS	—veronica	GERMANDER SPEEDWELL
bell-flower	CAMPANULA, RAMPION	boat lily	RHOEO
Beloperone	SHRIMP PLANT	Bocconia	MACLEAYA, PLUME POPPY
Bengal fig	FICUS	bog	
benne	BEN(N)I, SESAME	—myrtle	MYRICA, SWEET-GALE
benth(e)	GROUND-IVY		SWEET-WILLOW
Bergamot	MONARDA	—pimpernel	ANAGALLIS
bilberry	BLAEBERRY, WHORTLEBERRY	—plant	BOG ASPHODEL, DROSERA
bindweed	BEARBINE, BELLBIND		SUNDEW, WATER-PURSLANE
	CONVOLVULUS	borage	BUGLOSS, COOL-TANKARD
bird of paradise	STRELITZIA		COMFREY, HELIOTROPE
bird's			HOUND'S-TONGUE, LITHOSPERMUM
—foot trefoil	LOTE, LOTOS, LOTUS		LUNGWORT, SYMPHYTUM
—nest	MONOTROPA	bottle	
bromeliad	NIDULARIUM	—brush	POTERIUM
birthwort	ASARABACCA	—plant	CALLISTEMON
Bishop's		Bougainvillea	PAPER FLOWER
—cap	SAXIFRAGE	Bouteloua	MOSQUITO GRASS
—weed	GOUTWEED, GOUTWORT	Bouvardia	JASMINE PLANT
—wort	BETONY, STACHYS	bowstring-hemp	SANSEVIERIA
bistort	ADDER('S-)WORT	bramble	LAWYER, RUBUS
	(PATIENCE-)DOCK	brassica	CABBAGE, KALE, TURNIP
	SNAKEROOT, SNAKEWEED	brassock	FIELD MUSTARD
bitter		brier	LAWYER
—herb	GERMANDER	brookweed	WATER PIMPERNEL
—vetch	ERS	broom	CYTISUS, HAG-WEED
bittersweet	DULCAMARA, SOLANUM	—parasite	BROOM-RAPE
	WOODY NIGHTSHADE	—rape	OROBRANCHE
black		Browallia	BUSH VIOLET
—cummin	FITCH	brown spiderwort	SIDERASIS
—currant	QUINSY-BERRY, RIBES	Brunella	SELF-HEAL
—hellebore	BEAR'S-FOOT, MELAMPODE	Brunnera	FORGET-ME-NOT
—medick	SHAMROCK	buck	
—salsify	SCORZONERA, VIPER'S GRASS	—bean	BOGBEAN
—saltwort	GLAUX	—thorn	RHAMNUS, RHEINBERRY
black-eyed Susan	THUNBERGIA		RHINEBERRY
bladder		—wheat	SARRASIN, SARRAZIN
—campion	CATCH-FLY, WHITE-BOTTLE	buck's-horn	
—senna	COLUTEA	plantain	STAR-OF-THE-EARTH
bladderwort	LENTIBULARIACEAE	Buddhist pine	PODOCARPUS
	UTRICULARIA	buff-coloured turnip	SWEDE
blanket flower	GAILLARDIA	bugle	AJUGA

bugloss	BORAGE	candytuft	IBERIS
bunch of keys	COWSLIP	Cannabis	HEMP
bur		Canterbury bell	CAMPANULA
—marigold	XANTHIUM		THROATWORT
—reed	SPARGANIUM	Cape	
—thistle	SPEAR THISTLE	—cowslip	LACHENALIA
—weed	BURDOCK, BUR-REED	—gooseberry	GROUND-CHERRY, PHYSALIS
burdock	CLOTBUR, XANTHIUM	—grape	RHOICISSUS
burnet	PIMPERNEL, PROTERIUM	—ivy	SENECIO
—rose	SCOTCH ROSE	—primrose	STREPTOCARPUS
—saxifrage	PIMPINELLA	Capsella	SHEPHERD'S PURSE
burning-bush	EUONYMUS, WAHOO	caraway	AJ(O)WAN
bush violet	BROWALLIA	Cardamine	CORAL-ROOT, TOOTHWORT
busy lizzie	IMPATIENS	carduus	MUSK-THISTLE
butcher's broom	JEW'S MYRTLE	Carex	SEDGE
	KNEE-HOLLY, RUSCUS	carnation	DIANTHUS
	SHEPHERD'S MYRTLE	Carolina	
Butomus	FLOWERING-RUSH	—jasmine	GELSEMIUM
buttercup	BACHELOR'S BUTTONS	—pink	SPIGELIA
	GIL(T)CUP, HELLEBORE	carrion-flower	STAPELIA
	KINGCUP, RANUNCULUS	cassava	ADAM'S NEEDLE, YUC(C)A
—type	MEADOW-RUE	Cassia	SENNA
butterfly flower	SCHIZANTHUS	Castilleja	PAINTED CUP
butterwort	LENTIBULARIACEAE	castor-oil plant	ARALIA, FATSIA
	PINGUICULA		PANAX, RICINUS
cabbage	BRASSICA, COLE(-WORT)	cat's	
	COLLARD, KALE	—ear	GROUND IVY
—rose	PROVINCIAL-ROSE		MOUNTAIN EVERLASTING
—tree	CORDYLINE	—foot	GROUND IVY
cactus	(*see* **cacti**)		MOUNTAIN-EVERLASTING
Cakile	SEA-ROCKET	—tail	REED-MACE
Caladium	ANGEL'S WINGS	catmint	CATNEP, CATNIP, NEP(ETA)
calamint	BASIL-THYME	Ceanothus	RED-ROOT
calceolaria	SLIPPER FLOWER	celery type	ALEXANDERS
	SLIPPERWORT	Celosia	COCKSCOMB, PLUME FLOWER
Calendula	MARIGOLD	Centaurea	STAR-THISTLE
Californian poppy	ESCHSCHOLTZIA	Centranthus	RED VALERIAN
calla lily	ZANTEDESCHIA		SPUR VALERIAN
Callistemon	BOTTLEBRUSH PLANT	Centunculus	BASTARD PIMPERNEL
Callistriche	WATER-STARWORT	Cerastium	MOUSE-EAR CHICKWEED
Calluna	HEATH(ER)	Cereus	CACTUS, TORCH-THISTLE
Caltha	KINGCUP	Cestrum	NIGHT JESSAMINE
Camelina	GOLD-OF-PLEASURE	cetywall	SETUALE, SETWALL, VALERIAN
camomile	ANTHEMIS, FEVERFEW	chalk plant	GYPSOPHILA
Campanula	BELLWORT	Chamaenerion	WILLOW-HERB
	CANTERBURY BELL	charlock	WILD MUSTARD
	(GIANT) BELLFLOWER	Cheiranthus	WALL (GILLY-)FLOWER
	NETTLE-LEAVED BELLFLOWER	Cheirinia	WALL (GILLY-)FLOWER
	STAR OF BETHLEHEM	chenille plant	ACALYPHA
	THROATWORT	Chenopodium	WORM-SEED
campion	CATCH-FLY, LICHNIS	chervil	CICELY, COW-CHERVIL
	FLOWER OF JOVE, LYCHNIS		COW-PARSLEY, COW-WEED
	RAGGED ROBIN	chestnut vine	TETRASTIGMA
Canada rice	ZIZANIA	chicken gizzard	IRESINE
Canadian pondweed	ANACHARIS	chick-pea	CHICH, CHICKLING VETCH
	WATER THYME		EGYPTIAN PEA, GRAM

chickweed	STELLARIA, STITCHWORT		columbine	AQUILEGIA
—wintergreen	TRIENTALIS		Columnea	GOLDFISH PLANT
chicory	ENDIVE, SUCCORY, WITLOOF		Colutea	BLADDER SENNA
Chimaphila	WINTERGREEN		comfrey	BORAGE, SYMPHYTUM
Chincherinchee	ORNITHOGALUM		common	
Chinese			—arum	CUCKOO-PINT
—balloon flower	PLATYCODON			LORDS AND LADIES
—lantern	PHYSALIS		—burnet	SALAD BURNET
Chionodoxa	GLORY OF THE SNOW		—daisy	DOG-DAISY
Chlorophytum	ST BERNARD'S LILY		—polypody	POLYPODIUM
	SPIDER PLANT		—ragwort	YELLOW-WEED
Christmas			condiment	DILL
—pepper	CAPSICUM		coneflower	RUDBECKIA
—rose	BLACK HELLEBORE		Convallaria	LILY OF THE VALLEY
cibol	WELSH ONION		coral	
Cicuta	WATER-HEMLOCK		—berry	AECHMEA, ARDISIA
cigar plant	CUPHEA		—root	CARDAMINE, TOOTHWORT
cinnamon	CANELLA		Cordatum	PHILODENDRON
cinquefoil	FIVEFINGERS, MARSH-LOCKS		Cordyline	CABBAGE TREE
	POTENTILLA			FLAMING DRAGON TREE
	MINIATURE GRAPE IVY			GRASS PALM, TI PLANT
Cirsium	CNICUS, SPEAR-THISTLE		corn	
Cissus	BEGONIA VINE, KANGAROO VINE		—bluebottle	BLAWORT, BLEWORT
	MINIATURE GRAPE IVY		—feverfew	MAYWEED
clary	ORVAL, SAGE		—flower	BLUEBOTTLE
Claytonia	SPRING-BEAUTY		—marigold	OX-EYE
cleavers	GOOSE-GRASS		—salad	LAMB'S-LETTUCE
clematis	TRAVELLER'S-JOY		—spurrey	YARR
	VIRGIN'S-BOWER		corncockle	AGROSTEMMA
Clerodendrum	BLEEDING HEART VINE		cornfield	
	GLORY BOWER		—plant	POPPY
Clianthus	GLORY PEA		—weed	KNAWEL
climbing	NASTURTIUM, PHILODENDRON		Coronaria	ANEMONE
	WISTARIA, WISTERIA		Coronopus	SENEBIERA, SWINE'S-CRESS
—evergreen	IVY		Corrigiola	STRAPWORT
—gourd	BRYONY		Cortaderia	PAMPAS GRASS
Clivia	KAFFIR LILY		cotton thistle	SCOTCH THISTLE
clog plant	HYPOCYRTA		cough remedy	HOARHOUND
clotbur	SEA-BURDOCK, XANTHIUM			WHITE HOREHOUND
cloudberry	MOUNTAIN-BRAMBLE		cow	
clove	EUGENIA		—bane	CICUTA
—pink	SOPS-IN-WINE		—berry	VACCINIUM
clover	ALSIKE, HARE'S-FOOT(TREFOIL)		—parsley	LACE CURTAINS, KECK(S)
	TRIFOLIUM			KECKSY(E), KEDLOCK, KEX
club-moss	STAGHORN MOSS		—parsnip	PIGWEED
club-rush	BULRUSH, SCIRPUS		—pea	CHERRY-BEAN
Cnicus	CIRSIUM, (SPEAR-)THISTLE		cowslip	BUNCH OF KEYS
coarse weed	HEMP-NETTLE			CULVER-KEY, HERB-PETER
Cobaea	CUP AND SAUCER VINE			PA(I)GLE
cock's-comb	CELOSIA, YELLOW RATTLE		—x primrose	POLYANTHUS
cockle-bur	CLOTBUR		cranberry	FEN-BERRY, VACCINIUM
Codiaeum	CROTON, JOSEPH'S COAT		cranesbill	DOVE'S-FOOT, GERANIUM
Colchicum	MEADOW SAFFRON		Crassula	ROCHEA
coleseed	NAVEW		creeping	
Coleus	FLAME NETTLE		—Jenny	LOOSESTRIFE, MONEYWORT
coltsfoot	HORSE-FOOT			PILEA

—moss	SELAGINELLA
Crepis	HAWKSBEARD
cress	CARDAMINE, CORAL-ROOT
Crithmum	SAMP(H)IRE
crocus	SAFFRON
Crossandra	FIRECRACKER FLOWER
Croton	CODIAEUM, JOSEPH'S COAT
crowberry	CRAKEBERRY
crowfoot	ANEMONE
crown of thorns	EUPHORBIA
Cryptanthus	EARTH STAR
	PHEASANT LEAF
	RAINBOW STAR, STARFISH PLANT
cuckoo	
—flower	CARDAMINE, LADY'S SMOCK
—pint	ARUM, WAKE-ROBIN
cucumber	COLOCYNTH, COLOQUINTIDA
Cucurbita	GOURD, SQUASH
cudweed	COTTON-WEED
cup and saucer vine	COBAEA
Cuphea	CIGAR PLANT
Cupid's bower	ACHIMENES
Cyanotis	TEDDY BEAR VINE
cyclamen	SOW-BREAD
Cynanchum	SWALLOW-WORT
Cyperus	UMBRELLA PLANT
daffodil	NARCISSUS
daisy	BELLIS
dame violet	HESPERIS, ROCKET
dandelion	TARAXACUM
Dane's blood	DANEWORT, DWARF ELDER
	WALLWORT
darnel	TARE
Datura	THORN-APPLE
day-lily	FUNKIA, HEMEROCALLIS
dead nettle	ARCHANGEL, DAY-NETTLE
deadly nightshade	ATROPA
	BELLADONNA, DWALE
deep-blue gentian	GENTIANELLA
Delphinium	LARKSPUR
desert privet	PEPEROMIA
devil's ivy	SCINDAPSUS
devil-in-a-bush	NIGELLA
(Devon and Cornwall)	ILLECEBRUM
Dianthus	(CHEDDAR-)PINK
	SWEET WILLIAM
Dicentra	DUTCHMAN'S BREECHES
Dieffenbachia	DUMB CANE, LEOPARD LILY
Digitalis	FOXGLOVE
dill	ANISE, FENNEL
dinner plate Aralia	POLYSCIAS
Dionaea	VENUS'S FLY-TRAP
Dipladenia	PINK ALLAMANDA
Diplotaxis	WALL-MUSTARD
	WALL-ROCKET
dittander	DITTANY, PEPPERWORT

dittany	BURNING BUSH
	SWEET HORSEMINT
Dizygotheca	FINGER ARALIA
dock	POLYGONUM, RUMEX
	SORREL
dog	
—bane	APOCYNUM, FLY-TRAP
—tooth violet	ERYTHRONIUM
—violet	VIOLA CANINA
—wood	HOUNDS-BERRY
dog's mercury	MERCURIALIS
Doronicum	LEOPARD'S-BANE
Dracaena	(MADAGASCAR) DRAGON TREE
	RIBBON PLANT
dragon	DRACONTIUM
—tree	DRACAENA
dragon's head	DRACOCEPHALUM
Drosera	SUNDEW
Dryopteris	MALE FERN
Duchesnea	INDIAN STRAWBERRY
duckweed	DUCK'S-MEAT, LEMNA
dumb cane	DIEFFENBACHIA
Dutch rush	SCOURING RUSH
Dutchman's	
—breeches	DICENTRA
—pipe	ARISTOLOCHIA
dwarf	
—elder	DANE'S BLOOD, DANEWORT
	WALLWORT
—marguerite	SHASTA DAISY
—poppy	ICELAND POPPY
dyer's rocket	MIGNONETTE, WELD
earth star	CRYPTANTHUS
Echinops	GLOBE-THISTLE
Echium	VIPER'S BUGLOSS
edible roots	(see vegetables)
eggplant	BRINJAL, BROWN JOLLY
Egyptian star cluster	PENTAS
Eichhornia	WATER-HYACINTH
Eleagnus	OLEASTER
elecampane	GOLDEN SAMPHIRE
elephant's	
—ear	PHILODENDRON
—foot	TORTOISE-PLANT
enchanter's nightshade	CIRCAEA
endive	ESCAROLE
Ephedra	SEA-GRAPE
Epilobium	WILLOW-HERB
Epipactis	HELLEBORINE
Episcia	FLAME VIOLET
	LACE FLOWER
Eranthis	WINTER ACONITE
Erica	HEATH, HEATHER
Erigeron	FLEA-BANE
Erodium	STORK'S-BILL
eryngo	SEA-HOLLY

Erysimum	TREACLE MUSTARD
	TREACLE WORM-SEED
Erythronium	DOG'S-TOOTH VIOLET
eschalot	ALLIUM, SHAL(L)OT
Ethiopian gladiolus	ACIDANTHERA
Eupatorium	HEMP-AGRIMONY
Euphorbia	(SUN-)SPURGE
euphrasy	EYE-BRIGHT
evening primrose	CLARKIA, GODETIA
	ENCHANTER'S NIGHTSHADE
	FUCHSIA, OENOTHERA
evergreen cherry	CHERRY-LAUREL
everlasting flower	IMMORTELLE
everlastings	XERANTHEMUM
evil-smelling	CARRION FLOWER
	DANE'S BLOOD, DANEWORT
	DWARF ELDER, FETID IRIS
	ROAST-BEEF PLANT
	SKUNK-CABBAGE, STAPELIA
	SYMPLOCARPUS, WALLWORT
Exacum	PERSIAN VIOLET
eye-bright	EUPHRASY
fat-headed Lizzie	FATSHEDERA
Fatshedera	FAT-HEADED LIZZIE
	IVY TREE
Fatsia	ARALIA, CASTOR-OIL PLANT
fennel-flower	LOVE-IN-A-MIST
ferns	(*see separate entry*)
Ferraria	TIGRIDIA
Ferula	GIANT FENNEL, LASERWORT
fetid iris	ROAST-BEEF PLANT
feverfew	BACHELOR'S BUTTONS
	PELLITORY, PYRETHRUM
Ficus	BENGAL FIG, FIDDLE LEAF FIG
	MISTLETOE FIG
	RUBBER PLANT, WEEPING FIG
fiddle	
—fig	FICUS
—leaf	PHILODENDRON
field mustard	BRASSOCK
figwort	ACANTHUS, MIMULUS
	NEMESIA, SCROPHULARIA
finger	
—aralia	DIZYGOTHECA
—nail plant	BLUSHING BROMELIAD
	NEOREGELIA
fingers and thumbs	GORSE
firecracker	
—flower	CROSSANDRA
—plant	MANETTIA
fire	
—thorn	PYRACANTH(A)
—weed	ROSE-BAY(WILLOW-HERB)
Fittonia	NERVE PLANT, MOSAIC PLANT
	PAINTED NET LEAF
	SILVER NET LEAF, SNAKESKIN PLANT

five-leaved clover	CINQUEFOIL
flagflower	IRIS
flame	
—nettle	COLEUS
—of the woods	IXORA
—violet	EPISCIA
flaming	
—dragon tree	CORDYLINE
—Katy	KALANCHOE
—sword	VRIESIA
flamingo flower	ANTHURIUM
flax	LINUM
flea-bane	ERIGERON
fleur-de-lis	IRIS
floating plant	BLADDERWORT
	UTRICULARIA
Florentine iris	ORRIS
flowering-rush	BUTOMUS
flowerless plant	CRYPTOGAM
	PTERIDOPHYTE
fodder-plant	SAIN(T)FOIN
fool's parsley	DOG-PARSLEY
forest lily	VELTHEIMIA
forget-me-not	BRUNNERA
	MOUSE-EAR
	MYOSOTIS
	SCORPION-GRASS
four-leaved clover	TRUE-LOVE GRASS
foxglove	DEADMEN'S BELLS
	DIGITALIS
	WITCHES'-THIMBLE
Fragaria	STRAWBERRY
Frankenia	SEA-HEATH
frankincense	LASER(WORT)
freckle face	HYPOESTES
French bean	HARICOT
friendship plant	PILEA
fritillary	CROWN-IMPERIAL
	SNAKE'S-HEAD
frogbit	HYDROCHARIS
fumitory	FUMARIA
Funkia	HOSTA, PLANTAIN LILY
furze	FINGERS AND THUMBS
	GORSE, ULEX, WHIN
Gaillardia	BLANKET FLOWER
Galanthus	SNOWDROP
Galucium	HORNED POPPY
garden	
—cress	LEPIDIUM
—daisy	HEN-AND-CHICKENS
gardener's garters	PHALARIS
garlic	ALLIUM
—mustard	JACK-BY-THE-HEDGE
garlic-like plant	ROCOMBOLE
Gaultheria	WINTERGREEN
gay feather	LIATRIS

genista	DYER'S-BROOM
	DYER'S-GREENWEED
	PETTY WHIN, GREENWEED
gentian	BALDMONEY, FELWORT
	YELLOW-CENTAURY
	YELLOW-WORT
geranium	PELARGONIUM
geum	AVENS
giant	
—bellflower	CAMPANULA, THROATWORT
—fennel	FERULA
gigantic mare's tail	GUNNERA
gillyflower	CLOVE-GILLYFLOWER
	STOCK-GILLYFLOWER
	WALLFLOWER
giving yellow dye	XANTHIUM
gladiolus	CORNFLAG
glasswort	KALI, MARSH SAMPHIRE
	MARSH-SAMPHIRE, SALICORNIA
Glaux	SEA-MILKWORT
globe thistle	ECHINOPS
Gloriosa	GLORY LILY
glory	
—bower	CLERODENDRUM
—lily	GLORIOSA
—of the snow	CHIONODOXA
—pea	CLIANTHUS
Gloxinia	SINNINGIA
goat's	
—beard	ASTILBE
	JACK-GO-TO-BED-AT-NOON
	SALSIFY
—weed	BISHOP('S) WEED
	GOUTWEED, GOUTWORT
Godetia	EVENING PRIMROSE
gold dust	ALYSSUM
golden	
—garlic	ALLIUM
—Pothos	SCINDAPSUS
—rod	AARON'S ROD
—samphire	ELECAMPANE
—seal	YELLOW-ROOT
goldfish plant	COLUMNEA
goose	
—flower	PELICAN-FLOWER
—foot	BLITE, FAT-HEN
	GOOD-KING-HENRY
	ORACH(E), PIGWEED
	SYNGONIUM
gorse	FINGERS AND THUMBS
	FURZE, ULEX, WHIN
gourd	CUCURBITA, SQUASH
goutweed	BISHOP('S) WEED, GOATWEED
grape	
—hyacinth	MUSCARI
	STARCH-HYACINTH
—ivy	RHOICISSUS
—vine	VITIS
grass	(see separate entry)
Gratiola	HEDGE-HYSSOP
great mullein	HAG-TAPER
	SHEPHERD'S CLUB
greater	
—celandine	SWALLOW-WORT
—knapweed	MAFELON
Greek valerian	JACOB'S LADDER
green	
—dragon	DRACUNCULUS
—weed	GENISTA
green-flowered orchid	LISTERA, TWAY-BLADE
Grevillea	SILK OAK
gromwell	SALFERN
ground ivy	BENTH(E)
groundsel	SENECIO
Guernsey lily	NERINE
Gypsophila	SOAP-ROOT
gypsywort	WATER HOREHOUND
Haemanthus	BLOOD LILY
hag	
—taper	(GREAT) MULLEIN
—weed	BROOM
hair-capped mosses	POLYTRICUM
harebell	BLAWORT, BLEWORT
	BLUEBELL, CAMPANULA
	HAIRBELL, HEATH BELL
	SCOTCH BLUEBELL
hare's ear	BUPLEVER
harlequin flower	SPARAXIS
hawksbeard	CREPIS
hawkweed	HIERACIUM
hazelwort	ASARABACCA
healing plant	PANACEA
heart's-ease	PANSY
heath	ANDROMEDA, BELL-HEATHER
	ERICA, GAULTHERIA
heather	CALLUNA, ERICA
—bell	HEATH BELL
hedge	
—hyssop	GRATIOLA
—mustard	FLIX-WEED
—plant	GARLIC MUSTARD
Hedera	IVY
Helenium	SNEEZEWEED
Helianthemum	ROCK-ROSE, SUN ROSE
Helianthus	SUNFLOWER
Helichrysum	EVERLASTING(-FLOWER)
Heliocharis	SPIKE-RUSH
Heliotrope	CHERRY-PIE
hellebore	CHRISTMAS FLOWER
	CHRISTMAS ROSE
Helxine	BABY'S TEARS
	MIND YOUR OWN BUSINESS

Hemerocallis	DAY-LILY	indoor oak	NICODEMIA
Hemigraphis	RED IVY	insectivorous plant	BUTTERWORT
hemp-agrimony	EUPATORIUM		DARLINGTONIA, DROSERA
henbane	HYOSCYAMUS		NEPENTHES, PITCHER-PLANT
Hepaticae	LIVERWORT		SARRACENIA, SUNDEW
Heptapleurum	PARASOL PLANT	Ipomoea	JALAP, MORNING-GLORY
herb	(*see* **herbs**)	Iresine	BEEFSTEAK PLANT
herb lily	ALSTRO(E)MERIA		BLOOD LEAF, CHICKEN GIZZARD
Herniaria	RUPTUREWORT	iris	GLADIOLE, GLADIOLUS
herringbone plant	MARANTA	Irish heath	ST DABEOC'S HEATH
Hesperis	DAME VIOLET, ROCKET	Isatis	WOAD
Hieracium	HAWKWEED	Ismene	PERUVIAN DAFFODIL
high taper	MULLEIN	Isoetes	QUILLWORT
Hippeastrum	AMARYLLIS	itchweed	FALSE HELLEBORE
hogweed	COW-PARSNIP		WHITE HELLEBORE
hollyhock	ALTHAEA, MALVA	ivy	ARALIA, HEDERA
	ROSE-MALLOW		LOVESTONE
honesty	BOTRYCHIUM, MOONWORT	—bush	TOD
hop-trefoil	SHAMROCK	—tree	FATSHEDERA
horse-tail	BOTTLEBRUSH, DUTCH RUSH	ivy-leaved speedwell	HEN-BIT
	EQUISETINAE, EQUISETALES	Ixia	AFRICAN CORN LILY
	MARE'S-TAIL	Ixora	FLAME OF THE WOODS
Hortensia	HYDRANGEA	Jacob's ladder	GREEK VALERIAN
hosta	FUNKIA, PLANTAIN LILY		POLEMONIUM
hot water plant	ACHIMENES	Jacobinia	KING'S CROWN
Hottonia	WATER-VIOLET	jalap	IPOMOEA
house		Japanese sedge	CAREX
—leek	JUPITER'S BEARD, SENGREEN	jasmine	JESSAMINE
—lime	SPARMANNIA	—plant	BOUVARDIA
Hoya	WAX PLANT	Jasione	(SHEEP'S-BIT) SCABIOUS
Humulus	HOP		SHEEP'S-BIT
husk tomato	GROUND-CHERRY		SHEEP'S SCABIOUS
hybrid rose	NOISETTE	Jerusalem	
hydrangea	HORTENSIA	—artichoke	SUNFLOWER
Hydrophyllum	WATER-LEAF	—sage	PHLOMIS
Hyoscyamus	HENBANE	jewel-weed	IMPATIENS
Hypericum	AARON'S-BEARD	John-go-to-bed-at-noon	GOAT'S-BEARD
	ROSE OF SHARON	Joseph's coat	CODIAEUM, CROTON
	ST JOHN'S WORT	Juncus	TOAD-GRASS, TOAD-RUSH
	ST PETER'S WORT	jute	CORCHORUS
Hypocyrta	CLOG PLANT	Kaffir lily	CLIVIA, SCHIZOSTYLIS
Hypoestes	FRECKLE FACE	Kalanchoe	FLAMING KATY
	POLKA DOT PLANT	kale	BOECOLE
Iberis	CANDYTUFT	kalmia	MOUNTAIN-LAUREL
ice-plant	MESEMBRIANTHEMUM	Karatus	SILKGRASS
Impatiens	BALSAM, BUSY LIZZIE	kidney	
	JEWEL-WEED, NOLI-ME-TANGERE	—bean	FLAGEOLET, FRENCH BEAN
	PATIENT LUCY, TOUCH-ME-NOT		HARICOT, (SCARLET-)RUNNER
Indian		—vetch	ANTHYLLIS, CENTAUREA
—corn	MAIZE, ZEA		JUPITER'S BEARD
—cress	LARK'S-HEEL, TROPAEOLUM		LADIES'-FINGERS
—pink	SPIGELIA		LADY'S-FINGERS
—pipe	MONATROPA	kingcup	CALTHA, MARSH-MARIGOLD
—poke	AMERICAN HELLEBORE	king's crown	JACOBINIA
—rice	ZIZANIA	knapweed	CENTAURY, HARD-HEAD
—strawberry	DUCHESNEA		ST BARNABY'S THISTLE

knawel	SCLERANTHUS
Kniphofia	RED-HOT POKER, TORCH-LILY
knot-grass	PERSICARIA, POLYGONUM
knotted	
—pearlwort	SAGINA
—spurrey	SAGINA
Labrador tea	LEDUM
lace curtains	COW PARSLEY
—flower	EPISCIA
Lachenalia	CAPE COWSLIP
lady's	
—fingers	KIDNEY-VETCH
—mantle	PARSLEY-P(I)ERT
—pincushion	THRIFT
—slipper	CYPRIPEDIUM
	MOCCASIN-FLOWER, ORCHID
—thistle	MILK-THISTLE
lake margin plants	LITORELLA
	SHORE-WEED
lamb's ear	STACHYS
larkspur	BLUE-ROCKET, DELPHINIUM
	LARK'S-HEEL, MONK'S HOOD
	STAVESACRE
Lathraea	TOOTHWORT
Lathyrus	SWEET-PEA, VETCHLING
laurel	LAURUS, SWEET-BAY
Lavatera	TREE-MALLOW
lavender	ASPIC, LAVANDULA
leafless parasite	DODDER
legume grown for forage	GUAR
lentils	PULSE
Leontodon	HAWKBIT
Leonurus	MOTHERWORT
leopard lily	DIEFFENBACHIA
Lepidium	PEPPER-GRASS
lesser yellow trefoil	SHAMROCK
Leucojum	SNOWFLAKE
levantine madder	ALIZARI
Liatris	GAY FEATHER
Ligusticum	LOVAGE
Ligustrum	PRIVET
like clover	MELILOT
lily	AMARYLLIS, ASPHODEL
	FRITILLARY
—of the	
Nile	AGAPANTHUS
valley	CONVALLARIA
—turf	OPHIOPOGON
—type	HYACINTH
Lima bean	SUGAR-BEAN
Limosella	MUDWORT
Linaria	BACON AND EGGS, TOADFLAX
Linum	FLAX
lipstick vine	AESCHYNANTHUS
Listera	TWAY-BLADE
Lithospermum	GROMWELL

Litorella	SHORE-WEED
liverwort	AGRIMONY, HEPATIC(A)
	MARCHANTIA, RICCIA
lollipop plant	PACHYSTACHYS
Lomeria	HARD-FERN
London pride	NANCY-PRETTY
	NONE-SO-PRETTY
	ST PATRICK'S CABBAGE
	SAXIFRAGA
Lonicera	HONEYSUCKLE
loosestrife	MONEYWORT
lousewort	PEDICULARIS
love	
—apple	TOMATO
—in-a-mist	DEVIL-IN-A-BUSH, NIGELLA
—lies-bleeding	AMARANT(H)US
lucerne	ALFALFA
lucky clover	OXALIS
Lunaria	HONESTY
Luzula	WOOD-RUSH
Lychnis	ROSE-CAMPION
Lycopus	GYPSY-WORT
Lysimachia	LOOSESTRIFE
Lythrum	PURPLE LOOSETRIFE
Macleaya	BOCCONIA, PLUME POPPY
Madagascar	
—dragon tree	DRACAENA
—jasmine	STEPHANOTIS
madder	GARDENIA, RUBIA
maize	INDIAN CORN
	SWEET-CORN, ZEA
Malcomia	VIRGINIA STOCK
mallow	ABUTILON, LAVATERA
	MALVA
mandrake	MANDRAGORA, SPRINGWORT
Manettia	FIRECRACKER PLANT
Maranta	HERRINGBONE PLANT
	NEVER NEVER PLANT
	PEACOCK PLANT, PRAYER PLANT
	RABBIT TRACKS
	RATTLESNAKE PLANT
	ZEBRA PLANT
mare's tail	BOTTLEBRUSH, HIPPURIS
marigold	CALENDULA
marjoram	AMARACUS, OREGANO
	ORIGAN(E), ORIGANUM
marsh	
—gentian	BUCKBEAN
—grass	REED
—lily	CALLA
—lousewort	RED-RATTLE
—mallow	ALTHAEA
—marigold	KINGCUP
—plant	MARE'S-TAIL, PENNY-WORT
	WATER-FERN
—samphire	GLASSWORT, SALICORNIA

martagon lily	TURK'S CAP
marvel of Peru	FOUR O'CLOCK, MIRABILIS
masterwort	ASTRANTIA
Matricaria	FEVERFEW
Matthiola	STOCK
matweed	NARD
mayweed	DOG'S-FENNEL
meadow	
—rue	THALICTRUM
—saffron	COLCHICUM, NAKED LADY
—sweet	QUEEN-OF-THE-MEADOW(S)
	SPIRAEA
Meconopsis	POPPY
medicinal plant	BETONY, BIRTHWORT
	CAR(R)AWAY
medick	MEDICAGO, SNAIL
melampode	BLACK HELLEBORE
melitot	FENUGREEK
Mentha	MINT, PENNYROYAL
	PEPPERMINT, SPEARMINT
Mercurialis	(DOG'S) MERCURY
mermaid vine	RHOICISSUS
Mertensia	OYSTER-PLANT
Mesembrianthemum	ICE-PLANT
Meum	BALDMONEY, SPIGNEL
	SPICKNEL
Michaelmas daisy	ASTER
mignonette	DYER'S ROCKET
	RESEDA, WELD
milfoil	ACHILLEA, YARROW
milk	
—root	POLYGAEA
—thistle	LADY'S-THISTLE
—vetch	ASTRAGALUS
	WILD LIQUORICE
—weed	ASCLEPIAS
—wort	POLYGALA, SNAKEROOT
Mimosa	TOUCH-ME-NOT
Mimulus	MONKEY-FLOWER
	MUSK-PLANT
mind-your-own-business	HELXINE
Ming Aralia	POLYSCIAS
miniature grape ivy	CISSUS
mint	CALAMINT, PENNYROYAL
Mirabilis	MARVEL OF PERU
mistletoe	VISCUM
—fig	FICUS
Mitella	BISHOP'S-CAP
mock privet	PHILLYREA
Monarda	BERGAMOT
moneywort	CREEPING JENNY
monk's	
—hood	ACONITE, BLUE-ROCKET
	LARKSPUR
—rhubarb	PATIENCE DOCK
monkey-flower	MIMULUS

Monstera	SPLIT LEAF PHILODENDRON
	SWISS CHEESE PLANT
Montbretia	TRITONIA
moon	
—seed	MENISPERMUM
—wort	BOTRYCHIUM, HONESTY
moorland plant	GRASS OF PARNASSUS
morning-glory	IPOMOEA, JALAP
mosaic plant	FITTONIA
moschatel	ADOXA
Moses in the cradle	RHOEO
moss	ACROGEN, CRYPTOGAM
mossy saxifrage	LADY'S-CUSHION
mother	
—in-law's tongue	SANSEVIERIA
—of thousands	STRAWBERRY GERANIUM
mountain	
—bramble	CLOUDBERRY
—laurel	KALMIA
—sorrel	OXYRIA, ROMAN SORREL
mourning-bride	SWEET SCABIOUS
mouse	
—ear chickweed	CERASTIUM
	SNOW-IN-SUMMER
—tail	MYOSURUS
mudwort	LIMOSELLA
mugwort	WORMWOOD
mulberry	MORUS
mullein	AARON'S ROD, ADAM'S FLANNEL
	HAG-TAPER, HIGH TAPER
	SHEPHERD'S CLUB, VERBASCUM
Muscari	GRAPE HYACINTH
	STARCH HYACINTH
musk	MIMULUS
—scented	MIMULUS, MUSK-MALLOW
—thistle	CARDUUS
mustard	SENVY
Myosotis	FORGET-ME-NOT
Myosurus	MOUSE-TAIL
Myriophyllum	WATER-MILFOIL
Myrrhis	SWEET-CICELY
myrtle	MYRTUS
naked lady	MEADOW-SAFFRON
Nancy-pretty	LONDON PRIDE
narcissus	JONQUIL, PHEASANT'S-EYE
nasturtium	INDIAN CRESS, LARK'S-HEEL
	TROPAEOLUM
Natal plum	CARISSA
navelwort	PENNYWORT
Neapolitan violet	PARMA VIOLET
needle-furze	PETTY WHIN
Nelumbium	LOTE, LOTOS, LOTUS
Nemesia	FIGWORT
nenuphar	WATER-LILY
Neoregelia	BLUSHING BROMELIAD
	FINGERNAIL PLANT

Nepenthe	PITCHER-PLANT
Nepeta	CATMINT, GROUND-IVY
Nephthytis	SYNGONIUM
Nerine	GUERNSEY LILY
Nertera	BEAD PLANT
nerve plant	FITTONIA
nettle	URTICA
—leaved bellflower	CAMPANULA
	THROATWORT
—with female flowers	ROMAN NETTLE
nettle-type	PELLITORY
never-never plant	MARANTA
New Zealand flax	PHORMIUM
Nicodemia	INDOOR OAK
Nicotiana	TOBACCO PLANT
Nidularium	BIRD'S NEST BROMELIAD
Nigella	DEVIL-IN-A-BUSH
	FENNEL-FLOWER, FITCH
	LOVE-IN-A-MIST, RAGGED-LADY
night	
—jessamine	CESTRUM
—shade	HENBANE, MOREL, SOLANUM
none-so-pretty	LONDON PRIDE
northern fern	HARD-FERN
nose-bleed	YARROW
Nuphar	WATER-LILY
Nymphaea	LOTE, LOTOS
	LOTUS, WATER-LILY
oat-shooter	ANGELICA, AIT-SKEITER
Oenanthe	WATER-DROPWORT
	WATER-HEMLOCK
Oenothera	EVENING PRIMROSE
offensive-smelling	DANE'S BLOOD
	DANEWORT, DWARF ELDER
	WALLWORT
oil-producing	RAPE
old-fashioned rose	MOSS-ROSE
oleander	NERIUM, RHODODAPHNE
	ROSE-BAY(LAUREL)
	ROSE-LAUREL
oleaster	ELEAGNUS
olive	OLEA
Ononis	REST-HARROW
Ophiopogon	LILY TURF
Opuntia	PRICKLY-PEAR
orange-flowered lily	TIGER-LILY
orchid	CORAL-ROOT, FLY ORCHIS
	LADY'S-SLIPPER
Ornithogalum	CHINCHERINCHEE
	STAR-OF-BETHLEHEM
orpine	LIVELONG
orval	CLARY
oshac	AMMONIAC
ox	
—eye daisy	MARGUERITE
—tongue	PIERIS

oxlip	FIVEFINGERS
Oxalis	WOOD-SORREL
Oxyria	MOUNTAIN SORREL
oyster-plant	GROMWELL, MERTENSIA
	SALSIFY
Pachystachys	LOLLIPOP PLANT
padma	SACRED LOTUS
painted	
—cup	CASTILLEJA
	PAINTED LADY
—lady	PAINTED CUP
—net leaf	FITTONIA
—tongue	SALPIGLOSSIS
painter's palette	ANTHURIUM
pampas grass	CORTADERIA
Panamiga	PILEA
Panax	ARALIA
pansy	HERB-TRINITY
	LOVE-IN-IDLENESS, VIOLA
Papaver	POPPY
paper	
—flower	BOUGAINVILLEA
—reed	PAPYRUS
parasitic plant	MISTLETOE, VISCUM
parasol plant	HEPTAPLEURUM
Paris quadrifolia	HERB-PARIS
parkleaves	ST JOHN'S WORT, TUTSAN
Paronychia	WHITLOW-GRASS
	WHITLOW-WORT
parsley-fern	ROCK-BRAKE
parsnip-type	MASTERWORT
parti-coloured	PAINTED LADY
paschal-flower	ANEMONE, PULSATILLA
pasque-flower	ANEMONE, PULSATILLA
Passiflora	LOVE-IN-A-MIST
	PASSION-FLOWER
	WATER-LEMON
patience-dock	MONK'S RHUBARB
patient Lucy	IMPATIENS
peace lily	SPATHIPHYLLUM
peacock	
—fern	SELAGINELLA
—plant	MARANTA
pearlwort	SAGINA
Pedicularis	LOUSEWORT
Pelargonium	GERANIUM, STORK'S-BILL
pelican-flower	GOOSE-FLOWER
pellitory	FEVERFEW, YARROW
	WALL-WORT
pennywort	NAVELWORT
Pentstemon	BEARDED TONGUE
Pentas	EGYPTIAN STAR CLUSTER
penthia	ASTROPHEL, STARLIGHT
pepper-grass	LEPIDIUM
pepperwort	DITTANDER, DITTANY
	SPANISH CRESS

perennial	
—herb	LASERPICIUM
—saxifrage	LONDON PRIDE
—weed	WILD(-)OAT
periwinkle	APOCYNUM, STROPHANTHUS
	VINCA
Persian violet	EXACUM
persicaria	KNOT-GRASS
Peruvian daffodil	ISMENE
petty whin	GENISTA, NEEDLE-FURZE
Phalaris	GARDENER'S GARTERS
pheasant leaf	CRYPTANTHUS
pheasant's eye	ADONIS, NARCISSUS
Phillyrea	MOCK PRIVET
Philodendron	CORDATUM
	ELEPHANT'S EAR, FIDDLE LEAF
	SWEETHEART PLANT
phlox	POLEMONIUM
Phormium	NEW ZEALAND FLAX
Physalis	CAPE GOOSEBERRY
	CHINESE LANTERN
	GROUND-CHERRY
	WINTER-CHERRY
Phytolacca	POKEWEED
pickling cabbage	RED CABBAGE
Pieris	OX-TONGUE
piggyback plant	TOLMIEA
pigweed	ARAMANTH, COW-PARSNIP
	GOOSEFOOT
Pilea	ALUMINIUM PLANT
	ARTILLERY PLANT
	CREEPING JENNY
	FRIENDSHIP PLANT, PANAMIGA
pilewort	CELANDINE, FIGWORT
pillwort	PILULARIA
Pilularia	PILLWORT
Pimpinella	ANISE, BURNET-SAXIFRAGE
pincushion	
flower	SCABIOUS
pineapple	ANANA(S), BROMELIA
—weed	(RAYLESS) MAYWEED
Pinguicula	BUTTERWORT
pink	CLOVE-GILLY-FLOWER
	CLOVE PINK, DIANTHUS
—Allamanda	DIPLADENIA
—root	WORM-GRASS
pipewort	ERIOCAULON
pitcher-plant	NEPENTHE
Plantago	RIBWORT(-PLAINTAIN)
plantain	RIBGRASS, WAYBREAD
—lily	FUNKIA, HOSTA
Platycerium	STAGHORN-FERN
Platycodon	CHINESE BALLOON FLOWER
Plectranthus	SWEDISH IVY
pleurisy-root	BUTTERFLY-WEED
Plumbago	SEA-LAVENDER, SEA-PINK

plume	
—flower	CELOSIA
—poppy	BOCCONIA, MACLEAYA
Podocarpus	BUDDHIST PINE
poisonous plants	CUCKOO PINT
	FOOL'S PARSLEY
	LORDS AND LADIES
	NIGHTSHADE
pokeweed	PHYTOLACCA
Polemonium	PHLOX
Polianthes	AMARYLLIS, TUBEROSE
polka dot plant	HYPOESTES
Polyanthus	PRIMULA
Polygala	MILKWORT
Polygonatum	SOLOMON'S SEAL
Polygonum	KNOT-GRASS, KNOTWEED
	PURPLE LOOSESTRIFE
	WILLOW-WEED
Polypodium	COMMON POLYPODY
Polyscias	DINNER PLATE ARALIA
	MING ARALIA
pomegranate	PUNICA
pond plant	ACORUS, SWEET-FLAG
pondweed	EELGRASS, FROG'S-LETTUCE
	GRASSWRACK
	HYDROCHARITACEAE
	PICKEREL-WEED
	POTAMOGETON, ZOSTER
poor man's	
—orchid	SCHIZANTHUS
—weather-glass	PIMPERNEL
poppy	MECONOPSIS, PAPAVER
Portulaca	PURSLANE
pot-herb	PURSLANE, PURSLAIN
potato	SOLANUM
Potentilla	CINQUEFOIL, SEPT-FOIL
	TORMENTIL, WILD STRAWBERRY
	BARREN STRAWBERRY
	SILVERWEED
Poterium	BOTTLE-BRUSH
prayer plant	MARANTA
prickly pear	INDIAN FIG, OPUNTIA
—poppy	ARGEMONE
—saltwort	KALI
—samphire	SALTWORT
primrose	BIRD'S-EYE, PRIMULA
Primula	OXLIP, PRIMROSE
prince's feathers	AMARANTHUS
	LONDON PRIDE
privet	LIGUSTRUM
producing red dye	MADDER
provincial-rose	CABBAGE-ROSE
Prunella	SELF-HEAL
Pulicaria	FLEA-BANE
Pulmonaria	LUNGWORT
Pulsatilla	PASQUE-FLOWER

pulse	CALAVANCE, CARAVANCE	resinous plant	STYRAX
	(*see separate entry*)	rest-harrow	LICORICE, LIQUORICE
Punica	POMEGRANATE		RASTIBOW
purple		Resurrection plant	ROSE OF JERICHO
—heart	SETCREASEA	Retama	SPANISH BROOM
—loosestrife	KNOTWEED	Rhamnus	BUCKTHORN
	WILLOW-WEED	rhapontic	RHUBARB
	LONG-PURPLES, LYTHRUM	Rheinberry/Rhineberry	BUCKTHORN
—medick	LUCERN(E)	Rheum	RHUBARB
—orchis	LONG-PURPLES	rhododaphne	OLEANDER
—passion vine	VYNURA	rhododendron	ALPINE ROSE, AZALEA
purslane	PORTULACA		ROSE-BAY
Puschkinia	STRIPED SQUILL	Rhoeo	BOAT LILY
pyracanth(a)	FIRETHORN		MOSES IN THE CRADLE
Pyrethrum	FEVERFEW	Rhoicissus	CAPE GRAPE, GRAPE IVY
Pyrola	WINTERGREEN		MERMAID VINE
queen-of-the-meadow(s)	MEADOW-SWEET	rhubarb	RHAPONTIC, RHEUM
quillwort	ISOETES	Rhus	SUMACH
quinsy-berry	BLACKCURRANT	ribbon plant	DRACAENA
rabbit tracks	MARANTA	Ribes	BLACK CURRANT, GOOSEBERRY
radish	RAPHANUS		RED CURRANT
ragged		ribgrass	PLANTAIN
—lady	NIGELLA	ribwort(-plaintain)	PLANTAGO
—robin	CAMPION, CUCKOO-FLOWER	Riccia	LIVERWORT
	WILD-WILLIAMS	Richardia	LILY OF THE NILE
rag		Ricinus	CASTOR-OIL PLANT
—weed	AMBROSIA, RAGWORT, SENECIO	roadside weed	HEDGE-MUSTARD
—wort	AMROSIA, RAGWEED		HEDGE-PARSLEY, SILVERWEED
	SENECIO, TANSY	roast-beef plant	FETID IRIS
rainbow star	CRYPTANTHUS	Rochea	CRASSULA
rampion	BELL-FLOWER	rock	
ramsons	WILD GARLIC	—brake	PARSLEY-FERN
Ranunculus	BUTTERCUP, SPEARWORT	—cress	ARABIS, AUBRIET(I)A
Rapa	SUGAR-BEET		WALL-CRESS
rape	NAVEW	—rose	CISTUS, HELIANTHEMUM
Raphanus	RADISH	rocket	DAME VIOLET, HESPERIS
rastibow	REST-HARROW	roe-blackberry	ROEBUCK-BERRY
rattlesnake plant	MARANTA		STONE-BRAMBLE
rayless mayweed	PINEAPPLE-WEED	roebuck-berry	ROE-BLACKBERRY
reate	WATER-CROWFOOT		STONE-BRAMBLE
Rechsteineria	CARDINAL FLOWER	rose	
red		—campion	LYCHNIS
—currant	RIBES	—laurel	OLEANDER
—ivy	HEMIGRAPHIS	—mallow	HIBISCUS, HOLLYHOCK
—rattle	MARSH LOUSEWORT	—of	
—root	CEANOTHUS	Jericho	RESURRECTION PLANT
—valerian	CENTRANTHUS	Sharon	HYPERICUM
	SPUR VALERIAN	—root	STONECROP
red-hot		rosebay (laurel)	OLEANDER
—catstail	ACALYPHA		RHODODENDRON
—hot poker	KNIPHOFIA, TORCH-LILY	—willow herb	SLINKWEED
	TRITOMA	Rubia	MADDER
reed-mace	BULRUSH, CAT'S-TAIL, TYPHA	rubber plant	FICUS
Reseda	DYER'S-ROCKET, DYER'S-WELD	Rudbeckia	CONEFLOWER
	DYER'S-YELLOWWEED	rue	HERB-(OF)-GRACE
	MIGNONETTE		HERB-OF-REPENTANCE

Ruellia	ACANTHUS, MANY-ROOT
Rumex	DOCK, SORREL
rupturewort	HERNIARIA
Ruscus	BUTCHER'S-BROOM
rutabaga	SWEDISH TURNIP
Saccharum	SUGAR-CANE
sacred lotus	NELUMBIUM, NELUMBO
	PADMA
safflower	BASTARD SAFFRON
saffron	CROCUS
sage	CLARY, SALVIA
Sagina	KNOTTED PEARLWORT
	KNOTTED SPURREY, PEARLWORT
Sagittaria	ARROW-HEAD
sainfoin	COCKSCOMB
Saint	
—Barbara's cress	YELLOW ROCKET
—Barnaby's thistle	KNAPWEED
—Bernard's lily	CHLOROPHYTUM
	SPIDER PLANT
—John's wort	AARON'S BEARD
	HYPERICUM, PARKLEAVES
	TUTSAN
—Patrick's cabbage	LONDON PRIDE
—Peter's wort	HYPERICUM
Saintpaulia	AFRICAN VIOLET
salad	
—herb	PURSLANE, PURSLAIN
—plant	CUCUMBER, LETTUCE, LOVAGE
	RADISH, ROCKET, WATER-CRESS
salfern	GROMWELL
Salicornia	GLASSWORT, MARSH-SAMPHIRE
	SALTWORT
saligot	WATER-CHESTNUT
sallow-thorn	SEA-BUCKTHORN
Salpiglossis	PAINTED TONGUE
salsify	GOAT'S-BEARD
	OYSTER-PLANT
Salsola	GLASSWORT, SALTWORT
salt	
—marsh plant	SEA-BLITE
	SEA-LAVENDER, STATICE
—wort	PRICKLY SAMPHIRE
	SALICORNIA, SALSOLA
Salvadora	MUSTARD-TREE
salvia	SAGE
Salvinia	WATER-FERN
samp(h)ire	CRITHMUM
sand	
—spurrey	SPERGULARIA
—wort	ARENARIA, SEA PURSLANE
Sansevieria	BOWSTRING-HEMP
	MOTHER-IN-LAW'S TONGUE
	SNAKE PLANT
Santolina	LAVENDER-COTTON
Sapindus	SOAP-BERRY

Sapium	TALLOW-TREE
Saponaria	SOAP-ROOT, SOAPWORT
Sarcostemma	SOMA
Sarracenia	SIDE-SADDLE FLOWER
sarrasin	BUCKWHEAT
Saussurea	SAW-WORT
Savoy	WINTER CABBAGE
saw-wort	SAUSSUREA, SERRATULA
saxifrage	AARON'S BEARD
	BISHOP'S CAP, STONE-BREAK
scabious	DEVIL'S-BIT
	PINCUSHION FLOWER
scammony	ANATOLIAN CONVOLVULUS
Scandix	SHEPHERD'S NEEDLE
	VENUS'S COMB
Scarborough lily	VALLOTA
scarlet	
—pimpernel	SHEPHERD'S GLASS
	WINK-O-PEEP
—runner	KIDNEY-BEAN
scentless mignonette	DYER'S-ROCKET
	WELD
Schefflera	UMBRELLA TREE
Schizanthus	BUTTERFLY FLOWER
	POOR MAN'S ORCHID
Schizostylis	KAFFIR LILY
Scilla	BLUEBELL, SQUILL
	WOOD-HYACINTH
Scindapsus	DEVIL'S IVY, GOLDEN POTHOS
	SILVER VINE
Scirpus	CLUB-RUSH
scorpion-grass	FORGET-ME-NOT
scorzonera	BLACK SALSIFY
Scotch	
—bluebell	HAREBELL
—rose	BURNET-ROSE
—thistle	COTTON THISTLE
scouring rush	DUTCH RUSH
Scrophularia	FIGWORT
scurvy-grass	HORSE-RADISH
Scutellaria	SKULLCAP
sea	
—buckthorn	SALLOW-THORN
—burdock	CLOTBUR, XANTHIUM
—gilliflower	THRIFT
—grape	EPHEDRA, GLASSWORT
	GULFWEED
—heath	FRANKENIA
—holly	ERINGO, ERYNGO
—lavender	PLUMBAGO, STATICE
—milkwort	GLAUX
—pink	ARMERIA
	LADY'S PINCUSHION
	PLUMBAGO, THRIFT
—purslane	SANDWORT
—rocket	CAKILE

seaside plants	CORRIGIOLA
	ENTEROMORPHA, FRANKENIA
	GLASSWRACK, MARRAM-GRASS
	SEA-COLEWORT, SEA-HEATH
	SEA-GILLIFLOWER, SEA-GRASS
	SEA-KALE, SEA-ORACH(E)
	SEA-REED, STRAPWORT, THRIFT
—shrubs	SEA-BUCKTHORN
	TAMARISK
sedge	CAREX, CLUB-RUSH, SPIKE-RUSH
—type	XYRIS
Sedum	STONECROP, WALL-PEPPER
Selaginella	CREEPING MOSS
	PEACOCK FERN
self-heal	BRUNELLA, PRUNELLA
Sempervivum	HOUSE-LEEK
Senebiera	CORONOPUS, SWINE'S-CRESS
Senecio	CAPE IVY, CINERARIA
	GROUNDSEL, RAGWEED
	RAGWORT
sengreen	HOUSE-LEEK
senna	CASSIA
senvy	MUSTARD
sept-foil	POTENTILLA, TORMENTIL
Serratula	SAW-WORT
sesame	BENNIE, BENN(I)
	TEEL, TIL
Seseli	MEADOW-SAXIFRAGE
Setcreasea	PURPLE HEART
setterwort	STINKING HELLEBORE
setwall	CETYWALL, SETUALE
	VALERIAN
shadbush	AMELANCHIER
shal(l)ot	ALLIUM, ESCHALOT
shamrock	LESSER YELLOW TREFOIL
Shasta daisy	(DWARF) MARGUERITE
sheep's	
—bit	JASIONE, SHEEP'S SCABIOUS
—scabious	JASIONE
shepherd's	
—club	HAG-TAPER, (GREAT) MULLEIN
—cress	TEESDALIA
—glass	SCARLET PIMPERNEL
—myrtle	BUTCHER'S BROOM
—needle	SCANDIX, VENUS'S COMB
—purse	CAPSELLA
—rod	SMALL TEASEL
Sherardia	FIELD MADDER
shield fern	ASPIDIUM
shore-weed	LITORELLA
showy flowers	SILENE, STRELITZIA
shrimp plant	BELOPERONE
shrubs	(see separate entry)
shrubby plant	HYDRANGEA
side-saddle flower	SARRACENIA
Siderasis	BROWN SPIDERWORT

silk	
—grass	AGAVE, KARATUS, YUCCA
—oak	GREVILLEA
silver	
—net leaf	FITTONIA
—vine	SCINDAPSUS
—weed	GOOSE-GRASS
	POTENTILLA, TANSY
single chrysanthemum	MARGUERITE
Sinningia	GLOXINIA
Sison	STONEWORT
Sium	SKIRRET, WATER-PARSNIP
skirret	SIUM, WATER-PARSNIP
skullcap	SCUTELLARIA
skunk-cabbage	SYMPLOCARPUS
slinkweed	ROSE-BAY WILLOW HERB
slipper	
—flower	CALCEOLARIA
—wort	CALCEOLARIA
sloe	BULLACE
small teasel	SHEPHERD'S ROD
smallage	WILD CELERY
smart-weed	WATERPEPPER
Smithiantha	TEMPLE BELLS
snail	MEDICK
snake	
—plant	SANSEVIERIA
—root	ARISTOLOCHIA
	BISTORT, MILKWORT
—skin plant	FITTONIA
—weed	ADDER('S) WORT, BISTORT
snake's-head	FRITILLARY
snapdragon	ANTIRRHINUM, FROG'S-MOUTH
sneeze	
—weed	HELENIUM
—wort	WHITE HELLEBORE, YARROW
snow	
—ball-tree	GUELDER-ROSE
—berry	SYMPHORICARPUS
—drop	GALANTHUS
—flake	LEUCOJUM
—in-summer	MOUSE-EAR CHICKWEED
soap	
—berry	SAPINDUS
—root	GYPSOPHILA, SAPONARIA
—wort	SAPONARIA
Solanum	BITTERSWEET, POTATO
	(WOODY) NIGHTSHADE
	WINTER CHERRY
Solidago	GOLDENROD
Solomon's seal	POLYGONATUM
soma	SARCOSTEMMA
Sonchus	SOW-THISTLE
sops-in-wine	CLOVE-PINK
sorrel	DOCK, RUMEX
southernwood	BOY'S LOVE

sow	
—bread	CYCLAMEN
—thistle	SONCHUS
Spanish	
—bayonet	YUCCA
—broom	RETAMA, SPART(IUM)
—cress	PEPPERWORT
Sparaxis	HARLEQUIN FLOWER
Sparganium	BUR-REED
Sparmannia	HOUSE LIME
spart(ium)	SPANISH BROOM
Spathiphyllum	PEACE LILY
spear	
—thistle	BUR-THISTLE
	CIRSIUM, CNICUS
—wort	RANUNCULUS
speckled carnation	PICOTEE
Specularia	VENUS'S LOOKING-GLASS
speedwell	BIRD'S-EYE
	FLUELLIN, VERONICA
Spergula	SPURREY
Spergularia	SANDWORT-SPURREY
sphagnum	BOG-MOSS
spider	
—plant	CHLOROPHYTUM
	ST BERNARD'S LILY
—wort	TRADESCANTIA
Spigelia	CAROLINA PINK
	INDIAN PINK
spignel	BALDMONEY, MEUM
	SPICKNEL
spike-rush	HELIOCHARIS
spikenard	NARD
spinach	SPINAGE
spinage	SPINACH
spineless thistle	KNAPWEED
spiny-leaved fern	HOLLY-FERN
Spiraea	DROP-WORT
	MEADOW-SWEET
spleenwort	ASPLENIUM, MAIDENHAIR
	WALL-RUE
split leaf Philodendron	MONSTERA
spotted orchis	WAKE-ROBIN
spring	
—beauty	CLAYTONIA
—start flower	TRITELIA
—wort	MANDRAKE
spur valerian	CENTRANTHUS
	RED VALERIAN
spurge	ALEURITES, EUPHORBIA
	POINSETTIA, WARTWEED
—laurel	DAPHNE
spurrey	SPERGULA
squash	CUCURBITA, GOURD
squill	SCILLA
squinancy-wort	QUINSY-WORT

Stachys	BETONY, BISHOP'S WORT
	LAMB'S EAR
staghorn	
—fern	PLATYCERIUM
—moss	CLUB-MOSS
Stapelia	CARRION-FLOWER
star	
—fish plant	CRYPTANTHUS
—light	ASTROPHEL, PENTHIA
—of Bethlehem	CAMPANULA
	ORNITHOGALUM
—of-the-earth	BUCK'S-HORN PLANTAIN
—thistle	CENTAUREA
—wort	ASTER, STITCHWORT
starch hyacinth	GRAPE HYACINTH
	MUSCARI
Statice	SEA-LAVENDER
stavesacre	DELPHINIUM, LARKSPUR
Stellaria	CHICKWEED
Stephanotis	MADAGASCAR JASMINE
stinking	
—camomile	MAYWEED
—crane's bill	HERB-ROBERT
—hellebore	SETTERWORT
stitchwort	ASTER, CHICKWEED
	STARWORT
stock	MATTHIOLA
Stoke's aster	STOKESIA
stone	
—bramble	ROEBUCK-BERRY
	ROE-BLACKBERRY
—break	SAXIFRAGE
—crop	ORPIN(E), ROSE-ROOT
	SEDUM, WALL-PEPPER
	WALL-WORT, WORM-GRASS
—wort	SISON
stork's-bill	ERODIUM, PELARGONIUM
strapwort	CORRIGIOLA
Stratiotes	WATER-SOLDIER
strawberry	FRAGARIA
—geranium	MOTHER OF THOUSANDS
—tomato	BLADDER-CHERRY
Strelitzia	BIRD OF PARADISE
Streptocarpus	CAPE PRIMROSE
striped squill	PUSCHKINIA
Strophanthus	PERIWINKLE
sub-Alpine	SPIGNEL
succory	CHICORY
sugar	
—bean	LIMA BEAN
—beet	RAPA
—cane	SACCHARUM
—grass	SWEET-SORGHUM
sumach	RHUS
sun	
—dew	DROSERA

—facing plant	TURNSOLE
—flower	HELIANTHUS
type	RUDBECKIA
—rose	HELIANTHEMUM
—spurge	EUPHORBIA
swallow-wort	ASCLEPIAS, CELANDINE
	CYNANCHUM
	GREATER CELANDINE
Swedish	
—ivy	PLECTRANTHUS
—turnip	RUTABAGA
sweet	
—bay	LAUREL, LAURUS
—brier	EGLANTINE
—Cicely	CHERVIL, MYRRHIS
—corn	MAIZE
—flag	ACORUS, CALAMUS
—gale	BOG-MYRTLE, MYRICA
	SWEET-WILLOW
—pea	LATHYRUS, VETCHLING
—scabious	MOURNING-BRIDE
—sorghum	SUGAR-GRASS
—William	DIANTHUS
—willow	BOG-MYRTLE, SWEET-GALE
sweetheart plant	PHILODENDRON
swine's	
—cress	CORONOPUS, SENEBIERA
	WART-CRESS
—succory	ARNOSERIS
Swiss cheese plant	MONSTERA
Symphoricarpus	SNOW-BERRY
Symphytum	BORAGE, COMFREY
Symplocarpus	SKUNK-CABBAGE
Syngonium	ARROWHEAD VINE
	GOOSEFOOT PLANT
	NEPHTHYTIS
Syrian rue	HARMALA, HARMEL
Tagetes	AFRICAN MARIGOLD
	FRENCH MARIGOLD
tallow-tree	SAPIUM
Tanacetum	TANSY
tansy	RAGWORT, SILVERWEED
	TANACETUM, YARROW
Taraxacum	DANDELION
tare	DARNEL, VETCH
taro	COLOCASIA
tarragon	STARAGEN
teasels	DIPSACUS
teddy bear vine	CYANOTIS
teel	SESAME, TIL
Teesdalia	SHEPHERD'S CRESS
telegraph-plant	DESMODIUM
temple bells	SMITHIANTHA
Tetrastigma	CHESTNUT VINE
Thalictrum	MEADOW-RUE
Thapsia	LASERWORT

thin-leaved ferns	FILMY FERNS
thistle	CARLINA, CNICUS
thorn-apple	DATURA
thrift	ARMERIA, SEA-GILLIFLOWER
	SEA-PINK
throatwort	CAMPANULA
Thunbergia	BLACK-EYED SUSAN
thyme	CALAMINT, THYMUS
Ti plant	CORDYLINE
tiger-flower	TIGRIDIA
Tigridia	FERRARIA
til	SESAME, TEEL
toad	
—flax	AARON'S BEARD
	BACON AND EGGS, FLUELLIN
	LINARIA, MOTHER OF MILLIONS
—grass	JUNCUS, TOAD-RUSH
tobacco	NICOTIANA
Tolmiea	PIGGYBACK PLANT
tomato	LOVE-APPLE, WOLF'S-PEACH
toothwort	CARDAMINE, CORAL-ROOT
	DENTARIA, LATHRAEA
torch	
—lily	KNIPHOFIA
	RED-HOT POKER, TRITOMA
—thistle	CACTUS, CEREUS
tormentil	POTENTILLA, SEPT-FOIL
tortoise-plant	ELEPHANT'S FOOT
touch-me-not	BALSAM, MIMOSA
Tradescantia	INCH PLANT
	SPIDERWORT, WANDERING JEW
tragacanth	ASTRAGALUS
traveller's joy	CLEMATIS
	OLD MAN'S BEARD
	VIRGIN'S-BOWER
treacle-mustard	ERYSIMUM
tree	
—mallow	LAVATERA, VELVET-LEAF
—peony	MOUTAN
trees	(see separate entry)
Treucrium	WOOD-GERMANDER
Trifolium	CLOVER
Trigonella	FENUGREEK
Tritelia	SPRING STAR FLOWERS
Triticum	WHEAT
Tritoma	KNIPHOFIA, RED-HOT POKER
	TORCH-LILY
Tritonia	MONTBRETIA
Trollius	GLOBE-FLOWER
Tropaeolum	NASTURTIUM
true-love	HERB-PARIS
trumpet flower	INCARVILLEA
tuberose	POLIANTHES
Turk's cap	MARTAGON LILY
tutsan	PARKLEAVES, ST JOHN'S WORT
tway-blade	LISTERA

two-flowered		wall	
daffodil	PRIMROSE PEERLESS	—cress	ARABIS, ROCK-CRESS
Typha	REED-MACE	—flower	CHEIRANTHUS, CHEIRINIA
Ulex	GORSE		GILLYFLOWER, JILLY-FLOWER
umbrella		—mustard	DIPLOTAXIS, WALL-ROCKET
—plant	CYPERUS	—pepper	SEDUM, STONECROP
—tree	SCHEFFLERA		WALL-WORT
urn plant	AECHMEA	—plant	THALE-CRESS
Urtica	NETTLE	—rocket	DIPLOTAXIS, WALL-MUSTARD
Utricularia	BLADDERWORT	—rue	SPLEENWORT
uva-ursi	BEAR-BERRY	—wort	DANE'S BLOOD, DANEWORT
Vaccinium	COWBERRY, CRANBERRY		DWARF ELDER, PELLITORY
	WHORTLEBERRY		STONE-CROP, WALL-PEPPER
valerian	ALL-HEAL, CENTRANTHUS	wandering Jew	TRADESCANTIA, ZEBRINA
	CETYWALL, SETUALE, SETWALL	wart	
Vallota	SCARBOROUGH LILY	—cress	SWINE'S-CRESS
variegated grass	GARDENER'S GARTERS	—weed	LICHEN, SPURGE, WARTWORT
vase plant	AECHMEA	water	
Veltheimia	FOREST LILY	—chestnut	HORN-NUT, SALIGOT
velvet plant	VYNURA	—crowfoot	REATE
Venus's		—dropwort	OENANTHE
—comb	SCANDIX, SHEPHERD'S NEEDLE	—fern	PILLWORT, SALVINIA
—fly-trap	DIONAEA	—flag	YELLOW IRIS
—looking-glass	SPECULARIA	—grass	REED
Veratrum	WHITE HELLEBORE	—hemlock	CICUTA, COWBANE
Verbascum	MULLEIN		OENANTHE
Verbena	VERVAIN	—hyacinth	EICHHORNIA
Veronica	SPEEDWELL	—leaf	HYDROPHYLLUM
vervain	LANTANA, VERBENA	—lemon	PASSION-FLOWER
vetch	FITCH, TARE, VICIA	—lily	CANDOCK, NELUMBIUM
vetchling	LATHYRUS, SWEET-PEA		NELUMBO, NENUPHAR
Viburnum	GUELDER-ROSE		NUPHAR, NYMPHAEA
Vicia	VETCH	—milfoil	MYRIOPHYLLUM
Vinca	PERIWINKLE	—parsnip	SIUM, SKIRRET
Viola	PANSY, VIOLET	—pepper	SMART-WEED
violet	VIOLA	—pimpernel	BROOKWEED
viper's		—plant	ANACHARIS, HORN-WORT
—bugloss	BLUE WEED		HYDROPHYTE, MYRIOPHYLLUM
	BLUE THISTLE, ECHIUM		PIPEWORT
—grass	BLACK SALSIFY	—plantain	ALISMA
virgin's bower	CLEMATIS	—rice	ZIZANIA
	TRAVELLER'S-JOY	—soldier	STRATIOTES
Virginia		—speedwell	BROOKLIME
—creeper	AMPELOPSIS, WOODBIND	—starwort	CALLITRICHE
	WOODBINE	—thyme	CANADIAN PONDWEED
—stock	MALCOMIA	—violet	HOTTONIA
Viscum	MISTLETOE	—weed	ANACHARIS
Vitis	GRAPE-VINE	waterside plant	PURPLE LOOSESTRIFE
Vreisia	FLAMING SWORD	wax	
Vynura	PURPLE PASSION VINE	—myrtle	CANDLE-BERRY
	VELVET PLANT	—plant	HOYA
wahoo	BURNING BUSH	waybread	PLANTAIN
wake-robin	ARUM, CUCKOO-PINT	weeping fig	FICUS
	FRIAR'S COWL	weld	DYER'S ROCKET, MIGNONETTE
	LORDS AND LADIES	Welsh onion	CIBOL
	SPOTTED ORCHIS	wheat	TRITICUM

whin	FINGERS AND THUMBS
	FURZE, GORSE, ULEX
white	
—bottle	BLADDER CAMPION
—bryony	MANDRAKE
—clover	DUTCH CLOVER, SHAMROCK
—hellebore	SNEEZEWORT, VERATRUM
—lily	MADONNA-LILY
whitlow-grass	PARONYCHIA
	WHITLOW-WORT
whortleberry	BILBERRY, COWBERRY
	HUCKLEBERRY, HURTLEBERRY
	VACCINIUM
wild	
—aster	MICHAELMAS-DAISY
—celery	MARSHWORT, SMALLAGE
—chrysanthemum	CORN-MARIGOLD
	OX-EYE
—crab-apple	WILDING
—fig	CAPRIFIG, GOAT-FIG
—flax	LINUM, PURGING FLAX
—garlic	RAMSONS
—geranium	CRANESBILL
—hyacinth	CULVER-KEY
—marjoram	ORIGAN(E)
—mint	HORSEMINT
—mustard	CHARLOCK
—olive	OLEASTER
—pansy	KISS-ME
—pink	MAIDEN PINK
—rice	ZIZANIA
—rose	DOG-ROSE, EGLANTINE
	SWEET-BRIAR, SWEET-BRIER
—strawberry	POTENTILLA
—Swedish turnip	NAVEW
—Williams	RAGGED-ROBIN
willow	
—herb	CHAMAENERION, EPILOBIUM
	FIRE-WEED, ROSE-BAY
—weed	KNOTWEED
	PURPLE LOOSESTRIFE
wind-flower	(WOOOD-)ANEMONE
wink-o-peep	SCARLET PIMPERNEL
winter	
—aconite	ERANTHIS
	WINTER HELLEBORE
—cabbage	SAVOY
—cherry	CHINESE LANTERN PLANT
	PHYSALIS, SOLANUM
—cress	BARBAREA, YELLOW-ROCKET
—green	CHIMAPHILA, GAULTHERIA
	MONOTROPA, PYROLA
witches'-thimble	FOXGLOVE
with	
—long spikes	LUPIN(E)
—red bracts	POINSETTIA

—ribbed leaves	HOSTA, PLANTAIN
witloof	CHICORY
woad	ISATIS
wolf's	
—bane	ACONITE, FRIAR'S CAP
	MONKSHOOD
—peach	TOMATO
wood	
—anemone	WIND-FLOWER
—bind/woodbine	HONEYSUCKLE
	VIRGINIA CREEPER
—germander	TREUCRIUM
—hyacinth	BLUEBELL, SCILLA
—land plant	SANICLE
—loosestrife	YELLOW PIMPERNEL
—rush	LUZULA
—ruff	QUINSY-WORT
	SQUINANCY-WORT
—sorrel	OXALIS
woody-nightshade	BITTERSWEET, SOLANUM
worm-grass	PINKROOT, STONECROP
wormwood	ARTEMISIA, MUGWORT
	SOUTHERNWOOD
Xanthium	CLOTBUR, SEA-BURDOCK
Xeranthemum	EVERLASTINGS
yarr	CORN SPURREY
yarrow	ACHILLEA, MILFOIL
	NOSE-BLEED, PELLITORY
	SNEEZEWORT, TANSY
yellow	
—centaury	GENTIAN, YELLOW-WORT
—clover	HOP-TREFOIL
—flowered narcissus	DAFFODIL
—iris	WATER-FLAG
—jasmine	GELSEMIUM
—loosestrife	LYSIMACHIA
—pimpernel	(WOOD) LOOSESTRIFE
—poppy	WELSH POPPY
—rattle	COCKSCOMB
—rocket	BARBAREA
	ST BARBARA'S CRESS
	WINTER-CRESS
—root	GOLDEN-SEAL
—weed	COMMON RAGWORT, GROUNDSEL
—wort	GENTIAN, YELLOW CENTAURY
yuc(c)a	ADAM'S NEEDLE, CASSAVA
	SILK-GRASS, SPANISH BAYONET
	SPANISH DAGGER
Zantedeschia	ARUM-LILY, CALLA LILY
	LILY OF THE NILE
Zea	INDIAN CORN, MAIZE
zebra plant	AECHMEA, APHELANDRA
	MARANTA
Zebrina	INCH PLANT, WANDERING JEW
Zizania	CANADA RICE, INDIAN RICE
zoster	EELGRASS, GRASSWRACK

plant diseases
  including: pests

corky scab	OEDEMA
diseases	
—affecting	
apple trees	APPLE BLOSSOM WILT
	BROWN ROT, CANKER
	CORAL SPOT, LEAF SCORCH
	MILDEW, SCAB, WITHER TIP
beans	POD CANKER, RUST
cabbage	ANBURY, BLACK ROT
	CLUB ROOT
cereals	SMUT
citrus, etc	LEAF SPOT
currant bushes	BIG BUD, CORAL SPOT
	LEAF SPOT
cuttings	DAMPING OFF, DIE-BACK
fruit trees	AMERICAN BLIGHT
	CROWN GALL, DIE-BACK
	WOOLLY APHIS
onions	MILDEW, SMUT
peach trees	PEACH-LEAF BLISTER
	PEACH-LEAF CURL
palms, etc	ANTHRACNOSE
pear trees	PEAR LEAF BLISTER
	SCAB
plum trees	PLUM REE RUST, SCAB
	SILVER LEAF
potatoes	BLIGHT, (CORKY) SCAB,
	LEAF ROLL, POTATO MOSAIC
	POWDERY SCAB
	STORAGE DISEASE
	WART DISEASE
roses	BLACK SPOT, CROWN GALL
	DIE-BACK, MILDEW, RUST
rye	ERGOT
seedlings	DAMPING OFF, DIE-BACK
soft-leaved plants	BLACKLEG
	BOTRYTIS, RUST
trees	DUTCH ELM DISEASE
	HONEY FUNGUS
turnip	ANBURY, CLUB ROOT
various plants	BRAND, WILT
wheat	PUCCINIA, RUST
—oedema	CORKY SCAB
—producing	
anbury	SLIME FUNGUS
black	
—powder	SOOTY MOULD
—spots	ANTHRACNOSE
brown	
—spores	RUST
—spots	LEAF SPOT
cork-like growths	CORKY SCAB
	OEDEMA
grey mould	BOTRYTIS

rotten parts	BLACKLEG, CROWN ROT
	ROOT ROT, STEM ROT
	TUBER ROT
white powder	(POWDER)MILDEW
—rust fungus	UREDO
pests	
—affecting	
apple trees	APHIS
	APPLE BLOSSOM WEEVIL
	BARK BORER, CAPSID BUG
	CODLIN MOTH, LACKEY MOTH
	(OYSTER-SHELL)SCALE
	RED-FOOTED BEETLE, RED SPIDER
	SAWFLY, SMALL ERMINE MOTH
	SUCKER, TRUNK BORER
all plants	APHIS, CATERPILLAR
	EARWIG
asparagus	BEETLE FLY
beans	AMERICAN BEETLE, APHIS
	BEAN BEETLE, BEAN WEEVIL
	SPANISH BEETLE
	THRIP
bulbs	BULB MITE
cabbage	CABBAGE MOTH
	CABBAGE ROOT FLY
	CABBAGE WHITE BUTTERFLY
	DIAMOND-BLACK MOTH
carrots	CARROT FLY
celery	CELERY (STEM) FLY
	LEAF MINER
cherry trees	CHERRY MOTH SCAB
	CHERRY SAWFLY
	LACKEY MOTH, SLUGWORM
currant bushes	CURRANT MOTH
	MAGPIE MOTH, SAWFLY
	SCALE
cyclamen, etc	CYCLAMEN MITE
flowers	EARWIG, LEAF MINER
fruit trees	BROWN-TAIL MOTH
	CHAFER BEETLE
	GOAT MOTH
	LEAF-ROLLER MOTH
	LEAF TORTRIX
	SHOT-BORER BEETLE
	VAPOURER MOTH
	WINTER MOTH
	WOOD LEOPARD MOTH
gooseberry bushes	GOOSEBERRY MOTH
	MAGPIE MOTH
	SAWFLY
grape vines	BLACK WEEVIL
	MEALY BUG, VINE WEEVIL
greenfly	APHIS(APHIDES)
greenhouse plants	GHOST FLY
	WHITE FLY
nut trees	NUT SAWFLY

onions	ONION FLY
parsnips	LEAF MINER
pear trees	BARK BORER
	LACKEY MOTH, MIDGE
	(OYSTER-SHELL)SCALE
	PITH MOTH
	RED-FOOTED BEETLE
	RED SPIDER, SAWFLY
	SMALL ERMINE MOTH
	SOCIAL PEAR MOTH
	TRUNK BORER
peas	PEA BEETLE, THRIP
pines	PINE BEAUTY (MOTH)
plum trees	BARK BORER
	LACKEY MOTH, MAGPIE MOTH
	MOTTLED UMBER MOTH
	(OYSTER-SHELL)SCALE
	SMALL ERMINE MOTH
	TRUNK BORER
potatoes	ROSY RUST MOTH
raspberries	CLAY-COLOURED WEEVIL
	RASPBERRY BEETLE
	RASPBERRY MOTH
	RASPBERRY SHOOT BORER
	RASPBERRY WEEVIL
roots	EELWORM, FUNGUS
	VINE WEEVIL
roses	GALL-FLY, GOLDEN CHAFER
	LEAF-CUTTER BEE
	ROSE BEETLE
	ROSE MAGGOT, ROSE TORTRIX
trees	GOAT MOTH, LACKEY MOTH
	LEAF-ROLLER MOTH
	MARCH MOTH, SHOT-BORER BEETLE
	SWIFT MOTH
	TORTRIX MOTH
turnips	SAWFLY, TURNIP BEETLE
	TURNIP FLY, TURNIP MOTH
	YELLOW UNDERWING MOTH
various plants	CENTIPEDE, EARWIG
	LEATHER-JACKET, MILLIPEDE
	SLUG, SNAIL, SWIFT MOTH
	WOODLOUSE
—aphis	GREENFLY
—brown, disc-shaped	SCALE
—causing	
fluffy patches	MEALY BUG
pale patches	VIRUS
—sap-sucker	APHIS, RED SPIDER MITE
	WHITE FLY
—small black flies	THRIPS

poetic
old words used by various poets
not covered elsewhere:
act

—like a fugleman	FUGLE

—noisily	OBSTREPERATE
active	SPRINGE
accomplished	ARCH
adopt native ways	GO FANTI
adorn	BEDIGHT
affording redress	REDRESSIVE
again	AGEN
against	GAINST
alabaster	ALABLASTER
appeal	PROVOKE
are	ART
array	BEDIGHT
art of painting	PEINTURE
assembly	DIVAN
attack in the rear	REAR
attentive	INTENTIVE, LISTFUL
auxiliary power	UNDER-POWER
avalanche	LAUWINE
avowed lover	PROTESTANT
bank	RIVAGE
base	GROUNDLING
be	
—flooded	FLOAT
—languorous	SWOON
—non-existent	UNBE
—soaked in blood	WELTER
beautiful	SHEEN
beneath	NEATH
bestially	BEASTILY
betray	CONFESS
bevel-wheel	BEDEL
bird's love-song	VALENTINE
bittern	BITTO(U)R, BITTUR
black	SABLE
—tincture	BUFO
blushing girl	BLUSHET
board	BO(O)RD, BORDE
body of	
—knights-errant	KNIGHTHOOD ERRANT
—water	WAVE
boiled fat beef	GAG
boorish	SWAINISH
border	MARGENT
born under unpropitious	
star	EVIL-STARRED
bowstring	NERVE
brainy	INTELLECTED
break in pieces	TO-BREAK
bright	SHEEN
capable of being clothed	HABILABLE
carry a message	MESSAGE
cease to be	UNBE
chariot	CAR
cicada	BALM-CRICKET
city urchin	TOWNSKIP
clad in purple	PORPORATE

close-fitting	SUCCINCT
clumsy	UNHEPPEN
collection of wagons	WAGONAGE
compelled	FAIN
complaining	MUTTERATION
content for want of better	FAIN
contrary of wealth or well-being	ILLTH
corpse	CORSE
cottage	COT
council	DIVAN
current	TIDE
curse	MALISON
daffodil	DAFFADOWNDILLY
	DAFFODILLY
dash	VIRETOT
day other than birthday	UNBIRTHDAY
dead-leaf colour	PHILOMOT
decoration of flowers	GARLANDAGE
den of iniquity	DOMDANIEL
denial of right to	
private property	ASPHETERISM
depict in pavement	IMPAVE
deprived of the appearance	
of a prince	DEPRINZED
desolate	WASTEFUL
despondency	DESPOND
detached	UNDIVESTED
did	GAN
discomfit	SHEND
disfavour	DISGUST
disgrace	SHEND
disorderly	RAGMATICAL
disorganise	UNMECHANISE
displeasure	DISGUST
distaste	DISGUST
divulge	UNCONFINE
domain	BOURN(E)
double limerick	TWINER
downcast	DOWN-LOOKED
dreamy	DREAMFUL
drummer	DRAKE
dullness	YAWN
dwelling	BOWER
eager to	FAIN
elicit	SWEEP
embroidered	SET-STITCH'D
empty region of air or water	WILD
emulate	EMULE
enchanted	FATED
enjoyment	PLEASANCE
equip	BEDIGHT
even	EEN
evening	EVE, EVEN
excellent	LUMMY
excess of formality	WIGGERY
face bravely	BIDE

fainting fit	SOUND, SWOUN
fancy	FANGLE
feathery	FLEDGY
field of battle	PLAIN
fiery red gem	PYROPUS
flash of fire or lightning	FIRE-FLAG
	FIRE-FLAUGHT
flourished	ARCH
flow in again	REINFUND
flushed	HECTIC
foaming	SPOOMING
follow	UPFOLLOW
forehead	FRONT
forgetfulness	OBLIVION
fortify	MUNITE
fount(ain)	FONT
fragment	FRUST
fray	FRIDGE
free from yoke	DISYOKE
frisky	WANTON
full of springs	FOUNTFUL
furnish	BEDIGHT
gad	VIRETOT
gay	WANTON
girded up	SUCCINCT
glad	FAIN
glance	ASPECT
gloomy	DARKSOME, DOWN-LOOKED
go native	GO FANTI
good news	EVANGEL
green woodpecker	YAFFINGALE
greet	DOLE
grotto	GROT
ground	MARL
growing luxuriously	WANTON
guardianship	WARDENRY
hall under sea	DOMDANIEL
halloo	HALLALOO
having	
—intellect	INTELLECTED
—the form of a tent	TENTING
heaven	SWERGA
heavenly spirit	GLENDOVEER
heed	HEARKEN
idleness	IDLESSE
illimitable	EXTERMINABLE
illumine	ILLUME
imaginary animal	WHANGAM
immaterial	UNESSENTIAL
impair	EMPERISH
impatient of	RESTLESS
imperfectly formed	UNDERSHAPEN
in	
—another way	ANOTHERGUESS
—strong words	IRON-WORDED
—the dark	DARKLINGS

India	IND	not	
industrious	WORKSOME	—burdensome	UNIMPOSING
inferior	UNDERRATE	—held back	UNWITHHOLDEN
—devil	PUG	—in agreement	UNCONSENTANEOUS
infernal cave	DOMDANIEL	—known	UNWIST
informal evening		—made noisy	UNBEDINNED
party	SMALL-AND-EARLY	obviate	MEET WITH
innkeeper	INNHOLDER	of	
inquiry	INQUIRATION	—another kind	ANOTHERGUESS
instrument		—the eye	VISUAL
—for bending		open	OPE
crossbow	WINDAC, WINDAS	—country	WEALD
—of torture	TRIP-HOOK	overcome by drowsiness	O'ER-DROWSED
intensify	INTENSATE	owl	GLIMMER-GOWK
interpretation	REDE	owlishness	OWLERY
interregnum	INTERREIGN	painted woman	PICT
it seems to me	MESEEMS	palmist	CH(E)IROGRAPHIST
it's	TIS	pamper	POMPEY
joyful	FAIN	paradise	SWERGA
joyous	FRABJOUS	pass tediously (time)	WEAR
kindle	TEEND	pay	SOLDE
knot	GORDIAN	—attention to	HEARKEN
last	DURE	peak	PIQUE
late mint	LATTER-MINT	peasant	SWAIN
level	STROW	perched aloft	UP-PERCHED
light	ILLUME	period of the night	WATCH
like prison	PRISONOUS	piercing	PERCEANT
listen	LIST	place as if in jelly	INJELLY
—to	HEARKEN	place one visits	VISIT
little god	GODLING	please	ARRIDE
look	ASPECT	pleasantness	PLEASANCE
lose colour	UNFLUSH	pleasure	PLEASANCE
love-making	SWAINING	poet	MINSTREL
lover	SWAIN	Poland	SARMATIA
lower sky	UNDERSKY	ponder beforehand	PREPONDERATE
make		postpone	WITHHOLD
—manifest	CONFESS	power of quelling	QUELL
—purring sound	CURR	prayer	BENE
maker of idols	GOD-SMITH	pre-eminence	SOVRANTY
margin	MARGENT	previous king	FOREKING
marked by deeds	DEEDFUL	prodigal	PROFUSER
meadow	MEAD	prow	PRORE
medical	MEDIC	punish	SHEND
melting away	DELIQUIM	pure	UNDROSSY
Milky Way	MILKEN-WAY	put	
moving		—in tune	STRING
—capriciously	WANTON	—to shame	SHEND
—freely	WANTON	rapacity	VULTURISM
mumbling speech	MUMBLEMENT	redeless	UNREADY
music	NOTE	reformed person	REFORMADO
musical instrument	SLUGHORN(E)	reformer	REFORMADO
named	NEMPT	remark following another	SUBJOINDER
nauseous mouthful	GAG	remuneration	SOLDE
necessity	NEEDYHOOD	reprisal	REPRISE
nimble	SPRINGE	reproach	SHEND
north country	NORLAN(D)	retrogression	REGREDIENCE

reveal	CONFESS
rich cake	ROUT-CAKE
rind	RINE
ring	CIRQUE
riotous	RAGMATICAL
riven	RAFT
river(-water)	TIDE
roll like the sea	WELTER
romantic setting	PLAIN
rub	FRIDGE
rue	REW
rush	VIRETOT
rustic	SWAIN
sail	SHEET
savage	SALVAGE
sceptred	SCEPTRY
Scotland	SCOTIA
scramble	SWERVE
sea	FOAM, WAVE
—serpent	ELLOPS
separate	UNCOMBINE
serenade	WAKE
sewing	SEAMSTRESSY
shady retreat	HERBAR
sharp-edged	VORPAL
shining	SHEEN
shiny-pated	GLASSYHEADED
ship	PRORE
shore	RIVAGE
—crab	OCHIDORE
sly trick	UNDER-CRAFT
smooth	SOOTH
smote	SMIT
soft	SOOTH
sorrow-lulling drink or drug	MANDRAGORA, NEPENTHE
spend time	WEAR
spendthrift	PROFUSER
spiritual	AERIE, AERY
state of floating	FLOAT
stately building	DOME
staying in one place	LOCORESTIVE
steep	STEEPY
stick of pipe-clay	PIPE
stomach	LITTLE MARY
strengthen	MUNITE
study of artillery	PYROBALLOGY
subconscious thirst	UNDERTHIRST
subside	SWOON
summons to war	WAR-NOTE
supporter	UNDERSTANDER
surpassing	FRABJOUS
swarm	SWERVE
swell of the sea	WALLOW
sword	VORPAL
swung	SWANG
tear	RANCH
tears	RHEUM
that	YON
—which underlies surface	UNDER-COUNTENANCE
the thing you know of	YON
thirsty	ADRY
thorough-going	UNENDING
those	YON
tie-up	GORDIAN
tip-cat	TIP-CHEESE
trilled high	UPTRILLED
tuft	TUZZ
turquoise	TURKIS
unaccustomed	UNWONT
undertaken	UNDERTA'EN
undutiful	UNDUTEOUS
unfortunate	EVIL-STARRED
unfrequented	WASTEFUL
unfriendly	INIMICITIOUS
unhomelike	UNDOMESTIC
uninhabited	WASTEFUL
unrestrained	UNWITHHOLDEN
unwary	UNAWARE
upriseth	UPRIST
using archaic language	TUSHERY
utter poetry	POESY
venturous	VENTROUS
village	VILL
visibility to the mind	VISUALITY
visitor's book	VISITING-BOOK
wagon	WAIN
warrior who cannot be wounded with metals	WARLOCK
winded	WIN'T
windlass for crossbow	WINDAC, WINDAS
window	WINDORE
without being	UNESSENTIAL
wood-sorrel	SHAMROCK
wooded country	WEALD
write bombastically	FUSTIANISE
yesterday evening	YESTREEN
yonder	YON
young man	SWAIN
zealot	ZE(A)LANT

(*see also* **Burns, Milton, old, Scott, Shakespeare, Spenser**)

poets

American	AIKEN, BLACKMUR, BLY BURROUGHS, CORMAN, CORSO CRANE, CREELEY, CUMMINGS DICKINSON(f), DOLITTLE ELIOT, FERLINGHETTI FROST, GINSBERG, HULSENBECK KEROUAC, LINDSAY, LONGFELLOW LOWELL, MACLEISH, MONROE(f)

	MOORE(f), OLSEN, OPPEN, PLATH(f)
	POE, POUND, RANSOM, REXBOTH
	REZNIKOFF, ROBINSON, SANDBERG
	SNYDER, STEVENS, TATE
	WHITMAN, WHITTIER
	WILLIAMS, WINTERS, ZUKOFSKY
Argentinian	BORGES
Australian	BRENNAN, GORDON, MURRAY
	PATTERSON, PORTER
Austrian	RILKE, TRAKL, WERFEL
Brazilian	XISTO
British	AE, AMIS, ARNOLD, AUDEN
	BARNFIELD, BETJEMAN, BLAIR
	BEARDSLEY, BEATTIE, BEERBOHM
	BLAKE, BRETON, BRIDGES
	BRONTE\:, BROOKE, BROWNING
	BROWNING(f), BUNYAN
	BYRON, CAMPION, CAREW
	CHATTERTON, CHAUCER, CIBBER, CLARE
	CLOUGH, CONQUEST, COLERIDGE
	COLLINS, COWLEY, COWPER
	CRABBE, CRASHAW, CRICHTON-SMITH
	DAVIE, DAVIES, DE LA MARE
	DONNE, DOWSON, DRYDEN, DUNNE
	ELIOT, EMPSON, ENRIGHT, EUSDEN
	FENTON, FLECKER, FLINT
	FULLER, GASCOYNE
	GOLDSMITH, GOWER, GRAVES
	GRAY, GUNN, HARRISON, HEANEY
	HENDRY, HENRI, HERBERT, HERRICK
	HOBSBAUM, HODGSON, HOOD, HOPKINS
	HUGHES, JAMES, JENNINGS(f)
	JOHNSON, JONSON, KEATS
	LANDOR, LANGLAND, LARKIN
	LEAR, LEWIS, LOGIE, LOVELACE
	LUCIE-SMITH, MACBETH
	MACNEICE, MARSH
	MARVELL, MASEFIELD, MCGOUGH
	MEREDITH, MEYNELL(f)
	MILTON, MONRO, MORGAN
	MORRIS, NOYES, OWEN
	PAMORE, PATTON, POPE, PYE
	RAINE(f), RALEIGH, REDGROVE
	RICHARDS, ROCHESTER, ROGERS
	ROSENBERG, ROSSETTI, ROSSETTI(f)
	ROWE, SASSOON, SHADWELL
	SHAKESPEARE, SHELLEY, SITWELL
	SKELTON, SMART, SOUTHEY
	SPENDER, SPENSER, STEPHENS
	SUCKLING, SURREY, SWIFT
	SWINBURNE, SYDNEY, SYMONS
	TATE, TENNYSON, THOMAS
	THOMSON, TREECE, VAUGHAN
	WAIN, WARTON, WATKINS
	WHITEHEAD, WILMOT, WORDSWORTH
	WYATT, YOUNG
Chilean	HUIDOBRO
Cuban	RODRIGUEZ
French	APOLLINAIRE, ARP
	BAUDELAIRE, CLAUDEL, ELUARD
	GARNIER, HUGO, ISOU, LAUTREAMONT
	LEMAITRE, MOREAS, NERVAL
	PREVERT, PONGE, RIMBAUD
	RONSARD, TZARA, VALERY
	VERLAINE, VILLON
Gaelic	OSSIAN
German	BALL, BENN, BRECHT
	CELAN, CELTES, CELTIS
	ENZENSBERGER, GERSHON(f)
	GOETHE, HEINE, HEYM, HOLZ
	HULSENBECK, NOVALIS, RILKE
	SCHLEGEL, SCHILLER, SCHWITTERS
	STEFAN, STAMM, TIECK
	VAN HARDENBERG
	ZUCKMEYER
Greek	HESIOD, HOMER, MOREAS
	PINDAR, RITSOS, SAPPHO(f)
Guatemalan	ASTURIAS
Hungarian	CELAN
Irish	AE, HEANEY, MOORE
	SYNGE, WILDE, YEATS
Indian	TAGORE
Italian	ARIOSTO, DANTE, GATTO
	LUZI, MARINETTI, MARINI
	MONTALE, ONOFRI, QUASIMODO
	SERENI, UNGARETTI
Japanese	SOSEKI
Lake School poet	LAKER, LAKIST
Martinique	CESAIPE
Mexican	PAZ
New Zealand	ADCOCK, BAXTER, CAMPBELL
Nicaraguan	DARIO
Nigerian	SOYINKA
one who writes doggerel	WATER-POET
Persian	HAFIZ, KHAYYAM
petty poet	POETASTER, POETICULE
Roman	CATULLUS, HORACE, JUVENAL
	MARTIAL, OVID
	TERENCE, STATIUS, VIRGIL
Romanian	CELAN, ISOU
Russian	AKHMATOVA(f), BELY, BLOK
	IVANOV, KHLEBNIKOV
	KRUCHENYKH, MANDELSHTAM
	MAYAKOVSKY, PASTERNAK
	POSNER, PUSHKIN
	RATUSHINSKAYA(f), TZARA
Scottish	BURNS, DOUGLAS, DUNBAR
	MACCAIG, MACDIARMID
	SCOTT
Senegalese	DIOP
Spanish	CERNUDA, LORCA
Swiss	CENDRARS

Uganda	P'BITEK
Welsh	MORGANWG, ORMOND, THOMAS
West Indian	BRAITHWAITE, BROWN
	JOHNSON, MORRIS, SCOTT
	WALCOTT
would-be poet	POETASTER, POETICULE
poison	TOXIN
antidote	ANTITOXIN, ANTIVENIN
	MITHRIDATE, SERUM
attacking	
—cells	CYTOTOXIN
—entire body	SYSTEMIC
—nervous system	NEUROTOXIN
bacterial	EXOTOXIN, PTOMAINE
buttercup	HELLEBORE
castor-oil bean	RICIN(E)
cereal fungus	ERGOT
conium	HEMLOCK
curare	CURARINE
deadly nightshade	ATROPOPINE
	BELLADONNA
dogbane	OUABAIN, WABAIN
element	ANTIMONY, ARSENIC
	STRONTIUM, THALLIUM
fly agaric	MUSCARINE
food poison	BOTULISM, LISTERIA
	PTOMAINE, SALMONELLA
	SALMONELLOSIS
fungus	AMANITIN, MUSCARINE
	PHALLOIDIN
hellebore	VERATRIN(E)
hemlock	CONIA, CONI(I)NE
henbane	HYOSC(YAM)INE
hydrocyanic acid	PRUSSIC ACID
immunity to poison	MITHRIDATISM
in stomach	ENTEROTOXIN
Java	UPAS
laburnum	CYSTISINE
lilies	HELLEBORE
Madagascar	TANGHIN
maize	AFLATOXIN
monkshood	ACONITE, ACONITUM
mushroom	MUSCARINE, PHALLIN
nux vomica	STRYCHNINE
opium	THEBAINE
peanuts	AFLATOXIN
periwinwkle	STROPHANTHIN
poppies	PAPAVERINE
putrefying flesh	NERINE, NUPINE
quick-acting	(HYDROGEN) CYANIDE
	HYDROCYANIC ACID
	PRUSSIC ACID
rat poison	WARFARIN
rye	ERGOT
sabadilla	VERATRIN(E)
snake	ECHIDNINE

South American	
—arrow poison	CURARA, CURARE, CURARI
—fish poison	SURINAM POISON
	TEPHROSIA, TIMBO
study of poisons	TOXICOLOGY
Tephrosia	SURINAM POISON
thorn-apple	DATURINE
tobacco	NICOTINE
weedkiller	DIOXIN, HERBICIDE
	PARAQUAT
wolfsbane	ACONITE, ACONITUM
wood	METHANOL, METHYL ALCOHOL
	WOOD SPIRIT
—sorrel	OXALIC ACID
Poland	PL, POL
cap	CHAPKA, CZAPKA, SCHAPSKA
capital	WARSAW
carriage	BRITSKA, BRITZ(S)KA
castle	GROD
coins	GROSZY, ZLOTY
dance	CRACOVIENNE, KRAKOWIAK
	MAZURKA, POLONAISE
dynasty	JAGELLON
forest	BOR
hill	GORKA
Jews	ASHKENAZIM
mountain	GORA
mountains	GORY
noble	SAROSTA
officer	HETMAN
reverse notation	RPN
town	GROD, MIASTO
police	CID, FORCE, FUZZ
	MET, THE BILL
police car	BLACK MARIA, PANDA
	PROWL CAR
Police Constable	PC
Police Corps	RMP
police district	MANOR
policeman	BIZZY, BLUEBOTTLE
	BOBBY, BOG(E)Y, BUSY
	COP(PER), MR PLOD, MP
	PC, ROZZER
Polynesian	
apple	KEVI
arrowroot	PIA
assembly	HUI
burial-place	AHU
chestnut	RATA
cloth	TAP(P)A
dance	HULA(-HULA), SIVA
demigod	AITU, MAUI
drink	(K)AVA
fern	TARA
garment	MALO, PAREU
labourer	KANAKA

paved court	MARAE	sandbank	BARRA
pepper	(K)AVA	sea	MAR
platform for statue	AHU	ship	LORCHA, MULETTE
pottery	LAPITA WARE	sir	DOM
skirt	LAVA-LAVA	Timor	P
sky	LANGI	title	DOM
tree	BELAH, TO(O)A, TI, TAMANU	town	VILA
wrap	PAREU	valley	VALE
porcelain	(*see* **china**)	water	
Portugal	LUSITANIA, P	—course	ARROIO
bay	BAIA, ZALEW	—fall	CACHOEIRA, SALTO
beach	PRAIA	weight (25lb)	ARROBA
cape (headland)	CABO	wine	(*see separate entry*)
capital	LISBON	wood	LAS
coins		**potato**	(*see* **vegetables**)
—unit	CENTAVO	**poultry dishes**	
—100 centavos	ESC, ESCUDO	including: game	
—1000 escudos	CONTO	animals	DEER, HARE, RABBIT
—old	PORTAGUE, PORTIGUE	bird split and cooked	SPATCHCOCK
	REE, REAL, REI(S), TESTOON	breastbone of bird	WISHBONE
—1000 reis	MILREIS	chicken dishes	A LA KIEV, A LA KING
—gold	CRUSADO, JO(H)ANNES		CHASSEUR, CHAUDFROID
	MOIDORE		COQ AU VIN, DEVILLED POUSSIN
country house	QUINTA		EVERGLADES, KORMA, MARENGO
dance	FADO		MARYLAND, PETTO DI POLLO
dam	REPRESA		SUPREME
depression	KOTLINA	cut into pieces and	
drowned valley	RIA	served in sauce	FRICASSEE
dynasty	AVIZ, BRAGANZA	deer meat	VENISON
epic poem	LUSIAD(S)	duck in orange	
folk song	FADO	sauce	CANARD A L'ORANGE
forest	LAS	duckling in cherry	
gentleman	FIDALGO	sauce	CANETON AUX CERISES
Guinea	P	edible organs	
harbour	PORTO	—birds	GIBLETS
island	ILHA	—deer	(H)UMBLES
Jews	SEPHARDIM	fat cockerel	CAPON
lady	DONA	game stew	SALM
lagoon	LAGAO	—Mexican	FAJITAS
lake	JEZIORO	hare	
man	DOM	—dish	CIVET DE LIEVRE
measure	MEIO, MOIO, PIPA		JUGGED HARE
mountain	MONTE	—stew (Greek)	STIFADO
—pasture	COXILHA	hens	(*see separate entry*)
—range	SERRA	game birds	BUSTARD, DUCK, GOOSE
mouth	BOCA		GROUSE, GUINEA-FOWL, MALLARD
no	NAO		PARTRIDGE, PHEASANT, PIGEON
parliament	CORTES		PLOVER, PTARMIGAN, QUAIL
plant	SERRADELLA, SERRADILLA		SNIPE, TEAL, TINAMOU, TURKEY
plateau	PLANALTO		WI(D)GEON, WOODCOCK
prince	INFANTE	—Europe	HAZEL HEN
princess	INFANTA	—USA	CANVASBACK
punishment of heretics	AUTO DA FE	large grouse	CAPERCAILLIE
river	RIBEIRAO, RIO	lower leg of bird	DRUMSTICK
—mouth	RIA	pheasant dish	A L'AMERICAINE
saint	SAN(TA), SANTO, SAO	pigeon pie	SQUAB PIE

prepare game	DRESS	mill-owners	MILLOCRACY
quail dish	QUAILS IN ASPIC	mob	MOBOCRACY, OCHLOCRACY
red grouse	MOORFOWL	money	DOLLAROCRACY
remove feathers	PLUCK	mothers	MATRIARCHY
rump of bird	PARSON'S NOSE	natural order	PHYSIOCRACY
	POPE'S NOSE	old people	GERONTOCRACY
set in jelly	GALANTINE	one man	AUTOCRACY
turkey	CACCIATORA	paternal right	PATRIARCHY
young		paupers	PTOCHOCRACY
—chicken	BROILER, FRYER	people	DEMOCRACY, ETHNARCHY
	POUSSIN, SPRING CHICKEN	priests	HIERARCHY, HIEROCRACY
—duck	DUCKLING	privileged class	ARISTOCRACY
—goose	GOSLING	prominent people	MERITOCRACY
—hare	LEVERET	property owners	TIMOCRACY

power

rich — PLUTOCRACY, PLUTO-DEMOCRACY

meaning: authority of
government by
power of
rule by

1 person	AUTARCHY, AUTOCRACY	saints	HAGIARCHY, HAGIOCRACY
	DESPOTISM, DICTATORSHIP	scientists	TECHNOCRACY
	MONARCHY, MONOCRACY	self-governing state	DOMINION
2 persons	DIARCHY, DUUMVIRATE	self-government	AUTONOMY
3 persons	TRIARCHY, TRIUMVIRATE	slaves	D(O)ULOCRACY
4 persons	QUADRUMVIRATE	small group	OLIGARCHY
5 persons	PENTARCHY	sovereignty of the seas	THALASSOCRACY
6 persons	HEXARCHY		THALATTOCRACY
7 persons	HEPTARCHY, SEPTARCHY	squires	SQUATTOCRACY
8 persons	OCTARCHY		SQUIR(E)ARCHY
10 persons	DECADARCHY, DEKADARCHY	teachers	PEDANTOCRACY
absolute power	AUTARCHY, IMPERIUM	technical experts	TECHNOCRACY
actresses married to		wealth	CHRYSOCRACY
peers, etc	ACTRESSOCRACY	wealthy	PLUTOCRACY
all people	PANTISOCRACY		PLUTO-DEMOCRACY
army	STRATOCRACY	Whigs	WHIGGARCHY
beggars	PTOCHOCRACHY	women	GYN(AEC)OCRACY
central and regional	FEDERALISM	workers	ERGATOCRACY
cotton planting or manu-		world ruler	COSMOCRAT
facturing interests	COTTONOCRACY	worst	KAKISTOCRACY
demons	DEMONOCRACY	worthy	MERITOCRACY
dictatorship	ABSOLUTISM, DESPOTISM	young people	YOUTHOCRACY
	TOTALITARIANISM	**prayer**	
divine rulers	THEARCHY, THEOCRACY	at specific times	
élite	MERITOCRACY	of day	CANONICAL HOURS
equal political powers	ISOCRACY	calling for	
exclusive class	OLIGARCHY	transubstantiation	EPICLESIS
experts	TECHNOCRACY	canonical hours	
god	THEOCRACY, THEONOMY	—1st, dawn	MATINS
holy persons	HAGIARCHY, HAGIOCRACY	—2nd, 6am	PRIME
joint sovereignty	SYNARCHY	—3rd, 9am	TERCE
land-owners	SQUATTOCRACY	—4th, noon	SEXT
	SQUIR(E)ACHY	—5th, 3pm	NONES
law	NOMOCRACY	—6th, early evening	VESPERS
many	POLYARCHY	—7th, late evening	COMPLINE
men	PATRIARCHY	commemorating Annunciation	ANGELUS
military despot	STRATOCRACY	confessing sins	CONFITEOR
		during three days	
		before Ascension	ROGATION
		evening prayers	COMPLINE, VESPERS

for
—God's help	INVOCATION
—souls of the dead	REQUIESCAT
Hail Mary	AVE MARIA
Islamic	FATIHA
Jewish	ALEINU, AMIDAH
	KADDISH, KOL NIDRE
	SHEMA
Lamb of God	AGNUS DEI
Lord have mercy	KYRIE ELEISON
Lord's prayer	PATERNOSTER
morning prayers	MATINS

of
—praise	GLORIA
—supplication	ROGATION
on behalf of another	INTERCESSION
Our Father	PATERNOSTER
Roman Catholic	ANGELUS, AVE MARIA
	CANONICAL HOURS
	CONFITEOR
short prayer	COLLECT
three-part prayer	AGNUS DEI
with responses	LITANY
precious stones	(*see* **gems, minerals**)
presidents (US)	ADAMS, ARTHUR
	BUCHANAN, BUREN, BUSH
CARTER, CLEVELAND, CLINTON, COOLIDGE	
EISENHOWER, FILLMORE, FORD	
GARFIELD, GRANT, HARDING	
HARRISON, HAYES, HOOVER	
JACKSON, JEFFERSON, JOHNSON	
KENNEDY, LINCOLN, MADISON	
MCKINLEY, MONROE, NIXON, PIERCE	
POLK, REAGAN, ROOSEVELT	
TAFT, TAYLOR, TRUMAN, TYLER	
VAN BUREN, WASHINGTON	
	WILSON
prime ministers (UK) ABERDEEN, ADDINGTON	
ASQUITH, ATTLEE, BALFOUR	
BALDWIN, BATH, BEACONSFIELD	
BUTE, CALLAGHAN	
CAMPBELL-BANNERMAN	
CANNING, CHAMBERLAIN, CHATHAM	
CHURCHILL, DERBY, DEVONSHIRE	
DISRAELI, DOUGLAS-HOME, EDEN	
GLADSTONE, GODERICH, GRAFTON	
GRENVILLE, GREY, HEATH, LAW	
LIVERPOOL, LLOYD-GEORGE	
MACDONALD, MACMILLAN	
MAJOR, MELBOURNE	
NEWCASTLE, NORTH, PALMERSTON	
PEEL, PELHAM, PERCEVAL, PITT	
PORTLAND, ROCKINGHAM, ROSEBERY	
RUSSELL, SALISBURY, SHELBURNE	
THATCHER, WALDEGRAVE, WALPOLE	
WELLINGTON, WILMINGTON, WILSON	

printing

adjustment of spacing	
between lines	CARDING, FEATHERING
accents	ACUTE, BOLLE, BREVE
	CARON, CEDILLA, DI(AER)ESIS
	DOT, DOUBLE ACUTE, DOUBLE GRAVE
	GRAVE, HACEK, HOOK, LATVIAN TAIL
	MACRON, OGONEK, STREG, STOKE
	TILDE, TREMA, UMLAUT, UPVEE
alignment of print	
on page	REGISTRATION
apprentice	DEVIL
arrangement of pages of	
type in a forme	IMPOSITION
blemish	MACKLE
brackets	ANGLE BRACKETS, BRACES
	PARENTHESES
	SQUARE BRACKETS
calculation of space that	
manuscript will occupy	
when set in type	CAST-OFF
capital letters	UPPER CASE
character with	
—2 letters making one sound	DIGRAPH
—2 or more letters joined	LIGATURE
—2 vowels joined	DIPHTHONG
—3 letters joined	TRIGRAPH
—3 vowels joined	TRIPHTHONG
copies of a book printed	
at one time	IMPRESSION
dots	
—indicating omission	
of words	ELLIPSES
	SUSPENSION POINTS
—or dashes linking	
separated words	LEADERS
double imprint on page	MACKLE
early printers	
—Antwerp	PLANTIN
—Basle	FROBEN
—Britain	CAXTON
—France	GARAMOND
—Germany	GUTENBERG
—Venice	ALDUS
embossed print for	
the blind	BRAILLE, MOON-TYPE
errand-boy	DEVIL
exclamation mark	GASPER, GASP MAR
	SCREAMER
frame holding type	CHASE
group of printed pages	
folded from one sheet	GATHER, SECTION
heavy print	BOLD, DOUBLE
imp of printing-house	RALPH
ink blot	MONK
inserted in space left in text	INCUT

insertion mark	CARET
inset from margin	INDENT
instruction to ignore correction	STET
left-hand page	VERSO
letter	
—or numeral at foot of page	SIGNATURE
—sloping	ITALIC
—upright	ROMAN
—written	
above the line	SUPERSCRIPT
below the line	SUBSCRIPT
lie flush at end of line	JUSTIFY, RANGE
line of cast type	SLUG
machine which sets a complete line of type	LINOTYPE
measure of	
—letter width	EL, EM, EN
—line length	ENNAGE
—print area	EM(M)AGE
misprint	LITERAL, TYPO
mould of papier-mâché	FLONG
old comma	VIRGULE
ornamental line on letter	SERIF
page number	FOLIO
paper	
—for newspapers	NEWSPRINT
—thick	BOND
—thin	BANK
papier-mâché sheet	FLONG
phonetic type	PHONOTYPE
photo-engraving	
—in intaglio	PHOTOGRAVURE
—using rotary press	ROTOGRAVURE
piece of type	
—bearing two or more characters	LOGOTYPE
—blank for spaces	QUAD(RAT)
—projecting beyond body or shank	KERN
plain letter	SANS SERIF
plate	
—cast from papier-mâché mould	CLICHE, STEROTYPE
—for casting type-faces	MATRIX
print	
—worker	COMPOSITOR, TYPESETTER
—union branch	CHAPEL
printed sheet from letterpress	IMPRESSION
printer's	
—marks	AMPERSAND, ARROW OUT ASTERISK, ASTERISM BACK-SLASH, BOX, BULLET CARET, CIRCLE DOT, CROSS

	DIAMOND, DIESIS, (DOUBLE) DAGGER (DOUBLE) GUILLEMOT, ELLIPSIS FILLED BOX, HASH, MARS OBELISK, OBELUS, OBLIQUE, ORDINAL PARAGRAPH MARK, PILCROW PRESA, SLASH, SOLIDUS, STAR SUSPENSION POINTS SWING DASH, TICK, VENUS, VIRGULE
—measure	VIRGULE DIDOT, EL, EM, EN, PT, POINT
—proof	GALLEY
—symbols	(*see* punctuation marks *below*)
printing	TYPOGRAPHY
—error	LITERAL, TYPO
—from stone	LITHOGRAPHY
—house imp	RALPH
—in several colours	STENOCHROMY
—left to right and right to left	BOUSTROPHEDON
—machine	BUBBLE JET, CYCLOSTYLE DAISY WHEEL, DOT MATRIX DUPLICATOR, FAX, FLATBED INKJET, LASER, LINE PRINTER MIMEOGRAPH, PHOTOCOPIER ROTARY, TELEPRINTER, TELEX
publisher's imprint	COLOPHON
punctuation marks	APOSTROPHE BRACKETS, COLON, COMMA DASH, EXCLAMATION MARK FULL-STOP, HYPHEN INVERTED COMMAS OPEN QUERY, OPEN SHRIEK POINT, QUESTION MARK QUOTATION MARKS, SEMI-COLON STIGME
right-hand page	RECTO
set of type characters	FO(U)NT
short last line at end of paragraph or top of column	ORPHAN, WIDOW
sloping print	ITALIC
small	
—letters	LOWER CASE
—tray in which type is set	COMPOSING STICK
spacing	
—between lines	LEADING
—of words to fill a column	JUSTIFICATION
tool	SHOOTING-STICK
technique of printing	
—from plate of which only parts accept ink	LITHOGRAPHY
with incised surface	GRAVURE INTAGLIO

with raised surfaces	LETTERPRESS
—from an inked cylinder	OFFSET
three stars	ASTERISM
title printed at head of every (alternate) page	RUNNING HEAD
tray holding set type	GALLEY
trial sheet of print	(GALLEY-)PROOF
trivia for filling odd spaces in newspaper	BALAAM
two pages of open book	SPREAD
type	
—10 letters per inch	PICA
—12 letters per inch	ELITE
—$^1/_{72}$ inch	POINT
—3½ point	MINIKIN
—4 point	BRILLIANT, MINION
—4½ point	DIAMOND
—5 point	PEARL
—5½ point	AGATE, RUBY
—6 point	NONPAREIL
—7 point	MINION
—8 point	BREVIER
—9 point	BOURGEOIS
—10 point	LONG PRIMER
—11 point	SMALL PICA
—12 point	PICA
—13 point	CICERO
—14 point	ENGLISH
—16 point	COLUMBIAN, TWO-LINE BREVIER
—18 point	GREAT PRIMER
—20 point	PARAGON
—22 point	DOUBLE PICA
—24 point	TWO-LINE PICA
—28 point	TWO-LINE ENGLISH
—36 point	TWO-LINE GREAT PRIMER
—40 point	TWO-LINE PARAGON
—48 point	CANON, FOUR-LINE PICA
—60 point	FIVE-LINE PICA
—72 point	SIX-LINE PICA
—assembled in a chase	FORME
—black letter type	FRAKTUR, GOTHIC
—dark Gothic	TEXTURA
—heavy-faced	CLARENDON
—large	CANON
—rounded script	RONDE, UNCIAL
—sloping	ITALIC
—special type	ELZEVIR
—upright	ROMAN
—without serifs	SANSERIF
typesetters	PICA THUMPERS
typograph(y)	TYP(O)
wedge for locking type	QUOIN
white space between facing pages	GUTTER

word	
—indicating literal quotation	SIC
—printed at the top of page to indicate content	CATCHWORD
wrong font	WF
	(see also **write**)

proteins

acting as	
—catalyst	ENZYME
—gene inhibitor	HISTONE
affecting cells	INTERLEUKIN
anti-viral substance produced by infected cell	INTERFERON
basic protein	HISTONE
coagulating blood	FIBRIN, FIBROGEN
containing carbohydrate	GLUCOPROTEIN
	GLYCOPROTEIN
	MUCOPROTEIN
dissolved in blood	PLASMA PROTEIN
elastic fibre in connective tissue	ELASTIN
fibrous protein in surface coatings of animals	SCLEROPROTEIN
forming	
—fibrin	FIBRINOGEN
—gelatine	COLLAGEN
grains of protein stored in plants	ALEURONE GRAINS
group of soluble proteins	GLOBULIN
in	
—almonds	AMANDINE
—amniotic fluid	ALPHA-FETO PROTEIN
—barley	HORDEIN
—blood	FIBRIN(OGEN), GLOB(UL)IN
	HAEMOGLOBIN
	IMMUNOPROTEIN
—bones	GELATIN(E)
—cells	
after viral infection	INTERFERON
of living organisms	GLOBULIN
—cereal	GLUTEN
—chromosome	HISTONE
cell nucleus	CHROMATIN
—collagen	GELATIN(E)
—connective tissue	COLLAGEN
—egg	
white	(EGG-)ALBUMEN
yolk	VITELLIN
—eye	CRYSTALLIN
—fat	LIPOPROTEIN
—fibrous tissue	COLLAGEN, ELASTIN
—gluten	GLIADIN, PROLAMINE

—haemoglobin	GLOBIN
—hair, skin, etc	KERATIN
—Indian corn	ZEIN
—keratin, collagen, etc	SCLEROPROTEINS
—ligaments, etc	COLLAGEN
—liver and spleen	FERRITIN
—milk	CASEIN, LACTALBUMEN
	LACTOGLOBULIN
	LACTOPROTEIN
—mucus	MUCIN
—muscle	ACTIN, ACTOMYOSIN
	DYSTROPHIN, MYOGLOBIN
	MYOSIN
—nails	KERATIN
—saliva	MUCIN
—seeds	ALEURONE
—silk	FIBROIN
—skin	GELATIN(E), KERATIN
—sponges	SPONGIN
—thyroid gland	THYROGLOBULIN
—wheat flour	GLUTEN
—wool, hair, horn etc	KERATIN
including a lipid	LIPOPROTEIN
insoluble	FIBRIN
not denatured	NATIVE PROTEIN
nucleic acid with	
protein	NUCLEO-PROTEIN
part of enzyme	APOENZYME
plant protein acting	
as antibody	LECTIN
produced by action of	
virus in cell	INTERFERON
producing luminosity	LUCIFERIN
scleroprotein	COLLAGEN
	ELASTIN, KERATIN
simple protein	HISTONE
soluble in	
—alcohol	PROLAMIN(E)
—salt	GLOBULIN
—water	ALBUMIN
stopping gene activity	HISTONE
storing iron	FERRITIN
used	
—as protection	
against virus	INTERFERON
—in adhesives, foods, etc	GELATIN(E)
psychology	PNEUMATOLOGY
including: psychiatry	
absence of emotion	APATHY
act of will	VOLITION
adaptation to frequent	
stimuli	HABITUATION
Adler school	INDIVIDUAL PSYCHOLOGY
adoption of female	
dress and manners	
by male	EONISM, TRANSVESTISM

aggression	ANTAGONISTIC BEHAVIOUR
alternation between	
extreme	
moods	MANIC-DEPRESSIVE PSYCHOSIS
analysis of	
—differences between	
mental and	
physical	MIND-BODY PROBLEM
—social	
exchanges	TRANSACTIONAL ANALYSIS
arrangement of	
mental	
states and	
processes	STRUCTURAL PSYCHOLOGY
attachment to idea,	
person, etc	FIXATION
attempt to control	
behaviour	CONDITIONING
attribution of one's	
own feelings to others	PROJECTION
automatic behaviour	
not recalled	FUGUE
awareness of the future	PRECOGNITION
based on study	
—from	
parts to whole	ELEMENTARISM
whole to parts	
	ORGANISMIC PSYCHOLOGY
behaviour	
—establishing hierarchy	DOMINANCE
—inward-looking	INTROVERSION
—likely to	
satisfy some desire	APPETITIVE
elicit epimeletic	
response	ETEPIMELETIC
—outward-looking	EXTRAVERSION
—relating to care	
of young	EPIMELETIC
—reverting to earlier	
stage	REGRESSION
body	
—and temperament type	SOMATYPE
—muscular and aggressive	SOMATONIA
—types	
long and thin	ECTOMORPH
muscular	MESOMORPH
round	ENDOMORPH
bonding to parent	ATTACHMENT
character analysis	BIOENERGETICS
charge of mental energy	CATHEXIS
condition	
—of	
bodily rigidity	CATALEPSY
immobility emotionally	
caused	CATAPLEXY
schizophrenic stupor	CATATONIA

—where
  physical symptoms
  have mental
  origin   CONVERSION HYSTERIA
  relationships seem
  to be threatening   ENGULFMENT
connecting principle in
  coincidence   SYNCHRONICITY
conscious part of the
  personality   EGO
consideration of
  psychology   METAPSYCHOLOGY
control of behaviour by
  results of previous
  behaviour   INSTRUMENTAL CONDITIONING
              OPERANT CONDITIONING
death-wish   THANATOS
defence mechanism   IDENTIFICATION
                           PROJECTION
                           RATIONALISATION
              REGRESSION, REPRESSION
                           SUBLIMATION
delusions of
  —grandeur   PARANOIA
  —self-importance   MEGALOMANIA
depression   MELANCHOLIA
device used for
  —communication with
    spirits   OUIJA BOARD
                            PLANCHETTE
  —spirit-writing   PSYCHOGRAPH
disorder
  —affecting communication
    with others   AUTISM
  —caused by excessive
    wealth   AFFLUENZA
  —of mood with
    high spirits   ELATION
    low spirits   DEPRESSION
disruption of self-
  image   IDENTITY CRISIS
doctrine/theory
  —based on
    first year of life   KLEINIAN THEORY
    individual
    responsibility   EXISTENTIALISM
    response to
    environment   LEARNING THEORY
  —of
    Adler   PSYCHOANALYSIS
    Freud   DYNAMIC PSYCHOLOGY
    Galton   DIFFERENTIAL PSYCHOLOGY
                            PSYCHOANALYSIS
    insanity as a
    social problem   RADICAL THERAPY
    Jung   PSYCHOANALYSIS

Maslow   HUMANISTIC PSYCHOLOGY
McDougall   HORMIC PSYCHOLOGY
                           PURPOSIVISM
Skinner   BEHAVIOURISM
universal soul   PSYCHISM
—that
  man is responsible
  for his actions   PURPOSIVISM
  mental states exist
  independently   MENTALISM
  only minds exist   PANPSYCHISM
dreamlike state   FUGUE
estrangement from the
  real world   ALIENATION
exacted reaction   COMPENSATION
excessive
  —fear   PHOBIA
                           (see also fear)
  —love of self   EGOMANIA, NARCISSISM
                           (see also love)
  —preoccupation with
    some subject   OBSESSION
expression of repressed
  feelings   CONVERSION
father-fixation in
  girl   ELECTRA COMPLEX
fear of
  —being destroyed   IMPLOSION
  —loss of ability to
    feel pleasure   APHANASIS
                           (see also fear)
feeling of
  —inadequacy   INFERIORITY COMPLEX
  —unreality   DEPERSONALISATION
feminine side of male   ANIMA
fixed idea   DELUSION
flow of mental
  activity   STREAM OF CONSCIOUSNESS
formation of complete
  personality   INTEGRATION
Freudian school   PSYCHOANALYSIS
front shown to
  the world   PERSONA
goal-directed behaviour   HORME
highest moral
  example   CATEGORICAL IMPERATIVE
hypothesis basing
  natural science
  on psychology   PSYCHOLOGISM
hypothetical governing
  principle   PSYCHOID
idealised impression   IMAGO
illusion of movement   PHI-PHENOMENON
imagined illness   HYPOCHONDRIA(SIS)
inability to
  —decide   AB(O)ULIA

—experience pleasure	ANHEDONIA
—remember	AMNESIA
particular	
event	PSYCHOLOGICAL BLOCK
increased performance	
based on expectation	ROSENTHAL EFFECT
induction to rules	
of society	SOCIALISATION
inherited idea	ARCHETYPE
inkblot test	RORSCHACH TEST
insanity	
—starting in childhood	HEBEPHRENIA
—with loss of mental	
powers	DEMENTIA
interpretation of	
philosopical problems in	
psychological terms	PSYCHOLOGISM
investigation	
—into paranormal	PSYCHICAL RESEARCH
—of	
hidden motives	PSYCHOANALYSIS
personality	PSYCHODIAGNOSTICS
involuntary reaction	INSTINCT
IQ scale	BINET-SIMON SCALE
	STANFORD-BINET SCALE
irrational fear	ANXIETY, PHOBIA
Jungian school	ANALYTICAL PSYCHOLOGY
Laing's school	RADICAL THERAPY
learning	
—by rewards	OPERANT CONDITIONING
	INSTRUMENTAL LEARNING
—from	
entire patterns	GESTALT PSYCHOLOGY
stimuli	CLASSICAL CONDITIONING
	PAVLOVIAN CONDITIONING
life-force	ORGONE
loss of memory	ANMESIA
masculine side of	
female	ANIMUS
measure of	
intelligence	INTELLIGENCE QUOTIENT, IQ
mental	
—action directing	
physical	PSYCHOMOTOR
—and emotional energy	LIBIDO
—condition caused by	
withdrawal of all	
stimuli	SENSORY DEPRIVATION
—deficiency	AMENTIA
—derangement	PSYCHOPATHY
—disease without	
physical cause	PSYCHONEUROSIS
—disorder	NEUROSIS, PSYCHASTHENIA
	PSYCHOSIS
—illness	
affecting body	PSYCHOSOMATIC

alternate depression	
and elation	
	MANIC-DEPRESSIVE PSYCHOSIS
based on anxiety	HYSTERIA
following	
shock	TRAUMATIC NEUROSIS
with	
—delusions of	
greatness	MEGALOMANIA
persecution	PARANOIA
—euphoria, etc	MANIA
—inability to separate	
reality from	
delusion	SCHIZOPHRENIA
—reiteration of	
ideas, etc	OBSESSIONAL NEUROSIS
—processes with no	
connection	DISASSOCIATION
mild mania	HYPOMANIA
mind	PSYCHE
misinterpreted event	ILLUSION
morbid self-interest	EGOMANIA
mother-fixation	
in boy	OEDIPUS COMPLEX
movement of objects	
by paranormal force	PSYCHOKINESIS
natural response	INSTINCT
object as opposed	
to subject	NON-EGO
obsession	COMPLEX
one	
—interested in	
both himself and the	
external world	AMBIVERT
self only	INTROVERT
the external world	EXRAVERT
	EXTROVERT
—qualified in mind	
sciences	PSYCHIST
	PSYCHOLOGIST
—suffering from	
behavioural disorder	PSYCHOPATH
	SOCIOPTAH
—who	
trains the mind	PSYCHAGOGUE
shows pathological	
degree of instability	PSYCHOPATH
	SOCIOPATH
—treats mental illness	ALIENIST
	PSYCHIATRIST
—with power of	
divination by contact	PSYCHOMETER
part of mind	
—holding thoughts	
which cannot become	
conscious	UNCONSCIOUS

—outside awareness	SUBCONSCIOUS	—Danish	LANGE
partially unconscious		—French	BINET, COUE, JANET, LACON
part of personality	SUPEREGO		SARTRE, SIMON
period of development		—German	BERGER, ERIKSON, FECHNER
between childhood			FICHTE, FROMM, HERBART
and puberty	LATENCY PERIOD		HERING, HORNEY, KOFFKA
persistent attachment	FIXATION		KOHLER, KRAEPELIN
personality			KRAFT-EBBING
—test	RORSCHACH TEST		KRETSCHMER, TOLMAN
—types doing well in			WEITHEIMER, WINDT
orthodox situations	CONVERGER	—Italian	ASSAGIOLI
unorthodox situations	DIVERGER	—Martinician	FANON
physiological outcome		—Polish	LEWIN
of mental disturbance	ACTUAL NEUROSIS	—Russian	LURIA, PAVLOV
pleasure			VELIKOVSKY, VIGOTSKY
—enhancing principle	ID	—Scottish	LANG
—from		—Swiss	BLEULER, JUNG
mental activity	CEREBROTONIA		PIAGET, RORSCHACH
pain to		psychotic condition	PSYCHOPATHY
—others	SADISM		SCHIZOPHRENIA
—self	MASOCHISM		SOCIOPATHY
and others	SADO-MASOCHISM		
physical activity	SOMATOTONIA	purposive	
sensation	VISCEROTONIA	psychology	HORMIC PSYCHOLOGY
potential thoughts	PRECONSCIOUS	rapid conditioning	IMPRINTING
power		reaction to	
—of divination by		—conditioning	BEHAVIOURISM
contact	PSYCHOMETRY	—contrived stimuli	CONDITIONED REFLEX
—supposed to cause			CONDITIONED RESPONSE
paranormal phenomena	PSYCHIC FORCE		PAVLOVIAN REFLEX
problem solving by			PAVLOVIAN RESPONSE
intense discussion	BRAINSTORMING	redirection of feelings	DISPLACEMENT
psychiatrist	PSYCHIATER	relationship between	
psychic energy	LIBIDO	—child and step-	
psychical research	PARAPSYCHOLOGY	parent	PHAEDRA COMPLEX
psychologists/psychiatrists		—daughter and father	ELECTRA COMPLEX
—American BANDURA, BERNE, BRUNER		—older man and young	
CATTELL, CLYNES, ERIKSON		girl	LOLITA SYNDROME
HORNEY, HULL, JAMES, JENSEN		—son and mother	OEDIPUS COMPLEX
KANNER, KEELER, KOFFKA, KOHLER		release of repressed	
LARSEN, LEARY, LEWIN, LINDSLEY		feelings	CATHARSIS
MASLOW, MAY, MEAD, MILLER		restraint of impulse	INHIBITION
MORENO, MURRAY, OLDS, REICH		reversion to earlier state	REGRESSION
RHINE, ROGERS, ROSENTHAL		reward for behaviour	REINFORCEMENT
SHELDON, SKINNER, SULLIVAN		Rogers's school	HUMANISTIC PSYCHOLOGY
SZASZ, TERMAN, THORNDIKE		Sartre school	EXISTENTIALISM
THURSTONE, TITCHENER		self	
WATSON, WECHLER		—encouragement	AUTO-SUGGESTION
WOODWORTH		—interest	INTROVERSION
—Australian	MEAD		NARCISSISM
—Austrian ADLER, BREUER, FREUD		—preservation instinct	EROS
RANK, REICH, SAKEL		sensation without	
—British BOWLBY, BURT, CLARKE		physical cause	HALLUCINATION
DALTON, EYSENCK, GALTON		set of unconscious ideas	COMPLEX
MCDOUGALL, OGDEN, PEARMAN		severe	
STRACHEY, WINNICOTT, WOOD		depression INVOLUTIONAL MELANCHOLIA	
			INVOLUTIONAL PSYCHOSIS

sex drive	LIBIDO
showing	
—relationship between	
mind and body	PSYCHOSOMATIC
—tendency to	
schizophrenic	
behaviour	SCHIZOID
Skinner school	BEHAVIOURAL PSYCHOLOGY
social hierarchy	PECKING ORDER
soul	PSYCHE
specialist in mental	
illness	ALIENIST
spirit	PSYCHE
—writing	PSYCHOGRAM
	PSYCHOGRAPHY
spiritualist	PSYCHIC
—doctrine	ANTHROPOSOPHY
split personality	SCHIZOPHRENIA
statistical analysis	
of psychological	
data	MATHEMATICAL PSYCHOLOGY
strong attachment	
to object or idea	CATHEXIS
study of	
—abnormal phenomena	METAPHYSICS
	PARAPSYCHOLOGY
—bodily reflexes as	
affecting behaviour	REFLEXOLOGY
—body/mind	
relationship	PSYCHOBIOGRAPHY
	PSYCHOBIOLOGY
—brain diseases as	
affecting behaviour	NEUROPSYCHIATRY
—experiences and	
their effects	PHENOMENOLOGY
—extra-sensory	
perception	PARAPSYCHOLOGY
—human behaviour	CLINICAL PSYCHOLOGY
—measurable	
behaviour	BEHAVIOURISM
—mental	
illness	ALIENISM, PSYCHIATRY
problems of the	
aged	PSYCHOGERIATRICS
—mind	
and behaviour	PSYCHICS
	PSYCHOLOGY
in its	
environment	PSYCHONOMICS
—motivation	DYNAMIC PSYCHOLOGY
—origins of mind	PSYCHOGENESIS
—physical psychology	PSYCHOPHISIOLOGY
—private	
experiences	
	INTROSPECTIVE PSYCHOLOGY
—psychic theories	METAPSYCHOLOGY

—psychology of	
abnormal states	
of mind	HUMANISTIC PSYCHOLOGY
	PSYCHOPATHOLOGY
individual	DIFFERENTIAL PSYCHOLOGY
	EGO PSYCHOLOGY
measurable factors	PSYCHOMETRICS
	PSYCHOMETRY
—relationship of mental	
to physical	PSYCHOPHYSICS
substitution of one	
activity for one	
less acceptable	SUBLIMATION
suppression of function	INHIBITION
temperament	
—inclined to high and	
low spirits	CYCLOTHYMIA
—types	
ectomorph	CEREBROTONIC
endomorph	VISCEROTONIC
mesomorph	SOMATOTONIC
optimistic	SANGUINE
passionate	CHOLERIC
pessimistic	MELANCHOLIC
stolid	PHLEGMATIC
temporal displacement	UNCOUPLING
	DECALAGE
test used as experiment	AUFGABE
theory	
—emphasises the use	
of will	VOLUNTARISM
—of emotion	JAMES-LANGE THEORY
—that faculties	
are innate	NATIVISM
thinking part of personality	EGO
thought determined	
by motives	PSYCHIC DETERMINISM
total lack of response	STUPOR
transfer of emotion	
to another object	DISPLACEMENT
treatment	
—by	
acting out problems	PSYCHODRAMA
auto-suggestion	COUEISM
exposing the	
subconscious	PSYCHONALYSIS
hypnosis	PSYCHOTHERAPEUTICS
	PSYCHOTHERAPY
unpleasant	
stimuli	AVERSION THERAPY
—linking personality	
elements	PSYCHOSYNTHESIS
—of the whole	
person	GESTALT PSYCHOLOGY
	CONFIGURATIONISM
	(see also **treatment**)

true personality	ANIMA
unconscious	
—critical faculty	SUPEREGO
—movement of wishes etc	
from one person	
to another	TRANSFERENCE
—process to prevent	
thoughts becoming	
conscious	REPRESSION
—reaction to danger	DEFENCE MECHANISM
understanding of	
self	SELF-ACTUALISATION
public	
public address (system)	PA
public good	PB
pub(lic house)	INN, LOCAL, PH
public lending right	PLR
public library	PL
public record office	PRO
public relations (officer)	PR(O)
Public Service Vehicle	PSV
Public Services Authority	PSA
Puerto Rico	PR
capital	SAN JUAN
pulses	CALAVANCE, CARAVANCE
African	KENYA BEAN
American	BLACK-EYED PEAS, TEPARY
—green bean	SNAP BEAN
Asian	CHICKPEA, COWPEA
	MUNG BEAN, SOYA BEANS
bean curd	TOFU
black-eyed beans	COW-PEAS
broad bean	FAVA BEAN, FIELD BEAN
	HORSE BEAN
butter beans	LIMA BEANS
carob	ALGAR(R)OBA, ALGAR(R)OBO
	ST JOHN'S BREAD
cherry-bean	COWPEA
chick-pea	EGYPTIAN PEA
	GARBANZO PEA, GRAM
—flour	BESSAN
—Spanish	GARBANZOS
Chinese	MUNG
cow-pea	BLACK-EYED BEAN
	CHERRY BEAN
dried and halved	SPLIT PEAS

dry peas	MARROWFAT PEAS
eaten in pod	MANGE-TOUT
Egyptian pea	CHICK-PEA, GARBANZO PEA
field bean	BROAD BEAN, HORSE BEAN
French bean	FLAGEOLET, HARICOT
	WAX(POD) BEAN
Garbanzo pea	CHICK-PEA, EGYPTIAN PEA
great northern bean	HARICOT
green bean (US)	SNAP BEAN
Guiana seed	TONGA-BEAN, TONKA-BEAN
	TONQUIN-BEAN
haricot	FLAGEOLET, NAVY BEANS
	PINTO
horse bean	BROAD BEAN, FIELD BEAN
Indian	ARRAH, BLACK GRAM
	DA(H)L, DHAL, DHOLL
	MUNG, PALAS, PIGEON-PEA
	URD(-BEAN)
Italian	BORLOTTI, CANELLINI
Japanese	ADZUKI
kidney bean	CANELLINI, FLAGEOLET
lady's fingers	BHINDI, GUMBO, OKRA
large pea	MARROWFAT
Lima bean	BUTTER BEAN
Mediterranean	CAROB BEAN, LOCUST BEAN
Mexican	CHILLI
Middle East	FUL MESDAMES
mottled bean	PINTO BEAN
navy bean	HARICOT
other beans	BORLOTTI, BROAD BEANS
	BUTTER BEANS
	FIELD BEANS
parched Indian corn	ROKEAGE
red kidney bean	CHILLI BEAN
	MEXICAN BEAN
small	
—beans	HELIDA
—kidney bean	PEA BEAN
—seeded	SIEVA BEAN
snuff flavouring	TONGA-BEAN
	TONKA-BEAN
	TONQUIN-BEAN
South American	LIMA BEAN
Spanish	HELDA BEAN
sugar-pea	MANGETOUT
tropical bean	COW(H)AGE, COWITCH

Qatar	
capital	AD DAUHHAH, DOHA
coin	
—unit	DIRHAM
—100 dirhams	RIYAL
quarter	FRACTION, MERCY
	QR, QU(AR)
Jew's quarter	GHETTO
quartermaster(-general)	QM(G)
quartermaster(-sergeant	QM(S)
quarter-sessions	QS
quasi-stellar object	QSO, QUASAR
Quebec	Q, QUE
inhabitant	QUEBECOIS
measure (c. $1^1/_4$ acres)	ARPENT
queen	Q, QU, R
Queen Anne	AR
Queen Anne's Bounty	QAB
queen city	CINCINATTI
Queen Elizabeth	ER, ORIANA
—Hall	QEH
Queen Mary	MR
Queen of	
—Carthage	DIDO

—England	ANNE, ELIZABETH I & II
	JANE, MARY I & II
	MATILDA, VICTORIA
—France	REINE
—Germany	KONIGIN
—heaven	ASHTORETH
—Italy	REGINA
—Navarre	MARGUERITE
—Scotland	MARGARET, MARY
—Sheba	AAZIZ, BALKIS
—spades	BASTA
—Spain	REINA
—the	
dead	ERESHKIGOL, HEL
	PERSEPHONE, PROSERPINE
fairies	MAB, TITANIA, UNA
Nile	CLEO(PATRA)
Queen Victoria	VIR, VR(I)
Queen's Bench	QB
queen's carriage	VICTORIA
Queen's College	QC
Queen's Counsel	QC
Queensland	Q

R

rabbit

diseases	COCCIDIOSIS, MYXOMATOSIS
types	ALASKA, ANGORA, ARGENTE
	ASTREX, BEAVER KING, BELGIAN HARE
	BEVEREN, BLANC DE BUSCOT
	BLANC DE HOTOT, BRITISH GIANT
	CALIFORNIAN, CASTOR (REX)
	CHINCHILLA (GIGANTA)
	CHINESE SACRIFICIAL, DUTCH
	ENGLISH LOP, FLEMISH, FOX
	FRENCH DWARF, HARLEQUIN, HAVANA
	HIMALAYAN, LILAC
	LINCOLNSHIRE SPRIG, MARTEN SABLE
	NETHERLAND DWARF, NEW ZEALAND
	POLISH, REX, RHINELANDER, SATIN
	SIAMESE SABLE, SIBERIAN
	SILVER SPRIG, SMOKED PEARL
	TAN, THURINGER

radio

radiation protection adviser	RPA
radio	
—frequency	RF
—telephone	RT
radiological safety officer	RSO

railway

	RWY
railway	
—region	GWR, LMS, LNER, SR
—sorting office	RSO
—sub-office	RSO
Railway Traffic Officer	RTO
railwaymen	NUR

rearing

including: breeding	
cultivation	
animals	ZOOCULTURE
bees	APICULTURE
birds	AVICULTURE
fish	PISCICULTURE
flowers	FLORICULTURE
fruit	POMICULTURE
hair	CRINICULTURE
oysters	OSTREICULTURE
plants	HORTICULTURE
—stimulated by	
electricity	ELECTROCULTURE
sea animals and plants	MARICULTURE
silk worms	SERICULTIRE
single crop	MONOCULTURE

snails	HELICULTURE
trees	ARBORICULTURE
vines	VINICULTURE, VITICULTURE
voice training	VOCICULTURE
without soil	HYDROPONICS
woods	SILVICULTURE
Red Indian	COPPERSKIN
	MOUNDBUILDER
	NATIVE AMERICAN, REDSKIN
arum root dish	TUCKAHOE
baby	PAPOOSE
bark canoe	WOOD-SKIN
beads from shells	WAMPUM(PEAG)
belt of shell-beads	WAMPUM-BELT
birch-bark box or basket	MOCOCK
blanket	MACKINAW
brave	SANNOP, SANNUP
carved pole	TOTEM (POLE)
chief	MUGWUMP, SACHEM
	SAGAMORE
child	PAPOOSE
communal house	LONG-HOUSE
confederacy of tribes	FIVE NATIONS
confer	POWWOW
conference	PAWAW, POWWOW
conjuror	PAWAW, POWWOW
currency	WAMPUM
dish	SUCCOTASH
drag	TRAVAIL, TRAVOIS
dried meat	PEM(M)ICAN
dwelling	HOGAN, HUT, LODGE, TEEPEE
	TENT, WICKIUP, WIGWAM
famous chiefs	BIG FOOT, COCHISE
	CRAZY HORSE, GERONIMO
	PONTIAC, SITTING BULL
	TECUMSEH
feast	PAWAW, POWWOW
Great Spirit	MANITO(U)
interjection	WAUGH
litter	TRAVAIL, TRAVOIS
liquor	HOO(T)CH
paradise	HAPPY HUNTING-GROUND
peace pipe	CALUMET
poetry	HIAWATHA
pole used in	
house-building	LODGE-POLE
pony	CAYUSE
porridge	HOMINY, SAMP, SUP(P)AWN
religious dance	CANTICOY, KANTIKOY
shaman	PAWAW, POW-WOW
shell money	PEAG, PEAK, WAMPUM(PEAG)
shoe	MOCCASIN, MOCASSIN
smoking mixture	KINNIKINICK
snakebite medicine	SENEGA
stew	SUCCOTASH
tent	TE(E)PEE, WIGWAM

tribes	ABENAKI, ALGONQUI(A)N
	ALGONKI(A)N
	APACHE, ARAPAHO, BANNOCK
	BLACKFOOT, BLOOD
	CADDO, CALUSA, CHEROKEE
	CHEYENNE, CHINOOK, CHIPPEWAY
	CHOCKTAW, CHUMASH, COCHIMI
	COMANCHE, CREE, CREEK, CROW
	DAKOTA, DELAWARE, ERIE
	FOX, HOPI, HUICHOL, HURON
	ILLINOIS, IROQUOIS, KAROK, KIOWA
	MANDAN, MASSACHUSET, MODOC
	MIAMI, MICMAC, MENOMINEE
	MOHAVE, MOHAWK, MOHEGAN
	MOHICAN, MOHOCK, MUSKOGE
	NARRAGANSET, NATCHEZ, NAVAHO
	NAVAJO, NEZ PERCES, NOOTKA
	OGLALA, OJIBWA(Y), OMAHA
	OSAGE, OTTOWA, PAIUTE, PAPAGO
	PAWNEE, PIMA, POMO, POTAWATOMI
	POWHATAN, PUEBLO, SAC, SARCEE
	SAUK, SENECA, SEMINOLE
	SHASTA, SHAWNEE, SHOSHONE
	SHOSHONI, SHUSWAP, SIOUX
	SIWASH, SNAKE, SUSQUEHANNOCK
	TARAHUMARA, TIMUCUA, UTE, WICHITA
	WINNEBAGO, YOKUTS, YUROK, ZUNI
	(*see also* **America, Canada**)
utensil used in war ceremony	WAR-KETTLE
village	PUEBLO
war	
—axe	TOMAHAWK
—cry	WHOOP
white man with Indian wife	SQUAW-MAN
wife	SQUAW
winter	
—feast	POTLA(T)CH
—festival	POTLATCH
woman	SQUAW
religion	(*see* **belief**)
resident	
Resident Medical Officer	RMO
Resident Surgical Officer	RSO
resident magistrate	RM
resin	(*see* **gum/resin**)
respiratory system	
branch(es) of windpipe	
—main	BRONCHUS(BRONCHI)
—small	BRONCHIA
—very small	BRONCHIOLE
breathing-hole	SPIRACLE
cavity at end of bronchiole	AIR-SAC
compartment(s) of air-sac	ALVEOLUS(ALVEOLI)
flap over gill	GILL-COVER
hair(s) in bronchi	CILIUM(CILIA)
membrane covering lung	PLEURA
opening for gill	GILL SLIT
respiratory organ	
—fish, etc	GILL
—spiders, etc	LUNG-BOOK
—vertebrates	LUNG
rudimentary gill slit	GILL POUCH
section of lung	LOBE
upper part of	
—gullet	PHARYNX
—trachea	LARYNX
windpipe	TRACHEA
rhetoric	
including: grammar	
speech	
words	
2 letters, 1 sound	DIGRAPH
2 vowel sounds as one	DIPHTHONG
3 letters, 1 sound	TRIGRAPH
3 vowel sounds as one	TRIPHTHONG
academic introduction	ISAGOGE
adage	PAROEMIA
added as finishing touch	EPIPHONEMA
addition	
—of words to clarify meaning	EPEXEGESIS
—to end of word	EPITHESIS
	PARAGOGE
adjective or verb applied to two nouns	ZEUGMA
affected style	EUPHUISM, GONGORISM
affirmation by	
—negation of contrary	ENANTIOSIS
	LITOTES
—substitution of contrary	ANTIPHRASIS
	ENANTIOSIS, IRONY
analyse	PARSE
anapaestic catalectic	PAROEMIA
anti-climax	BATHOS
anticipation	PROLEPSIS
apparent but not real absurdity	PARADOX
apposition	PARATHESIS
arch disparagement	DIASYRM
argument	
—of probability	ENTHYMEME
—to one point	DIALLAGE
arrangement in order of greater strength	CLIMAX
assigning human feelings to non-human objects	PATHETIC FALLACY
attack with words	INVECTIVE
attributive used as proper name	ANTONOMASIA

avoiding repetition	ANAPHORA	description by	
balancing of opposing		—analogy	METAPHOR
ideas	ANTITHESIS	—likening to something	
beginning		else	SIMILE
—and ending sentence		—negation	ENANTIOSIS
with same word	EPANADIPLOSIS	desultory talk	DISCURSION
—successive sentences		development of vowel	ANAPTYXIS
with the same word	(EP)ANAPHORA		SVARABHAKTI
boldness of speech	PARRHESIA	diacritical sign over	
bombastic style	EUPHUISM	letter n	TILDE
breach of syntax	SOLECISM	diaeresis	TREMA
breaking of sentence	APOSIOPESIS	digression in speech	APOSTROPHE
burlesque mixture of words	MACARONIC		ASIDE, ECBOLE, EXCURSION
change			EXCURSUS, PARENTHESIS
—in form of word to		direct address to one	
indicate tense, etc	INFLECTION	present or absent	APOSTROPHE
—of		disingenuous	
letter	PARAGRAM	—denial	APOPHASIS
relation of words		—mention of a subject	METASTASIS
in sentence	HYPALLAGE	diversion	APOSTROPHE
—to an r-sound	RHOTACISE, RHOTACIZE	downbeat	THESIS
child-talk	GAMMACISM	drawing attention to a point	
	HYPOCORISM(A)	by apparently ignoring it	PARAL(E)IPSIS
childish speech	LALLATION	elision	ECTHLIPSIS
circumlocution	PERIPHRASIS	end of speech	PERORATION
clauses without		ending of successive	
connectives	PARATAXIS	clauses with same word	EPISTROPHE
combination of		erroneous quotation	MISCITATION
contradictory terms	OXYMORON	exaggeration	HYPERBOLE
comparison of		exclamation	ECPHONESIS, EPIPHONEMA
—unlike ideas or objects	SIMILE	exhortation	ALLOCUTION
—using transferred name	METAPHOR		PARAN(A)ESIS
compound words	TATPURUSHA	explanatory note	SCHOLION, SCHOLIUM
compounding of words	PARATAXIS	explicit comparison	SIMILE
—without change	PARATHESIS	expression conveying	
concession	SYNCHORESIS	opposite meaning	IRONY
concise		faulty syllepsis	ZEUGMA
—saying	EPIGRAM	figurative	
—style	LACON(IC)ISM	—analogy	METAPHOR
concurrence of vowel		—language	TROPOLOGY
sounds	HIATUS	—resemblance	SIMILE
condensed expression	BRACHYLOGY	figure of speech	TROPE
conditional clause	PROTASIS	flattery of judge	
confusion of meaning	SYNCHYSIS	or audience	COMPROBATION
containing figures		formal speech	ADDRESS, ALLOCUTION
of speech	FIGURATIVE		DISCOURSE, DISQUISITION
contrast by parallelism			LECTURE, ORATION
in reversed order	CHIASMUS	formation of new word by	
correct expression		wrong derivation from	
displacing an		an existing word	BACK FORMATION
incorrect one	SUMPSIMUS	freedom of speech	PARRHESIA
corresponding in		funeral oration	ELOGE
arrangement of syllables	TAUTOMETRICAL	grammatical construction	SYNTAX
coupling of opposites	SYNOECIOSIS	having	
descent from sublime		—acute accent on	
to ridiculous	ANTI-CLIMAX, BATHOS	penultimate syllable	PAROXYTONE

third last syllable	PROPAROXYTONE
—an additional syllable	PERISSOSYLLABIC
—circumflex accent on the penult	PROPERISPOMENON
—full number of syllables	ACATALECTIC
—one more syllable in cases other than nominative	IMPARISYLLABIC
high-flown expression	EUPHUISM
hinting at	INNUENDO
idiomatic expression	IDIOTISM
imitation of sound	ONOMATOPOEIA ONOMATOPO(I)ESIS
immediate repetition	EPIZEUXIS
important speech	KEYNOTE SPEECH
inconsistent comparison	MIXED METAPHOR
incorrect use of words	CATACHRESIS MALAPROPISM
indeclinable noun	APTOTE
insertion	PARENTHESIS
—of sound	EPENTHESIS
interchanged relation-ship of words	HYPALLAGE TRANSFERRED EPITHET
introduction	EXORDIUM, ISAGOGE PROLEGOMENON
inversion	ANASTROPHE HYSTERON-PROTERON
—of	
antithesis	ANTIMETATHESIS
meaning	ANTIPHRASIS
jumbling of words	SYNCHYSIS
lack of syntactical sequence	ANACOLUTHIA ANACOLUTHON
last but one syllable	PENULT(IMA)
lengthening of short syllable	ECTASIS
list of words to be avoided	ANTIBARBARUS
litotes	M(E)IOSIS
logical argument	SYLLOGISM
marrowsky	SPOONERISM
meiosis	LITOTES
melting of final vowel	SYNALOEPHA
metaphor	IMAGE, PARABOLE
metaphorical	FIGURATIVE
metonymy	METALEPSIS
milder term for unpleasant thing	EUPHEMISM
misapplication of words	CATACHRESIS MALAPROPISM
modification of sound caused by context	SANDHI
more than two words	POLYONYMIC

much talk with little to say	MACROLOGY
mutual interchange of relationships	HYPALLAGE TRANSFERRED EPITHET
narration of facts	DIEGESIS
non-literal expression	TROPE
noun	SUBSTANTIVE
obfuscation	SERMOCINATION
omission of	
—conjunctions	ASYNDETON
—first sound or syllable	APH(A)ERESIS
—last sound or syllable	APOCOPE
—sound or syllable from middle of word	HAPLOLOGY SYNCOPATION, SYNCOPE
—vowel	
at beginning of word	APHESIS
or syllable	ELISION
—word(s)	ELLIPSIS
oration	DIEGESIS
overstatement	HYPERBOLE
palatalised	MOUILLE
panegyric	ELOGE, ENCOMIUM EULOGY, EULOGIUM
perissology	PLEONASM, VERBIAGE
personification	PROSOPOEIA
pert speech	DICACITY
phrase found once only	HAPAX LEGOMENON
phrases describing different aspects of something	SYSTROPHE
pithy saying	ADAGE, APHORISM APO(PH)THEGM, EPIGRAM, GNOME LACON(IC)ISM, MAXIM PROVERB, SAW
play on words	PARAGRAM, PARONOMASIA PARONOMASY, PUN
pleasant pronunciation	EUPHONY
pleonasm	PERISSOLOGY
pompous language	BOMBAST, EUPHUISM FUSTIAN GRANDILOQUENCE
pretended neglect	PARAL(E)IPSIS
process by which word acquires	
—less favourable meaning	DETERIORATION PEJORATION
—more favourable meaning	AMELIORATION ELEVATION
professed doubt	APORIA
prolixity	MACROLOGY
pronounced in liquid manner	MOUILLE

pronouncing `r' as `l'	LALLATION	ridicule	IRONY, SATIRE, SCORN
pronunciation with		round-about expression	PERIPHRASE
wide-open mouth	PLATEASM		PERIPHRASIS
proper name used		running together of vowels	SYN(A)ERESIS
as attributive	ANTONOMASIA	—in separate words	SYNAL(O)EPHA
proverb	PAROEMA	same	
question to oneself	HYPOPHORA	—notion in two	
raillery	DICACITY	expressions	HENDIADYS
recapitulation	EPANADOS	—relationship but	
redundant expression	PLEONASM	different sense	SYLLEPSIS
refined irony	ASTEISM	sarcasm	INVECTIVE
relationship of		satirical remark	SARCASM
—two words side by side		self-evident truth	AXIOM, TRUISM
one explaining		sentence	
the other	APPOSITION	—begins and ends	
—word to other words		with same word	EPANADIPLOSIS
in a sentence	CASE	—ending	CLAUSULA
repetition		separation of parts of	
—at beginning and end		compound words	TMESIS
of clauses	SYMPLOCE	series of syllogisms	POLYSYLLOGISM
—in reverse order	ANTIMETABOLE	setting down	THESIS
—of		short clause at end	
connectives	POLYSYNDETON	of period	CLAUSULA
important word or		shortening of syllable	SYSTOLE
phrase	ANADIPLOSIS	simile	IMAGE, PARABOLE
occurrence of sounds	ASSONANCE	similitude	PARABOLE
sound	TAUTOPHONY	solo speech	MONOLOGUE, SOLILOQUY
word or clause		speech	
for emphasis	PALLILOGY	—of	
—at the beginning		appeal	EXHORTATION, PLEA
of words	ALLITERATION	denunciation	DIATRIBE, HARANGUE
word	PALILLOGONY		PHILIPPIC, TIRADE
—at		emotion	EFFUSION
begining		farewell	VALEDICTION, VALEDICTORY
and end of sentence	EPANADIPLOSIS	lamentation	JEREMIAD
—of successive		opening	INAUGURAL
clauses	(EN)ANAPHORA	praise	ENCOMIUM, EULOGY
end of successive			PANEGYRIC
clauses	EPISTROPHE	—sound	PHONEME
—immmediately	EPIZEUXIS	—with	
—or clause		enemies	PARLEY, POW-WOW
after parenthetic text	EPANALEPSIS	others	COLLUQUY, DIALOGUE
at end of one clause		splitting of word by	
and beginning		insertion of another	TMESIS
of the next	ANADIPLOSIS	Spoonerism	MARROWSKY
—useless	BATTOLOGY, TAUTOLOGY	study of verse	PROSODY
reproachful accusation	INVECTIVE	stuttering	GAMMACISM
responding alternately	AMOEBAEAN	suggestion wihout assertion	INNUENDO
resumption	EPANALEPSIS	suppression of	
retracting in order to		—sound	ECTHLIPSIS
correct or intensify	EPANORTHOSIS	—vowel or syllable	ELISION
reversion after a		symbol with more than	
parenthesis	HYPOSTROPHE	one phonetic value	POLYPHONE
rhetorical question	EROTEMA, EROTEME	syntax relating to meaning	SYNESIS
	EROTESIS	three letters, one sound	TRIGRAPH
riddle	LOGOGRIPH	time	TENSE

tirade	LAISSE
transference of	
—adjective	HYPALLAGE
—meaning	METALEPSIS, METONYMY
—name	METAPHOR
to related object	METALEPSIS
	METONYMY
transposition of	
—initial sounds	MARROWSKY
	SPOONERISM
—order	HYPERBATON
—sounds or letters	METATHESIS
trema	DIAERESIS
trite statement	TRUISM
turning away from	
main theme	APOSTROPHE
two	
—speaking	DUOLOGUE
—vowels pronounced	
as one	DIPHTHONG
understatement	LITOTES, M(E)IOSIS
ungrammatical	ASYNTACTIC
union of two vowels	SYNECPHONESIS
	SYNIZESIS
unprepared speech	AD LIB(ITUM)
	EXTEMPORISATION
	IMPROMPTU, IMPROVISATION
use of	
—adjective to apply to	
two words when appropriate	
only to one	ZEUGMA
—another's imagined words	MIMESIS
—I in excess	IOTACISM
—less offensive word	EUPHEMISM
—more offensive word	DYSPHEMISM
—personal name to	
refer to class	ANTONOMASIA
—redundant words	MACROLOGY
—synedoche	SYNEDOCHISM
—word	
in	
—place of another	
related to it	METONYMY
—anticipation	PROLEPSIS
—sense opposite to	
literal sense	ANTIPHRASIS
	ENANTIOSIS, LITOTES
	IRONY
to apply in different	
ways to two others	SYLLEPSIS
used in three cases	TRIPTOTE
useless repetition	BATTOLOGY
	TAUTOLOGY
using part for whole	
or whole for the part	SYNECDOCHE
valediction	APOPEMPTIC

variation of vowel	ABLAUT
verbiage	PERISSOLOGY
violent censure	INVECTIVE
vivid description	HYPOTYPOSIS
vocabulary of a dialect	IDIOTICON
vowel	
—pronunciation mark	DI(A)ERESIS
	UMLAUT
—sound	MONOPHTHONG
without	
—conjunctions	ASYNDETON
—the article	ANARTHROUS
word	
—containing more	
than 3 letters	PLURILITERAL
—expressing sentence	
or phrase	HOLOPHRASE
—found once only	HAPAX LEGOMENON
—having	
more than one meaning	POLYSEME
same	
—meaning	SYNONYM
—sound but	
different	
meaning	HOMONYM, HOMOPHONE
—spelling but	
different meaning	HETERONYM
	HOMOGRAPH
two constructions	SYLLEPSIS
—imitating sound	ONOMATOPOIEA
—of	
1 syllable	MONOSYLLABLE
2 syllables	DISYLLABLE
3 syllables	TRISYLLABLE
4 syllables	QUADRISYLLABLE
	TETRASYLLABLE
5 syllables	PENTASYLLABLE
6 syllables	HEXASYLLABLE
7 syllables	HEPTASYLLABLE
8 syllables	OCTOSYLLABLE
10 syllables	DECASYLLABLE
11 syllables	HENDECASYLLABLE
12 syllables	DODECASYLLABLE
many syllables	POLYSYLLABLE
—represented by single	
sound	GRAMMALOGUE
—riddle	LOGOGRIPH
—that reads alike	
backward and forward	PALINDROME
	(*see also* **language**)
Rhodesia	RSR
	(*see also* **Zimbabwe**)
rice	
dishes	
—East Indian	NASI GORENG
	RIJST(T)AFEL

—Indian	BIRIANI, BIRYANI
	PILAU, PULAO
—Italian	RISOTTO
—Japanese	SUSHI
—Middle East	PILAF(F), PILAU, PULAO
—rice and fish	KEDGEREE
—Spanish	PAELLA
types	
—American	CAROLINA
—Indian	BASMATI, PATNA
—Italian	ARBORIO
—long grain	PATNA

rivers

Afghanistan	AB-I-PANJA, AMUDHRYA
	BANDIHALA, FARAH RUD
	HARI RUD, HELMAND, KOULM
	KUNDUZ, MURGHAB, OXUS
Alaska	YUKON
Albania	DRINI, SEMANI, VJOSA
Algeria	CHELIFF
Andorra	VALIRA
Angola	CUANDO, CUANZA, CUNENE
	KUANZA, KUNENE, KWANDO
Argentina	BERMEJO, CHICO, CHUBUT
	COLORADO, DE LA PLATO
	DULCE, LIMAY, NEGRO
	PARANA, PILCOMAYO
	PLATE, SALADO, URUGUAY
Australia	ASHBURTON, BARCOO, BARWAN
	BRISBANE, CULGOA, DALY
	DARLING, DAWSON, DE GREY
	DIAMANTINA, FINKE, FITZROY
	FLINDERS, FORTESCUE, GASCOYNE
	GEORGINA, GILBERT, HAY, LOCHLAN
	MITCHELL, MURCHISON
	MURRAY, MURRUMBIDGEE, ORD
	ROPER, SWAN, VICTORIA
	WARREGO, YARRA-YARRA
Austria	DANUBE, DONAU, INN, MUR
Bangladesh	GANGA, GANGES
	JAMUNA, JUMNA, MEGHNA
Belgium	ESCAUT, MEUSE, SAMBRE
	SCHELDT, YSER
Belize	HONDO, NEW
Bhutan	AMO-CHU, MACHU
	MANAS, WANG CHU
Bolivia	BENI, BENICTO, GUAPAY
	MADIDI, MAMORE
	PILCOMAYA, PARAGUAY
Botswana	CHOBE, SHASHI
Brazil	AMAZON, ARAGUAIU, DESEADO
	DOLCE, IRIRI, JAPURA
	JEQUITINHANHA
	JURUA, MADEIRA, NEGRO
	PARAGUAY, PARANA, PARAPANEMA
	PARNAIBA, PURUS

	SAO FRANCISCO, SOLIMOES
	TAPAJOS, TOCANTINS
	TROMBETAS
Brunei	BRUNEI
Bulgaria	DANUBE, DUNAN, ISKAR
	ISKUR, MARITZA, TUNDZHA
Burkina Faso	VOLTA BLANCHE
	VOLTA NOIRE, VOLTA ROUGE
Burma	CHINDWIN, IRRAWADDY
	MEKONG, NU CHIANG
	SALWEEN, SITTANG
Burundi	KAGERA, RUZIZI
Cambodia	MEKONG
Cameroon	NYONG, SANAGA
Canada	ALBANY, ASSINIBOINE
	ATHABASCA, CHURCHILL
	COLUMBIA, FRASER, MACKENZIE
	MOOSE, NELSON, PEACE, RED
	ST LAWRENCE, SASKATCHEWAN
	SEVERN, SLAVE, SNAKE
	TESLIN, YUKON
Central African Republic	KOTTO
	OUBANGUI
Ceylon	KELANI GANGA
	MAHAWELI GANGA
Chad	BAHR, CHARI, KEITA, LAGONE
Chile	BIO-BIO, LAO, MAULE, VALDIVA
China	ARGUN, CHANJIANG
	CHANG KIANG
	HAN KIANG, HUANGHE
	HUNGSHUI HO, HWANG HO
	IRRAWADDY, KHOTAN
	KIALING KIANG, MEKONG
	SALWEEN, SI KIANG, SIANG KIANG
	TARIM, TATU HO, TSANGPO, WEI HO
	YALUNG KIANG, YANGTZE KIANG
	YARKAND, YELLOW RIVER
Colombia	AMAZON, CAUCA, CAQUETA
	GUAVIARE, MAGDALENA
	META, NEGRO
Costa Rica	RIO GRANDE
Cuba	CAUTO
Cyprus	PEDIEAS, SERANHIS
Czechoslovakia	DANUBE, DUNAJ, ELBE
	HRON, LABE, MORAVA
	NITRA, VAH
Denmark	GUDENA
Dominica	LAYOU
Dominican Republic	YAQUE DEL NORTE
Ecuador	CURARAY, DAULE
	NAPO, PASTAZA
Egypt	NILE
El Salvador	LEMPA
encircling	
—earth (myth)	OCEAN
—Hela's domain (myth)	GYOLT

England	AIRE, ARUN, AVON, CAM
	CHERWELL, DEE, DOVE, EDEN, EXE
	ISIS, KENNET, LEA, LUNE, MERSEY
	NENE, OUSE, PARRETT, RIBBLE
	ROTHER, SEVERN, SOW, STOUR
	SWALE, TAMAR, TAME, TARE, TAW
	TEES, TEST, THAMES, TRENT, TYNE
	USK, WEAR, WELLAND, WEY, WHARFE
	WITHAM, WYE
Equatorial Guinea	BENITO, CAMPO, MUNI
Ethiopia	ABBAY, AWASH, JUBA
	OMO, SAGAN, TEKEZE
	WEBBE SHIBELI, WEBI SHEBELE
Fiji	BA, NADI, NAVUA
	RIWA, SIGATOKA
Finland	KEMIJOKI, LEVOJOKI
	KORKIMAENJOKI
	PAATSJOKI, TORNIOJOKI
France	RIVIERE, DORDOGNE
	GARONNE, GIRONDE, LOIRE
	MARNE, MOSELLE, OISE
	RHINE, RHONE
	SAONE, SEINE, SOMME
Gabon	OGOOUE, OZOUE
Gambia	GAMBIA
Germany	FLUSS
	DANUBE, DONAU, ELBE
	EMS, HAVEL, MOSEL, ODER
	RHEIN, RHINE, WESER
Ghana	OTI, VOLTA
Guatemala	MOTAGUA, USUMACINTA
Guinea	BAFING, KOGON
	KONKOURE, NIGER
Guinea-Bissau	CACHEU, CORUBEL
	GEBA, MANSOA
Guyana	BERBICE, COURANTYNE
	DEMERARA, ESSEQUIBO
	MAZARUNI
Hades (myth)	
—fire	PHLEGETHON
—forgetfulness	LETHE
—lamentation	COCYTUS
—oath of gods	STYX
—woe	ACHERON
Haiti	ARTIBONITE
Honduras	PATUCA, ULUA
Hungary	DANUBE, DRAVA, DUNA
	RBA, TISZA
Iceland	SKJALFANDAFLJOT, THJORSA
India	BHADRA, BHIMA, BOLAN
	BRAHMAPUTRA, CAUVERY, CHAMBAL
	GANGA, GANGES, GHAGHARA
	GODAVARI, HUGLI, JUMNA, KISTNA
	KRISHNA, MAHANADI, NARBADA
	NARMEDA, PENNER, SON, SUTLEJ
	TAPTITUNGA, YAMUNA

Indonesia	BARITOS, DIGUL, HARI
	KAJAN, KAPUAS, MAHAKAM
Iran	ATRAK, KARKHEH, KARUN
	SAFID, SEFID RUD
	ZAYANDEH
Iraq	EUPHRATES, TIGRIS
Ireland	ALLEN, BANN, BARROW
	BLACKWATER, BOYNE, ERNE
	LAGANLEE, LIFFEY, SHANNON
	SLANEY, SUIR
Israel	JORDAN, QISHON
Italy	FIUME, ADIGE, AGRI, ARNO
	BALTEA, BIFERNO, BORMIDA
	BRADANO, BRENTA, DORA
	GARIGLIANO, ISONZA, LIRI, MAIRA
	METAURO, OMBRONE, PANARO
	PIAVE, PO, RENO, SANGRO
	SECCHIO, SELE, SERCHIO, SESIA
	STURA, TAGLIAMENTO, TANARO
	TARO, TEVERE, TIBER, TICINO
	TREBBIO, TRONTO
	VALDI-FIEMME, VOLTURNO
Ivory Coast	BANDAMA, KOMOE
	SASSANDRA
Jamaica	BLACK
Japan	ISHIKARE, KITAKAMI
	SHINANO, TONE
Java	SOLO
Jordan	JORDAN
Kenya	ATHI, MATHIOYA, TANA, UMBA
Korea	CHONGCHON, HAN, IMJIN
	KUM, NAKTONG, NAM
	SOMJIN, YALU, YONGSAN
Laos	MEKONG
Lebanon	JORDAN, LEONTES
legendary (Hebrew)	SAMBATION
	SANBATION
Lesotho	CALEDON, ORANGE
Liberia	CESS, ST JOHN, ST PAUL
Libya	WADI EL-FARIGH
Liechtenstein	RHEIN, RHINE, SAMINA
Luxembourg	ALZETTE, MOSEL(LE)
	OUR, SURE
Madagascar	IKOPO, MANGOKY, MANIA
Malawi	SHIRE
Malaya	KELANTAN, PAHANG
Mali	FALEME, NIGER, SENEGAL
Mauritania	SENEGAL
Mexico	BALSAS, BRAVO, CONCHOS
	FUERTE, GRANDE, GRIJALVA
	PANUCO, SONORA
Mongolia	HERELENG, KERULEN, KHODASIN
	NUN, OB, ORHON, SELENGA
	SELENGE, SUNGARI, URUNGU
Morocco	OUED DRA, OUED MOULOUYA
	OUED OUM-ER-RBIA, SEBOU

Mozambique	LIMPOPO, LUGENDA, RUVUMA	
	SAVE, SHIRE, ZAMBEZI	
Namibia	CUNENE, OKAVANGO	
Nepal	KARNALI, KOSI, NARYANI	
Netherlands	IJSSEL, MAAS, MEUSE	
	RHINE, WAAL	
New Zealand	AWATERE, BULLER	
	CLARENCE, CLUTHA, HOKITIKA	
	HURUNUI, MANAWATU, MOKAU	
	MOTUEKA, ORETI, RAKAIA	
	RANGITAIKI, RANGITATA	
	RUNGITIKEI, TAIERI, THAMES	
	WAIAPU, WAIHOU, WAIKATO	
	WAINOA, WAIRAU, WAITAKI	
	WANGANUI, WHAKATANE	
Nicaragua	COCO, ESCONDIDO, GRANDE	
	SAN JUAN, SEGOVIA	
Niger	DILLIA, NIGER	
Nigeria	ANGERMA, BENUE, CROSS	
	INDALS, NIGER	
North America	ALABAMA, ALLEGHENY	
	ARKANSAS, BRAZOS, CHEYENNE	
	COLORADO, COLUMBIA, GILA	
	HUDSON, MISSISSIPPI, MISSOURI	
	NORTH PLATTE, OHIO, POTOMAC	
	PECOS, RED, RIO GRANDE	
	SACRAMENTO, SAN JOAQUIM, SNAKE	
	SOUTH PLATTE, ST JOHN, ST JUAN	
	SUSQUEHANNA, YELLOWSTONE	
Norway	GLAMA, GLOMMA, LAGEN	
	TANAELV, UME	
oblivion	LETHE	
Pakistan	BEAS, CHENAB, DASHT	
	GANGES, INDUS, JHELUM	
	RAVI, SOAN, SUTLEJ	
Panama	BAYANO, CHUCUNAQUE	
	SANTA MARIA, TUIRA	
Papua New Guinea	FLY, SEPIK	
	STRICKLAND	
Paraguay	HONDO, PARAGUAY	
	PARANA, PILCOMAYO, SALGADO	
Peru	AMAZON(AS), PURUS, TAMBORYACU	
	UCAYALI, URUMBAMBA	
Philippines	ABRA, AGNO, AGUSAN	
	CAGAYAN, LAOANG, MAGAT	
	PAMPANGA	
Phrygia	MEANDER	
Poland	NAREW, ODER, ODRA	
	VISTULA, WISLA	
Portugal	LIMA, TAGUS, TEJO	
Romania	DANUBE, DUNAREA, MURES, PRUT	
Russia	ALDAN, AMGUN, AMUR, ANADYR	
	ANGARA, ANYUY, ARRAKS, BARGUZIN	
	BIRYUSA, BOLSHAYA, CHUNA	
	DNEIPER, DON, DVINA, EMBA, ILIM	
	IRTYSH, ISHIM, KAZYM, KHROMA	

	KIRENGA, KOLYMA, KORKODON
	KOTUY, KURA, KUREYKA, LENA
	MAYA, NADYM, OLEKMA, OLENEK
	OLOY, OKA, OMOLON, PECHORA
	PRIPYAT, SUGAI, TAZ, TOBOL
	TUNGUSKA, UNZHA, URAL, VETLUGA
	VITIM, VOLGA, YANA, YENISEY
	YUDOMA, ZEYA
Rwanda	LUVIRONZA
Scotland	CLYDE, DEE, DON, FORTH
	NITH, SPEY, TAY, TEVIOT
	TWEED
Senegal	CASAMANCE, GAMBIA
	GAMBIE, SENEGAL
Sierra Leone	JONG, ROKEL, SIWA
Somalia	GIUBA, JUBA
	SHEBELE, SHEBELI
South Africa	ORANGE, VAAL
Spain	RIO
	DOURO, DUERO, EBRO
	GUADALQUIVIR, GUADIANA
	TAGUS, TAJO
Sudan	ATBARA, LOL, NILE
Suriname	COMMEWIJNE, COPPENAME
	CORANTIJN, MARONI
	MAROWIJNE, NICKERIE
	SARAMACCA, SURINAME
Swaziland	INGWAVUMA, KEMATI
	UMBULZI, USUTU
Sweden	ANGERMAN, DAL, KLARALVEN
	MJOSA, TORNE, UME
Switzerland	AARE, INN, RHEIN
	RHINE, TICINO
Syria	ASI, EL FURM, ORONTES
Taiwan	CHOSHUI CHI, HSIA-TAN-SHUI
	TANSHUI, WU CHI
Tanzania	PANGANI, RUAHA, RUFIJI
	RUVU, RUVUMA
Tasmania	DERWENT, GORDON, TAMAR
Tempe (myth)	PENEUS
Thailand	CHAD PYHA, MEKONG
	PING, YOM
Trinidad	CORONI, OROPUCHE, ORTOIRE
Tunisia	MEDJERDA
Turkey	DICLE, EUPHRATES, FIRAT
	HALYS, IRMAK, KIZILIRMAK
	MURAT, SAKARYA, TIGRIS
Uganda	NILE, SEMLIKI
Uruguay	URUGUAY
Venezuela	APURE, META, ORINOCO
Vietnam	BLACK RIVER, MA, MEKONG
	RED RIVER, SONG BO
	SONG KOI
Wales	CLEDDAU, CLWYD, DYFI
	TAFF, TAW, TEIFI, TOWY
	USK, VYRNWY, YSTWITH

Yugoslavia	DANUBE, DRAVA, DUNAU
	MORAVA, SAVA, VARDAR
Zaire	CASSAI, CONGO, KASAI, KWA
	KWILU, LUALABA, LUBILASH
	LUKENIE, LUKUGA, LULUA
	LUVUA, SANGA, SANKURU
	TSHUPA, UBANGUI, UELE, ZAIRE
Zambia	LUANGWA, LUAPULA, KAFUE
	ZAMBESI, ZAMBEZI
Zimbabwe	LIMPOPO, LUNDI, NUANETSI
	ODZI, SABI, SHANGANI
	UMNIATA, UMZINGWANI
	ZAMBESI, ZAMBEZI

rock

above fault-plane	HANGING WALL
aggregate of loosened	
fragments	DETRITUS
angle in rock-face	DIEDRE
balanced on another	LOG(G)AN(-STONE)
	LOGGING-STONE
banded	GNEISS
below fault-plane	FOOT WALL
body of rock enclosing	
an intrusion	COUNTRY ROCK
boulder transported by glacier	ERRATIC
calcium carbonate as	
stalagmite or stalactite	DRIPSTONE
cave-dweller	TROGLODYTE
cavity	
—containing crystals	DRUSE
	DRUSY CAVITY, GEODE
—in rock	CAVE, GEODE, VESICLE
Cornwall	VUG
change in shape	DEFORMATION
	METAMORPHISM
—due to	
pressure	DYNAMIC METAMORPHISM
reaction with	
enclosing rock	ENDOMORPHISM
—involving chemical	
composition	METASOMATISM
character of rock	LITHOLOGY
clay rock	SHALE
column with grooves	STYLOLITE
composed of	
—angular fragments	AGGLOMERATE
	BRECCIA
—calcium-containing	
minerals	TESTACEOUS
—fragments	CLASTIC
—lime silicates	HORNFELS
—mixed minerals	AGGREGATE
—pebbles	PSEPHITE
—rock	RUPESTRIAN
—rounded fragments	CONGLOMERATE
	PUDDING STONE

—separable fragments	AGGREGATE
—sand grains	PSAMMITE
—volcanic fragments	AGGLOMERATE, TUFF
containing	
—carbon	CARBONACEOUS
—crystalline and	
glassy material	HEMICRYSTALLINE
—diatom skeletons	DIATOMACEOUS
—grains	GRANULAR
	GRANULOSE
	GRANULOUS
—graphite	PLUMBAGINOUS
—gravel	GLAREOUS
—less than 10% silica	INTERMEDIATE
—little silica	BASIC
—more than	
10% silica	ACID ROCK
one material	COMPOSITE
—ore	GANGUE, LODE
—plate-like crystals	TABULAR
—sand	ARENACEOUS
—shell-like material	TESTACEOUS
—silica	SILICEOUS, SILICIOUS
—steam cavities	AMYGDALOID
conversion of	
—loose material to rock	CEMENTATION
—sediment to rock	DIGENESIS
Cornish	ELVAN
crack in	
—horizontal limestone	GRIKE, GRYKE
—rock	CHIMNEY, CREVICE
	FAULT, FISSURE
	JOINT, RIFT
crest of fold	ANTICLINE
debris	
—at	
foot of	
—glacier	MORAINE
—slope	SCREE, TALUS
side of glacier	LATERAL MORAINE
—produced by	
weathering of rock	ELUVIUM
decomposed rock at outcrop	GOSSAN
	GOZZAN
deposited by	
—hot springs	CALC-TUFF
	SINTER, TRAVERTINE
—water	SEDIMENTARY
description of rocks	PETROGRAPHY
displaced by folding	NAPPE
distinguishing features	FACIES
division of rock	
formation	SERIES, SYSTEM
easily split into lamina	SCHIST, SLATE
exposed on surface	OUTCROP
extrusive rock	BASALT

fall of rock	BERGFALL	—round hot springs	GEYSERITE
flat limestone block	CLINT	fragment(s) of rock	CLAST, DEBRIS
flowing			DETRITUS, RUBBLE
—into cracks	INTRUSIVE	—angular	GRAVEL
—out at surface	EXTRUSIVE	—at base of cliff	SCREE, TALUS
fold		—embedded in another	XENOLITH
—at constant angle	MONOLINE	—rounded	COBBLE, PEBBLE
—dipping outward in			SHINGLE
all directions	PERICLINAL	—small	GRIT
	QUAQUAVERSAL	frothy lava	PUMICE
—downward	SYNCLINE	greywether	SARSEN
large	GEOSYNCLINE	hard broken rock	RAG
—highly folded		having	
geoanticline	ANTICLINORIUM	—crystalline structure	AUTOMORPHIC
geosyncline	SYNCLINORIUM	—no	
—overturned anticline	OVERFOLD	crystalline structure	ANHEDRAL
—parallel to surrounding		regular arrangement	AMORPHOUS
rocks	RECUMBENT	hole (Australia)	GNAMMA HOLE
—upward	ANTICLINE	igneous	PYROGENIC
large	GEOANTICLINE	—fine-grained	VULCANITE
—with almost parallel		—in	
sides	ISOCLINE	horizontal sheet	SILL, TRAP
formation		mound below surface	LACCOLITE
—exposed at Earth's			LACCOLITH
surface	OUTCROP	vertical sheet	DIKE, DYKE
—from fragments	LITHIFICATION	—injected into fissure	DIKE(-WALL)
formed			DYKE(-WALL)
—at depths below		—intrusive mass	BATHOLITE, BATHOLITH
the surface	HYPOGENE		BATHYLITE, BATHYLITH
—after enclosing rock	EPIGENETIC	—lens-shaped mass	PHACOLITH
—by			SADDLE-REEF
accretion	OOLITH	—not reaching surface	HYPABYSSAL
alteration of limestone	DOLOMITE	—rocks	AMYGDALOID, BASALT
altered composition due			BASANITE, BATHOLITE
to high temperature			DOLERITE, GABBRO, GRANITE
and pressure	METAMORPHIC		MONZONITE, PERMATITE
change of molecular			PERIDOTITE, PHONOLITE
structure	PARAMORPH		PORPHYRY, RHYOLITE
compression of clay	SLATE		SPILITE, TRACHYTE
cooling of lava			VARIOLITE, WHINSTONE
or magma	EXTRUSIVE	isolated rock	
	IGNEOUS	—pillar in sea	STACK
deposit of calcium etc		—standing above	
from moving water	FLOWSTONE	ice	NUNATAK
deposition	SEDIMENTARY	its surroundings	MONADNOCK
evaporation of sea-water	EVAPORITE	large rounded lump of rock	BOULDER
hardening of silt	SILTSTONE	layer(s) of rock	STRATUM (STRATA)
outpouring of lava	EFFUSIVE	lens-shaped mass of	
subterranean heat	ABYSSAL	igneous rock	PHACOLITH
	PLUTONIC		SADDLE-REEF
—in volcanoes	(see **volcano**)	limestone	
—from		—coarse	PISOLITE
clay or mud	PELITE	—crystalline	MARBLE
organic material	BIOLITH	—decomposed	ROTTENSTONE
—of thin layers	FOLIACEOUS	—deposited from	
	FOLIATED	solution	TRAVERTIN(E)

—Dorset	PURBECK MARBLE	overlying rock	OVERBURDEN
	PURBECK STONE	painting or inscription	
—granular	OOLITE	on rock	PETROGLYPH
—India	KUNKAR, KUNKUR	paramorphic change	METASTASIS
—needle		partially decomposed	SAPROLITE
growing upward	STALAGMITE	particle	GRAIN, GRANULE
hanging down	STALACTITE	peak	CRAG
—patterned	LANDSCAPE MARBLE	permitting passage	
—soft and crumbly	MALM	of water	PERMEABLE ROCK
living in rocks	LITHODOMOUS		PERVIOUS ROCK
	RUPICOLINE, RUPICOLOUS	pile of rock	CAIRN, TOR
long rounded rock	ROCHE MOUTONNEE	pillar of limestone	
looking like another		—hanging	STALACTITE
which it has replaced	PSEUDOMORPH	—standing	STALAGMITE
loose rock at		plateau	MASSIF
—foot of cliff	SCREE, TALUS	plutonic rock	GRANITE, SYENITE
—surface	MANTLEROCK, REGOLITH	pointed mass of rock	AIGUILLE, CRAG
magnetic rock	LOADSTONE, LODESTONE	porous	TUFA, TUFF, PUMICE
mantle rock	REGOLITH	preventing passage	
mass of		of water	IMPERMEABLE ROCK
—igneous rock			IMPERVIOUS ROCK
formed by intrusion		production of different	
of magma	BATHOLITE, BATHOLITH	rocks from common	
	BATHYLITE, BATHYLITH	mother base	DIFFERENTIATION
lens-shaped	PHACOLITH, SADDLE-REEF	radioactive rock	AUTONITE, CARMENITE
—plutonic rock	PLUTON		PITCH-BLENDE, RADIUM
—rock balanced on slender			TORBANITE, URANIUM
neck	PEDESTAL ROCK	ridge running into sea	PROMONTORY
—carried away by		rock	
natural phenomena	BOULDER, ERRATIC	—boring	LITHOPHAGOUS
—sandstone		—building	LITHOGENOUS
in Alps	FATSCH	—dwelling	RUPICOLINE, RUPICOLOUS
left after erosion		—guano	SOMBRERITE
of layer	GREYWETHER, SARSEN	—oil	PETROLEUM
—wall rock		rocky	
interrupting lode	HORSE	—crust of Earth	LITHOSPHERE
—with convex sides	LENS	—desert	HAM(M)ADA, REG
mechanical breakup	CATACLASIS	—edge of mountain	ARETE
metamorphic rocks	GNEISS, MYLONITE	—height	TOR(R)
	PORPHYROID, SCHIST	—island	SKERRY, STACK
	SLATE	—mound (Scot.)	SCALP
mineral composition		—recess	COVE
of rock	MODE	—valley	GULCH, RAVINE
mining from surface	OPENCAST	rudaceous rock	SEDIMENTARY
—US	STRIP MINING	sandy	
molten rock	MAGMA	—ironstone	DOGGER
moved by glacier	ERRATIC	—shale	FA(I)KES
new rock surrounded		sarsen	GREYWETHER
by older	OUTLIER	sedimentary rocks	BRECCIA, CHACK, CLAY
non-crystalline rock	AMORPHOUS		COAL, GRIT, IRONSTONE
old rock surrounded			LIMESTONE, MUDSTONE
by newer	INLIER		QUARTZITE, SANDSTONE
on			SHALE, SLATE
—ice in glacier	GLACIER TABLE	series of rocks	FORMATION
—or near surface	EPIGENE ROCK	shaly sandstone	FA(I)KES
outcrop	BASSET	sheet of rock	NAPPE

sloping	
—area of scree	TALUS
—bedrock at foot of	
steeper slope	PEDIMENT
small lump of rock	NODULE
splitting into layers	CLEAVAGE
	LAMINATION
standing above ice	NUNATAK
steep rock(-face)	CRAG, CLIFF
stone polished by wind	VENTIFACT
streaks in igneous rock	SCHLIEREN
stretching of rock into	
sausage shape	BOUDINAGE
study of	
—rocks	GEOLOGY, LITHOLOGY
	PETROLOGY
—rock strata	STRATIGRAPHY
subterranean mass of	
solidified rock	PLUTON
thin layer(s) of rock	LAMINA(E)
through which vein of	
ore runs	WALL ROCK
transported from original	
site by glacier	ERRATIC
under sea	LEDGE, REEF
underlying	
—rock	BEDROCK
—surface	BEDDING PLANE
—stratified rocks	BASEMENT (COMPLEX)
useless	GANGUE
vertical face formed	
by erosion	RIMROCK
volcanic rock	(*see* **volcano**)
water-bearing	AQUIFER
without crystalline	
structure	GLASS
worthless	GANGUE
(*see also* **geography, mineral, stone**)	
rockets	(*see* **missiles, space**)
Roman	ROM
acquisition by occupation	USUCAPTION
actor	ROSCIUS
—in dumb show	PANTOMINE
actor's mask	PERSONA
additional name	AGNOMEN
administrative building	BASILICA
administrator	PROCURATOR
agate	MURR(H)A
amphitheatre	COLOSSEUM, COLISEUM
ancient kingdom	PONTUS
apartment house	INSULA
assemblies	
—for laws	COMITIA
—of	
centuries	COMITIA CENTURIATA
patricians	COMITIA CURITA

tribes	COMITIA TRIBUTA
assembly	FORUM
auxiliary soldier	FOEDERATUS
awning	VELARIA
axe	DOLABRA
barrack-room	CONTUBERNIA
barracks	CAN(N)ABA
bathing establishment	THERM
block of buildings	INSULA
blood-sucking witch	LAMIA
body of soldiers	LEGION
boring engine	TEREBRA
boundary	LIMES
brickwork	OPUS LATERICUM
bridge builder	PONTIFEX
building	INSULA
—where senate met	CURIA
bundle of rods	FASCES
calendar	FASTI
camp gate	PR(A)ETORIAN GATE
cap of free slave	PHRYGIAN CAP
capital	ROME
catapult	BAL(L)ISTA
Catholic	RC
centurion's badge	VINE ROD
chair	CURULE
chariot	BIGA, QUADRIGA
chief	
—magistrate	CONSUL
—priest (Syria)	SYRIARCH
—secretary of chancery	PROT(H)ONOTARY
children's ornament	BULLA
church	
—basin	CANTHARUS
—office	NONES
circus barrier	SPINA
citizen	QUIRITES
clan	GENS
cloak	TOGA, TOGE
—for travelling	PAENULA
—military	ABOLLA
—of manhood	TOGA VIRIUS
—woman's	PALLA
coin metal	POTIN
coins	
—copper	AS, SEMUNCIA
—1/6 as	SEXTANS
—1/4 as	KODRANTES, QUADRANS
—1/2 as	SEMIS
—2 asses	DUPONDIUS
—2½ asses	SESTERCE
—10 asses (silver)	DENARIUS
—2 denarii	ANTONINIANUS
—12 denarii (silver)	SOLIDUS
—1000 sesterces	SESTERTIUM
—old	DUPONDIUS

—gold	AUREUS, SOLIDUS
college of heralds	FETIALES
colonial governor	PRO-CONSUL
comedy	PALLIATA
commander of	
—10 soldiers	DECURION
—100 soldiers	CENTURION
commoner	PLEB
company of soldiers	MANIPLE
	VEXILLIUM
conquered ally	FOEDERATUS
consul's robe	TRABEA
cooling room	FRIGIDARIUM
couch	TRICLINUM
councillor	DECURION
country house	VILLA
court	CURIA
—official	LICTOR
—(yard)	AULA
cross	TEN, X
curved tile	IMBREX
cushioned seat	PULVINAR
dagger	SICA
dance	TRIPUDIUM
daring conspirator	CATALINE
dates	
—1st of each month	CALENDS
—9th before ides	NONES
—13th/15th	IDES
days	
—Monday	DIES LUNAE
—Tuesday	DIES MARTIS
—Wednesday	DIES MERCURII
—Thursday	DIES JOVIS
—Friday	DIES VENERIS
—Saturday	DIES SATURNI
—Sunday	DIES SOLIS
—when business	
legal	FASTI
not legal	NEFASTI
decree of senate	SC
	SENATUS CONSULT(UM)
deities	(*see* **gods, goddesses**)
descendant of original	
Roman people	PATRICIAN
digest of law	PANDECT
dining-room	TRICLINUM
dish	PATERA
ditch round amphitheatre	EURIPUS
diviner	AUGUR, AUSPEX
	HARUSPEX
division of tribe	CURIA
divorce	DIFFAREATION
dominion governor	PRO-CONSUL
drinking cup	CANTHARUS
dual officials	DUUMVIR

early Roman empire	PRINCIPATE
earth mound	AGGER
earthenware jar	DOLIUM
election canvass official	NOMENCLATOR
emperor's	
—bodyguard	PR(A)ETORIAN GUARD
—decree	INDICTION, NOVELLA
engine of war	TORMENTUM
entrance hall	ATRIUM
epic poem	AENEID
exit door	VOMITORIUM
family name	COGNOMEN
farmstead	VILLA
fastening of woman's sash	VIRGIN KNOT
favourite food	MUR(A)ENA
felt cap	PILEUS
festival of	
—boundaries	TERMINALIA
—cornfields	AMBARVALIA
—exorcism	LEMURIA
—fertility	LUPERCALIA
—Pales	PALILIA
—Saturn	SATURNALIA
—Vulcan	VULCANIA
—wine	VINALIA
fifteen-year cycle	INDICTION
financial agent	PROCURATOR
fish sauce	GARUM
flask	AMPHORA, AMPULLA
flat dish	PATERA
forename	PRAENOMEN
former master of slave	PATRON
forming friendship	
by dividing stone	CONTESSERATION
fort	CASTELLUM
freeman	AERARIAN
galley	BIREME, TRIREME
	QUADRIREME, QUINQUEREME
games	SECULAR GAMES
general's	
—cloak	PALUDAMENT(UM)
—quarters	PRINCIPIUM
—tent	PR(A)ETORIUM
ghost(s) of the dead	LEMUR(ES)
gift	CONGIARY
gladiator	SAMNITE
—armed with net	RETIARIUS
god	DEUS
god's head-dress	MODIUS
governor's residence	PR(A)ETORIUM
grappling hook	CORVUS
hall	ATRIUM, AULA
headband	VITTA
headquarters	PR(A)ETORIUM
	PRINCIPIA
heavy javelin	PILUM

heraldic	FECIAL, FETIAL
Hermes's rod	CADUCEUS
hill of Rome	QUIRINAL
himation	PALLIUM
historian	LIVY, TACITUS
hospital	VALETUDINARIUM
household gods	LARES AND PENATES
imperial	
—official	COUNT
—standard	LABARUM
internal quadrangle	COMPLUVIUM
jar	AMPHORA, DOLIUM, OLLA
javelin	PILE
judge	CENTUMVIR, QU(A)ESTOR
kill every tenth man	DECIMATE
knight	EQUES
land tax	INDICTION
lapsing (law)	CADUCOUS
large hall	BASILICA
law	LEX
—digest	PANDECT
leader	DUX
leather armour	LORICA
legal transfer	MANCIPATION
legion	COHORT
low-class citizen	PROLETARIUS
magistrate	(A)EDILE, (PRO)PR(A)ETOR
	PRO-CONSUL, QU(A)ESTOR
	TRIBUNE
—whose ancestors had	
never held office	NOVUS HOMO
magistrate's	
—attendant	LICTOR
—badge	FASCES
—chair	CURULE
man	VIR
man's undergarment	SUBUCULA
mantle	PALLIUM, TOGA, TOGE
manuscript style	RUSTICA
market	
—day	NUNDINE
—place	FORUM
marriage	CONFAR(R)EATION
mausoleum	MOLE
measures	
—58 inches	PACE
—1000 double paces	MILE
—1.4 miles	LEAGUE
—1 gallon	CONGIUS
—1 peck	MODIUS
milestone	MILIARY
military	
—cloak	ABOLLA, PALUDAMENT(UM)
	SAGUM
—earthwork	AGGER
—shelter formed by shields	TESTUDO

—standard	LABARUM
—wheeled shelter	TESTUDO
missile-thrower	TORMENTUM
monarch	CAESAR
monster	LAMIA, TYPHON
moray	MUR(A)ENA
mortuary	SPOLIARY
mound	AGGER
name	NOMEN
—without description	NOMEN NUDUM
noble	PATRICIAN
oak wreath	CIVIC CROWN
officer's cloak	PALUDAMENT(UM)
official	LICTOR
—scrivener	TABELLION
one of	
—board of	
two men	DUUMVIR
three men	TRIUMVIR
four men	QUADRUMVIR
five men	QINQUEVIR
six men	SEXTUMVIR
seven men	SEPTEMVIR
ten men	DECEMVIR
—two divisions of	
Roman people	PLEBS
open area in middle of	
house	COMPLUVIUM
orator	CICERO
patrician	PATRON
—marriage	CONFARREATION
—virgin	VESTA
perpetual right in land	EMPHYTEUSIS
platter	LANX
pledge in lawsuit	SACRAMENT
poet	(see writer below)
porridge	PULS
pound	LIBRA
precious metal	MURR(H)A
precluding debate	PEREMPTORY
	PLAUTUS, PLINY
priest	FLAMEN, PONTIFEX
—foretelling future	AUGUR, AUSPEX
	HARUSPEX
—of field deities	ARVAL BRETHREN
privy council (chamber)	CONSISTORY
prize to first to mount	
wall of besieged city	MURAL CROWN
procession in honour	
of victorious general	TRIUMPH
prosecutor	QU(A)ESTOR
province (ancient)	PONTUS
provincial governor	PROPRAETOR
public	
—baths	THERMAE
—hall or court	BASILICA

—square	FORUM
purification ceremony	LUSTRE, LUSTRUM
rain-water receptacle	IMPLUVIUM
rampart	VALLUM
ramps	ASCENSI
reclining couch	TRICLINUM
register	ALBUM
religious	
—ceremony	LECTISTERNIUM
—dance	TRIPUDIUM
—festival	LUPERCAL(IA)
	QUIRINAL(IA)
—head-band	INFULA
—offerings	INFERIAE
repository for Penates	SACRARIUM
richest booty	SPOLIA OPTIMA
road	VIA
Roman people	PR
royal palace	BASILICA
ruler	CAESAR
ruling body	SENATE
rural deity	FAUN
sacrifice	INFERIAE
—of animals	SUOVETAURALIA
satirist	JUVENAL(IS)
score	DOUBLECROSS
scroll	STEMMA
sea-fight	NAUMACHIA, NAUMACHY
second name	NOMEN
senate	CURIA
senators	CONSCRIPT FATHERS
	PATRES CONSCRIPTI
shallow pan	PATINA
shield	SCUTUM
—from heaven	ANCILE
sleeveless garment	EXOMIS, PAENULA
soldier(s)	
—company	MANIPLE, VEXILLATION
of	
—10	DECURIA, DECURY
—100	CENTURY
—300-600	COHORT
—3000-6000	LEGION
—in charge of	
10 men	DECURION
100 men	CENTURION
—lightly-armed	VELITE
—tenth of legion	COHORT
soldier's oath	SACRAMENT
soothsayer	AUGUR, AUSPEX
	HARUSPEX
spear	PILUM
spirits of the dead	MANES
staircases	ASCENSI
standard	LABARUM, VEXILLUM
—bearer	VEXILLARY

stool	CURULE
straight trumpet	TUBA
stripe on senator's tunic	LATICLAVE
surplice	STOLA
surveying instrument	GROMA
swimming-pool	PISCINA
sword	GLADIUS, SPATHA
symbol of authority	FASCES
tax-collector	PUBLICAN
temple of	
—all gods	PANTHEON
—Jupiter	CAPITOL
tenth part of	
—legion	COHORT
—tribe	CURIA
third (family) name	COGNOMEN
three-pronged weapon	TRIDENT
tile	TEGULA
training ground	CAMPUS MARTIUS
travelling-cloak	PAENULA
tribe	GENS
triple officials	TRIUMVIR
trumpet	BUCCINA
underfloor space	
for heating	HYPOCAUST
undergarment	SUBUCULA, TUNIC
veteran	VEXILLARY
wall decoration	TOPIA
warm room in baths	TEPIDARIUM
weights	
—½ ounce	SEMUNCIA
—12 ounces	AS
—pound	AS, LIBRA
white tablet	ALBUM
wine	
—festival	VINALIA
—jar	DOLIUM
woman's	
—mantle	PALLA
—robe	STOLA
workshop	FABRICIA
writer	APULEIUS, CATULLUS, HORACE
	JUVENAL, LUCRETIUS, OVID
	PLAUTUS, PLINY, TERENCE, VIRGIL
	(*see also* **Latin, mythology**)
Romania	R(O)
capital	BUCHAREST, BUCURESTI
coins	BANI, LEU
newsagency	AGERPRES
secret police	SECURITATE
stew	TOCANA
room	
alcove for private study	CARREL(L)
artist's room	STUDIO
bedchamber (Fr.)	ROUELLE
behind stage	GREEN ROOM

circular	ROTUNDA
council chamber	DIVAN
court of justice	DIVAN
dining room	
—in college etc	REFECTORY
—Roman	TRICLINIUM
dungeon with opening	
only in the top	OUBLIETTE
entrance	ANTECHAMBER, ANTEROOM
	HALL, LOBBY, VESTIBULE
	FOYER
—college etc	(PORTER'S) LODGE
—Roman	ATRIUM
for	
—conversation	LOCUTORY
—domestic work	KITCHEN, SCULLERY
	UTILITY, WASH-HOUSE
—manoeuvre	LATITUDE, LEEWAY
	PLAY, SCOPE
—meals	DINER, DINETTE
	DINING ROOM, REFECTORY
—parties (Amer.)	RUMPUS ROOM
—prayer	ORATORY, PROSEUCHE
—private use	DEN, SANCTUM
	SNUG, STUDY
—sleeping	BEDROOM, DORMITORY
garret	SOL(L)AR, SOL(L)ER
hot-room	
—Roman	SUDATORIUM
—Swedish	SAUNA
in	
—roof	ATTIC, GARRET
—synagogue	GENIZAH
ladies' private room	BOUDOIR, BOWER
library	ATHENAEUM
living room	LOUNGE
	PARLOUR, SITTING ROOM
	(WITH)DRAWING ROOM
meeting room	HALL
—of coterie	CENACLE
open, central room	ATRIUM
photographer's room	DARK ROOM, STUDIO
reception room	(WITH)DRAWING ROOM
	PRESENCE CHAMBER, SALON
reading room	ATHENAEUM, LIBRARY
retiring-room	(WITH)DRAWING ROOM
—in theatre	GREEN ROOM
room on	
—ship	CABIN, CUDDY
	STATEROOM
—train	COMPARTMENT
rooms linked together	SUITE
sitting-room (military)	ANTEROOM
small	
—compartment	CUBICLE
—room	CAMARILLA

—storeroom	BOXROOM, CUBBY HOLE
	GLORY HOLE
smoking-room	DIVAN
staffroom	COMMON ROOM
store for	
—bones	CHARNEL HOUSE, OSSUARY
—books	ARCHIVE, LIBRARY
—clothes	DRESSING-ROOM
	GARDEROBE, WARDROBE
—documents	ARCHIVE
—medicines etc	DISPENSARY
—provisions	BUTTERY, PANTRY
	LARDER, STILL-ROOM
—vestments	SACRISTY, VESTRY
sun-room	SOLARIUM
supper room	CENACLE
upper room	SOL(L)AR, SOL(L)ER
where	
—cardinals meet to	
select Pope	CONCLAVE
—privy council of Roman	
Empire met	CONSISTORY
writing room	LIBRARY, SCRIPTORIUM
rope	
circus rope	JEFF
coil	HANK
cowboy's rope	LARIAT, LASSO
	REATA, RIATA
fastener	TOGGLE
groove between strands	CANTLINE
—clockwise	Z-LAID
—counter-clockwise	S-LAID
halter for horse-breaking	HACKAMORE
handrail on ship	MANROPE
hanging noose	HALTER
hoisting sling	PARBUCKLE
joint in rope	SPLICE
knotted rope for	
calculating (Peru)	QUIPO, QUIPU
ladder	ETRIER, JACOB'S LADDER
lashing round	
bowsprit	GAMMON
loop	CAT'S-PAW, BIGHT, HANK
neck-cord	LANIARD, LANYARD
picket-rope	HOBBLE, LARIAT
rigging	CORDAGE, TACKLE
—below	
bowsprit	BOBSTAY
yard	FOOTROPE
—for	
fastening	
—bowline to sail	BRIDLE
—furled sail to yard	GASKET
furling square sails	CLEW-LINE
	CLEW-GARNET
hoisting	GANTLINE

raising sail or flag	HALLIARD	Canadian Academy	RCA
	HALYARD	College of	
setting yards	BRACE	—Art	RC, RCA
—from		—Music	RCM
boom to deck	KICKING-STRAP	—Organists	RCO
	VANG	—Physicians	RCP
lower corner of sail	SHEET	—Preceptors	RCP
	TACK	—Science	RCS
sail to bow	BOWLINE	—Sculptors	RCS
—guy rope for gaff	VANG	Corps of	
—on reef-band for furling	REEF-POINT	—Signals	RCS
—round edge of sail	BOLT-ROPE	—Transport	RCT
—step in shrouds	RATLIN(E)	Dublin Society	RDS
	RATTLIN(E), RATTLING	Engineers	RE
—supporting		Exchange	RE
awning	CROWFOOT	Flying Corps	RFC
masts	SHROUD, STAY	Geographical Society	RGS
—to prevent bellying		Grenadier Guards	RGG
of sail	BUNTLINE	Highness	RH
rope-making material	COIR, HEMP	Horse Artillery	RHA
	MANILA, NYLON	Hibernian Academy	RHA
	JUTE, SISAL	Highland	
rope-soled shoe	ESPADRILLE	—Fusiliers	RHF
rope's-end (navy)	COLT	—Show	RHS
running noose	LASSO	Historical Society	RHS
securing gun to ship	BREECHING	Horse Guards	RHG
short rope		Horticultural Society	RHS
—for fastening	LANIARD, LANYARD	Humane Society	RHS
—with metal ring inside	CRINGLE	Institute	RI
small cable	HAWSER	—of Chemistry	RIC
strong rope	CABLE	Institution of Painters	RI
tent-rope	GUY, STAY	Irish	
trailing from balloon	DRAGROPE	—Academy	RIA
used for		—Constabulary	RIC
—leading animal	HALTER	Mail	RM
—mooring boat	PAINTER	—Steamer	RMS
—mooring ship	CABLE, HAWSER, WARP	Marines	*(see separate entry)*
—towing ship	CABLE, TOWROPE	Microscopical Society	RMS
	HAWSER	Military	
—tying		—Academy	RMA
animal	HOBBLE, TETHER	—Police	RMP
or binding	CORD, LASHING	National Lifeboat Institution	RNLI
	MARLIN(E), STRING	Naval Reserve	RNR
	WHIPPING	Navy	*(see separate entry)*
weighted rope (S. Amer.)	BOLAS	Observer Corps	ROC
Royal		Order of Victoria and Albert	VA
Academician/Academy	RA	Philharmonic Orchestra	RPO
Academy of Music	RAM	Photographic Society	RPS
Air Force	*(see separate entry)*	Radar Establishment	RRE
Artillery	RA	School of Music	RSM
Australian Navy	RAN	Scottish	
Automobile Club	RAC	—Academician/Academy	RSA
Arch Charter	RAC	—Water Colour Society	RSW
Armoured Corps	RAC	Society	
Asiatic Society	RAS	—for Prevention of	
Astronomical Society	RAS	Accidents	ROSPA

Cruelty to Animals	RSPCA	—commissioned	SECOND LIEUTENANT
—of			ACTING LIEUTENANT
Antiquaries	RSA		LT, LIEUTENANT
Arts			CAPT, CAPTAIN
British			MAJ, MAJOR
—Artists	RBA		LT-COL, LIEUTENANT-COLONEL
—Sculptors	RBS		COL, COLONEL
Edinburgh	RSE		BRIG, BRIGADIER
Etchers and Engravers	RE		MAJ-GEN, MAJOR-GENERAL
Literature	RSL		LT-GEN, LIEUTENANT-GENERAL
Medicine	RSM		GEN, GENERAL
Painters in Water Colours	RWS		RN

Royal Navy

Portrait Painters	RP	common names	
Statistical Society	RSS	—air engineer	GRUBBER
Ulster Constabulary	RUC	—first mate	NUMBER ONE
Yacht Squadron	RYS	—leading seaman	KILLICK
Yachting Association	RYA	—master-at-arms	JAUNTY
Zoological Society	RZS	—midshipman	SNOTTY
	RAF	ranks (lowest first)	

Royal Air Force

common names		—other ranks	(ORDINARY RATING
—aircraftman	ERK		(ORDINARY SEAMAN
—rear gunner	TAIL-END CHARLIE		AB, ABLE RATING, ABLE SEAMAN
ranks (lowest first)			LEADING RATING
—non-commissioned	AC, AIRCRAFTMAN		LEADING SEAMAN
	LAC, LEADING AIRCRAFTMAN	—non-commissioned	PETTY OFFICER, PO
	SAC, SENIOR AIRCRAFTMAN		CHIEF PETTY OFFICER, CPO
	JUNIOR TECHNICIAN		FLEET CHIEF PETTY OFFICER
	CORPORAL		MIDDY, MIDSHIPMAN
	SERGEANT	—commissioned	ACTING SUB-LIEUTENANT
	CHIEF TECHNICIAN		SUB-LIEUTENANT
	FLIGHT SERGEANT		LT, LIEUTENANT
	WARRANT OFFICER		LIEUTENANT-COMMANDER
—commissioned	PILOT OFFICER, PO		COMMANDER
	FLYING OFFICER, FO		CAPT, CAPTAIN
	FLIGHT LIEUTENANT		COMMODORE
	SQUADRON LEADER		REAR-ADMIRAL
	WING COMMANDER		VICE-ADMIRAL
	GROUP CAPTAIN		ADM, ADMIRAL
	AIR COMMODORE		ADMIRAL OF THE FLEET
	AIR VICE-MARSHAL		

rubber

	AIR MARSHAL	Central American rubber	(H)ULE
	AIR CHIEF MARSHAL	latex	
	MARSHAL OF THE RAF	—from rubber trees	CAOUTCHOUC
royal family	(*see* **house**)		GUM ELASTIC, INDIA RUBBER
Royal Marines	RM	—producing dandelion	KOK-SAGHYZ
common name - marine	JOLLY	natural	GUTTA PERCHA, (H)ULE
ranks (lowest first)			JELUTONG, PONTIANAC
—other ranks	MARINE I		PONTIANAK
	MARINE II	rubber-like polymer	THIOKOL
—non-commissioned	CORPORAL, CPL	rubber-producing fluid	LATEX
	SERGEANT, SGT	synthetic	BUTYL RUBBER, NEOPRENE
—warrant officer {	COLOUR-SERGEANT		NITRILE RUBBER
{	WARRANT OFFICER II		SILICONE RUBBER
{ REGIMENTAL SERGEANT-MAJOR			STEREO-REGULAR RUBBER
{	RSM		STYRENE-BUTADIENE RUBBER, SBR
{	WARRANT OFFICER I		TRANS-POLYCHLOROPRENE

with sulphur	VULCANISED RUBBER
	VULCANITE
rug	BAKU, BERGAMA, BERGAMOT
	BOKHARA, BUKHARA, CHICHI
	DAGESTAN, DERBENT, HAMADAN
	HEREKE RABJIK, KABISTAN, KALI
	KASHAN, KILIM, KIRMAN
	LEZGIAN, NUMBAH, PANEDERMA
	RABJIK, TABRIZ
British	AXMINSTER, WILTON
Chinese	TIENTSIN
French	AUBUSSON
Greek	FLOKATIS
Indian	RABJIK
Pakistani	BOKHARA, BUKHARA
Spanish	CORDOBA
Rugby football	
area between scrum and touchline	BLIND SIDE
deflection of tackle	HAND-OFF
famous players	
—Australian	BURGESS, CAMPESE
	CATCHPOLE, CUTLER, ELLA
	GOULD, HIPWELL, POIDEVIN
	SLACK
—English	BEAUMONT, BENNETT
	COTTON, DALTO, DUCKHAM
	GREGORY, HANLEY, HARE
	HELME, HILL, HILLER, IRO
	IRVING, LOCHORE, LYDON
	MOORE, OBOLENSKY, ROGERS
	SHARP, TEAGUE, UNDERWOOD
	UTTLEY, WHEELER, WOODWARD
originator	ELLIS
—French	BERRANNE, BLANCO, DAUGA
	FOUROUX, PAPAREMBORDE
	RIVES, SPANGHERO
	VILLEPREUX
—Irish	CAMBELL, GIBSON
	KIERNAN, MACBRIDE, MCGANN
	SLATTERY, WARD
—New Zealand	DAVIS, FITZGERALD
	FRASER, GOING, HADEN
	HEWSON, KIRKPATRICK, LAIDLAW
	LOVERIDGE, MEADS, MOURIE
	NORTON, REID, ROBERTSON
	SHELFORD, WILLIAMS, WILSON
—Scottish	BROWN, CALDER
	CARMICHAEL
	MCLAUCHLAN, MOURIE
—South African	BOTHA, DE VILLIERS
	DU PREEZ, GERBER
	PLESSIS, VISAGTE
—Welsh	DAVIES, DAWES, EDWARDS
	HOLMES, JOHN, PRICE
	RICHARDS, WILLIAMS

famous teams	BARBARIANS, HARLEQUINS
	SARACENS, WASPS
high kick downfield	GARRYOWEN
kick dropped ball	DROP-KICK, PUNT
lines on field	GOAL LINE, TOUCH LINE
	TWENTY-FIVE YARD LINE
mass of forwards around the ball on the ground	SCRUM
national teams	
—Australian	WALLABIES
—Argentine	PUMAS
—British	LIONS
—New Zealand	ALL BLACKS
—South African	SPRINGBOKS
playing positions	(BLINDSIDE) FLANKER
	CENTRE, FLY-HALF, FORWARD
	FULL-BACK, HOOKER
	LEFT CENTRE, LEFT WING
	LOCK, NO 8, PROP, RIGHT CENTRE
	RIGHT WING, SCRUM-HALF
	STAND-OFF (HALF), WING
restart of play	DROP-OUT
result of	
—ball out of play	LINE-OUT, SCRUM
—foul	PENALTY (KICK)
score	CONVERSION, DROP GOAL
	PENALTY, TRY
seize an opponent	TACKLE
teams	
—Rugby League	THIRTEEN
—Rugby Union	FIFTEEN
venues	
—England	TWICKENHAM
—Ireland	LANSDOWNE ROAD, DUBLIN
—Scotland	MURRAYFIELD
—Wales	CARDIFF ARMS PARK
rule	(*see* **power**)
Russia	SU, USSR
includes: former USSR	
administrative division	GUBERNIYA
	OBLAST
agreement	DA
airline	AEROFLOT
alphabet	CYRILLIC
approval	DA
aristocrat	BOYAR
association	COMINTERN
	KOMINTERN
bay	BUKTA, GUBA, ZALIV
beef	GOVYADINA
bleached sand soil	PODSOL, PODZOL
blizzard	BURAN
bog	BOLOTO
bureaucrat	APPARATCHIK
	CHINOVNIK

cabbage	KAPUSHTA
—soup	SHTCHI, SHCHI
cakes	TORTI
canal	KANAL
cape (headland)	MYS
capital	MOSCOW
card game	VINT
carriage	DROS(H)KY, TROIKA
cart	TELEGA
castle	GRAD
cathedral	SOBOR
cavalry	COSSACKS
caviar	IKRA
channel	PROTOKA, VOROTA
cheese	SYR
chicken	KURITSA
Christian	UNIAT
citadel	KREMLIN
cloth	SERGE
coins	
—unit	COPEC(K), KOPEC(K), KOPEK
—100 kopeks	R(O)UBLE
collective farm	KOLKHOZ
Committee for State Security	KGB
Commonwealth of Independent States	CIS
—members	AZERBAIJAN, BELARUS
	GEORGIA, KAZAKHSTAN
	KYRGYZIA TADJIKISTAN
	TURKMENISTAN, UKRAINE
Communist party machine	APPARAT
comrade	TOVARI(S)CH
concierge	DVORNIK
Cossack	
—headman	ATAMAN, HETMAN
—troop	SOTNIA
council	D(O)UMA, SOVIET
country-house	DACHA
covered cart or sled	KIBITKA
croquette fried in bacon or calf's udder	KROMESKY
dance	GOPAK, KOLO
	ZIGANKA
dandelion	KOK-SAGYZ
Decembrist	DEKABRIST
decree	UKASE
department store	GUM
depression	KOTLOVINA, VPADINA
desert	PESKI, TUNDRA
dish	BLINI, KASHA, KNISH
	KROMESKY, PELMENY
dissident	RASKOLNIK, REFUSENIK
district	OKRUG, RAYON
—assembly	ZEMSTVO

drink	KVASS, QUASS, VODKA
dog	BORZOI, SAMOYED(E)
	WOLF-HOUND
duck	UTKA
dynasty	ROMANOV, VARANGIAN
Easter cake	KULICHPASHKA
edict	UKASE
eggs	YAITZA
emperor	CZAR, TSAR, TZAR
emperor's	
—daughter	CZAREVNA, TSAREVNA
—eldest son	CESAREVI(T)CH
	CESAREWI(T)CH
	TSESAREVI(T)CH
—son	CZAREVI(T)CH
	TSAREVI(T)CH
—wife	CZARINA, TSARINA
	CZARITSA, TSARITSA
estuary	USTYE
exploiter	KULAK
extinct horse	TARPAN
extreme Socialist	BOLSHEVIK
farmer	KULAK
fellow-traveller	POPUTCHIK
fermented milk	K(O)UMISS
fertile soil	CHERNOZEM
fish	RYBA
—L Baikal	GOLOMYNKA
—soup	UKKA
forced labour camp	GULAG
forest	LES
former USSR states	ARMENIA, AZERBAIJAN
	BELARUS, ESTONIA
	GEORGIA, KAZAKHSTAN
	KYRGYZIA, LATVIA, LITHUANIA
	MOLDOVA, TADJIKISTAN
	TURKMENISTAN, UKRAINE
fox	KARAGAN
gallery	HERMITAGE
glacier	LEDNIK
government department head	COMMISSAR
grandmother	BABUSHKA
ground squirrel	S(O)USLIK
gulf	LIMAN
gypsy woman	TSYGANKA
head-scarf	BABUSHKA
hemp	RHYNE
highlands	NAGORYE
hill	SOPKA, UVAL
hollow wooden dolls	MATRIOSHKA
holy man	STARETS, STARETZ
hood	BASHLYK
hors d'oeuvres	ZAKUSKI
house	DACHA, ISBA, IZBA
hut	ISBA, IZBA

illicit vodka	SAMOGON
information bureau	COMINFORM
	KOMINFORM
insectivore	DESMAN
isinglass	CARLOCK
island(s)	OSTROV(A)
Jewish area	JEWISH PALE
kebab	SHASHLYK
lake	KUL, OZERO
lamb	BARASHEK
launching site for	
spacecraft	COSMODROME
leather	YUFT
legislature	D(O)UMA, PR(A)ESIDIUM
	SUPREME SOVIET
letters	AS, BUKI, DOBRO, FERT
	GLAGOL, ISHE (BREVE), KAKO
	KHERR, LIUDI, MUISLETE, NASH
	ON, POKOI, RTSUI, SHA, SHTSHA
	SLOVO, TSHERV, TSUI, TVERDO
	YA, YER, YERUI, YEST, YU
	ZEMLA, ZHIVETE
little pies	PIROSHKI, PIROSHKI
local	
—council	ZEMSTVO
—government division	VOLOST
marsh	BOLOTO
marshy forest	TAIGA, URMAN
massacre	POGROM
measures	
—28 inches	ARSHEEN, ARSHIN(E)
—7 feet	SAGENE, SAJEN(E), SAZHEN
—²/₃ mile	VERST
—2.7 acres	DESSIATINE, DESSYATIN(E)
—quart	S(H)TOFF
—3 galls	VEDRO
meat	MYASA
—pie	PIROG, PIROSHKI
	PIROZHKI, PIROZHOK
minister	COMMISSAR
mink	KOLINSKY
moderate	
—liberal	OCTOBRIST
—Socialist	MENSHEVIK
mole-like amphibian	DESMAN
mountain	GORA, TAU
—range	KHREBET
mountains	GORY
mushroom	GRIBI
Muscovite guard	STRELITZ
musical instrument	BALALAIKA, DOMRA
	GUSLA, GUSLE, GUSLI
musk-shrew	DESMAN
news	
—agency	NOVESTI, TASS
—paper	ISVESTIA, PRAVDA

oil fuel	ASTATKI
one refused permission	
to emigrate	REFUSENIK
openness	GLASNOST
outstanding worker	STAKHANOVITE
pancake	BLINI, BLINY
parliament	D(O)UMA
partly-trained doctor	FELDSHER
party executive	POLITBUREAU
	POLITBURO
pass	PEREVAL
peace	MIR
peak	PIK
peasant	M(O)UJIK, MUZHIK
—cloak	SARAFAN
peninsula	POLUOSTROV
pheasant	FAZAN
plain	RAVNINA, RAZLIVY
	STEPPE
plateau	PLATO, PLOSKOGORYE
poem	BYLINA
pole-cat	KOLINKSY
poor soil	PODSOL, PODZOL
pork	SVININA
porridge	KASHA
porter	DVORNIK
principality of Moscow	MUSCOVY
Protestant	STUNDIST
province	OBLAST
provincial council	ZEMSTVO
race	COSSACK, SAMOYED(E)
rapids	POROGI, SHIVERA
reconstruction	PERESTROIKA
refusal	NIET, NYET
region	KRAY
religious	
—dissenter	RASKOLNIK
—teacher	STARETS, STARETZ
republics	AMUR, BAROVSK
	BASHKORKTOSTAN, BURYAT
	CHECHENYA, CHUVASH, DAGESTAN
	KABARDINO-BALKAR, KALMYK
	KAMCHATKA, KARELIA, KOMI
	LITVA, MAGADAN, MARI
	MORDOVIA, NORTH OSSETIA
	RUSSIA, SAKHA, TATARSTAN
	TUVA, UDMURT, YAKUTSK
rice	RIS
rich peasant	KULAK
ridge	GREBEN, GRYADA, KRYAZH
rock	KAMEN
ruling committee	POLITBURO
rye beer	KVASS, QUASS
sable	SOBOL
salt-lake	SOLONCHAK
sandpiper	TEREK

sandy desert	KUM
satellite	SPUTNIK
sea	MORE
secret	
—police	GRU, KGB, MVD, NKV
	OGPU, (T)CHEKA
—printing	SAMIZDAT
sect	D(O)UKHOBOR
settlement	POSELOK
shore	BEREG
sledge	KIBITKA
small pie or pastry	PIROG, PIROZHOK
snack	ZAKUSKA
snow-ridge	SASTRUGA, ZASTRUGA
soldier	STRELITZ
soup	BORSCH(T), BORTSCH(T)
sour cream	SMETANA
soviet of rural district	VOLOST
special troops	SPETSNA(T)Z
spermophile	S(O)USLIK
	SPERMOPHILUS
spider	KARAKUT
spirit	VODKA
spring of water	BULAK, KUDUK
standing committee	PR(A)ESIDIUM
state	
—farm	SOVKHOZ
—store	GUM
stew	RAGU
strait	PROLIV, VOROTA
sturgeon	BELUGA
tea urn	SAMOVAR
team of three (horses)	TROIKA
title of respect to foreign men	GOSPODIN

tomb	KURGAN
travelling companion	SPUTNIK
underground printing	SAMIZDAT
union of states	SOVIET UNION, SU
	UNION OF SOVIET SOCIALIST REPUBLICS
	USSR
vehicle	DROS(H)KY
	TARANTAS(S)
	TROIKA
village	
—community	MIR
—headman	STAROSTA
violent revolutionary	BOLSHEVIK
wagon	AR(A)BA, KIBITKA
	TELEGA
water-nymph	RUSALKA
weight	ZOLOTNIK
—1 pound	FUNT
—36 pounds	POOD, PO(U)D
wheat meal	SASHA
whip	KNOUT
wild ass	K(O)ULAN
wind storm	BURAN
woman's cloak	SARAFAN
worker	STAKHANOVITE
workers' guild	ARTEL
world	MIR
youth organization	COMOSOOL
	KOMOSOL
zizel	S(O)USLIK
Rwanda	RWA
capital	KIGALI
coin	CENTIME, FRANC

S

sacred
book
—Christian — BIBLE
—Hebrew — (T)HORAH
—Hindu — MANTRA(M), PURANA
SHASTER, S(H)ASTRA
—Moslem — ALCORAN, KORAN
QORAN, QURAN
bull (Egypt) — APIS
character — HIEROGLYPH(IC)
drink
—Sikh — AMRIT
—Zoroastrian — HAOMA
enclosure in temple — SEKOS
fish — OXYRHYNCUS
flower — LOTUS
fountain — ZEMZEM
language — PALI
law (Islam) — SHARIA
lotus — PADMA
monkey — HANUMAN
mountain — OMEI
part of temple — ADYTON
person — SHAMAN
river — ALPH
scriptures — SHRUTI
snakes — NAGA
stone — BLACK STONE
syllable — OM
symbol — HIEROGRAM, HIEROGRAPH
text
—Buddhist — SUTRA
—Hindu — AVESTA, MANTRA(M), PURANA
SHASTER, S(H)ASTRA
TANTRA, VEDA
—Jain — KALPA-SUTRA
—Zoroastrian — AVESTA
tree — BO, BODHI, PEEPUL
verse — MANTRA
word — OM
sailor — AB, BLUEJACKET
SALT, TAR
bed — HAMMOCK
biscuit — HARDTACK
—softened in water and
baked — DUNDERFUNK
boiled oatmeal, etc — BURGOO
captain — OLD MAN, SKIPPER

carousing — MALLEMAROKING
carving in whalebone etc — SCRIMSHAW
chapel — BETHEL
clothing and bedding — SLOPS
dance — HORNPIPE
experienced — WATER-DOG
famous sailors
—American
WW1 — BENSON, SIMS
WW2 — DOORMAN, FLETCHER, HALSEY
HART, KIMMEL, KING, LEAHY
MITSCHER, NIMITZ, OLDENDORFF
POWNALL, SPRAGGE, SPRUANCE
—Austria/Hungary
WW1 — HAUS, HORTHY
—British
American revolution — GRAVES, HOOD
Elizabethan — DRAKE, GRENVILLE
Napoleonic wars — NELSON
WW1 — BACON, BEATTY, CARDEN
CRADOCK, DE ROBECK, FISHER
JACKSON, JELLICOE, KEYES
MADDEN, MILNE, MOUNTBATTEN
OLIVER, STURDEE, TROUBRIDGE
TYRWHITT, WEMYSS
WW2 — CUNNINGHAM, MOUNTBATTEN
PHILLIPS, RAMSAY
—Dutch — DE RUYTER, VAN TROMP(E)
—French
Napoleonic wars — DE BARRAS
DE GRASSE, VILLENEUVE
WW1 — DARTIGE, GAUCHET, LACAZE
RONARCH
WW2 — DARLAN
—German
WW1 — ARNAUD, BACHMAN, BULOW
HIPPER, HOLTZEDORFF, REUTER
SCHEER, SOUCHON, SPEE
TIRPITZ, TROTHA
WW2 — DO(E)NITZ, RAEDER
—Italian
WW1 — ABRUZZI, THAON DI REVEL
—Japanese
WW2 — KOGA, KURITA
NAGUMO, NISHIMURA, NOMURA
OZAWA, SHIMA, SUZUKI, TAKAGI
TOGO, YAMAMOTO
—Russian
WW1 — EBERHARDT, ESSEN
GRIGOROVICH, KOLCHAK
(*see also* **explorers**)
—Spanish — GRAVINA
first mate — NUMBER ONE
force or trick
into service — CRIMP, COMMANDEER
(IM)PRESS, PRESS-GANG, SHANGHAI

goods	
—found floating	FLOTSAM
—thrown overboard	JETSAM
grave	DAVY JONES'S LOCKER
gruel	LOBLOLLY
Indian	CLASHEE, LASCAR
inexperienced	LANDLUBBER
lascar	
—bosun	SERANG
—petty officer	TINDAL
master-at-arms	JA(U)NTIE
	JA(U)NTY, JONTY
meat and biscuit stew	LOBSCOUSE
midshipman	REEFER, SNOTTY
old sailor	SHELLBACK
officers	UPPER DECK
ordinary sailor(s)	DECKHAND, LOWER DECK
Oriental	
—bosun	SERANG
—petty officer	TINDAL
—sailor	LASCAR
plug leak with canvas etc	FOTHER
punishment	FLOGGING, KEELHAULING
	WALKING THE PLANK
rope's end	COLT
sailors	CREW, NUS, RN
salt beef	JUNK
sea-bred officer	TARPAULIN
song	SHANTY
stew	LOBSCOUSE, LOB'S COURSE
trousers	BELL BOTTOMS
Turkish	GALIONGEE
waterproof hat	SOU'WESTER, TARPAULIN
	(*see also* **Royal Navy**)
St Lucia	WL
St Vincent	WV
Saint's day	(*see* **holidays**)
salad	(*see* **vegetables**)
Sanskrit	SANS
book of fables	PANCHATANTRA
law	DHARMA
righteousness	DHARMA
sacred text	PURANA
script	NAGARI
unrighteousness	ADHARMA
	(*see also* **Hindu, Indian**)
Sao Tome	P
capital	SAO TOME
coin	CENTAVO, DOBRA
satellites	
artificial	(*see* **space**)
natural	(*see* **astronomy**)
sauce	
bechamel and	
—aspic	CHAUDFROID
—cheese	MORNAY

—eggs	TARTARE
—tomato paste	AURORE
berries, fruit	APPLE, CHESTNUT
	CRANBERRY, GOOSEBERRY
breadcrumbs	BREAD SAUCE
—and stock	PANADA
brown sugar, brandy, etc	BRANDY BUTTER
butter and	
—sugar	BUTTERSCOTCH
with flavouring	HARD SAUCE
capers, vinegar, etc	CAPER SAUCE
cheese and	
—mustard	CHEESE SAUCE
—wine	FONDUE
Chinese	HOISIN
cocoa	CHOCOLATE SAUCE
curry	DANSAK, KORMA, MADRAS
	ROGAN JOSH, VINDALOO
demi-glaze and	
—truffles	PERIGEUX
—Madeira wine	MADEIRA
—Marsala wine	MARSALA
—mushrooms	MUSHROOM SAUCE
—port	PORT WINE SAUCE
eggs and	
—cream, butter, sherry	NEWBURG(H)
—herbs	REMOULADE
—mayonnaise	TARTARE
—sugar	SABAYON
—vinegar	HOLLANDAISE
	MAYONNAISE
—white sauce	EGG SAUCE
espagnole and	
—aspic jelly	CHAUDFROID
—gravy	DEMI-GLAZE
—onions	ROBERT
—orange peel	BIGARADE
—redcurrants	REFORME
—stock	PEPPER
fish (Roman)	GARUM
garlic mayonnaise	AIOLI
German	GREEN SAUCE, GRUNE SOSSE
herb	HORSERADISH, MINT
	PARSLEY, SALSA VERDE
hollandaise with cream	MOUSSELINE
hot	HORSERADISH, HP
	PICCALILLI, WORCESTER
jam, arrowroot, etc	JAM SAUCE
Japanese	TAMARI
mayonnaise with tomato	
puré	ROUILLE
mushrooms, peppercorns, etc	VELOUTE
oil and vinegar	FRENCH DRESSING
	VINAIGRETTE
olive oil and lemon	
juice	SALMORIGLIO

onions and		—short	VIENNA SAUSAGE
—bacon, etc	ESPAGNOLE	French	
—breadcrumbs	BREAD SAUCE	—large	TOULOUSE SAUSAGE
—butter, etc	BECHAMEL	pork	ANDOUILLE(TTE)
—coconut	SAMBAL	—salami	SAUCISSON
—curry powder	CURRY SAUCE	German	BIERWURST, BLUTWURST
—eggs, etc	BEARNAISE		BOCKWURST, BRATWURST
—mushrooms	CHASSEUR		CERVELATWURST
orange and			FRANKFURTER, HAMBURG(H)ER
—cornflour	ORANGE SAUCE		(KNACK)WURST, LEBERWURST
—lemon	CUMBERLAND		SCHINKENWURST, WIENER(WURST)
parsley, butter, etc	MAITRE D'HOTEL		ZUNGERWURST
	MEUNIERE	—boiled	KOCHWURST
peanuts, etc	SATAY	—preserved	BOHWURST
peppers	TABASCO	—scalded	BRUHWURST
raspberries	MELBA	Greek	KOKORETSI, LUKANIKA
redcurrants	OXFORD	Hebrew	VIENNA SAUSAGE
roux and stock	BROWN SAUCE, VELOUTE	highly-seasoned	CHORIZO, SALAMI
salad dressing	(FOAM) MAYONNAISE		SAVELOY
	FRENCH, GOLDEN	in	
	OLIVE OIL, RUSSIAN DRESSING	—bread roll	HOT DOG
	SOUR CREAM	—pastry case	SAUSAGE ROLL
	THOUSAND ISLANDS	—Yorkshire pudding	TOAD-IN-THE-HOLE
	VINEGAR, VINAIGRETTE	Italian	BOLOGNA, CERVELLATA
seaweed	LAVER		MORTADELLA, PEPPERONI
shallots	PIQUANT		POLONY, SALAMI
—and wine	BERCY, BORDELAISE	large sausage	CUMBERLAND
	BOURGUIGNONNE		HAMBURG(H)ER, TOULOUSE
shrimps, lemon peel	SHRIMP SAUCE	liver (Ger.)	LEBERWURST
Sicilian	SALMORIGLIO	long thin sausage	CABANO, KABANO
sour cream	GRADVALAK, GRADVALAX	partly cooked	POLONY
soya beans	SOY SAUCE	Polish	KIELBASA, KRAKAUER
—Japanese	TAMARI		KRAKOWSKA, ZYWIECKA
spicy	CURRY SAUCE, HOISIN	pork meat and fat	WHITE SAUSAGE
thickened meat juices	GRAVY	pre-cooked	FRANKFURTER, SALAMI
tomatoes, etc	CATCHUP, CATSUP		SAVELOY
	KETCHUP, TOMATO SAUCE	salted	SALAMI
velouta with		sausage sandwich	HOT DOG
—eggs and cream	ALLEMANDE	small sausage	CHIPOLATA
—vinegar	RAVIGOTE		COCKTAIL SAUSAGE
Welsh	LAVER	smoked	
white sauce and		—German	CERVELATWURST
—anchovies	ANCHOVY SAUCE		FRANKFURTER
—cream	SUPREME	—Italian	SALAMI
—eggs	EGG SAUCE	—pork	CERVELAT
—lemons	LEMON SAUCE	South African	BOEREWORS
—onions	ONION SAUCE, SOUBISE	Spanish	CHORIZO, SALCHICA
—parsley	PARSLEY SAUCE	**Scandinavian**	
Saudi Arabia	(*see* **Arabia**)	ancient	NORSE
sausage		casserole	NORRLANDS PUDDING
Australian	SNAG	dynasty	VARANGIAN
blood sausage	BLACK PUDDING	fish dish	GRAVADLAX
—German	BLUTWURST	frost giant	YMIR
British	BANGER, BLACK PUDDING	goblin	NIS
	CUMBERLAND	hors d'oeuvres	SMORGASBORD
Frankfurter	WIENER	magistrate	AMMAN, AMTMAN

old coin	SKILLING		controlling	
open sandwich	SMOR(RE)BROD		—electrical resistance	RHEOSTAT
parliament	THING		—current flowing in one	
pirate	VIKING		circuit by current	
soup	LAPSKAUS		in another circuit	RELAY
spirit	AKVAVIT, AQUAVIT		converting	
stew	LABSKAUS		—alternating current to	
toast	SKO(A)L		direct current	CONVERTER

scientific instruments

absorption of light	ABSORPTIOMETER		—direct to alternating	
accurate			current	INVERTER
—clock	CHRONOMETER		—electrical	
—recording clock	CHRONOGRAPH		impulses to sound	(LOUD)SPEAKER
amplifying			to mechanical energy	SOLENOID
—microwaves	PARAMETRIC AMPLIFIER		—frequency modulation to	
—small sounds	PHONENDOSCOPE		amplitude modulation	DISCRIMINATOR
analysing spectra	SPECTROSCOPE		—optical image to	
apparatus for gas			electrical signal	ICONOSCOPE
analysis	EUDIOMETER		—sound to electrical	
atom-smasher	(*see* particle accelerator *below*)		impulses	MICROPHONE
automatically replying			—vapour to liquid	(LIEBIG) CONDENSER
to received signal	TRANSPONDER		—X-rays to	
balloon carrying			visual image	IMAGE CONVERTER
instruments measuring			correcting chromatic	
—electrical data	ELECTROSONDE		aberration	TEINOSCOPE
—meteorological data	RADIOSONDE		counting	
calculating ruler	SLIDE RULE		—alpha particles	SPINTHARISCOPE
carrying sound	PHONOP(H)ORE		—drops	STACTOMETER
cathode-ray tube with			—flashes from	
four screens	CHROMATRON		scintillator	SCINTILLATION COUNTER
	CHROMOSCOPE		—ionised	
chamber			particles	GEIGER(-MULLER) COUNTER
—controlled at very low			—neutrons	BORON COUNTER TUBE
temperature	CRYOSTAT		cup for melting	
—for heating under			substances	CRUCIBLE
pressure	AUTOCLAVE		cuts very thin slices	MICROTOME
changing voltage of			detecting	
alternating current	TRANSFORMER		—air pressure changes	STATOSCOPE
combining coloured images	CHROMOSCOPE		—electric currents	ELECTROSCOPE
comparing				GALVANOSCOPE
—series of astronomical			—electric waves by	
photographs	BLINK COMPARATOR		reduced resistance	COHERER
	BLINK MICROSCOPE		—radio frequencies of	
—structure of			celestial bodies	RADIO TELESCOPE
spectral lines	INTERFEROMETER		—temperature changes	THERMISTOR
compass based on				THERMOSCOPE
spinning wheel	GYRO-COMPASS		—underwater sound	HYDROPHONE
	GYROSCOPIC COMPASS		—water	HYDROSTAT
concave reflector	DISH AERIAL		determining	
	PARABOLIC REFLECTOR		—amount of flue gases	ORSAT APPARATUS
	PARABOLOID REFLECTOR		—decrease in temperature	
condenser	DEPHLEGMATOR, RECTIFIER		due to evaporation	CRYOPHORUS
—in microscope	ABBE CONDENSER		—freezing points	CRYOSCOPE
—to collect components			—mass of atoms	MASS SPECTROGRAPH
boiled off at different				OMEGATRON
temperatures	FRACTIONATING COLUMN		dialysis machine	DIALYSER
			diffracting lens	FRESNEL LENS

displaying polarised light phenomena	POLARISCOPE
distilling	
—apparatus	RECTIFIER, STILL
fractional	COFFEY STILL
—flask	RETORT
(old)	ALEMBIC
drying chamber	DESICCATOR
dual prism	NICOL PRISM
electron-tube in which beam is modified	KLYSTRON
electrostatic accelerator	TANDEM GENERATOR
emission tube with ten cathodes	DEKATRON
estimating temperature of furnace	SEGER CONE
eye-piece with two plano-convex lens	RAMSDEN EYEPIECE
filtering by suction	BUCHNER FUNNEL
flask	RETORT
—flat-bottomed, conical	KERLENMEYER FLASK
—for estimation of nitrogen	KJELDAHL FLASK
focusing light into parallel beams	COLLIMATOR
gas burner	BUNSEN BURNER
glass	
—container with two or more necks	WASH BOTTLE
	WOULFE BOTTLE
—cover	BELL JAR
—graduated tube	PIPETTE
with tap	BURETTE
—vessel with narrow neck	RETORT
high	
—speed separator	CENTRIFUGE
—temperature thermostat	PYROSTAT
interferometer	ETALON
ionisation chamber	BORON CHAMBER
isotope separator	ISOTRON
jar lined with tinfoil	LEYDEN JAR
locating objects by reflected	
—radio waves	RADAR
—sound waves	SONAR
liquefying gas	CASCADE LIQUEFIER
maintaining	
—electric resistance	RHEOSTAT
—humidity	HYGROSTAT, HUMIDISTAT
—low temperature	CRYOSTAT
—pressure	BAROSTAT
—temperature	THERMOSTAT
measuring	(*see* **measuring instruments**)
microscope using	
—electron beam	ELECTRON MICROSCOPE

—reflected and transmitted light	PHASE CONTRAST MICROSCOPE
—ultraviolet light	ULTRAVIOLET MICROSCOPE
microwave amplifier	PARAMETRIC AMPLIFIER
observing star passage	ALMACANTAR
	ALMACANTUR
optical projector	EPIDIASCOPE
—double	STEREOPTICON
particle	
—accelerator	BETATRON, BEVATRON
	COSMOTRON, CYCLOTRON
	ELECTRON-POSITRON COLLIDER
	ELECTRON SYNCHROTRON
	LARGE ELECTRON-POSITRON COLLIDER
	LEP, LINAC, LINEAR ACCELERATOR
	PHASOTRON, SUPERCOLLIDER
	SYNCHROCYCLOTRON
	ZETA
—counter	SPINTHARISCOPE
—detector	BUBBLE CHAMBER
	(DIFFUSION) CLOUD CHAMBER
	HODOSCOPE, SPARK CHAMBER
	STREAMER CHAMBER
passing light in one plane	NICOL PRISM
photographing	
—spectra	SPECTROGRAPH
—sun	(SPECTRO)HELIOGRAPH
porcelain filter cup with small holes	GOOCH CRUCIBLE
producing	
—alternating current	ALTERNATOR
—direct current	DYNAMO, GENERATOR
—electricity from heat	THERMOPILE
junction of dissimilar metals	THERMOCOUPLE
—gas from action of liquid on solids	KIPP'S APPARATUS
—high-voltage oscillation	TESLA COIL
—image of electrical quantities	OSCILLOSCOPE
—interference in light patterns	INTERFEROMETER
—nuclear fusion	TORUS
	TOROIDA
	KAMERA MAGNETIC
	TOKAMOK, STELLERATOR
	SCYLLAC
—output after a specified number of inputs	SCALER
	SCALING CIRCUIT

—polarised light   ROCHON PRISM
     WOLLASTON PRISM
—reactance in a circuit   REACTOR
—reducing amount of
   current passing   SHUNT
—resistance
   in a circuit   RESISTOR
   varying with
     temperature   THERMISTOR
—sound waves   OSCILLATOR
—spectrum of beam
   of ions   MASS SPECTROMETER
—static electricity   ELECTROPHORUS
     VAN DER GRAAF GENERATOR
     WIMSHURST MACHINE
quartz prism   WOLLASTON PRISM
radar screen   CATHODE RAY OSCILLOSCOPE
     CRO
rapidly flashing
   light source   STROBE, STROBOSCOPE
recording
—atmospheric pressure   BAROGRAPH
—cloud patterns   NEPHOGRAPH
—earthquakes   SEWISMOGRAPH
—electric currents   OSCILLOGRAPH
—electrical action
   in muscles   ELECTROMYOGRAPH
—enlarged or reduced
   image   PANTOGRAPH
—humidity   HYGROGRAPH
—intensity of sun   HELIOGRAPH
—over a distance   TELEMETER
—particle tracks   BUBBLE CHAMBER
—pressure   BAROGRAPH
—short time interval   CHRONOGRAPH
—sound vibrations   PHONAUTOGRAPH
—speed and time of use
   of vehicles   TACHOGRAPH
—temperature   THERMO(METRO)GRAPH
     (*see also* **write**)
reducing current in
   circuit   (ELECTRICAL) SHUNT
reflecting sun in
   constant direction   HELIOSTAT
restoring coherer   DECOHERER
semiconductor with
   negative resistance
   in part of range   TUNNEL DIODE
separating substances by
   rotation   CENTRIFUGE
shallow glass dish   PETRI DISH
showing effects of
   electrical discharge
   through gases   GEISSLER TUBE
signalling by reflected
   sunlight   HELIOGRAPH

small sighting telescope   COLLIMATOR
steriliser   AUTOCLAVE
storage bottle   WINCHESTER (QUART)
sub-dividing measuring
   scale   VERNIER
suction filter   BUCHNER FUNNEL
switch based on
   superconductivity   CRYOTRON
television screen   CATHODE RAY TUBE
     CRT
testing
—lenses and prisms   INTERFEROMETER
—vacuums   TESLA COIL
thermionic valve used
   as switch   THYRATRON
tracking charged
   particles   BUBBLE CHAMBER
     CLOUD CHAMBER
     HODOSCOPE
transferring power
   between systems   TRANSDUCER
transmitting data   TELEMETER
     TRANSPONDER
—from balloon   RADIOMETEOROGRAPH
     RADIOSONDE
tube
—condenser   LIEBIG CONDENSER
—used to centrifuge
   blood   HAEMATOCRIT
used in switching
   circuits   TUNNEL DIODE
vacuum
—flask   DEWAR FLASK
—pump   CONDENSATION PUMP
     DIFFUSION PUMP
—tube
   displaying cathode
   rays   CATHODE RAY TUBE, CRT
   with electrodes   CROOKES TUBE
     GEISSLER TUBE
variable resistor   RHEOSTAT
viewing
—crystal structure   STAUROSCOPE
—distant objects   TELESCOPE
—electric current   OSCILLOSCOPE
—fast movement   STROBE, STROBOSCOPE
—fermentation   ZYMOSCOPE
—heavens   TELESCOPE
—high-energy particles   BUBBLE CHAMBER
     HODOSCOPE
—meridian passage   DIPLEIDOSCOPE
—objects
   above eye-level   PERISCOPE
   under water   HYDROSCOPE
—optical spectra   SPECTROSCOPE
—short-lived images   TACHISTOSCOPE

—small objects (ELECTRON)	MICROSCOPE
—sun	HELIOSCOPE
—temperature at remote distance	TELETHERMOSCOPE
—tissues on fluorescent screen	FLUOROSCOPE
in 3-dimensions	STEREO-FLUOROSCOPE
—two-dimensional photographs in three dimensions	STEREOSCOPE
—radar signals	RADARSCOPE
—X-ray images	FLUOROSCOPE

(see also astronomy)

weighing very small amounts	TORSION BALANCE
wire rheostat	RHEOCHORD

(see also measuring instruments)

Scotland CALEDONIA, SCOTIA

(see also Scottish)

Scott

words found in his writings:

ace of trumps	TIB
akin	SIBB
arrogance	SURQUEDY
astute	ASTUCIOUS
backgammon	VERQUIRE
bad luck	WANION
bag-piping	SACK-DOUDLING
bank-notes	SNUFF(-PAPER)
blood relation	SIBB
bough used as torch	ROUGHIE
brandish	WAMPISH
brisket	BREASKIT
brother or sister	SIBB
brown bread roll	SOUTER'S CLOD
byrlawman	BIRLIEMAN
cajole	BEFLUM
club	TRUNNION
commotion	STEERY
coward	VILLAGIO
cross-grained	FRAMPAL
cudgel	SOUPLE
curse	WANION
cut out	SNECK
dash	VIRETOT
dilapidated house	HURLEY-HOUSE
dry bough	ROUGHIE
eldin	YEALDON
enchanter/enchantress	REIM-KENNAR
endearment	YARTO
excited by moon	MOON-RAISED
falcon	TERCEL-GENTLE
favouritism	PEATSHIP
fierce warrior	WAR-WOLF
fiery	FRAMPAL
fish-roe	RAUN, RAWN

flighty	WEATHER-HEADED
flourish	WAMPISH
fool	BEFLUM
fortified site	KAME, KAIM
four of trumps at gleek	TIDDY
friar with short frock	CURTAL-FRIAR
fuel	YEALDON
gad	VIRETOT
give landlord information leading to raising of rent	WHISTLE
half-guinea	SMELT
hawk's turn	CANCELEER, CANCELIER
heart	YARTO
help in need	BEETMASTER
horn-blast	PRYSE
hypochrondriac	PHRENESIAC
infantry regiment	TERTIA
interjection of derision	QUEP
irascible	TOUSTIE
jacket	RAILLY
kinship	SIBB
knob	NOOP
law	LAUCH
literary style	BOW-WOW
loop	LOUP
low collar	RABATINE
Lowlander	SASSENACH
maddened by moon	MOON-RAISED
make a display	PROPALE
Moon	MACFARLANE'S BUAT
nick	SNECK
not —bruised or crushed	UNBRIZZED
—to be molested	SACLESS
note of assault	WAR(R)ISON
official who searched for stolen goods	RANZELLAAR
old card-game	PENNEECH, PENNEECK
overweening	OUTRECUIDANCE
pardoner	QUAESTIONARY
pear	QUEEZ-MADDAM
peaty	TURBINACIOUS
pedlar	PEDDER-COFFE
peevish	FRAMPAL
pigment	PIMENT
pinnacle	PINNET
plate	VASSAIL, VESSAIL
presumption	OUTRECUIDANCE
private	SINGLE SOLDIER
probationer	STIBBLER
prophetess	VOLUSPA
proportion of malt	STRAIK
pursuit of moss-troopers	HOT TROD
rabble	RASCAILLE
racked	RECKAN
rascal	RASCAILLE

ransack	RANSHA(C)KLE
ricked	RECKAN
riding-hood	TROT-COSEY, TROT-COZY
rush	VIRETOT
scoundrelly	HOUNDS-FOOT
scree	SCRAE
search	RANSHA(C)KLE
shawl from goat hair	TOZIE
sibyl	VOLUSPA
slash	SCORCH
small curiosity	GABION
snick	SNECK
snip	SNECK
spiced, sweetened wine	PIGMENT
stay as guest	GUESTEN
state official	BARON-OFFICER
steal	CONDIDDLE, MAG
stick	TRUNNION
subordinate spy	UNDER-ESPIAL
subterranean prison	MASSYMORE
sulky	GUMPLE-FOISTED
sun-dried	TILED
supporter of popish prelates	PAPAPRELATIST
tall raw-boned woman	RANDLE-TREE
talon	TALENT
tarred rags	HARDS, HURDS
tern	PICTARNIE
tip (of elbow)	NOOP
tithes	PARSONAGE
trace of a fact	REMNANT
trinket	TRANKUM
trouserless	BARE-BREACHED
twist about	WELK
unchallengeable	SACLESS
unguarded	LIPPEN
unsaluted	UNHALSED
vengeance	WANION
vessels	VASSAIL, VESSAIL
wave about	WAMPISH
wench	GOUGE
wheel-barrow	MONOTROCH
worn out	OVERSCUTCHED
young gull	SCOURIE, SCOWRIE
Scottish	SCOT
including: legal terms	
a	ANE
—moment ago	ENOW
abandon	FORHOO(IE), FORHOW
—proceedings	DESERT THE DIET
abate	FAIK
abbacy	ABTHANE
ablaze	ALOW(E)
able	FERE
above	ABUNE
above-ground	
—part of potato	TATTIE-SHAW

—parts of plant	SHAW
absconding from justice	FUGITATION
absolve	ASSOILZIE
abundance	FOUTH, FOWTH, ROUTH
	ROWTH, SONCE, SONSE
	STOUTH AND ROUTH
abundant	ROUTHIE, ROWTHIE
abuse	SNASK
abusive language	SNASH
accusation	THREAP, THREEP
accused person(s)	PANEL
accustom oneself	USE
acquisition	CONQUEST
acrobat	SPEELER
across	YONT
act of dragging	HARL
action to	
—declare false or forged	IMPROBATION
—prove witness perjured	
or biased	REPROBATOR
active	BIRKIE, YA(U)LD, YANKNG
—fellow	SWANK(E)Y
addition	EIK
adept	DEACON
adjust	SORT
advancing	ONCOMING
adze	EATCHE
affair	EFFEIR, EFFERE
affected person	PRICK-ME-DAINTY
afflicted	WAESOME
afoot	AGAIT
afraid	FEARED, RAD
afternoon refreshment	FOUR-HOURS
afterwards	SYNE
against	ANENT
aggressively outspoken	RANDIE, RANDY
agile	SWANK
agitation	CARFUFFLE, CERFUFFLE
	KEFUFFLE
—of water	JABBLE
ago	SYNE
agony of death	DEAD THRAW
agree	GREE, SORT
agreement	AYE
ague	EXIES
aim	ETTLE, MINT, VISIE, VIZY, VIZZIE
air	LIFT
ajar	AGEE, AJEE, JEE
akin	SIB
alarm	GLIFF, GLIFT
alas	EWHOW, WAESUCKS, WALY
alderman	BAIL(L)IE
ale	YILL
—brewing (Islands)	BUMMOCK
—house	CHANGE-HOUSE
alert	GLEG

alive	TO THE FORE	approach(ing)	ONCOMING
alley-way	VENNEL	April Fool	GOUK, GOWK
allodial (Islands)	UDAL	apt	GLEG
allowance to mill		—to feel chilly	CAULD-RIFE
servants	SEQUEL	arbiter	BYRLAWMAN, ODDSMAN
alms	ALMOUS, AWMOUS	arch	COOM
alone	HIMSELF, HIS LANE	area of operation	SUCKEN
	MY LANE	armpit	OXTER
along	ENDLANG	argue snappishly	NYAFF
aloof	ABEIGH, SKEIGH	arranged	RED(D)ED
also	ALS	array	EFFEIR, EFFERE
alternately	TIME ABOUT	arts student	MAGISTRAND
amber	LAMMER	as soon as	WHENE(V)ER
amiable	COUTHIE	ascent	UPGANG
ample	WAL(L)Y	ash bucket	BACKET
amuse	PLAY	ashes	AIZLE, EASLE
amusing		ask	SPEER, SPEIR
—person or thing	DIVERT	askew	AGLEE, AGLEY, SKIVIE
—story	BA(U)R, BAWR	aslant	ASKLENT
an	ANE	aspire	ETTLE, MINT
ancestor	FOR(E)BEAR	assault	STOUND, STOWND
ancient	AULD-WARLD	—in own house	HAMESUCKEN
—castle	BROCH, BR(O)UGH	assertion	THREAP, THREEP
—race	PICT	assess	MODIFY
ankle	COOT, CUIT, CUTE, QUEET	assess(ment)	STENT
annat	ANN	assistant	SERVITOR
annoy(ance)	FASH	associate with women	WINCH
annual payment under feu	FEU-DUTY	assuage	MEASE
annul	REDUCE	assume	HECHT
any	ARY	assuming	UPSETTING
anything		astir	AGAIT
—beaked	KIP(P)	astray	WILL, WULL
—built	BIGGIN	astride	STRIDE-LEGS
—eaten as relish	KITCHEN		STRIDE-LEGGED
—frightful	WIRRICOW	at	
	WORRICOW, WORRYCOW	—a loss	WILL, WULL
—small	PINK	—all	AVA, OUGHTLINGS
—stunted	SCRUNT	—present	PRESENTLY
apiece	THE PIECE	—the big house	UPBY(E)
apology	OFFCOME	—times	WHILES
apothecary	POTTINGAR	attack	ONFALL
apparatus	GRAITH	attempt	MINT
apparition	TAIS(C)H	attend to	SORT, TENT
appeal	RECLAIM	attercop (spider)	ETHERCAP, ETTERCAP
appear	CAST UP	auction	ROUP
—above ground	BRAIRD, BREER	avail	DOW
—and disappear	COOK, KOOK	availed	DOCHT, DOUGHT
—ignorant	MISKEN	avaricious	GRIPPY
—in court	COMPEAR	awake	WAKEN
appearance	EFFEIR, EFFERE, SHAW	award	MODIFY
appendage	POFFLE	away	AWA
appetising	GUSTY	awkward	BLATE
applaud/applause	RUFF	—person	BUCKIE
appliance for winding yarn	WINNLE	awl	BROG, ELS(H)IN, STOB
appointed deputy	DEPUTE	awnless	HUMBLE, HUMMEL
apprentice	SERVITOR	awry	AGLEE, AGLEY

back	
—of	
knee-joint	HOUGH
shoulder	BACK-SPAUL(D)
—passage	DUNNY
backward and forward	BUT AND BEN
bad luck	WANION
bag	POCK
—pudding	POCK-PUDDING
bagged	BAGGIT
bagpipe music	LUTHA, PIBROCH, URLAR
bail	CAUTION
bailiff (Islands)	FOUD
bailiff's jurisdiction	FOUDRIE
baker's grater	RISP
balk	HEN
ball	BA
ballad	BALLA(N)T, BALLET
bamboozle	BUMBAZE
bank	BINK, SUNK
bankrupt(cy)	DYVOUR(Y)
bankruptcy	SEQUESTRATION
—process	CESSIO BONORUM
banter	TROCK, TROKE
bar	RANCE, SPAR
—across condemned cell	GAD
—in chimney	RANDLE-TREE
	RANDLE-BALK
	RANDLE-PERCH, RANNEL-TREE
	RANNLE-TREE, RANTLE-TREE
—of grate	RIB
barefoot Highlander	GILLIE-WHITE-FOOT
	GILLIE-WET-FOOT
bargain	WANWORTH
barge	GABBARD, GABBART
bark like snarling dog	YAFF
barley	BERE, BIGG
barrel projection	LAGGEN, LAGGIN
barren	HI(R)STIE, YELD
barrister	ADVOCATE
barter	COUP, NIFFER, TROCK, TROKE
basement	DUNNY
bashful	BLATE
basket	MURLA(I)N, MURLIN
bathe	DOOK
baulk	REEST, REIST
bawdy talk	SCULDUDD(E)RY
	SKULDUDDERY
bay (Islands)	VOE
be	
—able	CAN, DOW
—active or excited	STEER
—frightened	FLAY, FLEY
—gaudy	SKYRE
—good for a purpose	DOW
—half asleep	DOVE

—hanged	STRING, WALLOP IN A TOW
	WALLOP IN A TETHER
—ignorant	MISKEN
—in training	BREED
—out of bed	STEER
—perverse	THRAW
—restive	FLISK
—smoke-dried	REAST, REEST, REIST
—stupefied	DOVE
—tamely submissive	SNOOL
—undecided	SWITHER
—vexed	FASH
beacon-fire	BALE-FIRE
beam	TREST
—of a balance	WEIGH-BANK
bear	BERE, BIGG, DREE
beat	DUNT, FIRK, LOUNDER
	PHEASE, TOUK
beating	LOUNDERING, PAIK
—the bounds	COMMON-RIDING
beautiful	WALY
become	SET
bed	
—of mussels	MUSSEL-SCAUP
—valance	PAND
bedaub	SLAISTER
bedraggle	TRAUCHLE
bee's nest	BINK
beetle	CLOCK
befit	SET
befool	BEGUNK
before bedtime	FORENIGHT
beg	FLEECH, THIG
beggar's pouch	GABERLUNZIE
begged	THIGGIT
begging	FLEECHING, FLEECHMENT
—for eggs	PACE-EGGING
begin to move	STEER
behave riotously	GIL(L)RAVAGE
	GIL(L)RAVITCH, GALRAVAGE
	GALRAVITCH
behaviour	HAVING
beheading machine	MAIDEN
behind	AHIND, AHINT
being facile	FACILITY
bell-rope	TOW
bellow	BULLER
belly	KITE, KYTE, WAME
beloved one	JO(E)
bench	BINK
beneath	ANEATH
benefit society	MENAGE
bent	
—double	TWAFALD
—spade	CASCHROM, CAS CROM
bequeath to charity	MORTIFY

bequest to charity	MORTIFICATION	—Islands	YARFA, YARPHA
beside	ASIDE	boggy	
besides	BY, FORBY	—place	SLACK
besom	COW, KOW	—water-channel	LATCH
bespatter	JAUP	boisterous	GOUSTROUS
best	WALE	—girl or boy	GILP(E)Y
bestir oneself	JEE ONE'S GINGER	boldly	CROUSE
	JOW ONE'S GINGER	boorish vulgarian	KEELIE
bewildered	MOIDERT, WILL, WULL	booth	BOTHAN
bewitch	FOR(E)SPEAK	—for selling	CRAME
beyond	AYONT, OUTWITH	booty	CREACH, CREAGH
—the bounds of	FURTH OF	border	ROON
bid	BODE	borough	BROGH, BURGH
big knife	GULL(E)Y	botch	CLATCH
bilberry	BLAEBERRY	—up	CLAMPER
bind with thread or cord	OOP, OUP	botched work	CLATCH
birch	BIRK	bother	FASH
biscuit	BAKE	bottom upward	TAPSALTEERIE
bishop	PRIMUS	bought	COFT
—who transmitted		bounce	STOT(TER)
revenues	TULCHAN BISHOP	bound	SCOUP, SCOWP, SPANG
bit of doggerel	RAT-RHYME		STEN(D)
biting	TOOTHY	—along	SKELP
bittern	BULL-OF-THE-BOG	boundary	MEITH
	MOSSBLUITER	—mark	DOOL
black		—stone	HARE-STANE
—berry	BRAMBLE	bow	JOUK
—clothes	BLACKS	box	BUIST
—eye	KEEKER	boy	LOON(IE)
—headed gull	PICKMAW	brain-pan	HARN-PAN
—smith	BURN-THE-WIND	brains	HARNS
blackish	BLAE	brand	BUIST
blame	WITE, WYTE	—new	SPLIT-NEW
blast	SCAITH, SKAITH, WAP	brandish	WAMPISH
blaze	LOW(E), LUNT	brat	GYTE
bleak	BLAE	brawl	FLITE, FLYTE
bleeding nose	JEELY NOSE		TUILYE, TUILZIE
blemish	TASH	breach	SLAP
blight	SCOUTHER, SCOWDER	—of chastity	SCULDUDD(E)RY
block	DIT		SKULDUDDERY
—head	TUMPHY	bread	LOAF
—of tenements	LAND	breakfast	DISJUNE
blood	BLUDE, BLUID	—roll	BAP
blow	CLA(U)TLOUNDER, PAIK	breathing space	BARLEY
	WHAMPLE, YANK	breeches	BREEKS
—on the head	CRUNT	brewing	BROWST
blue	BLAE	bridesmaid	BESTMAID
—bell	HAREBELL	bridge	BRIG
—gown	GABERLUNZIE	—centering	COOM
board	BROD	bridle	BRANKS
bob	HOD	brigand	CATERAN
bobbin	PIRN	brimming	REAMING
bodice	JIRKINET	bringing misery or calamity	WAESOME
body	BOUK, BUIK, BUKE	brisk	CANT
—of vassals	MANRENT	bristle	BIRSE
bog	MOSS	bristly	BIRSY

brittle	BRICKLE, BRUCKLE, FRUSH
broad	BRAID
—Scots	LALLANS
—valley	STRATH
broil	BRU(I)LZIE, STRAMASH
broken	
—branch	SCROG
—ground in bog	HAG(G)
brood	CLOCK, CLECKING
—of children	BAIRN-TEAM, BAIRN-TIME
brooding hen	CLOCKER
brook	BURN
—lime	WATER-PURPIE
brother	BILLIE, BILLY
—in-law	GUDE-BROTHER
brow	BROO
browse	MOOP
brushwood	HAG(G)
budge	JEE
buffet	YANK
build	BIG
building-site	STANCE
bulk	BOUK, BUIK, BUKE
bumble bee	BUM-BEE
bump	CLOUR, DUNCH, DUNSH
bun	COOKIE
bunch of twigs	COW, KOW
bundle	DORLACH
bung	DOOK
bungle	BAUCHLE, BLUNK
	MIS(H)GUGGLE
burden of a song	O'ERCOME
	O'ERWORD, OWREWORD
burial fee	GR(O)UND MAIL
burly	BUIRDLY
burn	SCOUTHER, SCOWDER
burrow	HOWE, HOWK
burst	LOUPEN, LOUPIT, LOWP
—of anger	FUFF
bushy place	SCROG
busy	EIDENT
butt	DUNCH, DUNSH
buttermilk and water	
(Islands)	BLAND
buttocks	DOUP, FUD, HINDER-END
	HINDERLAN(D)S, HURDIES
buxom	GAUCY, GAWSY, SONCIE
	SONCY, SONSIE, SONSY
buy	COFF
by	
—my faith	HAITH
—stealth	STOW(N)LINS
—the time of	GIN
cabbage	
—broth	KALE, KAIL
—patch (Islands)	PLANTIE-CRUIVE
—seller	KAILWIFE
—stock	CASTOCK, CUSTOCK
cackle	KECKLE
cajole	CUITTLE
cake	BANNOCK, BUTTER-BAKE
	FARL(E), FARTHEL
—Shrove Tuesday	CARCAKE
call	CA
—by an ill name	MISCA(LL)
—to	
cows	PROO, PRUH
horse	HIE, HIGH
calm	LOUN(D), LOWN(D)
cannot	CANNA
—be bothered	DOWNA
cap	KILMARNOCK
—Highland Regiment	HUMMEL BONNET
capacity	BIND
caper	SCOUP, SCOWP
—about	FLISK
capital	AULD REEKIE, EDINBURGH
capricious	CAPERNOITED, CAPERNOITIE
	CAP(P)ERNOITY
caraway	CARVY
card	FLAUGHT
care	K(I)AUGH, SUSSY
careful look	VISIE, VIZY, VIZZIE
carefully	HOOLY
careless	UNTENTY
carouse	BIRL(E)
carriage	HURLY-HACKET
carrion	KET
—crow	HOODIE
case-law	PRACTIC
cast an eye around	GLEDGE
castle-goblin	RED-CAP, RED-COWL
casual	ORRA
casual(ly)	OVERLY
cat	BAUDRONS
catch	CLAUGHT, KEP, TACK
—fish with seine-net	TRAWL
—word	O'ERWORD
catechism	CARRITCH
catgut	THAIRM
cattle	BESTIAL, KY(E), NOUT, NOWT
—disease	MOOR-ILL
—Islands	KYLOES, LUING CATTLE
—farm	STORE-FARM
—lifting	SPREAGHERY, SPRECHERY
—theft	HERSHIP
caught	KEPPIT
cause to	
—bounce	STOT(TER)
—flee	FLAY, FLEY
cause(d)	GAR(T)
cease	DEVALL

Celt	GADHEL
certain	SICCAR, SICKER
certainly	CERTES, CERTIE, CERTY
cesspool	JAWHOLE
chaffinch	SNABBY
chairman	PR(A)ESES
challenge to act of daring	HEN(NER)
change one's	
—abode	FLIT
—mind	TAKE THE RUE
charge	DITTAY
charlock	RUNCH
charm	WEIRD
chat	CRACK
chatter	CHITTER, CLASH, GABNASH,
	NASHGAB, YATTER
cheat	JINK
cheerful	CANT(Y)
cheerfully	
—complacent	JOCO
—confident	CROUSE
cheese	CABOC, KEBBOCK, KEBBUCK
chemise	SARK
chest	BUNK, KIST
—for holding meal	MEAL-ARK
chide	QUARREL
chief	
—herald	(LORD) LYON
—magistrate	PROVOST
cities	LORD PROVOST
chief's	
—barge (Islands)	BIRLINN
—heir elect	TANIST
child	BAIRN, CHIEL(D)
	GAIT, GEITA, GYTE
	LITTLEANE, LITTLIN, SMOUT
	SMOWT, WEAN
—beginning to walk	GANGREL
child's garment	POLONAISE
children's	
—entitlement	BAIRN'S-PART, LEGITIM
—game	NIEVIE-NICK-NACK
chill	OORIE, OURIE, OWRIE
chilling	CAULD-RIFE
chimney	LUM
—cap	OLD WIFE
—corner	LUG
—top	LUM(-HEAD)
chip	SPALE
choice	WALE
choke	WORRY
choose/choosing	WALE
chore	TROCK, TROKE
church	KIRK
—court	KIRK-SESSION
—government system	PRESBYTERIANISM

—of Scotland	AULD KIRK
—officer	BEADLE, BED(E)RAL
—yard	KIRK-YA(I)RD
churl	BODACH
cibol	SYBOE, SYBO(W)
circle of hunters	TINCHEL
circular stone tower	BROCH
cite	SIST
cithern (Islands)	LANGSP(I)EL
claim	CRAVE
clamber	SPRAICKLE, SPRAUCHLE
clamour	RAIRD, REIRD
clasp-knife	JOCKTELEG
clatter	HOTTER
clause in charter specifying	
vassal's service	REDDENDO
claw	CLA(U)T
clean out of money	RUMP
clear up	RED(D)
cleavage	SLOT
cleft	CLOFF
—between hills	SLACK
—in rock (Islands)	RIVA
clerical function	DIET
clever	GLEG, SOUPLE
cleverness	CLEVERALITY
cliff	CRAIG
climb	SCLIM, SKLIM, SPEEL
climbing-iron	SPEELER
clock	KNOCK
—wise	DEASIL
clods	MOOLS, MOULS
clog	CLAG
close	
—fitting garment	JEISTIECOR
—look	VISIE, VIZY, VIZZIE
closed	LUCKEN
clot	LAPPER
—of dirt or colour	SPLATCH
cloth	CLOOT
clothes	CLAES, TROGGS
—horse	SCREEN
cloud-drift	CARRY
cloven-hoof	CLOOT
club-moss	BURR
cluck	CLOCK
clumsy	
—girl	TAUPIE, TAWPIE
—person	BAUCHLE
clutch	CLAUCHT, CLAUGHT
	GLAUM
coal	
—bin	BUNK
—bucket	BACKET
—fish	SAITH(E), SILLOCK
	STENLOCK

coaly fireclay	TUMPHY
coarse	RUDAS
—cloth	KELT
—file	RISP
—grained	CURN(E)Y
—woollen (Orkney)	WADMA(A)L
	WAFDMALL
coarsely outspoken	RANDIE, RANDY
coax	CUITTLE, FLEECH
coaxing	FLEECHING, FLEECHMENT
cobbler	SOUTAR, SOUTER, SOWTER
cock	
—crow	SKREIGH OF DAY
—that will not fight	FUGIE
cocker	CUITER
codfish	KEELING
coffin	KIST
coiffure	COCKERNONY
coil	FANK
coins	
—small copper (old)	PLACK
—¹/₆ penny	BOD(D)LE
—farthing (old)	TURNER
—halfpenny	BAUBEE, BAWBEE
—3d bit (old)	BAUBEE, BAWBEE
—2p (old)	QUADRUPLE
—1³/₄d	MERK
—18/-	UNICORN
—£1	PISTOLE
—74/-	LION
—£12 (old)	PISTOLE
—eighth of mark (Islands)	URE
—gold coin (old)	BONNET-PIECE
—silver coin (old)	SWORD-DOLLAR
cold	FRAIM, FREMD, FREMIT
	WEED, WEID
colic	BATTS
collar-bone	HAUSE-BANE
collect (parcel)	UPLIFT
collection	
—of small things	SMYT(E)RIE
—plate	BROD
colt	STAIG
comb	KAME, KAIM, RED(D)
come	
—across	MEET IN WI(TH)
—to light	SPUNK OUT
comely	SONSIE, SONSY
comfortable	BEIN, BIEN, CANNY
	COUTHIE, TOSH
—looking	SONSIE, SONSY
coming on	ONCOME
common sense	RUMGUMPTION
	RUM(M)EL-GUMPTION
	RUM(M)LE-GUMPTION
	RUMBLE-GUMPTION

commotion	CARFUFFLE, CURFUFFLE
	KEFUFFLE, HOTTER
	TIRRIVEE, TIRRIVIE
communion service	OCCASION
companion-in-arms	BILLIE, BILLY
compel	GAR
compel(led)	GAR(T)
complain peevishly	GIRN, WHEENGE
	WHINGE
complete	
—set	STAND
—sum	SOLIDUM
completely	STOOP AND ROOP
comply with	OBTEMPER
concerned with fate	WEIRD
concerning that matter	THEREANENT
concurrence	CONCOURSE
condition	FID, PLISKIE, PLISKY
	PLY
conduct sheep into fold	WEAR
conductor of	
festival (Islands)	SCUDDALER, SCUDLER
	SKUDLER
cone of damp gunpowder	PEEOY, PIOY(E)
confidential	PACK
confirmation by	
subsequent act	HOMOLOGATION
confound	BUMBAZE
confuse	MOIDER
confused	
—disturbance	BRU(I)LZIE
—jumble	MIXTER-MAXTER
	MIXTIE-MAXTIE
	MIX(T)Y-MAX(T)Y
confusedly mixed	THROUGH-OTHER
confute	REDARGUE
connecting ridge	HAUSE, HAWSE
connivance at adultery	LENOCINIUM
considerable	GAY, GEY
—number	HANTLE
considerably	GAY, GEY
conspicuous	KENSPECKLE
contemptible fellow	SMAIK
contend strongly with	PINGLE
contention	STURT
continue to wait	WAIT ON
contradict	THREAP, THREEP
contrary to course	
of sun	WID(D)ERSHINS
	WITHERSHINS
controlling fate	WEIRD
conundrum	GUESS
convey in wheeled vehicle	HURL
cool	CALLER
cormorant	SCART(H), SKART(H)
corn	OATS

—dolly	KIRN-BABY, KIRN-DOLLIE	crease	LIRK
—maiden	MAIDEN	creature	CRATUR
corporation of royal burgh	GUILDRY	credit	MENSE
corpse	LIKE	creek (Islands)	GEO, GIO, VOE
cosy	COSH	creep (of the flesh)	GREW, GRUE
cottage	BOTHIE, BOTHY	crested	TAPPIT
—room	END	criminal intention	DOLE
cottager	MAILER	cringe	SNOOL
cottar's-house	COT-HOUSE	cripple	LAMETER, LAMITER
cottars	COT-FOLK	crisp	CRUMP
cotton-grass	CANNA(CH), MOSS-CROP	crook-handled	
cough loudly	KINK	walking-stick	KEBBIE
counter for casting lots	CAVEL	crooked	CAMSHO(CH), CAMSHEUGH
country			THRAWARD, THRAWART
—dance	PETRONELLA	crop	CRAP, STOW
—lass	JENNY	cross	THRAW
—talk	CLASH	—examine	TARGE
court		—grained	ILL-HAIRED, THRAWN
—judgement	DECREET	—question	BACKSPEER, BACKSPEIR
—official	DEMPSTER, DOOMSTER	crow steps	CORBIE-STEPS
—sitting	SEDERUNT	crowd of children	SMYRTIE
—usher	MACER	crowded	PANG
Covenanter	WHIGGAMORE	crown of head or causeway	CANTLE
Covenanters	HILLFOLK, HILLMEN	crumb	NIRL
cover		crumble	MURL
—by drifting (snow)	WREATH	crupper	CURPEL
—of pot	PAT-LID	crush	CHACK, CHECK
cow		cry	GLEET, GOWL, SPRAICH
—dung	SHA(I)RN	—fretfully	WHEENGE, WHINGE
—house	BYRE	cupboard	AWMRIE, AWMRY
—man	BYREMAN	cuckoo	GOUK, GOWK
	NOWT-HERD	cudgel	KEBBIE
—or ox killed and		cuff	GOWF
salted	MART	cunning mischief	PAWK
cow's yield	MELTITH	cup	QUAICH, QUAIGH, TASSIE
coward	FUGIE	cur	MESSAN
cower down	CROODLE	curdle	LAPPER
cows	KY(E), NOUT, NOWT	—(of blood)	GREW, GRUE
coy	SKEIGH	curdled milk	LAPPER(ED)-MILK
crab	PARTAN	cure with smoke	REAST, REEST, REIST
—apple	SCROG	curlew	(GREAT)WHAUP
crabbed	CAPERNOITED, CAPERNOITIE	curry favour	CUITTLE
	CAP(P)ERNOITY, CRABBIT	curse	WEARY, WINZE
crafty	LOOPY	—of Scotland	QUEEN OF DIAMONDS
—person	SNECK-DRAWER	curtailed	CUTTY
—twist	W(H)IMPLE	cushion	COD
crag	HEUCH, HEUGH	cut	
cram	CRAP, PANG, STAP	—and dry peat	CAST
crammed	PANG	—on something	INSCULP
crane-fly	JENNY-LONG-LEGS	—turf	FLAUGHTER
cranky	FIFISH	cutter on plough	CO(U)LTER
crash	FRUSH	cutting of last sheaf	KERN, KIRN
cravat	OVERLAY	dabble in	
crazy	DOILED, DOILT, DOTTLE(D)	—liquid	PLOTTER, PLOUTER
	GYTE, WOWF		PLOWTER
cream	REAM	—miry matter	CLATCH

dabbling	PLOTTER, PLOUTER, PLOWTER
dagger	DIRK, SKEAN, SKENE
	WHINGER, WHINIARD
	WHINYARD
dainty	GENTY, SUNKET
dally	PINGLE
dam	STANK
—in stream	CAULD
damage	SCAITH, SKAITH
damson	PLUMDAMAS
dance	BOB, HIGHLAND FLING
	LOWP, PETRONELLA, REEL
	STRATHSPEY
—tune	SPRING
dandle	DOODLE
dangerous	MISCHANCY, NO'CANNY
	UNCHANCY, WANCHANCIE
	WANCHANCY
dangle after	TRAIK AFTER
dapple-grey	LIART, LYART
dare	DAUR
dark blue	BLAE
dart	
—obliquely	SKITE, SKYTE
—of pain	STEN(D)
dash	JABBLE, SPANG
—of pen	SCART
daub	CLATCH, SLAKE
daunt	DANTON
day's work	DARG
daybreak	SKREIGH OF DAY
days of merriment	
(New Year)	DAFT DAYS
dazzling	GLAIK
dead	DEED, DEID
deafen	DEAVE
deal out sparingly	TAPE
dealer	COUPER
dealings	TROCK, TROKE
dean's warrant	JEDGE
death	DEID
—throe	DEID-THRAW
debt under £20	SMALL-DEBTS
deceive	MISLIPPEN
decent	WISE-LIKE
decisive movement	UPCOME
deck out	DAIKER
declare	
—heir	SERVE
—to be an idiot	COGNOSCE
decline in health	TRAIK
decorous	MENSEFUL
decree	DECERN, MODIFY
deed of qualification	BACK-BOND
deep	
—draught	WILLIEWAUGHT

—sea fishing ground	
(Islands)	HAF
defamation	SLANDER
defeat	WA(U)RST
defile	FILE, HAUSE, HAWSE
deformed	ILL-FAURD
delay	SIST
delicate	DORTY
deliveryman	POSTIE
dell	DARGLE, HOWE
demure	MIM(-MOU'D), PRIMSIE
departing	WAY-GOING
depend	LIPPEN
dependent interest	RIDING-INTEREST
deplorable	WAESOME
deprive	TWIN(E)
deranged	SKIVIE
derisive gesture	GECK
derived	EXTRACT
desert	FORHOO(IE), FORHOW
desolate	GOUSTY
despicable fellow	FOOTRA, FOUTRA
destine	WEIRD
devastated place	WASTAGE
Development	
—Agency	SDA
—Department	SDD
devil	AULD MIS(C)HANTER
	CLOOT(IE), CLOOTS, DEIL
	HORNIE, NICKIE-BEN
	WIRRICOW
	WORRICOW, WORRYCOW
devour ravenously	WORRY
dialect of islands	NORN
dib-stones	CHUCKIE-STANES, CHUCKS
die	DEE
died	DEED
difference	DIFFER
dig	HOWK
diligent	EIDENT
din	RAIRD, REEL, REIRD
	STOUND, STOWND
dingy	OORIE, OURIE, OWRIE
dinner	KALE, KAIL
dip in hot water	PLOT
direction	AIRT
dirge	CORANACH, CORONACH
dirt	GUTTERS
disappoint	MISLIPPEN
disarray	TASH
disaster	MIS(C)HANTER
disciplinarian	
in University	HEBDOMADAR
	HEBDOMADER
disease coming without	
known cause	INCOME

disentangle	RED(D)
disfigure	BLA(U)D, TASH
disgust	SCOMFISH, SCUNNER
dish	ASHET, BRO(U)GH, HAGGIS
	HOWTOWDIE, (PEASE-)BROSE
dismal	DOWIE
disorder	CARFUFFLE, CURFUFFLE
	KEFUFFLE
dispatch unceremoniously	SHANK
disperse	SCALE, SCAIL, SKAIL
dispirited	SACKLESS
displacement	JEE
dispute	THREAP, THREEP
disputed	THREAPIT, THREEPIT
distort	THRAW
distorted	THRAWN
distrain	POIND
distraint	POINDER, POINDING
distress	PUT ABOUT
distressed	ILL
district thirled to mill	SUCKEN
distrust	MISLIPPEN
disturb	JEE, STEER
disturbance	COLLIESHANGIE
	STRAMASH, STURT
disturbed	MISTRYSTED
ditch	SHEUCH, SHEUGH, SIKE, STANK
divination	TAGHAIRM
divine	SPAE
diviner	SPAER, SPAEMAN
division of county	WARD
dizziness	MIRLIGOES
do	DIV
document produced in court	PRODUCTION
dodge	JINK, JOUK
doggerel	RAT-RHYME
dolphin	CA(A)ING-WHALE
dominate	O'ERGANG
donkey	CUDDIE, CUDDY
doom	WEIRD
door	YETT
—catch	SNETCH
—knocker	RISP
dotard	DOTTLE
double	
—feu-duty	DUPLICAND
—handful	GOWPEN
dove	DOO
—cote	DOOCOT, DOOKET
dower	TOCHER
down-and out	FORFAIRN
down-at-heel	SHAUCHLE
dowry	TOCHER
doze	DOVER
drag	
—along ground	HARL
—oneself	HARL
draggle	TRACHLE, TROLLOP
drain	POUR, SHEUCH, SHEUGH
	SIVER, SYVER
draining-board	BUNK
dram	TIFT
drank	DRUCKEN
draught	WAUCHT, WAUGHT
—animal	AVER
—board	DAMBOARD, DAMBROD
—man	DAM
draw (money)	UPLIFT
dreary	DREICH, GOUSTY
	OORIE, OURIE, OWRIE
drench	DROOK, DROUK
drenched	DROOKIT, DROUKIT
dress	BOUN, GRAITH
—neatly	DINK
dresser	AUMRIE, AWMRIE, AWMRY
dried	
—heath	ROUGHIE
—meat (Islands)	VIFDA, VIVDA
drily humorous	PAWKY
drink	ATHOLL BROSE
	HEATHER ALE, TIFT
—cup out	BEND THE BICKER
—hard at	BEND
—in large draughts	WAUCHT, WAUGHT
drinking	
—bout	BEND
—cup	QUAICH, QUAIGH
drive	CA
driver of horses at plough	GADSMAN
drizzle	SCOUTHER, SCOWDER
	SMIR(R), SMUR
drizzling mist	DROW
drone or play, as bagpipe	DOODLE
drooping	OORIE, OURIE, OWRIE
drub(bing)	PAIK
drudge	SCOGIE
drudgery	SLAISTERY
drunk	FOU, STOTIOUS
drunkard	SAND-BED
drunken	FOU, WAT
drunken(ness)	DRUCKEN(NESS)
dry	EILD, HI(R)STIE
	REEST, REIST
—in the	
sun	RIZZAR, RIZZER, RIZZOR
wind	WIN
—stone	
wall	DRY-STANE DIKE
waller	COWAN
—with smoke	REAST, REEST, REIST
duck	JOOK, JOUK
dull	DOWF, DOWIE

—witted	DONNERD, DONNERED
	DONNERT, FOZY
dunce	SUMPH
dunderhead	GOMERAL, GOMERIL
dung-fork	GRAIP
dupe	GECK
dust	STOOR, STOUR, STOWRE
dusty	STOURY
dwarf	DROICH
dwell	STAY
dynasty	STEWART, STUART
each	ILK(A)
—other	OTHER
eager	FRACK, FRECK
ear of corn	ICKER
Earl Marshal	EARL MARISCHAL
early dram	MORNING
earnest of bargain	ARLES
	ARLE(S) PENNY
earth	(Y)EARD, YERD, YIRD
—house	PICTS' HOUSE
—hunger	(Y)EARD)-HUNGER
	YERD-HUNGER
	YIRD-HUNGER
earthenware (crock)	PIG
earwig	HORNIE-GOLOCH
easily	
—recognised	KENSPECKLE
—tickled	KITTLY
Easter-egg	PACE-EGG
easterly	EASSEL(GATE), EASSIL(GATE)
	EASTLIN(G)
eastwards	EASSEL, EASSIL
easy enough	GEY AND EASY
eat with	
—a spoon	SUP
—feeble appetite	PINGLE
eatables	VIVERS, VIVRES
eccentric	SHKITE, SKTE
ecclesiastical function	DIET
ecstasy	EXIES
edge sheep into fold	WEAR
edible	
—crab	PARTAN
—seaweed	BADDERLOCK
Education	
—Certificate	SCE
—Department	SED
Educational Institute	EIS
effeminate man	JENNY, JESSIE
efficacy	FECK
eke	ECHE, EIK
elder	PRESBYTER
—tree	BOUNTREE, BOURTREE
elderly woman	LUCKIE, LUCKY
elegant	JIMP(Y), JINTY

elude	JINK
emaciated	WANTHRIVEN
emblem	THISTLE
embrace	HAUSE, HAWSE
emerge	CAST UP
empty	BOSS, GOUSTY, TOOM
enable to last	WEAR
enclosure	HAINING
end of eggshell	DOUP
ends of ribbon	FATTRELS
endearment	BURD(IE), LEEZE ME
—Island	JARTA, YARTA
endure	DREE, THOLE, WEAR
English	SOUTHRO(U)N
—man	POCK-PUDDING, SASSENACH
enough	ENOW, SAIRING
entail	TAILLIE, TAILYE, TAILZIE
entangle	FANKLE, TAIGLE
entreat	PRIG
equipment	GRAITH
escapade	SPLORE
essential virtue	FIZZEN, FUSHION
established church	AULD KIRK
estranged	FRAIM, FREMD, FREMIT
Evangelical	HIGH-FLIER, HIGH-FLYER
even if	SUPPOSE
evening	FORENIGHT
—party	ROCKING
every day (but Sunday)	ILKADAY
everything	HALE HYPOTHEC
ewe	YOW(E)
—after lambing	KEB
exacting person	FIKE, FYKE
examine	COGNOSCE
exclamation	TOOTS, TUTS
excavation	HEUCH, HEUGH
excel	WA(U)RST
excellent	WAL(L)Y
excessive	NIMIOUS
exchange	EXCAMB, NIFFER
	SCORSE, TROCK, TROKE
—of	
goods	TROCK, TROKE
lands	ESCAMBIUM, EXCAMBION
excite loathing in	SCUNNER
excuse	FAIK
exempt	EXEEM, EXEME
exert oneself	PINGLE
exhausted	FORFAIRN
	FORFEUCHEN
	FORFOUGHEN
—from travelling	WAYGONE
expect	LIPPEN
expenses for catching	
rogues	ROGUE-MONEY
experience a pang	STOUND, STOWND

experienced	USED
expert	SKEELY, SKILLY, USED
expiry	ISH
extinguish	SLO(C)KEN
extract	HOWK
extraordinary	BY-ORDINAR, BYOUS
eye	EE, KEEKER
eyebrow	BREE
eyes	EEN, EYNE
face	GIZZ
fail	MISGIVE
—in health	DWALM, DWAUM
—to	
keep appointment	MISTRYST
recognise	MISKEN, TARTLE
faint	DWAMY, SWERVE
fairly	GAY, GEY
faithful	AEFA(U)LD, AFA(W)LD
fall	FA
—of snow	STORM
false hair piece	COCKERNONY
familiar jog-trot	HEICH-HOW
famous	NAMELY
fantastic	
—ornamentation	WHIGMALEERIE
	WHIGMALERY
—round ornament	CURLIEWURLIE
farm	
—cottage	BOTHIE, BOTHY
—in joint tenancy	TOWNSHIP
—overseer	GRIEVE
—song	CORN-KISTER
—stead	FARM-TOUN, FERMTOUN
	ONSTEAD, TOWN
—worker	HIND
fasten	STEEK
fastened	SNECKED
fat	FOZY
fate	WEIRD
father-in-law	GUDE-FATHER
faulty state	VICIOSITY, VITIOSITY
favoured	FA'ARD, FAURD
fearless	RAUCLE
fearsome	UNCO
feathered legs	COOTIE
feeble	FIZZENLESS, FUSHIONLESS
	SACKLESS, SHILPIT
	SOBER, WERSH
—person or animal	WALLYDRAG
	WALLYDRAIGLE
feebleness in intelligence	WANT
feed with corn	CORN
female	
—auctioneer	ROUPING-WIFE
—fish	RAUN, RAWN
—outworker	BONDAGER

ferrule	VIRL
feudal service	ARRIAGE
few	WHEEN
fibre	TAIT, TATE
fictitious dwarf	PICT
fiddle	ITCH
—(Islands)	GJO, GJU, GU(E), GOU
fidget	FIDGE, FIKE, FYKE
—with eagerness	HOTCH
field	PAIRK
fierce	WUD
fiery person	SPUNKIE
fight	TUILYE, TUILZIE, WAP
—in heat of passion	CHAUD-MELLE
fight(er)	FECHT(ER)
filled full	PANGFU(LL)
find by skilful means	EXPISCATE
fine	GRASSUM, UNLAW
—misty rain	SMIR(R), SMUR
—powder	SMEDDUM
finely dressed	BRAW
finger-hole of wind	
instrument	LILL
finical	PERJINK(ETY), PREJINK
fire-screen	HALLAN
fireside disputation	KILFUD-YOKING
firm	SICCAR, SICKER
	STEEVE, STIEVE
—place in bog	HAG(G)
first	
—attendance of magistrate	
after election	KIRKIN(G)
—church attendance after	
marriage	KIRKIN(G)
—furrow	FEERING
—shoots of crop	BRAIRD, BREER
fish	
—roe	RAUN, RAWN
—spawn	REDD
—trap	CRU(I)VE
—with the hands	GUDDLE, GUMP
fit of	
—hysterics	EXIES
—passion	TIRRIVEE, TIRRIVIE
—perversity	THRAW
—stubbornness	REEST, REIST
—the sulks	TOUT, TOWT
fitting	WISE-LIKE
flagstones	PLAINSTANES
flake	FLAUGHT
flame	LOW(E)
flannel undervest	WYLIE-COAT
flap	FLACK, FLAFF(ER), WAP
—about	WALLOP
flapping	FLAUGHT
—rag	WALLOP

flash	FLAUGHT, GLAIK
flat	
—bonnet	BALMORAL
—cake	BANNOCK
—fish	CRAIGFLUKE
—moist land	FLOW
flatter	FLEECH, PHRASE
flattering	FLEECHING, FLEECHMENT
flaunt	SKYRE
flax (seed)	LINT (SEED)
fled	LOUPEN, LOUPIT
flee	LOWP
fleece	KET, PLOT
flicker	FLAUGHTER
flicking with thumbnail	SPANG-COCKLE
flight	FLAUGHT
flighty	HELLICAT
	LOUP-THE-DYKE
flock of sheep	HIRSEL
flourish	WAMPISH
flow lumpily	SLUMP
fluff	OOZE
fluffy	PLUFFY
flurry	SWITHER
flutter	FLAUGHTER, FLICHTER
—of wings	FLAFF
fluttering motion	FLAUGHTER
flying shower	SCOUTHER, SCOWDER
fold	LIRK
—back	FLIPE
food	BROSE, SCAFF, VIVERS
	VIVRES
—scraps	BROCK
fool	DOTTLE, GOUK, GOWK
foolish	DOILED, DOILT, DOTTLE(D)
	FOOL, GLAIKIT
—fellow	GOMERAL, GOMERIL
—person	HAVEREL
—talk	HAVER(ING)S
foot-stamping	RUFF
football game	BA'ING, BA'SPIEL
footballers	SFA
footless stocking	HOGGER, MOGGAN
for	ON
—the express purpose	ONCE ERRAND
	ANCE ERRAND
	YINCE ERRAND
foray	CREACH, CREAGH, SPREAGH
forcible	VIVE
ford	LIRK, RACK
foreign	FRAIM, FREMD, FREMIT
foreman	TOPSMAN
forenoon	FOREDAY
foretell	SPAE
forewarn	WEIRD
form of Scots	LALLAN
formerly	UMQUHILE
foreseeing the future	FAY, FEY, FIE
forth	FURTH
fortified	
—house	BASTEL-HOUSE
—island	CRANNOG
forward	FORRIT, THRAWARD
	THRAWART
—girl	YIP
foster-child	DA(U)LT
foul-mouthed old woman	RUDAS
found	FAND
fourth part	FORPET, FORPIT
fowl	BRISSEL-COCK
—house manure	HEN-PEN
fox	LOWRIE(-TOD)
	TOD-LOWRIE, TOD
fragment	BLA(U)D
freckle	FAIRNYTIC(K)LE
free	
—defendant of charge	ASSOILZIE
—hold estate	BARONY
Islands	UDAL
—of claim	ASSOILZIE
—range	SCOUTH, SCOWTH
freebooter	CATERAN
freeholder (Islands)	UDALLER
Free Church of Scotland	WEE FREES
frequency	COMMONALTY
fresh	CALLER
—man	BAJAN(T), BEJAN(T)
friable	CRUMP
fried dish	SKIRL-IN-THE-PAN
friendly	COUTHIE, TOSH
fright	FLEG, GLIFF, GLIFT
frighten	FLEG, FLAY, FLAY
	FRICHT, SCAUR
frivolous excuse	WHITTIE-WHATTIE
frog	PADDOCk
—spawn	REDD
frolic	SPLORE
from	FRAE, THRAE
froth	REAM
fuddled	TA(I)VERT
fuel	EILDING
fulfilment	IMPLEMENT
full	FOU, SKELPING
funeral banner	GUMPHION
furious	WUD
furnace cinders	DANDER
furnish	PLENISH
furniture	INSIGHT, PLENISHING
	STOUTH(E)RIE
furrow	FUR(R), SHEUCH, SHEUGH
further on or up	UPBY(E)
fuss	FIKERY, FYKERY

fussy	FIKISH, FIKY, FYKISH, FYKY
—talk	PHRASE
gable	GAVEL
gad	TRAIK
Gael	GAHDEL, GOIDEL
Gaelic-speaking	
districts of Scotland	GAIDHEALTACHD
gag	BRANKS
gaiter	COOTIKIN, CU(I)TIKIN
	QUEET
gallows	DULE-TREE, WOODIE
game	SHINNY, SHINTY
gamekeeper	GILLY, G(H)ILLIE
gap in fence	SLAP
garb	THRATCH
garish	ROARIE, ROARY
garret	ROOST
gasp for breath	KINK
gate	YATE, YET(T)
—crash	SORN
gave	GAE, GIED
genealogist	SEANNACHIE, SEANNACHY
	SENNACHIE, SHANACHIE
generous	MENSEFUL
gentle	CANNY
get	
—by	
begging	THIG
groping	POWTER
—lost	TRAIK
—over	OVERCAST
gey and...	GEYAN
ghastliness	GASHLINESS
ghastly	GASH(FUL), GASHLY
ghost	CHAPPIE, WAFF
giddy	GLAIKIT
—headed	HELLICAT
gift	PROPINE
—given on last day of year	HOGMANAY
—of escheat	SUBREPTION
gig	HURLY-HACKET
girdle	GRIDDLE
girl	CUMMER, CUTTY, KIMMER
	LASSIE, QUEAN, QUEYN(IE)
	QUIN(I)E
give	GID, GIE
—and take	GIFF-GAFF
—judgement on	COGNOSCE
—security for another	CAUTIONRY
—up the charge	DESERT THE DIET
given	GIEN
giving possession	SASINE
glance	GLEY
glancing blow	SKITE, SKYTE
gleam	SHEEN
—of sunshine	SUN-BLINK

glen	HOWE
glide	SCRIEVE, SKITE, SKYTE
—obliquely	SKITE, SKYTE
glimmer	STIME, STYME
glimpse	GLEDGE, GLIFF, GLIFT
	GLIM, GLISK, GLIST
	STIME, STYME, WAFF
globe-flower	LUCKENGOWAN
gloom	DOOL
gloomy	DRUMLY
glower	GLAUR
gluttonous	GUTSY
go	GAE, GANG
—about or forth	STEER
—arm-in-arm	CLEEK
—counter	THRAW
—easy	CA'CANNY
—on crutches	STILP
—slowly	WEAR
—to sleep	FALL OVER
—wearily	TRAIK
go-by	GANG-BY
goal	DOOL, DULE
—(in games)	HAIL
gob	GAB
goblin	BODACH, BROWNIE
	RED-CAP, RED-COWL
godmother	CUMMER, KIMMER
going	GAUN
gold	GOOL, GULE, GOWD
—finch	GOUDIE, GOWDIE, GOWDSPINK
golf	GOWF
—ball	GOWF-BA
gone	GANE
good	GUID, GUDE
—condition	PLY
—deal	HANTLE
—fortune	SEIL
—health!	SLAINTE
—looking	WEEL-FAIRED, WEEL-FA(U)R'D
	WEEL-FA(U)RT
—luck	SONCE, SONSE
—manners	HAVING
—many	HANTLE
	SONSY
—turn	CAST
good-for-nothing	NE'ER-DO-WEEL
goodly	FAIR-FARAND
good-natured	SONCIE, SONCY, SONSIE
goodness!	(MY) CONSCIENCE
gooseberry	GROSER(T), GROSET, GROSSART
gore	GAIR
gossip	CLASH, CLATTER, CLAVER
	CLISH-CLASH, CLISHMACLAVER
	CUMMER, JAUNDER, KIMMER
got	GOTTEN

—off lightly with	CHEAP OF
grace	MENSE
graceful	GENTY
graceless	MENSELESS
gracious	MENSEFUL
grain	CURN
—chest	CORN-KIST
—crops, cut or ready	VICTUAL
—due to miller's servant	KNAVESHIP
—measure	WECHT
—of corn	PICKLE
granary	GIRNEL
grand	
—child	OE, OY(E)
—father	GUDESIRE, GUTCHER
	LUCKIE-DAD
—mother	GUDE-DAME
grantor's warranty	WARRANDICE
granular	CURN(E)Y
grasp	CLA(U)T, GLAUM
grass field	PARK
grate	CHIRK, RISP
grating over drain	SIVER, SYVER
gratuity	MAG(G)S
grave	GRAFF
—digger	BEADLE, BED(E)RAL
gravel	CHANNEL
grazing blow or	
movement	SKIFF
grease	CREESH
great	FELL, UNCO
—stride	STEN(D)
greedy	GARE
gridiron	BRANDER
grief	VEX
grim	DOUR, GURLY
grimace	MURGEON
grin	GIRN
groove in masonry	RAGGLE
grope	GRAPE, RIPE
gross amount	SLUMP
ground	
—floor house	MAINDOOR
—for one grave	LAIR
ground-rent	GROUND ANNUAL
group of	
—cot-houses	COT-TOWN
—houses	TOWN
growl	GURL
gruel	BROCHAN, CROWDY
grumble	GIRN
grunt	GRUMPH
guarantee	WARRANDICE
guarantor	OBLIGANT
guard	WEAR
guardian of minor	TUTOR

guess	ETTLE
guide	
—in certain direction	W(E)ISE, WEIZE
—sheep into fold	WEAR
guileless	SACKLESS
guillemot	LUNGIE
gull	SCAURY, SCOURIE
	SCOWRIE, SEA-MAW
gully (Islands)	GEO, GIO
gulp	SUILK
gun-sight	VISIE, VIZY, VIZZIE
gurgle	BULLER, RUCKLE
gurgling sound	GOLLAR
gust	FLAUGHT
gutsiness	GREEDINESS
gutter	STRAND
guttural bawl	GOLLAR
gypsy	CAIRD, TINK(LER)
habitual saying	O'ERWORD, OWREWORD
habituate	USE
hack	HAG
haddock	HADDIE, SPELD(R)IN(G)
hag	RUDAS
haggle	NIFFER, PRIG
hair	
—comb	REDDING-COMB
	REDDING-KAME
—piece	COCKERNONY
—powder	M(O)UST, MUIST
halberd	LOCHABER-AXE
hale	FRACK, FRECK, RAUCLE
half	HALFLIN(G)S
—a silver penny	HALFLIN(G)
—grown person	HALFLIN(G)
hall	HA
ham	HOUGH
hand over to as one's fate	WEIRD
handful	GOWPEN, LOOFFUL
	RIP(P)
handkerchief	NAPKIN
handsome	BRAW
hang	STRAP
hanging clock	WAG-AT-THE-WALL
	WAG-BY-THE-WALL
hangman	LOCKMAN
hangman's rope	TOW
happening	WEIRD
happiness	SEIL
harass	PINGLE
harbour	RESET
—due	SHORE-DUE
harbouring of criminal	RESET
hard blow	DEV(V)EL
hardened clay	BLAE
hardly	JIMPLY
hare	BAUDRONS, MALKIN, MAWKIN

—bell	BLAWORT	high tea	TOUSY TEA
hare's tail	FUD	Highland	HIELAND
harm	SCAITH	—dancer's shout	HOOCH
—physically	WRONG	—dagger	DIRK
harmless	CANNY	—festival	MOD
harry	HERRY	—gentleman of	
harvest	HAIRST	inferior rank	DUN(N)I(E)WASSAL
—field	HAIRST-RIG	—whisky	PEAT-REEK
—home	KERN, KIRN	Highlander	NAINSEL(L), PLAIDMAN
hasp	HESP	Highlander's cap	GLENGARRY
hatch eggs	CLECK	hill	LAW, BRAE
haughty	PAUGHTY	—pass	SLAP
haul	RUG	hinder	TAIGLE
haunch	HAINCH	hint	MINT
haunt	HOUFF, HOWFF	hire	FEE
have	HAE	hired mourner	SALLIE, SALUIE, SAULIE
—a holiday	PLAY	hitch	HOTCH
—dealings	INTROMIT	hoar frost	CRANREUCH
—done	BE THROUGH	hoarse	ROOPIT, ROOPY, ROUPIT
—lustre	SHEEN	hoarseness	ROOP, ROUP
having a certain		hoary old stone	HARE-STANE
appearance or manner	FAR(R)AND	hoax	GEGG
	FARRANT	hob nail	TACKET
hawk	KEELIE	hobble	HILCH
hawker	YAGGER	hobgoblin	WIRRICOW, WORRICOW
hazard	NIFFER		WORRYCOW
hazy	URY	hobnail	TACKET
head	POW	hock	HOUGH
—of hair	POW	hoe	CLA(U)T
—to foot	HEADS AND THRAWS	hog's lard	SAIM
headland in field	HEAD-RIG	hoist	HEEZE
headlong	RAMSTAM	hold	CLAUCHT, CLAUGHT
health	HEAL		HAD, HAU(L)D
heap of mortar	BINK	holder of	
heard	HARD	—document	HAVER
heart (Islands)	JARTA, YARTA	—land under feu	FEUAR
heave up	HEEZE	—small feu	PORTIONER
heavens	LIFT	—underlease	SUBTACKSMAN
heavy	DOWF	holding	HADDIN
—blow	LOUNDER	holiday	PLAYING
—impact	DUSH	hollow	BOSS, CORRIE, HOWE
heed	TENT	—of two hands	GOWPEN
heifer	QUEY	homage	MANRENT
held	HADDEN, HUDDEN	home	HAME
helmet	KNAPSCAL, KNAPSCULL	—farm	MAINS
	KNAPSKULL	—made firework	PEEOY, PIOY(E)
hemp-nettle	DAE-NETTLE, DAY-NETTLE	—spun	RAPLOCH
herald	UNICORN	homeward	HAMEWITH
hesitate	TARROW	honey	HINNY
hew	HAG	hoof	CLOOT
hide	FLAUGHT	hoop	GIRD, GIRR
hideous	GASH(FUL), GASHLY	hooped dish	LUGGIE
hideousness	GASHLINESS	hop-scotch	PEEVERS
hiding place	HIDLING(S), HIDLINS	horizontal tombstone	THROUGH-STANE
	HIDY-HOLE	hornless	
higgledy-piggledy	THROUGH-OTHER	—cow	DODDY, HUMLIE

—(stag)	HUMBLE, HUMMEL		—tempered	GIRNIE
horse	CUDDIE, CUDDY, GALLOWAY		—treat	DEMEAN, MISGUIDE
—backband	RIGWIDDIE, RIGWOODIE		illegal drinking-place	BOTHAN
—collar	BRECHAM		impediment in speech	HALT
—dealer	HORSE-COUPER		impervious clay	TILL
—disease	WEED, WEID		impetuosity	BIRR
—feeding on stubble	STIBBLER		importune	PRIG
—fever	WEED, WEID		impound	POIND
—fly	CLEG		improvised sledge	HURLY-HACKET
—old	AVER, YAUD		impudent	BARDY
—shoe	PANTON-SHOE		in	INTIL
hot	HET		—arrear	BACK-GANGING
—pursuit	HOT-TROD		—being	TO THE FORE
—water bottle	PIP		—confusion	HIRDY-GIRDY
house	BIGGIN		—contrary direction	WID(D)ERSHINS
—agent	HOUSE-FACTOR			WITHERSHINS
—leek	FOUAT, FOUET		—dotage	DOITED, DOITIT
—of turf	BLACKHOUSE		—indiscriminate	
—one room deep	SINGLE HOUSE		mixture	THROUGH-OTHER
—the harvest	LEAD IN		—the country	LANDWARD(S)
—warming	INFARE		—turns	TIME ABOUT
household goods	INSIGHT		into	INTIL
hovel	CRU(I)VE		incipient movement	MINT
howl	GOWL		incline to think	DOUBT
huff	STRUNT		inclined to	
hug	OXTER		—avarice	GRIPPY
hum softly	SOWF(F), SOWTH		—shiver or shudder	OORIE, OURIE, OWRIE
hungry	YAUP		increase in stipend	AUGMENTATION
hurl	BUM		indecision	SWITHER
hurry off	WHIRRY		indeed	ATWEEL, DEED
hurt	MIS(C)HANTER		indictment	DITTAY
	SCAITH, SKAITH		indoors	THEREIN
husband	GUIDMAN		indulge	PETTLE
hush!	WHEESHT		inert	THOWLESS
hussy	LIMMER		infield	INTOWN
hut	BOTHAN, BOTHIE, BOTHY		infuse	MASK
	SHEAL(ING), SHEEL(ING)		inhabitant	RESIDENTER
	SHEIL(ING), SHIEL(ING)		injure	SCAITH, SKAITH
—Islands	SKEO, SKIO		injury	MIS(C)HANTER
hysterics	EXIES			SCAITH, SKAITH
I shall	ISE		inn-keeper	STABLER
ice-cream between wafers	SLIDER		inner room	BEN, SPENCE
idiot	TUMPSHIEHEID		innocent	SACKLESS
idle			inquire	SPEER, SPEIR
—about	DAIDLE		insignificant person	SCOOT
—talk	CLAVER		insinuating person	SNECK-DRAWER
if	GIF, GIN		insist	THREAP, THREEP
ignorant of	UNACQUAINT		insisted	THREAPIT, THREEPIT
ignore	MISKEN		insolence	SNASH
ill			insolent	BARDY
—conditioned	MISLEARED		inspector of coal	KEEKER
—favoured	ILL-FAURD		inspiration	TAGHAIRM
—grown	WANTHRIVEN		instalment selling	MENAGE
—looking	ILL-FAURD		instant	WHIP
—natured person	ETHERCAP, ETTERCAP		instrument for winnowing	WECHT
—omened	UNCHANCY		instrumental tune	PORT

intent	ETTLE
intercourse	TROCK, TROKE
interdict	INJUNCTION
interfere	INTROMIT
interjection	OCH
—deploring	AICH WOW
	(EH) WHOW, EWHOW
—of	
concession	OU, OW
irritation	HOOT, HOOT(S)-TOOT(S)
	HOUT, HOUT(S)-TOUT(S)
lamentation	O(C)HONE
surprise	HECH
interpose	INTERPONE
intestine	THAIRM
intimate	CHIEF, PACK, TOSH
—friend	FAR BEN
intractable	KITTLE
intricate	TIRLIE-WIRLIE
invest with heritable	
property	INFEFT
inwards	INBY(E)
Irish stew	STOVIES
iron	AIRN
—mould	IRON-MAIL
irregular Highland troops	WATCH
island	INCH
issue	ISH
it does not matter	IT MAKSNA
jabber	YAB, YATTER
Jack	JOCK
jackdaw	KA(E)
jade	LIMMER
jaded	DISJASKIT
jam sandwich	JEELY PIECE
jape	BEGUNK
jaw	CHAFT
jelly	JEELY
jest	BA(U)R, BAWR
Jew's harp	TRUMP
jog	DUNCH, DUNSH, HOD, HOTCH
—along	WHIG
join	OOP, OUP
joint-heiress	HEIR-PORTIONER
joint on hind leg	HOUGH
jollification	SPLORE
jolly	GAUCIE, GAUCY, GAWCY
	GAWSY
jolt	HOTTER
jostle with shoulder	HOG-SHOUTHER
journey in wheeled vehicle	HURL
joust	GIOUST
judge	DECERN
—of Court of Sessions	LAW-LORD
judge's	
—decree	INTERLOCUTION
—private consideration	AVISANDUM
	AVIZANDUM
judicious	WISE-LIKE
jumble	JABBLE
jurisdiction	FOUDRIE, SUCKEN
jury	ASSIZE
keen	GLEG, SNELL
keep in subjection	SNOOL
kestrel	KEELIE
kick strongly	BLOOTER
kill in fit of passion	CHAUD-MELLE
kilt	FILABEG, FIL(L)IBEG
	PHIL(L)ABEG, PHIL(L)IBEG
kind	ROUTHIE
kindle	LUNT
kindly	COUTHIE
kine	KY(E)
King's evil	CRUEL(L)S, CREWELS
kiss	PREE
kitchen	BUT
—boy	GALOPIN
—garden	KAILYARD
(Islands)	PLANTIE-CRUIVE
knave	JOCK
knick-knack	WHIGMALEERIE
	WHIGMALERY
knife	GULLEY
knob of hair	TOORIE
knock	CA, CLOUR, DAUD, DAWD
—at door	CHAP
—down	DING DOUN
—off work	LOWZE
knocked off work	LOWSIT
knotty	NIRLIE, NIRLY
know	KEN
—not	KENNO
knowing	CANNY
—look	GLEDGE
lace	PEARLIN(G)
lack of spirit	FOZINESS
lacking freshness	FOZY
lad	CALLANT
ladder to loft	TRAP
laid aside in store	PAST
lake	LOCH
—dwelling	CRANNOG
lament	GLEET
lamp	CRU(I)SIE, CRUSY
—lighter	LEERIE
land	(Y)EARD, YERD, YIRD
—holder	F(E)UAR
—owner	LAIRD
—paying feu-duty	
(Islands)	URE
—tenure	RUNDALE, RUNRIG
landed proprietor	LAIRD

landholder liable to public burdens	HERITOR
landmark	MEITH
lane	LOAN(ING), VENNEL, WYND
language	GADHELIC, GAELIC
	LALLANS, SCOTS
languid	DWAMY
lank	SCRANKY
lantern	BOWAT, BOWET, BUAT
lap-dog	MESSAN
lapwing	PEASEWEEP, PEESWEEP
	PEEWEE, TEUCHAT
large	
—beetle	CLOCKER
—cravat	O'ERLAY
—draught	WAUCHT, WAUGHT
—hook	CLEEK
last	
—clause of deed	TESTING CLAUSE
—day of year	HOGMANAY
—night	YESTREEN
—of	
cow's milk	JIBBINGS
family	BIRD-ALANE
	BURD-ALANE
—three days of March	BORROWING-DAYS
latch	SNECK
latched	SNECKED
late	UMQUHILE
later	SYNE
Latin prose	VERSION
latter end	HINDER-END
laugh	LAUCH
laughed	LEUCH(EN), LEUGH(EN)
laughing-stock	OUTSPECKLE
lawsuit	PLEA
lawyer's clerk	SERVITOR
lay	
—blame on	WITE, WYTE
—eggs in out-of-the-way places	LAY AWAY
—out (corpse)	STRAUCHT, STRAUGHT
	STREEK, STREAK
lazy	SWEER, SWEIR
lead pencil	KEELIVINE, KEELYVINE
leader of mummers (Islands)	SCUDLER, SCUDDALER
	SKUDLER
leaky	GIZZEN
lean and tough	RIGWIDDIE, RIGWOODIE
leap	LOWP
—over	OWERLOUP
leaped/leapt	LAP, LOUPEN
	LOUPIT, LUPPEN
leaping-pole	KENT
learning	LEAR(E), LEIR, LERE

lease	SET, TACK
leased tenement	TACK
ledge	SCARCEMENT
left	
—handed	FISTY
—over	ORRA
—thumbhole in bagpipe	BACK-LILL
legal	
—practitioner	WRITER
—restriction	BURDEN
—usage	PRACTIC
lengthwise	ENDLANG
lessee	TACKSMAN
let	LITTEN, LOOT(EN)
	LUIT(EN), LUTTEN
letters in the sovereign's name requiring payment	LETTERS OF HORNING
levity	GLAIKITNESS
levy	STENT
liar	LEEAR
liberty of going out	ISH
licensed beggar	BEAD(S)MAN
	BEDE(S)MAN
lichen (dye)	CORKIR, KORKIR
lick	SLAKE
lie	LEE, WHID, YANKER
lief is me	LEEZE ME
lien on goods for debt	HYPOTHEC
lifeless	CAULD-RIFE
lift	HEEZE, HEEZIE
light	LICHT
—and soft	FUFFY
limb	SPALL, SPAUL, SPA(U)LD
limp	HILCH
limping gait	HIRPLE
line	LING
linen	LIARN
linger	TAIGLE
linnet	LINTIE, LINTWHITE
liquor	SKINK
—from boiling	BROO
liquorice	SUGAR-ALLIE, SUGAR-ALLY
list	ROON, RUND
—of	
candidates	LEET
court cases	SUMMAR ROLL
nobles pledged to Edward I	RAGMAN ROLLS
persons for trial	PORTEOUS ROLL
poor litigants	POOR'S-ROLL
listless	THOWLESS, UPSITTING
	WAFF
listlessness	UPSITTING
little	
—amount	CURN

—auk	DOVEKIE
—bit	BITTOCK, KENNING
—drop	DRAPPIE, DRAPPY
—finger	PINKIE, PINKY
—hat	HATTOCK
—lamb	LAMBIE
—star	STARNIE
—way over	O(W)ERBY
live on alms	THIG
lively	CANT(Y), CROUSE, VIVE
livid	BLAE
load	LADE, LAID
loaf made in pan	PAN-LOAF
loan	LEN(D)
loathing	SCUNNER
loathly	LAIDLY
local jurisprudence	BOURLAW, BYRLAW
lock of hair	TAIT, TATE
lodging and entertainment	UP-PUTTING
loft	ROOST
—ladder	TRAP
lofty	BRENT
log transporter	JANKER
loin	LUNGIE, LUNYIE
loiter	TAIGLE
lone	LANE
long	DEE, GREEN, GREIN, LANG
—ago	(AULD) LANG SYNE
—drawn out	DREICH
—for	WEARY
—frost	STORM
—handled spade	PATTLE, PETTLE
—since	LANG SYNE
look cunningly	GLEDGE
looking-glass	KEEKING-GLASS
loose	LOWZE
—heap	RICKLE
—young woman	GILLET, JILLET
loosed	LOWSIT
lord	LOSH
lore	LAIR
lose	TINE, TYNE
—courage or resolution	HEN
loss	TINSEL
—(of sheep)	TRAIK
lost	AMISSING, TINT
lot	CAVEL, KAVEL, WEIRD
loth	LAITH, SWEER(ED)
	SWEERT, SWEIR(T)
loud rattling	REEL
lounge	DA(C)KER, DAIKER
lout	COOF, CUIF, GOMERIL, KEELIE
love	LEAR(E), LEIR, LERE
	LO'E, LOO
lover	LAD
low	LAW

—born person	GUTTERBLOOD
—lying (land)	LAIGH
—lying meadow	INCH
—price	WANWORTH
—spirited	DOWIE
lowering	GURLY
lowland	LALLAN, LAWLAND
luck	SONCE, SONSE
—bringing	SONSIE, SONSY
lucky	CANNY, SONCIE, SONCY
	SONSIE, SONSY
lumbering thing	CLATCH
lump	CLA(U)T, NIRL, SLUMP
—sum paid on lease	GRASSUM
lumpsucker	PADDLE, PA(I)DLE
—female	HEN-PAIDLE
—male	COCK-PAIDLE
lunch	DISJUNE, TIFT
lurch	STOIT
lurk	SNOWK
lurking with	
treacherous purpose	FELL-LURKING
lusty	FRACK, SKELPING
mad	DOILED, DOILT, GYTE
	WOWF, WUD
magician	WARLOCK
magistrate	BAIL(L)IE
magpie	PIET, PYAT, PYET, PYOT
maid-servant	LASS
maintain persistently	THREAP, THREEP
maintained persistently	THREAPIT
	THREEPIT
make	MA(C)K, MAIK
—a	
grating sound	RISP
groove in masonry	RAGGLE
hoarse sound	ROOP
long-drawn-out cry	WHEEPLE
low sound	CHIRL
scratchy sound	SCRAICH, SCRAIGH
squawk	SCRAUCH, SCRAUGH
—afraid	FRICHT
—faces at	MURGEON
—known	KITHE, KYTHE
—one's way quietly	SLIP ONE'S WAYS
—over to another	DISPONE
—palatable	KITCHEN
—ready	GRAITH
—tidy	RED(D)
—to last	KITCHEN
—trial of	PREE
—void	IRRITATE
maker	WRIGHT
male sheep	DINMONT
man	CHIEL(D), MAN-BODY
	MON

—covered in seaweed (Orkney)	TANGIE
man's skirt	KILT
manifestation of loathing	SCUNNER
manner of doing	GATE
many	MONY
mar	MIS(H)GUGGLE
marble	BOWL
mare	YAUD
mark with ruddle	KEEL
market	MERCAT
—for hiring farm-servants	FEEING-MARKET
—place	TRON(E)
marriage settlement	DOWN-SITTING
marry	WAD
marshal	MARISCHAL
Martinmas	REMOVAL TERM
masonry groove	RAGGLE
master	MAISTER
—of company	DEACON
mat	TAUT, TAWT
matted	TATTY, TAUTIT, TAWTIE
—wool	KET
matter	MAKE
May 28th	REMOVAL TERM
meal	MELTITH
—and water mixed	DRAMMACH
	DRUMMOCK
	DRUMMOCK, WATER-BROSE
—chest	GIRNEL
—time	MELTITH
sponger	SCAMBLER
means of	
—compelling	COMPULSITOR
—ignition	LUNT
measures	
—37 inches	ELL
—1976 yards	MILE
—6150 sq. yds (old)	ACRE
—variable land area	PLOUGHGATE
—¼ pint (Scottish)	MUTCHKIN
—³/₄ pint (imperial)	MUTCHKIN
—1 quart	CHOPIN
—3 pints	(SCOTTISH) PINT
—½ gallon	LIPPIE, LIPPY
—¼ peck	LIPPIE, LIPPY
—1 bushel	FOU
—¼ boll	FIRLOT
—2-6 bushels	BOLL
—16 bolls	CHALDER
—40 bottles of hay or straw	KEMPLE
meat	
—pie	BRIDIE
—plate	ASHET
—turnover	BRIDIE

meatless broth	MUSLIN-KALE
meeting-point in front of mansion	COVIN-TREE
mentally weak	FACILE
merry	VOGIE
messenger	SEND
—returning late or not at all	CORBIE-MESSENGER
metal knitting-needle	WIRE
mettle	SMEDDUM
mettlesome	METTLE
—person	SPUNKIE
mickle	MUCKLE
midday dram or nap	MEDRIDAN
midwife	HOWDIE, HOWDY
	WISE WOMAN
mighty	FELL
mild explosion	PLUFF
milk	
—can	PITCHER
—cheese	CROWDIE
—closely	JIB
—strainer	MILSEY
milking-pail	LEGLAN, LEGLEN
	LEGLIN, SKEEL
mill	
—district	SUCKEN
—race or tail-race	MILLDAM
—servant's quantity of meal	LOCK
—stream	LADE
miller	MULLER
minced meat	MINCED COLLOPS
mine own	MINE AIN
minimum (of vision)	STIME, STYME
minister	PRESBYTER
minister's house	MANSE
mire	GLAUR, LAIR, LATCH
mirror	KEEKING-GLASS
mischievous	ILL-DEEDY, SCATHY
—boy	NICKUM
—girl/woman	CUTTY
—trick	PLISKIE, PLISKY
miser	SCRUNT
miserly	GARE, HOODOCK
misfortune	MIS(C)HANTER
mishap	MIS(C)HANTER
missing	AWANTING
mistaught	MISLEARED
mistress of house	HERSELF
mitigate	MEASE
mixed	
—confusedly	THROUGH-OTHER
—grain	MASHLIN, MASHLOCH
	MASHLUM, MASHLAM
	MASHLIM

mixture of foods	POWSOWDIE
	POWSOWDY
mobbing of curates	RABBLING
mock with grimaces	MURGEON
mocking deception	GLAIK
moisten	SLO(C)KEN
mole	MOUDI(E)WART
	MOUDI(E)WORT
	MODIWORT, MOULDWARP
moment	GLIFF(ING), GLIFT
monastic territory	ABTHANE
money	SILLER
—box	PENNY-PIG
—to be paid by vassal	REDDENDO
mongrel	MESSIN
monkey	PUGGY
mood	FID
moor	MUIR
moorland pool	FLOW
morass	FLOW
more	MAE
morning	FORENOON
mortgage	HERITABLE SECURITY
	WADSET(T)
mortgagee	WADSETTER
moss	FOG
mostly	FECKLY
mother-in-law	GUDE-MOTHER
mouldy	MOOL, MOUL
mountain over 3000ft	MUNRO
mounting-stone	LOUPING-ON-STANE
mouth	GAM, MOU
—music	PORT A BEUL
move	STEER
—along briskly	SKELP
—around or to activity	STEER
—nimbly	LINK
—quickly	WHID, WHIRRY
—slowly	WEAR
—with whizzing sound	WHEESHT
much	MUCKLE
mud	DUBS, GUTTERS
muddle	FANKLE
muddled	MOIDERT, TA(I)VERT
muddy	DRUMLY, SLASHY
mule	MUIL
multitude	HIRSEL
multure	MOUTER
murmur like a dove	CROODLE
musical instrument	BAGPIPES
	STOCK-AND-HORN
	THAIRM
musk	M(O)UST, MUIST
must	MAUN
—not	MAUNNA
mutter	WHITTIE-WHATTIE

mutton from sheep that died from disease or accident	TRAIK
nag	YAFF
named	HECHT
nap	OOZE
napkin round infant's hips	HIPPING
narrow	
—alley	WYND
—strait	KYLE
national	
—emblem	THISTLE
—Orchestra	SNO
—Party	SNP
native of the town	TOWN'S BAIRN
natural death in bed	STRAE-DEATH
nauseate	SCOMFISH, SCUNNER
ne'er-do-well	SKELLUM
near	EWEST, INBY(E)
—the	
farmhouse	INTOWN
house	INBY(E)
nearly	FECKLY, NEAR-HAND
neat	DINK, DONSIE, GENTY
	JIMP(Y), NOUT, SNOD, TOSH
necessity	MISTER
neck	CRAIG, HAUSE, HAWSE
—ring	JOUGS
need	MISTER
neglect	MISLIPPEN
neglected	WAIF
neigh	NICHER, NICKER
neither one thing nor the other	NEITHER HUP NOR WIND
nest of bees/wasps	BIKE, BYKE
nevertheless	STILL AND ON
new	
—ale	SWATS
—pupil in Edinburgh	GAIT, GEIT, GYTE
news	SPEERINGS, SPEIRINGS
New Year gift	NE'ERDAY
New Year's Day	NE'ERDAY
next	STANCHEL, SYNE
nibble	MOOP
nicety	PERJINKITY
nickname for Scotsman	SAWN(E)Y
niggard	CARL, SCRUNT
niggardly	NEAR-(BE)GAUN
	NIRLIE, NIRLY
nightcap	KILMARNOCK COWL, PIRNIE
nightdress	WYLIE-COAT
nimble	SWACK, YA(U)LD
no	NA(E)
—laughing matter	NAE MOWS
nobody	NAEBODY
noddle	CAPERNOITIE
	CAP(P)ERNOITY

noise of frying	SKIRL-IN-THE-PAN	odour	WAFF
noisy	ROARIE, ROARY	of good omen	CANNY
—frolic	GALRAVAGE, GALRAVITCH	offer	BODE, PROPINE, SHORE
	GIL(L)RAVAGE	—and acceptance	MISSIVES
	GIL(L)RAVITCH, RANT	offspring	BURD
—musician	RANTER	old	AULD
—quarrel	BRULYIE, BRULZIE	—fashioned	AULD-FARAND
—wrangling	COLLIESHANGIE	—horse	AVER, YAUD
none	NAE	—man	BODACH
nonsense	CLAMJAMPHRIE	—rusty sword	SHABBLE
	CLANJAMFRAY, HAVER	—woman	CAILL(E)ACH, CAILLIACH
noonday meal	TWALHOURS		CARLINE, LUCKIE
noose	FANK	—world	AULD-WARLD
north country	NORLAN(D)	omen	FREET, FREIT
not	NA, NO	on one's feet	UPSTANDING
—akin	FRAIM, FREMD, FREMIT	once	ANCE, ENE, YINCE
—altogether absurd	NO SAE HIELANT	one	AE, ANE, YIN
—dangerous	CANNY	—in nervous state	HEN ON A HOT GIRDLE
—frosty	FRESH	—licensed to preach	PROBATIONER
—giving milk	YELD	—nominated to benefice	POSTULATE
—matched	ORRA	—of a pair	NEIGHBOUR
—of gentle birth	SEMPLE	—receiving lands	
—so bad as might be	NO SAE HIELANT	escheated to the	
—subject to feudal		Crown	DONATORY
superior (Islands)	UDAL	—roomed dwelling	SINGLE-END
—to mention	LET BE	—sent to fetch a bride	SEND
—yielding milk	EILD	—to whom feu-duty is paid	SUPERIOR
notch edges of	LIP, MUSH	—who	
nothing	NAETHING	cuts the corn left	
notice	TENT	by the reaper	STIBBLER
notorious	NOTOUR	lets go	LETTER-GAE
—rumour about minister	FAMA CLAMOSA	lifts the latch	SNECK-DRAWER
November 28th	REMOVAL TERM	presents graduates	PROMOTOR
now	PRESENTLY	submits tamely to	
nozzle	STROUP	wrong	SNOOL
nudge	DUNCH, DUNSH	talks nonsense	BLETHER(AN)SKATE
number	FECK	onion	FOUAT, FOUET, INGAN
O yes	OU AY	only	ANERLY
oak	AIK	onset of disease	ONCOME, ONFALL
oat	AIT	onslaught	ONFALL
—cake	BANNOCK, FARLE	onward rush	RACE
—meal	GRITS	ooze	GLEET
dish	BROWSE, CROWDIE	open	
	FLUMMERY, SOWANS, SOWANS	—stitching	OPEN-STEEK
object of		—weather	FRESH
—loathing	SCUNNER	opponent of Protester	REMONSTRANT
—scorn	GECK	opportune time	SEIL
obligation to		opportunity of reading	READ
entertain (Islands)	WATTLE	opposite to	FORNENT
observant	TENTIE	ordinary	ORDINAR
obstinate	DOUR, THRAWART	—plain bread	LOAF-BREAD
obtrude oneself	SORN	organ	KIST O' WHISTLES
occasional	DAIMEN, ORRA	ornament	MENSE
odd	ORRA	other than heritable	MOVABLE
—job man	ORRA-MAN	ounce	UNCE
—looking	ODD-LIKE	ousting of curates	RABBLING

out of doors	OUTBY(E), THEREOUT		—of	
outdoor possessions	OUTSIGHT		carcase of beef	SEY
outlaw	BROKEN-MAN, HORN		flail	SOUPLE
—by three blasts of			—the hair	SHADE
the horn	PUT TO THE HORN		partially	HALFLIN(G)S
outside	FURTH OF		particle	CURN
—of	FURTH, OUTWITH		parting cup	DEOCH-AN-DORUIS
—stair	FORE-STAIR		partition	HALLAN
—wc	CLUDGIE		partridge	PAITRICK
outward appearance			Pasch	PACE
of promise	UPCOME		pass	HAUSE, HAWSE
outward	OUTWITH		—judgement	DECERN
oven	OON		passage	
over	O'ER, OUT-OWRE, OWER		—in salmon cruive	SLAP
	OWRE		—left between fields	
—bearing assumption	UPSETTING		of corn	LOAN(ING)
—flow	REAM		Passover	PACE
—hanging bank	HAG(G)		pasture (for one cow)	SOUM, SOWM
—heat	SCOUTHER, SCOWDER		pasty thing	CLATCH
—look	MISLIPPEN		pat	CLAP
—plus	O'ERCOME		path	GATE
—precise	PRICK-ME-DAINTY		patron	STOOP, STOUP
—turn	COUP, COWP		—saint	ANDREW
own	AIN, NAIN		paunch	KITE, KYTE
—self	NAINSEL(L)		pavement	PLAINSTANES
owner of estate	HERSELF		pawky	CANNY
owner's mark	BUIST		pawn	WADSET(T)
ox-eye daisy	(HORSE-)GOWAN		pay penalty	PAY THE CAIN
oxen	OWSEN		payment	MAIL
pact	PACTION		—in goods	TROCK, TROKE
pad	SUNK		—to miller by those	
paddling	PLOTTER, PLOUTER		compelled to have	
	PLOWTER		grain ground	INTOWN MULTURE
paddock	PARK		peaceable	DOUCE
pains	FASH		peacock	PAWN, POW(I)N
pair of scales	WEIGH-BANKS		peasant	BLUEBONNET, COTTAR
pale	WHITELY			COTTER
—blaes	CA(L)M, CAUM		peat	VAG
palm of hand	LOOF		—hole	HAG(G)
paltry	WAESOME, WAFF		—spade (Islands)	TUSKAR, TUSKER
pamper	CUITER			TWISCAR
panel	BOX		peaty soil (Islands)	YARFA, YARPHA
pang	STOUND, STOWND, THRAW		pedlar	PEDDER, PETHER, YAGGER
pant	FLACK, FLAFF, PECH, PEGH		peep	COOK, KEEK, KOOK, PEEK
pantry	AWMRIE, AWMRY		peewit	PEASEWEEP, PEESWEEP
parched grain	GRADDAN			PEEWEE, TEUCHAT
pare	FLAUGHT		peg-top	PEERIE
paring of turf	FLAUGHTER		pellicle of ice	GREW, GRUE
parish	PARISCHAN(E), PARISHEN		pen	CRU(I)VE
	PAROCHIN(E)		penalty	UNLAW
—minister	MAS(S)-JOHN		—drink	KELTIE, KELTY
	MES(S)-JOHN		pendant	POFFLE
park	PAIRK		pendicle	POFFLE
parlour	SPENCE		penny (sterling)	TWALPENNY
paroxysm	THRAW		peppermint sweet	PAN-DROP
part	TWIN(E)		perhaps	A(I)BLINS, YIBBLES

periodical gathering to check weaponry	WAP(P)ENS(C)HAW
	WAPINS(C)HAW
	WEAPON-S(C)HAW
pernickety person	FIKE, FYKE
peroration	PIRLICUE, PURLICUE
perplex	FICKLE
persevere	STICK IN
person	WYE
—first nominated as heir	INSTITUTE
—in disguise	GUISARD, GUISER
—sued or accused	DEFENDER
pert	CROUSE
—chatterer	GABNASH, NASHGAB
—girl	YIP
pertaining to	
—a sucken	INSUCKEN
—will	TESTAMENTAR
perverse	CAMSTAIRY, CAMSTEARY
	CAMSTEERIE, DONSIE
	THRAWN
pet	DAUT(IE), DAWT(IE)
	MAKE OF, PETTLE, TOUT, TOWT
petticoat	WYLIE-COAT
pettish	DORTY
petty possessions	SPREAGHERY, SPRECHERY
petulant	TOUTIE
pick	WALE
Pict	PECH(T), PEGH(T)
philosopher	HUME
piece of	
—news	UNCO
—property	SUBJECT
—slate	SCLATE-STANE
pierce	SLAP, STEEK
pigswill	BROCK
pile up	BIG
pilfering	PICKERY
pillory	JOUGS
pillow	COD
pimple	PLOOK
pin	PREEN
—of door-latch	TIRLING-PIN
pinch	CHACK, POOK, POUK
	TATE, TAIT
—of snuff	SNEESH(AN), SNEESHIN(G)
—with cold	NIRL
pinched	POOKIT, POUKIT
pink	CLOW-GILLIEFLOWER
pinnacle	PINNET
pipe-clay	CA(LM), CAUM
pit in a bog	MOSS-HAG(G)
pitch-dark	PIT-MIRK
pithless	THOWLESS
pitiful	WAEFU(L), WAESOME

place	
—for milking cows	LOAN(ING)
—of punishment	TRON(E)
plaid	MAUD
plain needlework	WHITE-SEAM
plaintiff	PURSUER
plant	
—refuse	ROSS
—temporarily	SHEUCH, SHEUGH
plantation	PLANTING
plaster	CLATCH, PLAISTER
plate-rack	BINK
play	
—fool	DAFF
—marbles	BOWL
—truant	KIP
playing card	CARTE
pleaded	PLED
pleasure-grounds round mansion	POLICY
pledge	WAD
—in drinking	PROPINE
plentiful	FOUTH, FOWTH, ROUTH
	ROWTH
plenty	SCOUTH, SCOWTH
	STOUTH AND ROUTH
pliant	SWACK, SWANK
plight	PLISKIE
plough	PLEUCH, PLEUGH
—cleaning tool	PATTLE, PETTLE
—up	RIVE
pluck	POOK, POUK
plucked	POOKIT, POUKIT
plug (of tobacco)	DOTTLE
plump	BONNIE, BONNY, SONCIE
	SONCY, SONSIE, SONSY
plunder	HERSHIP, REAVE, REIVE
	SPREAGH(ERY), SPRECHERY
	SPU(I)LZIE, SPULY(I)E
ply with drink	BIRL(E)
pochard	SCAUP-DUCK
pocket in end of plaid	PLAID-NEUK
poet	MAKAR
pointed hill	KIP(P)
poke	POCK, POWTER
pole	CABER, KENT
poll	POW
pollack	LYTHE
polled cow	HUMLIE
pollute	FILE
pond	LOCHAN, POUND
pool	STANK
—of foul water	DUB
—or hole in bog	HAG(G)
poor	PUIR, SOBER
—thin beer	SWANK(E)Y

popgun	BOURTREE-GUN
—made of quill	PEN-GUN
population thirled	
to mill	SUCKEN
porpoise	PELLACH, PELLACK
	PELLOCK
porridge	BROCHAN, CROWDIE
	PARRITCH
—stick	SPURTLE
portly	GAUCIE, GAUCY, GAWCY
	GAWSY
portmanteau	POCKMANKY, POCKMANTIE
possession	SASINE
post	STELL
posthumous stipend	ANN, ANNAT
potato	TATTIE
—fork	GRAIP
—haulms	TATTIE-SHAW
—soup	TATTIE-CLAW
potatoes served in	
their jackets	PEEL-AND-EAT
potsherd	PIG
potter	DA(C)KER, DAIDLE, DAIKER
	PLOTTER, PLOUTER, PLOWTER
pouch	SPORRAN
poult	POOT, POUT
pour	TOUT, TOWT
—out	BIRL(E)
—unsteadily	JIRBLE
powder	M(O)UST, MUIST, POUTHER
—puff	PLUFF
power of pump-suction	FANG
powerlessness	DOWNA-DO
praise	ROOSE
prattle	GABNASH, NASHGAB
precentor	LETTER-GAE
precise	PRECEESE
precocious	AULD-FARAND
prejudice	SCUNNER
preliminary examination	
of witnesses	PRECOGNITION
premature birth of lamb	KEB
premium	GRASSUM
prepare	BOUN
Presbyterian	WHIGGAMORE
—transgressor	DIKE-LOUPER
present	PROPINE
presently	ENOW
preserve	HAIN
president	PR(A)ESES
presiding bishop	PRIMUS
press eagerly	THREAP, THREEP
pressed eagerly	THREAPIT, THREEPIT
presumption	UPSETTING
pretentious display	PARAF(F)LE
preternatural	NO'CANNY

pretext	OFFCOME
pretty	BONNIE, BONNY
prey	SPREAGH
price of grain	FIARS
prick	BROG, JAG
priest with no parish	STICKIT MINISTER
prim	MIM(-MOU'D)
	PERJINK(ETY)
	PREJINK, PRIMSIE
private agreement among	
creditors	SUPERSEDERE
proceedings in criminal libel	DIET
proclaim banns	CRY
procure	SORT
prodigality	WAST(E)RY
progeny	BURD
projection of building	OUTSHOT
promise	HECHT
promontory	MULL
prompt	FRACK
promptly	BELIVE
proof	PRIEF(E)
prop	RANCE
propel	CA
property	
—given as dowry	TOCHER-GOOD
—which may be bequeathed	DEAD-PART
proportion of sheep	
or cattle suitable	
for pasture	SOUM, SOWM
propose	PROPONE
propound	PROPONE
propriety	MENSE
prosecute	PURSUE
prosecuting solicitor	CROWN AGENT
prosecutor	(PROCURATOR-)FISCAL
prosperous	WELL-TO-LIVE
protection	BEELD, BIELD
Protestor	REMONSTRANT
prove	PREE, PRIEF(E)
proved/proven	PREE
provide	PLENISH, SORT
provision	STOUTH(E)RIE
prowl about	SNOWK
pshaw!	OCH
public	
—knowledge	HABIT AND REPUTE
—notice	PROGRAMME
—weighing-machine	TRON(E)
puddle	DUB
puff	FLAFF, FUFF, PLUFF, SKIFF
puffed up	PLUFFY
puffin	TAMMIE NORIE
puffy	PLUFFY
pull roughly	RUG
punch	KNEVELL, NEVEL

pungency	NIPPING
pungent	FELL
punt(ing pole)	KENT
purblind person	STIMIE, STIMY, STYMIE
purport	FECK
purpose	ETTLE, MINT
purse	SPLEUCHAN
purslane	PURPIE, PURPY
pursuer's reply	TRIPLY
put	PAT, PIT, PITTEN, PUTTEN
—before a court	PROPONE
—forward	PROPONE
—in order	RED(D)
—into goal	HAIL
—out	MISTRYSTED, SMORE
of humour	MISSET
of shape	SHAUCHLE
—to	
flight	FLEME
rights	SORT
puzzle	FICKLE, KITTLE
—game	GLAIK
quaint	AULD-FARAND
quantity of liquid	JABBLE
quarrel	CAST OUT, OUTCAST
	WAP, WHID
quarry-face	HEUCH, HEUGH
quarter	AIRT
—days	BELTANE, CANDLEMAS
	HALLOWMAS, LAMMAS
—evil	SPAULD-ILL
—of round cake of	
flour or oatmeal	FARL(E)FARTHEL
queer	FIFISH
—person	SKITE, SKYTE
quench	SLO(C)KEN
quick turn	JINK
quickly	BELIVE
quiet	LOUN(D), LOWN(D), SACKLESS
quite	REAL
—alone	LEE(SOME)-LANE
quiver	DIRL, TIRL
quoth	CO, QUO
rabbit's tail	FUD
rabble	CLAMJAMPHRIE
	CLANJAMFRAY
race at wedding	BROOSE, BROUZE
rail	SPAR
rain suddenly	PLUMP
rainy	SODDEN
—blast	BLATTER
raise a bump	CLOUR
rake	CLA(U)T
rampage	RAMPAUGE
ramshackle structure	
or collection	RICKLE

randy	RUDAS
range	
—of cattle pasture	GANG
—over	SCUR, SKER, SKIRR
	SQUIRR
ransack	RIPE
rap	YANKER
rapid noiseless movement	WHID
rascal	SMAIK
rasp	RISP
rather	GAY, GEY, LOOR
ratification of executor	CONFIRMATION
rattle	TIRL
—in throat	RUCKLE
raucous squawk	SCRAUCH, SCRAUGH
rave	TA(I)VER
ravine	CLEUCH, CLOUGH, HEUCH
	HEUGH
raw (weather)	WERSH
—hide shoe	RULLION
ray	STIME, STYME
reach	RAX, RYKE
—out	RAX
real property	HERITABLE PROPERTY
really	REAL
reap with sickle	SHEAR
reaping contest	KEMP
rear premises	BACKSIDE
rebound	STOT(TER)
rebuke	THREAP, THREEP
rebuked	THREAPIT, THREEPIT
receive knowing to	
be stolen	RESET
receptacle	LOOM
recess	BOLE
—in wall of room	OUTSHOT
reckless	RAMSTAM
reclaimed wastelands	NOVALIA
Records Office	REGISTER HOUSE
recover	OVERCAST
red	
—currant	RIZZAR(D), RIZZART, RIZZER
—ochre	KEEL
rede	RED(D)
redeem	LOWZE
redeemed	LOWSIT
reel	PIRN
refrain	O'ERWORD
refusal	NAE, REEST, REIST
refuse	RED(D)
—to	
move (horse)	REEST, REIST
recognise	MISKEN
refute	REDARGUE
rehabilitate	REPONE
reign	RING

reinstatement	REPOSITION
relapse	WEED, WEID
related by common descent	SIB
relating to Argyll	ARGATHELIAN
relative	FRIEND
—on mother's side	COGNATE
release	EXEEM, EXEME
—from outlawry	RELAXATION
religion	PRESBYTERIANISM
relish	SA(I)R
reluct	TARROW
reluctant	SWEER, SWEIR
rely	LIPPEN
remainder	LAVE
remarkable (thing)	UNCO
remarkably	UNCO
remedy	REMEAD, REMEDE, REMEID
remember	MIND
remind	MIND
rendering void	IRRITANT
rent	MAIL(ING)
—in	
kind	CAIN, KAIN
money	PENNY MAIL
rented farm	MAILING
repentance fine	BUTTOCK-MAIL
replication	REPLY
reply to a	
—duply	TRIPLY
—triply	QUADRUPLY
reprimand	TARGE
reproach	UPCAST
reproof	SLOAN
residence	HADDIN
resist law officer	DEFORCE
resort	HOUFF, HOWFF
resourceful	FENDY
respectable	MENSEFUL
restive	FLISKY
restless	WANRESTFUL
restlessness	FIKE, FYKE
restore to office	
or status	REPONE
restrain	COMPESCE, HEFT
resume in conclusion	PIRLICUE
	PURLICUE
retain (milk or urine)	HEFT
return	RETOUR
—of the feu	RECOGNIZANCE
revival of an action	WAKENING
Reynard	TOD-LOWRIE
rickety structure or	
collection	RICKLE
riddle	GUESS
ridge of land for oats	CORN-RIG
riding hood	TROTCOSY, TROTCOZY

right	
—opposite	FOREANENT, FORNEN(S)T
—to	
cut sods	FEAL AND DIVOT
use for life	LIFE-RENT
rigmarole	RAGMAN, RAGMENT
rigorous in morals	UNCO GUID
rill	SIKE
rim	ROON
ring	JOW
—dove	CUSHAT
ringing in	JOWING IN
rinse	SIND, SYND
riotous merrymaking	GALRAVAGE
	GALRAVITCH
	GIL(L)RAVAGE
	GIL(L)RAVITCH
rippling	JABBLE
rise	PLUFF
rived	RAVE
river	CLYDE, FORTH, TWEED
—horse	KELPIE, KELPY
	WATER-HORSE
riverside	
—meadow or flat	HAUGH
—plain	CARSE
rivulet	STRAND
road	RAID
—junction	TOLL
rob	REAVE, REIVE, RUB
robbed	RUBBET, RUBBIT, RAFT, REFT
robber	CATERAN, REAVER, REIVER
rock	JOW
rode	RADE, RAID
Rogation Days	GANG DAYS
rogue	HEMPY
roguery	JOOKERY, JOUKERY
	JOUKERY-PAWKERY
roll	ROW
—the eyes	WAUL, WAWL
rolling pace eggs	PACE-EGGING
roof	
—gutter	ROAN, R(H)ONE
—of loft or garret	ROOST
rope	TOW
rose	RA(I)SE
rosin	ROSET, ROSIT, ROZET, ROZIT
rough	GURLY, RAMGUNSHOCH
	RAUCLE
—justice	JEDDART
roughcast	HARL
roughened bar	RISP
round	
—flat stone	PENNY-STANE
—hillock	KNOWE
rounded hill-top	DOD

rouse	FIRK, STEER
routine	HEICH-HOW
row	SPLORE
rowan	RODDIN
royal steward	MAORMAR
rubbish	BROCK, CLAMJAMPHRIE
	RED(D), TROCK, TROKE
	CLANJAMFRAY
—tip	TOOM
ruddle	KEEL
rude	GOUSTROUS
Rugby Union	SRU
ruined place	WASTAGE
rummage	POWTER
rump	RUMPLE
run	RACE, RIN, SCOUP
—as if lame	HIRPLE
—jauntily	LAMP
—wild	LAMP
runaway	FUGIE, LOUP-THE-DYKE
rush	RASH, THRESH
rustle	. FISSLE
rusty sword	SHABBLE
sackless	SAIKLESS
sad	DOWIE
sadness	WAENESS
safe	AWMRIE, AWMRY
sagacious	AULD-FARAND
sailor	TARRY-BREEKS
saint	SAUNT
sale by auction	ROUP
salmon-curing house	CORF-HOUSE
salmon spear	LEISTER, WASTER
salt	SAUT
salutation	BECK
salute by raising hat	HAT
salve	SAW
same	AE, SAMEN
sample	SWATCH
sand-lark	SANDY-LAVEROCK
sandstone	KINGLE
sated	STAWED
satisfy	SAIR
saucepan	GOBLET, KAIL-PAT
saucy	NEBBY
saunter	DA(C)KER, DAIKER
	DA(U)NDAR, DAUNER, DAWNER
save	HAIN
savour	SAIR
savoury	GUSTY
Saxon	SASSENACH
say	
—be quiet!	WHEESHT
—nothing of	LET BE
scald	SCAUD
—and pluck	PLOT

scales	WEIGHT
scallop edges	MUSH
scalp	SCAUP
scamp	SKELLUM
scamper	LAMP, SCAUP, SCOUP, SCOWP
scant	JIMP(Y), JINTY
scare	GLIFF, GLIFT, SCAR(RE), SCAUR
scarecrow	TATTIE-BOGLE
scatter	SCALE, SCAIL, SKAIL
scavenger	SCAFFIE
scholarship	BURSARY
school fight	BICKER
schoolmaster	DOMINIE
scold	FLITE, FLYTE, RAGE, YAFF
scolding	DIRDUM, DURDUM
	THROUGH-GAUN
	KAILWIFE, SCAUD
—match	FLYTE, FLYTING
scold's bridle	BRANKS
scope	SCOUTH, SCOWTH
—of choice	WALE
scorch	BIRSLE, SCOUTHER, SCOWDER
score	RIT(T)
—(goal)	HAIL
scorn	GECK, SCOUTHER
scour	SCUR, SKER, SKIRR, SQUIRR
scowl	GLOOM
scramble	SPRATTLE
scrap	GLIM
scrape	SCART, SNAPPER, SPLORE
scraping of anything	HARL
scratch	CLA(U)T, RIT(T), SCART
screech	SCRAICH, SCRAIGH, SCREICH
	SCREIGH, SKRIECH, SKREIGH
screen between door	
and fireplace	HALLAN
scrofula	CRUEL(L)S, CREWELS
scrubby wood	SCRODG
scruff	CUFF
scuff	CUFF
scuffle	TUILYE, TUILZIE
sea basin or sound	FLOW
seahorse (Orkney)	TANGIE
seal	SEALCH, SEALGH, SELKIE
	SILKIE, SILKY
search	RIPE, SCUR, SKER
	SKIRR, SQUIRR
—for stolen goods	
(Islands)	RANCEL, RANZEL
searching of gutters	STRAND-SCOURING
season	SEIL
seaweed	WARE
second	
—reply in law case	DUPLY
—sight	TAIS(C)H
—year student	SEMI-BAJAN

secrecy	HIDLING(S), HIDLINS
secret	HIDLING(S), HIDLINS
—hoard	POSE
sect (extinct)	BEREAN
security	CAUTION, WAD
—on goods in respect of a debt	HYPOTHEC
sedate	DOUCE
seed-time (Islands)	VOAR
seek	SIK
seer	SPAEMAN, SPAER SPAEWIFE
seethe	BULLER
seisin	SASINE
select list of candidates	SHORT-LEET
selection of verse	BLA(U)D
self	SEL(L)
selvage	ROON, RUND
sensible	WISE-LIKE
sensitive	KITTLY
sentence of outlawry	FUGITATION
sentimental story writers	KAILYARD SCHOOL
separate	RED(D), TWIN(E)
separation of churches	DISRUPTION
serve	SAIR
—as relish	KITCHEN
served right	CHEAP OF
service to be rendered by a vassal	REDDENDO
serving-dish	ASHET
session	DOWN-SITTING
set	STELL
—in motion	STEER
order	SNOD
—off	MENSE
—on one side	JEE
—things in order	RED(D)
—to work	YOKE
setting in order	REDDING-UP
severe	ILL, SNELL
shabby	OORIE, OURIE, OWRIE
shadow	SCO(O)G, SCOUG
shake	WAP
shaky	COGGLY
shallow ford	RACK
shamble	BAUCHLE
share	RUG
sharp	GLEG, SNELL
shavings	RISPINGS
sheaf	DORLACH
shed (Islands)	SKEO, SKIO
sheep	
—disease	BRAXY, LOUPING-ILL
—fold	FANK

—shelter	SHEAL(ING) SHEIL(ING), STELL
shelf	BINK
shellfish	BUCKIE
shelter	BEELD, BIELD, SCO(O)G SCOUG, SHEAL(ING) SHIEL(ING)
sheltered	LOUN(D), LOWN(D)
shepherd's	
—crook	KEBBIE
—own sheep	PACK
—plaid	MAUD
sheriff	SHIRRA
sheriff's messenger	SHELLYCOAT
shilling	TWALPENNY
shilly-shally	WHITTIE-WHATTIE
shin-bone soup	SKINK
shine	SHEEN, SKYRE
shinty-stick	CAMAN
ship	LYMPHAD
shirt	SARK
shiver	CHITTER, GREW, GRUE
shock	STOUND, STOWND
shoemaker	SOUTAR, SOUTER, SOWTER
shoemaker's thread	LINGEL, LINGLE
shoot	PLUFF
—like a pang	STOUND, STOWND
shore	RANCE
short	CUTTY
—clay pipe	CUTTY
—connecting-pipe	HOGGER
—distance	WEE
—dumpy girl	CUTTY
—shift	CUTTY-SARK
—time	WEE
—winded	PURFLED
shot	PLUFF
shoulder	SHOUTHER, SPALL, SPAUL SPA(U)LD, SPEAL, SPULE
—blade	SPULEBANE
—of hill	DOD
shovel	SHOOL
show	EFFEIR, EFFERE, SHAW
—perturbation	JEE ONE'S GINGER JOW ONE'S GINGER
shower	SCOWTHER
showy	BRANKY, BRAW
shred	TA(I)VER
shrewd	CANNY
shriek	SCRAICH, SCREICH, SCREIGH SKIRL, SKREICH, SKREIGH SKRIECH, SKRIEGH, SPRAICH
shrill cry	SKIRL(ING)
shrink	CRINE, NIRL
—from dryness	GIZZEN
shrivel	NIRL

shrivelled	GIZZEN	sledging	HURLY-HACKET
Shrove Tuesday	BROSE AND BANNOCK DAY	sleek	SNOD
	FASTE(R)N('S)-E'EN	sleepy	SLEEP(E)RY
shudder	GREW, GRUE	slender	JIMP(Y), JINTY, SWANK
shuffle	SHAUCHLE	slice of	
shut	STEEK	—beef	RUNNER
shy	BLATE, SKEIGH	—bread	SHIVE
	WILLYARD, WILLYART	slid	SLADE, SLAID
sickly	DONSIE, DWAMY, WERSH	slide	HIRSLE
—looking	SHILPIT	slight	LICHTLY
side		—attack of illness	BRASH
—by side	HEADS AND THRAWS	—fit of ill-humour	DOD
—glance	GLEDGE	—shower	SCOUTHER, SCOWDER
sieve	SILE, SYLE	—slap	SCLAFF
sift	SEARCE	—touch	SKIFF
signal	WAFF	slip	SKITE, SKYTE
silence!	WHEESHT	—in conduct	SNAPPER
silly person	DOTTLE	—suddenly	SCOOT
silver	SILLER	slipper	MUIL, PANTON
simple	AFA(W)LD, AEFA(U)LD	slippery	GLID(DERY)
	SACKLESS, SEMPLE	slit	RIT(T)
simpleton	GOMERAL, GOMERIL	slobbery mess	SLAISTER
since	SIN(E), SYN(E)	sloe	SLAE
—that time	SINSYNE	sloping-ceilinged	COOMCEILED
sing shrilly	SKIRL	sloppy	
singe	SCOUTHER, SCOWDER	—drink	SWANK(E)Y
single	AFA(W)LD, AEFA(U)LD	—thing	CLATCH
sink	JAWBOX	slops	CLATS, SLAISTERY
sinner	DIKE-LOUPER	slothful	SWEER(ED), SWEERT, SWEIR(T)
sip	SOWP, TIFT	slough in a bog	MOSS-HAG(G)
sir	STIR	sloven	HACHEL
sirloin	(BACK-)SEY	slovenly	
sirrah	STIRRA(H)	—person	WALLYDRAG, WALLYDRAIGLE
sister	TITTY	—work	SLAISTER
—in-law	GUDE-SISTER	slow	
sit	CLOCK	—match	LUNT
sitting	DOWN-SITTING	—moving stream	POW
six	SAX	sluggish stream	LANE
sketch	SKIFF	slush	LAPPER
skilful	CANNY, SKEELY	slut	CLATCH
skilled	SKEELY, SKILLY	sly	CANNY, SLEE
skim	REAM, SKIFF	—person	TOD
skimming	SKIFF	slyly	PAWKILY
skin	FLAUGHT	smacking	SKELPING
skip about	FLISK	small	PINKIE, PINKY
skittish	SKEIGH	—amount of bread	PIECE
—young woman	GILLET, JILLET	—cake	NABKET
skua (Islands)	BONXIE	—creek	POW
sky	LIFT	—cup	TASSIE
slabbery daub	SLAKE	—drawer	SHOTTLE, SHUTTLE
slake	SLO(C)KEN	—drink	SOWP
slant	SKLENT	—drop	DRAPPIE, DRAPPY
slap	CLATCH, SCUD, SKELP	—goods	TROCK, TROKE
slate	SCLATE, SKLATE	—heap	TOORIE
—pencil	CA(L)M, CAUM	—inn	CHANGE-HOUSE
slatternly woman	BESOM	—job	TROCK, TROKE

—landowner	BONNET LAIRD
—person	NYAFF, SMOUT, SMOWT
—portion	KENNING, TATE, TAIT
—quantity	CURN, HARL, PICKLE, WHEEN
—thing	NYAFF
—tree	SCROG
—wage	PENNY-FEE
—wares	TROCK, TROKE
smash	STRAMASH
smear	SLAKE
smell about	SNOWK
smelt	SPARLING, SPIRLING
smithy	SMIDDY
smoke	SMEEK, SMEIK, SMEKE
	SMOOR
—tobacco	LUNT
smoky	REEKIE
smolt	SMOUT, SMOWT
smooth	BRENT, SLEEKIT, SNOD
—tongued	SLEEKIT
smother	SMORE
smothered laugh	SNIRT
snack	CHACK
snap	CHACK, SNACK
—at	HANCH
snare	GIRN
snarl	GIRN
snatch	CLAUCHT, CLAUGHT
snicker	SNIRTLE
snigger	SNICHER, SNICKER
snipe	HEATHER-BLEAT(ER)
	HEATHER-BLUITER
	HEATHER-BLUTTER
sniveller	SNOOL
snob	SNAB
snooze	DOVER
snub	SLOAN, SNIB, SNOOL
snuff	NABKET
	SNEESH(AN), SNEESHIN(G)
—about	SNOWK
—box	MILL, MULL, SNEESHIN-MULL
snug	COSH, COUTHIE, SNOD
snuggle	CROODLE
so	SAE
soap suds	SAPPLES
sob	SAB
sober	DOUCE
sock	HUSHION
sod	FAIL
—for roofing	DIVOT
soft, sheepish fellow	SUMPH
softly	HOOLY
softness	FOZINESS
soil	TASH
solely	ALLENARLY
solicitor	LAW-AGENT

somehow	SOMEGATE
something	
—of slender importance	SHEEP-SHANK
—pledged or pawned	WADSET(T)
somewhere	SOMEGATE
son of	MAC
song	SANG
soon	BLIVE, ENOW
sore	SAIR
sorrel	SOUROCK
sorrow	DOOL, TEAN
sorrowful	WAE(SOME)
soul	SAUL
sound	FERE
—of liquid from bottle or cork drawn	CLUNK
sound of slap	SCLAFF
soundness	HEAL
soup	COCKALEEKIE, COCKIELEEKIE
	COCKILEEKY
—ladle	DIVIDER
sour liquor	TIFT
southern	SOUTHRO(U)N
southernwood	APPLERINGIE
sow	SAW
sowens	FLUMMERY
space	
—before kiln fire	LOGIE
—in front of kiln	KILLOGIE
spare	HAIN
sparing (with money)	CANNY
spark	FLAUGHT, SPUNK
sparrow	SPRUG
spasm	THRAW
spatter	JA(U)P
spawning-place	REDD
spear with leister	LEISTER
specify	CONDESCEND
specious	FAIR-FARAND
spectacle	OUTSPECKLE
spell	TACK, WEIRD
spend	BIRL, MOIDER, WARE
—thriftlessly	WASTER
spiced hot drink	PLOTTIE, PLOTTY
spider	ETHERCAP, ETTERCAP
spill	SCALE, SCAIL, SKAIL
spin	BIRL
spinning party	ROCKING
spirit	SMEDDUM
spiritless(ness)	DOWF(NESS)
spirituous liquor	STRUNT
spitting of cat	FUFF
splash	BLASH, JABBLE, JA(U)P
—of dirt or colour	SPLATCH
splashing sound	CLATCH
splinter	FRUSH, SPALE

split and	
—dried fish	SPELD(R)IN(G)
—lay open	SPELD(ER)
splotch	SPLATCH
spoil	BAUCHLE, BLUNK
	SPUILZIE, SPULYE
spoliation	HERRIMENT, HERRYMENT
	REIF, SPU(I)LZIE, SPULY(I)E
spongy	FOZY
spool	PIRN
spoonful	SOWP
spot (of iron-mould)	MAIL
spout	STROUP
sprain	STAVE, WREST
sprat	GARVIE, GARVOCK
spread open	SPELD(ER)
spree	SKITE, SKYTE, SPLORE
spring	
—in a marsh	WELL-HEAD
—(Islands)	VOAR
—time	WARE
sprinkle	STRINKLE
—of snow	SCOUTHERING, SCOWDERING
sprout	BREER, BRERE
spruce	SPRUSH
spur-leather	SPUR-WHANG
squall	DROW
squat	SQUATTLE
squint	GLEDGE, GLEE, GLEY, SKELLY
—eyed	GLEED, GLEYED
squirt	SCOOT
stable-keeper	STABLER
stagger	DAIDLE, WINTLE
	STOITER, WINTLE
stake	STOB
stale liquor	TIFT
stallion	COOSER, CU(I)SER, STAIG
stalwart	BUIRDLY, PRETTY
stamp	STRAMP
stanchion	STANCHEL, STANCHER
standing	
—place	STANCE
—stone	HARE-STANE
star	STARN, STERN
starched cap	COCKERNONY
stark mad	RED-WOOD, RED-WUD
start with fear	STURT
state	
—of anger or displeasure	KIPPAGE
—the object	CONCLUDE
statement of case	CONDESCENDENCE
station	STANCE
stay	STAW, SIST
—as guest	GUESTAN, GUESTEN
steelyard (Islands)	BISMAR
steep	BRENT, MASK, STEY

—in hot water	PLOT
—sided valley	HEUCH, HEUGH
stew	STOVE
stewardship	STEWARTRY
stewed potatoes	STOVIES
sticky and dirty	CLARTY
stiff	STEEVE, STIEVE
—clay	TILL
stiffly	STEEVELY
stifle	SCOMFISH
still	ALWAY
stir	JEE, STEER
stirrup-cup	DEOCH-AN-DORUIS
stitch	STEEK
stock	PLENISH
—and goods in lease	STEELBOW
—farm	STORE-FORM
stocking-shaped net	HOSE-NET
stoke	TOUK
stole	STAW, STEALED, STEALT
stolen	STOWN, STEALED, STEALT
stomach	GEBBIE
stone hammer	KNAPPING-HAMMER
stood	STOODEN, STUDDEN
stool	BUFFET, SUNKIE, TREST
—of repentance	CREEPIE, CUTTY-STOOL
stop	DEVALL, DIT, SIST
storm	WAP
stout	STUFFY
straight	STRAICHT, STRAUCHT, STRAUGHT
—on	ENDLANG
—staircase	SCALE-STAIR(CASE)
strain	RAX, SEIL, SILE, SYLE
strainer	SEIL, SILE(R)
strait	KYLE
strange	FRAIM, FREMD, FREMIT, UNCO
—folk	FRAIM, FREMD, FREMIT
stranger	FRAIM, FREMD, FREMIT, UNCO
strangle	THRAPPLE
strap	TAWS(E)
straw	STRAE
stray	TRAIK, WAFF
streaked	HAWKIT
stream	BURN
streamer	PINNET
street	GATE
—fight	BICKER
—leading to water	WATER-GATE
—sweepings	POLICE-MANURE
—swindler	MAGSMAN
strength	FIZZEN, FUSHION
strenuous contest	PINGLE
stress (pronunciation)	BIRR
stretch	RAX, STRAUCHT
	STRAUGHT
strict examination	EXPISCATION

stride	
—along	LAMP
—vigorously	STEN(D)
strife	BICKER
strike	BLA(U)D, GOWF
—(clock)	CHAP
—heavily against	DUSH
striking part of flail	SUPPLE
string round leg	
below knee	NICKY-TAM
strip	JIB, TIRL, TIRR
—of thread or cloth	ROON, RUND
—off	TIRR
—worn over shoulder	PLAID
striped	PIRNIE, PIRNIT
—woollen nightcap	PIRNIE
strive	BARGAIN, PINGLE
stroke	STOUND, STOWND, STRAIK
—of	
bell	JOW
pen	SCART
—received in trying to	
separate fighters	REDDING-STRAIK
stroll	DA(U)NDER
	DAUNER, DAWNER
strolling beggar	GABERLUNZIE
strong	YA(U)LD
struck	STRA(C)K
struggle	TUILYE, TUILZIE
—with difficulties	PINGLE
strut	STRUNT
stub	STOB
stubble	STIBBLE
stubborn	RIGWIDDIE, RIGWOODIE
—insistence	THREAP, THREEP
stuck	STACK, STICKIT
stuff	CRAP, PANG, STAP
stuffed	PANG
—haddock's head	CRAPPIT-HEAD
	CRAPPIT-HEID
stumble	SNAPPER, STOIT
stump	STOB
—and rump	STOOP AND ROOP
stumpy	NIRLIE, NIRLY
stun with a blow	DEV(V)EL
stunned	DONNERD, DONNERT
stunt	NIRL
stunted	WANTHRIVEN
—bush	SCROG(-BUSS)
—child	URF
—person	NIRL
—tree	SCRUNT
stupefy	DOZEN
stupid	TA(I(VERT
—fellow	HASH
—person	CUDDIE, CUDDY
sturdy	STEEVE, STIEVE, STUFFY
—beggar	HALLAN-SHAKER
stutter	HABBLE
sty	CRU(I)VE
subdue	DANTON
subject to pangs	THRAW
submerge	TAKE
substance	FECK
substitution of one	
obligation for another	INNOVATION
subterfuge	OFF-COME
subterranean dwelling	WEEM
such	SICCAN
sudden	
—blow	SPANG, WHAMPLE
—fall of rain	PLUMP
—flame	LUNT
—illness	TOUT, TOWT, WEED, WEID
—movement	SPANG
—sickness	DWALM, DWAUM
—storm	ONCOME, ONFALL
suddenness	SUDDENTY
sue	PURSUE
—for	PLEAD
suet pudding	CLOOTIE DUMPLING
suffer pangs	THRAW
suffocate	SMORE
suit of clothes or armour	STAND
sulk	DORT
sulks	DORTS, STRUNTS
sulky	STUNKARD
sullen	DOUR, STUNKARD
—look	GLOOM
summary	SUMMAR
summer pasture	SHEALING, SHIELING
summon	SIST
sunken	LAIGH
sunrise	DEASI(U)L, DEASOIL
	DEIS(H)EAL
supernumary	ORRA
superstition	FREET, FRIET
superstitious	FREETY, FREITY
supervise strictly	TARGE
supplement	EIK
support under arm	OXTER
supporter	STOOP, STOUP
sure	SICCAR, SICKER
surety	CAUTIONER, VADIUM
surfeit	STAW
surge of liquid	JAW
surly	GURLY
surpass	DING
surplice	SARK
suspect	J(E)ALOUSE, MISLIPPEN
swaggerer	BIRKIE
swarm	BIKE, BYKE, HOTTER

swarming	HOTTER
sway	SWEE, THRAW
sweated	SWAT
sweep	SOOP
sweetheart	JO(E)
swell	HOVE
swelling	CLOUR
swig of liquor	SCOUR
swim	SOOM
swine	GRUMPHIE
swing	SWEE
swingle	SUPPLE
swipple	SOUPLE, SUPPLE
swoon	DWALM, DWAUM
sword	CLAYMORE, SPURTLE(-BLADE)
—blade	ANDREA FERRARA
	ANDREW FERRARA, ANDRO FERRARA
—rusty	SHABBLE
symbolical occupation	INFEFTMENT
system of	
—succession	TANISTRY
—weights	TRON(E)
table linen	NAPERY
tailor	PRICK-(THE-)LOUSE
take	TA(C)K
—a loathing to	SCUNNER
—copy of	EXTRACT
—heed	TENT
—no trouble in	
the matter	NEVER FASH YOUR THUMB
—pains	FASH
—trouble	FASH
—under the arm	OXTER
—up for burial	LIFT
taking of evidence by judge	PROOF
tale of fate	WEIRD
talk	
—frivolously	NYAFF
—impudently	SNASH
—nonsense	BLETHER, HAVER
talkative	GASH
talker of nonsense	BLETHER(AN)SKATE
tall hat	LUM(-HAT)
tangle	FANK(LE), TAUT, TAWT
tangled	TATTY, TAUTIT, TAWTIE
tantrum	TIRRIVEE, TIRRIVIE
tap	TOUK
tar barrel	CLAVIE
task	DARG
taste	PREE
tasteless	SAURLESS, WERSH
tattle	GASH
tavern reckoning	LAW
tax	STENT
—assessor	STENTO(U)R, STENTMASTER
(Islands)	WATTLE

tea-urn	KITCHEN
teach	LEAR(E), LEIR, LERE
tear	TIRR
tease	TEAN
tedious	DREICH, EDI(OU)SOME
television	STV
tell tales	CLIPE, CLYPE
temples	HAFFET, HAFFIT
tenant	SUCKENER
—bound by thirlage	SUCKENER
—of	
crown	THANE
same stock as landlord	
or whose family has held	
land in succession	KINDLY TENANT
tenure	FEU, HOLDING, TACK
—watching	BURGAGE
term-day (11th November)	MARTINMAS
territorial jurisdiction	REGALITY
Text Society	STS
than	BY, NOR
thank God!	BE THANKIT, BETHANKIT
thatch	THACK, THEEK
thaw	FRESH
the	
—bulk	FECK
—one	TA(N)E
—sulks	THE DODS
theft	STOUTH(E)(RIE)
—with violence	STOUTHRIEF
them	THAIM
then	SIN(E), SYN(E)
theological college	DIVINITY HALL
these	THIR
thick	
—bawling noise	GOLLAR
—witted Highlander	TEUCHTER
—woollen (Islands)	WA(AD)MAL
	WADMOL(L)
thin	SKINKING
—broth	MUSLIN-KALE
—liquor	TIFT
—porridge	WATER-BROSE
third reply in law case	TRIPLY
thistle	THRISSEL, THRISTLE
thorn	STUG
thorough-going	THROUGH-GANGING
those	THAE
thrash	TARGE
thrashing	LICKS
threaten	SHORE
—by movement	MINT
—rain or snow	SCOUTHER, SCOWDER
threatening	SHORE
—gesture	MINT
threw	THRAWN

thrifty	FENDY	toe	TAE
thrill	DINDLE, DINNLE, DIRL	together	THEGITHER
throat	CRAIG, HAUSE, HAWSE, THRAPPLE	toil	MOIDER
throe	THRAW	told	TAULD, TELD, TELL'D, TELT
throng	THRANG	toll	JOW
thropple	THRAPPLE	tomboy	GILP(E)Y
throttle	THRAPPLE	tomorrow	THE MORN
through	YONT	—morning	THE MORN'S MORN
—passage	TRANCE, TRANSE	—night	THE MORN'S NICHT
throw	CLOD, THRAW	too	TAE
—down	DING DOUN, DUSH	—bright	ROARIE, ROARY
—into a lump	SLUMP	tooth	GAM
thrust	STAP	top	TAP
—onward	STAVE	—of chimney	LUM-HEAD
thump	DAUD, DAWD, DUNT	toper	SAND-BED
	LOUNDER, PAIK	topsy-turvy	REEL-RALL
thwart	THRAW		TAPSALTERIE, TAPSIETEERIE
tickle	KITTLE	torrent of words	BLATTER
—trout	GUDDLE	toss	BUM
ticklish	KITTLE	—coin	BIRL
tidal race (Islands)	ROOST, SWELCHIE	totter	HOTTER
tidied	REDDED	tough	TEUCH, TEUGH
tidy up	RED(D)	towards	ANENT
tight	ANG	—the	
timber transporter	JANKER	coal face	INBY(E)
time	STOUND, STOWND	interior	INBY(E)
—long past	LANG SYNE	town (burgh)	BURROWSTOWN
—of		tractable	TAWIE
day	SEIL	trade	TREAD
trial	HOUR OF CAUSE	traditional	
trouble	STOUND, STOWND	—belief	THREAP, THREEP
timid	BLATE	—dish	HAGGIS
tingle	DINDLE, DINGLE, DIRL, TIRL	trample	STRAMP
tingling after a blow	DIRL	tranquil	LOWN
tinker	CAIRD, TINK(LER)	transient experience	GLIFF, GLIFT
tiny	WEE	transmitter of	
tip	MAG(G)S, PROPINE	family lore	SEANNACHIE, SEANNACHY
—up	COUP, COWP		SENNACHIE, SHANACHIE
tired out	FORJASKIT, FORJESKIT	trash	TRASHTRIE
tiresome	DREICH	tread	TRAMP
—chatter	YATTER	—in a tub, washing	
tirl	RISP	clothes	TRAMP
tithe	TEIND	treason	PURDELLION
titlark	MOSS-CHEEPER	treat in return	ARCHILOWE
to	ON, TAE	tree-trunk	CABER
—be lost	TINE, TYNE	tremble	HOTTER
—debar the unworthy		trench	SHEUCH, SHEUGH
from communion	FENCE THE TABLES	trews	SKILTS
toad	PADDOCK	trial	
toadstool	PADDOCK-STOOL	—at instance of	
toast	BIRSLE	Lord Advocate	INDICTMENT
—slightly	SCOUTHER, SCOWDER	—without jury	PROOF
tobacco		tribute	CAIN, KAIN
—pipe stem	PIPE-STAPPLE	trick	BEGUNK, CANTRIP, GEGG
	PIPE-STOPPLE		GLAIK, PAWK, SHAVIE
—pouch	SPLEUCHAN		SKITE, SKYTE

trickery	JOCKERY, JOUKERY	—year old animal	TWINTER
	JOUKERY-PAWKERY	—years old	TWINTER
trifle	DAIDLE, PINGLE	ugly	ILL-FAURD
trim	DINK, DONSIE, SNOD	umpire	BYRLAWMAN, ODDSMAN
	TOSH		OVERSMAN
trinket	WHIGMALEERIE	umwhile (formerly)	UMQUHILE
	WHIGMALERY	unacquainted	UNACQUAINT
trip along briskly	LINK	uncanny	ELDRITCH, WANCHANCIE
troll for fish	HARL		WANCHANCY, WEIRD
—Islands	DROW, TROW	uncared for	UNTENTED
troth	TROGGS	uncivil	MENSELESS
trouble	FASH, K(I)AUGH, STURT	uncommon	UNCO
troublesome	BRICKLE, FASHIOUS	under a liability	PASSIVE
trouser braces	GALLUSES	undergo one's	
trousers	BREEKS, TREWS	destiny	DREE ONE'S WEIRD
truce	BARLEY	underground	
truck	TROCK, TROKE	—dweller	PICT
trudge	TAIGLE	—dwelling	WEEM
truss	DORLACH	underlease	SUBTACK
trust	LIPPEN	undershirt	SEMMIT
try to beat down price	PRIG DOWN	unearthly	WEIRD
tub	SKEEL	unevenly wrought	PIRNIE
tuft	TATE, TAIT	unfriendly	FRAIM, FREMD, FREMIT
—on a bonnet	TOORIE	ungainly person	CLATCH
tug	RUG, TIT	unheeded	UNTENTED
tumult	HIRDY-GIRDY	unite closely	WAD
	STRAMASH, STRAMASH	unlucky	DONSIE, MISCHANCY
turbid	DRUMLY		UNCHANCY, WANCHANCIE
turbulence in water	BULLER		WANCHANCY
turf	FAIL, FLAUGHT	—chance	MIS(C)HANTER
—seat	SUNK	unmanageable	NEITHER HUP NOR WIND
—wall	FAIL-DIKE	unmannerly	MISLEARED
turkey-cock	BUBBLY-JOCK	unmusical	TIMBER
turn	THRAW, TIRl	unnecessary outcry	HUMDUDGEON
—down a bed	MAKE DOWN	unpleasantly severe	UNCANNY
—edge of	LIP	unproductive	YELD
—to left	HIE, HIGH	unqualified mason	COWAN
—up	CAST UP	unruly	CAMSTEARY
turnip	TUMPSHIE, NEEP		CAMSTEERIE
turnstile	TIRL		CAMSTAIRY
tusk	GAM	unsafe	UNCANNY
tut	OCH, TOOT(S), TUTS	unsalted	WERSH
tutor	DOMINIE	unstable	BRUCKLE
twelve	TWAL	untilled patch to	
—month	TOWMON(D), TOWMONT	avert Devil's	
twill	TWEEL	malice	GOODMAN'S CROFT
twirl(ed)	TIRLIE-WIRLIE	unto	INTIL
twist	THRAW, TWISTLE	unusual	UNCO
twisted	THRAWN	unworthy	WANWORDY
twitch	TIT, TWIRK	unyoke (horses)	LOWZE
two	TWA(E), TWA(Y)	unyoked	LOWSIT
—fold	TWAFALD	up	
—roomed house	A BUT AND BEN	—the way	UPBY(E)
—some	TWASOME	—there	UPBY(E)
—storied	TWA-LOFTED	—to	UP-TILL
—wheeled barrow	HURLY	uphold	UPHAUD

upright beam	STANCHEL, STANCHER
uproar	COLLIESHANGIE, RAIRD, REIRD
	DIRDUM, DURDUM
upset	UPCAST, WHEMMLE
—plans	COUP (THE CRAN), COWP
upside down	HEELS O'ER GOWDY
urchin	HURCHEON
urge	THREAP, THREEP
—forward	WHIG
urged	THREAPIT, THREEPIT
use	
—sparingly	KITCHEN, TAPE
—thriftlessly	WASTER
useful	WAKERIFE
useless person	BAUCHLE
usher in court	MACER
utter volubly	BLATTER
vacated	RED(D)
vagabond	RINTHEROUT, WAIF
vagrant	CAIRD, RINABOUT
	GANGREL, GANG-THERE-OUT
	RINTHEROUT, TINK(LER)
vague language	WHITTIE-WHATTIE
vain	VOGIE
valance	PAND
valise	DORLACH, WALISE
valley	CLEUCH, CLOUGH, CORRIE
	GLEN, STRATH
valuation	STENT
value	APPRIZE
variegated	BROCKED, BROCKIT
vault	COOM
vaulted passage	PEND
venture	MINT
veritably	REAL
very	AE, UNCO
—big	SKELPING
—hard rock	KINGLE
—much	FELL
vessel with spout	POURIE
vex	FASH, TEAN
vexatious	FASHIOUS
—detail in work	FIKE, FYKE
vibrate	DIRL, TIRL, HOTTER
vibration	DIRL, HOTTER
victuals	VIVERS
vigilant	WAKERIFE
vigorous	RAUCLE
village	CLACHAN
—with parish church	KIRKTO(W)N
violent push	BIRR
violin (Islands)	GJO, GJU, GU(E), GOU
virago	RUDAS
viscera	HARIGAL(D)S
vitality	FIZZEN, FUSHION
vivid	VIVE

voice of one about	
to die	TAIS(CH)
voracious hunger	(Y)EARD-HUNGER
	YERD-HUNGER
	YIRD-HUNGER
vow	HECHT
waddle	DAIDLE
wag	LICK
wainscot	BOX
wait	BIDE
—at appointed place	BIDE TRYST
wakeful	WAKERIFE
waking	WAKEN
walk as if lame	HIRPLE
walker	GANGER
wall	DIKE, WA
—opening	BOLE
—plug	DOOK
wander	STRAVAIG, TRAIK, TA(I)VER
wandering	WAFF
want of spirit	FOZINESS
wanting	AMISSING
wanton girl	GILLFLIRT, JILLFLIRT
warble	CHIRL
ward off	WEAR
warn	SHORE
warning cry	GARDELOO, JORDELOO
warrant to	
—apprehend fugitive	
debtor	FUGIE-WARRANT
—arrest debtor	CAPTION
—produce witnesses etc	DILIGENCE
was	
—able	DOCHT, DOUGHT
—good for a purpose	DOCHT, DOUGHT
washy	SHILPIT
wasps' nest	BINK
waste away	DWINE
wasteful	WASTERIFE
wasteland	REESK
watch over dead	LIKEWAKE, LIKEWALK
	LYKEWAKE
water	
—bailiff	WATER-BAILIE
—goblin	SHELLYCOAT
—plant (Islands)	PIPEWORT
—spirit (Orkney)	TANGIE
—sprite	KELPIE, KELPY
	RIVER-HORSE
watery	SKINKING
—bog	MOSS-FLOW
—stuff	BLASH
wave	WAFF
waxed thread	LINGEL, LINGLE
way	GATE
wayward	LOUP-THE-DYKE

weak	BRICKLE, FIZZENLESS
	FUSHIONLESS
wean	SPANE, SPAIN, SPEAN
wearer of	
—kilt	KILTIE, KILTY
—short shift	CUTTY SARK
weary with drudgery	TRAUCHLE
weasel	WHIT(T)RET
	WHITTERICK
weaver	WABSTER
wed	WAD
week	OU(L)K
weep	GLEET, GREET
weighing machine	TRON
weight	
—12-34lbs (Islands)	LISP(O)UND
—80 stone	SERPLATH
weir	CAULD
weird	ELDRITCH
weld	WALD
welfare	HEAL
well	A(T)WEEL, WEEL
—favoured	WEEL-FA(U)R'D
—known	NOTOUR
—off	BEIN, BIEN, WELL-TO-LIVE
—wishing	GOOD-WILLY
went	GAED
wept	GRAT, GRUTTEN
western	WESTLIN
wet	WAT
—slovenly work	SLAISTER
what!	SICCAN
—does it matter?	WHAT RECK
—kind of?	WHATEN, WHATNA
wheedle	CUITER, PHRASE
wheel	HURL
—barrow	HURL-BARROW
wheeze	WHAISLE, WHAIZLE
where	WHAUR
which	QUHILK, WHILK
whilom	UMQUHILE
whim	FLISK, WHIGMALEERIE
	WHIGMALERY
whimbrel	LITTLE WHAUP
whimper	PEENGE
whine	PEENGE, WHEENGE
	WHINGE
whinstone	WHUNSTANE
whip	FIRK
whirl	BIRL, TIRL
whirlpool (Islands)	SWELCHIE
whirring sound	BIRR
whisk	WHID
whisky	AULD KIRK, THE CRATUR
	USQUEBAUGH
—bottle	AULD KIRK

whisper	HARK, WHEESHT
	WHITTIE-WHATTIE
whistle	FISSLE, SOWTH
—feebly	WHEEPLE
—softly	SOWF(F), SOWTH
whit	HAET, HAIT
white	
—faced	HAWKIT
—pudding	WHITE-HASS, WHITE-HAWSE
whitening-stone	CAMSTA(U)NE, CAMSTONE
whitish	WHITELY
Whitsuntide	REMOVAL TERM
whiz	WHIDDER
whole	HALE
—affair	HALE HYPOTHEC
wholesome	HEALSOME
whooping-cough	KINK-H(O)AST
whortleberry	BLAEBERRY
why yes	OU AY
wicked creature	HELLICAT
widow's right to a third	TERCE
wife	GUIDWIFE
wig	GIZZ, JIZ
wild	
—daisy	GOWAN
—radish	RUNCH
wilful	WILLYARD, WILLYART
will not	WINNA
Will-o'-the-wisp	SPUNKIE
willow	SAUCH, SAUGH
wind (clock)	ROLL
winding stair	TURNPIKE(STAIR)
window	WINDOCK, WINNOCK
—seat	BUNK
windpipe	THRAPPLE
winter sport	CURLING
wipe	DICHT
wish	WISS
witch	CARLINE, GYRE-CARLIN, WEIRD
witch's spell	CANTRIP
wither	GIZZEN, SCAITH, SKAITH
within	BEN, INWITH
without	
—dowry	UNTOCHERED
—feudal superior (Islands)	UDAL
—injury	SCAITHLESS, SKAITHLESS
—intermission	EVEN ON
—orderliness	THROUGH-OTHER
—scratches	SCART-FREE
woe	DOOL(E), DULE, WAE
woeful	DOLENT, WAEFU(L), WAESOME
woman	CUTTY, CUMMER, KIMMER
	WOMAN-BODY
—(contemptuously)	GIMMER
—keeping ale-house	LUCKIE, LUCKY

—practising witchcraft	WITCH-WIFE
—who buys at auction	ROUPING-WIFE
woman's	
—cap	MUTCH
with side flaps	TOY
—loose jacket	SHORTGOWN
—short cloak	ROCKLAY, ROKELAY
womanish man	JENNY, JESSIE
wonder	FERLY
wood	WUD
wooden	
—bowl	COG, COG(G)IE
—drinking-cup	CA(U)P
—in tone	TIMBER
—leg	PIN-LEG
—peg-top	PEERIE, PEERY
—vessel	COG(UE)
wool	OO
—of sheep's neck	HAUSE-LOCK
word	WHID
—of reproach	RIGWIDDIE, RIGWOODIE
work	WARK
—contest	KEMP
—house	POOR'S-HOUSE
	PUIR'S-HOOSE
—ineffectually	PINGLE
—into miry matter	CLATCH
—into paste	CLATCH
worker's free allowance	MAG(G)S
worn out	DISJASKIT
	FORFAIRN, TRAIKIT
—shoe	BAUCHLE
worry	DEAVE, FASH, PHEESE, PINGLE
worse	WAR(RE), WAUR
worst	WA(U)RST
worthless	ORRA, WAFF, WANWORDY
—fellow	FOOTRA, FOUTRA
—person	NYAFF, WALLYDRAG
	WALLYDRAIGLE
—thing	NYAFF
wot	WAT
wound	DUNT
wrack and ruin	PIGS AND WHISTLES
wrap	HAP
wreck	STRAMASH
wrench	THRAW, TWISTLE
wrest	THRAW
wrestle	WARSLE
wretched	WAESOME
wriggle	HIRSLE
wring	THRAW
wrinkle	LIRK
writ requiring security	
against doing violence	LAW-BURROWS
writhe	THRAW, WINTLE
written	WRATE

—assertion	TESTIFICATE
wrong way	WID(D)ERSHINS, WITHERSHINS
wry	THRAWN
yap	NYAFF
yarn-winding appliance	WINNLE
yawn	GA(U)NT
yearn	GREEN, GREIN
yell	SKELLOCH, YELLOCH
yelp	NYAFF
yeoman	COCKLAIRD
yes	AYE
—(Islands)	JOKOL, YOKUL
yesterday evening	YESTREEN
yon(der)	THON(DER)
young	YOUTHY
—animal	BURD
—bird	BURD
—coalfish	PODLEY
—ewe	GIMMER
—gull (Islands)	SCAURY
—hen	EIRACK
—onion	SYBOE, SYBO(W)
youngest of family	WALLYDRAG
	WALLYDRAIGLE
youth	HALFLIN(G)
script	(*see* **alphabet**)
sculpture	
bas relief gemstone	CAMEO
broad chisel	BOASTER, BOLSTER
bronze-casting	
technique	CIRE PERDUE
	LOST-WAX PROCESS
bust	
—and pedestal in one	
piece	TERM
—on square base	HERM(A)
carving	
—of basket of fruit	CORBEIL
—in	
bas relief	ANAGLYPH
intaglio	DIAGLYPH
—not free-standing	RELIEF
chip from stone	SPALL
clay mould	MANTLE
curved file	RIFFLER
decorated with gold	
and ivory	CHRYSELEPHANTINE
form a rough shape	BOAST
incised stone	INTAGLIO
later impression from mould	RESTRIKE
metal skeleton	ARMATURE
moving sculpture	KINETIC SCULPTURE
	MOBILE
plaster/glue mixture	GESSO
pointed hammer	BOUCHARDE
pose with torso twisted	CONTRAPPOSTO

raised carving	BAS RELIEF	—Spanish	CANO, GONZALEZ
	BASSO-RELIEVO	—Swedish	MILLES, OLDENBURG
	BASSO RILIEVO	—Swiss	BILL, GIACOMETTI, ITTEN
	(LOW) RELIEF		POERRI, TINGUELY
rough model	BOZETTO, MAQUETTE	stationary sculpture	STABILE
sculptors		statue	
—American	CALDER, KIENHOLZ, KIESLER	—as column	
	LEWITT, LIPCHITZ, MORRIS	female figure	CARYATID
	OLDENBURG	male figure(s)	ATLAS(ATLANTES)
—Austrian	DONNER, KIESLER	—cherub	PUTTO
—British	ADY(E), ARCHER, BANKS	—crucifixion	CALVARY
	BUTLER, CARO, CHANTREY	—Cupid	AMORINO
	CHADWICK, CHERE, EPSTEIN	—Greek	
	FLAXMAN, GAUDIER-BRZESKA	female	KORE
	GIBBONS, GIBSON	male	KOUROS
	GILBERT, GILL, HEPWORTH	—Mary and Jesus	PIETA
	HEWETSON, JOSEPH, MOORE	support frame for model	ARMATURE
	PAOLOZZI, SMITH, WILTON	workbench	BANKER
—Danish	THORWALDSEN	**seaweed**	ALGA, (BLADDER)WRACK
—Dutch	DE VRIES		OARWEED, ORE(WEED)
—Flemish	DELVAUX, NOLLEKENS	SEA-TANG(LE), SEA-WARE, TANGLE	
	RYSBRACK, SHEEMAKERS	Ascophyllum	SEA-WHISTLE
	SLUTER	bladderwrack	FUCUS, ROCK-WEED
—French	ADAM, ARP, BONHEUR		SEA-BOTTLE
	BOURDELLE, BRANCUSI	blue-green	NOSTOC
	DAVID, DEGAS, FALCONET	brown	KELP, KILP, LAMINARIA
	GAUDIER-BRZESKA, LACOMBE		PHAEOPHYCEAE
	LAURENS, LE MARCHAN		SEA-FURBELOW, WRACK
	MAILLOL, PEVSNER, PIGALLE	carrag(h)een	SEA-MOSS
	RODIN, ROUBILIAC	cast ashore	WRACK
—German	BARLACH, GUNTER	Channel Islands	VRAIC
	HECKEL, HOELZEL	Chorda(ria)	WHIPCORD
	MACKENSON, MODERSOHN	coarse seaweed	TANG(LE)
—Greek	GLYCON, PHIDIAS	coralline	NULLIPORE
	PRAXITELES, SCOPAS	dialect	ORE, WARE
—Hungarian	FLEISCHMAN	edible	DULSE, LAMINARIA, LAVER
—Italian	ALGARDI, AMMANATI		PORPHYRA, TANGLE
	BANDINELLI, BARISANUS	Fucaceae	WRACK
	BERNINI, BOCCIONI	grasswrack	EELGRASS, EELWRACK
	BRUNELLESCHI, BUGATTI	green	CHLOROPHYCEAE
	CANOVA, CELLINI, DANTI		ENTEROMORPHA
	DELLA ROBBIA, DESIDERIO		GREEN ALGAE, IKODONT
	DONATELLO, GHIBERTI	growing on shore	WRACK
	GIAMBOLOGNA	gulf-weed	SARGASSO, SARGASSUM
	GUELFI, LEONARDO		SEA-GRAPE, SEA-LENTIL
	MASTROIANNI, MICHELANGELO	kelp	VAREC(H)
	MUNARI, PISANO	Laminaria	SEA-GIRDLE, TANGLE
	SANSOVINO, VITTORIA	laver	PORPHYRA
—Latvian	LIPCHITZ	olive-brown	GULF-WEED
—Nigerian	ENENWEOUN	pink	CORALLINE
—Norwegian	VIGELAND	Porphyra	(PURPLE) LAVER
—Romanian	BRANCUSI	purple	CARRAG(H)EEN, IRISH MOSS
—Russian	ARCHIPENKO, GABO		LAVER, PORPHYRA
	GONCHAROV, PEVSNER	red	CHONDRUS, FLORIDEAE, LAVER
	ZADKINE		PORPHYRA, RHODOPHYCEAE
—Scottish	PAOLOZZI		RHODYMENIA

ribbon-weed	SUGAR-WRACK		sergeant-at-law	SL
rock-weed	BLADDERWRACK		sergeant-major	SM
Sargassum	GULFWEED, SEA-GRAPE		**servant**	
sea-			acolyte (old)	ACOLOUTHITE
—girdle	LAMINARIA, TANGLE		agent	BAILIFF, COMMIS, FACTOR
—grape	GULFWEED, SARGASSUM			REEVE, STEWARD
—lentil	GULFWEED		American	
—lettuce	GREEN LAVER, ULVA		—hotel page or porter	BELL-HOP
—moss	CARRAG(H)EEN		—messenger (Congress)	PAGE
—whistle	ASCOPHYLLUM		—railway porter	REDCAP
sugar-wrack	RIBBON-WEED		apprentice chef, waiter	
tangle	LAMINARIA, SEA-GIRDLE		or steward	COMMIS
translucent	BLADDERWRACK, SEA-BOTTLE		assistant	ACOLYTE, ACOLYTH
Ulva	GREEN LAVER, SEA-LETTUCE		—to official	YEOMAN
varec(h)	KELP, WRACK		attendant	ACOLTE, ACOLYTH
whipcord	CHORDA, CHORDARIA			FAMULUS, VARLET
wrack	FUCACEAE, VAREC(H)			WAITING-VASSAL
secret			—armed (Turkey)	CAVASS, KAVASS
Secret Intelligence Service	MI, SIS		—at races	STEWARD
secret jargon of vagrants	SHELTA		—for horses	GROOM, OSTLER
secret police				STABLE-BOY, STABLE-LAD
—East Germany	STASI		—on	
—Nazi Germany	GESTAPO		aeroplane	STEWARD(ESS)
—Romania	SECURITATE		Highland chief	G(H)ILLIE, GILLY
—Russia	(T)CHEKA, GRU, KGB, MVD			GILLIE-WETFOOT
	NKVD, OGPU			GILLIE-WHITEFOOT
—South Africa	BOSS		knight	ARMIGER, (E)SQUIRE
—Sweden	SAPO			SCUTIGER, VARLET
secret printing	SAMIZDAT		ship	STEWARD
secret script (Greek)	SCYTALE		boy attendant	BUTTONS, PAGE
secret society	FRATERNITY		carrier	BEARER, PORTER
—Algerian French	OAS		Chinese labourer	COOLIE
—American	KU-KLUX KLAN		cook	CHEF
mafia	BLACK HAND, COSA NOSTRA		doing all kinds	
—Chinese	BOXER, HOEY, TONG		of work	FACTOTUM
	TRIAD			GIRL FRIDAY, HOUSEKEEPER
—claiming mystical				MAN FRIDAY
knowledge	ROSICRUCIANS		door-keeper	CONCIERGE, PORTER
—French	MAQUIS		driver	CHAUFFEUR, CHAUFFEUSE
—German (18th c)	ILLUMINATI		Eastern	
—international	(FREE)MASONS		—harem servant	EUNUCH
—Italian			—(nurse)maid	AMAH
Calabrian	NDRANGHETA		factor	CHAMBERLAIN, SENESCHAL
Neapolitan	CAMORRA		factotum	CIRCAR, FAMULUS
Sicilian	MAFIA			SIRCAR, SIRKAR
republican	CARBONARI		family servant	RETAINER
—Japanese	YAKUZA		female servant	HANDMAID(EN)
—Kenyan	MAU MAU		—suckling child for mother	WET-NURSE
—Muslim	ASSASSINS		—working for board and	
—South African	BROEDERBOND		lodgings	AU PAIR
Senegal	SN		foreman	STEWARD
senior	SENR, SR		footman	FLUNKEY, LACKEY, LACQUEY
senior common room	SCR		French	
Senior Deacon	SD		—doorkeeper	CONCIERGE
Senior Medical Officer	SMO		—maid	BONNE
sergeant	NCO, SERG(T), SGT		gatekeeper	CONCIERGE, PORTER

general steward	MAJOR DOMO, SENESCHAL
group of servants	RETINUE, TRAIN
hotel or inn	
—bootblack	BOOTS
—page	BELL-BOY, BUTTONS
—pulling off guests'	
boots	BOOT-CATCHER
—serving drinks	BARMAN
	POT-BOY, POT-MAN
house servant	DOMESTIC
Hungarian	HAIDUK, HEYDUCK
Indian	
—domestic	WALLAH
—groom	SYCE
—hotel servant	BEARER
—household servant	BEARER
—maid	AYAH
—nursemaid	AYAH
—personal servant	BEARER
—porter	SHERPA
—rajah's servant	CHOBAR
—waiter	K(H)IDMUTGAR
	K(H)ITMUTGAR
Irish boy-servant	GORSOON, GOSSOON
janitor	CONCIERGE
Jewish temple servants	NETHININ
ladies' maid	ABIGAIL, SOUBRETTE
	TIRE-WOMAN, TIRING-WOMAN
land steward	BAILIFF
liveried servant	FLUNKEY
maidservant	SOUBRETTE
manservant	
—attending to clothes etc	VALET
—in charge of food	
and drink etc	BUTLER, PANTLER
—liveried	FOOTMAN
—serving at table	SEWER, WAITER
menial servant	DOGSBODY, DRUDGE
	MINION, SCULLION
	SKIVVY, SLAVE(Y)
messenger	BEARER
military servant	BATMAN
native	BEARER
officer of court (old)	APPARITOR
one in charge of	
building	CONCIERGE
	JANITOR, SUPERINTENDENT
overseer	STEWARD
page	BELL-BOY, BELL-HOP
	BUTTONS
personal assistant	PA
porter	CONCIERGE, BELL-BOY
Scottish	
—barefoot messenger	GILLE-WETFOOT
	GILLIE-WHITEFOOT
—guide	G(H)ILLIE, GILLY

secretary	AMANUENSIS, FAMULUS
shoe cleaner	BOOTBLACK
slave	BOND(S)MAN, HELOT
	VASSAL
South African (nurse)maid	AYAH
Spanish governess	DUENNA
steward	CHAMBERLAIN
	SENESCHAL
university servant	BEDDER, FAG, GYP
	SCOUT, SKIP
valet	LACKEY, LACQUEY
warden	CONCIERGE
witch's servant	FAMILIAR
seven	VII, S
against Thebes	ADRASTUS, AMPHIARAUS
	CAPANEUS, HIPPOMEDON
	PARTHENOPAEUS
	POLYNICES, TYDEUS
based	SEPTENARY, SEPTIMAL
books of OT	HEPTATEUCH
champions	ST ANDREW, ST ANTHONY
	ST DAVID, ST DENIS
	ST GEORGE, ST, JAMES
	ST PATRICK
Christmas presents	SWANS
cleft	SEPTEMFID
combining forms	HEPTA-, SEPT(I)-
	SEPTEM-
creations	ANIMALS, EARTH, FIRE, HUMANS
	PLANTS, SKY, WATER
daughters of Atlas	PLEIADES
days	HEBDOMAD, WEEK
Deadly Sins	ANGER, COVETOUSNESS
	ENVY, GLUTTONY, LUST
	PRIDE, SLOTH
Dwarfs	BASHFUL, DOC, DOPEY
	GRUMPY, HAPPY
	SLEEPY, SNEEZY
fold	SEPTIFORM, SEPTUPLE
groups	HEBDOMAD, HEP, HEPTAD
	SEPTENARY, SEPTET(T
	SEPTETTE, SEPTUOR
having seven	
—angles	HEPTAGONAL, SEPTANGULAR
—cusps	SEPT-FOIL
—faces	HEPTAHEDRONAL
—feet	HEPTAPODIC, SEPTEMPEDAL
	SEPTIPEDAL
—languages	HEPTAGLOT
—leaflets	SEPTEMFOLIATE
—measures	HEPTAMETER
—parts	HEPTAMEROUS
	SEPTEMPARTITE
—sides	HEPTAGONAL, SEPTILATERAL
—stamens	HEPTANDRIAN, HEPTANDROUS
—styles	HEPTAGYNIAN, HEPTAGYNOUS

—syllables	HEPTASYLLABIC
Heptateuch	**Pentateuch** *plus*
	JOSHUA, JUDGES
hills of Rome	AVENTINE, CAELIAN
	CAPITOLINE, ESQUILINE
	PALATINE, QUIRINAL, VIMINAL
hundred	PSI
hundredth anniversary	SEPTINGENTENARY
hundred thousand	PSI
in government	HEPTARCHY
	SEPTEMVIRATE
Magnificent	FILM
notes	SEPTIMOLE, SEPTUPLET
one of seven	
—at one birth	SEPTUPLET
—men	SEPTEMVIR
Sages	BIAS, CHILON, CLEOBOLUS
	PERIANDER, PITTACUS
	SOLON, THALES
Seas	ANTARCTIC, ARCTIC
	N & S ATLANTIC, INDIAN
	N & S PACIFIC
senses	*as* **five** *plus* SPEECH
	UNDERSTANDING
sevens	RUGBY
Sisters	ROCKS
sleepers	CHRISTIAN YOUTHS
Stars (of Pleiades)	GREAT BEAR, PLOUGH
	SEPTENTRION(ES)
	TRIONES, PLOUGH
stories told in 7 days	HEPTAMERON
thousand	Z
times as much added to stake	SEPTLEVA
tones	HEPTACHORD
virtues	CHARITY, FAITH
	FORTITUDE, HOPE, JUSTICE
	PRUDENCE, TEMPERANCE
Wonders of World	COLOSSUS
	HANGING GARDENS
	MAUSOLEUM, PHAROS
	PYRAMIDS, STATUE OF ZEUS
	TEMPLE OF ARTEMIS
works	SPIRITUAL MERCY
year ...	ITCH
years	PROPHETIC WEEK
	SEPTENATE, SEPTENNIUM
seventy	O, OMICRON, S
seventy-eight	DISC, RECORD
The Seventy	JEWISH COUNCIL
	SANHEDRIN
thousand	O, OMICRON, S
year old	SEPTUAGENARIAN
sewing	
including: embroidery	
needlepoint	
applied decoration	APPLIQUE

blunt needle	BODKIN
border on clerical vestment	ORPHREY
diagonal line	BIAS
edging	PURL
embroider on edge	PURFLE
embroidery	
—frame	TAMBOUR
—needle	CREWEL
—with padding	QUILTING, TRAPUNTO
gathering	SHIRRING, SMOCKING
knotted threadwork	MACRAME, MACRAMI
narrow braid	SOUTACHE
non-fraying edge	SELVAGE, SELVEDGE
open pattern	BRODERIE ANGLAISE
overlapping seam	MONK'S SEAM
patterns stitched	
on fabric	EMBROIDERY
	NEEDLEPOINT
	TAPESTRY
perforated shapes	BRODERIE ANGLAISE
pre-shrunk	MERCERISED
raised	
—strip	RIB(BING)
—surface	NAP
round strip	PIPING
seam stitched on both sides	FRENCH SEAM
slit in garment	PLACKET
spool	BOBBIN
stitches	BARGELLO, BLANKET
	BUTTONHOLE
	CABLE, CHAIN, CLOUD FILLING
	CRETAN FLY, CROSS, DARNING
	FEATHER, FISHBONE, HERRINGBONE
	HOLBEIN, JAPANESE, LAZY-DAISY
	MOSS, RAISED, RUNNING, SQUARE
	VANDYKE, WAVE, WEAVING
	WHIPPED WEB, WOVEN
stitching	
—diagonally	TENTWORK
—heavy thread	COUCHING
—over weft	TRAMMING
—with two threads	COUCHING
superimposed materials	APPLIQUE
tapestry stretcher	BLOCKING BOARD
temporary stitching	BASTING, TACKING
triangular insert	GORE, GUSSET
trimming	GIMP
wavy	
—braid	RICKRACK
—edge	LETTUCE EDGE
weft in embroidery	TRAM(MING)
woven edge	SELVEDGE
zigzag needlepoint	BARGELLO
Seychelles	SY
capital	(PORT) VICTORIA
coin	CENT, RUPEE

Shakespeare

words found in his works:

a thing discovered	DESCRY
abate	PLUCK OFF
abhorred	HELL-HATED
abide	REMAIN
able to perform wonders	WOND(E)RED
abode	BEING, REMAIN
abominable	EXSUFFLICATE
abounding in rooks	ROOKY
about	SOON AT
abreast	AFRONT
absence	REMOVE
—of restraint	LET-ALONE
abstain from	REFRAIN
absurd medley	GALLIMAUFRY
abundance	TALLENT
abundant of produce	INCREASEFUL
abuse with violence	LANDDAMNE
abusive language	ROPE TRICKS
acceptance	ADMITTANCE
accident	UPCAST
accompanied by a woman	WOMAN'D
accompany	ASSOCIATE, ASSIST
	SERVE
accomplice	FEDAR(AR)IE, FEDERARY
	FOEDARIE, FOEDAIRE
accomplishment	COMPLIMENT, EXERCISE
accord	CONGREE
accost	ASSAY, BOARD
account	RENDER
accountant	ONEYER
accusation	CAUSE
accuse	APPEACH, APPEAL
	DETECT, PEACH
accustomed	TAME
accruing	GROWING
accumulation	ENGROSSMENT
accuse	APPEAL
achieve by kneeling	KNEE
acid	AYGRE, EAGER
acquit	UNCHARGE
act	ISSUE
—according to one's nature	DO ONE'S KIND
—as	
a boy	BOY
regent for	PROTECT
—lazily and stupidly	DRUMBLE
—of	
aiming	LEVEL
devising	FRAME
extending	EXTENT
seizing	PREY
standing	STATION
—up	EVEN

—upon	SALUTE
acting as a procurer	PANDERLY
actions	EFFECTS
active	FACTIOUS, QUIVER
—youth	LEAPING-TIME
actor's profession	QUALITY
actual	BODILY
adapt measures	ORDER
add up	PARCEL
addicted	FREQUENT
—to looking in a mirror	GLASS-GAZING
addition	VANTAGE
additional title or designation	SURADDITION
address	BOARD, SUPERSCRIPT
adjudge to one side or the other	SIDE
adjustment in ratio	PROPORTION
admission to office	ENTERTAINMENT
admonition	ADVERTISEMENT
adorn with a brooch	BROOCH
adorned	CROWNED
adroit	QUAINTLY
adulterate	CARD
—wine with lime	LIME
adulterer	BED-SWERVER
advantage	COMMODITY, EMINENCE
	PRISE, PROCEEDING
—yielded	PRIVILEGE
advent	INCOME
adventurous	DAREFUL
adverse	AWKWARD
advisement	VIZAMENT
affair	CAUSE
affect	SALUTE
affectation	AFFECTION
affirmed before	FOREVOUCHED
afflict with apoplexy	APOPLEX
afflictions at sea	SEA-SORROW
affright	GHAST
afraid	AF(F)EARD
against proper feeling	UNKINDLY
aggressive person	SQUARER
agitate	BETOSS, JUMP
agree	ATONE, CONGRUE, CONVENT
	GREE, HIT
—to	CONGREE, UNDERWRITE
agreement	COMART
alarm	TIRRIT
alas!	WELLANEAR
alchemist's elixir	TINCT
alembic	LIMBEC(K)
Algiers	ARGIER
all	
—destroying	NONE-SPARING
—night drinkers	CANDLE-WASTERS

—round	FULL-FRAUGHT	appraisal	PRISE
allege	LEGE	appraise	PRAISE
allot	SORT	approach	COST(E)
allotment	DOLE, LOTTERY	approaching the sky	SKYISH
allow	BETEEM(E)	approbation	ALLOWANCE, APPROOF
allowed three-suits p. a.	THREE-SUITED	appropriate	PROPERTY
allusion	POLLUSION	apt to learn	SPACKT, SPRAG
always opening	UNSISTING	arbitration	COMPROMISE
amazed	AGAZED	ardour	WRATH
Amazon	HIPPOLYTA, PENTHESILEA	arithmetician	COUNTER-CASTER
ambitious	EMULATE	armour for arm	BRACE
amorous	LOVELY	army	BATTLE
amount	SUBSTANCE	aromatic herb	NOSE-HERB
amulet	PERIAPT	arrange	SCEDULE
ancient	FANS	arrest	REST
anger	INCENSEMENT	arrogance	OPINION
animal's		arrow	BIRD-BOLT
—bed	CABINET	art of fencing	DEFENCE
—entrails	CHAWDRON	artful	ARTIFICIAL
animated	AUDACIOUS		CAUTELOUS, FINE
—by lust	LUST-BREATHED	as it may happen	HEREBY
annoyance	NOYANCE	ashamed	SHENT
annul with a kiss	UNKISS	ask for writ	
anoint	BALM	delivering	
answer	REIN	freehold to heir	SUE ONE'S LIVERY
antagonism	OPPUGNANCY	askance	ASCONCE
antecedent happening	PREMISE, PREMISS	aspire to	SPEAK TO
anticipating	FOREHAND	assail	ASSAY
antipodes	UNDER-GENERATION	—with	
any odds	LOTS TO BLANKS	rattling	RATTLE
anything		words	TONGUE
—calculated to arouse	HUNT'S-UP	assailant	OFFERING
—displayed for show	FLAUNT	assault	ASSAY
—engraved	SCULPTURE	assay	SAY
—of value	WORTHY	assayer	SAY-MASTER
—human	CIVIL	assemble	CONDUCE
—protuberant and		assembled	DREW
hanging loosely	WALLET	assembly	DISSEMBLY
—that dashes hopes	COOLING-CARD	assign	SORT
—very small	HALFPENNY	—to one side	SIDE
anyway	ALL-THING	—value to	PRAISE
apparently true	TRUE-SEEMING	assistant tapster	UNDERSKINKER
apparitor	PARITOR	associate	COMPETITOR, COMPLICE
appear	EYE, LOOK OUT	assume	UNDERTAKE
appearance	OSTENT, PORT	assurance	SURANCE
—of life	LIVELIHOOD	assure	PASS, SECURE
appendages	ASSIGNS	assured	THOUGHTEN
appendix to bill	SCEDULE	assuredly	PARDIE, PARDY, PERDIE
apple	LEATHER-COATS		PERDY
	POMEWATER, SWEETING	astonishment	ADMIRATION
apply mouths	MOUTH	astride	COLOSSUS-WISE
appoint	LIMIT, SCEDULE	at	
—a time for	SET DOWN	—an end	EXPIATE
—by writing	PAPER	—any rate	AT ANY HAND
appointment	MATCH	—night	ANIGHT
apposite	PREGNANT	—peace	WHIST

—the	
beginning	AT HAND
present time	THE WHILE
—this very time	INSTANTLY
—variance	ODD
atmosphere	REGION
atone	ABIDE, ABY(E)
atrociously wicked	FACINERIOUS
attack	BOARD, EXTENT
attend	TEND
—as servant	STAY
attend to	RECK
attendants	TENDANCE
attentive	ADVERTISING, ATTENT
attraction	FAVOUR
auburn	ABRAM
augment	ECH(E), EECH, ICH
auspicious	FAIR-BODING
avarice	MISERY
avaricious	CHUFF
avenge	VENGE
avenging	REVENGE
averse to conversation	UNQUESTIONABLE
avoid	EVITATE
avowed	BARE-FACED
awry	CAM, KAM(ME)
back up	VERIFY
backbiting	BACK-WOUNDING
backward fall	TAILOR
bad luck	WANION
badge of dignity	GUARD
badly tempered	ILL-TEMPERED
bailiff	BUM-BAYLIE
	SHOULDER-CLAPPER
bait	STALE
balance	PEASE, PEAZE, PEISE
	PEIZE, PEYSE
—evenly	WEIGH
—of an account	REMAINDER
ball of thread	BOTTOM
balsamic liquor	MUMMY
baneful	BATEFUL
banish	ABANDON
bank	RIVAGE
—of river	WHARF
banker	ONEYER
bankrupt	TRADE-FALNE
bar	MAKE
—tailed godwit	SCAMEL
bargain	COMPOSITION
barrel	BOMBARD, BUMBARD
base	CULLIONLY
—tyke	HUNT-COUNTER
basket	MAUND
baste	ENLARD
bathed	BALKED

batter by violence	
of weather	OVERWEATHER
battle	WAGE
baubles with fool's head	FOOLS ZANIES
bawd	GREEK
bawl	GAPE
be	BIN
—a	
guest	HOST
pattern for	PATTERN
widow	WIDOW
wooer	SUE
—amends for	PURCHASE
—an accessory	BE OF CONSENT
—conciliatory	MAKE FAIR WEATHER
—consistent	ADHERE
—daunted	DISMAY
—deluded with hopes	EAT THE AIR
—dilatory	FORESLOW
—distasteful	DISTASTE
to	RESIST
—equal in value	WAGE
—equivalent to	REANSWER
—imprisoned	LIE
—in	
fashion	WEAR
service	DEPEND
waiting	TEND
—inconstant	BLENCH
—intent	TIRE
—intimately mixed	LARD
—lodged	LIE AT HOST
—married	GO TO THE WORLD
—over-punctilious	STRAIN COURTESY
—perverse	BE OPPOSITE WITH
—security for	SURETY
—silent	PEACE
—sluggish	DRUMBLE
—suitable	CONVENT
—surety for	UNDERTAKE
—the better	AVAIL
—transacted	PROCEED
been	BIN
bear	
—in mind	REMEMBER
—like a crest	UNDERCREST
beard	EXCREMENT
beardless	UNRUFFE
bearing	CONCERNANCY
bearing	PORTANCE
beast of the chase	VENISON
beat	COMB, FIRK, PAY, PRAT
	SWINDGE, SWITS
beater	SWITS
beauty	FAIR
because	THAT

beckoning	WAFTURE
become	BESORT
—an informer	PEACH
—lank	LANK
—mouldy	HOAR
bedcover	COUNTERPOINT
bedraggle	BEMOIL
beetle for clothes	BATLET, BATLER
befall	BEFORTUNE
befit	BESORT
befooled	POUPT
before	TOFORE
beforehand	FORMER
beggar	BEZONIAN
begging bowl	CLACK-DISH
begone	AROINT, AROYNT
behaving like a fop	FASHION-MONGING
behaviour	GESTURE, PORTANCE
beholden	BEHOLDING
being in a passion	PASSIONING
belated	LATED
beldame	TROT
believe	WIS(T)
belladonna	INSANE ROOT
beloved	TENDER
belt	CENTER
bend	COMPASS, CURB
—one's course	SWAY
beneficiary	BENEFIT
bent	CRISP
—upon prey	PREYFUL
benumb	PROROGUE
beset	LAY
beshrew	SHREW
best	DEAR, WHIP
bestially drunk	SWINE-DRUNK
bet	LAY
bethink	REMEMBER
betide	BETIME
betray	PEACH
betroth	ASSURE, TROTH
betrothal	ASSURANCE
betrothed	COMBINATE
	TROTH-PLIGHT
between sand-blind	
and stone-blind	HIGH-GRAVEL-BLIND
bewitchment	TAKING
beyond description	UNEXPRESSIVE
bias	PARTIALISE
Bible	TEXT
biliousness	CHOLER
bind	COMBINE
—as in gratitude	ENDEAR
—in fetters	ENFETTER
—weed	WOODBIND, WOODBINE
bird of ill-omen	NIGHT-CROW

bird's nest	CABINET
biting in tongue	WASP-STUNG
	WASP-TONGUE
bitter	AYGRE, EAGER
—end	UTTERANCE
black	COLLIED, ROOKY
—as hell	HELL-BLACK
—bird	WOOSEL(L)
—jack	BOMBARD
blandishment	SOOTH
blast	STRIKE, TAKE
—by lightning	THUNDER-STROKE
blasted	DEROGATE
bleacher of linen	WHITSTER
bleaching-time	WHITING-TIME
blight	BLASTMENT, STRIKE
blind	BEESOME, BISSON
	C(O)URB, WINKING
—fold	W(H)IMPLE
—man's buff	HOODMAN-BLIND
blinding	BISSON, SEELING
blinking	PINK
blockhead	CLOTPOLL, SNIPE
bloodhound	LYM
blooming	PRIMY
blow	PASH
—in fencing	MONTANTO
blundering word	NON-COME
blunt	DISEDGE
—arrow	BIRD-BOLT
blusterer	RUDESBY, SWASHER
boarded	PLANCHED
boasting	MAGNIFICENT
—of	REPUTING
bodge	BUDGE
bodily	
—constitution	COMPLEXION
—pain	GRIEF
—quality	THEW
body	
—of people owing allegiance	SUBJECT
—servant	GENTLEMAN
boggled	BODGED
boiling pot	STEW
boldness	DARE
bookish man	INKHORN-MATE
boredom	SPLEEN
born	
—in dung	SHARD-BORNE
—to a procuress	BAUD-BORN
borne by scaly wings	SHARD-BORNE
bosky	BUSKY
bosom friend	CATER-COUSIN
botcher	COSIER, COZIER
bout	VENEW
bowl-beating	BOLD-BEATING

bowsprit	BEAK
boy	CRACK, JACK-A-LENT
	KNAVE
brabble	PRABBLE
brain	PIA MATER
—sick	BRAINISH
brand	WIPE
—with infamy	INFAMONISE
bravery	HARDIMENT
bravest	BEST
brawl	BRABBLE, PRAWLE
breach of amity	FRACTION
break	FRACT, FRUSH
bred in heat of passion	MAD-BRED
brevity	FEWNESS
bright red	WAX-RED
brimming with tears	WATER-STANDING
bring	PROCURE
—back to better state	RECURE
—forth young	EAN, KINDLE
—into plot	PACK
—on	INFER
—safely	SAFE
—to	
an end	FINE
me	DUCDAME
broach	STRIKE
broad linen tape	INKLE
broken with care	CARE-CRAZED
brood	KINDLE
—in nest	AERIE, AERY, AYRIE
	EYRIE, EIRY
brothel	HOTHOUSE, LEAPING-HOUSE
bruise	FRUSH
bruised	PASHED
brushing blow	SWITS
bubonic plague	RED-MURRAIN, RED-PLAGUE
buck of fourth year	SOAR(E), SORE
bucket	STO(O)PE
budge	BOUGE
bully	CUTTLE
bullying	SWASHING
bumblebee	DRUMBLEDOR
burden	CARRIAGE
—of a song	FADING, HOLDING
	WHEEL
burdensome	CHARGEFUL
burdock	HARDOKE, HORDOCK
burnt torches used	
as blacking	LINK
bury	INHEARSE, INHERCE
but slightly	SMALL
butt of the company	
at table	TABLE-SPORT
buy too dear	OVERBUY
buzzard	PUTTOCK

by	
—all means	OF ALL LOVES
—common report	REPORTINGLY
—God!	BEGAD, BEGAR
—scent of the foot	DRY-FOOT
—starts	STARTINGLY
—word of mouth	VERBATIM
bystander	STANDER-BY
byword	AYWORD
Caesar	KEISAR
cake	BAKE
calamity	BALE
call	
—a whore	BEWHORE
—to account	TAKE-UP
calling	
—for haste	RASH
—in question	IMPEACH
camp follower	BOY
candlestick	CANSTICK
cane	SWITS
cannot be	
—cloyed	CLOYLESS
—wounded	INTRENCHANT
canon	SQUIER, SQUIRE
canto	CANTON
cap worn on Sundays	STATUTE-CAP
capable	DELIGHTED
—of taking oath	OATHABLE
capacious	CAPTIOUSWOMBY
caparisoned	BARBED
caprice	SPLEEN
captiousness	CURIOSITY
card	TOAZE
care	TENDER
careful of	OBSEQUIOUS
carefully chosen	CHOICE-DRAWN
caress	COY
carpenter's square	SQUIER, SQUIRE
carriage	PORTANCE
carried by itself	SELF-BORNE
carry	
—away in spirit	
or with joy	RAP
—foolish appearance	FACE
—off	TRANSPORT
carted	SCUTCHED
carve(d)	INSCULP(T)
case	SHALE
cast	
—a	
light	REFLECT
spell	TAKE
—down	DEJECT
—of the eye	ELIAD, ILLIAD, OEILIAD
—off	CASTED

castrate	GLIB
cataract	PIN AND WEB, WEB AND PIN
catch	FANG, GYVE, PHANG
—in	
a lapse	LAPSE
the act	WATCH
—of the voice	SNATCH
catchword	NAYWORD
catgut string	CATLING
casually dropped	SCATTERED
cause to	
—act	COMMAND
—be remembered	MEMORISE, MEMORIZE
—contract or wrinkle	WARP
—mourn	YEARN
—start	FIT
—tremble	QUAKE
caused by soreness	
of heart	HEART-SORE
causing	
—drowsiness or sleep	YAWNING
—numbness	NUMB
cautious	ADVISED
—in speech	CLOSE-TONGUED
—person	ACHITOPHEL, AHITHOPHEL
cave	ANTAR
cease to exist	DETERMINE
censure	APPEACH
centre	CENTRY
certain	PERFECT
cesspool	DRAUGHT
chaffering	BARGAIN
chain	CARKANET
challenge	ASSAY
chamber	LONDON
—pot	JORDAN
chance	UPCAST
change to a worse state	DISTASTE
changeover	SWITS
character	COMPOSURE, OPINION
—of fox	FOXSHIP
charm worn round neck	PERIAPT
chaste	GRACED
chastise	FIRK, SWINDGE
chastity	HONESTY
chatterer	CHEWET
cheat	BOB, COLT, CONY-CATCH
	GULL-CATCHER, HARLOT
check	TRASH
cheese-rind	CHEESE-PARING
cherub	CHERUBIN
chided	ACOLD
chief	ARCH
child	BA(I)RN, COLLOP
	CRACK, EYAS-MUSKET, KIND
children	IMAGES

children's game	PU PIN
chin	SHINNE
chlorosis	WHITE DEATH
chop (logic)	BA(U)LK
church service	MASS
churl	CARLOT
cincture	CENTER
circle	OE, RONDURE, ROUNDER
circlet	RIGOL(L)
cite	CONVENT
civilised	INLAND
clad in armour	IRON
claim	PLEA
clamour	UTIS
clandestine visiting	TRUNK-WORK
clasp	TASSEL
claw	CLOYE
clever	QUAINTLY
close	SEAM
—connection	IMMEDIACY
—covering	MODEL
—in approach	UPON
closed	WINKING
closely interwoven	THICK-PLEACHED
cloth made in Wales	FRIZE
clothed	SUITED
clothes	
—hung round ship	
to hide crew	FIGHTS
—washing implement	BATLER, BATLET
clouded	NIGHTED
clover-stalk	HONEY-STALK
clown	CARL, LOWT, NORTHERN MAN
club	BAT
coarse	UNBOLTED
—beef	BULL-BEEVES
cobbler	COSIER, COZIER
cockboat	COCK
cockchafer	DRUMBLEDOR
coign	COIN
coin	G(U)ILDER, STAMP
colour	LEER
comb	PHEEZE
combat	OPPOSITION
combination	QUILL
combustible	COMBUSTIOUS
come	
—down the scale	PLUCK OFF
—to a head	HEADED
—with me	DUCDAME
comedy	COMMONTY
coming	
—close upon	THICK-COMING
—in	INCOME
command	CHECK, IMPOSE
commanding battalion	HYE-BATTEL'D

commit adultery	ADULTERATE	confessional	SHRIFT
common	MODERN, UNPROPER	confidence	INWARDNESS
—sewer	FILTH	confine	BALE
—woman	CUSTOMER	—as in hoop	INHOOP
commonalty	COMMON	confinement	PRISONMENT
commonness	COMMUNITY	confirm	AFFEAR, AFFEER
commonplace	MODERN		COMPACT, STABLISH, TIE
commotion	GARBOILS, ROMAGE	confirmation	APPROBATION
communicative	INTELLIGENT	confirmed	AFFEARD
companion	COMATE, COPES-MATE	—possession	STABLISHMENT
	SKAINES MATE	—state of manhood	PROOF
—devil	YOKE-DEVIL	confoundedly	PLAGUY
—in study	BOOK-MATE	confused sound	WHOOBUB
	INKHORN-MATE	confutation	REPROOF
companionable	FELLOWLY	confute	CONTROL, PUT DOWN
company	HAUNT, HEAP	conjecture	CONJECT, ESTIMATION
—arriving	ARRIVANCY	conjoin	COJOIN
compare	LIKE	connected consistency	DEPENDENCY
compartment	SQUARE	connecting link	COMMA
compassionate feeling	REMORSE	conquer	HARROW
complain	MEAN(E), MEIN, MENE	conscious of	WITTOL
complaint	PLAINING	consciousness	CONSCIENCE
complete	PARCEL, REPLENISHED	consent	GRANT
completely	HOME	consequence	COLLECTION
—contented	PERFECT	considerate	RESPECTIVE
complexion	HAIR, LEER	consideration	CONSIDERANCE
complimentary	BREATHING	constant	STILL
composed of ribaldry	RIBAUDRED	consume	CONFOUND
composition	COMPOSTURE	consummate	MADE UP, REPLENISHED
compost	COMPOSTURE	contemplation	BEHOLDING
compound	TAKE UP	contemptible	EXSUFFLICATE
compounded	CREATE		PELTING
comprehensive	CAPABLE	—person	SNIPE
compulsory	COMPULSATIVE	contend	WAGE
conceal	OVERGREEN	contention	BATE
conceit	OPINION	contents	ARGUMENT
conceited fellow	PRINCOX	—of bag or satchel	SCRIPPAGE
conceive	ENWOMB	continue chaste	VIRGIN
—of	BRAIN	continuously	AN-END
conception	HENT	contradict	TAKE-UP, FORESPEAK
concern	CERNE, TENDER	contrariety	ADVERSITY
concerted music	BROKEN MUSIC	contrary	RETROGRADE
conclude	CROWN, INCLUDE	control	CHECK, DANGER
concordancy	COMPOSITION	controversy	DEBATEMENT
concupiscence	CONCUPY	convene	CONVENT
condescend	YIELD	convent	COVENT
condescended unwillingly	COYED	conversation	QUESTION
conduce	SHAPE	converse	DIALOGUE, PROPOSE
conduct	GOVERNMENT, ORDER, PASS		QUESTION, REASON
—itself	CONDUCE	conveyance	ASSURANCE
confederate	COMPETITOR, FEDAR(AR)IE		TRANSPORTANCE
	FEDARARY, FOEDARIE	convict	APPROVE, CONVINCE
	FOEDAIRE		INDITE
confederates	QUALITY	convinced	PERFECT
confession	EXERCISE, RENDER	cool	KEEL, RESPECTIVE
	SUBMISSION	cope with	TAKE UP

copy	TAKE OUT	—artful device	DAWBRY
corner	COIGNE	cruel through holiness	HOLY-CRUEL
—stone	COIN	crush	PASH
corollary	COLLECTION	crust of a pie	CUSTARD-COFFIN
coroner	CROWNER	cry triumph over	ORECROWE
corporal	NYM	cuckold-maker	HORN-MAKER
corpulent	GORBELLIED	cudgel	BALLOW, BAT(TERO)
corrected	ATTASKED, ATTASKT	cunning	FOXSHIP, SKILL
	CORRIGIBLE		SUBTILE-WITTED
corroded	CORROBORATE	Cupid	BOW-BOY
corrupt	CORROBORATE, DISTASTE	cur	CURTAIL, TYKE
Cotswold	COTSALE	curdle	POSSET
cough	TISICK	cure	RECURE
countenance	PATRONAGE	curry	PHEEZE
counterpane	COUNTERPOINT	curse	VENGEANCE, WANION
course	STERNAGE	cursory	CURSELARIE, CURSENARY
—of events	OCCASION	curtail	ABATE
courtesan	BONA-ROBA, GUINEA-HEN	curtains	CHAMBER-HANGINGS
courtesy	GENTRY	curve	COMPASS
cover		cut	SLISH
—ground	RID WAY	—notches in	NICK
—to real purpose	STALE	—slightly	SCOTCH
—up	HOODWINK	—to pieces	MAMMOCK
—with red colour	OVERRED	cutpurse	BUNG
covered with		cutting	SECT
—high growth	HIGH-GROWN	cynic	CRITIC
—wickerwork	TWIGGEN	dabchick	DIVE-DAPPER
cow	ROTHER(-BEAST)	daily	JOURNAL
—dung	SHARD	dainties	CATES
coward	VILIACO, VILLIAGO	dairymaid	DAY-WOMAN
—cock	COSTREL, CONSTRIL	dance	CINQUE-PACE, SINKE-A-PACE
	COYSTRIL	—tune	LIGHT-O'-LOVE
cowardice	COWARDSHIP	—with much leaping	LAVOLT(A)
cowardly	COWISH, MEACOCK	Dane	DANSHER
	MILK-LIVERED	dark	
coxcomb	PRINCOX	—as night	NIGHTLY
coyness	NICETY	—complexioned person	WOOSEL(L)
cozened	POUPT	—spot on horse's face	CLOUD
crabbed	CURST	darken	COLLY
crack	WHIP	darkened	NIGHTED
cradle	LULLABY	darling	SWEETING
craft	CAUTEL	dart in	ENDART
craftiness	FOXSHIP	dash	PASH
crafty	BRAID(E)	dastardly creature	MEACOCK
cram	FRANK	daubed with blood	BLOOD-BOLTERED
crazy	WOOD	daubing	DAWBRY
creative	FORGETIVE	Dauphin	DOLPHIN
crewel	INKLE	day for settling disputes	LOVE-DAY
crime	MALEFACTION	daze	ASTONISH, DARE
critic	CARREN	dead	
crone	TROT	—body	GHOST
crooked	CAM, KAM(ME)	—dog	DITCH-DOG
crowd	VARLETRY	deaden	PROROGUE
crowfoot	CROW-FLOWER	deal with a pimp	BROKE
crown	PALE	dealing	MERCHANDISE
crude	CRUDY	dear	CHARITABLE

—to the heart	HEART-DEAR	edge	DISEDGE
dearest	LIEFEST	horse	UNCOLT
death	DEFUNCTION, FUNERAL	life	UNLIVE
	LETHEE	possession	DISPROPERTY
decay	BRUSH	state or dignity	UNSTATE
deceitful	BRAIDE, DECEPTIOUS	wits	UNWIT
	PROPER-FALSE	deprived of orb	DISORBED
deceive	BLEAR, MISUSE	deputation	ATTORNEY
decency	GOVERNMENT	deranged	BRAIN-SICKLY
decide	MAKE UP, PASS	description	ADDITION, DEFINEMENT
—to go to a place	RESOLVE ON	design	INTENDMENT, PRETENCE
decipher	CIPHER, CYPHER		SKILL
decisive	EFFECTUAL	desire	AFFECTION, BOSOM
defend by bars	SPERR(E)	—strongly	EARN
declare	DISCUSS	despatch	EXPEDIENCE
decorations	FURNITURE	destination	LIST
deed	ISSUE	destitute of kindness	KINDLESS
deer	VENISON	destroy	CONFOUND, LANDDAMNE
—out of condition	RASCAL		QUELL, RUINATE, SPOIL
defame	INFAMONISE		STROY, UNLACE
defect	DECIPHER	destruction	DEFEAT
defence	PROPUGNATION	detachment	DISTRACTION
defend	ENGUARD	detail	SEVERAL
—from the weather	WEATHER-FEND	—item by item	PARCEL
defer	REJOURN	determine	DETERMINATE
defile	ENSEAM, FILE, RAY	determined	FAST
deft	FEAT	—person	RESOLUBLE
deftest	EFTEST	detractor	SUBTRACTOR
degenerate	DEROGATE, RECOIL	detrition	BRUSH
degraded	DEROGATE	device	IMPRESS, PLATFORM
degrees about court	MESSES		PRETENCE
deify	GOD	devil	GOODYEAR, SETEBOS
deign	DAINE	devolve	SUCCEED
delay	FOR(E)SLOW, FORSLOE	devotion	DEVOTEMENT
	INDURANCE	devouring	MOUSING
delegation	SUBSTITUTION	dexterously	FEATLY
delicacy	CATE	diadem	CIRCUIT
delicate	INCONIE, INCONY	dice game	NOVUM, TRAY-TRIP
	KONY	didapper	DIVE-DAPPER
delightful	DELIGHTED	die	CEASE, GO OFF
delineated	STEELD	difficulty	STRAIN
deliver back	RELIVER	dignified	CROWNED
demeaned	BORE	dilate	DELATE
demolish	RUINATE	dilatory	PROLIXIOUS
demure	PRENZIE	dim-sighted	THICK-SIGHTED
den	ANTRE	diminutive figure	AGLET BABIE
dentist	TOOTH-DRAWER		AGLET BABY
departure	DEPART	din	UTIS
depending on negotiation	LITIGIOUS	direct	REFLEX
depict	IMPAINT	—one's course	INTEND
depravity	FOLLY	direction	
depress	ABATE	—by mute signs	ACTION
deprive	UNPROVIDE	—of the eye	BEND
—of		dirty	RAY
all chance	LURCH	—drab	PUSSEL
beauty	UNFAIR	—woman	MALKIN, MAWKIN

disarmed of his senses	UNQUALITIED	diurnal	JOURNAL
disavow	DISVOUCH	divert	SWITS
disburse	DISPURSE	divided	DIVIDABLE
discandying	DISCANDERING	dividing	MEER'ED
discoloured by smoke	RE(E)CHIE, REECHY	divinitary agitation	MOTION
discharge		division of atmosphere	REGION
—as if with rending	RIVE	do	
—from		—battle	DARRAIGN(E), DARRAIN(E)
a sponge	DISPUNGE		DARRAYN, DERAIGN
nose	SALT-RHEUM	—homage	VAIL
disclosure	OVERTURE	—it	DICH
discontent	DISEASE	—up	DUP
discourse	ENTREATMENT, PROPOSE	—without	MISS
	REASON	doctor	BODY-CURER
discourteousness	KILL-COURTESY	dog	LYM, SHOUGH
discover	SMOKE		SHOWGHE, TYKE
discovered by fire-light	UMBERED	—rose	CANKER
discovery	DENOTEMENT	doing	OCCASION
discuss	EXPOSTULATE, QUESTION	domestic office	STRACHY
discussion	QUESTION	domestics	MEINIE, MEIN(E)Y
discussed too much	OVERHANDLED	dominion	EMPERY
disdain	COY	done	SPED
disdainful	DISDAINED	—for	POUPT
	ORGILLOUS, ORGULOUS	dotard	DOTANT
disfigure	DEFEAT	doubt	STRAIN
disfigurement	DEFEATURE	down in a feather	DOWL(E)
disgrace	REPROOF	down(y)	DOWLNE(Y)
disguise	DAUB, IMMASK	dragged by the head	HEAD-LUGGED
disguised	SELF-COVERED	draught of merriment	ROUSE
dishearten	UNHEART	draw	
dishonest	LOZEL(L)	—advantage	AVAIL
—practice	INDIRECTION	—in	INSHELL
dismal	TRISTFUL	—out	EXHALE, TOAZE
dismiss	CAST, DAFF	drawn	
dismissal	AVAUNT	—by doves	DOVE-DRAWN
dismissed from the		—in a just cause	RIGHT-DRAWN
world in peace	PEACE-PARTED	—out of bogs	FEN-SUCKED
disorder	DEFUSE, GARBOIL	dread	GASTNESS(E)
disordered	BETUMBLED	—of evil to come	MISDREAD
disparage	DISVALUE	dreadful	DE(A)RN
dispel	RESOLVE	—event	STRATAGEM
dispersal	SEGREGATION	dreamy fellow	JOHN-A-DREAMS
dispirited	PALE-HEARTED	dregs of the people	LEGGE
display to view	IMBARE	dress	TRICKING
dispose	SORT	—of	
disposed	PREGNANT	knights on horseback	BASE
disposition	AFFECTION, INTENDMENT	new-born child	SWATH
disregard	OMIT	dressed	SUITED
dissembling	BRAIDE	drift	HULL, RACK
disseminate	SCALE	drinking	
dissolution	CRACK	—between meals	BY-DRINKING
dissolve	RESOLVE	—cry	RIVO
—from candy	DISCANDIE, DISCANDY	—vessel	STO(O)PE
distempered	ILL-TEMPERED	drive	RACK
distinction	DISTINGUISHMENT	—away	OVERBLOW
distinguishable	DIVIDANT	from habitation	DISHABIT

—by fits	FIT
—mad	MAD
—out of roost	UNROOST
droop	LOB
drown the voice of	OUTVOICE
drub with bloodshed	DRYBEAT
drudge	DRUG
drunk	FAP, PAID
drunken fellow	COYSTRIL
dry up	ENSEAR
due	FITMENT
—performance	PROPERTY
dull	BARREN, BLUNT-WITTED
	DISEDGE, FAT
	ILLUSTRIOUS, MULL
dung	SIEGE
dutiful	OFFICIOUS
dwarfish person	AGATE
dwell	REMAIN
dying young	TENDER-DYING
eager	AYGRE, PRONE, WATERY
—to rival	EMULATE
eagerness of desire	INTENTION
earnest	DEAR
earnestly	WISTLY
easily	LIGHTLY
easy work	BEDWORK
eat one's words	EAT THE LEEK
echo	CHIDE, REPLICATION
	RESPEAK, REWORD
edict	PROCESS
efface	DISLIMN
effeminate	MEACOCK
—person	CARPET-MONGER
effusion	EFFUSE
eggs	PULLET-SPERM
eke out	ECH(E), EECH, ICH
elicit	TOAZE
emanate	VANISH
emasculated	NICKED
embark	INSHIP
embassy	EMBASSADE
embed in sand or ooze	DOCK
emblem	IMPRESS(E)
embrace	CHAIN, EMBRASURE
	INCLIP
emergence from egg	DISCLOSE
emotion	GIRD
empiricutic	EMPIRICKQUTIQUE
employ	EXECUTE
employment of exercise	EXECUTION
empty	CAST
enactment	ENACT
encamp	SET DOWN
encamped	FIELDED
encircle	ENWHEEL, PALE

enclose	EMBOSS, EMBOUND
	RIB, WOMB
—as in hearse	INHEARSE, INHERCE
enclosing wall	EMURE
encounter	CLOSE, COPE
encouragement	AIM
encroach	JET
end	LOOSE, SPOIL, UTMOST
—and purpose of	
coming	PROFESSION
—of all	EXIGENT
endanger	DANGER
endearing	CHARITABLE
endless	FINELESS
endow with widow's rights	WIDOW
endowed with	FULL-FRAUGHT
—grace	GRACED
—parts	PARTED
endowments	BELONGINGS
endue	DUE
endurable	PORTABLE
endure	ABROOKE, PERDURE
enduring	UNDERGOING
enema syringe	CLYSTER-PIPE
enemy of mankind	PREGNANT ENEMY
enfold	INCLIP
engage in fight	MEDDLE
engineer	ENGENER
engrave(d)	INSCULP(T)
engraving	SCULPTURE
enigma	EGMA
enjoy carnally	TASTE
enjoyment	SUFFIGANCE
enormously wicked	HIGH-VICED
enough	BASTA
enrich	RICH
enriched	MADE
enseam	INSEEM
enshelled	ENSHIELD
entangle	ENROOT
—hair	ELF
enter into articles	ARTICULATE
entered upon manhood	MAN-ENTERED
enterprise	DESIGNMENT
	EXPEDIENCE
entertainment	ENTERTAIN
entice(ment)	TICE
entire	MEERED
entrails	CHAUDRON
entrance	INDUCTION
entreaty	BESEECH, TREATY
entry on probation	APPROBATION
epithet(on)	APATHATON
equal	COMPEER, EGAL
—rank	RIVALITY
equality	RIVALITY

equipment	FURNITURE, TIRE
equipped	FULL-FRAUGHT
erect	STRAIGHT-PIGHT
ergo	ARGAL
escort	TEND
essential detail	PROPERTY
establish	APPROVE, STABLISH
estimated amount or value	RATE
estimation	RATE
evade by trick or lie	FUB OFF
evening just past	OVERNIGHT
evenness of temper	GOVERNMENT
evens	MEET
event	LOOSE, SPEED
—foretold	OMEN
events	OCCASION
everlasting	PERDURABLE
everyday	MODERN
evidence	ARGUMENT, AVOUCH
	INSTANCE
evident	PREGNANT
evil	SHREWD
—usage or behaviour	MISUSE
exact	COMMAND
exactly	JUMP
exaggerate	RACK
exale	VANISH
exalted	HAUGHT, HAU(L)T
examine	QUOTE
—on oath	DEPOSE
example for imitation	SAMPLE
exceed in	
—addiction to	
mistresses	OUT-PARAMOUR
—beauty	OUTBRAG
—boldness	OUTBRAVE
—clamour	OUTVOICE
—cunning	OUTCRAFTY
—estimation	OUTPRIZE
—poisonousness	OUTVENOM
—splendour	OUTBRAG, OUTBRAVE
—value	OUTWORTH
—villainy	OUTVILLAIN
exceedingly	VENGEANCE
excel	OUTPEER
excellence	WORTHY
excelling	PASSED
except	ABATE
excess	VANTAGE
excessively	OUT OF ALL CESSE
exchange	COUNTERCHANGE
excite	ACCITE, SOLICIT, TARRE
execute	OVERSEE
executioner	EXECUTOR
exercise	
—of power	FACULTY

—office over	O'REOFFICE
—one's craft	CRAFT
exhausted	EMBOWELLED
exhibited in articles	ARTICULATED
exhilaration preceding	
death	LIGHTNING
exhortation	EXERCISE
existent	ESSENTIAL
expectation	EXPECT, SUPPOSE
expediency	COMMODITY
expeditious	EXPEDIENT
expend	CONFOUND
expensive	CHARGEFUL
experience	ASSAY
expired	EXPIATE
explain	UNBOLT
exploit	TOUCH
express	
—in writing	PRINT
—purpose	NONCE
expression	EXPRESSURE
—of contempt	COBBY
exquisite	PICk
exterminate	EXTERMINE, EXTIRP
	KILL-UP
external appearance	OUTWALL, OUTWARD
extinguished	EXTICTED
extracted	EXTRAUGHT
extractor of teeth	TOOTH-DRAWER
extravagant	DIFFUSED, FANATICAL
extremely	VENGEANCE
extremity	UTTERANCE
eye	
—disease	PIN AND WEB
	WEB AND PIN
—lids	WINDOWS
face	PROPOSE
—down	OUTLOOK
—in profile	HALF-CHEEK
—out with scorn	OUTSCORN
facinorous (wicked)	FACINERIOUS
fade	VADE
fail to check	UNCHECK
faint	SWELT
fair	PROPER FALSE
fairy	OUPH(E)
—ring	ORB
faith	FAY
faithful	HOLY
falcon	TASSEL-GENTLE
falconer	ASTRINGER
fall	
—headlong	PRECIPITATE
—short of	SHORT
falling	CADENT
fallow deer, second year	PRICKET

false			—infant	CHILD
—friend	MOUTH-FRIEND		—messenger	WOMAN-POST
—hood	DAUBERY, DAWBRY		—offender	OFFENDRESS
—in religion	IRRELIGIOUS		feminine	EFFEMINATE
—pretence	DAWBRY		fencer	SCRIMER, SCRIMURE
—step	MISTREADING		fencing	
falsify	COG		—term	HAY
falsifying	FALSING		—thrust	PASSADO, STUCK
familiarity	INWARDNESS		ferry	TRANECT
fanciful head-dress	TIRE-VALIANT		fervent	PRONE
fancy	LOVE, TOY		festivity	CARPET CONSIDERATION
fanfare	SENNET		fetched from a depth	DEEP-FET
fang	PHANG		few	PAUCAS
fantastic	FANTASTICO		—words	FEWNESS
—person	PHANTASIM(E)		fickle person	CHANGING-PIECE
far from observing	WIDE OF		fickleness	CHANGE
far-fetched	EXQUISITE		fiend	OBIDICUT
farcin/ farcy	FASHIONS		fierce	WALL-EYED, WOOD
fashion	FEAT		fig	FICO, FIGO, FOOTRA, FOUTRA
fasten	LATCH		fight	STRIKE
—by rein	REIN		—against	REPUGN
—talons on	TIRE		fighting person	SQUARER
fastening	TASSEL		figure and rank	SORT AND SUIT
fastidious	CHARY		fill with	
fat			—horror	ABHOR
—bellied	GOR-BELLIED		—lies	BELIE
—of ox or cow	TALLOW KEECH		filthy	SCALD
father	MALE		final throw at bowls	UPCAST
fatigued	WAPPEND		fine	INCONIE, INCONY, KONY
fatten	ENGROSS, FRANK		—collector	CHEATER
faucet-seller	FOSSET-SELLER		—fellow	BAWCOCK
favour done	LOVE		—filament	SLEAVE
favoured	GRACED		—velvet	THREE-PILE
favouring	SECOND		finger	
favours	ENTREATMENT		—as on a virginal	VIRGINAL
fawn on	SPANIEL		—hole	VENTIGE
fawned on	PANELLED, SMOOTHED		—nails	TEN COMMANDMENTS
feast together	CONVIVE		finical	NEAT
feather	DOWLE		—delicacy	CURIOSITY
feature	LEER, TOUCHE		fire for trying or proving	TRIAL-FIRE
features	FAVOUR		firm in belief	THOUGHTEN
fed to repletion with			firmly	FASTLY
empty promises	PROMISE-CRAMMED		firmness	FIXTURE
feeble old man	PANTALOON		first	
feed	REPAST		—act of military	
—greedily	TIRE		service	FLESHMENT
—one's thoughts or desires	TIRE		—in procession	WHIFFLER
feel tenderness for	TENDER		—of women	PRINCIPALITY
feign	TAKE UPON ONESELF		—part	VAUNT
feigned	SUPPOSED		fish on land	LAND-FISH
fellow	COMPANION, COMPETITOR		fist	NEAF(F)E
	RIVAL, SEMBLABLE		fit	FADGE, RAPTURE
felt	APPROVED		—of lunacy	LUNE
female			—to be shaved	RAZORABLE
—child	MAID-CHILD		fits of bad temper	LINES
—fox	FIXEN		fitting	LIABLE

five-spotted	CINQUE-SPOTTED	—shooting point-blank	FOREHAND
fix firmly	CONFIX	forbear compliance	STAND OFF
fixed	PIGHT, STEELED	force	
flake	FLAW	—back against the current	RESTEM
flap wings impatiently	BATE	—from	OUTFACE
flash	FLAKE	forefront	VAWARD
flat		forehead	FRONTIER
—buttock	QUATCH-BUTTOCK	foreign	STRANGE
—pancake	FLAPJACK	foremost	FORMER
flatter	MAKE FAIR WEATHER, WORD	forenamed	PRENOMINATE
fleece	FETCH OFF	forerunner	PRECURRER
flesh-eating	CARNAL	forfend	SHIELD
fleshing	FLESHMENT	form	
flew	FLEWED	—of particulars	SCEDULE
flexible twig	SWITS	—the freight of a vessel	FRAUGHT
flighty person	MINUTE-JACK	formed	FEATED
float	HULL	—into	
flock bed	QUILT	ridges	ENRIDGED
flood	RAGE	stars	STEELED
florid	TAFFETA(S), TAFFETY	formulate	PROPOSE
flourish	SWINDGE	forsaken	
—on a trumpet	TUCKET	—by mistress	LASS-LORN
flout	LOUT	—person	FORLORN
flow	RECOURSE	fortune	HAVING
flowed	FLOWN	foul	REEKY
fluke	UPCAST	found	STAY
flushed	ROSED	four inches wide	FOUR-INCHED
flutter	BEAT	fowl	BIDDY
—like a hawk	BATE	fragment	FLAW, QUANTITY
fly		frame of mind	TEMPERALITIE
—off	BLENCH	frantic	WOOD
—over	OREPEARCH	free	LARGE
—up and perch on	OREPEARCH	—from domestic cares	UNHOUSED
flying cloud	RACK	—school	CHARGE-HOUSE
foam on water	YEAST	freedom	LET-ALONE
fodder	STOVER	French disease	GOOD-JER
fold	PLEACH		GOODYEAR
folding of tops of boots	RUFF	frenzy	LUNES
follow like a spaniel	SPANIEL	frequent	OLD
followed as by spaniel	PANELLED	frequenter of theatre pit	GROUNDLING
follower	SEQUENT	freshness	YOUTH
food	REPASTURE	friend	LOVER
fool	ASINICO, CHIPOCHIA	friendliness	FRIENDING
	COLT, GECK, LACK-BRAIN	fright	TIRRIT
	PIED NINNY, SNIPE	frighten	DARE, GALLOW, GAST
fool's word	IMPETICOS	frightened at oneself	SELF-AFFRIGHTED
foolhardy	DARING-HARDY	fringed with a beard	VALANCED
foolish person	BAUBLE	frolicsome person	GAMESTER
foolishly	SHALLOWLY	from	ON
footing	FEET	—time to time	STILL AND END
footpad	FOOT-LAND-RAKER, STRIKER	front	FOREWARD, VAWARD
fop	BARBER-MONGER	fruitful	CONCEPTIOUS
foppish	FANGLED	fruiting	CHILDING
—megalomaniac	MONARCHO	fuddled	FAP
for		fulfil in substitution	STEED UP
—any sake	OF ALL LOVES	fulfilment	ENACTURE

full	
—of	
daring	DAREFUL
faults or crimes	FAULTFUL
honest zeal	TRUE-DEVOTED
obstructions	BAR(RE)FUL
small openings	LOOPED
—speed	RANDON
—to the brim	TOPFULL
—with acorns	FULL-ACORNED
fully	BY WEIGHT, IN WEIGHT
	WITH WEIGHT
—completed	EXPIATE
fully-charged	FULL-FRAUGHT
fumitory	FEMETARY, FEMITER
	FENITAR, FUMITER
furious	BRAINISH, WOOD
furnish	STUFF
—supper for	SUP
furniture	TIRE
gain	
—advantage over	RECOVER (THE WIND)
—money	COIN
gallant	CHAMBERER
gallantry	GAME
gallants	GALLANTRY
gallery of theatre	SCAFFOL(D)AGE
galligaskins	GASKINS
gallows	GALLOWSES
gallows-bird	HEMP-SEED
game	
—killed in hunt	HUNT
—like bagatelle	TROLL-MY-DAME
	TROU-MADAME
—running figure	
of eight	QUAINT-MAZES
—with dice	TRAY-TRIP
gamester	CHEATER
gaming	DIE
gaoler	ADAM
gap in fence	MUSET, MUSIT
gape with astonishment	YAWN
gash	SCOTCH
gay fellow	CAVALERO
gelded	UNPAVED
genuflection	KNEE
get married	GO INTO THE WORLD
ghostly	SPRIGHTLY
gibberish	LINSEY-WOOLSEY
gibe	GLEEK, GLIKE
gift of no value	NOTHING-GIFT
gild	ENGILD
gillyflower	GILLYVOR
gimmal	GIMMOR
gimmalled	JYMOLD
ginger rootstock	RACE

gipsy	TURLEYGOOD, TURLUPIN
give	BETEEM(E)
—a share of	PARTAKE
—away	LEAVE
—freedom to	ENFREEDOM
—new life to	REQUICKEN
—place	BACCARE, BACKARE
—up by signing	SUBSCRIBE
given due consideration	WELL-RESPECTED
giving	
—attention	ATTENT
—no help	HELPLESS
—offence	OFFENCE-FUL
glade	LAUND
glance	ELIAD, ILLIAD, OEILIAD
glaring	WALL-EYED
glittering	CLINQUANT
glorying	MAGNIFICENT
glutted with prey	RAVINED
go	PATH
—hang	SNECK UP, SNICK UP
—on	CONDUCE
—to the deuce	GO WHISTLE
—between	RING-CARRIER
in romantic affairs	LOVE-BROKER
goblin	OUPH
God's	
—foot	'SFOOT
—pity	OD'S-PITIKINS
gold-thread made in Venice	VENICE GOLD
golden	
—money	GILD
—russet	LEATHER-COAT
—tresses	TALLENT
gone	
—by	BY-PAST
—equal distance with	FILED
good	
—manners	GENTRY
—sense	MATTER
gorged	RAVIN'D
gorgeously variegated	PROUD-PIED
gorging	MOUSING
gorse	GOSSE
grace	DUE, FAVOUR
graduation on a dial	PRICK
grant	BETEEM(E)
grasping	LARGE-HANDED
grassy place	LAUND
gratification	SUPPLIANCE
gratify with a sixpence	TESTERN
gratifying	GRATULATE
gratuity	GRATILLITY
grave	CIVIL
—digger	GRAVE-MAKER
—import	STATE

grease	ENLARD, SEAM(E)	hat fringed with thrums	THRUMMED-HAT
greasy	RE(E)CHIE, REECHY	hatch	DISCLOSE
great		hated as hell	HELL-HATED
—event	STRATAGEM	haughty	HAUGHT, HAU(L)T
—expanse	MAIN		SURLY
—gun	CHAMBER	haul out	EXHALE
greet (again)	REGREET	haunt	SPRIGHT
greeting	COMMEND	have	
greetings	REGREET	—a holiday	PLAY
grieve	CONDOLE, TAKE THOUGHT	—engagement	BE PROMISED
grievous	DEAR(E), DERE	—done	BE THROUGH
grimace	MOE	—ill-will towards	BEAR HARD
grip	FANG, VICE	—in the womb	ENWOMB
gross	SALT-BUTTER	—value	WEIGH
grossly	GREASILY	having	
—covered	MABLED, MOBLED	—a	
grotesque		child	CHILDED
—endearment	PRINCOX	lover	LOVERED
—pageant	ANTIC	—abilities	PARTED
grow cold	QUENCH	—chaps of a hound	FLEWED
guarantee legal		—curly hair	CURLED-PATE
possession	VOUCH	—died at a natural time	TIMELY-PARTED
guard	ENGUARD, FORTRESS	—dislocated shoulder	SHOULDER-SHOTTEN
guess	AIM	—ejected spawn	SHOTTEN
guilt	FACT	—fewer customers	CUSTOM-SHRUNK
guilty	GUILTY-LIKE	—fiery eyes	FIRE-EYED
guinea(-hen)	GYNN(E)Y	—literary knowledge	LITERATURED
gull	ZANY	—mind of	
gun (30lb)	DEMI-CANNON	a puppy	PUPPY-HEADED
habit of frequenting	HAUNT	mixed contents	MOTLEY-MINDED
hale	EXHALE	—nailed soles	CLOUTED
half		—performed wonders	WOND(E)RED
—gallon drinking-pot	POTTLE-POT	—power to do many things	MULTIPOTENT
—wolf	DEMI-WOLF	—protuberances	WHELKED
halloo	SO-HO	—right to	CAPABLE
hamstring	HOX	—skin eruptions	TETTEROUS
hand	PICKER	hawk-keeper	ASTRINGER
handkerchief	HANDKERCHER	hawklike	HAWKING
handsome	GOOD-FACED	hazard	JUMP
handsome and deceitful	PROPER-FALSE	he-ass	ASSINEGO
hanging		head	COCKSCOMB, MAZ(Z)ARD
—in rags	TOTT'RING		NOLE, NOWL, PASH
—like fetters	DOWN-GYVED	—dress shaped like	
hangman's noose	HEMPEN CAUDLE	soup-dish	PORRENGER
happen	PROCEED		PORRINGER
—to	BEFORTUNE	heal	RECURE
happening once a minute	MINUTELY	healthy	LUSTICK, LUSTIQUE
hard-hearted	FLINT-HEART(ED)		WHOLESOME
harden by cold	BAKE	heap up	UPHOORD
hardship	DISGRACE	hear over again	OVERHEAR
hare	BAUD	hearken	TEND
harlot	HIREN	heart	BOWER
harm	VENGEANCE	—in medical astrology	TAURUS
harsh	AYGRE, EAGER	heartily	AGOOD
haste	EXPEDIENCE, POST	heart's desire	BOSOM
hasty	FESTINATE	hearty eater	TRENCHER-MAN

heaving	HEFT
heavy galley	GALLEASS
Hecate	HECAT
hedged in with poles	POLE-CLIPT
height	BROW
—of mockery	ARCH-MOCK
heir	
—apparent	APPARENT
—to much wealth	RICH-LEFT
held	HILD
hell	TARTAR
helm	STERN
helpful	SECOND
hemlock	INSANE ROOT
henbane	HEBENON, HEBONA
	INSANE ROOT
hen-pecked	WOMAN-TIRED
hesitate	MAMMER
hiccough	WAXEN, YEXEN
hide	ENCAVE, HOODWINK
high	
—crowned	COPATAINE
—spirits	SPLEEN
highly accomplished	ABSOLUTE
hill where grain is	
winnowed by the wind	SHEALING-HILL
	SHEELING-HILL
	SHIELING-HILL
	SHILLING-HILL
hinged	JYMOLD
hiss	HIZZ
hist	PEACE
hit	PAY
—in fencing	VENEWE, VENEY
ho!	WHOOP
hoard	UPHOORD
hold up as example	PARAGON
holiday	PLAYING
hollow	COVERED, WOMBY
holy-water vessel	STO(O)PE
homely	FOUL
homicidal (error)	HON(E)Y-SUCKLE
homicide (error)	HON(E)Y-SEED
honest fellow	TRUEPENNY
hope	ESPERANCE
honorary ornaments	CEREMONIES
hook fastening clothes	POINT
horn-call to assemble	
hounds	RECHATE, RECHEAT
horned	FORKED
horoscope	FIGURE
horse	CUT
horse's	
—canine tooth	TUSH
—disease	FIVES
horseback journey	RODE

hot	
—and passing like	
a summer	SUMMER-SEEMING
—headed	BRAINISH
	WASPISH-HEADED
—spiced	
gingerbread	PEPPER-GINGERBREAD
hour-point on a clock	PRICK
house made gloomy	
by discontent	DARK HOUSE
how does it happen that?	HOW CHANCE
howl at	BEHOWL
hubbub	WHOOBUB
human	
—creature	CIVIL
—feet	PETTITOES
humbled	PLUME-PLUCKT
humid	HUMOROUS
humour	COMPLEXION
humorous	CAPRICIOUS
hunchback	CROOKBACK
hungry	HUNGERLY, SHARP
hungrily	HUNGERLY
hurried	FESTINATE
hurry away with whizzing	
sound	WHIR(R)
hurtful	SHREWD
husk	SHALE, SHEAL, SHEEL
	SHIEL, SHILL
husky	CORKY
hyena	HYEN
hypocrisy	COUNTENANCE
I	CHE
—tell fortunes	DUCDAME
idle chatter	BIBBLE-BABBLE
ignoble	UNNOBLE
ignominy	IGNOMY
ignorant	UNCONFIRMED
ill	
—conditioned	SHREWD
—mixed	ILL-TEMPERED
—natured	SHREWD
—regulated	INCORRECT
illumine	OVERSHINE
image	MODULE, SHRINE
imaginary	AIR-DRAWN
imagination	AFFECTION
imaginative	FORGETIVE
imagine	PROPOSE
—expectantly	WEEN
imbued with properties	PROPERTIED
immature	PUPPY-HEADED
—peascod	SQUASH
immoderately	OUT OF ALL CESSE
immodest woman	TOMBOY
immortal	EVER-LIVING

immure	EMURE
impact	POISE
impart	PARTAKE
impatient of question	UNQUESTIONABLE
impeach	APPEACH
impede	RUB
impending evil	IMMINENCE
importunacy	IMPORTANCE
importunate	IMPORTANT
importunity	IMPORTANCE
imposition	DAUBERY, DAWBRY
impossible to undo	UNRECALLING
imprecation	GOODYEAR
impregnated with	
bitumen	BITUMED
impresa	IMPRESS(E)
impression	CHARACTERY, CICATRICE
	(IM)PRESSURE
imprint	SET
imprisonment	PRISONMENT
improve	PROFIT
imprudent fellow	JACK SAUCE
impulse	SPLEEN
in	
—a	
body	IN SORT, IN THE QUILL
derogatory manner	DEROGATELY
moment	UPON A THOUGHT
	WITH A THOUGHT
—any case	IN ANY HAND
—concert	IN THE QUILL
—custody	FORTHCOMING
—consequence of that	THEREUPON
—full	
bloom	FLUSH
extent	HOME
—good earnest	A-GOOD
—like manner	SEMBLABLY
—most thought	CONSCIENCE
—my name	IN MY VOICE
—one's	
prime	PRIMY
right mind	WELL-ADVISED
—rapid motion	RACKING
—readiness	ALL POINTS
—state of just	
proportion	WEAL-BALANCED
—succession	SUCCESSANTLY
—the	
field of battle	FIELDED
least	IN THE SMALLEST
meantime	THE WHILE
night	ANIGHT
inattentive	UNRESPECTIVE
incapable of retaining	INTENIBLE
incite to fight	TARRE

inclination	CARE
incline	PROPEND
incomprehensible	UNCOMPREHENSIVE
inconsiderable	EASY, PELTING, WEAK
inconsiderate	UNWEIGHING
inconsistent medley	GALLIMAUFRY
inconstant	GIGLET, GIGLOT
incontinent	UNSTANCHED, WAPPEND
incorporate	INCORPSE
—one's own share	PIECE UP
increasing	CRESSIVE
incredible	INCREDULOUS
incurable	UNRECURING
incursion	RODE
indecent	UNACCUSTOMED
indebted	DEBTED
indeed	GOOD-DEED
indicate	DESIGN
indication	DENOTEMENT
indifferent to	WIDE OF
indignation	MOTIONS
indirect course	INDIRECTION
individual person	SEVERAL
individuality	PROPERTY, PROPRIETY
indivisible	INDIVIDABLE
	INTRENCHANT
induce to come	PROCURE
indulge	ALLOW
indulged in	EMBRACED
ineffective	UNPREGNANT
inevitable	UNSHUN'D, UNAVOIDED
inexorable	INEXECRABLE
inexperienced	PUNY, UNEXPERIENT
inexpressible	TERMLESS
infant	EYAS MUSKET
infection	ATTAINT
inference	COLLECTION
inferior	IMPAIR
infested by thieves	THIEVISH
infix strongly	CHARACTER
inflammable	COMBUSTIOUS
—as tinder	TINDER-LIKE
inflated	BOMBAST
—as with pride	HIGH-BLOWN
inflict pain on	SUFFER
inform	RECOMMEND, YIELD
—against	PEACH
ingoing	ENTER
inhabitant	CONFINER
initiated	WELL-ENTERED
initiating excitement	FLESHMENT
initiation	ELEMENT
injunction	IMPOSE
inquiry	ENQUIRE, INQUIRE
insanity	INFAMIE, INSANIE
inscrutable	INVIS'D

insensible	BLUNT, IRON-WITTED	invigoration by resting	REST
—to shame	SHAME-PROOF	invisible	SIGHTLESS
insert in a schedule	ENSCHEDULE	invite	INDITE
inshelled	COCKLED, ENSHIELD	inviting	COASTING
inside	INWARD	invoke	SWEAR
insidious	CAUTELOUS	involved	PLIGHTED
—purpose	CAUTEL	involving trust	TRUSTY
insignificant	PICKING, PUISNY	ironical endearment	PRINCOX
—person	QUAT, WATER-FLY	irregular	DIFFUSED
insincere	MOUTH-MADE	irresistible	OPPOSELESS
insincerity	MOUTH-HONOUR	irretentive	INTENIBLE
insinuate	SUGGEST	irritated	RAG'D, RAGDE
insist	CONSIST	is of no importance	SKILLS NOT
—upon	STRAIN	jack	
insisting	UNSISTING	—at bowls	MISTRESS
inspection	OVERVIEW	jack-in-office	JACK GUARDANT
instigator	PUTTER-ON	jade	NAG
instruct	STUDY	jagged	RAG'D, RAGDE
—in Gospel	GOSPEL	jaunt	JAUNCE, JAUNSE
instructed	WELL-ENTERED	jealous of higher authority	EMULOUS
insult	INSULTMENT	jerk	PECKE, SWITS
—by gesture	FIG	jest	GLEEK, GLIKE
intangible	UNFELT	jester	MOTLEY, PIED NINNY
intensive	AND TWENTY	jilt	HUSWIFE
intention	DESIGNMENT, HENT	jocular endearment	PRINCOX
	INTENDMENT, REGARD	jog-trot	RANKE
—of going	PURPOSE	join	INJOINT, SPLINTER
interchange	CONVERSE	—as partner	PARTNER
interest	MEANS	—together	INTERJOIN
interjection	CAESE, CEAS(E)	joined as with sinews	INSINEW
	HANDY-DANDY	joining again	REIOYNDURE
	SESE(Y), SESSA	joint	
—boisterous	HOO	—bargain	CO-MART
—imitating arrow sound	HEWGH	—in mechanism	GIMMOR
—of		jointed	JYMOLD
impatience	TILLY-FALLY	jolly	
	TILLY-VALLY	—cock	BAWCOCK
surprise	GEMINI, GEMINY	—companion	EPHESIAN
	GEMONY, JIMINY	journey	GEST
—to call a person	WHY	Jove	THUNDER-BEARER
interest	USANCE, USE		THUNDER-DARTER
interested	INTEREST		THUNDER-MASTER
interpret	SCAN	judge by evidence	TESTIMONY
intertwine	IMPLEACH	judgement	DIRECTION
interval	BETWEEN	juicy	MOIST
interwoven	ENTERTISSUED	just	JUMP, TRUE-DISPOSING
intimacy	INWARDNESS	justify	APPROVE
intimate friend	INWARD	keen	HAWKING, PARLOUS
intoxication	DISTEMPER	keenly	SHREWD
intricate	INTRINCE, INTRINSE	keep	
	INTRINSICATE	—a hawk from sleep	WATCH
introduction	INDEX	—busy with scruples	TASK
inured by practice	BREATHED	—from exertion	PROROGUE
inventive	FORGETIVE	—good watch or	
inventory	SCEDULE	order	KEEP GOOD QUARTER
invested with power of destiny	FATED	—head to wind	TRY

—in suspense	PEIZE
—off	EXPEL, OVERBLOW
keeping	
—back knowledge	IGNORANT
—off the sun	SUN-EXPELLING
kestrel	STALLION, STANYEL
kettle-drum	KETTLE
key on musical instrument	CHIP, JACK
kindness	LOVE
kindred	KINDLY
kite	PUTTOCK
—of infernal breed	HELL-KITE
knack	QUIRK
knave	COISTREL, COISTRIL
	COYSTREL, COYSTRIL
knavery	PATCHERY
kneel	KNEE
knight's stall	INSTALLMENT
know	WEET(E), WIS(T), WOT
—how to behave	UNDERSTAND
knowing	ACKNOWNE, WITTOL
knowledge	KNOW
known by heart	RECOLLECTED TERMS
knurled	GNARLED
lace tag	AGLET BABIE
ladykin	LAKIN
laid	
—by the wind	LODGED
—waste	BARE
lame	MAIN
lament	MEAN(E), MEIN, MENE
large	WIDE-STRETCHED
lark-song	TIRRA-LIRRA, TIRRA-LYRA
lascivious	CAPRICIOUS, SAUCY
lash	SWINDGE, SWITS
—made of wire	WIRE
last	LATTER
—night	TONIGHT
—purpose	CROWNET
—strait	EXIGENT
latrine	BENCH-HOLE
latter part	POSTERIOR
lattice-work on stomacher	WINDOW-BARNE
laugh	LOFFE
lawless	IRREGULOUS
lawn	LAUND
lay	
—bare	SCALE
—claim to	SPEAK TO
—man	TERRESTRIAL
—open	IMBARE
—under water	ENSTEEP
lazy fellow	BED PRESSER
league	COMPACT
leaky	UNSTANCHED
lean person	BARE-BONE

learned	AUTHENTIC, LITERATURED
leave	AVOID, LET, PART
—off	OMIT
lecherous	CODDING
lecture	EXERCISE
led in divisions	WING-LED
left	BESTOWED
legend	LEGION
legitimate	LOYAL
lending at interest	USANCE
lens of the eye	EYE-GLASS
leopard	LUBBAR
leprosy	MEAZEL, MESEL
let	
—go	OMIT
—me understand	TAKE ME WITH YOU
—slip	DELAY
letter	CAPON
levy	TAKE-UP
lewd	
—person	GAMESTER
—woman	CALLET, MALKIN
	MAWKIN
liable to schoolboy	
punishment	BREECHING
licentious	IRREGULOUS, LIBERAL
	LARGE, UNMASTERED
lick over	LATCH, LETCH
lie	COG
—to	TRY
life of pleasure	PRIMROSE PATH
	PRIMROSE WAY
life-blood	LETHEE
lift up	DUP, RELIEVE
light	
—giver	TORCHER
—on a beacon	CREDIT
like	SEMBLABLE
—a	
contented cuckold	WITTOLLY
surgeon	CHIRURGEONLY
vault	VAULTY
—the sky	SKYISH
liken	LIKE
limb by limb	LIMBMEAL
line of trees	LINE-GROVE
lineage	DESCENDING
liquor jug	BOMBARD
list	FILE, SCEDULE
—of actors and parts	SCRIPT
litigious	ACTION-TAKING
litter	KINDLE
little	PRETTY
—by little	BY SMALL AND SMALL
—gentleman	FRANKLIN
—heart	HEARTIKIN

—smile	SMILET
lively dance	UPSPRING
liver, brain and heart	PERFECTIONS
load	BALLAST
loading	FRAUTAGE
lodestone	MAGNESSTONE
lodge	HOST
lofty	HIGH-STOMACHED, SKYISH
loiter	FORESLOW
lonely	DEARN
long	LONGLY, SIDE
—continued	PERDURABLE
—delayed end	LAG-END
—distance arrow	FLIGHT
—for	EARN
longingly	WISTLY
look	
—demurely	DEMURE
—of one destined to hang	GALLOWS
looking upwards	HIGH-SIGHTED
loop in sword-belt	CARRIAGE
loose	
—and frivolous person	HOBBY-HORSE
—part of a coat	FORESKIRT
—vicious person	PAGAN
loosen	TOAZE
lose	LEESE
lost	LORE, LORN
lot	SORT
love	FANCY
—of	
oneself	SELF-CHARITY
youthful pleasures	COLT'S TOOTH
—sick	FANCY-SICK
	SICK-THOUGHTED
lovelock	LOCK
lover of malted liquor	MALT-WORM
loving	BELOVING, LOVELY
low-born	
—fellow	LOWNE
—prostitute	STALE
—servant	JACK SLAVE
—wretch	VASSAL
luck	ISSUE
lug out	EXHALE
lump of	
—fat	KEECH
—tallow	TALLOW-CATCH
lunacy	LUNES
lurking thief	MICHER
lustful	LUXURIOUS, RANK
lustreless	PALE-DEAD
lusty	LUSTICK, LUSTIQUE
lute-string of catgut	CATLING
mad	FOOLBEGGED, WOOD
—house	DARK-HOUSE

made	
—neat	FEATED
—of	
brands	PLANCHED
ropes	TACKLED
straw	SHEAVED
thread	THREADEN
wickerwork	TWIGGEN
—pensive	PENSIV'D
—up of	COMPACT
madness	ECSTASY
magpie	MAG(G)OT-PIE
maiden's funeral garland	CRANTS
maim	MAIN
maintain	ESCOT
maintenance	KEEPING
make	
—a	
fool of	BOB(B)
head	CAPITULATE
pattern	PATTERN
whore of	BEWHORE
—amorous advances	CARVE
—an agreement	CLAP HANDS
—away with	FETCH OFF
—believe	TAKE UPON ONESELF
—childless	UNCHILD
—clear	SCALE
—common cause	PARTAKE
—difficulties	MAKE IT STRANGE
—dishonest	
arrangement with	PACK CARDS WITH
—drunk	CUP
—faces	MOO
—fair	FLOURISH
—feat	FEAT
—grotesque	ANTIC
—happy	HAPPY
—haste	DESPATCH, DISPATCH
—heir	INHERIT
—hoary	HOAR
—known	DISCUSS
—lank	LANK
—lazy	SLUG
—much of	MAKE ON
—neat	FEAT
—pay dear	SAUCE
—plain	PLAIN
—progress	PROFIT, RID WAY
—rents in	WINDOW
—secret arrangement	PACK
—stable	STABLISH
—terms	DISPOSE
—to	
fail	SHORT
pass quickly	FLEET

—unlike	DISLIKEN	meddle	TEMPER
—up into total	PARCEL	medicinal virtue	FACULTY
maker of sport	GAMESTER	meditation	COMMENT
making		meet	COPE
—maps	MAPPERY	melancholy	ALLICHOLY, ALLYCHOLY
—no exception	EXCEPTLESS		SPLEEN, THOUGHT
male puppet	MOTION GENERATIVE	—strain	DUMP
malignant		memoranda	TABLES
—composition	HELL-BROTH	mercenary	COSTER-MONGER
—influence	TAKING	merchant	MARCATANT, MERCATANTE
Malvolio	BIDDY	mermaid	SEA-MAID
man		merry	
—killer	MAN-QUELLER	—and impetuous	HURTLING
—like	MANKIND	—festival	UTIS
—of the world	TERRESTRIAL	—meeting	ALE
—who busies himself		messenger	MISSIVE
with woman's affairs	COT-QUEAN	middle-age	MID-AGE
mandrake	MANDRAGORA	mien	MINE
mangle	MAMMOCK	mighty	MIGHTFUL
mangy	ROYNISH	mild	SARCENET, SARS(E)NET
manner	QUALITY	military pioneer	PIONER, PYONER
—of meeting	ENCOUNTER	milksop	COCKNEY, MEACOCK
many	MUCH	mind	MINE, NOTION
mark	CICATRICE	mine	MINERAL
marriage contract	CONTRACTION	—uncle	NUNCLE
marzipan	MARCHPANE	minute's time	MINUTE-WHILE
mask	CARACT, IMMASK	mirror	STONE
mast-head	HIGH-TOP	misanthrope	MISANTHROPOS
match	BESORT, MEET	miscellaneous gathering	GALLIMAUFRY
	PATTERN	mischief	MALICHO, MALLECHO
matchmaker	BROKER		VENGEANCE
mate	COMATE	mischievous	SHREWD
matted hair	ELFLOCKS	misdeed	MISTREADING
matter	CAUSE	misfortune	WRO(A)TH
—of		misgiving	GAINGIVING
conscience	REMORSE	mistake	MISTAKING
responsibility	OCCASION	mistaken	VICIOUS
matterful	MATERIAL	mistress	DOXY
mature	FLUSH	mitigation	REMORSE
may it		mix	CARD
—do	DICH	mixed	BLENT
—profit you	PROFACE	—badly	MISTEMPERED
meal of fish	FISH MEAL	mixture	COMPOSTURE
mean	CULLIONLY, FOXSHIP	moan	MEAN(E), MEIN, MENE
	ROYNISH, SCALL	model	MODULE
—fellow	COYSTRIL	moderation	MODESTY
meanest persons	LAG	modesty	PUDENCY
meaning	INTELLECT, INTENDMENT	moment	POIZE
meanly	COSTER-MONGER	moist	HUMOUROUS
—pretty	MODERN	moisten	BEWET, LATCH, MOIST
means	MEASURE	moment	POIZE
measure	CESS, HOOP, WHOOPING	momentum	SWAY
—½ gall.	STOUP	money	CHINKS, GILT
—of corn	MOY	moon's influence	
measured by sand	SANDY	on plants	PLANTAGE
mechanic	MECHANICAL	Moorish pike	MORRIS-PIKE

moral	L'ENVOY	necessary	NEEDY
more	MOE	negative side	NAYWARD
—execrable	INEXECRABLE	necklace	CARKANET
—fish than man	LAND-FISH	negligence	NEGLECTION
—quickly	RATHER	Negro	THICK-LIPS
—serious	SLOWER	neighbouring	SISTERING
—than enough	OLD	neither one thing	
morning	MATIN	nor another	ODD-EVEN
most		new-born lamb	EANLING
—beloved	ALDER-LIEFEST	never at rest	UNSISTING
—efficacious part	VIRTUE	newly	
—rascally	RASCALLIEST	—introduced	UPSTRING
—valuable part	HEART	—baptised child	CHRISOM-CHILD
motion of		nibble all over	OVEREAT
—contempt	FICO, FIGO	nightmare	CACOD(A)EMON, MARE
—horse	CAREIRES	nimble	QUIVER
motionless	STONE-STILL	—witted	VOLABLE
motto	IMPRESS(E)	nipping	SNEAPING
mould	MODEL	no alternative	NO REASON BUT
mournful elegy	DUMP	noise of clock pendulum	JAR
mouser	MOUSE-HUNT	noisy	BLUSTROUS, SWASHING
moustache	EXCREMENT	north	SEPTENTRION
movable rail	SWITS	—wind	AQUILON
move in zigzag course	INDENT	Norwegian	NORWEYAN
moving part of body	MOTIVE	not	
much		—adorned with holes	UNPINKT
—good may it do you	PROFACE	—artificial or counterfeit	UNCOYNED
—sought after	WELL-ADMIRED	—blown	UNBLOWED
muffled	MOBLED	—brought into action	UNEXECUTED
murderer	MAN-QUELLER	—bruised or crushed	UNBRUSED
murderous	CARNAL	—contradicted	UNCHECKED
murky	ROOKY	—controlled	UNSWAI'D
muscle	THEW	—dealt with	UNTRIDE
music	NOISE	—despised	UNCONTEMNED
musket	CALIVER	—dressed	UNREADY
muster-roll	MUSTER-FILE	—exercised	UNBREATHED
mutation	REVOLUTION	—having	
mutineer	MUTINE	a body	INCORPORAL
mutiny	MUTINE	bloomed	UNBLOWED
my lady	MADONNA	received sacrament	UNHOUSLED
name			UNHOUZZLED
—before	FORE-RECITED	—in	
—beforehand	PRENOMINATE	common use	UNTRACED
—of plant	CUCKOO-BUD	the secret	OUTWARD
nameless	TITLELESS	—marked off as paid	UNCROSSED
narrative	PROCESS	—noticed	UNTRIDE
native		—one's own	UNPROPER
—born	SELF-BORNE	—pinked	UNPINKT
—goodness	SELF-BOUNTY	—practised	UNBREATHED
—of Denmark	DANSKER	—produced by ordinary	
natural	UNCOYNED	generation	UNGENITURED
—spirit	SELF-METTLE	—quickened by lively	
nature of a child	CHILDNESS	sense	UNPREGNANT
navel	NAVE	—regulated	INCORRECT
neat(ly)	FEAT(LY)	—restrained in movement	FREE-FOOTED
necessarily	NEEDLY	—rustic	INLAND

—strongly timbered	UNTIMBERED
—swung	UNSWAI'D
—to be	
blunted	BATELESS
recalled	UNRECALLING
—ventured upon	UNTRIDE
—wielded	UNSWAI'D
—willed	UNWILLING
—yet born	UNBRED
notify	FRUTIFY
notion	PROJECT, SUPPOSAL
number of	
—fish together	SCUL(L), SCULLE
—individuals	POLL
nun	CLOISTRESS
nursing	NURSERY, SICK-SERVICE
oaf	OUPH(E)
oath	BY COCK AND PIE
—on the Bible	BOOK-OATH
obedient	BUXOM
object for flouting	FLOUTINGSTOCK
obliged	DEBTED
obliterate	DISLIMN
obscure	
—dungeon in prison	HELL
—word	AN HEIRES, BRAKE
obseqious	
—attendant	OBSERVANT
—bowing	FLEXURE
observed	COTED
observer	SPECULATION
obstinacy	OPINION
obstinate	HIGH-STOMACHED
	OBSTACLE
obtain on credit	TAKE UP
occupy oneself	TIRE
occurrences	CURRENTS
oeillade (glance)	ELIAD, ILLIAD
of	
—a jovial turn	GOOD-LIFE
—anticipation	FOREHAND
—good stock	WELL-DERIVED
—great importance	OF GREAT ARTICLE
—necessity	NO REMEDY
—no value	IMMOMENT
—partiality	PARTIAL
—the air	REGION
offence	MALEFACTION
offer	PROPOSITION
office	FACULTY
officer of	
—(bishop's) court	PARITOR
—the Exchequer	HEATER
officious	SUPERSERVICEABLE
—fellow	PLEASEMAN
oil of consecration	BALM

omission	OMITTANCE
omit	LET
on	
—account	LONG
—purpose	NONCE
—the spur of the moment	UPON THE GAD
—what grounds	WHEREUPON
one	
—administering	
correction	CORRECTIONER
—and the same	ONE SELF
—bound by the same vow	VOW-FELLOW
—deformed	STIGMATIC
—deserving hanging	CRACK-HEMP
	CRACK-ROPE
	CRACK-HALTER
—in charge of provisions	PANT(L)ER
—making progress	PROFICIENT
—on a quest	QUESTANT, QUESTER
	QUESTRIST
—only	ONE SELF
—partly a bawd	PARCEL-BAWD
—who	
affects wit	WIT-SNAPPER
breaks engagements	CRACK-TRYST
can keep secrets	COUNSEL-KEEPER
concerns himself	
with love	FANCY-MONGER
deserves gallows	GALLOWS
draws with	
confederate	COACH-FELLOW
entreats	IMPLORATOR
foments argument	BREED-BATE
hunts counter	HUNT-COUNTER
incurs punishment	FORFEITER
is	
—ill	SICKMAN
—suntanned	TANLING
rides in front	FORE-SPURRER
seeks for another	QUESTRIST
sells taps	FOSSET-SELLER
settles business of	PHEAZAR
takes on another's	
quarrel	UNDERTAKER
travels post	POSTER
with pasty face	TALLOW-FACE
one's own utterances	SELF-BREATH
open	DUP, RAZE
—mouthed	WIDE-CHAPPED
opening	PORTAGE
—up	OVERTURE
operating suddenly	RASH
opinion	DEEM
opportunity	HENT, VANTAGE
oppose	REPUGN
opposition	REPUGNANCY

oppress by bulk	OVERBULK	—fellow	HILDING
oppressive supervisor	SHEEP-BITER	pamper	ENGROSS
orange-seller	ORANGE-WIFE	pampered by lust	LUST-DIETED
ordain	FOR(E)SAY	pander	GREEK
ordaining	ORDINANT	pang	THROW(E)
ordinary experience	USE	paper of conditions	BOOK
orifice	ORIFEX	parallel	PATTERN
original of a copy	PRECEDENT	parasite	TRENCHER-FRIEND
ornament	FLOURISH, GARLAND		TRENCHER-KNIGHT
	GUARD	parcel	COMMODITY
—for the neck	RABATO	paroxysm	THROW(E)
—with puffs	BLISTER	parson	SOUL-CURER
ostentation	OSTENT	part	SQUARE
ostentatiously dressed	CURLED	—of an army, camp, etc	QUARTER
out of breath	OUTBREATH'D	partake	PERTAKE, UNDERGO
outdo	LURCH	particular	SEVERAL
outer garment of leather	PILCHER	—nature	PROPRIETY
outgrowth	EXCREMENT	—purpose	NONCE
outlying sentinel	PERDU(E)	parting	DEPART
outshine	OUTLUSTRE, OVERSHINE	partner	RIVAL
outside garb	CASE	pass	
outstare	ORE-STARE	—by	COTE
outward	WITHOUT-DOOR	—in succession	SUCCEED
outweigh completely	WEIGH TO THE BEAM	—over on knees	KNEE
outwork	FRONTIER	—time	ENTREAT
over		passionate	WASPISH-HEADED
—dainty	SUPERDAINTY	passive	PRONE
	TAFFETA(S), TAFFETY	patched	CLOUTED
—come	CONVINCE	patronise	EMPATRON
by jesting	OUTJEST	pattern	SPOTTE
—grown with wild		pawn	FINE
orchises	PIONED	pay	
—power	CONVINCE, THRONG	—for	ESCOT
—reached	OE'R-RAUGHT	—of an army	ENTERTAINMENT
	ORE-RAUGHT	—ready-money	PITCH AND PAY
	ORE-WROUGHT	—up	COME OFF
—ridden	SUR-REYN'D	peace	
—subtle	SUPERSUBT(I)LE	—maker	MAKE-PEACE
—take	COTE	—officer	FARBOROUGH
—value	OVERHOLD		THARBOROUGH
—worked	SUR-REINED, SUR-REYNED	peacock	PAIOCK(E), PAJOCK(E)
—worn	OVERSCHUTCH	pearl	UNION
—wrested	ORE-RESTED	peasant	CARLOT
own affairs	SELF-AFFAIRS	peculiar sorrow	FEE-GRIEF
ox	ROTHER(-BEAST)	pedant	PEDASCULE
pace	RANK	peep under	UNDERPEEP
pain	MEAN	peer	SQUINNY, TWEER, TWIRE
painful	PANGING	people	MEINIE, MEIN(E)Y
paint	IMPAINT	perceive	SURVEY
—face	GAUD, GAWD	perform	
painted in	TRICK	—by proxy	ATTORN
pair (eyes)	GEMINI, GEMINY	—sleight of hand	CONVEY
	GEMONY, JIMINY	performance of promise	DEED OF SAYING
pale-faced	PALE-VISAGED	peril	APPERIL
—like a sick girl	MAID-PALE	perjured person	PERJURE
paltry	BARE, PELTING	perjury	OATH-BREAKING

perky	PERT
petty	PELTING
persistent	PERSISTIVE
person with a tail	TAILOR
personal	
—identity	PROPERTY
—relation	PARTICULAR
personality	CHARACT
persuasion	INDUCEMENT
pert	
—boy	CRACK
—woman	FLIRT-GILL
pertaining to the dead	DEFUNCTIVE
perverse	PEEVISH
perversity	ADVERSITY
pestilence	MURREN, MURRION
petard	PETAR
petty	PUISNY
phrase	COMMA
—appropriated to	
pilgrims	WOOLWARD
—in combat	UTTERANCE
physician	MEDICINE
physiognomy	FISNOMIE
piano key	JACK
picked	RECOLLECTED TERMS
pickthank	PLEASEMAN
picture giving	
fantastic effect	PERSPECTIVE
piddling	PICKING
pie-crust on	
custard-pie	CUSTARD-COFFIN
piece	SPLINTER
—of	
cow-dung	SHARD
fluff	DOWL(E)
money	MOY
needlework	SPOTTE
pierced with grief	GRIEF-SHOT
pig-sty	FRANK
pilchard	PILCHER
pile-driver	THREE-MAN-BEETLE
pious	ZEALOUS
pip	PEEP(E)
pirate	WATER-THIEF
pish!	PUSH
pitch	PECKE, SET DOWN
pity	BOWEL, REMORSE
place	BIDING
—in	
order	ENRANK
the sky	ENSKY
—noted for brothels	PICKT-HATCH
—on lee side	BELEE
—where pastry is made	PASTRY
placed in a window	WINDOWED

plague	GOODYEAR
—spot	DEATH-TOKEN
—spots	THE LORD'S TOKENS
plan	SCEDULE
—of action	PLATFORM
planning	MAPPERY
plants in general	PLANTAGE
plausible	PLAUSIVE, PROBALL
play	
—part in a mask	JEST
—trick on	GLEEK, GLIKE
plebeian	PLEBEAN
pleasant	LUSTICK
please	FREET
pleasing	PLAUSIVE
pleasure	LUST
pledge	FINE
plenty	FUL(L)NESS
plot	PRACTISE
pluck	RASE, TO(A)ZE
plume	PRANK
pluming oneself	REPUTING
plump	PLUMPIE, PLUMPY
pocket	POAKE
point in tennis	CHASE
poison	BANE, MINERAL
poke	POAKE
Pole/Polish	POLACK
pole for carrying baskets	COWL-STAFF
polished	INLAND
politeness	COMPLEMENT
pollute	FILE
poltroon	POULTROONE
pomander	POUNCET
pooh	POWWAW, PUH
poor	SCALD, SINGLE
popular	WELL-GRACED
porcupine	PORPENTINE
portent	AUGUR
portholes	PORTAGE
portion	COMMODITY, SCANTLE
position	FIXTURE
—for being observed	PROSPECT
post-horse	POST
postpone	PROLONG, PROROGUE
	REJOURN
pot-thumping	BOLD-BEATING
potentate	POTENT
pound	PUN
pour	INFUSE
—out	BETEEM
power of overcoming	PREVAILMENT
powerful	MIGHTFUL
practice arrow	BUTT-SHAFT
practised	TRADED
praise	COMMEND

—excessively	SUPERPRAISE
prance	JAUNCE, JAUNSE
precedent	PRESIDENT
precipice	PRECEPIT
precipitate	STEEP(E)-DOWN(E)
	STEEP(E)-UP
precisely	BY THE SQUIRE
precondition	PREMISE, PREMISS
preface	INDEX
pregnant	GREAT-BELLIED
premature	TIMELESS
preparation	APPOINTMENT, INDUCTION
	PREPARE
prepare	ADDRESS
presage	ABODE
present with sixpence	TESTERN
preserve from decay	SEASON
press	
—for	STRAIN
—hard	THRONG
pressure	OPPRESSION
pretend	INTEND
pretty	INCONIE, INCONY
prevail over	CARRY
prevent	UNDO
previous practice	ELEMENT
prey to mournful	
sensations	PASSIONATE
price	ESTIMATE
prim	PRENZIE
primer	ABSEY BOOK
primogeniture	PRIMOGENIT
prince	HAMLET, POTENT
princely	PRENZIE
principal	ARCH, CAP
prison	CONFINE
private	REMOVED
—grief	FEE-GRIEF
—person	PRIVATE
—room	BY-ROOM
privilege	COMMODITY, PRISE
privy	AJAX, JAKES, DRAUGHT
prize	PRICE, PRISE, REPRISAL
problem	CONCLUSION
proceed	SWAY
proclaim	PROTEST
procrastination	INDURANCE
produced in heaven	HEAVEN-BRED
profit	COMMODITY
prognostication	PRECURSE
programme	SCEDULE
project	REFLEX
—beyond	JUTTY
prologue	INDEX
prolong	LINGER, RESPITE
prompt	PRIME

proof	ASSAY, INSTANCE
propensity	PROPENSION
propitious	WHOLESOME
proportion	QUANTITY
prosperous	WELL TO LIVE
prostitute	CUSTOMER, GUINEA-HEN
	LACED MUTTON, POLECAT
	QUAIL, RODE, STALE
	VENTURE
protect plant from cold	WINTER-GROUND
protected against	
floods by plaited	
osiers	TWILLED
protract	LINGER
proud	ORGILLOUS, ORGULOUS
—in the highest degree	TOP-PROUD
—spirited	HIGH-STOMACHED
prove	CITE
—by	
evidence	TESTIMONY
testing	TRY
provender	PROVAND, PROVEND
	PROVIANT
provocation	PROVOKEMENT
provoke	TARRE
proxy	SUBSTITUTE
	PREWYN, PROIN(E), PROYN(E)
	PRUINE, SWITS
public	GENERAL
pudding with many	
ingredients	HODGE-PUDDING
puff in scorn	BLURT
puffed	
—out	EXSUFFLICATE
—sleeve	TRUNK-SLEEVE
puffy	EMBOSSED
pull	TOZE
—by the ears	SOLE, SOWL
pulse	PULSIDGE
punctilious	PICK
puny	PUISNY
puppet	MOTION
—thrown at in Lent	JACK-A-LENT
purblind	BEESOME, BISSOM
purport	PURPOSE
purpose	DESIGNMENT, MIND
purposeless	SHAPELESS
put	
—an end to	PERIOD
—aside	DAFF, DOFF
—forward repeatedly	VIE
—in	
gaol	ENGAOL
pocket	IMPETICOS
shelter	ENSHELTER
splint	SPLINTER

the stocks	STOCK-PUNISHT	—at hand	AT AN INCH
—off	FUB OFF	—for tears	WEEPING-RIPE
by	DAFF	—to sink	SINKING-RIPE
with contempt	SLIGHT OFF	real	BODILY, ESSENTIAL
—on oath	DEPOSE		UNCOINED, UNCOYNED
—to death	TRANSPORT	rear	CATASTROPHE, HAUNCH
putting under embargo	EMBARQUEMENT	reason	SKILL
pygmy	ATOMY	reasonable	WHOLESOME
quadrangular space		reassemble	RE-ENFORCE
on hand	TABLE	rebel	MUTINE, REVOLT
qualify	ABLE	rebuke	SAUCE
quality	AFFECTION, ASSAY	rebuked	SHENT
qualm	CALM	recall of pursuers	RETREAT
quarreller	QUARREL	receiving ball	EMBALLING
quarrelsome	QUARRELOUS	recently made sad	NEW-SAD
—person	CHIDER, SQUARER	receptacle for	
quarrelsomeness	QUARREL	—meal	BOLTING-HATCH
question propounded	PROPOSITION	—tallow	TALLOW-CATCH
quibble	SNATCH	recipient	CAPTIOUS
quick!	YARE	reciprocation	COUNTERCHANGE
—minded	BAVIN-WITS	recital	RECOUNTMENT
—to understand	APPREHENSIVE	recited before	FORE-RECITED
quickest	RATHEREST	reck	WREAK(K)
quit	AVOID, PART	reckon up	PARCEL
quite		reckoning	ICK, WHOOPING
—alone	HIGH-LONE	reckoner	COUNTER-CASTER
—new	FRE NEW	recoil	REQUOYLE
quits	MEET	recollect	ADVISE
quoin	COIN	recompense	REGUERDON
quote	COAT(E), COTE	red	CAIN-COLOURED
rabble	VARLETRY	reduce to	
race	RAZE	—poverty	RUINATE
rage	VIOLENT	—subjugation	ASSUBJUGATE
raged	RAG'D, RAGDE	re-echo	REWORD
ragged	RAG'D, RAGDE	refer	PUT OVER
raid	RODE	refined	INLAND, PICK
raise	ADVANCE	reflecting the	
—from the dead	ARAISE, ARAYSE	sentiments of another	GLASS-FACED
raising of a siege	REMOVE	reflection	REGARD
rally	RE-ENFORCE	refresh	REPAIR
rank	ORDINANCE	refuse-basket	SIEVE
rarely shown	SELDSHOWN	regale in the cook-room	KITCHEN
rascal	COMPANION, FAITO(U)R	regard	COTE, TENDER
rashness	GUST	regarded without awe	AWELESS
ravening	RAVEN, RAVIN(E)	regardful	RESPECTIVE
ravished	YRAVISHED	region	CLIMAT(UR)E
reach	DANGER, MEASURE	register of soldiers	
read	SCAN	or sailors	MUSTER-BOOK
readiest	EFTEST	reinforcing	SUPPLIANT
read(ing) over	SUPERVISE	reins halfway up side-	
readily	LIGHTLY	piece of bit	HALF-CHECKED
—inclined	PROMPT	reject	ABHOR
ready	ADDRESSED, ADDREST	rejoining	REIOYNDURE
	FEAT, PREGNANT	relation in detail	RECOUNTMENT
	PREST, PRONE	relevance	CONCERNANCY
—apprehension	RECEIVING	religious recluse	ANCHORET

relinquish	GIVE OUT
relish	SAY
rely	STAY
remain in a certain place	CLIMATE
remark	REASON
remedial	REMEDIATE
remedy	RECURE
remit a debt or offence	FORGIVE
remoteness	REMOTION
removal	REMOTION
remove a covering	DISCASE
render	
—destitute	DISFURNISH
—dumb	DUMB
—spiritless	CRAVEN
—trivial	TRIFLE
repairing	STILL-PEERING
	STILL-PIECING
repeat	REWORD
repetition of same rhyme	RANKE
replenishment	SUPPLYMENT
repletion	PLURISIE, PLURISY
report	NOISE, QUEST, YIELD
—the words of	REDELIVER
reporting	REPORT
reposing	REPOSALL, REPOSURE
reprehended	ATTASKED, ATTASKT
represent anew	REFIGURE
representation	EXPRESSURE
representative	IMAGE
reprieve	REPREEVE
reproach	AYWORD, BRAID
reproachfully	INVECTIVELY
reprobation	REPROBANCE
reproduce	REFIGURE
reprove	TAKE UP
reputation	ESTEEM, OPINION, PASS
requital	QUITTAL
requited	REQUIT(TED)
resembling	SEMBLABLE, SEMBLATIVE
residence	BIDING, MASONRY
resist	REPUGN
resolved	PIGHT
resort	HAUNT, TRADE
resorting to law	ACTION-TAKING
restlessly	DISQUIETLY
restore	REPAiR
restrict	COMBINE
retain	CONTAIN
retard	TARDY
retching	HEFT
retinue	MEIN(E)Y, MEINIE
retrace	UNTREAD
return	REGUERDON, REPAIR
reveal	DECIPHER
revel at night	NIGHT-RULE

revengeful	VENGEABLE, VINDICATIVE
reverberation	REPLICATION
revival preceding death	LIGHTNING
revivify	REPAIR
revocation	REVOKEMENT
revoke by contrary shout	UNSHOOT
revolution	INNOVATION
revulsion	REVOLT
reward	REGUERDON
—with sixpence	TESTERN
rheum	RUME
rich	CHUFF
riches	TAL(L)ENT
riddle	CONCLUSION
ride	RODE
—hastily	SKIRR
riding-whip	SWITS
right of sanctuary	PRIVILEGE
riot	RUFFLE, WHOOBUB
ripe	FLUSH
—for tears	WEEPING-RIPE
rising on high	MOUNTANT
risk	JUMP
river-bank	WHARF
road	RODE
roam	WHEEL
roar	RORE
robe	PALLIAMENT
robed in fire	FIRE-ROBED
rod	SWITS
roguery	PATCHERY
roll	FILE
Roman robe	PALLIAMENT
rondure	CIRCLE
root	RAZE
rope-torture	STRAPPADO
rose tree	ROSIERE
rotation	SWAY
rote	ROATE
rough	
—coated apple	LEATHER-COAT
—mannered fellow	TYKE
round	COMPASSED
—off	PARCEL
roundure	RONDURE
rousingly defiant	ROISTING, ROYSTING
rowdy gang	TRIBULATION
rub with oil or grease	LIQUOR
ruck	ROOK
ruddock	RADDOCKE
rudiment	GERMAIN(E)
ruin	RUINATE
ruined	SHENT
rule	SQUIER, SQUIRE
ruled with difficulty	HARD-RULED
rummage	ROMAGE

rumour	MURMUR	scurvy	ROYNISH, SCALL
run		—woman	RONYON, RUNNION
—through from first		scythe	SIETH, SITHE
to last	DECLINE	sea bird	SCAMEL, SEA-MELL
—over as in race	HEAT	seal with others	COUNTERSEAL
rush	RANDON	seam	LARD
rustic	BACON	search-party	SEARCH
—game	(PRISON-)BASE	season	BESPICE
said	FAINE, SAINE	seat	
sailor	CANVAS-CLIMBER	—in church porch	CHURCH-BENCH
sailor's private venture	PORTAGE	—of dignity	STATE
salacious	SALT	secret	INWARD
salt hake	POOR JOHN	—council	CHAMBER-COUNCIL
salutation	REGREET	—going or passage	STEALTH
salute mutually	CONGREET	—message	PRIVATE
salutiferous	VIRTUOUS	secretary	CHANCELLOR
sanctities	SONTIES	seeming	SEMBLATIVE
sane	FORMAL	seen	SAWN
sanity	WISDOM	seigneur	SIGNIEUR
sated	RAVIN'D	seize	CEAZE, EXTEND, SEASE, SEAZE
satiety	CLOYMENT	—upon	PHANG
satire	TAXATION	seizure	EXTENT, SEYSURE
satisfaction	SUFFIGANCE	self	
satyr	SALTIER	—confidence	OPINION
savage	SALVAGE	—deception	SELF-ABUSE
—practices	FELL-FEATS	semblance	ASSEMBLY
savouring of the		senior	SIGNEUR
ale-house	RED-LATTICE	seniority	SIGNEURIE
scabby	ROYNISH	sense	SENT
—fellow	SCROYLE	sensible	WHOLESOME
scaffolding	SCAFFOLAGE	sensitive	COUNTABLE
scapegrace	SKAIN(E)S MATE	sent before due time	PREMISED
scar	WIPE	sentence	CENSURE
scare	GALLOW, SCAR(RE)	sententious saying	REASON
scarecrow	CROWKEEPER	sentry-box	WATCH-CASE
scattering silver	SILVER-SHEDDING	separable	DIVIDANT
scent	SENT	separate	DISTRACT
schedule	SCEDULE	—body	DISTRACTION
scheme	PLATFORM	sequence	SEQUEL
school	CHARGE-HOUSE, SCUL(L)	serge	SURGE
	SCULLE	serious	OBSEQUIOUS
—fellow	BOOK-MATE, INKHORN-MATE	serpigo	SAPEGO, SUPPEAGO
—master	PEDANT	serve	CONVENT
scion	S(E)YEN, SIEN	serviceable	COMMODIOUS
scissors	CIZERS	set	
scoff	GALL	—aside	REPEAL
scold	CALLET	with contempt	SLIGHT OFF
Scotsman	BLUECAP	—astray	STRAY
scour	SKIRR	—at defiance	BEARD
scout	DISCOVERER	—before the mind	PROJECT
scramble	MUSS(LE)	—crosswise	TRAVERSED
—for	SCAMBLE	—forth	PROJECT
scrap	QUANTITY	—free	ENFREE
scrawl	MARTIAL-HAND	—in	
screech-owl	SCHREECH-OWL	battle array	DARRAIGN(E), DARRAIN(E)
scurry	SCUR, SKER, SKIRR, SQUIRR		DARRAYN, DERRAIGN

tender frame	TENDER-HEFTED	—reluctance	MAKE IT STRANGE
—mark of folly on	NICK	shower	ASPERSE, ASPERSION
—of		showing	
anchors	ANCHORAGE	—marks of travel	TRAVEL-TAINTED
four	MESS	—part of face	HALF-FACED
—on	TARRE	shrew	SHROW
—squatting	ROOK	shrewd	PARLOUS, SHROWD
—up	STABLISH	shrewdly	UNHAPPILY
setting	VAIL	shrewish	SHREWD, WASP-STUNG
settle	TAKE UP		WASP-TONGUE
—a dispute	TAKE UP A QUARREL	shriek	SHREEK, SHRIKE
—the business of	FEEZE	shrill in throat	SHRILL-GORGED
	PHE(E)SE, PHEEZE	shuffle	PALTER
severe	WEIGHTY	shut	MAKE
—in manner	OVEREARNEST	—up	SPERR
sewer	COMMON-SHORE	in sty	FRANK
shaft	FIL(L)	shy	CHARY
—horse	P(H)ILHORSE	sick with the thought	THOUGHT-SICK
shaggy	RAG'D, RAGDE	sidesman	STICKLER
—lapdog	SHOWGHE	sigh	HEAVE
shame	REPROOF	sight	BEHOLDING
shamefacedness	PUDENCY	sign	CARACT, DENOTEMENT
shameless	UNBASHFUL	—of ale-house	RED LATTICE
shape	PROJECT	silence	CLAMOUR
shapeless	UNFASHIONABLE	silent	LANGUAGELESS
share	COMMON	silk	SAY
sharing	IMPARTMENT	silver coin	PLATE
sharp	AYGRE, EAGER	similar	SEMBLABLE
—pointed buttock	PIN-BUTTOCK	simply	SHALLOWLY
shaven	PIEL'D	simulative	SEMBLATIVE
she		since	SITH(ENS), SITHENCE
—cat	TIB-CAT	sincerely beloved	HEART-DEAR
—physician	MEDICINE	sing in chorus	CHOIR
sheathed	BREACHED	singing a simple theme	PLAINSONG
shed in small drops	DRIZZLE	singular	UNTRACED
shedding	EFFUSE	sink down	SWAGG
sheer drop	PRECIPITATION	sixpence	TESTRIL(L)
shekel	SICKLE	Sium	CYME
shell	SHALE, SHEAL, SHEEL	skeleton	ATOMY
	SHIEL, SHILL	skewer	PRICK
shelter	WEATHER-FEND	skilful	QUAINT
sheltered under dung	SHARDED	skill	DIRECTION, DOCTRINE
sheriff's officer	YEOMAN		MISTERY, MYSTERY
sherry	SHERRIS	skin disease	SAPEGO, SUPPEAGO
shine upon	OVERSHIRE	—eruption	TETTER
shining through	TRANSPARENT	skull	MAZ(Z)ARD
shiplike head-dress	SHIP-TIRE	sky-blue	WELKIN
shoal	SCHOOLE	slacken	QUAIL
shock	SHOUGH	slaked	YSLAKED
—headed	RUG-HEADED	slanderous	VENOM'D-MOUTH'D
shoot	GERMAIN(E)	slash	RACE, SCORCH
—up	SPIRT	slaying	QUELL
short-sleeved garment	SEA-GOWN	sleaved	SLE(I)DED
show	CITE, LOOK OUT	sleeping house	LULLABY
	OSTENT, PORT	slice	SCANTLE
—in glory	TRIUMPH	slight	EASY, SINGLE

—salute	HALF-CAP	sounding	SONUANCE
slink about	PEAK	sour	AYGRE, EAGER
slow		sourness	RANCOUR
—dance	PAVAN(E), PAVEN, PAVIN	souse	SOUCE, SOWS(S)E
	PADUAN	soused	SOUCT
—flying	FLY-SLOW	sovereign command	EMPERY
—witted	UNPREGNANT	sowing	SEEDNESS
sluggish	RESTY	sown	SAWN
small	PINK, SINGLE	space under gable	BAY
—box for perfumes	POUNCET-BOX	Spanish wine	BASTARD, SHERRIS-SACK
—cannon	CHAMBER	sparrow	PHILIP
—coin	SOLIDARE	spasm	THROW(E)
—freeholder	FRANKLIN	speak	
—French coin	DENIER	—against	FOR(E)SPEAK
—gratuity	GRATILLITY	—ill of	MISREPORT, MISUSE
—herb	HERBELET	—louder than	OUTTONGUE
—hole	VENTIGE	speaker	DISCOURSER
—shade of colour	EYE	specify	FRUTIFY, LIMIT
—share	MOIETY	specious nobleman	COUNT CONFECT
—stream of water	FRESH	speechless	LANGUAGELESS
—tusk	TUSH	speedy	SOON
smeared	TRICK	spend time	ENTREAT, CONTRIVE
smell	SENT	spent by time	TIME-BEWASTED
smile	SMOILE, SMOYLE	spermaceti	PARMACITIE
smutted with coal	COLLIED	sphere	SPHEAR(E)
snap	SNATCH	spinner	SPINSTER
snatch	RASE, RUFFLE	spirited	SPRIGHTFUL
sneak about	PEAK	spiritless	MUDDY-METTLED
snort	BLURT	spite	SPIGHT
so let it be!	WHY, SO	splendid phraseology	FESTIVAL TERM
social class or order	ORDINANCE	splinter	FLAW
soft	LITHER	spoil taste of	DISTASTE
soften	TEMPER	spoilt child	PRINCOX
soldier	MILITARIST	sport beyond the limits	OUTSPORT
sole	MEER'ED	spots (plague)	DEATH-TOKENS
solicitation	INSUIT	spotted	MEAL'D
solicitous	CURIOUS	sprang	SPRONG
solid		spray	ASPERSE, ASPERSION
—lump or mass	KEECH	spread	SCALE
—thing	SOLIDITY	spring	WHITING-TIME
something		sprinkle	DISPUNGE
—fitted to an end	FITMENT	sprinkling	ASPERSION
—needed	NEEDMENT	sprite	SPRIGHT
—savoury	SALAD	sprout	SPIRT
—showing anger	INDIGNATION	spume	YEAST
—to fill up time	SUPPLIANCE	spy	SURVEY
—waved	WAFTURE	square	SQUIER, SQUIRE
—with poisonous juice	HEBONA	squat	
sometimes	SOME	—buttock	QUATCH-BUTTOCK
—humble	PRONE	—down	ROOK
sooner	RATHER	squatting position	TAILOR
soonest	RATHEREST	squint	SQUINNY
soothe	COY	stab	BORE
sorrowful	TRISTFUL	stability	FIXTURE
sound	CHIDING	stage	GEST
—to call back dogs	RECH(E)ATE, RECHEAT	—fanfare	SENNET

stagger along	REEL	strictness	STRICTURE
stained	MEAL'D	strife	BATE
—with neighbour's		strike	PASH
blood	NEIGHBOUR-STAINED	—aghast	GHAST
stake	IMPONE	—off the roll	UNROLL
stalking-horse	STALE	—with	
stamp	PRESSURE	switch	SWITS
stand		violence	PASH
—as godfather	GOSSIP	strip	DISFURNISH, UNCASE
—back	BACCARE, BACKARE	—naked	CASE
—erect (hair)	ROUSE	stripped of plumes	PLUME-PLUCKT
—muttering	MAMMER	strive	PURCHASE
—under	UNDERSTAND	stroke	COY
—upon	CONSIST	—of lightning	THUNDER-STROKE
standstill	STILL-STAND	—with claw	CLOYE
stank more than	ORE-STUNCK	strong	BONNIE, BONNY
stanza	STANZE, STANZO	—liquor	TICKLE-BRAIN
start		stubborn	IMPERSEVERANT
—aside	BLENCH	—foe	WRANGLER
—off	BLENCH	studied	RECOLLECTED TERMS
state	PORT	stuffing for cooked	
—beforehand	PRENOMINATE	carcase	PUDDING
—of defence	BRACE	stumble	PECKE
statesman	WEALSMAN	strumpet	BONA-ROBA, TIB
stay	REMAIN	stun	ASTONISH
—beyond	OUTDWELL	stunted	SCRUBBED
stead	STEED	stupefy	MULL
steadfast	STEDFAST	stupid	BARRED, CLAY-BRAINED
steep	ENSTEEP		CONCEITLESS
steerage	STERNAGE	sty	FRANK
steering-gear	STERN	subdue	ABATE, CONVINCE, HARROW
steersman's place	STERN	subject	LIABLE
sterile	HUNGRY	—by need	NECESSITIED
stiff collar	RABATO, REBATER, REBATO	—to	
stigmatise	SEAR	pangs	THROW(E)
stimulate	TARRE	whipping	BREECHING
stir	COIL, GARBOILS	submission	SUBSCRIPTION
stock of children	AERIE, AERY	submissive	COMPTIBLE
	AYRIE, EYRIE, EYRY	submissiveness	DEPENDACIE
stocking	BOOT-HOSE	submit	SUBSCRIBE
stolen goods	EQUIPAGE, PURCHASE	subside in passion	QUENCH
stool	SIEGE	substance of the thing	MATERIAL
stoop to supplicate	C(O)URB	substitutions	SUPPOSES
stop		subtitles	QUIDDITS
—in a machine	STICKING-PLACE	success in conclusion	ISSUE
—ringing of	CLAMOUR	sucking rabbit	RABBIT-SUCKER
store	STUFF	suffer	BETEEM
stout	BONNIE, BONNY	—pangs	THROW(E)
stoutness	HARDIMENT	sufficiency	SUFFIGANCE
straight	STRAIGHT-PIGHT	suffusion	EYE
—path	FORTHRIGHT	suggest	INCENSE
strand	STROND	suggestion	PROMPTURE
strange	MUCH	suitable	LIABLE
strength	THEW	—company	BESORT
strengthen	FORSE	summer-house	GARDEN-HOUSE
strewings	STREWMENT	summon	CONVENT

superabundance	PLURISIE, PLURISY	talon	TALENT
supercilious	HIGH-SIGHTED	tame	ENTAME
superscription	SUPERSCRIPT	—a hawk	MAN
superstitious	CEREMONIOUS	—spirited	SOFTLY-SPRIGHTED
supplementary	SUPPLIANT	tamper	TEMPER
—document	SCEDULE	tape	INKLE
supplementing	SUPPLYMENT	tapestries	CHAMBER-HANGINGS
supply	IMP	tapster	UNDER-SKINKER
supplying	SUPPLIANCE	tattered	TOTTERED
support	KEEPING, SUPPORTANCE	tax	TASK
—for ruff	RABATO, REBATER, REBATO	tear	EYE-DROP
suppose	PROPOSE	—and tug	TIRE
suppositions	SUPPOSES	—away	RASE
surface	BREAST	—off	RASE
surfeit	CLOYMENT	—to pieces	MAMMOCK
surpass	COME OVER, OUTPEER	tease	PHEEZE
	PARAGON	—out	TOAZE
—in work	OUTWORK	teeming	CHILDING
surrender	SUBSCRIBE	temper	CO-MEDDLE, TEMPERALITIE
surround	ENROUND	temperament	COMPOSURE
sustain	UNDERBEAR	tempered	
swaddling-clothes	SWATHLING-CLOTHES	—badly	MISTEMPERED
	SWOTHLING-CLOTHES	—for evil	MISTEMPERED
swaggerer	RUDESBY, SQUARER	tempt	SUGGEST
swallow	GULF	temptation	PROMPTURE
swashbuckler	SWINDGE-BUCKLER	ten at cards	SINGLE TEN
swashing	WASHING	tenderness	BOWEL
sway	SWINDGE	tending	
swayed	WAID(E)	—in sickness	SICK-SERVICE
sweet	HONEYED	—sheep	SHEEP-WHISTLING
—juicy apple	POM(E)WATER	tenor	TENURE
—wine	CHARNECO	—of a discourse	SAW
sweetness	SOOTH	tenth or tithe	DISME
swell out	FARCE	tenure at fixed rent	FEE-FARM
swift	FLIGHTY	term	
swiftly fierce	TIGER-FOOTED	—in	
swinge	SWINDGE	fencing	HAY, VENEWE, VENEY
switch	SWITS	tennis	CHACE
swollen	BOLLEN, EMBOSSED, RANK	the manege	HOLLA
table	SCEDULE	—of	
—cloth	CARPET	abuse	CUT, FUSTILARIAN
tailor	COSIER, COZIER		FUSTIL(L)IRIAN, PILCHER
take			RAMPALLION
—by cheating	BOB	contempt	CASTILIANO VULGO
—counsel	RESOLVE		COBLOAF, COBBY, DRIBBLING
—in			NIT, RAG, SCALD, SPRAT
hand	UNDERGO		TILLY-FALLY, TILLY-VALL(E)Y
security	ARREST		TWANGLING
—shape or form	INFORM	contemptuous dismissal	AVAUNT
—to highway	HACK	disdain	MUCH
taken	TANE	endearment	CHUCK
—possession of	PROPERTIED	highest reproach	COLLIER
tale-bearer	CARRY-TALE	opprobium	CASTILIAN
	MUMBLE-NEWS	reproach	BEZONIAN, GIB-CAT
talk	PROPOSE		PATCH, RONYON, RUNNION
—endearingly	HONEY		SCALL, SKAINES-MATE

terrify	GAST
test	APPROVE
—by evidence	TESTIMONY
testimony	ATTEST, REPORT
tetter	SAPEGO, SERPIGO
	SUPPEAGO
than	AND
thank with ill-will	GRUDGE A THOUGHT
thanks	THANKINGS
that which	
—cannot be cut	INTRENCHANT
—crowns or accomplishes	CROWNET
—is	
characterised	CHARACTERY
distilled	DISTILMENT
loaned	LENDER
—stares fatally	MORTAL-STARING
thatch	STOVER
theft	CONVEYANCE, STEALTH
theme	COPY
thence	SITHENCE
thereafter	UPON
thickly interwoven	THICK-PLEACHED
thief	LIFTER, NUTHOOK, PRIG
	TROJAN
thieving	PUGGING
thigh-armour	CUSH
thill	FIL(L)
—horse	P(H)IL-HORSE
thin	
—as a lath	LATTEN
—faced	PAPER-FACED
thing	
—imported	IMPORTANCE
—seen	REGARD
think ill of	MISTHINK
third	TRIPLE
thistle	CARDUUS
thoughtless	UNWEIGHING
thrash	PAY
threatened with death	DEATH-PRACTISED
three-cornered	THREE-NOOKED
threnody	THRENOS
throat	GULF
throe	THROW(E)
throw	
—at bowls	UPCAST
—into uproar or confusion	UPROAR
—open	WIDEN
thrown from its sphere	DISORBED
thrust	HAVE-AT-HIM, POTCH(E)
—in fencing	FOIN, STOCK
—with quick motion	YERK
thunderbolt	THUNDER-STONE
tick	JAR
ticklish	SUBTLE

tie by rein	REIN
tight	STRAIT, STRICT
tighten	RESTRAIN
till this time	HERETO
time	
—fixed for stay in place	GEST
—for	
confession	SHRIVING-TIME
giving rings	RING-TIME
—of	
beginning	SPRING
midday meal	UNDERTIME
silence	SILENT
—server	MINUTE-JACK, TIME-PLEASER
—table	SCEDULE
timorous	MEACOCK
tincture	SMATCH
tinge	EYE
tinselly	CLINQUANT
tiny	TINE, TYNE
tipple	POT
tippler	MALT-WORM
tired	WAPPEND
—as a dog	DOG-WEARY
—by day's work	DAY-WEARIED
—of life	LIFE-WEARY
title	ADDITION
to	
—be heir	INHERIT
—condescend to take	DEIGN
—go over to enemy	FALL OVER
—make aghast	GAST
—put into dialogue	DIALOGUE
—the smallest detail	TO POINT
—too great an extent	OVERFAR
—what	WHEREUNTIL
token	PRECEDENT
tokens of respect	CEREMONIES
told before	FOREVOUCHED
tom-cat	GIB-CAT
tonsured	PIEL'D
toothless	BROKEN
top	UPWARD
—of head	NOLE
toper	EPHESIAN
toss	
—contemptuously	SLIGHT
—in blanket or canvas	CANVASS
touching the	
—clouds	CLOUD-KISSING
—sky	HEAVEN-KISSING
toy	GAUD
trace	TRACT
track	TRACT
traffic	MART, PASSAGE
—in	MERCHANDISE, MERCHANDIZE

traitor	FAITOR	typical woman's name	TIB
transcendent in glory	TRIUMPHANT	ugly	FOUL
transfixed	BROACHED	unaching	UNAKING
transform	TRANSPOSE, TRANS-SHAPE	unadapted	UNSQUARED
transformed person	TRANSFORMATION	unadorned	UNCOINED, UNCOYNED
transport	TRANSPORTANCE	unassisting	UNSISTING
travel		unbearded	UNROUGH, UNRUFFE
—stained	TRAVEL-TAINTED	unbecoming	ILL-SEEMING
—worn	SEASICK	unblunted	UNBATED
tread back	UNTREAD	unbounded	UNCONFINABLE
treat		unbroken	CONTINUATE
—as property	PROPERTY	uncertain	INCERTAIN
—tenderly	TENDER	uncharitable	INCHARITABLE
—with		unchaste	WAPPEND
contempt	JADE, LOUT, LOWT	uncivil	INCIVIL
scant courtesy	STRAIN COURTESY	unconciliating	UNTEMPERING
treatment by fasting		unconsidered	UNSKAN'D
and sweating	TUBFAST	under-butler	BREAD-CHIPPER
trenched	PIONED	under command	BUXOM
tress	SWITS	under-constable	THIRDBOROUGH
trick	BOBB, COLT, GLEEK	underpraise	UNDERPRISE
	GLIKE, PASS, QUIRK	understanding	CONCEIT
—deserving the gallows	ROPE-TRICK	undertaken	UNDERTA'EN
tricky	SUBTLE	undervalue	DISABLE
tried	TOUCHED, TRIDE	undeserving	UNMERITABLE
trifles befitting a lady	LADY-TRIFLES	undiscriminating	UNRESPECTIVE
trifling	BAUBLING	undo	DEFEAT, DUP, UNLACE
trim	GUARD	undone	POUPT
triple time	TRIPLEX	undress	DEVEST, DISCASE, UNCASE
trite	MODERN	undressed	UNREADY
triumphal	TRIUMPHANT	uneasily	DISQUIETLY
triumvirate	TRIUMPHERY	unexpected	UNWARIE
Trojan	TROYAN	unfaded	UNBRAIDED
troublesome person	WATER-FLY	unfavourably	UNHAPPILY
trousers	STROSSERS	unfeeling	IRON-WITTED
truckle	CURB	unfit	IMPAIR
trull	CALLET	unfledged bird	GULL
try to have restored		unfortunate	MISADVENTURED
to favour	REPEAL	unfurnish	UNPROVIDE
tuft	TUFFE	unhackneyed	UNTRADED
tumult	ROMAGE, RORE	uninfluenced	UNSWAI'D
tune to arouse hunters	HUNT'S-UP	unintentional	UNWILLING
turban	TURBAND, TURBOND	unknowingly	UNWARES
turbulent	COMBUSTIOUS	unknown word	HACK, SCARRE
turn	INTEND, SWITS, WAFT	unlawfully	FORBIDDENLY
—aside	ASKANCE, ASKANT, DAFF	—begotten	MISBEGOT(TEN)
—round	RETURN	unlikely	UNLIKE
—to stone	STONE	unlikeness	DISLIKENESS
turned awry	TORTIVE	unlimited	CONFINEIESS
turquoise	TURKIES	unlucky	WICKED
tusk	TUSH	unnatural	KINDLESS
tutor	SCHOOLMASTER	unobtrusive going	
twenty paces	SCORE	or passage	STEALTH
twilight	COCKSHUT	unowned	UNOWED
twisted	WEALK'D, WELKT	unpolished person	HOMESPUN
type of apple	BITTERSWEET	unprepared	DISAPPOINTED

unprolific	HUNGRY	vast	WASTE
unready	REDELESS, UNDRESSED	veiled	MABLED, MOBLED
	UNPREGNANT	velvet	VELURE
unrefined	UNCOINED	—trimmings	VELVET-GUARDS
unreliable person	BREAK-VOW	vend	MART
	BREAK-PROMISE	vengeance	WAN(N)ION
unresisting	UNSISTING	venture	JUMP
unresting	UNSISTING	venue	VENEWE, VENEY
unrestrained	UNYOKED	verbal intercourse	ENTREATMENT
unripe peascod	SQUASH	verbose	VERBAL
unruly	RAG'D, RAGDE	verse	STANZE, STANZO
unsated	UNSTANCHED	versed	TRADED
unsearchable	UNTENTED	very	
unseasonable	UNSEASONED	—durable	PERDURABLE
unseasonably pregnant	CHILDING	—famous	WELL-FAMED
unseeing	IMPERSEVERANT	—rude or uncivil	GIANT-RUDE
unseemly	UNACCUSTOMED	—small person	MINIMUS
unseen	INVIS'D	viands	CATES
unshaven	UNBARBED	vigorous	LUSTICK, LUSTIQUE
unsightly	SIGHTLESS	vile	VILD(E)
unstable person	MINUTE-JACK	village people	VILLAGREE
unsuccessful in trade	TRADE-FALNE	villages	VILLAGREE
unsuitable	IMPAIR	villainy	PATCHERY
unthinking	UNRESPECTIVE	vindictive	VINDICATIVE
unthinkingly	LIGHTLY	viola da gamba	VIOL-DE-GAMBOYS
until	WHILE(S)	violate	FRACT
untilled	UNEARED	violation of promise	PROMISE-BREACH
untrimmed	UNBARBED	violence	EXTENT
unused in any action	UNDEEDED	—beyond measure	OUTRAGE
unwounded	UNGORD	violent	ROBUSTIOUS
upheaval	ROMAGE	viragoish	MANKIND
uphold	ABLE	virtuous	GRACED
upper		visor	SIGHT
—air	REGION	vives	FIVES
—hand	EMINENCE	vixenish	SHREWD
—part of shoe	OVERLEATHER	vizier	PHEAZAR
upright	AN END	void of guile	SINGLE
uproar	GARBOIL(S), WHOOBUB	voluntarily	BY MY WILL
uproot	SUPPLANT	vote	TONGUE
upshot	LOOSE	vow	PROTEST
upstart	START-UP	voyage	SHIPPING
urge	PERSUADE, STRAIN	vulgar	GENERAL
urine	CHAMBER-LYE	—fellow	JACK-SLAVE
use		wafting	WAFTURE
—ceremony	COMPLY	wager	IMPONE
—roughly	HARRY	wait	STAY
usury	EXCESS	walking so that legs	
utmost degree of any passion	BENT	interfere	NEAR-LEGGED
utter ringingly	TANG	wall	MORALL, MURAL, MURE
vagrancy	EXTRAVAGANCY	—in	CIRCUMMURE
vagrant	VAGROM	wander	WHEEL
valuation	PRISE, PRIZE	wandering	WINDRING
value	PRAISE, PRICE	want of respect	NON-REGARDANCE
—a thing	RESPECT	wanting	
vanguard	VA(U)NT, VAWARD	—linen	LACK-LINEN
varlet	VARLETTO	—spontaneity	RECOLLECTED TERMS

wanton	GAMSTER, NICE, RIGGISH	wholly decayed	DIRT-ROTTEN
—woman	FLIRT-GILL	whore	QUAIL
wantonness	LUXURY	—monger	FLE MONGER
wappered	WAPPEND	—son	HORSON
warble	REL(L)ISH	whoring	DRAB
wardship	GUARDAGE	wicked	FACINERIOUS, NAUGHTY
warn	VOR		SPOTTED
warrant	WARN	wickered	TWIGGED, TWIGGING
waste time	BURN DAYLIGHT	wide-mouthed	STRETCH-MOUTH'D
wasted	CONFOUNDED	widow's right	WIDOWHOOD
watchful	OPEN-EYED	wife	KICKIE-WICKIE
—heed	OBSERVANCE		KICKSY-WICKSY
watchword	NAYWORD	wild mustard	HARLOCKS
water		willing	WILFUL
—colours	WATER-WORK	wilt	WO(O)T
—parsnip	CYME	win	LURCH
watering	WATERY	wind	BOTTLE
waterspout	HURRICANO	winding	WINDRING
waving	WAFTURE	wink	ELIAD, ILLIAD
way	QUIRK	winter	HIEMS
—worn	JOURNEY-BATED	wintry	HIEMAL
weak	FOND, SINGLE	wise	WINNOWED
wealth	FUL(L)NESS, TALLENT	—in folly, foolish	
wear out	CONTRIVE	in wisdom	FOOLISH-WITTY
wearing a toga	TOGED	wish	BOSOM
weasel	MOUSE-HUNT	—not to be	UNWISH
weigh down	PEASE, PEAZE	wit	WEET(E)
	PEISE, PEIZE, PEYSE	witch-goddess	HECAT
weight	POIZE	with	
weird	WEY(W)ARD	—a	
well		face like tripe	TRIPE-VISAG'D
—balanced	WEAL-BALANCED	sense of loss	MISSINGLY
—off	WELL TO LIVE	slant	ASCAUNT, ASLANT
—proportioned	CLEAN-TIMBERED	sweep of the stakes	SOOPSTAKE
wencher	CORINTHIAN		SWOOP-STAKE-LIKE
wet	BEWET	vengeance	WITH A WITNESS
what		—downcast eyes	PRONE
—if	WHAT AN IF	—eyes shut	WINKING
—the devil	WHAT A PLAGUE	—moral right	UPRIGHTEOUSLY
—though	WHAT AN IF	—promise of success	SUCCESSFULLY
—went before	VAUNT	—the speed of thought	UPON A THOUGHT
when times are getting			WITH A THOUGHT
better	TIME-BETTERING	—well-nourished rump	RUMP-FED
whereunto	WHEREUNTIL	—wide strong wings	FULL-WINGED
whip	FIRK	—young	IN KINDLE
whipped at cart tail	OVERSCHUTCH	withdraw	INSHELL
whippersnapper	WHIPSTER	withered	CORKY
whisk	SWITS	without	
whispered	EAR-BUSSING	—bounds	CONFINELESS
	EAR-KISSING	—consequence	IMPORTLESS
whisperer	BUZZER	—good repute	REPUTELESS
whit	FICO, FIGO	—means of generation	UNSEMINAR(IE)D
Whitsun	WHEESON		UNGENITURED
whoever	WHAT	—possessions	UNPOSSESSING
whole weight	SWAY	—shrubs	UNSHRUBD
wholesome	PHYSIC	—sinews	UNSINNOWED

—superior	TOPLESS	youth	JUVENAL
witness	ATTEST		LEAPING-TIME
woman	PLACCAT, PLACKET		SALAD DAYS
—of bad character	CALLET	youthful freshness	MAY-MORN(ING)
womanish	FEMALE	**Shakespeare's people**	
womb	VENTRICLE	abbess of Ephesus	AEMILIA
wonder	ADMIRATION	agent for Silvia	EGLAMOUR
—struck	WONDER-WOUNDED	ambassador	EUPHRONIUS
wonderful	MIRABLE, MUCH	—Charles V	CAPUCIUS
wonted	TAME	—France	CHATILLON
woo	SUE	ancient	IAGO, PISTOL
wooded	BUSKY	archbishop	
wooden funnel	TUN-DISH	—Canterbury	BOURCHIER, CRANMER
word of any meaning	HUMOUR	—York	ROTHERHAM, SCROOP
worked secretly against	UNDERWROUGHT	armourer	HORNER
working-horse	CUT	attendant to	
worn	CONFOUNDED	—Antipholus	DROMIO
—in winter	WINTERED	—Cleopatra	ALEXAS, CHARMIAN
—with armour	ARMGAUNT		DIOMEDES, IRAS, MARDIAN
worsted	INKLE		SELEUCUS
—ribbon	CADDYSS	—Duke of Illyria	CURIO, VALENTINE
worthless	JADED, LOZEL	—exiled Duke	AMIENS, JAQUES
—dog	HUNT-COUNTER	—Hero	MARGARET, URSULA
—person	TRASH	—Horner	PETER
worthy of respect	RESPECTIVE	—Imogen	HELEN
wound	BATTERY, BORE	—Katharine	ALICE
—with spur	SPUR-GALL	—King of Navarre	BIRON, DUMAIN
wrap up	MAIL		LONGAVILLE
wrench	FIT	—Olivia	MARIA
wretch	MISER, SCROYLE	—Princess of France	BOYET, MARIA
wristband	SLEEVEHAND		KATHARINE, MERCADE
write	CHARACTER		ROSALINE
—down	PAPER	—Queen Katharine	PATIENCE
—on scroll	INSCROLL		
writing	CHARACTERY	bawd	DOLL TEARSHEET
written			MRS OVERDONE
—music	PRICK-SONG	bellowsmender	FLUTE
—securities	PAPER	betrothed to Angelo	MARIANA
wrong-doing	MISS	bishop	
wry face	MOO	—Ely	MORTON
yearn	EARN	—Winchester	BEAUFORT, GARDINER
yellow	CAIN-COLOURED, SANDED	brother of	
yet in the bud	UNBLOWED	—Agamemnon	MENELAUS
yew	EUGH	—Brabantio	OTHELLO
yewen	EUGHEN, EWGHEN	—Don Pedro	DON JOHN
yield	COME, SUBSCRIBE	—Edward IV	CLARENCE
yielding	LITHER	—exiled duke	FERDINAND
—up life	LIFE-RENDERING	—Henry	GLOSTER
yoke	BOW	—Henry V	BEDFORD, GLOSTER
—of garment	SQUARE	—Isabella	CLAUDIO
Yorkshireman	TYKE	—King	
young		John	ARTHUR
—fox	KID-FOX	of Naples	SEBASTIAN
—lamb	EANLING	—Lady Grey	RIVERS
—thoughtless person	SKIPPER	—Leonato	ANTONIO
younger	LATTER-BORN	—Marcus	TITUS

—Menelaus	AGAMEMNON	—Simonides	THAISA
—Othello	BRABANTIO	—Titus	LAVINIA
—Saturninus	BASSANIUS	—widow	DIANA
—Titus	MARCUS ANDRONICUS	dauphin	CHARLES, LOUIS
—Viola	SEBASTIAN	deputy to Duke of Vienna	ANGELO
butler	STEPHANO	duchess of Gloster	ELEANOR
carpenter	QUINCE	duke of	
chamberlain to		—Anjou	REIGNIER
King John	DE BURGH	—Athens	THESEUS
clown	COSTARD, TOUCHSTONE	—Clarence	GEORGE
—Greek	ACHILLES, AJAX	—Ephesus	SOLINUS
	DIOMEDES, NESTOR	—Exeter	BEAUFORT
	PATROCLUS, ULYSSES	—Gloster	HUMPHREY, RICHARD
—Trojan	AENEAS, ANTENOR	—Illyria	ORSINO
conjurer	BOLINGBROKE, PINCH	—Lancaster	JOHN OF GAUNT
conspirator		—Milan	ANTONIO, PROSPERO
—English	CAMBRIDGE, GREY	—Norfolk	BIGOT, MOWBRAY
	SCROOP	—Vienna	VICENTIO
—Roman	CASCA, CASSIUS, CIMBER	—York	EDMUND, PLANTAGENET
	CINNA, DECIUS BRUTUS		RICHARD
	LIGARIUS, MARCUS BRUTUS		
	TREBONIUS	earl of	
constable	DULL, ELBOW	—Douglas	ARCHIBALD
corporal	NYM	—Essex	FITZ-PETER
councillor of Naples	GONZALO	—March	MORTIMER
count-Rousillon	BERTRAM	—Norfolk	BIGOT
countess	OLIVIA	—Northumberland	PERCY, SIWARD
country fellow	WILLIAM	—Pembroke	MARESHALL
courtier	CORNELIUS, CURAN	—Richmond	HENRY
	GUILDENSTERN, LE BEAU	—Rutland	EDMUND
	OSRIC, ROSENKRANTZ	—Salisbury	LONGSWORD
	VOLTIMAND	—Somerset	BEAUFORT
cousin of		—Worcester	PERCY
—Henry V	YORK	emperor-Rome	SATURNINUS
—Justice Shallow	SLENDER	executioner	ABHORSON
creature	BAGOT, BUSHY, GREEN	fairy	COBWEB, MOTH
curate	NATHANIEL		MUSTARDSEED
daughter of			PEASBLOSSOM, PUCK
—Baptista	BIANCA, KATHARINA	fantastic	LUCIO
—Calchas	CRESSIDA	—Spaniard	DON ADRIANO
—Capulet	JULIET	father of	
—Charles VI	KATHARINE	—Arviragus	CYMBELINE
—Cymbeline	IMOGEN	—Cordelia	LEAR
—Duke of Milan	SILVIA	—Fleance	BANQUO
—Egeus	HERMIA	—Florizel	POLIXENES
—exiled duke	ROSALIND	—Goneril	LEAR
—Frederick	CELIA	—Guiderius	CYMBELINE
—Glendower	LADY MORTIMER	—Hector	PRIAM
—Hermione	PERDITA	—Helenus	PRIAM
—King Lear	CORDELIA, GONERIL, REGAN	—Hermia	EGEUS
—Leonato	HERO	—Hero	LEONATO
—Pericles	MARINA	—Imogen	CYMBELINE
—Polonius	OPHELIA	—Jaques	DE BOIS
—Prospero	MIRANDA	—Jessica	SHYLOCK
—Reignier	MARGARET	—Juliet	CAPULET
—Shylock	JESSICA	—Lady Mortimer	GLENDOWER
		—Laertes	POLONIUS

—Lavinia	TITUS
—Lucentio	VINCENTIO
—Mamillius	LEONTES
—Marcius	CORIOLANUS
—Margarelon	PRIAM
—Margaret	REIGNIER
—Marina	PERICLES
—Martius	TITUS
—Miranda	PROSPERO
—Mutius	TITUS
—Oliver	DE BOIS
—Ophelia	POLONIUS
—Orlando	DE BOIS
—Paris	PRIAM
—Proteus	ANTONIO
—Publius	MARCUS
—Quintus	TITUS
—Regan	LEAR
—Richard	PLANTAGENET
—Romeo	MONTAGUE
—Thaisa	SIMONIDES
—Troilus	PRIAM
follower of	
—Bertram	PAROLLES
—Cade	DICK, GEORGE, JOHN
	MICHAEL, SMITH
—Don John	BORACHIO, CONRADE
—Falstaff	BARDOLPH, GADSHILL
	NYM, PETO, PISTOL, POINS
Franciscan	JOHN, LAWRENCE
friar	JOHN, LAWRENCE
	PETER, THOMAS
friend of	
—Antonio	BASSANIO, GRATIANO
	LORENZO, SALANIO, SALARINO
—Antony	DEMETRIUS, DERCETAS
	ENOBARBUS, EROS
	PHILO, POMPEIUS
	SCARUS, VENTIDIUS
—archbishop of York	MICHAEL
—Bassanio	GRATIANO, LORENZO
	SALANIO, SALARINO
—Brutus	CATO, LUCILIUS, MESSALA
	TITINIUS, VOLUMNIUS
—Caesar	AGRIPPA, DOLABELLA
	GALLUS, MAECENAS
	PROCULIEUS, THYREUS
—Cassius	CATO, LUCILIUS
	MESSALA, TITINIUS
	VOLUMNIUS
—Coriolanus	AGRIPPA
—Cymbeline	POSTHUMUS
—Demetrius	HELENA
—duke of Illyria	VIOLA
—Hamlet	HORATIO
—Henry IV	BLUNT, WESTMORELAND

—Hermione	DEMETRIUS, LYSANDER
—Philario	IACHIMO
—Pompey	MENAS, MENECRATES
	VARRIUS
—Posthumus	CYMBELINE
—Romeo	MERCUTIO
—Shylock	TUBAL
—Virgilia	VALERIA
general	
—Antony	CANIDIUS
—Athenian	ALCIBIADES
—fighting	
Goths	TITUS
Volscians	CORIOLANUS
—Caesar	TAURUS
—Greek	AGAMEMNON
—Roman	ANTONY, CAIUS
	CORIOLANUS, COMINIUS
	JULIUS CAESAR
	TITUS ANDRONICUS
—Scottish	BANQUO, MACDUFF
—Volscian	AUFIDIUS
gentleman (of)	
—foolish	FROTH
—Kent	IDEN
—Padua	BAPTISTA
—Pisa	VICENTIO
—Sicilian	ROGERO
—Venetian	RODERIGO
—Verona	PETRUCHIO, PROTEUS
	VALENTINE
—Windsor	FORD, PAGE
—young	CLAUDIO, FENTON
gentlewoman	HELENA
goldsmith	ANGELO
governor of	
—Cyprus	MONTANO, OTHELLO
—Messina	LEONATO
—Mitylene	LYSIMACHUS
—Tower	SCALES
Greek - deformed	THERSITES
heiress	PORTIA
herald - French	MOUNTJOY
hostess of tavern	DAME QUICKLY
husband of	
—Emilia	IAGO
—Helen	MENELAUS
—Imogen	POSTHUMUS LEONATUS
—Mrs Quickly	PISTOL
—Octavia	ANTONY
—Paulina	ANTIGONUS
—Portia	BRUTUS
—Virgilia	CORIOLANUS
imposter	SIMPCOX
jester	TRINCULO
Jew	SHYLOCK, TUBAL

joiner	SNUG
justice	SHALLOW, SILENCE
king of	
—Antioch	ANTIOCHUS
—Bohemia	POLIXENES
—Britain	CYMBELINE, LEAR
—Denmark	CLAUDIUS
—fairies	OBERON
—France	CHARLES VI, LOUIS XI
	PHILIP
—Henry IV	BOLINGBROKE
—Naples	ALONSO
—Navarre	FERDINAND
—Pentapolis	SIMONIDES
—Scotland	DUNCAN, MACBETH
—Sicilia	LEONTES
—Troy	PRIAM
kinsman of Brabantio	LODOVICO
lady	EMILIA
—of Verona	JULIA
legate - Pope	PANDULPH
lieutenant of the Tower	BRAKENBURY
	WOODVILLE
lord (of)	
—Antioch	THALIARD
—banished	BELARIUS
—Bohemian	ARCHIDAMUS
—chamberlain	POLONIUS
—Ephesus	CERIMON
—flatterer of Timon	LUCIUS, SEMPRONIUS
—Florentine	CLAUDIO
—French	GRANDPRE, MELUN
	RAMBURES
—Naples	ADRIAN, FRANCISCO
—old	LAFEU
—Padua	BENEDICK
—Sicilian	ANTIGONUS, CAMILLO, DION
—Tyre	ESCANES, HELICANUS
—Vienna	ESCALUS
lover - Jessica	LORENZO
master of the revels	PHILOSTRATE
merchant	BALTHASAR
—Syracuse	AEGEON
—Venice	ANTONIO
messenger - from Venice	SALERIO
mistress	
—Alcibiades	PHRYNIA, TIMANDRA
—Cassio	BIANCA
Moor	AARON, OTHELLO
mother of	
—Arthur	CONSTANCE
—Coriolanus	VOLUMNIS
—King John	ELINOR
—Perdita	HERMIONE
neighbour to widow	
of Florence	MARIANA, VIOLENTA

nephew of Capulet	TYBALT
niece of	
—King John	BLANCH
—Leonato	BEATRICE
—Pandarus	CRESSIDA
—Toby Belch	OLIVIA
noble	
—Athenian	TIMON
—Roman	AEMILIUS, CORIOLANUS
—Scottish	ANGUS, CAITHNESS
	LENNOX, MACDUFF
	MENTEITH, ROSS
—young	PARIS
nun	FRANCISCA
nurse-Marina	LYCHORIDA
officer	BERNARDO
—attending Macbeth	SEYTON
—foolish	DOGBERRY, VERGES
—in army	ERPINGHAM, FLUELLEN
	GOWER, JAMY, MACMORRIS
	MARCELLUS
—in Ventidius's army	SILIUS
page to	
—Armado	MOTH
—Falstaff	ROBIN
parson - Welsh	EVANS
philosopher	APEMANTUS
physician	CORNELIUS
—French	CAIUS
—Henry VIII	BUTTS
poet	CINNA
predecessor - Othello	MONTANO
priest	HUME, SOUTHWELL
	URSWICK
—Trojan	CALCHAS
prince of	
—Arragon	DON PEDRO
—Denmark	HAMLET
—Gloster	HUMPHREY
—Lancaster	JOHN
—Norway	FORTINBRAS
—Tyre	PERICLES
—Verona	ESCALUS
—Wales	EDWARD
prisoner	BARNARDINE
prophet	PETER
prophetess	CASSANDRA
protector	GLOSTER
queen of	
—Amazons	HIPPOLYTA
—Denmark	GERTRUDE
—Edward IV	ELIZABETH
	LADY GREY
—England	ANNE
—fairies	TITANIA
—France	ISABEL

—Goths	TAMORA
—Henry VI	MARGARET
—Sicilia	HERMIONE
rebel	CADE
recruit	BULLCALF, FEEBLE
	MOULDY, SHADOW, WART
regent of France	BEDFORD
rival of Valentine	THURIO
rogue	AUTOLYCUS
schoolmaster	HOLOFERNES, PINCH
sea captain	ANTONIO
senator - Roman	BRABANTIO, CICERO
	LENA, PUBLIUS
servant (of)	BOULT, CAPHIS
	HORTENSIUS, PHILOTUS
—Antonio	PANTHINO
—Bassanio	LEONARDO
—Brutus	CLAUDIUS, DARDANIUS
	LUCIUS, STRATO, VARRO
—Capulet	CHAPMAN, GREGORY
—Cassius	PINDARUS
—clownish	SPEED
—Cressida	ALEXANDER
—Dionyza	LEONINE
—Don Pedro	BALTHAZAR
—Dr Caius	MRS QUICKLY, RUGBY
—duke of Vienna	VARRIUS
—Lady Faulconbridge	GURNEY
—Leonato	IMOGEN
—Lucentio	BIONDELLO, TRANIO
—Luciana	LUCE
—Montague	ABRAHAM
—Mrs Overdone	CLOWN
—Northumberland	MORTON, TRAVERS
—Oliver	ADAM, DENNIS
—Olivia	CLOWN, FABIAN
—Petruchio	CURTIS, GRUMIO
—Polonius	REYNALDO
—Portia	BALTHAZAR, STEPHANO
—Posthumus Leonato	PISANIO
—Proteus	LAUNCE
—Romeo	BALTHAZAR
—Shallow	DAVY
—Shylock	GOBBO
—Slender	SIMPLE
—Timon	FLAMINIUS, LUCILIUS
	LUCIUS
—Wolsey	CROMWELL
shepherd	CORIN, SILVIUS
shepherdess	DORCAS, MOPSA, PHEBE
sheriff's officer	FANG, SNARE
shrew	KATHARINE
sister of	
—Adriana	LUCIANA
—Claudio	ISABELLA
—Katharine	BIANCA

—Luciana	ADRIANA
—Queen of France	BONA
—Sebastian	VIOLA
slave	CALIBAN
soldier	BARDOLPH, BATES
	CASSIO, COURT, FRANCISCO
	IAGO, NYM, PISTOL, WILLIAMS
son of	
—Aegeon	ANTIPHOLUS
—Banquo	FLEANCE
—Coriolanus	MARCIUS
—Cymbeline	ARVIRAGUS, GUIDERIUS
—De Bois	JAQUES, OLIVER, ORLANDO
—Duke of York	AUMERLE
—Duncan	DONALBAIN
—Edward IV	RICHARD, YORK
—Gloster	EDMUND, EGDGAR
—Henry IV	CLARENCE, THOMAS
	HUMPHREY, JOHN
	THOMAS
—Henry VI	EDWARD
—King	
Duncan	MALCOLM
John	HENRY
of Naples	FERDINAND
—Lady	
Faulconbridge	PHILIP, ROBERT
Grey	DORSET
—Leontes	MAMILLIUS
—Marcus	PUBLIUS
—Montague	ROMEO
—Northumberland	HOTSPUR, PERCY
—Plantagenet	EDWARD, RICHARD
—Polixenes	FLORIZEL
—Polonius	LAERTES
—Priam	DEIPHOBUS, HECTOR
	HELENUS, MARGARELON
	PARIS, TROILUS
—Richard I	FAULCONBRIDGE
—Tamora	ALARBUS, CHIRON
	DEMETRIUS
—Titus	MARTIUS, MUTIUS
	QUINTUS
—Vincentio	LUCENTIO
—Volumnia	CORIOLANUS
sophist	ARTEMIDORUS
spirit	ARIEL, CERES, IRIS, JUNO
steward to	
—Goneril	OSWALD
—Olivia	MALVOLIO
—Timon	FLAVIUS
suitor	
—Bianca	GREMIO, HORTENSIO
—Katharine	PETRUCHIO
—Portia	PRINCE OF ARRAGON
	PRINCE OF MOROCCO

Shakespeare's people

tailor	STARVELING
tinker	SLY, SNOUT
tribune	FLAVIUS, JUNIUS BRUTUS
	MARCUS ANDRONICUS
	MARULLUS, SICINIUS, VELUTUS
triumvir	AEMILIUS LEPIDUS
	ANTONIUS LEPIDUS
	MARK ANTONY, OCTAVIUS
uncle of	
—Cressida	PANDARUS
—Duke of York	MORTIMER
—Henry V	EXETER
—Henry VI	GLOSTER
—Olivia	BELCH
—Richard II	LANCASTER, YORK
—Tybalt	CAPULET
usher to Queen Katharine	GRIFFITH
vicar	MARTEXT
waiting-maid to Portia	NERISSA
weaver	BOTTOM, SMITH
wench	AUDREY, JAQUENETTA
widow	
—Henry VI	MARGARET
—Prince of Wales	ANNE
wife of	
—Antigonus	PAULINA
—Antipholus	ADRIANA
—Antony	OCTAVIA
—Brutus	PORTIA
—Caesar	CALPURNIA
—Cleon	DIONYZA
—Coriolanus	VIRGILIA
—Hector	ANDROMACHE
—Henry VIII	KATHARINE
—Hotspur	LADY PERCY
—Iago	EMILIA
—Leonatus	IMOGEN
—Menelaus	HELEN
—Othello	DESDEMONA
—Pistol	MRS QUICKLY
—Posthumus	IMOGEN
witch	HECATE, JOURDAIN
wrestler	CHARLES
youth	HENRY

Shakespeare's plays
titles and characters:
A Midsummer Night's
Dream   BOTTOM, COBWEB, DEMETRIUS
EGEUS, FLUTE, HELENA, HERMIA
HIPPOLYTA, LYSANDER, LION
MOONSHINE, MOTH, MUSTARDSEED
OBERON, PEASBOTTOM, PHILOSTRATE
PUCK, PYRAMUS, QUINCE
ROBIN GOODFELLOW, SNOUT
SNUG, STARVELING, THESEUS
THISBE, TITANIA, WALL

Shakespeare's plays

All's Well That
Ends Well   BERTRAM, COUNTESS
DIANA, DUKE, HELENA, KING
LAFEU, MARIANA, PAROLLES
VIOLENTA
Antony and
Cleopatra   AGRIPPA, ALEXAS, ANTONY
CANIDIUS, CHARMIAN, CLEOPATRA
DEMETRIUS, DERCETAS, DIOMEDES
DOLABELLA, ENOBARBUS, EROS
EUPHRONIUS, GALLUS, IRAS
LEPIDUS, MARDIAN, MECAENAS
MENAS, MENECRATES, OCTAVIA
OCTAVIUS, PROCULEIUS, POMPEIUS
PHILO, SCARUS, SELEUCUS
SILIUS, TAURUS, THYREUS
VARRIUS, VENTIDIUS
As You Like It   ADAM, AMIENS, AUDREY
CELIA, CHARLES, CORIN, DENNIS
DUKE, FREDERICK, HYMEN, JAQUES
LE BEAU, MARTEXT, OLIVER
ORLANDO, PHOEBE, ROSALIND
SILVIUS, TOUCHSTONE
WILLIAM
Coriolanus   AGRIPPA, AUFIDIUS
BRUTUS, COMINIUS, CORIOLANUS
LARTIUS, MARCIUS, VALERIA
VELUTUS, VIRGILIA, VOLUMNIA
Cymbeline   ARVIRAGUS, BELARIUS
CLOTEN, CORNELIUS, CYMBELINE
GUIDERIUS, HELEN, IACHIMO
IMOGEN, LEONATUS, LUCIUS
PHILARIO, PISANIO, QUEEN
Hamlet, Prince
of Denmark   BERNARDO, CLAUDIUS
CORNELIUS, FORTINBRAS
FRANCISCO, GERTRUDE
GUILDENSTERN, HAMLET
HORATIO, LAERTES
MARCELLUS, OPHELIA, OSRIC
POLONIUS, REYNALDO
ROSENCRANTZ, VOLTIMAND
Julius Caesar   ANTONIUS, ARTEMIDORUS
CALPURNIA, CASCA, CASSIUS
CATO, CICERO, CIMBER, CINNA
CLAUDIUS, CLITUS, DARDANIUS
DECIUS BRUTUS, FLAVIUS
JULIUS CAESAR, LENA, LEPIDUS
LIGARIUS, LUCILIUS, LUCIUS
MARCUS BRUTUS, MARULLUS
MESSALA, OCTAVIUS, PINDARUS
PORTIA, PUBLIUS, STRATO
TREBONIUS, VARRO, VOLUMNIUS
King Henry IV
(Part I)   ARCHIBALD, BARDOLPH
BLUNT, FALSTAFF, GADSHILL

GLENDOWER, HOTSPUR, KING HENRY
MICHAEL, MORTIMER, PERCY
NORTHUMBERLAND, PETO, POINS
PRINCE JOHN, PRINCE OF WALES
QUICKLY, SCROOP, VERNON
WESTMORELAND, WORCESTER
(Part II)   BARDOLPH, BULLCALF
COLEVILLE, DAVY, FALSTAFF
FANG, FEEBLE, GOWER, HARCOURT
HASTINGS, KING HENRY, MORTON
MOULDY, MOWBRAY, NORTHUMBERLAND
PAGE, PETO, PISTOL, POINS
PRINCE HUMPHREY, PRINCE JOHN
PRINCE OF WALES, QUICKLY
SCROOP, SHADOW, SHALLOW
SILENCE, SNARE, SURREY
TEARSHEET, THOMAS, TRAVERS
WART, WARWICK, WESTMORELAND
King Henry V   ALICE, ARCHBISHOP
BARDOLPH, BATES, BEDFORD
BOURBON, BURGUNDY, CAMBRIDGE
COURT, ELY, ERPINGHAM, EXETER
FALSTAFF, FLUELLEN, GLOSTER
GOWER, GRANDPRE, GREY
ISABEL, JAMY, KATHARINE
KING CHARLES, KING HENRY
LOUIS, MACMORRIS, MONTJOY
NYM, ORLEANS, PISTOL
QUICKLY, RAMBURES, SALISBURY
SCROOP, WARWICK, WESTMORELAND
WILLIAMS, YORK
King Henry VI
(Part I)   ALENCON, BASSET
BEAUFORT, BEDFORD, BURGUNDY
CHARLES, COUNTESS OF AUVERGNE,
EXETER, FASTOLFE, GARGRAVE
GLANSDALE, GLOSTER, JOAN OF ARC
KING HENRY, LUCY, MARGARET
MORTIMER, ORLEANS, PLANTAGENET
REIGNIER, SALISBURY, SOMERSET
SUFFOLK, TALBOT, VERNON
WARWICK, WOODVILLE
(Part II)   BEAUFORT, BOLINGBROKE
BUCKINGHAM, CADE, CLIFFORD
DICK, EDWARD, ELEANOR, GEORGE
HORNER, HUME, HUMPHREY, IDEN
JOHN, JOURDAIN, KING HENRY
MARGARET, MICHAEL, MORTIMER
PETER, PLANTAGENET, RICHARD
SALISBURY, SAY, SCALES
SIMPCOX, SMITH, SOMERSET
SOUTHWELL, STANLEY, STAFFORD
SUFFOLK, VAUX, WARWICK
WHITMORE
(Part III)   BONA, CLIFFORD
EDWARD, EXETER, GEORGE

HASTINGS, HENRY, KING HENRY
LADY GREY, LOUIS XI, MARGARET
MONTAGUE, MONTGOMERY, MORTIMER
NORFOLK, NORTHUMBERLAND, OXFORD
PEMBROKE, PLANTAGENET, RICHARD
RIVERS, RUTLAND, SOMERSET
SOMERVILLE, STAFFORD, STANLEY
WARWICK, WESTMORELAND
King Henry VIII   ABERGAVENNY, ANNE
BRANDON, BUCKINGHAM, BUTTS
CAMPEIUS, CAPUCIUS, CRANMER
CROMWELL, DENNY, GARDINER
GRIFFITH, GUILDFORD, KATHARINE
KING HENRY, LINCOLN, LOVELL
NORFOLK, PATIENCE, SANDS
SUFFOLK, SURREY, VAUX, WOLSEY
King John   ARCHDUKE, ARTHUR
BIGOT, BLANCH, CHATILLON
CONSTANCE, DE BURGH, ELINOR
FAULCONBRIDGE, FITZ-PETER
GURNEY, KING JOHN, LONGSWORD
LOUIS, MARESHALL, MELUN
PANDULPH, PETER, PHILIP
PRINCE HENRY
King Lear   ALBANY, BURGUNDY, CORDELIA
CORNWALL, CURAN, EDGAR
EDMUND, GLOSTER, GONERIL, KENT
KING LEAR, KING OF FRANCE
OSWALD, REGAN
King Richard II   AUMERLE, BAGOT
BERKLEY, BOLINGBROKE, BUSHY
CARLISLE, DUCHESS OF GLOSTER
DUCHESS OF YORK, FITZWATER
GAUNT, GREEN, KING RICHARD
LANGLEY, MOWBRAY
NORTHUMBERLAND
PIERCE, PERCY, QUEEN, ROSS
SALISBURY, SCROOP, SURREY
WILLOUGHBY, WESTMINSTER
King Richard III   ANNE, BOURCHIER
BRACKENBURY, BUCKINGHAM
BLOUNT, CATESBY, CLARENCE
DORSET, DUCHESS OF YORK
ELIZABETH, GLOSTER, GREY
HASTINGS, HERBERT, KING EDWARD
LOVEL, MARGARET, MORTON, NORFOLK
OXFORD, PRINCE OF WALES
RATCLIFFE, RICHMOND, RIVERS
ROTHERHAM, STANLEY, SURREY
TYRREL, URSWICK, VAUGHAN
YORK
Love's Labour's
Lost   BIRON, BOYET, COSTARD
DON ADRIANO, DULL, DUMAIN
FERDINAND, HOLOFERNES
JAQUENETTA, KATHARINE

LONGAVILLE, MARIA, MERCADE
MOTH, NATHANIEL, PRINCESS
ROSALINE,
Macbeth   ANGUS, BANQUO, CAITHNESS
DONALBAIN, DUNCAN, FLEANCE
HECATE, LENNOX, MACBETH
MACDUFF, MALCOLM, MENTEITH
NORTHUMBERLAND, ROSS
SEYTON, SIWARD

Measure for
Measure   ABHORSON, ANGELO
BARNARDINE, CLAUDIO, CLOWN
ELBOW, ESCALUS, FRANCISCA
FROTH, ISABELLA, JULIET
LUCIO, MARIANA, OVERDONE
PETER, THOMAS, VARRIUS
VICENTIO

Merry Wives of
Windsor   BARDOLPH, CAIUS, EVANS
FALSTAFF, FENTON, FORD
NYM, PAGE, PISTOL, QUICKLY
ROBIN, RUGBY, SHALLOW
SIMPLE, SLENDER

Much Ado About
Nothing   ANTONIO, BALTHAZAR
BEATRICE, BENEDICK, BORACHIO
CLAUDIO, CONRADE, DOGBERRY
DON JOHN, DON PEDRO
HERO, LEONATO, MARGARET
URSULA, VERGES

Othello, The Moor
of Venice   BIANCA, BRABANTIO
CASSIO, DESDEMONA, DUKE
EMILIA, GRATIANO, IAGO
LODOVICO, MONTANO
OTHELLO, RODERIGO

Pericles, Prince
of Tyre   ANTIOCHUS, BOULT
CERIMON, CLEON, DIANA
DIONYZA, ESCANES, GOWER
HELICANUS, LEONINE
LYCHORIDA, LYSIMACHUS
MARINA, PHILEMON, PERICLES
SIMONIDES, THAISA
THALIARD
Romeo and Juliet   ABRAHAM, BALTHASAR
BENVOLIO, CAPULET, ESCALUS
GREGORY, JOHN, JULIET, LAWRENCE
MERCUTIO, MONTAGUE, PARIS
PETER, ROMEO, SAMPSON, TYBALT

The Comedy
of Errors   ADRIANA, AEGEON, AEMILIA
ANGELO, ANTIPHOLUS
BALTHAZAR, DROMIO
LUCIANA, LUCE
PINCH, SOLINUS

The Merchant of
Venice   ANTONIO, BALTHAZAR
BASSANIO, GOBBO, GRATIANO
JESSICA, LAUNCELOT, LEONARDO
LORENZO, NERISSA, PORTIA
PRINCE OF ARRAGON
PRINCE OF MOROCCO
SALANIO, SALARINO
SALERIO, SHYLOCK
STEPHANO, TUBAL, VENICE

The Taming of
The Shrew   BAPTISTA, BIANCA
BIONDELLO, CURTIS, GREMIO
GRUMIO, HORTENSIO, KATHARINA
LUCENTIO, PETRUCHIO, SLY
VINCENTIO

The Tempest   ADRIAN, ALONSO, ANTONIO
ARIEL, CALIBAN, CERES
FERDINAND, FRANCISCO, GONZALO
IRIS, JUNO, , MIRANDA, PROSPERO
SEBASTIAN, STEPHANO, TRINCULO

The Winter's
Tale   ANTIGONUS, ARCHIDAMUS
AUTOLYCUS, CAMILLO, CLEOMENES
DION, DORCAS, EMILIA, FLORIZEL
HERMIONE, LEONTES, MAMILLIUS
MOPSA, PAULINA, PERDITA
POLIXENES
Timon of Athens   ALCIBIADES, APEMANTUS
CAPHIS, FLAMINIUS, FLAVIUS
HORTENSIUS, LUCILIUS, LUCIUS
LUCULLUS, PHILOTUS, PHRYNIA
SEMPRONIUS, SERVILIUS, TIMANDRA
TIMON, TITUS, VENTIDIUS
Titus Andronicus   AARON, AEMILIUS
ALARBUS, BASSIANUS, CHIRON
DEMETRIUS, LAVINIA, LUCIUS
MARCUS, MARTIUS, MUTIUS
PUBLIUS, QUINTUS, SATURNINUS
TAMORA, TITUS
Troilus and Cressida   ACHILLES, AENEAS
AGAMEMNON, AJAX
ALEXANDER, ANDROMACHE
ANTENOR, CALCHAS, CASSANDRA
CRESSIDA, DEIPHOBUS, DIOMEDES
HECTOR, HELEN, HELENUS
MARGARELON, MENELAUS, NESTOR
PANDARUS, PARIS, PATROCLUS
PRIAM, THERSITES, TROILUS
ULYSSES

Twelfth Night
or What You Will   AGUECHEEK, ANTONIO
BELCH, CURIO, FABIAN
MALVOLIO, MARIA, OLIVIA
ORSINO, SEBASTIAN
VALENTINE, VIOLA

Two Gentlemen	
of Verona	ANTONIO, DUKE, EGLAMOUR
	JULIA, LAUNCE, LUCETTA
	PANTHINO, PROTEUS, SILVIA
	SPEED, THURIO, VALENTINE

shapes

all shapes	OMNIFORM
almond	AMYGDALOID
almost circular	PENANNULAR
anchor ring	TORIC, TOROID)AL)
appearing to be halved	DIMIDIATE
approximately circular	ORBICULAR
arch	ARCUATE, FORNICATE
arrow	SAGITTAL
—head	SAGITTIFORM, SAGITTATE
awl	SUBULATE
axe	SECURIFORM
bacillus	BACILLAR(Y), BACILLIFORM
bag	CYSTIFORM
ball	ORB, SPHERE
basin	PELVIFORM
bell	CAMPANIFORM
berry	BACCIFORM
bilaterally symmetrical	ZYGOPLEURAL
bird	AVIFORM
bladder	CYSTIFORM
boat	SCAPHOID
bow	ARCUATE
brain	CEREBRIFORM
breast	MAMMIFORM
bristle	STYLIFORM
—tail	CAMPODEIFORM
brush	PENICILLATE, PENICILLIFORM
buckler	CLYPEATE, CLYPEIFORM
	PELTATE, SCUTATE, SCUTIFORM
bull	TAURIFORM, TAUROMORPHOUS
buttocks	NATIFORM
C-shaped	SIGMOID
cake	PLACENTIFORM
calyx	CALYCIFORM
cap	PILEATE(D)
capital lambda	LAMBDOID(AL)
caterpillar	ERUCIFORM
chisel	SCALPRIFORM
circular	
—pyramid	CONE
—rod	CYLINDER
cirrus	CIRRIFORM
claw	UNGUIFORM
cleaver	DOLABRIFORM
cloud	NUBIFORM
club	CLAVATE, CLAVIFORM
	ROPALIC
—somewhat	CLAVULATE
coin	NUMMULAR
comb	CTENIFORM, CTENOID

cone	CONIFORM
constant intercept of	
tangent and fixed line	TRACTRIX
coral	CORALLIFORM
	CORALLOID(AL)
cord	RESTIFORM
—hanging between	
two points	CATENARY
corolla	COROLLIFORM
	COROLLINE
cowl	CUCULLATE
crab	CANCRIFORM, CANCROID
crescent	CRESCENTIC, LUNATE(D)
	LUNULAR, LUN(UL)ATE
crest	CRISTIFORM
cross	CRUCIATE, CRUCIFORM
crow's beak	CORACOID
crustacean larva	NAUPLIFORM
cube	CUBIFORM
cumulus	CUMULIFORM, CUMULOSE
cup	CRATERIFORM, COTYLOID
	CUPULAR, CUPULATE
	CYATHIFORM, POCULIFORM
	SCYPHIFORM
—in front	PROCOELOUS
curve	CURVIFORM
cushion	PULVILLIFORM
cylindrical and	
smooth	TERETE
cyst	CYSTIFORM
diamond	LOZENGE, RHOMBOID(AL)
disc	COTYLIFORM, DISCOID(AL)
doughnut	TORIC, TOROID(AL)
drop(let)	GLOBULAR, GUTTATE
	STILLIFORM
drum	TYMPANIFORM
eagle's beak	AQUILINE
ear	AURIFORM, AURICULATE
eel	ANGUILLIFORM
egg	OBOVATE, OBOVOID, OOIDAL
	OVATE, OVIFORM, OVOID(AL)
fan	FLABELLATE, RHIPIDATE
feather	PENNIFORM, PINNATE
fiddle	PANDURATE(D)
	PANDURIFORM
figure of eight	LEMNISCATE
finch	FRINGILLIFORM
finger	DIGITATE, DIGITIFORM
fish	PISCIFORM
flask	LAGENIFORM, VASIFORM
flattened circle	ELLIPSE, OVAL
	(see also egg above)
flattened sphere	OBLATE
flower	ANTHOID, FLORIFORM
foot	PEDIFORM
fork	FURCATE(D), FURCULAR

funnel	INFUNDIBULAR		points	PENTACLE, PENTAGON
	INFUNDIBULATE			PENTAGRAM, PENTALPHA
	INFUNDIBULIFORM		sides	PENTAGON
globe	GLOBATE(D), GLOBED, GLOBOID		—6	
	GLOBOSE, GLOBOUS, GLOBULAR		angles	HEXAGON
gnat	CULICIFORM		faces	HEXAHEDRON
goat	CAPRIFORM			PARALLELEPIPED
granule	GRANULIFORM		—rhombi	RHOMBOHEDRON
hair	PILIFORM, VILLIFORM		lines	HEXAGRAM
half			points	HEXAGON, HEXAGRAM
—arrowhead	SEMI-SAGITTATE		sides	HEXAGON
—cylinder	SEMITERETE		—7	
—moon	SEMI-LUNAR, SEMI-LUNATE		angles	HEPTAGON, SEPTANGLE
—sphere	HEMISPHEROID		faces	HEPTAHEDRON
halved	DIMIDIATE		ranges of six	
hammer	MALLEIFORM		faces	HEPTAHEXAHEDRON
hand	MANIFORM, PALMATE		sides	HEPTAGON, SEPTILATERAL
hatchet	DOLABRIFORM		—8	
having			angles	OCTAGON
—1 form	MONOMORPHIC		faces	OCTAHEDRON
	MONOMORPHOUS		sides	EIGHT-SQUARE, OCTAGON
—2			—9	
faces	DI(H)EDRAL, JANIFORM		angles	ENNEAGON
	JANUFORM		faces	ENNEAHEDRON
—hollow each side	BICONCAVE		sides	ENNEAGON, NONAGON
—convex each side	BICONVEX		—10	
feet	BIPEDAL		angles	DECAGON
forms	DIMORPHIC, DIMORPHOUS		faces	DECAHEDRON
sides	BILATERAL		sides	DECAGON
—equal	ISOSCELES		—11 sides	(H)ENDECAGON
—3			—12	
angles	TRIANGLE		faces	DODECAHEDRON
faces	TRIGONAL, TRIHEDRAL		sides	DODECAGON
feet	TRIPEDAL		—18 faces	TETRAKISHEXAHEDRON
forms	TRIMORPHIC, TRIMORPHOUS		—20 faces	ICOSAHEDRON
lines	TRIGRAM		—24 faces	ICOSITETRAHEDRON
prongs	TRINACRIAN			TRIAKISOCTAHEDRON
radiating curves	TRISKELE			TRISOCTAHEDRON
	TRISKELION		—90 faces	ENNEACONTAHEDRON
sides	TRIANGLE, TRIGON		—1000	
	TRILATERAL		faces	CHILIAHEDRON
—4			sides	CHILIAGON
angles	QUADRANGLE		—full number of faces	HOLOHEDRON
faces	PYRAMID, TETRAHEDRON		—many	
forms	QUADRIFORM, TETRAMORPHIC		faces	POLYHEDRON
lines	TETRAGRAM		—like trapezoids	TRAPEZOHEDRON
sides	DIAMOND, LOZENGE		forms	POLYMORPHIC
	PARALLELOGRAM			POLYMORPHOUS
	QUADRANGLE, QUADRILATERAL		sides	POLYGON
	RECTANGLE, RHOMB(US), SQUARE		—various forms	VARIFORM
	TRAPEZIUM, TRAPEZOID		—varying forms	VERSIFORM
—5			head	CAPITATE
angles	PENTAGON, PENTANGLE		heap	CUMULIFORM
	QUINQUANGLE		helmet	GALEATE(D)
faces	PYRAMID		heart	CARDIOID, CORDATE
lines	PENTAGRAM			CORDIFORM

honeycomb	FAVEOLATE, FAVOSE	pentagonal	PYRITOHEDRON
hood	CUCULLATE	pine-cone	PINEAL
hook	UNCIATE(D), UNCIFORM		STROBILIFORM, STROBILOID
—beak	RHAMPHOID	pitcher	ARYT(A)ENOID
horn	CORNICULATE, CORNIFORM		URCEOLATE
horse-shoe	HIPPOCREPIAN	pointed	ACULEATE(D), FASTIGIATE
hump-back	GIBBOUS	potato	SOLANOID
indented	CRENELLATE(D)	pouch	BURSIFORM, SACCATE
intersection of cone			SACCIFORM
and plane		prism	PRISMOID
—parallel to side	PARABOLA	pyramid	PYRAMIDAL, PYRAMIDIC(AL)
—cutting both branches		rectangle	QUADRATE
of cone	HYPERBOLA	relationship of angle	
irregularly notched	EROSE	to its sine	SINE CURVE
jellyfish	MEDUSIFORM	rhombus	LOZENGE, RHOMBOID
keel	CARINATE		SECURIFORM
kidney	NEPHROID, RENIFORM	ribbon	CESTOID, T(A)ENIATE
kite	DELTOID		T(A)ENIOID
knife	CULTRATE, CULTRIFORM	ring	ANNULAR, CIRCINATE, CRICOID
ladder	SCALARIFORM		TOROID
lance	LANCEOLATE, LANCIFORM	rod	BACILLAR(Y), BACILLIFORM
lance-head	LANCEOLATE		VIRGATE, VIRGULATE
larvae	LARVIFORM	roof	TECTIFORM
lattice	CLATHRATE	root	RADICIFORM
leaf	(see leaf²)	rounded teeth	CRENATE(D)
lens	LENTICULAR, LENTIFORM	—finely crenate	CRENULATE(D)
	PHACOID(AL)	S-shaped	OGEE, SIGMOID
lentil	LENTICULAR, PHACOID(AL)	saddle	HYPERBOLIC PARABALOID
letter		saucer	PATELLATE, PATELLIFORM
—C	SIGMATE, SIGMOID(AL)	saw tooth	RUNCINATE, SERRATE
—H	ZYGAL	scale	SQUAMIFORM
—S	OGEE, SIGMATE, SIGMOID(AL)	scalpel	SCALPELLIFORM
—upsilon	HYOID	scimitar	ACINACIFORM
—ypsilon	YPSILIFORM, YPSILOID	screw	HELICOID(AL)
lily	CRINOID(AL)	sesame seed	SESAMOID
limpet	PATELLATE, PATELLIFORM	shell	CONCHATE, CONCHIFORM
long			CONCHOID
—and narrow	LINEAR	shield	CLYPEATE, CLYPEIFORM, PELTATE
—spiral	TURRICULATED		SCUTATE, SCUTIFORM
lozenge	RETICULATE(D), RHOMB(US)		THYR(E)OID
lyre	LYRATE(D)	shovel	SPATULATE
mitre	MITRIFORM	sickle	FALC(UL)ATE, FALCIFORM
mushroom	FUNGIFORM	sieve	COLIFORM, CRIBIFORM
needle	ACEROSE, ACICULAR, ACIFORM	slipper	CALCEOLATE
net	RETIFORM	sloping to point	FASTIGIATE
nipple	MAMILLAR(Y), MAMMILATE(D)	slug	LIMACIFORM
	PAPILLIFORM	small fragments	LAPILLIFORM
obelisk	OBELISCAL, OBELISCOID	snail shell	COCHLEATE
olive	OLIVARY	snake	ANGUIFORM, SERPENTIFORM
orange	OBLATE	socket	GLENAL, GLENOID
oval	VULVIFORM	solid	
	(see also egg above)	—catenary form	CATENOID
palm	PALMATE(D)	—parabola	PARABOLOID
partition	SEPTIFORM	spade	SPATULATE
pea	PISIFORM	spear	HASTATE(D)
pear	PYRIFORM	spike	SPICATE(D)

spindle	CLOSTRIDIAL, FUSIFORM
spine	SPINIFORM
spiral	COCHLEATE(D), HELIX
	HELICAL, TURBINAL
	TURBINATE, VOLUTE(D)
spoon	COCHLEAR(IFORM)
	COCHLEATE(D)
spur	CALCARATE, CALCARIFORM
	CALCARINE
stalactite	STALACTIFORM
star	STELLAR, STELLATE(D)
	STELLIFORM
stem	CAULIFORM
strainer	COLIFORM
strap	LIGULATE
style	STYLIFORM
suspended chain	CATENARY
sword	ENSATE, ENSIFORM
	GLADIATE, XIPHOID
tapering to a point	ACUMINATE
	APICULATE, CUSPIDATE
tapeworm	CESTOID
thin plate	LAMELLIFORM
thorn	SPINIFORM
tongue	LINGUIFORM, LINGULATE
tooth	DENTIFORM, DENTOID
top	STROMBULIFORM
torus	TORIC, TOROID(AL)
trapezium	TRAPEZIFORM
tree	DENDRIFORM, DENDROID
triangle	DELTOID, TRIANGULAR
tube	TUBIFORM, TUBULAR, VASIFORM
tuber	TUBERIFORM
turnip	NAPIFORM
twig	VIRGATE
umbrella	UMBRACULIFORM
undifferentiated into	
root, stem and leaves	THALLIFORM
urn	URCEOLATE
vase	VASCULIFORM
violin	PANDURATE(D), PANDURIFORM
wand	VIRGATE
watch-glass	MENISCOID
wavy-edged	CRENULATE, REPAND
	SINUATE
wedge	CUNEAL, CUNEATE
	CUNEIFORM, SECURIFORM
	SPHENIC, SPHENOID
wheel	ROTATE, TROCHAL, TROCHATE
whip	FLAGELLATE, FLAGELLIFORM
wing	ALARY, ALARIFORM
woman	GYNAECOMORPHOUS
worm	HELMINTHOID, LUMBRICIFORM
	LUMBRICOID, VERMICULAR
	VERMIFORM
yoke	ZYGOMORPHIC, ZYGOMORPHOUS

sheep

Angolan	ZUNA
Asian	AMMON, ARGALI
	CARACUL, KARAKUL
Australian	JUMBU(C)K
British	BORDER LEICESTER
	CANNOCK GREYFACE
	CANNOCK HEATH
	CHEVIOT, COTSWOLD
	HERDWICK, ROMNEY
	SHROPSHIRE DOWN, WENSLEYDALE
Corsican	MUS(I)MON, M(O)UF(F)LON
diseases	GID, SCRAPIE, STURDY
	WATERBRAIN
female	EWE, KEB, TEG(G)
flock-leader	BELLWETHER
hand-reared	COSSET
Himalayan	BHARAL, BLUE SHEEP
	BURREL(L), BUR(R)HEL
	NAHOOR, NAHOUR
	OORIAL, URIAL
horned	JACOB (SHEEP)
Lake District	HERDWICK
male	DINMONT, RAM, TUP, WETHER
North African	AOUDAD
	BARBARY SHEEP
old ewe	CROCK
second-year	HOG(-SHEEP), TEG(G)
short-legged	ANCON
South American	ALPACA, GUANACO
	HUANACO, LLAMA, PACO
Spanish	LATXA, MERINO
Tibetan	SHAPO, SHAHPU
woolly-faced	MUG
yearling	HOG(G), HOGGEREL, HOGGET
young	LAMB, YEANLING
—ewe	GIMMER, THEAVE

shellfish

abalone	EAR-SHELL, ORMER, SEA-EAR
—New Zealand	PAUA, PAWA
American clam	BUTTER CLAM, COHOG
	QUAHOG, QUAHAUG
	ROUND CLAM
arthropod with	
hard shell	CRUSTACEAN
Australian	PIPI
bivalves	CLAM, COCKLE, LAMELLIBRANCH
	MUSSEL, OYSTER, RAZOR CLAM
	RAZOR SHELL, SCALLOP
clam	SCALLOP(-SHELL)
clinging to ships, rocks etc	BARNACLE
crab	PARTON
Crangon	SHRIMP
crawfish	CRAYFISH, LANGOUSTE
	NORWAY LOBSTER, ROCK LOBSTER
	SPINY LOBSTER

decapod crustacean	BRACHYURA, CRAB	—part of temple	HONDON
edible		outer shrine of temple	HAIDEN
—crustacean	LOBSTER, SHRIMP	purification	HARAI
—gasteropod	(PERI)WINKLE	ritual prayers	NORITO
French		truthfulness	MAKOTO
—mussel	MOULE	underworld	YOMI
—winkle	VIGNETTE	*(see also* **Japanese**)	
freshwater decapod	CRAYFISH		
highest class of molluscs	CEPHALOPOD	**ship**[1]	
Homarus	LOBSTER	includes: types	
langoustine	DUBLIN BAY PRAWN	1 hull	MONOHULL
	KING PRAWN	2 hulls	CATAMARAN
large oyster	CHAMA	3 hulls	TRIMARAN
like small lobster	CRAYFISH, LANGOUSTE	American	DORY, SHOWBOAT
	LANGOUSTINE, PRAWN, SHRIMP		STERNWHEELER
marie snail	(PERI)WINKLE, WHELK	Annamese	GAY-YOU
New Zealand	PAUA, PIPI	ancient galley	BIREME, TRIREME
Norway lobster	LANGOUSTINE, SCAMPI		QUADRIREME, QUINQUEREME
ormer	ABALONE, EAR-SHELL	—oars and sails	GALLEAS, GALLEY
	SEA-EAR	Arab	*(see* Egyptian *below)*
oysters on toast	ANGELS ON HORSEBACK	argosy	CAR(R)ACK, CARRACT
Pacific Ocean	COCONUT CRAB		CARRECT
pearl producing	OYSTER	armed merchantman	Q-SHIP
Pecten	SCALLOP(-SHELL)	Baltic	
sea-ear	ABALONE	—1-masted	COG
segmented	ARTHROPOD	—2-masted	NEF
single-shelled	UNIVALVE	—3-masted	CHEBECK, SHEBECK
small		barge	GABBARD, GABBART
—clam	COQUINA		WHERRY
—shrimps	KRILL	British	
Solen	RAZOR-CLAM, RAZOR-FISH	—coal lighter	KEEL
spiny lobster	LANGOUSTE, ROCK LOBSTER	—coal-vessel	CAT
squid-like	CUTTLEFISH	—flat-bottomed	KEEL
ten-legged	CRAB, CRAWFISH, CRAYFISH	—small yacht	KNOCKABOUT
	LOBSTER, SHRIMP	cargo	COASTER, FREIGHTER, TRAMP
unsegmented		cargo-warship	CAR(R)ACK, CARRACT
invertebrate	MOLLUSC, MOLLUSK		CARRECT
Venus mollusc	COHOG, QUAHOG	carrying	
	QUAHAUG, ROUND CLAM	—cargo	FREIGHTER, TRAMP
West Indies	CONCH	in crates	CONTAINER SHIP
whalefood	KRILL	—coal	COLLIER, GEORDIE, KEEL
with		—oil	OILER, TANKER
—broad foot	GAST(E)ROPOD	—passengers	CRUISE SHIP, LINER
—ear-shaped shell	ABALONE, ORMER	—vehicles and passengers	FERRY, RORO
—fan-shaped shell	SCALLOP	Chinese	JUNK, SAMPAN, SANPAN
—hinged shells	BIVALVE	corvette	SLOOP
—spiral shell	NAUTILUS, (PERI)WINKLE	cut-down	RAZEE
	WHELK	despatch boat (Spanish)	AVISO
		disguised warship	Q-SHIP
Shinto		dismantled	HULK
ancient texts	KOJIKI	dredger	PETER-BOAT
code of moral principles	BUSHIDO	Dutch	BESANT, BEZANT, KOFF
domestic shrine	KAMI-DANA		PINK(IE), PINKY
goddess	AMATERASU	—1-masted	HOY
gods and their powers	KAMI	—2-masted	BILANDER, BYLANDER
holy			BUSS, DOGGER
—object in temple	SHINTAI		HOOKER, HOWKER, KOFF

—3-masted	FLUYT
—cargo	GAL(L)IOT
—flat-bottomed	
lighter	PRA(A)M
	SCOW, SCHUIT, SCHUTT
—privateer	CAPER
Eastern coaster	GRAB
Egyptian	DAHABEEAH
	DAHABIYAH, DAHABIYEH
	FELUCCA, NUGGAR, SAMBOOK
	SAMBUC(C)O, SAMBUK, ZARUG
escort	CORVETTE
excavator	DREDGER
European	
—1-masted	BILLY-BOY, COG, CUTTER
	DANDY, SHALLOP, SLOOP, YAWL
—2-masted	BRIG(ANTINE)
	KETCH, LUGGER
	PINNACE, SNOW
—2-6 masted	SCHOONER
—3-masted	CLIPPER, CORVETTE
	FRIGATE
—3-4 masted	BARK(ENTINE)
	BARQUE(NTINE)
—4-masted	JACKASS-BARK
—trading	CAR(A)VEL, CAR(R)ACK
	CARRACT, CARRECT, CRARE
	CRAYER, GALLEON, LUGGER
famous ships	
—American battleships	DELAWARE
	NEVADA, OKLAHOMA
	NEW JERSEY
—Amundsen	FRAM
—Anson	CENTURION
—balsa raft	KON TIKI
—Beatles	YELLOW SUBMARINE
—British battleships	ARK ROYAL, BROKE
	DREADNOUGHT
	DUKE OF YORK
	HOOD, INVINCIBLE, IRON DUKE
	ORION, PRINCE OF WALES
	QUEEN ELIZABETH, RENOWN
	REPULSE, RODNEY
	ROYAL SOVEREIGN
—Captain	
Bligh	BOUNTY
Cook	ENDEAVOUR
Nemo	NAUTILUS
Scott	DISCOVERY
—Chichester's yacht	GIPSY MOTH
—clipper	ARIEL, CUTTY SARK
	SERICA, TAIPING
—Columbus	SANTA MARIA
—crewless	MARIE CELESTE
—Darwin	BEAGLE
—Drake	GOLDEN HIND

—first nuclear-powered	
cruiser	LONG BEACH
merchant ship	SAVANNAH
oil-fired battleship	ROSTISLAV
submarine	NAUTILUS
—French battleships	BRETAGNE, COURBET
	LORRAINE, PROVENCE
—German battleships	BISMARCK, BLUCHER
	DEUTSCHLAND, EMDEN
	GOEBEN, GNEISENAU
	GRAF SPEE, HIPPER
	SCHARNHORST
—Gilbert and Sullivan	HMS PINAFORE
—Greenpeace	RAINBOW WARRIOR
—Heyerdahl	KON TIKI, RA, TIGRIS
—Italian battleship	ANDREA DORIA
—Japanese fishing-boat	
contaminated by first	
atomic explosion	LUCKY DRAGON
—leather boat	BRENDAN
—liner sunk by iceberg	TITANIC
—Longfellow's schooner	HESPERUS
—Magellan	VITTORIA
—Mountbatten	KELLY
—mystery ship	MARIE CELESTE
—Nelson	VICTORY
—oceanographic	CHALLENGER
—paddle steamer	COTTON BLOSSOM
—Pilgrim Fathers	MAYFLOWER
—reed boat	RA, TIGRIS
—royal yacht	BRITANNIA, OSBORNE
—Russian battleship	POTEMKIN
—salvaged woodenwall	MARY ROSE
—Shackleton	QUEST
—Showboat	COTTON BLOSSOM
—Slocum's yacht	SPRAY
—Sopwith's yacht	ENDEAVOUR
—spectral	FLYING DUTCHMAN
—Tudor battleship	MARY ROSE
	ROYAL SOVEREIGN
—Weddell	JANE
fast sailer	CUTTER, SLOOP
	(TEA-)CLIPPER
fishing-boat	BANKER, DOGGER, DRIFTER
	(HERRING-)BUSS, LUGGER,
	PETER-BOAT, SMACK, TRAWLER
flat-bottomed	KEEL
Flemish sloop	BOYER
French carrack	NEF
galleon	GALLOON
galley	
—beaked	DRAKE
—Greek	(see Greek below)
—heavy	GALLEAS
—old	(see ancient above)
—Scottish	LYMPHAD

—small	GAL(L)IOT
Greek	
—30 oars	TRIACONTER
—50 oars	PENTECONTER
guard-boat	VEDETTE
heavy galley	GALLEAS
Indian	BUDGERO(W), LANCHA
	PATAMAR, PUTELI, SAMBOK
	SAMBUC(C)O, SAMBUK
jointed ship	CONNECTOR
Italian merchant	ARGOSY
Japanese	MARO, MARU
largest	SEAWISE GIANT
Levantine ketch	SAIC(K), SAIQUE
Malay	COROCORE, COROCORO
	GALLIVAT
	PRA(H)U, PROA
Mediterranean	SANDAL, SET(T)EE
	TARTAN(E)
—2-masted	CAR(A)VEL, FELUCCA
—3-masted	CAR(A)VEL, CHEBEC(K)
	SHEBEC(K), XEBEC(K), ZEBEC(K)
	POLACRE, POLACCA
—coaster	MISTICO
—warship	DROMON(D)
Newfoundland	BANKER
non-fighting naval ship	AUXILIARY
Norse	
—magic ship	SKIDBLADNIR
—merchant ship	KNORR
—Viking ship	LONGSHIP
old ship fitted as place	
of worship	BETHEL
passenger	CRUISER, LINER
plying across rivers, etc	FERRY
Portuguese	CAR(A)VEL, LORCHA
	MULETTE
prefabricated	LIBERTY SHIP
	VICTORY SHIP
prison-ship	BRIG, HULK
privateer	CORSAIR, CRUISER
refuelling ship	OILER
river-boat	PADDLEBOAT, PADDLER
	SHOWBOAT, STERNWHEELER
Scottish	
—barge	BIRLINN
—flat-bottomed	COB(B)LE
—galley	LYMPHAD
shallow, fast	WHERRY
small	LUGGER, PINK, PINNACE
—galley	GAL(L)IOT
Spanish	CAR(A)VEL, GALLEASS
	GALLEON, ZABRA
spectral	FLYING DUTCHMAN
state barge	GALLEY-FOIST
supply	MAILBOAT, PACKET, TENDER

supported on	
—air cushion	HOVERCRAFT
—runners	HYDROFOIL
Thames fishing	BAWLEY, BORLEY
Tigris ferry	GUFA
trader	INDIAMAN
Turkish	CAIC, CAIQUE
underwater	SUBMARINE
unwieldy	HULK
Venetian	ARGOSY, FRIGATOON
	VAPORETTO
warship	AIRCRAFT CARRIER, CORVETTE
	CRUISER, DESTROYER, DREADNOUGHT
	FRIGATE, IRONSIDE, MAN-O(F)-WAR
	MINELAYER, MINESWEEPER
	MONITOR, Q-SHIP
	(MOTOR)TORPEDO BOAT, MTB
	SLOOP, SUBMARINE
—old	SHIP OF THE LINE
	WOODENWALL
—used in harbour defence	BLOCK-SHIP
West Indian coaster	DROG(H)ER
yacht	(see **yachting**)

ship²

includes: terms	
access panel	HATCH
across the ship	(A)THWARTSHIPS
adjust sails to catch	
the wind	TRIM
adjustable stay for mast	(LEE) RUNNER
	WEATHER RUNNER
after part of	
—bow	LOOF, LUFF
—ship	POOP, STERN
anchor	KILLICK, KILLOCK
—at bow	BEST BOWER, SMALL BOWER
—rope	MESSENGER
apparatus for determining	
speed of ship	LOG
arms for raising and	
lowering lifeboats	DAVITS
beam for raising anchor	CATHEAD
beat to windward	LAVEER
body of ship	HULL
bottom member of hull	KEEL
bracket carrying rowlock	OUTRIGGER
break over stern (waves)	POOP
bring ship to standstill	HEAVE-TO
built with	
—flush planking	CARVEL-BUILT
—overlapping planking	CLINKER-BUILT
call to exertion	HEAVE-HO
capstan bar	NORMAN
cargo space	HOLD
carousing on icebound	
ship	MALLEMAROKING

cast the log into the water	HEAVE THE LOG
change course	
—by swinging sail to other side	JIBE, GYBE
—close to another boat	SLAM DUFF
clean ship's bottom	BREAM
close-hauled to the wind	FULL AND BYE
coastal trading	CABOTAGE
cover over opening in deck	(COMPANION-)HATCH
	SCUTTLE
deck	
—high at rear	POOP
—housing main armament	GUN DECK
—lowest	ORLOP
deviate temporarily from a straight course	YAW
distance between tacks	REACH
doctor	SURGEON
examine ship's papers	JERK, JERQUE
eyelet in sail	CRINGLE
fasten sail securely	FRAP, LASH
fix a mast	STEP
front of	
—keel	FOREFOOT
—ship	BOW, CUTWATER, FOC'S'LE
	FORECASTLE, STEM
fulcrum for oar	ROLLOCK, ROWLOCK
	RULLOCK
galley	CABOOSE
haul	TRICE
high deck at stern	POOP
hijack a ship	SEAJACK, SHIPJACK
hole	
—in	
bows for cable	HAWSE-HOLE
stern for cable	CAT-HOLE
—to drain deck	SCUPPER
immersion while hanging over side	TEABAGGING
in a vertical position (anchor)	ATRIP
inferior sailor	GREENHAND
inner keel	KE(E)LSON
inward slope of ship's side	TUMBLEHOME
kitchen	CABOOSE, GALLEY
lashing round bowsprit	GAMMON
launching ramp	SLIPWAY
let the wind out of sail	SPILL
loading mark	PLIMSOLL LINE
lower sail, flag, etc	STRIKE
lowest deck	ORLOP
movable keel	CENTREBOARD
on duty	ON WATCH

opening in deck	HATCHWAY, SCUTTLE
part of	
—boat between thwarts and stern or bow	SHEETS
—bows	HAWSE
—deck abaft the mainmast	QUARTER-DECK
—sail (that can be) rolled up	REEF
pig-iron ballast	KENTLEDGE
pin	
—for keeping oar in place	THOLE(-PIN), THOW(E)L
—for securing rope	BELAYING PIN
plate taking strain of rigging	CHAIN-PLATE
platform on mainmast	MAINTOP
pole supporting sail	SPAR, YARD(ARM)
props supporting ship before launch	DOGSHORES
projecting float	OUTRIGGER
race meeting	REGATTA
raised and secured (anchor)	CATTED AND FISHED
rail round table etc	FIDDLE
rear part of	
—deck	TRANSOM
—ship	STERN
record of voyage, etc	LOG
rig	
—chief sails square	SQUARE-RIGGED
—mainsail on one side, foresail on the other	GOOSE-WINGED
—mixed rig	HERMAPHRODITE RIG
—one large	
fore-and-aft sail	CAT-RIGGED
square sail	LUG(GER)-RIGGED
—three or more masts	FULL-RIGGED
—triangular mainsail	BERMUDA RIG
	GENOA RIG
	MARCONI RIG
rigging	(*see* **rope**)
roll up part of sail	FURL, REEF
rope	(*see separate entry*)
rower's bench	THWART
run before the wind	SCUD, SPOON
sail	
—close to the wind	LUFF
—hoisted ready for trimming	ATRIP
—into wind	BEAT
on zigzag course	TACK
—slightly sideways to offset drift	CRAB
—with wind from	
behind	RUN
one side	REACH

sailing rhumb lines	LOXODROMY	—facing wind	WEATHER SIDE
sailor	(*see separate entry*)	—sheltered from wind	LEE (SIDE)
sails		socket receiving mast	TABERNACLE
—above		spar	
lower topsail	UPPER TOPSAIL	—of fore-and-aft sail at	
mainsail	LOWER TOPSAIL	foot	BOOM
royal	SKYSAIL	head	GAFF
skysail	MOONSAIL	—for extended sails	OUTRIGGER
topgallant	ROYAL	—projecting from	
upper topsail	TOPGALLANT	bows	BOWSPRIT
—asymmetric spinnaker	GENNAKER	mast	CROSSTREE, YARD(ARM)
	GENNIKER	—set diagonally to	
—attached to another	BONNET	extend sail	SPRIT
—at end of yard	STUNSAIL	—under bowsprit	MARTINGALE, SNOTTER
—between		speed recorder	LOG
foremast and bowsprit	FLYING JIB	staircase	COMPANION-WAY
	FORESTAYSAIL	steering mechanism	RUDDER, TILLER
	INNER JIB, OUTER JIB	storage compartment	HOLD
masts	STAYSAIL	strap for fastening	
—corner of sail	CLEW, TACK	furled sails to yard	GASKET
—extended by a sprit	SPRIT-SAIL	swing sail to other side	JIBE, GYBE
—four-sided sail on		take soundings	HEAVE THE LEAD
diagonal spar	LUG(SAIL)	temporary mast, etc	JURY RIG
—front edge of sail	LEADING EDGE	tie up sails to yards	CLEW (UP)
	LUFF	tilt when sailing into wind	HEEL
—headsail	YANKEE	to the rear of	ABAFT
—lower corners of mainsail		top plank of bulwark	GUNNEL, GUNWALE
or foresail	GOOSE-WING	tube for anchor-chain	HAWSE-PIPE
—lowest on mast	COURSE, MAINSAIL	turn	
—mid-section of sail	BAG, BUNT	—into the wind	BROACH, LUFF
—on		—vessel on its side	
foremast	SPENCER	for repair, etc	CAREEN
mainmast	SPENCER	upper part of	
mizzen mast	CRO(SS)JACK	—side	GUNELL, GUNWALE
	DRIVER, SPANKER	—stern	TAFFEREL
—rigged along line			TAFFRAIL
of vessel	FORE-AND-AFT	watches	
—side edge of sail	LEECH	—midnight-4am	MIDDLE WATCH
—small sail set high on mast	KITE	—4am-8am	MORNING WATCH
—storm sail	HULLOCK	—8am-noon	FORENOON WATCH
—strengthening strip	REEF-BAND	—noon-4pm	AFTERNOON WATCH
—triangular mainsail		—4pm-6pm	FIRST DOG WATCH
slung from diagonal		—6pm-8pm	LAST DOG WATCH
spar	LATEEN (SAIL)		SECOND DOG WATCH
used on racing		—8pm-midnight	FIRST WATCH
vessels	BERMUDA, GENNAKER	windward side of ship	LUFF
	GENNIKER, GENOA	wooden block	
	MARCONI, SPINNAKER	—for lanyard	DEADEYE
scrub deck with sandstone	HOLYSTONE	—holding lines of crowfoot	(E)UPHROE
search ship	JERK, JERQUE	written record of events	LOG
seat set across boat	THWART	**shoes**	(*see* **footwear**)
sheltered side of ship	LEE	**showjumping**	
ship over the stern	POOP	dressage movements	
short spell of duty	DOGWATCH	—backward	REINBACK
side of ship		—balancing on hind legs	LEVADE
—above deck	BULWARK	—curvet	FALCADE

—diagonal	CANTER- HALF-PASS
—fast showy walking	RACK, SINGLE-FOOT
—half turn	CARACOLE
—high-stepping trot	PASSAGE
—leap with rear legs under-belly	CROUPADE
—low prancing jump	CURVET, GAMBADO
—sideways walk	PASSAGE
tracing circle	VOLTE
—slow trot	PIAFFE
—standing on hind legs	PESADE
—turn on haunches	PIROUETTE
—upward jump	CAPRIOLE
famous horses	BARBERRY, BENTON
	BOOMERANG, CHAGALL
	CHARISMA, DEISTER
	FOXHUNTER, GRANAT
	HALLA, METEOR, MILTON
	PINOCCHIO, RYAN'S SON
	WAYFARER
high-jumping event	PUISSANCE
no faults	CLEAR ROUND
penalties	
—exceeding time	1/4 FAULT PER SECOND
—failing to finish	ELIMINATION
—fall	8 FAULTS
second	ELIMINATION
—foot in water	4 FAULTS
—knocking down fence	4 FAULTS
—landing on tape marker	4 FAULTS
—omitting an obstacle	ELIMINATION
—refusal	3 FAULTS
second	6 FAULTS
third	ELIMINATION
—starting too soon	ELIMINATION
penalty point	FAULT
raised poles for jumping	CAVALLETTI
riders	
—American (m)	COFFIN, DAVIDSON, MATZ
	STEINKRAUS, THOMPSON
	TUTTLE
(f)	STIVES
—Australian (m)	MCVEAN
(f)	LEONE, ROYCROFT
—Austrian (m)	FRUHMANN, SIMON
	VANGEENBERGHE
—Belgian (m)	HAEGEMAN, PHILIPPAERTS
	VAN DEN BROECK
—Brazilian (m)	PESSOA
—British (m)	BROOME, EVANS, HEFFER
	HUNT, LLEWELLYN, MEADE
	ROBESON, SKELTON
	SMITH, STARK, TODD, TURI
	WELDON, WHITAKER
(f)	BRADLEY, CARRUTHERS
	GREEN, HOLGATE, HUNT

	LENG, LORISTON-CLARKE
	MCIRVINE, MAC, MASON
	PRIOR-PALMER
	THOMSON, WINTER
—Canadian (m)	GREENOUGH
(f)	MILLER
—Dutch (m)	LANSINK, MORTANGES
—French (m)	DOLLAND, DURAND
	GODIGNON, JOUSSEAUME
	MARLON, ORIOLA, ROZIER, TOPS
(f)	BOST, CREPIN, D'ESME
—German (m)	BECKER, BEERBAUM
	HAFEMEISTER, KIMKE, MOHLE
	ROTHENBERGER, SCHOCKE
	SLOOTHAACK, TEBBEL
	WINKLER, THIEDEMANN
(f)	LISENHOFF, UPHOFF
—Irish (m)	DARAGH, MACKEN, MULLINS
—Italian	CHECCOLI, ROMAN
—New Zealand (m)	TAIT, TODD
(f)	LATTA
—Russian	FILTOV, KILATOV, MENKOVA
—Swedish	ST CYR, SANDSTROM
	MORNER, NORLANDER
—Swiss (m)	GALBATHULER
venues	
—Britain	BADMINTON
	GATCOMBE PARK
	HICKSTEAD, OLYMPIA
	WHITE CITY
—France	DINARD
—Germany	AACHEN, BERLIN, DORTMUND
—Ireland	DUBLIN
—Luxemburg	MONDORF LES BAINS
—Netherlands	GEESTERN
	'S HERTOGENBOSCH
—Sweden	FALSTERBO
—USA	MADISON SQUARE GARDEN
shrubs	
acacia	MIMOSA
Actinidia	CHINESE GOOSEBERRY
Alexandrian laurel	DANAE
Aloysia	LIPPIA
Ampelopsis	PARTHENOCISSUS
	VIRGINIA CREEPER
Andromeda	PIERIS
Aristolochia	DUTCHMAN'S PIPE
azalea	WINTER-BLOOM
barberry	BERBERIS, PODOPHYLLUM
beauty bush	KOLKWITZIA
berberis	BARBERRY, PODOPHYLLUM
Berberidopsis	CORAL PLANT
Bignonia	CAMPSIS, TRUMPET VINE
blackberry	DEWBERRY, RUBUS
—x raspberry	BOYSENBERRY
	LOGANBERRY

bladder	
—nut	STAPHYLEA
—senna	COLUTEA
box	BUXUS
bramble	RUBUS
broom	CYTISUS, GENISTA
Buddleia	BUTTERFLY BUSH
burning bush	EUONYMUS, WAHOO
butcher's broom	RUSCUS
buttercup shrub	POTENTILLA
butterfly bush	BUDDLEIA
Buxus	BOX
Californian lilac	CEANONTHUS
Calluna	HEATHER
Campsis	BIGNONIA, TRUMPET VINE
Cape jasmine	GARDENIA
castor oil plant	FATSIA
Ceanothus	CALIFORNIAN LILAC
Ceratostigma	PLUMBAGO
Chaenomeles	CYDONIA
	FLOWERING QUINCE
	JAPONICA
Chilean firebush	EMBOTHRIUM
Chimonanthus	WINTER SWEET
Chinese	
—gooseberry	ACTINIDIA
—hawthorn	PHOTINIA
—sacred bamboo	NANDINA
Choisya	MEXICAN ORANGE BLOSSOM
Cistus	ROCK ROSE
clammy azalea	SWAMP AZALEA
	WHITE HONEYSUCKLE
Clerodendron	GLORY TREE
Clianthus	LOBSTER-CLAW PLANT
	PARROT'S BILL
Cneorum	DAPHNE (MEZEREUM)
	MEZEREON, WIDOW-WAIL
Colutea	BLADDER SENNA
coral plant	BERBERIDOPSIS
Cornus	DOGWOOD
Cotinus	SMOKE TREE
cranberry	FEN-BERRY, VACCINIUM
Cydonia	CHAENOMELES
Cytisus	BROOM
Daboecia	IRISH HEATH
daisy bush	OLEARIA
Danae	ALEXANDRIAN LAUREL
daphne	SPURGE-LAUREL
—mezereum	CNEORUM, MEZEREON
	WIDOW-WAIL
Diervilla	WEIGELA
dogwood	CORNUS
double-flowered gorse	ULEX
Dutchman's pipe	ARISTOLOCHIA
Easter rose	JEW'S MALLOW, KERRIA
elder	SAMBUCUS

Embothrium	CHILEAN FIREBUSH
Erica	HEATHER
Exochorda	PEARL BUSH
Fatsia	CASTOR OIL PLANT
firethorn	PYRACANTHA
flowering	
—currant	RIBES
—nutmeg	LEYCESTERIA
—quince	CHAENOMELES
forsythia	GOLDEN BELL BUSH
gardenia	CAPE JASMINE
Genista	BROOM, SPANISH GORSE
glory tree	CLERODENDRON
golden bell bush	FORSYTHIA
guelder rose	GELDER('S)-ROSE
	ROSE-ELDER, VIBURNUM
Halesia	SNOWDROP TREE
Hamamelis	WITCH HAZEL
heather	CALLUNA, DABOECIA, ERICA
Hebe	VERONICA
Hedera	IVY
Hibiscus	ROSE-MALLOW, ROSE OF CHINA
	TREE HOLLYHOCK
holly	ILEX
—leafed Berberis	MAHONIA
honeysuckle	CAPRIFOLE, LONICERA
	WOODBIND, WOODBINE
Hypericum	ST JOHN'S WORT
Ilex	HOLLY
Irish heath	DABOECIA
ivy	HEDERA
Japanese	
—bitter orange	PONCIRUS
—spurge	PACHYSANDRA
japonica	CHAENOMELES
Jerusalem sage	PHLOMIS
Jew's mallow	KERRIA
Kerria	EASTER ROSE
	JEW'S MALLOW
Kolkwitzia	BEAUTY BUSH
Lantana	SHRUB VERBENA
Laurus	SWEET BAY
Laurustinus	VIBURNUM
lavender	LAVANDULA
lemon-scented verbena	LIPPIA
Leycesteria	FLOWERING NUTMEG
Ligustrum	PRIVET
lilac	SYRINGA
Lippia	ALOYSIA
	LEMON-SCENTED VERBENA
lobster-claw plant	CLIANTHUS
	PARROT'S BILL
Lonicera	HONEYSUCKLE
magnolia	TULIP TREE
Mahonia	HOLLY-LEAVED BERBERIS
Mexican orange blossom	CHOISYA

mezereon	CNEORUM
	DAPHNE (MEZEREUM)
	WIDOW-WAIL
mile-a-minute vine	POLYGONUM
	SILVER LACE
mimosa	ACACIA
mock orange	PHILADELPHUS, SYRINGA
Myrica	TAMARISK
myrtle	MYRTUS
Nandina	CHINESE SACRED BAMBOO
naseberry	NEESBERRY, SAPODILLA PLUM
Nerium	OLEANDER
Oleander	NERIUM
Olearia	DAISY BUSH
Pachysandra	JAPANESE SPURGE
parrot's bill	CLIANTHUS
	LOBSTER-CLAW PLANT
Parthenocissus	AMPELOPSIS
	VIRGINIA CREEPER
pearl bush	EXOCHORDA
periwinkle	VINCA
Perovskia	RUSSIAN SAGE
Philadelphus	MOCK ORANGE, SYRINGA
Phlomis	JERUSALEM SAGE
Photinia	CHINESE HAWTHORN
Pieris	ANDROMEDA
plumbago	CERATOSTIGMA
Polygonum	MILE-A-MINUTE VINE
	SILVER LACE
Podophyllum	BARBERRY, BERBERIS
	RACCOON-BERRY
pomegranate	PUNICA
Poncirus	JAPANESE BITTER ORANGE
Potentilla	BUTTERCUP SHRUB
privet	LIGUSTRUM
Punica	POMEGRANATE
Pyracantha	FIRETHORN
raccoon-berry	PODOPHYLLUM
raspberry	RUBUS
Rhus	SMOKE TREE
Ribes	FLOWERING CURRANT
rock rose	CISTUS
rose-elder	GUELDER-ROSE
rose of China	HIBISCUS
rosemary	ROSEMARINUS
Rubus	BLACKBERRY, BRAMBLE
	RASPBERRY
Ruscus	BUTCHER'S BROOM
Russian sage	PEROVSKIA
sage	SALVIA
St John's wort	HYPERICUM
Sambucus	ELDER
Sapodilla plum	NASEBERRY, NEESBERRY
Scotch creeper	TROPAEOLUM
sea buckthorn	HIPPOPHAE
shrub verbena	LANTANA

shrubby germander	TEUCRIUM
silver lace	POLYGONUM
	MILE-A-MINUTE VINE
smoke tree	COTINUS, RHUS
snowball tree	VIBURNUM, WHITSUN ROSE
snowberry	SYMPHORICARPUS
snowdrop tree	HALESIA
Spanish	
—broom	SPARTIUM
—gorse	GENISTA
Spartium	SPANISH BROOM
Staphylea	BLADDER NUT
swamp azalea	CLAMMY AZALEA
	WHITE HONEYSUCKLE
sweet bay	LAURUS
Symphoricarpus	SNOWBERRY
syringa	LILAC, MOCK ORANGE
	PHILADELPHUS
tamarisk	MYRICA
Teucrium	SHRUBBY GERMANDER
Trachycarpus	CHUSAN PALM
tree hollyhock	HIBISCUS
Tropaeolum	SCOTCH CREEPER
trumpet vine	BIGNONIA, CAMPSIS
tulip tree	MAGNOLIA
Ulex	DOUBLE-FLOWERED GORSE
veronica	HEBE
Viburnum	LAURUSTINUS
Virginia creeper	AMPELOPSIS
	PARTHENOCISSUS
Weigela	DIERVILLA
white honeysuckle	CLAMMY AZALEA
	SWAMP AZALEA
Whitsun rose	SNOWBALL TREE
	VIBURNUM
widow-wail	CNEORUM
	DAPHNE (MEZEREUM)
	MEZEREON
winter	
—bloom	AZALEA, WITCH HAZEL
—sweet	CHIMONANTHUS
witch hazel	HAMAMELIS, WINTER-BLOOM

Siamese

bay	AO
canal	KLONG
cape (headland)	LAEM
capital	BANGKOK
coin	BAHT, SATANG, TICAL
creek	KLONG
dynasty	CHAKKRI
island	KO
language	THAI
measure	
—1"	NIU
—20"	SAWK
—80"	WAH

—44 yards	SEN
—⅓ acre	RAI
mountain	DONG
river	(MAE) NAM
town	NAKHON
twins	PARBIOTIC
weight (3 lb)	CHANG
Sierra Leone	WAL
capital	FREETOWN
coin	CENT, LEONE
Sikh	
baptism ceremony	AMRIT
fanatic	AKALI
holy	
—book	GRANTH (SAHIB)
—person	SANT
knife	KIRPAN
law of causality	KARMA
nectar	AMRIT
organiser of worship	GRANTHI
script	GURMUKHI
sugar-and-water drink	AMRIT
temple	GURDWARA
	(*see also* **belief, Indian**)
Singapore	SGP
six	
at dice	SICE, SIZE
balls	OVER
books of OT	HEXATEUCH
Christmas presents	GEESE
cleft	SEXFID
combining forms	HEX(A)-, SEXA-
counties (of Northern	
Ireland)	ANTRIM, ARMAGH
	FERMANAGH, DOWN
	(LONDON)DERRY, TYRONE
daily	SEXTAN
day fever	SEXTAN
days of creation	HEXAEMERON
fold	SEXTUPLE(X), SEXTUPLICATE
groups	HEXAD, SENARY, SESTET(T)
	SESTETTE, SEXTET(T)
	SEXTETTE, SEXTUOR
having six	
—angles	HEXAGONAL, SEXAGONAL
—columns	HEXASTYLE
—compartments	SEXLOCULAR
—feet	HEXAPODAL
—fingers	HEXADACTYLIC
	HEXADACTYLOUS
	SEXIDIGITAL
	SEXIDIGITATE(D)
—languages	HEXAGLOT
—leaves	SEXFOIL
—lines	HEXASTICH(AL)
—lobes	SEXFOIL

—metrical feet	HEXAMETER
	HEXAMETRIC(AL)
—notes	HEXACHORD
—parts	HEXAMEROUS
	HEXPARTITE
—pistils	HEXAGYNIAN, HEXAGYNOUS
—plane faces	HEXAHEDRON
—rays	HEXACT(INAL)
—sides	HEXAGONAL
—stamens	HEXANDRIAN, HEXANDROUS
—styles	HEXAGYNIAN, HEXAGYNOUS
—times normal number	
of chromosomes	HEXAPLOID
—toes	HEXADACTYLIC
	HEXADACTYLOUS, SEXIDIGITAL
	SEXIDIGITATE(D)
—valencies	SEX(I)VALENT
—vascular strands	HEXARCH
—versions	HEXAPLAR(IC)
	HEXAPLARIAN
headed monster	SCYLLA
hours	QUARTER-DAY
hundred	BALACLAVA, DC
	LIGHT BRIGADE, VIC
—years	SEXCENTENARY
notes	SEXTOLET
nymphs	HYADES
on die	CISE, SICE, SISE
one of six at a birth	SEXTUPLET
pence	SICE, TANNER
six-footer	ANT, BEE, INSECT
yearly	SEXENNIAL
sixteen	
sixteen leaves per sheet	SEXTODECIMO
	SIXTEENMO
sixteenth note	SEMIQUAVER
verse of sixteen lines	SIXTEENER
sixth	
sixth (music)	SEXT
sixth of circle	SEXTANT
sixth-sense	ESP
sixty	LX
sixty grains	DRAM
sixty-year-old	SEXAGENARIAN
	SEXAGENARY
sixtieth	SEXAGESIMAL
skating	
arena	RINK
events	COMPULSORY FIGURES
	FIGURE SKATING, FREE STYLE
	ICE DANCING, SPEED SKATNG
movements	AXEL, CAMEL-SPIN, CHOCTAW
	LUTZ, MOHAWK, SALCHOW
	TOE-LOOP
on	
—blades	ICE SKATING

—boards with wheel	BOARDSKATING
	SKATEBOARDING
—wheels	ROLLER SKATING
skaters	
—American (m)	BUTTON, JENKINS
(f)	ALBRIGHT, FLEMING
	HAMILL
	HEISS, TRENARY
	YAMAGUCHI, YOUNG
—Austrian (m)	BOCKL, SCHAFER
	SCHWARTZ
(f)	SCHUBA
—British (m)	COUSINS, CURRY, DEAN
(f)	ALTWEGG, TORVIL
—Canadian (m)	BROWNING, PAUL, STOKJO
(f)	SCOTT, WAGNER
—Czech (m)	DIVIN, NEPELA
—Dutch (m)	SCHENK, VERKERK
(f)	BORCKINK, DIJKSTRA
	SCHUT
—Finnish(m)	THUNBERG, SKUTNABB
	VASENIUS
(f)	MUSTONEN
—French (m)	BRUNET
(f)	BRUNET
—German (m)	FALK, KELLER
	SCHNELLDORFER
(f)	BECKER, FALK
	POTZSCH, WITT
—Norwegian (m)	BALLANGRID, MAIER
(f)	HENIE, JENSEN
—Russian (m)	GRISHIN, PETRENKO
	PROTOPOPOV, ULANOV
	ZAITSEV
(f)	AVERINA, BELOVSOVA
	LEBEDEVA, RODNINA
	SKOBLIKOVA
—Swedish (m)	GRAFSTROM, SALCHOW

skiing

Alpine ski touring	RANDONNEE
bicycle on skis	SKIBOB
climbing with skis	
pointing outward	HERRINGBONING
cross-country events	NORDIC (SKIING)
—skiing	LANGLAUF
downhill	
—fast run	SCHUSS
—run with skis parallel	WEDELN
—slalom racing	ALPINE
—zigzag	(GIANT) SLALOM, SUPER G
freestyle skiing	HOT-DOGGING
hardest run	BLACK
jump in downhill run	GELANDESPRUNG
jumpers	
—Austrian	VETTORI
—Finnish	NYKA(E)NEN

—German	THOMA
—Norwegian	HUGSTEAD, RUUD
leaning foward on skis	VORLAGE
marked slopes	PISTE
most direct line	FALL-LINE
mound of compacted snow	BOSSE, MOGUL
off-piste skiing	RANDONNEE
paragliding with skis	PARAPENTE
ski suit	SALOPETTE
skiers	
—American (f)	ROFFE
—Austrian (m)	AAS, HOEFLEHNER
	KLAMMER, MADER, NIERLICH
	OSTREIN, SAILER, TRITSCHER
(f)	BUDER, HECHER
	KRONBERGER
	STANGASSINGER, WACHTER
—British	BELL
—Canadian	VILLIARD
—Finnish (m)	HAKULINEN, MANTYRANTA
—French (m)	ALPHAND, KILLY
	PICCARD, REY
(f)	CHAUVET, GOITSCHEL
	MASNADA, MERLE
—German (m)	BITTNER, KRAUSS, ROTH
	SCHICK, STUFFER, WASMEIER
(f)	GERG, MITTERMAIER
	WEHLING
—Italian (m)	GEROSA, GHEDINA, MAIR
	POLIG, RUNGGALDIER
	THOENI, TOMBA
—Japanese	OKABE
—Luxemburg	GIRARDELLI
—Norwegian (m)	BRENDEN, FURUSETH
	GRONNINGEN, HAUG
	SKAARDAL, THORSEN
(f)	KNUTSEN
—Russian (m)	BAJUKOV, VEDENIN
(f)	BOYARSKIKH, KULAKOVA
	SMETANINA, ZELENSKAJA
—Swedish (m)	ERIKSSON, HENNING
	STENMARK
(f)	ANDERSSON, JERNBERG
	NILSSON, WIBERG
—Swiss (m)	BESSE, MAHRER
	ZURBRIGGEN
(f)	FIGINI, NADIG
	SCHNEIDER, WALLISER
—Yugoslav (f)	BOKAL, BENEDIK, SVET

skiing

—and shooting competition	BIATHLON
—behind horse or vehicle	SKIJORING
—diagonally across slope	TRAVERSE
—disciplines	AERIALS, BALLET, MOGULS
—on single ski	SKI-SURFING
	SNOW BOARDING

skiing

—over rough ground — BUMP-SKIING
slowing by turning
  skis inwards — SNOW-PLOUGHING
slope prepared for aerials — KICKER
stationary turn — KICK-TURN
turn
  —by pushing out
    heel of ski(s) — STEM TURN
  —high speed — SWING
  —jump-turn — QUERSPRUNG
  —medium-fast — CHRISTIANIA
       CHRISTIANSEN
       CHRISTIE, CHRISTY
  —on outer ski — TELEMARK
  —short zigzag — WEDELN
  —stationary — KICK-TURN
unmarked slopes — OFF-PISTE
venues
  —Australia — THREDBO
  —Austria — HAUS, HINTERSTODER
     INNSBRUCK, KITZBUHEL
     LECH, MINTER GLEMM, ST ANTON
     ST CHRISTOPH, SALBACH
     SCHLADMING, STUBEN, ZURS
  —Britain — AVIEMORE
  —Canada — BLACKCOMB, CALGARY
     LAKE LOUISE, MOUNT ST ANNE
     NORQUEY, SUNSHINE PEAK
     WHISTLER MOUNTAIN
  —Czechoslovakia — JASNA
  —France — ARGENTIERE, CHAMONIX
     GRENOBLE, LES ARCS
     MARIBEL
  —Germany — BADWEISSEE
     BORSCHTESGADEN
     GARMISCH-PARTENKIRCHEN
     LENGGRIES, PFRONTEN
  —Italy — CORTINA D'AMPEZZO
     COURMEYEUR
     MADONNA DI CAMPIGLIO
     IANCAVALLO, SESTRIERE
  —Japan — SAPPORO
  —North America
    California — HEAVENLY VALLEY
     MAMMOTH
     SQUAW VALLEY
    Colorado — ARAPAHOE BASIN, ASPEN
     BEAVER CREEK
     BRECKENRIDGE
     COPPER MOUNTAIN, CRESTED BUTTE
     KEYSTONE, TELLURIDE
     STEAMBOAT SPRINGS, VAIL
    Nevada — MOUNT ROSE
     SLIDE MOUNTAIN
    New Mexico — TAOS VALLEY
    New York — LAKE PLACID
    Utah — ALTA, BRIGHTON
     DEER VALLEY, PARK CITY
     SNOWBIRD, SOLITUDE
    Vermont — KILLINGTON
    Wyoming — GRAND TRAGHEE
     JACKSON HOLE
  —Norway — GEILO, HEMSEDAL
     OSLO, STRANDA, TROMSO
  —Romania — POIANA BRASOV
  —Sweden — ARE, KLOVSJO, SALEN
     VEMDALEN
  —Switzerland — ADELBODEN, ANDERMATT
     BRIGELS, HINTERTUXM LAAX
     MURREN, ST MORITZ
     VAL D'ISERE, VAL GARDENA
     VAL THORENS, VERBIER
     WENGEN, ZERMATT
  —Yugoslavia — KRANJSKA GORA
     MARIBAR, SARAJEVO

snakes

snakes — ANGUIFAUNA, OPHIDIA
adder — VIPER
Africa — BERG-ADDER, COBRA
     MAMBA
  —garter-snake — ELAPS, HOMORELAPS
  —horned-viper — CERASTES
  —tree-snake — BOOMSLANG
  —viper — RIVER_JACK
America — BLACK-SNAKE, BULLSNAKE
     COPPERHEAD
  —coral-snake — ELAPS, MICRURUS
  —non-venomous — GARTER-SNAKE
     GREEN SNAKE, RING-SNAKE
  —rattlesnake — PIT-VIPER
  —viper — RATTLER, RATTLESNAKE
  —venomous — MOCASSIN, MOCCASIN
  —water-moccasin — COTTONMOUTH
Asiatic — KING-COBRA
Australia — BLACK-SNAKE
     CARPET-SNAKE
     DEATH-ADDER
     TAIPAN, TIGER-SNAKE
Britain — ADDER, GRASS SNAKE
     RING(ED) SNAKE, VIPER
coach-whip snake — MASTICOPHIS
coral-snake — SCYTALE
East Indies — BOIGA
Egypt
  —juggler's snake — NAGA, NAIA, NAJA
Eryx — SAND-SNAKE
fabulous snake — AMPHISBAENA
fer-de-lance — YELLOW VIPER
flying — CHRYSOPELEA, COLOBRIDAE
green — BOIOBI
Hydrophidae — SEA-SNAKE
India — BONGAR, HAMADRYAD
  —boa — JIBOYA

—cobra	COBRA DA CAPELLO
	NAGA, NAIA, NAJA
—rock-snake	KAA, K(A)RAIT, PYTHON
krait	ROCK-SNAKE
legless lizard	GLASS-SNAKE
Madagascar	LANGAHA
Masticophis	COACH-WHIP SNAKE
non-venomous	COLUBER, DIPSAS
	HOOP-SNAKE
puff-adder	CLOTHO
python	ROCK-SNAKE
rattlesnake	CROTALUS, CROTALIDAE
sand snake	ERYX
sea-snakes	HYDROPHIDAE
serpent	ASP, BOYUNA
short-tailed	SAND-SNAKE
snakes	OPHIDIA
South America	
—anaconda	SUCURUJA
—bushmaster	SURUCUCU
—python	(A)BOMA, BOA
—venomous	BUSHMASTER
	EYELASH VIPER
	FER-DE-LANCE, JARARACA
	JARARAKA, LACHESIS
	SURUCUCU
—water-boa	ANACONDA, SUCURUJU
spitting cobra	RINCHAL
tree-snake	DENDROPHIS
two-headed (myth)	AMPHISBAENA
venomous	ASP, ASPIC(K), KOKOB, SEPS
viper	ADDER
West Indies	FER-DE-LANCE
yellow viper	FER-DE-LANCE

snooker

balls	BLACK, BLUE, BROWN
	GREEN, PINK, RED
	WHITE, YELLOW
cue ball	WHITE
game	FRAME
line across table	BAULK LINE
obstruction by another	
ball	SNOOKER
opening in cushions	POCKET
padded edge of table	CUSHION
players	
—Canadian	CHAPERON, DOLNALDSON
	ROBIDOUX, THORBURN
	WERBINUK
—English	CORR (f), DAVIS, FISHER (f)
	JAMES, PARROTT
	PULMAN, TAYLOR, WHITE
—Irish	HIGGINS
—Scottish	HENDRY
—Thai	WATTANA
—Welsh	GRIFFITHS, MOUNTJOY

rod for striking ball	CUE
score made in one turn	
at the table	BREAK
start of play	BREAK OFF
stroke with cue held in	
vertical position	MASSE
venues	
—County Kildare	GOFFS
—Derby	ASSEMBLY ROOMS
—Preston	GUILD HALL
—Reading	THE HEXAGON
—Sheffield	THE CRUCIBLE
—Stoke-on-Trent	JOLLEES
soccer	(*see* **football**)

Society

for Psychical Research	SPR
of	
—Antiquaries	SA
—Arts	SA
—Engineers	SE
—Incorporated Accountants	SAA
—Jesus	SJ
—the Holy Cross	SSC

soldier

Albanian	ARNA(O)UT, PALIKAR
African	
—infantryman	VOETGANGER
—native warriors	IMPI
—soldier	ASKARI
Algerian	
—cavalry	SPAHEE, SPAHI
—infantry	GOUM, TURCO, ZOUAVE
American	
—commanders	
Civil War	
—Confederate	BEAUREGARD, BRAGG
	EARLY, HOOD, JACKSON
	JOHNSON, JOHNSTON, LEE
	LONGSTREET, PICKETT
—Federal	GRANT, HALLECK, MEADE
	LEE, MCCLELLAN, SCOTT
	SHERIDAN, SHERMAN
Indian Wars	CUSTER
Mexican War	HOUSTON
Revolution	ALLEN, ARNOLD, CLARK
	GATES, GREEN, HERKIMER, HOWE
	LAFAYETTE, LEE, LINCOLN
	MARION, MONTGOMERY, MOULTRIE
	MORGAN, PHILLIPS, PICKENS
	ST CLAIR, SCHUYLER, SULLIVAN
	SUMTER, WASHINGTON
WW1	BLISS, BULLARD, LIGGETT
	MARCH, PERSHING
WW2	BEDELL-SMITH, BRADLEY
	BUCKNER, CLARK, COLLINS
	DEVERS, EAKER, EISENHOWER

	GAVIN, HODGES, KENNY, KING
	KRUEGER, LEMAY, LUCAS
	MACARTHUS, MARSHALL, PATCH
	PATTON, STILWELL, SULTAN
	TRUSCOTT, WEDEMEYER
—civil war soldier	ZOUAVE
—Confederate	GREY-COAT
—ex-serviceman	VET(ERAN)
—militiaman	MINUTEMAN
—of both World Wars	RETREAD
—soldier	DOUGHBOY, GI, JOE
	SAMMY
Arab commando(s)	FEDAYEE(N)
armed with short rifle	CARABINEER
artilleryman	GUNNER
—old	BOMBARDIER
assistant to	
commanding officer	ADJUTANT
Australian	ANZAC, DIGGER
—commander - WW1	MONASH
Austrian	PANDOOR, PAND(O)UR
Austro-Hungarian	
—commanders - WW1	BOHM-ERMOLLI
	BOROEVIC, CONRAD
	DANKL, EUGEN
	JOSEPH, KOVESS
Belgian commander - WW1	LEMAN
bomb-thrower (old)	GRENADIER
British	LOBSTER, REDCOAT
	TOMMY
—commanders	
American Revolution	BURGOYNE
	CARLETON, CLINTON
	CORNWALLIS, GAGE
	HAMILTON, HOUSE
	PARKER, RAWDON
Canada	WOLFE
India	CLIVE, WELLESLEY
Napoleonic wars	WELLESLEY
	WELLINGTON
old	BOADICEA (f)
	BOUDICCA (f)
Spanish Succession	MARLBOROUGH
WW1	ALLENBY, BYNG
	CRADDOCK, FRENCH, FULLER
	GOUGH, HAIG
	HAMILTON, KIGGELL, KITCHENER
	MARSHALL, MAUDE, MILNE
	MONRO, MURRAY, NIXON, PLUMER
	RAWLINSON, ROBERTSON
	SMITH-DORRIEN, TOWNSHEND
	WILSON
WW2	ALEXANDER, AUCHINLECK
	BROOKE, CUNNINGHAM, DILL
	GORT, HARDING, IRONSIDE
	ISMAY, LEESE, MONTGOMERY

	PLATT, RITCHIE, SLIM
	WAVELL, WILSON, WINGATE
Carthaginian	HANNIBAL
cavalryman	TROOPER, YEOMAN
—Cromwellian	IRONSIDE
—French	CHASSEUR
—French-Algerian	SPAHEE, SPAHI
—heavy	DRAGOON
—light	HUSSAR, LANCER, H(H)LAN
—officer	CORNET
—Turkish	SPAHEE, SPAHI
Circassian slave	MAMELUKE
Croat in Austrian service	PANDOOR
	PAND(O)UR
commando(s)	GREEN BERETS
—Arab	FEDAYEE(N)
—in	
boats	SBS, SPECIAL BOAT SERVICE
Burma	CHINDIT
desert	LONG RANGE DESERT GROUP
	LRDG
planes	PARATROOPS, SAS
	SPECIAL AIR SERVICE
Cromwellian	ROUNDHEAD
—cavalryman	IRONSIDE
Czech commander	SVOBODA
East African	ASKARI
Egyptian	
—commander	SIRDAR
—officer	BIMBASHI, BINBASHI
—soldier/slave	MAMELUKE
Eighth Army	DESERT RAT
élite troops	COMMANDOS, SAS
	SPECIAL AIR SERVICE
engineer	SAPPER
enrolled compulsorily	CONSCRIPT
European mercenary	CONDOTTIERE
fighting for	
—money	MERCENARY
—the Holy Land	CRUSADER
	KNIGHT TEMPLAR
foot soldiers	INFANTRY, YEOMANRY
force men to serve	COMMANDEER
	CONSCRIPT, DRAFT
	LEVY, IMPRESS
	PRESS(GANG)
French	SOLDAT
—cavalryman	CHASSEUR
Algerian	SPAHEE, SPAHI
—commanders	
18th-19th c	NAPOLEON
WW1	ANTHOINE, BERTHOLET
	CASTELNAU, DE GAULLE, DUBAIL
	FAYOLLE, FOCH, GALLIENI, GOURAUD
	GUILLAUMAT, JOFFRE, LANREZAC
	MAISTRE, MANGIN, MAUNOURY

	MICHELER, NIVELLE, PAL, PETAIN	—commander of	
	ROQUE, SARRAIL, WEYGAND	10	DECADARCH
WW2	BILOTTE, CORAP, DE GAULLE	1000	CHILIARCH
	DENTZ, DOUMENC, GAMELIN	10000	MYRIARCH
	GEORGES, GIRAUD, GUINGAND	cavalry	HIPPARCH, PHYLARCH
	FOCH, HUNTZINGER, JOFFRE	division	TAXIARCH
	JUIN, LATTRE DE TASSIGNY	sub-division	TETRARCH
	LECLERC, NEY, PETAIN	—commanders	
	RUBY, WEYGAND	old	ALEXANDER
—guerrilla	FRANC-TIREUR	modern	METAXAS, PAPAGOS
—light infantryman	CHASSEUR		TSOLAKOGLU
	VOLTIGEUR	—heavily armed	HOPLITE
—in North Africa	LEGIONNAIRE	—lightly armed	PELTAST
—infantryman	POILU	—military commander	POLEMARCH
—private (slang)	PIOU-PIOU	—soldier	EVZONE
—rifleman	TIRAILLEUR	group of soldiers	DETACHMENT, DETAIL
—sniper	FRANC-TIREUR		PATROL, SQUAD
German	SOLDAT	—in increasing size	SECTION, TROOP
—army reserve	LANDWEHR		PLATOON, BATTERY
—commanders			COMPANY, SQUADRON
WW1	ARZ, AUFFENBERG, BOTHMAN		BATTALION, COMMANDO
	BULOW, EICHHORN, EINEM		REGIMENT
	FALKENHAIN, GOLTZ, GROENER		BRIGADE
	HINDENBURG, HOFFMAN, HUTIER		CORPS
	GLUCK, KRAFT, LEOPOLD, LIMAN		ARMY
	LINSINGEN, LOSSBERG, LUDENDORFF		ARMY GROUP
	MACKENSEN, MARWITZ, MOLTKE	guards	
	PRITTWITZ, SEECKT	—cavalry	HORSE GUARDS
WW2	ARNIM, BALCK, BAYERLEIN		HOUSEHOLD CAVALRY
	BOCK, BLOMBERG, BLUMENTRITT		LIFE GUARDS, THE BLUES
	BRAUCHITSCH, BUSCH, CHOLTITZ	—infantry	COLDSTREAM, GRENADIER
	DIETL, DIETRICH, DOLLMAN		IRISH, SCOTS, WELSH
	EBERBACH, FALKENHORST, FRANK	home-based troops	HOME GUARD, MILITIA
	FRIEDBURG, FROMM, GOERING	horse soldiers	CAVALRY
	GUDERIAN, HALDER, HARPE	Hungarian	
	HAUSSER, HINDENBURG, HOEPNER	—cavalryman	HUSSAR
	HOTH, JODL, KEITEL, KESSELRING	—guerrilla	HAIDUK, HEYDUCK
	KLEIST, KLUGE, KREBS, KUCHLER	in	
	LEEB, LIST, LOSSOW, LUDENDORFF	—full suit of armour	CATAPHRACT
	MANSTEIN, MARCKS, MILCH, MODEL	—leather armour	JACKMAN
	NEHRING, PAULUS, REICHENAU	Indian	JAWAN, SIKH
	REINHARDT, ROMMEL, SCHLIEBEN	—captain	SUBA(H)DAR
	SCHWIFFEN, SCHORNER, SPEIDEL	—cavalry commander	RESSALDAR
	SPERRLE, STUDENT, VIETINGHOFF		RISALDAR
	WELCHS, WEIDLING, WENCK	—corporal	NAIK
	WESTHAL, WIESE, WOLFF	—foot-soldier	JAWAN
	ZANGEN, ZEITZLER	—in British service	SEPAHI, SEPOY
—emergency force	LANDSTURM	—irregular	SEBUNDEE, SEBUNDY
—Hitler's bodyguard	SCHUTZSTAFFEL, SS	cavalryman	SILLADAR
—lancer	U(H)LAN	—mercenary	PINDAREE, PINDARI
—mercenary	HESSIAN, LANDSKNECHT	—military leader	SIRDAR
	LANZNECHT, LANSQUENET	—mounted	SOWAR
—rifleman	JA(E)GER	—officer	JAMADAR, JEMADAR
Greek			JEMIDAR
—at siege of Troy	MYRMIDON	—Nepalese	GURKHA
—captain of guards	PROTOPATHARIUS	—sergeant	HAVILDAR

—staff officers	OMLAH
—troop of armed tribesmen	LASHKAR
—trooper	SOWAR
infantryman	BROWN JOB, PRIVATE
	(PERCY) PONGO, SQUADDIE
	SQUADDY, TOMMY (ATKINS)
—armed with	
axe-like weapon	HALBERDIER
bow	ARCHER, BOWMAN
spear	PIKEMAN
irregular soldier	GUERRILLA, PARTISAN
Irish	
—ancient	FIANN, GALLO(W)GLASS
—expatriate	WILD GEESE
—foot soldier	KERN(E)
—freebooter	RAPPAREE
Italian	SOLDATO
—commanders	
WW1	CADORNA, CAPELLO, DIAZ
WW2	BADOGLIO, BERGONZOLI
	GRAZIANI
—mercenary leader	CONDOTTIERE
—mountain troops	ALPINI
—rifleman	BERSAGLIERE
	CARABINIERE
Japanese	
—commander	
WW1	KAMIO
WW2	ADACHI, HOMMA, IIDA
	IMAMURA, MATSUI, MUTAGUCHI
	USHIJIMA, YAMASHITA
Knights of St John of	
Jerusalem	
—commander	TUCOPOLIER
—soldier	TURCOPOLE
loyalist	CAVALIER
mercenary (16th c)	LANDSKNECHT
mounted	
—sentry	VEDETTE, VIDETTE
—soldiers	CAVALRY, DRAGOONS
	HUSSARS
Muscovite guard(s)	STRELITZ(STRELZI)
Muslim	GHAZI
Nepalese in British army	GURKHA
New Zealand	
—commander	FREYBERG
—soldier	ANZAC, KIWI
newly enlisted	RECRUIT, ROOKIE
Norse	BERSERKER
officer	
—acting as administrative	
assistant	ADC, ADJUTANT
	AIDE (DE CAMP)
—below captain	SUBALTERN
—commanding	COMMANDANT
—in training	CADET

—of	
high rank	BRASS-HAT
Yeomen of the Guard	EXON
—on duty	ORDERLY OFFICER
—responsible for	
planning strategy	GENERAL STAFF
—responsible for	
provisions	QUARTERMASTER
old	
—names	CENTINEL(L), MAN-OF-WAR
	MILITARY, SOULDIER
—soldier	RETREAD, SWEAT, VET(ERAN)
on	
—guard duty	SENTRY
—ship	MARINE
Oriental	LASCAR
Parachute Regiment	RED DEVILS
part-time troops	MILITIA
	TERRITORIALS
persecution by soldiers	DRAGONNADE
	DRAGOONING
police	REDCAPS, (R)MP
Polish commander	SKORZENY
private	SQUADDIE, SQUADDY
	SWAD(DY)
professional	REGULAR
quarters	BARRACKS, BILLET
	CANTONMENT, CASERN(E)
ranks	
—private	FUSILIER, GUARDSMAN
	GUNNER, RIFLEMAN
	TRAINED SOLDIER, TROOPER
—non-commissioned officer	NCO
	BOMBARDIER
	(LANCE) CORPORAL
	(LANCE) SERGEANT
—warrant officer	WO
	COMPANY QUARTERMASTER-SERGEANT
	CQMS
	COMPANY SERGEANT-MAJOR, CSM
	DRILL SERGEANT
	STAFF SERGEANT
	REGIMENTAL QUARTERMASTER-
	SERGEANT
	RQMS
	REGIMENTAL SERGEANT-MAJOR, RSM
—officer	CORNET, ENSIGN
	SECOND LIEUTENANT
	LIEUTENANT
	CAPTAIN, MAJOR
	LIEUTENANT-COLONEL
	COLONEL
	BRIGADIER
	MAJOR-GENERAL
	LIEUTENANT-GENERAL
	GENERAL, FIELD MARSHAL

recruit	NIG-NOG, ROOKIE, ROOKY	—in Mexico or Peru	CONQUISTADOR
rifleman (old)	FUSILIER, MUSKETEER	—infantry regiment	TERCIO
Roman		special	
—auxiliary	FOEDERATUS	forces	(*see* commando(s) *above*)
—company	VEXILLATION	standing in front of	
—emperor's		squad drilling	FUGLEMAN, MARKER
bodyguard	PR(A)ETORIAN GUARD	trained to drop	
—infantry		from aircraft	PARA, PARATROOP(ER)S
company	MANIPLE	Turkish	NIZAM
regiment	TERCIO	—armed attendant	CAVASS, KAVASS
—lightly-armed	VELITES	—army officer	BIMBASHI, BINBASHI
—officer in charge of			SPAHEE, SPAHI
10	DECURION	—cavalryman	SPAHEE, SPAHI
100	CENTURION	—commander	AG(H)A
—soldier	LEGIONARY	Crusades	SALADIN
—squad of		-in-chief	SERASKIER
$^1/_{10}$ legion	COHORT	WW1	ABDUL KERIM, DJEMEL PASHA
10	DECURIA, DECURY		ENVER PASHA, IZZET PASHA
100	CENTURY	—footguard	JANISSARY, JANIZARY
—standard-bearer	VEXILLARY	—irregular	BASHIBAZOUK
Royalist	CAVALIER	—militiaman	TIMARIOT
Russian		—palace guard	BOSTANGI
—commanders		using heavy guns	ARTILLERY
WW1	ALEKSEEV, BRUSILOV	volunteer serving	
	DANILOV, EVERT, GURKO	as officer	REFORMADO
	IVANOV, KORNILOV, KUROPATKIN	**solicitor**	SOL(R)
	PLEHVE, RENNENKAMPF, RUZSKI	Solicitor at Law	SL
	SAMSONOV, SHCHERBACHEV	solicitor before superior court	SSC
	SUKHOMLINOV, YANUSHKEVICH	Solicitor General	SG
	YUDENICH, ZHILINSKY	**Somalia**	
WW2	ANTONOV, BUDENNY, CHUIKOV	capital	MOGADISCIO, MOGADISHU
	GOLIKOV, KIRPONOS, KONIEV	coin	CENTESIMO, SHILLING
	LELYOSHENKO, MALINOVSKY	**son of**	
	POPOV, ROKOSSOVSKY, ROMANENKO	a	
	SHTEMENKO, SOKOLOVSKY	—bitch	SOB
	TIMOSHENKO, TOLBUKHIN	—Scot	MAC
	TUKHACHEVSKY, VATUTIN, VLASOV	—Welshman	AP
	VORONOV, VOROSHILOV, YEREMENKO	an Englishman	FITZ
	ZHUKOV	**soup**	
—guard(s)	STRELITZ(STRELZI)	African - okra pod soup	GUMBO
Serbian nationalist	CHETNIK	American - shellfish	CHOWDER
servant	BATMAN, ORDERLY	Asian	BIRD'S-NEST SOUP
serving		barley and vegetables	SCOTCH BROTH
—at sea	MARINE	beef broth	BREWIS
—for money	MERCENARY	beetroot	BORSCHT, BOR(T)SCH
—with another nation	AUXILIARY	bread and tomato	POPPO AL POMODORO
sharpshooter	SNIPER, TIRAILLEUR	brown	WINDSOR SOUP
slang name	BROWN JOB, GALOOT	calf's head	MOCK TURTLE
	PONGO, TOMMY	chicken/leek	COCK-A-LEEKIE
small mounted group	COSSACK POST	chilled cream soup	VICHYSSOISE
South African		clear soup	CONSOMME, JULIENNE
—commanders	BOTHA, SMUTS	crayfish	BISK, BISQUE
—soldier	VOETGANGER	cream	VICHYSOISSE
Spanish	SOLDADO	curry-soup	MULLIGATAWNY
—commanders	CORTES, CORTEZ	East Indian	MULLIGATAWNY
	PIZARRO	egg-Spanish	TONILLO

Egyptian	MELOKHIA
fish	BISQUE, BOUILLABAISSE
	CHOWDER, TURTLE
—Russian	UKKA
Florentine	RIBOLLITA
French	BISQUE, CREME DUBARRY
	MADRILENE
German	LEBERKNODELSUPPE
Greek	AVGOLEMONO
—fish	BARASOUPA, KAKAVIA
Hungarian	GOULASH, GULYASLEVES
Indian	MULLIGATAWNY
Italian	MINESTRE IN BRODO
	MINESTRONE
	POPPO AL POMODORO
leeks, potatoes, etc	VICHYSSOISE
lobster	BISQUE DE HOMARD
meat with	
—curry	MILLIGATAWNY
—dumplings (US)	PEPPER POT
mutton	SCOTCH BROTH
New Zealand	TOHEROA
oatmeal gruel	BURGOO
Philippines dumpling soup	TANCIT MOLO
Polish	ZUPA
Russian	
—beetroot	BORSCHT, BOR(T)SCH
—cabbage	SHCHEE, SH(T)CHI
—fish	UKKA
Scandinavian	LAPSKAUS
Scottish	COCKALEEKIE, PUNCHNEP
	MUSLIN-KALE
shark's fin	YU TSI TANG
shellfish	BISQUE, TURTLE
Spanish	GALICIAN
—cold	BOURRISE, GAZPACHO
—egg	TONILLO
—fish	CALDO DE PESCADO
strong broth	BOUILLON, CULLIS
thick soup	POT(T)AGE, SCOTCH BROTH
thin soup	BOUILLON, BROTH
	CONSOMME, GRUEL, SKILLY
tomato-flavoured	MADRILENE
Turkish yoghurt	YAYLA CORBASI
various meats and vegetables	STOCKPOT
without solid pieces	PUREE
with pasta	MINESTRE IN BRODO
South Africa	RSA, SA, ZA
capitals	CAPE TOWN, PRETORIA
coin	CENT, RAND, RD
homelands	BOPHUTHATSWANA
	CISKEI, TRANSKEI, VENDA
provinces	CAPE PROVINCE, NATAL
	ORANGE FREE STATE
	TRANSVAAL
	(*see also* **African**)

South America	SA
alligator	CAIMAN, CAYMAN
ant	SAUBA-ANT, UMBRELLA-ANT
—bear	TAMANOIR
—eater	ARMADILLO, TAMANDUA
—thrush	ANT-BIRD
armadillo	PEBA, TATOU
aromatic kernel	PICHURIM BEAN
arrow-poison	CURARA, CURARE
balsam	COPAIBA, COPIAYA
bat	DESMODUS
beetle	HERCULES BEETLE
beetles	PYROPHORUS
bird	AGAMI, ANT-THRUSH, ARAPUNGA
	BELL-BIRD, CAMPANERO
	COCK-OF-THE-ROCK, CONDOR, COTINGA
	CURASSOW, , HOA(C)TZIN, JABIRU
	JACAMAR, MANAKIN, MOTMOT
	MUSK-DUCK, OVEN-BIRD
	PUFF-BIRD, QUETZAL, RHEA, SERIEMA
	STINK-BIRD, SUN-BITTERN, TAPACOLO
	TAPACULO, TERU-TERO, TOPAZ
	TOUCAN(ET), TROGON, TRUMPETER
	TURCO, UMBRELLA-BIRD, URUBU
	YNAMBU, ZOPILOTE
—catching spider	TARANTULA
birthwort	ARISTOLOCHIA
brome-grass	RESCUE-GRASS
burrowing armadillo	PICHICIAGO
butterfly	MORPHO
butternut	S(A)OUARI(-NUT)
cactus	CHRISTMAS CACTUS
canoe	PERIAGUA, PIRAGUA
	PIROGUE
Cape gooseberry	STRAWBERRY-TOMATO
capybara	RIVER-HOG
carica	PA(W)PAW, PAPAYA
catfish	HASSAR
cattle	
—farm	ESTANCIA
—farmer	ESTANCIERO
cavy	GUINEA-PIG
cereal	QUINOA
chain	ANDES
climbing plant	AYAHUASCO
	CANARY CREEPER
	INDIAN CRESS, MARCGRAVIA
	PASSION-FLOWER, PHILODENDRON
	SMILAX, SARSAPARILLA, TIMBO
	TROPAEOLUM, WAX-FLOWER
cloak	PONCHO
coin	PESO
coral-flowered plant	EASTER CACTUS
corkwood	BALSA
cowboy	GAUCHO, VAQUERO
crab-tree	CARAPA

—fruit	CARAP-NUT
crested screamer	CHAUNA, , CARIAMA
	SERIEMA
crocodile	CAIMAN, CAYMAN
dance	PAVANE, ZAPATEO
dorado	GOLDEN SALMON
dormouse	ECHIMYD
drink	ASSAI, AYAHUASCO, CHICHA
	MATE, YERBA (DE MATE)
drug	PAREIRA BRAVA
early civilisation	HUARI, TIAHUANACO
edentate	SLOTH
edible	
—grub	GROO-GROO, GRU-GRU
—tuber	ARRACACHA, OCA
eel	CARAPO
epiphyte	TILLANDSIA
estate	HACIENDA
establishment	HACIENDA
factory	HACIENDA
finch	TANAGER
fireflies	PYROPHORUS
fish	ANGEL-FISH, ARAPAIMA
	CARIBE, CHICHLID, PERAI, PIRAI
	PIRANHA, PIRARUCU, PIRAYA
	SWORD-TAIL
—poison	SURINAM POISON, TIMBO
flea	CHIGGER, CHIGOE
	CHIGRE, JIGGER
flooded forest	(I)GAPO
flowers	ALSTROEMERIA, ANTHURIUM
	GLOXINIA, TAGETES
fox	ZORRO
fruit	A(C)KEE, ASSAI, CASHEW-APPLE
	CASHEW-NUT, GUAVA, LUCUMA
	SOUR-SOP, SUGAR-APPLE
	SWEET-SOP
game bird	GUAN
garment	TAYO
golden	
—breasted trumpeter	AGAMI
—salmon	DORADO
goosefoot	QUINOA
gourd	CACOON
grass	PASPALUM
gum	ANGICO, CONIMA
hare-lipped bat	NOCTILIO
hawk	CARACARA
hoatzin	STINK-BIRD
holly	MATE
Honduras bark	CASCARA
horned screamer	PALAMEDEA
horseman	GAUCHO, LLANERO
humming-bird	SWORD-BILL, SYLPH
hut	TOLDO

Indians	GUARANI, TUPI
indigo	COBRES
jacaranda	PALISANDER
kinkajou	HONEY-BEAR, POTTO
landmark	SENAL
language	CARIB, GURANI, TUPI
lapwing	TERU-TERO
large eagle	(HARPY) EAGLE
laurel tree	PICHURIM
leaf-carrying ant	SAUBA
leopard	JAGUAR
liquor	CHICA
lizard	AMPHISBAENA, BASILISK
	(I)GUANA, TEGUEXIN
lion	COUG(U)AR, PUMA
maize drink	CHICHA
marmalade-tree	MAMMEE-SAPOTA
marmoset	JACCHUS
measure (33"-43")	VARA, VARE
missile	BOLAS
mortgage	CEDULA
moth	OWL-MOTH
mountain-sickness	PUNA
mud-fish	LEPIDOSIREN
mulberry tree	CONTRAYERVA, CRECOPIA
nest-building	
catfish	HASSAR
night-ape	DOUROUCOULI, DURUKULI
non-Spaniard	GRINGO
oil-bird	GUACHARO, GUACHERO
opossum	MARMOSE
orchid	ONCIDIUM
ostrich	NANDOO, NANDU, RHEA
pack animal	ALPACA, PACO
	GUANACO, HUANACO, LLAMA
palisander	JACARANDA
palms	(see **palms**)
papaya	CARICA, PA(W)PAW, PAPAYA
parrot	AMAZON, MACAW
pineapple	TILLANDSIA
Pithecolobium	RAIN-TREE
plain	CAMPOS, LLANO, PAMPA(S)
	PARAMO, SAVANNA(H)
—dweller	LLANERO
plant	ARTILLERY-PLANT, BIXA
	DUMB-CANE, FURCRAEA
	PAREIRA, PETUNIA
—yielding	
curare	(O)URALI, (O)URARI
	WOORALI, WOURALI
snakebite antidote	GUACO
poison	CURARA, CURARE
pouch-toad	NOTOTREMA
purgative nut	PHYSIC-NUT
quail	TINAMOU
rabbit-squirrel	CHINCHA

racoon	COATI(MONDI)
	COATI(MUNDI), KINKAJOU
rail	COURLAN
rain forest	SELVA
ranch	HACIENDA
red jasmine	FRANGIPANI
rescue-grass	BROME-GRASS
resin	CARANNA, CARAUNA
riding-whip	QUIRT
river	AMAZON
—hog	CAPYBARA
rodent	ACOUCHY, AG(O)UTI
	AG(O)UTY, BISCACHA
	CAPYBARA, CAVY
	CHINCH(ILL)A, COYP(O)U, PACA
	DILOCHOTIS, GUINEA-PIG, MARA
	PATAGONIAN HARE, TUCOTUCO
	TUCUTUCO, TUKUTUKU
	VISCACHA. VIZCACHA
—colony	VISCACHERA
rosewood	PALISANDER
rubber substitute	BALATA
screamer	KAMICHI
settlement	PUEBLO
shrub	ESCALLONIA, JABORANDI
	PILOCARPUS, RHATANY
	SIMARUBA, TREE-0TOMATO
skunk	ATOC, ATOK, ZORILLO
sloth	AI, UNAU
spiny fish	DORAS
spirit	DEMERARA
strainer for juice	TIPITI
tableland	MESETA, PUNA
three-toed sloth	AI
tiger-cat	MARGAY
timber	*(see separate entry)*
tinamous	PARTRIDGE
town	PUEBLO
tree	ACACIO, ACAJOU, A(C)KEE, ANGICO
	BEBEERU, BOMBAX, CACAO, CALABASH
	CANDLE-TREE, CANNONBALL-TREE
	CASHEW, CHINA(CHINA), COW-TREE
	DALI, FIDDLEWOOD, FUSTIC, FUSTOC
	GRAPETREE, GREENHEART, GUAIACUM
	GUAVA, JACARANDA, KINA(KINA)
	LEOPARD-WOOD, LETTER-WOOD
	LIMA-WOOD, LOGWOOD, LUCUMA
	MAHOGANY, MASSARANDUBA
	MILK-TREE, MISSEL-TREE, OITICICA
	OMBU, PAPAYA, PALISANDER
	QUASSIA, QUEBRACH, RAIN-TREE
	S(A)OUARI, SAVANNA-WATTLE
	SNAKEWOOD, SOAP-BARK, SOUR-SOP
	SUGAR-APPLE, SWEET-SOP
	SWEETWOOD, TRUMPET-TREE
	WALLABA, XYLOPIA

—frog	NOTOTREMA
—yielding quinine	CHINA(CHINA)
	CINCHONA, KINA(KINA)
	QUINA(QUINA)
	QUINQU(INA
turtle	MATAMATA
two-toed sloth	UNAU
ungulate	TAPIR
uplands	CUCHILLA
village	PUEBLO
vine	AYAHUASCO
vulture	CONDOR, URUBU
walking fish	DORAS
water-opossum	YAPO(C)K
weasel	GRISON, TAIRA, TAYRA
weevil	DIAMOND-BEETLE
wet forest	SELVA
wild	
—cat	EYRA, JAGUAR(ONDI)
	JAGUARUNDI
	MARGAY, OCELOT
	PUMA
—llama	GUANACO, HUANACO
	VICUNA
—pig	PECCARY, TAPIR
—turkey	CRAX, CURASSOW
	PENELOPE
wood-sorrel	OCA
Yankee	GRINGO
South Australia	SA
South Island	SI
South Pole	SP
Soviet Union	*(see* **Russia***)*
space	
capsule	
—USA	APOLLO, AURORA, FAITH
	FREEDOM, FRIENDSHIP
	GEMINI, LIBERTY
	MERCURY
	SIGMA, SKYLAB
—USSR	SOYUZ, VOSHKOV
	VOSTOK, ZOND
probe	
—Halley's comet	GIOTTO
—Jupiter	GALILEO, PIONEER
	VOYAGER
—Mars	MARINER, ORBITER
	VIKING
—Mercury	MARINER
—Moon	LUNA, LUNIK, ORBITER
	RANGER, SURVEYOR
	ZOND
—Neptune	VOYAGER
—Saturn	VOYAGER
—Sun	HELIOS
—Uranus	VOYAGER

—Venus	MAGELLAN, MARINER	—Russian	BURAN, ENERGIA
	VENERA	station	FREEDOM, MIR, VOSTOK
rocket		traveller	ASTRONAUT, COSMONAUT
—fuel	HYDYNE, LIQUID OXYGEN	velocity required	
	LOX	to overcome gravity	ESCAPE VELOCITY
—launching site			(*see also* **astronomy**)
American	CAPE CANAVERAL	**Spain**	E
French	KOUROU, GUIANA	**Spanish**	HISPANO-, IBERIAN, SP
Japanese	KAGOSHIMA	act	AUTO
Russian	BAIKANOUR, COSMODROME	agreement	SI
—pioneers		almond	ALMENDRA
American	GODDARD	American half-caste	MESTIZO
German	OBERTH, VON BRAUN	anchovy paste	ANCHOIADE
Russian	MOLCHANOFF, TSIOLKOVSKY	apple	MANZANA
—range	WOOMERA	articles	EL, LA, LAS, LOS
—small rocket controlling		baby	NENE
direction, etc	VERNIER ENGINE	barracks	CASERNA
	VERNIER MOTOR	Basque	
	THRUSTER	—ball game	PELOTA
—types		—separatists	ETA
American	ARROW, ALAS, CRUISE	bar	CANTINA
	DELTA, HAWK, LANCE	bay	BAHIA, GOLFO
	MINUTEMAN, PEGASUS, PERSHING	bazaar	ALCAICERIA
	POLARIS, REDSTONE, SATURN	beach	PLAYA
	STINGER, TRIDENT	beer	CERVEZA
	WAC CORPORAL	black	NEGRO
British	BLOWPIPE, BLUE STEEL	—pudding	MONDONGO
	BLUESTREAK, LANCE, THOR	blanket	MANTA
Chinese	LONG MARCH	blusterer	CACAFOGO, CACAFUEGO
French	ARIANCE	boundary-house	POSADO
German	V1, V2	boy	MUCHACHO
Indian	AGNI, PRITHVI		NINO
Israeli	JERICHO	brazier	BRASERO
Russian	AMOS, ARCHER, ATOLL	bread	PAN
	SAM	bridge	PUENTE
South African	SKERPION	brother	HERMANO
satellite	ARABSAT, ASIASAT, AST	—hood	HERMANDAD
	ASTERIX, ASTRA	bullfighting	(*see separate entry*)
	BSB, CHINA, COBE, COSMOS	cabal	JUNTA, JUNTO
	DELTA STAR, EARLY BIRD	cabinet	VARGUENO
	EINSTEIN OBSERVATORY	canape	TAPA
	EXPLORER, EUTELSAT, EXOSAT	canyon	CANON
	GORIZONT, HIPPARCHUS	cape	CAPA, MANTILLA
	INTELSAT, IRAS, LANDSAT, LACROSSE	—(headland)	CABO, PUNTA
	MARCO POLO, METEOR, METEOSAT	capital	MADRID
	MUSES-A, NIMBUS, NOAA	cask	BARRICA
	OLYMPUS, OPEK, OSUMI	chalk	SOAPSTONE
	PALAPA, PEGASUS, PROSPERO, RADUGA	chamber	CAMARA
	ROHINI, RORSAT, SKYLAB	champion	CAMPEADOR, CID
	SOLAR MAX, SPOT 2, SPUTNIK	chaperone	DUENNA
	SYNCOM, TELECOM, TELSTAR	cheer	OLE
	TIROS, TRANSIT, VANGUARD	cheese	QUESO
	VELA, WESTAR, ZIRCON	chicken	POLLO
shuttle		chickpeas	GARBANZOS
—American	ATLANTIS, CHALLENGER	chief	CID
	COLUMBIA, DISCOVERY	—magistrate	CORREGIDOR

child	NINO
Christian	MOZARAB
city	CIUDAD
cloak	CAPA, CAPOTE, MANTA
clown	GRACIOSO
cliff	PENA
coast	COSTA
code of law	FUEROA
coins	
—unit	PESO, PESETA
—½ peseta	REAL, RIAL, RYAL
—2 reals	PISTAREEN
—8 reals	PIECE OF EIGHT
—5 pesetas	DURO, PESO
—dollar	PIECE OF EIGHT
—old	
2 pistoles	DOUBLOON
copper coin	MARAVEDI, VELLON
gold coin	PISTOLE
silver coin	COB
cold soup	GAZPACHO
collection of songs	CANCIONERO
commander	ENCOMENDERO
commandery	ENCOMIENDA
conqueror	CONQUISTADOR
constitution	FUERO
council	JUNTA
—meeting	CONSULTA
country house	QUINTA
courtyard	PATIO
covered wagon	TARTANA
cress	PEPPERWORT
dance	BALLE
dances	BOLERO, CACHUCHA, FANDANGO
	FARRUCA, FLAMENCO, JOTA
	PASO DOBLE, PASSACAGLIA
	SARABAND, SEGUIDILLA
	ZAPATEADO
danger warning on chart	VIGIA
deep valley	CUENCA
desert plateau	PUNA
desk	VARGUENO
despatch boat	AVISO
dialect	CASTILIAN, CATALAN
	LADRINO
dish	PAELLA, SALPICON
district	BARRIO
doctor	MEDICO
donkey	BURRO
drama	AUTO
drunken fellow	BORACHIO
dynasty	BOURBON
—Moorish	NASRID
egg	HUEVO
—soup	TONILLO
estuary	ESTERO

fan	AFICIONADO
fascist	FALANGE, PHALANGE
father	PADRE
favoured	GRACIOSO
festival	FIESTA
few words	POCAS PALABRAS
fish	PESCADO
—soup	CALDO DE PESCADO
—stew	ZARZUELA DE PESCADO
fleet	ARMADA, FLOTA
fly	BLISTER-BEETLE, CANTHARID
folk-dance	SARDANA
forest	SELVA
fortress	ALCAZAR
gap	PORTILLO
garlic	AJO
—mayonnaise	AIOLI
gentleman	CABALLERO, DON, HIDALGO
girl	NINA
glazed tile	AZULEJO
good	
—afternoon	BUENAS TARDES
—day/morning	BUENOS DIAS
—night	BUENAS NOCHES
goodbye	ADIOS
gorge	CANADON, CAN(Y)ON
governor	ADELANTADO
	ALCA(I)DE, ALCAYDE
governess	DUENNA
grandee	ADELANTADO, GRANDE
	HIDALGO, PROCER
grape	UVA
grass	ESPARTO
gulf	GOLFO
gypsy	
—man	ZINCALO
—song	FLAMENCO
—woman	ZINCALA
gypsies	ZINCALI
ham	JAMON
hamlet	ALDEA
harbour	PORTO, PUERTO
hare	LIEBRE
head	
—covering	MANTILLA
—of state	CAUDILLO
headman	CAPITANO
hero	(EL) CID
highness	ALTEZA
highway	CAMINO REAL
highwayman	BANDOLERO
hill	CERRO, COLLADO, LOMA
holiday	FIESTA
horseman's cap	MONTERO
hostel	PARADOR
hotel	PARADOR, POSADA

hunter	MONTERO	naked	EN CUEROS
I kiss your hands	BESO LAS MANOS	nap	SIESTA
ice cream	HELADO	narrow	
icing	ALCORZA	—canyon	CANADA
in close-fitting dress	EN CUERPO	—pass	PUERTA
infantry regiment	TERCIO	narrows	ANGOSTURA
inlet	ESTERO	noble	DON, GRANDEE
inn	POSADA	notary	ESCRIBANO
insectivore	DESMAN	nothing	NADA
intriguers	CARARILLA	oil	ACEITE
interjection of annoyance	CARAMBA	olive paste	OLIVADE
island	ISLA	on	
jar	OLLA, TINAJA	—horseback	EN CABALLO
Jews	SEPHARDIM	—the contrary	AL CONTRARIO
judge	ALCALDE	open area in town	PLAZA
kebab	PINCHO	orange	NARANJA
kidney bean	FRIJOL(E)	otter	NUTRIA
knife	CUCHILLO	palace	ALHAMBRA, ALCAZAR
lady	DON(Y)A, HIDALGA	parliament	CORTES
lake	LAGO, LAGUNA	partridge	PERDIZE
language	BASQUE, CATALAN	pass	PASO, PORTILLO
	CASTILIAN, LADINO	peak	CERRO, CORNO
large			PICACHO, PIC(O)
—cigar	PERFECTO	peas	GUISANTES
—jar	TINAJA	penal settlement	PRESIDIO
leader	CAUDILLO, (EL) CID	pheasant	FAISAN
liquor	AGUARDIENTE	plain	LLANO, PLANA, PLANICIE
little	POCO	police	GUARDIA CIVIL
madam	DONA, SENORA		RURALES
man	HOMBRE, SENOR	—officer	ALGUACIL, ALGUAZIL
manifesto	PRONUNCIAMENTO	political boss	CACIQUE, CAZIQUE
mantle	MANTILLA	port	PORTO, PUERTO
market-place	PLAZA	potato omelette	TORTILLA
marsh	BANADO	pot	OLLA
matador	ESPADA	poultry	AVES
mayor	ALCALDE	prairie	LLANO
measure		priest	CURA, PADRE
—yard	METRO	prince	INFANTE
—4.2 miles	LEAGUE	princess	INFANTA
—2¼ pints	LITRO	proclamation	PRONUNCIAMENTO
meat and fish pie	EMPANADILLA	province	ANDALUSIA
military post	PRESIDIO	public	
milk and egg pudding	CREMA CATALANA	—square	PLAZA
miracle-worker	SALUTER	—walk	ALAMEDA
miss	SENORITA	punishment of heretics	AUTO DA FE
mister	DON, SENOR, SR	rabbit	CONEJO
mixed stew	OLLA-PODRIDA	race	BASQUE
Moslem lawyer	ALFAQUI	rapids	TORRENTE
mounted bullfighter	PICADOR	ravine	ARROYO, CANADA
mountain	MONTE	reservoir	EMBALSE
—range	CORDILLERA, CUCHILLAS	restaurant	HOSTERIA
	SIERRA	reward (for good news)	ALBRICIAS
muleteer	ARRIERO	river	RIO
municipal council	AYUNTAMIENTO	—mouth	RIA
musical instrument	TENORA, VIHUELA	road-house	PARADOR
	ZAMBOMBA	robber	LADRON

rock	CAYO, PENA	—fish	ESPADA
rotten	PRODRIDA	tableland	MES(ET)A
royal road	CAMINO REAL	talk	PALABRA
saddle	COLLADO	tavern	FONDO
saddlebag	ALFORGA	telephone company	TELEFONICA
saint	SAN(TA), SANTO	title	DON
saint's day	FIESTA	tomorrow	MANAN(Y)A
salad	ENSALADA	town	CIUDAD
saloon	CANTINA	treaty	AS(S)IENTO
salt		trooper	GINETE
—lake	SALADA	turkey-buzzard	GALLINAZO
—pan	SALAR, SALINA	until we meet again	HASTA LA VISTA
sandal	ALPARGATA	urn	OLLA
sandbank	BANCO	valley	VAL(L)
sauce	SALSA	vaudeville	ZARZUELA
sausage	CHORIZA, SALCHICA	veal	TERNERA
sea	MAR	vegetable soup	GAZPACHO
see you		vehicle	VOLANTE
—later	HASTA LUEGO	village	ALDEA, PUEBLO
—tomorrow	HASTA MANANA	volcano	VOLCAN
serenade	RONDENA	waiter	MOZO
shawl	MANTILLA, MANTON	walk	PASEO
sheep	MERINO	war	GUERRA
—skin coat	ZAMARRA, ZAMARRO	—to the knife	GUERRA AL CUCHILLO
sherry	AMONTILLADO, JEREZ	watch-tower	ATALAYA
shop	TIENDA	water	
shore	COSTA	—cooler	ALCARRAZA
shrub	CNEORUM, WIDOW-WAIL	—course	ARROYO
sir	DON, SENOR, SR	—fall	CATARATA, SALTO
slaughtering and freezing		well	FUENTE
establishment	FRIGORIFICO	weight	
sleep	SIESTA	—gram	GRAMO
small		—25lb	ARROBA
—fumarole	HORNITO	who knows?	QUIEN SABE?
—room	CAMARILLA	wild marjoram	OREGANO
smoked pilchard	FUMADO	window	VENTANA
snack	TAPA	wine	VINO
soldier	SOLDADO		(*see also separate entry*)
song	CANCION	—shop	BODEGA, CANTINA
soup	BOURRIDE	—skin	BORACHIO
source	FUENTE	woman	MUJER, SENORA
spitfire	CACAFOGO, CACAFUEGO	wood	SELVA
sponge roll	BRAZO DE GITANO	word	PALABRA
square	PLAZA	**special**	
squid	CALAMAR	Special Air Service	SAS
standard bearer	ALFEREZ	Special Constable	SC
steak	BISTEC	special drawing right(s)	SDR
stew	OLLA-PODRIDA	special order	SO
strait	ESTRECHO, PASO	**speech**	(*see* **language, rhetoric**)
strangulation	GAR(R)OTTE	**Spenser**	
street	CALLE, PASEO	words used in his works:	
sun-dried brick	ADOBE	abandon	ABAND
swamp	ESTERO	abash	QUELL
sweetmeat	ALCORZA	abate	APPAL, QUELL, RELENT
sword	BILBO, ESPADA, ESTOQUE	abiding place	GRANGE
—blade	TOLEDO	able	HABLE

abounding	RANK	appeal	PEAL
absolve	QUIGHT, QUYTE	appearance	HEW
accomplish	COMPLISH	appease	DEFRAY
accusation	CRIME	approach	CO(A)ST, COST(E), SUCCEED
accuse	APPEAL	—death	FIT
acquit	QUIGHT, QUYTE	arbour	HERBAR
act		arm	EMBATTLE
—amiss	MISDONNE	arrange	ENRAUNGE
—of seizing	PREY	arranged	COMPACT
active	WIMBLE	array	ATTRAP, PLIGHT
adjudge	BEHIGHT, BEHOTE	arrear	AREAR, ARERE
adjudicator	DAYES-MAN	arrogance	SURQUEDRY
adjust	CONCENT	arrowhead	FORKHEAD
admiration	ADMIRA(U)NCE	art	FEAT
adorn	ADORE, ATTRAP, DITE	artifice	GIN
adorned	DITE	as	
advance	AVAUNT	—conveying an impression	PURPORT
—in hostility	SWAY	—soon	ALSOON(E)
advancing	VAUNCING	assail	ASSAY
advantage	VAUNTAGE	assault	ASSAY, STOUND, STOWND
advise	AVISE, AVIZE, AVYSE, REED(E)	assay	SAY
affect	ASSAY	assayer	SAY-MASTER
—disagreeably	UNSEASON	assembled	ACCOYLD
affectedly nice or prim	QUAINT	assembly	ASSEMBLA(U)NCE
afflict	ASSAY	assuredly	PARDIE, PARDY, PERDIE
affliction	TINE, TYNE		PERDY
afraid	ADRAD, ADRED	astound	STOUND
aged	SHOT	astounded condition	STOUND
ago	YGO(E)	astray	ABORD
agreed upon	COMPACT	astronomy	STAR-READ
aim	UPSHOT	Astrophel	PENTHIA, STARLIGHT
air	DEMAINE, DEMAYNE	at a distance	WIDE
	DEMEANE	athletic contest	PRISE
akin	SYBBE	atone	ATTONE
alembic	LIMBEC(K)	attack	BODRAG, BORDRAGING
alike	YLIKE	attain	SEISE
allegiance	FOY	attempted	FOND
alleviate	AL(L)EGGE	attendance at court	COURTING
alleviation	AL(L)EGGAUNCE	attention	ATTENT
allot	TEENE	attentive consideration	INTENDIMENT
allow	BETEEM(E)	augury	SOOTHE
almost	UNE(A)TH, UNEATHES	avenger	VENGER
	UNNETHES	avowal	AVOURE
altogether	ALGATE	await	REMAIN
amaze	AWHAPE	award	ADDOOM, ADWARD
ambush	AWAIT	away	AWAYES
amerced	AMERST	axis	HENGE
amice	AMIS	back	CHINE
amount	MOUNTENA(U)NCE	—up	ABET
anew	OF NEW	bait	BAYT
anger	TINE, TYNE	balance	LAUNCE, PEASE, PEAZE
animated	EMPASSIONED		PEISE, PEIZE, PEYSE, POUND
annoy	NOY	baldric(k)	BAUDRICKE
annoyance	NOYANCE	ban	BAND
antagonist	PEER	banderol	BANNERALL
anvil	ANDVILE	bandy	CHAFFER

banish	BAND, FOR(E)SAY
bar	SPARRE, SPERRE
barren	BLUNT
basket	FLASKET
bate	BAYT
bathe	BAY(E), EMBAY
battle	BATTIL
be	
—a guest	HOST
—abashed	BASH
—active or excited	STIRE, STYRE
—filled	REDOUND
—flooded	FLOAT
—it how it may	HOWBE
—necessary	MISTER
—on	
guard	WAITE
the side next	SIDE
—out of bed	STIRE, STYRE
—painful	TINE, TYNE
—sorry for	FORTHINK
—spoken of	HEAR
—stopped by	STAY
beak	BECKE
bear	BIER
bearing	AMENAUNCE, DEMAINE, DEMAYNE
	DEMEANE, DEMAINE, DEMAYNE
	DEMEANE, PORTANCE
—towards another	DEMEASNURE
beaten by cold	WINTER-BEATEN
beautiful and good woman	BELLIBONE
because	BY MEANS
becoming	BESITTING
bed	BID
bedyed	BEDIDE
befit	BEFALL
beforehand	PARAVA(U)NT
begin to move	STIRE, STYRE
begot	KYNDED
beguile	GUILE
behaviour	COMPORTANCE, DEMEASNURE
	HAVEOUR, HAVIOUR
beheaded	TRUNKED
behest	HEAST(E)
belabour	LAY ON LOAD
believe wrongly to be	MISTAKE
bellow in return	REBELLOW
beloved	BEL(L)AMOURE
bend	BOUGHT
benefit	VANTAGE
bent	CORBE
beseech	BESEEKE
beset	EMPEACH
—by	BESTAD(D)E
besides	FOREBY
besiege	ASIEGE

besprinkle	SHED
bestow part of	EMPART
betroth	SPOUSE
between whiles	ATWEEN
bid	BED
bight	BOUGHT
bind	EMBRACE
bistort	POLYGONY
bit	WHAT
bite	REMORSE
bitten	GRYPT
bittern	BITT(O)UR
bitterness	FELL
black hellebore	MELAMPODE
blameless	UNREPROVED
blast	SCATH
blatant	BLATTANT
blemish	BLEMISHMENT
blockhead	MOME
blood	
—relation	SYBBE
—relationship	KINDRED
blossom	BLOOSME
blow	PEASE, PEAZE, PEISE
	PEIZE, PEYSE
blue	BLEW
boast	CRAKE
body	SOYLE
boiling pot	STEW
bolt	SPERRE
—for cross-bow	QUAR'LE
bonny lass	BON(N)ILASSE
border	BOARD, FRONTIER
borrowed	STRAUNGE
bought provisions	ACHETES
bound up	UPBOUND(EN)
boundaries	OUTBOUNDS
boundary water	SHARD, SHERD
brace	EMBRACE
braid	EMBRAID
brandish	BLESS, HURTLE
breaded	BREDE
break	CESURE
—mail from	DISMAYL
bright	SHERE
bring	
—back	RELATE, REVERSE
to better state	RECURE
—discredit on	BLAME
—down	EMBACE
—into being	REAR
—on	INFER
—reproach on	UPBRAY
—to	
an end	EXPIRE
bear	SERVE

mind	MIND	—to whirl or roll	REEL
—together	COMPILE, UPKNIT	cave	DELVE
—up	NOUSELL, NOU(R)SLE	cease	BLIN, CESSE, LIN
	NUZZLE	—to	
—urgently	COMPEL	occupy	QUIGHT, QUYTE
brittle	BRICKLE	put forward	DISADVANCE
broken		ceiled	SIELD
—pottery	POTSHARE	ceiling	SEELING
—up	TO-BRUSD	centre of target	MARK-WHITE
brother	SYBBE	certainly	SICCAR, SICKER
brought down	EMBASTE	chafe	CHAUFE, CHAUFF
bruise	INTUSE	champion	DOUCEPERE, DOUZEPER
—with walking	SURBATE	chapiter	CHAPTER
bruised severely	TO-BRUSD	charge with	
—with walking	SURBATED, SURBET	overwhelming force	SURCHARGE
bubble	ROWNDELL	charged with	ENFOULDERED
budget	BOUGET	—passion	EMPASSIONED
burden	BEARE	chariot	CHARET
burdensome	CHARGEFUL	chase	SCORSE
burning	SEARE	chastise	DISPLE, REFORM
—within	INBURNING	check	REVOKE
burst	BRUST, DISTRAIN	cheer	CHERRY
bush	TODDE	chest for records	SCRINE, SCRYNE
—of hair over eyes	GLIB	chief magician	ARCHIMAGO
busy in traffic	TRADEFUL	choice	TRYE
by	FOREBY	choicest	PRIMROSE
call	CLAME, ENQUERE, ENQUIRE	choke	ACCLOY
	INQUERE, INQUIRE	circumstances	STEAD
—by an ill name	MISCALL	cite	CONVENT
called	HOTE, NEMPT	claim	CLAME
camlet	CHAMELOT	clamour	OUTRAGE
canal superintendent	ZANJERO	clamorous	BLATTANT
cannot be helped	HELPLESS	clear	CLEAN, NEAT
canon	SQUIER, SQUIRE	—of blame	QUIGHT, QUYTE
canto	CANTICLE	—off	QUIGHT, QUYTE
cap	CALL	clemency	CLEMENCE
captain	CAPITAYN	climb	STIE, STYE
captive	CAITIVE	climbed	CLAMBE, SCAND
captivity	CAPTIVA(U)NCE	clog	ACCLOY
career	CARIERE	close	STRAIT
careful	HEEDY	—fight	GRAPLEMENT
carpenter's square	SQUIER, SQUIRE	cloth covering	DRAPET
carriage	PORTANCE	clothe	EMBOSS
carve	KERVE	—again	REVEST
case	STEAD	clown	PATCHC(H)OCKE
cast about	THROW ABOUT	coach	COCH
castaway	WEFT(E)	coast	BOARD, COST(E)
casually dropped	SCATTERED	coil	BOUGHT
caterwaul	WRAWL	cold	FRENNE
caught	KEIGHT	colour	HEW
caul	CALL	coltsfoot	COLTSWOOD
cauldron	CAUDRON	combatant	BATTEILANT
cause	ENCHEASON, GARRE	come	
—of		—forth alone	SINGLE
grief	HEART-SORE	—to grief	MISWEND
wrongdoing	CRIME	comedown	AVALE, AVAIL(E)

comer	COMMER	cuirass	CURAT, CURIET
command	HEAST(E)	cunning	PRACTIC
—a view of	SURVEW	cup of maple wood	MAZER
commit	ARRET(T)	cur	KURRE
companying	COMPANING	curdle	CRUDDLE
comparison	PARAGON	curdy	CRUDDY
compassionate feeling	REMORSE	cure	RECURE
compel	GARRE	curse upon	MA(U)LGRE
competition	PARAGON	curtal-axe	CURTAXE
complain	MEAN(E), MEIN, MENE	custody	BAIL
completeness	COMPLEMENT	cut	
compose	COMILE	—asunder	DISCIDE
conceal	HEAL, HEEL, HELE	—into	ENTRENCH, INTRENCH
concealing	COVERT	chines	CHYND
conceive	CONTRIVE	—off	SHARE
conclude	UPKNIT	cutting	TRENCHAND
condition	HOOD, STEAD	daily	ADAYS
conference	EMPARLAUNCE	dairy	DAYR-HOUSE
confound	AWHAPE	damage	EMPEACH, SCATH
congratulate	GREET	danger	DOUBT
conned	COND	dare	DARRE
consent	AFFOORD	dark/darken/darkly	DIRK(E)
constant	SAD	darling	DEARLING
consummateness	COMPLEMENT	dastard	HYLDING
contemptuous	DESPITEOUS	daunted	QUAYD
contradict	UNDERSAYE	day of ill omen	DISMAL DAY
contrivance	GIN	daze	DARE
controversy	DEBATEMENT	dealt mercifully with	MERCIFIDE
convene	CONVENT	dearth	DERTH
conversation	BOARD	death	FUNERAL
conversation(al speech)	PURPOSE	debase	EMBACE
converse	COMMON	debased	EMBASTE
convey	REPORT	deceit	MALENGINE
corbel	CORBE	deceiver	FALSER, TREACHETOUR
coronation	CARNATION	decline	WELKE
could not	NOTE	decorate	EMBRAVE
counsel	AREAD, AREDE, ARREEDE	decrease	DECREW
	READ, REED(E)	decree	SAW
counterfeit	IDOL	deemed	DEMPT
counterplot	COUNTERCAST	defaced	DEFAST(E)
courageous	STOMACHOUS	defame	DEFACE
course	FARE, TRACE	defence	MUNIFIENCE
cover	HEAL, HEEL, HELE	deformed	DISMAYD
covered	COURD	degenerate	DEGENDER
—over	OVERDIGHT	degrade	EMBACE
—with sweat	FORSWATT	degraded	EMBASTE
coward	COWHE(A)RD	deify	GOD
coward(ly)	HYLDING	delay	FOR(E)SLOW, FORSLOE
cowardice	COWARDREE	delight in	FAIN
coyness	NICETY	dense	RANK
crew together	CONCREW	depart	QUIGHT, QUYTE
crimson	CREM(O)SIN	—from	QUIGHT, QUYTE
cross-bow bolt	QUAR'LE	departure	DEPART, PARTURE
cry		depression	DELVE
—like a cat	WRAWL	deprive of armour	DISMAYL
—triumph over	OVERCRAW	deserving	CONDIGN

design	DESINE, DESYNE, SLEIGHT
designate	INTEND
desire	FAIN
—strongly	EARN
desk	DESSE
despairing	DESPAIRFUL
despised	CONTEMPT
detention	DETAIN
determine	HIGHT
dethrone	DISTHRONISE
detriment	EMPEACH
device	SLEIGHT
devour	ENGORGE
dew	DEAW
dewy	DEAWIE, DEWAY
dexterously	FEATEOUSLY
dialect	LEDDEN
die	QUELL, STERVE
difficult to wield or move	UNWELDY
dig beneath	UNDERMINDE
digest mentally	ENDEW, INDEW
dilute	DELAY
diminish	BAYT
din	DEEN, STOUND, STOWND
direct	AVENTRE, HIGHT
disapprove	DISPROOVE
discern	SCERNE
discharge	QUIGHT, QUYTE
discipline	DISPLE
disclose	UNHEAL, UNHELE
disclosed	DISCLOST
discomfit	YSHEND
discouraging onslaught	DISMAY
discourse	PURPOSE
discourteous	DISCOURTEISE
discover	DISCOURE, DISCURE
disdain	SDAINE, SDAYN, SDEIGNE
	SDEIN
dishearten	DISPARAGE
dishonourable	DISLEAL
disinherit	DISHERIT
disloyal	DISLEAL
dismal	GASTFULL
dispense	DISPENCE, SHED
dispersed	SPERST
displeasure	DISPLEASANCE
disposed	DISPOST, DITE
dispute	CONTROVERSE
dissemble	FEIGN
dissuade	DISCOUNSEL
distance	MOUNTENA(U)NCE
distract	FORHAILE
distracting	DIVERSE
distress	DISMAY
disturb	STIRE, STYRE
ditty	DIT

divide	DEPART, DISCIDE
do	DOEN, DONE, DONNE
—amiss	MIS
—battle	DARRAIGN(E), DARRAINE
	DARRAYN, DERRAIGN
—service	SUE
—wrongly	MISDONNE
doff	UNDIGHT
doing daring deeds	DER-DOING
domain	REAME
doom	DOME
doubtless	DREADLESS
drag	TRAYNE
draw	
—back	DISADVANCE
—over	OVERHA(I)LE
drawn	
—aside	DISTRAUGHT
—away	MISTRAYNED
dread(ed)	DRAD
dreariness	DRE(A)RE, DRERYHOOD
	DRERYMENT
dreary	GASTFULL
dress	AGUISE, AGUIZE, ATTRAP
drifter	DROVER
drive	
—improperly	WREST
—with thunderbolts	THUNDER-DRIVE
drove	DRIVE
drowned	DRENT, DROWNDED
drowsiness	DROWSIHE(A)D
drum	DROOME
due	DEWFULL
dwelling-place	HABITAUNCE
dye	HEW
earlier	RATHER
earn	ERNE
easily	EATH(E), EATHLY, ETHE
easy	EATH(E), ETHE
ebony	HEBON
echo back a loud noise	REBELLOW
efts	EWFTES
elegant	DAINT(Y), DAYNT
embrace	BRACE
embraced	HAULST
embraid	EMBREAD
emerald	EMERAUDE
emulate	AEMULE
emulation	PARAGON
encircle	STEMME
encircled	EMBAYLD
enclose	EMBOSS
encompass	BRACE
encounter	COUNTER
encourage	ACCO(U)RAGE
encouraged	UPCHEARD

encumber	ACCLOY	exterminate	EXTIRP
endeavour	ENDEAVOURMENT	extolled	EXTOLD
endow	ENDEW	extort	OUTWREST, RACK
endue	ENDEW, INDEW	extraction	EXTREAT
enduring	DUREFUL	fabulous	
enflame	ENFIRE	—beast	ANTELOPE
enfold	IMPLY	—bird	WHISTLER
enlarge	ENLARGEN	—fish	SCOLOPENDRA
enquire	ENQUERE	faced	FAST
enrage	ENRANCKLE	fail	MIS
enrolled	ENTROLD, INTROLD	failure to value	MESPRISE, MESPRIZE
enslave	BETHRALL		MISPRIZE
ensue	ENSEW	faint	STANCK, SWELT
entangle	ENSNARL	fainting fit	SOWND, SWOUND
entanglement	ENTRAIL	falcon	TASSELL-GENT
entertain	ACCOURT	fall back	RECOYLE, RECU(I)LE
—guest	HOST	fallen unluckily	MISFALNE
entertainment	ENTERTAIN	false	
entrails	ENTRALLES	—appearance	MISSEEMING
entrance	INGATE	—religious belief	MISCREAUNCE
entrap	UNDERFONG	familiar friend	GOSSIB
entreat	INTREAT	familiarly	COMMONLY
entreating	ENTREATFULL	far	FAR-FORTH
entreaty	IMPLORE	fasten	EMBRACE
entrust	ARRET(T)	—with a spar	SPERRE
entwine	ENTRAIL	favour	GREE
enviable	ENVIOUS	fear	AFFRAY
enwrap	ENROL(L)	feign	FAIN(E), FAYNE
equality	EQUAL	fell	FELONOUS
equip	AGUISE, AGUIZE, DITE	female	
equipment	PURVEYANCE	—animal	SHIDDER
erase	RACE	—dolphin	DOLPHINET
error	MESPRIZE	—poet	POETRESSE
establish	STABLISH	festivity	JOYANCE
esteem	PRISE, STEEM, WAY	feud	FOOD
estranged	FRENNE	fewter	ENCHASE
everywhere	OVERALL	fiat	FIAUNT
evil device	MALENGINE	fickle	CHOICEFUL
exalted	HAUGHT, HAU(L)T	fierce	BREEM, BREME, STOUT
examine	APPOSE	figure	AUMAIL
example for imitation	SAMPLE	find	INVENT
excellently	GOODLY	fine	QUAINT
excess	OUTRAGE	first	PARAVA(U)NT
exchange	CHAFFER, SCORSE	—fruits	PRIMITIAS
excite	EMMOVE, ENMOVE	—year's revenue	PRIMITIAS
excuse	ESSOIN, ESSOYNE	fish-basket	HASK
exile	EXUL	fishing boat	DROVER
exit	OUTGATE	fit	CONCENT, DEWFULL, DUEFUL
expectation	TENDANCE		QUEME, CONCENT
expensive	CHARGEFUL	—for war	WARHABLE
experience	ENTERTAIN, EXPERT	fling headlong	RUINATE
—a pang	STOUND, STOWND	flitted	FLITT
explain	UPKNIT	flock of birds	FLUSH
expound	COMMENT, REED(E)	flow	FLEET, RAILE, RAYLE
extended	DISTENT	foam	FRY
extension in time	PROTENSE	foes	FOEN, FONE

foil	FOYLE	futility	VAINESSE
foin	FOYNE	gaiety	JOYANCE
fold	PLIGHT	gain	EXCHEAT
food	PASTURE	—anew	REPRIZE
foolhardiness	FOOLHARDISE	gained	WAN
	FOOLHARDIZE	gall	FELL
footing	TROAD(E), TRODE	gape	GERNE
for		garb	VESTIMENT
—a long time in the past	LONG SIN	garment	VESTIMENT
—that	FORTHY	gate	YATE
foray	FORRAY	gear	GEARE, GERE
force		Genoese coin	JANE
—away	WREST	gentle	GENT
—back	RECOYLE, RECU(I)LE	get	COMPARE
forced again	RENFORST	—back	RECURE
foreign	FRENNE, STRAUNGE	—out of	OUTWIN
forester	FOSTER	—the better of	CONVINCE
foretokening	SOOTHE	ghastly	GREISLY, GRIESLY
forgery	COUNTERFEASAUNCE		GRISELY, GRYESLY
form		gibbet	CROOK
—anew	REALLIE	gilded	GILDEN, GUILT, GYLDEN
—into roll	ENROL(L)	—leather	CHECKLATON
forsaken	FORLORE	gillyflower	GELLIFLOWRE
fortalice (fortress)	FORTILAGE	gilt	GELT, GUILT
for the most part	MOSTWHAT	girl	GERLE
fortification	MUNIFIENCE	give	
foster	NOUSELL, NOU(R)SLE	—excuses for	CAUSEN
	NUZZLE	—out as if on hire	OUTHYRE
foul person	DREVILL	—over	LIN, OVERGIVE
found	FOND	—up	FORGIVE, OVERGIVE
fountain-basin	LAVER	—vent to	DISCLOSE
free	QUIGHT, QUYTE	—way	RELENT
freedom	RANDON	given	YEVEN
frigate	FRIGOT	giving attention	ATTENT
frighten	AFEAR, AFFEAR(E), DARE	glad	GLADFUL
frightful	GRIESLY, GRISELY, GRYESLY	gladly	FAIN
frisk	COLT	glanced	YGLAUNST
from being fordone	FROM FORDONNE	glided	GLODE
frosty	FRORY	glittering	GLITTERAND
frozen	FRORY	gloom	DRE(A)RE
fulfil a term	EXPIRE	glory	GARLAND
full		go	GOE, YEAD, YEDE, YEED
—of		—about or forth	STIRE, STYRE
air or fragrance	BREATHFUL	—astray	MISWEND
devices	DEVICEFUL	—back	RECOURSE
life	LIFULL, LYFULL	—over in one's mind	RECORD
moans	GRONEFUL	—up	AMOUNT
—speed	RANDON	goat	GATE
fulminate	FULMINE	gold	GOOLD
funeral service	HERSE	gondola	GONDELAY
furious	YOND	gone	GOE, YGO(E)
—onset	AFFRET	good	
furnish with		—and fair maid	BON(N)IBELL
buildings	EDIFY	—day	GOD DAY
furnishing	FURNIMENT, PURVEYANCE	—for the heart	HARTIE-HALE
fury	DREAD	—for-nothing	LORRELL, LOZEL

—friend	BELAMY	hard-pressed	STRAIT
—health or fortune	WELL	harden	ENDURE
—reception	BEL-ACCOYLE	harnessed in a team	TE(E)MED
goodness	GOODLIHEAD	harsh	RIGOROUS
	GOODLYHEAD	hastened	HIDE
goodwill	GREE	haughty	HAUGHT, HAU(L)T
gore	ENGORE		STOMACHOUS
got at	ARRAUGHT	have	
government	GOVERNALL	—need	MISTER
graced	GRASTE	—(plural)	HAN
graciously	GOODLY	—wrong opinion	MISWEEN
grant	BETEEM(E)	having	
granted beforehand	FOR(E)LENT	—many layers	MANY-FOLDED
grapple	CRAPPLE, GRAPLE	—power	VERTUOUS
grasp	ENGRASP, HEND	hazard	HAZARDIZE
grasping	GRIPLE	heal	G(U)ARIS, RECURE
gravel	GRAILE, GRAYLE	healthy	HARTIE-HALE
great knight	DOUCEPERE, DOUZEPER	heap up	COMPILE, UPHOORD
greedy	GRIPLE	heaped	HEPT
greeted	SALUED, SALVE'D	heard	HARD
grey	BLONCKET, GRIESIE, GRYSESY	hearse	HERSE
grief	TINE, TYNE, WAYMENT	heart(en)	HART(EN)
grieve	ENGRIEVE, WAYMENT	heartily	HARTELY
grievous	CAREFUL, DEAR(E), NOYOUS	heartless	HARTLESSE
grin	GERNE, GIRN, GREN	heat	BEATH
grinned	GRIND	heaved	HEFT(E)
griped	GRYPT	heavily awkward	UNWELDY
griping	GRIPLE	heed	RESPECT
gripped	GRYPT	heedful	HEEDY
grisly	GREISLY, GRIESLY	height	LOFT
ground tackle	GROUND-HOLD	held	HILD
growl	ROYNE	hell	TARTAR(E), TARTARIE, TARTARY
grudge	GRUTCH	herd	HEARD
guard	SAVEGARD	hest	HEAST(E)
guess	DEVISE, GESSE, GHESSE	hide	HEAL, HEEL, HELE
guild	GYELD	hie	HYE
guile	GUYLE	high	HAUGHTY, HYE
guise	GUYSE, PURPORT	hind	HYNDE
gullet	WEASAND-PIPE	hinder	EMPEACH
gush	RAILE, RAYLE	hindrance	IMPEACH
gypsy	GIPSEN	hither(ward)	HETHER(WARD)
hacking	HEW	having shoulders that	
haggling	CHAFFER	displace the sea	SEA-SHOULD'RING
hailed	SALUED, SALVE'D	hoar	HORE
hair	HEARE	hoard	UPHOORD
hairy	HEARIE	hold	
hale	HAYLE	—down	SUPPRESS
half	HALFEN(DEALE)	—together	COMPRISE
halloo	BLEW	hole	DELL, DELVE
hammer	MARTEL	hollow	DELVE
handle	STEAL(E), STEEL, STEIL	holly	HOLM
	STELE	home	HAEME
hang in clusters	SHAG	honeysuckle	CAPRIFOIL
happen		hood	CAPUCCIO
—ill	MISHAPPEN	hooped in	EMBAYLD
—to	BEHAPPEN	hot	WHOT

hover	HO(O)VE
however	HOWBE
hue	HEW
humble	AFFLICTED, DEMISS
humbleness	HUMBLESSE
hurt	NOY, SCATH
hush	WHIST
husk	PILL
hyacinth (stone)	HYACINE
idea	CONCEIT
ignoble	UNNOBLE
ignorant person	IGNARO
ill	
—arranged	MISDIGHT
—gotten	MISGOTTEN
—shaped	MISHAPT
—tempered	GIRNIE
—treat	DEMEAN
—will	MALTATENT
illumine	ENLUMINE
imagined character	PERSONAGE
imbrue	EMBREWE
imbue	EMBAY
imp	YMP
impair	EMPA(I)RE, EMPAYRE
	EMPERISH
impairment	EMPEACH
impeach	EMPEACH
imped	YMPT
impede	EMPEACH
implant	ENRACE
improper feeding	MISDIET
in	
—a row	AREW
—averse direction	FROWARD
—complete confusion	UPSIDEOWNE
—front	PARAVA(U)NT
—some degree	SOMEDELE
—sorry plight	MISDIGHT
—time	TIMELY
inadvertent	UNADVISED
inasmuch	IN SORT
inattention	MISREGARD
incisive	TRENCHAND
increase	ACCREW
incursion	RODE
indecorous	SEEM(E)LESS(E)
indeed	SOOTHLICH
Ind(ia)	YND
indicate	DESIGN
indue	INDEW
ineffectual	RESTY
infamy	DEFAME
infatuated	ASSOTT(ED)
inflamed	FLAMED
inform	ENFORM, PARTAKE

infusion	INFUSE
inglorious	IRRENOWNED
ingots	INGO(W)ES
ingress	INGATE
inhabitant	INHOLDER
inhabiting woods	WOODY
inhospitable	HOSTLESSE
injure	SCATH
injured by cold	WINTER-BEATEN
injurious	NOYOUS
injury	BLAME, EMPEACH, SCATH
	TINE, TYNE, TORT
—to oneself	SELFE-DESPIGHT
inner	ENTIRE
innermost thoughts	PRIVITY
innocent	SEELY
inoperative	RESTY
inquire	ENQUERE, INQUERE
Irish chieftaincy	CHEVERYE
inscribe	ENDOSS
instruction	DOCUMENT
instrument of torture	GIN
insult	REPRIEFE
integument	PILL
intend	HIGHT
intention	ATTENDEMENT
intercourse	ENTERDEALE
interest in property	STATE
interlace	ENTRAIL
interpretation	READ
interruption	CESURE
intimately	COMMONLY
intrigue against	UNDERMINDE
inward	ENTIRE
irresistible	INSUPPORTABLE
irrigating canal	ZANJA
is not	NIS, NYS
ivy-bush	TODDE
jasper	JASP
jaw	CHAW
jealous	GEALOUS
jealousy	GEALOUSY, GELOSY
jeer	GEARE
jellied	GELLY
journey	WAY, WENT
joust	GIOUST
joyousness	JOYANCE, JOVYSAUNCE
	JOUISANCE, JOUYSAUNCE
judge wrongly	MISWEEN
judged wrongly	MISDEMPT
junket	JUNCATE
jurisdiction	BAIL
keen	BREEM, BREME
keep	
—head to wind	TRIE
—in subjection	UNDERKEEP

—watch	WAITE	letter of introduction	BENEFICIAL
keeping time	TIMELY	levy	LEAVE
keyhole	CLINK	liar	FALSER
kick	RECOYLE, RECU(ILE)	lie	LIG(GE), LIGGEN
killed	KILD, KILT	—down	SEAT
kind	KYND(E)	—in folds	W(H)IMPLE
—look	BELGARD	—out of the way	BA(U)LK
kindled	TIND, TYND(E)	—to	TRIE
kindly	GOODLY	lift up	EXTOL
kine	KYNE	light	LITE
kingdom	REAME	like	LICH
kinship	SYBBE	—a Centaur	HALF-HORSY
kite	KIGHT	—lightning	ENFOULDERED
knew	KOND	likeness	LIKELINESS
knob	SNUBBE	limb	SPALLE
know	CON(NE), KON, WEET(E)	limiter	LYMETER
	WEETEN, WOT	lineage	LIGNAGE, LYNAGE
knowest	KYDST	linen	LYNE
ladder	STIE, STYE	linger	HO(O)VE
laid before	FORELAY	list(en)	LEST
lair	LARE	listless	LUSTLESS
lame	ACCLOY	lithe	LYTHE
lament	MEAN(E), MEIN, MENE	little bush	BUSKET
	WAYMENT	livelihood	LIVELO(O)D
lamentation	WAYMENT	living thing	QUICK
lance	LAUNCE	load	TODDE
lancing	LA(U)NCH	loam	LOME
language	LEDDEN	loathsome	LOTH(E)FULL
lasting	DUREFUL	lodge	BOWER, HOST
latch	CLINK	lodging	BRAME, FERM, HOSTRY
launch forth	OUTLAUNCE	loiter	HO(O)VE
lawless	RULESSE	loll (the tongue)	LILL
lay		long	LENG, SIDELONG
—about one	THROW	—for	EARN
—in a cradle	ENCRADLE	longer	LENGER
—on	POUND	longest	LENGEST
lazy	LAESIE	look over	SURVEW
leak	LEKE	loop	LOUP
lean	LEANY	loose	LOAST, LOSE(N)
leaped/leapt	LEPPED, LOPE	—(hair)	UNDIGHT
learn	CON(NE), KON, LEAR(E)	—robe	CAMIS, CAMUS
	LEIR, LERE	—woman	FRANION
lease	FARM	lose	LEESE
leave off	QUIGHT, QUYTE	lost	LOAST, LOS'TE
lecher	LEACHOUR	lout	LOORD
leech	LEACH	lovingly	LOVELY
left	LORE, LORN, OTHER	lower	AVALE, AVAIL(E), EMBACE
leg armour	GAIMBEUX	lowered	EMBASTE
leisure	LEASURE	lumpish	LOMPISH
lest	LEAST	mad	YOND
—by chance	ENAUNTER	made footsore	SURBATED, SURBET
let		madman	GELT
—forth as from entrails	DISENTRAIL	mail	MALE
	DISENTRAYLE	make	
—go	QUIGHT, QUYTE	—a show of	COUNTENANCE
—out for pay	WAGE	—amends	DISPENSE

—busy	EMBUSY	misshapen	DISMAYD, MISSHAPT
—divine	DIVINE	misused	MISUST
—feeble	FEEBLE	moan	MEAN(E), MEIN, MENE
—fierce	EFFIERCE, ENFELON, ENFIERCE	moderate	RELENT
—footsore	SURBATE	moiety	MOYITY
—fortunate	FORTUNIZE	moil	MOYLE
—happy	FORTUNIZE	momentum	POISE
—known	READ	monster	ROSMARINE, SEASATYRE
by display	VAUNT		ZIFFIUS
—little or less	MINISH	month	MONETH
—pregnant	ENWOMB	mostly	MOSTWHAT
—showy	EMBRAVE	mount	STIE, STYE
—thick	ENGROSS	movable front of	
—uneasy	DISEASE	helmet	VENTAILE
mannered	THEWED		VENTAYLE
many-coloured	DISCOLOURED	move	EMMOVE, ENMOVE, MIEVE
marked	DISTINCT		QUICH, QUINCHE
—with spots	EYE-SPOTTED	—around or to	
marred	MARD	activity	STIRE, STYRE
massive	TIMBERED	much	MOCHELL, MUCHELL
master	MAISTERDOME, MAYSTER	—worn	FORWORN
mastering	MAISTRING	muscle	BOWR
match	AMATE, PRISE	must	MOT(E)
mate	PARAGON	muster	HOSTING
may	MOT(E)	musty	FROUGHY, FROWIE, FROWY
—(past tense)	MOUGHT	mutter	ROYNE
meadow-sweet	MEDAEWORT	mutual dealings	ENTERDEALE
mean person	HYLDING	name	BEHIGHT, BEHOTE, READ
meaning	INTENDIMENT	named	HOT(E), NEMPT
means of living	LIVELO(O)D	narrow	STRAIT
meantime	MEAN	narwhal	MONOCEROS
meet	ENTERTAIN	nathless	NETHELESS
meeting place of guild	GYELD	near	FOREBY
melted	YMOLT	nearer	NARRE
mention	HIGHT	neatly	FEATEOUSLY
mercenary soldier	WAR-MONGER	needy	STRAIT
merciful	MERCIABLE	negotiations	ENTERDEALE
mere	MEARE	never the more	NATHEMO(RE)
mered	MEAR'D	new thing	NEWELL
merriment	JOLLIMENT	newly weaned child	
merrymaking	MERIAMKE	or animal	WEANEL
meted	MOTT	nimble	WIMBLE
mews	MEAWES	nobility	NOBILESSE
middle(most)	IDDEST	noble	DOUCEPERE, DOUZEPER
military expedition	HOSTING		GENT
misbecome	MISSEEM	—youth	INFANT
misbegotten	MISGOTTEN	noise	NOYES
miscarry	MISWEND	not	
misconception	MISCONCEIT	—akin	FRENNE
misfortune	MISFARE	—braced	UNBRASTE
mishap	DISAVENTURE, DRE(A)RE	—challenged	UNDEFIDE
misled	MISTRAYNED	—civilised	UNCIVIL
mislike	MISLEEKE	—clear in the head	ILL-HEDDED
mismade	DISMAYD	—defied	UNDEFIDE
mismanagement	MISGOVERNAUNCE	—dressed	UNDIGHT
misshaped	MISSHAPT	—favouring	FAVOURLESS

—known	UNWIST	pansy	PA(U)NCE, PAWNCE
—lamented	UNPLAINED	parleying	EMPARLAUNCE
—marred	UNMARD	paroxysm	THROW(E)
—matching	MATCHLESS	partake	PERTAKE
—prayed for	UNBID	pass	
—provided with	UNPURVAIDE	—away	VADE
—the more	NATHEMO(RE)	—like a fever	SWELT
—to be appeased	IMPACABLE	passage	FARE
notwithstanding	HOWBE	passion	BRAME
object gazed at	GAZEMENT	past	FOREBY
oblique	OBLIQUID	pasture	LARE
occasion	ENCHEASON	path	STIE, STYE, TROAD(E)
occupy	EMBUSY		TRODE, WENT
—oneself with	ENTREAT	pattern	SLEIGHT
ochre	OAKER	pay	QUIGHT, QUYTE, SOLD
of		—for	PRYSE
—a tree	TREEN	—the price of	PRICE
—straw	STRAWEN	payment	HAN(D)SEL
—the same		peacock	PAVONE
province	COMPROVINCIAL	peal	PELE
time of day	TIMELY	pease	POUSSE
offer up	APPEAL	pebble	PUMY(STONE)
omen	SOOTHSAY	peep	TOOT
one who proclaims	BLAZER	peer	PEARE
only	ONELY	—about	TOOT
onset	SALIAUNCE	peised	PAYSD
open place	OVERTURE	pen	PENNE
orbit	SPHERE	penal retribution	VENGEMENT
ordain	BEHIGHT, BEHOTE	penalty	HAN(D)SEL
ore	OWRE	penetrate	SEIZE
originate	REAR	penny	PENI(E)
ornament	GARLAND	penthia	ASTROPHEL, STARLIGHT
ostrich	OSTRIGE	perceive	UNDERTAKE
out of condition	RAW	perch (of land)	LUG
outcry	STEVEN	performance	CHEVISANCE
outlet	OUTGATE	perilous	PERLOUS
outward appearance	FORESIDE, PURPOST	perish	QUELL, TINE, TYNE
overcast	OVERKEST	perplex	DISTROUBLE
overcome	CONVINCE, UNDERFONG	personality of beast	BEASTLY-HEAD
—by wrestling	OVERWRESTLE	pestilence	MURRIN
overflow	REDOUND	phantom	PHANTOSME
overlay	SPILL	piece of tapestry	TAPET
overspread	OVERDIGHT	pierce	EMP(I)ERCE, LA(U)NCH
overtake	OVERHENT		PEARCE, PERCE, PERSE
overtaken	OVERCAUGHT, OVERHENT	pierced	GRYPT, PEARST, PIERST
overtook	FORHENT	piercing	THRILLANT
overworked	FORSWONCK	pinion	PENNE
ownerless property	WAIFT, WEFT	pinioned	PINNOED
ox	STEARE	pioneer work	PYONINGS
painful experience	FIT	pitch	PRICK
pains	TINE, TYNE	pitched	PIGHT
paint	DEPAINT	pitied	MERCIFIDE
painted	IMPICTURED	pity	REMORSE
paltry fellow	SQUIB	placed	PLAST(E)
panacea	PANACHAEA	—above	OVERPLAST
pang	STOUND, STOWND, THROW(E)	plant (unknown)	TETRA

plash	PLESH
playing games of hazard	HAZARDRY
pleaded	PLED
please	QUEME
pleasure	LUST
pledge	BANK
plight	TAKING
pluck	RACE
plunder	BEROB, EXCHEAT, HERRIMENT
	HERRYMENT, PREY
plundering	SPOYLEFULL
plunge	EMPLONGE, PLONG(E)
plunged	PLONGD
poetess	POETRESSE
poignant	POYNANT
point	PRICK
—out	PRESAGE
poise	PEASE, PEAZE, PEISE
	PEIZE, PEYSE
poised	PAYSD
poisonous plant	SAMNITIS
policy	POLLICIE, POLLICY
politeness	COMPLEMENT
pollute	BLEND
pompous	STATE
pool	PLESH
poplar	ASPINE
porpoise	PORCPISCE
portable breviary	PORTAS, PORTESS(E)
	PORT(E)OUS, PORTHORS
	PORTHOS, PORTHOUSE
portion	WHAT
portrait(ure)	RETRAITT, RETRATE
portrayed	POURTRAHED
possessing virtue	VERTUOUS
postpone	PROLONG
pot	CREWE
potsherd	POTSHARE
pour	POWRE
praise	HERRY, HERY(E)
prance	PRAUNCE
precarious	T(R)ICKLE
precedent	PRESIDENT
precepts	SCHOOLERY
precisely	BY THE SQUIRE
predicted	FORESHEWED
pre-eminently	PARAVA(U)NT
preferred	PREFARD
preparation in advance	PURVEYANCE
press	PEASE, PEAZE, PEISE
	PEIZE, PEYSE
	PREACE
—down	SUPPRESS
pressure	STRAINT
pretended	COUNTERFECT
prey	PRAY, RAVEN, RAVIN(E), SOYLE

price	PRISE
prick	ACCLOY
private counsels	PRIVITY
prize	PRISE
proceed	YEAD, YEDE, YEED
proceeded	FOND, YOD(E)
process of combat	DISCOURSE
profit	VANTAGE
prognostication	PREJUDIZE
promise	BEHIGHT, BEHOTE
promptly	B(Y)LIVE
proof	ASSAY
proper	DEWFULL, DUEFUL
proportion	REASON
prosper	THEE
protect	SAVEGARD
protection	PATRONAGE
prove	TRIE
provide	COMPARE
province	REAME
pry	TOOT
puddle	PLESH
pull apart	DISTRAIN
punching	POUNCING
punish	YSHEND
purified	TRYE
purpose	DEVISE, PROPOUND
purse	CRUMENAL
purslane	PERSELINE
pursue	POURSEW, POURSUE, PURSEW
pursuit	POURSUIT(T), SUIT
put	
—at a distance	DISLOIGN
—down	UNDERLAY
—far apart	DISLOIGN
—forth as shoot or fruit	SPIRE
—into	
action	SERVE
operation	ENURE
—on	INVEST
—out of countenance	DEFACE
—to shame	YSHEND
—together	COMPILE
putting to death	DEAD-DOING
quagmire	WAGMOIRE
quaint	QUEINT
quaked	QUOOKE
quality	ASSAY
quarrel	QUAR'LE
quarrelsome	DEBATEFULL
quarter	QUART
quash	REPEAL
quenched	QUEINT
question	APPOSE
quickly	B(Y)LIVE
quickness	NIMBLESSE

quince	QUEENE-APPLE
quit	QUIGHT, QUYTE
quite	QUIGHT
race	RAUNCH
raced	RAST
raid	BODRAG, BORDRAGING
rail	SPARRE
raise	LEAVE
—in front	FORELIFT
rancid	FROUGHY, FROWIE, FROWY
rang	RONG
range about	DISPACE
rapt	YRAPT
rapture	ENRAGEMENT
rare	GEASON, SE(E)LD
rashness	HAZARDRY
ravish	SUPPRESS
ray	RAYON
raze	RACE
reach	SEISE
read	RAD, RED(D)
ready	PREST
realm	REAME
reason	ENCHEASON
rebound	RECOYLE, RECU(I)LE
rebuild	RE-EDIFY
recapture	REPRIZE
receive	ENTERTAKE
reck	REKE, WREAK(E)
recognised character	PERSONAGE
recoil	REBUT, RECOYLE, RECU(I)LE
reconcile	UPKNIT
reconciled	AFFRENDED
recover	RECOURE, RECOWER, RECURE
rede	REED(E)
reduce	DEDUCT, MINISH
refreshment of sleep	REPAST
refund	REDISBURSE
refuse	NILL
—to agree	DISACCORD
refused	NILLED, NOULD(E)
regard as holy	HERRY, HERY(E)
region	QUART, REAME
regret	FORTHINK, RELENT
rehearsal	HERSALL
reign	RAIN(E)
—to the end of	OUTRAIGNE
reinforced	RENFORST
reinstate	RESEIZE
rejoined	RELIDE
relate	REED(E)
relax	RELENT
relaxed	UNBRASTE
release	
—from obligation	QUIGHT, QUYTE

—on payment by instalment	STAL'D
relied	RELIDE
remedy	RECURE
remembrance	SOVENA(U)NCE
remit	QUIGHT, QUYTE
remove	DISLOIGN
—wrongly	MISTAKE
removed	REMOUD
—from hearse	UNHERST
remuneration	SOLD
renewed efforts	RENFORST
renounce	FOR(E)SAY
rent (cuddy)	CUDDEEHIH
repay	QUIGHT, QUYTE
repeat from memory	RECORD
repent	RELENT
repentance	REPENT
reprehend	SPOT
represented beforehand	FORESHEWED
repress	REPEAL
reprieve	REPRIVE, REPRYVE
reproach	REPRIEFE, YSHEND
reproof	REPRIEFE
reprove	REPRIEVE
require	REQUERE
requite	QUIGHT, QUYTE, REQUIGHT
requited	REQUIGHT, REQUIT
rescue	RESKEW
resentful	STOMACHOUS
resigned beforehand	FOR(E)LENT
resistless	IMPORTUNE
response	RESPONDENCE
rest one's weight	UPLEAN
restitution	RESTORE
restore to its position	REPAIR
restrain	ABSTAIN, BEHOLD
rethink	FORTHINK
retrace	REMEASURE
retreat	RECOYLE, RECU(I)LE, RETRATE
return	RECOURSE, REVERSE
reveal	DESCRY, PRESAGE
reversed	RENVERST
revert	RECOYLE, RECU(I)LE
—in the mind	RECOURSE
revive	RELIVE
ribald	RIBAUD, RYBAULD
ribaldry	RYBAUDRYE
rid	QUIGHT, QUYTE
rife	RYFE
rightly	ARIGHTS
rigorous	STRAIT
rind	RINE
rise	HOVE, STIE, STYE
—one above another	REDOUND

riven	RIFTE
—fragment	RIFT
river	LEE
road	RODE
roar	ROYNE
rod (of land)	LUG
rode	RAD
roll about wallowing	ENWALLOW
root out	OUTWEED
rounded	COMPAST
rouse	ABRAY, AMO(O)VE
	STIRE, STYRE
rove over	ENRAUNGE
ruby	RUBIN(E)
ruff	RUFFIN
ruffle	RUFF
rule	SQUIER, SQUIRE
ruleless	RULESSE
run	RENNE, RONNE
running	RONNING
runt	RONT(E)
rush	RANDON
rustic	HOBBINOLL
sacramental	HOUSLING
saddle	SEL(LE)
safeguard	SAUFGARD
sage	SAULGE
salience	SALIAUNCE
saluted	SALEWD, SALUED
sate	ACCLOY
satisfy	DEFRAY
savage	SALVAGE
save	SAFE
say	SAINE, SAYNE
—in answer	UNDERSAYE
sayest	SAIST
saying	READ
scale	SCAND
scaly sea-monster	PHOCA
scanned	SCAND
scarified	SCARIFIDE
scent	SENT
scheme	GIN
scimitar	CEMITARE
scion	SIENT
scorch	SCATH
scorn	MESPRISE, MESPRIZE, MISPRIZE
screech-owl	SHRIECH-OWL, STRICH
screen	SCRIENE, SKREENE
scuffle	CUFFLE
scutcheon	SCUCHI(O)N
scythe	SITHE
sea	
—horse	HIPPODAME
—monster	ROSMARINE
	SEA-SATYRE, ZIFFIUS

secret proceeding	COVERTURE
seemliness	SEEMLYHED
seize	HEND, SEASE, SEAZE, CEAZE
seized	ARRAUGHT, FORHENT
sell	CHAFFER
send downstream	POUR
sense	SENT
sentinel	CENTONEL(L)
set	PIGHT
—about by	BESTAD(D)E
—in	
battle array	DARRAI(G)N(E)
	DARRAYN, DERRAIGN
motion	STIRE, STYRE
—on fire	ENFIRE
—spear in rest	ENCHASE
—up	ADDRESSED, ADDREST
	FEUTRE, FEWTER
settle downward	PEASE, PEAZE
	PEISE, PEIZE, PEYSE
shade	OVERCAST
shadow forth	SHADE
shaft	STEAL(E), STEEL
	STEIL, STELE
shaken off	OFF-SHAKT
shallow pool	PLESH
shame	REPRIEFE, YSHEND
shank	STEAL(E), STEEL
	STEIL, STELE
shaped	SHOPE
share	CO-PORTION
—out	EMPART
shared	SHARD
sheer	SHERE
shining	NEAT
—obscurely	GLOOMING
shiver in pieces	DISSHIVER
shock	STOUND, STOWND
shoot like a pang	STOUND, STOWND
shoulder	SPALLE
shout	CLAME
showed beforehand	FORESHEWED
shower	POUND
showing	
—much white (eye)	WHALLY
—through the skin	RAW
shriek	SCRIKE, SHREEK
	SHRIECH, SHRIGHT, SHRIKE
shrine	SCRINE, SCRYNE
shrink from	RECOYLE, RECU(I)LE
shrive	SHRIEVE
shy	LOFT
sic	SIKE
silence	WHIST
similar	LIKELY
simple	SEELY

simplicity	SIMPLESSE
since	SENS, SITHENS, SITHENCE
sing in measure	MEASURE
singe	SWINGE
sister	SYBBE
sit down	SEAT
skill	FEAT
skilled	PRACTIC
skirmish	SCARMOGE
skirt worn by knight	BASE
skull	PANNIKELL
sky-blue	CAERULE
slacken (pace)	RELENT
slant	RASH
sleep	SWOON
sleepiness	DRWOSIHE(A)D
slight	MESPRISE, MESPRIZE
	MISPRIZE
slow down	RELENT
small boat	COTT
smeared in blood	BEGORED
smell	SENT
smite	SMIGHT
snag	SNUBBE
snarl	GIRN, SNAR
snatch	RACE
snub	SNIB
solve	LOOSE
something	WHAT
—taught	SCHOOLERY
somewhat	SOMEDELE
song	CANTION, CHARM
soot	SOUT
soothe	ACCOY
sorrow	REPENT
sorrowful	CAREFUL
sorry scamp	LORRELL, LOZEL
souse	SOUCE, SOWS(S)E
soused	SOUCT
space of time	STEAD
spared	SPARD
sparing in giving	STRAIT
sparingly	NIGHLY
spasm	THROW(E)
spawn	BLOT
speak to	BEHIGHT, BEHOTE
speech	LEDDEN
spire	SPYRE
spirited	STOMACHOUS
spiritless	HYLDING
spite	SPIGHT
spot (of iron-mould)	MOLD
spray of water	WATER-SPRINKLE
spread	SPRAD
—out below	SUBJECT
sprite	SPRIGHT

spur	SPURNE
spy	SPYAL
squeeze	SCRUZE
stagger back	RECOYLE, RECU(I)LE
stain	STAYNE
stair	STAYRE
stand	STANDEN, STOND
standing on end	UPSTART
start	
—back	RECOYLE, RECU(I)LE
—up	ASTART
startled bird	FLUSH
starvation	PINE, PYNE
starve	STERVE
stayed	STAID
stead	STED(D), STED(D)E
steadfast	SAD
steam	STEEM
steep	EMBAY
steer	STEAR(E), STIRE
steerage	STEARAGE
steered	STEARD
stir	STIRE, STYRE, QUICH
	QUINCHE
stone	PUMY(STONE)
—or earthenware vessel	STEANE
stop for	STAY
stoppage	BLIN
stoutly	STATE
straight	STREIGHT
strain	STRENE
strait	STREIGHT
strand	STROND
strange	FRENNE, SELCOUTH
	STRAUNGE
stray far	FORWANDER
strayed	
—animal	WAIFT, WEFT
—over	MISWANDRED
strengthening band	BEND
stretch forth	INTEND
—or in front	PRETEND
strict	STRAIT
strife	CONTECK
strifeful	STRYFULL
strike	AFFRAY
stripe	STAKE, STRAIK
strive	ENFORCE
stroke	STOUND, STOWND
—in return	COUNTERSTROKE
struck	
—by thunderbolt	YTHUNDERED
—with downward	
blow	OVERSTROOKE
stub	SNUBBE
stun	STOUN, STOUND

stunned	STOUND
—condition	STOUND
stupid	DOTED
stupidity	BRUTENESS
subdue	ADAW, SUBDEW
subject	CAITIVE
—to pangs	THROW(E)
submerge	EMPLONGE
subside	QUELL
successively	BY-AND-BY
such	SICH, SIKE
suddenly	UNWARELY
sue	SEW
suffer pangs	THROW(E)
suing	SEWING
suit	QUEME
sullen	SOLEIN
sum up	UPKNIT
summon	CONVENT
support	LIVELO(O)D
suppose	DEVISE
surely	SICCAR, SICKER, YKER
surge	REDOUND
surly	SYRLYE
surpass	UNDERLAY
surround with border	EMPALE
survey	SURVEW
surview	SERUEWE, SERVEWE
suspected	MISDEMPT
swaddling-band	SWEATH-BAND
sweated	SWAT
sweating-sickness	STOOPE-GALLAUNT
sweetly	SOOT(E)
sword	BRONDYRON, SWEARD
swordfish	MONOCEROS
tabor player	TABRERE
take	
—away	REAR
—in	ENDEW, INDEW
—off	UNDIGHT
taken	TANE
tale	SCORE
talon	TALA(U)NT
tambourine	TAMBURIN
tame	AMENAGE
tar	TARRE
teamed	TE(E)MED
tear	
—away	RACE
—off	RACE
teen	TINE, TYNE
temper	DELAY
tender	FRAIL
terrace	TERRAS
terrify	AGRISE, AGRIZE, AGRYZE
territory	RIGHT

that which humbles	
gallants	STOOPE-GALLAUNT
thatch	THETCH
theft	STEALTH
then	THO
therefore	FORTHY
thicket	GRE(A)VE
thing aimed at	LEVEL
thirst	THRIST, THRUST
those	THO
thou art	THOUS
thought wrongly	MISDEMPT
thoughtful	CONCEITFUL
thread	RID
thrive	THEE
throat	WEASAND-PIPE
throe	THROW(E)
throw off	DISCUSS
thrust	AVENTURE
—in the bowels	EMBOWEL
thunder	FOULDER
ticklish	T(R)ICKLE
tied	TIDE, TIGHT, TYDE
tier of guns	TIRE
time	SITH(E), SYTHE
	STOUND, STOWND
—of trouble	STOUND, STOWND
tinged	TINCT
tingle	TICKLE
tint	HEW
tired animal	TYRELING JADE
titmouse	TITMOSE
to	
—be at discord	DISACCORD
—burn with anger	EMBOIL
—carve	CARVEN
—catch	CATCHEN, KETCH
—pierce	PERCEN
—the smallest detail	TO POINT
—toss	TOSSEN
together	SAM, YSAME
told	TELD
tomb	FUNERAL
took	WAN
top of head	NOULE
torch	TEAD(E)
torn	ENRIVEN
—to pieces	TO-RENT
tossed	YTOST
total number	SCORE
trace	TRACT
track	CHALLENGE, TRACT, TRADE
	TROAD(E), TRODE
—of blood	PERSUE
trail	TRADE, TRAYNE
train	TIRE

traitor	TREACHETOUR	unformed	INFORMED
transferred	TRANSFARD	unfriendly	FRENNE
transform	DISCLOSE	ungovernable	IMPOTENT
transmute	TRANSMEW, TRANSMOVE	unguarded state	RANDON
traverse	WEAR	unidentified plant	ASTROFELL
treading	TRADE		ASTROPHEL
treat	DEMEAN	unjustly held	WRONGFUL
—insultingly	INDIGNIFY	unknowing	UNWIST
treatment	DEMAINE, DEMAYNE	unlaced	UNLAST(E)
	DEMEANE	unlikly	UNLIKE
tree used for carving	CARVER	unmanageable	UNWELDY, WEELDLESSE
tree-trunk	STUD	unobserved	UNSPIDE
trenching	PYONINGS	unpierceable	IMPERCEABLE
trick	COUNTERCAST	unprepared	UNPURVAIDE
	COUNTERPOINT	unprovided	UNPURVAIDE
tried	FOND, TRIDE	unread	UNRED
trod	TROAD(E), TRODE	unruliness	UNRULIMENT
Trojan	TROYAN	unruly	RULESSE
trouble greatly	DISTROUBLE	unseemly	SEEM(E)LESS(E)
troublesome	BRICKLE	unshed	UNPARTED
truce	TREAGUE	unstable	UNSTAYED
truly	SOOTHLICH	unsweet	UNSOOTE
truncated	TRUNKED	unthriftiness	UNTHRIFTYHE(A)D
try expedients	THROW ABOUT	untired	ENTIRE
turban	TURRIBANT	untold	UNRED
turn		unusual	UNACQUAINTED
—aside	DIVERSE, REVERSE	unweave	UNREAVE
—back	RETURN	upbraid(ing)	UPBRAY
—out	TRIE	upheld	UPHILD
twain	TWAY	upper region	LOFT
twist	BOUGHT	upriseth	UPRYST
twisting	ENTRAIL	upset	RENVERST
twit	TWIGHT	upside down	UPSIDEOWNE
ugly-faced	ILL-FASTE	urge earnestly	PROCURE
umpire	DAYES-MAN	urgent	IMPORTUNE
unaccustomed	UNWONT	utter in measure	MEASURE
unbecoming	MISSEEMING	utterly	RANK
—a knight	KNIGHTLESS	vagrant	SCATTERLING
uncommon	SE(E)LD	valuation	PRIZE
uncontrolled state	RANDON	vanity	VAINESSE
uncounted	UNRED	variegate	AUMAIL
uncover	UNHEAL, UNHELE	variegated	DISTINCT
uncurdled	UNCRUDDED	veil	VEALE, VELE
undergrowth	SPRING	velvet	VELLET
underlying	SUBJECT	vengeance	VENGEMENT
understand	CONTRIVE	venturous	VENTROUS
understanding	INTENDIMENT	verdict	VERDIT
undertake	UNDERFONG	vervain	VERVEN
undertaken	UNDERTANE	vestment	VESTIMENT
undo	UNDIGHT	vex	NOY
undoing	DEFEATURE	vexatious	NOYOUS
undress	DISATTIRE	view	ADVEW
undue divergence from mean	OUTRAGE	vile	VILD(E)
unequal match	DISPARAGE	villeinage	VELLENAGE
unexpectedly	UNWARELY	violent	RIGOROUS
unfledged	EYAS	violently	RANK

visor	UMBREL, UMBR(I)ERE, UMBRIL
vitiate	BLEND
vulgar	BLATTANT
wafted	WEFT
waif	WAIFT, WEFT(E)
waist-belt	TAWDRY-LACE
wait	WAITE
waived	WEFT(E)
walk about	SPACE
wall-eyed	WHALLY
walrus	ROSMARINE
wane	WELKE
want	PINE, PYNE
wariness	WARIMENT
warlike	BATALIOUS
warn	AWARN
was	
—accustomed	DID WON
—called	HOT(E)
waste	
—away	FORPINE
—utterly	FORWASTE
watch	AWAIT
watchful	AVIZEFULL
wax faint	APPAL
waxed	WOX(EN)
way	TRACE
—in	INGATE
weak	BRiCKLE
weaken	DEDUCT, DELAY
—gradually	UNDERMINDE
weapon	SPARKE
weary out	FORWEARY
weave	WIND
weep	GREET
weigh	WAY
weight of	
—blows	LOAD
—wool	TODDE
welfare	HAYLE
well-knit	PIGHT
went	YOD(E)
while	THROW
whole(some)	HOLE(SOME)
wick	WEEKE
wicker	SALE
wide as a basin	BASEN-WIDE
wield	SOWND
wifehood	WIVEHOOD
will	WULL
—not	NILL
windpipe	WEASAND-PIPE
wit	WEET(E), WEETEN, WOT
with	
—clothing unfastened	UNBRASTE
—tension relaxed (drum)	UNBRASTE

withdraw	REVOKE
wither	SCATH
without	
—knowing	UNWARE
—luxury	BARE
—possibility of escape	UNREDREST
—redress	UNREDREST
—rules	RULESSE
woe	WAE
won	WAN, WOON
wont	FAIN
woo	WOW
worn out	TO-WORNE
worse	WAR(RE)
worthless	
—beast	HYLDING
—fellow	JAVEL
—scamp	LORRELL, LOZEL
worthy	CONDIGN
wot not	NOTE
would not	NOULDE
wound	ENTRENCH, INTRENCH
wrap	EMBOSS
wreaked	(Y)WROKE, YWRAKE
wreathe	WRETHE
wretch	MISER
wrinkled	WRIZLED
wrong	TORT
—doing	MISFARING
wrongful challenge	MISCHALLENGE
yearn	EARN, ERNE
yet	HOWBE
yew	EUGH
yewen	EUGHEN, EWGHEN
young	YOUTHLY
—female sheep	SHIDDER
—gentleman	YOUNKER
—knight	YOUNKER
—male sheep	HIDDER
youth	SPRING, YOUNGTH
youthful	YOUNGTHLY, YOUTHLY
spice	
allspice	PIMENTO
amaracus	MARJORAM
aniseed-flavoured	DILL
Artemisia	TARRAGON
black berries	JUNIPER, PEPPER
cardamon	AMOMUM
Carum	CARAWAY
cayenne pepper	PIM(I)ENTO
chilli	
—dried	ANCHO, CHERRY-TYPE
	CHIPOTLE, RAT-DROPPINGS
	SANNAM
—green	ANAHEIM, LION
	JALAPENO, SHISHI-TO

—large	ANAHEIM, CAYENNE	zingiber	GINGER
	PEPPERONCINI	**spirit**	MONAD
—red	WESTLANDSE LANGE	including: apparition	
coarse cinnamon	CASSIA	demon	
condiment	MUSTARD, PEPPER, SALT	ghost	
	VINEGAR	spectre	
curcuma	TURMERIC	African	ZOMBI(E)
curry		appearance of ghost	APPARITION
—mixture	GARAM MASALA		MATERIALIZATION
—spices	CORIANDER, CUMIN		VISITATION
	TURMERIC	apparition	EIDOLON, FETCH, PHANTASM
decorative	POPPY SEED		WRAITH
from		Arab	AFREET, AFRIT
—Africa	FRESNO CHILLI, MALAGUETTA		(*see also* Moslem *below*)
—capsicum	CAYENNE PEPPER	between man and god	D(A)EMON
	CHILE, CHIL(L)I	bog(e)y	BOGLE, GOBLIN
	PAPRIKA, PIM(I)ENTO	brownie	HOB
—China	CHERRY-TYPE CHILLI	Buddhist	
—climbing orchid	VANILLA	—fertility	YAKSHA, YAKSHI
—crocus	SAFFRON	—tree	YAKSHA, YAKSHI
—East Indies	CASSUMUNAR, NUTMEG	Caribbean	DUPPY
—Europe	CORIANDER	causing mechanical trouble	GREMLIN
—Holland	WESTLANDSE LANGE	devil	DEMON, INCUBUS
—Hungary	PAPRIKA		SCRAT(CH)
—India	SANNAM CHILLI	—Scottish	(*see* **Scottish**)
—Indonesia	GALANGAL(L), GALENGALE	disembodied soul	SHADE, SPIRIT
	GALINAGLE	dog-like goblin	BARGAIST, BARG(H)EST
—Japan	LION CHILLI	domestic goblin	BROWNIE
	SHISHI-TO CHILLI	double	ALTER EGO, DOPPELGANGER
—Mediterranean	CAPER, CUM(M)IN		FETCH
—Mexico	VANILLA	Eastern demon	GH(O)UL
—Moluccas	CLOVE, CORIANDER	emanation	ECTOPLASM
—Sri Lanka	CINNAMON	evil spirit	DEMON, INCUBUS
—Thailand	BIRD('S EYE) CHILLI	fairy	HOB
—West Indies	ALLSPICE	—Irish	LEPRECHAUN
	JAMAICAN PEPPER, PIMENTO	—malignant	ELF
	SCOTCH BONNET CHILLI	female attacking	
ginger	AMOMUM, CARDAMON	sleeping men	SUCCUBA, SUCCUBUS
	CASSUMUNAR, TURMERIC	frightful apparition	(HOB)
	ZINGIBER	German	
Grains of Paradise	AMOMUM	—domestic brownie	KOBOLD
	MALAGUETTA	—king of the elves	ERL-KING
Hebrew	STACTE, STORAX	—mountain	BERGGEIST
Jamaican pepper	PIM(I)ENTO	imp	RUBESZAHL
liquorice	ANISEED	—spirit of the mines	KOBOLD
malaguetta	GRAINS OF PARADISE	—water-spirit	NIX
marjoram	AMARACUS	—wraith	DOPPEL-GANGER
mild	CORIANDER	ghost	APPARITION, BOGEY, BOGLE
mixture	GARAM MASALA, TAMARA		GYTRASH, LARVA, PHANTASM
nutmeg	MACE		PHANTOM, REVENANT, SHADE
pimento	ALLSPICE		SPECTRE, SPIRIT, SPOOK
piper nigrum	PEPPER		WRAITH
red pepper	CAYENNE, PAPRIKA	gnome	GOBLIN, SPRITE
Sinapis	MUSTARD	goblin	BOG(E)Y, BOGLE, GNOME
Spanish paprika	PIMIENTO		PUCK, SPRITE
turmeric	CURCUMA	—in mine	KNOCKER

good spirit	D(A)EMON	sprite	GOBLIN, GNOME
Greek	DAIMON	supernatural visitor	VISITANT
guardian	ANGEL	voodoo spirit	ZOMBI(E)
Hebrew evil spirit	DYBBUK	water	
Hindu	PURUSHA	—demon	NICKER
Indian	PURUSHA	—spirit	ARIEL
—evil	RAKSHAS(A)	West Indies	DUPPY, JUM,BIE
—good	DEVA		JUMBY, ZOMBI(E)
—spirit of place	BONGA	wicked	IMP
Irish	BANSHEE, LEPRECHAUN	wraith of living person	FETCH
malignant fairy	ELF	**sport**	*(see* **games***)*
mischievous		**square**	
—fairy	ELF, HOBGOBLIN	Berlin	ALEXANDERPLATZ
—spirit	POLTERGEIST		MARX-ENGELS PLATZ
—sprite	PUCK		POTSDAMERPLATZ
Moslem spirit	(D)JINNI, GENIE	Brussels	GRANDE PLACE
	JINNEE	Bucharest	PALACE SQUARE
—(plural)	GINN, (D)JINN		UNIVERSITY SQUARE
—jinni		Cairo	ARABA SQUARE
less powerful	JANN		REPUBLIC SQUARE
powerful	MARID		TAHRIR SQUARE
nocturnal (Shak.)	PONK	France	PLACE
Norse goblin	NIS, TROLL	Germany	PLATZ
nymph	*(see separate entry)*	Italy	PIAZZA
one returned from the dead	REVENANT	London	BERKELEY SQUARE
Persian	AHRIMAN, DEEV, DIV		GROSVENOR SQUARE
phantom	EIDOLON		OXFORD CIRCUS
presiding spirit	GENIUS		PICCADILLY CIRCUS
Red Indian	MANITO(U)		RUSSELL SQUARE
Roman			TRAFALGAR SQUARE
—ghost(s) of the dead	LEMUR(ES)	Madrid	PLAZA DE CASTELAR
—spirit investing			PLAZA DE CASTILLA
everything	GENIUS		PLAZA DE ROMA
—spirits of the dead	MANES		PLAZA DE TOROS
Scandinavian goblin	NIS, TROLL		PLAZA MAYOR
Scottish		Milan	PIAZZA DEL DUOMO
—apparition	TAIS(C)H	Moscow	DZERZHINSKY SQUARE
—goblin	BODACH, BODRACK,		RED SQUARE
	BROWNIE, RED-CAP, RED-COWL		PUSHKIN SQUARE
—water		New York	TIMES SQUARE
goblin	SHELLYCOAT		WASHINGTON SQUARE
spirit	TANGIE	Paris	PLACE DE LA BASTILLE
sprite	KELPIE, KELPY, RIVERHORSE		PLACE DE LA CONCORDE
Shakespeare			PLACE DE LA NATION
—nocturnal	PONK		PLACE DE LA REPUBLIQUE
—spirits	ARIEL, CERES		PLACE DE L'ETOILE
	IRIS, JUNO		PLACE D'ITALIE
soul	PNEUMA, PSYCHE	Peking	TIANANMEN SQUARE
spectre	*(see* ghost *above)*	Prague	WENCESLAS SQUARE
spirit	PNEUMA, PSYCHE	Rome	PIAZZA COLONNA
—attending at call	FAMILIAR		PIAZZA DEL POPOLO
—dwelling in all things	ARCH(A)EUS		PIAZZA DI PORTA CAPENA
—matter	ECTOPLASM		PIAZZA SANTA PIETRA
—of the			PIAZZA VENEZIA
air	ARIEL, SYLPH	Siena	PIAZZA DEL CAMPO
woods	FAUN, SATYR	Spain	PLAZA

Venice	PIAZZA SAN MARCO	red	
	ST MARK'S SQUARE	—dwarf	BARNARD'S STAR, ERIDANI
Vienna	HELDEN PLATZ		PROXIMA CENTAURI, ROSS
	KARLS PLATZ	—giant	ANTARES, BETELGEUSE
	MESSE PLATZ		BETELGEUX, BETELGEUZ, CRUCIS
	MORZIN PLATZ		MIRA, RAS ALGETHI, SCHEAT
	OTTO WAGNER PLATZ	seven stars	PLEIAD(E)S
	SCHWARZENBERG PLATZ	—Plough	SEPTENTRION(E)S
Sri Lanka	CL	shooting star	METEOR(ITE)
	(*see* **Ceylon**)	star in	
standard	STD	—Andromeda	ALMACH, ALPHERATZ
Standard Book Number	SBN		MIRACH
standard deviation	SD	—Aquila	ALTAIR
Standard Serial Number	SSN	—Aries	HAMAL
standard temperature and		—Argo	CANOPUS
pressure	STP	—Auriga	CAPELLA
Standard Wire Gauge	SWG	—Boötes	ARCTURUS, IZAR
stars		—Cancer	ALTARF
always visible	CIRCUMPOLAR STAR	—Canis Major	ADHARA, SIRIUS
brightest star	SIRIUS	—Capricornus	ALGEDI
brightness	MAGNITUDE	—Carina	AVIOR, MIAPLACIOUS
classification	HARVARD CLASSIFICATION	—Cassiopeia	RUCHBAH
	SPECTRAL CLASS	—Centaur	ALPHA CENTAURI, RIGIL
	SPECTRAL TYPE		HADAR-KENT, MENKENT
constellations	(*see separate entry*)	—Cetus	DIPHDA, MENKAR, MIRIA
Day Star	VENUS	—Columba	PHAET
developing from interstellar			HADAR-KENT, MENKENT
matter	PROTOSTAR	—Cetus	DIPHDA, MENKAR
Dog Star	CANICULA, SIRIUS	—Corvus	ALGORAB, ALKES, GIENAH
Evening Star	HESPER(US)	—Crux	ACRUX, BECRUX, GACRUX
	VENUS, VESPER	—Cygnus	DENEB
exploding star	NOVA	—Delphinus	ROTANEV
	PLANETARY NEBULA	—Draco	ELTANIN, THUBAN
	SUPERNOVA	—Eridanus	ACAMAR, ACHERNA(R)
five stars	HYADES	—Gemini	CASTOR, POLLUX
flaring star	NOVA	—Grus	AL NAIR
group of stars	ASTERISM, GALAXY	—Hydra	ALPHARD
	CONSTELLATION	—Leo	DENEBOLA, REGULUS
halo	CORONA	—Lesser Dog	PROCYON
high red luminosity	RED GIANT	—Libra	ZUBENELGENUBI
large red star	RED GIANT	—Lyrae	VEGA
largest star	ALPHA HERCULIS	—Mensa	NUBECULA MAJOR
lode star	NORTH STAR, POLARIS	—Ophiuchus	RASALHAGUE
low			SABIK, YED
—luminosity	WHITE DWARF	—Orion	ALNILAM, BELATRIX
—red luminosity	RED DWARF		BETELGEUSE
Morning Star	DAYSTAR, LUCIFER		BETELGEUZE, RIGEL
	PHOSPHORUS, VENUS	—Pavo	PEACOCK
most massive	PLASKETT'S STAR	—Pegasus	ENIF, MARKAB, SHEAT
nearest star	PROXIMA CENTAURI	—Perseus	MIRFAK
North Star	TYRIAN CYNOSURE	—Phoenix	ANKAA
pair of stars	BINARY STAR	—Piscis Austrinus	FORMALHAUT
Pole Star	LOADSTAR, LODESTAR	—Plough	MIZAR, SEPTRION(E)S
	NORTH STAR, POLARIS		TRIONES
pulsating star	PULSAR	—Pleiades	MAIA
quasi-stellar object	QUASAR	—Puppis	NAOS

—Sagittarius	KAUS AUSTRALIS, NUNKI
—Scorpio	ANTARES, SHAULA
—Southern Fish	FOMALHAUT
—Taurus	ELNATH, HYADES
	PLEIADES
—Toucan	NUBECULA MINOR
—Triangulum Australe	ATRIA
—Ursa Major	ALIOTH, ALKAID
	DUBHE, MERAK
	MIZAR, PHECDA
—Ursa Minor	KOCHAB
—Vela	SUHAIL
—Virgo	SPICA
Star of David	MAGEN DAVID
	MOGEN DAVID
symbol	ASTERISK
system	CONSTELLATION, GALAXY
types	BINARY, BROWN DWARF
	(CEPHEID) VARIABLE
	FLARE, NEUTRON, NOVA, PULSAR
	QUASAR, RED DWARF
	RED (SUPER-)GIANT
	SUB-GIANT, SUPERNOVA
	WHITE DWARF, X-RAY
variable star	MIRA, VIRGINIS STAR
white dwarf	PROCYON, THE PUP
	VAN MAANEN'S STAR

state[1]

State Certificated Midwife	SCM
State Enrolled Nurse	SEN
State Registered Nurse	SRN

state[2] (USA)

official names and abbreviations:

Alabama	AL, ALA
Alaska	ALAS
Arizona	ARIZ
Arkansas	ARK
California	CAL
Colorado	COL(O)
Columbia (District)	DC
Connecticut	CT
Delaware	DEL
(District of Columbia)	DC
Florida	FLA
Georgia	GA
Hawaii	HAWAII
Idaho	ID, IDA
Illinois	ILL
Indiana	IND
Iowa	IA
Kansas	KAN, KS
Kentucky	KEN, KY
Louisiana	LA
Maine	ME
Maryland	MD
Massachusetts	MASS

Michigan	MICH
Minnesota	MINN
Mississippi	MI, MISS
Missouri	MO
Montana	MONT
Nebraska	NEB(R)
Nevada	NEV
New Hampshire	NH
New Jersey	NJ
New Mexico	NM(EX)
New York	NY
North Carolina	NC
North Dakota	ND(AK)
Ohio	O
Oklahoma	OKLA
Oregon	OR(E), OREG
Pennsylvania	PA, PENN
Rhode Island	RI
South Carolina	SC
South Dakota	SD, S DAK
Tennessee	TEN(N)
Texas	TEX
Utah	U(T)
Vermont	VT
Virginia	VA
Washington	WASH
West Virginia	WVA
Wisconsin	WIS
Wyoming	WY(O)

unofficial names:

Aloha State	HAWAII
Apache State	ARIZONA
Badger State	WISCONSIN
Baked Bean State	MASSACHUSETTS
Bay State	MASSACHUSETTS
Bayou State	LOUISIANA
Battle born State	NEVADA
Beef State	NEBRASKA
Bear State	ARKANSAS
Beaver State	OREGON
Beehive State	UTAH
Blue Grass State	KENTUCKY
Buckeye State	OHIO
Cavalier State	VIRGINIA
Centennial State	COLORADO
Chinook State	WASHINGTON
Constitution State	CONNECTICUT
Cornhusker State	NEBRASKA
Cotton State	ALABAMA
Coyote State	SOUTH DAKOTA
Creole State	LOUISIANA
Diamond State	DELAWARE
Elephant State	WASHINGTON
Empire State	NEW YORK
—of the south	GEORGIA
Equality State	WYOMING

Evergreen State	WASHINGTON	American	BURGOO, SUCCOTASH
First State	DELAWARE	beans and meat	CASSOULET
Flickertail State	NORTH DAKOTA	beef with	
Free State	MARYLAND	—beer	CARBON(N)ADE
Garden State	NEW JERSEY	—red beans	CHILLI CON CARNE
Gem State	IDAHO	—vegetables	POT-AU-FEU
Golden State	CALIFORNIA	bread (Portugal)	ACORDA
Gopher State	MINNESOTA	East Indian	MULLIGATAWNY
Grand Canyon State	ARIZONA	Egyptian	FOUL MEDAMES
Granite State	NEW HAMPSHIRE	fish and vegetables	CHOWDER
Green Mountain State	VERMONT		MATELOT(T)E
Hawkeye State	INDIANA		MULLIGAN
Heart of Dixie	ALABAMA	—French	BOUILLABAISSE
Hoosier State	INDIANA	—Swedish	GRAVADLAX
Jayhawk State	KANSAS	French	BOUILLABAISSE, DAUBE
Keystone State	PENNSYLVANIA		NAVARIN, POT-AU-FEU
Land of			RATATOUILLE
—Enchantment	NEW MEXICO	game	SALMI(S)
—Opportunity	ARKANSAS	Greek	STIFADO
—the Midnight Sun	ALASKA	Hebrew	
Last Frontier	ALASKA	—brisket and vegetables	CHOLENT
Little Rhody	RHODE ISLAND	—vegetables and	
Lone Star State	TEXAS	dried fruit	TZIMMES
Magnolia State	MISSISSIPPI	highly seasoned	RAGOUT
Mountain State	WEST VIRGINIA	Hungarian	GOULASH, PORKOLT
North Star State	MINNESOTA	Italian	BRODETTO, BURIDDA
Nutmeg State	CONNECTICUT		CACCIUCCO
Old		lamb and vegetables	LANCASHIRE HOTPOT
—Colony State	MASSACHUSETTS	—French	NAVARIN (PRINTANIER)
—Dominion	VIRGINIA	meat	
—Line State	MARYLAND	—highly seasoned	GOULASH
—North State	NORTH CAROLINA	—in	
Palmetto State	SOUTH CAROLINA	red wine (French)	DAUBE
Panhandle State	WEST VIRGINIA	stock	FRICASSEE
Peach State	GEORGIA	—with	
Pelican State	LOUISIANA	beer	CARBONADE
Peninsula State	FLORIDA	biscuit	LOBSCOUSE
Pine Tree State	MAINE	potatoes, etc	HOTPOT, IRISH STEW
Prairie State	ILLINOIS	vegetables	HASH, MULLIGAN
Sagebrush State	NEVADA		RAGOUT
Show Me State	MISSOURI	—French	POT-AU-FEU
Silver State	NEVADA	—Indian	DHANSAK
Sioux State	NORTH DAKOTA	—Spanish	OLIO, OLLA PODRIDA
Sooner State	OKLAHOMA	Mexican	CHILLI CON CARNE
Sugar State	LOUISIANA	mutton and vegetables	IRISH STEW
Sunflower State	KANSAS	rabbit	HASENPFEFFER
Sunshine State	FLORIDA, NEW MEXICO	ragout in cream sauce	BLANQUETTE
	SOUTH DAKOTA	Romanian	TOCANA
Tar Heel State	NORTH CAROLINA	Russian	RAGU
Treasure State	MONTANA	sailor's	(LOB)SCOUSE
Tree Planter's State	NEBRASKA	Scandinavian	LABSKAUS
Volunteer State	TENNESSEE	seafood	(CLAM) CHOWDER
Wolverine State	MICHIGAN	shellfish	CLAM CHOWDER
Wonder State	ARKANSAS	ship's	
Yellowhammer State	ALABAMA	—gruel	LOBLOLLY
stew	HOTPOT, RAGOUT	—stew	LOB'S COURSE, LOBSCOUSE

Spanish
—beans and sausage   FABADA ASTURIANA
—chicken, rice, etc   PAELLA
—lentils   COCHIDA DE LENTEJA
—meat and vegetables   OLLA-PODRIDA
Swedish fish stew   GRAVADLAX
tomatoes, aubergines etc   RATATOUILLE
thick   BURGOO
tinned meat and vegetables   MACONOCHIE
two meats and vegetables   BRUNSWICK
vegetables and biscuits   LOB'S COURSE
         (LOB)SCOUSE
West Indian   PEPPERPOT
white meat in sauce   BLANQUETTE

stone
amulet (Australia)   CHURINGA
artificial   RECONSTRUCTED STONE
         TABBY
at Delphi   OMPHALOS
balanced on another   LOG(G)AN(-STONE)
         LOGGING-STONE
band of stone   CORDON, STRING-COURSE
bare rock projecting
   above ground   GREY-WEATHER
         SARACEN'S-STONE
     SARS(D)EN, SARSEN-STONE
becoming stone   LAPIDESCENT
building stone   BATH, FLINT, GRANITE
     IRONSTONE, LIMESTONE
     MARBLE, PORTLAND
     RAG, SANDSTONE, YORK
—American   BROWNSTONE
centre stone of arch   KEYSTONE
change to stone   PETRIFICATION
circle of standing
   stones   CROMLECH, CYCLOLITH
     HENGE, PERISTALITH
coffin made of stone   SARCOPHAGUS
column   OBELISK
corner stone   QUOIN
crushing (in body)   LITHOLAPAXY
cutter   LAPIDARY
cutting   LITHOTOMY
         STEREOTOMY
dressed stone   MASONRY
—lining opening   RYBAT
drystone waller   COWAN
engraving on stone   LITHOGLYPH
fastener for stonework   AGRAFFE, GUDGEON
four-sided pillar   OBELISK
fragment of stone   SPALL
gall-stone   CHOLELITH
having
   —magical properties   ELIXIR
     PHILOSOPHER'S STONE
   —magnetic properties   LODESTONE

imitation stone
—limestone chips and cement   SCAGLIOLA
—stone dust
   cement   RECONSTRUCTED STONE
in
—animal cell   LITHITE
—body   CALCULUS
—ear   OTOLITH
—gall-bladder   GALL-STONE
—kidney   KIDNEY-STONE
—intestines   ENTEROLITH
—nose   RHINOLITH
—protozoa   RHABDOLITH
—stomach (goats, etc)   BEZOAR
—urinary tract   UROLITH
inscribed with Egyptian
   hieroglyphics   ROSETTA STONE
irregular stone   RUBBLE
Italian limestone   SCAGLIA
jetty   MOLE
large stone   MEGALITH
like marble   MARMOREAL
lintel   SUMMER(BEAM)
living in
—rocks   LITHODROMOUS
—stones   LAPIDICOLOUS
Lydian stone   TOUCHSTONE
marble
—Dorset   PURBECK MARBLE
         PURBECK STONE
—Italy   CARRARA
megalith
—England   AVEBURY, STONEHENGE
—France   CARNAC
memorial
—heap   CAIRN
—stone   EBENEZER
meteoric stone   AEROLITE, AEROLITH
         ASTROLITH
mound of stones   CAIRN
of the sun (Greek)   PANTARBE
old stone implement   EOLITH
on top of wall   CAPSTONE, COPESTONE
         COPING STONE
paving slab   FLAG(STONE)
painting on stone   LITHOCHROMATICS
polished by the wind   VENTIFACT
prehistoric monument   CROMLECH, DOLMEN
     MEGALITH, MENHIR
—Balearic Islands   NAVETA
     TALAYOT, TAULA
ring of stone pillars   CROMLECH, HENGE
rocking stone   LOG(G)AN(-STONE)
     LOGGING-STONE
rounded stone   BOULDER, COBBLE
         PEBBLE

rubble in masonry	MOELLON
sacred stone (Mecca)	BLACK STONE
	KAABA
slab	LEDGER
small fragments	AGGREGATE, GRAVEL
spout	GARGOYLE
standing stone	MEGALITH, MENHIR
	MONOLITH
Stone Age	
—Old	PALAEOLITHIC
—Middle	MESOLITHIC
—New	NEOLITHIC
stone-eating	LITHOPHAGOUS
stony	LAPIDEOUS
—organism	LITHOPHYTE
—sponge	LITHISTID
through a wall	PARPANE, PARPEN(D)
	PARPENT, PARPOINT
	PERPEND, PERPENT
throw stones at	LAPIDATE
tomb in form of chest	CIST
tool	NEOLITH
—small	MICROLITH
touchstone	LYDIAN STONE
transparent	PHENGITE
turn to stone	LAPIDIFY, PETRIFY
undressed stone	RUBBLE
upright stone	ORTHOSTAT
—slab	STELA, STELE
—with crossbeam	DOLMEN, TRILITH(ON)
wedge-shaped (in arch)	VOUSSOIR
worker in stone	MASON, SCULPTOR
	(*see also* **building construction**)
	(*see also* **minerals, rock**)

street

Berlin	KURFURSTENDAMM
	UNTER DEN LINDEN
	WILHELMSTRASSE
Dublin	O'CONNELL STREET
Edinburgh	PRINCES STREET
France	RUE
Germany	STRASSE
Italy	STRADA, VIA(LE)
London	BOND STREET
	DOWNING STREET
	FLEET STREET
	OLD KENT ROAD
	OXFORD STREET
	PARK LANE
	REGENT STREET
	THE MALL
	THE STRAND
Los Angeles	SUNSET BOULEVARD
Madrid	CALLE MAYOR
	PASEO DE LA CASTELLANA
Moscow	GORKY STREET

New York	BROADWAY
	FIFTH AVENUE
	PARK AVENUE
	WALL STREET
Naples	VIA CHIARA
New Orleans	SOUTH RAMPART STREET
Oxford	BROAD STREET
	CARFAX
	HIGH STREET
Paris	AVENUE VICTOR HUGO
	CHAMPS ELYSEES
	RUE DE RIVOLI
	RUE LAFAYETTE
Rome	CORSO VITTORIO EMMANUELE
	VIA DEI FORI IMPERIALI
	VIA DEL CORSO
	VIA DEL QUIRINALE
	VIA NATIONALE
	VIALE TRASTEVERE
Spain	CALLE
Washington	ARLINGTON BOULEVARD
	PENNSYLVANIA AVENUE
	THE MALL

student   L

Student Christian Movement	SCM
Student of Civil Law	SCL
Student Representative Council	SRC
student's union	NUS

study

including: knowledge of
    science of
    study of

abnormal	
—growths	TERATOLOGY
—working of the mind	PSYCHOLOGY
	PSYCHOPATHOLOGY
action of	
—forces	MECHANICS
—ice	GLACIOLOGY
adages	PAROEMIOLOGY
adaptation of machinery	
to suit humans	ERGONOMICS
	BIOTECHNOLOGY
aerial navigation	AERONAUTICS
aerolites	AEROLITHOLOGY
ageing	GERONTOLOGY
agricultural pests	PESTOLOGY
agriculture	GEOPONICS
airborne organisms	AEROBIOLOGY
alchemy	HERMETICS
algae	ALGOLOGY, PHYCOLOGY
amphibia	HERPETOLOGY
anatomy of fleshy parts	SARCOLOGY
ancestry	GENEALOGY
ancient	
—blood groups	PALAEOSEROLOGY

—customs	FOLK-LORE	birds'	
—environment	PALAEOECOLOGY	—eggs	OOLOGY
—geography	PALAEOGEOGRAPHY	—nests	CALIOLOGY
—human remains	PALAEOPATHOLOGY	blood	HAEMATOLOGY
—Italians	ETRUSCOLOGY	bodies affected by forces	DYNAMICS
—magnetism in rocks	PALAEOMAGNETISM	body	
—man	PALAEOETHNOLOGY	—and mind	
—papyri	PAPYROLOGY	relationship	PSYCHOBIOGRAPHY
—soils	PALAEOPEDOLOGY		PSYCHOBIOLOGY
—things	HIEROLOGY	—movement	
—weather	PALAEOCLIMATOLOGY	conveying information	KINESICS
—writing	PALAEOGRAPHY	mechanics of	KINESIOLOGY
animal		—reflexes	REFLEXOLOGY
—behaviour	ETHOLOGY	bones	OSTEOLOGY
—diseases	ZOOPATHOLOGY	books	BIBLIOLOGY
—life	ZOOLOGY		BIBLIOGRAPHY
—pathology	ZOOPATHY	botany	PHYTOLOGY
—tissues	HISTOLOGY	brain	
animals	THEROLOGY	—disorders as affecting	
	ZOOGRAPHY	human behaviour, etc	NEUROPSYCHIATRY
—resembling plants	ZOOPHYTOLOGY		NEUROPSYCHOLOGY
antibiotics	SEROLOGY	—functions	NEUROPHYSIOLOGY
ants	MYRMECOLOGY	brambles	BATOLOGY
apples and pears	POMOLOGY	breeding	
applied		—animals	ZOOTECHNY
—nuclear physics	NUCLEONICS	—domestic animals	THREMMATOLOGY
—thermodynamics	HYDRAULICS	brewing	ZYMURGY
—sciences	TECHNOLOGY	building	ARCHITECTURE
aquatic animals	CETOLOGY		ARCHITECTONICS
aqueous vapour	ATMOLOGY	—as an art	TECTONICS
arrangement of atoms	STEREOCHEMISTRY	bumps on head	PHRENOLOGY
artillery	PYROBALLOGY	butterflies	LEPIDOPTEROLOGY
assaying	DOCIMOLOGY	calculation	LOGISTICS
assisting memory	MNEMONICS	cancers	ONCOLOGY
	MNEMOTECHNICS	casting nativities	GENETHLIALOGY
astronomical measurement	URANOMETRY	causation	AETIOLOGY
astronomy	URANOLOGY	causes at work	
atmosphere	AEROLOGY	in development	EPIGENETICS
atomic nuclei	ATOMIC PHYSICS	caves	SPELEOLOGY
bacteria	BACTERIOLOGY	cells	CYTOLOGY
ballet	CHOREOLOGY	—nuclei	KARYOLOGY
bathing	BALNEOLOGY	—shed from internal	
beasts	THEROLOGY	body surfaces	EXFOLIATIVE CYTOLOGY
behaviour of		centres of spatial	
—genes	MENDELISM	distribution	CENTROGRAPHY
—radioactive substances		changes associated	
in living tissues	RADIOBIOLOGY	with chemical	
being	METAPHYSICS	reactions	PHYSICAL CHEMISTRY
bells	CAMPANOLOGY	chaos	CHAOLOGY
biological		character	ETHOLOGY
—effects caused by light	PHOTOBIOLOGY	—from face	METOPOSCOPY
—forms	MORPHOLOGY	charged particles	THERMIONICS
—rhythms	CHRONOBIOLOGY	charters, diplomas, etc	DIPLOMATOLOGY
biology by cine film	CINEBIOLOGY	chemical	
bionomics	ETHOLOGY	—composition of Earth's	
birds	ORNITHOLOGY	crust	GEOCHEMISTRY

—methods applied to radioactive materials	RADIOCHEMISTRY
—reactions caused by light	PHOTOCHEMISTRY
chemistry	
—applied to agricultural products	CHEMURGY
medical theory	IATROCHEMISTRY
—dealing with very small quantities	MICROCHEMISTRY
—of	
carbon compounds	ORGANIC CHEMISTRY
living things	BIOCHEMISTRY
radioactivity	RADIOCHEMISTRY
substances under high pressure	PIEZO-CHEMISTRY
the	
—body	ZOOCHEMISTRY
—Earth	GEOCHEMISTRY
tissues	HISTOCHEMISTRY
children	P(A)EDOLOGY
children's	
—development and growth	P(A)EDOLOGY
—diseases	PAEDIATRICS
—teeth	PAEDODONTICS
China	SINOLOGY
Christ	CHRISTOLOGY
chromosomes and genetics	CYTOGENETICS
church forms and practices	ECCLESIOLOGY
ciphers	CRYPTOLOGY
citizenship	CIVICS
classification	TYPOLOGY
—laws	BIOSYSTEMATICS
—of	
animals	ZOOTAXY
diseases	NOSOLOGY
organisms	CLADISTICS
plants and animals	TAXONOMY
climate	AEROGRAPHY
	CLIMATOLOGY
	METEOROLOGY
—in relation to life	BIOCLIMATOLOGY
—of restricted areas	MICROCLIMATOLOGY
clocks	HOROGRAPHY, HOROLOGY
clouds	NEPHOLOGY
cockroaches etc	ORTHEROPTOLOGY
codes	CRYPTOLOGY
coins	NUMISMATICS
	NUMISMATOLOGY
collective biographies	PROSOPOGRAPHY
colour	CHROMATICS
—change	PHOTOCHROMICS
communications in man and machine	CYBERNETICS

communities	DEMOLOGY
—of plants and animals	SYN(O)ECOLOGY
comparative	
—measurements of parts of animals	ZOOMETRY
—philology	GLOSSOLOGY
	GLOTTOLOGY
composition of substances	STOICHIOMETRY
conditions in towns	URBANOLOGY
congenital abnormalities	TERATOLOGY
conservation of energy	THERMODYNAMICS
constitution of universe	COSMOGRAPHY
control mechanisms	CYBERNETICS
cooking	GASTROLOGY
correct pronunciation	ORTHOEPY
cosmetics	COSMETOLOGY
crime	CRIMINOLOGY
crustaceans	CARCINOLOGY
crystals	CRYSTALLOGRAPHY
—using X-rays	X-RAY CRYSTALLOGRAPHY
cultivation using mineral solutions	HYDROPONICS
cyphers	CRYPTOLOGY
data obtained by touch	HAPTICS
dates	CHRONOLOGY
—from growth-rings	DENDROCHRONOLOGY
death	ESCHATOLOGY
	THANATOLOGY
deformation and flow of matter	RHEOLOGY
demons	DEMONOLOGY
dentistry concerned with gum diseases	PERIODONTICS
	PERIODONTOLOGY
deposits	SEDIMENTOLOGY
derivation of words	ETYMOLOGY
descent of families	GENEALOGY
descriptive	
—astronomy	URANOGRAPHY
—botany	PHYTOGRAPHY
determination of chemical equivalents	STOICHIOMETRY
development of Earth's crust	GEOLOGY
devil-lore	DIABOLOLOGY
diagnosis	DIAGNOSTICS
dialects	DIALECTOLOGY
dictionaries	LEXICOLOGY
dietetics	SIT(I)OLOGY
dining	ARISTOLOGY
diseases	NOSOLOGY
	PATHOLOGY
—as influenced by environment	GEOMEDICINE
—classification of	NOSOLOGY

—of	
man	ANDROLOGY
mind	PSYCHIATRY
plants	PHYTOPATHOLOGY
rectum	PROTOLOGY
women	GYNAECOLOGY
—widespread	EPEDEMIOLOGY
disorder	CHAOLOGY
distilling	ZYMORGY
distribution of	
—animals	ZOOGEOGRAPHY
and plants	BIOGEOGRAPHY
—chemicals in tissues	HISTOCHEMISTRY
—currents	ELECTROKINETICS
—human groups	GEOANTHROPOLOGY
—ice	GLACIOLOGY
—living things	BIOGEOGRAPHY
—mankind	ANTHROPO(GEO)GRAPHY
—plants	PHYTOGEOGRAPHY
—population	DEMOGRAPHY
—races	ETHNOLOGY
dogma	DOGMATOLOGY
domestication of animals	ZOOTECHNY
dosage	POSOLOGY
dreams	ONEIROLOGY
drugs	PHARMACOLOGY
ductless glands	ENDOCRINOLOGY
dust in air	KONIOLOGY
duty	DEONTOLOGY
dynamic forces within	
the Earth	GEODYNAMICS
dynamics of gases	AERODYNAMICS
ear	OTOLOGY
—nose and	
throat	OTORHINOLARYNGOLOGY
early history	PREHISTORY
	PROTOHISTORY
Earth	CHOROLOGY, GEOSCIENCE
—measurement	GEODESY
—quakes	SEISMOGRAPHY
	SEISMOLOGY
—sciences	NATURAL HISTORY
Earth's	
—atmosphere	AERONOMY
—surface	CHOROGRAPHY, GEOGRAPHY
	PHYSICAL GEOGRAPHY
	PHYSIOGRAPHY, TOPOGRAPHY
echoes	PHONOCAMPTICS
ecology of	
—groups	SYN(O)ECOLOGY
—individual organisms	AUTOECOLOGY
econometrics in history	CLIOMETRICS
economic data	ECONOMETRICS
effects of	
—disease on body	
tissues	HISTOPATHOLOGY

—dissolved substances	
on freezing points	CYROSCOPY
—drugs on	
behaviour	PSYCHOPHARMACOLOGY
—radiation on	
living tissue	RADIOBIOLOGY
—space travel on	
organisms	BIO-ASTRONAUTICS
eggs	OOLOGY
Egypt	EGYPTOLOGY
election results	PSEPHOANALYSIS
	PSEPHOLOGY
electric	
—charges in motion	ELECTRODYNAMICS
	ELECTROKINETICS
—technology	ELECTROTECHNICS
electrical	
—circuits	ELECTRONICS
—measurements	ELECTROMETRY
—phenomena in living	
organisms	ELECTROBIOLOGY
	ELECTROPHYSIOLOGY
electricity	ELECTROLOGY
—and	
chemical change	ELECTROCHEMISTRY
electromagnetic	
radiation	PHOTO-ELECTRONICS
heat	ELECTROTHERMICS
	ELECTROTHERMY
magnetism	ELECTROMAGNETISM
—at rest	ELECTROSTATICS
—generated by	
plasma flow in	
magneticfield	
	MAGNETOTHERMODYNAMICS
—in	
ore separation	
	ELECTROMETALLURGY
motion	ELECTRODYNAMICS
	ELECTROKINETICS
electronic	
communication	INFORMATION TECHNOLOGY
	IT
electronics in aviation	AVIONICS
electrons emitted from	
heated substance	THERMIONICS
elements	
—and their	
compounds	INORGANIC CHEMISTRY
—of animal tissue	STOECHIOLOGY
	STOICH(E)IOLOGY
embryos	EMBRYOLOGY
emotional forces	PSYCHODYNAMICS
endemic diseases	ENDEMIOLOGY
energy	
—laws	ENERGETICS

—using spectroscope	SPECTROSCOPY	forecasting	FUTUROLOGY
engraved gems	DACTYLIOGRAPHY	force producing motion	KINETICS
	DACTILIOLOGY	form	MORPHOLOGY
environment	(O)ECOLOGY	—of land	GEOMORPHOLOGY
environmental pollution	ECOTOXICOLOGY	formation of Earth	GEOGENY, GEOGONY
enzymes	ENZYMOLOGY	fossil(s)	ORYCTOLOGY
epidemic animal diseases	EPIZOOTICS		PALAEONTOLOGY
epidemics	EPEDEMIOLOGY	—animals	PALAEOZOOLOGY
esoteric science	HERMETICS	—fishes	PALAEOICHTHYOLOGY
ethics	DEONTOLOGY	—plants	PALAEOBOTANY
—of medical research	BIOETHICS		PALAEOPHYTOLOGY
evolution	GENETICS	freshwater life	LIMNOLOGY
exercise	PHYSIOTHERAPEUTICS	friction	TRIBOLOGY
excrement	SCATOLOGY	fruit	CARPOLOGY, POMOLOGY
experimental		—growing	POMOLOGY
psychology	PSYCHOPHYSIOLOGY	functioning of living	
extraterrestrial life	BIO-ASTRONOMY	organisms	PHYSIOLOGY
	EXOBIOLOGY	fungi	MYC(ET)OLOGY
eyes	OPHTHALMOLOGY	future developments	FUTUROLOGY
eyesight	OPTOLOGY	gases	AEROMETRY, AEROSTATICS
fathers	PATRISTICS, PATROLOGY		PNEUMATICS, PNEUMATOLOGY
faulty pronunciation			PNEUMODYNAMICS
or vocabulary	CACOLOGY	gem-engraving	GLYPTICS
features of limited area	TOPOGRAPHY	general structure	
feet	PODOLOGY	of Earth	GEOGNOSY
fermentation	(EN)ZYMOLOGY	genetic	
	ZYMURGY	—basis of nervous	
ferns	PTERIDOLOGY	system	NEUROGENETICS
fevers	PYRETOLOGY	—control	EUGENICS
figures	GEOMETRY	genetics in relation	
final		to cells	CYTOGENETICS
—causes	TELEOLOGY	geological	
—things	ESCHATOLOGY	—distribution	CHOROLOGY
finger		—time	GEOCHRONOLOGY
—prints	DACTYLOGRAPHY	geology	
	DACTYLOLOGY	—from air photographs	PHOTOGEOLOGY
—rings	DACTYLIOGRAPHY	—of Moon etc	ASTROGEOLOGY
	DACTYLIOLOGY	geometry of changing shapes	TOPOLOGY
—talking	DACTYLOGRAPHY	germ-free animals	GNOTOBIOTICS
	DACTYLOLOGY	gesture	CH(E)IROLOGY
fireworks	PYROTECHNICS	ghosts	SPETROLOGY
first principles	METAPHYSICS	giants	GIGANTOLOGY
fishes	ICHTHYOLOGY	glaciers	GLACIOLOGY
fishing	HALIEUTICS	glands	ENDOCRINOLOGY
flags	VEXILLOLOGY	god	THEOLOGY
fleshy parts	SARCOLOGY	good eating	GASTROLOGY
floras	FLORISTICS		GASTRONOMY
flow		government	ARCHOLOGY
—and change of shape			POLITICAL SCIENCE
of matter	RHEOLOGY	gramophone records	DISCOGRAPHY
—of fluids	FLUIDICS	grasses	AGROSTOLOGY
flowers	ANTHOECOLOGY	ground plans	ICHNOGRAPHY
	FLORISTICS	growing plants in water	HYDROPONICS
folk-lore	STORIOLOGY	growth	
food and nutrition	BROMATOLOGY	—and development	
footprints	ICHNOLOGY	of children	P(A)EDOLOGY

—of embryos	EMBRYOLOGY	inland water	LIMNOLOGY
—rings in trees	DENDROCHRONOLOGY	insects	ENTOMOLOGY
guns	BALLISTICS		INSECTOLOGY
hair	TRICHOLOGY	instruction	PEDAGOGY
hand	CH(E)IROLOGY	integrated	
—writing	GRAPHOLOGY	circuits	SOLID STATE PHYSICS
hearing	AUDIOLOGY	interconversion of	
heart	CARDIOLOGY	chemical and	
heat	THERMOLOGY	electrical energy	ELECTROCHEMISTRY
	THERMOTICS	interpretation of	
—as mechanical agent	THERMODYNAMICS	—Scripture	HERMENEUTICS
—in chemical		—text	EXEGETICS
reactions	THERMOCHEMISTRY	interrelationship of	
heavenly bodies	ASTROLOGY, ASTRONOMY	environment and	
	COSMOGONY, URANOLOGY	organisms	BIONOMICS, ECOLOGY
heredity	(CYTO)GENETICS, MENDELISM	ions in solution	POLAROGRAPHY
heresies	HERESIOLOGY	iris	IRIDOLOGY
high-frequency		jets of fluids to	
pressure waves	SUPERSONICS	perform tasks	FLUID LOGIC, FLUIDICS
	ULTRASONICS	kidneys	NEPHROLOGY
history	HISTORIOLOGY	knowledge	EPISTEMICS, EPISTEMOLOGY
—from psychological		labels	PHILATELY
viewpoint	PSYCHOHISTORY	lakes	LIMNOLOGY
—of		land management	AGRONOMICS
languages	GLOTTOCHRONOLOGY	language	LINGUISTICS, PHILOLOGY
proper names	ONOMASTICS	—detail	MICROLINGUISTICS
words	LEXICOLOGY	—in relation to	
horse diseases	HIPPIATRICS	culture	ETHNOLINGUISTICS
horses	HIPPOLOGY	gesture	METALINGUISTICS
human		literature	STYLISTICS
—antiquity	ARCHAEOLOGY	locality	DIALECTOLOGY
—biology	ANTHROPOBIOLOGY	meaning	METALINGUISTICS
—body	SOMATOLOGY	other features of	
—muscles	KINESIOLOGY	behaviour	META-LINGUISTICS
—population	DEMOGRAPHY	society	SOCIO
—settlements	EKISTICS	larynx	LARYNGOLOGY
—society	SOCIOLOGY	last or final things	ESCHATOLOGY
humour	HUMOROLOGY	law	JURISPRUDENCE, NOMOLOGY
hydrodynamics	HYDRAULICS	laws of energy	ENERGETICS
	HYDROMECHANICS	life	
hymns	HYMNOLOGY	—and work of Christ	CHRISTOLOGY
hypnotism	NEUR(OH)YPNOLOGY	—processes	PHYSIOLOGY
hypothetical creatures	CRYPTOZOOLOGY	—without germs	GNOTOBIOTICS
ice movements	GLACIOLOGY	light	OPTICS
icons	ICONOLOGY	—as affecting	
ideas	IDEOLOGY	chemical reactions	PHOTOCHEMISTRY
illness diagnosed from		organisms	PHOTOBIOLOGY
marks on iris	IRIDOLOGY	limits in sets	TOPOLOGY
images in art	ICONOGRAPHY	liquids	HYDRAULICS
immunity	IMMUNOLOGY	—at rest	HYDROSTATICS
improvement in living		—in motion	HYDRODYNAMICS
standards	EUTHENICS	liver	HEPATOLOGY
industrial chemical		liverworts	HEPATICOLOGY
processes	CHEMURGY	living	
influence of the stars	ASTROLOGY	—things	BIOLOGY, BIOMETRY
inheritance	GENETICS, MENDELISM		BIOMETRICS, BIOSCIENCE

in relation to	
chemistry	BIOGEOCHEMISTRY
—tissues	HISTOLOGY
logic of reasoning	DIALECTICS
low temperatures	CRYOGENICS
	CRYOPHYSICS
lubrication	TRIBOLOGY
lying	PSEUDOLOGY
lymph vessels	ANGIOLOGY
magnetism	
—and electricity	ELECTROMAGNETISM
—of ancient rocks	PALAEOMAGNETISM
malaria	MALARIOLOGY
malformations	TERATOLOGY
man	ANTHROPOLOGY
managing fermentation	ZYMO-TECHNICS
manoeuvring	TACTICS
maps	CARTOLOGY
mathematical drawing	GRAPHICS
matter	
—in solid state	SOLID STATE PHYSICS
—using spectroscope	SPECTROSCOPY
—with motion	KINETICS
—without motion	STATICS
Maya people	MAYOLOGY
meaning	SIGNIFICS
—of words	LEXICOLOGY
meanings	SEMANTICS
	SEMASIOLOGY
measurable psychological	
factors	PSYCHOMETRICS
	PSYCHOMETRY
measurement	
—and recording of stars	ASTROMETRY
—of	
height above Earth's	
surface	HYPSOMETRY
social phenomena	SOCIOMETRY
time	HOROLOGY
very small things	NANOTECHNOLOGY
measurements	METRICS, METROLOGY
mechanics of the	
electric circuit	ELECTROMECHANICS
medals	NUMISMATICS
	NUMISMATOLOGY
mediaeval chemistry in	
medicine	IATROCHEMISTRY
medical problems of	
old people	GERIATRICS
medicines	PHARMACEUTICS
mental	
—attributes of historical	
figures	PSYCHOHISTORY
—disorders	PSCYHOPATHOLOGY
—faculties	PHRENOLOGY
—forces	PSYCHODYNAMICS

—illness	ALIENISM, PSYCHIATRY
—problems of the	
aged	PSYCHOGERIATRICS
—states quantified	PSYCHOMETRICS
meteor stones	AEROLITHOLOGY
	ASTROLITHOLOGY
meteors	METEORITICS
metrical theory	STICHOLOGY
metals	METALLURGY
	METALLOGRAPHY
metaphysics	IDEOLOGY
methods and rules	METHODOLOGY
micro-organisms	BACTERIOLOGY
	MICROBIOLOGY, VIROLOGY
microscopically	
small things	NANOTECHNOLOGY
midwifery	OBSTETRICS
mind	NOOLOGY
—and behaviour	PSYCHICS, PSYCHOLOGY
—in its environment	PSYCHONOMICS
—measurement	NOOMETRY
mineral	
—fossils	ORYCTOLOGY
—springs	BALNEOLOGY
minerals	MINERALOGY
missiles	BALLISTICS
mites	ACAROLOGY
moisture content of	
the atmosphere	HYDROMETEOROLOGY
molecules in living	
organisms	MOLECULAR BIOLOGY
molluscs	CONCHOLOGY
	MALACOLOGY
monads	MONADOLOGY
Moon	SELENOGRAPHY
	SELENOLOGY
—surface	SELENOMORPHOLOGY
morals	DEONTOLGY, ETHICS
mosses	BRYOLOGY, MUSCOLOGY
	SPHAGNOLOGY
moths	LEPIDOPTEROLOGY
motion	
—involving force	KINETICS
—not involving force	KINEMATICS
—of	
air or other gases	AERODYNAMICS
bodies in	
—air	AERODYNAMICS
—space	ASTRODYNAMICS
fluids	HYDRAULICS
	HYDRODYNAMICS
	HYDROKINETICS
	OR(E)OLOGY
mountains	STOMATOLOGY
mouth (disorders)	
movement	
—and supply of troops	LOGISTICS

—of		pecuniary management	ECONOMICS
humans	KINESIOLOGY	personal	
living creatures	BIOMECHANICS	—appearance	PROSOPOGRAPHY
mud	PELOLOGY	—interrelationships	SOCIOMETRY
muscles	MYOLOGY	personality traits	CHARACTEROLOGY
museums	MUSEOLOGY	phenomena	PHENOMENOLOGY
music	HARMONICS, MUSICOLOGY	phonological shapes	MORPHO(PHO)NEMICS
—of primitive			MORPHO(PHO)NOLOGY
peoples	ETHNOMUSICOLOGY	physical	
myths	MYTHOLOGY	—condition of	
natural		heavenly bodies	PHYSICAL ASTRONOMY
—agents in shaping		—features of	
the Earth's crust	DYNAMICAL GEOLOGY	an area	TOPOGRAPHY
—science	PHYSICS	Earth	PHYSIOGRAPHY
nature	PHYSIOGRAPHY	—geography	PHYSIOGRAPHY
—and essence	ONTOLOGY	—properties of	
navigation	NAUTICS	chemicals	PHYSICAL CHEMISTRY
nervous system	NEUROLOGY	—state of Earth and	
neurological		atmosphere	GEOPHYSICS
—disorders	NEURO(PATHO)LOGY	physics	NATURAL PHILOSOPHY
—factors in language		—of	
development	NEUROLINGUISTICS	heavenly bodies	ASTROPHYSICS
nose	RHINOLOGY	living things	BIOPHYSICS
nuclear physics	NUCLEONICS	the Earth	GEOPHYSICS
numbers	NUMEROLOGY	physiological	
numerical		psychology	PSYCHOPHYSIOLOGY
—data	STATISTICS	pigs	PORCINOLOGY
—proportions in which		place-names	TOPONYMICS, TOPONYMY
substances react	STOICH(E)IOMETRY	plant	
nutrition	TROPHOLOGY	—anatomy	PHYTOTOMY
obstetrics	TOCOLOGY, TOKOLOGY	—communities	SYNOECOLOGY
old age	GERONTOLOGY	—diseases	PHYTOPATHOLOGY
ontology	METAPHYSICS	—distribution	PHYTOGEOGRAPHY
optics	PHOTICS	—nutrition	AGROBIOLOGY
—and electronics	OPTOELECTRONICS	plant(s)	BOTANY, PHYTOLOGY
orbits and		—and	
trajectories	CELESTIAL MECHANICS	animals in relation	
organic molecules	MOLECULAR BIOLOGY	to environment	ECOLOGY
organised whole	GESTALT PSYCHOLOGY	geography	GEOBOTANY
organisms	BACTERIOLOGY	—population and	
—as affected by climate	PH(A)ENOLOGY	habitats	GENECOLOGY
origins of		—sociology	PHYTOSOCIOLOGY
—man	ANTHROPOGENY	—tissues	HISTOLOGY
	ANTHROPOGONY	plastic surgery	COSMETOLOGY
—proper names	ONOMASTICS	plays	DRAMATICS
—things	ARCHOLOGY	pleasure	HEDONICS
—universe	COSMOGONY	poisons	TOXICOLOGY
—words	ETYMOLOGY	political	
parasites	PARASITOLOGY	—economy	PLUTOLOGY, PLUTONOMY
particular place	TOPOLOGY	—science	ECONOMICS
pathology of nervous		pollen grains	PALYNOLOGY
system	NEUROPATHOLOGY	pollutants	ECOTOXICOLOGY
pauses, etc in		population	DEMOGRAPHY, LARITHMICS
conversation	CHRONEMICS	portraits	ICONOGRAPHY
pears	POMOLOGY	postcards	DELTIOLOGY
peat-mosses	SPHAGNOLOGY	pottery	CERAMOGRAPHY

practical application of science	TECHNOLOGY
preaching	HOMILETICS
precious stones	GEMMOLOGY
prediction	HOROSCOPY
pressure of gases	AEROSTATICS
primitive customs	AGRIOLOGY
prison management	P(O)ENOLOGY
probability	STATISTICS
problems of states	GEOPOLITICS
processes leading to invention	SYNECTICS
production of wealth	POLITICAL ECONOMY
prognosis	FUTUROLOGY
prolonging life	MACROBIOTICS
pronunciation	PHONETICS, PHONOLOGY
proper names	ONOMASTICS
properties of	
—angles	TRIGONOMETRY
—figures unchanged by deformation	TOPOLOGY
—heavenly bodies	ASTROPHYSICS
—large masses of particles	STATISTICAL MECHANICS
—lines, surfaces and solids	GEOMETRY
—matter	PHYSICS, SOMATOLOGY
protozoa	PROTOZOOLOGY
proverbs	PAROEMIOLOGY
psychic phenomena	
—extraordinary	METAPHYSICS
—theorising	METAPSYCHOLOGY
psychical research	PARAPSYCHOLOGY
psychological factors affecting physiology	PSYCHOSOMATIC MEDICINE
psychology	PSYCHICS
—of	
abnormal mental states	PSYCHOPATHOLOGY
animals	ZOOPSYCHOLOGY
—measurable factors	PSYCHOMETRICS
public institutions	ESTABLISHMENTOLOGY
punishment	PENOLOGY
pure being	ONTOLOGY
purposelessness	DYSTELEOLOGY
quantity	POSOLOGY
race	
—deterioration	CACOGENICS
—improvement	EUGENICS
races	ETHNOGRAPHY ETHNOLOGY
radiation on tissues	RADIOBIOLOGY
radioactivity	RADIOLOGY
rainfall	HYETOLOGY
reaction of matter to forces	MECHANICS
reality	AXIOLOGY
reasoning	LOGIC
reflected light	CATOPTRICS
reflection and refraction of light	GEOMETRICAL OPTICS
reflexes	REFLEXOLOGY
refracted sounds	DIACOUSTICS
refraction	DIOPTRICS
refuse collection and disposal	GARBOLOGY
relationship of	
—electrical and mechanical forces	ELECTRODYNAMICS
—languages	GLOTTOCHRONOLOGY
—living things	BIOSYSTEMATICS
to their surroundings	BIONOMICS ECOLOGY, ETHOLOGY
—mental to physical	PSYCHOPHYSICS
—perceived and actual characteristics of stimuli	PSYCHOPHYSICS
—workers to their environment	ERGONOMICS
religion	DIVINITY, THEOLOGY
religious feasts	HEORTOLOGY
replication of animal movements by machine	BIONICS
reptiles	HERPETOLOGY
rhythm	RHYTHMICS
rhythmic movement	EURHYTHMICS
rivers	LIMNOLOGY, POTAMOLOGY
rock masses	STRUCTURAL GEOLOGY
rocks	LITHOLOGY, PETROGRAPHY MINERALOGY, ORYCTOLOGY PETROLOGY
—layering	STRATIGRAPHICAL GEOLOGY STRATIGRAPHY
rural economy	AGRONOMY
Russian politics	KREMLINOLOGY
sacred things	HIEROLOGY
sailing on rhumb lines	LOXODROMICS LOXODROMY
saints' lives	HAGIOLOGY
salvation	SOTERIOLOGY
sanitary principles	HYGIENICS
seals	SPHRAGISTICS
seas	HYDROGRAPHY, OCEANOLOGY THALASSOGRAPHY
seasons	PH(A)ENOLOGY
seaweeds	ALGOLOGY, PHYCOLOGY
secret writing	CRYPTOLOGY
secretions	ECCRINOLOGY
seeds	CARPOLOGY

self	AUTOLOGY
—regulating systems	AUTONOMICS
semantics	SEMASIOLOGY
semiconductors	SOLID STATE PHYSICS
senility	NOSTOLOGY
serums	SEROLOGY
sexual behaviour	SEXOLOGY
shape	MORPHOLOGY
shaping metals by electrical means	ELECTROMETALLURGY
shells	CONCHOLOGY
signets and seals	SPHRAGISTICS
significance of	
—terms	SIGNIFICS
—values	AXIOLOGY
signs and signals	SEM(E)IOLOGY
—in language	SEMIOTICS
skin	DERMATOLOGY
—patterns	DERMATOGLYPHICS
skull	CRANIOLOGY, PHRENOLOGY
small	
—electronic systems	MICROELECTRONICS
—objects	MICROLOGY
—organisms	MICROBIOLOGY
—quantities of chemicals	MICROCHEMISTRY
—scale weather systems	MICROMETEOROLOGY
—worlds	MICROCOSMOGRAPHY
smell	OLFACTOLOGY
snakes	HERPETOLOGY, OPHIOLOGY
social	
—anthropology	ETHNOLOGY
—behaviour	SOCIOBIOLOGY
	SOCIOMETRY
—groups	SOCIOLOGY
—types	TYPOLOGY
Socratic art	MAIEUTICS
soil	AGROLOGY, EDAPHOLOGY
	PEDOLOGY
—yields	AGROBIOLOGY
sound	ACOUSTICS, PHONICS
—applications	SONICS
—beyond human hearing	ULTRASONICS
—echoes	CATACOUSTICS
	CATAPHONICS
space travel	ASTRONAUTICS
spectra	SPECTROSCOPY
speech	
—sound in writing	GRAPHEMICS
—sounds	PHONEMICS
	PHONETICS, PHONOLOGY
spiders	ARACHNOLOGY
spiritual beings	PNEUMATOLOGY
spoken sounds	PHONICS
sponges	SPONGOLOGY

spores	PALYNOLOGY
spread of disease	EPIDEMIOLOGY
stamps	PHILATELY, TIMBROLOGY
standing water	HYDROSTATICS
stars	ASTRONOMY
static electricity	ELECTROSTATICS
statics of rigid bodies	GEOSTATICS
statistical	
—analysis of economic data	ECONOMETRICS
—biology	BIOMETRY
stomach and intestines	GASTRO-ENTEROLOGY
stones (in body)	LITHOLOGY
strata	STRATIGRAPHY
structural geology	(GEO)TECTONICS
structure of	
—metals and alloys	METALLOGRAPHY
—organisms	MORPHOLOGY
—soil, etc	AGROLOGY
	MICROMORPHOLOGY
—tissues	HISTOLOGY
subatomic particles	MICROPHYSICS
	NUCLEAR PHYSICS
sugars	GLYCOBIOLOGY
Sun	HELIOLOGY
—dials	HOROGRAPHY
surface	
—features of Earth	GEOMORPHOLOGY
—tension	STALAGMOMETRY
surfaces	TOPOLOGY
—in contact	TRIBOLOGY
symbols	SYMBOL(OL)OGY
symptoms	SEM(E)IOLOGY, SEM(E)IOTICS
	SYMPTOMATOLOGY
systems	SYSTEMATOLOGY
teaching	PEDAGOGY
technology of metals	METALLURGY
teeth	ODONTOLOGY
terrestrial magnetism	GEOMAGNETISM
theological explanations	ISAGOGICS
theory of knowledge	EPISTEMOLOGY
thermionic valves	THERMIONICS
three-dimensional vision	STEREOSCOPY
	STEREOPTICS
ticks	ACAROLOGY
time	CHRONOLOGY
—by sundial	GNOMONICS
—pieces	HOROGRAPHY, HOROLOGY
tissues	HISTOLOGY
—in relation to disease	HISTOPATHOLOGY
—round teeth	PERIDONTIA
	PERIDONTICS
	PERIDONTOLOGY
—using chemical reactions	HISTOCHEMISTRY

trajectory of missiles	BALLISTICS
transmitting messages	TELEGRAPHY
treatment of	
—diseases	THERAPEUTICS, THERAPY
—prisoners	PENOLOGY
—the aged	GERONTOTHERAPEUTICS
tree-rings	DENDROCHRONOLOGY
trees	DENDROLOGY, FORESTRY
triangles	TRIGONOMETRY
tumours	ONCOLOGY
Turin shroud	SINDONOLOGY
types	TYPOLOGY
ultimate nature	AXIOLOGY
unchanging properties	
of figures	TOPOLOGY
unclean things	COPROLOGY
unidentified flying objects	UFOLOGY
universal benevolent	
interference	PANTOPRAGMATICS
universe	COSMOLOGY
unpredictable behaviour	
in systems	CHAOLOGY
urine	UR(IN)OLOGY
variations in language	STYLISTICS
variety of humans	ETHNOLOGY
venereal disease	SYPHILOLOGY
	VENEREOLOGY
versification	PROSODY
veterinary surgery	ZOIATRICS
vines	VINOLOGY
viruses	VIROLOGY
visibility	ENTOPTICS
vision	OPTOLOGY, OPTOMETRY
volcanoes	VULCANOLOGY
wars	POLEMOLOGY
wasps	VESPOLOGY
water	
—bodies	HYDROGRAPHY
—inland	LIMNOLOGY
—resources	HYDROLOGY
wealth	CHREMATISTICS
weapons	HOPLOLOGY
wear in machinery from	
iron in lubricants	FERROGRAPHY
weather	AEROGRAPHY
	METEOROLOGY
weights and measures	METROLOGY
whales	CETOLOGY
wind	ANEMOLOGY
wine-making	ZYMURGY
wines	OENOLOGY
wisdom	PHILOSOPHY
with microscope	MICROGRAPHY
women's diseases	GYNAECOLOGY
wood	XYLOLOGY
woodlands	FORESTRY

word origins	ETYMOLOGY
working of things	BIONICS
worms	HELMINTHOLOGY
writing hymns	HYMNOGRAPHY
X-rays and gamma rays	RADIOLOGY
	ROENTGENOLOGY
	(*see also* **pertaining, write**)

Sudan

capital	EL KHARTUM, KHARTOUM
coin	
—unit	MILLIEME
—10 milliemes	PIASTRE
—100 piastres	POUND

sugar

aldehyde	ALDOSE
arabinose	PECTINOSE
artificial sweetener	SACCHARIN
beet sugar	SUCROSE
blood-sugar deficiency	HYPOGLYCAEMIA
brown crystallised	
sugar	DEMERARA
cane sugar	SUCROSE, SACCHAROSE
—residue	BAGASSE
coarse	
—Indian	GOOR, GUR, JAGGERY
—Mexican	PANOCHA, PANOCHE
common sugar	BEET SUGAR, CANE SUGAR
	SUCROSE, SACCHAROSE
compound	
—from which sugar can be	
derived	GLYCOSIDE
—with one hydrogen	
atom replaced	GLUCOSIDE
containing several	
simple sugars	POLYSACCHARIDE
converted cane-sugar	INVERT SUGAR
dextrose	GLUCOSE
disaccharide	LACTOSE, MALTOSE
	SUCROSE
excess of blood-sugar	HYPERGLYCAEMIA
finely-ground sugar	CASTER SUGAR
	CASTOR SUGAR
from	
—aldehyde	ALDOSE
—arabin	ARABINOSE
—beet	BEET SUGAR
—cane	CANE SUGAR
—cells	(DEOXY)RIBOSE
—cereals	MALTOSE
—fruit	FRUCTOSE, LAEVULOSE
—glucose	ARABINOSE, PECTINOSE
—gum	ARABINOSE, PECTINOSE
—honey	FRUCTOSE, LAEVULOSE
—lactose	GALACTOSE
—maple	MAPLE SUGAR
—nectar of flowers	FRUCTOSE, LAEVULOSE

—ribonucleic acid	RIBOSE	syrup	MOLASSES, TREACLE
—starch	DEXTROSE, GLUCOSE	trisaccharide	RAFFINOSE
	MALTOSE	used for culture medium	ARABINOSE
—various plants	DULCOSE		PECTINOSE
fructose and glucose		unrefined	BROWN SUGAR, CASSONADE
mixed	INVERT SUGAR		GOOR, GUR, MUSCOVADO
fruit sugar	FRUCTOSE, L(A)EVULOSE	wood sugar	XYLOSE
grape-sugar	DEXTROSE, GLUCOSE	**Sun**	(see **astronomy**)
	GLYCOSE	**surfing**	
having		crest of wave	LIP
—five carbon atoms	PENTOSE	cylinder formed by	
—molecules with		curling wave	TUBE
more than one		froth of foam	SOUP
monsaccharide	POLYSACCHARIDE	moving from back of	
two monosaccharides	DISACCHARIDE	board to front	BOARDWALKING
three		put toes over edge	
monosaccharides	TRISACCHARIDE	of board	HANG FIVE, HANG TEN
—six carbon atoms	HEXOSE	reverse direction	CUTBACK
hexose	DEXTROSE, GALACTOSE	ride	
	GLUCOSE	—down breaking wave	FLOATER
malt sugar	MALTOBIOSE, MALTOSE		GO OVER THE FALLS
milk sugar	LACTOSE	—over edge of wave	AERIAL
monosaccharide	FRUCTOSE, GALACTOSE	shoot off top of wave	OFF-THE-LIP
	GLOCUSE, HEXOSE, KETOSE	surfers	
	PENTOSE, SIMPLE SUGAR	—Australian	ELKERTON, HORAN
palm sugar	JAGGERY		MACAULAY
pectinose	ARABINOSE	—British	HARDMAN, LYNCH, POTTER
pentose	RIBOSE		WILLIAMS
polysaccharide	GLYCOGEN	—Hawaiian	BURNS, DAVID, GARCIA
—in			HO, OCEAN PACIFIC PRO
fruit	PECTIN	tournaments	BILLABONG, MARUI MASTERS
insect cuticle	CHITIN	turn full circle	THREE-SIXTY
plants	PECTIN	venues	
—plants	XYLAN	—Britain	CORNWALL
—stored as food in		—California	BIG SUR
algae	(CHRYSO)LAMINARIN		HUNTINGTON BEACH
	LEUCOSIN	—France	BIARRITZ, COTE SAUVAGE
plants	INULIN		LACANAU, LA SAUZAIE
powdered	ICING SUGAR		LE ROZEL, LES CAVALIERS
pressed into lumps	CUBE SUGAR		SEIGNOSSE, SIOUVILLE
refined in cigar shape	LOAF SUGAR	—Hawaii	NORTH SHORE, PIPELINE
residue of cane sugar	BAGASSE		SUNSET BEACH, WAIMEA BAY
simple sugar	(MONO)SACCHARIDE	—Portugal	COXOS, MACHO LESTE
study of sugars	GLYCOBIOLOGY		RIBIERA D'ILHAS
substitute	ACESULFAME POTASSIUM	—South Africa	BAY OF PLENTY
	ASPARTAME, CYCLAMATE	—Spain	LOS LOCOS, MUNDACO
	GLUCOSE SYRUP, ISOMALT	**surgery**	
	MALTITIOL, SACCHARIN(E)	including: medical instruments	
	SORBITOL, THAUMATIN	surgical instruments	
	XYLITOL	atomiser	NEBULISER
—proprietary	CANDEREL, HERMESETAS	brain surgery	PSYCHOSURGERY
	NUTRASWEET, SWEETEX	crushing of bladder stone	LASERTRIPTY
sugar-coated	CRYSTALLISED, GLACE		LITHOLAPAXY
sugar-regulating		cutting into	
hormone	INSULIN	—2 parts	BISECTION, DICHOTOMY
sugar-splitting	SUCROCLASTIC	—3 parts	TRISECTION, TRICHOTOMY

—4 parts	QUADRISECTION	—windpipe	TRACHEO(S)TOMY
	TETRACHOTOMY	—womb	HYSTEROTOMY, UTEROTOMY
—abdominal wall	LAPAROTOMY	cutting out	
—animals	ZOOTOMY	—adenoids	ADENOIDECTOMY
—artery	ARTERIOTOMY	—appendix	APPEND(IC)ECTOMY
—beard	POGONOTOMY	—bladder	CYSTECTOMY
—bladder	CYSTOTOMY	—bone	OSTECTOMY
—bodies of animals	ZOOTOMY	of middle ear	STAPEDECTOMY
—bone	OSTEOTOMY	—bony plate	LAMINECTOMY
—bowel	ENTERO(S)TOMY	—bowel	ENTERECTOMY
—brain	ENCEPHALOTOMY, LEUCOTOMY	—breast	MASTECTOMY
	LOBOTOMY	—cerebral cortex	TOPECTOMY
—chest cavity	THORACTOMY	—duodenum	DUODENECTOMY
—colon	COLOTOMY	—Fallopian tubes	SALPINGECTOMY
—cornea	KERATOTOMY		TUBECTOMY
—ear-drum	MYRINGOTOMY	—gall-bladder	CHOLECYSTECTOMY
—front of brain	LEUCOTOMY, LEUKOTOMY	—gland	ADENECTOMY
	LOBOTOMY	—gums	GINGIVECTOMY
—gall-bladder	CHOLECYSTO(S)TOMY	—intestines	ENTERECTOMY
—head	CEPHALOTOMY	—iris	IRIDECTOMY
of foetus	CRANIOTOMY	—kidney	NEPHRECTOMY
—human anatomy	ANTHROPOTOMY	—larynx	LARYNGECTOMY
—inner ear	FENESTRATION	—liver	HEPATECTOMY
—iris	IRIDOTOMY	—lobe (of lung)	LOBECTOMY
—intestine	ENTERO(S)TOMY	—lump in breast	LUMPECTOMY
—kidney	NEPHROTOMY		TYLECTOMY
—larynx	LARYNGOTOMY	—lung	PNEUMONECTOMY
—living animal	VIVISECTION	—nerve	SYMPATHECTOMY
—lobe of organ	LOBOTOMY	—organ	ABLATION, EXCISION
—lung tissue	PNEUMONECTOMY		EXTIRPATION
—nerve	NEUROTOMY	—ovaries	OOPHORECTOMY
fibres in neck	CORDOTOMY		OVARIECTOMY
roots	RHIZOTOMY	—part of body	ABLATION, AMPUTATION
—ovary	OVARIOTOMY		EXCISION, EXTIRPATION
—perin(a)eum	EPISIOTOMY	—pituitary body	HYPOPHYSECTOMY
—pharynx	PHARYNGOTOMY	—prostate gland	PROSTATECTOMY
—plant	PHYTOTOMY	—root of tooth	APICECTOMY
—pleura	PLEUROTOMY	—specimen	BIOPSY
—pubic junction	SYMPHYSEOTOMY	—sperm duct	VASECTOMY
	SYMPHESIOTOMY	—spleen	SPLENECTOMY
—skull	CRANIOTOMY	—stomach	GASTRECTOMY
—solids	STEREOTOMY	—sympathetic nerve	SYMPATHECTOMY
—spine	CORDOTOMY	—testicle	ORCHIDECTOMY
—stomach	GASTROTOMY	—tongue	GLOSSECTOMY
—tendon	TENOTOMY	—tonsils	TONSIL(L)ECTOMY
—thorax	THORACOTOMY	—uterus	HYSTERECTOMY
—to			UTERECTOMY
cure squinting	STRABOTOMY	—wrinkles	RHYTIDECTOMY
make opening	SYRINGOTOMY	delivery of foetus	
remove stones	LITHOTOMY	surgically	CAESARIAN SECTION
—tonsils	TOLSIL(L)OTOMY	destruction of	
—trachea	TRACHEO(S)TOMY	—brain tissue using	
—tumour	ONCOTOMY	electricity	STEREOTAXIA
—uterus	HYSTEROTOMY, UTEROTOMY	—tissues by burning	CAUTERY
—vagina	EPISIOTOMY	drainage of fluid	
—vein	PHLEBOTOMY, VENESECTION	from eye	GONIOPUNCTURE

facelift	RHYTIDECTOMY
forming	
—artificial anus	COLOSTOMY
—opening	SYRINGOTOMY
fracture of bone	OSTEOCLASIS
instrument for	
—artificial respiration	IRON LUNG
—auscultation	STETHOSCOPE
—breaking bones	OSTEOCLAST
—collecting cells from	
cervix	CYTOBRUSH
—cutting	BISTOURY, ECRASEUR
	FLEAM, LANCET, SCALPEL
bone	OSTEOTOME
brain tissue	LEUCOTOME
discs of bone	
from skull	TREPAN, TREPHINE
skin for grafting	DERMATOME
stones	LITHOTOME
—crushing stones in body	LITHOCLAST
	LITHO(N)TRI(P)TOR
	LITHOTRITE
—delivery of babies	FORCEPS, RONGEUR
—destruction of tissues	
by burning	CAUTER(Y)
—dilating	BOUGIE
—draining or injecting fluid	CANNULA
—examination of	
bladder	CYSTOSCOPE
bronchi	BRONCHOSCOPE
ear	OTOSCOPE
eardrum	MYRINGOSCOPE
eye	OPHTHALMOSCOPE
	RETINOSCOPE
interior of stomach	GASTROSCOPE
internal	
—cavities	ENDOSCOPE
—organs	LAPAROSCOPE
—parts	FLUOROSCOPE
joints	ARTHROSCOPE
lower colon	SIGMOIDOSCOPE
lungs	STETHOSCOPE
neck of uterus	COLPOSCOPE
nose	RHINOSCOPE
tissues and organs	FIBRESCOPE
—examination using	
ultra-sound	SOMASCOPE
—fracturing bone	OSTEOCLAST
—holding open incisions	RETRACTOR
—incision	LANCET, SCALPEL
—injecting	CANNULA, CATHETER
	HYPODERMIC NEEDLE
—lifting and holding	
blood vessels	TENACULUM
—measuring	
blood pressure	SPHYGMO(MANO)METER

field of vision	PERIMETER
oxygen in blood	PULSE OXIMETER
sharpness of hearing	AUDIOMETER
—opening a body	
passage	SPECULUM
—percussion	PLESSOR, PLEXOR
	PLESSIMETER, PLEXIMETER
—piercing	TROCAR
—pressing down	DEPRESSOR
—recording	
brain	
activity	ELECTROENCEPHALOGRAPH
changes in heartbeat,	
breathing and blood	
pressure	POLYGRAPH
heartbeats	ELECTROCARDIOGRAPH
muscle activity	ELECTROMYOGRAPH
variations in blood	
pressure	KYMOGRAPH
—removing	
liquids from	
body cavity	ASPIRATOR, CATHETER
obstruction in	
—bronchi	BRONCHOSCOPE
—throat	PROBANG
stones from bladder	GORGET
tumours	ECRASEUR, SNARE
—resuscitation	DEFIBRILLATOR
—scraping	CURETTE
bones	RASPATORY, XYSTER
uterus	RESECTOSCOPE
—stretching canals	BOUGIE
—three-dimensional	
X-ray photographs	CAT SCANNER
	(*see also* **X-ray**)
listening (to lungs etc)	AUSCULTATION
opening artifically made	FISTULA
piercing	PARACENTESIS
—intestine	ENTEROCENTESIS
—uterus	AMNIOCENTESIS
—vein	VENEPUNCTURE
	VENIPUNCTURE
plastic surgery	(*see* repair *below*)
reflex separation	AUTOTOMY
removing	
—dead tissue	DEBRIDEMENT
	NECROTOMY
—gall stones	CHOLELITHOTOMY
—kidney stones	LITHONEPHROTOMY
—stones in the body	LITHOTOMY
repairing or reshaping	
—artery	ARTERIOPLASTY
—bone	OSTEOPLASTY
—breast	MAMMOPLASTY
—chest wall	THORACOPLASTY
—cornea	KEROTOPLASTY

—damaged tissue	ALLOGRAFT
	AUTOGRAFT
	AUTOPLASTY, HOMOGRAFT
	HOMOPLASTY
—ear	OTOPLASTY
—mouth	STOMATOPLASTY
—nose	RHINOPLASTY
—roof of mouth	URANOPLASTY
removal of tissue for examination	BIOPSY
scraping	CURETTAGE
self-amputation	AUTOTOMY
separation after fracture or wound	ABDUCTION
sew up wound	SUTURE
spray	NEBULISER
sterilisation	
—female	TUBAL LIGATION
—male	CASTRATION, VASECTOMY
stitch in wound	SUTURE
surgeon	VET
surgeons	RCS
	(*see also* **physician**)
surgical thread	LIGATURE
tapping (fluids)	PARACENTESIS
	(*see also* piercing *above*)

Surinam(e)

capital	PARAMARIBO
coin	CENT, GULDEN
	GUILDER, FLORIN

swamp

	BOG, FEN, MARSH, MORASS
	(QUAG)MIRE, SLOUGH
	SWALE, WASH
American	BAYOU, EVERGLADES
	VLEI, VLY
Canadian	MUSKEG
exhalation from marsh	MIASM(A)
light hanging over marsh	FRIAR'S LANTERN
	IGNIS FATUUS
	JACK-O'-LANTERN
	WILL-O'-THE-WISP
marsh-gas	METHANE
South African	VLEI, VLY

Swaziland SZD

capital	MBABANE
coin	CENT, LILANGENI

Sweden S

aeroplane	SAAB
airline	SAS
bay	BUKT(EN)
beach	STRAND
cape (headland)	UDDEN
capital	STOCKHOLM
chief magistrate	LANDAMMAN(N)
clover	ALSIKE

coin	
—unit	ORE
—100 øre	KR, KRONA
complaints officer	OMBUDSMAN
farm	TORP
harbour	HAMN
hors d'oeuvres	SMORGASBORD
manual training	SLOID, SLOYD
measure (2/3 acre)	MORGEN
moor	MYR
mountain	BERG, FJALL
parliament	RIKSDAG
province	LAN
provincial council	LANDST(H)ING
river	ALV(EN)
saint	SANKT
secret police	SAPO
strait	SUND
swamp	MYR
toast	SKOAL
turnip	RUTABAGA
valley	DAL
wild turnip	NAVEW

sweets

almond	
—flavoured	MACAROON
—paste	MARZIPAN
aromatic	COUGH DROP, LOZENGE
	PASTIL(LE), PEPPERMINT
chewy	BUBBLE GUM, CHEWING GUM
	NOUGAT, TOFFEE
chocolate	
—coated	BONBON
—disc	CHOCOLATE DROP
covered with coloured sugar balls	NONPAREIL
—drop	DRAGEE
coconut and sugar	COCONUT ICE
crystallised sugar	CANDY
flat	
—boiled sweet	LOLLIPOP, LOLLYPOP
—liquorice	POMFRET CAKE
	PONTEFRACT CAKE
flavoured boiled sweet	SUGARPLUM
frozen	ICE CREAM
—between biscuit layers	WAFER
—covered in chocolate	CHOC-ICE
—in conical biscuit	CORNET
—on a stick	ICE LOLLY
hard	BOILED SWEET
ice-cream	(*see* **desserts**)
jelly cubes, dusted with sugar	LOK(O)UM
	TURKISH DELIGHT
large round sweet	BULLSEYE, GOBSTOPPER
	JAWBREAKER

liquorice	
—sweet	POMFRET CAKE
	PONTEFRACT CAKE
mixture	LIQUORICE ALLSORTS
lozenge	CACHOU
medicated	COUGH SWEET, LOZENGE
	PASTIL(LE)
mixed sweets	DOLLY MIXTURE
nougat (Italian)	TORRONE
nuts	
—fruit, etc, in sugar	SWEETMEAT
—in	
boiled sugar	BRITTLE
sugar paste	NOUGAT
on a stick	TOFFEE APPLE
scented	CACHOU
silvered ball	DRAGEE
small	HUNDREDS AND THOUSANDS
soft and spongy	MARSHMALLOW
spun sugar	CANDY FLOSS
stick of boiled sugar	ROCK
—America	ROCK CANDY
stickjaw	TOFFEE
sticky	CARAMEL, TOFFEE
sugar-coated nut	COMFIT, DRAGEE
	PRALINE, PRAWLIN
	SUGARED ALMOND
sweetened cocoa block	CHOCOLATE
toffee	STICKJAW, TOM-TROT
—butter	BUTTERSCOTCH
—chewy	CARAMEL
thin piece of	
chocolate	LANGUE-DE-CHAT
tom-trot	TOFFEE
Turkish delight	LOK(O)UM
swimming	
including: divers	
diving	
divers	
—American (m)	DESJARDINS, GALITZEN
	LOUGHANIS, LEE, PINKSTON
	TOBIAN, WEBSTER, WHITE
(f)	BECKER, COLEMAN
	MCCORMICK, POYNTON-HILL
	RIGGIN
—British (m)	PHELPS
(f)	FERRIS
—Canadian (f)	BERNIER
—Chinese (f)	JIHONG
—Czech (f)	DUCHKOVA
—German (f)	ENGEL-KRAMER
—Italian (m)	DIBIASI
—Japanese (m)	OHTSUBO
—Mexican (m)	CAPILLA, PEREZ
—Russian (m)	PORTNOV, VASIN
(f)	KALININA

diving	
—events	HIGH BOARD, SPRINGBOARD
—movements	PIKE, SOMERSAULT
	TUCK, TWIST
strokes	BACKSTROKE, BREAST STROKE
	BUTTERFLY, CRAWL, FREESTYLE
swimmers	
—American (m)	BURTON, GAINES
	GOODELL, HENCKEN, HICKOK
	KAHANAMOKU, KEALOHA
	NABER, SCHOLLANDER
	SPITZ, LUNDQUIST
	WEISSMULLER
(f)	ANDREWS, BABASHOFF
	CAULKINS, COHEN, HOGSHEAD
	KOLB, LUNDQUIST, MCFARLANE
	MEAGHER, MEYER, NORELIUS
	ROTHHAMMER, STEINSEIFER
	WAITE
—Australian (m)	BAILDON, ROSE, SIEBEN
	THIELE, WENDEN
(f)	CRAPP, FORD
	FRASER, GOLD
—British (m)	GOODHEW, HOLMAN
	JARVIS, MOORHOUSE
	ROBINSON, TAYLOR, WILKIE
(f)	BROWNSDON, COOMBES
	DAVIES, FOOT, GRINHAM
	LONSBOROUGH
	SCARBOROUGH
—Canadian (m)	BAUMANN, DAVIS
	DRAXINGER, KELLY
	TEWKSBURY
(f)	DUGGAN, GIGWERE
	OTTENBRITE
—Chinese (m)	JIANGIANG
—Cuban (m)	HERNANDEZ
—Danish (m)	JENSEN, JACOBSEN
—Dutch (m)	ELZERMANN
(f)	DE ROVER, MASTENBROEK
	MUIS, NORD
—German (m)	AROSS, HACKMAN
	HASE, HERMANN
	HOFFMEISTER, MATTHES
	PYTTER, SITT, WARNECKE
	WEBER, WOITHE
(f)	ENDER, FRIETSCHE
	JAHNICHEN, KRAUSE
	ORTWIG, OSYGUS, REINECH
	RICHTER, STEVENS
	STRAUSS, THURMER
—Italian (m)	LAMBERTI
(f)	DALLAVALLE
—Japanese (m)	KIYOKAWA, SUZUKI
	TAGUCHI, TAKASE
	TSURUTA, YAMANAKA

(f)	NATSUME, SHITO
	TANAKA, TSURUTA
—Norwegian (f)	DALBY
—Russian (m)	FESENKO, KOPLIAKOV
	SALNIKOV, VOLKOV, ZULPA
(f)	KASKUSHITE, KOSHEVAIA
—Swedish (m)	ARVIDSSON, BORG
	HENNING, HOLMERTZ
	LARSSON
(f)	CEDERQUIST
team	
—game	AQUAPUSH
	UNDERWATER HOCKEY
	WATER POLO
—swimming	SYNCHRONISED SWIMMING
underwater swimming	SCUBA DIVING
	SNORKELLING
Swiss	HELVETIAN
alpenhorn melody	RANZ-DES-VACHES
cabin	CHALET
cantons	AARGAU, BASELLAND, BERN(E)
	FRIBOURG, GLARUS, GRABUNDEN
	JURA, NEUCHATEL, NIDWALDEN
	ST GALLEN, SCHAFFHAUSEN, SCHWYZ
	SOLOTHURN, THURGAU, TICINO
	UNTERWALDEN, URI, VAUD
	WAADT, WALLIS, ZURICH
capital	BERN(E)
coin	FRANC, RAPPEN
dish	BERNERPLATTE, MUESLI
division	CANTON
dried potatoes	RO(E)STI
herdsman's song	RANZ-DES-VACHES
hero	TELL
magistrate	AM(T)MAN
measure (small)	LIGNE
sled	LUGE
Switzerland	CH
sword	BRAND, GLAIVE
	WHITE ARM
arm of cross-guard	QUILLON
Arthur's sword	CALIBURN, EXCALIBAR
	EXCALIBUR
blunted sword	CURTANA, CURTA(E)
	CURTEIN(E), CURTEYNE
broad-bladed	BACKSWORD
	BROADSWORD
—curved sword	SEAX
—sword (short)	CURTAL-AX
bullfighter's sword	ESTOQUE
cavalry sword	SABRE
Celtic	CLAYMORE, CLEDDYO
ceremonial sword	CURTEIN
Charlemagne's sword	FLAMBERGE
concealed	JACOB'S-STAFF
	SWORD-CANE, SWORD-STICK

curved sword	SABRE, S(C)IMITAR
Damascene	DAMASCUS BLADE
Doge's bodyguard's	
sword	SCHIAVONE
duelling-sword	SHARP, SMALL-SWORD
engraved	DAMASCE(E)NE, DAMASKEEN
	DAMASKIN, DAMASQUIN
—sword	DAMASCUS BLADE
fencing weapon	EPEE, FOIL, SMALL-SWORD
fighting sword	ESPADRON, SPADROON
fight with swords	DIGLADIATE
German	SCHLAGER
Indian	TULWAR
Lewis Carroll's sword	VORPAL
long slender sword	RAPIER
King Edward's	
sword	(*see* sword of mercy *below*)
knob on hilt	POMMEL
naval sword	CUTLASS
—short	HANGER
Norse myth	BALMUNG, GRAM
obsolete	FOX
old sword	GLAIVE
part of	
—guard	KNUCKLE-BOW
—rapier blade	RICASSO
Persian	S(C)IMITAR
rapier	BILBO
—(Shak.)	TUCK
rare	GLADIUS
Roland's sword	CO(U)RTAIN
Roman	GLADIUS, SPATHA
St George's sword	ASCALON, ASKELON
Saxon	SEAX
Scots	CLAYMORE
	SPURTLE-BLADE
—rusty	SHABBLE
short sword	ESTOC
—curved	FALCHION, FAULCHI(O)N
—naval	HANGER
Siegfried's sword	BALMUNG
Siegmund's sword	GRAM, NOTHUNG
Sir Bevis's sword	MORGLAY
small sword	SHARP
Spanish	BILBO, ESPADA
	ESPADIN, ESTOQUE
suspended	SWORD OF DAMOCLES
sword of mercy	CURTANA, CURTAN(E)
	CURTEIN(E), CURTEYNE
sword-bearer	BALDRIC(K), SELICTAR
swordsman	SPADASSIN
Turkish	SCIMITAR
two-edged sword	PATA
wooden sword	WASTER
Syriac	
alphabet	ESTRANG(H)ELO

bishop	ABBA	—100 piastres	POUND
testament	PESHITTA, PESHIT(T)O	dynasty	SELEUCID
Syrian	SYR	garment	AB(B)A, ABAYA
abbess	AMMA	hyrax	DAMAN
Aramaic dialect	SYRIAC	newspaper	AL-THAWRA
bishop	ABBA	nomad	SARACEN
capital	DAMASCUS, DIMASHQ	plant	ROSE OF JERICHO
chief priest (Roman)	SYRIARCH	pot-herb	JEW'S MALLOW
cloth	AB(B)A, ABAYA	rue	HARMALA, HARMEL
coin		sect	DRUSE, DRUZ(E)
—unit	PIASTRE	society	REMOBOTH
		tobacco	LATAKIA

T

Taiwan RC
capital TEIPEI
coin CENT, DOLLAR
Tanganyika EAK
tanks
American ABRAMS, BULLDOG
CALLIOPE, CHAFFEE
CHRISTIE, GRANT, LEE, PERSHING
PRIEST, SHERMAN, WALKER, WHIZBANG
British ARTHUR, BIG WILLIE
CARDEN-LLOYD, CENTAUR, CENTURION
CHALLENGER, CHIEFTAIN
CHURCHILL, COMET, CONQUEROR
COVENANTER, CROMWELL, CRUSADER
FIREFLY, HONEY, INDEPENDENT
INTERNATIONAL, LIBERTY, MATILDA
MORRIS-MARTEL, MOTHER, SCORPION
VALENTINE, VICKERS, WARRIOR
—with 6-pdr gun MALE
—with machine-guns only FEMALE
French CHAR D'ASSAUT
CHAR ST CHAMOND, RENAULT
SCHNEIDER
German ELEFANT, FERDINAND
KOENIGSTIGER, LEOPARD
(JAGD) PANTHER
PANZERBEFEHLSWAGEN
PANZERJAGER, PANZERKAMPWAGEN
ROYAL TIGER, STURMMORSER
STURMPANZER, STURMTIGER
(JAGD) TIGER, (KING) TIGER,
Tanzania EAT, EAZ
capital DODOMA
coin CENT, SHILLING
tea
black CAPER-TEA, OOTAK
China BOHEA, CAPER-TEA, CONGO(U)
DIMBULA, GUNPOWDER
HYSON, JASMINE, KEEMUN
LAPSANG SOUCHONG, LYCHEE
NUWARA ELIYA, OOLONG, OULONG
PADRA, PEKOE, POUCHONG
TWANKAY, YUNNA, UVA
flavoured
—bergamot EARL GREY
—lemon LEMON TEA
—rose petals ROSE PUCHONG
green HYSON, TWANKAY

herbal CAMOMILE, PEPPERMINT
ROSE-HIP
hot water, milk, etc CAMBRIC TEA
India ASSAM, DARJEELING
NILGIRI
Labrador LEDUM
Mexico CHIA
Paraguay MATE
purgative SENNA
small leaves DUST, FANNINGS
South America YERBA (DE MATE)
Sri Lanka CEYLON, DIMBULA, URA
teeth CHOPPERS
artificial teeth CAP, CROWN
DENTURES, FALSE TEETH
bone holding teeth DENTARY
PREMAXILLA
broken tooth SNAGGLETOOTH
care of teeth DENTISTRY
cavity
—in tooth PULP CAVITY
—into which tooth fits ALVEOLUS
cell forming dentine ODONTOBLAST
cleaning materials DENTAL FLOSS
DENTIFRICE, TOOTH PASTE
TOOTH POWDER
corrective wiring BRACE
crushing tooth MOLAR
—with deciduous
predecessor PREMOLAR
cusp of molar METACONE
cutting
—of teeth DENTITION, ODONTIASIS
—tooth INCISOR
decay (DENTAL) CARIES
dental x-rays BITE-WING, PANORAMIC
PERIAPICAL
dentist ODONTIST
description ODONTOGRAPHY
diagram of arrangement
of teeth DENTAL FORMULA
false teeth DENTURES
film of bacteria etc on teeth PLAQUE
first set of teeth DECIDUOUS TEETH
MILK TEETH
fossil tooth ODONTOLITE
gum disease GINGIVITIS, PYORRHOEA
hard film SCALE
having
—crescent-shaped ridges
in teeth SELENODONT
—cutting back teeth SECODONT
—more than two dentitions POLYPHYDONT
—nodules on teeth BUNODONT
—rounded teeth CRENATE
—teeth DENTIGEROUS

all the same	HOMODONT
like a shrew	SORICIDENT
of different kinds	HETERODONT
on inside of jawbone	PLEURODONT
—toothed jaws	ODONTOSTOMATOUS
—transverse ridges on teeth	LIPHODONT
horse's canine	TUSH
in pharynx of wheel-	
animalcules	TROPHI
long pointed tooth	CANINE, DOG-TOOTH
	EYE-TOOTH, FANG
	TUSH, TUSK
molar	MOLENDINAR, WANG(-TOOTH)
origin of teeth	ODONTOGENY
premolar	BICUSPID
projection on tooth	CUSP
repair	BRACE, BRIDGE, FILLING
scissor-tooth in	
carnivore	CARNASSIAL TOOTH
second set of teeth	PERMANENT TEETH
small	
—toothlike structure	DENTEL
	DENTICLE, DENTIL
—tusk	TUSH
socket	ALVEOLUS
space between teeth	DIASTEMA
sprouting of teeth	DENTITION
sticky film	PLAQUE
study	ODONTOLOGY
substance	
—covering teeth	ENAMEL
—of which teeth are made	DENTIN(E)
third molar	WISDOM TOOTH
tooth	CRENA
—ache	DENTAGRA
	ODONTALGIA, ODONTALGY
toothed whale	ODONTOCETE
toothlike	
—decoration	DENTELLE
—projection	DENTATION
treatment of	
—teeth	DENTISTRY
—tissues round teeth	PERIDONTIA
	PERIDONTICS
	PERIDONTOLOGY
tumour	ODONTOMA
types	CANINE, EYETOOTH, INCISOR
	(PRE-)MOLAR, WISDOM
upper	
—canine	EYE-TOOTH
—tooth (fish)	VOMERINE TOOTH
telescope	(*see* **observatory**)
temple	(*see* **church—buildings**)
ten	
based	DECIMAL, DENARY
cents	DIME

combining form	DECA-
groups	DECAD, DECADE, DENARY
having 10	
—arms	DECAPODAL, DECAPODAN
	DECAPODOUS
—columns	DECASTYLE
—faces	DECAHEDRON
—feet	DECAPODAL, DECAPODAN
	DECAPODOUS
—lines (poem)	DECASTICH
—parts	DECAMEROUS
—pistils	DECAGYNIAN, DECAGYNOUS
—sides	DECAGON
—stamens	DECANDRIAN, DECANDROUS
—syllables	DECASYLLABLE
Christmas presents	LORDS
Commandments	DECALOGUE, FINGERNAILS
dollar bill	SAWBUCK, TENSPOT
events	DECATHLON
fold	DECUPLE
gallon hat	SOMBRERO
gram(me)s	DECAGRAM(ME)
Green...	BOTTLES
litres	DECALITRE
Little...	NIGGERS
Lost Tribes	ASHER, EPHRAIM, DAN, GAD
	ISSACHAR, MANNASEH
	NAPHTALI, REUBEN
	SIMEON, ZEBULUN
men (Roman)	DECEMVIR
metres	DECAMETRE
steres	DECASTERE
thousand	MYRIAD, TOMAN, X
years	DECADE, DECENNARY
	DECENNIUM

tennis

area within which served	
ball must land	SERVICE-COURT
ball served and	
—landing outside	
service area	FAULT
—striking net but landing	
in service court	LET, NET
championship of Australia,	
France, UK and USA	GRAND SLAM
courts	CLAY, GRASS, HARD
	INDOOR
first stroke	SERVICE
four major championships	GRAND SLAM
group of	
—games	SET
—sets	MATCH
line at	
—end of court	BASELINE
	SERVICE-LINE
—side of court	SIDELINE, TRAMLINE

officials	LINE-JUDGE, REFEREE
	UMPIRE
put ball into play	SERVE
players	
—American (m)	AGASSI, AUSTIN, CHANG
	CONNORS, FALKENBURG, FLACH
	FLEMING, GERULAITAS, GILBERT
	GONZALES, GOTTFRIED, KRAMER
	MCENROE, MAYER, MCKINLEY
	MULLOY, OLMEDO, PARKER
	PATTY, RALSTON, REISSEN
	SAVITT, SCHROEDER, SEGUSO
	SEIXAS, SMITH, TILDEN
	TRABERT
(f)	ARTH, AUSTIN, BROUGH
	CAPRIATI, CASALS, CONNOLLY
	EVERT, FRY, GIBSON, HARD, HART
	JORDAN, KING, KIYOMURA, LLOYD
	MICHEL, MOFFITT, RICHEY
	RUSSELL, SHRIVER, SMITH
	SUSMAN, TODD
—Argentinian (m)	MANICINI
(f)	SABATINI
—Australian (m)	BROMWICH, CASE, CASH
	COOPER, DAVIDSON, EMERSON
	FLETCHER, FRASER, HARTWIG
	HEWITT, HOAD, HOWE, LAVER
	MASTERS, MCGREGOR, MCNAMARA
	MCNAMEE, NEWCOMBE, QUIST
	ROCHE, ROSE, ROSEWALL
	SEDGMAN, STONE
(f)	CAWLEY, COGHLAN, COURT
	GOOLAGONG, REID, SMITH
	SMYLIE, TEGART, TURNBULL
	TURNER
—Brazilian (m)	BUENO
—British (m)	BATES, LLOYD, PERRY
(f)	BUXTON, DURIE, JONES
	MOODY, MORTIMER, SCRIVEN
	SHILCOCK, WADE
—Bulgarian	MALEEVA
—Czech (m)	DROBNY, KODES
	LENDL, MECIR
(f)	MANDLIKOVA, NAVRATILOVA
	SUKOVA
—Dutch (m)	SCHAPERS
(f)	STOVE
—Ecuadorian	GOMEZ
—French (m)	BOROTRA, NOAH, LECONTE
	PARADIS, PETRA
(f)	DURR, LENGLEN
—German (m)	BECKER, VON CRAMM
(f)	GRAFF, KOHDE-KILSH
—Hungarian (m)	TAROCZY
—Japanese (f)	SAWAMATSU
—Mexican (m)	OSUNA, PALAFOX, RAMIREZ

—Romanian	NASTASE
—South African (m)	CURREN, HEWITT
	MCMILLAN, STURGESS
(f)	STEVENS, SUMMERS
—Spanish (m)	SANCHEZ, SANTANA
(f)	MARTINEZ
—Swedish (m)	BORG, EDBERG
	GUNNARSSON, JARRYD
	NYSTROM, WILANDER
—Swiss	GUNTHARD
—Yugoslav (f)	SELES
playing area	COURT
rebound	BRICOLE
scores	
—nil	LOVE
—first point	FIFTEEN
—second point	THIRTY
—third point	FORTY
—three points each	DEUCE
—point after deuce	ADVANTAGE
—final point	GAME
scoring unit	POINT
service with foot in front	
of baseline	FOOT FAULT
short game to decide winner	
of tied game	TIE-BREAK
strokes	BACKHAND, FOREHAND
	HALF-VOLLEY, LOB, SERVICE
	SMASH, (STOP-)VOLLEY
venues	
—America	BOSTON, FLUSHING MEADOW
	KEY BISCAYNE, INDIAN WELLS
	MADISON SQUARE GARDEN
	NEWPORT, PHILADELPHIA
—Australia	MELBOURNE
—Britain	BECKENHAM, BRIGHTON
	DEVONSHIRE PARK
	EASTBOURNE, EDGBASTON
	QUEEN'S CLUB, TELFORD
	WEMBLEY, WEST KIRBY
	WIMBLEDON
—France	ROLAND GARROS STADIUM
	PARIS
—Germany	DUSSELDORF, FRANKFURT
	HAMBURG, STUTTGART
—Monaco	MONTE CARLO
—Switzerland	GSTAAD
tenth	
tenth in methane series	DECANE
tenth of	
—are	DECIARE
—bel	DECIBEL
—franc	DECIME
—gram(me)	DECIGRAM(ME)
—litre	DECILITRE
—metre	DECIMETRE

—normal concentration	DECINORMAL
—stere	DECISTERE
Thailand	T
	(see also **Siamese***)*
theatre	
accommodation for	
prompter	PROMPT BOX
acting	
—production or study	
of plays	DRAMATICS
—style identifying	
with character	METHOD (ACTING)
actor(actress)	
—delivering	
closing speech	EPILOGUE
opening speech	PROLOGUE
—in	
comedy	COMEDIAN(-ENNE)
folk drama	MUMMER
tragedy	TRAGEDIAN(-ENNE)
actors	
—American	STRASBERG
—British	BARKWORTH, BUCHANAN
	CHARLESON, CONTI, COWARD, COWEN
	DENNISON, DEVINE, DU MAURIER
	FINLAY, GODFREY, GUINNESS, HARRIS
	HARRISON, HORDERN, IRVING
	JOHNS, KEMBLE, MCCOWAN
	MCKELLAN, MILLER, MILLS
	NEVILLE, OLIVIER, QUAYLE
	QUILLEY, SCOFIELD, SUTHERLAND
	TREE, USTINOV, VAN GYSEGHEM
	WOLFIT
—French	ARTAUD, BARRAULT
	COREAU, DASTE, DULLIN
	JOUVET, GERARD, PITOEFF
	TALMA
—German	HILPERT
—Irish	HARRIS, MAC LIAMMOIR
—Roman	ROSCIUS
—Russian	MEYERHOLD, OKHLOPKOV
	PITOEFF, STANISLAVSKY
	VAKTANGOV
	(see also **cinema***)*
actors' trade union	EQUITY
actresses	
—American	HAYES, MALINA
—British	ASHCROFT, ASHER
	BENNETT, CAMPBELL
	COURTNEIGE, DENCH, EVANS
	GRAY, HIRD
	JACKSON, KENDAL, LANGTRY
	LAYE, LEIGH, MILES, PLOWRIGHT
	SCALES, SEYLER, SMITH, THORNDIKE
	TUTIN, TEMPEST, WORTH
—Canadian	LILLIE
—French	BERNHARDT, FEUILLERE
	SIGNORET
—German	MALINA, WEIGEL
—Greek	MERCOURI
—New Zealand	PORTER
	(see also **cinema***)*
allegorical play	MORALITY PLAY
American repertory	
company	STOCK COMPANY
ancient farcical play	MIME
astonishing piece of	
stagecraft	COUP DE THEATRE
back-stage rest-room	GREEN ROOM
climax or unravelling	CATASTROPHE
	DENOUEMENT
characters in play	CAST
	DRAMATIS PERSONAE
	ENSEMBLE
chief actor	LEADING MAN
	PROTAGONIST
—actress	LEADING LADY
comedy of hopelessness	BLACK COMEDY
	PIECE NOIRE
contrived solution	DEUS EX MACHINA
copy of script used	
by prompter	PROMPT-BOOK
	PROMPT-COPY
courtly spectacle	MASQUE
curtain drawn upward	
and outward	TABLEAU CURTAIN
—hiding scene changes	DROP CURTAIN
	DROP SCENE
—to contain fire	SAFETY CURTAIN
curved backcloth	CLYCLORAMA
deliberate effect of	
reducing audience	
involvement	A-EFFECT
	ALIENATION EFFECT
dialogue in alternate	
lines	STICHOMYTHIA
dramatists	*(see separate entry)*
entertainment between	
acts	DIVERTISSEMENT
	ENTR'ACTE, INTERLUDE
first part of play	PROTASIS
forget one's lines	
on stage	DRY (UP)
German theatre	
association	PEOPLE'S STAGE
	VOLKESBUHNE
god brought in by	
mechanical device	DEUS EX MACHINA
Greek theatre	ODEON
group of	
—3 related dramas	TRILOGY
—4 related dramas	TETRALOGY

—actors chanting comment　CHORUS
—supporting actors　ENSEMBLE
guild comedy of Italian
　Renaissance　COMMEDIA DELL'ARTE
height of drama　CATASTATIS
humorous play　COMEDY
horror play　GRAND GUIGNOL
imitation blood　KENSINGTON GORE
incidental actions
　by actor　BUSINESS
Japanese play　KABUKI
　　NOGAKU, NO(H)
laugh on stage at
　inappropriate time　CORPSE
lights
　—at front of stage　FLOATS
　　FOOTLIGHTS
　—overhead　FLOODS, SPOTS
living picture　TABLEAU (VIVANT)
London theatre group　THEATRE WORKSHOP
　　UNITY THEATRE
main action of Greek
　drama　EPITASIS
method acting　STANISLAVSKY METHOD
monologue by character
　to himself　SOLILOQUY
motionless
　representation　TABLEAU (VIVANT)
movement of chorus
　to one side　STROPHE
narrative style　EPIC THEATRE
one
　—in charge of
　　costumes　DRESSER
　　furniture, etc　PROPERTY MANAGER
　　　PROPS
　　set, etc　STAGE MANAGER
　—reminding forgetful
　　players　PROMPT(ER)
outdoor theatre　AMPHITHEATRE
part
　—before entry of chorus　PROLOGUE
　—played by female
　　in male dress　BREECHES PART
piece of scenery　FLAT
　—in wings　TORMENTOR
play
　—based on
　　humour and terror　THEATRE OF PANIC
　　improvisation and
　　　aggression　LIVING THEATRE
　　pain and
　　　suffering　THEATRE OF CRUELTY
　　threats as comedy　COMEDY OF MENACE
　　use of lights,
　　　movement, etc　TOTAL THEATRE

—dealing with
　dreadful events　BLACK COMEDY
　　PIECE NOIRE
　events in the Bible
　　or lives of saints　MIRACLE PLAY
　　　MYSTERY PLAY
　sordid domestic
　　life　KITCHEN-SINK DRAMA
　the faults of
　　society　COMEDY OF MANNERS
—emphasising futility
　of modern life　THEATRE OF THE ABSURD
—with
　gestures but no speech　MIME
　musical accompaniment
　　(old)　MELODRAMA
　no artistic
　　merit　BOULEVARD THEATRE
　one speaking part　MONOLOGUE
　sad ending　TRAGEDY
　two speaking parts　DUOLOGUE
playwrights　(*see* **dramatists**)
purification of emotions　CATHARSIS
reappearance of actor(s)
　on stage at end of play　CURTAIN CALL
recognition leading to
　dénouement　ANAGNORISIS
retiring room　GREEN ROOM
returning dance
　of chorus　ANTISTROPHE
revolving prism giving
　scene changes　PERIAKTOS
Roman theatre　ODEUM
romantic and sensational
　drama　MELODRAMA
room
　—behind stage　GREEN ROOM
　—below stage　MEZZANINE
　—for resting actors　GREEN ROOM
seating area　AUDITORIUM
　—balcony　LOGGIA
　—box　LOGE
　—high　BALCONY, GALLERY, GODS
　—low　FAUTEUILS, PIT, STALLS
serious drama　LEGITIMATE (THEATRE)
short comic piece　COMEDIETTA
situation where irony is
　apparent to audience
　but not to characters　DRAMATIC IRONY
sound-effect devices　THUNDERSHEET
　　WIND MACHINE
speech
　—at end of play　EPILOGUE
　—introducing the action　PROLOGUE
stage
　—3 sided set　BOX SET

—arch framing stage	PROSCENIUM (ARCH)	thirty-three	DISC, LP, RECORD
—area		thirty-nine	
above stage	FLIES	—Books	OLD TESTAMENT, OT
at side of stage	COULISSE, WINGS	—in	
behind proscenium		novel	STEPS
arch	PICTURE-FRAME STAGE	religious belief	ARTICLES
in front of curtains	APRON STAGE	thirty thousand	L, LA(M)BDA
	FORESTAGE	**thousand**	CHILIAD, G, K, M, X
over proscenium	LOGUM	combining form	KILO-
used by chorus	ORCHESTRA	group	CHILIAD
—back of stage	UPSTAGE	thousand and one	MI
—front of stage	DOWNSTAGE	thousand million	BILLION, MILLIARD
	PROSCENIUM	thousand years	MILLENARY, MILLENNIUM
—left side of stage	OPPOSITE PROMPT	thousandth	MILLESIMAL
—open		—anniversary	MILLENARY, MILLENNIUM
front of set	FOURTH WALL	**three**	CROWD, GAMMA
on all sides	OPEN STAGE	B's	BACH, BEETHOVEN, BRAHMS
	THEATRE IN THE ROUND	canons of classical	
—right side of stage	PROMPT SIDE	drama	UNITIES
—room under stage	MEZZANINE	cards	P(AI)RIAL, PAIR-ROYAL
—scenery	DECOR, SET	choices	TRILEMMA
—slide	COULISSE	Christmas presents	FRENCH HENS
—slope of stage	RAKE	cleft	TRIFID, TRIPARTITE
—surrounded by		combining form	TER-, TRI-
audience	ARENA THEATRE	cornered hat	TRICORN(E)
	THEATRE-IN-THE-ROUND	days	TRIDIUM
—trapdoor	SCRUTO	Estates of the Realm	COMMONS
—wings	COULISSES		LORDS SPIRITUAL
—with audience on			LORDS TEMPORAL
three sides	PLATFORM STAGE	F's	FAIR RENT, FAIR SALE
stock of pieces that a			FAIR TENURE
company can perform	REPERTOIRE	Fates	(see separate entry)
	REPERTORY	feet	YARD
storage building	SKENE	fold	TRI(N)AL, TRIPLEX, TRIPLICATE
story of life and action	DRAMA	Furies	(see separate entry)
sudden		Graces	(see separate entry)
—change of fortune	PERIPET(E)IA	grooved tablet	TRIGLYPH
—turn of events	COUP DE THEATRE	groups	P(AI)RIAL, PAIR-ROYAL
theatre company with			TERN(ION), TERZETTO
stock of plays	REPERTORY (COMPANY)		TRIAD, TRILOGY, TRINE
three canons of			TRINITY, TRIO, TRIPLE
classical drama		Harpies	(see separate entry)
(action, time, place)	UNITIES	having three	
tragedian's boot	BUSKIN, COTHURN(US)	—apses	TRIAPS(ID)AL
young		—atoms	TRIATOMIC
—actor	JUVENILE	—axes	TRIAXIAL, TRIAXONIC
—actress	INGENUE	—beats	TRICOTIC, TRICOTOUS
theologian	BD, DD	—bodies	TRICORPORATE
(see also **church—personnel**)		—branches	TRICHOTOMOUS
thirteen	BAKER'S DOZEN, DEVIL'S DOZEN		TRIFURCATE(D), TRIGEMINAL
	LONG DOZEN, RL TEAM		TRISULCATE
	UNLUCKY NUMBER	—bundles of stamens	TRIADELPHOUS
thirteen witches	COVEN	—carpels	TRICARPELLARY
thirteenth loaf	MAKEWEIGHT	—cells	TRILOCULAR
thirty	L, LA(M)BDA	—colours	TRICHRO(MAT)IC
thirty requiem masses	TRENTAL		TRICOLOUR(ED)

—consonants	TRICONSONANTAL
—corners	TRICORN(E)
—cusps	TRICUSPID, TRITUBERCULAR
—days	TRIDUUM
—dimensions	TRIDIMENSIONAL
—electrodes	TRIODE
—ethyl groups	TRIETHYL
—extremities	TRINACRIAN
	TRINACRIFORM
—faces	TRIFACIAL, TRIHEDRAL
—feet	TRIPEDAL
—fingers	TRIDACTYLOUS
—focal lengths	TRIFOCAL
—forks	TRIFURCATE(D)
—forms	TRIFORM(ED)
	TRIMORPHIC, TRIMORPHOUS
—furrows	TRISULCATE
—heads	TRICEPHALOUS, TRICEPS
—horns	TRICERATOPS, TRICORN(E)
—hydrogen atoms	TRIACID, TRIBASIC
—hydroxyl groups	TRIHYDRIC
—interlaced arcs	TRIQUETRA
—languages	TRIGLOT, TRILINGUAL
—leaflets	TERNATE, TRIFOLIATE
—leaves	TRIFOLIATE, TRIPHYLLOUS
—legs	TRIPOD(AL)
—letters	TRILITERAL
—lines	TRIGRAM, TRILINEAR
—lobes	TREFOIL, TRILOBATE(D)
	TRILOBE(D)
—marriages	TRIGAMOUS
—measures	TRIMETER, TRIMETRIC
—methyl radicals	TRIMETHYL
—oxygen atoms	TRIOXIDE
—parts	TRIMEROUS, TRIPARTITE
—petals	TRIPETALOUS
—phenyl groups	TRIPHENYL
—pistils	TRIGYNIAN, TRYGYNOUS
—points	TRICUSPID(ATE)
	TRINACRIAN, TRINACRIFORM
—prongs	TRIDENT(AL), TRIDENTATE
	TRIDENTED, TRINACRIAN
	TRINACRIFORM
—rays	TRIACT(INAL), TRIACTINE
	TRIRADIAL, TRIRADIATE
—ribs	TRICOSTATE
—rings	TRICYCLIC
—rows	TRIFARIOUS, TRISTICHOUS
—sides	TRILATERAL
—stamens	TRIANDRIAN, TRIANDROUS
—strings	TRICHORD
—styles	TRIGYNIAN, TRIGYNOUS
—sulphur atoms	TRISULPHIDE
	TRITHIONIC
—teeth	TRIDENTATE, TRIDENTED
—terms	TRINOMIAL, TRIONYM

—times	
haploid number	
of chromosomes	TRIPLOID
molecular mass	TRIMERIC
—toes	TRIDACTYL(OUS)
—tubercles	TRITUBERCULAR
—unequal axes	TRICLINIC
—use of 3 elements	TRIPHIBIOUS
—valencies	TERVALENT, TRIATOMIC
	TRIVALENT
—valves	TRIVALVE(D)
	TRIVALVULAR
—ways	TRIFARIOUS
—whorls	TRICYCLIC
—wings	TRIPLANE, TRIPTEROUS
—wives	TRIGAMOUS, TRIGAMY
	TRIGYNIAN, TRIGYNOUS
—words	TRINOMIAL, TRIONYM(AL)
—xylem strands	TRIARCH
—yearly occurrences	TRIENNIAL
hulled boat	TRIMARAN
hundred	B
—years	TERCENTENARY
in	
—one	TRINITY, TRIUNE
—the fountain	COINS
Jerome characters	MEN IN A BOAT
Jewels	RIGHT CONDUCT
	RIGHT FAITH
	RIGHT KNOWLEDGE
legged race	MANX
letter word	TRILITERAL
lines	TERCET, TERZETTA
lobed fossil	TRILOBITE
men in office	TRIUMVIRATE
monthly	TRIMONTHLY
months	TRIMESTER
Musketeers	ARAMIS, ATHOS
	PORTHOS
one of three at birth	TRIPLET
people	CROWD
	ETERNAL TRIANGLE
persons	
—ruling	TRIARCHY
—speaking	TRIALOGUE
pipped card or domino	TREY
pronged spear	TRIDENT
tablets	TRIPTYCH
thousand	B
times	TREBLE, TRIPLE
—a day	TID
tragedies	TRILOGY
under par	ALBATROSS
wheeled vehicle	TRICAR, TRICYCLE
	TRISHAW
winged aeroplane	TRIPLANE

Wise Men (Magi)	BALTHAZAR
	GASPAR(CASPAR), MELCHIOR
yearly	TRIENNIAL
Tibetan	
abominable snowman	YETI
animal	(GIANT) PANDA
antelope	GOA
barley dish	TSAMBA
Buddhist sect	GELUK PA, SAKYA PA
capital	LHASA
cloth	KATA
dog	LHASA APSO, SHIH TZU
goat	TAKIN
hybrid cattle	DSO(MO), DZO, JOMO, Z(H)O
	ZHOMO, ZOBO, ZOBU
language	PALI
leader	LAMA
mysterious beast	YETI
monastery	LAMASERY
monument	STUPA
ox	SARLAC, SARLAK
	YAK, Z(H)O
—pannier	YAKHDAN
pony	TANGUN
porch	TORAN
priest	LAMA
religious leader	DALAI LAMA
	PANCHEN LAMA
scarf	KATA
sheep	SHAHPU, SHAPO
tribe	SHERPA
wild ass	KIANG, KYANG
timber	
from	
—conifers	SOFTWOOD
—deciduous trees	HARDWOOD
hardwood	
—Andaman Islands	BOMBWAY
	BULLET-WOOD
	CANARIUM, CHUGLAM, HOKKO
	MARBLEWOOD, PADAUK, PADOUK
	PAPITA, PYINMA, RED DHUP
	THINGAN
—Angola	AVODIRE, COPALWOOD
	MUNINGA
—Argentina	QUEBRACHO
—Asia	BOXWOOD, MAPLE
	PAULOWNIA, WALNUT
—Asia Minor	BOXWOOD, HORNBEAM
—Australia	ALPINE ASH, BLACK BEAN
	BLACKBUTT, BLACKWOOD, BLUE GUM
	BRUSH BOX, CEDAR, COACHWOOD
	IRONBARK, JARRAH, KARRI
	MULGA, NEGRO-HEAD BEECH
	QUEENSLAND MAPLE, (RED) SATINAY
	ROSE GUM, ROSE MAHOGANY

	SALIGNA GUM, SHE-OAK
	SILKY OAK, SILVERTOP ASH
	SPOTTED GUM, TALLOWWOOD
	TASMANIAN MYRTLE, TASMANIAN OAK
	TURPENTINE, WALNUT, WANDOO
	WHITE ASH, WHITE OAK
	YELLOW STRINGBARK
	YELLOW WALNUT
—Borneo	KAPUR, LAUAN, MENGKULANG
	MERANTI, MERBAU, SEPETIR
	SELANGAN(BATU), SERAYA
—Botswana	MUGONGO
—Brazil	ARARACANGA, BASRALOCUS
	BICUIBA, BRAZILWOOD, CANELLA
	CURUPAY, EMBUIA, FREIJO, IMBUYA
	IPE, JEQUITIBA, KABUKALLI, KINGWOOD
	LOURO, MAHO, MAHOGANY, MANDIO
	PALISANDER, PEROBA, QUARUBA
	QUEBRACHO, RED LOURO, ROSEWOOD
	SUCUPIRA, TULIPWOOD, VINHATICO
	ZEBRAWOOD
—Burma	ANAN, CEDAR, CHICKRASSY
	ENG, GURJUN, GMELINA
	HALDU, HOKKO, IRONWOOD
	KATON, KAUNGHMU, KERUING
	LAUREL, MERSAWA, PADAUK
	PADOUK, PAPITA, PYINMA
	PYINKADO, TEAK, THINGAN
	THITKA, TULIPWOOD, YON
—Canada	ASPEN, BEECH
	BALSAM POPLAR, BASSWOOD, BIRCH
	BUTTERNUT, CHERRY, COTTONWOOD
	HICKORY, HORNBEAM
	PACIFIC MAPLE, PAPER BIRCH
	RED OAK, ROCK ELM, ROCK MAPLE
	SOFT MAPLE, WALNUT, WHITE ASH
	WHITE ELM, WHITE OAK
	WHITEWOOD, YELLOW BIRCH
—Celebes (Sulawesi)	EBONY
—Central and	
tropical Africa	AFZELIA, ALBIZZIA
	ALSTONIA, ANTIARIS, BOMANGA
	DITSHIPI, ERIMANDO, GABOON
	MISSANDA, MUGONGO, MUKANGU
	MUKULUNU, MUSIZI, M(U)TONDO
	MUGONGO, MUTOBO, OLON
	WAIKA CHEWSTICK
—Central and	
tropical America	ALCANTOR, ANGELIN
	BALSA, BANAK, BITTERWOOD
	BLACK CABBAGE-BARK, CAOBA
	CATIVO, CEIBA, CEDAR
	(CEDRO) COLORADO, CELTIS
	COCOBOLO, COURBARIL, DALLI
	DEGAME, EBONY, ESPAVEL, FUSTIC
	FUTUI, GLASSY WOOD, HOGPLUM

	HURA, JIGUA, LAPACHO, LETTERWOOD
	LIGNUM VITAE, LONGUI ROUGE
	LOURO PRETO, MAHOE, MAHOGANY
	MANGLE, MASTIC, MAYFLOWER, PILON
	PARTRIDGE-WOOD, PRIMAVERA
	PURPLEHEART, SALMWOOD
	SANTA MARIA, SAPAN DE PALOMA
	SAPODILLA, SATINE, SIMARUBA
	SNAKEWOOD, WAIKA CHEWSTICK
—Chile	COIGUE BEECH, LAUREL
	LINGUE, OLIVILLO, RAULI BEECH
	ROBLE BEECH, TEPA, ULMO
—China	KATSURA
—Colombia	KABUKALLI
—Congo	MUTENYE, TCHITOLA, WENGE
—Cuba	COCUS WOOD, DEGAME
	MAHOE, MAHOGANY, SABICU
—East Africa	BLACKWOOD, CANARIUM
	CANDELABRA-WOOD, CELTIS
	DAHOMA, ELGON OLIVE, EBONY
	GEDU, GREENHEART, IROKO, MAFU
	LOLIONDO, MAHOGANY, MECODZE
	MOBURA, MSANDARUSSI, MTONDO
	MUERI, MUHUHU, MUKALI, , MUKEO
	MUKUMARI, MUSINE, MUTOBO
	M(U)TONDO, MVULE, NKUNYA, NOHOR
	OTU, PANGA, PILLARWOOD
	RAPANEA, SILKY OAK, WALNUT
—East Indies	BELIAN, MERBAU, MERANTI
	ROSEWOOD, SEPETIR, SERAYA
—Ecuador	ALCANTOR, FERNAN SANCHEZ
—Ethiopia	OLIVE
—Europe	ALDER, APPLE, ASH
	ASPEN, BEECH, BIRCH
	BLACK POPLAR, BOXWOOD
	CHERRY, CHESTNUT, ELM
	HOLM OAK, HORNBEAM, LIME
	MAPLE, OAK, PEAR, PLANE
	ROBINIA, ROWAN, SWEET CHESTNUT
	SPINDLEWOOD, SYCAMORE
	TURKEY OAK, WALNUT
	WHITEBEAM
—Ghana	AFRORMOSIA, ANOPYXIS
	AVODIRE, MAKORE, WHIMAWHE
—Guatemala	GUANACASTE, NARANGO
—Guyana	BAROMALLI, BASRALOCUS
	GREENHEART, HIARIBALLI
	(ITURI)WALLABA, KABUKALLI
	KUROKAI, MAHO, MANDIO
	(MORA)BUKEA, RED LOURO
	VIROLA, WAIKA CHEWSTICK
	WARAMA, YARURU
—Honduras	CRAMANTEE, MAHOGANY
	NARGUSTA, ROSEWOOD, YEMERI
—India	ANAN, APITONG, AXLEWOOD
	BENTEAK, BIJASAL, CALAMANDER

	CEDAR, CHICKRASSY, COROMANDEL
	EBONY, ELM, GARDENIA, GMELINA
	GURJUN, HALDU, HOKKO, KERUING
	KINDAL, KUMBAR, KUMBUK, LAUREL
	PALO, POON, PISSUR, PYINMA
	ROSEWOOD, SAL, SANDALWOOD
	SATINWOOD, SISSOO, TEAK
	THINGAN, YANG, YON
—Indonesia	JELUTONG, NYATOH
	PUNAH, PYINMA
—Iran	OAK
—Ivory Coast	AVODIRE
—Jamaica	COCUS WOOD, HOGPLUM
—Japan	ASH, BEECH, ELM
	HORSE CHESTNUT, KATSURA
	MAPLE, OAK, SEN, WALNUT
—Java	ROSEWOOD
—Kenya	CAMPHORWOOD, OLIVE
—Malaya	APITONG, GURJUN
	JELUTONG, KAPUR, KERUING
	LAUAN, MACHANG, MELAWIS
	MENGKULANG, MERANTI, MESUA
	NEMESU, RAMIN, TEAK, YANG
—Malaysia	ANAN, BALAU, BINTANGOR
	CANARIUM, GERONGGANG, GURJUN
	JELUTONG, KAUNGHMU, KEMPAS
	KERENTAI, KERUING, KUNGKUR
	MATA ULAT, MERBAO, MERANTI
	MERAWAN, MERSAWA, NYATOH
	PUNAH, SATIN ASH, SELANGAN
	SEPETIR, SERAYA, TEAK
	TERENTANG
—Mexico	PRIMAVERA
—Mozambique	AFZELIA, BANGA WANGA
	BEKUNGU, KNOBTHORN
	MECRUSSE, MUNINGA
	MZIMBE, PAU FERRO
—New Guinea	PALDAO
—New Zealand	HARD BEECH, RED BEECH
	SOUTHLAND BEECH, TAWA
—Nigeria	AFZELIA, CEIBO, CORDIA
	HOMALIUM, OMO, OPEPE, TEAK
—North America	ALDER, APPLE, ASH
	ASPEN, BALSAM POPLAR
	BASSWOOD, BEECH, BIRCH
	BLACK WILLOW, BUCKEYE
	BUTTERNUT, BUTTONWOOD
	CELTIS, CHERRY, CHESTNUT
	COFFEETREE, COTTONWOOD
	DOGWOOD, ELM, GREEN ASH
	GUM, HACKBERRY, HICKORY, HOLLY
	HONEYLOCUST, HORNBEAM, KOA
	MAGNOLIA, MANGROVE, MAPLE, MYRTLE
	OAK, PACIFIC MAPLE, PAPER BIRCH
	PECAN, PERSIMMON, PLANE, RED OAK
	RED GUM, RED OAK, ROBINIA

	ROCK ELM, ROCK MAPLE, SOFT MAPLE
	SYCAMORE, TUPELO, WALNUT
	WHITE ASH, WHITE ELM
	WHITE OAK, WHITEWOOD
	YELLOW BIRCH
—Pakistan	CHICKRASSY, SISSOO
—Peru	MAHOGANY
—Philippines	APITONG, GURJUN, LAUAN
	KERUING, PALDAO
	PALOSAPIS, SERAYA, YANG
—Sabah	BINUANG, GAGIL, KAPUR(MERAH)
	KEMBANG, RANGGU
	SELANGAN BATU, SERAYA
—Sarawak	JONGKONG, RAMIN
	MELAWIS, MENGKULANG
—Sierra Leone	TOFEE
—Siam	(see Thailand below)
—South Africa	BOXWOOD, CAPE BEECH
	COPALWOOD, KAMASSI, MULGA
	MUNINGA, WHITE ELS
—South America	AMARILLO, ANDIROBA
	BALSA, BASRALOCUS, BITTERWOOD
	CANGERANA, CEDAR, CIRUELILLO
	CRABWOOD, DALLI, DEGARLE
	FREIJO, GREENHEART, IMBUYA
	LANCEWOOD, LETTERWOOD, LOURO
	MAHOGANY, PADDLEWOOD
	PARTRIDGE-WOOD, PAU MARFIM
	PURPLEHEART, QUEBRACHO
	ROSEWOOD, SANTA MARIA
	SNAKEWOOD, TINEO, VERA WOOD
	ZEBRA-WOOD
—South-east Asia	BALAU, GERONGGANG
	KAPUR, KERUING APITONG
	LAUAN, MENBAU, MENGKULANG
	MERANTI, NYATOH
	SERAYA, SEPETIR
—Sri Lanka	CALAMANDER, COROMANDEL
	EBONY, HORA, KATABODA
	KUMBUK, LUNUMIDELLA
	PALU, SATINWOOD
—Sudan	HARAZ, HEGLIG, NEEM
	SEYAL, SUNT
—Sumatra	KAPUR(MERAH)
—Tanzania	BUSSEI, CAMPHORWOOD
	MAHOGANY, MCHENGA, MEGUZA
	MFUNE, MGONGO, MJOMBO
—Thailand	ANAN, APITONG
	CHUMPRAK, ENG
	GURJUN, HALDU, KAPONG, KATON
	KAUNGHMU, KERUING, MAIDU
	MERSAWA, PADAUK, PADOUK
	TEAK, TASUA, THINGAN
	PYINMA, YANG, YOM HIN, YON
—Trinidad	NARGUSTA, SERRETE
—Uganda	MUCHENCHE, MUHIMBI

—United Kingdom	APPLE, ASH, ASPEN
	BEECH, BLACK POPLAR, BOXWOOD
	CHERRY, CRACK WILLOW
	CRICKET-BAT WILLOW, DUTCH ELM
	EUROPEAN ELM, EUROPEAN OAK
	GREY POPLAR, HAZEL, HOLLY
	HOLM OAK, HORNBEAM, LABURNUM
	LIME, LUCOMBE OAK, PEAR
	PLANE, RED OAK, ROBINIA
	ROWAN, SMOOTH-LEAVED ELM
	SWEET CHESTNUT, SYCAMORE
	TURKEY OAK, WALNUT
	WHITEBEAM, WHITE POPLAR
	WHITE WILLOW, WYCH ELM
—Venezuela	MAHOGANY, MARACAIBO
	PATRIDGE-WOOD, SUCUPIRA
—West Africa	ABURA, ADJOUOBA, AFARA
	AFINA, AFRORMOSIA, AFZELIA
	AGBA, AKAK, APOME, AVODIRE, AYAN
	AZOBE, BERLINIA, BOMBAX, BUBINGA
	CAMWOOD, CANARIUM, CASSINE
	CELTIS, COUL ATTAI, DAHOMA
	DANTA, DIFOU, DOUKA, DOUSSIE
	EBIARA, EBONY, EDINAM, EKKI
	EKOP, ESSIA, GEDU, GUAREA, IDIGBO
	IROKO, LANDA, LIMBA, MOBURA
	MAHOGANY, MAKORE, MANSONIA
	MOABI, NIA(N)GON, NIOVE, NOHOR
	NYANKOM, OBECHE, ODOKO, ODUDU
	OLON, OKAN, OKWEN, OMU, OPEPE
	OSOL, OTU, PADAUK, PADOUK, POGA
	PTERYGOTA, PYCNANTHUS, RIBI
	RIKIO, SAPELE, SIBO, SOUGUE
	STERCULIA, TENDRE, UTILE
	WALNUT, ZEBRANO
—West Indies	ANGELIN, BALSA
	CANDLE-WOOD, CATIVO, CEDAR
	COCO(A)-WOOD, COCUS-WOOD
	COURBARIL, CRABWOOD, FUSTIC
	HURA, JAMAICA EBONY, KOKRA-WOOD
	LANA, LANCEWOOD, LIGNUM VITAE
	MAHOGANY, MAYFLOWER, PILON
	SABICU, SALMWOOD, SANTA MARIA
	SAPAN DE PALOMA, SATINWOOD
	YACCA
—Zambia	MUGONGO, MUNINGA, TEAK
—Zimbabwe	COPALWOOD, MUGONGO
	MUNINGA, TEAK
softwood	
—Argentina	PARANA PINE
—Asia Minor	CEDAR
—Australia	BUNYA PINE
	CELERY TOP PINE, HOOP PINE
	HUON PINE, KAURI PINE
	KING WILLIAM PINE
	RADIATA PINE

—Borneo	SEMPILOR
—Brazil	PARANA PINE
—Canada	ALPINE FIR, AMABILIS FIR
	BALSAM FIR, BLACK SPRUCE
	DOUGLAS FIR, ENGELMANN SPRUCE
	GRAND FIR, HEMLOCK, INCENSE CEDAR
	JACK PINE, LODGEPOLE PINE
	PONDEROSA PINE, RED PINE
	RED SPRUCE, TAMARACK LARCH
	WESTERN LARCH, WESTERN RED CEDAR
	WHITE CEDAR, WHITE PINE
	WHITE SPRUCE, YELLOW PINE
—Central America	PITCH PINE
—Chile	ALERCE PINE, MANIO
—China	JAPANESE CEDAR
—Cuba	PITCH PINE
—Cyprus	ALEPPO PINE
—East Africa	CEDAR, CYPRESS
	MANIO, PODO
—East Indies	KAURI
—Europe	AUSTRIAN PINE, CEDAR
	CORSICAN PINE, LARCH
	MARITIME PINE, REDWOOD
	SCOTS PINE, SILVER FIR
	(SITKA) SPRUCE, WHITEWOOD
—Fiji	KAURI PINE
—Guatemala	CYPRESS
—Honduras	YELLOWWOOD
—India	BLUE PINE, CEDAR
	HIMALAYAN SPRUCE
	SILVER FIR
—Japan	LARCH, CEDAR
—Kenya	PODO, YELLOWWOOD
—Malta	THUYA
—Manchuria	SIBERIAN PINE
—New Guinea	HOOP PINE
—New Zealand	KAURI PINE, KEWAKA
	MATAI, MIRO, RIMU
	SILVER PINE, TOTARA
	WHITE PINE
—North Africa	THUYA
—North America	ALPINE FIR
	AMABILIS FIR, BALSAM FIR
	BLACK SPRUCE, CYPRESS
	DOUGLAS FIR, ENGELMANN SPRUCE
	GRAND FIR, HEMLOCK
	INCENSE CEDAR, JACK PINE
	LODGEPOLE PINE, NOBLE FIR
	PITCH PINE, PONDEROSA PINE
	PORT ORFORD CEDAR, RADIATA PINE
	RED PINE, RED SPRUCE, SEQUOIA
	SITKA SPRUCE, SUGAR PINE
	TAMARACK LARCH, WESTERN LARCH
	WESTERN RED CEDAR, WHITE CEDAR
	WHITE PINE, WHITE SPRUCE
	YELLOW CEDAR, YELLOW PINE

—Russia	SIBERIAN LARCH
—Sarawak	SEMPILOR
—Siberia	LARCH, SCOTS PINE
	SIBERIAN PINE
—South Africa	RADIATA PINE
—Tanzania	PODO, YELLOWWOOD
—Uganda	PODO, YELLOWWOOD
—United Kingdom	AUSTRIAN PINE
	CEDAR, CORSICAN PINE
	DUNKELD LARCH, EUROPEAN LARCH
	EUROPEAN SPRUCE, JAPANESE LARCH
	LEYLAND CYPRESS, NOBLE FIR
	SCOTS PINE, SILVER FIR
	SITKA SPRUCE, WELLINGTONIA
	YEW
Titans	*(see* **gods***)*
toasts	
Austrian	PROST
Chinese	GUN-BEI
Danish	SKAL
Dutch	PROOST, SANTJES
English	BOTTOMS UP, CHEERS
	CHIN-CHIN, GOOD HEALTH
	MUD IN YOUR EYE
Finnish	KIPPIS, SKAL
French	A VOTRE SANTE
	BONNE SANTE
German	GESUNDHEIT, PROS(I)T
Irish	SLAINTE
Israeli	L'CHAIM
Italian	CIAO, SALUTE
Japanese	KAMPAI
naval	SANDY BOTTOMS
Norwegian	SKOAL
Portuguese	SAUDE
Roman	BENE VOBIS
Scottish	SLAINTE MHATH
South African	GELUK, GESONDHEID
Spanish	SALUD
Swedish	SKAL
Welsh	IECHYD DA
toes	
1-toed	MONDACTYLOUS
2-toed	DIDACTYLOUS
3-toed	TRIDACTYLOUS
4-toed	TETRADACTYLOUS
5-toed	PENTADACTYLOUS
6-toed	HEXADACTYLOUS
even-toed	ARTIODACTYLOUS
many-toed	POLYDACTYLOUS
Togo	TG
Tonga	
capital	NUKU'ALOFA
coin	
—unit	SENITI
—100 seniti	PA'ANGA

tools

blacksmith's tools	ANVIL, DUFT, FILE
	FLATTER, FULLER, HARDY
	LEAF HAMMER, MANDREL
	PINCERS, RASP, SETT HAMMER
	SWAGE, TONGS
bricklayer's tools	BOASTER, BOLSTER
	HAWK, HOD, PLUMB-LINE
	POINTING TOOL, SPIRIT LEVEL
	TROWEL
butcher's tools	CLEAVER, KNIFE
	STEEL, SAW
carpenter's tools	ADZE, BRACE (AND BIT)
	BROACH, CHISEL, CLAMP
	FILE, GAUGE, GIMLET, GOUGE
	HAMMER, HAMMER-DRILL
	MALLET, MITRE-BOX
	PINC(H)ERS, PLANE, PLIERS
	PROTRACTOR, PUNCH
	QUANNET, RASP, REAMER, RIMER
	ROUTER, RULE(R), SAW, SCORPER
	SCRAPER, SCREWDRIVER, SCRIBER
	SET SQUARE, SHAPER
	SHOOTING BOARD
	SPIRIT LEVEL, SPOKESHAVE
	T-SQUARE
chisels	COLD CHISEL, FIRMER CHISEL
	GOUGE, MORTICE CHISEL
	MORTISE CHISEL, SCORPER
concretor	MIXER, TAMPING BOARD
	TREMIE, TROWEL
	VIBRATOR
contractor's plant	BACKHOE
	CONCRETE MIXER, DIGGER
	DRAGLINE, DUMPER
	EXCAVATOR, HIMAC
	JACK HAMMER
	JCB, PILEDRIVER, ROAD DRILL
	ROLLER, SCAFFOLD(ING)
	(TOWER-)CRANE, TREMIE
	VIBRATOR
cultivating	(CHAIN) HARROW
	DISC HARROW
	MUCKSPREADER, PLOUGH
	ROTAVATOR, ROTOVATOR
	SCUFFLER, SEED-DRILL
digging	CROW-BAR, FORK, LOY
	MATTOCK, PICKAXE
	SPADE, TROWEL
drilling	AUGER, (BRAD-)AWL
	BRACE AND BIT, BROACH
	COUNTERSINK BIT, GIMLET
	REAMER, SHELL DRILL
	TWIST DRILL, WIMBLE
engraving tool	BURIN
enlarging tool	FRAISE, REAMER, RIMER

excavator	BONING ROD
	JACK HAMMER, PICK(-AXE)
	PNEUMATIC DRILL, SHOVEL
	SIGHT RAIL, SPADE
file	
—mounted like a plane	QUANNET
—with curved ends	RIFFLER
garden tools	BESOM, DIBBER, DIBBLE
	DRAW HOE, DUTCH HOE, EDGING TOOL
	FORK, PRUNER, RAKE, SECATEURS
	SHEARS, SPADE, TROWEL
glazier	(*see* painter *below*)
gouging chisel	SCORPER
grass-cutting	CLIPPERS
	(CYLINDER-)MOWER, (EDGINS-)SHEARS
	FLAIL-MOWER, FLYMO, GANG-MOWER
	HOVER MOWER, ROTARY MOWER
	SCYTHE, SICKLE, STRIMMER
grooving tool	ROUTER
hammers etc	BALL-PANE HAMMER
	BALL-PEIN HAMMER
	BEETLE, CLAW HAMMER
	CROSS-PEIN HAMMER
	KNAPPING HAMMER
	LUMP HAMMER, MADGE
	MALLET, SCABBLING HAMMER
	SLEDGE HAMMER, TACK HAMMER
	WALLER'S HAMMER
harvesting	BALE FORK, BINDER
	(COMBINE) HARVESTER
	FLAIL, HAY-FORK
	HAY-KNIFE, PITCHFORK, RAKE
	TEDDER, THRESHING MACHINE
hedge-cutting	AXE, BILLHOOK
	HATCHET, SLASHER
hide scraper	SLATER
locksmith	OUSTITI, OUTSIDERS
	SKELETON KEY
mason	CHISEL, DRAG COMB
	MALLET, SCABBLING HAMMER
	WALLER'S HAMMER
metal-working	CALLIPERS, DIE, DRILL
	FILE, HAMMER, HAMMER DRILL
	MOLE GRIP, PINC(H)ERS
	PLIERS, PUNCH, REAMER
	RIMER, RASP, SHEARS, SPANNER
	SWAGE, TAP, TIN SNIPS, WRENCH
narrow spade	LOY
painter and glazier	BUCKET
	DISTEMPER BRUSH
	PAINT BRUSH
	PAPERHANGER'S BRUSH
	PASTE TABLE, PLUMB BOB
	PUTTY KNIFE, SCISSORS
	SCRAPER, SPIRIT LEVEL
	STRAIGHT-EDGE, TACK HAMMER

planes	BADGER PLANE
	BENCH PLANE, BLOCK PLANE
	FILLISTER(PLANE)
	GROOVING PLANE, JACK PLANE
	MOULDING PLANE, RABBIT PLANE
	REBATE PLANE, SMOOTHING PLANE
	TONGUING PLANE
plasterer's tools	HAWK, LARRY
	MOULDING TOOL, PLUMB-LINE
	SIEVE, SPIRIT-LEVEL, TROWEL
printer's tool	SHOOTING-STICK
pulverising tool	MULLER
saws	BACK SAW, BAND SAW, BOW SAW
	CHAIN SAW, CIRCULAR SAW
	COMPASS SAW, COPING SAW
	CROSSCUT SAW, FLOORING SAW
	FRET SAW, HACK SAW, HAND SAW
	JIG SAW, KEYHOLE SAW
	PANEL SAW, PIT SAW, RIP SAW
	SCROLL SAW, TENON SAW
sculptor's tools	BOASTER, BOLSTER
	BOUCHARDE, CHISEL
	FILE, MALLET, RIFFLER
shipwright's tool	CAULKING IRON
shovel	MAIN
slater's tools	RIPPER, SAX, ZAX
spade	
—narrow	LOY
—Scottish	CAS CROM, CASCHROM
—turf-cutting	SLANE
spanners etc	ADJUSTABLE SPANNER
	ALLENBY TOOL, BOX SPANNER
	MOLE GRIP, RING SPANNER
	SOCKET SPANNER
	STILLSON (WRENCH)
	STRAP WRENCH, TORQUE WRENCH
thatching	EAVES HOOK, EAVES KNIFE
	REED KNIFE, REED LEGGETT
	SHEARING HOOK, SPAR HOOK
	STRAW RAKE, YOKE
watchmaker's tool	FRAISE
wheelwright's tools	AUGER
	BOXING ENGINE, BRUZZ
	JARVIS, SAMSON, SPOKESHAVE
	TRAVELLER
woodturner's chisel	BRUZZE

trade

trademark	TM
trade name	TN
Trade Union	TU
Trade Union Congress	TUC

treatment

by/of/with:

acting out one's problems	PSYCHODRAMA
acupressure	SHIATSU
acupuncture	STYLOSTIXIS

animals	ZOOTHERAPY
antigens	IMMUNOTHERAPY
association with	
unpleasant thoughts	AVERSION THERAPY
auto-suggestion	COUEISM
balanced diet	MACROBIOTICS
bladder diseases	UROLOGY
blood	
—disorders	HAEMATOLOGY
—serum	SEROTHERAPY
bodily reflexes	REFLEXOLOGY
body-energy radiated	
as colours	COLOUR THERAPY
bone and muscle disorders	ORTHOPAEDICS
burning herbs	MOXIBUSTION
chemicals	CHEMOTHERAPY
children's diseases	PAEDIATRICS
climatic environment	CLIMATOTHERAPY
combining chemicals	CHELATION THERAPY
control by electronic	
monitoring	BIOFEEDBACK
crafts or hobbies	OCCUPATIONAL THERAPY
crystals	CRYSTAL THERAPY
deafness in babies	NATURAL AURALISM
deep	
—massage	ROLFING
—X-rays etc	DEEP THERAPY
defective eyesight	ORTHOPTICS
deformities in children	ORTHOP(A)EDICS
	ORTHOP(A)EDY
	ORTHOP(A)EDIA)
diet	
—exercise, etc	POLAR THERAPY
—meditation, etc	AYURVEDA
diseases	THERAPEUTICS
—or injury of bones	ORTHOP(A)EDICS
	ORTHOP(A)EDY
	ORTHOP(A)EDIA
disturbed children	ORTHOGENICS
drawing metal bars over	
affected parts	TRACTORATION
drug-induced sleep	NARCOTHERAPY
drugs	
—having opposite	
effects to symptoms	ALLOPATHY
	HOM(O)EOPATHY
—in small doses	HOM(O)EOPTAHY
electric shocks	AVERSION THERAPY, ECT
	ELECTRO-CONVULSIVE THERAPY
	SHOCK THERAPY
electricity	ELECTROLOGY
	ELECTRO-THERAPEUTICS
	ELECTRO-THERAPY
essential oils	AROMATHERAPY
exercise	PHYSIOTHERAPY
exposing subconscious	PSYCHOANALYSIS

extracts from animal		needles	ACUPUNCTURE
organs	OPOTHERAPY		STYLOSTIXIS
	ORGANOTHERAPY	nervous system	NEUROLOGY
extreme cold	CRYOTHERAPY	neurosis	BEHAVIOUR THERAPY
eye muscles	ORTHOPTICS	own blood	
faulty position of		cells	ADOPTIVE IMMUNOTHERAPY
teeth	ORTHODONTICS	pendulums	RADIESTHESIA
feet	CHIROPODY, PEDICURE	plant extracts	HERBALISM
	PODIATRY	pleasant mental images	IMAGING
finger pressure	ACUPRESSURE, SHIATSU	posture	ALEXANDER TECHNIQUE
foot massage	REFLEXOLOGY	psyche	RADIONICS, PSIONICS
	ZONE THERAPY	psychosomatic	
hands and nails	MANICURE	disorders	DIANETICS
heat from electric		radiation	RADIOTHERAPEUTICS
currents	DIATHERMY		RADIOTHERAPY
herbs	HERBALISM	radium	CURIETHERAPY
high		'reliving' early years	PRIMAL THERAPY
—body temperature	PYRETOTHERAPY	rhythmic	
—pressure	HYPERBARIC TREATMENT	exercise	CURATIVE EUR(H)YTHMICS
Hindu	AYURVEDA	salts of gold	CHRYSOTHERAPY
homeopathy treating		skin	DERMATOLOGY
chemical imbalance	BIOCHEMICS	small doses of drugs	HOM(O)EOPATHY
hypnosis etc	HYPNOTHERAPY	spinal manipulation	CHIROPRACTIC
	PSYCHOTHERAPEUTICS	spiritual	CHANNELLING
	PSYCHOTHERAPY		FAITH HEALING
illumination in		stylostixis	ACUPUNCTURE
colour	COLOUR THERAPY	Sun	HELIOTHERAPY
Indian (yoga)	AYURVEDIC MEDICINE	sweet-smelling oils	AROMATHERAPY
	STRUCTURAL INTEGRATION	tree chemicals	FORESTRY THERAPY
induced current	FARADISM	ultra-violet rays	ACTINOTHERAPY
ionised air	NEGATIVE ION THERAPY	unpleasant stimuli	AVERSION THERAPY
interferon	CYTOKINE TREATMENT	vitamins	MEGAVITAMIN TREATMENT
light	PHOTOTHERAPEUTICS	water	HYDROPATHY
	PHOTOTHERAPY		HYDROTHERAPEUTICS
low temperatures	CRYOTHERAPY		HYDROTHERAPY
manipulation	CHIROPRACTIC	women's diseases	GYNAECOLOGY
	OSTEOPATHY	X-rays	RADIOTHERAPEUTICS
many different drugs	POLYPHARMACY		RADIOTHERAPY
massage	OSTEOPATHY	**treaty**	ASSIENTO
	PHYSIOTHERAPEUTICS	America/England	ASHBURTON, JAY
	PHYSIOTHERAPY, ROLFING	anti-nuclear	RORATONGA
medicines introduced		anti Warsaw Pact	ATLANTIC TREATY
by electricity	CATAPHORESIS		BAGHDAD PACT
	ELECTROPHORESIS		BRUSSELS TREATY
meditation	TM	Austria/England	VIENNA
	TRANSCENDENTAL MEDITATION	/France	ARRAS, LUNEVILLE
mental illness	ORTHOPSYCHIATRY		VERSAILLES
	PSYCHODRAMA	/France/England	VERSAILLES
	PSYCHOTHERAPEUTICS	/France/Prussia	DRESDEN
	PSYCHOTHERAPY	/Prussia	BRESLAU
monitoring responses	BIOFEEDBACK	/Turkey	PASSAROWITZ
Moslem	UNANI		ZSITVA TOROK
movement	KINESIPATHY	Britain/Austria	ST GERMAIN
	KINESITHERAPY	/France	AIX-LA-CHAPELLE
mud baths	PELOTHERAPY	/Germany	NEVILLY, VERSAILLES
natural processes	NATUROPATHY	/Hungary	TRIANON

/Italy	LONDON TREATY	apple	PYRUS
	ST JEAN DE MAURIENNE	Araucaria	CHILE(AN) PINE
/Malaya	YANDABU		MONKEY-PUZZLE
/Maoris	WAITANGI	arbor vitae	THUJA, THUYA, TREE OF LIFE
/Russia	NYSTAD	Arbutus	STRAWBERRY-TREE
/South Africa	COLENSO	Aria	WHITEBEAM
	VEREENIGING	Arundinaria	BAMBOO
/Turkey	SEVRES	ash	FRAXINUS
	(see also England below)	—sapling	GROUND-ASH
Burgundy/France	ARRAS	aspen	ABELE, POPULUS
	CENTO, BAGHDAD PACT		TREMBLING POPLAR
Communist bloc	WARSAW PACT	Aucuba	JAPANESE LAUREL
Denmark/England	WEDMORE	Aucuparia	MOUNTAIN ASH
England/China	NANKING	balsam poplar	TACAMAHAC
/France	AMIENS, BASSEIN, CALAIS	bamboo	ARUNDINARIA
	CHATEAU CAMBRESIS	baobab	ADANSONIA
	CHAUMONT, DOVER, GHENT	Barbados cedar	JUNIPER
	LOCARNO, PARIS	bastard cedar	CEDRELA
	TROYES, UTRECHT	bay	LAUREL
/France/Holland	BARRIER	beech	FAGUS
/France/Russia	HANOVER	Betula	BIRCH
/France/Spain	SEVILLE	birch	BETULA, BIRK
/Ireland	KILMAINHAM	bird-cherry	HACKBERRY, HAGBERRY
/Russia	PARIS	bitter oak	CERRIS
/Scotland	EDINBURGH	black	
France/Holland	NIMWEGEN	—larch	AMERICAN LARCH, TAMARACK
/Prussia	BASEL	—mulberry	MORUS
/Russia	TILSIT	—thorn	SLOE
/Spain	CAMBRAI, PYRENNEES	box	BUXUS
Germany/Romania	BUCHAREST	Buxus	BOX
/Russia	BREST-LITOVSK	Brazil-wood	SAP(P)IAN
Greece/Rome	PHOENICE	buckthorn	JUJUBE
Italy/Spain	BARCELONA	Carpinus	HORNBEAM
	NATO, ATLANTIC TREATY	cashew-tree	ACAJOU
Rome/Syria	APAMEA	Castanea	CHESTNUT
Russia/Turkey	ADRIANOPLE	Casuarina	SWAMP-OAK
slave treaty	ASSIENTO	cedar	CEDRUS, DEODAR
trees[1]		—gum	EUCALYPTUS
including: species		Cedrela	RED CEDAR
Abele	ASPEN, POPLAR	Celtis	NETTLE-TREE
Abies	FIR	Cercis	JUDAS TREE, REDBUD
acacia	WATTLE	Cerris	BITTER OAK
acajou	CASHEW-TREE	chestnut	CASTANEA
Adansonia	BAOBAB	Chile(an) pine	ARAUCARIA
alder	ALNUS		MONKEY-PUZZLE
almond	AMYGDALUS	Chinese Dove tree	DAVIDIA
Aesculus	HORSE-CHESTNUT	classification	
amboyna	WALAN	—alder	BETULACEAE
Amelanchier	JUNE-BERRY, SHADBUSH	—ash	OLEACEAE
	SNOWY MESPILUS	—Austrian pine	PINACEAE
American		—bay	LAURACEAE
—larch	BLACK LARCH, TAMARACK	—beech	FAGACEAE
—willow	PUSSY WILLOW	—birch	BETULACEAE
Amur cork tree	PHELLODENDRON	—bird cherry	ROSACEAE
Antarctic beech	NOTHOFAGUS	—blackthorn	ROSACEAE
Antiar	UPAS	—box	BUXACEAE

—buckthorn	RHAMNACEAE	Conium	HEMLOCK
—bullace	ROSACEAE	conker-tree	HORSE CHESTNUT
—cedar of Lebanon	PINACEAE	cornelian cherry	CORNEL, CORNUS
—Chile(an) pine	PINACEAE	Corylus	HAZEL
—cornel	CORNACEAE	cottonwood	POPULUS
—crab	ROSACEAE	cowrie pine	COWDIE, KAURI
—deodar	PINACEAE	crab	MALUS
—dogwood	CORNACEAE	Crataegus	HAWTHORN
—Douglas fir	PINACEAE	Cydonia	QUINCE
—elder	CAPRIFOLIACEAE	cypress	CUPRESSUS
—elm	ULMACEAE	damson	DAMASK-PLUM
—gean	ROSACEAE	Davidia	CHINESE DOVE TREE
—guelder rose	CAPRIFOLIACEAE		GHOST TREE
—hawthorn	ROSACEAE		HANDKERCHIEF TREE
—hazel	BETULACEAE	deodar	HIMALAYAN CEDAR
—holly	AQUIFOLIACEAE	dogwood	CORNEL(IAN), CORNUS
—hornbeam	BETULACEAE		PRICKWOOD
—horse chestnut	HIPPOCASTANACEAE	Douglas fir	PSEUDOTSUGA
—Indian cedar	PINACEAE	dragon-tree	DRACAENA
—juniper	PINACEAE	dwarfed	BONSAI
—laburnum	LEGUMINOSAE	elm	ULMUS
—larch	PINACEAE	—rock	WAHOO
—Lawson's cypress	PINACEAE	—winged	WAHOO
—lime	TILIACLEAE	Eucalyptus	CIDER GUM
—locust tree	LEGUMINOSAE	evergreen oak	HOLM-OAK
—magnolia	MAGNOLIACEAE	exudes	
—maple	ACERACEAE	—latex	MILKWOOD
—medlar	ROSACEAE	—sugar	ALHAGI, MANNA-ASH
—monkey-puzzle tree	PINACEAE		MANNA-LARCH, TAMARISK
—mountain ash	ROSACEAE	false acacia	LOCUST-TREE, ROBINIA
—oak	FAGACEAE	fir	ABIES
—plane	PLATANACEAE	—with white marked	
—poplar	SALICACEAE	needles	SILVER-FIR
—rowan	ROSACEAE	forest tree	DRYAD
—Scots pine	PINACEAE	fustet	YOUNG FUSTIC
—service tree	ROSACEAE	ghost tree	DAVIDIA
—silver fir	PINACEAE	golden rain	LABURNUM
—sloe	ROSACEAE	great sallow	GOAT-SALLOW, GOAT-WILLOW
—spindle-tree	CELASTRACEAE	gum	SAPOTA
—spruce fir	PINACEAE	handkerchief tree	DAVIDIA
—stone pine	PINACEAE	horse-chestnut	AESCULUS, CONKER TREE
—strawberry tree	ERICACEAE		HIPPOCANASTACEAE
—sweet chestnut	FAGACEAE	hawthorn	CRATAEGUS, THORN-TREE
—sycamore	ACERACEAE		WHITETHORN
—tulip tree	MAGNOLIACEAE	hazel	CORYLUS
—walnut	JUGLANDACEAE	hemlock	CONIUM
—wayfaring tree	CAPRIFOLIACEAE	Himalayan cedar	DEODAR
—whitebeam	ROSACEAE	holly	ILEX
—wild		holm-oak	HOLLY-OAK, ILEX
apple	ROSACEAE	hop hornbeam	OSTRYA
cherry	ROSACEAE	hornbeam·	BETULA, CARPINUS,
pear	ROSACEAE		WITCH-HAZEL
plum	ROSACEAE	incense cedar	LIBOCEDRUS
—willow	SALICACEAE	Japanese laurel	AUCUBA
—yew	TAXACEAE	Judas tree	CERCIS, REDBUD
cluster-pine	PINASTER	jujube-tree	ZIZYPHUS

June-berry	AMELANCHIER, SHADBUSH
juniper	BARBADOS CEDAR, JUNIPERUS
	PENCIL-CEDAR, SAVIN(E)
Kauri pine	COWDIE, COWRIE
laburnum	GOLDEN RAIN
larch	LARIX
Larix	LARCH
lentisk	MASTIC(H)
Librocedrus	INCENSE CEDAR
lilac	SYRINGA
lime	LIND(EN), TEIL, TILIA
linden	LIME, TEIL, TILIA
liquidambar	SWEET GUM
Liriodendron	TULIP-TREE
locust	ALGAR(R)OBA, ALGARROBO
	CAROB, ROBINIA
magnolia	UMBRELLA-TREE
maidenhair	GINGKO, GINKGO
Malus	CRAB
maple	ACER, MASTEL
mastic(h)	LENTISK
medlar	MESPILUS
Mespilus	MEDLAR
mesquite	ALGAR(R)OBA, ALGARROBO
miniature	BONSAI
monkey-puzzle	ARAUCARIA
	CHILE(AN) PINE
Morus	BLACK MULBERRY
mountain-ash	QUICKEN (TREE)
	QUICK-BEAM, RODDIN, ROWAN
	SORB(IN), SORBUS, WICKEN
	WICKY, WITCHEN
mulberry	SYCAMINE
—fig	SYCAMORE, SYCOMORE
nettle-tree	CELTIS, HOOP-ASH
Nothofagus	ANTARCTIC BEECH
nut-pine	STONE-PINE
oak	DURMAST, QUERCUS
—sapling	GROUND-OAK
oil-palm	ELAEIS
oldest species	BRISTLE CONE PINE
osier	SALIX, SALLOW, WILLOW
	WIDDY, WITHE, WITHY
Ostrya	HOP HORNBEAM
pagoda-tree	SOPHORA
palm	(see separate entry)
palmetto	SABAL
Pandanus	SCREW-PINE
papaw	CARICA, PAPAYA
pear	PYRUS
Phellodendron	AMUR CORK TREE
Picea	FIR, (NORWAY) SPRUCE
pinaster	CLUSTER-PINE
Pinus	(SCOTS) PINE
pitch-tree	AMBOINA, KAURI PINE
	SILVER FIR, SPRUCE
plane	BUTTONWOOD, MAPLE
	PLATAN(E), PLATANUS
poplar	ABELE, ASP(EN), POPULUS
Populus	ASPEN, COTTONWOOD, POPLAR
prickly ash	TOOTHACHE TREE
prickwood	DOGWOOD
Pseudotsuga	DOUGLAS FIR
Pterocarya	WING NUT
Pyrus	APPLE, PEAR, WHITEBEAM
Quercus	OAK
quince	CYDONIA
red	
—cedar	CEDRELA, VIRGINIAN JUNIPER
—gum	EUCALYPTUS
—pine	NORWAY PINE
—wood	SEQUOIA, WELLINGTONIA
Rhus	SMOKE-BUSH, SMOKE-TREE
	SUMACH
Robinia	LOCUST-TREE, FALSE ACACIA
rock elm	WAHOO
rowan	SORBUS, MOUNTAIN-ASH
—like	SERVICE
Sabal	PALMETTO
sacred	BO(DHI)
Salix	SALLOW, WILLOW
sallow	SALIX, WILLOW
sambuca	ELDER
Sapota	GUM
savin(e)	JUNIPER
screw-pine	PANDANUS
Sequoia	MAMMOTH-TREE, REDWOOD
	WASHINGTONIA, WELLINGTONIA
service tree	SORB
shadbush	AMELANCHIER, JUNE-BERRY
Siberian cedar	AROLLA
silk-cotton tree	ERIODENDRON
sloe	BLACKTHORN
smoke-tree	RHUS, SUMACH
Snowy Mespilus	AMELANCHIER
Sophora	PAGODA-TREE
sorbus	MOUNTAIN-ASH, WHITEBEAM
Spanish oak	ROBLE
spindle-tree	EUONYMUS, PRICKWOOD
spruce	PICEA
—fir	PICEA
stone-pine	NUT-PINE
strawberry-tree	ARBUTUS
sumach	RHUS, SMOKE-BUSH
	SMOKE-TREE
swamp	
—cypress	TAXODIUM
—oak	CASUARINA
sweet gum	LIQUIDAMBAR
Swiss stone pine	AROLLA, CEMBRA
sycamine	MULBERRY-TREE
sycamore	ACER, PLANE, MULBERRY-FIG

Syringa	LILAC
tacamahac	BALSAM POPLAR
tallow-tree	ALEURITES, PENTADESMA
	SAPIUM
tamarack	BLACK LARCH
	AMERICAN LARCH
Taxodium	SWAMP-CYPRESS
Taxus	YEW
teil	LIME, LINDEN
terebinth	TURPENTINE-TREE
thorntree	HAWTHORN
Thuja	ARBOR VITAE, THUYA
	TREE OF LIFE
Tilia	LIME, LINDEN
toothache tree	PRICKLY-ASH
tree of	
—heaven	AILANTO
—life	ARBOR VITAE, THUJA, THUYA
trembling poplar	ASPEN
tulip-tree	LIRIODENDRON
Turkey oak	CERRIS
turpentine-tree	TEREBINTH
Ulmus	ELM
umbrella-tree	ELKWOOD, MAGNOLIA
upas	ANTIAR
Venetian sumach	FUSTET
Viburnum	WAYFARING-TREE
Virginian juniper	RED CEDAR
Vitex	AGNUS CASTUS
walan	AMBOYNA
walnut	JUGLANS
Washingtonia	REDWOOD, SEQUIOA
wattle	ACACIA
wax-tree	JAPANESE SUMAC
	WAX-MYRTLE
wayfaring tree	MEAL-TREE, VIBURNUM
Wellingtonia	REDWOOD, SEQUIOA
whitebeam	ARIA, SORBUS, PYRUS
whitethorn	HAWTHORN
wild	
—apple	CRAB
—cherry	GEAN
willow	OSIER, SALIX, SALLOW
	WIDDY, WITHE, WITHY
wing nut	PTEROCARYA
winged elm	WAHOO
witch-hazel	HORNBEAM, WYCH-ELM
with crown cut off	POLLARD
wych-elm	SCOTCH ELM, WITCH-ELM
	WITCHEN, WITCH-HAZEL
yew	TAXUS
Zizyphus	JUJUBE-TREE
trees[2]	ARBOR
including: relating to terms	
stem of tree	CAUDEX, TRUNK

tree-carving	DENDROGLYPH
tree cultivation	ARBORICULTURE
	SILVICULTURE
tree-dweller	SILVAN
tree dwelling	ARBOREAL
tree garden	ARBORETUM
tree growth of region	SILVA
tree-like growth	ARBORESCENCE
tree-measuring instrument	DENDROMETER
tree-planting day	ARBOR DAY
tree-worship	DENDROLATRY
Trinidad and Tobago	TT
capital	PORT OF SPAIN
coin	CENT, DOLLAR
trophy	
acting	(*see* theatre *below*)
agricultural machinery	BURKE TROPHY
air	
—race	KING'S CUP
—speed record	SCHNEIDER TROPHY
American football	LOMBARDI TROPHY
	SUPERBOWL TROPHY
athletics	
	JESSE OWENS INTERNATIONAL TROPHY
Atlantic crossing	BLUE RIBAND
	HALE TROPHY
	VIRGIN ATLANTIC CHALLENGE TROPHY
arts	PRAEMIUM IMPERIALE
Australian football	PREMIERSHIP CUP
badminton	
—ladies	UBER CUP
—men	THOMAS CUP
baseball	CY YOUNG AWARD
bowls	MIDDLETON CUP, WALKER CUP
	WATERLOO CUP
boxing	LONSDALE BELT
broomball	TAITTINGER TROPHY
chemistry	NOBEL PRIZE
college football	HEISMAN TROPHY
cookery	GLENFIDDITCH AWARD
coursing	WATERLOO CUP
cricket	
—Australia	GILLETTE CUP
	MCDONALD'S CUP
	SHEFFIELD SHIELD
	SHELL TROPHY
v West Indies	FRANK WORRELL TROPHY
—England	
v Australia	ASHES
v West Indies	WISDEN TROPHY
—county matches	GILLETTE CUP
	NATWEST TROPHY
—fastest century	LAWRENCE TROPHY
—India	DEODHAR TROPHY
	DULEEP TROPHY
	MOIN-UD-DOWLAH GOLD CUP

	NEHRU TROPHY, RANJI TROPHY
	WILLS TROPHY
v Sri Lanka	GOPLANAN TROPHY
—New Zealand	PLUNKET SHIELD
—Pakistan	QUAID-E-AZAM TROPHY
	WILLS CUP
—South Africa	CASTLE BOWL, CURRIE CUP
	NISSAN SHIELD
—West Indies	SHELL SHIELD
croquet	MACROBERTSON SHIELD
	PRESIDENT'S CUP
curling	STRATHCONA CUP
cycling	BIDLAKE PLAQUE
	SAUNDERS TROPHY
darts	BRITISH GOLD CUP
	NATIONS CUP
debating	SILVER QUAICH
fashion design	GOLDEN THIMBLE
films	
—American	OSCAR
—British	BAFTA AWARD
—European	FELIX
—French	CAESAR
—international	PALME D'OR
—TV and cinema	GOLDEN GLOBE AWARD
—Venice	GOLDEN LION
football	
—Footballer of the Year	BALLON D'OR
—highest scorer	GOLDEN BOOT AWARD
—World Cup	JULES RIMET TROPHY
golf	CANADA CUP, CURTIS CUP
	HARRY VARDON TROPHY
	HOPMAN CUP, MURPHY'S CUP
	RYDER CUP, VAGLIANO TROPHY
	WALKER CUP, WORLD CUP
greyhound racing	SCURRY GOLD CUP
hockey	INTERCONTINENTAL CUP
horse-racing	
—Australia	MELBOURNE CUP
—England	ASCOT GOLD CUP
	CHELTENHAM GOLD CUP
	CORONATION CUP, GOODWOOD CUP
	ONE THOUSAND GUINEAS
	TWO THOUSAND GUINEAS
—France	CHALLENGE D'OR PIAGET
	GRAND PRIX DE DEAUVILLE
	PRIX JACQUES LE MAROIS
	PRIX KERGORLAY
	PRIX MAURICE GHEEST
	PRIX MORNY
	PRIX STAVROS NIARCHOS
—Ireland	GALLOWAY PLATE
ice hockey	CANADA CUP, HART TROPHY
	JAMES NORRIS TROPHY
	ROSS TROPHY, STANLEY CUP
jazz	BIRD PRIZE

jargon	GOLDEN BULL AWARD
literature	BOOKER PRIZE
	WHITBREAD PRIZE
—Britain	BRITISH BOOK AWARD, NIBBIE
—crime stories	DIAMOND DAGGER AWARD
	GOLD DAGGER AWARD
—economics	FISHER PRIZE
—fiction	HIGHAM AWARD
	PULITZER PRIZE
—first novel	BETTY TRASK AWARD
over 40	MCKITTRICK PRIZE
over 60	SAGITTARIUS PRIZE
—international	NOBEL PRIZE
—non-fiction	SILVER PEN AWARD
—science-fiction	HUGO AWARD
	NEBULA AWARD
—USA	NATIONAL BOOK AWARD
	PULITZER PRIZE, TURNER AWARD
medicine and	
psychology	NOBEL PRIZE
moto-cross	COUPE DES NATIONS
motor-cycle racing	TOURIST TROPHY
	EUROLANTIC TROPHY
motor racing	BRITISH EMPIRE TROPHY
	GORDON BENNETT TROPHY
	ULSTER TROPHY
	VANDERBILT CUP
musical composition	BRITTEN TROPHY
newspaper reporting	PULITZER
officialese	GOLDEN BULL AWARD
painting	TURNER PRIZE
peace	NOBEL PRIZE
physics	NOBEL PRIZE
play	SAMUEL BECKETT AWARD
polo	ABERA TROPHY, CARTIER GOLD CUP
	CHAMPION CUP, CHELTENHAM CUP
	CICERO CUP, COWDRAY PAR
	GOLD CUP, CUP OF THE AMERICAS
	DAVIDOFF GOLD CUP, DOLLAR CUP
	DUKE OF SUTHERLAND'S CUP
	HORSE AND HOUND CUP
	PRINCE OF WALES TROPHY
	POLO TROPHY, QUEEN'S CUP
	RALPH LAUREN TROPHY
	ROYAL WINDSOR CUP
	TEXACO TROPHY
	WESTCHESTER CUP
pop music	DIAMOND AWARD
powerboat racing	CETREK NEEDLES TROPHY
	HARMSWORTH TROPHY
recording	
—American	GRAMMY
—British	BRITS AWARD
rock music	ELVIS
rowing	BRITANNIA CUP
	DIAMOND SCULLS

	DOUBLE SCULLS CHALLENGE CUP
	GRAND CHALLENGE CUP, LADIES' PLATE
	NICKALL'S CUP, PRINCE PHILIP CUP
	PRINCESS ELIZABETH CUP
	QUEEN MOTHER CUP, SILVER GOBLETS
	STEWARD'S CUP, THAMES CUP
	VISITOR'S CUP, WYFOLD CUP
Rugby League	CHALLENGE CUP
	HARRY SUNDERLAND TROPHY
	JOHN PLAYER SPECIAL TROPHY
	LANCE TOOD AWARD
	PREMIERSHIP TROPHY
	REGAL TROPHY
—Australia	WINFIELD CUP
Rugby Union	WORLD CUP
—Australia/New Zealand	BLEDISLOE CUP
—England/Scotland	CALCUTTA CUP
—New Zealand	RANFURLY SHIELD
—South Africa	CURRIE CUP
science	NOBEL PRIZE
shinty	CAMANCHD CUP
	KEYLINE MACAULAY CUP
	MACDONALD CUP
shooting	ALEXANDRA CUP, BISLEY CUP
	CONNAUGHT CUP
	DUKE OF CAMBRIDGE TROPHY
	EYRE MEMORIAL CUP
	GENERAL'S CUP, GOLDFIELD CUP
	HUTTON TANKARD
	KING GEORGE V CUP
	QUEEEN'S CUP, QUEEN'S PRIZE
	RAVEN CUP, SIMBANG CUP
	TIMES CHALLENGE CUP, TURNER CUP
	VIZIANAGRAM TROPHY
	WINAN'S CUP, WOOD CUP
	WHITGIFT CUP, WYNESS CUP
show jumping	DUBAI CUP
	KING GEORGE V GOLD CUP
	NATIONS CUP, PRESIDENT'S CUP
	QUEEN ELIZABTH II CUP
	WORLD CUP
snooker	EMBASSY CUP, POT BLACK CUP
soccer	CHARITY SHIELD
	FOOTBALL ASSOCIATION CUP
	FOOTBALL LEAGUE CUP
	FREIGHT ROVER CUP
	UEFA CUP, WORLD CUP
—amateur	FOOTBALL ASSOCIATION VASE
—South America	LIBERATORES CUP
song writing	IVOR NOVELLO AWARD
speedway racing	GOLDEN HELMET AWARD
stage	
—American	TONY
surfing	TRIPLE CROWN, WORLD CUP
table tennis	CORBILLON CUP
	SWAYTHLING CUP

tennis	DAVIS CUP, FEDERATION CUP
	NATIONS CUP, WORLD CUP
—Germany	LUFTHANSA CUP
—ladies	MAUD WATSON TROPHY
	WIGHTMAN CUP
television	BAFTA AWARD
—acting, programme,	
etc	EMMY
—advertising	GOLDEN BREAK AWARD
—science programme	SCI-TECH AWARD
theatre	IAN CHARLESON AWARD
	LARRY OLIVIER AWARD
transport	
(air, land or water)	SEGRAVE TROPHY
writing	(see literature above)
yachting	ADMIRAL'S CUP, AMERICA CUP
	ASTRID CUP, BATHSHEBA TROPHY
	BIRKETT CUP, BONES TROPHY
	BRABAZON TROPHY, BRITANNIA CUP
	CAMROSE MEMORIAL TROPHY
	CARRITT CUP, CAYLEY CUP
	CELLINE VASE
	CHAMPAGNE MUMM TROPHY
	CHISHOLM CUP
	CORONATION CHALLENGE BOWL
	CORUM TROPHY, COURTNEY TROPHY
	CREIGHTON TROPHY, DE MAAS CUP
	DOWSON TROPHY, DUNELM TROPHY
	FITZPATRICK-ROBERTSON CUP
	FREEMANTLE SALVER, GRENFELL TROPHY
	GRETTON CUP, HAYLES BOWL
	HAYLING HULL TROPHY
	HEWITT TROPHY, HYLAND TROPHY
	PAMELA SNAGGE TROPHY
	PRESTON CUP, PURDY CUP
	QUARTER-TON CUP, RATSEY CUP
	RAYMOND TROPHY, REDWING CUP
	RYS TROPHY, SOUTHERN CROSS CUP
	SUNBEAM SALVER, TOMAHAWK TROPHY
	WHITBREAD CUP

tropical

American	(see **South America**)
bean	COW(HAGE), COWITCH
	LABLAB
bird	BARBET, DRONGO(-SHRIKE)
	HONEY-EATER, HUMMING-BIRD
	JACANA, KING-CROW
	KING-VULTURE, SALAGANE
	SUN-BIRD, SWIFTLET
	TROCHILUS, TROGON
cashew-nut tree	LENTISK
climber	COCCOLUS, COW(H)AGE
	COWITCH, LIANA
dal	PIGEON-PEA
dish	DA(H)L, DHOLL
fern	DICKSONIA, ELKHORN-FERN

—genus	SCHIZAE
fever	(*see* **disease**)
fish	CHAETODON, CORAL FISH
	DANIO, SEA-SURGEON
	TRIGGERFISH
flower	ANTHURIUM
fruit	ANANA, CHINESE GOOSEBERRY
	MANGO(STAN), MANGOSTEEN
	TAMARIND
gourd	LOOFA(H), LUFFA
grass	SORGHUM
gum	KINO
herb	ZINGIBER
humming-bird	RUBY-THROAT, SABRE-WING
	SAPPHIRE-WING
	SWALLOW-TAILED BIRD
leaf-climbers	GLORIOSA
mallow	GOSSYPIUM, URENA
narcotic fruit	INDIAN BERRY
nut	BEN(-NUT)
orchid	DENDROBIUM
papyrus	CYPERUS
pigeon-pea	DA(H)L, DHOLL
plant	BATATA, BIGNONIA, CROTON
	DERRIS, HIBISCUS, FALSE PAREIRA
	LAPORTEA, SWEET-POTATO
	VELVET-LEAF, YAM
potato	YAM
resin	ELEMI
seabird	PHAETON, TROPIC-BIRD
sedge	CYPERUS
shrub	CAPSICUM
tree	CARAPA, GNETUM, MACACO
	RAUWOLFIA, TAMARIND
—anchovy-pear	LECYTHIS
—Brazil-nut	LECYTHIS
—cannon-ball tree	LECYTHIS
—dragon-tree	CORDYLINE
—erythrina	CORAL-TREE
—flamboyant	POINCIANA
—flowering	COMBRETUM
—Kigelia	SAUSAGE-TREE
—mangosteen	GARCINIA
—mahogany	CARAPA, CEDRELA
—monkey-pot	LECYTHIS
—Moringa	HORSE-RADISH TREE
—Poinciana	FLAMBOYANTE, FLAME-LEAF
	PEACOCK-FLOWER
Tunisia	TN
capital	TUNIS
coin	DINAR, MILLIME
governor	BEY
Turkey	TR
administrative official	VAIVODE
	VOIVODE, WAIVODE
admiral	CAPITAN

ambassador	ELCHEE, EL(T)CHI
armed attendant	CAVASS, KAVASS
army officer	BIMBASHI, BINBASHI
band	METHER
bath	HAMMAN, HUMM(A)UM
bay	KORFEZI
boat	PERMAGY
brazier	MANGAL
cap	MARTAGAN
cape (headland)	BUR-UN, BUR-NU
capital	ANGORA, ANKARA
carpet	CADANE
cart	AR(A)BA
castle	HISAR
cavalryman	SPAHEE, SPAHI
clotted cream	KAYMAK
coin	
—unit	KURUSH
—100 kurush	LIRA
—$^1/_{40}$ piastre	PARA
—silver	PIASTRE
obsolete	ASPER
commander	AG(H)A
—in-chief	SERASKIER
cymbal	CROTALO
dagger	ATAGHAN, YATAG(H)AN
dam	BARAJ
dancer	CENGHI
decree	FIRMAN, HATTI-SHERIF
	IRADE
division	SANJAK
dog	ANATOLIAN
drink	AIRAN, BOZA, MASTIC(H)
dulcimer	SANTIR, SANT(O)UR
dynasty	OSMANLI, OTTOMAN, SELJUK
emblem	CRESCENT
execution	GANCH
felt cap	CALPA(C)K, KALPAK
female slave	ODALISK, ODALI(S)QUE
fermented milk	YAOURT, YOGH(O)URT
feudal militiaman	TIMARIOT
filo pastry	YUFKA
flag	CRESCENT
forest	ORMANI
governor	BASHAW, BEGLERBEG
	BEY, CAIMAC(AM), KAIMAKAM
	PASHA, PACHA, VALI, WALI
grape-juice syrup	PEKMEZ
guard house	DERBEND
gulf	KORFEZI
harbour	LIMAN
harem	SERAGLIO, SERAI(L)
head of division	MUTESSARIF
headgear	FEZ
hors d'oeuvres	HUMMUS, MEZE
hot drink	SALEP

ice cream	KAYMAK, SALEP	porter	HAM(M)AL
imperial government	PORTE	power	CRESCENT
infidel	GIAOUR	prime minister	GRAND VIZIER
inn	CAFENET, (CARAVAN)SERAI	property dedicated to God	WAQ'F
	KHAN	province	EYALET, VILAYET
instrument	SAZ	ravioli	MANTI
irregular soldier	BASHI-BAZOUK	reform bill	TANZIMAT
island	ADASI	river	IRMAK, NEHRI
javelin	JEREED, JERID	robe	CAFTAN, DOL(L)MAN
jurisdiction of pasha	PACHALIC		KAFTAN
	PASHALIK	rug	KHILIM, KONIA
land division	SANJAK	ruler	ATABEG, ATABEK, CALIPH
lake	GOL(U)		KHAN, PADISHAH, SULTAN
language	OSMANLI, OTTOMAN	sailor	GALIONGEE
law	MULTOCA	savoury pie	BOREK
manna	TREHALA	sea	DENIZI
measures		seed paste	HUMMUS, HOUM(O)US
—25"	ENDAZE		TAHINA, TAHINI
—30"	ARSHEEN, ARSHIN(E)	servant	HAM(M)AL
—2½ acres	DJERIB	ship	CAIC, CAIQUE, PATAMAR
—1 bushel	KILEH		SAIC(K), SAIQUE
meat		smoking (hookah)	CHILLUM
—dish	CABOB, KABAB, KABOB	soldier	JANISSARY, JANIZAR(Y)
	KEBAB, KEBOB		NIZAM
—on skewer	SHISH KEBAB	standard	CRESCENT, HORSETAIL
—pizza	LAHMACUN	strait	BOGAZI
men's quarters	SELAMLIK	stream	CAYI
military		street	CADDESI
—chief	BASHAW, PACHA	stuffed	
	PASHA, ZAIM	—aubergines	IMAM BAYILDI
—district	ZIAMET	—vineleaves	DOLMA(DE
—music	JANIZARY MUSIC	sultan	GRAND SIGNIOR
milk pudding	TAVUK GOGSU	sweetmeat	BULBUL, HAL(A)VA(H)
minced lamb	CIG KOFTE		LOKUM, LOUKOUM
minister	WAZIR, WESIER	sword-bearer	SELICTAR
	VESIR, VISIER, VIZI(E)R	theologian	ULEMA
Moslem	SALAR	title	AG(H)A, BASHAW, BEG, BEY
—sect	BEKTASHI, KARMATHIAN		DEY, GHAZI, PACHA, PASHA
	MEVLEVI, (WHIRLING) DERVISH	—of respect	EFFENDI
mountain	DAG		HODJA, KHO(D)JA
—range	SILSILESI	Turk	OSMANLI, OTTAMITE
non-Moslem	RAYAH		OTTOMITE, SELJUK
officer	AG(H)A	vest	YELEK
order of knighthood	MEDJIDIE	village	KOY
orchid root drink	SALEP	vine	SOMA
palace	SERAGLIO	wagon	AR(A)BA, AROBA
—guard	BOSTANGI	walnut salad	MUHAMARRA
pass	GEDIGI	war minister	SERASKIER
pastry	KADAYIF	water-pipe	CHILLIM, HOOKA(H)
—with nuts, etc	BACLAVA, BAKLAVA		NARG(H)ILE, NARGILEH
pavilion	KIOSK		NARG(H)IL(L)Y
pipe	CHIBOUK, CHIBOUQUE	weight	
plain	OVASI	—1½ drams	MUSCAL
policeman	CAVASS, KAVASS	—2¼lb	OKE
	ZABTIEH, ZAPTIAH, ZAPTIEH	—17lb	BATMAN
port	LIMAN	—125lb	CANTAR, KANTAR, QUANTAR

—509lb	CHEKI
women's quarters	SERAGLIO, SERAIL
yoghurt soup	YAYLA CORBASI
twelve	DOZ(EN), XII
12½ cents	BIT
Apostles	ANDREW, BARTHOLEMEW, JAMES
	JAMES (brother of John), JOHN
	JUDAS, MATTHEW, PETER, PHILIP
	SIMON, THADDEUS, THOMAS
base	DUODECIMAL
Christmas presents	DRUMMERS
combining form	DODECA-
having 12	
—columns	DODECASTYLE
—faces	DODECAHEDRON
—leaves per sheet	DUODECIMO
—sides	DODECAGON
—stamens	DODECANDRIAN
	DODECANDROUS
—styles	DODECAGYNIAN
	DODECAGYNOUS
—syllables	DODECASYLLABIC
—tones	DODECAPHONIC
—yearly intervals	DUODECENNIAL
E(E)C members	BELGIUM, DENMARK
	FRANCE, GREAT BRITAIN
	GREECE, IRELAND, ITALY
	LUXEMBURG, NETHERLANDS
	PORTUGAL, SPAIN
	WEST GERMANY
fold	DUODENARY
Glorious Twelfth	AUGUST
hours	AM, PM
hundred	MCC
in Norse mythology	GODS
inches	FOOT
jobs	LABOURS OF HERCULES
men	JURY
peers of Charlemagne	DOUZEPERS, PALADIN
signs of Zodiac	(see **Zodiac**)
tables	ROMAN LAW
tribes	ISRAELITES
twelfth	DUODECIMAL, DUODENARY
twenty	SCORE, XX
combining form	ICOS(A)-
having	
—20	
faces	ICOSAHEDRONAL
stamens	ICOSANDRIAN, ICOSANDROUS
—24 faces	ICOSITETRAHEDRONAL
Twentieth Century	
Dictionary	TCD
twenty-five pounds sterling	PONY
twenty-six in Norse	
mythology	GODDESSES
twenty-seven Books	NEW TESTAMENT, NT

twenty-twenty	VISION
twenty thousand	K
two	COMPANY, PAIR, PR, TWAIN
a penny	CHEAP, TRIVIAL
alternative courses	DILEMMA
choices	DILEMMA
Christmas presents	TURTLE DOVES
cleft	BIFID, BIPARTITE
combining form	BI-, DI-
companies monopolising trade	DUOPOLY
eyed steak	KIPPER
faced	HYPOCRITICAL
—god	JANUS
fold	BINAL, DOUBLE, DUAL, DUPLEX
	DUPLICATE, TWIFOLD
for his heels	JACK, KNAVE
grooved tablet	DIGLYPH
groups	BIS, BRACE, COMPANY
	COUPLE, DOUBLE, DUAD
	DUAL, DUO, PAIR
	TWAIN, TWOSOME
having two	
—adductor muscles	DIMYARIAN
—amyl groups	DIAMYL
—ancestral groups	DIPHYLETIC
—at one birth	DITOKOUS
—atoms	DIATOMIC
—axes	DIAXIAL, DIAXON(IC)
—beats	DICROTIC
per bar	DUPLE
—branches	BIFURCATE(D), BISULCATE
	DICHOTOMOUS, DIVARICATE
	TWIFORKED, TWYFORKED
—breeding seasons p.a.	DIGONEUTIC
—bundles of stamens	DIDELPHOUS
—butyl groups	DIBUTYL
—carpels	DICARPELLARY
—cells	BICAMERAL, BILOCULAR
—chromium atoms	BICHROMATE
	DICHROMATE
—claws	DIDACTYL
—colours	DICHROM(AT)IC
—cotyledons	DICOTYLEDONOUS
—cusps	BICUSPID
—double	
refractive power	BIREFRINGENT
serrations	BISERRATE
—ears	BINAURAL
—electrodes	DIODE
—ethyl groups	DIETHYL
—eyes	BINOCULAR
—faces	BIFACIAL, DIHEDRAL
—feet	BIPED(AL)
—fibres	BINERVATE
—fingers	DIDACTYLOUS
—focal lengths	BIFOCAL

—forms	DIMORPHIC, TWIFORMED	—sets of teeth	DIPHYODONT
	TWYFORMED	—sexes	BISEXUAL
—furrows	BISULCATE	—sides	BILATERAL
—gills	DIBRANCHIATE	—sheaths	DITHECAL
—gods	DITHEISTIC	—spore cases	DITHECAL
—halves	DIMIDIATE	—stable states	BISTABLE
—hands	BIMANAL, BIMANOUS	—stamens	DIANDROUS
—heads	BICEPS, BICIPITAL	—stomachs	DIGASTRIC
	DICEPHALOUS	—styles	DIGYNIAN, DIGYNOUS
—husbands	BIGAMOUS, DIANDROUS	—sulphur atoms	BISULPHIDE, DISULPHIDE
	DIGAMOUS	—syllables	DISYLLABLE, DISYLLABIC
—hydrogen atoms	DIACID, DIBASIC	—terms	BINOMIAL
—hydroxyl groups	DIHYDRIC	—thecae	DITHECAL
—independently heritable		—threads	BIFILAR
characters	DIHYBRID	—toes	DIDACTYLOUS
—keys	BITONAL	before and two	
—languages	BIGLOT, BILINGUAL	behind	ZYGODACTYL(IC)
	DIGLOT	—types of spore	HETEROSPOROUS
—legs	BIPOD(AL)	—use of two	
—letters	BILITERAL	elements	AMPHIBIAN, AMPHIBIOUS
—lips	BILABIAL	hands	AMBIDEXT(E)ROUS
—leaflets	BIFOLIOLATE	—valencies	BIVALENT, DIATOMIC
—leaves	BIFOLIATE		DIVALENT
—lobes	BILOBAR, BILOBATE	—valves	BIVALVE, DIVALVULAR
	BILOBED, BILOBULAR	—variants	BIVARIATE, DIVARIATE
	DITHECAL	—ways	BIVIOUS
—lines	DIGRAM	—wheels	BICYCLE
—loculi	BILOCULAR, DITHECAL	—whorls	DICYCLIC
—marriages	BIGAMOUS, DIGAMOUS	of stamens	(OB)DIPLOSTEMONOUS
—measures	DIMETER	—wings	BIPLANE, DIPTERAL
—metals	BIMETALLIC		DIPTEROUS
—methyl radicals	DIMETHYL	—wives	BIGAMOUS, DIGAMOUS
—months' duration	BIMESTRIAL		DIGYNIAN, DIGYNOUS
—oxygen atoms	DIOXIDE	—wombs	DIDELPHIC
—pairs of stamens	DIDYNAMIAN	—words	BINOMIAL
	DIDYNAMOUS	—xylem strands	DIARCH
—parts	BIPARTITE, DIMEROUS	—yearly occurrences	BIANNUAL
	DIDYMOUS	—zones	BIZONAL
—perianth whorls	DI(PLO)CHLAMYDEOUS	hulled boat	CATAMARAN
—petals	BIPETALOUS	hundred	CC, H, S, SIGMA
	DIPETALOUS	—and fifty	E, K
—phenyl groups	DIPHENYL	thousand	E
—pistils	DIGYNIAN, DIGYNOUS	—thousand	H, S, SIGMA
—planes	DIHEDRAL	—years	BICENTARY, BICENTENNIAL
—points	BICUSPID(ATE)	in song	LILLYWHITE BOYS
—poles	BIPOLAR, DIPOLAR	letter word	BILITERAL
—prongs	BIDENTAL, BIDENTATE(D)	letters, one sound	DIGRAPH
	BIFURCATE(D)	men in office	DUUMVIR(RATE)
—rays	DIACT(INAL), DIACTINE	month period	BIMESTER
—rings	DICYCLIC	notes	DUPLET
—rows	BIFARIOUS, BISERIAL	one of two at a birth	TWIN
	DISTICHOUS	penny	CHEAP, WORTHLESS
—sacs	DITHECAL	performers	DUET(T), DUETTO, DUO
—sepals	DISEPALOUS	persons	COMPANY, DUO
—separate sexes	DIOECIOUS		TWOSOME
—series	BISERIAL	—ruling	DIARCHY

Scottish	TWA(E), TWAY	time	CROSS, DECEIVE
speaking	DIALOGUE	times	DUPL(ICAT)E
	DUALOGUE	under par	EAGLE
spots	DEUCE	vowels sounded as one	DIPHTHONG
stars	GEMINI	winged plane	BIPLANE
thousand	Z	**type**	(*see* **printing**)

Uganda	EAU
capital	KAMPALA
coin	CENT, SHILLING
Ulster	NI
Defence Association	UDA
Defence Regiment	UDR
Freedom Fighters	UFF
Unionists	UU
Volunteer Force	UVF
united	
United Arab Emirates	UAE
—capital	DUBAI
—coin	FILS, DIRHAM
United Arab Republic	ET, UAR
United Dominions Trust	UDT
United Free Church	UF
United Kingdom	UK
United Nations	
—Association	UNA
—(Organisation)	UNO
United Presbyterian	UP
United Press	UP
United States	US, USA
—Army	USA
—(Army) Air Force	US(A)AF
—Navy	USN
—Ship	USS
universal	
Universal Decimal Classification	UDC
universal organisation	UN
Universal Postal Union	UPU
universal set	E
Universal Time	UT
university	U, UNIV
academic dress	GOWN, MORTARBOARD
—Oxford	SUBFUSC, SUBFUSK
accounts for food	BATTELS
administrator	VICE-CHANCELLOR
	RECTOR
American	CALTECH, HARVARD, YALE
annual feast	GAUDY, RAG
at university	UP
basic degree	BACCALAUREATE
body of senior members	CONGREGATION
brochure	PROSPECTUS
built in recent years	REDBRICK
business representative	SYNDIC
class	SEMINAR, TUTORIAL

course (half-year)	SEMESTER
degree ceremony (Amer.)	COMMENCEMENT
department	FACULTY
entrance examination	MATRICULATION
expel from university	RUSTICATE
	SEND DOWN
fellow	DON
first-year student	FRESHER, FRESHMAN
food shop	BUTTERY
former student	ALUMNA, ALUMNUS
four branches of	
mathematics	QUADRIVIUM
fraternity (Amer.)	PHI BETA KAPPA
governing body	SENATE
—Scotland	SENATUS ACADEMICUS
governor (Amer.)	REGENT
graduate	ALUMNA, ALUMNUS
	BA, BSC
graduates' conference	CONVOCATION
Grants Committee	UGC
grounds	CAMPUS
higher degree	MASTER, DOCTOR
—Europe	LICENTIATE
honours examination	
—Cambridge	TRIPOS
—Oxford	GREATS, MODS
instructor	LECTURER, TUTOR
liberal arts	TRIVIUM
member	BA, DON, F, FELLOW
	MA, PROF(ESSOR)
men's club (Amer.)	FRATERNITY
non-resident student	EXTRAMURAL
official responsible for	
—ceremonies	BEADLE
—discipline	PROCTOR
—financial matters	BURSAR
—records	REGISTRAR
old American universities	IVY LEAGUE
one	
—awarded	
a degree	GRADUATE
first-class honours	
in mathematics (Camb.)	WRANGLER
—holding professorship	
created by royal grant	REGIUS PROFESSOR
—representing university	
at sport	BLUE
—studying for degree	UNDERGRADUATE
—waiting to receive degree	GRADUAND
paid leave for research	
or travel	SABBATICAL
place of those who pass	
without honours	GULF
press	CUP, OUP
principal	VICE-CHANCELLOR, RECTOR
—German	RECTOR MAGNIFICUS

proctor's assistant	
(Oxford and Cambridge)	BULLDOG
second-year student (Amer.)	SOPHOMORE
Senate committee	
—member (Camb.)	SYNDIC
senior lecturer	READER, PROFESSOR
servant	BEDDER, FAG, GYP
	SCOUT, SKIP
steward	MANCIPLE
student (Cambridge	
and Dublin)	(SUB-)SIZAR, (SUB-)SIZER
teacher	DON, LECTURER
	PROFESSOR, READER
	TUTOR
teachers' union	UAT
term	SEMESTER
the university that	
one attended	ALMA MATER
titular head of	
university	CHANCELLOR
universities	
—America	CALTECH, COLUMBIA
	DUKE, HARVARD
	PRINCETON, STANFORD, YALE
—England	ASTON, BATH, BIRMINGHAM
	BRADFORD, BRISTOL
	BRUNEL, BUCKINGHAM
	CAMBRIDGE, CITY, DURHAM
	EAST ANGLIA, ESSEX, EXETER
	HULL, KEELE, KENT, LANCASTER
	LEEDS, LEICESTER, LIVERPOOL
	LONDON, LOUGHBOROUGH

	MANCHESTER, NEWCASTLE
	NOTTINGHAM, OPEN, OXFORD
	READING, SALFORD, SHEFFIELD
	SOUTHAMPTON, SURREY, SUSSEX
	WARWICK, YORK
—France	SORBONNE
—Ireland	DUBLIN
—Japan	KOKUGAKUIN
—Northern Ireland	BELFAST
—Scotland	ABERDEEN, DUNDEE
	EDINBURGH
	GLASGOW, HERIOT-WATT
	ST ANDREWS, STIRLING
	STRATHCLYDE
—Wales	WALES
vice-chancellor's	
mace bearer	BEADLE
—(Oxford and Cambridge)	BEDELL
women's club (Amer.)	SORORITY
Uruguay	ROU, U, URU
capital	MONTE VIDEO
coin	CENTESIMO, PESO
US(A)	(*see* **America, states**)
USSR	(*see also* **Russia**)
republics of the former USSR	
—now in CIS	AZERBAIJAN, BELARUS
	GEORGIA, KAZAKHSTAN
	MOLDOVA, RUSSIA(N FEDERATION)
	TADJIKISTAN, TURKMENISTAN
	UKRAINE, UZBEKISTAN
—not in CIS	ARMENIA, ESTONIA
	LATVIA, LITHUANIA

V

Vanuatu

capital	PORT VILA
coin	CENTIME, FRANC, VATU
old name	NEW HEBRIDES

vegetable

beans	(*see* pulses)
Belgian endive	CHICORY
black salsify	SCORZONERA
Brassica	CABBAGES
bulb	GARLIC
cabbages, etc	BRASSICA
chard	LEAF BEET
chicory	BELGIAN ENDIVE
Chinese cabbage	PAKCHOI
corn etc	(*see* cereals)
courgette	ZUCCHINI
edible seaweed	LAVER, SEA LETTUCE
endive	ESCAROLE
flowers, leaves	ARTICHOKE, ASPARAGUS

BORECOLE, BROCCOLI, CABBAGE
CALABRESE, CARDOON, CAULIFLOWER
CELERY, CHARD, CHICON, CHIC(C)ORY
CHINESE CABBAGE, CHINESE LEAVES
COLE(WORT), COLLARD, CORN SALAD
COS, CURLY KALE, DWARF FENNEL
ENDIVE, FENNEL, FINNOCHIO
FINOC(C)HIO, FLORENCE FENNEL
FRENCH FENNEL, FRISE(E), GLASSWORT
GLOBE ARTICHOKE, GOOD KING HENRY
GOOSEFOOT, KALE, KAIL, KOHLRABI
, LAMB'S LETTUCE, LEAF BEET
LEEK, LETTUCE, MARSH SAMPHIRE
MUNG BEANSHOOTS, ORACH(E)
OYSTER PLANT, POKEWEED
RADICCHIO, RAMSON, RAPE, ROMAINE
SALAD BURNET, SALSAFY, SALSIFY
SAMPHIRE, SAVOY, SAXIFRAGE
SCORZONERA, SEAKALE(BEET)
SILVER BEET, SORREL
SPINACH(BEET), SPROUTING BROCCOLI
SUCCORY, SWEET FENNEL
SWISS CHARD

fresh fruit and vegetables	CRUDITES
fruit pod	AUBERGINE, BRINJAL

BREADFRUIT, BREADNUT
CAPSICUM, CHAYOTE, CHOWCHOW
CUCUMBER, CUSTARD MARROW, DOODY

EGG-PLANT, GOURD, KARELA
LADIES' FINGERS, MANGETOUT
OKRA, PIMIENTO, PEPPER
PUMPKIN, SQUASH, SUGAR PEA
TOMATO, ZUCCHINI
(*see also* fruit, pulses)

Good King Henry	GOOSEFOOT
ladies's fingers	OKRA
leaf beet	CHARD
leafy vegetables	GREENS, POTHERB
—America	POKEWEED
leek	ROCAMBOLE, SCALLION
mushroom	(*see* fungus)
okra	LADIES' FINGERS
oyster plant	SALSIFY
	VEGETABLE OYSTER
peas	(*see* pulses)
potatoes	ARRAN PILOT, ASPERGES

BELLE DE FONTENAY, BRODICK
BINTJE, CARA, CARLINGFORD, CATRIONA
CHARLOTTE, CORNICHON, DESIREE
DUKE OF YORK, ELVIRA, EPICURE
ESTIMA, FOREMOST, FRENCH CHARLOTTE
HOMEGUARD, JERSEY MIDS
KING EDWARD, LA RATTE, MAJESTIC
MARFONA, MARIS PEER, MARIS PIPER
PENTA, PENTLAND DELL
PENTLAND JAVELIN
PENTLAND SQUIRE, PINK FIR APPLE
RECORD, ROMANO, SHARPES EXPRESS
ULSTER CHIEFTAIN, WILJA

—American	RUSSET BURBANK
—Irish	MURPHY, PRATIE
—Scottish	TATTIE, TATTY
—slang	SPUD
pulses	(*see separate entry*)
rocambole	LEEK
root	AHIPA, ARTICHOKE, BEETROOT

CARROT, CASSAVA, CELERIAC
CHINESE WATER-CHESTNUT
COCOYAM, DASHEEN, EARTHNUT
EDDO, FINNOCHIO, FLORENCE FENNEL
JERUSALEM ARTICHOKE
MANDIOC(C)(A), MANI(H)OC
MANIHOT, MOOLI, OCA, ONION
SALEP, SALOOP, SCALLION
SHALLOT, PARSNIP
PIGNUT, POTATO, RUTABAGA
SUGAR BEET, SWEDE, SWEET POTATO
TARO, TURNIP, YAM

salad	ALEXANDERS, CABBAGE LETTUCE

CELERY
CHICORY, CHINESE LETTUCE
CHIVE, COS LETTUCE, CRESS
CUCUMBER, ENDIVE, ESCAROLE
ONION, RADISH, RAMPION, PEPPER

	SPRING ONION, TOMATO
	WATERCRESS, YARROW
salsify	OYSTER PLANT
	VEGETABLE OYSTER
scallion	LEEK, SPRING ONION
scorzonera	BLACK SALSIFY
sedge tuber	WATER CHESTNUT
spring onion	SCALLION
squashes	ACORN, BUTTERBALL
	BUTTERCUP, BUTTERNUT, CALABAZA
	CHRISTOPHINE, COURGETTE
	CUSTARD, DELICATA
	GEL REUZIN, GOLDEN DELICIOUS
	GOLDEN NUGGET, GREEN DELICA
	HOKAIDO, KARELA, KOBOCHE
	LITTLE APPLE, LITTLE GEM
	ONION, PATTYPAN, PUMPKIN
	RED KURI, SCALLOP, SPAGHETTI
	SWEET DUMPLING, SWEET POTATO
	TABLE QUEEN, TURBAN
	(VEGETABLE) MARROW, ZAPALLO
sweet	
—potato	YAM
New Zealand	KUMARA
—turnip	RUTABAGA, SWEDE
turnip	
—Scottish	NEEP
—Swedish	RUTABAGA, SWEDE
vegetable oyster	OYSTER PLANT
	SALSIFY
young	
—cabbage	SPRING GREENS
—onion	GREEN ONION
—turnip tops	RAPPINI
zucchini	COURGETTE
vegetable dishes	
beans	BAKED BEANS
cabbage	BUBBLE AND SQUEAK
	CAULIFLOWER AU GRATIN
	COLESLAW
candied	SUCCADE
carrot	CARROT CAKE
chick-peas and spices	FALAFEL, FELAFEL
diced vegetables	
—battered and fried (Ind.)	PAKORA
—salad	MACEDOINE
French	PISSALADIERE
	RATATOUILLE, TIAN
—fries	POTATO CHIPS
garnish of vegetable	
strips	JARDINIERE
	JULIENNE
German	
—cabbage	ROTKOHL, SAUERKRAUT
—potatoes	KARTOFFELKNODEL
	KARTOFFELPUFFER

Greek	DOLMA(DE), FASIOLA
	TSATSIKI, TZATZIKA
in	
—syrup	SUCCADE
—thin pancake	SPRING ROLL
Indian	RAITA
Indonesian	GADO-GADO
Irish	CHAMP, COLCANNON
Italian	GNOCCHI, PEPERONATA
Jewish	FALAFEL, FELEFEL, LATKE
lentil cake	CHILLADA
mashed potatoes	
—and cabbage	BUBBLE AND SQUEAK
Irish	COLCANNON
—piped and browned	DUCHESSE
maize dish (US)	SUCCOTASH
Mexican	CAESAR SALAD
	GUACAMOLE
Middle Eastern	BABA GOUNASH
	DOLMA(DE)
	FALAFEL, FELAFEL
	HUMM(O)US
mixed, diced	MACEDOINE, MIREPOIS
	MIREPOIX
peas	A LA FRANCAIS
	MUSHY PEAS
	PEASE PUDDING
pickled cabbage	SAUERKRAUT
potato	ANNA, BOULANGERE, CHIPS
	CRISPS, CROQUETTE
	DAUPHINOIS, DUCHESSE
	FONDANT, HASH BROWN
	HUNTER'S PIE, LYONNAISE
	MASHED, PARISIENNE, SCALLOPS
	SHEPHERD'S PIE, TORTILLA
—cake	GALETTE
—chips	FRENCH FRIES
—sliced and fried	GAME CHIP
—stewed (Scot.)	STOVIES
salad	CALIFORNIAN SALAD
	COLESLAW, EGG MAYONNAISE
	LOBSTER MAYONNAISE
	PATIO SALAD, ROMA SALAD
	RUSSIAN SALAD, SALADE NICOISE
	TAHITIAN SALAD, WALDORF SALAD
salad dressing	(see **sauces**)
Scottish	STOVIES
Singapore	GADO-GADO
small green peas	PETIT POIS
Swiss	RO(E)STI
Turkish	IMAM BAYILDI
vehicle	
amphibious	DUCK, DUKW, WEASEL
—tracked	AMTRACK
amusement vehicle	DODGEM (CAR)
	DUNE BUGGY

articulated	
—bus	BENDIBUS
—vehicle	RIG
cab	CABRIOLET
car	(*see* **motor-car**)
carriage	(*see separate entry*)
cross-country	
vehicle	ALL-TERRAIN VEHICLE, ATV
	SCRAMBLER
delivery vehicle	
—American	PANEL TRUCK
—milk	FLOAT
flat-bottomed	FLOAT
general-purpose	
vehicle	LORRY, PICK-UP
	TRUCK, UTILITY, VAN
hired vehicle	MINICAB, (TAXI)CAB
	TAXI
horse-drawn vehicle	(*see* **carriage**)
large box-van	PANTECHNICON
lunar	MOON BUGGY
man-powered vehicle	BICYCLE
	HOBBY-HORSE, JAMPAN
	JINRICKSHA(W), JINRIKISHA
	LITTER, MONOCYCLE, PALANQUIN
	PEDICAB, PENNY-FARTHING
	RICKSHA(W), SCOOTER, SEDAN CHAIR
	TRICYCLE, TRISHAW, UNICYCLE
	VELOCIPEDE
military	(BREN-GUN)CARRIER
	HALF-TRACK, JEEP
	PERSONNEL CARRIER
	SCOUT CAR, TANK
motor-car	(*see separate entry*)
motorised pedal-	
cycle	MOPED
one-wheeled	MONOCYCLE, UNICYCLE
open coach	CHARABANC
public transport	
vehicle	COACH, MINBUS, (OMNI)BUS
	TRAM, TROLLEY-BUS
—American	GREYHOUND, STREET-CAR
police vehicle	BLACK MARIA, HOOLIVAN
	PATROL CAR
railway vehicle	BOGIE TRUCK, CABOOSE
	DANDY CART, (FLY-)COACH
	FREIGHTLINER, LOCOMOTIVE
	PONY ENGINE, PULLMAN
	SLEEPER, (TANK-)ENGINE
	TENDER, WAGON-LIT
small	
—bus	MINIBUS
—car	MINI(CAR)
—taxi	MINICAB
snow vehicle	(BOB)SLEIGH, DRAG, LUGE
	KIBITKA, SKIBOB, SKIDOO

	SKIMOBILE, SLED(GE), SNOCAT
	SNOWMOBILE, TOBOGGAN
	WEASEL
three-wheeled	TRICYCLE, TRISHAW
touring coach	CHARABANC
tractor	CRAWLER
two-wheeled	BICYCLE, JINRICKSHA(W)
	JINRIKISHA, MOTOR-CYCLE
	(MOTOR-)SCOOTER, RICKSHA(W)
very large	JUGGERNAUT
with	
—removable top	CONVERTIBLE
	RAGTOP, SOFT-TOP
—two doors	COUPE
veins	(*see* **circulation**)
Venetian	
boat	GONDOLA
boatman	GONDOLIER
bridge	RIALTO
coin	BETSO, DUCATOON, SEQUIN
	ZECCHINE, ZECCHINO
	ZECHIN, ZEQUIN
dance	FORLANA, FURLANA
magistrate	DOGE, PODESTA
merchant	ANTONIO, POLO
mosaic	TERRAZZO
noble	DOGE, MAGNIFICO
prosecutor	AVVOCADORE
resort	LIDO
rose	SIEN(N)A
ship	ARGOSY, FRIGATOON
state barge	BUCENTAUR
sumach	FUSTET
sword	SCHIAVONE
Venezuela	YV
capital	SANTIAGO
coin	BOLIVAR, CENTIMO
	LOCHO, MEDIO
verse	V
additional syllable	HYPERCATALEXIS
ancient Phrygian metre	GALLIAMBIC
answering	
—alternately	AMOEBAEAN
—stanza	ANTISTROPHE
anthology	FLORILEGIUM
apparent rhyme	EYE-RHYME
Arabic	G(H)AZAL, GHAZEL
burlesque poem	DOGGEREL, MACARONIC
Byzantine verse	POLITICAL VERSE
canto	DUAN
choliamb	SCAZON
classic hexameters	HEROIC VERSE
closed rhyme	RIMA CHIUSA
collection of poems	ANTHOLOGY, DIVAN
combining	
—dactyls with trochees	LOGAOEDIC

—parallel sentences	REPORTED VERSES
competition in verse	TENSON, TENZON
concise poem	EPIGRAM
concluding lines	EPILOGUE
continuation of sense	
beyond end of line	ENJAMB(E)MENT
continuity of verses	SYNAPHE(I)A
corresponding in	
arrangement of syllables	TAUTOMETRIC
couplet	DISTICH
—burlesque	HUDIBRASTIC
—heroic	RIDING-RHYME
—with 12 and 14	
syllables	POULTER'S MEASURE
dactyl and	
—spondee	ADONIC
—three trochees	GLYCONIC VERSE
—trochee	ADONIC
dactylic hexameter	DOLICHURUS
	PYTHIAN VERSE
division of	
—foot	SEMEION
—line	HEMISTIC
—poem	DUAN
double	
—foot	DIPODY
—limerick	TWINER
—spondee	DISPONDEE
downbeat	THESIS
duration of	
—half of long syllable	MORA
—short syllable	MORA
eight strophes	OCTASTROPHIC
emphasising	
—sound of words	PHONETIC POETRY
—the word itself	HERMETIC POETRY
	POESIA ERMETICA
—verbal imagery	IMAGISM
—visual effect of	
words	CONCRETE POETRY
feet	
—½ foot	SEMIPED
—1 foot	MONOMETER
—1½ feet	SESQUIPEDAL(IAN)
—2 feet	DIMETER, DIPODY
combined	SYZYGY
—2½ feet	PENTHEMIMER
iambi	DIAMB
—3 feet	TRIMETER, TRIPODY
—4 feet	GLYCONIC, TETRAMETER
	TETRAPODY
—5 feet	PENTAMETER, PENTAPODY
—6 feet	HEXAMETER, HEXAPODY
	SENARIUS, SENARY
—7 feet	HEPTAMETER, HEPTAPODY
	SEPTENARIUS, SEPTENARY

—7 half-feet	HEPHTHEMIMER
—8 feet	OCTAMETER, OCTAPODY
	OCTONARION
final	
—letters of lines	
spell word	TELESTICH
—stanza	ENVOI
foot of	
—1 syllable	MONOSYLLABLE
—2 syllables	DISYLLABLE
long:short	CHOREE, CHOREUS
	TROCHEE
long:long	SPONDEE
short:long	IAMB(US)
short:short	PYRRHIC
—3 syllables	TRISYLLABLE
long:long:long	MOLOSSUS
long:long:short	ANTIBACCHIUS
long:short:long	AMPHIMACER, CRETIC
long:short:short	DACTYL
short:long:long	BACCHIUS
short:long:short	AMPHIBRACH
short:short:long	ANAP(A)EST, IONIC
short:short:short	TRIBRACH
	TRISEME
—4 syllables	QUADRISYLLABLE
	TETRASYLLABLE
long:long:long:short	EPITRITE
long:long:short:short	IONIC
long:short:short:long	CHORIAMB
long:short:short:short	PAEON
short:long:long:short	ANTISPAST
short:short:long:long	IONIC
short:short:	
short:short	PROCELEUSMATIC
	TETRASEME
—5 syllables	PENTASYLLABLE
dactyl and spondee	ADONIC
short:long:long:	
short:long	DOCHMIUS
—6 syllables	SEXISYLLABLE
—7 syllables	HEPTASYLLABLE
	SEPTASYLLABLE
—8 syllables	OCTASYLLABLE
—10 syllables	DECASYLLABLE
—11 syllables	HENDECASYLLABLE
—12 syllables	DODECASYLLABLE
6 iambs	ALEXANDRINE
—14 syllables	FOURTEENER
—15 syllables	FIFTEENER
—16 syllables	SIXTEENER
free verse	VERS LIBRE
French	
—alexandrine	HEROIC VERSE
—epic	CHANSON DE GESTE
—lyrical poem	RONDEAU, RONDEL

—medieval poem	PASTOURELLE	—six lines of sonnet	SESTET(T), SESTETTE
funeral		Latin verse	LEONINE
—ode	EPICEDE, EPICEDIUM	light verse	VERS DE SOCIETE
—oration	ELOGE, ELOGIUM, ELOGY	line	STICH
—song	ELEGY	—½ line	HEMISTICH
Greek style	ALCAIC, ADONIC	—1 line	MONOSTICH
group of		—2 lines	COUPLET, DISTICH
—Greek verses	SYSTEM	—2 couplets	CLERIHEW
—lines	STANZA	—3 lines	TERCET, TERZETTA
half			TRIAD, TRISTICH
—a line	HEMISTICH	—4 lines	CLERIHEW, QUATRAIN
—foot	SEMIPED		SAPPHIC, TETRASTICH
—of long syllable	MORA	Welsh	ENGLYN
having		—5 lines	CINQUAIN, LIMERICK
—additional syllable	HYPERMETRICAL		PENTASTICH
—different rhythms	ASYNARTETE	—6 lines	HEXASTICH, SIXAINE
—each word a syllable longer		—7 lines	RHYME-ROYAL
than the one before	RHOPALIC	—8 lines	HUITAIN, OCTASTICH
—eight			OCTAVE, SPENSERIAN
feet	OCTAPODAL	—10 lines	DECASTICH, DIZAIN
strophes	OCTASTROPHIC	—13 lines	RONDEAU, RONDEL
—equal number of		—14 lines	RONDEL, SONNET
time-units	ISORHYTHMIC		PYTHIAN VERSE
—full number of syllables	ACATALECTIC	—19 lines	VILLANELLE
—same		lines	
stanza structure		—beginning and ending	
throughout	MONOSTROPHIC	with same word	SERPENTINE VERSE
syllable		—ending with same word	KYRIELLE
arrangement	TAUTOMETRIC(AL)	—repeated at intervals	REFRAIN
heavily accented verse	SPRUNG RHYTHM	long	
heroic		—narrative	EPIC, SAGA
—couplet	RIDING-RHYME	—treated as short	IRRATIONAL
—poem	EPIC, ODE	longer verse followed by	
humorous poem		shorter one	EPODE
—4 lines	CLERIHEW	love poem	AMORET
—5 lines	LIMERICK	lyrical poem	IDYLL
—in jumbled language	MACARONIC VERSE	Malay verse	PANT(O)UM
iambic trimeter	CHOLIAMB, SCAZON	mark of division	SEMEION
in form of a letter	EPISTLE	metrical	
initial letters		—pattern	SCANSION
—forming word	ACROSTIC	—stress	ICTUS
—reproducing first verse	PARACROSTIC	—tale	FABLIAU
introduction	PROLOGUE	mixed with prose	MENIPPEAN
introductory syllable	ANACRUSIS	modern Greek verse	POLITICAL VERSE
irregular verse	DOGGEREL	monologue in verse	MONOPOEM
irregularly divided	ALLOIOSTROPHOS	mournful ode	MONODY
Italian		mourning song	ELEGY
—stanza	OTTAVA RIMA	narrative poem	BALLAD
—triplet	TERZA RIMA	natural metre	SPRUNG RHYTHM
Japanese verse	HAIKAI, HAIKU, HOKKU	nonsense verse	AMPHIGORY
	LINKED VERSE, RENGA	occasional verse	VERS D'OCCASION
	TANKA	ode	
lacking one syllable	CATALECTIC	—of lamentation	THRENE, THRENODY
laisse	TIRADE	—to victory	EPINICION, EPINIKION
last		old	
—part of ode	EPODE	—Latin verse	SATURNIAN

—lyrical poem	SONNET
—six-lined six-stanza poem	SESTINA
—two-rhyme poem	VILLANELLE
part of ode	STROPHE
pastoral poem	BUCOLIC, ECLOGUE
	GEORGIC, IDYL(L)
patchwork of verses	CENTO
patterned by syllables	SYLLABICS
	SYLLABLE VERSE
pause	
—in line	C(A)ESURA
—of one mora	LIMMA
pensive verse	ELEGY
Persian	G(H)AZAL, GHAZEL
Phrygian metre	GALLIAMBIC
pithy and sententious saying	GNOME
poem	
—about returning	NOSTOS
—celebrating wedding	EPITHALAMION
	EPITHALAMIUM
	PROTHALAMION
—honouring victory	EPINICION
	EPINIKION
—in triplets	BALLADE
Italian	TERZA-RIMA
—lamenting death	ELEGY
—made up from unconnected	
fragments of poems	CENTO
—of retraction	PALINODE
—on	
husbandry	BUCOLIC, GEORGIC
rural life	IDYLL
—without metre	
or rhyme	BLANK VERSE
	FREE VERSE, VERS LIBRE
poet	RHYMESTER, VERSIFIER
poetic dialogue	AMOEBEUM
poets	(see separate entry)
printed in specific	
shape	CALLIGRAM(ME)
prose into verse	METAPHRASE
quatrain	COMMON METRE
	SERVICE METRE
	SHORT METRE
quatrains of eight-	
syllable lines	LONG-MEASURE
redundant word	CHEVILLE
reversed dactyl	ANAP(A)EST
rhyme of	
—final syllables	MALE RHYMES
—two or more syllables	FEMININE RHYME
sandwich rhyme	RIMA CHIUSA
scazon	CHOLIAMB
section of long poem	CANTO, STANZA
series of	
—rhyming lines	MONORHYME

—stanzas (Italian)	CANZONE
short	
—clause in Latin prose	CLAUSULA
—epic	EPYLLION
—form (Italian)	STORNELLO
—hymn	CATHISMA, TROPARION
—lines ending with	
same word	KYRIELLE
—narrative	LAY
—pastoral poem	ECLOGUE, IDYL(L)
—poem	DITHYRAMB
—simple verses	JINGLE
—syllable	MORA
song of victory	EPINICION, EPINIKION
spondee, choriamb,	
iambus	ASCLEPIAD
stanza	STROPHE, TROPARION
stress	ICTUS
string of verses	
on one rhyme	LAISSE, TIRADE
stringing together	
of poems	RHAPSODY
syllable(s) introductory	
to rhythm of line	ANACRUSIS
test for one claiming	
benefit of clergy	NECK VERSE
tetrameter in tonics	SOTADEAN, SOTADIC
three stanzas	TRIAD
tribrach, iamb, trochee	TRISEME
triple rhyme	SDRUCCIOLA
trochaic dipody	DITROCHEE
two-rhymed	
—French verse	VIRELAY
—ten-syllable lines	HEROIC COUPLET
typographic	CONCRETE POETRY
unequal strophes	HETEROSTROPHIC
unit of	
—metre	FOOT
—time	SEMEION
unrhymed poem	BLANK VERSE
	FREE VERSE, VERS LIBRE
upbeat	ARSIS
use of gods in poetry	THEOTECHNY
using	
—letter-juggling	EMERGENT POETRY
—symbols	SEMIOTIC POETRY
verse into prose	METAPHRASE
visual	CONCRETE POETRY
wedding ode	EPITHALAMION
	EPITHALAMIUM
	PROTHALAMION
Welsh improvised verse	PENNILL(ION)
with extra syllables	ROVE-OVER
work omitting words	
containing a particular	
letter	LIPOGRAM

worthless	DOGGEREL	P	CITRIN
would-be rhyme	EYE-RHYME	PP	NICOTINIC ACID
vestments	(*see* **church—garments**)	X (now P)	(*see* P *above*)
Victoria		in yeast	TORULIN
Victoria Cross	VC	**volcano**	
Victoria Medal of Honour	VMH	apex	CONE
video		cavity in lava	AMYGDULE
video cassette recorder	VCR	cloud of hot gas etc	NUEE ARDENTE
video frequency	VF	crater outside lava cone	MAAR
video tape recorder	VTD	cylindrical channel	PIPE
Vietnam	VN	extinct (France)	PUY
bay	DAM, VINH, VUNG	formed from fragments by	
cape (headland)	MUI	volcanic action	PYROCLASTIC
capital	HANOI	goddess	PELE
coin		lake in extinct volcano	CRATER LAKE
—10 xu	HAO	large crater	CALDERA
—10 hao	DONG	lava flow	COULEE
gulf	VUNG	liquid lava	PYROCLASTIC ROCK
hill	DEO	mineral-filled cavity	AMYGDULE
island	CU LAO, DO, HON	mud volcano	PAINT POT, SALSE
mountain	BONOM, DEO, NGOC	natural phenomena	VOLCANISM
	NUI, PHU		VOLCANICITY, VULCANISM
New Year	TET	pertaining to	VOLCANIC, VULCANIAN
river	DA, IA, NAM, SONG	pillar of solidifed	
virtues		lava	VOLCANIC NECK
Christian	CHARITY, FAITH, HOPE	rocks, etc	EJECTA, TEPHRA
	HUMILITY	—angular rocks	AGGLOMERATE, BLOCKS
	FORTITUDE, JUSTICE	—banded	EUTAXITE
	PRUDENCE, TEMPERANCE	—basalt lava	TOADSTONE
violin	AMATI, CREMONA	—black and shiny	OBSIDIAN, PITCHSTONE
	STRAD(IVARIUS)	—broken by volcanic	
—strings	A, D, E, G	action	PYROCLASTIC
vitamin		—compacted mixture	TUFF
A	AXEROPHTHOL, BIOTIN	—coarse material	CINDER
	CAROTENE, ERGOSIA, RETINOL	—cooled magma	IGNEOUS RAOCK
B	ADERMIN, ANEURIN, BIOTIN	—dust	POZZ(U)OLANA
	COBALAMINE, CYANOCOBALAMIN(E)		PUZZOLANA
	FOLIC ACID, INOSITOL	—earthy tuff	TRASS
	LACTOFLAVIN, NIACIN	—ejected by Vesuvius	IDOCRASO
	NICOTINAMIDE, NICOTINIC ACID		VESUVIANITE
	OROTIC ACID, PANTHENOL	—fine	
	PANTOTHENIC ACID, PTEROIC ACID	grained ash	HORNSTONE
	PTEROYLGLUTAMIC ACID	material	ASH
	PYRIDOXIN(E), RIBOFLAVIN	textured rock	PUMICE, RHYOLITE
	THIAMIN(E)	—fragments	TUFF
C	ASCORBIC ACID	—fused	GLASS
	CEVITAMIC ACID	—glass	PE(A)RLITE, PITCHSTONE
D	CALCIFEROL, CHOLECALCIFEROL	—lava fragments	SCORIA, SLAG
E	TOCOPHEROL	—molten material	LAVA, MAGMA
F	LINOLE(N)IC ACID	—mud	MOYA
G (now B)	LACTOFLAVIN, RIBOFLAVIN	—porous	PUMICE, TUFA, TUFF
H	BIOTIN	—ropy lava	PAHOEHOE
K	MENADIONE, PHYLLOQUINONE	—rough	
	PHYTONADIONE	cindery lava	SLAG
M (now B)	FOLIC ACID	lava	AA, SCORIA
	PTEROYLGLUTAMIC ACID	—rounded rocks	BOMBS, PILLOW LAVA

—small rocks	LAPILLI
—smooth lava	PAHOEHOE
—soil (India)	BLACK COTTON EARTH
—split lava	PILLOW
—stopping vent	NECK, PLUG
—tuff	TARRAS, TERRAS, TRASS
—vitreous	OBSIDIAN, PALAGONITE
—with	
plagioclase	ANDESITE
steam holes	SCORIA
steam or gas hole	FUMAROLE, HORNITO
	MOFETTE, SOLFATARA
	SUFFIONE
stream of lava	COULEE
study	VOLCANOLOGY
	VULCANOLOGY
subordinate cone	MONTIC(U)LE
	MONTICULUS
volcanic rock	EXTRUSIVE ROCK
—glassy	VOLCANIC GLASS
volcanoes	
—Aegean	SANTORINI, THERA
—Alaska	MOUNT KATMAI, REDOUBT
—America	CRATER LAKE, GLACIER PEAK
	LASSEN, MOUNT ADAMS
	MOUNT BAKER, MOUNT HOOD
	MOUNT JEFFERSON, MOUNT MAZAMA
	MOUNT MCLOUGHLIN, MOUNT RANIER
	MOUNT ST HELENS, MOUNT SHASTA
	MOUNT SPUR, NEWBERRY CRATER
	SUNSET CRATER
—Antarctic	EREBUS
—Argentina	MOUNT SIDLEY
	OJOS DEL SALADO
—Azores	FAIAL
—Cameroon	MOUNT CAMEROON
—Chile	GUALLATIRI, LASCAR
	TUPUNGATITO
—Colombia	PURACE
—Costa Rica	IRAZU, MOUNT ARENAL
—Ecuador	CHIMBORAZO, COTOPAXI
	SANGAY
—enclosing Pacific	
Ocean	RING OF FIRE
—Greece	SANTORINI, THIRA
—Guatemala	TACANA, TAJUMULCO
—Hawaii	AIRI, HALEMAUMAU
	HUALALAI, KILAUEA (IKI)

	MAUNA KEA, MAUNA LOA
—Iceland	EDFELL, GJASTYKKI
	GRIMSVOTEN, HAIMAEY
	HELGAFELL, HEKLA
	MOUNT LAKI, SURTSEY
—Indonesia	ANAK KRAKATAU, KELI MUTU
	KELUT, KRAKATOA
	MOUNT LAMINGTON
	MOUNT MERAPI, MOUNT RIN(D)JANI
	RAOENG, SEMERU, SLAMAT
	TAMBORA, TOBA
—Italy	SALSA, STROMBOLI
	VESUVIUS, VULCANO
—Japan	FUJIYAMA, SAKURAJIMA, USU
—Java	RAOENG
—Lipari Islands	VULCANO
—Martinique	MONT PELEE
—Mexico	EL CHICHON
	NEVADA DEL RUIZ
	PARICUTIN, POPOCATEPETL
—New Zealand	RUAPEHU
—Nicaragua	CONCEPCION
—Réunion	
Island	PITON DE LA FOURNESSE
—Russia	KLYUCHEVSKAYA SOPKA
	KORYAKSKAYA
	MOUNT TOLBACHIK
—Sicily	ETNA
—Solomon Islands	TINAKULA
—Spain	PICO DE TEIDE
—Tristan da Cunha	THE PEAK
—Virgin Islands	GROS PITON
	HODDER'S VOLCANO
	KICK-'EM-JENNY, MORNE AU DIABLE
	MORNE DIABOLOTIN, MORNE PATATES
	MOUNT MISERY, MOUNT ST CATHERINE
	NEVIS PEAK, PETIT PITON
	QUALIBOU(LA), SOUFRIERE
	THE MOUNTAIN, THE QUILL
—with wide base	SHIELD VOLCANO
—Zaire	NYIRAGONGO

volunteer

Voluntary Aid Detachment	VAD
Voluntary Defence Corps	VDC
Voluntary Service Overseas	VOS
Volunteer (Officers') Decoration	VD
Volunteer Reserve Decoration	VRD

W

Wales	CYMRU
waterfall	CATARACT, CHUTE
	FORCE, LIN(N), RAPID
Africa	VICTORIA
Argentina	DEL IGUAZU
Austria	KRIMMLER FALLE
Brazil	GUIARA, GLASS, IGUAZA
	PATOS-MARIBONDO
	PAULO ALFONSO, SEVEN FALLS
	URUBU-PUNGA
Canada	CHRUCHILL, GRAND
	HORSESHOE, NIAGARA
	TAKKAKAW
cascade pool	LIN(N)
England	CA(U)LDRON SNOUT
	SCALE FORCE, STANLEY FORCE
	SCALEBER FORCE, THE STRID
France	GARVARNIE
Guyana	KAIETEUR, KING GEORGE VI
	KOITUOK, RORAIMA
highest	ANGEL
Ireland	POWERSCOURT
New Zealand	CLEVE-GARTH, SUTHERLAND
North America	NIAGARA, RIBBON
	SILVER STRAND, YOSEMITE
Norway	ITIGARD, KILE, KVELLFOSSEN
	MONGEFOSSEN
	OSTRE MARDOLA FOSS
	TYSSESTRENGANE
Paraguay	GUAIRA, SEVEN FALLS
Scotland	CROMACH, FALLS OF BRUAR
	FALLS OF CLYDE, FOYERS
	EAS-COUL-AULIN
	GREY MARE'S TAIL
South Africa	TUGELA, VICTORIA
steep	CATARACT
Tanzania	KALAMBO
Uganda	OWEN FALLS
Venezuela	ANGEL, CUQUENAN
	KUKENAAM
Wales	PISTYLL RHAIADR
	PISTYLL-Y-LLYN
	SWALLOW FALLS
where water atomises	BRIDAL VEIL
Zaire	STANLEY
Zambia	RAINBOW, VICTORIA
weapon	
African spear	ASSAGAI, ASSEGA(A)I,

anti	
—submarine	DEPTH-CHARGE, MINE
	TORPEDO
—tank	BEEHIVE, (LAND)MINE
	STICKY BOMB
axe	
—2-edged	TWIBILL
—Bronze Age	PALSTAFF, PALSTAVE
—long-handled	BROWNBILL, GISARME
	GLAIVE, HALBERD, HALBERT
	LOCHABER AXE, PARTISAN
	SPARTH(E), SPONTOON
	VOU(L)GE, WELSH HOOK
—long-headed	JETHART STAFF
—Red Indian	TOMAHAWK
blowpipe	SARBACANE
buried	LANDMINE
burning	FLAMETHROWER
	INCENDIARY BOMB, NAPALM
bow	FOOTBOW, CROSSBOW, LONG-BOW
—crossbow	ARB(A)LAST, ARBALEST
	AR(CU)BALIST
catapult	(E)SPRINGAL(D)
cavalry	LANCE, SABRE
club	(*see* **club**)
dagger	(*see* **knife**)
device for	
—cocking crossbow	CRANEQUIN
	GOAT'S FOOT, MOULINET
	WINDAS, WINDLASS
—testing gunpowder	EPROUVETTE
dropped from aircraft	BOMB, TORPEDO
engines of war	
—boring	TEREBRA
—cutting	SIEGE SCYTHE
—large crossbow	BAL(L)ISTA
—moveable tower	BELFRY, SIEGE TOWER
Roman	MUSCULUS
—stone-throwing	BAL(L)ISTA, BRICOLE
	CATAPULT, MANGONEL
	ONAGER, PERRIER, PETRARY
	SCORPION, STONEBOW
	TORMENTUM, TREBUCHET
fired from	
—aircraft	MISSILE
—air-pistol/rifle	DART, PELLET
—blowpipe	DART
—bow	ARROW
—crossbow	BOLT, QUARREL
—gun	BULLET, SHELL
—launcher	MISSILE
—ship	BAR-SHOT, CASE-SHOT
	CHAIN-SHOT, DEPTH-CHARGE
	GRAPE(-SHOT), LANGRAGE
	LANGREL, LANGRIDGE
	MISSILE, TORPEDO

—shotgun	CARTRIDGE, PELLET, SHOT
—silo	MISSILE
fixed to	
—fingers	KNUCKLEDUSTER
—rifle	BAYONET
floating	MINE
for killing	
—fish	PRIEST
—salmon	LEISTER
—whales	HARPOON
fragment of shell, etc	SHRAPNEL
gavelock	JAVELIN
grenade	MILLS BOMB, PINEAPPLE
gun	(*see separate entry*)
halberd	BROWNBILL
harpoon	(GRAIN)STAFF
Indian	LATHI, PATA
iron-tipped staff	QUARTER-STAFF
javelin	GAVELOCK
—Oriental	JEREED, JERID
—Roman	PILE, PILUM
—Turkish	JEREED, JERID
knife	(*see separate entry*)
mortar	
—British	STOKES, TOC EMMA
—German	MINENWERFER
	MOANING MINNIE
mine	ACOUSTIC, CONTACT
	MAGNETIC
officer's halberd	SPONTOON
rocket-propelled	MISSILE
Roman javelin	PILE, PILUM
Scottish salmon spear	WASTER
Siva's trident	TRISUL(A)
spear	
—3-pronged	TRIDENT
—African	ASSAGAI, ASSEGA(A)I
—cavalry	LANCE
—infantry	PIKE
—old	GADE, GALING, GAID
	GLAIVE, LA(U)NCEGAY(E)
—Roman	PILE, PILUM
—salmon	LEISTER
Scottish	WASTER
—throwing	GAVELOCK, JAVELIN
—whales	HARPOON
spear-thrower (Australian)	WOOOMERA
spiked	
—ball	CALTRAP, CALTHROP
—club	MACE
—shaft	PIKE, LANCE, SPEAR
swinging bar	FLAIL
sword	(*see separate entry*)
Turkish javelin	JEREED, JERID
undersea	DEPTH CHARGE, MINE
	TORPEDO

war-hammer	MARTEL
weather	(*see* **meteorology**)
weight	
0.06 grams	GRAIN
3 scruples	DRACHM
8 drachms	OUNCE TROY
$^1/_{16}$ ounce	DRAM, DRACHM
1.1 ounce	OUNCE TROY
16 drams	OUNCE
20 grains	SCRUPLE
24 grains	DWT, PENNYWEIGHT
480 grains	OUNCE
8 ounces (gold, silver)	MARK
12 ounces Troy	POUND
16 ounces	POUND
4lb	
—(loaf)	QUARTERN
—on 104lb allowance	TRET
7-10lb (wool or cheese)	CLOVE
14lb	STONE
16lb (cheese)	STONE
22lb (hay)	STONE
24lb (wool)	STONE
25lb (US)	QUARTER
28lb	QUARTER
—(wool)	TOD
32lb	SLUG
36lb (straw)	TRUSS
56lb	
—(butter)	FIRKIN
—(old hay)	TRUSS
60lb (new hay)	TRUSS
100lb	CENTAL, QUINTAL
112lb	CWT, HUNDREDWEIGHT
120lb (glass)	SEAM
140lb (flour)	BOLL
240lb	PACK
—(wool)	WOOL-PACK
750-1200lb (tobacco)	HOGSHEAD
4000lb	LAST
13 stone	WEY
2 weys	SACK
½cwt (hops)	HOP-POCKET
cwt (old)	QUINTAL
19½cwts (lead)	FOTHER
25½cwts (coal)	CHALDRON
atomic weight of element	GRAM-ATOM
litre of hydrogen	CRITH
nylon, rayon, silk	DENIER
silver and gold	TROY
	(*for* metric weights *see* **French**)
Welsh	CAMBRIAN, CYMRIC
bards' assembly	GORSEDD
beloved	BACH
boat	CORACLE
burial chamber	CISTVAEN, KISTVAEN

Welsh

capital	CARDIFF
char	TORGOCH
congress of bards	EISTEDDFOD
dish	LAVER BREAD
divine inspiration	HYWL
dog	CORGI
druids' meeting	GORSEDD
emblem	LEEK
fervour	HYWL
fiddler	CROWDER
fish (Lake Bala)	GWINIAD, GWYNIAD
four-line stanza	ENGLIN
giant	IDRIS
hill	DUN
hollow in hillside	CWM
improvised verse	PENNILL(ION)
lament	PLANXTY
liquor	METHEGLIN
mountain	MYNNYDD
Nationalist Party	PLAID CYMRU, WNP
patron saint	DAVID
payment to new king	MISE
porch	GALILEE
riots	REBECCA
sea	MOR
stanza	PENNILL
the Welsh	CYMRY
tribe	SILURES
valley	CWM
violin	CROUD, CROUTH
	CROWD, CRWTH

West Indian

allspice	JAMAICAN PEPPER
ball of dough	FLOAT
Barbados cherry	MALPHIGIA
bark	CARIBBEE-BARK
	CASCARILLA
belief in snake deity	ZOMBIISM
birch	SAMYDA
bird	GREEN SPARROW
	SOLITAIRE
	TODY, TREMBLER
bobolink	BUTTER-BIRD
bread	COO-COO
cake	BAMMIE
Canna	TOUS-LES-MOIS
capsicum	CHERRY-PEPPER, PIM(I)ENTO
cassava	MANIOC, TAPIOCA
—juice	CASSAREEP, CASSARIPE
chief	CACIQUE, CAZIQUE
clay	BARBADOS EARTH
climbing plant	SCOTCH ATTORNEY
compressed dika	
seed	DIKA-BREAD
dance	BEGUINE, CHA-CHA(-CHA)
	LIMBO, MAMBO, R(H)UMBA

West Indian

demoiselle fish	COW-PILOT
dish	PEPPER-POT
drink	CURACAO, CURACOA
	EAU DE CREOLES, MOBBIE
	MOBBY, RUM, SANGAREE
	SANGRIA, TAFIA
drum	BONGO
durra	NEGRO-CORN
edible	
—frog	CRAPAUD
—starch	TOUS-LES-MOIS
—tuber	YAM
extinct tribe	TAINO
farm	PEN
fibre	ABACA, MANIL(L)A-HEMP
fish	BARRACOUTA, BARRACUDA
	COBIA, CRAB-EATER, GUPPY
	MILLIONS, SERGEANT-FISH
—dish	ACCRA
flea	CHIGGER, CHIGOE, CHIGRE
	JIGGER
flycatcher	SOLITAIRE
folk-song	CALYPSO
freshwater tortoise	HIC(C)ATEE
fruit	A(C)KEE, ANANA(S)
	ANCHOVY-PEAR, BARBADOS CHERRY
	BARBADOS GOOSEBERRY, BULLOCK'S
	HEART, COCO PLUM, CUSTARD-APPLE
	GENIPAP, GRANADILLA, GRENADILLA
	MAMMEE(-APPLE), NASEBERRY
	PASSION FRUIT, PENGUIN
	PINGUIN, SAPODILLA-PLUM
	STAR-APPLE
ghost	DUPPY, JUMBIE, JUMBY
groundnut	PINDA
gum	ANIME, COURBARIL
hog-rat	HUTIA, MUSK-CAVY
insectivore	AGOUTA
Jamaican	
—birthwort	CONTRAYERVA
—pepper	ALLSPICE
language	CARIB, TAINO
lizard	GALLIWASP
locust tree	COURBARIL
magic	MYALISM, OBEAH, OBI(A)
	OBY, VAUDOO, VAUDOUX
	VOODOO, VOUDOU
manioc	CASSAVA, TAPIOCA
marmalade-tree	MAMMEE-SAPOTA
mesquite	CASHAW
mulberry	RAMOON
music	CALYPSO, REGGAE
Negro	QUASHEE, QUASHIE
oil from dika	DIKA-BUTTER
orange dye	AN(N)ATTA
	AN(N)ATTO, ARNOTTO

passion-flower	BULL-HOOF
	LOVE-IN-A-MIST
peanut	PINDA
pepper	PIM(I)ENTO
pineapple	KARATAS
pirate	BUCCANEER, BUCCANIER
	FILIBUSTER
plant	BIKA, SAVANNA FLOWER
plantation	PEN
poinciana	PEACOCK-FLOWER
potatoes	EDDOES
prickly-pear	TUNA
pumpkin	CALABAZA
race	CARIB
resin	ANIME
rock music	REGGAE
rodent	HOG-RAT, HUTIA
rum	TAF(F)IA
ship	DROG(H)ER
shrub	BARBADOS-PRIDE
spice	PIMENTO
spiny cactus	DILDO
spurge	MANIHOT, MANIOC
squash	CHRISTOPHINE
stew	PEPPERPOT
superstition	VAUDOO, VAUDOUX
	VOODOO, VOUDOU
sweet potato	BATATA
tapioca	CASSAVA, MANIOC
taro	DASHEEN
thrush	SOLITAIRE
thunderstorm	HOUVARI
timber	(see separate entry)
tortoise	HIC(C)ATEE
tree	A(C)KEE, BARBADOS CHERRY
	BLACKBULLY, BOLLETRIE, BULLY-TREE
	BULLET-TREE, BULLETRIE, CANELLA
	COCO-PLUM, COCUS-WOOD, GAUZE-TREE
	GENIPAP, GRANADILLA, GRENADILLA
	HERCULES CLUB, HOG-PLUM, MALPHIGIA
	LACE-TREE, LOCUST-TREE, MAMMEE
	PIMENTO, PRICKLY ASH, QUASSIA
	SAPODILLA, SWEETWOOD
	TOOTHACHE-TREE, XANTHOXYLUM
	YACCA
tree-nesting termite	DUCK-ANT
voodoo priestess	MAMBO
white man	BUCKRA
wild mango	DIKA
witchcraft	OBEAH, OBI(A), OBY
	MYALISM
Western Samoa	WS
capital	APIA
coin	
—unit	SENE
—100 sene	TALA

whale	GRAMPUS
baleen whales	MYSTACOCETI
finback	RORQUAL
group	POD, SCHOOL
order	CETACEA
rorqual	FINBACK SEI
types	BLUE, BOTTLENOSE, BOWHEAD
	BRYDE'S, FIN, GREY, HUMPBACK
	KILLER, MINKE, RIGHT, SEI, SPERM
	SULPHUR BOTTOM
toothed	ODONTOCETI
whale food	KRILL, PLANKTON
which	
which	
—is	QE
—see	QV
—was to be	
done	QEF
found	QEI
proved	QED
wind	
Aegean	ETESIAN
Africa	BERG WIND, CHILI
	HARMATTAN, LESTE
anticlockwise round low	
pressure (North)	CYCLONE
Argentina	ZONDA
Asia	KARABURAN
Australia	
—cyclone	WILLY-WILLY
—north-easter	BRICKFIELDER (WIND)
—south wind	SOUTHERLY BU(R)STER
—stormy	BUSTER
autumn winds	EQUINOCTIAL GALES
Beaufort scale	

No.	mph.	
0	<1	CALM
1	1-3	LIGHT AIR
2	4-7	LIGHT BREEZE
3	8-12	GENTLE BREEZE
4	13-18	MODERATE BREEE
5	19-24	FRESH BREEZE
6	25-31	STRONG BREEZE
7	32-38	NEAR GALE
8	39-46	GALE
9	47-54	STRONG GALE
10	55-65	STORM
11	66-75	VIOLENT STORM
12	>75	HURRICANE

brief	FLURRY, GUST
California	NORTHER, SANTA ANNA
Cape Horn	WILLIWAW SQUALL
carrying particles	DUST-STORM
	SAND-STORM
caused by	
—avalanche	AVALANCHE WIND

—convection currents	THERMAL
downwards	KATABATIC
on slopes	MOUNTAIN WIND
upwards	ANABATIC
—insolation	PLANETARY
Central America	NORTE, TEMPORALES
change direction	
—anticlockwise	BACK
—clockwise	VEER
China Sea	TYPHOON
clockwise round low	
pressure (North)	ANTICYCLONE
cold	
—Andes	NEVADOS, PUNA
—Australia	SOUTHERLY BUR(S)TER
—down glacier	GLACIER BREEZE
—France	BISE, MISTRAL
—from Arctic or Antarctic	POLAR WIND
—Italy	BISE
—off mountains to sea	WILLIWAW
—Switzerland	BISE
—with snow	BLIZZARD
consistent winds	
at sea	ANTITRADES
	TRADE WINDS, WESTERLIES
convection wind	ANABATIC, KATABATIC
	VALLEY WIND
cool sea breeze	DOCTOR
Cuba - squall	BAYAMO
desert wind	DUST STORM, SAND STORM
	S(C)IROC(CO)
diagram of wind direction	
and speed	WIND ROSE
direction	
—from which wind is	
blowing	UPWIND, WINDWARD
—of wind	SET
—towards which wind	
is blowing	DOWNWIND, LEEWARD
east	EURUS
—Mediterranean	LEVANT(ER), SOLANO
—Spain	SOLANO
European	HELM
force measurement	BEAUFORT SCALE
frequently changing	
direction	BAFFLING WIND
gentle breeze	ZEPHYR
high altitude	JET STREAM
hot	
—Africa	BERG WIND, CHILI, HARMATTAN
—Andes	ZONDA
—Arabia	HABOOB, SAMIEL, SHAMAL
	SIMOOM, SIMOON
—Argentina	ZONDA
—Asia	TEBBAD
—Australia	BRICKFIELDER
—Egypt	K(H)AMSIN
—Iran	SAMOON, SAMUN
—Italy	S(C)IROC(C)O
—Java	KOEMBANG
—Kurdistan	RESHABAR
—mountain	FO(E)HN
—North Africa	GIBLI
—Rockies	CHINOOK
—South America	NEVADOS, ZONDA
—Sudan	HABOOB
—Sumatra	BOHOROK
hurricane	BAGUIO
increase in strength	FRESHEN
indicator	WEATHER VANE
	WIND SOCK, WIND VANE
Iran	SAMOON, SAMUN, SEISTAN
Iraq	SHAMAL
Italy	S(C)IROC(CO), TRAMONTANA
Java	KOEMBANG
land breeze (Peru)	TERRAL
law governing wind	
direction	BUYS BALLOT'S LAW
light breeze	CAT'S-PAW
	MACKEREL-BREEZE
localised whirl of dust	DUST DEVIL
	WIND DEVIL
Madeira	LESTE
measuring instrument	ANEMOMETER
Mediterranean	ETESIAN, GREGALE
	LEVANTER, MAESTRO
	PONENTE, SOLANO
Mexico	NORTE, PAPAGAYO
most frequent from a	
particular direction	PREVAILING WIND
New Zealand	NOR'-WESTER
north	AQUILO(N), BOREAS
—Asia	SEISTAN
—Central America	NORTE
—France	BISE
—Iran	SEISTAN
—Italy	BISE, TRAMONTANA
—Mediterranean	ETESIAN
—Mexico	PAPAGAYO
—North America	NORTHER
—South America	ZONDA
—Switzerland	BISE
—Turkey	MELTEMI
North Africa	CHILI, GIBLI
	S(C)IROC(CO)
North America	NORTHER
north-east	IMBAT, TRADE
—Adriatic	BORA
—Aegean	ETESIAN
—Africa	HARMATTAN
—Asia	KARABURAN, PURGA
—Australia	BRICKFIELDER

—Central Asia/Siberia	BURAN
—Europe	HELM
—Indian Ocean	MONSOON
—Mediterranean	GREGALE
—Switzerland	BISE
north-west	
—Iraq	SHAMAL
—Mediterranean	MAESTRO
—Milton	ARGESTES
off shore	LAND BREEZE
on shore	SEA BREEZE
Peru	TERRAL, VIRAZON
Philippines - hurricane	BAGUIO
planetary winds	
—north and south of horse	
latitudes	WESTERLIES
—towards Equator	TRADE WINDS
region of light winds	CALMS OF CANCER
	CALMS OF CAPRICORN
	DOLDRUMS
	HORSE LATITUDES
Rocky Mountains	CHINOOK
rotating	ANTICYLONE, CYCLONE
	HURRICANE, TORNADO
	TYPHOON, WHIRLWIND
Russia - windstorm	BURAN
sand-storm	HABOOB, TEBBAD
sea breeze	
—Arabian Sea	BAT FURAN
—Peru	VIRAZON
seasonally reversing	
system	MONSOON
short violent storm	(LINE)SQUALL
Sicily	S(C)IROC(CO)
side	
—away from wind	LEEWARD
—facing wind	WINDWARD
slight breeze	MACKEREL-BREEZE
south	AUSTER, NOTUS
—Africa	LESTE
—Australia	SOUTHERLY BUSTER
—Egypt	K(H)AMSIN
—Italy	S(C)IROC(CO)
—North Africa	CHILI, GIBLI, S(C)IROC(CO)
—Sicily	S(C)IROC(CO)
south-east	EURUS, TRADE
—Africa	CAPE DOCTOR
—Indian Ocean	MONSOON
—Spain	SOLANO
south-west	AFER, LIBECC(H)IO
—Central America	TEMPORALES
—Indian Ocean	MONSOON
—South America	PAMPERO
—Spain	LEVECHE, VENDEVALES
Spain	LEVECHE, SOLANO
	VENDEVALES

speed	
—scale	BEAUFORT SCALE
—measuring instrument	ANEMOMETER
—record	ANEMOGRAM
—recording instrument	ANEMOGRAPH
spring winds	EQUINOCTIAL GALES
squall	BLIRT, BLORE
—Cuba	BAYAMO
—East Indies	SUMATRA
—India	NOR'-WESTER
—Magellan Strait	WILLIWAW
—Scotland	DROW
storm	GALE, HURRICANE
	TEMPEST
Sumatra	BOHOROK
tempest	BOURASQUE
tempestuous	EUROCLYDON
	EURAQUILA
through mountain passes	STOWED WIND
tornado	
—America	TWISTER
—at sea	WATERSPOUT
transitory breeze	SLANT
tropical thunderstorm	TORNADO
violent gust	BLORE
west	FAVONIUS, TRADE(S)
	ZEPHYR
—Mediterranean	PONENTE
—southern	
hemisphere	BRAVE WEST WINDS
ocean	ROARING FORTIES
West Indies -	
thunderstorm	HOUVARI
whirlwind	TORNADO, TOURBILLION
	TYPHON, TWISTER
	WHITE SQUALL
wind	
—of 120 days	SEISTAN
—scale	(see Beaufort Scale above)
wine	
add sugar to grape	
juice	CHAPTALIZE, GALLIZE
	GALLISE
at room temperature	CHAMBRE
champagne and	
—orange juice	BUCK'S FIZZ
—stout	BLACK VELVET
claret	
—India	LOLL-SHRAUB
	LOLL-SHROB
—with soda-water, etc	BADMINTON
classification	
—Corsican	
guaranteed	
standard	APPELLATION CONTROLEE
ordinary standard	VIN DE CORSE

—French
excellent　　　　(GRAND) CRU (CLASSE)
　　　　　　　　　LES GRANDS VINS
good　　　　　　　CRU BOURGEOIS
　　　　　　　　　CRU EXCEPTIONEL
　　　PREMIER (GRAND) CRU (CLASSE)
　　　　　　　　　VDQS
guaranteed
　standard　APPELLATION CONTROLEE
　ordinary　　　　　VIN DE PAYS
　　　　　　　　　VIN DE TABLE
　　　　　　　　　VIN ORDINAIRE
—German
excellent　AUSLESE, BEERENAUSLESE
　　　　　　EISWEIN, KABINETT
　　　QUALITATSWEIN MIT PRADICAT
　　　QUALITATSWEIN MP, SPATLESE
　　　TROCKENBEERENAUSLESE
good　　　　　QUALITATSWEIN BA
ordinary　　　　　TAFELWEIN
superior table wine　　LANDWEIN
—Greek
ordinary　　　　　EPITRAPEZIO
mature　　ENDIKOS DIATIRIMENON
—Hungarian
best wine　　　　MINOSEGI BOR
ordinary wine　　　KIMERT BOR
table wine　　　　ASZTALI BOR
—Italian
aged for 3 years　　RISERVA
good　　　　　　VINO TIPICO
guaranteed standard　DOC, DOCG
　　　　　　　GARANTITA
ordinary　　　VINO DA BANCO
　　　　　　　VINO DA PASTA
　　　　　　　VINO DA TAVOLA
　　　　　　　VINO ORDINARIO
—Portuguese
best quality　　　GARRAFEIRA
good　　　　　　RESERVA
guaranteed
　quality　DENOMINACAO DE ORIGEN
ordinary　VINHO DE CONSUMO
　　　　　　VINHO DE MESA
—Romanian
light wine　　　　VIN USOR
ordinary　　　　VIN DE MASA
superior　　　　VIN SUPERIOR
—Russian
dessert wine　　DESERTNOE VINO
Georgian wine　GRUZINSKOE VINO
ordinary wine　STOLOVOE VINO
—Spanish
aged
　—3 years　　　RESERVA
　—5 years　　GRAN RESERVA

guaranteed
　standard　DENOMINACION DE ORIGEN
　ordinary　　　VINO CORRIENTE
　　　　　　　VINO DE MESA
　　　　　　　VINO DE PASTO
sherry types
　—dry　　　　　　FINO
　—dry, light　　MANZANILLA
　—medium　　AMONTILLADO
　—pale, rich　CORTADOR, PALO
　—sweet　　　　OLOROSO
—Yugoslav
dessert wine　　DESERTNO VINO
selected wine　　CUVENO VINO
table wine　　　STOLNO VINO
crust on port　BEESWING, FLOR
divination from wine　OENOMANCY
draw off, leaving sediment　DECANT
fragrance　　　　BOUQUET
freezing before
　pressing　　CRYOEXTRACTION
general terms
—Austrian
　estate　WEINGARTEN, WEINGUT
　estate-bottled　ORIGINALABFULLUNG
　group of vineyards　EINZELLAGE
　semi-sparkling　　SCHLUCK
　small vineyard area　　REID
　wine bar　　　　HEURIGE
　without added sugar　NATURWEIN
—Bulgarian
　dry　　　　　　　SUHO
　red　　　　　CHERVENO
　sparkling　　ISKRIASHTO
　sweet　　　　SLADKO
　vineyards　　　LOZIA
　white　　　　BJALO
　wine　　　　　VINO
—French
　at room temperature　CHAMBRE
　blend　　　　　CUVEE
　cellar　　　　　CAVE
　cool　　　　　FRAIS
　crop　　　　　RECOLTE
　dry　　　　　　SEC
　early　　　　PRIMEUR
　field in vineyard　CLIMAT
　from white grapes　BLANC DE BLANC
　group of vineyards　COMMUNE, CRU
　half-dry (sweet)　DEMI-SEC
　hillside　　　COTE(AU)
　house-name
　—Bordeaux　　CHATEAU
　—Burgundy　　DOMAINE
　manager　　RECOLTANT
　merchant　NEGOCIANT

method of making sparkling wine	METHODE CHAMPENOISE	—areas	FRANCONIA MOSEL-SAAR-RUWER, NAHE RHEINGAU, RHEINPFALZ
noble rot	POURRITURE NOBLE	—district	BEREICH
owner	PROPRIETAIRE	winery	WEINKELLEREI
parish	COMMUNE, FINAGE	—Greek	
pink	ROSE	dry	XIROS
pinkish	PELURE D'OIGNON	factory	OINOPOIEION
red	ROUGE	old wine	PALAION
slightly sparkling	CREMANT, PERLANT	pink	KOKKINELI, ROSE
still	NATUREL	producer	OINOPARAGOGAS
storage building	CHAI	red	ERYTHROS, MAVROS
sweet	DOUX	resin flavoured	RETSINA
very dry	BRUT	sparkling wine	AFROTHES
vat	CUVE	white	LEFKOS
vineyard(s)	CLIMAT, CRU VIGNOBLE	wine	OINOS
—under one owner	MONOPOLE	—Hungarian	
—walled	CLOS	bottled	PALACKOZOTT
vintage	RECOLTE	dry	SZARAZ
white	BLANC	from very ripe grapes	ASZU
wine	VIN	natural Tokay	SZAMORODNI
—grower	VITICULTEUR	red	VOROS
—growing areas	ALSACE, BORDEAUX BURGUNDY CHAMPAGNE LOIRE, RHONE	sweet white	EDES FEHER
		—Italian	
		aged in cask	RISERVA
		association of growers	CONSORZIO
—German		bar	CANTINA
bottle (Franconia)	BOCKSBEUTEL	bitter	AMARO
bottler	ABFULLER	company making wine	CASA VINICOLA
cafe wine	SCHOFFENWEIN	concentrated	COTTO
carbonated	PERLWEIN	cooked	COTTO
cellar	KELLER	co-operative	CANTINA SOCIALE CONSORZIO
commune	GEMEINDE		
cooperative	WINZERVEREIN	dark red	NERO
dry	TROCKEN	dry	AMARO, SECCO
estate-bottled	ERZEUGER ABFULLUNG	estate	TENEMENTI
Franconian	STEINWEIN	firm	CASA
from frozen grapes	EISWEIN	flask	FIASCO
group of vineyards	GROSSLAGE	fortified	VINO LIQUOROSO
half-dry	HALBTROCKEN	from	
parish	GEMEINDE	—dried grapes	PASSITO VIN(O) SANTO
pink wine	ROSEWEIN, SCHILLERWEIN WEISSHERBST	—finest area	CLASSICO
red wine	ROTWEIN	holding	TENEMENTI
rural district	KREIS	house	CASA
semi-sparkling	PERLWEIN	light red	CHIARETTO
sparkling	SCHAUMWEIN, SEKT SPRITZIG	medium sweet mellow	ABBOCCATO, AMABILE STRAVECCHIO
unfermented juice	SUSS RESERVE	pink	ROSATO
vineyard	EINZELLAGE	red	ROSSO
white wine	WEISSWEIN	ripe	STRAVECCHIO
wine	WEIN	slightly sparkling	FRIZZANTE
winery	WEINKELLEREI	sparkling	SPUMANTE
wine-producing		sweet	DOLCE
—area	GEBEIT, LANDE	very dry	AMARO

vintage	VENDEMMIA	red	KRASNOE
white	BIANCO	white	BELOE
wine	VINO	wine	VINO
—cellar	CANTINA	—Spanish	
winery	CANTINA	aged	CON CRIANZA
—Portuguese		bar	BODEGA
dry	BRUTO, SECO	cask	BOTA
estate	QUINTA	controlling body	CONSEJO REGULADOR
—bottled	ENGARRAFADO NA ORIGEM	crop	COSECHA
farm	QUINTA	dry	SECO
legally-defined		good	FINO
area	REGIAO DEMARCADA	light red	CLARETE
light red	CLARETE	not aged	SIN CRIANZA
matured	MADURO	pink	ROSADO
pink	ROSADO	range of sherry casks	SOLERA
port terms		red	TINTO
—dark port	RUBY	sparkling	ESPUMOSO
—from		sweet	ABOCADO, DULCE
one good year	VINTAGE	very dry (sherry)	FINO
white grapes	WHITE PORT	vineyard	VINA, VINEDO
—good non-vintage	CRUSTED	vintage	COSECHA, VENDIMIA
	VINTAGE CHARACTER	warehouse	BODEGA
—pale from ageing	TAWNY	white	BLANCO
—trough for crushing		wine	VINO
grapes	LAGAR	—cellar	BODEGA
—warehouse	LODGE	young wine	VINO VERDE
red	TINTO	—Swiss	
sparkling	ESPUMANTE	from maker's own	
sweet	ADAMADO, DOCE	vineyards	PREMIER CRU
vineyard	VINHA	pink wine	OEIL DE PERDRIX
vintage	COLHEITA	—Yugoslav	
white	BRANCO	dry	SUHO
wine	VINHO	medium dry	POLSUHO
—cellar	ADEGA	natural	PRIRODNO
young wine	VINHO VERDE	pink	RUZICA
—Romanian		red	CRNO
bottled	IMBUTELIAT	sparkling	BISER
dry	SEC	sweet	SLATKO
grape	STRUGURE	white	BIJELO
pink	ROSE	inferior wine	PLONK
red	ROSU	kept too long	MADERISED
sparkling	SPUMOS	make sparkling wine	CHAMPENISE
state farming		—method	METHODE CHAMPENOISE
organisation	GAS, IAS	peach-flavoured	PECHER
sweet	DULCE	science of wine	OENOLOGY
vine	VIE	sediment	LEES
vineyard	VILE	sequence at tasting	FLIGHT
vintage	RECOLTA	slightly sparkling	PETILLANT
white	ALB	sweet wine from partially	
wine	VIN	dried grapes	STRAW-WINE
—cellar	PIVNITA	types	
—Russian		—Algerian	PINARD
champagne	SHAMPANSKOE	—American	
dry	SUKHOE	California	AHLGREN, BARBERA
factory	VINOZAVOD		BEAULIEU, BRANDER
pink	ROSOVOE		BUENA VISTA

CALLOWAY, CHAPPELLET
CHATEAU ST JEAN, CLOS DU BOIS
CRESTA BLANCA, CRIBARI, ESSENSIA
GALLO, HEITZ, INGLENOOK, FETZER
FELTON-EMPIRE, FIRESTONE, MARTINI
MASSON, MONDAVI, MONTICELLO
MOUNT PALOMAR, PARDUCCI, RIDGE
ROUDON-SMITH, SANFORD
SIERRA VISTA, SONOMA, ZACA MESA

East CATAWBA
CHATEAU GRAND TRAVERS
HENRI MARCHANT, HERON HILL
LABRUSCA, LAKE COUNTRY
SCUPPERNONG

North-west HAVILAND, QUAIL RUN
SALISHAN, ST CHAPELLE

—Australian BLEASDALE, BUNDARRA
CHATEAU REMY, GRAND HERMITAGE
LAKE'S FOLLY, MOUNT BARKER
ORLANDO, PORPHYRY, ROTHBURY
ROXBURGH, RUTHERGLEN
QUELLTALER, SEPPELT
VASSE FELIX

—Austrian GUMPOLDSKIRCHEN
HEURIGE, SCHLUCK

—Bulgarian GAMZA, HEMUS, MELNIK
MISKET

—Corsican MUSCATELLU, PATRIMONIO

—Cypriot AFAMES, BELLAPAIS
COMMANDARIA
DOMAINE D'AHERA
NEGRO, OTHELLO
SEMELI, SHERRY

—Egyptian CRU DES PTOLEMEES
OMAR KHAYYAM
REINE CLEOPATRE

—French ANJOU, BARSAC, BEAUJOLAIS
BEAUNE, BORDEAUX, BURGUNDY
CHABLIS, CHAMBERTIN, CHAMPAGNE
CHATEAUNEUF-DU-PAPE, CHENAS
CHINON, FLEURIE, GIGONDAS, GRAVES
HERMITAGE, JULIENAS, LIRAC
MACON, MARGAUX, MEDOC, MERSAULT
MUSCADET, NUIT ST GEORGES
POMEROL, POMMARD, POUILLY-FUISSE
POUILLY-FUME, SANCERRE, SAUTERNES
ST EMILION, ST ESTEPHE, ST JULIEN
TAVEL, VOLNAY, VOUVRAY

—German BACHARACH, BADEN
BERNKASTELER, FRANKEN
HOCK, JOHANNISBERGER
LIEBFRAUMILCH, MOSELBLUMCHEN
MOSEL(LE), MARCOBRUNNER
NIERSTEINER, PIESPORTER
RHEIN-WINE, RHINE(-WINE)
RUDESHEIMER, STEINBERGER

—Greek AMINTAION, CHATEAU CARRAS
DEMESTICA, KOUTAKIS, KRASSI
LINDOS, MALVASIA, MALVASIE
MANTINIA, MAVRODAPHNE, METAXIS
NAOUSSA, RETSINA, RHODITIS
RO(M)BOLA, VERDEA

—Hungarian BIKAVER, BULL'S BLOOD
ESSENCIA, HARSLEVELU
KEKFRANKOS, TOKAY

—Italian ASTI (SPUMANTE), BARBERA
BARDOLINI, BAROLA, CHIANTI
FALERNIAN, FRASCATI, FRIULI
LACHRYMA CHRISTI, LAMBRUSCO
ORVIETO, SOAVE, TRENTINO
VALPOLICELLA, VERDICCHIO

—Lebanese CHATEAU MUSAR

—Madeira BUAL, MADEIRA
MALMSEY, SERCIAL, VERDELHO

—new wine MUST

—New Zealand BABICH, MONTANA
NOBILO

—North African CHANTEBLED
CHATEAU FERIANI
CHATEAU MORNAG
CHATEAU THIBAR, CHELLAH
COTEAUX DE CARTHAGE
CUVEE DU PRESIDENT, GHARB
GRIS DE BOULAOUANE, MAGON
MUSCAT DE KELIBIA, RENAULT
SIDI SELEM, TARIK
ZAER, ZEMMOUR

—pink wine BLUSH WINE, ROSE

—Portuguese BUCELLAS, DAO, DOURO
LISBON, MADEIRA
MATEUS ROSE, PORT, SANTOS

—Romanian BABEASCA, COTNARI, PERLA
SEGARCEA, SADOVA

—rosé BLUSH WINE

—Russian CHUMAI, GRATIESTI
GURDZHAANI, NAPAREVIL
NEGRU DE PURKAR, ROMANESTI
TETRA, TRIFESTI

—Sicilian MARSALA, SETTESOLI

—South African CONSTANTIA
FLEUR DU CAP
MEERLUST, ZANDVLEIT

—Spanish ALICANT(E), JEREZ, MALAGA
MONTILLA, PETER-SEE-ME, RIOJA
SACK, SHERRY, TARRAGONA, TORO
VALENCIA, XERES

—sparkling wine ASTI SPUMANTE
CHAMPAGNE, LAMBRUSCO
MOUSSEC, POMAGNE
VALPOLICELLA

—Swiss DOLE, DORIN, ERMITAGE
FENDANT, GORON, HUMAGNE

	MALVOISIE, NOSTRANO
	PERLAN, SALVAGNIN
	SCHAFISER, TWANNER, VITI
—Turkish	BUZBAG, DIKMEN
	KOROGLU, TRAKYA
—Yugoslav	BOGDANUSA, GRK, DINGAC
	MALVASIA, MARASTINA, OPOL
	PLAVAC, PLAVINA, POSIP
	POSTUP, PROSEK, VUGAVA
	VRANAC, ZILAVKA
unfortified wine	TABLE WINE
warm wine drink	BISHOP, MULL
wine	
—waiter	SOMMELIER
—with	
blackcurrants	KIR
eggs, etc	FLIP, FUSTIAN, NOG
honey	OENOMEL
juniper berries	GENEVRETTE
lemon, etc	COBBLER
milk	POSSET
spices	AQUA MIRABILIS
	BISHOP, HIPPOCRAS, SANGAREE
	SANGRAI, WASSAIL
—Scott	PIGMENT
spirit, eggs, etc	EGG-FLIP
spirits added	FORTIFIED WINE
sugar and soda-water	BADMINTON
unpleasant taste	CORKED
wormwood	VERMOUTH
Wise Men	MAGI, BALTHAZAR,
	GASPAR(CASPAR), MELCHIOR

without

meaning: absence of
   deficiency of
   failure of
   lack of
   lacking
   loss of
   minus
   want of, etc

absence of	
—brain	ANCEPHALY
—emotion	APATHY
—feeling	ANAESTHESIA
—law	ANARCHY
—oxygen	ANAEROBIC
—pain	ANALGESIA
—passage in body	ATRESIA
—pulsation	ACROTISM
—thyroid gland	ATHYRIA
abstinence from food	ABROSIA
absolute silence	ANACOUSTIC
calmness	ATARAXIA, ATARAXY
cessation of breathing	APNOEA
deathlessness	ATHANASY

defect of vision	ASTIGMATISM
defective vision	ANOPIA
deficiency	
—in oxygen	ANOXIA
—of CO^2	ACAPNIA
disinclined to read	ALITERATE
dwarfism without	
disproportion	ATELEIOSIS
failure to	
—menstruate	AMENORRHOEA
—secrete	
milk	AGALACTIA
urine	ANURIA
having short stem	ACAULESCENT
hopelessness	ANOMIE, ANOMY
illiterate	ANALPHABEIC
imperfect development	AGENESIS
—of organ or part	APLASIA
impermeability to	
radiant heat	ATHERMANCY
inability	
—of heart to empty itself	ASYSTOLE
—to	
co-ordinate	
movements	ATAXIA, ATAXY
express thought in	
words	APHASIA
speak	ALOGIA
swallow	APHAGIA, APHAGY
understand spoken	
or written words	APHASIA
intermission of fever	APYREXIA
lack of	
—blood	ANAEMIA
—co-ordination	ASYNERGIA
in walking	ABASIA
—nervous energy	ANEURIA
—power	ADYNAMIA
—sense of	
smell	ANOSMIA
touch	ANAPHIA
—strength	ADYNAMIA
—syntactical sequence	ANACOLUTHIA
—understanding	ANOESIS
—vitamins	AVITAMINOSIS
lawlessness	ANOMIA
little or no change	AMETABOLOUS
loss of	
—ability to manipulate	
objects	APRAXIA
—appetite	ANOREXIA, ANOREXY
—feeling	ANAESTHESIA
—hair	ALOPECIA
—honour	ATIMY
—memory	AMNESIA
—power	

of
—voluntary movement AKINESIA
AKINESIS
—writing AGRAPHIA
to read ALEXIA
—sense of smell ANOSMIA
—speech ALALIA, APHEMIA
—taste AGEUSIA
—voice APHONIA, APHONY
making no angle AGONIC
mental defectiveness AMENTIA
never meeting ASYMPTOTE
non-moral AMORAL
not
—arranged in belts AZONAL
—conforming to type ATYPICAL
—connected ASYNARTETE
—cyclic ACYCLIC
—divided into cells ACELLULAR
—in rows ASTICHOUS
—joined AZYGOUS
—liable to decay ASEPTIC
—local AZONIC
—periodic APERIODIC
—political APOLITICAL
—social ASOCIAL
—standing in a
fixed position ASTATIC
—typical ATYPICAL
—yoked AZYGOUS
opposed to theology ATHEOLOGY
reducing sexual desire ANAPHRODISIAC
rejection as spurious ATHETESIS
sexless ASEXUAL
stoppage of pulse ASPHYXIA, ASPHYXY
straight ATROPOUS
ungrammatical ASYNTACTIC
unknowableness ACATALEPSY
unleavened AZYMOUS
want of
—power ADYNAMY
—strength ADYNAMY
wasting away ATROPHY
weakness of digestion APEPSIA, APEPSY
without
—a
day fixed SD, SINE DIE
head ACEPHALOUS
placenta APLACENTAL
septum ASEPTATE
skin APELLOUS
tail AN(O)UROUS
—accent ATONIC
—albumen EXALBUMINOUS
—alteration INVARIABLE
—anthers ADESPOTA

—animation INANIMATE
—astigmatism ANASTIGMATIC
—awns MUTICIOUS
—beak EROSTRATE
—being an image ANICONIC
—belief in God ATHEISM
—blame INCULPABLE
—blood EXSANGUINOUS
—body INCORPOREAL
opening ATRESIA
—bracteoles EBRACTEOLATE
—bracts EBRACTEATE
—care (sloth) ACEDIA
—cause ACAUSAL
—central cylinder ASTELY
—change INVARIABLE
—children ISSUELESS
SINE PROLE, SP
—chromatic aberration ACHROMATIC
—coelom ACOELOMATE
—colour ACHROMATIC
—columns ASTYLAR
—congruousness INCONCINNOUS
—conjunctions ASYNDETON
—consideration (law) NUDE
—date SA
—defective vision ANASTIGMATIC
—desire INAPPETENT
—distinct
joints ANARTHROUS
margin IMMARGINATE
—disturbance ATARAXIA, ATARAXY
—doubt SINE DUBIO
—echo ANECHOIC
—effect INSIGNIFICANT, INVALID
—end ETERNAL, INFINITE
—energy ATONY
—equality IMPARITY
—faith NULLIFIDIAN
—fault IMPECCABLE
—fear IMPAVID
—feeling INSENSATE
—feet APODOUS
—fever APYREXIA, APYREXY
—fingers ADACTYL
—flavour INSIPID
—flowers ANANTHOUS
—foresight IMPROVIDENT
—form or shape INFORM
—free oxygen ANAEROBI(OTI)C
—fruit ACARPOUS
—gills ABRANCHIATE
—gravity AGRAVIC
—hands AMANOUS
—harmony ANHARMONIC
—hinges ECARDINATE

—hope	ANOMIE, ANOMY
—horns	ACEROUS, MOOLY
	MUL(L)EY
—importance	INDIFFERENT
—inclination	ACLINIC
—indication	INDESIGNATE
—infection	ASEPTIC
—interest	INSIPID
—irises	ANIRIDIA
—issue	SP, SINE PROLE
—knowledge	NESCIENT
—leaves	APHYLLOUS
—lens (eye)	APHACIA
—lid	INOPERCULATE
—life	AZOIC, EXANIMATE
	INANIMATE
—light	APHOTIC
—limbs	AMELIA
—liquid	ANEROID
—logic	ALOGICAL
—male issue	SMP
—means of	
communication	INCOMMUNICADO
—method	IMMETHODICAL
—milk	AGALAXY
—mitosis	AMITOSIS
—modesty	IMPRUDENT
—money	BROKE, IMPECUNIOUS
—morals	IMMORAL
—mouth	ASTOM(AT)OUS
—movement	IMMOBILE
—name	INNOMINATE
—nerves	ANEURIN
—nodes	ENODAL
—nucleus	ENUCLEATE
—offspring	ATOCIA
—operculum	INOPERCULATE
—opposition	NEM CON
—pain	ANODYNE
—parasites	AXENIC
—perception	AGNOSIA
—perianth	ACHLAMYDEOUS
—permanence	IMPERMANENT
—personality	IMPERSONAL
—petals	APETALOUS
or sepals	ACHLAMYDEOUS
—placenta	IMPLACENTAL
—point	ASTIGMATIC, MUTICIOUS
—polarity	ASTATIC
—power	IMPOTENT
—probity	IMPROBITY
—proportion	INCONCINNOUS
—qualification	LAY
—rays	ABACTINAL
—religion	IRRELIGIOUS
—restraint	IMMODEST

—reverberation	ANECHOIC
—ribs	ECOSTATE
—sap	EXSUCCOUS
—sensation	INSENSATE
—sepals	ASEPALOUS
—settled dwelling	NOMADIC, VAGRANT
—sex	ASEXUAL
—sexual desire	ANAPHRODISIAC
—shadow	ASCIAN
—shame	IMPRUDENT
—smell	INODOROUS, ANOSMIC
—sound	ANACOUSTIC
—speech	OBMUTESCENT
—spherical	
aberration	APLANATIC
—spine	MUTICIOUS
—spirit	EXANIMATE, INANIMATE
	INSIPID
—stalk	SESSILE
—stamens	ANANDROUS
—stipules	EXSTIPULATE
—stomach	AGASTRIC
—strength	ASTHENIA
—surviving issue	SPS
—symmetry	ASYMMETRY
—synchronism	ASYNCHRONOUS
—tail	ECAUDATE
—taste	INSIPID
—teeth	EDENTATE, EDENTULOUS
—the article	ANARTHROUS
—thematic vowel	ATHEMATIC
—thought	IMPROVIDENT
—tone	ATONIC
—tongue	AGLOSSAL
—transparency	OPAQUE
—turning	ATROPOUS
—understanding of	
numbers	INNUMERATE
words	ILLITERATE
—validity	INVALID
—voice	ANAUDIA
—water	ANHYDROUS, NEAT
—weight	IMPONDERABLE
—will	INTESTATE
power	AB(O)ULIA
—willingness	NOLITION
—wings	APTERAL, APTEROUS
—wisdom	INSIPIENT

woman

Australian woman	ADELAIDE, SHEILA
Dutch woman	FROW, VROUW
Egyptian woman	BINT
French woman	FEMME
German woman	FRAU
Italian woman	DONNA
Spanish woman	MUJER

Women's		sun	HELIOLATRY
—Institute	WI	symbols	SYMBOLOLATRY
—Land Army	WLA	trees	DENDROLATRY
—Liberal Federation	WLF	Virgin Mary	MARIOLATRY
—Rural Institute	WRI	wealth	PLUTOLATRY
—Voluntary Service	WVS	wonders	THAUMATOLATRY
	(*see also* **girls**)	words	EPEOLATRY, LOGOLATRY
		world	COSMOLATRY

word

word of four letters	QUADRILITERAL
	TETRAGRAM
word processor/processing	WP
words per minute	WPM
	(*see also* **language**)

world COSMOLATRY

(*see also* **belief**)

write

including: description of
engraving
drawing (of)
photograph (of)
record (of)
writing (about)

world

world bank	BIS
World Boxing Association	WBA
World Boxing Council	WBC
World Championship Tennis	WCT
World Council of Churches	WCC
World Health Organisation	WHO
World Meteorological Organisation	WMO
World Wildlife Fund	WWF
worldwide	MONDIAL

3-D image	HOLOGRAPHY
accidental omission	
of letter(s)	LIPOGRAPHY
adages	PAROEMIOGRAPHY
ancient inscriptions	EPIGRAPHY
atmospheric conditions	AEROGRAPHY
	METEOROGRAPHY

worship

including: reverence for
worship of

animal/human forms	THERIANTHROPISM
animals	THERIOLATRY
	ZOOLATRY
angels	ANGELOLATRY
books	BIBLIOLATRY
Christ	CHRISTOLATRY
church forms and	
traditions	ECCLESIOLATRY
dead	NECROLATRY
devil	SATANISM
Earth	GEOLATRY
fetishes	FETICHISM, FETISHISM
fire	PYROLATRY
fish	ICHTHYOLATRY
heavenly host	SABAISM
horses	HIPPOLATRY
idols	IDOLATRY, IDOLISM
images	ICONOLATRY
Luther	LUTHEROLATRY
man	ANTHROPOLATRY
nature	PHYSIOLATRY
nobility	LORDOLATRY
one god	MONOLATRY
sacred things	HIEROLATRY
saints	HAGIOLATRY, HIEROLATRY
self	AUTOLATRY
Shakespeare	BARDOLATRY
snakes	OPHIOLATRY
stars	ASTROLATRY
stone	LITHOLATRY

bad	
—spelling	PSEUDOGRAPHY
—writing	CACOGRAPHY
biography	PROSOPOGRAPHY
blood pressure	KYMOGRAPH
bones	OSTEOGRAPHY
books	BIBLIOGRAPHY
burnt-in photograph	PYROPHOTOGRAPH
calculation chart	ABAC, NOMOGRAM
	NOMOGRAPH
ceramics	CERAMOGRAPHY
cervix	CERVICOGRAPHY
character representing	
sound	PHONOGRAPH
chemical anaylsis by	
electrolysis	POLAROGRAPHY
ciphers	STEGANOGRAPHY
colour	
—analysis	CHROMATOGRAPHY
—frequencies	SPECTROGRAPH
—printing	CHROMOLITHOGRAPHY
	CHROMOTYPOGRAPHY
	CHROMOXYLOGRAPHY
contour feathers	PTERYLOGRAPHY
copying	MIMEOGRAPH
	PANTOGRAPHY
—drawings	EIDOGRAPHY
correct writing	ORTHOGRAPHY
dancing	CHORE(O)GRAPHY
death	THANATOGRAPHY
description of	
—nature	PHYSIOGRAHPY
—skin	DERMATOGRAPHY

descriptive	
—astronomy	URANOGRAPHY
—biography	PROSOPOGRAPHY
dictionaries	LEXICOGRAPHY
diseases	NOSOGRAPHY
	PATHOGRAPHY
distant thunderstorms	KERAUNOGRAPHY
document wholly	
written by author	NOMOGRAPH
drawing spirals	HELICOGRAPHY
Earth	CHOROGRAPHY
	GEOGRAPHY
	TOPOGRAPHY
electrically-charged	
powder	XEROGRAPHY
electrolytic	
determination of	
ion concentration	POLAROGRAPHY
electrotype copying	GLYPHOGRAPHY
elevation drawing	ORTHOGRAPHY
ellipses	ELLIPSOGRAPH
engraving	
—from stone	LITHOGRAPHY
—on	
brass	CHALCOGRAPHY
copper	CHALCOGRAPHY
gemstones	GLYPTOGRAPHY
stones, etc	EPIGRAPHY
	LITHOGRAPHY
wood	XYLOGRAPHY
—photographically	HELIOGRAPHY
	HELIOGRAVURE
enlarged photograph	PHOTOMICROGRAPHY
exact copy	APOGRAPH
false writing	PSEUDOGRAPH
features of Mars	AREOGRAPHY
fine writing	CALLIGRAPHY
fishes	ICTHYOGRAPHY
fluid pressure	KYMOGRAPH
fossils	ORYCTOGRAPHY
gamma-ray photography	SCINTIGRAPHY
geography	CHOROGRAPHY
—of living things	BIOGEOGRAPHY
ground plans	ICHNOGRAPHY
handwriting	CH(E)IROGRAPHY
heart movements	CARDIOGRAPHY
heat	THERMOGRAPHY
height of land	HYPSOGRAPHY
	TOPOGRAPHY
—and depth of water	BATHYOROGRAPHY
human	
—population	DEMOGRAPHY
—races	ETHNOGRAPHY
hymns	HYMNOGRAPHY
ideography	PASIGRAPHY
illustration	ICONOGRAPHY

image using radio-isotope	
in specimen	AUTORADIOGRAPH
inscriptions	EPIGRAPHY
interwoven letters	MONOGRAM
laws	NOMOGRAPHY
life	
—and writings	BIOBIBLIOGRAPHY
—of individual	BIOGRAPHY, BIOSCOPE
	PROSOPOGRAPHY
light image	PHOTOGRAPHY
lithography in	
colour	CHROMOLITHOGRAPHY
magnetic variations	MAGNETOGRAPH
magnified photograph	MICROPHOTOGRAPH
many copies	POLYGRAPH
map-making	CARTOGRAPHY
—from aerial	
photographs	PHOTOGRAMMETRY
meteorological records	AEROGRAPHY
	METEOROGAPHY
mimes	MIMOGRAPHY
minerals	ORYCTOGRAPHY
Moon	SELENOGRAPHY
motion pictures	CINEMATOGRAPHY
	KINEMATOGRAPHY
—through	
microscope	CINEMICROGRAPHY
mountains	OR(E)OGRAPHY
movement	
—or duration	CHRONOGRAPHY
—of heart	CARDIOGRAPHY
muscular contractions	MYOGRAPHY
myths in art	MYTHOGRAPHY
natural wonders	THAUMATOGRAPHY
nature	PHYSIOGRAPHY
notation for dances	ORCHESOGRAPHY
obituaries	NECROGRAPHY
old manuscripts	PALAEOGRAPHY
oil paint on stone	LITHOCHROMATICS
omission of letters	LIPOGRAPHY
one subject	MONOGRAPH
opinions of	
philosophers	DOXOGRAPHY
organs of plants	
or animals	ORGANOGRAPHY
original manuscript	AUTOGRAPH
perspective drawing	SCENOGRAPHY
phonetic typewriting	STENOTYPY
photograph of sun by	
monochromatic light	SPECTROHELIOGRAPH
photographic	
—engraving	HELIOGRAPH
	HELIOGRAVURE
—impression on	
wood block	PHOTOXYLOGRAPHY
zinc plate	PHOTOZINCOGRAPHY

photography	
—by	
gamma rays	SCINTIGRAPHY
short wave	RADIOGRAPHY
split laser	HOLOGRAPHY
—of	
cyclic	
movement	CHRONOCYCLOGRAPHY
manuscripts	ROTOGRAPHY
moving objects	CHRONOPHOTOGRAPHY
	(*see also separate entry*)
physical geography	PHYSIOGRAPHY
picture-writing	HYPERGRAPHY
	IDEOGRAPHY, PICTOGRAPHY
planet Mars	AREOGRAPHY
poker work	PYROGRAPHY
population	DEMOGRAPHY
pottery	CERAMOGRAPHY
printing	TYPOGRAPHY
—from	
photograph	PHOTOLITHOGRAPHY
stone	LITHOGRAPHY
—with whole words	
cast in type	LOGOGRAPHY
private mark	IDIOGRAPH
proverbs	PAROEMIOGRAPHY
quick writing	STENOGRAPHY
radiography	ROENTGENOGRAPHY
reproduction of	
transmitted drawings	TELAUTOGRAPHY
reversed image	ROTOGRAPH
rocks	ORYCTOGRAPHY
	PETROGRAPHY
relationship between	
members of a group	SOCIOGRAM
sacred symbols	HIEROGRAM
	HIEROGRAPH
scene painting	SCENOGRAPHY
seas	OCEANOGRAPHY
secret writing	CRYPTOGRAPHY
	STEGANOGRAPHY
sexual perversion	PORNOGRAPHY
shape of mouldings	CYMOGRAPH
shorthand	BRACHYGRAPHY
	STENOGRAPHY
	TACHYGRAPHY
showing	
—resemblances of	
individuals in group	DENDOGRAM
—wear in machinery	FERROGRAM
sign for whole phrase	PHRASEOGRAPH
signature	AUTOGRAPH
signed by all parties	SYNGRAPH
silk-screen printing	SERIGRAPHY
skin	DERMATOGRAPHY
sound vibration	PHONOAUTOGRAPH

spirit-writing	PSYCHOGRAPHY
spoken sound	PHONOGRAPHY
stars and galaxies	URANOGRAPHY
still-life pictures	RHYPAROGRAPHY
Sun	CORONAGRAPHY
	CORONOGRAPHY
symbol representing	
thing itself	IDEOGRAM, IDEOGRAPH
symbolic writing	IDEOGRAPHY
	SYMBOLOGRAPHY
teeth	ODONTOGRAPHY
three	
—dimensional picture	STEREOGRAPH
	VECTOGRAPH
—letters, one sound	TRIGRAPH
tides	MARIGRAPHY
topography	CHOROGRAPHY
trade mark	IDIOGRAPH
transmission of	
—drawings etc, by	
telegraphy	PHOTOTELEGRAPHY
—messages by electric	
impulses	TELEGRAPHY
two letters, one sound	DIGRAPH
unintentional repetition	
in copying	DITTOGRAPHY
using oil-film	EVAPOROGRAPH
vibrations	VIBROGRAPH
voluminous writing	POLYGRAPHY
wind pressure and speed	ANEMOGRAPHY
world	COSMOGRAPHY
woven in coloured silk	STEVENGRAPH
writing	
—on	
both sides	OPISTHOGRAPHY
one subject	MONOGRAPH
wax	CEROGRAPHY
—with stylus	STYLOGRAPHY
written	
—character	IDEOGRAM, IDEOGRAPH
—cyphers	CRYPTOGRAPHY
wrong words	PARAGRAPHIA
X-rays	(*see separate entry*)

writers
American (m)   ARDREY, ASIMOV, BALDWIN
BELLOW, BRODSKY, BRZEZINSKI
BURROUGHS, CAPOTE, CHANDLER, COHN
CREELEY, DE VRIES, DICK, DOS PASSOS
FAULKNER, FIEDLER, FITZGERALD
GARLAND, GINSBERG, GOODMAN
HAMMETT, HAWTHORNE, HEMINGWAY
HIGGINS, HOWELLS, JAMES, KENEALLY
KEROUAC, KNIGHT, KRISTOL
LONDON, MACDONALD
MAILER, MELVILLE, MENCKEN, MILLER
NORRIS, O'HARA, POE, POHL, POIRIER

ROBBINS, ROSENBERG, ROTH, RUMAKER
RUNYON, SANTAYANA, SAROYAN
SILVERBERG, SINCLAIR, SINGER
SONTAG, SPILLANE, STEINBECK, STOW
THOREAU, TOFFLER, TRILLING
TWAIN, UPDIKE, VIDAL, WATTS, WHITMAN
WILLIAMSON, WILSON, WOLFE
(f)   GARNER, HANRAHAN
JOLLEY, STEIN

Argentinian   BORGES, TORRE
Australian (m)   CLARKE, FURPHY
LAWSON, PATTERSON
RICHARDSON, WHITE
(f)   ASTLEY, FRANKLIN
MCCULLOUGH, STEAD
Austrian   ARTMANN, BAYER, FRIED, KAFKA
RUHM, WERFEL
Belgian   MAETERLINCK, SIMENON
British (m)   ADDISON, ALDINGTON, ALDISS
AMIS, ARCHER, ARNOLD, BALLARD
BARSTOW, BENNETT, BIRRELL, BLAIR
BRADBURY, BRAINE, BROPHY, BUCHAN
BURGESS, BURNS, CALDER, CARLYLE
CHAUCER, CHESTERTON, CHURCHILL
CHUTE, CLARKE, COLLINS, CONGREVE
CONNOLLY, CONRAD, CREASEY, DAHL
DEFOE, DENNIS, DICKENS, DRYDEN
DURRELL, FIELDING, FLEMING, FORD
FORSTER, FORSYTHE, FOWLES
GALSWORTHY, GARNETT, GISSING
GOLDING, GOLDSMITH, GRAY
GREEN, GREENE, HAGGARD, HARDY
HAZLITT, HEPPENSTALL, HIGGINS
HOPKINS, HUXLEY, INNES, ISHERWOOD
JOHNSON, KENT, KINGSLEY, KIPLING
KOESTLER, LAMB, LANG, LAWRENCE
LE CARRE, LEE, LEHMANN, LEWIS
LODGE, LUDLUM, MAUGHAM, MACLEAN
MEREDITH, MILNE, MILTON, MOORE, NAIRN
NORMAN, ORWELL, PAUL, PEACOCK
PEAKE, PEPYS, POWELL, PRIESTLEY
READE, RUSKIN, RUSSELL, SANSOM
SCOTT, SHAKESPEARE, SILLITOE
SMOLLETT, SNOW, SPENSER, STERNE
STEVENSON, STOREY, STRACHEY
STRONG, SWIFT, THACKERAY, THWAITE
TOLKIEN, TROLLOPE, VERNE, WAIN
WALLACE, WALPOLE, WARNER, WAUGH
WELLS, WILSON, WODEHOUSE
(f)   ALLINGHAM, AUSTEN
BAINBRIDGE, BOWEN, BRONTE
CARTLAND, CHRISTIE, CROMPTON
DU MAURIER, ELLIOT, GASKELL
HEYER, HIGHSMITH, INNES, JAMES
LEHMANN, LESSING, MURDOCH
POTTER, RENDELL, RICHARDSON

SAYERS, SPARK, TAYLOR, WELDON
WEST, WOOLF
Bulgarian   CANETTI
Chilean   NARUDA
Cuban   RODRIGUEZ
Czech   CAPEK, HASEK, HAVEL, SEIFERT
Danish   ANDERSON
dramatists   (*see separate entry*)
Egyptian   MAHFOUZ
Finnish   SILLANPAA
French (m)   ARAGON, ARRABAL, BALZAC
BAUDELAIRE, BENDA, BERNANOS
BRETON, BUTOR
CAMUS, CHAMFLEURY, CHAMSON
COCTEAU, CORNEILLE, DAUDET
DE MAISTRE, DE SADE
DU JARDIN, DUGARD, DUHAMEL
DUMAS, D'URFE, FLAUBERT
FONTANELLE, FRANCE
GAUTIER, GENET, GIDE, GIRAUDOUX
GONCOURT, HUGO, HUYSMANS, LARBAUD
LAUGIER, MALRAUX, MARTIN
MAUPASSANT, MAURIAC, PERSE, PICABIA
PONGE, PROUST, RABELAIS, RACINE
RIMBAUD, ROBBE-GRILLET, ROLLAND
ROMAINS, ROUSSEL, SARTRE
SIMON, SOLLERS, SOREL, STENDAHL
VOLTAIRE, ZOLA
(f)   COLETTE, SAND, SAGAN
SARRAUTE
German   BALL, BENJAMIN, BENN
BOBROWSKI, BOLL, DOBLIN
FALLADA, FONTANE
GOETHE, GRASS, HARDENBERG
HERDER, HESSE, HOFFMANN, JENS
JOHNSON, JUNGER, LEWIN, KAFKA
KASTNER, KIPPHARDT, KISCH
LESSING, MANN
NOVALIS, PAQUET, PFEMFERT
RAABE, RENN, RICHTER, SCHILLER
SCHREYER, SPENGLER, SUDERMANN
TIECK, WALDEN, WEISS, WILLE
Ghanaian   ARMAH
Greek   AESCHYLUS, ARISTOPHANES
ELYTIS, EURIPIDES
SEFERIS, SOPHOCLES
Guatemalan   ASTURIAS
Hungarian   KOESTLER, NORDAU
Icelandic   LAXNESS
Irish (m)   BEHAN, JOYCE, MOORE
(f)   O'BRIEN
Israeli   AGNON
Italian   CALVINO, CAPUNANA
D'ANNUNZIO, LAMPEDUSA
MACHIAVELLI, MONTALE
MORAVIA, QUASIMODO, SILONE

	TRANQUILLI, VERGA
Japanese	KAWABATA, MISHIMA
Kenyan	THIONG'O
Martinician	CESAIRE
Mexican	FUENTES, MARQUEZ, RULFO
New Zealand (m)	CURNOW, DAVIN, GEE
	HULME, HYDE, IHIMAERA
	SARGESON, SHADBOLT
(f)	FRAME, MANSFIELD, MARSH
Nigerian	ACHEBE, EKWENSI
	OKIGBO, SAYINKA, TUTUOLA
poets	(see separate entry)
Polish	BRZEZINSKI, MILOSZ
Puerto Rican	JIMINEZ
Russian (m)	ANDREYEV, BELY, BUGAKOV
	CHEKHOV, DOSTOEVSKY
	EHRENBURG
	FEDIN, GASTEV, GOGOL, GORKY
	GRUZDEV, IVANOV, KAVERIN
	LUNACHARSKY, LUNTS, NABOKOV
	NIKITIN, OSTROVSKY, PASTERNAK
	POZNER, PUSHKIN
	SELYUNIN, SHKLOVSKY, SHOLOKHOV
	SLONIMSKY, SOLZHENITSYN
	TIKHONOV, TOLSTOY, TURGENEV
	ZAMYATIN, ZOSHCHENKO
(f)	POLONSHAYA
Somali	FARAH
South African (m)	COETZEE, FUGARD
	PATON, SMITH
(f)	GORDIMER, HEAD
Spanish	ALEXANDRE, CARRERE, CELA
	CERVANTES, GOYTISOLO, LORCA
	PARMENO, PINILLOS, TORRE
Swedish	IBSEN, JOHNSON, LAGERQUIST
	MARTINSON, STRINDBERG
	WEISS, ZACHS
Swiss	CENDRARS, SISMONDI
West Indian (m)	DE BOISSIERE, HARRIS
	HEARNE, JAMES, LAMMING
	LOVELACE, MAIS, MCKAY, MENDES
	MITTELHOLZER, REID, SELVEN
	STOMER
(f)	BENNETT
Yugoslav	ANDIC

X-ray	RADIOGRAM, SKIAGRAPH
of	
—bile ducts	CHOLANGIOGRAPHY
—blood vessels	ANGIOGRAPHY
	ARTERIOGRAPHY
—bones	OSTEOGRAPHY
—brain	ENCEPALOGRAPHY
	VENTRICULOGRAPHY
—breast	MAMMOGRAPHY
—gall bladder	CHOLANGIOGRAPHY
—kidneys	PYELOGRAPHY
—layer of body	TOMOGRAPHY
—lymph glands	LYMPHOGRAPHY
—salivary duct	SIALOGRAPHY
—spinal cord	MYELOGRAPHY
—urinary tract	UROGRAPHY
photography	ROENTGENOGRAPHY
xerography	XERORADIOGRAPHY
xanthium	BURDOCK, BUR-MARIGOLD
	CLOTBUR, CLOTE
Xantippe	SHREW
Xeres	SHERRY

yachting
classes   CENTAUR, CHS, CONTESSA
DARING, DRAGON
ETCHELL'S, FLYING DUTCHMAN
FLYING FIFTEEN, FOLKBOAT, FOURTEEN
HALF-TONNER, IOR, J-CLASS
LIGHTWAVE, MERMAID, MINI-TWELVE
OYSTER, REDWING, SEVEN
SIGMA, SIX-METRE
SOLING, SONATA, SPRING, SQUIB
SUNBEAM, SUNBIRD, SWALLOW, TOPPER
TORNADO, TWELVE-METRE
TYPHOON, ULTRA
VICTORY, XOD
races   AMERICA'S CUP, FASTNET
RORC CHANNEL RACE
WHITBREAD ROUND THE WORLD
WHITBREAD TRANSATLANTIC
round-the-world
sailors   BLYTH, CHICHESTER
EDWARDS(f), JAMES(f), FRANCIS(f)
KNOX-JOHNSTON, SLOCUM
venues
—Australia   SYDNEY
—England   COWES, HAYLING ISLAND
LYMINGTON, POOLE, SWANSEA
—Ireland   COUNTY DOWN, DUBLIN
DUNLOGHAIRE

—Italy   PONTECERVO
—Mediterranean   SARDINIA
—Netherlands   HOORH
—Pacific   HAWAII
—Sweden   MARSTRAND
yacht-club president   COMMODORE
Yemen   ADEN
capital   SANA'A
coin   DINAR, FILS, RI(Y)AL
Yiddish   (*see* **Hebrew**)
Yugoslavia   YU
capitals   BELGRADE, BEOGRAD
LJUBLJANA, SARAJEVO
SKOPJE, ZAGREB
coins   DINAR, DNR, PARA
countries (former
republics)   BOSNIA(-HERZEGOVINA)
CROATIA, MACEDONIA
SLOVENIA
republics   KOSSOVO, MONTENEGRO
SERBIA, VOIVODINA
federation of villages   ZUPA
governor   ZUPAN
kebabs   CEVAPCICI
newsagency   TANJUG
parliament   SKUPSHTINA
province   BANAT

Z

Zaire	ZR	crab	CANCER
capital	KINSHASHA, LEOPOLDVILLE	fishes	PISCES
coins	LIKUTA, SENGI, ZAIRE	goat	CAPRICORN(US)
Zambia	Z	lion	LEO
capital	LUSAKA	ram	ARIES
coins	KWA(T)CHA, NGWEE	scorpion	SCORPIO
Zamenhof's language	ESPERANTO	twins	GEMINI
Zantippe (Zentippe)	SHREW	virgin	VIRGO
Zanzibar	EAZ	water-carrier	AQUARIUS
Zimbabwe	ZW	**zoological regions**	
capital	HARARE, SALISBURY	Arctic region	ARCTOGAEA
coins	CENT, DOLLAR	Australasian region	NOTOGAEA
Zodiac (signs)		Neotropical region	NEOGAEA
archer	SAGITTARIUS	region of the bear	ARCTOGAEA
balance	LIBRA	southern region	NOTOGAEA
bull	TAURUS	tropical America	NEOGAEA

Other Crossword books

Sunday Express Complete Guide to Cryptic Crosswords
J. A. Coleman

The ideal book for the crossword puzzler, from the novice who knows in theory what cryptic puzzles are all about to more expert practitioners. It covers the whole subject of cryptic crosswords in detail with the different types of cryptic clue and shows how to interpret and solve them.
£12.99

Sunday Express Crossword Dictionary
Gillian Clark

Designed to allow you to compete with compilers on equal terms, this dictionary is a valuable aid to solving all types of crossword: cryptic, definitional and general knowledge. It contains approximately 70,000 words organised in 125 major thematic categories.
£4.99

Eric Dobby Reference Books